Best Practices in School Psychology–III

Best Practices in School Psychology–III

Edited by

Alex Thomas
Miami University
Oxford, Ohio

Jeff Grimes
Iowa Department of Public Instruction
Des Moines, Iowa

The National Association of School Psychologists
Washington, DC

First Printing, 1995

Published by the National Association of School Psychologists
Washington, DC

ISBN   0-932955-99-1

Printed in the United- States of America

From NASP Publications Policy Handbook

The content of this document reflects the ideas and positions of the
authors. The responsibility lies solely with the authors and does not
necessarily reflect the position or ideas of the National Association
of School Psychologists.

Preface

Best Practices in School Psychology–III, like the two preceding editions published by NASP, is designed to provide a comprehensive reference for school psychologists with contemporary research and perspectives related to quality professional services. The third edition establishes a theme that is reflected in most of the chapters, emphasizing a problem-solving approach to professional practice.

A problem-solving orientation is distinguished by its purpose: to improve student performance and enhance educational success in a demonstrable manner. Problem solving is a systematic process that includes the assessment of children and their environments, identification of needs, development and implementation of supports to meet needs, and the monitoring and evaluation of outcomes. This orientation permits any theoretical approach in the design of interventions, but uses improved student performance and educational functioning as a criterion for measuring success. This commitment to improving students' performance and well-being is in harmony with NASP's mission of serving the mental health and educational interest of all children and youth.

As an aid to the reader, the book is divided into four parts with chapters clustered around identified concepts. Part 1 establishes a professional focus. Chapters in this section are related to enhancing professional services with topics ranging from the shifting paradigm in school psychology to mainstay themes within a profession such as ethics, legal issues, governmental relationships, and maintaining professional effectiveness. These chapters present content that potentially influences all other professional services. Part 2 presents a systems focus. System approaches include orientations related to collaboration and adopting prevention programs. Also in this section are systems used by school psychologists in supporting broad based educational interventions such as peer tutoring and school discipline. Part 3 considers individualized services for students, families, and schools. Not surprisingly, this is the bulk of the book. The chapters include topics related to problem solving such as progress monitoring, designing interventions, measuring intervention effectiveness, as well as assessment approaches and concepts for working with special populations. Part 4 provides a set of appendices that will be a useful professional reference including NASP ethics, standards and position statements, state certification and licensing standards, a listing of training programs across the country, as well as medications commonly used to treat children and adolescents.

Also as an aid to the reader, most chapters follow a common framework of headings. Each chapter, in addition to a list of citations from the professional literature, also includes an annotated bibliography with up to five additional readings to extend one's learning related to the chapter topic.

We hope that this organizational structure and the content of this publication will assist the profession in advancing the quality of services to educational systems, students, parents, and families. That is the intent and spirit of this publication. It is through your individual efforts that the profession collectively advances and we hope this resource will be useful in that endeavor.

Acknowledgments

Best Practices in School Psychology–III is an ambitious project that has been touched by many people. We would like to take this space to acknowledge them.

First, acknowledgments go to the cadré of reviewers who read draft chapters, provided valued feedback to authors, and shared their perspectives of the topics. Reviewers for this book include:

Carolyn Allen
Tom Barry
James Batts
Karen Boyce
Jo Kay Boyle
Steve Breckheimer
Rhonda Broadwater
Mei Mei Burr
Servio Carroll
Chuck Catania
Arlene B. Crandall
Stefanie Currington
Marcia Davidson
Carl DiMartino
Lynn Durham
Sharon Ehas
Kristal Ehrhardt
Jean Fankell
Ervi Farkas
Gwen Fecht
Barbara Fischetti
Jim Fuhrman
Amy Glaser
Susan Green
Shelley Greggs
Debra Grilly
Fred Grossman

Leslie Hale
Steve Haskell
Bill Hillebrand
Liz Horwitz
Lee Huff
Joe Jackson
Steve Jackson
Gloria Johnson
Mike Juskelis
David Ketchum
Chuck Klein
Carla Lendrum
Dick Mace
Clare Marsh
Dale E. Matson
Marlene Merrill
Holly Middleton
Thomas Miele
Pat Mullaney
Randy Olley
Susan Page
Leslie Paige
Edward Perreault
William Pfohl
Beth Poe
Kelly K. Powell-Smith
Fred Provenzano

Pam Read
Gary Ross-Reynolds
Edward Saegel
Chuck Saltzman
Ed Schlossman
Ann Schmitt
Robbie Sharp
Agnes Shine
Tracy Simonson
Diane Smallwood
Douglas K. Smith
Lori Sortino
Julie Staresnick
Bob Stark
Brenda Stevens
Stephanie Stollar
Trish Sullivan
Hedwig Teglasi
Deanna Thursby
Michele Turner
Nancy Waldron
Jim Weaver
Christin Weyn
Jon Williams
Ray Witte
Don Wuerstl

Much of the editorial work of tracking draft changes, final manuscripts, copyedited versions of final manuscripts, and galleys, were done by very capable Miami University graduate students in school psychology: Kelli Kazmier, Crista Chenoweth, Holly Heaviland, Cara Eichenlaub, and Kristie Dietrich.

The support of the NASP Publications Board is appreciated and Leslie Hale is to be particularly commended for providing support through the proposal to printing process.

Thanks are certainly due to Susan Gorin, NASP Executive Director, for ably clearing paths which allowed for efficient completion of this ambitious project. As usual, Rosemary O'Donnell provided inordinately competent ombudspersonship for the myriad details and problems associated with getting this task completed. NASP publications fulfillment guru, Betty Sommerville, deserves the vintner's recognition award for assuring that no book will be served before its time.

Special recognition to Paul Mendez, NASP Director for Publications, who has ably shepherded this project on the production end and he deserves credit for the final look and feel of the book. His even temper and good humor is always valued.

Kudos must also be extended to Mary Fitzhimmons and Lawrence Moran, copyeditors extraordinary. Their timeliness, incisiveness, and commitment to this project is appreciated.

All the typesetting and page layout for this book, and previous editions of this book, have been done by a remarkably energetic and efficient Judy Fulwider. Considerable, if not most, of the credit is extended to her for the timely completion of this publication.

The "anything is possible if you don't worry who gets the credit" award goes to Bonnie Thomas who did much of the detailed proofing of galleys, corrected galleys, and a thousand other details in the final preparation of this gargantuan manuscript. She has perused many words.

Acknowledgment is also extended to Doris Bergen (Chair, Department of Educational Psychology, Miami University) and Jeanne Hagen (Chief, Bureau of Special Education, Iowa Department of Public Instruction), for fostering a professional environment supportive of the editorial involvement necessary for this book's completion.

On a personal note, most heartfelt appreciation goes to the continued support received from Bonnie and Sue.

Alex Thomas and Jeff Grimes

Contents

PROFESSIONAL ISSUES

The Profession

Professional Supervision and Leadership

Focus on Systems

Suporting System Functioning

System Level Interventions

FOCUS ON INDIVIDUALIZED SERVICES

Problem Solving Approach

Assessment Domains for Intervention Planning

Student Interventions

Specific Populations

APPENDICES

Professional Issues

School Psychology Paradigm Shift

Daniel J. Reschly
Iowa State University

James E. Ysseldyke
University of Minnesota

In this third edition of one of the most successful volumes in school psychology, the shifting paradigm toward services guided by problem solving and evaluated by the achievement of positive outcomes is increasingly apparent. In contrast to the first two editions, the authors of nearly every chapter treat problem solving as the foundation for school psychological services with an outcomes criterion used as the basis for determining the success of problem-solving efforts. In this introduction, we describe and contrast different paradigms for the design and delivery of school psychological services, analyze problems in the traditional delivery system, and review major policy and reform statements. This introduction concludes with a discussion of the knowledge base, underlying principles, and strategies that form the basis for psychological services that emphasize problem-solving and outcomes criteria.

SCHOOL PSYCHOLOGY AND CRONBACH'S TWO DISCIPLINES

In 1957 Cronbach suggested that a merger of the two disciplines of scientific psychology would produce maximum benefits to consumers. The two disciplines, correlational and experimental, were described as differing in terms of (a) philosophical assumptions, (b) research methodology, (c) key variables and causal inferences, and (d) methods of promoting human welfare.

Correlational Discipline

The correlational discipline emphasizes assessment of the natural variations among people in cognitive, physical, and social-emotional domains. These variations are then related to actual performance in academic or employment settings. If there are significant relationships (correlations) between these natural variations and performance, increased efficiency in the use of resources and enhanced overall performance can be produced by differential selection or placement. The correlational discipline attempts to advance human welfare by selecting the best qualified persons for different careers, training programs, or instructional procedures. Cronbach suggested that the correlational tradition was more consistent with political conservatism in that the individual differences are typically seen as relatively immutable to change and the main outcome is to fit persons to existing programs.

Experimental Discipline

In contrast, the experimental discipline was seen as more liberal politically because the fundamental aim is to create higher levels of performance through, first, discovering the best interventions and then, second, disseminating and implementing the best interventions. Different treatments or interventions are carefully contrasted so that causal statements can be made about which had the highest average effects for groups of participants or, in single subject designs, for individuals. Careful control of experimental conditions is extremely important so that valid comparisons can be made between experimental conditions (i.e., treatments).

The fundamental differences between the two disciplines becomes more apparent in considering what each does with individual differences. The experimentalist attempts to create variations among persons receiving different treatments and to minimize variations among persons receiving the same treatments. Variation among persons receiving the same treatment is error, something to be controlled to the greatest extent possible. Experiments are rarely entirely successful. Some degree of variation among persons receiving the same treatment is virtually inevitable.

These more or less "natural" variations among persons — the error variance for the experimentalist — are the fundamental phenomena studied in the correlation discipline. It is this natural variation that makes differential prediction possible. Nonsignificant or attenuated prediction accuracy results from the absence of variations among persons or artificially reduced variations. Interestingly, variations among persons or individual differences are fundamental to both disciplines; however, the predictor variables in the correlation tradition contribute to the error terms in the experimental discipline. One science attempts to produce differences while the other attempts to predict performance from existing individual differences and to select more appropriate placements. In many ways the traditional and modern trends in school psychology parallel the approaches in the two disciplines.

Aptitude by Treatment Interactions

Use of aptitude by treatment interactions (ATI) was seen by Cronbach (1957) as the means to use the strengths of each of the two disciplines to maximize human welfare: "For any potential problem, there is some best group of treatments to use and some best allocation of persons to treatments" (p. 680). The ATI approach would involve study of (a) differences among treatments, (b) aptitude differences among persons, *and* (c) the interaction of aptitudes and treatments. Based on the interactions, individuals would be assigned to treatments producing the best results. The educational application suggested by Cronbach, greater emphasis on individual prescriptions, was the basis for much of school psychology over the past two decades: "We should *design* treatments, not to fit the average person, but to fit groups of students with particular aptitude patterns. ... We should seek out the aptitudes which correspond to [interact with] modifiable aspects of the treatment" (Cronbach, 1957, p. 681).

ATI is one of the most attractive ideas in all of basic and applied psychology (Arter & Jenkins, 1977, 1979; Ysseldyke, 1973). It is an idea that "should" work in the laboratory and in practice. The idea of matching treatment to naturally occurring characteristics of the person makes inherently good sense; clearly, it is consistent with our humanistic commitments of individualizing instruction and psychological treatments in order to maximize opportunities. ATI is especially attractive in school psychology where most of the work traditionally has been with individual children referred for learning and behavior problems. However, what "should" work, what is inherently appealing, is not always a sound basis for practice. Such is the case with the efforts to use ATI as the foundation for applied psychology.

ATI Failure and Short-Run Empiricism

In less than two decades, Cronbach's frustration with ATI as a basis for applied psychology was palpable in another *American Psychologist* article, "Once we attend to interactions, we enter a hall of mirrors that extends to infinity" (Cronbach, 1975, p. 119). In the ensuing years between 1957 and 1975, Cronbach and colleagues conducted many studies in which attempts were made to identify interactions of aptitudes and treatments. Unfortunately, the hypothesized interactions often did not occur, were extremely weak when they did appear, and were entangled in intractable and hopelessly complex higher order interactions that were virtually impossible to study in laboratory settings, let alone use in practical situations. Furthermore, potent interaction effects, when they did exist, were for prior achievement or skill levels within the domain(s) of behavior that was/were the dependent variable(s) in the ATI experiments. Indeed, level of prior knowledge or skills is an important variable in subsequent learning or performance; however, the effect of prior knowledge was not the kind of aptitude envisioned in Cronbach's grand design or in the school psychology applications of ATI.

In the 1975 article Cronbach abandoned ATI as the basis for applied psychology. The strategy he suggested to replace ATI was remarkably similar to the outcomes criteria and problem-solving strategies that will be discussed in more detail later in this chapter and in many of the chapters that follow. In place of ATI, Cronbach suggested context-specific evaluation and short-run empiricism, "One monitors responses to the treatment and adjusts it" (p. 126). Two realistic goals were proposed by Cronbach for applied psychology, "One reasonable aspiration is to assess local events accurately, to improve short-run control. The other reasonable aspiration is to develop explanatory concepts, concepts that will help people use their heads" (1975, p. 126). The use of short-run empiricism (problem-solving) and the selection of behavior change or instructional design principles from the available literature (selecting explanatory concepts and using our heads) is the contemporary application of Cronbach's suggestions for moving beyond the rigidity and insufficiency of the two disciplines of scientific psychology.

School Psychology Applications

Parallels to Cronbach's two disciplines in traditional and modern school psychology are easily identified. Although experimental trends were apparent in the earliest roots of school psychology (Sandoval, 1993), most of school psychology's history has been devoted to practice consistent with the correlational and ATI bases for practice (Ysseldyke, 1973). The relatively infrequent use, until recently, of single-subject designs and behavioral interventions represent the clearest applications of the experimental discipline.

The correlational parallel occurs with traditional placement services in which referred children are assessed to determine if they meet the criteria for classification as disabled. Children with low scores on measures of current intellectual functioning and academic achievement, or large discrepancies between the scores on intellectual and achievement measures, are often placed in different educational programs for part or all of their school day. The differential placement is seen as necessary to allow children to benefit educationally because the general education program is inappropriate to their naturally occurring aptitudes, a classic application of the correlational discipline described by Cronbach in 1957. The earliest roots of school psychology (Fagan, 1992; Fagan & Wise, 1994) and a substantial proportion of current practice involves assessment of children's aptitudes and achievement as the basis for placement decisions. This application of the correlational science is valid to the degree that the placements are different and beneficial for individuals, groups, or systems, an issue to which we will return in a subsequent section.

UNRESOLVED PROBLEMS IN CURRENT PRACTICE

Concerns about and alternatives to the traditional practice of school psychology have become increasingly prominent over the last 20 years. These problems and suggested solutions closely parallel the different applications of the two disciplines of scientific psychology, the ATI movement, and Cronbach's endorsement of practice that is informed by theory and research and guided by a methodology of short-run empiricism.

Nature of Current Practice

Survey studies of the practice of school psychology yield consistent results (Reschly & Wilson, 1995; Smith, 1984). School psychologists devote about two-thirds of their time to activities related to special education classification and placement, with slightly over half of the time devoted to individual assessment activities, usually with standardized measures of ability and achievement. These surveys also indicate that current practitioners prefer to spend more time in direct and indirect activities related to interventions such as individual counseling and problem-solving consultation. The value of the current time allocations depends heavily on the benefits to students associated with classification as disabled and placement in special education programs. Do differential diagnoses such as mild mental retardation (MMR) or specific learning disability (SLD) lead to different treatments, and are those treatments differentially effective depending on the student's diagnosis?

Effectiveness of Special Education

The single greatest problem with current practice is the uncertain benefits of special education classification and program placement for students with mild disabilities (mild disabilities constitute approximate-ly 85% to 90% of the students in special education programs; Algozzine & Korinek, 1985; Reschly, 1987). This is an old problem (e.g., Dunn, 1968). Yet recent evidence provides little confidence in the utility of current diagnostic categories or in treatments based on aptitudes (Kavale, 1990).

In Table 1 the outcomes of program placement and aptitude-based treatments are summarized based on Kavale's 1990 review. The first two rows contain the average effect of being classified as MMR or SLD and placed in special education. These meta-analyses are consistent with the interpretation that classification as MMR or SLD and special education placement produces negligible effects in the former case and weak effects in the latter case. Traditional aptitude-based treatments also fare poorly in the meta-analyses (see the third and fourth rows in Table 1). Matching instructional methodology to visually based or auditorially based aptitudes has no positive effects. The disappointing outcomes associated with traditional diagnoses such as MMR and SLD and with matching intervention methodology to aptitudes is part of the "push" toward system reform.

Nonfunctional and Stigmatizing Labels

In most states, a specific disability must be designated as part of a classification and placement process whereby children and youth with learning and behavior problems receive special education and related services. School psychologists usually are the key players in determining which disability is most appropriate for a specific student. The critical question is, "Do the mild disability categories make any difference to treatment?" (Reschly, 1987, 1988; Ysseldyke, 1973, 1988; Ysseldyke, Algozzine, Regan, & McGue, 1981; Ysseldyke, Algozzine, Shinn, & McGue, 1982; Ysseldyke, Thurlow, Christenson, & Weiss, 1987).

Substantial evidence indicates that the same treatment goals and teaching strategies are adopted regardless of the category of mild disability (Reynolds & Lakin, 1987). For example, the top IEP goals typically are reading, then math, then written expression regardless of whether the disability is MMR, SLD, or behavior disorder (BD), and the same teaching strategies are used regardless of disability category. Furthermore, programs for low achieving students (e.g., Chapter I) and special education for students with mild disabilities are highly similar in terms of the needs of the students served and the intervention methodology used. Despite these similarities, markedly different levels of financial support are provided in special education and Chapter I, often on the basis of a few points on a test or a pair of tests. Some students are called disabled (and lots more money spent on their education) while others remain in regular education with little assistance. Do these distinctions make sense? It is difficult to justify the

TABLE 1
Summary of Effect Sizes in Meta-Analyses of Placements and Interventions

Placement/Intervention	Effect Size[a]
MMR Diagnosis/ Special Education Placement	−.14
SLD Diagnosis/Special Education Placement	.29
Modality Matched Instruction (Auditory Strength)	.03
Modality Matched Instruction (Visual Strength)	.04
Behavior Modification/Behavior Therapy (Social Behavior Goals)	.93
Curriculum-Based Progress Monitoring with Formative Evaluation	.70
Curriculum-Based Progress Monitoring with Formative Evaluation and Systematic Use of Reinforcement	1.00

Note. The results in this table are abstracted from results reported by Fuchs and Fuchs (1986) and Kavale (1990). Interested readers are referred to those sources for more information.

[a]Effect size expresses in standard deviation units the average results of interventions, placements, or treatments from many studies.

labeling process if program benefits are not clearly documented (Gallagher, 1972) and if differential treatment is not related to the category assigned (Cromwell, Blashfield, & Strauss, 1975; Heller, Holtzman, & Messick, 1982). System reform efforts often involve noncategorical special education, with less emphasis on finding the right category, or differential diagnosis among disabilities, and more emphasis on determination of programming needs and design of interventions (Reynolds & Lakin, 1987; Ysseldyke, 1988).

The Special Problem of Specific Learning Disabilities

Nearly every system reform discussion focuses more attention on SLD than any other area. Why? Because of the "Willie Sutton" reason. Sutton, a notorious bank robber in the 1930s, was asked, "Why do you rob banks?" His reply was, "That's where the money is." Similarly, the reason for the focus on SLD is that although SLD is only 1 of 13 categories of disability recognized in federal legislation, slightly over half of all students with disabilities are classified as SLD.

Although there are many tantalizing findings in the LD research, few generalizations can be made beyond the observation that students with LD have low achievement, most often in reading. The same conclusion applies to students in Chapter I programs. Notably absent in the LD research and practice is evidence for validated differential treatment based on the LD diagnosis or the identification of reliable subtypes of LD for whom matching treatment to subtype produces better outcomes (Epps, Ysseldyke, & McGue, 1984; Shinn, Tindal, Spira, & Marston, 1987; Shinn, Ysseldyke, Deno, & Tindal, 1986; Sleeter, 1986; Ysseldyke & Algozzine, 1983; Ysseldyke, Algozzine, & Epps, 1983; Ysseldyke, Algozzine et al., 1982;

Ysseldyke, Thurlow, Graden, Wesson, Algozzine, & Deno, 1983).

Treatment Validity of Assessment Procedures

In Table 2 the most frequently used assessment procedures by school psychologists in a 1991–1992 survey are listed. Two rather dramatic conclusions are apparent from examination of this list. First, many of the instruments have mediocre to poor technical characteristics (Christenson & Ysseldyke, 1989; Reschly, 1980; Salvia & Ysseldyke, 1978, 1995; Witt, 1986; Ysseldyke, Algozzine, Regan, & Potter, 1980; Ysseldyke & Thurlow, 1984). Second, the instruments with strong technical characteristics (Wechsler Scales and Woodcock-Johnson Achievement) have relatively little application to the determination of specific treatment needs or to monitoring and evaluating the effects of treatments. As noted in a *Buros Mental Measurements Yearbook* review, the Wechsler Scales have excellent technical characteristics related to determining relative standing in a normative group, information useful for classification but largely irrelevant to treatment: "In short, the WISC-R lacks treatment validity in that its use does not enhance remedial interventions for children who show specific academic skill deficiencies" (Witt & Gresham, 1985, p. 1717).

Aptitude by Treatment Approaches

The original ATI applications in school psychology and special education involved *training* weak areas in perceptual-motor or psycholinguistic domains, or *matching* instructional methodology to strong areas in these domains (Mann, 1979). By the early 1980s these approaches generally were viewed as ineffective (Arter & Jenkins, 1977, 1979; Hammill & Larsen, 1974, 1978; Kavale, 1981; Kavale & Mattson,

TABLE 2
School Psychologists' Self-Report of Assessment Instruments' Use Per Month

Instrument	Times Used Per Month
Structured Observation Procedures[a]	10.64
Wechsler Scales[b]	10.08
Bender Motor Gestalt Test	7.06
Draw-A-Person	5.30
Anecdotal or Unstructured Observation	4.84
House–Tree–Person	4.13
Developmental Test of Visual-Motor Integration	3.71
Kinetic Family Drawings	3.65
Woodcock-Johnson Achievement	3.59
Wide Range Achievement	2.59

Source: Wilson & Reschly, (1994).

[a]Total of duration, event, interval, and time sampling observations.

[b]Includes WISC–R, WAIS–R, and WPPSI.

1983; Ysseldyke, 1973; Ysseldyke & Mirkin, 1982). Despite this negative evidence and the more general complications of ATI research (Cronbach, 1975), the practice of attempting to match instruction to aptitude strengths continues to be prominent in some recommendations for school psychology practice. Recent aptitude constructs used in the matching process involve cognitive processing strengths such as successive or simultaneous processing or neuropsychologically intact areas (Hartlage & Reynolds, 1981; Hartlage & Telzrow, 1986; Kaufman, Goldstein, & Kaufman, 1984; Kaufman & Kaufman, 1983; Reynolds, 1981, 1986, 1992). These aptitude-by-treatment constructs have been no more successful than their information-processing-modality predecessors (Ayers & Cooley, 1986; Ayers, Cooley, & Severson, 1988; Good, Vollmer, Creek, Katz, & Chowdhri, 1993). Indeed, the major barrier to the use of these more recent aptitude constructs in school psychology is the near total absence of treatment outcome results wherein the aptitudes are assessed, intervention methodology is matched and mismatched to these aptitudes, interventions are implemented, and results are carefully examined (Teeter, 1987, 1989). Whether aptitude is conceptualized as cognitive processes, information processing modalities, or intact neurological areas, Cronbach's (1975) characterization of ATI is still accurate, "Once we attend to interactions, we enter a hall of mirrors that extends to infinity" (p. 119).

Disjointed Incrementalism

Disjointed incrementalism refers to the increasingly separate general and special education systems and the myriad of special programs with separate funding streams and eligibility criteria but similar goals and clientele (Reynolds, Wang, & Walberg, 1987). The consequences of the current organization of services is inefficient use of funds, uncoordinated programs, curricular discontinuity, and limited generalization of effects across settings. System reform plans typically attempt to combine various services and achieve better integration of general and special education programs.

Quality of Interventions

One of the greatest concerns is the quality of current interventions (Flugum & Reschly, 1994; Gresham, 1989; Gresham, Gansle, Noell, Cohen, & Rosenblum, 1993). Basic intervention principles often are not implemented in IEPs, special education programs, and prereferral interventions, and these interventions typically are not evaluated using individualized, treatment sensitive measures. Absence of high quality interventions coupled with poor evaluation of individual progress may alone account for the undocumented benefits of special education.

Disproportionate Minority Placement

Disproportionate minority placement may be the quintessential special education issue in the last quarter of this century, an issue that has not gone away (U.S. Department of Education, 1992). Most analyses of this issue have focused on testing and placement processes. Such analyses answer some questions but miss the main issue: specifically, the effectiveness of special education programs for students with mild disabilities and the development of effective alternatives that meet the enormous needs of economically disadvantaged students who are now overrepresented in special education (Reschly, Kicklighter, & McKee, 1988a, 1988b).

Consider these facts. More money is spent on the student's education in special education. There is a lower student–teacher ratio. The program is individualized and the teacher typically has additional training. Yet plaintiffs representing minority students overrepresented in special education programs clearly did not see special education as a good bargain. Why? Was it because of overrepresentation? That is a simple answer, but it is as wrong as it is simple! Consider other programs such as Head Start and Chapter I. More overrepresentation exists in those programs than in special education and those programs involve many more students. But there has been scant concern raised about overrepresentation in these areas.

If overrepresentation is not the answer, then what explains the motivation of minority plaintiffs? Scrutiny of the evidence presented by plaintiffs, judicial decisions, and other writings by plaintiffs provides clear evidence that overrepresentation was a symptom associated with critical assumptions about classification as disabled and placement in special education. Plaintiffs asserted that classification was stigmatizing and associated with few if any benefits because of the ineffectiveness of special education programs and that biases in referral, assessment, and decision making caused the overrepresentation. Although some of these assumptions are incorrect, or at least arguable, defending the effectiveness of special education was the most difficult challenge for the defendant school districts and state departments of education in the overrepresentation litigation (Reschly et al., 1988a, 1988b).

SYSTEM REFORM

Attention to the most effective ways that school psychologists can promote the mental health and educational interests of children and youth has been prominent in the modern school psychology literature (e.g., Cutts, 1955; Gray, 1963). The current Zeitgeist in school psychology began about 15 years ago with two national conferences on the future of psychology in the schools (Ysseldyke, 1982). Interested readers are referred to several papers from these conferences that appeared in special issues of the *School Psychology Review* (see especially Grimes, 1981; Trachtman, 1981).

One of the most influential documents developed soon after the conferences was *School Psychology: A Blueprint for Training and Practice* (Ysseldyke, Reynolds, & Weinberg, 1984). Key recommendations in *Blueprint* have been incorporated in other policy statements and reform documents. The most important themes in *Blueprint* were:

1. Eliminating the categorical classification of students with mild disabilities and replacing those classification and placement practices with interventions in natural settings guided by problem-solving procedures with curriculum-based and behavioral assessment measures.

2. Greater emphasis on systems to manage challenging behaviors rather than individual, within-child studies to identify disorders.

3. Greater emphasis on increasing the capabilities of general education to provide appropriate programs for children with learning and behavior problems rather than diagnosis of disabilities and placement outside of general education.

4. Transformation of psychologists' roles from individual diagnoses of disabilities to support of classroom instruction in academic and social behaviors through problem-solving consultation and direct interventions.

5. Closer working relationships among parents and teachers to capitalize on opportunities to develop interventions designed and implemented simultaneously by parents and school officials.

In 1985 the policy statement, "Advocacy for Appropriate Educational Services for All Children" was passed unanimously by the Executive Board and Delegate Assembly of the National Association of School Psychologists (NASP). One year later that body unanimously adopted the policy statement, "Rights Without Labels." Both statements rejected the traditional methods of classifying children as disabled in order to provide services and strongly advocated development of systems that provided services and supports needed by children and youth without labeling them "disabled." Both statements proposed establishment of experimental system change programs that would investigate ways to provide services without labeling and, at the same time, maintain rigorous protection of the rights of parents and students.

In the late 1980s the knowledge base for school psychologists' roles in reformed systems was significantly improved by the publication of an alternative delivery systems monograph (Graden, Zins, & Curtis, 1988), followed a few years later by a monograph on interventions (Stoner, Shinn, & Walker, 1991). Parallel to these developments was the special education research synthesis project culminating in a two-volume compendium of research reviews (Wang, Reynolds, & Walberg, 1987, 1988) and a synthesis of these reviews (Wang, Reynolds, & Walberg, 1990). Several of the major system reform recommendations in the synthesis were reminiscent of the classification project led by Hobbs (1975). Common to both was the concern about the usefulness of traditional disability designations such as SLD, MMR, and BD. Common to both was the commitment to providing necessary instructional and support services to children and youth with learning and behavior problems in natural settings to the greatest extent possible and to better implementation of the available knowledge base regarding instructional design and behavior change principles.

A recent policy statement on assessment and eligibility in special education goes still further in delineating the system changes needed to capitalize optimally on the current knowledge base regarding assessment and intervention (NASP-NASDSE-OSEP, 1994). Again, the first step emphasized is to change the categorical classification system and to fund services and supports needed by children and youth without disability categories. This statement establishes the context for applying the knowledge base on system reform (see Graden et al., 1988) and principles of instructional design and behavior change (see Stoner et al., 1991) through describing a comprehensive problem-solving approach that would be used to determine eligibility for services, to organize and provide those services, to monitor progress and change programs as needed, and to evaluate outcomes.

Summary

We are *pushed* by problems in the current system to consider alternatives to conventional referral, assessment, classification, and placement practices. These pushes provide the motivation to consider alternatives. Policy statements over the past decade have described the necessary changes in the delivery system that will permit the delivery of psychological services more closely related to the needs of children, youth, and families. Although the way to a reformed and more effective practice of school psychology has been charted in a general way, descriptions are still needed of specific bodies of knowledge, assessment skills, and intervention competencies.

ADVANCES IN ASSESSMENT AND INTERVENTION

We are *pulled* to delivery system alternatives by advances in assessment and intervention techniques that have the promise to substantially improve the outcomes of special education. Implementation of these alternatives has the potential for creating a revolution in how school psychology is practiced in the United States (Reschly, 1988; Ysseldyke, Reynolds, & Weinberg, 1984).

Assessment has been, and will continue to be, a salient activity in the roles of school psychologists; however, vast changes will occur with system reform in assessment purposes, techniques, and outcomes (Christenson & Ysseldyke, 1989; Reschly, 1980, 1986; Ysseldyke, 1984; Ysseldyke & Christenson, 1988; Ysseldyke & Thurlow, 1984). Purposes will focus more on interventions, specifically, what can be changed in environments to produce improved learning and behavior. In the first edition of *Assessment in Special and Remedial Education*, Salvia and Ysseldyke (1978) described five purposes for assessing students: screening, classification, instructional planning, pupil evaluation, and program evaluation. Fifteen years later developments in assessment practices required expansion of that characterization to recognition of 13 kinds of decisions made with assessment information (Salvia & Ysseldyke, 1995). These 13 decisions are organized into four areas: pre-referral classroom-based decisions, entitlement decisions, postentitlement classroom decisions, and accountability/outcomes decisions (see Figure 1). Assessment practices are expanding; they are moving to earlier stages of intervention and to new kinds of decisions.

Techniques will increasingly involve gathering information in natural environments with direct measures of behaviors that can be used frequently as interventions are implemented. These measures will be used to define problems, to establish intervention goals, to monitor progress, and to evaluate outcomes. These measures also will be used as the basis for classification of students as eligible for more intensive instructional or social/emotional intervention programs, including special education (Deno, 1985; Germann & Tindal, 1985; Marston & Magnusson, 1988; Reschly, 1986; Shapiro, 1989; Shapiro & Kratochwill, 1988; Shinn, 1989; Shinn & Marston, 1985; Shinn, Tindal, & Stein, 1988).

Outcomes Orientation

A major shift to a focus on outcomes rather than intervention inputs or processes is apparent in the reform literature. An outcomes orientation has been applied to analyses of overrepresentation of minority students in special education (Reschly, 1979; Reschly & Tilly, 1993). Greater attention to documentation of outcomes is pervasive in general and special education (Ysseldyke, Thurlow, & Bruininks, 1992). The push to document the outcomes of education has its roots in concern by business and community leaders about the relatively low-level skills exhibited by the people they hire and in concern about the relatively low standing of American students in international comparisons. It used to be the case that directors of special education described their special education programs by talking about numbers of students, categories of students, settings in which they were educated (e.g., resource rooms), and kinds of teachers and instructional programs. Now the scene is shifting and administrators are being asked about the extent to which students reach outcomes (read, write, and cipher).

State education agencies are specifying standards, goals, or outcomes students are to achieve and are devising ways to measure attainment of out-

FIGURE 1. **Assessment decisions (Salvia & Ysseldyke, 1995).**

Assessment Decisions

Pre-Referral Classroom Decisions
Decisions to Provide Special Help or Enrichment
Referral to an Intervention Assistance Team
Decision to Provide Intervention Assistance

Entitlement Decisions
Screening Decisions
Referral Decisions
Exceptionality
Document Special Learning Needs
Eligibility Decisions

Post-Entitlement Classroom Decisions
Instructional Planning Decisions
Setting Decisions
Progress Evaluation Decisions

Accountability/Outcome Decisions
Program Evaluation Decisions
Accountability Decisions

comes. The national education goals panel is reporting on the extent to which students are achieving national education goals. Some states include students with disabilities in their outcomes assessment practices, others exclude these students. Approximately 40% to 50% of school-age students with disabilities are excluded from some of the most prominent national educational-data-collection programs (McGrew, Thurlow, & Spiegel, 1993). School psychologists are increasingly involved in the business of helping specify indicators and measures of outcomes that stakeholders believe are important. As they do so, a number of conceptual and technical issues arise (Thurlow & Ysseldyke, 1994).

Problem-Solving Orientation

Several problem-solving approaches have appeared in the literature, with slight variations related to intended population or type of problem (Bergan, 1977; Bergan & Kratochwill, 1990; Gutkin & Curtis, 1990; Knoff & Batsche, 1991; Rosenfield, 1987). All have common features involving problem definition, direct measures of behaviors, design of interventions, monitoring of progress with intervention revisions as necessary, and outcomes evaluation. All are more consistent with the experimental tradition in psychology as well as the short-run empiricism described by Cronbach (1975) as a promising replacement for interventions guided by aptitude-by-treatment interactions.

Problem solving is an essential component of implementing advances in assessment and interventions. We caution against superficial versions of problem solving, particularly those that do not involve precisely defined problems, direct measures of behavior, preintervention data collection, intentional application of instructional design and behavioral change principles, frequent progress monitoring with program changes as needed, and evaluation of outcomes through comparisons to initial levels of performance. As Fuchs and Fuchs (1992) noted, "feel good" consultation is likely to make the participants (e.g., psychologist and teacher) feel good, with little benefit to students.

Problem solving provides the overall structure for an alternative delivery system. Different levels of problem solving are illustrated in Figure 2, which represents the system developed by the Heartland Area Education Agency in Iowa. The four levels of problem solving involve different degrees of intensity and different levels of special education and support services involvement. The first two levels are conceived as occurring entirely within general education with occasional involvement of related services providers such as psychologists. Level III problem solving, involving related services personnel, is a rigorous, data-driven, intervention effort that must meet exacting standards for parent involvement, problem definition, systematic data collection, problem analysis, goal, intervention plan development, intervention

FIGURE 2. Heartland Area Education Agency Levels of Problem Solving.

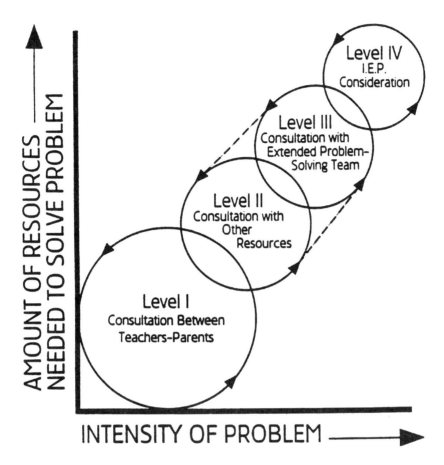

PROBLEM SOLVING APPROACH

Source: *Program Manual for Special Education,* pp. 17. (Heartland Area Education Agency, 6500 Corporate Drive, Johnston, IA 50131)

plan implementation, progress monitoring, and decision making. Detailed standards have been developed for each of these problem-solving components (Bureau of Special Education, 1994). Interventions meeting these quality indices must be implemented for a reasonable period of time and found to be insufficient according to progress monitoring data before Level IV problem solving is initiated.

In Level IV problem solving, classification of the student as needing special education may be considered based on documentation of (a) substantial discrepancies from average levels of classroom performance that are not resolved to a sufficient degree by high quality interventions in general education or (b) behavioral discrepancies that require programming elements or instructional intensity beyond the resources that reasonably can be provided in general education. This system depends heavily on problem

solving, curriculum-based and behavioral assessment, and high quality interventions. A critical eligibility criterion is resistance to intervention (Gresham, 1991), with rigorous standards established for quality of interventions. Further discussion of each of these areas appears in other chapters in this volume.

Assessment Technology and Decision Making

Significant advances in assessment technology permit greater emphasis on measures functionally related to interventions. Most of these advances can be classified as behavioral assessment procedures (Shapiro & Kratochwill, 1988). The knowledge base for practice has improved substantially with the development of curriculum-based assessment and curriculum-based measurement (Deno, 1985; Howell,

Fox, & Morehead, 1993; Shapiro, 1989; Shinn, 1989). Advances in the assessment of instructional environments provides further technological support to academic and behavioral interventions (Christenson, Ysseldyke, & Thurlow, 1989; Ysseldyke & Christenson, 1987a, 1987b, 1993; Ysseldyke, Christenson, & Kovaleski, 1994; Ysseldyke & Marston, 1990). Parallel advances in behavioral assessment of social and emotional phenomena have led to equally substantial improvements in practice in these areas (Alessi & Kaye, 1983; Shapiro & Kratochwill, 1988). Technologically sophisticated assessment methods, Ecobehavioral Assessment Systems Software (EBASS; Greenwood, Carta, Kamps, Terry, & Delquadri, 1994) have been developed to aid in the detailed collection of observational data in classrooms.

The assessment technology to support practice guided by an outcomes criterion is now available for the first time in the history of school psychology. Behavioral assessment measures also can be used in decisions about eligibility for various special programs and in decisions about placement (Gresham, 1985, 1991; Shinn, 1988; Shinn et al., 1988). It appears that virtually the same students will be identified as needing specialized instruction and social-emotional interventions using behavioral assessment procedures; however, the behavioral assessment procedures yield information useful for intervention planning and evaluation as well as eligibility determination.

Instructional Design

Behavior assessment and instructional analysis are inextricably related in functional assessment of academic behaviors. The marriage of instructional design principles (e.g., Englemann & Carnine, 1982) with behavioral intervention technologies have produced impressive outcomes for students (Becker & Carnine, 1980; Kavale, 1990). As noted in the last three rows of Table 1, the effects of interventions based on behavior therapy principles, combined with progress monitoring and changes in programming based on results (Fuchs & Fuchs, 1986; recall Cronbach's short-run empiricism), produce strong effects according to the meta-analysis evidence. Use of this knowledge base produces results markedly superior to traditional special education programs or instruction based on matching teaching methods to presumed strengths in cognitive style, information processing, or neuropsychological status. Much of system reform is driven by the desire to implement more effective interventions.

Behavior Change

Behavior change principles are well established (Stoner et al., 1991; Sulzer-Azaroff & Mayer, 1991). In addition, characteristics of effective schools and effective teaching are well represented in the school psychology literature (e.g., Bickel, 1990). There is a solid knowledge base for assessment and intervention; however, the remedial programs for most children and youth do not apply all, or even most, of this knowledge base.

Summary

One of the main themes in system reform is improved application of the available knowledge on assessment, instruction, learning, and behavior change. Improved application of this knowledge base will be facilitated by the movement toward noncategorical classification and integration of diverse programs intended to serve children and youth. Reductions in the amount of time devoted to standardized testing to determine eligibility will permit greater opportunities for school psychologists to be involved in new roles related to functional assessment, interventions, and evaluation of student progress.

POLITICAL VALIDITY OF SYSTEM REFORM

The major statements on system reform emphasize the importance of the *process* whereby reforms are designed and implemented. The system reform statement endorsed unanimously by the NASP Delegate Assembly in March 1985 stressed, "the development and piloting of alternatives" as well as the "need to assure that no child is put at risk for loss of services while the change process is occurring" (National Association of School Psychologists, 1985). Since 1985, NASP has devoted considerable resources to critical elements of system reform including policy advocacy and continuing education of school psychologists (Cobb & Dawson, 1989; Graden et al., 1988; Stoner et al., 1991). Politically valid reforms have the critical elements of fair and equitable distribution of resources, involvement in decision making, protection of jobs, and continuing education opportunities (Jenkins, Pious, & Peterson, 1988).

Resource Allocation

System reform often involves development of different ways to fund programs. Two protections are critical. First, system reform cannot be allowed to become a way to reduce financial support of special and remedial programs for children and youth. The legitimacy of system reform requires at least stable resources. Second, alternative methods of funding programs and alternative resource allocation procedures should first be pilot tested in smaller units (e.g., a few districts, or regional units in a state) before application to the entire system.

Involvement in Decision Making

Constituents of the present system should be involved in decision making regarding the design of alternative delivery systems. Constituents should be viewed broadly, including related services professionals, special educators, general educators, parents, and children and youth. Leadership by psychologists is essential to successful system reform; indeed, the major advances in assessment and interventions on which reforms are based originated in basic and applied psychology! Ensuring that the available knowledge base is implemented is a crucial role for psychologists in system reform.

Protection of Jobs

Practitioners in the current system are asked in system reform to support significant changes that affect the way they do their jobs and the kinds of professional roles that are valued. The roles of some practitioners may change dramatically. The legitimacy of system reform depends on guaranteeing the employment of these persons, at least in the short term, and providing for them ample continuing education opportunities to acquire skills needed in the new system. Each individual should get a fair shot at continuing his or her employment in a valued role if they are willing to acquire the skills needed in the new system.

Continuing Education

Continuing education opportunities are perhaps the single most important feature of system reform. Most of us have ample continuing education needs, expressed eloquently by one of our leading scholars, "I have saved my course notes from graduate school. With the exception of statistics, everything I was taught no longer is true" (Bardon, 1981, p. 202). The advances in assessment and intervention are not well represented in all graduate school psychology programs; indeed, it is our observation that many of us who are university faculty have continuing education needs that equal and, in most cases, exceed those of typical practitioners!

Traditional school psychology training provides an essential foundation for system reform that can be used as a base in meeting our continuing education needs. The knowledge base in learning, normal and exceptional patterns of development, sensitivity to cultural differences, measurement, assessment, counseling methods, and relationship skills is unique among related services personnel and essential to successful performance of roles in new systems. To this traditional knowledge base, systematic problem solving, consultation, principles of behavior change, principles of instructional design, and functional assessment need to be added.

The design of continuing education is crucial (Reschly & Grimes, 1991). Most current continuing education can be characterized as "train and hope" because actual supervised practice with feedback in implementation of new skills is not provided. Effective continuing education that leads to persistent changes in professional services requires a multistep process, that is,

1. Awareness and knowledge acquisition.

2. Demonstration.

3. Simulated try-out with feedback.

4. Implementation in the work setting with feedback.

5. Additional training opportunities to overcome problems that emerge in implementation.

6. Support and incentives for changing roles through performance evaluation and other mechanisms.

PARADIGM SHIFTING AND LEADERSHIP BY PSYCHOLOGISTS

The paradigm shift is occurring at different rates and in varying forms throughout the United States. There are, however, few states that have not been involved in special education reform and the pace of change is anticipated to quicken in the later part of the 1990s. We acknowledge that a paradigm shift does not occur quickly or easily; indeed, many unanticipated barriers have been encountered and there are undoubtedly more to come. Despite the necessity to acknowledge significant impediments to reform, we remain optimistic about the delivery system and role changes described in this and other chapters in this volume. Our faith is based on a conviction that the delivery system and role changes are in the best interests of children, youth, and families and that application of the outcomes criterion will increasingly invigorate and strengthen the support for a paradigm shift from the correlational science of prediction and placement to an experimental science of interventions designed to maximize learning guided by short-run empiricism. This paradigm shift means making differences in, rather than predictions about, students' lives.

REFERENCES

Alessi, G., & Kaye, J. (1983). *Behavioral Assessment for School Psychologists.* Washington, DC: National Association of School Psychologists.

Algozzine, B., & Korinek, L. (1985). Where is special education for students with high prevalence handicaps going? *Exceptional Children, 51,* 388–394.

Arter, J. A., & Jenkins, J. R. (1977). Examining the benefits and prevalence of modality considerations in special education. *Journal of Special Education, 11,* 281–298.

Arter, J. A., & Jenkins, J. R. (1979). Differential diagnosis — prescriptive teaching: A critical appraisal. *Review of Education Research, 49,* 517–555.

Ayers, R., & Cooley, E. J. (1986). Sequential versus simultaneous processing on the K-ABC: Validity in predicting learning success. *Journal of Psychoeducational Assessment, 4,* 211–220.

Ayers, R. R., Cooley, E. J., & Severson, H. H. (1988). Educational translation of the Kaufman Assessment Battery for Children: A construct validity study. *School Psychology Review, 17,* 113–124.

Bardon, J. I. (1981). A personalized account of the development and status of school psychology. *Journal of School Psychology, 19,* 199–210.

Becker, W. C., & Carnine, D. W. (1980). Direct instruction: An effective approach to educational intervention with the disadvantaged and low performers. In B. B. Lahey & A. K. Kazdin (Eds.), *Advances in clinical and child psychology* (vol. 3; pp. 429–473). New York: Plenum.

Bergan, J. R. (1977). *Behavioral consultation.* Columbus, OH: Charles E. Merrill.

Bergan, J. R., & Kratochwill, .T. R. (1990). *Behavioral consultation and therapy.* New York: Plenum.

Bickel, W. E. (1990). The effective schools literature: Implications for research and practice. In T. B. Gutkin & C. R. Reynolds (Eds.), *The handbook of school psychology* (2nd ed.; pp. 847–867). New York: Wiley.

Bureau of Special Education, Iowa Department of Education. (1994). *Professional Practices in Problem Solving.* Des Moines, IA: Author.

Christenson, S. L., & Ysseldyke, J. E. (1989). Assessing student performance … An important change is needed. *Journal of School Psychology, 27,* 409–426.

Christenson, S. L., Ysseldyke, J. E., & Thurlow, M. L. (1989). Critical instructional factors for students with mild handicaps. *Remedial and Special Education, 10,* 21–31.

Cobb, C. T., & Dawson, M. M. (1989). The evolution of children's services: Approaching maturity. *School Psychology Review, 18,* 203–208.

Cromwell, R., Blashfield, R., & Strauss, J. (1975). Criteria for classification systems. In N. Hobbs (Ed.), *Issues in the classification of children* (pp. 4–25). San Francisco, CA: Jossey-Bass.

Cronbach, L. J. (1957). The two disciplines of scientific psychology. *American Psychologist, 12,* 671–684.

Cronbach, L. J. (1975). Beyond the two disciplines of scientific psychology. *American Psychologist, 30,* 116–127.

Cutts, N. E. (1955). *School psychology at mid-century.* Washington, DC: American Psychological Association.

Deno, S. L. (1985). Curriculum-based measurement: The emerging alternative. *Exceptional Children, 52,* 219–232.

Dunn, L. (1968). Special education for the mildly retarded: Is much of it justifiable? *Exceptional Children, 35,* 5–22.

Englemann, S., & Carnine, D. (1982). *Theory of instruction: Principles and applications.* New York: Irvington.

Epps, S., Ysseldyke, J., & McGue, M. (1984). Differentiating LD and non-LD students: "I know one when I see one." *Learning Disability Quarterly, 7,* 89–101.

Fagan, T. K. (1992). Compulsory schooling, child study, clinical psychology, and special education: Origins of school psychology. *American Psychologist, 47,* 236–243.

Fagan, T. K., & Wise, P. S. (1994). *School psychology: Past, present, and future.* White Plains, NY: Longmans Publishing Group.

Flugum, K. R., & Reschly, D. J. (1994). Pre-referral interventions: Quality indices and outcomes. *Journal of School Psychology, 32,* 1–14.

Fuchs, D., & Fuchs, L. S. (1992). Limitations of a feel-good approach to consultation. *Journal of Educational and Psychological Consultation, 3,* 93–97.

Fuchs, L. S., & Fuchs, D. (1986). Effects of systematic formative evaluation: A meta-analysis. *Exceptional Children, 53,* 199–208.

Gallagher, J. (1972). The special education contract for mildly handicapped children. *Exceptional Children, 38,* 527–535.

Germann, G., & Tindal, G. (1985). An application of curriculum-based measurement: The use of direct and repeated measurement. *Exceptional Children, 52,* 244–265.

Good, R. H., Vollmer, M., Creek, R. J., Katz, L., & Chowdhri, S. (1993). Treatment utility of the Kaufman Assessment Battery for Children: Effects of matching instruction and student processing strength. *School Psychology Review, 2,* 8–26.

Graden, J. L., Zins, J. E., & Curtis, M. J. (Eds.). (1988). *Alternative educational delivery systems: Enhancing instructional options for all students.* Washington, DC: National Association of School Psychologists.

Gray, S. W. (1963). *The psychologist in the schools.* New York: Holt, Rinehart, & Winston.

Greenwood, C. R., Carta, J. J., Kamps, K., Terry, B., & Delquadri, J. (1994). Development and validation of standard classroom observation systems for school practitioners: Ecobehavioral Assessment Systems Software (EBASS). *Exceptional Children, 61,* 197–209.

Gresham, F. M. (1985). Behavior disorder assessment: Conceptual, definitional, and practical considerations. *School Psychology Review, 14,* 495–509.

Gresham, F. M. (1989). Assessment of treatment integrity in school consultation and prereferral intervention. *School Psychology Review, 18,* 37–50.

Gresham, F. M. (1991). Conceptualizing behavior disorders in terms of resistance to intervention. *School Psychology Review, 20,* 23–36.

Gresham, F. M., Gansle, K. A., Noell, G. H., Cohen, S., & Rosenblum, S. (1993). Treatment integrity of school-based interventions. *School Psychology Review, 22,* 254–272.

Grimes, J. (1981). Shaping the future of school psychology. *School Psychology Review, 10,* 206–231.

Gutkin, T. B., & Curtis, M. J. (1990). School-based consultation: Theory, techniques, and research. In T. B. Gutkin & C. R. Reynolds (Eds.), *The handbook of school psychology* (2nd ed.; pp. 577–611). New York: Wiley.

Hammill, D., & Larsen, S. (1974). The effectiveness of psycholinguistic training. *Exceptional Children, 41,* 5–14.

Hammill, D., & Larsen, S. (1978). The effectiveness of psycholinguistc training: A reaffirmation of position. *Exceptional Children, 44,* 402–414.

Hartlage, L. C., & Reynolds, C. R. (1981). Neuropsychological assessment and the individualization of instruction. In G. W. Hynd & J. E. Obrzut (Eds.), *Neurological assessment and the school age child: Issues and procedures.* New York: Grune & Stratton.

Hartlage, L. C., & Telzrow, C. E. (1986). *Neurological assessment and intervention with children and adolescents*. Sarasota, FL: Professional Resource Exchange.

Heartland Area Education Agency. (1994). *Program manual for special education*. Johnston, IA: Author. (Available from author, 6500 Corporate Drive, Johnston, IA 50131.)

Heller, K., Holtzman, W., & Messick, S. (Eds.). (1982). *Placing children in special education: A strategy for equity*. Washington, DC: National Academy Press.

Hobbs, N. (1975). *The future of children*. San Francisco: Jossey-Bass.

Howell, K. W., Fox, S. L., & Morehead, M. K. (1993). *Curriculum-based evaluation teaching and decision making* (2nd Ed.). Columbus, OH: Charles E. Merrill.

Jenkins, J. R., Pious, C. G., & Peterson, D. L. (1988). Categorical programs for remedial and handicapped students. *Exceptional Children, 55*, 147–158.

Kaufman, A., Goldsmith, B. Z., & Kaufman, N. L. (1984). *K-SOS: Kaufman sequential or simultaneous*. Circle Pines, MN: American Guidance Service.

Kaufman, A., & Kaufman, N. (1983). *Kaufman Assessment Battery for Children* (K–ABC). Circle Pines, MN: American Guidance Service.

Kavale, K. A. (1981). Functions of the Illinois Test of Psycholinguistic Abilities: Are they trainable? *Exceptional Children, 47*, 496–510.

Kavale, K. (1990). The effectiveness of special education. In T. B. Gutkin & C. R. Reynolds (Eds.), *The handbook of school psychology* (2nd ed.; pp. 868–898). New York: Wiley.

Kavale, K. A., & Mattson, P. D. (1983). "One jumped off the balance beam": Meta-analysis of perceptual-motor training. *Journal of Learning Disabilities, 16*, 165–173.

Knoff, H. M., & Batsche, G. M. (1991). Integrating school and educational psychology to meet the educational and mental health needs of all children. *Educational Psychologist, 26*, 167–183.

Mann, L. (1979). *On the trail of process*. New York: Grune & Stratton.

Marston, D., & Magnusson, D. (1988). Curriculum based measurement: District level implementation. In J. L. Graden, J. E. Zins, & M. J. Curtis (Eds.), *Alternative educational delivery systems: Enhancing instructional options for all students* (pp. 137–173). Washington, DC: National Association of School Psychologists.

McGrew, K., Thurlow, M. L., & Spiegel, R. (1993). An investigation of the exclusion of students with disabilities in national data collection programs. *Educational Evaluation and Policy Analysis, 15*, 339–352.

NASP/NASDSE/OSEP. (1994). *Assessment and eligibility in special education: An examination of policy and practice with proposals for change*. Alexandria, VA: National Association of State Directors of Special Education.

National Association of School Psychologists. (1985). Advocacy for appropriate educational services for all children. *School Psychology Review, 19*(4).

Reschly, D. J. (1979). Nonbiased assessment. In G. Phye & D. Reschly (Eds.), *School psychology: Perspectives and issues* (pp. 215–253). New York: Academic Press.

Reschly, D. J. (1980). School psychologists and assessment in the future. *Professional Psychology, 11*, 841–848.

Reschly, D. J. (1986). Functional psychoeducational assessment: Trends and issues. *Special Services in the Schools* (Special Issue on Emerging Perspectives on Assessment of Exceptional Children), *2*, 57–69.

Reschly, D. J. (1987). Learning characteristics of mildly handicapped students: Implications for classification, placement, and programming. In M. C. Wang, M. C. Reynolds, & H. J. Walberg (Eds.), *The handbook of special education: Research and practice* (Vol. I; pp. 35–58). Oxford, England: Pergamon Press.

Reschly, D. J. (1988). Special education reform: School psychology revolution. *School Psychology Review, 17*, 459–475.

Reschly, D. J., & Grimes, J. P. (1991). State department and university cooperation: Evaluation of continuing education in consultation and curriculum based assessment. *School Psychology Review, 20*, 519–526.

Reschly, D. J., Kicklighter, R. H., & McKee, P. (1988a). Recent placement litigation Part II, Minority EMR overrepresentation: Comparison of *Larry P.* (1979, 1984, 1986) with *Marshall* (1984, 1985) and *S-1* (1986). *School Psychology Review, 17*, 20–36.

Reschly, D. J., Kicklighter, R. H., & McKee, P. (1988b). Recent placement litigation, Part III: Analysis of differences in *Larry P., Marshall*, and *S-1* and implications for future practices. *School Psychology Review, 17*, 37–48.

Reschly, D. J., & Tilly, W. D. (1993). The WHY of system reform. *Communiqué, 22*(1), 1, 4–6.

Reschly, D. J., & Wilson, M. S. (1995). School psychology faculty and practitioners: 1986 to 1991 trends in demographic characteristics, roles, satisfaction, and system reform. *School Psychology Review, 24*.

Reynolds, C. R. (1981). Neuropsychological assessment and the habilitation learning: Considerations in the search for aptitude x treatment interaction. *School Psychology Review, 10*, 343–349.

Reynolds, C. R. (1986). Transactional models of intellectual development, Yes. Deficit models of process remediation, No. *School Psychology Review, 15*, 256–260.

Reynolds, C. R. (1992). Two key concepts in the diagnosis of learning disabilities and the habilitation of learning. *Learning Disability Quarterly, 15*, 2–12.

Reynolds, M. C., & Lakin, K. C. (1987). Noncategorical special education for mildly handicapped students. A system for the future. In M. C. Wang, M. C. Reynolds, & H. J. Walberg (Eds.), *The handbook of special education: Research and practice* (Vol. I; pp. 331–356). Oxford, England: Pergamon Press.

Reynolds, M. C., Wang, M. C., & Walberg, H. J. (1987). The necessary restructuring of special and regular education. *Exceptional Children, 53*, 391–398.

Rosenfield, S. A. (1987). *Instructional consultation*. Hillsdale, NJ: Erlbaum.

Salvia J., & Ysseldyke, J. E. (1978). *Assessment in special and remedial education*. Boston: Houghton-Mifflin.

Salvia, J., & Ysseldyke, J. E. (1995). *Assessment* (6th Ed.). Boston: Houghton-Mifflin Company.

Sandoval, J. (1993). The history of interventions in school psychology. *Journal of School Psychology, 31*, 195–217.

Shapiro, E. S. (Ed.). (1989). *Academic skills problems: Direct assessment and intervention*. New York: Guilford Press.

Shapiro, E. S., & Kratochwill, T. R. (Ed.). (1988). *Behavioral assessment in schools: Conceptual foundations and practical applications*. New York: Guilford Press.

Shinn, M. R. (1988). Development of curriculum-based norms for use in special education decision-making. *School Psychology Review, 17,* 61–80.

Shinn, M. R. (Ed.). (1989). *Curriculum-based measurement: Assessing special children.* New York: Guilford Press.

Shinn, M., & Marston, D. (1985). Using curriculum-based measures to identify mildly handicapped students. *Remedial and Special Education, 6*(2), 31–45.

Shinn, M. R., Tindal, G. A., Spira, D., & Marston, D. (1987). Practice of learning disabilities as social policy. *Learning Disabilities Quarterly, 10,* 17–28.

Shinn, M. R., Tindal, G. A., & Stein, S. (1988). Curriculum based measurement and the identification of mildly handicapped students. *Professional School Psychology, 3,* 69–85.

Shinn, M. R., Ysseldyke, J. E., Deno, S. L., & Tindal, G. A. (1986). A comparison of differences between students labeled learning disabled and low achieving on measures of classroom performance. *Journal of Learning Disabilities, 19,* 545–552.

Sleeter, C. (1986). Learning Disabilities: The social construction of a special education category. *Exceptional Children, 53,* 46–54.

Smith, D. K. (1984). Practicing school psychologists: Their characteristics, activities, and populations served. *Professional Psychology: Research and Practice, 15,* 798–810.

Stoner, G., Shinn, M. R., & Walker, H. M. (1991). *Interventions for achievement and behavior problems.* Washington, DC: National Association of School Psychologists.

Sulzer-Azaroff, B., & Mayer, G. R. (1991). *Behavior analysis for lasting change.* New York: Holt, Rinehart, & Winston.

Teeter, P. A. (1987). Review of neuropsychological assessment and intervention with children and adolescents. *School Psychology Review, 16,* 582–583.

Teeter, P. A. (1989). Neuropsychological approaches to the remediation of educational deficits. In C. R. Reynolds & E. Fletcher-Janzen (Eds.), *Handbook of clinical child neuropsychology* (pp. 357–376). New York: Plenum Press.

Thurlow, M. L., & Ysseldyke, J. E. (1994). Focusing on outcomes: Challenges for special education personnel. *Special Services in the Schools, 8,* 167–184.

Trachtman, G. M. (1981). On such a full sea. *School Psychology Review, 10,* 138–181.

U.S. Department of Education, Office of Special Education Programs. (1992). *Fourteenth Annual Report to Congress on the Implementation of the Individuals with Disabilities Education Act.* Washington, DC: Author.

Wang, M. C., Reynolds, M. C., & Walberg, H. J. (Eds.). (1987, 1988). *The handbook of special education: Research and practice* (Vol. 1–3). Oxford, England: Pergamon Press.

Wang, M. C., Reynolds, M. C., & Walberg, H. J. (Eds.). (1990). *Special education research and practice: Synthesis of findings.* Oxford, England: Pergamon Press.

Wang, M. C., & Walberg, H. J. (1988). Four fallacies of segregationism. *Exceptional Children, 55,* 128–137.

Wilson, M. S., & Reschly, D. J. (1994). The times they are a'changin': Assessment training and practice are not. Manuscript submitted for publication.

Witt, J. C. (1986). Review of the Wide Range Achievement Test–Revised. *Journal of Psychoeducational Assessment, 4,* 87–90.

Witt, J. C., & Gresham, F. M. (1985). Review of the Wechsler Intelligence Scale for Children Revised. In J. Mitchell (Ed.), *Ninth mental measurements yearbook* (pp. 1716–1719). Lincoln, NE: Buros Institute.

Ysseldyke, J. E. (1973). Diagnostic-prescriptive teaching: The search for aptitude–treatment interactions. In L. Mann & D. Sabatino (Eds.), *The first review of special education.* New York: Grune & Stratton.

Ysseldyke, J. E. (1982). The Spring Hill Symposium on the future of psychology in the schools. *American Psychologist, 37,* 547–552.

Ysseldyke, J. E. (Ed.). (1984). *School psychology: The state of the art.* Minneapolis, MN: University of Minnesota, National School Psychology Inservice Training Network.

Ysseldyke, J. E. (1988). Classification of handicapped students. In M. C. Wang, M. C. Reynolds, & H. J. Walberg (Eds.), *The handbook of special education: Research and practice* (Vol. 1; pp. 253–271). Oxford, England: Pergamon Press.

Ysseldyke, J. E., & Algozzine, B. (1983). LD or not LD: That's not the question! *Journal of Learning Disabilities, 16,* 29–31.

Ysseldyke, J. E., Algozzine, B., & Epps, S. (1983). A logical and empirical analysis of current practice in classifying students as handicapped. *Exceptional Children, 50,* 160–166.

Ysseldyke, J. E., Algozzine, B., Regan, R., & McGue, M. (1981). The influence of test scores and naturally occurring pupil characteristics on psychoeducational decision making with children. *Journal of School Psychology, 19,* 167–177.

Ysseldyke, J. E., Algozzine, B., Regan, R., & Potter, M. (1980). Technical adequacy of tests used by professionals in simulated decision making. *Psychology in the Schools, 17,* 202–209.

Ysseldyke, J. E., Algozzine, B., Shinn, M., & McGue, M. (1982). Similarities and differences between low achievers and students classified learning disabled. *The Journal of Special Education, 16,* 73–85.

Ysseldyke, J. E., & Christenson, S. L. (1987a). *The instructional environment scale.* Austin, TX: Pro-Ed.

Ysseldyke, J. E., & Christenson, S. L. (1987b). Evaluating students' instructional environments. *Remedial and Special Education, 8,* 17–24.

Ysseldyke, J. E., & Christenson, S. L. (1988). *Linking assessment to intervention.* In J. L. Graden, J. E. Zins, & M. J. Curtis (Eds.), *Alternative educational delivery systems: Enhancing instructional options for all students* (pp. 91–110). Washington, DC: National Association of School Psychologists.

Ysseldyke, J. E., & Christenson, S. L. (1993). *The Instructional Environment System–II.* Longmont, CO: SOPRIS West.

Ysseldyke, J. E., & Christenson, S. L., & Kovaleski, J. (1994). Identifying students' instructional needs in the context of classroom and home environments. *Teaching Exceptional Children, 26*(3), 37–41.

Ysseldyke, J. E., & Marston, D. (1990). The need of assessment information to plan instructional interventions: A review of the research. In T. B. Gutkin & C. R. Reynolds (Eds.), *The handbook of school psychology* (2nd ed.; pp. 661–682). New York: Wiley.

Ysseldyke, J. E., & Mirkin, P. K. (1982). The use of assessment information to plan instructional interventions: A review of the research. In C. R. Reynolds & T. B. Gutkin (Eds.), *The handbook of school psychology.* New York: Wiley.

Ysseldyke, J. E., Reynolds, M. C., & Weinberg, R. A. (1984). *School psychology: A blueprint for training and practice.*

Minneapolis, MN: National School Psychology Inservice Training Network, University of Minnesota.

Ysseldyke, J. E., & Thurlow, M. L. (1984). Assessment practices in special education: Adequacy and appropriateness. *Educational Psychologist, 19,* 123–137.

Ysseldyke, J. E., Thurlow, M. L., & Bruininks, R. H. (1992). Expected educational outcomes for students with disabilities. *Remedial and Special Education, 13*(6), 19–30.

Ysseldyke, J. E., Thurlow, M., Christenson, S. L., & Weiss, J. (1987). Time allocated to instruction of mentally retarded, learning disabled, emotionally disturbed, and nonhandicapped elementary students. *Journal of Special Education, 21,* 43–55.

Ysseldyke, J. E., Thurlow, M., Graden, J., Wesson, C., Algozzine, B., & Deno, S. (1983). Generalizations from five years of research on assessment and decision making: The University of Minnesota Institute. *Exceptional Education Quarterly, 4,* 75–93.

2

Best Practices in Professional Conduct: Meeting NASP's Ethical Standards

Philip B. Bowser
Roseburg (Oregon) Public Schools

OVERVIEW

Ethos, the Greek root for "ethics," refers to "the characteristics and distinguishing attitudes, habits, beliefs, etc. of an individual or of a group" (Guralnik, 1974). Over the years, the word transformed into *ethics*, the branch of philosophy that deals with conduct and character, and the concepts of right and wrong (Singer, 1993). Professional groups eventually applied the term to rules and regulations that limit the range of acceptable behavior for members of the group. There should be a central core of commonly shared beliefs applicable to all school psychologists (including graduate students, university professors, research specialists, internship/practicum supervisors, etc.), regardless of job site, and pertinent to the manner in which they conduct themselves.

This is particularly important for a profession that does not speak to consumers with a single voice about what is "best practice." Over the course of several years, teachers and parents are likely to meet school psychologists who approach problems from the behavioral, Freudian, neurological, collaborative/consultative, or systems point of view. How could service consumers recognize a school psychologist unless there was some common thread connecting the various training backgrounds?

The development of a set of ethics is a common task for a professional association. The National Association of School Psychologists described the benefits in the introduction to the *Professional Conduct Manual* (National Association of School Psychologists [NASP], 1992b):

> By virtue of joining the Association, each NASP member has agreed to act in a manner that shows respect for human dignity and assures a high quality of professional service. Although ethical behavior is an individual responsibility, it is in the interest of an association to adopt and enforce a code of ethics. If done properly, members will be guided towards appropriate behavior, and public confidence in the profession will be enhanced. Additionally, a code of ethics should provide due process procedures to protect members from potential abuse of the code. (p. 5)]

To develop this code of ethics, NASP's Ethics and Professional Conduct Committee systematically obtained recommendations from the ethics committees of state school psychology associations. Practicing school psychologists, university trainers, students, administrators, and a wide range of NASP leaders commented on the rough drafts. The NASP Delegate Assembly approved the document in 1984, making it the standard for individual NASP members and the state affiliates. Following the same tradition of working collaboratively at the grass roots level, *Principals for Professional Ethics* (hereafter *Ethics*) was revised in 1992 with the intent of representing "a national consensus regarding the professional behavior required of school psychologists in any setting (NASP, 1992a, p. 3).

The individual student or practitioner of school psychology who studies NASP's *Ethics* will find what seems to be mostly common sense advice. For example, school psychologists are told to be advocates for their students/clients, to provide only services for which they have achieved a recognized level of competency, and to refrain from sexual exploitation. This sounds easy enough in the abstract, from the comfort of one's favorite reading chair. But the "real world" is full of organizational pressures, conflicting regulations, and personal challenges that can very quickly make fuzzy and grey the sharp, black-and-white distinctions found in a book.

People expect ethical challenges to be rather rare and obviously large, such as the offer by a parent of a $50 bribe to make sure a child receives an IQ score high enough to assure entry into a talented and gifted program. In fact, opportunities to act unethically tend to be more subtle, and appear almost daily. Take, for example, the supervisor who says "We are out of funds for materials — just make a photocopy of the test protocol." Unless one had carefully studied NASP's *Ethics*, it would be rather easy to succumb to the pressure to complete work in a timely manner, to follow orders in a "good soldier" spirit. The probability of penalty is low; the probability of praise is high. By acting quickly, one might even help bring some relief to a suffering student — yet it would be a clear violation of the ethical principles.

Time magazine recently surveyed 285 therapists across the United States. Forty-six percent reported "feeling so angry with a client that you do something you regret later" and 20% reported "flirting with a client" (Therapists and Their Patients, 1993). These are people who were trained to know better, and yet the numbers are too high. Evidently the human condition is such that we need to be in a state of constant alertness for potentially unethical behavior.

The intent of this chapter is to describe for the reader several sources of guidance about appropriate professional behavior. The author will attempt to distill the basic themes, which should make it easier to recall general ethical principles. Case studies will provide a model of a problem-solving approach to the analysis of an "ethical dilemma."

BASIC CONSIDERATIONS

For each employment situation, the school psychologist will find a variety of potentially conflicting sources of advice regarding appropriate behavior. NASP, the American Psychological Association (APA), and the National Education Association (NEA) all publish principles for professional ethics, which present the particular view of the organization. These rules are binding on their respective members, and some professionals may belong to all three associations, or more. NASP, as well as other publishing firms, prints *Best Practices* books, such as this one. NASP also releases several standards documents and occasionally the NASP Delegate Assembly issues a "position statement." Most employers have an employee handbook that describes policies and procedures. Then there are state laws, federal laws, and the rules that implement them. The application of the statutes are modified by case law, and there are various attorneys and university professors who earn additional money by promoting their latest opinions. Since these were all developed independently of each other, chances are good that they will fail to agree in many areas. What to do?

For NASP members the answer is relatively simple. As noted in the *Principles for Professional Ethics* (NASP, 1992a):

> As a general rule, the Association will seek to enforce the *Ethical Principles* upon members. The *NASP Standards for the Provision of School Psychological Services* are typically not enforced, although all members are encouraged to work towards achieving the hallmarks of quality services delivery that are described therein. Similarly, "position statements" and "best practices" documents are not adjudicated. (p. 5)

(Readers are advised that NASP standards also apply to nonmembers who hold National Certification.)

Therefore, NASP's *Ethics* should be the basic reference document for NASP members. It is typical for ethics documents to provide a series of relatively general principles instead of an exhaustive list of rules. This is done to provide stability across time; general procedures are not as likely to be influenced by current fads. It also prevents individuals from claiming they cannot be charged with an ethical violation because there was not a specific item in the text that deals with a unique situation. It does place a responsibility on the individual member to study NASP's *Ethics*, reflect on the intent of the sections, and determine how those principles apply to a particular employment setting or a specific sequence of events.

Let's turn to the NASP documents now, and search for common themes running throughout. Drawing on the work of several writers, Jacob and Hartshorne (1992) found four basic motifs repeated in the scores of the helping professions.

Welfare of Client

This theme refers to respect for the dignity and human rights of the individual, including "self-determination and autonomy . . . privacy and confidentiality . . . the values of fairness and nondiscrimination" (Jacob & Hartshorne, 1992, p. 12). A quick scan of the *Ethics* finds phrases such as "This objective is pursued in ways that protect the dignity and rights of those involved" (III-A-1); "School psychologists respect all persons and are sensitive to physical, mental, emotional, political, economic, social, cultural, ethnic, racial, gender, sexual preference, and religious characteristics" (III-A-2). School psychologists are also called upon to respect the wishes of those who object to their services (III-C-3). A nondiscrimination statement can be found in III-E-3. Respect for individual integrity and individual differences is required by IV-B-1-a, specifically with regard to assessment and intervention practices. Similar sections are found in *Standards for the Provision of School Psychological Services* (NASP, 1992c; hereafter *Standards*), particularly in regard to respect for the contribution of cultural groups.

Even though one may feel proud of one's rigorous training, unique experiences, and understanding of the schooling process, this theme requires humility. Achieving the rank of school psychologist is supposed to imbue one with a greater understanding of individual differences and a profound respect for human rights. Arrogance is antithetical to the goals and purposes of the profession.

Professional Competence

Mastery of one's craft should lead to a high proportion of correct decisions. When parents or teachers ask for assistance, competent school psychologists should be able to deal with such requests in a manner that leads to improvement in their students' condition; at the very least, they should do no harm. This will require that they be certain which skills are fully developed, and which are not yet ready for presentation to the public. Supervision and continuing professional development are assumed under this theme, as is one's ability to accept total responsibility for actions taken (Jacob & Hartshorne, 1992, p. 14).

The second paragraph of the introduction to *Ethics* clearly calls for school psychologists to do no harm and to provide only competent services. Section II deals with this theme in greater detail, and a number of statements in the other sections provide some suggestions for how to "maintain the highest standard" (IV-B-1).

There may be times when agencies or individuals apply pressure to the school psychologists to reduce the quality of services in order to see more students in a shorter time. Or perhaps there is a desperate need for a particular type of service, one that some specifically trained school psychologists could provide, but the school psychologist assigned to the area lacks the competence. According to *Ethics*, and the principle of "responsible caring" (Jacob & Hartshorne, 1992, p. 14), the only course of action is to resist the pressure. One must provide only high-quality services; one must reach a recognized level of relevant training before providing a given service.

Integrity of Professional Relationships

In dealing with other professionals, this tenet implies that school psychologists are open, honest, and fair. Their actions are based on principles, not defensive emotions. School psychologists are aware of conflict of interest situations, and do not allow their special place in the school system and the community to bring them unfair advantage.

In *Ethics*, there are many references to avoiding conflicts of interest and maintaining professional relationships at the highest level. The entirety of Section III-F specifies actions for dealing with related professions. Section III-D-4 recommends: "As much as possible, the stance of the school psychologist is made known in advance to all parties to prevent misunderstandings." Perhaps the easiest way to prevent misunderstandings is to explain school psychology services *a priori*. In that way, any potential conflicts can be revealed and an agreeable solution developed before any difficulties arise.

Responsibility to Community/Society

This section recognizes school psychologists' status as citizens, and that they are not denied their rights to participate in the political process because of their training or employment. Section III-E-1 of *Ethics* cautions that political activism should not compromise one's professional effectiveness. Section III-E-2 prescribes making certain that attempts to bring about social change should be accomplished lawfully, and further requires that individual actions

not be presented as representing the profession of school psychology.

Special additional responsibilities fall on those who perform research with human subjects (*Ethics* III-A-6, IV-D-1, IV-D-2; *Standards* 4.3.5.1). Individual practitioners conducting private practice also need to be especially careful to avoid providing diagnosis or therapy through public channels (*Ethics* V-B-4). Announcements and advertising are also limited to presentation in a formal, professional manner (*Ethics* V-C-1 through V-C-7). State licensing boards will undoubtedly have additional restrictions for those in private practice. These would make interesting reading for the public sector practitioner who collaborates with the private sector.

These common themes provide a relatively easy way to summarize the major points in NASP's *Ethics*. One should always place the welfare of the student/client over one's own interest or convenience. One must achieve competence in an area before offering it to the public and must continually upgrade skills to maintain that competence. Relationships with other professionals should be based on openness, honesty, and the logical consideration of facts over defensive emotions. As a member of the larger community, one may press for change through the political process, but only in a lawful, conservative manner that does not reflect badly on school psychology.

If this sounds rather difficult and one-sided . . . it is! The intention is to protect the public, and all of the responsibility falls on the individual school psychologist. As summarized so clearly by Jacob and Hartshorne (1992), "Professionals do not have rights under a code of ethics, only obligations" (p. 21).

BEST PRACTICES

Prepare in Advance

As mentioned above, it is preferable to prevent problems than to deal with them. Colleagues and one's hiring agency need to be fully informed regarding one's training, experience, theoretical orientation, personal limitations, and ethical beliefs. For example, NASP's *Ethics* calls on school psychologists to act as advocates for their students/clients. This position can cause the school psychologist to function as the "conscience of the school" (Dawson, 1992), perhaps in the face of pressure from colleagues to recommend what would be easiest for the educational system. If all parties knew in advance that the school psychologist would take this role, there would be less of a surprise and a better chance to resolve any conflicts in a manner that benefits the student.

NASP documents, such as the *Professional Conduct Manual* (1992b), are relatively inexpensive and may be used during the "prior notice" phase. Colleagues and supervisors, particularly those who are not school psychologists or not NASP members, should have copies of *Ethics* and of *Standards* on their desks for reference. Should one be forced by circumstances to take a stance based on principle, it would be nice for one's employer to understand and support the action because of discussions and manuscripts provided in advance. Another publication that may be helpful is the *Self-Evaluation Manual*, created by Virginia Smith-Harvey (1991) which is based on NASP's *Standards*. This document can assist a school psychology department in conducting an evaluation of services to see how well current practice matches NASP's recommendations. The resulting report may help administrators to better understand how a school psychology unit should operate, and to provide a clear direction for the improvement of services.

Always Be on the Alert

As mentioned before, situations that can draw one into unethical practice tend to arise suddenly and may initially appear benign. First of all, school psychologists need to study NASP's *Ethics* thoroughly to gain an understanding in depth of what is required. Second, they need to be always on the alert for detrimental practice. Finally, they need to act conservatively, thoroughly evaluating situations before taking action.

Seek Assistance

There may be times when the proper course of action is unclear. A school psychologist may find himself or herself caught in a web of conflicting loyalties, laws, and policies. Under these conditions, it is proper to write the Ethical and Professional Standards (E&PS) Committee for an opinion. Simply describe the situation in detail, and ask the committee for an opinion about the best way to proceed. Sometimes a more experienced school psychologist on your staff, a qualified supervisor of school psychological services, or the chairperson of the Ethical Standards committee of your state affiliate association can provide the guidance you seek.

If You Suspect Unethical Practice

A time may come when the actions of a fellow school psychologist appear to be in violation of professional ethics. NASP members, and members of the National Certification System, are required to take steps in an attempt to correct such a situation. It is never easy to face a colleague with a serious concern. But if the potentially unethical practice is allowed to continue, it may result in damage to students and the reputation of the profession. Uncomfortable as it may be, the concerns must be raised.

Several sections of NASP's *Ethics* explain how to proceed. In Section III-A-7, school psychologists who suspect "detrimental or unethical practice" (p. 7) are told to attempt to rectify the situation informally. This means having a private, serious talk with the individual engaged in the practice. Whether the practitioner is a NASP member or not, bring along the appropriate sections of the *Professional Conduct Manual*. If often helps to begin and end a difficult conversation with statements of appreciation, thus placing the "bad news" in the middle. This is sometimes known as the "sandwich method." Using this technique, a hypothetical discussion might begin like this:

> Joe, I've worked with you here at the Anytown School District for 10 years or so, and I've always admired your work. You might say I've used you as a role model and tried to match your high standards. But I've noticed that you are dating a high school student — somebody young enough to be your daughter — and what's more, she is somebody that you see in counseling. I'm worried about how all of this might turn out; both you and the student could be hurt very badly. Plus, I've been reading the ethical standards for both NASP and that counseling association you belong to — based on those standards I'm convinced this type of behavior is unethical. You are too valuable to this school district and you do too many good things for the students you see. And I would hate to lose you as a colleague . . .

If the situation of concern is not a clear violation of ethical principles, it may be helpful for both individuals to jointly approach the Ethical and Professional Standards Committee for an opinion. By asking for an opinion together, one avoids the adversarial aspects of filing a formal complaint. The atmosphere is more one of collegiality, with individuals of two opposing viewpoints seeking resolution through consultation with an outside party. Should the situation deteriorate to the point that a complaint would need to be filed, that step is still available.

Should all informal attempts prove unfruitful, the process would move to the next level. The school psychologist who had observed the detrimental practice would file a written complaint with the appropriate professional association (*Ethics* III-F-7). These procedures vary across groups, so some background investigation into the proper method may be required. If the person in violation does not belong to a professional organization, one should complain to the hiring agency. The complaint should be in writing, provide explicit examples of offenses instead of generalities, and reference the sections of the ethical standards that seem to have been violated. The complaint will need to be signed, as anonymous complaints cannot be accepted.

The filing of an ethical complaint is an extremely serious step. It should be done to help a recalcitrant colleague to understand the seriousness of the malfeasance and take corrective actions. The purpose is to protect the public and the profession by policing a wayward member. Whenever possible,

NASP's Ethical and Professional Standards Committee attempts to resolve such situations by educating the member regarding appropriate practice. If this is not possible, a variety of sanctions may be imposed, including expulsion from the Association.

The full process is rather involved and will not be described in detail here. The adjudication proceedings are based upon providing complete due process for members, so there are checks, balances, and appeals at every step of the way. The E&PS committee has a good record of rectifying conflicts at the educative level, with very few complaints needing to go to expulsion. In situations in which the committee believes that the welfare of the public is at stake, NASP will notify other interested parties about the final outcome of the case. For example, NASP could notify one's employer or the state certification/licensure board, which implies a potential loss of employment.

On occasion, school psychologists may experience strong conflicts with colleagues or parents. If the individual leaves feeling angry and helpless, s/he may cast about for a way to get even. Filing a complaint of ethical misconduct, even an unfounded complaint, will fill some individuals' need for revenge. Since school psychologists as professionals are jealous of others' good opinion of their conduct, simply having charges brought against them can be a shocking experience that creates self-doubt, embarrassment, and fear of wrongful punishment. We cannot prevent members of the public from taking this course of action; we can only trust that the truth will be revealed as the E&PS committee follows the prescribed procedures. There is a section in *Ethics* (III-7-b) that forbids NASP members from filing a charge "that is frivolous or motivated by revenge" (p. 7).

Special Responsibilities of Private Practice

School psychologists who provide services through a private practice take on additional responsibilities designed to protect the public. This is especially critical for simultaneous practice in both the public and the private sectors. Section V-A-1 of *Ethics* requires private practitioners to take full responsibility, and to inform the consumer of any potential difficulties. Under these guidelines, if any ethical problems arise, it is always the fault of the private practitioner.

Although this rule may seem excessively harsh, it is built on a simple premise: The consumer enters the market with vastly less knowledge and information than the private practitioner. In order for the consumer to make an informed judgment about services, the critical facts must be provided by the private practitioner. Full disclosure to such a high degree will undoubtedly upset those who incline to high-pressure sales, and will ultimately cause the ethical private practitioner in effect to turn away clients.

For example, a school psychologist working in the private sector may not charge a client for the same service that a school psychologist would provide free of charge through the public sector (*Ethics* V-A-2). In fact, the private sector school psychologist is required to inform the client that the same services are available free of charge through the public schools (*Ethics* (V-A-3). Just imagine the pressure on a new, "hungry" private practitioner who has to tell a potential customer that the same service is available free!

Private practice and public service are required to be kept separate (*Ethics* V-A-4, 5). Great difficulty in following this standard is possible if one's private practice is physically near one's public service. Even though the private practice may be conducted on weekends or evenings in another town, the private clients could very easily know how to contact the school psychologist during the day. Even if they were instructed not to call during working hours, a crisis might require private clients to call the school psychologist at the public school. Now we have an unethical conducting of private business on public time! Despite all efforts to avoid this situation, it is almost impossible unless practice sites and the nature of the services are widely separated.

CASE STUDIES

Thinking analytically about ethics is a skill that is developed with practice. To provide members with a model for this type of problem solving, the NASP newsletter, *The Communiqué* occasionally presents an Ethical Dilemma column. The feature describes a "sticky situation" and then invites NASP members to render an opinion regarding the appropriate course of action. Reviewing another person's thinking in a case study can be a fun and informative way to become more knowledgeable about professional conduct. Summarized below are two examples.

Blanket Permission for Services

In an attempt to be efficient, a school psychologist hired to provide counseling and consultation sends a letter to all parents announcing the availability of services. The letter asks all those who would object to services to contact the school psychologist. Hearing no complaints, the school psychologist will assume that permission is granted.

For this column, Lane Roosa, John H. Correll, Carol Osip, and John Reinhardt provided opinions. They all began their responses by determining the key elements of the situation — in this case, whether informed consent was obtained through the use of a general announcement. They then studied NASP's *Ethics* and *Standards* for sections that would pertain. Although the exact wording and section numbering has changed a bit over the years, all of the respondents found passages that require the active involvement of the parents. They also considered relevant laws, such as the Family Educational Rights and Privacy Act (Rules and Regulations, 1982). They considered crisis situations, and involvement in the reporting of potential abuse. Putting all of that information together, the authors all concluded that the "call me if you object" shortcut is unwise, does not necessarily lead to the provision of high-quality service, and could actually create more time-consuming trouble than was saved (Canter, 1989, p. 9). In terms of our four broad themes, the blanket permission does not adequately protect the welfare of the client, and it suggests reduced professional competence. The intent — increased efficiency — is laudable, but the practice falls short of attaining that goal.

Pressure to Provide a New Service

Fred Grossman responded to a situation posed in a *Communiqué* Ethical Dilemma column, which involved an administrator who insisted that a school psychologist provide a new service. The problem: The school psychologist has had no training or experience in that area. The administrator insists and suggests that the school psychologist's job is at stake if the service is not provided.

Grossman quickly pinpointed the issue of professional competence. He consulted NASP's *Ethics* and *Standards*, and a position statement recently issued by the Oregon School Psychologists' Association, "On Performing Within the Bounds of One's Competence" (Professional Standards Committee, 1992). These documents clearly forbid providing services for which a recognized level of competence has not been achieved. Expanding on his assignment, he then produced four suggestions for dealing with the situation: (a) Notify all relevant parties in advance of areas of competence; (b) make referrals to trained professionals for those services that are outside of one's own area of training; (c) consult and collaborate with practitioners in other professions to supplement one's own training; and (d) obtain the training necessary to ethically provide the requested service. This example touches upon all four of the broad themes noted above: welfare of the client, professional competence, integrity of professional relationships, and responsibility to the community/society.

These case studies demonstrate a particular style of problem solving. It involves thinking very specifically about the critical aspects of a problematic situation in order to describe the problem concisely. In the context of a broader focus of attention, relevant documents relating to ethics, standards, and statutes are studied in a hunt for applicable sections. The final analysis attempts to apply logic and reason to a human predicament that might be fraught with emotion. The end result should meet the standard recommended by Haas and Malouf (1989):

1. The decision is *principled*, that is, based on generally accepted ethical principles.

2. The action is a *reasoned* outcome of a consideration of the principles.

3. The decision is *universalizable* [sic], that is, the psychologist would recommend the same course of action to others in a similar situation. (pp. 2–3).

SUMMARY

Many of the actions that help to identify a professional as a school psychologist are specified in NASP's *Professional Conduct Manual*, a publication that contains the *Principles for Professional Ethics*, and the *Standards for the Provision of School Psychological Services*. There are other sources of advice, such as "best practices" publications, school district policies and procedures manuals, and state and federal laws. When the guidance is conflicting, NASP considers the general principles described in *Ethics* to be the authority, and will take alleged violators through an adjudication process to enforce prescriptions in *Ethics*. *Standards* documents are not enforced, but NASP encourages all members "to work towards achieving the hallmarks of quality services delivery that are described therein" (NASP, 1992b, p. 5).

Although many of the principles seem to be simply common sense, they require study and reflection. The injunctions in *Ethics* are written in general terms, for the most part, and their application to a specific situation in a particular place of employment may not be immediately clear. Furthermore, is it more likely that school psychologists will encounter several subtle situations on a daily basis than the occasional blatant disregard for ethics. This requires us to be constantly evaluating our performance in respect to what is considered to be ethical.

By announcing our capabilities and ethical responsibilities in advance, school psychologists can avoid many of the smaller problems that are caused when others make inaccurate assumptions about the role and function of school psychologists. NASP prints several reference books that are often valuable for informing supervisors and for providing support for appropriate, but perhaps unpopular, actions (Knoff, 1989).

Ethical behavior tends to be that which (a) places the welfare of the client above the convenience of the practitioner; (b) is limited to the provision of services for which the school psychologist has achieved a recognized level of competence; (c) maintains honest and respectful relationships with other professionals; and (d) works to improve conditions within schools, the profession, and the community in general. When circumstances are murky, assistance in determining what is ethical is available from the NASP Ethical and Professional Standards Committee, or the Professional Standards committees of the state affiliates of NASP. Case studies provide a means for learning how to apply a problem-solving methodology when analyzing an ethical dilemma.

When potentially unethical practice occurs, the school psychologist should attempt to resolve the conflict by using informal means. If this proves to be unsuccessful, a formal complaint should be filed with the appropriate professional association. NASP's complaint procedures attempt to educate rather than adjudicate, and they are characterized by a respect for maintaining a member's confidentiality and due process rights.

This chapter deals very briefly with professional ethics, providing only a starting point for study. This may not be the most entertaining or exciting reading in the professional literature, but every practitioner will regularly encounter situations requiring a decision based on ethical principles. By preparing in advance for these situations, we will be confident in our ability to proceed in a manner that protects clients, ourselves, and ultimately ensures high-quality school psychology services.

REFERENCES

Bowser, P. (1992). Ethical dilemma: What do you do when your boss asks you to do something you're not trained for? *The Communiqué, 21*(4), 18.

Canter, A. (1989). Ethical dilemma: Is parental permission always necessary? *The Communiqué, 18*(3), 9.

Dawson, M. (1992). Comment during subcommittee meeting of the Ethical and Professional Standards Committee.

Guralnik, D. B. (1974). Webster's New World Dictionary of the American Language. Cleveland: William Collins & World.

Haas, L. J., & Malouf, J. L. (1989). *Keeping up the good work: A practitioner's guide to mental health ethics.* Sarasota, FL: Professional Resources Exchange. Reprinted in Jacob, S., & Hartshorne, T. (Eds.). (1992). *Ethics and law for school psychologists.* Brandon, VT: Clinical Psychology Publishing Co.

Jacob, S., & Hartshorne, T. (Eds.). (1992). *Ethics and law for school psychologists.* Brandon, VT: Clinical Psychology Publishing Co.

Knoff, H. M. (1989). NASP's "forgotten" standards documents. *The Communiqué, 18*(5), 3.

National Association of School Psychologists. (1992a). *Principles for Professional Ethics.* Silver Spring, MD: Author.

National Association of School Psychologists. (1992b). *Professional Conduct Manual.* Silver Spring, MD: Author.

National Association of School Psychologists. (1992c). *Standards for the Provision of School Psychological Services.* Silver Spring, MD: Author.

Professional Standards Committee. (1992). *On performing within the bounds of one's competence.* Portland, OR: Oregon School Psychologists' Association.

Rules and Regulations for PL 93-380 Implementing Section 438 (The Family Educational Rights and Privacy Act). (1982). In C. R. Reynolds & T. B. Gutkin (Eds.), *Handbook of school psychology.* New York: John Wiley.

Singer, M. G. (1993). *Grollier's on-line electronic encyclopedia.* GEnie Information Service.

Smith-Harvey, V. (1991). *Self-evaluation manual.* (Ethical and Professional Standards Committee Document.) Silver Spring, MD: The National Association of School Psychologists.

Therapists and Their Patients: Anger, Hate, Fear and Sex. (1993, May 17). *Time,* p. 25.

ANNOTATED BIBLIOGRAPHY

American Psychological Association. (1989). *Ethical Principles of Psychologists.* Washington, DC: Author.
This is the APA's stand on ethics; it is interesting to notice the similarities to and differences from NASP's positions.

Jacob, S., & Hartshorne, T. (1992). *Ethics and law for school psychologists.* Brandon, VT: Clinical Psychology Publishing Co.
An excellent, comprehensive textbook. This book was in publication prior to NASP's most recent revision of *Ethics,* so an outdated version appears in the appendix.

National Association of School Psychologists. (1992). *Professional Conduct Manual.* Silver Spring, MD: Author.
This booklet contains both the *Principles for Professional Ethics* and the *Standards for the Provision of School Psychological Services.* It is your primary reference. Supervisors and administrators, particularly those who do not have a background in school psychology, should have a copy.

Various editions of the NASP newsletter, *The Communiqué,* contain the Ethical Dilemma column. These provide good examples of the application of a problem-solving approach to the analysis of difficult ethical situations.

Your school board and state board of psychology examiners may have policy documents that describe their interpretation of ethical professional behavior. Even though NASP believes its documents supersede all others, it is in your best interest to be knowledgeable about them.

3

Best Practices in School Psychology and the Law

David P. Prasse
Governors State University

OVERVIEW

School psychology has been influenced by various legal sources including legislation and judicial decision. Such influences are on the rise and bringing with them an inevitable professional and public scrutiny of the disciplines' practices and policies. While many components of psychology and education are subject to legally defined parameters, school psychology, due in part to historical ties to special education, has realized a significant legal impact that has modified roles, responsibilities, and the overall delivery of school psychological services.

As the programs and practices of education have undergone radical change as a result of judicial and legislative influence, so too has the service delivery components of school psychology. Courts, in their role as mediator between the rights of students and parents and the rights/responsibilities of schools, have moved to protect and define procedural and substantive due process for students, especially students with disabilities. Courts have instructed school systems to provide special education programs where there has been an absence of programs or where inappropriate programs have not met the educational needs of students. The legislative influence of Public Laws 94-142 and 99-457 and Section 504 of the Rehabilitation Act and, more recently, PL 101-476, the Individuals with Disabilities Education Act, are known to us all. Much of the legal influence on the discipline of school psychology is a result of these federal acts and similar state-based legislation. Recognizing the sources of legal influence on school psychology is fundamental to a comprehensive knowledge of "best practices."

As the legal parameters change, so too does the school psychology/law relationship. This constant state of flux means that what is mandated or required today may change tomorrow. A practice or process followed yesterday may be judged inappropriate or illegal in the future! As societal priorities change and individual rights are further defined, legal requirements change and the parameters of influence expand and/or constrict. While there exists "fundamentals" of law that mostly remain stable across time, the daily practices and service delivery approaches are susceptible to legislative and judicial interpretation of those fundamentals.

What follows is a foundation for best practice. The purpose is to indicate what is known about the influence of law on school psychology and therefore what all school psychologists are expected to know and understand. The intent is not to provide detail about the specifics of best practice. Rather it is to highlight the areas of knowledge regarding school psychology and the law that should be known to all who practice school psychology.

BASIC CONSIDERATIONS: SOURCES OF LEGAL INFLUENCE

There exists a sequential nature to sources of law that reflect (in most cases) application of broad principles to specific situations. It is expected that specific laws, practices, and procedures be consistent with broad principles. Understanding the broad principles provides the foundation upon which we problem solve specific situations. The sources of law are for the most part hierarchical and are pictured as follows:

Federal Constitution

Federal Statute

State Constitution

State Statute

Administrative Rules

Local Policy and Procedure

Sources of law are more influential (i.e., having greater impact) the higher they are in the hierarchy. They are also sequentially subordinate, and those that exist beneath others are narrower in scope and applicability. However, on occasion these lower order sources may be no less important than those sources higher in the hierarchy.

Constitution

The cornerstone of all law is the Constitution of the United States. Sources of law (federal and state statutes, judicial decisions, etc.) are subject to the provisions of the Constitution. Laws, practices, and procedures not congruent with principles established by the Constitution are eventually judged (usually by a court) as unacceptable.

The U.S. Constitution has nothing directly to say about education yet everything to say about the manner in which education (including school psychological services) is provided to the public. There is no constitutional right or guarantee to an education. Providing an education to the public is a matter left to the individual states by way of the Tenth Amendment which states:

> The powers not delegated to the United States by the Constitution, nor prohibited by it to the States, are reserved to the States respectively.

Therefore, states may provide a public education to its citizens. In so doing, the state must do so in a manner that is compatible with the principles established by the Constitution.

It is this requirement that impacts the delivery of school psychological services. As an aspect of public education, school psychological services must adhere (as education in general) to established constitutional principles. When the practices and procedures of school psychology violate those principles, they will likely be viewed as unacceptable. Knowledge of these fundamental constitutional principles and the legislation and litigation that builds on them is necessary to effective problem solving when weighing the legal parameters associated with delivering school psychological services.

Legislation

Legislation, or statute, is the most influential source of law affecting the delivery of educational and school psychological services. Enacted by Congress or state legislatures, legislation is created to provide the mechanism for implementing constitutional guarantees or for the purpose of initiating specific programs. Federal legislation important to school psychology is either program legislation or civil rights legislation. Program legislation provides funds for delivering specific programs (e.g., Chapter I, Special Education) and in providing these funds mandates that agencies delivering the services do so in a manner prescribed by the legislation. The Individuals with Disabilities Act of 1990 (PL 101-476, IDEA) is among the most widely known. Its precursor was the Education for All Handicapped Children Act of 1975 (PL 94-142, EAHCA or EHA). Through IDEA funds are made available for educating children with disabilities. The procedures by which these educational services are delivered are specified by the leg-islation and recipients are obligated to comply with the requirements. Civil rights legislation differs in that requirements are usually not tied to program funding; that is, procedures mandated by the law must be adhered to even in the absence of funds tied directly to a program. Section 504 of the Rehabilitation Act of 1973 is a relevant example of this type of legislation.

State statutes serve to enact the principles established by a state constitution or federal mandate and may be quite specific and detailed. For example, most states have a compulsory school attendance law and a law that provides for educating children with disabilities. The later must be compatible with constitutional principles and requirements delineated in IDEA and Section 504. State laws affecting education are wide ranging and differ from state to state. For example, mandatory child abuse reporting laws may or may not detail the precise steps necessary for reporting suspected abuse. Direct and indirect impact on school psychology will vary accordingly.

Administrative Rules

When a law is enacted, a specific governmental agency is charged with implementing the requirements of the statute. Inasmuch as the legislation may not include all the specific details necessary for successful implementation, the appropriate governmental agency is empowered to write rules to accompany the newly enacted law. When adopted, these rules are equivalent in importance and influence as the statute itself. At the federal level, a statute pertaining to education is usually administered by the Department of Education, which is then responsible for developing corresponding rules. At the state level, the relevant agency is frequently the Department of Public Instruction or Education which has similar responsibilities to those found at the federal level. These governmental agencies will usually "propose" rules, hold public hearings, and finally adopt the rules. Paying close attention to the rule-making process as well as possessing a thorough knowledge of the final rules is a necessary and crucial component for understanding the intent and specific requirements of a particular law.

Litigation

Litigation is the source of and knowledge base for law referred to as case law, and the influence of judicial decision making is predicated, in part, on the judicial structure itself. There exists a federal court system and individual state court systems. The federal system includes three levels: U.S. District Courts (trial courts), U.S. Court of Appeals (11 circuits), and the U.S. Supreme Court (Court of last resort). Generally, the federal judicial system is used when the question involves a constitutional issue or a federal statute. Each state has its own judicial system and each system varies greatly. Like the federal system, states have different levels often including circuit courts, one or two levels of appellate courts, and a "supreme" court.

The import of a judicial decision depends, in part, on the level of court in which the issue is adjudicated. Generally, the higher a court is in the system, the greater the impact or influence. For example, a state supreme court decision is applicable to that particular state, while a decision rendered by a U.S. Court of Appeals is applicable to that entire district which, except for the District of Columbia and one dealing with special patents and copyright issues, includes several states. Decisions of the Supreme Court are applicable to all states and effectively become the law of the land. So the higher the court in the judicial hierarchy the more authoritative its decision and accompanying opinion.

The fundamental purpose of judicial decision is to resolve conflict — conflict that arises from two different interpretations of a statute or from questions embodied in a state or the federal Constitution. Judicial decisions involve determining the intent of the legislature and the compatibility of that intent and/or practices with constitutional principles. Statutes or practices that violate constitutional principles are then overturned or modified by the court. The potential impact or influence of case law is thus twofold. First, the jurisdiction of the court (where it is in the hierarchy) determines the influence of the decision. Second is the cumulative influence established through a series of decisions that when taken together establish a clear and unequivocal trend, pattern, or precedent.

Professional Standards and Ethical Code

Professional standards or ethical codes represent an additional (albeit indirect) source of legal influence on the discipline of school psychology. (See Bower this volume for coverage of ethical practice.) The standards that directly bear on school psychology include the National Association of School Psychologists (NASP) *Principles for Professional Ethics* (1992), *Ethical Principles of Psychologists and Code of Conduct* (American Psychological Association [APA], 1992), *Specialty Guidelines for the Delivery of Services by School Psychologists* (APA, 1981), and *Standards for Educational and Psychological Testing* (APA, 1984). In addition, most state school psychology associations have adopted professional practice codes.

Although important to the overall process of shaping and monitoring behavior of school psychologists, professional standards are not, at least in the traditional sense, "the law" and therefore do not carry similar weight, or influence as statutes or case law. Professional standards interface with the law and in so doing are not free to develop from discipline preferences alone. The existence of a standard in the NASP *Principles* that states, "School psychologists avoid any action that could violate or diminish civil and legal rights of clients" is clear acknowledgment of this interface.

Nonetheless, standards are important to the profession (including the consumers of services) in that they represent consensual thinking with respect to "best practices." They become the means by which professional behavior is judged by both peers and on occasion the courts. Courts have and continue to refer to professional standards when reviewing the behavior of an individual psychologist and when reviewing the procedures and policies of service delivery systems. In the legal arena, the "clout" of professional standards may be described as a dynamic state of potential. That is, if a court considers professional standards during deliberations and bases decisions (even in part) on professional standards, then those standards become (at least in that particular case) like the law. The more times that occurs, the stronger is the "legal" influence of professional standards.

BASIC PRINCIPLES: FOUNDATIONS FOR PROBLEM SOLVING

Attempts to define or describe best practice with respect to school psychology and the law is challenging for two reasons. First, as stated earlier, law or legal influence is dynamic. Requirements, restrictions, and parameters around professional practice change, sometimes with short notice. Second, legal influence on practice is subject to interpretation. Professional opinions (both psychologists and lawyers) differ with regard not only to basic legal principles but also to how specific requirements should be implemented. The "correct way" to deliver services is then open to debate.

What should be known by school psychologists about the law is traced to a few important sources. They are fundamental, for they serve as the basis for day-by-day problem solving. They include an understanding of specific components of the Constitution, certain procedures and principles that flow from it, an understanding of children's rights, and finally, specifics of relevant legislation and litigation. We turn first to the Constitution.

The Constitutional Foundation

A theme that permeates discussion with respect to legal requirements and mandates for school psychology is "May we do this?" or "Will I be held liable for this?" Problem solving is, in large part, dependent on understanding the *intent* of the law (case or statute) which emanates from fundamental constitutional principles. To understand these principles is to know the foundation for judicial decision, which provides a base on which specific practice questions are answered.

The constitutional principles relevant to judicial decisions and legislation are relatively few in number. As indicated earlier, it is the Tenth Amendment that establishes education as a state function. Other relevant Amendments include the First and Fourteenth. The Fourteenth Amendment has been most influential with respect to special education and school psychological services, for many court decisions that have clarified the rights of children and educational practice have, in large part, been based on this Amendment. The Fourteenth Amendment states, in part:

> No state shall make or enforce any law which shall abridge the privileges or immunities of citizens of the United States; nor shall any State deprive any person of life, liberty, or property without due process of law, nor deny to any person within its jurisdiction the equal protection of the laws.

Application of the Fourteenth Amendment to education and school psychology is understood through a brief elaboration of two clauses: the *due process* clause and the *equal protection* clause. Application of the Fourteenth Amendment by courts means that most actions respecting children with disabilities (or suspected disabilities) must guarantee procedural and substantive due process and equal protection. Procedural due process guarantees a person the right and meaningful opportunity to protest and be heard before government (in this case schools) may take action with respect to them. Substantive due process establishes that there are certain rights and privileges that a state may not arbitrarily take from a citizen (in this case student or parent) and that the state may not act unreasonably, arbitrarily, or capriciously in dealing with a citizen. Equal protection guarantees to a person the same rights and benefits all other citizens enjoy with respect to their government (e.g., schools) unless the withholding of those rights and benefits is for a valid reason that justifies the state in singling out the person for differential treatment.

Judicial application and interpretation of the Fourteenth Amendment is a continuous and dynamic process. Court decisions range from establishing an equal educational opportunity for persons with disabilities to mandating assessment practices that do not result in disproportionate placement or overrepresentation of minorities. Among the procedures affecting school psychological services required by dint of the Fourteenth Amendment are

- Written notice to parents if a school proposes to change, or refuses to change, the identification, evaluation, or educational placement of the child.

- Providing parents an opportunity to present complaints with respect to any matter relating to the identification, evaluation, or educational placement of their child.

- Procedural requirements of informed written consent prior to assessment and special class programming.

- All requirements specific to nondiscriminatory assessment.

Application of the Fourteenth Amendment to the educational arena for children with disabilities resulted in dramatic change: It opened the schoolhouse doors to children with disabilities. However, children with disabilities would not see those doors open wide until a broader "right to an education" was established under our Constitution for all children.

The right to an education. As stated earlier, there is no federal constitutional right to an education. However, when states choose to provide an education to its citizens (as all states do), they must do so in a manner acceptable to fundamental constitutional provisions. Judicial intrusion into the educational arena has been mixed. However, the cornerstone for providing an equal educational opportunity for all children, including those with disabilities, is *Brown v. Board of Education* (1954). Reversing almost 60 years of judicially supported segregation, (*Plessy v. Ferguson*, 1896), *Brown* addressed the applicability of the equal protection clause to public education. The *Brown* decision established that educating minority children in separate but "equal" facilities violated the equal protection clause of the Fourteenth Amendment and therefore denied them an equal educational opportunity. The thinking of the Supreme Court was that education became a property interest when states made it available to its citizens and separate but equal was inherently unequal.

When the Court found this practice violated the equal protection clause, it established the foundation upon which the exclusion of children with disabilities from school would subsequently be challenged. That challenge was helped by the Court's decision in *Brown* which made clear the applicability of the Fourteenth Amendment to the public school arena. Indeed, the rationale and precedent established by the Court should be critically considered as potentially applicable to the current debate surrounding inclusion. It was against the backdrop of *Brown* and the political promise of equality and equal opportunity emerging in the 1950s and 1960s that the hope for educating children with disabilities emerged.

Program availability. Legal influence on educational programming is an outgrowth of litigation involving the provision of educational services to children with disabilities. It was litigation and later legislation that resulted in various mandates to provide an education to children, particularly the child with disabilities. The legal foundation for requiring equal educational opportunity for children with disabilities is the equal protection clause. By applying the equal protection clause of the Fourteenth Amendment to education, courts created the fundamental concept of an equal educational opportunity, thereby precluding states from excluding from its schools children with disabilities. For many years children with disabilities were excluded from public schools — often shut out of school altogether or shunted to inappropriate institutions.

The precedent-setting cases challenging school systems and states that systematically denied a free public education to individuals with disabilities include PARC (*Pennsylvania Association for Retarded Citizens [PARC] v. Commonwealth of Pennsylvania* [1972]) and *Mills v. Board of Education of the District of Columbia* (1972). *PARC* challenged the exclusion from school of children deemed to be uneducable or unable to profit from an education on the basis that such exclusion violated their equal protection and due process rights. Settled by consent decree in favor of the children, the case, receiving national media attention, served as an impetus for similar litigation throughout the country.

The children represented in *Mills* were denied an equal educational opportunity as a result of their various handicapping conditions and the District denied them an education by utilizing procedures of suspension, exclusion, and class reassignment. In addition, their due process rights were denied when the District assigned them to special classes, precluding them from access to regular education programs. In finding for the plaintiffs the court dismissed limited financial resources as a basis for the denial of equal educational opportunity and ordered an equal expenditure of funds so that no child would be excluded from a publicly supported education. *Mills*, unlike *PARC*, applied not only to mental retardation, but to other handicapping conditions as well. Together these cases served as a basis for the development of federal legislation, particularly PL 94-142, requiring equal educational opportunity for children with disabilities. Indeed it was the due process provisions of *Mills* that served as the foundation for the specific requirements that were to emerge in the Education for All Handicapped Children Act of 1975 (EAHCA).

The Legislative Foundation

Although pervasive in their impact on school psychological services, the federal laws that shape daily practice are actually few in number. They are however comprehensive and detailed in coverage and, more so than any other source, have influenced the practices and procedures of school psychology. Earlier program or funding legislation was distinguished from civil rights or antidiscrimination legislation. The statutory provisions of Section 504 of the Rehabilitation Act, for example, are requirements that attempt to ensure disabled persons are not discriminated against.

Section 504 of the Rehabilitation Act. Adopted in 1973 as an amendment to an older law that focused on vocational rehabilitation regarding employment, the 1973 Rehabilitation Act provided that recipients of federal financial assistance could not discriminate on the basis of a handicap. Although adopted in 1973, the implementing regulations were not approved until 1977. Section 504 (as it is often referred to) is civil rights legislation and similar therefore to other antidiscrimination legislation such as that dealing with race (Title VI) and gender (Title IX). Ensuring compliance is then the responsibility of the Office of Civil Rights, not the U.S. Department of Education. The overarching requirement is that *all* recipients of federal funds not discriminate against an otherwise qualified disabled individual on the basis of disability. As such, requirements extend to many institutions (public and private) including business, health care, and of course schools.

Section 504 defines a disabled person as follows:

any person who (i) has a physical or mental impairment which substantially limits one or more of such person's major life activities, (ii) has a record of such an impairment, or (iii) is regarded as having such an impairment. [29 U.S.C. Sec. 706(7) (B)].

Physical or mental impairment includes physiological disorders or conditions, including cosmetic disfigurement, and mental or psychological disorders include mental retardation, organic brain syndrome, emotional or mental illness, and specific learning disabilities. Major life activities are "functions such as caring for one's self, performing manual tasks, walking, seeing, hearing, speaking, breathing, learning and working" (34 C.F.R. Part. 104.3).

Section 504 (Subpart D) requires that districts provide a "free appropriate public education" (FAPE) to each qualified person with a disability, regardless of the nature or severity of the disability. Districts are required to provide a full range of special accommodations and services necessary for students with disabilities to participate in and benefit from public education programs and activities.

Under Section 504 a free appropriate public education requires districts to follow procedures that ensure

- Nondiscriminatory evaluation and placement procedures.

- Periodic re-evaluation of students with disabilities.

- Educational services that meet individual educational needs.

- Educational services equal in quality to that provided for nondisabled students.

- To the maximum extent possible, the education of disabled students with nondisabled students.

• Due process procedures that ensure parent participation in evaluation and placement decisions and provide for an impartial hearing with parent representation by counsel.

A determination under Section 504 that a student has a disability does not necessarily mean that the student would be deemed disabled according to the criteria specified under IDEA. In those cases, students' educational needs must be provided for by regular education programs and their specific individualized educational needs met through the resources of regular education.

Individuals with Disabilities Education Act (IDEA). Triggered, in part, by the litigation of *PARC* and *Mills*, Congress, in 1974, passed a funding bill that required states to adopt goals that would ensure providing full educational opportunities to all handicapped children. Establishing such goals was a condition for receiving federal funds (PL 93-380). The following year Congress passed the Education for All Handicapped Children Act (EAHCA) which became effective in 1977. Finally, in 1990, Congress amended the EAHCA and retitled the law as the Individuals with Disabilities Act (IDEA; PL 101-476, 20 U.S.C. Sec. 1400 [a]).

The adoption of legislation mandating an equal educational opportunity to students with disabilities brought with it cornerstones of service delivery that continue to shape the practice and procedures for delivering both special education and school psychology services. These cornerstones remain the foundation for problem solving many of the questions that arise about delivering services to disabled students. These broad principles help us understand what is operationally meant by a free appropriate public education.

Zero reject. IDEA (as well as Section 504) makes it clear that all children are to be afforded an equal educational opportunity and states may not deny an education on the basis of a disability. Further, the law requires that states be affirmative in seeking out those who are disabled through "child find" activities. Extending an education to all disabled students today means those eligible individuals from birth through age 21. In addition, the severity of the disability is not a reason to deny an otherwise eligible student an education. As a result, the definition of education has been expanded to include even basic and fundamental life skills such as feeding and toilet training. Students may not be excluded from school only on the basis of a disability, and if a student's behavior at school is disruptive yet caused by the disability, schools remain obligated to provide for the student's education (Buesing & Prasse, 1991).

Appropriate education. Since the adoption of the federal law requiring public schools to provide an equal education opportunity to students with disabilities, the notion of what is an appropriate education has proven to be one of the most dynamic and evolving principles of the law. Professionals have debated issues of appropriate education in the literature while courts have rendered increasingly specific decisions that further define what is meant by appropriate.

To help determine what is appropriate, courts have turned to two key components required of districts when implementing FAPE. They are the *Individualized Education Program* (IEP) and *Least Restrictive Environment*. As a requirement of IDEA, the legal definition of an IEP means a written statement for a child with a disability that includes specific statements about a student's current educational level, annual goals, specific educational and related services, dates for initiation and anticipated duration, objective criteria for measuring the annual goals, and evaluation procedures. Least restrictive environment requires "that to the maximum extent appropriate, handicapped children, including children in public or private institutions or other care facilities are educated with children who are not handicapped" (34 C.F.R. Sec. 300.551[b] [1]). The legal definition continues with a requirement that "special classes, separate schooling or other removal of handicapped children from the regular educational environment occurs only when the nature or severity of the handicap is such that education in regular classes with the use of supplementary aids and services cannot be achieved satisfactorily" (34 C.F.R. Sec. 300.551[b] [2]).

Individualized Education Program. The requirement that a school district develop a plan unique (individualized) to the student's educational needs that includes goals, objectives, and time lines for implementation has been used by the Supreme Court as one basis by which to judge the congressional intent of the meaning of an appropriate education. In *Board v. Rowley* (1982) the Supreme Court dealt for the first time with the question of what constitutes an appropriate education. Deciding whether a deaf child required an interpreter (as a related service) the Court ruled that the interpreter was not required under the law. In reaching this decision the Court emphasized the legislative history of P.L. 94-142 and concluded that the intention of Congress was not to maximize development of students with disabilities. Rather it was to grant access to educational opportunity and provide a reasonable opportunity to learn. Noting that the student had learned and progressed from grade to grade the Court concluded the district had satisfied the intent of what is referred to as the "open door" policy, or in other words provide comparable treatment. Therefore, in the opinion of the Court the intent of IDEA is to provide a reasonable opportunity for a student to learn, not necessarily to maximize their potential.

The relevance of *Rowley* to the IEP and an appropriate education is noted when the Court affirmed what might be termed a process definition of the IEP. That is, if the IEP is developed procedurally in a manner compatible with the requirements of IDEA it will be deemed appropriate. An IEP developed by a group of professionals and parents is the basis or cornerstone for individualizing an education program. The *Rowley* decision affirmed that what was meant by appropriate education is gleaned from an overall understanding of IDEA which emphasizes process and inputs rather than results and outputs (Turnbull, 1986).

The relevance of the IEP to judging an appropriate education was strengthened in *Irving Independent School District v. Tatro* (1984). The fundamental question involved was whether Clean Intermittent Catheterization (CIC) was a necessary related service, or was it excluded as a medical service as is provided under IDEA. The child in question had spina bifida with orthopedic impairments. She required CIC assistance during the school day. The requirement was not mentioned as a component of the IEP and the district refused to administer it.

The Court affirmed the Tatro's claim that their child was entitled to CIC. The Court ruled that CIC is a related service as defined under IDEA, for it is a service which provides a meaningful access to an education. Necessary to the decision was to rule CIC a school health service and not a medical service.

With regard to an appropriate education the implication of the *Tatro* decision is two fold. First the decision affirms judicial review regarding the appropriateness of the IEP. Going therefore a step beyond *Rowley*, the Court made clear their intent to judge the appropriate education standard not only on the basis of adherence to procedural safeguards but on the basis of substance and content as well. The Court did review the content and substance of the IEP and found it wanting. Second, the decision serves to broaden the construct of related services to enable the child not only to benefit from but also to obtain access to educational services.

Least restrictive environment. The judicial cornerstone for educating children with disabilities with children who are not is over 40 years old, for it was *Brown v. Board of Education* (1954) that applied the equal protection clause of the Fourteenth Amendment to the issue of racial segregation in our public schools. Holding that separation is inherently unequal, the Supreme Court set forth the argument that education, when guaranteed by a state, is a property interest and must therefore be delivered in a manner that affords due process of law and equal protection of the laws. The principles set forth in *Brown* became the basis for subsequent litigation that forced the public schools to extend an equal educational opportunity to children with disabilities (*PARC v. Pennsylvania*, 1972; *Mills v. Board of Education*, 1972).

Separating children (either on the basis of race or disability) became then a practice that was considered unacceptable, if not illegal, and at both the state and federal level, legislation emerged that not only required an equal educational opportunity for the disabled student but also required that it be delivered in a "least restrictive environment." The requirement is nested in the judicial holding that separate is not equal and separation stigmatizes. In addition, interacting with nondisabled peers is considered an essential activity in the education and development of disabled students.

The consideration of the least-restrictive-environment variable in the appropriate education equation has proven to be one of the most challenging and continuously changing professional requirements. Even the language and concepts have changed markedly in the past 10 years, from *mainstreaming* to *inclusion.* The program and philosophical initiatives reflected in the Regular Education Initiative (Will, 1986) speak directly to this change.

In recent years several significant decisions have been reached by trial and appellate courts which have increased the significance of the least-restrictive-environment requirement in judging the appropriate education standard. Each has served to further interpret those sections of IDEA that bear heavily on the least restrictive environment/inclusion mandate. In *Daniel R. R. v. State Board of Education* (1989), the Fifth Circuit Court of Appeals constructed from the language of IDEA a two-part test for deciding whether a school district is in compliance with IDEA's least restrictive requirement. First, a determination must be made "whether education in the regular classroom, with the use of supplementary aids and services, can be achieved satisfactorily" (874 F. 2d. at 1048). Second, if a court determines that placement outside a regular classroom is necessary for the child's educational benefit, it must then decide "whether the school has mainstreamed the child to the maximum extent appropriate" (874 F.2d at 1048).

With *Daniel R. R.* in place the parents of Rafael Oberti sued the school district to move Rafael from a separate classroom to a regular classroom. Rafael is a Down's Syndrome child. In *Oberti v. Board of Education* (No. 92-546, 1993), the Third Circuit Court of Appeals found in favor of the Oberti family and identified three factors that should be considered in deciding whether a child can be educated satisfactorily in a regular classroom with supplementary aids and services. First, what steps has the school taken to try and include the child in a regular classroom? Second is a comparison between the educational benefits the child will receive in a regular classroom (with supplementary aids and services) and the benefits the child will receive in the segregated, special education classroom. Third, what is the possible negative effect the child's inclusion may have on the education of the other children in the regular classroom? Only after a consideration of these three questions can the question of including the child in school programs with nondisabled children to the maximum extent appropriate be considered.

The judgment of an appropriate education is then a complex and changing issue. The fundamental constitutional, legislative, and judicial requirements allow for the delineation of some general practice considerations, including:

- IEPs are created by a team (professionals and parents).

- The process followed by the team is an important legal consideration in judging the appropriateness of the school based decision.

- The content of the IEP is equally important, from the perspectives of what is stated, what is not stated, and what is missing that should be stated.

- Programming must proceed on the basis of what is articulated in the IEP.

- There must be measureable goals and objectives for each student and evaluation of a student's progress is required so that results are realized, not just services provided.

- Parental participation is absolute at every stage.

- Appeal of school district decisions is permitted, first through the administrative hearing process and second through the court. Appeals may be based on either alleged procedural violations or alleged content/substance violations.

The Family Educational Rights and Privacy Act

The Family Educational Rights and Privacy Act (FERPA, 1974, also referred to as the Buckley Amendment) was adopted by Congress at the same time it passed the original legislation providing an education for disabled students. Adopted as a result of many complaints from parents and students about record inaccessibility and inaccuracy, the law established rules regarding access and inspection, copying, and release. Many of the requirements were repeated in later legislation (e.g., IDEA). Although the law is over 20 years old, questions remain and some disagreement over the accessibility of certain records continues.

Questions focus on which records are accessible, which, if any are exempt, and whether the procedures and principles of confidentiality, privileged communication, and test security relate in any way to the records-access law. Frequently the questions focus specifically on accessibility of test protocols, and "private notes." The answer to such questions is partially found in the law's definition of a record *and* through a study of congressional intent regarding the law. An education record is defined as follows:

A. For the purposes of this section the term "education records" means, except as may be provided otherwise in subparagraph (b), those records, files, documents, and other materials which

    i. contain information directly related to a student and;

    ii. are maintained by an educational agency or institution, or by a person acting for such an agency or institution.

B. The term "education records" does not include:

    i. records of instructional, supervisory, and administrative personnel ancillary thereto which are in the sole possession of the maker thereof and which are not accessible or revealed to any other person except a substitute.

Where psychologists have questioned the right of parents to access certain records, they usually have referred to Part B. In claiming that a protocol is not an accessible record some school psychologists have claimed that a protocol is in their sole possession and that they are the exclusive maker, or that the protocol is a private note.

When the meaning of legislation is unclear the intent may be learned through a review of the congressional debate and/or accompanying statements of explanation. It is here that the intent of the law is found and in this case helps clarify the issue of accessibility of protocols. It is in the Joint Statement in Explanation of Buckley/Pell Amendment (Congressional Record at S.21488, December 13, 1974) that the intent of the definition and exception is partially clarified.

> An individual should be able to know, review, and challenge all information — with certain limited exceptions — that an institution keeps on him, particularly when the institution may make important decisions affecting his future, or may transmit such personal information to parties outside the institution. This is especially true when the individual is a minor. Parents need access to such information in order to protect the interests of their child.
>
> The amendment makes certain reasonable exceptions to the access by parents and students to school records. The private notes and other materials, such as a teacher's daily record book, created by individual school personnel (such as teachers, deans, doctors, etc.) as memory aids would not be available to parents or students, provided they are not revealed to another person, other than in the case of a substitute who performs another's duties for a temporary period.

Continuing, the statements go on to say:

> If a child has been labeled as mentally or otherwise retarded and put in a special class or school, parents would be able to review materials in the record which led to this institutional decision . . . to see whether

these materials contain inaccurate or erroneous evaluations about their child.

The Congressional intent is affirmed in *John K. and Mary K. v. Board of Education for School District 65* (1987). This Illinois appellate court decision held that raw psychological test data is part of a student's temporary record subject to disclosure. The school psychologist who had administered the Rorschach argued that the verbatim responses were raw data and not subject to disclosure. The court was not persuaded either by professional standards or by federal regulations that the psychologist cited in support of nondisclosure.

Of relevance to the question of accessibility are the requirements of PL 94-142 that provide parents the right to inspect and review their children's records collected, maintained, and used by the school in its special education decision making. It would be difficult to argue that test results are not used by psychologists in this process and therefore inaccessible. Certainly a parental challenge to placement (either at the hearing or judicial level) would result in a request to review test protocols. To refuse would be to deny parents the right to review important records on which the school's decision was based. Finally, access does not necessarily mean obtaining a copy. With respect to test protocols publishing companies have made it clear that such material is protected by copyright restrictions. So while parents or their legal representatives might have access, indiscriminate or wholesale copying is not allowed. Clearly the access-to-records requirements necessitate a delicate balance between the public right to be informed and the psychologist's responsibilities to the student and accepted professional standards.

SUMMARY

As a profession we have come to experience ongoing changes that affect our practices and procedures. The sources of change come from both within and outside the discipline. The legal influence has been pervasive and constant. As school psychologists we understand the mandates of parental participation, notice and consent, the requirement that all children with disabilities be afforded an education, and the necessity to ensure valid and reliable assessments that address educational needs. There are constitutional foundations and statutory requirements for these and other practices and any change in our practice will require adherence to these.

Many of the emerging reforms in school psychology are compatible with sound legal practice — practice that honors not only the technical requirements of the law — but the intent as well. Some examples include

- Curriculum-based assessment faces fewer problems associated with cultural differences than does norm-referenced assessment.

- Greater emphasis on classroom-based instruction responsive to the individual needs of disabled students who are educated as a matter of first course with nondisabled students invites (if not demands) integration in the least restrictive environment.

- Meaningful evaluation of short-term objectives and long-term goals increases the likelihood of achievement-oriented results and is more readily accomplished when using curriculum-based assessment.

In the end our challenges should be focused more on successful educational interventions than conformity to procedural due process. The more success we have with the former the less we will need to be concerned about the latter.

REFERENCES

American Psychological Association. (1981). *Speciality guidelines for the delivery of services by school psychologists*. Washington, DC: Author.

American Psychological Association. (1992). *Ethical Principles of Psychologists and Code of Conduct*. Washington, DC: Author.

American Psychological Association, American Education Research Association, & National Council on Measurement in Education. (1984). *Standards for educational and psychological tests*. Washington, DC: Author.

Board of Education of the Hendrick Hudson Central School v. Rowley, 102 S.Ct. 3034 (1982).

Brown v. Board of Education, 347 U.S.483 (1954).

Buesing, D. A., & Prasse, D. P. (1991, August). *Expelling handicapped children: Judicial review and psychological practice*. Paper presented at the American Psychological Association Annual Convention, San Francisco.

Daniel R. R. v. State Board of Education, 874 F. 2d 1048 (1989).

Education of All Handicapped Children Act of 1975, 20 U.S.C. Sec. 401 (1975).

Family Educational Rights and Privacy Act. Implementing Regulations, 34 C.F.R. Sec. 99.3 (1976).

Individuals with Disabilities Act, 20 U.S.C. Sec. 1400 (1990).

Irving Independent School District v. Tatro, 104 S.Ct. 3371 (1984).

John K. and Mary K. v. Board of Education for School District No. 65, 504 N.E.2d. 797 (1987).

Mills v. Board of Education of the District of Columbia, 384 F. Supp. 866 (1972).

National Association of School Psychologists. (1992). *Principles for Professional Ethics*. Washington, DC: Author.

Oberti v. Board of Education, No. 92-546, Third Circuit Court of Appeals (1993).

PARC v. Commonwealth of Pennsylvania, 343 F. Supp. (1972).

Plessy v. Ferguson, 163 U.S. 537 (1896).

Rehabilitation Act of 1973, 20 U.S.C. Sec. 794.

ANNOTATED BIBLIOGRAPHY

Hart, S., & Prasse, D. (Eds.). (1991). Children's rights and education. *School Psychology Review, 20,* 331–440.

This theme issue of the *School Psychology Review* provides perspectives on the historical evolution of children's rights, clarifies the significance of core rights and issues, and indicates their relevance for education and school psychology. The articles react to the United Nations Convention on the Rights of the Child and are conceptual as opposed to empirical, often surfacing themes of the dignity of children as persons.

Jacob, S., & Hartshorne, T. (1991). *Ethics and law for school psychologists.* Brandon, VT: Clinical Psychology Publishing.

The authors present a comprehensive overview of legal influences on the practice of school psychology. Coverage includes both statutory and judicial review and ethical standards. Important issues such as privacy, confidentiality, research, and consultation are all covered. The book is well organized and includes many original references to the relevant issues affecting special education and school psychology.

Keith-Spiegel, P., & Koocher, G. (1985). *Ethics in psychology: Professional standards and cases.* New York: Random House.

Excellent coverage of applied practice and ethical issues. This book uses text and cases adjudicated before various ethics committees. Comprehensive chapters are included on record keeping, assessment, therapeutic intervention, dual-role relationships, and others. Each chapter begins with a definition and thorough explanation of the topic followed by application drawing on different cases and professional standards.

Melton, G. (Ed.). (1989). *Reforming the law: Impact of child development research.* New York: Guilford.

This compilation of chapters drawing on years of child development research in a wide range of areas assesses the impact of research on children's competence in decision making. Chapters provide coverage of the broader areas of applied psychology, scientific knowledge, and judicial decision making. Drawing from a research foundation, authors provide suggestions for influencing the legal system.

Prasse, D. (1988). Licensing, school psychology and independent private practice. In T. R. Kratochwill (Ed.), *Advances in school psychology: Volume VI* (pp. 49–80). Hillsdale, NJ: Lawrence Erlbaum Associates.

This chapter provides an overview of regulation and licensing. Scope and authority of licensing is presented and coverage is given to legal and ethical considerations in professional practice. Examples of specialty licenses in school psychology are presented along with definitions of scope of practice. Emergent problems associated with delivering school psychological services in the private sector are discussed.

Best Practices in System-Level Consultation and Organizational Change

Michael J. Curtis
Stephanie A. Stollar
University of South Florida

OVERVIEW

Consider four situations seemingly quite different, but each of which might very well confront a school psychologist:

- A fifth-grade team is concerned about an increase in the number of incidents involving aggressive behavior among their students and wants to work with parents in addressing the problem.

- An elementary school wants to implement an intervention assistance program to provide more support to classroom teachers in their efforts to respond to the needs of their students.

- The Board of Education decides to establish local school improvement teams in each of the schools throughout the district.

- The Child Development Council is faced with numerous logistical problems resulting from the anticipation of a dramatic increase in enrollments in its Head Start programs.

Each of these cases represents a system-level problem. At the very least, each situation is likely, directly or indirectly, to impact the school psychologist (e.g., requests for help with incidents of aggressive behavior, participation as a member of an intervention assistance team, operational changes in the school resulting from the work of the local school improvement team, problems experienced by both teachers and children when a Head Start Center opens despite many unresolved logistical issues). On the other hand, each is a situation in which the school psychologist, through system-level consultation, could serve as a valuable resource in facilitating change at a classroom, grade, building, district, or county-wide level.

The frequency of discussions and reports of activities relating to school reform efforts all across the United States suggest a tremendous need for the involvement and support of individuals highly skilled in problem solving and in understanding and facilitating organizational change. Consequently, this may be an opportune time for school psychologists to consider expanding typical roles and functions into this new area of professional service, a service that could indirectly benefit many more students than typically can be impacted through direct services to individual students (e.g., assessment, counseling).

Although system consultation has not been among the services emphasized by many school psychologists, it is an area to which many school psychologists could bring valuable knowledge and expertise. The foundation of psychology is understanding human behavior. A special strength of school psychology is understanding human behavior, that of children as well as adults, within the context of schools and educational institutions.

BASIC CONSIDERATIONS

There are some circumstances in which a school psychologist might function in the role of a system consultant from outside the organization. In other words, he or she would be specifically employed to deliver system-level consultation. However, in most cases, the school psychologist will be an employee of the organization and system consultation will represent only one of a variety of direct and indirect services offered. To engage effectively in system-level consultation, school psychologists need to call upon three areas of expertise in addition to their foundation of knowledge regarding human behavior: (a) understanding human behavior from a social systems perspective, (b) ability to use collaborative-planning and problem-solving procedures, and (c) familiarity with principles for organizational change.

Schools as Social Systems

Although schools usually can be identified by their physical appearance, without the students, teachers, special services professionals, administrators, and other personnel who work there, they are very much like any other building. Bricks, mortar, steel beams, and glass, regardless of their configuration, do not indicate much about the character of a school; it is the people within who give it life and make the school a living social system. Thus, if 10 school buildings were exactly the same in terms of physical structure, no 2 among them would be functionally alike because of the uniqueness of the individuals who inhabit each school building.

Understanding systems. System-level intervention and organization development are founded in general systems theory. Initially, the application of systems theory was confined largely to military and industrial settings. The relevance of systems theory to the behavioral sciences did not emerge until the mid-1950s. Consideration of this theory in schools as a framework for analyzing complex organizational problems and developing solutions did not begin until the mid-1960s.

What is a system? It is important to clarify the meaning of the term *system*. Simply stated, a system is an orderly combination of parts that interact to produce a desired outcome or product. An automobile engine is an example of a system. It consists of a number of specific parts that interact to produce power and motion. However, in contrast to a living system, an automobile engine is an example of an *inert* system; that is, as long as the parts continue to function, the engine should continue to produce power in essentially the same way.

Schools are *living* systems because, as noted previously, it is people who give schools their real meaning. Technically, living systems exist on a continuum beginning with individual cells within a human being and extending all the way to the entire population of the earth. For the purposes of this chapter, however, a somewhat narrower spectrum is appropriate. For our purposes, *a system is the orderly combination of two or more individuals whose interaction is intended to produce a desired outcome.*

Consistent with this definition, a school is a system because it consists of component parts (e.g., students, teachers, school psychologists, cafeteria workers, parent volunteers, principal) that are organized in some fashion and interact for the purpose of producing a definable outcome, educated children. As is true of all systems, the school is also part of a larger system, the school district. Individual classrooms, grade-level teams of teachers, local school-improvement committees, and intervention assistance teams are also examples of systems. Each consists of component parts that interact for the purpose of attaining desired outcomes, and each exists within a larger system.

Reciprocal influence. A critical feature that differentiates a living system from an inert system is its ability to interact with and to react to its environment, both internally and externally. Because of their capacity to interact with the environment, all living systems are *open systems.* Each of the parts of a system influences all of the other parts as well as the performance of the system as a whole. A change in one part will cause change in other parts of the system. For example, if the building principal (one component of the school) is replaced by a new principal, that change is likely to effect classrooms, students, teachers, the school psychologist, cafeteria workers, and so forth. Although changes in one component of the system may tend to have more impact than do others because of the role played by that particular part (a principal versus one student), *each part*, regardless of role or size, influences the system to some degree. There also can be circumstances that significantly alter the influence normally expected by a change in one part (e.g., a tragedy involving one student that impacts everyone in the school). Similarly, changes in the larger surrounding environment (called the suprasystem) influence the system as well as the components (called subsystems within). For example, the enactment of a new district policy on discipline would influence the individual school as well as its teachers, students, and other personnel to varying degrees.

A systems perspective involves the ability to understand the reciprocal influence that the various parts of a system, the system itself, and the surrounding system or environment exert on one another. Bandura (1978) suggested viewing the individual child within a systems framework. From the systems or ecological perspective, the child is one element in a larger environment. Personal characteristics, behavior, and forces within the environment are all interrelated and influence each other. The child influences and is influenced by various forces in the system of which she or he is a part.

The capacity of the system to solve problems. One of the ways in which systems differ is the extent of their openness to environmental influences. Systems deemed healthy, based on their identified goals screen environmental information, accepting what is important, rejecting what is not, and responding in a manner appropriate for the information received. In other words, healthy systems demonstrate the capacity to analyze problems and to solve them in a manner that facilitates the attainment of their goals.

Of course, some systems lack the capacity to solve problems effectively. In some cases, they are not sufficiently open to accept important information. Or they may have been open at an earlier time, but because they did not have the ability to solve problems confronting them, they became closed (somewhat like the ostrich with its head in the sand). The inability to interact with influential forces, internally as well as externally, creates tremendous tension in closed systems. If the tension reaches a high enough level, a crisis occurs which causes some type of change in the system.

Rigidity Elementary School, Anywhere, U.S.A., offers one illustration of a closed system. An increasing number of discipline problems are occurring on school buses transporting students to and from the school. As a result, several parents have called the school to express their concerns. Initially, the principal tells the parents that these are isolated incidents and that such problems rarely occur. As the problems continue to increase, the principal has the receptionist screen his calls, telling parents that he is in a meeting and will return their calls later. However, the calls are never returned. Angry parents show up at the school, asking to see the principal, but he is unavailable. Frustrated and fearful for their children, the parents show up and voice their anger at a meeting of the district board of education. Eventually, the principal is forced to respond to the parental concerns or is replaced.

On the other hand, some systems are too open and are unable to screen environmental forces. They essentially accept all input and try to respond to everything, often with the same level of intensity. They are overwhelmed and operate in a constant state of crisis. Everything must be done immediately! Crisis Elementary School, Elsewhere, U.S.A., serves as an example of this type of system. In this case, every time a parent calls the school to express a concern, the principal responds by writing a memorandum to the entire staff or creating a new policy that impacts the entire school. The result is that the school is in a constant state of change. In such systems, because there is a lack of stability and continuity, it is exceedingly difficult to set goals, make plans to attain them, and monitor progress.

The primary goal of system-level consultation is to increase the problem-solving capacity of the system so that it can deal with all problems more effectively. In this way, system-level consultation is exactly like one-to-one consultation. While the immediate objective in one-to-one consultation is to help the consultee (the person requesting assistance) solve the problem causing the concern, the primary objective is to help that person become more effective in solving similar problems in the future In system-level consultation, the system is the consultee. While the immediate goal is to help the system solve a specific problem, the primary goal is to facilitate the development of the system as an effective problem solver. In both cases, although involvement in consultation is likely to result in improved problem solving for the consultee(s), direct consultee training in problem-solving methods will result in greater and more immediate skill development.

Collaborative Planning and Problem Solving

Collaboration serves as the foundation for system-level consultation. In simple terms, collaboration means working together to achieve a common objective. *For the purpose of consultation, whether one-to-one or system level, collaboration means two or more people working together, using systematic planning and problem-solving procedures, to achieve desired outcomes.*

The principles of collaborative planning and problem solving that apply to individual consultation are directly relevant to system-level consultation as well. In fact, collaborative one-to-one consultation and system level consultation are directly parallel in almost every respect. Although we will not discuss one-to-one consultation skills in depth here, it would be helpful to note very briefly some of the fundamental characteristics of effective consultation.

Interpersonal relationships. Effective consultation is based on mutual respect, trust, and coordinate power status among the participants. The role of the system consultant is to facilitate the efforts of the group to achieve the goals that *the group* has decided upon, in a manner that *the group* chooses. Effective communication skills are essential for a consultant. The ability to listen, ask open-ended questions, paraphrase, and summarize and synthesize information, all within a nonjudgmental climate, are especially important. While these skills are important for all consultants, they take on added significance when attempting to facilitate change from *within* the system. Group members often are not very tolerant of a member whose behaviors tend to alter the coordinate power status among members (e.g., giving advice or feedback to the group or to individual members).

Planning and problem-solving skills. It is essential to remember that consultation is a problem-solving process and that attention to *both* interpersonal relationship skills *and* problem-solving procedures are critical in determining success. Curtis and Van Wagener (1988) demonstrated that despite highly effective interpersonal skills, consultation was not effective in resolving student-related concerns when problem-solving procedures were not employed. Effectiveness in each area is necessary but insufficient by itself.

Fundamentally, planning and problem-solving procedures are very similar, with the major difference being one of direction, that is, desired outcome. Whereas planning is intended to achieve a desirable goal, problem solving is intended to alleviate an undesirable condition.

There are literally hundreds of articles and other works in which authors have discussed planning and/or problem solving. Many models have been proposed that apply such procedures in different ways and incorporate varying numbers of steps or stages. Although the number of steps may vary, most models reflect, implicitly if not explicitly, the inclusion of four major stages:

1. Problem/Situation Analysis.

2. Goal Identification

3. Strategy Development and Implementation.

4. Evaluation.

Regardless of the model chosen, effective consultation must include all four of these stages. However, it also should be noted that although such models typically describe a specific sequence of stages, actual problem solving during individual consultation often does not proceed in such a mechanical, lockstep manner. Rather, it is common for there to be movement back and forth among the stages. Nevertheless, the general sequence of stages typically should occur as described and *all* stages must be included. For a comprehensive review of the consultation literature and a discussion of the core characteristics of different consultation models (including interpersonal relationships) and problem solving, the reader is referred to Gutkin and Curtis (1990).

Principles for Organizational Change

Applying system-level analysis and organization development to schools received little if any attention until the mid-1960s so the area remains relatively new. Nevertheless, a considerable amount of organizational change research and conceptual literature regarding other social systems has been published. This work, when combined with the research and conceptual literature generated specific to educational settings, has yielded a useful knowledge base to guide system-level consultation in schools. Fullan, Miles, and Taylor (1980) have provided an excellent comprehensive review and synthesis of the organization development literature available up to that time. Although other relevant work has been published since then, the review by these authors still probably represents the best single resource on the state of the art regarding organization development in schools.

BEST PRACTICES

Best practices in system-level consultation can be illustrated through an examination of key concepts and practices addressed in the organizational change literature. Furthermore, it is important to remember throughout the following discussion that system-level consultation is a problem-solving process and, therefore, directly parallels the steps of individual problem solving. Key concepts and principles for organizational change through systems consultation will be identified and discussed.

Planning for Change

A definition of organization development provides fundamental principles to guide the practice of system consultation. Although a number of definitions have been suggested, for our purposes, *organization development is the planned and sustained effort to bring about system-level improvement through self-analytic and problem-solving methods.* System-level change must be planned and pursued in a systematic manner over time. It does not just happen. Furthermore, it is not an event or activity, but an ongoing process. The definition presented above also emphasizes the critical point discussed earlier; that is, the primary goal of system consultation is for the system to become more effective in solving all problems. Solving a specific, precipitating problem should be considered only a short-term goal. However, it typically is the precipitating problem that provides an opportunity to engage in a longer, sustained effort for system-level change. In this way, system consultation parallels individual consultation. A specific concern causes the consultee to seek assistance. But the resultant involvement in consultation is intended to increase the general problem-solving skills of the consultee as well as to address the precipitating concern.

The Uniqueness of Each System

The same intervention methods would not be employed to address different concerns relating to different students. The intervention would have to fit the specific problem in each situation. Yet, in system consultation, there sometimes seems to be a tendency to use the same change strategies, regardless of the specific characteristics and needs of different systems.

System consultation is built upon careful analysis of the organization and of the resulting plan that is designed to address the unique needs and characteristics of a particular system. Two types of procedures that are useful at this stage include *diagnostic evaluation* and *input evaluation*. Diagnostic evaluation is helpful for identifying the needs of the system through multiple sources. It might be conceptualized as a multifactored evaluation at the system level. Formal techniques such as surveys and questionnaires may be combined with informal measures such as interviews and observations to provide a complete understanding of the organization. Needs assessments are particularly useful not only for gathering information about the organization but for involving all members of the system in the change process (Curtis & Metz, 1986).

Once the needs of the system have been clearly identified, available resources that may be relevant to addressing those needs are examined through input evaluation. The skills and resources of the staff, support of parents and district personnel, and financial resources are some of the factors to be considered. Focusing on problems can sometimes make it easy to overlook the importance of acknowledging and building upon the existing strengths, resources, and successes of the system. Attitudinal factors may be just as important as tangible resources. The planning stage of system-level consultation is directly parallel to the intent of the problem analysis stage of the problem-solving process used in individual consultation. A thorough understanding of all relevant factors, both negative and positive, must be developed before moving forward.

Commitment of Key Personnel

Because successful change requires a large investment of staff time and effort, voluntary participation is desired. In addition, the high level of involvement necessitates the commitment of key personnel. At the very least, such persons cannot be obstacles if the change effort is to succeed.

Gatekeepers. It is essential to identify all *gatekeepers* before any aspect of the change process, including diagnostic evaluation, is initiated. The role of the gatekeeper is characterized by decision-making power, ability to distribute resources, and authority within the system. Gatekeepers must not only give sanction for the change process but, optimally, provide support and fully participate with all other members of the system. Sometimes, just the nonparticipation of the gatekeeper can be a negative factor warranting consideration. The role of gatekeeper is most commonly held by personnel such as the principal or superintendent. However, staff in less obviously powerful positions, such as the school secretary or specific teachers, can function as gatekeepers and be influential in determining the success or failure of change efforts.

Involvement of all stakeholders. In addition to securing the commitment of gatekeepers, those involved in organizational change must see that all *stakeholders* in the system participate in every stage of the change process. This is a fundamental principle for oganizational change. Stakeholders are all members of the system who will be impacted by the change. Decisions about system-level change in schools are often made at the administration level. Failure to involve important stakeholders, such as classroom teachers, will negatively impact the organizational change effort.

Many efforts to implement intervention assistance programs in schools have violated this fundamental rule. Typically, the discussions, planning, and even implementation have involved seemingly everyone *but* classroom teachers. Principals, special education personnel, school psychologists, and other related services professionals then "inform" teachers about the new procedures. Confusion and frustration result when teachers do not participate regardless of the good intentions of the change agents. Common sense suggests that classroom teachers are *the* primary stakeholders among a school's professional staff who will be impacted by the implementation of intervention assistance programs. They should be meaningfully involved in every aspect of such change efforts, beginning with initial discussions regarding

potential change and continuing through implementation.

Demonstrating change strategies. Because an organizational change effort must be planned and sustained over time, it is important that not only key personnel, but all stakeholders, have a realistic understanding of what may be involved. Otherwise, the absence of immediate change (an unrealistic goal to begin with) could lead to the loss of commitment and investment in the process. Therefore, it may be helpful to demonstrate change methods so the group can gain familiarity as well as experience success in addressing real concerns. Curtis (1982) suggested that teaching group problem-solving techniques is helpful in securing the commitment of the school staff. This activity could involve having the participants identify real concerns and establish goals for change. Then, group problem-solving skills are used to develop strategies to address the concerns. This exercise serves to teach the problem-solving skills necessary for planning change as well as confirms the commitment of the staff to the goals for change. Curtis and Metz (1986) provide a case study in system-level change that employs this type of strategy.

Goal Identification

Based on the diagnostic evaluation and input evaluations, specific desirable outcomes should be identified. It is critical that these goals reflect information derived during the problem-analysis procedures. These goals will determine the types of system-level intervention considered, and specifically those chosen for implementation. It is at this stage that groups often discover that they have identified several different, although related, goals. Refinement of goals and the selection of one goal at a time to pursue through specific change strategies will enhance the likelihood that the group will be successful in their efforts.

It also is important to *establish realistic, concrete, system-level goals*, especially during the early stages of an organizational change effort. When seeking organizational change, planners can get lost in an "all-or-nothing" view of the system. The consultant needs to break larger goals down into more reasonable steps by which change can be measured. Even a small initial change has the potential to create a ripple effect that leads to more significant change later. For example, one school psychologist began by regularly scheduling only 15 minutes each week to talk with the building principal about building-level issues. After a few weeks of such talks, an interesting journal article related to one of the issues discussed would occasionally be given to the principal. Over time, the school psychologist came to be viewed by the principal as a source of information and expertise regarding a broader range of issues, particularly as they pertained to organizational concerns.

Strategy Development and Implementation

System-level consultation involves ongoing activities to address long-term goals. Intervention is not conceptualized as a single event. Therefore, it is helpful to have a staff member who will serve as facilitator of the change process. Although school psychologists may be well suited for this role, the itinerant nature of many school psychology assignments may preclude involvement in the ongoing monitoring of change.

The overall plan for change may involve intervention methods which target the cognitive, affective, and/or structural components of the organization. Interventions that address cognitive aspects would include instructional activities such as training staff in new technology or practice. Affective interventions are those that address the interpersonal relationships among the staff. Examples include training in communication and effective listening skills. Structural interventions focus on the way the organization is put together and its relationship to the various sub- and suprasystems. Because these components are somewhat interrelated, system-level intervention plans that address all three may be most effective. The intervention activities should be carefully selected to achieve aspects of the overall goal of the system.

Teaching Planning and Problem-Solving Procedures

As noted previously, the development of problem-solving skills by system members is the primary goal of system-level consultation. The most effective method for achieving this goal is through direct instruction, practice, and follow-up. Therefore, the consultant should provide training to as many of the major stakeholders in the system as possible. The effectiveness of the system will increase as the proportion of its members who are effective problem solvers increases.

It may be necessary to begin by training only a few members; however, providing all members with training in problem-solving skills should still be maintained as an eventual goal. For example, in working at the building level, a school psychologist may begin by training a specific group such as the local school improvement team. Once the group has been trained, had an opportunity to practice using collaborative planning and problem-solving procedures, and then refined their use of such methods through feedback, discussion, and perhaps further training, they can become a vehicle for planning training for the remainder of the staff. However, improving the problem-solving skills of any members of the system represents progress, even if training the entire staff is not possible. Any improvement should be recognized as a positive outcome of system-change efforts.

Although many different approaches to problem solving might be used, the model described in the next section has been used by this chapter's authors to train a wide range of individuals and groups in a variety of settings, including schools, agencies, and professional organizations. Each of the steps is explained briefly. Then an example is provided based on the actual work of a school-based intervention assistance team.

A Model for Collaborative Planning and Problem Solving

The effectiveness of this model is dependent on conscientious adherence to following the steps described in sequential order and thoroughly completing one step before moving on to the next. For ease of presentation, each step is explained in terms of *problem-solving* procedures. However, the same steps may be used to achieve goals identified for the purpose of *planning*.

1. *Describe the problem or concern as concretely and as specifically as possible. Once the problem has been defined, identify the desired outcome of your problem-solving efforts, again using concrete, descriptive terms.*

Often, what initially is thought to be a problem, once analyzed, is recognized to be several distinct, although perhaps related problems. Record all problems identified. Although all of them may not be dealt with during a particular session, once recorded, they can be addressed during subsequent sessions. Identify the specific problem that will be addressed *first.* Then, define the desired outcome that would result from resolution of only that specific problem. It is essential that all members of the problem-solving team have the same understanding of the problem to be addressed and of the desired outcome.

2. *Analyze the specific problem chosen in terms of factors that might help in addressing it (resources)* and *factors that serve as obstacles to its resolution.*

Using a "brainstorming" process, all members of the group participate in generating a list of resources and obstacles. The use of only concise statements should be encouraged. It is essential that ideas are not discussed, evaluated, or even clarified at this point. The intent is to produce as much information as possible by involving all members of the group in a free flow of ideas. Record only enough about each idea to allow clarification by its originator after brainstorming is completed. This should be recognized as an "idea" stage. There have been no decisions made regarding actions to be carried out.

3. *Select* one *obstacle that is significant in terms of its hindrance to resolving the specific problem identified in Step 1.*

The obstacle selected should be viewed as the first obstacle to be addressed, not as the only one. It is best to avoid trying to identify the most important obstacle to reduce concerns that may be associated with ownership according to who generated specific ideas. Other important obstacles can be noted for future attention.

4. *Focusing only on the one obstacle selected in Step 3, brainstorm resources and activities that might be used to reduce or eliminate that obstacle.*

The list of resources identified in Step 2 serve only as a stimulus for the generation of ideas. Again, because a brainstorming process is being used, the intent is to generate and record as many ideas as possible. Specific ideas can be clarified after brainstorming is complete. Remind participants that this is only an *idea* stage and that no decisions have been made regarding actual action plans.

5. *Design a concrete plan of action that reflects accountability for completion (i.e., who, what, when).*

If possible, several action plans should be developed to address the same obstacle. In that way, if one plan is not carried out or does not attain the desired results, the identified obstacle still may be reduced or eliminated through other actions. Each plan should clearly identify *who* (by name) is responsible for carrying out *which* specific activity (include as much detail as possible) by *what* date. Avoid stating any aspect of a plan in general terms; the greater the detail provided in a plan, the greater the likelihood that it will be carried out as intended and on time. Sometimes, it is desirable to try out an action plan on a limited scale before proceeding with full implementation.

6. *Establish a procedure for follow-up and review.*

Consider interim reporting dates and procedures to check on the progress of an action plan, rather than waiting until the deadline for its conclusion. This stage also is used to evaluate the effectiveness of action plans and for modifying them or even recycling to an earlier stage in the process.

Example of the Six-Step Problem-Solving Model

To clarify the problem-solving process within the limits of the space available, the following example includes only selected entries for some steps.

Original concern: The teachers are not using the Intervention Assistance Team as a means for helping them respond to the special needs of their students.

Statement of problem/concern: Many of the staff are unaware of the benefits they can receive from intervention assistance.

Resources:

- Some staff have used the process and realized benefits.
- Resource people have worked with other schools where process is working well.

Obstacles:

- Intervention assistance is viewed as a barrier to testing.
- We haven't communicated very effectively with our staff about process and results.

Obstacle selected: We haven't communicated very effectively with our staff about the intervention assistance process and the results.

Brainstormed ideas:

- Conduct an in-service on the benefits.
- Report regularly during staff meetings.
- Disseminate written reports on process and results.

Action Plan 1: Sue, Anne, and Mr. Allen will make a presentation at the staff meeting on March 10th about the process and how it is intended to be a resource for teachers.

Action Plan 2: Jim will contact several teachers who have used the process and ask if they will report during the March 10th staff meeting on the benefits they experienced. He will contact them by March 3rd.

Action Plan 3: Mr. Allen will contact Jan Smith, a school psychologist who works in several schools, to ask if she will also make a brief presentation during the staff meeting regarding the benefits being realized in some other buildings. He will contact her by March 3rd.

Follow-up: The intervention assistance team will meet March 3rd at 3:00 p.m. to review the plans for the in-service program and to make any final arrangements.

Evaluation

Measuring progress can be achieved on two levels: (a) progress toward the objectives of specific intervention activities and (b) progress toward the long-term goal. As with individual consultation, frequent evaluation is essential for determining progress and identifying the need for adjustments to the plan.

SUMMARY

Many opportunities exist for school psychologists to expand their role to include indirect service to students through system-level consultation. By building on current competencies, school psychologists can increase participation in system-level change efforts by viewing behavior from a systems perspective, using collaborative-planning and problem-solving procedures, and becoming familiar with principles for organizational change. The fundamental components and goals of individual consultation are directly parallel to system-level consultation. Any planned change effort, no matter how small, can be an important step toward improved services for students.

REFERENCES

Bandura, A. (1978). The self-system in reciprocal determinism. *American Psychologist, 33,* 344–358.

Curtis, M. J. (1982, March). *Gaining access to schools through a demonstration of organization development techniques.* Paper presented at the annual meeting of the National Association of School Psychologists, Toronto.

Curtis, M. J., & Metz, L. W. (1986). System level intervention in a school for handicapped children. *School Psychology Review, 15,* 510–518.

Curtis, M. J., & Van Wagener, E. (1988, April). *An analysis of failed consultation.* Paper presented at the annual meeting of the National Association of School Psychologists, Chicago.

Fullan, M., Miles, M. B., & Taylor, G. (1980). Organization development in schools: The state of the art. *Review of Educational Research, 50,* 121–183.

Gutkin, T. B., & Curtis, M. J. (1990). School-based consultation: Theory, techniques, and research. In T. B. Gutkin & C. R. Reynolds (Eds.), *The handbook of school psychology* (2nd ed., pp. 577–613). New York: Wiley.

ANNOTATED BIBLIOGRAPHY

Fullan, M., Miles, M. B., & Taylor, G. (1980). Organization development in schools: The state of the art. *Review of Educational Research, 50,* 121–183.
Although somewhat dated, this article provides the most comprehensive theoretical and empirical review of the use of organization development (OD) in schools. The authors present the defining characteristics of OD in general and as applied to education, the various models of OD in practice, an assessment of the outcomes of OD, and suggestions for future applications.

Gutkin, T. B., & Curtis, M. J. (1990). School-based consultation: Theory, techniques, and research. In T. B. Gutkin & C. R. Reynolds (Eds.), *The handbook of school psychology* (2nd ed., pp. 577–613). New York: Wiley.
An excellent resource for information on the components of individual consultation. This chapter provides a comprehensive review of the core characteristics of school-based consultation. The steps of problem solving are outlined within the framework of a systems orientation. Also reviewed are the major approaches to school-based consultation including the ecological and mental health models. Critical research and professional practice agendas are presented for closing the gap between real and ideal roles for school psychologists.

Schmuck, R. A., & Runkel, P. J. (1985). *The Handbook of Organization Development in Schools.* Palo Alto, CA: Mayfield Publishing Co.
The third edition of *The Handbook* reflects 15 years of collaboration and research on organization development at the University of Oregon. The book was designed to be used as both a college text and as a resource for practitioners. Each chapter is written so that it can be read and understood independently of the rest of the book. The chapters are grouped by major themes which cover theory, communication and problem solving, decision making and conflict, and diagnosis and evaluation. Ideas, exercises, and procedures are offered for each section.

Snapp, M., Hickman, J. A., & Conoley, J. C. (1990). Systems interventions in school settings: Case studies. In T. B. Gutkin & C. R. Reynolds (Eds.), *The handbook of school psychology* (2nd ed., pp. 920–934). New York: Wiley.
This chapter provides nine case studies that illustrate systems-level interventions by school psychologists. Examples of school psychologists expanding their role as consultants, both internal and external to the school system, are provided. The idea that change at any level in one subsystem affects change in other interrelated subsystems is emphasized.

5

Trends in the History of School Psychology in the United States

Thomas K. Fagan
University of Memphis

OVERVIEW

This chapter is not a chronological or topical treatise about the history of school psychology, such as those appearing in Fagan (1990), French (1990), and Fagan and Wise (1994). Instead, it expands upon previous work by providing brief descriptions of trends in selected aspects of the history of school psychology over the past century. Trends in practice settings, roles and functions, and other areas of the field are changing. We may be entering a period in which many aspects of school psychology will be revised; this period of revision would follow earlier periods of uncertain identity, unprecedented growth, and stabilization. Historical trend analyses, revealing the stability of some professional developments and the changeability of others, help us understand questions about our present by reflecting on our past. For example, is the organizational growth since 1970 unprecedented? Is the literature of school psychology more diverse than in earlier times? Is the practice of school psychology different than it was 50 years ago? Have school psychologists always had children as their primary clients? These and other questions will be addressed in this chapter. The discussion is not intended to be comprehensive, but rather to provide an overview of some important trends in school psychology. Certain trends are discussed in detail because they have not been surveyed in other sources, while some are treated only briefly because they have been discussed elsewhere.

Number of School Psychologists

The earliest survey of psychological practitioners serving school settings was undertaken in1913, and identified only 115 persons. Growth in the number of school psychologists was gradual but persistent, and by 1950 there were about 1,000. The post-World War II baby boom, with its growth in school attendance, and the enactment of comprehensive special education laws entailing mandatory psychological services were dominant forces affecting the rapid growth of practitioners observed after 1950. By 1970 the field had about 5,000 practitioners; current estimates

range from 22,000 to 25,000. In recent years, growth can also be attributed to the expansion of settings in which school psychological services are delivered. Estimates of the size of the work force usually include trainers and state government personnel as well as practitioners. However, trainers comprise a very small proportion of the work force, perhaps three to five percent; and government personnel such as state consultants account for about .3%. The size of the work force at different times is estimated as follows:

1920	200	1970	5,000
1940	500	1975	8,000
1950	1,000	1980	10,000
1960	3,000	1985	15,000
1965	4,000	1990	22,000

For all the studies and estimates, no reliable count of the number of school psychologists has ever been accomplished. Even the term "school psychologist" has eluded consistent definition — adding to problems of whom to count and with whom past and future comparisons should be made. Recent estimates are probably more accurate than early estimates, but exactitude is still lacking, with estimates off by perhaps 10% or more. Despite problems of accuracy, the trend in upward growth nevertheless has been significant. Continued growth is expected in the future, but not of the magnitude witnessed in the past 25 years. The number of school psychologists will probably not exceed 30,000 to 35,000 in the coming 20 years.

Gender Trends

Public school teaching was a male-dominated field early in the history of American education, but has been dominated by women throughout the twentieth century, ranging from 86% (1919–1920) to approximately 65% in recent years. Throughout this century school psychologists have been drawn in large numbers from the ranks of teachers. Even in recent years many school psychologists hold teaching credentials and have teaching experience. Although early survey data are not available, it is known that several women were among the early practitioners of school psychology (e.g., Norma Cutts, Helen Thompson Woolley, Leta Hollingworth); that women held several prominent district-level administrative positions in school psychology (e.g., in Cleveland, Chicago, Cincinnati, Detroit), state department of education positions (e.g., Wisconsin, New York), and university positions (e.g., Columbia, Purdue); and comprised one-fourth of the Thayer Conference participants (French, 1988). Division 16–APA data indicate that women accounted for more than 60% of the membership and elected leadership in 1949, and 54% of its 600 members in 1956–57. The figures appear to have declined to less than 50% by the 1960s, a period when men gained proportionally in leadership positions (Hagin, 1993). A more representative survey by Farling and Hoedt (1971) found an overall female representation of 40%, including 35% of the APA member respondents and 47% of the NASP member respondents. A 1976 survey reported female representation of 45% (Ramage, 1979). By 1982 a NASP survey found women comprising 58% of the membership, and just three years later this had grown to 61% of the membership. Surveys in the early 1990s place the membership representation of women at 65%.

Given the representativeness among school psychologists of NASP's membership, the data suggest a substantial feminization of the field in recent years. It is probable that the proportion of women in school psychology has varied across the century, from perhaps 30% at some point early in the century to half or more during the period 1940–1960, perhaps experiencing a brief proportional decline in the 1960s and 1970s, and then rising to its present high of about 60–65%.

Female representation has varied by the types of positions held. For example, female representation is highest among practitioners (65%), while among trainers it is 30% (Reschly & Wilson, 1992). Women's representation on the Executive Board of NASP has improved from one-third to two-thirds during the period 1970–1993. A less discernible trend appears in the data for Division 16 elected leadership, although women held half or more of the positions on several occasions in the past twenty years (Fagan, 1993b). Although regional variations likely exist, there are probably few states where men are in the majority. Despite women's proportional advantage, a woman has never been appointed to the editorship of a school psychology journal, though several have served in associate editorship positions.

The feminization of school psychology is among the more predictable and significant influences on the field for the next two decades. The proportion of women in school psychology may rise to as high as 75%. While men more often have held leadership positions in the past twenty years, the trend will change dramatically at all levels, including state and national associations, academia, editorships, and state education agencies. The trend could be attenuated by recruiting more men into the field and/or by men continuing to be successful in obtaining leadership roles. With increased female presence in the leadership, the future of school psychology will be influenced by their efforts even more than in the past.

Service Ratios

The ratio of school psychologists to children served — the service ratio — has been reported many times in our history. The ratio has improved from 1:60,000 in 1934, to 1:36,000 in 1950, to 1:10,500 in 1966, to 1:4,800 in 1974, to 1:2,100 in 1986 (Fagan, 1988). In large and urban school districts the median ratio has improved from 1:18,500 in 1950, to 1:9,000 in 1966, to 1:2,000 in 1991 (Fagan & Schicke, in press). These figures are consistent with a recent report that the ratio for rural school psychologists (1:2,184) was not significantly different from that of urban (1:1,931) or suburban (1:1,892) school psychologists. Practitioners in combined settings (e.g., rural and urban) had significantly worse ratios (1:2,283) (Reschly & Connolly, 1990). The trend throughout the century, then, has been to improve ratios in various settings. Gradual improvements are anticipated for the future, but the 1992 NASP recommended ratio of 1:1,000 will remain an elusive goal.

Practice Settings

School psychologists have worked in several settings throughout history, although their primary identification has been with public and private schools. In the early decades of practice (1890–1920) they also worked in clinics and research bureaus affiliated with charitable agencies, juvenile courts, colleges and universities, and medical settings. Data by setting do not exist, but it is possible that nonschool-setting practitioners outnumbered school-based practitioners in the early years. Prominent early "school psychologists" such as Lightner Witmer and Arnold Gesell worked in the schools but from external agencies. This pattern probably changed in the 1920s. Founded in 1945, Division 16–APA (School Psychology) was originally intended for school-based practitioners, not practitioners in other settings. The Division's restrictiveness reflected a conceptualization of school psychology as applied clinical and/or educational psychology, with the school being the primary applied setting. A 1960 Division 16–APA survey found that among 233 respondents, 12 (5%) were from private schools, 11 (5%) from state school systems, 42(18%) from county school systems, and 168 (72%) from city schools (Results of Questionnaire, 1960). Setting expansion has been more noticeable since 1980, following a rapid growth of practitioners and increased interest in nonschool and independent practice. The shifting interest appears related to opportunities encouraged by PL 94–142 (e.g., second opinion evaluations), the rapid growth of third-party insurance reimbursements for psychologists, the success of other psychologists in the private sector, increased numbers of school psychologists holding the doctoral degree, and a general maturing of the field of school psychology. Recent survey data indicate the following percentage distribution of employment settings for school psychologists: public school settings (86%), private practice (4%), one percent each in hospital, college or university, institutional/residential, and clinic, and five percent in "other" settings (Reschly & Wilson, 1992).

Throughout our history we have maintained school psychology's identity with school settings despite gradual increases in nonschool practice. What does the future hold? There will be an increase in both the number of practice settings and the percentage of school psychologists serving nonschool settings. Postsecondary educational setting practice will be more available, as will agency and private practice. The expansion of practice settings depends on the growth in the percentage of practitioners holding the doctoral degree.

Clientele

The issue of clienthood is complex, but most agree that children and their parents or guardians are the primary clients of school psychologists. School psychologists came into practice in order to directly serve children while working less directly with their teachers and parents. This primary client relationship with school-aged children has been maintained throughout our history. Surveys of practice, research studies on assessment and intervention, and other descriptive reports consistently reveal that school-age children have been the most common clients of school psychologists. However, growing provision of consultation will increase the extent to which teachers and parents are the primary service recipients and clients. School-age children will continue to be the most common direct service recipients, as well as the primary target of indirect services delivered through other recipients. Although the definition of "school-age" has expanded in recent decades to include ages 3 to 21, some school psychologists provide services to persons outside this age range.

Practitioner Salaries

Salary data are practically nonexistent for the first half of the twentieth century. Nevertheless, some trends can be inferred from archival sources, from limited surveys conducted by state and national associations between 1940 and 1970, and from more comprehensive recent surveys. Early salaries can be inferred from the salaries of positions held by selected practitioners. For example, when the Chicago Public School's Department of Scientific Pedagogy

and Child Study was founded in 1899, its Director was paid $2,000/year and his assistant was paid $100/month ($1,200/year) (Slater, 1980). Between 1915 and 1919, Arnold Gesell was paid $2,000 for his half-time, nine-month position with the State of Connecticut and he was reimbursed for travel, meals, postage, and telephone expenses. Finally, archival sources reveal that Gertrude Hildreth was paid $1,850 for her full-time, nine-month position in "mental testing" with the Okmulgee, Oklahoma, public schools in 1921. I suspect that the range of salaries in the period 1890–1930 was from $1,000 to $4,000 for full-time practitioners, and that a typical figure was probably $2,000 or less. Among the earliest known surveys is the 1939 State of New York survey (based only on the eight districts having a salary schedule), which found that "the range reported was from $1,400 to $4,000 – the median being about $1,600 to $2,800" (Cornell, 1942, p. 25).

The 1954 Thayer Conference survey identified an overall salary range of $3,000 to $15,000, with minimum salaries ranging from $3,000 to $4,600 and maximum salaries ranging from $3,600 to $15,000. Benefits and transportation allowances were mentioned (Cutts, 1955). A 1960 Division 16–APA survey (N = 67) revealed a median salary in the range of $7,000 to $7,999. More than half (55%) were paid $7,000 to $8,999. One-third to one-half of all respondents were given full expenses and time for attending professional growth meetings, and an additional one-third received partial expenses (Results of Questionnaire, 1960).

A reworking of Farling and Hoedt's (1971) survey data yielded a median salary in the range of $12,000 to $14,999.[1] Regional data suggested higher salaries in the Northeast and West than in the Midwest and South (p. 75). The overall upper salary range was significantly greater than in the 1960 Division 16 survey, with 84% reporting salaries of $10,000 or more compared to only 8% in the earlier survey. A 1976 survey of Division 16–APA and NASP members revealed the median salary to be in the range of $16,000 to $18,999 (Ramage, 1979).

Surveys of the NASP membership reported in its 1982 and 1985 membership directories found the median salary in the range of $22,000 to $24,000 and $25,000 to $27,000, respectively. An independent survey of practitioners (Smith, 1984) revealed a median salary range of $20,000 to $24,999. A 1990 survey of a random sample of NASP members (N = 1,781) indicated that the median salary was in the range of $35,001 to $40,000 (Graden & Curtis, 1991). Reschly and Wilson (1992) reported a median income of $35,800 for practitioners and $44,500 for academicians, but the academicians had a median age six years older.

Salaries have increased sharply in the past 30 years following small but persistent increases in the previous 50 years. The large recent increases are reflected in the 1990 data, which suggest that 40% of NASP members had salaries of $40,000 or above compared to just 8% five years earlier. Sampling methods and the effect of rapid membership increases associated with NASP's system of national certification might partially explain discrepancies in surveys from 1985 to present. Additionally, recession has slowed the rate of salary growth since the late 1980s.

Salaries by gender have not been reported, though a survey by Hall (1949) mentioned that one city had a differential between the salaries paid men and women psychologists; Smith's (1984) data suggest higher salaries for males, but this may have been a result of slightly greater levels of experience and degree attainment (see Table 2, p. 801). Teacher salary schedules, with some adjustments for psychological personnel, were reported in early and more recent surveys. No doubt, benefits also have improved in recent decades in comparison to the first half of the century.

Preparation Programs

The earliest programs were designed to prepare "clinical" psychologists to provide services in the schools. The programs were not titled specifically "school psychology" until the 1920s, when the first so-titled program was established at New York University. The second formal program appears to be the doctoral program founded at Pennsylvania State University in the late 1930s. By the time of the 1954 Thayer Conference there were 18 programs, including five at the doctoral level (Cutts, 1955). Institutions offering training in school psychology grew from 28 in 1954, to 79 in 1964, to 147 in 1974, to 211 in 1984 (Fagan, 1986b). The 1989 edition of the NASP training program directory identified 231 institutions, while the most recent edition identifies 233 program institutions (see appendix on training programs in this book). A leveling of growth in the number of training program institutions has occurred since the early 1980s. Future growth in the number of participating institutions will remain modest. The number is unlikely to exceed 250; and conceivably will decrease. The most predictable increase is in the number of institutions offering a doctoral program in school psychology.

Characteristics of Preparation

In the early part of the century, school psychology programs were oriented toward clinical psychology, educational psychology, or a combination thereof. Even the earliest training programs created specifically for school psychologists tended to take these orientations. Perhaps the earliest unambiguous joint orientation of educational and clinical psychology was the University of Illinois program, founded in 1951. Programs have been developed in both education and psychology administrative units with few

apparent differences (Fagan, 1990; Reschly & McMaster-Byer, 1991).

The content of training programs was largely unregulated until the 1960s, in what might be called a long period of "diversity of necessity" in which training emerged from programs designed for a variety of educational and psychological personnel. Many of the programs established in that era combined traditional core psychology or core education courses with specialty training, including psychoeducational evaluation but with limited emphasis on interventions. With the establishment of APA and NCATE/NASP accreditation, the profession entered a period of "restriction for identity" in which very specific standards for preparation were developed to give school psychology training its own identity. Accrediting and credentialing standards also have brought about broader and more specific content in programs. The standards have significantly raised the expectations for entry-level training and have broadened preparation to include various types of assessment and intervention. The current entry-level expectation of the specialist degree or its equivalent is more than twice the expectation published in the original NASP training guidelines of the early 1970s. However, in raising the expectations to meet job demands and establish a separate training identity in school psychology, nondoctoral programs have been forced to become highly prescriptive. Doctoral programs have tended to follow the broader scientist-practitioner or professional models of preparation.

The past several decades have seen an improved balance of psychology and education-related content. Very noticeable changes have been the expansion of field experience requirements, including practica and internships, and the infusion of faculty specifically prepared as school psychologists. While a sharp increase in training standards is not expected for several years, the upward trend will continue. This may appear first at the doctoral level, where national forces are driving accrediting and credentialing toward the postdoctoral level. The nondoctoral standards will likely remain much the same for the coming decade. We should encourage a future of "diversity for maturity," where many forms of preparation will be available in order to better prepare persons for practice in a future of increasing diversity of settings and clients.

Credentialing

Although the New York City Board of Education had provisions for examining and approving school psychological personnel in the 1920s, the earliest state education agency credentials for school psychologists were granted by New York and Pennsylvania in the mid-1930s. Licensing for nonschool practice by state boards of examiners in psychology was initiated in 1945 (Connecticut). By 1960,

15 states licensed psychologists, and all states did so by 1977 (Missouri was the final state). State board of education certification was available in at least 7 states by 1946, 11 states by 1949, 20 states and the District of Columbia by the time of the Thayer Conference, 24 states (including DC) by 1960, 37 states by 1965, 42 states (including DC) by 1973, and all states (including DC) by 1977 (Brown, Horn, & Lindstrom, 1980; Pryzwansky, 1993). A historical analysis of specific changes in credentialing requirements over the past 60 years has not been undertaken and is beyond the scope of this chapter. However, a discernible trend has appeared requiring greater amounts of graduate education and supervised field experiences, and program approval or accreditation. Teaching credentials and/or experience were not required in the original certification in New York and Pennsylvania, and such requirements have declined from 12 of the 20 states certifying school psychologists at the time of the Thayer Conference (1954) to only a few states at present.

Literature

Until the appearance of the first issue of the *Journal of School Psychology* in 1963, the field had no direct journal outlet for its research and professional literature. Before then, the field relied upon an assortment of journals in psychology and education, including *American Journal of Psychology, American Psychologist, Journal of Educational Psychology, Journal of Consulting Psychology* (now *Journal of Consulting & Clinical Psychology*), *Pedagogical Seminary* (now *Journal of Genetic Psychology*), *Psychological Bulletin, Psychological Clinic*, and *Psychological Review* (Fagan, 1986a). Attending the growth of school psychologists since 1960, the growth of school psychology journals was rapid and included the publication of *Psychology in the Schools* in 1964, *School Psychology Digest* (now *School Psychology Review)* in 1972, *School Psychology International* in 1979, and *Professional School Psychology* (now *School Psychology Quarterly)* in 1986. Related journals, including those mentioned earlier, have continued to be important, including *Exceptional Children, Journal of Learning Disabilities, Journal of Psychoeducational Assessment, Professional Psychology: Research & Practice*, and *Special Services in the Schools*, as well as a growing number of journals on specific techniques or disorders.

Trends in the publication of books about school psychology appear in French (1986) and Whelan and Carlson (1986). These surveys identify the chronological order and significant content changes of books in the field. In brief, the earliest book specifically about school psychological services was published by Gertrude Hildreth in 1930; a period followed in which few books were published, including the Thayer Conference proceedings, and then a surge of books occurred beginning in the 1960s. The number and diversity of books published follow the growth pattern for journals from 1960 to the present. Despite a paucity of school psychology books and journals before the 1960s, the field has been served by many literary sources throughout the century (Fagan, Delugach, Mellon, & Schlitt, 1985).

Organizations

Organizational entities exclusively serving school psychologists originated with the Division of School Psychologists of the American Psychological Association (Division 16–APA) established in 1944–45, which evolved from the Educational Section of the American Association of Applied Psychologists (AAAP), established in 1937. Prior to the existence of these organizations, school psychologists appear to have been members of various groups, including the American Psychological Association (founded in 1892) and its offshoot the American Association of Clinical Psychologists (founded in 1917), which became the APA Section of Clinical Psychology in 1919; and the Association of Consulting Psychologists (founded in 1930), which evolved into the AAAP. Although some school psychologists were members of the National Education Association, throughout the first half-century most did not belong to any professional organization for psychologists (Fagan, 1993a). Division 16–APA was the only national-level organization for school psychologists until the founding of the National Association of School Psychologists (NASP) in 1969. For the past 25 years, both Division 16 and NASP have served as national representatives of school psychology's interests. The founding of the American Psychological Society in 1988 and the American Association of Applied and Preventive Psychology in 1990 represent increasing organizational diversity. Their effect on school psychology remains to be seen, and only a small percentage of school psychologists have become members.

The earliest state association for school psychologists appears to be that founded in Ohio in 1943. The growth of such groups was gradual, and by 1969 there were only 17 state associations, several of which were sections of their respective state psychological associations and affiliates of the APA. Growth in the number of states having separate school psychology associations that affiliated with NASP was rapid in the 1970s and 1980s (Fagan, Hensley, & Delugach, 1986). At present, every state has some form of association, and in some states more than one group exists.

Roles and Functions

Twentieth-century American education has been characterized by increased segmentation and sorting of children, presumably to intervene in their lives in more meaningful ways. The sorting function of education has a long tradition dating to the acceptance of compulsory schooling and the employment of experts, including psychologists, to assist in the segmentation of students. The sorting for interventions has ranged from school lunch programs, Title I, vocational education, advanced placement or honors classes, to nearly a dozen categories of special education. It is common for large school systems today to have numerous specialized programs operating concurrently.

As part of this growing bureaucratic process, school psychologists have served two primary functions (Fagan & Wise, 1994). The first has been a role of sorter, in which the most visible function has been the psychoeducational assessment of children for placement in special education programs. In earlier decades, this role was predominantly psychometric, although the conceptualization and practice of assessment has broadened in recent decades as a result of legislative and litigational initiatives and shifting problem-solving strategies. School psychologists now work as members of service teams in which a more comprehensive approach to assessment is taken.

A second role, that of repairer, has engaged school psychologists in individual and group interventions. In earlier decades this often involved academic remediation and counseling. More intensive interventions, such as psychotherapy, were often restricted, prohibited, or considered too time consuming or too costly to be done by district-based practitioners. This practice has changed in the past 30 years as a result of broader training, supervised internships, greater availability of school-based practitioners, and a gradual shifting of administrators' thinking in the direction of serving children's mental health as well as academic needs.

A third role, consultation, could be considered a special case of the repairer role, but it has received so much attention since the 1960s that usually it is considered a separate role. There are many instances of consulting in the early literature of our field, but the in-depth consultation characteristic of recent times was only occasionally practiced and seldom researched. All school psychologists occasionally consult with others, but that does not mean they are engaged in consultation. To function effectively in the consultant role, a practitioner now requires specialized preparation and experience.

A fourth role is that of engineer, in which the practitioner works with overall service delivery schemes. This extension of the consultation role to systems analysis and development focuses its assessment and interventions at systemic needs, not the needs of individual children, parents, or educators. Until recent times, this role was rarely performed by school psychologists.

Many school psychologists enjoy broader roles and functions than others did in earlier decades. However, most continue to practice the two traditional roles of sorter and repairer, with attendant functions of traditional psychoeducational assessment and one-to-one or group interventions with children. The similarity of roles over time gives a false impression that little has changed in the practice of school psychology. The technical quality and knowledge about assessment and intervention functions (e.g., cognitive and achievement tests, behavior modification, or behavioral consultation) have strengthened the roles of school psychologists. Perhaps the most striking changes have occurred in the context of practice. Just 25 years ago most school psychologists worked without requirements for parent/guardian permission, multidisciplinary teams, annual reviews and IEPs, and least restrictive environment placements. The category of learning disability, now the largest area of exceptionality, was just gaining official recognition. Public laws 93–380, 94–142, and 99–457 were far off in the future. Most special education services were provided in segregated programs. Among the more frequently given tests were the WISC, Stanford-Binet (1960 edition), Illinois Test of Psycholinguistic Abilities, Frostig Developmental Test of Visual Perception, and the Bender Motor Gestalt Test. The school psychologist typically held a Master's degree with a practicum and little or no internship experience. In some settings the school psychologist served in a dual capacity as psychoeducational assessment specialist and coordinator of special education. He/she was a one-person M-Team. Although some aspects of role and function have persisted, there has been considerable change in our field.

Problem-Solving Strategies

Although their approach to the task has varied over the century, school psychologists have been employed to help alleviate the problems of children and their schooling. This discussion of problem-solving approaches will focus only on the sorter and repairer roles — that is, the traditional child study approach to services. Early descriptions of practice reveal a problem-solving strategy that focused exclusively on the individual child. This strategy sought solutions to children's school problems by studying their identifiable skills and the presumed underlying abilities, traits, or personality characteristics. Problems were considered to rest with the skills and characteristics associated with the child, and the solutions rested with their alteration. Diagnosis and intervention were child-centered. Assessment methods included questionnaires, interviews of the child, parent, or teacher, tests (both standardized and unstandardized, normed and unnormed), inspection of the child's work, school and health histories, and occasional classroom observations. The rapid acceptance of the Binet and Simon intelligence scales and standardized norm-based achievement tests was attributable to the apparent objectivity they brought to an assessment process fraught with varying opinions about classification and degrees of symptomatology. The new tests added scientific respectability to problem solving by quantifying the extent of a problem and contributing to greater objectivity in classification. Interventions included brief counseling, remediation of academic skills, and an expanding array of instructional and community-based programs in special education.

In part as a result of debates over nature and nurture, as well as the increasing influence of behavioral psychology, the problem-solving strategy of school psychologists gradually expanded to include the assessment and intervention of persons and factors beyond the individual child. The most obvious shift of focus was from the child to the parents and guardians. For example, for many years it was believed that certain child problems (e.g., autism) were etiologically linked to inadequate parenting (often construed to mean inadequate mothering in an era when societal consensus held that mothers were the primary child caretakers). The focus also expanded to classroom variables, including teacher characteristics and the characteristics of their teaching. As this strategy continued to expand, the notion of problem-solving assessment broadened to the concept of ecological assessment. The child continued to be the focus of study, but only in relation to the other variables in the child's environment and especially the child's unique interaction with this environment. Logically, the etiology of children's problems expanded as well. Failure was no longer viewed in terms of child variables but in terms of other factors, separately or in combination with child variables (e.g., ineffective teaching with children having specific learning deficits).

The methodology continued to include standardized and unstandardized, normed and unnormed tests. Also included were an array of measures, formal and informal, of peer relationships and sociograms, attitude toward school, parenting, classroom climate and teaching, socioeconomic status, and formalized observations of child and peer behaviors (e.g., event and time sampling). Interventions continued to include the earlier forms, though with greater sophistication in special education programs and diversified therapeutic techniques (e.g., client-centered, rational-emotive therapies, and behavior modification) applied to groups as well as to individuals. Problem solving was still focused on the child, although increasingly school psychologists relied upon indirect interventions such as teacher and parent consultation (see Kehle, Clark, & Jenson, 1993; Sandoval, 1993).

The ecological viewpoint (including reciprocal determinism), with its contention that variables external to the child are worthy of study and intervention, has strongly influenced school psychology for the past three decades (see, e.g., Elliott & Witt, 1986). In recent years, the problem-solving task has shifted some of its focus back to the child in the form of directly measured observable skills and corresponding direct interventions. At least where the "high incidence" problems of children are concerned (e.g., learning disability, educable mental retardation, emotional and behavioral disturbance), the shift has been toward disavowing underpinning normative characteristics in favor of direct interventions in observable academic and social behaviors. A long-standing paradigm of assessing skills through underlying supportive characteristics (e.g., intelligence) has shifted to a paradigm of direct assessment of skills and direct remedial instruction irrespective of underlying abilities or traits. The current conceptualizations are identified with an "outcome education" orientation under various names, including authentic-, curriculum-, performance-, and portfolio-based assessment. These are variations on earlier themes of criterion-based assessments that have been popular at different times in our history. Other shifts in problem solving have focused on parent and teacher effectiveness, and the child's family constellation. It is now common for school psychologists to consider family variables in both their diagnostic and intervention efforts, and systems have been developed for family assessment and therapy.

In summary, school psychologists have always been identified with one or more problem-solving strategies, the nature of which has shifted over time. Although it is easy to look back with disdain on the practices of earlier eras, earlier practices were influenced as much by broad societal ideologies of the period as by professionals' lofty aspirations. For example, the recent clamor of interest in the family has occurred after an era of governmental, societal, and professional alarm over family deterioration. There was less focus on the family in the 1950s, an era often viewed nostalgically as one of family strength. The irony points to our tendency to draw attention to phenomena for study after the fact. The shifting strategies toward child study are probably less "on the cutting edge" of practice than they are on the backside of educational and psychological research, and societal acceptance of the changing spheres of child influence.

In retrospect, we observe stages of development in problem-solving approaches associated with a broadening recognition and acceptance of the spheres of influence on children. While clear-cut temporal or strategy demarcations cannot be specified, the expansion of spheres generally has been from child, to parents and teachers, to family and school, to community and society. Even though the stages overlap and continue to be observed in the varied practices of professional psychologists, comprehensive assessment and intervention practices have expanded accordingly.

Critics of traditional school psychology contend that it was not based on a problem-solving model at all. However, all problem-solving models involve assessment and intervention. The traditional model identified the school psychologist primarily with assessment to determine eligibility for interventions most often provided by others via special classrooms and programs. Most traditional school psychologists were, and many still are, not effectively linked to the intervention side of problem solving. But that does not mean the overall process is outside the realm of problem solving. Employing an assembly line approach to automaking, instead of having each worker build the entire car, does not make the assembly line outside the realm of automaking. Further, the shift from processing assessment to functional assessment does not mean that the former was outside the realm of a problem-solving model. What has changed is simply the nature of the assessments advocated and the involvement of the school psychologist throughout the assessment and intervention. Some advocates of the "new" problem-solving approaches have chosen to dissociate themselves from the earlier approaches to practice, preferring reform to transition in practice. However, even the current *zeitgeist* is historically linked to earlier approaches known as diagnostic teaching during Witmer's time, and precision teaching, directive teaching, and mastery learning in the last two decades. The recent shifts in problem-solving strategy could benefit services in the long run if they successfully drew greater attention to the importance of interventions and recognized the complementary relationship between child-centered and ecological assessment approaches, and normative-based and criterion-based measurement. The shift toward collaborative inclusion of parents and teachers as peers in the problem-solving process could also have positive implications. Finally, perhaps the school psychologist will earn a more balanced role than in the past, as "repairer" instead of "sorter" of children's problems.

REFERENCES

Brown, D. T., Horn, A. J., & Lindstrom, J. P. (1980). *The handbook of certification/licensure requirements for school psychologists*. Washington, DC: NASP.

Cornell, E. L. (1942). *The work of the school psychologist*. Albany: Division of Research, New York State Education Department.

Cutts, N. E. (Ed.). (1955). *School psychologists at mid-century*. Washington, DC: American Psychological Association.

Elliott, S. N., & Witt, J. C. (1986). Fundamental questions and dimensions of psychological service delivery in schools. In S. N. Elliott & J. C. Witt (Eds.), *The delivery of psychological services in schools: Concepts, processes, and issues* (pp. 1–26). Hillsdale, NJ: Erlbaum.

Fagan, T. K. (1986a). The evolving literature of school psychology. *School Psychology Review, 15*, 430–440.

Fagan, T. K. (1986b). The historical origins and growth of programs to prepare school psychologists in the United States. *Journal of School Psychology, 24*, 9–22.

Fagan, T. K. (1988). The historical improvement of the school psychology service ratio: Implications for future employment. *School Psychology Review, 17*, 447–458.

Fagan, T. K. (1990). A brief history of school psychology. In A. Thomas & J. Grimes (Eds.), *Best practices in school psychology–II* (pp. 913–929). Washington, DC: National Association of School Psychologists.

Fagan, T. K. (1993a, April). A critical appraisal of NASP's first 25 years. Annual Convention, National Association of School Psychologists, Washington Hilton Hotel, Washington, DC.

Fagan, T. K. (1993b). Separate but equal: School psychology's search for organizational identity. *Journal of School Psychology, 31*, 3–90.

Fagan, T. K., Delugach, F. J., Mellon, M., & Schlitt, P. (1985). *A bibliographic guide to the literature of professional school psychology 1890–1985*. Washington, DC: National Association of School Psychologists.

Fagan, T. K., Hensley, L. T., & Delugach, F. J. (1986). The evolution of organizations for school psychologists in the United States. *School Psychology Review, 15*, 127–135.

Fagan, T. K., & Schicke, M. C. (1994). The service ratio in large school districts: Historical and contemporary perspectives. *Journal of School Psychology, 32*, 305–312.

Fagan, T. K., & Wise, P. S. (1994). *School psychology: Past, present, and future*. New York: Longman.

Farling, W. H., & Hoedt, K. C. (1971). *National survey of school psychologists*. Washington, DC: National Association of School Psychologists.

French, J. L. (1986). Books in school psychology: The first forty years. *Professional School Psychology, 1*, 267–277.

French, J. L. (1988). Grandmothers I wish I knew: Contributions of women to the history of school psychology. *Professional School Psychology, 3*, 51–68.

French, J. L. (1990). History of school psychology. In T. B. Gutkin & C. R. Reynolds (Eds.), *Handbook of school psychology* (pp. 3–20). New York: Wiley.

Graden, J., & Curtis, M. (1991, September). *A demographic profile of school psychology: A report to the Delegate Assembly of the National Association of School Psychologists*. Washington, DC: National Association of School Psychologists.

Hagin, R. A. (1993). Contributions of women in school psychology: The Thayer report and thereafter. *Journal of School Psychology, 31*, 123–141.

Hall, M. E. (1949). Current employment requirements for school psychologists. *American Psychologist, 4*, 519–525.

Kehle, T. J., Clark, E., & Jenson, W. R. (1993). The development of testing as applied to school psychology. *Journal of School Psychology, 31*, 143–161.

Pryzwansky, W. B. (1993). The regulation of school psychology: A historical perspective on certification, licensing, and accreditation. *Journal of School Psychology, 31*, 219–235.

Ramage, J. (1979). National survey of school psychologists: Update. *School Psychology Digest, 8*, 153–161.

Reschly, D. J., & Connolly, L. M. (1990). Comparisons of school psychologists in the city and country: Is there a "rural" school psychology? *School Psychology Review, 19,* 534–549.

Reschly, D. J., & McMaster-Beyer, M. (1991). Influences of degree level, institutional orientation, college affiliation, and accreditation status on school psychology graduate education. *Professional Psychology: Research & Practice, 22,* 368–374.

Reschly, D. J., & Wilson, M. S. (1992). School psychology practitioners and faculty: 1986 to 1991–92, trends in demographics, roles, satisfaction, and system reform. *School Psychology Review, 24,* 62–80.

Results of questionnaire on working conditions of school psychologists. (1960). *Division 16 Newsletter, 14*(2), 4.

Sandoval, J. (1993). The history of interventions in school psychology. *Journal of School Psychology, 31,* 195–217.

Slater, R. (1980). The organizational origins of public school psychology. *Educational Studies, 2*(1), 1–11.

Smith, D. T. (1984). Practicing school psychologists: Their characteristics, activities, and populations served. *Professional Psychology: Research and Practice, 15,* 798–810.

Whelan, T., & Carlson, C. (1986). Books in school psychology: 1970 to the present. *Professional School Psychology, 1,* 279–289.

FOOTNOTE

[1]The original results (which totaled only 70%) reflected percentages based on the total sample of survey respondents, not just those who answered this question. The percentages were recomputed to reflect a distribution based only on the 70% who had responded (i.e., for an N = 2,197 instead of 3,138).

6

Best Practices in Planning School Psychology Delivery Programs

Mel Franklin
Amphitheater Public Schools, Tucson, Arizona

OVERVIEW

The increasing complexity of society has placed greater demands upon the school, the school psychologist, and school psychology delivery programs to add to their repertoire of "traditional" services (Franklin & Duley, 1991). School psychology delivery programs that are predicated on refer-and-test models of service, school psychologists as gatekeepers for special education, a search for pathology, or a commitment to reactive versus preventive services, which perpetuate a static approach to delivery, may find their future survival at best questionable. It is imperative that school psychologists make choices in their professional services that match the needs of the children and youth that we serve and "enhance the likelihood of effective intervention" (Reschly & Grimes, 1990, p. 425). Oakland (1986) suggests that school psychologists must work to ensure that their services are cost-effective, have community support, and are demonstrated to be beneficial compared with what occurs without school psychology services.

The purpose of this chapter is to provide direction for school psychologist practitioners or individuals responsible for establishing or redesigning school delivery programs for psychology services. This chapter will include (a) a review of programs that work, (b) organizational considerations, (c) program administration and supervision, (d) comprehensive service delivery, and (e) considerations for the future.

BASIC CONSIDERATIONS

The National Association of School Psychologists (NASP) *Standards for the Provision of School Psychological Services* (NASP, 1992b) provides the position of the Association "regarding the delivery of appropriate and comprehensive school psychological services." It is suggested that individuals who are establishing or modifying existing school psychological services possess a thorough working knowledge of these NASP standards.

To successfully establish or modify a program of school psychology service delivery, the school psychologist may benefit from sensitization to programs that work. Although there exist numerous exceptional school psychology programs, few have recently been described in the literature. A review of six award-winning innovative school psychology delivery programs is provided.

Beginning in 1982, Division 16 (School Psychology) of the American Psychological Association (APA) and the National Association of School Psychologists (NASP) initiated an award to recognize exemplary school psychology service units (Telzrow, 1989). "The award represents a positive public citation for excellence in providing comprehensive psychological services in the school" (Telzrow, 1989, p. 59) and recognizes a psychology services unit that is "exemplary in the range and quality of services offered in the schools" ("Division Spotlight," 1988). Recipients of the APA Division 16–NASP Award for Excellence have included (1) Memphis (Tennessee) City Schools Mental Health Center (1982); (2) Gwinnett County Schools Psychological Services (Lawrence, Georgia) (1985); (3) Amphitheater Unified School District School Psychology Department (Tucson, Arizona) (1987); (4) Broward County Schools Psychological Services (Florida) (1990); (5) Cherry Creek School District Mental Health Team (Englewood, Colorado) (1990); and (6) Cypress–Fairbanks Independent School District Psychological Services (Houston, Texas) (1990) (Telzrow, 1989; L. W. Roosa, personal communication, May 24, 1993).

Memphis City Schools Mental Health Center

The Memphis City Schools Mental Health Center (MCSMHC) is a service unit to the Memphis City Schools as well as an incorporated not-for-profit mental health center (Paavola, Hannah, & Nichol, 1989). The unit is led by the director, who is a licensed psychologist with competencies in school psychology. The director reports to the same assistant superintendent as do the heads of special education, guidance, and research (Paavola et al., 1989). The MCSMHC is committed to prevention and prereferral intervention through the use of school support teams (S-Teams); this has yielded a 25% drop in initial special education referrals. The MCSMHC requires each staff member to obtain a minimum of 50 staff development hours each year. The MCSMHC provides mental health services that include parent/teacher consultation; prevention activities; individual, family, and group counseling; and psychological assessment (Nichol, 1993). The MCSMHC is also involved in the provision of alcohol and drug prevention and intervention activities, violence reduction efforts, an adolescent parenting program, and treatment services for abused and neglected students. Paavola et al. (1989) recognize that many issues will come to prominence in future years that will impact on the well-being of children and youth. Although it may be difficult to anticipate appropriate responses to each of these issues, the MCSMHC appears to be addressing these issues as they arise by maintaining its focus on providing a comprehensive array of services.

Gwinnett County School Psychological Services

Bush et al. (1989) reported that Gwinnett County (Lawrence, Georgia) has experienced tremendous growth in their student population without a concomitant increase in psychological services staff. Historically the Gwinnett County School Psychological Services program has been responsible for assessment of students for possible eligibility for special education programs. This diagnostic model of service delivery was found to be inadequate owing to the increasingly diversified population. Following a needs assessment, the program formulated a more comprehensive model of services that combined traditional assessment functions with consultation activities. The mission of the program was to provide comprehensive psychological service. The program utilizes a school-based model of consultation proposed by Gutkin and Curtis (1982) with emphasis on collaborative problem solving and the use of student study teams. The Gwinnett County program is directed by a licensed/certified professional psychologist and uses a process of peer review. Bush et al. (1989) report that the program has established a goal to include research and publication. Bush et al. (1989) also state that by more effectively managing the assessment aspects by the department and focusing on prevention, the perceived role of the psychologist has changed from gatekeeper of special education to that of child advocate with expertise in many areas.

Amphitheater School District School Psychology Department

In the Amphitheater School District in Tucson, Arizona, the School Psychology Department head is a certified professional school psychologist who holds a supervisory school psychologist certificate and is licensed by the State Board of Psychologist Examiners. The department head provides school psychology services to two district schools and reports directly to an associate superintendent. The program adheres to a model of behavioral consultation based upon the work of Bergan (1977). If initial consultation is not successful or more formal intervention appears warranted, a student study team (SST) model is employed to generate alternative intervention strategies. The primary function of the school psychologist is advocacy for the student to attempt resolution of the referral problem in the least restrictive setting (Franklin & Duley, 1991). Use of the SST has allowed the development of an additional creative and dynamic problem-solving process with a multidisciplinary team approach. Each school psychologist is expected to participate in research activities as well as the dissemination of applied research. The Amphitheater School Psychology Department, through the use of a consultative model, has utilized a growing research base across a number of fields of psychology to address concerns of students in an educational setting. The use of this model has led to a decrease in per capita referrals during a period of increasing student population. The staff has been better able to provide increased levels of behavioral consultation, direct service, in-service, and related efforts.

Broward County Schools Psychological Services

The Broward County School District is the nation's eighth largest school system, serving a diverse population of over 180,000 students and employing approximately 75 school psychologists (L. W. Roosa, personal communication, June 11, 1993). Psychological Services is a department within Student Services, which is a component of the Division of Instruction and Program Services. The Psychological Services Unit is headed by a director who is an experienced school psychologist. The director administers the program and is responsible for the programmatic aspects of the services. The direct supervision of school psychologist is provided by Area Coordinators of Student Services who are experienced school psychologists. The Psychological Services Department provides a comprehensive range of services that focus upon prevention and consultation activities. School psychologists participate on school-based child study or intervention assistance teams. Collaborative problem-solving consultation activities are available to teachers, principals, and parents. The special features of the department also include a minority/bilingual traineeship program, involvement in a program for young socially maladjusted students, the use of a computer data base to monitor assessment cases, biweekly professional development activities, and a departmental newsletter, distributed to each school, members of the school board, district administrators, and state school psychology trainers, that is designed to articulate the role and the accomplishments of the staff members. As a function of the size of the department and the staff selection procedures, the diverse staff has school psychologists with expertise in low-incidence handicaps (e.g., autistic and motor-sensory-impaired) and bilingual evaluations. Bilingual school psychologists have participated in the development of informal academic assessment instruments in both Creole and Spanish.

Cherry Creek School District
Mental Health Team

The Cherry Creek Schools Mental Health Team (CCMHT) consists of approximately 50 psychologists and social workers who serve a population of 28,000 students in a suburban area near Denver, Colorado (W. M. Porter, personal communication, November 4, 1993). The CCMHT pairs a psychologist and a social worker in a building as a mental health team. The mental health team determines the needs of an individual school and tailors services to these identified needs. The services may include consultation with teachers, parents, and administrators; curriculum-based assessments and environmental and biological assessments; direct services to students through individual and group counseling and crisis intervention; and counseling and support for the mental health needs of teachers and staff with a connection to an employee assistance program. The CCMHT utilizes a comprehensive community approach in an attempt to develop strategies to meet the needs of the individuals and systems it services. The CCMHT is directed by a coordinator who reports directly to the director of Pupil Services. The CCMHT demonstrates a commitment to the training and supervision of future school psychologist practitioners. The CCMHT offers weekly seminars for school psychology interns and practicum students completing placements in the district. The CCMHT also demonstrates a strong commitment to the professional growth of its mental health team members. Psychologists are encouraged to pursue cultural and international exchanges with psychologists from other settings and to conduct research projects that foster individual and professional growth.

Cypress-Fairbanks I.S.D. Psychological Services

The Cypress-Fairbanks Independent School District Psychological Services in Houston, Texas is overseen by a director of psychological services, who is a licensed psychologist and a certificated school psychologist and the director reports directly to the associate superintendent in charge of administration (K. A. Young & K. S. Grier, personal communication, May 28, 1993). The district has grown from a population of 7,000 in 1968 to approximately 46,000 in 1993.

The unit employs five doctoral interns annually and is approved as an APA Professional Psychology internship site. The program uses a combination of psychologists and educational diagnosticians. In psychoeducational assessments the psychologists are responsible for the emotional and personality components of the assessment, while the diagnosticians evaluate the intellectual, academic, and adaptive behavior components. The department involvement throughout the district has significantly expanded in response to the behavioral and emotional needs of the district's ever-growing population. The Department of Psychological Services mandate is to "provide quality, broadly based psychological services to the entire school district through a comprehensive psychological service delivery system." The department has targeted primary prevention, indirect service through consultation, the provision of direct services, and coordinating and complementing the community mental health and education system as vehicles to meet the mandate (K. A. Young & K. S. Grier, personal communication, May 28, 1993). The staff demonstrates a commitment to continuing professional development by participating in weekly training colloquiums and program development meetings.

A seventh program, described in the literature, is presented for your information.

Minneapolis Psychological Services

Canter (1991) outlines a comprehensive database model of school psychological service delivery for all 44,000 children and youths within the Minneapolis public schools. Centralized administrative supervision for psychological services is provided by a chief psychologist. However, since the 22 full-time-equivalent school psychologists in the Minneapolis School District have traditionally been assigned to specific schools as building staff, they are responsible directly to principals (Canter, 1991). Canter (1991) reports that a delivery model that was largely assessment-driven was replaced with a new model for service delivery that emerged from a change in focus to indirect services, which was stimulated by the changing character of the student population, the loss of revenue from declining enrollment, and the interests and allocation of staff. School psychology services became an "increasingly consultation-based system providing services to the teacher and administrator at least as often as those directly provided to the student" (Canter, 1991, p. 53). The department provides a proactive system of accountability that enlists a systematic process of documenting and evaluating the delivery model. Procedures have been developed to enable school psychologists "to monitor their roles in service delivery, examine referral issues, document staff development needs, and measure the effectiveness of interventions, as well as track changes in these areas over time" (Canter, 1991, p. 56). The district uses a curriculum-based measurement (CBM) model for measuring the students' progress and for determination of eligibility for special education. A focus upon indirect service delivery has allowed school psychologists to be actively involved in curriculum planning, research, staff training, development of educational programs and policy, and maintaining professional visibility (Canter, 1991). The delivery model is not seen as static, but as a "continuing evolution of theory and practice" that is constantly being "modified in response to internal and external needs and changes" (Canter, 1991, p. 73).

The aforementioned innovative school psychology delivery systems appear to possess in aggregate the following characteristics:

1. Highly qualified generalist/specialist practitioners and a wide range of expertise within each department.

2. The delivery of expanded and comprehensive school psychology services to meet the needs of *all* students.

3. A commitment to prereferral intervention/prevention activities.

4. The use of school-based collaborative consultation.

5. Linking assessment to instructional intervention rather than to classification alone.

6. Articulating departmental successes.

7. Accountability through efficacy data.

8. Malleability.

9. A focus on continuing professional development.

10. Departmental autonomy and clinical supervision and evaluation by a school psychologist.

11. Involvement in research.

12. A commitment to the training of future school psychologist practitioners.

BEST PRACTICES

There is no unitary ideal delivery system of school psychology services. A best practices model for an individual practitioner requires careful consideration of numerous variables. This section reviews organizational considerations, program administration and supervision, and ten basic components of comprehensive service delivery for a successful school psychology program.

Organizational Considerations

Placement of the school psychology delivery program within a school district's organization pattern (Talley, 1990) is seen as a critical issue for considera-

tion. Talley (1990) provides a review of four basic *within-district* models of service delivery to school psychology: (a) as a separate program, (b) within special education services, (c) within special education, and (d) building-based. School psychology as a separate department allows for greater professional autonomy and visibility as a means to facilitate the delivery of comprehensive school psychology services. This model allows for practice that is less encumbered by traditional association with special education. The director can provide both administrative and clinical supervision and often reports to an assistant or associate superintendent. In a second model of school psychology service delivery, staff reports to a director of student services, who may not be a school psychologist. Some independence from special education may be available in this model; however, there often exists a lack of appropriate school psychology leadership and administration, as well as appropriate clinical supervision of practice. In a third model, presented by Talley (1990) and commonly encountered, the school psychology program is subsumed within the special education department. In some districts school psychologists are chosen to direct the school psychology program, but often nonpsychologists are asked to assume this supervisory role. Among the problems that might arise from the choice of a nonpsychologist director is a lack of knowledge of practice guidelines, professional standards and ethics, and the comprehensive nature of school psychology services that can be provided. Staunch advocacy for expanded school psychology services may also be absent. The fourth model, building-based psychology, provides for a school psychologist assigned to one school or based in one school with the provision of services to several schools. Supervision and evaluation of practice is provided by the building principal. In this model, school psychologists generally lack appropriate clinical supervision and may experience a sense of isolation from fellow district school psychologists. Talley (1990) outlines a fifth model of regional service delivery (often found in rural school districts) in which the school psychologists are employed by a regional service center or cooperative.

Program Administration and Supervision

The provision of appropriate supervision of school psychologists is *required* by professional associations (APA, 1981; NASP, 1992b), is *desired* by practitioners (Zins, Murphy, & Wess, 1989), and is an *integral component* to the success of a school psychology delivery program. NASP has proposed that supervision be made available to all practicing school psychologists "to an extent sufficient to ensure the provision of effective and accountable services" (NASP, 1992b, p. 39). NASP suggests that a ratio of one supervisor for every ten school psychologists be maintained with an equivalent ratio for part-time supervisors, and that school psychologists receive one hour per week of face-to-face supervision during the first 3 years of full-time employment (NASP, 1992b). Following the first 3 years all school psychologists are to continue under supervision and/or peer review (NASP, 1992b). A supervising school psychologist is defined by NASP as a professional psychologist who has completed three years of supervised experience as a school psychologist and has met credentialing requirements (NASP, 1992b). Coursework or other training in the supervision of school personnel is seen as desirable (NASP, 1992b) and as needed (Ross & Goh, 1993).

APA suggests that supervision should be provided by a doctoral school psychologist at a ratio of one supervisor per 15 full-time school psychology personnel, that all nondoctoral school psychologists should be supervised, and that all school psychology services staff should receive face-to-face supervision (APA, 1981; Talley, 1990). Although one might assume that these supervisory standards are commonly followed by most employers, such a commitment to supervision may be the exception rather than the rule. Zins et al. (1989) have reported that less than one in four school psychologists actually received clinical supervision. How often have practitioners observed supervisors with little or no formal training or practical school psychology experience providing clinical supervision for school psychologist practitioners? Zins et al. (1989) reported that clinical supervision was often provided by individuals whose terminal degree was not in school psychology and that less than 50% of supervision met NASP or APA professional practice standards.

The supervisor should be responsible for providing evaluation of the school psychologist practitioner with data pertaining to their personal effectiveness, as well as data pertaining to the effectiveness of the department as a whole. This evaluation should be both formative and summative. Such evaluation can assist the school psychologist practitioner in determining his or her current development level and professional strengths and weaknesses (Knoff, 1986). It is also suggested that the supervisor assess the effectiveness of the service delivery by the department and determine the match with the needs of the local constituency.

The nature, magnitude, and frequency of problematic situations in the schools seems to be changing at a rapid pace in most communities. Therefore, it continues to be the school psychologist practitioner's responsibility to assess these problematic situations and provide timely and appropriate intervention. The nature and breadth of these problems make it at times difficult, if not impossible, to possess every technical and practical skill to deal with every facet of practice demanded in the field (Knoff, 1986). It becomes the responsibility of the supervisor to match the practitioner's relative strengths with the identified needs of the constituency. It is important for the supervisor of school psychologists to provide liaison activities with other professionals in related fields. The federal and state rules, regulations, and standards to which school psychologists must adhere may be different from the rules that are applied to practitioners in related areas. It may therefore be necessary for the supervisor to define these differences to appropriate agencies or private practitioners to facilitate the continued delivery of quality school psychological services.

Supervisors of school psychologists can be most effective when they also function as school psychologist practitioners. Ideally they should "walk in the shoes" of fellow practitioners. They should always be seen as striving for individual and departmental excellence while keeping one foot in the camp of the school psychologist practitioner. Without such a frame of reference, one's supervisory effectiveness can be greatly diminished (Franklin, 1989). Any best practices model for school psychology services delivery requires adherence to the provision of appropriate school psychology practitioner supervision.

In the establishment of modification of a delivery program it is necessary that we recruit qualified practitioners. Although most school psychologist practitioners have received training as generalists (Fagan, 1990b), there may be a need to recruit individuals within specialty training to include early childhood, neuropsychology, and curriculum-based assessment. Prior to hiring a new school psychologist practitioner it may be useful for the department to assess its present needs and establish a rubric for the replacement psychologist. The supply-and-demand gap for school psychologist practitioners appears to continue to be problematic (Connolly & Reschly, 1990). Ongoing networking with state professional organizations and graduate training programs, maintenance of competitive salary schedules, and work environments that allow for school psychologists to use their diverse skills can improve both the quantity and quality of applicant pools of school psychologists. As individuals in training programs seek higher levels of required training and employment in more diverse practice settings (Fagan, 1990a), as well as a "graying" of the profession, shortages of school psychologist practitioners likely will continue in the future.

The school psychology department should foster the establishment of short-term and long-range departmental direction through the use of strategic planning to include a needs assessment, a mission statement, and specific departmental goals and objectives with measurable criteria (Franklin & Wasserman, 1992). This process allows the department to know where it needs to go, how it plans to get there, and when it has arrived.

NASP (1992b) provides guidelines suggesting a ratio of at least one full-time school psychologist for each 1,000 children and youths served. NASP recognizes that the ratio vary with the needs of the children served, the type of program served, the resources that are available, the distance between schools, and other unique characteristics (NASP, 1992b). School psychology programs should advocate at the state and local levels for a practitioner-to-student ratio that allows for the provision of comprehensive school psychological services.

In light of higher caseloads, the lack of sufficient funding in public education to provide appropriate compensation or appropriate salary increases, and increasing expectations from school psychologist practitioners (Fagan, 1990a), it can be anticipated that retaining qualified practitioners will continue to be a demanding issue. In addition issues surrounding burnout of school psychologist practitioners should also be given consideration (Huebner, 1992).

Comprehensive Service Delivery

All school psychological practice should be in full accordance with NASP *Principles for Professional Ethics* (NASP, 1992a) and *Standards for the Provision of School Psychological Services* (NASP, 1992b). The purpose of the *Standards* is to help "ensure the delivery of comprehensive services by school psychologists" (NASP, 1992b, p. 43). The following components are seen as essential to a comprehensive program.

Consultation. Central to most successful school psychology delivery programs is the use of problem-solving behavioral consultation with parents, teachers, and students themselves. "The school psychologist usually does not personally provide the intervention," but rather guidance for those that do (NASP, 1992b). Behavioral consultation generally incorporates a four-stage process in which problem identification, problem analysis, plan implementation, and plan evaluation are carried out to address students' difficulties. A basic concept of the consultation model is the collaborative interaction between the psychologist and the consultee in which the latter (most frequently a teacher) acquires novel skills to address students' needs (Franklin & Duley, 1991). It is then hoped that these efforts will provide generalization of those skills across other cases in the educational setting. In this way psychologists can use their skills more effectively in their service as mental health practitioners and team leaders in comparison with more reactive, psychometrics-based practice (Franklin & Duley, 1991). Batsche (1991) reports that consultation/intervention services can reduce special education placements by as much as 50% without adversely affecting the progress of individual students.

Assessment. Another significant component of school psychology service delivery may be psychological and psychoeducational assessment. School psychologist practitioners must employ multifaceted psychological and psychoeducational assessments of children and youths according to current best practices (NASP, 1992b). School psychologists should utilize a variety of observational, behavioral evaluation, and interview techniques, as well as the traditional use of both normative and criterion-referenced instrumentation. All assessment should be linked to instructional intervention. Reschly (1988) cautions that assessment for classification will be replaced by assessment for the express purpose of developing interventions to be implemented in the classroom. Direct assessment techniques such as curriculum-based assessment (CBA) are seen as important competencies for school psychologists (Reschly, 1988).

Direct services. Direct service to students is traditionally seen as "techniques supplied in a face-to-face situation, which are designed to enhance the mental health, behavior, personality, social competency, academic, or educational status of the student" (NASP, 1992b, p. 45). Both individual and group counseling activities would fall under this heading. It seems that school psychologists are consistently dealing with crisis intervention situations that result in the "interrupted day." Often they are the front-line mental health professionals in the schools and are therefore called upon to provide intervention services on an as-needed basis. Thus, the best devised schedule for a school psychologist practitioner can go out the window on any given day, although the demands of the existing case load and mandated timelines continue in force.

Prevention. Primary and secondary prevention rather than tertiary prevention (treatment) should also be seen at the heart of a successful school psychology delivery program. Primary prevention seeks to change the incidence of new referrals by intervening proactively before a disorder occurs (Hightower, Johnson, & Haffey, 1990). For example, prosocial competencies can be increased through education and environments can be modified to reduce or counteract harmful circumstances. Primary prevention efforts call for proactive efforts to prevent problems from occurring, rather than attempts to reduce existing problems (Hightower et al., 1990). Secondary prevention is generally seen as identification of problems during the earliest stages and intervention before the problems become severe. This paradigm shift from treatment to prevention (Hightower et al., 1990) is seen as a critical strategy for practicing school psychologists who desire to provide a successful school psychology delivery program. The present need for more school psychology services and the continuing shortage of school psychologist practitioners suggest the need for further adoption of effective prevention programs (Hightower et al., 1990). School psychologists must continue to place their energy on the "front end" of the prevention–treatment continuum rather than on the "back end" of reactive crisis intervention.

Research. NASP suggests that school psychologists "design, conduct, report, and use the results of research of a psychological and educational nature" (NASP, 1992b, p. 45). Keith (1990) defines such research as "activities designed to produce new scientific knowledge or to use the knowledge to improve school psychological practices" (p. 207). Keith (1990) sees the need for school psychologist practitioners to be competent consumers of research and to act as distributors of research, and for some school psychologists to conduct research. For practitioners involved in conducting research, the use of quasi-experimental research, single-case designs, reversal designs, and multiple baseline designs holds promise (Keith, 1988). School psychologist practitioners should be involved in one or more levels of research to bring about a quality school psychology delivery program. Stoner and Green (1992) suggest that 100% of a school psychologist practitioner's time should be involved in doing research, in that practice and research should become one and the same.

Kratochwill, Schnaps, and Bissell (1985) describe four general types of research in school psychology: historical research, descriptive research, passive observational methods, and experimental research. They also provide some explanation and possible solutions for school psychological practitioners who have not been actively involved in research or the use of research findings. Franklin and Sabers (1987) have suggested that active participation in research is almost certain to be accompanied by additional learning and professional development. Reading and discussing the literature during the planning stages of a study are likely to produce a better-informed practitioner. The credibility one gains for oneself, the service unit, and the district should not be minimized. In this day of static or decreasing budgets for school psychology, it becomes more important for the practicing school psychologist to maintain high visibility and become more indispensable. The school psychologist as researcher can become more clearly indispensable, both as disseminator of research findings and as one who can provide answers to questions needing investigation.

Anything that is worth doing in the school setting warrants consideration for sharing with fellow professionals (Franklin & Sabers, 1987). This sharing may take the form of oral presentations to district staff, papers presented to local, state, or publications in national professional groups, papers in state and regional publications, book chapters, or publications in national refereed journals. "If it is worth doing, it is worth telling your fellow psychologists about it."

During routine assessment, Franklin (1983) observed consistently lower subtest scores obtained on a subtest of a commonly utilized individually administered reading achievement test. This concern led to a decision to study this subtest within the psychoeducational role of the practicing school psychologist. Questions surrounding design, random assignment, and statistical analysis were quickly resolved through consultation with colleagues at a local university. This effort led to a publishable article based on data that were gathered as part of routine reevaluations of a relatively small number of students. The reading subtest was subsequently modified by the instrument's author. This revision led Franklin, Fullilove, and Sabers (1985) to further assess the author's modifications. Again, this research was accomplished as part of a routine pre–post testing battery for development of individual education plans and made use of a school psychology practicum student. NASP's initial efforts to match school psychologist practitioners' research questions with graduate students seeking research topics appear to hold great promise of increasing the body of research data in the profession.

Liaison and coordination. NASP advocates that school psychologists establish and maintain relationships with other professionals who provide services to children and families and "collaborate with these professionals in prevention, assessment, and intervention efforts as necessary" (NASP, 1992b, p. 43). School psychologist practitioners can assist in coordinating the services of mental health providers from other agencies to provide a continuum of service for students (NASP, 1992b). It is likely that these liaison and coordinating roles for psychologist practitioners will become increasingly important.

Supervision, training, and mentorship. School psychology departments have a responsibility to provide training and development of new school psychologists. In the provision of training sites for introductory school psychology students, practicum students, and internship students, such an emphasis allows for continued sharing of existing expertise with a school psychology practitioner as well as the learning provided to the practitioner by students in training. It is also important for school psychology departments to work with university trainers in the area of supervision of students participating in school psychology practicums and internships. These activities help ensure the existence of a future pool of quality school psychologist practitioners (Franklin, 1989). New school psychologist practitioners should be assigned to school psychologist mentors to assist in shepherding them into the politics and nuances of the school district.

Continuing professional development. There is a constant shift in the needs of our constituency. These needs may in part be met through the provision of continuing education and professional training to the school psychologist practitioner. This can be accomplished through the dissemination of information between professionals within a school's psychological services department, through contracting with experts for in-service training, and through the participation of practitioners in conferences and workshops that teach new, or hone existing skills (Franklin, 1989). McKee, Witt, Elliott, Pardue, and Judycki (1987) suggest that talking to colleagues, exploring local needs, and requesting and sharing specific information may be as useful in obtaining information as employing outside consultants, having school psychologists attend workshops, and using professional development materials. It may be necessary for the supervisor of school psychology services to inform or educate central office and building administrators, as well as members of the governing board, of the importance of continuing professional education and professional training activities for school psychologist practitioners.

"The practice of school psychology will continue to change significantly over the course of the next years as new knowledge and technological advances are introduced" (NASP, 1992b, p. 46). It will therefore be necessary for the school psychologist practitioner to remain knowledgeable about these changes in practice. It is suggested that school psychology service programs that require or encourage school psychologist practitioners to acquire and maintain credentialing by the National School Psychology Certification System (NASP, 1988) assist in the continued training and honing of the existing skills of its practitioners. Continued training and the reinforcement of existing skills are critical to the maintenance of quality school psychology delivery programs (Franklin, 1989).

Accountability. Accountability of the service delivery program is an important component as well (NASP, 1992b). Zins (1984) defines accountability as an

> evaluative effort designed to gather systematically information relevant to the performance assessment of school psychologists. It enables them to demonstrate the effectiveness of their services to others, and it provides an evaluation of how well they have met their performance objectives. It is concerned with both quantitative and qualitative aspects of practice and addresses both individuals and groups. It is particularly useful in improving service delivery and enhancing professional development. (p. 58)

Batsche (1991) suggests that school psychological practitioners collect data regarding efficacy in relation to costs and consumer satisfaction, as well as the effectiveness of service delivery. "If you are a supervisor or a school psychologist in a district hard hit by financial difficulties, ask yourself whether or not you are providing information that convinces superintendents and boards of education of the worth of school psychological services" (Batsche, 1991, p. 2). In the Minneapolis Psychological Services Program previously described, accountability data brought about modifications in school psychology practice as a function of the outcome of the accountability system (Canter, 1991). As individual school psychological practitioners and as a profession we cannot ignore the need to regularly evaluate our services (Zins, 1990). Providing accountability data must become a routine component of school psychology services.

High visibility. It is also important to report the accomplishments of the school psychology department to the teachers, administrators, governing board members, and constituents of the district (Franklin, 1989). Maintaining high visibility for a successful school psychology delivery program can generate future support for the acquisition of additional staff positions, the provision of continuing education and professional training, and the delivery of nontraditional practice opportunities for the school psychologist (Franklin, 1989). Attention to public image must be seen as a major factor in the role of the school psychologist and the services that are provided (Kelly, 1990). The advice, attributed to the late Congressman Adam Clayton Powell, that "you will never hear any music, if you don't blow your own horn" (K. P. Dwyer, personal communication, March 8, 1994) should be seriously considered by school psychologist practitioners.

Future Considerations

Hutton, Dubes, and Muir (1992) report that school psychologists spend 40%–60% of their time in assessment activities. Will (1988) suggests that the traditional role of school psychologists as gatekeepers for the entry to special education and reentry to regular education needs to shift from reactive to proactive, in which learning and instructional problems are prevented. "This shift will require greater emphasis on instructional variables that include the curriculum, task features, teaching functions, and instructionally based assessment procedures" (Will, 1988, p. 478).

Reschly (1988) believes that the "character of school psychology at the dawn of the 21st century will be markedly influenced by how we manage the challenge of special education reform and the necessary revolution" (p. 472). Kavaleski (1988) is of the opinion that

> school psychologists have a unique opportunity to alter contingencies that influence their own practice. Accepting this challenge can lead to the establishment of school psychology in a reformed system. Ignoring the opportunity will lead at best to business as usual and at most the demise of a discipline. (p. 483)

Continued professional development will be a component necessary to the future delivery of school psychological services. As practitioners "shift in focus from a search for pathology to educational attainment" (Myers, 1988, p. 167), it will be advantageous to acquire and hone skills in curriculum-based assessment for both formative and summative purposes.

As school psychology service delivery programs continue to experience static or declining budgets, five issues will demand scrutiny.

1. Overcoming resistance by school psychologists, teachers, and administrators as practitioner roles change from refer-and-test to prereferral intervention and prevention.

2. The need to preserve school-based school psychologist positions (NASP, 1993).

3. The provision of efficacy data for school psychology services (Batsche, 1991).

4. Attracting and retaining qualified school psychologist practitioners.

5. The hiring of individuals with less comprehensive training as educational diagnosticians or psychometrists.

SUMMARY

As school psychology delivery programs are asked to constantly reexamine their roles, functions, and skills, they must resist the temptation to remain locked into models of delivery that are "comfortable." There is no single best way to deliver effective school psychological services. However, the NASP *Standards for the Provision of School Psychological Services* (NASP, 1992b) provides exceptional direction for individuals who are planning or modifying existing school psychology delivery programs. The chapter reviewed organizational considerations, program administration and supervision, and components of comprehensive service delivery for a successful school psychology program. A review of seven innovative school psychology programs reveal that they appear to possess in aggregate a series of characteristics: (a) highly qualified practitioners and a wide range of expertise within each department, (b) delivery of comprehensive services to all students, (c) commitment to prereferral intervention/prevention activities, (d) use of school-based collaborative consultation, (e) linking of assessment to intervention, (f) articulation of departmental successes, (g) accountability through efficacy data, (h) malleability, (i) continuing professional development, (j) departmental autonomy and supervision by a school psychologist, (k) involvement in research, and (l) commitment to training future school psychologist practitioners.

It is hoped that school psychology services delivery programs that are fixated on traditional roles and functions for school psychologist practitioners will strive to move from what is "real" to what may be seen as more "ideal" (Stewart, 1986).

ACKNOWLEDGMENTS

I would like to express my sincere appreciation to Darrell L. Sabers for his comments and suggestions on the initial drafts of this chapter.

REFERENCES

American Psychological Association. (1981). Specialty guideline for the delivery of services by school psychologists. *American Psychologist, 36,* 670–681.

Batsche, G. (1991). School psychological services: Can we prove their worth? *Communiqué, 20*(3), 2.

Bergan, J. R. (1977). *Behavioral consultation.* Columbus, OH: Merrill.

Bush, K., Carter, D., Dickerson, C., Evans, G., Martin, F., Raskind, L., & Thomas, A. (1989). Gwinnett County: Changing its service delivery in response to population growth. *Professional School Psychology, 4,* 189–200.

Canter, A. (1991). Effective psychological services for all students: A data-based model of service delivery. In G. Stoner, M. Shinn, & H. Walker (Eds.), *Interventions for achievement and behavioral problems* (pp. 49–78). Washington, DC: National Association of School Psychologists.

Connolly, L. M., & Reschly, D. (1990). The school psychology crisis of the 1990's. *Communiqué, 19*(3), 1, 12.

Division Spotlight. (1988, July). *APA Monitor,* p. 6.

Fagan, T. K. (1990a). A brief history of school psychology in the United States. In A. Thomas & J. Grimes (Eds.), *Best practices in school psychology–II* (p. 913–929). Washington, DC: National Association of School Psychologists.

Fagan, T. K. (1990b). Best practices in the training of school psychologists: Considerations for trainers, prospective entry-level and advanced students. In A. Thomas & J. Grimes (Eds.), *Best practices in school psychology–II* (pp. 723–741). Washington, DC: National Association of School Psychologists.

Franklin, M., & Wasserman, H. M. (1992). *Establishing effective parental partnerships with school psychology: Responsibilities and pitfalls.* Paper presented at the annual convention of the National Association of School Psychologists, Nashville.

Franklin, M. R., Jr. (1983). The effort of practice and instruction on the word comprehension subtest of the Woodcock. *Journal of Psychoeducational Assessment, 1,* 197–200.

Franklin, M. R., Jr. (1989). Field-based supervision offers many benefits. *Communiqué, 17*(5), 16, 21.

Franklin, M. R., Jr., & Duley, S. M. (1991). Psychological services in the Amphitheater School District. *School Psychology Quarterly, 6,* 61–80.

Franklin, M. R., Jr., Fullilove, R. M., & Sabers, D. L. (1985). Woodcock analogies: Effect of additional practice and instruction for learning disabled students. *Journal of Learning Disabilities, 18,* 521–523.

Franklin, M. R., Jr., & Sabers, D. L. (1987). The school psychologist's role as researcher. *Intervention, 19,* 1, 6, 8. (Available from AASP, 3900 E. Camelback, Suite 200, Phoenix.)

Gutkin, T. B., & Curtis, M. J. (1982). School based consultation: Theory and techniques. In C. R. Reynolds & T. B. Gutkin (Eds.), *The handbook of school psychology* (pp. 796–828). New York: Wiley.

Hightower, A. D., Johnson, D., & Haffey, W. G. (1990). Best practices in adopting a prevention program. In A. Thomas & J. Grimes (Eds.), *Best practices in school psychology–II* (pp.

63–79). Washington, DC: National Association of School Psychologists.

Huebner, S. E. (1992). Burnout among school psychologists: An exploratory investigation into its nature, extent, and correlates. *School Psychology Quarterly, 7,* 129–136.

Hutton, J. B., Dubes, R., & Muir, S. (1992). Assessment practices of school psychologists: Ten years later. *School Psychology Review, 21,* 271–284.

Kavaleski, J. (1988). Pragmatic obstacles to reform in school psychology. *School Psychology Review, 17,* 479–484.

Keith, T. Z. (1988). Research methods in school psychology: An overview. *School Psychology Review, 17,* 508–526.

Keith, T. Z. (1990). Best practices in applied research. In A. Thomas & J. Grimes (Eds.), *Best practices in school psychology–II* (pp. 207–218). Washington, DC: National Association of School Psychologists.

Kelly, C. (1990). Best practices in building-level public relations. In A. Thomas & J. Grimes (Eds.), *Best practices in school psychology–II* (p. 171–181). Washington, DC: National Association of School Psychologists.

Knoff, H. M. (1986). Supervision in school psychology: The forgotten or future path to effective services? *School Psychology Review, 15,* 529–545.

Kratochwill, T. R., Schnaps, A., & Bissell, M. (1985). Research design in school psychology. In J. Bergan (Ed.), *School psychology in contemporary society: An introduction.* Columbus, OH: Merrill.

McKee, W. T., Witt, J. C., Elliott, S. N., Pardue, M., & Judycki, A. (1987). Practice informing research: A survey of research dissemination and knowledge utilization. *School Psychology Review, 16,* 338–347.

Myers, J. (1988). School psychology: The current state of proactive and future practice of the specialty. *Professional School Psychology, 3,* 165–176.

National Association of School Psychologists. (1988). *National School Psychology Certification System.* Washington, DC: Author.

National Association of School Psychologists. (1992a). *Principles for professional ethics.* Washington, DC: Author.

National Association of School psychologists. (1992b). *Standards for the provision of school psychological services.* Washington, DC: Author.

National Association of School psychologists. (1993). *Preserving school-based positions: Ideas and resources for school psychologists.* Washington, DC: Author.

Nichol, G. T. (1993). Memphis City Schools Mental Health Center. *Communiqué, 22*(3), 17–18.

Oakland, T. (1986). Further thought on professionalism in school psychology. *Professional School Psychology, 1*(1), 47–49.

Paavola, J., Hannah, F., & Nichol, G. (1989). The Memphis City Schools Mental Health Center: A program description. *Professional School Psychology, 4,* 61–74.

Reschly, D. J. (1988). Special education reform: School psychology revolution. *School Psychology Review, 17,* 459–475.

Reschly, D. J., & Grimes, J. P. (1990). Best practices in intellectual assessment. In A. Thomas & J. Grimes (Eds.), *Best practices in school psychology–II* (pp. 425–439). Washington, DC: National Association of School Psychologists.

Ross, R. P., & Goh, D. S. (1993). Participating in supervision in school psychology: A national survey of practices and training. *School Psychology Review, 22,* 63–80.

Stewart, K. J. (1986). Innovative practice of indirect service delivery: Realistic and idealistic. *School Psychology Review, 15,* 466–478.

Stoner, G., & Green, S. K. (1992). Reconsidering the scientist–practitioner model for school psychology practice. *School Psychology Review, 21,* 155–166.

Talley, R. C. (1990). Best practices in the administration and supervision of school psychological services. In A. Thomas & J. Grimes (Eds.), *Best practices in school psychology–II* (pp. 43–62). Washington, DC: National Association of School Psychologists.

Telzrow, C. (1989). Award of excellence for school psychological services programs series. Introduction. *Professional School Psychology, 4,* 59.

Will, M. (1988). Educating students with learning problems and the changing role of the school psychologist. *School Psychology Review, 17,* 476–478.

Zins, J. E. (1984). A scientific problem-solving approach to developing accountability procedures for school psychologists. *Professional Psychology: Research and Practice, 15,* 56–66.

Zins, J. E. (1990). Best practices in developing accountability procedures. In A. Thomas & J. Grimes (Eds.), *Best practices in school psychology–II* (pp. 323–337). Washington, DC: National Association of School Psychologists.

Zins, J. E., Murphy, J. J., & Wess, B. P. (1989). Supervision in school psychology: Current practices and congruence with professional standards. *School Psychology Review, 18,* 56–67.

ANNOTATED BIBLIOGRAPHY

Bush, K., Carter, D., Dickerson, C., Evans, G., Martin, F., Raskind, L., & Thomas A. (1989). Gwinnett County: Changing its service delivery in response to population growth. *Professional School Psychology, 4,* 189–200.
This article describes how the Gwinnett County Psychological Services Unit altered its service delivery model from one with a primary emphasis on psychoeducational assessment to a focus upon consultation and prevention services.

Canter, A. (1991). Effective psychological services for all students: A data-based model of service delivery. In G. Stoner, M. Shinn, & H. Walker (Eds.), *Interventions for achievement and behavior problems* (pp. 49–78). Washington, DC: National Association of School Psychologists.
This chapter provides a detailed description of the Minneapolis schools' Psychological Services Department data-based accountability model of service delivery. This model has allowed the department to avoid "a retreat from excellence."

Franklin, M. R., Jr., & Duley, S. M. (1991). Psychological services in the Amphitheater School District. *School Psychology Quarterly, 6,* 66–80.
This article reviews the delivery of a traditional and nontraditional school psychological services to at-risk and low-risk students by means of a collaborative consultation model and student study teams.

Paavola, J., Hannah, F., & Nicol, G. (1989). The Memphis City Schools Mental Health Center: A program description. *Professional School Psychology, 4,* 61–74.
This article describes the Memphis City Schools Mental Health Center, which has demonstrated emphasis on prevention, prereferral consultation, and screening in the provision of comprehensive school psychological services from "prevention to therapy."

Talley, R. (1990). Best practice in the administration and supervision of school psychological services. In A. Thomas & J. Grimes (Eds.), *Best practices in school psychology–II* (pp. 43–62). Washington, DC: National Association of School Psychologists. This chapter provides distinctions between administrative and clinical supervision, organizational models for the delivery of school psychology services, and guidelines for school psychology leaders who are charged with translating theory into real-world school psychology services.

7

Best Practices in Continuing Professional Development for School Psychologists

Evelyn Fowler
Patti L. Harrison
University of Alabama

Continuing professional development (CPD) is a dynamic process that flows from the intrinsic motivation, interest, learning history, and professional context of the individual. In regard to school psychologists, it is the process by which they "actively participate and engage in activities designed to continue, enhance, and upgrade their professional training and skills and to help ensure quality service provision" (National Association of School Psychologists, 1992a, p. 46). The purpose of this chapter is to present suggested guidelines for individualizing CPD for school psychologists

OVERVIEW

In order to put CPD in an appropriate perspective so that it may be more fully appreciated, a brief history and rationale will be presented. Following that will be a discussion of CPD requirements for school psychologists, including state certification/licensure, school accreditation, and qualifications as a nationally certified school psychologist (NCSP).

Historical Background and Rationale

CPD was a rather loosely held concept prior to World War II, when it received its first official recognition under the Engineering, Science, Management War Training Act (Tucker & Huerta, 1984). Following World War II, as professionalism grew and expanded, CPD emerged as the means for assuring competence. CPD remained largely unorganized and received little emphasis until the accountability movement of the 1960s. Consumer dissatisfaction with professional inadequacies and criticism from within professional ranks themselves contributed to its revitalization. A recognition of the need for CPD by professionals grew out of introspection about competition, failure, uncertainty about how to solve a problem, and accountability demands by the public. Professionals viewed CPD as a panacea for diffusing rising public criticism, malpractice suits, loss of certification, and compulsory recredentialing. The creation of the continuing education unit (CEU) in 1970 by a national task force of the National Advisory Commission on Health Manpower and its subsequent adoption in 1971 by the Southern Association of Colleges and Schools added impetus to the CPD movement (National League for Nursing, 1974; Tucker & Huerta, 1984).

In addition to accountability and quality control, another important reason that contributed to the growth of CPD is the modern notion of professionalism as a dynamic process entailing lifelong learning. According to Houle (1980), "Every occupation . . . seeks constantly to improve itself. . . . Therefore, a lifetime of learning is required . . ." (p. 10). Houle's statement suggests that professionalism is not a static entity that is achieved on completion of a formal educational program. Rather, it should be an ongoing process, maintained by motivation for learning throughout one's professional lifetime. Professionalism should be an evolving process, expanding and taking new and more complex forms as the professional oscillates between theory and practice with each reinforcing the other (Houle, 1980).

The need to maintain skills and keep abreast of new ideas and technology have contributed to the growth of CPD as well. In recent years, the knowledge bases of professional fields have rapidly and extensively developed and expanded (Houle, 1980; Rosenfield, 1985). Numerous advances have been made in technology, medicine, pharmacology, and research methodology, to name only a few. In a rapidly developing society such as ours, skills quickly erode and become dated. The term *half-life* has been used to describe the continuous obsolescence of professional competence. The half-life concept raises the notion that professionals quickly become only half as competent to meet professional demands as they were upon graduation. In particular, the half-life of a school psychologist's training has been estimated as ranging from 3 years to 5 years (Rosenfield, 1985; Hynd, Pielstick, & Schakel, 1981).

Research has also contributed to the growth of CPD by documenting its many benefits. Some of the more salient social and professional advantages to be derived from CPD participation are self-satisfaction, documented changed behavior that has translated into improved service provision, enhancement of knowledge, improved attitude, improved skills and techniques, greater confidence, increased awareness and abilities in dealing with others, better job performance, increased salary/fringe benefits, promotion on the job, and better reputation for the employing agency (Cervero & Rottet, 1984; Houle, 1980).

Continuing education is now a recognized necessity across professions and is embraced as the means for assuring quality control, competence, and accountability among professionals (Houle, 1980; Tucker & Huerta, 1984). CPD requirements are in place nationwide for relicensure or professional standing of doctors, lawyers, nurses, school psychologists, counselors, and others (e.g., American Nurses Association [AMA], 1984, 1992; National Association of School Psychologists [NASP], 1992a, 1992b; Goldberg, 1990; Wilcoxon & Hawk, 1990).

CPD Requirements for School Psychologists

Ethical standards for school psychologists, as well as requirements for certification and renewal of licensure, emphasize the need for CPD. In its ethical standards and specialty guidelines, the National Association of School Psychologists emphasizes the obligations a school psychologist assumes for CPD and ethical behavior when initially engaging in the practice of school psychology. NASP (1992b) ethical standards state:

> School psychologists engage in continuing professional development. They remain current regarding developments in research, training, and professional practices that benefit children, families, and school. (p. 6)

NASP ethical standards specifically state that participation in CPD activities is part of the continuing obligation of a school psychologist.

The *American Psychologist*'s (1992) "Ethical Principles of Psychologists and Code of Conduct" also emphasizes psychologists' obligations for ongoing education:

> They maintain knowledge of relevant scientific and professional information related to the services they render, and they recognize the need for ongoing education. (p. 1599)

Many school psychologists employed in school districts are required to document CPD activities for renewal of their individual state certificates or continued employment in their system. Among other requirements, school system accreditation often hinges on individually documented CPD activities for all

school professionals within the system. For example, in 1971 the Southern Association of Colleges and Schools implemented the CEU requirement for school professionals in order for schools to receive regional accreditation (Tucker & Huerta, 1984). Many states have CPD requirements for renewal of psychology licensure; currently, 27 states require CPD for psychology licensure renewal, compared with five or six states in 1981 ("Growth of CE Program," 1992).

Nationally certified school psychologists (NCSPs) must complete CPD requirements for national certification renewal. The CPD requirements include the completion of 75 CPD credits or contact hours (actual clock hours) in at least three of the following six skill areas: consultation, psychological and psychoeducational assessment, intervention, supervision, research, and program planning and evaluation. CPD requirements for renewal of national certification are described in NASP's CPD program, located in Appendix V of this volume.

BASIC CONSIDERATIONS

Consideration of the CPD needs of school psychologists must address three important issues. First, the educational level of school psychologists vary. Next, school psychologists perform wide and varied job functions. Finally, school psychologists serve the entire range of environments — from rural to urban to large metropolitan areas. Consequently, their knowledge base, training, skill level, and professional role are multidimensional (NASP, 1992a). Only an individualized approach to CPD can address such multifaceted needs. This section describes an individualized CPD process for use by school psychologists.

The individualized CPD process described here shares elements across professions and involves five steps (ANA, 1992; Baker, 1981; Houle, 1980; Kaplan, Geoffroy, Pare, & Wolf, 1992; Kathrein, 1990; Rosenfield, 1985). The elements that are emphasized in the CPD process are a problem-solving approach in seeking solutions to skills deficits and to updating skills, self-directedness in launching new learning, and recognition of both internal and external contexts of the individual professional. The five steps are (a) assessing needs, (b) selecting goals, (c) stating objectives, (d) selecting learning options, and (e) making evaluations.

Self-Evaluation of CPD Needs

A needs assessment is a basic aspect of a self-evaluation and is the first step in the suggested individualized CPD process. A school psychologist's needs assessment involves an analysis of professional knowledge and skills relative to NASP CPD skill areas. The CPD skill areas should be considered in conjunction with the current role/function, the expanded role/function, the professional interest, and/or the anticipated career change of the school psychologist. Skills relative to improved performance in one's current position typically should receive priority attention. Skills relative to an expanded role or function in one's present situation and those relative to a future role or career change can be addressed as long-range goals. If the latter two are imminent, they may be a greater priority. Naturally, consideration of one's professional interest is an important additional element in analyzing professional needs.

Table 1 presents a rating scale that can be used for assessing a school psychologist's professional needs. Skill areas are taken from the NASP CPD program (see Appendix V, this volume, for more details about the skill areas). Completion of the scale involves three steps: (a) reviewing skills and knowledge areas relative to NASP CPD standards, (b) rating each area according to predetermined competence, and (c) weighting each area relative to individual needs.

A variety of sources are available for assessing professional competence. Input from supervision is one source. In situations in which supervisory input is not available, peer appraisal is another option. Peer appraisal may be formal or informal. The formal peer group appraisal process involves an organized network of professionals who observe, objectively measure performance, and provide feedback to members. An informal peer group appraisal process involves a group of professionals who get together to critique and share observations about shared needs. Consumer feedback obtained from parent, teacher, and student surveys is yet another means of assessing professional competence. Questionnaires, rating scales, and interviews are additional sources of feedback data.

Directions for completing the needs assessment featured in Table 1 are as follows:

1. Review each specific skill and knowledge area.

2. Record a rating for your knowledge/skill in each area by indicating if your skill/knowledge in the area is satisfactory (S), questionable (Q), or needs improvement (NI) for one or more of the following:

   a. the roles and functions required in your current position;

   b. the roles and functions that would be required if your position were expanded to include new activities and responsibilities;

   c. the roles and functions for a new career or new position;

   d. your own professional interest in an area.

Note: Your skill/knowledge rating is considered in conjunction with your current or expanded role/function, career change and/or professional interest. For example, if you have limited skill or knowledge in a specific area listed in Table 1 but your current job

does not require the skill/knowledge, record (S). If your current job does require the skill/knowledge, record (NI).

3. The ratings of knowledge/skill can be recorded by one or more of the following:

   a. yourself (self-assessment);

   b. supervisor;

   c. peer;

   d. consumer (school principal, teacher, etc.).

4. Following completion of the ratings of your skill/knowledge, record "CPD priority weights" to identify the skill/knowledge areas that should be the focus of your CPD activities. First, determine which of the following is most important in regard to improvement of skills — current role/function, expanded role/function, career change, personal interest. Then, for knowledge/skill rated as NI or Q, assign CPD priority weights according to the following scale:

1 = Priority — My immediate CPD goals should definitely include this area.

2 = Relevant — This area may be included in immediate or long-range goals.

3 = Somewhat Relevant — This area may be an appropriate long-range goal.

4 = Not Very Relevant — This may not be an appropriate area for my CPD goals.

Developing and Implementing Personal CPD Plans

Once a determination has been made concerning areas of skill and knowledge needs, the goal selection process begins. Individual ratings of the CPD skill areas determine CPD goals. Areas receiving NI or Q ratings and priority weights of 1 should represent immediate goals. Skills receiving lesser ratings/weights might represent distant or long-range goals. Next, objectives (tasks) designed to meet selected goals are specified. Consideration of learning options or avenues is the next step in the individualized CPD process.

Traditional and Nontraditional Avenues for CPD

Research indicates that participation in CPD activities is an effective means for promoting positive change in professional knowledge, skills, attitudes, beliefs, and performance (Cervero & Rottet, 1984; Cooley & Thompson, 1992; Reschly & Grimes, 1991). A number of learning options or avenues are available. These include traditional and nontraditional methods.

TABLE 1
Knowledge/Skills Rating Scale

Skill Knowledge Area	Current Role Function	Expanded Role Function	Career Change	Professional Interest	CPD Priority Weight[b]
	Rating of Knowledge Skill for:[a]				
Consultation					
Mental health consultation					
Behavioral consultation					
Educatonal consultation					
Promotion of mental health and learning					
Promotion of preventon of disorders					
Promition of improving educational systems					
Professional inservice					
Skills to enhance collaborative relationships					
Other					
Assessment					
Multifactored assessment					
Personal-social assessment					
Intellectual assessment					
Scholastic aptitude assessment					
Adaptive behavior assessment					
Language and communication assessment					
Academic achievement assessment					
Sensory and perceptual-motor assessment					
Environmental-cultural assessment					
Vocational assessment					
Observation					
Behavioral assessment					

(Table 1, continued)

Skill Knowledge Area	Rating of Knowledge Skill for:[a]				
	Current Role Function	**Expanded Role Function**	**Career Change**	**Professional Interest**	**CPD Priority Weight**[b]
Non-biased assessment					
Ethical considerations in assessment					
Other					
Interventions: Interventions for individuals					
Interventions for groups					
Interventions for systems					
Interventions for cognitive development					
Interventions for social development					
In-service					
Organizational development					
Parent counseling					
Parent education					
Other					
Supervision Supervision					
Administration					
Provision of practicum/ internship					
Other					
Research On psychological functioning					
On assessment tools and procedures					
On educational programs/techniques					
On educational processes					

(Table 1, continued)

Skill Knowledge Area	Rating of Knowledge Skill for:[a]				
	Current Role Function	Expanded Role Function	Career Change	Professional Interest	CPD Priority Weight[b]
On social systems and organizational factors					
On psychological treatments					
Other					
Program Planning and Evaluation Program planning					
Decision making					
Developing educational activities					
Other					

[a] Rating scale for knowledge skills: S = satisfactory; Q = questionable; NI = needs improvement.
[b] CPD priority weights: 1 = priority; 2 = relevant; 3 = somewhat relevant; 4 = not very relevant.

Traditional programs include formal coursework, workshops, institutes, and in-service programs. In situations in which the professional has little or no knowledge to serve as a base for a needed skill, formal coursework is the preferred learning option. Formal coursework has the advantages of guaranteed supervision, guided practice, and feedback (Houle, 1980). Workshops and institutes also provide a means for acquiring needed skills and knowledge, but they may not have the aforementioned advantages (Rosenfield, 1985). In-service programs are the traditional means of providing CPD for school personnel, but they have been severely criticized as ineffective (Spitzer, 1979). Effective in-service programs exhibit cooperatively planned institutional and individual needs, participant involvement, personal and professional relevance, and they provide reinforcement, feedback, and follow-up (Cooley & Thompson, 1990; Truesdell, 1985). Other traditional educational methods are participation in discussion groups and reading professional journals, monographs, books, manuals, and digests (Houle, 1980).

A number of less traditional options are also available. The peer group, a number of individuals organized to meet a shared need, is also an effective learning option (Zins, Maher, Murphy, & Wess, 1988). Their purposes may be varied. As explained earlier, they can be formally or informally organized. The peer group can use a teaching–learning mode in which members teach and learn from one another; a problem-solving mode, in which members focus on mutual problems and use collective problem-solving techniques to resolve the difficulty, or the practice mode, in which members practice a new technique with each other. A fourth option is that of invited guest lecturers. A professional conference can be viewed as an extended peer group meeting (Rosenfield, 1985). Some advantages of the peer group process cited in the literature are increased morale, increased networking, greater familiarity with community resources, increased participation in professional organizations, motivation to continue one's education, and development of professional skills (Zins et al., 1988).

Facilitation, mentoring, and supervision are other less traditional learning options. Facilitators are individuals who can guide continuing professional growth of colleagues by acting either as models, by demonstrating aspects of a skill, or as teachers, by providing instruction on an interactive basis directly related to the professionals' needs. Mentors are individuals who act as counselor/learning facilitators, giving moral support and encouragement. A supervisor could act as a facilitator or mentor (Houle, 1980; Rosenfield, 1985). Another option might be purchased supervision. This could be especially advantageous for those who have no direct supervision but need to develop skill in different areas. Supervisors with different areas of expertise could be hired to accommodate varying needs (Rosenfield, 1985).

The above types of activities can be carried out through a number of technologies, making long-distance learning feasible. Distance education includes the more nontraditional electronic media such as the telephone and speaker phone; taped digests of current literature; audio- and videotapes of lectures, workshops, conventions, and even formal coursework; closed-circuit, cable, and satellite television; computer-mediated communication; and written correspondence study. Research shows the academic effectiveness of distance education to be compatible with that of conventional classroom instruction (Clark & Verduin, 1992).

Self-supervision methods such as recording or videotaping interventions, counseling, and consultation sessions, and later critiquing them according to personal standards of performance, provide additional learning opportunities. Peer groups can be used in this process and in developing checklists to monitor performance in certain areas (Rosenfield, 1985).

Additional means of professional development are supervising interns in the field (NASP, 1992a), and holding a position of leadership in a local, state, or national professional organization. Teaching, research, and program development are other sources of professional development, since all three involve a considerable amount of preparatory study and learning.

Exchange programs, or "trading places," offers another means of professional development. One way to overcome the boredom and the eroding of the sharpness of one's skills is to exchange places with colleagues for a given period of time. This can result in renewed interest, motivation, and new learning (Rosenfield, 1985).

Evaluation

Evaluation is an integral part of ethical professional practice, and numerous reasons have been cited for it (Rosenfield, 1985). The purposes that are most relevant to the individualized CPD process are assessment for accountability and improvements in service, collection of information about strengths and needs, and charting of progress toward goals. By engaging in goal-driven CPD activities that have been developed from the knowledge/skills rating scale (Table 1) and by assessing progress toward or attainment of each, the school psychologist accomplishes all three purposes.

Again, initial development of priorities and goals is the basis for all evaluations in the individualized CPD process. Assessment of goal attainment should follow completion of each CPD activity. Informally charting, graphing, checking, or noting anecdotally such activities as number of professional meetings attended, journals read, workshops presented, and college courses completed are examples of enumerative data that are useful for charting progress toward goals and documenting their attainment. Questionnaires and surveys completed by peers and consumers can provide documentation about improvements in services. Checklists completed by peers, consumers, and/or supervisors can provide feedback about professional strengths and needs that is useful for guiding future CPD plans. Equally important, evaluation in the individualized CPD process should be ongoing, and adjustments should be made as dictated by the circumstances. For example, should a chosen CPD activity prove unsatisfactory in meeting a particular goal, it should be abandoned and replaced with an alternative activity.

Taken collectively, the evaluative data provide the means for certifying CPD participation and attainment of or progress toward, individually selected CPD goals. The need on the part of the profession to monitor CPD activities for maintenance of credentials is addressed by the documentation of completed CPD activities by means of the CPD summary sheet (see Appendix V).

Constraints on CPD Activities

Though obstacles to participation in CPD activities have not been as extensively researched as have been factors that impel it, several deterrents have been identified (Houle, 1980; Scanlon & Darkenwald, 1984; Tucker & Huerta, 1984). The following constraints must be recognized by school psychologists and considered when developing individualized CPD plans.

1. Time. The number 1 deterrent cited by professionals, it includes time away from the job, course schedule, and length of formal coursework.

2. Administrative constraints. Centers around concerns about program quality and/or poor reputation of the sponsoring agent.

3. Expense. Professionals and adults in general cite cost (travel, food, lodging, loss of income while away from work, tuition, registration fees) as the most frequent deterrent.

4. Family. Deterrents such as time away from family, childcare, and family/spousal objections.

5. Disposition. Attitudes and values such as age and family biases, uncertainty, and resistance to chance affect participation.

6. Attitude/motivation. Lack of involvement in the program selection and/or planning, implementation, and evaluation process, as well as program relevance, affects involvement.

Accountability for CPD Activities

Professionalism carries with it the responsibility of maintaining competence. This is done at the level of the individual and through professional requirements to obtain and retain credentials. From the perspective of the individual professional, competence involves the responsibility for maintaining a current knowledge base, preserving sharpened skills and techniques, and providing quality service. From the perspective of the profession as a whole, certification and/or recertification requirements are accountability standards for assuring competence and quality control within its own ranks.

BEST PRACTICES

1. School psychologists must acknowledge their obligation of continually engaging in CPD activities. In a field in which initial training has an estimated half-life of 3–5 years, school psychologists must recognize that preservice training will not take them far. A commitment to lifelong learning is a solution to the problem of continuous skills obsolescence. School psychologists must make such a commitment.

2. School psychologists must approach CPD as a problem-solving activity that must be part of professional practice.

3. School psychologists must not wait until CPD activities come to them, but must plan and organize ways to set up CPD projects that meet their professional goals.

4. School psychologists should systematically assess CPD needs and develop CPD goals, instead of using a hit or miss approach. Effective CPD cannot be obtained by simply engaging in the activities that happen to be provided by an employer or that happen to be available in the local community. School psychologists must continuously monitor their knowledge and skill, identify needs, and develop plans to enhance or increase knowledge and skill.

5. School psychologists should not select CPD activities just for convenience. Rather, activities that will meet goals and promote the most learning should determine selection.

6. School psychologists should consider new avenues for CPD beyond traditional workshops, courses, and in-service. School psychologists should also consider nontraditional activities such as peer support groups, peer supervision, distance education, and computer-mediated communication.

7. Each individual school psychologist should evaluate the effectiveness of a CPD activity, asking the questions: Has the activity really increased my skill/knowledge? Has the activity enhanced job performance? School psychologists who judge that an activity has not been effective in enhancing a skill

area should select new options for learning. They should also inform CPD organizers about the effectiveness or ineffectiveness of CPD activities.

8. School psychologists should use problem solving to address constraints to CPD. For example, courses, lectures, or workshops via satellite television or computer-mediated communication provide flexibility in time and schedule. Organizing local peer groups, supervising interns, and engaging in research all promote learning and allow flexibility in time, cost, and schedule.

SUMMARY

Skills erosion, obsolescence, and accountability for effective, competent service provision are recognized concerns among school psychologists. Research shows CPD to be an effective means for addressing these problems. In this chapter the rationale, requirements, and process for CPD of school psychologists were discussed. An individualized, five-step problem-solving procedure was described. Methods, activities, and options for addressing each of the five steps were suggested. Frequently cited constraints on CPD were listed so that school psychologists might recognize and consider each when developing individualized CPD plans. School psychologists must take a proactive stance toward CPD and make it an integral part of professional practice. Such a stance requires a commitment to lifelong learning.

REFERENCES

American Nurses Association. (1984). *Standards for continuing education* (COE-8). Washington, DC: American Nurses Publishing.

American Nurses Association. (1992). *Roles and responsibilities for nursing continuing education and staff development across all settings* (COE-16). Washington, DC: American Nurses Publishing.

American Psychological Association. (1992). Ethical principles of psychologists and code of conduct. *American Psychologist, 47,* 1597–1611.

Baker, S. B. (1981). *School counselor's handbook.* Boston: Allyn and Bacon.

Cervero, R. M., & Rottet, S. (1984). Analyzing the effectiveness of continuing professional education: An exploratory study. *Adult Education Quarterly, 34*(3), 135–146.

Clark, T. A., & Verduin, J. R., Jr. (1992). Distance education: Its effectiveness and potential use in lifelong learning. *Lifelong Learning: An Omnibus of Practice and Research, 12*(4), 24–26.

Cooley, V. E., & Thompson, J. C., Jr. (1990). An English perspective on inservice: A comparative analysis of practices and views in the United States. *Educational Research Quarterly, 14*(3), 51–56.

Goldberg, M. Z. (1990). Continuing legal education is mandatory in 35 states. *Trial, 26*(8), 76–79.

Growth of CE program shows no sign of abating. (1992, December). *APA Monitor,* p. 36.

Houle, C. O. (1980). *Continuing learning in the professions.* San Francisco: Jossey-Bass.

Hynd, G. W., Pielstick, N. L., & Schakel, J. A. (1981). Continuing professional development in school psychology: Current status. *School Psychology Review, 10*(4), 480–486.

Kaplan, L. S., Geoffroy, K. E., Pare, P., & Wolf, L. (1992). Using an individual action plan to enhance the professional development of elementary school counselors. *School Counselor, 39*, 164–170.

Kathrein, M. A. (1990). Continuing nursing education: A perspective. *Journal of Continuing Education in Nursing, 21*(5), 216–218.

National Association of School Psychologists. (1992a). *Continuing professional development program.* Silver Spring, MD: Author.

National Association of School Psychologists. (1992b). *Professional conduct manual.* Silver Spring, MD: Author.

National League for Nursing. (1974). *Outdate update continuing education: Who, what, where, when, how?* (Pub. No. 52–1579). New York: Author.

Reschly, D. J., & Grimes, J. P. (1991). State department and university cooperation: Evaluation of continuing education in consultation and curriculum-based assessment. *School Psychology Review, 20*(4), 522–529.

Rosenfield, S. (1985). Professional development management. In C. A. Maher (Ed.), *Professional self-management* (pp. 85–104). Baltimore: Paul H. Brookes.

Scanlan, C. S., & Darkenwald, G. G. (1984). Identifying deterrents to participation in continuing education. *Adult Education Quarterly, 34*(3), 155–166.

Spitzer, D. R. (1979, November). Continuing professional education: A critique of a new challenge for the educational technologist. *Educational Technology,* pp. 26–28.

Truesdell, L. A. (1985). Assessing the quality of inservice training for special education. *Teacher Education and Special Education, 8*(1), 25–32.

Tucker, B. A., & Huerta, C. G. (1984). *Continuing professional education* (Report No. CE 040 445). Washington, DC: National Institute of Education. (ERIC Document Reproduction Service No. ED 252 674)

Wilcoxon, S. A., & Hawk, R. (1990). Continuing education services: A survey of state associations of AACD. *Journal of Counseling and Development, 69*, 93.

Zins, J. E., Maher, C. A., Murphy, J. J., & Wess, B. P. (1988). The peer support group: A means to facilitate professional development. *School Psychology Review, 17*(1), 138–146.

ANNOTATED BIBLIOGRAPHY

Houle, C. O. (1980). *Continuing learning in the professions.* San Francisco: Jossey-Bass.
This text presents a historical overview of continuing professional development, discusses its goals, and outlines specific strategies that are useful for designing, implementing, and evaluating continuing professional development programs.[TO]

Rosenfield, S. (1985). Professional development management. In C. A. Maher (Ed.), *Professional self-management* (pp. 85–104). Baltimore: Paul H. Brookes.
This chapter presents a rationale for and outline of a four-stage model for continuing professional development. A variety of engaging options are presented for each stage. It is a detailed guide to self-managed continuing education for school psychologists.

8

Best Practices in Government Relations

Kevin P. Dwyer
National Association of School Psychologists

The first step in bringing about change is caring. But caring is not enough . . . One must proceed step by systematic step to mold and assemble the pieces until the whole is positively affected.

Marian Wright Edelman (1987), p. 103

OVERVIEW

• School psychologists are the best trained mental health professionals in the schools

• Children need our services.

• School restructuring and reform will be lost without our involvement.

Most policy makers and stakeholders in educational reform are either unaware of these beliefs or do not understand the role of school psychology in reaching national education objectives. They have not seen the effective and wide range of services that school psychologists can provide to help children reach world-class standards. How can we rectify this gap in knowledge and influence? How can we become more involved in restructuring and reform to make sure that children's social, emotional, and learning needs are met? And how can we make sure that the policy makers understand the value of integrating our services into the restructured school?

School psychologists have the knowledge and skills to effectively advocate for children and for the profession. This chapter will provide basic information on ways in which each and every school psychologist can help shape public policy through involvement in government relations activities at the local, state, or national level.

BASIC CONSIDERATIONS

Within a decade of passage of the landmark Education for All Handicapped Children Act (P.L. 94-142) in 1975, the number of school psychologists more than doubled. Now, another decade later, about 20,000 school psychologists serve 45 million public school children in about 16,000 school systems, at an estimated cost of more than $9 billion a year (Fagan, 1994). Although growth in the profession has been dramatic, our professional standards document the need for another 25,000 school psychologists just to provide minimal educational and mental health services for our nation's children. The cost of the increase nationally is estimated to be about $11.5 billion. How do we persuade the community and taxpayers to pay the additional $11.5 billion for needed school psychological services?

The National Mental Health Association (Koyanagi & Gaines, 1993) reported that only one state in the nation (Connecticut) had the adequate ratio of school psychologists to students, with an adequate ratio being defined as 1 school psychologist to 1,000 students, or 1 to 100 for students identified as disabled and needing special education. The national average of 1:2221 explains why some school systems were given a "D" grade on the national report card of children's mental health services and two states — with ratios of 1:25,000 — received an "F–."

The U.S. Congress Office of Technology Assessment (1986) estimated that almost eight million children have significant emotional or behavioral problems blocking educational success and warranting mental health services within the schools. This means that for every school psychologist employed in the United States there are about 450 students with serious emotional and behavioral problems. This does not include the psychological needs of all other disability groups or children at risk for social, emotional, or learning problems or victims of abuse or crises. The report also stated that almost none of the students with serious emotional problems are receiving needed psychological services. A recent report (McInerney, Kane, & Pelavin, 1992) indicated that only 16% of children with serious emotional disturbance receive psychological services through the Individuals with Disabilities Education Act (IDEA) and only 42% of local public school districts provide any psychological services beyond assessment.

Although these survey and research data are not new to most school psychologists and have peppered the nation's legislative bodies, their impact has been minimal in stimulating a national policy for this critical service shortfall in school-based services. Therefore, research alone will not work. It must be combined with political power (of school psychologists) to influence public policy for the benefit of children, families, and schools.

Poor administrative policies and priorities have made the situation even worse for school psychological services. Existing services are prioritized to serve special education regulations rather than children. School psychologists spend less than one-third of their time providing direct service or consultation services to children's teachers and parents. Most of their time is dedicated to mandated special education eligibility evaluations and procedural meetings, resulting in a lack of service to many needy students. Students placed in special education and those at risk account for a high percentage of school dropouts and adult unemployment. An extensive five-year study of outcomes of special education programs (Wagner & Shaver, 1989) noted that only 36% of students identified as "seriously emotionally disturbed" graduated from high school. After high school age, those emotionally disturbed youth who drop out are much more likely to be unemployed and, according to the study, an astounding 75% are arrested within five years of leaving school.

No one in the community wants these problems to remain unsolved, yet few are willing to support increased taxes to pay for unproven school psychological services programs. Whether it be the local school site-based decision-making committee or the U.S. Congress, service implementation requires proof of improved outcomes. The community will support services that result in increased graduation rates, employment, and independence and reduced violence and drug abuse. Accountability must be improved and information must be conveyed to the right stakeholders, parent advocates, and policy makers.

BEST PRACTICES

Whatever the effort, be it local, state, or national, it is important to evaluate existing and needed resources as they relate to any government relations mission. Several critical factors in this analysis are parallel to the information gathering and analysis that school psychologists use within their professional lives. They include problem identification, goal setting, and analysis of strengths and weaknesses as they relate to a stated mission. School psychologists are experts in team work, measurement, research, and communication. These skills should be utilized in all government relations activities.

Forming a Government Relations Committee

A successful government relations effort requires the time and effort of several people and the commitment of some financial resources. Members of a Government Relations Committee (GRC) must be knowledgeable, dedicated school psychologists who can "think on their feet" and who have the time to share the burden of the numerous tasks required to make the committee work. Because continuity is critical, they must have the ability to sustain the effort over several years.

The tasks of the GRC include:

- Choosing a chairperson.

- Choosing committee members.

- Establishing a vision or mission statement.

- Establishing a network that enhances rapid responses to GRC issues.

- Establishing an information system that increases the association leadership's awareness of the GRC mission and the current critical issues.

- Building relationships with advocates and related professionals.

- Organizing coalitions of education, pupil services, mental health professionals, and other organizations supporting education and children's issues.

- Establishing an information-dissemination system to inform policy makers about the work of school psychologists in the community or state, including highlighting effective programs.

Once you have accomplished the groundwork it is easier to get to the GRC tasks of monitoring local, state, and/or national legislative and agency activities.

Choosing a committee chairperson. The GRC chairperson must be an excellent communicator and facilitator with a strong commitment to the profession and children. The chair guides the committee and the association leaders in communicating with the legislature and agencies. The chair must always follow the guidelines of the approved mission statement and legislative agenda. It is the chair's responsibility to provide feedback to the association's leadership and to the members. Strong public relations, human relations, and cooperative, team-building skills are critical. The chair must be familiar with laws and agency policies that affect the practice of school psychology, education, mental health, and human services. The chair must be an able leader who can delegate, appropriately use committee members' skills, and ensure that committee members receive the information they need to carry out their responsibilities. The committee chair must also use good reinforcement procedures.

When there is a professional staff available, it is imperative that the chair be able to work cooperatively with the association's government relations staff. It is helpful for the association's leadership to establish descriptors for the responsibilities of both volunteers and staff.

Characteristics of committee members.

- Personal Characteristics
  - Action-oriented, assertive personality.
  - Good oral and written communication skills.
  - Strong human relations skills.
  - Interest in or desire to learn the political process.
  - Experience (work or volunteer) in legislative/political process.
  - Personal ties to legislative/political/governmental circles.
  - Willingness to "carry the water."
  - Patience.
  - Knowledge of the legislative process.
  - Enthusiasm and sense of humor.
  - Pride in work and professional role.
  - Involvement supported by spouse and family.
  - Access or geographic proximity to government activity.
- Professional Characteristics
  - Comprehensive knowledge of the practice of school psychology.
  - Representative of professional interests in the organization.
  - Representative of the various geographical and community interests.
  - A client advocate.
  - An advocate of professionalism and program development.
- Work-Related Characteristics
  - Freedom to leave work setting for governmental relations activities.
  - Access to a computer and/or secretarial support.
  - Access to telephone and fax machine.
  - Access to photocopying equipment and materials.
  - Involvement supported by colleagues, supervisors, and administration.

Generating Solutions: Building Coalitions

How can school psychologists prove the merits of their services and gain the support of community leaders to increase these services? The answer requires long-term strategic plans, significant time, dedicated professionals, and financial resources.

A coalition is a union of organizations seeking similar ends. A strong source of information and power, a coalition unifies groups and prevents the fragmentation of forces that share common goals. Building coalitions with groups supportive of school psychological services is critical in getting the message across. The consumers of our services, particularly parents, can become our strongest allies. Other allies with whom to form coalitions include pupil service personnel such as counselors, social workers, nurses, and others who provide services similar or complimentary to those of school psychologists.

Purpose of a public policy coalition.

- Act as an ombudsman.
- Serve as an information source on legislative issues.
- Critique federal, state, and local policy and legislative proposals.
- Propose actions to achieve the desired political action at the federal and state levels.
- Coordinate consensus and unified action among the organizations.

Example of coalition building: School-linked health services. Many communities are forming coalitions among parents, health and education agencies to meet the mental health and other health needs of children. It is valuable to join or interact with existing coalitions which may have a role to play in the community-wide delivery of psychological services to children and their families. Education leadership sees mental health as a "health agency" issue and is frequently relieved to have that agency take the lead in generating solutions.

"Communities Can," a Georgetown University Child Development Center project, sponsored by the Maternal and Child Health Bureau of Health and Human Services and the American Academy of Pediatrics, is a community-based, coalition-building plan being developed in almost every community. It may become a mechanism for change in the delivery of services, including mental health services to children and their families. Being a catalyst for or, becoming part of, a "Communities Can" coalition can ensure that school psychology will remain a viable service among services.

Example of coalition building: Gray Panthers. It is important to broaden the scope of allies and include other groups interested in children.

Sometimes coalitions do make for "strange bedfellows," but it is helpful to have the support of disparate groups to show that your issue has broad-based consensus. In one recent budget-cutting Board of Education meeting, the local senior citizens' chapter of the Gray Panthers came out in support of school psychologists because they believed that violence against the elderly could be reduced by better school-based preventive mental health services. Most community organizations are interested in reducing violence, drug abuse, and vandalism and increasing the employability and social responsibility of youth. These groups may recognize the hidden costs of youth violence and related problems. The National Commission on Children provides excellent data on the long-range costs of neglecting these needs. Community organizations and leaders want to hear about solutions and are consistently supportive of cost-effective intervention plans and services. It is imperative to document solutions and share these with community leaders who have the clout that school psychologists may not have. Building coalitions and allies for school psychological services is as important as establishing a legislative mission.

Monitoring the Legislature and Agencies

Too frequently school psychologists wait to communicate with the legislature and agencies only to respond to a professional crisis or to get a "guild issue" bill sponsored or passed. Although these are necessary activities of a GRC, the outcomes in these and other circumstances will be much more successful when the groundwork has been laid and relationships established between the association, legislators, and legislative staff. Over time these relationships will result in invitations to give input on developing legislation and regulations rather than "putting out fires" after the legislation is drafted.

It would be ideal for the GRC to monitor members from every legislative district, but when funds and dedicated members are limited, the GRC should focus upon specific legislative committees that deal with education, mental health, related social and health services, and — do not forget — the appropriations committee(s)! Legislation without funding is useless. Appropriations committees are usually less sympathetic to increasing services to solve human problems and are generally more responsive to proven money-saving programs and to coalitions that speak with political clout.

To maintain these relationships, your association needs an accurate roster of all legislative and agency officials, including those key staff persons who are the legislator's right hand. Quite frequently the most important persons in the office are the long-term secretaries who screen most incoming communication and who often know the schedule better than any other person in the office.

Agency Contacts

It is advisable to establish permanent professional links with state agencies that have direct and indirect control over school psychological services and the health, education, and social services needed for children and families. Getting on state and local committees that provide advisory support, evaluate programs, and have decision-making power can be invaluable. These committees frequently provide the guidelines for future legislation and the setting of agency policies, rules, and priorities. Being involved in local and state agencies and executive functions can result in having school psychologists appointed to state boards that control education or certification and licensure.

Forms of Communication

Information is a two-way system: Providing information to others is as important as receiving it. Local and state (elected and appointed) leaders should be kept informed about your activities. One way is to include them on your state newsletter mailing list. Other publications and information about effective best practices should be passed on to legislative and agency staff members. And do not forget the governor!

Remember to send any news releases about school psychology to local board of education members and local representatives of your state legislature. Your congressional representatives should also be informed of effective services. Build a file on the legislators' offices to be reviewed when your association seeks those legislators' support. Relationships and follow-up communications are best formed when legislative or agency deadlines are not pressing and staff have time to listen to the valuable information that your association and coalitions can provide.

Legislators also appreciate it when their names and recognition of their accomplishments supporting professional practice and children's issues appear in your publications.

Telephoning. If immediate action on specific legislation is necessary, telephoning can be very effective. You probably will not be put through directly to your legislator, but instead your call may be routed to the Legislative or Administrative Assistant who specializes in education or human service issues. This aide will pass your message on to the legislator for consideration. Call the Capitol Operator at (202) 224-3121 to be connected to a particular office.

Be prepared for the call: Write down important points beforehand and the specific steps you want the legislator to take. Be certain to identify yourself and your location (where you live or are calling from), your professional position (including the names of the schools you serve in the legislator's district), and your purpose for calling. Be prepared to bring the staff person up to date because staff sometimes know little abut the specifics unless their member is on a committee dealing directly with that issue. To help the staff person focus upon your concern, have the bill name and number available. Make sure that the person with whom are are talking can repeat your concern. Use your communication skills, keeping in mind that you are probably speaking to a busy, sometimes underpaid lawyer or professional postgraduate who has several deadlines and many, many important issues on which to focus. Yet, this staff person is usually very interested in your concerns as a constituent. Also, have appropriate questions prepared. Following your conversation, write a "thank you" to the legislator. Mention the staff person's name and any positive comments you can make about the exchange. Appreciation will be remembered.

Telegrams and E-mail. The telegram or mailgram is another quick way to communicate with legislators. It is relatively inexpensive and will usually be sent to the legislator's office within two hours. Although it is quick, it is not as effective as a phone call. Generally, telegrams and mailgrams are best used when you can generate several hundred within a short period of time to show broad support for an issue.

Modern technology provides us with many new methods of communication including the fax machine, voice mail, and electronic mail. Like telegrams, the faxed message may not be as effective as a telephone call, but is useful when a quick response is necessary. The fax is also valuable when it is a specific follow-up to a phone call. Send the fax to the attention of a specific person and remind that person of the previous contact, your detailed identification, the reason for the fax, and the specific action requested. Remember, the name and number of the bill are important ways to jog the memory of the staff person.

Electronic mail (E-mail) is becoming a widely used quick-response method for reaching members of Congress. E-mail addresses for U.S. Senators or Representatives can be obtained by calling their office directly or through the Capitol Operator at (202) 224-3121.

Writing letters. Most legislators' offices use mail as the largest single gauge of public and voter sentiment. Some insiders have noted that many letters to Congress are primarily read for the identifying data and the "side" of the issue the writer is taking on a bill. At the state level, mail is likely to be read with more scrutiny. Personal face-to-face contacts are almost always more effective at the national as well as at the local level. However, a carefully thought out one-page letter which represents an individual's point of view is an effective method of communication. The letter should be clear and simple and express exactly how the measure being proposed will affect the member's constituents. As with the phone call, a letter should refer to a policy or bill specifically by its title and number. Almost all government officials answer their mail.

Timing is important. One can exert greater influence by writing as early as possible before a bill or policy will be voted on and by continuing to correspond with legislators as the bill progresses. If it is possible to identify with a group or cause, do so. Also try to state and document reasons for the position you have taken. A letter simply thanking a member for his or her support is greatly appreciated. Members of Congress who take on difficult issues or who seek additional funds for needed services receive lots of negative mail and your "thank you" can be a significant counterblance.

Send "blind" copies (no cc:) of all correspondence to the national headquarters GPR staff and your state legislative committee chair or state staff. This helps them monitor the level of grassroots activity and to obtain a measure of interest in a particular issue. A sample letter and some pointers are included in this chapter to assist you in corresponding with your state legislator or member of Congress (see Figures 1 and 2).

Visiting. A very effective method of communication is meeting with your legislator either individually or as part of a group. Your objectives are to convey a particular message and also to establish a dialogue. Over subsequent visits, a relationship will develop that can be nurtured through further correspondence and discussions. The member will have a personal awareness of you and your child-centered concernns after such a meeting.

For the visit, know your issues and be prepared with concise "talking points." Be prompt and ready to cover your points in 15 minutes. If possible, learn the legislator's views beforehand. Highlight the legislative issues that concern you and relate their impact on the children you serve. Personalize the issue. Ask for the legislator's feedback — does he/she share your concerns? Try to gain a commitment — what is he/she willing to do? Do not ever threaten or cajole if the legislator does not agree with you. Establishing a good working relationship is important to future contacts. Leave brief written materials as supplemental information and offer to provide further data, if necessary. As soon as possible, send a thank-you letter summarizing your concerns and reminding the official of any actions that he or she agreed to take. Pass along any information you agreed to provide. Finally, offer to arrange for the legislator and his or her staff to visit your work place. This is an excellent way to familiarize them with a "real world" view of the issues faced by school psychologists each day.

Some strategies for successful individual and group visits with government officials are to:

• Make your appointment in advance.

FIGURE 1. Sample letter.

January 1, 1995
8524 Carlynn Drive
Bethesda, MD 20817-4308

The Honorable Connie Morella
U.S. House of Representatives
Washington, DC 20515

Dear Congresswoman Morella:

I am a school psychologist in Montgomery County, Maryland. I serve about 200 students with complex disabilities at Walter Johnson High School in Bethesda. I urge you to support the bipartisan effort to increase mental health services within the schools by co-sponsoring the *Pupil Services Demonstration Act* (H.R. 1234).

A critical component in the total array of services for mental health, wellness, and prevention is school psychological services. School psychologists assist teachers and parents in helping children who are frustrated or angry learn alternatives to violence. At Walter Johnson High, I have worked with counselors and the school nurse to involve staff in supporting peer conflict resolution, social skills training, and anger control. Prevention is a cost-effective service model and the schools are the best place to teach social and behavioral skills. I have enclosed information on a program called "Project Achieve" that demonstrates the cost-effectiveness of the pupil services model. H.R. 1234 will provide the funding to replicate such programs and help meet the unique needs of each community. Please let me know your position on this legislation. I am available at (301) 229-8251 if you wish more detailed examples of successful school psychology programs. Your commitment to the welfare of children is recognized and appreciated.

Sincerely,

Kevin P. Dwyer, MA, NCSP

° Be on time.

° Be flexible. If the legislator must cancel, be willing to reschedule.

° Cancel your appointment only when you have a very good reason and inform the office as early as possible.

• Dress in a businesslike fashion.

• Approach the actual face-to-face meeting in the following manner:

° Be friendly, polite, and businesslike.

° Provide those visited with a brief background sketch of your organization and the persons who are present.

° State the purpose(s) of your visit.

° Present rationale and opinions for your positions. Be prepared to present clear, relevant facts and statistics.

° Distribute position papers, resolutions, and other relevant documents.

° Stress the impact of legislation, regulations, and other governmental/legislative actions on local schools and mental health and human service agencies. Emphasize the impact on children, adolescents, parents, teachers, and the community.

° Listen to opinions and concerns presented by those visited, giving the legislator a chance to ask questions.

° Stay on the subject. Be specific about what you want such as seeking support, assistance, sponsorship of legislation, and/or other actions.

° Speak factually. Answer questions to the best of your ability. If you do not know the answer, say so and promise to obtain any information or data that you do not have readily available. Never promise what you cannot deliver, and be certain to follow up on any promises made during your visit. If you find that you cannot provide the information, make sure you say so.

° If asked, be ready to talk about the opposition to your position. This can help the official become aware of the political factors in supporting your position and can ready that person for answers to the opposition.

FIGURE 2. Writing elected officials: Basic rules.

- Prepare handwritten letters for all personal communication. Letters from associations and institutions should be typed on official stationery and signed by the appropriate officer, chairperson, or the like.

- Personalize the letter as much as possible. Tell the addressee what position you have and where you live and work. This is especially important if you are a constituent of the person whom you are contacting.

- Begin your letter with the proper salutations, including title, name, and address. The clerk of the state legislature can provide a current list of members and the governor's office can provide a listing of key people in the executive branch. For a list of federal legislators and government officials, consult the various references contained in your local library. Some states have computer software or electronic bulletin boards which contain this information.

- Construct a letter that is clear in purpose and offers concise arguments for your personal position. Attempt to keep your letter to a single page.

- Identify any legislation, law, or regulation by name and number. This will allow staff aides to link your letter to specific issues and record your concerns accordingly. Legislators often refer to such records of public concerns prior to voting on a piece of legislation.

- Provide constructive criticism. Cite the strong points in a bill, law, or set of regulations. Address weak points and areas of omission.

- Offer your personal assistance and that of your association to gather additional information or prepare formal testimony. Such gestures of volunteer assistance can have immediate and long-range impact as legislators and government officials solicit expert opinion on pending legislation and government regulations.

- Make certain that your letter reaches the right person(s) in timely fashion. Do not procrastinate. Your letter is like a vote, and you cannot vote after the polls close.

- Ask the addressee for a response. Most legislators and government officials will acknowledge personal letters. A simple question, inserted in the text of your letter, can ensure this response is more than a routine acknowledgment.

- Approach the addressee in a positive nonthreatening manner. Negative, threat-ridden letters have little impact in the legislative world.

- Identify your organization and the size and nature of its membership. If you are writing on behalf of a branch, state division, or local chapter, be certain that the addressee is aware of the organization, its composition, and the number of persons that it represents.

- Address "blind" copies (no cc:) of your correspondence to key people in the GRC and leadership of your association. This will allow the Government Relations Committee to monitor the breadth and quantity of communication on an issue. Keep a copy of your letters for a personal file. You may wish to refer to a particular letter at some future point or in follow-up correspondence.

- Write a "thank you" letter to those legislators and government officials who act on your behalf. Too many officials only hear from the public and from professional groups when there is a problem or need. They like to hear from you when they have appropriately presented your personal and professional interests.

- Read the nonverbal signals and do not make the meeting too long. Summarize your concerns and arguments, and offer your personal assistance and that of your organization to aid the official in obtaining a better understanding of your professional concerns.

- Thank host/hostesses and close visit. Remember the staff and secretary in the office. They can be key to future contacts.

- Write a thank-you letter to the person(s) with whom you visited, reminding them of your position and enlisting their support.

Testifying. Committee hearings provide an excellent opportunity to present a case for the mental health and educational needs of children and to attract legislative, media, and public support. Spoken testimony by someone knowledgeable in the field of school psychology can be very effective and influential. Most legislators do not have the time to learn about many issues in depth and therefore rely on others to provide the information on which they will make decisions. School psychologists have a perfect opportunity to use their expertise in helping to educate and guide policy makers. In addition, practitioners (by virtue of their experience) are often able to "breathe life" into messages about how policies actually affect children, conveying a greater sense of urgency than these messages might otherwise possess.

Testimony may be presented orally or in writing. Written testimony may be submitted to support an individual's oral testimony or may be proffered on its own to become part of the documentation compiled for a legislative hearing.

Witnesses should know specifically what the committee is considering and what the opposing viewpoint consists of. The witness should be prepared to answer questions from those opposed to the school psychologist's point of view. The witness's statements should be backed up with coalition support, research, and statistics. If your organization is testifying on behalf of several groups, that should be acknowledged. Because politicians think in terms of votes, generally the more numbers you represent the stronger your position will be considered. If others are testifying in support of your position, try to coordinate the testimony prior to the hearing to avoid contradictions, data discrepancies, and redundancies.

The title page of written testimony should be on association stationery and include the name and number of the bill, the name and title of the witness, the name of the legislative body or committee, and the date. The testimony should begin with the name and credentials of the witness as well as his or her organizational affiliation or the group on whose behalf he or she is presenting the testimony. The witness should then:

- Mention the bill number, title, and subject of the hearing.
- Introduce any persons who have accompanied the witness.
- State his or her reasons for supporting or opposing the proposed measure.
- If in opposition, suggest positive alternatives to the legislation in question.
- Provide specific and graphic examples that support his or her position. Personal and professional experience supported by factual data presents a strong case.
- End by summarizing his or her position.
- Make additional information available if so requested.

Developing Your Own Government Relations Program

Activities of a Government Relations Committee. As noted previously, the activities of a successful Government Relations Committee are numerous and require dedicated members willing to work hard for their profession. Both proactive and reactive actions are required; working with a legislator to get new legislation introduced is no less important than working to change legislation already in existence.

There are several "musts" when working as an effective Government Relations Committee. The following can be used as a checklist to ensure that nothing of importance is being overlooked:

- Monitor legislative and governmental activity.
- Establish a working relationship in the name of the profession with legislators and their staff personnel. Present psychology and pupil service viewpoints by engaging in direct lobbying and personal communication, including
  - ○ Telephone calls and electronic mail.
  - ○ Letters.
  - ○ Visits.
  - ○ Information dissemination (i.e., honorary subscriptions to state and national school psychology publications, reports, news releases and articles, and research data).
- Organize and conduct communication campaigns, including
  - ○ Letter-writing campaigns.
  - ○ Telephone contacts.
- Organize and conduct group visits (i.e., "Day at the Capitol") with legislative and government officials.
- Prepare legislation. Work for its introduction and passage.
- Prepare and offer written and/or oral testimony to those charged with preparing relevant legislation.
- Develop and maintain accurate rosters of legislative and governmental officials.
- Conduct government relations training workshops for members.

On the state level, it is advisable to be involved in the administrative process as much as possible. Work to install a member of the profession on official state boards, committees, and task forces concerned with school psychology and the pupil service professions.

1. Involvement with Other Professional and Public/Consumer Organizations.
   - Organize and participate in coalitions of educational, mental health, and related human service organizations.
   - Organize and participate in coalitions of public and consumer organizations.
   - Assist groups in legislative concerns of mutual interest.
   - Enlist support of groups for legislative concerns of mutual interest.

- Prepare and disseminate information, including
  - ° General public relations pieces.
  - ° Issue and position papers.
  - ° Summaries of model programs.
  - ° General legislative platform.
  - ° Research documents.

2. Working within the Government Relations Program of the National Association of School Psychologists (NASP).

- Establish and maintain linkages with your state government relations representatives. Maintain a system of two-way communication.
- Establish and maintain linkages with the NASP government relations staff. Make sure that you are a member of the School Psychologists Action Network (SPAN).
- Respond to *all* calls for support and information (i.e., written and/or personal contact with legislators).
- Participate in NASP Government Relations training programs whenever possible. Keep yourself educated and informed about the legislative process.

Government Relations Committee budget concerns. Because the amount of money available for government relations activities will vary markedly from state to state, it is difficult to produce a sample budget for Government Relations Committee work. However, in developing a budget, each committee should allow for the following expenditures:

- Communications: newsletters, telephone calls, postage, telegrams, and subscriptions.
- Travel: committee meetings, testimony presentation, governmental/legislative visits, NASP training and related activities.
- Supplies and materials.
- Printing and reproduction: brochures, reports, testimony, training materials, and legislative updates.
- Special activities: "Day at the Capitol," training programs, convention activities, and audio/visual materials.

Job description of the governmental relations chairperson. The following should be among the responsibilities of the government relations chairperson:

- Government Data: The chair seeks to become thoroughly familiar with individuals, agencies, and programs operating within the state which can affect local and/or national school psychology and pupil service activities.
- Communications: The chair serves as a link between (a) the agencies of government that shape policies and direct funds within the state and (b) members of the school psychology and pupil service professions. The chair is also responsible for maintaining or appointing a committee member to maintain an effective communications network.
- Public Relations: The chair seeks to establish, sustain, and maximize a continuing dialogue between government contacts and the membership.
- Information Dissemination: The chair ensures that high quality information representing the best interests of the school psychology and pupil service professions is offered to appropriate government sources.
- Decision Making: The chair serves as the expert in his or her state concerning which agency or individuals receive information and the form in which it is best submitted.
- Follow-through: The chair monitors the use of information given to governmental sources and offers suggestions to these sources for possible usage.
- Feedback: The chair strives to ensure that any information generated by governmental contacts is properly received, acknowledged, and directed to NASP government relations staff and interested state and regional representatives.

SUMMARY

All school psychologists can be effective advocates for children and the profession. Successful government relations efforts require the proactive and reactive actions of dedicated members willing to expend the time and effort necessary in bringing about positive change.

School psychologists can influence public policy by monitoring legislative and government activity; communicating with elected officials through phone calls, letters, and visits; preparing and presenting testimony; working in coalition with groups having mutual interests; and preparing and disseminating information on relevant legislation.

REFERENCES

American Association for Counseling and Development. (1987). *Government relations training manual.* Alexandria, VA: Author.

Edelman, M. W. (1987). *Families in peril: An agenda for social change.* Cambridge, MA: Harvard University Press.

Fagan, T. (1994). *School psychology: Past, present, and future.* New York: Longman.

Koyanagi, C., & Gaines, S. (1993). *All systems failure.* Alexandria, VA: National Mental Health Association.

McInerney, M., Kane, M., & Pelavin, S. (1992). *Services to children with serious emotional disturbance.* Washington, DC: Pelavin Associates.

National Association of School Psychologists. (1991). *Government relations handbook.* Silver Spring, MD: Author.

National Commission on Children. (1992). *Beyond rhetoric: A new American agenda for children and families.* Washington, DC: U.S. Government Printing Office.

U.S. Congress, Office of Technology Assessment. (1986). *Children's mental health: Problems and services — Background paper* (OTA-BP-H-33). Washington, DC: U.S. Government Printing Office.

Wagner, H. M., & Shaver, D. (1989). *Educational programs and achievements of secondary special education students: Findings from the National Longitudinal Transition Study.* Menlo Park, CA: SRI International.

ANNOTATED BIBLIOGRAPHY

SPAN Update is a quarterly newsletter produced by NASP staff and sent to all School Psychologists Action Network (SPAN) members. *SPAN Update* provides current information on legislative issues of concern to school psychologists. Available to all NASP members free of charge by calling (301) 608-0500. *Legislative Alerts* will be sent as needed to NASP members when an issue arises that demands immediate attention or action.

Congressional Newsletters and Press Releases are issued regularly by most U.S. Representatives and Senators; constituents can receive them upon request.

Copies of Congressional Legislation can be requested from the document rooms of both houses by subject and bill number. For House bills, send a stamped, self-addressed envelope to:

House Document Room
Room B-18
House Annex #2
3rd and D Streets, SW
Washington, DC 20515
(202) 225-3546

For Senate bills, send the same to:

Senate Document Room
SH-BO4
Washington, DC 20510
(202) 224-7860

The U.S. Congress Handbook contains biographical and statistical information on all members of the U.S. Congress, all committees and subcommittees, the executive and judicial branches, tips on communicating with legislators, and explanations of how Congress is organized and operates. This book may be purchased from Capitol Advantage, P.O. Box 1223, McLean, VA 22101. (703) 734-3266.

The Congressional Record is published daily when Congress is in session and contains the record of floor proceedings plus any additional information inserted by members of Congress on particular issues. The *Record* may be obtained from the Superintendent of Documents, U.S. Government Printing Office, Washington, DC 20402.

The Federal Register is published daily and contains regulations and legal notices issued by federal agencies. These include Presidential proclamations, executive orders, and federal agency documents required to be published by Acts of Congress. The *Register* may be obtained from the Superintendent of Documents, U.S. Government Printing Office, Washington, DC 20402.

Education Daily focuses on national, state, and local events pertinent to primary and secondary education. Includes pending court decisions, legislative updates, federal budget charts, and other resources. Published by the Educational News Services Division of Capitol Publications, Inc., 1101 King Street, Alexandria, VA 22314.

Special Education Report covers new laws, regulations, court cases, and funding issues related to educating children with disabilities. Published by the Education News Services Division of Capital Publications, Inc., 1101 King Street, Alexandria, VA 22314.

The Special Educator offers news and analysis of federal laws, rules, and programs concerning the education of disabled individuals. Published by the LRP Publications, P.O. Box 980, Horsham, PA 19044-0980.

9

Best Practices in Facilitating Professional Effectiveness and Avoiding Professional Burnout

Alex Thomas
Miami University

OVERVIEW

There are an estimated 22,000 to 25,000 school psychologists in the United States (Fagan & Wise, 1994). At a minimum, with each school psychologist having contact with at least 125 students through consultation, assessment, or other direct or indirect service activities, a conservative estimate of 2.5 million students receive some type of professional activity from school psychologists every year. Professional activity is also likely to encompass involvement with these students' families (parents, guardians, siblings, grandparents). Additionally, with increasing emphasis on the delivery of indirect services through consultation, collaboration with ancillary agencies, and greater community involvement regarding social and demographic issues, there is an ever increasing number of people affected by school psychologists' services. There is an individual and collective "spread of effect" which is remarkable and frequently undetected by outcome measures. School psychology represents the most widespread, multifaceted, and available mental health service delivery system for this nation's youth.

The feeling of individual impact of efficacy, however, can often be blunted by the enormity of the problems faced. There may also be frustration with systemic characteristics perceived to provide barriers to more effective services. Additionally, there may be idiosyncratic perceptions of being confined to a rather narrow channel of professional activity despite training and personal choice leading to hoped for expansiveness of service provision.

Most school psychologists enter the profession with high optimism, a hearty work ethic, and genuine enthusiasm for applying psychological knowledge and principles to aid children and their families within the educational enterprise. Some school psychologists maintain that same attitudinal fervor throughout their careers. Some do not. Most, in the course of a career, experience ups and down relative to professional enthusiasm, involvement, and effectiveness.

That school psychologists have an effect on children, families, and systems is not startling news. What is startling, however, is the extent to which professionals in the mental health field, such as school psychology, frequently lose sight of the impact they can have in their respective endeavors. It is often difficult to maintain a positive focus to deliver optimum professional service when there may be personal problems interfering with job functioning, economic and political pressures within the school system, a feeling of futility or uselessness with one's work, or a perception that the organization does not value or use the skills that one has. The frequency, duration, and intensity of such feelings over a long period of time can negatively affect professional growth and effectiveness.

Though there has been no established research linking higher levels of job satisfaction with greater professional effectiveness (presumably, one can be effective and still be dissatisfied with what one does), it is likely that most people would prefer to be rich than poor, healthy than unhealthy, contented rather than discontented, and effective rather than ineffective. As the aphorism states, "Optimists and pessimists are right an equal amount of time but optimists are more enjoyable to be around."

The purpose of this chapter is to review strategies school psychologists can use to maintain or improve an upward trajectory encouraging professional growth and effectiveness.

BASIC CONSIDERATIONS

Job Satisfaction and Professional Stresses

The concept of professional burnout is not necessarily synonymous with low job satisfaction but it is related. Burnout can be defined as feeling emotionally exhausted, feeling a sense of depersonalization or lack of meaningful connection, and having a low sense of personal accomplishment (Maslach & Jackson, 1981). The construct of burnout has existed for some time and comes in and out of fashion as a term related to low job satisfaction, which may also be coupled with an accompanying attitude that may negatively affect a person's nonprofessional life. Huebner (1992) and others (Huberty & Huebner, 1988; Levinson, Fetchkan, & Hohenshil, 1988; Pierson-Hubeny & Archambault, 1987; Solly & Hohenshil, 1986; Wise, 1985) have explored issues of burnout and job satisfaction specifically related to school psychologists.

Huebner (1992) found a strong relationship between burnout and job related stresses such as incompetent or inflexible supervisors, unavailability of resource or testing materials, inadequate secretarial help, lack of contact with colleagues, and feeling caught between children's needs and administrative constraints. Other stresses were noted to be issues related to time management (backlog of referrals, report writing), high risk to self and others (dealing with potential suicide cases, child abuse cases, threats of a due process hearing), and interpersonal conflict (working with uncooperative administrators, conferences with resistant teachers or parents). Among a sample of school psychologists, Huebner (1992) found that one-third met the Maslach and Jackson (1981) criterion for emotional exhaustion, one-quarter met the criterion for reduced sense of personal accomplishment, and almost 10% met the criterion for high sense of depersonalization.

Wise (1985) rank ordered the job stresses identified by survey responding school psychologists (see Table 1). The 35 stress areas were subject to factor analysis and nine clusters were identified. They were, in order of importance:

- Interpersonal conflict (conferences or staffings with resistant teachers, working with uncooperative administrators).

- High risk to self and others (crises situations, due process hearings, child abuse cases, teacher's strike).

- Obstacles to efficient job performance (inflexible supervisors, inadequate secretarial help, feeling caught between child's needs and administrative constraints).

- Public speaking (in-service workshops, parent groups, public speaking engagements).

- Time management (not enough time, backlog of reports or referrals).

- Keeping the district legal (due process, compliance issues).

- Hassles (carrying materials between schools in inclement weather, driving).

- Professional enrichment (inability to keep up with literature in the field).

- Insufficient recognition of work.

Each school psychologist can provide a personal configuration of perceived stressors or barriers to maximum effectiveness based on his or her own circumstance. A conscious acknowledgement of these personal stresses and specific barriers to optimum professional functioning is a first step in developing a plan to minimize them at best, or at worst, place these realities in perspective.

Taking a Personal and Organizational Inventory

Lack of professional morale or feelings of low effectiveness are due to a combination of factors related to personal and organizational characteristics. Personal characteristics are those temperamental or enduring traits brought to all situations including family, vocational, and avocational. For example, are things viewed positively when unfortunate things happen? Put simply, is the glass of water seen as half full or half empty, is the weather described as partly cloudy or partly sunny? Adjectives like "moody," "cheerful," "energetic," "phlegmatic," "unhappy," "depressed," "positive," "excited," and so forth, may be consistently used to describe personalities independent of context. There are people who bring energy and verve to the most difficult circumstances and those who bring a sullen defeatist attitude to the most positive circumstances. It is important for an individual to know what his or her own tendencies are. There will probably always be people who say they are "burned out" and spend much time bemoaning circumstances conspiring against them. In some instances, however, colleagues would argue that being burned out is impossible for these people have never been on fire. Others can, with an advantageous situation, find reasons to complain and find fault ("Have a nice day!" "No thank you, I have other plans.") Yet some people are capable of making the best of any situation, however adverse it may be.

A large component of professional growth and effectiveness is the personal orientation that is brought to any endeavor. Each individual needs to understand his or her own nature and predisposition independent of organizational or environmental circumstances.

Organizational characteristics are those inherent within a school or district unit. Even the school psychologist of the century may not thrive in some organizational climates. A competent, well-trained school psychologist may, nevertheless, be poorly compensated, not released for professional development activities, forced to do routine assessments, and offered little administrative support within their district. In an adjoining district, a school psychologist of less distinction may be well compensated, allowed significant freedom for professional growth, and have the possibility to engage in a variety of role functions. Some of the factors influencing the specific organizational climate, which are independent of personal characteristics, would be size of the district, the type of supervision provided, the organization of special

TABLE 1
Ranks and Means of Stressful Events for School Psychologists

Stressful Event	Rank	Mean
Notification of unsatisfactory job performance	1	7.1
Not enough time to perform job adequately	2	6.6
Potential suicide cases	3	6.5
Working with uncooperative principals and other administrators	4	6.4
Feeling caught between child's needs and administrative constraints (i.e., trying to "fit" a child into an existing program)	5	6.3
Threat of a due process hearing	5	6.3
Lack of appropriate services for children	7	6.1
Child abuse cases	8	6.0
Incompetent or inflexible "superiors"	8	6.0
A backlog of more than 5 reports to be written	8	6.0
Working in physically dangerous situations (e.g., gang-rule high schools)	11	5.8
A backlog of more than 10 referrals	11	5.8
Pressure to complete a set number of cases (e.g., you must test at least 100 children a year)	13	5.7
Conferences or staffings with resistant teachers	14	5.6
Conferences or staffings with resistant parents	15	5.4
Teacher dissatisfaction with your recommendations	16	5.2
Report writing	17	5.1
Conducting in-service workshops	18	5.0
Keeping your district "legal" (i.e., in compliance with federal, state, and local regulations)	19	4.9
Public speaking engagements (e.g., P.T.A.)	20	4.8
Insufficient recognition of your work	20	4.8
Telling parents their child is handicapped	20	4.8
Lack of consensus in a staffing	23	4.6
Inadequate secretarial help	24	4.3
Being told that you "have it easy" by classroom teachers	25	4.2
A change in the schools or districts which you serve	26	4.1
Lack of contact with professional colleagues	26	4.1
Screening bilingual children	26	4.1
Conducting parent groups	26	4.1
Lack of availability of appropriate assessment materials	30	4.0
Impending teachers' strike in your district	31	3.9
Supervising an intern or school psychology graduate student	32	3.5
Keeping up with current professional literature	33	3.4
Carrying testing equipment around in unfavorable weather conditions	34	3.1
Spending time driving between schools	35	2.4

Note. From "School Psychologists' Ratings of Stressful Events," by P. S. Wise, 1985. *Journal of School Psychology, 23,* p. 36.

education and pupil personnel services, and the district's history and philosophical orientation. School psychologists need to understand the organizational unit in which they are embedded independent of their own personal characteristics. Often the quality of the setting is unrelated to the abilities of the school psychologist.

In addition to stable personal and organizational characteristics, time can bring changes to professional outlook. Discussing stages of development in the original manuscript for the Vineland Social Maturity Scale, Doll (1953) outlines the dietary stages of life which can be adapted to the stages of career as well (see Table 2).

TABLE 2
Stages of Life and Career

1. Milk.
2. Milk and bread.
3. Milk, bread, eggs, and spinach.
4. Oatmeal, bread and butter, apples, and an all day sucker.
5. Ice cream soda and hot dogs.
6. Burger, french fries, coffee, and apple pie.
7. Sirloin tip, baked potatoes, creamed broccoli, fruit salad, cherries jubilee, Brazilian coffee.
8. Pate de foie gras, wiener schnitzel, potatoes Parisienne, egg plant a l'oppera, demi-tasse and Roquefort cheese.
9. Soft boiled eggs, toast, and milk.
10. Milk and bread.
11. Milk.

Note. Adapted from Philadelphia Rotary Club as cited in *Measurement of Social Competence* (p. 27) by E. A. Doll, 1953, Circle Pines, MN: American Guidance Service.

School psychologists need to acknowledge in which stage their professional careers are. The goal is to spend most, if not all, of one's professional career in a nutritious stage with a well balanced diet.

A Personal Inventory

My own personal inventory of practitioner stresses encompassing organizational and personal characteristics included, in no particular order:

• Interpersonal conflicts with one or two ancillary professionals that persisted despite earnest ameliorative efforts.

• Too many winter days with travel to three or more locations (which meant I was always chilled).

• Schlepping "stuff" between buildings.

• Discovering, after heroic efforts to be at a specific school at a specific time, that the youngster to be seen was absent or on a field trip.

• The need to be poised at the most vulnerable time of the day for me (late afternoon staff meetings or conferences).

• Due process procedures that appeared more akin to "endless process."

• An increasingly adversarial nature of first meetings due to the influence of the media and well-meaning advocacy groups.

• What I saw as time wasted with meaningless assessments to meet rigid state mandates.

It is important for school psychologists to conduct an inventory of the personal and organizational characteristics that contribute to high and low levels of professional satisfaction and effectiveness. If there is minimal enjoyment or satisfaction, little sense of wonder or discovery, or low or nonexistent feelings of efficacy, a need exists for developing a realistic plan to deal with these conditions.

Expending energy on problems over which one truly has no control is pointless. If an individual has attempted to positively address a source of stress and not been successful, there is no need to create more discomfort by worrying about the inability to deal with the stress. A saying goes "In the desert, it is dry and hot." The implication is that being thirsty and hot is an expected condition of being in a desert so why complain. School psychologists would do well to identify their own professional deserts, that is the barriers to their professional growth and effectiveness, and determine which ones are workable and which are not. Diligently work on those that are workable. However, it is quixotic and a sure path to frustration to continually confront situations when there is no likelihood of success.

Once personal and organizational strengths and weaknesses have been assessed, you can develop a plan (a practitioner's Individualized Effectiveness Plan) for yourself which includes current levels of performance, measurable goals in areas of assessed need, and planned interventions to achieve those goals.

BEST PRACTICES

Maintaining or facilitating professional growth and effectiveness requires a conscious effort much like maintaining interpersonal relationships, maintaining or developing skill at a sport, or developing and maintaining expertise at a hobby. One cannot rely on serendipity. Paraphrasing a sports or work aphorism, when a person complimented another on being lucky enough to enjoy what she did and also lucky to be very effective at it, the response was: "The harder I work at it the luckier I get." Rarely does anything of value come easy.

It is important to develop a personal individual development plan which incorporates the current level of professional effectiveness, describes the personal and organizational barriers to increased levels of effectiveness, and outlines a plan to increase professional effectiveness. Any implemented plan can also facilitate attaining continuing professional development requirements for state certification and be credited for NCSP renewal. The following areas of attention should be considered in formulating a professional and personal development plan.

Maintaining Physical and Psychological Health

Obviously, one's physical and psychological health extends to all life activities, including vocational. Maintaining physical health means taking care of one's body with respect to nutrition and exercise. Those likely to be reading this already know resources related to exercise and nutrition and already know the importance of maintaining the body. It is unlikely that the more subtle best practices suggestions that follow would have any merit if this basic dictum is not considered.

Psychological health related to employment means maintaining a delicate balance between the realistic possibilities of using one's training and individually developed skill to help others while simultaneously not developing unrealistic expectations of either the impact to be made or the appreciation of others for such expenditure. Admittedly, this is a delicate balance. If you become discouraged and disenchanted, then your personal effectiveness may diminish. On the other hand, falsely high expectations can lead to disappointment in the outcomes.

Related to personal characteristics is the notion of the impostor phenomenon (Harvey, 1985). This construct refers to the psychological anxiety created by high-achieving professionals who feel that they have arrived at a certain level of perceived expertise by subterfuge and that, at any moment, someone is going to find out they are a fraud. The continued feeling of anxiety accompanying professional activities is a function of the impostor phenomenon: that at any moment the "high-achiever" will be unmasked and announced as an impostor. These high levels of self-expectation do equate to high professional productivity but also to increased stress. However laudable the goal to be all things to all people, it may be unrealistic to maintain quality consultation services to scores of teachers, complete 75 or more quality assessments in a year, implement and monitor 50 yearly interventions of high quality, participate actively in curriculum and other system level committees, be sought for counsel by principals and other administrators, participate actively in school related social activities, conduct research on district problems, while simultaneously maintaining a fulfilling family and civic life.

Peer Support

It is possible to feel isolated and alone even in a large system, to feel as if you are the only person having to deal with an angry teacher, uncooperative administrator, belligerent colleague, immovable school system, overwhelming number of referrals and reports yet to be written. For those school psychologists who practice in rural or small suburban districts and have no colleagues, the sense of isolation may be even more dramatic.

A peer support group can assist in providing a sense of camaraderie and connection. It does not have to be formal. It can be a group of professionals who meet on a periodic basis to talk about common problems, discuss professional developments, share stories or anecdotes, and provide a supportive environment for each other regarding professional endeavors. At a minimum, peer support could mean monthly luncheons or a "happy hour" with colleagues, or even being part of an electronic network. It could extend to weekly formal meetings with established agendas, presentations, and minutes. Additional perspectives and specific details for establishing a peer-support group can be found in Zins, Mayer, Murphy, and Wess (1988), who also list key elements of establishing these groups (see Table 3).

Involvement in Professional Associations

Professional association involvement is important in maintaining a sense of professional identity, providing opportunities for continuing professional development, and communicating contemporary information about political and professional activities related to the discipline. Involvement in these associations can be viewed on a continuum from membership (receiving notices of conferences and various publications) through attendance and participation at association meetings, to committee membership, to election to the executive board or as an officer.

There are associations for school psychologists at the international, national, and state levels. Some states are divided into regions and regional association membership is available which may provide some of the peer-support activities referred to previously. In larger states, the regions may be further divided into county or city associations. Within most associations, there are numerous possibilities for involvement that would coincide with an individual's particular interest or skill. Most associations have committees dealing with professional issues (e.g., children's services, special education), legislative activities (e.g., legislative or governmental affairs), or organizational maintenance (e.g., membership, elections). In addition, there is ample opportunity to participate in communications (e.g., public relations efforts, association newsletter) or professional devel-

TABLE 3
Key Elements of an Effective Peer Support Group

- Establish a nonthreatening, supportive environment and norms that encourage participation and openness.
- Involve all participants in agenda setting.
- Identify a highly relevant, broad range of topics for meetings.
- Build member commitment and enthusiasm.
- Maintain group camaraderie, trust, and support.
- Facilitate a networking process that continues outside of group meetings.
- Vary learning formats.
- Select members who share common professional goals.
- Rotate leadership.
- Include participants who are diverse in terms of employment settings, educational backgrounds, and professional experiences.

Note. Adapted from "The Peer Support Group: A Means to Facilitate Professional Development" by J. E. Zins, C. E. Mayer, J. J. Murphy, and B. P. Wess, 1988, *School Psychology Review, 17,* p. 144.

opment (e.g., annual conventions, workshops) activities.

Most school psychology associations maintain a regular newsletter containing professional information, notices of future meetings, and discussions of contemporary issues. Associations provide the opportunity to place individual endeavors in a larger context and to influence local, state, or national policy in areas where a practitioner may have a particular interest. Associations provide the opportunity to work collectively on issues where there may be individual frustration. This collective effort when successful allows individual endeavors to be seen in a more positive context.

There are also professional and non-professional groups in related fields such as parent teacher associations, learning disability or autism groups, and so forth. Association involvement can increase a sense of efficacy, provide some peer-support opportunities, and also be a source of personal and professional friendships.

School and Community Involvement

It is a rare occasion that a child is referred because of a long attention span, inordinate scholastic persistence, or achievement greater than ability would dictate. By the nature of the discipline, and despite earnest efforts to promote a preventative model of service delivery, most students seen and services provided are based on the perception or the reality of problems. This can contribute to an unrealistic view of the schools, the community in which the schools are located, or the larger society in which the community is embedded. Just as involvement in the local or school community is perceived as healthy for families and for children, such involvement can also promote positive outcomes for professionals.

Being a coach or club advisor for a school group can provide access to students, parents, and teachers whom the school psychologist may never meet under professional circumstances. Not only can these contacts provide a positive spread of effect in activities more directly related to professional roles, but also they provide an opportunity to view a different side of the school system. Volunteering to be part of a school committee, to chaperone for a field trip or student venture, or even to substitute (where possible) for a teacher taking a professional development day can reap unforeseen benefits in improving access to students, teacher rapport, parental acknowledgment, and administrative support. Being seen in a non-psychologist light can also lead to vulnerability and establish a different relationship with staff who may be accustomed to seeing the psychologist in a specific role. Even participating in school sports pools or joining with the staff in their lottery ticket purchase can increase the sense of community with a school and certainly provide topics of conversation removed from routine business. Although these frivolous or non-focused conversations may seem irrelevant, they may lead to greater receptivity and satisfaction when business is discussed.

A perennial question emerging in most introductory role and function classes is whether the school psychologist is a guest in the school or an integral part of the school family. Whatever the circumstances the feeling of distance can be minimized with increased participation by the school psychologist within the school community. The chapter by Kelly (this volume) on school-oriented public relations activities has numerous suggestions on how this can be accomplished. By initiating these activities, the school psychologist may come to be viewed as part of the school family, an unintended, positive benefit.

Within the community, there is also ample opportunity to participate depending on your interests. Joining and participating in service clubs, offering to write monthly articles about timely topics for the local paper (most communities have free papers advertising local businesses and providing information on local events), or volunteering for a community activity increases visibility within the community and, like activities discussed within the schools, has potential unintended benefits.

Just as the family's involvement in ongoing community events can be important to their health and the health of the children, so does the school psychologist's involvement in the life of the school and community portend greater receptivity for services that he or she has to offer. Community support is good for personal morale and effectiveness and can bolster the often-voiced desire of school psychologists to expand their professional roles.

Using Positive Professional Metaphors

The use of cognitive reframing can affect the delicate relationship between thought and reality. Given the circumstances with which many school psychologists deal, it is easy to view the world with jaundiced eyes and skeptical ears. If metaphors of war and battle are used to describe activities — "on the front lines," "in the trenches," "escaped that bullet," "won that battle" — then that school psychologist views his or her role within a war-like context. Even natural activities can be shaded and seen in this harsh way. Examine the metaphors used when working within schools. If negative metaphors like those involving war or drowning (e.g., "up to the neck in alligators," "throw me a rope," "going down for the last time," "sink or swim") permeate the conversation, then it might be time to review personal and professional descriptions.

Reframing will not change the objective reality of a situation, but it may change an individual's perspective on it. Try viewing service delivery as the preparation of a gourmet meal: Things must be ready at the same time, some dishes need to be on the back burner, some do not turn out as planned, some are over-cooked, some half-baked, and some need more time to simmer. Or service delivery can be turned into an investment or financial metaphor: need to invest more in this project, must look at assets and liabilities, need better returns for the investment. The school psychologist as gardener is another metaphor (e.g., nurturing, needing more sun or water to thrive, prune back for optimum growth).

Initially, the metaphors used may describe one's feelings but eventually they shape one's thinking as well. Maintaining maximum professional effectiveness requires as positive an outlook as possible within the circumstances, and use of language can assist in shaping that reality.

Professional Activity That is Prized

Most everyone has a prized project that they would like to undertake but often feel there is not the luxury of time for such indulgence. It is vital for school psychologists to have an ongoing project that is not routine and which represents a potential professional service. Even though this often involves risk-taking, it can enhance overall satisfaction.

This volume of *Best Practices* contains numerous topics and offers annotated bibliographies where additional resources can be found within each topic. In every setting there is usually a receptive teacher and often a receptive school where initiatives on your part will be appreciated. Organize a parent program or a group on an important topic for students or teachers, conduct a research study to answer local questions, or develop specific expertise and experience with a population with which you have had interest. Make it a goal to spend part of each day, if only 5 minutes, immersed in the topic: to read about it, talk about it, plan it, or implement it. If you do not find the time for this activity, you must make the time.

Maintain a Sense of Humor and Perspective

The practice of school psychology is a serious business and can be fraught with numerous frustrations. Maintaining a sense of humor and perspective while delivering professionally competent services is essential for continued professional effectiveness. Whether it is the funny things that students say during interviews or assessments, the seemingly Catch-22 administrative or bureaucratic dictums by state or school policies, or the sometimes absurd expectations of service desired by colleagues, an element of humor and a heightened perspective can usually be found. Maintaining a degree of involved and committed distance is facilitated through maintaining a sense of humor and perspective.

Activities to facilitate humor might include keeping a log of favorite student responses, a top-10 list of frustrations or impossible requests for service, or a doodle sketch pad of caricatures for the artistically inclined, or develop creative acronyms. I can recall inadvertently asking a student "what is the thing to do if you cut a finger that belongs to someone else?" That experience initiated an off-beat interest in creating very brief assessment techniques by combining several questions. Such activities would provide good conversation among colleagues or be a welcome addition to an association newsletter.

Such humorous diversions in no way detract from the seriousness of professional activities but can help place daily frustrations and stresses in perspective. Humor, it is important to note, should never be used to disparage people. Humor, however, used optimally, assists in gaining perspective and maintains social contact without diminishing quality service delivery.

Taking the Larger View

In many places, a frustration inherent in contemporary service delivery is the systemic expectation of making a binary (yes/no, eligible/not eligible) decision regarding students. There is no assurance that being or not being in a specific program would be good for the child. The line of children to see will always go out the door and extend down the hall. However fast school psychologists consult, test, or assess the line goes on.

Decisions and procedures are established at the national, state, school district, and school levels to provide parameters within which services are provided. Although the service delivery level where most psychologists operate is the most important level of decision making, latitude at that level is limited by these policies and procedures. Because the strictures of these parameters can be frustrating, it may help to extend one's point of view. For example, having to do automatic intelligence testing for re-evaluations of high school students who have received similar assessment five times over 12 years can be inordinately frustrating as well as futile. Such frustration can be attributed to the notion that it is a federal regulation, that decisions were made higher up the professional hierarchy or food chain, and that they have filtered down through state and local systems in the form of regulations and policies. As long as school psychologists *only* deliver direct services, then their influence on policy that guides and informs direct service delivery will be limited. For example, administration of an intelligence test for re-evaluation is not specifically stated in any federal regulation. These regulations are interpreted by state and school district officials as a requirement. This interpretive rigidity may also apply to retention policy, structure of special education services, use of corporal punishment, or other programs for students experiencing school problems.

School psychologists can work individually and collectively at policy levels to eventually impact practice at the most important level, direct service delivery. This is not only an issue of empowerment but also one of morale. If an individual has no control of his or her destiny, then it becomes inevitable to feel robotic and to lack a sense of professional efficacy.

Whether the individual school psychologist feels frustrated about the retention policy in the district, the lack of programming options for children with specific learning characteristics, or the manner in which the district chooses to use discretionary federal or state funds — all those decisions made apart from the service-delivery level yet certainly affecting its outcome — these barriers at other levels of the professional food chain must be identified and dealt with. The chapters by Curtis and Stollar (this volume) on system-level consultation and by Dwyer (this volume) on influencing public policy can aid in suggesting strategies to assist in thinking and acting systemically.

SUMMARY

Maintaining quality professional services requires that each school psychologist inventory the personal and organizational characteristics that are barriers to a heightened sense of effectiveness and professional growth. Most school psychologists know what to do in this regard but the key is to actually develop and consciously work toward implementing activities that promote growth and effectiveness, and by implication, avoid professional burnout.

These activities include maintenance of both physical and psychological health, involvement in the professional and school communities, ongoing peer-support in some form, awareness of the language used to describe activities and frustrations, maintenance of a sense of humor and perspective, and thinking systemically as well as individually.

Anyone trained in a helping profession is aware of the concept of intervention adherence. Most school psychologists can identify specific personal and organizational barriers to optimum professional effectiveness. It is further likely that there are specific activities that have the potential to overcome these barriers. Just as losing weight is simple (eat less, exercise more) or raising responsible children is simple (provide love, structure, and consistency) school psychologists may similarly know what can be done to promote professional growth and effectiveness. The challenge is to integrate these activities into a daily routine and to adhere to the plan.

REFERENCES

Doll, E. A. (1953). *Measurement of social competence.* Circle Pines, MN: American Guidance Service.

Fagan, T. K., & Wise, P. S. (1994). *School psychology: Past, present, and future.* New York: Longman.

Harvey, J. C. (1985). *If I'm so successful, why do I feel like a fake?* New York: St. Martin's Press.

Huberty, T. J., & Huebner, E. S. (1988). A national survey of burnout among school psychologists. *Psychology in the Schools, 25,* 54–61.

Huebner, E. S. (1992). Burnout among school psychologists: An exploratory investigation into its nature, extent, and correlates. *School Psychology Quarterly, 7,* 129–136.

Levinson, E. M., Fetchkan, R., & Hohenshil, T. H. (1988). Job satisfaction among practicing school psychologists revisited. *School Psychology Review, 17,* 101–112.

Maslach, C. M., & Jackson, S. E. (1981). The measurement of experienced burnout. *Journal of Occupational Behavior, 2,* 99–113.

Pierson-Hubeny, D., & Archambault, F. X. (1987). Role stress and perceived intensity of burnout among school psychologists. *Psychology in the Schools, 24,* 244–253.

Solly, D. C., & Hohenshil, T. H. (1986). Job satisfaction among school psychologists in a primarily rural state. *School Psychology Review, 15,* 119–126.

Wise, P. S. (1985). School psychologists' ratings of stressful events. *Journal of School Psychology, 23,* 31–41.

Zins, J. E., Maher, C. E., Murphy, J. J., & Wess, B. P. (1988). The peer support group: A means to facilitate professional development. *School Psychology Review, 17,* 138–146.

ANNOTATED BIBLIOGRAPHY

School Psychology Associations

There are school psychology associations at the international, national, and state levels. Some states have regional associations. To gain more information about these organizations, contact:

International School Psychology Association: ISPA, Hans Knudsens Plads 1 A, 1. tv., 2100 Copenhagen 0, Denmark.

National Association of School Psychologists: NASP, 4340 East West Highway, Suite 402, Bethesda, MD 20814.

Division of School Psychology (Division 16), American Psychological Association: Division 16 Member Services, APA, 750 First St., NE, Washington, DC 20002.

State School Psychology Association: contact NASP, Membership Services (address above), for the specific address of your state association.

Regional School Psychology Association: contact your state association president or the state association office.

Publications

Ohio School Psychologists Association. (1993). *Hermobilia.* Columbus, OH: Author.
This is a collection of whimsy related to school psychology: over 150 cartoons, flow charts, humorous articles, and drawings. Most were done by Herm Zielinski whose work has been featured in the *Communiqué* and in Sattler's *Assessment of Children.* Available (until July, 1998) as nonprofit service ($8 check covering postage and handling) from the Ohio School Psychologists Association, 750 Brooksedge Blvd., Westerville, OH 43081.

Zins, J. E., Maher, C. E., Murphy, J. J., & Wess, B. P. (1988). The peer support group: A means to facilitate professional development. *School Psychology Review, 17,* 138–146.
The peer support group is described and illustrated with a case example. A description of goals, structure, and composition, activities, and professional outcomes are outlined. Though it is likely that most school psychologists would find it impractical to implement this model in total, it is an excellent resource for considering the advantages, structure, and prospective barriers in developing peer support activities.

10

Best Practices in Supervision of Interns

Jane Close Conoley
Theresa Bahns
University of Nebraska-Lincoln

OVERVIEW

Though largely unexplored in the research and conceptual literature of school psychology, the role of supervision of psychology interns is of vital importance for the welfare of clients and the welfare of the profession (Ross & Sisenwein, 1990; Zins, Murphy, & Wess, 1989). Supervisors must be concerned about their interns' knowledge and behavior in terms of ethics, competence, and personal functioning (Lamb, Cochran, & Jackson, 1991). In consequence, this is a very complex and demanding role.

Supervision of interns is conceptualized from a number of perspectives (Bartlett, 1983; Blocher, 1983) and may be seen as a sequence of learning objectives or as a developmental sequence of self-perceptions and other perceptions by the supervisor and the supervised (Stoltenberg & Delworth, 1987). In addition to conceptual understandings, the process of supervision is regulated by the National Association of School Psychologists (1992, 1994) and the American Psychological Association (1981, 1992).

However one defines and implements the process, supervision is a key factor in the construction of critical attitudes and skills in new professional psychologists. Despite its importance, most supervisors report limited academic training in supervision or access to peer supervision (Zins et al., 1989). herefore, an important first step in exploring the supervisory process is for supervisors to attend to their own skills, knowledge, and vision for the supervisory relationship.

Part of this self-assessment deals with developing a theoretical model to guide supervisory behavior; another deals with constructing standards of behavior between supervisor and supervised; and finally, part has to do with creating a plan to engage the intern in complex ethical decision making in regard to the complicated problems facing school psychologists in the 1990s.

This chapter will consider the needs of the supervisor, the intern, and the client from a number of perspectives. Supervision is carried out with overlapping responsibilities to the intern, the host training context, the intern's academic program, and the clients. It is not a role to be taken without careful study and continuing refinement of skills. A first step for supervisors is to identify which existing supervisory model is closest to their theoretical orientation and to begin a process of study.

MODELS OF SUPERVISION: BASIC CONSIDERATIONS

There are several models of supervision that are based on various theoretical orientations: psychodynamic, client-centered, behavioral, and developmental. Brief comments on each of the models follow.

Psychodynamic Supervision

The primary focus of psychodynamic supervision is on supervisees' learning to use themselves effectively in helping relationships. This is accomplished primarily by concentrating on the dynamics of the supervisory relationship to monitor constructive or destructive ways of reacting to others. It is assumed that understanding the relationship dynamics of the supervisor and supervisee will generalize to understanding the dynamics between supervisees and their clients.

Supervisors must build a working alliance with their interns. This alliance is based on a willingness to work together to improve the effectiveness of the supervisee. Proponents of this model suggest that any unresolved personal issues of supervisees and supervisors are major impediments to development and growth (Thorenson, Miller, & Krauskopf, 1989).

There is little research to support this model. The danger of creating therapeutic rather than supervisory interactions has been suggested (Doehrman, 1976). However, national studies of clinical psychologists state that between 2% and 60% of the respondents admit to working sometimes when they are too distressed to be effective (Farber, 1985). Such findings suggest the need to train interns to reflect upon their own issues as a necessary ingredient to competent professional functioning.

Client-Centered Supervision

Growing from Rogers's (1958) seminal work, client-centered supervision seeks to establish conditions between supervisor and intern that mirror the conditions that are necessary for effective psychotherapy. The therapeutic conditions of psychological contact — congruence, unconditional positive regard, empathy, and warmth — are the necessary and sufficient conditions in any relationship based on increased self-exploration. Interns must be taught how to create and communicate each of these conditions in their relationships with clients. Interns' professional development depends on the supervisor's skills in creating and communicating these therapeutic conditions.

Tapes, modeling, role-plays, and live demonstrations are often components of client-centered supervision. Personal therapy is seen as a very important way of increasing supervisees' expertness in interpersonal relationships. Research indicates that supervisors must teach specific techniques and skills as well as facilitate a supportive environment to increase supervisees' effectiveness (Forsyth & Ivey, 1980).

Behavioral Supervision

Proficient performance is based on learned skills. Supervisors must teach appropriate behaviors and extinguish inappropriate ones. Each intern's job can be broken into identifiable tasks with associated skills. The supervisor should use the same behavioral principles with the intern as are used in all professional interactions with colleagues and clients (Delaney, 1972).

Mutual assessment of skill deficits and strengths are followed by a shared commitment as to the steps to be taken to meet measurable goals. Frequent feedback is provided regarding current progress toward attainment of goals. Supervision is conducted through an individualized contract of specific behavioral goals and identification of the means for attaining these goals. The key steps of supervision are as follows: (a) Establish a relationship between supervisor and supervisee; (b) assess skills; (c) set supervision goals; (d) generate and implement strategies to accomplish goals; (e) evaluate strategies and generalization of learning.

The failure to provide feedback and provide for remedial activities is often the basis for ethical complaints between supervisor and interns (Freeman, 1985; Keith-Spiegel & Koocher, 1985). A strength of the behavioral approach is the demand for clear communication and careful monitoring of skill development.

Developmental Supervision

Supervisees pass through predictable stages of levels on their way from being apprentices to masters (Stoltenberg & Delworth, 1987). Beginning supervisees lack confidence and are dependent on the supervisor for advice and direction. At this early stage, interns may be more concerned about how to do things the right way and not have much insight into their own behavior or impact.

With some experience, many interns begin to experience a conflict between dependence and autonomy. Thus, feelings of confidence are quickly replaced by feelings of being overwhelmed. Supervisors and interns may have disagreements over the right way to handle situations.

Eventually a firmer sense of identity and self-confidence evolves. The intern becomes more tolerant of differences and is increasingly more flexible in choosing approaches to solve problems. In addition, the supervisee seeks help and advice without feeling too dependent on the supervisor.

Excellent supervisors change their behaviors (from advice giving to support) according to the needs of their interns. They do not overreact to predictable conflicts or testing behaviors and are patient with interns' early feelings of helplessness.

Synthesis

The personal style of the supervisor and intern, the supervisor's and the intern's characteristics, and previous experiences with supervisors will all interact in choosing a particular model of supervision. The best supervisors may be those who have been able to manage a flexible blending of the above perspectives. They provide structured resources for interns in terms of goals and learning experiences while making sure to emphasize the personal impact of the intern. The personal impact of the intern is a function of his or her ability to carry interventions through to successful completion through careful planning, evaluation, and coordination of the efforts of other persons involved. Experience has indicated that powerful technologies are wasted if psychologists cannot gain the investment of staff members and families in their intervention efforts. Furthermore, the intensity of the supervisory relationship demands that the supervisor have some framework to use in sorting out dynamics.

BEST PRACTICES IN THE SUPERVISION OF INTERNS

Assessment of Supervisory Skills

In addition to meeting the requirements for being a supervisor from the relevant professional organizations (e.g., school psychologists with continuing credentials; doctoral, licensed psychologists), supervisors should reflect upon their own supervisory skills and experience in order to prepare for the supervisory role.

Appendix A is a suggested format for rating the supervisor's skills. Completing this assessment may provide supervisors with some important learning goals and information about blind spots in their own behaviors.

For example, the supervisor's comfort with allowing independence among interns is very important to analyze. Interns in the Nebraska Internship Consortium in Professional Psychology (Kramer, Conoley, Bischoff, & Benes, 1991) often describe supervisors as too laissez-faire (i.e., tending to allow for too much independence) or as too controlling. Given the developmental issues raised above (Stoltenberg & Delworth, 1987), it is vital that supervisors be aware of their general stance toward the autonomy of the intern and the ways this stance may be modified according to intern or client situations.

Evaluating Supervisee Skills

A successful supervisor must develop a number of strategies for evaluating the level of intern skills so that appropriate teaching plans can be made and assessment activities accomplished. The critical issues for the supervisor to investigate are as follows.

1. *Competence.* Does the intern have the necessary skills, techniques, and abilities to take appropriate action? Psychologists must be expert in implementing and interpreting numerous assessment procedures, performing direct interventions with children and their families such as counseling and behavior modification, and indirect interventions (e.g., consultation, research, and evaluation).

2. *Emotional awareness.* Can the intern use his or her own emotions and reactions to understand others? Supervisors must target interns' communication skills, interpersonal relationships, and personal stability as potential areas for change if problems are apparent.

3 *Identity.* Does the intern develop a consistent way of thinking about problems and planning actions?

4. *Respect for individual differences.* Does the intern make an active effort to understand and appreciate cultural or ethnic (or other) differences? Is basic respect present for alternative lifestyles and choices?

5. *Purpose and direction.* Can the supervisee formulate plans, identify short- and long-term goals, and map progress? Research training should have had the outcome of preparing interns to complete $N = 1$ studies, collect data, and evaluate outcomes. Intervention or assessment without outcome-based evaluation is questionable practice.

6. *Autonomy.* Can the supervisee make choices and decisions independently? Is there an appropriate degree of self-management?

7. *Ethics.* Are ethical issues, values, and standards integrated into practice?

8. *Motivation.* Is the intern internally motivated, finding work rewarding and meaningful?

Making informed judgments along these dimensions will demand that the supervisor meet individually with the intern, observe the intern's professional functioning, and collect evaluations from others who are directly involved with the intern. The evaluation instrument used by the Nebraska Internship Consortium in Professional Psychology is reproduced as Appendix B. This device is completed twice each year. The completion of the instrument serves as a way for the supervisor and intern to discuss progress at the end of the first five months of the internship and again close to the end of the experience.

It is also of great importance to develop ways to provide ongoing feedback to interns and give them help in organizing their work. Appendix C is an example of a Progress Monitoring Sheet used to give interns information about their cases and about the success of their interventions. The form is designed to be done in duplicate so the intern has a record of suggestions developed during supervision, and the supervisor has a record of what issues and strategies deserve follow-up attention.

Ethics and Equity Issues

Though rarely the target of litigation, school psychologists have enormously complex ethical dilemmas to face. In addition, supervisors must clearly understand the boundaries that delimit supervisory relationships in terms of exploitation and equity (e.g., appropriate work expectations, gender equity issues, etc.).

Interns. Although the entire practice of psychology is governed by law and ethics, the practice of school psychology has additional demands from laws specific to education and the ethical dilemmas posed by continuous interactions with minor clients. It is clear that intern supervisors should always determine the intern's level of knowledge about current ethical standards and educational laws and regulations as well as associated state mental health laws. Supervisors need to assess this knowledge at the very start of the internship experience, so that interns can be given any needed information immediately.

Beyond knowledge, however, is the ability to apply these principles to daily decision making. Although research supporting the effectiveness of didactic training in ethics is mixed (Welfel, 1992), the efficacy of positive modeling by the supervisor and careful monitoring of the intern's behavior must be accepted as a powerful force influencing interns. Supervisors might find it useful to study Kitchener (1984) and Rest (1984) for information (beyond mere listings of principles) that is useful in developing the ethical decision making and moral development of their interns.

Rest (1984) suggests that an ethical person must have (a) empathy; (b) well-understood rationales for deciding which of the options in a dilemma is morally right or comes closest to one's ideals; (c) ways of selecting among competing values and motivations so that a plan of action can be made; and, finally; (d) the characteristics that allow plans of action to be implemented, such as resoluteness and perseverance.

Kitchener (1984) provides assistance for ethical decision making, especially for deciding among options. She delineates five critical ethical principles for the evaluation of ethical dilemmas in psychology. These principles are autonomy, beneficence, nonmaleficence, justice, and fidelity. Although each of these principles has many applications, a few examples may suggest the richness of Kitchener's (1984) thinking.

Interns should know that a commitment to autonomy underlies our pledge of confidentiality and carefulness in dealing with records. Respecting and promoting others' control of their lives is a key element of establishing therapeutic relationships. Dealing with autonomy concerns with children is quite sensitive. For example, how does the intern handle disclosures from adolescents that implicate family members as abusers but are unlikely to result in the child's removal from the home? How is confidentiality protected when so many professionals have a "need to know" about children?

Nonmaleficence means a promise to "above all, do no harm" and beneficence is associated with psychology as a science and practice dedicated to promoting human welfare. Trainees and supervisors must examine their competencies, the potential negative impact of assessments and interventions, and the client's and client family's civil rights when choosing treatment and assessment options. Unfortunately, there is frequently a price associated with every positive change and interns are often unaware that their interventions or assessments may inadvertently do harm. It is critical to be able to sort through the likely harm and good associated with our professional intrusions into other people's lives.

Justice means being dedicated to fairness. School psychologists are necessarily concerned that each child access an appropriate education. How are situations resolved when one child's access is deleterious to another's? Can a common good be discerned in every situation?

Finally, fidelity refers to honesty in fulfilling commitments and being consistent. Fidelity is owed to children, teachers, school systems, and families, and to personal ethics. Each of these may have differing demands upon the intern — often with compelling rationales.

Too often supervisors and interns may believe that knowing the lists of ethical principles from the National Association of School Psychologists (NASP, 1992) and the American Psychological Association (APA, 1992) may suffice in respect to ethical competencies. It seems clear, however, from the rising numbers of complaints about psychologists that attention to high-level ethical thinking is warranted. In addition, challenges raised by AIDS, teenage health and sexuality decision making, culturally sensitive assessment and intervention efforts, and the changing expectations regarding school psychologists all suggest that ethical training is of critical importance.

Supervisors. Supervisors have many ethical responsibilities toward their interns. Paramount among these may be the management of the supervisory relationship to ensure it is equitable. Although romantic and sexually intimate relationships between female psychology students and their male educators is a well-known fact, nothing is known concerning this issue specifically among school psychology supervisors (Bartell & Rubin, 1990; Pope, 1989). All dual relationships with supervisees are problematic (e.g., intimate friendships, business ventures) but sexual relationships are expressly forbidden. Whatever the experience of the intern or the supervisor at the moment, both should be aware of societal norms that contribute to power differentials between men and women and the great likelihood that sexual relationships will be viewed later by the woman as having been exploitative (Kitchener, 1988). At the very least, the supervisor has failed to model appropriate professional interactions and so has failed to fulfill an important element of his or her contract with the intern.

Sexual and racial harassment are present in most (all?) of our major societal institutions. Supervisors must be alert to even subtle instances of such in their own and their interns' behaviors. Disentangling personal history and social constructions is a very complicated business that may demand outside consultation (e.g., on ethnic/cultural/racial issues) and an ability to be nondefensive. It may be useful for supervisors to consult the *Guidelines for Providers of Services to Ethnic, Linguistic, and Culturally Diverse Populations* (APA, 1990).

Interns' Perspectives on the Process

The interns in the Nebraska Consortium have been asked for the past several years to provide input regarding the quality of their internship experiences. In addition, the second author of this chapter interviewed students who had completed field placements regarding critical incidents in their experience of being supervised. Several themes emerged from these written evaluations and interviews.

Supervisor availability. Interns are sensitive to the accessibility of their supervisors. Even when they perceive the supervisor to be talented and competent, difficulties in contacting a supervisor during a critical period or in arranging for regular supervision result in poor evaluations and a diminished experience. Two hours each week of individual supervision must be given to the interns in addition to other group staffing and educational experiences. Supervisors are permitted to have only two interns and must be organized to have supervisory time available.

Time management. Although all interns expect to work hard, most are unprepared for the intensity of the internship experience. Interns commonly report feeling overwhelmed by the demands on their time and unaware they should take some responsibility for controlling their assignments. They report feeling unwilling to refuse any assignment. This occurs sometimes because they (ambitiously) want to learn everything and sometimes because they fear a negative evaluation if they demur. Very often they lack basic time management and assertiveness skills. These predictable problems sometimes result in interns' engaging in activities that are inappropriate for their role. Not only do they fail to set limits with supervisors, they set no limits with anyone else! Supervisors should be ready to teach these professional management skills to interns.

Exploitation of skills. Some institutions use interns as cheap sources of labor for repetitive or unpopular tasks without a concomitant commitment to training. This attitude is easily discerned by the interns, who resent that their work for the organization is not met with a return of training opportunities. Internships are organized training experiences, not mere on-the-job experiences. This basic fact about internships is often not well understood at the internship site. Careful cooperation between university and internship faculty must be maintained to be sure that everyone stays invested in teaching the interns.

Negative supervisor attitudes. Interns are disillusioned by supervisors who are pessimistic or cynical about professional functioning. Often, under the guise of teaching the intern what the real world is like, supervisors fail to model enthusiasm and optimism in their work. Supervisors may act like victims in their systems rather than instructing interns on how to approach the long and difficult processes of organizational change. Interns may learn more negative information than positive steps to create change.

Personal concerns. The 9-month internship for educational specialist students (1,200 hours) or the 12-month experience for doctoral students (1,500–2,000 hours depending on the state) occurs in the context of family, financial, health, and academic concerns for many interns. The stress on family may be significant because of the intern's time commit-ments at the site. The internship, even though paid, may represent a serious financial hardship on the intern's family. Many intern programs do not provide health insurance. All of these and a host of other everyday hassles need some attention from supervisors. Although few of such problems, if any, can be solved by a supervisor, all interns seem to appreciate being known in their complexity by their supervisors. Some mutual appreciation of what the training site is offering the intern and what the intern is sacrificing to finish the demanding degree program can help both sides keep ultimate goals in view.

SUMMARY

All supervisors must be well versed both in current guidelines from their professional organizations (APA, 1981, 1992; NASP, 1992, 1994) that speak to basic expectations regarding state-of-the-art training of interns, and in the research supporting supervisory processes (Robiner & Schofield, 1990). Furthermore, they must be cognizant of their own competencies in assuming an educative role with others. These competencies include knowledge, ethics, and personal functioning. The exact sequence of activities offered to interns should be well articulated and responsive to the intern's strengths and weaknesses and academic program expectations. Interns should be offered experiences in the best of professional functioning if the field is to progress. Tired, old, and invalid test batteries should not be imposed on interns, who may arrive at their sites with information new and useful to the supervisors. Enthusiastic, "book-smart" interns should be schooled in the complexities of working in systems that have yet to understand the great potential of psychology.

The vitality of psychology in the schools depends on every supervisor who mentors an intern to high levels of skill, compassion, and the certainty that school psychologists can make a huge contribution to children, families, and the educational enterprise.

REFERENCES

American Psychological Association. (1981). Specialty guidelines for the delivery of services by school psychologists. *American Psychologist, 36,* 670–681.

American Psychological Association. (1990). *Guidelines for providers of services to ethnic, linguistic, and culturally diverse populations.* Washington, DC: Author.

American Psychological Association. (1992). *Ethical principles of psychologists and code of conduct.* Washington, DC: Author.

Bartell, P. A., & Rubin, L. J. (1990). Dangerous liaisons: Sexual intimacies in supervision. *Professional Psychology: Research and Practice, 21,* 442–450.

Bartlett, W. E. (1983). A multidimensional framework for the analysis of supervision in counseling. *Counseling Psychologist, 11,* 9–17.

Blocher, D. H. (1983). Supervision in counseling: II. Contemporary models of supervision: Toward a cognitive developmental approach to counseling supervision. *Counseling Psychologist, 11,* 27–34.

Carifio, M. S., & Hess, A. K. (1987). Who is the ideal supervisor? *Professional Psychology: Research and Practice, 18,* 244–250.

Delaney, D. J. (1972). A behavioral model for the practicum supervision of counselor candidates. *Counselor Education and Supervision, 12,* 46–50.

Doehrman, M. J. G. (1976). Parallel process in supervision and psychotherapy. *Bulletin of the Menninger Clinic, 40,* 3–84.

Farber, B. A. (1985). Clinical psychologists' perceptions of psychotherapeutic work. *Clinical Psychologist, 38,* 10–13.

Forsyth, D. R., & Ivey, A. E. (1980). Microtraining: An approach to differential supervision. In A. K. Hess (Ed.), *Psychotherapy supervision: Theory, research, and practice* (pp. 242–261). New York: Wiley.

Freeman, E. (1985). The importance of feedback in clinical supervision: Implications for direct practice. *Clinical Supervisor, 3,* 5–26.

Heppner, P. P., & Handley, P. G. (1981). A study of the interpersonal influence process in supervision. *Journal of Counseling Psychology, 28,* 437–444.

Keith-Spiegel, P., & Koocher, G. P. (1985). *Ethics in psychology: Professional standards and cases.* New York: Random House.

Kitchener, K. S. (1984). Intuition, critical evaluation and ethical principles: The foundation for ethical decisions in counseling psychology. *Counseling Psychologist, 12,* 43–55.

Kitchener, K. S. (1988). Dual role relationships: What makes them so problematic? *Journal of Counseling and Development, 67,* 217–221.

Kramer, J. J., Conoley, J. C., Bischoff, L., & Benes, K. (1991). Providing a continuum of professional training. *School Psychology Review, 20,* 551–564.

Lamb, D. H., Cochran, D. J., & Jackson, V. R. (1991). Training and organizational issues associated with identifying and responding to intern impairment. *Professional Psychology: Research and Practice, 22,* 291–296.

National Association of School Psychologists. (1992). *Principles for professional ethics.* Washington, DC: Author.

National Association of School Psychologists. (1994). *Standards for training and field placement programs in school psychology.* Washington, DC: Author.

Pope, K. S. (1989). Sexual intimacies between psychologists and their students and supervisees: Research, standards, and professional liability. *Independent Practitioner, 9,* 33–41.

Rest, J. R. (1984). Research on moral development: Implications for training counseling psychologists. *Counseling Psychologist, 12,* 19–29.

Robiner, W. N., & Schofield, W. (1990). References on supervision in clinical and counseling psychology. *Professional Psychology: Research and practice, 21,* 297–312.

Rogers, C. (1958). Characteristics of a helping relationship. *Personnel and Guidance Journal, 37,* 6–16.

Ross, R. P., & Sisenwein, F. E. (1990). Best practices in internship supervision. In A. Thomas & J. Grimes (Eds.), *Best practices in school psychology–II* (pp. 441–454). Washington, DC: National Association of School Psychologists.

Stoltenberg, C. D., & Delworth, U. (1987). *Supervising counselors and therapists.* San Francisco: Jossey-Bass.

Thorenson, R. W., Miller, M., & Krauskopf, C. J. (1989). The distressed psychologist: Prevalence and treatment considerations. *Professional psychology: Research and Practice, 20,* 153–158.

Vasquez, M. J. T. (1992). Psychologist as clinical supervisor: Promoting ethical practice. *Professional Psychology: Research and Practice, 23,* 196–202.

Welfel, E. R. (1992). Psychologist as ethics educator: Successes, failures, and unanswered questions. *Professional Psychology: Research and Practice, 23,* 182–189.

Zins, J. E., Murphy, J. J., & Wess, B. P. (1989). Supervision in school psychology: Current practices and congruence with professional standards. *School Psychology Review, 18,* 56–63.

ANNOTATED BIBLIOGRAPHY

Bernard, J. M., & Goodyear, R. K. (1992). *Fundamentals of clinical supervisor.* Boston: Allyn and Bacon.

Integrated review of supervision literature from several disciplines addresses professional responsibilities of evaluation, dealing with ethical and legal issues, and developing administrative and organizational skills. Personal and cultural attributes that affect the supervision process are discussed with a special focus on multicultural interactions. The text concludes with transcripts of supervision featuring several eminent psychologists.

National Association of School Psychologists. (1993). *Standards for the credentialing of school psychologists.* Washington, DC: Author.

This revision provides a continuum of supervision including face-to-face supervision, mentoring, and a continuing professional development plan. Two new standards are included: One lists the competencies required in the areas of professional work characteristics, knowledge base, and applied professional practice; the second provides requirements for receiving the NCSP credential.

National Association of School Psychologists. (1994). *Standards for training and field placement programs in school psychology.* Washington, DC: Author.

These standards reflect significant emphasis on knowledge-based and outcome-based training. Students should be prepared for the delivery of comprehensive, intervention-based services. One comprehensive standard for practica is included; practicum experiences are proposed in areas not previously required.

Stoltenberg, C. D., & Delworth, U. (1987). *Supervising counselors and therapists: A developmental approach.* San Francisco: Jossey-Bass.

Developmental levels of trainees are described over eight dimensions: intervention skills, assessment techniques, interpersonal assessment, client conceptualization, individual differences, theoretical orientation, treatment goals and plans, and professional ethics. Progress is traced by using three structures: awareness of self and others, motivation, and autonomy.

Vasquez, M. J. T. (1992). Psychologist as clinical supervisor: Promoting ethical practice. *Professional Psychology: Research and Practice, 23,* 196–202.

Supervisors are responsible for training in three areas: ethical knowledge and behavior, competency, and personal functioning. Vasquez provides a structure for ethical decision making. Supervisor ethics for provision of training and ethical interactions with supervisees are also presented.

APPENDIX A
Self-Assessment of Supervisor Skills and Knowledge

	Needs			Expert	
Teaching Skills					
Identify learning needs	1	2	3	4	5
Write learning goals	1	2	3	4	5
Devise instructional strategies	1	2	3	3	5
Present material didactically	1	2	3	4	5
Present material experientially to explain rationale of intervention	1	2	3	4	5
Evaluate learning	1	2	3	4	5
Comfort in authority role	1	2	3	4	5
Give constructive feedback	1	2	3	4	5
Intervention Skills					
Possess appropriate knowledge bases	1	2	3	4	5
Establish rapport	1	2	3	4	5
Create motivation	1	2	3	4	5
Challenge existing knowledge and attitudes	1	2	3	4	5
Facilitate exploration of skills	1	2	3	4	5
Facilitate exploration of feelings	1	2	3	4	5
Knowledge of interpersonal dynamics	1	2	3	4	5
Model appropriate skills	1	2	3	4	5
Respond with flexibility	1	2	3	4	5
Integrate data into case conceptualization	1	2	3	4	5
Consultation Skills					
Assess problem situation	1	2	3	4	5
Provide alternative interventions or case conceptualizations	1	2	3	4	5
Facilitate brainstorming	1	2	3	4	5
Encourage choices, responsibility	1	2	3	4	5
Function in collegial, collaborative manner	1	2	3	4	5
Manage group/team process	1	2	3	4	5
Commitment to Ethics and Equity					
Knowledge of current ethical standards	1	2	3	4	5
Skills in application of ethics to complex situations	1	2	3	4	5
Skills in enhancing the moral development of interns	1	2	3	4	5
Commitment to creating nonexploitative relationships	1	2	3	4	5
Commitment to equal opportunity	1	2	3	4	5

The following questions may be helpful in framing some of the important issues.

1. In which supervisory role do you have the most experience? Teacher, consultant, counselor? In which do you have the least experience?

2. What is your preferred style?

3. What feedback have you received about your supervision? For example, do you overexplain, are uninvolved, are too verbose, can give examples, are challenging as well as facilitative.

4. What strengths and limitations do you see in your supervision style? How might the strengths be used and the weaknesses by addressed?

5. With what types of learners (interns) are you most comfortable? Consider ethnic/cultural/racial/sexual preference/disability groups when you reflect upon this answer.

6. Can you remember an event of effective supervision you experienced during your training? Do you remember an ineffective incident? Describe the critical dimensions of each.

7. What did you look for in a supervisor? What worked best for you?

APPENDIX B
Psychology Intern Evaluation
Nebraska Internship Consortium in Professional Psychology

Date of Evaluation _____

Intern _____

Training Director _____

Directions: The ratings of the intern should be based upon actual observation and/or reports from staff, clients, families, etc. Circle the number of the scale that best describes the intern's competence. A description of scale points is provided below.

1 – Competence is considered to be in need of further training. Intern seems to lack basic professional maturation in this area. Skill development seems doubtful.

2.– Competence is currently considered below average, but supervision and experience are expected to develop the skill. Close supervision is required.

3 – Competence is at an average level for functioning with moderage supervision.

4 – Competence is assessed to be above average suggesting only a minimal need for supervision.

5 – Competence is very well developed and reflects a capacity for independent functioning with little or no supervision required.

No data – Insufficient information to make a rating at this time.

General Competencies

Rating   **Strengths/Comments**

1. Evaluation — Assessment

_____ Intellectual _____

_____ Social Emotional _____

_____ Interviewing Skills _____

_____ Behavioral Assessment _____

_____ Personality Assessment _____

_____ Curriculum-Based Assessment _____

_____ Environmental Assessment _____

_____ Neuropsychological Assessment _____

_____ Family Assessment _____

_____ Ability to Integrate Data _____

_____ Other _____

2. Intervention

_____ Practicality _____

_____ Appropriateness to Problems _____

_____ Specificity of Recommendations _____

_____ Conceptual Clarity _____

_____ Provision for Follow-up _____

_____ Implementation _____

_____ Actual Follow-up _____

_____ Flexibility _____

3. Communication and Collaboration

_____ Staff Conferencing   _____

_____ Parent Conferencing   _____

_____ Administrative Conferencing   _____

_____ Case Staffing   _____

_____ Report Writing   _____

_____ Use of Supervisory Input   _____

4. Consultation

_____ Problem/Need Identification   _____

_____ Plan Formulation   _____

_____ Plan Implementation   _____

_____ Follow-up and Evaluation   _____

_____ Family Consultation   _____

_____ Primary Caregiver Consultation   _____

_____ Staff Consultation   _____

5. Teaching/Workship Presentation Skills

_____ Planning   _____

_____ Implementation   _____

_____ Evaluation   _____

6. Interpersonal Skills

_____ Confidentiality   _____

_____ Enthusiasm   _____

_____ Dependability   _____

_____ Promptness   _____

_____ Creativity   _____

_____ Productivity   _____

Rapport with:

_____ clients   _____

_____ staff   _____

_____ parents   _____

7. Research/Program Evaluation

_____ Planning   _____

_____ Implementation   _____

_____ Provision for Subject Rights   _____

_____ Provision for Confidentiality   _____

8. Overall Rating of the Intern   1   2   3   4   5

Please summarize any intern strengths or weaknesses not mentioned on the above rating scale. Note any training experiences that should be planned for this intern.

_____
_____
_____
_____
_____
_____
_____
_____

I have read and understand this evaluation.

_____   _____

Psychology Intern   Date

APPENDIX C

Supervision Progress Notes

Notes to _____

From   _____

Date   _____

Regarding _____

_____

_____

_____

_____

_____

We discussed these concerns _____

_____

_____

_____

Possible strategies _____

_____

_____

_____

_____

	Effective	Not Effective
Tried 1.	_____	_____
2.	_____	_____
3.	_____	_____
4.	_____	_____

Comments on concern? New problem definition? or new information? _____

_____

_____

_____

_____

_____

11

Best Practices in Implementing a Staff Development Program

Susan K. Green
School District 5 of Lexington
and Richland Counties, South Carolina

OVERVIEW

Scope of Staff Development

Staff development is a concept that covers a wide variety of efforts in the schools to encourage education professionals to improve job performance. Definitions of staff development by a number of authorities have ranged from the relatively narrow concept of single in-service programs for teaching a particular skill, to comprehensive systems change efforts addressing basic philosophical shifts and redistribution of power in educational institutions. Griffin (1991), for example, suggests that "staff development is a serious and systematic effort to engage a group of professional educators who work together, a staff, in activities designed to increase the power and authority of their shared work" (p. 244).

The staff in staff development can involve educators from superintendents to teachers' aides. In this chapter, staff will refer to educators with direct, daily involvement with children such as teachers and school psychologists. A school psychologist might consult this chapter in a variety of situations — during change efforts such as when a broad school improvement effort is initiated by the district administration, when the school psychologist is asked to develop an in-service on classroom management techniques for teachers, when the school psychologist is asked to help plan a program to improve school management, or when a special education director wants to encourage an outcomes orientation among staff using curriculum-based measurement (CBM) and other progress-monitoring tools. This chapter can also be of use as school psychologists contemplate changes they would like to make toward best practices advocated in this volume. Whether the contemplated change is large or small, similar principles underlie efforts to encourage, instruct, support and evaluate changes in individual or organizational performance.

Justification for Staff Development

The need for staff development in the schools is indisputable. New knowledge about effective instruction, interventions, and content areas increases almost daily, so even the best-trained professional will need frequent updates over the years to stay current in best practices. In addition, the nature of students and the type of problems faced by educators is changing. Teachers are facing an increasing diversity of students with an incredible range of skills from the severely disabled to the gifted. More families are in financial difficulty and their communities are suffering economic recession. Schools are more and more responsible for their students' social as well as academic competence.

In addition, individuals and organizations need to change and learn if they are to succeed in accomplishing their goals or missions. This need is formally recognized by the increasing number of mandates in many states and national organizations (e.g., the NASP certification program) that require continuing education. Effective staff development can refresh and rekindle enthusiasm as new practices are implemented and found to solve problems. Many have argued that schools must foster learning for staff as well as students to be more effective institutions and to model the importance of lifelong learning.

It is also important to highlight that, whether using staff development to attempt broad or narrow changes within a school or a school system, the ultimate justification for any staff development effort is enhancing students' learning. As staff development projects are conceived and carried out, details and logistics can obscure or water down this goal. Keeping in mind the ultimate purpose from the beginning of any discussion of staff development, including this one, is crucial.

Importance of Context in Staff Development

In examining the staff development literature, it is clear that merely providing professionals with information about new knowledge or practices is woefully inadequate for producing behavior change in educators or improved learning in students. Since the early 1980s, authorities on staff development have called attention to the critical influence that context has on the success of change initiatives (Fullan, 1991; Hall & Hord, 1987). For example, because the in-service context is so different from the classroom context, skills needed for transferring learning that take into account these differences have recently been emphasized. Other contextual variables such as degree of administrative support and organizational climate are also seen as important for success. Changes in rewards and norms in the school context must accompany individual learning so that change toward new practices is seen as desirable. It is also contextually important to take into account the needs and experiences of the staff members involved in any staff development effort. Modifying a new program to fit these needs, which vary from school to school, can also help strengthen it. Considerable research and experience across disciplines have demonstrated that context must be taken into account for change to be lasting and successful (e.g., Rogers, 1983).

This chapter will address the issues involved in constructing a successful staff development program, emphasizing those elements of context that are important for producing lasting change. It will also describe basic issues to consider before initiating a staff development program, including taking account of the nature of adult learning, establishing a clear need for staff development, and securing administrative support. Next, the broad steps that many authorities have proposed as a sequence for optimal staff development efforts will be delineated. These include (a) identifying needs and priorities, (b) goal setting, (c) training and feedback, and (d) implementation, evaluation, and maintenance.

BASIC CONSIDERATIONS

Nature of Adult Learning

Before embarking on a staff development program, it is essential that the initiators acquire a background in the nature of adult learning. Moore (1988) has described factors that differentiate adult learning from children's learning that have implications for the design of staff development programs. She indicated that as people get older they are more frequently involved in self-directed learning efforts. That is, they can and do determine their own areas of weakness and take appropriate action to remedy them. Thus, staff developers should design programs that acknowledge and incorporate individuals' capacity for self-direction by encouraging participants to be in-

volved in determining the goals and content of a new program. She also suggested including program components that encourage independent study and, in general, create a collaborative atmosphere. Each of these suggestions is meant to establish a climate of respect for staff members' capacity for independent, self-motivated learning.

A second observation about adult learning with implications for staff development is the prominence of experiential learning for adults. As people get older, they accumulate countless experiences that are often drawn upon as a source of new learning and as a vivid context to which other sources of learning must be connected to be meaningful. Educators' first-hand experience with educating children is a valuable asset in any staff development program. Staff development programs should take advantage of participants' experiences, using them as basic building blocks in developing new skills and incorporating them into exercises or demonstrations. For example, staff members could be asked to use one of the students they have difficulty with in their class as an example to work on throughout an in-service on classroom management techniques. Such efforts can also help keep the new knowledge oriented toward action in the familiar context with an emphasis on problem solving.

On the other side of the coin, however, adult learners often are not willing to question or examine their implicit assumptions and the world view they may have constructed as a result of their sometimes insular learning path. Moore (1988) pointed out the need for staff development programs to encourage critical self-examination of educators' implicit assumptions and values related to their profession.

Perceived Need as a Foundation for Staff Development

Self-perceived needs of staff. Another basic consideration to address before a staff development effort is undertaken is clear evidence of a strongly felt need for it from the perspective of the target staff. A clear picture of these needs and the early incorporation of them whenever possible will help ensure success of a staff development effort by taking advantage of natural interest and motivation. Taking into account these needs does not imply limiting any staff development effort to what the staff wants, which might therefore implicitly endorse the status quo. However, if an effort is undertaken that is more ambitious than currently self-perceived needs would suggest, it is important to consider likely staff concerns and show how they can be addressed by the effort. The school psychologist or other change agent can also work to help identify a need that staff members may not have realized exists. For example, school psychologists who view the assessment for eligibility services that they provide as too narrow may wish to change their role. They could begin emphasizing useful prereferral services, discussing and providing such services to such a point that their success triggers a desire for more formal staff development to create a strong prereferral team and services.

Cultural values. Understanding the cultural values within the school or district targeted for staff development is another element of grounding staff development in the context of self-perceived staff needs. Kantor (1992) pointed out that it is important that staff developers examine their own implicit assumptions and make sure they are not diametrically opposed to those of the staff they are working with. As an example he contrasted "skills" versus "personal growth" approaches to writing instruction, pointing out how difficult it is for an adherent of one approach to work with advocates of the other. Kantor implied that a skills or a personal growth writing instruction model can pervade the way a school is organized, making a new model impossible to adapt. Even if staff are attracted to new approaches, they may sense that those approaches will not work in their present school context. Differences in unspoken beliefs, assumptions, and values can be uncovered and addressed if careful assessment of a staff's needs is undertaken before a staff development effort begins.

Organizational climate. Assessing the school's organizational climate — the effectiveness of its formal and informal procedures, communication processes, and norms — is another element to consider when examining the need for staff development. Research has shown that students' achievement is higher and innovations are more effective in schools with a more positive climate, as measured by good problem-solving and renewal capabilities, opportunities for teachers to learn and collaborate, and workplace commitment (Rosenholtz, 1989). It is useful for the staff developer to assess the organizational climate to see if the school or district has structures already in place to solve problems, make decisions, deal with conflict, and clarify communication. If a poor organizational climate exists, efforts to improve it can be built into the staff development project as they are relevant to the content of training. Organizational development, which is a conceptual framework for developing strategies to improve the functioning of organizations, has been used in schools and other organizations for many years (Schmuck, 1990). Schmuck and Runkel (1994) have reported that a recent trend promoted by the National Council on Staff Development is to integrate organizational development activities that improve climate with professional development related to acquiring new skills or changing educational procedures. For example, if a staff wants to develop a schoolwide discipline program, the staff developer can include exercises and information on improving decision making related to discipline and on effective conflict resolution. If a

staff wished to institute a weekly prereferral intervention team meeting, a staff developer could include components on running effective meetings and on techniques for successful role clarification.

Schmuck and Runkel (1994) have suggested a number of ways to assess organizational climate that are based on extensive research in organizational development. Informal observations can illuminate many aspects of the communication process, such as whether unpleasant feelings are shared only privately rather than at general staff meetings, whether trivial issues are discussed at length while important ones are ignored, and whether conflicts are appropriately resolved. More formalized methods such as systematic interviews and questionnaires can also be used to develop an overall picture of communication and organizational climate at a school. Schmuck and Runkel (1994) have suggested that school organizations that are most adaptable in constructively managing change exhibit four metaskills: *diagnosis*, which involves frequent formal and informal monitoring of organizational functioning; *gathering information and resources*, which involves searching out additional resources when information is not available to solve current problems; *mobilizing synergistic action*, which involves having staff members coordinate their actions in new patterns rather than initiating changes individually; and *monitoring the first three metaskills*, which involves frequent overall assessment of whether the staff is using the first three skills to move in the direction they would like to go.

Administrative Support as a Foundation for Staff Development

Another important preliminary consideration is determining the extent of administrative support for any staff development effort. The need for a multi-level orientation to staff development is essential, according to many staff development experts (e.g., Pink & Hyde, 1992). Pink and Hyde, in analyzing a group of staff development case studies, recommended that representatives at the levels of principal and central office staff — as well as targets of staff development efforts who will be working directly with students — be involved at the outset of every staff development effort. They provide the support necessary to sustain a change effort, such as smoothing logistical problems and providing incentives. Also, if principals and other administrators are not involved, it communicates that the staff development effort has a low priority, so staff are unlikely to view the changes being sought as important. The important role of supervisors such as principals is dramatically illustrated in a study of implementation of problem-solving consultation conducted by Reschly and Flugum (1993). They found that if staff development participants had supervisors who expected them to complete cases by the new methods and if these expectations were incorporated into their annual personnel evaluations, 84% of the participants incorporated the new procedures. If there was no such support and operationalized expectation, only 13% incorporated new procedures. These findings highlight the need for administrative support clearly specified in concrete ways. The best time to secure that support is to build it in from the inception of any new change effort.

Attending to perceived need on the part of the staff and securing strong administrative support are both crucial to successful staff development. Sometimes such a broad base of support is not possible and a more informal person-by-person approach is the only alternative. However, staff developers agree that the changes needed in norms and incentive patterns to make change desirable entail a supportive organization as well as enhanced individual skills. A great deal of research on school change suggests that successful change requires both "top-down" and "bottom-up" efforts and support (e.g., Bullard & Taylor, 1993), and this dual approach should be pursued whenever possible.

Time as a Basic Consideration

Change takes time, usually more time than people estimate. Pink and Hyde (1992) concluded from their analysis of staff development case studies that providing sufficient time for planning and implementing staff development efforts is central to success. They have suggested that for serious change, people should adjust their estimates from months to years. Developing a clear sense among all involved of exactly what should change and how it can best be accomplished is necessary — what Fullan (1991) termed "shared meaning." Collaboration, reflection, practice, and preparation all contribute to the development of shared meaning and occur only gradually over time. For changes to be long-lasting and successful, ideas and practices from outside must be incorporated into and adapted to the context in which the staff work and the practices the staff already have.

BEST PRACTICES IN IMPLEMENTING A STAFF DEVELOPMENT PROGRAM

This section will be organized according to broad steps many authorities have described as a logical sequence for staff development efforts. The principles to consider as well as the general activities involved will be discussed within each of these steps. Table 1 presents an overview of the steps, the issues involved at each step, and sample activities.

Step 1: Identification of Needs and Priorities

Identifying the needs and priorities for a new staff development effort must be handled with care but also with efficiency. A staff developer must balance the needs of the staff, the administration, and

other interested groups, whose perspectives are very different and, therefore, whose ideas about what is needed may conflict. Involving staff members is essential in this process because it helps them "own" the staff development effort, and it gives them an appreciation for the kinds of conflicting ideas that must be melded into one program that has as its ultimate goal enhancing students' learning. Self-perceived needs of the staff, organizational climate and philosophy, and administrative support are issues that must be explored thoroughly in the identification of needs and priorities step.

Schmuck and Runkel (1994) have described a systematic problem-solving technique that can be used as part of the process of identifying needs and priorities for a staff development effort. They have suggested that a problem exists when there is a discrepancy between the present circumstances or situation and the ideal situation the staff would like to achieve. The problem is solved — or, in this case, the focus of the staff development effort is clarified — when a path is chosen between the present situation and the target.

The following are the steps relevant to the process of identifying needs and priorities.

Come to agreement on the problem. Staff members come to consensus on the nature of the present situation (e.g., that discipline is inconsistent at their school, that rates of student infraction of discipline rules are too high, and that staff members feel the need for additional training in classroom and playground management). They must also agree on feasible targets (e.g., to increase the management skills of the staff, to implement a schoolwide discipline program, and to increase students' rule following). Systematic gathering of data is important at this step. To assist in this process, devising a questionnaire that asks the staff to rate their own degree of competency and their degree of interest in a list of skills, for example, is one technique that could systematically provide input from many people (Frase, 1992). Oldroyd and Hall (1991) also have suggested staff development interviews, which can be more flexible and personalized, a consideration that is especially important in more comprehensive staff development efforts. At the school level, holding group discussions can provide illuminating information. In summarizing both qualitative and quantitative data, Oldroyd and Hall have cautioned that the criteria for analyzing information and establishing priorities should be developed and agreed upon by everyone beforehand so that the outcome will be seen as fair.

Generate alternative paths. Staff members come up with alternative plans for moving from the present situation to the target. Brainstorming and using outside resources can be especially helpful at this step. For example, staff members may suggest several types of discipline techniques they would like

TABLE 1
Steps, Issues, and Activities in a Staff Development Program

Steps	Issues	Activities
1. Identify needs and priorities	Staff self-perceived needs Organizational climate Organizational philosophy Administrative support	Gather and summarize data (e.g., surveys, interviews, staff meetings)
2. Goal setting	Specific goals Staff participation in goal setting Frequent feedback	Quantify goals Specify measurement Specify time frame
3. Training and practice	Executive control Shared meaning	Present effective techniques Present specific information Incorporate practice and feedback Build in choice and control Incorporate stages of concern
4. Implementation, evaluation, and maintenance	Formative and summative evaluation Nonjudgmental follow-up Change as a process not an event	Schedule group meetings that incorporate regular feedback Express administrative support Celebrate

to study in small groups; alternatively they may suggest attending professional conferences and workshops. They might also suggest examining schoolwide discipline plans from other schools in their state.

List helping and hindering forces. Staff members describe forces that will foster or interfere with efforts to reach the target. For example, helping forces could include technical assistance from faculty at a local university, administrative support, or skills some members of the staff already have. Hindering forces could include lack of skill on the part of staff members, a vacillating principal, or a poor organizational climate.

Choose action steps. Staff members choose helping forces to mobilize and they work on eliminating or reducing hindering forces. For example, the staff could decide to hold a series of in-services on classroom management that focuses on the skills the group feels they need most. They could also decide to stage a series of meetings with the principal to clarify discipline policy and to have an organizational development expert serve as facilitator.

The examples involving school discipline described above illustrate the process of identifying needs and priorities from within a school. This process can also be undertaken by an outside staff developer. As part of the process, it is crucial for the staff developer, whether an insider or an outsider, to have a good picture of the environment in which the staff development program will take place. Awareness of the organizational climate and the philosophies of the staff, knowledge of who the opinion leaders (or influential people) are among the staff, and a

clear understanding of the administration and its priorities as they may affect the topic of the staff development program can be keys to ensuring success.

Step 2: Goal Setting

After forming a clear picture of the needs to be addressed in the staff development program, setting concrete goals that provide focus is essential. Effective goal setting at the level of the district, the school, and especially the individual is the step that ensures that staff members will focus on outcomes related to tangible changes in behavior rather than viewing inservices or other staff development efforts as largely a more vague broadening of horizons. Goals should be developed in the context of district priorities, and they should be established with a clear connection to daily work. For teachers, goals can be developed relating to their own actions in the classroom (e.g., incorporating a review of classroom rules in morning opening exercises each day; monitoring at least three students' reading progress using CBM or other means). Schoolwide goals can also build on and interweave with individual goals (e.g., reduce office referrals for rule breaking by 50% by June; increase the number of third graders reading over 100 words per minute by 20% by December). To be effective, these goals must later be used for evaluation to determine whether the program has been successful. They can also be incorporated into performance evaluations and other naturally occurring assessments in the school context.

Principles of effective goal setting. Much research on the effectiveness of goal setting has been conducted by industrial/organizational psychologists.

Research on organizations has shown unequivocally that specific goals improve performance on the job. Locke and Latham (1984) have summarized this research by highlighting the most effective principles involved in successful goal setting. First, having a *specific goal* provides a clear objective to pursue that is not available with vague exhortations to "Do your best." Second, *participation* in goal setting by the staff greatly increases acceptance of the goal. If people participate in setting a goal, they are more likely to accept the goal as legitimate than if it is assigned by their supervisor. People are more committed to choices in which they have a say. Third, *feedback* on progress toward goals improves performance because feedback provides a benchmark for judging behavior.

Procedures for successful goal setting. Locke and Latham (1984) have recommended that goal setting procedures involve (a) choosing a difficult but attainable goal and quantifying it, (b) specifying how performance will be measured, and (c) specifying the time span involved. From extensive research, they have concluded that "goals facilitate performance in four ways: they direct attention and action, they mobilize energy, they increase persistence, and they motivate the development of appropriate task strategies" (p. 26).

Use of specific goals helps a staff come up with measurable and verifiable actions and outcomes that should flow from the staff development program. Spending time on goals up front makes implementation, evaluation, and maintenance of change much easier because criteria for success have already been established. As people gradually move toward their goals their progress can be monitored, and the gap between the goal and current performance can be used for continued training and improvement. Also, clear expectations can reduce anxiety and misunderstanding among staff who are learning new techniques and behaviors.

Step 3: Training and Feedback

Several principles have proven effective in the design of training for successful staff development. Perhaps the most important of these is the need to ensure that the training transfers from the training context back to the everyday school context. To elaborate this principle, Joyce and Showers (1983) have discussed the important concept of "executive control," which they define as

> understanding the purpose and rationale of the skill and knowing how to adapt it to students, apply it to subject matter, modify or create instructional materials attendant to its use, organize students to use it, and blend it with other instructional approaches to develop a smooth and powerful whole. (p. 8)

Joyce and Showers maintain that in many jobs (the military, the factory assembly line) standard operating procedures are developed so that workers exercise their own judgment as little as possible. In education professions, however, people are called upon to use their own judgment frequently and there are few standard operating procedures; thus "executive" skills are required. As a result, any staff development training cannot simply enumerate a set of skills or standard operating procedures. Transferring skills in which judgment and adaptation must be relied upon must also be explicitly trained.

Executive control is developed by first working on a skill, then practicing it in the workplace while feedback and coaching are provided. These kinds of additional activities allow staff members to develop the conceptual framework for integrating new skills into current practice, to alter or eliminate other practices that interfere with them, and to exercise judgment effectively. For example, in the early stages of developing a schoolwide discipline program, after deciding what behaviors represent following school rules, teachers might collaborate in pairs at recess, taking turns at working with children (e.g., providing behavior-specific praise, using agreed-on correction procedures) and observing (e.g., providing feedback on the consistency and fairness of the other teacher's actions).

In a comprehensive review of the literature on staff development, Showers, Joyce, and Bennett (1987) concluded that the most effective staff development efforts did indeed involve not only presentation of information, but also demonstrations and opportunities for practice and feedback. They suggested that the practice and feedback components give staff members more of a chance to develop the judgment skills that permit them to use new methods appropriately and adapt them to their needs. The concept of executive control echoes the principle of shared meaning. Both highlight the complexity involved in the gradual process of incorporating new ideas and practices into a preexisting system.

Within the broad framework of developing executive control as a goal, several principles are useful in designing staff development presentations. It is important to note that the major responsibility for designing and conducting such presentations should rest with the presenter, because research has shown that training is more effective when presenters rather than participants are in charge.

Present effective techniques. Given the high investment of time and resources in staff development training, it is essential that any new techniques the staff learns have been proven effective through appropriate research. Education has been prey to many fads, and it is important that new practices be grounded in careful research showing positive effects on students' learning. In addition, Guskey (1985) and others have pointed out that changes in educators' attitudes toward specific new practices occur only after they have seen them improve their own students' outcomes. Thus, for comprehensive attitude change to take place, the new strategies being learned must work. Guskey's model also suggests that spending too much time on getting commitment from staff before the staff development effort is under way can be fruitless. Comprehensive commitment to any particular new methods comes only after the staff sees that they work in their own school. Guskey's perspective particularly emphasizes the need for teaching only well-documented, effective techniques in staff development training.

Present well-defined, concrete, and specific information. The staff development literature suggests that the more explicit and concrete the material presented, the more clearly it is understood and assimilated by staff (Duttweiler, 1989; Hinson, Caldwell, & Landrum, 1989). Vague concepts end up even vaguer as they go through the complex process of interpersonal communication that is intended to foster shared meaning. The first elements of every staff development training should involve demonstration and presentation of information. Demonstration can include descriptive case examples, videotapes, and modeling of sample problems and their solutions. For example, when teaching educators to make graphs for monitoring students' reading progress over time, it is important to explicitly describe the rationale, to lay out the measurement system, to explain the scale used for labeling the graph, and to walk through several examples. One should not automatically assume that everyone is familiar with the conventions of graphing. Similarly, when designing and implementing a schoolwide discipline program, it is important to provide concrete steps for teaching the rules to children by demonstrating the use of examples of appropriate and of inappropriate behaviors. Detailed presentations of information and demonstrations are a necessary building block for later steps in staff development training. Before techniques and strategies can be used effectively, the foundations and actual procedures involved must be unambiguously established.

In this regard it is helpful to provide written materials and worksheets to accompany any presentation. It can also be helpful to solicit oral and written feedback from staff development participants. If participants write down their questions, concerns, and reactions to presentations, in regular "reaction papers," the staff developer can get a clearer picture of how they are thinking about the material and can plan future sessions to address appropriate concerns and reexplain difficult concepts.

Provide opportunities for practice and feedback. In a comprehensive review of the effectiveness of in-service education, Wade (1984) concluded that four types of in-service instruction are significantly more effective than others: observation of actual classroom practices, microteaching, video/audio feedback, and practice. (Instructional methods that appeared to be much less effective included discussion, lecture, games/simulations, and guided field trips, which perhaps have the potential to stray more easily from the goals of the training to something more rambling and less focused.) The first of these — observation — is important for clear, concrete presentation of new techniques, as discussed in the previous section. The other three techniques identified by Wade provide structured, task-oriented opportunities for educators to experiment with new practices and reflect on them in their typical context, prerequisites for developing executive control. An example of a somewhat casual use of such opportunities is trying out techniques in the classroom or other setting and informally noting the effects on students. Microteaching, in contrast, involves teachers preparing and teaching a short lesson (5–20 min.) to a small group of students, which is taped to provide feedback. Structured peer critiquing in which constructive feedback is provided after a staff member is observed while trying out new strategies in the typical context also can be helpful in integrating new techniques into everyday practices.

Other authors have recommended coaching (e.g., Joyce & Showers, 1982), in which a more experienced colleague assists a less experienced colleague in learning new practices, providing companionship, feedback, and analysis. Such coaching must have structured and goal-oriented sessions, a mutually respectful relationship, and built-in efforts to foster the independence of the trainee. In any case, most authors agree that practice and feedback arranged through opportunities for structured interaction are crucial for effective training that promotes executive control.

Research has also shown that one-shot in-services are rarely as effective as ongoing staff development efforts. The need for practice and feedback before new techniques can be incorporated into a staff's everyday practice explains why one-session efforts can fail. Building on experience and encouraging cumulative learning over time enhances stronger commitment and deeper learning of new skills.

Build in staff choice and control. Because adult learners have the capacity to be self-directed in pursuing their own learning needs, some element of choice and control needs to be built into staff development training efforts to convey respect and to take into account expressed interests. Once the overall goals of the staff development effort are chosen and agreed upon, staff participation comes into play in the process of practice and feedback. For example, in staff development training on classroom management, teachers could choose which students in their rooms or periods of the day to focus on while in practice and feedback phases. In an effort to implement cooperative learning, teachers could choose which subject area and how diverse a group they will work with in implementing a new group activity. These types of choice allow staff members to set their own level of challenge and to decide where current practice can best be modified.

In addition, staff choice and control can be incorporated into broader types of change in a district. For example, in developing a new districtwide special education effort to monitor students' progress, teachers could choose monitoring material and the form the graphs will take. Getting staff feedback on new procedures can help improve the procedures and adapt them to the needs of the school or district as well as help make the staff members feel included. The perception of choice and control has been shown in extensive psychological research to be an important determinant of a sense of well-being (e.g., Yates & Aronson, 1983). The types of choice and control, however, need not always be major or dramatic. For example, energy conservation researchers have found that consumers are much more willing to install automatic day–night thermostats if they are designed to allow people to override the system temporarily, even if the override system is never actually used.

Incorporate staff stages of concern. Hall and Hord (1987) have developed the Concerns-Based Adoption Model, a conceptual model describing the process educators go through as they experience change. Their model is based on the assumption that the point of view of the participants in the change process is crucial to success, and it is up to staff developers to systematically probe and understand these concerns. One element of their model, the stages of concern, is particularly helpful in designing staff development training.

Hall and Hord have suggested that change is a personal experience for each individual involved, and people go through predictable developmental stages as they respond to it. At each stage different perceptions, motivations, and feelings predominate, so it is important for staff developers to address the appropriate concerns and adjust their presentations to them. The first stage of awareness involves *self concerns*. The early level of this stage involves general awareness and interest in learning about new practices. Concerns at this level can also be defensive — doubts about one's adequacy to handle new techniques, potential conflicts generated, and status implications of the change. *Task concerns*, the next level of the model, involves focusing on managing new procedures, such as scheduling and logistics, efficiently. At the last level, *impact concerns*, staff members become concerned primarily with cooperating with others to implement the change and impacting students in the most effective way.

To learn about the concerns participants have and to classify them into stages, staff developers can analyze written answers to open-ended questions (e.g., When you think about this change, what are your concerns? How does this change affect you?), or engage in "one-legged conferences." One-legged conferences involve brief, informal checks (e.g., passing in the hall or lunchroom) on how the new program is going that provide an opportunity to get a sense of the staff member's concerns. The questioner then follows up by doing something to respond to the concerns expressed. One-legged conferences take advantage of typical casual encounters that staff developers often have with staff. This kind of work is especially important when the staff development effort is starting to focus on practice and feedback elements. For example, if a teacher mentions in passing that he or she is having difficulty helping students understand the rule "Respect others," the consultant working on a schoolwide discipline plan with the staff could jot down a few suggestions that had been effective for other teachers and put them in the teacher's mailbox. Hall and Hord (1987) have reported that success or failure of staff development programs can hinge on the use of one-legged conferences to encourage and support the staff who are initiating the new projects. Such conferences can be especially helpful for providing quick feedback related to the change, for correcting erroneous impressions, or for adding a crucial piece of information that could have been missed in the first exposure to the new material.

Perhaps the most crucial stage for this kind of personalized interaction is the self concerns stage, when individuals may be feeling uncertain or inadequate about the change and have the potential to respond defensively and reject the change to maintain self-esteem. In the competition between familiar and new patterns, the familiar usually wins out unless the incentives to embrace the new are potent. Frequent interpersonal contact can help keep the incentives salient. Also, when encouraging people to adopt new behaviors, personal contact is more effective than more impersonal means because it can target the concerns that have surfaced at the moment. Change is always accompanied by ambiguity, and it is important to keep track of people's concerns so that the uncertainty doesn't mushroom into elaboration of worst-case scenarios and rejection of the new ideas.

Step 4: Implementation, Evaluation, and Maintenance

Implementation. When new procedures are ready to be implemented after early rounds of training, practice, and feedback, mechanisms for continued interaction and feedback must be in place. A nonthreatening, nonjudgmental stance is essential for such support to be effective. Continuation of one-legged conferences can be helpful, but more formalized procedures may also be called for. Regular small-group meetings in which problems are discussed and solved or a mentor system in which more experienced colleagues meet regularly with newer staff members to work on implementation issues are two possibilities. Incorporated in such a process should be regular feedback to staff members on the individual and group goals chosen at the beginning of the staff development effort. For example, once a school-wide discipline plan has been implemented, teachers should continue meeting regularly to review patterns in data collected on playground referrals to make sure they are moving toward target rates. They can also review teaching and correction procedures that prove to be problematic, and they can deal with other issues that arise in day-to-day practice. A key element of such efforts is to encourage an atmosphere of collaborative problem solving at the school to reduce staff isolation.

As new practices are implemented, it is also important for administrators to demonstrate support for the new activities. Such support can be shown by providing participating staff members access to resources such as additional materials or release time for planning. Administrators can also offer encouragement and recognition by keeping abreast of the changes, showing an interest in how things are going, and providing incentives for goal attainment.

Evaluation. With implementation comes the need for evaluation. An obvious source of information is *summative evaluation:* examining whether the goals defined when the project was first developed have been met. For example, determining whether classroom and schoolwide discipline referrals have decreased would be useful at a school where the staff development effort focused on teaching children schoolwide rules. Examining whether students are reading more fluently would be useful at a school where the staff development effort focused on implementing a new progress-monitoring system.

In addition, *formative* evaluation also is needed to address how and to what degree new practices are being implemented and adapted by the staff and whether progress toward ultimate goals is being made. Direct observation of the extent to which new practices are in place can be helpful. For example, observing in the classroom how often teachers discussed, modeled, or taught classroom rules or examining graphs of students' academic data to determine whether progress was being correctly monitored would provide information on the extent of implementation of new procedures in the examples above. To get the most accurate information, such data should be gathered directly through observation rather than second-hand through questionnaires.

Gathering formative evaluation data is important for diagnosing weak spots that need improving. It also provides reinforcement to participants who can profit from formative feedback showing they are making progress toward their goals. It can also be used to show that the new procedures were, in fact, implemented with fidelity and that any outcomes can truly be attributed to the staff development effort rather than to extraneous variables.

Maintenance. Many staff development writers cite Hall and Hord's (1987) basic assertion that change is a process not an event. Implementation of a staff development effort is not an event that abruptly grinds to a halt after objectives have been met. The staff development effort that has been well integrated into the school's, or the school district's, mission should move easily to a maintenance phase in which new practices are integrated into the staff's daily behavior and monitoring continues. This phase involves continuing support for staff. For example, Killion and Kaylor (1991) have described follow-up techniques that involve regular group meetings focused on problem solving, feedback, and assistance for implementers. These kinds of groups can also provide a mechanism for monitoring or enhancing organizational climate. They can help people feel they are an important part of the project's success and can promote job satisfaction. Continuing leadership and enthusiasm by administrators is also important. Regular supervision and evaluation of staff incorporates goals developed as part of the staff development effort. In addition, particular attention to the continuing impact on the students' learning is important.

Finally, at the maintenance phase (and at other phases as well) it is important for the staff to celebrate its successes. Recognizing people for their accomplishments with, for example, a round of applause at staff meetings, a letter from the principal, an announcement in the newspaper or school newsletter, or special certificates, can go a long way toward validating people and their efforts to improve the schools they work in. It is important to recognize and honor staff members who go the extra mile and take on the challenges that staff development can bring into the already complex world of the school.

SUMMARY

Staff development covers a wide variety of efforts in the schools to encourage education professionals to improve job performance. The ultimate justification for any staff development effort is to enhance the students' learning. Since the early 1980s, educational leaders have come to understand that the overall context in which staff development occurs influences the success of any effort. For example, it is crucial to establish a clear need for staff development on the part of the staff involved, and it is essential to secure strong administrative support for staff development efforts.

The preliminary steps in implementing a staff development effort include (a) Identifying needs and priorities of the staff, and (b) Setting goals for feedback and evaluation. Designing and implementing the training is the next step. A major consideration when designing staff development training is the need to address the transfer of new knowledge from the training back to the everyday context. To this end, staff development experts have suggested that specific, effective techniques be presented in training with plenty of structured and informal opportunities for practice and feedback. It is also important to build in choice and control for the staff during training activities and to tailor training to the needs and concerns that staff express at different stages of the learning process. The final (but ongoing) step in staff development efforts combines implementation, evaluation, and maintenance activities. Ongoing formative and summative evaluation is encouraged at this step as well as continued administrative and collaborative peer support. As the new staff development program is maintained, an emphasis on celebration and recognition of accomplishments is helpful.

ACKNOWLEDGMENTS

The author gratefully acknowledges the assistance of Lisa Habedank, Dan Johnston, William Kentta, Mollie McKibben, William Mills, Kelly Powell-Smith, Richard Schmuck, and three anonymous reviewers in the preparation of this chapter.

REFERENCES

Bullard, P., & Taylor, B. (1993). *Making school reform happen.* New York: Allyn and Bacon.

Burke, P., Heidman, R., & Heidman, C. (1990). *Programming for staff development.* London: Falmer.

Duttweiler, P. C. (1989). Components of an effective professional development program. *Journal of Staff Development, 10*(2), 2–6.

Frase, L. (1992). *Maximizing people power in schools.* Newbury Park, CA: Corwin.

Fullan, M. (1991). *The new meaning of educational change.* New York: Teachers College Press.

Griffin, G. A. (1991). Interactive staff development: Using what we know. In A. Lieberman & L. Miller (Eds.), *Staff development for education in the 90's* (pp. 243–258). New York: Teachers College Press.

Guskey, T. (1985). Staff development and teacher change. *Educational Leadership, 42*, 57–60.

Hall, G., & Hord, S. (1987). *Change in schools: Facilitating the process.* Albany, NY: State University of New York Press.

Hinson, S., Caldwell, M., & Landrum, M. (1989). Characteristics of effective staff development programs. *Journal of Staff Development, 10*(2), 48–52.

Joyce, B., & Showers, B. (1982). The coaching of teachers. *Educational Leadership, 40*, 4–10.

Joyce, B., & Showers, B. (1983). *Power in staff development through research on training.* Alexandria, VA: Association for Supervision and Curriculum Development.

Kantor, K. (1992). Cultural conflicts in staff development of the teaching of writing. In W. Pink & A. Hyde (Eds.), *Effective staff development for school change* (pp. 139–151). Norwood, NJ: Albex.

Killion, J. P., & Kaylor, B. (1991). Follow-up: The key to training for transfer. *Journal of Staff Development, 12*(1), 64–66.

Locke, E., & Latham, G. (1984). *Goal setting: A motivational technique that works!* Englewood Cliffs, NJ: Prentice-Hall.

Moore, J. (1988). Guidelines concerning adult learning. *Journal of Staff Development, 9*(3), 2–5.

Oldroyd, D., & Hall, V. (1991). *Managing staff development: A handbook for secondary schools.* London: Paul Chapman.

Pink, W., & Hyde, A. (1992). Doing effective staff development. In W. Pink & A. Hyde (Eds.), *Effective staff development for school change* (pp. 259–292). Norwood, NJ: Albex.

Reschly, D., & Flugum, K. (1993). *Effects of protocol-based problem solving on intervention quality and resolution of classroom learning and behavior problems.* Paper presented at the National Association of School Psychologists convention, Washington, DC.

Rogers, E. (1983). *Diffusion of innovations.* New York: Free Press.

Rosenholtz, S. (1989). *Teachers' workplace: The social organization of schools.* New York: Longman.

Schmuck, R. (1990). Organization development in schools: Contemporary concepts and practices. In T. Gutkin & C. Reynolds (Eds.), *The handbook of school psychology* (3rd ed.; pp. 899–919). New York: Wiley.

Schmuck, R., & Runkel, P. (1994). *The handbook of organization development in schools* (4th ed.). Palo Alto, CA: Mayfield.

Showers, B., Joyce, B., & Bennett, B. (1987). Synthesis of research on staff development: A framework for future study and a state-of-the-art analysis. *Educational Leadership, 45*, 77–80, 82–87.

Wade, R. (1984). What makes a difference in inservice teacher education? A meta-analysis of research. *Educational Leadership, 42*, 48–54.

Yates, S., & Aronson, E. (1983). A social psychological perspective on energy conservation in residential buildings. *American Psychologist, 38*, 435–444.

ANNOTATED BIBLIOGRAPHY

Brandt, R. S. (1989). *Coaching and staff development.* Alexandria, VA: Association for Supervision and Curriculum Development. This book contains readings from the journal Educational Leadership that pertain to staff development. Articles are divided into sections on building a culture for professional growth, research on teaching, research on staff development, collegiality, and coaching.

Caldwell, S. J. (1989). *Staff development: A handbook of effective practices.* Oxford, OH: National Staff Development Council. This book provides discussions of basic issues in staff development organized around themes of process, content, and context. Chapters on process address how training is designed and how enthusiasm is sustained. Chapters on content address use of research methods and content. Chapters on context discuss the interplay of district, school, and individual needs.

The *Journal of Staff Development*, which appears quarterly, provides many interesting, timely articles on a wide variety of aspects of staff development. Two recent articles provided general themes for effective staff development programs (see Duttweiler, 1989, and Hinson et al. 1989 in the reference section). The journal also provides descriptions of successful staff development programs (e.g., on multicultural education or instructional changes), think pieces on general issues (e.g., the balance between process and content; influencing decision makers), and articles on specific elements of staff development (e.g., follow-up activities, in-service presentations).

Locke, E., & Latham, G. (1984). *Goal setting: A motivational technique that works!* Englewood Cliffs, NJ: Prentice-Hall.
This book summarizes the goal-setting literature in organizational psychology and lays out the most effective methods for goal setting. The chapters on how to set goals, how to obtain commitment to goals, and how to implement goal setting are particularly helpful for implementing goal-setting techniques as part of a staff development effort.

Schmuck, R. A., & Runkel, P. J. (1994). *The handbook of organizational development in schools* (3rd ed.). Palo Alto, CA: Mayfield.
This thorough handbook provides a guide to using organizational development techniques to improve communication and help schools solve interpersonal problems. Step-by-step techniques are provided with sample exercises and interesting examples of these techniques in action in schools. Helpful chapters on improving meetings, working with conflict, and clarifying communication can assist in improving organizational climate.

12

Best Practices in Applied Reseach

Timothy Z. Keith
Alfred University

Why bother with a chapter on research? Conventional wisdom is that school psychologists are not interested in conducting research and that many are antagonistic toward research. Yet my experiences teaching and conducting workshops on research and writing about research for the practitioner-oriented journal, *School Psychology Review*, lead me to believe that the conventional wisdom may be conventional but it is not wise. Many school psychologists have expressed an interest in conducting research in applied settings and many more want to do a better job of incorporating others' research into their daily practice. Both of these are appropriate research roles for school psychologists.

For the purpose of this chapter, research is defined as activities designed to produce new scientific knowledge or to use that knowledge to improve school psychological practice. Three hierarchical research roles for school psychology are indicated:

1. All school psychologists should strive to be competent *consumers* of research. The types of people we serve, our methods and our instruments, and our roles are constantly changing. At the same time, there are always plenty of bandwagons tempting us to hop aboard. The best way to stay abreast of current developments while avoiding bandwagons is the careful reading of research. Research tells us which good ideas really *do* work.

2. There is also a need for a smaller number of school psychologists to act as *distributors* (or synthesizers or disseminators) of research. They may read research relevant to a topic of interest and summarize and draw conclusions from it for other interested groups, such as other psychologists or a Board of Education.

3. Some school psychologists are interested in performing the role normally considered research: *conducting* research of interest to themselves, their colleagues, or their employers.

The three roles are hierarchical because one needs to be an effective consumer of research to summarize and distribute it effectively, and one needs to be able to summarize research to be an effective conductor of research.

As an example, consider three school psychologists interested in the effectiveness of study-skills instruction. John, a research consumer, is interested in study-skills instruction as an educational intervention for a low-achieving child. He reads research to find out if study-skills instruction is generally effective in improving achievement, which methods of instruction are available, and whether some methods are generally more effective than others, particularly with children similar to the one John is working with. Elaine, a research distributor, is asked by her superintendent to investigate whether it would be worthwhile to teach study skills to incoming high school students and, if so, which approach would be most effective. Finally, Carolyn conducts research comparing the achievement of students in her district who were taught study skills to those who were not.

BASIC CONSIDERATIONS

The Consumer of Research

Although social science research is often contradictory, it is also the one way we have of putting aside our hopes and prejudices and testing whether an intervention works or not. To serve children well, psychological practice needs to be consistent with research findings. Yet research is contradictory, and much research is of poor quality and limited applicability. School psychologists thus need to evaluate the research they read in order to separate the good from the bad.

To evaluate research, one asks two essential questions. Did the research demonstrate anything, and is it applicable to my situation? The training needed to become a competent consumer of research is not extensive and is probably included in most specialist-level school psychology programs. Basic statistics, research, and measurement courses, which focus on a *conceptual* at least as much as a numerical understanding, are needed. Unfortunately, many such courses continue to be taught as if most students were going to be conducting research rather than reading and evaluating it: More attention is needed toward the *evaluation* and use of others' research. Single-case research methods also need more coverage; this is one research method that practitioners need to use, but its coverage is spotty. The primary resource needed by consumers of research is access to relevant journals.

The Distributor of Research

Although all school psychologists should strive to incorporate research results into their practice, all do not need to integrate and distribute research to others nor conduct research. Whether one becomes a distributor or conductor of research should be a matter of choice and job description.

Research distributors first need to be good research consumers and they additionally need experience sifting through and integrating research findings which may be rather diverse and inconsistent. Their formal training should also include at least basic courses in research, statistics, and measurement and, at least as important, guided experience in integrating and summarizing research. All doctoral and many specialist-level psychologists should have this level of training and at least some experience, at minimum, when writing a thesis or dissertation.

Research distributors need access to a wider range of journals and other sources of research: conferences at which research is presented, the ERIC Document Reproduction Service, and *Psychological Abstracts*. Electronic data bases such as ERIC and PsycLit — to be discussed in more detail later in this chapter — can enhance greatly the effectiveness of research distributors by providing the ability to search a broad range of journals. Access to a university library is also extremely useful.

The Conductor of Research

It is well known that not all school psychologists are interested in conducting research, but this role should — and often is — available to psychologists with the appropriate interest and training. Again, these roles are seen as hierarchical; one needs to be a competent distributor of research in order to be a good conductor of research, because the conclusions drawn from previous research should guide the research conductor's efforts.

The formal training of those who plan to conduct research needs to be more extensive and should include a series of research methods and statistics courses. Nevertheless, most doctoral level and some specialist level psychologists have completed such coursework, to interest and experience tend to be more limiting. Probably the best training for this role is to assist someone else in several research projects or to conduct several research projects under supervision (in addition to a thesis or dissertation). A graduate research assistantship or some sort of research apprenticeship can be extremely valuable.

The conductor of research needs access to the same resources as the distributor of research: research publications and a good library. In addition, most psychologists who conduct research need access to a computer with a good statistical analysis program.

BEST PRACTICES

Consumers

Reading and evaluating research. Consumers of research read and evaluate research as a means of improving their practice. To perform this role one must, of course, have access to relevant research. Consumers must also be able to evaluate the research they read. Much research in the social sciences is contradictory, and an effort to find the research answer to a question of practice can be quite frustrating. I do not believe this inconsistency means that research cannot inform practice. It does mean however, that *evaluation* of the research is necessary.

Journals, the primary source of research, accept only a fraction of the articles submitted for publication, thus supposedly ensuring that the research they do publish is of high enough quality to deserve our trust. Nevertheless, much research, even that published in good journals, is not good research:

- Research problems are poorly conceived or are trivial.

- Samples are small and poorly selected.

- Inappropriate statistics are used or mistakes are made in calculating and reporting statistics.

- Research designs are weak and do not rule out plausible alternative hypotheses.

- Designs do not fit the purpose of the research or do not test the hypotheses the researcher wants to test.

Even when research is well-conceived and conducted, there are problems of interpretation. Most researchers have been guilty of overblown conclusions that extend well beyond what might reasonably be concluded by the results, but more subtle problems are common as well. It is not unusual, for example, for a discussion to address a different issue than that addressed by the research! This problem is common when a mismatch occurs between the intended purpose of the research and the research as actually conducted. For all of these reasons, much research is of poor quality, and consumers of research need to evaluate carefully the research they do read.

Fortunately, one does not have to be a statistician to evaluate research. Instead, what is needed is a *conceptual* understanding of research methods and what those methods can tell you. What is the purpose of a representative sample? Of random assignment to groups? When is research experimental and when is it nonexperimental? What threats to validity does a multiple-baseline design control? What does significance mean? What does analysis of variance, or multiple regression, or factor analysis tell us? Being able to answer these conceptual questions will help one evaluate research much more so than being able to calculate *t*-tests by hand. One also needs to read research articles carefully — even skeptically.

Research evaluation focuses on a number of different aspects of the research, but there are three very important considerations. First, are the internal features of the research conducted well enough so that the research consumer can have confidence in the results? This consideration is generally referred to as the internal validity of the research (Campbell & Stanley, 1963) but may also be thought of as the "power" of the research design (Keith, 1988). In other words, is the research design powerful enough so that we can be confident that it was the *treatment, and not something else*, that caused the resulting change in behavior?

Second, how generalizable or applicable are the results? This consideration — external validity — focuses primarily on the subjects used in research and the treatments. Are the people used in the research study similar to those one might encounter during normal practice? Are the treatments used similar to those that might be used in applied settings, or have they been modified drastically to fulfill the requirements of the experiment? There is often a trade-off in these two aspects of research. For example, a school-based study in which various classes were assigned differing amounts of homework would likely be less powerful (more threats to internal validity) than a lab-based experiment in which college freshmen were assigned randomly to groups and given different amounts of time to study nonsense words. On the other hand, many would probably feel more comfortable generalizing the results of the first study to a middle school student who does not complete his homework. The second study is more powerful but less generalizable.

Third, is the article written well enough so that readers can understand what was done and the implications of the results? It does not matter how technically sophisticated research is if the writing is unclear and confusing.

Although skepticism is necessary in evaluating research, it should not be carried to an extreme. Be warned: *No research is perfect!* Conducting research consists, in large part, of making decisions and compromises, and there are weaknesses in any piece of research. When evaluating research, one needs to weigh its strengths and weaknesses and decide whether the results obtained are trustworthy and whether the treatment described really resulted in the behavioral change found. When research evaluation leads the consumer to conclude that the weaknesses are insurmountable and the results suspect, these studies should be ignored. The rest will fall along some continuum from merely adequate to excellent. Research that is strong in all areas can be applied with more confidence than that with many weaknesses.

Figure 1 includes a list of questions that may be useful in evaluating research articles. Various sources useful in gaining a conceptual understanding of the issues involved in research are listed in the annotated bibliography.

For research that is well-conducted and well-described, the next problem is application. It is obviously easier to apply applied research than research that is highly theoretical. Intervention studies and psychometric research are often directly applicable to daily practice. But basic and theoretical research may also be quite applicable, especially if it helps us understand how or under what conditions a treatment (or intervention) may be useful. Basic research comparing the effectiveness of various mnemonic devices for different types of subjects might be quite applicable to a student with poor memory skills, for example. The connection is not as direct, but a good mix of applied and basic research may be very useful in understanding a problem.

Sources for consumers of research. The primary source of research reports is journals with relevance to school psychology. A useful list of such journals is presented in Reynolds, Gutkin, Elliott, and Witt (1984, Appendix G). Conferences, conference proceedings, and the ERIC Document Reproduction Service are other outlets for relevant research, but these manuscripts are generally not as carefully reviewed as are those submitted to journals, so consumers of this research need to be even more critical than of journal articles. Research reviews and book chapters are another good source for both consumers and distributors of research. If well done, they provide a concise, objective summary of research knowledge in an area and their reference lists can provide good sources of the original research. These reviews and chapters may also provide a good conceptual introduction that will be useful when reading the original research. But like original research, the quality of reviews and chapters varies considerably; it is best to have some familiarity with at least some of the original research to be able to ascertain that the writer of the review did a competent job of summarizing the research.

If most school psychologists are to be consumers, rather than conductors, of research, then their concern when taking research courses should

FIGURE 1. Questions for evaluating research articles.

Is the purpose well defined?

Is the literature adequately summarized?

Does the introduction establish the need for the study?

Is the research design appropriate? Is it powerful enough so that you can trust the results?

Does the research design fit the purpose?

What type of research design is used (experimental, quasi-experimental, nonexperimental, single-case, etc.)?

Does the analysis fit the design?

How was the sample collected? Is it representative? Is it large enough to allow a good statistical test?

Is there evidence to support the reliability and validity of any tests or questionnaires used?

Are the results presented consistent with the purpose, the design, and the analysis?

Does the discussion flow from the results? Is it consistent with the purpose of the study?

Are the conclusions consistent with the results or do they go well beyond them?

Are the limitations of the research discussed?

What are the major strengths and weaknesses of the study?

Is the article well written?

Are the results of the study generalizable to your population? Are the treatments generalizable into interventions?

Is this research applicable to your work?

Note. These questions provide an overview of those aspects which may be important in evaluating research articles. They will not all be equally applicable for all articles.

---

be for a conceptual understanding of research. I believe there is one exception to this rule. All school psychologists should be able to develop rudimentary single-case research designs. It may not be feasible to expect all school psychologists to conduct complex single-case research (although such research is more applicable to applied settings than are most types of research), but knowledge of such designs is useful because they can be used to evaluate the effectiveness of virtually *any intervention* — behavioral or otherwise.

An example: Using research to develop an intervention. As an example, a school psychologist is referred a fifth-grade boy, Sam, who is having trouble keeping up with his peers. The teacher does not think Sam is a candidate for special education but does want assistance in helping him deal with what appears to be a relatively mild learning problem. Assessment and a review of records supports the teacher's suspicions: Sam has never been a star student but he has never experienced serious problems before either and has not previously been referred. He appears to have slightly below-average abilities and achievement in a generally high-achieving school. Assessment also suggests that Sam, his teacher, and his parents are all fairly motivated and would be willing to cooperate with some sort of intervention.

The school psychologist has read several articles recently on the effects of homework, and it occurs to her that homework might provide the basis for a cooperative home/school intervention. A cursory review of research suggests that homework is effective for this age group, especially so when it is commented on by the teacher and when current homework demands are small (e.g., Keith, 1987). Further investigation reveals that the teacher currently assigns little homework, and thus a homework intervention seems a likely possibility. Additional reading suggests worthwhile features of effective homework interventions (Miller & Kelley, 1991).

The psychologist begins conducting curriculum-based assessments in Reading (e.g., Deno, 1986) and charting Sam's weekly quiz grades in math and spelling. In cooperation with the teacher and the parents she plans a homework intervention: The parents will provide a quiet place for Sam to study at a regular time each day; the teacher will eventually provide daily, individualized homework in at least two of the three areas being charted and, on a daily basis, will check the homework, comment on it, and provide feedback to the parents about its accuracy. The parents, in turn, will provide reinforcement at home for homework that meets an agreed upon, adjustable criterion of accuracy (as reported by the teacher).

Because the psychologist wants to ensure it is the intervention, rather than some other, uncontrolled influence that causes any subsequent change in Sam's achievement, she designs the intervention as a multiple-baseline design across school subjects. Homework in reading is introduced first, although performance in all three areas continues to be charted. If the intervention is effective, she might expect to see improvement in reading after a few weeks of the homework intervention while spelling and math grades stay at about the same level. Homework could next be introduced in spelling and, after progress was shown, in math. Of course, if the homework seemed effective in reading, the teacher and parents might be tempted immediately to begin homework in the other two areas, but they would need to be cautioned against jumping the gun. By conforming to the multiple-baseline plan, the psychologist can feel confident that the intervention, not something else, is causing any change in Sam's behavior. This knowledge is important because it provides information that may be useful in future interventions with Sam and other students and because it ensures that Sam, his parents, and his teacher are not completing all of this additional work for no purpose. This approach has the added benefit of introducing the intervention gradually and of providing data that may be used to make needed changes in the intervention. The approach is not a sophisticated single-case design, but it would provide evidence of the effectiveness — or lack of effectiveness — of the intervention. It also illustrates the connections among research, assessment, intervention, and evaluation. It should also be noted that a wide range of outcome measures (behavioral and otherwise) are possible in single-case designs. For example, if we were interested in the teacher's impressions of Sam's preparation for class, we could assess this possible outcome using a simple rating scale. These daily ratings of preparedness in the three subjects would also fit well in the multiple-baseline design.

Improving skills: Consumers. Most school psychologists have had all or most of the training necessary to become effective *consumers* of research; what they need is to improve and use the skills they have. The books and articles in the annotated bibliography may help refresh that training, and they approach research more from a conceptual than a numerical level. Consumers should also read research regularly and attend research presentations at conferences. We should be interested in the results of research, but always approach it skeptically. As Reynolds and Kaiser reminded us, our attitude should be "In God we trust; all others must have data" (1990, p. 487).

Of course, if school psychologists are to be effective consumers of research, their employers must recognize this as a part of the job. In my experience, many employers are pleased when their psychologists try to base their practice on solid research, provided that the knowledge (a) does not cost a lot of extra money and (b) is not used as a weapon with which the psychologist battles policies of the administration (as in, "Well, the research says this program the superintendent started up last month is not very effective"). As with any new role, this process might have to be started through an investment of one's own time rather than the employer's: When you can show some payoff — for example, through effective interventions — your employer will be much more willing to recognize the value of the research consumer approach.

Distributors

Integrating research findings. Distributors of research consolidate and integrate research findings in order to draw conclusions from that research and make recommendations based on those conclusions. To do so, distributors first need access to a body of research, and probably a wider access than do consumers of research. Distributors need to be able to define their research topic so that their review is neither too broad nor too narrow. I find it helpful to organize research topics as a group of overlapping circles. For example, if I were interested in the effects of cooperative learning strategies on the math achievement of students with learning disabilities (LD), I would want to read and evaluate research that directly addressed that question as comprehensively as possible. Thus, my central topic — and the central circle in Figure 2 — is research addressing the effects of cooperative learning on LD students' math achievement.

I would also be interested in several related topics, such as the effects of cooperative learning on other types of exceptional children's achievement, the effects of cooperative learning on normal children's math achievement, and other important aspects of math learning in LD children: These topics are represented by circles that overlap the central circle. Although each of these related topics is of interest, they are less central to the main topic of interest and therefore my reading of research in these areas would not need to be as comprehensive. Much of my information about these topics could even rely on review articles, if they were well done, comprehensive, and recent. The next set of circles from the center might include such topics as the effects of cooperative learning strategies on other subject areas and the design of cooperative learning strategies: while these topics should be considered, they might receive only a cursory review. Thus, although my reading should cover all important aspects of the problem, I would spend less time on research less central to my research question.

Like consumers, distributors of research need to be able to evaluate the research they read. In fact, this

FIGURE 2. Topics included in a review of the effects of cooperative learning on the math achievement of students with learning disabilities (LD). The farther the circle is from the center, the less extensive the review.

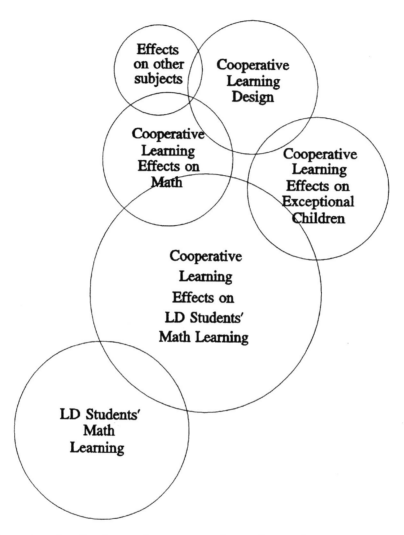

skill is even more important for distributors because they need to cover the research more thoroughly and are therefore more likely to encounter contradictory research findings. Distributors need to weigh better research more heavily in making conclusions. That is, they should base their conclusions primarily on the better research, only using the medium-quality research when it addresses important questions unanswered by better conducted studies.

Probably the most difficult part of consolidating research is *integrating* diverse research findings. The least useful review of research is one which simply lists in separate paragraphs the findings of each research study. Instead, the goal of a research review should be to combine and *integrate* the various research findings in order to draw one or several conclusions (with appropriate caveats) from the research. One rule of thumb is to avoid making the *researchers* the subject of a sentence or a paragraph,

but rather to focus on the *findings* of research and make most citations to researchers parenthetical. For example, a hypothetical sentence might read that "coursework appears an important influence on student learning (Anderson, 1991), whether learning is measured by test scores (Smith, 1988) or by grades (Jones, 1987)." This sentence integrates the findings of three hypothetical studies. In contrast, I might have written: "Smith (1988), in a regression analysis of 867 high school students, found that the coursework taken by those students had a strong effect on their subsequent achievement test scores. Jones (1987) studied students in academic versus general high school tracts and found that . . ." and so on. The first method integrates the findings; the second method treats them separately.

Quantitative research synthesis, or meta-analysis, is becoming increasingly common and can be a valuable tool for research distributors. Even those who do not use the quantitative methods of meta-analysis can profit from a discussion of the considerations necessary for valid research synthesis (e.g., Wolf, 1986).

The steps listed previously as important in distributing research are the same steps involved in a literature review: review an appropriate body of research, integrate the findings, and make conclusions. Distributors of research need to take this process one step further, however. They are presumably conducting a research review because they wish to bring research findings to bear on some practical problem; they also are conducting the review to share with others. As a final step in such a review, a research distributor should be able to make recommendations for action based on the conclusions drawn from research.

Sources for distributors of research. Research distributors need a wider access to journals and other sources of research than do most consumers. In addition to school psychology journals, distributors need access to journals from educational psychology, special education, behavioral, and counseling and clinical psychology. Distributors also need access to other sources of research (e.g., conferences, ERIC abstracts, books) and they should be able to integrate basic, theoretically oriented research with applied research.

Fortunately, the "legwork" required of research distributors — conducting searches of the literature, finding relevant articles and books — is becoming easier and easier. Most university libraries now have data bases of research articles on CD-ROM. For example, ERIC and PsycLit on CD contain 10 years or more of abstracts and publication information from education and psychology journals. It is easy to search multiple journals quickly for keywords of interest; the results of the search can then be downloaded to floppy disk or printed. Obviously, these new "instant" searches can be a great starting place for research distributors.

Much of the work involved in distributing research can be completed before a visit to the library. Research distributors with access to the *Internet* computer network can search the holdings of most university libraries in the U.S. (and many outside the U.S.) from their home or office. ERIC and PsycLit searches are available through the Internet, as is a service (CARLUNCOVER) that allows the search of the titles of articles from over 14,000 journals. With CARLUNCOVER one can also order articles of interest, for a fee. Research distributors interested in such services should contact a local university library for more information. Most universities are connected to Internet, and access to Internet is also available through most commercial electronic networks (e.g., Compuserve).

Improving skills: Becoming a research distributor. Psychologists interested in improving their research distributing skills may also profit from the books and articles listed in the bibliography. Also, they should develop the practice of critically reviewing the research they read and study research reviews written by others. One excellent way to practice reviewing research is to serve as a referee for articles submitted to journals. Most journal editors are eager to find colleagues willing to serve as occasional reviewers for research and review articles submitted for publication in their journals (and editors of school psychology journals are often especially eager to find practitioners willing to review articles). Most journals use anonymous reviewing (the reviewer does not know the identity of the author) in order to ensure honesty in reviews; however, courtesy should not be sacrificed as a result of anonymity. Serving as a reviewer provides practice and often feedback; most editors send each reviewer the comments of the other reviewers in addition to their own blinded letter to the author.

Without realizing it, most psychologists hear questions amenable to research review constantly, from parents, teachers, and administrators. Do you think young boys should wait an extra year before starting kindergarten? Should I give homework to second graders? Does ability grouping harm low-achieving students? Should we institute a cooperative learning program in the elementary schools? All of these questions address educational topics that have been the focus of research, and answering those questions may be easier with a solid understanding of what research says about the effectiveness of the programs in question. Psychologists who wish to add the role of research distributor to their jobs can begin by volunteering to help provide answers to questions of interest to their school district or other employer, or by volunteering to serve on policy-making committees. For example, district-wide policies on homework are becoming popular; a psychologist serving as a research distributor could provide valuable information to a policy-making committee on the effects of homework on student learning.

Conductors

Designing and conducting research. Conductors of research first need to be competent consumers and distributors of research. Beyond that, they of course need to be competent in research design and analysis. Arguably, they also need another, often overlooked skill: They should be able to transform vague questions of practice and policy into general research questions. In my experience, the most common mistake made by inexperienced researchers is that they tend to focus immediately on the details of a study (the sample, the statistics to be used); a common mistake made even by experienced researchers is that they have vague or poorly defined research questions. The missing step in both cases is to go beyond the vague questions that led to an interest in the topic being studied and to derive *general, testable* research questions. Do you wonder what can be done to best educate disadvantaged youth or whether low-achieving first graders should be retained? These vague questions of policy can be phrased as research questions is a variety of ways, each of which would lead to a slightly different research design. I find it helpful to force myself to phrase these vague questions as questions of 10 words or less, usually in the form of does *x* affect (or improve or influence) *y*? Does grade retention improve later achievement? Does an academic curriculum affect disadvantaged students' future economic success?

Once the general question has been phrased, conducting research is simply a matter of making choices (how do we define disadvantaged?) and compromises (should we use a small, but intensively interviewed local sample or a larger regional sample with less information per person?) With practice, you will find research questions popping up everywhere — as a result of normal conversations, articles in journals, newspaper stories and editorials, and other unlikely sources (for example, the seed for my question about educating disadvantaged youth was planted by an article in *Reader's Digest*).

Conductors of research also need competence in a variety of research designs to ensure that the design chosen indeed tests the research question asked. *Expertise* in research design is not necessarily needed if you are willing to collaborate or seek the advice of someone with that expertise, but a broad understanding of research designs is needed. In particular, competence is needed in research methods that are appropriate in applied settings but which may not be stressed in a typical graduate program: quasi-experimental, single-case, and nonexperimental designs, along with psychometric methods.

Similarly, conductors of research need a general, broad competence in analysis to ensure that the method of analysis is congruent with the research design and the research question. For any sort of statistical analysis one needs access to a good statistics computer program. There are a multitude of programs available for personal computers, ranging from simple to complex and from cheap to expensive. Reviews of programs are one source for help in choosing a program and are becoming more commonplace in professional journals and computer magazines. For example. *PC Magazine* recently reviewed and compared 13 statistical programs ranging in price from $125 to several thousand dollars (Canter, 1993). Beyond reviews, one needs to look for a program that computes the statistics wanted, is easy to use, is widely used, and is regularly revised.

One option is to use one of the major programs derived from mainframe statistics packages (e.g., SAS or SPSS). These programs are widely used and regularly updated, and so one may have confidence that any errors will be quickly spotted and remedied. Unfortunately, these packages also tend to be the more expensive and largest programs available. Fortunately, there are many less expensive programs available but, again, care is needed in choosing a program that is accurate and easy-to-use. Statistical programs are increasingly becoming required purchases in statistics classes and are often available at a considerable discount through such classes; the opportunity to purchase a good program at a low cost may be an extra benefit for anyone planning to take a new or refresher research class.

Conductors of research also need competence in communicating the findings of research orally and in writing. Nothing spoils a good piece of research faster than a report of that research that is poorly written, vague, or full of jargon.

Improving skills: Becoming a research conductor. Many psychologists have the knowledge necessary to conduct research, and most have, or could easily have, access to data that would be useful for research purposes. School psychologists are awash in data — test scores, ratings, observations — much of which would be ideal for research purposes with a little prior planning. What is generally missing is *practice* doing research; even school psychologists who have completed a thesis or dissertation often do not feel comfortable with the process of doing research. If this assessment is correct, what psychologists — those with the necessary requisite skills — need is to work with, or even serve as apprentices to, others who actively are conducting research.

Probably the easiest way to develop a research apprenticeship is to contact faculty in school psychology or related areas at a local university. Most faculty at universities with graduate programs are expected to carry on a program of research as a part of their jobs; most would welcome help in data collection, analysis, writing, and the other tasks of research, especially if you can provide a source of data and are interested in answering research questions that are of interest to them. Another option is to work with others at a local level who are doing research. For those interested in serving as an apprentice, proximity is important in order to experience all aspects of research. For those who already have research experience and who are looking for research collaboration, proximity may not be as important. With computers and electronic mail (even with regular mail), long distance collaboration is quite possible and increasingly common.

The best way to have the role of conductor included as a part of your job description is essentially the same as for a research distributor: Volunteer to find the answer to a research question that evolves from a problem facing your school system (or mental health center, etc.). If your research will answer a question of interest to your employer, not cost a lot of money, and not interfere with your other responsibilities, you will probably be welcome to conduct it. It may take a commitment of your own time in the beginning, but if you can prove your worth as a research conductor, your employer will begin to see this role as a part of your job.

SUMMARY

All school psychologists should be involved in research, although there is little need for most actually to conduct research. All psychologists need to be effective *consumers* of research; they should be able to read critically research that has implications for their practice and incorporate the findings of that research into their practice. A smaller number of psychologists are needed to serve as research *distributors:* They summarize the findings of relevant research and convey those findings to their colleagues and employers. A still smaller number may be interested in actually *conducting* research: They should be able to design and conduct studies that answer research questions of interest to themselves and their employers. It is not particularly difficult to serve in any of these roles, and advances in computers, software, and electronic networks have made these research roles available to a much wider audience. As with any new role, the hardest part is getting started.

REFERENCES

Barlow, D. E., & Hersen, M. (1984). *Single case experimental designs: Strategies for studying behavior change* (2nd ed.). New York: Pergamon.

Campbell, D. T., & Stanley, J. C. (1963). *Experimental and quasi-experimental designs for research.* Chicago: Rand McNally.

Canter, S. (1993). Statistical analysis: Stat of the art. *PC Magazine, 19*(3), 227–287.

Deno, S. L. (1986). Formative evaluation of individual student programs: A new role for school psychologists. *School Psychology Review, 15,* 358–374.

Huck, S. W., Cormier, W. H., & Bounds, W. G., Jr. (1990). *Reading statistics and research.* New York: Harper Collins.

Keith, T. Z. (1987). Children and homework. In A. Thomas & J. Grimes (Eds.), *Children's needs: Psychological perspectives* (pp. 275–282). Washington, DC: National Association of School Psychologists.

Keith, T. Z. (1988). Research methods in school psychology: An overview. *School Psychology Review, 17,* 508–526.

Kerlinger, F. N. (1986). *Foundations of behavioral research* (3rd ed.). New York: Holt, Rinehart & Winston.

Miller, D. L., & Kelley, M. L. (1991). Interventions for improving homework performance: A critical review. *School Psychology Quarterly, 6,* 174–185.

Phillips, B. N. (1990). Reading, evaluating, and applying research in school psychology. In T. B. Gutkin & C. R. Reynolds (Eds.), *The handbook of school psychology* (2nd ed., pp. 53–75). New York: Wiley.

Reynolds, C. R., & Kaiser, S. M. (1990). Test bias in psychological assessment. In T. B. Gutkin & C. R. Reynolds (Eds.), *The handbook of school psychology* (2nd ed., pp. 487–525). New York: Wiley.

Reynolds, C. R., Gutkin, T. B., Elliott, S. N., & Witt, J. C. (1984). *School psychology: Essentials of theory and practice.* New York: Wiley.

Wolf, F. M. (1986). Meta-analysis: Quantitative methods for research synthesis. *Sage University Paper Series on Quantitative Applications in the Social Sciences, 59.* Beverly Hills, CA: Sage.

ANNOTATED BIBLIOGRAPHY

Barlow, D. E., & Hersen, M. (1984). *Single case experimental designs: Strategies for studying behavior change* (2nd ed.). New York: Pergamon.
This comprehensive book is an excellent reference for single case research methods.

Huck, S. W., Cormier, W. H., & Bounds, W. G., Jr. (1990). *Reading statistics and research.* New York: Harper Collins.
This fine book was originally published in 1974; it was reprinted, but not revised, in 1990. The book is intended primarily for people who want to read and understand the research of others (here called research conductors and distributors). It presents statistics and research designs from a conceptual standpoint and, although quite dated, does a nice job of demystifying research. It also contains a nice introductory chapter on single case research.

Keith, T. Z. (1988). Research methods in school psychology: An overview. *School Psychology Review, 17,* 508–526.
This article provides a conceptual overview of diverse research methods used in school psychology, with a particular emphasis on understanding the power of different methods for inferring that a research treatment produces an outcome.

Kerlinger, F. N. (1986). *Foundations of behavioral research* (3rd ed.). New York: Holt, Rinehart & Winston.
Kerlinger's book is probably the best single book on research; his is primarily a conceptual, theoretical approach, although he does not shy away from numbers. Despite some unevenness of coverage (single-case designs are not discussed; the presentation of LISREL is overly-enthusiastic), this is a very thorough book.

Phillips, B. N. (1990). Reading, Evaluating, and applying research in school psychology. In T. B. Gutkin & C. R. Reynolds (Eds.), *The handbook of school psychology* (2nd ed., pp. 53–73). New York: Wiley.
Phillips presents a variety of issues pertinent to research in school psychology, written primarily for consumers and distributors.

13

Best Practices in Maintaining an Independent Practice

Steven L. Rosenberg
PSI Associates, Inc.
Twinsburg, Ohio

OVERVIEW

Many school psychologists are loath to consider such economic concepts as "cash flow," "market niche," and the "law of supply and demand." Even in our free-enterprise open-market economy, considered a touchstone symbol of our Western civilization, to think of a *return on investment* is often viewed as somewhat distasteful and distant from "professional psychology." Success in the independent practice of school psychology demands a realistic view of the free enterprise system. Would-be practitioners must come to terms with these forces if they are to succeed. One prerequisite requires the psychologist to shrug off the baggage of emotions that equates independent practice with something that is somehow unclean, dishonorable, and parasitic. This may well overstate some public providers' disdain for private practice. Yet, the successful independent practitioner recognizes that it is equally as worthy and "professional" to provide services for fair and direct remuneration, as it is to be paid indirectly from the public purse through service to schools. Medicine, for example, has come to terms with dual systems of public and private service without any implications of hierarchy. (However, where a hierarchy is assumed, then independent practice is frequently seen as *higher status* than service as a hospital doctor.) Psychology would come a long way by emulating the mature perceptions of independent practice as seen in accounting, medicine, and law.

With a PSI Associates, Inc. colleague, Donald M. Wonderly, I prepared a chapter for *Best Practices in School Psychology–II* dealing with the early stages of developing an independent practice (Rosenberg & Wonderly, 1990). That chapter describes some of the pitfalls awaiting the psychologist naive in business matters and offers suggestions for hurdling problem areas. "Establishing an Independent Practice" describes some of the considerations basic to setting up a business selling professional services, including *finances*, *planning*, selecting the *product* of the service, *promoting* the business to referral sources, and *locating* the business. Space was given to the issue of

price and *fees:* How much should I charge, and how do I collect the fees? Many psychologists new to business are frankly uncomfortable with anything to do with collecting a fee for the work they do. However, these same people are adept at spending the very dollars they find tough to collect. For example, many psychologists learn to their chagrin the extraordinarily high costs of engaging front office help (such as a receptionist and secretary); office, furniture, and equipment lease fees; and similar expenses of initiating a business. Consequently, in that chapter I detailed many of these costs, including

- Payroll taxes, rent, utility and telephone charges.
- Tax and legal representation and consultancy.
- Insurance (general liability, professional liability, fire, theft), professional membership, salaries for employees, health and life insurance, retirement contributions, postage, printing and travel.
- Furniture, equipment and office supplies.
- Interest costs (lost or incurred) on funds used to float the business.

Thus, the chapter "Establishing an Independent Practice" provides a starter kit for the psychologist considering a venture into the business arena. This present chapter develops on the earlier discussion about creating a viable business by considering issues that have increasing importance as the business matures.

BASIC CONSIDERATIONS

Entrepreneurship: Can It *Ever* Be "Professional"?

An independent practitioner's attitude towards entrepreneurship is a key ingredient if an independent practice is to grow (or even be maintained successfully). Unfortunately, most school psychologists are unfamiliar with the principles of business and finance and are disinclined to accept conceptualizations associated with the *business* operation of an independent practice. In fact, an entrepreneurial orientation many times conflicts with values held by publicly employed school psychologists.

Unless the would-be practitioner plans to open the office and merely wait for the phone to ring, he or she must reckon with such concepts as market niche, competition, profit margin, "bottom line," and salespersonship. Many of these concepts can be learned. A bounty of legal and financial consultants (caveat emptor) are available to "assist" in all these matters. Their help notwithstanding, it is imperative that the practitioner be prepared to cope with an entirely new set of demands upon time. Business considerations *must* be successfully dealt with if financial and professional goals are to be realized, and commitments honored.

Independent practitioners of school psychology must also be prepared for the reactions of peers, especially as the enterprise becomes successful. It is as common as it is ironic that publicly employed personnel are critical of their private sector counterparts. Unlike private practitioners in medicine, dentistry, and law, independent practitioners of school psychology are generally *not* held in high regard by their peers. This is especially true of the practitioner who works in nontraditional settings. Contractual, and similarly innovative delivery models typically ruffle the feathers of conservative colleagues.

Such criticism is certainly common in the worlds of industry and commerce. Yet, it is more difficult for the entrepreneurial helping-professional to be the recipient of criticism and rumoring. This problem is compounded because there is no readily available forum to explain actions which are in question. High profile cases (e.g., custodial and forensic evaluations) and situations involving large numbers of individuals (e.g., employee assistance programs) can be particularly difficult, requiring skills foreign to school psychology preparation.

The practitioner must be ready and willing to deal squarely and responsively with many nonprofessional issues. What percentage of assessed fees are noncollectible? How are employees to be compensated? What employee benefits are appropriate? Which of these are affordable? Are employees to be paid whether or not fees are collected? What is the competition doing and how does it impact upon already established plans? What are the overhead costs (secretarial, rent, payroll rates, postage, printing, supervision, advertising, taxes, etc.)? How long can financial commitments be met with a lower than expected income stream?

These are but a few of the innumerable issues independent practitioners must address. Ignoring them, with a focus only on the professional issues associated with school psychology, has destined many an enterprise to fail. Competent and efficient professional services are a necessary but insufficient recipe for developing and maintaining a successful practice. Such skills must be blended with a sound business and financial orientation to increase the probability of success. Only in this way can the entrepreneur avoid many of the common trapdoors which cause an inordinate number of young professional businesses to fail.

Targeting Your Marketplace

It is critical for the "would-be independent practitioner" to clarify the "market niche" to be served. As the supply of qualified psychological personnel grows, it becomes more important to narrow the scope to serve an otherwise unserved or poorly served population. While historically the traditional "Jack-of-all-trades" psychological provider has been successful (and still may be successful in high-demand situations), one's chances for success are enhanced by offering a clearly delineated specialty that is in demand. Paradoxically, such a specialty must, of course, also be broad enough to generate sufficient referrals to satisfy cash flow requirements.

The best and perhaps only genuine way to determine your specialty is to analyze your talents, training, and skill levels in every way possible. Introspection and feedback from fellow professionals that identifies with which of your clients you were most successful are critically important first steps. Self-critique can save the possibility that you will target a market which seems novel, attractive, and of high interest — but one where your skills are insufficient to generate the reputation needed to develop a niche. Once this professional focus is narrowed, you must investigate whether there is a local market which demands your services.

Common sense, professional propriety, and ethical canons clearly demand that your final determination of a specialty be demonstrably within your areas of training and expertise. Further investment in academic and professional experience is rarely justifiable to help make the final decision as to your area of service.

One of the principal difficulties in maintaining success in independent practice is attracting a steady flow of clients. Contributing factors include (a) inadequate or inaccurate information about your services, (b) clients' prior negative experiences with mental health providers, (c) clients' resistance to the notion that one benefits from psychological service, and (d) its cost. The impact of this last factor becomes more severe as third-party payors reduce, restrict, or even eliminate coverage to school psychological services. The first and last of these four factors are perhaps most amenable to your creative problem-solving efforts, while solutions to the other two result from your growing positive reputation.

Even those practitioners who rely on the relatively conservative marketing stratagem of accepting referrals from other professionals discover obstacles. Referring parties may fear the competition your services seem to represent. School psychologists suffer from a poorly-defined image. The assumption is often made that your services are unnecessary, unimportant, or redundant with the services of providers in related fields. Already-established referral patterns to other professionals can also interfere and will persist as a barrier to the success of your practice unless you can market your services to other professionals as uniquely responsive to their clients' needs. Growing a successful independent practice depends in large part on the quality and dependability of your referral sources. This often misunderstood concept causes many fledgling practices to falter and fail. Rather than concentrating on office color schemes and floor plans, the wise entrepreneur cultivates appropriate and reliable sources of referral.

The neophyte independent practitioner must diligently develop a viable network of referring sources. Once the targeted client population has been identified, an exhaustive list should be developed of all available sources of referral. Many of these potential sources will be easily accessible; others may demand more creative approaches to establish contact. Sufficient time and energy must be invested to explore every available avenue: Family doctors and pediatricians, the family dentist, and attorneys with whom you are acquainted are examples of ready contacts as are speech and hearing therapists who work independently or who are part of an agency or center, and social workers employed by government agencies to work with children. Publicly employed school psychologists represent potential and valuable sources of referral. Each of these professionals should be encouraged to suggest others in their network for contact.

Even for a part-time practitioner, no single referral source can be depended on to keep a practice busy. A variety of referral sources must be garnered for the independent practitioner to be successful. Many components are necessary if a potential referral source is to become viable. However unfortunate it may seem, competency itself is insufficient to ensure the success of an independent practice.

There are a number of other factors every entrepreneur must consider. First and foremost, the purchaser of services, or the referring professional, must have confidence in the provider. There must be a belief that valuable services will be forthcoming. Confidence develops slowly. Trust is on a shaky foundation when it's based on an embellished claim of prior therapeutic successes. Rather, such assertions are usually transparent; for they plant seeds of mistrust that are, at the very least, counterproductive and unethical. The practitioner needs to present a menu of services in a responsible and accurate manner that engages the interest of a would-be referral source.

What services can be provided that differ from those offered by others? Can more in-depth follow-up be provided? Can office hours be tailored to client needs? Can the geographic distribution of other independent practitioners be exploited so that your office location will offer greater ease and convenience? Can the services of a variety of related professionals (e.g., speech, nursing, medical) be offered within the same office complex, enhancing the ease of referral by busy physicians, school administrators, and the like? Are your service costs comparable to competitors' rates? Can fees be structured to be appealing to potential clients (per hour, no charge initial consultation, etc.)? Consider in what form referring sources would most prefer feedback. Are they inclined to participate in your treatment, or do they wish to be "out of the loop"? Are there special financial considerations (e.g., graduated payment schedules)? When a referral source is satisfied with the services, can that individual be gently encouraged to pass your name on to other colleagues? The importance of developing competent referral systems cannot be overstated.

A thorough evaluation of the competition offers the innovative psychologist innumerable ways to position an independent practice. What is "the other guy" providing that can be done better? Why should potential referral sources select your practice instead of more established ones? In what ways can your services be distinguished from others?

While these questions are difficult, success depends upon the quality of your answers. In a world of ever increasing privatization, deregulation, and free enterprise, school psychologists wishing to break into the potentially rewarding world of independent practice must cope successfully with these issues.

Learning from Colleagues

During 1987–89 I chaired the Independent Practice Task Force of the National Association of School Psychologists (NASP). As a "flagship" activity for this group we conducted a NASP preconvention program, part of which provided insights into some of the reasons why independent school psychology businesses fail. The obstacles are many and varied; nonetheless, there are patterns to be discerned and overcome, regardless of states' regulations and the specific limitations on particular professionals.

Issues associated with insufficient client recruitment, excessive financial commitment, an oversupply of service providers, and a lack of business acumen are of greatest concern. These must be squarely confronted for an independent practice to become successful. Failed endeavors usually faltered because of one or more of the following pitfalls: Poorly constructed goals and objectives; nonspecific service models; prematurely terminating secure employment to pursue potential independent practice income; and incurring unnecessary expenses.

It is common for school psychologists to initiate an independent practice without a clear and concise foundation of goals and objectives. Which client population shall be served? How will referrals be obtained? Can potential sources be relied upon? What is the minimum number of billable client-hours each week needed to generate sufficient net income? What income can reasonably be expected after 12 months, 24 months, 36 months, and so forth?

It is also common for new practitioners to assume that the traditional fee-for-service paradigm is the delivery system of choice. However, successful entrepreneurs have first considered all the available options before committing themselves to one specific approach. Perhaps contractual services, of which there are many variations, can be an innovative and successful tactic. Novice independent practitioners as well as established practitioners wishing to expand their operations must consider all the available service models before committing to one. The invested time and effort inevitably pay dividends.

It *should* be surprising to learn about individuals who prematurely sacrifice secure employment to risk the rewards of independent practice. But that is not the case. This phenomenon is all the more astonishing since opportunities exist to establish a practice on a part-time basis without terminating school-based employment. Given the failure-rate for new businesses in general, and the independent practice of psychology in particular, every opportunity to learn about independent practice should be examined before walking away from a guaranteed income.

"Delusions of grandeur" among neophyte practitioners are not unusual. Upon obtaining the appropriate licensing credentials, school psychologists are often convinced that wealth and fame are just around the corner. Business cards and a "Yellow Page" listing seem all that stands in the way of success. However, the repeated stories of disappointment are indicative of the significant obstacles facing would-be independent practitioners.

The prospect for disappointment is reduced in direct proportion to the accumulation of business knowledge and experience. Since most school psychologists are unaccustomed to the intricacies of the hidden costs of doing business (e.g., payroll taxes, utilities, telephones, service contracts, secretarial costs, postage, general and professional liability insurance, employee benefits, rent, etc.), consulting knowledgeable individuals is an essential step. While well trained accountants and lawyers can be expensive, they may save untold dollars and aggravation. Other resources can be tapped. Older, more experienced psychologists can serve as consultants. The Council of Small Business Enterprises (COSE) provides a link to low-cost or no-cost "senior" consultants willing to mentor fledgling entrepreneurs. The time involved in meeting with a successful professional to learn about reliable strategies and methods can be very valuable. Being an "apprentice" for such a practitioner on a full or part-time basis can be exceptionally educational. Finally, your public library has a wealth of books devoted to entrepreneurship, many of which have sections relevant to the independent practice of school psychology.

Rent is one of the main expenses to consider. Perhaps office sharing, an "incubator office" (i.e., per hour rental), or working from your home should be the first approach. Fancy offices with secretaries come *after* success, not before. While the appeal of paneled offices is understandable, independent practice should be approached with the utmost caution. Far more important is the analysis of expected income and expenditures. The number of clients needed per week to pay the bills must be calculated. Will the necessary number of clients continue indefinitely? How many of those clients will pay their bills in full? In a 40-hour week how many "billable hours" of client contact are possible? (Incidentally, even the most successful independent psychologist averages fewer than 25 billable hours weekly.)

The world of independent practice can be exciting, fulfilling, and rewarding. It can be entered with low risk and relatively low cost. It is crucial, however, for the practitioner to be a cautious business person.

Methods for Growing the Independent Practice:

Public exposure. One of the most common methods for building the practice is to actively seek opportunities to address the public. Well-prepared presentations on topics within one's expertise is a low cost but potentially highly productive method of gaining appropriate recognition. Presentations to public service groups are easily arranged. Radio and local television (i.e., cable) stations often look for articulate guests who are knowledgeable about high-interest topics. Hospital and philanthropic associations (e.g., Kiwanis, Lion's Club) often have Speaker Bureaus who may be receptive to your presentations. For the professional who is a satisfactory speaker, only time, energy, and initiative are necessary to arrange for many public speaking engagements.

Telephone directory advertisements. Most "Yellow Page" directories contain a lengthy section devoted to psychology. The entries range from discrete announcements to global claims of "anything cured." While the significance of phone directory advertisements is often overstated, they can provide for easy and convenient advertising. It is important to carefully review the cost of these ads and to consult with the appropriate state agency (e.g., your State Board of Psychology) to ensure that your entry is in accord with current professional standards and regulations.

Workshops. Constructing and implementing a successful workshop is very challenging. Enrollment and cost factors are difficult to overcome. However, if the practitioner is able to discover a niche previously unserved — but one in need of attention — then there are multiple professional and financial benefits from presenting workshops. The odds of successfully operating an independent practice are greatly enhanced if the practitioner's skills and reputation are widely known. It is wise first to contact family doctors, lawyers, and other well-placed professionals to learn what issues would be of greatest benefit to their clients. Workshops are an ideal way to match areas of expertise with community needs at a relatively low cost.

As many practitioners will agree with these notions as will disagree. Review them, adjust them, and then implement those with which you agree. Successful entrepreneurship demands affordable innovation and experimentation. After careful consideration, aggressively execute your chosen plans and methods to determine their viability.

Can Ethics and Business Goals Conflict?

Every business enterprise entails an element degree of risk. One ever-present danger concerns the possibility of litigation resulting from charges of malpractice. Although we rarely hear of cases actually brought to court and even less frequently of actual verdicts against a school psychologist, even one legal judgment can, if not ruin a career, seriously damage financial assets and impugn professional reputations.

It is impossible for a professional to be completely protected from legal action. The popular adage "anyone can sue anyone over anything" is well worth remembering. Whether a case can be won, of course, is a different matter. Yet, the legal fees, the inconvenience, and the harm to one's reputation can be very discouraging — even for those who win! While there are many steps that an independent practitioner can take to minimize legal risks, they can never fully be eliminated. All independent practitioners must face the fact that any professional contact may result in some form of legal action.

The obvious first step to reduce the chances of sustaining severe damage from litigation is to secure a competent and appropriate professional liability insurance policy. The premier ethical rationale for obtaining such coverage is that the policy protects our clients from our own misdeeds. In addition, it may save an unfortunate psychologist from incurring a ruinous debt which can wreck a family's financial security. While many attorneys (and even insurance agents in a candid moment) will admit that the very existence of professional liability insurance policy is an inviting target encouraging litigation, most professionals obtain some form of coverage. Independent school psychological practitioners must be careful to ensure that their policy covers work in a private setting. Policies utilized by publicly employed school psychologists typically exempt from coverage private practice.

Although it is always helpful to listen to the insurance agent's explanation of the benefits being purchased, it is vital to remember that insurance companies are not bound by the agent's assertions. Therefore, the entire policy must be read thoroughly. If you are unsure of its meaning, obtain written clarification from the underwriter. The onus is on the purchaser to be secure that the policy covers what is important. Examine the limits of the policy: Both the maximum paid for any individual claim, and the aggregate maximum that can be paid for all claims. Each practitioner must be comfortable with the limits purchased. It may be wise to discuss these issues with an objective third party such as a trusted attorney, accountant, or an established and experienced independent practitioner.

Secondly, every practitioner must remain vigilant to limit professional work to his or her area of expertise. While it may be occasionally challenging and/or opportune to provide service beyond one's own specialty area, to do so is not only unethical and unprofessional but also invites legal action by dissatisfied consumers.

Thirdly, each practitioner can alleviate a wide range of difficulties by being thoroughly and appropriately candid with clients: By comprehensively reviewing costs, the nature of the proposed treatment, and the expected length of time the treatment is intended to take. In this way, each client knows exactly what to expect. It is not uncommon for psychologists (as well as medical, legal, and other professionals) to provide clients with billing and other pertinent information in written form. Regardless of the method ultimately chosen, it is vital that clients are fully informed, thereby reducing the odds that any client will be surprised or angry — incentive enough to initiate litigation. Candor and honesty will serve any therapist well. High bills, excessive time commitments, and even less-than-successful therapy are *not* what angers the typical client. Instead, it is the client who feels he or she has been duped or taken advantage of. Hence, while it may feel awkward, it is essential to share appropriate information with every client early in the relationship.

The value of documentation cannot be overstated. Note when and what financial and prognostic information was shared with the client. Record the progress of treatment and any other important data shared with the client. These records can become an integral part of any legal defense. Many attorneys advise, however, that practitioners be circumspect in the information recorded in such "Clinical Notes." Many an unsuspecting therapist has had to review their "private" (sic) documents in the full and public light of the courtroom. However, there is no substitute for the appropriate recording of pertinent and relevant data.

Independent practitioners are guided by the profession's codes of ethics, state-level licensure requirements and laws, and published standards for service providers. A primary purpose of these guidelines is the protection of client welfare. In addition, practitioners find that adherence to such standards affords a degree of protection from claims of unsatisfactory of irresponsible service. Beyond familiarity with these principles, practitioners rely primarily on experience and advice to avoid the pitfalls associated with work whose success is so clearly dependent on the quality of the relationship between client and provider.

A recent article entitled, "Professional Liability Aspects of the Doctor/Patient Relationship" published by the American Dental Association Council on Insurance, discusses methods for fostering rapport and developing trust with clients. It contends that when the provider–client relationship is characterized by effective communication, the likelihood of client dissatisfaction — and potential legal action against the provider — is greatly reduced. However, this preventive philosophy does not always protect against dissatisfaction with, or failure of, treatment or client perception of case mismanagement. The report notes that certain types of clients and client behavior are associated with eventual legal action. Clients who pay their own bills, for example, or those who have been associated with providers for a short period of time, are more likely to sue. Client behaviors can also serve to warn practitioners of potential litigation. The article lists examples of such behavior: "Taking issue with . . . fees; Offering cash for a discount, particularly when a third party carrier is involved; Extra demands of time and attention . . . or the expectation of never having to wait for an appointment; The 'shopper'; The 'expert' (they see articles describing a particular technique and *that* is what they will get, either through you or through someone else who will do it)."

While providers need to be aware of these "warning signs," the solution to the problem of potential legal action does not lie in terminating relationships with clients exhibiting such behavior. On the contrary, such behaviors suggests a need for careful and extensive communication to ensure that misunderstandings or dissatisfaction are minimized or effectively managed. Risk management skills include several that are the psychologist's "stock in trade" such as listening skills (eye contact, body language, elimination of distracters, encouragement of questions) and speaking skills (avoidance of "psychobabble" and the use of clear examples). Other factors influencing the professional relationship are:

- The efficiency with which appointments are made, kept, or adjusted when emergencies arise.

- The style in which the provider's office is designed and decorated (outmoded furniture can suggest outmoded techniques; clutter suggests sloppy treatment and records management; expensive decor bespeaks exorbitant fees).

- The nature of written information (use of follow-up letters summarizing findings and plans; availability of newsletters or self-help/wellness pamphlets; provisions for telephone contact during crises; follow-up calls to referring colleagues).

- Record-keeping practices (procedures to safeguard confidentiality, including the removal of files from the view of waiting clients; preparation of neatly-typed and clear reports; release of reports in a timely fashion).

Finally, we must consider the importance of terminating the relationship responsibly and sensitively, regardless of the reason. If the relationship is terminated "prematurely," for example, the provider should help the client find alternative care and make records available to facilitate the transition. All clients should be prepared for the termination of services, with clear information about follow-up plans and recommendations. Truly capable and professional independent practitioners view the growing trend toward consumerism not as an annoyance or threat, but as an impetus for monitoring the effectiveness of their own policies and practices.

Certain types of intervention may seduce the psychologist into overstepping professional boundaries and ethical limitations either because of the hoped-for financial reward, or the thrill of engaging in more extensive work than is normally experienced within the parameters of traditional school psychology. Providing psychological services to children from disintegrating families is an example of "gray area" involvement.

Independent practitioners are often asked to intervene with children of separating, divorcing, or otherwise disintegrating families. In these circumstances children present a variety of diagnostic and therapeutic opportunities. Some of these interventions can be very valuable to the client. Others are more problematic. Evaluating the child's academic and personality factors associated with these familial difficulties are well within the areas of expertise typically included in school psychology training programs. Diagnosing the child's feelings toward his or her parents, their impact on the child's self-concept, and the ramifications these issues may have on school work, interpersonal development, and family interactions are equally appropriate and consistent with standard training programs.

For the child from a disintegrating family there are many issues that require training and experience additional to that normally received by the nondoctoral school psychologist. School psychology cannot be transmuted into "family therapy" simply because it is both needed and being provided independently. The decision to enter into such clinical areas should be made on a case-by-case basis, because situations and training programs differ dramatically. It is essential, however, for the practitioner to be keenly aware of his or her areas of expertise while remaining vigilant to continually steer clear of those interventions which may extend beyond formal levels of training and previously supervised experience.

The problem with treating children encountering divorce is that many *nonschool* psychological issues are liable to be associated with the child's problems (e.g., parental and familial dysfunctions). In addition, the school psychologist working privately with these children is likely to be vulnerable to legal entanglements in what are becoming virtually obligatory custody battles. While some school psychologists report that they feel challenged by the idea of engaging in "combat" with legal advocates, psychologists ill-prepared or operating beyond their areas of expertise frequently wish they had never allowed themselves to become entwined with the judicial system. Serving as an expert witness requires careful preparation and consultation with texts on the "how to" of expert testimony, in addition to a thorough clinical knowledge of the client.

Families undergoing divorce represent enormous opportunity for independent practitioners of school psychology. Offering therapeutic support groups, coping skills programs, and teaching parents methods they can use to reduce their children's anxiety, can be extremely valuable. Practically, however, it can be difficult for the clinician to have access to enough eligible children with similar problems within the right age range to make group arrangements successful.

Cultivating contacts with those directly involved with divorcing families can be very valuable. Divorce attorneys and domestic relations judges and referees, as well as mental health professionals within the justice system (e.g., those working in court-sponsored reconciliation facilities) can be good sources of referral. Approaching domestic relations attorneys, however, can be a challenging and daunting task, especially high powered lawyers with large divorce practices. The school psychologist should carefully select the attorneys to be contacted, always investigating reputations and specialties (e.g., women's issues), in an attempt to discover ways to complement the attorney's task or help provide their clients with a needed service. Clearly, finding a respected mutual acquaintance or professional known by both the psychologist and the attorney can only serve to strengthen the "referral bond."

While most "helping professionals" claim they feel capable of working with children of divorce, few specialize in this field. Therefore, one's professional persona may be enhanced by limiting to this work. Attorneys will respect this choice. A specialty concentrates the prospects for professional and financial success. Not only does it allow the practitioner to be-

come truly expert, but affords the opportunity to be able to present oneself as a true specialist in an important and difficult field. Such specialization can provide the competitive edge, helping the psychologist become known as a skilled practitioner within this growing, but well defined subgroup — a very effective way to build a successful practice.

SUMMARY

Independent practice offers many intriguing and fascinating opportunities to the school psychologist who may be interested in working in nontraditional settings. The expansion of the role of the school psychologist and the chance to further develop professional skills are among the many benefits independent practice offers. Challenges are encountered on every front: ethical, professional, and financial. The rewards, however, can be substantial. To break away from the traditional psychometric mold, to operate with increased autonomy, to ply a wide variety of skills, and perhaps to reap financial reward are among the most desirable aspects of independent practice.

It is unfortunate that novice practitioners tend to focus on the glamorous rather than the essential components of independent practice. Without careful review, the psychologist risks far more than simply time and convenience. Reputation, personal assets, and self-esteem can be jeopardized. Only through diligence and knowledge is one apt to succeed.

Many psychologists attempting to grow their practice are overly concerned with such trivial issues as business cards and office color schemes. All one needs, they believe, are a signed lease, an ad in the telephone yellow pages, and of course, a secretary with a large appointment book. Data on failed businesses indicate that such an approach is foolhardy and dangerous. Many practitioners have found themselves with an exorbitant overhead and few, if any, paying clients. Such circumstances are both professionally embarrassing and financially draining. The tragedy is that such predicaments are generally avoidable. With foresight and knowledge, the school psychologist can be prepared and positioned to vastly improve the chances of success, while limiting risk.

Psychologists contemplating independent practice must evaluate their own attitude toward business. The concept of taking money in return for psychological services is anathema to many. However, unless one intends to offer services solely on a *pro bono* basis, receiving payment for service is crucial. The process becomes more difficult when clients already suffering from emotional distress are also of poor economic means. It is essential that the school psychologist growing an independent practice be fully prepared for what are considered the more unattractive aspects of the business. While exceptions can always be made in difficult situations, tough decisions must be faced.

The issues associated with independent practice are as varied as they are demanding. Regrettably, most school psychologists are ill-prepared competently to enter this field. Surveys of school psychology training programs' curricula demonstrate that it is rare indeed for programs to address independent practice. Yet with foresight, planning, and the necessary knowledge, the independent practitioner of school psychology can innovatively blend professional skills with entrepreneurship for the mutual benefit of the school psychologist and the client. Independent practice is a challenging, exciting, and sometimes remunerative field for appropriately prepared school psychologists.

REFERENCE

Rosenberg S. L., & Wonderly, D. M. (1990). Best practices in establishing an independent practice. In A. Thomas & J. Grimes (Eds.), *Best practices in school psychology–II* (pp. 339–351). Washington, DC: National Association of School Psychologists.

ANNOTATED BIBLIOGRAPHY

Author Note: I know of no academic or technical treatise in the psychological literature on this topic. Academic libraries will rarely carry the following titles. However, most large bookstores carry them in a **Business** section of "how to" *trade books.* For this reason, I have provided ISBN numbers and current costs.

General:

Harper, S. C. (1991). *Starting your own business: A step-by-step blueprint for the new entrepreneur.* New York: McGraw-Hill. ISBN 0-07-026687-5. $12.95.

Sotkin, J. (1993). *Starting your own business: An easy-to-follow guide for the new entrepreneur.* Laguna Hills, CA: Build Your Business. ISBN 1-881002-84-5. $11.95.

Both are packed with explicit and specific recommendations based on proven experience from beginning business people. Best read in combination, they truly provide the step-by-step building blocks sought by the neophyte entrepreneur.

Hawken, P. (1987). *Growing a business.* New York: Simon & Schuster. ISBN 0-67167164-2. $9.95.
Companion to the 17-part PBS series of the same name — which is probably still available on video tape. Folksy and motivational in style, the book is not a "how to," rather, it illustrates business possibilities and pitfalls through experiences of individuals from widely differing fields. Emphasis is on marketing, customer-focus, and working to maintain repeat and referral business.

Witmyer, C., Rasberry, S., & Phillips, M. (1989). *Running a one-person business.* Berkeley, CA: Ten Speed Press. ISBN 0-89815-237-2. $12.00.
Comprehensive and practical for those planning on initiating or sustaining a solo business venture. While *not* restricted to *professional* businesses, most of the lessons are readily applicable by a creative school psychologist. Includes bookkeeping and financial strategies, information and time management, "setting up shop" (e.g., home vs. office base), the benefits and costs of solo business status, etc.

Incorporation:

Davidson, R. L. (1993). *The small business incorporation kit.* New York: John Wiley. ISBN 0-471-57652-2. $12.95.

McGuown, J. H. (1992). *Inc. yourself.* New York: Harper Business. ISBN 0-88730-611-X. $12.00.

Nicholas, T. (1992). *How to form your own corporation without a lawyer for under $75.00.* Dearborn, MI: Enterprise. ISBN 0-79310-419-X. $19.95.

Storey, M. J. (1993). *Taking money out of your corporation: Perfectly legal ways to maximize your income.* New York: John Wiley. ISBN 0-471-58043-0. $17.95.

In most states *professional corporations* do not have unlimited liability. Nonetheless, there are many benefits to incorporating the fledgling venture, including: In the case of economic failure the "loss" can be carried against other income, there are tax-reducing strategies unavailable to the sole proprietor, and several favorable tax-shelter retirement plans are only available to the corporation. Clearly, it is essential to get advice and oversight by a lawyer and accountant when deciding about incorporation; however, the information in these books can help you ask informed questions of your advisors.

14

Best Practices in Facilitating Team Functioning

Steven R. Shaw
Mark E. Swerdik
Illinois State University

OVERVIEW

In education, different types of teaming serve different purposes, including eligibility for special education services, development of individualized education plans (IEPs), periodic review of progress of children receiving special education services, co-teaching, site-based management, and problem-solving intervention teams. Each of these types of meetings can be collaborative problem-solving teams. This chapter will focus on increasing collaboration and improving the effectiveness of all team meetings. Collaborative teaming involves face-to-face interaction, shared leadership, effective communication, and individual and group accountability (Thousand & Villa, 1992). Most, if not all, types of team meetings can improve in creativity, productivity, and satisfaction if a collaborative approach is adopted.

Despite its intuitive appeal, the history of collaborative educational teaming for problem solving, planning, and program implementation is short. Its roots are found in legislated school improvement reforms, including site-based decision making (Glickman, 1990), ad hoc problem-solving teams (Skrtic, 1987; Thousand & Villa, 1992), teacher assistance teams (Chalfant, Pysh, & Moultrie, 1979), and collaborative planning and teaching teams (Thousand & Villa, 1992). Teaming recently has been promoted by those who advocate school restructuring and teacher empowerment. Some believe that teacher empowerment is increased through participatory decision making (Schlechty, 1990). Educational futurists, who have identified collaborative problem solving as a critical life skill for the twenty-first century, also have encouraged teaming in the schools (Wiggens, 1989). Students will then be able to observe educators value and model collaboration, and in many cases, participate in teaming. However, collaborative problem-solving teams are not common in today's schools.

Teaming has evolved over the past 50 years. Initially, the common approaches to service delivery were unidisciplinary; professionals became as competent as they could and served children without input from other professionals. Intradisciplinary teams developed as individuals within professions contributed to students' education. For example, a group of special education teachers may help each other to develop new intervention ideas for a child with a unique set of educational problems. Multidisciplinary teams (MDTs) involve a variety of professions (Maher & Pfeiffer, 1983). The members of MDTs recognize the importance of other professions in providing special services to children. However, each profession provides services individually, without integration. Most teams currently functioning in schools would be classified as MDTs. In most cases, traditional MDTs would not be classified as collaborative problem-solving teams. Interdisciplinary teams involve a variety of professions working together to develop jointly planned and implemented programs. Transdisciplinary teams involve a number of professions teaching, learning, and working with one another across professional boundaries. In a transdisciplinary team, a contact person handles most direct assessment, intervention, and parent contacts. The contact person may need to learn to administer curriculum-based assessment, conduct parent counseling, engage in occupational therapy, and conduct speech and language therapy. Other members of the team share their expertise by training the contact person to perform all of these roles (Patterson, D'Wolff, Hutchinson, Lowry, Schilling, & Siepp, 1976). In many states, the transdisciplinary model of teaming is not possible because roles are restricted by certification requirements and licensing laws. As models of teaming grow increasingly sophisticated, collaboration among and between professionals increases.

School psychologists have been involved in teaming primarily through the special education system. Special education has stimulated teaming in the schools through the MDTs mandated to conduct preplacement case studies, to determine eligibility, and to develop individualized education programs (IEPs) for students in special education. Multidisciplinary teams were required as part of legislation mandating free and appropriate public education for all children regardless of handicapping condition — namely the Education for All Handicapped Children Act of 1975 (PL 94–142), since reauthorized as the Individuals with Disabilities Education Act of 1990 (PL 101–476). However, MDTs that focus on classification and placement issues have been plagued by a variety of problems. The most significant problem is the lack of equal participation in decision making by some disciplines. Assessment personnel are given the most time and influence in these programs; educators participate relatively little in developing interventions (Ysseldyke, 1983). Many MDTs consist of cataloguing the student's problems and reciting standardized test scores and behavioral observations (Huebner & Hahn, 1990; Ysseldyke, Algozzine, & Mitchell, 1982). Instead of problem solving, MDTs frequently engage in problem admiring.

The Regular Education Initiative (REI), originating out of special education, emphasizes the value of building-based problem solving teams. The REI movement assumes that special education policies have created a fragmented system and that the regular educational environment has failed to meet the needs of a sizable group of students (Will, 1986). The REI movement has led to the idea of inclusive schools, where all children are taught in what has traditionally been called regular education (Ohio Department of Education, 1989). However, educational environments will need to be sensitive to the needs of children previously served by special education. A primary characteristic of successful inclusive schools has been a strong teaming approach for problem solving, planning, and program implementation (Schattman & Benay, 1992).

BASIC CONSIDERATIONS

Effective and Ineffective Teams

While team meetings can produce greater job satisfaction, more reliable educational decisions, reduce the likelihood of biased decisions, and are more likely than individual decision making to develop creative solutions to educational problems, this method also contains pitfalls. Team meetings present a host of potential problems: hidden agendas, chronically late or absent members, role rigidity, lack of trust, competitiveness, dominant or submissive members, a hierarchical structure of the team, diffusion of responsibility, and many other factors can dramatically reduce a team's effectiveness. Often a member of an ineffective team may believe that he or she can perform a task alone more effectively, without the team as a burden.

Members of effective teams report that team meetings are the highlights of their work day, cannot imagine having to perform individually the complex tasks addressed by the team, and believe that children receive better education due to the efforts of the team. Effective teaming requires more than collecting several educators in one room, however. Developing an effective team demands planning, patience, knowledge of small-group dynamics, interpersonal skills, unity of purpose, and continuous assessment of team effectiveness. Only by investing time in an effective team will creative and constructive work be accomplished.

Team Development

The Ohio Department of Education (1989) identifies five stages in group development. Teams that have been working together can expect to spend some time in each stage. These stages include (a) orientation stage — members are eager to begin and have positive expectations; (b) dissatisfaction stage — members may become frustrated that their early expectations have not been met and feel incompetent as a team and as individuals; (c) resolution stage — members develop realistic expectations and acquire more effective collaborative skills; (d) production stage — leadership is shared, and a sense of mutual interdependence with other members grows; and (e) termination stage — members feel a strong sense of accomplishment and are sorry that the team's work is ending. Effective collaboration demands a great deal of patience and effort. Understanding that all teams go through a period of frustration before becoming truly productive can be an incentive for continuing to invest in teaming.

Philosophical Orientation

Shared values and assumptions are important for effective teaming, although team members do not necessarily have to hold the same theoretical orientations (e.g., all behaviorists). These values and assumptions should be articulated and agreed upon before collaborative teaming is instituted in a building, and all building staff should participate in these discussions. The following lists assumptions that were adopted in a building in which one of the authors consulted; they are based on the work of Graden (1993).

1. All children can learn.

2. All students can experience some degree of success in school.

3. Learning does not require that all students complete all the tasks or even all of the same tasks of any particular unit.

4. Children's learning and behavior problems reflect the interaction between their own personal characteristics and their environment.

5. All children have a need to be a member of their peer group.

6. All children have a right to be included as a valued member of their family, school, and community.

7. Teachers play an important role in collaborative problem-solving to develop effective intervention strategies for students.

8. Teachers can develop new skills, acquire new knowledge, and with assistance develop intervention strategies to address the needs of students.

9. Team members can effectively plan interventions to address the needs of students.

10. A wide range of interventions should be available to meet a variety of student needs, facilitate student participation, and maximize student achievement.

11. Both assessment and intervention should relate directly to the needs of students and be classroom-based.

Whether the team decides to adopt these assumptions or some of its own does not matter. However, if members do not share the same assumptions about teaching and learning, then resistance to some interventions and poor integrity of treatment implementation will likely result (Elliott, 1988).

BEST PRACTICES

Process Variables

Leadership is important to the success of team meetings. However, we recommend a distributed functions approach unlike that of many traditional teams; here, the functions of the classic lone leader are distributed among all members. The tendency for one member to become automatically the coordinator of the team may not be entirely negative in the early stages of team development, but teams function most effectively when leadership roles are dispersed. Such roles include the praiser, who administers positive feedback; the harmonizer, who reduces tension with humor and nonjudgmental explanations; the conflict resolver, who identifies emerging conflicts and signals the group to begin to resolve conflict; the equalizer, who regulates flow of discussion to make sure all members have a chance to participate; the parity checker, who makes sure work loads are evenly distributed among members; the "but" watcher, who monitors discussion that blocks creative ideas by using such as language as, "yes, but . . ."; and the jargon buster, who signals when members are using specialized terms that may not be understood by all members of the group (Thousand & Villa, 1992; Zins, Curtis, Graden, & Ponti, 1988). These roles may rotate from meeting to meeting. Distributing leadership roles lets each team member know that each is valued equally and everyone on the team has valuable and unique expertise. Even the important elements, developing agenda and setting goals, are reached by team consensus. Such a leadership system also confirms that all team members are "in this together." If building administrators also join the team, they need to share leadership rather than maintain a traditional hierarchical style of leadership. Hierarchical relationships discourage creativity and consensus building among team members.

For teams to work effectively they must meet face-to-face frequently and regularly to encourage camaraderie and team work. Team functions such as goal setting and agenda development are managed more easily when groups meet frequently. Teams that meet irregularly tend to focus on too many items at each meeting or on the crisis of the week. Regular meetings give the group sufficient time and energy to address a few important agenda items per meeting. Sixty minutes is the maximum time for effective meetings; beyond that the attention and productivity of the participants decrease rapidly. Further, a proactive approach to addressing problems often results from regular meetings. However, teams trying to meet frequently face the problems of conflicting schedules and individuals who tend to arrive late or depart early. Setting strict time limits for the beginning and ending of meetings is often helpful. If the team has the support of building administrators, perhaps teachers can be released from classes, having substitutes or volunteers take over during the regular team meeting periods. Team members may agree on group norms to help reduce attendance problems: "All meetings will start and end exactly on time"; "Meetings will not be interrupted to update late members"; and "No other activities will preempt meeting times."

A second problem is that teams often are too large: Teams of 15 to 20 educators are common. Large teams find it difficult to reach consensus, have all members participate, schedule times, communicate effectively, and make members accountable. A core team of four to seven members is most efficient. While two heads may be better than one, 20 heads are not necessarily better than four. A smaller team has enough members to present a variety of viewpoints and expertise, yet also allows each member to provide a unique and valued perspective. In addition, relationships among team members grows best when the team is small. Teams can be expanded temporarily to include physical therapists, physicians, translators, educational specialists, parents, peer advocates, or students as needed for input on a specific problem, but four to seven should be the core team size. The core team should be comprised of people who are most immediately and directly involved with a specific student, and the following questions should be asked when deciding who should be on the core team: Who is most expert in the area? Who will be most affected by the team's decisions? Who will be implementing the team's interventions? Who is an effective collaborator? In addition, to keep the teams small, members may represent a larger group. For example, a team may be made up of a teacher representative, a special education teacher representative, an administrator, a parent representative, a school counselor, and a school psychologist. Representatives should solicit ideas from their constituents and inform them of the activities of the last meeting. Because school psychologists' expertise includes communication, leadership, assessment, intervention, and preventative mental health strategies, we recommend that school psychologists serve on the core team in their buildings.

Whether a group of educators becomes a creative, effective team or a resentful, dysfunctional group depends on how well they address process issues. Time and energy must be spent on group functioning and on developing methods of increasing team efficiency. The authors have observed some teams investing time in processing during the initial stages of team development, but that time wanes as the work load becomes greater. This approach is penny-wise and pound-foolish. Content is obviously important, but it is worthwhile to spend 10 minutes of every hour-long meeting on comments concerning team member satisfaction, ideas for making the team run with increased efficiency, methods of opening communication, and other process components. The payoff will be an effective, creative, and satisfied team.

An important first step in becoming an effective team is for members to state their goals for the team and their individual goals as honestly as possible. To create trust, members should accept and support other members' goals. Individual goals might be "I need to get out of my classroom for an hour"; "I like to talk with adults for a change"; "I need to feel that I have a voice in some of the decisions at this school." All are acceptable reasons for being a part of a team. Honest goals that are accepted will help make openness, acceptance, and sharing part of the team norms. The norms of trust and trustworthiness will reduce the likelihood that members will have hidden agendas.

A frequent problem is that few educators have been trained to function on an egalitarian team. Many professionals are fixed in their roles by training and are uncomfortable with others impinging on their turf. Discomfort is not necessarily bad. However, strict role differentiation is unlikely in an effective team. Although team members will have various areas of expertise, some professional overlap is to be expected and encouraged. If openness to professional overlap is encouraged and agreed upon as a group norm, then a variety of problems can be addressed at team meetings. Teachers may help school psychologists to create more relevant and realistic academic interventions based upon identified learning strengths and weaknesses. School psychologists may help teachers to individualize curriculum for students with special needs. Principals may help counselors with efficient administration of services. Relying on the unique and varied expertise of team members by sharing knowledge through open communication produces creative, effective problem solving.

Perhaps the most important process variable is conflict management. In a climate of trust and open communication conflict is inevitable. If appropriately addressed, conflict leads to creative and useful solutions to problems. However, many conflicts arise from past interpersonal problems or current power struggles. Such conflicts must be resolved as soon as they occur. Thousand and Villa (1992) present four approaches to diminish conflict in team meetings.

1. Dysfunctional behaviors that occur infrequently or in isolated situations should be ignored.

2. Humor might be used to call attention to the behavior.

3. Attention may be called to these behaviors by noting the alternative or more appropriate behaviors of other team members. For example, if a team member frequently interrupts, other team members who wait their turn or build on the ideas of others are identified for the team.

4. If the team member's behavior becomes frequent and distracting, direct confrontation should be used. Comments regarding these distracting behaviors are uncomfortable for both the giver and the receiver. However, if it is believed that the feedback will be received positively, it can be given by any team member. If a negative response is anticipated, the feedback should be given in private by someone who enjoys a positive relationship with the person.

Inappropriate behaviors that violate group norms can be confronted using these five steps (Schmuck & Runkle, 1988): (a) observe the problem member's and other's responses to the behavior; (b) try to understand why the member may be persisting in the behavior; (c) describe to the member the behavior and its effect on the team, using nonjudgmental language; (d) establish rules for minimizing future disruptions; (e) turn the unfavorable behavior into a favorable one (e.g., assign an "aggressor" the role of devil's advocate for certain issues, have the "joker" open each meeting with the funny story, assign a "dominator" the role of encourager or equalizer, have the person who wanders from the topic signal whenever anyone gets off track [Corey & Corey, 1984; Thousand & Villa, 1992]).

A common observation in team meetings is that 10% of the people do 90% of the work (Rainforth, York, & Macdonald, 1992). These teams are often characterized by a lack of trust and failure to collaborate. Equity of work is essential for group trust and harmony. This is so important that we recommend that each team have a member assigned the role of parity enforcer, who would make sure that work is distributed fairly and all members have a chance to participate. Some of the dreaded roles, such as completion of paperwork and secretarial tasks, may need to be rotated each meeting. To minimize freeloading, each member should be asked to report on the progress of agreed-upon tasks from the past meeting. Thus, members are held publicly accountable for their roles and responsibilities. When work is distributed equally and each member has ownership of the groups' goals, accountability is rarely a problem.

Most educators learn collaboration while on the job, with little formal training. A wise investment would be in-service training for all administrators, teachers, parents, and other appropriate contributors to problem-solving teams. Anderlini (1983) developed an in-service program for improving team participation in MDTs. Clearly, preservice training and supervised field experience would be the best methods of training team members. For example, the University of Cincinnati requires course work and supervised fieldwork in teaming for regular and special education teachers, and other related service personnel, including school psychologists (University of Cincinnati, 1992). If collaborative problem-solving teams are to become a part of education in the twenty-first century, the new generation of educators will need formal training.

Teams need to have a systematic approach to problem solving. An effective approach to problem solving appears in the literature on behavioral consultation (Bergan & Kratochwill, 1990). The first stage, problem identification, determines the strengths and weaknesses of systems or individuals to be targeted, ascertains discrepancies between current and desired performance, sets goals, and finally, collects baseline data to verify the problem. This first stage is the most important step in problem solving. All team members must have a clear definition of the problem in order to solve it. During the problem-identification stage, the team must separate facts from opinions, focusing only on the facts that are most conducive to problem-solving. Although this stage may appear easy to accomplish, it is often the most difficult, and it demands a great deal of time.

A commonly forgotten stage is the second step, problem analysis. The goal of this stage is to identify factors that affect the development of problem solutions. Some of the issues addressed at this stage are legal consequences, administrative issues, antecedents and consequences of behaviors (e.g., prerequisite skills, environmental conditions surrounding the behavior), sequential conditions (e.g., what time of day does the behavior occur?), and how much time individuals are willing to invest in solving the particular problem.

Solutions to the problem can be generated in the third stage. Brainstorming is an effective and commonly used method of creating possible solutions. In this technique, all members are encouraged to submit ideas before the suggestions are evaluated. Members share interventions that have proven effective with children exhibiting problems similar to those of the target child.

Given a suitable number of suggestions, members discuss the strengths and weakness of each solution until they reach consensus. Important considerations are the effectiveness of the intervention based on previous experience, the ease of use and implementation, the possible negative effects on others, the intrusiveness of the intervention, and cost and time effectiveness. The person primarily responsible for its implementation must make the final choice as to which intervention to select. If this person is pleased with the intervention selected and believes that it can work, the intervention is more likely to be executed as planned (Elliott, 1988).

When a single solution or set of solutions is agreed upon, an individual or subcommittee forges the details of the solution. At this stage, members most closely involved in the problem examine exactly what tactics are to be used and make sure that the intervention is feasible. A rehearsal of the plan may even be attempted. The members should then ask, Who will implement the plan? When is the intervention to occur? Where is the intervention to occur? How will it be implemented? How and when will the outcomes be evaluated?

The solution is then implemented. Because many plans are not executed as designed, at least one member of the team must follow-up to make sure that the solution is being performed as planned.

Finally, after a suitable period of time, the solution or plan is evaluated. Members of the team compare, through data collection, the behaviors of systems or individuals with the goal established during problem identification. Often plans need to be modified or even abandoned entirely. In the latter case, the entire process may need to be repeated, starting with problem identification. When goals are reached, it is important to congratulate all team members.

Evaluating Effectiveness

Assessing a team's effectiveness demands a two-pronged approach. Providing specific feedback on team and individual performance improves both individual and collective effectiveness. Further, evaluating the productivity and effectiveness of the team's decisions yields outcome data that the team may use for improvement. The team may also wish to catalog outcome data for an external audit. Both process and outcome measures require a data-based approach to evaluating effectiveness.

Assessment of group process must take place for both individuals and team. Thousand and Villa (1992) have developed a useful self-report scale to assess individual and team functioning, which consists of four clusters of skills: trust building, communication and leadership, decision making and creative problem solving, and conflict management. Members assign a score of 1 (I/we never do) to 5 (I/we always do) for themselves and the team for each item. Members may also note two to four items that they believe they need to improve individually or as a team. Sample items are "I/we arrive at meetings on time"; "I/we do not use putdowns"; "I/we relieve tension with humor"; "I/we ask team members' opinions"; "I/we criticize ideas without criticizing people." These items focus on 47 specific competencies upon which all teams can improve. Frequent administration of this instrument can help determine group and individual improvement on certain skills, and help create process goals for the future. In addition, informal assessment of each team member's satisfaction provides information that can produce open discussion of how team functioning can be made increasingly enjoyable and productive. Such ideas can be added to Thousand and Villa's checklist for future assessment of team improvement.

Maintaining and developing effective communication and teamwork is a necessary, but not a sufficient condition for a team to be considered effective. Teams must also create effective products. From a management perspective, meetings are extraordinarily expensive in money and personnel. Thus, teams must demonstrate that they are doing more than communicating effectively. Two measures of outcome can demonstrate whether a team is effective: the number of solutions generated and the efficacy of these solutions. Expectations for the number of solutions vary depending on the purpose of the team. For example, a MDT designed to determine special education eligibility for students should be able to address more individual problems than should a team that is creating a new reading curriculum. Using the number of solutions as one accountability variable helps keep the agenda full and meetings moving at a reasonable pace. As an outcome measure, the effectiveness of each intervention is clearly more important than number of solutions generated. Six educators functioning independently would likely create more solutions than one team of six members. However, the solutions might not be as comprehensive, creative, thoughtful, or effective as team problem solving. To test effectiveness, each solution must also have a plan for collecting data to demonstrate the efficacy of the solution. Data should be collected using such approaches as curriculum-based measurement for a student's reading problems, direct observation of a student's behavior problems, or a survey of teacher satisfaction on the newly developed lunch supervision schedule, as well as number of grade retentions, number of special education referrals, pupil achievement on standardized test scores, tardiness, discipline referrals, parental satisfaction, teacher absences and requests for transfers, student grades, number of students failing, and reasons for referrals for special education. Efficacy data may be written up in a one-page report and stored in the team portfolio. In the event of an administrative accountability review, the team can provide brief reports of successes and ongoing projects. These data will demonstrate that educational teams are more than just meeting legal mandates and finding an excuse for socializing, but are an efficient use of resources for creative educational problem solving.

SUMMARY

As the population of children in the schools becomes increasingly diverse and the concept of inclusion gains favor in many school districts, the need for comprehensive, creative, and effective educational strategies grows stronger. Further, teachers, more than ever, are receiving public criticism, and may feel powerless to make any significant changes in the way their profession conducts itself. One answer to both problems is to institute collaborative problem-solving teams. These teams, made up of professionals with a variety of skills, can develop and implement a wider variety of interventions than any single individual. Also, greater empowerment and control over what happens in the classroom can be achieved by including educators and parents on these teams. However, a collected group of people who care about children and education does not constitute a collaborative team. Before they can call themselves a team, the people involved must develop common assumptions about children and learning, as well as common goals and expectations. Leadership, group norms, processes, conflict management techniques, equity in work, training, and systematic approaches to problem solving must continually be cultivated. The patience and effort demanded to turn a group into a team can have powerful rewards for school personnel, parents, and children.

REFERENCES

Anderlini,\cih\e L. S. (1983). An inservice program for improving team participation in educational decision-making. *School Psychology Review, 12,* 160—167.

Bergan, J. R., & Kratochwill, T. R. (1990). *Behavioral consultation and therapy.* New York: Plenum Press.

Chalfant, J., Pysh, M., & Moultrie, R. (1979). Teacher assistance teams: A model for within building problem solving. *Learning Disability Quarterly, 2,* 85–96.

Corey, G., & Corey, M. (1984). *Groups: Process and practice.* Monterey, CA: Brooks and Cole.

Elliott, S. N. (1988). Acceptability of behavioral treatments in educational settings. In J. C. Witt, S. N. Elliott, & F. M. Gresham (Eds.), *Handbook of behavioral therapy in education* (pp. 121–150). New York: Plenum Press.

Glickman, C. D. (1990). *Supervision of instruction: A developmental approach* (2nd ed.). Newton, MA: Allyn and Bacon.

Graden, J. L. (1993, February). *Problem solving assessment within an intervention assistance process.* Workshop presented at the Annual Convention of the Illinois School Psychologists Association, Rockford, IL.

Huebner, E. S., & Hahn, B. M. (1990). Best practices in coordinating multidisciplinary teams. In A. Thomas & J. Grimes (Eds.), *Best practices in school psychology – II.* Washington, DC: National Association of School Psychologists.

Maher, C. A., & Pfeiffer, S. I. (1983). Multidisciplinary teams in the schools: Perspectives, practices, and possibilities. *School Psychology Review, 12*, 2.

Ohio Department of Education. (1989). *Intervention assistance teams.* Columbus, OH: Author.

Patterson, E. G., D'Wolff, N., Hutchinson, P., Lowry, M., Schilling, M., & Siepp, J. (1976). *Staff development handbook: A resource for the transdisciplinary process.* New York: United Cerebral Palsy Association.

Rainforth, B., York, J., & Macdonald, C. (1992). *Collaborative teams for students with severe disabilities.* Baltimore: Paul H. Brooks.

Schattman, R., & Benay, J. (1992, February). Inclusive practices transform special education in the 1990s. *The School Administrator*, 8–12.

Schlechty, P. C. (1990). *Schools for the 21st century: Leadership imperatives for educational reform.* San Francisco: Jossey-Bass.

Schmuck, R., & Runkel, P. L. (1988). *Handbook of organizational development in schools.* Prospect Heights, IL: Waveland Press.

Skrtic, T. (1987). The national inquiry into the future of education for students with special needs. *Counterpoint, 4*, 6.

Thousand, J. S., & Villa, R. A. (1992). Collaborative teams: A powerful tool in school restructuring. In R. A. Villa, J. S. Thousand, W. Stainback, & S. Stainback (Eds.), *Restructuring for caring and effective education* (pp. 73–108). Baltimore: Paul H. Brooks.

University of Cincinnati. (1992). *Cincinnati Initiative for Teacher Education.* (Available from College of Education, Teachers College, Cincinnati, OH 54221–0002.)

Wiggens, G. (1989). The futility of trying to teach everything of importance. *Educational Leadership, 47*, 44–59.

Will, M. (1986, November). *Educating students with learning problems – A shared responsibility.* Washington, DC: Office of Special Education and Rehabilitation Services.

Ysseldyke, J. E. (1983). Current practices in making psychoeducational decisions about learning disabled students. *Journal of Learning Disabilities, 16*, 226–233.

Ysseldyke, J. E., Algozzine, B., & Mitchell, J. (1982). Special education team decision making: An analysis of current practice. *Personnel and Guidance Journal, 60*, 308–313.

Zins, J. E., Curtis, M. J., Graden, J. L., & Ponti, C. R. (1988). *Helping students succeed in the regular classroom.* San Francisco: Jossey-Bass.

ANNOTATED BIBLIOGRAPHY

Ohio Department of Education. (1989). *Intervention assistance teams.* Columbus, OH: Author.

This is a comprehensive "how to do it" booklet on developing and implementing intervention teams from initial ideas to final evaluations. It also includes detailed lists of strategies and preventative approaches to address various barriers to effective operations of teams. It is available from The Ohio Department of Education, Division of Elementary and Secondary Education, 65 Front Street, Columbus, OH 43215.

Rainforth, B., York, J., & Macdonald, C. (1992). *Collaborative teams for students with severe disabilities.* Baltimore: Paul H. Brooks.

Although this book is concerned primarily with serving severely disabled students, it contains several excellent chapters on the benefits of a collaborative relationship among parents, medical personnel, and educational personnel. Nearly all of the authors' recommendations for collaboration serve as best practices models for mildly as well as severely handicapped students.

Schmuck, R., & Runkel, P. L. (1988). *Handbook of organizational development in schools.* Prospect Heights, IL: Waveland Press.

This handbook provides a detailed treatment of processes and issues in team meetings, and may be most useful for its presentation of team building activities. These activities are effective in building team cohesion and communication.

Thousand, J. S., & Villa, R. A. (1992). Collaborative teams: A powerful tool in school restructuring. In R. A. Villa, J. S. Thousand, W. Stainback, & S. Stainback (Eds.), *Restructuring for caring and effective education* (pp. 73–108). Baltimore: Paul H. Brooks.

This comprehensive chapter addresses many issues and problems in developing a collaborative problem solving team, as well as presenting specific strategies, including self-evaluation tools for teams. The chapter also provides excellent coverage of process variables necessary to maintain productive collaborative teams.

Zins, J. E., Curtis, M. J., Graden, J. L., & Ponti, C. R. (1988). *Helping students success in the regular classroom.* San Francisco: Jossey-Bass.

This book includes a discussion of the need, important goals, benefits, and rationale for intervention assistance teams. Unique to this source is extensive coverage of intervention designs for common academic and behavioral problems in the schools. The book includes a rationale for how intervention assistance teams can be incorporated as a system of service delivery. There is also a valuable section on evaluating the effectiveness of an intervention assistance program.

15

Best Practices in a Problem-Solving Approach to Psychological Report Writing

James M. Surber
Knox-Warren Special Education District
Galesburg, Illinois

OVERVIEW

Report writing has traditionally been one of the least attractive aspects of a school psychologist's job responsibilities. Avoidance can be attributed to a variety of reasons, beginning with the fact that it generally occurs after the interventions are in place, after the multidisciplinary conference, after the information has been verbally communicated and demonstrated to the referring teacher, and after eligibility and placement decisions have been made. Repeating such information in writing "after the fact" then becomes a very low priority item in the school psychologist's schedule. Since most school psychologists value and emphasize direct services to children, parents, and teachers, they often delay their report writing in favor of more professionally rewarding activities such as consultation, counseling, research, and even testing. Teachers, parents, and administrators also directly communicate their desire for the school psychologist to delay report writing in favor of providing these direct services. Many school psychologists refer to report writing as an onerous burden, to be undertaken only when forced by the end of the semester or the school year. Witness the traditional picture of the school psychologist, dictaphone in hand, attempting to decipher his/her notes and recall key information about a student who was evaluated several months earlier.

Notwithstanding their limited popularity, written reports fulfill a variety of important functions in the school. They have historical significance for other professionals and other school districts by providing a longitudinal portrait of the child. Such information is particularly helpful at the time of reevaluation when the effectiveness of a program is being evaluated. The psychological report also provides written documentation and accountability when the primary purpose of conducting an evaluation is to gather information sufficient to permit the multidisciplinary team to determine whether the student is disabled and in need of special education and related services.

In probably no other profession or specialty do legislative regulations have such an important effect on the information presented in a written report. The psychological report for a student must address the source of the interference in learning, the child's unique educational needs, the answers to specific referral questions, and a determination of whether the child is disabled and in need of specialized educational services. However, we must keep in mind that the report is simply a vehicle to convert the assessment data into faithfully designed and executed interventions that lead to improved student performance.

This chapter will offer school psychologists an overview of a referral question/problem-solving mode of report writing. The emphasis will be on (a) clarifying referral questions during the consultative interview; (b) tailoring assessment procedures to answer specific referral questions; (c) ensuring that low-inference procedures precede high-inference procedures; (d) integration of the information into the report as the referral questions are addressed; and finally (e) development of interventions that assist in reducing the discrepancy between teachers' expectations and the student's performance. The first section reviews some of the problems inherent in traditional assessment and subsequent reports. Second, a problem-solving framework in the form of a referral question model of report writing is then described as a best practices approach. A discussion of methods for reducing bias during the data collection and decision-making process follows; and the final section addresses the mandated triennial reevaluation.

BASIC CONSIDERATIONS

Ysseldyke (1979) suggests that many educational personnel engage in assessment for no apparent purpose and with no clearly defined outcome for their findings. This lack of direction in assessment is most evident in the use of a standard battery in the identification of disabled students. Standard batteries typically include the administration of an intelligence test, a standardized achievement battery, and a measure of visual–motor coordination. Reschly and Wilson (1990) report that school psychologists devote approximately 65% of their time to various activities related to determining special education eligibility. Typical services often reflect a refer–test–place–forget sequence in which intellectual assessment is the prominent source of data collection. However, these standardized tests are relatively useless and potentially harmful to children if their use does not emphasize interventions and recommendations for reducing the interference to the child's learning. To date, there is no empirical support for the use of standard batteries in answering specific referral questions or planning appropriate instruction for students. In fact, they miss the key referral concerns in a majority of cases.

The use of these so-called standard batteries have been criticized for a variety of reasons, ranging from fairness to students to concerns about validity of the assessment and placement decisions (Reschly & Wilson, 1990). More specifically a standardized battery makes it extremely difficult, if not impossible, to address a variety of potential referral concerns. Second, such practice does not lend itself readily to an integrated approach. Third, the traditional report often presents intellectual, educational, fine-motor, and behavioral/emotional data in a compartmentalized format with each area assigned its own heading. This format typically places the burden of determining what information is relevant on the reader, rather than the author. Finally, the last paragraph, often titled "Summary," is left for the integration of all the separate sections. Consequently, the reader typically pages ahead to the summary section without gaining the benefit of an integrated approach. Integration of the assessment data should occur throughout the report, not just in the summary (Batsche, 1983).

In response to heavy caseloads or in an attempt to provide written feedback in an expedient manner, many school psychologists feel restricted in the amount of time they can devote to the development of a report. As a result, the psychologist's report is limited to 1–$1\frac{1}{2}$ pages, addressing instruments used, test scores, and special education eligibility. This format tends to be generic, not providing the reader with a clear picture of the referred student. At the opposite end of the continuum, some of the more lengthy reports include every detail of the evaluation process, whether relevant or not. Both novice and experienced readers are left to wade through the jargon, attempting to ferret out the key elements that have relevance for the student and the teacher in the classroom. Consequently, items of greatest relevance become diluted in the sea of information being washed ashore. Tallent (1993) noted that the longer the report, the less significant any given item becomes, causing the relevance of the content to gradually fade. During the process of report writing, the school psychologist must give as much consideration to what information

should be left out of the document as to what should be included.

Computer-assisted reports also have the inherent weakness of so-called information overload. Although such programs have an initial lure for time-strapped psychologists, Matarazzo (1986) reported that "With almost no exception, today's software produces only a single, typically very lengthy, clinical narrative." As anyone who has used them can attest, computer-generated reports, with their limited bank of canned phrases and interpretations, result in a "horoscope" of oversimplified conclusions.

Readability is also a source of concern when reports serve as the primary mode of communication with the referral agent. Consequently the rule of thumb is that psychological and educational jargon must always be avoided. If not, statements may not be understood, which reduces the psychologists' credibility, making the report nothing more than a source of frustration for the classroom teacher. Thus, the writer is left with the problem of reporting the assessment in such a way as to exclude common terms for explaining the meaning of the data, such as "visual-motor coordination," "verbal/performance discrepancies," and so forth (Ownby, 1987). However, this dilemma can be avoided if such terms are followed with a detailed explanation of how the identified strengths or weaknesses are manifested and demonstrated by the student in the educational setting. These explanations take on added significance if we consider survey research in which school psychologists report continuing concerns with insufficient time devoted to formulating intervention plans during multidisciplinary conferences (Huebner & Gould, 1991). Considering the limited time available at staffings to explain evaluation results and recommendations, the report may take on greater significance in detailing the interventions that were developed as a part of the assessment process. In general reports must be child-centered, objective, positive, integrated, concise, and outcome-based, and they must be completed in a timely fashion.

BEST PRACTICES

Tallent (1993) points out that the psychological report is clearly a reflection of the role that the psychologist has assumed within the school environment. If the psychologist's role is limited to that of "tester–technician," the document produced will reflect this narrow focus and will be restricted to the reporting of test results. On the other hand, if the psychologist functions as a consultant, the format of the report takes a markedly different direction. When the psychologist's role is expanded to include consultative services, the approach to assessment becomes "related to a distinctive prescription for educational practices . . . that leads to improved outcomes for students" (Heller, Holtzman, & Messick, 1982). The resulting document moves beyond the simple reporting of test scores to the development of educationally relevant interventions that can be understood by parents and put into practice by school personnel. Although many school psychology training programs are incorporating this consultative model into all aspects of training, a large number of practicing psychologists have made this transition on their own through preservice training, in-service presentations, and other self-initiated professional development activities. This transition has been fueled by the fact that most school psychologists find the model professionally rewarding because of its relevance and direct benefits to both the student and school personnel.

With this shift from assessment for classification decisions to assessment for intervention purposes (Gresham, 1983), practicing school psychologists need to examine their roles in the school to determine if their style of report writing is consistent and current with a problem-solving theoretical model. The most likely match for this current best practices approach to assessment is a problem-solving report-writing model. From examining this model, it also becomes evident that it includes many built-in safeguards that will assist the psychologist in avoiding many of the pitfalls associated with more traditional models.

Problem-Solving Report-Writing Model

The premise of the problem-solving report-writing model is that the collection of assessment data is for the purpose of developing quality interventions. As Batsche (1983) suggests, a problem-solving report-writing model responds to a variety of weaknesses inherent in traditional reports. First, it ensures that both the assessment and the report are individualized and address the specific referral questions. Second, the report is intervention-oriented and clarifies the reasons for the referral. Third, it increases the treatment validity of the assessment procedures; and finally, the report is tailored directly to the referral source.

Conceptually, a problem-solving model utilizes the selection of assessment devices that are geared to answering specific referral concerns, which in turn lead to relevant classroom interventions. However, the relevance of any intervention cannot be determined adequately in the absence of defensible levels of adherence to the intervention plan and of treatment integrity (Gresham, 1991). Meichenbaum and Turk (1987) define intervention adherence as the degree to which the classroom teacher is committed to implementing a specific intervention and actively demonstrates behaviors directed toward this end. Treatment integrity, a term closely related to intervention adherence, describes the degree to which an intervention is planned and implemented in good faith (Gresham, 1989). Zins and Ponti (1990) point out

that these two variables are clearly the critical issue in producing successful outcomes for students in a problem-solving model (see Telzrow in this volume for more information regarding intervention adherence).

Failure of such documented interventions would then be the basis for initiating the case study evaluation process. If the child does not respond to the interventions at his/her instructional level in curricular areas, the probability increases that a learning or behavioral deficit exists. The results of these interventions should be used as the basis for making decisions regarding further educational recommendations and/or establishing the need for initiating a referral. To ensure treatment integrity, it is recommended that there be documented evidence of at least three attempted interventions in the regular classroom. Such a procedure is critical to ensure appropriate referrals and to rule out academic or behavioral problems that are not the result of a disability. Resistance to training may be a better indicator of a disability than present levels of performance that have been generated by a battery of standardized tests. Since there are many reasons for learning and behavior problems in the school environment, it is essential to have a plan for studying children systematically before referring them for comprehensive case study evaluations. Such a model emphasizes a preventative approach with modified instruction to assist children who are experiencing difficulty. This process takes advantage of existing professional skills and helps to eliminate problems that may be related to factors other than disability. This procedure is consistent with the concept of least restrictive environment and may help reduce the number of children who are too quickly referred, evaluated, classified as disabled, and placed in a special education program. Such a procedure should not be used or misinterpreted as an approach for delaying the provision of services to disabled children. In fact, the purpose of such preliminary data collection is to expand available assistance to students in the regular classroom, not to deny needed services (Zins, Graden, & Ponti, 1988).

The generic problem-solving model described in this chapter should be thought of as a continuum that begins with preliminary data collection in the regular classroom that may or may not lead to a case study evaluation. The following are recommended steps in the process:

Steps in the Problem-Solving Model

Request for services. When a student's academic and adjustment problems are a persistent concern, the classroom teacher should submit a request for assistance to the school psychologist, building-based team, and so on. Parents are always informed of the associated concerns and encouraged to be active participants in the process.

Preliminary data collection. Following receipt of a request for services, the first step is to review and/or collect available information regarding the student. This may involve a review of records, test scores, grades, discipline reports, work samples, primary mode of communication, language proficiency data, information from parent conferences, classroom observations, and any other relevant information. This data will ensure that the school psychologist and the building team are informed partners during the consultative interview.

Consultative interview. The development of appropriate interventions begins with a consultative interview with the referral source. The goal of the interview is to strategize the problem-solving process by focusing on prior interventions, desired outcomes, student's strengths and a definition of the referral concerns in a behavioral theory-specific and discrete form. This process is metacognitive in that it allows the participants to think about their own thinking. Teachers are given time to think about what they know, what they do not know, and what they need to know about solving the problem (DeBoer & Ciello, 1990). Listed below are recommended points that should be addressed during the interview. The areas do not necessarily need to be reviewed in the order in which they are presented. Rather they should be answered at naturally occurring times during the consultative interview.

1. *Problem statement:* The interview will begin with a general statement/overview of the concerns expressed by the referral agent.

2. *Problem analysis:* In this step the referral questions are behaviorally defined. Typically the majority of the interview is spent on clearly identifying the problem. This follows from the thesis that the best interventions are more obvious and acceptable to teachers once the problem is clarified and framed.

3. *Prior interventions:* The teacher will discuss the success or lack of success of interventions that have already been attempted in the classroom. This may serve as the basis on which to build subsequent solutions.

4. *Desired outcomes:* Here it is important to have the teacher identify the desired replacement behaviors. In other words what they would like the student to be doing that she or he is currently not doing.

5. *Student's strengths:* This step actually serves two purposes. First, it requires the participants to focus on the student's assets in addition to the deficit areas. Second, interventions can be centered around the child's strengths. This strategy assists in move-

ment away from a deficit-oriented model and builds on existing skills and abilities.

6. *Interventions to be implemented:* In collaboration with other team members, the school psychologist should not have preconceived notions of how to solve the problem. Solutions tend to evolve as the problem is clarified. No suggestions should be offered by the consultant(s) until the referral agent has explored all of his or her own ideas, resources, and possible options. Offering possible solutions too early in the process is a guarantee of failure. Until teachers have ownership of the problems they report, they are not likely to focus all of their energy on solving them. Interventions must be predicated on teaching new behaviors not just reducing or eliminating undesirable behaviors. If the intervention does not involve a teachable skill, it will not be an effective intervention.

7. *Monitoring system:* Before the interview is brought to a close, there must be some agreed-upon method of monitoring the student's progress. For example, nonobtrusive documentation may take the following forms: percentage of work completed; percentage of time in seat; comparison of work samples; event recording; time sampling; percentage of correct work; and so forth.

8. *Follow-up date:* A follow-up date should always be set. This provides for a specified amount of time to evaluate the effectiveness of the interventions.

Development of Referral Questions

As early as 1967 Rucker reported on the results of teachers' ratings and the usefulness of reports written by experienced and by less experienced school psychologists. Although the results were statistically nonsignificant, the teachers completing the ratings judged that the most useful reports were those that clearly answered the referral questions (Ownby, 1987). Consequently, the key element of defining the referral concern behaviorally provides not only the rationale for data collection, but also the means by which the school psychologist can successfully link assessment data to clearly defined interventions.

Best practice requires that referral questions be limited to those that are definable, measurable, and relevant to the educational concerns of the child, and that are agreed-upon and prioritized. The continued use of standard batteries can be attributed in part to the lack of clearly defined referral questions. Questions that lend themselves only to classification concerns are inappropriate and not considered relevant for the development of classroom interventions. The referral question is generated during Step 2 of the interview process. Other questions can be added at the discretion of the school psychologist, after limited success with the interventions or when it is decided to go to a case study evaluation. The questions should be listed individually throughout the report with the source of the question identified. Examples: (a) Why is it difficult for Richard to complete his independent seatwork successfully? (Ms. Schmidt, classroom teacher); (b) How good are Sarah's reading fluency and comprehension skills compared with her current grade placement and measured intelligence? (Ms. Jones, Chapter 1 reading teacher); (c) Why is Mike noncompliant during direct instruction; what precipitates the inappropriate behavior and what maintains the behavior? (Mr. Hall, second-grade teacher); (d) Are Johnny's poor attending skills interfering with his academic performance? If so, how can his productivity in the classroom be increased? (Ms. Becker, fifth-grade teacher).

Selection of Assessment Procedures

When choosing assessment procedures, it is important to keep in mind that the selection of each procedure must be purposeful in seeking an answer to a referral question, not merely serve as an essential element of a standard battery or so-called multifactored assessment.

There are primarily five types of data that may be utilized by school psychologists in answering referral questions and formulating educational interventions:

1. Reviews of available information.

2. Interviews with significant persons who have direct contact with the child.

3. Observations, both anecdotal and standardized.

4. Testing, which may include norm-referenced, criterion-referenced, and/or curriculum-based measurement.

5. Vision and hearing screening.

Review of available information. Both temporary and permanent records paint a very good picture of a child's educational history. This information can be extremely useful in determining if present levels of performance are consistent with reported and observed behavior in the current school environment. If the current behavior is divergent from the child's previous behavior, it may indicate a situational or instructional variable (e.g., a recent traumatic event or a conflict with an individual teacher or subject area) rather than an established pattern of performance over time.

Interviewing. Interviewing persons who have direct contact with the student is extremely important in gaining an understanding of the child from the people that know her or him the best. As outlined in the section above, interview information is extremely important, even vital in determining present patterns of behavior, gaps in learning, effective reinforcers, ef-

fective consequences, and the basis for hypothesis testing of unknown information.

Observations. Sattler (1988) suggests that behaviors recorded over a sufficient period of time will reflect a representative sample of the behaviors under observation in the school. Observational data, both anecdotal and standardized, are an important source of information to be considered prior to the consultative interview and before the development of interventions. Such information is objective, reliable, verifiable, clear, and complete and can serve as a direct link between the formal test data and the actual classroom behavior. It is also helpful in quantifying behavioral characteristics and establishing a baseline for the development of interventions.

Testing. *Testing* is often used interchangeably with the term *assessment*. However, testing is only one component that falls under the umbrella of assessment. Testing can be formal in the case of norm-referenced tests, which are used primarily in the classification of disability areas. Criterion-referenced testing, on the other hand, is used in the determination of instructional levels and the development of educational interventions.

Vision and hearing screening. Although listed last, this information may be the most important because it rules out any sensory impairment that may be contributing to the difficulties a student is experiencing in the classroom. It is extremely important that a sensory deficit not be incorrectly interpreted as a skill deficit in an academic subject area.

Selection of Assessment Devices

After the school psychologist has developed specific referral questions, the assessment devices must be selected and tailored to answer the specific questions. These assessment techniques are not rank-ordered and no single method should be considered more important than another. Rather, the choice will vary depending on the referral question and the desired information. For example, it is not necessary that every child referred for a case study evaluation be routinely administered a standardized intelligence test. If a child is acting out in the classroom despite a demonstration of above-average academic and abstract reasoning skills, an intelligence test is clearly not warranted. In this case, the most relevant information may be standardized observations, behavior rating scales, and interviews with the parents and teacher. These data collection methods have a much better chance of answering the referral concern, which in turn leads to relevant interventions.

Sequence of Assessment

An important step in minimizing outcome bias is making sure that the assessment sequence proceeds from low-inference to high-inference items. Low-inference methods are objective and require a minimum of subjective judgment or psychological interpretation to reach consensus. Such data collection methods include observation, review of records, interviews, student work samples, and so on, which will ultimately influence the selection, administration, and interpretation of high-inference procedures. The collection of these objective data should lead to the development of hypotheses for developing predictions that can and should be tested through the collection of high-inference procedures. It is through the development of relevant, predictive, and testable hypotheses that the school psychologist moves beyond merely accumulating and reporting facts into an evaluation of the linkages among the facts. For example, the teacher may express a concern about the poor quality of a student's independent seatwork. The school psychologist might immediately question whether the student has the necessary reading skills to complete the work. If the teacher is unsure, this could be checked out by suggesting that he or she establish an instructional level through the use of curriculum-based measurement. Skills deficits in other areas and slow rates of learning may suggest the need to move to data collection procedures that require a higher degree of inference, such as cognitive batteries or intelligence tests. These methods are obviously much more hypothetical and require higher degrees of subjective interpretations to confirm or deny the predictions about the student. The point is that if the high-inference procedures are conducted first (as often is the case), conclusions may be incorrectly drawn about the student that are not consistent and convergent with the student's performance in the classroom. When such methods are put into practice, biased outcomes for students often result. To minimize this as a source of bias, it is recommended that assessment proceed in the following manner: review of records; vision and hearing screening; determination of language dominance; classroom observation(s); interview with teacher; interview with the parents; review of work samples; determination of educational achievement through the curriculum; completion of behavior checklists; and assessment of adaptive behavior, achievement, intelligence, learning processes, and personality.

Answering Specific Referral Questions and Converging Multifactored Assessment Information

The answers to specific referral questions must begin with an analysis and integration of the diverse sources of information. As Gresham (1983) suggests, the most meaningful way to integrate evaluation information is through the use of a multitrait–multimethod approach. Such an approach utilizes numerous methods (tests, interviews, observations, re-

views, etc.) to assess multiple traits (intelligence, adaptive behavior, academic achievement, etc.), in order to determine the consistency of the results across methods and traits. This requires the school psychologist to shift assessment efforts away from a simple description of the results to an integration of the data that requires a high level of agreement between and within assessment methods. When convergence of the results exists and all the data are pointing toward the same conclusions, the school psychologist and other team members can feel much more confident about the answers to the referral questions and subsequent recommendations. If there is a lack of agreement between or within these methods of assessment, then further investigation of the referral questions is mandatory. For example, if the results obtained from the standardized tests are not consistent with the teacher's reports, parents' reports, work samples, and classroom performance, then additional investigation is needed to determine the reasons for the divergence of the information. In such a case there may be several reasons for the lack of consistency between data sources. First, the standardized procedures may be invalid and not constitute a true representation of the student's ability. Second, the variation in scores may be due to the different response patterns in a group versus an individual setting. Or the differences may represent the lack of curriculum validity between what is being taught and what is being tested by the norm-referenced tests. Regardless of the reasons, additional referral questions must be generated and answered before one proceeds with further analysis, integration, classification, recommendations, or interventions. Without such careful scrutiny children will continue to be inappropriately labeled and placed in special programs without a clear understanding of the reasons for the interference in learning, the necessary interventions to reduce the interference, and the best educational setting for implementing the recommendations. It is important to remember that placement of a child in special education is not an intervention; it is merely a change in location. There must be clearly defined reasons for the placement and evidence that the interventions can be accomplished only in a setting outside of the regular classroom.

RECOMMENDATIONS/INTERVENTIONS

Recommendations for the development of school-based interventions that are directly linked to the referral concerns will conclude the formal process. While this framework relates to observable aspects of the student's behavior, it does not imply that the only treatments that are appropriate are behavioral. The treatment technologies may be as varied as the ingenuity of the people involved in designing interventions. When interventions are agreed-on and definitively chosen, the rule of thumb is to "think big and begin small." In other words, easy-to-implement solutions are preferable to grandiose interventions that may be disruptive to the classroom, time-consuming, and difficult for the teacher to monitor. It is also important that recommended interventions be developed in such a manner that they can be implemented with a minimum of guidance from the school psychologist or other team members. New interventions should be built on existing structures, or ideas previously implemented by the teacher, that may have been abandoned too early. Always plan for maintenance and generalization of skills and get students involved in monitoring their own progress. Each recommendation should be taught and/or demonstrated to the teacher in the classroom if it is an unfamiliar technique. The effectiveness of interventions should be data based rather than subjectively determined by teacher observation.

REEVALUATIONS

Reports of reevaluations will be approached from the perspective of determining individual education plan (IEP) relevance, measured progress of goals and objectives, appropriateness of setting, and needed interventions or changes. From a legal perspective, the reevaluation process must address all components of the initial or most recent regulatorily complete case study evaluation. The nature and thoroughness of each component will vary depending on the individual needs of the student and the pertinent information already available in the student's educational record. It is reasonable to expect that certain types of information may not change significantly during the time period between the most recent case study evaluation and the reevaluation. The evaluation team must demonstrate professional judgment regarding the amount and type of evaluation to be performed based on available information. Under certain circumstances a reevaluation need only be a review of records and current progress with appropriate recommendations. On the other hand, circumstances may indicate the need for a complete assessment of all case study components.

Best practices would suggest that the student be reevaluated by utilizing the four following problem-solving steps.

Review of All Existing
Data Available on the Student

This should include a review of the child's permanent and temporary school records and any pertinent information (work samples, test results, etc.) collected by the classroom teacher(s). In evaluating the child's confidential file, particular note should be made of the IEPs for the last 3 years. The IEPs should be reviewed to determine to what extent the student has met the goals over the past 3 years.

Interview with the Child, Parent(s), and Teacher to Develop New Referral Questions

The purpose of the interview is to gain information about the student, to clarify what additional information is desired by the parent and/or teacher(s), and to develop definable and measurable referral questions.

Selection of Appropriate Assessment Procedures for the Referral Questions

There are basically four methods of collecting data for assessment purposes: observation, reviewing, interviewing, and testing. The method of choice will be determined by the individual needs of the student and the pertinent information already available.

Selection of Intervention Strategies

Recommendations and interventions should be organized from the information that was gathered during the interview process. Once sufficient information in the form of specific referral questions has been gathered, the school psychologist must select assessment procedures designed to answer those questions. This will help to ensure meaningful outcomes for the student.

The primary intent of the reevaluation is to ensure that the continuing individual needs of the student are identified and that the relevant information for present and future programming is available. As the student progresses through his or her specific program, referral questions will continually be generated, information gathered, and interventions implemented.

SUMMARY

In brief, psychological reports are a reflection of how the school psychologist practices. If the majority of time is spent testing children and determining eligibility for special education, the report will convey such an approach. In turn, if the school psychologist operates within a consultative, problem-solving, referral question model, the written results, recommendations, interventions, and ultimate outcomes for the student will be graphically represented in the psychological report. Consequently, a review of best practices in report writing must be preceded by a discussion of best practices in the delivery of services. It is the intent of this chapter to demonstrate how report writing and practice are inextricably intertwined.

Psychological reports must continue to evolve by moving beyond the simple reporting of individual test scores and determinations of eligibility for special education. It is important to keep in mind that placement of a child in a special education program is not an intervention; rather special education is a setting in which appropriate services may or may not be delivered. The environment in which these services can best be delivered depends on the needs of the individual student. We have all heard of special education referred to as a "deficit model" and the psychological report as a search for the pathology. Consequently, it is vitally important to avoid the reporting of assessment data that emphasize only deficits and negative aspects of the child. The positive aspects of the child must be emphasized as well, with the building of interventions on strengths, rather than weaknesses. In order to do this, reports must be more than a review of scores generated from a standard battery of tests. Such an approach incorrectly encourages a shotgun approach in which an effort is made to report every conceivable characteristic of the child. This produces a document that is poorly integrated and focuses on test results rather than the student's needs. It is common in this type of report to interpret each test individually with limited attention to how the results from one area may affect the outcomes in other areas. Reports written in this style tend to be a very broad review of nonspecific and irrelevant information (Tallent, 1993). Rather, the mission of the psychological report should be a review of answers to referral questions that lead to faithfully executed interventions that assist in reducing the interference in learning.

The appropriateness of interventions is contingent upon the collaborative problem-solving team's having a thorough understanding of the student's needs. The standard of excellence in a problem-solving approach is whether the referral question has been behaviorally defined and is consistent with recommended interventions and desired outcomes. The linking of assessment to intervention continues to be one of the most complex and challenging demands placed upon today's school psychologist. However, it is important that this link be established and the challenge be met in order for the student to be the beneficiary of appropriate school-based interventions.

Psychological reports represent one of the key components of a case study evaluation. Although reports are often criticized for their jargon and lack of relevance for classroom interventions, the psychological report remains an important communication link between the psychologist and regular and special education teachers, parents, administrators, community agencies, pupil personnel staff, and all other staff involved with the student.

In a practical sense, it is important that the report be clear, concise, meaningful, integrated, and well-organized. It is imperative that the turn-around time for reports be short in order for them to be a useful tool for the school personnel engaged with the student on a daily basis. Teachers are pleased to receive shorter, more timely, reports that will assist them immediately with their intervention efforts.

The model outlined in this chapter defines assessment as a problem-solving process with a focus on the reasons for assessment and outcome-based interventions. The identified problem(s) cannot be solved and the team cannot collaboratively contribute to the solution until questions and referral concerns relevant to the child's educational problems are behaviorally formulated, specifically defined, in measurable terms, and agreed upon by all participants. Clearly defining the referral concern provides the only rationale for any assessment or data collection by the school psychologist. The report evolves naturally as a part of this consultative process by addressing relevant background information, giving specific answers to referral questions, describing the interference in learning, and tailoring interventions to answer the specific concerns. Such an orientation precludes the school psychologist's role as the administrator of standard batteries and recognizes that not all school-based concerns are dealt with in the same manner. By attending to the sequence of assessment and incorporating a multimethod, multitrait approach, the school psychologist can better ensure that the outcomes for students are nondiscriminatory.

It is hoped that this chapter will assist school psychologists in understanding the importance and value of providing integrated, data-based reports that respond to identified concerns and lead to positive outcomes for students, teachers, and parents.

REFERENCES

Algozzine, B., & Ysseldyke, J. E. (1986). The future of the LD field: Screening and diagnosis. *Journal of Learning Disabilities, 19*(7), 394–398.

Batsche, G. M. (1983). The referral oriented consultative assessment report writing model. In J. Grimes (Ed.), *Communicating psychological information in writing* (pp. 27–43). Des Moines, IA: Iowa Department of Public Instruction.

DeBoer, A., & Ciello, M. (1990). *Collaborative problem solving: A video training program.* Copyright 1990 by DeBoer-Haller Company.

Gresham, F. M. (1983). Psychoeducational reports: Converting multifactored assessment. In J. Grimes (Ed.), *Communicating psychological information in writing* (pp. 47–61). Des Moines, IA: Iowa Department of Instruction.

Gresham, F. M. (1989). Assessment of treatment integrity in school consultation and prereferral intervention. *School Psychology Review, 18,* 37–50.

Gresham, F. M. (1991). Whatever happened to functional analysis in behavioral consultation? Journal of Educational and Psychological Consultation, 2, 387–392.

Grimes, J., & Ross-Reynolds, G. (1983). On skinning cats, choking dogs, and leaving lovers. In J. Grimes (Ed.), *Communicating psychological information in writing* (pp. 3–7). Des Moines, IA: Iowa Department of Public Instruction.

Gutkin, T. B., & Curtis, M. J. (1990). School-based consultation: Theory, techniques, and research. In T. B. Gutkin & C. R. Reynolds (Eds.), *The handbook of school psychology* (2nd ed.). New York: Wiley.

Huebner, E. S., & Gould, K. (1991). Multidisciplinary teams revisited: Current perceptions of school psychologists regarding team functioning. *School Psychology Review, 20,* 428–434.

Kavale, K. A., & Glass, G. V. (1982). The efficacy of special education interventions and practices: A compendium of meta-analysis findings. *Focus on Exceptional Children, 15*(4), 1–14.

Kellerman, H., & Burry, A. (1991). *Handbook of psychodiagnostic testing: An analysis of personality in the psychological report* (2nd ed.). Boston: Allyn & Bacon.

Lloyd, J. S., Keller, C. E., Kaufman, J. M., & Hallahan, D. P. (1988, January). *What will the regular education initiative require of general education teachers?* Report submitted to Office of Special Education and Rehabilitative Services, U.S. Department of Education. Washington, DC: U.S. GPO.

Matarazzo, J. D. (1986). Computerized psychological test interpretations: Unavailable dated plus all mean and no sigma. *American Psychologist, 41*, 14–24.

Ownby, R. L. (1987). *Psychological reports: A guide to report writing in professional psychology.* Clinical Psychology Publishing Co.

Phye, G. D., & Reschly, D. J. (1979). *School psychology: Perspectives and issues.* New York: Academic.

Reschly, D. J., Genshaft, J., & Binder, M. S. (1987). *The NASP survey: Comparison of practitioners, NASP leadership, and university faculty on key issues.* Washington, DC: National Association of School Psychologists.

Reschly, D. J., & Wilson, M. S. (1990). Cognitive processing v. traditional intelligence and treatment validity. *School Psychology Review, 19*, 443–458.

Reynolds, M. C. (1989). An historical perspective: The delivery of special education to mildly disabled and at-risk students. *Remedial and Special Education, 10*(6), 7–11.

Ross-Reynolds, G. (1990). Best practices in report writing. In A. Thomas & J. Grimes (Eds.), *Best practices in school psychology–II.* Washington, DC: National Association of School Psychologists.

Sattler, J. M. (1988). *Assessment of children* (3rd ed.). San Diego: Jerome M. Sattler, publisher.

Shellenberger, S. (1982). Presentation and interpretation of psychological data in educational settings. In C. R. Reynolds & T. B. Gutkin (Eds.), T*he handbook of school psychology* (pp. 51–81). New York: Wiley.

Shepard, L. A. (1989). Identification of mild handicaps. In R. L. Linn (Ed.), *Educational measurement* (3rd ed., pp. 545–572). New York: Macmillan, for the American Council on Education.

Tallent, N. (1993). *Psychological report writing* (4th ed). Englewood Cliffs, NJ: Prentice-Hall.

Thurlow, M. L., Ysseldyke, J. E., Lehr, C. A., & Nania, P. A. (1988). Diagnostic assessment in early childhood special education programs. *Special Services in the Schools, 4*(314), 1–22.

Ysseldyke, J. E. (1979). Issues in psychoeducational assessment. In G. Phye & D. Reschly (Eds.), *School psychology: Perspectives and issues.* New York: Academic.

Zins, J. E., & Barnett, D. W. (1983). Report writing: Legislative, ethical, and professional challenges. *Journal of School Psychology, 21*, 219–227.

Zins, J. E., & Graden, J. L. (1988). Prereferral intervention to improve special services delivery. *Special Services in the Schools, 4*(314), 109–130.

ANNOTATED BIBLIOGRAPHY

Grimes, J. (Ed.). *Communicating psychological information in writing.* Des Moines, IA: Iowa Department of Public Instruction.

This resource guide describes approaches and considerations involved in school psychologists' communication of information in reports. Following an initial tongue-in-cheek discussion of principles of report writing by J. Grimes and G. Ross-Reynolds, the same writers focus on "Three Counter Proposals to the Traditional Psychological Report," in which revised formats of the same report are presented. G. Batsche describes the "Referral-Oriented Consultative Assessment Report Writing Model" and F. Gresham reviews the multitrait--multimethod approach to test validation and applies the approach to psychoeducational assessment and decision making. In the final chapter Ross-Reynolds reviews the "Three-Year Reevaltion: An Alternative to the Reevaluation–Means–Retest Model."

Ownby, R. L. (1987). *Psychological reports: A guide to report writing in professional psychology.* Brandon, VT: Clinical Psychology Publishing Co.

This book does a very good job of addressing the difficulty of translating assessment results into writing. Ownby does this by developing a theory-based outline of report-writing practices and a structure for considering the problems associated with report writing. This resource has a strong clinical orientation with the exception of a brief section in Chapter 7. However, this would still be an excellent resource for the experienced practitioner desiring a refresher and a must for the school psychologist in training.

Ross-Reynolds, G. (1990). Best practices in report writing. In A. Thomas & J. Grimes (Eds.), *Best practices in school psychology–II.* Washington, DC: National Association of School Psychologists.

Ross-Reynolds does an excellent job of reviewing a variety of alternative report-writing models from which psychologists may choose to make their reports more effective. The models reviewed include the traditional report; psychological reports—revised format; letter and memo formats; referral-oriented, consultative assessment reports; translated reports; graphs in reports; and computer-assisted reports. The chapter also includes a self-assessment checklist that serves as an excellent self-monitoring device for the school psychologist with all levels of training and experience. Any psychologist writing reports on a regular basis should periodically review this chapter.

Sattler, J. M. (1988). *Assessment of children* (3rd ed.). San Diego: Jerome M. Sattler, publisher.

Sattler provides an essential reference as well as an excellent text for all professionals involved in the assessment of children and the writing of reports. Several examples of both correct and incorrect report-writing models are provided as learning tools. The pitfalls common to psychological reports are reviewed and an outline for a best practices approach to report writing is recommended. This book is a requirement for all professional libraries.

Tallent, N. (1993). *Psychological report writing* (4th ed.). Englewood Cliffs, NJ: Prentice-Hall.

In his fourth edition Tallent does a masterful job of providing an overview of all aspects of psychological report writing. Although greater emphasis is given to clinical report writing, Chapter 10 is devoted to psychological report writing in the school setting and provides a great deal of insight into the difficulties encountered in schools. This is an excellent reference for school psychologists.

16

Best Practices in Training School Psychologists

Karen T. Carey
Marilyn S. Wilson
California State University, Fresno

OVERVIEW

This chapter is intended for school psychology students, practitioners, and trainers. Changes in the field are forced by shifts in the constituency (students and schools) and facilitated by ongoing research on learning and behavior. Ongoing evaluation of school psychologists' personal skills and training programs are needed to evaluate congruence with the history of school psychology, current roles, and challenges of the future. A brief history of school psychology training is presented first in this chapter, followed by information on skills needed for the 21st century. Training standards promulgated by the National Association of School Psychologists (NASP) and the American Psychological Association (APA) are reviewed and questions related to training that require reflection and resolution are raised. Future directions for training in school psychology are then presented.

Early Training in School Psychology

Psychological, educational, and relevant medical services to assist school-age children in making academic progress have been provided on varying levels for nearly 100 years. In 1896, Lightner Witmer founded the first psychological clinic at the University of Pennsylvania. Others soon followed Witmer's lead and clinics were established in Chicago, Detroit, and other cities. As time went on, school psychologists were employed by school districts and began to travel to schools in order to provide services to students (Fagan, 1986; French, 1990).

During the period 1900 to 1940 the majority of these early school psychologists obtained applied training in university clinics. In the mid-1920s New York University started the first training program. Training programs and courses were soon developed at other universities in New York as well as at universities in Pennsylvania and Ohio in the 1930s. By 1940, 500 school psychologists were providing services to students (Fagan & Wise, 1994). In many states training in school psychology was initially provided

through credentialing programs in adjunct fields (e.g., special education, counseling). By 1970 more than 100 universities were training school psychologists, and 40 states were credentialing school psychologists. The 1975 passage of Public Law 94-142, the Education for All Handicapped Children Act, provided the impetus for tremendous growth in training programs explicitly in school psychology, from approximately 33 programs in 1964 to 230 training programs today (Fagan & Wise, 1994; see Figure 1; also see Appendix IX).

Development of Training Standards

The issues of accreditation of programs and entry level for practitioners have been debated from the beginning days of the field. In the early 1970s, school psychology programs gained some recognition from the National Council for the Accreditation of Teacher Education (NCATE); however, the training standards developed by NASP in 1972 were not enforced in a strict and structured manner. NASP was established as an affiliate of NCATE in 1976 and in 1978 the NASP standards for school psychology training were revised. In 1978 NASP recommended that school psychology students complete a 60-hour program and a 1-year internship as minimum level of entry. As an affiliate of NCATE, NASP now approves programs and program accreditation is granted by NCATE (Brown, 1990). APA has traditionally supported only doctoral-level psychology, and in 1969 APA developed standards for accrediting doctoral programs in school psychology. The first programs were evaluated and accredited in 1971. There are currently 44 APA-approved school psychology programs and 5 joint (e.g., school, clinical, counseling) APA-approved programs (APA, 1993, 1994).

A joint APA/NASP Task Force was formed in 1978 to resolve areas of overlap and conflict in NASP and APA training and professional standards. The Spring Hill Symposium, held in 1980, was an attempt by NASP and APA to partition responsibilities for doc-

FIGURE 1. Number of school psychology programs by decade.

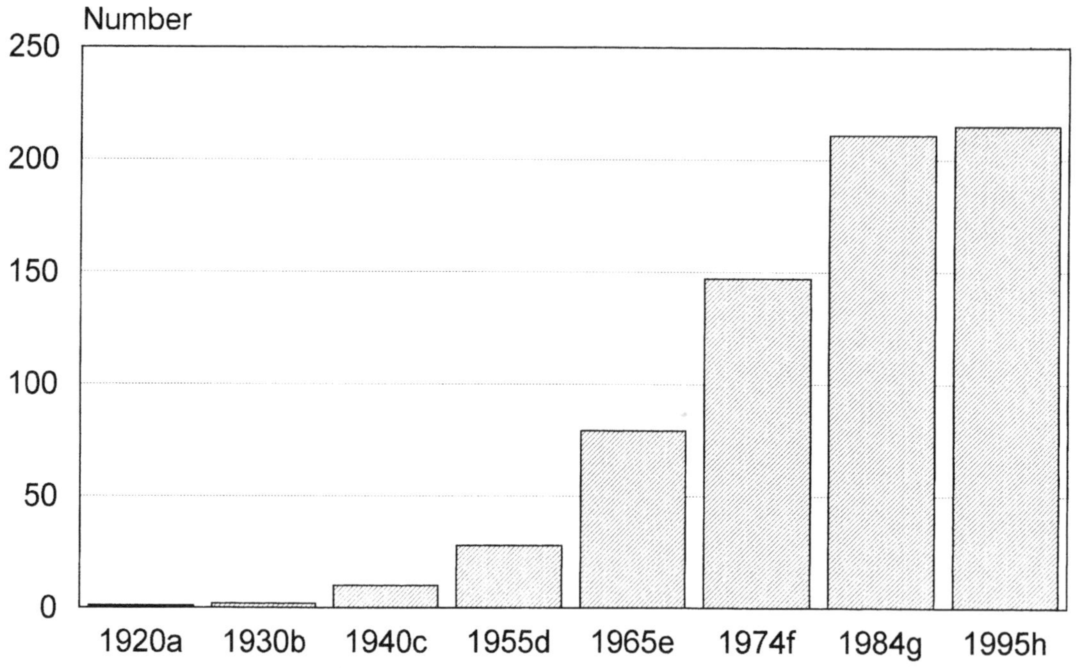

aNYU; bNYU & PA State U; cFarber, 1956; dCutts, 1955; eSmith,1964-65; f
Bardon & Wenger, 1974; gBrown & Minke, 1984; hSmith, 1995

toral and nondoctoral training (Trachtman, 1981). Multiple models of training were endorsed: entry-level nondoctoral (specialist) programs, practitioner-focused doctoral (PsyD) training, and traditional doctoral (PhD) training. The ongoing issue of specialization-versus-a-generalist model of training was also considered, resulting in support for the generalist model.

Training continues at the nondoctoral and doctoral levels, with nondoctoral programs continuing to train the majority of school-based practitioners. A doctoral program requires one to two years additional academic coursework plus dissertation or major project, written and oral exams, and a 1500-hour internship. The opportunity to develop a specialization is frequently a motivation for pursuing doctoral studies. However, documentation of actual program content reveals that much of the actual coursework may involve research and design rather than an area of specialization (McMaster, Reschly, & Peters, 1989). Therefore, the role of, and training for, doctoral-level school psychologists continues to be debated. Students should choose doctoral programs that are congruent with career goals (e.g., school practitioners, academic, or private practice).

Conferences have played an important role in guiding psychology training. In 1949, the Boulder conference on clinical psychology was held in Boulder, Colorado. Although this conference was not specific to school psychology, issues related to training and credentialing were discussed. The outcome of the conference was to recommend that all students in applied psychology be trained as scientist-practitioners. The Thayer conference, held in 1954, was sponsored by APA. Resulting recommendations for school psychology training included a 2-year program and a 6-month internship at the subdoctoral level with a 4-year program recommended for the doctoral degree.

Two major conferences related to the training of doctoral-level psychologists were subsequently sponsored by APA. At the 1987 Utah conference, resolutions on the requirements of the structure and core-curriculum content for undergraduate through postgraduate training in psychology were developed (Lambert, 1993). In 1990, the Gainesville Conference on the Education and Training of Scientist-Practitioner Psychologists for the Professional Practice of Psychology was held. This conference resulted in recommendations for identifying and training scientist-practitioners. Future conferences related to training and practice are in the planning stages at the time of this writing and focuses include the means by which training programs can meet all areas of current training standards, the development of future training standards, and the evolving roles of women in the field.

Another endeavor to maintain high standards for programs and individual practitioners was the establishment of standards for the National Certification of School Psychologists (NCSP) developed by NASP in 1985 (Batsche, Knoff, & Peterson, 1991). Goals of the NCSP included national recognition of professional development and reciprocity between states. Thus, a student trained in Minnesota who was NCSP certified could relocate to Arizona without the need to complete additional coursework. In 1988–89 school psychologists currently practicing in the field took a national examination in order for cut-off scores to be determined. Anyone taking the exam could then apply for NCSP status through grandparenting regardless of the score obtained. Cut-off scores are revised regularly. Students completing NASP-approved programs may now apply to take the certification exam and, upon passing the exam, receive the NCSP.

The NASP standards for training and field placement in school psychology were revised in 1984 and the National School psychology Inservice Training Network published *School Psychology: Blueprint for Training and Practice.* School psychology was envisioned as a broad field encompassing roles in educational, intellectual, and interpersonal assessment and consultation; in academic skills, instruction, and classroom management; in home–school–community relations in an increasingly multicultural context; and in legal, ethical, and professional issues relevant to schools, students, and the profession. Phillips (1990) also advocated new roles for school psychologists. His vision was oriented toward doctoral-level school psychologists with specialization in behavior and learning. Others (Epstein, 1992; Woody, LaVoie, & Epps, 1992) have recently visualized school psychologists of the future as psychologists serving the mental health needs of entire school populations, students, and their families. The scope of these predictions is exciting but overwhelming for the currently already rigorous school psychology training program.

Training School Psychologists for the 21st Century

The populations of America's schools are becoming more multifarious. School psychologists are increasingly assisting teachers and parents of children with severe disabilities and medical problems to determine and construct least restrictive environments. As special education legislation expands and emphasizes services to youngsters with disabilities from infancy to young adulthood, a concomitant need exists

to augment skills in areas such as assessment of young children and their families and to delineate transition programs. Many children are coming to school from poverty or diverse cultures. School psychologists are involved in planning and implementing classroom and home–school interventions to support children, families, and teachers. More practitioners are finding it imperative to determine how best to assess children whose backgrounds do not match most standardization samples and to advise schools on how and where (regular or special education) to provide appropriate educational services. As practitioner roles expand, so should training. Planners and educators cannot anticipate all the skills psychologists of the 21st century will need but must provide students with a strong foundation in psychological and educational principles, knowing that will not be sufficient. A focus of graduate school should be to provide students with critical thinking and evaluation skills. As formative evaluations and problem solving become ever more critical to the practice of school psychology, so should they be stressed in training.

Historically, training programs have both led the charge to aid children with learning and behavior problems and reflected specific practices deemed fitting by legislation. However, Curtis and Batsche (1991) ask whether school psychology training programs are leading the field or following it. Training programs operate within the constraints of accreditation and credentialing systems and the pragmatic pressures of graduating students who met the needs of the job market. School psychology programs struggle to maintain quality training in assessment courses and expand the content of assessment to include areas such as bilingualism and preschool materials, while increasing emphasis on intervention and consultation coursework (McMaster et al., 1989). Program faculty can direct students to resources and insist on excellence in knowledge of test construction, statistics, and legal and ethical issues in order that students have the skills to evaluate the adequacy of new and future technologies.

The array of student populations and needs today mandates recruitment into the field of school psychology of persons from various backgrounds and ethnic groups and persons with disabilities and greater balance in gender and race within training programs. School psychology practitioners currently in the field are very unbalanced ethnically (approximately 92% are Caucasian) and increasingly lopsided in gender (70% of current NASP members are female). Rogers, Ponterotto, Conoley, and Wise (192) surveyed training programs regarding multicultural training in psychology. Approximately 80% of the faculty and students in their survey were Caucasian. Minority faculty seemed to attract minority students; both were more likely to be at universities in urban areas. In discussing the need to include multicultural experiences in training for all school psychology students, Rogers et al. (1992) make the astute recommendation that students in more rural areas may need to arrange practica or internships that include opportunities to work with diverse populations. More research is desperately needed to determine how to interest, retain, and retrain more males, persons of color, bilingual students, and persons with disabilities in becoming school psychologists.

BASIC CONSIDERATIONS

Professional Knowledge

Historically school psychologists have been trained in normal and abnormal child development, learning and remedial techniques, assessment, consultation, intervention, and counseling, research and evaluation, and professional roles. The increasingly chaotic lives of many children necessitate additional content on prevention, educational reform, and crisis intervention. Furthermore, both NASP and APA require that students have a foundation base in traditional psychology as well as in education. Coursework requirements include biological bases of behavior, social bases of behavior, psychopathology, human exceptionalities, organization and operation of schools, and instructional and remedial techniques. Professional school psychologists also must have knowledge of the history of psychology as well as of school psychology, an understanding of ethical and legal issues, the skills to perform diverse roles and functions, and the knowledge and skill to work with increasingly complex technologies. Staying current in any of these areas is demanding. School psychology program faculty must continuously update their knowledge base and skill level in all areas to ensure that students are prepared to make decisions on best practices in their own fieldwork.

Personal Qualifications

School psychologists will be unable to use the knowledge they possess if they do not have good interpersonal skills. Training needs to include *content* and *process* (Conoley & Gutkin, 1986). School psychologists work in an indirect service model; for the most part services are not directly provided to children but behaviors are assessed and recommendations made for others to implement (e.g., special education or general education teaches, parents, administrators). Therefore, training should include how to effectively interact with others through coursework in consultation and social and organizational psychology. In addition, practice through practicum and internship experiences and role modeling by trainers can help students become competent agents for change. Written reports and annual Individualized Education Program (IEP) meeting are not necessarily effective methods of communication, if effectiveness is judged by changes in students' behaviors. Far more

footwork, collaboration, sharing of responsibilities, and follow-up are required to target specific problems, design interventions, and evaluate progress. Perseverance, reliability, and interpersonal skills cannot necessarily be instilled during a training program; recruitment of persons demonstrating high levels of these qualities, training them extensively in *what* they need to know, and then modeling and supervising *how* to work effectively with others is most apt to ensure competent graduates.

Practical Experience

School psychologists work in schools; therefore, their practicum and internship experiences should occur in schools, at least at the nondoctoral level (Carey, 1994a). At the doctoral level other settings for internships may be available for experienced practitioners. However, regardless of level of training, to be prepared for the future, school psychologists should be trained to work with preschoolers, families, students of diverse cultures, and students with severe and challenging disabilities. Practicum and internship experiences require close supervision, accountability by both students and trainers, and evaluation by students, trainers, and field-based practicum supervisors.

Furthermore, as Curtis and Batsche (1991) state

Trainers of school psychologists must become more actively involved with both supervision and professional practice. … Trainers must work in school and other settings, side by side with students as well as with parents, teachers, administrators, and other professionals. In this way, trainers will be able to engage in necessary retraining along with field-based practitioners. … Conversely, this shift would facilitate research programs that better meet the needs of the consumers of school psychological services. The link between training and practice would be strengthened. (p. 575)

NASP training standards require faculty to hold doctorates and certification or licensing in school psychology. Faculty are also to have at least two years experience as school psychology practitioners in school settings. They are expected to remain current in the field by professional development and to contribute to the field by research, service, consultation, or field experience. We concur with Curtis and Batsche (1991) that faculty need to continue to work in schools, at least periodically, to remain aware of the challenges practitioners face. However, we would take the practical experience component one step further in that we believe trainers should also practice in the field *as* school psychologists in addition to working alongside students. In this way trainers would be personally involved in seeking and evaluating solutions to challenges, rather than operating as outside experts or "consultants" to schools.

Guild Guidance

Credentialing of school psychologists and accreditation of school psychology programs, while separate processes, are related. Credentialing of school psychologists generally occurs at the State Department of Education while accreditation may occur at the state level or in conjunction by the state with NCATE and NASP or APA. The rules and regulations for the required documentation in the process of accreditation require significant amounts of time and paperwork.

The standards for training and field placement programs in school psychology (NASP, 1994) endorse entry at a 60-hour/3year masters/specialist level "at least 54 hours of which are exclusive of credit for the supervised internship experience." To receive NASP/NCATE approval, a school psychology training program must meet these training standards. The NASP training standards require specific coursework content, a designated number of hours for practicum and internship, ad continuous program evaluation. NASP Training Standards can be found in Appendix III of this volume. Training at the doctoral level, based on APA standards, also requires specific coursework content, training in professional ethics and standards, and training in research and design. Credentialing requirements as well as state-level accreditation often vary significantly from that demanded by the professional organizations (Curtis & Zins, 1989). Thus, obtaining accreditation status from the professional organization and the state-level body can require separate processes. For example, in California the state requirements for accreditation of School Psychology Programs are less than those required by NASP. To obtain accreditation at both the national and state levels separate documents must be submitted for review.

BEST PRACTICES

The Scientist-Practitioner

APA and NASP training standards emphasize the scientist-practitioner model. However, training in the scientist-practitioner model has often presented the roles as separate (and perhaps not equal), thereby minimizing the field of applied psychology (Martens & Keller, 1987). Whereas psychologists trained in this model are presumably scientists *and* practitioners, most practitioners utilize their training to evaluate professional practices and rely on faculty and other researchers to actually produce research. Hoshmand and Polkinghorne (1992) suggest a more functional synthesis could be attained, along with enhancing the mutual respect of practitioners and researchers, by examining and modifying the view that research is generated only in formal settings using standard procedures and statistical analyses. Those in Academe might consider expanding the repertoire of accept-

able techniques to include qualitative methodology and clinical expertise. This shift would allow practitioners to contribute more fully to the expert base of knowledge and to more readily assimilate research-based knowledge into their practices.

Whereas training in traditional statistical analyses and research design is essential for critically reviewing the literature, practitioners are unlikely to actually implement large *N*-group comparisons. Yet single-case design is not only feasible but an integral part of intervention evaluation. Training programs could emphasize applied psychology as science and include single-case methodology. School psychologists trained in time-series methodology (Barlow, Hayes, & Nelson, 1984; Cooper, Heron, & Heward, 1987) are able to engage in hypothesis testing, contribute to the database on treatments that benefit children, and empirically verify their work.

The Practitioner-Scientist

Best practices charges practice based on scientific research. The greatest controversy in Standards for Training and Field Placement in School Psychology centers around practice issues: Standard 2.4: Interventions/Problem-Solving. Most of the actual daily tasks and requests that school psychologists confront deal with these areas. The orientation of the training program, and the concomitant content of coursework in interventions and problem solving, will guide fledgling practitioners as they venture into the field. In fact, research indicates that practitioners and trainers tend to rely throughout their careers on the techniques and tests learned in their training program (see Lambert, 1993).

In the current NASP training standards, assessment is now termed "Assessment for Intervention," emphasizing the link between problem identification ad problem solving. The *range* and *variability* of assessment courses and content in a program must be evaluated. For example, do courses cover behavioral methods such as structured observations and curriculum-based measurement in as much depth as traditional norm-based academic measures? Are students trained to utilize multimethod and multisource assessment? Is supervision provided on interviewing parents and teachers and on using behavior rating scales? Are assessment instruments designed for use with infants, toddlers, preschoolers, and their families covered? Are students trained to work with multicultural, bilingual students? Is one specific model (e.g., curriculum-based assessment or neuropsychology) emphasized in training versus exposing students to a wide variety of models? Conversely a program can be so eclectic that students have little theoretical focus or orientation to guide practice.

Consultation and intervention, as the core of service delivery, need corresponding emphasis in training programs. A spiraling sequence building on observation, interviewing, consultation, intervention, and therapy techniques is recommended. Training needs to build on prior coursework and incorporate expanded skills in practicum experiences. Students need a conceptual framework, examples of applications, and personal confrontation with the barriers and accomplishments associated with a consultation-based model of service delivery.

A number of programs were founded in counseling, and training in these areas continues to be important. School psychologists trained in social skills, organization, problem solving, or conflict resolution would be welcomed by many teachers. Program faculty need to ensure that counseling training is relevant to the practice of school psychology. Thus, counseling methods with empirical support for use with children need to be taught and practicum experiences provided with children and adolescents rather than adults. Finally, students need an awareness of the limitations of direct counseling with younger children and the feasibility of using parent or teacher consultation and intervention instead.

Practicum and Internship

Standard 3 of the NASP standards, the practicum requirement, addresses the experiences and systematic evaluations in the "practitioner" part of the model, that is, assessment, intervention, consultation, and counseling. Students must be given opportunities to use the knowledge obtained from coursework in applied settings. Internship, addressed in Standard 4 of the document, requires integrated and thorough experiences under careful supervision and evaluation. NASP practica and internship standards term assessment as "assessment for intervention" and include behavior management as a component of intervention. This requirement is consistent with the emphasis on outcome-based services that became a part of the 1994 NASP training standards. In fact, programs are now deemed accountable via outcomes. Students must be able to verbally explain components of school psychological practice, cite legal precedents for services, and defend practices with empirical evidence. Furthermore, students should demonstrate integration of this knowledge throughout practicum and internship by delivering services to children, families, and schools in a skillful and professional manner.

At the specialist level, NASP requires 1,200 hours of internship experience occurring over 1 academic year full-time or over 2 years part-time and 1,400 hours at the doctoral level. APA doctoral level requirements call for a 1,500-hour internship, with at least half of those hours to be completed in a school setting, unless the school requirement has been met through prior internship or experience.

According to the Association of Psychology Postdoctoral and Internship Programs (APPIC;

1991–1992) 123 of the 494 APA-approved internship sites accept school psychologists as interns. Few of these sites are in school districts because districts rarely can provide the licensed supervision required by APA standards. The Nebraska Internship Consortium in Professional Psychology is one of the few internship sites approved by APA that is designed primarily for school psychologists (Kramer, Conoley, Bischoff, & Benes, 1991). Most internships are agreements between school districts and training programs that meet NASP internship standards.

Professional School Psychology

Professional school psychology, Standard 2.6 of the NASP training standards, requires a knowledge base of the professional speciality. This section encompasses the history of school psychology, legal and ethical issues, and the role and functions of school psychologists under various models of service delivery. Ensuring that school psychologists are well prepared to enter the field is only a good start. An important area often overlooked is that of continuing education. (For additional information, see the chapter by Fowler in this volume.)

Bandwagons seem to come along frequently in education and as professionals, school psychologists should have the skills and knowledge to carefully evaluate the usefulness of innovative practices. We must remain open to new ideas and techniques and to antithetic points of view throughout our careers and make decisions about training and practice based on research and experience rather than rigidity or naïveté.

Surveys over the years have found new changes in the assessment tools practitioners are using (Carey, 1994b; Goh, Teslow, & Fuller, 1981; Hutton, Dubes, & Muir, 1992; Wilson & Reschly, under review). Actually, it is unethical to use instruments and techniques with students without adequate training in their use. Therefore, continuing education is not only desirable but necessary.

Curtis and Batsche (1991) recommend more flexibility in university training programs to facilitate ongoing training for practitioners. The NASP standards are designed to both require and offer opportunities for the updating of skills through workshops, conventions, and the like. In-service training may be the most efficacious way to train psychologists in working with low incidence populations, such as individuals with severe disabilities (Mar, 1991). Reschly and Grimes (1991) describe a model of statewide in-service used to update practitioners in the areas of consultation and curriculum-based assessment. Postservice training must involve more than listening on the part of the trainees; actual practice and follow-up are necessary for skills to be mastered.

Future Directions

Entry-level preparation, in terms of level and specialization, continues to be debated. Phillips (1990) asks

> Will school psychology be an occupation that continues to play a role limited largely to assessment and determinations of special education eligibility? Will school psychology become a two-tiered occupation, consisting of doctoral school psychologists increasingly engaged in a variety of nontraditional (and nonschool) roles and nondoctoral school psychologists who continue to be engaged in the traditional assessment role? Or will school psychology become a speciality and profession that reaches for new roles, that raises the academic standards of training programs and the practical competence of its members, thus engendering prestige, compensation, and working conditions good enough to be recognized as a specialty and profession of first class? (p. 252)

We consider school psychology presently to be a first-class specialty and profession. However, to meet the needs of children today and the challenges of tomorrow, we agree that our roles, at both the subdoctoral and doctoral levels, must expand beyond that of special education gatekeepers.

Epstein (1992) provides a model for school psychology in the 21st century in which school psychology is responsive to the needs of students, families, and schools. This is analogous to a new NASP Training Standard, 1.2, which states that programs should train school psychologists to deliver services sensitive to the needs of families and schools. Thus, school psychologists must be knowledgeable in the areas of child development and educational practices and able to advise parents, facilitate workshops for educators, and serve as coordinators for multiyear plans, communicators and coordinators with parents, and evaluators of programs and school climate. Only through comprehensive training will school psychologists be partners with teams of educators and parents. As psychologists of the school, we will be responsible for developing environments that prevent problems and promote mental health. This must be the focus of our training: a view of the future that actually takes us back to our roots (Fagan & Wise, 1994; French, 1990; Woody, LaVoie, & Epps, 1992).

SUMMARY

The challenge of providing services to students in schools is becoming extremely complex. Increasingly children are entering our schools "at risk" for academic, social, and emotional difficulties due to a multitude of societal changes and problems. To meet the needs of children we must, as school psychologists, continually update our skills and stay current in the field. To facilitate this, trainers of school psychologists must remain active in the field through practice, service, and conducting and evaluating research; practitioners must engage in continuing professional development through workshops, training programs, and readings; and students must be provided with state-of-the-art education with an understanding that training today will not be sufficient for serving children tomorrow. Change and learning are life-long processes.

REFERENCES

American Psychological Association. (1993). APA-accredited doctoral programs in professional psychology: 1993. *American Psychologist, 48,* 1260–1270.

American Psychological Association. (1994). Supplement to listing of APA-accredited doctoral and predoctoral internship training programs in psychology. *American Psychologist, 49,* 671–672.

Association of Psychology Postdoctoral and Internship Programs (APPIC). (1991–1992). *Directory of internship and postdoctoral programs in professional psychology.* Washington, DC: Author.

Bardon, J. I., & Wenger, R. D. (1974). Institutions offering graduate training in school psychology: 1973–1974. *Journal of School Psychology, 5,* 70–83.

Barlow, D. H., Hayes, S. C., & Nelson, R. O. (1984). *The scientist practitioner: Research and accountability in clinical and educational setting.* New York: Pergamon Press.

Batsche, G. M., Knoff, H. M., & Peterson, D. W. (1991). Trends in credentialing and practice standards. *School Psychology Review, 18,* 193–202.

Brown, D. T. (1990). Professional regulation and training in school psychology. In T. B. Gutkin & C. R. Reynolds (Eds.), *The handbook of school psychology* (2nd ed.; pp. 3–20). New York: Wiley.

Carey, K. T. (1994a). Internships in school psychology. *Communiqué, 22*(6), 8–9.

Carey, K. T. (1994b). *School psychologists' perceptions of current roles and functions.* Unpublished study.

Conoley, J. C., & Gutkin, T. B. (1986). Educating school psychologists for the real world. *School Psychology Review, 15,* 457–465.

Cooper, J. O., Heron, T. E., & Heward, W. L. (1987). *Applied behavior analysis.* Columbus, OH: Merrill.

Curtis, M. J., & Batsche, G. M. (1991). Meeting the needs of children and families: Opportunities and challenges for school psychology training programs. *School Psychology Review, 20,* 565–577.

Curtis, M. J., & Zins, J. E. (1989). Trends in training and accreditation. *School Psychology Review, 18,* 193–202.

Cutts, N. E. (Ed.). (1955). *School psychology at mid-century.* Washington, DC: American Psychological Association.

Epstein, J. L. (1992). School and family partnerships: Leadership roles for school psychologists. In S. L. Christenson & J. C. Conoley (Eds.), *Home–school collaboration: Enhancing children's academic and social competence.* Silver Spring, MD: National Association of School Psychologists.

Fagan, T. K. (1986). The historical origins and growth of programs to prepare school psychologists in the United States. *Journal of School Psychology, 24,* 9–22.

Fagan, T. K., & Wise, P. S. (1994). *School psychology: Past, present, and future.* New York: Longman.

Farber, N. (1956). The psychologist in the school system. *Merrill-Palmer Quarterly, 2,* 173–178.

French, J. L. (1990). History of school psychology. In T. B. Gutkin & C. R. Reynolds (Eds.), *The handbook of school psychology* (2nd ed.; pp. 3–20). New York: Wiley.

Hoshmand, L. T., & Polkinghorne, D. E. (1992). Redefining the science-practice relationship and professional training. *American Psychologist, 47,* 55–66.

Kramer, J. J., Conoley, J. C., Bischoff, L. G., & Benes, K. M. (1991). Providing a continuum of professional training: The Nebraska psychology of schooling project and the Nebraska internship consortium in professional psychology. *School Psychology Review, 20,* 551–564.

Lambert, N. M. (1993). Historical perspective on school psychology as a scientist-practitioner specialization in school psychology. *Journal of School Psychology, 31,* 163–199.

Mar, H. H. (1991). Retooling psychology to serve children and adolescents with severe disabilities. *School Psychology Review, 20,* 510–521.

Martens, B. K., & Keller, H. R. (1987). Training school psychologists in the scientific tradition. *School Psychology Review, 16,* 329–337.

McMaster, M. D., Reschly, D. J., & Peters, J. M. (1989). *Directory of school psychology graduate programs.* Washington, DC: National Association of School Psychologists.

National Association of School Psychologists. (1994). *Draft — Standards for training and field placement programs in school psychology.* Washington, DC: Author.

Phillips, B. N. (1990). *School psychology at a turning point: Ensuring a bright future for the profession.* San Francisco: Jossey-Bass.

Reschly, D. J., & Grimes, J. P. (1991). State department and university cooperation: Evaluation of continuing education in consultation and curriculum-based assessment. *School Psychology Review, 20,* 522–529.

Rogers, M. R., Ponterotto, J. B., Conoley, J. C., & Wise, M. J. (1992). Multicultural training in school psychology: A national survey. *School Psychology Review, 21,* 603–616.

Smith, D. C. (1964–65). Institutions offering graduate training in school psychology. *Journal of School Psychology, 3,* 58–66.

Trachtman, G. (1981). On such a full sea. *School Psychology Review, 10,* 138–181.

Wilson, M. S., & Reschly, D. J. (under review). *The times they are a changin': Assessment practices and training are not.*

Woody, R. H., LaVoie, J. C., & Eps, S. (1992). *School psychology: A developmental and social systems approach.* Boston: Allyn & Bacon.

ANNOTATED BIBLIOGRAPHY

Fagan, T. K., & Wise, P. S. (1994). *School psychology: Past, present, and future.* New York: Longman.
This book provides an excellent overview of the field of school psychology for students entering the field or those persons wanting more information about school psychology. Topics include the employment of school psychologists, professional evaluation and accountability, and considerations for practica and internships.

McMaster, M., Reschly, D. J., & Peters, J. M. (1989). *Directory of School Psychology Programs.* Washington, DC: National Association of School Psychologists.
Th Directory of School Psychology Graduate Programs is currently undergoing revision. The edition by McMaster et al. is the most complete summary of information available on school psychology training programs. Program entries include degrees offered, accreditation status, faculty, and admission requirements.

Smith, D. (in press). *Directory of School Psychology Programs.* Washington, DC: National Association of School Psychologists.
This book will contain information on 215 programs. Programs are in place in 46 states and Washington, DC. Of these programs, 82 offer doctorates. See Appendix IX for listing.

17

Best Practices in
Serving as an Expert Witness

James M. Stumme
Heartland Area Education Agency
Johnston, Iowa

OVERVIEW

School psychologists are becoming increasingly involved in the legal system and are called upon to testify regarding psychological evaluations, treatment procedures, and special education programs, and to make recommendations regarding particular cases. School psychologists have testified in a variety of legal arenas, such as, due process administrative hearings, state civil courts, state criminal courts, and federal district courts. This testimony has been rendered on a wide range of issues, such as, disability eligibility, appropriateness of placement options, appropriateness of IEPs, degree to which responsibility for criminal acts was diminished by disability conditions, test bias, alleged discrimination against minority students, and many others, In addition, school psychologists are involved in less direct legal matters such as giving professional opinions on what constitutes acceptable professional practice (Shapiro, 1984). For example, a school psychologist may be requested to evaluate for a malpractice suit whether a mental heath practitioner demonstrated acceptable professional practice. Similarly, another related role the school psychologist can serve is that of consultant to the legal system in the form of reviewing and critiquing a psychological evaluation/intervention performed by another professional for the specific purpose of furnishing the opposing attorney with information for cross-examination.

Whether or not school psychologists appear in court on any of the above topics will likely depend on the kind of assignment and population they serve and what someone else wants to do with or about these clients. Professional preferences or even selected areas of expertise occasionally do *not* determine the issues that school psychologists may be required to address in court.

Unfortunately, traditional school psychology training programs do not provide practitioners with knowledge or practice that will prepare them to provide competent court interventions. Graduate course-work on professional issues and ethical concerns tends not to present more than perfunctory treatment of the role of the school psychologist in the legal system, the psychologist/lawyer/client relationship, or the expert witness role. Tymchuk et al. (1982) concluded from a survey of clinical psychologists that only 37% of the survey participants received formal, structured modes of learning in professional issues and ethics. The naive practitioner may unknowingly plunge from the relative safety of daily routine and familiar school territory into the unknown legal arena and threatening environment of the witness stand. Once on the witness stand, school psychologists can potentially have their credentials belittled, their testimony rigorously interrogated, their opinions subject to ridicule, and if not thoroughly prepared and schooled in the ways of the court, their self-esteem and professional credibility tarnished. It is in this context that this chapter has been written.

The purpose of this chapter is to acquaint the school psychologist with the special procedures, techniques, and considerations necessary for providing effective courtroom interventions. More specifically, this chapter will address the most common court interventions rendered by school psychologists, namely, the provision of expert testimony and how to construct and submit written reports.

BASIC CONSIDERATIONS

The essential purpose of any testimony is to provide useful and relevant information to the court to assist it in making an informed legal decision (Schwitzgebel & Schwitzgebel, 1980). Hopefully this process can be accomplished with a minimum amount of stress on the expert witness. This is possible only when the expert witness is knowledgeable of the court process and is adequately prepared. An uninformed and unprepared witness is in the unforgiving hands of the adversarial counsel. The following information, suggestions, and considerations are presented to assist school psychologists in their preparation to assume the role of the expert witness.

The Lay Witness Defined

There are two distinct categories of witnesses, lay witnesses and the expert witnesses. Lay witnesses may testify only to phenomena which they have legitimately seen, heard, felt, tasted, or smelled directly. The general rule is that the lay witness is prohibited from testifying about anything other than that gained from personal perception (Westphal & Kohn, 1984). A lay witness may not in testimony express opinions or draw inferences unless the court finds that these can be rationally based on the perception of the witness and that they are helpful to understanding the witness' testimony. "Thus, lay opinion evidence as to distance, time, speed, size, weight, direction, form and identity are admitted; if such opinions are of a type which a normal person forms constantly and correctly" (Cook, 1964, p. 459). Expressing conclusions is not within the scope of lay witness testimony and is, in fact, the function and burden of the court.

The Expert Witness Defined

In contrast to the lay witness, who may testify primarily only on first-hand perceptual knowledge, the expert witness may in testimony formulate and express professional opinions and can draw inferences from data. Experts are asked to testify because they have special knowledge, training, and experience beyond that of a lay person. They possess something unique to contribute. The expert witness is limited, however, to opinions or inferences about matters which are perceived by, or personally known to, the witness. The information presented must also be within the scope of the witness' special training, skill, and experience to interpret, and be of direct aid to the court (Cook, 1964). For an example of the professional specificity of such testimony, consider the expert witness who was requested in a criminal case to testify on "how the development, adaptations, and function of [the] defendant's behavior processes may have influenced his conduct" (*Washington v. United States*, 1967). Or consider the expert who was, in a civil commitment hearing, asked to "explain the development and manifestations of the alleged mental illness and also probably to make a prediction about the individual's 'dangerousness' to self or others" (Schwitzgebel & Schwitzgebel, 1980, p. 238). Although specificity is necessary to address many professional issues, it should be tempered with explanations that the lay public can understand. Simply asserting a professional conclusion (e.g., the individual suffers from schizophrenia) is not, in and of itself, adequate (*Carter v. United States*, 1957). In essence, expert testimony is admitted only when it assists the trier of fact (a jury or judge in a nonjury trial) to understand and analyze evidence or to determine a fact (Federal Rules of Criminal Procedure, Rule 702).

Brodsky (1991) and Brodsky and Robey (1973) describe and examine two extremes of expert witness behavior exhibited by mental health care professionals. They dichotomize these two distinct groups as the courtroom-oriented expert witness and the courtroom-unfamiliar expert witness. The courtroom-oriented witnesses are portrayed as behaving in desirable ways, while the courtroom-unfamiliar witnesses conduct themselves in comparatively undesirable ways. Gorlow (1975) summarizes the former as possessing some legal training, having some knowledge of the law, displaying minimal emotional reaction to subpoena, speaking in clear and concise language avoiding jargon, and representing their position with restrained advocacy. Gorlow characterizes the courtroom-unfamiliar witness as possessing no relevant legal training and as being unaware of law and evidence rules, showing personal distress in response to subpoenas, representing their findings in technical jargon, demonstrating fierce advocacy, and responding with resentment and anger to cross-examination.

Prior to authorizing an expert witness to express an opinion, inference, or conclusion, the court must be assured of two prerequisite conditions: (a) the expert testimony is necessary to fully understand the evidence or to determine a fact in evidence, and (b) the expert witness possesses the necessary credentials to adequately form an opinion, inference, or conclusion (Westphal & Kohn, 1984). The requirements needed by a school psychologist to meet the specific qualifications of an expert witness differ from case to case and range from the most rigorous credential inquiry to a cursory review. In a case cited by Schwitzgebel and Schwitzgebel (1980), the conviction of an accused murderer was reversed in part because the prosecution's psychologist did not possess a PhD degree, 5 years of postgraduate training in clinical psychology, and a 1-year American Psychological Association-approved internship. Nonetheless, since each case is handled differently, the chief factor in determining the credentials required of the expert witness is the matter before the court. If, for example, the case involves expertise in the area of the most appropriate and least restrictive alternative in special education placement, the school psychologist might be deemed by the court to have specialized qualification and, indeed, an expert worthy of providing testimony.

Even if a particular psychologist is considered the utmost authority for a given case, she or he must be adequately prepared for a courtroom appearance. If not, the results could be disastrous. The court system is not kind or sympathetic to the unprepared.

BEST PRACTICES

Pretrial Preparation

Optimal courtroom performance is accomplished through the combination of implementing competent best practices in the delivery of all pretrial professional services and thoroughly preparing testimony material prior to taking the witness stand. Diligent pretrial preparation greatly alleviates harmful courtroom stress, is ethically responsible, and can have a potentially positive impact on the esteem others hold for the profession of psychology. Adequate pretrial preparation covers a wide diversity of activities, which are examined in the following discussion.

Selection of the expert witness. A psychologist may be requested to testify as an expert by the court system or by attorneys representing either the plaintiff or the defendant. Experts may be chosen because of past work with a client or because of their area of specialization, such as assessment of chemical abuse, assessment of child abuse, or knowledge about developmental disabilities. Some jurisdictions even retain organized pools of mental health experts, which they reimburse on a fee-per-case basis (Schwitzgebel & Schwitzgebel, 1980).

Information gathering. Just a word of caution. No pretrial preparation is complete without scrutinizing all gathered information for possible trouble spots or holes. Any questions that are unanswered should be answered. It is better to tackle these during preparation than during cross-examination. Any information gaps can furnish the opposing counsel with ammunition to contest the expert's credibility and ensuing testimony. A cursory reading of a record can cause the expert to miss some important point(s), which can greatly discredit testimony on the stand (Shapiro, 1984). In addition to checking records and other gathered material, the expert witness must make sure the person seen is the person who was referred. There are examples of mistaken identity. The expert providing testimony should never leave the session during an assessment, nor should an associate, assistant, practicum student, or intern be allowed to administer an examination. The expert witness must be confident of the source of information to avoid any suggestion by the opposition that an outsider wrongfully prejudiced the results (Schwitzgebel & Schwitzgebel, 1980).

Information dissemination. In both civil and criminal cases, all parties are allowed the opportunity to receive the names of expert witnesses and their findings prior to their testimony, which eliminates any unexpected revelations. In fact, some court systems require the attorney to list their witnesses, a summary of their evidence, an estimate of the time required for witnesses' testimony, and the intended order in which the witnesses will be called — all in written form to be submitted to the court prior to even a pretrial conference (Cook, 1964). Although it may be appropriate for an expert witness to dialogue with the opposing lawyer, it is imperative that the expert witness contact the client's attorney prior to the meeting to allow the client's attorney the option of attending. Conservative practice would dictate that all communication with the opposition's attorney should be conducted through the client's attorney. In the case of a school hearing, the school attorney would need to be notified. No written correspondence should be delivered to the opposition without the express written consent of the client's lawyer (Westphal & Kohn, 1984).

Since there are few limitations for restricting the dissemination of expert witnesses' findings, there is some danger that information harmful to the client's case will be obtained by the opposition. This information could potentially help the opposition both build a case against the client and find weak areas in the expert witness' testimony. However, it should be noted that there is a thin line between professional conduct as an expert witness and advocacy. It is unethical for a psychologist to misrepresent testimony for a client's cause. By concealing information, the expert witness becomes an advocate of the client rather than an advocate of the facts. The former constitutes questionable ethical practice.

Utilization of files, records, and the face sheet. Any files, records, or personal notes that are brought to the witness stand by the expert witness can be obtained by counsel for the opposition and used as fuel for cross-examination. The opposition simply asks to have the expert's files and records admitted as an exhibit so that the court may more thoroughly examine them. Because of this open-record policy, expert witnesses should bring with them only file and record information that will assist them in their testimony and that will hold up under the most exhaustive adversarial scrutiny. File information that is not relevant to the case should not be brought to the witness stand, as it can be a source of potential embarrassment to the client and make it difficult for the expert witness to stay within ethical boundaries. According to Shapiro (1984), one of the favorite ploys in cross-examination is to ask expert witnesses if the notes they have on their person are all of the notes that they took during the examination. The cross-examining attorney will then obtain the notes and compare them to the written report submitted by the expert. Any notes left out of the report will then be attacked in a highly accusatory manner in which the expert witness will be requested to state why some notes were included and interpreted in the report and others were not. One defense strategy for this tactic is for the expert witness to take only carefully selected handwritten notes on the file to court. Another defense when discrepant material is found between personal notes and the written report is to state that only that information which, in the expert's opinion, is clinically significant is included in the report (Shapiro, 1984).

Although handwritten notes are preferred by most expert witnesses, there are circumstances when entire files must be taken to the witness stand (i.e., the subpoena of school records). In such situations, it is imperative that the expert witness thoroughly know the files and how to quickly locate every piece of information within them. Moreover, the expert witness must be prepared to defend how opinions and inferences are supported by the documentation within the files and why discrepant information within the files is not considered clinically relevant.

A good tool for organizing written files, records, and personal notes is the face sheet. The face sheet is a 1- to 2-page outline that summarizes quantitative data such as the number of sessions with the client, beginning and ending dates, etc., along with a brief summary of findings, impressions, opinions, conclusions, and recommendations. In addition, it is helpful for expert witnesses to list on the face sheet all information they feel is important to bring out in court. The face sheet can be of great assistance for quick reference when, under the stress of cross-examination, the mind goes blank.

Legal consultation and preparation. An important pretrial preparation that should not be overlooked is the consultation between the expert witness and the attorney of the client. This is an educational process. The attorney has been schooled to carefully prepare the expert witness for testimony but may not know how to deal with psychological data. In juvenile cases, chances are good that the expert witness will have a young, inexperienced lawyer. The expert witness may need to educate the lawyer on the best ways to present the data. Do not assume the client's legal counsel knows what questions to ask or even the best way to ask them. This may not be the case. And a lawyer who does not know to ask might ask questions that could harm the expert witness' testimony. An expert witness' testimony might be potentially compelling, but unless the correct material is prompted by the lawyer's questions, it will not be heard. Moreover, an expert witness can appear foolish. It is therefore imperative that the expert witness outline for the attorney the information the expert wants to get across. A list of tentative questions to the attorney is certainly appropriate but not if the list contains answers. If answers are included, it is considered scripting, and scripted dialogue could find its way to the opposition's counsel. The list of questions should allow for responses to be elaborated and systematically build toward the desired culmination. Although it is not appropriate to script dialogue, there is nothing wrong with role-playing possible courtroom scenarios that could occur with the client's counsel.

One problem that must be addressed with respect to consultation with the client's counsel is the accusation that may be made that the lawyer somehow influenced the expert witness' findings. Shapiro (1984) suggests that the expert witness should respond to this by stating that, in the course of the pretrial consultation, the expert witness communicated his or her findings to the attorney after completing an evaluation and reaching an opinion. It is best practice to document the exact dates of services to the client, establishing an opinion, and consulting with the client's lawyer.

Presentation of professional credentials. Prior to asking the psychologist to give expert testimony, the court must establish that the witness does, in fact, possess the necessary educational credentials and experience to qualify as an expert witness. This will be done on the witness stand and requires careful preparation prior to being sworn in.

The expert witness should meet with the client's attorney and provide an outline of credentials or a vita that carefully lists:

- formal education and degrees

- specialized training including practica and internships

- areas of research and publication

- professional affiliations and offices held

- assistantships, fellowships, and work experiences

Often the attorney will review the expert's credentials one at a time in court to give the expert an opportunity to tell of his or her expertise and accomplishments. The manner of presentation will in no small way determine the credibility of the expert witness. According to Westphal and Kohn (1984), the psychologist does not need to be world famous or the author of a book on the subject to be admitted as an expert. But the psychologist's evaluation methodology and resulting opinions should generally be similar to the conclusions of others in the same field.

The lawyer for the opposition will be afforded an opportunity to cross-examine the expert witness about credentials in order to invalidate or limit the expert's testimony. A strategy for limiting the expert's testimony is to call for a stipulation of qualifications. When an opposing lawyer asks to stipulate, she or he is probably trying to keep the trier of fact from knowing the breadth of the expert witness' qualifications (Shapiro, 1984). This tactic avoids giving the expert witness too much credibility. The psychologist should request the client's attorney not to allow stipulation should it be requested, in order to allow the court to hear the expert witness' full credentials.

When actually presenting credentials to the court, it is important not to understate or to minimize qualifications, because the credibility and effectiveness of one's testimony is reliant on them. Likewise, overstatement and arrogance can be detrimental to one's effectiveness as an expert witness.

Use of visual aids. Like the clarity and visual impact provided to psychological reports by graphs and charts, visual aids can assist in explaining data to the court system. The salient difference is that the visual aids utilized in the courtroom must be targeted at a lay population and free from technical jargon. Other than that, courtroom visual aids can run the gamut from large poster presentations to individual handouts.

Courtroom conditioning. The more familiar the expert witnesses are with the courtroom environment and principal actors in that environment, the better their performance will be. Under ideal conditions, it is helpful to visit the specific courtroom and become familiar with the location of the judge's bench, jury box, and witness stand. It is good practice (conditioning) for expert witnesses to sit where they will probably sit before being called to testify and to practice walking to the witness stand. Sadly, some expert witnesses have adequately prepared their presentation, worn their most professional suit, and then had their confidence shaken and their credibility questioned when, as they approached the witness stand, they could not open the gate separating the observers from the trial participants. The unknown can be unnerving! It is important to learn as much about courtroom procedures as possible before the day of the hearing. For example, if expert witnesses are Jewish and are asked to place their hand on the Bible and to tell the truth, they will be facing their first dilemma. Another piece of information the expert witnesses would want to know is whether reporters will be present or any other media coverage is planned. Expert witnesses can handle almost anything as long as they are informed of possible scenarios ahead of time.

Along with knowledge of the physical environment, it is equally important for expert witnesses to have information on the identities, roles, and personalities of the other principal actors that they will interact with in court. For example, in a jury trial the judge will act as referee, the jury will be the decision makers, the lawyers the advocates and persuaders, and the witnesses the information providers. In a nonjury trial, the judge will be both referee and decision maker. More than just knowing the roles people will play, it is extremely important to know how the specific judge and representing attorneys are likely to conduct themselves in court. If, for example, expert witnesses know that an attorney typically tries to intimidate a witness, they can be prepared and not take it personally. Likewise, knowing that a lawyer typically sets witnesses up by trapping them with apparently simple questions will alert the witness to the need for caution. In determining how to present information in a way the judge will consider effective

and determining the person to whom responses should be presented, law clerks and bailiffs can be an excellent source of information.

Dress and demeanor in court. An expert witness' acceptability and credibility are contingent on numerous easily overlooked variables. One influential variable is dress. Expert witnesses apparel and accessories should add to their role as competent experts, not diminish the impact of their testimony. A dark suit or dress is traditional and desirable. Outlandish, eye-catching clothing should be avoided. Dress is like a billboard and advertises the wearer's role, status, and personality. The more uniform the clothing, the more it emphasizes the person's role and decreases the importance of personality. The image the expert witness wants to portray for role is professional and competent, for status is middle class, and for personality is pleasing, objective, empathetic, and intelligent.

Another powerful variable, one apart from the substantive issues covered during testimony, is the expert witness' demeanor. The witness should be confident but not cocky. The expert witness is not on trial, but the expert's opinions and inferences will be questioned, and this can be unnerving. It is best to try not to show too much emotion. Exaggerated displays of emotion are unprofessional and give the appearance of a personal investment in the outcome of the case. The expert witness is an advocate of the facts, not the client.

Although dress and demeanor can potentially add to or subtract from an expert's credibility, the expert witness should be aware that the most important aspect of testimony is to help the court system by providing accurate, understandable data. An expert witness can look good and sound professional, but not help anyone.

Expert Testimony: The Direct Examination

The school psychologist at this point has implemented best clinical practices; formulated opinions, conclusions, and recommendations; and painstakingly prepared to present data in understandable lay terminology. The clinician is then called to the witness stand, sworn in, and questioned by the attorneys representing both the defendant and the plaintiff to establish the witness as an expert witness for the specific case at hand. It is now time to proceed with the direct examination of the expert witness.

The adversarial process. The adversarial process is a concept foreign to the mode of operation of most school psychologists. The range of acceptable behavior for attorneys is distinctly dissimilar to that of practitioners in behavior sciences. The adversarial process places a much different expectation upon lawyers than upon mental health professionals (Schwitzgebel & Schwitzgebel, 1980). "Psychologists

TABLE 1
Ethical Code and Principles for Psychologists and Lawyers

Psychologists	Lawyers
Goal:	*Goal:*
Gather all data in as unbiased a manner as possible.	Present facts as one sidedly as possible. Represent client as aggressively as possible.
Present all facts (data), even data dhat are seemingly contradictory.	Use any part of law that will help client.
Present limitations of evaluations and findings.	Make client look good and right and the opposition look bad and wrong.
Present information accurately and in an unbiased manner.	Single focus on winning.
Basis of Reputation	*Basis of Reputation*
Being impartial	Being partial

present the science of psychology and offer their services, products, and publications fairly and accurately, avoiding misrepresentation through sensationalism, exaggeration, or superficiality" (American Psychological Association, 1981, p. 635). The ethical code of lawyers is much different and charges them to present evidence as one-sided as possible to win their case. Attorneys will use any part of the law that will be most beneficial to their case; it is their absolute duty. Within the confines of the law, an attorney will attempt to force the expert witness to make definitive specific statements about behavioral data. This holds for the client's lawyer as well as the opposition's counsel. School psychologists, in the role of the expert witness, know there is a range of accuracy in behavioral science that does not allow absolute specificity. This impasse is where lawyers and psychologists clash. Psychologists must be on constant guard to maintain their ethical standards within the adversarial framework of the courtroom. Table 1 contrasts the ethical codes and concomitant principles for the professions of psychology and law.

Advocacy. If the school psychologists believe that they are, in fact, scientists, then they must not be advocates of a client, a school, or a state agency, but rather advocates of the data. The expert witness is an advocate of objective facts. The practitioner as an expert witness should be emotionally tied only to providing impartial facts. It is an irrational belief that the expert witness must defend one side or the other. When independent witnesses for the court have strong emotional feelings about a client, they frequently respond differently to defendant and prosecution questions, which inevitably harms their credibility as an expert witness. Table 2 highlights the substantive differences in the advocacy role for psychologists and lawyers.

One aspect of advocacy must be clarified. It is generally not considered good practice for a psychol-

ogist to become an examiner for a client he or she is seeing or has seen, for therapy. As a therapist, the practitioner is an advocate for the client, but in the courtroom the school psychologist must become an advocate of the facts. Discussing these facts impartially in public could destroy the therapist–client relationship and ultimately harm the client. Referral at this juncture is usually deemed most prudent. Clarification with the client of the psychologist's role and parameters of confidentiality prior to rendering any professional services is ethically responsible.

Responding to questions. Under direct examination it is appropriate for the expert witness to look directly at the person asking the questions and respond verbally back to the person in a direct, honest, and candid manner. It is sometimes difficult to talk about defendants when they are physically present in the courtroom. This can be rectified by occasionally talking to them during testimony as if giving them feedback on the evaluation. On long responses it is desirable to make eye contact with the judge and jury. On short answers, eye contact with all courtroom actors is awkward and experts could find themselves continually glancing around the courtroom.

The expert witness is required to respond verbally. Hand or head gestures are not acceptable and the court will ask the witness to emit a verbal response.

In giving testimony, experts should be concise to avoid lessening the importance of their information through too many words. To promote communication, they should minimize technical jargon and explain technical terms when their use is absolutely necessary. Professional terminology that has a different lay meaning should be carefully defined. Examples include depression, deterioration, and within normal limits (Shapiro, 1984). The judge is a trained listener, and any condescending or patronizing comments will not be well received. Likewise, the expert

TABLE 2
Advocacy Roles for Psychologists and Lawyers

Psychologists	Lawyers
Advocacy for facts and data	Fierce advocacy for client
Detached from emotion	Strive to use emotion for client's benefit
Impartial	Partial

witness should refrain from flippant remarks or attempts to be amusing. The expert witness wants to be seen as professional and competent, not as a witty comic.

The best verbal response in the world is useless if it is not directed to the question that was asked. The expert witness must listen diligently to the question posed before responding. If the question is unclear, the expert should request that it be repeated, explained, or rephrased. The expert witness has the right to have questions repeated and words or phrases explained.

There are different opinions as to whether an expert witness should answer only the specific questions asked or volunteer additional information. The former opinion is based on the thought that the lawyer has a specific order of questions and will use that order to most effectively utilize expert testimony. Breaking that sequence by volunteering information will be detrimental to the impact of the testimony. The latter view holds that expert witnesses should use questioning as a guide for their responses and present, within general boundaries, that information which they feel is most relevant. At any rate, if expert witnesses are asked an open-ended question, they should use that opportunity to build, fortify, and elaborate on their findings and conclusions. Lawyers are frequently taught to never ask "why" questions. According to Shapiro (1984), "why" questions are an opportunity for the expert witness to take as much time as necessary to explain something as fully as possible. The expert witness who would like to cover more information than requested can ask for permission to elaborate on the subject. If the attorney says yes, it is permissible to proceed. If the attorney says no, it signals the opposing attorney and judge that the questioning attorney is not being fair, and that the judge or opposing attorney can follow up with questions or directions to the expert to elaborate. Expert testimony is not like that which is exemplified in television drama. The expert does not have to answer just the question posed. The judge will not allow the lawyers to control the type of information that is introduced. The judge is interested in knowing whatever helpful information the expert has and this information will be allowed to be aired. Likewise, the judicial system will not stipulate that the expert respond with only a

yes or no answer if that response would be misleading (Cook, 1964).

When expert witnesses do not know the answer to a question or do not have an opinion, they should not speculate or render a haphazard guess. Rather, they should attempt to rephrase the question so it becomes one to which they can respond. In regard to giving an opinion, expert witnesses should only give opinions when they have carefully considered all available evidence. There is nothing wrong with requesting time to consider new information. To respond without careful deliberation sets the expert witness up for potential difficulties. In addition, making seemingly quick decisions undermines the validity of the professional's carefully thought out and considered opinions.

The expert witness should be cautious about answering questions with one-word responses. One-word responses, although simple, are open to too many interpretations and assumptions. For example, if the witness responds with yes to a question, does this mean yes for every situation like this one or just yes for this specific instance? In addition, one-word answers can build a response set that allows the lawyer to ask many questions very rapidly and allows the lawyer too much control over the direction and rate of questioning. An alternative method of responding for the expert witness would be to simply repeat or rephrase the question before responding. This provides the expert with more control.

If at a later time in their testimony, expert witnesses feel they have given misleading or inaccurate information, they should amend their statements as quickly as possible.

Presenting limitations and contradictory data. Expert witnesses should make a substantial endeavor to anticipate in advance of their testimony the areas of testimony in which they appear weakest and could be challenged (Shapiro, 1984). They should then present the limitations of their evaluation and findings and any seemingly contradictory data in a very orderly manner during the direct examination. This is a much preferred mode of operation to appearing bewildered and distressed by challenges during cross-examination. Handling potential trouble spots during direct examination is more comfortable and controlled than during cross-examination, gives the professional more credibility, and adds to the potential strength of the testimony.

Expert witnesses should present the limits of their involvement with the client by describing the dates they saw the client, the number and length of their sessions, and their relationship with the client prior to, during, and after the evaluation. In addition, they should further specify the exact nature of their intervention. If, for example, they did a chemical dependency evaluation on a child, they would not address questions about whether a particular parent should have custody of the child, nor would the court expect them to. Expert witnesses should not render an opinion on a subject unless they have done an evaluation on that particular subject.

When there are apparent contradictions in the data, expert witnesses will want to present these contradictions and explain how they have reconciled contradictions with their findings during the direct examination. This will demonstrate to the court their awareness of the issues and that they have carefully considered the issues, evaluated their significance, and assimilated that information into their findings and opinions (Shapiro, 1984).

Expert Testimony: The Cross Examination

Cross examination is without question the most feared of all courtroom experiences, and for good reason. Graduate students in their oral defense are treated better and challenged less than an expert on the witness stand. There is no collegial status within the courtroom for a mental health practitioner as an expert witness. The adversarial environment of the legal system is engineered so that at all times one side carefully listens to testimony for evidence of support while the other listens to systematically tear the testimony down. Some attorneys in their cross-examinations use blatant ridicule, while others are more effective in methodically weakening or destroying an expert's testimony by more subtle means (Ziskin, 1975). Either way, expert witnesses must be prepared and aware of typical attacks, common traps, and strategies in order to successfully hold their own during cross-examination.

The attack. There are many different techniques attorneys use in cross-examination. While some prefer to berate the expert witness personally, other lawyers choose to not assault the opposing professional too adamantly because the repercussion could undermine their own expert witness' testimony. Thus, most lawyers tend to be very discriminating about how they cross-examine the expert witness (Shapiro, 1984).

To keep the expert witness from becoming defensive and taking cross-examination too personally, Shapiro (1984) has offered the following guideline. The attorney's first inclination will be to attack the expert's opinion. If that opinion is strongly supported, the attorney will attack the expert's credentials. If the expert's credentials are beyond approach, the attorney will then be forced to attack the expert personally. So if experts feel they are being attacked personally they can feel reasonably confident that their credentials and opinions are sound. This frame of reference will allow expert witnesses to assess the strength of their case by the level of attack of the cross-examining lawyer.

Common traps. Cross examining attorneys occasionally trap expert witnesses by baiting them with questions about tangential and unrelated information in an attempt to undermine the expert's credibility and testimony. One common trap is for the lawyer to present the expert witness with an obscure article or research study and ask the expert if she or he is familiar with it and how it relates to the particular case. When this happens, if experts are aware of the article they should acknowledge it and discuss the findings of the study. If the findings are different than the expert has concluded, the expert should cite other research which supports their findings, and be prepared to analyze the study and state why the findings are not applicable in this case (Shapiro, 1984). If experts are not aware of the study, they should simply say so.

Another typical ploy by the cross-examining lawyer is to pose a hypothetical situation and ask the expert to comment about it in regard to the expert's findings and conclusions on the case at hand. This is a trap. As was stated before, experts should not render an opinion on an evaluation they did not do. The expert witness should state that any hypothetical situation would contain too many unknown quantities and that the professional does not make decisions without careful research, study, and evaluation. Speculation is simply speculation and should not be made by a behavioral scientist without data.

A closely related trap employed by a cross-examining lawyer is to ask the expert witness to make a generalization based on data the expert compiled during evaluation. For example, the attorney might say to an expert, "Isn't it possible, based on your observations, that . . . could happen?" Once experts go along with this line of questioning, they will have a difficult time at where to draw the line and stop. Taken to extremes, these generalizations can greatly harm the expert's carefully thought-out, considered opinions. One response might be for the expert to declare, "Anything is possible." But this brash comment may be counterproductive, antagonize the lawyer and judge, and not help with the professional image the expert hopes to project. An alternative response that could potentially strengthen the expert's credibility would be, "Although that is possible, given the evaluation which I conducted, it is my opinion that . . ." (Shapiro, 1984).

Cross-examining lawyers will also try to isolate one symptoms, behavior, or specific test variable and ask the expert witness how that piece of evidence contributed to the expert's opinion. To avoid this trap, the expert witness should respond by stating that their opinion on the individual client was derived by assimilating the totality of information available to them from many various sources and not based on any one specific piece of data.

Expert witness strategies. In direct examination, the lawyer cannot lead the expert witness, but during cross-examination the attorney can and will lead the witness. The expert witness must therefore have a ready supply of proactive strategies to cope with the onslaught during cross-examination. The following strategies and suggestions are offered to aid the school psychologist preparing for cross-examination.

Preparation, preparation, preparation. The expert witness should know their theoretical orientation, know the related literature and research, and be able to adequately describe the assessment process they conducted. The cross-examining attorney will probably not attack the expert's conclusions, but rather the scientific adequacy of the method used to derive those conclusions (Schwitzgebel & Schwitzgebel, 1980). It is important to remember during cross-examination that it is the expert who has the knowledge of the field, and that knowledge can be used to the expert's advantage. Here is an example of cross-examination interchange from Shapiro (1984, p. 81).

Attorney: Now, then, doctor, hasn't research shown that the MMPI is invalid?

Expert: I really cannot answer that question; would you be able to define what you mean by validity?

Attorney: Come now, you're a doctor, don't you know what valid is?

Expert: Certainly, counselor, but there is predictive validity, construct validity, and face validity — to name only a few. You will have to define your terms more precisely before I can respond to the question.

Attorney: I withdraw my question.

Expert witnesses should acknowledge their beliefs, weaknesses, and sympathies honestly and without undue hesitation. They need not appear embarrassed by them. Admitting weaknesses will not undermine their credibility and can, in fact, make them more creditable and believable.

The expert witness should respond in terminology that is easily understood by the courtroom participants and resort to esoteric jargon only when absolutely necessary. Many people are skeptical about experts anyway, so the less jargon, the more acceptable the expert's testimony will be.

As in the direct examination, expert witnesses will need to listen to questions carefully during cross-examination. If a question cannot be answered as asked, experts should say so and ask to have it rephrased or rephrase it themselves. This latter option gives the experts more leeway; they can shape the question to fit their response. If the question has more than one part, experts will need to be sure to answer each part specifically, and if they have additional information that would be helpful to the case, they should also try to work it in.

Cross-examining attorneys will attempt to intimidate and control the pace of their questioning. To counter this, expert witnesses should set their own tempo by pausing to carefully think before responding, and by restating or rephrasing the question. In addition, sustained periods of time testifying can be fatiguing, can contribute to nervousness, and can produce anger, carelessness, and a willingness to say anything to get off the stand (Westphal & Kohn, 1984). If experts sense any of these symptoms, they should request a short recess.

The best preparation of all for cross-examination is to thoroughly use direct examination to the fullest. This involves the client's attorney and the psychologist spending time together planning how to most effectively present the data in order to achieve the greatest clarity and most persuasive presentation possible. The expert should instruct the attorney to follow up any stated opinions with a question to the expert asking the expert to state the grounds and basis for the opinion (Shapiro, 1984). This will allow, hopefully in the direct examination, the expert to present as much information as possible to fortify and explain their inferences, interpretations, and conclusions. If this information is not presented in the direct examination and only brought out during cross-examination, experts appear defensive and their testimony weaker. The more comprehensive the testimony during direct examination, the less stressful and challenging the cross-examination will be.

Other Considerations

Sometimes it is the little pieces of information that separate the good expert witness from the excellent expert witness. The following information is presented to promote the latter.

Rule on witnesses. It is usual practice during lay testimony for the lawyer to ask the judge for a "rule on witnesses," which means that everyone else testifying on the same concern is to be excluded from the courtroom to avoid one testimony influencing another. It is entirely within judges' discretion to determine if they will apply this rule to expert testimony (Shapiro, 1984). If a judge should apply the rule on witnesses to expert testimony, the expert should not be insulted or upset but rather just accept this as standard courtroom practice and gracefully leave the courtroom chambers.

Fee considerations. To avoid any misunderstandings, a fee for the expert's evaluation, report writing, preparation, and testimony should be established and paid before actual testimony takes place. This will eliminate any possible implication that the fee is contingent upon the expert's testimony, which could be challenged in court (Schwitzgebel & Schwitzgebel, 1980). However, it is certainly appropriate for experts to submit a bill for their time in court afterward, as they would for any professional service they provide.

Unexpected outcomes. Sometimes court rulings are hard to understand. No matter how prepared expert witnesses are and how impressive their court performance, the court can rule in a seemingly unpredictable and incomprehensible manner. This can happen for a number of questionable and uncontrollable reasons. For one thing, judges are only human. The particular judge may have had previous contact with the defendant or plaintiff either in or out of the legal system, which could be either beneficial or detrimental to the case. Or the person on trial could be a well-known personality in town. This too could be good or bad.

Also, facts today are not facts tomorrow. History is laden with examples of things considered undeniably true, scientifically proved and backed by the best minds, that were ridiculed, abandoned, and scientifically disproved at a later date. It is for this reason that the field of law is extremely cautious about accepting something as absolutely, ultimately true until it has been demonstrated to be unquestionable by the passage of time (Cook, 1964).

In addition, even if the court does accept a scientific opinion from the expert, it may rule against the expert's recommendations because other facts that came out during the trial, possibly concealed from the expert, make it improbable that the expert's information is prevalent or valid. Usually the trier of fact does not totally neglect the expert's information, but rather exerts that the expert has not carried their burden of proof to the degree stipulated by law (Cook, 1964). In civil cases, the law requires that the preponderance of evidence be demonstrated, while in criminal law the data must be shown to be beyond a shadow of doubt. Furthermore, in regard to child welfare cases, the hearing officer is an advocate for the child and may elect to recommend a course of action different from the positions recommended by any of the parties involved. This can lead to some creative and unanticipated resolutions.

Whatever the outcome, expert witnesses should remember that it is their charge to function as advocates of the facts as they have perceived them, and to present this information in as clear and meaningful terms as possible. The rest is out of their hands and the charge of the court system.

The Written Court Report

Just as in the expert's textimony, the fundamental purpose of the expert's written report is to provide useful and relevant information to the court to assist the legal system in making an informed judicial decision. When expert witnesses provide testimony along with their submitted written report, they can expound upon any aspects of the document that are unclear and answer directed questions that may be elicited. However, when the expert does not testify and is represented only by a written court report, that document must be comprehensive in scope and balanced with concise and forthright content. The following information, suggestions, and considerations are presented to assist the school psychologist in constructing and submitting a written court report.

The comprehensive report. In their day-to-day practice, most school psychologists are involved in multidisciplinary team approaches to assessment, decision making, program planning, and recommendation implementation. The team approach as specified in the Individuals with Disabilities Education Act (IDEA), formerly known as the Education for All Handicapped Children Act of 1975 (Federal Register, 1977), provides protection and an assurance of checks and balances by drawing on a variety of perspectives from different disciplines. In addition, when there is a multidisciplinary team approach the individual written reports are seen as fragments of information that converge to give an overall comprehensive picture of the individual client. But in many civil and criminal law cases, the psychologist does not have the luxury of the multidisciplinary team assessment and resulting written documentation. In fact, in many such cases the psychologist's written report is entered into court as the only input from an expert mental health practitioner. This can greatly increase the potential impact and importance of the psychologist's report and the responsibility of the school psychologist in court interventions.

The court report versus the traditional psychological report. There are as many acceptable court report writing formats and styles as there are traditional psychological report writing formats and styles. It is of utmost importance that the written report be tailored to the individual client and case, rather than attempting to fit the client to a predetermined model of reporting.

The comprehensive court report utilizes most of the typical sections of the traditional report with the addition of several distinctive features. The first distinctive feature of a good court report is that it clearly identifies the reason for referral by specifying in detail what questions the report will address. After specifying the questions to be addressed, the court report should delineate the purpose and scope of the evaluation. This sets the structure for the intervention which is conducted and the format for how data will be presented in the report.

Another important feature of the court report is the review of relevant history and current data. The word *relevant* should be highlighted, because as a comprehensive report the psychologist should exhaustively search for relevant background information but not pad the document with unnecessary information. It is considered unethical to provide the court with interesting or unusual information that is not relevant to the court's disposition. A client's right to confidentiality should be protected even when authorization to release information has been granted; thus information released should be directly pertinent to the case. Since this report may be the only professional opinion entered into the court record, a complete psychosocial history should be taken but again only with pertinent information presented. This section should carefully list the sources and informants consulted to gather the background information.

The next section of the court report usually contains the clinical interview and notes about the client's behavior during the evaluation. The distinction between this section and that usually reported in a school psychological report is the additional reporting of a client's mental status. A mental status examination consists of assessing the client's dress, grooming, and general appearance, degree of cooperation; emotional responses, affect and mood; thought content; orientation as to person, place, and time; memory and attention; language usage; and the professional's general impression of the client.

The assessment section should use as comprehensive a battery of formalized assessment instruments as are necessary to obtain the appropriate data without overevaluation. In addition, functional assessment data including relevant progress monitoring data can be useful.

The final and most important section of the written court report is the summary and recommendations. It is most important because it is often the first, and sometimes only, section thoroughly read. The whole report should be written to support and focus on this section. The summary should synthesize and converge all the relevant information into a concise and forthright presentation. The recommendations should answer each of the questions posed in the reason for referral section in terms of conclusions, opinions, and specific recommendations.

The evaluation report versus the data report. When a psychologist is retained by the judicial system the court is asking for an expert opinion. A data report that clerically reports uninterpreted data is of little use and does not meet the needs of the legal system. The expectations of a professional court report is that it will make specific recommendations that will answer the referral questions. The court demands an expert's professional opinions, inferences, and recommendations, and that is what school psychologists should include in their evaluation report.

Technical specificity. It is very helpful to know in advance the target audience for the written court report. In most instances court reports should be straightforward and free of technical jargon. There are situations, however, such as when there is a nonjury trial and the judge is particularly sophisticated in psychological testimony and terminology, that it is appropriate to present data in a more technical report-writing style. Even so, the psychologist should keep in mind that any good written report should meet the criterion of communicating well.

Clarity through graphs and charts. To aid in communicating psychological data to the court in the written report, the visual impact of graphs and charts can be very helpful. This means of presentation can be especially advantageous in comparing the referred client to a normative population and to demonstrate changes over time through, for example, progress-monitoring data.

Submitting the written court report. To alleviate any difficulties or misunderstandings, the intended recipients of the written court report should be clarified and stipulated prior to expert's initiating their evaluation of a client. In addition, it is ethically responsible for the psychologist to notify the client prior to the evaluation how the information obtained during the evaluation will be utilized and what parties will be exposed to it. After the evaluation has been completed and the report written, it should then be delivered to the specified recipients in keeping with the timetable previously established.

SUMMARY

Optimal courtroom performance is accomplished through the combination of implementing competent best practices in the delivery of all pretrial professional services and thoroughly preparing testimony material prior to taking the witness stand. Diligent pretrial preparation greatly alleviates courtroom stress, can keep the school psychologist from getting beat up in the courtroom, is ethically responsible in terms of the client's welfare, and can have a potentially positive impact on the esteem others hold for the profession of psychology.

The school psychologist assists the court in two major ways: through the delivery of verbal testimony and through the creation of tangible evidence for the court to consider (e.g., psychological reports, videotapes, work samples, charts of progress-monitoring). The fundamental purpose of verbal testimony and tangible evidence is to provide useful and relevant information to the court to help the legal system in making an informed judicial decision. These legal decisions not only impact the individual case being tried but can also generalize to define the work environment for all school psychologists practicing in an educational setting.

This chapter discussed (a) the process of pretrial preparation (gathering and disseminating of information, utilizing files and constructing a face sheet, obtaining legal consultation and preparation, presenting professional credentials effectively, and acquiring courtroom conditioning); (b) the direct examination procedure (the adversarial process, providing appropriate advocacy, responding to questions effectively, and presenting limitations and contradictory data); (c) surviving and making points through the cross-examination (preparing for the attack, understanding common traps, and investigating expert witness strategies); and (d) other considerations (fee considerations and tolerating unexpected outcomes). In addition, the written court report was examined and the differences between a court report and a traditional psychological report written for school purposes were delineated.

REFERENCES

American Psychological Association. (1981). Ethical principles of psychologists. *American Psychologist, 36*, 633–638.

Brodsky, S. L. (1991). *Testifying in court: Guidelines and maxims for the expert witness*. Washington, DC: American Psychological Association.

Brodsky, S. L., & Robey, A. (1973). On becoming an expert witness: Issues of orientation and effectiveness. *Professional Psychology, 3*, 173–176.

Carter v. United States, 252 F2d 608,617 (D.C. Cir. 1957).

Cook, C. M. (1964). The role and rights of the expert witness. *Journal of Forensic Sciences, 9*, 456–460.

Federal Register. (August 23, 1977). *Part II. Rules and regulations for amendments to Part B, Education of All Handicapped Children Act of 1975, Public Law 94-142, Education for handicapped children*, 24274–42518.

Federal Rules of Criminal Procedure, 18 U.S.C.A., Rule 702.

Gorlow, L. (1975). The school psychologist as expert witness in due process hearings. *Journal of School Psychology, 13*, 311–316.

Schwitzgebel, R. L., & Schwitzgebel, R. K. (1980). *Law and psychological practice*. New York: Wiley.

Shapiro, D. L. (1984). *Psychological evaluation and expert testimony: A practical guide to forensic work*. New York: Van Nostrand Reinhold.

Tymchuk, A. J., Drapkin, R., Major-Kingsley, S., Ackerman, A. B., Coffman, E., & Baum, M. (1982). Ethical decision making and psychologists' attitude toward training in ethics. *Professional Psychology, 13*, 412–421.

Washington v. United States, 390 F2d 444,457 (D.C. Cir. 1967).

Westphal, K., & Kohn, S. (1984). The school psychologist as a witness: Techniques and skills. *Communiqué, 12*(7), 1–2.

Ziskin, J. (1975). *Coping with psychiatric and psychological testimony* (2nd ed.). Beverly Hills, CA: Law and Psychology Press.

ANNOTATED BIBLIOGRAPHY

Brodsky, S. L. (1991). *Testifying in court: Guidelines and maxims for the expert witness*. Washington, DC: American Psychological Association.

Brodsky's book concentrates on educating the psychologist on the cross-examination process. Brodsky highlights the questions often asked, the power and control gambits attorneys use, the lines of questions, the nonverbal parrying, and the special limitations of courtroom rules. The basic lessons are directed at allowing the witnesses to comply with the oath of honesty, to be responsive to the questions asked and to the witness role, and to be able to defend themselves, their opinions, and their integrity. This book is intended to do one thing: to present a way of thinking about court testimony and to offer a series of choices and alternatives for thinking about testifying in court.

Schwitzgebel, R. L., & Schwitzgebel, R. K. (1980). *Law and psychological practice*. New York: Wiley.

The purpose of this book is to lead human service professionals and interested clients through the unfamiliar territory of law and psychological practice. Included in the book is a wide variety of helpful information for the school psychologist, including chapters on patients' rights, punishment, psychological testing, school law, confidential communications, malpractice, and many others. Another helpful aspect of this book is the inclusion of a multitude of appendices, including a sample contingency contract for therapy, an intervention contract, a behavior management program consent form, a consent form for a minor to participate in research, and many more.

Ziskin, J. (1975). *Coping with psychiatric and psychological testimony* (2nd ed.). Beverly Hills, CA: Law and Psychology Press.

Ziskin's book is useful for school psychologists because it reveals how their testimony can be potentially torn down. The book is written to provide lawyers with the tools they need to bar psychiatric or psychological testimony in most cases and to dilute or destroy its effect in those cases where it is admitted through utilizing scientific literature to have evidence not admitted or to systematically and methodically reduce the credibility of psychiatrists and psychologists.

18

Best Practices in APA Policy and Advocacy for School Psychology Practice

Ronda C. Talley
American Psychological Association
Center for Psychology in Schools and Education

OVERVIEW

Policy and *advocacy* may sound like terms that have relevance only for the Washington lobbyist or the state association legislative chair. However, nothing could be further from the truth. Whether it is realized or not, each psychologist engages in policy and/or advocacy activities every single day, whether by design or default. The development, implementation, or expression of policy and advocacy take place at the local level through such simple acts as offering an opinion based on scientific data, interpreting an assessment report according to state or district guidelines, or assisting a parent or guardian to access needed services. Concomitantly, policy and advocacy initiatives occur at the state or federal levels through the expression of positions which inform relevant decision makers in those arenas. Psychologists are needed at each of these levels to articulate considered and consistent positions and to coordinate activities that emphasize psychology's expertise in providing solutions to the issues facing America's schools and its students in this century and beyond.

Why should policy and advocacy initiatives be a concern for the school psychology practitioner? One compelling reason is that these issues affect the daily practice of psychology at the local level. Policy positions developed at the district, state, or national levels may have a profound influence on *what* psychologists are allowed to do and *how* it may be done.

An example of this need for coordination in advocacy activities recently occurred at the national level but has implications for state and local practice. In this case, when the Elementary and Secondary Education Act was before the U.S. Congress for reauthorization, the American Psychological Association (APA) suggested inclusion of a definition for "supervisor of pupil services" which would allow years of experience as a school psychologist to count in lieu of teaching experience for that administrative credential. If this addition is retained in the final draft of the legislation, which has been renamed the Improving America's Schools Act of 1994 (IASA), then school

psychologists in each state could use this federal model to advocate for school psychological practice experience to qualify them for the supervisory credential. This is important because in many states, school psychologists are not allowed to move into supervisory positions unless they have a specific number of years of teaching experience. While some states have formulated advocacy plans to remedy this situation, parallel activities at the federal level may help support all states' efforts. This change would open up a career ladder for school psychologists and allow them to supervise their own school psychology programs in states where currently they may be prohibited from doing so by the teaching experience requirement. This example illustrates that the school psychology practitioner should be concerned about policy and advocacy because *the psychologist's employment and ability to function as a professional is affected.*

Secondly, psychologists have a tremendous range and breadth of knowledge and experience which should be brought to bear on current social issues. For example, psychologists are critical experts on issues such as violence affecting children and youth, the impact of television and other media on youngsters, public health issues in the schools, and education reform. Psychologists address these concerns and others by assisting in the development of school-based or school-linked prevention and intervention activities, including leading services integration activities, initiating programs to help students successfully negotiate challenging developmental hurdles (i.e., preschool development ad middle school transition), and developing community/family outreach and involvement components. Psychologists' advocacy in social issues serves to inform the larger school community and public, including policy makers. It also provides a scientific foundation to the development, implementation, and evaluation of programs designed to ameliorate societal problems related to the education of America's youth. Thus, the school psychology practitioner should be concerned about policy and advocacy issues because *the psychologist has something to give back to society and society needs the skills of psychologists.*

While there are many other reasons, such as our relevance to society, our identity, and our employment and practice, for psychologists to be actively involved in policy and advocacy activities, an overriding and compelling reason for our involvement is the *opportunity to positively influence the futures of children.* Psychologists, as professionals and often parents, are personal stakeholders in the mission of effecting positive social change. The lives of children can be enhanced through policy and advocacy efforts. As psychologists, we must act proactively, responsibly, and skillfully in leading advocacy efforts which contribute to the positive development of the nation's most precious resource, its children.

In this chapter, issues related to policy and advocacy for school psychology practice will be explored. Four prominent reform movements and their implications for psychology will be discussed and examples of advocacy efforts for each movement will be presented. It is hoped that the illustrations of advocacy activities at the federal level will provide examples or blueprints of action for initiatives which may also occur at state and local levels.

BASIC CONSIDERATIONS

Getting Started

While some professionals think of the *activities* initiated to address policy development and advocacy concerns as a central focus, they are really one of the last steps to be implemented in the process. As noted by Johnson (1994), "important changes do not occur at the margins, but rather when the social structures in which we live our lives are re-made" (p. 117). Therefore, before engaging in policy and advocacy initiatives, the psychologist or group should consider its characteristics, assumptions, philosophies, and goals. These should be clearly articulated in an organizational description and mission statement. The following is an example of such an organization description and mission statement by the Psychology in the Schools Program of the American Psychological Association (APA).

APA Organizational Statement

The American Psychological Association (APA) is the largest scientific and professional organization representing psychology in the United States and is the world's largest association of psychologists. APA's membership includes more than 118,000 clinicians, researchers, educators, consultants, and students. Through its divisions in 48 subfields of psychology and affiliations with 57 state and Canadian provincial psychological associations, APA has worked for more than 100 years to advance psychology as a science, as a profession, and as a means of promoting human welfare. APA publishes 21 psychological journals, 7

secondary journals, *Clinicians Research Digest*, and numerous books and monographs. APA headquarters operations and programs are managed through the Executive Office, the Office of Publications, and Communications, and four Directorates — Education, Practice, Public Interest, and Science.

Psychology in the Schools Program Mission Statement

The Psychology in the Schools Program of the American Psychological Association is a point within the association where issues pertaining to the practice of psychology in school settings are addressed. Furthermore, since the majority of psychological practice in schools is conducted by school psychologists, this group represents a key constituency for the program. In addition, the issues faced by school psychologists who practice in hospitals, mental health centers, agencies, universities, or other settings, including private practice, are areas of concentration. Th program engages in political and professional advocacy and policy development in response to both guild ad professional practice issues that face practicing psychologists who seek to provide quality services to children, youth, families, school and agency staff, and systems (Talley, 1992).

After these characteristics are specified and advocacy goals are articulated, work then focuses on development of a formal or informal strategic plan for their accomplishment. For example, with the APA Psychology in the Schools Program, a strategic plan was written (Talley, 1992) and disseminated to relevant stakeholders for review and feedback. The plan addressed all major areas of program responsibility in relation to the identified goals and specified activities for each area. Actions formed the last area of the plan and emanated from the program assumptions and goals. For additional projects to be considered for action, they had to prove pertinent to the identified goal areas and complementary to existing program activities.

Considering the Issues

When considering which policy and advocacy goals should be considered in developing a strategic plan, planners must explore the major issues affecting practice. In this section, four prominent social issues which may dramatically impact school practice are highlighted (see Figure 1). Following a discussion of the four major reform issues that influence American education, examples of advocacy efforts implemented in each area are presented.

In American society today, there is a massive convergence of social issues which affect the schools. The most well known of these for educators is, of course, the education reform movement. This movement embodies both the eight national education goals and a wider array of structural and procedural

FIGURE 1. Reform movements of the 1990s.

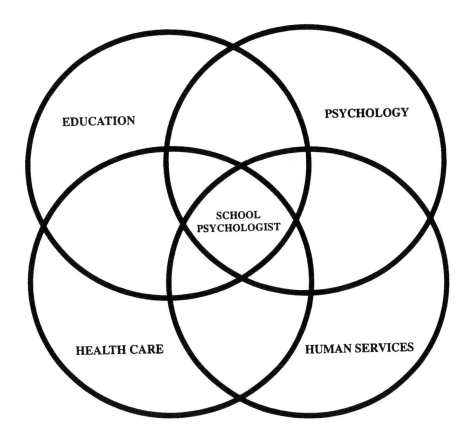

issues pertaining to the way schools work and the definition of their mission.

A parallel and sometimes overlapping reform movement may be found in the health care system. With many schools throughout the nation adding school health clinics to their list of basic services, it is unclear where the delivery of health promotion as well as mental health services fits into the new service delivery paradigms

A third and less widely discussed social movement is occurring in human services. The human services reform movement has two parts: services integration and welfare reform. While school psychologists are not consistently involved in welfare reform issues, the services integration movement appears to be sweeping the nation. Schools are seeking personnel with the consultative and processing skills to lead teams who integrate services between schools and communities.

The fourth reform movement impacting school psychologists is primarily an internal one: Psychology is changing. There is dialogue and debate concerning, to name a few issues, the minimal training required for practice, the redefinition of specialties, the training of psychologists who can prescribe medication, and appropriate credentialling bodies for training programs and individuals. Qualitatively, it seems a time of bold visions and new opportunities. Advocacy efforts associated with this and the other three reform movements will be considered next.

Education Reform

The national education goals have been promoted as a standard for American education. However, the education reform movement as embodied by the goals actually constitutes a broad pattern for comprehensive services for children and adults that addresses health, social needs, mental health, and development as well as education. Whereas American education traditionally has occurred within the confines of the school building, education reform cannot be achieved without a coordinated, integrated, and interdisciplinary effort that also includes parents, social and health agencies, and communities. In fact, service delivery within education reform and the proposed health care reform may share many mechanisms and objectives. These two reform movements, sometimes overlapping and sometimes parallel, may provide psychology with an unprecedented opportunity to redefine psychological service delivery for the 21st century.

However, psychology has been conspicuously absent in policy and program development for educational reform. Short and Talley (1993) describe this as an important reason for the lack of progress in education reform initiatives. They note that although psychological theory and research underlie much of educational practice, education policy and the educational literature seldom cite psychological contributions to the improvement of education. Frank Farley, Past-President of the APA, cogently noted this disparity:

> In my view, a central reason for the slow progress in reform is the relative absence of psychology in the equation for educational change. The principle target for education reform should be the *minds of kids*. If the minds of kids are to the bull's eye, then we're not going to much improve education. We will simply be rearranging the deck chairs on the Titanic. No discipline is more sure-footed on the mindscape of kids than psychology. Psychology is the core science of mind, and without psychology's signature on the blueprint of education reform, reform will fail. Therefore, it is imperative that we advocate for a *psychology of education reform*. (Farley, 1993, p. 15)

Health Care Reform

America is witnessing a clear change in direction in health care and education policy (Short, 1993). Of the numerous pieces of health care reform legislation introduced in Congress, only the Health Security Act of 1994 proposed by President Clinton contained a specific section devoted to schools. In Title III, Subtitle G, two dimensions of school health care were addressed: comprehensive school health education and school-related health services. Health, prevention, and education rather than disease, intervention, and mental health were emphasized. This is one sign that, within the health care reform movement, emphasis on specialized care for clinical populations is yielding to a more preventive, comprehensive orientation that addresses specific social and health problems such as intentional injury and substance abuse. Schools and educational agencies are primary settings for the delivery of services with this orientation, and psychologists are uniquely prepared to provide comprehensive preventive services in schools and communities.

As health care reform initiatives are considered at the state and federal levels, schools will no longer be in the exclusive purview of education. Psychologists who practice in schools need to prepare for a new reality in terms of school-based health service provision and would do well to consider how their services will be viewed and valued. Indeed, legislation may provide a challenge and an opportunity to recast psychological service delivery to children and youth (Talley & Short, 1994a, 1994b).

Human Services Reform: Services Integration

While education and health reform have been highly touted in the last few years, a third revolution — in the human services area — has been brewing. This new movement, called *services integration*, has provided an opportunity for psychology to position itself for the delivery of services across multiple settings in a teaming fashion with other health service providers. Services integration is defined by the National Alliance of Pupil Services Organizations as "the process by which a range of education, health, and psycho-social services are delivered in a coordinated way to individuals and family systems" (1992b).

Current legislation defining comprehensive school health services emphasizes the education of the individual student in the school and classroom. However, the prevention of many childhood health problems requires a much broader and more coordinated educative focus, in other words, a services integration approach. Failure to address behaviors and characteristics of parents, peers, and communities minimizes the potential effectiveness of school-based educational interventions. Because parents, peers, and communities are critically important to the development, prevention, and treatment of the problems addressed in legislation, involvement of these groups in health education is crucial. The skills and expertise of psychologists provide a productive tool for pulling together various constituencies for effective planning and services for children.

Within the services integration movement, psychologists will be impacted in four ways. In the area of training, psychologists will need greater breadth and flexibility, with opportunities for training as team members with other health service professionals. Psychologists will be asked to assume leadership roles within integrated services programs providing program administration ad supervision, building collaborative teams, and facilitating planned change in the direction of more integrated services. Practitioners will be able to exercise greater flexibility in the range of activities with which they engage and not be constrained in regard to funding source and eligibility considerations. And finally, psychological research on the efficacy of integrated service delivery approaches for children and families represents a unique contribution for psychology.

The Reform of Psychology

As mentioned earlier, a number of changes are either occurring or being considered within America psychology. With the convergence of these major issues, psychology may find an opportunity to consider new ways of viewing the profession and what constitutes psychological service delivery. For example, for services integration initiatives to be successful, psychologists increasingly find themselves working in teams of human service providers across a variety of disciplines with services occurring both on and off school grounds. Increasing numbers of psychologists may choose to acquire additional training in order to prescribe medications as this idea becomes more accepted both within the profession and in society. Both education reform and health care reform with their many overlapping features, will call for new and creative ways for psychologists to work with teachers, administrators, parents, agencies, and the community. The reform of the profession of psychology will challenge psychologists to be consumer oriented and responsive to system needs. Agencies, associations, and credentialling bodies must also be responsive to changing consumer demands. Psychologists with the social, process, and content skills needed in these changing paradigms will thrive.

BEST PRACTICES

In beginning a program of policy development and advocacy, it may be useful to examine a range of strategies and activities successfully implemented by other groups. The following section treats each of the four areas previously discussed and highlights activities which the American Psychological Association has initiated to address social reforms on behalf of American psychology.

Education Reform

Legislative/regulatory advocacy. In 1993, APA's Education Directorate formed the Schools Advisory Group in Education (SAGE) to promote the role of psychology in improving American schools and education in the national legislative and policy agenda, including applications, practice, training, and research. SAGE was designed to address all major education and education-related legislation and policy, including all major social issues impacting education: education and education reform; schools, education, and prevention in health care reform; educational technology; schools and education in welfare reform; education and training of psychologists in schools and education; and the role of schools in crime and judicial legislation. Most recently, SAGE has provided recommendations to Congress promoting psychology's role in Goals 2000: The Educate America Act, the Improving America's Schools Act, and recent crime and safe schools legislation.

APA Task Force on Psychological Principles and School Psychological Services in Education Reform (TFER). The TFER was established in 1994 to promote psychology's role in the education reform movement; to articulate psychology's contribution to children, families, and systems in advancing the national education goals; and to develop model psychological service delivery systems to promote these goals in states and local school systems. The Task Force was charged with developing a proposal for an APA-wide action plan to promote the role of psychology and psychologists in education reform. In accomplishing their mission, the Task Force examined models for education reform and school change and specified the roles psychology and psychologists can play in influencing the legislation to be developed and in designing and providing services to support reform objectives.

APA/NEA collaboration. The APA/NEA (National Education Association) collaboration was begun in 1991 as a means to promote a number of psychological and educational issues (" APA, NEA work …" 1994). The collaboration, formalized in a December 1993 meeting between the two associations, continues to promote the common concerns and mutual interests of both groups. The goal is the establishment of collaborative mechanisms between the two groups with the intention of culminating in the joint approval of a formal memorandum of collaboration. The American Psychological Association brings to the collaboration expertise in psychological issues related to the education and health of individuals and systems as well as information pertaining to the practice of psychology in schools. The National Education Association brings to the collaboration its representation of over 2.2 million teachers, psychologists, and other education personnel and its expertise on critical issues in American education. The APA/NEA collaboration promotes the common agendas of both associations through the development of joint policy/position statements; publications, legislative/lobbying activities; research, training, and practice activities; and positions on state and local collective bargaining efforts.

APA/National Education Goals Panel collaboration. The APA has played a leadership role in representing psychology to the nation's governors, the President's education staff, and education members of Congress. This group, as represented by the National Education Goals Panel (NEGP), invited APA to draft its definitional paper on Goal Seven of the national education goals, commonly referred to as the "safe schools" goal. The NEGP is a bipartisan group comprised of governors, members of the Clinton administration, and members of Congress which has as its mission "to build a nation of learners" (NEGP, 1993).

APA/NAPSO collaboration. In addition, the NEGP and the National Alliance of Pupil Services Organization (NAPSO), of which APA is a member, sponsored a national conference on Goal Seven of the national education goals in October 1994. The conference, targeted to education policy makers and pupil services practitioners, focused on solutions to school violence, substance abuse, and highlighted the creation of environments conducive to learning. The conference offered a unique opportunity to present the case for pupil services, including school psychology, as an essential ingredient in addressing educational, health, and safety issues pertaining to America's children and youth. The NAPSO is a coalition of 23 national professional organizations whose members provide "a variety of primary, preventive, developmental, remedial, and supportive services which are required to assist children and youth to benefit fully from their education" (NAPSO, 1992).

Health Care and Human Services Reform

Schools as health service delivery sites work group. This group was established in 1993 and charged with producing a report on schools as health service delivery sites in national health reform. Specific areas addressed in the report include (a) a historical perspective on the role of schools as settings for the provision of primary health care, (b) clarification of the definition of a health care setting and rationale regarding how the schools and/or school-based clinics meet these criteria; (c) clarification of the schools as appropriate health service delivery settings for the psychology internship; (d) identification of legislative and educational structures that support or limit the roles of schools as health care provider settings; (e) an examination of existing and potential roles for psychologists in the public school health care delivery system; (f) identification of models of comprehensive and coordinated services for children that currently exist in public schools with an analysis of evaluation data regarding their effectiveness in meeting the mental health needs of children; (g) an examination of reimbursement issues for psychologists in school settings; and (h) a description of how psychologists in schools provide an essential function in the delivery, coordination, and integration of a variety of children's mental health services. After completion, the report will be used to design a number of additional advocacy initiatives around health service delivery in schools and the roles which school psychologists have in this process.

APA Task Force on Comprehensive and Co-ordinated Psychological Services for Children Age 0–10 (TFCCPS). The TFCCPS was established in 1991 and charged with assessing the current array of services available to met the psychological and mental health needs of children from birth through age 10 with particular emphasis placed on the delivery of services within school settings. Further, after identification of the current service delivery needs, the TFCCPS was charged with analyzing available resources, comparing service needs with resources to determine gaps in service delivery, and recommending how these gaps should be addressed to provide a comprehensive and coordinated array of services to meet the psychological and mental health needs of children. In fulfilling its charge, the TFCCPS built on the work of many leaders, including Melville and Blank (1991) and NAPSO (1993) to produce a report entitled *Comprehensive and Coordinated Psychological Services for Children: A Call for Service Integration* (Paavola et al., 1995), a two-page fact sheet on "Children's Mental Health Needs: Reform of the Current System" (1993), a book prospectus on service integration, and a draft "Children's Agenda" for APA. Additionally, in the spring of 1993, the TFCCPS hosted a meeting of over 50 children's issues groups to discuss psychology's contributions to and advocacy in this area.

The Reform of Psychology

Leadership development. To establish a dialogue with school psychology leaders in the field and to provide key leaders with an opportunity to discuss reform issues in their states and at the federal level, the APA and the Administrators of School Psychological Services (ASPS) group of the Division of School Psychology joined forces in 1994 to offer the first Institute for Administrators of School Psychological Services. The Institute was held in conjunction with the APA convention and carried the theme "Advocacy for School Psychological Services Practice: Challenges for the Year 2000." The superintendent of the Los Angeles Unified School District, Sidney A. Thompson, and Dr. Cindy Carlson, President of the APA's Division of School Psychology, were keynote speakers. In addition, sessions were offered on the following topics: school psychologists in education and health care reform, school violence and crisis planning, services integration and interagency collaboration, school psychological services program evaluation and student outcomes, and continuing professional development for changing service needs.

Networking. In 1993, APA christened its electronic communications system, the School Psychology Leaders Network (SPLN). Leaders in the field of school psychology were added to this electronic mail network and receive regular updates from the APA Center for Psychology in Schools and Education on legislative progress, new publications, pertinent announcements from the federal government, and other items of interest.

In both 1993 and 1994, the APA Center for Psychology in Schools and Education produced the *APA Leaders in School Psychology Directory* ("New Directory," 1994). The *Directory* lists all school psychology leaders who serve the association or work with the Division of School Psychology. Division task force chairs are also included. The following information is available for each person in the *Directory;* name, title, mailing address, telephone and fax numbers, two primary ares of expertise, and major professional affiliations and offices. Copies are available free of charge.

Print advocacy. In December 1993, the APA announced the publication of two new documents related to school psychology practice. The first document, *Guide for the School Psychologist: A System for the Promotion of Diversified Psychological Services in Schools* ("Guide for," 1993), is designed to aid practicing school psychologists in providing information on the myriad of services which they deliver. The second publication, *Delivery of Comprehensive School Psychological Services: An Educator's Guide* (Jackson et al., 1993), explains school psychologists and their work to school administrators.

In addition to formal reports, APA has produced numerous articles and other publications related to reforms occurring in psychology and psychological practice (APA, 1994a, 1994b; De Angelis, 1994; de Groot, 1994a, 1994b) as well as articles to address general advocacy issues (Allen, 1993; *Federal Advocacy Handbook*, 1993; *Psychology in the Public Interest*, 1992). APA affiliates, such as the Pennsylvania Psychological Association (1992), have also been active in advocacy issues through the publication of political handbooks.

Division of school psychology. The APA Division of School Psychology has also shown leadership in the reform of psychology through publications (Carlson, 1994; DeMers, 1993), and the establishment of task forces to study reform issues as they specifically apply to school psychology. For example, the Division has established a group to review the APA draft document, *Learner-Centered Principles for School Redesign and Reform* (1993), develop a report on psychopharmacology and children, and redraft the school psychology specialty guidelines.

SUMMARY

Policy and advocacy in school psychology is one of the most challenging and exciting areas of professional practice. It requires patience, determination, knowledge, social skills, negotiation abilities, key contacts, and time. And, of course, it requires that one views the cause as significant in terms of potential benefit to a long-range program of political advocacy. Policy and advocacy initiatives must engender a sense of focus and dedication which allow the advocate to set aside other peripheral concerns and implement a plan to accomplish a set of recognized and valued goals.

School psychologists have a vested interest in influencing policy and advocacy positions. They should be key players in the reform movements of the 1990s: education reform, health care reform, human services reform (including services integration), and the reform of psychology. Initiatives in this area affect school psychologists' practice and employment, their relevance and professional identity, and, most importantly, the lives of children and youth. Because psychologists have the scientific knowledge and techni-

cal expertise to inform policy decisions and to lay the foundation for well researched advocacy proposals, it is a critical part of their responsibility to the profession and to society to use their training and experience to positively shape social policy. Each psychologist should seek ways through which this challenge may be met.

ACKNOWLEDGEMENT

The author wishes to acknowledge her collaboration with Dr. Rick Jay Short, Assistant Executive Director for Education in the APA Education Directorate, on many of the school psychology advocacy efforts described in this article. Dr. Short's equal contribution to these is greatly appreciated and fully acknowledged.

REFERENCES

Allan, M. (1993, Fall). APA national school psychology intern report. *The School Psychologist*, pp. 8, 12.

American Psychological Association. (1994a, April). *Improving American schools: Psychology's role in health care.* (Available from the American Psychological Association, 750 First Street, NE, Washington, DC.)

American Psychological Association. (1994b, June). *The future of America's schools: Psychology's role in education.* (Available from the American Psychological Association, 750 First Street, NE, Washington, DC.)

APA, NEA work together on mutual issues, concerns. (1994, May). *APA Monitor*, p. 23.

Carlson, C. (1994, May/June). Make a new friend at school: What your school psychologist can do for you. *The Psychology Teacher Network*, p. 5.

Children's mental health needs: Reform on the current system. (1993). (Available from the American Psychological Association, 750 First Street, Washington, DC 20002-4242.)

DeAngelis, T. (1994, January). APA redoubles its efforts to lead education reform. *APA Monitor*, pp. 38–39.

deGroot, G. (1994a, June). Psychologists are key to school reform. *APA Monitor*, pp. 38–39.

deGroot, G. (1994b, June). APA advocacy team touts the value psychology adds. *APA Monitor*, p. 38.

DeMers, S. T. (1993, August). *School psychology in the second century of American psychology.* Division 16 Presidential address presented at the meeting of the American Psychological Association, Toronto.

Farley, F. (1993, November/December). The education reform summit: Psychological science goes to school. *APA Psychological Science Agenda*, 6(6), 15.

Federal advocacy handbook: A guide to grassroots lobbying. (1993). (Available from the Practice Division, American Psychological Association, 750 First Street, NE, Washington, DC 20002-4242.)

Guide for the school psychologist: A system for the promotion of diversified psychological services in schools. (1993). (Available from the American Psychological Association, 750 First Street, NE, Washington DC 20002-4242.)

Jackson, J. H., Balinky, J. L., Lambert, N. M., Oakland, T D., DeMers, S. T., Alpert, J. L., Reynolds, C. R., & Talley, R. C. (1993). *Delivery of comprehensive school psychological services: An educator's guide.* Washington, DC: American Psychological Association.

Johnson, D. (1994, May). Education reform Clinton-style. *Psychological Science*, pp. 117–121.

Learner-centered principles for school reform (draft.). (1993). (Available from the American Psychological Association, 750 First Street, NE, Washington DC 20002-4242.)

Melaville, A. I., & Blank, M. J. (1991). *What it takes: Structuring interagency partnerships to connect children and families with comprehensive services.* Washington, DC: Institute for Educational Leadership.

National Alliance of Pupil Services Organizations. (1992a). *Mission statement.* (Available from the National Alliance of Pupil Services Organizations, c/o American Psychological Association, 750 First Street, NE, Washington, DC 20002-4242.)

National Alliance of Pupil Services Organizations. (1992b). *Policy statement on school-linked integrated services.* (Available from the National Alliance of Pupil Services Organizations, c/o American Psychological Association, 750 First Street, NE, Washington, DC 20002-4242.)

National Education Goals Panel. (1993). *National education goals report.* (Available from the National Education Goals Panel, 1850 M Street, NW, Washington, DC 20036.)

New directory lists school psych leaders. (1994, May). *APA Monitor*, p. 22.

Paavola, J. C., Cobb, C., Illback, R. J., Joeph, H. M., Torrmella, A., & Talley, R. C.. (1995). *Comprehensive and coordinated psychological services for children: A call for service integration.* (Available from the American Psychological Association, 750 First Street, NE, Washington, DC 20002-4242.)

Pennsylvania Psychological Association political handbook. (1992). (Available from the Pennsylvania Psychological Association, 416 Forster Street, Harrisburg, PA 17102-1714.)

Psychology in the public interest: A psychologist's guide to advocacy. (1992). (Available from the Public Policy Office, American Psychological Association, 750 First Street, NE, Washington, DC 20002-4242.)

Short, R. J. (1993, December). *The role psychology can play in improving America's schools.* (Available from the American Psychological Association, 750 First Street, NE, Washington, DC 20002-4242.)

Short, R. J., & Talley, R. C. (1993). *A psychology of education reform.* Paper prepared at the request of the APA Board of Educational Affairs. (Available from the American Psychological Association, 750 First Street, NE, Washington, DC 20002-4242.)

Talley, R. C. (1992, August). *Psychology in the Schools program: Strategic plan.* (Available from the American Psychological Association, 750 First Street, NE, Washington, DC 20002-4242.)

Talley, R. C., & Short, R. J. (1994a, Spring). Health care reform and the schools: Just the facts. *The School Psychologist*, pp. 1, 7, 11.

Talley, R. C., & Short, R. J. (1994b, Summer). Health care reform and school psychology: A wake up call from school psychologists to school psychologists. *The School Psychologist*, pp. 1, 3, 15.

ANNOTATED BIBLIOGRAPHY

American Psychological Association. (1994). *Psychology's role in health care: Psychological services for the 21st century.* (Packet available from the American Psychological Association, 750 First Street, NE, Washington, DC 2002-4242.)

The American Psychological Association has developed a packet of individual documents on a variety of health care topics which are designed to inform the public about what psychology has to contribute to health care. Individual flyers with the following titles are included: improving America's schools, preventing youth violence, promoting women's health, making work places safer and more productive, educating and training the next generation of psychologists, mental health services cut overall health costs, psychological services address a range of health concerns, psychological research: vital to health care reform, and psychological services: integral to a new health care system. The packet's overall theme focuses on how psychologists promote health services, and save health care dollars. A limited number of packets are available free of charge.

Jackson. J. H., Balinky, J. L., Lambert, N. M., Oakland, T. D., De Mers, S. T., Alpert, J. L., Reynolds, C. R., & Talley, R. C. (1993). *Delivery of comprehensive school psychological services: An educator's guide.* Washington, DC: American Psychological Association.

This booklet, referred to as "the educator's guide," was produced by the APA Task Force for Psychology in the Schools and is now in its second printing. The publication, directed to school administrators, attempts to provide basic information on what a school psychological services program should look like at the local district level. The first chapter, "Your School Psychologist," offers information on how psychologists work and with whom they do their work. It also addresses what type of services psychologists provide: support of school-wide or district-wide programs and services to individual students, groups, and families. Next, "Planning and Developing a School Psychological Services Program" provides an outline with which a district can build or refine a program. The third chapter, "Enhancement of School and District Goals Through Use of School Psychological Services," addresses general contributions of school psychologists to the enhancement of school goals. It also offers a section on research and program evaluation as they are used to support school goals. The final chapter, "Legal, Ethical, and Professional Issues in the Delivery of Psychological Services in Schools," targets litigation and legislation that affects school psychologists in schools. Copies of this document are available for $10.

Psychology in the public interest: A psychologist's guide to advocacy. (1992). (Available from the Public Policy Office, American Psychological Association, 750 First Street, NE, Washington, DC 20002-4242.)

The *Psychologist's Guide to Advocacy* is a brief primer on the legislative process. Its topics are organized under three major headings: APA advocacy for psychology, a short course in the legislative process, and effective communications. Within these major areas, topics include understanding the legislative process, selecting committees and subcommittees to target for advocacy efforts, determining how a legislator decides to vote, and examining the regulatory process. A separate section provides details on identifying and locating our legislators, understanding the role of Congressional staff, writing a constituent letter, making a constituent telephone call, meeting with your legislator, and inviting your legislator to visit. Copies of the document are available free of charge from the APA Public Policy Office.

Short, R. J. , & Talley, R. C. (1993). *A psychology of education reform.* Paper prepared at the request of the APA Board of Educational Affairs. (Available from the American Psychological Association, 705 First Street, NE, Washington, DC 20002-4242.)

This document was developed to inform psychologists of the importance of being involved in education issues. It begins by highlighting how education reform extends far beyond the schoolhouse and moves to focus on why psychology is important to eduction reform. The article documents the importance of psychology to education by addressing each of the national education goals and provides examples of how psychology impacts each goal. The document concludes by stating the case for why education reform is important to school psychology: It affects our practice, our relevance and identity, our children, and our employment. Copies are available free of charge.

Focus on Systems

19

Best Practices in Fostering School/Community Relationships

Susan M. Sheridan
University of Utah

Schools cannot provide all the needed resources for educating children today, nor can communities themselves — both must begin to collaborate to improve the schools of our nation.

National Association of State
Boards of Education, 1992

Today's youth soon will be responsible for sustaining America's work force, for enhancing the economic climate of the country, and for enriching the social resources of society. Our future in large part rests on the ability of youth to fulfill the tasks necessary to support the economic, political, and social structures of our country. To ensure that students are equipped with skills to carry out this daunting responsibility, communities *must* become actively involved in education. This is not simply a "nice idea" — it is a necessity.

Communities have a myriad of resources. A vast number of assets is available outside of the school walls, and it is becoming more and more important to tap these resources and establish meaningful and productive school/community partnerships. The purposes of this chapter are to provide an overview of school/community partnerships; identify basic considerations for establishing effective relations; and review various models of school/community partnerships.

OVERVIEW

Definition of School/Community "Partnerships"

Over time, the relationship between schools and communities has changed. In the early days of formal education, the "social and physical distances between teachers and the community" were minimal (Tangri & Moles, 1987, p. 519). As schools adopted a central educational responsibility in society, however, the notion that schools should be separate and isolated from the community became rigidly reinforced. This isolation from the community has contributed to several problems faced by schools, such as limited resources, lack of community confidence in schools, and little communication. The barriers between schools and communities must be overcome, and the most fruitful way to begin this process is to conceptualize the relationship as a partnership.

Webster (1981) defines "partnerships" and "partner" as the "state of being a partner . . . one who shares" (p. 829). A partnership assumes a close, cooperative relationship wherein all parties (students, teachers, and community representatives) have specific and joint rights and responsibilities. The objectives of educational partnerships include (a) pooling and sharing of talents, resources, and efforts to achieve a commonly defined mission in the education of students; (b) empowering educational personnel to access, refine, and/or develop new, creative approaches; (c) developing and refining professional skills through the exchange of ideas, knowledge, and expertise; and (d) enhancing educational services to *all* students (Welch & Sheridan, in press). In this framework, all participants in the partnership benefit.

Various partnerships are possible in educational environments, ranging from student–student cooperative structures to home–school partnerships to community-based instruction and training. A pragmatic schema for conceptualizing various forms of partnerships appears in Figure 1. This chapter is concerned with the broadest level of partnership cutting across the greatest number of settings, individuals, and functions: that of school/community partnerships.

Benefits of School/Community Partnerships

Several advantages lie in developing and strengthening the relationship between schools and communities. Community agencies and businesses often can provide a unique educational experience that is unavailable in traditional, isolated school buildings. Community involvement can increase students' awareness of means by which to contribute to society. It can enhance students' understanding of citizenship and social commitment. It can also help develop such important values as respect for others and civic responsibility (National Association of State Boards of Education, 1992). Work experiences, vol-

FIGURE 1. Spectrum of educational partnerships.

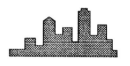

Community – based

Business – school partnerships
Functional life skills programs
Vocational education

Home – school

Parent education
After school programs
Latch key programs
Parent – teacher collaboration

School – based

Staff development
Curriculum mapping
Teacher assistance teams
Collaborative consultation
Team teaching

Classroom – based

Strategic intervention
Peer – mediated intervention
Instruction/curricula modification
Grading modification

unteer or other community service practices, and field-based learning opportunities also provide effective, hands-on educational possibilities beyond the classroom walls.

Besides these obvious immediate benefits to students, productive partnerships also provide advantages to communities and schools. An important benefit is the improvement of skills in the labor pool from which businesses and communities will draw their work force. Community and business participants often report a boost in morale from their involvement with students and a renewed sense of pride and value in their own work (Tangri & Moles, 1987).

Schools also derive benefits from active school/community partnerships. Most obvious is the time, expertise, and equipment that businesses and the community donate to educational programs. Direct assistance in the form of personnel development, food assistance, management, and purchasing also have become available to schools through community involvement. Schools involved with successful programs also report lower absenteeism, truancy, and dropout rates (Bucknam, 1976).

When teachers are actively involved in the development or implementation of school/community programs, they benefit through career exploration, expanded roles, and increased involvement with the community. Ideally, teachers receive formal training or internships to enhance their position as a community liaison.

CONSIDERATIONS

Perhaps more important than any other consideration, it is essential that efforts to build, strengthen, and maintain school/community relationships be well thought out and planned. It is not sufficient that school and community persons have good intentions to forge a working partnership; rather, they must have a clear vision of what the partnership will achieve and an operational plan for accomplishing that mission.

A report of the National Association of State Boards of Education (1992) outlined several principles of community involvement. The first suggested that programs be well managed and skillfully organized. This requires the development of an appropriate and adequate management plan, which should include specific details about activities (what?), responsibilities (who?), time lines (when?), locations (where?), and procedures (how?).

Second, effective school/community partnerships are flexible. The organization and implementation of the management plan must be based on the needs of the school involved and the local community. Each school, community, and school/community interaction is unique; therefore, the goals, objectives, and program guidelines must be specific to local issues. Further, aspects of the community (e.g., socioeconomic status, size, nature of businesses and organiza-

tions, community strengths) must be considered, to realize maximum benefits.

A third characteristic of successful school/community partnerships is an adequate time commitment. Quality relationships require a significant amount of time to develop, strengthen, rework, and evaluate. Partnerships will not form overnight and will not maintain themselves without concerted effort and a long-term commitment. Likewise, the needs and resources of local schools and communities will change over time. Therefore, the partnership requires continued creativity and reconceptualization of the means by which its efforts can produce the best results.

Finally, formal preparation of teachers, administrators, and community representatives is essential in successful programs. In many areas, the formalization of school/community relations is novel, and necessary skills and strategies are unfamiliar to the key participants. The persons who provide training will vary across situations, but will likely involve some combination of school and community personnel. It is hoped that attention to establishing school/community partnerships will become an integral component in preservice professional preparation programs across colleges of education and business. Until this time, however, comprehensive and integrated in-service training will be necessary.

BEST PRACTICES

Identifying Resources and Establishing Partnerships: A Problem-Solving Approach

School/community partnerships can be operationalized and implemented in a number of ways. Just as no two schools and no two communities are alike, no two partnerships are identical in structure, purpose, or procedure. Although several examples are now available to schools and communities interested in forging a productive relationship, the means by which the partnership actually takes shape must be determined by the needs of the participants. Thus, a structured, ecological problem-solving approach (Kratochwill & Bergan, 1990) may be beneficial in developing, implementing, and evaluating school/community programs.

Problem Identification and Goal Formulation

When establishing a partnership of any kind, participants must clarify the scope, purpose, and objectives of the relationship. This entails specifying clearly why the partnership is necessary (i.e., the "problem" it is meant to prevent or resolve), and what the partnership is intended to accomplish (i.e., the goals). Although school/community programs may be desirable in their own right, they will not sustain themselves if they do not serve a specific and concrete purpose. Therefore, members of the partnership must establish clear lines of communication and jointly determine the primary areas of need, estimated prevalence rates, and appropriate goals for the school/community program.

One can identify problems at an individual classroom, school, or district level. As with all prevention programs, the broader the level at which a need can be defined, the more far-reaching are the effects. A comprehensive needs assessment should take place during the problem identification stage. For example, as a school psychologist working in an inner-city, overcrowded high school, you may recognize that student achievement in your school is significantly lower than in other district high schools. By investigating characteristics of the school (e.g., technological and material resources, instructional opportunities in technical skills, volunteerism, neighborhood businesses) and those common to several students in the school (e.g., computer literacy, after-school activities, later life aspirations), you will be in a position to specify salient school and student needs and develop objectives for school/community programs. The likely goals of such programs in this school would be to raise student achievement, equip students with meaningful life skills, and prevent current and future problems (e.g., dropping out, delinquency, academic failure).

Ecological Analysis

To truly understand problems in the school or community, one must carefully analyze environmental strengths and limitations, examining variables within the school and community that perpetuate existing problems. For example, the existence of a significant gang culture in the high school described above may foster lack of interest in academic achievement and school programs by students and community persons alike. Likewise, the school historically may have been isolated from the community due to lack of confidence in the school's ability to teach basic skills and prepare its students to compete in the work force. By generating hypotheses about the nature and function of the problem (in other words, *why* it occurs), one can explore appropriate and meaningful partnerships.

An important aspect of ecological analyses is identifying resources that can help solve the problem. It is essential that human, material, technological, financial, and informational resources be explored before committing to any one type of partnership. Likewise, a multisource, multisetting consideration of resources should be invoked, including those available within student, home, school, and community agencies. A matrix such as the one depicted in Figure 2 can be employed when considering the various resources that may be available in developing school/community partnerships. Note that a discussion of home/school partnerships and use of home re-

sources is beyond the scope of this chapter; readers should consult Christenson (this volume) for extensive coverage of this important topic. Suffice it to say that consideration of the home environment and parental involvement in the development of school/community linkages should not be overlooked.

Plan Development and Implementation

The actual development of a school/community program should occur via brainstorming with all key persons from schools and communities. When brainstorming, participants should think creatively, withhold judgment, and pool ideas and options to create even more alternatives. Possible programs may include aspects of or entire models available in the literature, such as those described later in this chapter. On the other hand, novel and unique alternatives may be generated when individuals from various constituencies pool their ideas and expertise. Indeed, the ability to share responsibility and offer varied options is a cornerstone of school/community partnerships. In the example above, increased involvement of volunteers in the school may be desirable to students with academic difficulties and teachers, and to change the perceptions of community persons. Likewise, an after-school sports program, staffed by coaches at the local community college and supported with equipment donated by a neighborhood sporting goods store, may decrease gang activity and keep students and local agencies interested and active in the school setting. Finally, community-based training in such skills as computer programming, gourmet cooking, mechanics, or child care can be instrumental in extending the formal educational experiences of students into meaningful, lifelong vocations.

Implementing a school/community program requires a great deal of organization and leadership. It is best to identify a key person in the school and a key person in the community to ensure that the details of the program are clear to all participants, the strategies are followed with integrity, and communication remains open. Specific written guidelines in the form of a management plan maximize smooth operation of the program. As mentioned earlier, the components of the management plan should specify what, why, where, how, and by whom the tactics will be instituted.

Plan Evaluation

Best practices of any school-based service delivery model dictate that the effects of the model be evaluated. School/community partnerships are no exception. When promoting and implementing these types of educational programs, one should evaluate benefits, limitations, and intended and unintended side effects; reassess prevalence rates; and examine

FIGURE 2. Resource matrix.

	Physical	Technological	Information	Financial	Human
Student					
Home					
School					
Community					

attainment of the concrete goals of the partnership. Both formative (process) and summative (outcome) evaluation practices can be instrumental in the overall assessment of the effects of school/community partnerships. Participants should also assess consumer satisfaction with the program (i.e., students, parents, schools, businesses, other community participants), and finally explore long-term benefits and liabilities.

MODELS OF SCHOOL/COMMUNITY PARTNERSHIPS

Although several models of school/community partnerships are available in the literature, research on the effectiveness of the various approaches is extremely limited. In general, programs can be based within the school (with community agencies entering school buildings and providing training or support), or within the community (with instruction and training occurring outside the school building). The objective of the various programs differ, as do the required resources and the expected outcomes. To reiterate a point made earlier, the needs of the school, students, community, and other educational patrons must be considered in determining the most appropriate type of partnership.

School-based Approaches

Although attention to school/community partnerships has increased drastically over the last decade,

most programs continue to be school-based. Examples of models involving community persons or resources in the school building itself include volunteerism and Adopt-a-School programs.

School volunteers. The most common form of community involvement in education takes the form of school volunteers (Gonder, 1981). Trained volunteers can provide several important functions in the school building, including conducting vision, hearing, and developmental screenings; providing individualized tutoring for students with special academic needs; monitoring behavioral programs; and helping to develop curricular materials. When directly involved in academic and instructional activities, volunteers lower the pupil–adult ratio in classrooms.

An important variable in the effectiveness of volunteer programs is recruitment. In a review of several volunteer programs, Gonder (1981) emphasized that "successful volunteer programs place a high priority on recruitment. The sensitive school district tries to recruit volunteers from all races and ethnic groups to serve the needs of their students. Another rich source is the retired community. Students and employed persons are also willing to volunteer" (p. 300). Indeed, the days are gone when volunteers involved only white, middle-class, nonworking mothers serving as "room mothers" and providing baked goods for the bake sale.

Adopt-a-School programs. Adopt-a-School programs match a particular school with a particular business according to teacher-identified student needs. While most Adopt-a-School programs involve primarily school-based activities, educational field trips to businesses allow for important community experiences. Such programs are especially successful in large cities with a well-organized business community (Tangri & Moles, 1987).

An important consideration of Adopt-a-School programs is that through such partnerships, both schools and community agencies benefit. For example, students have opportunities to hear guest speakers, tour facilities, and participate in innovative programs. Likewise, businesses enjoy a positive public image while their employees obtain community service experience. Such programs also enable employees to demonstrate leadership skills, creativity, and other desirable traits that may not be readily observable in their day-to-day job responsibilities (Gonder, 1981). Although one barrier to Adopt-a-School programs is the lack of teacher involvement, teachers also can benefit greatly by establishing professional contacts in the community.

Community-based Approaches

An exciting alternative to school-based programs are those that provide training and instruction in the community itself. In essence, these programs extend the walls of the school building to incorporate businesses, community agencies, and other work settings. These types of instructional experiences promote generalization of academic learning to the actual setting in which it is used. Examples of community-based approaches include vocational and career education programs, experience-based career education, and community as classroom programs.

Vocational and career programs. The defining characteristic of vocational and career educational programs is that students are taken off campus for part of their schooling. The programs vary tremendously, from those that provide occasional field trips to those that provide a steady, paid job to students. Common to all programs is that they ensure adult supervision for the activity, integrate the activity with the students' academic requirements, and elicit participation of members of the larger community (Tangri & Moles, 1987). Objectives of vocational programs include enhancing students' performance in traditional academic subjects; increasing students' knowledge about vocations and methods of coping in the real world; and improving the satisfaction of educators, parents, students, and the general community.

In general, students in vocational programs are involved for two years. They work at their own pace to master objectives set by the business community in jobs such as computer technology and cosmetology. In their second year, they seek on-the-job training that may lead to paid jobs (Gonder, 1981).

The vast majority of vocational and career programs are implemented at the secondary school level. Little or no attention to such programs at the elementary level appears in the literature. To receive federal funding, programs are required to enroll at least 15% educationally disadvantaged and 10% handicapped students. Sex discrimination in federally funded programs is also prohibited.

Experience-based Career Education. Experience-based Career Education (EBCE) was designed to bridge the gap between high school coursework and experience, and between the classroom and the community (Bucknam & Brand, 1983). In EBCE programs, students move off campus for firsthand experiences in such community settings as offices, stores, factories, hospitals, and government agencies. Off-campus sites become the primary setting in which curriculum is delivered, via planned experiences as bases for learning academic subjects. Such a program differs from others in which community visits are brief. Students in EBCE programs earn academic credit rather than pay; thus all learning experiences in the community lead directly to a regular high school diploma.

For EBCE programs to be successful, policy directives are provided by an advisory board comprised of individuals from business and labor, parents, students, and other community interests. However, the programs require students to take a greater role in shaping their own educational plans. They are also designed to integrate a variety of student populations.

Whereas little or no empirical studies have addressed most school/community programs discussed thus far, EBCE has received some attention in the research literature. In a meta-analysis of 80 evaluations of EBCE, Bucknam and Brand (1983) found that in the majority of studies (a) EBCE students made large gains not only in career skills and life attitudes, but also in academic skills; (b) EBCE students gained more than students who received the typical high school curriculum; (c) greater gains were noted in programs with high fidelity (i.e., those that followed standard procedures) than those with low fidelity, although students in these latter programs also made gains; and (d) students at all socioeconomic levels from all types of residential areas profited from EBCE experiences.

Community as classroom. Programs that fall under the class of "community as classroom" deliver important academic curricula outside of the school building, but the nature of the work is not vocational, career, or work education. However, they do use donated community resources (such as church basements) to hold regular classes, and both the school and community benefit. Some instruction may be delivered in settings specific to the subject matter, such as nature centers, arboretums, or historical parks. Some students are also able to take courses for col-

TABLE 1
Recommendations for Breaking Down Interagency Barriers

Create interprofessional programs for training professionals.

Create solutions that bring diverse groups together for a period of time.

Find legitimate ways to deal with confidentiality problems.

Examine existing categorical program structures and make changes if necessary.

Link information systems in a systematic fashion.

Adapted from Kirst, 1991.

lege credit from a community college (Tangri & Moles, 1987).

A potential difficulty with community-as-classroom programs is the logistical problems of securing a location and gaining entrance. Likewise, some high school students are not responsible enough to enjoy their autonomy and still complete the academic requirements of off-campus programs. Nevertheless, most of these programs have yielded positive results. For example, many students are able to complete their high school graduation requirements in less than the traditional four years in community-as-classroom programs (Gonder, 1981).

INTERAGENCY COLLABORATION: THE SCHOOL'S ROLE IN COORDINATED SERVICES DELIVERY

A different, albeit critically important form of school/community partnership consists of collaborative relationships between multiple agencies, including the school, all bearing some level of responsibility for meeting the needs of children. Several factors have arisen in recent years contributing to the need for schools to work more closely with health, social services, and other youth-related institutions. Current societal conditions include homelessness, AIDS, family dissolution, adolescent pregnancy, alcohol and drug abuse, and suicide. However, at least 25% of children are not covered by any form of health care. Two-thirds of the children and adolescents who need mental health services receive either no services or those inappropriate to meet their needs (Knitzer, 1982; Saxe, Dougherty, Cross, & Silverman, 1987). Cutbacks in social services have produced counselor caseloads of 250–500 students. Medical attention in schools, once available through school nursing services, has also been cut, and many nurses now visit a different school each day (Achievement Council, 1988).

Many agencies, institutions, and organizations exist in communities, most of which should be available to children and families. Existing educational legislation (e.g., Public Law 94–142; Public Law 99–457) mandates that students with special needs *must* be provided with those services necessary to meet their unique educational and related needs. Ac-

cording to Apter (1992), "nothing in the law prohibits the school from utilizing other nonschool community services and funding where they are available" (p. 490). The reality, however, is that coordination of the multitude of services some children require is haphazard, incomplete, or nonexistent. Services that are offered often do not meet the complex needs of children and families (Knitzer, 1982, 1993).

Several factors evident in schools, families, agencies, and communities limit linkages. These include funding policies at the local, state, and national levels; lack of communication networks between families and agencies; little training of school personnel in establishing collaborative relationships; issues of "turfism"; unstructured referral mechanisms; and allegiances to employing agencies, rather than to families and children (Apter, 1992; Bucci & Reitzammer, 1992; Hazel, Barber, Roberts, Behr, Helmstetter & Guess, 1988). Recommendations for breaking down barriers are presented in Table 1.

Regardless of the reasons why these barriers exist, the fact remains that parents have extreme difficulties identifying and accessing services on their own (Featherstone, 1980). Schools have been suggested as appropriate settings to function as a "hub" of service delivery (Knitzer, 1993). Given that children with special needs often are identified initially by school personnel, and that schools are one societal agency available to everyone (Apter, 1992; Kirst & McLaughlin, 1989; Shedlinn, Klopf, & Zaret, 1989), it may be most appropriate for the locus of systems coordination to occur in the school setting. According to Ascher (1990), "because all children have to attend schools . . . [and] because schools are supposed to be concerned with their students' overall development, it is logical for them to coordinate students' contact with human service agencies." In keeping with the correlates of collaborative partnerships, "not only will access to health, employment, and social services be improved if they are located in schools, but . . . school policies can be influenced positively by professionals from these disciplines" (p. 1).

Schools, and particularly school psychologists, *can* play a primary role in coordinating services for students and families. However, few clearly defined, operationally specific models exist to provide struc-

TABLE 2
Characteristics of Successful Interagency Collaborations

Successful interagency collaborations:

1. Are both top-down and bottom-up;

2. Involve parents and children from the start;

3. Make clear that the school is a partner, but is not in charge;

4. Link services to additional school restructuring efforts;

5. Offer a wide array of services or provide easy entry to services;

6. Move beyond crisis management and early intervention to prevention and development;

7. Cross professional and bureaucratic boundaries to offer coherent services, often at nontraditional hours in nontraditional settings;

8. Provide staff with the time, training, and skills necessary to build relationships of trust and respect;

9. Hire one staff member from the local community to act as facilitator;

10. Deal with the child as part of the family, and the family as part of the neighborhood or community; and

11. Utilize a new system of accountability.

Adapted from Ascher (1990) and Kirst (1991).

ture and guidance in the development and implementation of this complex service delivery model. As emphasized earlier, a solutions-oriented problem-solving approach may be most appropriate for coordinated services. In this type of model, the specific needs of a target child and family determine the manner in which resources are identified and accessed. Characteristics of successful collaborative partnerships, which relate also to the types of school/community relationships discussed in the first part of this chapter appear in Table 2.

A number of formats can be used to implement a coordinated services approach. As suggested, it may be most appropriate for services to be "school-linked" (Kirst, 1991). This does not mean that the school dominates the organizations of delivery of services, or that the school is financially responsible for the coordinated care. Rather, it means that the school is the location in which services come together. The program defined as an "interagency system linking schools and local and private human service agencies with the support of business, higher education and other community resources to meet the interrelated educational, social and psychological needs of children" (Kirst, 1991, pp. 6–7). In the spirit of collaboration, such programs benefit all who are involved by empowering the various constituencies (i.e., parents, schools, agencies) to become more effective and efficient service providers and consumers.

Various types of school-linked models are possible. For example, a "case management" model can be used, wherein an individual within the school (e.g., teacher, social worker, psychologist, counselor) is assigned to help a student receive needed services. A "programmatic integration" approach requires that a school and agency link to deliver a particular service or range of services. A third model is that of "co-loca-

tion," where necessary service providers (e.g., nurses) are brought into the school, often at the expense of a foundation or agency. "Community coordinating councils" are councils that integrate mental health, social services, education, and employment. These councils typically are appointed at the city level (McLaughlin, 1989).

The Early Childhood Direction Model (Apter, 1992) is a New York state network of information, support, and referral centers that offer technical assistance to families and children from birth to age five. The operative mechanisms of Early Childhood Direction Centers (ECDCs) may serve as a model for establishing smaller-scale coordination programs in schools. According to Apter (1992), "the concept of 'direction service' has to do with a family-centered, single coordinating entity designed to assist families in negotiating the maze of services and developing a coordinated plan to meet their needs and those of their disabled child" (p. 490). Centers involved in the network are each responsible for several functions, including conducting active-finds, maintaining current resource information, assisting parents with transition between various educational programs (from preschool to elementary school and beyond), and providing information, referral, support, and follow-up to parents and professionals.

In the spirit of a problem solving orientation, ECDCs are charged with assisting families to identify their own specific issues and problems, locating appropriate support agencies, making timely referrals, helping parents access those services, and following up over brief and lengthier time intervals. Although such programs can be costly, there is some evidence to support their utility (Musumeci & Koen, 1982). Readers interested in obtaining more information about ECDCs are referred to Apter (1992) and Zeller (1980).

SUMMARY: SCHOOL PSYCHOLOGISTS AND SCHOOL/COMMUNITY PARTNERSHIPS

In the current zeitgeist of educational restructuring and reform, the role of the school psychologist can change drastically. One function that school psychologists should strive to adopt is that of liaison between homes, schools, and communities. A number of strategies by which schools can be linked productively with communities have been explored in this chapter. Clearly, the role of the school psychologist in these programs will vary. School psychologists are perhaps the most logical and best-trained individuals in educational settings to establish and implement school/community programs. However, the degree to which school psychologists take on leadership functions must be in line with individual levels of interest, time, and training. A particularly important consideration is the amount of administrative and staff support available in psychologists' work settings. Specifically, the development of such programs will take a great deal of time and effort, and hence should not be considered an "add on" responsibility. Rather, the manner in which psychological services are defined must change. Case loads, assessment tasks, and direct service responsibilities should be shifted to allow the school psychologist to function adequately and effectively as program developer. Likewise, given the systemic structure of schools, families, and communities, the roles and relationships of all individuals within the educational community must be redefined. Indeed, this is no easy task. Perhaps the most pragmatic approach is to "think big, start small, go slow" (Welch & Sheridan, in press).

REFERENCES

Achievement Council. (1988). *Unfinished business: Fulfilling our children's promise.* Oakland, CA: Author.

Apter, D. (1992). Utilization of community resources: An important variable for the home-school interface. In S. L. Christenson & J. C. Conoley (Eds.), *Home-school collaboration: Enhancing children's academic and social competence* (pp. 487–498). Silver Spring, MD: National Association of School Psychologists.

Ascher, C. (1990). Linking schools with human service agencies. *ERIC Digest, 62,* (February).

Bucci, J. A., & Reitzammer, A. F. (1992). Collaboration with health and social service professionals: Preparing teachers for new roles. *Journal of Teacher Education, 43,* 290–295.

Bucknam, R. (1976). The impact of EBCE: An evaluator's viewpoint. *Illinois Career Education Journal, 33,* 32–37.

Bucknam, R., & Brand, S. G. (1983). EBCE really works: A meta-analysis on experience based career education. *Educational Leadership,* 67–71.

Featherstone, H. (1980). *A difference in the family.* Middlesex, England: Penguin.

Gonder, P. O. (1981). Exchanging school and community resources. In D. Davies (Ed.), *Communities and their schools* (pp. 297–329). New York: McGraw-Hill.

Hazel, R., Barber, P. A., Roberts, S., Behr, S., Helmstetter, E., & Guess, D. (1988). *A community approach to an integrated service system.* Baltimore: Paul H. Brooks.

Kirst, M. W. (1991). The different worlds of preschools, elementary schools, and children's service agencies: Breaking down barriers and creating collaboration. *Proceedings of the NCREL Early Childhood Connection* (pp. 5–8), North Central Regional Educational Laboratory No. ECE–921.

Kirst, M. W., & McLaughlin, M. (1989). *Rethinking children's policy: Implication for educational administration.* Paper presented for the National Society for the Study of Education (NSSE) Yearbook.

Knitzer, J. (1982). *Unclaimed children: The failure of public responsibility to children and adolescents in need of mental health services.* Washington, DC: Children's Defense Fund.

Knitzer, J. (1993). Children's mental health policy: Challenging the future. *Journal of Emotional and Behavioral Disorders, 1,* 8–16.

Kratochwill, T. R., & Bergan, J. R. (1990). *Behavioral consultation in applied settings: An individual guide.* New York: Plenum Press.

McLaughlin, M. W. (1989). A child resource policy: Moving beyond dependence on school and family. In *Expanding the role of the school: Elementary School Center Conferences, 1987–1989.* New York: Elementary School Center.

Musumeci, M., & Koen, S. (1982). *New York State Early Childhood Direction Centers: 1981–82 evaluation report.* Yorktown Heights, NY: Center for Resource Management.

National Association of State Boards of Education. (1992). *Partners in educational improvement: Schools, parents, and the community.* Alexandria, VA: Author.

Saxe, L., Dougherty, D., Cross, T., & Silverman, N. (1987). *Children's mental health: Problems and services.* Durham, NC: Duke University Press.

Shedlinn, A., Klopf, G. L., & Zaret, E. S. (1989). *The school as locus of advocacy for all children.* New York: Elementary School Center.

Tangri, S., & Moles, O. (1987). Parents and the community. In V. Richardson-Koehler (Ed.), *Educator's handbook: A research perspective* (pp. 519–552). New York: Longman.

Webster, M. (1981). *Webster's new collegiate dictionary.* Springfield, MA: Merriam-Webster.

Welch, M., & Sheridan, S. M. (in press). *Educational partnerships: Serving students at-risk.* San Francisco: Harcourt-Brace Jovanovich.

Zeller, R. (1980). Direction service: Collaboration one case at a time. In J. O. Elder & P. R. Magrab (Eds.), *Coordinating services to handicapped children: A handbook for interagency collaboration* (pp. 69–82). Baltimore: Paul H. Brooks.

ANNOTATED BIBLIOGRAPHY

Apter, D. (1992). Utilization of community resources: An important variable for the home-school interface. In S. L. Christenson & J. C. Conoley (Eds.), *Home-school collaboration: Enhancing children's academic and social competence* (pp. 487–498). Silver Spring, MD: National Association of School Psychologists.
This chapter provides an extensive overview of models and programs for school/community linkages. The focus of the

chapter is assisting families to identify and access appropriate, integrated, and comprehensive services. The chapter provides a detailed description of a "direction model," which can serve as a framework for school psychologists. It also includes case examples with helpful guides and other strategies for linking families to resources.

Knitzer, J. (1993). Children's mental health policy: Challenging the future. *Journal of Emotional and Behavioral Disorders, 1,* 8–16.

In this timely article, Knitzer provides a historical overview of issues in children's mental health, outlines the need for a paradigm shift in the delivery of services, and describes various considerations in the development of integrated service models. In particular, the author examines issues surrounding research, training, and legislation regarding children and families.

This is a very comprehensive and important essay for school psychologists interested in restructuring children's mental health services at the policy and practitioner levels.

National Association of State Boards of Education. (1992). *Partners in educational improvement: Schools, parents, and the community.* Alexandria, VA: Author.

This concise overview of parent and community involvement in education describes various benefits, models, and principles of successful partnerships in a pragmatic, succinct manner. Further, the report discusses important implications for policy and leadership and provides resources for parent and community involvement and contacts for several states. The report is available from the National Association of State Boards of Education, 1012 Cameron Street, Alexandria, VA 22314.

20

Best Practices in Preschool Screening

Betty E. Gridley
Lynn Mucha
Bobby B. Hatfield
Ball State University

OVERVIEW

The term "screening" can have a variety of meanings. In this chapter, screening refers to brief, global, relatively low-cost procedures used to obtain preliminary information about a wide range of behaviors for large groups of children. In turn, this restricted sample of information is used to roughly estimate a child's skills and abilities, characteristics of the child's environment, and ways these may interact. The focus will be on screening during the period when children customarily make the transition to traditional school experiences. Many of the procedures discussed are geared to "kindergarten roundup" where children are screened just prior to school entrance or to screening conducted early in the kindergarten year. Such screening may have more than one purpose including:

1. Early identification of potential learning problems.

2. Referral of children for further evaluation/assessment.

3. Obtaining essential health and background information.

4. As an aid to development of programming and/or experiences based on individual children's needs.

5. Engagement of parents to ensure appropriate development of their children through recognition of individual strengths and weaknesses.

Including purposes 4 and 5 in the above list may cause some consternation for clinicians concerned lest screening replace more thorough assessment. However, there is no cause for alarm. The authors of this chapter certainly do not advocate that screening be used to replace complete evaluation where such assessment is warranted. Screening procedures are typically less reliable and valid than those used for in-dividual assessment and should not be used to make diagnoses nor to label children. However, it should be recognized that for a great majority of children such individual assessment is neither feasible nor necessary. Information from screening can be valuable to help increase the chances of early school success for all children by providing tools for parents and teachers to tailor experiences and curricula to individual needs.

The value of early intervention has been well established (see Harrison, 1992, for a good review). Indeed, Dunst (1986) argued that the time has come to stop asking if intervention works and to start exploring how to better identify problems in order to improve therapeutic and educational services. Only through early identification, effective family involvement, and intervention can real behavior change be expected to occur.

Obvious problems which may interfere with learning are usually hard to ignore and may have been identified long before a child reaches kindergarten entry. This should become increasingly true as the impact of Public Law 99-457 is felt. Once "child-find" procedures for children from birth to age five are universally instituted, screening just prior to or soon after school entrance will no longer play as important a role as it currently does in initial identification of children with disabilities and/or who are at risk for school failure. However, it is expected that such screening will remain important (a) to identify children missed earlier, (b) to determine "hidden" problems which may not be easily identified, (c) to serve as a quick check of previously instituted interventions, and (d) to help provide information for developing programming and individualizing instruction for all children. The latter purpose becomes more important as efforts towards inclusion and restructuring take form during the next few years.

One often overlooked advantage of early screening programs is the opportunity to engage parents in the education of their children and in a positive relationship with school systems. By soliciting the help of parents during this early introduction, school personnel have a golden opportunity to emphasize how essential it is for parents to be involved in the education of their youngsters. Parents can help their children to be more effective in school, both through focusing on strengths and weaknesses identified during screening, and through increased involvement and communication with the school. This process also provides a vehicle for the beginnings of conversation dealing with acceptance of problems and subsequent positive attitudes toward amelioration of these. Indeed, screening may be the first time that parents have been faced with realities involved with youngsters whose development lags behind others of their age group.

The use of screening to determine inclusion or exclusion in kindergarten seems to have become prevalent. Yet many, including these authors, do not recommend such practice because of their belief that excluding children from kindergarten based on screening is not sound. For example, kindergarten curricula are becoming increasingly academic in their orientation. This trend is counter to that recommended by early childhood educators and to the position taken by the National Association of School Psychologists (NASP). All too often accompanying such practices may be a failure to recognize the individual nature of learners which in turn mediates against making appropriate adaptations in curriculum and instruction to accommodate individual differences. The practice of excluding youngsters deemed "unready" is also an extension of the philosophy that difficulties are primarily child centered rather than the result of the interaction between characteristics of the child and his or her environment.

The purposes of this chapter are to (a) discuss advantages and disadvantages of early screening, (b) present an ecological problem-solving model of screening, (c) present guidance in using this model for developing and implementing screening, (d) present suggestions for instruments and procedures to be included, and (e) highlight ways in which to engage parents in screening and the subsequent education of their children. An ecological-problem solving model which takes into consideration not only child variables but also the environment is presented in the Basic Considerations section which follows.

BASIC CONSIDERATIONS

Many school districts are able to use screening results to make informed decisions to help children become better learners as well as engaging parents and teachers in the process. Unfortunately, in spite of its many benefits, there are some pitfalls connected with early screening. First, care must be taken to ensure that the results of screening are used appropriately. Indeed, screening measures and procedures should not be used for diagnosis or for attaching labels to children (see NASP position paper on Rights Without Labels).

Second, preschoolers differ both quantitatively and qualitatively from school-age children. Care should be taken to select procedures developmentally appropriate for preschoolers (Peterson, 1987). Additionally, even under the best of circumstances, many preschool instruments have lower reliability than those used for school-age youngsters.

Third, it is normal for behaviors of children in this age group to change dramatically from one time period to the next and from situation to situation. These children are not stable responders for a number of reasons. For example, they may have underdeveloped social skills, be wary of unfamiliar adults and situations, be anxious at being separated from parents, be distractable, have short attention spans and lack concentration skills, have limited verbal skills, and lack knowledge about the purpose and the importance of testing. For the most part, these children have as yet not learned to be "students." Therefore, care must be exercised in selecting procedures and interpreting results.

Prevailing procedures used for screening too often focus on a strictly child-oriented model. Unfortunately, even the best child-centered measures leave a great deal to be desired when their ability to predict outcomes is considered. For example, setting cut-off scores for determining those at risk versus those not at risk has been found to be, at best, questionable. Even with the best predictors, only about 45% to 65% of students predicted to have difficulties based on preschool screening really did have problems in learning by second grade. Generally, results of follow-up studies indicate that while those students who generally do well on screening measures can be predicted to succeed, those who do poorly may or may not be successful. Cut-off scores can be adjusted to eliminate some of these "false positives." However, it is not clear how many youngsters with real difficulties will be overlooked in the process.

Because of the inability to determine which children will succeed or not through examining child behaviors, school psychologists increasingly have sought answers through consideration of home and school variables. Indeed, a child's success or failure in school can be conceptualized as a function of the interaction between individual characteristics such as developmental status, temperament and motivation, and specific environmental factors found in the home and classroom. Such an interactional or ecological model results in goals for screening incorporating the view that school success is due not only to the skills and behaviors of the child but the congruence between these and the characteristics of the classroom situation. This has resulted in an accompanying shift of focus from problem persons to problem environments and allows for models which take into account not only the child and his or her environment but the interaction of the two.

If the primary goal of a screening program is to enhance early school success, such a program must incorporate important knowledge about characteristics of the child's environment. A major advantage of using an ecological model is the implication that problems can be potentially resolved through a range of alternative strategies such as: (a) modifying the problem behavior, (b) changing the expectations of parents and teachers, and/or (c) altering the situation (Barnett & Paget, 1988). Another important ramification of studying whole systems is that if the child does not "own" the problem, then a significant number of problems may never need to be assessed because they can be prevented through appropriate modification of environments (Adelman, 1982).

In spite of the emphasis placed on earlier identification, it is possible that during screening children may be identified who have significant delays. In this case referral for further assessment is mandatory. In addition, this may provide an opportunity for school personnel to help parents begin to deal with the changes necessary to accommodate youngsters with difficulties. It is very possible that these parents have been denying that a problem exists.

The following outline represents one problem-solving approach based on an ecological model. The Best Practices section following this list examines each step in detail.

1. Determine the purposes of screening and decide how the results will be used.

2. Select domains to be sampled.

3. Select assessments and procedures that provide for collection of useful information from and about important individuals in each environment.

4. Choose personnel and plan logistics.

5. Analyze data within and across contexts comparing data from and about various sources.

6. Provide feedback for parents and recommend experiences designed to enhance the child's chances for success.

7. Evaluate and revise procedures where changes might result in more efficiency, greater communication, and/or smoother integration of systems.

BEST PRACTICES

Step 1. Determine the Purposes of Screening, and Decide How the Results Will Be Used

As mentioned earlier, screening may be conducted for a number of purposes. If the aim of screening is merely to differentiate those students who need further evaluation from those who do not, a low-cost, quickly administered multipurpose screen may be ad-

equate. However, the best screening programs include information from a variety of domains, across a variety of environmental settings, and from a variety of sources (Bailey & Wolery, 1989; Lichtenstein & Ireton, 1991). At a minimum, arrangements should be made to see the child and to obtain information from the parent(s), preschool teacher, and/or other professionals involved with the child, and about home and school/preschool environments. While integration of these data may be time consuming, actual collection from a variety of sources may be accomplished quite expediently.

Once the purposes for screening have been determined, the task is to choose specific areas to be screened. Some domains often sampled are described in Step 2.

Step 2. Select Domains to Be Sampled.

Whatever its intended purpose, screening should include information about behaviors from a number of different domains. Decisions about which domains should be emphasized and which information should be collected depends on the purposes of the screening as well as other factors. However, cognitive, language, and social/adaptive behavior information has been shown to be most predictive of school success. Speech, fine and gross motor, and perceptual abilities have been found to be related to a lesser degree and are usually not predictive unless problems are severe. The following nine domains represent the most common areas screened.

Health. Screening for visual and auditory acuity may accompany or precede screening. Such information is essential in helping evaluators rule out physiological bases for behaviors. Parental input is essential in providing information about perinatal history, developmental milestones, immunizations, health problems, and the like.

Cognitive/basic concepts. This area includes a wide range of mental abilities including association, reasoning, memory, and understanding of basic concepts. Basic concepts are rudimentary, functional vocabulary terms that refer to general ideas or characteristics which are applicable to several objects or events and help us mentally organize our world. Children must learn many basic concepts before they can be successful in school. Some examples are relationships of objects one to another (e.g., over, under, beside, next to, and behind), size, texture, quantity, time, shapes, colors, letters, numbers, and social relationships. It is better to focus on basic concepts rather than the more general aspect of cognitive or intellectual ability because of the potential for abuse of such terms and information. Too often parents and teachers may make unwarranted assumptions about a child based on presumed ability information. By the time they are four or five, youngsters are learning about time and weather, likenesses and differences, and categorization. They can answer "why" and "how" questions and are becoming aware of community people and places.

Speech and language. The development of speech and language is a remarkable accomplishment. Each child must learn speech sounds, words and their meanings, to combine words to make understandable sentences, and to use sentences to communicate with others. Ordinarily, by the time a child is four or five years old, she has mastered all of the sounds of her language, has a vocabulary of approximately 2,000 words, can follow conversations, and use polite forms such as please and thank you appropriately.

Gross and fine motor. Motor skills include large motor movements, coordination, balance and equilibrium, eye-hand coordination, manipulation of objects, use of paint brushes and scissors, grasping patterns, and imitation of body movements by visual cues. By the time children are ready to enter kindergarten, they can move quickly and purposefully in many ways. They are strong and confident and quickly follow directions. Many are able to ride bicycles with the use of training wheels. Most can trace their own names and print several letters. They draw simple persons with three or four body parts, copy simple shapes, color within the lines, and put together simple puzzles.

Behavior/temperament/socioemotional. Some useful components in screening of this domain include the child's activity level, social interactions, relations with same-age peers, typical affect, ability to follow directions and focus attention, play style, anger control, and sleep and eating patterns. A typical five-year-old is fairly independent, respects authority, and is interested in group activities. She can share with others and wants to go to school.

Self-help. In order to be successful in kindergarten, children must be self-sufficient in caring for their everyday needs. By the time a child is ready to enter school, he often can tie his shoelaces, can be given two or three tasks to do, and will carry them out in order. He dresses himself and is semi-independent at clean-up and grooming tasks.

Visual perception/motor integration. Visual perception refers to the process of interpreting what is seen. This goes beyond the acuity information obtained through health screening to include such areas as recognition of similarities and differences (discrimination); seeing a figure as distinct from its background (figure ground); ability to orient oneself in space (spatial relations); recognition of images when they vary in context such as size, shape, color, or placement (constancy); and integration of visual and motor skills. Items measuring visual motor and per-

ception skills may overlap with those used to measure motor functioning, because fine motor control and eye-hand coordination are included. Also important are the ability to remember visual sequences, draw two-dimensional forms, reproduce three-dimensional visual structures, visually discriminate among common objects, and demonstrate visual-spatial analysis and synthesis. Children entering kindergarten generally must be able to sustain visual attention, discriminate, remember, and use visual closure skills quickly enough to produce comprehension.

Auditory perception. Auditory perception refers to the ability to understand speech sounds given that one can hear comfortably. Auditory perception includes the ability to listen and to repeat information given, to receive and process auditory stimuli, to respond to questions heard, and to discriminate among speech sounds. Most five-year-olds are able to discriminate most of the sounds and patterns common in their native language. Problems with auditory perception are often manifested in delayed language acquisition, poor oral expression, difficulties in remembering sequences, and the like.

Home environment. This domain includes aspects of the home environment and parent–child interactions. For example, questions might be asked about types of play materials; kinds of books in the home; the frequency with which parents read, talk, and play with the child; and the amount of responsibility given to the child. Other areas might include the importance placed on work, achievement, and success; the extent to which education and school-related activities are encouraged and supported; interest placed on intellectual, ethical, and cultural activities; and the extent to which exchanges of ideas and decisions are encouraged and valued. Sample questions to guide information gathering include:

- What kinds of communication exist among family members?

- Does the family function as a support system?

- What is the organization of roles and responsibilities?

- What is the nature of the interaction of child and parents?

In order to tap at these domains, a number of strategies may be chosen. Information about procedures that can be used to gather this information is given in the following section.

Step 3. Select Assessments and Procedures that Provide for Collecting Useful Information from and about Important Individuals in Each Environment

The model for selecting screening procedures given here follows suggestions made by Bagnato and

Neisworth (1991) for their protypical assessment battery for preschoolers. They suggest gathering norm-based, curriculum-based, judgment-based, and eco-based information. This framework is used in the following section; for more information about specific instruments and/or procedures, the reader is directed to Bagnato and Neisworth, 1991, Paget and Barnett, 1990, and Bracken, 1991.

Norm-based. Norm-based assessments compare a child's performance with the performance of a given group thought to be typical or similar to that child. Although national norms are useful for comparing children with their peers throughout the U.S., local norms also compare them with their more immediate peers. This can be an important consideration when the characteristics of standardization samples do not closely match those of your group. Even with difficulties associated with norm-based instruments, they remain one of the most reliable and efficient ways to collect information. They provide for quick collection of broad-based information about a number of important domains. The number of instruments designed specifically for screening of preschoolers has increased rapidly over the past few years. Not only are there more choices available, but the instruments themselves have been improved greatly. Although norm-referenced instruments should not be used in isolation from other factors in the child's environment, it can be useful to include at least one in the screening battery. In fact, because a number of the newer instruments provide for gathering information in judgment- and eco-based contexts, it might be wise to reexamine norm-based screening procedures in light of the improvements made in the past few years. To aid in such a reevaluation, the following list of selection criteria was culled from suggestions by a number of authors (e.g., Bailey & Wolery, 1989; Lichtenstein & Ireton, 1984) as well as the authors' personal experiences.

1. Screening should include information about behaviors across a wide variety of environmental settings and from a variety of sources.

2. A profile of outcomes is preferable to a single score.

3. Evidence for adequate standardization and assessment of psychometric properties such as reliability and validity is provided.

4. The screening must be acceptable to its primary users. Those using the instrument must feel confident about its use both from a practical point of view and from the confidence they feel about its usefulness.

5. The focus is on developmental tasks rather than those that tap at learned information that is influenced a great deal from experiential opportunities not available to all children.

6. Procedures include provision to systematically gather information from parents.

Curriculum-based. Curriculum-based procedures are referenced to skills and competencies expected for kindergarten success. Criterion-referenced tests are developed from curriculum content, and skill attainment is compared to the child's previous performance rather than to that of a group. Criterion-referenced tests extend from a task-analytic perspective and emphasize individualized instruction. Criterion-based instruments are not without their problems. For example, too much emphasis on the acquisition of skills with which the child has had little experience may lead to the erroneous conclusion that the child is not ready for the demands of school. One must always seek to ascertain whether a child has been unable to attain certain skills because of some difficulty in learning or because he or she lacked appropriate experiences and/or instruction.

Some representative criterion-referenced tests include the Brigance Inventory of Early Development (Brigance, 1979), the Brigance K and 1 Screen (Brigance, 1987), Beginning Milestones (1986), and the Portage Guide to Early Education (Bluma, Shearer, Frohman, & Hilliard, 1976).

Judgment-based. Judgment-based procedures include parent and professional perceptions of child status and progress. Judgment-based measures are useful for many reasons. Examples of formal measures used to provide information include the Child Behavior Checklist (Achenbach, 1991), Personality Inventory for Children (Wirt, Lachar, Klinedinst, & Seat, 1984), Social Skills Rating Inventory (Gresham, F. M., & Elliott, S. N., 1990), and Temperament Assessment Battery (Martin, 1988). As mentioned earlier, many of the multidomain screening instruments also include a brief measure of parent and/or clinician judgment of behavior.

Perhaps the most essential ingredient of any successful screening program is the parent(s) or other caregiver. Parental involvement is critical for a program's success from a number of different perspectives. Parents see their children on a day-to-day basis and know behavioral patterns over the years. Thus parents' descriptions are of behaviors as they occur naturally and are therefore more reflective of what youngsters can actually do. Information and observations garnered during the actual screening process may be influenced by the strange situation phenomenon whereby youngsters are forced into environments unlike those they know and understand. Table 1 provides an overview of research validating the importance of parental input in preschool screening.

Input from others is also important. For example, preschool teachers and other caregivers can give important information to help explain other screening results. Observations and ratings by those administering the screening also provide important informa-

TABLE 1
What Research Indicates About Using Parent Input in Preschool Screening

Research Study	Sample Description	Instrumentation	Research Findings
Bagnato (1984)	54 infants and preschool children with multiple disabilities and their mothers	Multiple clinical judgment and performance measures	1. Mothers have extreme sensitivity to subtle changes in their children's behavior 2. Including mothers on the diagnostic intervention reduced parental anxiety. 3. Team approach improved mother's motivation to be involved in intervention
Harrington (1984)	3008 black and white children from urban areas in Indiana and Washington state	Mother's report from Developmental Profile	A correlation of .84 between the Stanford-Binet mental age and the Developmental Profile academic age
Colligan (review of 7 students, 1982)	1,413 children from seven studies	Subjective and objective performance criteria	The use of parent questionnaires in preschool screening as a means of obtaining useful, economical information about the potential difficulty of prekindergarten children in the early school years was supported in each of the seven studies
Lichtenstein (1982)	391 preschool children aged 49 to 64 months and their parents	1. Minnesota Preschool Screening Instrument. 2. 28-item developmental inventory to parents 3. Teacher ratings of kindergarten performance one year after screening	1. Positive relationship between parent reports of developmental functioning and early school performance 2. Although validity rates for parent report measures were promising, this study did not suport the sole use of parental information in preschool screening as a substitute for direct testing.
Eisert, Spector, Shankaran, Falgenbaaum, and Szego (1980)	Children aged 2 to 5 years	Minnesota Child Development Inventory (MCDI) completed by parents	1. High correlation was found between the parents' perceptions on the MCDI and results of objective cognitive tests (McCarthy Scales of Children's Abilities and Stanford-Binet)

tion about a child's approach to a particular task, general activity level, and the like.

Eco-based. Eco-based procedures characterize the social and physical qualities of the child's developmental context, especially the family. Currently available eco-based measures that examine either the context or the interaction of the child in the environment include Home Observation for Measurement of the Environment (Caldwell & Bradley, 1978), Early Childhood Environment Rating Scale (Harms & Clifford, 1980), and the Parenting Stress Index (Abidin, 1986). Although these instruments are not designated primarily as screening instruments, many are relatively easy and quick to administer.

Summary. In choosing instruments and procedures, it is preferable to collect information from a variety of sources and across a number of settings. A profile of outcomes is probably preferable to a single score. Tasks and procedures must be brief and easily administered. It is best to make choices based on a developmental rather than a psychometric perspective.

It is often difficult to distinguish between developmental screening and readiness tests. However, school readiness tests usually focus on skill acquisition and are product oriented, whereas developmental screening tests focus on the ability to acquire skills and are process oriented. Typically, readiness tests are used for class placement and planning of school curriculum and express a child's present level of skill performance rather than a child's developmental potential.

Examples of a number of commonly used screening instruments are given in Table 2. Evaluations concerning time and ease of administration and how comparisons of each with selection criteria are also provided.

Step 4. Choose Personnel and Plan Logistics

Personnel. It is important to choose a coordinator who has a thorough knowledge of normal development. Professionals who do not deal with preschoolers on a regular basis may have a tendency to underestimate the competence of youngsters of this age. The coordinator must also be able to function effectively within the system and work well with everyone involved in the program. A screening program's success depends a great deal on the cooperation of professionals, volunteers, parents, and various agencies who may be involved with preschoolers.

A school psychologist, early childhood specialist, and/or kindergarten teacher should be included in the planning team. In addition, personnel taking part in the actual screening must be carefully chosen and trained. Preferred characteristics for those persons include flexibility, organization, patience, thorough knowledge of procedures, confidence, ingenuity (who knows what will happen), experience and skill, and, perhaps most importantly, a good sense of humor. Do not discount the value of using parents and other volunteers. The authors have found fifth and/or sixth graders mature enough to be valuable "screening buddies." In this system, each preschooler being screened has his/her special buddy for the time actual screening takes place. These older students help to make sure each child progresses through all aspects of the screening. In addition, they are invaluable in entertaining those children not currently actively engaged in the screening process. This occurs when the number of children invited to participate exceeds the number of available stations or activity centers (more on these later).

Logistics. Outreach communication is essential in involving as many eligible youngsters as possible. Professionals should inform the community about the rationale for offering the program and its importance for children entering school. Additional information to be disseminated includes answers to

- Where and when will screening occur?
- Who will be screened?
- Who will perform the screening?
- Who will have access to the results?
- How will the results be utilized?

This information can be conveyed to parents and other agencies and service providers through special mailings, school newsletters, parent-teacher meetings, local newspaper articles, and special topic school programs. However, do not neglect personal contact with parents, which has been found to be more effective than mass media efforts. A special effort may be needed to contact parents whose first child is entering school. They generally are not attuned to local newspapers and other school information. They may be a little hesitant or just not know that such services are available. An important consideration during this phase is sensitivity by the school to parents.

Logistically, screening can be a nightmare unless carefully orchestrated. For example, the first time the authors screened youngsters in a particular school, the school nurse decided that this would be a good time for children to receive tuberculosis (TB) tests. After they had received the TB test, many children cried, setting off a chain reaction among those still waiting or going through screening. While it is an admirable goal for the school to ensure that children have adequate immunizations, screening is not the best time to offer those services.

Careful thought to physical arrangements and to progression through screening is also important. A first-time screening can make or break the program (as well as the program director and staff). It is amazing how little things make a difference. For mass screening such as that done during kindergarten roundup, a "station" type approach where each child is screened on particular tasks and then progresses to others seems to work best. This active system allows for children to move about physically and reminds examiners that attention spans are short. While some may question whether meeting a variety of screeners might be problematic for some "shy" youngsters, this system's advantages tend to override any disadvantages. As an example, important information may be gained if it is apparent that a youngster warms up more quickly with one examiner than another. Stations also allow for screeners to become "experts" in their screening procedures. This is extremely important because of the repertoire of behaviors common in this age group. The more practiced and automatic the examiner is the better. This arrangement also allows for better training of paraprofessionals and volunteer helpers.

If at all possible, it is a good idea to obtain, in advance, a list of youngsters being screened. The list should have the children's names as well as their birthdays. Each staff person participating in screening can then receive a list. Name tags, specifically designed for children, can be prepared ahead of time. The list and corresponding name tags make routing children through the system much easier. The authors have also found that rewarding each child with a sticker for each task completed is not only popular

TABLE 2
Commonly Used Screening Instruments

Instrument[a]	Time and Ease[b]		Age Range	Domains Evaluated	Standardization	Criteria Met[c]
				Screening Across Domains		
Brigance K & 1 Screen (1982)	10–20 min.	1	Kindergarten/ First Grade	Motor, auditory, visual, and 14 other domains	Field test; 14 states	4, 5
DDST (1975)	20 min.	1	Birth to 6	Personal-social, fine motor, adaptive, gross motor	Denver area only; white, black, Hispanic; children with disabilities excluded	2, 4, 5, 6
DIAL-R (1983, 1990)	20–30 min. Parent questionnaire is completed in 10–15 min.	3	2–0 to 5–11	Motor, concepts, language, family/behavior	National norms, 1980 census; white, non-white; Hispanic; children with disabilities included	1, 2, 3, 4, 5, 6
EPSF	60 min.	3	4 to 6	Receptive language, auditory, visual memory, visual discriminitation, fine motor, gross motor	Components of the battery include: The Peabody Picture Vocabulary Test–Revised, The Developmental Test of Visual Motor Integration, Draw-a-Person, Motor Activity Scale–Revised, The Preschool Language Scale. The first 3 have natonal norms. There are no standardized data available on the battery	2, 4, 5
ESI (1988)	15 min.	1	4–0 to 5–11	Visual-motor, adaptive, language, cognition	465 from one urban community, all white; national norms in progress	2, 4, 5, 6
ESP (1990)	20–25 Min.	2	2–0 to 6–11	Cognitive/language, motor, self-help/social, Home, Health	National norms, 1990 census estimate; norms 1987–1988; children with disabilities included	1, 2, 3, 4, 5, 6
First STEP (1992)	15 min.	3	2–9 to 6–2	Cognition, communicaton, physical, social/ emotional, adaptive functioning	National norms, demographics, match U.S. census, 1,433 children. Norms available for 6-month intervals for each of seven age groups. Children with developmental delays accurately identified (72% to 85% accuracy)	1. 2. 3. 4. 5. 6
MST (1978)	20 min.	3	4–0 to 6–5	Right-left orientation, verbal memory, Draw-a-Design, number memory, concept grouping, leg coordination	MSCA national norms applied to MST; white, black, American Indians, Asians, Hispanics by race; Children with disabilities excluded	4, 5

(... Table 2, continued)

Instrument[a]	Time and Ease[b]	Age Range	Domains Evaluated	Standardization	Criteria Met[c]
MAP (1982)	20–30 min. 3	2–0 to 5–8	Sensory/Motor, cognitive ability, and combined abilities in five areas	National norms; 1,204 "normal" children; 86% white, 12% black, 2% othr; additional 90 children with disabilities included	2, 5
MPI (1979)	15–20 min. parent completes	4 to 5	Self-help, fine motor, expressive language, comprehension, memory, letter recognition, number comprehension, adjustment	The norms of the MPI were based on a sample of 360 white, suburban children ages 56–67 months. The hit rate of identification of children at risk for not having a successful school experience was 75%	2, 4, 5, 6
PDI (1984, 1988)	Untimed 1	3 yrs. to 6 yrs.	General development/ symptoms, behaviors	220 children in South St. Paul, Minnesota, who were in regular public school program	5, 6
MCDI (1974)	Untimes 1	6 months to 6 years	General development, gross motor, fine motor, expressive language, conceptual self-help, personal social	Norms compiled from a suburban sample distinctly different from the U.S. population	2, 5, 6
BDI (1984)	Untimed	Birth to 8 years	Personal–social, adaptive, motor, language cognitive	Research with the BDI is scarce and norms have not yet been obtained	2, 5
Screeening of a Single Domain					
BBCS (1984)	20–30 min. 2 complete scales	2–6 to 7–11	Basic concepts	Sample follows U.S. census. Total of 1,109 children. Southern and northern sections overrepresented	Screening Version not recommended 2, 3, 4, 5 Supplementary teaching materials
TABC (1988)	15_20 min. parent, teacher, clinician complete	3 to 7	Temperament (activity, adaptability, approach/withdrawal, emotional intensity, distractibility, and persistence)	National sample, overrepresented by Southeast	1 (if all forms are given) 2, 5

[a]DDST = Denver Developmental Screening Test–Revised. DIAL–R = Developmental Indicators for the Assessment of Learning–Revised. ESI = Early Screening Inventory. ESP = Early Screening Profiles. MST = McCarthy Screening Test. MAP = Miller Assessment for Preschoolers. PDI = Preschool Development Inventory. MCDI = Minnesota Child Development Inventory. BDI = Batelle Developmental Inventory Screening Test.

[b]Ease of Administration: 1 = easier to administer than most preschool instruments; 2 = administration ease is average as compared to others; 3 = more difficult to administer and score than many.

[c]Criteria are designed to aid in the selection of appropriate instruments for the reader's specific task.
1. Includes information about behaviors across a variety of environmental settings and from a variety of sources.
2. Profile of outcomes is available.
3. Evidence for adequate standardization, psychometric properties.
4. Accepted by primary users.
5. Contains brief tasks and procedures.
6. Focuses on developmental rather than readiness tasks.

TABLE 3
Practical Activities for Parents to Help Work with Young Children

Area of Weakness	Suggested Activities
Language Skills	1. Talk with your children, not just to them.
	2. Ask open-ended questions.
	3. Read to your children each day.
	4. Slow down speech so children will understand sounds and words.
	5. Discourage baby talk.
	6. Help children categorize objects by color, shape, size, texture, use, etc.
	7. Teach children to use functional language.
Gross Motor Skills	1. Encourage outdoor play with running, hopping, and jumping activities.
	2. Engage children in throwing and catching of objects (bean bags, balls, balloons).
	3. Have children walk on a line to help balance.
Visual Motor Skills	1. Provide opportunities for children to work with clay or play dough.
	2. Practice using scissors and paint brushes.
	3. Manipulate puppets.
	4. Practice buttoning, zipping, tying, tracing, and coloring/drawing.
Auditory–Memory	1. Have children identify common sounds with their eyes closed.
	2. Give children a series of two- or three-part instructions orally.
	3. Have children reproduce tapped patterns.
	4. Encourage listening and following oral directions.
Basic Concepts	1. Let the children practice locating parts of the body.
	2. Have children complete partially drawn figures.
	3. Work with colors, one at a time.
	4. Begin letter recognition, starting with upper case first.
	5. Point out letters on signs and books.
	6. Cut out letterforms; have the children trace and color letters.
	7. Introduce numbers with activities similar to those for letter recognition.
	8. Model shapes with clay; have the children trace and color shapes and cut shapes from different materials.
	9. Reinforce through conversation concepts such as size, texture, quantity, time, and social relationships.

with the children but provides a quick check of whether they have completed each task. It is helpful, and fun, to use stickers that correspond to the stations. For example, a particular favorite of these authors is the sunglasses sticker to use for visual screening.

In establishing the routines of screening, it is wise to keep in mind that many of the normal characteristics of preschoolers call for special "accommodations." Parents may need to stay in the room or close at hand. Extra time may be needed to establish rapport and examiners should be cautioned to allow children to warm up to the situation rather than coming on too strong. Limits need to be set and gently, but firmly, reinforced. Preschool children need plenty of reinforcement and tangible reinforcers produce good results. However, reinforcement must focus around the effort rather than correctness of answers. Compared to school-age children, preschoolers respond better to shorter testing periods and more frequent breaks. Providing for adequate space to move around and play is essential. It is a great help to have a number of active games and videotapes available for children who are waiting or between stations.

When screening is connected to kindergarten roundup, orientation for the parents can be scheduled during the time when their children are being screened. This usually consists of presentations by the principal, kindergarten teacher, latch key coordinator, and other professionals with whom the children may be involved. Parents also fill out rating scales and information sheets that become part of the

FIGURE 1. The role of the parent: You are very important!

Consistently	support the behavior you ask your child to demonstrate.
Read	to your child often.
Experience	and share short trips with your child. The zoo, store, and a farm are good places to begin.
Ask	and answer questions about what your child sees or does.
Talk	to and with your child often.
Encourage	your child to carry out simple duties at home.
Supply	your child with crayons, paper, and scissors to be used in a constructive manner.
Understand	good and poor behavior, and explain limits when it is necessary.
Count	and add small objects with your child.
Create	an interest in doing things for fun.
Encourage	your child to speak distinctly.
Sing	and play children's songs. Use records and help your child select TV programs with music.
Show	your love and affection for your child for no apparent reason other than for being your child.

data to be analyzed in Step 5. Some programs encourage parents to actively participate with the child during screening. In fact, some procedures allow for screeners to evaluate parent-child interaction during an instructional task. When parents are observing in the room where screening occurs, it may sometimes be better to have them sit out of the direct line of vision of the child. On the other hand, parents should never be *required* to observe and in some cases may have to be asked not to observe if anxiety on the part of either parents or child is observed.

Step 5. Analyze Data within and across Contexts Comparing Data from and about Various Sources

Many available screening instruments provide information about the desired areas of interest, although not every instrument will sample behavior from each of the domains. Although there may be a tendency for some to rely primarily on scores, it is important when working with preschoolers to look beyond scores. Other relevant pieces of data must be included in interpretation of screening results for young children. In some cases it may be more important to recognize the *how* and *why* of a child's performance than in scores per se. Examiners must not only be skilled in administering tests but also be good observers and interpreters of children's behaviors. These observations then become part of the data analyzed during this step. Poor performance may be the result of many factors, including the possibility that a child does not possess the skill. However, with these youngsters, it may be just as possible that the lack of performance is due to any one of several other factors such as attention span or lack of understanding about the parameters of the task.

Interpretation of scores from screening instruments should include consideration of other data collected. One specific example illustrating the importance of auxiliary data is a phenomenon the authors have often noticed on the *Bracken Basic Concepts Scale*. It is not unusual for children to score fairly well in the average range on most of the basic concepts scales except for the School Readiness Composite (SRC). This composite consists of five scales which tap at such things as letter and number recognition, shape recognition, and the like. Performance on these tasks seems to be fairly vulnerable to previous experiences; that is, they are tied more closely to actual experiences, such as exposure to preschool or enriched home environments than the other tasks. The net effect is that low performance on the SRC with average or above average performance on the other scales may indicate that the child has not had adequate training and/or experiences. On the other hand, if this same pattern exists for children who have had preschool experiences and adequate environmental stimulation, the chance is greater to develop the types of school-related problems connected with learning disabilities. This interpretation is very dependent upon the other information garnered about the child. Of course, one could go on forever with specific instances of where interpretation based on all the available data is important. However, the hypothesis-testing framework that school psychologists use in their assessment procedures provides a good structure for analysis of these data as well.

One goal of analysis must be to determine which children to refer for more complete assessment. A three-tier system has proven useful: Children who have obvious problems can be referred for further evaluation; those who have some delays or difficulties may be rescreened or watched for problems, and those who have few or no problems are "passed."

Step 6. Provide Feedback for Parents and Recommend Experiences Designed to Enhance the Child's Chances for Success

Parents should receive feedback about their children's performances. Whether children are progressing normally or display weaknesses, parental follow-up should be prompt. Parents of children designated to be rescreened or referred for further assessment should be contacted personally and individually. An important consideration during this time is making parents aware that screening results are not final diagnoses or outcome measures for this child's development.

Even normal development may be inconsistent. Through screening, various strengths and weaknesses among different domains may be identified. Often parents are unaware of exactly what they can do to help their children. Practical and easy activities for parents to do with their children are given in Table 3 and Figure 1. Remember, parents may be the most important teachers their children will ever have.

Step 7. Evaluate and Revise Procedures Where Changes Could Result in More Efficiency, Greater Communication, and/or Smoother Integration of Systems

Only if we are willing to learn from what we have done, can we improve our practice. What works for one school psychologist may not work for another. New instruments and procedures are developed all the time, and programs and philosophies change. In order to continue having the best program possible, periodic review is necessary. A debriefing session as soon after screening as possible is especially helpful. Consider including several parents in this session to solicit their impressions as well as those of staff.

SUMMARY: PUTTING IT ALL TOGETHER

The application of a comprehensive model for preschool screening should not result in simply labeling of children. Instead, these procedures should aid teachers and committees in the planning of curricula and developmentally appropriate programs for young children. Teachers need to convey clearly to parents the importance of program development and the ways information obtained through screening can aid in this process. Models that incorporate the relationships between the child and the various settings

within which he or she interacts represent an ecological perspective (Paget & Nagel, 1986).

All the suggested components recommended in the formation of a screening program require advance planning. Meisels (1989) suggests making the following decisions prior to the formation of a screening program:

1. Determine funding sources.

2. Identify a coordinator for screening program.

3. Set up a screening planning and implementation committee.

4. Determine the purposes and goals of the screening program.

5. Identify the population of children to be screened.

6. Select the appropriate screening instruments and procedures.

7. Arrange the location and time of screening.

8. Arrange the medical examinations, vision and hearing tests.

9. Engage parent and community cooperation for child identification.

10. Recruit and train screening staff.

11. Conduct in-service training for kindergarten and other early childhood teachers.

12. Implement screening program.

13. Request information from teachers and parents/caregivers.

14. Monitor all components of the program.

15. Communicate results and impressions with parents.

16. Provide recommendations to parents if necessary.

17. Notify assessment teams of follow-up on individual children.

18. Evaluate screening program effectiveness.

REFERENCES

Abidin, R. R. (1986). *The Parenting Stress Index*. Charlottesville, VA: Pediatric Psychology Press.

Achenbach, T. M. (1991). *Child Behavior Checklist*. Burlington, VT: University of Vermont.

Adelman, H. S. (1982). Identifying learning problems at an early age: A critical appraisal. *Journal of Clinical Child Psychology*, *11*(3), 255–261.

Bagnato, S. J., & Neisworth, J. T. (1991). *Assessment for early intervention: Best practices for professionals*. New York: Guilford.

Bailey, D. B., & Wolery, M. (1989) *Assessing infants and preschoolers with handicaps.* Columbus, OH: Merrill.

Barnett, D. W., & Paget, K. D. (1988). Alternative service delivery in preschool settings: Practical and conceptual foundations. In J. Graden, J. Zins, & M. C. Curtis (Eds.), *Alternative educational delivery systems: Enhancing instructional options for all students* (pp. 291–308). Washington, DC: National Association of School Psychologists.

Bluma, S., Shearer, A., Frohman, A., & Hilliard, J. (1976). *Portage Guide of Early Education Checklist.* Portage, WI: Portage Project, Cooperative Educational Services.

Bracken, B. A. (1991). *The psychoeducational assessment of preschool children* (2nd ed.). Boston, MA: Allyn and Bacon.

Brigance, A. H. (1979). *Brigance Diagnostic Inventory of Early Development.* North Billerica, MA: Curriculum Associates.

Brigance, A. H. (1987). *K & 1 Screen for Kindergarten and First Grade.* North Billerica, MA: Curriculum Associates.

Caldwell, B., & Bradley, R. (1978). *Home Observation for Measurement of the Environment (HOME).* Little Rock, AR: University of Arkansas, Human Development.

CTB/McGraw-Hill. (1977). *Comprehensive Test of Basic Skills.* Monterey, CA: McGraw-Hill.

Dunst, C. J. (1986). Overview of the efficacy of early intervention programs. In L. Bickman & D. L. Weatherford (Eds.), *Evaluating early intervention programs for severely handicapped children and their families* (pp. 79–148). Austin, TX: PRO-ED.

Gresham, F. M., & Elliott, S. N. (1990). *Social Skills Rating System (SSRS).* Circle Pines, MN: American Guidance Service.

Harms, T., & Clifford, R. (1980). *Early Childhood Environment Rating Scale (ECERS).* New York: Teachers College Press.

Harrison, P. L. (1992). Planning and evaluating preschool screening and assessment programs. *Child Assessment News, 2*(3), 1, 8–12.

Lichtenstein, R., & Ireton, H. (1984). *Preschool screening: Identifying young children with developmental and educational problems.* Orlando, Fl: Grune & Stratton.

Martin, R. P. (1988). *The Temperament Assessment Battery for Children.* Brandon, VT: Clinical Psychology.

Meisels, S. J. (1989). *Developmental screening in early childhood: A guide* (rev. ed.). Washington, DC: National Association for the Education of Young Children.

National Association of School Psychologists. (1987). *Position paper on rights without labels.* Silver Spring, MD: Author.

Nurss, J. R., & McGauvran, M. E. (1986). *Metropolitan Readiness Tests.* Cleveland, OH: The Psychological Corporation.

Paget, K., & Barnett, D. W. (1990). Assessment of infants, toddlers, preschool children, and their families: Emergent trends. In T. B. Gutkin & C. R. Reynolds (Eds.), *Handbook of school psychology* (2nd ed.; pp. 458–486). New York: John Wiley & Sons.

Paget, K. D., & Nagel, R. J. (1986). A conceptual model of preschool assessment. *School Psychology Review, 15,* 154–165.

Peterson, N. L. (1987). *Early intervention for handicapped and at-risk children: An introduction to early childhood-special education.* Denver: Love Publishing.

Wirt, R. D., Lachar, D., Klinedinst, J. K., & Seat, P. D. (1984). *The Personality Inventory for Children.* Los Angeles: Western Psychological Services.

ANNOTATED BIBLIOGRAPHY

Bracken, B. (Ed.). (1991). *The psychoeducational assessment of preschool children.* Boston: Allyn and Bacon.
This comprehensive book on assessment of preschoolers has a single chapter devoted exclusively to screening. However, this chapter's authors recommend this book as a definite inclusion in the professional library because it addresses so many important issues in working with youngsters in early childhood.

Bagnato, S. J., & Neisworth, J. T. (1991). *Assessment for early intervention: Best practices for professionals.* New York: Guilford.
Best available treatment of alternative models for assessment, especially curriculum based issues. Provides a philosophical model yet has much to offer in the way of implementation and practical aspects. While a majority of the book deals with assessment in general, there is an entire chapter devoted to screening.

Harrison, P. L. (1992). Planning and evaluating preschool screening and assessment programs. *Assessment News, 2*(3), 1, 8–11.
A short article that provides a succinct overview of the whole process. Many important issues are outlined and discussed including reasons for assessment/screening, usefulness of early intervention, inherent dangers in identification, and discussion of limitations of instrumentation often used.

Lichtenstein, R., & Ireton, H. (1984). *Preschool screening: Identifying young children with developmental and educational problems.* Orlando, FL: Grune & Stratton.
This little book probably still remains *the* classic in this area. A book that must be read by anyone involved in implementation of a screening program. Includes information on parent involvement, screening instruments, and establishing programs.

Meisels, S. J. (1989). *Developmental screening in early childhood: A guide* (3rd ed.). Washington, DC: The National Association for the Education of Young Children.
A practical, hands-on treatment of screening. Deals with many of the nuts and bolts and procedural issues connected with implementation. Copy of the *Early Screening Inventory Parent Questionnaire* is included.

21

Best Practices in Implementing Intervention Assistance Programs

Roslyn P. Ross
Queens College of the City University of New York

OVERVIEW

Intervention assistance programs go by a number of names in the schools where they are found (e.g., prereferral intervention, prereferral consultation, mainstream assistance teams, teacher assistance teams, teacher support teams, student assistance teams, instructional consultation teams). All are support systems for solving problems within the regular classroom. They are intended to provide immediate assistance to students and teachers, to enhance the ability of teachers to effectively serve difficult-to-teach students within regular classrooms, and to reduce inappropriate referrals to special education. They are often called prereferral programs because they are used to assist teachers in generating and implementing intervention strategies *prior* to seeking referral for consideration of a more restrictive placement. The model of service delivery common to intervention assistance programs is consultation; in this respect, they do not introduce a new type of service delivery. Readers interested in implementing such programs also will find much that is useful in the chapters on School Consultation and Behavioral Consultation in this volume.

Intervention assistance programs first began to be described in the literature in the late 1970s and early 1980s (e.g., Chalfant, Pysh, & Moultrie, 1979; Graden, Casey, & Christenson, 1985). They represent the most concerted and organized effort to date to correct a number of problems associated with service delivery under PL 94-142, The Education for All Handicapped Children Act of 1975. Too often, the only pathway to service for students having behavioral and learning difficulties is a "referral-test-place" sequence. This has resulted in overreferrals to special education (Research for Better Schools, 1986) and misclassification of students as disabled. It also has resulted in identification procedures that are costly and time consuming. One-half of all school psychologists, for example, devote more than 40% of their time to identification for learning disabilities, with about one in five devoting more than 60% of their time to

this activity (Ross, in press). Despite their cost, current diagnostic procedures, which emphasize standardized testing, usually yield little more than placement–no placement decisions. They must be followed by alternative types of assessment to develop intervention plans. These factors have led many professionals to question the amount of time devoted to "gate keeping" in our current service-delivery system as well as the particular gate that is being kept.

Intervention assistance programs propose consultation as an alternative framework for delivering service. Although the role of consultation is not new in school psychology, its implementation often depends upon the initiative of a particular individual and may fade away when that person leaves (Graden, Casey, & Bonstrom, 1985). A number of the programs currently being developed are attempts to implement a school-wide consultation service model. These programs often include teams of professionals, all of whom are trained in consultative, problem-solving methods. Team composition is a variable that distinguishes two types of intervention assistance programs currently in existence. One type, the one that school psychologists are involved in, has multidisciplinary teams. The second type is composed solely of regular classroom teachers, although others may be asked to participate when necessary. Teacher Assistance Teams, problem-solving groups composed of regular classroom teachers, were originally introduced as an alternative to traditional in-service training in the early 1970s (Chalfant, Pysh, & Moultrie, 1979). They emphasize teacher initiative, communication, and effective decision making. Teacher empowerment through self-help is an underlying assumption.

Clearly, intervention assistance programs have much to recommend them. Pugach and Johnson (1989a) argue they are an extraordinarily progressive concept and a clear improvement to legislated practice because they (a) remediate unnecessarily restrictive parts of PL 94-142; (b) appropriately redirect special education resources toward the immediate solution of problems in the classroom; (c) provide resources for students not identified as disabled; (d) are consistent with important task-force recommendations for reforming both the operation of schools and the preparation of teachers (e.g., the need for building-level responsibility shared among professionals in the schools, encouragement of collaborative problem-solving characterized by collegial professional relationships, increased professionalism for classroom teachers). You may well recognize the consonance of these goals with those of mainstreaming and the Regular Education Initiative (Will, 1986).

The great appeal of intervention assistance programs is shown by the extent to which they have been endorsed by state education agencies. A survey conducted in 1987 by Carter and Sugai (1989) indicated that prereferral interventions for students suspected of having a disability were required by 23 state education agencies and recommended by 11. Information is lacking, however, on how local educational agencies actually implement states' recommendations; the prevalence of such programs within schools is unknown.

Carter and Sugai (1989) noted that prereferral intervention became a common component of state educational agency policy even before there was much empirical support for its effectiveness. Currently, promising evidence indicates that intervention assistance programs can reduce the number of students referred for formal assessment and then placed in special education *if* there is appropriate administrative support, sufficient time and resources invested in the program, staff willingness to be involved, and well designed interventions faithfully executed (e.g., Chalfant & Pysh, 1989; Graden, Casey, & Bonstrom, 1985; Fuchs, Fuchs, & Bahr, 1990; Fuchs, Fuchs, Bahr, Fernstrom, & Stecker, 1990). The programs also can yield high teacher and student satisfaction and appear to improve teacher attitudes toward and tolerance of students experiencing difficulties. Outcome studies generally show implemented strategies can produce desired student performance, but this is frequently assessed by having the same person implement the strategy and rate its perceived effectiveness in the absence of data-based measures. Interventions have tended to focus more on management and maintenance of student behavior (e.g., work habits, classroom and interpersonal behavior) than on academic performance. Chalfant & Pysh (1989) suggest that this will change with time. They report observing that as a program matures, teachers shift from seeking assistance for behavior management problems, usually first priority issues, to seeking assistance for academic skill problems.

An adequate data base does not yet exist to evaluate the extent to which intervention assistance programs lead to increases in academic skills, class management skills, teaching skills, consulting skills, and professional collaboration. This is not so surprising given the time and effort that first must go into developing a program and the extreme difficulties that doing research in this area entail (see, e.g., Fuchs, Fuchs, Dulan, Roberts, & Fernstrom, 1992; Rosenfield, 1992).

Despite these difficulties, we do have "encouraging notes on preliminary findings" (Sindelar, Griffin, Smith, & Watanabe, 1992, p. 245) to add to the enthusiasm found in the literature and at the state education agency level. Currently, the efforts of practitioners and researchers, who work in the area, are being devoted to identifying and creating the conditions necessary for successful implementation. These conditions as well as the obstacles to creating them are given major attention in the next section on basic considerations. Following this, guidelines are presented for best practices in developing a program and providing intervention assistance.

BASIC CONSIDERATIONS

Controversial Issues

The emergence of intervention assistance programs presents psychologists with exciting opportunities to focus more of their efforts on trying to help resolve student problems when they first start. Most school professionals would agree that this is a worthy goal. Controversy arises, however, from the fact that intervention assistance programs also have come to represent a strategy for implementing educational reform. This reform involves changes in the way resources are deployed as well as changes in the way educational professionals function and relate to each other. It should come as no surprise, therefore, that there is considerable debate in the professional literature about reform issues and that these issues are likely to surface whenever an intervention assistance program is considered. Differences arise on how comprehensive the reform effort can be and how professionals should collaborate.

Who owns mainstreaming? As Davis (1989) points out, mainstreaming was not the idea of general education teachers, but they own the potential burden of instructing more difficult-to-teach students. Usually, they must do so without appropriate reductions in teacher–student ratios. It has been argued (e.g., Friend & Cook, 1990; Evans, 1990) that mainstreaming is unlikely to become enthusiastically owned by general teachers if it is oversold, underfunded, unrealistically expands roles and responsibilities, or is directed by others. Questions about the advisability of reducing or eliminating some traditional special educational services, without better evidence of its potential for success, are raised by other educational professionals and community groups as well.

Furthermore, as Friend and Cook (1990) point out, general and special educators historically have had different overriding goals for their students. Special education's requirement for extensive individualization (of instruction and mastery standards) may well conflict with regular education's goal of getting a relatively large number of students to master specified content within a specified time period. Requiring extensive individuation also is incompatible with other current educational reform proposals. Concern with the quality of public education and teacher training has lead to calls for placing greater emphasis on achievement. This call would have teachers increasing homework and stepping up the educational pace for their students.

Who owns prereferral intervention? Even when education professionals agree upon the need to find ways to maintain difficult-to-teach students within the classroom, they may disagree upon whose purview this is or who should be doing the consultation. This disagreement may take the form of recommending different kinds of support systems.

As stated earlier, intervention assistance programs currently fall into two types based on team composition, and team composition tends to determine who the consultant is. Those who advocate a multidisciplinary team, where the consultant more often than not is a specialist, often stress the collaborative nature of consultation (see, for example, Graden, 1989; Idol, Paolucci-Whitcomb, & Nevin, 1986). Those who advocate teacher teams, where the consultant is a teacher and specialists are invited to participate when necessary, may question whether consultation between general educators and special educators or psychologists can be truly collaborative with equal value given to each person's input. Pugach and Johnson (1989a, b) for example, argue that prereferral consultation as it is commonly practiced involves classroom teachers receiving assistance from specialists; it is an expert, rather than a collaborative, model of consultation that is implemented, despite assertions to the contrary. The danger that this presents, according to Pugach and Johnson, is that it reduces independence on the part of classroom teachers and subverts teacher empowerment. They contend that true collaboration, involving parity or equal value given to each person's input, can only exist when general educators help one another. They further argue that because mainstreaming is part of the general teaching environment, teachers, rather than special educators, should own the resources for problem solving (time and training) that prereferral structures grant. "In the context of prereferral interventions, the proprietary role specialists now play only defers a consideration of what constitutes the proper boundaries of special education in the schools" (Pugach & Johnson, 1989a, p. 225).

Prescriptive or collaborative consultation? This issue involves questions about the popular view that consultation should be collaborative, that is, involve a reciprocal arrangement "that enables people with diverse expertise to generate creative solutions

to mutually defined problems" (Idol, Paolucci-Whitcomb, & Nevin, 1986, p. 1). (The reader who is interested in a discussion of conditions necessary for collaboration is referred to Friend & Cook, 1990.) Fuchs, Fuchs, Bahr, Fernstrom, and Stecker (1990), for example, argue that there is a justifiable place for prescriptive approaches to prereferral intervention and school consultation:

> In schools in which stress is high, expertise in consultation is low, and consultation time is non-existent, prescriptive approaches appear better suited for success than collaborative ones. We have no doubt that, in different situations, more collaborative approaches may represent a better choice. . . . The nature of consultation activity should be determined more by the circumstance in which consultants find themselves than by an a priori belief system. (p. 511–512)

Fuchs et al. (1990) drew these conclusions from their well-researched effort to implement Mainstream Assistance Teams (MAT), a behavior consultation model with specialists as consultants. At the end of the first year of the program, which followed a multidisciplinary, collaborative model, they found that in-class interventions produced unimpressive results. During the second year they changed to a prescriptive model. MAT consultants and teachers selected among a small group of carefully detailed interventions with prescriptive instructions; multidisciplinary teams no longer were involved in the process. Results were much more impressive. Fuchs et al. (1990) reported:

> [At the end of year 1] many teachers complained they had insufficient time for the give-and-take nature of collaborative problem solving. Instead, they wanted helpful suggestions. In contrast, during debriefings and on questionnaires administered after more directive Year 2 activity, teachers from the same school district expressed satisfaction with the MAT interventions and consultation process. No one described the project experience as coercive or implicitly denigrating of his or her knowledge or skill. (p. 511)

While prescriptive plans appear to increase the efficiency of implementation, questions have been raised about whether such "packaged" plans may deprive the staff of a necessary sense of ownership and disappear when the program designer departs (Rosenfield, 1992).

Potential Obstacles and Disincentives

Any decision to adopt a program as a solution to identified problems involves weighing relative advantages and disadvantages. Factors that may be perceived as potential disadvantages of an intervention assistance program follow. These potential disadvantages or disincentives can be thought of as obstacles to successful implementation that need to be overcome through creative problem-solving.

- *Loss of funding resulting from reduced student enrollment in special education classes.* Successful prereferral intervention threatens a loss of state funding based on the number of students serviced within special education. It certainly cannot be rewarding for school district administrators to contemplate finding themselves with significantly less funds to accomplish the same goals with difficult-to-teach students, albeit in a less restrictive environment. Models have been proposed for compensating school districts for implementing effective programs (e.g., Fry, 1990; Idol, 1988); appropriate financing is critical.

- *Cost of intervention assistance programs.* Considerable resources have to go into starting intervention assistance programs if they are to have a chance to succeed. Time needs to be appropriated for the process and workloads have to be adjusted appropriately. Personnel need training in consultative problem-solving procedures. Given current estimates that it takes about 3 years to implement programs (Chalfant & Pysh, 1989; Fullan, Miles, & Taylor, 1980; Ponti, Zins, & Graden, 1988), some districts may be reluctant to support a program whose promised cost containment will take some time to realize. Many of the programs described in the literature have coped with this problem by obtaining special start-up funding in the form of grants from state or federal agencies. Gifts from individuals, corporations, or foundations also may be solicited.

- *Scaled-down costs may involve scaled-down expectations.* It is reasonable to expect that gains in professional productivity can result from investing in training and improving organizational structure. It seems less realistic, however, to expect that problem-solving skills of education professionals will increase enough to bear the entire cost of providing a full range of services to difficult-to-teach students in less restrictive settings. The cost-containment expectations for intervention assistance programs are at odds with expectations that "the public school [is] responsible for remediating virtually the entire range of physical, cognitive, and emotional conditions that can affect students" (Evans, 1990, p. 73). One or the other of these expectations may have to be scaled down.

- *Loss of jobs.* Part of the reason for the popularity of prereferral intervention is that it promises to contain the burgeoning costs of special education. Many special education and special services professionals fear that, if successful, this may translate into lost jobs rather than new opportunities for better service delivery. Similar fears may arise if prereferral activities are perceived to lead to a redeployment of scarce resources from special education to regular education; protecting one's turf

may take precedence over building collegial problem solving under such circumstances. The development of a more efficient and effective service delivery system, however, can serve as an impressive validation of the effectiveness of the service providers. This, in turn, could lend credence to the importance of providing financial support for other services.

- *Changed job roles and responsibilities.* While this may be described as an advantage in the reform literature, it does not always feel like one to professionals who have spent much time and effort to develop certain competencies. Even when convinced of the need for change, they may find it unpleasant to replace (temporarily, though it may be) a feeling of mastery with the inevitable anxiety and uncertainty that accompanies learning new skills and ways of functioning. Inservice training and ongoing support systems for participating staff are essential components of any intervention assistance program.

- *Increased job responsibilities.* If the demands of the program are added to the demands of traditional roles (e.g., caseloads remain the same, individualized instruction for some students is added to the regular teaching environment, no release time is given teachers for the problem-solving process), this can be quite a disincentive and barrier to successful implementation. Indeed, a shortcoming frequently reported by participants evaluating their prereferral program is that they lacked enough time to consult. Sufficient resources have to be marshalled to make sure that participants are not overloaded with work.

- *Commitment to special education services under PL 94-142.* While most education professionals acknowledge problems connected with service delivery under PL 94-142, many may believe that the advantages outweigh the disadvantages or alternatively that it is premature to restructure schools to eliminate some traditional special education services without better evidence of the effectiveness of prereferral intervention and mainstreaming. The benefits of change may be perceived as doubtful or not worth the risks. The prereferral model may be perceived as withholding beneficial special education services to students. Parents too may pressure for special education services under PL 94-142. Continuing research is needed to settle what are essentially empirical questions about the relative effectiveness of different service delivery systems.

- *Commitment to other programs.* New program implementation may already be taking place or a school may not have enough resources to introduce additional programs. Additionally, if the new program (e.g., curriculum reform) reflects a proposed solution for the same problems that intervention assistance programs address, the one already being implemented may be seen as a more appropriate solution.

- *More bureaucracy.* An intervention assistance program runs the risk of becoming another layer of bureaucracy. If too complex, it may detract from the immediate resolution of problems.

- *Resistance to change.* This disincentive does not refer to legitimate opposition to change. Rather, it refers to the natural tendency of people to protect themselves from uncomfortable feelings of anxiety and uncertainty, typically stirred by changes to anything perceived as important, by resisting such change. Examples of particular dangers that prereferral programs may represent are (a) threats to esteem because of implied failure of previous efforts or because of shifts in focus from child-as-the-problem to instructional and organizational factors, (b) decreases in self-esteem that inevitably accompany learning new skills, (c) loss of status associated with needing help, (d) threats to independence and control, and (e) threats to job security. Certainly, people differ in the ease with which their anxiety or defenses are stirred, but such reactions are to be expected. Awareness of the ongoing concerns of participants needs to be maintained so that concerns can be addressed through training and support processes. Readers interested in an indepth discussion of resistance and strategies for working with resistance are referred to Margolis, Fish, and Wepner (1990) and Zins, Curtis, Graden, and Ponti (1988), Chapter 9.

- *Poorly conceived plans.* This is a rather obvious disincentive and ways to avoid it will be discussed in the best practices section of this chapter.

- *Well conceived plans.* This is a not so obvious disincentive. Well conceived plans include a strong evaluation component (e.g., whether the model is actually being implemented as designed, effectiveness of staff training, effectiveness of intervention assistance). Rosenfield (1992) describes why this is likely to be seen as a disincentive from the point of view of the school:

> The intolerance of school personnel for extensive research procedures is legendary. Even with excellent working relationships, there were many kinds of research designs that were not possible for [Instructional Consultation] IC-Team . . . because the school culture does not find research a meaningful use of its precious resources of time and personnel. (p. 43)

Rosenfield recommends that research in school settings be kept short, cheap, and simple.

Resources Needed

Now that the long list of potential obstacles that may have to be handled is past, the reader may well wonder what the bottom line is. What resources are needed to give one a fair chance of doing useful intervention assistance? This next section identifies resources (or facilitators) mentioned consistently in the literature (see, e.g., Chalfant & Pysh, 1989; Graden, Casey, & Bonstrom, 1985; Idol & West, 1987). A subsequent section focuses on the specific skills that a practitioner needs to become involved in different aspects of intervention assistance programs.

- *Planning, patience, persistence, and perspective.* Developing and implementing intervention assistance programs is a complex and demanding process. This message is sounded time and again in descriptions of the process found in the literature. A great deal of careful planning is required to set the stage for change. Unforeseen challenges must be faced during implementation which require recycling to earlier stages of problem solving and program formulation. It has been reported (Chalfant & Pysh, 1989; Rosenfield, 1992) that it takes about three years to get programs implemented and another year or two for them to become institutionalized (an integral, accepted, and effective part of a building system).

- *Time to consult.* Consulting has to be a legitimate activity, not something squeezed in for a few minutes in the hallway, or whenever time can be spared from regular responsibilities. Insufficient time to consult is one of the most cited criticisms in program evaluations. Teachers need to be given release time with coverage for their classes if they are to make use of consultation services. Consultants need schedules which make them available during appropriate times. Idol (1988) describes a number of scheduling possibilities that have been used successfully for varying grade levels. She also gives guidelines for determining appropriate caseloads for consultants, including teachers, who have both direct and indirect service delivery responsibilities.

- *Administrative support.* The need for substantial administrative support is invariably included in program descriptions and evaluations. The foremost need is administrative support in the form of providing time for personnel to consult on a regular basis (e.g., Chalfant & Pysh, 1989). Administrative support also takes the form of providing policy initiatives for prereferral intervention, encouraging and publicizing program efforts, engaging in thoughtful planning, and mobilizing resources. Whether administrative support should take the form, as it has in some programs, of leading team problem-solving meetings remains controversial. Professionals may be reluctant to reveal problems to a principal who also has to evaluate their job functioning.

- *Staff development and training.* An obvious need is staff with good consultation skills. Practitioners who already have these skills represent an invaluable resource. However, staff development is consistently included as a major, needed component of intervention assistance programs. All faculty need an orientation to the concepts and techniques of the program. Staff who elect to participate in the program need considerably more training, not only to enhance (or develop) their consultation skills but to function effectively in teams. Without training, teams tend to be inefficient and ineffective (Hayek, 1987; Schram & Semmel, 1984). Training for skill development requires opportunities for observing of effective practice, feedback, and guided practice. It is an ongoing process and provides staff with continued technical assistance and support systems (e.g., opportunities for peer supervision and for networking) after the period of initial skill development.

- *Faculty support.* Without sufficient faculty support, there can be no program. Indeed, program effectiveness is often measured in terms of the willingness of faculty to be involved. This resource has to be cultivated through involving faculty in needs assessment and planning, providing orientation to the program, providing training and appropriate support for change, allowing for voluntary participation, and coming through with perceived benefits.

- *Parent support.* Outcome studies have tended to ignore the role played by parent support, so little empirical data exist demonstrating its importance. However, most program developers consider it quite important and devote effort to gaining the support and sanction of all interested parties, including parents. This is done through providing information at orientation meetings, involving representative groups in planning, sharing information on an ongoing basis, and coming through with perceived benefits.

- *Financing.* Funding is particularly crucial during the start-up period. There are expenses for planning, training, inservice presentations, release time to consult, evaluation, and publicity. These expenses precede potential cost savings. Funding sources have included bootstraps, local schools, school districts, bureaus of cooperative educational services (BOCES), state education agencies, the federal government (e.g., Office of Special Education Programs), and private foundations. These are temporary solutions and workable funding plans for ongoing programs need to be developed at the state level.

Skills and Knowledge Needed

School psychologists may function in many different roles in intervention assistance programs. They may be involved in program development, program oversight, team leadership, team problem solving, and provision of individual consultation services. It is hoped they are not attempting to function in all of these roles at the same time.

These roles all require knowledge of and skill in engaging in the various phases of a problem-solving consultative process. Idol and West (1987) describe the consultation process as involving both a communicative/interactive component and an underlying knowledge base. The first component refers to the good interpersonal and communication skills that must be in place to engage clients in the process. The second component refers to having something of value to share once clients are engaged. Psychologists draw on the wide knowledge base required to be a school psychologist in the first place for this "something of value to share." Special emphasis, however, is placed on some knowledge domains.

Most obviously, a knowledge of systematic steps to be followed in a problem-solving process is required for all consultation. (These steps are described later in the chapter and are fully detailed in other chapters on consultation in this volume.) Intervention assistance programs additionally require a particularly strong knowledge base in the domain of effective classroom intervention technology. In addition to the many relevant chapters in this volume, the reader may consult Cohen and Fish (1993), Martens and Meller (1990), and Shapiro (1988) for information on intervention technology and Gresham (1989) for information on treatment integrity.

An analysis of existing intervention assistance programs by Idol and West (1987) indicated a common requirement for knowledge of and skills in assessment focused on curriculum-based assessment and diagnostic/analytic teaching. Rosenfield (1992) stresses that this should also include being able to monitor student progress by providing data-based measures (e.g., graphing). Intervention assistance programs seem to rule out the possibility that assessment based on standardized testing is useful in analyzing problems at a prereferral stage; such assessment is restricted to formal evaluation procedures associated with special education consideration.

Knowledge of systems theory ad change techniques is included as an important requirement by those who propose that consultants function as change agents at the system or school level (e.g., Zins et al., 1988). This is the role assumed by consultants during program initiation and development. Some interesting evidence suggests that gender-associated attitudes about engaging in leadership behaviors may be as influential, if not more so, as possessing requisite knowledge in determining whether consultants attack problems at a system level. Conoley and Welch (1988) found, from their analysis of consultation logs, that young, female psychology trainees concentrated on individual problem solving, mainly with same-sex consultees of relatively low status in the organization. In contrast, young male trainees (with the same training and qualifications) were more likely to be involved with administrative staff, often male, and tended to use more risk-taking or systemic models of consultation. Thus, positive attitudes about exhibiting leadership behaviors and relating in an authoritative manner with (primarily male) administrative personnel have to be added to the skills and knowledge necessary to initiate and develop intervention assistance programs. Women who are concerned that they may be disadvantaged in this regard will find the Conoley and Welch (1988) article of interest.

Finally, psychologists who assume team leadership roles require knowledge of group dynamics and skill in facilitating team problem solving. The interested reader is referred to Arends and Arends (1977) for their discussion of task and maintenance functions in leading groups, All members of problem-solving teams need knowledge of effective teaming strategies; training in teaming strategies should be part of program development.

BEST PRACTICES

Problem solving is the essential characteristic of consultation and intervention assistance programs. A number of steps are followed systematically in dealing with problems whether they concern individuals or systems. Bergan (1977) describes the steps as including problem identification, problem analysis, plan implementation, and plan evaluation. Gutkin and Curtis (1982) further divide the stage of plan implementation into generating alternative strategies through brainstorming, evaluating alternative strategies, clarifying implementation procedures and responsibilities, and implementing the strategy.

Some of the intervention assistance programs in existence favor the behavioral model of consultation which tends to focus on developing interventions for individuals or small groups of students. The interventions thus developed are based on social learning theory and behavior modification and might involve, for example, increasing or decreasing the frequency of a targeted behavior. Other programs favor a process model of consultation which tends to focus on organizational analysis and interactions among people in work groups — the teacher's skill in handling a group of students, for example, rather than on the student's behaviors per se. Interventions are based on research on small groups, organizational effectiveness, and social psychology, and are designed to restructure the setting so that individuals can make progress (e.g., improving the teacher's skill in pacing instruction in order to increase students' academic engaged time;

restructuring a management system within the school to be more collaborative).

A third model, mental health consultation, focuses more on discerning what is blocking the teacher's problem-solving skills (e.g., lack of knowledge, skill, self-confidence, or objectivity). Mental health consultation has its roots in psychodynamic psychology which includes an interest in unconscious dynamics. Interventions might involve providing information (e.g., recommending how the teacher should deal with a student, arranging for inservice training), modeling skills, providing support and reassurance for blocks coming from lack of self-confidence, or helping the consultee improve objectivity through techniques which Caplan (1970), the developer of this approach, called theme-interference reduction and indirect confrontation. Consultants also pay attention to organizational realities and group difficulties. According to Conoley and Conoley (1988), the mental health consultation model is foreign to the style of most school-based consultants and least likely to be accepted by school organizations. Indeed, intervention assistance programs described in the literature do not appear to be favoring this model.

The reader interested in learning more about how the different models effect the routine activities and problem-solving formulations of the consultant should read the analysis by Conoley and Conoley (1988), which served as the basis for the preceding description. West and Idol (1987) also present an excellent review of consultation theory.

Few detailed descriptions of how programs were actually developed and implemented currently exist. Notable exceptions are the handbook by Fuchs and his colleagues and the guide by Zins and his colleagues, both listed in the annotated bibliography. As program development proceeds, handbooks are likely to become more available; some state education agencies (e.g., Ohio) seem to be developing them. Professionals who are involved in this early stage will find it helpful to share information with their colleagues informally and at professional meetings. The overview of practices that follows is based on a review of the literature.

Program Development and Initiation

During this step, decisions must be made about the need for an intervention assistance program, as well as the type of program to adopt, resources must be mobilized and committed, and an operating plan for implementing the program must be developed (Rosenfield, 1992; Zins et al., 1988). The tasks often overlap and influence each other. Talking to school members about whether they see the need for intervention assistance, for example, also may have the effect of interesting some in working on perceived problems — certainly a valuable resource to mobilize during problem clarification and analysis.

Deciding to adopt a program. An intervention assistance program imposed just because someone wishes to have consultation services available or has a vision of change not shared by others, starts off on very shaky grounds. Efforts have to go into clarifying the need for a program and the school's willingness to consider one. Talking to colleagues is one of the ways of starting this effort. Zins et al. (1988) recommend a systematic organizational assessment and describe procedures that include surveys, observations, review of records, interviews, and analyses of various elements of the system. This recommendation reflects their process, or systems, perspective. The material on potential disincentives presented earlier in this chapter also provides information relevant to understanding factors influencing the decision-making process.

If the process of problem clarification and analysis yields sufficient consensus to proceed, it will also provide a basis for clarifying program goals and tailoring them to identified needs. Alternative options for structuring intervention assistance programs are then evaluated in terms of the organization's needs and resources. A frequent recommendation in the literature is to start with a small program or pilot project.

Mobilizing resources and gaining commitment. Substantial administrative support is repeatedly described as necessary for program success. It needs to be mobilized rather early in the decision-making process. The importance of obtaining the sanction and support of *all* relevant stakeholders is stressed by Rosenfield (1992) and Zins et al. (1988). Included among the stakeholders they mention are teachers, the teachers' union, building and district administrators, special services staff, and parents. Organizational analysis may reveal others as well. Support may be obtained by involving representative groups in problem analysis and planning. All should be kept informed of program status and have an opportunity to provide input. Mobilizing resources also involves finding ways to fund the program.

The operating plan. Careful team planning goes into producing an operating plan for implementing the program. The team who works on this has to prepare a working document and addresses a multitude of practical issues. This working document should include

1. Program purpose.

2. Specific goals, clearly defined so they can be evaluated.

3. Program description.

4. Recipients of the services.

5. Program cost and ways resources will be provided, including funding.

6. Operational procedures for providing intervention assistance to individuals and for coordinating the service delivery program (e.g., what actually will be done and who will do it, staff roles, leadership, meeting times, record keeping).

7. Plan for sharing information about the program with identified stakeholders.

8. Plan for staff development and training in consultation and teaming strategies.

9. Plan for ongoing program evaluation (integrity of model implementation as well as outcome data).

10. Time table for the various tasks that have to be accomplished.

Program Implementation

During this second stage, the program is actually put into practice. Intervention assistance is provided, training now moves to skill development, support structures for addressing faculty concerns are put in place, and evidence is gathered to evaluate program effectiveness. The effectiveness of the structures put in place and refined during this stage impacts strongly on whether the program eventually reaches the third stage of change, institutionalization, to become part of the structure and fabric of the school (Rosenfield, 1992).

The multidisciplinary team model. Many intervention assistance programs have adopted a model in which multidisciplinary teams are used for consultation and problem solving. The rationale for their use is that they increase the breadth of knowledge and skills available for problem solving and, further, that they serve as models for collaborative professional functioning. Rosenfield (1992) suggests that their popularity may be enhanced by their similarity to the structure common in schools under current special education law. These teams may include an administrator, special services personnel (e.g., psychologist, guidance counselor, nurse, social worker, speech and language specialist), a special education consultant or teacher, and a regular education teacher, all of whom receive training in consultation and team strategies. Zins et al. (1988) recommend that such teams be standing, rather than ad hoc, teams and that the number convened for any group decision making be seven or fewer.

Some ingenuity is needed to fix upon the time that a team can meet because of the number of people involved. Once found, it seems preferable to make this a standing, weekly time so that it becomes an integral part of school functioning. Zins et al. (1988) suggest 60 minutes weekly to allow the team to meet with two teachers or hold in-depth discussions. Chalfant and Pysh (1989) warn that care must be taken to establish efficient procedures lest meetings be perceived as burdensome and wasteful. They recommend clearly identified agendas and verbal economy practiced by team members.

In general, multidisciplinary teams reserve group problem solving for the most complex cases or circumstances when communication among a number of people needs to be facilitated. Intervention assistance is primarily provided by individual consultants. While this reflects a parsimonious use of resources, the balance between individual consultation and team problem solving also may be influenced by team composition — specifically, whether or not an administrator is a team member. Zins et al. (1988, p. 179) seem to be alluding to this when they comment that individual sessions for problem solving may minimize difficulties stemming from the reluctance of school personnel to discuss problems when the principal is present. Descriptions in the literature (e.g., Chalfant & Pysh, 1989) suggest that group problem solving may be a more typical service delivery system when teams are composed entirely of teachers. Currently no data exist to evaluate whether one or the other model is more effective or whether administrative participation is best sought in team membership or leadership.

Someone has to have responsibility for directing the team and facilitating the problem-solving process during meetings. Responsibility also has to be assigned to someone to "organize team meetings, receive referrals, and monitor the status of all cases" (Rosenfield, 1992, p. 36). The selection of a "systems manager" to perform this function was identified as a critical dimension of Instructional Consultation teams. The various leadership responsibilities may or may not be assigned to the same individual.

Intervention assistance process. Graden, Casey, and Christenson (1985) provide the following (multidisciplinary team) model for stages of the pre-referral intervention process:

- *Stage 1: Request for consultation.* The classroom teacher requests consultation. This can be an informal process in which the teacher requests problem-solving assistance from a building consultant or a formal process in which all initial referrals are screened by a building team and then assigned to a consultant.

- *Stage 2: Consultation.* Collaborative consultation takes place to (a) identify problems in behavioral, measurable terms; (b) set priorities for action; (c) analyze relevant variables, including classroom variables; (d) collaboratively design an intervention; (e) implement the intervention; (f) evaluate the intervention; and (g) provide follow-up. Intervention plans may include the student, parents, or other school personnel.

- *Stage 3: Observation.* If the intervention plan is not successful, the consultant collects additional data through detailed observation of the student and the instructional/teaching environment. Based on this data, further interventions are planned collaboratively by consultant and teacher, and a meeting is held with the student and/or parent to discuss instructional/behavioral changes. Interventions are implemented and evaluated. If successful, the process ends with provision for follow-up.

Gresham (1989) recommends that this stage of observation also include monitoring whether the treatment is being implemented as planned and describes procedures for doing so. One of these procedures involves rating each component of an intervention for its occurrence/nonoccurrence and computing percent integrity. Fuchs et al. (1990) provide evidence that oversight (e.g., explicit written instructions and monitoring) may be needed to insure fidelity of implementation.

- *Stage 4: Conference.* The consultant and teacher meet with the team to decide whether to continue with the intervention, try another one, or refer the child for psychoeducational assessment and consideration of special education eligibility. (Although parent participation is recommended, a large team can be overwhelming; other ways of involving parents may be more appropriate in many circumstances.)

- *Stage 5: Formal referral.* If appropriate, the student is formally referred for evaluation and enters the child study process with due process regulations. This evaluation should use data collected from Stages 1–4.

- *Stage 6: Formal program meeting.* The formal review meeting, traditionally used in school programs, is held to determine eligibility and the extent of special education services. If mandated, the instructionally relevant data that has already been obtained through trying different interventions is used to develop the Individualized Education Plan (IEP).

Maintaining records of the process. Records of the intervention assistance process need to be maintained. Such records provide accountability data (documenting the amount and nature of services being provided) in addition to data needed to monitor individual case status. Well developed forms also help guide the process by specifying information needed to assess problems and successive stages of contact. Those developed by Fuchs and Fuchs (1989, p. 280), for example, include written "scripts" to orchestrate the stages of behavioral consultation. Forms compatible with the process described by Graden and her colleagues can be found in Salvia and Ysseldyke (1991, chap. 25).

Evaluation

Evaluation should be an essential, ongoing component of all aspects of intervention assistance programs. Data needs to be collected to evaluate (a) implementation, that is, whether the program is being implemented as intended; (b) the effectiveness of individual interventions; and (c) program outcomes. Examples of the kind of data that might be collected for each of these respective categories are:

1. Implementation: checklists to see whether critical dimensions of the program are in place, interviews with team members and teachers, reviews of records, analysis of tapes of the consultation process.

2. Effectiveness: frequency of target behavior, teacher ratings, single-subject and multiple-baseline designs, teacher satisfaction with intervention results.

3. Program Outcomes: referral and placement patterns, number of requests for consultation, changes in teachers' attitudes, changes in teachers' classroom management skills, consumer satisfaction, outcome of individual interventions, student academic achievement.

One can easily see that it is a major undertaking to plan evaluation procedures. It is no less an undertaking to collect data and analyze it so that it provides useful information about what works well and what should be changed. Effective efforts to evaluate programs (as well as individual interventions) require collaboration between program participants; it is important that participants perceive the evaluation system as responsive to their needs and to their suggestions for changes.

SUMMARY

The emergence of intervention assistance programs presents psychologists with exciting opportunities to use consultation as a framework for delivering services and to focus more of their efforts on resolving student problems within regular classrooms. The programs are support systems intended to assist teachers in generating and implementing intervention strategies *prior* to seeking referral for consideration of a more restrictive program. As such, they represent the most concerted and organized effort to date to correct a number of problems associated with service delivery under PL 94-142. They come in for their share of controversy, however, because they may be seen as "a vehicle for or obstacle to special education" (Zins et al., 1988, p. 63). State education agencies, for example, have seized upon the programs as a strategy for containing spiraling special education placements and costs. Friend (1988) also cautions:

> The impact of the REI on consultation may thus eventually be either positive or negative. It will be positive if it results in the clarification and refinement of the concepts and practices of consultation. It will be negative if consultation and the Regular Education Initiative come to be perceived as synonymous. (p. 10)

Currently, the efforts of practitioners and researchers working in this area are devoted to identifying and creating the conditions necessary for successful intervention assistance programs. These conditions as well as the obstacles to creating them are given major attention in this chapter. Best practice guidelines are given both for developing a program and for providing intervention assistance in individual cases.

REFERENCES

Arends, R. E., & Arends, J. H. (1977). *Systems change strategies in educational settings.* New York: Human Sciences Press.

Bergan, J. R. (1977). *Behavioral consultation.* Columbus, OH: Merrill.

Caplan, G. (1970). *The theory and practice of mental health consultation.* New York: Basic Books.

Carter, J., & Sugai, G. (1989). Survey on prereferral practices: Responses from state departments of education. *Exceptional Children, 55,* 298–302.

Chalfant, J. C., & Pysh, M. V. D. (1989). Teacher assistance teams: Five descriptive studies on 96 teams. *Remedial and Special Education, 10,* 49–58.

Chalfant, J. C., Pysh, M. V. D., & Moultrie, R. (1979). Teacher assistance teams: A model for within-building problem solving. *Learning Disability Quarterly, 2,* 85–96.

Cohen, J. J., & Fish, M. C. (1993). *Handbook of school-based interventions: Resolving student problems and promoting healthy educational environments.* San Francisco: Jossey-Bass.

Conoley, J. C., & Conoley, C. W. (1988). Useful theories in school-based consultation. *Remedial and Special Education, 9*(6), 14–20.

Conoley, J. C., & Welch, K. (1988). The empowerment of women in school psychology: Paradoxes of success and failure. *Professional School Psychology, 3,* 13–19.

Davis, W. E. (1989). The regular education initiative debate: Its promises and problems. *Exceptional Children, 55,* 440–446.

Evans, R. (1990). Making mainstreaming work through prereferral consultation. *Educational Leadership, 47,* 73–77.

Friend, M. (1988). Putting consultation into context: Historical and contemporary perspectives. *Remedial and Special Education, 9*(6), 7–13.

Friend, M., & Cook, L. (1990). Collaboration as a predictor for success in school reform. *Journal of Educational and Psychological Consultation, 1,* 69–86.

Fry, D. (1990, April). *Prereferral funding: A model for promoting system level change.* Paper presented at the meeting of the National Association of School Psychologists, San Francisco, CA. (ERIC Document Reproduction Service No. ED 337 971)

Fuchs, D., & Fuchs, L. S. (1989). Exploring effective and efficient prereferral interventions: A component analysis of behavioral consultation. *School Psychology Review, 23,* 260–283.

Fuchs, D., Fuchs, L. S., & Bahr, M. W. (1990). Mainstream assistance teams: A scientific basis for the art of consultation. *Exceptional Children, 57,* 128–139.

Fuchs, D., Fuchs, L. S., Bahr, M. W., Fernstrom, P., & Stecker, P. M. (1990). Prereferral intervention: A prescriptive approach. *Exceptional Children, 56,* 493–513.

Fuchs, D., Fuchs, L. S., Dulan, J., Roberts, H., & Fernstrom, P. (1992). Where is the research on consultation effectiveness? *Journal of Educational and Psychological Consultation, 3,* 151–174.

Fullan, M., Miles, M. B., & Taylor, G. (1980). Organization development in schools: The state of the art. *Review of Educational Research, 50,* 121–183.

Graden, J. L. (1989). Redefining "prereferral" intervention as intervention assistance: Collaboration between general and special education. *Exceptional Children, 56,* 227–231.

Graden, J. L., Casey, A., & Bonstrom, O. (1985). Implementing a prereferral intervention system: Part II. The data. *Exceptional Children, 51,* 487–496.

Graden, J. L., Casey, A., & Christenson, S. L. (1985). Implementing a prereferral intervention system: Part I. The model. *Exceptional Children, 51,* 377–384.

Gresham, F. M. (1989). Assessment of treatment integrity in school consultation and prereferral intervention. *School Psychology Review, 18,* 37–50.

Gutkin, T. B., & Curtis, M. J. (1982). School based consultation: Theory and techniques. In C. R. Reynolds & T. B. Gutkin (Eds.), *The handbook of school psychology* (pp. 796–828). New York: Wiley.

Hayek, R. A. (1987). The teacher assistance team: A pre-referral support system. *Focus on Exceptional Children, 20,* 1–7.

Idol, L. (1988). A rationale and guidelines for establishing special education consultation programs. *Remedial and Special Education, 9*(6), 48–58.

Idol, L., Paolucci-Whitcomb, P., & Nevin, A. (1986). *Collaborative consultation.* Austin, TX: PRO-ED.

Idol, L., & West, J. F. (1987). Consultation in special education (Part II): Training and practice. *Journal of Learning Disabilities, 20,* 474–494.

Margolis, H., Fish, M., & Wepner, S. (1990). Overcoming resistance to prereferral classroom interventions. *Special Services in the Schools, 6,* 167–187.

Martens, B. K., & Meller, P. J. (1990). The application of behavior principles to educational settings. In T. B. Gutkin & C. R. Reynolds (Eds.), *The handbook of school psychology* (2nd ed.; pp. 612–634). New York: Wiley.

Ponti, C. R., Zins, J. E., & Graden, J. L. (1988). Implementing a consultation-based service delivery system to decrease referrals for special education: A case study of organizational considerations. *School Psychology Review, 17,* 89–100.

Pugach, M. C., & Johnson, L. J. (1989a). Prereferral interventions: Progress, problems, and challenges. *Exceptional Children, 56,* 217–226.

Pugach, M. C., & Johnson, L. J. (1989b). The challenge of implementing collaboration between general and special education. *Exceptional Children, 56,* 232–235.

Research for Better Schools. (1986). *Special education: Views from America's cities.* Philadelphia: Author.

Rosenfield, S. (1992). Developing school-based consultation teams: A design for organizational change. *School Psychology Quarterly, 7,* 27–46.

Ross, R. P. (in press). The impact of state guidelines for evaluating underachievement on psychologists. *Learning Disability Quarterly.*

Salvia, J., & Ysseldyke, J. E. (1991). *Assessment* (fifth ed.). Boston: Houghton Mifflin.

Schram, L., & Semmel, M. I. (1984). *Problem solving teams in California: Appropriate responses by school site staff to students who are difficult to teach and manage.* Santa Barbara: University of California, Graduate School of Education. (ERIC Document Reproduction Service No. ED 225 485)

Shapiro, E. S. (1988). Preventing academic failure. *School Psychology Review, 17,* 601–613.

Sindelar, P. T., Griffin, C. C., Smith, S. W., & Watanabe, A. K. (1992). Prereferral intervention: Encouraging notes on preliminary findings. *The Elementary School Journal, 92,* 245–259.

West, J. F., & Idol, L. (1987). School consultation (Part I): An interdisciplinary perspective on theory, models, and research. *Journal of Learning Disabilities, 20,* 388–408.

Will, M. (1986). Educating students with learning problems: A shared responsibility. *Exceptional Children, 52,* 411–416.

Zins, J. E., Curtis, M. J., Graden, J. L., & Ponti, C. R. (1988). *Helping students succeed in the regular classroom: A guide for developing intervention assistance programs.* San Francisco: Jossey-Bass.

ANNOTATED BIBLIOGRAPHY

Cohen, J. J., & Fish, M. C. (1993). *Handbook of school-based interventions: Resolving student problems and promoting healthy educational environments.* San Francisco: Jossey-Bass.
This handbook describes interventions for major problem behaviors students may exhibit from kindergarten through grade 12. The interventions are research-based and drawn from the literature.

Fuchs, D., Fuchs, L. S., Reeder, P., Gilman, S., Fernstrom, P., Bahr, M., & Moore, P. (1989). *Mainstream Assistance Teams: A handbook on prereferral intervention.* Available for $12.00 from the MAT Project, John F. Kennedy Center, Box 40, George Peabody College, Vanderbilt University, Nashville, TN 37203.
This handbook describes a well-researched effort to implement a behavioral consultation model of intervention assistance.

Rosenfield, S. (1992). Developing school-based consultation teams: A design for organizational change. *School Psychology Quarterly, 7,* 27–46.
This article describes how an Instructional Consultation Team model was developed and presents a model for change consisting of three stages — initiation, implementation, and institutionalization.

Zins, J. E., Curtis, M. J., Graden, J. L., & Ponti, C. R. (1988). *Helping students succeed in the regular classroom: A guide for developing intervention assistance programs.* San Francisco: Jossey-Bass.
This is an excellent guide and provides many detailed and practical recommendations. It describes a systems-level process model and includes chapters on intervention technology and ethical and legal issues.

22

Best Practices in Facilitating School-Based Organizational Change and Strategic Planning

Howard M. Knoff
University of South Florida

OVERVIEW

Today's children are coming to the schoolhouse door significantly at risk for both educational and social failure. According to the Children's Defense Fund (1990), "the mounting crisis of our children and families is a rebuke of everything America professes to be. It also will bring America to its economic knees and increase violence and discord within this country unless we confront it" (p. 3). As examples of the broad-based problems currently facing our children and families, this report highlights the devastating statistics regarding school dropouts, child runaways, abuse and neglect, teenage parents, drug and alcohol abuse, children killed by guns, and the effects of poverty and homelessness on America's children (p. 3–5). On a positive note, the decade of the 1990s may turn out to be one of the most important relative to rededicating ourselves to the educational and social needs of children and youth in America, but only if our nation's schools are prepared to respond to the challenges described above. Significantly, when the divorce rate, the number of two-parent working families, and our nation's health care crisis are factored in, virtually every student in this country is potentially at risk.

Starting with the 1982 National Academy of Sciences report (Heller, Holtzman, & Messick, 1982) addressing the fundamental problems that exist in the provision of services to handicapped and at-risk students, continuing with the 1983 *Nation at Risk* report of the National Commission on Excellence in Education, and finishing with the National Governors' Association educational summit in the Fall of 1989 to specify the nation's educational goals for the coming 10 years, the commitment to educational reform has been sounded at national, state, and local levels. With our National Education Goals and the Goals 2000 legislation now in place, all of our schools have benchmarks recognizing the importance of children's academic, social, and learning readiness skills to their educational success. The question that now remains is, Do our individual schools have the skills, resources, motivation, and wherewithal to plan for and actually effect organizational change such that these goals can be attained? This is the focus of this chapter, a chapter whose primary assumption is that school psychologists need to be primary players *and facilitators*, at the school level, in organizational change, strategic planning, and school reform.

Introductory Assumptions

Prior to a discussion of how to facilitate organizational change and strategic planning, a number of assumptions must be reviewed and accepted as follows:

1. Organizational change and strategic planning are natural, necessary, and ongoing processes in any healthy organization.

2. Organizational change and strategic planning initially involve a number of people working together as representatives of the larger organization. Eventually, all members of the organization work together in a dynamic partnership with defined goals, roles, and activities to bring about change.

3. Even with this representative group working together, organizational change and strategic planning generally involve one or two individuals who oversee, guide, and facilitate the process.

4. In the schools, some seemingly child-focused problems are actually building, systems, or community problems that must be addressed at multiple levels using a problem-solving process that results in systematic, multifaceted intervention and substantive change.

5. The facilitator of organizational change and strategic planning need only be skilled in overseeing the process — no specific school-based profession has primary ownership of this facilitator role.

Unfortunately, until recently individual schools have rarely engaged in systematic organizational development and strategic planning processes. Thus they have not recognized that these activities are natural, necessary, and ongoing processes in any healthy organization, nor have they learned how to carry them out efficiently and effectively. Significantly, the vast majority of the early initiatives resulting from the *A Nation At Risk* report, from 1983 to approximately 1990, were federal- or state-imposed legislative or administrative top-down mandates that increased the oversight, standards, and accountability of schools, teachers, and students, but did not provide a blueprint for successful programs and interventions — or funds, for that matter — to attain this accountability (Bacharach, 1990; Sergiovanni & Moore, 1989).

From 1990 to the present, however, the school reform movement has recognized that substantive change will come only with school-level change, and thus, the focus has shifted to encouraging (or mandating) schools to organize comprehensive, bottom-up grass-roots initiatives that involve parents, community leaders, and school personnel as equal and responsible partners. Yet at this level numerous hurdles — such as financing, time availability, and needed staff training and supervision — exist that potentially will limit and frustrate the school reform process. Indeed, a recent publication by Seymour Sarason, *The Predictable Failure of Educational Reform* (1990), highlights a number of additional reasons why school-based reform may never reach expected levels and what we can do to avoid continued failure. Specifically, Sarason expects today's school reform process to fail for the following reasons:

1. Many of the people writing school reform reports and passing legislation have never worked in school systems, do not understand school systems, and have no idea what will work and what will fail.

2. School and communities do not understand how unique the United States is in its racial, ethnic, and cultural composition, and how we will need to adapt to the social and academic realities of this composition both as adults working together and as adults working to help children.

3. The individuals "facilitating" the reform process do not understand their schools or the reform process in the context of either their schools' history or larger social systems. They are looking for the causes and solutions of system problems rather than for the resources needed to reconceptualize and redesign new systems. Further, they want guarantees ahead of time that change will work.

4. School leaders do not understand that schools exist to facilitate on an equal basis the development and growth of both students and educational personnel.

5. School leaders really do not understand that this process requires changes in thinking and behavior. They do not know how to effect these changes,

and they do not recognize the difference between power and influence.

6. School personnel do not want to confront and change the existing power relationships among administration, teachers, other staff, and parents such that true collaboration and shared decision making can exist.

7. School leaders do not understand that, left unchecked, schools will respond to reform in ways that minimize the effort needed and the degree of real change required. This avoidance response, however, is directly correlated with the degree of powerlessness felt by those most responsible for the change.

School reform means change. And without a guided organizational change and strategic planning process that involves parents, community leaders, *and* school personnel, building-based change will be extremely difficult to accomplish. As a first step in this process, all of the participating parties need to learn how to collaborate and strategically plan for school-based reform. This learning may take from 3 to 5 years, it may require an outside consultant or a full-time staff facilitator, and it may be made even more difficult if the school is required, as many are, to implement the change process at the same time that the school-based management or advisory team is learning it. But it must be done, it must be focused on increasing students' social and academic learning and development, and school psychologists must be involved — potentially as the primary facilitators of the process. By way of summary, Goodlad (Quinby, 1985) concludes:

> Cosmetic changes can be legislated and mandated; the ways children and youth acquire knowledge and ways of knowing cannot. These depend on the knowledge and creativity of teachers. Better preparation of principals and teachers along with help and time for designing programs *at the site*, are necessary ingredients of school improvement. This message is at best only at the rhetorical level of acceptance at policy makers seeking to improve schooling. Unless it becomes a guiding principle of action as well as faith, little more than peripheral changes in the central curricular and instructional functioning of schools is likely to occur. (p. 19)

BASIC CONSIDERATIONS

In order to coordinate and facilitate a school-based organizational change and strategic planning process, school psychologists must understand and have expertise in three primary areas: (a) the problem-solving and planning cycles of a school from an organizational perspective, (b) the characteristics of an operating school district from a systemic perspective, and (c) the steps in a strategic planning process. Each of these will be discussed in detail below.

Planning and Problem-Solving from a District Perspective

Problem solving is needed and occurs in virtually every area of our personal and professional lives. Similarly, problem solving is used in virtually every area of business, politics, education, human services, and civic planning. Although some use more or fewer stages, problem solving typically is divided into four sequential stages: problem identification, problem analysis, intervention, and evaluation.

1. The problem identification stage involves actions that help (a) to operationally define the referred problem, whether it is of an individual nature or an organizational nature; (b) to specify the goals of the consultation, problem-solving, and/or planning process; and (c) to begin to verify the existence and extent of the problem and to generate hypotheses to explain why the problem is occurring.

2. The problem analysis stage involves actions whereby (a) the referred and operationalized problem is fully investigated in all of its ecological, organizational, situational, and behavioral contexts; (b) the hypotheses generated to explain the problem are assessed and confirmed or rejected; and (c) interventions related to the confirmed hypotheses are identified and developed while their potential acceptability, social validity, treatment integrity, and generalizability are concurrently evaluated.

3. The intervention stage involves (a) the development of the organization and its members' capacity to implement the intervention plan; (b) the identification of criteria to determine whether the intervention has been successful or not, the methods to evaluate this success, and an estimate of the amount of time needed to begin to see this success; (c) the actual implementation of the intervention plan; and (d) a determination of whether revisions or adaptations of the intervention are necessary to increase its effectiveness or to respond to unexpected outcomes.

4. Finally, the evaluation stage determines (a) formatively and summatively whether the goals of the problem-solving process and the intervention have been met; (b) how the intervention's implementation process was qualitatively perceived; (c) how long the intervention plan should be continued and if it needs to be changed, faded out, or discontinued as a function of continuing success; and (d) the degree to which the organization and its members can independently continue the intervention and whether ongoing consultation and problem solving are needed.

Significantly, individual schools attempting school reform must recognize that different parts of the school system use the same problem-solving process, yet they use this process in different time cycles (see Figure 1). This not only makes school-based reform a more complex process, especially if the school district is larger and more bureaucratic, but it reinforces the need for strategic planning. As an example, most schools do their budgeting and grade-level planning in 1-year, action-planning cycles. Often this planning begins by January or February at the latest and is completed no later than March, when the school must submit its budget to an assistant or area superintendent or to a business manager. From a school reform perspective, it is important to recognize the symbiotic relationship between school improvement goals and the budgeting process. While the ideal situation would be to have the goals determine how much of the total budget is dedicated to instruction and student progress, reality dictates that a lower than desired percentage of a school's budget will go to school reform and that schools must prioritize their goals according to the limited dollars provided. Another reality that must be integrated into the school reform process is that individual schools typically budget themselves on an annual basis. While businesses can set 5-year goals and budget accordingly, the annual nature of each school's budget and the lack of carryover funds make long-term goal setting and attainment very difficult.

Within a school, most grade-level teams (e.g., in an elementary school) or departments (e.g., in a high school) can respond to specific problems within 1 or 2 months (so long as they don't involve major financial expenditures), and they can determine the success of their problem solving often within 3 to 5 months. Moreover, most *teachers* in a classroom can respond to a situation, through effective problem solving, in a matter of 1 or 2 weeks, and then see the impact of their efforts within a month's time. The point here is that the closer one gets to the classroom level, the faster the problem-solving or action-planning cycle can occur. At a building level, problems are typically more complex: they often have budget, scheduling, or personnel implications, and thus the problem solving often requires many months and sometimes can only be addressed across school years.

At a district level, problem solving and action planning typically occur in 3- to 7-year cycles. Essentially, this means that school-based problems that require district-level change have to wait until the planning, budgeting, and implementation cycle phases in, and that some problems may be addressed by the district only if they occur across a significant number of schools. As an example, a school may find that the newly adopted reading series is not sensitive to the background and culture of its lower SES and at-risk students. Since most districts purchase their basic academic textbook series (e.g., in reading, math, and spelling) in at least 7-year cycles, this problem is likely to exist until the next series is adopted, unless the school chooses to expend a great deal of time and money to review and buy a new series. Even from a policy level, most school districts take from 2 to 4 years to implement any new policy if it involves acceptance, dissemination, training, and execution.

For a summary of this section, please refer to Figure 1, which diagrammatically shows the problem-solving process across the multiple time cycles that exist within a school district. From an organizational perspective, the strategic sequencing and integration of these cycles are critical, as is the district's capacity to streamline some of these cycles at times, while recognizing that not all change can occur immediately. Finally, the importance of the evaluation stage must be emphasized once again. If the desired outcomes of problem solving are not occurring, all four stages must be reviewed. More specifically, the wrong problem may have been identified or it may have been analyzed incorrectly, the wrong interventions may have been chosen or they may have been implemented without treatment integrity, or the evaluation methods themselves may be providing false negative readings when acceptable results actually have occurred.

Characteristics of an Operating School District

In order to facilitate organizational change and do strategic planing, school psychologists must understand the characteristics and interdependencies within an operating school district. With this understanding and an understanding of the developmental and critical events history of the school district, certain processes (such as specific power relationships, how decisions are made and by whom, and how particular people were appointed to their current positions) become more comprehensible, and others that are critical to the change process become more predictable. In the end, however, organizational change is not always a systematic, cause-and-effect process. Clearly it is always easier for a strong leader to facilitate change when entering a system in crisis, or near-crisis, or a system frustrated because of chronic inertia and mismanagement. Similarly, a well-developed strategic plan can be thwarted by a crisis event (e.g., a community's rejection of a bond issue, the death of an important staff person, or a natural crisis like a hurricane or a flood), which may completely derail the process for many years.

Below, the characteristics of an operating school district will be briefly described (see Figure 2). These have been adapted from Egan (1985), and they are organized in four major systems: the receiving system, the performance system, the human resources and people system, and the pervasive system variables. In total, the school system must be viewed as an ecological system that includes the home and the community, and it must be recognized that this ecological system both creates and identifies its own problems *and* has the resources and capacity for innovations to solve these problems.

The receiving system. The receiving system is comprised of our primary clients, the schoolchildren whom we serve, and our primary goal is to create and maintain an operating system that maximizes their social and academic development and progress. Critically, however, the organizational change and strategic planning process may identify secondary goals and interventions that involve other clients, such as families and younger preschool students, and that preventively help to support our primary goals. In fact, given our current poverty rate, the number of teenage and single parents, the increasing number of students who are not socially or academically prepared when they enter school, and the increasing number of full service schools, the inclusion of families and younger siblings in the school's receiving system makes eminent sense.

In analyzing the receiving system, the answers to a number of questions beyond "Who are our primary or targeted clients?" become critical. These questions include the following: What are our clients' needs? What do *they* identify as their own needs? What are their prescribed versus *felt* needs? What are their goals? How attainable do they feel that these goals are? From a strategic planning perspective, the answers to many of these questions will require both a client needs assessment and an analysis of at least the home and community environments, including their demographic histories. From an advocacy perspective, we need to make sure that we are integrating and reflecting the real needs, goals, and desires of our clients into our organizational change process, and that we are not choosing only those goals that are convenient or expedient. Significantly, advocates often are not members of the group they advocate for and thus sometimes never fully understand the group, remaining unaware of the group's subtle needs and reasons behind those needs.

The goals for this system are (a) to identify those client groups most related to the social and academic progress of the students in the school; (b) to understand the historical and environmental characteristics that impact this progress; (c) to analyze the client groups' strengths, weaknesses, resources, and limitations; and (d) to determine especially why the weaknesses exist, so that school reform goals can be targeted to them. In doing this, primary, secondary, and tertiary prevention interventions likely will emerge. Ultimately, however, the organizational change process should focus on primary and secondary interventions at system and building levels, and on providing educational personnel the skills and resources to implement the tertiary prevention interventions.

The performance system. The performance system involves the organizational and strategic planning aspects of a building's system that help it to reach its student-focused academic and social goals. Minimally, there are five elements to this system: the building's mission; the major aims or goals of the building that are consistent with and operationalized

FIGURE 1. Problem solving within school districts as correlated with time and planning cycles.

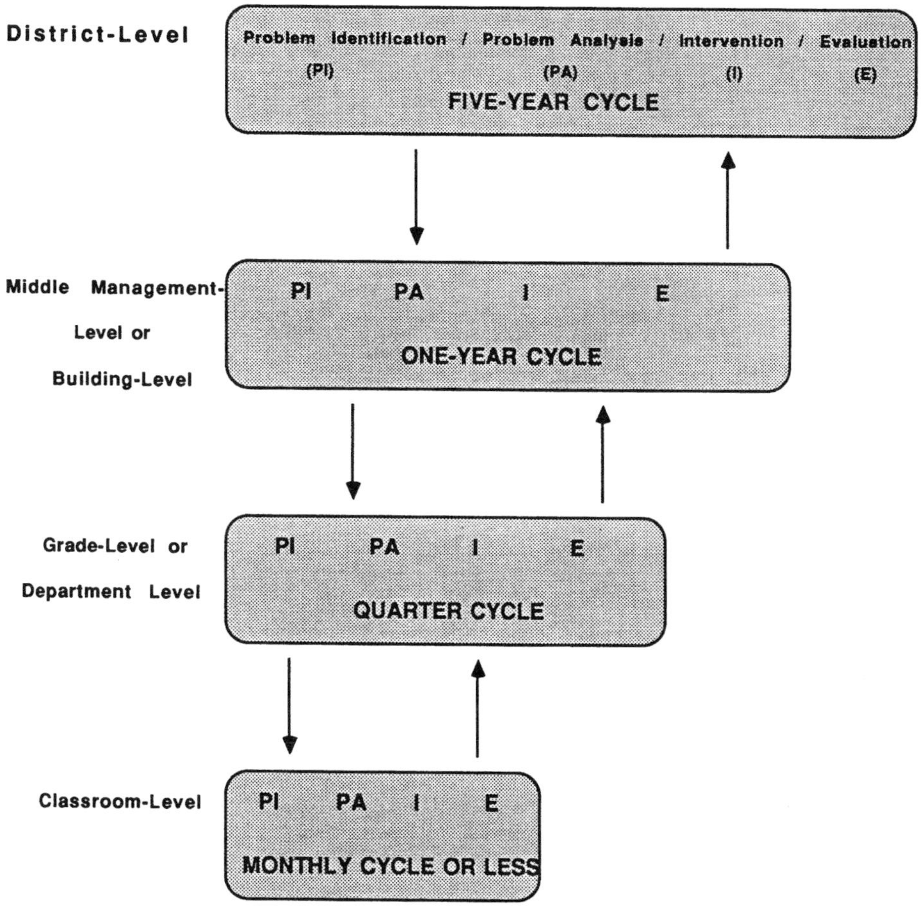

from the mission; the tasks, programs, or activities that will lead to the attainment of the aims; the materials and resources needed by the school's personnel to implement the programs or activities; and the specific outcomes that each program will accomplish, which again should cumulatively lead to the realization of the building's overall goals and the accomplishment of its mission.

A building's mission statement should identify the purpose for the organization's existence, its targeted "consumers," its desired outcomes, and how, within a particular philosophical framework, those outcomes will be attained. This mission statement should be brief, specific, and clear, but given its importance to the strategic planning process, it should not sacrifice length for its ability to communicate. Indeed, the mission statement should be the statement that all within the organization point to as their defining purpose, and it should be the crystallizing perspective that integrates the performance system with the receiving system. As such, in the strategic planning process the (re)development of the mission statement most often follows the organizational and needs assessment and

situational and environmental analysis steps. Below are two examples of mission statements, one from a school district and the other from a school building. Note that the building statement is somewhat more specific and tailored to its distinct population and circumstances.

> The General County School District is dedicated to enabling students to develop their individual capabilities for a lifetime of learning and for responsible, productive participation in a diverse and changing world.

> The Specific Elementary School will prepare each child to meet life's challenges by providing the best possible learning environment with the most effective methods and resources to ensure that each child will develop academically, socially, and aesthetically.

Often underlying the mission statement are a number of visions, philosophies, or beliefs agreed upon by the school as essential to everyone's acceptance of the mission statement. One set of beliefs, adapted from the Council of Administrators of Special Education's 1992 report, *A Future Agenda for*

FIGURE 2. A whole-system perspective for organizational assessment, strategic planning, and systems change. From *Change Agent Skills in Helping and Human Service Settings* (p. 51) by G. Egan, 1985, Monterey, CA: Brooks/Cole. Copyright 1985 by Brooks/Cole. Adapted with permission.

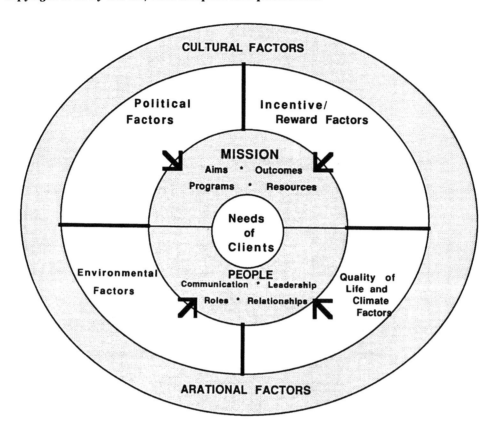

Special Education: Creating a Unified Education System, is as follows:

1. Everyone is responsible for the education of all students.

2. A unified system of education integrating regular and special education must prevail.

3. Accountability for all students is guaranteed through a system of unified outcomes.

4. All educators are prepared to educate all students.

5. Funding must support a unified system.

6. Site-based management is key.

7. A unified system requires a unified, yet flexible, curriculum that is shared among and with educators and that has specified outcomes.

8. Staff development encourages problem-solving, shared resources, and continuous improvement.

9. All families feel welcome and are involved in the schooling of their child.

10. All students and staff have access to and training in appropriate technology (p 2).

Clearly the development of the mission statement and the generation of the goals that operationalize the mission statement will come more easily to the staff that embraces many or all of these details.

As noted above, once the mission statement has been developed, the building should identify the major aims, programs, needed resources, and specific outcomes that will ensure building success. Often it makes sense to develop 3- or 5-year plans, specifying the major aims and outcomes only, and then a series of 1-year plans that, if implemented, will sequentially lead to the 3- or 5-year outcomes. The generation of these plans will be discussed below in the Strategic Planning Process section. For now, it is important to emphasize the importance of identifying a priori outcomes that are relevant, observable, and measurable so that formative evaluations can be applied periodically to determine whether the programs chosen are meeting their intermediate goals or if problem solving and special intervention for these programs, due to less-than-successful outcomes, are needed.

The human resources and people system. This system involves all of the human resources within a school that are needed to implement the programs and accomplish the work that the school has identified in its strategic plan. Significantly, however, human resources also include the personnel and process management of the individuals needed, so that the whole is greater than the sum of its parts. To this end, then, schools must evaluate and coordinate their staff people, their respective roles and responsibilities, their relationships both to each other and to the school's goals and programs, and the process variables (e.g., leadership, communication, and decision-making approaches) that make it all work together. Much of this, moreover, should be driven by the specific programs identified within the performance system, so that the entire school operating system becomes more integrated and better planned.

To expand briefly, the important components of the human resources and people system are as follows:

1. The necessary people in the system are identified by the client, program, and management needs of a building. Client needs typically involve both the educational and mental health needs of the students and related family needs. These needs may necessitate both a strong cadre of primary educators and an equally strong support network of support professionals — educational specialists in particular curricular areas and health and mental health specialists like school psychologists, social workers, and nurse practitioners. While program needs may involve both educational and mental health specialists, the point here is that the programs identified in the performance system must be staffed by individuals who can best meet the specified outcomes. At times, this will require hiring staff with special backgrounds and credentials; at other times, this will necessitate training the existing staff so that the programs have the highest probability of success.

Finally, the management needs of the building are also critical to the overall success of the building. These include personnel management and supervision, office and data management, transportation and food management, and grounds and security management. Once again, personnel to address the building's management needs could overlap with those dedicated to client and program needs. The issue ultimately becomes how these individuals are organized and the degree to which they are integrated and satisfied with the level of integration required.

2. As noted above, the specification of building, program, and activity roles and responsibilities is important to determine whether the knowledge and skills needed for success exist in the building. Two points are especially important here. First, relative to the academic and social progress of students, the professional title of the individual providing a program is basically irrelevant. What is relevant is that the individual has the ability to provide the desired skills. More specifically, if a building decides that an anger control group is needed for certain students, it mat-

ters little whether it is provided by a guidance counselor, a clinical social worker, a school psychologist, or a teacher with special training so long as an appropriately trained professional fulfills the need.

The second point is that staff training should always have three outcomes: the mastery of knowledge, the translation of that knowledge into functional skill, and the attainment of a high enough level of staff confidence for both the knowledge and skill levels to be maintained over time. Unfortunately, staff training often is limited to 1-day in-services that provide some knowledge but very little skill development and/or transfer into appropriate settings. Successful staff training provides both the foundation knowledge necessary to understand the topic at hand and the skill development and supervision in the settings where the knowledge will be applied. While this may involve a significant investment in staff time, it also will reinforce the importance of the in-service area, ensure that staff have the skills needed to independently use the information with, for example, their students, and develop a high enough level of staff confidence for them to be able to apply the skills to new situations and to train new staff over the years in the lessons learned.

In the end, the specification of the functional roles and responsibilities that a school needs to accomplish its goals is critical to both the building's personnel planning and development and to staff confidence and morale. While the division of labor and tasks could result in establishing new job descriptions, the use of broad and flexible job descriptions is recommended over those that link particular professions to stereotyped and overly specific jobs and activities. Ultimately, the skills, commitment, and personal interactions of the staff will more powerfully determine the building's success than the technical adequacy of the job description.

3. The relationships and process variables part of the human resources system qualitatively involves the monitoring and reinforcement of (a) the processes that integrate the needs of the client groups, the goals of the performance system, and the personnel who will get the job done; (b) the processes that create positive school and working climates; and (c) the processes that ensure good group interactions, sound communication, strong leadership, and appropriate decision making. In essence, the school psychologist working here is functioning as a process consultant (Schein, 1969) or a human relations specialist, but clearly this is not outside of any psychologist's area of expertise. To accomplish any task, one must always attend both to process and to content and outcomes. While content and outcome often determine whether a building has the skills or capacity to complete a goal, the process typically determines whether the skills are ever applied and the degree to which they are applied. The issue here is

productivity — does a staff have the motivation and coordination to accomplish more than would be predicted by their raw skills alone, or will they accomplish only the bare minimum without regard for the loss that entails for the students?

The pervasive system variables. The pervasive system variables are building, district, and community variables that impact the performance and human resources and people systems in both positive and potentially negative ways. In essence, these are the macro-level variables that can affect system morale, motivation, and satisfaction. At the same time, many buildings are able to insulate themselves from these variables as they impact at a district level, and create their own building-level variables so that they can accomplish far more than the dysfunctional district within which they exist. In total, there are six pervasive system variables. Briefly, they are:

1. The *incentive and reward factors* are those formal and informal factors that motivate teachers and other building and district staff people to accomplish their educational goals. The most formal of these factors are the contracts that staff people are working under, and the conditions under which those contracts were negotiated and accepted. Numerous studies and public polls over the years have found that salary schedules are not the most important motivating factor keeping our teachers and other educators in the classroom and profession (usually salary ranks anywhere from 4th to 7th). However, when appropriate raises are not forthcoming, when union-administration tension over a contract exists, and when strikes or other work stoppages occur, staff motivation can decrease and the collaborative relationship between teachers and administrators (including building principals) may suffer. Overall, this can significantly interfere with the organizational change and strategic planning process, and its residual effects may persist for many years after the original contractual conflict has ended.

On an informal level, building staff are most motivated by their own collaboration and accomplishments, their feeling that they are making a difference in their students' lives, their belief that they have some autonomy in determining what and how they want to teach, the building-level recognition that they receive from their peers, and the incentives available to them — for example, opportunities to participate in advanced training, district-level leadership activities, and innovative classroom and other programs. Critically, many of these informal yet powerful incentives and rewards should be identified by and integrated into the strategic planning process. One important incentive is the incentive of time. Many organizational change programs require in-service training and high levels of cooperation, and provide this training (through the use of substitute teachers and release days) during the school day with follow-up

grade-level and cross-grade-level team meetings that also meet during the school day. This provides teachers with both incentives and built-in rewards. Not only are they motivated by training that is specifically tailored to their needs, but they are rewarded when the training is successful and helps them to accomplish their goals more effectively and efficiently.

2. *Quality of life and climate factors* coexist, to a large degree, with the incentive and reward factors. Elements of these factors include those tangible and intangible needs that must be present in order to get the work of the building done (e.g., books, sufficient desks, supportive teacher-principal relationships, appropriate provisions for safety). All of these elements ultimately converge to create a positive (or negative) school climate that creates or supports the motivation and morale necessary for the incentive factors above. While there are many operational definitions of positive school climate and many, many school climate scales, a synthesis of the school climate areas most identified and used include (a) a safe and orderly environment, (b) a clear school mission with appropriate levels of planning and action and a good use of resources, (c) instructional leadership and smooth administration of the school, (d) opportunities for students to learn and stay on-task and high expectations for student social and academic achievement, (e) positive home–school relations and parent involvement, (f) student involvement and influence, (g) good teacher and staff morale, and (h) positive race relations.

3. *Environmental factors* include those community-based factors that directly or indirectly impact the management and organizational atmosphere of the school. These community-based factors include (a) the demographic and social, economic, governmental, and political status and circumstances of the neighborhood or broader community around the school and (b) issues related to population age and growth, families and households, minorities and race/ethnicity/gender status, crime, health, attitudes and values, personal income and employment, economic growth, housing, transportation, government income and expenditures, government support of the community and education, political participation, and philanthropy. In the context of strategic planning, many of these factors are evaluated in the context of an environmental scan or analysis. When doing this, the strengths, weaknesses, opportunities, and threats within the community, from the school's perspective, need to be appraised. Ultimately, the positive and negative impacts of the environment on the school must be determined and integrated into the strategic planning process. Clearly the environment potentially impacts the school's quality of life and available resources, as well as the needs of both the clients and the staff.

Mention must be made of special events and circumstances that concurrently impact a community and its schools. Unfortunately, the best examples of these events tend to be catastrophic, but clearly less intense circumstances also can be significant. As examples, one might recognize the economic, personal, and emotional impacts of such events as hurricanes Hugo and Andrew, the San Francisco/Oakland earthquakes, the Midwest floods of 1993, and other such natural disasters, and the more generic but now-too-frequent killings of and violence against schoolchildren in our classrooms and on our school grounds. These "environmental" events affect the day-to-day and year-to-year lives of our students and schools as much as the ever-present demographic and economic factors within our communities. In fact, many of these events have a more long-standing and subtle impact over time, and thus, it is important for us to strategically address and plan for them so that we can prevent their long-term effects and turn their presence into opportunities for learning and prevention.

4. *Political factors* occur both within a school district or building and outside of district or in the community. While the within-district factors are implicit in the incentive and climate factors above, the out-of-district facets are particularly pertinent here. These political factors involve ways that outside stakeholders in the system utilize their formal and informal power (in overt and covert ways) to influence the status and direction of the schools. At a macrosystem level, these political factors include local governmental (e.g., financial or morale) support, the impact of school boards and their elections, the selection or election of the superintendent, the participation of the business community indirectly or through, for example, business partnerships, and the involvement of advocacy and special interest groups. At a building level, they additionally include the involvement of the Parent Teacher Association, influential parents and community leaders, and specific client groups to the degree that they are organized or command attention.

It must be noted that while politics often is considered negative and intrusive, this does not have to be the case. In fact, through a strategic planning process, government, business, and other community leaders can be integrated into a comprehensive and integrated plan of action so that the political system can be directly used to support the broader goals of the school and school district. In the end, most communities are willing to commit time, funds, and energy to a process when clear goals are identified and important outcomes are (potentially) realized. This is the typical and expected outcome of the organizational change process, and this process often can rise above a political system bent more on power and influence than equity and excellence.

5. *Cultural factors* within a school or school system involve the stated and unstated values, beliefs, assumptions, norms, policies, and rules that affect the productivity of the school or system and its quality of life. Like any complex organization, a school goes through specific life stages that reflect its development, personnel, clients, and goals and objectives. With the introduction of a new principal, with the turnover of significant staff members, with shifts in demographics, with new mandates from state or district levels, the school adjusts, develops new norms and procedures, and redefines its culture or way of doing business. Without the understanding of a school's culture, organizational change is more difficult, random, and tenuous. With this understanding, the positive aspects of the culture can be utilized and the weaker aspects isolated, minimized, or changed.

6. The *arational factors* within a system involve those dysfunctional, skewed, and unchangeable characteristics that interfere with the system's progress if allowed. While these characteristics typically can be identified and understood, they cannot be changed — or at least their change will take a monumental effort. These characteristics include system resistance, inertia, self-interest, unpredictability, emotionality, rejection of data, hidden agendas, and many more. At the very least, arational factors must be identified so that people within the system can agree to ignore or circumvent them and not be frustrated by their presence. At the very most, arational factors might be so strong within a system that organizational change should not be attempted. Given the latter situation, one organizational option is to literally dismantle the system so that a new and improved system can replace it.

Strategic Planning Process

Strategic planning is a systematic process that increasingly is being used in education to help schools and school districts to anticipate and plan their future directions while considering both internal and community-based strengths, weaknesses, threats, and opportunities. Designed to promote and encourage teamwork, strategic planning involves a number of systematic activities that initially may take a year or more to get into place. Nonetheless, once implemented, strategic planning often takes considerably less time as it (a) develops and monitors the programs and activities designed to meet the system's mission and goals, (b) tracks their progress over time, (c) makes midcourse adjustments, and (d) attempts to anticipate other, future events that may impact the school or school district in its pursuit of educational excellence. Ultimately, strategic planning introduces a systems perspective to education that emphasizes planning, cost- and time-efficiency, and maximum resource utilization. In the long run, it can help a school or school district identify and rededicate itself to its primary mission and goals, and ensure that these goals are met effectively and efficiently.

Cook (1990) and Valentine (1993) provide two overlapping perspectives on how strategic planning should occur. Cook divides the strategic planning process into five phases: Phase I, creating a base for planning and change; Phase II, developing the strategic plan; Phase III, developing the implementation plan; Phase IV, implementing and monitoring the plan; and Phase V, renewing the plan. During Phase I, the school or district engages in the following activities:

1. An external environmental scan and analysis through which (a) economic, demographic, social, political, and education trends are analyzed; (b) national, state, regional, and local patterns in the trend areas above are evaluated; (c) scenarios that predict future environmental events and their impact on the school are created; and (d) school-based responses to the most likely scenarios, consistent with the school's resources and capabilities, are generated.

2. An internal organizational scan and analysis through which the strengths (or assets), weaknesses (or limitations), resources (or opportunities), and barriers within the school are identified, guided by the organizational map described above and depicted in Figure 2.

3. An analysis of stakeholder perceptions and expectations (as described earlier) whereby client needs and community (political) goals are identified.

4. A community education process that ties the entire process together (a) by helping the community to understand the data collected, the trends and scenarios identified, and the need for strategic planning and change; and (b) by involving the community and its stakeholders as equal partners in the remaining phases of this planning and change process.

In Phase II, the strategic plan is written by taking the results of the external and internal scans and sequentially developing a vision statement, a mission statement, strategic goals, and an outline of the implementation plan. This plan is then reviewed by members of the planning team, by critical client and stakeholder groups, and by others who might be either politically or functionally important to the implementation process. Ultimately, the feedback from this review process is synthesized and evaluated, and a revision of the strategic plan is "finalized." According to Cook (1990), the Phase II process should take approximately 3 months, and even then it is to be expected that the plan will be adapted over time.

In Phase III, the implementation plan is formalized through the development of districtwide and building-level plans. It is at this point that the coordination of the planning and budgeting time cycles shown in Figure 1 become critical. Relatedly, the implementation plan actually involves three components: a 3- to 5-year strategic operational plan, an annual operational plan, and a series of individual performance plans for each personnel unit involved in the implementation process (United Way of America, 1989). More specifically, the strategic operational plan should contain a series of operational goals and goal statements, a prioritization of these goals, the organizational unit(s) or department(s) responsible for each goal, the 3- to 5-year time frame for the completion of each goal, and the 3- to 5-year costs of the activities needed to accomplish each goal. The annual operational plan should identify, for each operational goal or subgoal, the action steps needed to accomplish the goal, the key results expected, the individuals responsible for taking the action steps, the resources and budget needed, the timelines (including beginning and end dates) required, and the evaluative process to determine the goal's attainment. Finally, an individual performance plan should involve (a) a performance planning section with areas of responsibility, operational goals, action steps to achieve the goals, and goals priorities specified; and (b) a performance review section to document actual achievements, levels of goal achievement, continuing responsibilities, and overall performance ratings.

In Phase IV, the strategic plan is implemented and monitored using the annual operational plans and the individual performance plans. As activities are completed and subgoals are accomplished, it may be necessary to adapt some timelines, budgets, responsibilities, or even some operational goals. This should be expected, and the revisions should be made with as much care paid to planning as when the original strategic plan was developed.

Finally, in Phase V, the renewal of the strategic plan is addressed. At this point, the school typically has accomplished a great deal, and yet it must determine whether its strategic direction is still valid. To do this, the school and planning team should review changes in the external and internal environmental conditions, review the mission statement and strategic goals, refocus the strategic plan as necessary, and renew the organization's commitment and energies toward the next level of accomplishment.

Valentine (1991) organizes her strategic planning process into five levels: Level 1, the preplanning stage of the planning process; Level 2, redefining the organization's direction; Level 3, developing the strategic mind-set; Level 4, implementing goals, objectives, and strategies; and Level 5, reassessing and institutionalizing the change process (see Figure 3). While Valentine's strategic planning process appears more complex and comprehensive than Cook's (1990), hers is actually just a descriptive expansion. Thus, it is instructive to review her process as shown in Figure 3 and compare it to Cook's approach above. In the end, every facet of Valentine's model has already been described. It does, however, provide a good summary to this section of the chapter.

FIGURE 3. Valentine's strategic management and planning model. From *Strategic Management and Education: A Focus on Strategic Planning* (p. 64) by E. P. Valentine, 1991, Boston: Allyn & Bacon. Copyright 1991 by Allyn & Bacon. Adapted with permission.

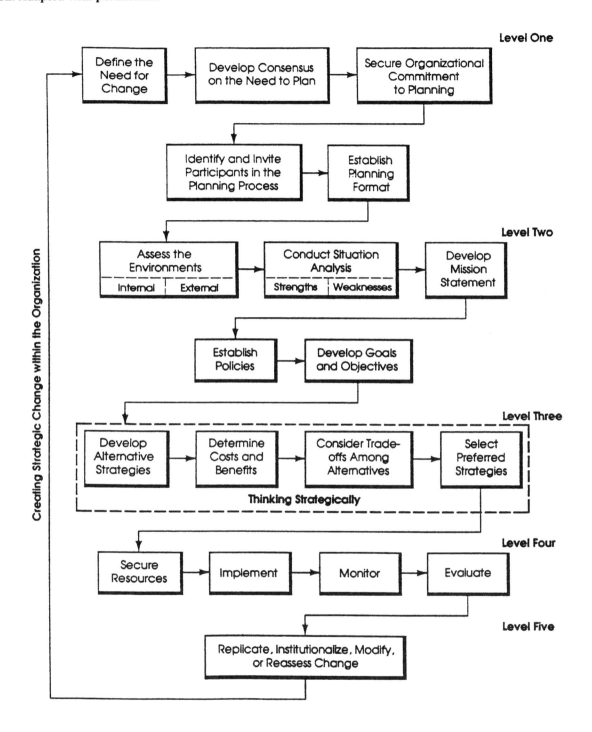

BEST PRACTICES IN THE AREA

From a strategic planning perspective, much of the discussion above has identified the critical steps and best practices in facilitating school-based organizational development and change. From a school psychological perspective, what remains is a discussion of the steps that school psychologists need to take in order to actually implement the change process. This will be discussed in five phases: Phase I, initiating the strategy; Phase II, preparing for implementation; Phase III, training for program implementation; Phase IV, implementing the planned change process; and Phase V, evaluating the planned change process.

In Phase I, the school psychologist makes an administrative entrance into the school with the express goal of facilitating the strategic planning and organizational change process. While this process often requires a series of meetings for relationship building and the clarification of change goals and objectives, it can move more quickly when the administration has a sound grasp of the organization's strengths and weaknesses and a commitment to true change. In accomplishing the tasks of this phase, the school psychologist should do the following:

1. Meet with the principal and/or the administrative team

2. Orient the administrative staff and other key personnel to the conceptual underpinnings of strategic planning and organizational change and describe its goals, strategies, and likely outcomes

3. Obtain administrative approval to proceed with the process and contractually agree on the official goals, outcomes, and timelines needed

4. Identify the key participants who, with the principal, will facilitate the planned change process

5. Begin to learn as much as possible about the organization, including its organizational structure and personnel, formal and informal rules and norms, policies and procedures, and organizational history and environment

During this phase, the school psychologist must determine (a) whether the building is ready for strategic planning, (b) whether she or he has the skills and resources to facilitate this particular change process, and (c) whether she or he wants to be the facilitator. In making these decisions and in managing the entry process embedded in Phase I, the school psychologist should do the following:

1. Assess his or her personal skills and the organization's history of change efforts before agreeing to lead the consultation process

2. Specify, at least informally, the amount of time, effort, and money that may be needed to complete different parts of the planning and change

3. Clarify potential goal differences (e.g., administrative- versus staff-driven change, crisis- versus prevention-motivated change, outcome versus process change) between the school psychologist and the administration

4. Establish a written or verbal contract with the administration, making sure that outcomes, timelines, and areas of responsibility are explicit

5. Emphasize that change is sequential and time-oriented, and that the ultimate goals are system efficacy and the ability to anticipate and prevent future problems

6. Emphasize and communicate the complexity of the consultation relationship relative to both staff and administration, discussing especially issues of dependency, authority, confidentiality, and competence

In Phase II, the school psychologist begins the preparations for implementing the planned change process by making a formal entry with the building staff. At this point, the staff complete the same groundwork done earlier with the administration, and the process from the environmental analysis and organizational assessment through the development of action plans is begun. In accomplishing the tasks of this phase, the school psychologist does the following:

1. Reenters the building at the staff level

2. Orients the staff to the concepts, goals, and strategies of the planned change process

3. Obtains staff agreement as to their participation, desires, and expected outcomes

4. Identifies formal and informal key stakeholders and organizational gatekeepers

5. Does a preliminary study of the building's organizational climate and climate change potential and its current mode of operation and functioning

6. Establishes a strategic planning team that represents a cross section of the staff to facilitate the organizational change process

7. Completes the environmental analysis, organizational assessment, and other facets of the strategic planning process

By Phase III, the annual operational plans should be complete, and the school psychologist has identified the training needed by the building in order for the strategic plan to succeed. For example, given the goal of improving the social and academic skills of students in an elementary school, the staff may identify the need for social skills training, a curriculum-based assessment process tied to curricular interventions, and a parent-involvement program. At this point the training program must be delivered so that staff have the knowledge, skill, and confidence to implement the various facets of the plan. During this process, the school psychologist also should monitor the staff's commitment and reactions to the training and the building's changing group climate. Critically, the school psychologist *should not* proceed to the actual implementation of the planned change process until all of the staff are trained in the needed skills and components.

In Phase IV, the planned change process is fully implemented, and in Phase V the process is formatively and summatively evaluated, looking at both outcome variables (e.g., increases in student achievement, decreases in student retentions and suspensions) and process variables (e.g., satisfaction with the change process, improvements in school climate). During these phases, the school psychologist should attend and respond to potential staff and administrative resistance, while ensuring that building personnel develop skills in the planned change process itself so that they are able to independently manage and renew the process over time. In the end, three questions become critical: Are we accomplishing our goals? Are we doing our job? How are we doing the job?

SUMMARY

This chapter has focused on the important steps and procedures that facilitate school-based organizational change and strategic planning. After providing a context and the assumptions reinforcing the need for such change and planning, the stages of problem solving were described, focusing on both the individual school and the school district. The importance of coordinating the change process with a district's various planning and budgeting cycles was emphasized, and the characteristics of an operating school district were described by analyzing the receiving system, the performance system, the human resources and people system, and the pervasive system variables. Two perspectives of strategic planning were introduced with five phases being typical: Phase I, creating a base for planning and change; Phase II, developing the strategic plan; Phase III, developing the implementation plan; Phase IV, implementing and monitoring the plan; and Phase V, renewing the plan. The chapter concluded with a discussion of the steps that school psychologists need to consider as they implement organizational change and strategic planning at the building level.

Throughout this chapter, it has been assumed that school psychologists can and should be primary facilitators in the organizational change and strategic planning process. As noted in the introduction, today's children are coming to the schoolhouse door significantly at risk for both educational and social failure. School psychologists are the best trained mental health and educational specialists in the

schools today. We must take the responsibility for guiding our schools through the reform process begun in 1983. We must make sure that the next generation of schoolchildren is prepared to succeed — not only at the schoolhouse door, but when passing through that door and entering the workforce and our communities.

REFERENCES

Bacharach, S. B. (1990). *Education reform: Making sense of it all.* Boston: Allyn & Bacon.

Children's Defense Fund. (1990). *Children 1990: A report card, briefing book, and action primer.* Washington, DC: Author.

Cook, W. J. (1990). *The planning discipline.* Cambridge, MA: Cambridge Management Group.

Council of Administrators of Special Education. (1992). *A future agenda for special education: Creating a unified education system.* Albuquerque, NM: Author.

Egan, G. (1985). *Change agent skills in helping and human service settings.* Monterey, CA: Brooks/Cole.

Heller, K., Holtzman, W., & Messick, S. (Eds.). (1982). *Placing children in special education: A strategy for equity.* Washington, DC: National Academy Press.

National Commission on Excellence in Education. (1983). *A nation at risk: The imperative for educational reform.* Washington, DC: Author.

Quinby, N. (1985). Improving the place called school: A conversation with John Goodlad. *Educational Leadership, 42,* 17–21.

Sarason, S. B. (1990). *The predictable failure of educational reform: Can we change before it's too late?* San Francisco: Jossey-Bass.

Schein, E. H. (1969). *Process consultation: Its role in organization development.* Reading, MA: Addison-Wesley.

Sergiovanni, T. J., & Moore, J. H. (1989). *Schooling for tomorrow: Directing reforms to issues that count.* Boston: Allyn & Bacon.

United Way of America. (1989). *Strategic management and the United Way.* Alexandria, VA: Author.

Valentine, E. P. (1991). *Strategic management in education: A focus on strategic planning.* Boston: Allyn & Bacon.

ANNOTATED BIBLIOGRAPHY

Bacharach, S. B. (1990). *Education reform: Making sense of it all.* Boston: Allyn & Bacon.
An important edited summary and analysis of the historical elements of the school reform movement since the *Nation at Risk* report, with some interesting and critical projections as to where we will be in the next decade. Written by over 30 of the best minds in school reform, the book is separated into seven units. An Overview of Education Reform; Actors in Reform; Defining Good Education: A Political Battleground with Too Many Casualties; Redefining Good Education: Preparing Students for Tomorrow; One Structural Remedy: Public Choice; Creating Better Choices within Schools; The Role of Teachers; What Hath Reform Wrought?

Egan, G. (1985). *Change agent skills in helping and human service settings.* Monterey, CA: Brooks/Cole.
A little-known book for anyone who hopes to intervene strategically in the schools. Based on the problem that "professionals often intervene in systems and manage them without ever having been trained to do so" (p. vi), the book provides a compre-

hensive picture and analysis of the functioning parts of the school, school district, and school culture. In order, Egan describes the performance system, the people, and the pervasive variables that impact the school, along with ways to assess the school and community environments, to manage school personnel for success, and to create the reward and incentive systems that help schools to work.

Sarason, S. B. (1990). *The predictable failure of educational reform: Can we change before it's too late?* San Francisco: Jossey-Bass.

Sarason, in his inimitable style, analyzes the American school system and its culture to determine whether the school reform process has any hope of success. Based on his experiences and interactions in the schools and with his typical incisive and no-holds-barred style, Sarason identifies the many pitfalls at the school level that, if left unattended, predict the failure of the current reform process. He maintains that educators do not understand the reform process, they are not willing to change the entire system, they do not want to deal with the issue of power between teachers and administrators, and they do not recognize that, unless pushed, individuals will do the least amount of reforming to get by.

Valentine, E. P. (1991). *Strategic management in education: A focus on strategic planning.* Boston: Allyn & Bacon.

This "book" (which is actually sold in a three-ring binder) provides a comprehensive strategic management model that is de

signed to assist the reader in guiding a school district through the strategic planning process. Supported by case studies and citations from the management literature, the book has three parts: Strategic Management – Its Role in Education, Planning for Strategic Change, and Creating Strategic Change Within the Organization. In addition, the book has over 30 step-by-step worksheets that operationalize the process and make the author's approach an easy one for anyone who understands the interdependent components of the school system to implement. This is a useful book that can help a reader to more completely understand the inner workings of strategic planning.

United Way of America. (1989). *Strategic management and the United Way.* Alexandria, VA: Author.

If you ever wondered why the United Way is so successful, this will answer your question. In this systematic eight-booklet set, the United Way describes in detail how to apply strategic management to communitywide planning and nonprofit administration. The booklets divide strategic planning into a six-step process that includes environmental analysis, organizational assessment, strategic direction setting, the formation of strategic plans, implementation, and performance evaluation. Supplemented by the introductory and the final "putting it all together" booklets, the set provides the reader with a comprehensive and practical resource that provides important insight and sequential procedures to the design and implementation of organizational analysis, strategic positioning, and change.

23

Best Practices in Supporting Home–School Collaboration

Sandra L. Christenson
University of Minnesota

Families and teachers might wish that the school could do the job alone. But today's school needs families, and today's families need the school. In many ways, this mutual need may be the greatest hope for change.

Dorothy Rich
p. 62, *Schools and Families:
Issues and Actions*

There are no pat answers — developing partnerships between parents and schools was found to be a difficult task requiring organizational, interpersonal, and training skills. The process of joining schools and parents requires that each school ask: What forms of parent participation are desirable; and what strategies can be employed to achieve them? Schools failed to realize they needed to ask and to answer those questions based on their particular school's needs, history, and resources. Schools came to understand that there were no "pat" answers and that parent participation needed to have parent-school collaboration as its ultimate goal in order to be effective.

Sharon Lynn Kagan
p. 21, *Parent involvement Research:
A Field in Search of Itself*

One of the best-kept secrets in Washington is that families are educators' most powerful ally.

Theodora Ooms
p. i, *The Family-School Partnership: A Critical
Component of School Reform*

Developing partnerships between home and school to enhance the competence of children and youth takes a concerted effort. Positive family-school connections are not automatic; however, they are essential to children's optimal success in school and must become a major focus within educational restructuring efforts. There are new directions in parent involvement, which often require schools to change their practices. The quotes by Rich (1987a) and Kagan (1984) illustrate the current rhetoric about family-school relationships, that is, the need for mutual sup-

port and collaborative problem solving to address educational and developmental concerns for children and youth. Oom's quite (cited in Ooms & Hara, 1991), suggests that educators' perceptions of family power may be challenged by these new directions. To help meet these challenges, this chapter provides (a) a definition and rationale for home-school collaboration; (b) barriers to home-school collaboration and challenges for parents and educators, which are framed as essential partnership principles; and (c) *content* knowledge, such as guidelines for supporting home-school collaboration and examples of home-school collaboration strategies and *process* or "how-to" knowledge for developing home-school partnerships. The literature on home-school partnerships has expanded tenfold in the last 5 years; therefore, information in this chapter must be considered a summary, and the reader is encouraged to consult the resources listed in the annotated bibliography.

OVERVIEW

Home-school collaboration is an attitude, not simply an activity. It occurs when parents and educators share common goals, are seen as equals, and both contribute to the process. It is sustained with a "want-to" motivation from all individuals rather than an "ought-to" or "obliged-to" orientation (Christenson, Rounds, & Franklin, 1992). Hence, home-school collaboration is not (a) parents only in schools as volunteers, who are directed by the school's agenda; (b) parents serving on advisory councils and educators not listening to their needs or concerns; (c) parent-teacher conferences that are a one-way exchange of information; (d) school-to-home contacts only when a student is failing or no home-to-school contact when the parent is concerned; (e) co-location of services with no collaboration; or (f) parent education programs determined by educators to be important for parents (Collins, Moles, & Cross, 1982). Nor is home-school collaboration the one-way delivery of services to parents. Rather, home-school collaboration or meaningful parent participation in education is the establishment of a mutual goal or shared agenda between educators and parents to improve educational outcomes for students. Ideally, home-school collaboration assumes parents and educators act as advocates and decision makers in the schools and that parents are key resources to improve their own children's education and the schooling of all children (Fruchter, Galletta, & White, 1992).

Home-school collaboration requires recognition by all involved that educational outcomes are influenced by events in the home, by events in school, and by the continuity between home and school environments (Hansen, 1986). Thus, the child's opportunity to learn includes what goes on in home and school, and the goal of home-school collaboration is to create an ethos for learning across these environments. Peter Usdan, President of the Educational Development Institute, has provided the most focused rationale for educators to create home-school partnerships for student productivity in school. At the 1989 Presidential Summit, Usdan reported that 91% of children's time from birth to age 18 is spent outside of school (cited in Ooms & Hara, 1991). In addition, educators know that there is "no pure" family or school time; a reciprocal, mutually influencing quality exists between children's home and school experiences.

The empirical basis for developing home-school partnerships to enhance student learning is strong (Christenson et al., 1992). First, benefits for all key stakeholders — students, teachers, parents, and schools — have been described in numerous integrative literature reviews; however, student outcomes are the primary reason for parents and educators to form a partnership. The literature supports the correlation between parent involvement and the following student outcomes: improvement in grades, test scores, attitudes, self-concept, and behavior; increased completion of assigned homework; higher rates of academic engagement and attendance; and a reduction in suspension rates (Henderson, 1989). Home support for learning — or what Walberg (1984) has labeled the curriculum of the home — "predicts academic learning twice as well as the socioeconomic status of families" (p. 400). The curriculum of the home includes informed parent-child conversations about everyday events, encouragement and discussion of leisure reading, monitoring and joint analysis of television viewing, expression of affection, interest in children's academic and personal growth, delay of immediate gratifications to accomplish long-term goals, realistic expectations and use of effort attributions, and structuring learning opportunities at home. Sloane (1991) succinctly described the conclusion by researchers about the effect of parent involvement on children's educational performance when she stated: "It is now well accepted that the home plays an important role in children's learning and achievement. *Some* [italics added] children learn

values, attitudes, skills, and behaviors in the home that prepare them well for the tasks of school" (p. 145).

The issue of equity is apparent. We know that home-based learning programs have been successful in improving the educational status of children across different grade and income levels (Graue, Weinstein, & Walberg, 1983). Furthermore, the benefits of home support for learning are evident for a large nationally representative sample of students who participated in the National Educational Longitudinal Study. In their analysis of that study's data, Keith et al. (1993) found that parent involvement correlated with eighth graders' success in all academic areas, in part due to the increased homework completed by students whose parents were involved in their schooling. Because much of the literature is correlational in nature, it is important to remember that families are potential facilitators, not determinants, of their children's success. Nor does parent involvement in education entail shifting educational responsibilities from the school to the home. Rather, schools are more successful when they involve the home and also teach effectively. Seeley (1985) ably describes this concept of partnership as a common effort toward a common goal and contends that the product of education is not produced by schools — but by students with the support of parents, teachers, peers, and community professionals. How then can school psychologists work with families as partners to enhance students' active engagement and productivity in schools? A primary theme of this chapter is that the elements of collaboration and a problem-solving approach between parents and educators are essential.

BASIC CONSIDERATIONS

Researches have shown that today's most effective schools are those that emphasize a respect for family diversity and a desire to connect with *all* families for greater student success (Swap, 1992). Parents and educators are just beginning to learn about essential partnership characteristics. School psychologists who facilitate home-school collaboration need knowledge about the functioning of systems, family-school partnership principles, and home-school collaboration strategies as well as the ability to facilitate problem solving. Respect for family diversity and a belief that parents are partners in — not problems for — intervention are essential. In this section, four broad features of the field, barriers for parents and educators, and home-school partnership principles are described.

Features

Four features characterize home-school collaboration:

1. Home and school are two microsystems that are used to operating autonomously. This, in part, explains the blaming that occurs between the two systems when a child is having difficulty in school. It is much easier to point "the finger of blame" at the other microsystem when one knows only about the child's behavior in his or her own microsystem. Plus, one does not need to live with the consequences of the recommendations made for the other microsystem.

2. Home-school collaboration is not restricted to a specific area. Rather, home-school collaboration can be used to address a child-specific academic, behavioral, or social concern, as well as systems-level concerns such as homework, discipline, and school violence.

3. Home-school collaboration is considered primarily a preventive activity. Although the best practices articulated in this chapter are applicable to conflicting situations between home and school, the focus of home-school collaboration is ongoing dialogue and support between parents and educators to increase student success and, therefore, prevent conflict and alienation.

4. Home-school collaboration is not synonymous with parent-teacher relationships. Clearly the parent-teacher relationship is critical to student success and an important part of home-school collaboration. However, home is conceived of broadly and refers to the primary caregiver or the school contact individual in a student's home, which may be a parent, grandparent, older sibling, or neighbor. Similarly, school refers to educators, such as teachers, principals, and support personnel, all of whom contribute to the success of students.

Barriers

A basic consideration in supporting home-school collaboration is to identify barriers for parents and educators. Liontos (1992) has identified several barriers for parents and educators. Barriers for parents include feelings of inadequacy; previous bad experiences with schools; suspicion about treatment from institutions; limited knowledge about school policies, procedures, or ways to assist with schoolwork; and economic (e.g., transportation, daycare) and emotional (e.g., daily survival) constraints. Barriers for educators include inadequate commitment to parent involvement; dwelling on family problems (e.g., "These parents have too many problems of their own to get involved"); crisis-oriented or negative communication with parents; stereotyping parents as uneducated or dysfunctional; and lack of training in ways to work with families as partners. It is also important to consider other barriers for the partnership, such as limited time for communication; frequency of ritualized contact (e.g., parent-teacher conferences, back-

to-school nights); differences in parent-professional perceptions; lack of funding; and lack of clarity about parents' and educators' roles and responsibilities (Leitch & Tangri, 1988; Mendoza & Cegelka, cited by Chrispeels, 1987; Swap, 1993).

Educators' practices for involving parents are crucial. Educators can invite parents into the school or reach out to parents by going to their home or community. Too often, educators will want parents to come to them, rather than going to the parents (Davies, 1991). According to Epstein (1992), if schools do not work to involve parents, then parent education and income level are important for deciding which parents become involved. If schools reach out to all parents, income level and parents' level of education decrease or disappear as important factors. Based on her research, Epstein speculates that "only a relatively small percentage of parents have personal problems so severe that they cannot work cooperatively with educators, given the proper assistance" (cited in Jennings, 1990, p. 21). To develop partnerships between parents and educators, barriers must be identified, acknowledged, understood, and systematically removed. Barriers should be reframed as challenges for parents and educators, who need time to engage in ongoing dialogue and problem solving about children's needs.

Home-School Partnership Principles

The five factors supported by the National School Public Relations Association (Ross, 1988) and found in successful parent involvement programs are climate, relevance, convenience, publicity, and commitment. In these successful programs, educators (a) welcomed all parents and, essentially, gave them the VIP treatment; (b) developed programs, such as workshops, based on parent input and need; (c) removed transportation and daycare barriers, making it more convenient for parents to be involved; (d) communicated with parents in multiple ways, such as a prearranged telephone chain, personal invitations, flyers, and newsletters; and (e) were committed to working with parents, which meant it was a priority school goal. Grassroots efforts to create partnerships consistently find relevance of the program or parent ownership to be a critical variable in parental involvement (e.g., Menning, 1993). Parents are involved because it is their program and meets their needs with their child.

The nine family-school partnership principles delineated by Ooms and Hara (1991) from the Family Impact Seminar in Washington, DC, underscore the seminal importance of commitment by educators. Each principle is illustrated with examples of school practices from the League of Schools Reaching Out Project (Davies, 1991):

1. *Every aspect of the school building and general climate is open, helpful, and friendly to parents.* Examples include use of "Parents are Welcome" signs and a parent center where parents meet and obtain information on child development, schools, and home learning support.

2. *Communications with parents — whether about school policies and programs or about their own children — are frequent, clear, and two way.* Examples include wall calendars with important school-related information and home-learning activities, teachers calling home to introduce themselves and giving parents a phone number and time when they can be reached, and Friday folders sent home weekly and returned with parental comments. Communication strategies are explained to all parents, not merely implemented.

3. *Parents are treated by teachers as collaborators in the educational process. Parents' own knowledge, expertise, and resources are valued as essential to their children's success in school.* Examples include schools developing learning contracts for students in collaboration with and signed by parents and parents monitoring homework after parent workshops on the topic have been conducted.

4. *The school recognizes its responsibility to forge a partnership with all families in the schools, not simply those most easily available.* Examples include varying times for conferences or open houses to accommodate needs of employed parents, conducting home visits and church visits in minority and immigrant communities, and providing interpreters.

5. *The school principal and other administrators actively express in words and deeds the philosophy of partnership with all families.* Examples include one in-service day per year to help educators learn to work with families as partners or provision of daycare for special events so parents can attend.

6. *The school encourages volunteer support and help from all parents by providing a wide variety of volunteer options including those that can be done from home and during nonwork hours.* For example, a school principal announces that parents are necessary for student success and that parents should provide some kind of volunteer assistance to the school. A list of 30 different options for parent choice is provided, and follow-up phone calls are made to obtain optimal parent participation.

7. *The school provides opportunities for parents to meet their needs for information, advice, and peer support.* Examples include parent support groups developed with PTA/PTO support and district funding of parent centers.

8. *Parents' views and expertise are sought in developing policies and solving school-wide problems; in some schools parents are given important decision-making responsibilities at a policy level.* Examples include a parent-educator committee to review and monitor the development of a broad-based health and sexual education program and the school-site council, as part of school-based management, to administer the school's discretionary funds.

9. *Schools recognize that they can best help parents provide a home environment conducive to children's learning if they facilitate their access to basic and supportive services.* Examples include collaboration with community agencies for before- and after-school care on site and a family services center in the school, which provides basic health screening, counseling, adult literacy and education courses, and clothing exchanges.

In closing, it should be apparent from these principles that educators need to examine their current practices with parents. *The partnership principles emphasize schools reaching out to all parents and initiating efforts at every grade level to involve parents in learning activities, school programs, and school-related decisions.* Furthermore, a no-fault model, where blame is not placed on either the home or school, is emphasized. New beliefs about parents and families are evident: All families have strengths, parents care about their children and can learn new techniques, and parents have important perspectives about their children (Liontos, 1992). By fostering collaboration — or the forming of a relationship with parents where parents and educators agree to work together and share responsibility for student outcomes — school psychologists can turn those beliefs into action.

Successful programs require an infrastructure. For home-school collaboration, this means the formal connection of schools to the rest of society — family, home, and environments outside of school in which children spend most of their time (Rich, 1988). Rich suggests ways to build this infrastructure: Launch a media campaign about parents as educators, train teachers to work with families as partners, provide ways for families to help each other (e.g., parent-support groups supervised by school psychologists), involve senior citizens and the larger community, and provide learning activities that families can use with children. Clearly, the way families and educators presently interact will need to be altered. And, because there have been few links between home and school, collaboration will not be easy. School psychologists interested in developing and supporting home-school collaboration to increase student success in school will find they need both content and process knowledge.

BEST PRACTICES

Content Knowledge: Guidelines for Supporting Home-School Collaboration

Based on intervention studies designed to develop home-school partnerships (Christenson, Thurlow, Sinclair, & Evelo, 1993; Davies, 1991), five essential guidelines for supporting home-school collaboration are evident. Although both parents' and educators' attitudes are integral to the success of the partnership, researchers have shown that the school's attitudes and practices are the stimulus for partnerships. School practices, or how schools reach out to parents, were determined by Epstein and Dauber (1991) to be more important determinants of parent participation in education than were parents' educational, socioeconomic, or ethnic backgrounds. Jean Krasnow (1990), who is associated with the League of Schools Reaching Out Project, has described how schools — more than the families — are in a position to create the conditions that erect barriers to greater parental involvement. The guidelines illustrate the importance of educators thinking of parents as partners in — not problems for — instruction and intervention.

A belief in shared responsibility. Home-school collaboration depends on a belief in shared responsibility for educational outcomes. Hulsebosch (1989) defined the characteristics of both teachers who are high involvers of parents in education and those who are low involvers. She showed that low involvers believed that home and school have separate responsibilities in the socialization of children, described the negative influence of home events on school life, and saw parent involvement activities as auxiliary to the real world of the classroom. In contrast, high involvers believed classroom activities should fit with children's homes and experiences, described parents in positive terms, and saw parents as an asset and basic element of a child's education. Both high and low involvers indicated the effort was a necessary and important part of their work, whereas low involvers implied the effort was an unnecessary add-on to the real world of teaching.

Because few schools have a policy that clarifies the essential role of families in the education of school-age children and because little consensus exists about the roles and responsibilities between parents and educators, school psychologists must determine whether educators at their school site believe in parents' meaningful participation in education. These questions need to be asked of the educators:

- How would you characterize the belief system about the relationship between parents and educators with respect to children's school performance?

- Do you believe in shared or separate responsibilities between home and school?

Should the belief in shared responsibility for educational outcomes not be present, the school psychologist may want to conduct a staff in-service on the empirical basis for parent participation (Henderson, 1989) and the curriculum of the home (Christenson, Rounds, & Gorney, 1992) as well as discuss Coleman's (1987) theory of families and schools vis-a-vis the socialization of children.

Coleman (1987) proposed that home and school provide different inputs for the socialization process of children. One class of inputs — opportunities, demands, and rewards — comes from schools. The second class of inputs — attitudes, efforts, and conception of self — comes from the social environment of the household. Educational outcomes result from the interaction of qualities that the child brings from home with qualities of the school. Schools do make a difference for children; however, they do not have an equal effect on children. According to Coleman (1987): "Schools, of whatever quality, are more effective for children from strong family backgrounds than for children from weak ones. The resources devoted by the family to the child's education interact with resources provided by the school — and there is greater variation in the former resources than the latter" (p. 35). Schools can reward, demand, and provide opportunities for children to learn; however, Coleman views families as providing the building blocks that make learning possible. Families provide the "social capital" needed by schools to optimize learners' outcomes.

Coleman argues that the social capital in homes is shrinking, in part due to the reduced availability of human capital because of single parenting and multiple demands on adult lives (e.g., two-working-parent households). Where this occurs, school achievement will not be maintained or increased without influencing home environments. According to Coleman's theory, the child's attitude toward learning is influenced predominantly by messages and experiences provided in the home setting. Therefore, educators must support and strengthen parents (parents used broadly to include adults in the home) as they assume the vital role of participant in their children's educational lives.

Finally, educators need to remember that parents do not want a hierarchical "professional-client" relationship with schools (Lindle, 1989). Parents indicated a dissatisfaction with school personnel who are "too business-like" or "patronizing," or "who talk down" to them. Parents want (a) information about their child's development and educational needs; (b) educators as partners, which means parents and educators are equals, share information about the child's performance and development, and share resources to solve concerns; (c) a support network or an opportunity to learn from and share with others; (d) training; and (e) informal contact with educators or a chance to build a trusting relationship (Peterson & Cooper, 1989).

Importance of perspective taking. The degree to which parents and educators engage in perspective taking and nonblaming influences the effectiveness of the home-school partnership. Parents and educators have multiple demands in their lives, are very busy, and often are not available to each other at a convenient time or in a convenient way (e.g., telephone). Swap (1987) has pointed out that the other's lack of availability is too often interpreted as a lack of concern for the student. In addition, typical parent-school contacts are ritualized and ineffective in achieving the goals sought in home-school collaboration: meaningful dialogue and sharing of resources to enhance student learning. Parent-educator contact at the 15-minute conference or back-to-school night does not permit the development of relationships or contribute to effective problem solving. Finally, differences in perceptions, as a function of the unique aspect of the parent or educator role interfere with communication and collaboration but are to be expected and need to be understood (Mendoza & Cegelka, cited in Chrispeels, 1987). For example, educators are expected to be fair to all children, whereas parents adopt an individualized perspective, wanting what is best for their child. Educators become "specialized experts," noting one aspect of a child's development, while parents adopt a more diffuse orientation, focusing on the child's ongoing development. Educators are expected to be effectively neutral, to be able to distance themselves from the child. The parent role is the antithesis of the educator role; emotional involvement is expected. Rather than blaming each other for their perceptions, they need to use their different perspectives to construct a more complete picture of the child's performance/behavior in both home and school contexts.

Differences in attributed patterns may account for some of the difficulty parents and educators have in dealing with school problems, delineating parent-teacher responsibilities, and arriving at mutually agreeable solutions. Guttmann (1982) found that teachers attributed causes for problem behavior to the child first, the parents second, and minimized or dismissed any reasons associated with themselves. In contrast, parents attributed responsibility almost equally to the child, teacher, and themselves. Rich (1987b) interpreted the emphasis teachers place on home life as a recognition of the significance of the home as an educational environment rather than as a deficit view of the child or blaming of the family. This is most encouraging. The key in collaboration is to shift from an emphasis on who is responsible for the problem to who is responsible for the solution. This will occur when parents and educators think about

their relationship differently, when they move from the concept of relationships in terms of service delivery — of "provider" and "client," of "professionals" and "target populations" — to one of complementary efforts toward common goals. Seeley (1985) argues:

> *Partners may help one another in general or specific ways, but none is ever a client, because the relationship is mutual. Providers and clients can deal with one another at arm's length; partners share an enterprise, though their mutuality does not imply or require equality or similarity. Participants in effective partnerships may be strikingly different, each contributing to the common enterprise, particular talents, experiences, and perspectives, and sometimes having different status within the relationship and control over aspects of the work to be done.* (p. 65)

Negative stereotypes about parents are destructive. Sometimes educators have fixed ideas about what constitutes a good family and proper child rearing. Most often middle-class families' behaviors and attitudes are preferred — educators see these children as coming to school with the "right stuff." Often educators perceive parents who are low income or nonwhite as deficient (Heleen, 1989). It has been shown that working-class or poor parents want their children to be successful in school but often do not understand school procedures, expectations, and how to assist their children. Consequently, these parents wait to be guided by educators. Educators have interpreted parents' behavior from a deficit-oriented model and coined these parents as apathetic or hard to reach. These parents see the school as hard to reach.

How do you think about families? Do you call them dysfunctional, or do you understand that they are affected by adverse living conditions? Do you identify family deficits or family strengths? All families have strengths; however, families differ in their energy, time, knowledge, and skills for assisting children (Christenson et al., 1993). Similarly, it is time for parents to understand the tremendous variability in student performance and that the solution for school success does not reside in the microsystem of the classroom.

School psychologists will find reframing, developing programs to reach out to all families, and increasing communication and contact between families and educators helpful tools for addressing the need for perspective taking in the partnership. Above all, they need to work actively to stop stereotypes and negative attributions to home life. These conditions, should they exist, suggest the need for information sharing and problem solving between home and school.

The importance of shared language. The degree to which the language of schooling is shared with parents must be examined by educators. The language of schooling includes grading practices, teacher expectations, curriculum goals, and homework policies. Joyce Epstein (1992), Co-director of the Center on Families, Communities, Schools, and Children's Learning, has advocated a similar approach. She suggests that parent involvement programs must make a strong connection with schooling and with the child as a student. Results from a pilot parent-interview study sponsored by the National Association of School Psychologists indicated parents needed information on specific ways to help their children at home (how to help with homework, talk about school, monitor progress), on what is happening at school (school activities, child's progress, teacher expectations), on school policies (sex education, testing, grading, discipline), and on how to be involved at school (how to communicate with teachers and help with specific problems, Christenson & Garrettson, 1992).

Also, the means by which the language of schooling is shared with parents must be checked by educators. Exclusive use of printed materials must be abandoned or equity issues vis-a-vis educational outcomes will persist. Even if parents can read, they often do not know how to apply the information to their situation. The result is that parents may know they should do something but not know how to do it. Parents are often told what to do (e.g., help your child with homework) but not told how. Likewise, educators provide parents with grades, but little information about how grades are determined. It is time to share information about child and adolescent development, school practices, home influences on learning, and ways to promote children's progress and development with parents and educators in multiple ways: printed materials (newsletters, handouts, lending library), classes/workshops, personal contact (home visit, school consultation), technology (audio, video, cable, telephone), and parent support groups. Sharing of information begins to create an infrastructure for education.

Parents need to be socialized for their role as facilitators of their child's school performance. Ames (1993), a researcher at the University of Illinois with the Center on Families, Communities, Schools, and Children's Learning, has shown that elementary school teachers who were high users of school-to-home communications reported they more often felt they could reach difficult students and help all students make progress. The school-to-home communications included strategies and practices in three categories: information about classroom learning activities (goals, curriculum, materials), information about their child's progress (accomplishments, improvement, effort), and direction to enable parents to help their children on learning activities at home. Information was communicated through newsletters, phone calls, personal notes, and work folders. Teachers' communications influenced parents' feelings of com-

fort with the school which then influenced parents' involvement in their children's learning. A similar study found that middle school educators' communication influenced parents' feelings of comfort with the school which then influenced parents' involvement in their children's learning; the practices enhanced the parents' belief that they could help their children, which then influenced their involvement (Christenson et al., 1993).

The focus of partnerships. Parents and educators come together when a child becomes a student; therefore, education and development are the natural link. Rich (1987a), Director of the Home and School Institute in Washington, DC, has shown "that parent participation is most widespread and sustained when parents view their participation as directly linked to the achievement of their children" (p. 63). Numerous interventionists and researchers have found that parents are more interested and involved when they learn ways to increase their child's success in school and when contacts are personal. The focus of home-school collaboration should, therefore, be to resolve school-based concerns about the educational life of the child. Parents, teachers, and/or students can initiate communication and a problem-solving dialogue about the educational concern. Based on a systematic investigation of home-school collaboration, Christenson et al. (1993) found it helpful to (a) invite parents to help solve a teacher's educational concern for their child; (b) be tolerant of and nonjudgmental about the ways parents indicate they can help; and (c) provide information, ongoing support, and consultation to parents as they learn how to assist their child's school performance. Ongoing communication between home and school is focused on the degree to which parents and educators, as facilitators of children's performance, are achieving their mutual goal: improving the child's school performance.

Vosler-Hunter's (1989) work on the Families as Allies Project is extremely relevant. Parents of children with emotional and behavioral disorders and educators participated in a number of training activities, out of which emerged key elements of collaborative relationships: mutual respect for skills and knowledge, honest and clear communication, two-way sharing of information, mutually agreed upon goals, and shared planning and decision making. These elements were most evident when problem solving was focused on those links between parents and educators — the child and the goal of their efforts — that increased the child's competence.

Options and flexibility. Home-school collaboration works best when many ways for parents to get involved exist and flexibility is encouraged. Epstein (1992) describes six kinds of activities and illustrates that parents can be involved in their child's education at school, at home, and at home and school. Because of the multiple demands on parents' lives, home-school collaboration has been more successful by negotiating educational responsibilities with parents that can be completed at home rather than expecting parents to participate at school (see next section). Herein lies the problem: Educators still quite often want parents to come to school rather than educators going to the parents.

Best practices in home-school collaboration are based on the belief that parents and educators share a goal, information directed to attaining the goal, decision making, and accountability for outcomes. This means educators need (a) to ask parents to become involved and share in the responsibility for their children's education, and (b) to admit parental help is required to resolve some educational concerns (e.g., school violence, destructive behavior). It means that parents may need to understand why their participation is encouraged by educators but not be *told* how they must help the school; rather they should be offered several options from which to select. In short, best practices in home-school collaboration set an expectation that parents will be involved; however, shared decision making will direct how they are involved.

Five variables — a belief in shared responsibility, a high degree of perspective taking, sharing the language of schooling, establishing the mutual goal of student success in school, and options for parent participation for learning — *exemplify the attitude in which all activities must be delivered.* In the next section, home-school collaboration strategies are illustrated.

Content Knowledge: Home-School Collaboration Model and Strategies

Epstein's typology. Epstein (1992) developed a well researched model of home-school collaboration characterized by six types of activities. It is critically important for school psychologists to recognize that these six activities, if all implemented, would constitute a comprehensive home-school collaboration program. Epstein found that implementing such a program involves planning and ongoing support over a 3- to 5-year period. Careful attention must be paid to implementation at each grade level. Typically parent participation declines dramatically after their children pass through the fourth grade, despite evidence that successful parent participation at secondary levels occurs when schools reach out to parents (Collins et al., 1982). The following paragraphs begin with Epstein's definitions verbatim (1992, pp. 503–505, in italics). Then ways school psychologists could provide ongoing support for home-school collaboration through either direct or indirect services are provided.

Type 1 — Basic Obligations of Families refers to the responsibilities of families for their children's health and safety, parenting and child-rearing skills at each age level, and positive home conditions for learning at each grade level. It is critical for educators to be sensitive to families' customs and cultures and provide information with the understanding that families differ in their energy, time, knowledge, and skill level for applying the information. Indirect service activities provided by school psychologists could include: Help schools provide information on parenting skills, child development, grade-level expectations, homework policies, and ways to build positive home learning conditions through printed materials, videotapes, workshops, parent support programs, and a lending library. Help schools to create a parent/family center (Johnson, 1993). Direct service activities provided by school psychologists could include: Consult with parents about specific ways to support students' learning and behavior in school, make home visits to reinforce home-based learning programs, and conduct workshops on ways to maintain healthy child development and school success across grade levels.

Given the diversity of America's families, school psychologists should not expect families to automatically understand their basic obligations or the curriculum of the home. To establish a shared responsibility for learning outcomes for students, schools must communicate this direct message: (a) children achieve more with home support for learning; (b) home support for learning can be provided in a variety of ways, and these are some examples (e.g., the restaurant menu approach); and (c) we want to work with you to increase our communication about your child's school progress and schoolwork. Schools must allow parents to decide how they can participate — or what role they can play. Finally, educators must remember that some families need only information, and others need information and ongoing support as they learn how to assume an active role in their child's schooling. For some families it is essential to determine what resources and support the family will need to fulfill their responsibility (Christenson et al., 1993).

Type 2 — Communications from the School refers to the responsibilities of schools for communications from school to home about school programs and children's progress in forms and words all families can understand and for options for home-to-school communications. Indirect service activities provided by school psychologists could include: Help develop frequent, efficient, and varied forms of all communication that are understood by all parents (memos, good news phone calls, report cards, conferences). Develop a structure for effective parent-teacher conferences, a routine phone calling/contact system, and a structure for contacting parents at the first sign of a problem. Direct service activities provided by school psychologists could include: Meet with parents to explain school programs and children's progress. Develop unique communication strategies for non-literate parents and communicate in parents' first language. Facilitate conferences and family-school meetings to develop interventions to improve the child's school success and grades, and create cooperative relationships between parents and educators.

Maintaining effective lines of communication is the most basic element of supporting home-school partnerships. The following list, which illustrates ways schools have changed their practices, is noticeably oriented to educators emphasizing the positive:

- The welcome sign is inviting.

- Educators emphasize goals for or skills they want to teach the child rather than the problems or deficits of the child in the school context.

- Parents are invited to help solve the school-based concerns, and parental input is actively encouraged throughout the process.

- Educators do not tell parents what to do (e.g., help your child with homework) but are prepared to guide and show parents (e.g., how to structure study time at home).

- Educators communicate at the first sign of a concern. Canter and Canter (1991) provide a helpful structure for teachers to use when contacting parents at the first sign of a concern. The structure includes six steps: statement of concern described using specific, observable behaviors; steps taken by the school to solve the concern; parental input about the concern; summary of new ways to approach the concern; expression of confidence about resolving the concern if home and school work together; and establishment of a follow-up time for contact.

- Ask teachers to provide four positive contacts to parents in varied areas: curriculum, good deed, child's progress, and child's strengths. Parents are invited to visit the classroom.

- Establish an ongoing contact system for *all* families. Examples include homework hot lines; use of electronic technology, such as the TransParent School Model (Bauch, 1989); and school-to-home progress reports/newsletters that provide parents with information about the classroom activity; child's progress, and ways parents can help reinforce child's learning (Ames, 1993). Some schools have used a notebook system for all students to increase communication between school and home. Assignments and teachers' and parents' comments are recorded. The power of the notebook system is that it is used school wide.

- Provide ways for all parents to learn about school policies and teachers' expectations. Strategies include orientation nights offered at multiple times, handbooks with designated policies, personal contacts for families who do not attend, and monthly workshops to discuss the language of schooling (testing, grading practices, discipline, monitoring students' progress).

- Reach out to families who do not attend or whose children are considered potential problems. Schools can conduct home visits or make phone contacts to invite parents to participate, to determine reasons for their lack of attendance (e.g., work conflicts, transportation), and to articulate that children produce more in school when parents and educators work as a team (Together Everyone Achieves More). Canter and Canter (1991) provide a structure for teachers to use when contacting a parent whose child is considered a potential problem student. Teachers are encouraged to call after a few weeks of school and to use this structure: statement of concern (e.g., I want this to be the best year for Tom); parental input about last year; parental input about this year; explain parental support is valued and critical; and express confidence that working together will help the student.

Type 3 — Volunteers refers to those who assist teachers, administrators, and children in classrooms, parent rooms, or other areas of the school; to those who assist at home; and to those who come to school to support student performance and events. Indirect service activities provided by school psychologists could include: Organize parent volunteer program to assist teachers, administrators, and children in classrooms. Ensure that schools vary schedules so all families can participate as volunteers or audience. Direct service activities provided by school psychologists could include: Train volunteers to increase their effectiveness. Ensure that transportation and daycare are provided for families. Encourage parents to attend school performances or other events. Contact parents who do not attend scheduled conferences or need follow-up contacts. Develop a buddy system to remove the barriers of transportation or alienation for some parents.

Volunteering by parents in schools is a traditional form of parent involvement and one which schools value highly, but parents' working schedules may require educators to alter their practices slightly (e.g., create volunteer activities to be done at home). Also, it is important to differentiate volunteering from establishing a shared responsibility for children's learning. At the beginning of the school year, schools often send home a list of needed volunteer activities in the hopes of recruiting parents. This approach indicates parent involvement is desirable but does not emphasize partnership. When schools invite parents to share in the responsibility for their child's school performance by indicating that efforts from school and home toward a common goal are known to produce better outcomes for students, schools are saying parents are essential, not merely desirable, to promote student success. Therefore, when schools send home the list of volunteer activities, a simple introductory sentence emphasizing the essential roles parents play in achieving positive outcomes turns the volunteer list into an example of a partnership effort.

Type 4 — Learning Activities at Home and Connections to Curriculum refers to parent-initiated, child-initiated, or teacher-initiated ideas to monitor, discuss, or assist children at home on learning activities that are coordinated with children's class work. Indirect service activities provided by school psychologists could include: Provide inservice training to teachers on home learning activities and other ways to involve parents with children's class work. Help schools provide information on how to monitor homework, grade-level expectations, and practice and enrichment activities. Teachers Involve Parents in Schoolwork (TIPS) is a helpful resource (Epstein, Jackson, Salinas, & Associates, 1991). Direct service activities provided by school psychologists could include: Meet with groups or individual parents to share strategies to increase student success in school. Plan, coordinate, and monitor interventions implemented by parents and teachers. The positive evidence for home-based learning programs (Graue et al., 1983) is strong, and parent-educator problem-solving meetings (see next section, this chapter) often serve as an entree for additional consultation and case management by the school psychologist.

Type 5 — Decision Making, Committee, Advocacy, and Other Leadership Roles refers to parent participation in decisions in PTA/PTO, advisory councils, other committees or groups at school, or independent advocacy groups. Indirect service activities provided by school psychologists could include: Help schools create participatory roles for parents and community members in PTA/PTO, advisory councils, Chapter I, and committees. Direct service activities provided by school psychologists could include: Train parent representatives in decision-making skills, collaboration, and ways to communicate with other parents about school improvement activities. Facilitate development of basic policies on curriculum, homework, and assessment. Successful home-school collaborative efforts often use these activities. In a review of programs, Kagan (1984) noted that the realization by both parents and educators that home-school collaboration must be a goal of their efforts is another essential element for success. Schools have implemented home-school teams to plan school events, to develop policies that require home and school support for successful implementation (homework, discipline), and to resolve school-based, system-level concerns (e.g., school violence). For these teams to be successful, a problem-solving orientation is necessary.

Two examples illustrate the power of a home-school team to focus on educational concerns. Referred to as the Comer Process, The School Development Program was developed in 1968 by James Comer, a psychiatrist at Yale, in collaboration with other colleagues at Yale and educators in the New Haven Public Schools (Conner, 1980). Because of the dramatic success of this project in terms of improving academic and social outcomes for students, the program has been replicated in over 100 public schools. Critical components of the program include: School Planning and Management Team (SPMT), Mental Health Team, Parent Participation Program, and Curriculum and Development. The SPMT is comprised of two teachers, three parents, and one mental health specialist and directed by the principal to establish policy and strategic planning across the key stakeholders in the school. The team coordinates school functions and maintains the focus on partnership and problem solving. The Mental Health Team is composed of a school psychologist, a social worker, and a regular and special education teacher. This team meets to address referrals and concerns, and also provides systematic training to parents *and* teachers about ways to promote social and behavioral competence in students. The Parent Participation Program offers many family-school events, employs parents as classroom assistants, and helps establish school policy by electing three representatives to the SPMT. Finally, curriculum and child development needs are met by providing monthly seminars in ways parents and educators can emphasize the academic and social skills acquisition of students. Parents and educators engage in mutual learning experiences on this project. A true partnership means the partners listen to each other, engage in ongoing dialogue about improving student success and development, and realize that problems can be solved by working as a team.

On the Partnership for Success Program (Christenson et al., 1993), a home-school team referred to as PATHS, Parent and Teachers Heading to Success, was developed for parents and educators to share information and perspectives, engage in ongoing dialogue about ways for parents and educators to assist each other, and to maintain a shared agenda for their efforts; the success of children in school. The team has developed a parent center and techniques to increase and improve home-school communication, developed and implemented a sex education program, and discussed homework policies. After 2 years, signs of finger pointing between home and school temporarily surface when a new concern is addressed. What is encouraging is that team members realize mutual support, sharing of information, and problem solving, not blame, are the answer, and with this realization, the finger pointing ceases.

Type 6 — Collaboration and Exchange with Community Organizations refers to school actions and programs that provide or coordinate student and family access to community and support services. Also, collaboration with businesses, cultural organizations, and other groups to improve school programs for children and services for families to support their child rearing and guidance of children as students, and to improve the effectiveness of the other types of involvement are included. Indirect service activities provided by school psychologists could include: Consult with teachers and administrators about forming business partnerships and community linkages to promote student success in school and family resource centers of school-linked services to meet children's needs through health and social service agencies. For example, Education Sunday refers to workshops for parents, delivered at church, about school issues. Direct service activities provided by school psychologists could include: Develop resources and a referral
network. Develop/coordinate a family resource center to provide family education, counseling, tutoring, food and clothing, or routine medical care. These services are often provided by community-based professionals in collaboration with schools.

Trust-building events. Because of barriers that may exist for parents and educators, trust-building activities may be essential before other collaborative efforts can be successful. Trust-building activities allow parents and educators to "find friendly faces in the crowd" and provide socializing experiences for parents and educators. Weiss and Edwards (1992) refer to these activities as climate-building activities. Examples of activities include: grade-level bagel breakfasts, multicultural potluck dinners, and family's evening out (movies, skating, gym night). There is no limit to the kinds of activities (except for lack of creativity!) that allow educators and parents to get to know each other on an information-sharing, non-problem-oriented basis. Many of the communication strategies qualify as trust-building activities, also.

Parent-educator problem solving. Maintaining a problem-solving, nonblaming interaction style with parents is essential. Parents and educators need to meet to share information of common concern at a system level (e.g., school violence) and on an individual level (e.g., child's academic or behavioral performance). Effective meetings are based on nonblaming interactions and a problem-solving orientation and structure (Sheridan & Kratochwill, 1992; Weiss & Edwards, 1992). The structures provided by these individuals have been used to develop a parent-educator problem-solving sequence that was implemented in elementary and middle schools to design collaborative interventions between home and school. This structure can be used to address a myriad of school-based concerns (attendance, academics, behavior),

thereby moving from problem admiration to problem solution. Although the steps are clearly delineated, recognize that problem solving is a concept more than a structured sequence that must be adhered to as delineated. School psychologists may wish to make some modifications while retaining the essential characteristics of information and resource sharing to achieve a goal. The stages are:

- **Introduction Stage**

  1. *Rapport Building.* This step is critical and, in a sense, related to trust building. Know the student, know the concerns, and know several positive attributes of the student. Welcome parents to the school. Mention a positive attribute of the student.

  2. *Describe the school-based concerns.* These concerns can be teacher-, parent-, or student-initiated; however, most often they are teacher-initiated. The concern is described in specific, behavioral, observable language. This statement reflects the child's current level of performance, which is usually considered to be problematic.

     - *Reframe the problematic behavior.* Reframing is a helpful strategy for building a partnership with parents. We know that parents wait to be directed by schools and want to know how to help their child be successful in school. By reframing problematic behavior to a learning goal, the desired behavior from the child has been specified. At this point, invite parental assistance. Educators indicate they will work to teach the student (Tom) the academic, social, or behavioral skills; however, they believe Tom will learn these skills faster if the parents can join the team of educators to support Tom's learning. Parents indicate whether they want to be involved.

     - *Focus on solutions.* The facilitator of the meeting (usually the school psychologist) states that the purpose of this meeting is to come up with a doable plan of action, something all participants agree with and help to implement. The tone is "we aren't here to blame anyone or look for responsibility for the problem. Rather, we are here to determine responsibilities for solutions" to the school-based concern.

- **Identification Stage**

  1. *Identify all concerns and perceptions.* Parent, student, and teacher perceptions as they relate to the school-based concern need to be shared. There needs to be a realization that perceptions will differ or what Jim Maddock, in Family Social Science at the University of Minnesota,

refers to as "truth comes in versions." Individuals observe the student in different settings. It is possible that other concerns will surface.

2. *Identify a mutual goal for the student.* After the information-sharing session, several goals may be expressed. It is important to arrive at consensus. Which goal will both parents and educators work on? There may be goals that either partner will take sole responsibility for and merely inform the other partner.

3. *Check for understanding.* Because many issues will be discussed, it is important to recap the discussion by describing the discrepancy between problematic behavior and desired behavior for the child (i.e., learning goal). Parents' and educators' efforts now focus on ways to work together to teach the desired behavior.

- **Solution Stage**

  1. *Possibilities for a solution.* Because parents generally wait to be guided by educators, they are usually relieved when educators are prepared to mention several possibilities for solution. These should include what can be done at school and home and should be presented as a restaurant-style menu. Brainstorming should be used to expand this original menu. The key is to find what parents and teachers can realistically implement.

  2. *Select an idea.* It is important for parents and teachers to indicate what they want to try to resolve the concern. After their selection, the school psychologist should ask, "What resources or support would you like to have as you try this idea?" For example, the school psychologist should be prepared to offer consultation, reading materials, contact with other parents, and the like. This question is important because it normalizes the notion of parents needing help around schooling issues (e.g., structuring learning time, supporting reading at home). It is an empowering statement because the focus is on promoting opportunities for parents to recognize their strengths, set their own agendas, and make constructive changes in their lives.

- **Implementation Stage**

  1. *Describe the doable plan.* It is important to recap the roles and responsibilities of teachers, parents, students, the school psychologist, and others.

  2. *Implementation phase.* During this time, it is important for the school psychologist or another individual to systematically contact the parents to discuss any concerns and to provide ongoing support and consultation.

  3. *Evaluate the plan.* The intervention plan is successful if the discrepancy between problematic and desired behavior is closed or if the learning goal is achieved. If the goal is not achieved, *no one is to blame.* It simply was a lousy plan, and the team needs to reconvene to modify the intervention. If the goal was achieved, find a way to celebrate!

In summary, content knowledge for developing effective home-school partnerships for learning includes partnership variables, home-school collaboration and trust-building activities, and parent-educator problem solving. Problem solving is the systematic tool to alter the interface between home and school in a way to increase connectedness and minimize distance.

Process for Developing Home-School Partnerships

Time is a factor when implementing a home-school collaboration intervention versus a home-school collaboration program. Training and leadership are required for both; however, to develop a comprehensive home-school collaboration program takes 3 to 5 years. In contrast, school psychologists working with individual parents could more quickly develop home-school collaboration interventions.

Kagan (1984) reminds us that best practices for developing programs are characterized by site-specific development and leadership. Each school must ask two questions: What forms of parent participation are desirable and feasible? and What strategies can be employed to achieve them? Other questions that schools must consider throughout the development phase appear in the literature. Examples include

- What is the school's definition of parent involvement?

- Is this the same as parents and community professionals?

- Do teachers recognize the family as a system for teaching and learning?

- What are high-priority problems in the school climate, and how can parents and educators address them?

- Has the school district made a fiscal commitment (within existing resources) to development of programs?

- Does the majority of the staff believe in the benefits of home-school collaboration?

- For which groups of parents would educators say, "You will never get them involved!"?

Best practices suggest that schools need to create a team of parents and educators who are interested in answering these questions.

Epstein (personal communication, 1991) recommends a helpful process for developing home-school partnerships. First, educators, with parental input, are encouraged to identify strong school practices that involve parents at each grade level. Second, educators are encouraged to specify the kind of involvement that will be developed in Year 1, 2, or 3 (or 4 or 5 if the process is lengthened). Throughout the development process, educators must ask, "How might *more* parents, *different* parents, or *all* parents be involved or better informed?" Effective home-school collaboration programs and policies are based on the notion of shared responsibility for educational outcomes; therefore, the roles of the state department of education, school district administration, educators, parents, and students are specified. It is essential for school psychologists who provide the necessary leadership in this area to be knowledgeable about different strategies. These strategies need to be tailored to the needs of parents and educators at each school site. Furthermore, according to Epstein (1992), school psychologists would have to draw upon several roles and skills, including synthesizer of information about home-school collaboration at each grade level; disseminator of good ideas to assist the team to improve practice; coordinator of plans for action, including multiyear plans; facilitator/trainer to support educators' implementation of new programs; demonstrator of promising and successful practices; communicator with parents; and evaluator of programs. Throughout the process, parents and educators must realize that home-school collaboration is not an end but a means to the end of promoting student success and positive attitudes towards learning.

Training of teachers and administrators in practices that reach out to all families is an essential prerequisite and a viable role for school psychologists. The major point is that for home-school partnerships to promote student success a concerted effort and leadership are required. While they do not happen automatically, there is solid literature base and resources to provide the basis for successful implementation of such programs.

In closing, a question must be addressed: *What do school psychologists need to support home-school collaboration?* Two responses come to mind: administrator support and personal interest. The commitment and support of the building administration (principal) is essential. School psychologists would be wise to inform principals and administrators of the importance of developing meaningful parent involvement in education as a way to increase students' learning opportunities and progress. The eighth National Educational Goal is: Every school will promote partnerships that will increase parental involvement and participation in promoting social, emotional, and academic growth of children. Therefore, school psychologists' discussions with principals would be timely, and perhaps a fortuitous way to expand one's role. The degree to which the principal is supportive will influence both the teacher's perceptions and time availability of the school psychologist to these efforts.

Second, personal interest and commitment by the school psychologist is integral to the efficacy of home-school collaboration. To move from talk to action requires more than a knowledge base about implementation of programs. It will, at a minimum, require administrative support for and personal interest by school psychologists for home-school collaboration.

SUMMARY

Although home-school partnerships to enhance student learning are not the norm, there is much rhetoric and interest in developing partnerships. In this chapter, the positive outcomes for all key stakeholders, particularly students, were used to provide the rationale for creating home-school partnerships for the success of all students. Features of, barriers to, and principles of home-school cices were described in terms of (a) *content* knowledge for guidelines supporting home–school collaboration were described. Best practnowledge for guidelines supporting home-school collaboration and home-school collaboration strategies, and (b) *process* knowledge for developing programs. Best practices are characterized by viewing parents as partners in — not problems for — the success of students. To this end, educators are challenged in this chapter to view parents as their allies, which requires them to (a) ask parents to become involved and share responsibility for their children's education, (b) admit help is needed to resolve some school-based concerns, (c) change their beliefs about parents described as at-risk or uninvolved, (d) overcome barriers that maintain distance, and (e) engage in strategies that reach out to families. Home-school partnerships to enhance student learning will become the norm when a concerted effort is made to engage parents and educators in sharing goals, information, decision making, resources, and accountability for students' educational progress.

REFERENCES

Ames, C. (1993). How school-to-home communications influence parent beliefs and perceptions. *Equity and Choice, 9*(3), 44–49.

Bauch, J. P. (1989). The TransParent School Model: New technology for parent involvement. *Educational Leadership, 47*(2), 32–35.

Canter, L., & Canter, M. (1991). *Parents on your side.* Santa Monica, CA: Lee Canter & Associates.

Chrispeels, J. A. (1987). The family as an educational resource. *Community Education Journal, 14*, 10–17.

Christenson, S. L., & Garrettson, B. (1992, March). *What do families want from schools?* Paper presented at the National Association of School Psychologists Annual Meeting, Nashville, TN.

Christenson, S. L., Rounds, T., & Franklin, M. J. (1992). Home–school collaboration: Efforts, issues, and opportunities. In S. L. Christenson & J. C. Conoley (Eds.), *Home–school collaboration: Enhancing children's academic and social competence* (pp. 19–51). Silver Spring, MD: National Association of School Psychologists.

Christenson, S. L., Rounds, T., & Gorney, D. (1992). Family factors and student achievement: An avenue to increase students' success. *School Psychology Quarterly, 7*(3), 178–206.

Christenson, S. L., Thurlow, M. L., Sinclair, M., & Evelo, D. (1993). *The Partnership for School Success Project.* Unpublished manuscript.

Coleman, J. S. (1987, August–September). Families and schools. *Educational Researcher,* 32–38.

Collins, C. H., Moles, O., & Cross, M. (1982). *The home-school connection: Selected partnership programs in large cities.* Boston, MA: Institute for Responsive Education.

Comer, J. P. (1980). *School power: Implications of an intervention project.* New York: Free Press.

Davies, D. (1991). Schools reaching out: Family, school, and community partnerships for student success. *Phi Delta Kappan, 72*(5), 376–382.

Epstein, J. L. (1992). School and family partnerships: Leadership roles for school psychologists. In S. L. Christenson & J. C. Conoley (Eds.), *Home-school collaboration: Enhancing children's academic and social competence* (pp. 499–515). Silver Spring, MD: National Association of School Psychologists.

Epstein, J. L., & Dauber, S. L. (1991). School programs and teacher practices of parent involvement in inner-city elementary and middle schools. *The Elementary School Journal, 91*(3), 289–306.

Epstein, J. L., Jackson, V. E., Salinas, K. C., & Associates. (1991). *Manual for teachers: Teachers involve parents in schoolwork (TIPS).* Baltimore, MD: Center on Families, Communities, Schools, and Children's Learning, The Johns Hopkins University.

Fruchter, N., Galletta, A., & White, J. L. (1992). *New directions in parent involvement.* Washington, DC: Academy for Educational Development, Inc.

Graue, M. E., Weinstein, T., & Walberg, H. J. (1983). School-based home instruction and learning: A quantitative analysis. *Journal of Educational Research, 76*(6), 351–360.

Guttmann, J. (1982). Pupils', teachers', and parents' causal attributions for problem behavior at school. *Journal of Special Education, 76,* 14–21.

Hansen, D. A. (1986). Family-school articulations: The effects of interaction rule mismatch. *American Educational Research Journal, 23*(4), 643–659.

Heleen, O. (1989). Involving the "hard to reach" parent: A working model. *Equity and Choice, 4,* 60–63.

Henderson, A. (1989). *The evidence continues to grow: Parent involvement improves student achievement.* Columbia, MD: National Committee for Citizens in Education.

Hulsebosch, P. L. (1989, April). *Significant others: Teachers' perspectives on relationships with parents.* Paper presented at the annual meeting of the American Educational Research Association, San Francisco.

Jennings, L. (1990, August). Parents as partners: Reaching out to families to help students learn. *Education Week, 9*(40), 23–32.

Johnson, V. R. (1993, September). Parent/family centers in schools: Expanding outreach and promoting collaboration. *Research and Development Report No. 20.* Baltimore, MD: Center on Families, Communities, Schools, and Children's Learning, Johns Hopkins University.

Kagan, S. L. (1984). *Parent involvement research: A field in search of itself.* Boston, MA: Institute for Responsive Education.

Keith, T. Z., Keith, P. B., Troutman, E., Brickley, P. G., Trivette, P. S., & Singh, K. (1993). Does parent involvement affect eighth-grade student achievement? Structural analysis of national data. *School Psychology Review, 22*(3), 474–496.

Krasnow, J. (1990). *Building parent-teacher partnerships: Prospects from the perspective of the Schools Reaching Out Project.* Boston, MA: Institute for Responsive Education.

Leitch, L. M., & Tangri, S. S. (1988). Barriers to home-school collaboration. *Educational Horizons, 66,* 70–74.

Lindle, J. C. (1989). What do parents want from principals and teachers? *Educational Leadership, 47*(2), 8–10.

Liontos, L. B. (1992). *At-risk families and schools: Becoming partners.* Eugene, OR: ERIC Clearinghouse on Educational Management, College of Education, University of Oregon.

Menning, E. (1993). New Mexico's family development program and the crucial three steps to parent involvement. *Family Resource Coalition Report (No. 2).* Chicago, IL.

Ooms, T., & Hara, S. (1991). *The family-school partnership: A critical component of school reform.* Washington, DC: The Family Impact Seminar.

Peterson, J. L., & Cooper, C. S. (1989). Parent education and involvement in early intervention programs for handicapped children: A different perspective on parent needs and the parent-professional relationship. In M. J. Fine (Ed.), *The second handbook on parent education: Contemporary perspectives* (pp. 197–236). New York: Academic Press.

Rich, D. (1987a). *Schools and families: Issues and actions.* Washington, DC: National Education Association.

Rich, D. (1987b). *Teachers and parents: An adult-to-adult approach.* Washington, DC: National Education Association.

Rich, D. (1988). Bridging the parent gap in education reform. *Educational Horizons, 66*(2), 90–92.

Ross, V. M. (1988). *Helping parents help their kids.* Arlington, VA: National School Public Relations Association.

Seeley, D. S. (1985). *Education through partnership.* Washington, DC: American Enterprise Institute for Public Policy Research.

Sheridan, S. M., & Kratochwill, T. R. (1992). Behavioral parent-teacher consultation: Conceptual and research considerations. *Journal of School Psychology, 30,* 117–139.

Sloane, K. D. (1991). Home support for successful learning. In S. B. Silvern (Ed.), *Advances in reading/language research: Vol. 5. Literacy through family, community, and school interaction* (pp. 153–172). Greenwich, CT: JAI Press.

Swap, S. M. (1987). *Enhancing parent involvement in schools.* New York: Teachers College Press.

Swap, S. M. (1992). Parent involvement and success for all children: What we know now. In S. L. Christenson & J. C. Conoley (Eds.), *Home-school collaboration: Enhancing children's academic & social competence* (pp. 499–515). Silver Spring, MD: National Association of School Psychologists.

Swap, S. M. (1993). *Developing home-school partnerships: From concepts to practice.* New York: Teachers College Press.

Vosler-Hunter, R. W. (1989). Families and professionals working together: Issues and opportunities. *Focal Point, 4*(1), 1–4.

Walberg, H. J. (1984). Families as partners in educational productivity. *Phi Delta Kappan, 65*, 397–400.

Weiss, H. M., & Edwards, M. E. (1992). The family-school collaboration project: Systemic interventions for school improvement. In S. L. Christenson & J. C. Conoley (Eds.), *Home-school collaboration: Enhancing children's academic & social competence* (pp. 215–243). Silver Spring, MD: National Association of School Psychologists.

ANNOTATED BIBLIOGRAPHY

Christenson, S. L., & Conoley, J. C. (Eds.). (1992). *Home-school collaboration: Enhancing children's academic and social competence.* Silver Spring, MD: National Association of School Psychologists.

In this 24-chapter book, programs and models for the 1990s are provided in 8 chapters and practical approaches for use with different populations and concerns are described in 12 chapters. In the remaining chapters, the theoretical and empirical bases for developing partnerships, community resources, and leadership roles for school psychologists are described.

Fruchter, N., Galetta, A., & White, J. L. (1992). *New directions in parent involvement.* Washington, DC: Academy for Educational Development, Inc.

The results of a study examining new directions in parent involvement in school districts across the country are reported. Eighteen recently developed programs or reforms for preschool through grade 12 are described and include such programs as Comer's School Development Program, Levin's Accelerated Schools Program, Davies's League of Schools Reaching Out, Parents as Teachers (PAT) program, Megaskills Program, and others. Excellent reference and resource lists are provided.

Liontos, L. B. (1992). *At-risk families & schools: Becoming partners.* Eugene, OR: ERIC Clearinghouse on Educational Management, College of Education, University of Oregon.

This 150-page manual is an excellent, readable synthesis of theory, research, and specific programs about home-school collaboration for at-risk populations. Topics include communication, home as an educative environment, school readiness, home learning, and decision making. Particular emphasis is placed on early intervention, dropout prevention, and supporting and strengthening families. Elements of successful programs and information on reaching families is detailed.

Moles, O. C. (1993). *Building home-school partnerships for learning: Workshops for urban educators.* Washington, DC: U.S. Department of Education, Office of Educational Research and Improvement (OERI).

This sourcebook is designed to give educators new information and strategies for working with parents and to strengthen learning activities at home that support learning at school. It contains five workshops and related materials for local staff development activities in elementary and middle schools. Topics include family life, school programs and teacher practice, and district policies that facilitate home-school partnerships. Although the sourcebook is directed to urban educators, the material applies equally well to suburban and rural education.

Rioux, J. W., & Berla, N. (1993). *Innovations in parent and family involvement.* Princeton, NJ: Eye on Education.

This is an unusual and exciting resource for school psychologists who want to learn about school-based programs to involve families. Thirty-four programs, including preschool (N = 5), elementary (N = 11), middle school (N = 5), high school (N = 5), and district wide (N = 8) are described. Common characteristics of successful programs are explicated. They include, but are not restricted to, rejection of a deficit model outlook, expanding roles for professionals, and developing parents' skills and knowledge.

Swap, S. M. (1993). *Developing home-school partnerships: From concepts to practice.* New York: Teachers College Press.

Background information includes the benefits of parent involvement, barriers to parent involvement, and models of home-school relationships. Based on a new vision for a partnership model, Swap articulates two-way communication, conferencing, shared decision-making, and home-support-for-learning strategies. Strategies for developing partnerships on a limited basis and in a comprehensive fashion are also described.

24

Best Practices in Building-Level Public Relations

Carol Kelly
Jefferson County (Colorado) Schools

OVERVIEW

Ongoing public relations efforts at the building level are an integral, vital part of the school psychologist's role. Lack of clear communication can lead to misunderstanding, criticism, and poor support for important initiatives on behalf of children. This chapter provides the practitioner with ideas and information necessary for starting or improving building-level public relations efforts. The need for developing support for services, an explanation of fundamental concepts, a planning process, suggested activities, and skills for working with the media are discussed.

The purpose of public relations for school psychologists is to create understanding and good will between us and our various publics, upon whose support we are dependent. For us to continue to provide services to children, we must let parents, fellow educators, and community members know what we are doing and what we can do. Public relations provides knowledge that will allow us to effectively advocate for changes and impact education.

Public image is a major factor in determining the role we play and the services we can provide. In 1952 Edward Bernays, the father of public relations, pointed out that educational improvement efforts were dependent upon a better public understanding of schools. Pollster George Gallup (1982) stated that one of the biggest challenges educators faced was to let people know about the quality things being done in the schools.

The Need for Public Relations Efforts

Educators are all faced with "new realities" in relating to their communities. These include people with no credentials who have public credibility and credibility in the news media; highly trained professionals who must constantly prove their worth; reporters who seem intentionally to misuse facts and data; standards which are "unachievable"; and people who are "unconvincible" (Lukaszewski, 1992). Materials are increasingly being circulated critical of school programs, and in many communities citizens are becoming more vocal about initiatives to increase standards or improve student achievement. Programs to increase self-esteem or tolerance for multicultural diversity may be subject to special scrutiny.

Because confidence in public education is eroding and the competition for public funds is fierce, district budget allocations are under close public scrutiny. Services that decision makers know the least about are most often the first to go. Therefore, any position that is not solidified is in jeopardy.

People survive who add value to an organization. Adding value and being able to demonstrate accountability, however, are not enough. What is most critical are the perceptions that others have about a person's value. We must work to let others know how we are helping schools prepare children to be successful in the 21st century and find ways to productively involve our communities in designing services.

We cannot help children succeed if we are not around. As long as there are parents, board members, business people, legislators, and other members of the voting public who do not understand our goals, skills, and competencies, building support for our services is necessary.

Communicating with and involving a broad range of people leads to quality school psychological services. When lines of communication are open between us and our school communities, we are better able to ascertain local needs and issues and improve services to children accordingly.

Attitudes and perceptions about school psychologists are determined at the local building level. Public relations efforts at the district, state, or national level serve to reinforce attitudes that have been put in place by school psychologists in the buildings they serve.

Our profession will be perceived as a proactive contributing force in enhancing the overall quality of American education to the extent that we establish strong relationships with key audiences at the local level. It is incumbent that every school psychologist design a plan of action to gain public support. No one can do this for us.

Defining Planned Communication

Public relations begins with quality services to children. It is not a coverup or substitute for excellence. Communications efforts cannot convince anyone for very long that a good job is being done if it is not.

The National School Public Relations Association (1982) offers the following definition: *Public relations is a planned and systematic two-way process of communication between an educational organization and its internal and external publics. It is a plan of action to encourage public involvement and to earn public understanding and support* (p. 2).

John Wherry (1988), former executive director of the National School Public Relations Association, stated that the term *public relations* was synonymous with the *practice of social responsibility*, or doing the right thing in the public interest. He summed up public relations this way: *Do an effective job and let people know about the successes and challenges.*

BASIC CONSIDERATIONS

To implement successful public relations efforts, the school psychologist needs commitment along with understanding of fundamental concepts. This section covers identification of key publics, communication techniques, and issues management.

Identifying Key Publics

It is useful to think not in vague terms of *the general public*, but of essential audiences with whom relationships should be improved and maintained. The most effective approach can best be determined when considering the needs and interests of specific individuals or groups. As Lukaszewski (1992) put it, "the key to impact is audience focus — getting your message directly and clearly to the people who want and need to know your point of view."

Internal publics are those inside the school family: professionals and support staff including teachers, students, administrators, secretaries, substitutes, custodians, board members, teacher assistants, and student teachers.

According to public relations veterans, the initial step in initiating any public relations effort is to *start internally*. Community members listen to and trust information that comes directly from people who spend time working in the school. Plus, family members of educators and school psychologists can be indispensable resources. They often interact with a wide range of individuals and can help build support for services and children.

By involving and communicating with internal publics, we build a foundation that can increase our success in working on behalf of children with the larger community. Although audiences within the school family can lend invaluable support to efforts, they can just as easily undermine them. Credibility is established when quality services are provided and strong relationships are maintained with those you directly serve.

External audiences are those who work outside the school, or have a more indirect association. These include parents, community agencies, churches, legislators, civic organizations, senior citizens, the business community, and realtors. Most external public relations efforts focus on parents.

Though parents are a critical group, educators need to keep in mind that nearly three-fourths of American households have no children in school and that there are fewer school-age children than senior citizens. It should come as no surprise then that voters and taxpayers are increasingly interested in the costs associated with maintaining quality education and somewhat skeptical of teaching methods and services different from what they experienced when they were in school.

Communication efforts with external audiences will usually result in a more positive attitude toward support services in the schools. An informed public is more apt to support schools than not to support them (Kindred, Bagin, & Gallagher, 1984). Ledell and Arnsparger (1993) noted that communicating well and involving the community in restructuring efforts makes change less difficult for everyone.

Direct Personal Communication is Key

Interpersonal communication requires face-to-face interaction between two people and is necessary for influencing attitudes. Persuasion requires that direct person-to-person communication is maintained between us, school leaders, and influential publics. Studies show that people who acquire their information about the schools directly from board members and school employees tend to support the schools more than people who get their information from other sources (Kindred et al., 1984). When people think about planning a vacation to a new place, for example, they tend to rely more on a trusted neighbor's opinion than a glossy travel brochure. We have more confidence in people with whom a relationship has been established.

Examples of situations that involve interpersonal communication include child-study-team meetings, back-to-school night, parent conferences, faculty presentations, phone calls, and talks delivered to small groups. Settings where interpersonal relationships can be established include athletic clubs, beauty salons, civic organization meetings, social events, grocery stores, and golf courses. *Any* interaction with other people is an opportunity to build a relationship that can lead to invaluable support for services.

When using interpersonal communication, be aware of both your personal communication style and that of the receiver. Your approach should vary depending upon whether you are talking to a progressive administrator, a skeptical parent, an insecure teacher, or a school board member who does not understand the need for support services in the schools. Does the person have a hidden agenda or anger that must be diffused? Begin by listening to the other person's perceptions. Be sensitive to cultural differences.

Trusting relationships form the basis for mutually supportive behavior. Essential elements for such relationships include authenticity, credibility, and trust. People develop confidence in you when you demonstrate expertise in your field and display understanding of viewpoints different from your own.

Mass communication techniques are useful for imparting information, making people aware of a specific situation, or reinforcing attitudes. Examples include newsletters, public service announcements, radio and television appearances, advertising, parent handouts, films, posters, and brochures.

Relying extensively on such sources, as opposed to more direct communication approaches, is a major mistake of many districts and educational associations. These strategies inform people, but do little to influence opinions or change behavior.

Be an Issues Manager

Issues management is a concept that cannot be overlooked when building support for services. For us to be successful, we must be aware of our customers, the voting public, and keep up with their thinking. Radical shifts in society create dilemmas that become issues. It may be necessary to readjust services to coincide with shirting public interests.

Planning from the issues, rather than being managed by them, allows us to take more control over the future. It requires a decisive approach and awareness of relevant community problems and trends. Key issues are the vehicle through which we reach our audiences, and our response to issues strongly shapes perceptions others have about us.

To stay current with the issues, scan publications that are read in the school community, maintain links with parent groups, visit the faculty lounge, and subscribe to periodicals such as *Education Week* and the *Kappan*. Look for concerns that you can do something about and that will make you more effective in meeting the needs of children.

Form *issues applications* teams with other members of the school community. Individuals review topics covered in local papers or discussed in the neighborhood related to education and children. Issues being addressed in other districts or states that could be of concern to the local district are anticipated.

William Banach of the Institute for Future Studies regularly releases *Critical Issues Facing America's Public Schools*, many of which have direct relation to school psychological services. On the forefront of many school agendas are student violence, the change process, lack of family experience for children, national standards, tuition vouchers, economic inequities, accountability, racial tension, and school reform.

Look for issues that will make you more valuable to other educators and to children. Watch where education, your district, and your individual schools are headed, how schools are responding, and how leaders are managing change. Look at the unique competencies that you have to help schools reach their objectives. Link your skills with directions your schools and communities are taking.

With renewed interest in children and public education at the national level, there is a momentum to help our country and districts shift their priorities on behalf of children and defend educational quality for all children.

With an issues-management approach, we cannot be bound by the job description. Services are designed around community needs. Efforts could include organizing a conflict resolution program, offering a parenting class, working on a school improvement committee, or developing a plan with the principal to help the staff adapt to change. The best efforts are aligned with school goals to boost parent involvement, create a safe learning environment, or improve student achievement. Responding constructively to local needs will result in a positive attitude from the staff and community and help build support for services to children.

BEST PRACTICES

This section outlines a public relations planning process, presents suggested activities to communicate to various audiences, and offers tips for working with the media.

Getting Started

An ongoing 4-step planning process will ensure that time and energy are strategically directed to building essential relationships. Effective planning is required to secure the future of quality mental health services for children. A planned approach for reaching out to people will be more efficient than implementing ideas from someone else's list or, worse, responding only to difficult crisis situations such as a proposal to reduce support staff.

The likelihood of developing workable, effective plans is increased when others are involved in the process. Put together a team and consult with colleagues, your school principals, and your supervisor throughout the process.

Step One. The first step consists of listening and conducting an *analysis* of where you are now. What individuals and groups are you already talking to, what is important to them, and what are current perceptions? It is likely that you already are promoting school psychology in many ways.

Identify audiences being reached through current efforts. Consider why communication with these people is important and the effectiveness of present efforts. List additional audiences with whom you would like to communicate. Decide what they need to know, what current perceptions are, and what you would like them to be.

Think about people who can help you meet your goals as well as those that can hurt or stop efforts. Which audiences may be uninformed about how school psychology contributes to education? Are there groups that have negative preconceived attitudes toward the profession?

Establish ongoing avenues of communication to directly determine perceptions, priorities, and concerns others have about your services. Listen to what teachers, parents, students, administrators, and other consumers of our services have to say. What do they want from psychologists and what are they willing to pay for?

Among your targeted groups, be sure to establish two-way communication with *opinion leaders* in the school community who care about support services for children. Opinion leaders are those influential role models whom others seek out for advice and who lead public opinion.

A helpful tool in this beginning step is a *communication grid.* List target audiences across the top of a page. Write ongoing activities down the left side. Check all groups that are reached by each activity. For example, a regular article in the school's newsletter may be read by parents, teachers, administrators, and support staff. The grid will help you take inventory of current activities and reveal where special efforts are needed.

A brief needs assessment is essential for making appropriate decisions. Many schools conduct annual community surveys. Request that a question about psychological services be included. Or, your department might want to develop its own survey. What perceptions do people we work with and community members have? Are others aware of the broad range of services provided? What are major concerns and expectations? Survey results can provide a solid base for your plan of action and goals of service.

Before designing specific plans, find out all you can about your school community. Consider factors such as the number of residents without children in school, voting patterns, educational background, income levels, mobility and employment patterns. How does the community view the school?

Step Two. It is essential to *plan:* Determine which audiences to focus upon and how you can most directly communicate with them. Will you adequately influence your selected groups through newspapers and brochures, or will you need to meet personally with individuals?

Set measurable objectives. Do you want to impart knowledge, improve perceptions and attitudes, or change behaviors? Goals may be for the hiring of additional psychologists or more cooperation from teachers. Think about your desired future versus your predicted future.

Establish time lines and ascertain any costs associated with your plans. School district communications officers, state school public relations associations, and the National Association of School Psychologists (NASP) may be able to provide expertise and materials specific to your situation; use them to your advantage. It may be possible to coordinate your activities with plans that your building, district, or state association is already implementing.

It will not be possible to design strategies that meet every need. *"Supertarget"* audiences most affected by what you are doing and who are most critical for support. While efforts will focus on these key groups, you may be able to maintain relationships with others through less frequent contacts. These relationships will result in a better reputation and can ensure that your interests will be considered when decisions affecting services to children surface.

Consider a *marketing* approach. When you are interacting with members of identified audiences, emphasize how school psychological services can support their goals. We must understand what is important to people and describe ourselves in terms that relate to their priorities. Tell how school psychologists help teachers improve student achievement, help administrators implement conflict resolution programs, or help parents become effective partners with the school. When messages are *personalized* and *relevant* to an individual, they are listened to with more interest.

Determine which strategies will most likely help meet objectives for each group. Develop an organized plan about how you can best communicate your needs and improve services for children.

Step Three. The next step is *implementation,* or carrying out plans. The most effective plans emphasize face-to-face interpersonal relationships and minimize the role of the media. People programs beat paper programs every time. Persuasion comes through the time-consuming and hard work of meeting with staff and key influential audiences (Bagin, 1993). Persistent one-on-one efforts are what influence attitudes, develop better understandings, and change behaviors. Be sure to maintain interaction with supporters and find ways they can actively promote your objectives.

Step Four. Finally, communications efforts need to be *evaluated*. Look at your original objectives and determine how successful you were. Many schools may be used for obtaining feedback; for the most reliable information, use a variety of sources.

A rigorous scientific system is not necessary to get accurate information. Informally evaluate the success of your plans by analyzing behavior toward school psychological services. Do students refer classmates in need? Did the community oppose a district proposal to reduce psychological services? Do parents express appreciation of your services and give your name to friends whose children may be having difficulties? Are you invited to be present at school board meetings? Keep a file of written feedback you receive.

Attend to negative feedback and look for ways to address concerns in new plans. Invite those who have concerns to brainstorm alternative with you. Identify modifications that need to be made in the future. Based on your findings, activities may be maintained, deleted, added, or modified.

This cycle may be repeated each school year. When efforts have been evaluated, go back to Step One. Influencing attitudes is an ongoing process. Reevaluate and modify plans on a continuing basis.

A Menu of Suggested Ideas

The following activities are designed to build positive relationships with parents, administrators, teachers, support staff, students, and the local community. Though organized around selected audiences, much overlap exists. For example, an activity listed under the parent section may also reach teachers and administrators. Coordinate activities into your overall plan.

Psychologists.

- Start with your own group first. Prepare a district plan to increase support. Develop ongoing communication strategies such as regular meetings, newsletters, or phone trees.

- Select a cadre of district and community leaders. Establish relationships, ask for perceptions, and involve them in planning your services.

- Involve family members of school psychologists in building support and communicating your message.

Teachers.

- Greet teachers and other staff members each day by name.

- Eat lunch with teachers. Vary your lunch period to socialize with more staff.

- Introduce yourself at a beginning-of-the-year faculty meeting. In new assignments, let the staff know how best to serve your services.

- Involve teachers in plans relating to your services with students.

- Give presentations to the faculty. Consider topics such as parent conferences, teacher stress, and classroom meetings.

- During School Psychology Week, show others your appreciation of their support. Bring refreshment to the lounge or send notes of appreciation.

- Be a part of the school family. Attend faculty meetings and school social functions. Know your school's mission and find ways to help reach school goals.

- Hold regular, open office hours.

- Help teachers manage district- and school-change efforts.

- Volunteer to serve on building committees. Consider community relations or a school improvement group.

Parents.

- Cultivate a group of parent supporters. Meet with them regularly and seek opinions about your services. Third-party advocacy can be invaluable.

- Make yourself visible. Circulate at school functions such as back-to-school nights, open houses, special events, and social activities.

- Distribute handouts on common areas of interest such as self-esteem, study skills, and stress. Use NASP *Communiqué* parent handouts.

- Project a professional image: Use business cards, hang diplomas and awards, and dress in a professional manner.

- Make regular phone calls to parents of children on your caseload. Commend them for their efforts and keep them posted on their children's accomplishments.

- Be sensitive to the fact that parents from other countries may not understand everything you are saying. Learn about cultural norms of diverse community groups.

- Actively involve parents in your service delivery.

- Write a regular school newsletter column.

- Maintain a flexible schedule for meetings with parents unable to come in during school hours. Include fathers and stepparents.

- Make home- or work-site visits when parents cannot or will not come to the school.

- Return phone calls promptly — within 24 hours whenever possible.

- Establish a liaison with your parent-teacher organizations.

- Welcome opportunities to talk to parent groups. They are always interested in learning ways to help improve their child's school performance. Do not wait to be invited.

- Work with the PTA to develop a parent shelf in the school library. Write book reviews in the school newsletter.

- Offer a parenting class.

- Communicate in simple language. You will not build confidence when people cannot understand you. Avoid jargon in reports and in face-to-face meetings.

Students.

- Maintain quality services and positive, caring day-to-day relationships. Community opinions are largely reflective of student comments about school.

- Make presentations about your services to students.

- Sponsor a student group such as student council, honor society, or an athletics team.

- Help develop and participate in student recognition programs.

- Send congratulatory notes or "happy grams."

- Continue to develop yourself and your skills by attending classes, taking workshops, and consulting with colleagues.

- Make positive referrals to the principal when students have been successful.

- Greet students by name around the building and in the halls. Walk through the lunch room from time to time.

- Attend special events such as plays, field trips, assemblies, and award presentations.

- Consider alternative settings for sessions with students. Take a walk, sit on the swings, shoot baskets, or meet for lunch.

- Take students out to lunch when they have accomplished a major goal. Let them invite classmates.

School community.

- Become a visible, indispensable resource. Let community members know what the problems and issues are that children face and how your services help.

- Write letters to the editor, guest opinions, or editorials about community issues for the local newspaper.

- Patronize local businesses, including those run by students' parents.

- Volunteer to be a guest and answer questions on radio call-in shows.

- Know the facts about your schools and district: board members, demographics, board policies, test scores, and district strengths and weaknesses.

- Nominate individuals for district, state, or national recognitions.

- Develop a plan so district psychologists are represented in community organizations.

- Become involved in community activities such as crime-prevention programs, church groups, sports programs, or service groups.

- Integrate school psychology activities and information into American Education Week events.

- Arrange media or newspaper coverage of special projects or events.

- Work with other service providers to sponsor a Saturday family workshop with a selection of speakers on various topics of interest to the community.

Administrators.

- Establish a positive working relationship with your school's leaders. Find out their interests and strengths.

- Develop a relationship with your superintendent. Make sure that he or she knows your competencies and find ways to work together.

- Keep administrators abreast of your activities.

- Work with your principal in areas of mutual concern such as conflict mediation, effective discipline, crisis intervention, or improving student achievement.

- Do not set yourself up for failure. Underpromise and overdeliver. Meet deadlines early and anticipate school needs.

- Regularly attend school board meetings. Positively involve board members in meeting needs of students in your district. Coordinate your efforts with those of board directions.

Support staff.

- Keep in mind that the best-known people in the school are usually nonprofessionals: bus drivers, custodians, and secretaries who often live in the neighborhood.

- Secretaries talk to more people in a month than most people do in a year; they are the "voice" of your school. Develop good relationships.

- Offer a behavior management inservice for teacher assistants.

- Participate in appreciation days and events for support staff members.

- Recognize any special efforts.

Public Speaking and Interviews

An effective strategy for fostering positive relationships is making small-group presentations to teachers, parents, board meetings, or community groups. You may also decide that television or radio interviews will help tell your story to key publics. The following suggestions will help you present yourself as an effective and credible information source.

- Enroll in a public speaking course or group like Toastmasters to hone your skills. In the process, you will educate fellow members who can go forth and tell your story.

- Know your topic. Always take time to thoroughly prepare. Avoid *on the spot* interviews or presentations unless you are very knowledgeable about the subject.

- Learn the technique of *bridging:* taking the conversation from where the interviewer may try to direct it to where you want it to go.

- Consider factors relating to your audience such as education level, cultural diversity, age, and income level.

- Make presentations on topics of interest to your audience. A talk on school psychology, per se, will usually not be of much concern.

- Anticipate information your source will want to know. If possible, find out what questions will be asked. Prepare an organized information sheet.

- Even in a crisis situation, ask if you can call back in half an hour so that you can gather your thoughts and information. Outline the course of action being taken.

- Be honest. Admit problems and state what is being done to address them.

- Do say "I don't know" rather than bluff your way through a response. Offer to find the information.

- Maintain eye contact with your audience or interviewer, not a television camera.

- Never speculate or answer "what if" questions.

- Pause when collecting your thoughts. Ask to have any "uhs" or "ahs" you may inadvertently say edited from recorded interviews.

- Eliminate jargon, accusations, and negative comments.

- Respond to questions with positive, complete quotable statements. Prepare 3-second quotes before the interview.

- Do not say "no comment" or "off the record." Give a valid reason for declining to comment, such as safety or maintaining confidentiality. If you do not want to hear or read about it, do not say it.

- Smile. Be excited about your topic. Use a warm and caring tone. Keep your hands at your side. Gesture to emphasize points, but do not overdo.

- Tape yourself, both when you practice and when you present.

- Present yourself as a credible source. Do not wear clothes that might distract from your message.

- Recognize what is remembered in any presentation or conversation: appearance, 55%; voice, 38%; and content, 7%.

Working with the Media

Using the media to win people over is no substitute for working directly with those you want to influence. When you use the media, your message becomes at risk of being modified, taken out of context, or put into an emotional backdrop.

At times, however, it is likely that it may be in your best interest to communicate with the community through the media as part of a support strategy to provide information or reinforce attitudes. This is one of the primary ways parents and people without children learn about the school.

The first step in establishing a relationship with the local media is finding out who covers educational news in your community. Call local newspaper, television, or radio stations directly for this information. Your district public relations office may provide contacts, assist with news releases, or arrange for media coverage of events.

The media can build support for services by sending reporters to cover programs such as divorce groups, safe school programs, or social skills units. News sources can provide advance publicity about upcoming events such as parenting classes or talks to a local civic group. Academic success, learning difficulties, discipline, and other issues school psychologists address make for interesting feature story topics.

What is news? Good publicity depends on knowing what makes good news. You are the best judge of which issues are of interest to the community. A key concept in story ideas is *timeliness*. Think of stories that are related to the time of year. Summer vacation activities, holiday pressures, children's fears (Halloween), adapting to a new school at the beginning of the school year, and middle school adjustment are a few examples. Do not forget to tie into national events and trends. Let people know what school psychologists are doing to address issues.

You might send in news releases when you attend a convention, initiate a new program, receive a special award, or are elected to a position in your professional association.

News releases. The most common way of letting the media know about upcoming events is by sending a news release. Use the following guidelines to increase the likelihood of getting a favorable response.

- Send out releases 10 days to 2 weeks prior to any event. Mail it to a specific person.

- Send the release on school stationery or a district news release form.

- Keep your message brief and concise. Omit needless words. Use the active voice.

- Releases should be typewritten, double-spaced on standard size paper. Use only one side and keep the release to one page. Use wide margins to allow for editing.

- Indent paragraphs. Include no more than two to three sentences in each. Longer paragraphs lose readers. Justify the left margin only.

- Use the *inverted pyramid* style. Include the "who," "what," "when," "where," and "how" in the first paragraph. Following this quick summary of major facts, include information in descending order of importance. This allows editors to cut from the bottom without having to rewrite it.

- Use first and last names: "Dr. Pat Harrison received the award," not "Harrison" or "Dr. Harrison."

- Eliminate jargon and write out any acronyms.

- Write releases in the third person, avoiding the use of first-person references such as "we," "our," and "your."

- Include a fact sheet about your school or school psychology association.

- For best readability, write at or below the 9th grade level. Fewer than 10 words out of 100 should have more than three syllables.

- Sentences should be short. The average length for best readability is no more than 19 words.

- Designate the end of the release with "# # #" centered. Clearly indicate the name of a person to contact for further information along with home and work phone numbers. Reporters often work day and evening hours.

When coverage is provided, send a note of appreciation. Papers and news broadcasts often have limited space and competition is keen.

SUMMARY

Establishing strong personalized relationships with audiences within the school community is essential. Attitudes that parents, community members, and educators hold about school psychological services are determined at the local building level. Influencing public attitudes is a continual process. Our challenge is to carefully identify key decision makers and meet with them directly so that they can join us in taking action on behalf of children.

Planned two-way communication creates understanding and support of the assistance our profession provides to children and education. The delivery of quality services to students is a prerequisite for successful public relations efforts.

A development and implementation cycle should be an ongoing part of every school psychologist's yearly routine. As a first step, current efforts are examined and information about the local school community is gathered. Priority audiences are then targeted along with the information each group needs to know and supportive action they can take. After planning and executing programs, feedback is secured and effectiveness of efforts is evaluated.

Every school psychologist must communicate with and involve a variety of people in his or her local community. The profession will be able to assume a leadership role in helping schools better meet the needs of all children to the extent that we work with others and build confidence in the services we provide.

AUTHOR'S NOTE

Pat Jackson of Jackson, Jackson, and Wagner is acknowledged for his contributions.

REFERENCES

Bagin, D. (1972). *School communication ideas that work.* Woodstown, NJ: Communicaid, Inc.

Bagin, D. (1985). *Evaluating your school PR investment.* Arlington, VA: National School Public Relations Association.

Bagin, R. (1993). Better ways to market school reform. *The NSPRA Network, 8:8.*

Banach, W. J. (1994). *Critical issues facing America's public schools.* Ray, MI: Banach, Banach, & Cassidy.

The Benton Foundation. (1991). *Strategic Communications.* Washington, DC: Author.

Bernays, E. (1952). *Public relations.* Norman, OK: University of Oklahoma Press.

Canter, A., & Crandall, A. (1994). *Preserving school-based positions.* Silver Spring, MD: National Association of School Psychologists.

Davis, R. (1986). *School public relations: The complete book.* Arlington, VA: National School Public Relations Association.

Dilenschneider, R. L. (1990). *Power and influence: Mastering the art of persuasion.* New York: Prentice Hall Press.

Fitzpatrick, J. L. (1993). *The board's role in public relations and communications.* Washington, DC: National Center for Nonprofit Boards.

Foundation for American Communications. (1987). *Media resource guide.* (A guide for non-profit volunteer organizations sponsored by the Gannett Foundation.) Los Angeles, CA: Author.

Gallup, G. (1982, December). Address to Glassboro State College Chapter of Phi Delta Kappa, Glassboro, NJ.

Kindred, L. W., Bagin, D., & Gallagher, D. R. (1984). *The school and community relations.* Englewood Cliffs, NJ: Prentice-Hall.

Ledell, M., & Arnsparger, A. (1993). *How to deal with community criticism of school change.* Denver, CO: Educational Commission of the States.

Lukaszewski, J. E. (1992). *Influencing public attitudes. Strategies that reduce the media's power.* Leesburg, VA: Issues Action Publications.

National School Public Relations Association. (1982). *Participant workbook: School communication workshop building level.* Arlington, VA: Author.

National School Public Relations Association. (1986). *Planning your school PR investment.* Arlington, VA: Author.

National School Public Relations Association. (1972). *Evaluation instruments for educational public relations programs.* Arlington, VA: Author.

Peterson, M. P., & Poppen, W. (1993). *School counselors and the first freedom.* Ann Arbor, MI: ERIC Counseling and Personnel Services Clearinghouse.

Powell, J. (1984). *The other side of the story.* New York: William Morrow and Company.

Ruess, C., & Silvis, D. (1985). *Inside organizational communications: Internal association of business communicators.* New York: Longman, Inc.

Stern, G. J. (1992). *Marketing workbook for nonprofit organizations.* (Available from Management Support Services, 919 Lafond Avenue, St. Paul, MN 55104.)

Wade, J. (1992). *Dealing effectively with the media.* Menlo Park, CA: Crisp Publications.

Wherry, J. (1988, July). *Ten top for 1988–1989 and what to do about them.* Paper presented at the National School Public Relations Association National Seminar, New Orleans, LA.

ANNOTATED BIBLIOGRAPHY

Davis, R. (1986). *School public relations: The complete book.* Arlington, VA: National School Public Relations Association.
This practical how-to text covers developments in effective building-level public relations programs.

Kindred, L. W., Bagin, D., & Gallagher, D. R. (1984). *The school and community relations.* Englewood Cliffs, NJ: Prentice-Hall.
In addition to providing expanded explanations of essential public relations concepts, this authoritative textbook offers worthwhile sections on oral presentations, radio and television basics, and preparation of printed material.

Ledell, M., & Arnsparger, A. (1993). *How to deal with community criticism of school change.* Denver, CO: Educational Commission of the States.
Written in cooperation with the Association for Supervision and Curriculum Development, the American Association of School Administrators, and the National Association of State Boards of Education, this booklet provides sound communications guidelines for building support for school restructuring efforts. Strategies for dealing with attacks and common concerns are included.

Lukaszewski, J. E. (1992). *Influencing public attitudes. Strategies that reduce the media's power.* Leesburg, VA: Issues Action Publications.
Based on sound principles, this book provides a step-by-step process for how organizations can influence attitudes and illustrates how traditional public relations efforts are often counterproductive. Direct communication, issues management, and audience analysis are emphasized.

25

Best Practices in Communicating with Parents

Paula Sachs Wise
Western Illinois University

OVERVIEW

Imagine that you are invited to attend a meeting of the State Board of Education regarding the status of school psychology in your state. You are the only school psychologist invited to attend the meeting. In fact, you are the only non-board-member in attendance at the meeting. The board members have worked together for a long time. They throw terms around with which you are unfamiliar, tell "private jokes" that you don't understand, present data about school psychology that you are unprepared to substantiate or refute, and smile rather condescendingly at you when you make a comment. The board members unanimously conclude that school psychological services in the state are woefully inadequate and should either be improved or dropped. A paper is then passed around to be signed by the board members and by you to show consensus. Everyone watches you to see if you will sign. Feeling tremendous pressure to conform, even though you are also feeling uncomfortable and depressed, you go along with the board since you have no "cold hard facts" on hand to refute their findings.

Not a very comfortable feeling is it? Especially when the meeting is about the fate of something you hold near and dear to you, like the profession of school psychology. You leave the meeting disgusted with the board for being so strong and disgusted with yourself for being so weak. You feel as though you have let school psychology down.

Now imagine you are a parent at a multidisciplinary staffing. Around the table sit a group of professional educators, most of whom know each other well and have worked together for a long time. You are the only non-school person in attendance. The topic of discussion is your child's educational future. Test results are presented and discussed and everyone else at the table seems to understand the results, but you don't know a processing deficit from an attention deficit. If all of these educators think that your child belongs in a learning disabilities resource room, who are you to disagree? Such a staffing represents what we might call the "worst practices in com-

municating with parents" because there is little genuine communication occurring.

The focus of this chapter is on the usefulness, the feasibility, and the importance of improving school psychologists' communications with parents. Some of the topics to be discussed include

- Why good communication between school psychologists and parents can benefit children.

- How good communication between school psychologists and parents can benefit children.

- How school psychologist–parent communication fits into the various roles and functions of the school psychologist.

In addition, references will be provided to assist school psychologists in communicating more effectively with different "types" of parents (e.g., parents new to special education, angry parents). Finally, general guidelines will be provided to facilitate school psychologists' improved communication with parents.

BASIC CONSIDERATIONS

Communicating frequently and effectively with parents should be as important a part of the school psychologist's job as assessing students and consulting with teachers. The passage of PL 94-142 in 1975 was touted by parents, special educators, and school psychologists alike as having the potential to lead to dramatic improvement in parents' involvement in the educational placement and programming of their children with disabilities. Yet while parents of children with disabilities have become more identified as team members in multidisciplinary staffings over the last few years, they have lost some ground as well. Since 1975 when staffings replaced parent conferences as the primary forum for the presentation of assessment results and the discussion of intervention strategies, parents have lost some of their unique privileges as parents while gaining rights as multidisciplinary team members.

Several years after the passage of PL 94-142, participants at the Olympia Conference on the Future of School Psychology emphasized school psychologists' relationships with parents as a major area to address (Brown & Cardon, 1982). At that conference, "concern was expressed that school psychologists have not been clearly recognized by the public as parent advocates. It was recommended that in matters relating to child welfare that parents and school psychologists merge their efforts in legislative and political action" (Brown & Cardon, 1982, p. 195). Yet as recently as 1991, a random sample of school psychologists in New York State reported spending an average of only 39.4 minutes (or 8%) of their days with family members of children in their schools (Fish & Massey, 1991). Of the 39.4 minutes per day, 40% was spent in telephone conversations, 30% in meetings with other people present, and 4% was spent writing notes to family members. Only 24% of the 39.4 minutes (9.5 minutes) was spent in individual meetings between the school psychologist and a child's family members. Fish and Massey also noted that of the total number of contacts with family members, 71% involved the mother only, 16.6% involved both parents, and 6.6% involved the father only. Fish and Massey suggested that more efforts be made to include fathers and other family members, and to increase the number of direct school psychologist-family contacts (without others present) in order to enhance school psychologist-family working relationships.

Why Good Communication Between School Psychologists and Parents is Important

School psychologist–parent communication provides the opportunity for the school psychologist to share information with the parent. When a child is first identified as being in need of psychological services, it is important to answer the parents' questions and provide general information. Specifically, the school psychologist needs to inform the parents as to the reason for the referral, the types of procedures that will be followed, the timeline that the parents can expect, the possible outcomes of the assessment, and the parents' rights and responsibilities in the assessment process. Parents should also have an opportunity to ask questions about these procedural issues.

Following an individual assessment of a child, parents generally wish to know, "How did my child do? Is my child 'normal'? What are his strengths and weaknesses? What can I expect from her? What should I do when he misbehaves?" (Wise, 1986, p. 7). Again, parents should have an opportunity to ask questions, request clarification, and understand in general terms the possible implications of your findings, keeping in mind that decisions are actually made during the multidisciplinary staffing. Parents who are informed of assessment results prior to the multidisciplinary staffing may be better able to act as contributing members of the multidisciplinary team (Teglasi, 1985). They have had time to digest and to ponder the assessment information and to formulate questions beforehand so that during the staffing they can ask their questions and make well thought out comments and suggestions.

School psychologist–parent communication provides the opportunity for the parent to "size up" the school psychologist and for the school psychologist to "size up" the parents. This is a frequently overlooked but important reason for school psychologist–parent conferences. Parents want to know: Who is this "shrink" who will be talking to my child? Does the person seem honest and trustworthy? Will my child like working with this person? Do I have confidence in the school psychologist's judgments? Does the school psychologist seem genuinely interested in and concerned about my child and about me? Not only do positive initial impressions ease the parents' mind, but parents who believe that the school psychologist is sincere and cares about them are more apt to carry out any eventual recommendations (Teglasi, 1985).

At the same time, school psychologists may use their initial contacts with parents to assess informally the child's family background, the degree of parental cooperation to expect, the parents' attitude about the child and the difficulties the child is having, as well as the parents' attitudes about the classroom teacher, the school system, and education in general. What are the parent's expectations for the child? Do these expectations seem realistic based upon the information already known? Is this a parent who would easily be able to complete a behavior questionnaire about the child? Will this parent follow through if asked to participate in intervention strategies? Just as every school psychology graduate student is taught the importance of establishing rapport with children, it is also important for school psychologists to establish rapport with parents!

School psychologist–parent communication provides the opportunity for parents to share information and concerns with the school psychologist. Who is better able to provide the school psychologist with information about developmental milestones, childhood illnesses and accidents, family stresses, and inter-sibling comparisons than the parents? How does the parent view the child and the difficulties that she is experiencing? What does the parent think are the child's strengths and weaknesses? What does the child say about school when he comes home? Were the parents aware of any problems prior to the referral? What is the child like at home? What does she like to do? Who does he play with? What activities is she involved in? What are his eating habits and sleeping habits? Are there any unusual stresses or strains in the child's life at present? What questions and concerns do the parents have that the teacher or other referral agent may not have mentioned?

Parents are generally their children's primary care givers and may be the one constant throughout the child's life. In all likelihood, they know more about the child than a teacher or other "temporary person" in the child's life. Why not rely upon parents for valuable information about the child? As noted by Sattler (1992), "Parents have a wealth of information about their child. A well-conducted parental interview will serve as a valuable source of information about the child and family and will lay the groundwork for enlisting parental cooperation with intervention efforts" (p. 429). Of course, it must be recognized that parents are far from unbiased observers of their children. Their viewpoints, however, are vital input for a thorough understanding of the child's difficulties.

Often, parents may be uncertain as to the teacher's reasons for referring their child. In fact, in one study (Knoff, 1982) when parents and school personnel were asked independently to identify the reasons for referral of a particular child from a checklist of 17 reasons, agreement between the parents and school personnel was found in only 57% of cases. Meeting with the parents prior to the gathering of other types of assessment data can provide the forum for clarification of any misconceptions the parents might have.

School psychologist–parent communication provides opportunities for parents and school psychologists to cooperate and collaborate — to view each other as allies rather than adversaries. If school psychologists truly want to achieve cooperative and collaborative relationships with parents, we must spend more time meeting with parents by themselves, away from the presence of other school personnel. Particularly in cases in which multidisciplinary staffings will likely result from our efforts, parents tend to be comforted by the fact that they have met with the school psychologist ahead of time and that there is at least one familiar and "friendly face" around the table — one person they have met before and whom they regard as an advocate for their child. Also if parents are hearing for the first time that their child has a disability of some type, they have the right to hear that news in a one-to-one meeting with the school psychologist, not in a large meeting with many strangers present. Parents' reactions to such news run the gamut from crying to yelling to shock (Sattler, 1992) but while the nature of the reaction may differ, the impact of such news on parents nearly always elicits a strong emotional response. Such emotional displays warrant a certain amount of privacy rather than a public forum.

Much has been written about the clientage issue within school psychology. That is, who is the client of the school psychologist? Pantaleno (1983) put forth the relatively extreme but thought-provoking notion that parents should be considered the primary clients of the school psychologist while children should be viewed as secondary clients. After all, parents not only provide us with children in need of our services but they also pay our salaries through their tax dollars. While others within the school system might have ulterior motives in referring a child for psychological services (e.g., getting the child out of a classroom or a school building), school psychologists tend to share the parents' motive to do whatever can be done to help the child.

Parents can also work with school psychologists as change agents in schools (Simpson & Poplin, 1982). Working together as child advocates, school psychologists can contribute their knowledge of how schools work and their awareness of current developments in school-related legislation and practices. Parents can contribute political clout through putting pressure on school officials, lobbying for legislation, and supporting local, state, and federal legislation with favorable platforms and voting records.

School psychologist–parent communication (in conjunction with school psychologist–teacher communication) may help bridge the gap between parents and teachers. When parents and teachers meet together each party may bring to the meeting a certain amount of "baggage" based upon what the child has said or done. A child may tell his parents how mean the teacher is, how she picks on him when others in the class are to blame, and how she refuses to answer his questions. The same child may tell his teacher that his parents let him stay up late watching R-rated movies or that he has so many home responsibilities with such severe consequences for noncompliance that he is unable to complete homework assignments.

The parent and teacher come to conferences with one another armed with these preconceived notions and immediately may be inclined to blame the other for the problems the child is experiencing. Parents may be convinced that the child's learning problems are a result of the teacher's unreasonable expectations, while the teacher may attribute the child's difficulties to a home environment neither supportive of nor conducive to education.

The school psychologist who understands that from an ecological perspective, the child's behavior is influenced by and influences the school *and* the home environment, can remain relatively neutral (Power & Bartholomew, 1985). Meeting individually with each party, the school psychologist can listen carefully, clarify terms and concerns, empathize with both, while still addressing the concerns in a nondefensive, realistic manner.

School psychologist–parent communication is necessary for compliance with legal and ethical guidelines (e.g., informed consent). There are several issues involved in communicating with parents that involve legal and ethical principles. The first contact many school psychologists have with parents may concern the need for the parents to consent to having their child receive psychological services. Informed consent is needed when assessment procedures are performed, individual or group counseling services are offered, research projects involve children, records are sent from the school to another professional or another school district, and so forth. Simply put, parents have a right to know what is going on with respect to their child in school especially if the child is treated differently in any way than his/her classmates. Jacob and Hartshorne (1991) note that parents must be provided with information regarding

> the nature and scope of services offered, assessment-treatment goals and procedures, the expected duration of services, any foreseeable risks or discomforts for the student-client (including any risks of psychological or physical harm), the cost of the services to the parent or student (if any), the benefits that can reasonably be expected, the possible consequences/risks of not receiving treatment/services, and information about alternative treatments/services that may be beneficial (p. 53)

In addition, parents must be provided with this information in an understandable manner. If the parents are non-English-speaking, for example, efforts must be made to find a way to communicate the information to the parents in their native language.

Parents have other legal rights as well. They have a right to review their children's academic records, a right to privacy, a right to confidentiality of the information they do choose to share, and a right to share information with or withhold information from other individuals and agencies. (See Fischer & Sorenson, 1991, and Jacob & Hartshorne, 1991, for further clarification of legal and ethical issues surrounding communication with parents.)

School psychologist–parent communication is important from a public relations standpoint. Those of us who work for school districts or other local, state, or national agencies are public figures. Our salaries are paid from tax monies, and we are accountable to the public for our professional activities. The more positive contacts we can have with parents, the more support we can probably hope for if our jobs are on the line or if a school referendum is up for a vote.

How Good School Psychologist–Parent Communication Can Benefit Children

There are several ways in which good communication between school psychologists and parents can benefit children. First, parents tend to pass their feelings about things to their children. If the parents believe that the school psychologist working with their child is likely to have a positive impact on the child's learning or behavior, then through the "self-fulfilling prophecy" or the power of positive thinking, the impact is more likely to occur.

Second, if the parents feel as though they are partners with the school psychologist and other school personnel and that they can help to make a difference in their children's school experiences, the parents may work harder to achieve results. To use a popular buzzword of the 1990s, the parents are "empowered" by their relationship with the school psychologist to take a more active role in their children's education. Thus parents may be more consistent in rewarding a child's good behavior, put forth extra effort in ignoring a child's inappropriate behaviors, or even take extra care in applying consequences when the child disobeys an established rule.

The Importance of Good School Psychologist–Parent Communication in Each of the Roles and Functions of the School Psychologist

In the traditional *child study or problem-solving assessment role*, the school psychologist needs to communicate with parents to obtain informed consent and background information as well as to provide parents with information about the assessment process, the timeline to be followed, and the possible outcomes of the assessment. In addition, parents may be asked to participate actively in the assessment process through completing behavior rating scales, personality inventories, and/or adaptive behavior inventories and collecting actual student performance data. Some problems that students experience in school may also be observable in the home environment. In such cases, parents can collect relevant data such as reading at home, completion of homework assignments, study habits, and so forth. On a less formal basis parents can be useful sources of information about children's study habits, reading practices, and other social and behavioral observations. Parents also function as part of the multidisciplinary team and in that role they participate in the information-sharing and decision-making processes as team members.

Of course not all school psychologist–parent communication is oral; written communication — memos, reports, and notices — are also worthy of consideration. Ross-Reynolds (1990) notes that "the fundamental purpose of reports is to communicate information to the referring person in such a way that the latter's beliefs, feelings, and/or behaviors relative to the child are changed" (p. 621). Reports have many other uses as well, including presenting and summarizing assessment data in a (usually) succinct manner, and providing a "hard copy" of results for teachers and parents to read at their leisure away from the distracting presence of other people. Ross-Reynolds's approach to report writing might be called an "action-oriented" approach focusing on interventions, actions, and outcomes rather than on the traditional rehashing of the psychologist's findings. It is also active because through his approach the psychologist is attempting to influence or change the reader in some ways.

A second innovative approach to report writing is put forward by Sandy (1986) who calls his method a "descriptive-collaborative approach." Sandy suggests that if school psychologists genuinely wish to have parents communicate their thoughts and feelings to us, we should not include our own interpretations of the data in the written report. Rather we should present assessment data, including some of the actual responses of the child. We should then, in conferences and/or staffings, encourage the parents and other participants to interpret the results and to provide examples of home and school behaviors similar to the test results. Sandy maintains that his approach is much more likely to lead to parents and others becoming increasingly active in identifying problems and suggesting and implementing interventions and that the approach also strengthens alliances rather than adversarial relationships between parents and school psychologists.

In the *intervention role*, parents are needed to provide consent for suggested interventions. They may also play an active role through such practices as being involved in the completion of daily school–home notes or providing reinforcements for appropriate behavior. Further, parents may be asked to carry out interventions, collect performance data, and assist with intervention decision making. Simpson and Poplin (1981) suggest a number of ways in which parents can be involved in behavioral interventions and provide a review of many successful programs described in the research literature.

In the *consultation role*, the parents are partners with school psychologists and other school personnel in the collaborative problem-solving process (Sheridan, Kratochwill, & Elliott, 1990). They may provide input into the problem, elaborate on the nature and scope of the difficulties, help to generate solutions, and implement the home-based part of the plan. Parents may also be involved in collecting data, completing behavior check lists, and providing reinforcements. Finally, in the consultation role, parents may be excellent sources of feedback as to how a plan is proceeding and what changes should or could be made to improve the results.

In the school psychologist's role as a *liaison between the schools and community agencies*, the school psychologist can provide a link between the parents, the school, and the agency, trying to match the child or the family up with appropriate services. Under some circumstances it may be appropriate for the school psychologist to make the initial contact with an outside agency in order to ease the parents' way for future contacts. The school psychologist may be a valuable source of information to the parents and to the school in providing information about available services, fees, waiting lists, procedures, and

so forth. Parents who have had little experience with such services may not even know what questions to ask and thus may be intimidated from following through in order to receive much needed services.

In the school psychologist's role as a *researcher*, parental cooperation and involvement is often critical. Not only will parents be asked to give informal consent if their child is asked to participate in a research project, the parents may also be asked to complete questionnaires about the family background, the home environment, or school-related experiences depending upon the nature of the project. All school psychologists, whether or not they take an active role in conducting research, should be involved as consumers of relevant research. For example, relevant to the area of communicating with parents, recent research has identified family-related variables that relate to school achievement (Christenson, Rounds, & Gorney, 1992). Based upon this research it has been suggested

> that school psychologists need to (a) be knowledgeable about family influences on student achievement, (b) assess the degree to which children's home environments are characterized by factors correlated with achievement, (c) promote recommended practices for involving parents in education, and (d) design home-school interventions that address students' learning. (Christenson, Rounds, & Gorney, 1992, p. 198)

BEST PRACTICES IN COMMUNICATING WITH PARENTS

Be familiar with communicating with different types or groups of parents. Specific guidelines for communicating with particular groups or types of parents have been identified and discussed throughout the school psychology literature. The rationale for the provision of such guidelines was summarized by Jensen and Potter (1990) as follows: "Parents approach a meeting with school personnel from a variety of perspectives and backgrounds. The psychologist must be sensitive to the unique needs that parents bring to a communication setting and be responsive to those needs" (p. 192).

Suggestions for communicating with specific populations of parents can be found in the following resources:

- Parents new to special education (Flagg-Williams, 1991; Jensen & Potter, 1990; Ormerod & Huebner, 1988; Sattler, 1992; Simpson, 1982)

- Experienced parents (Jensen & Potter, 1990)

- Passive parents (Jensen & Potter, 1990)

- Assertive parents (Jensen & Potter, 1990)

- Angry parents (Jensen & Potter, 1990; Margolis, 1991)

- Alienated parents (Calabrese, Miller, & Dooley, 1987)

- Handicapped parents (i.e., parents with disabilities) (Jensen & Potter, 1990)

- Mobile parents (i.e., transient families) (Jensen & Potter, 1990)

- Culturally different and minority parents (Jensen & Potter, 1990; Li & Liu, 1993; Simpson, 1982)

- Non-English-speaking parents (Jensen & Potter, 1990)

- Single-parent families and reconstituted families (Burns & Brassard, 1982; Carlson, 1990; Simpson, 1982)

- Non-custodial parents (Jensen & Potter, 1990)

- Parents at various developmental stages (Pierson & Whaley, 1990)

Other articles have provided guidelines for parents of particular types or groups of children. Such articles include suggestions for parents of:

- College-bound students with learning disabilities (Aune & Johnson, 1992)

- Sexually abused children (Brassard, Tyler, & Kehle, 1983; Hillman & Solek-Tefft, 1988)

- Gifted children (Anderson, 1987; Brown, 1982; Sattler, 1992)

- Children with developmental disabilities (Harris & Fong, 1985)

- Rural children with disabilities (Latham & Burnham, 1985)

- Adolescent drug users (Severson, 1984)

- Children with elective mutism (Lazarus, Gavilo, & Moore, 1983)

- Socially withdrawn children (Sheridan, Kratochwill, & Elliott, 1990)

- Children with severe disabilities (Downing, 1989)

- Visually impaired children (Erchul & Turner, 1987)

In addition to the references listed above which address particular populations of parents, there are several general principles which relate to all school psychologist–parent communications. These principles are as follows:

Treat parents as you would wish to be treated if the situation were reversed! Most of us would expect to be treated courteously and kindly. Appointments should begin on time. Information should be presented candidly yet in an understandable manner. Ample time should be allowed for questions to be asked and adequately answered. Meetings should be held in rooms which allow for privacy and confidentiality of information shared. Interruptions of such meetings should not be allowed except in case of emergency.

In addition, parents should be recognized and treated as individuals. Some parents do not wish to be bothered with attending pre-assessment meetings, post-assessment meetings, and multidisciplinary staffings. Other parents wish to be as active and visible as possible in their children's educational planning and welcome any and all opportunities for involvement. Simpson and Fiedler (1989) on the topic of parental participation in IEP conferences noted that

> while PL 94-142 has effectively promoted an individualized perspective toward all children with disabilities, ironically it has not applied the same emphasis on individualization to parents . . . decisions about the degree of parent involvement in IEP conferences should be made on the basis of individual preferences rather than generalized expectations. (Simpson & Fiedler, 1989, p. 149)

Simpson and Fiedler go on to suggest that parents should be given a choice as to how involved they wish to be in the IEP process and that school personnel should not assume that more parental involvement is either better or worse than less involvement. School psychologists should make every effort to inform parents of their options. Parents, however, should have the final say in choosing from among the options.

Focus on the interpersonal aspects of school psychologist–parent communication. Treat parents with dignity, respect, honesty, and empathy. Reinforce parents for the efforts they make and for the positive things they do for their children. If parents confide in you, thank them for their trust and their honesty (Sattler, 1992). If parents make special efforts to attend a conference or staffing, acknowledge their efforts. Find positive and unique things about each child you work with and share those observations with the parents. Reassure parents, when appropriate, that they are "good parents." Make every effort to include parents in discussions during staffings just as you might try to "draw out" a reticent guest in your home. Keep in mind how strongly most parents identify with their children. When a negative comment is made about a child, the parents often take it as a personal criticism either of themselves or of their parenting skills.

Help teachers, principals, and other school personnel improve their communication skills with parents. School personnel often report that they were unprepared in their own training to communicate with parents (Fish, 1990; Strickland, 1982). Yet dealing with parents is a big part of the job for those who work with children. Volunteer to address communication skills with parents at a teacher or administrator inservice. Provide opportunities for participants to role-play potentially difficult cases (e.g., defensive parents, feuding parents) and then discuss the role-playing efforts. Provide guidelines for ways in which teachers can organize their conferences such that all of the important information is covered while making sure that time is allowed for parents to share their concerns or ask their questions. Suggest that an advisory group of parents be established in your schools in order to elicit opinions concerning parent–teacher conferences (e.g., length, frequency, structure). If the parents in such an advisory group are a relatively homogenous group and not representative of other parents in the school district, consider conducting a survey of all or of randomly selected parents to obtain more diverse opinions. Perhaps the improvement of parent–teacher conferences could be adopted as a goal of the local parent teacher organization. Also suggest that teachers communicate more often to parents through informal newsletters or notes. Children can be relatively poor "transmitters" of information as to classroom events and activities.

Provide parents with resources. Even if you meet with parents before and after assessing individual children, many parents want more of your time and expertise. Parenting generally is an isolated occupation. Parents are not provided with owners' manuals and the advice received from well-meaning relatives, friends, and strangers usually ranges from the inappropriate to the offensive. To make matters worse, it may take 20, 30, or more years for parents to find out how they did and whether or not they made the right decisions. Most parents are genuinely concerned about their children and want to do what is best for them. School psychologists can reach a large audience of parents through speaking engagements at school functions (e.g., PTA meetings); service organizations (e.g., Rotary, Lions); and more specialized groups (e.g., Parents without Partners). Many of these groups have regularly scheduled meetings and program chairs are often desperate for speakers. Volunteer! If public speaking does not appeal to you, consider offering advice or presenting new ideas to parents through newspaper or newsletter columns. The National Association of School Psychologists newsletter, *Communiqué,* has a feature entitled, "By-line School Psychology," with sample columns you can use or adapt.

School psychologists might also consider developing reading lists for parents who want more information about particular topics (e.g., attention deficit hyperactivity disorder [ADHD], learning disabilities, discipline). There are many such books available to the general public in libraries and/or bookstores. Make it a practice to read through these books on a regular basis to determine which might be most worthy of your recommendation. Such efforts on your part would not only be helpful to parents but also would count towards hours needed for Continuing Professional Development. Sattler (1992) provides a

list of "general sources of information for parents of handicapped children and for children" (p. 785–787) although most of the books listed were published prior to 1980. A few more recent references are suggested in the annotated bibliography at the conclusion of this chapter.

Another resource school psychologists can provide for parents is to help in establishing support groups of parents with children with similar difficulties. Parents of students with disabilities may feel as though they are the only ones whose children are experiencing difficulty in school. Schell (1981) noted that with all of the talk about teacher burnout, little attention has been paid to the phenomenon of "parent burnout." Parents of children with disabilities often need support systems desperately. Establishing a school-based group of parents of children with disabilities can meet some of these needs by providing a safe forum to share ideas and information and lessen feelings of isolation and burnout. Speakers can be brought in to address particular areas of interest (e.g., the impact of inclusion on students with disabilities, the use of medication for students with ADHD). School psychologists speaking to such groups can explain in general the types of assessment information we gather and the ways that information is used. Thus, parents will become more knowledgeable about assessment procedures overall prior to subsequent conferences in which their children's performance on specific tasks is discussed. Many parents may be more likely to try intervention strategies which other parents have implemented successfully.

School psychologists can also improve their communication with parents through running parent groups for parents experiencing problems with discipline, parents going through separation or divorce, and so forth. For school psychologists lacking the time, energy, or expertise for such groups, it may be helpful to act as a liaison with a local mental health center or other resource in order to find someone who is willing to provide such a service in the community.

Periodically assess your skills in communicating with parents. A study by Zins and Fairchild (1986) indicated that only 13.3% of a national sample of school psychologists gather accountability data from parents. Yet such data collection is certainly not only possible but desirable. Fairchild (1985) described a system in which parents as well as teachers were asked to complete questionnaires evaluating school psychology interns' skills in assessment and intervention. From a different angle, Wise (1986) provided an instrument designed to help school psychologists assess their own parent conference skills. Her "Self-Evaluation of Parent Conference" form focuses on such areas as the school psychologists' courteousness, openness, honesty, and organization during parent conferences. Medway (1989) summarizes the results of 27 studies examining the effectiveness of parent education programs and groups, by examining whether parents changed their attitudes or behaviors as a result of such training. Results were encouraging and demonstrate ways to assess effectiveness of yet another school psychologist-parent activity. Perhaps somewhat surprisingly, no studies were identified that examined the effectiveness of school psychologists' telephone conversations with parents. Yet as cited earlier, Fish and Massey (1991) found that the largest amount of time (40%) that school psychologists spend in parent communication involved telephone conversations. Certainly research is needed into this much-neglected mode of communication.

SUMMARY

Throughout this chapter, an effort has been made to demonstrate ways in which school psychologists can improve their communications with parents. Reasons were provided as to why improved communication with parents is desirable in terms of helping parents, helping children, and helping the professional image of the school psychologist. Improved communication with parents transcends the various roles and functions of the psychologist in the schools. It is difficult to imagine any professional function of school psychologists that is unrelated (at least indirectly) to working with parents. Assessment of students, for example, involves parental awareness, consent, cooperation, and collaboration while the planning and implementation of intervention strategies involves parental consent, cooperation, collaboration, and active participation.

There are many methods by which school psychologists can go about improving their communications with parents. Such methods include but are not limited to treating parents as you would want to be treated under similar circumstances; focusing on the interpersonal aspects of our communication with parents; helping other school personnel to improve their communication skills with parents; and providing parents with additional resources (e.g., readings, handouts, support groups, and parenting groups).

In order to improve communication skills with parents, it is important to assess realistically the current level of such skills and to identify, document, and measure, in some way, efforts made to improve such skills. Such assessment should be an integral part of one's total professional accountability plan.

REFERENCES

Anderson, M. A. (1987). Facilitating parental understanding of the "gifted" label. *Techniques, 3,* 236–244.

Aune, E. P., & Johnson, J. M. (1992). Transition takes teamwork: A collaborative model for college-bound students with learning disabilities. *Intervention in School and Clinic, 27,* 222–227.

Brassard, M. R., Tyler, A., & Kehle, T. (1983). Sexually abused children: Identification and suggestions for intervention. *School Psychology Review, 12,* 93–97.

Brown, D. T., & Cardon, B. W. (1982). The Olympia Proceedings, Section VIII. Synthesis and editorial comment. *School Psychology Review, 11,* 195–198.

Brown, P. P. (1982). The role of the school psychologist in gifted education. *Roeper Review, 4,* 28–29.

Burns, C. W., & Brassard, M. R. (1982). A look at the single parent family: Implications for the school psychologist. *Psychology in the Schools, 19,* 487–494.

Calabrese, R. L., Miller, J. W., & Dooley, B. (1987). The identification of alienated parents and children: Implications for school psychologists. *Psychology in the Schools, 24,* 145–152.

Carlson, C. (1990). Best practices in working with single-parent and stepparent family systems. In A. Thomas & J. Grimes (Eds.), *Best practices in school psychology–II* (pp. 837–857). Washington, DC: National Association of School Psychologists.

Christenson, S. L., Rounds, T., & Gorney, D. (1992). Family factors and student achievement: An avenue to increase students' success. *School Psychology Quarterly, 7,* 178–206.

Downing, J. (1989). Identifying and enhancing the communicative behaviors of students with severe disabilities. *School Psychology Review, 18,* 475–486.

Education of All Handicapped Children Act of 1975 (PL 94–142), 20 U.S.C.

Erchul, W. P., & Turner, B. D. (1987). Visually impaired children: II. Intervention strategies. *School Psychology International, 8,* 271–281.

Fairchild, T. N. (1985). Obtaining consumer feedback as a means of evaluating school psychology intern performance. *Psychology in the Schools, 22,* 419–428.

Fischer, L., & Sorenson, G. P. (1991). *School law for counselors, psychologists, and social workers* (2nd ed.). New York: Longman.

Fish, M. C. (1990). Best practices in family-school relationships. In A. Thomas & J. Grimes (Eds.), *Best practices in school psychology–II* (pp. 371–381). Washington, DC: National Association of School Psychologists.

Fish, M. C., & Massey, R. (1991). Systems in school psychology Practice: A preliminary investigation. *Journal of School Psychology, 29,* 361–366.

Flagg-Williams, J. B. (1991). Perspectives on working with parents of handicapped children. *Psychology in the Schools, 28,* 238–246.

Harris, S. L., & Fong, P. L. (1985). Developmental disabilities: The family and the school. *School Psychology Review, 14,* 162–165.

Hillman, D., & Solek-Tefft, J. (1988). *Spiders and flies: Help for parents and teachers of sexually abused children.* Lexington Books: Lexington, MA.

Jacob, S., & Hartshorne, T. (1991). *Ethics and law for school psychologists.* Brandon, VT: Clinical Psychology Publishing Co., Inc.

Jensen, B. F., & Potter, M. L. (1990). Best practices in communicating with parents. In A. Thomas & J. Grimes (Eds.), *Best practices in school psychology–II* (pp. 183–193). Washington, DC: National Association of School Psychologists.

Knoff, H. M. (1982). Evaluating consultation service delivery at an independent psychodiagnostic clinic. *Professional Psychology, 13,* 699–705.

Latham, G., & Burnham, J. (1985). Innovative methods for serving rural handicapped children. *School Psychology Review, 14,* 438–443.

Lazarus, P. J., Gavilo, H. M., & Moore, J. W. (1983). The treatment of elective mutism in children within the school setting: Two case studies. *School Psychology Review, 12,* 467–472.

Li, C., & Liu, T. C. (March, 1993). How to work effectively with Asian-American families. National Association of School Psychologists, *Communiqué,* pp. 23–26.

Margolis, H. (1991). Listening: The key to problem solving with angry parents. *School Psychology International, 12,* 329–347.

Medway, F. J. (1989). Measuring the effectiveness of parent education. In M. J. Fine (Ed.), *The second handbook on parent education: Contemporary perspectives* (pp. 237–255). San Diego, CA: Academic Press.

Ormerod, J. J., & Huebner, E. S. (1988). Crisis intervention: Facilitating parental acceptance of a child's handicap. *Psychology in the Schools, 25,* 422–428.

Pantaleno, A. P. (1983). Parents as primary clients of the school psychologist or why is it we are here? *Journal of School Psychology, 21,* 107–113.

Pierson, E. M., & Whaley, A. L. (1990). Implications of adult developmental stages for school psychologists' work with parents of school-age children. *Psychology in the Schools, 27,* 233–237.

Power, T. J., & Bartholomew, K. L. (1985). Getting uncaught in the middle: A case study in family-school system consultation. *School Psychology Review, 14,* 222–229.

Ross-Reynolds, G. (1990). Best practices in report writing. In A. Thomas & J. Grimes (Eds.), *Best practices in school psychology–II* (pp. 621–633). Washington, DC: National Association of School Psychologists.

Sandy, L. R. (1986). The descriptive-collaborative approach to psychological report writing. *Psychology in the Schools, 23,* 395–400.

Sattler, J. M. (1992). *Assessment of children* (3rd ed.). San Diego: Jerome M. Sattler, Publisher, Inc.

Schell, G. C. (1981). The young handicapped child: A family perspective. *Topics in Early Childhood Special Education, 1,* 11–19.

Severson, H. H. (1984). Adolescent social drug use: School prevention program. *School Psychology Review, 13,* 159–161.

Sheridan, S. M., Kratochwill, T. R., & Elliott, S. N. (1990). Behavioral consultation with parents and teachers: Delivering treatment for socially withdrawn children at home and school. *School Psychology Review, 19,* 33–52.

Simpson, R. L. (1982). *Conferencing parents of exceptional children.* Rockville, MD: Aspen.

Simpson, R. L., & Fiedler, C. R. (1989). Parent participation in Individualized Educational Program (IEP) conferences: A case for individualization. In M. J. Fine (Ed.), *The second handbook on parent education: Contemporary perspectives* (pp. 145–171). San Diego, CA: Academic Press.

Simpson, R. L., & Poplin, M. S. (1991). Parents as agents of change. *School Psychology Review, 10,* 15–25.

Strickland, B. (1982). Parental participation, school accountability, and due process. *Exceptional Education Quarterly, 3,* 41–49.

Teglasi, H. (1985). Best practices in interpreting psychological assessment data to parents. In A. Thomas & J. Grimes (Eds.), *Best practices in school psychology* (pp. 415–429). Kent, OH: National Association of School Psychologists.

Wise, P. S. (1986). *Better parent conferences: A manual for school psychologists.* Kent, OH: National Association of School Psychologists.

Zins, J. E., & Fairchild, T. N. (1986). An investigation of the accountability practices of school psychologists. *Professional School Psychology, 1,* 193–204.

ANNOTATED BIBLIOGRAPHY[B

Fine, M. J. (Ed.). (1989). *The second handbook on parent education: Contemporary perspectives.* San Diego: Academic Press.
Provides summaries of many current models of parent training. A good resource for professionals interested in conducting parent training groups.

Garber, S. W., Garber, M. D., & Spizman, R. F. (1987). *Good behavior: Over 1,000 sensible solutions to your child's problems from birth to age twelve.* New York: Villard Books.
A personal favorite to recommend to parents, the book begins with general behavior management principles and moves to suggestions for hundreds of specific concerns parents may have.

Jacob, S., & Hartshorne, T. (1991). *Ethics and law for school psychologists.* Brandon, VT: Clinical Psychology Publishing Co., Inc.
An excellent and easy-to-read guide to legal and ethical issues in the practice of school psychology including many aspects of school psychologist–parent communication.

McCullough, V. E. (1992). *Testing and your child.* New York: Penguin Books.
Describes 150 of the most common medical, educational, and psychological tests. For each of the tests, the author addresses whose permission is needed; what the test does and does not test; how results are recorded, evaluated, interpreted, and compared; and how reliable the test is.

Shore, M. F., Brice, P. J., & Love, B. G. (1992). *When your child needs testing.* New York: Crossroads.
While this book underemphasizes the role of the school psychologist, it is still a solid and up-to-date resource for parents whose children are referred for psychological testing.

26

Best Practices in Facilitating Services in Urban Settings

Joseph D. Perry
Cleveland Public Schools
and University of Akron

OVERVIEW

In contrast to Jackson's (1990) chapter on urban school psychology in *Best Practices–II*, this review is focused on facilitating services. The focus includes conceptual and practical issues for planning, developing, expanding, and implementing urban school psychology services. A primary rationale is that large urban schools present both opportunities and challenges to providing effective school psychology services that differ from those encountered in other types of school settings. The intent is to emphasize the necessity of developing comprehensive services that meet the unique challenges of serving urban youth within the at-risk ecology of large-city schools.

The general issue of facilitating services is highly relevant in view of recent legislative and professional developments that impact service delivery. For example, the American Psychological Association (APA) has recently developed a task force on an urban initiative as well as task forces on related topics of violence and substance abuse (Cantor, 1993). The urban task force was initiated by the APA president (Cantor) and is directed at the "crises" urban youth experience in adjustment and learning.

A major caveat for facilitating or even conceptualizing the challenges confronting school psychologists in urban settings is that a data-based needs assessment should initially be conducted. Urban schools are complex and vary not only in size of population but also in terms of organizational structure, special education services, demographics, risk factors, and a multiplicity of other variables. Hence, school psychology services should attempt to address the unique needs of a specific urban setting. The content of a needs assessment is reflected by the issues reviewed in the basic considerations section and will be described later in the practice guidelines. Facilitating program development for services needed in an urban school system often requires knowledge bases that the typical school psychologist lacks such as violence prevention and Comer's Yale Child Study Model (Cantor, 1993). Hence, facilitating services in urban settings is a complex process.

Best practice guidelines are provided concerning multiple topics such as facilitating the following: leadership, needs assessment, public relations, grant-funded programs, and alternative services. The last issue of alternative services is especially relevant for urban settings. There are typically special projects and multiple departments in urban schools that could benefit from involvement of school psychology services. Types of alternative services reviewed include the School Development Program (SDP); an intervention project in Chapter I programs; an intervention program for expelled students; and crisis/violence intervention services. The more specific nuances for implementation will be reviewed in the best practices section to provide the reader with practical examples for promoting services.

BASIC CONSIDERATIONS

Recent publications have pointed out the failure of large urban schools to address the needs of urban student populations (e.g., Bracey, 1993; Bullard & Taylor, 1993; Cantor, 1993). Indeed, youth living in urban settings have been found to present similar stress reactions to those living in "war zones" according to cross-cultural research findings conducted by Garbarino, Dubrow, Kostelny, and Pardo (1992). However, Cantor (1993) states "the science and profession of psychology, with the broadest understanding of human behavior of any science and profession, has not made a unified, concerted effort to address the urban crisis" (p. 5). To illustrate the uniqueness of the needs of inner city youth, a brief review of the characteristics of urban schools and the problems encountered are provided in this section. Other issues that have impact for facilitating services in urban public school settings are also reviewed.

Demographics

The 1990 census reported that about one-third of the U.S. population resides in the 488 cities with populations above 50,000. The demographics of cities have been changing during the past 25 years. Urban public school populations have been reduced due to families of all races with higher socioeconomic levels moving to the suburbs and increased enrollments of private and parochial schools (Bracey, 1993; Zero Population Growth, 1993). School districts of the nation's 25 largest cities now have student populations composed of cultural, ethnic, racial, and linguistic groups (Ponterrotto, 1990) leaving whites in the minority. The Greater Washington Research Center (1993) found that half of the nation's 488 largest cities also have poverty rates exceeding the national average of 13.14%. The 25 largest cities with the highest poverty rates also had populations that were composed of over half minorities. Typically, urban school populations have poverty rates and minority representations higher than the total city population in which they are located. For example, Jordan (1993) pointed out that Atlanta's general population is 67% African American but 92% of the public school's enrollment is composed of African Americans. Similarly, the Cleveland Public School's population has a poverty rate of over 70% as defined by school lunch status and is composed of about 76% minorities.

It is not just the concentration of minorities and poverty in urban schools that creates risks for youth, but rather an ecology characterized by high crime, gang involvement, single-parent families, unemployment, family mobility, and population density (Garbarino et al., 1992; Hammond & Yung, 1993). Moreover, as Hammond and Yung point out, current explanations are not adequate because many impoverished African American youth in urban settings do not present maladjustment.

Educational Deficits, Stress, and Violence

There is considerable evidence indicating that urban public school populations are increasingly at risk for negative sequelae to multiple stressors in all areas of development. For example, it is estimated that about 20% of first-grade students in large urban settings need remediation to master the initial reading curriculum (Madden, Slavin, Karweit, Dolan, & Wasik, 1991). The school dropout rate in large urban settings is reported to range from about 41% to 50% (Bullard & Taylor, 1993; Council of Great City Schools, 1987). Educational deficits for those who stay in school were also reported by a recent nationwide study conducted for the U.S. Department of Education by the Abt Associates (1993). Schools with demographics similar to large urban settings (e.g., low socioeconomic status [SES] as defined by at least 75% of students qualifying for free and reduced price lunch) had only 15% to 32% of students attaining a grade-point average (GPA) of 3.0 or higher while 35% to 47% of students in low-poverty schools attained this GPA. Moreover, students from high-poverty schools with the 3.0 or higher GPA scored lower on standardized tests in reading and math than students from low-poverty schools with a 2.0 GPA. Educational deficits may be related to other problems such as multiple stresses and especially violence which according to recent reports has dramatically increased for urban youth.

A recent nationwide study by Zero Population Growth (1993) reported that youth in the 195 largest U.S. cities experienced more stress than those in other geographical locations (i.e., 493 counties and 239 metropolitan areas). It was generally found that higher population density was associated with greater stress for children based on an index of 70 indicators such as crime, health care, educational outcomes, and community economics. Out of a top positive score of 100, the 8 worst cities in order of stress for children and their scores were Newark (27.4), Gary (29.1), Cleveland (29.4), Chicago (29.6), Detroit (30.5), Miami (32.5), Los Angeles (33.3) and Houston (33.3). This is in contrast to average ratings of about 65 for counties and metropolitan areas.

Garbarino et al. (1992) reported that violence is the major stress for urban youth. Hammond and Yung (1993) pointed out that homicide is now the leading cause of death for African American male adolescents with a 55% increase between 1985 and 1990. Sample statistics cited by Hammond and Yung include: (a) the majority of urban youth have witnessed stabbings and shootings and one-third have directly observed a homicide; (b) death rates are 5 times higher for inner-city youth than those in other settings; (c) urban African American male adolescents are most likely to be both perpetrators and victims of violence; and (d) 20% of urban youth are threatened with a gun and 12% have gunfire directed at them. Garbarino et al. (1992) reported that violence for urban youth is particularly stressful because the perpetrators are often persons familiar to the victims. Although Hammond and Yung (1993) reported a lack of adequate explanations for the increasing rate of violence, they also noted recent hypotheses including (a) racism and poverty with hostile responses due to resentment, hopelessness, and self-hatred; (b) drug and gang involvement with such cultural values as high status for violent offenders; (c) inner-city residence with family dysfunction, crowding, and community disorganization.

There are many other indicators of negative developmental sequelae and risks for urban youth that could impair school performance. These include increased rates of drug and alcohol abuse, adolescent pregnancy, gang involvement, suicide behavior, and sexually transmitted diseases. A recent text edited by Gaw (1993) indicated that the prevalence and nature of mental health problems varies for different cultures and types of residence with implications for differentiated interventions. Because of the stress and violence already prevalent in their lives, urban youth could be expected to present a high prevalence of adjustment problems to loss from death experiences and parent separation. School psychologists working in urban schools are in an opportune position to address these psychosocial factors as a foundation for facilitating psychological services.

Special Education Placements

Jackson (1990) noted that in urban schools "there is continuing confrontation over who needs and who does not need special education" (p. 759). A salient issue is the recent finding that a disproportionate number of students from minority backgrounds are placed in special education. The *Fourteenth Annual Report to Congress* (U.S. Department of Education, 1992) recently summarized the findings of a federally sponsored study on this topic entitled the National Longitudinal Transition Study of Special Education Students (NLTS). This study provided a demographic profile of a nationally representative sample of special education students 13 to 21 years of age. The findings were more definitive than previous literature such as the National Academy of Science Report in the 1970s and generally indicated that, in comparison to the general population, youth with disabilities were disproportionately male, African American, and from single-parent families with a low SES similar to that of most large urban school populations.

More specific findings regarding race indicated that African American youth were the most disproportionate of any racial group in total special education placements. African American students represented 24% of all special education students but only 12% of the general population studied. Hispanic students were found to be underrepresented (i.e., 8% with disabilities and 13% in the general population) as were white students (i.e., 65 and 70% respectively). African American youth were found to be most disproportionately represented in the disabilities of mental retardation (31%), speech and language impairments (28%), visual impairments (25.9%), and serious emotional disturbance (25%) with less in the high-incidence specific learning disability category (21.6%). The major concern is that African American students are disproportionately identified for special education and other remedial programs for students with "low ability" rather than the less stigmatizing specific learning disability program (Madden et al., 1991; Special Education Committee for the Council of Great City Schools, 1988). The NLTS report did include interpretive hypotheses for the disproportionate special education placement of African American students which could provide urban school psychologists with direction for services to address this issue.

The explanations regarding biased assessments and referral processes have been most frequently reviewed in the past and nondiscriminatory assessment as well as referral procedures continue to have relevance in addressing this issue. However, the increased disability prevalence for minority students due to low SES and early biological risks has not been typically addressed relevant to this issue. The SES explanation in relation to the overrepresentation of black students in special education appears to be supported by the NLTS data since 57% of the African American special education population were from households with incomes below $12,000.

The NLTS explanations regarding the higher prevalence of disabilities for low-SES minority students due to early biological risks may be especially salient for urban school psychologists' understanding of this issue. This was supported by Crosby (1993) who stated that "in major urban areas, it is estimated that one child in 15 has some congenital problem that can impair his or her behavior and learning" (p. 604). Crosby and the NLTS study cited such risks as poor prenatal care, low birth-weight babies, drug-damaged babies, head injuries, and poor health care as occurring more frequently in low-SES minority students residing in urban settings.

When these special education placement statistics are combined with the urban demographic and risk data reviewed earlier, it might be expected that urban public school populations would have disproportionately high special education placements. However, the limited evidence available does not support this projection. The Council of Great City Schools (1988) indicated that about 10% of large urban school populations based on Average Daily Membership (ADM) are placed in special education, a percentage similar to the national average. This possible disproportionality by type of disability and general decreased identification of total disabilities relative to risks for urban school populations may be associated with service delivery issues not typically considered such as the following:

- *Funding of Services.* The number of school psychologists and special services funded by state departments of education are typically based on ADM rather than need as in other countries such as Sweden (Bracey, 1993). The ADM in urban schools does not account for the number of students actually registered in comparison to non-urban schools due to relatively high absenteeism.

- *Time-Delays.* The time required by the tasks inherent in the process of identifying students for special education may be greater in urban than non-urban schools due to various issues (e.g., locating students with high absenteeism; locating parents with frequent address changes and limited phone access; and conducting nondiscriminatory assessments beyond the typical multifactored evaluation).

- *Referral Issues*. While referrals of urban students may be disproportionately high, the caseload capacity of the school psychologists employed probably results in only those with the most severe educational impairment receiving evaluation. This, in turn, may result in identification of a possibly higher prevalence of mentally retarded but not the higher prevalence that may also exist of the less severe specific learning disabled (SLD).

These service-delivery issues extend beyond traditional "gatekeeper" concerns. Clearly, the rates of placements by race and type of disability often have relevance for legal cases related to nondiscriminatory assessment/placement in desegregated urban schools.

Service Guidelines and Resources

Recent revisions to professional and ethical guidelines published by the National Association of School Psychologists (NASP) and the American Psychological Association (APA) have applications for facilitating services to urban settings. The APA *Guidelines for Psychological Practice with Ethnic, Linguistic, and Culturally Diverse Populations* (APA, 1991) generally require that psychologists have a "very thorough understanding" of how culture may affect the provision of services. The NASP position statement, *At Risk Students and Excellence in Education: The Need for Educational Restructuring* (1992), provides implications for school psychologists to broaden services for students who present risks typical of urban youth. The 1992 revisions to the NASP and APA ethical principles require that school psychologists attempt to identify the degree that services apply to youth when considering SES, race, ethnicity, and other factors. These generally indicate the need for expanded training and supervision in order to improve providers' competencies in serving students of diverse ethnic and cultural backgrounds.

Goals of Services

While not typically addressed, a conceptual foundation for providing support services to inner city youth relevant to the pessimism and apathy that can permeate an urban school system (i.e., "a nothing works attitude") was reviewed by Garbarino et al. (1992). It was recommended that early intervention should generally be directed at promoting children's ability to cope by preventing a "build-up" of stressors. This was based on studies illustrating that it is multiple stressors which predict negative developmental outcomes rather than a single stressor. Zigler (1990) stated that "no amount of counseling, early childhood curricula, or home visits will take the place of jobs

that provide decent incomes, affordable housing, appropriate health care, optimal family configurations, or integrated neighborhoods where children encounter positive role models" (p. xiii).

Thus, a conceptual foundation for facilitating school psychology services in urban settings could be viewed as helping children cope and preventing an accumulation of risks. For example, reducing academic failure and adjustment problems at school may reduce only one stress but this may help urban children avoid a total breakdown in adjustment. There is a particular need for school psychologists to address the impact of ecological and demographic variables (e.g., SES, stressors, and race) in outcome studies when evaluating services.

Summary

Many other basic considerations for facilitating services to meet the unique needs or urban youth could not be reviewed due to the space constraints of this chapter. Examples include such considerations as children's physical health, family issues, child abuse/neglect, mental disorder prevalence, and influences of various cultures on service delivery. Issues selected for emphasis in this section and their implications for facilitating services are provided in the best practices section.

BEST PRACTICES

Few conceptual and empirical foundations based on validated best practices for facilitating services in urban schools exist. Hence, this section offers suggestions based on recent experience in expanding school psychology services in an urban setting. The intent is to provide practical applications to address the organizational issues and actual nuances likely to be encountered when attempting to implement comprehensive school psychology services in a large-city school district.

General Implications of Basic Considerations

Influence of culture and disadvantage. Most urban school populations are now composed of cultural, racial, ethnic, and language minority students and thus school psychologists need a comprehensive understanding of how these factors influence learning and adjustment. Familiarity with influences of deprivation associated with low SES is also critical. Urban school psychologists should routinely indicate the degree that culture and deprivation influence a child's school performance relevant to nondiscriminatory assessment and culturally sensitive interventions. General implications include staff training on these topics and recruitment of culturally diverse school psychologists.

Prevention of school failure. About 20% of students lack the school-entry competencies needed for mastering the first-grade curriculum and as many as 50% do not graduate. School psychologists could assist schools in early academic intervention and prevention programs as well as drop-out prevention programs. "Success for All" (Madden et al., 1991) is a model program that could be applied for this need.

Services for stress and violence. Considering the evidence presented concerning the heightened stress and violence experienced by urban youth, school psychologists should target these areas for services.

Special education services. There is continuing confusion regarding the prevalence of urban students with disabilities and the need for special education services in urban settings. In view of the updated data and considerations reviewed, increased school psychology and special education services are needed. The referral process in urban versus non-urban schools may differ substantially in the determination of suspected disabilities. Rather than just increasing the number of students identified for special education, schools could provide a broader range of special services and improved programs within regular education. Early intervention and prevention programs are also needed. Consistent with the current trend of inclusion, an increased number of urban students with disabilities could be provided with services while attending regular education. However, students' needs should be identified.

Public Law 101-476 (Individuals with Disabilities Education Act, IDEA) targeted students with disabilities from minority backgrounds for improved services. One approach to addressing the needs of urban students with disabilities would be to expand the related service of direct counseling and mental health interventions by school psychologists. This could be directed at reducing the increased stresses that urban students with disabilities are likely to encounter which may impair their school performance.

Mental health services. Increased mental health interventions could be delivered by coordinating with special projects that often exist in urban schools and community agencies. Sample services that are most needed include crisis intervention, school team intervention policy for discipline, and prevention programs.

New guidelines and resources. Recently published professional developments and resources have particular applications for facilitating services in urban schools. New ethical and professional standards are more explicit in meeting the needs of diverse minority populations. School psychologists are in need of continuing education on these topics. The reader is referred to the Annotated Bibliography at the end of this chapter as a basic starting point.

Leadership Issues

An advantage for facilitating services in urban versus non-urban schools is the greater likelihood that supervision would be provided by an administrator who is a school psychologist. This is the result of the relatively greater number of school psychologists employed in urban settings with the need for supervision of this separate service. However, Talley (1990) pointed out that various administrative structures within the school's bureaucracy influence the effectiveness of leadership for facilitating psychological services. Moreover, there is a lack of data regarding the efficacy of various theoretical models for supervision (Iverson & Iverson, 1993). A recent review of the literature on this topic by Iverson and Iverson indicated the following inadequacies regarding supervision in school psychology: (a) only 30% of practitioners were supervised and most of this was on an "as needed basis" and (b) the majority of supervision was provided by nonpsychologists. Considering the complexity of supervision and these limitations, the best-practice guidelines on this topic are restricted to suggestions with explanations concerning applications for facilitating services in urban settings.

School district organization. If at all possible, school psychology services should be organized as a separate department in the school district with the director or supervisor reporting to higher administration such as an assistant superintendent. This would enable comprehensive services to both special and regular education students to be coordinated with the multiple school departments and community agencies needed for effective delivery of services. However, this is not typical, and the second most desirable organizational structure is placement of school psychology within a pupil personnel or student services department. While this alignment may help in coordination with other student services and still enable school psychologists to work in programs serving both regular and special education students, there is the possibility that leadership will be provided by an administrator without school psychology competencies. A less desirable organizational structure for facilitating services is placement in a special education department. This may impair the expansion of services beyond the narrow gatekeeper function for special education. The least desirable administrative organization is building-based where services are decentralized and supervision is provided by school principals. This has obvious limitations such as staff being assigned unrelated duties with possible violations of professional standards.

It is critical that higher administration be educated about the professional standards for school psychologists and the need for a school psychologist to provide leadership for this service. Recent urban-school reform trends that include such decentralized issues as site-based management (Bullard & Taylor,

1993) should not apply to the needs for effectively administering school psychologists (Bard & Hardy, 1991). The optimal time to develop a plan for expanding services is during the employment process of a supervisor of school psychologists: This is when the higher administration may be most available and receptive to suggestions for administrative structure reorganization based on a plan for facilitating optimal services applications.

Staff organization. A critical component of supervision for facilitating services is the manner in which a large urban staff is organized for assignment and service delivery. The relatively large number of school psychologists in addition to multiple types of service opportunities in large urban settings make assignment of staff a challenging task.

Guidelines for assigning the school psychology staff in a manner that facilitates services include the following:

1. Major criteria are the competencies of staff for the specific assignments. For example, those with training and experience in serving preschool students would be assigned to this service.

2. Consumers of services should be involved in decision making regarding assignments. For example, administrators of special projects may wish to interview staff with competencies and interest for that project.

3. While school psychologists' salaries may be funded by special projects, the administrators of these projects should be informed of the need for continued supervision by a psychologist administrator. A helpful approach is to fund staff only for part-time assignment to new programs with the remainder of time on regular assignment. This has several advantages such as enabling staff to maintain competencies for traditional roles while providing new services.

A strategy for planning new services is organizing staff committees. This involves encouraging school psychologists with special competencies to serve as co-chairs of committees and then requesting that the remainder of staff serve on committees. A critical issue is identifying the topics or areas that could facilitate services for the committees to consider. Committees for a large school-psychology staff have several advantages such as (a) staff training for advanced skills, (b) involvement of staff in decision making, (c) assistance for the administration in planning new services, and (d) peer support for developing the staffing competencies. The following are sample committees with possible applications for facilitating services in urban settings:

1. *Research and Grants.* This committee could help design and implement research studies and grants that could address facilitating services.

2. *Staff Development.* It is critical to gain the staff's input for providing staff development. This helps school psychologists gain the competencies needed for facilitating services.

3. *Crisis Intervention.* The need for ongoing refinement in policies, guidelines, and implementation of this challenging service could be addressed by this committee. While all staff in urban settings are expected to have competence in crisis intervention, committee leaders and members could provide support to staff when needed.

4. *Multicultural and Bilingual Services.* This committee could help plan and implement services and staff training to address the needs of minority and bilingual students.

Many other types of committees could be helpful for staff organization beyond those directly relevant to facilitating new services (e.g., newsletters, intervention handouts, and best practices in intervention and assessment). Ad hoc committees could also be formed as needed for short-term needs or opportunities relevant to facilitating services.

Another critical leadership task is the recruitment and employment of school psychologists for urban schools. Beyond recruiting cultural and ethnic minority staff, several other criteria that could help facilitate services include professional experience working with urban youth, competence for specific alternative school services, and other general qualities of positive employees.

Needs Assessment and Planning

It has already been stated in this chapter that needs assessment is the critical initial step for facilitating services in urban settings. It is within the competence of school psychology to facilitate not only psychological services but also general education programs and other services. A comprehensive assessment would be focused on the needs of students plus the existence of multiple risks and support systems. Considering the sample data reviewed earlier, the needs of students should reflect an index of problems, such as the prevalence of special education disabilities, mental health disorders, school failure, academic functioning, cognitive abilities, physical health, death/suicides, violent behavior, discipline/juvenile violations, school attendance/dropouts, drug abuse, and sex problems/pregnancies. Risk factors include stresses and other ecological characteristics that may increase the problems youth encounter. Support systems are protective factors that may reduce or prevent the problems youth experience.

To interpret the degree of need for services, data from national, state, and local metropolitan areas should be compared to that of the urban school district being served. Staffing by ADM could also be compared to other school settings, especially the metropolitan area or suburbs of the city. The data may resemble the information presented in the basic considerations section indicating greater problems and risks but less support for the urban population. It may also reveal that more school psychologists are employed per ADM in the metropolitan area, especially in suburbs with high SES, than in the city.

The following methods could be used in conducting a needs assessment that addresses the factors just described.

Kindergarten screening. Screening kindergarten students could provide indicators of the students' school-entry cognitive and social skills. Parents should be given an opportunity to have input regarding support systems, risk factors, social/behavior ratings, and health background. This information could serve as a basis to request general education support based on needs and as background for grant applications.

Demographic data. Total school district and city data could be requested from a research department such as exists in many large-city schools. Data regarding mental and physical health as well as education could be requested from local mental health boards, pediatric hospitals, local census offices, and state departments of education.

Surveys. Teachers, administrators, school psychologists, and other school personnel could be surveyed regarding relevant issues and the perceived need for psychological services. Parental input could best be gained through a telephone survey.

Annual reports. The services provided by school psychologists are typically summarized in an annual report. This report should include a comprehensive summary of services and aspects of the needs assessment data. Implications for facilitating services should be written in the report.

Application of the needs assessment for alternative and improved general services by school psychologists should be provided in written reports. For example, if stresses and risks are found to influence educational outcomes, implications for psychological services to address these problems should be specified. General implications for general school programs could also be provided.

It should be noted there may be resistance to a needs assessment due to concerns that this could be stigmatizing to the schools and that implications would be costly. One response is that the data would be used formatively to plan services and seek funding as well as to provide explanations for the existing stigmatizing information often cited about large urban schools. Helping the schools to be sensitive to students' needs and developing responses to meet those needs were recommended as major tasks for support services in urban settings (Garbarino et al., 1992).

Public Relations for Promoting Services

Urban schools have complex political and bureaucratic structures with various administrative and other units influencing system-wide change. To facilitate services, supervisors and school psychologists should study all school departments and convey an interest in applying psychological services to the mission and needs of these departments. This is especially possible when urban school districts form task forces to plan reform. School psychologists and supervisors should volunteer to serve on these groups. This must be conducted in a politically sensitive manner with recognition of both the explicit and implicit values of various school departments and disciplines.

There are many other ways of gaining visibility and seeking to be actively involved in as many levels of the school and community as possible. A brief summary of some examples include the following:

- *Staff Development.* Prepare a list of staff development topics that school psychologists could provide and distribute it to all schools, administrative units, parent groups, and community agencies. Some salient topics are discipline, violence prevention, and crisis intervention.

- *Newsletters and Intervention Handouts.* A staff committee and the supervisors could write these and distribute them on a district-wide basis to help school staff address students' needs.

- *Parent Support Groups.* Parents who demonstrate leadership abilities could be organized into various support groups (e.g., types of disabilities). School psychologists could serve these groups by providing parent education regarding the special needs of these students and interventions that could be provided at home. Parent leaders could be involved as mentors, and other parents in need of assistance could be referred to them.

- *Media Communication.* Supervisors and staff could work in cooperation with the school's community relations department to provide written reports and speeches when needed on special topics or situations that may arise.

- *Community Agency Boards.* Sending letters to relevant community agencies to express interest in serving on advisory and executive boards promotes involvement and knowledge of community services.

- *Annual Reports.* These reports could be written in a format that explains the nature of services provided and future needs. The annual report should be distributed to all relevant school personnel and agencies.

Grant-Funded Services

Grants can be sought to implement innovative programs and research. The needs assessment data described earlier could be used as the justification for funding typically required by grant applications. Here is an area where urban schools may have an advantage because of the many characteristics present that are enablers for seeking grants. These include: (a) a large, economically disadvantaged population; (b) availability of grant-funding sources such as large businesses; (c) community agencies for multidisciplinary approaches; and (d) the presence of universities for assistance in research.

Current trends or themes targeted by grant-funding sources are highly relevant to the needs of urban schools and school psychology services. Examples are: (a) special needs of students with disabilities from minority backgrounds; (b) case-management mental health interventions; (c) multi-agency services for students with emotional and behavioral disabilities; (d) improved services for preschool students with disabilities; (e) violence- and drug-prevention programs; and (f) recruitment of minorities in school psychology and development of culturally sensitive interventions. There are multiple types of grant-funding sources relevant to school psychology services including local philanthropists and state and federal agencies in not only education but also mental health and medicine.

Working collaboratively with multiple school departments and community agencies to seek grants increases the likelihood of success. School psychology services could be the major focus in some grants and secondary or supportive for other grants. School psychologists could provide not only assessment and data-gathering for grant-funded programs but also direct and indirect interventions.

Alternative Services

The term *alternative services* has recently been used to describe school psychology functions beyond those provided for special education students with disabilities. The NASP publication on this topic (Graden, Zins, & Curtis, 1988) provided an extensive review of multiple applications but not to urban settings specifically. In urban settings, there are typically many students with risks and needs beyond the criteria for special education who require more immediate psychological intervention services. Hence, a general theme of alternative school-psychology services would be providing direct and indirect intervention to minimize students' adjustment problems that may impair learning. In keeping with the school district's goals and programs, these could be conceptualized as failure-prevention services rather than special education identification and placement services. Examples of prevention, intervention, and other alternative school psychology services are briefly described below.

School Development Program (SDP). This primary and secondary prevention program has also been described as the Comer Yale Child Study Model and is intended to promote the school adjustment of urban minority students from disadvantaged backgrounds (Haynes & Comer, 1990). In the SDP, a school psychologist works with a school team that includes teachers and parents and is chaired by the principal. This team reviews the school's climate in terms of plans and activities as they relate to the prevention of students' behavior problems.

An Intervention Assistance Team (IAT) format addresses individual problems experienced by students and school staff. Parent involvement in all aspects including general curriculum planning and individual teams is emphasized. A major goal is to reduce the discontinuity between home and school which Jackson (1990) reported to be present for urban youth. Positive outcomes have been reported by Haynes and Comer concerning the general school climate as well as student criteria in the areas of self-concept, behavior, and academic achievement.

Crisis intervention. School psychologists could help urban schools develop policies and procedures for this secondary and tertiary prevention service which involves multiple school personnel and community agencies. Principals should have primary responsibility for the crisis referral in addition to notifying higher administration, parents, and involved school departments. Most urban schools have security departments that work with the police and these personnel should have responsibility for managing students experiencing crises. Local mental health boards may provide outreach programs and crisis services that could be involved when follow-up beyond school is needed.

School psychologists provide initial consultation to the principal and school crisis team. Direct intervention for students when life-threatening behavior is present should be provided in compliance with ethical and due-process principles. Consultation with parents and community agency staff in addition to staff development for school personnel are important roles for school psychologists. A major service is follow-up assessment and planning when the student returns to school after a crisis.

Violence prevention/intervention. Hammond and Yung (1993) reviewed recent school-based violence-prevention programs for African American inner-city youth. These apply cognitive-behavioral approaches to reduce violence by teaching prosocial behavior such as social problem solving, modeling, and group training of social skills. School psychologists are familiar with these types of interventions and continuing education could provide applications to violence prevention. The role of the school psychologist would be similar to that in crisis intervention, namely as consultant plus provider of staff development support and parent education services that promote prevention. Students who have experienced violence could be included in follow-up intervention and prevention services by school psychologists.

Alternative to expulsion program. Due to the problems associated with violence (reported earlier), the rates of expulsions as well as suspensions are typically high in urban schools. Absenteeism and eventual dropping out of school are related problems. A major need that school psychologists could address is helping the schools meet recent legal requirements for expulsions and suspension relevant to students with disabilities or suspected disabilities.

Recent pilot programs have been implemented in urban schools to provide an alternative to expulsion. School psychologists could assist in developing an educational and support program that could be housed in a separate facility or in a section of a school. Rather than being expelled, students along with their parents could elect to attend this program. Students would be provided with continuing education in addition to support services by school psychologists funded to serve in this program. The role of the school psychologist would involve not only assessment to rule out disabilities and mental health problems but also the provision of direct and indirect interventions for students.

Compensatory education. Recent developments in compensatory education programs funded by Chapter I have included decentralization to "school-wide" projects with school-building teams designing remedial education programs. Urban schools typically have extensive Chapter I programs due to disadvantaged school populations. Decision making regarding the budget for these programs is typically provided by a school building team. School psychologists could provide assistance to this team by designing failure prevention programs that include funding of psychological services.

The general theme of psychological services for these programs would be interventions for students with adjustment and learning problems that may impair their classroom performance. Sample services include: (a) screening students to identify risks; (b) helping school teams write individual intervention plans; (c) consulting with and educating parents about interventions that could be applied at home; (d) consulting with teachers and visiting classrooms to assist teachers in implementing intervention plans; and (e) providing direct individual and group interventions for students with adjustment problems. An additional need that school psychologists could help the school-wide project address is developing outcome indicators beyond standardized assessment as recently recommended for Chapter I. This could in-clude curriculum-based measures and assessment of students' adjustment.

Alternative discipline programs. School psychologists could offer services to school departments responsible for developing discipline policies and procedures. Many school districts have abolished corporal punishment and are in need of alternatives for administrators and classroom teachers. School psychologists could help by applying recent developments in cognitive-behavioral approaches to discipline programs. The content of this program could include such information as the following: (a) multiple theoretical and procedural models of discipline; (b) applications of behavioral assessment for prescriptive discipline techniques; (c) teaching positive social skills to prevent discipline problems; (d) cultural influences on behavior and culturally sensitive discipline techniques; and (e) applications for students with disabilities and special needs.

Beyond developing written plans, school psychologists could provide assistance in implementation through staff development and parent education. School psychologists could also encourage teachers to apply the alternative discipline techniques in IAT services.

Case-management mental health services. Case management, a model currently being implemented by many community mental health agencies, emphasizes coordination of services for an individual rather than provision of services in isolation. To provide a school liaison for this service delivery model, school psychology leadership could serve on children's mental health planning boards as the school district's representative. Funding for school psychologists to work as part of the mental health team could come from special projects related to this approach. This interagency approach has been recommended by PL 101–476 as a way to improve services for students with serious emotional disturbances (SED).

Many other types of alternative services could be provided by school psychologists in urban settings beyond those briefly described here. Written summaries could delineate how school psychology services are relevant to the missions and services provided by other professionals in programs administered by multiple school departments and/or community agencies. Examples include adult education, career education, health services, staff development, and various community agencies.

SUMMARY

The major approach recommended for facilitating services was adapting school psychology functions to meet the needs of inner city youth and urban schools. Considering the severity and nature of the problems experienced by the students as supported by the data briefly reviewed, this task should be approached with a spirit of "aggressive opportunism." That is, school psychologists cannot wait for the school administration or other entities to seek their services, but rather should seek opportunities to apply their services to students' needs.

Two general implications for services include nondiscriminatory assessment and culturally sensitive interventions. While knowledge concerning the influence of culture is at a rudimentary level, assessment and interventions could be directed at the major risks confronting urban youth (i.e., stress and violence). However, this is challenging because, as Garbarino et al. (1992) observed, "the run down, overburdened inner city school is locked into a rigid curriculum that makes it difficult to meet the special psychological agenda imposed by trauma" (p. 229).

Many of the needs for providing effective services implicit in this review may not be consistent with current "bandwagons." For example, such trends as decentralization, reduction of special education by inclusion, and privatization may not be as applicable to facilitating services in urban settings as compared to non-urban schools. This is especially relevant if service delivery and educational reform are driven by needs.

The demographics and risks of urban schools are projected to be increasingly applicable to the general public school population across the nation (e.g., the majority of the national school population will be comprised of minority students early in the next century). Hence, initiatives to improve services in the cities may prove to have more generalized relevance in the future. It is suggested that NASP develop an urban task force similar to APA but with emphasis on school psychology services. It is hoped that this chapter will help stimulate this development by sensitizing school psychologists to the needs of urban youth and implications for expanded services.

REFERENCES

Abt Associates. (1993). *Prospects: The congressionally mandated study of educational growth and opportunity.* Washington, DC: U.S. Department of Education.

American Psychological Association. (1991). *Guidelines for providers of psychological services to ethnic, linguistic, and culturally diverse populations.* Washingtin, DC: Author.

American Psychological Association. (1992). Ethical principles of psychologists and code of conduct. *American Psychologist, 47,* 1597–1611.

Bard, E. M., & Hardy, J. T. (1991). School psychological services within urban restructuring. *Mid-western Educational Researcher, 4,* 35–38.

Bracey, G. W. (1993). The third Bracey report on the condition of public education. *Phi Delta Kappan, 75,* 104–117.

Bullard, P., & Taylor, B. O. (1993). *Making school reform happen.* Boston: Allyn and Bacon.

Cantor, D. W. (1993). The challenge to psychology: A response to the crisis in the cities. *The School Psychologist, 47,* 5.

Council of the Great City Schools. (1987). *Challenge to urban education: Results in the making. A report of Great City Schools.* Washington, DC: Author.

Council of Great City Schools. (1988). *Special education in America's cities.* Washington, DC: Author.

Crosby, E. A. (1993). The "at-risk" decade. *Phi Delta Kappan, 74,* 598–604.

Garbarino, J., Dubrow, N., Kostelny, K., & Pardo, C. (1992). *Children in danger: Coping with the consequences of community violence.* San Francisco: Jossey-Bass.

Gaw, A. C. (Ed.). (1993). *Culture, ethnicity, and mental illness.* Washington, DC: American Psychiatric Press.

Graden, J. L., Zins, J. E., & Curtis, M. J. (Eds.). (1988). *Alternative educational delivery systems: Enhancing instructional options for all students.* Washington, DC: National Association of School Psychologists.

Greater Washington Research Center. (1993). *Poverty rates of U.S. cities.* Washington, DC: Author.

Hammond, W. R. (1991). *Dealing with anger: Givin' it, takin' it, workin' it out.* Champaign, IL: Research Press.

Hammond, W. R., & Yung, B. (1991). Preventing violence in at-risk African-American youth. *Journal of Healthcare for the Poor and Underserved, 2,* 369–373.

Hammond, W. R., & Yung, B. (1993). Psychology's role in public health response to assaultive violence among young African-American men. *American Psychologist, 48,* 142–154.

Haynes, N. M., & Comer, J. P. (1990). The effects of a school development on self-concept. *Yale Journal of Biological Medicine, 63,* 275–283.

Iverson, A. M., & Iverson, S. J. (1993). *A reinvestigation of supervision in school psychology.* Paper presented at the annual meeting of the National Association of School Psychologists, Washington, DC.

Jackson, J. H. (1990). Best practices in urban school psychology. In A. Thomas & J. Grimes (Eds.), *Best practices in school psychology–II* (pp. 757–772). Washington, DC: National Association of School Psychologists.

Jordan, M. (1993). In cities like Atlanta, whites are passing on public schools. *Washington Post,* A–1.

Madden, N. A., slavin, R. E., Karweit, N. L., Dolan, L., & Wasik, B. A. (1991). Success for all. *Phi Delta Kappan, 72,* 593–599.

Myers, H. F., Wohlford, P., Guzman, L. P., & Echemenda, R. J. (Eds.). (1991). *Ethnic minority perspectives on clinical training and services in psychology.* Washington, DC: American Psychological Association.

National Association of School Psychologists. (1992). *At risk students in education: A need for educational restructuring.* Silver Spring, MD: Author.

National Association of School Psychologists. (1992). *Professional conduct manual.* Silver Spring, MD: Author.

Ponterrotto, J. G. (1990). Affirmative action: Current status and future needs. In J. G. Ponterrotto, D. Lewis, & R. Bullington (Eds.), *Affirmative action on campus* (pp. 5–18). San Francisco: Jossey-Bass.

Talley, R. C. (1990). Best practices in the administration and supervision of school psychological services. In A. Thomas & J. Grimes (Eds.), *Best practices in school psychology–II* (pp. 43–62). Washington, DC: National Association of School Psychologists.

U.S. Department of Education. (1992). *Fourteenth annual report to Congress on the implementation of the Individuals with Disabilities Education Act.* Washington, Dc: U.S. Government Printing Office.

Zero Population Growth. (1993). *Children's stress index.* Washington, DC: Author.

Zigler, E. F. (1990). Foreword. In S. J. Meisels & J. P. Shonkoff (Eds.), *Handbook of early childhood education* (pp. i–xviii). Cambridge, England: Cambridge University Press.

ANNOTATED BIBLIOGRAPHY

Bullard, P., & Taylor, B. O. (1993). *Making school reform happen.* Boston: Allyn and Bacon.

This textbook is recommended for school psychologists working in urban settings in order to gain a comprehensive knowledge of urban school reform issues. School psychologists could plan to adapt services for involvement in the school reform programs. Especially relevant are new approaches to remediation in regular education.

Garbarino, J., Dubrow, N., Kostelny, K., & Pardo, C. (1992). *Children in danger: Coping with the consequences of community violence.* San Francisco: Jossey-Bass.

This textbook provides conceptual and empirical foundations for understanding the needs of urban youth as well as facilitating services. The early intervention program is especially relevant for developing school psychology services to address the stressors experienced by urban youth during preschool and the early elementary grade levels.

Gaw, A. C. (Ed.). (1993). *Culture, ethnicity, and mental illness.* Washington, DC: American Psychiatric Press.

Considering that new ethical guidelines require psychologists to have knowledge of how culture may impact services, this textbook is an excellent resource. Multiple authors who have expertise for working with various cultural and ethnic groups review mental health needs relevant to serving the different populations.

Hammond, W. R. (1991). *Dealing with anger: Givin' it, takin' it, workin' it out.* Champaign, IL: Research Press.

This school-based intervention program includes structured cognitive-behavioral techniques and videotaped modeling for aggression replacement training with adolescents. This approach emphasizes culturally sensitive content and can be applied to youth who are either perpetrators or victims of violence.

Hammond, W. R., & Yung, B. (1991). Preventing violence in at-risk African-American youth. *Journal of Healthcare for the Poor and Underserved, 2,* 359–373.

This article provides a model outcome study that is not typically available regarding school-based interventions for reducing aggressive behavior in urban adolescents. It was found that the treatment group evidenced significantly less indicators of aggression than a control group.

27

Best Practices in Facilitating Services in Rural Settings

Susan Jacob-Timm
Central Michigan University

OVERVIEW

Many Americans hold idealized images of rural America — images shaped by television, movies, and vacation excursions into the countryside. Country life is seen as "the good life," characterized by fresh air and scenic beauty, tightly-knit families, close ties with neighbors, freedom from crime, and freedom from the "constraints, pressures, and fast paced life of the cities" (Hobbs, 1992, p. 21). As Hobbs has noted, however, these idealized images "tend to be at substantial variance with current facts concerning rural America and its communities" (p. 21). Research comparing metropolitan and nonmetropolitan areas shows substantially higher rates of poverty in nonmetropolitan areas, and an increasing number of rural families in poverty (Hobbs, 1992). Studies show that a disproportionately high number of children in rural areas is at risk for school failure and mental health problems (Helge, 1990). Furthermore, most unserved or underserved children with disabilities live in rural areas (Helge, 1985).

There is currently a nationwide shortage of school psychologists, with shortages being most acute in rural areas (Fagan, 1988). Unfortunately, rural communities also often lack adequate numbers of nonschool health and mental health professionals to meet the needs of rural children and their families. One purpose of this chapter is to describe the benefits and special challenges associated with rural school psychology. It is hoped that this will prompt students-in-training and practitioners to consider future employment in rural schools. As Hughes and Fagan observed, "because a large number of handicapped rural children are not receiving the education and mental health services to which they are entitled, professional school psychology bears an ethical and moral responsibility to increase the availability of quality special education and mental health services to the children of rural America" (1985, p. 400).

A second purpose of this chapter is to provide an overview of "best practices" in the delivery of school psychological services in small, rural schools, particularly those located in sparsely populated and remote communities. As discussed later in the chapter, there is great diversity among rural communities and schools. Consequently, the goal here is to provide information and ideas that will encourage rural practitioners to formulate new approaches and solutions appropriate to each unique setting.

BASIC CONSIDERATIONS

This portion of the chapter explores the characteristics of rural communities, families, and schools, and the special benefits and challenges of rural school psychology. It is important to note that there is no widely accepted definition of the term "rural." The distinction between "rural" and "urban" have blurred with the rapid growth of urban sprawl on the periphery of major cities (Hobbs, 1992). For the purposes of this chapter, "rural schools" are those located in communities outside of a Standard Metropolitan Statistical Area, distant/remote from a large city, and in counties where the population density is low (see National Rural and Small Schools Consortium, 1986, for a more detailed discussion).

Rural Communities

As Helge (1985) has suggested, effective practice of rural school psychology is based on knowledge of the special characteristics of rural communities and the unique setting in which the practitioner serves. Rural communities tend to differ widely from one another. Rural New England is very different from rural Iowa, and both are quite different from rural Texas, Alaska, Alabama, Colorado, or West Virginia. Each rural community is shaped by its particular geography, its economic base, and the ethnic and religious makeup of community members (Hobbs, 1992).

Despite their diversity, rural communities often share some common characteristics. In 1988, the average per capita income in rural counties was $12,657.00, only 71% of the urban average (U.S. Bureau of the Census, 1991). Research comparing metropolitan and nonmetropolitan areas has found more unemployment, underemployment, and lower-paying jobs in nonmetropolitan areas. Rural communities historically have depended on natural resource-based sources of livelihood such as agriculture, mining, timber, or fishing. In some areas of the country these industries have declined or disappeared. Although some rural areas now have manufacturing or tourism as part of their economic base, rural communities typically lack the economic diversity of metropolitan areas. Because of this lack, rural areas are vulnerable to periods of economic instability and downturn. Rural communities today often must cope with economic uncertainty and instability, or chronic poverty (Hobbs, 1992).

Most rural communities have undergone marked change in the past 10–15 years. Technological advances and improved roads and transportation have created new links to metropolitan areas. Rural products now are more likely to be sold to national and international markets, creating a greater interface with the outside world (Hobbs, 1992). For better or worse, rural America is less isolated from mainstream America than in the past. Some communities have been quick to adapt to change; other communities are characterized by a heightened wariness of outsiders and resistance to new ideas.

Rural Families

Effective practice of rural school psychology is also based on an understanding of rural families (Helge, 1985). Media images portray the rural family as embracing traditional values, sheltered from crime, hard working and tightly-knit. Children are seen as benefiting from the support of a stay-at-home mother and an extended, multigenerational family. While seldom depicted as wealthy, rural families are nevertheless thought to enjoy the good life (Hobbs, 1992).

The reality of the rural American family may be very different from idealized images, however. As previously noted, there is a disproportionately high number of rural families in poverty. In impoverished areas, children are likely to live in substandard housing and suffer from poor nutrition. Rural residents are more likely than their urban counterparts to have serious and severe health problems (Gesler, Hartwell, Ricketts, & Rosenberg, 1992). Furthermore, the rise in economic problems experienced by rural families has been accompanied by an increase in mental health problems — particularly stress-related problems — in rural areas (Hobbs, 1992). Findings from a series of studies conducted in the 1980s indicated that rural families have experienced an increase in chronic depression, suicide, alcoholism and other substance abuse, and spouse and child abuse (Helge, 1992). In some communities, teen pregnancy rates are high. Unfortunately, many rural communities lack adequate medical and mental health services; and even when such services are available, families often can-

not afford treatment because they lack medical insurance (Hobbs, 1992). The lack of public transportation also makes it difficult for rural families to gain access to needed resources.

Once tightly-knit rural families also are unraveling in other ways. Economic dislocation in rural areas has caused an increase in separation and divorce, and a concomitant rise in the number of female-headed single-parent households. Many rural women have little formal job training, but must now support themselves and their children. As a result of these economic and societal changes, rural women are entering the paid work force in record numbers (Luther & Todd, 1992). Parents in rural areas may commute long distances to work, and consequently many rural districts have witnessed a dramatic increase in the number of latchkey children (Hobbs, 1992). Most rural communities lack adequate child care, preschools, and after-school programs (Luther & Todd, 1992).

It is also important to note that rural families are no longer isolated from the influences — positive or negative — of the media. Most families in rural areas now watch the same television shows and videotapes as their urban counterparts, and purchase the same products as do city dwellers (Hobbs, 1992).

Rural Schools

Besides understanding the characteristics of rural communities, effective practice of rural school psychology also requires knowledge of the characteristics and history of rural schools. In the late 1800s and early 1900s, school improvement efforts focused on urban schools, particularly the challenge of preparing large numbers of foreign immigrant children to work in industrialized America. During the first half of this century, many states attempted to impose an urban-industrial model of schooling on rural communities — a "one best system of education." Despite the absence of empirical data on the effectiveness of rural schools, the schools were nevertheless characterized as poorly organized and inefficient, offering an outdated curriculum, and lacking in intellectual stimulation. Bigger was seen as better. There was a push towards school consolidation and control of rural schools by professional educators, who were said to know more about the educational needs of rural youth than the lay people of the local community. Thousands of small rural schools were closed between 1900 and 1960, despite the protests of rural citizens (DeYoung, 1987; Nachtigal, 1982).

In the mid-1980s, educational researchers began to take a closer look at the strengths as well as the problems of rural schools. The view that small rural schools necessarily provide an inferior education began to be reevaluated. It was recognized that the poor academic achievement and high student dropout rates found in some rural areas must be interpreted in terms of the pervasive effects of rural poverty, not just in terms of the effectiveness of the school (DeYoung, 1987). Based on a study of school districts in New Jersey, Walberg and Fowler concluded that "generally, it appears that the smaller the district, the *higher* the achievement when the SES and per-student expenditures are taken into account" (emphasis added, 1986, p. 20).

As many writers have observed, small schools are now "being rediscovered as models for effective schools" (DeYoung, 1987, p. 135), and growing evidence supports the contention that "the quality of school life in many rural elementary schools equals and often exceeds that found in urban schools" (Muse & Thomas, 1992, p. 47). Some of the characteristics of effective schools often found in rural districts include high levels of teacher involvement in decision making, a sense of pride and "ownership" by the community, and little bureaucracy. Other strengths typical of small rural schools include small teacher–pupil ratios, high levels of individualized attention to pupils, and use of innovative problem solving. Furthermore, cooperative learning strategies and peer tutoring have a long history in multigrade classrooms (DeYoung, 1987; Muse & Thomas, 1992).

Small rural schools face unique and continuing challenges, however. Because of their geographic isolation, the cost of program delivery in rural areas typically is higher per pupil than in nonrural areas (Phelps & Prock, 1991). In many states, funding inequities between rural and urban schools favor schools in metropolitan areas. Local funds for rural schools are tied closely to the health of the local economy, which may be unstable or depressed. Many rural communities have experienced a shrinking tax base due to a loss of workers coincident with an increase in elderly residents (Phelps & Prock, 1992).

Rural schools also face problems of recruitment and retention of qualified teaching and support staff. Attrition rates for school personnel in rural districts are reported to be 30–50%, much higher than attrition rates reported for nonrural schools (Helge, 1984a). This difficulty of recruiting and retaining competent educators means that rural schools may sometimes have less qualified teachers, administrators, and support personnel than nonrural schools (Muse & Thomas, 1992).

In addition, rural districts face unique challenges in the delivery of special education services. Prior to 1975, there were typically no public school programs for children with severe disabilities in rural areas. Many children with severe impairments were institutionalized or simply kept at home. Children with mild disabilities, however, often were included in the regular classroom. After passage of the *Education of All Handicapped Children Act* in 1975, more programs and services became available for children with severe disabilities in rural areas, particularly through intermediate school units or other regional cooperatives. However, a shortage of special education teachers in rural schools continues to exist. Furthermore, because of the small numbers of children with diverse special needs, many rural districts are not able to offer the full continuum of special education alternatives found in nonrural areas (Helge, 1992).

Rural School Psychology

The last paragraphs of this section provide an overview of rural school psychology. Several studies have explored job role and job satisfaction of rural school psychologists. Unfortunately, much of the available research is flawed because of small samples, the failure to adequately operationalize the "rural" variable, and reliance on the respondent's self-report of employment setting (Reschly & Connolly, 1990). Findings from studies of rural school psychology must be viewed as tentative in light of these shortcomings.

Several benefits of rural school psychology have been suggested in the literature. Studies have suggested that, because of the limited availability of other specialists, school psychologists in rural areas are likely to assume a "generalist" rather than a "specialist" role — that is, they typically have the opportunity to assume a broader range of professional roles than their counterparts in suburban or urban schools (Cummings, McLeskey, & Huebner, 1985). In addition, when compared with their nonrural counterparts, rural school psychologists have reported greater influence on school policy, more time spent in consultation and less time devoted to assessment, and a greater emphasis on boundary-spanning functions (i.e., coordination of people and resources) (Huebner, McLeskey, & Cummings, 1984; Jerrell, 1984).

Rural school psychology, however, also poses special challenges. Rural practitioners may encounter poor travel conditions, few appropriate program alternatives for children with special education needs, and a shortage of teachers with specialized training for work with children with behavior or learning problems. Furthermore, the lack of mental health specialists in rural areas may make it difficult to ensure that children and families receive needed mental health services (Helge, 1990).

Recent studies of rural and nonrural school psychologists typically have found no significant differences in salary and other compensation (Ehly & Reimers, 1986; Reschly & Connolly, 1990). Interestingly, several studies have reported no differences in overall job satisfaction in comparisons of rural and nonrural school psychologists (Ehly & Reimers, 1986; Reschly & Connolly, 1990). Many practitioners, however, report professional isolation as a major source of dissatisfaction with the rural setting (Benson, Bischoff, & Boland, 1984). For example, rural practitioners may have limited access to professional libraries and up-to-date assessment and remediation materials, and they may be isolated from opportunities for consultation with peers. Entry-level practitioners in isolated rural schools may have difficulty finding qualified school psychologists to supervise their work. Although some studies suggest that rural practitioners participate in professional development activities as frequently as their nonrural counterparts do, those activities may be designed for teachers rather than psychologists. Thus, there may be few local continuing education opportunities specifically appropriate for the professional development needs of psychologists (Benson et al., 1984; Helge, 1985; Solly & Hohenshil, 1986).

In discussing the special challenges of rural school psychology, one must also consider the entry and adjustment of the new practitioner to rural community life. Personal isolation and dissatisfaction with community life may be more important factors than job role or satisfaction in determining retention of school psychologists in rural schools. Little research has appeared on practitioner adjustment to rural community life. The literature on teacher shortages, however, clearly suggests that "rural culture shock" is a key factor in teacher attrition in rural schools (Helge, 1992).

The benefits of rural community life may include scenic beauty, opportunities for outdoor recreation, high-quality family life, and lower levels of crime and violence. School psychologists who accept positions in rural schools may have difficulty finding adequate housing and gaining acceptance in tightly-knit communities, however. Some rural areas have no apartments and little available rental housing. In some communities, practitioners may be respected as professionals, but never gain full social acceptance. Teachers who stay in rural districts are likely to have been raised in rural communities and to be married. Unless school personnel make an active effort to create a social network, there may be few social opportunities, particularly for practitioners who are not married. Teachers in rural communities often report a loss of personal and family privacy because of the visibility and interdependence that characterize sparsely populated areas. There may also be limited access to shopping and cultural events, particularly if weather conditions make travel difficult (Helge, 1992). Rural school psychology is not for everyone.

BEST PRACTICES

Consistent with other chapters in this volume, this overview of best practices in rural school psychology focuses on the delivery of broad-based consultative services. Within this framework, practitioners are encouraged to adopt a collaborative problem-solving approach with the goal of planning effective interventions. The section begins by discussing how to establish effective consultative relationships in small rural schools. Best practices in the delivery of services to teachers and pupils, families, and schools

in rural communities are then discussed, including identification of technological advances that may enhance service delivery and create new educational opportunities for rural youth. The "best practices" portion of the chapter closes with a summary of strategies for continued self-renewal in rural settings, and identification of ways in which training programs might improve placement and retention of school psychologists in rural areas.

Establishing Effective Consultative Relationships

One key to establishing effective consultative relationships in rural schools and communities rests on an understanding of the role of the rural school principal. Urban schools typically employ a number of administrative specialists, including directors of special education, vocational education, transportation, personnel, and program evaluation and research. In contrast, the rural school principal often bears sole responsibility for educational leadership and ensuring quality programs and instruction for the students within his or her building.

In many rural areas, school psychologists are employed by an intermediate school unit or other regional cooperative. They may be housed within a rural district or provide itinerant services. Whether they are employed by a regional cooperative or by the school district, entering practitioners must recognize the significant role of the building principal in the functioning of rural schools. To establish effective consultative services, it is critically important for the rural practitioner to meet with each school principal to discuss the nature and scope of services he or she has to offer, to identify — and perhaps negotiate — professional roles and service priorities, and to seek agreement about procedural issues. It is also important to establish communication channels to ensure each principal is kept informed about services being provided within his or her building. In rural communities, parents and teachers with questions or concerns about the psychologist's activities are likely to contact the principal, and he or she must have the information necessary to respond to their concerns. Without the sanction and support of the principal, it is extremely difficult for a psychologist in a small rural school to gain and maintain credibility and acceptance among school personnel and the community.

A second key to maximizing consultation effectiveness in rural schools and communities rests on an understanding of social power. Interpersonal or social power is the potential of one individual to affect the attitudes, perceptions, and/or behavior of another (French & Raven, 1959). Two forms of social power are available to the school psychologist in consultative relationships: "expert power" and "referent power." With expert power, the consultee (usually a teacher or parent) perceives that the consultant (school psychologist) has the skills or knowledge that will help him or her accomplish goals. Teachers, parents, and other school staff are likely to seek the help of those they believe are expert in the area of a problem. Referent power, in contrast, is attributed to the consultant when the consultee identifies with him or her. This identification is likely to occur when the consultee perceives the consultant as someone with feelings, attitudes, and behaviors similar to his or her own (Martin, 1978).

The goal in consultative relationships is to achieve a balance of power between the consultant and the consultee. When the consultant and consultee share coordinate status, an open exchange of ideas is likely to lead to effective collaborative problem solving. The consultant brings his or her specialized knowledge of behavior and learning to the problem-solving situation; the consultee brings his or her specialized knowledge of the student(s), the setting, and his or her own role (teacher or parent). To be perceived as credible and approachable, the psychologist must have some measure of both expert and referent power.

As Fagan and Hughes (1985) observed, in many rural settings, the school psychologist must learn to rely more on his or her referent power than on expert power to maximize consultative effectiveness. School psychologists who enter schools in middle-class settings typically are afforded status and some measure of credibility — that is, expert power — on the basis of their graduate degree and specialized training. Personal characteristics (older, more experienced, professional demeanor and attire) may enhance their perceived expert status (Martin, 1978). In contrast, middle-class practitioners who enter schools in isolated, economically depressed rural settings may discover that many parents and some school personnel dislike, discount, and mistrust outsider-experts with "fancy" college degrees and titles. Consequently, knowledge of how to maximize referent power while building expert power is essential for success in some rural settings.

An important strategy for developing referent power is getting to know members of the school community, and allowing members of the school community to get to know you. This may involve spending time in the teachers' lunch room, engaging in small talk with the school secretary, and helping with school projects unrelated to job role (Martin, 1978). In addition, Helge (1992) encourages school professionals who are new to rural settings to take an interest in community events and accept invitations to social gatherings. These suggestions are based on the observation that person-to-person communication and informal power networks are highly important in rural communities (Helge, 1992), and the view that the school psychologist and members of the school community can best get to know each other in informal settings (Martin, 1978).

In interactions with school-community members, the entering school psychologist needs to emphasize ways in which his or her interests, attitudes, beliefs, values, and concerns are similar to those of school-community members. In addition to emphasizing commonalities, practitioners need to use empathetic listening techniques and convey acceptance and respect for others (Fagan & Hughes, 1985). First impressions are important, so the practitioner needs to dress in attire that is not too different from others in the school community. In informal interactions and in consultative relationships, referent power may be enhanced by acknowledging and emphasizing the expertise of others.

As Martin (1978) noted, fostering referent power requires time and opportunities for informal exchange. The itinerant school psychologist consequently faces special challenges in developing referent power. To facilitate entry and acceptance, practitioners need to identify the teachers who are the "opinion leaders" within the school buildings they serve, and seek to provide consultation to those teachers soon after initiating service delivery in the building. Effective work with one respected teacher can go a long way toward enhancing both referent and expert power within a small school. Similarly, establishing a positive rapport with the opinion leaders in the larger school community can facilitate collaboration with others in the community and acceptance among families (Meyer, Parsons, & Martin, 1979).

Working with Teachers

As noted earlier, rural schools often have difficulty attracting and retaining qualified teachers. In order to staff special education programs in rural areas, new teachers, marginal candidates, noncertified teachers and teachers with temporary out-of-field permits, or paraprofessionals may be hired (Ludlow, Bloom, & Wienke, 1990). Because of travel distances, regular education teachers may not receive adequate support from itinerant special education staff in planning individualized instruction for the pupils with disabilities in their classrooms. As a result, teachers in rural schools may feel unprepared to work with the pupils in their classes who have learning and behavior problems, particularly when those difficulties are severe. Rural school psychologists therefore can play an important role in providing instructional and behavioral consultation to teachers in rural schools.

The use of school-based teams to assist teachers in problem solving is gaining popularity in rural as well as nonrural schools (Alkire, 1990; Helge, 1988). School-based problem-solving teams have been given a number of different names, including "pupil assistance teams," "intervention assistance teams" (Alkire, 1990), "mainstream assistance teams" (Fuchs & Fuchs, 1988), and "instructional support teams"

(Rosenfield, 1992). These teams involve a systematic effort on the part of teachers, administrators, and support personnel to plan interventions for pupils with learning or behavior problems. Team goals are to assist teachers in problem solving so that students may be taught more effectively, and to ensure that the diverse educational needs of pupils are met within the regular classroom if at all possible. Pupil assistance teams provide a support system for teachers, encourage a problem-solving approach, and reduce special education referrals. They also provide an incentive for continued professional growth, as team members learn new strategies from each other to improve educational outcomes for children (Alkire, 1990).

Team membership and leadership are likely to vary according to the characteristics of the school and the nature of the referral problem. Based on his experiences in Ohio, Alkire (1990) observed that a key to effective pupil assistance teams in small schools is support and participation by the building principal.

The pupil assistance team literature (see citations above) generally encourages an ecological approach to problem resolution that involves consideration of many factors that affect learning and behavior, including characteristics of the classroom, instructional variables, characteristics of the referred pupil, and support available from the home (Fuchs & Fuchs, 1988). Because of their knowledge of systematic data collection and analysis and instructional and behavioral management, school psychologists have much to contribute to problem identification, planning interventions, and evaluating intervention effectiveness. The practitioner's knowledge of interpersonal communication and group dynamics can help teams function effectively. Furthermore, because of their training and experience in handling confidential and sensitive information, rural school psychologists may also help prevent unnecessary intrusion on pupil, family, or teacher privacy in data gathering and problem analysis.

As Rosenfield (1992) has observed, the development of instructional support teams requires an extended period of time. Psychologists who are interested in developing support teams must establish a positive working relationship with the school, garner principal and teacher support, organize staff training activities related to developing successful teams, plan strategies for ongoing evaluation of team functioning, and plan strategies for evaluating the effects of interventions on referred pupils. However, rural practitioners should be encouraged by the observation that there appears to be a "good match" between the use of pupil support teams and the characteristics of small schools. As noted previously, small schools often have a history of collaborative problem solving, there are fewer bureaucratic barriers to change, and individual professionals may have much influence on

school policy. Practitioners interested in developing pupil assistance teams may wish to consult the literature cited above.

In providing consultation to school-based teams or individual teachers, rural school psychologists are advised to recognize and build on the traditional strengths of small, rural schools. In some rural areas, there is a high level of community involvement with the schools and a strong tradition of volunteerism. Classroom interventions might involve the assistance of retirees or other community volunteers. Also, because of the interdependence of individuals in rural communities, children typically are taught to value cooperation in attaining goals. Cooperative group learning methods and cross-age tutoring have a long history in small rural schools, and their continued use should be encouraged.

Technological advances are seen as an important problem solver in rural schools. In a study conducted more than ten years ago, Helge (1984b) found that most rural school systems had at least some types of electronic technology available, with microcomputers available in 88% of the rural districts or cooperatives surveyed. In light of U.S. Department of Education and state-level initiatives (Jefferson & Moore, 1990), a marked increase has likely occurred in the availability of electronic technology in rural areas since Helge's study. From her survey, Helge (1984b) found that computers and other technologies were used to support instruction in a number of ways, including drill and practice, simulation, and educational diagnosis and prescription. School psychologists with expertise in computers and other technologies may have an important role to play in providing consultation to rural teachers. For example, practitioners might help locate and adapt computer programs to the instructional needs of pupils, locate and adapt assistive devices for children with sensory or motor impairments, and help pupils and teachers learn how to use new technologies.

In addition to classroom computers, distance education technologies now promise to break down existing geographic barriers to educational opportunity. Distance education technologies can provide up-to-date knowledge and specialized instruction to students and teachers in remote, isolated schools. Model distance education programs have been developed in Iowa, Kansas, and Utah and, with the anticipated support of the Clinton administration for further development of telecommunication networks, it is likely that all rural areas in the United States will have distance education service before the year 2000. Many different kinds of distance education are available, involving various technologies. Distance education links can be one way or two-way (interactive). If the link is interactive, the "feedback loop" from student to teacher may allow the student to interact with the teacher only by signal (striking a key), by audio only, or by audio and visual. The visual image may be produced by a "freeze frame" system, where still pictures are displayed, or involve a continuous-motion video system (Jefferson & Moore, 1990).

Distance education systems may allow rural teachers to instruct students in their homes or at distant community centers. This will help ensure instructional continuity in rural areas where weather causes frequent and long school closings, or when a serious health problem limits school access for a child during part of the year (Helge, 1984b).

Distance education will also link teachers and students around the state, making it possible for small rural schools to offer a more diverse curriculum. This technology may be particularly helpful for specialized instruction of children with disabilities. For example, close-captioned instruction available via distance education can expand learning opportunities for hearing-impaired students in rural areas. Specialized content available via distance technologies may also provide needed educational challenges for gifted and talented students in small schools. School psychologists may assist in matching instructional resources available via telecommunications to the learning needs of rural youth. Links among public schools and colleges and universities will also provide opportunities for consultation with experts regarding difficult classroom problems, and continued professional development opportunities for rural educators.

Working with Families

In recent years, most states have attempted to improve interagency cooperation in the delivery of human services in order to avoid duplication and cut costs. The school has traditionally been the hub of community life in rural areas, and it is now the center for interagency coordination of services to families in many areas of the country. Because of these changes, the rural school psychologist has an increasingly important role in creating and maintaining links among the school, community agencies and programs, and families to meet the needs of rural children and youth.

As noted previously, children in rural areas historically benefited from the support of an extended, tightly-knit family and high levels of parental involvement in the schools. However, with the increases in poverty and single-parent homes, many rural families now need support from the school and community in meeting their children's needs. In addition, the lack of job opportunities in economically depressed areas has lowered the educational expectations of many rural youth (MacBrayne, 1987). Consequently, in many rural communities, schools now must make a more active effort to work closely with families to raise educational expectations and ensure student success in school.

In all settings, school psychologists must be sensitive to local values and traditions in gaining acceptance among families. While there is ethnic diversity in some rural communities, in other rural areas — particularly those that are geographically isolated — an ethnic or religious minority may be a strong subculture (Helge, 1988, 1992). Some remote rural communities are composed of Hispanic migrants, African Americans, Native Americans, or a religious minority who have little experience interacting with those who are different. Depending on the characteristics of this group, there may be a dislike or mistrust of outsiders, or a high level of conservatism.

In gaining acceptance among rural families, practitioners must make a special effort to learn about the local culture, show respect for customs and mores, and provide opportunities for community members to get to know them in informal settings. Practitioners need to identify the individuals within the school community (e.g., a well-respected teacher or school nurse) who can smooth the way for work with families within the area. Home visits made with a well-liked teacher or school nurse and tours of local industries can often bring important insights into family and community life.

Helge (1992) cautions practitioners that the right to self-determination is highly valued in many rural cultures. Consistent with the literature on effective consultation, it is important that school psychologists working with rural families communicate respect for the family's right to make choices. For consultation with families to be effective, the consultant must provide alternatives and the knowledge necessary to make good choices, rather than imposing solutions.

There is now a growing understanding of family influences on student competence in school. As Epstein (1986) has observed, parents want their children to be successful in school, but many do not know how to help their children succeed in the school setting. Based on a review of the available literature, Christenson, Rounds, and Gorney (1992) identified a number of family factors that affect achievement in school, with special attention to those that can be altered through intervention. This literature shows how educators might work with families to improve school competence and learning. Interventions designed to raise parental expectations for the child's academic performance, improve home support of academic learning, increase parental involvement in schooling, and create a more supportive affective home environment all promise to improve student outcomes. Helge (1992) has suggested that it is also sometimes important to help families learn how to be effective advocates for their children. Rural families may not be aware of the legal rights of children with disabilities, and they may not know about available resources or how to access those resources within the school or community.

As noted earlier, rural families have experienced an increase in stress-related mental health problems, including substance abuse and child abuse, but there is often a shortage of health and mental health professionals in rural communities. In planning interventions to improve home conditions for children, school professionals need to recognize the important role of paraprofessionals and volunteers in providing assistance and support to rural families. Parent discussion and support groups led by paraprofessionals and volunteers often are more successful in rural communities than programs offered by professionals (Helge, 1992). As Helge observed (1988), rural family members will listen to friends and neighbors more easily than they will to professionals. Thus, it is important that rural school psychologists work to support, rather than supplant, existing helping relationships in rural communities (Keenan, Dyer, Morita, & Shaskey-Setright, 1990). School psychologists may play an important role by offering their expertise to the nonprofessionals involved in helping systems. In this way, the effectiveness of existing helping systems may be improved, providing greater benefits to rural children and families.

Consultation to Schools and the Community

Recent school reform efforts have produced greater emphasis on systematic evaluation of educational programs and student outcomes. Program evaluation results can be used to modify program design and instruction to improve student learning. As Helge has observed, systematic program evaluation is particularly important in rural schools because such efforts can "provide data to defend programs in an era of declining resources and school consolidation" (1987, p. 60). Unfortunately, rural schools typically lack staff trained in program evaluation. Because school psychologists are knowledgeable in research design, they may play a significant role in program evaluation.

School psychologists may also play a significant consultative role in rural schools by researching the availability of state and federal grants for improvement of educational programs. In 1978, Sher published an influential paper criticizing the lack of federal government attention to the problems of rural schools. Since that time, the U.S. Department of Education has made a greater effort to provide funds to improve rural education. Rural school psychologists who are (or become) knowledgeable in grantsmanship may be able to assist rural schools in obtaining funds for program improvement.

School psychologists also may have an important role to play in providing consultation to rural communities. In many rural areas, the school is the center of community revitalization efforts. Rural educators and businessmen have recognized that they must have an educated work force to attract much-needed industry, and jobs must be available to keep educated adults in the community (Hobbs, 1992). This interface between education and the economic development of the community can create exciting opportunities for rural school psychologists. Rural practitioners may become involved in various school-community improvement efforts, including the development of day care, preschool, and after-school services and the development of vocational training opportunities for youth and adults.

Strategies for Continued Self-Renewal

This section provides a brief overview of strategies to avoid job burnout, reduce professional isolation, and create opportunities for continued self-renewal in rural areas. One factor known to be associated with job burnout among school psychologists is role ambiguity (Huberty & Huebner, 1988). The role of the school psychologist may be misunderstood in rural schools and communities (Helge, 1988). In addition, psychologists who are employed by regional cooperatives may encounter conflicting role expectations from the regional office versus local districts (Benson, 1985). In order to avoid role ambiguity, rural school psychologists are wise to negotiate their job description during the hiring process, taking time to clarify roles and priorities in discussions with regional and local school administrators. Periodic review of job goals and priorities with supervisors and building principals is important to ensure continued role clarity and reduce the likelihood of burnout.

In many rural areas, poor travel conditions can add to job stresses, particularly for practitioners who provide itinerant services. Use of a C.B. car radio or a car phone can help reduce travel-related stress by allowing the school psychologist to communicate with schools or parents while traveling. Such devices ensure help will be received if travel emergencies arise, and allow for the timely rescheduling of appointments in the event of unforeseen delays. The current generation of laptop computers can also reduce job stress by facilitating the efficient handling of paper work at all work sites.

Although rural school psychologists report levels of job satisfaction similar to those of their nonrural counterparts, personal and professional isolation may be a source of dissatisfaction with the rural setting. Rural practitioners who provide itinerant services and/or work as the only psychologist within a district are advised to make a "conscious and deliberate effort" to form a professional support group (Presbury & Cobb, 1985). Support groups can help practitioners solve difficult professional problems and provide a stimulus for continued professional growth. Of equal or perhaps greater importance, however, such groups can be a source of emotional support and give the practitioner a sense of social belonging.

Technological advances also can reduce professional isolation and create continuing education opportunities. Computer bulletin boards can be used to create links to other school psychologists and rural educators (see Lipinski, 1991). Videotapes and the distance education technologies described above also promise to provide continued professional development opportunities specifically appropriate to school psychologists.

Training Programs for Rural School Psychologists

Only a few school psychology programs currently emphasize training of practitioners to provide services in rural schools. The University of Colorado at Boulder and Alfred University in New York have made special efforts in this area. In order to improve placement and retention of school psychologists in rural settings, the following are needed: (a) increased recruitment and training of students from rural areas who are likely to return; (b) increased recruitment of students who have a commitment to rural education and knowledge of the personal and professional challenges associated with rural settings; (c) improved training in skills and service-delivery models needed in rural schools, including supervised preservice field experiences in rural settings; (d) increased availability of quality supervision for entry-level rural practitioners; (e) the development of regional networks to provide professional support for psychologists in rural school settings; and (f) increased availability of professional development opportunities for psychologists in rural settings.

SUMMARY

Effective practice of rural school psychology is based on knowledge of the special characteristics of rural communities, schools, families, and the unique setting in which the practitioner serves. In order to gain and maintain credibility and acceptance, rural practitioners must understand the significant role of the principal in small schools, recognize the importance of establishing positive working relationships with school and community opinion leaders, and know how to maximize referent social power.

Rural school psychology offers a number of professional and personal challenges. Probably the most important broad professional challenge is to work with others in the school community to ensure that all rural children and youth have the best possible opportunities to succeed in school. The goals of providing educational opportunities and ensuring good school outcomes must be met despite many barriers commonly found in rural areas: inadequate funds for schools, a shortage of qualified teachers and other professional personnel, geographic and climatic barriers, cultural differences, and the pervasive effects of family poverty.

Rural school psychology also promises many unique opportunities, as educators rediscover the strengths of small schools and how to build on those strengths, and technological advances provide solutions to the problem of geographic isolation. In addition, in many rural communities, the school is the center of interagency coordination of services to families, and the hub of community economic revitalization efforts. This creates the possibility of many exciting boundary-spanning roles as schools and community join together to improve home conditions, community services, education, and vocational opportunities for rural youth and their families.

ACKNOWLEDGMENTS

A special thank you to Central Michigan University graduate student Christine Richey for her assistance with the library research.

REFERENCES

Alkire, P. (1990). Small school and IATs — A solution for at-risk students. *Rural Educator, 12,* 1–3.

Benson, A. J. (1985). School psychology service configurations: A regional approach. *School Psychology Review, 14,* 421–428.

Benson, A. J., Bischoff, H. G. W., & Boland, O. A. (1984, April). Issues in rural school psychology. (Survey Report). Philadelphia: National Association of School Psychologists.

Christenson, S. L., Rounds, T., & Gorney, D. (1992). Family factors and student achievement: An avenue to increase students' success. *School Psychology Quarterly, 7,* 178–206.

Cummings, J. A., McLeskey, J., & Huebner, E. S. (1985). Issues in the preservice preparation of school psychologists for rural settings. *School Psychology Review, 14,* 429–437.

DeYoung, A. J. (1987). The status of American rural education research: An integrated review and commentary. *Review of Educational Research, 57,* 123–148.

Ehly, S., & Reimers, T. H. (1986). Perceptions of job satisfaction, job stability, and quality of professional life among rural and urban school psychologists. *Psychology in the Schools, 23,* 164–170.

Epstein, J. L. (1986). Parents' reactions to teacher practices of parent involvement. *Elementary School Journal, 86,* 147–159.

Fagan, T. K. (1988). The historical improvement of the school psychologist service ratio: Implications for future employment. *School Psychology Review, 17,* 447-458.

Fagan, T. K., & Hughes, J. N. (1985). Rural school psychology: Perspectives on lessons learned and future directions. *School Psychology Review, 14,* 444–451.

French, J. R. P., & Raven, B. H. (1959). The bases of social power. In D. Cartwright (Ed.), *Studies in social power* (pp. 150–167). Ann Arbor: University of Michigan Institute of Social Research.

Fuchs, D., & Fuchs, L. S. (1988). Mainstream assistance teams to accommodate difficult-to-teach students in general education. In J. L. Graden, J. E. Zins, & M. J. Curtis (Eds.), *Alternative educational delivery systems: Enhancing instructional options for all students* (pp. 49–70). Washington, DC: National Association of School Psychologists.

Gesler, W. M., Hartwell, S., Ricketts, T. C., & Rosenberg, M. W. (1992). Introduction. In W. M. Gesler & T. C. Ricketts (Eds.), *Health in rural North America*. New Brunswick, NJ: Rutgers University Press.

Helge, D. I. (1984a). The state of the art of rural special education. *Exceptional Children, 50*, 294–305.

Helge, D. I. (1984b). Technologies as rural special education problem solvers. *Exceptional Children, 50*, 351–360.

Helge, D. I. (1985). The school psychologist in the rural education context. *School Psychology Review, 14*, 402–420.

Helge, D. I. (1987). Strategies for improving rural special education program evaluation. *Remedial and Special Education, 8*, 53–60.

Helge, D. I. (1988). *Serving at-risk populations in rural America. Teaching Exceptional Children, 20*(4), 17–18.

Helge, D. I. (1990). *A national study regarding at-risk students*. Bellingham, WA: National Rural Development Institute.

Helge, D. I. (1992). Special education. In M. W. Galbraith (Ed.), *Education in the rural American community* (pp. 107–135). Malabar, FL: Krieger.

Hobbs, D. (1992). The rural context for education: Adjusting the images. In M. W. Galbraith (Ed.), *Education in the rural American community* (pp. 21–41). Malabar, FL: Krieger.

Huberty, T., & Huebner, E. S. (1988). A national survey of burnout among school psychologists. *Psychology in the Schools, 25*, 54–61.

Huebner, E. S., McLeskey, J., & Cummings, J. A. (1984). Opportunities for school psychologists in rural settings. *Psychology in the Schools, 21*, 325–328.

Hughes, J. N., & Fagan, T. K. (1985). Guest editor's comments: The challenge of rural school psychology. *School Psychology Review, 14*, 400–401.

Jefferson, R. E., & Moore, O. K. (1990). Distance education: A review of progress and prospects. *Educational Technology, 30*(9), 7–12.

Jerrell, J. M. (1984). Boundary-spanning functions served by rural school psychologists. *Journal of School Psychology, 22*, 259–271.

Keenan, L. D., Dyer, E., Morita, L., & Shaskey-Setright, C. (1990). Toward an understanding of mentoring in rural communities. *Human Services in the Rural Environment, 14*(2), 11–18.

Lipinski, T. A. (1991). Resources in rural education. In A. J. DeYoung (Ed.), *Rural education: Issues and practice* (pp. 313–329). New York: Garland.

Ludlow, B. L., Bloom, L. A., & Wienke, W. D. (1990). Rural school services for students with severe disabilities: Changes in personnel and programs. *Rural Special Education Quarterly, 10*(2), 15–20.

Luther, V., & Todd, M. (1992). Educational needs of rural women. In M. W. Galbraith (Ed.), *Education in the rural American community* (pp. 241–254). Malabar, FL: Krieger.

MacBrayne, P. S. (1987). Educational and occupational aspirations of rural youth: A review of the literature. *Research in Rural Education, 4*, 135–141.

Martin, R. (1978). Expert and referent power: A framework for understanding and maximizing consultation effectiveness. *Journal of School Psychology, 16*, 49–55.

Meyers, J., Parsons, R. D., & Martin, R. (1979). *Mental health consultation in the schools*. San Francisco: Jossey-Bass.

Muse, I. D., & Thomas, G. J. (1992). Elementary education. In M. W. Galbraith (Ed.), *Education in the rural American community* (pp. 45–72). Malabar, FL: Krieger.

Nachtigal, P. (1982). *Rural education: In search of a better way*. Boulder: Westview.

National Rural and Small Schools Consortium. (1986). *Definitions of rural, small, and remote schools*. Bellingham, WA: Western Washington University.

Phelps, M. S., & Prock, G. A. (1991). Equality of educational opportunity in rural America. In A. J. DeYoung (Ed.), *Rural education: Issues and practice* (pp. 269–312). New York: Garland.

Presbury, J., & Cobb, H. (1985). Best practices in organizing professional support groups. In A. Thomas & J. Grimes (Eds.), *Best practices in school psychology*. Kent, OH: National Association of School Psychologists.

Reschly, D. J., & Connolly, L. M. (1990). Comparisons of school psychologists in the city and country: Is there a "rural" school psychology? *School Psychology Review, 19*, 534–549.

Rosenfield, S. (1992). Developing school-based consultation teams: A design for organizational change. *School Psychology Quarterly, 7*, 27–46.

Sher, J. P. (1978). A proposal to end federal neglect of rural schools. *Phi Delta Kappan, 60*, 280–282.

Solly, D. C., & Hohenshil, T. H. (1986). Job satisfaction of school psychologists in a primarily rural state. *School Psychology Review, 15*, 119–126.

U.S. Bureau of the Census. (1991). *State and metropolitan area data book, 1991*. Washington, DC: U.S. Government Printing Office.

Walberg, H. J., & Fowler, W. J. (1986). Expenditures and size efficiencies of public school districts. (ERIC Document Reproduction Service No. ED 274 4471)

ANNOTATED BIBLIOGRAPHY

Galbraith, M. W. (Ed.). (1992). *Education in the rural American community*. Malabar, FL: Krieger.
This book provides a framework for understanding the rural context for education. The chapters focusing on elementary, secondary, and special education are of particular interest to school psychologists.

Clearinghouse on Rural Education and Small Schools and National Rural Education Association. (1990). *Directory of organizations and programs in rural education*. Charleston, WV: Author. Available from ERIC/CRESS at AEL, P.O. Box 1348, Charleston, WV 25325.
This directory lists programs and resources helpful to practitioners and researchers in rural education. It includes national associations and networks, regional educational laboratories, national centers and clearinghouses, federal and state government agencies and programs, and titles of journals related to rural education.

28

Best Practices in Adopting a Prevention Program

A. Dirk Hightower
Primary Mental Health Project — University of Rochester

Deborah Johnson
Primary Mental Health Project — University of Rochester

William G. Haffey
Monroe Board of Cooperative Educational Services #1 — Rochester, New York

OVERVIEW

Defining primary prevention has proven to be difficult. Indeed, a consensus among authors has not been reached (Hightower & Braden, 1991). However, primary prevention efforts universally seek to change the incidence of new cases by intervening proactively, that is, *before* disorders occur. For example, (a) competencies may be increased through education; (b) training may be provided to help people develop coping strategies to short-circuit negative effects of stressful life events and crisis; (c) environments may be modified to reduce, or counteract, harmful circumstances; or (d) support systems may be developed more fully. Whole populations or groups considered to be "at risk," rather than individuals, are targets for such interventions. Primary prevention efforts do *not* attempt to reduce existing problems; rather they are proactive preemptive efforts to prevent problems from occurring.

Prevention in this chapter means secondary and primary prevention; tertiary prevention is referred to as *treatment*. The essence of secondary prevention is early identification of problems and intervention before problems become severe. By identifying problems in their initial stages, professionals can design interventions to shorten the duration of the problems and minimize their intensity, thus reducing the prevalence of disorders. Frequently, children are targets of secondary prevention because of their psychological malleability and flexibility. The younger the child, the less likely problems will be entrenched and the more favorable the prognosis.

In support of prevention programs, Bloom (1985) states that "if we insist on waiting until all direct treatment needs are met before allocating resources to prevention, we will doom our profession to continuation of the hopeless downward spiral in which we now find ourselves." While school psychology traditionally has not been in the forefront of working with prevention programs, the field's current movement supports and enables school psychologists to become more proactive in providing for a better educational system for our children. Realistically, school psychologists will have to divert more time, money, and energy from direct services, such as assessment and special education, toward working with school systems implementing prevention programs.

The paradigm shift from treatment to prevention can be a small, yet a logical, change for many school psychologists. Whereas many treatment and prevention technologies are, at times, surprisingly similar, conceptual and philosophical distinctions between treatment and prevention are important. In essence, treatment and prevention differ primarily in terms of the *time* of intervention in relation to the period of onset of difficulties and the *target* of such interventions. Treatment programs serve individuals experiencing problems, whereas preventive interventions focus on groups when problems are just starting to emerge or before they occur. The ever present need for more school psychology services, the continuing shortage of school psychologists, and the relatively small gains made in *treating* various learning problems, behavioral conditions, or mental disorders, all point to the need for further adoption of effective prevention programs.

BASIC CONSIDERATIONS

In this chapter, it is assumed that the school psychologist has identified a potential prevention program to adopt. If more information is needed regarding well-documented and available prevention programs for children of all ages and adults, the reader is referred to the end of this chapter, which contains an annotated bibliography, an abridged prevention bibliography, a list of prevention clearinghouses, and a list of journals that routinely feature prevention.

BEST PRACTICES IN ADOPTING A PREVENTION PROGRAM

This chapter considers concrete ways to introduce and conduct school-based prevention programs. The next section focuses on determining if a school is ready to implement a prevention program and introducing such programs into the school. The second section focuses on issues of implementation including program size, staffing, building support, training, and developing realistic goals and objectives. The third section provides suggestions for maintenance of prevention programs and quality control. The later two processes rest on successful system analysis and program introduction.

System Analysis and Prevention Program Introduction

Identifying needs. In any plan for change, the school psychologist must have a clear understanding of system needs and ways a prevention program might meet those needs. He or she must also understand the school system — a step required *before* a prevention program can be proposed.

Prevention programs, like all applied endeavors, must have relevance for, and address the needs of, those who are involved. For school-based prevention programs, this means the needs of the community, the central administration, the principal, the teachers, and students must be addressed. But, until a system's gatekeepers perceive a need, prevention programs cannot start, much less succeed.

How is need identified? One way is to conduct a formal needs assessment. For more information on formal needs assessments see the Nagle chapter in this volume. Hazards of such global needs assessments include (a) identifying more needs than can be addressed and (b) raising expectations unrealistically. If the resources or programs to address the identified needs are unavailable, then the relative good and harm resulting from global assessments should be weighed before starting such assessments.

An alternative to formal needs assessment is to follow one's "sense of the obvious" which is then confirmed by convergence across sources. To do this, the school psychologist must spend considerable time in open discussion and active listening with building staff so as to identify sources of repeated frustration. For example, a colleague conducting numerous individual psychoeducational assessments followed by teacher conferences observed that many elementary students had poor peer relationships and that teachers were aware of and especially concerned about these children. At almost the same time a high school teacher commented, "Kids these days don't even have

enough interpersonal skills to work together on a half-hour chemistry lab." In a research project it was noted that many young elementary school children believed it was against the rules to help other children with their work. In their words, "It's cheating!" These observations reflected a convergent message from independent sources and confirmed an obvious need: Many children lack important peer social and cooperation skills.

Delineation of a school's needs offers a framework for developing a hierarchy of concerns, identifying the most important ones, and selecting those that fit the *expertise* and *interest* of the school psychologist. Other relevant questions in this early exploration process include the following: Will staff require training within the selected "need" area? Which interventions have been tried in the past? How can the largest number of students be reached? Across which grades are there common needs?

Addressing such issues effectively through a prevention program will usually require major shifts in the thinking of school personnel. For example, the teaching staff and the school psychologist will need to move away from addressing problems and toward issues of wellness and the development of competencies. For a discussion of this needed change, as well as other resistances and excuses likely to be encountered, the reader is referred to Hightower and Braden (1991) and the chapter in this volume on Promoting Competence by McConnell.

Prevention program review. Once needs and prevention programs addressing those needs have been identified, as much information as possible should be obtained. Attending program workshops, visiting schools and communicating with school personnel who have implemented similar programs, and reading relevant journal articles and research reports are all important aspects of the initial review process. The goal of such inquiry is to thoroughly study each program and to conceptualize how it may best be adapted to a specific need in a specific school *before* it is recommended for adoption. Time spent in these activities will significantly improve the chances of successful program implementation and maintenance.

Introduction of the system. Once the review steps are well under way, the process of introducing any prevention program into the system begins. For school psychologists who (a) have worked for years in the same system, (b) have a good understanding of a school's governance and decision-making processes, and (c) are knowledgeable about the system's entry and negotiation procedures, the following section may be familiar. This section is written primarily for those who are new to the field, who come from an outside agency and are not familiar with the school system's way of operating, or who would like a review of practices and procedures appropriate for prevention program adoption.

Each system should be approached at its *safest* point. Identifying this safest point means that each system should be analyzed or, in clinical terms, *diagnosed* in relation to its functional structures and processes (see Schein, 1969). Gatekeepers, allegiances, managerial styles, and communication pathways exemplify some areas of diagnostic importance. System analysis, though often complex and time consuming, is always necessary. Whatever one's conceptual orientation, the diagnostic process remains surprisingly similar. The point to keep in mind is that an essential first step *before* approaching a system with a new idea is to find out as much as one can about the system, that is, a social history.

Talk to anyone who knows about the system; retired principals or teachers, for example, are often informative sources. Read documents about the system's lineage, strengths and weaknesses, key leaders, and power structures. Helpful documents in this process include minutes of board meetings, policy and procedure handbooks, superintendent's or director's "state of the school" or annual reports, and *budgets*, which are available for most public schools. As an example, one school psychologist, who works regularly in different schools, reads the school board minutes religiously. As a result, she often knows more about what is happening within her school district than the principals!

Remember everything or, better yet, record your impressions, because human memories are limited. Look for convergence. As a general rule, if something appears *once*, remember it; if it appears *twice* from different sources, recognize it is likely to be true and important; and if it appears *three* times from different sources, it is almost certain to be true and important.

In the absence of prior contacts with informed inside sources, starting with the highest levels of administration is one way to enter a system. But it may also be a very dangerous place to start because top administrators have the power to quash an idea immediately, or, worse yet, they may like an idea and proceed to force those below them to participate. For several reasons, the middle management in many school systems, that is, principals, supervisors, or directors of pupil personnel, may be the best place to make an initial contact. Although middle managers typically cannot give definitive approval to new proposals, they are often influential gatekeepers and decision shapers. In addition, middle managers are also familiar with the system's administrative concerns, style, and jargon; thus, they can provide useful cues about the best ways to proceed. For example, in talks with a principal about a new primary prevention program designed to teach third graders assertiveness, communication, relaxation, and problem-solving skills, it became clear that use of the word *assertiveness* made him squirm. During the discussion the

principal remarked that the superintendent's focus for the year was to develop students' "coping skills." On the basis of this visit, the initially named Assertiveness Training Program was retitled the Classroom Coping Skills Program. In that form it was eagerly adopted by the school district. Equally important is the fact that if middle managers like a prevention program they have the power to support it from within the system. Such support is a necessary, but not a sufficient, condition for adopting a prevention program.

Although it is often a good idea to begin discussions about new programs with middle managers, eventually others must be involved. A carefully conducted organizational assessment can often provide useful cues about when and how to take those next steps. Answers to the following questions may help in making good decisions about when and how to proceed:

- How do others perceive the principal? The superintendent?

- How and by whom are decisions made?

- Who are the real leaders? Who follows whose lead?

- How does communication take place within the system?

- Who are the "thinkers?" The "doers?"

In assessing a school system, it is helpful to understand a school's de facto power structure, how the system actually operates. Power can either support success or facilitate failure. Two examples follows. Figure 1 depicts a system with considerable potential for program implementation. In this model there are open lines of communication among teachers, the principal, the psychologist, and the pupil personnel director. However, with this or any other structure, negotiations must involve all school staff who will implement or be involved with the new prevention program. Whenever possible, a school psychologist should use a bottom-up mode of communication, that is, have the approval and input of the teachers, principal, and supervisor *before* a proposed prevention program is taken to the superintendent.

Unlike the system presented in Figure 1, Figure 2 depicts a divided system. The two teacher groups often bypass the prescribed structure and deal directly with the Board of Education, which apportions only superficial power to the central administration. The psychologist can be caught between the teacher groups, trusted by neither, and rendered powerless. Such a system, concerned as it is with internal power struggles, is typically not ready for any new programs.

In summary, system analysis is needed to establish either that a prevention program is potentially feasible and how best to proceed or that a system is not ready for the introduction of change. In the au-

FIGURE 1. Healthy school district organization.

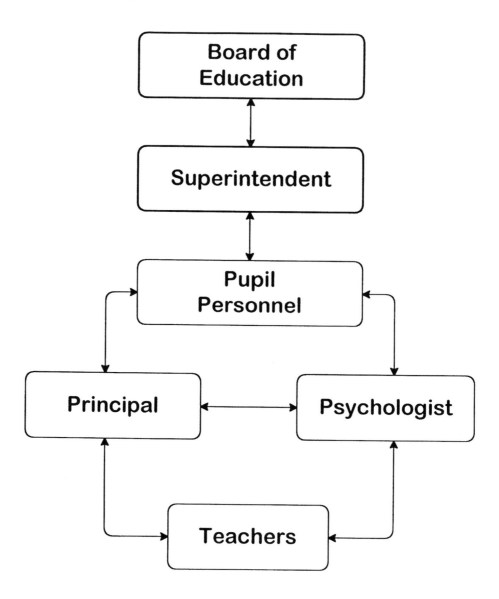

thors' experience the entry process works best if the school psychologist keeps three considerations in mind:

1. School systems do not always function as one might infer from their tables of organization. Knowing how a system actually functions helps the school psychologist proceed in ways that can best advance program objectives.

2. Getting a new program started requires considerable time and respect for district procedures. Patience, sensitivity, and persistence are necessary for the long run.

3. It is prudent to develop solid support from those who will be impacted by the program, as well as the system's middle managers.

In many ways the process of introducing a prevention program into a school is like introducing any other program. "Professional small talk" and the initial presentation, however, can be of particular importance in introducing prevention programs.

Professional small talk. In many situations, before a prevention program is introduced, the first order of business is professional small talk (PST). A goal of PST is to develop a professional relationship between the school psychologist and relevant school personnel that is characterized by trust, respect, good communication, and understanding. Developing such a strong professional relationship enhances the likelihood that a prevention program or even a pilot program can be started. Because prevention is an ab-

FIGURE 2. Unhealthy school district organization.

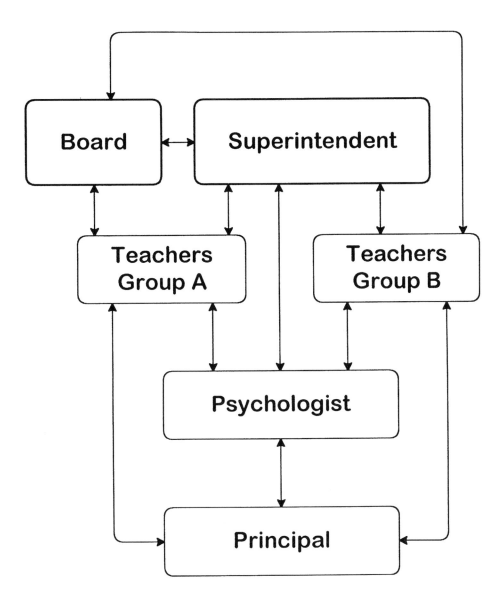

straction to many, the more specific the program description and its objectives, the more likely it will be understood and attempted. On the other hand, if the working relationship between the school psychologist and school staff is weak or poor, even the best prevention program does not have a chance of getting started. The point is that the time invested in establishing effective working relationships with school personnel can contribute importantly throughout the adoption processes of a prevention program.

Initial presentation. After the needs assessment, program selection, system analysis and entry processes, an initial program presentation is made. This is an important step, which, when properly taken, can set a positive tone for the entire program. The two main goals of such a meeting are to provide basic information about the program and to answer questions. Some guidelines that have been found useful in making such presentations follow.

It is important to anticipate which types of information will be relevant to the host and to address those points. These concerns typically center around the program's rationale, goals, objectives, target group(s), and specific procedures. One way to identify salient information is to formulate a list of likely questions from those involved in the presentation and to develop clear answers to all such questions. This procedure can be further enhanced by consulting with people who know the system well and soliciting other concerns from them.

The following are examples of questions frequently posed at meetings introducing new prevention programs.

- How will the new prevention program interfere with ongoing programs or curricula?

- Does this prevention program duplicate Ms. X's efforts?

- How will the program's effectiveness be assessed?

- Have others run similar programs? What did they find?

- Who will pay for this program?

- Who will be hired and what will be their credentials? Can we use Ms. G from our staff?

- What does the teachers' union think about this program?

- Whom should parents call if they have a question?

- Why implement this program now?

These questions are representative, not exhaustive. The key point to stress is that concerns should be anticipated to the greatest extent possible *before* starting. Also, essential consumer information should be provided, and false turns should be minimized. If unanticipated questions arise for which clear answers are not available, it is best to indicate that you will find out the answer and get back to the concerned individual than it is to make up an answer.

Another suggestion for the initial presentation is to limit the opening program statement to 10–15 minutes, and then say something like, "Let me stop here and answer your questions." This will enable the audience to clarify points they have missed, raise questions, and identify matters that may need more in-depth coverage.

It is not safe to assume that what is said during a presentation will be remembered *accurately*. Before making a presentation, a brief, two-page, written proposal should be developed. (A one-page proposal is probably too short to do the program justice, and more than two pages is too long for the reader's interest.) The clearly written proposal should be simple and straightforward and should answer: Why Who will doing What with Whom, When.

The proposal should include a catchy nonjargon program name appropriate to the host school. For example, "Wings," "Special Friends," "Growth Center," "Project Try," "Primary Intervention Project (PIP)," and "Primary Project" are all adaptations of "Primary Mental Health Project." The latter title, though descriptive, may include potentially negative associations. Given that a program's name is used more often than anything else associated with the program, it helps to choose a name with a positive connotation. Naming a program also expedites the transfer of program ownership.

Other points to include in the brief written description are succinct statements of (a) the program background and rationale, including brief references to past relevant research; (b) the program's central goals and objectives stated in concrete and specific terms; (c) a program description, including its basic structures and activities; and (d) a listing of responsibilities of relevant program and school staff. An appendix can include drafts of letters and permission forms for parents, sample curriculum materials, a reading list, and a budget. This does not necessarily mean that all audiences should receive all these documents; each audience should receive only a set of documents pertinent to it. Unless the written materials will be referred to in the verbal presentation, documents should be handed out *after* the presentation, so that attention can be focused on the presentation.

The authors have also found it helpful to assume that the middle manager *might* have useful notions about how best to proceed with a program. That assumption orients one to the following questions: "From your perspective, what would you suggest is the best way to proceed from here?" or "What next steps need to be taken?" Such questions put school staff in an active participant role and enhance their sense of project ownership. School people can respond to such queries in several directions: (a) "I'll take it and run with it" or (b) "You need to do X, Y, and Z." The confidence you place in your system analysis often structures how best to proceed. For example, before a meeting with a known and trusted pupil personnel director about implementing a prevention program, it was assumed that *he* would take the proposal to the superintendent. Instead, he recommended:

> I can take it to the chief, but then I would have to defend it. If you mail it to him, he will seek my advice and approval, which I have no problem giving. I think that's the way to go this time because I've been asking for a lot of things lately.

His suggestion was followed and the scenario unfolded as he predicted.

Another guiding principle is to recognize that systems move slowly and that due process and realistic timelines must be respected. After an initial presentation, several months lead time may be needed before a preventive program can actually start.

Although it is helpful to describe evaluation components as *part* of the program from the beginning, there may be points of conflict between evaluation and service components. In such instances, evaluation ideals may need to be modified to respect pressing service needs. In most cases, however, a compromise can be worked out that addresses both sets of concerns satisfactorily. Also, experience has shown that in an applied setting, the term *program evaluation* is better received than the term *research*.

Finally, before the initial presentation meeting ends, action steps to be taken should be specified and

TABLE 1
Processes of Implementing a Prevention Program

1. Understand the needs of the school.
   a. Formal needs assessment, and/or
   b. A "keen sense of the obvious."

2. Conduct a system analysis observing:
   a. Communication and interaction pattern.
   b. Leadership and decision-making styles.
   c. Staffs' conceptual and motivational strengths.
   d. The system's power structure.

3. Choose a well-documented validated program that meets the school's needs.

4. Develop internal allies who can assist in all stages of program development.

5. Allow enough time for the program to be understood.

a set of *contracts* (Cowen, 1985) about the responsibilities of all concerned parties should be established. In other words, it should be clear who will be doing what by when in order for the program to proceed smoothly.

The preceding paragraphs are practical rules for an initial presentation and an important step in the overall implementation process for a prevention program. Although it helps to think through these matters carefully before making the initial presentation, professional skill, wisdom, and sensitivity need to supplement these basics.

Summary of diagnostic and introductory steps. The essential processes during the early stages of implementing a new prevention program are reviewed in Table 1. In sum, the ultimate goal of these steps is to maximize the likelihood of successful program implementation by paying close attention to a system's characteristic ways of functioning, due process, procedures, and human sensitivities.

Implementing a Prevention Program

Although the diagnostic, implementation, and maintenance processes associated with prevention programs are considered in separate sections of this chapter, these processes occur simultaneously. Clearly, good system analysis will advance the introduction and implementation of a program, and effective implementation, in turn, facilitates program maintenance. In essence, however, all these processes are intended to advance the same goal: to develop a successful, durable prevention program. Some frequently asked questions about prevention programs' implementation processes are discussed next.

How big should the initial program be? It is best to start small. The main reason is that most schools have had little experience with such programs. The *paradigm* shift required to provide services to students *before* serious problems are evidenced takes time. Although school personnel may endorse the idea of prevention as an abstraction, concerns may develop, for example, when services are to be provided to a relatively healthy Nathan before a "problem ridden" William. Starting small, that is, targeting a single grade in one school instead of four grades in six schools, allows for careful program scrutiny and a focus on quality control. Smaller implementations permit the school psychologist a chance to address thoughtfully the inevitable "brush fires" associated with new programs and to give all parties involved the attention needed. Also, a successful pilot program can provide a solid foundation on which the school psychologist can build effective programming in future years. Starting small costs less, leaves more room to address mistakes, reduces administrative worries, provides valuable experience to program implementaters, and provides a basis on which to decide whether the program merits more widespread dissemination.

Who should be involved in a prevention project? It is important for the school psychologist to determine, as much as possible, who will participate in and staff a prevention program. The best school-based prevention programs available will fail if the wrong persons are involved. The persons who enhance the chances of success include those who (a) have a good understanding of school systems and their general operating procedures; (b) demonstrate good interpersonal skills with students, parents, faculty, and administrators; (c) understand the prevention program; (d) are motivated to learn and receive training in the skills needed to implement the prevention program; and, most importantly, (e) *want* to be involved.

If school faculty are involved in a prevention program, "wanting to be involved" may be the only variable over which a school psychologist will have control. Frequently, those faculty members who volunteer to participate embody the characteristics just described. Faculty should *not* be forced to participate.

In fact, forcing faculty to participate usually creates ill will and inspires program sabotage.

If new staff are to be hired for a prevention program, personnel with the attributes just listed should be sought. Most institutions have specific policies and procedures for hiring and these need to be consulted. In general, it is better to have flexibility in hiring. In addition, asking trusted faculty or colleagues for referrals is a good method: Over the years, we have found word of mouth to be more productive than newspaper ads in finding good staff. Of course, depending upon the strength of the various collective bargaining units, seniority may be an issue. If so, asking experienced staff with desirable virtues to apply for the prevention program position may be a solution.

Once applicants are identified, several independent interviews are recommended to finalize the selection process. For example, to select nonprofessionals to work individually with primary grade children as "special friends," the interview team frequently includes the project coordinator, the school principal, a teacher, and a school mental health professional. When consensus from different perspectives exists regarding the appropriateness of an individual, there is rarely dissatisfaction and the prevention program thrives. Of course, this process may consume a lot of time, even months, and many persons may have to be interviewed before consensus is reached. However, without consensus among interviewers, difficulties can develop. In sum, the time spent to recruit excellent staff, even if it seems excessive, is time well spent.

Communicate to whom, when? Communication regarding a prevention program should be planned, ongoing, and systemic. Plans should include appropriate communication with each level of the hierarchy. For example, school boards, superintendents, and other district administrators are typically interested in the program's general goals, efficacy, fiscal costs, school district liabilities, and responsibilities. These groups typically want the "big picture." They need yearly updates of the program's activities and accomplishments. Indeed more frequent updates are recommended during a program's first 2 or 3 years.

As much information as possible about a prevention program should be communicated to the principal. A principal's routine communications involve parents, teachers, district administrators, and the superintendent. As strategic gatekeepers, principals can enhance a program's support and success or increase the likelihood of foul-ups and failure. Program updates for the principal should occur at least weekly for new programs and monthly for more seasoned ones. Those implementing a prevention program need to communicate with their principal often enough to generate enthusiasm and support for their prevention program during budget crunches and brush fires. The more a principal perceives a prevention program as a necessary part of the school's continuum of services, the more likely the program will endure.

Teachers also need to know the basics of most school-based prevention programs. If they are not directly involved in implementing a prevention program, *their* students may be. Although teachers are directly responsible for only their respective classrooms, a loss of their support can jeopardize preventive services not only in that teacher's classroom, but also in the rest of the school. Accordingly, weekly and sometimes daily communication with teachers is advisable. Communicating with teachers is no less important than similar processes with the principal, but it may be of lower priority when competing demands limit available time.

Parents should be informed by mail and/or phone about all programs. At times parental permission will be required, so a letter sent home describing the program and asking for permission will be built into the program. If prevention programs are part of a formally adopted curriculum, parent permission for a child to participate may not be needed. Even so, good communication about the prevention program is needed. Parents can advocate for a prevention program, but only if they are informed about it. In the 50+ collective years of experience with prevention programs represented by this chapter's three authors, parents have *rarely* sabotaged an effective prevention program, *if* they have understood it. Hence, feedback to parents is needed from the time a program starts and while it is in progress.

Reporting prevention program elements in school and community newspapers, by way of letters home from the principal, and on local radio shows usually enhances community understanding and support. And, because a fundamental goal of many prevention programs is to enhance support from families, peers, the school, and the community, adequate information to these constituents increases the chances that program support, acceptance, and success will result.

How important are support networks for prevention practitioners? It is helpful, if not critical, to develop and maintain support networks among prevention practitioners both within and across programs. Support networks are defined here as groups, the smallest group being two people, who are able to support, encourage, inspire, assist, reassure, and strengthen each other in the face of day-to-day operations and during occasional, and even more formidable complications. Support networks that reflect these capabilities do not happen by chance; they take time and effort to develop.

Program support can be facilitated by planning and scheduling regular meetings. Meetings can be (a) formal, with participants sitting around a table and following an agenda; (b) informal, meeting in the hall or faculty room over a hot or cold liquid refreshment; or (c) via the telephone with someone who is experiencing or has experienced a similar situation. For those starting a program, it is recommended that formal meetings be regularly scheduled. Informal and telephone contacts should occur as needed but may also be scheduled as routines necessitate. Time spent over cups of coffee may seem like a luxury in a hectic schedule, but in reality it may be some of the most valuable time spent in building and maintaining support. It takes time to be supportive and to receive support, so it is necessary to plan for such time accordingly.

Timeliness is an important dimension that needs to be designed into a support network. At times almost instantaneous responses will be needed. The more critical an issue is *perceived*, the quicker the need for a response. For example, if someone is supposed to be available to answer questions or facilitate problem solving, but does not answer the phone, perceived support could easily be zero. In this case the support network may actually have a negative impact. In most cases, prevention program emergencies do not require immediate responses but do require timely responses. In sum, tardy responses produce insecurity and anger; timely responses build support and trust.

How important are consultation and problem-solving skills in implementing prevention programs? Consultation and problem-solving skills are key to building strong prevention programs as well as support networks. The saying, "Give me a fish and I eat for a day, teach me to fish and I eat for a lifetime," accentuates the philosophy needed. Most school personnel would rather be guided over rough spots than told how to accomplish certain tasks. A goal should be to develop a "we" versus a "they" orientation so the responsibility for the success or failure of a prevention program is not localized in a few (i.e., primarily the program school psychologist) but rather generalized across many: the school staff, parents, and the community. In addition, and almost paradoxically, the greater an individual's sense of responsibility, accomplishment, and control, which are processes accelerated by good consultation, the greater the perceived support from others.

How important is training? Quality training enhances the likelihood that a prevention program will succeed. When various program participants know *how, when,* and *why* they are supposed to do various tasks, they feel empowered.

Good training articulates needed materials and those for whom a program is appropriate. It also clarifies which program elements are: (a) *necessary* for successful program implementation, (b) *likely to improve* the chances of realizing the program's goals,

and (c) *open to modification* without detrimental outcomes. Adoption of a successful prevention program is not easy and requires careful attention to training those involved.

As much as possible, prevention program training should be relevant and fun. If training is boring or irrelevant, school staff will find excuses for not attending or leaving early. It is important to keep training meetings as short and as task oriented as possible. Even though school staff may be experts in providing instructional materials to others, they may not be experts in prevention programs. In fact, the more concrete and specific the training, the more effective it is likely to be. Good general teaching principles apply here: first *tell*, then *show*, and finally *let the trainees practice* what needs to be done before they return to their particular schools.

Prevention training should accentuate the positive. Prevention trainers should look for and mention first what has been accomplished best, no matter how difficult it is to find. Following the positive, assistance can be given as to what might be done better. Well-timed constructive criticism is a difficult diplomatic process that taxes consultation skills to their maximum.

Prevention program trainers must also be flexible and sensitive to important issues. Issues that may interfere with learning about how to conduct a prevention program may, at times, intrude and have to be addressed. An example of such a pressing issue might be a recent school board resolution limiting school personnel salaries. Like children with life stressors, school personnel may need to deal with vital matters before learning new material. On occasion, it is better to provide time for such discussions in order that productive time can be spent in prevention training.

A pleasant atmosphere can also help make a more conducive learning environment. Training is usually enhanced by refreshments and comfortable rooms.

How should prevention programs be integrated into schools? To whatever extent possible, prevention programs should be integrated into existing school structures and processes. For example, one structural component of the Primary Mental Health Project (PMHP) is early detection and screening to identify children who show early signs of school adjustment problems. Instead of having a separate screening process just for PMHP, many schools have incorporated PMHP screening into their existing kindergarten screening process. Both time and efficiency are maximized. The point to stress is that it can help, while reviewing a prevention program, to focus on how and where the program will fit into the totality of existing programs and services.

Should those adopting a "successful" prevention program evaluate their efforts? *Every* prevention program should incorporate an evaluation component. (See Keith, in this volume, "Best Practices in Applied Research.") Because adoption of a prevention program is at best difficult, both formative and summative evaluations are needed to determine if a program has been successful, if program goals have been attained, and where improvements might be made.

How can a prevention program be funded? Prevention programs are rarely, if ever, mandated by those who govern schools. Developing funding sources for such programs is, therefore, an important issue. Although seeking fiscal support from school boards is an obvious place to start, that does not always work initially. Recently, state departments of education and mental health have released Requests for Proposals (RFPs) for various types of prevention programs. In general, state agency applications for program support tend to be much shorter, less involved, and less time consuming than federal agency grants. Buzz words from states to look for include "Youth At Risk," "Drug and Alcohol Education," "FOCUS on Youth," "Primary Intervention Projects," "Early Mental Health Initiatives," and other, similar titles. If such RFPs are not available, state school psychological associations and members of the National Association of School Psychologists are well advised to advocate for such resources.

The private sector should also be considered. Private foundations, the United Way, community volunteer organizations, and for-profit corporations frequently look for ways to demonstrate community interest and involvement. Prevention programs that address important community needs have a good chance of being funded, at least on a start-up basis.

Prevention Program Maintenance

Maintaining a prevention program depends upon the many processes used to initiate and implement such a program. Assuming a program has been *successfully* introduced and implemented, primary goals are to foster system ownership and program integrity and efficacy.

System ownership. Fostering system ownership requires: (a) planning from the outset, (b) establishment of support and information networks, (c) integration of the program into the curricular structure, and (d) securing of school district commitment.

Planning from the beginning. Thoughtful planning to facilitate program maintenance should start when the program starts. Even if it proves relatively easy to get a school district to implement a prevention program on a short-term pilot basis, getting a district to maintain a prevention program beyond the initial funding period, past the tenure of the person who starts the program, and over an extended period of time is more difficult. For example, in one prevention project, the project school psychologist did not attend to how the project could be maintained until the final year of outside financial support. Only then did the school psychologist approach the district superintendent, who knew relatively little about the program, to request that project funds be incorporated in the district's budget for the following year. The project was discontinued.

Establishing system ownership of prevention programs takes time. It takes time for a program to become assimilated by the school staff and to be incorporated into the school system. To accomplish this goal there are no simple, how-to recipes available. There are, however, some guiding principles based upon observations of successfully maintained prevention programs.

Support and information networks. Support networks are built from information networks. The more teachers, principals, district administrators, and school boards know about a prevention program, the more they perceive the program to be theirs and the more likely the program will continue. Establishing formal, ongoing communication channels helps program continuity. In one school, for example, the school psychologist strategically requested, and was allowed to review, a prevention program with the school board each February, which also happened to be budget month. His presentation is now a standard part of the school board's February meeting. With little effort, this "institutionalized" progress report can continue after he leaves. Such reports help to keep concerned parties informed and to maintain program support.

Another formal communication channel is a program operations handbook. Such a handbook can be structured and standardized following a specific format, or it can be informal and nonstandardized. An informal handbook can start with a three-ring notebook in which are placed all relevant program memos, letters to parents, minutes of meetings, and copies of presentations to PTAs, school boards, and so forth. Such a notebook/handbook serves as a valuable resource not only for those currently involved with the program, but even more so for those who are beginning with the project and know little of its history.

Program support is also built upon relationships — relationships with positions as well as with people. Key project positions or roles, such as project coordinator, need to transcend the individual. While it is obvious that each person brings specific strengths and weaknesses to a position, essential program functions and relationships must continue when staff changes occur. This means knowledge of important program relationships and functions must be communicated clearly to those who become responsible for a position. This can be accomplished by written job descriptions detailing functional responsibilities enhanced and substantiated by planned briefings. Although the departure of a key person cannot always be foreseen, the codification of basic program information is the best insurance that a program will survive inevitable personnel changes.

Integration of the prevention program into the school's curricular structure. To be maintained in schools, a prevention program will eventually need to be integrated into the totality of school services, as well as the school's philosophies and policies. Prevention programs isolated from the rest of a school's program are not likely to last. Ideally, a prevention program should address some of the more broadly accepted goals of education, the school district, and the school in which it is implemented. One example might be improving classroom behavior and maximizing students' learning. Prevention programs considered to be frills or fads are more likely to be eliminated from school budgets and the school.

School district commitment. Essential to the maintenance of a prevention program is getting local school and district administration to allocate sufficient professional time for completing the program's responsibilities. Because school districts have limited resources, they must allocate those resources according to their priorities. Staff time is the most costly of all expenses. Therefore, when a school allocates staff time to a prevention program, one essential element of program maintenance has been established.

Once again, one obvious way to get support for a program is to ask for it. Although this may suffice as a short-term solution, more is needed for the long term. For continued support, prevention programs need to show concretely what they are preventing and/or which skills they are promoting or enhancing. The formative and summative evaluations suggested previously must address these issues. Nothing breeds support and program maintenance like documented success.

Short-term is defined here as less than 5 years. One critical issue in program maintenance is developing *a realistic time perspective* (Sarason, 1986). Because many prevention programs cannot realistically claim immediate and dramatic results, reasonable and achievable short-term expectations should be proposed.

Program integrity and program efficacy. Once realistic timelines have been established, both formative and summative program evaluations must assess how well the program adoption matches the model and how well the adoption has met its goals. Programs frequently stray from their original model, which can be associated with less than expected results and disappointing outcomes. Therefore, prevention programs need to be monitored to ensure that essential program elements are being implemented faithfully. If they are not, modifications will need to be made. Similarly, if implementation accurately reflects the original model, but the program does not meet its goals, then modification or termination of the program should be considered. Over time, nothing will hurt prevention program adoption and maintenance more than the continuation of inert, ineffective, or harmful programs.

None of these caveats are intended to suggest that a program should be rigid or inflexible, in fact quite the opposite is true. A program as initially implemented may not fully generalize to a different school environment, or it may operate successfully for a number of years and then become less successful. Prevention practitioners must recognize that all systems change. Systems experience internal and external pressures that require good problem-solving skills, flexibility, and alterations. Prevention program implementers must be sensitive to the need for change and plan for it by repeatedly assessing the efficacy of specific program elements and the overall results and by-products of the prevention program.

SUMMARY

Many of the processes involved in adopting a prevention program are similar to those involved in adopting any program. One important difference, however, is the change required in thinking about how best to approach a problem. In schools there is a tradition of working with the most seriously impaired first. School psychology has only recently begun to recognize the significant limitations of this tradition. Many schools and school psychologists, however, continue to focus on casualties of the system. Hence, for many school personnel a paradigm shift (Kuhn, 1970) in thinking is required. Although systems respond slowly to change, small changes in one part of a system can catalyze change throughout the system.

Another important difference in thinking required when adopting prevention programs is a new sense of appropriate "time." It takes time to *prevent* something or to know if something has been prevented. Contemporary society wants immediate results and today's schools are no different. For most prevention programs, immediate positive results are rarely possible. Although changing school professionals' expectations as to what should occur by when — that is, the "magic bullet" syndrome — will not be easy to accomplish; doing so is a major responsibility of those implementing a prevention program.

Finally, most prevention programs available are still in their infancy. Few have been validated across different settings, populations, or time. These realities dictate that restrained optimism should be used when introducing and implementing a program. It also suggests strongly the need for adequate program evaluation strategies to be part of every prevention program. Practitioners need to be innovative, yet not so foolish or naive to maintain programs or practices that produce questionable results or that simply do not work.

REFERENCES

Bloom, B. L. (1985). Psychiatric epidemiology and prevention: The possibilities. In R. L. Hough, P. A. Gongla, V. B. Brown, & S. E. Goldstein (Eds.), *New possibilities in prevention* (pp. 31–52). Los Angeles, CA: Neuropsychiatric Institute.

Cowen, E. L. (1985). Two little magic words. *Professional Psychology, 16,* 181–190.

Hightower, A. D., & Braden, J. (1991). Prevention. In T. R. Kratochwill & M. Morris (Eds.), *The practice of child therapy* (2nd ed.; pp. 410–440). New York: Pergamon.

Kuhn, T. S. (1970). *The structure of scientific revolutions* (2nd ed.). Chicago: University of Chicago Press.

Sarason, S. B. (1986, August). *And what is in the public interest?* Paper presented at the American Psychological Association annual convention, Washington, DC.

Schein, E. H. (1969). *Process consultation: Its role in organizational development.* Reading, MA: Addison-Wesley.

ANNOTATED BIBLIOGRAPHY

Felner, R. D., Jason, L. A., Moritsugu, J. N., & Farber, S. S. (Eds.). (1983). *Preventive psychology: theory, research, and practice.* New York: Pergamon.
Defines and describes the basic elements of prevention and reviews major topical areas in prevention.

Joffe, J. M., Albee, G. N., & Kelly, L. D. (Eds.). (1984). *Readings in primary prevention of psychopathology.* Hanover, NH: University Press of New England.
Provides a representative sample of papers published by the Vermont Conference on the Primary Prevention of Psychopathology and an overview of the field of primary prevention. Topics include factors that affect incidence, stress and stress reduction, increasing competence and coping skills, improving self-esteem, and fostering support systems and networks.

Lorion, R. P. (1989). *Protecting the children: Strategies for optimizing social and emotional development.* New York: Haworth.
Summarizes 10 preventive intervention strategies used successfully with children. Target groups for the various programs range from preschool through adolescents.

Price, R. H., Cowen, E. L., Lorion, R. P., & Ramos-McKay, J. (Eds.). (1988). *Fourteen ounces of prevention: A casebook for practitioners.* Washington, DC: American Psychological Association. Reviews 14 prevention programs judged to be exemplary and replicable. Early childhood, children and youth, and adult programs are discussed. Information needed to make the programs work is provided.

Rickel, A. U., & Allen, L. (1987). *Preventing maladjustment from infancy through adolescence.* Newbury Park, CA: Sage.
Describes representative preventive intervention approaches used with children at risk for maladjustment. It examines various risk factors and then intervention programs that deal with those risk factors.

PREVENTION BIBLIOGRAPHY

Albee, G. W., & Joffe, J. M. (Eds.). (1977). *The primary prevention of psychopathology: The issues.* Hanover, NH: University Press of New England.

Cowen, E. L. (1973). Social and community interventions. *Annual Review of Psychology, 24,* 423–472.

Cowen, E. L. (1982). The special number: A compleat roadmap. *American Journal of Community Psychology, 10,* 239–250.

Cowen, E. L. (1984). A general structural model for primary prevention program development in mental health. *Personnel and Guidance Journal, 62,* 485–490.

Cowen, E. L., & Hightower, A. D. (1982). The Primary Mental Health Project: Alternative approaches in school-based prevention interventions. In T. B. Gutkin & C. R. Reynolds (Eds.), *The handbook of school psychology* (2nd ed.). New York: Wiley.

Johnson, D. B., Carlson, S. R., & Couick, J. (1993). *Program development manual for the Primary Intervention Program.* Sacramento, CA: California Department of Mental Health.

Kelly, J. G., & Hess, R. E. (Eds.). (1987). *The ecology of prevention: Illustrating mental health consultation.* New York: Haworth.

Kessler, M., & Goldston, S. E. (Eds.). (1986). *A decade of progress in primary prevention.* Hanover, NH: University Press of New England.

Lorion, R. P., & Lounsbury, J. (1982). Conceptual and methodological considerations in evaluating preventive interventions. In W. R. Task & G. Stahler (Eds.), *Innovative approaches to mental health evaluation* (pp. 24–57). New York: Academic.

Prevention Task Panel Report. (1978). *Task Panel reports submitted to the President's Commission on Mental Health* (Vol. 4; pp. 1822–1863). Washington, DC: U.S. Government Printing Office, Stock No. 040-000-00393-2.

Price, R. H., & Smith, S. S. (1985). *A guide to evaluating prevention programs in mental health.* Rockville, MD: National Institute of Mental Health.

Roberts, M. C., & Peterson, L. (Eds.). (1984). *Prevention of problems in childhood: Psychological research and applications.* New York: Wiley.

Sarason, S. B. (1971). *The culture of the school and the problem of change.* Boston: Allyn-Bacon.

Shaw, M. C., & Goodyear, R. K. (Eds.). (1984). Primary prevention in the schools. *Personnel and Guidance Journal, 62,* 443–495.

Strayhorn, J. M. (1988). *The competent child: An approach to psychotherapy and preventive mental health.* New York: Guilford.

Zins, J., & Forman, S. G. (Eds.). (1988). Mini-series on primary prevention: From theory to practice. *School Psychology Review, 17*(4).

CLEARINGHOUSE FOR MATERIAL ON PREVENTION

VCPPP Prevention Training Clearinghouse
Department of Psychology
University of Vermont
Burlington, VT 05405
(802) 656-4069

Ontario Prevention Clearinghouse
984 Bay Street, Suite 603
Ontario M5S 2A5, Canada
(416) 928-1838

JOURNALS THAT FEATURE PREVENTION

American Journal of Community Psychology
Plenum Publishing Corporation
233 Spring Street
New York, NY 10013

Prevention in Human Services
Haworth Press, Inc.
28 East 22nd Street
New York, NY 10010

Journal of Community Psychology
Clinical Psychology Publishing Company
4 Conant Square
Brandon, VT 05733

The Journal of Preventive Psychiatry
Mary Ann Liebert, Inc.
1651 Third Avenue
New York, NY 10128

The Journal of Primary Prevention
Human Sciences Press
72 Fifth Avenue
New York, NY 10011

The Journal of Public Health Policy
Milton Terris, MD., Editor
208 Meadowood Drive
South Burlington, VT 05403

29

Best Practices in Defining, Implementing, and Evaluating Educational Outcomes

Carolyn T. Cobb
Division of Innovation and Development Services
North Carolina Department of Public Instruction

OVERVIEW

The theme underlying *Best Practices–III* is problem solving, with most chapters likely emphasizing practice with individual and groups of students. The intent of this chapter is to overview the nature of and reasons for dramatic changes in public education in this nation, especially in the types of outcomes or goals that must be addressed. The paradigm of schooling is subtly but surely changing from an emphasis on the resources and inputs of education to accountability for the outcomes and achievement levels attained by students. Inherent in this shift is the importance of the *types* of outcomes for which schools are to be held accountable. As schools explore the types of outcomes to set for their students, seek to apply new knowledge about learning, and search for more valid direct (e.g., low-inference) assessment strategies for accountability purposes, the potential roles for school psychologists will expand. The orientation, knowledge, and skills for these roles may be different from traditional areas of training in school psychology. They will require, at least, different types of application.

Some of the greatest opportunities will be helping schools and districts to identify exactly what the problems are — perhaps the most critical step in the problem-solving process. Defining, implementing, and evaluating outcomes will offer considerable opportunity for school psychologists to identify problems, use low-inference assessment, establish interventions, monitor progress, and determine attainment of the goals/outcomes. The applications may be appropriate at the system and community levels as well as the classroom or student levels. In this chapter, I hope that school psychologists will identify future opportunities and challenges for new roles and realize how the knowledge and skills that they already possess can, with slight redirection, assist schools and districts in facing what some claim to be the most challenging time in educational history.

Why Schools Must Change: A Focus on Outcomes

Since *A Nation at Risk* (1983) was issued, American schools have been under serious scrutiny. Many observers and educators recognize that we are at a defining moment in American education. Poor rankings of American students compared to students of other industrialized nations are often used as evidence that schools are not producing high quality students. Our high dropout rate of 25% or more is cited as additional evidence that schools are failing students. Is it true that our schools are worse today than they used to be?

Some researchers have noted that schools are doing as well as or better than they did in previous decades. Standardized test scores are actually as good as they were in the 1960s, their highest point. While overall Scholastic Aptitude Test (SAT) scores have fallen slightly, a much higher percentage of diverse students now takes the SAT. When scores are analyzed by type of student subgroups, SAT scores have actually increased for every type of subgroup. (See Jaegger, 1992, for an overview of these issues and data.) The dropout rate was approximately 50% in the 1950s, much higher than it is today. In spite of evidence of increased academic success, critics maintain students are less well prepared to take their place in society. The answer to this seeming paradox lies at least partially in the changing requirements of society and the world of work.

Today one can hardly be ignorant of the evidence that the world is changing in fundamental ways and, along with it, our American society. We now refer to the economy in global terms, as we do much of our political life. Diverse cultures of the world are increasingly interdependent. America is especially marked by diverse racial and ethnic groups. Large segments of our youth culture are in turmoil, causing increased violence in schools. Our society is no longer characterized by "traditional" family structures of a working father, stay-at-home mother, and two children. Almost 1/4 of our youth live in single-parent families, and at least 1/5 of children live in poverty. Higher standards of living are no longer assumed for the next generation, and the economic gap between rich and poor seems to be increasing. In short, children coming to schools today are quite different from children of past generations.

Perhaps the most fundamental change is the nature of the economy and the world of work that our children will confront. Even now workplaces are increasingly characterized by high technology. Our era is referred to as the "Information Age." Manufacturing processes often replace human labor with robots or other computerized technology. This kind of economy requires workers who can think, solve problems, and be flexible. Workers are required to work together, often in teams, as well as independently. Drucker (1989) noted that an economy in which knowledge is the true capital and wealth-producing resource will make stringent demands on schools for education performance and accountability.

In this view of a changing society, there is no room for citizens and workers who cannot perform at high levels. Universal literacy that includes higher order skills is required. Thus, while a 25% dropout rate is much better than the 1950s rate, it is not acceptable if all students are to acquire complex knowledge and skills.

Schools today have not changed fundamentally from the way schools have been run for decades and, as such, are not likely to meet the demands of a new economic age. Schools were built to reflect the industrial age, with bureaucratic structures and "assembly line" operations of rigid age or grade promotions, where all students move at the same rate "ready or not." They often reflect "caste" systems where students are slotted into special programs or levels and never get out. Schools typically reflect an emphasis on teaching, not on learning; and the two are not the same.

The last 10 to 15 years of cognitive and educational research have yielded considerable gains in knowledge about how we learn. This new understanding of learning is consistent with the strategies needed to facilitate the types of outcomes deemed necessary for the 21st century society. The American Psychological Association has recently published "Learner-Centered Psychological Principles" (APA, 1992), which all school psychologists should read and study. These principles summarize the best of what is known about learning and reflect the tenets of a view of learning called "constructivism." Practices in schools today generally do not reflect new knowledge about learning.

A new era requires new types of learning and outcomes for all students. And new learnings require new kinds of schools. These new outcomes and how they are learned will drive the reform efforts.

New Types of Outcomes

Inherent in any discussion of restructuring or reinventing schools is the issue of the types of outcomes that schools must address. When outcomes are defined in terms of what is learned, the intended outcomes must be set forth with care (Finn, 1990). While educational reform has frequently focused on traditional norm-referenced test scores, educators and citizens increasingly express a desire for complex cognitive, social, and affective outcomes. Educators are being asked to address significant knowledge, skills, and attributes necessary to prepare students to live in an information society characterized by global economic interdependence, cultural pluralism, rapidly expanding technologies, and decentralized social structures. While the national education goals speak to excellence in traditional subject matter areas, they also reference the need for students to learn to "use their minds well" (Goal 3).

Schlecty (1990) proposes that a new era requires new purposes of schooling. "Knowledge work" should be the focus of schools — using ideas and symbols for some purposeful result. An information-based society relies on knowledge and the ability to put it to work to create, to invent, and to solve problems. The new literacy that requires fundamental and total restructuring of the educational system includes capacities once demanded only of a few: to think critically and creatively, solve problems, exercise judgment, and learn new skills and knowledge throughout a lifetime (Brown, 1991).

During the Bush administration, the U.S. Department of Labor established the Secretary's Commission on Achieving Necessary Skills (SCANS). This group of business and education leaders issued a report, *What Work Requires of Schools* (SCANS, 1991), defining the knowledge, skills, and attributes necessary in high performance workplaces. Under "Foundation Skills" they included *basic skills* of reading, writing, arithmetic and mathematics, speaking, and listening. But they also included *thinking skills* (ability to learn, reason, think creatively, make decisions, and solve problems), as well as *personal qualities* (responsibility, self-esteem, self-management, sociability, and integrity). "Workplace Competencies" were also defined for effective workers. These competencies included *using resources* (e.g., allocation of time, money, materials, space, and staff), *interpersonal skills* (e.g., work on teams, teach others, serve customers, negotiate, work with people from culturally diverse backgrounds), *information* (e.g., acquire and evaluate data, interpret and communicate, use computers to process information), *systems* (e.g., understand social, organizational, and technological systems; monitor and correct performance; design and improve systems), and *technology* (e.g., select equipment and tools, apply technology to tasks, maintain and troubleshoot equipment).

Clearly, the knowledge and skills reflected by these reports and writers exceed the areas measured by traditional indicators of student success and reflect the need for changes in what and how students are taught. We are not likely to attain these kinds of outcomes in the current schooling paradigm.

The Focus on Outcomes and Learning: A New Schooling Paradigm

The changes cited in the preceding sections are paradigm changes in our world. Systems that met needs in previous decades no longer meet today's problems or opportunities. The concept of paradigm helps to explain the powerful and fundamental shift in understandings, assumptions, and values now emerging in education. Paradigms are the rules and regulations, the stated and unstated assumptions, the "world view" that shape our understanding or ways of viewing something (Kuhn, 1970). Paradigms begin to crumble when they no longer help solve problems.

Paradigm shifts often are not evident to those participating in them. The outcome-focused paradigm has not been linear, but its emergence has been evident in numerous ways. For decades, we have assumed that if we provided enough resources, appropriate strategies, and equality of inputs, we would have equality of outcomes. The Coleman Report of 1966, which asserted that schools could not overcome the socioeconomic status of students, shattered the presumed link between inputs and outputs. Essentially, Coleman maintained that schools could not overcome the effects of social class.

Many researchers felt that Coleman's findings were flawed. They believed that if they could find schools that served all students well, including poor students, they could discover the causes and conditions that led these schools to be effective and, thus, refute Coleman's claims. They defined an "effective school" as one in which academic success could not be predicted by the student's socioeconomic status. Using scores on norm-referenced tests as their measure of academic success, they were able to identify effective schools, as well as correlates that appeared to account for their success. Effective schools, as defined by these researchers, are concerned with how schools can become effective for all learners; equity in excellence is a fundamental premise. Thus, effective-schools research was a major step in linking school process variables (e.g., leadership, instruction, time) to student outcomes and in moving toward an outcomes focus. Other evidence of the shifting paradigm to outcomes can be seen in an increasing number of meta-analysis studies and in Walberg's (1984) productivity research.

Emphasis on site-based management and flexibility in how outcomes are reached is part of the paradigm implying that it is no longer critical *to prescribe how* outcomes are reached, but *whether* outcomes are reached. The establishment of national educational goals by the Governors and the ensuing debate around the issues of a national curriculum, national assessment systems, and new forms of assessment are all a part of the emerging outcomes paradigm. Reform under the existing paradigm has meant trying to do the same things harder, more, or better. While previous reforms have focused on the need for higher standards in terms of traditional course structures, more time for learning, and increased emphasis on the "basics," the outcome paradigm implies

- Graduation requirements based on mastery of essential knowledge and skills rather than a predetermined number of hours in given grades or courses.

- Different mastery rates for different learners across various subjects.

- Multifaceted assessment systems for determining progress (e.g., portfolios, products, demonstrations).

- Transcripts of specific skills rather than courses and grades.

Outcome-based education is increasingly coming to mean a specific paradigm for transforming schools that focuses all of the school's instructional programs and operating structures around attaining important outcomes (Spady, 1992; Spady & Marshall, 1991). Outcome-based educators ask what knowledge, skills, and attributes students will need to work and live in the 21st century, and then redesign curriculum, learning, instruction, and assessment to ensure that these outcomes are reached. In existing schools, time is fixed for all students and achievement (e.g., outcomes) varies across students. In a results-oriented paradigm, outcomes are held constant across students and time for mastery is allowed to vary among students. Clock hours and Carnegie units have little meaning in schools based on performance and mastery.

Whereas the effective-schools movement emphasizes the school as the unit of change and its impact on the student in terms of school goals, outcome-based education starts from the perspective of the student in terms of the outcomes necessary for future success. In this system, everything in schools (e.g., curriculum, instruction, operations, structure) is driven by defined outcomes of significance and existing knowledge of the learning process. It is this understanding that requires fundamental changes in traditional school structures, such as time, credits, graduation units, grade levels, grading practices, student advancement, didactic instruction, and normative assessment.

Skeptics may assert that strategies associated with the outcome-based paradigm have been tried before, including mastery learning, ungraded classes, and continuous progress. If these strategies did not succeed then, why should they do so now? When the research is considered, it becomes clear that many of the previous innovations were, in fact, successful but were unable to be maintained in a system that was fundamentally input-based. A paradigm shift involves changes in every aspect of the framework, not just selected portions as has occurred in the past. In addition, the outcomes perspective is pervasive both inside and outside of education. The push for an outcomes focus derives more from business and the public than from educators. Previous reform efforts typically emanated from educators.

The desperate need for all of our citizens to perform at high levels to be successful in the 21st century and to shape a healthy society is widely recognized. Even noted news columnist, William Raspberry, has written columns that reflect outcome-oriented thinking. In one article (1991a) he questioned the absurdity of an educational system that allows the quality of student work to vary while keeping time fixed. In a second editorial (1991b) he attacked the pervasive academic competition in schools, grading on the curve, and the creation of winners and losers. He asks: "Doesn't it make more sense to make sure that every kid gets a chance — and more than one chance — at academics?"

All of the existing aspects of schooling support a time-based, input paradigm that results in inconsistent outcomes for students. Sorting, tracking, and classifying — system functions currently associated with school psychologists among others — are much less relevant in an outcome-based paradigm. Most aspects of schooling have to change to support a school where intended outcomes for all students drive everything else.

The Outcome Paradigm and School Psychology

School psychologists must reflect on the implications of these new education directions for their practice. A fundamental question is whether our history and training are in conflict with the emerging paradigm of schooling and the assumptions it embodies. While exact origins of school psychology are debated, the psychometric and assessment heritage has permeated our practice for decades. This heritage that evolved from the existing system includes training in ability differences and intelligence testing; assessment practices based on the normal curve; a focus on deficits and remediation; and roles of sorting, tracking, and classifying students for various programs and levels.

The new paradigm replaces an emphasis on ability with an emphasis on effort. It harbors the belief that all children can learn well. It does not assume that all children will learn to the same level or exactly the same things, but recognizes that we often have limited students' choices by labeling them with certain levels of "ability" or fearing that we might expect too much and damage their self-esteem. Cross-cultural studies of perceptions of success in school show that Japanese mothers are more likely to attribute different levels of achievement to effort, whereas American mothers tend to attribute differential success to ability. Our profession's early emphasis on normal distributions, intelligence testing, and placement for special education has likely contributed to the notion that ability is the key trait for success, not effort or hard work.

Most educational and psychological assessment has been based on normal distributions. Only recently have we moved into curriculum-based assessments and other low-inference procedures. We have not readily questioned the usefulness of the bell-shaped curve — which assumes as many students fail as succeed, with most being "average." The normal curve is often descriptive, but we have used it in our profession and education as "prescriptive" and "predictive." Larry Lezotte, noted effective-schools researcher, has observed that we could attain a normal curve of achievement without schools; it would merely reflect the population performance without intervention. If schools really are effective, they should not yield a bell curve of achievement (Lezotte, 1990). We should begin to see a "J-Curve," where most students achieve what schools intend that they learn. Figure 1 illustrates the difference in the theoretical distributions of the normal and J-curves. It should be noted that the J-curve can be obtained by setting low standards. But in schools that are restructuring around high-level outcomes for all students, the intent is that most students will attain satisfactory performance on these challenging outcomes (e.g., grade C or better).

Assessment in the Outcome-Based Paradigm: An Example.

Because assessment has always been fundamental to the school psychologist's role, examining that role in outcome-based education may be useful. Figure 2 illustrates assessment assumptions and practices along the dimension of "test inference." Inference refers to the extent to which the sample of behavior assessed by a particular instrument matches the behavior of concern in real life. Thus, projective personality assessments and intelligence tests may be referred to as "high inference," requiring a fair amount of interpretation between the sample of behaviors on the instrument itself as compared to the observation of those traits in daily life. "Low-inference" procedures, on the other hand, more closely approximate the actual behaviors of interest. In communicating with teachers, high-inference assessment might be referred to as indirect measurement and low-inference assessment as direct measurement.

A number of assessment dimensions, as well as elements or characteristics of each dimension, can be

FIGURE 1. Normal and J-curve expectations of success.

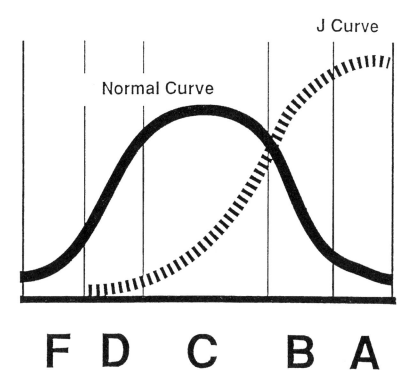

plotted along this inference continuum. While there is no exact point on the inference continuum where characteristics of each dimension fall, the location should be considered approximate and relative to other assessment characteristics on the same continuum. For example, the "domains of assessment" (the first dimension) included in high inference/indirect assessment typically include psychological traits, such as personality characteristics or intelligence. As we move along the continuum toward low inference/direct assessment, we are more likely to measure actual knowledge and, ultimately, skills. Similarly, the "types of assessments" (second dimension) associated with these domains begin with norm-referenced assessment (high inference) and move sequentially through criterion-referenced assessment, curriculum-based assessment, portfolios, and performances or demonstrations in moving toward lower inference procedures.

Typically, high-inference procedures occur in "decontextualized" or artificial settings. They frequently focus on discrete (some say trivial) skills or behaviors and are designed to sort, track, and classify. Thus, they require forced or high variance, resulting in normal distributions. Low-inference procedures are measured "in context" or in authentic (real-life) settings. They focus on culminating skills and are concerned with proficiency and instruction. As such, they reflect low variance and seek to attain a J-curve,

where most students are mastering culminating skills of significance.

Thus, the types of assessment built around norm-referenced, high-inference procedures typically focus on comparing students to each other. Low-inference procedures are more likely to compare individual performance to a target set of criteria. These criteria are set forth in advance so that students are "in on it" from the beginning. The focus is on mastery, not mystery, learning.

The depiction in Figure 2 is not meant to ascribe value only to high- or to low-inference assessment. Both types of assessment have a purpose and appropriate uses. However, assessment in the traditional schooling paradigm has been characterized by high to mid-level inference strategies, with the primary purposes of sorting and classifying students. Although there are examples to the contrary, this paradigm is where school psychology currently resides in the main. Increasingly, use of norm-referenced assessment to determine student achievement or to predict future achievement is under serious scrutiny.

Low-inference assessment is integral to an outcome-based paradigm of schooling. The focus is demonstrated mastery for most students; thus, low variance in scores is typical. If school psychologists are locked into a belief system holding that ability among students is normally distributed (therefore achievement among students must be normally dis-

FIGURE 2. Implications of high- versus low-inference assessment.

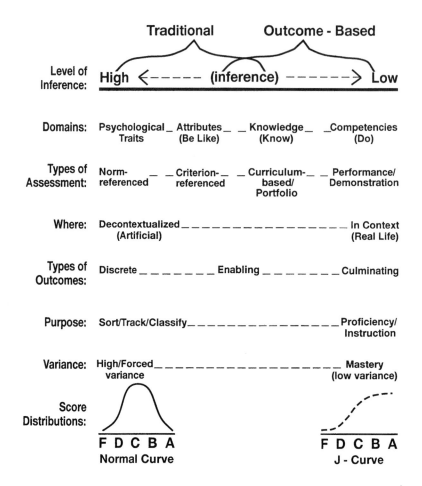

tributed), and students at the lower end of that curve cannot learn significant outcomes for the 21st century, then we will not be very useful to schools of the future. Even more germane to the point of this book, low-inference procedures are essential to effective problem-solving for students, classrooms, and systems. Understanding low-inference assessment in the context of schools that emphasize higher order outcomes for all students is essential.

The opportunities for school psychologists in an outcome-based paradigm of schooling are numerous. But we will need to reconsider our historical training, assumptions, and beliefs if we are to mesh with a system intent on all students learning successfully and attaining knowledge and skills necessary to live and work in the 21st century.

BASIC CONSIDERATIONS

Knowledge and Skills for a Shifting Paradigm

Fundamental to moving beyond our historical beginnings is a shift from a mental health and deficit model to one of educational attainment and develop-

ment for all students, from clinical to instructional terminology, and from a focus on the individual to a focus on increased systems interventions (Cobb, 1990). If we are to focus on educational attainment for all, school psychologists must

- Understand low-inference assessment procedures and move to assessment that facilitates achievement and measures accountability in terms of attained outcomes.

- Move away from comparing, sorting, and classifying students for programs defined by labels rather than by instructional needs.

- Be current with the research about learning and how higher order skills are acquired.

If students are to be proficient at understanding systems (SCANS, 1991), school psychologists can be among the most useful personnel in education to help students develop those skills. Of course, school psychologists have to be taught to think in systems terms as well.

Many skills that school psychologists currently have will be useful in an outcome-based paradigm of schooling. However, the reorientation of some of those skills (e.g., assessment) as well as the acquisition of new types of skills will be required in order for school psychologists to be relevant to mainstream instruction and reform in American schools of the future. A few areas of relevant knowledge and skills to be acquired by school psychologists, as well as incorporated into preservice training programs, are suggested here.

Understanding the future and work force needs. School psychologists must attend to discussions about the future and requirements of citizens in the 21st century. We must be able to help define the types of outcomes that will be relevant for student success in work and life. We must, at the very least, attend to news articles about such things as the changing world of work and new systems for society's challenges. More formal reading in these areas, including membership in organizations like the World Futures Society, may also be helpful. An extension of these skills would include vision-driven strategic planning, where school district plans are shaped by a vision of where they want to be in the future, what they will look like, and what external forces will impact them.

Systems theory and operation. Many school psychologists already study systems theory, but all need to do so. A systems view is useful because it

1. Helps examine external influences from other systems.

2. Highlights the impact of our "outputs" and services.

3. Helps us see that we are not helpless but can behave in alternative ways toward external influences.

4. Emphasizes that in order to change any system component in a substantive way, the entire system must be considered and possibly altered (Katz & Kahn, 1978).

Interestingly, the SCANS report identifies the understanding of how systems operate as a basic outcome to be required for all students. Psychologists need to know how systems operate and can be changed so that they can both effect change in the public schools and help ensure that students understand and can improve
or design systems. (See the chapter in this book by Michael Curtis on systems consultation.)

Organizational change and group process. Related to systems theory, knowledge of organizational change and group process skills are essential to implement new schooling paradigms, empower all

staff, and create effective organizational structures. Understanding and impacting organizational culture (e.g., roles, rules, relationships), reshaping organizational structures, understanding the change process, and facilitating work and decision groups in schools are all essential roles in the emerging school restructuring paradigm. These roles are particularly appropriate for school psychologists.

Constructivist principles of learning. It is critical that school psychologists are current in their understandings about how learning occurs. Many school psychologists have been well-schooled in a behavioral model of learning. While there are many useful behavioral principles, the behavioral view of learning that focuses on strengthening bonds between stimulus and response, breaking tasks into component parts, getting the "right" answer, and repetitive training is rapidly becoming outmoded. Learning has been studied in laboratory (artificial) settings, and cognitive psychologists assumed that knowledge and skills could be acquired independently of context (Berryman, 1991).

Today, the predominant view of learning among cognitive and educational psychologists is called "constructivism." Learning is viewed as a goal-directed process, where meaning is constructed from both information and experience. Learners construct representations of knowledge that make sense to them; they associate and connect new information with what they already know. Constructivist research contains important implications for how to teach. For example, it is not necessary that students learn basic skills before learning problem-solving skills. These skills are not necessarily sequential but rather are mutually reinforcing. Instruction should be reoriented away from mere mastery of facts and information and toward the recognition and solving of complex problems. Real "know-how" cannot be taught in isolation; students need practice in applying these skills in real-life contexts.

The American Psychological Association has produced "Learner-Centered Psychological Principles: Guidelines for School Redesign and Reform" (APA, 1992). These principles synthesize state-of-the-art research and knowledge about learning, including elements of the brief review presented here. The learner-centered principles address metacognitive and cognitive factors, affective factors, developmental factors, social factors, and individual differences. Implications for aspects of school redesign include instruction, curriculum, assessment, instructional management, teacher education, parent and community involvement, and policies. All school psychologists should read and study these principles. The principles reflect ways that school psychologists can be part of schools of the future, help schools set significant outcomes for students, develop classrooms and school environments to achieve these significant outcomes, and determine if the outcomes have been attained (i.e., problem-solving for school reform).

Research on instructional and school practices that improve outcomes. The success of school psychology in 21st-century schools requires that their work have greater relevance to the instructional elements of schooling, including curriculum, teaching processes, and the learning environment. To be effective problem-solvers at the individual student, classroom, and district levels, school psychologists must rely on an empirical base of knowledge about what works to improve achievement and other student outcomes. There is a growing base of research on effective classroom and school-level practices.

Constructivism, for example, supports the belief that curiosity, creativity, and higher order thinking are stimulated by learning tasks that are challenging, relevant, authentic, and novel. Learning and self-esteem are enhanced by interacting with others in flexible, respectful, and caring instructional settings and relationships (APA, 1992). Instruction that is consistent with constructivism and higher order outcomes requires that students be active rather than passive learners. Teachers are facilitators of learning rather than dispensers of information. While there is a place for didactic instruction, classrooms must facilitate hands-on activities, interaction, and collaboration. Teachers help students make interdisciplinary connections and provide a setting for risk-taking, experimentation, and active manipulation of physical structures and models. Learning units may be more extended and integrated through themes or projects.

Other effective practices include, to name a few, heterogeneous classes (vs. between-class ability grouping), functional grouping and regrouping, reduced grade retention, cooperative learning strategies, peer helping, integrated instruction, accelerated learning, and student-led conferences. Teachers will need to know how to use grouping and regrouping strategies in the classroom effectively. Cooperative learning, peer helping, and student-led conferences are appropriate strategies for classrooms where students are active and responsible learners. School psychologists should be familiar with various instructional strategies to help teachers problem solve for effective instruction of individuals and groups of students.

Research suggests the effectiveness of a number of school-level programs. The Stanford Accelerated Schools Project (Levin, 1991) is based on the premise that at-risk students must learn at a faster rate than more advantaged students — not at a slower, remedial rate that drags them down further. The intent is to bring them into the mainstream at grade level by the end of elementary school. The School Development Program (Comer, 1988) incorporates the elements of effective schools and builds on the needs of the whole child, including other community agencies and parents in the educational planning for children. The Coalition of Essential Schools (Sizer, 1992) emphasizes the need for rigor, disciplined habits of mind, integrated instruction, and problem solving at the high-school level. Success for All (Madden, Slavin, Karweit, Lawrence, & Wasik, 1991) uses a combination of strategies (e.g., cooperative learning, whole language) to bring the achievement of highly disadvantaged students up to grade level. While the school psychology literature may include some important information in these areas, school psychologists likely will need to refer to educational practice and research journals to acquire information particularly useful to school personnel and reform.

A key contribution of school psychologists is their skill in understanding the research and translating it for application and practice. Suggesting policy, program, and instructional implications of the research is one way psychologists can build the research base into teaching and program development in schools.

Authentic assessment strategies. Assessment has moved to center stage in the national debate on educational reform. High-stakes assessment has traditionally been defined by normed-referenced, standardized achievement tests that focus on discrete knowledge in given subject areas and that compare students to each other. New assessment practices that reflect the type of learning and instruction described previously are increasingly at the center of the discussion. These assessments are often referred to as "authentic" or based on real-world performances and tasks. Sometimes the terms "authentic" and "performance-based" are used interchangeably, because real life expectations require some demonstration of knowledge and skills. Compared to conventional assessments, new assessment practices

- Are ongoing and cumulative versus annual.
- Use open-ended versus multiple-choice formats.
- Draw upon a variety of settings versus a single setting.
- Are performance based versus paper and pencil.
- Are criterion-referenced versus norm-referenced.
- Are teacher mediated versus teacher proof.

Authentic tasks are becoming important aspects of instruction and assessment. Assessment in this paradigm is designed to be an integral part of instruction and is often not distinguished from it. Thus, teachers need considerable assistance in understanding how classroom instruction can be reliably and validly assessed. Authentic assessment in the classroom involves worthy tasks from the real world that require students to apply their knowledge and skills. Authentic assessment engages students, involves self-assessment and frequently peer assessment, and requires preset criteria to let students know "up front" what constitutes acceptable and exemplary performances. Students have an active role in determining the target learning criteria and learn to reliably assess the performance of self and peers. Examples of performance assessments include direct writing assessments, extended projects, presentations, investigations, open-ended questions, debates, and experiments. To be maximally helpful to teachers, school psychologists should expand their knowledge to include these types of assessments and skills.

The use of authentic assessments at district, state, or national levels for high-stakes decisions is still being debated. Issues of reliability and validity are central to the national debate. Some educational psychologists believe that new forms of validity will become important. Whether results from a single performance task can be generalized to the entire domain of concern is also questioned. Shavelson, Gao, and Baxter (1993) found that large numbers of tasks are necessary to get a generalizable measure of performance, regardless of the subject matter (math or science), domain (education or job performance), or level of analysis (individual or school). For example, they estimate that approximately 10 performance tasks in science would be necessary to get a reliable estimate of a child's understanding of science in general. Obviously, performance assessment is time-consuming and expensive, especially for decisions outside of the classroom as Vermont recently discovered when they used portfolios as part of their statewide assessment with discouraging results. Although reliability between raters was acceptable for groups of students, it was extremely low for individual student scores. Nevertheless, districts, states, and national groups are pursuing the possibilities of performance or authentic assessment for large-scale purposes. School psychologists must be informed about and participate in these debates to assist districts in developing appropriate and accurate assessments.

Understanding the "quality" issue. After being a pivotal issue driving many business reforms of the 1980s, the notion of "high quality" performance is infusing education. Total Quality concepts such as worker-level decision making, continuous improvement, and self-assessment based on clear criteria are being used by many teachers and districts. Teachers work with their students to establish the criteria or rubrics for quality work in the classroom. Likewise, principals work with teachers to determine criteria for quality teacher performance. The student and staff outcomes established by many districts and states often include the concept of quality work. School psychologists should have a basic understanding of Total Quality concepts as described by Deming (1986) and others to assist schools and districts in implementing new types of outcomes, as well as in carrying out restructuring efforts.

BEST PRACTICES

With a slight reshaping of the knowledge and skill base, school psychologists can be some of the best-trained professionals in schools to help teachers, schools, and districts implement and evaluate new types of educational outcomes. Opportunities for problem-solving roles exist at the community, system, school, classroom, and individual-student levels.

System- and Community-Level Roles

As school districts consider the desired types of student and staff outcomes and results and the types of restructuring changes necessary to achieve them, they often engage in vision-driven strategic planning. School psychologists can be instrumental in developing a constructive process for strategic planning, as well as the transition processes necessary to shift the district's focus and priorities. The existing problems and need for change must be clearly defined by staff and the community. Strategic planning involves assessment of the environment (often called environmental scanning), as well as the strengths and needs of the organization. From a problem-solving perspective, the steps to effect the desired changes are system "interventions." Mechanisms for continuous monitoring of progress toward attainment of desired goals is essential as are knowledge of systems, organizational change, and group processes if school psychologists are to help lead systems through this type of fundamental change.

Districts also need assistance in determining the types of outcomes that will drive their restructuring and instructional efforts. Facilitating the development of outcomes that meet the needs of living and working in the 21st century and that are based on what we know about learning is a critical role for school psychologists. Outcomes usually include knowledge, skills, and attributes desired for all students. Coalitions and consensus in the community around these outcomes, including involvement of citizens, parents, and students in the development process, is essential to the attainment of designated outcomes. If school psychologists understand the future work force and citizenship needs, current knowledge about learning, and group process skills, they will be able to be key players in this process.

As school psychologists work with parents around individual student problems or needs, they can help parents understand the outcomes expected of their children and ways that parents can further attain those outcomes. By linking specific interventions to district-level outcomes, school psychologists will help reinforce the importance of the outcomes and more likely ensure that all students attain them.

Developing and selecting performance-based assessments for district accountability systems that measure new types of outcomes also provides an important role for school psychologists. Their understanding of the issues involved in moving from sole reliance on norm-referenced achievement tests to performance assessments and other measures of outcomes is critical. While most educators maintain that instruction should drive assessment, in fact assessment often shapes the nature of instruction. In developing district-wide assessment procedures, schools must consider the various purposes for which assessment data are needed, as well as the impact of the assessment system on teaching and learning. A combination of low-to-moderate-inference assessments may be useful, and psychologists will need to help schools match assessments to purposes in meaningful ways. Specifically, psychologists might

- Study existing assessments.

- Assess gaps in what is needed to move in desired directions.

- Lead groups through a study of alternative assessments.

- Assist in development and/or selection of system-level assessments.

- Link results of assessments to district goals and outcomes.

- Evaluate the appropriateness and use of district accountability systems. (See Elliott, 1992 for a more complete description of one school psychologist's role in district-level assessment.)

School- and Classroom-Level Roles

Learning to teach to new types of outcomes, employing appropriate instructional strategies, working with groups in classrooms, and applying authentic assessments will be daunting challenges for most teachers and principals. Educators often cite the belief that all students can learn well, but real application of that belief requires changes in how students are taught, grouped, graded, and advanced. School psychologists can be valuable contributors to staff development or "capacity building" for teachers. Areas of training might include current principles of learning and their classroom applications, team work, effective instructional strategies, and strategies to address skills and attributes as well as content knowledge, and classroom assessment.

Collaborating with teachers to plan and implement new instructional practices in the classroom will require school psychologists to use careful problem-solving strategies. For example, the teacher's state of readiness and real goals (problem definition) should be determined. Strategies currently in use and the teacher's level of knowledge and skills regarding new instructional strategies that reflect constructivist learning principles and new types of outcomes also should be assessed. Specific measurable goals for implementation of new strategies should be established.

When appropriate, the psychologist should work closely with the teacher as new strategies are employed, providing feedback, coaching, modeling, or other support interventions.

Even consultation with teachers and other staff regarding individual students can be focused around the district's outcomes. If instruction and assessment are aligned with culminating student outcomes, then everything — including consultation goals — should be designed to help students reach these exit or culminating outcomes. Because many districts include outcomes that reflect desired attributes (e.g., responsibility, self-management, perseverance), even interventions for behavioral problems should be viewed in the light of facilitating district-level outcomes for all students.

"All" means all. The status of students with disabilities in outcome-based education is an important issue. When we say outcomes are to be specified for *all* students, do we mean to include students who are mentally or learning disabled or otherwise impaired? Many educators believe that exit outcomes or goals should be stated so that *all* students are included. An outcome that describes a "quality worker" or "contributing citizen" can apply to any student regardless of mental or emotional status. The specific levels of outcomes, the nature of instruction, and ways that outcomes are assessed may vary for students with disabilities. However, if culminating outcomes are stated in terms of subject matter content (e.g., algebra), then *all* will not mean all. In the state of Kentucky, exit outcomes are intended for all students. A statewide portfolio assessment system has been developed to assess severely disabled students on these outcomes at levels appropriate to their individual goals and abilities. Nevertheless, these individual goals are driven by the statewide exit outcomes. It should be noted that Kentucky expects the majority of students with disabilities to participate in the regular statewide assessment procedures.

It will be imperative that school psychologists guard against the excuse that these students are disabled and should not be pushed too hard. Helping to determine high-level *yet reachable* outcomes for students with disabilities may be one of the most difficult and crucial roles that school psychologists can play. This role will include understanding how exit outcomes apply to these students, using low-inference procedures to determine their status relative to these outcomes, developing instructional and behavioral strategies and interventions that facilitate learning these outcomes, and measuring student progress toward achieving these outcomes. Assisting school staff with inclusion practices and consulting for student success in regular classes will also be important. Perhaps even more critical will be helping more people believe that students with disabilities can attain high-level outcomes.

A Final Note

A single school psychologist probably will not perform all of the roles cited in this chapter. However, the opportunities to develop, implement, and evaluate high-level outcomes for all students exist in a myriad of ways. An attempt could be made within a district staff of school psychologists or within a regional consortium of school psychologists to provide many or most of the functions and roles suggested here, from those at the individual-student level to system level.

The opportunities described here are not necessarily all inclusive. For example, there are five trained school psychologists, including this author, who currently are employed in the North Carolina Department of Public Instruction. Only one of those is designated as the "school psychology" consultant. A second psychologist came to the Department in the personnel area that developed professional performance appraisal and career ladder systems. He later became chief consultant of the Student Services Team in the High School Division. The other three of us work in the Division of Innovation and Development Services, which I direct. Two of my three Development Unit staff are the other two school psychologists. They were interviewed and selected by teams; I did not make the decision alone to hire them. They each rose to the top of fairly large applicant pools, as did the psychologist in personnel services, because of their apparent understanding of systems, writing and presentation skills, collaboration skills, ability to understand research and translate it into implications for practice, and ability to contribute to our program evaluation efforts. The training of school psychologists, especially with some additions and shifts in focus, prepare them as well as any other professional to assist in defining and reaching important educational goals.

CONCLUSION

Schools in America are attempting more fundamental changes than ever in their history. Public demands for high performance are coming at a time when schools have the most diverse population of students in their history. Although schools appear to be doing as well as ever on traditional outcomes, the demand for graduates with new types of knowledge, skills, and attributes is driving the need for a new type of schooling. The challenges are formidable, but the opportunities are considerable for school psychology. The need for problem-solving skills will be greater than ever. School psychologists, mired in the paradigm of norm-referenced thinking, will not be able to seize these opportunities. We must operate within a paradigm driven by high-level outcomes for all students, a belief that all students can learn well, and the understanding that schools, in fact, control the conditions of success for students.

AUTHOR NOTE

I am particularly thankful to Delores Brewer for several substantive and editing suggestions, as well as to Bobbye Draughon and Judy White for their helpful editing comments. Delores Brewer and Judy White are both school psychologists in the Division of Innovation and Development Services. Bobbye Draughon is the chief consultant in the Division.

REFERENCES

American Psychological Association. (1992, September). Learner-centered psychological principles: Guidelines for school redesign and reform (draft). *Communiqué*, pp. 15–18.

Brown, R. G. (1991). *Schools of thought: How the politics of literacy shape thinking in the classroom.* San Francisco: Jossey-Bass.

Cobb, C. T. (1990). School psychology in the 1980s and 1990s: A context for change and definition. In T. B. Gutkin & C. R. Reynolds (Eds.), *Handbook of school psychology* (2nd ed.; pp. 21–31). New York: John Wiley and Sons.

Comer, J. P. (1988). Educating poor minority children. *Scientific American, 259,* 42–48.

Deming, W. E. (1986). *Out of the crisis.* Cambridge, MA: Massachusetts Institute of Technology.

Drucker, P. F. (1989). *The new realities.* New York: Harper & Row.

Elliott, S. N. (1992, October). Authentic assessment: A case report of system change. *Communiqué*, pp. 1, 4–5.

Finn, C. E. (1990). The biggest reform of all. *Phi Delta Kappan, 71,* 584–592.

Jaegger, R. (1992). World class standards, choice, privatization: Weak measurement serving presumptive policy. *Phi Delta Kappan, 74,* 118–128.

Katz, D., & Kahn, R. L. (1978). *The social psychology of organization* (2nd ed.). New York: John Wiley & Sons.

Kuhn, T. S. (1970). *The structure of scientific revolutions.* Chicago, IL: University of Chicago Press.

Levin, H. M. (1991). *Accelerating the progress of all students* (Special Rep. No. 31). Albany, NY: State University of New York at Albany, Nelson A. Rockefeller Institute of Government.

Lezotte, L. (1990). *Effective schools.* Presentation at a workshop of the North Carolina Department of Public Instruction, Raleigh, NC.

Madden, N., Slavin, R., Karweit, N., Lawrence, D., & Wasik, B. (1991). Success for all. *Phi Delta Kappan, 72,* 593–599.

Raspberry, W. (1991a, December 15). Fixed-time education process continues to produce inferior products. *The Winston-Salem Journal.*

Raspberry, W. (1991b, December 20). Teach academic success. *The Charlotte Observer.*

Schlecty, P. C. (1990). *Schools for the twenty-first century: Leadership imperatives for educational reform.* San Francisco: Jossey-Bass.

Shavelson, R. J., Gao, X., & Baxter, G. P. (1993, March). *Sampling variability of performance assessments* (CSE Technical Report 361). Los Angeles: University of California, Los Angeles, National Center for Research on Evaluation, Standards and Student Testing (CRESST).

Sizer, T. R. (1992). *Horace's school: Redesigning the American high school.* New York: Houghton Mifflin.

Secretary's Commission on Achieving Necessary Skills. (1991, June). *What work requires of schools: A SCANS report for America 2000.* Washington, DC: U.S. Department of Labor.

Spady, W. G. (1992, March). It's time to take a close look at outcome-based education. *Communiqué,* pp. 16–18.

Spady, W. G., & Marshall, K. J. (1991). Beyond traditional outcome-based education. *Educational Leadership, 49,* 67–72.

Walberg, H. J. (1984). Improving the productivity of America's schools. *Educational Leadership, 41,* 19–30.

ANNOTATED BIBLIOGRAPHY

American Psychological Association. (1992, September). Learner-centered psychological principles: Guidelines for school redesign and reform (draft). *Communiqué,* pp. 15–18.
These principles summarize psychological research and knowledge about learning and the implications for schools. They address metacognitive and cognitive factors, social factors, affective factors, developmental factors, and individual differences. Implications for instruction, curriculum, assessment, teacher education, and parent and community involvement are listed.

Brandt, R. S. (Ed.). (1993). The challenge of higher standards. *Educational Leadership, 50*(5).
With the current efforts underway to establish national standards in subject areas, this journal issue examines the potential impact, promise, and problems of such standards. In the search for new types of outcomes, school psychologists should be part of these issues and debates.

Elliott, S. N. (1992, October). Authentic assessment: A case report of system change. *Communiqué,* pp. 4–5.
Dr. Elliott describes how he became involved as a parent and school psychology trainer in helping his local school district explore and begin to develop evaluation and authentic assessment strategies for student outcomes, programs, and services. He explains the strategic planning process and delineates possible roles for school psychologists in the use of alternative assessment methods.

Spady, W. G. (1992, March). It's time to take a close look at outcome-based education. *Communiqué,* pp. 16–18.
Spady defines the meaning of "outcome-based" education (OBE), describes the evolution of the concept, and defines three types of OBE: traditional, transitional, and transformational. He clearly defines the implications for OBE, regardless of the type implemented, for our educational system.

Secretary's Commission on Achieving Necessary Skills. (1991, June). *What work requires of schools: A SCANS report for America 2000.* Washington, DC: U.S. Department of Labor.
This report from a Commission composed of educators, business representatives, and citizens delineates foundation skills and broad competencies necessary for students to work successfully in the 21st century. It also compares schools of today with those of tomorrow necessary to achieve these skills.

30

Best Practices in Considering the Role of Culture

G. Susan Mosley-Howard
Miami University

OVERVIEW: CONCEPTUALIZATIONS OF CULTURE

A Christian man in England shows respect for his religion by taking off his hat but keeping on his shoes, while a Muslim man in an Arab country will show similar respect by keeping on his hat and removing his shoes.

(Evans-Pritchard, 1962)

Before examining the role and impact of culture upon the practice of school psychology, and in the educational lives of children served by school psychologists, it is best if the reader understands how culture has been conceptualized. This chapter first presents a selected review of literature on culture, followed by perspectives of how culture can influence various aspects of a child's life and his or her educational experiences (identity, achievement, communication, and family). The chapter concludes with some discussion about how culture can be considered when attempting to understand and work with children from educational settings in the areas of assessment, intervention, or consultation.

For this chapter culture is defined as the varied patterns of living, traditions, and attitudes possessed by individuals. These patterns of living, traditions, or attitudes are developed out of the person's specific place of origin, and subsequent caste, yet are influenced by transmitted messages from parents/community. By defining culture in this way, one looks at groups such as women and people of color as cultural groups. To assist in this examination of culture, it might help to use a person by environment (PXE) interaction perspective (Lewin, 1935). From this frame of reference, the person's behavior must be evaluated within the setting/social context from which it originates. Lewin's view advocated the understanding of a person's behavior and perceptions by establishing a "definite form of structure in a definite sort of environment" (p. 43). That is, one must develop a view of both the individual-level and environmental-level (culture) of the "organism."

During the course of this chapter, as cultural contexts are being examined, the reader may notice statements about various environmental experiences attributed to groups of people. That is because being a part of a culture often means sharing certain experiences and possibly ways of being. These generalized notions are somewhat distinct from traditional stereotypes in that stereotypes are behaviors assumed to be unilaterally true for a person or a group of persons, without observation or experience of that person(s). In addition, it is often assumed that groups of people are homogeneous, or without variation within their cultural group. It is not the intent of the writer to perpetuate that notion in this chapter. Researchers and practitioners in education and psychology alike must constantly guard against making such assumptions. Generalized statements in this chapter, however, are statements taken from research or theoretical notions in an attempt to examine cultural issues from the perspective of the person-by-environment interaction theory.

A Review of Related Literature

An examination of social science literature illuminates the running dialogue about "what is culture?" Immediate culture is often considered to be the child's home and local community. This perspective seems to perceive culture as connected with values and norms inherent within the environment of socialization. Frisby (1992) presents and critiques six "connotative meanings" for culture. His presentation points out the range of definitions of culture from a pattern of living, customs, and traditions to race consciousness to a difference in outer appearance. Geertz (1973) defines culture as an "historically transmitted pattern of meaning" (p. 89) in a symbolic format by which humans perpetuate and communicate knowledge and attitudes. Another definition offered by Gordon and Armour-Thomas (1991) defines culture as "status phenomenon" (p. 87). This perspective enables one to determine the societal status of the individual along with the privileges available to him or her. The definition of culture that a person uses often guides his or her own mode of research and subsequent practices in social science and education as well as influences the assessment and consultative practices of school psychology.

In the United States, national identity has been filtered through our ethnic origin because cultural values and behavioral norms were transformed here. Race (a unique variable of ethnicity) differentiates people by their physical appearance. It is used as a social identifier in the United States of persons who have an African, Asian, Indian, or Hispanic as opposed to Caucasian origin through at least one ancestor. There are not always, however, one-to-one correspondence between ethnic origin and cultural practices. The connection between ethnicity and culture therefore is partly understood by examining acculturation.

The degree of acculturation has a strong impact on the adherence to original cultural norms (Ogbu, 1978). Acculturation is the extent to which values connected with one's culture of origin have been set aside or changed for the adoption of the dominant culture. An illustration of this phenomenon could be seen among those African Americans who may have adopted "American or European American" traditions above African or in concert with those traditions from some part of Africa. Malgady, Rogler, and Costantino (1987) describe the distinctions between acculturated Hispanics who accept and identify with Anglo interactive styles or conventions versus those who adhere to Hispanic cultural ways of interacting. They cite examples such as the use of English versus Spanish, thinking in the "here and now" versus having a "teleological" orientation. Another factor influencing acculturation level is socioeconomic status. Often the groups at low socioeconomic levels are those least acculturated into majority culture (Ogbu, 1978).

By bringing the issue of culture, acculturation, and ethnicity into the discussions about the school environment, cultural diversity has become one of several central issues for the educational system. Perhaps the first step in the process of examining this issue involves seeing culture as connected with traditions and attitudes held by the individual. The second step involves viewing culture in conjunction with place of origin (country, region) or the conditions under which a cultural group existed in this country. Third, the attitudinal messages adopted from parents and community, and the subsequent level of acculturation, is important to consider. It is the parental or community group message that often contains values/attitudes different from those of the psychologist and other persons within the school environment. For example, a Japanese American child will bring cultural attributes to the school setting if his or her parents and community stress those traditions and values specific to his or her region or continental place of origin (Kitano & Kikumura, 1976). So if the individual's view of competition is inconsistent with the use of competition in school, understanding these disparate views would be helpful for the child and those working with him or her. Understanding that, depending upon level of acculturation, this child might not make direct eye contact and may be very compliant will help both teacher and school psychologist work more effectively with the child. Borrowing once again from Lewin's perspective, it is the understanding of the dynamics between the individual and environment that becomes a key factor in this situation (see Figure 1). It is important to recognize the individual characters in concert with the influence of socialization within a family, cultural group, and a socioeconomic group, and impacted by an education system housed within a social mileu.

Even though the school environment typically creates an Anglo or European American atmosphere (competition, individualism, uniformity, materialism), the school environment, as a salient context for social exposure, should be charged with the responsibility of facilitating awareness of the contents of diverse "cultural systems" (Boykin, 1986; Ogbu, 1988).

Within the school setting, some school psychologists already serve a significant number of learners from culturally diverse backgrounds. According to the Department of Education's *Digest of Education Statistics* (National Center for Education Statistics, Office of Education and Improvement, 1993) some areas of New York, Florida, and California already have between 30% and 80% "minority" students in the schools. That number will increase dramatically over the next 10 years until there is a majority of non-white or non-European Americans within many school systems (Henry, 1990). It is imperative therefore to be mindful of what role culture plays in the lives of learners. School psychologists are not always adequately introduced to theory about the complexities of culture nor is there adequate time spent considering the impact of culture upon practice (Barona, de Barona, Flores, & Gutierrez, 1990; Rogers, Ponterotto, Conoley, & Wiese, 1992). In addition to general lack of information or exposure, some school psychologists have not clarified their thinking about the construct of cultural diversity. In this next section, basic issues are presented that may aid in the process of rethinking and solidifying notions around questions of cultural influences on identity, achievement, communication, community, and family systems.

Impact of Culture on Sense of Self

Often an area of interest in the research on "minority" children in schools are the factors that contribute to their sense of self. Research about the impact of same-sex and/or same-race schools generally points toward the enhanced sense of esteem, resulting from experiences that students have as they ma-

FIGURE 1.

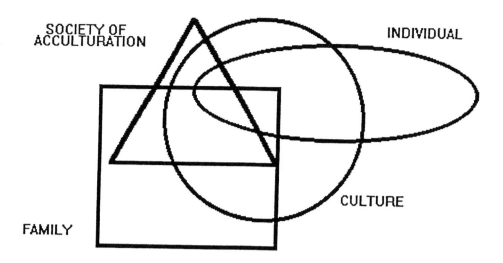

SOCIETY OF
ACCULTURATION

INDIVIDUAL

CULTURE

FAMILY

triculate within these culturally homogeneous settings as opposed to heterogeneous ones (Collison, 1991; Lee & Byrk, 1986). Students that attend same-sex or same-race schools tend to have higher levels of esteem and/or different school experiences (Sadker & Sadker, 1994). For example, in heterogeneous classes, girls are not asked as many probing questions during classroom discussions as boys and teacher wait-time differs between girls and boys. Also, disproportionate numbers of African American children experience pedagogical strategies that may be inconsistent with their optimum mode of learning (Allen & Boykin, 1992; Sadker & Sadker, 1994). However, despite the benefits of homogeneous settings, questions are raised about hidden disadvantages such as isolating children from settings that mirror the real world and evaluating whether homogeneous settings can truly be equal.

The issue of racial or gender identity development adds yet another factor inherent in the development of all culturally diverse youth (White & Parham, 1990). The struggle to balance culture of origin with the exposure to European American views or male cultural views plays a key role in the development and subsequent behavior of culturally diverse youth. Psychologists working with culturally diverse youth may need to understand their exposure to and struggle with these divergent cultural influences in order to understand the youth's need to "hold on" to role models from their culture of origin, to celebrate their cultural elements, and to affirm self. Cross (1991) and Helms (1985) have proposed that "minorities" move through stages of identity formation similar to Erikson's (1963) model of psychosocial development. Through these stages, youth will move from rejecting one's culture and often having a preference for the dominant culture, to rejecting the dominant culture,

to ultimately internalizing cultural influences and striking a balance between the culture of origin and the acquired culture. Recognizing this model of identity development might prove of value to the school psychologist helping culturally diverse youth with their socialization process.

Impact of Culture on Academic Achievement

A second area to consider in this examination of culture is school performance and social behaviors (interpersonal relationships) that often influence academic achievement. When considering the impact of culture upon the student, the psychologist may want to consider racial-social-economic attributes to gain a full understanding of how culture impacts academic performance and subsequent behaviors surrounding school life. To foster a clearer understanding of this connection, the work of Ogbu (1988, 1992), Boykin (1986), Allen and Boykin (1992), Sue and Okazaki (1990), Gopaul-McNicol (1992a), Asante (1987), and Hale-Benson (1986) is recommended. These writers discuss the connection between academic pursuits and the influence of cultural frames. Such connections can be found in Ogbu's (1992) approach of conceptualizing African Americans as a caste-like minority and trying to recognize the impact of involuntary citizenship in America, acquisition of one's status by birth, limited access to social goods because of group membership, and collective institutional discrimination. A focus on Native Americans and their life-long struggles for consideration as a people and their historical segregation might lead to a fuller understanding of the impact of these experiences upon the academic performance as well as acculturation of youths from these groups. Cultural elements greatly influence educational experience, self-perception, perception of the educational system and its members (including that of the psychologist), and subsequent achievement.

By examining another cultural frame, discrimination, one may see another connection to academic achievement. With systemic discrimination sometimes comes a disillusionment which often leads to anger and/or blaming of that system. Sometimes children of various cultures harbor unacknowledged anger toward the system that they perceive to have established barriers and lessened expectations for them. Others do not perceive barriers or discrimination with the social system but rather many opportunities afforded to them. They take these opportunities and through individual effort and social support turn them into successes. Responses to this situation are as varied as the perceptions of it: from dropping out or lashing out (Council of the Great City Schools, 1987), to proactive and creative strategies for systemic change, to demonstrating exceptional academic success in the face of barriers (Ogbu, 1992).

Another example of the impact of culture on academic experience is the low rate of minority children attending preschool. The *Digest of Education Statistics* (National Center for Education Statistics, Office of Education and Improvement, 1993) states that 37% of African American children and 27% of Hispanic American children 3 to 4 years of age attended any private or public preschool in 1992. This means that in many cases early cognitive learning and cultural indoctrination occur at home. Because of this "at-home" preschool education these children sometimes come to the European-American K–8 system with a culture-specific set of learning styles, learning goals, and expectations. Negotiating the new system on their own can be challenging. One useful strength comes from this experience, however: the valuing of education that most people of color possess (McAdoo, 1993). This value and others are shared by many people and it could be that these shared values can serve as a foundation upon which to build an academic experience where all can succeed. Using the person-by-environment perspective could help in identifying the elements both brought by the individual and existing within the academic environment that together contribute to potential success.

Impact of Culture on Communication

Within each culture exists various modes of communication. One difference that may manifest itself is the varying forms of direct and indirect communication used by different cultures. For some European-Americans and men, indirect communication is used as a way to make requests. For example, an European American teacher saying "it is chilly in here" could be a way of asking someone to close the window. Some children of color may interpret this statement as directly expressing that the teacher is cold and not see it as a request for them to close the window. This sce-

nario could result in the teacher's perceiving the child as unresponsive or even defiant. Some people of color use direct forms of communication even though the mode of delivery varies. For many Asians, Hispanics, and Native Americans, direct eye contact between adult and child could be a sign of disrespect, while a direct message is being delivered. It may not be unusual for a child socialized within these cultures to look down while communicating with an authority figure.

Disclosure during communication also often varies across cultures. African Americans often prefer to turn to indigenous support systems (e.g., family, friends, minister) when disclosing personal issues or seeking support (Hines & Boyd-Franklin, 1982; Neighbors & Jackson, 1984). This same preference was observed in a study of native Puerto Ricans and first generation Puerto Ricans socialized in this country (Zayas, 1988). Some Appalachians also divulge very little outside of the family circle, while other European American subgroups turn more readily to "professionals" and others outside of their immediate circle for contact or assistance.

In addition to the mode of communication, style could also be an issue. Dialect and bilingualism, as influenced by culture of origin, often affect ease of communication and subsequent learning. In addition, schools expect, advocate, and value the use of "standard English" while some minorities use both "standard English" and dialects or languages with which they identify. Some studies (Hudson, 1980; Penalosa, 1980; Ramirez, 1985) point out the negative attitudes that some teachers have toward children who communicate in "non-standard English" format. These researchers further point out that these negative attitudes foster in turn a negative perception within the child of his or her own form of communication. Of course, some children are able to adapt quite well to a variety of communication styles. They are able to make transitions from one style of communication to another depending upon the setting. It is this group of children who seem to function the best and ultimately succeed within the school environment.

Impact of Culture on Family Systems

Understanding the role of family is key to understanding the child: This is true for children from any cultural group. Families impact growth, values, and identity development as well as academic achievement. Taylor (1989) found that among a college sample of African American youth, parents seemed to be the key element in identity formation. In contrast, Taylor's data from "inner-city low income" African American youth indicate a lack of identification with familial role models and a general mistrust of "others" as resources. This contrast between the two groups points out the role of other variables within the cultural frame, like socioeconomic status (SES). When looking at the Taylor sample it is hard to discern whether SES impacted the family interaction to such a degree as to circumvent its impact or if the "low income" group found familial structure from other sources and therefore rejected their own family.

Within various cultures however, the role of the family system, the modes of interaction with children, and the male–female relationships vary. The notion of correcting the behavior of children takes on different dimensions. Within the context of some Appalachian and African American families, physical punishment may be acceptable and understood or interpreted by the child differently. Therefore, it has a different psychological effect (Gray & Cosgrove, 1985). Physical punishment is often linked to theological notions of atonement for wrongdoing, to alleviate guilt for the "crime," clean the slate, and start anew. Gray and Cosgrove (1985) studied the child-rearing styles of six ethnic groups: Filipino, Japanese, Samoan, Vietnamese, Mexican-American, and Blackfoot Indian. There was great misconception about these varied styles of child rearing. The protectiveness of the Japanese and Filipino mothers and the physical discipline of the Samoans was believed by observers/raters to be harmful to the child, perceptions no doubt influenced by the specific cultural backgrounds of the observers/raters. The reader is referred to the study as a useful illustration of various ways families handle child rearing and the ways these practices are interpreted by others.

As various cultural groups are studied, a number of differences, as well as some similarities, emerge (Boykin, 1983; Hale-Benson, 1986; Hilliard, 1976). As stated in an earlier section of this chapter, stereotyping people by generalized characteristics is something that all must ward against. But the information from these sources when considered in relationship to the level of acculturation within the person/group (and not used as a blanket truth for all persons of that group) can facilitate an understanding of the complex maze of influences operating within a child's life. Culture is multileveled and influenced by numerous factors, but there are some shared dimensions within cultures and across cultures that are experienced by many people.

BEST PRACTICES:
IMPACT OF CULTURE UPON PRACTICE

By considering and evaluating multiple environmental factors impacting a student, the school psychologist can better understand and work with that individual. There are several steps school psychologists can take and programs they can implement to better understand cultural factors and to enhance practice. First, school psychologists need to be informed about various perspectives on cultural differences and similarities. Reading critically the research suggesting quick solutions or one dimensional answers to complex cultural questions is important as is remaining flexible in thinking about the construct of culture. Careful selection of theories useful in practice is an important issue that should not be dismissed because of varied theoretical perspectives or differences of opinion nor because the cultural variability within groups often makes it difficult to conceptualize group characteristics. One key element in this whole notion of culture may be simply understanding the complexity of the issue and the multiple layers that impact it.

Second, school psychologists should examine critically their own ideologies about cultural diversity, revisit biased notions that may have been acquired during their upbringing, and tease out their own beliefs about culture that stem from training-program ideologies. Prejudices found within our society need to be carefully evaluated. In turn school psychologists can assist teachers and administrators in reframing their perspectives if needed. This can be done in a nonthreatening workshop or through in-service activities as well as in preservice clinical supervision experiences. Cultural diversity workshops that foster awareness, knowledge, and practice can also be beneficial.

Third, school psychologists could try to become familiar with the cultural experiences of the children with whom they work and the person-by-environment variables influencing the child's attitudes, beliefs, and behaviors. This requires a full examination of socioeconomic influence, gender, the family system, level of acculturation, traditions and customs, and the connections with ethnic communities or continents of origin of the families and children with whom they work. Suggestions for practice have recently been included in the "Guidelines for Providers to the Culturally Diverse" (American Psychological Association, 1993). To work effectively with diverse children, school psychologists could visit the various communities within their district, meet with families and/or leaders at community centers and churches, and treat the indigenous language (e.g., Spanish) with respect. School psychologists could gain insight into the numerous learner characteristics common to that culture. This process may also increase their chances of determining the degree to which instructional changes such as those offered by Hale-Benson (1986), Kunjufu (1984), and others is warranted (e.g., infusing culturally relevant tradition and material into the curriculum, changing teaching style).

Fourth, when prescribing interventions, school psychologists could use the family and community support systems inherent in the child's environment. These systems' agents could be involved in the assessment and intervention process and their recommendations should be requested and considered.

Fifth, school psychologists could identify how the systems of the larger society positively or adversely impact the child and should serve as advocates in ameliorating adverse conditions, whether this is the school, the family, or the criminal justice system. For example, if the classroom teacher is using a style inconsistent with the child's culturally influenced style, then the psychologist can help the teacher to change the way knowledge is presented to that child. On the other end of the spectrum, the system could be evaluated to determine its facilitative effect. These aspects of the child's experience should be fostered and expanded.

Sixth, school psychologists could become familiar with (a) assessment tools that address the multifaceted components of "intelligence" or "cognitive capability" and (b) various intervention issues. These are especially valid pursuits because research indicates that slightly more than half of the school psychologist's time is still used for assessment and a significant number of minority children are in special education or considered educationally at risk (Gopaul-McNicol, 1992b; Hutton, Dubes, & Muir, 1992; Reschly, Kicklighter, & McKee, 1988). For example, incorporating the Sternberg (1985) or Gardner (1983) view of multiple intelligence may be a more sensitive framework to use for conceptualizing the diverse capabilities present within individuals of nondominant cultural groups. Using assessment instruments normed with representative samples of cultural groups can also be helpful if those samples represent local numbers of ethnic and gender groups. This should not be the end point however; psychologists may need to go beyond this practice, to designing and using instruments conceptualized with cultural diversity in mind. It is possible that a more accurate assessment of learner capabilities may be produced by instruments that take into consideration possible brain-hemisphere-control differences. If cultural variations underlie the European-American analytical-left hemisphere and Native American holistic-right hemisphere epistemology, for example, assessment instruments should require students to demonstrate elements of both styles of knowing. Assessment tools that consider and accommodate culture/ethnicity to varying extents include

- Woodcock Johnson-R

- Escala de Inteligenica Wechsler para Ninos-R (WISC-1982)

- Kaufman Assessment Battery for Children (1983)

- Differential Ability Scale-5th Edition

- Test of Non-Verbal Intelligence-2

- Language Assessment Scales-Oral–Spanish and English

- Culture Free Self Esteem Inventory

- Vineland Adaptive Behavior Scales

- The "Who" and "U" Checklists (Hilliard, 1976)

Some of these tests are reported as being frequently used by school psychologists (e.g., Kaufman Assessment Battery for Children, Culture Fair Tests, Vineland, Test for Nonverbal Intelligence) (Hutton et al., 1992).

Because Native American learners have high creativity scores as measured by the Torrance Test of creativity, Tannehill (1992) suggests the use of creative instructional exercises for Native American children. Along these same lines, Florey (1986) outlines several issues to consider when working with Native American children and assessing them for "gifted" programs. For example, reliance on nonverbal communication, noncompetitiveness, and detailed verbal accounts can provide useful information. Mercer (1989) recommends the use of both an assessment tool and a curriculum that tap into the optimal ability of culturally diverse children. The notion behind this approach is the belief that optimal performance is developed and can be attained by all through practice. When using the Optimal Performer Locator, the child is introduced to materials culturally relevant to him or her. The tasks tap into all modes of functioning (e.g., tactile, kinesthetic, cognitive) and if the child's performance initially fails to match desired outcomes, behaviors are modeled and children are reevaluated to determine if skills have been acquired. The goal is to measure the highest level of functioning for that child. This same perspective is supported by the System of Multicultural Pluralistic Assessment (SOMPA; Matthew, 1992). The assumptions of this model are that (a) many normal curves for behavior are necessary for assessment, (b) one cannot compare people of different cultures, (c) multiple measures should be used, and (d) a multicultural perspective should be a part of the assessment philosophy.

Seventh, school psychologists could use qualitative as well as quantitative assessment tools with diverse groups of learners. These might include anecdotal records, observation, post facto work, and interviews. Again, using indigenous consultants during the assessment and intervention process is important during this phase.

Eighth, school psychologists should become acquainted with the use of a multidisciplinary team approach, such as the PACTS model (Savage & Adair, 1980) where children are examined from a cognitive, social, emotional, cultural, and behavioral perspective with an array of techniques including observation, interviews, and paper-pencil instruments. This provides a more holistic view of events and characteristics surrounding the child in question.

Programmatic Examples

Numerous programs have been developed to address the dilemma of facilitating rather than negating the diverse cultural influences on youth and their consequent behaviors. Most of these programs exist outside of the regular curriculum; however, psychologists working within school settings can be mindful of these successful programs and work toward cultural inclusion. A few programs are highlighted here:

Winners: The Key to Success is Effort (Murray & Fairchild, 1989). This 10-week program consists of workshops geared toward supporting the academic success of African American junior and senior high students. The program uses attribution therapy (Diener & Dweck, 1978), expectancy training, internal speech as a self-monitoring device (Meichenbaum & Goodman, 1971), and social modeling techniques (Sarason & Ganzer, 1973).

The 16 outcomes connected with this program range from identifying and understanding the causes of school difficulties to increasing self-confidence and image to establishing values and goals.

Cultural Enrichment Programs such as Simba Wachanza Program (Swahili for young lions), W.E.B. DuBois Program, and many other programs modeled after the suggestions of Kunjufu (1984). They advocate the use of African traditions, educating about African and African American culture, and validating the participants' sense of self. These programs (a) have a culturally sensitive mission, (b) emphasize leadership, (c) have high expectations, (d) frequently monitor student progress, (e) possess a positive learning environment, (f) provide sufficient opportunity for learning, and (g) support parent/community involvement.

Some schools (Marva Collins, African American boys schools, schools for girls, etc.) adhere to this framework. In communities where these schools are not available, after-school programs can be and have been created with this cultural slant in mind.

Kamehameha Early Education Project (KEEP). This program was developed to assist Hawaiian children with reading acquisition skills. It is infused with cultural-specific patterns of behavior and language characteristics (Foster, 1992).

Reading and Language Skills. A collaborative project sponsored by the University of Arizona and the Bureau of Applied Research in Anthropology and geared for Mexican American children focuses on reading and language skills (Foster, 1992).

SUMMARY

The role of the school psychologist in the lives of children is often crucial for their long-term school success. School psychologists should not forget the importance of knowing all children and the *whole* child. The challenges of understanding children from various cultural frames and helping to meet their needs may seem overwhelming at times. It may help, when considering cultural factors within the school system, to remember three basic words: balance, awareness, and context. As illustrated by the numerous authors cited here and elsewhere, culture may be viewed from several perspectives (Frisby, 1992). Psychologists may need to transform their own and others' thinking about culture from a fragmented and yet sometimes one dimensional view to a more diunital and integrated one. A balanced view that includes multiple aspects of the child's life increases the chances of generating appropriate assessments and interventions. In addition, being constantly aware of multiple cultures and the impact of these cultures may assist the school psychologist in providing effective consultation to teachers, families, and community agencies. And, the infusion of cultural sensitivity facilitates the development of *all* people as we strive to interface with a world that is truly diverse.

Finally, Lewin's (1935) notion of environmental context can provide a frame with which to examine the "cultural" picture. Examining multiple aspects of the person as well as the environment or context from which he or she came (as well as their present context) brings to light the complexity and importance of culture. In the practice of school psychology, it is critical to understand the multiple layers and interconnectedness of cultural influences: They cannot be ignored nor oversimplified. Attention must be paid to such environmental factors as

1. Messages passed on from generation to generation, coupled with the present day atmosphere in which those messages are received.

2. The pervasiveness of those messages.

3. The nature of those messages.

4. The ways they are connected to the culture of origin.

5. Conflicting messages from other sources.

6. The power of the other sources.

7. The child's own view and level of understanding.

8. The degree to which these messages are compared to, confirmed by, or discounted by the person's own experiences.

Weighing the various elements within the environment facilitates a deeper understanding not only of the child but of the connections between one's own experiences and those of the child (a good basis for developing relationships) and of the differences and similarities that may exist.

A few final issues to keep in mind are

1. Remain aware of the systemic impact upon the child (macrosystems to mesosystems to microsystems).

2. Evaluate the cultural milieu of the child and the degree of acculturation.

3. Evaluate strengths of the culture of origin and its adaptive characteristics.

4. Focus on development/readiness and all aspects of cognitive style.

5. Become aware of characteristics influenced by culture that may have an impact on assessment and intervention results.

6. Become aware of one's own view of culturally diverse populations and remain flexible in one's interactions with children from these populations.

7. Actively seek the input of family members of the child with whom one is working and work collaboratively as advocates for the child.

REFERENCES

Allen, B. A., & Boykin, A. W. (1992). A\\2|| children and the educational process: Alienating cultural discontinuity through prescriptive pedagogy. *School Psychology Review, 1*(4), 586–596.

American Psychological Association. (1993). Guidelines for providers of psychological services to the ethnic, linguistic and culturally diverse populations. *American Psychologist, 48,* 45–48.

Asante, M. K. (1987). *The Afrocentric idea.* Philadelphia, PA: Temple University Press.

Barona, A., de Barona, M., Flores, A., & Gutierrez, M. (1990). Critical issues in training school psychologists to serve minority school children. In A. Barona, & E. Garcia (Eds.), *Children at risk: Poverty, minority status and other issues in educational equity* (pp. 187–200). Washington, DC: National Association of School Psychologists.

Boykin, A. W. (1983). The academic performance of Afro American children. In J. Spence (Ed.), *Achievement and achievement motives* (pp. 324–371). San Francisco, CA: W. Freeman Press.

Boykin, A. W. (1986). The triple quandary and the schooling of the Afro-American children. In U. Neisser (Ed.), *The school achievement of minority children: New perspectives* (pp. 57–92). Hillsdale, NJ: Lawrence Erlbaum Associates.

Collison, M. (1991, February). Black male schools: Yes. *Black Enterprise,* p. 18.

Council of the Great City Schools. (1987). Challenge to urban education: Results in the making. A Report of the Council of Great City Schools. Washington, DC: Author.

Cross, W. (1991). *Shades of Black.* Philadelphia, PA: Temple University Press.

Culture Free Self Esteem Inventory. (1981). J. Battle (Ed.). PTS.

Diener, C. I., & Dweck, C. S. (1978). Analyses of learned helplessness: Continuous changes in performance, strategy, and achievement cognitions following failure. *Journal of Personality and Social Psychology, 36,* 451–462.

Differential Ability Scales. (1990). C. Elliott (Ed.). Psychological Corporation.

Erikson, E. (1963). *Childhood and society* (2nd ed.). New York: W. W. Norton.

Escala de Inteligencia Wechsler para Ninos-R (1982). D. Wechsler (Ed.). Psychological Corporation.

Evans-Pritchard, E. E. (1962). *Social Anthropology and other essays.* New York: Free Press.

Florey, J. E. (1986). Identification of gifted children among the American Indian Population: An inservice model. Unpublished manuscript.

Foster, M. (1992). Sociolinguistics and the African-American community: Implications for literacy. *Theory and Practice, 31,* 303–311.

Frisby, C. L. (1992). Issues and problems in the influence of culture on the psychoeducational needs of African American children. *School Psychology Review, 21,* 532–551.

Gardner, H. (1983). Frames of mind: The theory of multiple intelligences. New York: Basic Books.

Geertz, C. (1973). Interpretation of cultures. New York: Basic Books.

Gopaul-McNicol, S. (1992a). Implementation for school psychology: Synthesis of the mini series. *School Psychology Review, 21*(4), 597–600.

Gopaul-McNicol, S. (1992b). Understanding and meeting the psychological and educational needs of African American and Spanish speaking students. *School Psychology Review, 21*(4), 529–531.

Gordon, E. W., & Armour-Thomas, E. (1991). Culture and cognitive development. In L. Okagaki & R. J. Sternberg (Eds.), *Directors of development: Influences on the development of children's thinking* (pp. 83–90). Hillsdale, NJ: Lawrence Erlbaum.

Gray, E., & Cosgrove, D. (1985). Ethnocentric perception of childrearing practices in protective services. *Child Abuse and Neglect, 9,* 389–396.

Hale-Benson, J. E. (1986). Black children: Their roots, culture and learning styles. Baltimore, MD: Johns Hopkins University Press.

Helms, J. (1985). Cultural identity in the treatment process. In P. Pedersen (Ed.), *Handbook of cross cultural counseling and therapy* (pp. 240–245). Westport, CT: Greenwood Press.

Henry, W. A. (1990, April 9). Beyond the melting pot. *Time,* p. 28.

Hilliard, A. (1976). Alternatives to IQ testing: An approach to the identification of gifted minority children (Final Report to the California State Department of Education).

Hines, P., & Boyd-Franklin, N. (1982). Black families. In M. McGoldrick, J. Pearce, & J. Giordano (Eds.), *Ethnicity and family therapy* (pp. 84–167). New York: Guilford Press.

Hudson, R. A. (1980). Sociolinguistics. New York: Cambridge University Press.

Hutton, J. B., Dubes, R., & Muir, S. (1992). Assessment practices of school psychologists: Ten years later. *School Psychology Review, 21*(2), 271–284.

Katz, J. H. (1985). The sociopolitical nature of counseling. *The Counseling Psychologist, 13,* 615–624.

Kaufman Assessment Battery for Children. (1983). A. Kaufman & N. Kaufman. Psychological Corporation.

Kitano, H. L., & Kikumura, A. (1976). "The Japanese American family." In C. H. Mindel & R. W. Habenstein (Eds.), *Ethnic families in America.* New York: Elsevier.

Kunjufu, J. (1984). *Developing positive self images and discipline in black children.* Chicago, IL: African American Image.

Language Assessment Scales-Oral. (1990). E. DeAvila & S. Duncan (Eds.). CTB.

Lee, V., & Byrk, A. (1986). Effects of single sex secondary schools on students' achievement and attitudes. *Journal of Educational Psychology, 78*, 381–395.

Lewin, K. (1935). The conflict between Aristotlean & Galilean modes of thought in contemporary psychology. In K. Lewin (Ed.), *A dynamic theory of personality* (pp. 141–177). New York: McGraw-Hill.

Malgady, R. G., Rogler, L. H., & Constantino, G. (1987). Ethnocultural and linguistic bias in mental health: Evaluations of Hispanics. *American Psychologist, 42*, 228–234.

Matthew, J. L. (1992). Use of SOMPA in identification of gifted African American children. *Journal of Education of the Gifted, 15*, 344–356.

McAdoo, H. P. (1993). Family ethnicity: Strength in diversity. Newbury Park, CA: Sage Publishers.

Meichenbaum, D. H., & Goodman, J. (1971). Training impulsive children to talk to themselves: A means of developing self control. *Journal of Abnormal Psychology, 77*, 115–126.

Mercer, J. R. (1989). Alternative paradigms for assessment in a pluralistic society. In J. A. Banks & C. A. McGee Banks (Eds.), *Multicultural education: Issues and perspectives* (pp. 289–304). Boston: Allyn & Bacon.

Murray, C. B., & Fairfield, H. H. (1989). Models of black adolescent academic achievement. In R. L. Jones (Ed.), *Black adolescents* (pp. 229–245). Berkeley, CA: Cobb & Henry Publications.

National Center for Education Statistics, Office of Education and Improvement (NCE 593–292). (1993). Digest of education statistics. Washington, DC: U.S. Government Printing Office.

Neighbors, H. W., & Jackson, J. S. (1984). The use of informal and formal help: Four patterns of illness behavior in the black community. *American Journal of Community Psychology, 12*, 629–644.

Ogbu, J. U. (1978). *Minority education and caste*. Orlando, FL: Academic Press.

Ogbu, J. U. (1988). Black education: A cultural-ecological perspective. In H. P. McAdoo (Ed.), *Black families* (pp. 169–184). Newbury Park, CA: Sage Publishers.

Ogbu, J. U. (1992). Adaptation to minority status and impact on school success. *Theory into Practice, 31*, 287–295.

Penalosa, F. (1980). Chicano Sociolinguistics. Rowley, MA: Newbury House.

Ramirez, A. G. (1985). Bilingualism through schooling. Albany: State University of New York Press.

Reschly, D., Kicklighter, R., & McKee, P. (1988). Recent placement litigation, Part III, Minority EMR overrepresentation. *School Psychology Review, 17*, 22–38.

Rogers, M. R., Ponterotto, J. G., Conoley, J. C., & Wiese, M. J. (1992). Multicultural training in school psychology: A national survey. *School Psychology Review, 21*(4), 603–616.

Sadker, M., & Sadker, D. (1994). Failing at fairness: How America's schools cheat girls. New York: Charles Scribner & Sons.

Sarason, I., & Ganzer, V. (1973). Modeling and group discussion in the rehabilitation of juvenile delinquents. *Journal of Counseling Psychology, 20*(5), 442–449.

Savage, J. E., & Adair, A. (1980). Testing minorities: Developing more culturally relevant assessment systems. In R. Jones (Ed.), *Black Psychology* (3rd ed., pp. 196–200). New York: Harper & Row.

Sternberg, R. J. (1985). *Beyond IQ: A triarchic theory of human intelligence*. New York: Cambridge University Press.

Sue, S., & Okazaki, S. (1990). Asian American educational achievements: A phenomenon in search of an explanation. *American Psychologist, 45*, 913–920.

Tannehill, R. L. (1992, November). *Assessing creativity in Native American students using the Torrence tests of creative thinking, figural form A*. Paper presented at the Annual Meeting of the Mid-South Educational Research Association, Knoxville, TN.

Taylor, R. L. (1989). Black youth, role models and the social construction of identity. In R. L. Jones (Ed.), *Black adolescents* (pp. 155–174). Berkeley, CA: Cobb & Henry Publishing.

Test of Non-Verbal Intelligence–2. (1990). L. Brown, R. Sheribenou, & S. Johnson (Eds.). Pro-Ed.

Vineland Adaptive Behavior Scales. (1984). S. Sparrow, D. Balla, & P. Cicchetti. Circle Pines, MN: American Guidance Service.

White, J. L., & Parham, T. A. (1990). *The psychology of blacks*. Englewood Cliffs, NJ: Prentice-Hall.

Zayas, L. H., & Palleja, J. (1988). Puerto Rican familialism: Considerations for family therapy. *Family Relations, 37*, 260–264.

31

Best Practices in Promoting Alternatives to Ability Grouping

Margaret M. Dawson
Center for Learning and Attention Disorders

OVERVIEW

"To ensure educational equity and excellence for all America's youth, NASP supports the creation of inclusive classrooms that are based on the belief that *all* students can learn — a core value of all schools in a democracy. NASP believes that tracking, or whole class ability grouping, is not consistent with that core value" (NASP, 1993). Thus begins the Position Statement on Ability Grouping passed by the Delegate Assembly of the National Association of School Psychologists in April 1993. In so doing, NASP joined numerous other national associations, consortia, and task forces in issuing a call for alternatives to ability grouping. Among the groups that have called for an end to tracking are the following: the National Education Association, National Association of State Boards of Education, National Association of Elementary School Principals, National Advocates for Children, Committee on Policy for Racial Justice, Education Commission of the States, National Middle Schools Association, National Commission on Secondary Schooling for Hispanics, and the Children's Defense Fund.

Despite these widespread calls for change, ability grouping remains firmly entrenched in many schools throughout the United States. This failure on the part of local school districts to act to promote what has been called the single change that would produce higher student achievement in our schools (Paul, 1992) may be due to two reasons: (a) Members of the school and community at large fail to see the need to promote alternatives to ability grouping; and (b) they may see it as important but lack a blueprint to implement alternatives.

This chapter will provide the tools necessary for school psychologists to play an activist role in promoting alternatives to ability grouping within the school districts in which they are employed. To accomplish this, three major areas will be addressed: (a) a brief review of the research on ability grouping which establishes the negative effects of this practice; (b) an overview of a process that can be used to implement alternatives to ability grouping; and (c) de-scriptions of specific alternatives to ability grouping that have been implemented in schools throughout the country.

BASIC CONSIDERATIONS

Summary of Ability Grouping Research

Statistical evidence. Ability grouping has been the object of extensive research since the beginning of this century, with comprehensive reviews of the research appearing several times each decade since the 1920s. While early reviews were of a narrative nature, in recent years researchers have employed more objective meta-analyses as a means of synthesizing the findings and drawing conclusions about the effects of ability grouping. These reviews by Slavin (1986, 1990) and Kulik (e.g., Kulik, 1992; Kulik & Kulik, 1982) have generally reached similar conclusions, although the authors interpret the findings somewhat differently.

Slavin (1986) reviewed the effects of five grouping plans on achievement at the elementary level: ability-grouped class assignment, regrouping within grade levels for math and/or reading, cross-graded grouping, comprehensive nongraded plans (using a continuous progress program), and within-class ability grouping. Slavin concludes that there is no evidence to support ability-grouped class assignment, and the research on within-grade regrouping is inconclusive. Slavin's analysis finds support both for cross-graded grouping and for comprehensive nongraded programs. The use of within-class ability grouping is supported for math. No studies have been conducted on the use of within-class ability grouping for reading, despite the fact that this is likely the most widespread use of ability grouping at the elementary level.

At the secondary level, Slavin (1990) looked at studies comparing ability-grouped classes with heterogeneously grouped classes. Meta-analyses looking at a total of 29 studies, as well as various subgroups of those studies, yielded effect sizes of nearly zero in all comparisons. Thus, ability grouping at the secondary level does not have a positive effect on achievement. Slavin points out that very few of those studies were completed above the ninth grade, although he concludes that "the more limited evidence that does exist from studies in Grades 10–12 also fails to support any effect of ability grouping" (Slavin, 1990, p. 494).

Slavin draws several other conclusions from this review. First, there are no differences in outcomes whether students are assigned to classes based on one composite ability or achievement measure or are assigned to classes based on specific subject performance measures. Second, ability grouping appears to be equally ineffective in all subject areas, although there is some evidence that it is more detrimental in social studies. Finally, there are no consistent positive or negative effects of ability grouping on students of high, average, or low ability.

Kulik (1992) also conducted meta-analyses on ability grouping research, although he expanded his study to include programs for gifted and talented students. While he and Slavin reach similar conclusions on the studies they looked at in common, Kulik found support both for accelerated programming (either by compressing instruction or having students skip grades) and for enrichment programs. Slavin (1991) has pointed out that there are serious methodological problems with most of the studies of enrichment programs, and makes an added point that makes the research in this area questionable: "Even if enrichment programs were ultimately found to be effective for gifted students, this would still leave open the possibility that they would be just as effective for *all* students" (p. 69).

Sociological evidence. The research cited thus far are all experimental studies looking at controlled comparisons of students placed in homogeneously and heterogeneously grouped classes. These studies might lead one to conclude that while ability grouping does not appear to be particularly helpful, neither does it appear to be harmful to students of any ability level. Another body of research exists, however, that challenges that conclusion. Sociological studies have investigated the differences between high- and low-ability classrooms on a wide range of factors that are considered to be strongly associated with school achievement. These include teachers' expectations, classroom climate, peer group norms, curriculum content, and instructional practices. Reviews of this research led educational psychologist Lorrie Shepard to conclude recently, "These studies consistently show alarming differences in educational quality between high- and low-track classrooms" (Shepard, 1992). And Gamoran and Berends (1987) concluded from their review of over 50 ethnographic studies on the effects of stratification in secondary schools that "the balance of the evidence suggests to us that grouping and tracking do affect achievement, despite the inconsistencies in survey analyses" (p. 431).

A summary covering the scope of this research was completed by Dawson (1987). Examples from elementary and secondary research are provided by way of illustration here.

Reading research affords good examples that detail differences in instruction available to high and low achievers at the elementary level. While research studies comparing grouped versus ungrouped reading instruction are available, numerous studies (e.g., Eder, 1981; Gambrell, Wilson, & Gantt, 1981; Rist, 1970) have shown that students in low-reading groups receive poorer quality instruction, evidence less time on task, and spend less time engaged in those activities most strongly correlated with high reading achievement than students in high-reading groups. It is likely that these effects take their toll: Weinstein (1976), for instance, found that when initial reading ability was controlled for, the reading performance of students in low-reading groups declined significantly compared with the performance of students in high-reading groups over the course of first grade.

At the junior high school level, one large-scale study (Evertson, 1982) found that teachers in high-ability classrooms were more clear in their instructional presentation, more consistent in dealing with behavior, and were better able to maintain task orientation. Teachers in low-ability classrooms tended to spend more time on classroom management and were more likely to reinforce off-task behaviors of students. And at the high school level Oakes (1985) also found greater clarity of presentation, teacher enthusiasm, task orientation, and avoidance of strong criticism in high-track classes than in low-track classes. Other advantages that high-track students have include being assigned teachers who are more experienced and more skilled and having access to more of the knowledge that is required for college entrance exams (Gamoran & Berends, 1987). With respect to students' behavior, higher-ability classes and higher-ability students have been found to exhibit better work habits, motivation, persistence, and self-confidence, as well as greater participation (Veldman & Sanford, 1984), thus contributing to a classroom atmosphere that is more conducive to learning. By way of contrast, for a compelling picture of life in lower-track classrooms, see Page's (1991) extensive ethnographic study.

Recent years, however, have seen many schools and districts begin to tackle this difficult issue. Out of their experiences have come important lessons on how to achieve school- or district-wide change. The next section will discuss processes that have been found to be effective in helping schools adopt alternatives to ability grouping.

BEST PRACTICES

Educators involved in helping schools "untrack" have learned two important lessons: (a) Untracking is most successful when it is carefully planned — where input is sought from a variety of constituencies and where a process of gradual change is designed with full participation of those affected by the change; and (b) successful untracking requires changing the way classrooms are structured and the way learning takes place.

A Process for Change

Untracking can be implemented by individual teachers and schools and on a districtwide level. Within a classroom, teachers can explore alternatives to traditional reading group instruction by using a mix of homogeneous and heterogeneous grouping, placing children in groups based on interests rather than ability, encouraging students to visit other reading groups, and reassessing and reassigning students frequently. Cooperative learning is an effective way to untrack in math or other content area subjects. Individualized instructional approaches such as the writing process (Grave, 1983) and building in daily silent reading time also facilitate untracking.

When individual schools untrack, it is usually because the principal has a strong commitment to heterogeneous grouping. Slow and careful planning characterizes the most successful of these efforts. One elementary school principal reported that the process she followed included disseminating research and articles on ability grouping, putting together study groups to discuss the research, sending teachers in small teams to visit other schools in the area that used mixed-ability groups, and introducing the change gradually, starting in only *some* classes at the lower grade levels before expanding out to include all classes, first at the lower, then at the higher, grade levels.

The process is more difficult but the effect more profound when untracking takes place at a district level. For this to be successful, some key ingredients appear to be essential to make the process go smoothly. A brief outline of steps to follow to implement district-wide untracking, adapted from George (1992) is as follows.

Appoint a steering committee to study instructional grouping. Key individuals should be identified to head the steering committee — people who, based on their status within the community as leaders and opinion makers, can lend authority to the process just by nature of their participation. The steering committee itself should represent the key constituencies affected by the change process: school board members and administrators, teachers, parents, and other community leaders. Consideration should be given to including student representatives from both high- and low-track classes. George (1992) points out that two sets of parents, in particular, should be part of the process: those who believe their students benefit from tracking and those who feel their children are hurt by it. With the first group, the task is to reassure parents that their children's educa-

tional prospects will not be harmed by a move to heterogeneous grouping, while the second group of parents need to be encouraged to "speak out against what they believe to be unjust and unfair practices and be encouraged to insist on equity in the assignment of students, teachers, and school resources" (p. 27).

The task of the steering committee is to review research findings and legal decisions and, in combination with information about local grouping practices, to make recommendations to the school board for new grouping practices.

Establish local self-study to assess the impact of grouping practices within the local school community. Change is more effectively implemented if results of national research can be supplemented by local-level research that investigates conditions specific to the school district that is planning for change. Questions that such a self-study might address include the following (taken from George, 1992): (a) How are students assigned to classes? (b) Is there proportional representation in all ability groupings of all ethnic and social-class groups? (c) How flexible are the grouping arrangements — do students assigned to particular groups tend to stay there over the length of their school careers? (d) How does ability grouping affect students' perception of themselves, including measures of self-esteem and future aspirations? (e) Does track placement affect students' behavior, as measured by discipline referrals, detentions and suspensions, their participation in extracurricular activities, their rates of absenteeism, and so forth? (f) How are teachers assigned to different tracks — do all teachers share equally in teaching both high- and low-track groups? (g) Are there differences in how high- and low-track classes are taught — are lessons prepared differently, are different instructional strategies used, are there different expectations, and so on? (h) Is parent involvement in school programs equally distributed across ability groups? Looking at these issues can bring to light significant disparities between high and low tracks across a broad set of dimensions that can make a compelling case to support untracking.

Disseminate findings to a wide audience. The results of both published research and self-study need to be made available to as wide an audience as possible. George (1992) notes that well-educated parents can become valuable allies in promoting change when confronted with research that both demonstrates the inequities associated with grouping and assures them that their children will not be hurt by untracking.

Wheelock (1992) describes a workshop activity for parents that powerfully illustrates the inequities of ability grouping. Developed by the Right Question Project, in Somerville, Massachusetts, workshop participants are given two sheets of paper stapled together. On the first sheet is written "What Your Child Should learn: The Curriculum for All the District's Schoolchildren." The second page contains the sentence, "The full curriculum is 100 pages long." On half the papers, a second sentence reads, "Your child will be taught the full 100-pages," while on the other half a second sentence reads, "Your child will be taught only the first 50 pages." The project director reported that this exercise leads parents to ask important questions such as "Why is my child only being taught 50 pages?" "Who made that decision?" "Why was it made?" "Am I supposed to be involved? Can I be?" (Wheelock, 1992, p. 83). Raising and discussing these questions leads parents to new insights into how grouping decisions are made and the consequences of those decisions.

Develop a board-approved policy statement on grouping for instruction. Such a statement should be developed by using all the information collected by the steering committee, including results from national research and local self-study and with input from a broad spectrum of the school community. Such a statement becomes a values statement that then drives the development of a long-range strategic plan.

Design a long-range strategic plan. Such a strategic plan will likely be a multiyear plan and should identify broad goals for reorganization as well as define specific objectives and identify the strategies required to ensure success. A phase-in-process either may target certain aspects of grouping practices to be addressed first or may determine that regrouping shall occur at younger grade levels or in some schools before others. A process for monitoring progress, for trouble-shooting and problem solving, and for evaluating the outcomes of untracking should be incorporated into the plan.

Implement extensive staff development to help staff prepare for untracking. To be effective, staff development cannot be a one-shot overview. It must be ongoing, with components in place before, during, and after full implementation of untracking. George (1992) outlines a number of components to staff development that appear to be critical to the success of the process. Teachers must have (a) access to national and local research on the effects of ability grouping, (b) the opportunity to discuss moral and philosophical issues inherent in ability grouping, and (c) extensive training in instructional strategies and alternative grouping arrangements that ensure that less-able students are sufficiently supported while more-able students are sufficiently challenged in their learning efforts.

Change is never easy. Advocates for untracking may become impatient when confronted with the need for a multiyear plan in the face of the day-to-day inequities they see in schools that distribute re-

sources unequally to students of different ability levels. Experience has taught, however, that hasty change too often leads to failure, and the ensuing bad feelings act as a serious impediment to future reform attempts.

ALTERNATIVES TO ABILITY GROUPING

Goodlad, in his massive study of schooling reported in *A Place Called School* (1984) described schools as consisting predominantly of classrooms where teachers explain and lecture and where students listen to teachers, write answers to questions, and take tests and quizzes. For untracking to be successful, schools must find methods that more effectively engage students and make learning real, interactive, and relevant for future life outcomes. For heterogeneous grouping to be successful, diversity will not only need to be acknowledged, it will need to be embraced. As adults, we draw on the strengths, aptitudes, and interests of those around us to increase productivity on the job and harmony in the home. Surely, if we create classrooms that allow students to do the same, we will create a better match between what happens in schools and what happens in the world beyond the schoolhouse door.

Effective instruction in heterogeneous learning groups may best prepare today's students for life after high school, but it cannot be accomplished by continuing to use traditional teaching and learning models. Brief descriptions of alternative grouping patterns, instructional strategies, and curricula that support learning in mixed ability groups are presented below.

Alternative Grouping Arrangements

Partial untracking. If it is politically inexpedient to curtail tracking altogether, a first step in the process may be to reduce the number of tracks, eliminate the lowest tracks, or make it easier for students to enroll themselves in higher tracks. Many school districts encounter the strongest resistance from parents when attempts are made to eliminate honors courses; hence it may be unwise to do this in the early stages of untracking. At the same time, efforts can be made to ensure that enrollment criteria for honors courses are fair and that all ethnic and social-class groups have equal access to these courses.

Flexible grouping/team teaching. This is the practice of using different grouping arrangements for different purposes. It may mean a schedule of homogeneous grouping two times a week and mixed-ability grouping three times a week, for instance. Or it may mean clustering students differently for different teaching units (e.g., homogeneous grouping for a study skills component of a social studies class). Sometimes, flexible grouping is combined with team teaching — by combining large, whole-group activities with smaller-group activities, with more teachers available to work with smaller groups. The social studies department of a small junior high/high school in northern Vermont, for instance, arranged teaching schedules so that all seventh-grade social studies classes were taught simultaneously. This gave teachers great flexibility in how they taught the curriculum and grouped the students.

Mixed-ability grouping with additional support. Placing all students in mixed-ability classes but offering extra support to students who need it is one grouping strategy that recognizes that students have different needs and learn at different rates. When Parkway North High School, outside St. Louis, Missouri, untracked several years ago, teachers added English Skills and Skills Tutorial Programs to provide students the skills they needed to survive in the mixed-ability classes (Merina, 1990). The added class periods enabled teachers to fill in gaps, do preteaching to enable students to better participate in class discussions, and establish closer relationships with students. Other models provide before- or after-school assistance to students who need additional help. Some schools hire college students to provide tutorial services; peer tutoring is an additional way to provide supplemental help to students who need it.

Instructional teams. At the middle school or junior high level, heterogeneous grouping appears to be most successful when students are divided into clusters within a school, with a team of teachers assigned to each cluster. Often, specialists, special educators, and instructional aides join the teams to provide additional support. Each team has a common planning period that enables them to discuss students or management problems and to develop interdisciplinary or thematic units where appropriate. While teams can make heterogeneous grouping successful, when employed in ability-grouped schools such teams have led to untracking as teams of teachers begin to question the quality of instruction they are providing to low-track students (Wheelock, 1992).

Cross-graded grouping. Also known as the Joplin Plan, this approach has research support when it is done with one or two subject areas such as math or reading (Slavin, 1986). It is a form of heterogeneous grouping, since younger high achievers may be placed with older low or average achievers. However, it allows teachers to work with a narrower range of skill levels, enabling them to use more whole-class, teacher-directed instruction.

Nongraded schools Nongraded schools do not assign students to grades; rather, teams of teachers are assigned to groups of students who are heterogeneously mixed by age and ability and are frequently regrouped depending on the nature of the learning task. Progress is determined by tasks completed or skills learned. Learning activities consist predomi-

nantly of complex problem-solving tasks that are of an interdisciplinary nature. Students are active participants in their own learning process. A recent review of 57 studies (Pavan, 1992) found that in 91% of those studies, students in nongraded schools performed as well as or better than students in traditional, graded schools. Students in nongraded schools also performed higher on measures of self-esteem and attitudes toward school. Longitudinal studies show the positive effects of nongraded schools hold up over time. Additionally, at-risk students performed better in nongraded schools.

Alternative Instructional Strategies

Cooperative learning. Cooperative learning is an instructional strategy in which learning takes place in small, heterogeneous groups carefully selected to represent a diversity of learning abilities. As most commonly practiced, students are responsible for helping each other master material or complete learning activities, incorporating individual accountability (ultimately, each student must demonstrate that he/she has learned the material) and group rewards for performance. Often, the rewards, which may be as simple as a certificate of achievement, are based on *improvement* on previous week's performance. This allows students of all abilities to contribute equally to the group's accomplishments. Cooperative learning has been shown to improve achievement, enhance attitudes toward school and self-concept, and facilitate cross-ethnic friendships and the mainstreaming of handicapped students (Slavin, 1983). This approach, which is now widely used throughout the United States, perhaps holds the best promise for reducing reliance on ability grouping.

Peer tutoring/cross-age tutoring. The use of student tutors allows for more active learning, more opportunities for individual response, and more immediate feedback. Meta-analytic research (Cohen, Kulik, & Kulik, 1982) has demonstrated that peer tutoring has positive effects on academic performance and attitudes of both tutors and the tutored. This approach is one way to provide additional support to students who need it in mixed-ability classes.

Seminar discussions. Long the instructional method of choice in this country's exclusive college preparatory schools, the use of seminars to help students grapple with complex information and questions for which there may be no right answer is also applicable to mixed-ability classrooms. Used primarily for discussions involving text interpretation, it is most successful when teachers begin discussions by posing open-ended interpretive questions for which text material can be found to support several alternative answers. Students become enthusiastic participants when they see that the teacher is genuinely open to a variety of answers and is not pushing students toward predetermined responses.

A discussion format such as this can produce results that are surprising to teachers. Cushman (1992), in writing about seminars with mixed-ability groups, stated, "Higher-performing students who are more comfortable with written texts learn to accept that sometimes there is no one answer with which they can please the authorities as they are used to doing. Less skilled students learn that their candor and rich life experience are assets in an academic discussion" (p. 1). A teacher who taught a mixed-ability English class for the first time reported, "The honors and college bound students were simply repeating material they already knew, parroting back what I had said. The general track students questioned them, forcing these 'academics' to clarify what they meant and put their ideas in terms everyone could understand" (Steinberg & Wheelock, 1992).

Hands-on/experiential learning. Activity-oriented learning lends itself to heterogeneous classrooms, and a number of specific curricula have been developed explicitly for use in mixed-ability classes. Such approaches combine learning by doing with teaching higher-order and creative-thinking skills. As an example, one of the junior-high-level projects developed by FAST (Foundational Approaches in Science Teaching) requires students to create a model submarine that can "rest on top of the water in a fish tank for five seconds, submerge, remain on the bottom of the tank for one minute, rise to the surface, and repeat the cycle" (Wheelock, 1992, p. 174). See Wheelock (1992) or Steinberg and Wheelock (1992) for descriptions of additional resources.

Project-oriented learning. Having students create a class store or newspaper, put together audio interviews of community workers, or produce a video tape depicting a community's history are all examples of project-oriented learning. These approaches often tap important communication skills that allow learners who are weak in traditional academic skills to display their talents.

Individualized instruction. This does not have to mean that a teacher creates 25 separate lesson plans for each student in the classroom. It *does* mean building in opportunities for differentiated instruction depending on the needs and interests of students. The following are examples of ways to individualize instruction.

1. Defining desired learning outcomes and giving students choices about how they will demonstrate that they've achieved those outcomes. When teachers begin by defining broad learning goals that they expect students to accomplish, this allows for significant flexibility in how students will accomplish these goals and how they will demonstrate mastery.

2. Having students design their own homework assignments.

3. Preparing activities at different difficulty levels that students can choose from to reinforce or extend their skills. A learning-center approach to instruction lends itself to this.

4. Negotiating learning contracts with students to enable them to earn specific grades by completing specific tasks or demonstrating specific competencies. One teacher in a high school in New Hampshire lists a vast array of activities and responsibilities (both in class and out of class) with points attached to each item. Course grades are determined by how many points students accumulate.

5. Allowing students to retake tests until they demonstrate mastery. Tests can be individualized in other ways by adapting the format and content to meet the needs of individual students. Portfolio assessments lend themselves to the assessment of *progress*, perhaps the most relevant form of student assessment.

Curricular Modifications

A recent national study, conducted jointly by the American Society for Training and Development and the U.S. Department of Labor, that details the kinds of skills employers seek in employees offers a compelling reason why school reform must include a more relevant curriculum for life in the *twenty-first century. Published in a book entitled Workplace Basics: The Skills Employers Want* (Carnevale, Gainer, & Meltzer, 1991), the study is based on interviews with hundreds of employers from a wide array of companies and organizations. The study includes a list of skills that employers seek in new employees. As summarized in *Education Week* (Marshak, 1993), the desired skills fall into seven areas: reading, writing, and computation skills; listening and speaking skills; "learning to learn" skills; problem-solving and creative-thinking skills; personal-management skills; teamwork skills; and leadership skills and organizational effectiveness.

Traditionally, schools have been most explicit in defining the reading, writing, and computation skills expected to graduates. This study suggests that greater emphasis needs to be placed on developing creative-thinking and problem-solving skills and the skills required to work well with other people. These skills are best taught and nurtured in an environment that is defined by diversity, not homogeneity.

Many of the instructional strategies described above address these skills. Through cooperative learning, seminar discussions, project-oriented learning, and hands-on, experiential learning, students learn to think through problems, devise creative solutions, listen to alternative viewpoints, and tap into the skills of others to achieve common goals. Thus, many of the skills described above can be infused into an existing curriculum by altering the way that curriculum is taught. Examples of specific curricula that have been developed to facilitate students' acquisition of higher-order thinking and problem-solving skills, as well as the skills required to work well with people, are briefly described below:

The HOTS Project. As described by Wheelock (1992), the HOTS (Higher Order Thinking Skills) "is a general thinking program designed to help students deal with several concepts simultaneously, engage in dialogue about ideas, think in terms of general principles, and pursue ideas to their logical conclusions" (p. 163). This program uses computer games such as "Oregon Trail" or "Where in the World is Carmen San Diego" as a jumping-off point, with teachers posing questions about how students make choices and reach conclusions. Although it was designed originally as a pull-out program for at-risk students, many schools use it effectively in heterogeneous learning groups. For more information, contact HOTS Project, College of Education, Division of Educational Foundations and Administration, University of Arizona, Tucson, AZ 85721.

Philosophy for children. This is a 12-grade curriculum designed to teach critical-thinking skills through the discussion of philosophical issues raised in stories that can be incorporated into a language arts, reading, or study skills curriculum. Evaluation studies have documented gains in reading and reasoning skills in students of all ability levels (Wheelock, 1992). For more information, contact the Institute for the Advancement of Philosophy for Children, Montclair State College, Upper Montclair, NJ 07043.

Junior Great Books Curriculum. This is a thinking skills curriculum that uses good literature to enable children to explore open-ended, interpretive questions. Selections are limited in length to permit reading and rereading; they lend themselves to extended interpretation through ambiguity of meaning, and they raise puzzling questions for both teachers and students. In addition to improving thinking skills, school districts employing this curriculum report substantial improvements on measures of reading vocabulary and comprehension. One elementary school in Pennsylvania reported that after 1 year, 50% of students considered "remedial" tested out of that classification (Wheelock, 1992). This approach appears to be particularly successful in heterogeneous classes. Wheelock (1992) quotes a middle school teacher about its use in this kind of classroom: "In homogeneous groups, the discussions used to drag; there wasn't a spark. But in the discussions in heterogeneous classes, the best thing about them is the mix of perspectives. . . . The kids ask questions because they're really curious, not just for the grade" (p. 162).

Practical-Intelligence-for-School (PIFS). Practical intelligence refers to the ability to understand and apply "tacit" knowledge to learning situations. Tacit knowledge is "knowledge that is not explicitly taught or even verbalized, but is necessary for an individual to thrive in an environment" (Sternberg, Okagaki, & Jackson, 1990). Together with Howard Gardner at Harvard University, Robert Sternberg has developed a curriculum to teach students the tacit knowledge they need to succeed in school. Three kinds of tacit knowledge are covered in this one-semester course, which includes a student text and a comprehensive teacher's manual, along with curricular material on managing oneself, managing tasks, and working with others. Students learn the self-management skills that are necessary to take in new information, demonstrate learning, and use new skills. They learn how to get organized, seek help for problems, manage time, and apply study skills. They are also taught communication skills and how to make good choices in school. For more information, contact Robert Sternberg, Yale University, Department of Psychology, P.O. Box 11A, Yale Station, New Haven, CT 06520-7447.

Cognitive strategy instruction. A number of cognitive strategy curricula have been developed to help teachers teach students procedures for accomplishing academic tasks. Coming from the field of cognitive psychology, extensive research has been done over the years on cognitive and metacognitive strategies that can enhance performance in a variety of academic areas, including reading decoding, reading comprehension, spelling, written language, and math problem solving. Since these strategies teach students to become more active and self-directed in their learning, they suggest application to heterogeneously grouped classrooms. Examples of cognitive strategy curricula are those developed by Deshler and his colleagues (Deshler & Schumaker, 1988) and the Benchmark School (Gaskins & Elliot, 1991). See also Pressley et al. (1990) for a comprehensive research-based review of cognitive strategies.

Role of the School Psychologist in Promoting Alternatives to Ability Grouping

Many school psychologists do not see it as their role to become involved in influencing policy or promoting school reform. And yet school psychologists are often in a good position to do just that, either through informal sharing of information with teachers and school administrators or through more formal participation on task forces or strategic planning committees. Because school psychologists are in contact with students who are not succeeding in school, they are often in the best position to see how the way schools are structured contributes to learning failures. Ability grouping is one such structure that does not serve students well.

Students from lower-track classrooms are often referred to school psychologists for learning or behavior problems. In designing effective interventions or in making decisions about the need for special education, it is important for school psychologists to be aware of the effects of lower-track classrooms on students' behavior, effort, and motivation on teachers' and students' morale, and on classroom climate. When asked to facilitate the mainstreaming of students with disabilities into regular classrooms, school psychologists need to be aware that ability grouping makes mainstreaming decisions difficult, because the disparity between skill level and ability in many youngsters with disabilities makes assignment to appropriate classrooms difficult.

And school psychologists who engage in systems consultation need to be aware of the effect of grouping practices on discipline referrals, participation in school and extracurricular activities, and long-term career goals and aspirations. To look at individual students' problems, or even schoolwide problems such as discipline referrals, and fail to consider how grouping practices affect them may limit the options that schools have to address these problems. School psychologists, with their unique systems perspective, may be in an ideal position to help schools move toward untracking.

What are some actions school psychologists can take to promote alternatives to ability grouping? Here are a few suggestions.

1. Share with administrators the research on ability grouping and the NASP Position Statement on Ability Grouping (see Appendix A), as well as information about how schools can go about implementing alternatives to ability grouping.

2. Organize or participate in study groups to investigate grouping practices and discuss alternatives. There are usually some teachers in every school who are open to the idea of untracking. Bringing a group together to discuss issues and think about change can be a first step in bringing about significant changes in grouping practices.

3. Volunteer to serve on schoolwide or districtwide committees dealing with policy issues. Even if the focus of the committee is not on grouping practices, questions can be raised about how tracking or ability grouping may affect the issues under consideration. For instance, a task force assembled to study standardized achievement testing could prompt questions about the performance of different curriculum tracks and their rate of progress over time.

4. Conduct a self-study of grouping practices within the school district and share the findings with school administrators. Look particularly at issues of disproportionate representation of minority or lower-socioeconomic-status group membership in lower tracks, since concern about discrimination may prompt administrators and board members to take action where other findings may not.

5. Proceed with caution. There are certain "hot topics" in education that engender strong feelings and create tensions and conflict among diverse members of the school community. Ability grouping is one such topic. School psychologists will likely be most effective in facilitating change by taking a low-key approach — by sitting down with an administrator in a relaxed and collegial atmosphere, for instance, to have an open discussion about grouping practices and whether consideration has been given to pursuing alternatives, by sharing a few pieces of written material, such as brief summaries of the research, and arranging a follow-up meeting to discuss the administrator's reactions; or by gaining an administrator's support for assembling a study group to investigate the issue. If these approaches are not successful, school psychologists will need to make a personal decision to take a more activist stance. In our efforts to promote optimal learning conditions for all learners, school psychologists are sometimes forced to make difficult decisions regarding when to speak up and what tactics and strategies to employ for maximum effectiveness.

SUMMARY

Ability grouping has been widely practiced and extensively researched in the United States throughout this century. While controlled experimental studies have failed to find significant differences in achievement between students placed in homogeneously grouped classrooms and those in mixed-ability classrooms, sociological and ethnographic studies have consistently found substantial differences between higher- and lower-track classrooms. The conditions that are associated with high achievement are far more prevalent in higher-track classrooms, while lower-track classrooms are characterized by emphasis on classroom management, more off-task behavior, low student and teacher morale, and a classroom climate that is not conducive to learning. Furthermore, mixed-ability classrooms have been shown to more closely resemble average- or high-track classrooms on a variety of dimensions.

Schools and districts that have successfully moved away from ability grouping have planned for change carefully and have implemented change slowly, usually following a multiyear strategic plan. Involvement of key constituencies, including parents, teachers, and administrators, has been secured, and extensive staff development in alternatives to ability grouping is an integral part of the process.

Schools that successfully group children heterogeneously do not simply apply traditional teaching structures to mixed-ability groups. Rather, these schools recognize that regrouping for diversity requires changes in organizational structures, instructional models, and curricula in order to ensure that all students are both challenged and supported in an environment that promotes optimal learning for all. There are a wide variety of ways that schools can achieve this, and each untracked school is unique in the choices it has made. What these schools have in common is a sense of purpose and excitement and a realization that diversity is not an obstacle to learning, but a tool. School psychologists have an important role to play in sharing the research on ability grouping and its alternatives, participating in discussions to promote understanding of this research, and planning for a successful transition from tracked to untracked schools.

REFERENCES

Carnevale, A. P., Gainer, L. J., & Meltzer, A. S. (1991). *Workplace basics: The essential skills employers want.* San Francisco: Jossey-Bass.

Cohen, P. A., Kulik, J. A., & Kulik, C. L. (1982). Educational outcomes of tutoring: A meta-analysis of findings. *American Educational Research Journal, 19,* 237–248.

Cushman, K. (1992). Conversations in classrooms: Who are seminars for? *The Harvard Education Letter, 8,* No. 2, 1–4.

Dawson, M. M. (1987). Beyond ability grouping: A review of the effectiveness of ability grouping and its alternatives. *School Psychology Review, 16,* 348–369.

Dentzer, E., & Wheelock, A. (1990). *Locked in/locked out: Tracking and placement practices in Boston public schools.* Boston, MA: Massachusetts Advocacy Center.

Deshler, D. D., & Schumaker, J. B. (1988). An instructional model for teaching students how to learn. In J. L. Graden, J. E. Zins, & Michael E. Curtis (Eds.), *Alternative educational delivery systems: Enhancing instructional options for all students.* Washington, DC: The National Association of School Psychologists.

Eder, D. (1981). Ability grouping as a self-fulfilling prophecy: A micro-analysis of teacher–student interaction. *Sociology of Education, 54,* 151–161.

England, R. E., Meier, K. J., & Fraga, L. R. (1988). Barriers to equal opportunity: Educational practices and minority students. *Urban Affairs Quarterly, 23,* 635–646.

Evertson, C. E. (1982). Differences in instructional activities in average- and low-achieving junior high English and mathematics classes. *Elementary School Journal, 18,* 219–232.

Felmlee, D., & Eder, D. (1983). Contextual effects in the classroom: The impact of ability groups on student attention. *Sociology of Education, 56,* 77–87.

Gambrell, L. B., Wilson, R. M., & Gantt, W. N. (1981). Classroom observations of task-attending behaviors of good and poor readers. *Journal of Educational Research, 74,* 400–404.

Gamoran, A., & Berends, M. (1987). The effects of stratification in secondary schools: Synthesis of survey and ethnographic research. *Review of Educational Research, 57,* 415–435.

Gaskins, I., & Elliot, T. (1991). *Implementing cognitive strategy instruction across the school.* Cambridge, MA: Brookline Books.

George, P. (1992). *How to untrack your school.* Alexandria, VA: Association for Supervision and Curriculum Development.

Goodlad, J. I. (1984). *A place called school: Prospects for the future.* New York: McGraw Hill.

Grave, D. H. (1983). *Writing: Teachers and children at work.* Portsmouth, NH: Heinemann Educational Books.

Kulik, C. C., & Kulik, J. A. (1982). Effects of ability grouping on secondary school students: A meta-analysis of evaluation findings. *American Educational Research Journal, 19,* 415–428.

Kulik, J. A. (1992). *An analysis of the research on ability grouping: Historical and contemporary perspectives.* Storrs, CT: National Research Center on the Gifted and Talented.

Marshak, D. (1993, June 2). What employers know that educators may not. *Education Week,* p. 25.

Merina, A. (1990, December). Tracking down alternatives. *NEA Today.*

National Association of School Psychologists. (1993, June). Position Statement on Ability Grouping. *Communiqué,* Insert Section.

Oakes, J. (1985). *Keeping track: How schools structure inequality.* New Haven, CT: Yale University Press.

Page, R. N. (1991). *Lower-track classrooms: A curricular and cultural perspective.* New York: Teachers College Press.

Paul, G. (1992). *How to untrack your school.* Alexandria, VA: Association for Supervision and Curriculum Development.

Pavan, B. N. (1992). The benefits of nongraded schools. *Educational Leadership, 50* (No. 2), 22–25.

Pressley, M., Burkell, J., Cariglia-Bull, T., Lysynchuk, L., McGoldrick, J. A., Schneider, B., Snyder, B. L., Symons, S., & Woloshyn, V. E. (1990). *Cognitive strategy instruction that really improves children's academic performance.* Cambridge, MA: Brookline Books.

Rist, R. (1970). Student social class and teacher expectations: The self-fulfilling prophecy in ghetto education.

Shepard, L. (1992, May 31). Studies support both sides in school debate. *Daily Camera* (Boulder, CO).

Slavin, R. E. (1983). *Cooperative learning.* New York: Longman.

Slavin, R. E. (1986). *Ability grouping and student achievement in elementary schools: A best-evidence synthesis.* Report No. 1. Baltimore, MD: Johns Hopkins Center for Research on Elementary and Middle Schools.

Slavin, R. E. (1990). Achievement effects of ability grouping in secondary schools: A best-evidence synthesis. *Review of Educational Research, 60,* 471–499.

Slavin, R. E. (1991). Are cooperative learning and "untracking" harmful to the gifted? *Educational Leadership, 48* (No. 6), 68–71.

Steinberg, A., & Wheelock, A. (1992). After tracking – what? Middle schools find new answers. *Harvard Education Letter, 8* (No. 5), 1–5.

Sternberg, R. J., Okagaki, L., & Jackson, A. S. (1990). Practical intelligence for success in school. *Educational Leadership, 48* (No. 1), 35–39.

Veldman, D. J., & Sanford, J. P. (1984). The influence of class ability level on student achievement and classroom behavior. *American Educational Research Journal, 21,* 629–644.

Weinstein, R. S. (1976). Reading group membership in first grade: Teacher behaviors and pupil experience over time. *Journal of Educational Psychology, 68,* 103–116.

Wheelock, A. (1992). *Crossing the tracks: How "untracking" can save America's schools.* New York: New Press.

ANNOTATED BIBLIOGRAPHY

Dawson M. M. (1987). Beyond ability grouping: A review of the effectiveness of ability grouping and its alternatives. *School Psychology Review, 16*, 348–369.
  This review article offers a concise overview of the research on ability grouping, including effects on achievement, self-concept, and attitudes toward schools. Sociological research is also reviewed that documents grouping effects on classroom climate, teacher expectations, instructional practices, and student behaviors. Alternatives to ability grouping are also discussed, including suggestions for effective grouping patterns, reading instruction for low-reading groups, and communicating achievement expectations.

Murphy, J. (1988). Equity as student opportunity to learn. *Theory Into Practice, 27*, 145–151.
  This article discusses ability grouping as an equity issue. Research is cited to demonstrate that students in lower-track classes are discriminated against by depriving them of the same quality of instruction, restricting access to the same kinds of knowledge, and exposing them to less instructional time than is available to higher-track students. A useful table summarizes these differences between high- and low-track classes.

Paul, G. (1992). *How to untrack your school.* Alexandria, VA: Association for Supervision and Curriculum Development.
  This booklet offers a concise guide to untracking schools, including a brief review of the research, a discussion of practical alternatives, an implementation process, and a list of helpful references and resources.

Wheelock, A. (1992). *Crossing the tracks: How "untracking" can save America's schools.* New York: New Press.
  This book is a rich source of suggestions for untracking schools. The author provides numerous examples of schools that have untracked and includes countless examples of strategies, tactics, methods, and materials both for implementing a change process and for providing effective instruction in heterogeneous classrooms. In addition to providing documentation regarding effective practices with mixed ability classes, the book captures the excitement that teachers and students feel when they move to inclusive schools. It is highly recommended as a resource and is particularly compelling for readers who are skeptical about both the feasibility and the benefits of untracked schools.

APPENDIX A

Position Statement on Ability Grouping

To ensure educational equity and excellence for all America's youth, NASP supports the creation of inclusive classrooms that are based on the belief that *all* students can learn – a core value of all schools in a democracy. NASP believes that tracking, or whole class ability grouping, is not consistent with that core value.

Extensive research on ability grouping has documented the following negative effects:

- Students with lower ability achieve less in lower track classes than in mixed ability classes;

- Students with higher ability do not achieve more in tracked classes than in mixed ability classes;

- Placing students with lower ability in tracked classrooms reduces self-esteem, with a particularly negative effect on students' sense of their own academic competence;

- Tracking students reduces the likelihood that students placed in lower track classes will choose college preparatory courses;

- Tracking students reduces opportunities to develop relationships among students from other racial, ethnic, and socioeconomic groups and has a negative effect on race relations;

- The placement decision concerning ability grouping is often made very early in a student's school career, is often based on questionable data, and is enduring.

NASP believes that grouping students heterogeneously offers advantages unavailable in schools that track. When implemented appropriately, heterogeneous grouping:

- Gives all students equal access to an enriched curriculum and the highest quality instruction schools have to offer;

- Avoids labeling and stigmatizing students with lower ability;

- Promotes higher expectations for student achievement;

- Reduces in-school segregation based on socioeconomic status, race, gender or ethnicity, or disability;

- Encourages teachers to accommodate individual differences in students' instructional and social needs;

- Enables students to learn from their peers, including students whose background may be very different from their own;

- Emphasizes effort more than ability.

NASP recognizes that heterogeneous grouping will not automatically guarantee *all* students a quality education. "Watering down" the curriculum or "teaching to the middle" will create disadvantages for able students and should be avoided. While NASP believes that all students can benefit from a more challenging curriculum, we also strongly support the development of a curriculum which recognizes and accommodates individual differences in learning styles, abilities, and interests. To be successful, mixed ability grouping must occur within the context of such a curriculum.

NASP also recognizes that heterogeneous classes require instructional and organizational innovations to accommodate a wide range of learners. Such approaches include cooperative learning groups, peer tutors, flexible grouping practices, team teaching, multi-age groupings, and instruction in higher order thinking and problem-solving skills. Where teachers do not currently possess competencies to enable them to work effectively with mixed ability classes, a commitment to further training is essential.

NASP believes that "untracking" schools requires careful planning and collaboration among constituent groups, including teachers, administrators, support personnel, students, and parents. Planned change can best take place using a model that includes the following:

- A steering committee composed of educators, parents, community members and school board representatives whose task is to study grouping practices and make policy recommendations to the school board;

- Local self-study to assess the impact of grouping practices within the school community;

- Wide dissemination of local and national studies of ability grouping effects;

- A board-approved policy statement on grouping for instruction;

- Well-designed staff development that exposes staff to the research, gives them the opportunity to discuss philosophical issues, and provides sufficient training in instructional methods for heterogeneous classes;

- Implementation of a strategic plan that allows for a phase-in process and ensures monitoring, trouble-shooting, and evaluation.

NASP believes that school psychologists can play a central role in helping schools develop appropriate alternatives to tracking. School psychologists have access to research, understand good instructional practices that enhance learning for *all* students, and possess group problem-solving skills that make them valuable as members of steering committees and strategic planning groups and as staff trainers.

School psychologists can contribute to the process of untracking schools by:

- Making research available to administrators and central office personnel;

- Leading informal study groups to explore alternative grouping practices;

- Becoming members of steering committees assembled to study tracking and to develop policy recommendations;

- Participating in strategic planning and staff development to prepare for untracking.

NASP recognizes that schools cannot simply eliminate tracking but must develop viable alternatives. Developing alternatives to tracking will take patience and careful planning. In order for schools to live up to the promise of educating *all* students to become productive citizens of the 21st century, NASP believes these alternatives must be "characterized by fairness and challenge, with equity and excellence equally available to all learners."[1]

FOOTNOTE

[1]This position statement drew on material from George, P. (1992). *How to untrack your school.* Alexandria, VA: Association for Supervision and Curriculum Development.

32

Best Practices in Systems Influences on Children's Self-Concept

Marilyn S. Wilson
California State University, Fresno

OVERVIEW

Self-concept is one's perception of self, based on encounters with the environment and guided by maturation. Through our successes and failures and through comparison with others we form conceptions of our own abilities. These self-concepts can influence our willingness to attempt new or challenging tasks or to persevere. We do not develop self-concepts in isolation. For students the environment (e.g., successes and failures and peer comparison) which shapes self-concept exists largely within the school system. Most parents and educators hope for and work towards positive self-concepts for children. Feeling good about oneself is viewed as a prerequisite for self-confidence, risk taking, and good mental health.

This chapter briefly reviews self-concept and social comparison theory and then examines how school systems inadvertently influence children's self-concepts and how school psychologists can work within school systems to evaluate and develop programs that can have positive influences on students' self-concepts. For example, program evaluation might include the effects on self-concept, as well as on academic achievement, of alternative service delivery systems such as mainstreaming, team-teaching, or cooperative learning. School psychologists can develop intervention and prevention programs in which parents are partners with the school. Finally, programs can be implemented in which students with learning and/or behavior problems are the providers rather than the recipients of services, as in cross-age tutoring. If self-concept is partially formed from feedback on behavior, then competent actions which elicit positive feedback should lead to enhanced self-concept.

Theory of Self-Concept

The global construct of self is typically called self-concept or self-worth. Bandura (1986) proposed that self-efficacy, the "self" that combines self-concept with prediction, is composed from mastery experiences, visceral feedback, verbal persuasion, and vicarious experiences. Therefore, programs and practices that help children achieve (mastery experiences) and give them positive feedback (visceral feedback and vicarious experiences) and encouragement (verbal persuasion) promote positive self-concepts.

Personal accomplishment. The principal component of self-efficacy and self-concept is personal accomplishment; for children accomplishments are relative mastery of tasks presented in school, such as learning to read and to do math. An old motto says, "Success breeds success." Curricula and instructional techniques that allow children to master academic building blocks promote positive self-concepts and children who are willing to tackle escalating academic tasks. For children who find academic work difficult and not particularly reinforcing (or reinforced) other activities (e.g., sports, music, art, 4-H) can be available in which the child can succeed, perhaps even shine. Academic programs and extracurricular activities designed and evaluated with children's social-emotional development as a primary goal are examples of systems' influences on self-concept.

Visceral feedback. The second component of self-efficacy is visceral feedback. These are the messages our body gives us to indicate pleasure, pain, anxiety, and so forth. Children exhibiting somatic symptoms may not be happy, confident individuals. Again, the educational environment should be evaluated for conflicts and adverse conditions that may be provoking the physical symptoms.

Verbal persuasion. Verbal persuasion is powerful! Praise and encouragement can stimulate action and accomplishment. The teacher who uses a classroom management system that recognizes and rewards labor and progress has built a tautology. Verbal persuasion may come with a hidden message, for we are complex beings and attributions are linked to feedback. For example, "you're working hard" may lead to an attribution of "I'm not so good at this; I can only do it with lots of effort," while "you're good at this" implies high ability. In our culture, the latter attribution, of high ability, leads to higher self-efficacy than attributions of expended effort (Schunk, 1983, 1985). Parents of Caucasian children are more supportive of this belief that children do well because they are bright; Asian-American parents reinforce effort and believe success is the result of hard work (Stevenson & Lee, 1990). These beliefs and attitudes shape children's self-concepts and expectations regarding effort. Children who seem to feel that if something is hard for them they cannot do it, so why even try, may be reflecting cultural system messages.

Vicarious experiences. The final component proposed by Bandura (1986) is vicarious experiences. We learn by observing others; we also utilize others as standards for evaluating our own performances. Festinger (1954) proposed that social comparison was used to judge self-performance in the absence of objective standards. Schunk (1983) and Bandura (1986) found children to use social comparison to estimate self-efficacy. School is the primary setting for validating academic self-efficacious beliefs through social comparison; the type of class and classmates influence how competent children judge themselves to be. The development of self-concept through evaluation, feedback, comparison, and maturation is briefly reviewed in the next section.

Development of Self-Concept

Self-concept is developed from accomplishments as evaluated by ourselves or others. Small children receive feedback on their successes and their inabilities from the environment and from persons in their environment. The infant practices eye-hand coordination and is rewarded by reaching the desired object; when he or she waves bye-bye, Grandma responds with a wave, hug, or kiss. When the toddler turns the spoon upside down very little reaches the mouth; feedback is swift, direct, and informative. Young children typically see themselves as competent because they are gradually achieving mastery of developmental tasks (Dweck & Elliott, 1983; Harter, 1983). In well-functioning families, preschool children should feel like they are in the mythical Lake Woebeggon where "all the women were beautiful and all the children above average" (Garrison Keillor, *A Prairie Home Companion* radio show).

When children begin school, they leave the security of being judged on and rewarded for progress toward goals all normally developing children generally master and enter a more competitive domain. Self-concept is lowered during the elementary years as feedback from adults is both corrective and evaluative, and as children begin to compare their performance to that of others (Stipek & Daniels, 1988). Children are given grades on their academic work; they may be placed in groups or tracks for certain subjects. These processes allow and force children to compare their assignments and progress to that of their classmates and to evaluate their own abilities. Social comparison for normative purposes develops in the primary grades, around ages 7 to 9 years (Frey & Ruble, 1985). How social comparison is utilized in class or educational grouping practices to impact children's self-concepts will be discussed in the following section.

Due to developmental differences, children may have very different concepts of task difficulty and of their own abilities than adults. Children below the age of 6 years do not differentiate between ability and effort and, therefore, assume tasks on which they succeed are easy and those on which they fail are difficult (Dweck & Bempchat, 1983; Nicholls, 1984). Young children underestimate task difficulty and have unrealistically high expectations of their own ability (Dweck & Elliott, 1983). By 11 or 12 years of age, children can differentiate the parts played by luck, task difficulty, ability, and effort in success or failure (Nicholls, 1984; Stipek, 1988).

BASIC CONSIDERATIONS

The self-concepts of school-age children are molded by the instructional environment and their relative success in school. Students with mild disabilities frequently exacerbate their learning problems by demonstrating an apparent lack of motivation that can lead to less engaged time and result in lower levels of achievement. When students continually meet with failure in academic tasks or see their performance as less competent than other children to whom they are comparing themselves, they often exhibit less perseverance (Schunk, 1983). This eventual lack of effort created and/or fed by lack of success is learned helplessness (Peterson, 1992). Therefore, if setting controls curriculum and curriculum determines the possibility of success, the setting in which children are taught and the ensuing curriculum may designate how students perceive themselves academically.

Within most settings parents and teachers provide the verbal persuasion element of self-efficacy. Children should receive encouragement that, with effort, they can learn. Students respond to praise and reinforcers by continuing to work and to try, and the praise and reinforcers are usually controlled by the adults in their lives. Reinforcers can be offered on an individual basis or through a class management system or be system-wide and involve community resources, as in reading-for-pizza projects. This section examines some of the ways school systems influence children's self-concepts.

Grouping

School systems influence self-concept by the mere fact children are forced into groups at ages in which they are learning to estimate their "worth" by comparing themselves to others. School children are typically placed in classes by age; beyond that the grouping may be heterogeneous or homogeneous. A recent position paper on grouping by the National Association of School Psychologists (NASP, 1993) addresses the academic and emotional influences of homogeneous grouping. Regular education classes are usually heterogeneous; however, regular education students may be grouped within a class for a specific subject (e.g., reading) or between classes by level of the subject matter (e.g., Developmental English, Advanced Placement English). Placement into a special education program constitutes grouping with distinct implications for a student's self-concept. Special education students are usually part of two groups; their regular education peers and their special education class. The proportion of time and influence of each depends on the restrictiveness of the programming (Wilson, 1992). These groupings impel the curriculum, opportunities for mastery, and social comparison processes.

Heterogeneous groups offer confounds in curricula and self-concept results; the curriculum may be inappropriate for slower and brighter students. Social comparison theory predicts negative effects on self-concepts of slower students and positive effects for the gifted in the heterogeneous groups (see Figure 1). It is frequently argued that in heterogeneous groups slower students are provided with role models of more competent students. However, through social comparison slower students will view themselves as less competent. Ego-wise, good students can see themselves as very competent in a heterogeneous group (Kulik & Kulik, 1991).

A grade-level class is usually heterogeneous with a middle-of-the-road curricula. Slower students struggle and the brighter students are bored. To present a broader range of curricula and better match students' achievement levels, sometimes a leveled or tracked curriculum is offered within the class or between classes. With homogeneous grouping and appropriate curriculum, the slower students may be better able to master the material and the brighter students challenged. In homogeneous groups the slower students can compare themselves favorably to others in the group; however, they may suffer loss of esteem due to the lower status of the group. In gifted classes brighter students are now part of an elite group, but suddenly may find themselves as only equal or even "dumber" than others in their group.

The recent NASP position paper on grouping (1993) adopted a position endorsing heterogeneous classes. However, there is no one result of grouping on self-concept; the forces of curriculum, group membership, and social comparison oppose each other. For gifted students the "big frog in a little pond" effect can allow for a generous self-concept in a heterogeneous class, even if the curriculum moves a little slowly (Bachman & O'Malley, 1986). On the other hand, with the challenging curriculum and status of advanced placement of talented and gifted classes, comes the position of being an equal, or perhaps slightly less competent, student than the others in the group. The reverse is true for slower students; they are allowed a more manageable curriculum and similar peers in return for the stigma of special education placement.

Retention

The academic gains of retention are generally not large nor long lasting (see the chapter in this book on retention), but the effects on self-concept can be devastating. Negative effects have been found to social and emotional adjustment and to self-concept regardless of the age at which the child was retained (Holmes & Matthews, 1984). Students view retention as punishment and a sign of failure (Smith & Shepard, 1989). In addition, they are removed from their same-age peers and classmates. Following retention, students may receive failure feedback from parents, peers, and teachers.

Some children are retained prior to starting school. "Red-shirting" kindergartners (as with football players) so they will be older — for academic, athletic, or social reasons — amounts to retention before they even begin! Longitudinal evidence suggests few academic benefits to this practice nor for transition programs which provide for a developmental year between kindergarten and first grade (Dawson, Raforth, & Carey, 1990). If children have assumed they would start school with their preschool friends or peers, staying home or in preschool (or kindergarten) another year can be quite disappointing and result in feelings of failure, incompetence, and lower self-esteem unless handled very carefully.

Special Education Placement

Special education placement may combine the worst of both retention and low-status grouping. In fact, many of these children have already been retained before being placed in special education. The literature previously reviewed discussed the impact on self-concept of placement into a homogeneous, lower functioning group. Placement into special education may, at last, allow the student a manageable, functional, and appropriate curriculum, but at the price of the special education label and membership in a lower status group. Extensive research indicates that special education students view themselves as academically less competent than their peers (Bear, Cleaver, & Proctor, 1991; Renick & Harter, 1989).

Spending years in special education can exacerbate feelings of worthlessness. Because of slow progress the curriculum tends to be exceedingly redundant: year after year of Individualized Educational Program (IEP) goals on reading and spelling, years of minimal growth and little concrete evidence

FIGURE 1. Relationship of grouping and self-concept.

ABILITY	VARIABLES	HOMOGENEOUS GROUPING	HETEROGENEOUS GROUPING
Brighter Students	Curriculum Social Comparison Group Membership	Challenging Curriculum Equal or Upward Social Comparison = Lower Self-Concepts Membership in Elite Group = Higher Self-Concept	Bored by Curriculum Downward Social Comparison = Higher Self-Concept
Slower Students	Curriculum Social Comparison Group Membership	Manageable Curriculum Equal Social Comparison = Higher Self-Concept Membership in Lower Status Group = Lower Self-Concept	Frustrated by Curriculum Upward Social Comparison = Lower Self-Concept

of such. As students enter junior high and high school, the curriculum diverges and becomes vocational; there really is no going back for students in a special class. And unless carefully couched in encouragement both at home and school, a work-ability program is not going to be viewed as prestigiously as college preparation courses. Ways to make curriculum feedback more beneficial to self-concept will be presented in the Best Practices section.

Attributions re Parental and Teacher Feedback

Children can interpret comments and actions from adults in various ways and become discouraged, timid, or embarrassed. Brophy (1983) reviewed the effects of teacher praise on children's self-concepts. Teacher expectations can become self-fulfilling prophecies; expectations can be conveyed to students through praise for low effort or incorrect responses or less feedback and attention. Does the mainstreamed child participate in class or is she or he "just there?" Children who need help most in classes may be least likely to ask for it because they do not want to be noticed or perceived as incapable (Jenkins & Heinen, 1989). Receiving unsolicited help from the teacher may be even worse, for children then make causal inferences of low ability (Aberbach & Lynch, 1991). "If I can't figure this out by myself, I must be dumb/" "Is anyone else getting help?"

Parents can provide academic assistance so their children can do better in school and feel more confident and offer positive reinforcement for effort and achievement both at home and school (see Christensen & Conoley, 1992). Dunst and Trivette (1987) discuss models of enabling and empowering families and conclude that a compensatory model in which parents are seen with limited responsibility for their

history but primarily responsible for their future best promotes self-efficacy among parents.

School psychologists can provide research for decision making and evaluate the social-emotional aspects of instructional environments and programs as well as develop training programs for parents and teachers and prevention programs for students. The first step is awareness of system decisions and practices on students' self-concept.

BEST PRACTICES

Psychologists and mental health consultants for school-age children are involved in the promotion of good mental health. As interventionists or as program evaluators, school psychologists can be involved in working toward better self-concepts for students (individual assessment and intervention for children with low self-esteem is covered in a separate chapter in this volume). School psychologists can serve as advocates for children in decision-making processes regarding appropriate educational and developmental programs as well as present research, both national and local, on the efficacy of such programs and practices. Lastly, school psychologists can assist or lead schools in developing programs and practices that enhance children's self-concepts (see Figure 2).

School Psychologist as Child Advocate

As a child advocate, the school psychologist can

- Participate in evaluating which program and which curriculum within a program provides maximum chances for success, academically and social-emotionally.

- With the program decided on, discuss ways the student's self-concept can be enhanced.

FIGURE 2. Systems infuences on chileren's self-concepts.

	PROGRAMS	**PRACTICES**
ACHIEVEMENT	Peer Tutoring Cooperative Learning Grouping Prevention Programs	Individualized Curriculum Goal Setting "Home" Work witn Parents Interventions for Time on Task Instructional Strategies for Practice/Response
POSITIVE FEEDBACK	Promotion Mainstreaming Least Restrictive Environment Parent Training in Behavior Management Teacher Training in Classroom Management	CBM Progress Monitoring Praise (Parents, Teacher) Home–School Notes Token Economy

Decision making. Meetings where decisions are being made should perhaps begin with the warning that special education placement and/or retention can be hazardous to children's mental health. Concern over the stigma of labeling accompanied PL 94-142 (Hobbs, 1975). Litigation regarding test bias and overrepresentation of minority children in special education classes has been predicated by the assumption that placement in a special education program is detrimental socially and emotionally via lower self-esteem and that this supersedes academic benefits (Prasse & Reschly, 1986). Retention has been found to result in lowered self-esteem for many children. Obviously, it is not advocated that no students be placed in special education nor retained. But the school psychologist is generally the member of the multidisciplinary team best qualified to make recommendations on the relative benefits and anticipated problems for a particular child.

According to the NASP Position Statement on Student Retention (1988), the best candidates for retention are children with minor academic deficits due to lack of instructional opportunities, such as illness, and with high self-concepts and good social skills. However, it is cautioned that the predictability for individual cases is low: There is no way of knowing which few children will benefit from repeating a grade. The school psychologist can point out research supporting individualized instruction and the evidence that retention does *not* help exceptional children nor prevent special education placement at a later date. In this case the child's ego has received a double whammy; these are not decisions to be made lightly.

Curriculum. Curriculum is as linked to special education programs as is image. As students remain in special education programs or are placed in more restrictive options the split between the regular classroom and special education curricula widens. Young children with minor academic deficits may, indeed, "be remediated" and soon returned to or, for the most part, remain in regular education classes. Those with more serious learning or behavior problems may be embarking on a path that steadily narrows. Especially in junior and senior high school, course content in special classes is largely prevocational. As members of IEP teams, school psychologists need to urge teachers, students, and parents to develop goals that result in a functional and meaningful curricula and that teach and reinforce responsibility and independence. These characteristics are necessary for self-respect and employability; being able to get and hold a job is vital to self-esteem as an adult.

When sitting around the table making decisions about the most appropriate educational program for young children, the school team needs to take a long look at the future and picture where this youngster might be — and what program maximizes his or her potential. Are the parents aware of the curricular and social-emotional implications of the decision to be made? Has a fair presentation been made of the literature on placement and retention, the local school programs and options, and likely outcomes for this student? Once a decision has been made, strategies should be developed to promote healthy adjustment and self-concepts. Strategies that transcend educational borders and can be utilized within both regular and special education programs include home–school communication, frequent feedback, and student participation in goal setting.

Home–school notes. Home–school notes are used to assist parents and teachers to work as a team to support the student (see Kelley, 1990). This communication can be designed to encourage parents to praise and reinforce their child for success in school. Goals on home–school notes frequently focus on personal responsibility and work habits, precursors to successful employability and the concomitant satisfaction of being able to support oneself. Children are not expected to subscribe to such far away goals; they feel good *now* when their work and efforts are recognized.

A home–school note is really a contract between the parent and student which is facilitated by the teacher. Goals that focus on academic, study, or behavioral needs are established and objectively defined. Remember how self-efficacy was described as composed of mastery experiences, psychological states, verbal persuasion, and vicarious experiences? Home–school notes should be construed to provide verbal persuasion (praise) for mastery experiences; for that to occur the target behaviors must be reasonably obtainable. Collect data on a peer; gather baseline data for the target student. How often do other students perform the behavior; what was the rate of performance for this student? Peer data is useful for setting an aim line; use baseline data and decide what is reasonable to expect now. Set the goals low enough to be readily achievable at first; the child must obtain the reward for it to become reinforcing. Failure and recriminations are not going to improve self-concept.

Curriculum-based measurement. A similar philosophy should be followed for academic goals. Success — with some effort — builds self-concept and promotes self-efficacy. Curriculum-based measurement (CBM) is an excellent way to determine the level of curriculum that is attainable and a slight challenge (see Shapiro, 1989; Shinn, 1988). Baseline data can indicate where the student is, schoolwide norming provides local standards to determine where to set the aim line, and progress monitoring offers frequent feedback. It is both motivating and reinforcing to know on a regular and frequent basis how you are progressing. The most convenient way to provide this is with a computerized curriculum-based program (see Fuchs, 1986).

Computerized CBM sets individual goals, provides practices, monitors progress, and gives feedback via graphs on the screen. School psychologists can remind teachers of the motivational and educational aspects of frequent monitoring and train them to construct probes, gather data, develop norms, monitor progress, and make instructional change decisions. It is most efficient if CBM is adopted as part of system reform because of the need for administrative support for training and norming and the construction of materials.

Class spelling tests and other drill materials can also be individually graphed to provide information on growth. The efficacy of these programs was demonstrated by Pavchinski, Evans, and Bostow (1989). Students participated in daily drills on math or reading. They were given tokens for correct answers within a set period of time, and made to engage in positive practice to correct incorrect responses. Students found the plan enjoyable and made good academic progress.

As child advocates, school psychologists need to consider the best interests of the whole child in program decisions. Placement in special education or retention directly influences self-concept via stigma and indirectly through the curriculum and social comparison. Feedback and positive reinforcers can be provided with CBM and home–school communication interventions. CBM and behavioral strategies can be incorporated into school restructuring.

Role of the School Psychologist in Program Evaluation

School psychologists have the training to assist schools in program evaluation. Program evaluation related to students' self-concepts includes the effectiveness and efficacy of special education, mainstreaming, cooperative learning, and curricula. Special education efficacy has been criticized and alternative service delivery models proposed, for example, team teaching of regular and special education students or the special education teacher coming into the regular education classroom to work with special education and other low-achieving students.

Mainstreaming/team teaching. When looking at where best to serve students in need of extra assistance, the school team might consider student preferences as well as program efficacy. Jenkins and Heinin (1989) and Wilson (1992) found students to prefer to leave the regular classroom to obtain extra help rather than have the special classroom teacher come into their classroom. Reasons included embarrassment, convenience for the teacher, and "like to leave the classroom." Other possible explanations for this unexpected result are attention from the special teacher and more familiarity with the pullout model than team-teaching. The school psychologist could encourage caution and data collection on children's preferences and self-concepts if changes are planned for instructional models. Research on alternative systems needs to consider how children feel about themselves in various settings. The following letter was printed in the May 1993 *Communiqué:*

Dear Mainstream Students:

We would like to share with you our experiences in special education. We would like to let you know what we like and do not like about being special ed. students. We hope that by giving you this information, you will understand us better.

These are some of the reasons why we like being special ed students:

1. Learning is geared to our pace.

2. Classroom sizes are smaller, so we get extra attention from the teachers.

3. Material is explained so that we understand it.

These are the disadvantages of being a special ed student:

1. Mainstream kids tease us, and

2. They make us feel badly about ourselves.

We hope this helps you understand us better and please know that we are not so different from you after all. (Betensky, 1993, p. 22)

While team teaching is a recent innovation, main-streaming of students with special needs into regular classrooms has sufficient history for several empirical studies on self-concept of students in regular and special classes who are learning disabled and mildly mentally disabled (Madden & Slavin, 1983; Meisels, 1986). Lower academic self-concepts have usually been found in the mainstreamed settings; no differences were reported for social domains. The psychological construct of social comparison probably accounts for these findings. Students with learning problems are making comparisons with other mildly disabled students in special education classrooms, but comparing to regular education students in mainstreamed classes. Research over the past decade suggests ways to ameliorate social comparison. MacIver (1987) found students who received frequent grades were less likely to engage in social comparison. Rosenholtz and Rosenholtz (1982) also found the students with individualized assignments were less able to compare and evaluate on the basis of social comparison, and thus most saw themselves as very competent.

Curriculum, grouping, grading, and reports are educational practices in which the school psychologist can work with the school personnel to evaluate which methods or strategies optimize both achievement and self-concept. When students are working in individualized curriculum with individualized goals, the ability or need to compare is mitigated and children feel good about their own successes and progress, without making classwide comparisons. We currently have the technology with curriculum-based measurement to provide more individualized programs for students and possibly eliminate the detrimental effects of social comparison in mainstreaming. Children are mainstreamed to learn together, not to compete. Cooperative learning is another technique that appears to be good for children.

Cooperative learning. According to Madden and Slavin (1983), mainstreamed students need maximum contact with nondisabled peers, prefer not to be identified or singled out, and do best in a noncompetitive atmosphere. Cooperative learning can provide all this.

Cooperative goal structures have been found by Johnson and Johnson (1986) to promote positive self-concepts. Students feel good because they are part of the success of the group. However, the group must be structured so lower achieving students can feel they are making a contribution. The positive peer evaluations found in cooperative settings are very influential in promoting self-esteem. Overall, cooperative learning environments are (mentally) healthier compared to competitive environments.

Mainstreaming students with learning difficulties into the regular education classroom poses threats to self-esteem, mostly due to the embarrassment of doing worse than peers and of needing extra help. These problems can be minimized if help from special teachers is provided to a number of students who need assistance, regardless of special education status. Secondly, individualized curricula diminish the need and ability to make comparisons. Cooperative learning enhances self-concept by allowing all students to contribute and receive positive feedback.

Opportunities for School Psychologists in Program Development

Epstein and Dauber (1991) encourage school psychologists to take on the role of mental health psychologist for the school. As part of that role, increased involvement with the emotional well-being of all students is implied. Development or implementation of new programs may be required to maximize ways to enhance student self-esteem. Examples could include peer tutoring, buddy systems, parent education, and community-school programs.

Peer programs. Self-concept is enhanced if students feel competent about something they are doing. Peer programs allow students to work within areas of strength and earn the satisfaction of being the teacher — the giver — instead of always the needy recipient. Peer tutoring programs offer advantages to tutor and tutee. The tutee learns with extra practice opportunities in a social environment. The tutor has a chance to shine and feel good about helping. For many children the best opportunities are working with younger children. They can read to them, work with flash cards, or show them how to play a game. Regardless of the task, it is very rewarding to be the teacher! Being a buddy for a mainstreamed student with more severe disabilities is another area where mildly disabled students can become leaders. They can facilitate social interactions and assist with routines; working with others is an excellent way to build self-confidence and skills.

Parent training. Psychologists can also develop parent training programs to help parents learn how to work with and support their children. Research indicates parents are more involved in elementary than middle schools, and in self-contained classrooms rather than departmental (Epstein & Dauber, 1991). Communication is the most prevalent type of activity; home-learning the least (Epstein & Dauber, 1991). Programs for parents can be implemented that allow for ongoing, meaningful participation of parents in the educational programs of their children. According to Cochran and Dean (1991), "empowerment is a process rather than an end state" (p. 262). Based on almost 3 years of research on a program of family support, they found parents' self-concepts improved as well as their relationships with others in the family. Some groups focused on improving the neighborhood; other parents got involved in their children's school. The emphasis of the home-visit program was that parents were the most important influence in their child's life, and children whose parents were involved in the program were doing better in first grade than a control group.

Teachers involved in home-school programs report increase self-efficacy, possibly due to the fact they are more highly rated by parents who participate in the programs. Increased communication serves to improve the self-concepts of both parties. School psychologists are in an excellent position to facilitate communication between teachers and parents through collaborative consultation. School psychologists can emphasize benefits to all from a coordinated program focusing on child strengths and needs.

To start a home-school program the partners in education need to envision their school of the future and determine a plan and practices. Research is necessary to evaluate the efficacy and worthiness of a program. The members need to be committed to listening to parental concerns and feelings as well as reviewing empirical evidence of support and change. Finally, a school-community program needs leadership and vision by those who do believe that all children can learn and that sharing the responsibility improves the odds of that happening.

Community programs. Student pride and self-concept is increased when their culture is endorsed by the system. Don Davies of Boston University (1991) described a demonstration project for school and community interactions called "Schools Reaching Out." Workable components included (a) a parent center; (b) home visitors, and (c) research teams of teachers. The parent center was a place for parents to meet in the school, participate in English-as-second-language (ESL), and General Education Development (GED) classes, organize volunteer activities for both working in school classes and assisting other parents in need of social or health services. The parent center

was staffed by two paid parent coordinators and equipped with a telephone and a coffee pot.

Most parents want their children to do well in school but may not have skills to assist them with their learning or in managing their behavior. The home visitors were recruited from the community and trained to provide information, materials, and support. They each visited four to five families per week and were paid $10 per hour. Davies suggests Chapter I money as one source of funding and that training for the visitors might be provided by local universities (school psychology program trainers?).

An old African saying points out the shared responsibility schools, families, and community agencies have for raising children: "The whole village educates the child." Schools and children in rural communities often benefit from enormous community; the school is viewed as the social center of the town and school activities as vital events. Students bask in the care, concern, and encouragement of many members of the community outside their immediate or extended families. These are people who offer congratulations and summer jobs; who pitch in when a family suffers a crisis and let the members know they are important; and who provide comprehensive monitoring of the behavior of the town's young people, often to their dismay. Urban families battling poverty, unemployment, and language barriers particularly need the support of their communities. Schools, parents, students, and community agencies and businesses can work together to set up programs to prevent drugs and dropping out. Self-concept is improved both by knowing someone cares and by participating in positive actions.

Similarly, just as younger students can achieve an enhanced self-image by helping others through peer tutoring programs, secondary students involved in community service programs such as cleaning up graffiti or volunteering as a candystriper or in a nursing home have the satisfaction of providing meaningful service. Psychologists can provide a mental health perspective: Activities of this type not only develop skills and provide needed services, but through sharing students grow in self-respect.

Psychologists and counselors working in secondary settings can assist schools in finding local employment training positions for students in vocational programs, including lower achieving and special education students. Self-efficacy is based on prior achievements; what better personal predictor for future success than mastering the technical and interpersonal skills necessary to hold a workability job.

SUMMARY

Although school psychologists are mental health practitioners, most of school psychology work has focused on assessment and promotion of academic and social skills. This chapter discusses school psychology services and system influences from the perspective of student self-concept. Practices frequently engaged in, placement in special education and readiness/retention decisions, have grave implications for self-concept. School psychologists are in a position to advise multidisciplinary teams of research findings regarding short- and long-term effects of these practices on the child's academic progress and emotional well being.

Within the school system traditional methods of grouping and curriculum also influence how students perceive themselves. Program evaluation should include social-emotional, as well as academic, outcomes. Alternative service delivery systems, for example mainstreaming and team teaching, have also been found to be detrimental to student self-concept under certain conditions. Individualized curriculum and cooperative learning were suggested as two system-level reforms to reduce social comparison and increase self-concept.

Parents are also recognized as powerful influences on children's self-concepts. Parents can work with school personnel (a) to help their children improve their performance and thereby earn more internal and external positive feedback and (b) to provide recognition and reinforcement for achievement. Finally, communities can have an important role in supporting families. Through volunteer and service programs, students can increase prevocational skills, provide services to those in need, and learn responsibility and self-respect. Most of the activities, programs, and practices presented in this chapter are normally utilized to increase academic skills and that may be a sufficient reason to implement a program. However, competencies will be most wisely and energetically used by confident, mentally healthy children and adults. School psychologists should lead the development of practices to enhance the self-concept of the students with whom they work.

REFERENCES

Aberbach, A. J., & Lynch, S. (1991, April). *When getting help is helpful: Gender and grade differences in children's autonomous help-seeking.* Paper presented at the biennial meeting of the Society for Research in Child Development, Seattle, WA.

Bachman, J. G., & O'Malley, P. M. (1986). Self-concepts, self-esteem, and educational experiences: The frog pond revisited (again). *Journal of Personality and Social Psychology, 50,* 35–46.

Bandura, A. (1986). *Social foundations of thought and actions: A social cognitive theory.* Englewood Cliffs, NJ: Prentice-Hall, Inc.

Bear, G. G., Clever, A., & Proctor, W. A. (1991). Self-concepts of nonhandicapped children and children with learning disabilities in integrated classes. *The Journal of Special Education, 24,* 409–426.

Betensky, K. (1993). Dear mainstream students: An open letter from special education students to their counterparts in the mainstream. *Communiqué, 21,* 22.

Brophy, J. (1983). Research on self-fulfilling prophecy and teacher expectations. *Journal of Educational Psychology, 75,* 631–661.

Christenson, S. L., & Conoley, J. C. (Eds.). (1992). Home-school collaboration: Enhancing children's academic and social competence. Silver Spring, MD: The National Association of School Psychologists.

Cochran, M., & Dean, C. (1991). Home-school relations and the empowerment process. *The Elementary School Journal, 91,* 261–269.

Davies, D. (1991). Schools reaching out: Family, school, and community partnerships for student success. *Phi Delta Kappan,* 376–382.

Dawson, M., Raforth, M. A., & Carey, K. (1990). Best practices in assisting with promotion and retention decisions. In A. Thomas & J. Grimes (Eds.), *Best practices in school psychology–II* (pp. 137–146). Washington, DC: National Association of School Psychologists.

Dunst, C. J., & Trivette, C. M. (1987). Enabling and empowering families: Conceptual and intervention issues. *School Psychology Review, 16,* 443–456.

Dweck, C. S., & Bempechat, J. (1983). Children's theories of intelligence: Consequences for learning. In S. G. Paris, G. M. Olson, & H. W. Stevenson (Eds.), *Learning and motivation in the classroom* (pp. 239–257). Hillsdale, NJ: Lawrence Erlbaum.

Dweck, C. S., & Elliott, E. S. (1983). Achievement motivation. In P. H. Mussen (Ed.), *Handbook of child psychology: Socialization, personality, and social development: Vol. 3* (pp. 643–691). New York: Wiley.

Epstein, J. L., & Dauber, S. L. (1991). School programs and teacher practices of parent involvement in inner-city elementary and middle schools. *The Elementary School Journal, 91,* 289–305.

Festinger, L. (1954). A theory of social comparison processes. *Human Relations, 7,* 11–16.

Frey, K. S., & Ruble, D. N. (1985). What children say when the teacher is not around: Conflicting goals in social comparison and performance assessment in the classroom. *Journal of Personality and Social Psychology, 48,* 550–562.

Fuchs, L. S. (1986). Monitoring progress among mildly handicapped pupils: Review of current practice and research. *Remedial and Special Education, 7,* 5–12.

Harter, S. (1983). Developmental perspectives on self-esteem. In P. H. Mussen (Ed.), *Handbook of child psychology: Socialization, personality, and social development: Vol. 3* (pp. 136–182). New York: Wiley.

Hobbs, N. (1975). *The futures of children.* San Francisco: Jossey-Bass.

Holmes, C. T., & Matthews, K. M. (1984). The effects of non-promotion on elementary and junior high school pupils: A meta-analysis. *Review of Educational Research, 45,* 225–236.

Jenkins, J. R., & Heinen, A. (1989). Students' preferences for service delivery: Pull-out, in-class, or integrated models. *Exceptional Children, 55,* 516–523.

Johnson, D., & Johnson, R. (1986). Mainstreaming and cooperative learning strategies. *Exceptional Children, 47,* 90–98.

Kelley, M. L. (1990). *School-home notes: Promoting children's classroom success.* New York: Guilford Press.

Kulik, C. C., & Kulik, J. A. (1991). Ability grouping and gifted students. In N. Colangelo & G. A. Davis (Eds.), *Handbook of gifted education* (pp. 178–196). Boston: Allyn and Bacon.

MacIver, D. (1987). Classroom factors and students' characteristics predicting students' use of achievement standards during ability self-assessment. *Child Development, 58*, 1258–1271.

Madden, N., & Slavin, R. E. (1983). Mainstreaming students with mild handicaps: Academic and social outcomes. *Review of Educational Research, 53*, 519–569.

Meisel, C. J. (1986). *Mainstreaming handicapped children: Outcomes, controversies, and new directions.* Hillsdale, NJ: Lawrence Erlbaum.

National Association of School Psychologists. (1988). Position statement on retention. *Communiqué, 16*, insert.

National Association of School Psychologists. (1993). Position statement on ability grouping. *Communiqué, 21*, insert.

Nicholls, J. (1984). *Advances in motivation and achievement: The development of achievement motivation* (Vol. 3). London: JAI Press.

Pavchinski, P., Evans, J. H., & Bostow, D. E. (1989). Increasing word recognition and math ability in a severely learning-disabled student with token reinforcers. *Psychology in the Schools, 26*, 397–411.

Peterson, C. (1992). Learned helplessness and school problems. In F. J. Medway & T. P. Cafferty (Eds.), *School psychology: A social psychological perspective* (pp. 359–376). Hillsdale, NJ: Lawrence Erlbaum.

Prasse, D. P., & Reschly, D. J. (1986). Larry P: A case of segregation, testing of program efficacy. *Exceptional Children, 52*, 333–346.

Renick, M. J., & Harter, S. (1989). Influence of social comparisons on the developing self-concepts of learning disabled students. *Journal of Educational Psychology, 81*, 631–638.

Rosenholtz, S. J., & Rosenholtz, S. H. (1981). Classroom organization and the concept of ability. *Sociology of Education, 54*, 132–140.

Schunk, D. (1983). Developing children's self-efficacy and skills: The roles of social comparative information and goal setting. *Contemporary Educational Psychology, 8*, 76–88.

Schunk, D. H. (1985). Self-efficacy and classroom learning. *Psychology in the Schools, 22*, 208–223.

Shapiro, E. (1989). *Academic skills problems: Direct assessment and intervention.* New York: Guilford.

Shinn, M. R. (Ed.). (1988). *Curriculum-based measurement and special services for children.* New York: Guilford.

Smith, M. L., & Shepard, L. A. (1989). *Flunking grades: Research and policies on retention.* New York: Falmer Press.

Stevenson, H. W., & Lee, S. (1990). Contexts of achievement. *Monographs of the Society for Research in Child Development, 55*, Nos. 1–2.

Stipek, D. J. (1988). *Motivation to learn: From theory to practice.* Englewood Cliffs, NJ: Prentice-Hall.

Stipek, D. J., & Daniels, D. H. (1988). Declining concepts of competence: A consequence of changes in the child or in the educational environment? *Journal of Educational Psychology, 80*, 352–356.

Wilson, M. S. (1992). *Children's academic self-concepts: The influences of social comparison and classroom setting.* Unpublished doctoral dissertation, Iowa State University, Ames.

ANNOTATED BIBLIOGRAPHY

Christenson, S. L., & Conoley, J. C. (Eds.). (1992). *Home-school collaboration: Enhancing children's academic and social competence.* Silver Spring, MD: National Association of School Psychologists.
This edited book describes a number of successful home-school programs dealing with problems from involvement with parents of preschoolers, increasing homework completion to working with students from substance-abusing families. Barriers to home-school collaborations are addressed and solutions proposed.

Boggiano, A. K., & Pittman, T. S. (Eds.). (1992). *Achievement and motivation: A social-developmental perspective.* Cambridge, England: Cambridge University Press.
This text is a compilation of recent research on motivation and achievement in educational settings. The second section of the book deals with the relationship between motivation and perceived competence. Developmental and systems influences are addressed.

Covington, M. V. (1992). *Making the grade: A self-worth perspective on motivation and school reform.* Cambridge, England: Cambridge University Press.
The author links theory on achievement motivation to educational restructuring. The high drop-out rate and other social ills are attributed to failure in school. Solutions which could be implemented in the near future are suggested.

Meisel, C. J. (1986). *Mainstreaming handicapped children: Outcomes, controversies, and new directions.* Hillsdale, NJ: Lawrence Erlbaum.
This book provides excellent coverage of cooperative learning, social comparison, and efficacy of special education. The chapters are reviews of the literature and would provide a strong base from which to argue for consideration of social competence, as well as academic, outcomes in school program evaluations and decisions.

Turnbull, A. P., & Turnbull, H. R. (1986). *Families, professionals and exceptionality: A special partnership.* Columbus, OH: Merrill Publishing.

Seligman, M., & Darling, R. B. (1989). *Ordinary families, special children.* New York: Guilford Press.
These books address assessing family needs and mobilizing family resources and strengths. Self-concepts of both parents and their children with and without disabilities are discussed. These books provide various members of a multidisciplinary team with possible perspectives of the family members.

Zins, J. E., Curtis, M. J., & Ponti, C. R. (1988). *Helping students succeed in the regular classroom.* San Francisco: Jossey-Bass.
The use of consultation to design and implement interventions necessary for students with learning and/or behavior problems to survive and achieve in the regular classroom is covered in this book. These changes are viewed as systems-level interventions.

33

Best Practices in Substance Abuse Prevention Programs

Kathleen M. McNamara
Cleveland State University

OVERVIEW

The Need for School-Based Prevention Programs

The problem of alcohol and other drug (AOD) use among American youth is illustrated by results of The National Household Survey on Drug Abuse conducted by the National Institute on Drug Abuse (NIDA). This 1990 survey found that 48% of youth aged 12 to 17 had used alcohol, with 41% reporting use in the previous year and nearly one-quarter reporting use in the previous month (NIDA, 1990). Experience with illicit drug use was reported by 22.7% of this group.

According to NIDA's National High School Senior Drug Use Survey conducted in 1990, 47% of participating seniors reported past use of one or more illicit drugs, while 80.6% reported past use of alcohol (NIDA, 1991). Almost one-third of participating seniors reported having five or more drinks during a single drinking occasion within the preceding 2 weeks!

These statistics reflect only part of the problem, however, because the measures were limited by the voluntary and self-report nature of surveys. In addition, school dropouts and absentees, who are likely to be more heavily involved in AOD use, were not even represented in the National High School Senior Drug Use Survey.

The anti-drug-and-alcohol-abuse efforts spearheaded in recent years by federal, state, community, and private agencies have had a positive impact on this problem. However, although the nature of abused substances and patterns of use have changed among certain groups in the past decade, overall levels of AOD use and abuse are still unacceptably high, particularly among the youth served in our nation's schools.

Title V of the Elementary and Secondary Education Act (1988) fostered widespread acceptance of the notion that schools are an appropriate forum for prevention and intervention efforts. In addition to their role as a primary vehicle for transmitting academic, vocational, and civic knowledge and skills, schools have assumed increasingly greater responsibility for addressing a variety of problem behaviors and social concerns. In discussing preventive programming in schools, Milgram and Griffin observed that "the role of the school . . . is not a choice of action or inaction, but rather a choice of acting purposefully and systematically, or sporadically and inconsistently" (1986, p. 16). Clearly, schools have significant potential for impact on the AOD problem because they not only afford ready access to educational resources and expertise but also house the population requiring accurate information and guidance in making choices about use.

This chapter offers a model for comprehensive school-based prevention programs based on consideration of four principal prevention methods as applied to three distinct audiences in the school population.

Prevention Programs: Methods and Audiences

Alcohol and other drug abuse prevention may be viewed as comprising a matrix of four methods, each directed toward three audiences in the school population.

School *policy* initiatives are reflected in written documents developed by or for local education agencies, setting forth a statement of philosophy about AOD use, supported by a set of rules, administrative procedures, and consequences for rule violations. Policies often include a description of the school's comprehensive program for AOD prevention and intervention activities.

The second method, *education*, is prominent in school programs, particularly since the passage of Title V of the Elementary and Secondary Education Act (1988). The method of education includes the dissemination of information about the harmful effects of AOD use as well as instruction in skills promoting social competence, especially resistance to cultural pressure to use alcohol and other drugs. Education also includes awareness campaigns, such as the National Red Ribbon Celebration, which solicits broadly-based support for drug-free lifestyles.

The method of *alternatives* encourages students to engage in activities incompatible with AOD use. Commonly, schools offer open gym nights or sponsor alcohol- and drug-free prom and graduation activities. In recent years, the method of alternatives has been expanded to include efforts to promote "positive peer culture" and methods to engage students in schools as a protective force against AOD use.

Finally, *intervention, treatment, and support* methods, as implemented in schools, consist of preliminary identification, assessment, and referral of students whose behavior places them at risk for involvement with alcohol and other drugs. These methods also include support groups for at-risk students as well as those recovering from diagnosed AOD dependency.

Audiences for Prevention Programs

It is helpful to regard a school's student population in terms of three audiences, each reflecting a level of prevention. The *primary prevention* audience consists of those who have not yet used alcohol or other drugs. For this audience, prevention activities are designed to "either reduce the rate of occurrence or a particular problem, or strengthen the well-being of the individuals in the population as a form of inoculation against the causes of subsequent problems" (Pianta, 1990, p. 306–307).

The *secondary prevention* audience consists of students who are at high risk for AOD use. Secondary prevention activities are designed to interrupt, minimize, or protect against the influence of these risk factors, with the goal of reducing the likelihood of AOD involvement.

Finally, the *tertiary prevention* audience consists of those who have already engaged in AOD use. Experience in the schools shows substantial diversity in this audience, ranging from students whose use is experimental in nature, through those with regular patterns of use, to those whose use is of a dependent or addictive nature. The last group is further subdivided into those whose addiction has not yet been identified or treated and those who are in the process of recovery from addiction. The purpose of tertiary prevention is to reduce the adverse consequences of any level of AOD use through appropriate intervention and treatment activities.

Prevention methods are most effective when there is an appropriate "fit" between their message and the characteristics of their audiences in the school population. While an awareness campaign may be helpful in reducing the incidence of early first use of alcohol and other drugs, it is not likely to have an impact on students who are already engaged in regular use. Similarly, an educational program which features the testimony of a young adult or successful athlete recovering from addiction is not likely to address the needs of students who have never used drugs (and may, in fact, inadvertently promote such use) — although it may be effective with students who have entered a dangerous phase of regular use.

BASIC CONSIDERATIONS

A research-literature base for AOD prevention efforts that can serve as a resource for program design has only recently begun to develop. Throughout the 1980s, and particularly with the passage of the Drug Free Schools and Communities Act of 1986, schools were inundated with promotional literature for AOD prevention curricula and training programs. Recognizing the need to address the growing problem of AOD use, schools adopted programs despite a lack of validation of their effectiveness in actually reducing and eliminating AOD use. Programs commonly lacked an adequate evaluation component or failed to evaluate AOD use as a specific outcome measure. At present, in part because of funding provisions that specify program components and evaluation, the prevention field is undergoing a period of transformation. While the research has not yet yielded conclusive data to form guidelines for program design, there is a growing knowledge base which should serve as the basis for prevention efforts.

This knowledge base provides information about circumstances, characteristics, and events that place youth at greater risk for AOD involvement as well as those that appear to exert a protective influence. School-based programs seek to reduce or mitigate risk, while promoting protection, through activities with demonstrated potential for effectiveness. This section explores this knowledge base, considering research findings on risk, protection, and program effectiveness.

Knowledge Base: Audiences for Prevention Programs

Traditionally, school-based prevention programs have focused on the variable of AOD use or non-use. Policy, education, alternatives, and intervention activities were narrowly focused on the goal of reducing and eliminating use among adolescents.

In recent years, however, research has demonstrated that experimental AOD use, while undesirable, may nevertheless represent an aspect of normative adolescent development (Shedler & Block, 1990). In addition, research has increasingly focused on factors (identifiable in the early school years) associated with increased *risk* for AOD use as well as factors associated with a decreased likelihood of use. Very recently, researchers have also identified differences in factors contributing to levels of use, observing that factors contributing to initial and experimental use differ from those associated with escalations in use.

Risk factors. Research on factors associated with the initiation of AOD use has yielded extensive support for a number of correlates, including easy availability of illicit substances, disadvantaged socioeconomic status, lack of religious commitment, poor school performance, rebelliousness and lack of conformity with laws and norms, perceived adult drug use, low self-esteem, impulsivity, sensation-seeking, many deviant behaviors, poor and inconsistent family management practices, association with drug-using peers, and low commitment to school (Clayton, 1992; Newcomb & Felix-Ortiz, 1992). These factors place students at risk by creating a state of vulnerability or susceptibility to AOD use.

Glantz (1992), summarizing longitudinal research studies on risk, notes that, at age 7, future frequent AOD users were "unable to form good relationships, were insecure with evidence of low self-esteem, manifested numerous signs of emotional distress, which they denied, and had poor coping, adapting, and interpersonal problem solving skills" (p. 408). In late childhood, these characteristics were exacerbated, expressing themselves in poor school achievement and peer group integration, maladaptive problem solving and coping skills, affiliation with deviant peer groups, and proneness to behavior problems. Family problems and stresses, in addition to parent or sibling models of drug use, take on increased salience.

Austin (1992) argues for the importance of school failure factors as common precursors or antecedents of the initiation and escalation of AOD use. In reviewing research on correlates of AOD use, he observes that, while school failure factors do not have as strong or as direct an influence in AOD use as peer associations, they are often embedded in a developmental history characterized by disengagement and the adoption of unconventional behaviors. Patterns of school failure can be identified as early as second grade; Slavin and Madden (1987) note that, by fifth grade, many students are caught up in a permanent cycle of falling behind and remediation. Summarizing the relationship between school failure and AOD use, Austin concludes that "youth who are failing at school by mid-adolescence, and facing a bleak future, are likely to see little reason why they shouldn't use drugs and to have little motivation to resist pro-use messages" (1992, p. 25).

Glantz notes that high-risk children are less likely to be influenced by protective factors, and, because they have been unsuccessful in developing adequate coping skills and strategies, these skills are "generally less available in (their) repertoire even if the maladaptive ones are successfully discouraged from use" (1992, p. 409). As a result, vulnerability to AOD abuse is often well-established by the onset of adolescence. Recent research has demonstrated that factors associated with initiation differ substantially from those associated with escalation of use. Survey data indicate a high prevalence of experimental AOD use among students. Therefore, the nature of factors promoting *escalation* of AOD use requires special attention. It is important to identify and intervene on those factors associated with escalation.

For example, individuals whose initial AOD use results in negative social sanctions tend to escalate use. Those who label AOD use as deviant are also more likely to escalate levels of use. Males whose initial AOD use arises from a motivation to express anger or increase potency are likely to escalate use, as are females whose AOD use is intended to cope with disrupted relationships (Kaplan & Johnson, 1992). These findings, some of which contradict commonsense notions of the motives underlying AOD use, represent critical information for programs addressing the needs of the tertiary prevention audience.

Some risk factors, such as academic failure, are amenable to direct intervention efforts. Others, including environmental circumstances, are not amenable to direct intervention. For the latter group, intervention efforts generally focus on the introduction of protective factors to buffer the influence of the risk factor, thereby reducing the likelihood that it will lead to AOD use or abuse (Clayton, 1992).

Protective factors. Relative to research on risk factors, the literature on factors that protect against AOD use is sparse and inconclusive. McIntyre, White, and Yoast (1990) observe that "among the researchers using a risk paradigm, protection against substance abuse is greatly overshadowed by the clamor to identify risk factors. And when protective factors are discussed, it is often with the assumption that they are the opposite of risk factors, hardly a sophisticated analysis, and perhaps even wrong" (p. 23). The authors further caution against confusing protective factors and interventions, noting that laws and sanctions, which may reduce AOD use, represent interventions, not protective factors. They also note that a factor which is protective against problems in some behavioral domains may create risk in other domains.

Research has failed to demonstrate a conclusive relationship between academic failure or success and later AOD use. However, Austin (1992) noted that, while academic problems in the early years of school may not be predictive of later AOD use in the general student population, "school success may play an important protective role among those youth who are *otherwise at high risk* for AOD abuse" (p, 19, emphasis added). Furthermore, the potency of academic success as a *mitigator* of early risk factors demonstrates that the negative impact of risk factors can be ameliorated by protective factors emerging later in the child's experience. It is, therefore, essential to approach the emerging literature on protective factors with an appreciation for their complexity.

Protective factors include individual attributes or characteristics, as well as situational or environmental conditions that inhibit, reduce, or buffer the probability of AOD use or escalation of use. Their protective influence is often observed in interactions among several factors. For example, Brook, Cohen, Whiteman, and Gordon (1992) demonstrated that low childhood aggression, interacting with low peer deviance and low peer illegal AOD use, yields conditions which are protective in nature. The role of protective factors in discouraging AOD use is by no means clear. Other research demonstrates that certain factors, such as school success, may play a protective role for students who are otherwise at high risk, although they may not have a significant role as a predictor of abstinence in the general student population (Austin, 1992).

Attachment with significant adults (particularly parents), expressed in support, communication, responsiveness, affection, and identification with the adult, serves as a deterrent to AOD use (Brook, Brook, Gordon, Whiteman, & Cohen, 1990). Other protective factors identified by research include high levels of educational aspiration, high grade point average, low depression, high religiosity, internal locus of control, personal and social competence, high self-acceptance, effective coping skills, autonomy, positive social bonding with institutions, accurate perception of peers' AOD use, commitment to conventional societal norms, and high law abidance. Ecological conditions that deter use, and are therefore often viewed as protective in nature, include communicated and enforced family norms regarding AOD use, effective family management skills and greater family cohesion and intactness, parental disapproval of alcohol and other drugs, discouragement of AOD use by the community, low availability of illicit substances, and the presence of sanctions against use (McIntyre et al., 1990; Newcomb, 1992; Newcomb & Felix-Ortiz, 1992).

Knowledge Base: Effective Programs

Several sources have described common approaches to AOD prevention during the past two decades. *Information-dissemination* approaches convey information about alcohol and other drugs, including their harmful effects. Fear-arousal messages, moralizing, and objective information-giving are included under this category. Anderson (1988) described fear-arousal messages as ineffective because the everyday experiences of their audience (students) failed to support their veracity: "The mere use of drugs did not lead to the problems their elders predicted" (p. 2). Anderson further noted that objective information-giving sometimes had an unforeseen effect: It reduced many students' anxiety about using by providing accurate information about alcohol and other drugs, thereby increasing use levels; further, it was based on false assumptions: "that drug use is primarily a cognitively-based phenomenon, that kids use drugs because they don't know something, and that cognitive knowledge alone is preventive" (p. 3). Despite their intuitive appeal, information-dissemination approaches have been found to have little or no impact on actual or intended AOD use among students (Botvin & Dusenberry, 1989).

A second major AOD prevention approach is *affective education*, which emerged in the 1970s as a result of research showing correlations between drug use and social competencies. Without directly addressing the topic of AOD use, affective education programs focused on interpersonal and intrapersonal competence and environmental responsiveness to the emotional, social, and cognitive needs of children. Austin (1992), reviewing research on the effectiveness of affective education programs, concluded that "these programs did not result in any meaningful reductions in use and in some cases may have contributed to increasing it" (p. 26).

It has been hypothesized that the failure of affective education as an effective AOD prevention strategy lies in the absence of a clear focus in such programs, inadequacy in the number and frequency of interventions, and application of inappropriate methods for fostering skill acquisition among students (Austin, 1992; Botvin & Dusenberry, 1989).

In response to these criticisms, a third category of preventive programs evolved, aimed at the development of social competence through *skill-training*. Early versions of this approach were designed to "increase students' awareness of the various social influences to engage in substance use along with specific resistance skills for effectively coping with these negative influences" (Botvin & Dusenberry, 1989). Students are taught to recognize and respond to high-risk situations with refusal techniques. A key feature of these programs is their emphasis on specific skills, taught through modeling, rehearsal, and reinforcement. The Prepare Curriculum (Goldstein, 1988) and Skillstreaming approach (Goldstein, Sprafkin, Gershaw, & Klein, 1980; McGinnis & Goldstein, 1984) provide examples of skill-training models that have been applied in AOD prevention programs. Project SMART, or Self Management and Resistance Training (Hansen et al., 1988) uses peer leaders to teach students methods to resist pressures to use alcohol and other drugs, providing opportunities for modeling and practice of skills. It emphasizes intervention on external factors, such as peer and media pressure, negative parental influences, and normative expectations.

Other versions of the skill-training approach are more comprehensive in nature. The Life Skills Training program developed by Gilbert Botvin (1989; 1990), for example, incorporates an AOD-specific component (information on AOD use and abuse, social pressures to use, and techniques for resisting pressures to use), a personal skills component (building critical-thinking, decision-making, and anxiety-reduction skills), and a social skills component (communication, assertiveness, and relationship skills). The Life Skills Training curriculum has three levels which are generally offered in successive years to young adolescents. Project STAR (Student Taught Awareness and Resistance) is an example of a comprehensive, community-based program, representing a collaborative effort between researchers and the community (Pentz, Cormack, Flay, Hansen, & Johnson, 1986). This program, incorporating direct training of youth in resistance skills; training of teachers, parents, and other implementors; and ongoing support for youth and program implementors, serves as a model for uniting school, family, media, and community organizations in skill training and support activities.

Summarizing research on competence-building programs, McIntyre, White, and Yoast (1990) note that they hold promise for enhancing AOD protective factors but have been used primarily with white, middle-class audiences in grades six through nine and been the subject of only limited longitudinal studies of program impact beyond immediate and short-term effects.

Austin (1992) cited the most persistent criticism of programs as their failure to address the needs of high-risk youth. "This lack of success if rooted, in part, to the failure of past prevention and intervention efforts to impact on relevant risk factors and to address specific subgroup needs" (p. 25). Even programs that promote skills to resist peer and other social pressures to initiate use may overlook the need to interrupt the developmental sequence that is determined by, and results from, the influence and interplay of a host of risk factors. This position has led to a final phase of AOD prevention programs.

Contemporary approaches incorporate intervention at the individual, family, and environmental levels, with concomitant awareness of the different goals and tasks involved in primary, secondary, and tertiary prevention. The Interpersonal Relations strategy devised by Eggert, Seyl, and Nicholas (1990) is an example of a program in which high-risk students benefit from teacher modeling and structured peer group support to increase bonding to prosocial peer groups; strengthen commitment to the school and conventional norms of success; and reinforce AOD abstinence while teaching and remediating academic and social skills. Vorrath and Brendtro (1985) describe an approach for high-risk students that fosters bonding to a peer group whose purpose is to teach and practice problem-solving and coping skills.

The School Psychologist's Contributions

Apart from familiarity with the specialized AOD prevention knowledge base just outlined, school psychologists possess many of the skills required for program design and implementation. Following is a de-

scription of some of the areas in which school psychologists can offer expertise.

Needs assessment. School psychologists offer expertise in the assessment of needs for AOD prevention programs. A combination of methods, including surveys and interviews, can be used to learn the extent of the AOD problem in a school system and to develop specific target areas for prevention activities. Secondary benefits of needs assessment include the promotion of a common understanding of the problem; refutation of denial by community members, parents, and educators; and the establishment of a baseline for comparison following the implementation of programs.

Student surveys of AOD use should assess attitudes, perceptions, and risk factors in addition to information about AOD-use patterns and prevalence. Focus groups are recommended as an inexpensive and motivating format for collecting data from students and parents. Key informant surveys, or structured interviews with school and community experts, can provide information about resources and services.

Existing data can be gathered from school records (discipline referrals, expulsions and suspensions, attendance) and community agencies (law enforcement and treatment providers). Data available from community agencies include juvenile alcohol and drug arrests, juvenile drunk driving arrests, deaths caused by drugs or alcohol, hospital emergency room overdose admissions, and juvenile admissions to drug or alcohol treatment programs.

The results of a needs assessment are used to develop problem statements, citing prevalence data, student attitudes, and the prevalence and impact of identified risk factors. School psychologists can serve as a resource in this process by assisting with assessment design, data collection, and compilation and analysis of assessment results.

Comprehensive program planning. School psychologists can serve as key members of teams collecting data and analyzing assessment results, offering expertise in the development of long- and short-term goals, objectives, activities to meet objectives, and resources (personnel, time, space, equipment, and materials). In planning programs, each of the four methods described earlier should be considered (policy, education, alternatives, ad intervention/treatment/support) for each of three audiences in the school population (primary, secondary, and tertiary prevention).

Curriculum design. School psychologists can assist in curriculum selection, implementation, and evaluation by focusing attention on the need for developmentally sequenced programs which offer flexibility and adaptability to different teaching and learning styles, and by assisting in evaluating the success of curricula in meeting instructional goals.

Collaboration. Models for AOD prevention planning cite a team approach as the most effective and desirable vehicle for program design and implementation. Teams of parents, community representatives, educators, and students have been effective in designing prevention programs. Team models are also employed in the delivery of services by school personnel. School psychologists can serve as important team members, contributing expertise in team building, goal setting, intervention planning, interpersonal communication skills, problem-solving techniques, group process, and facilitating cooperation with team efforts by members of the school community.

Training. An effective AOD-prevention program requires training of school personnel, parents, and students themselves. School administrators, faculty, and staff require training to help them understand and identify risk factors, apply concepts of "protection" at every level of prevention, and intervene on problems in an effective manner. Parents require training in skills to enhance family management and develop effective support networks. Students involved in positive peer programs and student leadership groups require training in team-building and strategies to promote positive peer influence. School psychologists can serve as trainers, facilitators of skill and support groups, and links to training resources in the community.

Early identification. School psychologists bring a wealth of skill to the task of identifying students who are at risk for AOD involvement before the impact of risk factors becomes debilitating. Patterns of early school failure, rebelliousness, lack of commitment to school, deficits in interpersonal skills, behavior problems, and association with deviant peer groups can be identified as precursors to AOD involvement.

Intervention. Strategies for intervening on the circumstances or behavior of high-risk students address a range of personal and environmental factors. Traditional AOD intervention programs focused on tertiary prevention, in which efforts were made to interrupt the development of harmful
patterns of use. With growing understanding of the role of risk and protective factors, intervention efforts are now directed toward the amelioration of conditions creating *vulnerability* to AOD use, including academic failure, peer rejection, and poor coping skills. Intervention seeks to inhibit, reduce, or buffer the effects of risk factors by promoting skill development and creating an environment in which students can embrace normative values and behaviors such as school achievement, personal and social competence, and identification with positive role models and peer groups. School psychologists offer expertise in devis-

ing, implementing, and evaluating the impact of interventions.

Evaluation. The value of school-based AOD-prevention programs can be demonstrated through on-going evaluation activities. Summative evaluation, which describes program activities, participation levels, and the expenditure of resources, provides an overview of the prevention program itself. Impact or outcome evaluation, on the other hand, is oriented toward the measurement of the effectiveness of activities in meeting program goals.

School psychologists can participate in both forms of evaluation by helping to identify indicators of program *scope*, including number of student participants in programs, background characteristics of participants, activities included in the program, frequency and duration of activities, number of school staff and community members involved in programs, and resources allocated to programs. Indicators of program *impact* include data reflecting student knowledge and attitudes about AOD use; prevalence of use; feedback from students, teachers, and parents on program effects; student attitudes toward school and learning; student achievement; school climate; attendance; and disciplinary referrals related to AOD use.

Evaluation data can be collected through questionnaires and interviews, observations, and review of documents such as attendance and disciplinary records. With extensive training in data collection and measurement of behavior change, school psychologists should play a key role in evaluating the scope and effectiveness of AOD-prevention programs.

BEST PRACTICES

Recommended Program Components: Methods X Audiences

Comprehensive AOD-prevention programs consist of the following components:

- A system in which student behavior is monitored on a continuous basis by every member of the school staff, and which provides for prompt and effective action when student performance, characteristics, or circumstances (risk factors) signal the need for intervention.

- A coordinated plan for providing services to troubled and at-risk students, utilizing resources available in the school itself or in the community. Services are not limited to students known to be troubled by alcohol or other drug-related problems; rather, a "broad brush" program, addressing a range of problems and risk factors, is recommended.

- School curricula, activities, and climate which clearly and consistently support and convey a "no-

TABLE 1

Comprehensive School-Based Prevention Programs

AUDIENCES	METHODS			
	Policy	*Education*	*Alternatives*	*Intervention, Treatment/Support*

Primary Prevention	• Rationale for deterrence
	  - Sanctions against AOD use
	  - Reduced AOD availability
		• Awareness of consequences of AOD use
		• Skills to resist negative influence
		• Effective coping skills
			• Foster protective factors
			  - Bonding to school
			  - Positive peer affiliations
			  - Accurate perceptions of AOD use
				• Continuous monitoring of behavior and school performance
				• Abstinence support groups
				• Parents: Family management skills

Secondary Prevention	• Rationale for risk focus
	  - Early identification procedures
	  - Risk intervention procedures
		• Intensive focus
		  - Resistance skills
		  - Coping with stressors
		• Arrest school failure trend
			• Strengthen protective factors
			  - Relationships with caring adults
			  - Opportunities for responsible behavior
			  - Positive peer affiliations
			  - Foster school success
				• Early identification activities
				• Academic, behavioral, and social remediation
				• Issue focused groups
				• Concerned persons groups
				• Parents: Problem-solving, limit-setting, and communication skills

Tertiary Prevention	• Rationale for recovery focus
	  - Interruption of AOD use patterns
	  - Recovery support
	  - Abstinence enforcement
		• Skills to achieve and maintain abstinence
		• Skills for coping with personal distress
			• Serve "reclaiming" function
			  - Establish/restore positive peer and adult affiliations
			  - Provide AOD-free activities
				• Interventions and referral for services
				• Insight groups
				• Abstinence (recovery support groups)
				• Parents: Linkage with community resources and support networks

use" message and provide students with opportunities, experiences, and skills that afford protection against AOD involvement.

These components are reflected in the methods of policy, education, alternatives, and intervention/treatment/support, with varying emphases and content for the three prevention audiences in school populations (see Table 1).

Policy. The AOD Policy adopted by a school system should reflect goals developed on the basis of a preliminary needs assessment. It is recommended that policies reflect a broad emphasis on AOD prevention, coupled with specific regulations and procedures that clearly indicate that AOD use or sales (by students and school personnel) will not be tolerated. Policy should be preceded by a statement of philosophy which clearly conveys the school system's beliefs and values regarding the nature of AOD problems; the emphasis on prevention, risk, early intervention, and protection in the school's comprehensive AOD program; and the role of the school in helping students to resolve problems associated with AOD use.

School policy is most effective when it is developed, promoted, publicized, and enforced in commu-nity-based efforts that include students, parents, law enforcement officials, and community representatives. Sanctions against AOD use have been cited as an environmental factor offering protection against initial AOD use. School policy provides a vehicle for expressing and enforcing such sanctions. Similarly, the availability of illicit substances, cited as a risk factor for AOD use, can be addressed through communication and cooperation with community law enforcement agencies and businesses offering alcohol and drug paraphernalia for sale.

As a guide for action in helping students to resolve problems associated with AOD use, policy should address the following issues:

- Specification of what constitutes an AOD offense by defining illegal substances or paraphernalia, the area of the school's jurisdiction (including school property and surroundings as well as school-related events), and types of offense (possession, use, and sale).

- Procedures to be followed for first-time offenders and repeat offenders and sellers. Consequences for policy violation should be stated clearly, with punitive action linked to referral for corrective services. Procedures often include provisions for holding penalties in abeyance if students and parents agree to participate in corrective activities such as assessment or treatment.

- Circumstances under which incidents should be reported and a description of responsibilities and procedures for investigating and reporting incidents, with provisions for notifying parents and law enforcement officials.

Administrative regulations or enforcement procedures should be included or referenced in school AOD policies. These procedures describe the specific actions taken by schools to interrupt harmful patterns of behavior in ways that are likely to result in positive change.

For the *primary prevention* audience, policy serves as a deterrent to AOD use. For the *secondary prevention* audience, policy provides a rationale for early identification and intervention on risk factors. For the *tertiary prevention* audience, policy offers goals and procedures for interrupting use, supporting recovery, and enforcing abstinence. At every level of prevention, policy provides a clear statement of the school's commitment to foster protective factors through education, alternatives, and intervention/treatment/support methods.

Education. The role of education in a comprehensive AOD prevention program reflects a dual emphasis on reducing the prevalence and impact of risk factors while promoting and strengthening factors associated with protection from risk.

The United States Department of Education (1988) recommends that AOD prevention curricula reflect the following themes at all grade levels, K through 12:

- A clear and concise message that the use of alcohol, tobacco, and other illicit drugs is unhealthy ad harmful.

- Knowledge of all types of drugs, including what medicines are, why they are used, and who should (or should not) administer them.

- The social consequences of substance abuse.

- Respect for the laws and values of society.

- Promotion of healthy, safe, and responsible attitudes and behavior by correcting mistaken beliefs and assumptions, disarming the sense of personal invulnerability, and building resistance to influences which encourage substance abuse.

- Strategies to involve parents, family members, and the community in the effort to prevent use of illicit substances.

- Appropriate information on intervention and referral services, plus similar information on contacting responsible adults when help is needed in emergencies.

- Sensitivity to the specific needs of the local school and community in terms of cultural appropriateness and local substance abuse problems (p. 10).

Decisions about whether to purchase, adapt, or develop prevention curricula are based on several considerations, including state requirements. Most states require AOD prevention education, while some provide minimum curriculum standards and certification requirements for teachers. A number of states have adopted or designed their own AOD prevention curricula. The costs associated with "packaged" curricula, including materials and training, can be prohibitive. A recent and popular trend finds school systems working with law enforcement agencies to develop and implement aspects of the prevention curriculum.

Consistent with research findings on the effectiveness of educational programs and curricula, schools should develop or adopt programs that emphasize training in skills to resist negative peer, adult, media, and community influence, while promoting the development of adaptive general coping skills and social competence.

Education directed toward a *primary prevention* student audience should increase students' awareness of the influence of peers, media, and the culture in promoting AOD use and teach specific skills for resisting and coping with these negative influences. Instead of providing technical information about AOD use and its effects, education should counteract perceptions among youth that AOD use is commonplace, thereby weakening perceived social support for such use. Information about the consequences of AOD use should emphasize immediate, short-term effects on matters of interest to students (such as interpersonal relationships), rather than focus primarily on long-term adverse health consequences.

An example of a skill-focused curriculum suited to elementary and middle-school students can be found in materials developed by Sharon Scott (1985; 1988; 1992), which train students (beginning at age 5) to recognize and deal effectively with problem situations through assertiveness and refusal skills. Elias (1993) offers a comprehensive resource describing programs and activities to promote social decision making and life-skills development for students at the middle-school level. A similar resource (Elias & Clabby, 1989) is available for educators who work with children at the elementary level. The Life Skills Training curriculum (Botvin, 1989; 1990) is recommended as a comprehensive program for adolescents.

The *secondary prevention* student audience requires, in addition, specific skill-training and remedial activities designed to reduce or buffer the impact of identified risk factors. Because school failure is a key component of the developmental sequence that often leads to AOD problems, interventions aimed at correcting deficiencies and building a sense of academic competence should receive special attention. Disengagement from the mainstream, leading to exposure to unconventional behaviors such as AOD use and association with like-minded peers, is often an unforeseen consequence of pull-out remedial programs. Therefore, efforts should be made to draw at-risk students into the educational mainstream, where positive peer associations and commitment to normative standards are more likely to occur.

Cooperative learning strategies, described in an earlier edition of *Best Practices in School Psychology* (Peterson & Miller, 1990), hold special promise for students in the secondary prevention audience because of their potential for improving learning and fostering more prosocial associations between high-risk and low-risk peers.

The *tertiary prevention* student audience, those who have already engaged in AOD use, benefit from the educational strategies outlined for the secondary prevention audience. In addition, however, they require specialized assistance to enable them to abandon destructive patterns of use; replace identification with deviant, socially-rejected groups with positive peer group affiliation; and learn more effective personal coping techniques. These educational objectives are often accomplished in programs offered in schools under the method of intervention, treatment, and support.

Effective prevention programs address the educational needs of school personnel and parents, in addition to those of students. Education enables school personnel to understand the role of risk and protective factors in the development of AOD problems and to learn strategies for combating risk and fostering protection. Parents can be taught skills for effective and consistent family management, including methods for setting and enforcing rules regarding AOD use.

Alternatives. As a result of its expansion beyond a more traditional focus on AOD-free activities for youth, the method of alternatives provides students multiple opportunities for meaningful and responsible participation in school. The emphasis of this approach is on the promotion of factors that are protective in nature, including prosocial bonding with peers and the school; student involvement in activities in which they can assume responsibility and achieve success; and formation of caring, nurturing relationships between school staff and students. Unlike educational programs focusing primarily on information dissemination and skill development, the method of alternatives is uniquely effective in addressing motivational issues and enlisting student commitment to the goals of school-based prevention programs.

In many schools, participation in alternatives is reserved for students who have demonstrated a ca-

pacity for responsible behavior. As a result, programs often address only the needs of the primary prevention audience, with the secondary and tertiary prevention audiences relegated to the role of recipient or beneficiary of service. This practice overlooks the power of alternatives for at-risk and troubled students, for whom participation offers an opportunity to achieve success while establishing bonds with positive peer groups and caring adults.

A key consideration in developing alternatives, then, is the recruitment and engagement of students from all three audiences. For students in the *primary prevention* audience, alternatives afford opportunities to expand and strengthen existing skills and prosocial motivation. Students in the *secondary prevention* audience are encouraged to participate in alternatives in order to establish and strengthen motives and skills to protect against and buffer the influence of risk factors. For the *tertiary prevention* audience, alternatives serve a "reclaiming" function, breaking patterns of failure, disengagement from school, and identification with deviant peer groups.

Classroom meetings, peer mediation programs, and service on student-faculty committees provide opportunities for students to assume responsibility for decision making and problem solving. Peer assistance programs such as peer tutoring, peer counseling, peer facilitation, buddy systems, peer-led workshops, and cross-age teaching provide regular opportunities for students to make meaningful contributions to others while improving their own academic and social skills. The variety of peer helping programs is limited only by the creativity of students and school staff. Mentoring programs, in which students are assigned to trained adult staff, foster trust and stability in student relationships with caring adults.

Intervention, treatment, and support. The focus of intervention, treatment, and support activities differs for each of the three prevention audiences. The primary prevention audience, exhibiting no characteristics associated with increased risk for AOD use, generally receives less attention under this category of methods. Recognizing, however, that developmental events (such as transitions from middle to secondary school) and environmental circumstances create risk, schools address the needs of the *primary prevention* audience through strategies designed to make alcohol and other drugs less available; to create networks of informed parents, community members, and school personnel that discourage use through monitoring of youth activities; to support abstinence among students; and to create a school climate in which behavior and achievement problems are identified for early intervention purposes.

Student Assistance Programs provide a vehicle for identifying and addressing the needs of the *secondary* and *tertiary prevention* audiences. Many schools have abandoned the more traditional focus on AOD use as a criterion for referral to Student Assistance Programs in favor of referral for any problem having an adverse impact on school performance. This "broad brush" approach is recommended as a means for providing more effective early intervention to a wider range of at-risk and troubled students.

Muldoon and Crowley (1989) describe a model for Student Assistance Programs which includes six steps:

- *Identification*, which requires the recognition of cues and signs of personal, behavioral, social, or academic problems.

- *Initial Action*, which includes discussion with troubled students and referral for Student Assistance Services.

- *Pre-Assessment*, in which school performance data is gathered and analyzed to arrive at an initial determination of needs.

- *Referral to Needed Services*, whether school- or community-based.

- *Provision of Appropriate Care*, in which schools provide direct service or assist students in accessing community services.

- *Support for Change*, in which schools help students maintain new and healthy patterns of behavior.

Among the services most commonly offered in Student Assistance Programs are

- *Insight Classes*, which consist of a highly structured series of presentations, assignments, and discussions for students who have encountered problems with AOD use.

- *Abstinence Support Groups*, which support AOD-free lifestyles for abstainers and those who have been treated for AOD addiction.

- *Concerned Persons Groups*, which provide support and skill-training for students affected by the use of family members and friends.

- *Issue-Focused Groups*, which foster coping skills and emotional support for students whose characteristics or circumstances place them at risk for AOD problems.

To enlist support for the goals of the Student Assistance Program as a trustworthy and effective resource for at-risk and troubled students, information about the program should be made available in the form of written materials and presentations to student, faculty/staff, and parent groups.

School personnel require instruction in strategies for identifying, confronting, and correcting behavior problems in students. In addition, they should receive clear information about their role as referral agents

and facilitators of change for students involved in the Student Assistance Program.

Despite the fact that insufficient evidence has been gathered to demonstrate their effectiveness (Schinke, Botvin, & Orlandi, 1991), programs that foster parent involvement represent a promising vehicle for prevention. Programs that extend the role of parents beyond that of participant and supporter to one of teaching and leadership are growing in popularity. Parent-to-Parent, developed by the Parents Resource Institute for Drug Education (PRIDE; Oliver, Creagh, & Fonesca, 1988) is a peer-driven program providing parents with information about AOD use, barriers to change, and skills for preventing and intervening on AOD use among children and youth. A model for parent support based on a plan for attracting and organizing parents into prevention networks based on children's grade levels is offered by Houghton (1986). Talking With Your Kids About Alcohol (Daugherty & O'Brien, 1987), a parent training program based on a lifestyle risk-reduction model, encourages parents to provide children with information about risks associated with AOD use and teaches specific communication techniques for conveying parental expectations and setting limits and consequences for use.

Program Recommendations: Legal Considerations

This section offers general recommendations for school-based prevention programs based on a review of relevant laws, policies, and judicial precedents. A more comprehensive review of legal issues is available in material recommended in the Annotated Bibliography accompanying this chapter. School officials should consult with legal counsel to determine the application of legal principles in their schools and to ensure compliance with all legal requirements.

- *Develop, publish, and follow a written policy.* Adherence to written policy affords substantial protection to schools when claims of discrimination and failure to safeguard other student rights arise. The policy should address, at minimum, the school's position regarding the use, possession, and sale of alcohol and other drugs, and outline the steps that will be taken in the event of a policy violation. State and local laws usually determine the range of sanctions that is permissible. The use of suspension and expulsion are subject to federal and state due process safeguards, including notice and an opportunity to be heard.

- *Inform students of limits on confidentiality.* Initial interview sessions with students who have been referred for AOD-related services should include a candid discussion of issues related to confidentiality, particularly at the high school level. As a general guideline, it is advisable to inform students that, while the confidentiality of shared information will be protected, there are circumstances when such information must be shared. These circumstances vary depending on state law, but generally include situations where there is a suspicion of abuse and neglect; when there is danger to the student or others; and when there is reason to believe that a crime has been committed.

- *Review record-keeping procedures.* Conventional wisdom applies to AOD programs as it does to other school programs and activities:

> If you practice it, write it down;
> If you said it, write it down;
> When you act, write it down.

Actions are more easily defended when they arise from the provisions of written policies and procedures. Written documentation of statements or actions should include the date, time, location, nature of the incident, parties involved, and a description of the statements made or actions taken.

- *Monitor program-related communication within the school.* Disclosure of information about students to parties outside the school is subject to a variety of legal constraints beyond the scope of this chapter. With respect to within-school communication, however, several guidelines apply. Only program personnel and administrators directly responsible for the AOD prevention program may share information about students who have applied for or received AOD-related services. However, acknowledgment of referral and general information about the student's progress may be shared with referring teachers and involved school personnel, as long as the information does not identify the student (directly or by implication) as an alcohol or drug abuser. When information is needed to provide appropriate medical care in an emergency situation, it is permissible — and, often, advisable — to share information with a nurse or physician.

- *Notify parents and, when required, obtain consent for services.* School policies should describe the types of services for which parental notification and consent are required. As a general rule, consent should be obtained if the AOD prevention program is not directly related to academic instruction and is not a part of the school's required curriculum. A support or skill-development group, for example, to which students are referred and in which they are expected to share information about attitudes, traits, opinions, beliefs, or feelings, should have provisions for obtaining parental consent. Although formal consent is not required for programs which are part of the curriculum, parental notification provides an opportunity for parents to inquire about the program and to object to their child's participation.

- *Provide adequate training to program personnel.* Schools should always ensure that program personnel have experience and are competent to provide the specific type of service offered. For example, facilitators of support groups should have training in group techniques. Teachers and other staff who make referral should be trained to recognize signs of AOD involvement, and should understand the school's policy and procedures for referral.

- *Develop a plan for searches.* School policy should provide explicit guidelines for searches of students as well as their possessions and lockers. A landmark United States Supreme Court ruling (*New Jersey v. TLO*) provides that:

Those responsible for the search must clearly state which school rule or law was violated;

The information on which the search is based must be recent, credible, and link the student to the violation;

The scope of the search must be reasonable and in context, given the student's age, sex, and the nature of the infraction;

The search must be based on a reasonable suspicion that the student has violated rules or law.

Similarly, drug testing should be employed only when there is reasonable suspicion of drug use by a student, and not as a "blanket" procedure for groups of students.

- *Develop a plan for referral to outside agencies.* Because school personnel are not qualified to provide comprehensive care for AOD problems, schools have frequent occasion to make referrals to outside agencies. It is advisable to channel referrals through a designated party in the school (often the school counselor or school psychologist who may, depending on state law, have additional legal protection not available to teachers and other staff). Although students may be entitled to obtain outside services without parental notification, it is advisable to encourage students to discuss their situation with, and seek the advice of, their parents or guardians. When making a referral, school personnel should take care not to impose their views or advocate any particular agency outside the school. School officials should request authorization to release confidential information to agency personnel.

SUMMARY

Several factors support the feasibility of school psychologists' involvement in school-based alcohol and other drug (AOD) prevention programs. School psychologists possess training and expertise in the areas of needs assessment, program planning, curriculum design, collaboration, training, early identification, intervention, and program evaluation. Their familiarity with the structure and organization of schools serves as an asset in planning and enlisting support for programs. Myers (1989) notes that prevention approaches "will be most successful if they are viewed by teachers as consistent with the educational process, and if they can be implemented with minimal added expenses and intrusiveness" (p. 393). Because school psychologists are familiar with the ongoing structures, organizations, and routines of school functioning, they play a dual role of "inside expert" and "outside consultant," bringing knowledge of research on the role of AOD risk and protective factors and components of effective programs.

Prevention programs are most effective when they involve multiple levels of influence, including peers, school personnel, and community resources (parents, community leaders, media) in efforts to reduce the onset, use, and abuse of alcohol and other drugs (Kazdin, 1993). Similarly, interventions are most likely to succeed when they avoid a narrow focus on the variable of AOD use, in favor of approaches that address multiple risk factors at both individual and environmental levels (Lorion & Ross, 1992). Experience indicates that effective programs extend their scope beyond information giving and skill training to include strategies for promoting protective school environments and enhancing prosocial motivation.

Research suggests that the phenomenon of substance abuse is the produce of a developmental pathway characterized by early failure in personal, social, and academic tasks, leading to associations with negative peer groups in which initial AOD use is likely to occur. When initial use is followed by relief from personal distress and acceptance of a deviant identity, youth become trapped in a lifestyle which rewards and escalates deviant and nonconforming behavior, including AOD use.

An understanding of the interaction between program methods and prevention audiences provides a framework for program planning and evaluation. A theme of intolerance of AOD use, coupled with a commitment to facilitate and support recovery from harmful and destructive patterns of behavior, should be clearly and consistently expressed in every aspect of school programs. The purposes and content of policy, education, alternatives, and intervention/treatment/support activities should be tailored to the needs of students in the primary, secondary, and tertiary prevention audiences.

The purpose of school-based programs for the *primary prevention* audience is to foster the attainment of characteristics which afford protection against AOD use. Educational efforts should focus on the development of awareness of the negative short-term consequences of AOD use and the establishment of effective coping skills, including techniques for re-

sisting negative influence. School programs should focus on enhancement of student performance and bonding to school, formation of positive peer associations, promotion of accurate perceptions of AOD use, and policies providing sanctions against AOD use. Schools should work with parents to provide assistance in developing more effective family management skills and with community members to reduce the availability of alcohol and other drugs.

The *secondary prevention* audience is served through school programs which seek to reduce or buffer the impact of risk factors. Educational interventions should provide a more intensive focus on the development of coping and resistance skills, coupled with efforts to arrest emerging trends of school failure. School programs should foster caring relationships between students and adults and implement strategies which place school success and positive peer affiliation within reach of troubled and at-risk youth. Responses to behavior problems should extend beyond the provision of sanctions to the creation of opportunities for responsible and rewarding behavior. Interventions with families should be extended to include training in problem-solving and communication skills, enabling parents to set and enforce limits for behavior.

The purpose of school programs for the *tertiary prevention* audience is to interrupt and eliminate patterns of AOD use. In addition to the interventions recommended for the secondary prevention audience, educational programs for the tertiary prevention audience should provide opportunities for students to learn and practice specific skills for achieving and maintaining abstinence and for coping with personal distress. School programs also serve a "reclaiming" function for this audience by drawing them into the mainstream, thereby providing opportunities to establish or restore positive peer and adult affiliations and commitment to normative standards of behavior. Interventions with families may require linkages with community-based resources and support networks of concerned parents. Efforts to reduce AOD availability and disrupt use patterns are most successful when they involve communication with law enforcement agencies. For the tertiary prevention audience, the provision of AOD-free activities is of special importance, and efforts should be made to engage students' interest and commitment to such programs.

In a 1992 article entitled *America 2000 and the National Education Goals Panel: Contributions of School Psychology*, George Batsche, former president of the National Association of School Psychologists, described the role school psychologists can play in accomplishing the goal that *every school in America will be free of drugs and violence and will offer a disciplined environment conducive to learning.* Participation in school-based AOD prevention programs is encouraged as a means for school psychologists to assume meaningful leadership in efforts to combat a problem that is recognized as a significant threat to the welfare and future of the nation's youth.

REFERENCES

Anderson, G. (1988). *When chemicals come to school: The student assistance program model.* Greenfield, WI: Community Recovery Press.

Austin, G. (1992). *School failure and other drug use.* Madison, WI: Wisconsin Clearinghouse, University of Wisconsin.

Batsche, G. (1992, February). America 2000 and the National Education Goals Panel: Contributions of school psychology. *NASP Communiqué, 20,* 2.

Botvin, G. (1989; 1990). *Life skills training (Levels I, II, and III): Teacher's Manual and Student's Guide.* New York: Springfield Press.

Botvin, G., & Dusenberry, L. (1989). Substance abuse prevention and the promotion of competence. In L. Bond & B. Compas (Eds.), *Primary prevention and promotion in the school* (pp. 146–178). Newbury Park, CA: Sage Publications.

Brook, J., Brook, D., Gordon, A., Whiteman, M., & Cohen, P. (1990). The psychosocial etiology of adolescent drug use: A family interactional approach. *Genetic, Social, and General Psychology Monographs, 116.*

Brook, J., Cohen, P., Whiteman, M., & Gordon, A. (1992). Psychosocial risk factors in the transition from moderate to heavy use or abuse of drugs. In M. Glantz & R. Pickens (Eds.), *Vulnerability to drug abuse* (pp. 359–388). Washington, DC: American Psychological Association.

Clayton, R. (1992). Transitions in drug use: Risk and protective factors. In M. Glantz & R. Pickens (Eds.), *Vulnerability to drug abuse* (pp. 15–51). Washington, DC: American Psychological Association.

Daugherty, R., & O'Brien, T. (1987). *Talking with your kids about alcohol and other drugs.* Lexington, KY: Prevention Research Institute.

Eggert, L., Seyl, C., & Nicholas, L. (1990). Effects of a school-based prevention program for potential high school dropouts and drug abusers. *International Journal of the Addictions, 25,* 773–801.

Elementary and Secondary Education Act, 20 U.S.C. (1988).

Elias, M. (1993). *Social decision making and life skills development: Guidelines for middle school educators.* Gaithersburg, MD: Aspen Publications, Inc.

Elias, M., & Clabby, J. (1989). *Social decision-making skills: A curriculum guide for the elementary grades.* Rockville, MD: Aspen Publishers, Inc.

Glantz, M. (1992). A developmental psychopathology model of drug abuse vulnerability. In M. Glantz & R. Pickens (Eds.), *Vulnerability to Drug Abuse* (pp. 389–418). Washington, DC: American Psychological Association.

Goldstein, A. (1988). *The prepare curriculum: Teaching prosocial competencies.* Champaign, IL: Research Press.

Goldstein, A., Sprafkin, P., Gershaw, N., & Klein, P. (1980). *Skillstreaming the adolescent.* Champaign, IL: Research Press Co.

Hansen, W., Graham, J., Johnson, C., flay, B., & Pentz, M. (1988). *Project SMART.* Pasadena, CA: Institute for Health Promotion and Disease Prevention Research, University of Southern California.

Houghton, E. (1986). *Organizing parents into an effective prevention network.* Deerfield, IL: Informed Networks, Inc.

Kaplan, H., & Johnson, R. (1992). Relationships between circumstances surrounding initial illicit drug use and escalation of drug use: Moderating effects of gender and early adolescent experiences. In M. Glantz & R. Pickens (Eds.), *Vulnerability to drug abuse* (pp. 299–358). Washington, DC: American Psychological Association.

Kazdin, A. (1993). Adolescent mental health: Prevention and treatment programs. *American Psychologist, 48,* 127–141.

League, V., & Pump, S. (1988). *A policy development manual for drug free schools.* Oakland, CA: Vincente Associates.

Lorion, R., & Ross, J. (1992). Programs for change: A realistic look at the nation's potential for preventing substance involvement among high-risk youth. *Journal of Community Psychology,* OSAP Special Issue, 3–9.

McGinnis, E., & Goldstein, A. (1984). *Skillstreaming the elementary school child: A guide for teaching prosocial skills.* Champaign, IL: Research Press Co.

McIntyre, K., White, D., & Yoast, R. (1990). *Resilience among high-risk youth.* Madison, WI: Wisconsin Clearinghouse, University of Wisconsin.

Milgram, G., & Griffin, T. (1986). *What, when, and how to talk to students about alcohol and other drugs: A guide for teachers.* Center City, MN: Hazelden Foundation.

Muldoon, J., & Crowley, J. (1989). *Effective student assistance programs.* Minneapolis, MN: Community Intervention, Inc.

Myers, J. (1989). The practice of psychology in the schools for the primary prevention of learning and adjustment problems of children: A perspective from the field of education. In L. Bond & B. Compas (Eds.), *Primary prevention and promotion in the schools* (pp. 391–421). Newbury Park, CA: Sage Publications.

National Institute on Drug Abuse. (1990). *National household survey on drug abuse, 1990.* Rockville, MD: National Institute on Drug Abuse, Division of Epidemiology and Prevention Research.

National Institute on Drug Abuse. (1991). *Monitoring the future, 1990: National high school senior drug abuse survey, 1990.* Rockville, MD: National Institute on Drug Abuse, Division of Epidemiology and Prevention Research.

Newcomb, M. (1992). Understanding the multidimensional nature of drug use and abuse: The role of consumption, risk factors, and protective factors. In M. Glantz & R. Pickens (Eds.), *Vulnerability to drug abuse* (pp. 255–297). Washington, DC: American Psychological Association.

Newcomb, M., & Felix-Ortiz, M. (1992). Multiple protective and risk factors for drug use and abuse: Cross-sectional and prospective findings. *Journal of Personality and Social Psychology, 63,* 280–296.

New Jersey v. TLO, 469 U.S. 323, 339 (1985).

Oliver, B., Creagh, M., & Fonesca, J. (1988). *Parent to parent.* Marietta, GA: Parents Resource Institute for Drug Education (PRIDE).

Pentz, M., Cormack, C., Flay, B., Hansen, W., & Johnson, C. (1986). Balancing program and research integrity in community drug abuse prevention: Project STAR approach. *Journal of School Health, 56,* 389–393.

Peterson, D., & Miller, J. (1990). Best practices in peer-influenced learning. In A. Thomas & J. Grimes (Eds.), *Best practices in school psychology-II* (pp. 531–546). Washington, DC: National Association of School Psychologists.

Pianta, R. (1990). Widening the debate on educational reform: Prevention as a viable alternative. *Exceptional Children, 56,* 306–313.

Schinke, S., Botvin, G., & Orlandi, M. (1991). *Substance abuse in children and adolescents: Evaluation and intervention.* Newbury Park, CA: Sage Publications.

Scott, S. (1985). *Peer pressure reversal: An adult guide to developing a responsible child.* Amherst, MA: Human Resource Development Press.

Scott, S. (1988). *How to say no! And keep your friends: Peer pressure reversal for pre-teens and teenagers.* Amherst, MA: Human Resource Development Press.

Scott, S. (1992). *Too smart for trouble.* Amherst, MA: Human Resource Development Press.

Shedler, J., & Block, J. (1990). Adolescent drug use and psychological health: A longitudinal inquiry. *American Psychologist, 45,* 612–630.

Slavin, R., & Madden, N. (1987, April). *Effective classroom programs for students at risk.* Paper presented at the Annual Convention of the American Educational Research Association, Washington, DC.

Vorrath, H., & Brendtro, L. (1985). *Positive peer culture.* New York: Aldine Publishing Co.

United States Department of Education. (1988). *Drug prevention curricula: A guide to selection and implementation.* Washington, DC: U.S. Department of Education, Office of Educational Research and Improvement.

ANNOTATED BIBLIOGRAPHY

Anderson, G. (1988). *When chemicals come to school: The student assistance program model.* Greenfield, WI: Community Resource Press (P.O. Box 20979, Greenfield, WI 53220).

This book is a comprehensive and widely acclaimed resource for school-based AOD programs. A "must" for the professional library of educators responsible for program design and implementation, it provides detailed descriptions of components of Student Assistance Programs, including policy design, the role of school personnel and parents, team development, intervention and referral models, and student support group curricula.

League, V., & Pump, S. (1988). *A policy development manual for drug-free schools.* Oakland, CA: Vincente & Associates (2101 Webster Street, Suite 1700, Oakland, CA 94612).

This book serves as an invaluable source of step-by-step guidance through the process of school policy development. It includes a useful and comprehensive summary of legal issues pertinent to school-based programs as well as sample policies adopted by representative school systems.

Schinke, S., Botvin, G., & Orlandi, M. (1991). *Substance abuse in children and adolescents: Evaluation and intervention.* Newbury Park, CA: Sage Publications (2455 Teller Road, Newbury Park CA 91320).

This publication of Volume 22 of the journal *Developmental Clinical Psychology and Psychiatry* offers a comprehensive review of research on the effectiveness of various prevention programs, including information dissemination, affective education, and skill-training approaches. Intended for professional audiences, it also reviews formats for adolescent treatment programs and offers an excellent discussion of evaluation methods for prevention and intervention activities.

United States Department of Education. (1989). *What works: Schools without drugs.* Available from the National Clearinghouse for Alcohol and Drug Information (P.O. Box 2345, Rockville, MD 20852).

This booklet, available free of charge from NCADI, provides an overview of the AOD problem; offers action plans for parents, schools, students, and communities; describes specific drugs and their effects; provides general information about legal issues; and offers information about resources for prevention-related products and services.

Western Center for Drug-Free Schools and Communities. (1988). *Planning for drug-free schools and communities: Participant manual.* Portland, OR: Northwest Regional Educational Laboratory (101 S.W. Main Street, Suite 500, Portland, OR 97204).

This manual, consisting of materials employed in a 2-day training workshop for school personnel, offers extensive information and guidelines for promoting awareness of AOD problems and planning appropriate prevention efforts. It describes school team models, needs assessment methods, planning activities, policy issues, prevention curricula, evaluation procedures, and suggestions for working with parents and community members.

AUTHOR NOTE

The development of this chapter was supported by PSI Associates, Inc. (Twinsburg, Ohio).

34

Best Practices in Addressing HIV/AIDS Issues in the School

Katrine Haefli
John B. Pryor
Steven Landau
Illinois State University

Herbert Johns, superintendent of a medium-sized suburban school district, looked across his desk at the parents of Michael Tobin. They were young, relatively affluent, active in the Parent/Teacher Association — and their only child had AIDS . . . Not a soul, other than the three people in the room, knew. The Tobins wanted to keep it that way. They wanted Michael to enter second grade like any other child. "It will all end for him soon enough; just let him have a few months of normal life," they pleaded.

Johns scanned the youngster's school records again. A model first-grader, well-behaved, bright, verbal — what a tragedy! None of the three adults doubted that Michael's life would become a living hell once the story was out . . . : protests by parents, loss of friends, legal battles, media attention. What a way for a child to die, Johns thought to himself — isolated, feared, and guilt-ridden.

The adults decided to keep Michael's [medical] results confidential; only the president of the school board would be let in on the secret. And so, in early September, Michael entered second grade.

Shortly thereafter, it happened. During recess one afternoon, three boys fell from the monkey bars. It was not a big accident — just scraped hands and knees and a lot of blood. With only two antiseptic wipes for three little boys — one of them, Michael — an unknowing teacher used the same wipe on six bloody knees and six upturned hands.

Conscience-stricken and in a panic, Michael's parents told the school nurse about his condition when the nurse phoned them to report what she perceived to be an ordinary playground mishap. No one could have imagined the chaos that ensued. Michael's school was closed. Classrooms were washed down, and the restrooms were scrubbed by workers wearing gloves and face masks. Teachers and students refused to enter the building. Then came the lawsuits: three separate tort liability cases and two class-action suits citing prior knowledge, breach of duty, negligent standard of care, and proximate cause. (Keough & Seaton, 1988, p. 58)

This situation, although fictitious, is based on real cases. It highlights the possibility of having an unidentified HIV-carrier in the school — whether it be a student or staff member — and an uninformed, unplanned reaction to a crisis.

The purpose of this chapter is to provide school psychologists with information regarding HIV/AIDS as it pertains to children in the schools. Currently, there are few known HIV-infected children in the schools. However, with increasing prevalence of HIV among adults, youth, and infants, and with advances in medicine that prolong the lives of those with AIDS, there will be increasing numbers of students who either are infected with HIV or who have a family member infected with HIV. School psychologists, then, need to be aware of the current epidemiology of HIV/AIDS among youth and the legal and policy issues concerning the school attendance of HIV-infected children. School psychologists must also be prepared to address potential problems in mainstreaming the HIV-infected child and in providing appropriate consultative services to facilitate this process. Educating the community, students, and school personnel about HIV/AIDS is the key component in effectively addressing HIV-related issues in the schools. Therefore, school psychologists should take a proactive role in planning and implementing AIDS education and HIV-related services in the schools. In this way, students directly and indirectly affected by the HIV epidemic can be provided optimal educational and psychosocial services in the schools.

In the following overview, AIDS and HIV infection are described, and the prevalence of the disease is discussed. Under *Basic Considerations*, the legal and policy issues regarding children with HIV infection and the task of mainstreaming these children in the schools are presented. In addition, the necessary precautions that all school personnel and students should practice are provided, along with the accompanying AIDS education that is crucial in successfully dealing with the AIDS epidemic in the schools. Finally, best practices for school psychologists dealing with HIV in the schools are presented.

OVERVIEW OF HIV/AIDS

HIV infection refers to infection with human immunodeficiency virus, regardless of the presence of overt illness or clinical manifestations. *HIV-related disease* refers to the presence of HIV infection and the presence of clinical manifestations which may or may not be life threatening. *Acquired immunodeficiency syndrome* (AIDS) represents essentially the later stages of HIV disease. The HIV virus attacks and ultimately compromises a person's immune system. Persons with AIDS are subject to a variety of opportunistic diseases which rarely infect people with healthy immune systems. The onslaught of such opportunistic illnesses in a weakened immune system eventually results in death for the person with AIDS (Weiss, 1993). Clinical diagnosis of AIDS hinges in part upon the presence of these opportunistic infections. The National Centers for Disease Control and Prevention (CDC, 1993b) has revised its definition of AIDS three times: in 1985, 1987, and in 1992. The revisions have broadened the range of AIDS-indicator diseases and conditions, and have used HIV diagnostic tests to improve the sensitivity and specificity of the definition.

Transmission of HIV

There are three major ways in which HIV is transmitted: (a) perinatally from an infected mother, (b) from exposure to infected blood or blood products, and (c) from unprotected sex with an infected person. Although all babies born of HIV-infected mothers carry maternal antibodies to HIV, only about one third are actually infected with the virus. Reliable diagnosis is generally possible after about 15 months (Chambers & Lindenbaum, 1993). The primary means by which people are infected with contaminated blood is through intravenous drug use. Needle sharing is a common practice among many intravenous (IV) drug users. This practice permits the passage of the virus from one user to the next. Exposure to contaminated blood is also possible through transfusions, the use of clotting agents in treating hemophilia, and accidental needle pricks encountered by medical personnel. Systematic screening of the blood supply in the United States has greatly reduced the number of infections related to transfusions and the use of clotting agents. The institution of universal precautions has significantly reduced the risk of medical personnel. The primary means of transmission is still unprotected sex with an infected person. The HIV virus may be present in either the semen or vaginal secretions of an infected person. Sexual activity in which a partner comes in contact with either of these fluids runs a risk for HIV transmission. CDC (1993a) reports that 56% to 69% of adult/adolescent AIDS cases in the U.S. involved a sexual contact risk factor. Among adolescent boys with AIDS 33% to 41% involved this risk fac-

tor. Among adolescent girls, 50% involved a sexual contact risk factor.

HIV is not spread by casual contact. In studies of hundreds of households where family members have lived with and cared for AIDS patients (sometimes in circumstances where it was not known that the person was infected with HIV), there has never been a case of transmission through casual contact (CDC, 1993a). If HIV is not transmitted in circumstances where kitchen and bathroom facilities, meals, eating and drinking utensils, and even toothbrushes are shared repeatedly for prolonged periods of time, it seems even less likely that HIV could be casually transmitted in other social situations such as schools or offices. It also should be noted that studies in Africa and Florida have found no evidence for household HIV transmission in mosquito infested areas. So, there seems no danger of HIV transmission through insect bites.

Consequences of HIV Infection

In addition to its effects upon the immune system, HIV has been found to affect the nervous system directly (Fletcher et al., 1991; Navia, Cho, Petito, & Price, 1986). The dementia aspect of AIDS (e.g., brain atrophy, encephalopathy) is believed to be separate from the immunodeficiency aspects and may be caused by direct infection of the brain with HIV. It is estimated that between 30% and 60% of adults with AIDS evidence neurological complications, whereas 50% to 90% of children evidence such complications (Byers, 1989). Indicators of neurological involvement in adults include general mental slowness, impaired concentration, mild memory loss, and motor skills impairment (e.g., progressive loss of balance, leg weakness). Younger children, particularly those infected perinatally, seem especially susceptible to neurological damage from HIV infection (Epstein, Sharer, & Goudsmit, 1988). Neurological damage is one of the most common causes of death in pediatric AIDS cases (Plesser, Foster, & Siegel, 1987). The HIV virus appears to have a profound effect upon brain development in pediatric cases and subsequently upon the attainment of motor, intellectual, and developmental milestones (Byers, 1989). In some cases, young children with AIDS have been found to regress and lose milestones previously attained. Recent research indicates that treatment with AZT (Aziodothymidine) may alleviate some of the AIDS dementia effects found in children (Culliton, 1989).

Epidemiology of HIV/AIDS

In early 1993, CDC reported a cumulative total of 5,647 cases of AIDS in persons under the age of 20 in the U.S. Almost 64% of these were children under the age of 5. The vast majority of the children under 5 were infected perinatally by their mothers. Moving from childhood to adolescence, one finds a different characteristic pattern of infection. For example, for adolescents ages 13–19, 48% of the males and 73% of the females were infected either via intravenous drug use or sexual contact. Minority children and adolescents have been hardest hit in this epidemic. Almost three-fourths of the AIDS cases in persons under 20 have been among Black and Hispanic youth.

While the number of children and adolescents with AIDS represents less than 2% of the total number of known AIDS cases in the U.S., AIDS and other manifestations of HIV infection represent a growing problem for schools for at least four reasons. First, while the development of a vaccine for HIV seems on the distant horizon, symptomatic treatment drugs have been and continue to be developed. These will result in an increasing number of children who will live to school age (Byers, 1989). Second, the rates of HIV infection continue to grow among children and adolescents in the U.S. (Hein, 1992), particularly in urban areas. Third, more adolescents are probably infected with HIV than current statistics reveal. For adults and adolescents, current estimates suggest a typical latency period of about 10–11 years from infection with the HIV virus to the development of AIDS (Gayle, Manoff, & Rogers, 1989). This suggests that the majority of adolescents with HIV infection is asymptomatic and would not be reflected in CDC counts of AIDS cases. Since 18% of the male and 24% of the female AIDS cases reported to CDC through March of 1993 involved people aged 20–29, one can infer that many of these people became infected while adolescents. Fourth, HIV disease affects families. Although uninfected themselves, school-age children with siblings, parents, or other family members who are infected with HIV bear the stigma and the personal strains of living with someone who has this terrible illness (Pryor & Reeder, 1993).

BASIC CONSIDERATIONS

Legal and Policy Issues

In 1985, the CDC and the National Educational Association issued guidelines concerning the attendance of HIV-infected children in the schools (Kirkland & Ginther, 1988). For most infected children, CDC recommends continued attendance in unrestricted school settings. More restricted environments are recommended for preschool aged children and neurologically handicapped children who lack control over body secretions and those who display behaviors such as biting and drooling. Section 504 of the Rehabilitation Act of 1973 and the Education for All Handicapped Children Act of 1975 (EHA) have provided the basis for legal arguments concerning HIV-infected children's rights to attend public schools. An important legal precedent for considering AIDS a handicap was set in the case of *Thomas v. Atascadero Unified School District* (1987). This case involved an HIV-infected child who was barred from

kindergarten after he bit a classmate. The federal court ruled that the child's condition was a protected handicap and ordered that the child be readmitted to school. The court contended that the school had not shown that the child's presence in the classroom presented a significant risk for transmission.

The child in the *Thomas v. Atascadero Unified School District* case manifested some observable symptoms of AIDS. In other cases, the courts vacillated on whether simply being infected with HIV without any obvious symptoms also might be considered a handicap (for example, see *School Board of Nassau County, Florida v. Arline*, 1987). Fortunately, the Americans with Disabilities Act (ADA) of 1990 extended the definitions of disabilities offered in the Rehabilitation Act to explicitly cover both persons with symptomatic AIDS and asymptomatic carriers of HIV (Pyle, 1992). In the ADA, Congress recognized the power of the stigma associated with HIV/AIDS even when no obvious symptoms are present, and the importance of protecting persons with HIV/AIDS from discriminatory practices.

In addition to federal laws, the majority of states have developed policies concerning school attendance for HIV-infected children. Katisiyannis (1992) found that 41 of 46 states surveyed had school attendance policies for children with HIV. Eighty-three percent used CDC guidelines in developing their policies. However, only 39% mandated adherence to state policies by Local Education Agencies.

Some of the most complex issues faced by school officials in dealing with HIV-infected children concern confidentiality and the right of privacy. The CDC (1985) guidelines on school attendance for HIV-infected children warn of the potential problems of revealing a child's HIV status to his/her classmates. CDC urges school personnel and others involved in the care and education of these children to exercise sensitivity to the need for confidentiality and the right to privacy. Both the EHA and the Family Education Rights and Privacy Act contain prohibitions on unconsented disclosures of personally identifiable information about students (U.S. Department of Education, 1987). Under these acts, the disclosure of HIV status to appropriate school officials could be permitted, if justified by public health or other legitimate considerations. The states have developed their own laws and guidelines on these issues. Katisiyannis (1992) found that all of the states he surveyed had policies on disclosure of HIV status for school children. Despite the most sophisticated school policies, practical problems still exist for maintaining confidentiality. The most likely source of a breach of confidentiality is the child, parent, or guardian (Pyle, 1992). Once a person's HIV status is revealed, the potential exists for massive negative reactions from other children and parents (Pryor & Reeder, 1993). These include the social ostracism of the HIV-positive child and in some cases acts of violence against the child and his/her family. However, such reactions are avoidable if a proactive effort is made to educate children and their families about HIV/AIDS, and prepare them for dealing with the HIV-infected person in a realistic and humane manner (Schmitt & Schmitt, 1990).

Mainstreaming the Child with HIV/AIDS

In spite of media coverage of negative community reactions to mainstreaming children with HIV/AIDS in the schools, there has been a paucity of research on how parents and school personnel react to the prospects of an HIV-infected child in the classroom. However, given that children with AIDS will experience cognitive and developmental problems in the advanced stage of the illness and will, therefore, have frequent or prolonged absences from school, the research on disabled and chronically ill children may prove relevant to an understanding of what HIV-infected children may face in the schools.

Although advances in inclusion continue to be made, it has been known for some time that, in general, most regular education teachers still prefer special class placement for students with disabilities (O'Reilly & Duquette, 1988), educable mentally handicapped and behavior disordered students (Goupil & Brunet, 1984; Williams & Algozzine, 1979), and emotionally disturbed students (Shotel, Iano, & McGettigan, 1972). In addition, teachers report being uncomfortable with meeting the academic needs of chronically ill children (Johnson, Lubker, & Fowler, 1988).

There are various explanations for teachers' discomfort in teaching chronically ill or disabled students. First, teachers often perceive themselves as ill prepared to teach these students. This includes not having necessary information about a specific medical condition or not having the educational preparation to meet the needs of the student with a specific disability or chronic illness (Aksamit, 1990; Hannah & Pliner, 1983; Johnson et al., 1988). Second, teachers seem to worry about insufficient time to prepare individualized material for the student with disabilities and the student experiencing health-related absences (Morsink, Blackhurst, & Williams, 1979). Thus, the disabled or chronically ill student may be perceived as one who places an excessive demand on teacher time. Third, there is evidence that teachers are concerned about classroom management of disruptive behaviors presented by some disabled or chronically ill students (Aksamit, 1990; Johnson, Gold, & Vickers, 1982; Johnson et al., 1988). It seems probable that these same barriers to inclusion would also apply to the HIV-infected child. In addition, teachers have expressed concern for the safety of the health impaired child in the classroom (Johnson et al., 1988), which is clearly relevant to the child with AIDS who is more vulnerable to opportunistic infection.

There is limited research on teacher concerns about HIV-infected students, and few specific guidelines for appropriate educational services for these students. Few, if any, teacher training programs provide preservice teachers with information about the educational needs of HIV-infected students. In addition, limited information has been given to teachers about the HIV-infected student's potential to be injured or the probability of contracting opportunistic infections from other students. Most importantly, many misconceptions regarding the transmission of HIV are still prevalent. Students infected with HIV who are assaultive, bite other students, are incontinent, or who drool may elicit concern about HIV transmission to others. Transmission fears are also evident in the cafeteria (e.g., sharing of eating utensils) and on the playground (e.g., mosquito bites). Ballard, White, and Glascoff (1990) found that 30% of preservice elementary teachers would feel personally threatened by a student with AIDS in their class, 20% did not understand the basics of HIV transmission, and less than half knew how to protect themselves from infection.

Brucker, Martin, and Shreeve (1989) also found that many teachers do not think they should be required to teach HIV-infected students and do not agree that these students should be allowed to attend school. In addition, Peach and Reddick (1989) found that the majority of teachers and school administrators surveyed in rural Tennessee felt uncomfortable with their level of knowledge about AIDS, thought that students and school personnel are at risk for HIV infection when there is an HIV-infected person at school, and thought that school personnel or students with HIV should not be allowed to remain in school.

Reluctance towards mainstreaming an HIV-infected child may be further compounded by the fact that HIV and AIDS, even pediatric AIDS, evoke strong negative social connotations. From an epidemiological perspective, HIV was initially identified in the United States among the male homosexual community and IV drug users. Therefore, attitudes and beliefs regarding HIV may be the product of one's disposition towards these minority groups considered deviant by the majority. Thus, stigma, especially associated with sexual orientation, may be applied to any individual with HIV, regardless of how that individual contracted the virus (Pryor & Reeder, 1993).

If school psychologists examine the literature that describes how to facilitate mainstreaming of students with other disabilities and chronic illnesses, they may be better prepared to meet the mainstreaming needs of children with HIV/AIDS. Successful mainstreaming of the student with HIV will likely include a focus on positive attitudes toward persons with HIV/AIDS, adequate knowledge regarding AIDS and HIV transmission, appropriate psychoeducational interventions, and environmental engineering that offers support and resources to teachers and other school personnel servicing these students. Thus, successful mainstreaming of HIV-infected children requires a collaborative effort in which planning, training, and support are necessary.

AIDS Education

Education of students, school personnel, and the community about HIV/AIDS must precede any successful effort at mainstreaming the HIV-infected child in the school. School psychologists, along with teachers and other school personnel, play an integral role in ensuring the success of appropriate and comprehensive educational services to the student with HIV/AIDS. In addition, school psychologists' expanding consultative role places them at a significant advantage in disseminating accurate information to school personnel, as well as members of the community, and in dispelling myths regarding HIV/AIDS. It is therefore important for the school psychologist to take a proactive role in

- Sensitizing the school administrators, as well as the community, to the importance of AIDS education in the schools.

- Consulting on education programs for schools and the community which address both prevention of HIV infection and attitudes toward infected individuals.

- Designing and implementing a developmentally appropriate presentation of AIDS education at all grade levels.

- Ensuring that the medical, psychological, and social needs of HIV-infected students and their families are met.

- Meeting the psychosocial needs of classmates of a dying child with AIDS or of a child with an HIV-infected family member.

Universal precautions. It is likely that one will eventually interact with an HIV-infected student or staff member in the schools, whether or not that person is aware of his or her HIV status. From the extant literature, it is evident that school psychologists are not typically among those school personnel who need to know about a person's HIV status. According to the National Association of State Boards of Education (Fraser, 1989), the superintendent and the individual's personal physician are the only persons who *should* be informed of an individual's HIV status. A public health official should also be informed, but he or she does not necessarily need to know the identity of the affected individual. Disclosure of a student's HIV status to other school personnel need only occur if it is relevant to meeting the needs of the student. As presented earlier, transmission of HIV is extremely un-

likely in normal school interactions. However, the Centers for Disease Control recommend that the usual universal precautions for infectious blood and body fluids be taken to prevent any chance of transmission (Fraser, 1989). These precautions are summarized in Figure 1.

Universal precautions pertain to blood or body fluids containing blood products. These precautions are described as universal because they should be applied to all persons, situations, or conditions regardless of HIV status. Thus, these precautions are not specific to HIV. They are as important in preventing other infections, such as hepatitis, as they are in preventing the transmission of HIV. In addition, they are extremely important in preventing opportunistic infections in the immune-suppressed HIV-infected child. Thus, universal precautions should be used in handling all body fluids. The school psychologist, other school personnel, and students should be familiar with universal precautions and should incorporate these precautions into everyday practice.

In addition to these universal precautions, it is imperative that all persons who work in the schools be educated regarding the modes of transmission of HIV and behaviors that can transmit the virus. In this way, informed proactive measures, rather than emotional reactions, can guide the decisions regarding the admission and treatment of an HIV-infected child in the school.

School-based AIDS education. As the prevalence of HIV/AIDS increases in the United States, so does the number of children and adolescents who live with or know an HIV-infected person. These increasing numbers of youth affected by HIV/AIDS intensify the need for AIDS education programs directed to this population, specifically school-based programs. As of March, 1992, 33 states and the District of Columbia had mandated AIDS education in their respective school districts and 14 states had recommended it (Haffner, 1992). Ohio, Tennessee, and Wyoming are the only states that neither mandate nor recommend AIDS education in the public schools. A state mandate is a requirement that all school districts provide this education, and it is usually accompanied by suggested curricula for AIDS education programs. A state recommendation is a suggestion that local school districts provide this education to the students, but they are not required to do so.

Unfortunately, the existence of a state mandate for school-based AIDS education does not mean there is a program in every school in the state. Furthermore, although the CDC and individual states provide guidelines for AIDS education in the schools, there is a lack of universally accepted standards for education programs. Therefore, actual programs vary widely among states, and even among districts within a state, in terms of which grade levels participate in the program, the program length and content, and training of the persons designing and implementing the program. In addition, program evaluation is inconsistent and often absent.

Studies of students' knowledge of HIV reveal that, although most surveyed children and adolescents know that HIV is transmitted through behaviors frequently identified in the media (e.g., sexual contact and sharing of needles for IV drug use), misconceptions regarding other modes of transmission, and negative attitudes or fears towards having a classmate with HIV are prevalent. For example, Holcomb (1990) found that 94% to 99% of 4th-graders surveyed knew that HIV is transmitted by sexual contact and sharing needles with someone who has AIDS. However, 36% to 56% also thought one can get AIDS from the virus particles in the air, by food prepared by someone who has AIDS, by being sneezed or coughed on by someone with AIDS, by mosquito bites, by sharing the same glass as someone with AIDS, and from public swimming pools. Of these 4th-graders, 51% believed that everyone is at risk for getting AIDS, and 59% "worry a lot" about getting AIDS. Seventy-one percent agreed they should receive education about AIDS and learn how it is spread.

Brown, Nassau, and Barone (1990) found similar results with 5th-, 7th-, and 10th-graders. Of these students, 90% to 98%
knew the major modes of HIV transmission. However, 20% to 53% believed one can contract HIV by using a comb of an HIV-infected person, by having blood taken, and by mosquito bites. And 68% to 86% of these students reported they are nervous about AIDS; 51% to 53% favored keeping people with AIDS away from them. Overall 95% to 97% of these students favored AIDS education.

A study by Kann et al. (1991), involving a national survey of 9th- through 12th-graders, also found that, while 98% to 99% knew the major modes of HIV transmission, they held misconceptions about other modes of transmission. For example, 75% of these students thought HIV is transmitted by public toilets, and 12% thought they can reduce their risk of HIV infection by taking birth control pills. In addition 23% thought it was possible to tell if people are infected with HIV just by looking at them. Although 91% of the students believed they could not be infected by being in the same class with an HIV-infected student, only 51% thought students with AIDS should be allowed to attend their school, and only 56% indicated willingness to be in the same class as an HIV-infected student. While only about one-half reported having been taught about AIDS in school, almost all thought they should receive this education. In addition, these students were surveyed regarding their sexual practices. Fifty-nine percent of the students reported having had sexual intercourse; of those students, 40% reported having had four or more sexual partners.

Therefore, a significant number of adolescents are at risk for HIV infection.

Although other studies have found a substantial increase in condom use among adolescents, the proportion of adolescents who are sexually active, and the proportion of adolescents engaging in unprotected sex, has also increased (Hingson, Strunin, Berlin, & Heeren, 1990). Thus, adolescents are at risk, not only for HIV infection, but also for other sexually transmitted diseases and unintended pregnancies. Compared to all other age groups in the general population, 10- to 19-year-olds have the highest rates of gonorrhea and syphillis (Miller, Turner, & Moses, 1990). Furthermore, if one is already infected with a sexually transmitted disease, he or she is at greater risk for contracting HIV during unprotected sexual activity.

Collectively, these studies indicate that, although children and adolescents can articulate the behaviors that spread HIV, they do not understand the modes of transmission. Therefore, myths about HIV transmission prevail. However, the vast majority of youth desire AIDS education. In addition, though they state that HIV-infected students should be allowed in the classroom, they do not want to be around them. Finally, though they can state the behaviors that transmit HIV, they continue to engage in these behaviors. In response to these findings, schools must provide education that facilitates understanding regarding the modes of HIV transmission, positive attitudes toward HIV-infected individuals, and changes in behaviors to decrease one's risk of HIV infection.

Community involvement. There is reason to believe that community-based AIDS education facilitates effective AIDS education in the schools. This may be accomplished by increasing community members' knowledge and positive attitudes about HIV/AIDS and facilitating communication at home between parents and their children regarding HIV-related issues. Community members' knowledge and beliefs about AIDS, and community response to AIDS education in the schools, are important considerations in developing an effective AIDS prevention program for children and adolescents. Over a decade after HIV was introduced into the United States, opposition to essential components of a comprehensive prevention program still exist. In June of 1993, a news release stated, *Miss America, . . . using her reign as a national platform to teach about AIDS, ran into censorship problems in her native Florida. Some school officials told her not to use the word "condom" while talking to students. Others forbade the name of the disease itself* ("Miss America," 1993).

Reluctance to allow AIDS education in the schools may result from lack of accurate information regarding HIV transmission, negative attitudes toward AIDS and persons with AIDS, or a general discomfort or fear regarding the disease. However, com-

FIGURE 1. Universal precautions for blood and body fluids.

1. Wear gloves when contact with blood or body fluids is likely.

2. Wash hands thoroughly with soap and water after removing gloves and after any contact with blood or body fluids.

3. Keep all cuts and open wounds covered with clean bandages.

4. Avoid smoking, eating, drinking, nail-biting, and all hand-to-mouth, hand-to-nose, and hand-to-eye contact when working in areas contaminated with blood or body fluids.

5. Clean all possible contaminated surfaces and areas with a 1:10 household bleach dilution or an approved disinfectant.

6. Clean up any spills of blood or body fuilds thoroughly and promptly, using a 1:10 household bleach dilution or an approved disinfectant.

7. Place all possible contaminated clothing and other items in clearly identified, impervious plastic bags.

8. Avoid sharing toothbrushes, razors, or other items that might transmit blood.

9. Avoid needlesticks and other sharp instrument injuries.

Note. From "Recommendations for Prevention of HIV Transmission in Health Care Settings" by Centers for Disease Control, 1987, *Morbididy and Mortality Weekly Report, 36*(25). Reprinted by permission.

munity involvement in AIDS education may ameliorate these circumstances. For example, Temoshok, Sweet, and Zich (1987) found that, among adults in three major cities, increased knowledge about AIDS was significantly correlated with decreased fear about AIDS and less negative attitudes about homosexuals. In addition, Sheridan, Humfleet, Phair, and Lyons (1990) found that an AIDS education seminar for school administrators, school nurses, and pastors significantly increased knowledge about AIDS, realistic perceptions of personal risk, and willingness to work with persons with AIDS.

Because many people associate moral and sexual issues with AIDS, there are families in the community who have negative attitudes toward AIDS education in the schools. The most likely alternative to school-based AIDS education for youth is AIDS education via parents or other family members. However, there is scant literature regarding family communication in the home about AIDS. Crawford et al. (1990) studied the effects of a multimedia-based presentation (television, newspaper, and newsletter) of AIDS education on 8th-grade students and their parents. Those 8th-graders and their parents who were exposed to the educational program and materials demonstrated significantly greater AIDS knowledge at posttest than those who were not exposed to the program components. In addition, at both pretest and posttest, those parents willing to participate in the education program reported they talked more with their children about AIDS and other sexual topics than did the parents who did not participate in the education compo-

nents. However, in both groups, parents of 8th-graders who were identified as "at risk" for HIV infection (e.g., 8th-graders who engage in or know someone who engages in IV drug use, and/or who engage in or have friends who engage in sexual intercourse) had more difficulty discussing AIDS and other sexual topics with their children than parents of 8th-graders not at risk. These findings indicate that AIDS education directed toward the family enhanced parents knowledge of AIDS. However, communication about AIDS within the family was only enhanced if the child was not at risk.

Thus, based on these studies, community-based AIDS education can increase knowledge about HIV/AIDS, allay fears and facilitate positive attitudes toward HIV/AIDS and persons with HIV/AIDS, and facilitate communication in the home regarding HIV/AIDS. However, for children who are at risk for HIV infection and children whose parents are not willing to discuss AIDS at home, the importance of school-based AIDS education becomes even greater.

Communities with very low risk status may evidence more negative responses to AIDS education and persons with AIDS than a community aware of its high risk for HIV transmission. Therefore, to facilitate effective school-based AIDS education, the school psychologist must be aware of the community's risk status for the prevalence of HIV/AIDS. This can be accomplished by becoming familiar with the demographics of one's community. School psychologists must also be aware of the community's knowledge and attitudes regarding HIV/AIDS and persons with

HIV/AIDS, and the status of community-based AIDS education programs. Therefore, being actively involved in parent organizations such as the PTO and maintaining an active dialogue with public health personnel is important. School psychologists must also be knowledgeable of current medical interventions and their sequelae for HIV infection and AIDS, especially as they relate to children and adolescents. One should, therefore, become familiar with the pediatric AIDS literature and should develop a working relationship with a medical expert in the community who can serve as a resource when questions arise.

Guidelines for school-based AIDS education programs. Whenever one examines the various AIDS education programs, it is evident that the ultimate goal of school-based AIDS education is to get adolescents to abstain from sexual activity and illicit drug use. If an adolescent has already engaged in sexual intercourse or use of illicit drugs, school programs should enable and encourage discontinuance of these activities. For those adolescents who continue in these activities, school programs should provide education regarding protective behaviors recommended for persons at risk of acquiring HIV infection. Finally, there is a more recent trend to include social and psychological issues in the curricula, such as acceptance of HIV-infected individuals. This is an area where the school psychologist can make an important contribution.

The CDC, in consultation with other health and educational organizations, provides general guidelines to help school personnel develop AIDS education programs (see Figure 2). As discussed previously, it is extremely important that school personnel obtain broad community support and participation in the planning stage of program development. This ensures that the school's policies and programs regarding AIDS are consistent with community needs and values. The CDC recommends that community representatives who are involved in program planning include school board members, parents, school administrators and faculty, school health services, local medical societies, the local health department, students, minority groups, religious organizations, and other relevant organizations.

State guidelines and community values and needs should determine specific program content, degree of explicitness and teaching materials, format for education (e.g., lecture, guest presentation, skills training), and training procedures for AIDS educators. However, the CDC provides essential information to be included in any AIDS education program. This information is divided into three grade ranges designed to reflect differences in children's cognitive functioning at the various levels: early elementary school, late elementary/middle school, and junior/senior high school. Most of the current recommendations for AIDS education by various health and education or-

ganizations advocate for a similar developmental approach. Although these recommendations were not based on AIDS-specific research, recent research by Walsh and Bibace (1991) has found that children's conceptions of AIDS tend to follow a general developmental sequence, and it is similar to that of their conceptions of illness in general.

Because school psychologists may assist in the development and evaluation of school-based AIDS education programs, it is important that they are aware of age-related cognitive differences in children's understanding of illness. The following is a brief description of developmental differences in children's conception of illness and AIDS as identified by Walsh and Bibace (1991). In addition, the CDC recommendations for each developmental level are presented.

Preschool to early elementary school. Preschool and early-elementary-age children typically have an egocentric view of the world. They make little distinction between self and others. Therefore, they do not understand why one person has AIDS and another person does not. They focus on external, observable events and do not differentiate between cause and effect in explaining illness. Therefore, they tend to associate a specific behavior or person with AIDS without understanding the cause-effect relationship. In addition, they think in absolute terms regarding illness outcome. They have a limited understanding of the passing of time and do not understand the concept of long-term illness. In their view, illness causes death, which is immediate. Therefore, AIDS education for this age level should focus on reassuring the child of his or her remote chance of HIV infection. The CDC recommends that AIDS education focus on allaying children's fears of contracting HIV by explaining that HIV is difficult to get and that it does not commonly affect children.

Elementary school. Elementary-age children are less egocentric than younger children and can differentiate between self and others, although in somewhat absolute terms. They identify certain groups of people as those who have AIDS (e.g., "grown-ups," "homosexuals," "teenagers who do bad stuff"), and they differentiate themselves from these groups. In addition, they begin to differentiate between internal and external bodily events and cause-and-effect relationships. Although they have a limited understanding of physiology, they recognize physical symptoms, such as a headache or an upset stomach, and link them to an illness. The cause-effect relationship between a behavior and a physical symptom or illness is typically unidirectional and direct. They identify a specific behavior as causing AIDS, or a specific type of person as having AIDS, although they recognize that the behavior or type of person is not always associated with AIDS. The mechanism of contracting HIV (e.g., mode of transmission) is not understood.

FIGURE 2. Guidelines for school-based AIDS education programs.

1. Parents, teachers, students, and appropriate community representatives should be involved in developing, implementing, and assessing AIDS education policies and programs.

2. AIDS education should be developed as an important part of a more comprehensive school health education program.

3. Education about AIDS should be taught by regular classroom teachers in elementary grades and by qualified health education teachers or other similarly trained personnel in secondary grades.

4. AIDS education programs should help students acquire essential knowledge to prevent HIV infection at each appropriae grade.

5. AIDS education programs should describe the benefits of abstinence for young people and of mutually monogamous relationships within the context of marriage for adults.

6. Education about AIDS should be designed to help teen-age students avoid specific behavior that increases the risk of becoming infected with HIV.

7. Training about AIDS and AIDS education should be provided for school administrators, teachers, nurses, and counselors, especially those who teach about AIDS.

8. Sufficient program development time, classroom time, and educational materials should be provided for education about AIDS.

9. The processes and outcomes of AIDS education should be monitored and assessed periodically.

Note. From "Guidelines for Effective School Health Education to Prevent the Spread of AIDS" by Centers for Disease Control, 1988, *Journal of School Health, 58.* Reprinted by permission.

However, basic concepts of illness prevention are understood. According to the CDC, AIDS education should explain that viruses cause illness and decreased immunity. It should focus on general strategies for illness prevention such as hygiene in addition to causes and noncauses of HIV infection.

Junior high to senior high. Junior high and senior high school students view self as distinct from others. They also identify certain groups of people as those who have AIDS, and they differentiate themselves from these groups. However, they also recognize their relatedness to individuals in these groups even when they do not categorize themselves as belonging to the group. In addition, internal body processes and their relationships to external events are better understood. Therefore, they identify causes of HIV transmission and AIDS in relation to internal body processes. The CDC recommends that education at this level address detailed explanations of modes of HIV transmission and the specific effects of the virus on the body. Specific behaviors that transmit HIV should be presented, as well as protective measures besides encouraging abstinence from sexual intercourse and illicit drug use. In addition, the community can supplement school-based AIDS education by providing, outside of school, further information regarding HIV testing, counseling, HIV-transmission, or other related problems. These community re-

sources should be made known to students as part of the school curriculum.

Evaluation of AIDS education programs. Evaluation of AIDS education programs is an essential component in prevention education. However, few programs have been formally evaluated. CDC (1988) provides nine criteria by which local and state personnel can evaluate the process by which schools are providing effective health education about AIDS:

1. To what extent are parents, teachers, students, and appropriate community representatives involved in developing, implementing, and assessing AIDS education policies and programs?

2. To what extent is the program included as an important part of a more comprehensive school health education program?

3. To what extent is the program taught by regular classroom teachers in elementary grades and by qualified health education teachers or other similarly trained personnel in secondary grades?

4. To what extent is the program designed to help students acquire essential knowledge to prevent HIV infection at each appropriate grade?

5. To what extent does the program describe the benefits of abstinence for young people and mutually

monogamous relationships within the context of marriage for adults?

6. To what extent is the program designed to help teen-age students avoid specific types of behavior that increase the risk of becoming infected with HIV?

7. To what extent is adequate training about AIDS provided for school administrators, teachers, nurses, and counselors — especially those who teach about AIDS?

8. To what extent are sufficient program development time, classroom time, and educational materials provided for education about AIDS?

9. To what extent are the processes and outcomes of AIDS education being monitored and periodically assessed? (p. 146)

In addition, outcome evaluation should include measures of children's and adolescents' knowledge regarding HIV/AIDS, as well as measures of application of this information (e.g., decreased sexual activity and IV drug use among adolescents, and increased use of protective measures during sexual activity and IV drug use). Although studies have shown that children and adolescents can state the high risk behaviors associated with HIV infection (e.g., sexual intercourse, sharing IV drug needles), no education programs to date have been shown to significantly reduce these behaviors. There are numerous AIDS knowledge questionnaires currently available. The reader is encouraged to consult Brown et al. (1990) as an example. In addition, Kann et al. (1991) provide examples of self-report surveys that have been used to assess behavior change.

BEST PRACTICES IN DEALING WITH HIV IN THE SCHOOL

As early as 1988, the National Association of School Psychologists (NASP, 1988) presented a position statement regarding AIDS. This encourages all school psychologists to become knowledgeable about the disease and facilitate the provision of AIDS education and related services to students. Specifically, NASP advocates that the school psychologist, in collaboration with other professionals:

1. Assist in the development, implementation, and evaluation of AIDS education appropriate for age, gender, ability level, and cultural group.

2. Facilitate parental involvement in AIDS education in the school, home, and community.

3. Participate in the decisions about educational and related services for an HIV-infected child.

4. Address the educational and psychological needs of students, parents, and school personnel who are concerned about school attendance of a student

known to be HIV infected, at perceived high risk of infection, or who has a family member with HIV infection.

5. Provide supportive counseling for students who have a family member or friend with AIDS, students at high risk or perceived high risk of HIV infection, or students with AIDS.

6. Help teachers, administrators, and parents recognize and address the general feelings and personal concerns regarding HIV.

7. Work with other education and support personnel to establish and maintain appropriate AIDS-related behaviors and attitudes in students.

Consistent with the NASP recommendations, the following suggestions will assist school psychologists to become proactive members of the collaborative team that must address HIV-related issues in school:

1. School psychologists need to be aware of the epidemiology of HIV. The CDC periodically updates epidemiology statistics in the *HIV/AIDS Surveillance Report*. It is important to assume that HIV is present in every community. Adolescents, in particular, are known to be at increased risk for HIV infection. Thus, each district must make a commitment to address HIV- and AIDS-related issues in their schools.

2. School psychologists should become familiar with the school's policy and guidelines regarding the presence of HIV-infected students and staff in the school. If this policy has not been established, school psychologists should advocate for its creation. This policy should be established before an HIV-infected student is known to the district.

3. Related to the above issue, school psychologists should become familiar with legal issues surrounding school attendance of infected children. An HIV-infected child cannot be denied admission to school on the basis of his or her HIV status. In addition, this child has a legal right to privacy. In most circumstances, this means that only the school superintendent and a pubic health officer have a right to access the information regarding the student's medical condition. In other words, it is not necessary for most school personnel to know the identity of an HIV-infected child.

4. School psychologists should become familiar with the physical and cognitive sequelae of HIV/AIDS. The current literature indicates that memory, attention, language, and motor abilities are adversely affected by HIV/AIDS. However, pharmacological intervention with AZT has resulted in increased Verbal and Performance IQ scores (Levenson & Mellins, 1992). The extent and permanence of the effects of HIV-infection and pharmacological treatments are not fully known. Therefore, a multidisciplinary team approach involving close collaboration with teachers, occupa-

tional therapists, physical therapists, speech therapists, the school nurse, and other professionals is necessary in assessing and monitoring children with HIV/AIDS.

5. School psychologists should become familiar with the social-emotional correlates of HIV/AIDS. Parental illness and death, stigma-induced isolation from peers and adults, as well as the prospect of facing disability and death, will affect the HIV-infected child's functioning at home, school, and in the community. Siblings of HIV-infected children, and noninfected children of parents with HIV, also face similar psychosocial trauma. Supportive counseling is considered a critical component in school psychologists' comprehensive approach to the AIDS challenge.

6. School psychologists, as well as all students and other school personnel, should be familiar with universal precautions for blood and body fluids. These precautions should be incorporated into everyday practice.

7. School psychologists should advocate for community-based HIV education. Research in this area documents that AIDS education in the school can be enhanced by community-based AIDS education and support services. School psychologists should become actively involved in parent and community organizations to accomplish this end.

8. School psychologists should establish working relationships with key public health and medical professionals in the community who work with HIV-infected patients.

9. School psychologists should contribute to the development and implementation of school-based AIDS education by consulting with the school's health educators and nursing personnel. They should advocate that AIDS education be infused into the curriculum at all grade levels and that it be age-appropriate. This includes allaying the fears of preschool and young elementary-age children, providing elementary school children information about hygiene and illness prevention, as well as causes of AIDS, and providing specific information to the junior and senior high school students regarding modes of HIV transmission. For these older students, this involves addressing specific behavior changes to decrease their risk of HIV infection. In addition, HIV education must address the social and psychological sequelae of the disease. Finally, school psychologists should use their expertise to facilitate positive attitudes of students and school personnel toward HIV-infected individuals.

SUMMARY

In most schools in the United States, AIDS education promoting sexual abstinence among adolescents is the typical educational response to the AIDS epidemic. However, AIDS education must not only target children at a much earlier age, but also address attitudes towards infected individuals. With the increasing number of children who are directly or indirectly affected by HIV, there will be a greater demand to meet the special needs of these students. This means that schools and communities must work together. The seriousness of the HIV epidemic requires that every school psychologist be active in preventive education addressing HIV transmission, in ameliorating the repercussions of HIV in the school, and in meeting the needs of affected students.

REFERENCES

Aksamit, D. L. (1990). Practicing teachers' perceptions of their preservice preparation for mainstreaming. *Teacher Education and Special Education, 13*, 21–29.

Ballard, D. J., White, D. M., & Glascoff, M. A. (1990). AIDS/HIV education for preservice elementary teachers. *Journal of School Health, 60*, 262–265.

Brown, L. K., Nassau, J. H., & Barone, V. J. (1990). Differences in AIDS knowledge and attitudes by grade level. *Journal of School Health, 60*, 270–275.

Brucker, B. W., Martin, J. J., & Shreeve, W. C. (1989). AIDS in the classroom: A survey of teacher attitudes. *Early Child Development and Care, 43*, 61–64.

Byers, J. (1989). AIDS in children: Effects on neurological development and implications for the future. *Journal of Special Education, 23*, 5–16.

Centers for Disease Control. (1985, August 30). Education and foster care of children infected with HTLV-III/LAV. *Morbidity and Mortality Weekly Report, 34*, 517–521.

Centers for Disease Control. (1987, August 21). Recommendations for prevention of HIV transmission in health-care settings. *Morbidity and Mortality Weekly Report, 36*(2S), 3S–12S.

Centers for Disease Control. (1988). Guidelines for effective school health education to prevent the spread of AIDS. *Journal of School Health, 58*, 142–146.

Centers for Disease Control. (1993a, January 1). *AIDS information: HIV transmission.* (Document #320020). Atlanta, GA: National Centers for Disease and Prevention.

Centers for Disease Control. (1993b, May). *HIV/AIDS Surveillance Report* (Vol. 5, No. 1). Atlanta, GA: National Centers for Disease and Prevention.

Chambers, D., & Lindenbaum, S. (1993). Public policies on children and families. In A. R. Jonsen & J. Stryker (Eds.), *The social impact of AIDS in the United States* (pp. 201–242). Washington, DC: National Academy Press.

Crawford, I., Jason, L. A., Riordan, N., Kaufman, J., Salina, D., Sawalski, L., Ho, F. C., & Zolik, E. (1990). A multimedia-based approach to increasing communication and the level of AIDS knowledge within families. *Journal of Community Psychology, 18*, 361–373.

Culliton, B. J. (1989, October 6). AZT reverses AIDS dementia in children. *Science, 246*, 21–23.

Education for All Handicapped Children Act of 1975. (P.L. 94-142). 20 U.S.C. Sec. 1401.

Epstein, L. G., Sharer, L. R., & Goudsmit, J. (1988). Neurological and neuropathological features of human immunodeficiency virus in children. *Annals of Neurology, 23,* 19–23.

Fletcher, J. M., Francis, D. J., Pequegnat, W., Raudenbush, S. W., Bornstein, M. H., Schmitt, F., Brouwers, P., & Stover, E. (1991). Neurobehavioral outcomes in disease of childhood: Individual change models for pediatric human immunodeficiency viruses. *American Psychologist, 46,* 1267–1277.

Fraser, K. (Ed.). (1989). *Someone at school has AIDS: A guide to developing policies for students and school staff members who are infected with HIV.* Alexandria, VA: National Association of State Boards of Education.

Gayle, H., Manoff, S., & Rogers, M. (1989, June). *Epidemiology of AIDS in adolescents, USA* (Abstract #MD07 p. 696). Paper presented at V International AIDS Conference, Montreal, Canada.

Goupil, G., & Brunet, L. (1984). Attitudes and behaviors towards mainstreaming of exceptional children. *Canadian Journal for Exceptional Children, 1,* 28–31.

Haffner, D. W. (1992). 1992 report card on the states: Sexual rights in America. *Sex Information and Education Council of the U.S., 20,* 1–7.

Hannah, M. E., & Pliner, S. (1983). Teacher attitudes toward handicapped children: A review and syntheses. *School Psychology Review, 12,* 12–25.

Hein, K. (1992). Adolescents at risk for HIV infection. In R. J. DiClemente (Ed.), *AIDS and adolescents: A generation in jeopardy* (pp. 3–16). Newbury Park, CA: Sage.

Hingson, R., Strunin, L. Berlin, B., & Heeren, T. (1990). Beliefs about AIDS, use of alcohol and drugs and unprotected sex among Massachusetts adolescents. *American Journal of Public Health, 80,* 295–299.

Holcomb, T. F. (1990). Fourth graders' attitudes toward AIDS issues: A concern for the elementary school counselor. *Elementary School Guidance & Counseling, 25,* 83–90.

Johnson, A. B., Gold, V., & Vickers, L. L. (1982). Stress and teachers of the learning disabled, behavior disordered, and educable mentally retarded. *Psychology in the Schools, 19,* 552–557.

Johnson, M. P., Lubker, B. B., & Fowler, M. G. (1988). Teacher needs assessment for the educational management of children with chronic illnesses. *Journal of School Health, 58,* 232–235.

Kann, L., Anderson, J. E., Holtzman, D., Ross, J., Truman, B. I., Collins, J., & Kolbe, L. J. (1991). HIV-related knowledge, beliefs, and behaviors among high school students in the United States: Results from a national survey. *Journal of School Health, 61,* 397–401.

Katisiyannis, A. (1992). Policy issues in school attendance: A national survey. *Journal of Special Education, 26,* 219–226.

Keough, K. E., & Seaton, G. (1988, December). Superintendents' views on AIDS: A national survey. *Phi Delta Kappan,* p. 58.

Kirkland, M., & Ginther, D. (1988). Acquired immune deficiency syndrome in children: Medical, legal, and school related issues. *School Psychology Review, 17,* 304–310.

Levenson, R. L., & Mellins, C. A. (1992). Pediatric HIV disease: What psychologists need to know. *Professional Psychology: Research and Practice, 23,* 410–415.

Miller, H. G., Turner, C. F., & Moses, L. E. (Eds.). (1990). *AIDS: The second decade.* Washington, DC: National Academy Press.

Miss America is told by a Florida school board not to speak to children about AIDS. (1993, June 4). *New York Times,* sect. B, p. 4.

Morsink, C., Blackhurst, E., & Williams, S. (1979). SOS: Follow-up report to beginning learning disabilities teachers. *Journal of Learning Disabilities, 12,* 150–154.

National Association of School Psychologists. (1988). Position statement on AIDS. *Communiqué, 17,* (insert).

Navia, B. A., Cho, E. S., Petito, C. K., & Price, R. W. (1986). The AIDS dementia complex: II. Neuropathology. *Annals of Neurology, 19,* 525–535.

O'Reilly, R. R., & Duquette, C. A. (1988). Experienced teachers look at mainstreaming. *Education Canada,* Fall, 9–13.

Peach, L. E., & Reddick, T. L. (1989, November). *A study of administrators' and teachers' views concerning AIDS and related issues.* Paper presented at the annual meeting of the midsouth educational research association, Little Rock, AR.

Plesser, D. R., Foster, C. D., & Siegel, M. A. (1987). AIDS – The coming plague? In D. R. Plesser, C. D. Foster, & M. A. Siegel (Eds.), *The information series on current topics* (pp. 97–119). Plano, TX: Publication Information Aids.

Pryor, J. B., & Reeder, G. D. (1993). Collective and individual representations of HIV/AIDS stigma. In J. B. Pryor & G. D. Reeder (Eds.), *The social psychology of HIV infection* (pp. 263–286). Hillsdale, NJ: Erlbaum.

Pyle, C. R. (1992). *AIDS and government responsibility and/or liability.* Paper presented at the National College of District Attorneys, San Francisco, CA.

Rehabilitation Act of 1973 (P.L. 93-122), Section 504, 29 U.S.C. 794.

Schmitt, T. M., & Schmitt, R. L. (1990). Constructing AIDS policy in the public schools: A multimethod case study. *Journal of Contemporary Ethnography, 19,* 295–321.

Sheridan, K., Humfleet, G., Phair, J., & Lyons, J. (1990). The effects of AIDS education on the knowledge and attitudes of community leaders. *Journal of Community Psychology, 18,* 354–360.

School Board of Nassau County, Florida v. Arline, 43 FED Cases 81 (U.S. Sup. Ct. 1987).

Shotel, J. R., Iano, R. P., & McGettigan, J. F. (1972). Teacher attitudes associated with the integration of handicapped children. *Exceptional Children, 38,* 677–683.

Temoshok, L., Sweet, D., & Zich, C. (1987). A three city comparison of the public's knowledge and attitudes about AIDS. *Psychology and Health, 1,* 43–60.

Thomas v. Atascadero Unified School District. No. 886-609 AHS (BY) (C.D. Cal. 1987).

U.S. Department of Education. (1987). *AIDS and the education of our children.* Pueblo, CO: Consumer Information Center.

Walsh, M. E., & Bibace, R. (1991). Children's conceptions of AIDS: A developmental analysis. *Journal of Pediatric Psychology, 3,* 273–285.

Williams, R. J., & Algozzine, B. (1979). Teachers' attitudes toward mainstreaming. *The Elementary School Journal, 80,* 63–67.

Weiss, R. (1993). How does HIV cause AIDS? *Science, 260,* 1273–1279.

ANNOTATED BIBLIOGRAPHY

American Association for Counseling and Development et al. (1990). Guidelines for HIV and AIDS student support services. *Journal of School Health, 60,* 249–255.
This document provides guidelines for multidisciplinary HIV-related student support services. It also provides recommended resources for these services as well as resources for AIDS curricula and AIDS information in general. It can be obtained from

National Coalition of Advocates for Students, 100 Boylston, Suite 737, Boston, MA 02116.

Center for Disease Control, & Center for Health Promotion and Education. (1988). Guidelines for effective school health education to prevent the spread of AIDS. *Journal of School Health, 58*, 142–146.
These guidelines provide information on planning and implementing school-based AIDS education. They are reprinted from: Center for Disease Control. (1988). Guidelines for effective school health education to prevent the spread of AIDS. Morbidity and Mortality Weekly Report, 37 (suppl 2), 1–14.

Fraser K. (Ed.). (1989). *Someone at school has AIDS: A guide to developing policies for students and school staff members who are infected with HIV.* Alexandria, VA: National Association of State Boards of Education.

This publication is an excellent source for policy guidelines and resource information regarding HIV-infected persons in the school and AIDS curricula. It can be obtained from the National Association of State Boards of Education, 1012 Cameron Street, Alexandria, VA 22314.

Yarber, W. (1989). Performance standards for the evaluation and development of school HIV/AIDS education curricula for adolescents. *SIECUS Report*, August/September, 18–26.
This is an excellent resource for AIDS curricula for adolescents. It provides specific information regarding student and teacher material content for education programs as well as education resources.

AUTHOR NOTE

The preparation of this chapter was supported, in part, by a grant from the Ronald McDonald Children's Charities awarded to the second and third authors.

35

Best Practices in Planning for Emergency Management within the Schools

Theresa Hubbell Jozwiak
Carol Johnson
Elaine Petersen
Loess Hills (Iowa) Education Agency 13

Often in the literature on crisis intervention, authors mention the need for developing pre-crisis plans and the importance of identifying community resources for use during and after a crisis event. The focus of the writing (Nelson & Slaikeu, 1984; Poland & Pitcher, 1990; Sandoval, 1987; Smead, 1985) however, tends to describe the steps and skills necessary to doing crisis intervention services in the schools. The process for developing the district-level response plan appears to have received little attention until recently (Pitcher & Poland, 1992). The intent of this chapter is to provide school psychologists and other pupil services personnel (social workers, guidance counselors, and nurses) a general process to facilitate developing a district-level or building-level emergency-management plan. This process is presented in a problem-solving format, as a series of questions to be answered first by a building or district core team and then by a larger, multiagency emergency-management planning committee.

OVERVIEW

Emergency planning is proactive. Planing allows the emergency to be managed in an effective, efficient manner rather than mismanaged through benign neglect resulting in chaos. The need for schools and community to collaborate in establishing a community-wide plan is critical because in an emergency situation the *two* systems become *one*. Community agencies providing a variety of safety, medical, and emotional well-being and relief services will be called upon during an emergency. When all the players understand and own a piece of the plan there will be a more effective response to the emergency. Quick and efficient response reduces injury, loss of life, and emotional trauma for the victims. What better reason for emergency planning than to protect our children!

Although central information centers are not collecting data regarding school emergencies, there are indicators of an increasing need for emergency management planning. Everywhere in this country students and adults are exposed to natural disasters, such as tornadoes, hurricanes, floods, and the like. In addition, there is overwhelming documentation (National School Safety Center, 1993) that the schools in this country are the scenes of "unnatural" disasters (fires, vehicular accidents, etc.) and violent behavior.

In 1990, the nation experienced a record juvenile violent-crime arrest rate. Between 1980 and 1990, murder committed by juveniles increased 87% and aggravated assault by 64% (Uniform Crime Reports, 1991).

- One-half of all violent crimes (homicide, forcible rape, robbery, or aggravated assault) against teenagers occurs in school buildings, on school property, or on the street. Most of the crime involving weapons occur on the street rather than in the school building (37% compared to 12%; Bureau of Justice Statistics, 1991).

- Children do not feel safe within their neighborhoods or schools. Each day 135,000 children bring a gun to school (National Children's Defense Fund, 1993).

- Only 37% of the violent crimes taking place in school buildings and 32% of those on school grounds are reported to the police (Bureau of Justice Statistics, 1991).

Regardless of whether the disaster is the result of natural or unnatural causes, the effects are differentially experienced by members of the community. Planning must include both management of the emergency situation and an immediate response of crisis intervention.

The literature on crisis intervention defines *crisis* as a time when "an individual is faced with any problem he/she sees as serious and that has no immediate solution. The problem might seem hopeless because the individual is unable to solve the crisis with their customary problem solving skills" (Smith, 1978). A crisis is often the result of an emotionally hazardous situation in which the individual is unable to call upon his or her emotional supports or in which he or she loses confidence to act effectively (Sandoval, 1987).

While the literature on crisis intervention talks about responding to and providing services in an emergency situation, emergencies and crises are not the same. An *emergency* is a potentially hazardous event which might trigger crisis for some individuals and not others. Some individuals might not find the situation threatening and others might find that they can cope regardless of the hazards and problems (Smead, 1985). It implies a possible need for a system-wide or multisystem response as compared to the individual focus of crisis intervention.

Emergency Management is a comprehensive, systematic approach to handling unexpected hazardous events. The ultimate goal is to ensure the safety of individuals and to minimize the trauma of the hazardous situation. An emergency management approach includes a planning phase, the response during the emergency situation, and the identification and provision of services for long-term needs (Poland & Pitcher, 1990).

As indicated in the crisis intervention literature (Poland & Pitcher, 1990, 1992; Smead, 1985), the traditional point of entry for pupil services personnel is following an emergency situation to provide individual crisis-intervention services. Crisis intervention is viewed as occurring at three levels: primary prevention, secondary intervention, and tertiary prevention (Poland & Pitcher, 1992).

Primary prevention includes those activities designed to prevent or minimize emergency situations and the resulting trauma and crises. These might include curriculum modifications to teach children safety rules and to recognize potential hazards, and ways and timing to respond in a specific crisis situation. Making and testing the emergency plans for how a district or building would respond is also a primary prevention activity.

Secondary intervention, as developed in Caplan's (1964) model, are those activities designed to minimize the escalation of the crisis through quick response. These activities include conducting drills (Poland & Pitcher, 1992; South Dakota State Department of Military and Veterans Affairs, 1991) to have staff and/or students practice the emergency plans. This practice allows the individuals to respond quickly in an emergency situation and to carry the knowledge into other situations and environments. It also includes the immediate response of the pupil services personnel to work with children and adults to manage the effects of the hazardous situation so that individuals are able to cope more productively.

Tertiary prevention, or postvention, are those activities designed to provide follow-up assistance to reduce the negative long-term psychological effects on those experiencing a traumatic event. Follow-up activities might include crisis counseling provided either by the pupil services personnel or through referral to community agencies. Long-term follow-up counseling might be necessary for some individuals and is often provided by community agencies.

Emergency-management planing activities provide a base from which pupil services personnel can be part of the team to identify how to respond quickly in an emergency situation. Early response increases the likelihood that fewer children are traumatized by an event (Poland & Pitcher, 1990). The children most traumatized are those most directly affected by the hazardous event (Nader, Pynoos, Fairbanks, & Frederick, 1990). Early response facilitates minimizing the trauma for children and adults. Emergency-management planning also provides the network for follow-up services.

BASIC CONSIDERATIONS

School psychologists and other pupil services personnel (social workers, guidance counselors, and nurses) have many roles in emergency management. These roles include (a) planning for emergency management, (b) developing crisis or emergency response teams, (c) providing direct crisis or emergency services during the event or immediately after, and (d) providing postvention services to assist the victims to cope with the long-term effects. To effectively work with Emergency Response teams, the school psychologist and pupil services personnel need a knowledge base in crisis intervention strategies for

- Individuals and systems (Poland & Pitcher, 1990; 1992; Sandoval, 1987; Smead, 1985).

- Methods for conducting debriefing groups (Lazarus & Howard, 1993; Thompson, 1990).

- Posttraumatic stress syndrome (Lipovsky, 1991; Nader et al., 1990).

- Strategies for addressing the grief process (Morrow, 1987; Slaikeu & Lawhead, 1985).

This knowledge base permits school psychologists to provide individual and group crisis counseling or to advise others for providing the support services needed. It also provides the base from which to advocate for a comprehensive emergency-management program including planning, practices and drills, and follow-up services.

To be an effective advocate for emergency planning, the school psychologist and pupil services personnel must be familiar with the crisis- or emergency-response plans existing in a building or district. Identification of community resources and contact people within the community organizations (Sandoval, 1985) for long-term follow-up services is quite often a task which falls to the pupil services personnel because other educators have little contact with the medical and private counseling sector.

The building administrator is the key to any comprehensive plan within a building. As a knowledgeable professional, often outside the direct supervision of a building administrator, the school psychologist is in an excellent position for taking an objective look at what is working, what is not, and what is available in an effort to meet the emotional needs of the students and staff. Participation on a response team in a crisis or emergency situation and in postvention is helpful for understanding what is covered by the current plans and what needs to be included in comprehensive planning. It is critical to obtain administrative support for emergency management planning.

Because of the importance for the planning process to involve various community organizations, an understanding and appreciation for differing, mandates, perspectives, and policies is needed to facilitate coordination and collaboration for emergency management. Basic skills in group process and facilitation are necessary to accomplish the work of such a diverse committee. School psychologists and social workers are often trained in these skills, thus making coordination of the committee's efforts a reasonable role for either or both.

Part of a comprehensive emergency-management plan is to provide inservice and drills for students, teachers, and other staff as determined appropriate. Assisting with this inservice and practice is an appropriate role for the school psychologist and the pupil services personnel, particularly regarding the emotional needs of individuals during traumatic events.

Thus the school psychologist and the pupil services personnel have key roles as advocates of comprehensive planning and services, as facilitators of the multiagency planning process, as trainers of the plans, and as direct service providers.

BEST PRACTICES

All to often planning for an emergency situation, which might or might not occur, is the last thing on a person's "to do list." Historically (Poland & Pitcher, 1990), the opportunity to develop an emergency response plan has followed an emergency for which there had been little organized response. Most crisis- or emergency-response programs recommend a debriefing meeting for the response team. This often provides the foot-in-the-door opportunity for the school psychologist and other pupil support personnel to advocate for additional planning.

One useful strategy for expanding the concept of emergency management is introducing "what if" scenarios into formal or informal discussions. During the training of emergency-response teams, one might expand their paradigms beyond suicide or accidental loss of life through the use of such scenarios. A script might be similar to the following two examples:

In our district this past school year eight fires were set in school buildings by students experimenting with matches or other combustible items. In most of these cases the fire department was not called immediately because the building staff opted to extinguish the fire themselves. None of these fires got out of hand or resulted in evacuation of the students. Now close your eyes and picture this: "What if" the fire continues to burn, spreading to more flammable materials? The students and staff are evacuated from the building using the standard fire drill procedures. By the time the fire department arrives, the fire has spread to several nearby classrooms. The students are not able to return to the building for the remainder of the day. It is January and the temperature is five degrees above zero. (Remember, fire drill procedures usually call for the students and teachers to leave the building without their coats.) What will you do? Where will you shelter the students and their teachers until dismissal?

In the past few years, our city has seen an increase in gang-related violence, primarily among our youth. While on the playground during recess, an elementary student was shot by a stray bullet from a drive-by shooting. In another incident, a high school student was shot while walking home from school. Now, close your eyes and imagine: "What if" a person was in the building with a gun? What will you do to minimize the risk to the greatest number of students? What do you need to consider?

Because there is a natural inclination to believe certain events would not happen in "my building" or "my district," finding opportunities to introduce relevant information describing the need for emergency planning is important for developing awareness. It is also beneficial to use information from local sources that indicates an emergency *can* happen within the local setting.

As with many planning efforts, a *core team* needs to be identified and organized to serve as a coordinating body for planning activities and a catalyst for implementing the plan. The core team at the building level consists of a building administrator, a teacher, a parent, and at least one representative from the pupil services personnel. Logically the members of the core team coordinate and organize an expanded emergency-planning committee. They provide the link between the community emergency plans and the building's application of the plans.

One of the primary tasks of the core team is to identify persons to serve on or advise the emergency-planning committee. Because the school belongs to the community, the community must be an integral part of the planning process. Representatives of community organizations who might be invited to participate on the planning committee include law enforcement officials, fire fighters, businessmen, health care professionals, community religious leaders, media representatives, utilities representatives, civil defense personnel, Red Cross officials, and whoever else has the interest and time to assist the school or district in developing an emergency-management plan. Additional school district or building personnel who might be included on the committee are a board representative, school nurse, building custodial staff, bus driver, and/or district administration staff.

Because planning is essentially filling the gap between what is already available and what is needed, the school and community people need to meet together at least once to discuss and identify:

1. What are the potential emergencies and what are the probabilities of their occurrence in your geographic area/building?

2. What are the community and school disaster plans? How do the plans fit each other and what are the roles of the representative organizations in a variety of emergencies? What do school personnel do until emergency services arrive?

3. What are the gaps between what we have and what we might need for the potential emergencies identified in question one? In order to identify the "gaps" in the existing plans, the planning committee might consider the following questions:

   a. Where could we evacuate students if necessary? How do we get students there? What is an alternative route?

   b. What needs to be done to confine students if necessary? Where should they be confined given the possible emergency?

   c. How can students be cared for until emergency personnel can arrive or until parents can arrive to assume responsibility for their child? Under what circumstances might the students be released without direct contact with the parent?

   d. How will students be accounted for? What is the procedure for releasing them? How might this differ in varying circumstances?

   e. How can students be transported to their homes if not released directly to their parents?

   f. How should parents be informed and updated about a specific emergency situation?

   g. What alternative communication resources are available?

   h. What is your district's media policy? How can you keep the media updated? Who are the prescribed district contact people?

   i. How can others who must be kept informed be updated and apprised of the situation as needed? How do we identify an alternative coordinator of a local-building response plan if the designated administrator is unavailable or hurt?

   j. How should external emergency response organizations be contacted? At what point?

   k. How do we reassure those involved in protecting the children (I.e., teachers, counselors, etc.) about the welfare of their own families when the emergency is district wide or even if they have family members in a different part of the same building?

   l. Is an emergency box needed? This would be a portable, fire-proof box with critical information which might be needed during an emergency or evacuation of a building. If so, what might be put in it (e.g., class rosters — teachers typically do not take their class rosters with them when evacuating for fire drills, student emergency phone contacts, district emergency policy, etc.)? Where would it be kept? Who keeps the information current? Who is responsible to take it from the building and under what emergency conditions?

   m. How can the need for water, food, and bathroom be met under each disaster/emergency situation?

   n. What are building barriers or hazards? What are classroom barriers or hazards?

   o. Where are plans of the building stored? (These should include shut-off valves.)

   p. Is our insurance adequate? Is our inventory adequate? Are records (student, personnel, and property) in fire-proofed files? Are media materials insured and properly protected?

   q. What measures are needed to protect the building from looters?

   r. What training is needed within the district/local building? To whom will this training be provided?

   s. What preparedness and hazard awareness information might be included in the curriculum for students?

   t. How involved can/should the students be in preparing the plans for their building/the district?

   u. How could the planning team practice the plans to determine the effectiveness and efficiency of the plans? Which plans are most likely to be needed and therefore, most likely to require rehearsal?

Initially the Planning Committee's work can seem overwhelming. One very helpful document is the *Emergency Planning Guide for South Dakota School Administrators*, available through the South Dakota State Department of Military and Veterans Affairs,

Pierre Division of Emergency and Disaster Service. This guidebook is designed to help develop emergency plans for schools and gives detailed step-by-step descriptions of how to develop the team and the plans. Although there might be existing written outlines for emergency management, it is critical for school and community representatives to have discussions about each organization's roles and responsibilities in various emergency situations. Only through this discussion can the "players" know what can be expected from one another.

Obviously, the written plan cannot be operationalized within the building unless all staff members are familiar with specific plans and have the skills to do what is expected of them in an emergency situation. The core team, with the assistance of community representatives, identifies training needs and appropriate resources (people, time, and topics) for providing the training. Most comprehensive plans (Manitoba Department of Education and Training, 1991; South Dakota State Department of Military and Veterans Affairs, 1991) recommend knowledge of first-aid for all teachers and CPR for selected individuals in addition to training for *all staff* in implementing the plans. Be sure that there are individuals within each building trained in first-aid, CPR, and crisis-intervention skills — understanding loss and grieving, facilitating debriefing groups, knowledge of the effects of posttraumatic stress, and referral to external support agencies. Each of these areas require skills above and beyond implementing the plan and most professional preparation sequences have not included the development of these skills. These skills, like any new skill, require use to develop expertise and maintain confidence. If situations do not arise in which the skills are used, pupil services personnel will need to obtain information and practice through literature review and workshops. One of the best methods for acquisition and maintenance of skills is through practice and drills.

The importance of drills/practice cannot be over emphasized. The purpose of the drill is to help students and staff learn to react immediately and appropriately to an emergency. Without the emotionality associated with a traumatic event, drills will highlight the areas needing change and allow them to be made. The core team might choose to request a community safety agency to observe the drill to assist in identifying the areas of need and to make recommendations for improvement. Drills encourage "what if" thinking to improve the preventative measures of the plan and support the purpose for emergency planning.

Using the planning committee's recommendations, the core team makes the decisions about the timing, the breadth, and the content of the drill. Questions the core team might consider include

1. What is the probability of a particular emergency occurring (Sandoval, 1987)?

2. What would be the impact of this emergency if it occurs even once?

3. Should this drill include all building staff, or students and staff, and/or community participants?

For additional information on how to structure drills, consult South Dakota (1991), Poland and Pitcher (1992), and Pitcher and Poland (1992).

Emergency education as a curriculum component will help students manage themselves in an emergency, not only at school, but at home as well. Their training in how to remain calm and to know what to do will help them deal effectively with emergencies in their families and communities. This information provides a lifetime benefit (Manitoba, 1991) and is carried over when they establish their own families.

Information and experience are the keys to protection and have been demonstrated to reduce the trauma associated with many hazardous situations.

SUMMARY

School psychologists and other pupil services personnel have been working to develop crisis-intervention teams to assist in minimizing the long-term negative psychological effects of traumatic events. Now is the time for these same individuals, who have the background in consultation and group facilitation, to assist schools in recognizing the need for comprehensive emergency-management plans. Natural disasters (like Hurricane Andrew), man-made emergencies (like Desert Storm), and the violence in our schools exist and threaten the well-being of our children. The literature has many examples of the benefits of rapid response. Emergency-management planning eliminates the gaps in building and district plans to train adults and students to respond appropriately in emergency situations, to access emergency response organizations and crisis intervention teams quickly, and to identify and refer individuals needing intensive follow-up services. Planning ensures the safety of students and staff and reduces the negative aftereffects of trauma for the participants in hazardous situations.

REFERENCES

Caplan, G. (1964). *Principles of preventative psychiatry*. New York: Basic Books.

Lazarus, P. J., & Howard, P. (1993). The state crisis team response team: A humble and necessary beginning. *Communiqué, 21*(6), 18–20.

Lipovsky, J. A. (1991). Posttraumatic stress disorder in children. *Family Community Health, 14*(3), 42–51.

Manitoba Department of Education and Training. (1991). *Guidelines for emergency preparedness in schools*. Winnipeg: Author.

Morrow, G. (1987). *The compassionate school*. NJ: Prentice-Hall.

Nader, K., Pynoos, R., Fairbanks, L., & Frederick, C. (1990). Children's PTSD reactions one year after a sniper attack at their school. *American Journal of Psychiatry, 147*(1), 1526–1530.

National School Safety Center. (1993). *School crime and violence statistical review.* Malibu, CA: Pepperdine University.

Nelson, E., & Slaikeu, K. (1984). Crisis intervention in the schools. In K. Slaikeu (Ed.), *Crisis intervention: A handbook for practice and research* (pp. 247–263). Boston, MA: Allyn and Bacon.

Pitcher, G., & Poland, S. (1992). *Crisis intervention in the schools.* New York; Guilford Press.

Poland, S., & Pitcher, G. (1990). Best practices in crisis intervention. In A. Thomas & J. Grimes (Eds.), *Best practices in school psychology–II* (pp. 259–274). Washington, DC: National Association of School Psychologists.

Poland, S., & Pitcher, G. (1992). Expect the unexpected. *Communiqué, 20*(7), 7–10.

Sandoval, J. (1985). Notes on teaching school psychologists about community resources and agencies. *Trainers' Forum, 5*(2), 1–4.

Sandoval, J. (1987). Crisis intervention. In C. A. Maher & J. E. Zins (Eds.), *Psychoeducational interventions in the schools.* New York: Pergamon Press.

Slaikeu, K. A., & Lawhead, S. (1985). *Up from the ashes.* Grand Rapids, MI: Pyranee Books.

Smead, V. S. (1985). Best practices in crisis intervention. In A. Thomas & J. Grimes (Eds.), *Best practices in school psychology* (pp. 401–415). Kent, OH: National Association of School Psychologists.

Smith, L. L. (1978, July). A review of crisis intervention theory. *Social Casework.*

South Dakota State Department of Military and Veterans Affairs. (1991). *Emergency planning guide for South Dakota school administrators.* Pierre, SD: Division of Emergency Disaster Service.

Thompson, R. (1990). Post-traumatic loss debriefing: Providing immediate support for survivors of sudden loss. In *Highlights: An ERIC/CAPS Digest.* Ann Arbor, MI: University of Michigan.

ANNOTATED BIBLIOGRAPHY

Pitcher, G., & Poland, S. (1992). *Crisis intervention in the schools.* New York: Guilford Press.
    The authors discuss the theoretical basis for crisis intervention in the schools, and information on specific crises often encountered is provided. Various roles of the school psychologist ranging from consultant to trainer to interventionist are presented in detail. Information to assist in establishing a district-wide management plan is also included.

South Dakota State Department of Military and Veterans Affairs. (1991). *Emergency planning guide for South Dakota school administrators.* Pierre, SD: Division of Emergency Disaster Services.

The guidebook is designed to help principals, teachers, staff, parents, and students develop an emergency guide for their school. Besides preparing a response plan, emergency planners must identify hazards, conduct drills, and involve the school community in planning to provide care and shelter for students until they can be reunited with their parents. Appendices contain planning forms and worksheets, a teacher's package on drills, safety information, and information on children in disasters.

INFORMATION RESOURCES

Federal Information Centers, 1-800-788-2800. One toll-free call accesses seven different federal information centers: National Clearinghouse on Alcohol and Drug Information (NCADI), Drug Information and Treatment Line, Drug-Free Workplace Helpline, Drugs & Crime Data Center and Clearinghouse, Drug Information & Strategy Clearinghouse, National AIDS Clearinghouse, and National Criminal Justice Reference Service. The information centers generally have multilingual and multimodal information in the specific area of interest. The materials are usually free of charge or at minimal cost.

Federal Emergency Management Agency (FEMA), FEMA Publications, P.O. Box 70274, Washington, DC 20024. (202) 646-3484.
    FEMA offers a variety of information – all of it free of charge – that can assist with emergency planning. Information is available for business and industry and for family preparedness. Information specific to schools is limited to tornadoes. If information is requested, it comes in a variety of formats (i.e., print-English and Spanish, braille, audio and video). For further information, call Ralph Swisher, Program Manager for Emergency Public Information in FEMA's Office of Emergency Management, (202) 646-3561.

National Crime Prevention Council, 1700 K Street, NW, Second Floor, Washington, DC 20006. (202) 393-7141.
    The council has materials at different developmental levels which would be appropriate for curriculum use. The council sponsors the "Take a Bite Out of Crime" program and other neighborhood and community programs to prevent crime and improve public safety.

National School Safety Center, 4165 Thousand Oaks Blvd., Suite 200, Westlake Village, CA 91632. (805) 373-9977.
    The N.S.S.C. is supported by the United States Department of Education and Criminal Justice. The Center provides many written and video materials. Call or write for a complete listing.

Regional Educational Laboratories and Regional Centers for Drug-Free Schools.
    These agencies provide print and video resources such as curriculum, model programs, and proven community strategies. They also provide technical assistance for creating violence prevention programs, school safety training for personnel, and gang awareness and violence prevention workshops. Contact your state department of education office to obtain the phone number and address for the regional center serving your local area. For example, in Iowa, planning committees would access the North Central Regional Education Laboratory's Minneapolis office.

State and County Civil Defense Offices.
    These organizations have local and state disaster and evacuation plans. They also usually have information on alternative communication systems.

36

Best Practices in Facilitating Peer Tutoring Programs

Enedina García–Vázquez
Stewart Ehly
The University of Iowa

OVERVIEW

The use of the word "tutor" can be traced back centuries to societies in which more privileged members provided education in the home to their children (Gordon, 1990). More recent use of the term "peer tutor" reflects the modern perception of the importance of peers as influences on children's development. Peer tutoring represents one form of children's helping relationships, one that has been investigated extensively in the past three decades (Foot, Morgan, & Shute, 1990) and recommended to improve student productivity (Walberg, 1984). In *Best Practices in School Psychology–II*, Peterson and Miller (1990) list peer tutoring as a viable peer-influenced academic intervention. Class-wide peer tutoring (Delquadri, Greenwood, Whorton, Carta, & Hall, 1986) and class student tutoring teams (Maheady, Sacca, & Harper, 1988) have also received favorable consideration in the literature.

Thus, the use of the terms "tutor" and "peer tutoring" has varied over time and throughout the literature. For the purposes of this chapter, discussion will center on activities that involve children helping other children to acquire specific knowledge or skills while working one-to-one under the guidance of the teacher or support professional. While the history of tutoring extends well beyond the limits of children working with their peers, this chapter features activities that utilize the resources of a typical classroom.

Another distinction of terminology is worth presenting, that between cross-age and same-age peer tutoring. Information on cross-age arrangements differs little from that of same-age or true peer combinations as indicated later in this chapter. Both options can be utilized within a school or, in the case of cross-age programs, involve children from several schools. The school psychologist as problem solver can be the agent who alerts teachers to the potential benefits of peer tutoring and who, for larger scale programs, links clusters of teachers together into working groups.

A basic consideration that must be addressed is: Why use peer tutoring? What does peer tutoring offer that other instructional options cannot provide? Simply stated, peer tutoring builds on the social and instructional resources of the classroom, school, or district to address fundamental academic needs of children. In the school reform literature, writers such as Perkins (1992, see Annotated Bibliography) argue for the importance of embedding learning activities within natural and available social networks in the school. Peer tutoring, along with cooperative learning and other peer-mediated activities, provides an effective means by which to introduce students to concepts, skill-building or practice materials, and even social-skills content that can supplement the actions of the teacher and support professional — always with student learning as the intended outcome. Perkins' (1992) proposal for a community of learners working with their peers echoes the early 19th century "monitorial system" created by Joseph Lancaster in England. A modern application involving an entire school in a tutorial community was proposed by Melaragno and Newmark (1969/1970).

Again returning to the basic question — why peer tutoring instead of other instructional options? Gerber and Kauffman (1981), while supporting peer tutoring, caution that the peer tutor is not a free resource. Time to select, train, monitor, and evaluate the tutor and learner (often referred to in the literature as the *tutee*) requires the teacher's time and energy. Drawing both partners away from other activities must result in gains for both parties to convince parents that time has been well spent. Gerber and Kauffman (1981) consider peer tutoring to be a rational choice for teachers "*if* the resulting educational outcomes are improved with the expenditure of the same amount of teacher time, or *if* the educational outcomes remain the same with an investment of less time" (p. 162).

The following sections highlight the available literature to justify consideration of peer tutoring as a "best practice" strategy within schools, an option that school psychologists can recommend, develop, and implement knowing that the intervention is likely to produce desirable outcomes.

BASIC CONSIDERATIONS

Peer Tutoring Options

Programs involving peer tutoring have been conducted with virtually every combination of cross-age pairings, of tutor-tutee ability levels, with volunteer and paid participants, in all school subjects, and within many forms of community and school programs. Ehly and Larsen (1980) reported examples of high school and junior high school students tutoring elementary children, older elementary students working with young children, and multiple examples of projects involving content from every academic subject, including science and social studies. Studies in the 1960s and 1970s often focused on gains for tutees, with advantages noted for many tutors. Later efforts to assess the growing literature on tutoring's effects identified benefits for both parties (Cohen, Kulik, & Kulik, 1982).

More recent studies conducted with elementary school students have reported academic benefits for all participants. An abundance of studies has been done involving children from special education classes serving as tutees. In general, research has shown that peer tutoring is a viable alternative to teacher-directed instruction to increase the academic performance of students, whether assigned to a general education or a special education classroom. In addition to gains in achievement, recent studies have targeted social gains from peer tutoring interventions. Osguthorpe, Eiserman, and Shisler (1985), for example, paired fourth through sixth grade students who had been assigned a label of "mental retardation" with peers from regular education classrooms. Eiserman (1988) paired students assigned a learning disabilities label with regular classroom peers who served as tutees. Both studies reported gains in the participant's social attitudes on school and learning.

While application of peer tutoring arrangements is much more commonly used with a small number of dyads, other options are available. Although many of the reported instances of same-age peer tutoring have targeted academic gains, Greenwood et al. (1984) demonstrated that class-wide tutorials are effective. Class-wide peer tutoring produced higher weekly test scores and more student responding than did teacher-run procedures. The authors noted that the lowest performing students in the class experienced the greatest benefits from their experiences.

Class-wide peer tutoring provides opportunities within the classroom for students experiencing difficulties to be tutored in a structured way by students who have mastered those skills (Phillips, Hamlett, Fuchs, & Fuchs, 1993). Most recently, Phillips and colleagues (1993) combined class-wide curriculum-based measurement with class-wide peer tutoring to increase academic skills in mathematics. This combination yielded a data-based system that provided structure to the peer tutoring program, assisted in instructional goals, and significantly increased math skills. While gains were more notable for students identified as low achieving and average achieving than students with learning disabilities, the overall conclusion was that integrating curriculum-based measurement with instructional strategies such as peer tutoring positively influences general education (Phillips et al., 1993).

Greenwood, Carta, and Kamps (1990) support peer-mediated instruction such as peer tutoring as a supplement, even an alternative, to teacher-mediated instruction. Not only do peer-mediated arrangements relieve the teacher of direct instructional responsibilities, they offer more one-to-one contact between instructor and learner. Gerber and Kauffman (1981) cite several studies that support the viability of peer tutoring as an instructional alternative for teachers. It is evident that all tutoring options (same-age, cross-age, class-wide) can lead to positive academic and social outcomes for all participants.

Practical and Ethical Considerations

Arrangements such as peer tutoring are not without costs, both calculable and ethical. The costs of teacher time and energy in arranging for and monitoring all phases of tutorials have already been mentioned. When school psychologists consult with teachers and provide assistance with any phase of arrangements, teacher time and energy are important considerations. In addition, materials developed by school personnel, students, or parents for peer tutoring activities impose very real costs on the parties involved.

Out-of-pocket expenses for peer tutoring can be supported by the school district, PTA/PTO, or any of a number of funding sources. Although the obvious expenses of tutorials can be calculated, the ethical costs may be more difficult to estimate. Greenwood, Carta, and Kamps (1990) raise three areas of ethical concern relevant to peer tutoring: accountability, competence, and informed consent. Each concern must be addressed to be consistent with the Principles for Professional Ethics of the National Association of School Psychologists (Appendix I).

School psychologists can be valuable allies to teachers in evaluating the ethical costs of tutorials. For example, the psychologist can assist in evaluating the benefits that the tutor and tutee are deriving from activities. The literature would suggest that academic gains are quite possible; affective changes are less certain. The psychologist can work with the teacher or the students to develop and implement monitoring and evaluation procedures to place within tutoring arrangements.

Often parents challenge the alleged benefits from peer tutoring. Parents of tutors selected from high-ability classroom groups question the value of tutorials for their children's academic development. When tutees are selected from low-ability groups, their parents often unfavorably compare tutorials with teacher-directed instruction. The psychologist with a knowledge of the literature can respond to many such challenges and be available to work with school personnel to ensure adequate implementation of procedures that will lead to the best possible outcomes.

The concern relating to competence centers on the tutor's ability to rise to the requirements of the role. Consensus on the importance of training and monitoring peer helpers exists across the literature (Greenwood, Carta, & Kamps, 1990). Ehly and Larsen (1980) recommend evaluating tutor ability for mastering all requirements of the role *before* allowing dyads to meet.

Finally, the issue of informed consent must be addressed. Parents are important parties to any requests for permission to involve children in special activities; the students themselves must be afforded the opportunity to consider the potential benefits from working with peers and be permitted to enter or retire from activities without coercion. The psychologist and teacher must be sensitive to participants' concerns relating to reactions from the peer group: Peer tutorials may meet an adult's standards for productive work but, by singling out individual students, may fail miserably to motivate students to become involved.

BEST PRACTICES

Research on Academic Outcomes

Numerous studies have been conducted examining the effects of peer tutoring on the tutor, tutee, academic outcomes, and even social benefits. However, the majority of the investigations have focused on academic benefits. The research has shown that tutoring programs have significant benefits on students' academic achievement, whether in the tutor or tutee role. Not as conclusive, though, are the benefits on affective aspects.

By the late 1960s reviews to consolidate findings and examine overall effects were being conducted. In 1969 Rosenshine and Furst reviewed the literature on tutoring programs and concluded that these programs contributed to the academic growth of both the tutee and the tutor. However, according to the authors, these results were noted only in well-structured and cognitively oriented peer programs. Additionally, Rosenshine and Furst (1969) stated that review methods were lacking a stringent scientific approach. With the inception of the meta-analysis procedure, more powerful methods were available to employ in reviewing overall effectiveness of peer tutoring interventions.

Hartley (1977) applied meta-analysis to findings in math at both the elementary and secondary levels and found that the effects of peer tutoring were positive. In addition she found that tutoring effects were stronger than those found with individual learning programs or computer-based instruction. A review by Cohen, Kulik, and Kulik (1982) stated that Hartley's (1977) work advanced the knowledge of tutoring, though the scope of her project was somewhat limited. They pointed out that Hartley's (1977) analysis covered only mathematics teaching and thus could not determine whether these effects would be evident in other content areas. In addition she only studied achievement effects and did not determine whether tutoring had any effects on other instructional outcomes such as attitudes toward school and school subjects or self-concept.

Cohen et al. (1982) also noted methodological weaknesses in Hartley's study. They reported that she aggregated effects on both tutors and tutees and that her analysis was based more on the findings rather than actual studies, which in turn made it difficult to determine statistical error. Another methodological weakness was that her pool of studies included some which lacked adequate methodological considerations, such as a control group. Nonetheless, Hartley's (1977) work helped to extend the scope of reviews.

Cohen et al. (1982) conducted their own meta-analysis examining student achievement, attitudes toward the subject matter, and student self-concept. They defined 15 variables to describe the studies: four outlining types of tutoring programs, three concerning experimental design variables, six describing features of the course setting, and two describing the features of the publication.

They found that academic achievement of tutees was reported in the majority of the studies analyzed. They also indicated that tutored students often performed better than students in conventional classes. Of great import to student learning were the author's findings that certain program features produced stronger effects. If the programs were structured or had shorter durations, the effects on student learning were larger. Tutoring effects also were stronger when the skills taught and tested were of lower difficulty, when math rather than reading was the content, when tests of achievement rather than reading assessed the content, and when tests of achievement were locally developed (Cohen, Kulik, & Kulik, 1982).

In evaluating the effects on the student tutors, the authors found that in about half of the studies achievement effects on tutors were reported. Tutors performed better than did their control counterparts on tests of the subject matter being taught.

In addition to the many studies conducted with students in the regular education classroom, numerous investigations exist encompassing students with various designations of disability (learning disability, behavior disorders, intellectual deficiency). And reviews have been conducted to determine the overall effectiveness of peer tutoring programs incorporating the child with a disability. For example, Cook, Scruggs, Mastropieri, and Casto (1986) focused on studies involving students with learning disabilities, intellectual handicaps, and behavior disorders, as defined by Public Law 94-142. Their emphasis was on the student with a disability serving as tutor. However, social and academic benefits for both tutors and tutees were quantitatively evaluated using means to judge the studies.

In their article, Cook et al. (1986) did not list the studies they reviewed; however, the results of their meta-analysis indicated that performance levels for tutors and tutees increased over one-half of a standard deviation above the control groups. They also reported that greater gains were evident when objective nonstandardized instruments rather than norm-referenced tests were used and the length of the intervention did not affect the effect size.

Cook et al. (1986) concluded that tutoring is a feasible and potentially powerful technique for students receiving services under labels of learning disabilities, behavior disorders, and intellectual handicaps. They found several examples of these students functioning with success in the role of tutor. Areas cited by these reviewers as needing continued investigation included the examination of social and emotional benefits, specific components of tutoring, and the relation between tutor gains and the content taught.

Research on Affective Outcomes

The social benefits that might accompany the pairing of students in a teaching situation also have been studied. Of importance have been the studies exploring the change in social acceptance resulting from the tutoring process. Studies by Custer and Osguthorpe (1983) and Osguthorpe, Eiserman, and Shisler (1985) indicated that tutors with disabilities experienced substantially more positive social interactions with their nondisabled peers as a result of the tutoring intervention. The multiyear study conducted by Osguthorpe et al (1985) noted a lasting effect in social acceptance: Students with disabilities who tutored interacted more with regular class peers than those who did not tutor. This suggests that personal/social progress could be enhanced by scheduling time for peer tutoring interventions.

Social benefits have been more systematically investigated when determining benefits for the student with a behavior disorder than for the one with a learning disability. Csapo (1976) found that tutors assigned a behavior disorders' label showed an increase in social functioning by expressing more self-confidence and more responsibility. Csapo (1976) further reported that the tutors' number of positive remarks increased, they returned home earlier at night, and the

number of adjudicated delinquencies decreased. In a study of disruptive adolescents, Lane, Pollack, and Sher (1972) found that when these students became tutors, their disruptive behavior decreased and they expressed less anger. These tutors also reported increased self-confidence and responsibility.

Maher (1982) found that tutors with behavior disorders demonstrated improved behavior more often than did tutees with behavior disorders and than students with behavior disorders who were receiving counseling. Maher (1982) found substantial decreases in disciplinary referrals and rates of absenteeism among the tutors with behavior disorders. Additionally, Top (1984) reported that tutors with a behavior disorder showed an improvement in their perceptions of their own abilities. Osguthorpe et al. (1985) also reported that tutors demonstrated greater improvements in social acceptance than did controls. The findings of Maher (1982), Top (1984), and Osguthorpe (1985) are strengthened because of the use of control groups by these researchers.

Although many studies indicate positive findings related to social acceptance and benefits, others reveal inconsistent or negative findings. Franca (1983), using a tutorial model with adolescents with behavior disorders serving as tutors and tutees, found few and inconsistent changes in self-concept and teacher perceptions of behavior. However, tutors and tutees demonstrated improved attitudes toward math and increased social interaction.

A more theoretical review of the social benefits attained by peer tutoring was conducted by Leyser and Gottlieb (1981). The authors listed different types of approaches that have been used to improve the social status of students with disabilities: sociometric grouping, cooperation, student active participation and involvement, rewarding social interaction, coaching, and peer tutoring. They reported that social status may be improved by decreasing inappropriate behaviors. The authors contend that by pairing a shy or withdrawn child with a popular student, the shy student will begin to model the outgoing child's behavior. Additionally, Leyser and Gottlieb (1981) stated that given the role of teacher, the tutor has an opportunity to employ more socially appropriate behavior.

Siperstein, Bak, and Gottlieb (1977) conducted a study on the effects of group discussion on children's attitudes toward peers with disabilities. They found a negative shift in attitudes toward a child with a disability regardless of grouping (friends or nonfriends). The authors suggested that children's interactions in groups may be an important factor to consider in determining the extent to which a child with a disability is asked to participate. In 1980, Siperstein and Bak conducted a study to improve peer attitudes toward blind peers. They reported that although the children "felt better" toward their peers with visual impairments, they actually engaged less in activities with the peers. In general, the authors reported more negative outcomes regarding social acceptance when students were paired with students with visual impairments.

In a study by Ballard, Gottlieb, Corman, and Kaufman (1977) positive results were noted in social acceptance of students with educable mental handicaps when paired with nonhandicapped students. However, social acceptance was not measured by direct observation.

Shisler, Osguthorpe, and Eiserman (1987) investigated the effects of reverse-role tutoring on the social acceptance of students with behavior disorders, based on the idea of mainstreaming students who were diagnosed with behavior disorders. The authors introduced a tutoring intervention strategy placing the student with behavior disorders in a higher status role (tutor) and paired these students with peers in regular education classes. The authors measured the change in attitudes by the regular education students toward the group of students with behavior disorders with whom they worked. They also measured whether hypothesized attitude changes were generalized to a second group of students with behavior disorders in the same school.

Students with behavior disorders were trained in basic sign language vocabulary for about 6 weeks. The tutoring sessions lasted 15 to 20 minutes and were conducted in each of the two classes four times weekly. The tutors were taught to be effective tutors. Tutoring sessions lasted 7 school weeks.

Results of this study revealed that reverse-role tutoring produced significant changes in the tutees' attitudes toward their tutors with behavior disorders. However, the study did not indicate that tutee acceptance of their tutors was generalized to another class of students with behavior disorders. In addition no significant changes were noted for the control group. The tutees' responses to their tutors fluctuated and Shisler et al. (1987) contend that research is still necessary to determine if classmates will indirectly accept students with behavior disorders as a result of tutoring.

In a more recent study (García-Vázquez & Ehly, 1992), the authors of this chapter investigated the effects of a structured peer tutoring program on the social acceptance of students in regular education classes. Students perceived as not socially accepted were paired with students rated as well liked by their peers. Three conditions were tested: Students perceived as not socially accepted were either (a) tutors, (b) tutees, or (c) part of a control group. The results were significant for type of student, distinguishing between students who were rated as liked and those who were not. Significance was obtained for experimental groups on a time variable, suggesting that regardless of role, changes in acceptance would be obtained over time. Mean analysis, however, indicated that students who were rated as disliked and served

as tutors were rated higher on the "like" variable following the tutoring intervention.

As important as the studies involving peer tutoring effects on social and academic benefits are another area requiring more research is investigation of the interactions that occur in the peer tutoring process. Fogarty and Wang (1982), for example, conducted a study to obtain more descriptive information about the interactions within the peer tutoring dyads. The study examined the process from an analysis of the verbal interactions and documentation of academic and attitudinal progress. Of interest were the effects of peer tutoring on the give-and-take exchange between tutors and tutees as well as the motivational force that yields positive academic effects and attitudinal progress.

Another study by this chapter's authors and an associate (García-Vázquez, Ehly, & Vázquez, 1993) examined tutee and tutor verbal interactions to determine the extent to which peer tutoring affects the perceptions of students when the tutor was either accepted or not accepted socially by peers. The results indicated that students initially disliked were more liked at the conclusion of the tutoring intervention when serving as tutors. The findings also indicated that the tutors who were initially liked provided more positive feedback, suggesting that training tutors to provide adequate verbal comments may influence the outcome of tutoring.

Implications for Practice

From the articles reviewed, evidence has accumulated to suggest that both tutors and tutees benefit from the tutoring experience. More specific and definite results have been found in terms of academic gains. Tutors and tutees have shown increases in achievement in subjects such as math, spelling, and reading. Positive academic results in general subject concepts are noted in several studies while in others more specific academic skills were evaluated. Nonetheless, peer tutoring has been proven to work when academic gains are attempted. Studies of social benefits, on the other hand, have produced inconclusive data at best. While some studies note positive findings in social acceptance, others note negative results. Further, in several studies social gains have not been systematically evaluated.

Tutors and tutees receive specific academic gains when tutored by special education students, regardless of content areas (e.g., math, spelling, or reading) and regardless of disability. Students with learning disabilities, mental handicaps, or behavior disorders can serve as tutors of other disabled and nondisabled individuals.

Investigations involving students with behavior disorders have focused more on the social benefits of tutoring than have investigations of students with other disability labels. However, lack of stringent research methodology, control groups, and differences in intervention programs have resulted in inconsistent findings. In addition, the studies have focused on students with a diagnosed disability and not much attention has been given to students who demonstrate mild behavior problems or no diagnosed disability. Further, the tutoring with behavior disordered students has been conducted primarily in self-contained classes and not in regular education settings.

The overall implications of the research on practice relate to the procedures, type of program, length of program, and subject matter. Even though the research on the effectiveness of tutoring varies in quality, overwhelmingly the results have been positive with the major variation being on the degree of program effectiveness. In deciding to develop and implement a peer tutoring program, individuals can feel confident that when academic gains are the goal, a tutoring program can facilitate this objective. In terms of affective goals, continued research is needed and how the program to influence social variables is set up will be important. One critical finding is that students having an opportunity to serve in a tutor role may help to empower student participants.

The more specific implications related to program structure such as type of program, tutor training, length of program, and other factors, are addressed in the next section.

Implementing a Peer Tutoring Program

Once a decision to implement a tutoring program has been reached, the next step is to plan the best possible program. Seven areas to consider are

- Specifying goals and objectives.

- Developing a strategy for the assessment of outcomes.

- Specifying materials and procedures.

- Training tutors for their role.

- Developing a monitoring procedure.

- Conducting a small-scale program before implementing a large-scale effort.

- Considering time and cost factors. (Ehly & Larsen, 1980)

Tutoring programs that have succeeded involved one or more of the seven elements. Often, the chances for success are increased when all these elements are implemented into a peer tutoring program.

The best time to specify goals is before the development of any other component of the program. Defining goals involves deciding what will be gained from a tutoring program. The goals can be simple or complex and fulfill a variety of purposes. Perhaps the program could free the teachers' in-class time to develop instructional materials. A teacher may want to

have structured time set aside for one-to-one instruction and review with students who may require additional assistance. Tutoring sessions also can be used to reinforce short-range objectives or to increase the skills via tutoring in conjunction with classroom instruction (Ehly & Larsen, 1980).

The language of goal statements is general, providing a focus for the set-up of the tutoring project. While a goal statement could be similar across different projects (e.g., increase academic achievement), implementation of the program can be in divergent ways. Nonetheless, goal statements serve as the general structure within which specific objectives can be implemented.

Developing objectives for tutoring programs is a process that involves translating the intent of goals into observable, behavioral statements. To add an evaluation component, frequency of numerical total statements can be added to the objectives to determine the extent to which the goals have been met (Ehly & Larsen, 1980).

Developing specific objectives to reflect the tutoring goals leads directly to the need for a statement of evaluation standards. Specifying competency standards for the students during tutoring provides both tutors and tutees goals to achieve in their partnership.

The extent to which strategies for assessment are developed varies widely. Yet setting evaluation standards prior to tutoring is as important as setting goals for the tutors and learners. Learners could be tested only on the content of each session, providing a consistent flow of information on the success of individual tutoring sessions (Ehly & Larsen, 1980). However, daily student evaluations are time consuming and consideration must be given to the degree of energy to achieve success with the tutoring program. The time spent necessarily will vary with the goals set for the program. If the goal is to increase the degree of interaction among students, detailed daily evaluations may not be critical. However, if the goal is to document learning gains, a more detailed data-based assessment, like a paper/pencil test, may be helpful.

Finally, goals for the tutor are also important to consider. While tutoring programs generally are implemented with the student learner in mind, the research is overwhelmingly positive on the benefits of tutoring for the tutor. Strategies for evaluating tutor progress are warranted. Again, depending on goals for the tutor's participation, the procedures for assessment will vary. When the results indicate that both partners benefit from the tutoring, a stronger case is made for tutorials.

As decisions are made about the program, such as goals, objectives, and evaluation standards and procedures, deciding on which materials and procedures to use will flow naturally (Ehly & Larsen, 1980). Materials can reflect the intent of the program as well as provide the content for the tutoring sessions. Just as with every other step in implementing a tutoring program, making decisions about materials prior to the start of the program will facilitate the process of implementation. Time can be spent early in the process searching for ready-made activities or developing materials so that the tutoring program will flow effortlessly.

Materials similar to those used in regular classroom activities are easily accepted by tutees and do not require much training of the tutors. Previous research indicates that students learn best when the tutoring program supplements the regular classroom instruction (Ehly & Larsen, 1980).

Procedures for presenting materials will depend on the type of tutoring program developed. For example, programs in math and reading will differ on disciplinary lines defined by the subject areas (Ehly & Larsen, 1980). However, the goal in procedure-development is to select the simplest, most direct approach for presentation of information by the tutor.

Another important consideration is tutor training. While the extent of tutor training may vary, research underscores the importance of this element to the success of the program (García-Vázquez & Ehly, 1992). Instructions can be as simple as stating expectations or as complex as providing several sessions of training. In implementing tutor training, four elements need to be considered: students, scheduling, space, and resources (Ehly & Larsen, 1980).

Student academic, social, and other information can be useful in making a decision on whether the student will succeed as a tutor, given the tutoring program goals. Tutor training sessions will alert students to the demands that will be placed on their time and effort. The sessions can provide an indication of the student's readiness to assume the tutor role. When tutoring involves students with disabilities, it is important to plan training sessions that will maximize the experimental students' ability to participate successfully in the tutoring program (Ehly & Larsen, 1980). All students with motivation and the ability to work with a partner have something to contribute to tutoring programs. The key is determining in which way and with what type of program the student will be most successful.

Scheduling tutorials raises crucial considerations given the limited opportunities that teachers have to devote to programs outside of their regularly scheduled activities. Setting up a tutoring program may result in borrowing from planning time in order to develop and implement a program. Of course the goals and the complexity of the program will determine how much time will be required, with more complex tutorials demanding more time to prepare and implement. However, scheduling demands can be minimized by contributions from supportive colleagues and administrators.

In training tutors, sessions optimally will be conducted in an area that will accommodate all of the tutors in the program. In cases of limited space, however, a few tutors at a time could be trained, making sure that the information presented is consistent across sessions. In any case, it is important that enough room is allowed for students to handle materials and role play skills. Often training can be completed in the students' classroom.

Training can include giving the students an opportunity to use the materials prior to commencing the tutorials. Tutors can locate and become familiar with the materials they will use. However, it is the school psychologist's or the teacher's responsibility to make sure the materials needed are easily available (Ehly & Larsen, 1980). Other teachers, staff, former tutors, and parents can serve as resources for the tutors. It is important to point out these people, discuss their roles, and provide the students an opportunity to talk with them.

The bottom line with training tutors is that the success of the program often is determined by the effectiveness of training. Just as important is the teacher's success in monitoring tutors while teaching tutees. Ongoing monitoring provides information on progress, so that the tutors can be praised, retrained, or reminded of tutoring components.

Training sessions can be structured using the principles developed by Deterline (1970). Deterline (1970) points out that tutors can learn to (a) put the learning partner at ease, helping to set the tone of the tutorials; (b) clarify learning expectations, showing the tutee how to verify answers and direct the learner on response procedures; and (c) provide feedback contingent on responses as well as help the tutee verify responses. As demonstrated in previous research, training tutors to provide verbal praise (García-Vázquez & Ehly, 1992) and avoid punishment is highly desirable. When the structure of tutorials calls for providing tangible rewards when appropriate, it becomes necessary for the tutor to know when and how to do so. Finally, Deterline (1970) suggests that tutors need to evaluate all elements of mastery on designated problems.

Monitoring students in the tutoring sessions will indicate whether students are following the designated sequence and using the materials appropriately. Interventions can be made early in the program if students are having difficulty with the process. When students understand the expectations, they will work cooperatively and freely. In addition, monitoring will aid in determining which students need assistance and reinforcing tutors and tutees who demonstrate positive behaviors.

Monitoring the tutee's progress through observations of behavior during tutoring, results on pencil/paper tasks, and attitude toward the process are also critical aspects contributing to the success of the program. This monitoring of the tutee can become a database on tutorial processes so that effects of tutoring can be more clearly established. By coupling curriculum-based measurement with peer tutoring

(Phillips et al., 1993), program effectiveness and student learning can be monitored in a structured, data-based manner. Therefore, monitoring includes examining the progress of the program, the tutor, and the tutee.

Other information that can assist in the development and implementation of tutoring programs includes pilot projects, time and cost considerations, and sources of additional assistance. Often pilot projects will provide knowledge of how a program will work on a smaller scale, and, as a step in a larger program, can be used to refine materials, strategies, procedures, and structure (Ehly & Larsen, 1980).

Developing and implementing a tutoring program can take a lot of time, energy, and money. It becomes important to objectively note what has and has not worked with tutorials to prepare for future endeavors. Teachers can work with administrators to make efficient use of time and to seek financial support. The key is to facilitate the venture without adding on unnecessary hours of labor to an already exhausted profession. In addition, tutoring projects can be financed by schools so that the teacher does not have to use personal funds (Ehly & Larsen, 1980).

Anyone interested in developing and implementing a program can turn to others for assistance, the obvious individuals being other teachers and administrators. Many times if a group of teachers is interested in a project, assistance from principals can be obtained. Support from parents also can be sought. Many parents appreciate feedback on their children's learning experiences and may volunteer to help develop or implement the program. Assistance from parent, teacher, and student organizations can be pursued. Student councils can help put materials together, fill out forms, or perform other regular but time-consuming tasks. Students, in addition to being part of the program, can serve as monitors, pass out assignments, and perform other duties (Ehly & Larsen, 1980).

Other resources can be found in the community. Many community groups have strong interests in education and may provide financial support, materials, and volunteer help. If the school is located near a university, that faculty can be a valuable resource. Many are abreast of the current research, can serve as guides, and have access to students who may want to volunteer to work with a program. Many universities have outreach and precollegiate programs whose intent is to connect with schools.

Tutoring programs work. How they will work in specific situations will depend on the preparation conducted prior to commencing the program. The ideas just described serve as guidelines for developing and implementing a tutorial program. A person's theoretical orientation will determine which specific strategies and activities will be selected for the program.

SUMMARY

School psychologists, as consultants to educators and liaisons to the school for an array of service options, are in an ideal position to introduce peer tutoring activities. Examples exist of a wide variety of individual and group tutorials. At the most basic level, school psychologists can serve as a resource to teachers, administrators, and parents interested in adopting peer tutoring interventions.

At the level of problem solver within the schools, psychologists can add peer tutoring to their list of academic intervention options that can be pilot tested with individual students or groups of children. Peer tutoring also may be implemented in community agencies providing after-school or alternative education services and in the home with sibling involvement.

The school psychologist as consultant and resource for evaluation and research can fulfill additional roles in guiding and assisting educators to assess the benefits of peer tutoring. The training of most school psychologists prepares them for these responsibilities. The problem-solver approach to service is entirely consistent with the available evidence on the implementation and evaluation of tutoring.

Peer tutoring is not new; it has been implemented in thousands of classrooms. When educators and parents become familiar with peer tutoring and its benefits, it can become an attractive intervention option. If the educator or psychologist has not implemented any previous peer tutoring programs, the amount of time and effort needed to achieve the desired outcomes from tutorials add to start-up considerations. School psychologists can serve as catalysts in planning, implementing, and evaluating activities by educators and can provide the support necessary to ensure positive learning outcomes for all students.

REFERENCES

Ballard, M., Gottlieb, J., Corman, L., & Kaufman, M. J. (1977). Improving the social status of mainstreamed retarded children. *Journal of Educational Psychology, 69,* 605–607.

Cohen, P. A., Kulik, J. A., & Kulik, C. C. (1982). Educational outcomes of tutoring: A meta-analysis of findings. *American Educational Research Journal, 19,* 237–248.

Cook, S. B., Scruggs, T. E., Mastropieri, M. A., & Casto, G. C. (1986). Handicapped students as tutors. *The Journal of Special Education, 19*(4), 483–492.

Csapo, M. (1976). If you don't know it, teach it. *Clearinghouse, 12*(49), 365–367.

Custer, J. D., & Osguthorpe, R. T. (1983). Improving social acceptance by training handicapped students to tutor their non handicapped peers. *Exceptional Children, 50*(2), 175.

Delquadri, J., Greenwood, C., Whorton, D., Carta, J., & Hall, R. (1986). Classwide peer tutoring. *Exceptional Children, 52,* 535–542.

Ehly, S. W., & Larsen, S. C. (1980). *Peer tutoring for individualized instruction.* Boston: Allyn and Bacon, Inc.

Eiserman, W. D. (1988). Three types of peer tutoring: Effects on the attitudes of students with learning disabilities and their regular class peers. *Journal of Learning Disabilities, 21,* 249–252.

Fogarty, J. L., & Wang, M. C. (1982). An investigation of the cross-age peer tutoring process: Some implications for instructional design and motivation. *The Elementary School Journal, 82*(5), 451–469.

Foot, H. C., Morgan, M. J., & Shute, R. H. (Eds.). (1990). *Children helping children.* Chichester: John Wiley & Sons.

Franca, V. M. (1983). Peer tutoring among behavior disordered students: Academic and social benefits to tutor and tutee. *Dissertation Abstracts International, 44,* 459–A.

García-Vázquez, E., & Ehly, S. W. (1992). Peer tutoring effects on students who are perceived as not socially accepted. *Psychology in the Schools, 24*(3), 256–265.

García-Vázquez, E., Ehly, S. W., & Vázquez, L. (1993). Examination of tutor and tutee interactions and attitudes: What happens during peer tutoring. *Special Services in the Schools, 7*(2), 1–20.

Gerber, M., & Kauffman, J. M. (1981). Peer tutoring in academic settings. In P. Strain (Ed.), *The utilization of peers as behavior change agents* (pp. 155–188). New York: Plenum.

Gordon, E. E. (1990). *Centuries of tutoring: A history of alternative education in America and Western Europe.* Lanham, MD: University Press of America.

Greenwood, C. R., Carta, J. J., & Kamps, D. (1990). Teacher-mediated versus peer-mediated instruction: A review of educational advantages and disadvantages. In H. C. Foot, M. J. Morgan, & R. H. Shute (Eds.), *Children helping children* (pp. 177–205). Chichester: John Wiley & Sons.

Greenwood, C. R., Dinwiddie, G., Terry, B., Wade, L., Stanley, S. O., Thibadeau, S., & Delquadri, J. C. (1984). Teacher- versus peer-mediated instruction: An ecobehavioral analysis of achievement outcomes. *Journal of Applied Behavior Analysis, 17*(4), 521–538.

Hartley, S. S. (1977). *Meta-analysis of the effects of individually paced instruction in mathematics.* Unpublished doctoral dissertation, University of Colorado. Boulder.

Lane, P., Pollack, C., & Sher, N. (1972). Remotivation of disruptive adolescents. *Journal of Reading, 15,* 351–354.

Leyser, Y., & Gottlieb, J. (1981). Social status improvement of unpopular handicapped and non handicapped pupils: A review. *The Elementary School Journal, 81*(4), 228–234.

Maheady, L., Sacca, M., & Harper, G. (1988). Classwide peer tutoring with mildly handicapped high school students. *Exceptional Children, 55,* 52–59.

Maher, C. A. (1982). Behavioral effects of using conduct problem adolescents as cross-age tutors. *Psychology in the Schools, 19,* 360–364.

Melaragno, R. J., & Newmark, G. (1969/1970). A tutorial community works toward specified objectives in an elementary school. *Educational Horizons, 48,* 33–37.

Osguthorpe, R. T., Eiserman, W. D., & Shisler, L. (1985). Increasing social acceptance: Mentally retarded students tutoring regular class peers. *Education and Training of the Mentally Retarded, 20*(4), 235–240.

Perkins. D. (1992). *Smart schools: From training memories to educating minds.* New York: The Free Press.

Peterson, D. W., & Miller, J. A. (1990). Best practices in peer-influenced learning. In A. Thomas & J. Grimes (Eds.), *Best practices in school psychology–II* (pp. 531–546). Washington, DC: National Association of School Psychologists.

Phillips, N. B., Hamlett, C. L., Fuchs, L. S., & Fuchs, D. (1993). Combining classwide curriculum-based measurement and peer tutoring to help general educators provide adaptive education. *Learning Disabilities Research & Practice, 8*(3), 148–156.

Rosenshine, B., & Furst, N. (1969). *The effects of tutoring upon pupil achievement: A review of research.* Philadelphia: Temple University.

Shisler, L., Osguthorpe, R. T., & Eiserman, W. D. (1987). The effects of reverse-role tutoring on the social acceptance of students with behavioral disorders. *Behavioral Disorders, 13*(1), 35–44.

Siperstein, G. N., Bak, J. J., & Gottlieb, J. (1977). Effects of group discussion on children's attitudes toward handicapped peers. *The Journal of Educational Research, 70,* 131–134.

Top, B. L. (1984). *Handicapped children as tutors: The effects of cross-age, reverse-role tutoring on self-esteem and reading achievement.* Unpublished doctoral dissertation, Brigham Young University, Provo, Utah.

Walberg, H. J. (1984). Improving the productivity of American schools. *Educational Leadership, 41*(8), 19–27.

ANNOTATED BIBLIOGRAPHY

Ehly, S. (1984). *Peer tutoring in the regular classroom.* Des Moines: Iowa Department of Public Instruction. Distributed by National Association of School Psychologists, Silver Spring, MD, 301-608-0500.
A handbook and videotape describing the development and implementation of peer tutoring interventions. The role of the school psychologist in consulting with teachers on tutorial programs is featured.

Foot, H. C., Morgan, M. J., & Shure, R. H. (Eds.). (1990). *Children helping children.* Chichester: John Wiley & Sons.
A collection of 17 articles covering an historical perspective of children helping each other, peer tutoring and collaboration, cooperative learning, and social and clinical issues in peer relations.

Perkins, D. (1992). *Smart schools: From training memories to educating minds.* New York: The Free Press.
A proposal, drawing on research from the cognitive sciences, for the reform of schools. The author promotes cooperative approaches to learning, including peer tutoring.

Gibbs, J. (1987). *Tribes: A process for social development and cooperative learning.* Santa Rosa, CA: Center Source Publications.
A process-oriented program geared for educators and promoting the development of a supportive environment. While this program is within the cooperative learning sphere, a goal is that "peer support enables the achievement of the program."

Johns Hopkins Center for Social Organization of Schools. (1980). *Student Team Learning Kits.*
Kits have been developed at Johns Hopkins emphasizing team learning. Similar to tutoring programs, the kits are developed in a variety of subject matter like life sciences, nutrition, math, language arts, and geometry. These materials can be easily used in the classroom and include teacher's manuals, guide sheets, activities, and the like.

37

Best Practices in Assisting with Promotion and Retention Decisions

Mary Ann Rafoth
Indiana University of Pennsylvania

Karen Carey
University of California at Fresno

OVERVIEW

We often associate the month of May with a sense of relief that winter is over and that a school year has ended successfully. But in classrooms across the country May is a time when some students and parents receive the unsettling news that a retention is being considered. Teachers grapple with the difficult decision that can affect a child's future so dramatically. Consider these scenarios: (a) A preschool teacher tells the parents of a 4-year-old boy with a birthday just before the school cutoff date that they may want to have him spend another year in preschool before facing the demands of public kindergarten; (b) It is recommended to parents of a first grader that their daughter be retained in first grade — because she's slow picking up reading and appears younger than her classmates; (c) A teacher recommends that a boy in fifth grade repeat the year because, while he appears bright and capable of doing the work, he has done very little in class and has handed in virtually no homework assignments; (d) A group of eighth-grade teachers draw up a list of students they feel have not mastered the academic skills necessary to proceed to high school. Many of the students have already repeated one year in school; most are boys from lower socioeconomic classes who have been placed in the lower tracks since early in elementary school; (e) A high school sophomore with frequent absences from school is forced to repeat 10th grade because she has failed to accumulate sufficient credits to enter the 11th grade. Every year, approximately 2.3 million U.S. students are held back in school, many under circumstances similar to those described above. Frequently, school psychologists are involved in making retention decisions. The efficacy of retention, while it is a common educational practice, is not supported by research literature. For the most part, retention is of questionable educational benefit and may have negative effects on achievement, self-concept, and school dropout rates. Nevertheless, teachers continue to believe

in its efficacy. Tomchin and Impara (1992) found that surveyed teachers saw retention as a positive practice that acts to lessen daily school failure and to motivate students to work harder.

This chapter provides the school psychologist with a brief review of the research on student retention as well as discussion of the issues involved when schools make retention decisions. The concluding section will address the role school psychologists may play in making retention decisions and will suggest alternatives to retention that may better meet the needs of students experiencing failure at school. Of the many professionals involved either in developing districtwide retention policies, or in making retention decisions about individual students, the school psychologist is uniquely qualified to act as a consultant in generating alternatives. School psychologists should help to evaluate the reasons for school failure, plan appropriate instructional programs for the following year whether or not the child is retained, and act as consultants both to parents faced with retention decisions and to their school districts in developing programs that are viable alternatives. Best practices regarding nonpromotion center on a thorough understanding of the research and careful consideration of the needs of the individual student.

BASIC CONSIDERATIONS

Retention or nonpromotion is the practice of requiring a child to repeat a particular grade or requiring a child or appropriate chronological age to delay entry to kindergarten or first grade. With the introduction of graded schools in the nineteenth century, retention emerged as a response to the problem of students unprepared for the academic demands of the next grade. While concern about possible negative effects of retention has been expressed since the 1930s, the practice continues to be widespread. In fact, retention remains a common educational practice although little research exists to validate its effectiveness (Holmes, & Matthews, 1984; Medway &

Rose, 1986; Shepard & Smith, 1989). While these reviewers and others (e.g., Jackson, 1975) have concluded that much of the research is flawed or of poor quality, the use of statistical techniques such as meta-analysis and causal modeling can help overcome the weaknesses of individual studies and help establish more definitive relationships between retention and later achievement and social growth.

Kindergarten and Elementary Level

Children are often recommended for retention at the kindergarten level because they have failed to acquire basic readiness skills. Sometimes these determinations are made because of poor performance on a readiness test administered before entry into kindergarten or at the end of the year. Failure to display skills in the classroom that is coupled with low achievement scores is often the reason a child is suggested as a candidate for retention after completing a year of kindergarten. Some children enter kindergarten with little exposure to academics, the school routine, or prerequisite skills such as letter and number recognition, which are typically taught in most preschools. Children from home backgrounds in which such exposure is limited may find themselves candidates for delayed entry into kindergarten or retention.

Delayed entry or retention at the kindergarten level also occurs because some children are judged to be "developmentally immature." These children seem to be slightly delayed in social, motor, and/or readiness skills and in need of a year to grow or mature neurologically and thereby catch up with their peers. Likewise, children who are physically small or relatively young compared with their peers (because of cutoff dates for school entry) are often candidates for delayed entry or retention. Many parents and teachers believe that the extra year will allow the child to compete more effectively with peers the following year.

While late-birthdate children who are retained or held out of school for a year initially may do better than those enrolled in first grade at the prescribed age, longitudinal studies show that initial achievement gains do not hold up over time. For instance, Miller and Norris (1967) divided first graders into three groups based on age at school entrance. They found significant differences between young, middle, and old first graders on three of six readiness measures. At the end of 4 years, however, the average achievement of the young group did not differ significantly from the average achievement of the middle group. Similarly, some research suggests that retention in kindergarten or first grade may be associated with poorer academic and social functioning throughout the elementary grades (Armistead et al., 1992). In a similar study, Hauck and Finch (1993) noted that their results were consistent with earlier research;

differences in achievement related to age exist to some extent in elementary school but tend to diminish and even disappear by middle school. Additionally, May, Brogan, and Knoll (1993) found no relationship between children's birthdates and later classification as handicapped. Profiles of children who are retained in kindergarten indicate that they have multiple deficits and needs, making it unlikely that simple exposure to the same curriculum would be an effective intervention (Mantzicopoulos, Morrison, Hinshaw, & Carte, 1989).

Many schools have adopted transitional or developmental programs for children "not ready for first grade." However, these programs appear to be no more effective than retention (Ferguson, 1991; Gredler, 1992; Mathews, 1977; Talmadge, 1981). Zinski (1983) found no significant differences between children who attended a transitional program between kindergarten and first grade at the end of first grade and children who repeated first grade. Gredler (1983) reviewed seven studies that investigated the effects of transition room placement and concluded that "research indicates that transition room children either do not perform as well or are at most equal in achievement levels to transition room-eligible children placed in regular classrooms."

Perhaps the most comprehensive review of the effects of retention was conducted by Holmes and Matthews (1984). They conducted a meta-analysis of 44 studies, calculating 575 effect sizes to determine the effects of retention on a variety of factors, such as achievement, personal adjustment, self-concept, and so on. The authors defined effect size as "the difference between the mean of the retained group and the mean of the promoted group, divided by the standard deviation of the promoted group." Meta-analysis has become a popular way to aggregate a large number of studies that investigate a common research question.

All the studies selected by Holmes and Matthews compared a group of retained students with a group of promoted students. Thirty-three of the studies investigated achievement effects. These studies yielded an overall effect size of \\ell\37, indicating that retained students scored significantly lower than promoted students on achievement measures. While teachers believe that retention in the grades kindergarten through third grade is not harmful (Tomchin & Impara, 1992), when Holmes and Matthews analyzed the data by the grade level in which the retention took place (Grades 1–6), they again found negative effects at all grade levels. This calls into question the commonly held belief that the earlier a student is retained the greater the likelihood that retention will produce positive effects.

While proponents of retention maintain that promoting children when they are not ready can have a harmful effect on personal adjustment, the bulk of the research does not support this contention. In addition to achievement effects, Holmes and Matthews (1984) also calculated effect sizes on personal adjustment measures taken from 21 studies. They found negative effects for social adjustment, emotional adjustment, and behavior, as well as self-concept, as did another study on the long-range effects of retention (Armistead et al., 1992). Many studies have found that students' attitudes toward retention are negative. Byrnes and Yamamoto (1984) found that children who are retained recognize the change as failure and feel ashamed. In their study children rated retention behind only blindness and a parent's death as most stressful experiences. Smith and Shepard (1989) reported that clinical interviews with retained students indicate that these students saw their retention as "flunking" and as punishment. In this same study, parents of retained kindergartners reported that their children experienced teasing and adjustment problems because of their nonpromotion. Johnson (1981) argued that children who have failed in school show characteristics of learned helplessness. The students in his study were likely to attribute failure to themselves and to deny responsibility for success.

Secondary Level

At the secondary level (i.e., middle school, junior high school, and high school) students are most often retained for two reasons: (a) a lack of sufficient credits to be promoted to the next grade level or to graduate from high school, or (b) a failure to pass mandated minimum competency exams. Through the sixth grade, retention rates tend to decrease with each year. However, when students reach the seventh grade retention rates rise and continue to increase in subsequent years (Medway & Rose, 1986; Rafoth & Carey, 1991). Generally the increase in retention rates is due to students' inability to meet the school district's standards for promotion or to obtain sufficient credits to graduate from high school. Often these students have received failing grades, have demonstrated higher absenteeism than their promoted peers, have been retained in earlier grades, and have experienced higher rates of discipline incidents (e.g., suspensions) (Fleming & Zafirau, 1982). Alternative education is often not provided to these students, and for many life outside of school becomes more important.

Perhaps prompted by employers' doubts about the meaning of a high school diploma and society's current attitudes toward perceived deficiencies in the U.S. educational system, many states now require students to pass minimal competency exams in order to receive a high school diploma. However, many students are unable to pass these tests because of poor reading skills and/or academic performance, and retention becomes the "intervention" of choice. Once retained, remediation often does not occur during the student's retained year, and the student makes little, if any, gains in academic performance (Purkerson & Whitfield, 1981). Many school policymakers believe that retaining students unable to pass minimum competency tests will motivate those students to improve skills and complete the necessary requirements for graduation. However, students are often not motivated by retention and once they have experienced retention, they often equate the circumstance with failure, view themselves as failures, and thus drop out of school (Thompson, 1980). It appears that setting higher standards and administering competency testing do not improve the academic performance of students most at risk for school failure. Instead, these actions may result in an increase in the number of students who are retained and drop out of school (Hamilton, 1986).

Research on retention at the secondary level has generally examined the relationships between grade retention and attendance, suspension, and self-concept, with an emphasis on the correlation between retention and dropout rates (Rumberger, 1987; Wehlage & Rutter, 1986). Retention rates at the high school level have been found to be related to attendance and suspension rates (Fleming & Zafirau, 1982). Generally, students who are failing do not attend school on a regular basis. In addition, students who have been retained prior to the secondary level are less likely to attend school on a regular basis in junior and senior high school. Additionally, regardless of the grade in which retention occurs, secondary students who have been retained often exhibit low self-esteem. In a follow-up study of high school students with a history of grade retention, Hagborg, Masella, Palladino, and Shepardson (1991) found that retained students were lower on a number of variables, including achievement, intelligence, and grades, and were more often absent from school and scored lower on a measure of self-esteem than did nonretained peers. They did note that students retained later in their educational careers displayed even lower grades, less positive school attitudes, more discipline problems, lower self-control, and a more externalized locus of control. General conclusions drawn from many studies suggest that retention correlates negatively with students' self-concept, peer acceptance, and personal adjustment.

The majority of the research on retention at the secondary level has focused on the relationship between retention and dropping out of school. This relationship can be explained by two competing hypotheses: (a) Repeating a grade may increase the risk of dropping out, or (b) Poor achievement may account for both retention and dropping out.

In many early studies undertaken to analyze the relationship between retention and dropping out of school, the achievement variable was not controlled. However, in a number of more recent studies (e.g., Grissom & Shepard, 1989) the achievement variable was adjusted in order to focus only on the relationship between retention and dropping out. It has been found that the dropout rate of overage students (retainees) is appreciably higher than the dropout rate of regularly promoted students when reading achievement scores are equivalent for the two groups. Even in high-socioeconomic school districts, where students are less likely to leave school, a significant increase in dropout rates has been found for retained students.

Do Some Children Benefit from Retention?

Sandoval and Hughes (1981) found that the children who made academic and social gains after repeating first grade had not experienced serious academic deficits in the year prior to retention, had strong self-esteem and social skills, and had shown signs of difficulty in school because of lack of exposure to academic materials (e.g., because of high absenteeism, illness, or frequent family moves) rather than low ability. In a 5-year follow-up, Sandoval (1987) found that these same factors predicted success in the upper grades. However, Smith and Shepard (1989) make two points about this study: (a) The fact that relatively high achievement and high self-concept prior to retention correlated with positive outcomes implies that the most successful retainees are those who need it the least; also (b) even the most successful retainees are no better than promoted controls on a variety of outcome measures at the end of first grade.

At times, retention is employed in an attempt to postpone or supplant special education. However, there is little evidence to support the use of retention in this way (Carstens, 1985; Chandler, 1984; Lieberman, 1980). Cross (1984) found that the most important factors governing a teacher's decision to recommend retention were failure to complete a primer designated by the school district; general immaturity; and anticipated resistance from the child's parents. Cross found that there were no differences in the reading achievement test scores of the children recommended and those not recommended for retention, and none of these factors have been shown to be useful predictors of successful retention.

Some researchers have believed it possible to predict which students benefit from retention and have encouraged schools to develop decision-making procedures to aid in selecting likely candidates (Lieberman, 1980; Light, 1977). Others have rejected such a process. Smith and Shepard (1987) conclude from their own research and their review of the literature, "Although some small percentage of those retained may be helped, the evidence indicates that educators are simply unable to predict accurately which individuals these will be."

BEST PRACTICES

Alternatives to Retention

School psychologists' involvement with retention practices can occur on several levels. It can range all the way from participating in making retention decisions about individual students to influencing school or districtwide retention policies, to lobbying for change on a state level through the collective efforts of a state school psychology association. An important effort at each of these levels should be to promote the use of alternatives to retention that will be more effective in remediating the skill deficits of students.

Individual Retention Decisions

School psychologists can be important participants when decisions are made about retaining students in their schools. They should help evaluate the reasons for school failure by looking at the children's school and developmental histories, the effectiveness of the instruction they have received, and the remediation strategies or programs available to them. The school psychologist should help plan an appropriate instructional program for the following year, whether or not the student is retained, and should act as a consultant both to parents and to school personnel to help them make retention decisions.

Two case discussions may help illustrate the part the school psychologist can play in making retention decisions. In the first case, a child whose first-grade teacher recommended retention was referred by her parents to the school psychologist for testing to rule out the possibility of a learning disability. The teacher reported that the student was having difficulty getting beyond the primer level in reading, her attention span seemed somewhat short, she had some trouble completing work independently, and she also seemed to be exhibiting some "immature behaviors" such as fidgeting in her seat and putting her fingers in her mouth. The child, an attractive, petite girl, was assessed as having average intelligence with achievement commensurate with her ability. The school psychologist met with the child's teacher and parents. She reviewed the test results and then led a discussion about retention. She summarized the research on retention, stressing that there is little evidence that it helps over the long term. She indicated that initially students who are retained in first grade show some improvement over similar students who are not retained but that these gains tend to disappear by third grade. She noted that the child's teacher was trying to make the best decision for the child as she could precisely because she was worried about the child's progress in the coming year, thereby lending support to the teacher without necessarily espousing her recommendation.

The school psychologist reported that while some children do seem to benefit from retention, at present educators lack the ability to predict reliably just which children will benefit. Therefore, she stressed to the child's parents that it would be important that they feel comfortable with whatever decision they made, since undoubtedly the child would sense her parents' comfort or discomfort with the decision. This statement was emphatically echoed by the child's teacher. The decision was left in the parents' hands. The mother later reported to the school psychologist that she had decided not to have her daughter retained. She indicated that as a child she had matured at a young age and she was worried that the same would happen to her daughter. She was concerned about the effect of early maturation, particularly if her daughter were already a year older than most of her classmates. While this parent decided to have her child continue on to second grade, she wanted to be sure her child would be able to get supplemental reading services and that her teachers would continue to monitor her progress in reading.

In a second example, a school psychologist became involved in the case of a kindergartner being considered for retention. In this case, the school psychologist led a team discussion, first questioning why retention was being considered. The classroom teacher pointed out that the child had spent most of the year in kindergarten with an undetected hearing loss and hence it was unclear how much the student had been able to benefit from instruction. The school psychologist then referred to the section of the NASP Position Statement on Student Retention (see Appendix), which specifies when retention is less likely to be harmful. She went down the list: Does this student lack serious academic skills deficits? Does the student have positive self-esteem and good social skills? Has the student had difficulty in school because of lack of access to instruction? The group decided that the answer to these questions was yes, and hence this youngster might benefit from retention.

Most parents and educators are unaware of the research on retention. The school psychologist should be willing to share this research to help schools and parents make informed decisions. This information should not be imparted dogmatically or in a way that impairs working relationships with colleagues or parents. In some cases, this may mean recognizing that schools will make decisions to retain children when the school psychologist feels it is not in the best interest of those children. Especially in these cases, it will be important for the school psychologist to participate in developing a specific plan of action by which the student's skills deficits can be remediated. School psychologists are encouraged to gather follow-up data on children who have been retained and children of comparable achievement levels who are not retained, to help their school districts better understand the outcomes of retention decisions.

School District/System Level

School psychologists' participation at a school district or system level can take many forms. As within their own schools, they can publicize the research on retention to help guide the development of informed policies. They can also serve an evaluative role, using districtwide data to assess the outcomes of retention decisions. And they can monitor the progress of students to ensure that problems are identified and addressed early, before retention becomes a consideration. School psychologists can also promote the development of effective alternatives to retention at all grade levels, from preschool through high school. These can include both developing programmatic interventions that address the needs of failing students and expanding the capabilities of classroom teachers to meet the needs of students at different skill levels.

Programmatic interventions may include developing screening programs to identify children at risk for school failure and to ensure early access to programs already available in the school or community, such as Head Start, Chapter I services, and remedial programs. It may also include developing intervention programs such as after-school tutoring or summer school courses. At the secondary level, school psychologists should encourage the development of reentry programs for dropouts and alternative education programs, such as ones that combine teaching skills with job training. Successful programs at the high school level often have two characteristics: (a) one or more individuals who develop relationships with students individually and monitor their progress carefully; and (b) some mechanism to allow students who have failed courses and lost credits to regain these credits in quicker than normal time, allowing for graduation at the expected time.

One program that exemplifies this approach is Project Stay, developed in Charleston, Illinois. At-risk students are identified by school counselors and teachers and invited to join the program. The students must make a commitment to the program and then be "voted in" by current student members. The Project Stay coordinator develops a strong relationship with each student, giving them wake-up calls at home, checking homework, and meeting them at the school door. Project Stay students complete some coursework in the Stay classroom in small classes and at their own pace. The classroom is equipped with living room furniture and is generally appealing to students. Students who complete failed coursework in the Stay classroom may cover several courses in the time it would typically take to finish one in the regular school program, thus allowing them to make up lost time. The students must maintain passing grades and not pose discipline problems in their regular courses to remain in the program. They may also lose the privilege of remaining in the program if they do not cooperate, by being "voted out" by fellow students. The majority of students who enter Project Stay on the verge of dropping out stay in school and graduate on time.

The instructional technology that enables classroom teachers to meet the needs of students of different skills levels is already available, but in many cases teachers do not have access to that technology. School psychologists can assist their school districts in learning about this technology and arranging for in-service programs to bring this information into the classroom. Instructional approaches such as mastery learning, adaptive education, team teaching, cooperative learning, peer tutoring, and curriculum-based assessment are all methods that have been shown to produce academic gains in students of all achievement levels (see Graden, Zins, & Curtis, 1988, for further discussion of these approaches).

Two examples of such approaches are one school district's decision to respond to high numbers of retentions in the early grades by implementing a curriculum-based assessment and remediation program to correct basic reading problems. The district, with state support, secured an outside consultant, conducted intensive in-services for teachers, and allowed a local school psychologist to develop expertise in the area and become an on-site leader. Enlisting community support to volunteer to review "sandwich word drills" with students garnered both help and excitement in the community. Children made substantial progress, teachers were excited by a new intervention method, and requests for retention dropped dramatically.

Similarly, another district has begun a systemwide program to provide in-service instruction to teachers in fostering metacognitive awareness and learning strategies in students, by helping teachers learn about metacognitive development and study skills training and learn how to embed instruction in these areas into their everyday teaching. Collaborative monthly meetings with a consultant and the training of Chapter I teachers to become on-site experts proved essential to this program's success. The program having been established at the primary level, the teachers in this district now speak less of retention and more of enabling strategies that can be carried over from grade to grade with at-risk students.

To be taught and implemented effectively, the program must gain from school districts a commitment to providing sufficient in-service training. School psychologists are often effective lobbyists for such continuing professional development. In making arguments for such training, school psychologists should help school administrators recognize the economic benefits of reducing retention rates. The National Education Association recently estimated that the average cost per pupil in this country is $4,509 per year (*NEA Today,* May 1989). If a school district, for instance, retains 30 students annually, adding 1 year to those students' school careers will cost districts or state educational agencies in excess of $135,000 each year. There is no doubt that quality training for teachers can be obtained at a far lesser cost.

Another district (Somersworth and Rollinsford School Districts, Administrative Unit 56) reduced retentions dramatically by putting in place a collaborative, problem-solving team to deal with problems prior to the necessity of referral. Retentions dropped from a peak of over 40 in the 1983–84 school year to just six in the 1990–91 school year in three elementary schools with an enrollment of 1,500. In addition, after the new model was put into place (through efforts of the local school psychologist), inappropriate referrals (those not leading to special education placements) and out-of-district placements also declined from 30 to 5, and from over 100 to less than 50, respectively, in a 5-year period.

State Education Agencies

As advocates for children, school psychologists can often be most effective when they move beyond the realm of their own schools and school districts to work at a state level to bring about change. The discrepancy between what is known about retention and what is practiced is great enough to warrant action at a higher level. While a school psychologist acting alone cannot influence state policies and practices, through the efforts of a state school psychology association, change can be effected.

School psychology associations are encouraged to share the research on retention with their state education agencies and with other professional education associations (such as state principals' and superintendents' groups). They are also encouraged to use the lobbying resources available to them to influence legislation, including funding for alternative services delivery and legislation that affects policy, such as decreasing the rigidity of minimal competency requirements. Associations are encouraged to make use of the NASP Position Statement of Student Retention and the Supporting Paper (Rafoth, Dawson, & Carey, 1988) in these efforts.

SUMMARY

While the research on retention is voluminous and much of it is flawed, most recent reviewers have concluded that there are no clear benefits to retaining students and that the practice can have deleterious effects on students' achievement, self-concept, and attitudes, and can increase the likelihood of dropping out of school. Research conducted since the release of the NASP Position Statement on Student Retention has continued to support these findings. Although it is possible that a small percentage of students retained may benefit, it is impossible to predict which students those will be. Use of transition rooms prior to first grade are no more effective than retention, and whatever initial benefits may be derived from retention after kindergarten or first grade appear to be washed out by the end of third or fourth grade. School psychologists should assist in making retention decisions about individual students and should promote effective alternatives to retention. Working to change school practices in the area of retention will require sharing the research on retention with educators, conducting evaluations on the outcomes of retention decisions at the local level, and lobbying at the state level to promote changes in policy and to advocate for alternative service delivery systems that more effectively meet the needs of students experiencing school failure.

REFERENCES

Anderson v. Banks. 520 EI Supp. 472 (S.D. Ga. 1981).

Byrnes, D., & Yamamoto, K. (1984). *Grade repetition: Views of parents, teachers, and principals.* Logan, UT: Utah State School of Education.

Carstens, A. (1985). Retention and social promotion for the exceptional child. *School Psychology Review, 14,* 48–63.

Chandler, H. N. (1984). Retention: Edspeak for flunk. *Journal of Learning Disabilities, 17,* 60–62.

Cross, R. (1984). Teacher decision making on student retention. Paper presented at the annual meeting of the American Educational Research Association, New Orleans. (ERIC Document Reproduction Service No. ED 252 930)

Debra P v. Turlington. 644 F.2d 397 (5th Cir. 1981).

Ferguson, P. (1991). Longitudinal outcome differences among promoted and transitional at-risk kindergarten students. *Psychology in the Schools, 28*(2), 139–145.

Fleming, M., & Zafirau, J. (1982). *Grading issues in a desegregated system.* Paper presented at the annual meeting of the American Educational Research Association, New York. (ERIC Document Reproduction Service No. ED 215 051)

Graden, J. L., Zins, J. E., & Curtis, M. J. (1988). *Alternative educational delivery systems: Enhancing instructional options for all students.* Washington, DC: National Association of School Psychologists.

Gredler, G. (1983). Transition classes: A viable alternative for the at-risk child? *Psychology in the Schools, 21,* 463–470.

Gredler, G. (1992). *School readiness: Assessment and educational issues.* Brandon, VT: CPPC Publishing.

Grissom, J. B., & Shepard, L. A. (1989). Repeating and dropping out of school. In L. A. Shepard, & M. L. Smith (Eds.), *Flunking grades: Research and policies on retention.* New York: Falmer.

Hagborg, W. J., Masella, G., Palladino, P., & Shepardson, J. (1991). A follow-up study of high school students with a history of grade retention. *Psychology in the Schools, 28*(4), 310–316.

Hamilton, S. F. (1986). Raising standards and reducing dropout rates. *Teacher's College Record, 87,* 410–429.

Holmes, C. T., & Matthews, K. M. (1984). The effects of non-promotion on elementary and junior high school pupils: A meta-analysis. *Review of Educational Research, 45,* 225–236.

Howe, H., & Edelman, M. W. (1985). *Barriers to excellence: Our children at risk.* Boston: National Coalition of Advocates for Students.

Jackson, G. B. (1975). The *research evidence on the effects of grade retention. Review of Educational Research, 45,* 613–635.

Johnson, D. S. (1991). Naturally acquired learned helplessness: The relationship of school failure to achievement behavior, attributions, and self-concept. *Journal of Educational Psychology, 13,* 174–160.

Lieberman, L. M. (1980). A decision-making model for in-grade retention (nonpromotion). *Journal of Learning Disabilities, 13,* 268–272.

Light, H. W. (1977). *Light's Retention Scale.* San Rafael, CA: Academic Therapy.

Mantzicopoulos, P., Morrison, D. C., Hinshaw, B., & Carte, E. T. (1989). Nonpromotion in kindergarten: The role of cognitive, perceptual, visual-motor, behavioral, achievement, socioeconomic, and demographic characteristics. American Educational Research Journal, 26(1), 107–121.

Mathews, H. W. (1977). *The effect of transition education, a year of readiness, and beginning reading instruction between kindergarten and first grade.* Unpublished doctoral dissertation, St. Louis University.

May, D. C., Brogan, R., & Knoll, N. (1993). Relationships between children's birthdates and classification as handicapped: Do they exist? *Psychology in the Schools, 30*(2), 187–191.

May, D. C., & Kundert, D. K. (1993). Pre-first placements: How common and how informed? *Psychology in the Schools, 30*(2), 161–167.

Medway, F. J., & Rose, J. S. (1986). Grade retention. In T. R. Kratochwill (Ed.), *Advances in school psychology,* Vol. V. Hillsdale, NJ: Erlbaum.

Miller, W. D., & Norris, R. C. (1967). Entrance age and school success. *Journal of School Psychology, 6,* 47–59.

Purkerson, R., & Whitfield, E. (1981). *Failure syndrome: Stress factors for middle school children.* Washington, DC: National Institute for Education. (ERIC Document Reproduction Service No. ED 207 680)

Rafoth, M. A., & Carey, K. (1991). A survey of state level contacts for school psychology regarding retention/promotion practices: Are we evaluating the risks and benefits? *Psychology in the Schools, 28*(1), 35–42.

Rafoth, M. A., Dawson, P., & Carey, K. (1988, December). Supporting paper on Retention Position Statement. *NASP Communiqué.*

Rumberger, R. W. (1987). High school dropouts: A review of issues and evidence. *Review of Educational Research, 57,* 101–121.

Sandoval, J. (1987). *A five year follow-up of children repeating the first grade.* Paper presented at the 196h Annual Convention of the National Association of School Psychologists, New Orleans.

Sandoval, J., & Hughes, P. G. (1981). *Success in nonpromoted first grade children. Final report.* Davis, CA: University of California. (ERIC Document Reproduction Service No. ED 212 371)

Smith, M. L., & Shepard, L. A. (1987, October). What doesn't work: Explaining policies of retention in the early grades. *Phi Delta Kappan,* 129–134.

Smith, M. L., & Shepard, L. A. (1989). Flunking grades: A recapitulation. In L. A. Shepard & M. L. Smith (Eds.), *Flunking grades: Research and policies on retention.* New York: Falmer.

Talmadge, S. J. (1981). *Descriptive and predictive relationships among family environments, cognitive characteristics, behavioral ratings, transition room placement, and early reading achievement.* Unpublished doctoral dissertation, University of Oregon.

Thomas, A. M., Armistead, L., Kempton, T., Lynch, S., Forehand, R., Nousuaunen, S., Neighbors, B., & Tannebaum, L. (1992). Early retention: Are there long-term beneficial effects? *Psychology in the Schools, 29*(4), 342–347.

Tomchin, E. M., & Impara, J. C. (1992). Unraveling teachers' beliefs about grade retention. *American Educational Research Journal, 29*(1), 199–223.

Wehlage, G. G., & Rutter, R. A. (1986). Dropping out: How much do schools contribute to the problem? *Teacher's College Record, 87*, 374–392.

Zinski, J. P. (1983). *A study of the effects of a pre-first grade transitional class as compared with first grade retention on reading achievement.* (ERIC Document Reproduction Service No. ED 248 459)

ANNOTATED BIBLIOGRAPHY

Carstens, A. (1985). Retention and social promotion for the exceptional child. *School Psychology Review, 14*, 48–63.
This article reviews the theoretical and empirical support for retention, with particular focus on the exceptional learner. The assumptions and goals of retention are reviewed from several theoretical perspectives: Gesellian, behavior analysis, cognitive-developmental, and mastery learning. The author concludes there is a lack of empirical support for retention, nor is there basis for retention on theoretical grounds. Exceptional children, including slow learners, learning-disabled students, and students described as "immature" do not appear to benefit from retention, and the author urges schools to apply interventions that attempt to remediate specific skill deficits.

Gredler, G. (1992). *School readiness: Assessment and educational issues.* Brandon, VT: CPPC Publishing.
This book is divided into four sections which include (a) an introduction and review of the concept of school readiness; (b) an assessment of readiness through screening measures and their validity and usefulness; and the emotional and social adjustment of "young"-for-age children; (c) current practices in the schools such as variation in entry age and its effect on achievement; the use of transition rooms between kindergarten and first grade; retention, intervention/remediation programs for young children, and issues in early childhood education; and (d) related legal and ethical issues concerning readiness and early retention. It offers a comprehensive overview of all issues that touch on the practice of retention at the beginning of a child's education. He concludes that transition rooms and early retention are not effective and discusses alternatives.

Holmes, C. T., & Matthews, K. M. (1984). The effects of non-promotion on elementary and junior high school pupils: A meta-analysis. *Review of Educational Research, 45*, 225–236.
This study employed meta-analysis to integrate the findings of 44 studies investigating the effects of retention on elementary/junior high students. The results established consistently negative effects of retention on achievement, personal adjustment, and attitude toward school. The authors conclude, "Those who continue to retain pupils at grade level do so despite cumulative research evidence showing that the potential for negative effects consistently outweighs positive outcomes."

Medway, F. J., & Rose, J. S. (1986). Grade retention. In T. R. Kratochwill (Ed.), *Advances in school psychology* (Vol. 5). Hillsdale, NJ: Erlbaum.
This chapter on research considers the legal implications of retention and attempts to identify the best candidates for retention. It concludes with a discussion of the role of the school psychologist in making retention decisions.

Smith, M. L., & Shepard, L. A. (Eds.). (1989). *Flunking grades: Research and policies on retention.* New York: Falmer.
This volume provides a comprehensive review of the literature as well as a discussion of the editors' own research addressing policy and practice in student retention. Particularly noteworthy is their discussion of the relationship between retention and school dropout, in which they demonstrate that students of comparable achievement levels are more likely to drop out of school if they have been retained than if they have been promoted. The book concludes with recommendations for alternatives to retention.

38

Best Practices in Conducting Needs Assessments

Richard J. Nagle
University of South Carolina

OVERVIEW

School psychologists can play an active role in designing programs or services responsive to children's needs. Needs assessment is a systematic process of collecting and analyzing data in order to identify needs and problems to be addressed in program planning, development, and modification. School professionals must develop clear and comprehensive goals that are responsive to the realities of the school and community. Because services should be those that are required and desired, needs assessment serves as the foundation on which programs are formulated (Lewis & Lewis, 1983).

Definitional and Conceptual Issues in Needs Assessment

The most common model for identifying needs in the schools is the discrepancy between some current condition and some desired (or required) state (Kaufman & Zahn, 1993; McKillip, 1987). In comprehensive needs assessment, once these gaps or needs are identified, the evaluator must also identify and assess existing school and community services and other resources to meet these needs; develop priorities among identified needs; and determine which services should be maintained, altered, or newly developed.

A need also has been defined as a "value judgment that some group has a problem that can be solved" (p. 10, McKillip, 1987). In defining need in this manner, McKillip (1987) underscores several important considerations for those who conduct needs assessments. First, because needs involve values, different people may perceive different needs for the same situation. It is quite possible that those observing the needs may differ from the person experiencing them as to what the needs are. Nor is it uncommon for service providers to differ from service recipients in reported needs. Second, because needs may emerge for a particular "group," this implies there is an environmental context which will require careful description to facilitate needs analysis. This is particularly important in identifying groups which may be "at risk" for poor outcomes. Third, McKillip states that the definitional component of "problems" reflects an inadequate outcome that falls short of expectations. Lastly, McKillip suggests that recognition of a need implies a judgment that problems which are detected can be solved. Because problems may be created by multiple causes or factors, potential solutions must be judged by their probable efficacy in alleviating the problem, the general cost of the solution, and the feasibility and ease of implementation of the solution.

Bradshaw (1972) developed four distinct conceptual approaches in defining and measuring need. These categories are labeled normative need, relative need, perceived need, and expressed need. This categorization is useful in that it offers multiple perspectives of need as well as different but complementary approaches to comprehending need (Kettner, Moroney, & Martin, 1990).

A normative need implies the presence of some norm or standard, with need being evaluated against some standard. These standards are often set by experts, professional bodies, school boards, or governmental bureaus (Rothman & Gant, 1987). Normative expectations are particularly useful in program planning and in areas where there is a lack of prior experience (McKillip, 1987). Although normative information may be advantageous in providing program planners with objective targets, a potential shortcoming with this approach is that norms or standards may change.

Felt or perceived needs are what people think or perceive are their needs or expectations for services outcomes. Perceived needs are based on the presumption that individuals in the target population have insight into their own needs (McKillip, 1987). Whether that is the case or not, program planners may discover ways in which services can be designed to be responsive to client needs. Unlike normative need where a single standard exists, with perceived need the standard changes with each respondent (Kettner et al., 1990). Thus these data may be highly variable and individualistic. Also, once consumers are asked to report perceptions of their needs, expectations may be raised that program planners will implement programs that will meet their needs (Kettner et al., 1990).

An expressed need deals with the actual utilization of services. This approach provides an estimation of the percentage of people whose perception of need has been mobilized into action (Kettner et al., 1990); however not all those who need services seek them. Because the main focus of expressed need involves the utilization of current services or programs, they can result in solutions which maintain the status quo (McKillip, 1987). Waiting lists, requests for services that do not exist, and petitions are all indicators of expressed need.

Lastly, comparative or relative needs involve the comparison of one group with another. The disparity existing between the two groups is the criterion on which the existence and extent of need are established (Rothman & Gant, 1987). Unlike normative need, there is no standard comparison but rather group comparisons. These could involve comparisons between elementary schools within the same school district or grade-level differences within the same school building, with the revealed gaps between levels of services in these groups indicating need. Program planners who make group comparisons should be vigilant to the unique sociocultural variables or environmental context among different groups to accurately explicate these differences.

As can be seen, all of these conceptualizations of need have distinct strengths and limitations. In the coming sections of this chapter, the reader will see that different methods of needs assessment emphasize certain conceptualizations of need. Given the limitations of each conceptual approach to need, multiple methods or techniques of needs assessment are often recommended to reduce bias in the identification of population needs.

Purposes of Needs Assessment for School Psychologists

The scope of a needs assessment can be very broad based such as at school district and/or community level, or much narrower in focus such as at the school, grade, or department level. Despite the possible breadth of scope of needs-assessment activities, there are several general purpose of needs assessment for school psychologists. As previously discussed, needs assessment can serve as the foundation for program planning, development, and modification. Needs assessment data may also provide information to decision-making bodies such as a school board to justify budgeting priorities. When a strong link between allocation of money and other resources and needed services is observed, decision makers demonstrate strong accountability for their actions.

Additionally, identified needs among a target population in a school district may justify funding requests for internal funding or external sources of local, state, or federal grants.

Needs assessment may also be useful in promoting the professional development of school personnel. Training needs may be established and help design staff development activities (i.e., in-service training) which are both relevant and appropriate to improving job functioning among school personnel.

Lastly, dissemination of needs assessment data may serve an important informative function within the schools and/or community. This can serve as the basis for school and/or community awareness of what the needs are and which courses of action decision makers are considering in their problem solving.

BASIC CONSIDERATIONS

School psychologists may become aware of problems in service delivery in a variety of different ways. Because the role of a school psychologist will vary considerably from school district to school district, it also will differ relative to the psychologist's relationship with program planners.

Planning the Assessment Program

Establishing a need. One of the initial phases in conducting a needs assessment is to clarify the presenting problems or unsatisfactory state of affairs. According to Illback, Zins, Maher, and Greenberg (1990), these problem-clarification activities are aimed at providing "systematic information to place the problem(s) in context and to assure that appropriate planning occurs based on a clear understanding of service needs" (p. 807). This contextual analysis provides initial data regarding the nature and scope of these problem(s). Methods which have been suggested in the literature (Harrison, 1987; Illback et al., 1990) include review of school documents, reports, files, direct observations, and brief interviews with involved persons. These interviews should be conducted with program planners, as well as a diverse sample of school personnel in order to clarify the problem from different perspectives.

Another important dimension to the problem-clarification phase is that it allows the school psychologist to estimate how receptive the school and/or community will be to change. The opportunity and commitment for program planning by key persons must be present. The initiation of needs assessment without the prior commitment to use data for planning purposes is a waste of time and resources and will likely result in conflict within the school (Warheit, Bell, & Schwab, 1977).

Establishing a needs assessment team. A needs assessment team is a working group responsible for the planning, monitoring, and perhaps executing the needs assessment process (National Urban League, 1983). The size of the group is dependent upon the nature and scope of the needs assessment effort, but usually not more than 6 people is a manageable size, particularly if the project is at the school level. Furthermore, it has been suggested (National Urban League, 1983) that members of the needs assessment team be selected based on the criteria of familiarity and knowledge of the target population, community resources and institutions, and the organizational context in which the programs will operate.

The needs assessment team should appoint a director of the project. For purposes of this chapter, it is assumed that this role will be filled by a school psychologist. Because this person will be required to oversee the entire project, he or she should have sufficient technical expertise and leadership skills to fulfill this function. Other members should be individuals who work cooperatively in a group, are task oriented, are capable of making fair and objective decisions, and have a strong commitment for program planning in the area of demonstrated need (National Urban League, 1983).

In addition to personal characteristics, potential assessment team members should be considered from a variety of school and community institutions. This group may include teachers, parents, community leaders and decision makers, local university faculty, representatives from appropriate community agencies, school board members, school administrative personnel, or principals. If the needs assessment is being conducted at the school level, representatives from the Parent Teacher Organization or school advisory council should also be considered. The bottom line is that the assessment team should have sufficient breadth of viewpoint to comprehend the problem and be able to assess the feasibility of different assessment approaches. The inclusion of members who are decision makers, such as principals for school-level assessment or school administrators/board members for district-level assessments, is important to build in commitment and political influence for program development recommendations based on the final needs assessment report.

Once the needs assessment team has been established, the scope of the needs assessment must be determined. In addition to the scope of the project, the amount of resources available to conduct the project is an important consideration. Practical considerations of budget and personpower will influence the method and level of information which can be gathered during the assessment process. The team members also need to evaluate the degree of technical expertise necessary to carry out some of the tasks of the needs assessment. If none of the members has sufficient skills in research design and data collection and analysis, the hiring of a consultant with these skills should be considered. Alternatively, the assessment team may be able to recruit volunteers with these professional skills.

Frequently, the school psychologist may be the only person available to conduct the needs assessment. In the absence of an assessment team, the school psychologist may solicit input from individuals using the same selection criteria used to choose members of the assessment team.

Methodological Concerns

After the initial planning activities are completed, the assessment team must determine what information should be collected. Team members should specify critical issues to be studied and the information necessary to understand them. The information to be gathered should be both quantitative (e.g., percentage of target group children not receiving a particular service) and qualitative (e.g., possible barriers to receiving such services). It has been suggested (National Urban League, 1983) that this information should be sufficiently specific to indicate the extent of the problems, influences on the problems, community resources available to deal with the problems, and hypotheses about potential solutions. However, the gathered information should not be so overly complex that the assessment process becomes unmanageable, too time consuming, or beyond the resources or expertise available (National Urban League, 1983). If the assessment process becomes too burdensome in terms of time and energy, it may delay or detract from program development and implementation activities.

The next section of this chapter will describe methods of needs assessment with a discussion of strengths and limitations to each approach.

BEST PRACTICES

There are different methods of needs assessment. Each approach has its own set of advantages and disadvantages, which will be addressed, and each can be easily modified relative to the scope of the needs assessment (i.e., school level, school district level).

Resource (Program) Inventory

A resource inventory is a compilation of services available to the target group in a specific service area (McKillip, 1987). This information is typically gathered by surveying service providers in the local community and school district. The central aim of a resource inventory is to describe available services, with particular emphasis upon identifying who is providing services, what are the characteristics and eligibility criteria of clients receiving services, and what is the service capacity of the program. Programs are also characterized based on their geographical location and organizational setting.

Programs can also be described based on the utilization patterns of services offered by each program. The underlying assumption of this approach is that program participants are those in the population in need of services. Because utilization rates represent manifestations of problems that have already developed, they are not helpful in prevention planning (Rhodes & Jason, 1991). Likewise, resource inventories detail programs which have already been implemented; therefore, conclusions based on data drawn from this method may give a status quo, institutionalized orientation to program planning (McKillip, 1987).

An important outcome of a resource or program inventory is that it may reveal significant gaps in services as well as identify underutilized services. Furthermore, it may reveal that different agencies provide overlapping services. In times of limited resources and budgets within the schools, the reduction in the overlap of services will allow the allocation of resources into other areas of need.

Resource inventories are generally quick and inexpensive to conduct. Resource inventories are usually among the initial steps in a needs assessment. As already mentioned, the resource inventory can provide certain levels of information for program planning. When considered alone, a resource inventory does not indicate need. Gaps in programming may exist because such services are not needed. For this reason, resource inventories should be supplemented with measures of the extent of the problem and potential demand for services (McKillip, 1987).

Social Indicators

The social indicators approach to needs assessment presumes that need estimates can be inferred by considering selected social and demographic statistics that have been found to correlate highly with service utilization (Lewis & Lewis, 1983). These statistics are presumed to be "indicators" of need. Social indicators are particularly valuable in estimating "at-risk" populations.

Because many federal, state, and local agencies, including schools, are required to maintain statistical information (Illback et al., 1990), social indicator data tend to be readily available through government publications summarizing census and surveys. The *American Statistical Index* is a comprehensive guide to statistical publications of the U.S. Government (McKillip, 1987). Local governments, health organizations, schools, social services agencies, and law enforcement organizations may also be important sources of indicator information. Depending on the problem area being assessed, information from these sources may include socioeconomic status, racial composition, educational levels, health status, housing patterns, family integration, prevalence of delinquency, suicide rates, school dropouts, drug and alcohol abuse, special class placements, achievement test information, and the like.

A distinct advantage of the social indicator analysis is that information is readily accessible and generally can be gathered for low cost by persons with limited research expertise or technical skills (Warheit et al., 1977). Another advantage of the social indicator approach is that the local community or school district can be compared to other communities at the local, state, or national level. In large school districts or ones where individual schools serve diverse populations, it may be useful to compare schools on selected demographic, economic, educational, and social characteristics.

Despite the advantages of social indicator analyses, there are several limitations in this approach. Because this approach is inferential in nature, it assumes that certain social indicators are predictive of needs for services. To validate this assumption, substantial evidence based on the research literature and prior studies is essential. Data from large geographic areas may not pertain or generalize to smaller communities or rural areas of interest (Rhodes & Jason, 1991). Before rates can be compared, differences in population characteristics must be considered.

Although extensive indicator data are available, the form or extent of specific informational requirements may not be fully met. For example, the data you are interested in gathering about certain child characteristics is subdivided into age levels different than those you require. Can it be assumed that information for 6- to 16-year-olds is a valid comparison with the 6- to 12-year-olds in an elementary school?

School psychologists who use the social indicator approach to needs assessment must be vigilant to population shifts which may occur in the schools they serve. While social indicator information is reported over a long time interval, it is possible that some communities may undergo very rapid changes. For this reason, the initiation of indicator analysis can provide baseline data on school or school district demographic characteristics to monitor changes and help guide future needs assessment programs.

Surveys

Surveys are the most commonly used needs assessment methods. They are flexible in format and can be conducted as face-to-face interviews, phone interviews, or questionnaires with a wide range of respondents.

Methods. The school psychologist interested in using surveys to assess needs must determine which method is most appropriate for his or her purposes. The selection of which methodology to choose is generally based on the intended scope of the needs assessment, the technical expertise available to conduct the survey, and the time and resources needed to complete the project.

If the number of persons to be surveyed is relatively small, then interviews are probably the most efficient means of gathering information. Therefore, needs assessments conducted at the school level usually lend themselves to the interview format. The success of interviews is largely a function of the skillfulness of the interviewer. The interviewer must be able to establish trust and convey empathy in order for the respondent to answer questions without feeling self-conscious or suspicious. Additionally, the interviewer should be able to keep the respondent on subjects pertinent to the needs assessment. If skilled interviewers are not available, considerable time and expense can be incurred for training. A major advantage of interviews is that they can provide in-depth information (Kaman, 1986) about a broad range of topics, including demographic characteristics, needs, feelings, desires, and solutions to the problems the respondent is experiencing. The interview also allows the opportunity to explicate questions and to probe ambiguous answers given by the respondent. Interviews are particularly well-suited in surveying the needs of marginal individuals (McKillip, 1987).

There are several advantages and disadvantages in the use of interviews. They can be time consuming and expensive and do not lend themselves to sampling large numbers of respondents. Given the cost of face-to-face interviews, phone interviews may be a reasonable alternative. Conducting phone interviews tends to be faster, but generally speaking, establishing rapport tends to be more difficult. Research also indicates that the rate of refusal to participate is higher with phone interviews than personal interviews (Warheit et al., 1972). Phone interviews may be the method of choice when interviews need to be conducted over a geographically dispersed region. In this instance, traveling expenses may make face-to-face interviews prohibitive. All of these issues have different levels of importance depending on whether the school psychologist conducts interviews at the school, school district, or community level.

Questionnaires are generally the preferred survey method when large numbers of respondents are required. If the items are highly structured, the data are easily quantifiable. The development of an effective questionnaire requires a certain degree of technical expertise. There are a number of important considerations in writing questionnaire items. A basic assumption is that the questions will be understandable, elicit the desired information, and motivate respondents to participate. Several sources (Edwards & Thomas, 1993; Fowler, 1993; McKillip, 1987) provide excellent guidelines on writing and formatting questionnaire items. Because it is beyond the scope of the present chapter to provide an in-depth description of questionnaire construction, the reader is referred to these references. Some of the central concerns in questionnaire construction deal with ensuring an appropriate readability level of items for the respondents, controlling for social desirability of responding, selecting open- versus closed-ended questions, and the use of ranking versus rating questions (McKillip, 1987).

Once items have been written, the next step should be to pretest or pilot the items. This is usually accomplished by asking a small group of individuals from the proposed sample to complete the questionnaire. After this has been completed, respondents are asked to critique questions and wordings, to ascertain whether questions are providing the information for which they were intended. Failure to undertake item piloting may result in wasted time and resources. Poorly written and designed questions will also result in decreased response rates.

Questionnaires have a number of disadvantages. They can be quite costly when reproduction, transportation, telephone, and postage expenses are considered. Generally, respondent turnaround time is slow so that a significant amount of time may elapse before the completed survey is received. If the response rate is low, considerable time and effort will be spent in follow-up aimed at increasing questionnaire completion.

Whether interviews or questionnaires are selected as the survey method, an important methodological concern involves sampling. When the objective is to estimate the frequency of need in the general population, a representative sample of that population is required. In instances where information about a specific subgroup is required, purposive sampling is the methodology of choice (McKillip, 1987).

Key informants as respondents. Key informants are individuals presumed to be knowledgeable about the problem under consideration. It is assumed because of the nature of their work or position in the school or community they will have a good understanding of the needs of the target population. The selection of key informants is made by the assessment team. The scope of the needs assessment and the perceived problem area will determine who are the key informants. For community-based needs assessments, individuals may be selected from the areas of public office, welfare and social service, law enforcement, religion, health, mental health providers, and education. Needs assessments at the school and school district level may include school administrators, principals, department coordinators, guidance counselors, school psychologists, special education teachers, nurses, regular education teachers, and so forth.

In initiating the key informant approach, the assessment steering committee should construct an interview schedule or questionnaire which permits those conducting the survey to obtain comparable data from each of the informants (Warheit et al.,

1977). The committee should also select a single method of data collection. The most frequently used technique is the personal interview because it permits face-to-face contact, an open exchange of ideas, and the best response rate (Warheit et al., 1977). Questionnaires and phone interviews, although they result in lower response rates, can also be used effectively.

If the key informant approach is well planned and a diverse sample of key informants is used, the needs assessor can receive a comprehensive impression of the needs of the school or community. Some of the advantages of this approach include:

- It is generally simple and inexpensive to conduct.

- Assessment is based on professional judgment and actual experience with the problem (National Urban League, 1983).

- Because many community agencies or, in the case of school-based needs assessment, an array of school personnel are involved, the groundwork for cooperation and the development of coalitions between agencies or groups can be laid.

- It can serve as the basis for effective program planning by creating organizational readiness for change and support initiatives in program development (Illback et al., 1990).

The key informant approach allows for the input of many people with different perceptions of the problem situation. However, because their individual views on needs are based on their own organizational perspective, they may be biased. Key informants may be unaware of some of the needs of those they serve or may not comprehend the needs of those who are unserved or underserved. It is for this reason that those using the key informant approach should evaluate the adequacy of the number and type of informants used.

While the key informant approach has some inherent problems, it can be a valuable first step in the needs assessment process. A careful synthesis of information gathered from key informants can help narrow the focus of the assessment by ensuring that only appropriate group meetings, questionnaires, and social indicator approaches are designed (Lewis & Lewis, 1983).

Client/community respondents. Survey methods can be conducted on a specified sample or the entire population. Information gathered in a school- or district-based survey can provide valuable information regarding the (a) frequency of the problem or need, (b) demand for available services in the system, (c) client viewpoints of the problem and needed services, and (d) acceptability of solutions to the problem. The most important advantage of this approach is that it *directly* assesses the problems and needs of the sample surveyed. Thus the client/community survey can locate specific individuals or groups in need and determine the type of services required and desired by the population (Balacki, 1988). Demographic and other characteristics of the population in need can also be determined.

When surveys are conducted at the client/community level, they can raise expectations that the problem area will be addressed by the schools. The survey process can be reactive in a positive way by marshalling support for program initiatives.

Surveys at the client/community level can be quite costly and are not cost effective to use when every new program or service is being considered (Lewis & Lewis, 1983). It is probably best justified for the purpose of cyclical reassessment of changing schools needs. Appropriate sampling techniques can reduce costs. The main limitation encountered with client/community surveys is that they may lack a broad-based perspective of a problem or need (National Urban League, 1983).

Structured Groups

Structured groups provide a supplement and alternative methodology to other needs assessment approaches already reviewed in this chapter. Structured groups can be the most "active and informative" approaches to needs assessment because they involve people in systematic problem analysis and discussion (Illback et al., 1990). Focus groups, nominal group techniques, Delphi technique, and community forums will be discussed.

Focus groups. Focus group methodology is a commonly used qualitative research approach used for exploratory or hypothesis generation and confirmation of results from other needs assessment approaches. Focus groups are guided discussions intended to yield information on specific topics relating to feelings and beliefs about needs from a selected population (Sussman, Barton, Dent, Stacy, & Stag, 1991).

Focus groups are lead by a well-trianed facilitator knowledgeable about the problem under study. The discussion is typically begun by asking broad, open-ended questions about the problem with questions becoming increasingly more specific. The size of focus groups is usually 6 to 10 people. Homogeneous grouping is essential to allow free interaction among group members (McKillip, 1987). The criteria for selecting members (i.e., age, ethnicity, etc.) are determined by the objectives of the study; however, several groups with varied characteristics may be involved to learn more about subgroups in the population (Ward, Bertrand, & Brown, 1991).

Focus groups may be viewed as being quite similar to open-ended interviews. Research, however, indicates that focus groups are frequently superior to individual interviews because of the "synergistic group effect" which results in more identified needs and solutions (Sussman et al., 1991).

Focus groups are frequently used in conjunction with other needs assessment methods. They are useful in helping explicate differences between professional (key informant) and target (clients/community members) audiences. Many needs assessors use focus groups to aid in the construction of questionnaires by identifying issues to be addressed in the survey and to determine terminology and phrases used by the target population to describe their needs and solutions to those needs. Focus groups can also be used to gather responses to conclusions generated from other needs assessment methodologies.

Nominal group technique. The nominal group technique (NGT) was developed by Delbecq and Van deVen (1971) to overcome the common problems of group dynamics including domination of talking by high status group members, non-involvement of reticent members, evaluation of ideas impeding idea generation, and group tendencies to get off-task from the agenda (McKillip, 1987). The NGT was designed to give individuals with disparate interests, capabilities, information, or influence more equity in the decision-making and priority-setting process (Lauffer, 1982). The term *nominal* describes the process of bringing groups together but minimizing verbal communication (Miller & Hustedde, 1987).

The NGT requires a well-trained group leader or facilitator. The group can be comprised of key informants, clients, teachers, students, or service providers (McKillip, 1987). Although there are a number of variants in the NGT, most involve the following steps (Frankel, 1987; Miller & Hustedde, 1987).

1. Facilitator of group presents a problem or question that is clearly defined (e.g., How can we prevent school violence?).

2. Each group member is asked to write down independently and silently as many solutions on a piece of paper or index cards as they can think of. At this point, no discussion is permitted.

3. Each group member presents one solution or idea, one at a time in a round robin fashion. The facilitator records each idea on a flip chart until all are recorded.

4. After all solutions are recorded, they are clarified and evaluated through discussion.

5. Group members are asked to either secretly rate each proposed solution or to rank order their top five choices.

6. Ratings are tabulated and a summary of the results is presented.

7. If clear choices and/or priorities result from the vote, the NGT is complete. In the event of no choices, additional clarification, discussion, and voting are undertaken until a clear choice is obtained.

8. The cycle is repeated for each problem or solution area.

The priorities established by the group may not be accepted by others in the school or community. To minimize this possibility, the needs assessor should develop a plan that has adequate representation among subgroups in the school or community.

Delphi technique. The Delphi technique was developed to get group opinion among experts or individuals with exceptional knowledge about a particular subject area. This technique was developed at the Rand Corporation in the early 1950s to solicit opinion from military officials regarding the number of bombs needed in the event of war (Miller & Hustedde, 1987). Although educational decision making does not deal with such dire issues, the Delphi technique has been used successfully in school program-planning activities.

The Delphi technique typically starts with the assessment team determining which needs will be assessed, who will participate in the process, and how the information will be used. Based on what will be assessed, a questionnaire is developed.

The Delphi technique elicits expert opinion through the use of successive questionnaires administered to individual "panelists," selected on the basis of their expert knowledge or opinion (Lauffer, 1982). The process is designed to forecast or predict events when inadequate information exists. The format of the Delphi method is quite variable relative to the number of questionnaires sent to the panel. For most school applications, three questionnaires are probably adequate if using a panel of 8 to 12 experts.

Miller and Hustedde (1987) have outlined the basic steps in having panelists complete the series of questionnaires. In the first questionnaire, respondents are asked to answer questions regarding a problem situation. The questionnaire is returned and summarized and serves as the basis of the second questionnaire. Panelists are requested to rank their concerns, agree or disagree with the central tendencies of the group, and clarify their judgments. The purpose of this second questionnaire is to portray agreements and disagreements in priorities. A third questionnaire is then mailed asking respondents to reassess prior answers and to clarify their ratings relative to the group. They are again asked to vote by ranking the items listed on the questionnaire. This process is complete when there is general agreement among panelists. In the event of substantial differences among panelists, the questionnaire refinement-feedback cycle is continued. The central aim of the Delphi technique is to clarify problems and needs, not reach group consensus. Once the process is complete, respondents should be provided with a final report.

The Delphi technique is usually blended with other need assessment techniques. It can be effectively used to avoid confrontation when severe disagreement is likely to emerge among experts (Lauffer, 1982). This technique may also be a cost-effective way of gathering expert information by avoiding the high cost of travel.

The Delphi technique requires that respondents have well-developed writing skills as well as a high level of motivation because no facilitator is present to help stimulate responses (Miller & Hustedde, 1987). Although the length of time to conduct a Delphi panel will vary as a function of the number of questionnaire mailings, it typically takes about two months to complete the process.

Community forum. The community forum is similar to a town meeting in which the views and opinions of community members about their needs and problems are gathered. The community forum is appealing because it is generally easy to arrange and can be conducted inexpensively. The community forum can be easily adapted to the scope of the needs assessment in the schools. If the scope of the assessment is at the school level, the forum can be held at an individual school, while a district-wide needs assessment may involve a sample of schools or all schools within a given district.

To enhance the effectiveness of a community forum, a certain degree of planning is required. First, the needs assessment planning team should prepare questions designed to structure the meeting around the issues and, at the same time, provide sufficient flexibility to allow for spontaneous comments and candor among the participants (Warheit et al., 1977). The meeting should be highly publicized through advertising and the media and held at a convenient time and accessible location, because it is essential that a representative sample of the community attend. Early evening meetings at the local school in the community member's attendance area fit these criteria.

A leader for the forum should be appointed by the needs assessment team. This individual should have sufficient skills to keep the audience discussion on track. The leader must clearly state the purpose of the forum and explain any ground rules which will be used, such as time limits on talking by participants. In the event of very large turnouts for the forum, it may be necessary to divide the groups into smaller sections to facilitate discussion. Obviously, in these instances, several group leaders will be necessary. A person from the needs assessment team should also be present to record the proceedings of the meeting. The group leader may also wish to take a vote on priorities and concerns. A sign-up sheet for all participants should be used, so that follow-up mailings can be sent to those attending the meeting.

The advantages and disadvantages of the community forum approach have been discussed exten-

sively by several authors (Lewis & Lewis, 1983; McKillip, 1987; Warheit et al., 1977). The community forum is easy to conduct, quick, and cost effective. The community forum allows for input from many segments of the community. The needs assessor may, in fact, become aware of some highly unique or unanticipated needs when the source of information is directly from potential service recipients. The community forum builds rapport and trust with the community and can enhance community members' commitment to program planning. It also identifies citizens who may be valuable resources for the later implementation of programs.

The validity of data gathered from a community forum will largely be a function of the representativeness of the group. Only a partial view of the community's needs or problems will be portrayed if the group is not representative of the general community. It is quite common for community members with severe problems or impairment not to attend a community forum. The forum leader must keep participants focused on the agenda, or else the meeting will degenerate into a gripe and grievance session. The forum leader must also avoid the meeting becoming controlled by special interest groups who wish to espouse their viewpoints, at the expense of not allowing others to offer opposing or different viewpoints. Similar to other needs assessment methods, the community forum raises expectations that something will be done to solve problems or to satisfy unmet needs.

The community forum is frequently used in needs assessment activities in the schools and is commonly used in conjunction with questionnaires to assess the "felt" needs of the community. The community forum approach is impressionistic and assumes that citizens are aware of and knowledgeable about their own problems and needs.

Selection of Needs Assessment Methods

As this chapter illustrates, needs assessment methods vary considerably in terms of their comprehensiveness, cost, and time necessary to complete the project. Many believe that cost and time should be held to a minimum so as not to interfere with other goals in the program planning process (Hobbs, 1987; Steadham, 1989). In performing needs assessments, no component is more important than the clear specification of the purpose and what you wish to accomplish in the needs assessment. The purpose and who you wish to influence are the most central criteria in choosing methods (Hobbs, 1987).

There are a number of additional criteria to consider when choosing a needs assessment method. These include the resources required and available for needs assessment activities, the skills of the needs assessment team, characteristics of the client system, preferred methods of the decision makers, and the allowable time frame for the needs assessment project (Steadham, 1989).

Because all needs assessment methods have inherent strengths and limitations, many needs assessors have advocated the use of multiple methods. By adopting this strategy, the potential limitations of one approach can be minimized by the use of an additional, complementary method. Multiple activities will also help estimate the reliability and validity of the results of the needs assessment.

Communication of Needs Assessment Findings

A successful needs assessment provides information, via reliable and valid methods, that will be used for program planning, development, and modification (Aponte, 1983). The effective communication of the results of the needs assessment to decision-makers is important because it will determine if the findings are used for program planning (McKillip, 1987). Decision makers will not act upon needs assessment information that they do not understand.

The scope and framework of the final report of the needs assessment depends on the audience to be addressed. The communication must fit audience interests, keeping in mind that they are busy and often unsophisticated about research methodology (McKillip, 1987). In instances where the needs assessor will report the findings to several audiences with divergent interests, modifications in the report may be necessary. While needs assessors focus on the results of the project, program planners are concerned with the organizational consequences of their decisions (Aponte, 1983). The findings should be reported to correspond to the questions raised by the decision makers.

The findings of the needs assessment can be presented in written and/or oral form. Warheit et al. (1977) has suggested the following outline for the needs assessment report:

1. Statement of purpose.

2. Historical background.

3. Design and methods.

4. Presentation of findings.

5. Listing of priorities and recommendations.

Written reports should be free of jargon or technical terms and provide only necessary information which will facilitate decision making. Poor grammar, typographical errors, and the like should be avoided because they will detract from the credibility of the report. The visual display of the findings also tends to facilitate clarity and understanding.

If an oral presentation is used, the needs assessment team must be sure that the presenter will be articulate, knowledgeable, and enthusiastic about the findings. Oral presentations can be greatly enhanced by handouts of the major findings of the needs assessment. Overheads or slides are also a useful means of avoiding "information overload" by audience members. A distinct advantage of the oral presentation is that it allows for personal contact with the exchange of information and occurs at a specified time (McKillip, 1987). Written and oral briefings are typically combined in needs assessment activities.

Whether or not the school or organization accepts the recommendations generated by the needs assessment report will be determined if the proposed changes (a) are based on factual data from the needs assessment, (b) are rank ordered by time-cost benefits, (c) are achievable, and (d) reflect the best interests of the school (Warheit et al., 1977). The problems associated with resistance to change will need to be considered at this juncture. Excellent discussions of these issues can be found in Harvey (1990), Kaufman and Zahn (1993), and Warheit et al. (1977).

SUMMARY

This chapter sought to introduce the reader to the use of needs assessment in the schools. A number of different needs assessment methodologies were explored, with the strengths and limitations for each approach discussed.

Needs assessment serves as the foundation on which programs in the schools are designed. Depending on the resources available in the school districts in which they work, school psychologists can play an active role in needs assessment activities. The unique training of school psychologists makes them viable members of needs assessment teams in the schools.

REFERENCES

Aponte, J. (1983). Need assessment: The state of the art and future directions. In R. A. Bell, M. Sandel, J. F. Aponte, S. A. Murrell, & L. Lin (Eds.), *Assessing health and human service needs: Concepts, methods, and applications* (pp. 285–301). New York: Human Sciences Press.

Balacki, M. F. (1988). Assessing mental health needs in the rural community: A critique of assessment approaches. *Issues in Mental Health Nursing, 9,* 299–315.

Bradshaw, J. (1972). The concept of social need. *New Society, 30,* 640–643.

Delbecq, A. L., & Van deVen, A. H. (1971). A group process model for problem identification and program planning. *Journal of Applied Behavioral Science, 7,* 466–492.

Edwards, J. E., & Thomas, M. D. (1993). The organizational survey process: General steps and practical considerations. In P. Rosenfeld, J. E. Edwards, & M. D. Thomas (Eds.), *Improving organizational surveys: New directions, methods, and applications* (pp. 3–28). Newbury Park, CA: Sage Publications.

Fowler, F. J. (1993). *Survey research methods* (2nd ed.). Newbury Park, CA: Sage Publications.

Frankel, S. (1987). NGT & MDS: An adaptation of the nominal group technique for ill-structured problems. *Journal of Applied Behavioral Science, 23,* 543–551.

Harrison, M. I. (1987). *Diagnosing organizations: Methods, models, and processes.* Newbury Park, CA: Sage Publications.

Harvey, T. R. (1990). *Checklist for change: A pragmatic approach to creating and controlling change.* Boston: Allyn & Bacon.

Hobbs, D. (1987). Strategy for needs assessments. In D. E. Johnson, L. R. Meiller, L. C. Miller, & G. F. Summers (Eds.), *Needs assessment: Theory and methods* (pp. 20–34). Ames: Iowa State University Press.

Illback, R. J., Zins, J. F., Maher, C. A., & Greenberg, R. (1990). An overview of principles and procedures of program planning and evaluation. In C. Reynolds & T. Gutkin (Eds.), *Handbook of school psychology* (2nd ed.; pp. 799–820). New York: Wiley.

Kaman, V. S. (1986). Why assessment interviews are worth it. *Training and Development Journal, 40,* 108–110.

Kaufman, R., & Zahn, D. (1993). Quality management plus: The continuous improvement of education. *Newbury Park, CA: Corwin Press.*

Kettner, P. M., Moroney, R. M., & Martin, L. L. (1990). *Designing and managing programs: An effectiveness-based approach.* Newbury Park, CA: Sage Publications.

Lauffer, A. (1982). *Assessment tools for practitioners, managers, and trainers.* Beverly Hills, CA: Sage.

Lewis, J. A., & Lewis, M. D. (1983). *Management of human service programs.* Monterey, CA: Brooks/Cole Publishing.

McKillip, J. (1987). *Need analysis: Tools for human services and education.* Newbury Park, CA: Sage.

Miller, L. C., & Hustedde, R. J. (1987). Group approaches. In D. Johnson, L. Meiller, L. C. Miller, & G. F. Summers (Eds.), *Needs assessment: Theory and methods* (pp. 91–125). Ames: Iowa State University Press.

National Urban League. (1983). *A guide for developing non-instructional programs.* New York: Author. (ERIC Document Reproduction Service No. ED 272 597)

Rhodes, J. E., & Jason, L. A. (1991). Community needs assessment. In E. Schroeder (Ed.), *New directions in health psychology assessment* (pp. 159–173). New York: Hemisphere Publishing.

Rosenfeld, P., Edwards, J., & Thomas, M. (1993). *Improving organizational surveys: New directions, methods, and applications.* Newbury Park, CA: Sage Publications.

Rothman, J., & Gant, L. M. (1987). Approaches and models of community intervention. In D. E. Johnson, L. R. Meiller, L. C. Miller, & G. F. Summers (Eds.), *Needs assessment: Theory and methods* (pp. 35–44). Ames: Iowa State University Press.

Steadhan, S. V. (1989). Learning to select a needs assessment strategy. In F. H. Margolis & C. R. Bell (Eds.), *Understand training: Perspectives and practices* (pp. 21–33). Minneapolis, MN: Lakewood Publications.

Sussman, S., Barton, D., Dent, C. W., Stacy, A. W., & Stag, D. (1991). Use of focus groups in developing an adolescent tobacco use cessation program: Collective norm effects. *Journal of Applied Social Psychology, 21,* 1772–1782.

Ward, V. M., Bertrand, J. T., & Brown, L. F. (1991). The comparability of focus group and survey results: Three case studies. *Evaluation Review, 15,* 266–283.

Warheit, G. J., Bell, R. A., & Schwab, J. J. (1977). *Needs assessment approaches: Concepts and methods* (Publication No. ADM-77-472). Washington, DC: Department of Health, Education, and Welfare.

ANNOTATED BIBLIOGRAPHY

National Urban League. (1983). *A guide for developing non-instructional programs.* New York: Author. (ERIC Document Reproduction Service No. ED 272 597)
This reference provides an excellent step-by-step guide in designing school programs. It includes major sections on needs assessment, program planning, program implementation, and program evaluation. Using their experiences with Follow Through programs, the authors provide an actual case study on program planning.

Fowler, F. J. (1993). *Survey research methods* (2nd ed.). Newbury Park, CA: Sage Publications.
This book is among the best sources available on how-to-do surveys. There are particularly helpful chapters on sampling, item writing, interview methods, data analysis, and the ethical issues involved in survey research. This is an indispensable source for school psychologists interested in using surveys for research or program development.

Lauffer, A. (1982). *Assessment tools for practitioners, managers, and trainers.* Beverly Hills, CA: Sage.
This book was designed to acquaint professionals with the use of various structured group methods in needs assessment activities. Chapter 4 provides an excellent overview and case study of the nominal group method. Chapter 5 discusses the Delphi method as well as presenting several actual applications of this method.

Harvey, T. R. (1990). *Checklist for change: A pragmatic approach to creating and controlling change.* Boston: Allyn & Bacon.
This is an easy-to-read book dealing with the problems associated with organizational change. The author provides a step-by-step analysis of facilitating change with particular emphasis on how to overcome resistance to change and how to institutionalize change. The book contains many useful forms to evaluate the various steps in the change process.

Warheit, G. J., Bell, R. A., & Schwab, J. J. (1977). *Needs assessment approaches: Concepts and methods* (Publication No. ADM-77-472). Washington, DC: Department of Health, Education, and Welfare.
This U.S. Department of Health, Education, and Welfare publication continues to be one of the key sources on how to conduct needs assessments. Using a community emphasis, this publication provides many practical suggestions including how to form a team, select methods, construct questionnaires, do sampling, and supervise a needs assessment team. This book has stood the test of time and serves as an excellent introduction to needs assessment.

39

Best Practices in School Discipline

George G. Bear
University of Delaware

OVERVIEW

Since the onset of public schooling, school discipline has been a foremost concern among both educators and parents. The public has always demanded that schools *teach self-discipline*, the self-regulation of behavior, for the good of society. Upon reaching adulthood, individuals are expected to function autonomously — to assume responsibilities associated with citizenship in a democratic society. The public also has demanded that schools *use discipline*, not only to teach habits reflecting self-discipline, but also for the purposes of maintaining an orderly environment conducive to academic achievement and developing socially and morally responsible individuals.

Whereas these two societal expectations have changed little over the years, the nature of the socialization task has changed markedly. Teachers must still contend with children talking in class, getting out of their seats, not completing their work, and exhibiting many other violations of social conventions. But added to this list in recent years have been a growing number of much more serious problems: verbal and physical aggression against teachers, use of guns and knives, drug use, vandalism, gang violence, and the like. Teachers are now expected to teach self-discipline and to use discipline in dealing with these moral transgressions, and often to do so with little help from the traditional sources of social support outside of the school — the home, the church, and the community.

In this chapter, *discipline* refers to (a) instruction designed to teach *self-discipline* and (b) *disciplinary actions* used to deal with behavior problems when they occur. Self-discipline reflects internal motivation for one's behavior. It entails self-directed inhibition of antisocial behaviors, moral and social responsibility for one's actions, understanding of right from wrong, and appreciation of the importance of cooperative relationships in the classroom and society. Self-discipline is most evident when external regulators of behavior (e.g., presence of adults, clear rules) are absent.

Because children rarely demonstrate self-discipline across all behaviors and settings, it is well recognized that externally based disciplinary actions also must play a necessary and crucial role in the educational process. Too often, however, educators have failed to recognize that the teaching of self-discipline, not the external control of behavior, is the ultimate goal of social education. Externally based disciplinary actions, although necessary for achieving immediate objectives in the classroom, are not sufficient for achieving the more long-term goals of self-discipline.

In light of the wide range and complexity of behavior problems, it is clear that educators must adopt comprehensive and broad-based models of discipline if they hope to achieve the dual goals of teaching self-discipline and managing misbehavior. Included in a broad-based school-wide model of discipline should be a prevention-oriented component focusing on the teaching of self-discipline, an intervention component designed to deal with common disciplinary problems, and a treatment-oriented component. Whereas the first two components would be for all children, the treatment-oriented component would be for students experiencing serious behavioral/emotional problems and those at risk for such problems.

BASIC CONSIDERATIONS

The topic of discipline cuts across multiple literatures, including child development (primarily under the rubrics of socialization, child-rearing, aggression, juvenile delinquency, self-regulation, moral development, and prosocial behavior), education (under classroom management, school climate, and character education), guidance and counseling (counseling techniques, affective education, crisis intervention), and school psychology (personality assessment, consultation, intervention techniques, intervention acceptability). In addition to keeping abreast of recent developments in theory, research, and practice in these areas, school psychologists need to remain aware of current legal, ethical, and political issues pertaining to discipline. For example, school psychologists should recognize that participation in "psychological" or "affective" programs and activities has been challenged successfully by parents who argue that federal law (i.e., the Hatch Amendment) guarantees them the right to exclude their children from participating. Thus, parental permission may be necessary for students to participate in those preventive activities (e.g., values clarification and moral discussion activities) which have commonly been viewed by educators as being harmless.

Corporal punishment defined as the "intentional infliction of physical pain, physical restraint, and/or discomfort upon a student as a disciplinary technique" (National Association of School Psychologists [NASP], 1988) and, to a lesser degree school expulsion, also have generated increased controversy in recent years. Despite greater public recognition of its many limitations and the passage of state laws restricting its use, corporal punishment continues to be used in America. Indeed, half of the American public view corporal punishment favorably (Gallup & Elam, 1988). Clearly, a best practice in dealing with discipline problems is to first become familiar with the disadvantages of punitive approaches (see Hyman, 1990); NASP's (1986) position on the use of corporal punishment; and local school policies related to the use of suspension, expulsion, and other disciplinary procedures.

BEST PRACTICES

Models of discipline most commonly have been organized according to their underlying theoretical perspective. Hyman, Flanagan, and Smith (1982) grouped discipline models into five basic categories: psychodynamic-interpersonal, behavioral, sociological, eclectic-ecological, and human-potential. Others have organized models of discipline according to the processes, strategies, and techniques emphasized. For example, Wolfgang and Glickman (1986) provided a useful process-oriented framework in dividing popular models of discipline into three major categories.

Relationship-Listening models, such as Teacher Effectiveness Training (Gordon, 1974), Transactional Analysis (e.g., Harris, 1969), and Values Clarification (Raths, Harmin, & Simon, 1966) emphasize effective communications, interpersonal relations, and the importance of a classroom environment that fosters free expression of feelings, self-esteem, and self-directed problem solving. Active listening, nondirective statements, and questioning are the strategies of choice.

Confronting-Contracting models, such as Glasser's Reality Therapy (Glasser, 1969, 1975) and Dreikurs' model of discipline (Dreikurs, Grunwald, & Pepper, 1982) emphasize the reciprocal interaction of cognitions, feelings, environmental factors, and overt behavior. Strategies commonly used are questioning, directive and nondirective statements, modeling, reinforcement, and physical intervention or isolation.

Rules/Rewards-Punishment models, such as Assertive Discipline (Canter & Canter, 1976), emphasize environmental control of behavior. Behavior modification techniques are employed, including directive statements, modeling, reinforcement, punishment, physical intervention, and isolation.

Perhaps a more functional way to conceptualize the multiple models of discipline is to focus primarily on the goal(s) of each model and secondarily on the processes, strategies, and techniques used to achieve the goal(s). Three main categories of discipline models thus could be identified:

1. Preventive Discipline (models primarily intended to prevent misbehavior and develop self-discipline).

2. Corrective Discipline (models that primarily address ways to deal with acts of misbehavior).

3. Treatment Discipline (those models designed primarily to treat students with chronic behavior problems or to provide extensive services to those children who are "at-risk" for developing serious conduct problems). (Bear, 1990)

Preventive Models

If one's primary concern is the development of self-discipline and the prevention of misbehavior, then strategies and techniques associated with preventive models should be of primary focus. These models share a common purpose: To teach children behaviors, cognitions, and emotions which characterize democratic ideals, especially self-discipline, respect of self and others, social and moral responsibility, empathy, and caring. They differ, however, in goals, strategies, and techniques emphasized.

Preventive classroom management model. Advocates of this model (e.g., Bauer & Sapona, 1991; Emmer, Evertson, Sanford, Clements, & Worsham, 1989; Evertson, Emmer, Clements, Sanford, & Worsham, 1989) recognize that effective teachers curtail misbehavior and foster academic achievement by keeping students actively involved in appropriate academic activities. Activities are presented at the correct pace and instructional level, are motivating, and help promote norms for behavior and work.

Effective teachers manage the classroom successfully by creating and maintaining orderly learning environments (Doyle, 1986). Beginning with the first week of school they present clear rules and procedures and follow predictable routines. Throughout the year they frequently monitor classroom behavior and consistently enforce classroom rules. Many behavior problems are anticipated and thus avoided. When behavior problems do occur they are re-

TABLE 1
Popular Models and Techniques for Dealing with Discipline Referrals

Model	Techniques Emphasized
Models and Techniques That Focus on Prevention	
Classroom Management Model	Effective teaching practices, including frequent monitoring, clear rules and procedures, and social praise.
Prosocial Behavior Model	Systematic reinforcement, modeling of prosocial behaviors, verbal instruction, role-playing.
Moral Education Models	
Cognitive developmental	Classroom moral discussions, role playing, student participation in school government.
Character education	Reading of moral literature, direct teaching of values, practice of prosocial habits.
Social Problem-Solivng Model	Direct teaching of SPS skills such as Model alternative thinking, means-end thinking, and the like; self-instruction training, dialoguing.
Peer Mediation Model	Teching of conflict resolution skills, cooperative learning.
Affective and Communication Models	Values clarification activities, active listening, communication and interpersonal skills training for students and teachers.
Models and Techniques That Focus on Correction and Control of Misbehavior	
Behavior Management Model	Direct instruction; reinforcement techniques including social praise, material reinforcers, tokens; punishment-oriented techniques, including verbal reprimand, response cost, time-out; group contingency techniques; behavioral contracting; self-management.
Reality Therapy Model	Confrontational questioning; classroom meetings, classroom moral discussions, social problem-solving, behavioral contracting, logical consequences, time-out, preventive techniques such as democratic governance.
Models and Techniques That Focus on Treatment	
Social Skill Training Model	Direct instruction, modeling and rehearsal, coaching, self-instruction, manipulation of antecedents and consequences.
Aggression Replacement Training Model	Social skills training techniques, self-instruction (Anger Control Training), moral discussions.
Parent Management Training Model	Parent training in application of behavioral techniques.
Family Therapy Model	Variety of therapeutic and educational techniques, depending on particular model.
Behavior Therapy	Variety of cognitive-behavioral and operant techniques.

sponded to immediately and in a manner that causes the least amount of classroom disruption.

Effective classroom managers ensure that more public attention is paid to academic work than to misbehavior. As such, they praise children often and strategically, being sincere and not overly effusive (see Brophy, 1981). They also recognize that certain physical arrangements and activities tend to invite misbehavior, such as transitional periods, recess, lunch, long student presentations, and other activities in which students move about frequently. Monitoring of behavior is increased during these times.

It is clear that teachers can prevent frequent misbehavior by establishing and maintaining an orderly climate in which students are sustained in work-related behavior. However, it also is clear that teachers should not equate preventive classroom managemnet with authoritarianism. Goldstein and Weber (1981) found that whereas group process and socioemotional climate approaches to discipline (similar to the *confronting/contracting models*) were associated with appropriate classroom behavior, the authoritarian approach was not.

Prosocial behavior model. Preventive classroom management and prosocial behavior models share many strategies. However, rather than focusing on the ecology of the classroom and managerial procedures, the prosocial model emphasizes the use of specific behavioral techniques to teach and reinforce appropriate social behaviors. According to this model, which is largely derived from social learning theory, behavior problems are prevented by teaching and maintaining such prosocial behaviors as sharing, helping, caring, and cooperating. The ultimate goal is to teach students to behave prosocially in the absence of external rewards (i.e., for children to become self-disciplined). Three types of behavioral techniques most commonly are employed, typically in combination with one another:

- Systematic reinforcement of desirable behaviors (using either social-, material-, or self-reinforcement).

- Exposure to prosocial models.

- Strategic use of verbal instruction.

Although the prosocial model clearly provides effective classroom techniques for preventing and correcting discipline problems, its reliance on external monitors of behavior has caused many educators to question its value in the teaching of self-discipline (see Doyle, 1986).

Moral education models. Moral education is "whatever schools do to influence how students think, feel, and act regarding issues of right and wrong" (Association for Supervision and Curriculum Development, 1988). It includes nearly all aspects of discipline: The moral and social climate of the classroom, self-control, values and goals, moral reasoning and social decision making, and prosocial behavior. Most preventive models of discipline also can be considered moral education models, and vice versa.

Derived largely from the works of Dewey, Piaget, and Kohlberg, the *cognitive-developmental model* of moral education posits that children simply do not acquire normative behavior via reinforcement, punishment, and modeling, but do so by acting on their environments. That is, self-discipline evolves from within the individual — it is not only a consequence of external control: Although clearly influenced by one's environment, children think and reason for themselves. A major aim of the cognitive-developmental model of moral education is to facilitate children's development of mature moral reasoning. Immature moral reasoning, especially that reflecting an egocentric and hedonistic perspective, has been associated with juvenile delinquency (Blasi, 1980) and a variety of classroom behavior problems (Richards,

Bear, Stewart & Norman, 1992), and peer rejection (Bear & Rys, in press).

Moral discussion, role playing, and active participation in school decision making are the major educational strategies used to promote mature moral reasoning. Programs based on the cognitive-developmental model have been effective not only in fostering the growth of moral reasoning (see Bear, 1987) but also in improving the moral climate of the school (Power, Higgins, & Kohlberg, 1989). The moral discussion approach also has been a component of successful programs designed for the treatment of serious behavior problems (Arbuthnot & Gordon, 1986; Gibbs, Arnold, Cheesman, & Ahlborn, 1984; Goldstein & Glick, 1987).

The cognitive-developmental model of moral education recently has been challenged by a new model — the *character education* model of moral education. Critical of the cognitive-developmental model's focus on reasoning and its lack of emphasis on actual behavior, proponents of this model (e.g., Kilpatrick, 1992; Wynne & Ryan, 1993) argue for an old-fashioned emphasis on developing virtues or character traits (e.g., honesty, truthfulness, industry). This is achieved by means of literature that highlights such traits (i.e., modern-day versions of the *McGuffey Reader*), the practice of good habits (e.g., community and school service), ceremonies and assemblies that recognize values, and strict codes of discipline. Whereas the recent character-education model appears promising, it has yet to develop a research or theoretical base.

Perhaps the most exemplary model education project, one that incorporates major elements of the cognitive-developmental model and the character-education model, is the Child Development Project (Battistich, Watson, Solomon, Schaps, & Solomon, 1991), a program being implemented in several school districts across the country. This comprehensive program uses a combination of strategies, including moral discussion, moral literature, highlighting of prosocial values, and cooperative learning, to develop children's prosocial reasoning, interpersonal understanding, values, and prosocial behaviors.

"Developmental discipline," an important component of the Child Development Project, focuses on developing self-control and internalization of prosocial values. It balances the developmental needs of the students with the classroom management needs of the teacher. Whereas teachers use a wide variety of developmentally appropriate strategies to promote self-discipline and intrinsic motives for prosocial behavior, they also set clear standards for appropriate behavior and enforce these standards. Teachers strive to develop moral and social reasoning and to build a sense of school community which is characterized by warmth, sensitivity, and open communication. Research has shown that compared to students in nonprogram schools, children in the Child Development

Project exhibit more prosocial behavior, have better-developed conflict resolution skills, and hold more democratic views (Battistich, Watson, Solomon, Schaps, & Solomon, 1991).

Social problem-solving model. Targets for instruction in the social problem-solving model are specific thinking skills lacking in aggressive children (Asarnow & Callan, 1985). The skills most commonly taught are alternative thinking, consequential thinking, social-causal thinking, means-ends thinking, and sensitivity to problems (Spivack & Shure, 1982). Advocates of this model claim that social problem-solving skills mediate interpersonal behavior and that the teaching of these skills generalizes to multiple settings and behaviors.

Behavior modification and cognitive modeling techniques are used to teach students sequential problem-solving steps directly. For example, in Gesten and Weissberg's curriculum, students learn to apply the following eight steps when faced with interpersonal problems:

1. Look for signs of upset feelings.

2. Know exactly what the problem is.

3. Decide on your goal.

4. Stop and think before you act.

5. Think of as many solutions as you can.

6. Think ahead to what will probably happen next after each solution.

7. When you think you have a really good solution, try it.

8. If your first solution doesn't work, try again! (Gesten, Weissberg, Amish, & Smith, 1987)

An attractive feature of this process, and others like it, is that it integrates affective, cognitive, and behavioral dimensions of social problem solving.

An additional technique used in social problem-solving programs is *dialoguing*, an intervention process in which the instructor guides students through the social problem-solving steps via questioning and cognitive modeling during actual situations of interpersonal conflict. In Shure's (1992) *I Can Probelm Solve* program, which combines dialoguing with the direct teaching of thinking skills, the following steps are recommended during dialoguing: (a) Ask the child to define the problem; (b) elicit feelings; (c) elicit consequences; (d) elicit feelings about consequences; (e) encourage the child to think of alternative solutions; (f) encourage evaluation of the solution; and (g) praise the child's act of thinking.

Although several studies have indicated that social problem-solving training is effective, others have not (see Coleman, Wheeler, & Webber, 1993; Denham & Almeida, 1987). Not all social problem-solving skills have been shown to mediate social behaviors, nor have many programs been successful in producing improvements in behavior that generalize across settings. Nevertheless, in a comprehensive literature review Kazdin (1987) concluded that social problem-solving training is one of the most promising programs for treating antisocial children.

Peer mediation. Programs designed to teach students to play an active role in settling disputes and handling classroom disciplinary problems have increased in popularity over the past few years. These programs are grounded in the philosophy that self-regulation is more important than external control of behavior and that students can be trained and empowered to resolve conflicts on their own. Perhaps the most developed peer mediation program is the Peacemaker Program (Johnson & Johnson, 1991; Johnson, Johnson, Dudley, & Burnett, 1992) in which students are taught the conflict resolution skills of negotiation and mediation. In negotiating and mediating classroom conflicts a variation of the social problem-solving model is followed by teacher-appointed peer mediators who wear official T-shirts while assuming "peacemaker" duties. Their goal is to facilitate a joint decision-making process that will result in solutions that are acceptable and fair to all parties involved.

Although much research remains to be conducted on the Peacemaker program, the program appears promising. Johnson et al. (1992) report that it was effective in reducing both the incidence of a variety of behavior problems and the need for teacher-imposed interventions.

Affective and communication models. Affective and communication models are typically atheoretical or humanistic in orientation. These models focus on feelings, self-concept, interpersonal communication, and values. In addition, they emphasize the importance of a classroom climate in which teachers effectively communicate with students by demonstrating empathetic understanding, warmth, and acceptance. Values are addressed in a non-indoctrinative and non-judgmental fashion. The teacher functions as a therapist-like facilitator who wisely uses active listening skills that promote communication, expression of feelings, and clarification of values.

Affective and communication models have generated a wealth of popular curriculum materials and programs. Examples include *Developing Understanding of Self and Others* (Dinkmeyer & Dinkmeyer, 1982), *Teacher Effectiveness Training* (Gordon, 1974), and *Values Clarification: A Handbook of Practical Strategies for Teachers and Students* (Simon, Howe, & Kirschenbaum, 1972). These programs generally rely on the use of role-playing, classroom discussions, games, and activity worksheets. They vary greatly in terms of scope, comprehensiveness, and primary focus. Given their comprehensiveness and the methodological difficulties in measuring affective goals, it is not too surprising that only a few studies have demonstrated the effectiveness of these models (see Leming, 1981; Strein, 1988, for reviews).

Models for Dealing with Discipline Encounters

Disciplinary encounters are likely to occur whenever a teacher perceives misbehavior as disrupting or threatening the order of a classroom activity, especially if the behavior is highly visible and contagious (Doyle, 1986). What follows is an overview of three popular models that use a variety of practical techniques and strategies to deal with disciplinary encounters. Many of the preventive strategies and techniques cited previously can, and *should*, be used when dealing directly with discipline-related problems. This would include social problem solving (including dialoguing), active listening, modeling, role-playing, and moral discussion. Depending on the behavior problem, use of these techniques communicates to students that misbehavior is inappropriate and must be corrected. However, many disciplinary encounters call for additional measures, used alone or preferably in combination with preventive-oriented techniques. Thus, added here are those techniques that focus more on the correction and control of misbehavior, rather than its prevention. Because of limited space, only three models representing best practices in dealing with intervention during disciplinary encounters are highlighted.

Behavior management model. For years teachers have responded to classroom misbehavior with punishment-oriented behavioral techniques. The most popular among these techniques have been verbal reprimands, response cost (e.g., loss of earned recess time or privileges), and time-out (e.g., making the student sit alone or sending the student to the principal). To a lesser extent teachers also have used positive reinforcement techniques such as privileges, material reinforcers, and tokens to bring about behavioral change (Kazdin, 1982). In responding to disciplinary problems with a behavior management approach, the best practice is combining punishment-techniques to decrease inappropriate behavior with reinforcement techniques to increase desirable behaviors, while emphasizing use of the latter.

The choice of behavioral strategies and extent of their use obviously would depend on the type and severity of the behavior problem. For mild kinds of inappropriate behavior, Emmer (1987) recommends a four-step strategy, which is consistent with the preventive classroom management model's emphasis on minimal disruption of learning: (a) Look the student in the eye until the behavior stops, (b) move closer to the student, (c) use a nonverbal cue (e.g., a finger to the lips), and (d) state the student's name or ask the student to stop the behavior. Redirecting the students to appropriate behavior also is highly recommended.

For more serious classroom misbehaviors (e.g., fighting, verbal abuse, continual noncompliance, property damage) more punitive behavioral strategies such as time-out, response cost, and detention might be used. Emmer recommends that the following principles be considered when using punishment:

1. Whenever possible, the punishment should relate logically to the misbehavior.

2. Severe punishment is frequently no more effective than moderate punishment and at times less so.

3. Punishment procedures should be focused on helping the student understand the problem and make a commitment to change to more acceptable behavior.

4. When punishment is used, it should not be overused, with respect to either time or frequency.

5. Consistency is essential.

An interdependent group contingency technique called the "Good Behavior Game" (Barrish, Saunders, & Wolf, 1969) should be considered when dealing with classes in which several or more children are misbehaving. Like many other behavioral techniques, the "game" also can be used to prevent behavior problems. Different variations of the game have been used, but most share common features: (a) specific classroom rules are listed, (b) the class is divided into two or more "teams," (c) each team receives a mark on the board whenever a member of that team violates a rule, and (d) the team(s) receiving points below a predetermined criterion number are offered reinforcement (extra recess, less homework, other privileges and rewards).

In addition to being simple to use and effective, the Good Behavior Game is liked by teachers. However, school psychologists should be aware of its negative features, including the potential for undue and harmful peer pressure and ridicule of those students who cause their team to lose, and its emphasis on the reduction of inappropriate behavior. Unfortunately, the latter negative feature applies to most other punishment- or control-oriented contingency procedures in which students are not taught prosocial behaviors (see Graham-Clay & Reschly, 1987, for a review of legal and ethical issues). However, many of these problems can be overcome by basing points in the game on the presence of positive behaviors as opposed to the absence of negative behaviors (Darveaux, 1984).

Assertive Discipline. With over 500,000 teachers having been trained in its use, Assertive Discipline (Canter & Canter, 1976) is perhaps the most popular commercially available behavior management program used in the schools. Canter and Canter argue that teachers have the right to maintain classroom order and to obtain assistance in disciplinary matters from parents, principals, and others. In protecting these rights, teachers must be assertive. The best way to assert themselves in the classroom is to correct or control student misbehavior by means of the systematic use of an amalgamation of behavior management techniques. Such techniques include the continuous monitoring of behavior (a mark is put on the board when a child violates a classroom rule), behavioral contracting, response cost, verbal reprimands, sending the student to the principal, and suspending the student from school. Positive "assertions" (privileges, rewards, positive parent contacts, token reinforcement) also are employed, contingent upon the absence of misbehavior.

Each of the behavior management techniques described here, including those used in the Assertive Discipline program, has been shown to effectively increase or decrease behavior, at least on a short-term basis. Behavior management techniques are recognized widely as being a necessary, although not sufficient, component of most comprehensive programs of discipline. That is, although necessary for classroom management, they are not sufficient for teaching self-discipline. As noted earlier, it is important that models of discipline balance the teacher's need for control with the child's need for self-discipline. Programs that focus specifically on teacher control, such as Assertive Discipline, fail to offer such a balance (Render, Padilla, & Krank, 1989). Unless such balance is provided, Assertive Discipline should not be considered a best practice.

Reality Therapy model. Like Assertive Discipline, Reality Therapy (Glasser, 1965, 1969) is a popular school-wide systems model for discipline that uses specific behavior management strategies. However, the model is much more comprehensive, viewing discipline as entailing much more than the management of behavior. Reality Therapy emphasizes the importance of democratic school governance, student values and responsibility, avoidance of student failure, and the use of classroom meetings to develop social problem-solving skills and moral reasoning. As such, it could be considered a preventive model of discipline but is presented here under corrective models because Reality Therapy is one of the few models that offers specific and sequential steps for dealing with actual cases of discipline problems. Glasser provides educators with a practical 10-step procedure for dealing with discipline problems in a fashion which empowers both teachers and students. The ten steps are:

1. Teacher asks "What are you doing?"

2. The student evaluates the misbehavior and makes a commitment to stop it.

3. The teacher plans for student success.

4. When the problem reoccurs, the teacher directs the student to stop the misbehavior.

5. If step #4 is unsuccessful, the teacher questions the student about the misbehavior and describes appropriate behaviors.

6. If step #5 is unsuccessful, the teacher briefly repeats the questions in #5 and firmly tells the student that the misbehavior has to be stopped and a corrective plan developed. The plan is developed by the student and is approved and enforced by the teacher.

7. If misbehavior continues, in-class time-out is used.

8. If misbehavior continues, in-school time-out is used.

9. If misbehavior continues, out-of-school suspension is used. The student is not allowed to return until an acceptable plan has been made.

10. If #9 continues to be unsuccessful, the student is referred for homebound instructions and/or treatment. (Glasser, 1975)

Treatment Models

Students who exhibit a consistent pattern of antisocial behavior, or those who are "at risk" for developing such a pattern, often demand more than what a preventive program or standard disciplinary procedure can provide. At-risk indicators include: (a) poor parental management; (b) early onset of antisocial behavior; (c) reports of stealing, lying, or truancy; (d) antisocial behavior within the family; (e) poor educational achievement; and (f) rejection by peers (Loeber & Dishion, 1983; Parker & Asher, 1987). Presence of a combination of these indicators typically would warrant consideration of the need for a program that is more intensive, broadly based, and lasting than programs reviewed previously.

Treatment programs employ many of the same techniques presented earlier, but their application is more intensive and extensive. Researchers have shown that students with conduct disorders can benefit from programs based on the social problem-solving model (e.g., Kazdin, Esveldt-Dawson, French, & Unis, 1987), the cognitive-developmental model of moral education (e.g., Arbuthnot & Gordon, 1986), the behavior management model (Kazdin, 1982), and combinations of the above (e.g., Aggression Replacement Training, Goldstein & Glick, 1987; *Prepare Curriculum*, Goldstein, 1988). Additional models and techniques available for treating conduct disorders include individual and group psychotherapy, behavior therapy, pharmacotherapy, residential treatments, family therapy, and parent training.

In a comprehensive review of treatments for antisocial behaviors of children and adolescents, Kazdin (1987) concluded that the most promising treatments are parent management training, functional family therapy, cognitive problem-solving skills training (including social problem-solving and cognitive-developmental moral discussion techniques), and community-based treatment. Although behavior therapies such as behavior modification and social skills training were found to control effectively or decrease isolated antisocial behaviors, Kazdin noted that there is very little evidence that their effects are lasting or that the skills learned transfer beyond the training setting and to other domains. Therefore, he recommends broad-based programs in which alternative techniques are combined to address the multiple and complex factors influencing antisocial behavior. Kazdin also warns that these techniques should not be chosen haphazardly but rather on the basis of theoretical and conceptual justifications.

Selecting and Implementing Models and Techniques

It is not enough that school psychologists simply possess knowledge of models and techniques that prevent, correct, and treat discipline problems. They must also possess the process skills necessary to help teachers and parents select and apply such models and techniques. Several models of school-based consultation provide such a process, particularly for helping schools prevent and deal with disciplinary problems. The choice of consultation model, or combination of models, likely is influenced by many factors including the appropriate level of consultation (direct service to student or consultee, or indirect to the consultee or the organization), pervasiveness and nature of the problem, and the training and expected role of the school psychologist. Knoff (1985) suggests that the behavioral consultation model is most appropriate when examining environmental causes of misbehavior and when selecting among behavior modification techniques. The mental health model is used when the teachers are unable to deal effectively with student misbehavior due to lack of knowledge, experience, confidence, or objectivity. It also appears that the systems consultation model (see Curtis this volume) is applicable when assessing, developing, and implementing school-wide preventive policies and programs. When functioning as a member of a child study or intervention team, the school psychologist should find the collaborative consultation model provides useful direction.

Regardless which consultation model is used, sequential problem-solving steps should guide the consultation process. Knoff (1985) and Bear (1990) offered a four-step problem-solving process for dealing with discipline referrals, consisting of problem identification, problem analysis, intervention, and evaluation. A slightly different four-step process is presented next, one that devotes greater attention to the planning of interventions. Whereas the following

steps most directly relate to cases of corrective discipline involving the classroom teacher and a child, it should be clear that these same four steps could be applied when developing preventive or treatment programs. The same process would be used, but many of the guiding questions would change. Likewise, the same four-step process could be used when helping children solve disciplinary problems on their own.

Note that the "consultee" referred to while discussing this process likely is the classroom teacher, but depending on the case and level of consultation it might be the student's parent(s), administrator(s), or groups thereof. Given that discipline problems are influenced by multiple and complex forces, best practice involves as many parties as feasible, but almost always the teacher, parent, and child. In keeping with this best practice objective, it is recognized that at times services of the school psychologist must not be restricted by an indirect, consultee-centered service approach. More direct, as well as other indirect services either separate from or combined with consultation, often are called for when dealing with disciplinary problems. This would include individual or group counseling, parent education, and inservice education (see Frisby, 1990, regarding inservice programs on discipline).

Problem identification. The critical first step in the problem-solving process is for the school psychologist and the consultee to pinpoint and define clearly the disciplinary problem(s) that led the consultee to seek assistance. This would require the identification of observable behaviors in concrete behavioral terms, both those that are desired and those that are undesired. Ideally, the school psychologist should observe the child in the setting(s) in which the behavior occurs and have the teacher establish a baseline of the frequency of undesired and desired behaviors.

It is at this step that the consultant should determine, at least tentatively, the severity of the problem(s) and who "owns" the problem(s). Determination of severity and ownership is critical to decisions made at later stages in the process, particularly in selecting the method and intensity of the intervention warranted. Obviously, inappropriate behaviors that are developmentally "normal," such as getting out of one's seat and talking in class, call for different disciplinary methods than the more severe problems such as stealing or unprovoked fighting, particularly when the latter behaviors occur frequently. Likewise, the focus of intervention would differ if the probelm behaviors reflect the teacher's poor classroom management rather than the child's lack of self-discipline.

Problem analysis. During this phase problems tentatively identified during problem identification are now examined in greater depth. Who "owns" the problem becomes clearer upon analysis of environmental factors (including situational antecedents and consequences), and the cognitions and behaviors of the student, consultee, and perhaps others who might be influencing the problem behavior. This analysis would almost always require informal assessments of the student's social problem-solving skills, self-perceptions, moral reasoning, and self-attributions, as well as the skills, expectations, self-confidence, and attributions of the consultee.

An interview with the child (by the school psychologist, consultee, or other member of an intervention team), a review of records, and classroom observations generally should precede the meeting during which problem analysis occurs. Family and peer relations and their impact on discipline also should be explored in recognition of the critical (and reciprocal) role of parental discipline in children's antisocial behavior (Vuchinich, Gank, & Patterson, 1992; Walker, Stieber, Ramsey, & O'Neill, 1991).

Guiding questions at this step include the following:

- Does the primary problem lie in the student not having appropriate prosocial skills and inhibitory controls, or in the student possessing but not exhibiting them?

- To whom, or what, do the student, teacher, and parent attribute the disciplinary problem?

- To what extent are such attributions biased?

- Do the consultee's discipline-related expectations, self-efficacy beliefs, or lack of knowledge contribute to the misbehavior?

- Are current disciplinary practices fair and implemented correctly?

- Do forces beyond the teacher–student relationship impinge upon the behavior (e.g., school climate, peers, parents, etc.)?

- In what ways might the above factors be related reciprocally?

Bandura's (1978) model of reciprocal determinism provides a useful framework for problem analysis because it focuses on the continuous reciprocal interaction between a person's cognitions, behaviors, and environmental factors.

Planning. The ultimate choice of model(s) and techniques rests with the consultee. The school psychologist's primary role, particularly during the collaborative planning phase, is to facilitate the decision-making process and to offer information and advice that might influence the consultee's choice of intervention(s). While brainstorming and evaluating models and/or strategies with the consultee, the school psychologist should advocate for the ones with the greatest potential for solving the immediate problem and for teaching the child self-discipline. Choice of model and/or strategies should be linked to information gleaned from problem identification and problem analysis and to the specific goals of the consultee. Of particular importance is information that indicates the extent and breadth of the intervention needed to bring about changes in behavior that are consistent with the consultee's goals.

Lepper's (1983) "minimal sufficiency principle" provides some guidance for selecting techniques during this phase. According to this principle, the internalization of social and moral norms is fostered by disciplinary procedures that exert the least amount of pressure on a student to conform. If this principle were followed in the classroom, the use of external controls would be minimal and used only when necessary. Some practical support for Lepper's principle comes from studies showing that interventions with a large number of self-management components (as opposed to teacher-management components) yield the greatest effects in curtailing misbehavior (Fantuzzo, Polite, Cook, & Quinn, 1988).

Factors which enhance the likelihood of the intervention being implemented successfully also should be considered. Based on research (see Greenwood, Carta, & Hall, 1987; Gresham, 1991) on the effectiveness and acceptability of interventions the following questions should be addressed:

- Has previous research shown the intervention to be effective under similar classroom conditions?

- Is the intervention sufficiently comprehensive and systematic?

- Are procedures clear and likely to be followed by the interventionist(s)?

- Are attempts made to involve the student in planning and implementation of the intervention?

- Are parents involved?

- Is the intervention acceptable to the teacher, parent, principal, and student?

Negative answers to these questions are likely to suggest difficulties and perhaps failure.

Teachers prefer interventions that are positive, of brief duration, and easy and inexpensive to implement, but recognize that more serious offenses require aversive and longer-lasting interventions (see Reimers, Wacker, & Koeppl, 1987). A recent survey (King, Gullone, & Dadds, 1990) of over 3,000 teachers in Great Britain found that reasoning with the individual student was the strategy of choice in dealing with run-of-the-mill disciplinary problems. A smaller scaled study by Rosen, Taylor, O'Leary, and Sanderson (1990) of teachers in the United States also found verbal management techniques to be most preferred. In addition to reasoning with the individual student, two additional easy-to-use and effective interventions preferred by teachers were redirecting students toward appropriate behavior and manipulating rewards (Martens, Peterson, Witt, & Cirone, 1986).

Whereas the teacher's acceptance of an intervention is important for obvious reasons, the importance of the student's acceptance is less clear. Group questionnaires show that most students accept discipline techniques that traditionally have been used by teachers, such as teacher–student discussion, time-out, and sending the misbehaving child to the principal (Bear & Stewart, 1990; King, Gullone, & Dadds, 1990), but dislike class-wide discussion or meetings with a school counselor (Bear & Stewart, 1990). Private reprimands are preferred over public ones and whole-class interventions clearly are disliked when imposed for the misbehavior of a few class members (Lovegrove, Lewis, Fall, & Lovegrove, 1985). Studies also show that in evaluating the fairness and perceived effectiveness of interventions students consider behavior problem severity as well as transgressor's reputation (Bear & Fink, 1991). That is, they recognize that harsh measures are fair (although not necessarily effective) for repeated violators of moral transgressions but are unfair for those who rarely misbehave, particularly if the misbehavior is minor.

A problem with group studies of student acceptability, however, is that the results may not apply to individuals with whom the techniques are used. A best practice with respect to student acceptance is to implement interventions viewed most favorably by the student. This is especially true when dealing with adolescents. However, one should not let the consideration of the student's acceptance preclude implementation of an intervention that is acceptable to all others, fair, and likely to be effective.

Implementation and evaluation. The effectiveness of any discipline program largely is dependent on the manner in which it is implemented. Even the most well-planned and best designed interventions likely will be ineffective when they are poorly implemented. In addition to addressing and resolving implementation-related concerns during the planning phase, adhering to certain practices during actual implementation likely will enhance program effectiveness. Four such practices (adapted from Weissberg, Caplan, & Sivo, 1989) are: (a) Develop a structured and detailed curriculum for preventive programs and provide specific procedures for dealing with misbehavior; (b) offer individual- or school-wide teacher training before and during the program; (c) provide classroom assistance, supervision, and on-site coaching, when needed; and (d) organize system policies and supports that encourage program integrity.

In evaluating discipline programs, there are many evaluation models and designs from which to choose. Likewise, there is a multitude of instruments for measuring the objectives of most models (e.g., measures of classroom management, self-concept, values, attitudes, moral reasoning, self-efficacy, antisocial behavior). The matching of program objectives with evaluation measures is of critical importance. Many local intervention programs have been "ineffective" due to the use of instruments (e.g., self-esteem inventories) that indirectly measure, or fail to measure, intended outcomes.

The complexity of the evaluation design largely depends on the purpose of the evaluation and the level at which consultation services are provided. Whereas sophisticated experimental and quasi-experimental group research designs are necessary for most system-level projects, simpler case study designs are appropriate when the focus is on an individual student or a small group of students. Regardless of the level of complexity, however, both the process of planning and decision-making (i.e., formative evaluation) and the outcomes of interventions (i.e., summative evaluation) should be evaluated. "If" and "how" an intervention succeeds or fails are equally important (Scriven, 1967). Likewise, evaluation should be ongoing so that interventions can be revised when necessary. Evaluation also should include both objective and subjective data, examine intended and unintended effects, and allow for a follow-up period (Brown, Pryzwansky, & Schulte, 1987; Knoff, 1982). Moreover, in order to promote self-management the student should be included in the evaluation process.

SUMMARY

Responding to discipline problems requires knowledge and skills in many areas, especially child development, behavior management, classroom effectiveness, and consultation. To be effective, school-based discipline programs must be broad-based, incorporating a variety of techniques designed to prevent, correct, and treat varying degrees of misbehavior.

The ultimate goal of a discipline program should be the development of self-directed behavior that is socially and morally responsible. To achieve this goal, programs must focus not only on improving the abilities of significant others to prevent and deal with discipline problems, but also on developing the cognitions, affect, and behaviors among children that might prevent discipline problems.

REFERENCES

Arbuthnot, J., & Gordon, D. A. (1986). Behavioral and cognitive effects of a moral reasoning development intervention for high-risk behavior-disordered adolescents. *Journal of Consulting and Clinical Psychology, 54,* 206–216.

Asarnow, J. R., & Callan, J. W. (1985). Boys with peer adjustment problems: Social cognitive processes. *Journal of Consulting and Clinical Psychology, 53,* 80–87.

Association for Supervision and Curriculum Development. (1988). *Moral education in the life of the school.* Alexandria, VA: Author.

Bandura. A. (1978). The self system in reciprocal determinism. *American Psychologist, 33,* 344–358.

Barrish, A. H., Saunders, M., & Wolf, M. M. (1969). Good behavior game: Effects on individual contingencies for group consequences on disruptive behavior in a classroom. *Journal of Applied Behavior Analysis, 2,* 119–124.

Battistich, V., Watson, M., Solomon, D., Schaps, E., & Solomon, J. (1991). The Child Development Project: A comprehensive program for the development of prosocial character. In W. M. Kurtines & J. L. Gewirtz (Eds.), *Handbook of moral behavior and development, Vol. 3: Application* (pp. 1–34). Hillsdale, NJ: Erlbaum.

Bauer, A. M., & Sapona, R. H. (1991). *Managing classrooms to facilitate learning.* Englewood Cliffs, NJ: Prentice-Hall.

Bear, G. G. (1987). Children and moral responsibility. In A. Thomas & J. Grimes (Eds.), *Children's needs: Psychological perspectives* (pp. 365–371). Washington, DC: National Association of School Psychologists.

Bear, G. G. (1989). Sociomoral reasoning and antisocial behaviors among normal sixth graders. *Merrill-Palmer Quarterly, 35,* 181–196.

Bear, G. G. (1990). Best practices in school discipline. In A. Thomas & J. Grimes (Eds.), *Best practices in school psychology–II* (pp. 649–663). Washington, DC: National Association of School Psychologists.

Bear, G. G., & Fink, A. (1991). Judgments of fairness and predicted effectiveness of classroom discipline: Influence of problem severity and reputation. *School Psychology Quarterly, 6,* 83–102.

Bear, G. G., & Rys, G. S. (in press). Moral reasoning, classroom behavior, and sociometric status among elementary school children. *Developmental Psychology.*

Bear, G. G., & Stewart, M. (1990). Early adolescents' acceptability of interventions: Influence of problem severity, gender, and moral development. *Journal of Early Adolescence, 10,* 191–208.

Blasi, A. (1980). Bridging moral cognition and moral action: A critical review of the literature. *Psychological Bulletin, 88,* 1–45.

Brophy, J. (1981). Teacher praise: A functional analysis. *Review of Educational Research, 51,* 5–32.

Brown, D., Pryzwansky, W. B., & Schulte, A. C. (1987). *Psychological consultation: Introduction to theory and practice.* Boston: Allyn & Bacon.

Canter, L., & Canter, M. (1976). *Assertive discipline: A take-charge approach for today's educators.* Seal Beach, CA: Canter & Associates.

Coleman, M., Wheeler, L., & Webber, J. (1993). Research on interpersonal problem-solving training: A review. *Remedial and Special Education, 14*(2), 25–37.

Darveaux, D. X. (1984). The Good Behavior Game plus Merit: Controlling disruptive behavior and improving student motivation. *School Psychology Review, 13,* 510–514.

Denham, S. A., & Almeida, M. C. (1987). Children's social provlemsolving skills, behavioral adjustment, and interventions: A meta-analysis evaluating theory and practice. *Journal of Applied Developmental Psychology, 8,* 391–409.

Dinkmeyer, D., & Dinkmeyer, D., Jr. (1982). *Developing understanding of self and others: (DUSO) 1 and 2* (rev. ed.). Circle Pines, MN: American Guidance Service.

Doyle, W. (1986). Classroom organization and management. In M. C. Wittrock (Ed.), *Handbook of research on teaching* (3rd ed.; pp. 392–431). New York: Macmillan.

Dreikurs, R., Grunwald, B. B., & Pepper, F. C. (1982). *Maintaining sanity in the classroom: Classroom management techniques* (2nd ed.). New York: Harper & Row.

Emmer, E. T. (1988). Classroom management and discipline. In V. Richardson-Koehler (Ed.), *Educator's handbook: A research perspective* (pp. 233–258). White Plains, NJ: Longman.

Emmer, E. T., Evertson, C. M., Sanford, J. P., Clements, B. S., & Worsham, M. E. (1989). *Classroom management for secondary teachers.* Englewood Cliffs, NJ: Prentice-Hall.

Evertson, C. M., Emmer, E. T., Clements, G. S., Sanford, J. P., & Worsham, M. E. (1989). *Classroom management for elementary teachers.* Englewood Cliffs, NJ: Prentice-Hall.

Fantuzzo, J. W., Polite, K. C., Cook, D. M., & Quinn, G. (1988). An evaluation of the effectiveness of teacher- vs. student-management classroom interventions. *Psychology in the Schools, 25,* 154–163.

Frisby, C. L. (1990). A teacher inservice model for problem-solving in classroom discipline: Suggestions for the school psychologist. *School Psychology Quarterly, 5,* 211–232.

Gallup, A., & Elam, S. M. (1988). The 20th annual Gallup poll of the public's attitudes toward the public schools. *Phi Delta Kappan, 70,* 33–40.

Gesten, E. L., Weissberg, R. P., Amish, P. L., & Smith, J. K. (1987). Social problem-solving training: A skills-based approach to prevention and treatment. In C. A. Maher & J. E. Zins (Eds.), *Psychoeducational interventions in the schools: Methods and procedures for enhancing competence* (pp. 118–140). New York: Pergamon.

Gibbs, J. C., Arnold, K. D., Cheesman, F. L., & Ahlborn, H. H. (1984). Facilitation of sociomoral reasoning in delinquents. *Journal of Consulting and Clinical Psychology, 52,* 37–45.

Glasser, W. (1969). *Schools without failure.* New York: Harper & Row.

Glasser, W. (1976). *Reality therapy: A new approach to psychiatry.* New York: Harper & Row.

Goldstein, A. (1988). *The prepare curriculum.* Champaign, IL: Research Press.

Goldstein, A. P., & Glick, B. (1987). *Aggression replacement training: A comprehensive intervention for aggressive youth.* Champaign, IL: Research Press.

Goldstein, J. M., & Weber, W. A. (1981, April). Teacher managerial behaviors and on-task behaviors: Three studies. Paper presented at the annual meeting of the American Educational Research Association, Los Angeles.

Gordon, T. (1974). *TET: Teacher effectiveness training.* New York: McKay.

Graham-Clay, S. L., & Reschly, D. J. (1987). Legal and ethical issues. In C. A. Maher & S. G. Forman (Eds.), *A behavioral approach to education of children and youth* (pp. 289–309). Hillsdale, NJ: Erlbaum.

Greewnood, C. R., Carta, J. J., & Hall, R. V. (1987). The use of peer tutoring strategies in classroom management and educational instruction. *School Psychology Review, 17,* 258–275.

Gresham, F. M. (1991). Conceptualizing behavior disorders in terms of resistance to intervention. *School Psychology Review, 20,* 23–36.

Harris, T. A. (1969). *I'm OK – you're OK: A practical guide to transactional analysis.* New York: Harper & Row.

Hyman, I. A. (1990). *Reading, writing, and the hickory stick.* Lexington, MA: Lexington Books.

Hyman, I., Flanagan, D., & Smith, K. (1982). Discipline in the schools. In C. R. Reynolds & T. B. Gutkin (Eds.), *The handbook of school psychology* (pp. 454–480). New York: Wiley.

Johnson, D. W., & Johnson, R. (1991). *Teaching students to be peacemakers*. Edina, MN: Interaction Book Company.

Johnson, D. W., Johnson, R. T., Dudley, B., & Burnett, R. (1992, September). Teaching students to be peer mediators. *Educational Leadership*, 10–13.

Kazdin, A. E. (1982). Applying behavioral principles in the schools. In C. R. Reynolds & T. B. Gutkin (Eds.), *The handbook of school psychology* (pp. 501–529). New York: Wiley.

Kazdin, A. E. (1987). Treatment of antisocial behavior in children: Current status and future directions. *Psychological Bulletin, 102*, 187–203.

Kazdin, A. E., Esveldt-Dawson, K., French, N. H., & Unis, A. S. (1987). Problem-solving skills training and relationship therapy in the treatment of antisocial child behavior. *Journal of Consulting and Clinical Psychology, 55*, 76–85.

Kilpatrick, W. (1992). *Why Johnny can't tell right from wrong*. New York: Simon & Schuster.

King, N. J., Gullone, E., & Dadds, M. R. (1990). Student perceptions of permissiveness and teacher-instigated disciplinary strategies. *British Journal of Educational Psychology, 60*, 322–329.

Knoff, H. M. (1982). The independent psychodiagnostic clinic: Maintaining accountability through program evaluation. *Psychology in the Schools, 19*, 346–353.

Knoff, H. M. (1985). Best practices in dealing with discipline referrals. In A. Thomas & J. Grimes (Eds.), *Best practices in school psychology* (pp. 251–262). Washington, DC: National Association of School Psychologists.

Leming, J. S. (1981). Curricular effectiveness in moral/values education: A review of research. *Journal of Moral Education, 10*, 147–164.

Lepper, M. (1983). Social-control processes and the internalization of social values: An attributional perspective. In E. T. Higgins, D. Ruble, & W. Hartup (Eds.), *Social cognition and social development: A socio-cultural perspective* (pp. 294–333). New York: Cambridge University Press.

Loeber, R., & Dishion, T. J. (1983). Early predictors of male delinquency: A review. *Psychological Bulletin, 94*, 68–99.

Lovegrove, M., Lewis, R., Fall, C., & Lovegrove, H. (1985). Students' preferences for discipline practices in schools. *Teaching and Teacher Education, 1*, 325–333.

Martens, B. K., Peterson, R. L., Witt, J. C., & Cirone, S. (1986). Teacher perceptions of school-based interventions. *Exceptional Children, 53*, 213–223.

National Association of School Psychologists. (1988). *Supporting paper on corporal punishment position statement*. Washington, DC: Author.

Parker, J. G., & Asher, S. R. (1987). Peer relations and later personal adjustment: Are low-accepted children at risk? *Psychological Bulletin, 102*, 357–389.

Power, C., Higigns, A., & Kohlberg, L. (1989). The habit of the common life: Building character through democratic community schools. In L. P. Nucci (Ed.), *Moral development and character education: A dialogue* (pp. 125–143). Berkeley, CA: McCutchan.

Raths, L. E., Harmin, M., & Simon, S. (1966). *Values and teaching: Working with values in the classroom*. Columbus, OH: Merrill.

Reimers, T. M., Wacker, D. P., & Koeppl, G. (1987). Acceptability of behavioral interventions: A review of the literature. *School Psychology Review, 16*, 212–227.

Render, G. F., Padilla, J. M., & Krank, H. M. (1989). Assertive Discipline: A critical review and analysis. *Teachers College Record, 90*, 607–630.

Richards, H. C., Bear, G. G., Stewart, A. L., & Norman, A. D. (1992). Moral reasoning and conduct: Evidence of a curvilinear relationship. *Merrill-Palmer Quarterly, 38*, 176–190.

Rosen, L. A., Taylor, S. A., O'Leary, S. G., & Sanderson, W. (1990). A survey of classroom management practices. *Journal of School Psychology, 28*, 257–269.

Scriven, M. (1967). The methodology of evaluation. In R. Tyler, R. Gagne & M. Scriven (Eds.), *Perspectives of curriculum evaluations* (AERA Monograph Series on Curriculum Evaluation; pp. 39–83). Chicago: Rand McNally.

Shure, M. B. (1992). *I can problem solve: An interpersonal cognitive problem-solving program*. Champaign, IL: Research Press.

Simon, S. B., Howe, L. W., & Kirschenbaum, H. (1972). *Values clarification: A handbook of practical strategies for teachers and students* (rev. ed.). New York: Hart Publishing.

Spivack, G., & Shure, M. B. (1982). The cognition of social adjustment: Interpersona(Eds.), *Advances in clinical child psychology, Vol. 5* (pp. 323–372). New York: Plenum.

Strein, W. (1988). Classroom-based elementary school affective education programs: A critical review. *Psychology in the Schools, 25*, 288–296.

Vuchinich, S., Bank, L., & Patterson, G. R. (1992). Parenting, peers, and the stability of antisocial behavior in preadolescent boys. *Development Psychology, 28*, 510–521.

Walker, H. M., Stieber, S., Ramsey, E., & O'Neill, R. E. (1991). Longitudinal prediction of the school achievement, adjustment, and delinquency of antisocial versus at-risk boys. *Remedial and Special Education, 12*(4), 43–51.

Weissberg, R. P., Caplan, M. Z., & Sivo, P. J. (1989). A new conceptual framework for establishing school-based social competence promotion programs. In L. A. Bond & B. E. Compas (Eds.), *Primary prevention and promotion in the schools* (pp. 255–296). Newbury Park, CA: Sage.

Wolfgang, C. H., & Glickman, C. D. (1986). *Solving discipline problems: Strategies for classroom teachers* (2nd ed.). Boston: Allyn & Bacon.

Wynne, E. A., & Ryan, K. (1993). *Reclaiming our schools*. New York: Macmillan.l cognitive problem-solving thinking. In B. B. Lahey & A. E. Kazdin

ANNOTATED BIBLIOGRAPHY

Benninga, J. S. (1991). *Moral, character, and civic education in the elementary school.*
Provides an excellent introduction to moral education models, especially the cognitive-developmental and character education models. Chapters present a rationale for each model, issues of controversy, and specific strategies associated with the two models.

DeVries, R., & Zan, B. (1994). *Moral classrooms, moral children: Creating a constructivist atmosphere in early education*. New York: Teachers College Press.
Applies the constructivist theories of Piaget and Kohlberg to promoting self-discipline. Based on a solid theoretical framework, the approach emphasizes children constructing their moral understandings of everyday interactions. Includes practical material on conflict resolution and classroom atmosphere.

Evertson, C. M., Emmer, E. T., Clements, B. S., Sanford, J. P., & Worsham, M. E. (1989). *Classroom management for elementary teachers*. Englewood Cliffs, NJ: Prentice Hall.

This text presents a succinct review of current research on effective classroom management and offers many practical suggestions for preventing and dealing with various behavior problems in the classroom. Another version of this text is available for educators at the secondary school level (see Emmer et al., 1989).

Glasser, W. (1969). *Schools without failure*. New York: Harper & Row.

In this classic book Glasser applies Reality Therapy to education and addresses school practices contributing to children's failure in school. Three types of classroom meetings designed to promote self-discipline are described (social problem-solving, open-ended, and educational-diagnostic).

Sulzer-Azaroff, B., & Mayer, G. R. (1986). *Achieving educational excellence: Using behavioral strategies*. New York: Holt, Rinehart & Winston.

Presents the major principles and techniques of behavior modification used in schools. Practical examples of their application are given and issues related to their use are discussed.

Wolfgang, C. H., & Glickman, C. D. (1986). *Solving discipline problems: Strategies for classroom teachers* (2nd ed.). Boston: Allyn & Bacon.

Presents the major models of discipline and their classroom applications. Helpful guidelines for choosing among various discipline models and techniques are suggested.

40

Best Practices in Crisis Intervention

Scott Poland
Cypress–Fairbanks (Texas) Public Schools

Gayle Pitcher
Jakarta, Indonesia

Philip J. Lazarus
Florida International University

INTRODUCTION

Crisis intervention skills for school psychologists are becoming indispensable as the numbers of crises in our schools spiral upward. At present all schools are at risk for crises — even "successful" schools in prominent neighborhoods (Jay, 1989).

Although few of us feel completely prepared to face and manage shootings, kidnappings, emotionally out-of-control staff members, or assaults of teachers, the simple reality is that most of us will. Government figures for 1985 documented 450,000 violent crimes in our nation's schools and colleges. Assaults accounted for most of the incidents, followed by robbery and rape (Mayfield, 1986). Keen (1989) noted that three million children are attacked at school each year and that weapons were used in 70,000 assaults. A recent 50% increase has been cited in the number of attacks on teachers from 1973 to 1985, and youth homicide has doubled in the last 20 years (McEvoy, 1988). Memmot and Stone (1989) report that one child is killed every day in accidental shootings and 10 more are injured.

Several years ago our department of psychological services received a phone call from a superintendent requesting that psychologists be sent to the site of an in-school shooting. Precisely what had happened, who was in charge, or how exactly we might benefit the situation was completely undetermined. Nothing could have prepared us for what we found: Television news teams roamed the halls, large numbers of frightened students were unaccounted for, telephone lines were clogged with frantic calls from parents, teachers were rattled from the near hysteria, and administrators felt ill equipped to manage the barrage of problems that fell upon them in the course of a fleeting moment. It was generally felt that a psychologist ought to know what to do with an incident that carries with it such emotionality. Those of us who approached the scene, however, felt the same sense of helplessness, anxiety, and confusion.

Since administrators frequently see school psychologists as the "experts" in this area and since we may be the only school personnel trained in the management of strong emotions and preventive program planning, it is logical that the crisis intervention responsibility fall squarely on us. Our profession, however, has been slow to prepare us for such a role or to be proactive in establishing and organizing crisis intervention activities in the schools (Smead, 1985).

For example, Lazarus and Phelps (1993) noted at a recent meeting of the Trainers of School Psychologists that trainers had not received systematic coursework in crisis intervention nor been trained in basic skills such as debriefing or psychological first aid. Therefore, in recent years, much of the training for the profession has become the purview of practitioners who learn their crisis intervention skills in the field (e.g., Franzen, 1993; Kamins, 1993; Pando, Laska, & Grant, 1993; Poland, 1993; Reynolds, 1993; Young, 1993).

Perhaps as school psychologists expand their attention to providing school psychology services to all children and not just youngsters in exceptional student education, the focus may shift. In a recent position statement put forth by the National Association of School Psychologists (1993) entitled *On Advocacy for Effective School Psychological Services for All Children*, NASP convincingly argues for comprehensive psychological services to include "developing crisis intervention plans and providing services in reaction to crises (such as suicide attempts, school and neighborhood violence, natural disasters)."

Lazarus (in press-a) makes the point that by emphasizing crisis intervention activities, school psychologists can attest that they are essential services rather than support services.

At a recent workshop, Kamins (1993) explained how his district added school psychology positions at a time of financial cutbacks by emphasizing to the school board and the superintendent all the crisis activities his staff had engaged in on a weekly basis. They did this by sending a memo to the superintendent of schools every time they intervened to prevent a crisis from occurring or escalating and explained how they had responded during and in the aftermath of a traumatic event. When lives were saved as a result of their intervention, this became their most potent rationale for the creation of new positions.

Though Smead (1985) has correctly criticized our profession for being slow to establish and organize crisis intervention services, it appears that in the nineties workshops (e.g., Franzen, 1993; Kamins, 1993; Pando et al., 1993; Poland, 1993; Reynolds, 1993; Young, 1993) and symposiums (e.g., Busher, 1990; Dillard, 1990; Lipton, 1990; Poland, 1990), and texts (e.g., Pitcher & Poland, 1992; Slaikeu, 1990) have begun to educate practitioners on how to deliver crisis intervention services and develop crisis response teams (Alderman, 1989; Armstrong, 1989; Lazarus & Howard, 1993; Pitcher & Poland, 1992). Recently, NASP (1991) published a compendium entitled *Resources in Crisis Intervention: School, Family, and Community Applications.* Moreover, the number of NASP presentations at annual conventions that were directly related to crisis intervention has increased from 3 in 1983 to 17 in 1993. Therefore, it can be seen that the profession is moving forward in taking on this critical role. The title of a recent article, "Crisis Response Teams a Must for All School Districts" (Neuhaus, 1990), may become the norm at the beginning of the twenty-first century and exemplifies the primary assumption in this chapter.

This chapter will outline a practical model for crisis intervention in the schools that will enable school systems to organize and respond effectively in the face of a crisis. The role of the school psychologist ranges from that of manager to trainer to program planner. The overall model first establishes competent reaction to crises, then presses on to establish competent prevention of crises. It is our intent to pass along the information we have accumulated in nearly a decade of research and management of school crises (Pitcher & Poland, 1992).

BASIC CONSIDERATIONS

Probably the most pronounced aspect of a crisis in the schools is the intense emotional upset or "disequilibrium" experienced by the system. Much as in personal crises, staff members experience feelings of helplessness, denial, inadequacy, and confusion. If the crisis is not resolved, depression or burnout, physical symptoms, and disorganization of functional working relationships occur. It is for this reason that school psychologists are frequently seen as the most appropriate personnel to intervene and support staff in crises.

In inexperienced or unprepared districts, however, psychologists are typically summoned at the least advantageous moment. Traditionally, crises have been regarded as unfolding in four stages: First, there is an initial rise in tension due to the crisis event. Second, in the face of the continued impact of the stressing event, there is a lack of success in the usual problem-solving techniques. During the third stage other problem-solving resources are mobilized, and, following failure of these, tension mounts to the breaking point during the fourth and final phase of severe emotional disorganization (Caplan, 1964). All too often school psychologists are called during the last portion of the third or fourth phase. It is necessary, then, that we develop the arsenal of skills required to have a positive impact on the organization at that time.

However, there is a second and very significant aspect of crisis in the schools that we must prepare ourselves and our profession to embrace. During and just subsequent to crisis there is a reduced defensiveness or increased openness on the part of the system, again paralleling personal crisis. Crisis has been frequently recognized as a time of potential danger as well as potential opportunity (Wilhelm, 1967; Lidell & Scott, 1968, Slaikeu, 1984). If our profession is able to manage the danger — that is, manage the immediate crisis and quickly return the system to normal functioning — then there exists a tremendous opportunity to stimulate long-term systemic change. Once seen as effective and credible, the psychologist has infinitely more opportunity to move the system in the direction of prevention. Thus, the general intent of our approach is actually twofold:

1. To establish crisis management procedures that support effective coping/management behavior during extreme emotional states (which will return the system to normal functioning as quickly as possible).

2. To introduce crisis prevention activities that will reduce the probability of the reoccurrence of crisis.

As in public health, our concept of prevention can take three forms: primary prevention, secondary prevention, and tertiary prevention (Bloom, 1977; Caplan, 1964). Primary prevention includes activities that prevent crises from occurring altogether, secondary prevention includes activities that arrest potential crises from escalating, and tertiary prevention aims to repair damage from the occurrence of a crisis (i.e., crisis management). By way of illustration, then, primary prevention might be educating elementary school teachers regarding custody laws and establishing school policies and procedures to regulate authorized removal of a child from the school. Secondary prevention might involve effective implementation of such safeguards, while tertiary prevention would involve competent management of a crisis in which a child has been removed from school by an unauthorized person.

School psychologists who have been trained in organizational and community intervention will quickly recognize primary and secondary prevention as the mainstay of most systems-level interventions (Danish & D'Augelli, 1980; Rappaport, 1977; Reiff, 1975). However, school administrators, in the most-frequent-case scenario, are infinitely more amenable to primary or secondary activities once they have found themselves face to face with the tertiary prevention problems of managing a crisis. In reality, therefore, school psychologists are frequently faced with the somewhat illogical approach of beginning to intervene at the tertiary level of crisis management, and only later focusing on primary and secondary activities. Enter the tremendous opportunity for school psychologists in crisis intervention.

Administrative personnel who have managed an intense crisis are far more motivated to avoid having to do so again. Frequently this phenomenon occurs at the highest levels of administration and the school board. These individuals are scrutinized by the entire community for making the "right" decisions under pressure. The question rises from parents, children, the media, and faculty: What's being done? Those districts who can answer this question most convincingly and reassuringly are those who have planned activities and procedures along all three avenues of prevention, as stressed by the present model.

For example, in a recent series in the *School Administrator*, a number of administrative personnel, including superintendents, associate superintendents, and principals, emphasized the importance of crisis intervention in the schools (Barish, 1991; Caylor, 1991; Colley, 1991; Coonan, 1991; Dunne-Maxim & Underwood, 1991; Excel, 1991). Caylor, superintendent of Huntsville, Alabama, city schools described how her school district developed an emergency response plan several years *after* a middle school was destroyed by an arsonist (Caylor, 1991). A young boy had set a stage curtain on fire that engulfed the school in flames. She commented, "We learned about dealing with a crisis the hard way" (p. 17). Since then, plans have been developed to address many situations: fire; bomb threat; explosion; ice/snowstorm; severe weather; hazardous materials; building intruder; off-campus/emergency bus wreck; and injuries to students, nonstudents, and employees; as well as student evacuation from schoolgrounds. The major point she makes is that the importance of developing a crisis plan cannot be overstated.

Excel (1991), the principal of the Cokeville Elementary School in Cokeville, Wyoming, described how his school was taken hostage by a couple with guns and a homemade bomb. They herded 150 people into a first-grade classroom and held the group hostage. Excel mediated the hostage takers' demands with the police. However, the bomb accidentally exploded, blowing out the ceiling and setting the room and all the occupants on fire. Fortunately, no children or staff members died, though many were badly burned, and 86 students and teachers were sent to area hospitals. After this trauma, the area psychologists taught parents and teachers how to cope and in turn how to help the students deal with the aftermath of this tragedy. It appears that administrators are not only beginning to appreciate the importance of planning for crisis, but also the crucial role that school psychologists can take in facilitating the coping process. The most innovative districts are now beginning to recognize the value not only of tertiary prevention, but primary and secondary prevention as well.

BEST PRACTICES IN DEVELOPING A DISTRICT PROGRAM FOR CRISIS INTERVENTION

Nelson and Slaikeu (1984) pointed out that crisis intervention needs to be included in the job descriptions of school personnel such as administrators, counselors, and school psychologists. Guetzloe (1988) emphasized that educational associations are recognizing that more needs to be done in preparing schools to deal with a crisis. Guetzloe pointed out that California in 1982 mandated that schools be safe and stressed the following points:

1. Teachers and administrators should be trained in crime prevention and safety procedures.

2. School security engineers should approve of school construction and schools have a responsibility to keep students safe.

Historically, attempts to prevent a crisis from occurring at school have concentrated on evacuation procedures such as fire and natural disaster drills. The incidence of violence in our schools and society indicates that we have to prepare for violent behavior. As one teacher put it, "We have to be prepared for a violent intrusion from an outsider or violent behavior on the part of a member of our school."

An examination of a number of school district procedures on crisis intervention is enlightening. Most procedures address chain-of-command issues such as when to call the superintendent or security and whether to evacuate the building in the event of a bomb threat. These organizational issues are certainly important but a crisis team that can provide a range of services is needed.

There is little information about exactly how crisis teams are organized. Ruof and Harris (1988) described three options in setting up a crisis team:

1. An inside model, which includes only staff from one building on the crisis team.

2. An outside team, composed of community mental health professionals or itinerant school personnel such as school psychologists and special education personnel.

3. A combined model that utilizes building personnel and professionals who do not regularly work in the building.

Ruof and Harris point out that there are many advantages to the inside team format because students know the team members, and they are more immediately available. A disadvantage may be that a building may not have the necessary personnel or the personnel may not have crisis intervention skills. The outside model utilizes more trained personnel, but they do not know the students and must be called to the building. One outside crisis team reported to us that they were ready to assist in the aftermath of a student's death but that the principal did not call on them. Pelej and Scholzen (1987) and Schulman (1986) have cautioned against the school system's always calling in outside experts when a crisis occurs. Ruof and Harris cited two additional problems with this approach. There may not be enough itinerant school personnel to call on and the outside professionals may be too costly. Comstock (1985) stressed that outside mental health professionals are willing to assist at little or no cost if the school system will involve them in a meaningful way and listen to their recommendations. The combined model is recommended by Ruof and Harris because it utilizes personnel in the building who know the students as well as the expertise of itinerant school personnel or community mental health personnel.

Selecting crisis team members is very important. Ruof and Harris (1988) recommend that membership on the crisis team be voluntary. Team members should not only be willing but should have attributes and skills that will enable them to perform well. The question of how many school personnel should be on a crisis team was discussed by Ruof and Harris, who recommended a minimum of two and preferable one team member per 100 children. We recommend that teams be composed of four to eight. Fewer than four team members may not provide enough team members to manage a crisis and more than eight team members results in confusion. A team approach is needed because no single person can do everything; principals have commented that they could not be in the four or five places they needed to be at the same time during a crisis.

Theoretical Model

Crisis team members need to be familiar with Caplan's (1964) model. Most people think of crisis intervention only as what is done in the immediate aftermath of a crisis, but the most important issue is what can be done to prevent a crisis from happening. One principal who experienced a shooting at school feels very strongly that students must not keep a secret about life-threatening behavior. Many efforts have been directed towards improving and maintaining close communication between faculty and students. Too often students know about potential crisis events but keep the information to themselves. It is not possible to specify all the *primary prevention* activities that a crisis team could be involved in. Examples are high schools that decide to do something about drunk driving by establishing a safe ride program and to work to prevent teen suicide by establishing a school crisis helpline. A local teacher rehearsed a "secret signal" of danger with her class; her students followed her cue and violence was averted when a gunman entered her class. The following are the types of questions that crisis teams need to think about to prevent a crisis.

1. What is worrisome about the school or the neighborhood?

2. Is there a potentially violent student or parent?

3. How could we notify students to stay away from windows or to evacuate the playground or the school quickly?

4. If we evacuate the school, where do we go?

5. What has worked or not worked in handling a crisis situation in the past?

6. Is all playground equipment safe?

7. Do school personnel know CPR and first aid? Who will summon medical assistance? What if the nurse is not available?

8. How can a teacher summon help from the office?

9. Does the school offer a gun safety program?

10. Is the school system prepared to deal with the media?

11. Have school staff been provided with information on how to deal with a violent individual?

12. What communication systems are available to contact police and to inform the superintendent of schools?

Dillard (1989) made these additional recommendations for primary prevention.

1. Know how to call on mental health resources in your community.

2. Establish close cooperative relations between the school system and police and fire departments.

3. Be prepared to provide continuing assistance to students, their parents and school staff after a crisis. Group meetings held at school can convey factual information and dispel rumors.

Many issues concerning safety also need to be addressed in the curriculum. One of the most important involves educating students about gun safety. Ten children each day under the age of 18 are killed in handgun suicides, homicides or accidents (Memmot & Stone, 1989). One school system that is educating its students about gun safety is Dade County in Florida. Doup (1989) reports that the program begins in the first grade and is modeled after drug prevention programs.

The *secondary level* of intervention in Caplan's (1964) model emphasizes responding quickly to minimize the chance of long-lasting effects to a crisis. School buildings may want to form medical emergency teams and rehearse their response to various situations. Control of students is also very important. Plans need to be developed to direct students to classrooms or out of the building without mass confusion. One high school crisis team has made evacuation arrangement with local churches near the high school campus. The team also has ready a "crisis box" with materials that would be needed in the event that the school needs to be evacuated. The school faculty must also be told promptly when a crisis occurs. Thought needs to be given to how to accomplish that. The faculty needs to process the crisis event and their feelings about it as soon as students have gone home. This meeting to process the event can also be used to plan for the next school day.

Contacting law enforcement personnel is also part of secondary intervention. What law enforcement personnel will be called and what to expect when they arrive are important questions to be addressed. Contact with parents is also very important. The parents of injured and upset children need to be contacted. Parents might simply appear at the school and might be upset and make demands upon the school or they might come to help out. One crisis team elected to involve parents by contacting parents who lived near the school and were home during the day and making them a part of their crisis team. Communication to parents after a crisis also is very important. It is important to clarify how this communication will take place and who will do it.

The emotional effects of a crisis must also be dealt with immediately in order to minimize long-lasting debilitating effects. This point is well illustrated by Sandall (1986), who not only discussed immediate steps taken in the aftermath of a school bombing in Cokeville, Wyoming, but contrasted actions taken there with those taken in Chowchilla, California, in the 1970s. A school busload of children were kidnapped in Chowchilla and was buried in the desert for several days. The children escaped and were physically unhurt. Sandall reports the Chowchilla schoolchildren were told to go home and forget about the incident, and that only a small percentage of them would suffer permanent psychological effects. A follow-up study 5 years later found 100% with psychological problems as a result of their experience. Sandall described the steps taken in Wyoming to provide opportunities for children and faculty to discuss their feelings after a bombing incident at school. School was held the day after the bombing and all who could be released from the hospital were encouraged to attend. Sandall commented in part, "Those children who verbalized most effectively and in the greatest quantity have managed recovery best" (1986, p. 2). Common reactions by children who have witnessed a traumatic event, according to Pynoos and Eth (1986), are (a) reexperiencing the event through thoughts; (b) fearing that it will happen again; and (c) withdrawing from the outside environment and experiencing an extreme need to cling to family members.

Schulman (1986) discussed immediate steps taken in Concord, New Hampshire, to deal with emotionality following the Challenger shuttle disaster that killed Christa McAuliffe, a teacher at the high school. Schulman emphasized that having a crisis team already in place was of great benefit. Students and teachers were provided many opportunities to express their emotions and were given flexibility with regard to their schedule and movement around the building. Students had a number of choices: They could go to the gym and vent frustrations and anger through physical activity, they could go to the cafeteria to support and be supported by others, or they could go to the library, which was a quiet work area.

Tertiary prevention involves the long-term follow-up of those affected by a crisis. Sandall (1986) stressed the need for tertiary intervention and pointed out that counseling was provided over the summer in Cokeville, Wyoming. Follow-up questionnaires are also recommended. School psychologists are in a position to provide follow-up and monitoring to those most affected by a crisis. If we cannot provide the long-term assistance ourselves, we can recommend that the family seek it privately. Anniversary dates of losses and crisis events are important.

Training Issues for Crisis Team Members

Team members need to be able to recognize a crisis, which Jay (1989) pointed out is an event that is likely (a) to interrupt normal routine and escalate in intensity; (b) to draw attention to the school and jeopardize the school's image; or (c) to interfere with the students' and the staff's ability to focus learning. Smead (1985) discussed the importance of responding immediately to a crisis to minimize effects. The crisis team should meet if at all possible even if a threatening event does not seem to be of crisis proportions. What this immediate response should be was emphasized by Slaikeu (1984), who outlined the following principles of psychological first aid:

1. Make contact with the victim and give him/her permission to express thoughts and emotions.

2. Explore the problem in terms of the past, present, and future.

3. Identify possible solutions to assist victim.

4. Take definite actions to assist victim.

5. Provide follow-up assistance.

Psychological first aid addresses immediate concerns and helps the victim sort out such needs as welfare, safety, shelter, and so on. Ruof and Harris (1988) recommend that team members receive as much as 30 hours of training.

Dealing with death. Stevenson (1986) pointed out that one of every 750 young people will die each year. The most frequent cause of death for school age children in order of magnitude are accidents, suicides, and homicides. School crisis team members need to be trained to assist in the aftermath of a death. Verification of a death is essential. A second or third verification needs to be made before the death is announced. The principal is the logical person to direct the crisis team and to announce the death. Fitzgerald (1988) makes a number of recommendations in this area:

1. Announce the death over the intercom so that everyone gets the same information; then visit as many classrooms as possible, especially those most affected.

2. Provide opportunities for discussion of emotions, the grief process, and funeral arrangements.

3. Send a letter home to parents giving information about
the death and how parents can help their children.

4. Counseling grief groups may need to be provided on a continuing basis.

Pitcher and Poland (1992) recommend notifying teachers first about the specifics of the crisis through a calling tree or faculty meeting. A memorandum read to the students by the teacher is preferable to an intercom announcement. Educators often expect all children to react to a death in the same way, the typical expectation being that children should cry. Children should be given permission for a range of emotions. Children who state today that they don't care may cry tomorrow. Crabb (1982) suggested the following classroom guidance activities to assist students: (a) unfinished sentence writing; (b) drawing a picture to express feelings; (c) using music to express thoughts and emotions.

Do not rush to remove the desks and personal possessions of the deceased. Involve students in that process and encourage students to contact the family of the deceased in person or through cards and letters. It is recommended that a school psychologist follow the class schedule of the deceased. Stevenson (1986) recommends minimizing religious platitudes or symbolism and maintains that there is no correct response to a death. Physical contact may comfort some students. Students may be flooded with waves of emotions. The life history of each person will influence his or her ability to cope with the death. Stevenson states that it is appropriate to just let students sit but not to leave them unsupervised. The most common reaction is shock as students try to grasp the finality of the loss. It is important that all school personnel model expression of emotion; curriculum concerns may have to be set aside.

Oates (1988) recommends a model to determine the expected degree of trauma following a death. Oates points out that the popularity of the person who died and her or his length of time at a particular school are determinants. The circumstances of the death are also important. Suicide or murder result in more trauma than death by natural causes. A death that occurs at school also results in more trauma. These factors that address who, how, and where are very relevant to those dealing with death. It is also important to look at what other crisis events have impacted on a particular school population (Pitcher & Poland, 1992).

Team members will need to be advocates for giving school children and staff the opportunity to express their emotions. This point is illustrated by the following teacher comments: "I heard about the murder of R, a seven-year-old girl in my class the night that she was killed. I went to school early the next morning. My principal was just moving her desk out of my room. The principal said that all of her possessions had been removed and that I should avoid talking about her murder and concentrate on academics. I was angry and so were my students, we all felt robbed of a chance to express our emotions and to say our farewells to her. One student asked if we couldn't at least let a balloon ascend to heaven in her memory. I allowed that and it helped her classmates."

Crabb (1982) emphasized that children's emotional problems after a disaster continue until help is provided. Children need to be provided the facts in age-appropriate terms and rumors must be dispelled. Dillard (1989) recommended providing parents and children the opportunity to be together and share experiences after a tragedy. Dillard described meetings that were held over the summer following a shooting in Winnetka, Illinois. These meetings helped children achieve mastery of the shooting. Dillard stressed that a traumatic event is stored in active memory until mastered. Details fade from immediate memory when mastery occurs.

Implementing Crisis Intervention: Some Basic Skills

In implementing crisis intervention services in the schools, it is essential that school psychologists have the requisite skills. Unfortunately, many of our professional colleagues have not been systematically trained in crisis counseling and intervention. They may have implemented psychological first aid after a major crisis has occurred, but never received feedback on how to improve their competence nor been prepared prior to the occurrence of a traumatic event on how to respond to it.

As noted by Lazarus and Jackson (1993b, p. 16), "Disasters are inevitable. They can occur at any time, in any place. They can blindside anyone at any age. They hit communities large or small." Crisis will occur whether or not school psychologists are prepared; therefore, adequate training in crisis intervention is essential. This is fundamental to the model presented that emphasizes competent reaction to crisis and systematic prevention of crisis.

Crisis intervention has been defined as a "helping process aimed at assisting a person or family to survive an unsettling event so that the probability of debilitating effects (e.g., emotional scars, physical harm) is minimized, and the probability of growth (e.g., new skills, new outlook on life, more options in living) is maximized" (Slaikeu, 1990, p. 6).

This process can be conceptualized in two phases: first-order intervention, which may be thought of as psychological first aid, and second-order intervention, which may be termed crisis therapy. When school psychologists typically first arrive at a school that has experienced a crisis, they often offer immediate assistance. One type of first-order intervention is called debriefing.

Debriefing. The ability to conduct a debriefing should be considered a requisite skill for all school psychologists. Lazarus (in press-a) describes debriefing as "a process in which survivors or witnesses of a trauma have the opportunity to describe and discuss the impact the event had on their lives. It provides individuals an opportunity to tell their story, ventilate their feelings and have their emotional reactions validated." As explained by Lazarus and Howard (1993), the purpose of a debriefing is to help survivors regain some sense of control or mastery over their lives. It provides a forum to assist participants in predicting future events and reactions so that they can prepare for them in adaptive ways.

It needs to be emphasized that debriefing is not therapy (Bates & Freeman, 1992), though it is therapeutic. It may be better conceptualized as an educational and psychological experience designed to help participants "let some steam off the pressure cooker of disaster reactions" (NOVA, 1991, p. 147).

Debriefing can be conceptualized primarily as a *secondary level* of prevention according to Caplan's (1964) model. It emphasizes a quick response to a crisis in an effort to ameliorate long-lasting adverse effects. During the debriefing process, individuals most affected by a crisis can be identified for counseling, follow-up, and monitoring. Therefore, if done correctly, debriefing automatically leads into *tertiary prevention*. In some instances, the discussion of the impact of the trauma during a debriefing may later lead to policies, procedures, and practices designed to avert future crises. Therefore, debriefing may indirectly precipitate *primary prevention* activities.

An example will illustrate. Following a shooting on school grounds, the administration and faculty implemented specific written policies on what students should do if they suspect another student is carrying a weapon. Procedures were clearly articulated to assist students in alerting school personnel. An 11th-grade girl reported to the principal that a student was carrying a gun. She felt guilty about reporting, but told her friends that if she had not witnessed a previous shooting or participated in crisis counseling afterwards, she would have kept the secret to herself.

One of the advantages of conducting a debriefing is that it adds structure to a crisis, which helps contain the chaos and confusion. It can be comforting to administrators, faculty, and students to know that they will have the opportunity to discuss any crisis that occurs and be given the latest information. When conducted properly, a debriefing emphasizes open communication, honesty, and the expression of feelings. It can help being individuals together and assist in creating a support system.

In the same way that districts expect school psychologists to conduct psychoeducational assessments, they can expect that school psychologists be involved in crisis intervention. In this way practitioners can emphasize the essential nature of their services (Lazarus, in press-a). When school psychology positions are being threatened in tight financial times (see Steegmann & Harwood, 1992), this takes on added importance.

A Model for Debriefing

When conducting a debriefing, it is recommended that a structured model be followed. The National Organization for Victims Assistance (NOVA) has developed a model that can easily be followed by school psychologists. According to Lazarus (in press-b), training school psychologists in debriefing requires teaching the essence of active listening, empathy, and effective communication techniques. It also requires teaching the psychologist how to project a presence of competence, calmness, and compassion in the presence of confusion. The details of the NOVA model include team roles, ground rules, timing and logistics, and procedures and processes.

Team roles. The debriefing team consists of a minimum of two individuals, a leader and a scribe. If resources are available, then optional caregivers are recommended.

School psychologists can act as the debriefing *leaders* and assume the major responsibility for conducting the sessions. They introduce themselves and all team members and express sadness about the impact the trauma has had on the lives of the participants. They clarify the purpose of the debriefing and explain the ground rules. They give permission for all individuals to express their feelings and come and go as they please. If time is allowed, they may also discuss issues such as common reactions to crisis, coping mechanisms, long-term stress reactions, hints for coping with acute and chronic stress, and strategies for maintaining physical and emotional well-being.

The *scribes* provide emotional support to the debriefing leaders. Typically, they act as recorders by writing on a flip chart or blackboard the reactions and emotions of the group. They assist individuals in crisis by distributing kleenex and water, providing physical comfort when necessary, and helping individuals leave the room. Usually, they act like a supportive and unobtrusive partner contributing only when called upon by the group leader. Lazarus and Phelps (1993) emphasized that responding to crisis is a team effort: The leader, the scribe, and the caregivers are members of a team that need each other to function more effectively. By modeling this behavior, a set is stressed that participants should also rely on each other in a time of crisis.

Ground rules. The ground rules for debriefing are simple and straightforward. All communication is confidential: Nothing said during the debriefing leaves the room. Names of participants are not written down and the blackboard is erased or the flip chart pages destroyed after the session is over.

If individuals are willing, they may identify themselves when they speak. They are given permission to express how they feel. Participants are informed that this is not a critique of what happened, but instead a review of their reactions (NOVA, 1991). Carnes and Sorensen (1993) who conduct debriefings for emergency medical personnel, firefighters, and police officers also offer some suggestions that could be incorporated in the school setting. They emphasize that no one talks for another and that participants' should comment only about their own thoughts, feelings, and reactions. Mental health professionals who conduct debriefings advise that groups should be as homogeneous as possible. If individuals feel uncomfortable with anyone present, this will be deleterious to the process. Therefore, no school administrators or teachers should be present when students are debriefed. Most importantly, the media must be excluded from any debriefing involving students or school staff. If necessary, the media can be debriefed as a separate group.

According to NOVA (1991), there is both an announced and real agenda. The announced agenda is to ask participants now they have reacted, how they are all presently reacting, and what their expectations are for the future. The real agenda is to help the groups "define the crisis reaction, provide some crisis intervention and predict and prepare the groups for possible future events" (Lazarus, in press-a).

Timing and logistics. Debriefing should take place 24–72 hours after a trauma and should not interfere with events such as funerals and memorials. Day debriefings are usually better for students and school personnel. Night or weekend debriefings may be better for parents. Session should last no more than 2 hours.

As to logistics, the room needs to be accessible and comfortable. Debriefings should be conducted in a circle or horseshoe arrangement and need to be free from distractions and interruptions. Kleenex, water, and other necessities need to be available to all participants.

Process and procedures. Participants are asked to describe their experience during the crisis. Though participants are encouraged to speak as freely as possible, they should not be pressured to talk, and their privacy needs to be respected.

Typically, participants are asked specific questions such as: (a) where they were when the trauma occurred; (b) who they were with; (c) what they heard, smelled, tasted, or touched at the time; and (d) how they reacted.

According to Lazarus (in press-a), the leader listens to the reactions and underscores any statements that fit within the crisis reaction framework. The scribe writes down the emotions and recollections as they are generated from the discussion. Typically, recollections of any crisis may generate feelings of shock, disbelief, and denial. Further, reactions of anger and rage, fear and terror, grief and sorrow, confusion and frustration, and guilt and self-blame usually emerge. All throughout the process, the leader needs to listen and validate key emotional reactions and concerns.

Carnes and Sorensen (1993) describe the debriefing process as consisting of a series of phases. In practical terms, they are not distinct and include the intermeshing of these phases: (a) introduction; (b) discussing of facts, thoughts, reactions, and symptoms; (c) teaching; and (d) reentry.

The process can move from the introduction of the purpose of debriefing to the discussion by participants of the facts, and their thoughts, reactions, and symptoms related to the crisis. Near the end of the session, the leader can discuss issues such as coping with crisis and how to handle stress reactions. Effective strategies used by participants in handling crisis are validated. Future meetings at the school may be arranged as necessary.

Handouts may be distributed that provide information about crisis reactions and managing acute and chronic stress, and hints for maintaining physical and emotional well-being following a crisis (see Lazarus, 1992a). Authors such as Faberos and Gordon (1981), NOVA (1991), and Pitcher and Poland (1992) provide suggestions that are useful for creating handouts. Also, most school districts have available information that can be shared with participants. Organizations including Mothers Against Drunk Driving (1990) provide handouts for dealing with death at school. NASP also has made available brief handouts with such titles as Understanding Trauma and Grief and What to Do About It (Hyman, 1992) that are included in *Helping Children Grow Up in the 90s: A Resource Book for Parents and Teachers* (NASP, 1992).

Staff debriefing. Following a debriefing conducted by school psychologists, counselors, and mental health personnel, it is incumbent on the team to be informally debriefed. Staff need to ensure that they make time for themselves to go over the event and describe their own emotions and reactions. Anyone who has performed crisis intervention services knows that it can be an emotionally draining experience.

At the next team meeting, it is recommended that the group make a brief presentation to all members of the school psychology staff. One of the purposes of this presentation is to brainstorm ways to improve crisis intervention service and be better prepared for the next event.

One District's Approach to Crisis Intervention Planning

The development and implementation of a crisis intervention plan by one school district was assigned by the superintendent to psychological services. The following steps were taken:

1. The literature was surveyed and a few crisis plans from other school districts were located.

2. Principals were interviewed to get their input and to involve them in the process.

3. Directors of security, nursing, transportation, and public information were all interviewed.

4. A building crisis team approach was recommended with district personnel involved in a support role.

5. Building principals were designated as crisis coordinators and the media spokespersons. An in-service was provided to clarify their role.

6. Principals designated liaisons in the following areas: counseling, law enforcement, student, parent, campus and medical. These liaisons together with the principal formed the building crisis team. Training was provided to the various liaisons.

7. Principals were provided with training on dealing with the media, emphasis being placed on being cooperative but also containing the media.

8. District transportation personnel received training.

9. A tip sheet for teachers and aides for dealing with a crisis was developed and presented at an in-service in every school building. Teachers were encouraged to make plans to deal with such behavior as tantrums, fights, running away, and medical emergencies. A worksheet to address these was provided.

10. A basic premise emphasized was that this was a starting point and that the most important recommendation was for the building crisis teams to meet regularly and discuss their school.

11. Crisis intervention activities were publicized and shared with the community.

Crisis drills. The district had on paper an excellent crisis plan, but to make crisis intervention an integrated part of school more steps had to be taken. The superintendent authorized conducting crisis drills and gave the principals forewarning. A script for the initial crisis drill was written and various central administrators went to the mock scenes to role-play the crisis. To minimize school disruption the crisis drill took place outside the school building. A sample crisis scenario appears below.

> **Incident:** A female student has been shot in the foot by a pistol in front of the school by the flagpole. The pistol, which she had been carrying in her purse, discharged with students nearby. Your first notification of the incident is when several hysterical students rush into the office. The student has a younger brother who attends the same school. The superintendent's secretary will role-play the mother; please call her.

> **Task:** Please respond to this incident, following the district crisis intervention procedures. District personnel are on the scene to role-play and ask questions. This is a *practice drill* and district personnel should be alerted; however, it is *not necessary* to notify agencies outside the district.

Verbal and written feedback were provided to the crisis team. The importance of a team effort was stressed, along with indications of prior planning. The first two drills were videotaped and were shown at the principal's meeting. Numerous drills have since been conducted, including even a surprise crisis drill at the central office. No one has complained about the crisis drills and they serve the purpose of making crisis intervention a regular part of conducting school.

Improving Crisis Intervention Services

One of the best ways to improve crisis intervention services is to receive systematic feedback on the functioning of the crisis support team in delivering services to the schools. Broward County (Florida) schools has developed an evaluation team follow-up procedure that evaluates their effectiveness. In particular, these questions are asked:

1. Did the crisis support team (CST) assist you in developing a school-based plan of action for dealing with a crisis at your school?

2. Did the CST assist you in informing students (i.e., announcements by principal, etc.) about the crisis?

3. Did the CST assist you in informing parents (i.e., letter, etc.) about the crisis?

4. Did the CST provide assistance in communicating with the media?

5. Did a member of the CST assist you in meeting with members of your faculty?

6. Did the CST provide individual consultation services to teachers? If so, did that service assist teachers in dealing with the crisis?

7. Did the CST provide counseling to students individually or in groups? If so, did that service assist students in dealing with the crisis?

8. Did the CST provide follow-up services to students and staff in need of that service?

9. Were on-site materials provided by team members effective in dealing with the crisis?

10. What else could have been done to improve the team's effectiveness and helpfulness?

Moreover, crisis teams need to systematically document all their activities, including both individual and group contacts and their impression of the crisis and their interventions. By doing so, they can not only organize their services better, but also maintain a method for improving their delivery system.

Responding to Community Disasters and Schoolwide Crises

Within the past decade, the role of the school psychologist has changed, and it is now incumbent on our profession to provide leadership in the wake of disasters resulting from natural, social, or specific school district causes. As noted by Lazarus (in press-a), "disasters are inevitable. Appropriate preparation is not." Therefore, our profession needs to be better informed about crisis reactions, crisis theory, and crisis interventions in the aftermath of large-scale disasters.

A brief overview of postdisaster crisis intervention. As summarized by Cohen (1982, 1986, 1990), mental health journals and books are presenting theoretical formulations on stress effects and crisis theory and providing information on a variety of approaches that have been applied to postdisaster situations. Tyhurst (1951) originally pinpointed sequences and phases of behavior related to crisis resolution and began to specify intervention approaches applicable to each phase. Parad and Caplan (1966) described the mechanisms families used in adapting to crisis events.

R. Lazarus (1966, 1980) has expanded the knowledge of coping by identifying the significant role of the cognitive system as it affects the psychological interpretation of a trauma. He sees coping as defined by two major activities. The first involves changing the system — problem solving. The second involves managing the subjective components (feelings, thoughts, physical well-being, behavior) of the problem. A crisis state is characterized by a breakdown in these processes in which rational problem solving is difficult and the individual has difficulty managing the subjective components of the crisis situation. Horowitz (1986) has proposed a model of information processing for dealing with the aftermath of a tragic event. As discussed by Dillard (1989), Horowitz explained that until a traumatic event can be mastered through understanding and then integrated, its psychology is stored in active memory. As mastery occurs, the trauma is incorporated, the details fading from immediate memory. Until the mastery occurs, individuals are vulnerable to psychological overload such that normal ego coping mechanisms are not up to the stress produced by the disaster.

In dealing with children, Caplan (1964) views the prevention of mental disorders as a function of whether they have adequate physical, psychological, and cultural supplies for dealing with life's stresses. Children who are said to cope well following a crisis are those who have not only personal and psychological strengths, but also the social supports necessary for enduring disequilibrium and making appropriate accommodations.

Pynoos and his colleagues have studied life threat and posttraumatic stress in school-age children (Eth and Pynoos, 1985; Pynoos et al., 1987). They have provided strong evidence that acute posttraumatic stress occurs in school-age children within weeks of a life-threatening violent event. Age, sex, and ethnicity do not influence the type or severity of posttraumatic stress. The most important variable in relation to the number of posttraumatic symptoms reported appears to be the degree of exposure. This notion of proximity to the event as the most important variable has also been supported by Dillard (1989).

Many of the original formulations about crisis theory and intervention have come from researchers with a community psychology orientation who have studied adults. Recently, the school psychology literature has paid attention to the role of their practitioners in crisis intervention. Pitcher and Poland (1992) have effectively discussed what lessons can be learned from man-made school district disasters (Chapter 5). Here they discuss the traumas (also dealt with in the sources cited in parentheses) of Chowchilla, California (Terr, 1983); Cokeville, Wyoming (Sandall, 1986; Stevens, 1989); Winnetka, Illinois (Dillard, 1989; 1990); Greenwood, South Carolina (Greer, 1988; Stevens, 1990); and Stockton, California (Armstrong, 1989). A series of articles in the *Communiqué* has highlighted the role of school psychology staff in responding to natural disasters such as the San Francisco earthquake (Spicher, 1989), Hurricane Hugo (Alderman, 1989; Harlom, 1989), and Hurricane Andrew (Lazarus, 1992a; Lazarus, 1992b; Lazarus & Howard, 1993; Lazarus & Jackson, 1993a). Since there has been an unfortunate escalation in the number of crisis events, our profession has had to respond by focusing on crisis intervention activities.

Recommendations for dealing with stress in the schools following a natural disaster. Considerable research suggests that a fair percentage of children exposed to natural disasters will experience circumscribed, time-limited fears or behavioral problems (Auerbach & Spirito, 1986, p. 194). As noted by Pynoos et al. (1987), those most exposed will be the most vulnerable. In major disasters, such as that in parts of South Dade County that were directly hit by Hurricane Andrew, it has been estimated that 95% of the children experienced post-traumatic stress disorder (PTSD) symptomatology.

In treating the trauma of disasters, some points can be emphasized.

1. The family can be considered the first line of defense in helping children adjust. Benedek (1979), in reviewing the relevant literature, concluded that a caring and stable parent was probably the most essential element in a child's adjustment following a catastrophe. Raphael (1975) believes that family ties, reassurance, and open discussions are critically important elements.

2. Children separated from their families during a disaster will require a great deal of comfort and reassurance. Information about the family's well-being, phone calls, and so forth, should be provided as quickly as possible.

3. Disaster treatment and services mandate that professionals working with survivors of disaster seek out individuals in need rather than waiting for them to seek help. It has been noted by Tuckman (1973) that reaching out to disaster victims immediately after a trauma can minimize the development of post-traumatic symptoms.

4. School-age victims of a disaster should be encouraged to resume many of their daily activities. Children should also develop an understanding of their situation and confront rather than deny their thoughts and feelings. Crabbs (1981) emphasizes that

activities should provide opportunity for personal expression regarding the crisis event.

5. Schools can provide a bridge to the community and serve as a disaster assistance center. The school can provide a site that can help coordinate disaster relief. Information of legal, economic, insurance, food, health, shelter and safety issues can be disseminated by school staff, crisis workers and community volunteers.

6. The school can provide security and support to children whose lives were disrupted by a natural disaster (Lazarus & Howard, 1993). Here school psychologists and counselors can provide needed emotional support to children and their parents.

7. It is also important to remember that children are resilient (NIMH, 1975–1984) and that victims view themselves as anxious and under stress but not pathological.

Some lessons learned. On December 3, 1985, and January 28, 1986 Concord (New Hampshire) High School sustained two significant tragedies. The first occurred when a 16-year-old former student who had recently dropped out of school appeared at Concord High carrying a loaded shotgun. After taking students hostage and threatening school personnel, he was killed in an exchange of gunfire with the local police. Less than 2 months later, Christa McAuliffe (the first teacher selected for a mission in space) was killed in the shuttle disaster along with six astronauts. Mrs. McAuliffe had been a teacher at Concord High until her NASA appointment. The faculty and students were watching on television the shuttle launching in which she died.

Norman Shulman had been the Emergency Service Program coordinator and was involved in developing the school's response plans following both crises. In discussing the best way to achieve the objectives of intervention following major stressful events, Shulman (1990, p. 67) proposes some intervention responses that can be deemed useful in almost any school situation following a disaster.

1. Obtain, disseminate, and update information about the crisis.

2. Encourage ventilation about the event in an empathetic and accepting manner.

3. Strengthen awareness of the normalcy of the victims' reactions. Help them view themselves as normal individuals undergoing acute stress.

4. Help the victims accept and confront the reality of the event. Identify reality-based cause–effect relationships between events and reactions.

5. Arrange group discussions to relate thoughts and feelings about the impact of the trauma.

6. Resume activity to help reorder life in its new context as it is redefined by the disaster.

7. Explain to victims that certain reactions, though distressing, are to be expected, and that these, as well as specific symptoms, should be viewed as normal.

As a final thought, by reading the literature on crisis theory and crisis intervention, by serving on crisis response teams, and by continually updating their skills through in-service and consultation with colleagues, school psychologists will be in a position to offer significant help following a major disaster. However, it is important that school psychology service staff work with their district to develop plans to cover a wide range of traumatic events.

SUMMARY

There has been an increase in the number of crisis events that affect the schools. School psychologists are the logical personnel to respond. It is important that school psychologists respond to this opportunity to help all concerned and to broaden the role of school psychology. The initial intervention of school psychologists will be at the secondary or tertiary level. It is important that we advocate for opportunities for those who experience a crisis to express their emotions. The focus for the future needs to be on primary prevention activities in the schools. Crisis intervention is an area in which all our efforts need to be constantly improving and evolving in response to the needs of our schools and society.

There are numerous state and national initiatives that focus on school crisis and violence prevention. A national educational goal has been set to have violence-free schools by the year 2000. The Clinton Administration has just passed the Safe Schools Act of 1993 to provide federal grants to encourage schools to develop curriculum, safety, and security programs. One state, South Carolina, has passed legislation that requires schools to develop crisis plans. It is our belief that schools will be held increasingly accountable for crisis prevention and management plans. The single greatest resource for school psychologists in this area is the National School Safety Center (NSSC), which is a combined effort of the United States Department of Criminal Justice and Education. The NSSC published articles, newsletters, journals, and books on all aspects of school safety. The current director of the NSSC, Ron Stevens (1990) emphasized that school crisis planning is an inside job that involves the staff, students, and community.

The importance of making crisis prevention and management plans today cannot be overemphasized. A biblical quote illustrates this point: "I must work the works of him that sent me while it is day: the night cometh when no man can work" (Gospel of St. John, Chapter 9, Verse 4). We have been faced with crisis situations and have found it difficult to think clearly and we have been uncertain of who should do what. School psychologists must step forward to provide leadership in crisis planning and should seek out those who need our help after a crisis.

REFERENCES

Alderman, G. (1989, November). Disaster team works during crisis. *Communiqué*, p. 24.

Armstrong, M. (1989, December). Cross-cultural issues in responding to a tragedy: The Stockton school shooting. *Communiqué*, *18*, pp. 10–11.

Auerbach, S. M., & Spirito, A. (1986). Crisis intervention with children exposed to natural disasters. In S. M. Auerbach & A. Stolberg (Eds.), *Crisis intervention with children and families*. Washington, DC: Hemisphere.

Barish, S. (1991). I was there when tragedy struck: Three administrators describe how they coped: A senior's suicide. *School Administrator*, May/June, pp. 12–13.

Bates, F., & Freeman, P. (1992, December). *Debriefing*. Presentation to Dade County School Psychological Services. Miami, Florida.

Benedek, E. (1979). The child's rights in times of disaster. *Psychiatric Annals*, *9*(11), 58–61.

Bloom, B. L. (1977). *Community mental health: A general introduction*. Monterey, CA: Brooks/Cole.

Busher, F. (Chair). (1990). *Tragedy in Stockton schoolyard*. Symposium presented at the meeting of the National Association of School Psychologists, San Francisco.

Caplan, G. (1964). *Principles of preventive psychiatry*. New York: Basic Books.

Carnes & Sorensen. (1993). *Critical incident stress management for mental health professionals*. Unpublished manual.

Caylor, M. J. (1991). One district's crisis plan. *School Administrator*, May/June, p. 18.

Cohen, R. E. (1982). Intervening with disaster victims. In H. C. Schulberg & M. Killilea (Eds.), *The modern practices of community mental health* (pp. 397–418). San Francisco: Jossey-Bass.

Cohen, R. E. (1986). Developmental phases of children's reactions following natural disasters. *Journal of Emergency and Disaster Medicine*, *1*, 4.

Cohen, R. E. (1990). Post disaster mobilization and crisis counseling: Guidelines and techniques for developing crisis-oriented services for disaster victims. In A. R. Roberts (Ed.), *Crisis intervention handbook: Assessment, treatment and research* (pp. 279–299). Belmont, CA: Wadsworth.

Colley, G. S. (1991). Are you a caring colleague? *School Administrator*, May/June, p. 18.

Coonen, J. T. (1991). I was there when tragedy struck: Three administrators describe how they coped: A tornado strikes. *School Administrator*, May/June, pp. 16–17.

Crabb, A. (1982, February). Children and environmental disasters: The counselor's responsibility. *Elementary School Guidance and Counseling*, pp. 228–231.

Crabbs, M. (1981). School mental health services following an environmental disaster. *Journal of School Health*, *51*(3), 165–167.

Danish, S. J., & D'Augelli, A. R. (1980). Promoting competence and enhancing development through life development intervention.

In L. A. Bond & J. C. Rosen (Eds.), *Competence and coping during adulthood.* Hanover, NH: University Press of New England.

Dillard, H. (1989). Winnetka: One year later. *Communique, 17*(8), 17–20.

Dillard, H. (1990). Crisis in Winnetka. In S. Poland (Chair), *Crisis intervention in the schools.* Symposium presented at the meeting of the National Association of School Psychologists, San Francisco.

Doup, L. (1989, June 16). Children and guns can be a dangerous combination. *Houston Chronicle,* p. 6e.

Eth, S., & Pynoos, R. S. (1985). Developmental perspective on psychic trauma in childhood. In C. R. Figley (Ed.), *Trauma and its wake.* New York: Brunner/Mazel.

Excel, M. T. (1991). I was there when tragedy struck: Three administrators describe how they coped: A school explodes. *School Administrator,* May/June, pp. 13–16.

Faberow, N., & Gordon, N. (1981). *Manual for child health workers in major disaster* (DHHS Publication No. [ADM] 81–1071). Washington, DC: U.S. Government Printing Office.

Fitzgerald, H. (1988). Helping children when a classmate dies. *Communiqué, 16*(5), 19.

Franzen, A. M. (1993, April). *Crisis intervention: A total community experience.* Paper presented at the meeting of the National Association of School Psychologists, Washington, DC.

Greer, R. (1988, September 30). Shooting suspect kept thinking of own unhappy school days. *Houston Chronicle,* p. 7a.

Guetzloe, E. (1988). Suicide and depression: Special education's responsibility. *Teaching Exceptional Children, 20*(4), 24–29.

Harlom. (1989, November). Effects last even when sun shines. *Communiqué,* pp. 24–25.

Hoff, L. (1978). *People in crisis: Understanding and helping.* Reading, MA: Addison-Wesley.

Horowitz, M. J. (1986). *Stress response syndromes* (2nd ed.). New York: Aronson.

Hyman, I. A. (1992). Post traumatic stress disorder in children and youth: Understanding trauma and grief and what to do about it. In *Helping children grow up in the 90's. A resource book for parents and teachers.* Silver Spring, MD: National Association of School Psychologists.

Jay, B. (1989, January). Managing a crisis in the schools. *National Association of Secondary School Principals Bulletin,* pp. 14–17.

Kamins, J. (1993, April). *Crisis intervention: Responding and developing crisis intervention teams.* Workshop presented at meeting of the National Association of School Psychologists, Washington, DC.

Keen, J. (1989, February 2). USA schools wrestle with kid violence. *USA Today,* p. 1a.

Keen, J., & Fiest, P. (1989, January 18). Are our kids safe while at school? *USA Today,* p. 1a.

Kniesel, D., & Richards, G. (1988). Crisis intervention after the suicide of a teacher. *Professional Psychology: Research and Practice, 19*(2), 165–169.

Lazarus, P. J. (1992a). Hurricane Andrew and the aftermath. *Communiqué, 21*(2), pp. 1, 6–7.

Lazarus, P. J. (1992b). Hurricane Andrew: A parent's plea and suggestions for coping. *Communiqué, 21*(3), 24–26.

Lazarus, P. J. (in press-a). All the King's horses and all the King's men: Strategies for debriefing following a natural disaster. *Trainer's Forum.*

Lazarus, P. J. (in press-b). Training future school psychologists in the essence of debriefing. *Trainer's Forum.*

Lazarus, P. J., & Howard, P. (1993). Hurricane Andrew and the aftermath: The state crisis response team – A humble and necessary beginning. *Communiqué, 21*(6), 18–20.

Lazarus, P. J., & Jackson, J. (1993a, April). *Hurricane Andrew: Crisis intervention in the aftermath.* Paper presented at the annual meeting of the National Association of School Psychologists, Washington, DC.

Lazarus, P. J., & Jackson, J. (1993b). When the walls come tumbling down: Crisis issues following hurricane disasters. *Communiqué, 2*(7), 16–17.

Lazarus, P. J., & Phelps, J. (1993, April). *Expect the unexpected: Training trainers in debriefing.* Paper presented at the meeting of the Trainers of School Psychologists, Washington, DC.

Lazarus, R. S. (1966). *Psychological stress and the coping process.* New York: McGraw Hill.

Lazarus, R. S. (1980). The stress and coping paradigm. In L. A. Bond & R. C. Rosen (Eds.), *Competence and coping during adulthood.* New Hampshire: University Press of New England.

Lidell, H. G., & Scott, R. (1968). *The Greek-English lexicon.* Oxford: Clarendon.

Lipton, H. (1990). Crisis in New York City schools. In S. Poland (Chair), *Crisis intervention in the schools.* Symposium presented at the meeting of the National Association of School Psychologists, San Francisco.

Mayfield, M. (1986, December 8). Assaults top the list of classroom chaos. *USA Today,* p. 10a.

McEvoy, A. (1988). Shocking violence in schools. *School Intervention Report, 1*(7), 1–3.

Memmot, C., & Stone, A. (1989, June 15). Firearms and youngsters: Deadly, tragic mix. *USA Today,* p. 3a.

Mothers Against Drunk Driving. (1990). *Death at school: A guide for teachers, school nurses, counselors and administrators.* Dallas, TX: Author.

National Association of School Psychologists. (1991). *Resources in crisis intervention: School, family and community applications.* Silver Spring, MD: Author.

National Association of School Psychologists. (Eds.). (1992). *Helping children grow up in the 90's: A resource book for parents and teachers.* Silver Spring, MD: Author.

NIMH (National Institute of Mental Health). (1975–1984). *Final reports of crisis counseling projects.* Mimeographed materials on file. Rockville, MD: Center for Mental Health Studies of Emergencies.

NOVA (National Organization for Victim Assistance). (1991). *Community crisis response team training manual.* Washington, DC: Author.

Nelson, E., & Slaikeu, K. (1984). Crisis intervention in the schools. In K. Slaikeu (Ed.), *Crisis intervention: A handbook for practice and research* (pp. 247–263). Boston: Allyn and Bacon.

Neuhaus, A. (1990, December). Crisis response teams a must for all school districts. *Communiqué,* p. 22.

Oates, M. (1988, Fall). Responding to death in the schools. *Texas Association for Counselor Development Journal, 16*(2), 83–96.

Pando, J. L., Laska, M., & Grant, J. (1993, April). *Preparing for the unexpected: Managing the emotional consequences of trauma and crisis: A school based model for intervention.* Paper presented at the meeting of the National Association of School Psychologists, Washington, DC.

Parad, H. J., & Caplan, G. (1966). A framework for studying families in crisis. In H. J. Parad (Ed.), *Crisis intervention: Selected readings* (pp. 53–72). New York: Family Service Association of America.

Pitcher, G. D., & Poland, S. (1992). *Crisis intervention in the schools.* New York: Guilford.

Poland, S. (1993). *Crisis intervention manual for Alaska schools.* Juneau: Department of Education.

Poland, S. (Chair). (1990). *Crisis intervention in the schools.* Symposium presented at the meeting of the National Association of School Psychologists, San Francisco.

Pynoos, R., & Eth, S. (1986). Child psychiatrists describe children reactions to disaster. *Communiqué, 15*(2), 3.

Pynoos, R., Frederick, C., Nader, K., Arroyo, W., Steinberg, A., Eth, S., Nunez, F., & Fairbanks, L. (1987). Life threat and post-traumatic stress in school age children. *Archives of General Psychiatry, 44,* 1057–1063.

Raphael, B. (1975). Crisis and loss: Counseling following a disaster. Mental Health in Australia, 1(4), 118–122.

Rappaport, J. (1977). *Community psychology: Values, research, and action.* New York: Holt, Rinehart, & Winston.

Reiff, R. (1975). Of cabbages and kings. The 1974 Division 27 annual for distinguished contributions to community mental health. *American Journal of Community Psychology, 3,* 185–196.

Ruof, S., & Harris, J. (1988). How to select, train and supervise a crisis team. *Communiqué, 17*(4), 19.

Sandall, N. (1986). Early intervention in a disaster: The Cokeville hostage/bombing crisis. *Communiqué, 15*(2), 1–2.

Slaikeu, K. (1990). *Crisis intervention: A handbook for practice and research* (2nd ed.). Boston: Allyn and Bacon.

Smead, V. (1985). Best practices in crisis intervention. In A. Thomas & J. Grimes (Eds.), *Best practices in school psychology* (pp. 401–415). Kent, OH: National Association of School Psychologists.

Stevens, R. (1990, Fall). Don't get caught with your plans down. *National School Safety Journal,* pp. 4–8.

Stevenson, R. (1986, December). How to handle death in the schools. *National Association of Secondary Principals Bulletin,* pp. 1–2.

Wilhelm, R. (1967). *The book of changes or the I ching.* Princeton, NJ: Princeton University Press.

ANNOTATED BIBLIOGRAPHY

National School Safety Center, 4165 Thousand Oaks Boulevard, Suite 290, Westlake Village, CA 91632; (805) 375-9977.
Publishes resource papers, workbooks, and guidelines on school safety.

Pitcher, G., & Poland, S. (1992). *Crisis intervention in the schools.* New York: Guilford.
The authors discuss both theoretical and practical aspects of managing crises in the schools. The role of the psychologist ranges from that of consultant to trainer to provider of direct services. Practical information regarding staff in-services, managing organizational crises directly, and stimulating intrasystemic change is presented. Special emphasis on moving the system in the direction of providing preventive services is emphasized.

School Crisis Consultants, 12318 Amado Dr., Houston, TX 77065; (713) 890-5701.
Scott Poland provides workshops and publishes a 126-page *Crisis Training Manual* complete with overheads. This manual provides step-by-step practical guidelines for handling crisis situations.

National Association of School Psychologists. (1991). *Resources in crisis intervention: School, family and community applications.* Silver Spring, MD: Author.

National Organization of Victim's Assistance, Washington, DC.
School guidelines for dealing with crisis situations are currently being developed.

41

Best Practices in Suicide Intervention

Scott Poland
Cypress-Fairbanks (Texas) Public Schools

OVERVIEW AND SCOPE OF THE PROBLEM

Completed Suicides

Much has been written about the increasing numbers of suicidal youth and of completed suicides. It is important that school psychologists have accurate information about the extent of the problem. The Center for Disease Control (CDC) in Atlanta, Georgia, compiles data on suicides and publishes reports annually detailing the incidence rates by age categories and state of residence.

Berman and Jobes (1991) pointed out that the suicidal behavior of young people over the past 30 years has generated a great deal of public concern. They emphasized the high suicide rate for young people between the ages of 15 and 24. Specifically there has been a 312% increase in the youth suicide rate from 1957 to 1987 for youth ages 15 to 19. The CDC (1992) pointed out that the youth suicide rate remains at or near an all-time high. Over the past decade suicide has been either the second or third leading cause of death for young people. The leading cause of death for young people has remained accidents with suicide and homicide exchanging places from year to year. In 1992 the CDC listed suicide as the third leading cause of death for youth under the age of 19.

Suicide rates vary by age, sex, and race. School psychologists are logically the most concerned about the suicide rate for school-age youth 5 to 19. Suicide rates are reported per 100,000 for each age range. The United States had 30,906 completed suicides in 1990 of which 4,869 or 13.3% were completed by young people ages 15 to 24 with an incidence rate of 12.4 per 100,000 (National Center for Health Statistics, 1993). Berman and Jobes (1991) cited an incidence rate of .98 per 100,000 in the 10 to 14 age group, and no incidence figures for youth under the age of 10 reported for the same year, 1989. A national goal has been set to reduce the youth suicide rate by the year 2000 but there appears to be little progress and Pfeffer (1986) predicted a 94% increase in the 15- to 19-year-old category by the year 2000.

Suicidal Ideation

This chapter's author (Poland, 1989) reviewed a number of national surveys of high school students. They indicated that, across the nation, between 8% and 14% of all high school students reported an attempted suicide and 25% to 35% admitted to suicidal thoughts. The CDC (1992) found the following data on high school students:

- Eight percent had already attempted suicide.

- Twenty-seven percent had seriously contemplated it.

- Sixteen percent had made a plan to commit suicide.

Davis and Sandoval (1991) reviewed figures on incidence and attempts and estimated the following prediction for a high school of 2,000 students.

- One suicide every 5 years.

- 168 to 400 annual attempts.

There is not much information available on the extent of suicidal ideation of elementary- and middle-school-aged students. My earlier report (Poland, 1989) indicated that the suicide of young people under the age of 10 is rare and the most cited explanations for lower incidence when compared to adolescents are:

- Less depression, alienation, and loneliness.

[a] More involvement with parents.

- Less drug and alcohol involvement.

- Less access to firearms.

School psychologists are encouraged to become familiar with incidence figures from their county and state. It is also important to be aware of racial and regional differences in suicide rates. Suicide rates are higher in western states of the United States which have a high Native American population. Leenaars and Wenckstern (1991) also pointed out that many researchers feel that governmental figures are actually an underestimation of the problem. Added to that is the fact that schools can be greatly affected by the suicides of individuals other than students such as a parent, teacher, neighbor, or sibling (Poland, 1989).

BASIC CONSIDERATIONS

Youth suicide has many implications for the schools. Laws in 12 states address the role of the school in prevention (Nguyen & Siver, 1993), and most states are studying the problem of youth suicide. No national legislation has been passed although the federal government sponsored a national conference in 1985. The strongest proponent for national legislation has been U.S. Representative Ackerman (1993) who emphasized that the federal government must fund youth suicide prevention efforts and encourage cooperation at all levels of government.

The question of the responsibility of the schools with regards to youth suicide is not a new one. Stekel, a social scientist, commented on an outbreak of youth suicide in Europe in the early 1900s, "The school is not responsible for the suicide of its pupils, but it also does not prevent these suicides. This is its only, but perhaps its greatest sin" (quoted in Peck, Farberow, & Litman, 1985, p. 158). Few schools are prepared to deal with youth suicide, and not enough policies and procedures have been written to clarify the role of school personnel (Harris & Crawford, 1987; Poland, 1989). Ross (1985) stressed that it is fear and not lack of concern that results in school administrators being reluctant to work on this problem. Few school administrators have received any formal training in suicide prevention. They believe many misperceptions about youth suicide and see it as a problem that happens elsewhere.

School prevention programs began in California in the 1970s and have spread by a grassroots effort with each school re-inventing the wheel (Ryerson, 1988). It is evident that school psychologists are the first professionals school personnel are going to turn to when they feel that a student might be suicidal. Davis and Sandoval (1991) cited one study that found that 79% of teachers would turn to the school psychologist first for assistance. Therefore, school psychologists are in a position to clarify the schools' role and write policies and procedures to work on this problem. Several writers emphasize that intervention programs in the school are effective (Cantor, 1987; Guetzloe, 1989; Leenaars & Wenckstern, 1991; Ross, 1985; Ruof & Harris, 1988.

Case Example

A high-school English teacher read a theme by a ninth-grade girl containing many references to hopelessness and nonexistence. The teacher asked the girl to stay after school and directly inquired about how things were going for her. The girl shared many family, school, and romance problems that were bothering her. She stated, "My life is hopeless and not worth living." The teacher told her that help was available and that the teacher cared. The teacher escorted her to the school counselor's office. The school counselor spent a lot of time establishing rapport with the student and gathering a careful case history. The girl had attempted suicide 6 months ago by taking aspirin. She became ill but told no one what she had done. The girl's aunt had committed suicide by carbon monoxide poisoning, and the girl planned to utilize that method next time. She had carefully thought out when she could go into the garage without being detected and had imagined how others would react to her death. The school counselor called the school psychologist for assistance. The girl signed a no-suicide contract and was told that her parents would be called and that this was in her best interest and in accordance with school policy. She was told that many other students had been helped and that the school psychologist and counselor would solicit a supportive reaction from her parents.

The parents initially refused to come to school. When they did arrive, they were angry at their daughter for not telling them about her suicidal thoughts. A referral was made to a private practitioner who had experience working with suicidal teenagers. The parents were provided with specific suggestions about supervision and support of their daughter. A follow-up appointment was made at school with the student and the school counselor. The principal was informed of the situation and the referring teacher was complimented on her role. The girl was monitored closely over the next several years. She never attempted suicide again. Shortly before graduation she stopped in and thanked her English teacher for helping her. The student stressed that her life was not wonderful but she was glad to be alive.

Forces and Factors in Youth Suicide

Space does not permit a detailed examination of the numerous forces and factors that school psychologists need to be aware of (see, instead, Poland, 1989).

However, the following section indicates the major events and circumstances in youth suicide. A precipitating event may cause a young person to act on suicidal thoughts. The most common precipitating events involve arguments with parents, boyfriends or girlfriends, or the loss of a loved one (Eyeman, 1987; Porter, 1985). Shaffer (1988) stressed that discipline incidents and loss of face with peers are also factors.

Depression has long been considered the most important warning sign of suicide. Numerous researches stress that depression in children does exist but does not account for all youth suicides.

Conduct disordered adolescents are also at risk to commit suicide (Eyeman, 1987; Shaffer, 1988).

Substance abuse is now known to play an important role in youth suicide. Substance usage may cause a young person to lose contact with reality and increases the chance of a suicide attempt. Alcohol and many other drugs are depressants which only add to a young person's problems. Davis, Sandoval, and Wilson (1988) suggest that substance abuse be added as a major warning sign of suicide.

Students who run away also may be at risk for suicide. Researchers have found that runaways attempt suicide approximately 20% of the time (Engleman, 1987; Fortinsky, 1987).

How children develop their concept of death is important. The young child may view death as something that is either reversible or only happening to the very old (Davis, 1985; Pfeffer, 1986). Adolescents may also have some misperceptions about the finality of death. Young children who talk about life-threatening, risk-taking behavior need to understand the possibly fatal consequences. The school psychologist should inquire as to the beliefs that the suicidal young person has about death. The young person who has spent lots of time imagining the reaction of others to his or her suicide may be at high risk to commit suicide (Davis, 1985; Poland, 1989).

Some youngsters' suicidal behavior is attention getting and manipulative. Barrett (1985) stressed that parents need to recognize that the young person wants something to change and parents should let themselves be manipulated until they get professional help.

Other factors that may greatly influence a particular child include:

1. Suicidal statements or suicide attempts by a parent.

2. Motion pictures that deal with suicide.

3. Suicidal song lyrics.

4. News coverage that glamorizes or mysticizes a suicide.

There has been a dramatic change in the methods employed to commit suicide by young people. Females are increasingly committing suicide by using guns. A strong correlation has been found between gun ownership and suicide with guns involved in approximately 60% of all suicides (Lester, 1988; Loftin, C., McDowell, D., Wiersema, B., & Cottey, T. 1991). The dramatic three-fold increase in youth suicide since the 1950s is almost entirely attributable to the increase in suicide by firearms according to Perper, Allman, Moritz, Wartella, and Zelenak (1991). Many professionals believe the single greatest factor to reduce youth suicide would be decreasing handgun access to troubled youth. Loftin et al. (1991) cited growing research demonstrating that handgun con-

trol legislation reduces the youth suicide rate. The CDC (1992) reported that none of the youth suicide prevention programs surveyed addressed restricting access to guns despite the evidence of its effectiveness. School psychologists will be in a position to address gun availability with young people and their parents and need to be specific about the need to remove guns from troubled youth. One teenager in her good-bye note to her parents questioned why they made suicide so easy by leaving a gun available (Poland, 1989).

There is no single factor or cause that explains youth suicide. Siebel and Murray (1988) stress that there may be as many as 28 factors or causes. School personnel need to be aware of these factors, and if at all concerned about a particular student, they need to inquire further.

BEST PRACTICES

Developing a Suicide Intervention Program

Every school system needs a written policy to clarify the school's role. These procedures need to address the three levels of intervention outlined by Caplan (1964) and elaborated on by Poland, Pitcher, and Lazarus in the chapter in this volume on Crisis Intervention. These three levels — primary prevention, secondary intervention, and tertiary intervention — correspond well with the terms utilized in the suicidology literature of *prevention*, *intervention*, and *postvention*. Vidal (1986) stressed that help for a suicidal student is contingent on school personnel knowing the policy. The obligations of the school at a *minimum* are (see Poland, 1989, for more detail):

1. Detect suicidal students.

2. Assess the severity level of their suicidal symptoms.

3. Notify parents.

4. Secure the needed mental health services and supervision for the student.

5. Follow-up at school.

Detection

All school personnel including bus drivers and aides need information on the warning signs of suicide as identified by the American Association of Suicidology (AAS; 1977). These warning signs include the following verbal and behavioral clues:

1. Suicide threats or statements.

2. An attempt at suicide.

3. Prolonged depression.

4. Dramatic change of behavior or personality.

5. Making final arrangements.

School personnel should be encouraged to reach out to help suicidal students and should follow district policy in referring students. School personnel *must not* keep a secret about suicidal behavior and need to understand the situational nature of youth suicide. They should feel empowered that they could save a life as in the case example.

Assessment

School personnel must be skilled at assessing the severity level of a suicidal student's symptoms. The most logical personnel to do this are school psychologists. They need to be prepared for whenever suicidal issues may come up by working through personal issues and perceived inadequacies in this area and by investigating the various suicidal assessment scales. It may be advisable to rehearse with a colleague or even a drama student intervening with a suicidal individual.

There is no one scale or set of questions recommended for use with a suicidal student. Davis et al. (1988) reviewed the available instruments. Although they cautioned that more validation needs to be done, they noted the following instruments as the most promising ones:

1. The Hilson Adolescent Profile developed by Inwald, Brobst, and Morrisey (1987).

2. The Suicidal Ideation Questionnaire developed by Reynolds (1987).

3. The Suicide Probability Scale developed by Cull and Gill (1982).

Hoff (1978) questioned the effectiveness of lethality assessment scales and instead stressed communication and the establishment of rapport with the student. Barrett (1985) emphasized the importance of carefully gathering information from the student to guide actions and pointed out the distinction between assessment and prediction. McBrien (1983) stressed that practitioners must stay calm and ask a series of questions as if the student were planning a trip. The need for direct inquiry into suicidal thoughts and plans is essential.

A careful case history and thorough inquiry into the suicidal plans and actions can be outlined through sample questions (see Poland, 1989). A number of suicidal assessment scales classify students into the categories of low, medium, and high risk for suicide. The school psychologist needs to be careful not to categorize a student as low-risk based on the psychologist's need rather than on the information gathered from the student.

No-suicide contracts have been shown to be effective in preventing youth suicide. Figure 1 is a sample no-suicide contract. This type of contract helps the student take control over their suicidal impulses and reduces the anxiety of both the student and the school psychologist (Berman & Jobes, 1991; Davis & Sandoval, 1991; McGrien, 1983). However, contracts should not be used in isolation (Barrett, 1985). A student who refuses to sign a no-suicide contract should be supervised until parents can pick them up and hospitalization may be needed.

A number of assessment approaches were reviewed by Davis and Sandoval (1991). They emphasized the importance of school personnel following one of the available models and techniques which provide the practitioner with structure to follow in a very anxiety-provoking situation. They caution school personnel to recognize their limitations and cited research demonstrating the impulsivity of youth who committed suicide. School psychologists dealing with suicidal youth should seek support and collaboration from their colleagues (Poland, 1989).

Parent Notification

Parents must be notified any time it is believed that a child is suicidal. The question is not whether to call them but instead what to say to them. The goal of parent notification is to safeguard the welfare of the student. The school psychologist who notifies parents is also protecting himself or herself from liability. School districts and school employees have been sued for inadequate suicide prevention programs.

Slenkovitch (1986) has stressed that schools should never take a suicide threat lightly. Davidson (1985) and Henegar (1986) discuss the question of liability. They clarified the importance of one's duty to care and the foreseeability of a client's actions and stated that the primary issue is negligence. Henegar commented in part, "a negligence theory in a suicide case is not generally a claim that one caused the suicide but rather that one did not take reasonable steps to prevent it" (1986, p. 4). Henegar made several recommendations that have implications for school psychologists.

1. Increase supervision of the student.

2. Limit access to self-destructive instruments.

3. Obtain psychological treatment for the student.

Davis and Sandoval (1991) discussed several cases brought against the schools by the parents on the grounds that their child's death resulted from school personnel having inadequate training in suicide prevention. Texas has addressed this issue by recommending yearly training for all educators on the warning signs of suicide. It seems clear that school personnel need training and that parents must be notified when a student makes suicidal statements or engages in suicidal actions. A ruling by the Court of Appeals in Maryland held that school counselors may have a duty to intervene to prevent a suicide. The case involved a junior-high-school student who made

FIGURE 1. A sample no-suicide contract.

I _____ agree not to harm myself. If I am having thoughts
        (Student Name)

of harming myself or committing suicide, I will do the following until I receive help:

- Get assistance from an adult
- Call the Crisis Hot-Line at _____
- Call the school psychologist or school counselor at _____
                                            (Name and Phone Number)

I understand the contract that I am signing and agree to abide by it.

_____
(Student Signature)

_____
(School Personnel Signature)

suicidal statements to friends. The case *Eisel versus Board of Education, Montgomery County, Maryland,* was discussed in detail by Owens (1992). Eisel, when questioned by school counselors, denied any suicidal ideation, and the counselors chose not to notify her parents. Eisel was murdered in a murder-and-suicide pact one week later, and her father filed suit contending that counselors were negligent in not notifying him. The Court of Appeals ruled that the counselors did have a duty to warn the father and should have been able to foresee the suicide despite Eisel's denial. This case was appealed and a recently completed 2-week civil jury trial found that the school counselors were not liable for the one million dollars in damages sought by the father of the deceases (Jennings, 1994). This case takes school personnel into new territory with regards to parent notification. The safest course of action would be notifying parents that you heard that their son or daughter was suicidal but that the statements were denied by the student. This case and many others illustrate the need to notify parents when in doubt and to keep careful records of interactions with suicidal students.

Most suicidal students will be relieved that their parents will now know what has been on their mind. Parental reactions may range from extreme cooperation to extreme denial and anger at the school. A common initial parental reaction is one of being hurt that their child is thinking of suicide. Johnson and Maile (1987) recommend that parents do the following:

1. Be patient, show love, and seek out the help their child needs.

2. Take threats and gestures seriously.

3. Keep communication open and get help with no strings attached.

The challenge to the school psychologist is to notify parents in a way that elicits their support and to convince the parents to obtain the needed services for their child. Stanton and Stanton (1987) emphasized finding parental strengths and empowering the parent with the belief that their child can be helped. It is advisable to document parent notification and to have two school personnel present at the conference where parents are notified. A resistant parent should be asked to sign a form acknowledging that they have been notified of their child's suicidal state (see Figure 2).

Parents who refuse to follow through on the recommendation for community treatment services need to be told that it is neglectful not to get treatment for a suicidal child and that school personnel will call the child welfare department. A resistant parent might forbid the school psychologist to talk with their child. Some states, such as Texas, have passed legislation that allows psychologists to provide services to a suicidal minor without the parents' permission.

Working with suicidal students causes anxiety. Brown and Schroff (1986) recommended that school psychologists take care of themselves by

1. Getting the opinion and support of others and processing feelings.

FIGURE 2. A sample notification of emergency conference.

I, or we _____, the parents of _____
were involved in a conference with school personnel on _____.
We have been notified that our child is suicidal. We have been further advised that we should
seek some psychological/psychiatric consultation immediately from the community. School personnel have clarified the district's role and will provide follow-up assistance to our child to
support the treatment services from the community.

_____   _____
(Parent or Legal Guardian)   (School Personnel   Title)

_____   _____
(Parent or Legal Guardian)   (School Personnel   Title)

2. Recognizing that no one can assume the responsibility for the life of an individual who is threatening suicide.

The approach just described is only one aspect of youth suicide prevention described by the Center for Disease Control (1992). These activities fall in the category of what they refer to as School Gatekeeper Training. They also encourage that suicide prevention information be presented to parents and community members such as clergy, police, merchants, and recreational staff who are Community Gatekeepers. Peer Support Programs designed to foster competency, peer relations, and social skills are also recommended.

Community Services

School psychologists need to be familiar with community resources to assist suicidal students. A goal should be to establish a cooperative relationship between the school, the parent, and the community mental health provider so that maximum support is provided to the student. The school psychologist should not accept the primary responsibility of treating a suicidal student although he or she will need to continue to provide support and monitoring at school even though the student is receiving community services.

Summary of Intervention

The key points in the intervention process can be summarized as follows:

1. Try to remain calm and seek collaboration from a colleague.

2. Gather case history information from the student and approach the student as if he or she were planning a trip.

3. Ask specific questions about the suicidal plan and the frequency of suicidal thoughts and remove any lethal weapons.

4. Emphasize that there are alternatives and the student is not the first person to feel this way.

5. Do not make any deals with the student to keep the suicidal thoughts or actions a secret and explain your ethical responsibility to notify the parents of the student.

6. Have the student sign a NO-SUICIDE CONTRACT and provide the student with the phone number of the local crisis hot-line.

7. Supervise the student until parents have assumed responsibility. (Poland, 1994)

Postvention

Schools are frequently not prepared to deal with the aftermath of a suicide yet few events are more disruptive. Experts have emphasized that a series of planned steps must take place to minimize the chances of a second suicide and to help students and faculty deal with their grief (Kneisel & Richards, 1988; Lamb & Dunne-Maxim, 1987; Leenaars & Wenckstern, 1991). Postvention policies need to be in place prior to a suicide. Numerous writers have emphasized that the suicide must be acknowledged and discussed (Biblarz, 1988; Davis & Sandoval, 1991; Ryerson, 1988). Normal procedures in the event of a death should be followed with an emphasis on avoiding a dramatic, romantic, or mystic treatment of the suicide. The task facing most school survivors is grief resolution. Homeroom discussions need to provide an opportunity for students to express their grief. Lamartine (1985) pointed out that the suicide of a student increases the probability 300% that a second suicide will occur. School psychologists need to identify other students at risk to commit suicide and provide assistance to them. Everyone at school needs to know the warning signs of suicide and to feel empowered to prevent further suicides. The following postvention guidelines were developed by the American Association of Suicidology (AAS; 1991);

1. Don't dismiss school or encourage funeral attendance during school hours.

2. Don't hold a large-scale school assembly or dedicate a memorial to the deceased.

3. Do provide individual and group counseling.

4. Verify the facts and do treat the death as a suicide.

5. Do contact the family of the deceased.

6. Do emphasize that no one is to blame for the suicide.

7. Do emphasize that help is available and that suicide is preventable and everyone has a role to play in prevention.

The AAS Postvention Guidelines (1991) also contain a number of recommendations for the media. There is growing national awareness that dramatic media coverage of youth suicide may contribute to the cluster phenomenon. Specific AAS suggestions for the media are:

1. Avoid details of the method and front-page coverage.

2. Do not report the suicide as unexplainable or the results of simplistic causes.

3. Do not print a photograph of the deceased.

4. Include positive outcomes of suicidal crises and emphasize where suicidal youth may obtain help.

Youth suicide is not news in most of our large cities unless several suicides occur in the same school. The fact that it is not news is a blessing but a sad commentary on the times. Much is still not known about suicide clusters and contagion although the Center for Disease Control is in the midst of a several-year study.

School psychologists do need to know that not everyone agrees with guidelines developed by the AAS. In particular, recommendations made by the Phi Delta Kappa Organization (1988) are in conflict on key points. Phi Delta Kappa recommended that the death not be treated as suicide and suggested that all concerned be forbidden to use the word "suicide" in order to protect the privacy of the family. A school administrator who has not thoroughly researched this area might follow these guidelines which also call for having all students who want more information about the death to gather in a large assembly. This leads to dramatization and glorification of the suicide.

Curriculum Issues

Curriculum approaches to suicide prevention fall into two categories. The first approach emphasizes a positive school climate; affirms life; and promotes life skills for students, especially problem solving (Sowers, 1987). All professionals agree with the importance of this approach. The second approach involves directly talking in the classroom about suicide as a mental health problem (California State Department of Education, 1987). These classroom presentations emphasize the warning signs, befriending skills, friend intervention, and the situational nature of suicide. Also included are the relationship between suicide and substance usage and community services available to help a suicidal youth.

There is debate about whether such an approach is recommended. Shaffer (1988) and colleagues Vieland, Whittle, Garland, Hicks, and Shaffer (1991) called for a moratorium on such curriculum presentations and noted that they were developed because the schools felt a need to do something. Smith (1988) commented on Shaffer's research and noted that most students who participate in curriculum programs view them positively. Holtzman (1991) cautioned against prematurely stopping curriculum presentations to prevent youth suicide and emphasized the limitations of the research done by Shaffer and colleagues and that all concerned were upset about newspaper headlines that suicide preventive programs were harmful to young people. The central issue to this controversy seems to be that curriculum presentations somehow plant the idea of suicide. This point is at the basis of Schafly's (1985) objections to curriculum presentations. A logical question is, "Can teenagers translate information presented to them into life-saving behavior?" Numerous evaluators have said "yes" to this question.

The question of whether parent permission should be obtained prior to a student participating in a curriculum presentation has been raised as well as the relevance of the Hatch Amendment (Davis et al., 1988; Shafly, 1985). Florida requires parent permission, for example, while California does not. An unfortunate consequence of the curriculum debate is that many school districts have misinterpreted the debate to mean that professionals do not agree on schools needing to prepare and take systematic steps to prevent youth suicide. This is not the case and no debate exists about the basic role of the school in detecting and assisting suicidal youth.

School psychologists need to be involved in determining the need for curriculum presentation in their district and selecting materials if presentations are to be provided to students. My 1989 book describes in detail how a school psychologist can design a carefully integrated mental health unit on suicide which addresses the biggest professional frustration that friends always knew about the suicidal actions of the deceased but unfortunately did not look to adults for help. There is every indication that with adult professional assistance the majority of youth suicides could be prevented.

The Center for Disease Control (1992) reviewed curriculum approaches to prevent youth suicide and summarized the following research findings:

1. Participants had short-term increases in knowledge about suicide prevention and knew more about mental health referral sources.

2. There is no evidence of increased suicidal behavior on the part of program participants.

3. The highest risk is that students may react negatively, and school personnel should be ready to assist any student who finds the program upsetting.

CDC recommends that suicide prevention programs be incorporated into existing health curricula rather than a highly visible special program. Programs were typically only 1 to 3 hours in length, and professionals must be cautious about what can be expected from a brief presentation. No program surveyed sought to measure changes in behavior such as students referring themselves or friends for assistance.

SUMMARY

The problem of youth suicide is at or near an all-time high but is somewhat overshadowed by concerns about other problems that face young people today such as violence, drugs, poverty, teen pregnancy, and AIDS. Many of these problems are inextricably linked. School psychologists have historically not been trained in suicide intervention despite the fact that they are the first professionals school personnel turn to for assistance in this area. It is important that school psychologists provide leadership to help schools respond to the problem of youth suicide. The following recommendations from the Center for Disease Control (1992) should guide the actions of school psychologists.

1. School programs need to link up more with community resources.

2. More programs need to focus on reducing access to lethal weapons, especially guns.

3. To address high-risk youth, suicide prevention programs need to be linked with other programs such as alcohol, dropout, and pregnancy programs.

4. The lack of evaluative data on prevention programs is a great obstacle to improving prevention efforts.

5. Programs need to be developed to focus not only on school-aged youth but also on the 20 to 24-year-old population who have a suicide rate twice that of teens.

6. Schools need carefully written policies and procedures to address the problem of youth suicide, and school personnel need training on the warning signs of suicide.

REFERENCES

Ackerman, G. L. (1993). A Congressional view of youth suicide. *American Psychologist, 48*(2), 183–184.

American Association of Suicidology. (1977). *Suicide and how to prevent it.* West Point, PA: Merck, Sharp, and Dome.

American Association of Suicidology. (1991). *Postvention guidelines for the schools.* Denver, CO: Author.

Barrett, T. (1985). *Youth in crisis: Seeking solutions to self-destructive behavior.* Longmont, CO: Sopris West.

Berman, A. L., & Jobes, D. A. (1991). *Adolescent suicide assessment and intervention.* Washington, DC: American Psychological Association.

Biblarz, D. (1988, April). Not in my school: Entry issues. In S. Perlin (Chair), *Tackling the tough issues in school based suicide awareness programs.* Symposium conducted at the meeting of the American Association of Suicidology, Washigton, DC.

Brown, S., & Schroff, B. (1986). Taking care of ourselves. *The Network News, 4*, 5–6.

California State Department of Education. (1987). *Suicide prevention program for the California public schools.* Sacramento: Author.

Cantor, P. (1987, November). Communication with students at risk. In A. McEvoy (Chair), *Suicide prevention and the schools.* Symposium sponsored by Learning Publications, Orlando, FL.

Caplan, G. (1964). *Principles of preventive psychology.* New York: Basic Books.

Center for Disease Control. (1992). *Youth suicide prevention and resource guide.* Atlanta, GA: Author.

Cull, J., & Gill, W. (1982). *Suicide probability scale manual.* Los Angeles: Western Publishing Services.

Davidson, H. (1985). Legal issues. In N. Farberow, S. Altman, & A. Thorne (Eds.), *Report of the National Conference on Youth Suicide* (pp. 297–303). Washington, DC: Youth Suicide National Center.

Davis, J. (1985). Suicidal crises in schools. *School Psychology Review, 14*, 313–324.

Davis, J., & Sandoval, S. (1991). *Suicidal youth: School-based intervention and prevention.* San Francisco: Jossey-Bass.

Davis, J., Sandoval, J., & Wilson, M. (1988). Strategies for the primary prevention of adolescent suicide. *School Psychology Review, 17*, 559–569.

Engelman, R. (1987). Running away from home is a sign of suicidal bent. *The Network News, 7*, 9.

Eyeman, J. (1987, March). Pre-conference workshop. *Suicide prevention in schools.* Symposium presented at the meeting of the National Association of School Psychologists, New Orleans.

Fortinsky, R. (1987). U.S.M. study finds link between runaways and suicidal potential. *The Network News, 7,* 9.

Guetzloe, E. (1989). *Youth suicide: What the educator should know.* Reston, VA: Council for Exceptional Children.

Harris, M., & Crawford, R. (1987). *Youth suicide: The identification of effective concepts and practices in policies and procedures for Texas schools* (Monograph No. 3). Commerce: Center for Policy Studies and Research, East Texas State University.

Henegar, C. (1986). Suicides in the shelters: Liability in the runaway centers. *The Network News, 4,* 4–7.

Hoff, L. (1978). *People in crisis: Understanding and helping.* Reading, MA: Addison-Wesley.

Holtzman, A. (1991, Summer). School-based curriculum: Avoiding premature closure. *Newslink, 2,* 2.

Inwald, R., Brobst, K., & Morrissey, R. (1987). *Hilson adolescent profile manual.* Kew Gardens, NJ: Hilson Research, Inc.

Jennings, V. (1994, March 19). Montgomery county schools win suicide pact lawsuit. *Washington Post,* p. 5.

Johnson, S., & Maile, L. (1987). *Suicide and the schools.* Springfield, IL: Charles C Thomas.

Kniesel, D., & Richards, G. (1988). Crisis intervention after the suicide of a teacher. *Professional Psychology: Research and Practice, 19*(2), 165–169.

Lamartine, C. (1985). Suicide prevention in educational settings. In *After a suicide death* (pamphlet). Dayton, OH: Suicide Prevention Center.

Lamb, F., & Dunne-Maxim, K. (1987). Postvention in the schools: Policy and process. In E. Dunne, J. McIntosh, & K. Dunne-Maxim (Eds.), *Suicide and its aftermath* (pp. 245–263). New York: Norton.

Leenaars, A., & Wenckstern, S. (1991). *Suicide prevention in schools.* New York: Hemisphere.

Lester, D. (1988). Research note: Gun control, gun ownership, and suicide prevention. *Suicide and Life-Threatening Behavior, 18,* 176–181.

Loftin, C., McDowall, D., Wiersema, B., & Cottey, T. (1991). Effects of restrictive licensing of handguns on homicide and suicide in the District of Columbia. *New England Journal of Medicine, 325,* 1615–1620.

McBrien, J. (1983). Are you thinking of killing yourself?: Confronting students' suicidal thoughts. *The School Counselor, 31*(1), 79–82.

National Center for Health Statistics. (1993). *Advance report of final mortality statistics, 1990.* Denver: American Association of Suicidology data page.

Nguyen, P., & Silver, L. (1993). *Teen suicide: The hidden social problem and policy analysis.* Unpublished manuscript, University of Houston.

Owens, M. (1992, Summer). Eisel v. Board of Education. *Journal of Law and Education, 21*(3), 487–490.

Peck, M., Farberow, N., & Litman, R. (Eds.). (1985). *Youth suicide.* New York: Springer.

Perper, B., Allman, C., Moritz, G., Wartella, M., & Zelenak, J. (1991). The presence & accessibility of firearms in the homes of adolescent suicides: A case control study. *Journal of the American Medical Association, 266,* 2899–2995.

Pfeffer, C. (1986). *The suicidal child.* New York: Guilford Press.

Phi Delta Kappa International. (1988, September). Responding to student suicide: The first 48 hours. *Current Issues Memo.*

Poland, S. (1989). *Suicide intervention in the schools.* New York: Guilford.

Poland, S. (1994). The role of school crisis intervention teams to prevent and reduce school violence and trauma. *School Psychology Review, 23,* 175–189.

Porter, W. (1985). *Inservice and resource guide for children and adolescent suicide prevention.* Unpublished manuscript, Cherry Creek Schools, Denver, CO.

Reynolds, W. (1987). *Suicidal ideation questionnaire.* Odessa, FL: Psychological Assessment Resources.

Ross, C. (1985). Teaching children the facts of life and death: Suicide prevention in the schools. In M. Peck, N. Farberow, & R. Litman (Eds.), *Youth suicide* (pp. 147–169). New York: Springer.

Ruof, S., & Harris, J. (1988). Suicide contagion: Guilt and modeling. *Communiqué, 16*(17), 8.

Ryerson, D. (1988, April). The importance of school personnel and researchers collaborating. In K. Smith (Chair), *How do we know what we've done? Controversy in evaluation.* Symposium conducted at the Meeting of the American Association of Suicidology, Washington, DC.

Schafly, P. (1985). The school and youth suicide. In N. Farberow, S. Altman, & A. Thorne (Eds.), *Report of the National Conference on Youth Suicide* (pp. 269–275). Washington, DC: Youth Suicide National Center.

Seibel, M., & Murray, J. (1988, March). Early prevention of adolescent suicide. *Educational Leadership,* pp. 48–51.

Shaffer, D. (1988, April). School research issues. In K. Smith (Chair), *How do we know what we've done? Controversy in evaluation.* Symposium conducted at the Meeting of the American Association of Suicidology, Washington, DC.

Slenkovitch, J. (1986, June). School districts can be sued for inadequate suicide prevention programs. *The Schools' Advocate,* pp. 1–3.

Smith, K. (Chair). (1988, April). *How do we know what we've done? Controversy in evaluation.* Symposium conducted at the meeting of the American Association of Suicidology, Washigton, DC.

Sowers, J. (1987, November). Issues in curriculum and program development. In A. McEvoy (Chair), *Suicide prevention and the schools.* Symposium sponsored by Learning Publications, Orlando, FL.

Stanton, J., & Stanton, S. (1987). Family and system therapy of suicidal adolescents. *Family Therapy Today, 2*(11), 1–4.

Vidal, J. (1986, October). Establishing a suicide prevention program. *National Association of Secondary School Principals Bulletin,* 68–72.

Vieland, V., Whittle, B., Garland, A., Hicks, R., & Shaffer, D. (1991). The impact of curriculum-based suicide prevention programs for teenagers. An 18-month follow-up. *Journal of the American Academy of Child and Adolescent Psychiatry, 30,* 811–815.

ANNOTATED BIBLIOGRAPHY

California State Department of Education. (1987). *Suicide prevention program for the California public schools.* Sacramento: Author.

Provides the information needed to train school personnel to detect suicidal behavior. The lesson guide provided is appropriate to use in the curriculum for grades 9–12, emphasizing warning signs of suicide, community resources, and intervention by friends.

Pitcher, G., & Poland, S. (1992). *Crisis intervention in the schools.* New York: Guilford.
The authors discuss both theoretical and practical aspects of managing crises in the schools. The role of the psychologist ranges from that of consultant to trainer to provider of direct service. Practical information regarding staff in-service, managing, organizational crises directly, and stimulating intrasystemic change is presented. Special emphasis on moving the system in the direction of providing preventive services is emphasized.

Poland, S. (1989). *Suicide intervention in the schools.* New York: Guilford.
The role of the school is defined, and case examples provide step-by-step guidelines for setting up and maintaining a comprehensive program. Issues covered include forces and factors in youth suicide, assessment, parent notification, liability, legislation, curriculum, and dealing with the media. Detailed procedures for intervention following crises is provided.

Center for Disease Control. (1992). *Suicide prevention programs: A resource guide.* Atlanta: Author.
This resource guide was the result of a national networking effort to locate exemplary youth suicide prevention programs. Eight major prevention strategies are outlined with discussion of findings and recommendations for the future.

Poland, S. (1994). *Crisis intervention resource and training guide.* Author.
This guide gives a complete overview of all levels of crisis intervention and includes practical examples of program development. A variety of school crisis scenarios are covered in detail including suicide, violence, and gangs. This guide includes numerous overheads designed to assist school psychologists to give in-service presentations and help them develop district and building plans.

Davis, J., & Sandoval, S. (1991). *Suicidal youth: School-based intervention and prevention.* San Francisco: Jossey-Bass.
The authors review research and clinical practices in youth suicide. Guidelines are provided for determining suicide potential and developing suicide awareness school programs.

Focus on Individualized Services

42

School Psychologist as Problem Solver

Stanley L. Deno
University of Minnesota

OVERVIEW

Successful functioning in any role requires a clear image of the primary purposes of that role. A cursory review of the current literature in school psychology reveals that clarity of purpose is lacking in the school psychologist role (Kramer & Epps, 1991). While the primary purpose may not be clear, the predominant activity of school psychologists is easy to identify. Assessment — with its related ignominious responsibility as gatekeeper for special programs — remains the most conspicuous activity of school psychologists. The problem with restricting the role of school psychologist to that of psychometrician is that many school psychologists have broader training and interests and are eager to make a broader contribution to child and family development. In the present chapter a case will be made that a broader and more satisfying role for school psychologists is that of data-based problem solver.

Fostering Human Development as the Purpose of Schooling

In developing a conception of school psychologists as problem solvers consider first the context within which they work. As participants in school environments, school psychologists are committed to the general purpose of schooling, that is, facilitating human development. This means, of course, that school psychologists will embrace the cognitive, affective, social, and physical developmental outcomes around which schools are organized. Within this framework, the problems to be solved by school psychologists are those generated out of the schools' efforts to promote growth and development.

Intervention. If we view the purpose of schooling as fostering human development, we can cast the mechanism of schooling as intervention. The term "intervention" is appropriate in that society has vested educators with the responsibility to organize deliberate activities that affect the course of child development. Without the deliberate activities of schooling there is no doubt that the lives of children

and youth would be markedly different. The term intervention, then, can be used very broadly to refer to the mechanisms of schooling. These interventions of schooling are designed to have impacts on the developmental processes that would otherwise occur in their absence.

Problems. Just as the term intervention can be used broadly to refer to the mechanisms of schooling, the term "problem" may be used to refer to the question of how best to attain the specific outcomes toward which interventions are directed. Thus, when schools focus their activities on developing literacy and numeracy, the problems to be solved are how best to promote the development of performance at reading, writing, and arithmetic. When schools seek to foster personal and social development, the problems to be solved are how best to promote the levels of development desired in these domains. When students take courses in physical education, the problems are how to best effect the physical development of children and youth. Societal priorities for the outcomes of schooling, then, establish the developmental problems that serve as the focus of intervention.

As should be clear in the foregoing paragraph, problem solving is not a term reserved for activities focused on atypical development. From the perspective presented here, problem solving is defined by the approach taken to intervention rather than by the perception of failure or deviance. We are problem solving if we conceptualize the primary goal of our work as reducing the difference between a current state of affairs (for example, the student's current level of development) and some future state of affairs (for example, his or her development at some later point in time). Taking such a generic approach is useful because it avoids controversies surrounding a question of whether a problem "really" exists. Further, from this perspective the school psychologist is in a position to work both proactively and reactively — enhancing as well as remediating — when intervening to foster human development.

The current state of affairs with respect to American education is a good example of how arbitrary the argument can be over whether educational problems exist. Some educators argue that the schools are more effective than they have ever been, while others both inside and outside of the schools believe that the United States is experiencing a major crisis. Obviously, whether the developmental outcomes currently attained by the children and youth of our country is viewed as satisfactory depends upon the standards applied by the person making the judgment. Many education professionals have experienced situations where they viewed a child's development as being quite satisfactory while the child's parents were quite unhappy because they wanted more.

Controversy over whether "real problems" exist can be reduced if education is viewed from a developmental perspective where all children and youth are seen to move at an irregular pace along various continua. Any child's current level of performance in some developmental domain always will be the focus of interventions designed to effect whatever movement along those continua is specified, and education's problem is to determine how best to accomplish that movement. Operating from this perspective, school personnel are problem solving whether they or someone else sees the child as developing "normally."

APPROACHES TO PROBLEM SOLVING

If school is a set of interventions designed to foster human development, and school personnel are problem solvers, what, then, is problem solving?

Typical Elements of Problem Solving

While a variety of different perspectives exist regarding the nature of problem solving, all contain three basic elements:

1. Formulating the problem.
2. Generating and selecting potential solutions.
3. Testing the selected alternatives.

These basic elements were contained in the conceptual model of human behavior developed by Miller, Galanter, and Pribram more than thirty years ago (1960). In their book, *Plans and the Structure of Behavior*, they describe a consistent structure of human activity across person–environment interactions. Their view is that humans interact with the world through successive applications of a sequence identified as Test-Operate-Test-Exit or TOTE. Tote, in effect, describes the basic steps required in problem solving. More recently, the IDEAL model of problem solving has been outlined by Bransford and his associates (1984). IDEAL is an acronym for the steps typically required in problem solving:

- Identify the problem.
- Define the problem.
- Explore alternative solutions to the problem.
- Apply a solution.
- Look at the effects of that application.

Inherent in both of these models is the idea that problem solving involves sensing and perceiving the existence of a problem, clarifying and defining the problem, generating and trying different approaches to overcoming the problem, and observing and evaluating the effects of our efforts.

School-Based Intervention Models

The intervention activities organized by the schools are of two general types. One is the ordinary set of instructional activities available to all children attending regular classrooms in their home schools. This common set of experiences is organized and conducted as the general education program. A second smaller set of interventions that exists in the school falls under the heading of special and compensatory programs. Different from the general education interventions, this second set of interventions is intended for only a subset of the general student population. Although it is possible to consider the role of school psychologist as problem solver within the context of both of these sets of school-based interventions, in the remainder of this chapter the focus will be on the problem-solving activities of the school psychologist within the context of special and compensatory programs.

The Role of Assessment in Problem Solving

When Miller, Galanter, and Pribram (1960) pointed out in their TOTE model that ordinary human interaction with the environment can be conceptualized as a sequence of problem-solving activities, they placed emphasis on the role of testing to determine the current state of the environment. As might be expected, while the word "test" was used to describe a key element in those activities, they used the term to refer to probing informally, rather than formally, and observing effects. Perhaps a general definition of assessment as "information gathering" for purposes of decision making is closest to the sense in which they use the term test within the TOTE model. In the same vein, Bransford's IDEAL model of problem solving includes the terms "identify" and "look at" to refer to the informal processes of sensing and perceiving aspects of the world that constitute the activities called informal assessment. Despite the fact that these activities are viewed as informal and natural elements of ordinary human problem solving, it is important to recognize the key role played by these informal assessment activities in problem solving. Because assessment is always viewed as a key part of school psychologist training, the role of assessment in problem solving will be considered next.

Assessment and Measurement Defined

The general definition of assessment as information gathering for purposes of decision making is inclusive of all types of information — qualitative or quantitative, verbal or numerical — gathered through all means — highly structured deliberate efforts involving intrusive test administration or informal and naturalistic observation. Narrative reports, anecdotal records, test scores, and coded observational data are all encompassed by assessment. The key element in assessment is neither the information gathered nor the procedures used, but what decision is to be made.

Measurement is a subset of assessment activities. The purpose of measurement is a numerical description and representation of observations. Those observations can be organized and structured through activities called tests or through activities occurring in natural settings. In either case, the outcome of measurement is quantitative description. Another useful way to distinguish or contrast measurement with assessment is to identify the essential purpose of assessment as informing while the purpose of measurement is clarifying. Thus, the special function of measurement tends to increase the sharpness or precision of the information provided. While efforts to clarify through quantification would seem to be a gain in the information gathering process, some argue that this increased precision is gained at the expense of qualities that cannot be represented numerically (Hesushius, 1991).

Assessment During Problem Solving

Consider the possible contributions of assessment to problem solving.

Documenting impressions. Psychologists have theorized for some time that thought directed toward problem solving originates from experiencing cognitive conflict (Berlyne, 1965; Festinger, 1957). This conflict occurs when a disparity exists between two important elements in our perception of the world. In schools, the conflict typically arises when a difference exists between what education personnel want students to do and what the personnel observe them doing. At such times the education professional thinks and behaves so as to reduce the discomfort produced by that conflict.

Because ordinary problem solving originates in these perceptions of difference between what we want and what we get, assessment can play a role in verifying or documenting the basis of our impressions. We can measure to increase the clarity regarding the perception of difference between our expectations and current reality. Initial impressions are certain to be implicit; therefore, assessment can help to make that experience explicit. For example, the feeling that student is having difficulty learning in school will be based on natural interactions and observations. That feeling can be objectified through collecting data on the student's current level of performance and contrasting it with our expectations for that performance. The current popularity of alternative approaches to assessment, particularly observation-based approaches, might be attributable to the fact that these more naturalistic methods of assessment authenticate the intuitive perceptions of the stakeholders who experience, observe, and develop impressions through their interactions with the students. Indeed, the term "authentic assessment," though prejudicial in its common usage, underscores the desires of many to document their sense of real student competence.

Clarifying and defining discrepancies. A distinction often not made explicitly in problem-solving models is that between sensing and defining. While sensation is an intuitive process, definition is formal and explicit. The distinction can be clearly understood in the difference between the statements "I think something's wrong" and "I wonder what it is." While the former statement is a reflection of the feeling of discomfort or cognitive conflict, the latter statement directs us to explicitly formulate the conditions producing this discomfort. In defining and clarifying problems school psychologists need to identify the discrepancies at the basis of the cognitive conflict. The discrepancies of particular interest to professionals involved in developing human performance are those between what students are doing and what the significant others in those student's environments would have them do.

Assessment for purposes of clarifying a discrepancy requires a school psychologist to collect information documenting both the current level of student performance and the level of expectation desired by those significant others who sense and perceive the existence of a problem. Useful assessment within this framework requires as much attention to assessing the standards for performance by those whose expectations contribute to the discrepancy (typically teachers or parents) as to collecting data on the current level of student performance. This will mean that diplomatic and sensitive probing of both the subjective and objective dimensions will have to be undertaken. Whereas objective assessment will involve establishing the desired characteristics of student performance in terms of frequency, magnitude, latency, or topography, subjective scaling will require obtaining an expression of the perceived importance of the discrepancy from the person who believes the problem exists.

To illustrate how assessment is conducted to clarify and document the existence of a problem consider the example of work completion. We could begin our assessment by collecting objective data on the percentage of current work being completed by that student and find she is completing between 60%

and 70%. We might then explore carefully with the teacher to determine what his standard is for work completion by students in his classroom and find that he expects 90% to 100% of the work to be completed. By collecting this information we have established a quantitative difference in performance of 30% between what the teacher wants and what the teacher is getting from this student. At this point, however, we do not know how important that difference is to the teacher. For some teachers a difference as small as 15% between what is desired and what is obtained is extremely important while for others a difference of 30% is viewed as only moderately important. This distinction between the magnitude of a problem and its perceived importance is the difference between quantification and values.

Generating alternatives. Conducting assessments for purposes of developing alternative solutions to a problem, while widely undertaken, is still an uncertain technology. Assessment of this type is typically termed "diagnostic" and is organized on the assumption that information from student performance directed toward interventions will be more effective than not collecting this information. The reality is, however, that over a decade ago Arter and Jenkins (1979) found scant empirical evidence supporting the effectiveness of differential diagnosis, and little evidence has developed since that time. The limitations of diagnostic assessment for generating interventions is not limited to more traditional differential diagnostic procedures using ability and personality tests. Current interests in describing the ecology of the classroom as a basis for developing interventions have not yielded rich results with respect to the differential effectiveness of interventions created from these ecological assessments over more traditional diagnostic prescriptive approaches. The same can be said for using currently popular efforts to assess "learning styles" and develop strategies consistent with those styles. Finally, while a subskill assessment approach makes sense to some, it has been widely criticized by others. At present it is perhaps best to expect relatively low cost-benefits ratios from the use of assessment to generate solutions to problems.

Documenting interventions. It may seem surprising to consider the role of assessment in documenting that interventions are occurring as intended. However, the experience of school-based researchers has established the importance of determining treatment "fidelity" when exploring treatment effects. Equally clear is the need to ensure that problem solution alternatives have been implemented and are operating with sufficient intensity before it is possible to evaluate their effects. Many of us have had the experience of working as a collaborative consultant to identify and plan what seemed to be a reasonable and potent intervention for solving a problem only to find upon subsequent review that the intervention was only partially or incompletely implemented. In such cases we may not have solved the problem as intended, neither have we established whether the problem could have been solved had the intervention been implemented. To actually test the effectiveness of solution alternatives, every effort must be made to document that the alternative has been fully and completely developed and that the student experiences that intervention. We can only wonder how many potentially successful solution alternatives have been discarded because the intervention was insufficiently implemented.

Formatively evaluating solutions. For some time a distinction has been made between formative and summative evaluation (Scriven, 1967). The evaluation of a program during its implementation is formative; while summative evaluation occurs upon completion of a program to determine whether it has achieved its goals. The purpose of formative evaluation is to determine the likely success of an intervention during its implementation so that it can be modified or changed to increase the likelihood that intended results will be achieved. This distinction is useful within a problem-solving framework because it clarifies that assessment should occur during implementation to inform decisions about program adjustment. In the Miller, Galanter and Pribram (1960) TOTE model described earlier, formative evaluation occurs when cycling through a test-operate-test-operate-test cycle until testing reveals that one can or should exit the situation. The advice, "If at first you don't succeed, try, try again" well captures the essence of both TOTE and the purpose of formative evaluation. Not surprisingly evidence exists that formative evaluation of interventions increases their success. Indeed an argument can be made that along with conducting assessment to initially clarify the nature of a problem, assessment as a basis for formative evaluation contributes most significantly to problem solution. For that reason considerable attention will be given in the remaining sections of this chapter to the school psychologist's role in formative evaluation of intervention attempts.

Determining success. Assessment contributes to problem definition in much the same way it contributes to determining whether problem solution has occurred. In evaluating program success the same assessment procedures that were used initially to clarify the discrepancy are used to establish whether that discrepancy has now been eliminated. To do this requires the same degree of thoroughness in determining both the degree and importance of any difference between what is desired and what is actually occurring. Following from our earlier example of work completion, this means that we must once again determine the difference in percentage between the student's current level of work completion and the level specified by the teacher. In addition, the teacher's perception of the importance of that difference must be reassessed. In the best of all worlds no difference will exist. In reality, we may find that while the student's level of work completion has increased, the teacher's standards or his values regarding the importance of a difference may have changed. Although we may view this as negative in our efforts to solve the problem, evidence exists that "goal ambitiousness" and goal raising by teachers are important factors in increasing the level of achievement attained by students (Fuchs, Fuchs, & Deno, 1985). Indeed, the purpose of school psychology presented at the outset of this chapter was continuous solving of human development problems. While the TOTE model provides for exiting a problem when the test reveals that the problem has been solved, both our ambitiousness and that of the teacher's to optimize development should mean that exiting is a momentary vacation from work rather than a condition of our employment.

Solving the Problems Called Handicaps

In ideal circumstances school psychologists are free to act on the complete range of developmental problems encompassed by schools. In reality, however, most school psychologists are constrained to give priority to that set of problems called "handicaps." In this section the meaning of the term handicap is explicated by contrast with the related terms "disability" and "impairment."

Disabilities and handicaps. In 1976, Public Law 94-142 was passed as the Education of the Handicapped Act (EHA). When the revision of that law was passed almost 15 years later as PL 101-476, it did so as the Individuals with Disabilities Act (IDEA). The change from using the term "handicap" to the term "disability" occurred not only in the title, but also throughout the text. While it would be easy to assume that this was simply a cosmetic change having more to do with a shift in popular usage than with substance, people with disabilities and their advocates to not operate from that assumption. Indeed, people with disabilities see as central to their concerns the need for society to clearly understand the distinction between the concepts represented by the terms handicap and disability. What is this distinction?

Handicaps are problems. Thus, handicaps are a difference between what someone does (or can do) in a particular situation, and what is required for the person to be successful in meeting the demands of that situation. If a person can move about in the environment within a wheelchair, but to gain access to a building is required to climb a stairway, then a handicap exists. Similarly, if a person has low visual acuity but must see words projected on a screen or written on a chalkboard in order to take notes in a class, then the person is handicapped. A student in high school who cannot read a textbook well enough to complete the daily work assignments is handicapped. We can see in each of these examples that a discrepancy exists between what the individual can do and the task demands necessary for success in that situation.

Whereas handicaps are conditions defined by the relationship between what the individual can do and must do to succeed at a particular task, disabilities are conditions of the individual. In each of the examples just provided, the disability is defined by what the individual's level of performance is in that situation. Thus, difficulty or inability at performing to a level typical for that individual's peers defines the individual's disability. Disabilities, then, are defined by the normative differences in ability while handicaps are defined by the minimum standards for successful task completion in a particular situation.

Another important distinction between disabilities and handicaps is the degree to which the existence of the condition can be altered by changing the environment. In the foregoing examples, the existence of each handicap can be altered by changing the task demands. If wheelchair access to a building is created, the handicap no longer exists. If large print paper copy is provided at the student's desk, the note-taking handicap no longer exists. If the information required to complete daily work assignments is made available through audio tapes, then no reading handicap exists. While in these examples the handicap can be eliminated by altering the task demands, the same cannot be said for individual disabilities. In each instance, the individual's level of performance in walking, seeing, and reading is unaltered by the modifications made in the requirements for success. Normatively defined disabilities change only when the individual's performance changes or the norm group changes.

The role that norms have played in defining disabilities has been clear for quite some time. What has been less clear is the role that society plays in creating the handicapping condition. Even in acting as a caring society we have tended to view handicaps as problems possessed by the individual that we might try to help them to cope with or overcome. In changing the language of the law from handicap to disability, advocates for people with disabilities were trying to influence us to think more completely and carefully about our role and responsibility when we create the requirements for task success and then assume that those who do not succeed bear the full responsibility for their lack of success. They have tried to emphasize that handicapping conditions are created at least as much by society as they are by the level of an individual's competence.

The handicapping conditions created by the schools are many and not easily identified. When a student struggling to read connected discourse is required to do extensive reading in order to earn an "A" or a "B" in the classroom, a handicapping condition exists. The student may possess a reading disability but is not handicapped until required to use a level of reading beyond his or her current skill in order to be successful in the classroom. The same exists for a student who does not write well or compute fluently. If standards of success or conditions of performance are established that exceed the student's current level, then a handicapping condition is created. Thus, students who have difficulty learning a range of communication skills in the school might be viewed as learning disabled; however, their disability in learning school tasks will not be a handicap until certain standards of performance are imposed as requisite for them to be successful in the classroom.

The third concept related to disability and handicap is "impairment." Impairment is a term used in reference to dysfunction in a biological process or structure. Impairments may, or may not, be related to the level of an individual's ability or performance. Spinal nerve damage is an impairment that can affect the level of an individual's ability to move the lower extremities for purposes of ambulation. Similarly, damage to the optic nerve or the retina may be a biological condition underlying or affecting visual perception, and damage to auditory mechanisms may result in lowering an individual's ability to discriminate speech sounds. Historically, we as a society have written laws assuming that disabilities in performance were caused by specific and identifiable impairments, and strong arguments are made that all disability conditions funded under federal law should be clearly based in biological anomaly. This line of reasoning has proved particularly problematic for conditions such as learning disability, emotional disturbance, and mild mental disabilities where impairments are difficult to identify. Current research to map the brains of people who are "dyslexic" using advanced electronic techniques such as PEP scans and magnetic resonance imaging are viewed as useful not only because they may someday lead to the development of appropriate treatments, but also because an impairment justifying special education resource expenditures may be identified in the brains of individuals who have difficulty learning to read.

While fairly clear connections can be drawn between some biological conditions and specific levels of competence, the relationship between the biological condition and the level of functional performance obtained by the individual is typically not direct and is always very complex. When central nervous system trauma occurs through closed head brain injury or spinal cord injuries, the degree to which an individual will lose or recover functioning associated with those injuries is difficult to predict. While this is due in part to difficulty in estimating the degree of healing or damage, it is also due to the fact that the central nervous system is able to adapt in ways that produce improved functioning even when impairments exist. Considerable evidence exists that, when the dominant cerebral hemisphere is traumatized, the less dominant hemisphere will take over some of the functions normally associated with the dominant hemisphere. The same difficulty exists when attempting to estimate the performance consequences of sensory impairments. Audiometric and opthomological examinations cannot ascertain the degree of useful hearing or vision. Legal classifications of blindness based solely on sensory acuity often result in the apparently contradictory situation where someone who is "blind" can read ordinary print. Further, while some students classified as hard-of-hearing can complete their schooling without the use of technological aids or compensatory programs, others have such great difficulty developing oral language skills that they seem more likely to succeed in a residential school where the culture is based in American Sign Language.

In summary, disabilities are conditions of the individual referring to the fact that their level of competence, performance, or ability to do something is consistently and significantly lower than that of their peers. Impairments are biological conditions thought to underlie an individual's seemingly unalterable disability status. Handicaps are conditions that exist when successful functioning in an environment requires a level of ability beyond that possessed by the person. A neat, simplistic formulation of the relationship among these three terms is that biological impairments produce disabilities that often result in the existence of handicaps. While relatively simple and straightforward examples of this formulation might exist, the functional relationships among these three terms are typically very difficult to establish.

Severity of disability. No discussion of disabilities and handicaps is complete without consideration of the degree or severity of these conditions. Earlier in this chapter, the magnitude of a problem to be solved was described as having two parameters: its measured or objective dimension and its reported or expressed values dimension. The same two parameters apply to the concepts, disability and handicap. The objective or measured severity of a disability refers to the scaled difference between the individual's performance on a particular task and the typical performance of the peer group. If presented with text passages from the local newspaper and asked to read them aloud, students will vary in the number of words each reads correctly and incorrectly in a fixed period of time. The result is a dimension of performance from relatively lower to higher levels of accuracy per unit of time. The difference in individual performance on this particular task, then, is an objective measure of their ability to read aloud from connected discourse. Whether performance on this task is considered "disabled," however, will depend upon the application of another person's standards of performance. Performance standards are external to the task itself. The number of words read correctly and incorrectly is simply a fact about performance until a framework for interpretation is created. The most common standards for interpretation applied to human performance, of course, are normative. Informal normative standards are usually acquired by teachers in their work with students. These informal standards account for students being viewed as "able" on a task if they perform similarly to students of comparable age and exceptional if they perform much better or worse.

Norms provide a useful basis for objectively discriminating between levels of performance and thereby help to establish degrees of ability and disability. Yet it should be kept in mind that the value of performance on a particular task is not inherent in the fact that people perform differently on the task. The value of performance on the task derives from the need for competence on that task, especially within a social context. For example, being able to read words with the same speed and accuracy as one's peers only becomes important when the personal and social consequences of performance on that task are important. Thus, performing more than two standard deviations below the mean at "singing in tune" may be objectively quantifiable; however, it will not be identified as a severe disability. The same cannot be said for similarly low performance in reading and writing.

Severity of handicap. Like the severity of disabilities, the severity of handicaps is defined both objectively and subjectively. The measurable and the expressed values dimensions of handicaps are not identical to those of disabilities, however, The performance aspect of a handicap may be measured in the same way as a disability; however, the standard for successful performance may be established quite differently. Recalling that disabilities are most often defined on the basis of performance relative to norms, the performance standards or requirements denoting the existence of a handicap may be established independently from current norms.

This distinction is well illustrated in the current national furor over the performance of American students in math and science. Using normative standards to evaluate the performance of U.S. students indicates that nearly 85% of the students perform normally (i.e., at a level equal to, or greater than, one standard deviation below the mean). Although 85% may seem satisfactory to some, U.S. policy makers find this current level of performance insufficient and want it raised so that our students are performing better than the students from all other nations of the world by the year 2000. The basis for establishing these year-2000 standards may not be clearly evident, but they do indicate certain assumptions about what is both possible and desirable for students in American society. Because it has not yet been established whether it is possible to attain the desired level of performance, it can be assumed that such a goal is

both nonempirical and nonnormative in its origins. More common examples of how nonnormative standards are imposed to create handicapping conditions can be found in the examples of parenting. A parent may establish that a son or daughter must attain a particular grade-point average to drive the car. The son or daughter may already be performing "normally," but the parent may desire or value a higher standard of academic success. This standard is established out of the values of the parent without particular reference to normative grades. These examples illustrate that while disabilities are defined by normative standards, handicaps are defined by somewhat more arbitrarily established standards.

Consequences and handicaps. Handicaps are also distinguished from disabilities by the fact that an incentive condition is contingent upon performing at the requisite level. In the parenting example just given, if the parent establishes a grade criterion that exceeds the student's capability, then failure results in the loss of an important incentive for the student. In the earlier illustration of handicap, employability within a building depended upon access to the building by a person in a wheelchair. Thus, not only does loss of access to the building occur when the environmental conditions are beyond the individual's level of performance, but also the loss of rewards associated with employment in that building. Those low-performing readers described earlier who cannot read their subject-matter texts well enough to do their daily work are not only disabled but handicapped. This is so not simply because the requisite performance standards exceed their current capability, but also because in failing to attain those standards they will not achieve the desired grade outcomes. The severity of a handicap, then, is based both on the magnitude of the discrepancy between what the individual can do and what the task requires and the loss of an important incentive associated with inadequate performance.

Relationship of handicaps to problem solving. It should be clear from the foregoing discussions that the definition of "handicap" parallels the definition of "problem" developed at the outset. Problems are defined as the difference between the performance wanted in a particular situation and the actual performance gotten in that situation. Handicaps are a particular type of problem where environmental demands are created that exceed a person's current level of capability and then the individual is expected to meet those demands in order to receive a valued incentive. In ordinary cases these handicaps are created by imposing what are considered to be conventional standards for performance on individuals disabled in that area of performance. The problems called handicaps, then, must be solved by reducing the difference between disabled performance and the standards of performance required for success.

BEST PRACTICES

Identifying and Defining the Problem

As with problem solving in general, solving the problems called handicaps requires cycling through the process of identification and definition, exploration and implementation of alternative solutions, and evaluation of the effects.

The key to success. Perhaps the most significant contribution to be made by school psychologists to solving handicap problems is made through collaboration with others who are invested in the problem to clearly and explicitly define the problem to be solved. This contribution requires skill in working sensitively with those who have created environmental demands exceeding the individual's capabilities both to make explicit and establish the necessity of those standards. As noted earlier, clarity and precision in problem identification and definition are essential to successful problem solving. School psychologists are (or should be) uniquely capable of contributing to increasing clarity and precision through the application of their knowledge of assessment procedures, especially the alternative assessment procedures described earlier in this chapter. To significantly contribute to problem solution, school psychologists must be able to develop and select assessment procedures that aid in precisely defining both the individual's current level of ability and the environmental demands in excess of that ability.

As school psychologists collaborate with others invested in the handicap to use assessment procedures to clarify the existing discrepancy they must be particularly sensitive to the values at the heart of the performance requirements. They must be mindful that no assessment procedure alone is sufficient to establish the existence of a handicap. They must emphasize that, at best, scores from standardized tests reveal the performance differences that aid in defining disabilities rather than handicaps. They do not establish that a problem exists that must be solved. Differences within the norm group on a particular test are meaningless until the values context associated with the performance on that test are clearly explicated and agreed upon. As stated later in this chapter, this issue also becomes important in attempting to establish both the need for special education and the annual goals for an Individualized Education Program (IEP).

Cultural imperatives. When attempting to collaborate with others in examining the value context surrounding handicaps, the school psychologist may find the idea of cultural imperatives useful in identifying those performance discrepancies important enough to be referred to as handicaps and those that are not. The term "cultural imperative" refers to those types of competence so highly valued by a society that resources will be allocated to overcome develop-mental discrepancies in those areas. In the U.S., for example, considerable resources are allocated to support learning to read, write, and compute. The high priority placed on competence in these domains is easy to infer simply by examining both the daily schedule of lessons and the curriculum of the schools. Not only do the learning activities occupy "prime time" in the school day, but when students have difficulty in learning these tasks, additional resources are used to develop remedial and compensatory programs in an effort to overcome students' failure to develop essential competence in literacy and numeracy. Further, both federal and state policy initiatives have been created to ensure that American students excel in these areas.

Cultural imperatives are easily understood when contrasted with cultural electives. Cultural electives are those abilities that, while valued by society, are given lower priority for resources than cultural imperatives. Musical abilities are good examples of cultural electives. Students are often given the opportunity in school to develop some degree of competence in music; however, relatively small amounts of time in the schedule are provided and, when resources are short, these activities are among the first to be cut from the school curriculum. Indeed, while someone may be described as not musically inclined, it is unlikely that the individual would be referred to "musically disabled." While a performance discrepancy may be as large in music as it is in reading, no additional societal resources will be forthcoming to overcome that discrepancy. Clearly, it is the difference in value ascribed to these activities within the culture that established that one disability is important and the other is not.

Situational handicaps and chronic disabilities. A second set of concepts useful in making problem-selection decisions is the distinction between situational handicaps and chronic disabilities. It follows from earlier discussion that handicaps can be created in any situation and may exist for only a moment in time. That is because handicaps typically are created by society's members making performance demands that some individuals cannot meet. As pointed out earlier, handicaps can be created for people whose abilities are quite typical. Distinct from situational handicaps, chronic disabilities are trans-situational and enduring. An otherwise typical student, or group of students, can have great difficulty meeting the performance demands of a teacher because the teacher has not made work demands appropriate to their level of skill. This problem is quite different from the one where a student has had serious difficulty in learning to read for several years regardless of the teacher and is routinely handicapped in school. In the former case the handicap is situational, while in the latter case the disability is chronic. In both cases discrepancies exist between what the individual can do and must do in order to succeed, but in the case of situational handicaps the problems are relatively temporary or local. Students with chronic disabilities must routinely endure the consequences of failing to meet sociocultural demands.

While this distinction between situational handicaps and chronic disabilities may seem an obvious one, it is mentioned here to preempt questions regarding the priority that must be given to different discrepancies when selecting problems. Ultimately, the value system that underlies resource allocation and the rules related to those values will determine the priority among problems to be solved. As will be discussed later, however, the funding provided for solving special education problems is intended to assist those people whose disabilities are chronic rather than those with situational handicaps. This means that school psychologists must be able to develop assessment procedures that can aid in distinguishing between situational problems and those that define the individual as disabled. As before, norms are useful tools in making this judgment because they emphasize individual differences in ability rather than failure to meet societal standards.

Problems as relational. A point often overlooked when using the discrepancy model in defining and selecting problems is that problems are not possessed by the individual. Problems are defined by the relationship between an individual's performance and the performance level that must be attained in order for the individual to be viewed as successful. Nor does the problem reside in the standard or desired level of performance. Rather, using the discrepancy model clarifies that the problem is relational — residing in the difference between what the individual does and what must be done. A problem may well exist when a student's reading skill is insufficient to accurately complete daily work assignments. To attribute the problem to the student's lack of reading skill or to the standards of performance set by the teacher is neither necessary nor helpful in problem identification and definition. Sensitivity to this issue helps to avoid the problem of "blaming the victim."

Problem ownership. While defining problems relationally helps to avoid fixing blame by identifying what *is* the problem, it is useful to identify who *owns* the problem. Ownership of a problem is determined by identifying those individuals who view a performance discrepancy as being important and are initiating action to solve the problem. These individuals may indeed not be those who established the performance requirements that the student cannot meet but rather are concerned that a discrepancy exists. For example, classroom teachers may be relatively unconcerned that some students cannot do daily assignments accurately — believing that low ability makes this inevitable. Likewise, students may come to accept their failure as a part of life. Parents, however,

may be deeply concerned and may press the school for adaptations in their children's program. In such cases neither the parents' performance nor their standards define the problem, but they are the owners of the problem. To paraphrase a well-known expression, "problems are in the eye of the beholder." Once this is understood, it becomes clear that it is the owners of the problem whose desires and concerns must be made explicit to clearly identify and define a discrepancy and to establish its importance. Practically speaking, teachers and parents own most common school problems. They are the ones most often expressing concern and taking action. Although it is tempting to identify the students as owning the problems, this is typically not the case.

Defining discrepancies quantitatively. When a teacher expresses concern over a student's performance, the language used often represents the difference between what the student is doing and what the teacher expects the student to do in qualitatively different terms. Thus, for example, a teacher might say that a student is having "difficulty in reading" and, when asked for more details, that the student is "unable to complete his independent work accurately." In attempting to clarify this problem, the school psychologist is confronted with the fact that the teacher's initial statement implies that the student has a skill deficiency in reading, while the second statement points to a different type of performance — "doing work accurately." While discrepancies may exist both in reading skill and work completion and while failure to complete work accurately may be due to reading difficulty, assessment of a difference between what the teacher wants and what the student does requires scaling performance along the same dimension. Thus, the student's "reading difficulty" needs to be operationalized and the teacher's expectations need to be expressed in the language of that operationalization. For example, careful probing may yield specific information regarding the reading book or books used for instruction and the level of reading skill necessary to be considered performing acceptably in those reading materials. It may be ascertained that the teacher expects the student to be able to read from a fourth-grade literature book at approximately the same rate and accuracy as the average student in the class. The quantitative difference between the teacher's performance expectation and the student's actual performance in fourth-grade literature could then be obtained by comparing the student's performance to a normative sample of the class. The difference in the number of words read correctly and incorrectly by the peer sample and the target student could be used to represent a reading discrepancy along the same quantitative dimension. If the teacher wished to focus instead on work completion, then the same general approach could be used to scale performance difference in work completion along the same dimension.

Skill development problems, by definition, are discrepancies where the teacher's performance expectations exceed the student's level of performance. At the same time, this does not mean that the discrepancy always is one where the student's performance is lower than the performance that the teacher desires. Behaviors deemed inappropriate or incorrect often occur at a level higher than that desired by the teacher. These "intrusive" behaviors include such things as high error rates in reading, spelling, and computing. They also include high levels of social behaviors like hitting, making noise, or being out of an assigned place. Whether the performance discrepancy is one where the actual performance is perceived to be too high or too low relative to the teacher's standards will not alter the basic utility of defining the problem in terms of quantitative rather than qualitative difference.

In closing this discussion of problem identification and definition, it is useful once more to emphasize that the key to successful problem solving is careful identification and definition of the problem. In mobilizing problem solving, resources move to the specified problem. Inaccurate or inappropriate problem selection will mean that the resources will be focused on the wrong problem. Unfortunately, it is all too common to find after implementing a problem solution that the owner of the problem expresses dissatisfaction with the results not because the intervention plan has failed, but because it has been focused on the wrong problem. School psychologists must be careful not to limit teachers to defining discrepancies in the preferred terms of psychology. Defining a reading problem in terms of the difference between the speed and accuracy of a student reading from fourth-grade literature in contrast to a normative sample of that student's peers may be preferred by school psychologists. Yet this approach to assessment may miss completely the problem felt most strongly by the teacher, that is, the discrepancy between the work completion rates of the student and the teacher's desired level of work completion. The school psychologist may be more interested in focusing on reading skill problems when the teacher is more interested in developing good work habits. In such a case, a problem might be solved but not the one the teacher wanted.

Developing and Selecting Alternative Solutions

Once problems have been carefully defined, it is possible to proceed with generating alternative plausible solutions to reduce the discrepancy. Because most school-based performance problems involve skill discrepancies it is common to assume that a problem is best solved by changing student performance to conform to the implicit or explicit standards from which they differ. While improving development is the goal of school programs, it should be remembered that problems can also be solved by adjusting performance requirements to be congruent with individual student capability. Of course, particularly in the case of those problems called handicaps, changing performance is always more difficult than altering the environmental conditions necessary for success.

Discussions of whether to seek problem solution through changing performance or adjusting requirements are fraught with potential controversy and must be handled carefully. In most instances this will mean that the owners of the problem must become engaged in a constructive discussion of the benefits and costs likely to be incurred through modifying the performance or the environmental demands. Central to the developing and selecting of problem-solution alternatives should be the idea that discrepancies can be reduced by altering the performance, the task requirements, or both. Within the problem-solving framework provided here, a problem is eliminated when the owner no longer identifies an important discrepancy. Adjusting task demands to meet current student capabilities or moving performance standards to be congruent with current levels of performance result in problem solution. While the problem is solved for the previous "owner," however, the school psychologist continues to bear a moral obligation to consider the long-term consequences of that type of solution for the student.

Diagnosis: An undeveloped technology. Often, instead of adjusting task demands, those involved decide that the problem is better solved through an intervention designed to improve student performance. When this occurs it is important to remember that, in the language of cognitive psychology, problems are "situated" — that is, they are defined by the specific circumstances in which they exist. And because problems are situated, their solutions also are situated. Therefore, success in problem solving rises with increases in specific knowledge of the individual and the circumstances. To obtain this greater knowledge regarding the nature and circumstances of a problem, school psychologists often conduct testing for the purpose of diagnosis. The intended outcome of diagnostic testing, of course, is an interpretation of assessment data that provides a plausible explanation for the student's performance. In the case of chronic disabilities, the diagnostic question focuses on why students are performing at a level significantly lower than their age norms.

Despite the widespread use of diagnostic procedures, it is important to realize that in most cases problems are so specifically situated that it renders useful diagnosis virtually impossible. The problem of situation specificity in diagnosis may well be why a reliable and valid technology of differential diagnosis and prescriptive treatment is, as yet, unavailable (Snow, 1989). Unfortunately, a popular literature exists that learning problems can be overcome through greater attention to individual differences in "learning styles" (Snider, 1992), and school psychologists are too often cajoled into "going beyond the data" when meeting with others to solve problems.

Problem solving as experimenting. Twenty-five years ago Donald Campbell advised us in his presidential address to the American Psychological Association to treat "Reforms as Experiments" (1969). His thesis was that new or modified programs should be viewed as experiments that require systematic evaluation, because the outcomes of those new or renewed programs were always unpredictable. In general, then, people introducing changes in programs at any level should vigorously advocate for collecting data in such a manner that the effects of program changes can be determined. In taking such an experimental approach, decision makers can avoid being "trapped" into the position that the changes for which they are advocating are certain to be effective.

Those working to solve educational problems, at any level, would be well advised to take the position advocated by Campbell. Psychological knowledge at best can only be used to estimate probabilities. Like the National Safety Council's predictions regarding the number of people who will be fatally injured in auto accidents during a holiday weekend, generalizations about the effectiveness of education programs are more accurate for groups than they are for individuals. An intervention strategy with a 50% success rate in influencing student behavior may help increase the chance of selecting a successful strategy, but there is no certainty that the intervention will be effective in solving a particular problem. In their efforts to intervene in school programs, school psychologists are the decision makers who should avoid being "trapped" into acting as if they are sure that a particular intervention will solve a specific problem. Instead, all involved should be encouraged to view the proposed solutions as operational hypotheses that can be empirically tested. This approach encourages the development of assessment procedures that are problem specific and produce data that help evaluate the problem-solving efforts.

Progress Evaluation

When approaching interventions into student programs as experiments, a critical issue arises concerning the method to be used for empirically testing the effects of those interventions. The most common method used in education to evaluate programs is an arrangement where students are pretested prior to implementing a program change and then posttested at program completion. Pretesting is used to create a "snapshot" picture of the initial difference between

actual and expected performance, and posttesting provides a similar static picture at the completion of an intervention that aids in determining whether the discrepancy still exists. While a pre-post test arrangement makes an important contribution to evaluating problem-solving efforts, it actually constitutes a weak set of conditions for making valid judgments about the effectiveness of interventions (Campbell & Stanley, 1963). Recent developments in procedures that can be used for monitoring individual student progress now provide an alternative to pre-post testing arrangements.

Progress monitoring. In general, procedures for individual progress monitoring are based on direct and frequent observation of performance on the tasks or in the situations representing the essential outcome of the intervention. Within this approach, performance assessment occurs before, during, and at the end of interventions. This produces a series of data points across time that not only permits the usual estimate of current performance level, but also estimates of both trend and individual variability. Estimates of trend and variability prior to program reform are derived from repeated measurements to establish a baseline for these characteristics. Trend and variability in individual baseline performance are then combined with initial level to create a stronger database for testing intervention effects. Evidence exists that, when individual progress monitoring is used in a formative evaluation design, intervention effectiveness can be increased (Fuchs & Fuchs, 1986). The most probable explanation for this increased intervention success when progress monitoring occurs is that the empirical records of intervention effects are continuously available for use in deciding whether a program is producing intended effects and should be continued, or is ineffective and should be modified or abandoned.

An illustration of how individual progress monitoring can serve as an aid to testing successive intervention attempts is presented in Figure 1. As can be seen in the figure, the progress monitoring data reveal that initial efforts to improve the student's reading performance were relatively unsuccessful and that an alternative approach to teaching the student to read was needed. After a series of trials, a collaborative program involving direct instruction was created and the trend in the student's reading performance shifted upward. Such a graphic record is important because it clarifies many things for decision makers. First, it clearly represents the difference between the student's initial level of performance and the standard of performance desired by the teacher. Second, by projecting the trend from the student's baseline performance to the goal date at the end of the graph it is possible to estimate the magnitude of the difference that would obtain on the goal date if no program reform occurred. Third, when the rate of growth in per-

FIGURE 1.

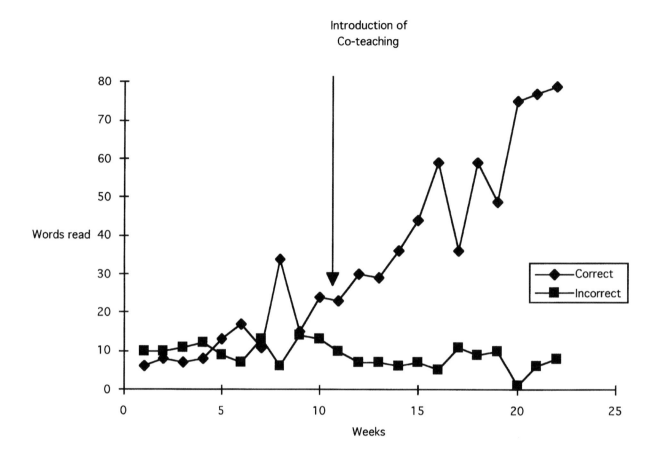

Introduction of
Co-teaching

Words read

Weeks

Correct
Incorrect

formance required to attain the desired level on the goal date is drawn on the graph it provides continuous feedback on progress toward the goal. Finally, the degree of program improvement produced by each successive reform can be estimated by contrasting the performance trends produced during successive reforms. This more dynamic picture of performance in relation to changes in student programs, then, creates a richer database for formatively evaluating program reforms than is available through pre- and posttesting of individual student performance.

Progress indicators. As with any effort to base decisions on measures of performance, successful use of individual progress monitoring necessitates that the data used for decision making validly represent the problems and goals of program intervention. Unfortunately, despite widespread interest in assessing educational outcomes, little agreement exists regarding which data are reliable and valid indicators of the culturally imperative outcomes of schooling. In the absence of a research basis for indicator selection, "authenticity" (Wiggins, 1993) and "social validity" (Wolf, 197) are currently the most highly touted characteristics of data on program outcomes. While these characteristics are not well defined, the essence

of authenticity seems to be that individual performance on tasks that are "real" and "meaningful" be observed as a basis for appraising competence. While this concept is laudable in the abstract, efforts to operationalize authenticity encounter both technical and logistical problems. Nevertheless, good reasons exist to consider the authenticity of the tasks used to appraise performance. Perhaps authenticity can be partly ensured through establishing social validity, that is, the degree to which significant others in the individual's environment agree that the data to be collected represent the important treatment goals.

When authenticity and social validity are used as criteria for evaluating the use of standardized achievement tests, it is easy to see why they have been subject to so much criticism. A standardized reading achievement test, for example, might include a variety of paper-and-pencil tasks such as recognizing isolated words, selecting definitions of words, and selecting multiple choice responses based on the content of short segments of text. While ample psychometric evidence may exist for the reliability and validity of the data produced through measuring student performance on such tasks, such tests are criticized on the grounds that the tasks are not authentic in that they are not what people do when reading. An argument can be developed that a more authentic reading task involves sharing or communicating reactions or feelings in regards to the content of a story. If so, then assessment should be structured around the social and communicative aspects of the reading experience rather than around arbitrarily selected words and questions from text not selected by students out of their own interests.

In contrast to authenticity, determining the social validity of such a standardized test is based on the values of those invested in student performance. If they are less interested in scores on such a test than whether the students are using their reading skills to successfully complete relevant school assignments, then, the socially valid information would be student performance on school assignments rather than their scores on the standardized test. At the same time, because social validity is based on shared values rather than independent judgments of authenticity, it would be possible for performance on such a standardized test to be judged as socially valid but inauthentic.

Another important set of characteristics with respect to useful progress indicators relates to practical and logistical concerns. If frequent measurement of progress is useful to ascertain intervention effects, then assessment procedures must be efficient and economical. That is one reason why the administration of commercially developed achievement tests cannot be used in progress monitoring. Frequent monitoring also necessitates that multiple equivalent forms be used so that practice effects on the test itself do not accrue. Thus far, direct observation and recording of relatively brief performance samples embedded within the context of ongoing classroom activities has proved to be the most practical and logistically feasible solution to these problems.

SUMMARY

Evidence has accumulated that program reforms are more successful when systematic data-decision rules have been used to make program improvement decisions (Fuchs & Fuchs, 1986). The research in this area seems to reveal that people will collect data on the existence of a problem and then monitor progress toward goals, but they tend not to use the data to make timely changes in unsuccessful interventions. Indeed, this failure to modify programs in response to performance data has been identified by supervisors as the primary barrier to effective system-level implementation of progress monitoring systems in special education programs (Yell, Deno, & Marston, 1992). At least two approaches to overcoming this barrier are available and may be effective. The first solution is based on the use of computer technology to provide more direction when using the data to modify student programs. In this approach a structure is created for determining when and how a program might be modified to increase the likelihood of it success. Evidence

has been produced revealing that the use of such a technology does, indeed, result in more effective programs (Fuchs, Fuchs, Hamlett, & Ferguson, 1992).

The second solution is to devote greater resources to developing and supporting professional practices consistent with effective use of progress-monitoring data to solve problems. This will require preservice and in-service training and accountability systems that encourage effective use of progress monitoring to formatively evaluate efforts to solve problems. As a relatively new practice, a data-based approach to problem solving must evolve as part of the natural practice of school psychology. As with any evolutionary outcome, the behaviors that become the "best practices" of school psychology will be determined by the degree to which those practices are adaptive for school psychologists. If survival in the culture of the schools requires the effective use of data-based problem solving, school psychologists must successfully adapt to that culture by learning and using effective data-based problem-solving procedures. System developers and managers must look to themselves if they want to identify the source of motivation for best practice.

REFERENCES

Arter, J. A., & Jenkins, J. R. (1979). Differential diagnosis-prescriptive teaching: A critical appraisal. *Review of Educational Research, 49,* 517–556.

Berlyne, D. E. (1965). *Structure and direction in thinking.* New York: John Wiley and Sons, Inc.

Bransford, J. D., & Stein, B. S. (1984). *The IDEAL problem solver.* New York: W. H. Freeman.

Campbell, D. (1969). Reforms as experiments. *American Psychologist, 24,* 409–429.

Campbell, D. T., & Stanley, J. C. (1963). In N. L. Gage (Ed.), *Handbook of research on teaching* (pp. 171–246). Chicago: Rand McNally.

Festinger, L. (1957). *A theory of cognitive dissonance.* New York: Harper and Row.

Fuchs, L. S., Fuchs, D., & Deno, S. (1985). Importance of goal ambitiousness and goal mastery to student achievement. *Exceptional Children, 52,* 63–71.

Fuchs, L. S., & Fuchs, D. (1986). Effects of systematic formative evaluation: A meta-analysis. *Exceptional Children, 53,* 199–208.

Fuchs, L. S., Fuchs, D., Hamlett, C. L., & Ferguson, C. (1992). Effects of expert systems consultation within curriculum-based measurement using a reading maze task. *Exceptional Children, 58,* 436–450.

Kramer, J. J., & Epps, S. (1991). Expanding professional opportunities and improving the quality of training: A look toward the next generation of school psychologists. *School Psychology Review, 20,* 452–461.

Miller, G. A., Galanter, E., & Pribram, K. H. (1960). *Plans and the structure of behavior.* New York: Holt, Rinehart, and Winston.

Scriven, M. (1967). The methodology of evaluation. In R. Tyler, R. Gagne, & M. Scriven (Eds.), *Perspectives of curriculum evaluation* (pp. 23–55). Chicago: Rand McNally.

Snider, V. (1992). Learning styles and learning to read: A critique. *Remedial and Special Education, 13,* 6–18.

Snow, R. E. (1989). Aptitude-treatment interaction as a framework for research on individual differences. In P. L. Ackerman, R. J. Sternberg, & R. Glaser (Eds.), *Learning and individual differences* (pp. 13–59). New York: W. H. Freeman and Co.

Wiggins, G. (1993). Authenticity, context, and validity. *Phi Delta Kappan, 75,* 200–214.

Wolf, M. (1978). Social validity: The case for subjective measurement, or how applied behavior analysis is finding its heart. *Journal of Applied Behavior Analysis, 11,* 203–214.

Yell, M., Deno, S., & Marston, D. (1992). Barriers to implementing curriculum-based measurement. *Diagnostique, 18,* 99–106.

43

Best Practices in
Ensuring Quality Interventions

W. David Tilly III
Iowa Department of Education

Kristi R. Flugum
Heartland Area Education Agency 11 (Iowa)

Those who fall in love with practice without science are like a sailor who enters a ship without a helm or a compass, and who never can be certain wither he is going.

Leonardo Da Vinci

In recent years, the trend in school psychology service delivery has shifted strongly toward providing intervention services to children, families, and schools. This direction is reflected in policy statements by professional organizations (e.g., National Association of School Psychologists & National Coalition of Advocates for Students, 1985; National School Psychology Inservice Training Network, 1985) as well as in major professional publications (e.g., Graden, Zins, & Curtis, 1988; Stoner, Shinn, & Walker, 1991). It is becoming increasingly possible for school psychologists to break out of the gate-keeper-for-special-education role and provide services with documentable benefits to students and teachers. With this shift has come the challenge and responsibility for school psychologists to expand the traditional role of disability-centered service delivery and move to an intervention and outcome-centered service delivery model.

OVERVIEW

The purpose of this chapter is twofold. First, the concept *intervention* will be defined and a structure for implementing educational interventions will be presented. Second, critical components of educational interventions will be discussed and a format for documenting these procedures will be described. Space limitations preclude a comprehensive treatment of each quality indicator of interventions. Many of the quality indicators could and do have complete chapters or books written on them elsewhere. Hence, this chapter will provide a brief discussion of each indicator, provide references to more complete sources for each indicator, and illustrate how the indicators work together within a problem-solving structure.

What Is an Intervention

In reviewing the literature on problem solving and intervention design for this chapter, the authors noted an elementary but important omission in much of the literature regarding educational interventions. Many of the studies and book chapters focusing on specific educational treatments or interventions do not define what is meant by the term intervention, nor do they describe a structure in which the intervention will be carried out and evaluated. Translating these practices into positive student outcomes is problematic because it assumes that (a) educators share a common definition of "intervention" and (b) a structure for implementing interventions in schools is present. In educational practice, our experience is that these may be unfounded assumptions.

For the sake of this chapter, the term "intervention" is defined as a *planned modification of the environment made for the purpose of altering behavior in a prespecified way.* Three components in this definition are critical. First, interventions are *planful* in that the procedures to be applied are specified clearly and completely. Often they are documented in writing using a plan that communicates clearly the intent and content of the program. Second, interventions are *environmentally focused* in that the actions taken modify the environment, not the individual. For example, a reading intervention might involve changing a student's reading curriculum or instructional arrangements for the purpose of improving his or her rate of skill acquisition. In this case, the goal is to improve individual performance, but the focus of teacher action is on the environment, not on the student's processing style or neurological makeup. Third, interventions are *goal directed* in that they alter behaviors in a prespecified way. By stating intervention goals prior to implementation, all interested persons can agree on a mutually desirable outcome.

FIGURE 1. Flow chart of educational problem-solving steps.

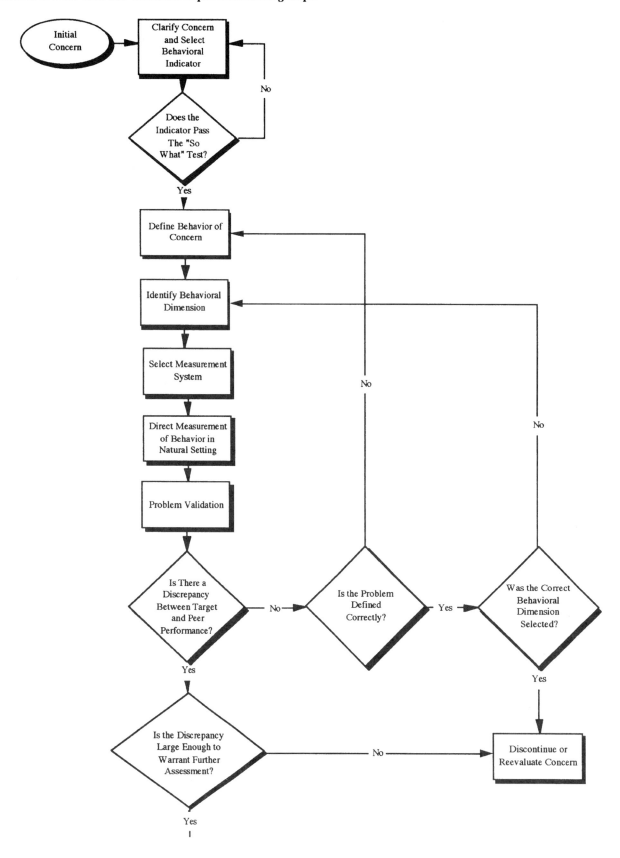

(Figure 1, continued)

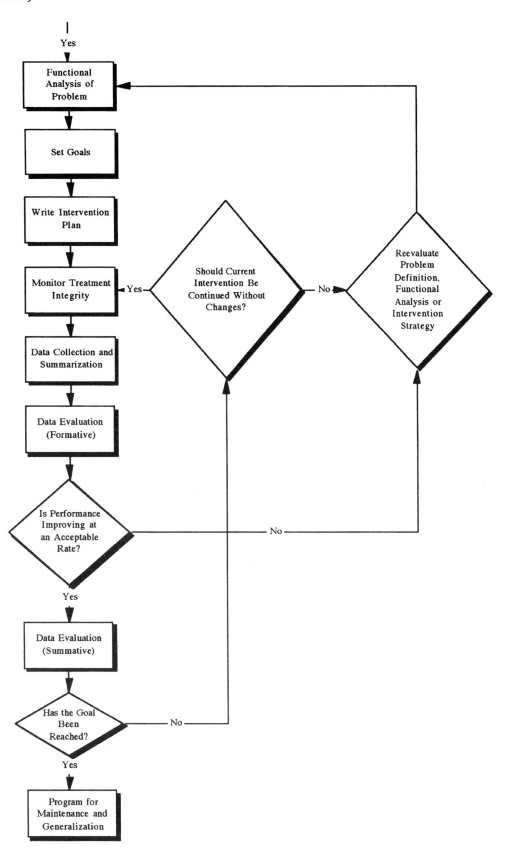

TABLE 1
Critical Dimensions for Defining School-Based Problems

Behavioral Dimensions
Frequency: How often a behavior occurs. This dimension is also referred to as Rate when frequency per time interval is the important cimension (e.g., hits per recess, words said per minute).
Latency: How long the time period is between the presentation of a prompt and the initiation of the behavior (e.g., how long it takes for a child to initiate compliance with a command).
Intensity: Refers to the strength of the behavior (e.g., how loud a shout is in decibels, how hard a punch is).
Topography: What the behavior looks like (e.g., if walking is the behavior, topography could refer to on one's toes, on one's heels, the bounciness of gate, etc.).
Accuracy: How correct the behavior is (e.g., correctness of math problems, free throws that go through the hoop).
Duration: How long the behavior lasts (e.g., how long a tantrum lasts, how long a student is out of seat).

Interventions as Part of Systematic Problem Solving

It is important to recognize that systematic interventions for school-based problems cannot stand by themselves. Instead, they should occur in the context of a problem-solving approach to educational service delivery. Adherence to this framework ensures the defensibility of intervention selection and ensures the intervention has a reasonable chance of remediating the identified problem.

The problem-solving model presented in this chapter combines aspects of behavioral assessment, behavioral consultation, and applied behavior-analytic models. This statement should not be interpreted to mean that behavioral approaches are the only ones that may be used with this model. Instead, this problem-solving approach provides a well articulated framework for examining problems, generating potential solutions, and monitoring outcomes without dictating treatment programs. The approach is pragmatic in that it focuses on providing effective interventions for individuals in applied settings. The approach is also dogmatic about not being dogmatic. That is, persons adopting this model must acknowledge two well-documented realities. First, the same intervention will not work with all persons in all situations. If this were the case, there would not be a need for individualized interventions. Second, there is no current technology that can predict with certainty the effectiveness of an educational intervention prior to its implementation. Therefore, professionals must monitor the effects of their interventions so changes can be made to ineffective programs in a timely manner.

The professional literature provides remarkable convergence on the components necessary to the successful implementation of this problem-solving model. The psychological (e.g., Barlow, Hayes, & Nelson, 1984), special education (e.g., Salvia & Ys-seldyke, 1991; Fuchs, Fuchs, Bahr, Fernstrom, & Stecker, 1990) and school psychology (e.g., Bergan & Kratochwill, 1990; Bergan & Neuman, 1980; Elliott, Witt, & Kratochwill, 1991; Kratochwill & Bergan, 1990; Shinn, 1989) literatures all provide examples of problem-solving models that contain these elements. One of the best summarizations of these components is provided in a recent paper by Flugum and Reschly (1994) examining quality indicators related to successful educational interventions. While the presence or absence of specific quality indices does not ensure an intervention's effectiveness, their presence increases the probability a positive outcome will result.

INDICES OF INTERVENTION QUALITY

As presented by Flugum and Reschly (1994), the indicators of quality interventions include (a) a behavioral (operational) definition of a problem, (b) a direct measure of the student's behavior in the natural setting prior to intervention, (c) a step-by-step intervention plan, (d) implementation of the intervention as planned, (e) graphing of intervention results, and (f) a direct comparison of a student's post-intervention performance to baseline data. Four additional problem-solving components implicit in the preceding six-step model have been identified in the literature (e.g., Bergan & Kratochwill, 1990; Deno, 1986; Shinn, 1989). These indicators are systematic problem validation, functional analysis of the problem, goal setting, and systematic formative evaluation of program effects. Because these steps are also crucial to successful implementation of a problem-solving system, they will be included as explicit components of the quality indices for the purposes of this chapter. Thus, a nine-component problem-solving model is proposed as a best practice standard for the development and documentation of educational interventions. A flow chart depicting these components and their relationships is contained in Figure 1.

To illustrate the use of the quality indices throughout this chapter, a case example will be presented. A. J. is a 6-year-old kindergarten boy who was referred by his teacher, Ms. Stein, to the school psychologist because of disruptive behavior in school. During a meeting between Ms. Stein, A. J.'s parents, and the school psychologist, "tantruming" was identified as the major behavior of concern in school. Throughout the chapter, information regarding the evaluation of this problem and subsequent intervention will be presented. An example of how data and decision making in this case were documented is provided in the Intervention Documentation Form at the end of the chapter (see Appendix A). As you read the remainder of the chapter, it may be helpful to place yourself in the role of the school psychologist and consider how the decision-making process used with A. J. could fit into your current role.

Operational Definition

The first step in the problem-solving process is to identify and define a problem operationally. Two critical components in this process are to select and define a behavior of concern. Appropriate selection of a behavior of concern ensures that a successful intervention will result in socially meaningful outcomes. A precise definition also ensures that all involved persons will share a common understanding of when the behavior is or is not occurring. The importance of this step cannot be underestimated because "even the best intervention strategy is doomed if it is applied to an improperly defined target behavior" (Reynolds, Gutkin, Elliott, & Witt, 1984, p. 186).

Selecting a behavior. During initial problem definition, a myriad of behaviors often are identified as concerns. When this happens, which behaviors are most problematic must be clarified and prioritized, usually through an interview. Questions such as "what does Jenny do when she is defiant?" and "How do you know when Scott is feeling withdrawn?" can help generate specific examples and assist in focusing attention on behaviors of most concern. Investing time in this clarification process both ensures accurate problem identification and establishes a shared responsibility for remediating the problem.

After generating and prioritizing specific problematic behaviors, a behavior or behaviors of concern must be selected for measurement and intervention. Two components are important to consider when selecting behavioral indicators: relevance and representativeness. Relevance refers to the importance of the behavior(s) selected for intervention. Stated plainly, behaviors targeted for intervention always must be subjected to and pass the "so what?" test. Professionals must ask, if a significant change were seen in this specific indicator(s), so what? — would that change represent a socially important outcome for the individuals involved? If the answer to this question is no,

then the problem must be reexamined and a different indicator or indicators selected.

Related to relevance is the issue of representativeness. In cases where a single behavior is problematic (e.g., hitting, thumb sucking), representativeness is a simple issue. The single behavior of concern can be defined directly. In cases where multiple behaviors are problematic, there are two general approaches to identifying a behavior of concern. First, in cases where a single behavior accurately reflects change in an important constellation of behaviors, a single indicator can be selected and defined. An example of this type of indicator is counting the number of words read correctly in 1 minute as an indicator of overall reading skill (i.e., Curriculum-Based Measurement). While counting words read correctly does not reflect everything about reading performance, oral reading fluency is an accurate indicator of many different components of reading, including comprehension (Shinn, Good, Knutson, Tilly, & Collins, 1992).

When a single behavior would not accurately represent the problem, it is often possible to define a group of behaviors by the effect they have on the environment. For example, if the concern is physical aggression against persons and there are multiple ways that aggression is perpetrated (e.g., hitting, biting, kicking), it may be inappropriate to choose a single behavior as reflective of aggression. In this case, it may be possible to define physical aggression as actions that could cause physical pain or discomfort to other persons in the environment and to use specific methods of aggression as examples in the definition.

Defining a behavior. The English language is full of inferential terms that appear to describe behavior but, upon closer scrutiny, could be inconsistently interpreted by different persons. Consider what is meant by the statements: Jamie acts depressed, Brett is hyperactive, and Marsha has low self-esteem. Each description appears to communicate something about an individual's behavior, but there are multiple actions or characteristics that could reflect each descriptor. As a result, two independent observers might have different understandings of the nature and severity of a concern based solely on a behavioral descriptor.

To remedy the problem of multiple interpretations, behaviors that are the subject of intervention must be described precisely. This process is called operationally defining a behavior. An operational definition must meet three criteria:

1. It must be objective, the definition should refer to observable characteristics of behavior or environmental events.

2. It must be clear, the definition should be so unambiguous that it could be read, repeated, and paraphrased by observers.

3. It must be complete, the definition should delineate both examples and non-examples of the behavior so that differences between occurrences and non-occurrences of the behavior can be discerned (Kazdin, 1982).

To write definitions with these characteristics, it may be helpful to use a standard format. A format that is particularly useful is:

(Target behavior) _____ means that *(target student action verbs)* _____.
Examples of *target behavior* include (1)_____, (2)_____, (3)_____ Non-examples of *target behavior* include (1) _____, (2) _____, (3) _____

This format requires that the intervention agent(s) attend directly to what an individual actually does when performing the behavior and provides a vehicle for efficient writing of definitions. This format also has the benefit of customizing and personalizing the description for a particular behavior, student, and setting.

In A. J.'s case, the term *tantrum* was used frequently during the initial interviews to describe the teacher's concerns. After following up these descriptions with the question "what does A. J. do when he tantrums?" it became clear that for A. J. crying was the major determinant of tantruming. He often did other behaviors along with his tantruming, but Ms. Stein could not identify an instance of a tantrum when A. J. did not cry. Moreover, there were very few cases where A. J.'s crying would not be considered as tantruming. Hence, an operational definition for A. J.'s "tantruming" in the format provided was written:

> Tantruming means A. J. **cries audibly after an adult answers "no" to one of his requests or after an adult gives him a direct command to do something.** Examples of tantruming include (a) crying when told to put away materials when it is time for lunch; (b) crying and tearing up papers when he is told by an adult to group his blocks by color; and (c) crying and throwing a toy after being told "no" when A. J. asks if he may play with a toy. Non-examples of tantruming include (a) crying after falling down at recess; (b) crying out loudly during outside activities; and (c) crying after someone says something that hurt his feelings.

This definition passes the "so what" test in that decreasing crying will allow A. J. to participate more fully in important class activities, will allow the teacher to spend more time teaching him other school-related behaviors, and may increase his opportunities for prosocial peer interaction. The definition is representative in that crying appears to be a major determinant of tantrums. Finally, this definition describes specific examples of what tantrums look like for A. J. and provides examples of what should not be counted as "tantruming."

Direct Measure of the Behavior in the Natural Setting Prior to Intervention

Once the target behavior has been defined, baseline data must be collected. This task involves establishing the relevant dimension(s) of the problem behavior, developing a method to systematically measure the behavior, and collecting data on the behavior prior to implementing an intervention.

Behavioral dimensions. Six dimensions of behavior are most frequently problematic in schools. The acronym FLITAD is a useful mnemonic device to assist in remembering these dimensions. The acronym comes from the first letter in the behavioral dimensions listed in Table 1.

To select the relevant behavioral dimension, a qualitative examination of the behavior in the natural setting must be completed. It may be helpful to ask the question "what exactly is it about this behavior that is problematic?" In some cases, the problematic dimension will be obvious. For example, the accuracy of Maria's math problems is very low or the frequency of Joe's hitting is too high. For some behaviors, there are multiple dimensions that may be problematic. For example, "tantruming" may include crying, using a loud voice, physical aggression, and noncompliance with adult directions. In some situations, the most problematic characteristic of tantrums may be their frequency; in others, duration of tantrums may be most relevant; in still others, the magnitude or intensity of the behaviors may be important. While "tantrum" might be operationally defined the same way in each of these situations, the way in which it will be measured will be different based on the most problematic dimension of the behavior.

In A. J.'s case, the most important dimension of his tantrums appeared to be duration. Ms. Stein, A. J.'s teacher, stated during an interview that the worst part of A. J.'s tantrums is sometimes they seemed to last "forever" and it made it difficult for her to teach. Moreover, when A. J. tantrumed, he did not usually become aggressive with other children, destroy significant property, or scream loudly in anyone's ear so intensity was probably not most problematic. She further stated that the number of tantrums varied on different days, but so did their duration. Thus, monitoring the number of times A. J. tantrumed probably would not have yielded meaningful results.

Behavioral measurement. Once the behavior has been defined and the relevant dimension of the behavior has been established, the behavior must be measured directly in the setting where it is perceived to be problematic. The measurement strategy used to collect information should be objective and related directly to the relevant dimension of the behavior.

TABLE 2
Five Components of the SORKC Model

SORKC Components
Stimulus — Any characteristics of or occurrence in the environment (both internal and external) that is or may be related to behavior (e.g., words on a page are a stimulus for reading).
Organism — Organismic variables that may influence behavior (e.g., hunger may influence the length of time a person attends to a reading task; learning history may influence whether a student answers a question correctly).
Response — An overt (e.g., reading out loud) or covert (e.g., reading silently) action that can be measured.
(K)Contingency — The rules of reinforcement specifying the relationships between stimuli (both S and O), responses and environmental consequences (e.g., the rule "when a reading comprehension question is answered correctly during reading group, the teacher praises the student who answered").
Consequence — The environmental events that are functionally related to the occurrence for non-occurrence) of the behavior (e.g., receiving a praise statement for a correct answer; receiving an F for not turning in one's homework.

This same strategy will be used throughout the intervention to monitor and evaluate its effectiveness at improving student performance. Therefore, the measurement strategy must be selected with care to ensure quality data collection. An extended discussion of behavioral measurement strategies is beyond the scope of the current chapter, but excellent resources are available (e.g., Alessi & Kaye, 1983; Bellack & Hersen, 1988; Epps, 1988; Shapiro & Kratochwill, 1988; Sulzer-Azaroff & Mayer, 1991).

In the initial discussion with Ms. Stein, the school psychologist suggested two different measurement strategies that might be used to monitor A. J.'s tantruming. The first option would require Ms. Stein to record how long A. J. tantrumed each day during the first 2 hours of school (the most problematic time of the day). This strategy had the advantage of only requiring measurement during part of the day but had the disadvantage of sampling A. J.'s behavior each day. The second strategy would require Ms. Stein to carry a stopwatch in her pocket and to turn it on when A. J. tantrumed and off when he stopped. This strategy's advantage was its comprehensiveness; its disadvantage was its intrusiveness on Ms. Stein's time, and the need for Ms. Stein to be present with A. J. throughout the day. Since she already spent most of the day with A. J., Ms. Stein chose to collect data on A. J.'s tantrums each day throughout the day. She was comfortable with the data-collection strategy because she "had lots of pockets to keep things in" and remembering to turn on the stopwatch would not be a problem because of how intrusive A. J.'s behavior was. The resulting data, collected across 1 week reflected the number of minutes each day A. J. had spent tantruming.

Pre-intervention data collection. After the behavioral dimension and measurement strategy have been identified, data collection can begin. Pre-inter-

vention observation should consist of repeated measures of the target behavior over several sessions, day, or even weeks, until a stable range of behavior has been identified (e.g., no new highs or lows for three data points in a row [Sulzer-Azaroff & Mayer, 1991]). Collection of these data has three major purposes in problem solving. First, they provide a pre-intervention summary describing characteristics of individual performance such as level, variability, and trend in behavior. This summary can be used to scale the magnitude of a problem and to document pre-treatment levels of behavior. Second, baseline data serve a predictive function by providing a database for predicting future performance in the absence of intervention. That is, an inference can be made about the future occurrence of the behavior if an intervention were not implemented. This prediction then serves as a standard for evaluating the effectiveness of an intervention. Third, collecting baseline data provides an opportunity to observe relationships between behavior and other environmental variables. These observations provide critical information that may be useful during functional analysis and intervention design.

To gather baseline data on A. J.'s tantruming, Ms. Stein collected data each day for 5 consecutive days. The data collected over the week ranged from 32 to 52 minutes of tantruming each day. Due to the variability during the first 5 days, data were collected for an additional 2 days, which resulted in a more stable summary of the typical length of A. J.'s tantrums. These data are depicted graphically on the intervention documentation form in Appendix A.

Problem Validation

At this point in the problem-solving process, a problem behavior has been defined and a direct measure of behavior has been obtained. A next step is to identify a context for evaluating the magnitude of the problem. In some cases, the severity of a problem will be obvious. For example, it would not take direct observation of peer performance to document that cutting other persons with a knife has a low base-rate in the typical population. In other (perhaps most) cases, the magnitude of a problem will not be apparent by examining the data alone. Whether being out of one's seat four times per hour in a fifth-grade classroom is a problem depends largely on that classroom's expectations and norms. Hence, the purpose of problem validation is to establish operationally the existence and magnitude of a problem.

A practical method for problem definition is to conceptualize problems as the difference between what is expected in an environment and what actually occurs. In practice, a discrepancy is determined by comparing an individual's current level of performance, documented during baseline data, to a performance standard representing acceptable performance. It should be noted at this point that an inference should not be made automatically that problems occur only as the result of poor student performance. Sometimes problems can occur as the result of inappropriate environmental expectations. The authors are reminded of a recent phone call from the mother of a 6-month-old who was concerned her son was not yet talking!

To address the problem of finding appropriate expectations, a most useful standard for both academic and social-emotional behaviors is based on typical peer performance. This standard is obtained by measuring typical peers' performance on a behavior of concern to find a range of typical performance. These data then can be used to quantify the magnitude of a problem, which is the difference between the target student's performance and peer performance. Using peer performance as a standard has clear advantages in educational settings. It encompasses many standards relevant to educational expectations. For example, typical peers' performance represents a standard accepted in a particular environment by a particular teacher. Typical peers' performance also takes developmental norms and expectations into account, thereby ensuring that developmentally inappropriate expectations are avoided. A response containing information about typical 6-month-old talking performance was all that was necessary to solve the problem of the non-verbal 6-month-old. Finally, a peer-performance standard is sensitive to local and regional differences in performance and expectations. Thus an individual's performance will not be evaluated in comparisons to regionally biased or unfair standards.

Though peer performance is often a useful standard in schools, other performance standards are also possible. For example, a standard set by the intervention team based on a logical analysis or on "expert judgment" might be needed in cases where typical peer performance is not available. Another standard sometimes used examines skills that an individual will need to perform satisfactorily in an anticipated future environment. The important components for all of these standards is that the desired level of performance is specified clearly, usually numerically in relation to the behavior of concern, and that the rationale for selecting a particular standard is compelling and defensible.

Once a standard is selected and operationalized, the existence and magnitude of the problem can be determined. At this point, two questions should be asked: (a) Is there a discrepancy between the target student's performance and the performance standard? and (b) If so, is the discrepancy large enough to warrant intervention? If the answer to either of these questions is no, then the existence of or severity of the problem should be questioned. The nature of the problem may need to be reexamined and redefined or further data may need to be collected to validate the problem. If the answer to both of these questions is yes, then the problem is validated and further assessment for the purpose of developing and evaluating interventions is needed.

In A. J.'s case, Ms. Stein stated that she expected no tantruming to occur during the school day but that some of A. J.'s peers also cried occasionally. During the pre-intervention data collection, the school psychologist collected data on both A. J.'s behavior and his peers' behavior. This information suggested that some of A. J.'s peers occasionally cried 3 to 5 minutes a day in a similar manner to A. J. Based on this information, there appears to be a meaningful difference between the duration of A. J.'s tantruming and his peers'. After reviewing these data with Ms. Stein and A. J.'s mother, it was agreed that further assessment and intervention appeared warranted.

Functional Analysis

Once a problem has been validated, a systematic analysis is needed to determine factors related to the occurrence, non-occurrence, and maintenance of problem behaviors. This analysis provides the critical link between assessment information and intervention procedures. Functional analysis requires careful examination of the behavior across different situations and consideration of multiple factors that may influence performance. This step is perhaps the most complex and most critical to the selection of appropriate interventions. Indeed, when an accurate functional analysis has been completed, the design of potentially effective interventions becomes less difficult.

A number of methods of functional analysis have been developed that can be used to examine human behavior (e.g., the ABC model developed by Reese, Howard, & Reese, 1977; the scatterplot method described by Touchette, MacDonald, & Langer, 1985). A particularly useful heuristic is based on the SORKC model developed initially by Lindsley (1964) and expanded by Kanfer and Phillips (1970). This model provides a conceptual structure for examining the "real world" behaviors and environments that school psychologists routinely observe in schools. Behavioral sequences are analyzed in the context of the naturalistic environments and relationships between behavior and the environment can be examined for the purpose of designing interventions. The five components in SORKC are defined in Table 2. To use the SORKC model in practice, multiple behavioral sequences are examined across time. Each sequence provides information used to summarize the environmental factors related to the occurrence and non-occurrence of behavior. As observational data are collected, patterns of relationships between behavior and the environment typically emerge. These patterns can then be analyzed and incorporated into intervention designs.

To illustrate the utility of the SORKC procedure, consider the situation surrounding A. J.'s problems. After Ms. Stein, A. J.'s parents, and the school psychologist operationally defined "tantruming" and identified the duration as the most problematic dimension, the school psychologist observed A. J. in the most problematic environment (during math activities, 25 minutes per period) and in the least problematic environment (art, 30 minutes per period) across 2 days. After observing many interactions between A. J. and adults, the following summary of the observational data was created by the psychologist (i.e., the summary comments are data-based descriptions and inferences). During the observations, three tantrums were observed during math.

- *Stimulus (Stimuli)* — Tantruming usually begins while A. J. is sitting at his desk; approximately one to two times per minute during teacher-led instruction (when all of the tantrums were observed) successive directions are given orally by the teacher usually to the whole group of 16 children; throughout math period, A. J. usually spends most of his time manipulating math materials (e.g., counting cubes, placing them in columns, grouping them, etc.); most of the time A. J. sits in the last row in the back of the classroom, typically, next to the teacher.

- *Organism* — Math activities are some of the first activities of the day and his mother stated that A. J. often does not eat breakfast (hunger could be related to current performance); A. J. has a history of having difficulty with counting and numbers (poor counting skills could be related to current performance).

- *Response* — Throughout the math class, A. J. usually does not perform the required math task correctly; when A. J. was observed to tantrum, he appeared to not understand directions; in these cases, after being given a specific direction related

to the activity, A. J. begins to cry, he stops performing the math task, he speaks in a loud voice, and one time threw a math cube (manipulative) at the back wall of the classroom; during his tantrums, he usually leaves his desk and walks to a part of the classroom away from his desk.

- *K(C)ontingency* — In this case, the contingencies appear to be the rules "begin to cry during math and the teacher will talk to you" and "begin to cry during math and you can stop working on the math for a short period of time."

- *Consequence* — In all three "tantruming" instances the teacher responded to A. J.'s behavior immediately by either walking over to him, talking to him (usually to ask him to stop and to redirect him), by helping him do the activity, or by talking to him loudly from across the room, or by asking him to move to the front of the class.

The psychologist also observed A. J.'s behavior during art, where no tantrums occurred.

The school psychologist functionally analyzed the observation data using the SORKC model, applied behavior analysis principles, and professional experience. The hypothesis was developed that A. J.'s tantruming was being reinforced by the teacher's attention and by tantruming A. J. escaped from a task that may be aversive to him. Moreover, it appeared that the teacher often was being reinforced for paying attention to A. J.'s inappropriate behavior (his crying appeared to become less loud when she talked to him), thereby making her more likely to attend to him when he cried. This information was used to guide the intervention decision to have the teacher attend to A. J.'s working during math period, to ignore his tantruming whenever it occurred (unless he posed a physical danger to himself or others), to have A. J.'s mother feed him breakfast in the morning, to directly instruct A. J. in how to complete the math assignments, to modify A. J.'s math assignments so that he could complete the majority of them during group work without assistance, and to provide stickers and behavior-specific praise (attention) frequently throughout the day contingent on his appropriate behavior.

Setting Goals

After validating the existence and magnitude of a problem, a performance goal should be set. The importance of setting a goal should not be underestimated. In the absence of a clearly articulated goal, the effectiveness of interventions can become obscured. In other words, as a colleague of ours often says, "The only wrong way to set a goal is not to set one" (Julie Schendel, 1993, personal communication).

Goals are general statements about the behavior targeted for change and the direction or level that change should take (Sulzer-Azaroff & Mayer, 1991).

Goal statements are based on the problem behavior(s) and should state clearly, in a measurable way, what the individual's performance will look like if the intervention is successful. In most circumstances, a goal statement can both be stated narratively and be represented graphically on a performance chart. For the narrative statement, it may be helpful to use a standard format. A format often used for stating goals is:

> In *(number)*_____ weeks, when *(condition occurs)*_____, *(learner)*_____ will *(behavior of concern to a specific criterion)*_____.

An example of using A. J.'s tantruming is:

> In 6 weeks, when he is at school, A. J. will tantrum for less than 10 minutes per day for 8 out of 10 consecutive school days.

This goal is represented on A. J.'s performance chart by the horizontal line drawn at the 10-minute mark (illustrated in Appendix A). For a comprehensive discussion of educational goal setting, the reader is referred to an excellent chapter by Lynn Fuchs (this volume).

Written Intervention Plan

At the point where an intervention has been designed, a goal has been set, and intervention implementation is ready to begin, creating a step-by-step intervention plan based on the results of the functional analysis is the next component. The intervention plan answers questions relevant to solving the identified problem, including who will do what, when will they do it, where will the plan be implemented, how will the steps be completed, and with whom will the plan be implemented. This plan (a) ensures that all parties involved with the intervention share the same understanding of the procedures to be used, (b) serves as a guide for implementors of interventions, and (c) serves as a record of the intervention. Just as an operational definition completely describes a behavior of concern, an intervention plan clearly describes the procedures to be used during an intervention. Indeed, an intervention plan should be clear enough that a trained reader could replicate the intervention and produce the same results (Baer, Wolf, & Risley, 1968).

Schendel and Ulman (1989) identified a series of components that should be included in a written intervention plan. For academic behavior, the intervention plan should define specific teaching procedures, physical arrangements, the time allotted to each teaching activity, the materials to be used in instruction, and motivational strategies to be employed. For non-academic behaviors the intervention plan should describe the settings where the intervention will occur, motivational strategies, specific behavior management procedures, and instructional strategies.

A final component in a written intervention plan is a statement of how decisions will be made. This component describes strategies that will be used for data collection, summarization, and evaluation. Specific issues to be addressed include frequency of data collection, which strategies will be used to summarize data for evaluation, the number of data points or the amount of time that should occur before data will be analyzed, and a statement describing the actions that will be taken by intervention agents based on the intervention data (decision made).

In A. J.'s case, the intervention plan followed directly from the functional analysis of the problem and the details were worked out in a second meeting with A. J.'s parents and teacher. Data were to be collected daily by Ms. Stein and decisions about the intervention were scheduled to be made at the end of each week. Specific intervention procedures, the persons responsible for implementing them, and specific decision-making strategies are contained in the Intervention Documentation Form in Appendix A.

Intervention Implemented as Planned

Once the intervention has been designed and a plan written, ensuring the intervention is implemented as intended is the next step (Peterson, Homer, & Wonderlich, 1982). This process is referred to in the professional literature as treatment integrity (Gresham, 1989; Telzrow, this volume). There are a number of different approaches that can be used to assess treatment integrity. A teacher may be interviewed regarding the steps followed during intervention. Direct observation of intervention implementation can be completed. Or the written step-by-step intervention plan could be used as a checklist after the intervention to determine the steps that were followed. The important component in assessing treatment integrity is determining the extent to which treatments were delivered as intended so that potential effects of treatment implementation can be factored into the evaluation of treatment effectiveness. If the intervention is not implemented as designed, progress (or lack thereof) cannot be attributed to the specific plan.

Evaluating treatment integrity in practice can be a sensitive issue. School psychologists are not typically responsible for evaluating teachers' competence or professional skills, nor would most be comfortable in that role. It may be, however, part of the psychologist's role to assist in evaluating the effectiveness of an intervention. In these cases, multiple sources of influence on student performance must be considered, including the integrity of the intervention.

When interventions are not implemented as planned, school psychologists may choose to use problem-solving strategies to identify components in their control that may lead to better compliance with the intervention. These variables can be held in mind when recycling through the problem-solving process and may help to fine-tune interventions the second (or third or fourth, etc.) time through.

In A. J.'s case, treatment integrity was promoted and assessed using interviews. Prior to intervention implementation, the school psychologist reviewed with Ms. Stein the procedures to be implemented in her classroom and encouraged her to ask any questions about scenarios that were not covered by the treatment plan. Also, the psychologist suggested that she and Ms. Stein jointly review the treatment plan together again in one week to make sure everything was going as planned. At this point, the psychologist also informed Ms. Stein that if their analysis of the problem was correct and their interventions worked as expected, A. J.'s behavior would likely get worse for a short period of time prior to its improving. The psychologist also scheduled two phone calls on the following Monday to Ms. Stein's classroom as a source of support for Ms. Stein and asked the principal to drop by periodically to see how the program was working.

Monitoring of Progress and Graphing of Intervention Results

Throughout intervention implementation, student performance should be assessed frequently and repeatedly so that continuous evaluation can occur and interventions may be modified as needed. Data are collected across time on the behavior identified during problem identification. These data are used to create a graphic display for the purpose of illustrating trends in student performance that can be analyzed and evaluated.

While graphs are but one of many methods for summarizing data, they are useful for at least four reasons. First, they provide a means of efficiently summarizing information about student performance such as current levels of performance, projected performance (a performance goal), and actual performance as it changes over the course of intervention. Second, trends in performance are more easily seen and communicated when data are graphically displayed. Third, graphing of results during monitoring may have an important impact on inferences made about the intervention effectiveness and student progress (Skiba, Deno, Marston, & Casey, 1989). For example, "When parents, teachers, and other agents can see visual evidence (i.e., a graph) that a procedure is bringing about the desired change, they are likely to find the evidence reinforcing. Such reinforcement helps to maintain the participation of those people in the treatment program, which is critical if objectives are to be achieved" (Sulzer-Azaroff & Mayer, 1991, p. 128). Fourth, graphing of student performance provides a measure of professional accountability demonstrating how behavior change is functionally related to the intervention being imple-

mented. For clarity of communication, a standard format should be used for graphs (see Parsonson & Baer, 1978; Sulzer-Azaroff & Mayer, 1991).

Formative and Summative Data Evaluation

The final component in intervention design and implementation is data evaluation and decision making. Two types of data evaluation should be conducted for each intervention: formative and summative. Formative evaluation occurs throughout the implementation of an intervention and requires the evaluator to answer the question "is this intervention working?" In most cases, effectiveness is evaluated by examining trends in performance data during intervention implementation and comparing these trends to the baseline data collected prior to intervention. Summative data evaluation typically occurs after an intervention procedure has been completed and requires the evaluator to answer the question "did the intervention work?" One systematic method of determining the effects of an intervention program is to directly compare baseline performance to post-intervention performance (Flugum & Reschly, 1994). In this case, the change in student performance across time can be determined and a comparison to the specified goal-level can be made. Again, specifics of data analysis for individual interventions are well beyond the scope of the current chapter, but a number of excellent sources are available (e.g., Kazdin, 1976; Kazdin, 1982; Marston & Tindal, this volume; Parsonson & Baer, 1978).

In A. J.'s case, the baseline data documented that his tantrums occurred an average of approximately 40 minutes a day and were somewhat variable in length. Throughout the intervention, A. J.'s performance was monitored daily and his data were recorded at the end of each day by Ms. Stein. As predicted prior to the intervention, A. J.'s tantrums increased in length immediately following intervention implementation and then reduced gradually across the next 2 weeks. After approximately 3 more weeks of intervention, A. J.'s tantrums had reduced in length on most days to below the goal level of 10 minutes per day and Ms. Stein began collecting data only 3 days per week. After 4 more weeks of intervention, a summative evaluation was conducted by holding a meeting with A. J.'s parents, the psychologist, and Ms. Stein, All persons present agreed the intervention has been successful and that A. J. appeared much happier at school. Ms. Stein agreed to continue providing positive feedback to A. J. during times when he was behaving appropriately, to informally monitor his performance, and to contact A. J.'s parents one time per week for the remainder of the semester to inform them of his progress.

QUALIFICATIONS AND CONCLUSIONS

It may seem through the illustrations presented in this chapter that school-based interventions occur in a linear, well articulated sequence. They do not. In school psychology practice, many intervention components may occur simultaneously and many of the procedures cycle back upon themselves. For example, if an initial intervention does not result in problem improvement, the intervention process may recycle back to a functional analysis for the purpose of determining how to modify the existing intervention. Another way the process is nonlinear is that some components of problem solving may occur simultaneously. The school psychologist might collect clues for a functional analysis even at the time when they are interviewing a teacher to identify a behavior to observe.

The important point in this chapter is not to prescribe a lock-step order in attending to the quality indices. Instead, it is critical that persons who provide intervention services attend to all of the quality indices *throughout* the process of service provision. Each component adds something significant to the overall picture and there are cases where the omission of any single quality index could render impotent an otherwise effective intervention.

As school psychology practitioners, the authors acknowledge that interventions are almost never as pristine as are the procedures presented in chapters such as this one. Data are often difficult to obtain or of dubious quality, persons implementing interventions may not implement them according to plan, time constraints may preclude data evaluation as frequently as would be optimal, and many other challenges will occur. Worse yet, providing these types of services may be incompatible with the structure of the service delivery model being implemented in a particular area or district.

Despite the challenges, however, using a problem-solving model to provide intervention services remains the best research-based alternative for improving individual student performance in schools. Whether students receive special education services or general education services, the procedures are equally applicable. The role of the school psychologist is changing and psychologists are increasingly being called upon to assist in problem resolution rather than problem classification. As a result, there is increasing incentive to focus more substantively on interventions and outcomes. Embracing this challenge now will both secure a place in future educational systems for school psychologists and result in improved outcomes for our constituencies.

REFERENCES

Alessi, G. K., & Kaye, J. H. (1983). *Behavior assessment for school psychologists*. Washington, DC: National Association of School Psychologists.

Baer, D. M., Wolf, M., & Risley, T. R. (1968). Some current dimensions of applied behavior analysis. *Journal of Applied Behavior Analysis, 1*, 91–97.

Barlow, D. H., Hayes, S. C., & Nelson, R. O. (1984). *The scientist practitioner: Research and accountability in clinical and educational settings*. New York: Pergamon Press.

Bellack, A. S., & Hersen, M. (Eds.). (1988). *Behavioral assessment: A practical handbook* (3rd ed.). Elmsford, NY: Pergamon Press.

Bergan, J. R., & Kratochwill, T. R. (1990). *Behavioral consultation and therapy*. New York: Plenum.

Bergan, J. R., & Neuman, A. (1980). The identification of resources and constraints influencing plan design in consultation. *Journal of School Psychology, 18*, 317–323.

Deno, S. L. (1986). Formative evaluation of individual student programs: A new role for school psychologists. *School Psychology Review, 15*, 358–374.

Elliott, S. N., Witt, J. C., & Kratochwill, T. R. (1991). Selecting, implementing, and evaluating classroom interventions. In G. Stoner, M. R. Shinn, & H. M. Walker (Eds.), *Interventions for achievement and behavior problems* (pp. 99–135). Silver Spring, MD: National Association of School Psychologists.

Epps, S. (1988). Best practices in behavioral observation. In A. Thomas & J. Grimes (Eds.), *Best practices in school psychology* (pp. 95–111). Washington, DC: National Association of School Psychologists.

Flugum, K. R., & Reschly, D. J. (1994). Pre-referral interventions: Quality indices and outcomes. *Journal of School Psychology, 32*, 1–14.

Fuchs, D., Fuchs, L. S., Bahr, M. W., Fernstrom, P., & Stecker, P. M. (1990). Pre-referral intervention: A prescriptive approach. *Exceptional Children, 56*, 493–513.

Graden, J. L., Zins, J. E., & Curtis, M. J. (Eds.) (1988). *Alternative educational delivery systems: Enhancing instructional options for all students*. Washington, DC: National Association of School Psychologists.

Gresham, F. M. (1989). Assessment of treatment integrity in school consultation and prereferral interventions. *School Psychology Review, 17*, 211–226.

Kanfer, F. H., & Phillips, J. S. (1970). *Learning foundations of behavior therapy*. New York: Wiley.

Kazdin, A. E. (1976). Statistical analysis of single-case experimental designs. In M. Hersen & D. Barlow (Eds.), *Single case experimental designs: Strategies for studying behavior change* (pp. 265–316). New York: Pergamon Press.

Kazdin, A. E. (1982). *Single-case research designs: Methods for clinical and applied settings*. New York: Oxford University Press.

Kratochwill, T. R., & Bergan, J. R. (1990). *Behavioral consultation in applied settings: An individual guide*. New York: Plenum.

Lindsley, O. R. (1964). Direct measurement and prosthesis of retarded behavior. *Journal of Education, 147*, 62–81.

National Association of School Psychologists, & National Coalition of Advocates for Students. (1985). *Position statement: Advocacy for appropriate educational services for all children*. Washington, DC: Author.

National School Psychology Inservice Training Network. (1985). *School psychology: A blueprint for training and practice*. Minneapolis, MN: Author.

Parsonson, B. S., & Baer, D. M. (1978). The analysis and presentation of graphic data. In T. R. Kratochwill (Ed.), *Single subject research: Strategies for evaluating change* (pp. 101–166). New York: Academic Press.

Peterson, L., Homer, A. L., & Wonderlich, S. A. (1982). The integrity of independent variables in behavior analysis. *Journal of Applied Behavior Analysis, 15,* 477–492.

Reese, E. P., Howard, J. S., & Reese, T. W. (1977). *Human behavior: An experimental analysis and its applications.* Dubuque, IA: William C. Brown.

Reynolds, C. R., Gutkin, T., Elliott, S. N., & Witt, J. C. (1984). *School psychology: Essentials of theory and practice.* New York: John Wiley.

Salvia, J., & Ysseldyke, J. E. (1991). *Assessment.* Boston: Houghton-Mifflin.

Schendel, J., & Ulman, J. (1989). *Performance monitoring of academic and non-academic behaviors.* Des Moines, IA: Bureau of Special Education, Iowa Department of Education.

Shapiro, E. S., & Kratochwill, T. R. (1988). *Behavioral assessment in schools: Conceptual foundations and practical applications.* New York: Guilford.

Shinn, M. R. (Ed.). (1989). *Curriculum-based measurement: Assessing special children.* New York: Guilford.

Shinn, M. R., Good, R. H. III, Knutson, N., Tilly, W. D.

III, & Collins, V. L. (1992). Curriculum-based measurement of oral reading fluency: A confirmatory analysis of its relation to reading. *School Psychology Review, 21,* 459–479.

Skiba, R., Deno, S., Marston, D., & Casey, A. (1989). Influence of trend estimation and subject familiarity on practitioners' judgment of intervention effectiveness. *Journal of Special Education, 22,* 433–446.

Stoner, G., Shinn, M. R., & Walker, H. M. (Eds.). (1991). *Interventions for achievement and behavior problems.* Silver Spring, MD: National Association of School Psychologists.

Sulzer-Azaroff, B., & Mayer, G. R. (1991). *Behavior analysis for lasting change.* Fort Worth, TX: Harcourt Brace Jovanovich College Publishers.

Touchette, P. E., MacDonald, R. F., & Langer, S. N. (1985). A scatter plot for identifying stimulus control of problem behavior. *Journal of Applied Behavior Analysis, 18,* 343–351.

ANNOTATED BIBLIOGRAPHY

Bergan, J. R., & Kratochwill, T. R. (1990). *Behavioral consultation and therapy.* New York: Plenum Press.
This book presents a problem-solving model within the framework of behavioral consultation. The four stages include problem identification, problem analysis, plan implementation, and program evaluation. Each of these stages is developed through a structured interview with a primary goal of developing and evaluating effective interventions.

Elliott, S. N., Witt, J. C., & Kratochwill, T. R. (1991). Selecting, implementing, and evaluating classroom interventions. In G. Stoner, M. R. Shinn, & H. M. Walker (Eds.), *Interventions for achievement and behavior problems* (pp. 99–135). Silver Spring, MD: National Association of School Psychologists.
This chapter provides an extensive review of behavioral approaches to classroom interventions. The presentation contains extensive citations to primary research and has an especially strong emphasis on factors influencing treatment selection, treatment acceptability, and teacher empowerment. Protocols for assessing treatment acceptability and treatment integrity are also included.

Graden, J. L., Zins, J. E., & Curtis, M. J. (Eds.). (1988). *Alternative educational delivery systems: Enhancing instructional options for all students.* Washington, DC: National Association of School Psychologists.
This edited book provides an excellent overview of the rationale and need for alternative approaches to educational delivery systems. Specific strategies are presented to address systems change efforts at all levels of educational systems from individual classrooms through organizational frameworks.

Stoner, G., Shinn, M. R., & Walker, H. M. (Eds.). (1991). *Interventions for achievement and behavior problems.* Silver Spring, MD: National Association of School Psychologists.
This book reflects the shift in school psychological practice toward interventions and outcomes. Chapters are written by experts in school psychology and special education. General intervention strategies are presented for a variety of academic and behavioral problems for a variety of ages (early childhood to secondary education).

Sulzer-Azaroff, B., & Mayer, G. R. (1991). *Behavior analysis for lasting change.* Fort Worth: Harcourt Brace Jovanovich College Publishers.
This book provides an extensive overview of applied behavior analytic techniques. Information concerning assessment and intervention and how to link the two are presented. Skills needed for increasing, decreasing, or maintaining behaviors or maintaining behaviors are a primary focus of the book.

APPENDIX A

Instructional Intervention Plan

Student **A.J. Jones**   Goal Area **Tantrums**

Decision Making Plan: Summarized during @ week by determining the median performance for the week. It is expected there will be an abrupt increase in A.J.'s tantruming then a rapid decrease (within the first 2 weeks) down to below 10 minutes per day. A.J.'s performance will be evaluated at the end of each week. If his performance does not match the predicted pattern, further analysis will be conducted to [see] the intervention changed. A.J.'s level of performance will be

Phase	Instructional Procedures	Materials	Arrangements	Time	Motivational Strategies
1	*Skills and Strategies* — teacher attention for appropriate working, teacher-led instruction on new materials/skills, modifications in math assignments (e.g. structured)	Holt Math	regular class arrangement	30-40 min. per day	verbal praise, ignoring of tantrums, contingent attention
2	*Skills and Strategies* — contingent teacher ignoring of tantrums, A.J. will be seed in a.m., behavior-specific praise contingent on appropriate behavior	Stopwatch	regular class arrangement	all day at school	Same as above
3	*Skills and Strategies*				
4	*Skills and Strategies*				
5	*Skills and Strategies*				

Definition of Behavior [Behavior– which is specific, observable, alterable and measurable– is defined then three examples and three nonexamples are provided]

Tantruming means A.J. cries audibly after an adult answers "no" to one of his requests or after an adult gives him a direct command to do something. Examples include (a) crying when told to put away materials when it is time for lunch; (b) crying & tearing up papers when he is told by an adult to group his blocks by color; & (c) crying & throwing a toy after being told "no" when A.J. asks if he may play w/a toy. Non-examples include (a) crying after falling down at recess; (b) crying out loudly during outside activities; and (c) crying after someone said something that hurt his feelings.

Dimension of Behavior [What about the behavior is problematic?] Duration

- Behavior happens too much or too little (Frequency)
- Behavior happens too long or too short (Duration)
- Behavior doesn't happen correctly (Accuracy)
- Behavior takes too long to begin after a prompt (Latency)
- Behavior occurs but is inappropriate or inefficient (Topography)
- Behavior is too loud, forceful, or too soft, passive etc. (Intensity)

Behavior DISCREPANCY BEFORE Intervention

- What is the student's current level of performance, the baseline? 40 min. (A)
- What level of student performance would be acceptable? <10 min. (B)
- What is the discrepancy between the level of A and B? 30 min (C)
- What standard is used to determine the acceptable level of performance in Item B: peer performance / teacher expectation
  Standards: • Local norms • Peer performance • Criteria for the next environment • Instructional placement standards • Developmental standards • Teacher expectation • School policy/standards • Medical • Other--please specify]

Intervention Considerations

Beginning Date 10 / 17 / 94
(Mo Dy . Yr)

Direction of Change (I,D,M) D
(Increase Decrease Maintain)

Intervention Mode (D,S,G) D
(Developmental, Supplemental, Generalization)

Measurement Strategy [Who's responsible for doing the actual data collection, method of data collection, measurement conditions, monitoring schedule--frequency of data collection per week]

Ms. Stein will collect observational data 2 times per week for the complete school day. The duration of A.J.'s tantrums will be measured using a stopwatch.

Behavior DISCREPANCY AFTER Intervention

- What is the student's current level of performance? _____ (A)
- What level of student performance would be acceptable? _____ (B)
- What is the discrepancy between the level of A and B? _____ (C)
- What standard is used to determine the acceptable level of performance in Item B:_____
  Standards: • Local norms • Peer performance • Criteria for the next environment • Instructional placement standards • Developmental standards • Teacher expectation • School policy/standards • Medical • Other--please specify]

Outcome Data Ending Date ____/____/____ # Intervention Phases_____ Discrepancy Conclusion (M,S,L) ____
(Mo Dy Yr)　　　　　　　　　　　　　　　　　　　(More, Same, Less)

Performance Conclusion _____ [See code with five options below]

(1) Goal met or exceeded: Trendline slope is at or greater than slope of the goal line. (2) Goal not met but performance improved: Trendline slope reflects improvement in performance, but at a rate less than that designated by goal line. (3) Goal not met and performance did not improve or got worse: Trendline slope reflects little or no change from baseline performance or is moving away from the goal in an undesirable direction. (4) Data is not available, but the student is in school. (5) Data is not available, student has moved from school.

APPENDIX B

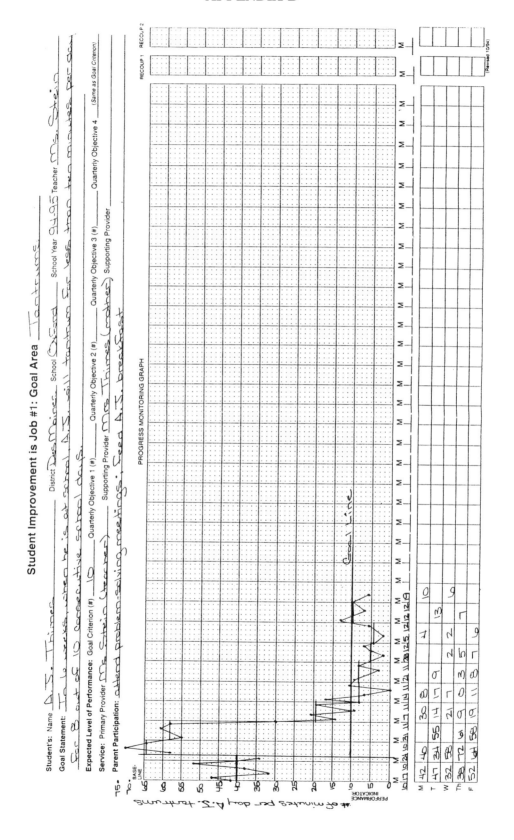

44

Best Practices in Facilitating Intervention Adherence

Cathy F. Telzrow
Cuyahoga Special Education Service Center, Ohio

OVERVIEW

Intervention adherence is the degree to which the consultee is committed to implement a specific intervention and actively demonstrates intervention-related behaviors (Meichenbaum & Turk, 1987). Closely related to intervention adherence is *treatment integrity*, a term that defines the degree to which a planned intervention is implemented as designed (Gresham, 1989). Intervention adherence and treatment integrity have been described as mutually dependent (Reimers, Wacker, & Koeppl, 1987), and together have been the critical variable in producing successful outcomes for students within a problem-solving model (Zins & Ponti, 1990). Even though "process variables," such as compliance with an approved problem-solving sequence, may be adhered to in designing an intervention, the effectiveness of that intervention cannot be determined adequately without a defensible level of intervention adherence and treatment integrity (Gresham, 1991). As stated succinctly by Reimers, Wacker, and Koeppl (1987), "treatments that are not implemented are actually not treatments at all. The same could be true for treatments which are not correctly implemented" (p. 222).

Intervention adherence encompasses a broad range of treatment arenas, including interventions developed for individuals and families in medical, therapeutic, or counseling settings. This chapter discusses intervention adherence by educational personnel in educational settings, particularly as delivered within the context of a problem-solving sequence.

BASIC CONSIDERATIONS

Intervention adherence within a problem-solving model has been conceptualized as having two major dimensions: the degree to which critical elements of the collaborative problem-solving process are adhered to, and the degree to which the designed intervention is implemented as planned (Fuchs, 1991; Gresham, 1991). Major variables associated with each of these dimensions will be described in greater detail below.

PERSONAL VARIABLES ASSOCIATED WITH INTERVENTION ADHERENCE

Consultee Variables

Hawryluk and Smallwood (1986) identified four major reasons why consultees seek assistance in educational settings: those related to knowledge (what to do), those related to skill (how to do it), the presence of certain thoughts, beliefs, or expectations (why it is important to do it), and the presence of facilitating or interfering affects (having the emotional resources to do it). Of these four variables, knowledge and skill deficits often may be addressed directly by the consultant's adopting an educative or modeling role. In contrast, adherence difficulties that are attributed to consultee cognitions or affects must be addressed through therapeutic techniques designed to help the consultee reframe beliefs or attributions about the concern and to develop a sense of competency and self-efficacy (Margolis & McGettigan, 1988).

Besides these four consultee variables, Sandoval, Lambert, and Davis (1981) identified several process variables that relate to the consultee's successful participation in school-based consultation: understanding how consultation differs from other contacts with mental health professionals; learning how to participate in a collaborative consultation; learning the consultant's role in a collaborative context; developing realistic expectations for consultation; and acquiring self-knowledge. Sandoval et al. (1981) caution that acquiring these skills is often time consuming, but can be facilitated by careful and intensive guidance by the consultant.

Consultant Variables

The literature on effective consultations repeatedly has identified the importance of both process and content skills (Gutkin, 1986), or what has been called the "artful science" of consultation (Idol & West, 1987).

Process skills: The art. A 100-number interdisciplinary, expert panel identified 47 collaborative competencies considered critical for regular and special educators interacting to meet the needs of disabled students in integrated settings (West & Cannon, 1988). Their top 10 competencies clustered into three areas: personal characteristics, interactive communication, and collaborative problem solving. Most of the frequently cited competencies involved effective interactive communication, such as clear oral and written communication, effective interviewing and listening skills, and the ability to manage confrontation successfully.

Similar emphasis on consultant process variables was demonstrated by Knoff, McKenna, and Riser (1991), who interpreted survey data from 177 university-based school psychology programs and 307 school psychology practitioners. They identified two somewhat different five-factor solutions of consultant variables. For both expert and practitioner samples, a factor sensitive to consultation process skills — comprising such characteristics as "able to confront without personal attacks," "prompt with feedback," and "documents for clear communication" — had the highest number of items. Pryzwansky (1989) reported that no linear relationship exists between the expression of such process skills and professional experience, suggesting that personal style characteristics may be a factor in the expression of such skills. Idol (1989) has argued that teaching the "art" of effective collaboration requires a different approach from instruction focusing on knowledge or content, and she recommends careful operationalization of desired behaviors and guided practice with feedback.

Content skills: The science. Transmission of content knowledge or information outside a collaborative context (i.e., the expert consultant model) may limit consultee investment in the intervention (Witt & Martens, 1988). Conversely, implementing an effective collaborative process without knowledge or content skills may produce a group of people who feel good, but don't know what to do (McConnell & Hecht, 1991). Some authors (e.g., Zins & Ponti, 1990) suggest that content skills have been underemphasized in the consultation literature, despite the fact that student-focused and organization-focused interventions are essential in order for consultation to be effective. Fuchs (1991) reported that lack of skill in identifying and implementing interventions was a major reason why consultations failed for difficult-to-teach students in the first year of a three-year Mainstream Assistance Team project.

McConnell and Hecht (1991) conceptualized school-based interventions as a dyad consisting of strategies to address social behavior problems and techniques to remedy academic difficulties. These authors have outlined a set of core competencies, in five areas, for school psychologists in instructional intervention: assessment for intervention; the organization and provision of educational activities; effective collaborative consultation; planning, implementing, and monitoring effective intervention; and research and evaluation competencies.

Ysseldyke and Christenson (1988) have summarized the literature on instructional design into a four-pronged system: planning procedures, management procedures, teaching procedures, and monitoring and evaluation procedures. These authors' assessment system (Ysseldyke & Christenson, 1993) is designed specifically to assess the instructional environment in order to match learner characteristics with the nature of instruction, including both task characteristics and the teacher's instructional and management style (Ysseldyke & Christenson, 1991). Their research emphasizes the complex, interactive nature of instructional design, and rejects a simplistic linear model for addressing student concerns.

SYSTEMIC VARIABLES RELATED TO INTERVENTION ADHERENCE

Besides personal variables involving consultants and consultees, systemic variables can influence intervention adherence. Examples of such variables include the nature of the intervention and the facilitating structures available.

Characteristics of Intervention

Intervention adherence is influenced to some degree by the nature of the intervention itself. Characteristics of the intervention that relate to intervention adherence include complexity, degree of positiveness, and perceived effectiveness (Reimers et al., 1987).

Martens, Peterson, Witt, and Cirone (1986) found that teachers prefer treatments they can implement independently over those requiring consultation with others. This "ease of use" variable also was identified by Gresham (1989), who reported that complex treatments requiring large amounts of time, materials, or staff members to implement usually are not delivered with the same treatment integrity as those that are less involved. However, some evidence shows that the complexity of the intervention plan may interact with the severity of the problem; teachers may demonstrate a preference for complex interventions where the demonstrated problem is severe (Elliott, Witt, & Kratochwill, 1991).

A second characteristic of the intervention plan that may affect treatment acceptability, and therefore adherence, is the degree to which it is perceived as educative or positive. Clark and Elliott (1988) reported that teachers consistently favored interventions using positive (e.g., modeling-coaching) over negative (e.g., overcorrection) approaches.

In addition to the complexity and positiveness of treatments, perceived effectiveness also relates to intervention adherence. Although actual effectiveness cannot be determined without a satisfactory trial, perceived effectiveness does relate to treatment acceptability. Specifically, low levels of intervention adherence typically follow if acceptability ratings of a proposed treatment are low (Elliott et al., 1991). Conversely, teachers rated interventions portrayed as being "strong and successful" higher than those presented as weak and comparatively unsuccessful (Clark & Elliott, 1988).

Support Structures

The presence or absence of adequate support structures is another important systemic variable for intervention adherence. Examples of such supports include building and classroom climate, human and material resources, and staff development opportunities. In their description of a six-year project to enhance student discipline by moving to consultation-based child study teams, Lennox, Hyman, and Hughes (1988) identified both organizational and individual facilitators and barriers to change. Besides these factors, an internal project manager who could convey and model expectations and assign essential resources was considered central to the success of this multiyear activity.

In a thoughtful discussion of ways to increase intervention adherence by teachers, Elliott et al. (1991) recommended adopting a systems orientation. This recommendation is based on several premises: that referrals for intervention typically arise from inappropriately arranged antecedents; that child-focused consultation may not reduce teacher concerns; and that the typical consultative relationship does not promote teacher empowerment. A systems orientation acknowledges the complex influences on an identified problem, and can manipulate those ecological and programming variables that contribute most to resolution of the concern (Witt & Martens, 1988).

BEST PRACTICES

Develop Shared Mission

Although intervention adherence is influenced by numerous variables, commitment to an intervention goal or purpose appears to be central (Gresham, 1989). Such commitment is often engendered through strategic planning that identifies a shared mission or purpose.

Henning-Stout and Conoley (1988) emphasize that "for real change to occur, the vehicles for change must be presented in a manner consistent with the values of the people within the system" (p. 472). They outline a process for influencing district-wide change, the "collective investment" approach. This process, a system-wide analog to collaborative problem solving, engenders commitment to a specified objective, while at the same time identifying actions necessary to achieve an outcome. In their description of a process for implementing consultation-based service delivery, Ponti, Zins, and Graden (1988) emphasize the importance of participatory planning.

Employ Collaborative Problem-Solving Process

Developing a shared vision or purpose is critical for collaborative problem-solving. Both the collaboration (the "art") and the problem solving (the "science") are crucial (Idol, 1989). Collaboration has several key features, including a nonhierarchical relationship among the parties involved, a climate of mutual trust and open communication, and shared responsibility for design and implementation of interventions (Zins & Ponti, 1990). Systematic problem solving — consisting of problem identification, goal setting, essential preintervention data collection, and progress monitoring — is considered critical for providing effective interventions for students (Fuchs, 1991). Data from an analysis of prereferral interventions in Iowa indicated a direct relationship between the presence of many of these "quality indicators" and the effectiveness of the intervention (Flugum & Reschly, 1992).

One resource to assist school personnel in applying a collaborative problem-solving process is displayed in Figure 1. I developed this Problem-Solving Assessment and Intervention Worksheet while providing technical support to four building-level teams as part of a statewide pilot project during the 1992–93 school year. This training tool, based on the work of Batsche (1990), Graden (1992), and resources from Iowa (*Understanding Components*, 1991), among others, outlines common pitfalls at each stage of the problem-solving process, and offers possible remedies or guiding questions that consultants might use to refocus the process and ensure the presence of key "quality indicators."

In implementing effective collaborative problem solving, careful consideration must be given to the systemic structures that can enhance its implementation. While investigating a three-year study of the effectiveness of Mainstream Assistance Teams on the academic and behavioral performance of difficult-to-teach students, Fuchs (1991) emphasized the importance of including intervention-oriented structures, such as role expectations, collaborative planning time, and an individual or team of individuals to direct such an effort. In addition, careful training of individuals in both the "art" and the "science" of consultation is essential (Fuchs, 1991).

FIGURE 1. **Problem-solving assessment and interventon worksheet.**

Student _____ Grade ____ Teacher(s) _____

Date of Referral _____ Date of Problem Analysis Meeting _____

Collaborators _____ _____

_____ _____

_____ _____

_____ _____

_____ _____

Step 1. Behavioral description of problem (including baseline data) _____

_____

_____

_____

_____

_____

_____

_____

Common Pitfalls	**Guiding Questions/Possible Remedies**
1. Concern is vague or general.	• What is it you would like _____ to do to be successful?
	• What would it be like if the problem weren't there?
2. Description is not behavioral.	• What does _____ look like?
3. Jumping to generating interventions before problem is analyzed.	• Do we fully understand the problem yet?
4. No baseline data on problem behavior.	• Knowledgeable team member assists in collecting data.

Step 2. Behavioral statement of desired goal or outcome _____

_____

_____

_____

_____

_____

_____

_____

_____

Common Pitfalls	**Guiding Questions**
1. Goal is vague, not in quantifiable terms.	• Would we have the goal if we reversed the description of the problem?
2. Stating the goal in "eliminative" or "dead person's" terms (i.e., absence of behavior).	• What are the replacement behaviors we would like to substitute for the problem behaviors?

Step 3. Analyze the problem by generating and testing hypotheses about why the behavior is occurring:

_____ occurs because _____
(Problem Behavior)   (Hypothesis)

Guiding Process

1. Generate hypotheses in all categories
 	
    a. Curriculum
    b. Instruction
    c. School/classroom environment
    d. Peers
    e. Home/Community
    f. Child characteristics
 	
2. Test the likelihood of each hypothesis by making prediction statements:
 	
    If _____, then _____
       (Positively phrased hypothesis)   (Desired outcome/goal)
 	
3. Determine need for collecting additional data to help analyze problem. *Collect only essential data.*
 	
4. If necessary, adjourn and reconvene after essential data are collected.

Step 4. Given hypothesized reason for problem, brainstorm possible interventions.

_____
_____
_____
_____
_____
_____

Common Pitfalls	**Guiding Questions**
1. Evaluating ideas as they are generated. 2. Limiting suggestions to what is currently in place.	• Let's just list ideas now, and evaluate later. • If we could do anything, what intervention would we design?

Step 5. Evaluate alternatives and select intervention. (Star alternative above)

Common Pitfalls	**Guiding Questions**
1. Tendency to see a specific place or person as an intervention. 2. Selecting interventions that are unrelated to the hypothesized reason for the problem. 3. Giving referring teacher sole responsibility for implementing interventions.	• Is that an intervention, or a place where intervention occurs? • Will that intervention address the cause of the problem? • How can we share responsibility for implementation?

Step 6. Clarify the intervention and develop action plan, goal, monitoring procedure, and review date.

By _____, student will _____
       (Review Date)   (Behavioral Goal)

as demonstrated by _____,
                      (Monitoring Procedure)

as a result of this intervention: _____
                      (What and how much)

to be implemented by _____, _____
                   (who)   (when)

and insured by _____
                  (treatment integrity procedure)

Common Pitfalls	Guiding Questions
1. Failure to specify goal or review data.	• What do we expect and when do we expect it?
2. Failure to thoroughly describe intervention.	• How will _____ (Social skills training, etc.) be implemented?
3. Failure to incorporate monitoring procedure.	• What data will we use to evaluate the effectiveness of this intervention on the review date?

Step 7. Implement the intervention and provide for long-term carryover as necessary.

Common Pitfalls	Possible Remedies
1. There is no commitment to implement plan (intervention adherence).	• Problem-solve about reasons why and develop plan to address (consider perceived effectiveness and ease of use).
2. Intervention is not implemented as planned (treatment integrity).	• Provide training, guided practice.
3. Intervention is restricted to a specialized service.	• Strategy is taught to others.

Step 8. Evaluate the effectiveness of the intervention, compare results to baseline or target goal, and continue or revise plan as necessary.

Summary of Intervention Effectiveness (Attached graphed data comparing results to baseline and target goal).

_____
_____
_____
_____
_____
_____

Common Pitfalls	Possible Remedies
1. Data from monitoring procedure are not available.	• Clarify/review monitoring procedure.
2. There is no evidence of treatment integrity.	• Provide for consistency in implementation through observation, self-monitoring.

Select and Specify Intervention

The literature suggests that intervention adherence may be fostered by selecting interventions that are relatively easy to implement (i.e., do not require excessive amounts of time, personnel, or materials); have perceived treatment effectiveness; and are constructive or educative, rather than reductive or eliminative (Elliott et al., 1991). Fuchs (1991) noted that for interventions to be effective they must be "feasible," a factor that varies from individual to individual, thus requiring continual redefinition. Working with other school personnel and parents, school psychologists may be in a unique position to convey information about interventions with demonstrated treatment effectiveness (Forness & Kavale, 1991).

Besides selecting interventions that are most likely to be implemented successfully, one must clarify the specifications of the intervention plan (Gresham, 1989). Intervention adherence and treatment integrity may be facilitated by completing a simple statement summarizing the planned intervention, such as that shown in Step 6 of Figure 1. A similar approach, specific to the use of contingency contract procedures, is illustrated by Fuchs (1991).

As is implied by the possible pitfalls and guiding questions associated with Step 6 in Figure 1, the specific nature of the intervention must be described and understood clearly by educational personnel (Fuchs, 1991). Generic descriptions of an intervention, such as "social skills training" or "differential reinforcement of other behavior (DRO)" are not adequate to ensure standardization of treatment (Gresham, Gansle, Noell, Cohen, & Rosenbaum, 1993). Some successful programs have developed specific treatment protocols for commonly employed interventions (Fuchs, 1991; Willis & LaVigna, n.d.). These protocols provide a written, step-by-step guideline for implementation of specific interventions. Often these should be accompanied by additional supports, such as those described in the following section.

Provide Support Structures

Successfully designing, implementing, and maintaining interventions to address students' academic and behavioral problems is a complex and sometimes fragile process. Zins and Ponti (1990) identified several characteristics of the process that, being nonreinforcing for consultees, may produce resistance. Part of the responsibility of effective consultants is to anticipate each barrier and to employ appropriate support structures (Margolis & McGettigan, 1988).

Physical/cognitive supports. One example of physical or cognitive supports that can enhance intervention adherence is the delivery of modeling and guided practice in implementing specific academic or behavioral interventions (Margolis & McGettigan, 1988; Zins & Ponti, 1990). In my experience, treatment integrity is often directly related to an incomplete or inaccurate understanding of how to implement a specific treatment. Even concepts that appear relatively straightforward (e.g., ignoring problem behaviors) may require demonstration and feedback so that they are implemented correctly.

A second consideration is the recognition and arrangement of systemic structures to facilitate effective school-based interventions. The provision of such supports relates directly to the first two elements, a shared mission and a collaborative process. Witt and Martens (1988) suggested that one cannot assume "that a clear cut solution exists for each and every classroom management problem, and can be applied independently of ongoing instructional practices" (p. 212). This view was expanded by Martens and Kelly (1993), who emphasized that desired student behavioral outcomes are fostered not through isolated treatment strategies, but through an effective instructional program that serves as a vehicle for stimulus control.

As Elliott et al. (1991) emphasized, effective interventions often require modification of system variables. These authors reject an intervention model that adopts a simplistic problem-to-treatment sequence, and advocate instead a system of teacher empowerment that recognizes the complex ecological framework in which educational interventions occur. One intervention model that incorporates systems change and teacher empowerment is the Comprehensive Classroom Management Project (*Strategies for Developing*, 1992). Developed by a statewide task force of educators and parents in Ohio, and piloted in several districts across the state during 1992–93, the Comprehensive Classroom Management Project "recommends that school districts adopt a systemic, positive, proactive, and instructional approach to classroom management" (p. 5). Development of school-community partnerships and systematic building-level collaborative problem solving are important components. The planning guide argues that rather than implementing short-term, reactive strategies to address behavioral concerns, schools should examine ecological variables that contribute to student discipline problems, such as school climate, aspects of curriculum and instruction, and formal discipline procedures.

Psychological/affective supports. Intervention adherence sometimes is impaired by the interventionist's beliefs or attitudes about the student, himself or herself, or the work setting. In such instances, the school psychologist may facilitate interventions by providing psychological or affective supports.

Analyzing the research on managing resistance in implementing interventions in mainstreamed classrooms, Margolis and McGettigan (1988) outlined several key considerations for consultants. Among these are the provision of interpersonal support, such as empathy and encouragement. Recognizing and understanding the enormous stress of working with students with significant academic or behavioral challenges may help overcome teachers' resistance. Offering concrete or therapeutic strategies for stress reduction, such as time for dialogue, relieving a teacher periodically, or occasional team teaching, goes a long way in conveying to teachers the true sense of "shared responsibility."

Employ Effective Monitoring Systems

By employing effective monitoring systems, such as those described below, the integrity of interventions can be enhanced (Elliott et al., 1991). Such mechanisms can help identify the need for additional supports for intervention adherence and treatment integrity.

Observation. Periodic structured observations during the course of intervention can identify barriers to intervention adherence and treatment integrity. Gresham (1989) delineates three steps to determine the integrity of interventions: explicit specification of the intervention components; direct observation to identify the occurrence and nonoccurrence of each component; and computation of the percent of intervention components implemented, to derive an index of treatment integrity. Additional considerations include the number of observations necessary and the effect of the observation itself on the implementation of the intervention.

Self-monitoring. Incorporating a self-monitoring strategy into the treatment program also may facilitate intervention adherence. Gresham (1989) provided an example of a self-monitoring procedure designed to assess and enhance treatment integrity. But he cautioned that such methods may be difficult to implement in some classroom setting because of competing activities.

Program Status Report. LaVigna, Willis, and Sweitzer (1990) have developed a specific strategy to enhance intervention adherence and treatment integrity for personnel working with individuals with moderate to profound developmental disabilities. This technique employs a systematic checklist of the program components considered important for the target student. Called the Program Status Report (PSR), this checklist is developed via consensus by interventionists, and is completed regularly through self-monitoring or through observation by a consultant. Illustrative program components incorporated into the PSR include current individualized education programs (IEPs), written behavioral plans, and regular monitoring data. The standards reflected on the PSR must be essential yet realistic program elements that are explicitly defined and verifiable through direct observation or permanent product (LaVigna et al., 1990).

Use of the PSR enables one to identify discrepancies between desired program components and actual characteristics of the intervention, and to seek remedies. LaVigna et al. (1990) have reported that systematic use of the PSR can enhance staff consistency in implementing interventions. Furthermore, they have identified a direct relationship between such staff consistency and client behavior. Specifically, if staff consistency ratings on the PSR are 85% or higher, problem behavior in populations of individuals with severe challenging behavior is reduced dramatically.

Incorporate Review/Trouble-Shooting Mechanism

When effective monitoring systems, such as those just described, are employed, problems with intervention adherence and treatment integrity often can be identified. However, without the inclusion of a review or trouble-shooting mechanism, it is difficult to design a viable remedy for the situation. The problem-solving process incorporates a review step to examine monitoring data and determine whether to continue or revise the intervention (see Figure 1, Step 8). This review must examine not only student outcome data (i.e., the progress toward the identified student goal), but also data describing the degree of intervention adherence.

SUMMARY

For the effectiveness of a given intervention to be determined, it must be implemented actively (intervention adherence) and correctly (treatment integrity). Inadequate attention to these two critical elements may produce erroneous conclusions about the effectiveness of specific treatments of students' school-related problems (Gresham et al., 1993).

In the context of educational consultation, intervention adherence may be influenced both by personal variables, such as the behavior of consultants and consultees, and by systemic variables, such as the nature of the intervention and the presence or absence of certain support structures. Intervention adherence and treatment integrity can be facilitated by the following practices:

- Employment of participatory planning to create a shared vision for the education of students and the design of intervention;

- Implementation of collaborative problem solving that engenders commitment to the intervention and incorporates key predictors of intervention effectiveness;

- Selection of interventions that are both feasible and effective and the careful specification of strategies so they are clearly understood by interventionists;

- Provision of both cognitive (e.g., information, training) and affective (e.g., encouragement, empathy) supports, preferably within an ecological framework;

- Incorporation of effective monitoring systems that can determine whether designed interventions have been implemented actively and correctly;

- Employment of formative and summative evaluation, to ascertain the need for revision in variables in order to improve intervention adherence and treatment integrity.

REFERENCES

Batsche, G. (1990). *Components of problem-solving: Defining and describing behaviors* [Videotape]. Des Moines: Iowa Department of Education.

Clark, L., & Elliott, S. N. (1988). The influence of treatment strength information on knowledgeable teachers' pretreatment evaluations of social skills training methods. *Professional School Psychology, 3,* 241–251.

Elliott, S. N., Witt, J. C., & Kratochwill, T. R. (1991). Selecting, implementing, and evaluating classroom interventions. In G. Stoner, M. R. Shinn, & H. M. Walker (Eds.), *Interventions for achievement and behavior problems* (pp. 99–135). Silver Spring, MD: National Association of School Psychologists.

Flugum, K. R., & Reschly, D. J. (1992, January 23). *Quality of prereferral interventions and outcomes for learning and behavioral problems.* Des Moines: Iowa Department of Education.

Forness, S. R., & Kavale, K. A. (1991). School psychologists' roles and functions: integration into the regular classroom. In G. Stoner, M. R. Shinn, & Walker, H. M. (Eds.), *Interventions for achievement and behavior problems* (pp. 21–36). Silver Spring, MD: National Association of School Psychologists.

Fuchs, D. (1991). Mainstream assistance teams: A prereferral intervention system for difficult-to-teach students. In G. Stoner, M. R. Shinn, & H. M. Walker (Eds.), *Interventions for achievement and behavior problems* (pp. 241–268). Silver Spring, MD: National Association of School Psychologists.

Graden, J. L. (1992, October 1). *Collaboration for educational reform.* Workshop presented for Cuyahoga Special Education Service Center, Maple Heights, OH.

Gresham, F. M. (1989). Assessment of treatment integrity in school consultation and prereferral intervention. *School Psychology Review, 18,* 37–50.

Gresham, F. M. (1991). Whatever happened to functional analysis in behavioral consultation? *Journal of Educational and Psychological Consultation, 2,* 387–392.

Gresham, F. M., Gansle, K. A., Noell, G. H., Cohen, S., & Rosenblum, S. (1993). Treatment integrity of school-based behavioral intervention studies: 1980–1990. *School Psychology Review, 22,* 254–272.

Gutkin, T. R. (1986). Consultees' perceptions of variables relating to the outcomes of school-based consultation interactions. *School Psychology Review, 15,* 375–382.

Hawryluk, M. K., & Smallwood, D. L. (1986). Assessing and addressing consultee variables in school-based behavioral consultation. *School Psychology Review, 15,* 519–528.

Henning-Stout, M., & Conoley, J. C. (1988). Influencing program change at the district level. In J. L. Graden, J. E. Zins, & M. J. Curtis (Eds.), *Alternative educational delivery systems: En-*

hancing instructional options for all students (pp. 471–490). Washington, DC: National Association of School Psychologists.

Idol, L. (1989). Reaction to Walter Pryzwansky's presidential address to the American Psychological Association on School Psychology. *Professional School Psychology, 4,* 15–19.

Idol, L., & West, J. F. (1987). Consultation in special education (Part II): Training and practice. *Journal of Learning Disabilities, 20,* 474–494.

Knoff, H. M., McKenna, A. F., & Riser, K. (1991). Toward a consultant effectiveness scale: Investigating the characteristics of effective consultants. *School Psychology Review, 20,* 81–96.

LaVigna, G. W., Willis, T. J., & Sweitzer, M. (1990). *Maximizing staff consistency in program implementation.* Los Angeles: Institute for Applied Behavior Analysis.

Lennox, N., Hyman, I. A., & Hughes, C. A. (1988). Institutionalization of a consultation-based service delivery system. In J. L. Graden, J. E. Zins, & M. J. Curtis (Eds.), *Alternative educational delivery systems: Enhancing instructional options for all students* (pp. 71–90). Washington, DC: National Association of School Psychologists.

Margolis, H., & McGettigan, J. (1988). Managing resistance to instructional modifications in mainstreamed environments. *Remedial and Special Education, 9*(4), 15–21.

Martens, B. K., & Kelly, S. Q. (1993). A behavioral analysis of effective teaching. *School Psychology Quarterly, 8,* 10–26.

Martens, B. K., Peterson, R. L., Witt, J. C., & Cirone, S. (1986). Teacher perceptions of school-based interventions. *Exceptional Children, 53,* 213–223.

McConnell, S. R., & Hecht, M. (1991). Instructional problems and interventions: Training needs for school psychologists. In G. Stoner, M. R. Shinn, & H. M. Walker (Eds.), *Interventions for achievement and behavior problems* (pp. 741–762). Silver Spring, MD: National Association of School Psychologists.

Meichenbaum, D., & Turk, D. C. (1987). *Facilitating treatment adherence: A practitioner's guidebook.* New York: Plenum Press.

Ponti, C. R., Zins, J. E., & Graden, J. L. (1988). Implementing a consultation-based service delivery system to decrease referrals for special education: A case study of organizational considerations. *School Psychology Review, 17,* 89–100.

Pryzwansky, W. B. (1989). School consultation: Some considerations from a cognitive psychology perspective. *Professional School Psychology, 4,* 1–14.

Reimers, T. M., Wacker, D. P., & Koeppl, G. (1987). Acceptability of behavioral interventions: A review of the literature. *School Psychology Review, 16,* 212–227.

Sandoval, J., Lambert, N. M., & Davis, J. M. (1981). Consultation from the consultee's perspective. In M. J. Curtis & J. E. Zins, *The theory and practice of school consultation* (pp. 174–183). Springfield, IL: Charles C Thomas.

Strategies for developing a comprehensive classroom management system. (1992). Columbus: Ohio Department of Education.

Understanding components of the problem-solving process: A collection of information papers to assist professionals. (1991, January). Des Moines: Iowa Department of Education.

West, J. F., & Cannon, G. S. (1988). Essential collaborative consultation competencies for regular and special educators. *Journal of Learning Disabilities, 21,* 56–63.

Willis, T. J., & LaVigna, G. W. (undated). *Assessment and intervention: A writing guide.* Los Angeles: Institute for Applied Behavior Analysis.

Witt, J. C., & Martens, B. K. (1988). Problems with problem-solving consultation: A re-analysis of assumptions, methods, and goals. *School Psychology Review, 17,* 211–226.

Ysseldyke, J. E., & Christenson, S. L. (1993). *The instructional environment system* (TIES-II). Longmont, CO: Sopris West.

Ysseldyke, J. E., & Christenson, S. L. (1988). Linking assessment to intervention. In J. L. Graden, J. E. Zins, & M. J. Curtis (Eds.), *Alternative educational delivery systems: Enhancing instructional options for all students* (pp. 91–109). Washington, DC: National Association of School Psychologists.

Zins, J. E., & Ponti, C. R. (1990). Best practices in school-based consultation. In A. Thomas & J. Grimes (Eds.), *Best practices in school psychology II* (pp. 673–693). Washington, DC: National Association of School Psychologists.

ANNOTATED BIBLIOGRAPHY

Elliot, S. N., Witt, J. C., & Kratochwill, T. R. (1991). Selecting, implementing, and evaluating classroom interventions. In G. Stoner, M. R. Shinn, & H. M. Walker (Eds.), *Interventions for achievement and behavior problems* (pp. 99–135). Silver Spring, MD: National Association of School Psychologists.
This chapter provides a review of research related to selecting, implementing, and evaluating the effectiveness of educationally-based interventions. It outlines variables associated with treatment acceptability and advocates a model for enhancing teacher empowerment and intervention compliance. The chapter concludes with a thorough discussion of issues related to treatment integrity.

Gresham, F. M. (1989). Assessment of treatment integrity in school consultation and prereferral intervention. *School Psychology Review, 18,* 37–50.
This article provides an excellent summary of the literature on treatment integrity. It describes factors associated with treatment integrity in educational settings, and illustrates strategies for evaluating treatment integrity.

Understanding components of the problem-solving process: A collection of information papers to assist professionals. (1991, January). Des Moines: Iowa Department of Education.
This resource consists of 10 information papers focusing on various aspects of problem solving. Developed by a council of instructional and support service representatives from the Iowa Area Education Agencies, this collection provides a concise but substantive introduction to the key indicators of effective student interventions.

Zins, J. E., & Ponti, C. R. (1990). Best practices in school-based consultation. In A. Thomas & J. Grimes (Eds.), *Best practices in school psychology-II* (pp. 673–693). Washington, DC: National Association of School Psychologists.
This chapter provides an excellent overview of school-based consultation, including sections devoted to collaborative problem-solving and intervention assistance process. Intervention effectiveness and follow-up are discussed, including a summary of the literature on intervention adherence and treatment integrity.

45

Best Practices in Program Modification and Exit Decisions

Julie Schendel
Joe Ulman
Iowa Department of Education
Lakeland AEA 3, Cylinder, IA

OVERVIEW

This chapter describes a strategy to determine when to alter special education programs and services in both academic and nonacademic areas. Decisions related to program modification represent extremely important judgments concerning the appropriateness of ongoing special educational programming. Included in those decisions are questions regarding when to modify the type or intensity of programming being offered as well as when to exit a student from all assistance. Guidelines in both areas will be offered.

The regulations of both Public Law 94-142 (the Education for All Handicapped Children Act of 1975) and the Individuals with Disabilities Education Act (IDEA, 1990, Public Law 101-476) provide limited assistance in program modification and exit decisions. Only initial placement decisions receive considerable attention (for example see Section 300.533, CFR or Section 1412 of IDEA). Other program modification issues, such as exit criteria or the basis for changes in the level of special education service a child should be receiving, are omitted. Instead it is only indicated that programs will be evaluated at least annually (IDEA stipulates they be "reviewed" every six months) with limited structure offered regarding what is to be contained in that effort (see Section 300.552, CFR or Section 1477 [b] of IDEA).

Likewise, little help is available in the educational literature regarding special education program modification and exit decision-making. An earlier document by the authors, *Performance Monitoring of Academic and Non-Academic Behaviors* (1990), provided methods for determining student change in both academic and nonacademic behaviors. Although useful in deciding when to change or modify a specific intervention, the document did not address program modification and exit issues.

Allen (1989) suggested two possible reasons why program modification and exit appear so infrequently in the literature. First, he hypothesized that data typically are not collected on student exit from special education because it is not a common event. A second hypothesis was related to the possibility that sufficient data were not available regarding student performance to allow program modification and exit decisions to be made reliably. Both explanations have been consistent with the authors' experience. For example, decisions related to program change have been based upon published achievement and ability tests. This information has been collected infrequently and analyzed unsystematically — typically during annual review meetings. Because of the lack of a curriculum match between published test content and classroom expectations, predictions of student success in a different environment have been impossible.

Although these hypotheses are plausible, it is the authors' opinion that a more problematic and pervasive explanation exists for the lack of information and guidance on program modification and exit issues. This hypothesis suggests that there is a fundamentally flawed philosophy within the educational community regarding the nature of student skill deficits and disability. Traditionally, disability has been viewed as an internal trait of the student and has provided the basis of eligibility and placement within special education programs and services. Within this philosophical viewpoint, disability has been seen as being within the child, permanent, and virtually unalterable. If appropriately identified (truly disabled), children have been expected to make limited growth and to require long-term assistance. Although remediation of the symptoms of the disability has been the focus, it has been accepted that, once identified, a student would in all likelihood, have the disability for at least his or her academic life and therefore would be continually eligible for (and therefore placed in) special education. Given the invariable nature of a disability in this type of belief system, significant effort has been focused upon initial eligibility issues, with complex formulas being developed to ensure that only the truly disabled are served. Also because of this orientation, sensitive data regarding student progress and special education exit criteria have not been a central issue. Actually, improvement in a student's skills to a level which put the student in "jeopardy" of losing special education eligibility often has resulted in Individualized Education Program (IEP) teams developing new and innovative areas of need which had less measurable criteria for eligibility (e.g., study/organizational skills) and would therefore allow the student to continue in the program.

In contrast, the model presented in this chapter views the issues of disability and need as being identical. Students' need for assistance defines their eligibility for service. There is no search for internal traits to determine disability. "Disability" status is assigned when a child's performance is found to be sufficiently different from peer performance to require specialized services not available in the regular education setting. Likewise, program modification and exit are based upon a similar analysis of the degree of need shown by the child when compared to peers. If, over a designated period of time, a student is found to be resistive to intervention attempts or, conversely, is found to reach a performance level acceptable within a less restrictive education setting, program modification or exit is initiated. The degree of special assistance is determined through analysis of the student's actual performance. This "performance monitoring" approach is consistent with, and discussed in depth in a chapter within this book (see Marston, Performance Monitoring).

BASIC CONSIDERATIONS

Why Are Students Continued in Special Programs?

There appears to be a number of reasons why students are maintained within a special education setting after they have made sufficient progress to have their programs modified. The following represent a partial listing.

1. *Lack of reliable data.* Perhaps the most frequent reason why students remain in a more restrictive setting than they require is simply that no one collects the correct data to determine their educational needs (Allen, 1989). Information about student performance most readily available to IEP teams at the time of program reviews is usually published, norm-referenced test results. This type of information has been found to be virtually useless in making significant program decisions about children (Jenkins & Pany, 1978; Good & Salvia, 1987), because it does not describe a student's growth over time and because the comparison group is a national sample rather than the more appropriate norm group of the less restrictive environment.

2. *Lack of communication systems between regular and special education staff.* In some circumstances, students are maintained in special education settings because there is a lack of systematic communication between regular and special education personnel. Often there is a perception by special education staff that if a child is exited from the special education program, coordination between programs will be limited and the techniques necessary for success will not be used. In these circumstances, a child is seen as needing to be completely able to function in a regular setting with no regular education modifications (a standard which is not met by many regular education students).

3. *Transitions.* Occasionally, students are maintained in special education due to an upcoming transition (elementary to junior high, movement from one building to another, change in teaching staff, etc.). There is a fear that if the child is exited at this critical time, progress may be lost and the child's skills may suffer. Rather than develop a support strategy to minimize the effects of the transition, teams determine that "now is not the time."

4. *Lack of clearly defined goals.* When goals for determining success are defined loosely (e.g., grade-level reading skills, recommendation of the IEP team, etc.), students are maintained in special education because any positive growth is seen as a measure of program success. In these circumstances, IEP teams may take an "if it ain't broke, don't fix it" orientation toward exiting students. Without criteria for successful re-entry into a less restrictive environment, the question of exit is never seriously discussed.

5. *Over protection/learned helplessness.* When special education programs take on the role of "protecting the disabled students" from the expectations of a less restrictive setting, students are placed into a circumstance that makes it difficult for them to return to such a setting. Goals for student performance must be anchored in functional skills demanded in the target setting.

6. *Current funding formulas.* Under the funding procedures in many states, school districts are provided added money to serve students within their districts who are identified as disabled. Special education teachers are often paid from those funds. If too many students are exited from a program, the amount of special education dollars available in the district might be less than the amount needed to hire the teacher. This procedure adds an unfortunate pressure to the decisions regarding the exiting of students from special education.

7. *Reinforcing nature of continued placement.* Those students currently being considered for exit from the special education setting are typically those evidencing a great deal of progress. These are usually

the same students who are the most rewarding for the special education teacher to maintain (achieving their goals, positive self attitude, etc.). This adds a disincentive for the special education teacher to exit the student from the program.

8. *Lack of knowledge of regular education expectations.* Typically, special education personnel do not know what is expected of a regular education student within a specific classroom. It is difficult to recommend exit from a special program entirely without a clear understanding of the typical performance level within the regular program.

9. *Parent request.* In some circumstances, parents will request that their child be maintained within the special program. Often this is because of the difficulties their child had in regular education prior to the provision of special education. Often, the data necessary to reassure parents by showing them how their child's performance compares to regular education classroom performance are lacking.

BEST PRACTICES

In the absence of specific legal guidelines and empirical research, the following procedures are suggested as an approach to program change.

When Should Program Change Be Considered?

One of the topics for discussion at annual review meetings is the pupil's need for continued special education placement. In the past, this annual review might have offered the only opportunity for considering a placement change due to the fact that it was the only time during the academic year when an attempt was made to formally measure a student's progress toward long-term goals. Although teachers might have regularly collected information on a student's acquisition of short-term objectives, a more comprehensive assessment of progress needed for placement decisions might have occurred only at annual review time. Under this traditional system, some students may have been maintained in special education placements longer than necessary simply because of a lack of comprehensive, long-term data at an earlier date.

The adoption of a performance-monitoring approach to evaluating student progress offers more frequent opportunities to consider a possible change in placement. Because student performance data are collected and analyzed continuously, recent information is always available about a student's progress toward long-term goals. If the data suggest that long-term goals have been achieved, consideration may be given to a change in placement at any time.

What Factors Should Be Considered in Determining Whether a Placement Change Is Warranted?

The evaluation which resulted in a student's placement into a special education program was multifaceted and comprehensive. Ideally, it should have examined not only student variables such as motivation and mastery of academic subskills but also characteristics of the curriculum and learning environment. These same factors need to be considered when making a decision about changing a student's placement. Each of these factors will be considered in turn.

Student variables. One important factor suggesting that a placement change is warranted is demonstration of improvement in the deficit area(s) that first prompted a student's placement in special education. For example, a placement change might be warranted for a student who has shown significant decrease in disruptive or aggressive behaviors, if these were the deficit areas originally identified as educational needs. Two questions need to be answered in order to determine whether sufficient improvement has been shown to warrant a change in placement:

1. Has the student met his or her IEP goals?

2. Is the student performance sufficient to meet the expectations of an alternate setting or, in other words, is the student functioning at a level similar to that of peers in the new setting?

The first question requires an individually referenced comparison that examines an individual student's rate and level of performance at different times under different instructional conditions (e.g., regular classroom instruction vs. resource room instruction). If a given instructional placement has been beneficial, then the student's level of performance should have changed to be similar to that prescribed by the IEP goal. In other words, the student's performance should be better than it was prior to the implementation of a given program.

A satisfactory response to the first question, however, is not enough to suggest that a change in placement is appropriate. The attainment of a specific IEP goal does not always mean that the student has sufficient skills to meet the expectations of an alternate setting. Most frequently, students are placed in special education programs because their performance is significantly discrepant from that of peers. For students who demonstrate very significant deficits in skills, the attainment of a given IEP goal may represent only a partial reduction of the initial discrepancy that warranted a special education placement. These students may continue to require special education services until their discrepancy in skills has been significantly reduced or eliminated.

The expectations of an alternate setting (i.e., the mainstream) are usually defined in terms of local norms. The second question, then, requires a norm-referenced comparison of an individual student's performance with that of a particular peer group. Don Allen (1989) describes two different comparisons which might be made to peer groups in the mainstream setting. First, the most common comparison might be made to "average" peers or the "average level of functioning" within a given classroom or grade level. It has been suggested, however, that this comparison might be too strict a standard because not all students in the mainstream perform exactly at the level of "average" peers. A more reasonable expectation might be defined by a comparison to lower functioning students within a classroom. For example, a reasonable performance expectation might be defined as an oral reading rate similar to that of students in the low reading group. While this level of performance is likely to be lower than the "average" for a given classroom, it may be viewed as describing the minimum level of performance necessary to be successful in the mainstream setting.

As student performance approaches that level of the IEP goal and mainstream expectations, the question arises as to how consistently or for how long a period of time the student must demonstrate this level of performance before a change in placement is considered. Unfortunately, at the current time, there is no empirical answer to this question. Obviously, it would be expected that the student demonstrate the appropriate level of performance with sufficient consistency to prove that its attainment was not just a fluke. At the same time, requiring the student to demonstrate a given level of performance for too long a time may delay an appropriate change in program. As a rule of thumb, IEP teams may wish to initiate consideration for a change in placement as soon as student performance begins to approximate defined levels. As the team formulates a plan for change, student performance can continue to be monitored and, if the team feels that a sufficiently stable pattern of behavior has been demonstrated, the program change can take place.

The attainment of a defined level of skill is probably the first variable that IEP teams will examine when considering a change in placement. However, it should not be the only one. Not only must a student have acquired a given skill, he or she must also be able to demonstrate that skill in the new setting. To demonstrate a given skill, the student must have acquired what are broadly termed "classroom survival skills" such as attention to task, organizational skills, and work completion rates. A data-based examination of student performance in comparison to peers will provide the IEP team with useful information about the degree to which a student might be successful in the mainstream setting and also about which skills the student needs to acquire and/or demonstrate consistently. Some students will require specific instruction in classroom survival skills as well as instruction in academic areas. Other students may be competent to perform a given skill but may have difficulty generalizing a given behavior to a different setting.

When considering whether deficits in classroom survival skills exist, the IEP team needs to consider the range of peer performance within a given setting. Some students will demonstrate a high level of functioning, while others will function at a much lower, but still acceptable, level according to classroom standards and teacher expectations. For example, some students may remain on task virtually 100% of the time, while others may be on task only 75–80% of the time. To avoid establishing unreasonably high standards for an individual student, the team may wish to define a minimum level of acceptable performance for a given behavior. This standard might not represent a high level of functioning or even an average level of functioning for peers but would still be within the range of acceptable performance.

If deficits in classroom survival skills exist, the IEP team is faced with the choice of either maintaining the student in special education until the appropriate skills have been acquired, or changing the student's program to an alternate setting and providing support and skill training in that setting. If the student enters the new environment without a given survival skill, not only will he or she require instruction and support, but also the new environment must be willing and able to make modifications for the student that will allow him or her to be successful until the new skill is acquired. It might be argued that many students would find it easier to learn a skill in the setting in which it is expected to be used rather than attempting to generalize a skill from one environment to another.

Some questions which need to be considered as the IEP team examines classroom survival skills are

1. How well is the student able to maintain attention on a given task and remain undistracted, not only in small-group settings but also in large-group activities and independent-study periods?

2. How well does the student make use of work time? Does the student begin work on a task promptly and without individual attention from the teacher?

3. What is the student's rate of work completion? Can the student complete a given task within a reasonable amount of time?

4. How is student performance in the area of assignment completion? Does the student take responsibility for completing assignments or are frequent reminders and monitoring necessary in order for the student to follow through?

5. Does the student ask for help when necessary, and is the student able to do so appropriately? Does the student attempt to resolve problems independently or does he or she ask for help excessively?

6. How are the student's organizational skills? Does the student remember to bring necessary books and supplies to class? Does the student keep track of assignments and remember to turn them in on time?

7. Does the student demonstrate appropriate classroom behavior? Does he or she follow rules about raising one's hand before speaking, cooperating with other students, and the like? Are there any problems with behavior in other settings such as the hallway, bathroom, lunchroom, or playground?

8. How well can the student follow oral and written directions? Does the student attend while directions are presented? Must directions be repeated, shortened, or somehow altered for the student to understand?

9. How are the student's social skills? Does the student interact appropriately with peers and adults? Can the student take turns, share materials, handle teasing or criticism, and so forth?

10. How appropriately does the student participate in group activities? Does the student attend during group discussions? Does the student volunteer pertinent ideas and answers? Does the student take an active role in group projects?

A final student variable necessary to consider when discussing a placement change is the student's attitude toward the change. Some topics to discuss with the student include expectations for success or failure in the alternate setting, concerns or fears about making the change, and the types of assistance the student might feel are necessary to be successful in the new program. A similar discussion with the student's parents might help to identify factors which need to be addressed prior to or after a change in placement.

Curriculum-instructional-environmental variables. Examining student variables alone is not sufficient to determine whether a placement change is appropriate or whether the student can be successful if such a change is effected. The IEP team also needs to assess the degree of similarity in the curriculum and instruction between the special education and regular education environments.

For some students, particularly those with more severe skill deficits, curriculum materials and instructional procedures used in the special education setting may be significantly different from those used in regular education. Alternate curriculum materials may introduce new skills in a different sequence or manner than the regular education curriculum, may provide more opportunities for practice of one skill before another is introduced, or may emphasize one approach to learning a skill rather than another (e.g., a phonetic approach to reading rather than a sight word approach). Instructional procedures used in the special education setting may involve more frequent teacher attention, behavioral prompts, and models and cues for a given skill. More immediate feedback about performance may be provided, along with error correction practice and a frequent schedule of reinforcement (Lentz & Shapiro, 1986). Even though a student may have made significant improvement in a skill, and even though performance monitoring using regular class curriculum materials may have indicated that this skill was generalizing, the student may not be able to maintain an appropriate rate of continued skill development if curriculum and instructional procedures are changed abruptly.

Caren Wesson (personal communication, January 9, 1990), Associate Professor at the University of Wisconsin-Milwaukee, has suggested that, prior to making a change in placement, efforts should be made to modify curriculum and instruction in the special education environment to more closely resemble those which will be found in the new environment. For example, instead of working in a special reading curriculum, the student may instead be placed in a specific level of the basal reading series used in the regular classroom. Instructional procedures may be altered to involve less one-to-one contact from the teacher and more small group and/or independent study activities instead. The schedule of reinforcement for assignment completion or accuracy may be significantly reduced. However, monitoring of student performance should continue to determine if the student's rate of progress slows or ceases with the new regimen. If such a decrease in improvement is demonstrated, the team may wish to examine the degree to which regular class instruction and/or curriculum materials can be altered to more closely approximate special education methods and better meet student needs. If such modifications are not feasible, the team may decide either that a slower rate of progress is acceptable, given the benefits of increased integration, or that a change in placement is not appropriate at this time.

Other environmental demands need to be assessed when considering a program change. The relationship between these environmental variables and classroom survival skills is of particular importance. Different classroom settings make different student demands and the survival skills necessary to be successful in one setting may be very different from those necessary to be successful in another.

Epps, Thompson, and Lane (1985) describe a number of factors which should be considered in evaluating a given environmental/classroom setting. They include the following:

1. Classroom routines and activities: What is the sequence in which specific classes are taught? What are the expectations for the appropriate use of free time? What are the procedures for changing from one activity to another or for preparing to go home in the afternoon?

2. Physical arrangement of the room and available materials: How are student desks arranged? Where is the teacher's desk? Where are storage spaces, study carrels, activity centers, chalk boards, bulletin boards, and other equipment used in the room such as computers, overhead projector, or tape recorders?

3. Behavioral expectations of the teacher: Which behaviors does the teacher emphasize and reinforce, and which does the teacher particularly dislike?

4. Types and amount of reinforcement available: Does the teacher use edible, tangible, token, social or activity reinforcers? For which behaviors are students reinforced? What is the schedule of reinforcement?

5. Methods used by the teacher to decrease or respond to inappropriate behavior: Does the teacher use time out, ignore inappropriate behavior, differentially reinforce appropriate behavior or use a response cost technique?

6. Goal setting: Are the goal structures cooperative, competitive, or individualistic?

7. Instructional materials and equipment: Does the teacher use a chalk board, overhead projector, chart, or map to illustrate points? Are other audiovisual materials used such as films, filmstrips, tape recorders, or records?

8. Instructional methods: What are the grouping patterns for various subjects, nature of assignments, manner in which directions are presented, opportunities for additional skill practice?

9. Basis of student evaluation: Are students graded on daily work, tests and quizzes, class participation, behavior, or some combination of these factors? How are assignments corrected and how soon does the student receive feedback on performance?

A careful examination of these environmental factors should assist the IEP team in identifying specific classroom survival skills which the student must possess to be successful in a given environment. If certain survival skills are lacking, efforts should be made to provide instruction and support in order to change student behavior to more closely match the expectations of the environment. Equal consideration should also be given to making environmental changes that will more closely match identified student needs. A change in placement is most likely to be successful if attention is devoted to student variables as well as curriculum/instructional/environmental variables.

How May the Transition from One Program to Another Be Accomplished?

As performance in the special education setting begins to approximate that described by IEP goals and the normative performance of peers, the IEP team should consider formulating a plan to transition the student from one program/environment to another. Consideration of the factors just described should enable the IEP team to determine the degree to which the student is ready for and likely to be successful in a different program. It should also enable the team to determine the degree to which the new environment is ready to receive the student and make accommodations for the student's needs.

In some cases, the results of an evaluation of student skills and environmental factors may make it clear that a change in program is appropriate and the transition can be made almost immediately. In this circumstance, the transition plan may involve little more than determination of the time line by which the change will occur. In other cases, an evaluation may indicate that the student and/or environment is not yet sufficiently ready for the transition. In this circumstance, the IEP team may choose either to continue the current program for the time being with no further consideration of a program change or to formulate a transition plan that will better prepare the student and the environment for the program change.

A transition plan is most likely to be successful if its formulation is a team effort involving the input of all concerned parties including the student, parents, special education teacher, receiving teacher, and all support staff who will provide assistance in one capacity or another. The transition plan should specify a period of time in which all parties will work on enhancing skills and environmental factors that will increase the likelihood of student success in the new environment. For some students, the team may choose to maintain the current environment while the transition plan is in effect.

As is the case throughout program planning, the transition plan should include objective, measurable goals to be accomplished by the student and/or the environment. With regard to student variables, these goals might include such factors as the maintenance or continued improvement of performance in IEP skill area(s) or improvement in specific classroom survival skills. With regard to the environment, goals might involve changes in instructional procedures or curriculum materials, the provision of a motivational strategy, or some alteration in the physical arrangement of the new setting. Time lines for the accomplishment of specific tasks should be established as well as a monitoring procedure that will facilitate data-based decision making about the plan's success. For a student who continues to be served in a special education program, the transition period may also provide opportunities to participate in the new environment. These experiences will not only allow the student to become more familiar with the new setting but also offer an opportunity for the team to assess skill generalization in the new environment.

At the conclusion of the transition period, the IEP team may use information from ongoing performance monitoring to determine the success of the transition plan. If transition goals have been accomplished, the team can then proceed with the program change.

How May the Success of the Program Change be Evaluated?

Unfortunately, at the current time it is not possible for IEP teams to predict with 100% accuracy that a program change will be successful. At best, teams can do a careful evaluation of the student and environment and use this information and their professional judgment to make what they consider to be an appropriate recommendation. A recommendation for a program change, like any other recommendation for a program placement or for a specific intervention procedure, should be treated as a hypothesis to be tested. Student performance should continue to be monitored and the IEP team should use this information to judge the success or failure of the planned change.

At the time that a program change is made, the IEP team should specify performance goals and a monitoring plan. They should also specify some points in time at which they will reconvene to evaluate the outcome of their recommendations for change. For some students, it may be important to conduct a follow-up review as the student transitions from one class to another at the beginning of a new academic year. This review might involve providing the student's new classroom teacher with information about instructional modifications used in the previous year and doing some evaluation and training in a new set of classroom survival skills for the student. In the Minneapolis Public Schools, a follow-up review of the student's performance is also conducted within one calendar year of termination from a special education program (Magnusson & Schuster, 1986).

When the IEP team convenes to evaluate the outcome of a program change, the following questions should be considered:

1. In comparison to the student's previous performance, has he or she continued to make progress in the specific deficit area(s) which initially prompted the provision of special education services? If so, is this progress at a satisfactory rate?

2. In comparison to peer performance, does the student continue to function within the normative range? That is, does student performance continue to be at a level similar to that of a defined peer group?

3. Does the student continue to demonstrate satisfactory performance with regard to important classroom survival skills?

4. What are the attitudes of the student, parents, teachers, and other staff members regarding the change? Are these parties satisfied that the change has been successful or do they have specific concerns which need to be addressed?

The answers to the first three questions should be data-based, allowing an objective evaluation of the degree to which a program change has been successful. Responses to the fourth question are also important, although more subjective, and the statement of specific concerns may provide ideas about factors which need to be addressed to make the program change more successful.

If it is the judgment of the IEP team that a program change has not been successful, a return to the original special education placement should not be the only option considered as a solution. The team needs to identify specific factors which led to the lack of success and then devise an intervention plan to address the factors. Once an intervention plan has been devised, it is up to the IEP team to determine the site(s) in which this intervention plan will be carried out. In some cases, this site may be the original special education program; in other cases, a less restrictive special education program may be recommended or even a continuation of the current program with additional support. Performance monitoring can continue to provide information about the success of any program changes recommended by the IEP team.

SUMMARY

Any program change represents an important milestone in a student's educational career. Although initial placement decisions have historically received significant attention, questions related to program modification and exit have lacked adequate answers. Too often, the minimal standards included in special education law have defined the time lines and content of program review procedures. We cannot continue to accept yearly inspection of student progress as the method for program decision making.

The strategies for program modification and exit described in this chapter offer a problem-solving approach as part of a larger system of data-based decision making. "Exit is linked to entrance as well as to monitoring of the effectiveness of instruction strategy" (Allen, 1989, p. 199). The time for isolated and infrequent data collection and problem solving regarding a student's program has passed. We must integrate our efforts throughout educational decision making (entrance, performance monitoring, and exit) to maximize impact on the student's educational experiences.

REFERENCES

Allen, D. (1989). Periodic and annual review and decisions to terminate special education services. In M. Shinn (Ed.), *Curriculum-based measurement: Assessing special children* (pp. 182–201). New York: Guilford Press.

Epps, S., Thompson, B., & Lane, M. (1985). *Procedures for incorporating generalization and maintenance programming into interventions for special education students.* Des Moines, IA: Iowa Department of Education, Bureau of Special Education.

Code of Federal Regulations. (1989). Regulations promulgated under Education of the Handicapped Act (P.L. 91-230), as amended by the Education of All Handicapped Children Act (P.L. 94-142).

Good, R., & Salvia, J. (1988). Curriculum bias in published, norm-referenced reading tests: Demonstrable effects. *School Psychology Review, 17,* 51–60.

Individuals with Disabilities Education Act. 20 U.S.C., Chapter 33, Sections 1400–1485, as amended by Public Law 101–470.

Lentz, F., & Shapiro, E. (1986). Functional assessment of the academic environment. *School Psychology Review, 15,* 346–357.

Magnusson, D., & Schuster, C. (1986) *Student identification procedures.* Minneapolis: Minneapolis Public Schools, Special Education Department.

Schendel, J., & Ulman, J. (1990). *Performance monitoring of academic and non-academic behaviors* (2nd ed.). Des Moines: Iowa Department of Education.

ANNOTATED BIBLIOGRAPHY

Allen, D. (1989). Periodic and annual review and decisions to terminate special education services. In M. Shinn (Ed.), *Curriculum-based measurement: Assessing special children* (pp. 182–201). New York: Guilford Press.
This book provides an in-depth review of behaviorally based methodologies to evaluate and improve instructional programs. The focus of Chapter 7 is normative and individually referenced decisions through the analysis of student outcomes. Both program modification and exit decisions are reviewed.

Deno, S. L. (1986). Formative evaluation of individual student programs: A new role for school psychologists. *School Psychology Review, 15*(3), 358–374.
The information in this article provides an excellent review of issues involved in assessment of student performance. It clarifies why assessment must be designed to develop and monitor educational interventions and how this might be done.

Schendel, J., & Ulman, J. (1990). *Performance monitoring of academic and non-academic behaviors* (2nd ed.). Des Moines: Iowa Department of Education.
The authors provide procedures for data-based performance monitoring of both academic and nonacademic behaviors critical for successful program modification and exit decisions. A checklist and work sheet are provided to assist in the development of performance monitoring strategies with individual students.

Reynolds, M. C., Wang, M. C., & Walberg, H. J. (1987). The necessary restructuring of special and regular education. *Exceptional Children, 53*(5), 391–398.
This article focuses upon basic but flawed beliefs within the current educational system regarding categorical programs and policies. It calls for a series of pilot programs which would focus upon child change and student progress rather than categorical labels.

Zins, J., Curtis, M., Graden, J., & Ponti, C. (1988). *Helping students succeed in the regular classroom: A guide for developing intervention assistance programs.* San Francisco: Jossey-Bass Publishers.
While the content of this book does not directly focus upon program modification and exit decisions, it does provide a model for an intervention program that includes evaluation of intervention effectiveness. It also contains a valuable discussion of why educators should increase their focus on data-based decision making.

46

Best Practices in
School-Based Behavioral Consultation

Thomas R. Kratochwill
Stephen N. Elliott
Pamela Carrington Rotto
University of Wisconsin–Madison

Consultation has become a major approach for providing psychoeducational services to children and adolescents. The three major models of consultation used most frequently are mental-health, organizational-development, and behavioral consultation, but many more have been identified (see Zins, Kratochwill, & Elliott, 1993). Although differences exist among these models, all emphasize an increase in the problem-solving expertise of the consultee within a triadic relationship (consultant-consultee-child). The behavioral model of consultation has emerged as an alternative to traditional service-delivery approaches in applied settings (Reschly, 1988).

While behavioral consultation traditionally has been affiliated with behavior modification and intervention techniques from this theoretical school (Kazdin, 1989; Sulzer-Azaroff & Mayer, 1977) a more current focus is to use a wide range of intervention technologies from diverse theoretical origins. For example, school psychologists may apply behavioral principles and techniques in developing intervention programs and use behavioral methodologies to evaluate the effectiveness of these services (see Martens, 1994). Likewise, school psychologists also may apply valid instructional principles such as pause time, pacing, teacher feedback, and/or homework instruction when developing an intervention plan to enhance the academic performance of underachieving students. Whereas specific intervention strategies may vary across presenting problems, two identifiable features are most frequently associated with behavioral consultation, namely, indirect service delivery and a problem-solving approach.

The most widely recognized feature of behavioral consultation is its *indirect service* delivery approach (Bergan & Kratochwill, 1990). Services are delivered by a consultant (school psychologist) to a consultee (teacher or parent) who, in turn, provides services to a child in the school or community setting. The indirect approach to service delivery generally is regarded as a distinct advantage of behavioral consul-

tation because it allows the psychologist to impact many more children than could be served by a direct service approach.

Behavioral consultation involves a collaborative relationship in which the consultant is viewed as a facilitator. Emphasis is placed on the collaborative *problem-solving process* which occurs during a series of interviews and related assessment activities. Throughout this process, the psychologist's role is to elicit a description of the problem, assist in analyzing the problem, devise a plan for intervention, and monitor the program once implemented. The teacher's or parent's role is to clearly describe the problem, work with the child to implement the intervention program, observe progress, periodically evaluate the plan's effectiveness, and supervise the child's actions (Elliott & Sheridan, 1992).

BASIC CONSIDERATIONS

Behavioral consultation has two important goals: (a) to provide methods for changing a child's behavioral, academic, or social problem and (b) to improve a consultee's skills so he or she can prevent or respond effectively to future problems or similar problems in other children. Given these goals, behavioral consultation can be both a proactive and a reactive service. Researchers indicate that behavioral consultation often has changed children's problem behaviors successfully (Gresham & Kendell, 1987). However, the more proactive goal of influencing a teacher's or parent's ability to handle future problems has not been observed consistently. The accomplishment of these goals requires consultees to participate in a general process for analyzing problems that results in an effective plan to resolve the problem. Successful behavioral consultants must demonstrate expertise both in coordinating and facilitating the problem-solving process and in behavior change methods. Although competence in problem identification, applied behavior analysis, and plan implementation are necessary conditions of behavioral consultation, they are not sufficient to facilitate effective consultative interactions. Integration of positive interpersonal skills and understanding with technical expertise are equally important to maximize consultant-consultee effectiveness. For example, characteristics such as acceptance through nonjudgmental statements, openness, nondefensiveness, and flexibility positively affect the interaction between consultant and consultee. In the remainder of this chapter, the basic components of problem solving in behavioral consultation, specific consultant-consultee relationship variables influencing the consultation process, and use of consultation with teachers and parents will be discussed.

The Structure and Process of Behavioral Consultation

Behavioral consultation has been conceptualized as a series of stages that structure and focus the problem-solving interaction between a consultant and consultee (Bergan & Kratochwill, 1990). A heuristic four-stage framework for behavioral consultation begins with *problem identification and problem analysis*, progresses to *plan implementation*, and concludes with *plan evaluation.*

Problem identification is the initial and perhaps most critical stage of consultation because it results in the design and implementation of an effective plan. The interview represents the primary assessment technology for defining the problem, although numerous other strategies assist in defining the problem or issue (e.g., tests, rating scales and checklists, direct observations). During the problem identification interview, the consultant and consultee focus on describing and operationally defining the child's behaviors which are of concern to the parent/teacher. In behavioral consultation a "problem" is a relative concept operationalized when the parent/teacher reports a significant discrepancy between the child's current level of performance and the desired level of performance. The determination of whether a significant discrepancy exists is not examined initially; however, once the current and desired levels of performance are defined objectively, this significant discrepancy becomes the focus. This approach to problem identification is based on the assumption that problems are the result of unsuccessful or discrepant interactions between persons (e.g., child and teacher, child and parent). Thus, the psychologist and parent/teacher first analyze the target problem within the ecological context of the child and his/her interactions with the environment. When baseline data support the existence of the specific problem, the psychologist and parent/teacher jointly begin to identify factors that might lead to behavior change and problem resolution.

Problem analysis, the second major stage of behavior consultation, focuses on the variables and conditions that are hypothesized to influence the child's behavior. Problem analysis is a natural extension of the problem identification stage, in that it essentially begins with the target behavior of concern and focuses on establishing functional relationships between it and the antecedent or consequent event. Questions about who, what, where, when, and under what conditions or contingencies all are relevant, and generally facilitate a better understanding of the problem behavior. In many cases, the problem analysis stage will require the psychologist to collect additional data about the child's target behavior. Thus, problem analysis may enhance refinement and, consequently, redefinition of the target problem and the factor(s) which influence it.

Plan implementation follows the problem analysis stage and has the dual objectives of (a) selecting an appropriate intervention and (b) implementing the intervention. Procedural details are essential at this stage, such as assigning individuals to various roles, gathering or preparing specific materials, and/or training individuals to implement the plan. The selection of interventions traditionally seems to have been based on the reported or assumed effectiveness of a particular method. Many consumers and providers of psychological services, however, are demanding that interventions also be acceptable (i.e., time efficient, least restrictive, fair and/or low risk to the target child; Elliott, 1988a, 1988b). Likewise, interventions consistent with the consultee's child-management philosophy and compatible with existing resources and the skills of the individual delivering the intervention also have gained recent consumer interest and empirical support (Witt & Martens, 1988). The design and selection of appropriate interventions should be based on empirically supportable treatments and requires attention to issues of intervention acceptability, intervention effectiveness, and consultee skills and resources. Plan implementation also involves discussing and actually carrying out the selected intervention. This substage may consume several weeks and is characterized by interactions between the parent/teacher and child. These interactions may occur through brief contacts in which the psychologist monitors intervention integrity and side effects (Gresham, 1989), and possibly brainstorms with the parent/teacher ways to revise the plan and its use. The school psychologist's role also may involve observations to monitor child and consultee behaviors or training sessions to enhance the skills of the individual who is executing the treatment plan.

Plan evaluation is the final stage of consultation. The objectives of this stage are to establish a sound basis for interpreting outcomes of the intervention for the targeted problem and to provide a forum for evaluating plan effectiveness. The rigor of evaluation involved in research may not be used in practice, but good evidence to verify outcomes should be routine in case consultation efforts. Single-subject or case study strategies and direct observations, which largely have been adopted as the methodology for applied behavioral psychology, provide one means for evaluating change in the child's behavior. When the reported discrepancy between the child's behavior and desired level of functioning is reduced significantly or eliminated, and the treatment is acceptable to both the teacher/parent and child, the consultant and consultee decide whether consultation should be terminated. Outcome criteria should include maintenance of the desired behavior over time and generalization across multiple settings and conditions. In theory, a consultative case is not concluded until the discrepancy between the child's existing and desired behavior is reduced substantively and an acceptable maintenance plan is in place. Criteria such as overall improvement in the quality of life (social and academic) can also be involved but may require a developmental focus to consultation interactions. Therefore, it often is necessary to recycle through previous stages of consultation and re-evaluate refined or newly implemented interventions.

In summary, behavioral consultation is a model for delivering psychoeducational assessment and intervention services to children via teachers or parents through a series of interviews. A heuristic problem-solving framework and behavioral principles provide structure for collecting information and affecting behavior change. Although the problem-solving structure is sequential and overt, it should not be interpreted as inflexible or irreversible. The activities of consultants and consultees are multifaceted, involving at least interviews, observational assessments, treatment of the target behaviors, and evaluation of the treatments. Such activities generally require several interactions between the consultant and consultee, as well as ongoing consultee and client collaborative interactions.

Consultant-Consultee Relationship

The interpersonal relationship between a psychologist and parent/teacher is assumed to play a major role in the use and effectiveness of behavioral consultation. Thus, as with psychotherapy, issues of trust, genuineness, and openness have been deemed important qualities for both consultants and consultees (Conoley & Conoley, 1982; Martin, 1978). These human qualities are magnified in a consultative model of service delivery due to the predominance of an interview mode of information gathering and sharing. The dynamics of communication, both talking and listening, are the medium through which psychologists display their attitudes about parents and teachers. Personal characteristics, professional competencies, and behavioral principles of reinforcement and modeling all are important elements in establishing and maintaining constructive and professional interactions.

Sensitivity to issues of importance to parents and teachers also contributes to the development of a positive consulting relationship. Variables commonly examined in treatment acceptability research (Elliott, 1988a; Witt & Elliott, 1985) and dimensions of helping emphasized by empowerment theorists (Dunst & Trivette, 1988; Witt & Martens, 1988) can be considered consistent with behavioral consultation because they are relevant to the enhancement of relationships with parents and teachers. Specifically, treatment acceptability researchers repeatedly have found that administration/management time and fairness of the treatment are important themes virtually to all teachers, and nonaversive approaches to intervention are valued highly by most teachers. Work by empowerment theorists applied to consultation suggests that (a) help is more likely to be perceived positively if it is offered proactively, (b) competence within teachers is best promoted by building upon their existing child-management strengths rather than remediating deficits, and (c) use of existing resources in the school environment is preferred over the intervention or purchase of new resources (Witt & Martens, 1988). Thus, it is concluded that effective behavioral consultants (a) overtly communicate awareness of issues central to teachers' daily functioning and (b) act cooperatively to design interventions. Such consultative actions may overcome many potential sources of resistance.

Resistance is a topic of considerable concern to practitioners and researchers alike and often has been conceptualized as something bad which resides within a person or institution. As observed by Wickstrom and Witt (1993), such a view of resistance is overly simplistic and unnecessarily negative. Within the context of a consultant-consultee relationship, they define resistance as "including those system, consultee, consultant, family, and client factors which interfere with the achievement of goals established during consultative interactions . . . [Resistance, then, is] *anything* that impedes problem solving or plan implementation and ultimately problem resolution" (Wickstrom & Witt, 1993, p. 160). This definition stresses that resistance is part of a system context and is multidirectional; that is, it does not reside in only one part of the system.

Behavioral consultation addresses resistance to consultation in terms of situational antecedents and consequences of the consultee's behavior (Bergan, 1985). Having reviewed the theoretical and empirical reports on resistance to treatment in both the psychotherapy and consultation literature, Wickstrom and Witt (1993) recommend two general tactics to responding to resistance. The first tactic they call "Joining the consultee" and the second they refer to as "Emphasizing referent power." Joining the consultee involves understanding a consultee's attribution system for explaining a problem of concern and then using that attributional framework to build a link to an intervention. Emphasizing referent power involves a consultant working to become more similar to a consultee. This tactic can be accomplished by using nonauthoritarian and noncoercive means of control, using cooperative modes of interaction, asking questions, and making suggestions for change tentatively (Parsons & Meyers, 1984). Efforts to use the consultee's existing skills and preferences for interaction activities, thereby reducing the number of "new" aspects of an intervention, also is likely to make suggestions more acceptable, and thus less resisted.

In closing this section, the reader might do well to remember that "once the door to the classroom is closed, there is little that any of the educational specialists can do to insure that occurrence of any event that the teacher does not want to occur" (Gutkin & Curtis, 1981, pp. 220–221). Hence, the interpersonal or therapeutic relationship skills of a psychologist are as important to the delivery of behavioral consultation as knowledge of assessment and intervention methods.

BEST PRACTICES IN THE
DELIVERY OF BEHAVIORAL CONSULTATION

As noted in the previous sections of the chapter, behavioral consultation consists of a series of stages or phases used to implement the process of consultation. These stages include problem identification, problem analysis, plan implementation, and plan evaluation. Each of these steps, with the exception of plan implementation, involves a formal interview resulting in specific objectives. Best practices in behavioral consultation suggest that psychologists adhere to specific objectives and activities within each phase. The major components for each of these phases are outlined next.

Problem Identification

Problem identification is achieved through an interview where the primary objectives are to specify the goals, assess the problem, and implement certain procedures. Behavioral consultation can involve a developmental or problem-centered focus. In developmental consultation the consultant establishes general, subordinate, and performance objectives. Usually these are obtained over a long period of time and in several series of interviews. In contrast, problem-centered consultation involves specification of problems that are specific and relate to one primary concern. Relative to the developmental consultation process, problem-centered consultation is time-limited.

Whether the nature of consultation is developmental or problem-centered, the psychologist needs to achieve clear specification of problems. Typically, this process involves generating precise descriptions of the student's behavior, carefully analyzing the conditions under which the problems occur, and estab-

lishing some indication of the level of persistence or strength of the problems. Another important objective is establishing an assessment technique. Together, the teacher and/or parent and psychologist agree on the type or kind of measure to be used, what will be recorded, and how this process will be implemented. Finally, certain procedural objectives must be met during the problem-identification phase. One of the first objectives involves establishing times, dates, and formats for subsequent interviews and contacts with the teacher or parent to examine procedural aspects of the consultation process. For example, the psychologist may agree to contact the teacher/parent weekly or biweekly to determine whether data are being gathered properly or if any unique barriers have occurred. Witt and Elliott (1983) outlined nine components that facilitate the problem-identification interview. These components were written as objectives and are briefly described as follows:

1. **Explanation of problem-definition purposes.** The parent or teacher should be told what is to be accomplished during the interview and why problem identification is important. (Example statement: "I would like to talk with you a few minutes about John and his behaviors that bother you most. We will need to assess his behaviors, when and how often they occur, and what factors in your classroom [or home] influence them.")

2. **Identification and selection of target behaviors.** The parent or teacher should be asked to focus attention on the problematic aspects of a student's difficulties. (Example statement: "Please describe exactly what John is doing that has caused you concern.") When individuals identify multiple problems, it is necessary to determine which to address. (Example statement: "Which of these concerns is most pressing to you now?")

3. **Identification of problem frequency, duration, and intensity.** After a target behavior has been defined, it is helpful to assess its basic characteristics: How often does it occur (frequency), how long does it last (duration), and how strong is it (intensity)? (Example statements: "How many times did John cry last week?" "How long does each crying session last?" "Does he cry loud enough for everyone in the room to hear him?") To interpret descriptions of frequency, duration, and intensity, the parent or teacher may be asked to compare the target child's behavior with that of other children. In addition, a psychologist should have knowledge of normative expectations to which the child's behavior can be compared.

4. **Identification of the conditions under which the target behavior occurs.** The assessment of environmental factors that occur in conjunction with a target behavior is essential in understanding

the problem. (Example statement: "How do you and the class react to John's crying?") Use of a simple model of behavior, such as the ABC model, can help unravel many problems. This model construes behavior (B) to be a function of antecedent (A) and/or consequent (C) events. Thus, once a behavior has been identified, a consultant looks at events that chronologically precede and follow it.

5. **Identification of the required level of performance.** Obtaining a description of the behavior required of a student is as important as obtaining a description of the student's problem behavior. (Example statement: "What would you consider to be an acceptable frequency for this out-of-seat behavior?") Once a desired or expected level of performance is identified, it serves as a goal.

6. **Identification of the student's strengths.** Learning what a child does well is often more useful than learning what a child does not do or does poorly. (Example statement: "What does John do best when interacting with his classmates?") Developing interventions that use a student's strengths helps to increase the probability of a successful treatment.

7. **Identification of behavioral assessment procedures.** All interventions require some assessment or recording of behavior. Thus, a consultant should help a teacher or parent decide what, how, when, and where behavior will be recorded and who will do the recording.

8. **Identification of consultee effectiveness.** Given that one major goal of behavioral consultation is to enable a consultee to solve his or her own problems in the future, it may be necessary to teach or model problem-solving skills and enhance the consultee's confidence in his or her ability to solve problems. The goal obviously is for the consultant to be helpful to the consultee. To accomplish this goal, Witt and Martens (1988) advocate an empowerment, rather than an advice-giving, philosophy of service for consultation. However, an empowerment philosophy assumes consultees basically are skilled individuals who can become more capable of solving their own problems by knowing what resources are available and how to gain access to them (Dunst & Trivette, 1988). If the consultee does not have the skills to provide services to the client, these skills should be taught or other treatment options considered. One can determine the consultee's potential effectiveness by asking about how similar problems have been handled in the past, assessing what methods the consultee already has used to remediate the target problem, and judging whether the consultee is self-reliant or dependent on others for reinforcement (Meyers, Liddell, & Lyons, 1977).

9. **Summary of the interview.** The final step in the problem identification stage should include a summary of the important points discussed and a review of the problem definition. This summary should include a statement of the specific target behavior(s) or clarification of any further assessment necessary to refine the target behavior(s).

Specific objectives associated with the consultation problem-identification interview are presented in Table 1. These are general objectives that need to be established in the consultation interview but typically correspond to features of the Consultation Analysis Record (see Bergan & Kratochwill, 1990).

Problem Analysis

After baseline data are collected on the areas of concern, the psychologist and teacher/parent meet to decide jointly on factors that might lead to some resolution of the problem. In this regard, the consultation process will focus on student, parent/teacher, and general environmental variables that may be of relevance.

The problem analysis interview includes five major steps: (a) choosing analysis procedures, (b) determining the conditions and/or skills analysis, (c) developing plan strategies, (d) developing plan tactics, and (e) establishing procedures to evaluate performance during implementation of any treatment program. Within the context of these phases, the psychologist might first analyze the factors that lead to potential solution of the problem and then develop a plan to solve the problem.

The psychologist focuses on conditions that facilitate attainment of the mutually agreed upon goals. Generally, it is necessary to accomplish the following:

1. Specify whether the goal of treatment is to increase, decrease, or maintain behavior.

2. Identify setting events and antecedent/consequential conditions associated with behavior.

3. Determine which current conditions affect the behavior by comparing the existing situation to related research findings.

4. Identify conditions not currently associated with behavior but which nonetheless could influence solving the problem.

During the problem analysis phase, the psychologist and teacher/parent, through mutual problem-solving efforts, must analyze the kinds of child skills necessary to achieve the consultation goals. Analysis of the child's skills can include both academic and social performance. Basically, the psychologist must work with the teacher/parent (and child if possible) to identify psychological and educational principles that relate to attaining the consultation goals. It is beyond the scope of this chapter to outline these procedures in great detail. Rather, the reader is referred to a number of sources that can be useful to analyze

TABLE 1
Problem Identification Behavior

Behavior Specification

Definition: The consultant should elicit behavioral descriptions of client functioning. Focus is on specific behaviors of the child interms that can be understood by an independent behavior. Provide as many examples of the behavior problem as possible (e.g., What does Cathy do?).

a. Specify behavior:

b. Specify examples of the problem behavior:

c. Which behavior causes the most difficulty? (i.e., prioritize the probelms from most to least severe):

Behavior Setting

Definition: A precise description of the settings in which the probelm behaviors occur (e.g., Where does John do this?).

a. Specify examples of where the behavior occurs:

b. Specify priorities (i.e., Which setting is causing the most difficulty?):

Identification of Antecedents

Definition: Events which precede the child's behavior. Provide information regarding what happens immediately before the problem behavior occurs (e.g., What happens right before Kristy hits other children?).

Sequential Conditions Analysis

Definition: Situational events occurring when the problem behavior occurs. Environmental conditions in operation when it occurs. For example, time of day or day of week when the problem behavior typically occurs. Sequential conditions are also defined as the patter or trend of antecedent and/or consequent conditions across a series of occasions (e.g., What is happening when the behavior occurs?).

Identification of Consequent Conditions

Definition: Events which occur immediately following the client behavior (e.g., What happens after the problem behavior has occurred?).

Behavior Strength

Definition: Indicate how often (frequency) or how long (duration) the behavior occurs. Behavior strength refers to the level or incidence of the behavior that is to be focused on. The question format used for each particular behavior strength will depend upon the specific type of behavior problem (e.g., How often does Shelly have tantrums? or How long do Brett's tantrums last?).

a. Frequency of behavior:

b. Duration of behavior:

Tentative-Definition-of-Goal Question

Definition: Appropriate or acceptable level of the behavior (e.g., How frequently could Matthew leave his seat without causing problems?).

Assets Question

Definition: Strengths, abilities, or other positive features of the child (e.g., What does Jane do well?).

Approach to Teaching or Existing Procedures

Definition: Procedures or rules in force which are external to the child and to the behavior (e.g., How long are Sue and other students doing seat-work problems?).

Data-Collection Procedures

Definition: Specify the target responses to record. This recording should include the kind of measure, what is to be recorded, and how to record. Specific details of data recording should be emphasized.

Date to Begin Data Collection

Definition: Procedural details of when to begin collecting baseline data.

overt behavioral and cognitive features relating to instructional and social functioning (e.g., Bergan & Kratochwill, 1990; Kazdin, 1989; Kratochwill & Morris, 1992).

The outcome of successful problem analysis is a plan to put into effect during the treatment implementation process. Development of this plan should begin with specifying broad strategies that can be used to achieve the mutually agreed upon goals. The plan typically includes *sources of action* to be implemented. Secondly, plan tactics are used to guide implementation of the strategy and outline principles to be applied during the intervention. For example, if reinforcement strategies are to be used, the person responsible for carrying out the plan and the conditions under which they will occur should be specified. During this phase psychologists might also assess treatment acceptability prior to its implementation. A number of scales have been developed for assessment of pretreatment acceptability and readers are encouraged to consult this material (Elliott, 1988b; Witt & Elliott, 1985). Appendix A is a sample rating scale that can be used in assessing treatment acceptability.

Finally, during problem analysis the psychologist and teacher/parent must establish performance and assessment objectives that will be used during plan implementation. Typically this procedure follows from a conditions analysis and involves specification of an assessment procedure previously used during baseline. For example, when plan implementation involves skill development, some agreed upon format for collection of data on performance related to the final objectives achieved is necessary.

Table 2 provides an example of the general objectives that should be met during the problem analysis interview. These objectives generally involve validating the problem, analyzing the problem and related variables, designing the plan, and developing the procedural goals.

Plan Implementation

The third stage in behavioral consultation involves implementing a treatment plan. Some initial activities are necessary to enhance the likelihood of intervention success. In this regard, the psychologist should maximize the probability that the intervention plan is put into effect by the teacher/parent and/or child during this part of the consultation process. This step will require collaborative decisions regarding role assignments, material assembly, and skill development, as needed during the process. Although there is no formal interview during the plan implementation phase, it is the responsibility of the psychologist to monitor the implementation of the intervention and work with the teacher/parent to revise procedures during plan implementation, if it is deemed necessary. It also may be desirable for the

consultant to observe the child and/or teacher or parent to monitor behaviors and determine the need for subsequent revisions in the plan.

During plan implementation the three major tasks that must be accomplished include skill development of the consultee (if necessary), monitoring the implementation process, and plan revisions. Typically, the psychologist must determine whether the teacher/parent has the skills to carry out the plan. If skill development is required, the consultee must be offered some type of training or guidance.

The second task, to monitor data, can determine if assessment is occurring as intended. Usually consultee records are examined to assess child outcome. This process indicates to the school psychologist when data are being gathered, how the performance of the child is being assessed, and what behaviors are being observed. It may also help the psychologist determine whether the plan is actually proceeding as designed. If little progress is observed, then it is advisable for the school psychologist to meet with the teacher/parent and revise the plan accordingly.

Monitoring plan implementation generally occurs in two ways. First, the child's behavior is monitored on an ongoing basis by the teacher/parent. This monitoring is a continuation from the problem identification and problem analysis phases of consultation. A second type of monitoring activity involves an evaluation of the strategies associated with the plan implementation itself. It is essential for the psychologist and teacher/parent to ensure that the plan agreed upon is being carried out as designed. The psychologist may monitor plan implementation and integrity by discussing the intervention plan with the teacher or parent, and, to complement this strategy, actually observe the plan in operation or to get the consultee to report integrity data periodically (Gresham, 1989). Although various individuals might serve in the role of treatment implementors, it is nonetheless likely that the agreed upon procedures to facilitate plan implementation are compatible with the resources and responsibilities of the school setting.

Finally, changes should be made in the plan when necessary. If the child's behavior is not changing in the desired direction, plan revision should occur. Generally, this outcome will require that the psychologist and teacher/parent return to the problem analysis phase to further analyze variables such as the setting, intrapersonal child characteristics, or skill deficits. Likewise, it may be necessary to return to the problem identification stage if it is determined that the nature of the problem has changed.

Plan Evaluation

Plan evaluation is implemented through a formal plan evaluation interview and typically is undertaken to determine whether the consultation goals have been reached. The process of evaluation includes as-

TABLE 2
Problem Analysis Interview

Strength of Behavior

Definition: Question or statement regarding behaviors, specific to the baseline data collected (e.g., It looks like Karen refused to do the assigned work except on Tuesday.).

Antecedent, Consequent, and Sequential Conditions

a. *Antecedent:* Events which precede the child's behavior. Information regarding what happens immediately preceding the problem behavior (e.g., Did you notice anything in particular that happened just *before* ...).

b. *Consequent:* Events which occur immediately following the child's behavior (e.g., What happened *after* Mary ...).

c, *Sequential:* Situational events or environmental conditions in operation when problem behavior occurs. Pattern or trend of conditions across occurrences such as day of week, time of day, etc. (e.g., What was happening *when* Jimmy ...).

Interpretation of Behavior

Definition: Consultant elicits the consultee's perception regarding the purpose of function of the behavior (e.g., Why do you think Justin is so disrespectful?).

Establishing a Plan

Definition: Consultant and consultee establish plan strategies and specific targets that might be used in treatment implementation. Consultant may ask for or provide strategies (e.g, What could be done to change the setting in which Charles gets into fights? OR We need to try something different. What could be done before Ron makes the abusive remarks?).

Continuation of Recording Procedure

Definitiona; Establish recording procedures to be used in treatment plan implementation.

---

sessment of goal attainment, plan effectiveness, and implementation planning.

Deciding whether the actual goals previously agreed upon have been met is determined through discussion with the consultee and observation of the client's behavior. The process of evaluating goal attainment was initiated during the problem-identification stage when the objectives and procedures for measuring mastery were specified. The data gathered since that phase should provide some evidence as to whether there is congruence between objectives and the problem solution. This congruence is essentially determined on the basis of the data collected; however, additional strategies, such as social validation criteria, might also be invoked. That is, the school psychologist will want to know whether the child reached some clinically established level of change and whether the intervention program brought the child's performance within a range of acceptable behavior as compared to normal or typical peers. Determination of the congruence between behavior and objectives generally leads the psychologist to conclude that no progress was evident, some progress was made, or the actual goal was obtained.

The mechanism for evaluating plan effectiveness can occur through one of several case-study strategies that have been used frequently in applied behavior analysis or single-case research. In this regard, a variety of clinical experimental procedures might be

implemented to facilitate decisions regarding progress in the consultation process. Again, it is beyond the scope of this chapter to outline these in great detail. Instead, the interested reader is referred to a primary source where these designs are reviewed (e.g., Barlow, Hayes, & Nelson, 1984). The recommended strategies basically involve a simple time-series design which includes an A/B format. Recent work by Busse, Kratochwill, and Elliott (in press) summarizes strategies for interpreting time-series data for consultation outcomes.

Advances in the evaluation of treatment effects and consultation outcomes continue to appear in the research literature. Several of these advances have been used in the evaluation of community mental health services and supplement the case-study and social-validation strategies traditionally used by consultants. Two of the most practical strategies are Goal Attainment Scaling (GAS; Lloyd, 1983) and the Reliable Change Index (RC; Gresham, in press; Jacobson, Follette, & Revenstorf, 1984).

Briefly, there are several different approaches to GAS. The basic tactic, however, is one where a consultee would be asked to describe five levels of treatment outcome. The most unfavorable outcome described is given a –rating, the expected outcome a 0 rating, and the most favorable outcome a +2 rating. Ratings of –1 and +1 are ascribed to descriptions of outcomes situated between the most unfavorable and expected outcome and the most favorable and expected outcome, respectively. This system of rating treatment outcomes can be used to get weekly measures on treatment progress, as well as final outcome perceptions from a consultee. GAS is a sensitive system because both over- and under-attainment of objectives can be rated. Both Lloyd (1983) and Rinn, Vernon, and Wise (1975) have developed GAS statistics to allow for comparisons across subjects.

The RC evaluation method was first proposed by Nunnally and Kotsche (1983). RC is defined as the difference between posttest scores and pretest scores divided by the standard error of measurement. Typically an RC of + 1.96 or greater is considered statistically significant, and more importantly it is inferred that the intervention produced a reliable change in a person's behavior. The RC is designed to be used with data from rating scales or individualized tests where total pretest and posttest scores can be calculated. Be cognizant, however, that this metric for reporting treatment outcomes is affected by the reliability of the dependent measures. Gresham (1991) noted that the dual criteria of social validation (social comparison and subjective evaluation) and RC should provide practitioners with a means for documenting educationally and statistically significant changes in behavior.

Once it has been determined that the problem has been solved, post-implementation planning occurs to help ensure that the particular problem does not occur again. This planning by the psychologist and teacher/parent can take several forms. One strategy is to leave the plan in effect. Typically, however, a plan that is put into effect will need to be modified (another strategy) to facilitate maintenance of behavior over time. There is considerable evidence in the treatment literature that specific tactics are needed to facilitate maintenance and generalization of behavior and these tactics must be accomplished during this phase of consultation. Generalization may occur naturally, but more likely it will need to be programmed. Several factors have been identified that have a bearing on the generalization of skills (Haring, 1988; White et al., 1988). Table 3 from White et al. (1988) lists the strategies for facilitating generalization along with a definition and example. The table is based on the seminal work of Stokes and Baer (1977) and can serve as a useful guideline for consultants.

Another major objective that should occur during the plan evaluation interview is discussion of post-implementation recording. Generally, this procedure refers to the process of continuing record-keeping activities to determine whether the problem reoccurs in the future. To facilitate this data collection process, the school psychologist and teacher/parent usually select periodic measures that are convenient to use and may maintain specific features of the original plan. Best practices also suggest that the psychologist consider conducting post-plan implementation ac-

ceptability assessment as well. These procedures can be implemented informally or more formally with acceptability instrumentation (Elliott, 1988b).

Finally, the teacher/parent should notify the school psychologist of any indications that the problem behaviors might be reoccurring. These usually can be brought to the psychologist's attention and specific tactics set up to establish a system to analyze the problems. Table 4 provides an overview of the general objectives of the plan evaluation interview.

USE OF BEHAVIORAL CONSULTATION WITH TEACHERS AND PARENTS

Traditionally, school psychologists have implemented consultation with classroom teachers in an effort to establish intervention programs in the regular classroom and thereby reduce the number of placements in special education programs. This emphasis on prevention and direct intervention with teachers advanced the development of a knowledge base to prevent more serious behavioral problems in children. Within the past decade, school-based consultation services have expanded to include work with special education teachers, particularly teachers of emotionally impaired children (Kratochwill, Sheridan, Carrington Rotto, & Salmon, 1991) and teachers from early intervention programs for preschool-age children (Kratochwill & Elliott, 1993). In addition, behavioral consultation also has been used successfully to remediate academic and socialization difficulties in school settings. Applications such as these have presented unique opportunities for school psychologists to increase contact with special education teachers while generally addressing more severe presenting problems in special needs children who often experience multiple difficulties. Hence, the role of consultation has become increasingly specialized, with unique time demands and treatment needs which may vary according to the child's presenting problems and the teacher's level of expertise in areas such as behavior management and individualized instruction.

Although behavioral consultation with teachers is an effective method of remediating school-based problems, this focus fails to address the broader context within which the child's problems may occur. For example, a withdrawn child who exhibits an absence of peer interactions at school likely would be unable to develop and maintain positive social relationships with neighborhood peers. Focusing exclusively on this child's social withdrawal in the school setting through teacher-only consultation restricts conceptualizations, analysis, and treatment of the problem to a single setting. The broader behavioral interrelationships across environments would not be considered. However, behavioral consultation has been extended to serve as a link among the significant settings in a child's life, primarily, the home, school, and commu-

TABLE 3
Strategies for Facilitating Generalization

Strategy	Definition	Example
Train & Hope	Providing simple instruction and then "hoping" that generalization will occur. Actually the *absence* of any special strategy.	Three preschool boys who were blind and severely or profoundly retarded were taught to reach for noise-making toys always presented at the midline. None of the boys generalized to objects presented on the right or left.
Setting Training in the Natural Setting	Training is conducted directly in at least one type of setting in which the skill will be used. Generalization is then probed in other non-training setting.	The social interaction skills of several individuals with severe handicaps were trained in the classroom and courtyard during class breaks.
Sequential Modification	Training is provided in one setting, and generalization is probed in other settings. If necessary, training is conducted sequentially in more and more settings until generalization to all desired settings is observed.	One girl with moderate handicaps needed articulation training in 3 settings before generalizing to all remaining situations of interest; a second girl only required training in two situations before generalizing.
Consequences Introduce to Natural Maintaining Contingencies	Ensuring that learner experiences the natural consequences of a behavior by: (1) teaching a functional skill which is likely to be reinforced outside instruction; (2) training to a level of proficiency that makes the skill truly useful; (3) making sure that learner actually does experience the natural consequence; and/or (4) teaching the learner to solicit or recruit reinforcement outside instruction.	Three teens who were multiply handicapped and severely retarded were taught to use symbols & pictures to request objects. Generalization was encouraged by using objects which would be regularly encountered outside instruction, making sure the boys always carried their communication boards, and that someone would always be present to provide any requested items.
Use Indiscriminable Contingencies	If natural consequences cannot be expected to encourage and maintain generalization, atificial consequences or schedules of natural consequences might be used. However, it is best if the learner cannot determine precisely when those consequences will be available, and so must behave as if they always are.	Two behavior disordered and five normal preschool children always generalized their interaction and study better when verbal praise by the teacher was provided after progressively greater delays, rather than immediately following each behavior.
Train to Generalize	The learner is only reinforced for performing some generalized instance of the target skill. Performing a previously reinforced version of the response is no longer reinforced.	Four youths with severe retardation were taught to name specific items. Contingencies were then altered so they were only reinforced if they named *untrained* items. After 3 sessions, all youths generalized well to untrained items.
Antecedents Program Common Stimuli	Selecting a salient, but not necessarily task-related, stimulus from the situation to which generalization is desired, and including that stimulus in the training program.	Stokes & Baer (1977) report a case in which an individual with severe retardation was taught exercise skills to facilitate integration in a physical education class. Music was played during the PE class, so music was also introduced into the individual's training sessions to make the two situations more similar.

(Table 3, continued)

Sufficient Exemplars	A strategy similar to Sequential Modification, involving sequential addition of stimuli to the training program until generalization to all related stimuli occurs.[2]	An adolescent with severe handicaps was taught to name objects, and probed with other objects from the same class. Some objects required only a single exemplar to produce generalized naming, while other objects required 5 exemeplars before generalization occurred.
Multiple Exemplars	Several examples of the stimulus class to which generalization is desired are trained at the same time.	Three adults with profound mental retardation were trained in three types of exercise. Generalization occurred to a group exercise program and to two untrained exercises.,
General Case Programming	The universe to which generalization is desired is analyzed and representative examples of positive stimuli (stimuli in the presence of which the skill should be used), negative stimuli (stimuli in the presence of which the skill should not be used), and irrelevant stimuli (stimuli which should not effect skill use, but might inappropriately do so) are selected for training.	Six young men with moderate to severe retardation were trained on three vending machines which reflected the range of machine-types found in community. Good generalization was obtained to 10 untrained machines in the community.
Other Train Loosely	Settings, cues, prompts, materials, response definition, and other features of the training situation are purposely varied to avoid a ritual, highly structured, invariate program which might inhibit generalization.	Mothers were taught to vary the type of stimuli and reinforcers they used in working with their children's motor skills. All children learned their skills quickly and generalized well to another setting.
Mediate Generalization	Teaching a secondary behavior or strategy which will help an individual remember or figure out how and when to generalize, or which will dispel the differences between the training and generalization situations.	Five adolescents with moderate or severe mental retardation were taught to self-instruct task completion using a picture sequence. They then used the self-instruction skill to generalize task completion of a new task with a new picture sequence.

[1]Stokes and Baer (1977) described this strategy as training in one situation and, if that fails to produce generalization, training in all remaining situations of interest. The more literally "sequential" nature of the procedure as described above seems better suited for describing current application of the strategy.

[2]Stokes and Baer used this label to describe the successive introduction of new stimuli or settings, but separating the two variations seemed more advisable for the current study (see note 2, above).

Note. From "Review and Analysis of Strategies for Generalization: by White et al., 1978. In N. R. Haring (Ed.), *Generalization for students with severe handicaps: Strategies and solutions* (pp. 15–51). Seattle: University of Washington. Copyright 1978 by the University of Washington. Reprinted by permission.

nity environments. This approach facilitates a comprehensive conceptualization of the problem while involving primary caretakers in the intervention process. In addition, although few investigators have assessed the generalization of treatment effects across settings, the potential benefits of broadening the focus of behavioral consultation to encompass the interacting system in the child's life are apparent.

One method of expanding behavioral consultation services beyond the school setting entails involvement or parent–teacher pairs. In conjoint consultation, parents and teachers together serve as consultees (Sheridan & Kratochwill, 1992; Sheridan, Kratochwill, & Bergan, in press). The primary goals of this approach are to bridge the gap between home and school settings, maximize positive treatment effects within and across settings, and promote generalization of treatment effects over time. Continuous data collection and consistent programming across settings also are inherent with this approach. Conjoint behavioral consultation has been found to be an effective method of service-delivery in enhancing social initiation behaviors across home and school settings (Sheridan, Kratochwill, & Elliott, 1990) as well as increasing the academic productivity of underachieving students (Galloway & Sheridan, 1992) and

TABLE 4
Plan Evaluation Interview

Goal Attainment
> *Definition:* Determine specifically if the goals of consultation have been attained. Question treatment outcome (e.g., How did things go?).

Plan Effectiveness
> *Definition:* Determine the effectiveness of the plan for the specific child. Was the specific plan effective in producing behavior change? What was the internal validity of the plan? (e.g., Would you say that the contract procedure was responsible for reducing John's profane language?).

External Validity of Plan
> *Definition:* Determine the effectiveness of the plan for another child who has a similar problem (e.g., Do you think this plan would have worked with another student?).

Post-Implementation Planning
> *Definition:* Decision is made regarding the advisability of leaving the plan in effect, removing the plan, or constructing a new plan. Selection of a post-treatment alternative may be made (e.g., Do you want to leave the point system in effect for another week to see if Bob's progress continues?).

Plan Modification
> *Devinition:* Establish new plan strategies to increase plan effectiveness. Consultant may suggest a change or question the need for change (e.g., How could we change the reinforcement procedure to make the plan more effective?).

Procedures to Facilitate Generalization and Maintenance
> *Definition:* Procedures to encourage continued progress. Goal is to encourage generalization to other settings, or maintain behavior over a long period of time (e.g., What procedures can be implemented to be sure that Sally continues to finish her homework?).

Follow-Up Assessment
> *Definition:* Discussion regarding follow-up recording procedures to monitor the behavior over time (e.g., Now that we have success in the program for George, how can we monitor his progress in the future?).

---

decreasing the irrational fears of a kindergarten student (Sheridan & Colton, in press). It also has been used to enhance the effects of parent training in managing the behavior of children diagnosed with attention deficit hyperactivity disorder (ADHD) across home and school settings (Johnson & Tilly, 1993).

Use of behavioral consultation has been extended beyond the schools to address problems with individuals other than teachers, such as parents. Parent-only consultation may be applicable when a child's problematic behaviors are observed predominantly in the home and/or community settings with little evidence of them in the school environment. For example, parent consultation has been used to decrease the noncompliant behaviors of school-age children whose difficult behaviors were displayed at home and in public places but were not observed in the more structured classroom setting (Carrington Rotto & Kratochwill, in press). In addition, behavioral consultation with parents has been advanced as a model of early intervention with the goal of decreasing noncompliant and aggressive behaviors of preschool-age children (Carrington Rotto & Kratochwill, 1993). In parent-only consultation, the traditional behavioral consultation framework provides structure for involving the parent(s) in the process of identifying and analyzing the problem, as well as observing and evaluating treatment effects over time. Use of behavioral technology consultation (i.e., parent training) provides structure for teaching parents specific skills which enhance plan implementation. Necessary preparations for plan implementation include teaching parents specific behavior management skills and ensuring that they are adept at implementing these skills. Further research is needed to examine specific methods of promoting generalization fo parent behaviors (i.e., skill implementation) across settings and situations to enhance specific child behaviors.

In sum, behavioral consultation provides a useful framework for working within and between family and school systems. This systematic problem-solving approach may be conducted with teachers, parents, or teacher-parent pairs to enhance child functioning across home, school, and community settings. Together with parents and teachers, school psychologists may develop and implement intervention plans to address diverse target problems in areas such as academic productivity, socialization, and behavioral difficulties. Future research should be directed toward replication of treatment effects with diverse subject populations and further examination of alternative parent and teacher roles and levels of involvement in consultation.

WRITING BEHAVIORAL CONSULTATION CASE REPORTS

At various times during the course of consultation, the consultant may wish to formally communicate the results of the intervention program to the parent and/or teacher. Indeed, it is the ethical and professional responsibility of the consultant to ensure that information concerning an intervention is communicated in a valid, clear, and concise manner. Although a variety of traditional report formats exist (see Gelfand & Hartmann, 1983; Martin, 1973; Ownby, 1987; for overviews), the present format provides a conceptual scheme for reporting interventions compatible with best practices in consultation. The consultant, however, is advised to modify this format to accommodate personal preferences and meet specific, institutional needs and standards. The reporting format that we present can readily be used for consultation activities that are part of a prereferral intervention or for specialized programs that are part of multidisciplinary team follow-up activities.

The present report format represents an outline for describing the activities of an entire consultation program (see Table 5). Psychologists reporting information prior of completion of the plan would find only parts of this report appropriate. General characteristics of the behavioral consultation report include (a) Background Information, (b) Problem Definition, (c) Intervention Plan, (d) Plan Evaluation, and (e) Summary and Recommendations.

The section on *Background Information* includes demographic information describing the child and details regarding the setting in which the problem occurs. For example, the child's name, date of birth, age, gender, school, parents, address, telephone, and teacher should be specified. The consultant should also include a description of the family, siblings, socioeconomic status, peers, teacher, and any other ecological features relevant to the case.

Many alternative ways exist to define a problematic situation. For example, problem behaviors may be described at various levels of specificity. Alternatively, a problem situation can be conceptualized in terms of reducing negative behaviors or increasing positive behaviors. The purpose of the *Problem Definition* is to provide a description and rationale for the problem as defined by the school psychologist (i.e., consultant) and teacher/parent during consultation. Information from the problem identification interview will be especially relevant. More specifically, details regarding the referral problem, target behavior(s), desired outcome behavior(s), critical setting or situations for change, and a preliminary analysis should be included.

Discussion of the initial referral issue should indicate the referral source and a description of the problem. The consultant also should note that consent for participation was obtained from the child's parents. An operational definition of the problem as agreed upon by the school psychologist and teacher/parent should be described in terms of deficits, excesses, frequency, intensity, and duration. Specifications of the target area(s) and a statement regarding desired outcome(s) also should be included. In addition, the consultant should discuss the critical setting where the child's behavior was expected to change and provide a detailed description of the situations necessary for such a change. Finally, a preliminary functional analysis should compare the antecedents and consequences surrounding the problem behavior to those necessary for attainment of the desired behavior.

The *Problem Analysis* discussion should be based on assessment procedures such as interview, direct observation, and/or standardized scales. Hence, the consultant integrates the baseline data, observational data, and problem identification interview to analyze the discrepancy between the existing behavior and desired behavior. A sample of each observational data sheet used during the case may be included in the report.

A description of any intervention programs or procedures implemented during the process of consultation should be included in the section entitled *Intervention Plan*. The consultant should characterize the basic design of the plan according to variables such as the (a) time needed for implementation, (b) contingencies, (c) criterion for delivery of contingencies, (d) setting and time, and (e) resources or materials. In addition, the consultant should specify clearly the procedures used for promoting new behaviors, increasing existing behaviors, and/or reducing interfering problem behaviors. A rationale describing why the particular intervention procedure(s) are relevant to the target problem is essential. In some cases, a treatment "package" consisting of many specific techniques (e.g., feedback, reinforcement, modeling) may be used. Identification of the individuals who are responsible for implementing the plan and a discussion of the degree to which the plan is acceptable to the teacher/parent and child also should be included. Finally, it is desirable to document the strategies used to facilitate generalization and to verify the intervention plan was implemented as intended.

This list is intended to serve as a resource and should be considered carefully. The consultant must determine the variables most pertinent to the specific case; thus, it may be necessary to generate additional dimensions that adequately describe the intervention. Likewise, some of the intervention variables listed may not apply to all cases. It may be helpful to use headings or an outline format similar to that in Table

TABLE 5
Outline for Writing a Behavioral Consultation Case Report

I. Background Information
   A. Demographic Information on the Child
   B. Ecological Context of the Problem

II. Problem Definition
   A. Referral Problem
   B. Target Behaviors
   C. Desired Outcome Behaviors
   D. Critical Setting/Situations for Change
   E. Preliminary Functional Analysis

III. Problem Analysis
   A. Description of Assessment or Data Recording Procedures
   B. Rationale for Use of Data Collection Procedures
   C. Presentation and Discussion of Data

IV. Intervention Plan
   A. Basic Design
   B. Contingencies
   C. Criterion for Contingencies
   D. Acceptability of Intervention to Teacher/Parent and Child
   E. Personnel Involved in Intervention Implementation
   F. Setting and Time
   G. Resources
   H. Procedures for Promoting New Behaviors
   I. Procedures for Increasing Existing Behaviors
   J. Procedures for Reducing Interfering Problem Behaviors
   K. Procedures for Facilitating Generalization
   L. Treatment Integrity Checks

V. Plan Evaluation
   A. Change in Behavior via Direct Observation
   B. Change in Teacher/Parent Performance Ratings
   C. Mainstreamed Peer Comparison
   D. Outcome Interview with Significant Adults
   E. Intervention Side Effects

VI. Summary and Recommendations
   A. Summary of Results Obtained
   B. Discussion of Effectiveness
   C. Suggestions for Increasing Program Effectiveness
   D. Suggestions for Future Follow-up

5 to facilitate notetaking during consultation interviews and post-treatment preparation of a clear and concise report.

A complete description of the *Intervention Evaluation Plan* should be provided, including methods used to evaluate the specific treatment components and document changes in the child's behavior. Especially relevant will be data from the plan evaluation interview. The school psychologist should present the results of the program in the context of the data collected over the duration of the program and during the generalization or follow-up phases. For example, direct observations and ratings of the child's performance may provide documentation of intervention outcome. In addition, the consultant may evaluate the performance of a mainstreamed peer for comparison

before and after the plan is initiated. At least one figure should be used to portray the data collected, and the school psychologist should acknowledge any unique features of the data (e.g., absence, program not followed) or challenges that may have occurred. The consultant should also provide details regarding any side effects which may have resulted from the intervention plan.

The *Summary and Recommendations* should begin with a brief overview of the results obtained and a rationale for program effectiveness or failure. The consultant also should include suggestions for increasing the effectiveness of the program. Recommendations may provide suggestions for (a) future follow-up, (b) enhancing maintenance/generalization, and (c) subsequent intervention plans. These suggestions should identify the involved socialization agents (e.g., parents, teachers, peers) and relevant materials that may be useful for the child or treatment personnel in future work.

SUMMARY AND CONCLUSIONS

Behavioral consultation is a four stage problem solving approach that uses behavioral technology as the basis for problem identification, analysis, intervention, and evaluation. The major features of behavioral consultation include its indirect service-delivery approach and problem-solving activity.

Behavioral consultation has two principal goals. The first goal is to produce change in the child's behavior indirectly through collaborative problem solving between a consultant (school psychologist) and consultee(s) (teacher/parent). A second, yet equally important, goal of behavioral consultation is to provide knowledge and skills that facilitate teacher/parent effectiveness with similar problems in the future. Behavioral consultation generally is recognized as a series of four stages that are used to implement the process of consultation (Bergan & Kratochwill, 1990). These include problem identification, problem analysis, plan implementation, and plan evaluation. Each of these steps, with the exception of plan implementation, is accompanied by a formal interview process and specific objectives.

Research and practice in behavioral consultation have expanded rapidly. Recent interest in consultative methods as they impact the delivery of psychological services in the schools has resulted in increased attention to this area in the literature. This growing enthusiasm over the potential benefits of behavioral consultation is apparent in the numerous articles on the topic published recently in both the psychological and educational literature (Zins, Kratochwill, & Elliott, 1993). As school psychologists have become interested in the integration of behavioral consultation with daily activities and child adjustment in schools and homes, questions regarding the process and outcome of consultation have surfaced. Studies have examined the application of behavioral principles in consultation to achieve changes in behavior and compared the effectiveness of behavioral consultation to other forms of service delivery.

Research documenting the effectiveness of behavioral consultation has been organized around four areas of investigation: (a) outcome research, (b) process research, (c) practitioner research, and (d) training research (Gresham & Kendell, 1987). Research addressing outcomes of behavioral consultation document its effectiveness in remediating academic and behavior problems manifested by children and youths in school settings (Bergan & Kratochwill, 1990). Likewise, these same studies suggest that changes result in the teacher's and parent's behavior, knowledge, attitudes, and perceptions. Although behavioral consultation traditionally has been directed toward a single client (i.e., teacher), it also has been applied successfully with parent groups.

Typically, much of the process research has focused on problem identification, since the consultant's ability to elicit a clear description of the problem has been identified as the best predictor of plan implementation and problem solution (Bergan & Tombari, 1975, 1976). Studies in this area also have focused on comparing behavioral consultation effectiveness with other forms of service delivery (Medway, 1979). It remains difficult to draw conclusions from the studies addressing variables associated with the process of consultation due to limitations in scope, theoretical base, and research methodology (Gresham & Kendall, 1987).

Studies on practitioner utilization have suggested that school-based consultation is a preferred activity for school psychologists (Gutkin & Curtis, 1981, 1990; Meacham & Peckam, 1978). Likewise, teachers and administrators view consultation as an essential aspect of school psychological services (Curtis & Zins, 1981). However, many practitioners identify limitations in actually implementing consultation due to time constraints and lack of consultee commitment (Gresham & Kendell, 1987).

Overall, behavioral consultation is a rapidly growing area with increasing empirical support. However, future studies must utilize more sophisticated designs and measurement strategies to evaluate variables in consultation. Careful scrutiny of behavioral consultation will impact its future use as an alternative to traditional assessment and intervention practices in educational settings and may result in an increased emphasis on the development of formalized training in school psychology programs. In turn, these developments would contribute to the practice of school psychology and positively impact the children, teachers, and parents receiving psychological and educational services.

AUTHOR NOTES

Preparation of this chapter was supported, in part, by Grant #G008730051 to the first author, Grant #H029F80013 to the second authors, and Grant #H023B10023 to the first and third authors, all from the U.S. Department of Education, Office of Special Education and Rehabilitative Services. The content of the chapter does not represent the views of the U.S. Department of Education.

REFERENCES

Barlow, D. H., Hayes, S. C., & Nelson, R. O. (1984). *The scientist-practitioner: Research accountability in clinical and educational settings.* New York: Pergamon Press.

Bergan, J. R. (1985). *School psychology in contemporary society: An introduction.* Columbus, OH: Charles E. Merrill.

Bergan, J. R., & Kratochwill, T. R. (1990). *Behavioral consultation in applied settings.* New York: Plenum Press.

Bergan, J. R., & Tombari, M. L. (1975). The analysis of verbal interactions occurring during consultation. *Journal of School Psychology, 14*, 3–14.

Bergan, J. R., & Tombari, J. L. (1976). Consultant skill and efficiency and the implementation and outcome of consultation. *Journal of School Psychology, 14*, 3–14.

Brown, D. K., Kratochwill, T. R., & Bergan, J. R. (1982). Training interview skills for problem identification: An analogue study. *Behavioral Assessment, 4*, 63–73.

Busse, R. T., Kratochwill, T. R., & Elliott, S. N. (in press). Meta analysis in single-case consultation outcome research. *Journal of School Psychology.*

Carrington Rotto, P., & Kratochwill, T. R. (in press). Competency-based parent consultation. Training parents to modify child noncompliance. *School Psychology Review.*

Carrington Rotto, P., & Kratochwill, T. R. (1993, April). *Competency-based parent consultation and training to modify noncompliance in young children.* Paper presented at the 25th Annual Meeting of the National Association of School Psychologists, Washington, DC.

Conoley, J. C., & Conoley, C. W. (1992). *School consultation: A guide to practice and training.* Elmsford, NY: Pergamon Press.

Curtis, M. J., & Zins, J. E. (Eds.). (1981). *The theory and practice of school consultation.* Springfield, IL: Charles C Thomas.

Dunst, C. J., & Trivette, C. M. (1988). Helping, helplessness, and harm. In J. Witt, S. N. Elliott, & F. M. Gresham (Eds.), *The handbook of behavior therapy in education* (pp. 343–376). New York: Plenum.

Elliott, S. N. (1988a). Acceptability of behavioral treatments: A review of variables that influence treatment selection. *Professional Psychology: Research and Practice, 19*, 63–80.

Elliott, S. N. (1988b). Acceptability of behavioral treatment in educational settings. In J. C. Witt, S. N. Elliott, & F. M. Gresham (Eds.), *The handbook of behavior therapy in education* (pp. 121–150). New York: Plenum Publishers.

Elliott, S. N., & Sheridan, S. M. (1992). Consultation conferencing: Problem-solving among educators, parents, and support personnel. *Elementary School Journal, 92*, 261–284.

Galloway, J., & Sheridan, S. M. (1992, March). *Parent-teacher consultation: Forging effective home-school partnerships in the treatment of academic underachievement.* Paper presented at the 24th Annual Meeting of the National Association of School Psychologists. Nashville.

Gelfand, D. M., & Hartmann, D. P. (1984). *Child behavior analysis and therapy* (2nd ed.). New York: Pergamon.

Gresham, F. M. (1989). Assessment of treatment integrity in school consultation and prereferral intervention. *School Psychology Review, 18*, 37–50.

Gresham, F. M. (1991). Moving beyond statistical significance in reporting consultation outcome research. *Journal of Educational and Psychological Consultation.*

Gresham, F. M., & Kendall, G. K. (1987). School consultation research: Methodological critique and future research directions. *School Psychology Review, 16*, 306–316.

Gresham, F. M., & Noell, G. H. (1993). Documenting the effectiveness of consultation outcomes. In J. Zins, T. R. Kratochwill, & S. N. Elliott (Eds.), *Handbook of consultation services for children* (pp. 249–273). San Francisco: Jossey-Bass.

Grimes, J. (Ed.). (1983). *Communicating psychological information in writing.* Des Moines, IA: Department of Public Instruction.

Gutkin, T. B., & Curtis, M. J. (1981). School-based consultation: Theory and techniques. In C. R. Reynolds and T. B. Gutkin (Eds.), *The handbook of school psychology* (pp. 796–828). New York: Wiley.

Gutkin, T., & Curtis, M. (1990). School-based consultation: Theory, techniques, and research. In C. R. Reynolds & T. B. Gutkin (Eds.), *The handbook of school psychology* (pp. 577–611). New York: Wiley.

Haring, N. G. (1988). A technology for generalization. In N. G. Haring (Ed.), *Generalization for students with severe handicaps: Strategies and solutions* (pp. 5–11). Seattle: University of Washington Press.

Jacobson, N., Follette, W., & Revenstorf, D. (1984). Psychotherapy outcome research: Methods for reporting variability and evaluating clinical significance. *Behavior Therapy, 15*, 336–352.

Johnson, T. L., & Tilly, W. D. (1993, March). *Using conjoint consultation to enhance the effects of parent training for children with ADHD.* Poster session presented for the 25th Annual Meeting of the National Association of School Psychologists, Washington, DC.

Kazdin, A. E. (1989). *Behavior modification in applied settings* (Revised ed.). Homewood, IL: The Dorsey Press.

Kratochwill, T. R., & Elliott, S. N. (1993). *An experimental analysis of teacher/parent mediated interventions for preschoolers with behavioral problems.* Unpublished manuscript, Office of Special Education and Rehabilitative Services, U.S. Department of Education, Wisconsin Center for Education Research, University of Wisconsin-Madison, Madison, WI.

Kratochwill, T. R., & Bergan, J. R. (1990). *Behavioral consultation in applied settings: An individual guide.* New York: Plenum Press.

Kratochwill, T. R., & Morris, R. J. (1992). *The practice of child therapy* (2nd ed.). New York: Pergamon Press.

Kratochwill, T. R., Sheridan, S. M., Carrington Rotto, P., & Salmon, D. (1991). Preparation of school psychologists to serve as consultants for teachers of emotionally disturbed children. *School Psychology Review, 20*, 539–550.

Lloyd, M. E. (1983). Selecting systems to measure direct outcome in human services agencies. *Behavioral Assessment, 5*, 55–70.

Martens, B. (1993). A behavioral approach to consultation. In J. E. Zins, T. R. Kratochwill, & S. N. Elliott (Eds.), *Handbook of consultation services to children* (pp. 65–86). San Francisco: Jossey Bass.

Martin, R. P. (1978). Expert and referent power: A framework for understanding and maximizing consultation effectiveness. *Journal of School Psychology, 16*, 49–55.

Martin, W. T. (1972). *Writing psychological reports.* Springfield, IL: Charles C Thomas.

Medway, F. J. (1979). How effective is school consultation? A review of recent research. *Journal of School Psychology, 17*, 275–282.

Meyers, V., Liddell, A., & Lyons, M. (1977). Behavioral interviews. In A. R. Ciminero, K. S. Calhoun, & H. E. Adams (Eds.), *Handbook of behavioral assessment* (pp. 117–152). New York: John Wiley.

Nunnally, J., & Kotsche, W. (1983). Studies of individual subjects: Logic and methods of analysis. *The British Journal of Clinical Psychology, 22*, 83–93.

Ownby, R. L. (1987). *Psychological reports: A guide to report writing in professional psychology.* Brandon, VT: Clinical Psychological Publishing Company.

Parsons, R., & Meyers, J. (1984). *Developing consultation skills: A guide to training, development, and assessment for human services professionals.* San Francisco: Jossey-Bass.

Reschly, D. K. (1988). Special education reform: School psychology revolution. *School Psychology Review, 17,* 465–481.

Rinn, R. C., Vernon, J. C., & Wise, M. J. (1975). Training parents of behaviorally-disordered children in groups: A three years' program evaluation. *Behavior Therapy, 6,* 378–387.

Sheridan, S. M., & Colton, D. L. (in press). Conjoint behavioral consultation and irrational fears: A case study. *Journal of Educational and Psychological Consultation.*

Sheridan, S. M., & Kratochwill, T. R. (1992). Behavioral parent–teacher consultation: Conceptual and research considerations. *Journal of School Psychology, 30,* 117–139.

Sheridan, S. M., Kratochwill, T. R., & Bergan, J. (in press). *Conjoint behavioral consultation: A procedural manual.* New York: Plenum Press.

Sheridan, S. M., Kratochwill, T. R., & Elliott, S. N. (1990). Behavioral consultation with parents and teachers: Delivering treatment for socially withdrawn children at home and school. *School Psychology Review, 19,* 33–52.

Stokes, T. F., & Baer, D. B. (1977). An implicit technology of generalization. *Journal of Applied Behavior Analysis, 10,* 349–367.

White, O. R., Liberty, K. A., Haring, N. G., Billingsley, F. F., Boer, M., Barrage, Connors, R., Forman, R., Fedorchak, G., Leber, B. D., Liberty-Laylin, S., Miller, S., Opalski, Phifer, C., & Sessoms, I. (1988). Review and analysis of strategies for generalization. In N. G. Haring (Ed.), *Generalization for students with severe handicaps: Strategies and solutions* (pp. 15–51). Seattle: University of Washington Press.

Wickstrom, K. F., & Witt, J. C. (1993). Resistance within school-based consultation. In J. Zins, T. R. Kratochwill, & S. N. Elliott (Eds.), *Handbook of consultation services for child* (pp. 159–178). San Francisco: Jossey-Bass.

Witt, J. C., & Elliott, S. N. (1983). Assessment in behavioral consultation: The initial interview. *School Psychology Review, 12,* 42–49.

Witt, J. C., & Elliott, S. N. (1985). Acceptability of classroom intervention strategies. In T. R. Kratochwill (Ed.), *Advances in school psychology* (Vol. IV, pp. 251–288). Hillsdale, NJ: Lawrence Erlbaum Associates, Inc.

Witt, J. C., & Martens, B. K. (1988). Problems with problem-solving consultation: A re-analysis of assumptions, methods, and goals. *School Psychology Review, 17,* 211–226.

Zins, J. E., Kratochwill, T. R., & Elliott, S. N. (Eds.). (1993). *Handbook of consultation services for children.* San Francisco: Jossey-Bass.

ANNOTATED BIBLIOGRAPHY

Barlow, D. H., Hayes, S. C., & Nelson, R. O. (1984). *The scientist-practitioner: Research and accountability in clinical and educational settings.* New York: Pergamon Press.

The authors outline specific assessment and measurement strategies that can be used in consultation. The text is especially useful in outlining assessment strategies and case-study techniques that can be helpful during the treatment implementation and treatment monitoring phase of behavioral consultation.

Bergan, J. R., & Kratochwill, T. R. (1990). *Behavioral consultation in applied settings.* New York: Plenum Press.

The authors provide an extensive overview of behavioral consultation research and practice. The text provides detailed information for researchers and practitioners in the conduct of behavioral consultation and accompanied by a companion self-instructional guide (see Kratochwill & Bergan, 1990, which follows).

Kazdin, A. E. (1989). *Behavior modification in applied settings* (revised ed.). Homewood, IL: The Dorsey Press.

The author presents an overview of behavior modification techniques in applied settings. It is extremely useful in consultation because it includes material directly relevant to implementing treatments in applied settings.

Kratochwill, T. R., & Bergan, J. R. (1990). *Behavioral consultation in applied settings: An individual guide.* New York: Plenum Press.

The authors present a practitioner guidebook devoted to behavioral consultation in applied settings. It details the problem identification, problem analysis, treatment implementation, and treatment evaluation phases of behavioral consultation. Specific formats for interviews are provided within the text.

Kratochwill, T. R., & Morris, R. J. (Eds.). (1992). The practice of child therapy (2nd ed.). Boston: Allyn & Bacon.

The editors provide an overview of various treatment approaches that is organized by the major childhood disorders. Although many of the treatments described are used in a direct therapy application, numerous approaches can be used by consultation mediators, especially with training.

APPENDIX A
Behavior Intervention Rating Scale

You have just read abut a child with a classroom problem and a description of an intervention for improving the problem. Please evaluate the intervention by circling the number which best describes *your* agreement or disagreement with each statement. *You must* answer each question.

	Strongly Disagree	Disagree	Slightly Disagree	Agree	Strongly Agree
1. This would be an acceptable intervention for the child's problem behavior.	1	2	3	4	5
2. Most teachers would find this intervention appropriate for behavior problems in addition to the one described.	1	2	3	4	5
3. The intervention should prove effective in changing the child's problem behavior.	1	2	3	4	5
4. I would suggest the use of this intervention to other teachers.	1	2	3	4	5
5. The child's behavior problem is severe enough to warrant use of this intervention.	1	2	3	4	5
6. Most teachers would find this intervention suitable for the behavior problem described.	1	2	3	4	5
7. I would be willing to use this intervention in the classroom setting.	1	2	3	4	5
8. The intervention would not result in negative side-effects.	1	2	3	4	5
9. The intervention would be appropriate for a variety of children.	1	2	3	4	5
10. The intervention is consistent with those I have use in classroom settings.	1	2	3	4	5
11. The intervention was a fair way to handle the child's problem behavior.	1	2	3	4	5
12. The intervention is reasonable for the behavior problem described.	1	2	3	4	5
13. I liked the procedures used in the intervention.	1	2	3	4	5
14. The intervention was a good way to handle this child's behavior problem.	1	2	3	4	5
15. Overall, the intervention would be beneficial for the child.	1	2	3	4	5
16. The intervention would quickly improve the child's behavior.	1	2	3	4	5
17. The intervention would produce a lasting improvement in the child's behavior.	1	2	3	4	5
18. The intervention would improve the child's behavior to the point that it would not noticeably deviate from other classmates' behavior.	1	2	3	4	5
19. Soon after using the intervention, the teacher would notice a positive change in the problem behavior.	1	2	3	4	5
20. The child's behavior will remain at an improved level even after the intervention is discontinued.	1	2	3	4	5

21. Using the intervention should not only improve the child's behavior in the classroom, but also in other settings (e.g., other classrooms, home).	1	2	3	4	5
22. When comparing this child with a well-behaved peer before and after use of the intervention, the child's and the peer's behavior would be more alike after using the intervention.	1	2	3	4	5
23. The intervention should produce enough improvement in the child's behavior so the behavior no longer is a problem in the classroom.	1	2	3	4	5
24. Other behaviors related to the problem behavior also are likely to be improved by the intervention.	1	2	3	4	5

From Elliott, S. N., & VonBrock, M. B. (1991). The Behavior Intervention Rating Scale: The development and validation of a social validity measure. *Journal of School Psychology, 29,* 43–52.

47

Best Practices in Defining Student Goals and Outcomes

Lynn S. Fuchs
Peabody College of Vanderbilt University

OVERVIEW

Definition of the Topic

The importance of goals in understanding human behavior is critical. Individuals organize their activities around goals that relate to their current levels of performance and their aspirations; the nature of an individual's goals and his or her daily strivings are intimately intertwined. Similarly schools are organized around goals related to age-appropriate societal expectations; the nature of those goals and the curricula of schools, or what teachers teach, are inextricably connected.

Clearly written, justifiable goals and procedures for evaluating goal attainment are potentially key factors for successful educational programs. Over the years, the pressure to specify clear, measurable outcomes for individual students has increased dramatically. The purpose of this chapter is to discuss the history, context, purposes, and applications of goals and to present alternative methods for accomplishing the specification of useful, manageable goal statements.

History and Rationale

Before the turn of the twentieth century, psychologists viewed the brain as a composite of general intellectual faculties that, when strengthened, could be applied to any area of human activity. Therefore, if educators identified faculties and strengthened them, they would expect concurrent educational growth.

At the turn of the century, however, Thorndike demonstrated the specificity of transfer, such that learning occurs when elements in the original context are relevant and similar to elements in other contexts. Applying Thorndike's work to the development of educational curricula, Bobbitt (1918) argued that human life consists of performing specific activities, and that the skills and knowledge required for successful adult life should constitute the curriculum of schools.

Consequently, psychologists began to develop the notion that general intellectual growth might be operationalized to include a series of learning products. This premise was central to Ralph Tyler's work in curriculum and instruction. Tyler argued that evaluation demonstrated the ways and extent to which students have changed in relation to a set of desired behaviors. While in charge of the eight-year study of secondary education for the Progressive Education Association, Tyler emphasized successfully the need to define educational goals in terms of student behaviors and specific content. A product of that study was Smith and Tyler's book, *Appraising and Recording Student Progress* (1942), which lists numerous behavioral objectives. As director of the National Assessment Project, Tyler required that educational objectives constitute the groundwork for developing curriculum materials and instructional procedures and in designing evaluation instruments to appraise the effectiveness of these newly developed materials and procedures (Bloom, Hastings, & Madaus, 1971).

Psychologists such as Gagne, Glaser, and Mager also attempted to develop clear statements of educational objectives. However, unlike Tyler, who was interested in evaluation, these investigators were interested primarily in the development of effective instruction. Their focus was on task analysis: the description of behavioral outcomes in terms of a repertoire of discrete behaviors that must be built sequentially to arrive at a terminal performance. The work of Gagne and others developed further the notion that school-related growth could be operationalized and segmented into very small units.

Perhaps one of the major effects of the use of distinct behavioral objectives in schools was to render local educational agencies more accountable to the public for the content and effectiveness of their programs. Similarly, in special education, accountability was one of the important rationales for mandating the development of Individual Educational Programs (IEPs), which include annual goals and short-term objectives. Developers of PL 94—142 intended that the IEP statement of goals, along with procedures and criteria for determining whether goals are being met, would assure that schools were accountable to students, parents, and taxpayers for the quality of the programs they provided to students with disabilities (Turnbull & Turnbull, 1978). Unfortunately, in the first two decades of PL 94–142's implementation, accountability focused almost exclusively on procedural compliance — documenting that goals and objectives were written and that services were provided.

Current Context

More recently, as concern about this country's academic and workplace competitiveness has increased, the demand for accountability for student outcomes has increased within special education and spread across the entire educational system. In September 1990, then-President George Bush convened a historic education summit with the nation's governors at the University of Virginia — the only time in our country's history that such a summit has been held to discuss issues pertaining to education. In his concluding remarks, President Bush discussed the overwhelming need to establish "accountability for outcome-related results."

This focus on student outcomes is reflected in a recent Gallup Poll, in which 70% of Americans favored requiring schools to conform to national standards and goals. Likewise, Ernest L. Boyer observed, "I think we've gone about as far as we can go in the current reform movement dealing with procedural issues. . . . Schools [should] be held accountable for outcomes rather than the current situation of heavy state regulation that 'nibbles' them to death over procedures."

This distinction between procedural and outcome accountability is particularly relevant to special education. As stated, since 1975, when PL 94–142 was passed, the field has witnessed a 20-year focus on procedural compliance. In 1995, however, in synchrony with the accountability movement in general education, the field has begun to refocus attention on what students are learning, rather than what services are being provided.

As we enter the second half of the last decade of the century — when resources are becoming tighter, when we increasingly are competing economically in an international marketplace, and when the disparities between the wealthy and poor are growing — accountability has become the operant word in justifying increased funds for schooling. The public requires that schools demonstrate student improvement — or results — to justify increased expenditures, including funds for special education.

Purposes

As the pressure to account for the effects of schooling continues to mount, the critical issue is how to define our goals so they represent the most important outcomes for our students to achieve. In considering alternative methods for specifying our goal statements, three purposes are critical: to direct teaching and curriculum development, to guide learners, and to structure evaluation and accountability.

Directing teaching and curriculum development. Studies indicate that teaching with goals fosters student academic growth and teacher success. In an early study, for example, McNeil (1967) randomly assigned 77 university teacher trainees to two groups. In the experimental group, trainees contracted with their cooperating teachers for the student changes that would constitute success; in the control group, practicing teachers familiarized themselves with class activities and prepared daily lesson plans. Both supervisors and cooperating teachers judged the experimental trainees' success in teaching by pupil achievement and the trainees' applications of learning principles. In a related experiment, McNeil (1967) added to these findings by demonstrating that student teachers effected superior student growth when their own grades depended on the appropriateness of the goals they selected for their students and on their students' mastery of those goals. Additional studies through the years have corroborated McNeil's early work, indicating that teaching with specific goals focused on student outcomes increases teacher success and student achievement.

Guiding learners. Industrial and social psychology studies of individual and group goals suggest that an individual functions better when clear about expected goals. Learning theory also supports the importance of students being aware of the goals toward which they strive: Such understanding theoretically helps learners recognize errors and improve performance, and this power to discriminate among responses affects their attainment of skills. In addition, a substantial number of studies has documented that student knowledge of goals enhances learning.

Structuring evaluation. As already discussed, a primary impetus for the use of goals in education has been to structure the evaluation, or accountability, process. Once a well-formulated goal has been specified, it structures the methods for assessment and evaluation.

Applications for School Psychologists

With changing demographics in the school-age population, school reform efforts that focus more on collaboration among professionals, and inclusion of disabled students within general education classrooms, the need for solving individual student problems should increase and school psychologists' roles should continue to become more varied. Consequently, the need for school psychologists to assume the role of problem solvers and to adopt a problem-solving approach to their professional activities should grow.

The concept of a problem-solving approach, as presented in this volume, is characterized by defining problem behaviors in behaviorally specific and discrete form, assessing those behaviors using low inference methods, setting goals in relation to baseline levels, formulating interventions to ameliorate problem behaviors, direct and frequent monitoring to gauge progress, and terminating services when goals have been realized. Central to guiding a successful problem-solving approach, consequently, is the definition of the problem and specification of the goal: With a well-specified goal, evaluation is structured, teaching and intervention are directed, and learners are guided toward problem solution. In school settings where a problem-solving approach is central to innovation, school psychologists must be prepared to assist fellow professionals in developing important, useful goal statements.

BASIC CONSIDERATIONS

Background for School Psychologists

Increasingly, school psychology training programs have broadened their focus from psychometric principles and test administration, interpretation, and reporting to preparing future school psychologists to assume critical roles in coordinating and improving academic and psychosocial treatments delivered within school settings. In preparing for their important role in helping schools delineate desired outcomes for their students, school psychologists must rely on consultation and collaboration skills, a thorough grounding in academic curricula, psychosocial treatments, workplace and community contexts, and complete understanding of alternative strategies for monitoring student progress toward anticipated outcomes.

Principles for Useful Goal Statements

This section reviews basic considerations for writing useful goal statements. Effective goals must be student-centered, clear and precise, ambitious, focused on long-term outcomes, descriptive of generalizable behavior within authentic settings, and developed through collaboration.

Student- versus teacher-centered goals. In useful goal statements, the verb does not describe teacher activities (e.g., the teacher will teach early civilization). Such statements of teachers' plans are helpful only after we have determined what we want students to accomplish. Consequently, outcomes that describe what we want students to accomplish should focus the direction and evaluation of instruction and, correspondingly, our goal statements.

The relationship between teacher- and student-centered goals is analogous to the relationship between learning processes and learning products. For Teacher A, learning might include having students trace letters in the air and complete Frostig worksheets; for Teacher B, learning might include provid-

ing phonics instruction and lots of opportunity for students to read literature. In both cases, however, the learning product — or goal — is identical: reading first-grade text proficiently.

As this example illustrates, goals should not outline the instructional methods or the content to be covered in a curriculum. Goals that do focus on instructional methods or content coverage are met when the instruction has been provided or the content has been presented — regardless of whether students have changed in any intended way. Unfortunately, in many school districts today, a strong emphasis on content coverage exists, pressing teachers to cover material in lockstep fashion, regardless of whether students are learning the material. Instead, goals should focus on student mastery.

Clear and precise goals. Research (e.g., Melton, 1978) indicates that the more clear goals are, the more likely participants are to attempt to meet them. Dales (1970) underscored this point by demonstrating that student performance was significantly better when students were given precisely rather than vaguely stated goals. This finding corroborates learning and measurement theory: Clear goals provide more useful information both to learners for discerning correct performance and to professionals for structuring instruction and evaluation.

Ambitious goals. If we accept the premise that goals are important in directing human behavior, then the ambitiousness of goal must be critical in determining how functional the goal will be. If goals are too easy to attain, they fail to sustain meaningful behavior. If, on the other hand, they are exceedingly difficult to achieve, they may discourage functional behavior.

Within educational settings, unambitious goals, which are relatively easy to achieve, may allow educators to appear more successful than they really are. By contrast, appropriately ambitious goals, which may reduce the appearance of success in the short run, may intensify programs and enhance outcomes in the long run.

In investigating goal ambitiousness, Fuchs, Fuchs, and Deno (1985) explored the relation between student achievement and goal ambitiousness and goal mastery. Participants were 58 special education students for whom teachers assessed baseline performance and set reading goals employing a standard format. On the basis of the relation between baseline and the stated goal, students were assigned to highly ambitious, moderately ambitious, and low goal groups. For 18 weeks, teachers worked to achieve their goals. Student achievement was measured at the beginning and end of the study; at the end, goal mastery was determined. Analyses revealed that the ambitiousness of the goals was associated positively with achievement. Goal mastery, however, was not. That is, teachers who geared their efforts toward more ambitious goals achieved better results, regardless of whether or not students actually met their goals.

In a related study, Fuchs, Fuchs, and Hamlett (1989) contrasted two decision-making structures used in conjunction with an ongoing assessment system, Curriculum-Based Measurement (CBM). Ten teachers participated in a contrast group in which CBM was not used. Ten teachers participated in a conventional CBM treatment in which, once the goal was specified at the beginning of the year, teachers were free to increase their goal at any time; the formal decision rules, however, never required them to increase the goal. The final group of 10 teachers participated in a CBM treatment in which the decision rules prompted an increase in the goal whenever the student's performance indicated that the student might be able to surpass the initially specified goal.

At the end of a 15-week treatment period, results indicated that teachers in the goal-raising treatment actually did increase goals more frequently than the conventional CBM treatment teachers. Moreover, as might be expected, the goals of the goal-raising teachers were more ambitious than those of the conventional CBM treatment teachers by the end of the study. Most important, however, the achievement of the students in the goal-raising treatment surpassed that of the contrast group, whereas the achievement of the conventional CBM treatment group did not.

Consequently, it appears important that practitioners specify ambitious goal statements. Unfortunately, guidelines for determining ambitious goals for individual students are difficult to identify. Later sections of this chapter will review some specific methods for monitoring goals and ensuring appropriate goal ambitiousness.

Long- versus short-term goals. A basic distinction between classes of goal statements is whether they focus on what the student will accomplish in a short time frame — within the next week or month — or on what the student will accomplish in a longer time frame — by the end of the year.

With a short-term goal approach, the teacher specifies a hierarchical curriculum, representing the sequence of skills to be mastered during the year. Each skill in this hierarchy then becomes the target of one short-term goal. For example, if the teacher planned for the student to master phoneme-grapheme associations at the beginning of the year, the teacher would specify a goal indicating mastery of phoneme-grapheme associations, and would focus on this goal until mastery was demonstrated. The teacher would then focus on the next goal in the hierarchy: perhaps reading consonant-vowel-consonant words. In this way, throughout the year, the teacher would periodically shift goal statements as skills in the hierarchy were sequentially mastered.

By contrast, with a long-term goal approach, the teacher specifies an annual goal and creates a large pool of related measurement items. For example, if the long-term goal were for the student to read third-grade text proficiently, a large pool of reading passages representing third-grade text would be prepared, from which passages could be drawn for frequent measurement of the student's reading proficiency. Regardless of the teacher's current instructional methods, the goal statement (and its related measurement strategy) would remain constant.

Short- and long-term goal approaches differ conceptually and practically. With a short-term goal approach, the goal focuses on the current instructional material and makes goal attainment relatively easy to realize. Because of these dimensions, short-term goals are relatively sensitive to the effects of instructional programs, and therefore can be satisfying for teachers and students.

However, a short-term goal approach also has distinct disadvantages. First, because the goal structure requires mastery of one goal before instruction on the next goal can begin, the validity of this hierarchy for an individual child is critical. Unfortunately, the hierarchy specified with a short-term goal approach almost always is hypothetically rather than empirically determined and, therefore, often of questionable relevance for an individual child. Second, because a short-term goal approach focuses on one skill at a time, it does not address cumulative mastery and coordinated use of multiple skills. Consequently, it is not unusual, especially for students with learning difficulties, for teachers to find that although students have mastered single skills sequentially through the year, those students have failed to demonstrate the capacity at the end of the year to integrate the multiple skills. Such a failure may explain the documented, relatively poor relation between number of skills mastered during the year and performance on end-of-year global achievement tests. Essentially, although it takes longer to see student improvement with a long-term goal approach, long-term goals better represent the ultimate desired outcome that we want to see students demonstrate.

At a practical level, a long-term goal approach offers additional advantages because, typically, only one goal statement is needed to describe the outcome we expect within a given domain. This translates into one elegant system for monitoring the student's acquisition of desired outcomes. By contrast, a short-term goal approach requires many different goal statements, and, for each statement, a different system for monitoring mastery. This can produce a complicated, unmanageable system. For example, Safer and Hobbs (1979) reported that nearly one-quarter of the IEPs they examined were at least 11 pages long, with goal statements comprising most of the documents. These goals covered small details that essentially outlined the components of the instructional programs the students were to receive. Numerous, specific goals render the task of monitoring progress cumbersome: With an excessive number of goals to track, teachers are faced with the overwhelming task of designing and administering measurement procedures for multiple goals, a situation that often leads to infrequent compliance with the IEP monitoring requirement (Thurlow & Ysseldyke, 1979). A long-term goal approach can streamline the process of monitoring goal attainment and thus enhance compliance.

Description of generalizable behavior within authentic settings. Related to a focus on long-term goals is the notion that, to the greatest extent possible, goals should describe generalizable behavior within authentic settings. To understand this principle, consider the following proposition: Goals that focus on reading connected text represent more generalizable behaviors and are more applicable to real-world tasks than are goals that focus on reading lists of r-controlled words. Similarly, goals that focus on spelling words correctly within naturally written compositions represent more generalizable behaviors and are more applicable to real-world tasks than are goals that focus on spelling lists of dictated words.

The extent to which we can focus our goals on the real-world outcomes we desire of students, the greater the probability that the instruction teachers provide and the evaluation methods they employ will enable students to acquire important, global skills. Consequently, goals should be statements about broad skills within even broader domains. They structure what broad skills a child will attain over a relatively long time. Relevant questions for practitioners to ask as they consider alternative goals are: Is this outcome necessary for students to function ultimately in complex heterogeneous community settings? Could students function as successful, employed adults if they did not accomplish this outcome? Do other, more important outcomes exist relating to overall academic or social competence?

Goals developed through collaboration. Useful goals are formulated through collaboration among multiple perspectives about what constitutes critical outcomes for an individual child. Relevant participants include current teachers across different subjects or settings; future teachers who will receive students at higher grades or in less restrictive settings; parents; community representatives, including potential employers, coaches, and church leaders, as well as current and former students. Because of their training in collaboration and consultation, school psychologists can be the ideal professionals for coordinating such a collaboration.

BEST PRACTICES

This section presents three practices for identifying and monitoring the attainment of critical outcomes: goal attainment scaling, curriculum-based measurement, and a standard core of outcomes. In addition, once the critical outcome has been identified, a level of desired performance typically must be specified. Therefore, this section also reviews three strategies for selecting performance levels: referencing goals to interindividual norms, employing intraindividual norms, and comparing an individual's own performance over time.

Practices for Identifying and Monitoring the Attainment of Critical Outcomes

Goal Attainment Scaling. Goal Attainment Scaling (GAS) (Carr, 1979) establishes goals and specifies a range of outcomes that would indicate progress toward achieving those goals. GAS comprises four essential steps. First, the teacher, student, parents, and principal decide mutually on general goals, such as "improved personal grooming" or "reduced errors in number facts." Second, each participant assigns a weight or number value to each general goal, so that the summed weight across all the general goals equals 100. Third, the teacher breaks down each goal into concrete behaviors. These behaviors represent a continuum of alternative behavioral outcomes, ranging from most to least desirable, within each general goal; a description of the likelihood that the behavioral statement will be achieved is attached. Finally, a student's functioning at any given time is described numerically: Within a goal, the best-fitting behavioral statement (with its corresponding numerical value) is identified; across goals, the products are summed.

In terms of the principles specified above, GAS satisfies some criteria for useful goals more than others. Its strengths include a focus on student outcomes rather than teacher outcomes; its clarity and precision; its potential for encouraging ambitious outcomes; and its deliberate emphasis on collaboration for formulating outcomes. Depending on how GAS is implemented, however, it does not necessarily satisfy the criterion for a long-term approach to goal setting, and it may fail to meet the critical condition that the goal behavior focus on generalizable behavior necessary in authentic settings. Nevertheless, if practitioners focus participants on long-term outcomes that require generalizable behavior in authentic settings, GAS can meet the multiple principles offered in this chapter for useful goals.

Curriculum-Based Measurement. Curriculum-Based Measurement (CBM) (Deno, 1985) is a set of procedures for monitoring student progress. Monitoring student progress requires identifying the goal toward which progress is aimed. Consequently, a major dimension of CBM methods is goal specification.

Within the CBM research program, questions about how to specify goals became subsumed under the larger question of "What to Measure" (see Deno &

Fuchs, 1987). In studying what to measure, CBM developers specified alternative procedures for measuring a student's proficiency within a domain (e.g., in reading: answering questions about the content read, reading list of words aloud, reading connected text aloud, or restoring missing words in text). Then the researchers investigated how well each procedure (a) related to other socially important measures of proficiency, (b) could be implemented accurately, (c) reflected student growth, (d) could be integrated for frequent measurement within the context of busy, complicated classroom settings, and (e) could be used by teachers to improve their instructional program and enhance student achievement.

In each content area (reading, spelling, written expression, and mathematics), one or two alternative formats for specifying annual outcomes satisfied for multiple criteria. For example, research (see Shinn, 1989, for synthesis) indicated that reading connected text aloud was a critical indicator of overall reading proficiency. Reading aloud from connected text (a) related well to many other socially agreed-upon indicators of reading proficiency, (b) was simple and straightforward so that it could be implemented accurately, (c) reflected student growth as it occurred, (d) could be integrated into busy classroom settings, and (e) could be used by teachers to improve their instructional programs and enhance student achievement.

This overall indicator of reading proficiency — reading connected text aloud — could be incorporated in end-of-year goal statements to represent the outcome teachers expect in literacy. Given the principles specified earlier, reading connected text aloud meets the requirements for useful goal statements: It specifies what students, rather than teachers, will accomplish; it communicates clearly and precisely about expectations; it can be used to frame ambitious levels of desired performance; it focuses students and teachers on the long-term outcome; that long-term outcome represents generalizable behavior, which requires integrated performances of multiple skills (e.g., reading words with different phonetic patterns, reading sight vocabulary, using comprehension to enhance fluency, and the like) and which is necessary in authentic settings; and the level of desired behavior or the text within which the performance will be expected can be specified through a collaboration of individuals with a variety of perspectives.

In addition, CBM provides an elegant system for monitoring students' goal attainment. Within an academic domain, it requires practitioners to measure only one, integrated system that simultaneously represents the multiple components of the teacher's curriculum and instructional program. Therefore, it can be used efficiently and feasibly.

Standard core of outcomes. The notion of a standard core of outcomes represents an extension of

CBM. The basic idea (Deno, 1993) is that within any behavioral domain, the field can identify standard tasks that (a) represent overall indicators of proficiency, (b) can be used to specify the outcomes of schooling that are critical to successful life-long adjustments, and (c) can structure a measurement process whereby practitioners can efficiently monitor a student's standing and attainment of critical outcomes.

Although a comprehensive system of standard outcomes has yet to be developed, the initial work on CBM in reading, spelling, written expression, and mathematics provides a model for subsequent development of such a system. A key distinction is that, unlike those for CBM, the goal statements within a comprehensive system of standard outcomes is not linked to the student's curriculum. An advantage of disconnecting the specification of goals or outcomes from the student's specific curriculum is that all students may be described in reference to the same standard; this facilitates comparisons across specific settings and contexts.

In all other ways, however, a system of standard outcomes should enjoy the benefits of a system such as CBM: The outcomes are student-centered, are clear and precise, can encourage ambitious expectations, and focus on long-term goals and generalizable behavior in authentic settings. Moreover, such a system requires collaboration among multiple perspectives.

Practices for Selecting Levels of Performance for Goals

Once a basic framework for specifying goals has been identified, the difficult task of selecting a level of desired performance remains. Consequently, if the school psychologist determines, in coordination with school staff, that a GAS framework will be adopted, he or she still must identify what levels of outcomes should be incorporated into, for example, the on-task goal statement (e.g., most unfavorable outcome: student is on task 10% of the time; less than expected outcome: student is on task 25% of the time; expected outcome: student is on task 50% of the time). If the school psychologist determines, in coordination with the school staff, that a CBM framework will be adopted, he or she still must identify what levels of outcomes should be incorporated into, for example, the reading goal statement (e.g., Given third-grade passages from the Holt curriculum, the student will read 125 words correctly in one minute). The next section reviews alternative strategies for identifying levels of performance for goal statements.

Referencing to interindividual norms. As illustrated in the early work of Deno and Mirkin (1977), one sensible strategy for selecting levels of performance for goals is to measure other, more proficient students' levels of performance in the relevant domain and to set the target student's goal so that he or she will demonstrate performance commensurate with that of the more competent peers.

In the most simple, manageable version of interindividual norm referencing, a school psychologist may sample several students within a general education classroom at the appropriate grade level. Let's say, for example, that Charlie, a student with a learning disability, is receiving reading instruction within the special education resource room. The special educator deems fourth-grade material a reasonable level of difficulty within which the student may achieve competence by the end of the year. The teacher specifies the goal as: Given fourth-grade passages from the Holt series, Charlie will read X words correctly within one minute. The teacher does not, however, have a concrete way of operationalizing "competence" for specification in the goal statement; that is, the teacher does not know how many words Charlie should read correctly to denote proficiency. The school psychologist can assist the teacher by sampling three to five students from two different fourth-grade classrooms: having each student read fourth-grade passages for one minute, averaging the scores, and using this number to denote proficiency for Charlie.

This method has the advantage of being empirically based, even as it focuses the teacher on a level of proficiency that should allow the target student to re-enter a less restrictive setting — should the goal be achieved. Nevertheless, this method is also problematic because while Charlie is striving toward the empirically derived criterion of performance, his general education peers also are improving. Therefore, when Charlie achieves the specified goal, his general education peers will have surpassed Charlie's achievement.

At least partly because of this problem, some school systems have established norms for their school district or schools, within their selected goal framework. Some districts that rely on CBM methods for goal specification, for example, have collected norms describing how many words per minute typical students in their schools read aloud from grade-level material at the beginning, middle, and end of the academic year. With such norms routinely available, practitioners have a data base that allows appropriate interindividual goal levels to be specified at any time. Shinn, Tindal, and Stein (1988) describe methods for collecting local CBM norms.

Referencing to intraindividual norms. Interindividual norms for setting goals are empirically defensible; they allow special educators to set their expectations in terms of how students within general education perform, and facilitate sound decisions about when students with disabilities may be moved across instructional settings. Unfortunately, this method of establishing performance criteria does not

consider a student's beginning-of-the-year performance: All third graders may have year-end reading goals set at the normatively appropriate level of 125 words read correctly per minute (WCPM). However, for a student with a beginning rate of 75 WCPM, this goal would represent an expected weekly increase of 1.67 WCPM ([125–65] + 30 weeks); for a student with an incoming rate of 25 WCPM, the expected weekly increase would be considerably larger ([125 –25] + 30 weeks = 3.33 WCPM). Consequently, relying on cross-sectional normative data can produce varying standards for weekly rates of growth.

One alternative method is to monitor intraindividual student progress over time and to calculate normative data directly from students' weekly rates of improvement. With such a method, students in a school district are monitored by the number of words they read aloud from text each week. At the end of the year, the average weekly rate of improvement is derived for typical students at each grade level within a performance domain. The weekly rate of improvement is then used to specify the performance criterion.

For example, as illustrated by Fuchs, Fuchs, Hamlett, Walz, and Germann (1993), second-grade students, when measured each week by the number of words read aloud from text in one minute, typically increase 1.46 words each week. Consequently, if a goal were specified for a student to read second-grade text, a teacher could select a performance criterion that establishes a weekly rate of growth commensurate with what we would expect normally achieving second graders to demonstrate — approximately 1.50 words per week. So, if the student initially read 35 WCPM from second-grade text, the performance criterion might be 80 WCPM ([1.5 x 30 weeks] + 35). Although this outcome may not place the student at a level commensurate with normally achieving second graders at year's end, it would denote a rate of progress commensurate with normally achieving second graders.

Interindividual comparisons over time. A third option for specifying the performance criterion also involves empirical determination. In contrast to an interindividual or an intraindividual normative approach, however, this third option does not rely on other children to derive the empirical determination. Rather, it relies on the student's own rate of improvement to formulate the end-of-year goal in a data-based, dynamic (i.e., ever-changing) way.

As illustrated by Fuchs et al. (1989), after a teacher relies on professional judgment to specify an initial performance criterion, he or she continuously monitors the student's progress. When the student's rate of progress matches or exceeds the rate of improvement specified in the initial goal, the teacher increases the end-of-year goal, in an attempt to maintain ambitious goals, relative to what the student is demonstrating he/she can achieve.

For example, let's say that the student's baseline performance is 35 WCPM in fourth-grade text and that the teacher's best judgment is that for the end-of-year goal (30 weeks away) the student would read 70 WCPM in fourth-grade text (a weekly rate of improvement of 1.16 words [70–35]/30 weeks). After six weeks of implementing the instructional program, the teacher finds that the student is increasing his/her weekly score by 1.6 words. At that time, the end-of-year goal would be reset to 83 (after six weeks, the student's current performance level is 44.6, i.e., [1.6 x 6 weeks] + 35 baseline; for the next 24 weeks, the teacher will not expect a continued weekly increase of 1.6: [1.6 x 24 weeks] + 44.6 = 83). The teacher continues to monitor the student's performance each week. Whenever the student's weekly rate of improvement increases, the goal is reset accordingly — always using the student's own best performance to determine an appropriately ambitious performance criterion for that student.

SUMMARY

This chapter focused on specifying student goals and outcomes, in order to direct teaching and curriculum development, guide learners, and structure evaluation. Goals should be student-centered, clear and precise, ambitious, focused on long-term outcomes, descriptive of generalizable behavior useful within authentic settings, and developed through a collaborative process. Given these considerations, three alternative frameworks for specifying goals — Goal Attainment Scaling, Curriculum-Based Measurement, and a Standard Core of Outcomes — are useful to varying degrees. Finally, three empirical strategies can be used to specify performance criteria: interindividual norms, intraindividual norms, and referencing to an individual's own ongoing performance.

REFERENCES

Bloom, B. S., Hastings, J. T., & Madaus, G. F. (1971). *Handbook on formative and summative evaluation of student learning.* New York: McGraw-Hill.

Bobbitt, F. (1918). *The curriculum.* Boston: Houghton Mifflin.

Carr, R. A. (1979). Goal attainment scaling as a useful tool for evaluating progress in special education. *Exceptional Children, 46,* 88–96.

Deno, S. L. (1985). Curriculum-based measurement: The emerging alternative. *Exceptional Children, 52,* 219–232.

Deno, S. L. (1993).Personal communicaton. April 12 1993.

Deno, S. L., & Mirkin, P. K. (1977). *Data-based program modification: A manual.* Reston, VA: Council for Exceptional Children.

Fuchs, L. S., Fuchs, D., & Deno, S. L. (1985). The importance of goal ambitiousness and goal mastery to student achievement. *Exceptional Children, 52,* 63–71.

Fuchs, L. S., Fuchs, D., & Hamlett, C. L. (1989). Effects of alternative goal structures within curriculum-based measurement. *Exceptional Children, 57,* 443–452.

Fuchs, L. S., Fuchs, D., Hamlett, C. L., Walz, L., & Germann, G. (1993). Formative evaluation of academic progress: How much growth can we expect? *School Psychology Review, 22,* 27–48.

McNeil, J. D. (1967). Concomitants of using behavioral objectives in the assessment of teacher effectiveness. *Journal of Experimental Education, 36,* 69–74.

Melton, R. F. (1978). Resolution of conflicting claims concerning the effect of behavioral objectives on student learning. *Journal of Educational Research, 48,* 291–302.

Safer, H., & Hobbs, V. (1979). Developing, implementing, and evaluating individualized educational programs. *JWK International.*

Shinn, M. R. (Ed.). (1989). *Curriculum-based measurement: Assessing special children.* New York: Guilford.

Shinn, M. R., Tindal, G., & Stein, S. (1988). Curriculum-based measurement and the identification of mildly handicapped students: A research review. *Professional School Psychology, 3,* 69–86.

Smith, E. R., & Tyler, R. W. (1942). *Appraising and recording student progress.* New York: Harper.

Thurlow, M. L., & Ysseldyke, J. E. (1979). Current assessment and decision making practices in model LD programs. *Learning Disability Quarterly, 2,* 15–24.

Turnbull, H. R., & Turnbull, A. P. (1978). *Free appropriate education: Law and implementation.* Denver: Love.

ANNOTATED BIBLIOGRAPHY

Carr, R. A. (1979). Goal attainment scaling as a useful tool for evaluating progress in special education. *Exceptional Children, 46,* 88–95.
This article provides a rationale and specific guidelines for implementing Goal Attainment Scaling. It provides examples of specific scales applicable to special education and methods for scoring.

Fuchs, L. S., Fuchs, D., Hamlett, C. L., Walz, L., & Germann, G. (1993). Formative evaluation of academic progress: How much growth can we expect. *School Psychology Review, 22,* 27–48.
This article reviews alternative methods for formulating performance criteria within goal statements. The authors outline methodology for collecting intraindividual normative data, and provide intraindividual norms for curriculum-based measurement in reading, spelling, and math.

Shinn, M. R., Tindal, G., & Stein, S. (1988). Curriculum-based measurement and the identification of mildly handicapped students: A research review. *Professional School Psychology, 3,* 69–86.
This synthesis specifies a methodology for collecting interindividual normative data for curriculum-based measurement, and reviews previous studies investigating the utility of such a framework for identifying students for special education services.

48

Best Practices in Curriculum-Based Measurement and Its Use in a Problem-Solving Model

Mark R. Shinn
University of Oregon

Curriculum-Based Measurement (CBM) is the use of standardized and validated short-duration fluency measures of basic skills by special education and general education teachers for the primary purpose of evaluating the effects of their instructional programs (Deno, 1985, 1986; Fuchs & Deno, 1991). Given this principal use, a logical question arises: Why should school psychologists be interested in CBM? The reasons are multi-fold and can be divided into two broad categories: (a) concerns about the programs and services for students with disabilities, and (b) concerns about the educational and psychological needs of all children. This chapter provides a rationale for use of CBM by school psychologists and other educators in a *problem-solving model* and details how CBM is used in decision making via a case study.

Special Education Concerns

Three major concerns related to school psychology practice can serve as compelling reasons why school psychologists should be interested in CBM: (a) effective special education programs, (b) the lack of quality for the Individualized Education Plan (IEP) goals and objectives, and (c) the misalignment of assessment and intervention. A survey of members of the National Association of School Psychologists (NASP) by Reschly, Genshaft, and Binder (1987) provides considerable information about some of these concerns. Reschly et al. (1987) surveyed 600 NASP practitioners, 139 leadership staff, and 166 faculty members on a variety of contemporary practice issues, including assessment practices and special education service delivery.

Lack of special education effectiveness. Among the Reschly et al. (1987) survey's findings is the striking discrepancy between the major activity of school psychologists, testing for special education eligibility (Hutton, Dubes, & Muir, 1992; Smith, 1984), and the perceived consequences of this activity for many students with disabilities, ineffective special education programs. Only about one-third (32%) of re-

sponding practitioners agreed with the statement that special education services are usually quite effective. Even fewer school psychology faculty (about one in 19) agreed with the effectiveness statement. These professional opinions are echoed by meta-analyses of special education effectiveness that provide little evidence of powerful special education programs (Carlberg & Kavale, 1980; Forness & Kavale, 1987; Kavale & Forness, 1985, 1987).

CBM can be used to improve special education students' achievement outcomes significantly. Repeated studies by L. Fuchs and D. Fuchs (e.g., Fuchs, Deno, & Mirkin, 1984; Fuchs, Fuchs, & Hamlett, 1989; Fuchs, Fuchs, Hamlett, & Allinder, 1991; Fuchs, Fuchs, Hamlett, & Ferguson, 1992; Fuchs, Fuchs, Hamlett, & Stecker, 1991) have shown that when teachers use CBM to write data-based goals, monitor the effects of their instructional programs, and adjust their interventions when the data show little outcome, student achievement improves. Typical effect sizes, the amount of standard deviation gains in achievement attained by members of the treatment group versus controls, exceed one half standard deviation. Because school psychologists are concerned about the limited or negligible effects of special education, they should be interested in implementing CBM to enhance student outcomes.

IEP goals and objectives. Another concern tied to the lack of special education outcomes is the quality of special education students' IEP goals and objectives. Without quality goals and objectives, evaluation of individual student's outcomes is problematic, and as a result, ineffective interventions will not be identified and modified. Special education legislation (e.g., the Individual Disabilities Education Act) recognizes the needs for evaluation of individual program outcomes and therefore mandates that each student with a disability have a statement as to what the intervention is designed to accomplish on at least an annual basis. However, 16 years after implementation of the landmark law ushering in the IEP mandates, the Education for All Handicapped Children Act, the quality of IEPs has not improved significantly (Smith,

1990). Typically, IEP goals are written without current student performance data; are vague and lack observable, measurable outcomes (e.g., "Will improve 1 year in reading"); or detail lists of isolated short-term instructional objectives (e.g., will master C-V-C words with 80% accuracy). Compounding the problem of difficult-to-measure goals is the lack of consensus as to what student goals should be. Too often, special education goals are procedurally driven (e.g., dictated by "district policy") as opposed to a meaningful discussion as to what an individual intervention program is designed to accomplish. This proceduralism may explain the apparent lack of substance in IEP goals and objectives, the observation that two-thirds of IEPs are written before or after the IEP meeting (Smith, 1990), and the reported problems in getting general education teachers and parents involved in the process (Huebner & Gould, 1991).

CBM is a technology that has been validated for use in writing data-based, observable and measurable IEP goals and objectives (Fuchs & Shinn, 1989). In fact, CBM's research-based development was supported by federal funds to identify a technology to assist in implementation of the original Education for All Handicapped Children Act, PL 94-142 (Deno, 1992).

Linking assessment and intervention. The third major special education concern for school psychologists is the lack of treatment validity of their assessment data. Information collected most often comes from published norm-referenced tests of aptitude and achievement (PNTs). Extensive discussion as to the limited treatment utility of PNTs is beyond the scope of this chapter. The reader is encouraged to see Marston (1989) or Howell, Fox, and Morehead (1993) for a more extensive discussion of this topic. In brief, although many PNTs are generally well constructed as *broad* measures of constructs or skills, the very nature of their broad-band precludes their usefulness for intervention planning. The tests have too few items, many of which are not tied to any particular curriculum and the limited number of items are spread across too large an age span. These problems lead to questionable conclusions about what a student can or cannot do correctly and what a student needs to learn to be successful in a *specific* classroom curriculum. Additionally, PNTs rely almost exclusively on selection-type response formats (e.g., pointing to one of four choices) that are not "authentic." These types of responses provide information only on correctness, not on what strategies or preskills a student brings to bear on a task (Howell et al., 1993).

CBM can be of use to school psychologists in special education intervention planning because it links what is measured to what is taught. CBM measures are very narrow band in test content; test items typically encompass only 1 year of a curriculum for each

level of the test. *All* items are derived from the curriculum used in general education classrooms, and thus maximize testing/teaching overlap. Finally, CBM relies heavily on production-type, authentic response modes. Students read aloud from text, write dictated spelling words, write answers to mathematics computational problems, and write stories. These types of responses allow for information to be gained not only about correctness, but *how* and *why* students answered in specific ways.

Educational and Psychological Concerns of All Children

Significant numbers of children, not all of whom receive special education, experience achievement and social-emotional problems in schools. The end result is high rates of school dropout and illiteracy. National dropout rates currently are around 30% for high school students (Center for the Study of Social Policy, 1991) and are even higher for students from minority backgrounds. The consequences of school dropout are serious, including limited earning power. For example, students without a high school education have twice the unemployment rate and have experienced a 42% decrease in earning power between 1973 and 1986 alone in constant 1986 dollars (Carnegie Council on Adolescent Development, 1989). Significant numbers of students also are exiting schools as functionally illiterate. Adams (1990) reports that nearly 85% of adjudicated youth are functionally illiterate. Estimates of illiteracy rates among minority youth are approximately 40%. High school dropouts and functionally illiterate adults are losing competitiveness in an ever more technological economy.

Unfortunately, special education has served as *the* primary mechanism for resolving the widespread achievement and social-emotional problems of children in schools. School psychologists are well aware of this situation. Reschly et al. (1987) reported that nearly two-thirds of school psychology practitioners and nearly 90% of the NASP leadership agreed that students are classified as learning disabled (LD) so that services can be provided even though they are not really handicapped. A similar proportion of practitioners (64%) and of the NASP leadership and school psychology faculty (80%) agreed with the statement that too many students are classified as LD and placed in special education. More than 70% of practitioners and faculty and 90% of NASP leaders agreed that better regular classroom instruction would prevent many students from being classified as LD.

Education must find more ways of contributing to *all* children's needs than assigning large numbers of students to special education. Increased school psychology assistance to general education teachers and parents can be one such resource (Curtis & Batsche, 1991). The primary obstacle to increased school psychology services to all children is school psychologists' heavy commitment to testing for special education eligibility. CBM can help school psychologists contribute to meeting the needs of more children by reducing these testing demands. When CBM is implemented in a problem-solving model, school psychology testing for special education eligibility is reduced significantly and corresponding increases in intervention services to all children are noted. Such changes were reported by Canter (1991) in Minneapolis Public Schools. Rather than routinely testing every referral for purposes of determining special education eligibility, when CBM was used in a problem-solving model, school psychologists tested students only when there were specific assessment questions. On average, this situation occurred in only half of the school psychologist referrals. Intelligence testing was reduced even further and involved only one-half of the cases where any specific testing was needed.

With this decrease in eligibility testing, changes were observed in school psychologists' intervention activities. Consultation to general education and special education teachers increased from 12% to 36% of cases within 3 years; within 5 years, this figure increased further to 52% of cases (Canter, 1991). This percentage is more than two-and-one-half to almost five times higher than the amount of consultation reported by school psychology practitioners (Costenbader, Swartz, & Petrix, 1992). Fewer than 5% of the national sample surveyed by Costenbader et al. (1992) exceeded the average consultation rates described in Canter's chapter. Canter (1991) also reported increases of direct services to students such as counseling or crisis intervention, an increase from 1.5% to 10% of caseloads.

What Makes CBM CBM?

Given these compelling reasons for school psychologists to be interested in CBM then, the question becomes "just what is CBM?" This question is important to answer because practitioners have encountered a virtual explosion of information in the professional literature on *curriculum-based assessment* (CBA). Among the numerous assessment techniques considered CBA are informal reading inventories, end-of-unit mastery tests, analysis of homework samples, Precision Teaching, and a variety of locally made tests that measure what students are learning. To reduce confusion, it is important for practitioners to discriminate the similarities and differences among the variety of approaches collectively entitled CBA. For more information on this topic, the reader is referred to Shinn, Rosenfield, and Knutson (1989) or Tindal (1993).

In brief, CBA is a very broad term that describes *any* testing strategy that uses a student's curriculum as the basis for decision making. CBM is one type of CBA. Testing is accomplished using a limited number of standardized and validated measures of student performance in the basic skill areas of reading, spelling, mathematics computation, and written expression. Specifically, CBM measures consist of the following core testing strategies:

1. In reading, students read aloud from basal readers for 1 minute. The number of words read correctly constitutes the basic decision-making metric. Maze, a multiple choice cloze reading technique, also has been validated as a CBM testing strategy (Fuchs & Fuchs, 1992). The number of correct word choices per 5 minutes is the primary metric.

2. In spelling, students write words that are dictated at specified intervals (either 5, 7, or 10 seconds) for 2 minutes. The number of correct letter sequences and words spelled correctly are counted.

3. In written expression, students write a story for 3 minutes after being given a story starter (e.g., "Pretend you are playing on the playground and a spaceship lands. A little green person comes out and calls your name and . . ."). The number of words written, spelled correctly, and/or correct word sequences are counted.

4. In mathematics, students write answers to computational problems via 2-minute probes. The number of correctly written digits is counted.

Upon first inspection, CBM may look like a number of other CBA approaches. For example, when reading is tested, students read text aloud in CBM, a process that looks much like an informal reading inventory. Similarly, students typically read aloud for 1 minute, a process that resembles precision teaching. However, these superficial "similarities" should not preclude a careful analysis of how CBM is different from other CBA approaches. CBM differs from other CBA approaches on a number of important features. Among its most obvious features is the short-duration (e.g., 1 to 3 minutes) of each of a limited number of test strategies. Usually, these short duration tests are not drawn from the exact point in a curriculum a student has been taught (e.g., a unit) but from the annual curriculum. A second obvious feature is CBM's reliance on fluency, a combination of accuracy and speed, as the behavior of interest.

CBM as DIBS. Why would a testing strategy place so much emphasis on short-duration fluency measures with such a limited number of different tasks? The best way to understand this approach to assessing student academic performance is to characterize CBM as a set of *DIBS*, or "dynamic indicators of basic skills." The measurement procedures are *dynamic* in that they are designed to be sensitive to the short-term effects (i.e., 4–6 weeks) of instructional interventions; they are designed to assess change. By using short-duration measures, these tests can be administered frequently, allowing change to be assessed on a routine basis. By using fluency, a metric is engaged that is more sensitive to change than other metrics such as accuracy.

The measurement procedures are *indicators* in that they were validated to be correlates of key behaviors indicative of overall performance in an academic area. The CBM measures were *not* designed to represent all behaviors that may be included in an academic domain such as reading. They will not provide direct information about whether a student can separate fact from fiction or identify the compellingness of an author's argument. Nor does their use preclude using other specific skill measures of interest. Should a teacher be interested in a student's fact versus fiction skills, a measure that assesses this specific skill would be appropriate.

Instead, CBM was designed to function like an educational thermometer. A thermometer can do two things especially well: (a) inform a person whether there is a health problem that warrants further investigation (e.g., a temperature of 104.5 F) and (b) tell a treatment provider whether a given intervention is effective (a reduced temperature to 100.3 after aspirin). It is important to note that indicators such as thermometers typically do not tell you directly what is wrong. For example, a thermometer would not inform a physician whether the cause of a high fever was a bacterial or viral infection or the result of appendicitis.

The use of academic "thermometers" requires that reliable and valid indicators be identified. Beginning in 1978, an extensive program of research was undertaken to identify key behaviors that would meet the technical requirements to serve as indicators of academic performance. The short-duration, fluency measures described previously are the results of this research program. Although a considerable body of information has been published on the technical adequacy of CBM in all four academic areas (see Marston, 1989, for an extensive summary), most research has been conducted on CBM reading measures. Results suggest strongly that for most students, oral reading works extremely well as an indicator of general reading proficiency, including comprehension. Evidence has been garnered with respect to construct validity (Shinn, Good, Knutson, Tilly, & Collins, 1992) as well as traditional conceptions of criterion-related validity, including correlations with other accepted published measures (e.g., Deno, Mirkin, & Chiang, 1982; Fuchs, Fuchs, & Maxwell, 1988) and teacher ratings (Fuchs, Fuchs, & Deno, 1982).

Finally, CBM are DIBS in that they are designed to quantify student performance in the *basic skill* areas of reading, spelling, mathematics computation, and written expression. They were not designed to draw inferences about a student's skill in content area courses such as science or health education. Although this basic-skills focus may appear limited in scope, it is important to note the importance of basic skills in the development of functional literacy (Adams, 1990) and the fact that nearly all students in special education are referred because of severe deficits in this area.

In sum, CBM's short duration, fluency measures were designed to fill a void in educational measurement. They were designed as dynamic indicators of basic skills (DIBS) to give educators a simple, straightforward way of determining the status of students' educational health in critical academic areas, and to provide a mechanism for evaluating the effects of efforts to improve any given student's academic health.

CBM and a tie to a Problem-Solving model. CBM can be set apart from other CBA models in that it is tied to an explicit decision-making model. It was stated in the first sentence of this chapter that CBM typically is used by teachers to evaluate the effects of their instructional programs. However, CBM is generally used to do more than accomplish this important endeavor. CBM implementation usually occurs in conjunction with implementation of a Problem-Solving model (Deno, 1989), a heuristic composed of the five major decisions presented in Table 1. Each of the problem-solving model decisions is associated with more familiar terms in special education decision-making jargon (e.g., Salvia & Ysseldyke, 1987). *Problem-Identification* and *Problem-Certification* decisions, for example, are related to the traditional processes of screening and eligibility determination, respectively. *Exploring Solutions* could be considered synonymous with instructional planning. With special education students, this process corresponds to the development of an individual education plan (IEP), including setting annual goals and determining intervention-plan content and process. *Evaluating Solutions* relates to pupil progress monitoring while *Problem Solution* is analogous to program termination or changes in placement to less restrictive settings.

Rather than broad-based undifferentiated data gathering activities and subsequent decision making, the Problem-Solving model dictates that specific information is collected for each step. The need for additional assessment information is decided on a sequential basis. Sometimes, when a problem not be validated, assessment activities stop after the first decision (i.e., Problem Identification). Other times, assessment and decision making may occur on a repeated basis throughout the years spanning a student's educational career. How CBM is used in the problem-solving model will be detailed later in the chapter.

As described by Deno (1989), the Problem-Solving model is predicated on three assumptions. First, a problem is defined as a discrepancy between *what is*

TABLE 1
CBM Problem-Solving Model Decisions, Measurement Activities, and Evaluation Activities

Problem-Solving Decision	Measurement Activities	Evaluation Activities	Specific Tasks
Problem Identification	Observe and record student differences, if any, between actual and expected performance	Decide that a performance discrepancy exists	Peer-referenced assessment
Problem Certification	Describe the magnitude of differences between actual and expected performance in the context of likelihood of general education alone solving the problem	Decide if discrepancies are important enough that special services may be required for problem resolution	Survey-Level Assessments and identification of alternative intervention options
Exploring Solutions	Determine options for annual goals	Decide on anual goal(s) and actual content of intervention to be implemented	Write annual goal based on Survey-Level Assessment; identify specific skill or strategy deficits
Evaluating Solutions	Monitor intervention mplementation and changes in student performance	Determine if intervention is effective or should be modified	Collect progress monitoring data and compare with aimline
Problem Solution	Observe and record student differences, if any, between actual and expected performance	Decide if current discrepancies, if any, are not enough and if special services may be reduced or eliminated	Repeat peer-referenced assessment and Survey-Level Assessment

expected and *what occurs*. In an academic context, a problem exists when a student does not perform the academic behavior(s) expected of him or her in a particular curriculum. The implication of this definition is that problems are situational and may not be the student's "internal problem." What is a problem in one context may not be in another. Consider the case of two third-grade students, Amy and Billy. Their classroom teacher would *expect* them to perform in the third-grade curriculum like other students in the classroom. The degree to which they vary from this achievement expectation may result in them being viewed as a problem.

With CBM, it is possible to use a data-based decision-making process to describe Amy and Billy's skills and determining whether there is a problem in a specific environment. Because the CBM measures are dynamic indicators and are of short duration, it is possible to describe the general achievement expectations in particular settings in a time-efficient manner by developing local norms. For more information on this process, see Habedank (this volume) or Shinn (1988; 1989). In Figure 1, Amy and Billy's reading skills relative to the achievement expectations in two school systems are compared. The foundation for the frequency distributions displayed in the Figure are the results of having all third graders, including Amy and Billy, read three randomly selected passages from the typical level of the third-grade general education

reading curriculum. Each student's median score is used for summary purposes. Imagine that Amy and Billy's median scores on the third-grade reading passages were 141 words read correctly for Amy and 39 words read correctly for Billy.

As displayed in Figure 1, reading skills in the third-grade curriculum in School A are distributed normally. Relative to these third graders, Amy is among the top quarter of the group in reading skills. Billy, however, is clearly the lowest performing reader in the curriculum. In this environment, although Amy's instructional needs may be similar to a number of other students, Billy may be considered by the classroom teacher as having a serious reading problem that may require additional accommodations.

In School B, reading skills in the curriculum are not distributed in the same way as School A. The distribution is positively skewed and a substantial proportion of students in the group are reading very poorly in their third-grade instructional curriculum. Therefore, problems may be defined differently. Amy, for example, is now the best third-grade reader and her skills may be so different from others that special accommodations may be necessary to meet her instructional needs. Billy is now no longer easily identifiable as having reading skill deficiencies. Out of 52 third-grade pupils, Billy reads as well or better than one-third (17) of the group. It would be most unlikely

FIGURE 1. A comparison of two students' scores relative to two different environments.

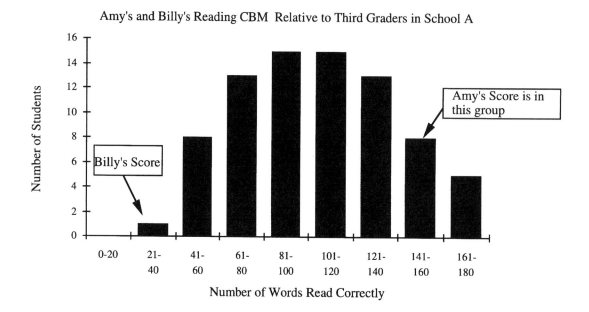

Amy's and Billy's Reading CBM Relative to Third Graders in School A

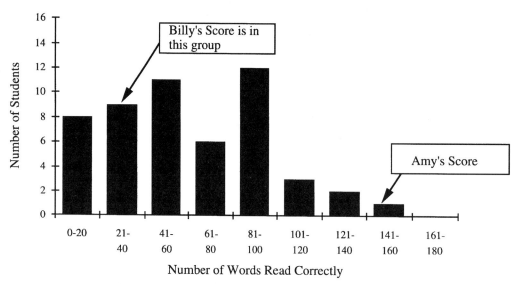

Amy's and Billy's Reading CBM Relative to Third Graders in School B

that Billy's general education teacher would consider him to have a reading problem that requires special remediation in this context.

In addition to problems being defined situationally as the discrepancy between what is expected and what occurs, the Problem-Solving model assumes that within specific environments, there is a subset of students whose discrepancies are so significant that

it may be unreasonable for the to achieve in general education unless their programs are modified (for more detail, see Deno, 1989; this volume). Currently, it remains a value judgment as to when the discrepancy is so severe that special services are warranted, despite repeated attempts to make it quantifiable using a battery of tests and regression formulas. Using CBM in a Problem-Solving model with local norms helps decision makers not only operationalize discrepancies, but also determine whether additional resources such as special education may be required to help students benefit from their education. For example, in School A, Billy has a reading discrepancy that may require additional resources; in School B, a discrepancy is not apparent, although it could be argued that significant numbers of third graders in this school need a change in their reading program because so many third-graders are reading so poorly.

The final assumption of the Problem-Solving model is that effective educators must "generate many possible plans of action prior to attempting problem solution" (Deno, 1989, p. 11) and evaluate the effects of the program actually implemented. Presently, the assessment technology is lacking to say with certainty which instructional program will work with any student. It is not clear whether Billy will benefit from special education (or peer tutoring or Chapter 1) in School A *before* it is tried. Therefore, all interventions should be treated as testable hypotheses that must be evaluated formatively for each individual student. Interventions that show strong positive effects when evaluated are maintained; ineffective interventions are discarded and/or modified.

USING CBM IN A PROBLEM-SOLVING MODEL

The core CBM test strategies are varied systematically and combined with other pieces of information to make one of five decisions in the Problem-Solving model. Depending on the decision to be made, for example, a student may be tested in different *levels* of a curriculum. For example, when making Problem Identification decisions, a student for whom there is a concern (e.g., a third grader) is tested in the level of the general education curriculum (i.e., third grade) in which the typical same-grade peer would be expected to perform satisfactorily. In contrast, when making Evaluating Solutions decisions, a student is tested on curricular materials corresponding to the level of the curriculum in which he or she would be expected to perform in 1 year (i.e., the instructional material that represents the annual goal of the IEP).

In addition to systematic differences in the level of the curriculum tested as a function of the decision to be made, the *decision-making standards* vary as well. Two major approaches are employed, *norm- or peer-referenced decisions and individually referenced decisions*. Some decisions in the Problem-Solving model (e.g., Problem Identification) use a norm- or peer-referenced approach. Decisions are made by comparing an individual student's test results to that of a local norm group. This local norm could represent students from the same class, same school, or same school district. For other decisions (e.g., Evaluating Solutions), an *individually referenced approach* is used. The standard is not how a student's performance compares to a group but how that student's performance compares to his or her previous performances.

Problem Identification

The first step of the Problem-Solving model is Problem Identification. The goal of Problem Identification is to determine in a systematic way if an academic problem exists that is important enough to warrant further assessment (Shinn & Hubbard, 1992). As presented in Table 1, the Problem-Identification process requires a data-based decision about whether a student's performance on academically important tasks (i.e., curriculum tasks) is *significantly discrepant* from that of same-grade peers. For example, in the case of Billy illustrated in Figure 1, at what point is his reading performance relative to other students considered to be so discrepant that it would be validated as a problem? In School A, his performance is the lowest of third graders, but is it *significantly* different? In School B, his performance was more like those of other students. How much like the other students did he perform? Problem Identification attempts to provide some quantification of the differences in curriculum performance to facilitate decision making.

Problem Identification begins like other school practices when someone, usually a general education teacher or a parent, considers a student's skills to be a concern. This concern usually translates into a referral. However, in contrast to prevailing practices where referral leads to special education eligibility testing, in a Problem-Solving model, referrals usually are made to a general education Child Study Team (CST) or Teacher Assistance Team (TAT). After collecting relevant information on student academic performance and school and medical history, the CST decides if a problem is validated and is one that may require significant changes in the student's general education program (e.g., special education; Chapter I) to be resolved. Only should a problem be identified, would more intensive assessment activities such as determining special education eligibility be conducted.

The Problem Identification process has a number of advantages. The first is one of philosophical approach. From the beginning of the process, not *every* potential problem is viewed as a potential special education problem. Referrals that are not validated as potentially significant problems may not necessitate a special education evaluation or special education intervention. Some referral concerns may be remedied based on interventions identified by the CST to occur in general education classrooms. The kind of data collected for Problem Identification is also useful for intervention planning in general education classrooms. The second advantage is that Problem Identification allows for a systematic verification of teacher or parent referral accuracy. Although teachers have been demonstrated to be highly accurate in identifying potential student achievement difficulties (Gerber & Semmel, 1984), they also have been shown to be susceptible to gender and ethnicity biases (Shinn, Tindal, & Spira, 1987). When there is a significant discrepancy, teacher perceptions of a problem are validated objectively. Parent referrals usually result in expensive assessment practices and lower rates of special education eligibility determination than teachers. By systematically collecting Problem-Identification information, the appropriateness of parental concerns can be examined objectively, without expensive special education testing. The third advantage is that the systematic Problem-Identification process can reduce overtesting, an expenditure of limited resources such as school psychologists' and other specialists' time. Those referred students for whom a problem is not identified are not tested. Terminating testing at this point frees up the persons who normally would collect eligibility information to help general education teachers address the student needs in the classroom.

In operation, Problem Identification relies on a norm- or peer-referenced approach. The referred student's level of performance is determined by repeated testing over a short period of time in grade-level curriculum materials in the academic area in which the student is considered to be experiencing difficulty. The student's scores then are compared to an expected achievement level derived from typical students using local norms. Depending on the degree of school system commitment to a Problem-Solving model, the local norms can be derived from students in the same classroom, building, or district. See Habedank (this volume) for more information on this topic. The discrepancy between the student's actual and expected performance (i.e., the achievement level of typical peers) is calculated and a decision regarding the need for further assessment is made via a cutting score.

A critical feature of Problem Identification is that repeated samples of the referred student's current performance are collected daily over a period of 3 to 5 days. Repeated samples provide information about the variability of the student's performance, reduce the effects of "good" days and "bad" days, reduce examiner familiarity effects, and allow for a broader sample of academic behavior.

For illustration of the Problem Identification procedures, consider the case of Sara, who was referred to a CST by her general education teacher during the Fall quarter of third grade because of concerns about her progress in reading and spelling. Because the CST found no obvious reasons for the teacher's concerns (e.g., poor school attendance, vision or hearing difficulties), Sara was tested by a trained member of the CST using a series of third-grade-level CBM probes derived from the general education reading and

spelling curricula. The levels of the reading and spelling curricula were the levels in which the typical third grader was expected to perform. In reading, there were two levels of third-grade readers; typical students were expected to be reading in Level 3–2. The CST member had Sara read three different randomly selected passages from Level 3–2 for 1-minute each every day for 5 days. The number of words read correctly and errors were recorded although, for simplification, errors are eliminated in this case study. Sara's reading scores were summarized daily using the median of the three passages.

In spelling, there was only one level of the spelling series. Sara completed a different 2-minute CBM spelling probe with words drawn randomly from all the words in the spelling book on each of the 5 days. The number of words spelled correctly and correct letter sequences, a precise measure of spelling skills, were recorded. For illustration, only correct letter sequence scores will be used here. Sara's 15 reading passage scores, daily reading medians, daily spelling scores, and summary median scores are displayed in Table 2. Table 2 also includes the median reading and spelling scores of 20 randomly selected third-grade students who had been tested using the same materials as part of a school norming process.

To facilitate decision making and increase communication, Sara's scores are displayed graphically in Figure 2. This figure shows Sara's daily median scores in reading and spelling as well as the median performance of other third-grade students in her school. The peer median is represented by the heavy solid line. To decide if a significant discrepancy exists, Sara's scores must consistently fall below a critical value or cutting score, which is represented in Figure 2 by the double line. In this example, the cutting score was based on a *discrepancy ratio* that is calculated by dividing the peer median score by the referred median student's score. Sara's reading discrepancy score was 3.7. The third-grade peer median of 100 words read correctly was divided by Sara's median score of 27 words read correctly. Her discrepancy ratio was 2.3 (123 Correct Letter Sequences/53 Correct Letter Sequences) in spelling. The most common discrepancy ratio used as a cutting score is equal to or greater than 2.0. This score indicates that a student performs at half the fluency (or less) of the typical student in a skill domain. A discrepancy ratio of this magnitude is sufficient to decide that a problem may exist that warrants further assessment.

Discrepancy ratios are used most commonly when local norms are developed for classrooms or schools. When district norms are used, a team has the advantage of more conventional decision-making scores, percentile ranks. Cutting scores based on percentile ranks are determined by finding the raw score that corresponds to an agreed-upon critical level such as the 10th percentile. When a referred student's

TABLE 2
Results of CBM Problem-Identification Testing for Sara

Academic Area Tested	Day					Overall Median	Peer Median
	1	2	3	4	5		
Grade 3–2 Reading Passages							
WRC Passage 1	33	16	32	26	29		
WRC Passage 2	40	27	42	38	24		
WRC Passage 3	38	33	30	25	27		
WRC Daily Median	38	27	32	26	27	27WRC	100WRC
Grade 3 Spelling Words							
CLS	55	45	56	53	49	53 CLS	123 CLS

Note. WRC = words read correctly.   CLS = correct letter sequences.

scores consistently fall below the value of scores at the 10th percentile, a problem is identified. If no obvious explanations exist to account for the discrepancy, the student may be assessed further in more detail. In the case of Sara, her median scores would be converted to percentile ranks and compared to the rankings of her third-grade peers from her school district. In reading, her scores fell below the 2nd percentile; in spelling, her scores were at the 5th percentile compared to school-district third graders.

Sara's Problem Identification data consistently were below the discrepancy ratio cutting scores in reading and spelling. Because the team ruled out educational or medical history as viable explanations for Sara's performance, they decided that further investigation of Sara's reading and spelling skills was warranted. For purposes of illustration, only the results of further assessment in reading will be reported.

Problem Certification

Once a problem is identified, a Problem Certification decision must be made. The major activity is to determine the magnitude or severity of the problem. As described in Table 1, Problem Certification is conceptualized as determining whether the difference between actual and expected performance is *serious* enough that a Multi-disciplinary Team (MDT) decides that it is unlikely that the academic problem will be resolved with general education resources alone. Once the magnitude of the discrepancy is known and the MDT decides that it is important, the team considers what resources may be available to resolve the problem (e.g., Chapter I, peer tutoring, special education). If the MDT decides that the student needs special education to succeed, eligibility is determined, assuming that procedural state and federal requirements are met (Shinn & Hubbard, 1992).

The Problem Certification process begins by conducting a Survey-Level Assessment using CBM for each academic area in which a problem has been identified. In a Survey-Level Assessment, the student is tested in successively lower levels in the curriculum sequence. For example, in Sara's school district's curriculum, there were two levels of third-grade text (3–2, 3–1), two levels of second-grade text (2–2, 2–1), and three levels of first-grade text, exclusive of pre-primers. The data from Level 3–2 were obtained already during Problem Identification so there was no need to repeat that testing. Sara was tested using a minimum of three randomly selected passages in each book, beginning with Level 3–1 until the level was reached in which she performed successfully. The Survey-Level Assessment was completed in one testing session of about 20 to 30 minutes. The difference between her grade placement and the level of the curriculum in which she could be defined as *successful* would indicate the magnitude of the problem. The results of Sara's Survey-Level Assessment are presented in Table 3.

Success can be operationalized in one of two ways, by using (a) instructional placement standards or (b) normative scores. The use of instructional placement standards requires that a set of criteria is used to determine which level of the curriculum appears to be best for purposes of instruction. For example, a standard recommended for reading when first- or second-grade levels are considered and students are to receive teacher-led instruction is that students are placed in the highest level in which they read between 40 to 60 words correctly per minute. Students also must have high accuracy, about 90% to 95% or 4 to 6 errors per minute. For third- through sixth-grade reading curriculum, students are placed in highest level in which they read between 70 and 100 words correctly per minute. A higher fluency standard is required because of the increased cognitive complexity of the reading materials. Again, students must have very high reading accuracy.

These reading instructional placement standards are represented in Figure 3 to facilitate communication. The placement standards are marked by the

FIGURE 2. Results of Sara's problem-identification testing in Gradd 3 reading and spelling probes compared to same-grade peers.

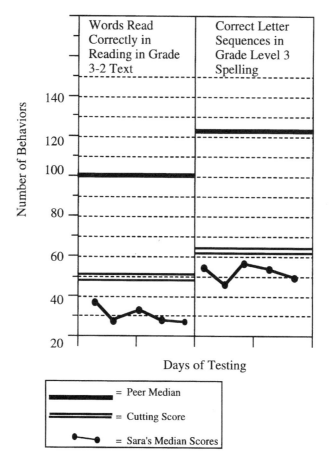

dark bands. Sara's scores relative to the bands also are displayed. Clearly, her reading performance in third- and second-grade levels of the curriculum is too low for her to be considered successful in that material. The highest level of the curriculum in which she meets the instructional standards is the Level 1–2 book. By comparing her expected grade placement, if she were considered a typical student, to her recommended instructional placement, it could be concluded that she is approximately 2 years behind according to the publisher's scope-and-sequence chart.

The second approach to operationalizing the severity of a problem is to determine the student's *normative score.* This index is obtained when the tested student's percentile rank score in material from a particular curriculum level falls in the average range of the local norm at that grade. Sara's percentile rank reading scores are also included in Table 3. For making Problem-Certification decisions, this local norm is based on a sufficient sample size to ensure stable, representative norms such as school district norms of at least 100 students per grade. The definition of "average" must be agreed upon in advance. Some districts have used a conventional definition of

performance between the 25th and 75th percentiles as average. Other districts have used a score from the 16th to 84th percentile (equal to plus or minus one standard deviation) as the definition of average. The latter definition was used in Sara's case. Sara earned reading scores that are clearly outside the normative range for students in third and second grade. Sara's score in reading first-grade material was better than most first graders who enter school as nonreaders (Shinn, 1988).

To facilitate decision making, the Survey-Level Assessment information can be graphed relative to the range of typical students reading scores in first-through fifth-grade-level materials at times similar to testing. Sara's scores are presented graphically this way in Figure 4.

To make Problem-Certification decisions, school leaders must establish a percentile-rank cutting score below which students can be considered for special education eligibility. One cutting score that has been used with some success is performance below the 16th percentile of students one grade below current placement. See Shinn (1989) for more detail on this topic. Using this criterion it was determined that Sara

TABLE 3
Reading Survey-Level Assessment for Sara with Curriculum Level and Performance Relative to Local Norms

Level of Ginn Curriculum	Sara's Median Performance	Grade-Level Peer Performance	Sara's Percentile Rank
3–2	27	100	2nd
3–1	27	NA	NA
2–2	32	NA	NA
2–1	37		15
1–3	49	NA	NA
1–2	55	**	**

Note. * = Local norms were developed only from 1 level of curriculum per grade level. Therefore, no norms are available for these curriculum levels.

**No first-grade students were tested in the Fall because most students entered with limited reading skills.

could be eligible because she performed at the 14th percentile in second-grade material compared to second-graders.

The second part of the Problem-Certification decision involves considering whether the student needs special education to benefit from their education. A student may not need special education services, even though they may meet the eligibility criterion (Rothstein, 1990; Shinn & Hubbard, 1992). Need is determined by examining the student's instructional needs in the context of resources available in general education that may resolve the problem. Only after considering Sara's reading performance in the context of the adequacy of her general education instructional environment, her behavior in that environment, other instructional opportunities available (e.g., lower reading group, peer tutoring), previous achievement, health, social and family factors, did the MDT determine that it was unlikely that the problem would be resolved with general education resources alone.

Exploring Solutions

If schools are well practiced in any assessment activity, it is in testing for purposes of determining special education eligibility. Thus far, this chapter has described the use of a Problem-Solving model to provide a needs-based assessment approach that arguably works as well or better than conventional eligibility determination activities (Shinn, 1989). Unfortunately, schools are less well practiced and proficient in assessing students for the purposes of intervention planning intervention and evaluation. Using CBM within a Problem-Solving model can remedy this situation when students have academic problems. The Problem-Solving model makes explicit the importance of assessment for intervention planning during the Exploring-Solutions decision. Using CBM in a Problem-Solving model allows a linkage between assessment for eligibility purposes and intervention

planning. As will be seen later in this chapter, the use of CBM also allows linkages between assessment for eligibility purposes and intervention planning to intervention evaluation.

As presented in Table 1, the purpose of Exploring Solutions is three-fold, to specify (a) the data-based goals of the intervention, (b) the *content* of the intervention or "what to teach," and (c) the *means* to deliver the intervention or "how to teach." CBM is most useful for the goal-setting component of Exploring Solutions. Although not useless for intervention planning, other CBA models are more suitable for determining intervention components and processes. Howell's Curriculum-Based Evaluation (e.g., Howell, Fox, & Morehead, 1993) is especially well-suited for making intervention planning decisions.

General goal-setting approach. CBM's linkage between eligibility assessment and intervention planning begins by using the data collected during Problem Identification and Problem Certification to *develop intervention goals* for the student (Fuchs & Shinn, 1989). The mechanism for goal setting is the annual goal of a student's Individualized Education plan (IEP). The basic *idea* is simple and works much like conventional practice; annual goals are based on identifying "where the student is now" and where the IEP team would like the student to perform in 1 year, if the intervention is successful. What differs from conventional practice is that when using CBM, it can be determined more directly "where the student is." This decision is not made using grade-equivalent scores from tests that may not measure a student's curricular skills. Instead, the decision is made by testing students *directly* in the curriculum they would be expected to learn in general education classrooms. Similarly, expectations about future performance are not gross extrapolations from a test's grade equivalent scores but are based on Survey-Level Assessment in curriculum-level materials a student would be expected to show mastery of in 1 year. This process can

FIGURE 3. Reading survey-level results for Sara.

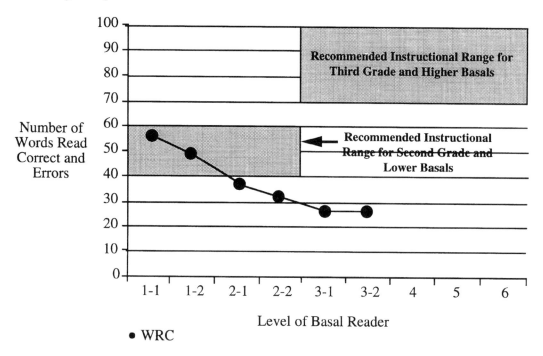

be illustrated using the case study. Sara's Survey-Level Assessment data showed her as "successful" in the Grade 1, Level 2 general education reading book. In 1 year, according to the publisher's scope-and-sequence, typical students would be expected to perform proficiently in Level 2 of the Grade 2 basal. The IEP team individualizes the annual goal by discussing the expectations for individual students. If the IEP team wanted to write a goal that facilitated Sara's "catching up" (i.e., reducing the discrepancy), they may want her to perform proficiently in a third-grade or even fourth-grade level of the basal series in 1 year. In Sara's case, the IEP team decided that they would consider the special education program to be successful if she performed proficiently in the Level 3–2 general education basal reader in 1 year.

Writing the annual goal. Annual IEP goals based on CBM data are written in the format of traditional behavioral objectives, and consist of a *behavior* to be measured, *conditions* for attainment, and *criterion* for success. The basic format in reading, math, written expression, and spelling is illustrated in Table 4.

CBM IEP goals use a long-term approach to goal setting. In a long-term goal approach, measurement of progress towards the goal is designed to answer the question, "Is the student becoming more proficient in reading, math, writing, or spelling in the general education curriculum?" This approach has an advantage over most common long-term goals (e.g., "Will improve 1 year in spelling") in that they are observable, measurable, and are tied directly to a vali-

dated way of *formative evaluation*. With formative evaluation, effective interventions identified during instruction are maintained; ineffective interventions are modified.

This long-term goal approach also avoids the numerous difficulties with short-term measurement (e.g., "Will master multiplication facts with 80% accuracy) that are problematic because they are tied to specific units or small skills within a curriculum. The advantages of using CBM and a long-term goal approach are discussed in more detail in Fuchs, this volume, and in Fuchs (1993) and Fuchs and Deno (1991).

The goal-setting process begins with identifying the academic area in which the goal is to be written. Once the academic area is specified, the dynamic indicator for that content becomes the behavior to measure. Therefore, because Sara requires an annual goal in reading, the IEP team knows that the behavior component of the goal is oral reading.

The second step is establishing the goal's *conditions*. The *time-frame* is the time at which the goal is expected to be accomplished. In Sara's school system, all IEP goals expired on their anniversary data, 1 year from the time of writing. Therefore, Sara's annual goal would begin "*In 36 weeks (1 academic year),* . . ." The next task is *specification of the level of curriculum* at which the student will be expected to perform proficiently in 1 year. This task requires knowledge of the general education curriculum scope-and-sequence, a judgment of how much is expected to be accomplished, and the ramifications on how the problem is defined. For example, writing an annual goal so that a special education student is ex-

FIGURE 4. Results of Sara's survey-level assessment in reading, comparing her performance to same- and other-grade general education students.

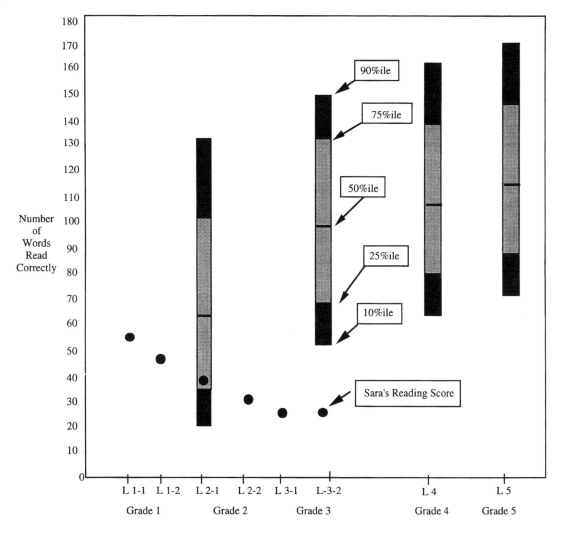

Curriculum Levels and Grade-Level Normative Ranges

pected to make less than 1 year's growth in general education curriculum is constructing an intervention that will leave a student further behind general education peers *and* the intervention would still be considered effective! Writing an annual goal so that a special education student is expected to make more than 1 year's growth in general education curriculum is constructing an intervention that, if successful, will make the student's skills more like general education peers. See Fuchs and Shinn (1989) for more detail on this topic. Because Sara's IEP team specified Level 3–2 as the annual goal material, when combined with the time frame and the behavior, her goal so far would read as follows: "*When given a randomly selected passage from Level 3–2 of the ABC Curriculum, Sara will read aloud . . .*"

The final task in setting annual goals requires specification of a *criterion for performance*. The question for Sara is "How well do we want her to read the Level 3–2 basal, if her intervention program is to be considered successful?" Two broad approaches can be used to identify a criterion for success, with or without local norms. When local norms are available, the IEP team can use the level of performance of typical students in the level of the curriculum identified in the conditions section as the criterion. For example, in Sara's case, because the IEP team distinguished book 3–2 as the level of the curriculum they desired in 1 year, they could expect that Sara read it as well as the typical third-grader in the Fall or 100 words read correctly. Alternatively, they could expect that Sara would read the Level 3–2 reader as well as an end-of-year third grader or 133 words read correctly.

In the absence of local norms, other strategies may be used to identify a criterion for success on the

TABLE 4
Basic Format for CBM Annual IEP Goals in Reading, Math, Written Expression, and Spelling

Academic Area	Conditions	Behavior	Criterion
Reading	In *(number of weeks until annual review)*, when given a randomly selected passage from *(level and name of reading series)*,	Student will read aloud	at *(number of words per minute correct / # of errors)*.
Math	In *(number of weeks until annual review)*, when given a randomly selected problem from *(level and name of math series)*, for two minutes,	Student will write	*(Number of correct digits)*.
Written Expression	In *(number of weeks until annual review)*, when given a story starter or topic sentence and 3 minutes in which to write,	Student will write	A total of *(number of words or letter sequences)*.
Spelling	In *(number of weeks until annual review)*, when dictated randomly selected words from *(level and name of spelling series)*, for 2 minutes	Student will write	*(Number of correct letter sequences)*.

Note. From "Writing CBM IEP Objectives" (p. 136) by L. S. Fuchs and M. R. Shinn, 1989. In M. R. Shinn (Ed.), *Curriculum-Based Measurement: Assessing special services for children.* New York: Guilford Press. Copyright 199 by the Guilford Press. Reprinted by permission.

annual goal. *Expert judgment* requires that IEP teams use an organizer that the student be expected to perform at a significantly higher level in a more difficult level of the curriculum in 1 year. The use of *instructional placement standards* is another strategy for goal setting without local norms. It is based on setting the criterion for success at a level of performance such that the curriculum is appropriate for instructional purposes for the student in 1 year. In reading, for example, the IEP team could use the instructional placement standards given earlier in the chapter. Using this approach in Sara's case, the criterion for success could be that, in 1 year, she would read a randomly selected passage from Level 3–2 between 70 to 100 words correctly. It is important that a more specific value is used rather than a range. If a high level of proficiency is expected, then the IEP team could select the upper end of the range (100 words read correctly) as the criterion for success. If a lower level of proficiency is satisfactory, then the IEP team could select the lower end of the range (e.g., 75 words read correctly). See Fuchs (this volume) and Fuchs and Shinn (1989) for more information on writing annual goals using CBM.

The actual IEP annual goal written by Sara's IEP team was as follows: *When given a randomly selected passage from Level 3–2 of the ABC Curriculum, Sara will read aloud 100 words correctly per*

minute. The team also added an accuracy criterion that she would read a randomly selected passage with 5 or fewer errors (approximately 95% accuracy). This goal was based on a rationale to have Sara proficient in an end-of-third-grade reader by the time she was in fourth grade. The team considered reading at 100 words correctly, the median level of third graders in that level in the Fall, as proficient.

Evaluating Solutions

The use of CBM Survey-Level Assessment data to write annual IEP goals links assessment for eligibility decision making to intervention planning. The use of CBM IEP goals links intervention planning to intervention evaluation by providing a standard for determining intervention effectiveness. As presented in Table 1, the purpose of Evaluating Solutions is to monitor student progress toward IEP goals and determine an intervention's effectiveness.

As with other decisions in the Problem-Solving model shown earlier, the annual goal can be represented graphically as shown in Figure 5 to clarify communication of expectations. In the figure, her initial Survey-Level data in Level 3–2, the annual goal material, represents her current performance. The intersection of the criterion for success (100 words read correctly) and the goal date (36 weeks) forms her *aim*. The line drawn from her current perfor-

FIGURE 5. Graphic display of Sara's IEP goal translated into expected rate of student progress.

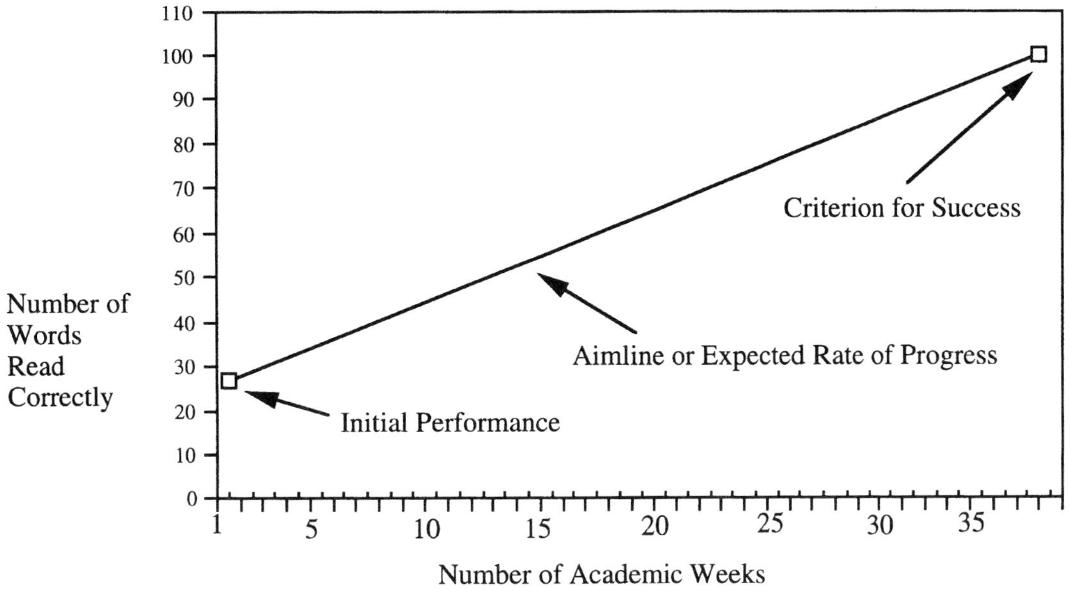

mance to her aim forms her aimline or *expected rate of progress*. By comparing her actual rate of progress, the *trendline*, determined by collected samples of her reading from Level 3–2 over time, with her expected rate of progress, decision can be made about treatment effectiveness and the need for program modification. When the actual rate of progress exceeds the expected rate of progress, the student's goal is raised. When the actual rate of progress is below the expected rate of progress, the student's intervention program is changed. See L. Fuchs (this volume) and the work of Lynn and Douglas Fuchs for more information on this topic.

Progress monitoring data usually are collected once or twice per week by a special education teacher delivering the intervention or via a microcomputer (Fuchs, 1988; Fuchs, Hamlett, & Fuchs, 1990). In reading, students read one probe each testing occasion. Testing items are selected from a pool that represents the domain of *all* the items from the goal level of the curriculum. With Sara, this would represent a sample from all passages in the Level 3–2 basal reader. Probes are created by randomly selecting subsets of items from this large pool and student progress is measured repeatedly on these probes. This process produces a set of parallel-form CBM probes with known technical adequacy.

The results of testing Sara one to two times per week using randomly selected reading probes from Level 3–2 are shown in Figure 6. The data are plotted soon after testing on an equal interval graph. A minimum of 10 data points are suggested before a reliable decision can be made about the effectiveness of an intervention program (Good & Shinn, 1990). On Sara's graph, after the first 10 data points, it is clear that she

is meeting or exceeding her expected rate of progress; 9 of the 10 data points are above the aimline. This is a good indication that the instructional intervention is effective and should be maintained. As the school year goes on, Sara's teacher continued to evaluate her progress routinely. At the end of the academic year, she had been tested 47 times during the 30-week-period. Her overall rate of progress, the trendline, is represented by the heavy black line that is calculated by drawing an ordinary least squares regression line through all the data. The trendline corresponds closely to the slope of the aimline, indicating an intervention program that is effective.

As mentioned earlier in the chapter, when the effects of instructional interventions are examined systematically and continuously, educators can make data-based decisions about whether to maintain or change interventions. Students need not receive instructional programs that do not meet their needs for long periods of time. Unsuccessful interventions can be changed to better meet students' needs. Educators need not discard or modify programs that may be working. The net result is that student achievement outcomes are improved significantly (Fuchs, Deno, & Mirkin, 1984; Fuchs & Fuchs, 1986).

Problem Solution

It can be argued persuasively that the kinds of testing activities that characterize long-term decisions about students' educational needs (e.g., annual reviews or special education exit) are little more than psychometric superstitious behavior. Annual reviews rely heavily on published achievements tests that

FIGURE 6. Graphic display of Sara's rate of progress relative to her IEP goal.

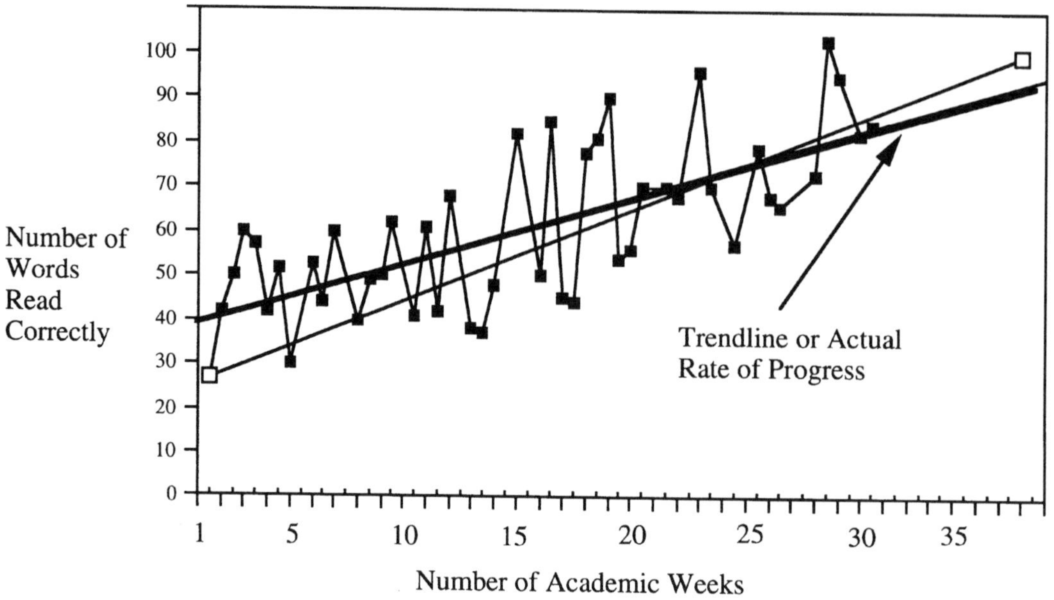

were not designed to evaluate the progress of individual students (Carver, 1974; Marston, 1989). Special education exit decisions occur so rarely that part of the problem must be related to measurement of outcomes. It is estimated that no more than 2% of special education students are exited each year (Fuchs, Fuchs, & Fernstrom, 1993). However, considerable numbers of these students have academic skills equal to those of general education students. For example, it has been demonstrated that in at least three school districts, 30% to 40% of special education students served more than 2 years in a pull-out program with an IEP objective in reading yet read as well or better than other low-performing readers in their general education classroom (Shinn, Baker, Habedank, & Good, 1993; Shinn, Habedank, Rodden-Nord, & Knutson, 1993). These students had not been considered for exiting special education.

A Problem-Solving model resolves some problems in determining students' long-term needs and the appropriateness of continued special education services. As presented in Table 1, Problem Solution decisions are tied conceptually to the assessment activities that defined the problem in the first place: Is there *still* a discrepancy between what is expected for the student and how the student performs? Procedurally, the discrepancy is measured again and is augmented by study of the special education student's rate of progress towards their IEP annual goal.

The logical time to make Problem-Solution decisions is during the periodic and annual reviews required by law (Rothstein, 1990). To date, periodic reviews rely heavily on informal subjective opinions of the teacher with responsibility for the intervention plan. Rarely are data collected or analyzed systemati-

cally specifically for this purpose. Annual review decisions usually are more structured and are oriented around the collection of student outcome information. CBM data can be collected efficiently at both periodic and annual reviews.

Periodic reviews. Periodic reviews are conducted with two pieces of CBM assessment data, the student progress graph and new peer-referenced testing results. These data are used to answer the questions: Is the student making progress? And if so, is the progress "important?" The first question is answered by examining the student's graph showing the rate of progress toward the IEP annual goal. As in making Evaluating-Solutions decisions, intervention effectiveness is determined by comparing the student's trendline to the aimline. If the trendline exceeds the aimline, two explanations are possible: (a) the intervention is effective; or (b) the annual goal is too low. If the trendline is below the aimline, two other explanations are possible: (a) the intervention program may be ineffective and need to be changed, or (b) the student's annual goal may be too high.

The second question about the importance of the student progress helps separate out issues of intervention effectiveness and goal appropriateness. Student change is defined as "important" if it results in *reduced discrepancies*. Data to make this decision is collected by testing the special education student in a norm-referenced manner as in Problem Identification. Again, random samples of the curriculum from the student's expected grade placement are used for testing. However, unlike Problem Identification, this testing takes place in one sitting rather than by collecting repeated samples over time. The student's

TABLE 5
Periodic and Annual Review of Reading Assessment as Part of Problem-Solution Decisions for Sara in Reading

Level of Curriculum	*Sara's Fall Median WRC	*Sara's Fall Percentile	**Sara's Winter Median WRC	Sara's Winter Percentile	*Sara's Spring Median WRC	*Sara's Spring Percentile
3–2	27	2nd	53	4th	69	6th
3–1	27	NA			66	NA
2–2	32	NA			81	NA
2–1	37	15			80	26th
1–3	49	NA			106	NA
1–2	55	NA			123	89th

Note. WRC = words read correctly.
*Based on SSurvey-Level Assessment
**Peer-Referenced Testing Compared to Same Grade-Students Only

scores are compared to same-grade peers, using the type of summary metric that was employed in Problem Identification.

Changes in discrepancy ratios or percentile ranks are noted. Reduced discrepancies indicate that the special education student has made meaningful, important growth. When combined with the student IEP graph information, the change in relative standing allows for an evaluation of a student's overall special education program, including intervention effectiveness and goal appropriateness. The use of these types of data is illustrated in the case study. A periodic review was conducted with Sara the first trimester after her special education certification (Winter), approximately 10 weeks after her special education placement. Her IEP progress graph at Week 10 showed her consistently scoring at or above her aimline (see Figure 6). Sara also was tested using three randomly selected passages from the same level of the reading series as her initial Problem Identification testing. This process took less than 10 minutes. Her scores, summarized in percentile ranks, are shown in Table 5. The number of words she read correctly increased to 52 and the magnitude of the discrepancy decreased from performance at the 2nd percentile compared to same-grade peers to the 4th percentile. Both pieces of data indicate that the progress she is making towards her IEP goal is educationally meaningful; she is reducing the reading skill discrepancy. If she were achieving her IEP goal, but not reducing the discrepancy, one could conclude that perhaps the IEP goal was not ambitious enough to result in real improvement. Conversely, if she were not making progress towards her IEP goal, but was reducing the peer discrepancy, it could be concluded that her goal was too ambitious and should be lowered.

Annual reviews. The annual review process is a more in-depth assessment of a student's skill level and rates of progress. Again, progress towards the

IEP annual goal is investigated by comparing actual-versus-expected student progress on the student performance graph. As can be seen in Sara's graph, at Week 30 when the annual review was conducted her actual rate of progress paralleled her expected rate. Overall, the annual review team believed the special education intervention to be effective and considered her to have attained the annual goal. Some concern was expressed over the current effectiveness of the program, however, as 7 of the last 10 data points fell below the aimline.

For annual review, more information is collected on the current severity of the problem with a new Survey-Level Assessment identical to the one conducted during Problem Certification. Not only are the Survey-Level Assessment data used to determine problem severity, but they are also used to write the annual goal for the next year. The results of Sara's annual review Survey-Level Assessment are also presented in Table 5. Sara's number of words read correctly improved again in third-grade material and the discrepancy from peers was reduced as she improved from the 4th to the 6th percentile. Her reading skills also improved significantly from Fall in all levels of the general education reading series.

Annual review Survey-Level Assessment results can be displayed graphically to show the growth relative to norm groups as shown in Figure 7. With adequate progress towards the IEP goal and a reduced discrepancy, the team considered the intervention successful and discussed Sara's continued *need* for the intervention.

A key decision in Problem Solution is determining when additional resources such as special education are no longer needed. In a Problem-Solving model, this decision is reached when the discrepancy is no longer important; that is, the special education student's skills are within the range of students in general education classrooms. In this instance, stu-

FIGURE 7. Fall and Spring survey-level assessment results for annual reviews.

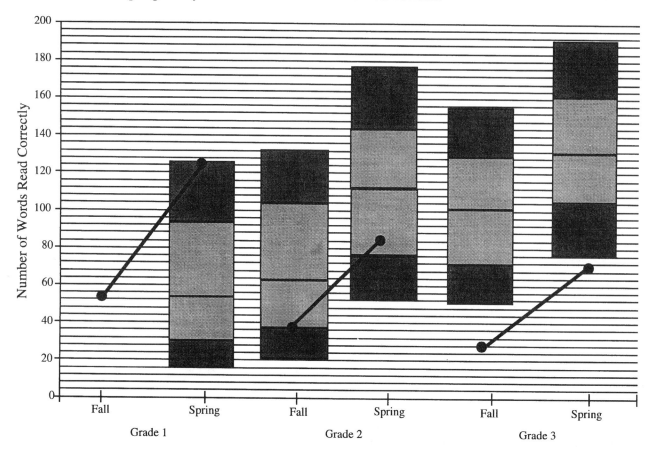

dents may be exited from special education and returned for instruction in less restrictive environments. For more detail on this topic, see Allen (1989) and Shinn, Habedank, Rodden-Nord, and Knutson (1993). Use of CBM to assist in making special education exit decisions resulted in an increase from 4% of special education students exited on an annual basis to 20% (Marston & Magnusson, 1988).

SUMMARY

Curriculum-Based Measurement (CBM) is a consistent and continuous measurement system that was designed to function as DIBS, dynamic indicators of basic skills. These DIBS are to be used as educational thermometers, tools to (a) identify an academic problem and (b) decide whether the intervention for that problem is effective. CBM is inextricably tied to a Problem-Solving model in which data are used to guide decision making. Decisions are tied to general education curricula and often to how typical students perform in that curriculum. However, the critical feature that defines CBM is the collection of data on repeated standard tasks for *individual* students. When used to evaluate and modify instructional intervention programs for individual students, research find-

ings consistently have found significantly improved outcomes. Programs for special education students are improved by allowing for validation and modification of individual interventions, better IEPs can be written, and assessment can be linked to intervention.

Because most CBM data are collected by trained special education and general education teachers, with consultation and supervision by school psychologists, the special education eligibility testing load for school psychologists can be reduced substantially. This reduction in testing load can be used to increase the amount of time school psychologists spend in indirect and direct service provision to all students in America's schools. One of my mentors once paraphrased an old saying, commenting that "school psychologists are trained to admire (i.e., identify) problems, not solve them." In more ways than one, CBM and its use in a Problem-Solving model allows for this conception of school psychology practice to change.

AUTHOR NOTES

The development of this chapter was supported, in part, by Grant No. 8029D80051-92 from the U.S. Department of Education, Special Education Programs, to provide leadership training in curriculum-based assessment and by Grant No. H023C10151 from the

U.S. Department of Education, Office of Special Education Research, to conduct research in using Curriculum-Based Measurement to facilitate reintegration of students with mild disabilities into general education classrooms. The views expressed within this chapter are not necessarily those of the U.S. Department of Education.

REFERENCES

Adams, M. J. (1990). *Beginning to read: Thinking and learning about print.* Cambridge, MA: MIT Press.

Allen, D. (1989). Periodic and annual reviews and decisions to terminate special education services. In M. R. Shinn (Ed.), *Curriculum-based measurement: Assessing special children* (pp. 184–203). New York: Guilford.

Canter, A. (1991). Effective psychological services for all students: A data-based model of service delivery. In G. Stoner, M. R. Shinn, & H. M. Walker (Eds.), *Interventions for achievement and behavior problems* (pp. 49–78). Silver Spring, MD: National Association of School Psychologists.

Carlberg, C., & Kavale, K. (1980). The efficacy of special versus regular class placement for exceptional children: A meta-analysis. *The Journal of Special Education, 14*(3), 295-308.

Carnegie Council on Adolescent Development. (1989). *Turning points: Preparing American youth for the 21st century.* New York: Carnegie Corporation of New York.

Carver, R. P. (1974). Two dimensions of tests: Psychometric and edumetric. *American Psychologist, 29*, 512–518.

Center for the Study of Social Policy. (1991). *Kids count data book.* Washington, DC: Author.

Costenbader, V., Swartz, J., & Petrix, L. (1992). Consultation in the schools: The relationship between preservice training, perception of consultative skills, and actual time spent in consultation. *School Psychology Review, 21*(1), 95–108.

Curtis, M. J., & Batsche, G. M. (1991). Meeting the needs of children and families: Opportunities and challenges for school psychology training programs. *School Psychology Review, 20*(4), 565–577.

Deno, S. L. (1985). Curriculum-based measurement: The emerging alternative. *Exceptional Children, 52*, 219–232.

Deno, S. L. (1986). Formative evaluation of individual student programs: A new role for school psychologists. *School Psychology Review, 15*, 358–374.

Deno, S. L. (1989). Curriculum-based measurement and alternative special education services: A fundamental and direct relationship. In M. R. Shinn (Ed.), *Curriculum-based measurement: Assessing special children* (pp. 1–17). New York: Guilford.

Deno, S. L. (1992). The nature and development of curriculum-based measurement. *Preventing School Failure, 36*(2), 5–10.

Deno, S. L., Mirkin, P., & Chiang, B. (1982). Identifying valid measures of reading. *Exceptional Children, 49*(1), 36–45.

Forness, S. R., & Kavale, K. A. (1987). De-psychologizing special education. In C. M. Nelson & S. R. Forness (Eds.), *Severe behavior disorders of children and youth* (pp. 2–14). Boston: College Hill Press.

Fuchs, L. S. (1988). Effects of computer-managed instruction on teachers' implementation of systematic monitoring programs and student achievement. *Journal of Educational Research, 81*, 294–304.

Fuchs, L. S. (1993). Enhancing instructional programming and student achievement with curriculum-based measurement. In J.

Kramer (Ed.), *Curriculum-based measurement* (pp. 65–104). Lincoln, NE: Buros Institute of Mental Measurements.

Fuchs, L. S., & Deno, S. L. (1991). Paradigmatic distinctions between instructionally relevant measurement models. *Exceptional Children, 58*, 232–243.

Fuchs, L. S., Deno, S. L., & Mirkin, P. (1984). The effects of frequent curriculum based measurement and evaluation on pedagogy, student achievement and student awareness of learning. *American Educational Research Journal, 21*, 449–460.

Fuchs, L. S., & Fuchs, D. (1986). Effects of systematic formative evaluation on student achievement: A meta-analysis. *Exceptional Children, 53*, 199–208.

Fuchs, L. S., & Fuchs, D. (1992). Identifying a measure for monitoring student reading progress. *School Psychology Review, 21*(1), 45–58.

Fuchs, L. S., Fuchs, D., & Deno, S. L. (1982). Reliability and validity of curriculum-based informal reading inventories. *Reading Research Quarterly, 18*, 6–26.

Fuchs, L. S., Fuchs, D., & Hamlett, C. L. (1989). Effects of instrumental use of curriculum-based measurement to enhance instructional programs. *Remedial and Special Education, 10*(2), 43–52.

Fuchs, L. S., Fuchs, D., Hamlett, C. L., & Allinder, R. M. (1991). The contribution of skills analysis to curriculum-based measurement in spelling. *Exceptional Children, 57*(5), 443–452.

Fuchs, L. S., Fuchs, D., Hamlett, C. L., & Ferguson, C. (1992). Effects of expert system consultation within curriculum-based measurement using a reading maze task. *Exceptional Children, 58*(5), 436–450.

Fuchs, L. S., Fuchs, D., Hamlett, C. L., & Stecker, P. M. (1991). Effects of curriculum-based measurement and consultation on teaching planning and student achievement in mathematics operations. *American Educational Research Journal, 28*, 617–641.

Fuchs, L. S., Fuchs, D., & Maxwell, L. (1988). The validity of informal reading comprehension measures. *Remedial and Special Education, 9*, 20–28.

Fuchs, L. S., Hamlett, C. L., & Fuchs, D. (1990). *Monitoring basic skills progress.* Austin, TX: PRO-ED.

Fuchs, L. S., & Shinn, M. R. (1989). Writing CBM IEP objectives. In M. R. Shinn (Ed.), *Curriculum-based measurement: Assessing special children* (pp. 132–154). New York: Guilford.

Gerber, M., & Semmel, M. (1984). Teachers as imperfect tests: Reconceptualizing the referral process. *Educational Psychologist, 19*, 137–148.

Good, R. H., & Shinn, M. R. (1990). Forecasting accuracy of slope estimates for reading curriculum-based measurement: Empirical evidence. *Behavioral Assessment, 12*, 179–193.

Howell, K. W., Fox, S. L., & Morehead, M. K. (1993). *Curriculum-based evaluation: Teaching and decision making* (2nd ed.). Belmont, CA: Brooks/Cole.

Huebner, E. S., & Gould, K. (1991). Multidisciplinary teams revisited: Current perceptions of school psychologists regarding team functioning. *School Psychology Review, 20*(3), 428–434.

Hutton, J. B., Dubes, R., & Muir, S. (1992). Assessment practices of school psychologists: Ten years later. *School Psychology Review, 21*(2), 271–284.

Kavale, K. A., & Forness, S. R. (1985). *The science of learning disabilities.* San Diego, CA: College-Hill Press.

Kavale, K. A., & Forness, S. R. (1987). Substance over style: Assessing the efficacy of modality testing and teaching. *Exceptional Children, 54*(3), 228–239.

Marston, D. (1989). Curriculum-based measurement: What is it and why do it? In M. R. Shinn (Ed.), *Curriculum-based measurement: Assessing special children* (pp. 18–78). New York: Guilford.

Marston, D., & Magnusson, D. (1988). Curriculum-based assessment: District-level implementation. In J. Graden, J. Zins, & M. Curtis (Eds.), *Alternative educational delivery systems: Enhancing instructional options for all students* (pp. 137–172). Washington, DC: National Association of School Psychologists.

Reschly, D. J., Genshaft, J., & Binder, M. S. (1987). *The 1986 NASP survey: Comparison of practitioners, NASP leadership, and university faculty on key issues.* Washington, DC: National Association of School Psychologists.

Rothstein, L. F. (1990). *Special education law.* New York: Longman.

Salvia, J., & Ysseldyke, J. E. (1987). *Assessment in special and remedial education* (4th ed.). Boston: Houghton-Mifflin.

Shinn, M. R. (1988). Development of curriculum-based local norms for use in special education decision making. *School Psychology Review, 17,* 61–80.

Shinn, M. R. (1989). Identifying and defining academic problems: CBM screening and eligibility procedures. In M. R. Shinn (Ed.), *Curriculum-based measurement: Assessing special children* (pp. 90–129). New York: Guilford.

Shinn, M. R., Baker, S., Habedank, L., & Good, R. H. (in press). The effects of classroom reading performance data on general education teachers' and parents' attitudes about reintegration. *Exceptionality.*

Shinn, M. R., Good, R. H., Knutson, N., Tilly, W. D., & Collins, V. (1992). Curriculum-based reading fluency: A confirmatory analysis of its relation to reading. *School Psychology Review, 21*(3), 458–478.

Shinn, M. R., Habedank, L., Rodden-Nord, K., & Knutson, N. (1993). The use of curriculum-based measurement to identify potential candidates for reintegration into general education. *The Journal of Special Education, 27*(2), 202–221.

Shinn, M. R., & Hubbard, D. D. (1992). Curriculum-based measurement and problem-solving assessment: Basic procedures and outcomes. *FOCUS on Exceptional Children, 24*(5), 1–20.

Shinn, M. R., Rosenfield, S., & Knutson, N. (1989). Curriculum-based assessment: A comparison and integration of models. *School Psychology Review.*

Shinn, M. R., Tindal, G., Spira, D., & Marston, D. (1987). Practice of learning disabilities as social policy. *Learning Disability Quarterly, 10*(1), 17–28.

Smith, D. K. (1984). Practicing school psychologists: Their characteristics, activities, and populations served. *Professional Psychology: Research and Practice, 15,* 798–810.

Smith, S. W. (1990). Individualized educational programs (IEPs) in special education: From intent to acquiescence. *Exceptional Children, 57*(1), 6–14.

Tindal, G. (1993). A review of curriculum-based procedures on nine assessment components. In J. Kramer (Ed.), *Curriculum-based measurement* (pp. 25–64). Lincoln, NE: Buros Institute of Mental Measurements.

ANNOTATED BIBLIOGRAPHY

Deno, S. L. (1986). Formative evaluation of individual programs: A new role for school psychologists. *School Psychology Review, 15,* 358–374.

In this article, problems associated with traditional assessment practices and functions of school psychologists are identified and a new role for school psychologists is proposed. The use of CBM formative evaluation is presented as a methodology that permits school psychologists to provide assessment information that is relevant in determining the effectiveness of educational interventions.

Deno, S. L. (1991). Individual differences and individual difference: The essential difference of special education. *The Journal of Special Education, 24*(2), 160–173.

In this article, the current aptitude-treatment interaction (ATI) instructional technology is examined and determined to be insufficiently responsive to individual differences of students. Instead, a formative evaluation model is proposed as an idiographic approach to building more effective programs for individual students. In this model, aptitude differences at the outset of a program are de-emphasized and methodology for tailoring programs to individual students during instruction becomes the focus.

Fuchs, L. S. (1986). Monitoring progress among mildly handicapped pupils: Review of current practice and research. *Remedial and Special Education, 7,* 5–12.

A review of research is presented in this article on the use of formative evaluation to improve instructional programs for mildly handicapped students. Critical issues discussed regarding this methodology for monitoring student progress are focus of measurement, frequency of measurement, data display, and data-utilization methods.

Fuchs, L. S., & Deno, S. L. (1991). Paradigmatic distinctions between instructionally relevant measurement models. *Exceptional Children, 58,* 232–243.

A comparison of the advantages and disadvantages of specific subskill mastery measurement (short-term goal approach) and general outcome measurement (long-term goal approach) progress monitoring is presented. General outcome measurement emerges as the most advantageous method for monitoring student progress. A case study is presented to illustrate the differences between approaches.

Kramer, J. (Ed.). (1993). *Curriculum-based measurement.* Lincoln, NE: Buros Institute of Mental Measurements.

In this book CBM is presented from the perspectives of a variety of scholars whose efforts have, in large part, defined the CBM approach to problem-solving assessment (Deno, Tindal, L. Fuchs, Lentz, Kramer, Shapiro, Shinn, & Good). CBM is defined, reviewed along with other assessment techniques that fall under the category of curriculum-based assessment, and presented as a method for enhancing instruction and student achievement. A prognosis for its future is discussed.

McKiggen, M., & Shinn, M. R. (1993). *CBM and problem-solving assessment: A self-instruction course.* Eugene, OR: University of Oregon School Psychology Program.

This continuing professional development (CPD) self-instruction course was designed for and researched with individual school psychology practitioners. Reading materials include Shinn (1989; see this annotated bibliography), a CBM skill-building workbook developed at the University of Oregon, and eight additional recently published articles. Course instructional materials include a six-unit syllabus, six unit quizzes, advance organizers for each assigned reading, and activity log forms to self- monitor progress through the course and maintain a record for CPD credits.

Shinn, M. R. (Ed.). (1989). *Curriculum-based measurement: Assessing special children.* New York: Guilford Press.

This book contains contributions of the work of the core-group of researchers and school practitioners (Deno, L. Fuchs, Marston, Shinn, Tindal, Allen) who developed and implemented CBM. Specific procedures for implementing CBM in school settings are detailed. General background information and conceptual issues surrounding the development and use of CBM as an alternative to traditional school psychology practice are also discussed.

49

Best Practices in Linking Assessment to Intervention

George M. Batsche
Howard M. Knoff
University of South Florida

OVERVIEW

Historical Perspective

With the 1975 passage of Public Law 94-142, the Education for All Handicapped Children Act, the number of practicing school psychologists grew dramatically. In fact, between 1970 and 1988, the number of school psychologists practicing in public schools quadrupled. Fagan (1988) identified this era (1970–present) as the "thoroughbred years." A review of the early history of school psychology indicates that "testing" was the primary function of those professionals identified as school psychologists. In the early 1970s, school psychologists began to add consultation, intervention, and organizational development activities to the existing assessment functions. However, the passage of Public Law 94-142 in 1975 resulted in an emphasis on the role of testing once again. The greatly increased number of school psychologists employed by school districts at that time were employed primarily to identify children and youth eligible to receive special education services.

P.L. 94-142 focused on the identification and placement of students with disabilities. As such, criteria were established for each of the handicapping conditions recognized in the act. School personnel were responsible for conducting assessments to determine the extent to which a student met the criteria for a handicapping condition and was eligible for special services. Because testing was, in and of itself, a required activity for determining eligibility for special programs, there was little or no pressure (from consumers or the profession) to expect more from the assessment process than an eligibility recommendation. The process of assessment for special education came under intense scrutiny, however, when litigation began over issues related to who (student demographics) was being placed (and more recently not placed) in special education. The *Larry P. versus Riles* case is but one example of litigation focusing on the appropriateness of psychological and educational assessment. However, the focus of the litigation was on the appropriateness of assessment relative to the *identification* of students for special education, not on its relevance to intervention.

During the heyday in the rise of special education services, intervention was linked to assessment only through the selection of a special education program for a student, not in the development of specific intervention strategies. *The special education placement was the intervention.* The outcomes of assessment were evaluated in terms of the appropriateness of the *placement* decision. Therefore, school psychologists were evaluated by supervisors and school district personnel on the basis of the number of students assessed, the number of staffings (teacher/parent conferences) conducted, and the number of students placed in special education. In fact, in many states, school psychologists (as well as special education teachers and other support personnel) were (and still are) paid out of special education funds available based on the number of students placed in special programs.

After the first 10 years following the implementation of P.L. 94-142, the focus of special services began to shift from the "child-find" function of the act to the efficacy of special education services. A number of researchers began to question whether placement in special education classes benefitted students with disabilities (Kavale, 1990). In the mid 1980s, advocacy began to place pressure on the U.S. Department of Education to conduct efficacy studies of special education services. The first report (National Council on Disability's *The Education of Students with Disabilities: Where Do We Stand?*) on the effectiveness of P.L. 94-142 appeared in 1989. The results of the report were not encouraging and recommendations were made that had significant implications for the profession of school psychology. Specifically, the report questioned the appropriateness of assessment (e.g., norm-referenced) that did not lead to the development and evaluation of intervention programs.

In recent years, there has been an increased focus on the link between assessment and intervention both in psychology and education (Batsche, 1992; Nelson & Hayes, 1979; Nelson, Hayes, & Jarett,

1986; Shapiro, 1988). In addition, the *outcome-based* education movement within the school reform process has triggered a general call for accountability in all aspects of education, including the profession of school psychology. Within school psychology one aspect of the accountability issue relates to the extent to which assessment procedures developed for *diagnostic* and eligibility determination can be used to develop and evaluate effective interventions. This is a healthy debate and has resulted in an increased focus (practice, research, teaching) on the link between assessment and intervention. More importantly, this focus has improved services to all students, resulted in new technologies for linking assessment to intervention, and provided an increased trust and integrity in the services provided by school psychologists.

An entire generation of school psychologists were trained in response to the unmet service delivery needs of students that resulted from P.L. 94-142. Training focused primarily on developing the skills necessary to conduct valid assessments of students with special needs from diverse backgrounds and to relating assessment results to program eligibility. There was little training provided in the areas of *functional assessment*, intervention development, and evaluation of interventions. Even today, the primary focus of training in the area of assessment remains on traditional norm-referenced assessment as it relates to diagnosis and placement concerns. However, if effective intervention plans for students with developmental, behavioral, and academic difficulties are to be formulated, assessment must relate to the development and evaluation of interventions, not to the process of diagnosis. The relationship between diagnosis and treatment (aptitude by treatment interaction) is not well established in psychology and education. Therefore, the link between assessment and intervention cannot occur through a problem-solving process designed to categorize disabilities. The link must be forged by understanding the relationship between the students and their needs and the environment and its resources. This requires a different approach to problem solving than the traditional "test-staff-place" approach. More appropriately, it will require developing assessment procedures designed to answer specific questions that relate to the academic, developmental, and behavioral difficulties of a particular student.

This chapter will present an empirically supported model of linking assessment to intervention, basic considerations of that model, and best practices associated with its implementation.

BASIC CONSIDERATIONS

Definition and Purposes of Assessment

Assessment designed to determine eligibility, placement, and diagnosis is *administrative* assessment. Assessment designed to develop and evaluate interventions is *functional assessment*. The problem-solving and decision-making processes of each are discrete. Attempting to "link" administrative assessment strategies to the development and evaluation of interventions is problematic.

The assessment/intervention debate in school psychology has been fueled, perhaps unnecessarily, by confusion over definitions. First, some would believe that assessment and testing are interchangeable terms. Nothing is further from the truth. This misnomer has developed from assessment practices that have, historically, relied primarily on "testing" (IQ, achievement, visual motor, emotional/behavioral). Assessment in psychology and education occurs primarily through four domains: *review* of records provided by school and family personnel, *interview* of persons familiar with the referral concern and/or responsible for interventions, *observation* of the student in assessment-appropriate settings, and *testing* the student directly. Any or all of these domains of assessment are appropriate when they are consistent with and valid for the purpose for which the assessment is being conducted.

Mash and Terdal (1988) have identified four common purposes of assessment: (a) diagnosis, (b) prognosis, (c) treatment/intervention design, and (d) evaluation of treatment/intervention effectiveness. Although the purpose of this chapter is to discuss the link between assessment and intervention, it is important to understand the "link" between assessment in school psychology to both diagnosis and prognosis as well as to intervention.

This chapter's authors believe that the debate over linking assessment to intervention (specifically testing) has been confounded by attempts to force assessment practices designed to yield data necessary for placement decisions to also function to develop and evaluate intervention programs. Assessment in special education has been conducted primarily for the *administrative* purposes of determining if a student is eligible for a special program. A concrete example of this would be the use of an audiometer (and the subsequent audiogram) to determine if a student meets the criteria for a hearing loss to be eligible for special services. A parallel example would be the use of an IQ test to determine if a student met the IQ criteria for eligibility for a program for students with mental disabilities. Although using an IQ test as a valid measure of the "mental ability" component of a mental disabilities diagnosis certainly has been debated, such use is an accepted practice and an IQ test is considered an appropriate measure to use when rendering such a diagnosis (as current diagnostic criteria exist). However, the use of an IQ test to develop educational interventions and then to evaluate the effectiveness of those interventions would be challenged vociferously within the profession.

School psychologists have attempted to justify the use of traditional tests to develop and evaluate interventions for a number of reasons, including: (a) discomfort with and lack of training in functional assessment; (b) lack of time and resources to conduct functional assessment; and (c) lack of time and support to evaluate program effectiveness. Traditional diagnostic tests have their most defensible "link" with the process of classification, not intervention. Using assessment practices designed for administrative purposes for the development and evaluation of interventions will be challenged.

The concept of *prognosis* has received little attention in the school psychology literature. If one equates prognosis with the severity of a problem (less severe, better prognosis, more severe, poorer prognosis) then Gresham's definition of severity proves useful. Gresham defines the severity of a problem as its *resistance to intervention*. If one accepts this definition, then the only assessment practices linked to the concept of prognosis are those that measure intervention efficacy. Therefore, *functional* measures of behavioral, emotional, developmental, and academic progress are valid measures for assessing the prognosis of a student. Assessment procedures that can be used both to develop and evaluate intervention programs serve the *multiple* functions of being used to design interventions, to evaluate their effectiveness, and to provide data to parents and teachers.

Shapiro and Kratochwill (1988) indicate that assessment and intervention procedures can be linked in three ways: (a) through the design of the intervention program, (b) by linking the assessment to the environmental conditions of the individual student's behavior, and (c) through treatment evaluation for the purpose of modification. To link assessment to intervention design, the school psychologist must develop hypotheses that relate (or link) the problem to potential causes. *Causes* are not defined here in the traditional medical model sense but rather are defined within the context of the student and his or her environment. Behavioral psychologists use the term, functional assessment, to denote this process. Taking Shapiro and Kratochwill's purposes of assessment further, one can only link assessment to environmental conditions if hypotheses can be developed regarding conditions under which the behavior will occur and can be assessed. The model of linking assessment to intervention presented in this chapter identifies six "conditions" that must be considered when developing an assessment plan for a student. These conditions are (a) child characteristics, (b) teacher characteristics, (c) peer characteristics, (d) curriculum issues, (e) school environment issues, and (f) family/community factors. Assessment practices that focus on the development of hypotheses that link the problem to the conditions under which the problem occurs, automatically provide a link with the desired intervention and the methods *Review, Interview, Observe, Test*—RIOT) required to assess the effectiveness of that intervention.

Focus of Assessment

The first step in successfully linking assessment to intervention is the development and identification of *replacement behaviors*. The primary focus of problem solving using an assessment-to-intervention paradigm should begin with the identification of replacement behaviors, not problem behaviors.

Traditionally, assessment has focused on describing the referral *problem* within a particular theoretical framework (psychological, educational). Typically, interventions for behavior problems have focused on the reduction of inappropriate behaviors. This focus on the behavior problem is inappropriate for two reasons and provides a direct threat to the development of the assessment-to-intervention link. First, interventions that focus on the reduction of a behavior assume that the negative behavior will be replaced, automatically, by a prosocial behavior. This assumption may not be true. If a student has not learned the appropriate behavior (skill deficit), then simply eliminating the inappropriate behavior will not "teach" the appropriate one. Unless the reductive intervention is continued, the negative behavior will return as soon as conditions warrant. As the reductive intervention becomes successful in reducing the problem behavior, the teacher or parent will have fewer prompts to use the intervention. As the use of the intervention declines, the probability that the negative behavior will return increases. This is a common outcome of school-based interventions.

Second, interventions designed to reduce behaviors are not educative and do not draw on the teaching skills of school personnel. Interventions that *teach* behaviors have a number of advantages. First, they use the same teaching processes of modeling, role play, performance feedback, and transfer of training that teachers use every day to teach academic skills. Therefore, the "behavioral regularity" (Sarason, 1985) of the teacher remains intact and the number of new skills required to implement interventions are minimized. This increases the probability that the intervention will be implemented appropriately and willingly (treatment integrity and treatment acceptability). Second, as the interventions are implemented, the skills o the student are improved, not reduced. This reinforces the continued use of the intervention by reinforcing the teacher or parent for intervention implementation. Third, the implementation of educative intervention requires the identification of *replacement behaviors* and building toward a positive focus early in the assessment-to-intervention-linkage process.

The identification of replacement behaviors is critical to the implementation of a process that links functional assessment to effective interventions and, as the focus of assessment and intervention, accomplishes a number of goals. First, the replacement behavior is, by definition, the *outcome goal* of the intervention. Clarification of the replacement behavior with the referral agent (teacher, parent, or student) increases the probability that the intervention will be linked to clinically significant outcomes. Second, assessment focuses on the behavior which is the target of intervention and may be different from the original referral behavior. For example, if a student is constantly out of seat and bothering others, the replacement behavior may be the development of self-instructional behaviors related to self-control rather than simply reinforcement and reductive strategies for "staying in the seat." Assessment will focus on the presence or absence of the skills necessary to develop self-control (such as self-monitoring and self-instructional strategies) and not necessarily on the referral problem (out-of-seat behavior). The intervention might lead to self-instructional strategies combined with social skills training. The result, of course, will be a reduction of out-of-seat behavior (the teacher's concern). If the focus was an out-of-seat behavior, then the assessment might focus on a frequence counting or observation of out-of-seat behavior with interventions focused on reinforcement for in-seat behavior and a reductive strategy (such as time-out) for out-of-seat behavior. The focus on replacement behaviors from the beginning results in assessment for problem analysis that is the same as for intervention.

The Development of Model Linking Assessment to Interventions

Any model linking assessment to intervention must include (a) a link between the referral problem, its desired replacement behavior, and the conditions that support the problem and prevent its replacement; (b) the development of hypotheses, grounded in theory and practice, that are known to relate to the referral problem and the desired replacement behavior; (c) the development of predictions that enable the hypotheses to be evaluated through a multifaceted assessment process; (d) the use of assessment data to evaluate hypotheses rather than develop them; and (e) the use of assessment strategies that serve as the basis for intervention evaluation as well as program development.

Traditionally, school psychologists have administered a wide range of assessment procedures to students, teachers, and parents. The problem-solving focus of traditional assessment is to develop hypotheses from the data collected *after* assessment is complete. This results in information that describes student performance in terms of the test administered and the hypotheses used to develop the test.

Using this approach, school psychologists often find themselves expected to interpret student performance and test results in areas about which they have little theoretical knowledge and few, if any, skills in the development of interventions. Examples of this might occur in the area of reading or childhood depression. School psychologists might be *trained* to administer tests of reading or tests that assess levels of depression. However, they may not *understand* the causes behind the reading problem or childhood depression and cannot develop hypotheses about why the problem is occurring or develop successful interventions.

The primary requirement for the use of the assessment-to-intervention model described in this chapter is the ability to develop hypotheses about the referral problem and the desired replacement behavior prior to the collection of assessment data. Assessment strategies are then selected based on the hypotheses developed and the referral questions asked. In this model, data are used to verify or nullify hypotheses developed *prior* to assessment rather than to develop hypotheses abut data *after* assessment. The use of this approach increases the probability that assessment strategies will be selected that assist in understanding the relationship between the problem, the replacement behavior, and the conditions under which they occur. Once this relationship is understood, the development of interventions (and their evaluation is the next logical step in the problem-solving process.

BEST PRACTICES IN LINKING ASSESSMENT TO INTERVENTION

The Referral Question Consultation (RQC) process (Batsche & Ullman, 1984; Batsche, 1984; Knoff & Batsche, 1991b) is an empirically based, generic, problem-solving model that can be used for specific academic and behavioral problems. More refined than the traditional generic problem-solving models that encourage problem identification, problem analysis, intervention, and evaluation steps (e.g., Curtis & Meyers, 1990), the RQC will require most school psychologists to make a paradigm shift as assessment truly is directly and functionally linked to intervention. The RQC process simply employs the scientific method in an empirically based, hypotheses-generating and -testing search for *why* a referred problem is occurring. The RQC process links functional assessment, focused on *explaining* and *confirming* why referred problems occur, with effective interventions for the purpose of facilitating the academic and social progress of referred students. Clearly, this is very different from the traditional refer-test-place approaches to psychoeducational assessment currently practiced in most of our schools (Gutkin & Conoley, 1990).

More specifically, the goal of the traditional psychoeducational assessment model is (a) to describe, often from a national, norm-referenced perspective, the referred problem in data-based (e.g., standard score) terms; (b) to investigate the extent to which a particular student may differ from same-age peers; and (c) to determine the referred student's eligibility, often using highly questionable criteria (especially in the case of learning disabilities, emotional disturbances, attention deficit disorders, and the like), for special education or other programs. Professionals who need to answer questions about the social and academic difficulties of students and to design effective interventions require a different approach to problem solving, one that goes beyond the eligibility-oriented decisions that result from standardized assessment. We feel that the RQC process fulfills this need.

The RQC method requires school professionals to comprehensively understand the types of social and academic problems referred to them. In too many instances, assessment teams rely on hypotheses derived from standardized assessment procedures, rather than on hypotheses based on (a) functional analyses of referral problems *in the environments where they occur* (e.g., Iwata, Vollmer, & Zarcone, 1990), and (b) reviews of empirical literature that relate to the referred problem. For example, there are multiple reasons why students experience reading, math, and written language problems or why they are aggressive, anxious, or withdrawn. Standardized psychoeducational assessment routinely answers the question "How much of a reading, math, or written expression problem exists?" but not *"What* potential conditions facilitate the existence of these problems?" Analogously, on a behavioral level, behavior rating scales and other personality assessment tools may indicate the type and level of a student's aggression, anxiety, or withdrawal, the teacher's or caregiver's perception of these difficulties, but not the reasons for their occurrence.

Expanding briefly, while three different students may exhibit the same frequency, duration, integrity, and typology of overt aggression, each student may be aggressing for a different reason. For example, one might be angry that his parents are getting divorced, another might be frustrated because academic work is too difficult, and the last might be reinforced for aggression by the gang members in his peer group. In each case, the strategic intervention will necessarily be different in that it focuses on the cause of the aggression (counseling, curriculum modification, group contingency procedures), taking the specific reason for the aggression into account. The RQC process provides the framework to validly assess "Why does this problem exist?" and links the answers to this question to procedures that lead to effective interventions. The method, however, does not independently generate the reason "why" a given problem exists. The *hypotheses* as to "why" a problem exists must be supplied by the professionals who are engaged in the RQC process as they functionally analyze the ecology and circumstances around the referred student and situation.

The RQC method is very rewarding for those individuals already aware of the potential reasons why a referred problem exists or willing to investigate those reasons. The RQC method is designed for the sole purpose of implementing effective interventions based on valid hypotheses that have been verified through functional assessment. It is not designed to provide additional information concerning special program eligibility or to diagnose children and adolescents. The authors believe that the processes necessary to determine program eligibility and those necessary to implement effective interventions are different. Each serves its own purpose well. As previously noted, problems arise, however, when one method is used to achieve the goals of the other.

The RQC Process

The RQC process typically involves any and all school professionals who interact with and might facilitate the problem-solving process relative to a referred student. It is assumed at the outset that all participants have expertise, each in their own professional area, and that the diversity of their perspectives will significantly enhance the problem-solving process and the search for reasons to explain a specific, referred behavior. After an individual student has been referred, the RQC process involves 10 interdependent steps:

1. *Review* all existing data available on the referred student and collect any additional background data as appropriate.

2. *Meet* with the referral source in a *consultative interview* to behaviorally define his or her initial concerns, to identify desired *replacement behaviors*, to identify the need for additional data to finalize the behavioral operationalization of these concerns, to informally test some initial hypotheses, and to determine the referral source's assessment goals and commitment to the RQC process.

3. *Develop hypotheses* to explain the initial concerns as behaviorally operationalized.

4. *Develop prediction statements* from the generated hypotheses to organize assessment strategies.

5. *Develop data-based referral questions* that will guide the assessment process and confirm or reject the generated hypotheses.

6. *Select multitrait, multimethod assessment procedures* that will specifically answer the referral questions and facilitate the link between assessment and intervention.

7. *Apply the assessment and background data* so as to answer the referral questions and to confirm or reject the generated hypotheses.

8. *Select and implement intervention strategies* consistent with those hypotheses that have been confirmed.

9. *Monitor and evaluate change* in the area of the initial concern to determine the impact of the intervention.

10. *Develop a written report* that documents the RQC process, the interventions tried, and the intervention outcomes as they relate to the resolution of the initial, referred concerns.

Review of the Data

When a multidisciplinary team or school psychologist receives a request for consultative services from a teacher, the first step in the RQC process is to review essential information about the referred student and to collect any additional background data that may be important to know before interviewing the teacher. The review of essential information typically centers around an analysis of four possible existing student areas or "folders": (a) the student's cumulative folder, (b) the administrative/discipline folder, (c) relevant teachers' academic work sample folders (student portfolios), and (d) the special education/remedial education (e.g., Chapter 1) folder. In addition to the information available in already-existing records and student folders, it may be time- and cost-efficient to collect other data from teachers and other sources prior to an initial consultation interview. This information may be collected through behavior checklists, behavior rating scales, ecological or developmental status surveys or questionnaires, or standardized inventories, and it may, for example, provide the answers to routine developmental status questions so that precious interview time can focus on areas more germane to the referral concerns. This information may facilitate a more accurate and in-depth behavioral or operationalization of the teacher's initial concerns, identify possible correlates of those concerns, identify possible student assets and strengths, generally prepare the school psychologist more thoroughly for the consultation interview and the teacher's (and others') perception of the referral problem, and provide content for hypothesis generation.

In all, a number of questions can be answered, even before the first consultative interview with the teacher, by reviewing existing student records and collecting rating scale and other information as appropriate. Among these questions are the following:

1. Is the student age-appropriate (young or old) for the grade?

2. Has the student been retained, received special services, or preschool services? How many schools has the student been in? How many school placement programs has the student experienced?

3. What has been the average yearly academic progress of the student?

4. Has the student had an unusual health history or have there been significant medical traumas or events in the student's life? Is the student currently taking medication? Is health or medication status related to the referral problem?

5. Are there documented effects of retention, special services, or other interventions on the student's academic or behavioral problems?

6. Has there been a documented history of behavior or disciplinary problems? If so, do behavior or disciplinary problems appear consistently over time?

7. What has the student's attendance record been over his or her academic career? Is there a relationship between attendance and the referred problem?

8. Are there documented family or developmental history factors that have contributed to any student problems?

9. What interventions have been tried with the student? What has been their effects?

10. What are the student's academic and social-emotional strengths from the perspective of teachers, parents, and other significant informants?

11. What are the student's academic and social-emotional weaknesses or problems from the perspective of teachers, parents, and other significant informants?

These last two questions can be answered most comprehensively, as noted previously, through the use of developmental scales and curricular scope and sequence charts, in the case of academic status, and behavior rating scales and objective personality assessment scales, in the case of social-emotional behavior. While school psychologists should ask teachers, they also should involve parents, students, and significant others so that (a) the broader ecology in which the referred child lives can be understood and (b) situation-specific versus more generalized academic and behavioral patterns can be discerned. While these data may be used and validated later during the multitrait, multimethod assessment process that focuses on hypothesis confirmation, the data collected from these tools, at this point in the RQC process, can only be considered teacher or parent perceptions.

The Consultative Interview

The consultative interview(s) involving those individuals referring and relevant to a specific child, is the most important activity in the RQC process. While the long-term impact of the consultation interview focuses on intervention planning and implementation, the interview has a number of goals as the second step of the RQC process:

1. To engage the teacher (and/or parents) in a comprehensive problem-solving consultation process such that they are committed to the process from beginning to end and to the service delivery directions that result from the process and fully understand (and feel) their importance to problem solving.

2. To obtain additional relevant information beyond that already collected during Step 1, Review of Data, and to integrate and apply all of the data to the next steps of the RQC process.

3. To clarify the initial concerns of the referral source, using all the data collected, resulting in a behavioral definition and operationalization of the behavior(s) of concern.

4. To identify replacement behaviors which will become the target of assessment and intervention.

5. To determine which interventions have already been attempted and to evaluate the treatment integrity and impact of those interventions.

6. To begin to generate tentative hypotheses that explain the clarified concern and to outline the remainder of the RQC assessment process for the consultee.

For the purpose of brevity, it is assumed that the consultative interview is done within a "best practices" context using effective consultation skills, methods, and processes (Gutkin & Curtis, 1990; Knoff, McKenna, & Riser, 1991). Pragmatically, then, the consultation interview addresses the following questions directly or indirectly:

1. To what extent can the referral source (e.g., the teacher) describe the referral concern (and other student liabilities) in behavioral terms, or is he or she only able to provide vague descriptions of concerns (e.g., "the child has a reading problem")?

2. What are the referred student's strengths across those domains relevant to the referral problem(s), across those domains that might be used in an intervention program for the referral problem, and across other domains that do not necessarily relate to the referral problem?

4. Where does the problem occur least often? Is the problem occurring more or less often than (a) last week, (b) last month, (c) the beginning of the year, (d) or at the onset of the problem? When did the problem behavior first occur? What is the teacher's preferred approach in solving the problem?

5. What is the function of the behavior for the student? for other students? for the teacher? What is the teacher's style, skill, and investment in dealing with the problem?

6. Is the problem a skill, performance, or self-management deficit for the referred student? Is the problem a skill, performance, or self-management deficit for the teacher?

7. How often can the behavior occur and still be tolerable for the teacher? How do other students in the setting behave and is their behavior acceptable/tolerable? If the student were unable to engage in the problem behavior, which other problem behaviors might occur as substitutes?

8. Which interventions have been tried before? What were the goals and characteristics of these interventions, how were they implemented, and what were the outcomes for the student and for the teacher, parents, and significant others?

9. What would motivate the teacher to work on this problem in the classroom setting? How would solving th problem behavior make the teacher's day easier? What is the teacher's commitment to work on the problem?

All of these questions can be expanded and individualized to the referred student, the referral problem, and the teacher, and some of these questions may be answered over the course of a number of consultation interview sessions. Nonetheless, all of these questions are asked (a) to clarify and behavioralize the consultee's initial concerns; (b) to identify the more positive or proactive behaviors needed to replace those deficit or maladaptive behaviors related to other initial concerns (called "replacement behaviors"); (c) to generate hypotheses that help to identify conditions under which the referral problem is occurring; and (d) to assess the acceptability , social validity, and treatment integrity of past interventions in preparation for future interventions. Relative to part (b), it is important to note that most interventions, when focused on the referred student, ultimately will focus not only on the alleviation of deficit or maladaptive behaviors, but also on the development, reinforcement, and maintenance of proactive replacement behaviors. Indeed, many students exhibit skill-deficit problems to the degree that even when their inappropriate behaviors decrease or cease, they still do not know how to enact the appropriate behavior. Thus, the RQC process needs to look especially at needed replacement behaviors and the reasons they are not present in the student's repertoire at the time of referral.

By the end of the initial consultation interview, the consultant should begin to organize the information collected into one of three categories and be ready to generate hypotheses. These three categories are (a) information that is relevant to the referred and operationalized problem and is known, (b) information relevant but unknown, and (c) information that is irrelevant. The first category involves information that is relevant to the referral situation as currently defined and understood by the consultant and consultees and that is known to exist and to be true. For example, if a fourth-grade teacher, who has referred a student with a reading comprehension problem, is asked the grade level where the student can identify a reading passage's main idea 100% of the time, and she responds that it is at the 3.2 reading level, then this information is relevant and known. From this information, a tentative hypothesis can be made that the student is unable to identify the main idea of passages at the 4.0 level because she has not yet learned the skills nor sufficiently experienced reading passages between the 3.2 and 4.0 levels to be successful.

The second category involves information that is relevant to the referral situation yet is unknown. Given the same example, suppose the classroom teacher does not know at which grade level a student can identify a reading passage's main idea 100% of the time. This information, then, is relevant but unknown, and it now becomes necessary to collect and analyze this information so that hypotheses related to this situation can be generated as needed.

The third category involves information that is irrelevant to the referral situation. For example, a new sibling at home may be used to explain why a student is suddenly having difficulty in reading, yet this information does not sufficiently explain why no student problems in math, spelling, and written expression are similarly observed. While it seems that the irrelevancy of certain information is in the eye of the beholder, the consultant can avoid some of this subjectivity by using research and the professional literature as a guide. In addition, the consultant can always collect data to determine the irrelevancy of any piece of information. At any rate, when information is determined to be irrelevant to a specific referral situation, it should simply be discarded or ignored. From a consultation perspective, however, this action should be explained to all consultees so that they understand the reasons why the information is irrelevant and so that this information will no longer be used to explain or understand the referred problem.

The Development of Hypotheses

After completing the needed consultation interviews and collecting the necessary relevant information, the RQC process proceeds to the development of hypotheses that explain the now-clarified and behaviorally operationalized referral concerns. At this point in the process, the school psychologist and others have a great deal of information about the referred behavior, the settings within which this behavior occurs, and other significant ecological environ-

ments and contexts related to the referred student and the referral situation. Now, it is time to integrate all of this information and generate hypotheses that answer the question, "Why is this referral situation happening?" These hypotheses may be generated from any professional perspective, use any theoretical (or other) orientation, and involve any number of settings, individuals, or conditions, *but* they must be relevant, predictive, and measurable.

Relative to format, hypotheses are organized into three components: (a) a restatement of the referral situation, (b) the word "because" to signify that a explanation of that referral situation is to follow, and (c) the explanation itself. Visually, this format looks like this:

"(The Referral Situation) occurs because (Hypothesis as to why)."

An example of a good hypothesis would be: "Johnny hits Lisa during unsupervised lunch times (the Referral Situation) because Johnny's friends (Dave, Mike, and Alex) reinforce him for doing so (the Hypothesis)."

It is through the development of relevant, predictive, and testable hypotheses that school personnel move from merely accumulating, describing, and reporting the facts related to, for example, a referred student's academic or social status to functional explanations as to why referred problems occur. Eventually, these hypotheses will help to directly link the RQC assessment process with specific and strategic interventions such that a high probability of successful interventions can be implemented.

The hypothesis domains. From a psychoeducational perspective, a number of empirically-devised models have been developed to integrate the research literature and to explain specific student outcomes (Centra & Potter, 1980; McKee & Witt, 1990; Rosenfield, 1987). These models have been synthesized into a single, summary model where student outcomes have been operationalized as (a) academic skill outcomes, (b) cognitive/metacognitive skill outcomes, (c) social skill outcomes, and (d) adaptive behavior skill outcomes. These outcomes are directly and indirectly impacted by eight different conditions or domains that exist in most students' worlds: family, neighborhood, community conditions; school/school district conditions; within school/classroom conditions; teacher characteristics or conditions; teacher performance/teacher effectiveness conditions; curricular characteristics and conditions; student characteristics and conditions; and student academic/learning support behavior conditions. The information in each of these eight domains can be used to generate hypotheses that explain why one of the four students outcomes is a problem for a referred student. For example, a student may be academically underperforming *because* the student–teacher ratio in the class-

FIGURE 1. Domains of hypotheses generation.

<hr>

Referral Question Consultation Problem Solving
(RQC)
Examples of Hypotheses Areas

I. Child Characteristics/Conditions

Cognitive Areas:

- Adequate short and long-term memory (auditory, visual)
- Length of attention span
- Self-monitoring skills
- Impulsivity (inability to delay long enough to think/behave)
- Inability to integrate visual/motor/auditory tasks
- Lacks prerequisite academic skills for task
- Other

Behavioral Areas:

- Self-control
- Attributions (beliefs — others out to get me, parents do not want me to do well in school, I expect to fail, if I do not fight first then I will be hurt, my parents want me to fight back, etc.)
- Social skills
- Other

Health Areas:

- Hearing, motor, vision skills
- Specific health condition related to referral problems
- Side effects of medication
- Speech/language difficulties
- Fatigue results in higher activity, less ability to focus, etc.
- Medication cycle not appropriate for school day/activities

Other

- Excessive absences
- Language other than English

II. Peer Characteristics/Conditions

- Peers reinforce inappropriate behavior
- Peers do not provide appropriate/adequate models
- Social/Academic skills of peers significantly higher (lower) than referred student
- Peers taunt/instigate student to engage in inappropriate behavior
- Expectations/values of peer group influence student

III. Curriculum Characteristics/Conditions

- Curriculum too easy or difficult
- Curriculum not relevant to child experiences/understanding
- Curriculum presented in a way that relates to child weaknesses (lecture/auditory, etc.)
- Curriculum presented too fast for student learning rate
- Insufficient opportunity to practice skills
- Length of curriculum assignments too long for attention/concentration skills of student
- Philosophy of curriculum presentation too narrow (e.g., phonics only)

IV. Teacher Characteristics/Conditions

- Teacher expectations too high for skills of student (e.g., reinforcers at end of week, student needs daily)
- Feedback to student not frequent enough
- Rate of reinforcement too low for student needs
- Student and teacher physically too far apart
- Insufficient rehearsal time, direct instruction time, teacher guided practice
- Teacher fatigue, tolerance results in higher negative, less frequent feedback
- Teacher unfamiliar with curricular methods necessary for child
- Level of supervision (frequency/rate) too low for student needs
- Teacher teaching style related to child weakness areas

V.   Classroom/School/District Characteristics/Conditions
- Classroom seating arrangement fosters problems (too close to peers, too far from teacher, near window or distractions, etc.)
- Rules/expectations in class/building far exceed skills of student to be successful
- Too many areas in building that are not supervised adequately
- Inconsistent discipline programs/philosophies/differences between staff who interact with same student
- Temperature
- Schedule of the daily activities
- Bus ride (length, problems on bus carry over to school, etc.)

VI.   Family/Neighborhood/Community Characteristics/Conditions
- Parent discipline inadequate/too severe/teaches child aggression
- Conflict/physical aggression between parents/guardians
- Lack of or low levels of supervision
- Different values/expectations between home/school
- Parent academic skills too low to help child
- Reading and related academic activities do not occur in the home
- Parent difficulties (substance abuse, etc.) result in inconsistent parenting, low levels of supervision, negativity
- Parent unable/unwilling to reinforce school-related academic/behavior strategies in the home
- Parent permits child to be around inappropriate adults/peers in community
- Parent expectations too high for child/too much pressure
- Parent unwilling/unable to meet health/nutrition/basic needs of child resulting in absences, inability of child to concentrate on tasks, tardiness, etc.

---

room is too high. Or, a student may be aggressively acting out *because* he is angry about and unable to cope with his parents' upcoming divorce.

To simplify the RQC process, the eight research-based domains have been reorganized into six areas (Figure 1) that are used to generate the hypotheses which drive the RQC process. These six areas have been described previously (Knoff & Batsche, 1991b, pps. 177–180) as follows:

1. Family, neighborhood, and community conditions. These involve characteristics or conditions of a referred student's family, neighborhood and community as they relate ultimately to effective teaching and student learning outcomes. They emphasize the importance of such factors as a healthy home environment, parenting style, levels of supervision and feedback, and their impact on a student's school readiness and success.

2. Within-classroom/school/district conditions. These involve favorable and/or unfavorable characteristics and conditions within a referred student's classroom and school building such as the physical plant, the pupil–teacher ratio, the presence of instructional resources (e.g., computers, audiovisual equipment), professional development opportunities for staff, the administrative and instructional organization of the building, and other conditions that explain teacher effectiveness. This area also extends to characteristics and conditions within the school district that impact classroom instruction and student achievement.

3. Teacher characteristics/performance/effectiveness conditions. These involve characteristics and conditions that teachers bring to the classroom that ultimately translate into effective instruction skills and behaviors that affect student learning (e.g., background characteristics, professional training). Also involved are those empirically identified skills, activities and conditions that teachers perform to make their instruction effective and impactful (e.g., use of curriculum, ability to adapt instruction).

4. Curricular characteristics/conditions. These involve characteristics and/or conditions of the curricula being used and include the curriculum's content as well as the processes used to ensure student learning and mastery.

5. Peer characteristics/conditions. These involve characteristics and/or interactions with a referred student's peer group that become either antecedent or consequent stimulus control conditions for specific behaviors. While these peer characteristics may be real or simply perceived by the referred student, they, nonetheless, do assert some level of control over a referred situation.

6. Student characteristics/conditions. These involve often pre-existing characteristics and conditions that relate primarily to a student's health/development, cognitive and academic ability, educational attitudes, and readiness for academic and social learning. These characteristics directly relate to those academic behaviors that support learning progress and achievement. These characteristics and conditions also involve those behaviors students exhibit that directly support their academic and social learning and progress such as self-competence skills, social skills, and the student's effective use of the teacher and teacher time.

A case study follows the complete description of the RQC process. This case study will provide examples in each of these six hypothesis areas. For now, it is important to note that hypotheses provide a possible explanation for a referred behavior or situation. This eventually sets the stage for the development of interventions. Hypotheses are developed by a variety of professionals representing different disciplines related to the behavior of concern. The hypothesis always follows the format, "The referral situation occurs *because* of a hypothesized reason."

The Development of Predictions

The next step in the RQC process is the development of predictions. Predictions are statements, developed from specific hypotheses, that identify what should or should not happen if a hypothesis is true or untrue, respectively. For example, if a hypothesis is "A child aggresses because his peers verbally taunt him," then prediction statements would be: "When peers verbally taunt the child, then the child will aggress to the peers," and "When peers do not verbally taunt the child, then the child will not aggress to the peers." Or, if it were hypothesized that "Mary is able to complete independent seat work in reading because her teacher makes sure that she masters the material during reading group time," then our prediction statements would be: "When Mary's teacher makes sure that Mary masters material during reading group time, then Mary is able to complete independent seat work in reading," and "When Mary's teacher does not make sure that Mary masters material during reading group time, then Mary is not able to complete independent seat work in reading."

It is important to note two things about these prediction statements. First, prediction statements are written in an "If … then" or "When … then" format. More specifically, prediction statements state that" *"When* … (the hypothesized reason for the referral concern occurs), *then* … (the referral concern will be exhibited or will not be exhibited)."

Second, prediction statements set up a situation whereby the hypothesis *and its converse* are both evaluated. That is, it is necessary to demonstrate that the referral concern exists when the explanatory hypothesis is true, and it is also necessary to demonstrate that the concern *does not exist* in the absence of the hypothesized conditions. For example, given the situations just described, it is necessary to demonstrate that the child aggresses only when his peers verbally taunt him. If he aggresses when the peers ignore him, then the hypothesis is not true. Similarly, it must be demonstrated that Mary completes her independent seat work in reading only when her teacher makes sure that she has mastered the material during reading group time. If Mary does not com-

plete her independent seat work even when her teacher makes sure that she has mastered the material during reading group, then the hypothesis is not true.

A final, important point about predictions is that they must be evaluated without changing the student's "natural" environment whenever possible. That is, predictions should be tested, as much as possible, without implementing new interventions and, thus, without changing the referral setting. If a student, for example, was referred because he was out of his seat a great deal of the time, and your hypothesis was that he gets out of his seat during unstructured times in the classroom, your prediction statements would say that "When unstructured time occurs in the classroom, then the student will get out of his seat," and "When structured time occurs in the classroom, then the student will stay in his seat." To evaluate these prediction statements in a naturally occurring way, a member of the group needs to observe the teacher during times when she or he routinely allows the classroom to be structured and unstructured, respectively. If the teacher were asked to plan special structured and unstructured times, for the purpose of observation, this would constitute an intervention that changes the normally occurring classroom routine. When such changes occur, in the absence of baseline data and a multiple baseline or reversal design, we can not truly be sure whether the referred student's behavior occurred due to the classroom's typical structure (or unstructure) or the change that we created in the classroom routine. To summarize, prediction statements functionally arrange specific hypotheses such that they can be confirmed or rejected. In addition, prediction statements are written in an "If … then" or "When … then" format. Finally, prediction statements are written such that the hypotheses can be evaluated in the student's "natural" environment whenever possible.

The Development of Referral Questions

Referral Questions are data-based questions, derived from specific prediction statements, that (when answered) will quantitatively confirm or reject hypotheses related to a referral concern. More specifically, Referral Questions are typically yes or no questions, or questions that relate to behavioral frequency, duration, latency, or intensity. Referral Questions are important for a number of reasons. First, Referral Questions actually drive the assessment and decision-making process. While assessment procedures must be reliable, valid, and psychometrically sound, the form and format of the Referral Questions actually determine which assessment methodologies must be used. Second, Referral Questions provide an internal check of the RQC process to ensure that a parent or teacher's referral concerns are still being addressed. Third, Referral Questions help to organize the report-writing process. In fact, reports documenting the confirmation of hypotheses, the development of interventions, and the successful results of those interventions can be structured in a question-and-answer format around the referral questions. Thus, reports should do more than describe the referred student; they should answer questions that lead to and relate to interventions.

1. They must be clearly defined, be directly related to the previous prediction statements, and require data that are observable and measurable.

2. They must be agreed upon by the referral source and other evaluation team members, and they must lead to or have the potential to lead to interventions, not labels.

3. They should result in clear, definitive answers. Referral Questions should be able to directly confirm or reject hypotheses generated to explain referred problems.

Writing Referral Questions. In general, Referral Questions are simply the prediction statements put into a question format. However, as prediction statements typically involve (a) a prediction statement and its converse, and each of these statements involves (b) a conditional statement (i.e., "if this condition occurs ...") and an outcome statement (i.e., " ... then this behavior will result"), then many times, two to four referral questions will be necessary to test a hypothesis. For example, if the prediction statements involve conditional and outcome statements that can be answered by yes/no questions, then two referral questions will be needed to address the original hypothesis. If the predictions involve two distinct conditions and two distinct outcomes, then four separate referral questions will be required. And, if the predictions involve a condition or outcome that can be answered by a yes/no question, with the remaining condition or outcome involving two distinct circumstances, then three separate referral questions will be required.

Using one of the earlier examples, the evaluation team predicted that "When peers verbally taunt the child, then the child will aggress to the peers," and "When peers do not verbally taunt the child, then the child will not aggress to the peers." Here, the referral question for the conditional part of the prediction should be: "Does the peer group verbally taunt the child?" The referral question for the outcome part of the prediction should be: "Does the referred child act aggressively with the peers?" Note how the two referral questions meet the characteristics of effective referral questions just stated. Note also that both the conditional and outcomes statements can be answered by a "yes or no" question, respectively. Thus, only two referral questions are needed for these prediction statements.

Using the second example, the team predicted that "When Mary's teacher makes sure that Mary masters material during reading group time, then Mary is able to complete independent seat work in reading," and "When Mary's teacher does not make sure that Mary masters material during reading group time, then Mary is not able to complete independent seat work in reading." Here, again, both the conditional and outcomes statements can be answered using "yes or no" questions, and thus, only two referral questions are needed. These referral questions should be: "Does Mary's teacher make sure that Mary masters material during reading group time?" and "Does Mary complete independent seat work in reading?"

Parenthetically, if prediction statements involving two distinct conditions and two distinct outcomes were desired, the predictions could be adapted to read: "When Mary's teacher spends 10 minutes or more of individual reading instruction per day with Mary, then Mary completes 90% or more of her independent seat work in reading," and "When Mary's teacher spends less than 10 minutes of individual reading instruction per day with Mary, then Mary completes less than 90% of her independent seat work in reading." In this situation, four separate referral questions will be required; "Did Mary's teacher spend 10 minutes or more of individual reading instruction today with Mary?" "Did Mary's teacher spend less than 10 minutes of individual reading instruction today with Mary?" "Did Mary complete 90% or more of her independent seat work in reading today?" and "Did Mary complete less than 90% of her independent seat work in reading today?"

Once Referral Questions are developed, assessment begins. This assessment can be done by anyone on the multidisciplinary team, but the school psychologist and the classroom teacher are typically the best candidates. Significantly, most RQC referral questions involve the direct assessment of the instructional process, academic work, or student/teacher/peer behavior *in the student's classroom*, the primary setting where the referred problem is occurring. These assessments involve low-inference procedures (e.g., the use of behavioral observation or curriculum-based assessment or measurement); they use multitrait, multimethod assessment procedures, and they directly link assessment and intervention. Assessment within the RQC process follows other best practices approaches (Shapiro & Lentz, 1985):

1. Assessment must reflect an evaluation of the behavior in the natural environment (i.e., the referral setting).

2. Assessment should be idiographic rather than nomothetic (that is, functionally related to the referred student, specifically).

3. What is taught (social or academic) should be what is tested.

4. Strong links must be present between the results of the assessment and the behavior targeted for intervention.

5. Assessment methods must be capable of providing ongoing evaluation of the intervention.

6. Methods chosen for use in assessment must be empirically validated and must reflect the multimethod, multitrait, multisetting criteria previously outlined.

7. Low-inference procedures should take preference over high-inference procedures.

Once data are collected, then the referral questions can be answered, and the original hypotheses can be confirmed or rejected. At this point, the multidisciplinary team can take the confirmed hypotheses, begin to develop intervention plans, and outline a formative report organized around the hypotheses tested, the referral questions generated, and the data collected.

Selecting and Implementing Interventions

As noted previously, referral questions are simply prediction statements placed into a question format. If the answers to the referral questions confirm the original hypothesis, then the intervention directions necessary are fairly obvious. For example, if the team confirms that the student is aggressive with peers only when (or most often when) the peer group verbally taunts him or her, then the intervention program should either (a) stop the peers from taunting the students (possibly through group dependent or independent procedures) and/or (b) teach the student to handle verbal taunts in a more appropriate manner (possibly through social skills training). If the team confirms that Mary completes her independent seat work in reading only when (or most often when) Mary's teacher makes sure that Mary masters material during reading group time, then the intervention program should (a) encourage and reinforce Mary's teacher for ensuring that Mary masters material during reading group time, (b) try to decrease the teacher-directed time that Mary needs toward reading mastery, and (c) increase Mary's self-monitoring and self-maintenance skills during independent seat work, once again, to facilitate the mastery process.

RQC Written Reports

For the typical referral, a great deal of work goes into problem solving, completing the RQC assessment process, and implementing interventions. To be completely meaningful, however, school psychologists and others must be able to effectively communicate the result and impact of these processes. While consultation with a teacher or parent often permits direct communication with the referral source, the written report is required to meet federal, state, and/or district requirements and to communicate with referral sources and significant others, when direct interaction is not possible. Reports can be quite lengthy when they are the only vehicle for communication. But, to be effective, they must communicate effectively.

When teachers receive a report, they look for information that relates, in a primary way, to the referral concern and intervention strategies. Thus, it is critical for school psychologists and others to organize a report in a way that makes it easy for teachers to find the information they need and to understand what they are reading. RQC reports typically use a "question and answer" format with the referral questions providing advanced organizers for each section of the report. Given this format, the assessment process is reported for each referral question, as are the specifics of what each team member did and which assessment procedures were used. Because RQC reports use Referral Questions that respond directly to teachers' concerns and avoid the use of psychological jargon, they often seem more "personalized" and "tailored" to the teachers' needs. That is, teachers see their own questions in print, thus increasing the relevance and their commitment to the contents of the report.

Ultimately, the RQC report discusses the data that answer the stated referral questions; the hypotheses that are confirmed and rejected; and interventions that are definitive, related to classroom behavior, and based on the completed process. Critically, the RQC report does not reveal out-of-context test scores that (a) referral sources often do not understand, and (b) usually require high levels of inference relative to the development of interventions. Thus, readers of the RQC report should have no difficulty understanding the data reported or its connection to the interventions suggested. Indeed, the entire RQC report is geared to the delivery of interventions and services, the ultimate goal of the RQC process.

The RQC report usually has three general sections: (a) Background Information; (b) Answers to Referral Questions, and (c) Intervention Plan. The *background information* section contains relevant and known information from the review of the student records and the various consultative interviews held throughout the RQC process. As with all referrals, a tremendous amount of information is available when a report is about to be written, and the school psychologist and others need to separate the relevant things that a teacher needs to know to implement successful interventions from the irrelevant. One rule of thumb in this regard is to include only information directly related to the referral questions asked or to the successful implementation of interventions. All other information should be considered confidential and/or unnecessary.

While the basic information in the *Answer to Referral Questions* section has been discussed previously, it is important to (a) use the actual referral questions from the consultative interview in the report; (b) include the name of the referral agent responsible for the development of each question; (c) include the assessment strategies and procedures used; and (d) answer the questions as briefly as possible, using information that employs the simplest language and that is directly focused on interventions.

The *intervention plan* section should be based on the actual answers to the Referral Questions. Typically, an intervention plan includes four components:

1. Assessment Outcomes: A brief summary of the assessment results so that a clear rationale for the intervention is provided.

2. Intervention Strategies: Very specific, "how-to-do-it" guidelines designed to improve the behaviors or problems relevant to the referral concern.

3. Expected Outcomes and Definitions of Success: Specifically, what will happen as a result of intervention, and what are the criteria (over time) that constitute "success"? In essence, this section answers the question, "Which behavior(s) or outcomes should the referral agent expect to see if the intervention is working?" and "How long must the intervention be in place before change is seen, and will the intervention need to be adapted as the referred student's behavior changes over time?"

4. Personnel Responsible: Specifically, who will be responsible for implementing the intervention? As this may involve a number of individuals, specific people (or positions) can be named along with the specific component(s) of the intervention that they will be responsible for.

To summarize, the purpose of the written report is to communicate essential information in a way that the referral source can use to implement interventions. In accomplishing this, the school psychologist should be able to (a) select appropriate information for the Background Section; (b) answer referral questions in a definitive manner by selecting only the information that is relevant and that contributes to the development of interventions; (c) identify the appropriate personnel necessary to implement the interventions; and (d) identify expected outcomes that are realistic, given the interventions recommended, and the timelines needed for full implementation in the classroom (or other) setting.

Case Study

To briefly review and reinforce the steps and utility of the RQC process in a functional way, a case study is presented. It must be noted that a fairly open-ended case vignette was chosen to demonstrate how hypotheses can be generated in each of the six areas discussed in the Development of Hypotheses section. In addition, the link between assessment and intervention, once again, is emphasized, as is the importance of pragmatically moving through Problem Identification and Operationalization; Replacement Behavior Identification; Hypothesis, Prediction, and Referral Question Generation; Assessment; and Intervention Plan Specification and Development.

Case vignette. Joe is in fourth grade. He gets out of school at 3:00 p.m. each day. During the past month, at around 2:30 p.m. Joe has begun to have behavior problems in the classroom, often ending up in the principal's office and missing the bus. These behaviors involve yelling at and pushing peers, not responding to teacher requests, and needing to be physically guided and accompanied down to the principal's office. He has been sent to the principal's office on eight occasions during the past 20 school days, and the teacher and the principal are upset both about the intensity of the behavior and the fact that it appears unprompted, unpredictable, and unresponsive to the interventions (i.e., sending him to the principal's office) thus far. Both of Joe's parents work, and thus, they have not yet been available for a home–school intervention program. In fact, Joe's mother has recently gone back to work part-time for the first time since Joe has been in school. Significantly, on a few occasions, the principal has had to drive Joe home after he missed the bus, leaving him with a neighbor until his parents come home from work. The principal has noted that Joe's neighborhood is not in one of the safest areas of town.

The teacher and principal decide to meet with the other fourth grade teachers to RQC this problem, hoping ultimately to develop an intervention plan that is more successful. Following are the hypotheses, predictions, and referral questions that they generated organized in the six hypotheses areas discussed earlier. Note that numerous hypotheses could be generated beyond those listed below and that, for some cases, hypotheses may not be generated or exist in all six hypothesis areas.

Hypothesis 1: Family/neighborhood/community condition. Joe acts out in class at 2:30 p.m. in order to avoid the bus because he does not want to go home to an empty house and be alone.

Prediction A: When Joe knows that his mother is not going to be home when he gets there, then he will act out at 2:30 p.m. in order to miss the bus.

Prediction B (Converse): When Joe knows that his mother *is* going to be home when he gets there, he will not act out at 2:30 p.m. and will take the bus home.

Referral Questions: Will Joe's mother be home when he gets home? (Yes/No?) Does he act out in class at 2:30 p.m.? (Yes/No?)

Assessment Approach: Observation; Parent or Student Self-Report.

Possible Interventions: Arrange for Joe's participation in an after-school program on days when his mother will not be home. Arrange for Joe to go to a friend's house on days when his mother will not be home. Help Joe to cope with his fear or anxiety about being home alone. Give him the 800-number after-school hotline number for latchkey kids.

Hypothesis 2: School/school district condition. Joe acts out in class at 2:3 p.m. in order to avoid the bus because he is being picked on and teased by some of the students on the bus.

Prediction A: When Joe gets picked on by students on the bus during the morning run, he will act out at 2:30 p.m. in order to miss the bus that afternoon.

Prediction B (Converse): When Joe does not get picked on by students on the bus during the morning run, then he will not act out at 2:30 p.m. in order to miss the bus that afternoon.

Referral Questions: Did Joe get picked on by students on the bus during the morning run? (Yes/No?) Does he act out in class at 2:30 p.m. (Yes/No?)

Assessment Approach: Observation; Student, Per, and/or Bus Driver Report.

Possible Interventions: Have the principal deal with the other students and their behavior. Role play with Joe ways to stop doing those behaviors that prompt the teasing and/or how to ignore it. Arrange for Joe to sit and interact with peers who are popular/accepted by the students doing the teasing. Help Joe to cope with his reactions to the teasing.

Hypothesis 3: Classroom condition. Joe acts out in class at 2:30 p.m. because this is an unsupervised time and his peers are teasing him such that he gets angry.

Prediction A: When there is little supervision and Joe's peers tease him, then he will act out at 2:30 p.m. and be sent to the principal's office.

Prediction B (Converse): when there is appropriate supervision and Joe's peers do not tease him, then he will not act out at 2:30 p.m. and not be sent to the principal's office.

Referral Questions: Is there appropriate supervision at 2:30 p.m.? (Yes/No?) Do Joe's peers tease him? (Yes/No?)

Assessment Approach: Observation; Student or Peer Report.

Possible Interventions: Have the teacher take better responsibility for the supervision of his or her classroom. Have the teacher deal with the other students and their behavior. Role play with Joe ways to stop doing those behaviors that prompt the teasing and/or how to ignore it. Role play more appropriate social interactions between Joe and those peers doing the teasing. Arrange for Joe to sit and interact with peers who are popular/accepted by the students doing the teasing. Help Joe to cope with his reactions to the teasing.

Hypothesis 4: Teacher condition. Joe acts out in class at 2:30 p.m. because the teacher is tired and begins to provide less positive reinforcement and more negative reinforcement for inappropriate student behavior than at other times during the day.

Prediction A: When Joe's teacher begins to provide less positive reinforcement and more negative reinforcement to Joe for inappropriate behavior at 2:30 pm., then he acts out and is sent to the principal's office.

Prediction B (Converse): When Joe's teacher provides the same amount of positive reinforcement and negative reinforcement to Joe for inappropriate behavior at 2:30 p.m. as during the rest of the day, then he does not act out and is not sent to the principal's office.

Referral Questions: How much positive to negative reinforcement does Joe's teacher provide him for inappropriate behavior during the day? Does the teacher's positive reinforcement decrease and negative reinforcement increase at 2:30 p.m.?

Assessment Approach: Observation; Student or Peer Report.

Possible Interventions: Help the teacher to maintain his or her level of positive and negative reinforcement throughout the entire day. Help Joe to cope with less positive reinforcement (e.g., via teaching him self-reinforcement) especially at 2:30 p.m.

Hypothesis 5: Curricular condition. Joe acts out in class at 2:30 p.m. because that is when his class does free reading, an activity that he does not like because of his low reading skills.

Prediction A: When Joe is expected to do free reading at 2:30 p.m. then he acts out and is sent to the principal's office.

Prediction B (Converse): When Joe is not expected to do free reading at 2:30 p.m. then he does not act out and is not sent to the principal's office.

Referral Questions: Is Joe expected to do free reading at 2:30 pm.? (Yes/No?) Does he act out in class at 2:30 p.m.? (Yes/No?)

Assessment Approach: Observation.

Possible Interventions: Arrange for Joe to do his free reading in books at his independent level of reading. Allow Joe to do his free reading with a peer willing to read to Joe. Allow Joe (and/or the class) to do a different activity that is less frustrating at 2:30 p.m. Use this 2:30 p.m. time for the teacher to work with Joe to increase his reading skills.

Hypothesis 6: Student condition. Joe acts out in class at 2:30 p.m. because he chose not to take his noontime dose of Ritalin.

Prediction A: When Joe does not take his noontime dose of Ritalin, then he acts out and is sent to the principal's office.

Prediction B (Converse): When Joe does take his noontime dose of Ritalin, then he does not act out and is not sent to the principal's office.

Referral Questions: Does Joe take his noontime dose of Ritalin? (Yes/No?) Does he act out in class at 2:30 p.m.? (Yes/No?)

Assessment Approach: Observation.

Possible Interventions: Make sure that the school nurse directly observes the administration of Joe's Ritalin. Provide Joe with an incentive to take the Ritalin every day. Consult Joe's doctor as to alternatives to address his need for noontime medication. Work with Joe's parents for a home–school collaborative intervention.

SUMMARY

While the sample case study may appear to be somewhat simplistic in its description, it clearly is able to generate a number of feasible, highly significant hypotheses. It is critical to note that each of these hypotheses, once confirmed, leads to different intervention recommendations and approaches. This reinforces the importance of using the scientific process that forms the foundation of the RQC process. Clearly, if there are so many potential intervention directions for a "simplistic" referral situation, then the clinician must introduce some level of empirical decision-making to the process such that the highest probability of successful intervention ultimately is implemented. To randomly attempt interventions is a disservice to both the teacher or parent involved and to the related student. And significantly, too many mismanaged intervention attempts will decrease the probability that teachers will continue to use the psychologist as a consultant, thus also decreasing the potential that future students will receive early and preventive services.

It also is critical to note that many referrals have large amounts of relevant and known information and that some of this information actually can be contradictory. Many clinicians attempt to integrate and reconcile every piece of information collected for a re-

ferred student, when this simply cannot be done. The RQC process recognizes that multiple hypotheses can be confirmed to help explain a referred situation but that, pragmatically, only so many interventions can be implemented at one time. Further, many times it is the *absence* of change that most burdens a referral situation, and the emergence of any change due to a planned intervention begins a process of even greater change. Thus, the one or two interventions that facilitate change are essential to many referral questions. The RQC process identifies these pivotal intervention directions in a way that is effective, efficient, and impactful.

School and other psychologists spend a great deal of their time in assessment and intervention activities yet, too often, they spend precious little time analyzing the impact and effectiveness of the problem-solving and decision-making approaches that they are using. Very little empirical work has been done, especially in school psychology, to compare and contrast different problem-solving and clinical judgment approaches and/or to investigate those variables that impact these processes primarily because few researchers have reviewed the various models and their attributes. The RQC process comes closest to an etiological model that uses behavioral decision theory approaches. A problem-solving model that parallels the scientific method, the RQC process, nonetheless, is antithetical to the approaches used today by many school psychologists. Thus, while RQC research to support a change in current field-based, clinical approaches clearly is important, the underlying foundation of the process has been shown to be valid for centuries. A paradigm-shift will be essential in order for the RQC process to be fully accepted in the field. The RQC process has a great potential to increase the clinical efficiency and effectiveness of field-based practices and, once again, to prove school psychologists' worth to their consumers. It is hoped that this article will help you, the reader, to revisit the origins and mechanisms of your decision-making processes and will initiate the paradigm shift needed to return school psychology practices to their empirical and scientific roots.

REFERENCES

Batsche, G. M. (1984). *Referral question consultation: A workbook and video tape.* Washington, DC: National Association of School Psychologists.

Batsche, G. M. (1992). School psychology and assessment: A future together? *Communiqué, 20*(6), 2–3.

Batsche, G. M., & Ullman, J. (1983). *Referral question consultation.* Des Moines, IA: Iowa Department of Public Instruction.

Centra, J. A., & Potter, D. A. (1980). School and teacher effects: An interrelational model. *Review of Educational Research, 50,* 273–291.

Curtis, M. J., & Myers, J. (1988). Consultation: A foundation for alternative services in the schools. In J. L. Graden, J. E. Zins, & M.

J. Curtis (Eds.), *Alternative educational service systems: Enhancing instructonal options for all students* (pp. 35–48). Washington, DC: National Association of School Psychologists.

Fagan, T. K. (1990). A brief history of school psychology in the United States. In A. Thomas & J. Grimes (Eds.), *Best practices in school psychology–II* (pp. 913–929). Washington, DC: National Association of School Psychologists.

Gresham, F. M. (1985). Behavior disorder assessment: Conceptual, definitional, and practical considerations. *School Psychology Review, 14,*(4), 495–509.

Gutkin, T. B., & Conoley, J. C. (1990). Reconceptualizing school psychology from a service delivery perspective: Implications for practice, training, and research. *Journal of School Psychology, 28,* 203–224.

Gutkin, T. B., & Curtis, M. J. (1990). School-based consultation: Theory, techniques, and research. In T. B. Gutkin & C. R. Reynolds (Eds.), *The handbook of school psychology* (2nd ed.; pp. 577–613). New York: Wiley.

Iwata, B. A., Vollmer, T. R., & Zarcone, J. R. (1990). The experimental (functional) analysis of behavior disorders: Methodology, applications, and limitations. In A. C. Repp & N. N. Singh (Eds.), *Perspectives on the use of nonaversive and aversive interventions for persons with developmental disabilities* (p. 301–330). Sycamore, IL: Sycamore.

Kavale, K. A. (1990). The effectiveness of special education. In T. B. Gutkin & C. R. Reynolds (Eds.), *The handbook of school psychology* (2nd ed.; pp. 868–898). New York: Wiley.

Knoff, H. M., & Batsche, G. M. (1991a). Integrating school and educational psychology to meet the educational and mental health needs of all children. *Educational Psychologist, 26,* 167–183.

Knoff, H. M., & Batsche, G. M. (1991b). *The Referral Question Consultation process: Addressing system, school, and classroom academic and behavioral problems.* Tampa, FL: Authors.

Knoff, H. M., McKenna, A. F., & Riser, K. (1991). Toward a consultant effectiveness scale: Investigating characteristics of effective consultants. *School Psychology Review, 20,* 81–96.

Mash, E. J., & Terdal, L. B. (1988). Behavioral assessment of child and family disturbance. In E. J. Mash, E. J. & L. G. Terdal (Eds.), *Behavioral assessment of childhood disorders* (pp. 3–65). New York: Guilford.

McKee, W. T., & Witt, J. C. (1990). Effective teaching: A review of instructional and environmental variables. In T. B. Gutkin & C. R. Reynolds (Eds.), *The handbook of school psychology* (2nd ed.; pp. 821–846). New York: Wiley.

Nelson, R. O., & Hayes, S. C. (1979). Some current dimensions of behavioral assessment. *Behavioral Assessment, 1,* 1–16.

Nelson, R. O., Hayes, S. C., & Jarett, R. B. (1986). Evaluating the quality of behavioral assessment. In R. O. Nelson & S. C. Hayes (Eds.), *Conceptual foundations of behavioral assessment* (pp. 463–503). New York: Guilford.

Rosenfield, S. (1987). *Instructional consultation.* New Jersey: Erlbaum.

Sarason, S. B. (1985). *Caring and compassion in clinical practice: Issues in the selection, training, and behavior of helping professionals* San Francisco: Jossey-Bass.

Shapiro, E. S., & Kratochwill, T. R. (Eds.). (1988). *Behavioral assessment in schools: Conceptual foundations and practical applications.* New York: Guilford.

Shapiro, E. S., & Lentz, F. (1985). Assessing academic behavior: A behavioral approach. *School Psychology Review, 14,* 325–338.

Ysseldyke, J. E. (1987). Classification of handicapped students. In M. C. Wang, M. C. Reynolds, & H. J. Walberg (Eds.), *The handbook of special education: Research and practice* (Vol. 3; pp. 213–243). New York: Pergamon.

ANNOTATED BIBLIOGRAPHY

Knoff, H. M., & Batsche, G. M. (1991b). *The referral question consultation process: Addressing system, school, and classroom academic and behavioral problems.* Tampa, FL: Author.
This workbook is a step-by-step training manual designed to present the conceptual and functional components of the RQC method and to provide practice exercises, with feedback, for the reader. The RQC method is a seven-step procedure beginning with problem identification and proceeding through hypothesis development, assessment to address hypotheses, and interventions linked to verified hypotheses. Assessment is used both to verify hypotheses and evaluate interventions. It is, in essence, a programmed learning text that provides the reader with the opportunity to acquire new skills in linking assessment to intervention.

Elliott, S. N., Witt, J. C., & Kratochwill, T. R. (1991). Selecting, implementing, and evaluating classroom interventions. In G. Stoner, M. R. Shinn, & H. M. Walker (Eds.), *Interventions for achievement and behavior problems* (pp. 99–138). Silver Spring, MD: National Association of School Psychologists.
This chapter provides an overview of the problem-solving process involved in intervention selection and evaluation. In addition, a review of treatment acceptability, teacher empowerment, and treatment integrity that are critical to the effective use of clasroom interventions is provided. Intervention evaluation is discussed in the context of intervention efficacy.

Kazdin, A. E. (1994). *Behavior modification in applied settings.* Pacific Grove, CA: Brooks/Cole.
Chapter three of this book provides an excellent review of methods to link behavior problems with assessment and intervention through a functional analysis of behavior. The functional analysis of behavior model is one method of develoing hypotheses about academic and social behavior that can be used in conjunction with the RQC method. This chapter reviews assessment methods that can be used both to validate the functional analyses as well as to evaluate intervention effectiveness.

50

Best Practices in Curriculum-Based Assessment

Edward E. Gickling
Pennsylvania Instructional Support Project

Sylvia Rosenfield
University of Maryland — College Park

Although it may seem unusual to compare fishing with curriculum-based assessment, the two do have a lot in common. To be successful in either endeavor, a person must be clear about the purpose of the activity, use the right equipment, and make a good presentation. For example, a well stocked fish and game store always carries a large variety of fishing tackle. Selecting the correct tackle depends upon where the person plans on fishing and what kind of fish are to be caught. Unless these purposes are clear, one can end up using the wrong equipment and bait, fishing in the wrong spot, and not catching any fish. The same is true for assessment. When the purpose of assessment is clearly defined, the equipment can be carefully chosen to meet the purpose, the process is carried out well, and the results are maximally useful. After individuals learn how to use the equipment and get the basics down, they have plenty of opportunities for challenge as novel situations present themselves and as the person tries to perfect various techniques. This analogy between fishing and assessment provides a useful metaphor for introducing curriculum-based assessment (CBA).

OVERVIEW

While there are different approaches subsumed under the general rubric of CBA (see Shinn, Rosenfield, & Knutson, 1989, for a discussion of these approaches), this chapter focuses on the approach originally developed by Gickling and Havertape (1981) and elaborated by Rosenfield and Kuralt (1990). In this chapter, however, two new issues are addressed: CBA's congruence with cognitively based instructional practices and its use as a peer-mediated learning strategy. Although clearly not limited to the practice of school psychologists, CBA provides useful and relevant instructional assessment information to psychologists working in the schools.

Instructional Assessment

CBA is a technique within the domain of educational assessment, which itself serves multiple purposes such as referral, screening, classification, instructional planning, and student progress monitoring (Salvia & Ysseldyke, 1985). However, assessment's most fundamental purpose is to design and deliver optimal instruction for all children (Johnston, 1987). In other words, instructional assessment's primary focus should be on providing relevant data to guide and manage student learning and to ensure that students are responding optimally to what and how they are being taught (Walker, 1992). Recognition of this essential purpose has evolved over the past decade, and CBA methods have played a major role as a technique for reaching the goal of this evaluation purpose.

Also related to the increased emphasis on instructional assessment has been a dramatic shift from an overreliance (and sometimes inappropriate reliance) on standardized/norm-referenced testing practices to more naturalistic and dynamic forms of student assessment. At its best, instructional assessment chronicles performance and development and sends a message that learning is not static but ever changing and evolving (Valencia, 1990). Therefore, assessment for instructional decision making requires a dynamic ongoing process rather than a yearly event, such as norm-referenced achievement testing. Unfortunately, instructional assessment can be misused when it is applied too narrowly, such as viewing it simply as another technique to obtain a set of scores as part of an assessment battery during a psychoeducational evaluation, rather than as a process which requires obtaining continuous snapshots of what students know and are able to do in response to what they are being taught. In this respect, CBA is very compatible with portfolio assessment, learning progress maps, student progress interviews, running records, and the like. Naturally, what goes into these snapshots must both be representative and directly and accurately reflect the student's actual work in the classroom.

Defining CBA

Descriptive terms such as "naturalistic" and "dynamic" reinforce the conclusion that the best possible instructional assessment practices occur as teachers observe and interact with students engaged in real tasks for real purposes (Valencia & Pearson, 1987). CBA, based on the same viewpoint, is defined as "a system for determining the instructional needs of a student based upon the student's on-going performance within existing course content in order to deliver instruction as effectively and efficiently as possible" (Gickling, Shane, & Croskery, 1989, pp. 344–345). It assumes that the most natural medium to use for instructional assessment is the day-to-day curriculum being taught in the classroom. The naturalness of the curriculum as the medium of assessment, along with a recognition of the importance of aligning assessment practices with instructional practices to favorably affect both learning and teaching, are the primary reasons for the development of curriculum-based assessment.

Basic Principles of CBA

Beyond meeting the basic requirements of being naturalistic and dynamic, CBA also meets requirements consistent with effective instruction, reading development, and learning theory. While the intent of the naturalistic assessment movement has been to bring assessment back into the classroom and to return the curriculum to a more central role within the assessment and instructional process, such changes cannot occur independent of effective instruction, meaningful content, and the active and interactive nature of learning and teaching. This view has resulted in a number of fundamental changes with regard to how assessment should impact instruction and how instruction should be delivered to improve the academic abilities of all students. These changes, which represent a departure from many of the traditional tenets of testing and teaching, are reflected in the following principles:

CBA complements prevailing curriculum approaches. CBA was designed for use with a variety of theoretical approaches to teaching reading, mathematics, and other content areas. It adheres to a generic set of principles applicable to any number of curriculum programs and practices. In this sense, the CBA process is content free or neutral, because it is not dependent upon the use of any specific materials, methodologies, practices, or theoretical orientations.

CBA has, however, been positively influenced by the rationale and philosophical bases of problem solving, strategic learning and teaching, and certain aspects of whole language instruction. CBA, as an assessment procedure, is congruent with emphases upon providing students with opportunities to reach mastery by integrating assessment and instruction within and across content areas, keeping learning connected and coherent rather than fragmented, capitalizing on the use of good literature, working within meaningful contexts, and developing strategic learners. In this vein, CBA can be used by teachers to create the types of conditions that enable students to interact with original texts and gain meaning that yet avoid the flawed practice of teaching isolated skills and hoping that the pieces will somehow magically connect to develop mature strategic learners. CBA can also be used to help students acquire essential word recognition, word study, and fluent reading skills using the context of meaningful texts as much as possible.

CBA aligns assessment practices with what is actually taught in the classroom. With the curriculum as the context for assessment, teachers are better able to assess both the performance of their students and the effectiveness of their teaching practices. Moreover, CBA places as much emphasis on assessing how students are thinking about and processing their work as it does on assessing what they produce.

CBA starts with what the student knows in building an integrated program. Assessment and teaching practices traditionally have focused on a student's deficiencies without due regard for what the student knows and can do. This practice has caused practitioners to become predisposed to identifying student deficiencies at the expense of determining and building on prior knowledge, yet this knowledge is essential if the student is to maintain an active role in learning (Bloom, 1976). Ignoring the entry-level skills of students frequently results in fragmented learning when students are asked to work assignments which contain excessive amounts of unknown information. As a result, academic learning time is diminished. CBA is structured to help teachers plan instruction based on the entry-level skills of students, thus maximizing on-task time during learning activities. Again this approach matches current definitions of good instructional design in reading, mathematics, and other academic disciplines, by acknowledging prior knowledge as an important prerequisite to learning (see, e.g., Ysseldyke & Christenson, 1993).

CBA addresses the need to regulate task variability, task demand, and the pace of instruction to ensure student success. A mismatch often occurs between the limited entry skills of at-risk students and the ever changing demands of their school work. Correcting this type of mismatch necessitates both curriculum and instructional changes to create an appropriate fit or instructional match for the student. This correction permits the practitioner to keep task variability and task demand within appropriate levels of challenge, while regulating the pace of instruction to match each student's learning rate. If this match is not continuously monitored as part of the instructional process, the "gap" is likely to widen between the entry skills of those students academically at risk and their ability to master each new learning task.

The *instructional match* is a widely acknowledged and fundamental concept of student learning. It reflects the types of optimum learning and teaching conditions under which both students and teachers thrive. Optimal conditions occur when the learner is provided with an appropriate level of challenge and a realistic opportunity for success on a frequent and continuous basis. The combination of these two factors provide students with the perception that they have the knowledge and skill to be successful and therefore the motivation to master the task (Borkowski, 1990; Meichenbaum & Biemiller, 1990). This combination of challenge and competence can be viewed as a comfort zone, or the level where the student can accomplish the task comfortably. These comfort zones have been extrapolated from the reading and teacher-effectiveness literature (see, for example, Archer et al., 1987; Betts, 1946) to reflect instructional levels for reading and practice-related activities. As such, these levels reflect the conditions where students are able to work comfortably without being excessively challenged or frustrated by each learning task. The use of these ratios is fundamental when applying CBA; they serve as guidelines for assessing what students know and are able to do and for problem solving in regulating task difficulty. As guidelines, they represent entry levels for instruction and not exit-level values representing mastery. The ratios for instructional levels for reading- and practice-related activities are:

Reading	Practice
93–97% Known Information	70–85% Known Information
3–7% Unknown Information	15–30% Unknown Information

This ratio system reinforces the importance of looking for and building upon what each student knows. Planning instruction so that the level of challenge does not exceed these guidelines and therefore so that a high level of known information exists within each learning task makes it possible for each student to maintain a more active role in his or her learning. By building upon what a student knows and

can do and by providing a student with an appropriate rather than excessive level of challenge, teachers can control for task variability while assuring the student of frequent and continuous success. By adhering to this process, teachers can take into account the natural variations in students' learning while still provide each individual with a high degree of task success.

CBA strives for high uniform scores among students. Traditional teaching practices have involved teaching students of differing abilities at the same pace using the same assignments, with the expectation that normal variations in students' scores will occur. Many schools continue to function under the premise that a single level of instruction is adequate and that those students unable to conform to this routine pace are somehow defective learners. Education has reinforced these perceptions through elaborate systems of screening, identification, labeling, and placement. The adverse effects of this process prompted Bloom (1976) to advocate for mastery learning. He recognized that the system of teaching was responsible for most defects in student learning rather than the students themselves. With mastery learning, and now with outcome-based and performance-based education, a student's progress is not compared against the calendar year; the pace of instruction is contingent upon the student's learning needs and the ability to master identifiable skills. Achieving mastery is contingent upon each student receiving and maintaining high uniform scores.

This approach does not deny that there will always be individual differences in student performance but rather assumes that the job of education is to reach students where they are and to teach them effectively and efficiently, not sort them along a normal distribution: "The normal curve is a statistical construct at odds with the purpose of education, which is to change a typical distribution of performance into a skewed curve of competence" (Wiggins, 1992, p. xi). To maintain high success rates for each student, educators must respect the differences among students by providing them with appropriate levels of challenge. This allows all students to earn high scores and enjoy the benefits which come from appropriately matched instruction.

CBA allows for the direct and continuous assessment of student progress. Concerns for accountability and for the assessment of ongoing performance are important to the CBA process. The dynamic features of instructional assessment permit users of CBA to constantly monitor how well students are processing instruction and progressing toward various outcomes, thus enabling detection of subtle changes in student learning. The analysis also permits evaluation of how successfully various classroom programs and support services are at maintaining students at instructional levels. Obtaining continuous snapshots of how the student is progressing and how instruction matches each student's learning needs is vital. Collections of work samples placed in portfolios, learning progress maps, and other relevant data are strongly encouraged. These and similar approaches facilitate the monitoring of student performance with respect to instructional goals.

The application of these basic principles in combination with current thinking in whole language and problem solving provides a coherent approach to instructional assessment and integrates assessment within the instructional design framework. Because control is maintained between curriculum difficulty and student entry-level skills, all students, including those at risk, can learn in a more optimal, less frustrating instructional environment. Thus, the CBA procedures contribute to effective instructional outcomes by determining where instruction should begin — based upon what each student knows and is able to do — and using this information to control for the excessive curriculum and instructional variance which fragment and frustrate learning for many students.

BASIC CONSIDERATIONS

Much concern exists today over the quality of classroom assessment in general and the classroom teacher's own assessments in particular. Stiggins and Conklin (1992) for example, noted that "teachers view instruction and assessment as separate activities. Integration of the two is done haphazardly and rarely to full advantage" (p. 148). They concluded that "most teachers either do not take the time or do not know how to make good use of assessment in presenting instruction, in evaluating it, and in making it more effective and meaningful" (p. 148). Regrettably, inadequate assessments lead to poor decision making in the classroom because the first stage of the problem-solving process is problem identification. The lack of identification leads to "inefficient instruction, and at worst . . . failure to learn and an attendant loss of student motivation to participate in the learning process" (p. 196).

Concern over the lack of adequate classroom assessment practices, coupled with the continuing concern over the inadequacies of traditional norm-referenced assessment in facilitating instructional outcomes for students (Reschly, Kicklighter, & McKee, 1988) has prompted school psychologists to integrate the concepts and procedures of different curriculum-based-assessment models into school psychology training and practice (Shapiro & Elliott, 1993; Shinn et al., 1989). This has led to increased acceptance of curriculum-based-assessment procedures by school psychologists. In a recent survey of school psychologists, Shapiro and Eckert (1993) documented that more than half of their sample agreed that the use of CBA in their practice results in less culturally biased assessments of students, is more accepted by teachers when assessing students with academic problems, and is more useful to parents and students than norm-referenced statements. Given that the formal history of CBA is less than 20 years old (Coulter, 1988), its current level of acceptance is encouraging.

Shapiro and Eckert (1993) noted, however, that the use of CBA is inconsistent and that there are insufficient training opportunities for school psychologists to develop real skills in applying CBA. While its literature base has been expanding, preservice and inservice training have lagged behind. Most training opportunities still resemble pull-out workshops rather than providing trainees with guided practice and feedback in real classroom settings and situations. Because of these training limitations, many school psychologists remain hesitant about fully participating in this new instructional assessment domain. Although they express considerable concern over the quality of classroom assessment, they remain uncomfortable embracing this new and changing role. They continue to wonder and raise questions about how best to be involved in working directly with the teacher within the classroom in conducting instructional assessment.

While classroom consultation and prereferral intervention are increasingly important facets of contemporary practice and an integral aspect of school service delivery options (Rosenfield, 1987), it should be stressed that reading about CBA, and other such practices, is only a beginning step. Receiving opportunities for guided practices as part of the instructional consultation process is crucial to feel comfortable and achieve mastery.

BEST PRACTICES

While it is important for practitioners to understand the theoretical basis of CBA and the need to align assessment practices with what is actually taught within the curriculum of the classroom, these concepts alone are insufficient to explain how the curriculum-based-assessment process is performed. The purpose of this section is to guide practitioners through the process and to provide them with a framework, using the assessment of reading as an example of the process. (For an example of how CBA can be used in mathematics, see Gickling et al., 1989).

Key Questions

Certain questions, which always need to be addressed when planning and guiding instruction, form the core of the curriculum-based-assessment strategy:

1. What does the student need to do in order to be successful within the curriculum? What does the teacher want the student to understand, develop, or demonstrate in relation to the curriculum being

taught? Specifically, which concepts, skills, strategies, procedures, or knowledge does the teacher want the student to acquire? The CBA process normally begins with clear expectations of the required curriculum goals of the classroom teacher. This process engages the teacher in selecting the appropriate outcomes for the student.

2. Which discrepancies, if any, exist between the anticipated outcomes established by the teacher and the performance of the student? An assessment of the student's performance within the actual classroom curriculum is used to determine whether an instructional match exists or not.

3. If an instructional mismatch exists, what prior knowledge and entry skills does the student need to develop to be successful? The assessment process proceeds to delineate what the student knows and is able to do in comparison to the specific skills, strategies, concepts, and knowledge which need to be acquired.

4. Are steps taken to match each learning activity or experience to the student's entry skills and learning needs as instruction progresses? The level of known to challenging information for each learning task is monitored using instructional ratios as a guide to sustain an instructional match. Fine-tuning of task difficulty is used throughout the instructional process.

5. Is instruction presented so that the student is learning as efficiently as possible? Is student learning managed so that both teacher and peer assistance is provided in a timely manner? Is there maximum use made of instructional time?

6. Is student progress regularly assessed, monitored, graphed, and used for instructional decision making? Is performance monitored to ensure that the student is actively engaged in the learning process?

Conducting Curriculum-Based Assessment

Unlike normative assessment practices which push students to the point of frustration during assessment sessions, the CBA process helps students to function comfortably. Conscientious efforts are made to activate the student's prior knowledge without creating frustrating experiences. The ratio concepts are used repeatedly to guide this process, and the evaluator is encouraged to look for what is known in the curriculum activity and to gradually incorporate or "fold in" what is unknown. Given the finite amount of time available for purposes of initial assessment, these rules have proven helpful:

1. Always look for what is known.

2. Never look for just the unknown.

3. Always build in success during assessment.

Although reading is used here to illustrate the CBA process, the four generic steps within the CBA process can be applied to any type of curriculum content. These steps are selecting, assessing, matching, and teaching. For example, after a teacher selects the objective and reading activity, the CBA process enables the practitioner to match the demands of the learning task with the student's entry skills on the basis of the assessment and to implement the instructional intervention. This 4-step process for reading involves the following activities.

Select a "workable passage." The concept of a *workable passage* is not to be confused with the concept of an *instructional level passage*. A passage well beyond the ability of a student to read comfortably can still provide valuable information from which to work — thus one use of the term "workable passage." The process begins with trying to gain some sense of the student's entry-level skills and to use that information to begin constructing reading activities on the student's instructional level. Most often the process begins with selecting a passage from the material which the teacher is using or has previously used with the student during reading instruction. In the early grades, this generally involves selecting a passage from a story in a basal reader, literature based text, anthology, and/or trade book. A few minutes may be spent discussing the story with the student to gain some sense of the student's prior knowledge and give the evaluator an indication of the student's oral skills.

To gain a measure of the student's ability to process print, a word search can be conducted by selectively pointing to words which the student has a high probability of knowing. Every fourth or fifth word, a more difficult word can be selected. The key to using this technique is to be selective and to maintain a lively pace. By keeping a lively pace, the word search should take no more than 2 or 3 minutes while covering 20 to 30 words. The process of searching for known, hesitant, and unknown words using this folding-in of difficult with easy words provides a measure of the student's working sight vocabulary without frustrating the student. If five or fewer errors occur, the student is asked to read the passage, since language and sight vocabulary should not be a hindrance to comprehension. If a greater number of errors is made, an easier passage may be selected. Another option is to modify the existing passage, making it easier for the student by taking into account the known, unknown, and hesitant words, and begin teaching at that point.

Assess contextual reading. The primary rationale behind having the student read the selection is to sample how the student interacts with the text. In an unobtrusive manner, the student's errors are marked. If there are any mis-called words or word delays, the student is provided with the correct response within

3 seconds so as not to disrupt comprehension. At the conclusion of passage reading, a dialogue with the student is conducted by asking unaided or general types of questions, such as "Tell me what the story was about." and "Can you tell me more?" If the student has difficulty, aided questions are used to help guide the student's ability to respond (Paratore & Indrisano, 1987). This process is similar to that used in informal reading inventories and some reading tests. However, the unique characteristic here is that the material used for the assessment is from the student's own classroom curriculum materials.

A second reason for asking the student to read the selection is to obtain a measure of reading fluency. This is done by taking one-minute time samples as the student reads. Fluency samples are used both for planning and for motivating students. They can be taken before and after reading practice and to measure progress at frequent intervals throughout the calendar year. They can also be used as measures of oral and silent reading depending upon the reading skills of the student and the purpose of the assessment. The time-sampling procedures developed in the curriculum-based-measurement literature can be used for this purpose (see, e.g., Deno & Fuchs, 1987).

Match reading instruction. The matching process involves three concurrent uses of decisions, each of which is essential to the design of good instruction. First, using the data from the word search and from the contextual reading sample, the teacher makes an initial decision concerning the types of reading support which should be provided. The reading framework helps to answer questions about whether or what kinds of mechanical and/or comprehension needs should be addressed. Specific questions concerning the language concepts and sight vocabulary, word-study skills, the recalling and retelling of information, oral and silent reading fluency, and the metacognitive processes used by the student are examined. Concerns for the interaction of these dimensions helps maintain a holistic picture of the reading process and of what is required to develop a more mature reader.

The second type of decision involves designing opportunities for the student to work at his or her instructional level. By assessing what the student knows, the teacher can select curriculum material that provides an appropriate level of challenge or can regulate the level of challenge by modifying existing materials so that they are matched to the student's entry-level skills. The most important point is to capitalize on the student's prior knowledge in order to maintain a comfort level (high success rate) during instruction.

The third set of decisions involves selecting appropriate strategies to develop the student's reading skills which have been targeted for instruction. Such strategies need to be used in a holistic framework to avoid the pitfalls of skill fragmentation. This can be accomplished efficiently by looking for both what the student knows and what the reading task requires. Based upon relevant instructional data, teaching strategies can focus on what is known and what is needed. The instructional integrity of the text is never sacrificed because the skills which need developing are taken directly from the text, taught and practiced, and folded back into the original text as part of the instructional design.

Teach the student. Knowing the student's skill level and ways to regulate the level of challenge within the material, the teacher can begin the teaching process. During the teaching session, appropriate instructional strategies are used with teaching moving at a pace which takes into account the student's learning rate (for example, the number of repetitions necessary to develop mastery, which varies among students). Feedback is provided continuously, progress is monitored and recorded, and the learner is positioned to achieve success.

Acquisition Rate, Retention Rate, and Degree of Need

Even though CBA's major role is in the instructional design process, it can also be used to provide relevant information about the learner's rate of acquisition and retention of new material as well as to help determine if any other resources are needed to help the student be successful. It is common knowledge that students learn differently, that they acquire knowledge and skill at different speeds, and that they require different amounts of repetition and practice to master various skills. The relative ease with which new information and skill is acquired is referred to as *acquisition rate*. A student's ability to retain and use information or skills in meaningful ways is referred to as retention rate. These two features constitute what is referred to as *student learning rate*.

A common misconception among educators is that if students are not keeping pace and learning at the same rate as other students, they have a slow rate of learning. Without CBA data, however, it is often unclear whether the student is failing to learn because of student-centered problems or because instruction is provided at an inappropriate level of difficulty. Until it can be determined that the student is working on an instructional level and can actively use his or her prior knowledge to an advantage in the instructional setting, it is difficult to gauge the student learning rate. This is one reason why the CBA process is so valuable early in the referral process. By regulating the level of challenge and maintaining the student at an optimal instructional level, educators can systematically determine the student's rate of learning on new curriculum tasks. Having created optimal learning conditions, the teacher is in a position to determine both the amount of support required to sustain the level of student's success within the regular classroom and the support (degree of need) necessary beyond what the classroom teacher can provide. In such cases, other resources within a continuum of services need to be explored.

Fostering Assessment Partnerships

In consulting with classroom teachers, the authors have come upon two frequently asked questions: "How can I do this with one child when there are 30 in my classroom?" and "Why single out one child when there are others just like him?" These two questions arise because teachers have responsibility for teaching 25 to 30 children and their focus is on group instruction. Consultants who apply techniques which enable teachers to change instructional assessment from a labor intensive one-on-one process to one which makes use of small-group learning and self-assessment increase the likely acceptability and implementation of critical instructional techniques. This transfer can be accomplished more easily if the questions are reframed to: "How can the focus be shifted to be more student centered and less teacher centered?" and "How can we get students to take a more active role in guiding their own learning through participation in a self-assessment process?"

Within the Pennsylvania Instructional Support Team (IST) project, with which one of the authors is associated, groups of teachers have collaborated to develop classroom routines to transfer much of the assessment process directly to their students. Keeping the instructional framework in mind, they selected grouping arrangements to facilitate the content and strategies they wanted their students to learn and apply. Their efforts concentrated on developing an instructional management system that supported active student involvement at each stage of learning. By integrating CBA with the principles of whole language and cooperative learning, they have provided for the continuous assessment of all their students, made certain that their students have been taught effectively and efficiently within their language arts curriculum, and have been accountable for the individual progress of each student. The motivating factors behind these changes included the desire (a) to use CBA in group classroom practices, (b) to capitalize on the support of an IST consultant, and (c) to eliminate student frustration and instructional fragmentation.

What follows is an abbreviated outline of how one creative set of teachers designed and implemented this group CBA process to fit their classroom routines, utilizing the four steps introduced earlier in this chapter.

Select. The teachers begin by selecting and then introducing a story during whole or small group instruction. They discuss the title and illustrations, and assess for prior knowledge. Teachers then assign readings — paragraphs or page(s). They provide cards and markers for students to conduct personal "word searches" for unknown words and word concepts.

Assess. Students silently skim their assigned readings, writing unknown words on cards as they identify them (approximately 2 minutes). In cooperative learning settings, group members assist each other in identifying and defining each unknown word. Teachers time each individual student's oral reading for one minute, provide unknown words after a 3-second delay, note how each student interacts with the reading passage, and record student's reading errors. Upon completion of the assigned reading, the teacher dialogues with the individual student to determine passage comprehension by first asking unaided questions followed by aided questions when necessary. Teachers record comprehension, note any reading strategies used by the student, and record fluency and accuracy rates including the number of words read correctly per minute (wpm) and the types of reading errors on a CBA Record Form. Fluency and error rates are charted on a Student Profile Form.

Match. Next the teachers address the three sets of decisions essential to the design of good instruction. First, they use the information acquired to determine the types of reading goals they need to set for the students. Secondly, they design opportunities for the students to work at their instructional levels. Finally, they select the appropriate strategies. For example, they identify and match appropriate word recognition, fluency, and comprehension strategies to be taught and used in cooperative groups. Students are paired with a partner to learn unknown words and word definitions. They are taught to fold-in or "sandwich" both known and unknown words, keeping a ratio of 70% to 80% known material. A sequence of known (K) to Unknown (U) words might be, for example, K-K-K-U-K-K-U-K-K-U. The new vocabulary is folded back into the actual reading passage where it is combined with strategies for developing fluency. Three to five minutes of this type of practice is provided each day. Comprehension is also taught in cooperative learning groups using, for example, "Think Aloud" and "Retelling" strategies. Writing activities are also integrated into the planning and practice process.

Teach. The final step is to implement in the classroom the instructional design they have developed. The students themselves are taught how to implement specific reading strategies, work with meaningful content in context, integrate reading and writing instruction, work at other students' instructional levels, and monitor and record reading and writing progress. The importance of ensuring the success of other students is also considered within the group teaching process.

FIGURE 1. Reading Comprehension Scores.

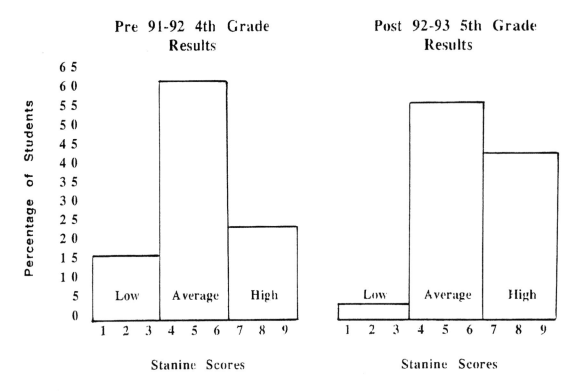

Evaluation of CBA Partnerships

Although it is premature to discuss in depth the results of this type of group CBA effort, the preliminary data are extremely encouraging. Results from a pilot school in northeastern Pennsylvania, for example, show a dramatic shift in both teacher acceptance and student performance as measured by reading comprehension. The data were collected toward the end of the fourth grade and again toward the end of the fifth grade on the same student population. There were 107 students in the initial sample at the beginning of the program, with 97 students remaining at the end of the study. Different grade level forms of the reading comprehension subtest of the Stanford Achievement Test were used as performance measures at the end of both grades. Figure 1 shows the comparative group changes, with the main intervening variable being the CBA small-group self-assessment and instructional intervention process.

SUMMARY

CBA represents best practice because it provides school psychologists, teachers, and other educational personnel with a method to assess student's academic needs and to link the information directly to instructional interventions. Unlike traditional assessment practices that test students on material disconnected from the context of the classroom, CBA uses actual classroom curriculum goals and materials to gauge student performance and to facilitate success-

ful instruction. It is based on the following set of principles:

• Although CBA is content free and can be used in any subject matter, it complements prevailing cognitively oriented curriculum and instructional approaches.

• The assessment process is performed using the natural context of the classroom curriculum, thus eliminating the need to translate assessment information back to the curriculum.

• CBA clarifies what the student knows and allows for the regulation of task variables, task demand, and the pace of instruction to ensure continued success in learning.

• CBA encourages the direct and continuous monitoring of student progress.

The CBA process includes four basic steps: the *selection* of goals and materials to help the student achieve success; the *assessment* of the student's entry skills as they relate directly to classroom materials; the decision-making process in which assessment information is used to *match* the student's entry level with appropriate instructional strategies; and finally, actual *instruction* — the outcomes of which are continually monitored to ensure that the instructional match is appropriate and that there is progress in learning the identified objectives.

Practicing school psychologists have shown increasing acceptance of CBA as part of their expanding role. For school psychologists involved in classroom-based consultation, the benefits of CBA continue to be apparent. It is hoped that the application of CBA peer- and self-assessment procedures and cooperative learning strategies, and their promising results, will make the assessment process even more attractive for use with school psychologists and classroom teachers in the future. If so, it will continue to be important to develop and provide access to skill training and guided practice in the application of CBA. Through the use of CBA procedures, school psychologists acquire an important set of skills for contributing to students' academic progress.

REFERENCES

Archer, A. L., Adams, A., Ellis, E. S., Isaacson, S., Morehead, M. K., & Schiller, E. P. (1987). *Working with mildly handicapped students: Design and delivery of academic lessons* (Academy for Effective Instruction Series). Reston, VA: Council for Exceptional Children.

Betts, E. A. (1946). *Foundations of reading instruction.* New York: American Book.

Bloom, B. (1976). *Human characteristics and school learning.* New York: McGraw Hill.

Borkowski, J. (1990, May). Moving metacognition into the classroom. Paper presented at the Conference on Cognitive Research for Instructional Innovation, University of Maryland, College Park, MD.

Coulter, W. A. (1988, November). Curriculum-based assessment: What's in a name? *Communiqué,* p. 13.

Deno, S. L., & Fuchs, L. S. (1987, April). Developing curriculum-based measurement systems for data-based special education problem solving. *Focus on Exceptional Children, 19,* 1–16.

Gickling, E. E., & Havertape, J. F. (1981). Curriculum-based assessment. Minneapolis: University of Minnesota, National School Psychology Inservice Training Network.

Gickling, E. E., Shane, R. L., & Croskery, K. M. (1989). Developing mathematics skills in low-achieving high school students through curriculum-based assessment. *School Psychology Review, 18,* 344–355.

Hargis, C. H. (1989). *Teaching low achieving and disadvantaged students.* Springfield, IL: Charles C Thomas Publisher.

Johnston, P. (1987). Teachers as evaluation experts. *The Reading Teacher, 40,* 744–748.

Meichenbaum, D., & Biemiller, A. (1990, May). In search of student expertise in the classroom: A metacognitive analysis. Paper presented at the Conference on Cognitive Research for Instructional Innovation, University of Maryland, College Park, MD.

Paratore, J. R., & Indrisano, R. (1987). Intervention assessment of reading comprehension. *The Reading Teacher, 40,* 778–783.

Reschly, D., Kicklighter, R., & McKee, P. (1988). Recent placement litigation. Part III: Analysis of differences in *Larry P., Marshall,* and *S-1* and implications for future practices. *School Psychology Review, 17,* 39–50.

Rosenfield, S. (1987). Instructional consultation. Hillsdale, NJ: Lawrence Erlbaum Associates.

Rosenfield, S., & Kuralt, S. (1990). Best practices in curriculum-based assessment. In A. Thomas & J. Grimes (Eds.), *Best practices in school psychology–II* (pp. 275–286). Washington, DC: National Association of School Psychologists.

Salvia, J., & Ysseldyke, J. E. (1985). *Assessment in special and remedial education* (2nd ed.). Boston: Houghton Mifflin Co.

Shapiro, E. S., & Eckert, T. L. (1993). Curriculum-based assessment among school psychologists: Knowledge, use, and attitudes. *Journal of School Psychology, 31,* 375–383.

Shinn, M. R., Rosenfield, S., & Knutson, N. (1989). Curriculum-based assessment: A comparison of models. *School Psychology Review, 18,* 299–316.

Stiggins, R. J., & Conklin, N. F. (1992). *In teachers' hands: Investigating the practices of classroom assessment.* Albany, NY: State University of New York Press.

Valencia, S. (1990). A portfolio approach to classroom reading assessment: The whys, whats, and hows. *The Reading Teacher, 43,* 338–340.

Valencia, S., & Pearson, P. D. (1987). Reading assessment: Time for change. *The Reading Teacher, 40,* 726–732.

Walker, B. J. (1992). *Diagnostic teaching of reading: Techniques for instruction and assessment.* Columbus, OH: Merrill Publishing Co.

Wiggins, G. P. (1992). Foreword. In R. A. Villa, J. S. Thousand, W. Stainback, & S. Stainback (Eds.), *Restructuring for caring and effective education* (pp. xi–xvi). Baltimore: Paul H. Brookes Publishing Co.

Ysseldyke, J. E., & Christenson, S. L. (1993). *The instructional environment system (TIES-II).* Longmont, CO: Sopris West Publishing Company.

ANNOTATED BIBLIOGRAPHY

Hargis, C. H. (1989). *Teaching low achieving and disadvantaged students.* Springfield, IL: Charles C Thomas Publisher.
This book describes how routine curriculum and grading practices contribute to the problems of low achievement. Procedures for developing CBA-related instructional procedures are included.

Rosenfield, S. (1988). CBA with Ed Gickling. Philadelphia, PA: Temple University School Psychology Program.
This videotape was produced for training purposes and includes instructional handout materials. Dr. Gickling demonstrates the process of conducting CBA with two elementary school children in reading and ways to build fluency with a young reader. This and additional tapes demonstrating CBA, including group CBA procedures, are available from the authors.

Rosenfield, S., & Shinn, M. R. (Eds.). (1989). Mini-series on curriculum-based assessment. *School Psychology Review, 18,* 293–370.
Two articles in this series contain information relevant to CBA. The article by Shinn, Rosenfield, and Knutson entitled "Curriculum-Based Assessment: A Comparison and Integration of Two Models" reviews and compares the various models of CBA and CBM on such dimensions as purpose, technical adequacy, and instructional design. Gickling, Shane, and Croskery's article "Developing Math Skills in Low-Achieving High School Students Through Curriculum-Based Assessment" describes the use of a CBA-based intervention in a secondary level math program.

51

Best Practices in Performance Monitoring

Doug Marston
Minneapolis Public Schools

Gerald Tindal
University of Oregon

OVERVIEW

It was Saturday morning and my young son and I were looking at his baseball card collection when he asked, "Why are all of these numbers on the back of the cards?" Seeing a chance to explain the importance of baseball statistics I began to explain that numbers such as "batting average" and "runs batted in" showed how well a player had performed and helped his team win. But before my discourse ran too long he interrupted and said, "If these numbers are so important, why aren't they on the front of the card?"

In some respects performance monitoring in education and psychology parallels the front and back of my son's baseball cards. All too often we assign the "back of the card" to the "statistics" needed to monitor pupil performance and the effectiveness of the interventions that we as psychologists and educators have crafted. Because we expend considerable effort developing interventions for students in need, the question arises as to why monitoring pupil performance and the effectiveness of our interventions frequently takes a back seat to other activities. The question is important because performance monitoring is a primary ingredient in the problem-solving approach (Iowa Department of Education, 1991).

> Progress monitoring is an essential aspect of any systematic approach to solving student problems. Whenever an intervention is implemented, student performance data should be collected on a regular and frequent basis. This on-going progress monitoring will yield objective data describing the student's progress toward goals. The data can be used to make decisions about the relative effectiveness of interventions. (p. 29)

Why is it so difficult to get educators to monitor pupil performance? Explanations for this occurrence fall into two categories. First, those who would monitor pupil performance are confronted with a variety of *external* difficulties and constraints within the educational environment. Second, many of the traditional assessment procedures used for performance monitoring possess *internal* technical problems.

Problems external to the measurement system that influence whether educators or psychologists implement performance monitoring include time constraints (Mirkin, 1980), cost (Mirkin, 1980), and at times, a negative attitude some educators have toward measurement (Bancroft & Bellamy, 1976). Frequently cited objections reported by Bancroft and Bellamy (1976) include

- Teachers think data are not necessary because they believe they already know where students are functioning.

- Classroom monitoring systems sometimes ignore essential characteristics of learning and development.

- The procedures are often too rigid and interfere with instruction.

Several problems internal to the traditional assessment procedures can also be identified. First, the technical adequacy of traditional assessments is often challenged. Ysseldyke, Algozzine, Regan, and Potter (1980) documented that many of the traditional instruments selected for measuring pupil performance do not possess adequate validity or reliability. Second, many available tests are not useful for instruction (Thurlow & Ysseldyke, 1982; Tindal, 1985), and third, in many cases assessments do not match the curricula used for instruction (Good & Salvia, 1988). A fourth problem is that most tests are not sensitive to real student improvement and an edumetric approach must be adopted if student learning is to be measured (Carver, 1974).

In reaction to these external and internal concerns new assessment models have emerged to provide instructionally relevant data to the teacher. Fuchs and Deno (1991) point out that many of these models are rooted in behavioral psychology, such as Individually Prescribed Instruction (Glaser, 1966),

Precision Teaching (White & Haring, 1980), and Data-Based Program Modification (Deno & Mirkin, 1977). An ingredient common to these types of models is systematic and objective quantification of behavior, typified by the guidelines Tawney and Gast (1984) described: "Basic steps or rules to be followed in the assessment process include (1) identifying what is to be measured, (2) defining the behaviors or event in observable terms, and (3) selecting an appropriate data-recording system for observing, quantifying, and summarizing behavior." Tucker (1985), in a review of curriculum-based assessment systems, delineated three major characteristics of these new instructionally relevant measurement systems: Use of items from the pupil's curriculum for monitoring, frequent measurement, and use of the data to evaluate instructional effectiveness. Marston and Magnusson (1988) labeled these three constructs as direct measurement, repeated measurement, and time series analysis.

Direct Measurement

Direct observation of student responses is paramount to performance monitoring. The notion of direct measurement fits nicely with Reynolds' (1982) analysis of how assessment is connected to the rights of children: "In general, behavioral assessments should be based heavily on direct observations rather than on presumed predispositional or underlying traits" (p. 105). Proponents reason that listening to a child read or examining a student writing sample is a more direct measure of performance than analyzing student responses on traditional achievement test items such as multiple choice or true/false questions.

The issue of directness is related to the extent to which the unit of measurement in the monitoring system allows one to examine actual student behavior. Johnston and Pennypacker (1993) argue the accuracy of measurement improves when the meaning of a unit of measurement is fixed or absolute. They make the distinction between idemontic units of measurement, whose meaning is absolute, and vaganotic units, where meaning varies. Idemontic units have a consistent form that makes observation from situation to situation more accurate. Vaganotic units, however, can differ across observations, meaning lowered reliability. Thus, observing idemontic units of behavior such as "words read correctly" or "letters correctly identified" is more accurate in monitoring performance than using vaganotic units such as "grade equivalent scores," "percentiles," or "Likert ratings."

Repeated Measurement

Another important element in performance monitoring is the use of repeated measurement. Frequently monitoring of pupil performance during the academic year increases the reliability of observation and allows for the examination of trends in student growth and quicker reaction to pupils who are falling behind. This dynamic approach to measuring student improvement exceeds the results of performance monitoring with achievement tests. A brief look at the "educational lifetime" of a typical student who attends school for 13 years (K–12), which is approximately 2,300 instructional days, confirms this. For example, using traditional achievement tests, at the rate of twice per year, means that the progress of the student would have been monitored 26 times during his or her "educational lifetime." However, if pupil progress were monitored on a weekly basis during these same 13 years of instruction, the result would be almost 500 measurements of student growth. Performance monitoring creates the latter condition and provides educators with timely assessment information that improves instructional decision making. The concept of repeated measurement is featured in Nazzaro's (1976) conclusion, "All evaluation procedures have potential biases and any 'one shot' sample of behavior, whether it be a test, an observation, or any other technique, tells little about a person's ability to learn. Only by sampling over time can one gain a fairly accurate picture of a child's potential" (p. 41).

Time Series Analysis

Time series analysis is the systematic examination of a student's direct and repeated measurement data in relation to implemented interventions. At the center of time series analysis is the graph upon which these data are recorded. By repeatedly plotting the frequency or duration of student behaviors the educator can evaluate the effectiveness of his or her strategy. Parsonen and Baer (1992) identify six advantages to be gained through graphic analysis:

1. It is visual, and thereby quick to yield conclusions and hypotheses.

2. Graphs can be quick and easy to make with no more technology than grid paper, pencil and straight edge. However, if the latest computer graphics technology is to be used, then speed and ease are recaptured only after an initial high cost of money, time, and training.

3. Graphing comprises a remarkably wide range of formats, even outside of the latest computer graphics technology.

4. Graphed messages are immediate, enduring, and accessible to students at unusually diverse levels of training.

5. In representing the actual data measured, graphs can and usually do transfer those data as minimally as possible. In those paradigms of knowing wherein the measurable data under study are the reality to be understood . . . , that is an obvious virtue.

6. The theoretical premises underlying graphs are minimal and well known — that what we are in-

terested in can be made visual, and that almost all of us are skilled in responding to visual isomorphisms of the world in ways that make the world useful. By contrast, the theoretical premises underlying the defensible use of statistical analysis are numerous, complex, diverse, and frequently arcane to the majority of their users. Thus, statistical analysis users find themselves relying on techniques subject to apparently endless debate about their suitability for given problems — a debate often accessible to only a small minority of the users.

Use of the graph is critical to time series analysis. However, Tawney and Gast (1984) point out data should not be collected for the sake of just collecting data: It needs to be used in the teacher's decision-making process. This notion is supported by Fuchs and Fuchs (1986) who demonstrated that when performance monitoring scores are graphed rather than recorded, student achievement improves about .5 standard deviations.

BASIC CONSIDERATIONS

Background Information

Many of the principles and concepts behind the performance monitoring approaches described in this chapter are grounded in applied behavioral analytic procedures theory. While not a requirement, a knowledge base in this area would obviously assist the school psychologist implementing performance monitoring procedures in the areas of inservice training, consultation and problem solving, and the development of new systems. Background sources that describe behavioral theory and single subject analysis include Kratochwill and Levin (1992), Johnston and Pennypacker (1993), and Tawney and Gast (1984).

The elements of performance monitoring presented here are found in the early work of Deno and Mirkin (1977) and are updated in Deno (1986). More recently, Fuchs and Deno (1991) clarified the role of Curriculum-Based Measurement when they examined instructionally relevant measurement models and identified two major models: specific-subskill-mastery measurement and general-outcome measurement. In the specific-subskill-mastery measurement model, general educational goals for the student are broken down into sets of subskills matched to short-term instructional objectives. Measurement in this model thus focuses on student performance on small sets of items specific to each objective. Thus, performance monitoring procedures are specific to the units of instruction and tend to be short term.

Fuchs and Deno (1991) note that while this approach provides flexibility and the opportunity to focus on specific instructional objectives it creates two problems. "First, freedom to select among a wide variety of alternatives resulted in ad hoc and idiosyncratic measurement with unknown reliability and va-

lidity. Second, the short-term objective focus of the mastery measurement did not prove useful for answering broad questions about student growth, such as 'How effective is my instructional program (a) in producing growth over time, or (b) in comparison to other instructional strategies I might have used with this child?' " (p. 489).

General outcome measurement procedures developed by Deno and associates were designed to solve these problems and answer these questions. To do so these researchers created a methodology of performance measurement that (a) prescribed the critical behaviors and procedures for monitoring and (b) could be used for long-term goal measurement, such as an academic year. The practices described in the next section conform to this *general-outcome measurement* model.

Equipment

Materials and equipment needs for implementing the performance monitoring approaches described in this chapter are minimal. Any school psychologist with access to the district's curriculum and a knowledge of district objectives can begin to create the materials necessary for monitoring. In addition, there are some commercially available products that would assist in measuring performance and graphing data.

Training

A key ingredient to the success of performance monitoring is training. The authors' experience has demonstrated that the traditional one-day workshop is not enough for training educators to begin and maintain implementation. Beyond initial training, learners need follow-up consultation on a regular basis. In the Minneapolis Public Schools, once-a-month meetings with lead teachers are provided throughout the school year after the initial one-day workshop.

Training should emphasize a conceptual understanding of the model and stress reliability during the implementation of procedures. The Minneapolis schools' training focuses on the rationale, the need, and the research basis for direct, repeated measurement and graph analysis. Once a philosophical framework is established, consistency and reliability in administration of procedures should be stressed. During initial training, an interrater agreement above 90% should be required for new trainees, with follow-up consultation and examination of reliability provided to avoid any drift away from standard practices.

BEST PRACTICES

Tawney and Gast (1984) have identified a sequence of important steps essential to any valid performance monitoring system:

1. Define the target behavior in observable terms.

2. Collect data only to the extent that the data will be used to guide instruction, that is, avoid the trap of collecting data on all programs and behaviors.

3. Measure that aspect of a student's objective which is of interest, that is, do not restrict data collection to simple responses and ignore more interesting and important aspects of student behavior.

4. Become thoroughly familiar with data collection and research design alternatives.

5. Select a measurement system which is practical and which can be consistently and reliably used within the constraints of the classroom.

6. Structure the classroom (daily schedule, staffing assignments, etc.) to facilitate data collection as well as teaching.

7. Evaluate data regularly and base instructional decisions so as to maintain or modify the program on the data.

8. Collect performance data frequently to yield an accurate measure of program effectiveness.

This section presents three examples of "best practice" in performance monitoring. These models conform to the basic principles set out by Tawney and Gast (1984) and are derived from the Curriculum-Based Measurement approach described by Deno (1986). These approaches include analyzing individual student growth in the Minneapolis Public Schools (Marston & Magnusson, 1988), analyzing classroom growth at Vanderbilt University (Fuchs, Fuchs, Bishop, & Hamlett, 1992), and performance monitoring in content areas at the University of Oregon (McCollum, Tindal, & Nolet, 1992).

Performance Monitoring: Analyzing Individual Student Growth

Performance monitoring has been an important component in the delivery of services to special education students in the Minneapolis Public Schools. Since 1983 the K–6 Resource Program has used Curriculum-Based Measurement (CBM; Marston & Magnusson, 1988) to continuously evaluate the impact of instructional interventions and measure progress toward the goals of the Individualized Education Program (IEP). An example of this type of performance-monitoring system is shown in Figure 1 which illustrates direct, repeated measurement and time-series analysis of pupil progress. For this student, Jason, CBM reading probes have been administered weekly during the school year. Jason's performance is plotted on an equal interval graph. Weeks are shown along the horizontal axis; the words read correctly are charted along the vertical axis. During "Phase A" in-

struction, it is clear that the reading progress of this second grader is minimal. However, during "Phase B" reading instruction, the student improves considerably.

How to develop probes. Because repeated measurement is essential to the performance-monitoring model, many equivalent probes must be created. In the Minneapolis schools, at least 30 different, but approximately equal, reading passages have been developed for each grade level. Passages are at least 200 words long and typed onto separate pages. The *student copy*, from which pupils read, contains only the text; the *examiner copy* includes a cumulative word count for each line to aid in scoring.

How to administer and score the probes. Students are asked to read aloud for 1 minute. During that minute the student is to attempt each word. If the student cannot correctly identify a word within 3 seconds, he or she is prompted to continue. The examiner follows along on the examiner copy and marks with an "X" those words incorrectly pronounced or omitted; self-corrections are scored as correct. At the end of the minute, the examiner counts the number of words read correctly. An interrater agreement coefficient of at least .90 is required during teacher training.

How to determine an appropriate measurement level. The next task in performance monitoring is the selection of the level of passages in which monitoring will occur. Let's assume that Jason, a sixth grader in need of special education, is instructed in a third-grade book. If a sixth-grade book were selected for performance monitoring, Jason would probably find the probes too hard to read. Most likely his scores would be close to the bottom or *floor* of the graph and the monitoring system would not be sensitive to pupil growth (White & Haring, 1980).

On the other hand, if we use Jason's third-grade reader, material in which he is receiving instruction, his scores may be toward the top or *ceiling* of the graph because of practice. The *ceiling effect* attenuates growth during performance monitoring.

Deno, Mirkin, and Wesson (1984) provide a procedure for eliminating floor and ceiling effects. They suggest a *sampling back* process in which observers listen to the pupil read in successively easier grade level readers. Marston and Magnusson (1988) provide empirical guidelines. For first- and second-grade students a reading level in which the student reads 10 to 30 words correctly per minute should be used for performance monitoring. The criteria for third to sixth graders is 30 to 60 correct words.

How to select a graph. Before plotting the student's performance the type of graph upon which it will be plotted needs to be selected. For most purposes the simple equal interval chart should be used. On this chart, time is measured along the horizontal axis and performance is scaled along the vertical axis.

FIGURE 1. An example of direct, repeated measurement and time-series analysis with Curriculum-Based Measurement procedures.

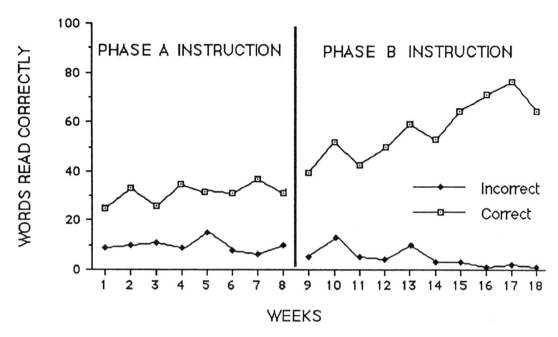

Precision-teaching proponents prefer the semi-logarithmic graph where performance along the vertical axis is measured on a logarithmic scale (White & Haring, 1985). Marston (1987), however, compared both types of graphs and found predictions of goal attainment were more accurate with the equal interval chart. He notes that this type of chart also possesses the advantage of easier communication with parents and other educators when discussing pupil performance .

Johnston and Pennypacker (1993) also provide relevant information on constructing graphs. These authors discuss how data ought to be presented, which measurement scales should be used, and the rules governing how a scale is applied and how data ought to be plotted.

How to set the long range goal. Once the measurement material for performance monitoring has been selected, it is time to set a goal and begin. The following paragraphs describe three approaches for determining the student goal:

1. **Normative tables.** A normative database was compiled in Minneapolis schools from testing approximately 7,200 students in Grades K–8 during the Fall, Winter, and Spring of an academic year. The data provide percentile ranks for each grade level for every month from September to June. This allows teachers to determine the typical performance at any level during the school year, and helps them select an appropriate goal for an individual student.

2. **Average learning rates.** Minneapolis has also examined hundreds of student charts in an effort to determine the typical learning rate of pupils at every grade on the various CBM measures. These rates can be used to set goals. For example, Minneapolis data demonstrate that each week the average first- and second-grade resource student gains about 1.5 correct words per minute (cwpm). Resource students in third to sixth grade improve about 1.0 cwpm per week. General education students, however, have higher weekly slopes: first and second graders improve 2–3 cwpm per week while third to sixth graders increase at about 1.5–2.5 cwpm per week. With this *average learning rate* database, teachers can determine goals by multiplying the number of weeks left in the school year by the selected weekly gain and add this to the student's baseline level.

Mastery criteria. A review of mastery criteria research by Fuchs (1982) and Starlin and Starlin (1974) indicates that appropriate goals are from 50 to 70 correct words for Grades 1 and 2, and 70 to 100 words correct for Grades 3 to 6.

How to use data-utilization strategies. Once the monitoring level is determined and a goal is set, performance monitoring is ready to commence. The question now is which type of data-utilization rules to use. This is important, because application of rules to time-series data significantly increases its usefulness in helping determine when to make changes in interventions. Fuchs and Fuchs (1986) have established that a .91 standard deviation increase in student achievement is associated with the systematic use of data-utilization rules.

FIGURE 2. An example of trend line analysis.

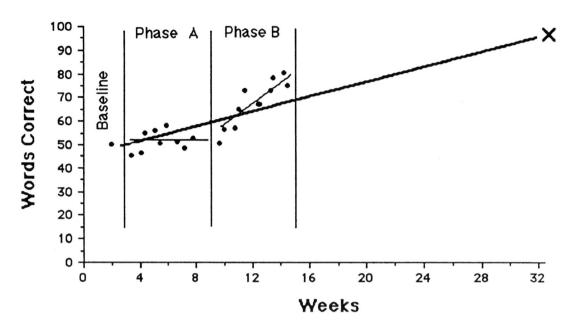

The Minneapolis Public Schools used two sets of rules: *trend-line analysis* and *data-point analysis*. In both approaches evaluations of intervention effectiveness are based on progress toward the goal.

- **Trend-line analysis.** Trend-line analysis uses the trend line or slope of the data points and is calculated by White and Haring's (1980) Quarter-Intersect method. After 9 to 12 data points are collected, typically 3 to 4 weeks of data collection, the trend line is drawn. If the trend line is higher than the aim line, only minor changes, if any, to the program should be considered. However, if the slope is lower than the aim line, major changes in the intervention are warranted. For example, the trend line in Figure 2 Phase A instruction indicates that the instructional program is not successful and a major change needs to be made. The trend line in Phase B, however, is higher than the aim line and indicates only minor modifications should be made, if at all.

- **Data-point analysis.** In data-point analysis no trend line is drawn. Instead, individual data points are analyzed in relationship to the aim line. These data points typically represent the median of three passages read during a week of instruction. If four consecutive data points fall below the aim line, a change in the instructional intervention should be made. Similar to trend-line analysis, it takes approximately 4 weeks to collect enough data to make a decision about instituting instructional changes. In Phase A of Figure 3 four consecutive medians fall below the aim line, indicating a need for change. However, in Phase B, the student's reading medians fall above and below the aim line

in equal fashion. In this case the intervention would continue as implemented.

Recent research by Fuchs, Fuchs, and Hamlett (1989) indicates higher levels of student achievement will occur if goals are increased during the school year. In this type of *dynamic* system of data utilization, teachers raise the student's goal if certain conditions are met. As a result the procedures correct for goals that might initially be set too low due to low teacher expectations, errors in measurement, or the like. In fact, Fuchs, Fuchs, and Hamlett (1989) found that "despite the importance of ambitious goals, special educators' typical goal-setting standards may under estimate many students' potential" (p. 436). This dynamic approach dictates that after a specified period of time, the teacher must make some type of change, either by raising the student's goal or making an instructional change.

Performance Monitoring: Analyzing Classroom Growth

Fuchs et al. (1992) have modified CBM procedures, which are typically used for individual assessment, for class-wide monitoring purposes. Relying on microcomputer technology, these researchers at Vanderbilt University have developed math and reading probes that can be used to monitor performance and help evaluate general education interventions in the classroom. They reason that while CBM is effective for evaluation at the individual level the diversity of public school classrooms demands assessment procedures that are useful for entire classrooms. "Unfortunately, despite the demonstrated efficacy of CBM within special education programs, few studies have

FIGURE 3. An example of data point analysis.

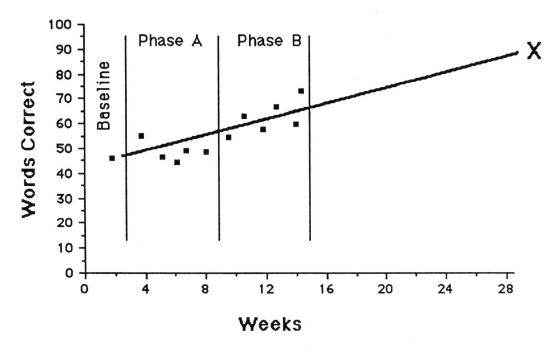

investigated the capacity of teachers to use this assessment methodology to design more effective programs within general education" (Fuchs et al., 1992, p. 40).

These reviewers created a set of equivalent monitoring probes that were keyed to basic math operations of addition, subtraction, multiplication, and division of whole numbers, fractions, and decimals. Each probe included 25 problems and was designed to be administered twice monthly by the teacher in a whole-class format or administered to the student working at a microcomputer setting. The computerized format offers several advantages: "The computer scores the test, keeps track of student mastery over time on the different skills incorporated in the annual curriculum, provides student feedback, and aggregates information across students to describe for teachers the class performance and to provide teachers with instructional recommendations" (p. 42).

The computerized performance-monitoring system provides individual feedback in the form of student growth, similar to those described in the previous section, and mastery feedback on specific skills for each student such as: adding with regrouping; subtracting with regrouping; subtracting with regrouping using 0; multiplying basic facts; multiplying 2-digit by 1-digit number with regrouping; and dividing basic facts. The computer also generates classwide teacher feedback in graphic and mastery form. On the class-wide graph the 25th, 50th, and 75th percentiles are plotted twice each month. As a result, the teacher is able to examine typical growth at each percentile over the entire year. The class-wide report

also presents a student list to show the degree to which a variety of skills have been mastered. Further, the report identifies groups of students for each skill area that need further instruction.

Research on this approach with students in Grades 2 through 5 showed that general educators were satisfied with the monitoring system and that "achievement data indicated a main effect (across different types of learners) favoring the growth of the students whose teachers used CBM with classwide reports that included instructional recommendations over each of the other conditions" (Fuchs et al., 1991, p. 49). They concluded that class-wide CBM decision-making was useful for general educators in planning for a wide range of students.

Performance Monitoring: Measurement in Content Areas

The ideas presented in the last two sections demonstrated how performance monitoring can be implemented for basic skills at the individual and classroom levels. This section provides some new ideas from the University of Oregon on how to monitor student performance in "content" areas using the principles of direct measurement, repeated measurement, and time-series analysis (McCollum et al., 1992). According to these authors, instruction and assessment in the content areas can be linked, providing continuous information about student progress. Problem-solving essays are used to assess the student and his or her ability to use the knowledge forms, concepts, or principles, in one of six intellectual operations: (a) reiteration, (b) summarization, (c) illustration, (d) prediction, (e) evaluation, and (f) application. A prompt is provided which poses a problem the student must solve by drawing on his or her understanding of specific knowledge forms. This same type of questioning and problem solving can be included in the instructional format so students are practicing using information in the service of solving some problem. Achievement is then based on the student's ability to manipulate the learned information. This type of classroom-based assessment, which links measures of performance with instruction, can be used to determine if the students have learned what the teacher wanted them to learn. Therefore, posing problems to students that require the use of intellectual operations becomes not only an important part of instruction but can be used in lieu of a typical assessment measure: It indicates meaningful use of information and success in instructional content.

Before instruction begins, the teacher reviews the material to be covered and identifies key *concepts* to be taught. Concepts are specific words or short phrases that refer to classes of objects or events sharing some common defining attributes. Concepts involve three parts: a label, key attributes, and a range of examples. For each concept, the teacher identifies key defining *attributes*, which enable discrimination of what is and is not an example of the concept. Examining the extent to which the student uses the concepts and attributes is critical to the assessment process. In addition, student essays are examined for the number of *thought units* expressed in the written composition.

In the case study presented here, Tom is a Chapter I student who is part of a seventh-grade social studies class. Instruction was designed to directly teach concepts and attributes related to (a) the geography, (b) the political systems, and (c) the economy of Greece and Rome. Significant emphasis was placed on examples and non-examples where the examples focused the students' attention on the dimensions of a concept, while non-examples acted as a means of discrimination. Principles were discussed and applied in different contexts. Graphic organizers were periodically used to provide a framework for teaching concepts and attributes in a simplified structure for delivering information and to assist the students in noting relationships among concepts and principles.

Every effort was made to challenge the student to think and draw on his knowledge and experience of a specific concept or principle. The student was provided repetitive instruction until a solid understanding of a concept or principle was gained, and then an effective questioning strategy was applied that prompted the use of information and personal background knowledge to solve a problem with some relevance to life and historical patterns. The result of this process was a student motivated to think and respond.

Student performance was assessed by analyzing work products and ascertaining their presence. As mentioned previously, an opportunity to practice using intellectual operations to manipulate knowledge forms was used as part of instruction. This practice resulted in a number of subproducts, or problem-solving essays, written by the case students over a 2-month period. Once Tom had an understanding of the critical concepts, he was asked to respond to a number of prompts that required the manipulation of knowledge forms in some intellectual operation.

In the following subproduct collected at the beginning of the instructional period, Tom was asked to make some decision and explain his reasoning about some specific concepts, in this case political systems. Although a decision was made, he gave minimal explanations for the concept selected.

- **Subproduct Prompt #1** — A group of people in one area of an empire are dissatisfied with the harsh rule of their king. They do not want their lives ruled by this strict king, but feel the need for some type of system (government) to help make decisions and solve problems for the people. What political system might they try to develop (assuming the king agrees)? Tell why that system (or government) would be better than the current rule by a king.

- **Tom's Written Response to Prompt #1** — *They might try to make a republic.*
  Because a king cant have his spot taken and you dont vote for king.
  if the elected person gets mouthy you can fire him
  republic people are involved

The essay was designed to reflect evaluation responding and Tom made a choice based on his knowledge of the concepts. He then attempted to make an argument for his choice, although his knowledge of the concept of republic is expressed in too vague a manner (don't vote for king/republic people are involved). This composition was scored as having 4 Thought Units, 1 Concept, and 0 Attributes. Tom wrote 35 words.

Toward the end of the 2-month instructional unit Tom responded to the following Subproduct Prompt.

- **Subproduct Prompt #2** — You are a merchant with a spice store in the township of Chestwick in the late Middle Ages. Many of the merchants in Chestwick have seen how well a charter has helped the people in the neighboring township and want to try this new system of self-governing. What happened to cause this movement toward writing charters in the late Middle Ages?

- **Tom's Written Response to Prompt #2** — *The early Middle ages. because the people were all was bosed around by the vassels, nobles. And so then they would want a charter so they won't get bosed*

FIGURE 4. Performance monitoring in content areas.

Changes over Time in Tom's Subproduct Essays

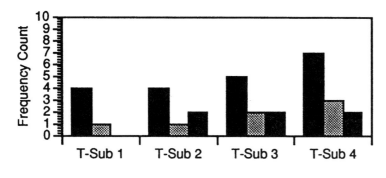
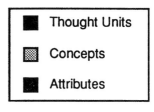

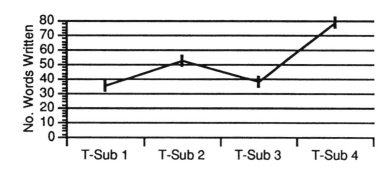

around. because they wanted to sell what they wanted to sell and sell it for the price they wanted to sell it, live where wanted. Becaus the loards don't know what there talking about as far as trade or the merchants buisnes\m\mthey want a charter so the can run themselfs.

In this composition Tom had 7 Thought Units, 3 concepts, and 2 Attributes, while writing 80 words.

The charts in Figure 4 depict Tom's performance over time. In the top graph, the number of thought units (one thought unit being a complete thought that could stand alone), concepts, and attributes are counted for each of Tom's subproduct responses (T-Sub 1–4). The bottom graph indicates the total number of words written for each subproduct response.

Notice that the number of thought units increases as Tom gains experience in responding to essay prompts. Also, his use of concepts within essays increases. Where the first two essays contain only one concept, subsequent essays contain an increase of one concept. Also, where concept attributes are non-existent in the first essay, later essays contain more than one attribute. In the bottom graph, the number of words increases despite a decrease for the third essay response. Although Tom has used fewer words in this response, the essay contains the use of two concepts and two attributes and indicates a clear understanding of both. Many students' essays contain

much superfluous information and indicate no truer understanding. Data for Tom indicate improvement in use of critical information for written responses.

Research on Barriers to Implementation

Yell, Deno, and Marston (1992) examined barriers to the implementation of performance monitoring with CBM procedures. They surveyed special education administrators from around the country using Delphi Probe techniques and identified the 10 greatest concerns:

1. Lack of repertoire of instructional strategies to use when data indicate teachers need to make an instructional change.

2. The practice by some teachers of mechanically measuring and charting but not using data to make instructional decisions.

3. Resistance to change: The use of CBM represents change and trying to implement change brings about resistance and anxiety.

4. Ongoing training system for special and regular education staff.

5. Applying CBM in secondary schools.

6. The logistics of evaluation and modification.

7. Difficulty in getting staff to use CBM to adjust their instructional strategies.

8. Time needed to monitor teacher's implementation of CBM.

9. Adequate district human resources to fully implement the program.

10. Concern over words read per minute, and if this realistically measures comprehension.

The first author's experience in the Minneapolis Public Schools is similar in many ways, particularly, barriers 1, 2, and 7. After Minneapolis first implemented performance monitoring, it was discovered that although the teachers were graphing student data, they made on the average approximately one instructional change per year in reading. Several reasons emerged as to why the student graphs showed few instructional changes. First, some teachers were unclear as to what constituted an instructional change or how significant a change should be to merit recording it on the graph. Second, some instructional changes for students may have been made independent of the data and not recorded on the graphs. For example, a teacher might react to the performance of one or two students in an instructional group and make a change for that entire group. Finally, in some cases it appeared that teachers did not make instructional changes because they were not equipped to provide an alternative.

The solution to this later problem was to increase inservice training on a variety of instructional interventions. Other approaches to countering barriers 1, 2, and 7 included pairing teachers with instructional specialists to discuss strategies or provide teachers with a forum to periodically discuss their data with other special education teachers. These "chart-share" sessions allowed teachers the opportunity to develop innovative ideas on how to teach individual students.

Time, barrier #8, is another frequent barrier but three approaches can help. First, teachers need to organize their materials in such a way that one-to-one monitoring of students can be conducted while other students are engaged in important instructional behaviors (Wesson et al., 1986). Second, teachers can decrease their standardized achievement testing, which makes more time available. Third, time for implementing the monitoring system in Minneapolis was decreased by changing to the data-point analysis approach. In this method three weekly probes are administered on the same day and the median is plotted. In addition, trend lines are not drawn, another time saver.

Many of the barriers to implementation of performance monitoring can be overcome by providing ongoing training activities and follow-up visits. For further discussion of ideas see Yell, Deno, and Marston (1992).

SUMMARY

Performance monitoring "statistics" should not take a back seat in educational practice. The measurement of pupil progress on an ongoing basis provides the educator with an opportunity to evaluate intervention effectiveness and truly link assessment to instruction. When such systems help guide instructional practice the assessment data is viewed as more meaningful. Further, such systems improve the skills of the school psychologist in his or her consultative roles.

To create the link between assessment and instruction, performance-monitoring procedures first need to be direct; that is, important academic behaviors ought to be directly observed so that accuracy and validity can be ensured. Second, assessment needs to be conducted on a repeated basis, rather than once or twice a year: Time is precious and educators can ill afford to wait to evaluate the effectiveness of the interventions. Third, time-series analysis can examine the relationship of student growth on direct, repeated measures of behaviors with the instructional interventions.

By implementing performance-monitoring procedures based on these three concepts the school psychologist has gained an important tool for improving the effectiveness of educational interventions with students. The practices described here can be used at the individual or classroom level of analysis. Further, these procedures, which were initially developed for basic skill areas, have been extended to content areas. Finally, barriers to implementation are described and some solutions presented. Attention to these issues will enhance the school psychologist's prospects for successfully implementing performance-monitoring procedures at the individual or systems level.

REFERENCES

Bancroft, J., & Bellamy, G. T. (1976). An apology for systematic observation. *Mental Retardation, 14*(5), 27–29.

Bijou, S. W. (1977). Practical implications of an interactional model of child development. *Exceptional Children, 44*(1), 6–14.

Carver, R. P. (1974). Two dimensions of tests: Psychometric and edumetric. *American Psychologist, 29*, 52–518.

Deno, S. L. (1986). Formative evaluation of individual student programs: A new role for school psychologists. *School Psychology Review, 15*, 358–374.

Deno, S. L., & Mirkin, P. K. (1977). *Data-based program modification: A manual.* Reston, VA: The Council for Exceptional Children.

Fuchs, L. S. (1982). Reading. In P. K. Mirkin, L. Fuchs, & S. L. Deno (Eds.), *Considerations for designing a continuous evaluation system: An integrative review* (Monograph No. 20). Minneapolis, MN: University of Minnesota, Institute for Research on Learning Disabilities.

Fuchs, L. S., & Deno, S. L. (1991). Paradigmatic distinctions between instructionally relevant measurement models. *Exceptional Children, 57*(6), 488–500.

Fuchs, L. S., & Fuchs, D. (1986). Effects of systematic formative evaluation: A meta-analysis. *Exceptional Children, 53,* 199–208.

Fuchs, L. S., Fuchs, D., & Hamlett, C. (1989). Monitoring reading growth using student recalls: Effects of two teacher feedback systems. *Journal of Educational Research, 83,* 103–111.

Fuchs, L. S., Fuchs, D., Bishop, N., & Hamlett, C. L. (1992). Classwide decision-making with Curriculum-Based Measurement. *Diagnostiqué, 18*(1), 39–52.

Glaser, R. (1966). *The Individually Prescribed Instruction Project.* Pittsburgh: University of Pittsburgh, Learning R & D Center Publications.

Good, R. H., & Salvia, J. (1988). Curriculum bias in published, norm-referenced reading tests: Demonstrable effects. *School Psychology Review, 17,* 51–60.

Iowa Department of Education. (1991). *Understanding components of the problem-solving process.* Des Moines, IA: Iowa Department of Education.

Johnston, J. M., & Pennypacker, H. S. (1993). *Strategic and tactics of behavioral research.* Hillsdale, NJ: Erlbaum Associates.

Kratochwill, T. R., & Levin, J. R. (1992). *Single-case research design and analysis: New directions for psychology and education.* Hillsdale, NJ: Lawrence Erlbaum Associates.

Kratochwill, T. R., Mott, S. E., & Dodson, C. L. (1984). Case study and single-case research in clinical and applied psychology. In A. S. Bellack & M. Hersen (Eds.), *Research methods in clinical psychology* (pp. 55–99). New York: Pergamon.

Marston, D. (1987). Measuring academic progress of students with learning difficulties: A comparison of the semi-logarithmic chart and equal interval graph paper. *Exceptional Children.*

Marston, D., & Magnusson, D. (1988). Curriculum-Based Measurement: District level implementation. In J. Graden, J. Zins, & M. Curtis (Eds.), *Alternative educational delivery systems: Enhancing instructional options for all students.* Washington, DC: National Association of School Psychologists.

McCollum, S., Tindal, G., & Nolet, V. (1992). *Content collaboration in middle schools: A case study supporting instruction in critical thinking skills* (Research Report No. 8). Eugene: University of Oregon Research, Consultation and Training Program.

Mirkin, P. K. (1980). Conclusions. In J. Ysseldyke & M. Thurlow (Eds.), *The special education assessment and decision-making process: Seven case studies.* Minneapolis: University of Minnesota Institute for Research on Learning Disabilities.

Nazzaro, J. (1976). Comprehensive assessment for educational planning. In F. Weintraub, A. Abeson, J. Ballard, & M. LaVor (Eds.), *Public policy and the education of exceptional children.* Reston, VA: The Council for Exceptional Children.

Reynolds, M. C. (1982). The rights of children: A challenge to school psychologists. In T. R. Kratochwill (Ed.), *Advances in school psychology* (Vol. II). Hillsdale, NJ: Lawrence Erlbaum Associates.

Parsonen, B. S., & Baer, D. M. (1992). The visual analysis of data, and current research into the stimulus controlling it. In T. R. Kratochwill, & J. R. Levin (Eds.), *Single-case research design and analysis.* Hillsdale, NJ: Erlbaum.

Scott, L., & Goetz, E. Issues in the collection of in-class data by teachers. *Education and Treatment of Children, 3*(1), 65–71.

Starlin, C., & Starlin, A. (1974). *Guidelines for continuous decision making.* Bemidji, MN: Unique Curriculums Unlimited.

Tawney, J. W., & Gast, D. L. (1984). *Single subject research in special education.* Columbus, OH: Charles E. Merrill.

Thurlow, M., & Ysseldyke, J. (1982). Instructional planning: Information collected by school psychologists vs. information considered useful by teachers. *Journal of School Psychology, 20*(1), 3–10.

Tindal, G. (1985). Investigating the effectiveness of special education: An analysis of methodology. *Journal of Learning Disabilities, 18,* 101–112.

Wahler, R., & Leske, G. (1974). Accurate and inaccurate summary reports: Reinforcement theory interpretation and investigation. *Journal of Nervous and Mental Disease, 156,* 386–394.

White, O., & Haring, N. (1985). *Exceptional teaching* (2nd ed.). Columbus, OH: Merrill.

Yell, M., Deno, S. L., & Marston, D. (1992). Barriers to implementing Curriculum-Based Measurement. *Diagnostiqué, 18*(1), 99–112.

Ysseldyke, J., Algozzine, B., Regan, R., & Potter, M. (1980). Technical adequacy of tests used by professionals in simulated decision-making. *Psychology in the Schools, 17,* 202–209.

ANNOTATED BIBLIOGRAPHY

Fuchs, L. S., & Deno, S. L. (1991). Paradigmatic distinctions between instructionally relevant measurement models. *Exceptional Children, 57*(6), 488–500.
Examines important differences between the specific subskill mastery measurement and general outcome measurement models. Describes how Curriculum-Based Measures fit into the general outcome measurement model and why this performance-monitoring approach is a more relevant educational practice.

McCollum, S., Tindal, G., & Nolet, V. (1992). *Content collaboration in middle schools: A case study supporting instruction in critical thinking skills* (Research Report No. 8). Eugene: University of Oregon Research, Consultation and Training Project.
Describes the importance of performance monitoring in the consultative relationship. These authors propose some new approaches to frequently monitoring pupil progress in content areas such as social studies.

Marston, D., & Magnusson, D. (1988). Curriculum-Based Measurement: District level implementation. In J. Graden, J. Zins, & M. Curtis (Eds.), *Alternative educational delivery systems: Enhancing instructional options for all students.* Washington, DC: National Association of School Psychologists.
Describes the implementation of the performance-monitoring system known as Curriculum-Based Measurement in a large, urban school district. The article provides a philosophical framework, explains procedures for administration and scoring, and provides data on a variety of psychoeducational decisions in which CBM is utilized.

Shinn, M. (1990). *Curriculum-Based Measurement: Assessing special children.* New York: Guilford Press.
A thorough review of the theory, research, and applications of Curriculum-Based Measurement in special and regular education. An excellent resource book for this topic.

Tawney, J. W., & Gast, D. L. (1984). *Single subject research in special education.* Columbus, OH: Charles E. Merrill.
Reviews the theory and practice of behavioral approaches to evaluating student performance. Describes the essential characteristics of single subject designs and demonstrates why it is an effective methodology for studying the behavior of individuals.

52

Best Practices in School Consultation

Joseph E. Zins
University of Cincinnati

William P. Erchul
North Carolina State University

OVERVIEW

Consultation has become one of the primary job functions of many school psychologists. This trend in practice is supported by a mounting body of empirical evidence demonstrating the efficacy of consultative services (e.g., Medway & Updyke, 1985), although there continues to be great need for further research on all aspects of the process.

Our goal in this chapter is a very practical one. We intend to present essential information about what a school psychologist needs to do to be an effective school consultant. Although considerable theoretical and empirical literature is cited, we have no aspirations about providing a thorough review of it, as such information is available elsewhere (e.g., Erchul, 1993; Zins, Kratochwill, & Elliott, 1993). Further, we assume that most readers already have at least an introductory-level understanding of consultation. For those who wish more detail than can be provided in this brief discussion, several recommended references are listed in the annotated bibliography at the end of the chapter.

The chapter begins with a presentation of our conceptualization of consultation, along with the prerequisite competencies and assumptions underlying practice. Next, practical guidelines for best practices in consultation are discussed, including a description of the consultative problem-solving process, and of individual and organizational factors that may exert influence. Finally, several emerging areas of practice are presented.

BASIC CONSIDERATIONS

Several approaches to consultation frequently employed in the schools have been described in the literature, namely, the behavioral, mental health, and organizational. Although universally accepted definitions for these approaches do not exist, and the models were not specifically developed for practice in the schools, the approaches have a number of elements in common. For instance, all stress the use of problem solving as the mechanism through which consultative interventions are developed, focus on work-related problems, and view participation in the process as voluntary. However, they differ in aspects such as the roles and relationships of consultants and consultees, the focus of consultative interventions, and the organizational level at which they are implemented. Despite the differences and lack of agreement in definition, the approaches are more similar than different, and consensus is emerging regarding key elements of the process (Zins et al., 1993).

The approach to consultation described in this chapter borrows heavily from a variety of models, but theoretically is most closely aligned with the ecobehavioral approach, which combines the behavioral and ecological/systems paradigms (Gutkin, 1993). It emphasizes the application of behavioral technology and utilization of the broad-based ecological/system perspective. We have extended the most salient aspects of a number of prior works, added some new ideas, and synthesized this information into a coherent framework specific to practice in the schools. Schools are different from other settings such as hospitals, correctional facilities, or business organizations, and because context is such an important aspect of consultation, it is desirable to limit the focus to school consultation. Such an approach also provides the latitude to discuss the various types of consultation that occur within schools, including consultation with individual teachers and parents, with groups of consultees, and systemwide consultation directed toward changing entire educational organizations.

Definition of School Consultation

In this chapter, school consultation is defined as a method of providing preventively oriented psychological and educational services in which consultants and consultees form cooperative partnerships and engage in a reciprocal, systematic problem-solving process within an ecobehavioral framework. The goal is to enhance and empower consultee systems, thereby promoting students' well-being and performance. A brief explanation of the essential components and underlying assumptions of this definition follows. Although ideas from many sources form the basis of this discussion, it is difficult to attribute original responsibility for many of the concepts. As Gutkin and Curtis (1990) note, these ideas have by now been so widely discussed that they are part of the basic assumptions typically made about consultation (even though not all have been empirically validated).

Preventive orientation. Consultation has a dual focus. It provides a mechanism through which the presenting problem is remediated, and secondarily, it attempts to increase consultees' skills and alter environmental variables and setting events that elicit and maintain problematic behaviors. These procedures are intended to prevent problems from becoming more severe and additional ones from arising.

The first goal is met by developing specific, empirically based interventions to deal with the presenting problem. The second is accomplished in a less direct manner by (a) ensuring that the consultant's expertise is readily available to the consultee system through encouragement of frequent interactions between consultants and consultees to facilitate the prevention and early identification of problem behaviors; (b) improving consultees' skills and knowledge so they can more effectively address similar problems in the future; (c) maintaining a systems perspective so that the broad array of conditions that might contribute to problem development and maintenance are considered and can be addressed; and (d) developing and implementing primary and secondary prevention programs. According to the literature, in most cases it is necessary for consultees to solve several problem situations successfully with the consultant's assistance before they apply these procedures independently, as training to a single exemplar is ineffective as a means of promoting generalization (Stokes & Baer, 1977). Even when consultation is applied in a clearly rehabilitative fashion, a primary intent is to minimize the possibility that more serious problems will arise. In practice, this preventive goal is not accomplished as often or as easily as the first; nevertheless, it should be pursued to enhance the overall value of the consultation process.

The increasingly preventive focus of consultation is gradually shifting the focus from individual children to entire systems — schools, school districts, the larger community, and even relevant state and federal policies, regulations, and legislation (Swift & Cooper, 1986). Practitioners, who are often frustrated by the limitations of focusing interventions on individual children are now recognizing the potential efficacy and long-term benefits of wide-scale interventions (see Knoff & Batsche, 1993, for illustration).

Method to provide services. Consultation is a means by which school psychological services are provided, or what Miller (1969) might describe as another way of "giving psychology away" to nonpsychologists. Indeed, consultation is often the foundation or overarching framework from which all other services are delivered and around which all other services are organized. The goal is to help clients (usually students) and the consultee system. Students are assisted indirectly through the process, in contrast to the direct method of providing service traditionally associated with psychoeducational assessment or counseling. However, we usually do not use the term *indirect* in discussions with educational decision makers because of a concern about the negative connotations that some occasionally attribute to it. These persons may mistakenly believe that all students benefit best from "direct" forms of help, and may not fully understand how consultation actually facilitates the provision of such assistance. Further, even when providing a direct service to a child, consultation with primary caregivers is crucial to ensure comprehensive assessment and treatment.

Cooperative partnership. Consultants and consultees work together to solve problems, and it is highly desirable for them to do so within a relationship that emphasizes trust, openness, and a sharing of responsibilities and expertise. In the phrase "cooperative partnership," *cooperative* implies that (a) participants work jointly on as equal a basis as possible (realizing that their levels of need are unequal and their areas of expertise are often divergent), and that (b) they have different contributions to make and varying responsibilities to uphold to maximize consultation effectiveness. *Partnership* implies that these responsibilities are clearly specified and mutually agreed upon to facilitate progress toward common goals.

In terms of specific responsibilities, consultees must provide contextual ecological information to help define problems and develop interventions. They also must assist in determining what interventions can be implemented in their setting and within their repertoire of skills. Both participants have responsibility for defining and analyzing problems, for establishing and maintaining the cooperative partnership, and for conducting follow-up activities.

Although consultants and consultees both contribute to problem solving, the consultant structures and guides the overall process, while consultees supply much of the content of the discussion. Consultee attempts to control the direction of the initial consultation interview have been linked to a variety of negative outcomes (Erchul & Chewning, 1990). However, because consultees (a) retain responsibility for the client, (b) can best judge treatment acceptability, and

(c) usually implement most interventions and thus can ensure treatment integrity, they make the final decisions regarding intervention implementation. Because the latter point is also a potential problem (Gutkin & Conoley, 1990), it is incumbent on consultants to work with consultees to ensure that these decisions are made in an informed and carefully thought-out manner. Finally, the consultant has primary (but not sole) responsibility for (a) ensuring that the atmosphere remains nonevaluative, (b) identifying and presenting interventions for possible implementation in many cases, and (c) developing the evaluation plan. Given these different responsibilities for consultees and consultants, a complementary and interdependent working relationship is needed.

The importance of the cooperative partnership is illustrated in a study by Erchul, Hughes, Meyers, Hickman, and Braden (1992), who studied 61 school consultant-consultee dyads. These researchers found that the more the consultant and consultee agreed on their respective roles, as well as on the process and goals of consultation, the more positive were consultee evaluations of various consultation outcomes, including consultant effectiveness. Although Erchul et al. used the term *teamwork* to characterize the nature of the desirable consultative relationship, their conceptualization is consistent with the cooperative partnership described here. In sum, in a cooperative partnership the possibilities that more creative solutions to problems will emerge are increased, consultee ownership of the intervention plan and commitment to carrying it out are enhanced, and consultee self-efficacy is improved.

Reciprocal interactions. The principles regarding the reciprocal nature of consultative interactions are derived from Bandura's (1977) social learning theory and philosophy of reciprocal determinism. Indeed, these two paradigms serve as a "meta-theory" underlying consultation practice (Zins, 1988). Unidirectional influence approaches usually have predominated descriptions of the interactions between psychologists and those they seek to assist (Tyler, Pargament, & Gatz, 1983), but they do not adequately reflect the complexity of the consultation process. According to Bandura's model, consultant, consultee, and student functioning result from the continuous and reciprocal interactions among behavioral, personal, and environmental factors. During the interpersonal exchanges that constitute consultation, participants exert influence on one another, and their personal perspectives and behaviors usually are altered as a result (Reardon, 1991). The challenge for consultants is to maintain a cooperative partnership while at the same time exerting interpersonal influence. Consultants accomplish this goal by establishing an atmosphere of mutual respect and trust, and by moving the process along through appropriate interviewing techniques. Consultees influence consultants

primarily by specifying the assets and constraints of their role, the students, and the setting. Students likewise influence consultants and consultees as well as the entire system. "Therefore, understanding and changing the functioning of a consultee or clients must focus on the interlocking relationship of these three [behavioral, personal, and environmental] factors, not on a single dimension" (Brown & Schulte, 1987, p. 283).

Systematic problem-solving process. Problem solving proceeds through an orderly, systematic sequence of steps as discussed in detail later in the chapter (see Table 1), and the process is dynamic, evolving, flexible, and cyclical in nature (Kurpius & Lewis, 1988). The consultant guides the overall process, but the active joint involvement of all participants is essential to maximize the potential for successful solutions to be developed and implemented. Moreover, formal, written documentation is kept regarding intervention development and outcomes to foster follow-up efforts and to increase accountability.

Ecobehavioral perspective. The behavioral paradigm has dominated the consultation field in recent years, but ecological/systems theories are now offered as means of expanding traditional behavioral approaches (Gutkin, 1993). Both make important contributions to understanding the process.

Behavioral theory provides the experimental rigor and methodology necessary to concisely identify and measure problems, analyze forces influencing problem situations, and evaluate intervention outcomes. In addition, there is an extensive array of behavioral interventions with documented success available for implementation through the consultation process (Elliott & Busse, 1993).

Ecological and systems perspectives offer a useful framework for more broadly conceptualizing the setting or organizational context in which consultation occurs, and they expand the goals of traditional case-centered consultation. The connection between a problem and the system variables that may be contributing to it or preventing its resolution must be examined. This perspective widens the focus beyond the individual child to also include peers, family, teachers, classrooms, curricula, schools, community, other system levels, and so forth. Consequently, a wide array of factors that may be contributing to the problem are always considered in identifying problems and in developing interventions.

Means of empowerment. The empowerment philosophy in consultation "requires different assumptions and behaviors on the part of the consultant than does traditional case-centered problem solving" (Witt & Martens, 1988, p. 213). This ideology recognizes more explicitly that consultees and con-

TABLE 1
Consultative Problem-Solving Process

1. **Establishment of Cooperative Partnership**

2. **Problem Identification and Analysis**
   Define problem in behavioral terms and obtain agreement with consultee.
   Collect baseline data regarding problem frequency, duration, and/or intensity and conduct task analysis as needed.
   Identify antecedent determinants of the problem behavior.
   Identify consequences that may maintain the behavior.
   Assess other relevant environmental factors.
   Identify all available resources.

3. **Intervention Selection and Development**
   Brainstorm range of possible interventions.
   Evaluate the positive and negative aspects of the interentions.
   Select intervention(s) from the alternatives generated.

4. **Intervention Implementation, Evaluation, and Follow-up**
   Clarify implementation procedures and responsibilities.
   Implement the chosen strategy.
   Evaluate intended outcomes and any side effects.
   Program generalization, plan maintenance, and develop fading procedures as appropriate.
   Recycle and follow-up as necessary.

sultee systems already possess or can readily develop most competencies necessary to deal with student-related problems, given the right opportunities and knowledge of available resources (Rappoport, 1981). They have a basic level of competence, but not necessarily the technical knowledge or skills to solve a particular problem. Thus, consultees' failure to solve problems is often a reflection of the system's failure to create opportunities or to provide support for them to exhibit these skills, rather than only an indication of their lack of knowledge about how to deal with the problem. The implications for consultants are significant. Their role becomes one of helping consultees to clarify needs and locate resources, and of ensuring that opportunities are available to enable consultees to engage in self-sustaining behaviors to resolve problems.

Enhancement of student well-being and performance. Although consultation usually focuses on improving consultees' skills and performance or changing their behavior, the ultimate beneficiary is always intended to be the student. To arrive at this goal, however, it is often appropriate for the entire school district or some segment of it to be the initial target of change, as in an organizational development program.

Other characteristics implicit in definition. The problems addressed are always work- or caregiving-related rather than personal. In addition, material discussed is considered confidential by consultants, consultation is entered into voluntarily by consultees, and the relationship is temporary. Gutkin and Curtis

(1990) have discussed these issues as well as other core characteristics of consultation in great detail.

Prerequisite Competencies and Assumptions of Consultation Practice

In addition to a general knowledge of psychological principles and techniques (e.g., human learning, ethics, social bases of behavior, research methodologies), there are other prerequisites to consultation practice.

Prerequisites and competencies. A sense of self-awareness with respect to one's feelings, beliefs, thoughts, and impact on others and personal clarity regarding one's values and theoretical biases are helpful to consultants (O'Neill & Trickett, 1982). Because a large aspect of the consultation process involves interpersonal interaction and influence, consultants must be cognizant of their own interpersonal styles, biases, and values, and of how these can impact consultees and influence problem solving.

Similarly, good interpersonal and communication skills are critical because consultation relies heavily on the interpersonal influence process to accomplish its goals. Consultants need, for instance, to be active listeners and to utilize effective questioning techniques to extract necessary information from consultees and to develop clear conceptualizations of problems. Further, the establishment of warm, caring, and understanding relationships is as important in consultation as it is in counseling.

Knowledge of intervention technology, both individually and organizationally focused, likewise is an essential competency, but one that has been largely neglected in the consultation literature. Gutkin (1981) found that over two-thirds of the reasons consultees sought assistance were related to their lack of knowledge and skills in resolving problems, although he did not use an empowerment framework for categorizing these reasons. The implication is that process skills are important but not sufficient for resolving most issues in consultation. Problem-solving and applied behavior analysis skills are also critical. Further, the goal of consultation is to promote application of effective interventions by consultees. Unless consultants are successful in this endeavor, schools will be less likely to use this technology to benefit students, no matter how potentially effective it is (Wolfe, 1978).

An understanding and knowledge of organizations and of organizational functioning is necessary for an ecological/systems perspective. Too often, school psychology training and daily practice tend to focus on the assessment and remediation of individual student-related problems, and consequently do not attend to more global and macro-level variables that exert significant influence. Thus, "consultants need an understanding of the workplace [school] not only as a technological system but also as a complex social organization" (Gallessich, 1982, p. 5). School norms, values, philosophy, and organizational climate can greatly facilitate or impede the consultative process.

An awareness of cultural, racial, ethnic, and gender issues and a sensitivity to them are important social dynamics in the consultative relationship. These various sociocultural factors, although not often discussed in the context of consultation, can exert considerable influence on the communication process, development of trust, reciprocal and mutual understanding, and overall relationship development. In addition, they have been found to affect help-seeking patterns and utilization of services, attitudes toward self-disclosure, duration of treatment, and outcome of treatment (Gibbs, 1985; Lorion, 1978). Further, the power-authority dimension of consultation can be affected by these issues, especially when one participant is a member of a minority and the other belongs to a majority group.

Assumptions. In addition to the above competencies, several assumptions underlie consultation. First is a belief that most parents, teachers, and other school personnel usually want to be involved in the problem-solving process. We recognize that there is a subset of people who (a) wish to be told what to do rather than jointly develop interventions; (b) do not want to deal personally with the presenting problem for some reason, but rather desire and expect someone else to do it (e.g., want a child placed in another classroom); (c) fail or refuse to recognize the existence of a problem situation and thus do not seek consultative assistance; (d) do not have the skills or interests necessary to implement various interventions; or (e) face organizational restraints that prohibit or minimize their participation in the process. In addition to these groups, there are potential consultees who expect the consultant to "tell them what to do" based on their previous experiences with helping professionals, when in fact they actually would like to be involved in the problem-solving process (Zins & Curtis, 1981). This group can best be dealt with through an educative process about consultation.

A second assumption is that prevention and early intervention are advantageous for most children. There is a growing, convincing body of literature that supports this assumption (e.g., Price, Cowen, Lorion, & Ramos-McKay, 1988), although there remains a clear need for additional research regarding the preventive aspects of consultation. Third, as noted earlier, vast intervention technology exists that can be applied to address the problems experienced by children. The challenge is how to apply it within the constraints of the school setting.

Finally, all school psychological services to children and schools are best provided through a consultative framework. That is, virtually all requests for assistance in dealing with a problem should begin with consultation. Thus, services such as psychoeducational assessment and counseling are viewed as components of problem clarification or as interventions developed to solve the problem.

BEST PRACTICES

Consultative Problem-solving Process

Problem solving is the essence of consultation. It includes a number of steps: relationship development, initial designation of the problem, development and implementation of an intervention plan, evaluation of goal attainment and plan effectiveness, and planning for generalization, maintenance, and follow-up (Bergan & Kratochwill, 1990). As indicated in the following pages, it is necessary to engage in multiple levels of problem analysis and intervention development during this process. Because consultation is an indirect service, it requires that changes be brought about on more than just the individual student level. Child-related difficulties often result, at least in part, from ineffective instructional or classroom management strategies or from other causes external to the child. Consequently, it is essential to remain aware of the link between changes in the environment or in consultees' behavior and changes in the target student(s) (Hawryluk & Smallwood, 1986). In addition, it is often necessary for consultative interventions to occur at several organizational levels.

An ecological/systems perspective provides participants with a framework for developing a broad conceptualization of problems and for examining the wide range of factors that could be contributing to a problem, enabling them to avoid developing simplistic explanations for problems. As stated above, problem analysis includes a thorough assessment of consultee variables as well as other factors affecting student behavior. For example, inaccurate perceptions or expectations of a child's behavior by the consultee may contribute to a problem. Research in the area of attributions has shown that teachers generally perceive problems to be caused by factors internal to a child or due to home variables (Medway, 1979). Although child or home issues may contribute to a problem, they should not automatically be considered the only cause. Student-related problems usually result from complex reciprocal interactions between the child's behavior and the environmental and/or instructional conditions that regularly exist in a particular classroom, school, or community. Therefore, as the participants in the consultation process define and analyze problems, information should be gathered not only about the child and the immediate contingencies affecting his or her behavior, but also about the ecology of the classroom, school, and community, or the home environment itself. Obtaining a broader perspective of the problem and reconceptualizing important variables as being within teachers' or parents' power to change will impact on their causal attributions and expectations for problem resolution, as well as on the types of intervention strategies considered.

Establishing a cooperative partnership. The overall consultation process begins with establishment of a cooperative partnership (Table 1). Relationship building is a critical element of the process, beginning with the consultant's initial entry into the school and continuing throughout the proceedings. When a consultant and consultee meet for the first time, each participant attempts to become better acquainted with the other, both strive to create an atmosphere of mutual respect and trust, and together they develop a "working contract" — a basic understanding of what will occur during consultation. The contract minimally specifies the roles and responsibilities of each party, expected activities, and anticipated timeline for the consultation.

Two points in the process require clarification. First, although the steps in the problem-solving process are presented separately in this chapter, they usually overlap and thus may not occur in the exact sequence described here. Also, because of space limitations, examples in this chapter primarily refer to one-to-one consultations occurring between a school psychologist and a teacher, but they are clearly applicable to a wide range of situations (e.g., group and organizational consultations).

Clarifying the problem. The second step is to clearly define the presenting problem(s) in clear, concise, complete, and measurable terms. Because there is a level of interdependence that exists between the

problem definition and the proposed intervention (Gutkin & Curtis, 1990), the following objectives need to be considered during this phase. First, consultants should help consultees describe concerns, goals, and expectations in a behaviorally specific manner. Consultees often do not have clear conceptualizations of problems when they request assistance, and they consequently present information in vague, global terms. Through skillful questioning, paraphrasing, and summarizing, a broad array of variables associated with a problem can be brought to their attention and then defined in measurable terms (see guidelines in Table 2). The collection of baseline data is an essential component of this step. Often it is expedient to divide a complex problem into its component parts, thereby helping to ensure that neither participant is overwhelmed, and that both can work toward a useful problem analysis.

At times, more than one problem may be designated, in which case they must be prioritized according to the perceived level of concern. With respect to an individual student, target behaviors can be ranked as (a) behaviors considered to be physically dangerous to self or others; (b) positive low-frequency behaviors in need of strengthening; (c) behaviors that can be naturally reinforced in the environment; (d) behaviors viewed as essential for development; and (e) behaviors that maximize functioning in a variety of settings. Further, all target behaviors selected should be consistent with developmental norms (see Kratochwill, 1985, for an excellent summary of issues in target selection). Although target behaviors are often some aspect of the child's behavior or performance, this does not imply that the child should be the only focus of the intervention. Consultees' perceptions or environmental and instructional variables are often what is changed. For example, use of teacher praise and feedback, or opportunities for students to respond in the classroom, may be altered. However, the effects of these changes are still measured in terms of student outcomes.

Questions may be raised during the problem identification (i.e., initial) interview that need to be answered by additional methods of assessment. Direct classroom observations, utilization of curriculum-based probes, analysis of student permanent products, or assessment of organizational communication or structure are among the procedures that may be considered to help answer these questions (Zins, Curtis, Graden, & Ponti, 1988).

Target behaviors must be defined in concise, measurable terms. Consultants and consultees should agree on the definition, and it should be worded in such a way that both parties (and others) can reliably record its occurrence. For instance, if lack of motivation is identified as a problem, it could be operationally defined in terms of "number of spelling assignments completed on time each day in school, and percent of correct responses." This defin-

TABLE 2
Guidelines for Behaviorally Oriented Problem Identification Interview

1. **Define the Problem.**

   Clarify vague general statements regarding the consultee's concerns. ("You say that Rob is aggressive toward other children. Can you give me some specific examples of his aggressive behavior?")

   Develop an operational definition of the problem. Define the problem in measurable terms. Make it specific enough that others will be able to recognize it when they see it.

   Collect information about the frequency and duration of the problem. ("How many times per day does Mary shout out in class? How long does each episode of behavior last and for what length of time has the problem been occurring?") Baseline data should be collected.

   Assess intensity or severity of behavior. ("Describe what types of things Brian does when he throws a temper tantrum.")

   If more than one problem is presented, prioritize and select one target behavior on which to work initially.

2. **Identify Antecedent Determinants of the Problem Behavior.**

   Identify temporal and situational antecedents. ("Are there times of the day when the behavior occurs most frequently? In which settings does the behavior occur?")

   Identify the behavior of others that may trigger or maintain the behavior. ("It seems that whenever you are paying attention to other children, John's disruptive behavior intensifies.")

   Identify and analyze conditions that alleviate the problem. ("Does Sue seem to work better when you have structured her independent seatwork time through the use of goal setting and a timer?")

3. **Identify Consequences That May Maintain the Behavior.**

   Explore positive consequences that currently are provided or could be instituted to improve behavior or performance. ("What do you do when Joe completes all of his homework?" "What things does Cindy really like to do?")

   Explore forms of inappropriate reinforcement or attention operating.

4. **Assess Other Relevant Environmental Variables.**

   Identify significant others in the child's environment and assess their attitudes, attributions, and expectations regarding the problem and the child in general.

   Assess the discrepancy between the child's behavior and expected behavior. ("Howard is out of his seat on an average of 15 times per half hour period. How many times would it be acceptable for him to be out of his seat within this time period in your classroom?")

   Assess relevant instructional variables and classroom or home routines.

5. **Identify All Available Resources.**

   Identify the strengths of the child. ("What types of things does Lisa do well?" "In what subject areas is William succeeding?")

   Identify materials and human resources available for intervention (e.g., peer tutors, parent volunteers, special instructional materials).

Note. Adapted from Peterson (1968).

ition is specific, easily measurable, and understandable to all.

   Problem analysis. Once the target behaviors have been identified, a comprehensive functional analysis of the interaction that exists between the child's behavior and the environment is conducted (see Gresham, 1991). The baseline data and results of the assessment procedures are key components of this step, as they provide a first-hand look at the complex interactions that occur between students, consultees, and their daily environments. Temporal and situational antecedents that appear to contribute to

the problematic behavior should be identified. In addition, situations in which the behavior of concern does not occur can be noted, and consequences operating to maintain the behavior can be recorded. When identifying consequences, consultants should obtain information on (a) appropriate positive reinforcement that is given, (b) forms of inappropriate reinforcement or attention gained by exhibiting the behavior, (c) the schedules of reinforcement in operation, and (d) reinforcement histories.

   Relevant environmental and instructional variables that operate regularly within a child's classroom or the larger context must also be identified and analyzed. For instance, a consultant could determine whether the teacher had developed a set of rules to establish consequences for particular behaviors, how consistently the rules are enforced, amount of reinforcement available to the child from sources other than the teacher, peer reactions to the target behavior, opportunities the student is given to respond (both oral and written), method and delay in providing instructional and behavioral feedback, and appropriateness of curriculum (Witt & Martens, 1988). For academic problems, a task analysis of student skills in a particular subject may be necessary through methods such as curriculum-based assessment/measurement, examination of permanent products, and think-aloud techniques. Teacher and/or parent perceptions and expectations also should be explored to help them understand the broad array of factors that could be influencing the child's behavior or performance. As a result, they must be more open to making needed changes in behavior management or instructional strategies. Finally, other variables such as peer interactions and school norms should be examined.

Instructional practices of teachers and daily classroom, school, and home routines also need to be clarified to obtain a broad ecological perspective. Many problems that appear to be individually based are not; on closer examination it may be seen that they require systems-level intervention. Traditionally, however, not much attention has been given to the environments of children and the adults who function in their environments. Nevertheless, it is the adults, not the child, who primarily control the environment in which a child functions (Saxe, Cross, & Silverman, 1988). In addition, teachers may require help in operationalizing what is acceptable behavior or performance in the classroom so that reasonable goals for the child can be developed.

Finally, all resources that potentially can be utilized in the development and implementation of interventions must be identified. These include student strengths, aspects of the system that are helping the child be successful in other situations, and material and human resources (teacher, time, parents, peer and volunteer tutors, community support systems) available for intervention.

Brainstorming and exploring intervention options. Once the problem is clearly defined and analyzed, the level of intervention must be determined. For example, a program could be developed for an individual student, the focus could be on helping a teacher change instructional practices or behavior management strategies used for an entire class, the district's reading curriculum could be altered, or its policy on corporal punishment could be modified. When participants agree on the level of intervention, they then generate as many treatment options as pos-

sible. The cardinal rule of this phase is to avoid evaluating ideas until the brainstorming process is completed. There often is more than one way to resolve a problem, and by generating a number of possible solutions, the probability is maximized of identifying an intervention that will be both effective and acceptable to the consultee.

Interventions usually consist of some form of environmental manipulation because (a) there is substantial research specifying what types of environments lead to effective teaching, parenting, and behavioral change; (b) all consultees routinely manipulate meaningful school and home environmental variables; and (c) most consultees do not have the skills to engage in nonenvironmental manipulations such as counseling. Examples of variables that can be considered for manipulation include reinforcement and punishment contingencies, curriculum content, instructional techniques, teacher behavior, peer and sibling behavior, physical arrangement of the home and classroom, and the school administration (Gutkin & Curtis, 1990).

Selecting an intervention. After a number of intervention ideas have been generated, each should be evaluated to determine potential benefits and risks for the child, unintended side effects, and feasibility of implementation. There generally are no "packaged" solutions to problems. A taxonomy of interventions related to a corresponding taxonomy of diagnoses does not exist (Gutkin & Curtis, 1990); therefore, treatments selected during consultation are simply high-probability hypotheses. After a careful analysis of the problem is conducted, hypotheses are formulated regarding what is eliciting and maintaining the behavior or situation, and intervention strategies are developed from this information. Although the consultant guides this problem-solving process and maintains primary responsibility for providing adequate information about the various intervention procedures identified, both contribute to the process and the ultimate selection of strategies rests with the consultee. The following guidelines are useful in generating and selecting interventions.

1. Implement positive intervention approaches before resorting to behavior suppression or reduction techniques in all but extreme cases.

2. Choose the least complex and least intrusive intervention possible. To the extent possible and appropriate, the focus should be on helping consultees to modify instructional variables or general behavior management strategies. Alterations in existing techniques usually are less intrusive or aversive to teachers than is learning a new procedure.

3. When a new skill must be developed by the consultee, design it to fit into the present structure and routines as much as possible.

4. Develop a pool of resources, such as peer and volunteer tutors or community resources, that can be utilized when changes in the classroom are not possible or not sufficient to resolve the presenting problem.

5. Provide support and reinforcement to consultees for implementing the intervention. Because a behavior change on consultees' part is often required, consultant support will encourage their continued enthusiasm and adherence in treatment implementation.

6. Promote interventions that require less time, are ecologically unintrusive, and are perceived by consultees to be effective. These types of interventions tend to be more acceptable to consultees (Elliott, 1988).

7. Finally, focus intervention efforts on promoting change at the highest organizational level possible.

Clarifying implementation procedures and responsibilities. Just as the nature of consultation was clarified in the initial meeting, the pragmatic aspects of implementation should be clarified once the intervention is selected. First, the roles and responsibilities of all participants with regard to the intervention must be delineated and agreed upon. The specific techniques should be outlined in a step-by-step fashion and potential reinforcers identified (often through a formal reinforcer assessment). The time(s) of the day and the settings or subject areas in which the intervention will be implemented must be decided. At this point, consideration should be given to programming for generalization. Specific suggestions for maximizing the probability that behavior change will generalize across time, persons, and settings are provided later in the chapter. All aspects of the plan should be put in writing at least in outline form (often in a written protocol format), so each person involved has a clear idea of her or his responsibilities. This written plan also serves as a record for accountability purposes.

Implementing the strategy. Once the intervention plan is developed, consultants should keep in close contact with consultees to aid in implementation, provide technical assistance, and reinforce consultees' efforts. Consultees often have questions about the details of the plan, unanticipated behaviors may arise, or there may be unintended reactions from other children. Consultants can enhance consultees' motivation by involving them in goal setting, establishing a trusting and warm relationship, and demonstrating personal competence (Brown & Schulte, 1987). Further, if an intervention requires the consultee to learn a new skill or to make substantial changes in current practices, it often is helpful for the consultant to model the procedure, observe the consultee implementing it, and provide constructive, supportive feedback. All of these elements — ongoing contact, adequate training, and support — are crucial for increasing and ensuring treatment integrity and success.

Consultees' resistance to a planned intervention may occur, although it can be minimized through establishment of a cooperative, supportive partnership. However, consultants must remember that the consultation process may (a) require considerable consultee effort and time, (b) focus on consultee failure, (c) involve differing perspectives of desirable outcomes, and (d) not result in immediate problem resolution (Piersel & Gutkin, 1983). Because each of these possibilities is nonreinforcing for consultees, at least on a short term basis, it is understandable that resistance is often encountered. By being aware of the potentially negative aspects of consultation, consultants may be better prepared to deal with any resistance. Further, there are many legitimate problems that consultees face that may prevent them from being able to carry out interventions as planned.

Evaluating intervention effectiveness and follow-up. There are several interrelated aspects of this stage of the problem-solving process, including evaluation of intervention effectiveness, generalization, fading, and follow-up.

Evaluation of intervention effectiveness. Once the intervention plan is implemented, it should be systematically and regularly monitored to ensure treatment integrity and to identify any unintended side effects. Of course, the evaluation plan should be agreed upon before intervention implementation begins. Generally, the same data collection procedures used to obtain baseline information can be applied again as a means of evaluation. These methods should be as simple and time-efficient as possible, so that a teacher, student, parent, or peer can easily use the system. Single-subject methodologies such as single phase, reversal, or multiple baseline designs are often used to evaluate intervention effectiveness. These evaluation procedures may suggest that (a) the intervention resulted in attainment of desired goals, thereby indicating that follow-up monitoring and/or generalization and fading procedures are needed, or (b) the intended outcomes were not reached entirely, suggesting the need to recycle through earlier problem-solving steps.

Generalization, facing, and follow-up. Evaluation data will indicate the degree to which the intervention is producing the desired outcome. Once an effective and reliable procedure has been identified, the intervention can be extended to other settings or systematically faded.

Although there are many well-developed, validated techniques for bringing about behavior changes, we know substantially less about how to maintain these gains. A number of suggestions, however, have been offered in the literature on how to program generalization as interventions are developed and as they are implemented (Meichenbaum & Turk, 1987). Selected reinforcers, for instance, should be naturally occurring events when possible, and techniques should be implemented that lend themselves to fading or to greater transfer of control to the student (i.e., self-management approaches). Students should take an active role in intervention development when possible, and efforts should be made to help them understand the usefulness and relevance of the intervention to their lives. Training should take place in a number of settings and should involve multiple tasks and trainers. Finally, opportunities to confront and deal positively with failure or mistakes also should be built into the intervention procedures.

Interventions that include specific prompts or reinforcement contingencies need to be faded systematically once the child is performing at desired levels. It is important to withdraw prompts or reinforcements in small steps rather than all at once to ensure maintenance of treatment gains. Fading can consist of increasing the amount of time before a child can earn a reinforcer, increasing task demands to earn a reinforcer, or decreasing the number of prompts given to children to elicit performance. If at any step in the fading process the student's behavior begins to deteriorate, reinforcement or prompting should revert to the previous level. Once the child's behavior stabilizes again for a period of time, fading can be continued.

The importance of follow-up by consultants during this stage is critical, although it is often neglected. Follow-up helps ensure that intervention procedures are being implemented correctly, and it can address the issue of unintended outcomes. When interventions provide ineffective or unreliable outcomes, consultants should observe them in operation and conduct a functional analysis of the current situation to determine what conditions might be contributing to the nonattainment of the desired goals. Oftentimes, modifications in the existing plan that are suggested through corrective feedback are all that is necessary to increase ease of implementation, improve intervention effectiveness, or counteract unanticipated student responses. If the alterations do not result in better outcomes, a new strategy should be sought, once again through the problem-solving process.

Influences on the Consultation Process

Central to the success of the consultation process are the issues of treatment acceptability, adherence, and integrity. Consideration of these issues, and the establishment of a cooperative partnership can be major factors in decreasing or avoiding resistance. Acceptability refers to judgments or beliefs of consultees and students about whether a treatment is "appropriate, fair, and reasonable for the problem or client" (Kazdin, 1981, p. 493). As Wolfe (1978) notes, if participants like the intervention (i.e., find it acceptable), they may be more likely to use it or to carry it out correctly. Adherence involves the willingness of (a) the consultee to carry out the intervention to its completion, and (b) the student to engage in certain behavior changes indicated in the intervention plan (Meichenbaum & Turk, 1987). Treatment integrity, on the other hand, refers to the extent to which the consultee implements the intervention plan as intended (Gresham, 1989). Elliott (1988) proposes that the elements of acceptability, adherence, and integrity are reciprocally dependent, that is, they influence and are influenced by one another. Adherence and integrity are the two elements that link intervention use with effectiveness.

Because consultation is an indirect service and interventions are almost always implemented by consultees, there are two levels of acceptability and adherence related to the process. The first involves the extent to which the consultee is actively involved in carrying out a mutually acceptable course of action to produce a desired behavior change in a child. The second level involves the extent to which the child is involved in the process and cooperates with the treatment plan implemented by the consultee (Meichenbaum & Turk, 1987). Further, there are certain factors related to treatment integrity that affect implementation, including the complexity of the intervention, time required to implement the plan, materials or resources needed, number of treatment agents involved, perceived and actual effectiveness of the intervention, and motivation of the consultees (Gresham, 1989).

When interventions are not followed or result in failure, consultants most often cite consultee variables such as motivation or skill as the cause (Martin & Curtis, 1981). Although consultee motivation may play a role in the success or failure of consultation outcome in some cases, it is not the predominant variable, nor is it within the consultant's sphere of control. As indicated in Table 3, there are numerous factors that influence both adherence and treatment integrity. Although correlational in nature, these factors can provide useful guidelines for consultants interested in enhancing both adherence and treatment integrity on both the consultee and the student levels. It is evident from the literature, for instance, that relationship variables are of crucial importance. Adherence can be improved and resistance decreased through the establishment of a supportive, cooperative partnership characterized by open communication. As mentioned previously, efforts should be made early in the process to clarify consultee beliefs and expectations about the consultation process and about intervention options and outcomes. In addition, discrepancies between consultant and consultee

TABLE 3
Examples of Factors Affecting Treatment Adherence and Integrity

Client (Student) Variables
    Belief that a problem exists
    Belief that the problem could have a negative impact on the student
    Belief that participating in the intervention will help the student
    Perceptions regarding not having a choice about being treated

Consultee Variables
    Beliefs about potential efficacy of the intervention
    Understanding of the consultative process
    Satisfaction with the relationship with the consultant
    Misconceptions held
    Cultural beliefs and values
    Opportunities available to exhibit skills
    Beliefs about ability to carry out the intervention
    Personal motivation to resolve the problem
    Skills in describing problem situations and carrying out interventions
    Perceptions of consultant's expertise and competence

Consultant Variables
    Theoretical orientation and values
    Skills in problem solving
    Technical competence in intervention development and evaluation
    Understanding of organizational functioning and change
    Motivation and enthusiasm
    Self-awareness and understanding

Relationship Variables
    Interpersonal and communication factors
    Discrepancies between consultant and consultee attributions
    Participant sensitivity to cultural, racial, ethnic, and gender issues
    Extent of cooperation or mutual participation in process
    Continuity of involvement
    Extent of support and follow-up provided

Treatment Variables
    Complexity of the intervention
    Time and resources required to carry out the interventions
    Intrusiveness of intervention relative to established regularities
    Duration of intervention
    Number of behavior changes that are made at once
    Number of treatment agents involved
    How soon behavior chnage is observed

Organizational Variables
    Openness of social/organizatioal climate
    Opportunities and support provided for change
    Length of time until assistance is provided
    Perception of organizational support
    Time and resource availability
    Principal's leadership behavior

Note. Adapted from Gresham (1989), Gutkin (1986), and Meichenbaum and Turk (1987).

causal attributions for the problem need to be resolved during problem clarification (Zins, 1985).

Other factors that affect treatment adherence include characteristics of the intervention procedures chosen and the extent to which the client is involved in the process. A related issue is that of consultant adherence (Meichenbaum & Turk, 1987). Consultants need to be aware of their own beliefs regarding their ability to improve consultee and client adherence, make efforts to monitor their own interactions with consultees, and develop the type of consultative relationship that maximizes the probability of adherence. Finally, because consultation often results in short-term negative outcomes for consultees, as noted earlier, the importance of providing support and encouragement is underscored.

Organizational Consultation

School consultation is not limited to one-to-one interactions between a consultant and a consultee, or to behavioral change in individual students (although those are the foci of this chapter). At times consultation is expanded to include groups of consultees (as discussed below), an entire school, or even a school district. Consultants increasingly are focusing on larger organizational issues to expand and maximize their influence, and to deal with problems that truly are systemic in origin. The same problem-solving procedures described above are followed in these instances, but of course there is a different focus and other types of interventions are developed. However, behavior-analytic and social-learning procedures continue to be relevant. Examples of organizational consultation include involvement in the evaluation of a districtwide program for gifted students, establishment of a smoking prevention program in a middle school, development of a program for senior high students to encourage safety belt use and avoidance of alcohol, implementation of a tutoring program that utilizes the services of volunteer senior citizens, and initiation of a health promotion program for school employees. There continues to be a need to develop new approaches that will expand opportunities to intervene to help students, and broad, systems-level approaches are essential in this respect.

Emerging Areas of Practice

Consultation practice in schools continues to grow and evolve rapidly. Below are four issues we believe will become more prominent in the future.

Group consultation. The "spread of effect" nature of consultation holds that a consultant, by working directly with a single consultee, can potentially affect the lives of numerous children (Gutkin & Curtis, 1990). Extending this approach, one can see the multiplicative impact of a consultant who sees many consultees over time. Taken one step further, if a consultant meets simultaneously with many consultees by using a group format, consultation's spread of effect may be maximized. Group consultation thus could be an efficient and cost-effective way of conducting school consultation. Also, to the extent the consultant is able to harness supportive elements of the group process, to keep a task focus, and to structure and organize the group, consultation outcomes may be more favorable than those resulting from a one-on-one approach (Wilcox, 1980).

Group consultation has rarely been discussed in the school psychology literature. However, given continuing and mounting demands on school psychologists' time, we believe greater attention should be, and will be, directed toward research and practice issues concerning school group consultation, perhaps in the context of intervention assistance programs.

Consultation vs. collaboration. When the consultant and consultee work in the same setting, many of the fundamental assumptions on which consultation is based are impractical or may prove difficult to follow. These assumptions include voluntary consultee participation (Harris & Cancelli, 1991), confidentiality of communications, complete consultee freedom to accept or reject advice, and lack of consultant responsibility for student outcome (Caplan & Caplan, 1993). In addition, school psychologists' frequently enhanced status (e.g., advanced degree, salary level) relative to that of consultees works against achieving equal relationships.

Given these circumstances, it may be advisable to reexamine aspects of the traditional consulting role of the school psychologist. As one alternative, Caplan and Caplan (1993) have proposed a model of mental health collaboration for internal consultants such as school psychologists. The primary differences between mental health consultation and mental health collaboration are that in collaboration (a) the school psychologist shares equal responsibility with the consultee for the overall outcome for the student, but primary responsibility for the mental health outcome; and (b) the consultee does not have the freedom to accept or reject advice, because the best possible course of action must be selected and implemented to improve the student's condition. Mental health collaboration involves not only direct intervention with the student by the school psychologist, but also efforts to educate and influence other school personnel with respect to the mental health aspects of their role in the case (Caplan & Caplan, 1993).

The potential utility of mental health collaboration is considerable, as collaboration has been consistently preferred over more indirect service approaches in studies of school personnel's service delivery preferences (Babcock & Pryzwansky, 1983). A collaborative approach, defined as consultation with an added direct service component, also has been shown to produce (a) favorable teacher perceptions regarding the effectiveness of consultation services, and (b) better academic outcomes for students with learning disabilities relative to pull-out programs (Schulte, Osborne, & McKinney, 1990).

Caplan (1993) proposes that collaboration ultimately should replace consultation as the preferred mode of interprofessional communication used by school psychologists. Whether this will occur will remain a matter of speculation for some time. However, based on early empirical evidence and the corresponding interest among other special services professionals (e.g., Morsink, Thomas, & Correa, 1991), there is good reason to explore the practice of mental health collaboration in school psychology.

Collegial support. Intervention assistance programs, which emphasize the development of interventions through consultation before a referral is made for special education assessment, are now recommended or mandated educational services in at least 70% of the states (Carter & Sugai, 1989). Descriptions of these programs typically include consultation involving a regular educator and a special services professional, and/or a team of special services staff (Zins, Curtis et al., 1988). Recently, however, there has been increased recognition of the importance of the consultative problem solving that occurs between regular educators, and suggestions to formally include such procedures (i.e., collegial support) as a component of intervention assistance programs have been made (Zins & Johnson, 1994). The fact is, such interactions between teachers have always occurred, even though the teachers may not have received preservice training in such skills and these activities are not encouraged by the structure of most school organizations. Rather, teachers traditionally have been accustomed to functioning in a somewhat isolated manner from their peers (Lieberman & Miller, 1984), and they have little time for reflecting on alternative means of meeting the diverse needs of their students. However, as there is increasing recognition of the need for teachers to engage in problem solving and reflection, and as the occurrence of collegial interactions among regular education teachers is increasing, school psychologists should support and encourage these efforts and view them as a component of the overall consultative approach to educational services. There are indications that the efficacy of the consultation process increases as teachers are trained in it (Anderson, Kratochwill, & Bergan, 1986).

Professional self-management and support. School psychologists often are the only mental health professionals in a school. Consequently, they may find themselves isolated from others with similar professional interests who deal with like problems on a daily basis. In addition, school psychologists are members of a profession that is rapidly changing and are faced with an explosion of new knowledge and techniques. For these reasons, it is becoming increasingly important for them to proactively manage their professional skill development (and thus their roles) and to have available the support of other school psychologists. To meet these challenges, many have joined peer
support groups. Participation in peer support groups enables them to learn from one another, to support one another, and to jointly solve problems (Zins, Maher, Murphy, & Wess, 1988). Thus, consultation with school psychology colleagues can play an important part in maintaining one's professional expertise and in addressing real-life problem situations.

SUMMARY

As consultation continues to become a major aspect of many school psychologists' jobs, it is critical for them to keep abreast of the latest theoretical and empirical knowledge of this emerging field. The knowledge base of effective consultative interactions, systems-level influences, and evaluation techniques is quickly expanding, and this chapter represents an integrative summary of many of the most important of these recent developments. Included was a review of the essential aspects of consultation practice, including its emphasis on a cooperative partnership, a preventive and empowering ideology, consideration of systems issues and of the reciprocal and interdependent nature of the interactions, and a review of the most important dimensions of the problem-solving process. It concluded with a forecast of issues considered to be significant to the development of the future practice of school consultation. Our intent was to succinctly review the essential information needed to effectively engage in consultation. Ultimately, it is hoped that improvements in consultation practice will result in school psychologists being identified with consultation-based services rather than with traditional IQ testing, so that successful outcomes for children occur with increasingly frequency.

ACKNOWLEDGMENTS

We would like to gratefully acknowledge the many contributions of Charlene R. Ponti, who was coauthor of the previous version of this chapter. In addition, we benefited from the helpful feedback of Jan N. Hughes on an earlier draft of the chapter.

REFERENCES

Anderson, T., Kratochwill, T. R., & Bergan, J. R. (1986). Training teachers in behavioral consultation and therapy: An analysis of verbal behaviors. *Journal of School Psychology, 24*, 229–241.

Babcock, N. J., & Pryzwansky, W. B. (1983). Models of consultation: Preferences of professionals at five stages of service. *Journal of School Psychology, 21*, 359–366.

Bandura, A. (1977). *Social learning theory.* Englewood Cliffs, NJ: Prentice-Hall.

Bergan, J. R., & Kratochwill, T. R. (1990). *Behavioral consultation in applied settings.* New York: Plenum.

Brown, D., & Schulte, A. (1987). A social learning model of consultation. *Professional Psychology: Research and Practice, 16*, 283–287.

Caplan, G. (1993). Epilogue. In W. P. Erchul (Ed.), *Consultation in community, school, and organizational practice: Gerald Caplan's contributions to professional psychology* (pp. 205–213). Washington, DC: Taylor & Francis.

Caplan, G., & Caplan, R. B. (1993). *Mental health consultation and collaboration.* San Francisco: Jossey-Bass.

Carter, J., & Sugai, G. (1989). Survey of prereferral practices: Responses from state departments of education. *Exceptional Children, 55*, 298–302.

Elliott, S. N. (1988). Acceptability of behavioral treatments: Review of variables that influence treatment selection. *Professional Psychology: Research and Practice, 19*, 68–80.

Elliott, S. N., & Busse, B. T. (1993). Effective interventions in behavioral consultation. In J. E. Zins, T. R. Kratochwill, & S. N. Elliott (Eds.), *Handbook of consultation services for children* (pp. 179–203). San Francisco: Jossey-Bass.

Erchul, W. P. (Ed.). (1993). *Consultation in community, school, and organizational practice: Gerald Caplan's contributions to professional psychology.* Washington, DC: Taylor & Francis.

Erchul, W. P., & Chewning, T. (1990). Behavioral consultation from a request-centered relational communication perspective. *School Psychology Quarterly, 5,* 1–20.

Erchul, W. P., Hughes, J. N., Meyers, J., Hickman, J. A., & Braden, J. P. (1992). Dyadic agreement concerning the consultation process and its relationship to outcome. *Journal of Educational and Psychological Consultation, 3,* 119–132.

Gallessich, J. (1982). *The practice and profession of consultation.* San Francisco: Jossey-Bass.

Gibbs, J. (1985). Can we continue to be color-blind and class bound? *Counseling Psychologist, 13,* 426–435.

Gresham, F. M. (1989). Assessment of treatment integrity in school consultation and prereferral intervention. *School Psychology Review, 18,* 37–50.

Gresham, F. M. (1991). Whatever happened to functional analysis in behavioral consultation? *Journal of Educational and Psychological Consultation, 2,* 387–392.

Gutkin, T. B. (1981). Relative frequency of consultee lack of knowledge, skill, confidence, and objectivity in school settings. *Journal of School Psychology, 19,* 57–61.

Gutkin, T. B. (1986). Consultees' perceptions of variables relating to the outcomes of school-based consultation interactions. *School Psychology Review, 15,* 375–382.

Gutkin, T. B. (1993). Moving from behavioral to ecobehavioral consultation: What's in a name? *Journal of Educational and Psychological Consultation, 4,* 95–99.

Gutkin, T. B., & Conoley, J. C. (1990). Reconceptualizing school psychology from a service delivery perspective: Implications for practice, training, and research. *Journal of School Psychology, 28,* 203–223.

Gutkin, T. B., & Curtis, M. J. (1990). School-based consultation: Theory, techniques, and research. In T. B. Gutkin & C. R. Reynolds (Eds.), *The handbook of school psychology* (2nd ed., pp. 577–611.). New York: Wiley.

Harris, A. M., & Cancelli, A. A. (1991). Teachers as volunteer consultees: Enthusiastic, willing, or resistant consultees? *Journal of Educational and Psychological Consultation, 2,* 217–238.

Hawryluk, M. K., & Smallwood, D. (1986). Assessing and addressing consultee variables in school-based behavioral consultation. *School Psychology Review, 15,* 519–528.

Kazdin, A. (1981). Acceptability of child treatment techniques: The influence of treatment efficacy and adverse side effects. *Behavior Therapy, 12,* 493–506.

Knoff, H. M., & Batsche, G. M. (1993). A school reform process for at-risk students: Applying Caplan's organizational consultation principles to guide prevention, intervention, and home–school collaboration. In W. P. Erchul (Ed.), *Consultation in community, school, and organizational practice: Gerald Caplan's contributions to professional psychology* (pp. 123–147). Washington, DC: Taylor & Francis.

Kratochwill, T. R. (Ed.). (1985). Mini-series on target behavior selection. *Behavioral Assessment, 7,* 1–78.

Kurpius, D. J., & Lewis, J. E. (1988). Assumptions and operating principles for preparing professionals to function as consultants. In J. F. West (Ed.), *School consultation: Perspectives on theory, research, training, and practice* (pp. 143–154). Austin, TX: Association for Educational and Psychological Consultants.

Lieberman, A., & Miller, L. (1984). *Teachers view their world and their work: Implications for school improvement.* Alexandria, VA: Association for Supervision and Curriculum Development.

Lorion, R. (1978). Research on psychotherapy and behavior change with the disadvantaged: Past, present, and future directions. In S. L. Garfield & A. E. Bergin (Eds.), *Handbook of psychotherapy and behavior change* (pp. 367–381). New York: Wiley.

Martin, R., & Curtis, M. (1981). Consultants' perceptions of causality for success and failure in consultation. *Professional Psychology, 12,* 670–676.

Medway, F. (1979). Causal attributions for school-related problems: Teacher perceptions and teacher feedback. *Journal of Educational Psychology, 71,* 809–818.

Medway, F., & Updyke, J. (1985). Meta-analysis of consultation outcome studies. *American Journal of Community Psychology, 13,* 489–504.

Meichenbaum, D., & Turk, D. (1987). *Facilitating treatment adherence.* New York: Plenum.

Miller, G. A. (1969). Psychology as a means of promoting human welfare. *American Psychologist, 24,* 1063–1075.

Morsink, C. V., Thomas, C. C., & Correa, V. I. (1991). *Interactive teaming: Consultation and collaboration in special programs.* New York: Merrill.

O'Neill, P., & Trickett, E. (1982). *Community consultation.* San Francisco: Jossey-Bass.

Peterson, D. R. (1968). *The clinical study of social behavior.* New York: Appleton-Century-Crofts.

Piersel, W., & Gutkin, T. B. (1983). Resistance to school-based consultation: A behavioral analysis of the problem. *Psychology in the Schools, 20,* 311–320.

Price, R., Cowen, E., Lorion, R., & Ramos-McKay, J. (Eds.). (1988). *14 ounces of prevention.* Washington, DC: American Psychological Association.

Rappoport, J. (1981). In praise of paradox: A social policy of empowerment over prevention. *American Journal of Community Psychology, 9,* 1–25.

Reardon, K. K. (1991). *Persuasion in practice.* Beverly Hills, CA: Sage.

Saxe, L., Cross, T., & Silverman, N. (1988). Children's mental health: The gap between what we know and what we do. *American Psychologist, 43,* 800–807.

Schulte, A. C., Osborne, S. S., & McKinney, J. D. (1990). Academic outcomes for students with learning disabilities in consultation and resource programs. *Exceptional Children, 57,* 162–172.

Stokes, T. F., & Baer, D. M. (1977). An implicit technology of generalization. *Journal of Applied Behavior Analysis, 10,* 349–368.

Swift, C., & Cooper, S. (1986). Settings, consultees, and clients. In F. Mannino, E. Trickett, M. Shore, M. Kidder, & G. Levin (Eds.), *The handbook of mental health consultation* (pp. 347–392). Washington, DC: U.S. Government Printing Office.

Tyler, F., Pargament, K., & Gatz, M. (1983). The resource-collaborator role: A model for interactions involving psychologists. *American Psychologist, 38,* 388–398.

Wilcox, M. R. (1980). Variables affecting group mental health consultation for teachers. *Professional Psychology, 11*(5), 728–732.

Witt, J. C., & Martens, B. K. (1988). Problems with problem solving consultation: A re-analysis of assumptions, methods, and goals. *School Psychology Review, 17,* 211–226.

Wolfe, M. M. (1978). Social validity: The case for subjective measurement or how applied behavior analysis is finding its heart. *Journal of Applied Behavior Analysis, 11,* 203–214.

Zins, J. E. (1985). Work-relations management. In C. A. Maher (Ed.), *Professional self-management* (pp. 105–127). Baltimore: Brookes.

Zins, J. E. (1988). Examination of the conceptual foundations of school consultation practice. In J. F. West (Ed.), *School consultation: Perspectives on theory, research, training, and practice* (pp. 17–34). Austin, TX: Association for Educational and Psychological Consultants.

Zins, J. E., & Curtis, M. J. (1981). Teacher preferences for differing models of consultation. In M. J. Curtis & J. E. Zins (Eds.), *The theory and practice of school consultation* (pp. 88–96). Springfield, IL: Thomas.

Zins, J. E., Curtis, M. J., Graden, J., & Ponti, C. R. (1988). *Helping students succeed in the regular classroom: A guide for developing intervention assistance programs.* San Francisco: Jossey-Bass.

Zins, J. E., & Johnson, L. J. (1994). Prereferral interventions for students with special needs. In T. Husen & T. N. Postethwaite (Eds.), *The international encyclopedia of education* (2nd ed., Vol. 8, pp. 4657–4662). Oxford: Elsevier Science.

Zins, J. E., Kratochwill, T. R., & Elliott, S. N. (Eds.). (1993). *Handbook of consultation services for children: Applications in educational and clinical settings.* San Francisco: Jossey-Bass.

Zins, J. E., Maher, C. A., Murphy, J. J., & Wess, B. P. (1988). The peer support group: A means of facilitating professional development. *School Psychology Review, 17*(1), 138–146.

ANNOTATED BIBLIOGRAPHY

Brown, D., Pryzwansky, W. B., & Schulte, A. C. (1991). *Psychological consultation: Introduction to theory and practice* (2nd ed.). Boston: Allyn & Bacon.
A very useful source for those who seek to develop the essential knowledge and skills of consulting, this text examines various models of practice and presents in detail the stages and processes of consultation. The chapters that concern consulting with teachers and parents seem especially germane to the practice of school psychology.

Caplan, G., & Caplan, R. B. (1993). *Mental health consultation and collaboration.* San Francisco: Jossey-Bass.
This book is a revision of Gerald Caplan's (1970) seminal work, *The Theory and Practice of Mental Health Consultation,* one of the most frequently cited books in school psychology. Besides updating the mental health consultation model, the Caplans describe mental health collaboration. They argue that internal consultants such as school psychologists should use collaboration rather than consultation.

Gutkin, T. B., & Curtis, M. J. (1990). School-based consultation: Theory, techniques, and research. In T. B. Gutkin & C. R. Reynolds (Eds.), *The handbook of school psychology* (2nd ed., pp. 577–611). New York: Wiley.
This well-referenced chapter provides a comprehensive overview of key issues associated with consultation in the field of school psychology. The authors' coverage of the rationale for consultation, major approaches to school consultation, and critical presentation of contemporary and future issues are particularly noteworthy.

Erchul, W. P. (Ed.). (1993). *Consultation in community, school, and organizational practice: Gerald Caplan's contributions to professional psychology.* Washington, DC: Taylor & Francis.
Contributors to this edited book describe and evaluate Caplan's innovative approach to consultation and related activities with respect to current and future practice of school, community, and organizational psychology. Caplan himself authors two chapters in this volume, which offers an intriguing historical perspective on the development of community mental health and school-based consultation.

Zins, J. E., Kratochwill, T. R., & Elliott, S. N. (Eds.). (1993). *Handbook of consultation services for children: Applications in educational and clinical settings.* San Francisco: Jossey-Bass.
Following the editors' overview of the history and current status of consultation, chapter authors review conceptual foundations, models, processes, evaluation considerations, practice issues, and training approaches pertaining to the field. The book is the most complete source of information for the school-based practitioner or researcher, and also contains extensive references that readers may consult for additional information.

53

Best Practices in Evaluating the Effectiveness of Applied Interventions

Mark W. Steege
University of Southern Maine

David P. Wacker
The University of Iowa

OVERVIEW

School psychologists, along with members of educational teams, share a critical responsibility for monitoring the effectiveness of interventions. There are three advantages to evaluating the effectiveness of interventions. First, the more precise and thorough we are in our evaluation procedures, the more information we will obtain about students. Second, by evaluating interventions across target behaviors, students, teachers, parents, and settings, the school psychologist will identify a wide repertoire of potentially useful interventions. Finally, ongoing monitoring of students' performance during the delivery of an intervention allows the school psychologist to identify specific procedural difficulties and to make necessary modifications to intervention components, thereby increasing the effectiveness of the intervention package.

The evaluation of the effectiveness of an intervention is a formidable task, but one that is frequently underestimated. At the most basic level, evaluating the effectiveness of an intervention involves answering a yes/no question: Did the student improve with intervention? Put in slightly more operational terms: Following intervention, did the behaviors targeted for intervention change in the desired direction? This type of question is really a two-part question that involves both an *outcome* and a *causal* relationship. Fairchild and Zins (1992) discussed the importance of outcome data as documentation of accountability, and as a measure of student progress, and of the performance of school psychologists. Outcome data provide information about behavior change (e.g., decrease in self-injury, increase in students' completion of homework, increase in prosocial behavior of students, increase in reading comprehension) as a direct result of interventions orchestrated by the school psychologist. In short, outcome data document behavior change, and indirectly document the performance of professional(s) responsible for the planning and implementation of the intervention. However, documentation of students' improvement is not sufficient. A best practices model must also demonstrate a causal relationship between the intervention and outcomes, a relationship in which the intervention (independent variable) is responsible for any change in outcome (dependent variable).

A causal relationship between an intervention and behavior change is determined through validating that the outcomes are attributable solely to the intervention and not to extraneous and/or confounding variables. While outcome data are derived by measuring students' behavior, causal relationships are validated through the use of specific methodology.

The best practices method of collecting outcome data is by direct and reliable measurement of students' behavior. Direct measurement of behavior enables the school psychologist to document significant, meaningful, and socially valid outcomes. The best practices method of determining a causal relationship between an intervention and an outcome is through the use of single-case experimental designs. Single-case experimental designs enable the school psychologist to conclude with a high degree of certainty that the intervention was responsible for a student's behavior change (Rush, Rose, & Greenwood, 1988). An evaluation methodology that involves direct, reliable measurement of student behavior, and single-case experimental designs that control for confounding variables, results in data that document both outcome and causation.

The following sections will discuss several issues that are of critical importance to the measurement of intervention outcomes and to the validation of the causal relationship between the intervention and outcomes. Methods of defining and measuring behaviors, and of using single-case experimental designs, to evaluate the effectiveness of interventions will be emphasized.

TABLE 1
Examples of Ambiguous and of Operationalized Definitions

Example 1:

Ambiguous definition — Appropriate hand raising.

Operationalized definition — Matthew raises his hand and, when called on to respond by the classroom teacher, verbally contributes to class discussion.

Example 2:

Ambiguous definition — Self-injurious behavior.

Operationalized definition — Self injurious behavior, such as Daniel's putting his hand or wrist to his mouth with his teeth contacting the skin.

BASIC CONSIDERATIONS

Defining and Measuring Behaviors

To evaluate the effectiveness of an intervention, the school psychologist needs to first develop clear, unambiguous, and concise definitions of specific behaviors upon which the intervention is intended to impact. Specifically, this means that after reviewing a written description of a target behavior, two observers would be able to observe a student and agree that the target behavior occurred. Behaviors are *operationalized* when they are clearly described. Operationalized definitions of student behavior allow for a reliable measurement of outcomes. The examples in Table 1 illustrate operationalized and ambiguous target behaviors.

Direct Observation

The most frequently used method of measuring behavior is direct observation. There are several methods of direct observation including event recording, duration recording, *and interval recording*. Each of these procedures has advantages and disadvantages. The selection of a measurement procedure is driven by the topography, frequency, and duration of the target behaviors. Therefore, it is recommended that, prior to deciding on an observation system, the school psychologist conduct a brief anecdotal observation to identify behavioral characteristics, setting events, and so forth, and select a method of observation that will yield the most reliable and valid data.

Event recording, or frequency recording, involves the tallying of discrete occurrences of the target behavior. Event recording is most applicable to recording behaviors that are discrete episodes or responses. For example, event recording could be used to measure the number of times a student raised her hand before contributing to class discussion, and the number of times she contributed to class discussion without raising her hand. Figure 1 illustrates the use of an event recording procedure to measure the frequency of handraising and of inappropriate verbalizations for one student in three classroom settings. These target behaviors were identified and defined during an interview with the classroom teacher prior to the intervention.

The school psychologist observed and recorded eight occurrences of appropriate handraising and 17 occurrences of inappropriate verbalizations across the three classroom settings. On the basis of these data and additional behavioral assessments, the school psychologist could collaborate with the classroom teacher in the design and implementation of an intervention to increase appropriate handraising and decrease inappropriate verbalizations in the classroom.

The disadvantages of event recording include the fragmentary view it gives of the stream of behavior, and the potential unreliability of observations when behavior onset and cessation are difficult to discriminate (Barlow & Hersen, 1984).

Duration recording notes the length of time that occurs between the onset of a specific behavior and the termination of the response. Duration recording is most applicable in measuring behaviors that involve persistence. For example, duration recording could be used to record the amount of time in which a student engages in social interactions (i.e., dyadic verbal exchanges) with peers. Duration recording is the least used of the measurement procedures, perhaps in part because of the apparent ease in estimation of duration by the use of interval recording procedures (Barlow & Hersen, 1984).

Interval recording involves measuring the occurrence or nonoccurrence of prespecified target behaviors during predetermined units of time. Whereas in event recording the observer records the number of times a behavior has occurred, in interval recording the observer is concerned with the number of intervals in which a behavior occurs. Because interval recording is applicable to a wide range of responses, and is particularly useful in measuring responses that

FIGURE 1. Event recording of appropriate handraising and inappropriate verbalizations.

Target Behaviors

1. Appropriate hand raising: raises hand and when calledon to respond by the classroom teacher, verbally contributes to class discussion (AHR)

2. Inappropriate verbalizations: offers verbal responses prior to raising hand and being called on by classroom teacher to participate in discussion (IV)

Classroom Activity	Frequency	
	AHR	IV
Language Arts Discussion	3	7
Social Studies Discussion	3	3
Science Discussion	2	7
Total	8	17

do not have clear distinguishable onset and termination, it is the most commonly used of the behavior measurement procedures.

There are three methods of interval recording: *partial interval*, *whole interval time sampling*, and *momentary time sampling*. In partial interval recording, the observer posts a response if it occurs at any time within a prespecified interval. For example, given a 10-second interval, an observer records as an occurrence of on-task behavior if the student was engaged in on-task behavior during as little as 1 second or as much as 10 seconds of the interval. With whole interval time sampling, the observer registers as an occurrence behaviors that persist throughout the *entire* interval. For example, given a 10-second interval, the observer records an occurrence of on-task behavior only if a student was engaged in on-task behavior during the entire 10 seconds. With momentary time sampling, the observer watches the student precisely at predetermined intervals, and notes whether a target behavior is occurring at the moment the observation occurs. The school psychologist could use momentary time sampling to record on-task behavior by observing the student at 1-minute intervals and recording on-task behavior if the student was actively engaged in the educational task. During a 15-minute observation session, a 10-second partial and whole interval procedure would result in continuous observation of the student's behavior and 90 recordings of the target behaviors. In contrast, a 1-minute momentary time sampling procedure would

result in 15 recordings of the target behaviors. Of these three methods, partial interval recording is preferred for measurement of high-frequency, and rapidly occurring (e.g., self-injurious headbanging) behaviors. Whole interval recording is recommended when continuous occurrence of the target behavior is expected (e.g., when recording sustained attention to tasks). Momentary time sampling is useful when continuous observation of a student is not practical, or when an observer is monitoring and measuring target behaviors with several students in one setting.

It should be noted that interval recording procedures provide only estimates of rate and duration of occurrence of target behaviors. The results of observations are reported in terms of the *number of percentage of intervals* in which target behaviors occur. Of the interval recording procedures, partial interval recording is the most frequently used.

Figure 2 displays a 6-second partial interval recording procedure that was used to measure the behavior of a student who had been referred to the school psychologist for behavioral assessment of self-injurious vis-a-vis appropriate behaviors.

To carry out this procedure, during an interview with the classroom teacher and support personnel, self-injury was defined as handbiting behaviors (i.e., student placed hand in mouth with teeth in contact with the hand) and appropriate behavior was defined as task participation (i.e., the student actively engaged motorically in functional and age-appropriate task). The results of this 5-minute observation

FIGURE 2. Partial-interval recording of self-injurious and of appropriate behaviors.

Target Behaviors

1. Self-injurious handbiting behaviors (SIB)
2. Appropriate behavior (AB)

	6	12	18	24	30	36	42	48	54	60
1	2	2	2	1 2	1	1	1	1	1	2
2	2	2	2	1	1	2	2	2	2	1 2
3	1	1	1	1 2	2	2	2	2	2	2
4	2	2	2	2	2	1	1	1	1	1
5	1	1	1	1	1	1	1	1	1	1

Percentage of Intervals in which Target Behaviors Occured

1. SIB = 28/50 = 56%
2. AB = 25/50 = 50%

demonstrated that self-injury occurred during 56% of the intervals and appropriate behavior occurred during 50% of the intervals. Note that during three of the intervals both self-injury and appropriate behavior occurred. This is possible in a partial interval recording procedure because the occurrence of one behavior during the interval does not preclude the occurrence of another behavior during the same interval.

Interobserver Agreement

An important consideration in measurement of student behavior is the accuracy of the recording method. Accuracy of measurement is defined in terms of *interobserver agreement*. Interobserver agreement refers to common findings by two or more observers or raters, on the occurrence and nonoccurrence of target behaviors, the ratings of behaviors, or the ratings of permanent products. There are several methods of determining the degree of interobserver agreement. The most commonly used method involves the use of the following formula:

Interobserver agreement = Number of agreements ÷ (Number of agreements + Number of disagreements) x 100

For example, suppose that using an event recording procedure to measure a student's social interactions during morning recess, two observers simultaneously and independently observed and recorded initiations of peer-directed social interactions. Observer 1 recorded 12 occurrences of the target behavior, while Observer 2 recorded 10. Interobserver agreement was calculated as follows:

Interobserver agreement = 10 ÷ 10 x 2
= 10 ÷ 12 = 83%

Generally, an interobserver agreement percentage of 80% or greater is considered the standard for concluding that the measurement of student behavior is reliable and valid. Interobserver agreement must be conducted for 25%–30% of the sessions/samples in order to document a trend. During the evaluation of the effectiveness of an intervention, the school psychologist could serve as the primary observer/rater to measure student behavior, and a trained secondary observer/rater could be enlisted to simultaneously, but independently, measure student behavior during the 25%–30% of the sessions.

BEST PRACTICES

Use of Single-Case Experimental Designs to Evaluate Interventions

Single-case designs are a powerful technique for discovering and validating effective interventions (Rush et al., 1988). Unlike group designs, which include an experimental and control group, in single-case designs, the student serves as his or her control. This means that the student's behavior is considered before, during, and following the intervention. The degree of variation in the student's behavior during these phases allows the school psychologist to determine the effectiveness of the intervention.

Single-case experimental methodology establishes a functional relationship between the independent variable (i.e., the intervention strategy: for example, a token economy program) and the dependent variable (i.e., the expected outcome; for example, an increase in prosocial behavior and a decrease in peer-directed physical aggression). Single-case experimental designs are able to control for rival explanations for changes in student behavior.

Repeated measurement of the target behavior(s) across the distinct phases of the intervention is a significant characteristic of single-case experimental designs. They are contingency-driven, meaning that the conditions within the design continue or are changed as a function of the behavior measured (Wacker, Steege, & Berg, 1988). This facilitates responsive adjustments to the intervention in order to effect positive change in target behaviors. Single-case designs begin with a baseline condition, in which no intervention is introduced. During this phase the student's behavior is measured for several sessions until a stable trend in behavior has been established. It is a mistake to discuss the length of baseline in an a priori fashion (e.g., baseline will continue for three sessions), because baseline must continue until stability in the rate of behavior occurs.

Figure 3 illustrates stable and unstable baseline. Generally, a baseline is considered to reflect a stable trend in behavior when the rate of behavior is steady or if it continues in a direction that is the opposite of the expected intervention outcome (e.g., a decreasing trend in rate of adaptive behavior when the intervention is designed to increase adaptive functioning). A minimum of three data points that indicate a definitive trend in responding is recommended. Baseline rates can at times be quite variable. In these cases it is important to continue collecting baseline data until either a definitive trend occurs or until a pattern of variability is established. There are ethical and practical limitations to extended baselines. For example, withholding an intervention designed to address severe aberrant behaviors until a stable baseline occurs may be problematic. The school psychologist needs to collect at least enough baseline data to demonstrate preintervention levels of responding.

The requirement for stability in the student's performance applies to all phases of an intervention. Thus the length of each phase and the changes from one phase to another are governed by the behavior measured. If changes in behavior occur and rival hypotheses are controlled, the influences that bear on a student's learning can be identified systematically.

Single-case experimental designs control for rival hypotheses in the following ways: (a) by introducing or withdrawing variables, (b) by immediately responding to and recording effects, and (c) by independently replicating effects (Rush et al., 1988). These factors control for rival hypotheses because the introduction of an intervention following baseline results in an immediate change in the level of student responding. Behavioral trends can also be influenced by withdrawing the intervention. Because both the introduction and the withdrawal of intervention result in behavior change, we can infer a cause–effect relationship between the intervention and the student's behavior change. Moreover, the introduction and/or withdrawal of the intervention must result in a relatively immediate impact on trends in the student's behavior. If behavior change only occurs after several intervention trials, then it is possible that extraneous variables have influenced the observed behavior changes. Finally, when the student's behavior change is replicated, one can be more certain that the intervention resulted in behavior change. With single-case designs, replication is demonstrated with the individual student across time, settings, behaviors, or personnel. In addition, the intervention may be replicated across students or classes of behaviors.

In the following sections we will review one case study method and three types of single-case experimental designs. The case study method, while lacking the experimental control found in single-case designs, is a useful method of documenting behavior change in students and is often the basis for a more formal and empirical evaluation of interventions. Single-case experimental designs can be classified into three major categories: (a) reversal; (b) alternating treatments; and (c) multiple baseline, multiple probe.

FIGURE 3. Stable and unstable trends during baseline.

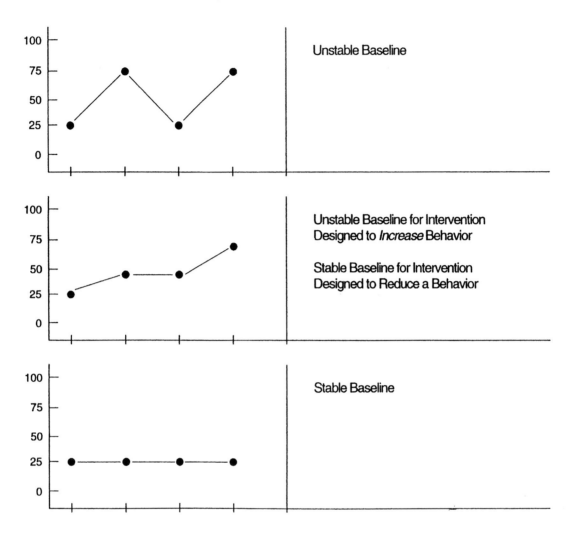

Case Study Method

The case study method involves a baseline (A) phase and an intervention (B) phase. With this method, baseline measures are repeatedly taken until stability is achieved. The intervention is then introduced and an appropriate number of measurements are made during this second phase. If behavior improves during the intervention phase, the effectiveness of the intervention is presumed to be demonstrated. Figure 4 illustrates an example of the case study (AB) method. The results of this intervention suggest that the improvement in spelling scores is directly related to the token economy intervention that was implemented beginning with session four. However, we don't know if the behavior change resulted from the treatment or from extraneous variables, or whether spelling skills would have increased naturally without the intervention. Thus, while the AB method may be useful for documenting a student's

progress, it does not allow us to evaluate the efficacy of the intervention. To control for rival hypotheses, to demonstrate intervention effectiveness, and to demonstrate accountability, the school psychologist needs to use single-case experimental designs to evaluate interventions.

Reversal Design

This design is identical to the case study method except that following the intervention phase a return to baseline phase is introduced (i.e., ABA). If the student's behavior is improved during the intervention phase and then deteriorates when the intervention is withdrawn, the effectiveness of the intervention has been demonstrated. In short, with a reversal design, positive intervention outcomes occur *only* when the intervention is being implemented. A major concern with this design is an ethical one, since the intervention is terminated with the student *not* receiving an

FIGURE 4. Case study method for documenting behavior change.

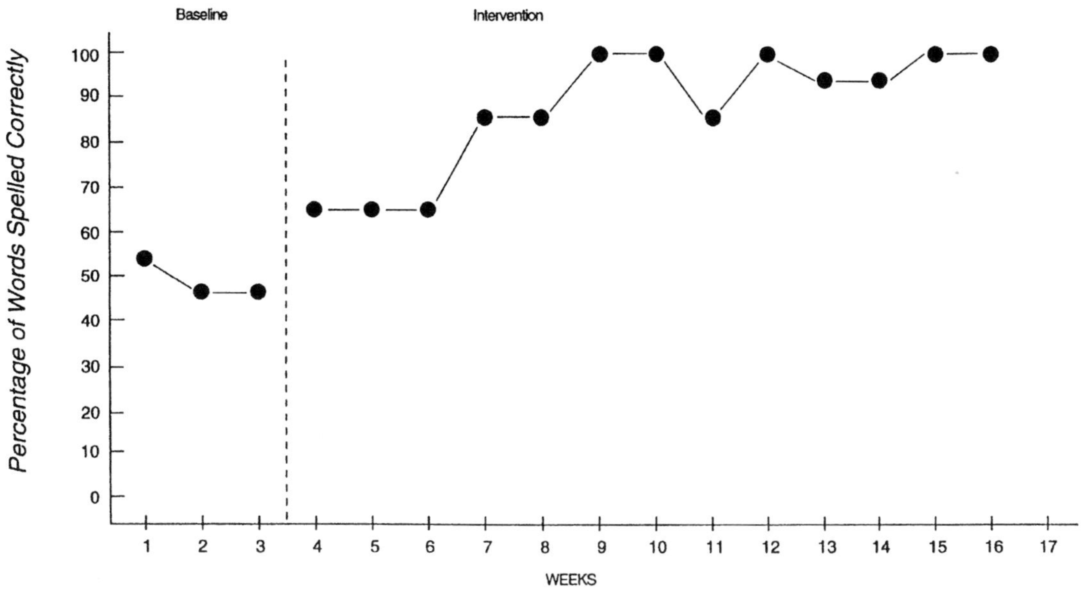

intervention that has been demonstrated to be effective. To address this issue, a return to the intervention phase is recommended (i.e., ABAB). In short, the ABAB design is identical to the ABA design with the addition of a replication of the intervention strategy. In addition to addressing ethical objections to an ABA design, the ABAB strengthens the conclusion about the effectiveness of the intervention by demonstrating positive treatment effects twice. Figure 5 illustrates the use of an ABAB design to evaluate the effectiveness of a picture prompt training procedure to teach two students with mild disabilities to operate a microcomputer.

In this example, through consultation with the classroom teacher and observation of the student, the school psychologist hypothesized that a picture prompt training procedure would increase the student's microcomputer skills. The school psychologist developed an intervention that taught the student how to perform a series of steps in operating a microcomputer (e.g., turn on computer, select appropriate software, etc.). The psychologist hypothesized that picture prompts would guide the student's performance and that without the picture prompts the student would need frequent instructional prompting from the teacher. To confirm these hypotheses, the school psychologist identified a series of steps and photographed each step of the task analysis.

During the 3 days of baseline, the student performed less than 20% of the steps of the task analysis independently. During the fourth session, the picture prompt training was initiated with the student, and by the tenth session the student was consistently using the picture prompt procedures to operate the micro-

computer. To determine if the intervention procedures were resulting in the gains in performance, *and* to determine if the intervention was continuing to maintain task independence, the school psychologist prompted the student to operate the microcomputer *without* the picture prompt strategy. When the picture prompts were removed (second A phase), the student's performance immediately decreased to baseline levels, suggesting that the increased performance during intervention was a result of the picture prompt strategy. Because it would be unfair to the student to discontinue the intervention, the school psychologist replicated the training phase of the intervention by reintroducing the picture prompt strategy (second B phase). This resulted in an immediate increase in microcomputer operation. The effect of the removal of the picture prompts on the student's behavior and the subsequent improvement in behavior following reinstatement of picture prompts demonstrated experimental control over the behavior, and thereby demonstrated empirically the effectiveness of the intervention.

Alternating Treatments Design

Alternating treatments designs are used to assess the relative effectiveness of two or more treatments (i.e., interventions) for a single subject. The basic strategy used in this design is the *rapid alternation* of two or more treatments, interventions, or conditions with a single subject (Barlow & Hersen, 1984). The alternating treatments design has been referred to by a variety of different terms: multiple schedule design, multielement baseline design, multielement manipulation design, and simultaneous treatment

FIGURE 5. Reversal design evaluating the effectiveness of picture prompt procedures.

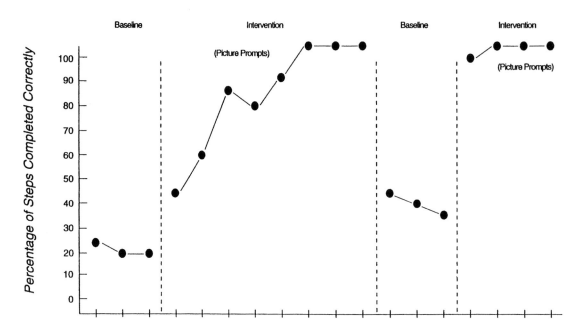

design. With an alternating treatments design, two or more treatments are presented to the student in a random or counterbalanced order. Because conditions are presented alternately, there should be no carry-over effects with respect to behavior from one treatment trial to the next. In the procedure illustrated in Figure 6, the school psychologist used an alternating treatments design to evaluate the relative effectiveness of three intervention strategies that were designed to increase a student's active participation in educational tasks. The student, Darrell, had previously been evaluated by the school psychologist and it was determined through a descriptive analysis that Darrell exhibited high rates of oppositional behavior (i.e., verbally refused to participate in activities, failed to attend to tasks, etc.) and low rates of active participation (e.g., as indicated by visual engagement in tasks, verbal contribution to class discussion, etc.) in assigned cooperative learning activities. The results of a functional analysis of oppositional behavior suggested that these behaviors were motivated by negative reinforcement (i.e., escape from academic demands). The school psychologist consulted with the classroom teacher and support personnel, and the team developed three treatments based on assessment results, that they hypothesized would increase Darrell's active participation in assigned cooperative learning activities. These three treatments were: (a) behavioral momentum, a strategy involving the presentation of a sequence of demands or requests with which Darrell is likely to comply, at brief intervals immediately preceding the situations in which oppositional behavior typically occurs (e.g., Mace &

Belifore, 1990); (b) differential reinforcement of incompatible (DRI) behavior, which consists of reinforcing the student for active participation in assigned task (e.g., Steege, Wacker, Berg, Cigrand, & Cooper, 1989); and (c) functional communication training (FCT), a procedure that teaches students, with subsequent reinforcement, to communicate a need for assistance from the classroom teacher (e.g., Carr & Durand, 1985).

The school psychologist began the intervention by determining a random assignment in the order of presentation of the three treatments. Next, the intervention team identified a specific context (e.g., classroom activity) that would be held constant across the presentation of the treatments. A 6-second whole-interval recording procedure was used to measure occurrences of active participation. The intervention team next implemented the three treatments in the following order: (a) behavioral momentum, (b) DRI, and (c) FCT. Following implementation of the three treatments, the team graphed the percentage occurrence of active participation relative to each of the treatments. The intervention team continued to implement the interventions across 5 days of evaluation as follows:

The results of the intervention clearly demonstrated that, relative to the other two treatments, the behavioral momentum strategy consistently resulted in higher rates of active participation. Thus, for this student, the intervention team could prescribe with confidence the use of behavioral momentum strategies as a method of increasing active participation.

FIGURE 6. Alternating treatments design to evaluate the relative effectiveness of interventions.

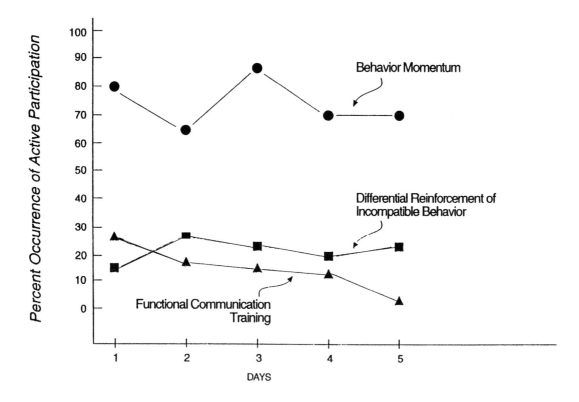

Multiple Baseline Designs

Multiple baseline designs are frequently used to evaluate the effectiveness of interventions, particularly for those interventions in which it is not practical to utilize a reversal, those in which the target behavior is not expected to reverse if the intervention is taken away, or those for which maintenance effects are anticipated.

Multiple baseline designs are an extension of the case study methodology. With multiple baseline designs, causal relationships between the intervention and its outcomes are inferred according to the following criteria: (a) continuous measurement of a behavior across a minimum of two baselines, (b) lagged introduction of treatment across baselines, (c) immediately measured effects of intervention, and (d) no observable effects in conditions in which the intervention has not been implemented (Rush et al., 1988).

There are three basic types of multiple baseline designs: across behaviors, across subjects, and across settings. Multiple baseline designs can also be used with groups of students. With multiple baseline designs, baseline data are collected on several behaviors for one student, one behavior for several students, or one student in several settings (Gay, 1992).

Multiple baseline designs can be used to evaluate the effectiveness of a variety of interventions across behaviors, students, or settings. For example, the

school psychologist may use a multiple baseline design across behaviors to evaluate the effectiveness of an intervention to sequentially teach a student with developmental disabilities three different community living skills (e.g., laundry skills, public transportation skills, personal grocery shopping skills). Utilizing a multiple baseline design across students, the school psychologist could evaluate the effectiveness of a social skills training intervention to increase prosocial behavior of five students in the context of a mainstream class. Similarly, the school psychologist could use a multiple baseline design across settings to evaluate the effectiveness of a social skills training intervention to increase prosocial behavior of one student in five educational settings.

A variation of the multiple baseline design is the multiple probe design. The multiple probe design involves the same components as the multiple baseline design except that fewer measures of the dependent variable are required. The multiple probe design is used as an alternative to extended baseline phases when repeated measurements would lead to possible changes in behavior, thereby resulting in an unstable baseline, or when repeated measures during extended baseline are potentially harmful to the student. Any combination of these designs is possible. For example, Steege, Wacker, and McMahon (1987) used a multiple baseline and multiple probe design across behaviors to evaluate the effectiveness of stimulus

TABLE 2
Order of Implementation

Day 1	Behavioral momentum	DRI	FCT
Day 2	DRI	FCT	Behavioral momentum
Day 3	FCT	DRI	Behavioral momentum
Day 4	DRI	Behavioral momentum	FCT
Day 5	Behavioral momentum	FCT	DRI

prompt strategies in teaching complex community living skills.

To illustrate the multiple baseline design, a case example is presented in which a school psychologist and a classroom teacher collaborated in the design of a self-monitoring intervention to increase on-task behavior during independent seatwork sessions for three students who displayed low rates of sustained attention.

The classroom teacher and the school psychologist piloted the intervention with three students (Lisa, Matt, and Daniel) to evaluate the efficacy of self-monitoring. They used a multiple baseline across students design because they hypothesized that since the students were expected to acquire self-monitoring skills, a reversal design was not applicable. Moreover, they reasoned that by sequentially replicating intervention effects across students following stable baselines, experimental control would be demonstrated. Figure 7 illustrates the components of the multiple baseline design across three students.

Using a 10-second whole-interval recording procedure, the school psychologist observed each of the students for 10 minutes during an assigned independent seatwork activity for three consecutive days. Beginning on the fourth day, the classroom teacher provided in vivo coaching with Lisa in the use of a self-monitoring procedure. Baseline measures of on-task behavior continued with Matt and Daniel. On the fifth day of the project, the classroom teacher again implemented the in vivo coaching of self-monitoring, and Lisa exhibited increased gains in on-task behavior. In contrast, and as a control, Matt and Daniel continued to maintain steady rates of on-task behavior. On the sixth day, the classroom teacher provided the third session of coaching in self-monitoring with Lisa and the first session of coaching in self-monitoring with Matt. This resulted in an increase in on-task behavior for both students. Daniel, who had not been exposed to the intervention, continued to display steady rates of on-task behavior. The seventh day of the project was identical to the previous day. Beginning with the eighth day, all three of the students were coached in the use of the self-control procedures. As for Lisa and Matt, the intervention resulted in an immediate increase in on-task behavior for Daniel. In vivo coaching by the classroom teacher continued through the 13th session, each of the stu-

dents maintaining high rates of on-task behavior. Beginning with the 14th session, the classroom teacher discontinued the intervention with each of the students. The school psychologist continued to measure rates of on-task behavior, during the 5-day maintenance and the 4-week follow-up phases. The students maintained high rates of on-task behavior throughout these phases. This intervention demonstrated that in vivo coaching in self-monitoring techniques resulted in increases in on-task behavior for Lisa, Matt, and Daniel.

DISCUSSION

This chapter introduced some of the underlying assumptions and strategies for reliably measuring change in students' behavior and for systematically evaluating the effectiveness of interventions. Systematic evaluations of interventions result in improved programming for students and increase the quality of school psychology services. School psychologists become accountable for their services by collecting data about student behavior and by establishing a causal relationship between an intervention and its outcome. This is becoming increasingly important, since consumers of school psychology services are no longer content to accept intervention services solely because the practitioner has been trained in their application, or because practitioners have had previous "success" using the intervention with other students, or because others provide testimonials about the skills of the practitioner. Consumers of psychological services are increasingly interested in objective measures of treatment efficacy (Sulzer-Azaroff & Mayer, 1991). Students, their families, and the professionals serving them deserve objective analyses that demonstrate that interventions are responsible for improvements in the students' behavior. The best practices method of documenting and confirming the effectiveness of interventions is through the use of direct measures of behavior and single case experimental designs.

REFERENCES

Barlow, D., & Hersen, M. (1984). *Single case experimental designs: Strategies for studying behavior change.* Elmsford, NY: Pergamon.

Carr, E., & Durand, V. (1985). Reducing behavior problems through functional communication training. *Journal of Applied Behavior Analysis, 18,* 111–126.

FIGURE 7. Multiple baseline design across students to evaluate the effectiveness of self-monitoring.

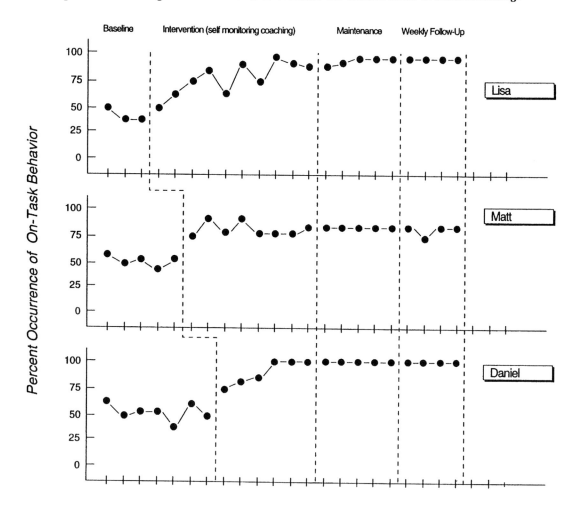

Fairchild, R., & Zins, J. (1992). Accountability practices of school psychologists: A national survey. *School Psychology Review, 21*, 617-627.

Gay, L. (1992). *Educational research: Competencies for analysis and application.* New York: Merrill.

Kazdin, A. (1982). *Single-case research designs: methods for clinical and applied settings.* New York: Oxford.

Mace, F., & Belifore, P. (1990). Behavioral momentum in the treatment of escape-motivated stereotypy. *Journal of Applied Behavior Analysis, 23*, 507–514.

Rush, F., rose, T., & Greenwood, C. (1988). Introduction to behavior analysis in special education. Englewood Cliffs, NJ: Prentice-Hall.

Steege, M., Wacker, D., Berg, W., Cigrand, L., & Cooper, L. (1989). The use of behavioral assessment to prescribe and evaluate treatments for severely handicapped children. *Journal of Applied Behavior Analysis, 22*, 23–33.

Steege, M., Wacker, D., & McMahon, C. (1987). Evaluation of the effectiveness and efficiency of two stimulus prompt strategies with severely handicapped children. *Journal of Applied Behavior Analysis, 20*, 293–299.

Sulzer-Azaroff, B., & Mayer, G. (1991). *Behavior analysis for lasting change.* New York: Holt, Rinehart, and Winston.

Wacker, D., Steege, M., & Berg, W. (1988). Use of single case designs to evaluate manipulable influences on school performance. *School Psychology Review, 17*, 949–956.

ANNOTATED BIBLIOGRAPHY

Barlow, D., & Hersen, M. (1984). *Single case experimental designs: Strategies for studying behavior change.* Elmsford, NY: Pergamon.

This volume offers a thorough review of the issues and procedures involved in the use of single-case experimental designs to evaluate clinical interventions that include an in-depth discussion of methodology and provides multiple examples of a wide variety of designs.

Kazdin, A. (1982). *Single-case research designs: methods for clinical and applied settings.* New York: Oxford.

This volume focuses on the application of single-case experimental designs in the evaluation of the effectiveness of clinical and educational interventions. Kazdin offers a variety of examples of single-case experimental designs that clearly demonstrate the use of these designs in applied settings.

Rush, F., Rose, T., & Greenwood, C. (1988). *Introduction to behavior analysis in special education.* Englewood Cliffs, NJ: Prentice-Hall.

This volume discusses the use of applied behavior analysis procedures in addressing the acquisition of adaptive behaviors and the decrease of maladaptive behaviors with students who evidence behavioral, developmental, and learning disabilities. Rush, Rose, and Greenwood devote two chapters to the measurement of student behavior and one chapter to strategies for evaluating student progress. They give particular attention to the application of reversal, multiple-baseline, alternating treatments, and changing-criterion single-case experimental designs in the evaluation of educational interventions.

Sulzer-Azaroff, B., & Mayer, G. (1991). *Behavior analysis for lasting change.* New York: Holt, Rinehart, and Winston.

Sulzer-Azaroff and Mayer offer a text in which they describe the scientific technological, and professional practice of applied behavior analysis in educational settings. They offer chapters that focus on issues related to the selection of intervention strategies, identification of goals and objectives, measurement, and analysis of student behavior, and methods of evaluating the effectiveness of interventions. Several chapters are devoted to methods of teaching skills to students and in reducing aberrant behavior.

54

Best Practices in Interviewing

Francis E. Lentz, Jr.
University of Cincinnati

Barbara A. Wehmann
Hamilton County (OH) Office of Education

OVERVIEW

"Interview ... a meeting face to face; usually a formal consultation." (Webster's Collegiate Dictionary)

Interviewing is one of the (if not the) most widespread and important procedures in the delivery of school-based psychological services. It plays a critical role in consultation, counseling, group problem solving, systems change efforts, and program evaluation. It is also the process through which the psychologist interfaces with consumers of services and must ultimately effect changes to solve problems. Traditionally psychologists have used interviews in both structured and unstructured ways, in diagnosis and classification, and as part of direct (counseling) and indirect (consultation) intervention processes.

All interviews have some common structure: verbal and nonverbal exchanges of information between an interviewer(s) and interviewee(s), content related to some purpose, and decisions resulting from the interview. These characteristics are clearly related to the basic characteristics of psychological assessment: the collection and analysis of information in order to make various decisions related to resolving problems.

Interviews are part of assessment and evaluation at the most basic level. However, for psychological services such as counseling or consultation, the goals of an interview may go beyond assessment processes and involve verbal attempts to change the behavior of the interviewee. For example, interviews within consultation may have objectives of changing interviewee behavior towards a referred child and counseling interviews usually include efforts at therapeutic changes in the client. These additional characteristics of interviews make writing a brief chapter on best practices in interviewing difficult.

This chapter will primarily examine interviews as methods of *assessment* within the problem-solving process: individual or group consultation, group problem-solving processes, and counseling. Even so, in a brief chapter it is impossible to discuss all aspects of interviews for every type of problem examined by school psychologists. The similarities among interviews used in different types of problem solving will be viewed within an ecological and behavioral framework.

It is important for school psychologists to consider the reliability and validity of interview information just as carefully as they consider how qualities of standardized tests (AERA, APA, & NCME, 1985) relate to meeting educational needs of students. Interviewing is sometimes treated too casually by practitioners, and this casual approach makes solving school problems even more difficult. This chapter's authors believe one of the best ways to avoid this casualness is by increasing knowledge about the important characteristics of a most basic tool, interviewing. Perhaps most importantly, interviews should be treated as carefully as any standardized assessment method.

COMPONENTS OF AN EFFECTIVE INTERVIEW

Effective interviewing, like all assessment procedures, is a multifaceted process. First, there must be some clear need for information during problem solving that the psychologist decides to partially meet by using an interview. (For the remainder of this chapter the terms psychologist and interviewer will be used interchangeably.) Secondly, groundwork must be laid within the school (system) so that other professionals understand the reasons for structured interviews and what information to expect from them. Understanding the reasons for structured interviews is seldom a naturally occurring event within a school building. Third, there must be an effective communication process so that interviewees and interviewers develop mutual trust, understanding, and the ability to collaborate (especially during consultative interviews). Without this type of relationship, interview data are likely to be inaccurate and probably not very useful.

Fourth, the content of an interview, especially questions and responses on the part of the interviewer, must be purposefully structured and made specific to both the interview purpose and type of presenting problem. Fifth, the psychologist must make explicit decisions on how to use the data from any interview, especially in regards to subsequent efforts with a case. Finally, the psychologist must understand the threats to inferences about necessary treatment that are influenced by interview information. These components will be explored in detail in the subsequent sections.

Principles for Effective Interviewing

Typically, the school psychologist is presented with some problem by teachers, parents, or students. It is difficult to imagine any school-based referral being satisfactorily processed without the use of one or more interviews. As part of the most traditional psychological service, namely classification for special education, the purpose of interviews has been to aid the classification decision. Interviews of adults and children, structured and unstructured, have been developed and studied in terms of reliability and validity specifically for this and related *diagnostic classification* (e.g., Hodges, Cools, & McKnew, 1989; Landau, Milich, & Widiger, 1991) with mixed results, especially in terms of often poor agreement across interviewers. Placing children in diagnostic categories has a long history in both clinical and school psychology. However, formal classification of problems has yet to demonstrate clear benefits to those who are classified. Discussion of interviews specifically related to this purpose will not be included in this chapter.

In terms of assessment for problem solving, however, there are several critical principles for conducting any type of interview that should be used as guidelines for best professional practice.

1. Interviews should always be ecological in nature (Barnett & Zucker, 1990) and directed toward the examination of variables in natural problem situations, the observable behaviors that resulted in a referral to a psychologist, and the beliefs and perceptions of the interviewee.

2. Before beginning the interview, the interviewer should set explicit desired outcomes, and these outcomes should be clearly related to making subsequent practice decisions.

3. Interviews must be focused and economical. This requires that the interviewer use questions and statements to control or direct the course of the interview. Control in this case does not mean telling the interviewee what to do and is not antithetical to collaboration. However, because school time for interviews is always limited, the maximum amount of information must be gleaned from an interview, and

rambling, disjointed interviews are unlikely to be productive.

4. When the objectives of any interview have been clearly established, best practice dictates the use of structured questions and responses clearly related to achieving those objectives. Interviewer questions or responses are similar for any interview with the same general purpose (e.g., problem identification, problem analysis, or evaluation of treatment integrity). The *specific content* of verbal behavior during interviews will vary widely depending on the nature of the presenting school problem that resulted in a referral. For example, the content of questions during problem identification interviews (during counseling, consultation, etc.) will be quite different for academic versus behavioral concerns or for other presenting problems (e.g., possible depression vs. suspected sexual abuse vs. poor social skills [e.g., Mash & Terdal, 1988]). The interviewer will have to select questions most relevant to making good decisions about the presenting problem.

5. The interviewer must be aware of being an active listener and practice the verbal and nonverbal aspects of this important communication skill.

6. There should be an explicit plan to connect interview information to decisions about what the next professional actions should be. These decisions can include selecting additional assessment activities to extend or confirm interview information, integrating different sorts of available information, or altering intervention plans.

7. The interviewer should clearly understand how interview data can threaten the validity of any problem-solving process. Validity should always ultimately relate to positive outcomes for clients of services.

Clarifying Purposes for Interviews During Problem Solving

Within problem-solving assessment, interviews as assessment procedures may be classified along two broad dimensions. The first has the interview viewed strictly as an assessment method, whose purpose is to measure relevant variables and provide information for problem identification, analysis, and resolution. In this category, interviews are employed just like any other assessment method, like interviewing a child to collect information related to analyzing a reading problem so that an intervention may be planned.

The second category involves interviews used as the procedure during which two individuals collaborate. They exchange information that will be *immediately* used to plan or analyze a problem and evaluate some intervention. The interviewer collects information (often soliciting interviewee opinions about data already collected), elicits interviewee input on prioritizing multiple problem behaviors, and guides planning for the type of intervention that may be appropriate.

A single interview may serve both of these functions. An example is a problem identification interview between a consultant and a classroom teacher who has referred a student. In this case, the interviewer is collecting assessment information that will subsequently be used to guide practice, to help analyze the problem, to plan an intervention, and/or to set treatment responsibilities. In short, the information from the interview is to be used like any other assessment data. At the same time, the interviewer is soliciting interviewee perceptions about the relative seriousness of various problems, ensuring that they both understand the nature of the referral, and soliciting interviewee acceptance of problem definitions. This information is immediately employed within problem solving.

Effective interviews are driven by clear assessment goals. It is useful to consider the sequential purposes of interviews as part of school-based problem solving. An interview used at any point within the problem-solving process would have specific objectives that are seen as common across both a variety of theoretical approaches to solving problems and types of service delivery (e.g., counseling or consultation).

Bergan and Kratochwill (1990) present a model for behavioral consultation, and Cormier and Cormier (1991) for counseling, that provide clear examples of objectives of sequential interviews during problem solving: problem identification; problem analysis; intervention planning; evaluation of treatment progress and treatment integrity; and treatment evaluation. To these is added an initial purpose, which is screening for disposition of a referral (Hawkins, 1979). An effective interview should be conducted with one or more of these objectives.

Table 1 provides a list of core (not all) objectives (and related decisions) for the most common types of interviews related to problem solving within school psychology (for a more complete list of objectives see Bergan & Kratochwill, 1990, and Gutkin and Curtis, 1990). For each type of interview, the focus is on the types of objectives that need to be met, and examples of interview purposes beyond information collection are included. These objectives are common for interviews of various people (teachers, students, etc.) and service delivery methods (e.g., counseling or consultation).

More specifically, each interview in the problem-solving process will provide information that will guide the psychologist/interviewer in making decisions about future actions. For example, when the school psychologist is conducting the initial interview of a referring teacher or student, the most immediate decision is whether the psychologist should continue

to be a prime change agent or whether the problem should be immediately referred to another source (as in the case of suspected child abuse). If the decision is for the interviewer to continue to have immediate responsibility for the referral, then a problem identification interview is begun immediately during the same meeting (or as soon as possible). Of course, even a decision about making a referral to another helping agent may require an interview of someone else to confirm critical information, and information could be received at any point in processing a referral that may require the psychologist to refer to another change agent.

In addition to the purpose of identifying the variables observed by the teacher that resulted in referral, information from the initial interview will be used by the psychologist to decide on which additional assessment procedures (including other interviews) may be needed (e.g., observations, child interviews, tests). The order for conducting more specific assessment (e.g., to observe in the class before interviewing the referred child) that will be needed to solve the referred problem must also be decided. These are critical decisions and may spell the difference between ineffective and inefficient psychological services and effective problem solution. Every interview will result in information being collected that will affect subsequent practice decisions. In this regard, psychologists need to limit the scope of questions during interviews to those relevant to helping the child, and not those about some issue in which the psychologist may have curiosity!

Failure to remain focused on objectives during the interview can have detrimental effects on the process of problem solving. This chapter's authors have been involved in training school psychologists and intervention assistance teams for a number of years, and it is their personal experience that one of the biggest barriers to effectiveness is for interviewers to lose sight of the purpose of an interview and "drift" aimlessly. This usually occurs during problem identification with the team, interviewer, and/or interviewee spending much valuable time "admiring" how "bad" a referred student is, even before defining the problem(s)! Everything is discussed endlessly, such as past transgressions, intransigence of parents, problems with previous siblings, and the like. However, no referring problems are clearly and specifically defined. The meeting ends with no objectives being met beyond agreeing that the referred child is the Mona Lisa of referrals.

In summary, the first step in using interviews effectively is for the psychologist to clearly understand the specific objectives of the interview and the types of decisions that will be influenced by interview information. Once these objectives and decisions are clearly understood, then the particular informational content needed for any type of referral, and the ver-

TABLE 1
Examples of Objectives and Decisions Related to
Typical Problem-Solving Interviews

Phase of Problem Solving	Type of Assessment[a]	Objectives/Decisions[b]
Screening	1	a. case disposal

Problem identification	2	a. define problem
		b. describe problem settings
		c. prioritize problems
		d. select baseline data/method
		e. initial quantification of defined problems
		f. establish baseline responsibilities
		g. set contact schedule
		h. establish relationship
		  • *what additional assessment is needed?*
		  • *schedule for assessment÷*

Problem analysis 1. Data collection interviews (could be multiple, different sources — parent, child, teacher)	1	a. collect interview data to help analyze problems

2. Problem analysis interview (consultation or counseling)	3	a. examine and clarify assessment data
		b. examine baseline data
		c. verify problem; set treatment goals
		d. form hypothesis
		e. select/plan intervention and responsibilities
		f. verify data collection
		g. set schedule
		  • *what are the reasons for the problem to exist?*
		  • *what are the most critical target behaviors?*
		  • *which acceptable treatment matches hypothesis?*
		  • *what is the treatment goal?*

Progress monitoring (brief contacts to review data and decide about needed change)	3	a. compare progress data to goals
		b. verify treatment integrity
		c. recycle if necessary
		  • *is intervention working?*
		  • *how well has treatment been implemented?*
		  • *If there were multiple objectives, do we start on next goal?*
		  • *should we continue as is or recycle to earlier phase?*

Plan evaluation	3	a. evaluate goals/data
		b. discuss general implications
		c. plan the fading of treatment
		d. establish ongoing data collection or terminate interview
		  • *should the intervention be stopped?*
		  • *how should it be ended?*

Note. This Table is adopted from several sources, including Barnett & Carey, 1992; Bergan & Kratochwill, 1990; Gutkin & Curtis, 1992.
[a]1 = prime assessment function, 2 = mixed function, 3 = interface for action.
[b]Decisions are in italics.

bal or nonverbal behavior that will be necessary to achieve goals, can be chosen.

Relationships and Interview Accuracy: Setting Expectancies, Effective Communication, and Active Listening

When interviews are considered as assessment procedures, it is important that interview data be accurate (related to actual events in problem environments or to real teacher/parent/student beliefs and attitudes) and that interference with accuracy be minimized. Practitioners need to understand the nature of forces that can prevent obtaining accurate or complete information. Likewise, they should both incorporate that understanding as they make decisions about interventions and take steps to minimize interference. Many variables can influence the accuracy of data from interviews: lack of trust, role conflicts, poor communication, and misunderstanding of reasons for a particular assessment technique. Perhaps the first step toward ensuring clear and accurate interview information is preparing interviewees for the interview.

Preparation and entry information. There is an increasingly strong Zeitgeist in school psychology toward practitioners becoming more heavily involved in practices directly benefiting school children (e.g., Graden, Zins, & Curtis, 1988); best practices in interviewing have clearly followed this path. To make interviewing the most effective force for such alternative services, practitioners should consider the preparations (interviewee, school, and district levels) necessary to effectively incorporate problem-solving interviewing into practice. This section will briefly describe preparing schools and individual interviewees so that interviewing is most effective.

First, it is important for practitioners to assist likely interviewees in understanding the purpose of typical interviews, the critical need for accurate timely interviews to solve school-based problems, and the likely interview structure. At the school level, this can at least partially be accomplished by teacher in-services designed to impart such knowledge. In-service workshops are particularly important when the nature of school psychological services changes or is in the process of changing, for example, from a refer-test-place practice to alternative problem-solving services. Failure to inform consumers of the nature of new methods, including the use of interviews that closely explore classroom environments, can result in teacher suspicions about psychologist motives and interfere with the accomplishment of interview objectives. If an interviewer is not careful, teachers may perceive the interviewer as critical of their teaching or even blaming them for the problem. Either of these will surely influence the interview outcomes!

Similarly, when interviewing someone (teacher, student, parent, administrator) it is critical to inform them of the goals and purposes of the interview, types of questions that will be asked, uses for interview information, and ways the interview may benefit the interviewee. Preparation for interviewing should be straightforward. See for example, suggestions for preparing consultees (Bergan & Kratochwill, 1990) or counseling clients (Cormier & Cormier, 1991). Not only is preparation important for producing good outcomes of interviewing, it is also the ethical thing for practitioners to do. This type of preparation is best done at the beginning of any interview and certainly can be modified for those who are interviewed repeatedly. Martens, Lewandowski, and Houk (1989a) demonstrated the positive effects of discussing the nature and purpose of problem identification prior to interviewing teachers to identify student problems.

Active listening and good communication. Interviewing is analogous to transmitting and receiving radio signals. There is some medium within which information is somehow encoded. In the interview, the "medium" includes all physical aspects of the interview situation, the problem situation, the characteristics of the interviewer and interviewee, and the communication process. Within this medium, specific types of information about a problem are sought, discussed, summarized, and eventually understood. This section will focus on the communication process and the variables that can distort information solicited during an interview. Unless the "medium" is ideal, a positive relationship between the interviewer and interviewee may never develop, and if not, then accurate information may never be transmitted.

A number of variables exist in a school setting prior to and during an interview that can have a negative impact on the usefulness of the interview. For example, a supervisor (principal) can direct a teacher to seek help from the psychologist about a child. Often this results in tension during the interview that prevents accurate information. Some problems are so disturbing to a teacher that perspective is lost, and again, information is distorted to the point of interfering with problem solving. Two general procedures can be used by a school psychologist to minimize these distortions. First, the psychologist needs to understand the culture of the school — and how it may have already "prejudiced" the information in the interview. Psychologists who actively seek to become part of the school community and who participate in school activities may already be trusted by staff and can, thus, circumvent this problem. Secondly, active listening and other effective communication processes should be part of interviews for any purpose.

Listening is a complex and surprisingly active process. The interviewer must not only be able to ask the correct questions to meet interview objectives but must discriminate and respond to interviewer feelings and emotions about the problem. Effective listening can create the warmth and genuineness that

TABLE 2
Brief Descriptions of Active Listening

1. *Decide* you are going to really listen prior to the interview.

2. Be alert, sit straight, lean forward slightly, maintain good eye contact, use appropriate facial expressions.

3. Make sure your goal is to clearly understand the message, not evaluate it immediately.

4. React with nods, comments, or questions when appropriate.

5. Let the interviewee finish before speaking.

6. Empathize with the interviewee both by actions/words and cognitively/affectively; try to put yourself in his/her shoes.

7. Ask questions when you do not understand or need clarification.

8. Concentrate on the person's nonverbal as well as verbal behavior (agitation, posture, facial expressions, etc.).

9. Do not start thinking about your personal reactions to the interviewee too soon.

10. Avoid hasty conclusions and *hypotheses* about the problem; you need all the information first.

11. Correct situational distractions (shut the door or window; request interviewee to talk louder if necessary).

most clinical theories agree are critical to helping relationships (but that almost no one is able to define clearly). Table 2 briefly summarizes the actions that an interviewer should take to appear more genuine and to solicit the most accurate information relative to the interview purposes (from Wehmann & Curtis, 1990; McKay, Davis, & Fanning, 1983).

Nonverbal behavior and detecting interviewee feelings. As Table 2 illustrates, it is important to detect the feelings of the interviewee concerning the presenting problem as well as to obtain more objective information. For example, if the purpose of the interview is to define the presenting problems, the interviewee could verbally agree to the interviewer's summarized definitions; however, voice tone and expression could indicate that the interviewee really did not agree. Additional questioning would clearly be in order. Also as will be discussed, generalizing conclusions across (and even within) cultures, different socioeconomic groups, gender, and combinations of these categories can be hazardous because the same nonverbal behavior may have drastically different meanings.

Other interview characteristics besides verbal content carry "messages" or affect the transmission and reception of assessment information. Nonverbal behavior, both on the part of the interviewer and the interviewee, will affect how well information is gleaned from the interview. Cormier and Cormier (1991) describe interviewer nonverbal behavior believed to be related both to interview success and to interviewees perceiving the interviewer as genuine. Despite the most carefully structured verbal behaviors, such variables as distance between people, interpersonal orientation, posture, eye contact, facial expressions, voice tone and level, rate of

speech, and even arrangement of furniture can also affect how interviewees respond.

Meanings associated with these various nonverbal aspects of interviews can be culturally, ethnically, economically, and even gender specific, and different interpretations of meaning can seriously affect data collected within interviews. The idea of culturally specific nonverbal messages is one that practitioners must carefully consider as they plan and conduct interviews.

Given the large number of cultures within the United States it is literally impossible for every practitioner to become "fluent" with differences across and within cultures in terms of communication characteristics; however, being at least aware of which cultures one is likely to encounter is critical. Perhaps the best advice to practitioners is to not be afraid to seek help from others when confronted with different cultural or ethnic groups. Similarly, ethical practice demands that practitioners carefully examine their own biases and ways these biases may effect practice. The notion of the effects of bias on interview outcomes will be more completely discussed in a later section.

It is also true that both verbal and nonverbal content need to be modified when the interviewees are children. For example, Garbarino and Stott (1989) suggest that child interviewers use the appropriate level of language and terms, interview the child in familiar settings, and always keep in mind the subject of the interview and its meaning to the child. Best practices would indicate that self-awareness of interviewing style and nonverbal content, as well as practice in improving these, are also critical. These issues should not be taken for granted, and careful observation of self, of others, and of the practitioner by others can be helpful.

Unfortunately, most systems of intervention that include elaborate interview procedures do not combine clear guidelines about both verbal and nonverbal behaviors. For example, Bergan and Kratochwill (1990) include little content on the nonverbal aspects of interviews, while being perhaps the best guide on verbal structures of effective problem-solving interviewing.

Finally, nonverbal behavior on the part of the interviewer can affect how the interviewee responds to questions and attempts to seek information. If the interviewee does not trust the examiner or is less likely to discuss issues with a person who does not have certain of the interviewee's personal characteristics, then the validity of the interview is seriously affected. For example, more positive responses of testees to familiar examiners have been documented for performance on standardized tests (see Fuchs & Fuchs, 1989) and there is no reason to believe that interviews will be exempt from such differential effects of interviewer characteristics. The effects on child performance of familiarity of the examiner were far greater for low-income minority students than for Caucasian middle-class children.

Verbal behavior required in all types of interviews. A number of interviewer verbalizations are used during almost any type of interview and to meet any type of interview objective: information-gathering questions, clarifying questions, paraphrasing statements, and summarizing statements. Clarifying (or verifying, Bergan & Kratochwill, 1990) requires the interviewer to state the information just received and verify that it is accurate ("So Ms. Smith, Betty turns in her homework about 40% of the time and is out of her seat about 5 times every 10 minutes?"), or to directly ask the interviewer to provide clarification ("Are you saying that John has no friends and that you have never seen another child invite him to play on the playground?").

Summarizing is one of the most important types of interviewer verbalizations; it allows both parties to be sure that they are on the same wavelength. For example, "Jody, this is what I hear you saying. You're frustrated because Tom has only completed 3 of his last 10 math assignments, and you're angry at Tom's parents because they ignore your phone calls. However, you're not sure what to do about it because they have even ignored your notes. Is that right?" Without periodic summarizations, the focus of interviews is often lost, which is one of the most common mistakes in school-based psychological interviews.

Because the focus of this chapter is on interviewing as assessment, information-gathering questions are of great importance. No matter what the interview's purpose is, the interviewer will be explicitly asking questions to get information related to the problem. For example, "John, what happens when you try to join a group in the cafeteria?" is an example of a likely question during problem identification. "Frank, after you finish your spelling homework, what happens next?" would provide information needed for problem analysis. Notice that both of these examples are *open-ended* questions; that is, they cannot be answered by a mere yes or no. This is always a best practice when seeking this type of information. Questions that can be answered yes or no could be appropriate, for example, when asking the interviewee to verify interviewer summarization of some issue.

Biases and Other Ecological Influences on Interview

Usefulness. Both interviewer and interviewee may possess biases or physical/cultural characteristics to which the other may respond in a biased manner. Race or ethnicity, gender, socioeconomic status, and even appearance of either party can influence the other. From the standpoint of desiring to collect accurate information from interviews, the issue of unwanted bias must be always considered. Some have suggested that behavioral interviewing, informing interviewees of the importance of accurate information, and clarifying the purpose of the interview may overcome any existing biases (Thomas, 1973). However, bias effects can even occur when interviewers or interviewees attempt to apply "knowledge" about general client characteristics (for example, from general research on African American culture) to a specific client to whom the characteristics do not in fact apply (Cormier & Cormier, 1991).

Other interview biases could manifest themselves during the course of an interview. For example, an interviewer with a negative bias toward homosexuals could be conducting a problem-identification interview with a student who has asked for help and realize that the interviewee may be experiencing a sexual-identity crisis. On the other hand, the interviewee could hold stereotypical beliefs about a group identity of the interviewer, and the interviewee bias could affect accuracy and completeness of information.

Perhaps the first issue for interviewers is to be aware of their own biases, make efforts to overcome them, be willing to seek assistance with a case where biases are likely to have an adverse effect, or even have someone else conduct the interview. The issue of bias in psychological services is an emotionally charged and important issue. Nevertheless, ethical practice requires service providers to be honest about the potential for bias and to be active in taking steps to ensure that bias does not adversely influence their professional practice which in this case involves conducting interviews. There are of course other aspects of service delivery beyond the scope of this chapter where cultural differences and/or biases can have serious negative impact on psychological service delivery. Any such problem would clearly impact the valid use of information data.

Negative interview situations. Finally, the ecology of the interview setting can seriously affect the ability to meet interview objectives. A good example of this may be seen in group interviewing of a referring teacher (usually within a building-level intervention assistance team or problem-solving team). If the team is not careful, teachers may become intimidated and feel like they are part of some inquisition as multiple teachers fire questions at them. Best practice may require teams to carefully orchestrate their questioning strategies, take special care to prepare referring teachers for the experience, or even have one team member conduct initial interviews. Subsequently, that member could act as the teacher's "advocate" during team meetings, assisting the teacher in clarifying problem issues to the team. One team known to the authors divides the types of questions to be asked among the team members (it is a small team); for example, one team member may summarize and another ask the information-gathering questions. (At a workshop in Louisiana, one team indicated that they even assigned a member the task of making empathetic statements to the interviewee to ensure that the interviewee felt validated for having asked for help.)

Matching Interview Content to Purpose

In any attempt to discuss best practices, the breadth of school psychological services unfortunately complicates things. School psychologists are expected to have an incredibly wide range of skills and knowledge related to the entire spectrum of school-based problems. They may encounter such different problems as reading or math difficulties, attention deficit disorder, childhood depression, school phobia, and sexual identity crisis. For each of these categories of difficulties, there are different aspects of the presenting problem and problem environments about which information is required. These special requirements require asking different questions during interviews.

As one example, consider the initial interview of a teacher who has concerns about a student's reading performance. Information allowing a clear definition and analysis of the conditions related to the reading problem is obtained through questions about issues typical to reading difficulties. In this case, information is needed about expected curriculum level, elements of the potent academic environment, student motivation, skill level, and various expected student academic behaviors (see Lentz & Shapiro, 1986). This content is at least partially different from the content necessary to analyze a student's refusal to go to school.

Another example of interview questions specific to a population and particular problem environment is found in the waking-day interview described by Barnett and Carey (1992). The general purposes of this interview are to define and prioritize problems of preschool children in both school and home. Additionally, the waking-day interview has the objective of identifying common family routines where problems are most prevalent and where natural intervention routines may be extended into an acceptable intervention. Table 3 summarizes the different content issues from these examples (no attempt is made to show every content issue, the table is illustrative only). It should be noted that within both of these examples, there are similar questions and other verbal behavior used by the interviewer — questions about immediate antecedents, frequency, and the like; summarization and feedback; and validation of concern.

Thus, best practices in interviewing require school psychologists to know and understand potentially important variables for an incredibly wide range of problems, even within their practice settings. Interviews related to different presenting problems are similar for the generic interview goals described in Table 1. For instance, questions about environmental variables surrounding a problem behavior or about attempted interventions are always asked by the interviewer. However, there will always be content questions specific only to particular types of presented problems.

Well-described systems for delivery of intervention-related services, such as the Bergan and Kratochwill (1990) model of behavioral consultation, describe interview objectives and consultant verbal behavior during interviews. However, mastering even the detailed process of behavioral consultation (including interviews) is insufficient without clear knowledge of potential types of interventions for particular problem situations. This knowledge is analogous to the necessity for knowledge about specific interventions for different types of school based problems.

Verbal behavior and interview purposes. Once objectives and needed information content are clarified, and the interviewer is prepared, best practices dictates that the interviewer use the means most likely to achieve the goals. The more general aspects of communication within an interview have already been discussed. Several additional characteristics define categories of interviewer verbal behaviors and their relationship to the purpose and effectiveness of interviews. Bergan and Kratochwill (1990) have one of the clearest conceptualization of interviewer verbalizations, and one for which some research data exist to help evaluate validity. Within this system, verbal "messages" are classified by source, content, process, and type of control.

For example, in one of the most extensive evaluations of interview-based behavioral consultation it

TABLE 3
Examples of Content Focus During Interviews
Related to Two Different Problems

Problem 1: Reading problem for elementary student; data needed for problem analysis collected in initial interview.

1. Expected curriculum placement
2. Appropriate curriculum level matching student skill
3. Current placement in curriculum
4. Type spent in direct instruction
5. Types of academic behaviors expected/required in curriculum
6. Specific behavior during group instruction (on task, oral answering of questions, reading rates, keeping place, etc.
7. Recent accuracy and completion of assignments
8. Typical feedback procedures
9. Typical contingencies for performance of curriculum tasks
10. Definition of competing/interfering behaviors
11. Available curriculum referenced assessment (chapter tests, etc.)

Problem 2: Behavioral referral of preschool student; data needed for problem analysis collected in initial interview.

1. If problems are identified sequentially by following the child through typical daily settings:
    a. waking up;
    b. getting dressed;
    c. eating breakfast;
    d. going to school/riding bus; entering building; independent activities; group activities; transitions; independent and group play; exiting school; riding home; entering home; chores; community settings; supper, with siblings or strangers; going to bed
2. Typical disciplinary style; specific for above problems
3. What change expected? How would it affect parent or teacher?

Note. examples are taken from Lentz and Shapiro, 1986; and Barnett and Carey, 1992.

was shown that meeting objectives of problem-identification interviews by specifically clarifying observable problem definitions (soliciting specific observable information, verifying understanding, etc.) had significant impact on the positive outcomes of interventions (Bergan & Tombari, 1976). Perhaps of greater relevance to practitioners, Miltenberger and Fuqua (1985) show that a carefully constructed self-help manual focusing on appropriate verbal behaviors can significantly improve interviewer skills in meeting objectives of behaviorally oriented assessment interviews. This source may be of interest to school psychologists who are interested in improving their interview skills related to problem solving.

While details are clearly beyond the scope of this chapter, practitioners should be aware that different types of questions, question content, summarization skills, and verbal feedback are associated with interview success. Success in solving problems results from structured, carefully controlled interviewer questions and statements. As stated early in this chapter, interviewing should not be informal and overcasual. Rather it should be goal driven and carefully structured.

Using Interview Data to
Help Make Valid Decisions

Table 1 outlines the specific decisions about psychological practice that are at least partially guided by interview information. Best practices in interviewing would have these decisions be made in a deliberate, explicit manner by psychologists and would require psychologists to clearly understand how interview data can affect the usefulness of treatment decisions. These decisions are always influenced by multiple sources of information and not just interview data. Part of best practices is to understand and to be able to clearly articulate how one has integrated information.

For example, if a decision is made to conduct classroom observations to verify teacher information given within a problem-identification interview, what will the psychologist do if information from the two sources is contradictory? An exact answer to this question would depend on the particular case. A decision would have to be made to actively collect more verification data (either interview or observation) or to go ahead and form an hypothesis about the reason for the problem, weighing one data source more heavily. However, the process of just collecting masses of data without a clear idea about how to integrate it is inefficient. It is perhaps analogous to the practice of giving five or six projective tests to "cover" all possible bases without any idea of what to do with the information or how to weigh the importance of the different tests.

Psychometric considerations of interview data. Psychologists are ethically bound to defend the selection and use of assessment procedures during practice (AERA et al., 1985). Thus, for any given purpose of conducting an assessment, the practitioner must clearly understand the reliability and validity of potential assessment methods prior to deciding which procedure is most appropriate. It is indeed unfortunate that the most widely used assessment practice, interviewing, is associated with a database quite sparse on the psychometric qualities of the information collected during interviews.

Arguably, one of the most important qualities of interview data is the degree of accuracy in relation to actual problem behaviors and ecological variables in problem situations. In terms of variables within environments, accuracy refers to the correspondence between collected data (in this case from interviews) and real-time events. Likewise, in terms of information concerning thoughts, beliefs, perception of interviewees, accuracy refers to the correspondence between interview data and the actual internal events (internal to the interviewee).

The behavioral assessment model seems the most appropriate for judging the qualities of interview data. For the problem-solving approach, this model is appropriate because the majority of interview data relates to behaviors and environmental variables within natural settings. Within this conceptual framework, interviews would usually be considered indirect because they almost always focus on retrospective measurement of events that have already occurred. The exception is when the focus is on the interviewee's current thoughts, perceptions, and the like.

In a behavioral assessment model, content validity is an issue (Linehan, 1980). Content validity for interviews relates to how well an interviewer samples the behaviors, settings, and ecological variables needed to resolve any particular problem. Lentz and Shapiro (1986) provide a description of the interview content related to academic problems.

Accuracy of interview information must be considered one of the most basic requirements, both technically and practically, in judging the adequacy of interviews. Treatment decisions cannot be made effectively in the absence of correct information or with distorted or inaccurate information. Data given by interviewees can be biased or not related to the actual events. However, if this is recognized, this knowledge becomes useful in understanding the dynamics of a referral. Note that to recognize such distortions assumes knowledge of what is actually true. Because data correctness is a prime issue for interviewing from a behavioral assessment model, the "truth" of data could be partially determined by examining the correspondence of data across interviewers and occasions and between interview information and other measures of the same behaviors. Of course, practitioners must make decisions about the reliability of interview data whenever they integrate information from different sources.

In a practical sense, integration of interview data can be conceived as a series of accuracy checks, although actual correctness of interview data is unlikely to be completely verified. At the end of any interview, a practitioner will make at least an implicit decision about whether to accept and act on the interview data or whether to employ other sources for extension or verification of information. This type of decision could be influenced by previous interactions with the interviewee and, unfortunately, by time constraints.

The final dimension of interview validity within the behavioral assessment model lies in the appropriateness of key treatment decisions: selection of treatment goals; formation of a hypothesis about why a presenting problem exists; correctly matching intervention characteristics to this hypothesis; making accurate decisions about whether treatment has been implemented with integrity; and correctly evaluating the significance of intervention results. Interview data will be involved to some extent in all of these decisions.

What is known about the validity of data collected from interviews used to make any of the decisions just listed? There are some data on appropriate content of interviews (actually on assessment packages) for a few types of problems (see Mash & Terdal, 1988, for examples). Some data exist on the relationships between specific interviewer verbal behavior within consultation and positive intervention results (Bergan & Tombari, 1976). For example, the clear definition of observable problems and verification of definitions by interviewees is related to success of problem-solving efforts. Amazingly, given the integral nature of interviews for any problem-solving approach, little other empirical guidance exists. The paucity of empirical knowledge was well described by Gresham (1984) and remains basically unchanged today.

In terms of social validity (for example, the acceptability of interview procedures, perceived significance of interventions developed through using interviews), a little more is known, primarily because existing research has focused on the process of interviewing rather than the outcomes. For example, Martens, Lewandowski, and Houk (1989b) identified several types of interviewer verbalizations significantly related to favorable ratings of interviews by interviewees. Generally, interviewer verbalizations primarily relating to being more directive in managing the course of the interview were viewed most favorably. While such social validity is important to understand, it does not necessarily clarify those types of interviewer behaviors most important in planning effective treatments.

Given the state of empirical information, how then may psychometric qualities of an assessment procedure (in this case interviewing) guide ethical school based practice? It seems reasonable to infer that structured interviews emphasizing well-defined goals and observable problem variables (even variables that may only be self-observed by the interviewee) rather than inferred constructs (psychological traits) are more likely to produce information that will assist in problem resolution. Content of interviews for specific problems has been published from successful treatment programs and may be used with more assurance of validity (see, for example, Barnett & Carey, 1992). Verbal and nonverbal behaviors that increase the acceptance of the change process (consultation for example) are partially identified, and guides such as Bergan and Kratochwill (1990) can be followed to increase the chances of success. Beyond this information, there are some other general guidelines that should increase the likelihood of both valid interview information and valid decisions made partially from interview data. These guidelines are summarized in the following sections.

Multiple sources and interview information. To ensure that information from interviews is accurate, practitioners need to carefully consider whether they need to actively verify interview information by examination and integration of data from other methods. An example is comparing information obtained from the teacher to information collected directly by observing in the classroom. Of course, interview data may be judged by the interviewer as accurate enough to be immediately used without such verification. It is likely that at times psychologist/teacher problem-solving teams may not even consider information other than that collected through interviews. This is not different from individual counseling where the psychologist/counselor relies on information from the therapeutic interviews to conduct ongoing therapy and does not collect independent verification.

The decision to use unverified interview information, or to employ multiple sources of information, is somewhat analogous to making a "leap of faith"; in fact psychological assessment must always involve such a leap. At some point, a psychologist must decide that sufficient information exists to make treatment decisions; it is in selecting this point that one must be careful. Some interview data are more easily checked than other types, for example, academic performance information (tests, homework completion, etc.) provided by teachers (i.e., Lentz, 1988). Other information may require more complicated efforts such as direct classroom observation (for example, information about the academic environment, regular classroom expectancies or contingencies).

Teachers may tend to report general rather than specific information about student classroom behavior and the referring problem. Part of the goal of a problem-identification interview is to clarify general descriptions into specific definitions. Likewise, teacher-reported information about student concern (or lack of) about the problems, or a child's willingness to change may be checked through student interviews.

In summary, best practice dictates that the psychologist make decisions about the necessity for multiple views of a problem in a conscious manner, idiosyncratically for the particular case at hand. Failure to make well-considered decisions about these issues likely will not enhance the success of problem solving.

Accuracy and inference. Of course, the fact that inaccurate information is collected during an interview may have its own significance in making treatment decisions. Teachers, parents, or other referring sources may well have a distorted view of actual behavior within real problem situations, and such a distorted view may have created the referral. However, unless the accuracy can be verified, the psychologist cannot make the inference that inaccurate perceptions are related to distorted views of a student by a referring source! Whether or not this type of distortion is suspected, the collecting of confirming information about the degree of reported behaviors may even assist the interviewer to change the perception of the referral source or to reframe expectancies about child behavior. Thus, to make valid inferences from interview data as to what actually occurs in problem settings, and to make valid use of interview data, accuracy must eventually be judged.

Treatment decision validity. Accuracy of any assessment data is necessary, but not sufficient, to make decisions about what actually needs changing, what level of change would satisfy the referring source and/or be developmentally appropriate, or which intervention may work the best. Examining the validity of these types of decisions has not received sufficient research. This is basically true from most types of assessment data, not just information from interviews. Within descriptions of such systematic procedures as behavioral consultation (Bergan & Kratochwill, 1990) or collaborative consultation (Gutkin & Curtis, 1990) are some suggested practices that will enhance the treatment validity of assessment practices including interviewing. For example, both of these approaches suggest that during interviews the consultant/interviewer solicits consultee understanding of information, validates target behavior selection by the consultee, and facilitates consultee willingness to make input into intervention design. These types of practical suggestions when incorporated into problem-solving processes are likely to produce more solved problems.

Finally, it should be clear that beyond assessing the accuracy of interview data, interviews are used as part of an assessment package and it is difficult to validate only a part of any package. The attempt to validate more traditional assessment procedures (for example, tests of cognitive ability) as stand-alone procedures seems also doomed to failure because such measures are almost never used alone in real practice.

Professional Development of Interviewing Skills

Use of effective interviewing procedures is neither natural nor simple. Unfortunately, it often seems that professionals who have not used structured interviews as part of the problem-solving process often assume that interviewing within this process will be easy and simple. Notwithstanding by using objective and behavioral procedures, psychologists can develop appropriate interview behaviors. Bergan and Kratochwill (1990) reviewed the research in training behavioral consultants, primarily in terms of interviewing skills, and concluded that structured and goal-directed training of interviewing skills was effective. Miltenberger and Fuqua (1985) demonstrated success with a majority of interview trainees by using clearly written instructions followed by practice; unsuccessful trainees with this method typically responded successfully to audio and/or written models. Both of these processes require practice and self-monitoring of clear observable behaviors as training goals. Mutual feedback between psychologists while practicing interviews can assist development of good skills, as can the use of videotapes. This chapter's authors have found both of these methods to be effective. In fact, without guided practice and feedback, *improvement* in interviewing procedures seems unlikely to occur.

Likewise, psychologists can develop skills necessary to integrate interviews into successful practice. As mentioned earlier, success in providing alternative intervention-oriented services requires development of many skills and a wide knowledge base: skills in integrating multiple data sources, skills in observation and alternative curriculum-reference assessment, skills in managing consultative problem-solving including interviews, and knowledge about a wide variety of often complex interventions for difficult problems. None of these skills by themselves will guarantee effective practice in the long run.

SUMMARY AND CONCLUSIONS

Interviewing has been presented as a major part of assessment and of intervention with school-based problems. Best practice with interviewing includes setting clear goals, structuring interviews to meet objectives, using appropriate verbal and nonverbal behavior to meet goals, and being aware of potentially biasing phenomena when interviewing. In spite of the importance of interviewing, it is a procedure without the support of an adequate research base. Because of the scanty database, empirical information that should normally guide ethical practice is lacking. However, there are procedures for psychologists to employ that will increase the chance of using interviews in a valid manner. Likewise, the means to acquire adequate interviewing skills are available if psychologists are willing to engage in structured professional development activities. Given the stakes involving misuse of such an important service component, developing and refining adequate interviewing skills and content knowledge related to typically encountered problems should be a priority.

REFERENCES

AERA, APA, & NCME. (1985). *Standards for educational and psychological testing.* Washington, DC: Author.

Barnett, D., & Carey, K. (1992). *Designing interventions for preschool learning and behavior problems.* San Francisco, CA: Jossey-Bass.

Barnett, D., & Zucker, K. (1990). *The personal and social assessment of children.* Boston, MA: Allyn and Bacon.

Bergan, J., & Kratochwill, T. (1990). *Behavioral consultation and therapy.* New York: Plenum Press.

Bergan, J., & Tombari, M. (1976). Consultant skill and efficiency and the implementation of outcomes of consultation. *Journal of School Psychology, 14,* 3–14.

Cormier, W., & Cormier, S. (1991). *Interviewing strategies for helpers: Fundamental skills and cognitive behavioral interventions.* Pacific Grove, CA: Brooks/Cole Publishing Co.

Fuchs, D., & Fuchs, L. (1989). Effects of examiner familiarity of Black, Caucasian, and Hispanic children: A meta-analysis. *Exceptional Children, 55,* 303–308.

Garbarino, J., & Stott, F. (1989). *What children can tell us.* San Francisco, CA: Jossey-Bass.

Graden, J., Zins, J., & Curtis, M. (1988). *Alternative educational delivery systems: Enhancing instructional options for all students.* Washington, DC: National Association of School Psychologists.

Gresham, F. (1984). Behavioral interviews in school psychology: Issues in psychometric adequacy and research. *School Psychology Review, 13,* 17–25.

Gutkin, T., & Curtis, M. (1990). School-based consultation: Theory, techniques, and research. In T. Gutkin & C. Reynolds (Eds.), *Handbook of school psychology* (2nd ed.; pp. 577–611). New York: Wiley.

Hawkins, R. (1979). The function of assessment: Implications for selection and development of devices for assessing repertoires in clinical, educational, and other settings. *Journal of Applied Behavior Analysis, 12,* 501–516.

Hodges, K., Cools, J., & McKnew, D. (1989). Test-retest reliability of a clinical research interview for children: The Child Assessment Schedule. *Psychological Assessment, 14,* 317–322.

Landau, S., Milich, R., & Widiger, T. (1991). Conditional probabilities of child interview symptoms in the diagnosis of attention deficit disorder. *Journal of Child Psychology and Psychiatry and Allied Disciplines, 32,* 501–513.

Lentz, F. (1988). Direct observation and measurement of academic skills: A conceptual review. In E. Shapiro & T. Kratochwill (Eds.), *Behavioral assessment in schools* (pp. 76–120). New York: Guilford Press.

Lentz, F., & Shapiro, E. (1986). Functional assessment of the academic environment. *School Psychology Review, 15,* 346–357.

Linehan, M. (1980). Content validity: Its relevance to behavioral assessment. *Behavioral Assessment, 2,* 147–160.

Martens, B., Lewandowski, L., & Houk, J. (1989a). The effects of entry information on the consultation process. *School Psychology Review, 18,* 225–234.

Martens, B., Lewandowski, L., & Houk, J. (1989b). Correlational analysis of verbal interactions during the consultative interview and consultees' subsequent perceptions. *Professional Psychology Research and Practice, 20,* 334–339.

Mash, E., & Terdal, L. (Eds.). (1988). *Behavioral assessment of childhood disorders* (2nd ed.). New York: Guilford Press.

McKay, M., Davis, M., & Fanning, P. (1983). *Message: The communication book.* Oakland, CA: New Harbinger.

Miltenberger, R., & Fuqua, R. W. (1985). Evaluation of a training manual for the acquisition of behavioral assessment interviewing skills. *Journal of Applied Behavior Analysis, 18,* 323–328.

Thomas, E. (1973). Bias and therapist influence in behavioral assessment. *Journal of Behavior Therapy and Experimental Psychiatry, 4,* 107–111.

Wehmann, B. A., & Curtis, M. J. (1990). *TEAMWORK: Together Early Childhood Agency Members Working on Resources for Kids.* Hillsboro, OH: Hopewell Special Education Regional Resource Center.

ANNOTATED BIBLIOGRAPHY

Bergan, J., & Kratochwill, T. (1990). *Behavioral consultation and therapy.* New York: Plenum.

This is the most complete and comprehensive guide to behavioral consultation (and general problem-solving consultation) that currently exists. Clear discussion of well-defined verbal behaviors within interviewing, the purposes of interviews, research into consultation, and consultative interviewing are included. This should be in the library of all practitioners.

Cormier, W., & Cormier, L. (1991). *Interviewing strategies for helpers: Fundamental skills and cognitive/behavioral interventions.* Pacific Grove, CA: Brooks/Cole.

While going far beyond interviewing skills, this book has excellent sections on interviewer characteristics, nonverbal aspects of interviewing, active listening, and the role of interviewing within a general problem-solving process.

Garbarino, J., & Stott, F. (1989). *What children can tell us: Eliciting, interpreting, and evaluating information from children.* San Francisco, CA: Jossey-Bass.

This is an excellent volume with extensive guidance about conducting interviews of children around a wide range of problems (sexual abuse, divorce, etc.). Settings and issues are covered that extend far beyond schools, but the content would be of extreme importance to any school psychologist who interviews children as part of assessment or during counseling.

Hughes, J. (1990). *The clinical child interview.* New York: Guilford Press.

An excellent addition to the school practitioner series that covers all aspects of child interviewing for school practitioners, this book includes interviews to collect information on internal events, discusses issues in interviewing across different age levels, and provides guidance on good strategies in dealing with common problems in interviewing children.

Shapiro E., & Kratochwill, T. (Eds.). (1988). *Behavioral assessment in schools.* New York: Guilford Press.

While this is a more general book about behavioral assessment (and a good one), it does have several excellent chapters directly relevant to interviewing (see chapters by Alessi and Witt). In addition, parts of many other chapters are relevant to understanding the use of interviews for many different school-based problems.

55

Best Practices in the Systematic Observation of Classroom Behavior

John M. Hintze
University of Connecticut

Edward S. Shapiro
Lehigh University

Gary's teacher, Mrs. Yotter, reports that Gary has extreme difficulty remaining in his seat during instructional periods. In addition, Gary has problems maintaining his attention and frequently does not seem to listen. As a result, his classwork has suffered terribly. Recently he has become a behavior problem by interrupting and distracting other students. In an attempt to reduce these behaviors, Mrs. Yotter reports that she has tried moving Gary's desk to the front of the room next to her own, reprimanding him, and taking away privileges, all without success.

Danielle, a third-grader, is reported to be extremely shy and withdrawn. Her teacher indicates that she avoids her peers and other social interactions. During free time, Danielle prefers to be alone rather than with her classmates and rarely initiates interactions with others. Her teacher has attempted to increase Danielle's involvement by structuring play and activity situations that would encourage opportunities for social interaction. More recently, Danielle has been involved in social skills training with the school counselor. Although Danielle is improving in some of her social skills, evidence for change in her classroom has been difficult to document.

Finally, Mr. Kramer reports that a student in his class for children with multiple handicaps engages in self-injurious face slapping. Neither Mr. Kramer nor the classroom aides have been able to determine a pattern to these occurrences or the frequency with which they occur. Several interventions have been attempted, including verbal reprimands, physical blocking, and time-out, without substantial effect. As a result, mainstreaming opportunities have been decreased and there has been consideration of alternative placement in a more restrictive setting.

All of these are situations in which the practicing school psychologist may be called upon to consult at any given time. One means of evaluating these problems would involve the use of a variety of behavioral assessment strategies which could include administration of behavioral checklists, interviews, and anecdotal observations. While such methods are less time-consuming to administer, they may not result in data that directly reflect the frequency, duration, or intensity with which the problem behaviors are occurring. Additionally, although indirect methods of assessment such as interviews and informant reports offer important information about the perceptions of significant others concerning the problem behavior, the inherent limitations with each of these measures can leave both the referring teacher and school psychologist feeling less than satisfied with the information gathered and any interventions that may be implemented.

More than any other method of behavioral assessment, systematic direct observation represents the most direct and desired approach to data collection (Shapiro, 1987). The distinguishing characteristics of such procedures requires noting the occurrence of the behavior of interest in the settings where the problem actually has been happening. As such, the data are empirically verifiable and do not require inferences from observations to other behaviors. With direct and systematic measurement, an ongoing assessment of the individual's performance is obtained in the actual environment. In contrast, indirect measurement (e.g., the use of teacher or parent reports, interviews, or anecdotal observation) requires that inferences be made concerning what the informant reports and the student's actual performance in the setting of interest (Cooper, 1987).

Individuals using systematic direct observations will often develop their own code for performing observations. After the target behavior(s) is defined, the observer may conduct the observations using any of the techniques to be discussed. The assessment may include event recording; interval recording; and the noting of frequency, rate, or duration of behavior. It also may include the recording of antecedents, consequences, and setting variables that may be related to the target behavior. The versatility of deriving one's own system makes this technique quite desirable and relevant for all types of assessments, including those done in the school.

BASIC CONSIDERATIONS: RATIONALE FOR SYSTEMATIC DIRECT OBSERVATION

As the role of the school psychologist continues to move toward service delivery through consultation, methods of assessment that offer direct linkages to intervention development are critical. In all of the cases presented at the beginning of this chapter, the school psychologist was being called upon to help teachers solve problems. Clearly, the use of assessment strategies useful in making diagnostic classifications for placement in special education programs (i.e., published standardized, norm-referenced tests such as WISC-III, Woodcock-Johnson Psychoeducational Battery, etc.) will not provide the information needed to identify specific behaviors to target for intervention, potential treatment procedures, nor ways of monitoring whether implemented interventions are effective. Direct and systematic observational measures were specifically designed for these purposes.

A number of advantages to school psychologists in using systematic observation can be identified. First, systematic observation measures focus on the observable behavior of the student. As such, they provide a clear operationalization of the problem concerning the teacher. Through these methods, it becomes possible to target specific behavior for change. The impact of altering these behaviors can be discussed with the teacher so that meaningful behavior change can be accomplished. This emphasis on functional importance has consistently been emphasized as a key to effective service delivery (Gresham, 1985).

Second, systematic direct observation allows the school psychologist to function in a much broader role than does the traditional diagnostic model. Because assessment and intervention are closely linked, the school psychologist's assessment provides an opportunity for direct consultation to teachers. Instead of simply providing diagnostic data that teachers rarely have found useful, the psychologist may offer a set of intervention techniques and direction on the implementation of these strategies. This places school psychologists in a position to draw on many additional skills and provides them with the much preferred role of consultant.

Third, use of systematic direct observation provides opportunities for accountability. The findings of school psychologists are increasingly being challenged. Court cases such as *Larry P.* and *PASE v. Hannon* are strong evidence that school psychologists must assume responsibility for their actions. Because systematic direct observation offers individualized analysis of behavior change due to intervention efforts, their accountability can be objectively measured.

In short, when one examines the types of decisions to be made from assessment, clearly direct systematic observation is most closely linked to decisions about intervention planning and pupil progress. Referrals for evaluation can be conceptualized as a request for the development of intervention strategies that can help ameliorate the referral problem. In using a systematic direct observational methodology, the school psychologist can not only answer the question raised, but can also provide ongoing consultation and evaluation of the recommendations. In this way, the school psychologist remains accountable and operates in a role preferred by all.

BEST PRACTICES

Considerations in Selection of Target Behaviors

Determining social significance of behavior. More often than not, consultation with teachers and other school personnel will reveal a wide range of student behaviors that might be candidates for modification. Assessment information gathered during problem identification must be examined to determine which elements of a student's behavioral repertoire might yield socially significant and ecologically valid target behaviors.

Any procedure that affects behavior of one or more persons in ways that increase the probability or magnitude of benefits (reinforcers) for them or others are considered to be socially valid targets for behavior change (Hawkins, 1986). Thus, teaching children to read, pay attention, or make friends with peers is likely to be habilitative, because these efforts generally increase benefits and decrease costs for both the individual learner and the rest of society (Hawkins, 1991). A goal, outcome, or procedure is valid to the extent that choosing it actually improves the benefit-to-cost ratio for the individual, for others, or for both. A consumer's or professional's opinion about a goal, outcome, or procedure is only valid to the extent that it is consistent with such improved benefit-to-cost ratio (Hawkins, 1991).

Nevertheless, judgments about how much a particular behavior change will contribute to a student's overall habilitation (adjustment, competence) are difficult to make. The school psychologist, however, must place the highest importance upon the specification and definition of target behaviors that are truly useful (Kratochwill & Bergan, 1990). Reliance on subjective judgment as the first and only criterion ignores other objective possibilities.

One objective validation strategy is the use of normative data to estimate which behaviors are likely to be adaptive. For example, observing the rates of academic engaged time of "average" or even "ideal" students will aid the clinician in determining the extent to which the behavior of the target child is discrepant (Hawkins, 1991). In a similar fashion, systematically observing specific behaviors thought to correlate with objective outcomes of performance from that of a normative group may assist in determining which behavior(s) are of critical importance for success. Such a method will not prove that the measured behaviors are functional but will certainly suggest possibilities (Hawkins, 1991). Finally, the best validation of which behavior is most adaptive is to test experimentally the outcomes produced by different behaviors and different levels of their performance (Fuqua & Schwade, 1986). By definition, the performance yielding the greatest benefit at the least cost is the most adaptive (Hawkins, 1986). For example, Warren, Rogers-Warren, and Baer (1976) assessed the effect of different frequencies of children's offers to share materials. Measuring peer reactions of accepting the offer indicated that such acceptance was maximal when the target child made offers at middle frequency, neither very often nor very seldom. In this case, peer reaction was a critical measure of the target behavior's appropriateness because it is peer acceptance that should eventually maintain the behavior.

Antecedents and consequences of behavior. Direct systematic observation allows the school psychologist to focus on examining the interdependencies among functional antecedents, behaviors, and consequences (Alessi, 1988). In their most simplistic form, such procedures involve observing what occurs just before and just after the problem behavior. Careful examination of functional response chains may help answer very telling questions such as

- Are there avoidance, escape, or termination behaviors made by the student to requests or demands made by the teacher?

- Do these behaviors escalate with certain tasks versus others?

- Does the student demand behaviors from the teacher or peers?

- Is there an escalating pattern here, as the teacher or peer attempts to avoid these demands?

- What are the functional outcomes of these interpersonal sequences?

- Do such exchanges occur primarily in one setting over another or during specific times of the day?

According to Alessi (1988), finding differences is one thing; however, finding out whether these differences make a difference is yet another. Once hypotheses regarding behaviors are formed, school psychologists may test these postulates by asking the teacher to change just one variable, the one most likely to be related to the behavior discrepancy. If a reduction or increase in behavior follows, then this factor may be the only change the teacher need make. However, if the problem behavior is unaffected, another change is then substituted for the first. Such

testing of hypotheses directly ties assessment to intervention and minimizes the teacher's burden by asking for only minimal changes in teacher behavior prior to the implementation of a formal intervention plan. Asking teachers to change the ecology of their classroom in a "least restrictive" fashion has been shown to increase the acceptability of proposed interventions (Witt, Martens, & Elliot, 1984) and to avoid the traditional comprehensive assessment process that usually consumes more staff resources and time merely to diagnose a problem than to resolve it using a strategic systematic assessment approach (Alessi, 1988).

Prioritizing possible target behaviors. In many intervention programs, decisions must be made about the relative priority of possible target behaviors. Sometimes the information produced by systematic observation methods points to one particular aspect of the student's behavioral repertoire in need of improvement. More often however, assessment reveals a constellation of related, and sometimes unrelated, behaviors in need of change. In most cases, all of these target behaviors cannot effectively be addressed at the same time. In other cases it is reasonable to expect that modifying one behavior will lead to multiple changes, both favorable and unfavorable. Thus, prioritizing is often appropriate. However, guidelines for prioritizing are not always clear.

Among the factors that might serve as guidelines, Nelson and Hayes (1979) have enumerated four: (a) alter the behavior that is most irritating to the mediator involved (Tharp & Wetzel, 1969); (b) alter a behavior that may be relatively easy to change (O'Leary, 1972); (c) alter behaviors that will produce beneficial response generalization; or (d) when responses exist as part of a longer chain, alter responses at the beginning of the chain (Angle, Hay, Hay, & Ellinwood, 1977). In addition, Hawkins (1986) has added a few others, some of which may overlap considerably with the four already listed. First, one should modify behaviors lower in skill hierarchy — the "keystone," "pivotal," or "foundation" skills — before modifying those higher in the skill hierarchy if there is, indeed, good evidence that one clearly depends upon the other. Second, one should give priority to behaviors that promise to have very general utility. For example, attention to task is useful in many aspects of a daily classroom functioning. A student who presents with difficulties in such areas should probably have that deficit remedied early in the intervention.

Third, the construction or acquisition of behavioral repertoires should take precedence over elimination of specific behaviors. In other words, it is important to focus on teaching new behavior rather than just eliminating unwanted behavior. Fourth, behaviors that gain the student access to natural environments where a variety of important behaviors will be taught or reinforcers made available should receive high priority. Such an approach maximizes the possibility that the behavior will be maintained over a long-term period after the specific intervention is completed. Fifth, behaviors given priority by the student should be preferred on the basis of the student's more extensive experience with the contingencies in his or her life. Clearly, the role of choice should play an important part in deciding which behaviors to target. Sixth, some behavior changes are urgent in the sense that the opportunity for a certain intervention may pass, the behavior may pose a serious risk to someone, or some temporally scheduled consequences of major importance (e.g., school suspension) may be imminent. Seventh, when a response chain is involved, one must sketch out alternative intervention plans and decide whether forward chaining or backward chaining appears more promising, and thus whether the first response or the last receives top priority.

Defining target behaviors and writing behavioral definitions. Before behavior can undergo systematic observation, it must be specifically defined. A good definition of a target behavior provides an accurate description of the behavior to be changed (and therefore measured), not an inference or an implication of behavior (Heward, 1987). Raising a hand to be called upon is an observable and measurable behavior. By comparison, being disorganized is not a description of any particular behavior; it merely implies a general class of responses. According to Hawkins and Dobes (1977), behavioral definitions must be explicit rather than implicit, and contain three essential characteristics:

1. The definition should be objective, referring only to observable characteristics of the behavior (and environment, if needed) or translating any inferential terms (such as "expressing hostile feelings," "intending to help," or "showing interest in") into more objective ones.

2. The definition would be clear in that it should be readable and unambiguous so that experienced observers could read it and readily paraphrase it accurately.

3. The definition should be complete, delineating the "boundaries" of what is to be included as an instance of the response and what is to be excluded, thereby directing the observers in all situations that are likely to occur and leaving little to their judgment. (p. 169)

Behavioral definitions must be objective, ensuring that specific instances of the defined target behavior can be reliably observed and recorded. Furthermore, a clear definition is a technological definition that enables others to use and replicate it (Baer, Wolf, & Risely, 1968). A complete definition identifies what is not the target behavior and aids observers in discriminating the target behavior from similar responses. It allows accurate recording of noninstances of the target behavior when of interest. Finally, behavioral definitions should be concise (Heward, 1987).

Measuring and Recording Behavior

There are various types of data that can be collected during direct systematic observation. The exact nature of the data is determined by the specific behavior observed, the frequency of its occurrence, or the particular interests of the observer (Shapiro, 1987). In addition, practical considerations such as the availability of observers, the amount of time the student is accessible, or any combination of these factors, all dictate the type of data collected. Because each of these data may yield different results, the method of data collection must be clearly understood.

Event recording. The type of data known as event recording involves counting the frequency of the occurrence of behavior (Shapiro, 1987). Typically, the observer records the number of times the behavior is observed within a specific time interval. The exact interval is kept constant throughout the observation period and can range from minutes to several days. Again, the time interval chosen is related to the specific type of behavior being observed as well as the availability of observation time and observers to collect the data.

Event recording is most successful when observing behavior that has a discrete beginning and ending. Throwing paper airplanes, the completion of a math problem, and the raising of one's hand are all examples of such behavior. Behaviors that are continuous or persist for longer durations are more difficult to observe using event recording. Examples of this type of behavior would be pencil tapping, talking out loud, or on-task behavior. For event recording to be used properly, an operational definition specifying the occurrence of each event is necessary. For example, an instance of pencil tapping may be considered to have ended after 10 continuous seconds of no pencil-tapping behavior. In this way, the frequency count for the behaviors actually represents the number of discontinuous instances of the behavior. Similarly, occurrences of talking out loud may be defined as ending after 30 seconds of silence. Although event recording is often used for such behavior, other methods more readily suited to nondiscrete types of behaviors are recommended and are discussed later.

The se of event recording is particularly helpful when observing low-rate behavior. Such behaviors often occur infrequently but are of interest because of their intensity or seriousness. For example, running out of the classroom may only occur once or twice a day but may represent significant difficulties for the student. In using event recording for such behaviors, the observer must be given specific definitions regarding the beginning and ending points of the behavior.

Behaviors that occur in response bursts are also good candidates for event recording. These behaviors usually occur in rapid succession with little or no discrete beginning or ending to each response. The entire set of responses is generally related to the same response class and thus can be counted as a single event. A good example of such behavior is aggression. A child who exhibits this class of behaviors may shout obscenities, hit other children, and then walk out of the classroom. Instead of counting each single behavior, the entire outburst can be defined as an aggressive incident. The observer must be instructed as to the dimension that designates the end of the outburst, for example, one aggression-free minute. Typically, response burst behaviors are of the low-frequency, high intensity type with the entire sequence of behavior counted as one single occurrence.

The methods for event recording are quite varied. Commonly, forms are provided for the observers on which the intervals are already delineated. Observers simply place a tally mark for the occurrence of each behavior (see Figure 1). However, other mechanical devices such as grocery store counters, golf wrist counters, and a wrist abacus can be used. Any device capable of keeping a frequency count can be used to perform event recording.

Duration recording. Another type of response that can be recorded is the duration of the behavior. The observer simply notes the length of time from the beginning of the response until it ends (Shapiro, 1987). For this measure to be useful, however, starting and finishing points of the behavior must be precisely defined.

Duration measures may be very helpful with certain types of school-related behaviors. Studying, temper tantrums, social isolation, and aggressive outbursts are good examples of responses in which the duration of the behavior is an important parameter. In each case, changing the duration of the response may in itself be the target for intervention.

Event and duration recording are usually combined to achieve effective assessment (Cooper, 1987). It is entirely possible with some behaviors that event or duration recording alone would not provide an accurate picture of the problem. If one child spends an entire play period and another, one 10-second observation interval in social isolation, both would be recorded as having a single occurrence of the behavior during the observation using event recording. The additional recording of duration, however, provides an accurate assessment of the difference between these students. Likewise, the recording of both frequency and duration may be quite important when examining study behavior. One student may be found to have numerous instances of study behavior all of a short duration, whereas another child may be found to have only a few instances of longer duration. In the former case, the goal for intervention would be to achieve more continuous instances of study behavior, whereas in the latter, to increase the frequency of studying. Finally, with disruptive behaviors, a child may have several very short disruptions each day whereas another child, one long, continuous disruption. By collecting both frequency and duration data, the target behavior for intervention can be precisely defined.

The most precise nonautomated instrument for duration recording is a stopwatch. A wall clock or wristwatch can also be used but will probably produce measures less precise than those obtained with a stopwatch. The procedure for recording total duration with a stopwatch is to start the stopwatch as the behavior begins and stop the timing at the end of the episode. Without resetting the stopwatch, the observer must start it again at the beginning of the second occurrence of the behavior and stop the timing at the end of the second episode. The observer continues to accumulate the durations of time in this fashion until the end of the observation period and then transfers the total duration of time showing on the stopwatch to a record sheet.

The procedure for recording duration per occurrence with a stopwatch is to start the stopwatch as the behavior begins and stop the timing at the end of the episode. The observer transfers the duration of time showing on the stopwatch to a data sheet and resets the watch. The stopwatch is started again at the beginning of the second occurrence of the behavior and is stopped at the end. The duration of time is again transferred to a data sheet and the procedure continued until the observation session ends. Figure 2 illustrates the use of a data sheet for recording duration per occurrence.

Latency recording. Latency recording is the measurement of elapsed time between the onset of a stimulus (e.g., verbal directive) and the initiation of a specified behavior (Cooper, 1987). Latency recording should be used when the major concern is the length of time between an opportunity to elicit a behavior (e.g., after the presentation of a verbal directive) and the actual time it takes to begin performing that behavior. The response latency would be the length of time between the end of the teacher's direction and the student's compliance. Concern also can focus on latencies that are too short. For example, a student may give incorrect answers because he or she does not wait for the teacher to complete the questions. The procedure for latency recording is similar to that for duration recording. Both report data on the temporal dimension of behavior, both use the same measurement procedure (e.g., use of some timing instrument such as a stopwatch), and both require precise definitions of the behavior to be recorded.

FIGURE 1. Example of frequency tally for hypothetical student. Instances of calling out, hitting, teacher approaches, and peer approaches are recorded during three time intervals.

BEHAVIORAL BASELINE

DATE: March 2, 1992

TIME	OBSERVER	CALL	HIT	T/A	P/A
9 - 10	George D.	/ / /	/	/ / / /	/ /
10 - 11	"	/		/	/
1 - 2	"	/ /		/ / / /	/

Time sampling. When behavioral observations are being collected, it is best if all instances of the behavior are recorded during the systematic observation periods. Unfortunately, practical concerns usually prevent this from being possible. Issues such as the availability of observers, the ability of the observer present in all settings in which the student interacts, and the lack of observer time to perform observations often prohibit continuous systematic observation. Unless the behavior is of low frequency, continuous event or duration recording is probably impossible. As a result, alternative methods of data collection must be employed.

In addition to the practical problems of continuous systematic observation, it is difficult to tell when some behaviors begin and end. Although event, duration, and latency recording can be used by precisely defining the parameters of the behavior, there are better and more useful methods for collecting data.

Time sampling is a technique that circumvents the difficulties just discussed. Instead of observing students continuously, the observation period is broken into a series of shorter timed intervals. Rather than record the frequency or duration, observers simply note whether the behavior occurred. From the recording of such data, an estimate of the actual frequency of behavior is obtained. When continuous observation is impossible, time sampling provides a method for collecting accurate and reliable data by only occasional observation. Similarly, with behaviors that are not discrete, time sampling allows the observer to make only a decision regarding the presence or absence of behavior, bypassing the problems of deciding whether it has begun or ended.

The use of time sampling represents one of the most frequently employed observation techniques in systematic observation. There exists a wide variety of ways in which time sampling can be performed.

When time-sampled data are collected, the entire observation period is divided into timed segments (Shapiro, 1987). The exact length of these segments varies according to the way in which the observation is being performed. For example, if an observer is able to sit in a classroom for a continuous amount of time, the intervals are usually short, around 10 to 60 seconds. If one is unable to perform continuous observations, the intervals may be lengthened to 30 to 60 minutes. Such long intervals may allow the teacher to collect the data with minimal intrusion on his or her instructional time. Likewise, if the behavior to be observed is of the high frequency, long duration type, short intervals may be more appropriate than the longer interval method. Regardless of the interval length, behavior is recorded as either present or absent. The various ways in which behavior is defined within the interval determines the type of recording procedure employed.

If a behavior is defined as present only when it occurs throughout a time interval, the *whole-interval* method of recording is being used. Such a definition requires the behavior to be evident from the beginning to the end of each interval or the interval would be scored as "behavior absent." For example, Ollendick, Shapiro, and Barrett (1982) in observing a child's appropriate block-play behavior in consecutive 10-second intervals, defined the behavior as "building towers or fences, making roads, and transporting blocks in trucks across the playroom" (p. 67). Children had to be engaged in this behavior for the entire 10-second period to be scored appropriate. Any instance of nonplay or inappropriate play resulted in the interval being scored as behavior absent. Although this technique could conceivably be used with long intervals, it is most applicable when short duration intervals are employed and to assess whether the behavior is continuous.

FIGURE 2. Sample data sheet for recording duration of behavior per occurrence.

DURATION OF BEHAVIOR

Student: ___Jeannine___ Observer: ___Carfagno___

Behavior: <u>scratching</u>

Date: <u>May 13, 1992</u>

Start Time: ___10:30___ Time Stop: ___10:40___

Behavior Number	Elapsed Time per Episode (in minutes ['] and seconds ["])
1	1' 17"
2	6' 5"
3	2' 1"
4	3' 35"
Total:	12' 58"

In contrast to whole interval recording, *partial interval* recording does not require the behavior to be present for the entire interval. Any single or multiple occurrences during the time interval will constitute that interval as being scored as behavior present (Shapiro, 1987). This procedure is particularly useful when recording noncontinuous behaviors that sporadically appear during the observation session.

Partial interval recording can also be helpful when using larger duration intervals. For example, a teacher may be asked to record throughout the day whether a particular student calls out. An easy method for time sampling this behavior would be to divide the day into 15-minute segments and have the teacher note if the behavior does or does not occur during each 15-minute period.

Another method of time sampling, called *momentary recording*, requires the observer to note whether a behavior is present or absent only during the moment when a timed interval begins (Shapiro, 1987). In this technique, the observer would not record any data regarding the period between intervals, only what was occurring during the instant of observation. For example, an observer asked to record the on-task behavior of a student would be using momentary recording if at the beginning of each 10-second interval they noted whether the student was on- or off-task at that instant. Like partial interval recording, this technique also can be used with longer duration intervals.

With any of the time sampling procedures, observers usually are provided with a form that has the intervals already marked sequentially. The type of form often used when making short interval, continuous observations is illustrated in Figure 3. An infinite variety of these forms exist and can include precoded behavioral categories or just blank space to record a "+" or "–".

Typically, observations of this type are done on an "observe-record" basis where a specified amount of time (usually 10–30 seconds) is allotted for observation and a shorter amount of time (5 seconds) to record the observation. In order to facilitate this process, the observer may use a small hand-held recorder with an earpiece in which a prerecorded tape specifies the beginning of each interval. It is recommended that prior to the observation this tape be made according to the interval specified, with prompts that cue the observer when and what interval to record (e.g., "observe 1," "observe 2," "observe 3," . . . "observe X"). Using such a system will provide a safeguard against "observer drift" and help ensure the correct recording of data.

FIGURE 3. Sample for conducting interval recording.

(Continuous / Non-Continuous) Intervals _____ Seconds

Person Observed: _____

Observer: _____

Date/Time: _____

Behavior: _____

1	2	3	4	5	6	7	8	9	10	11	12	13	14	15	16
17	18	19	20	21	22	23	24	25	26	27	28	29	30	31	32
33	34	35	36	37	38	39	40	41	42	43	44	45	46	47	48
49	50	51	52	53	54	55	56	57	58	59	60	61	62	63	64

Reporting Data Collected

The purpose of direct systematic observation is the collection of data which can then be used for program planning and decision making. To accomplish this purpose, it is necessary to compare performance over time. What a student does at a specific point in time is usually not important for decision making or analysis if that performance cannot be compared to performance at other points in time.

In addition, simply recording the amount of behavior is generally unacceptable. The amount of behavior should be converted to other units of measurement to allow for a comparison of behavior over time (Cooper, 1987). The major units of conversion are frequency, rate, and percentage measures.

Frequency of behavior. Frequency of behavior is the number of times a specific behavior occurs in some period of time (Cooper, 1987). Tallying, or counting, instances of behavior is possible when the behavior is readily observable and discrete. Frequency should be used only when time and opportunity for response are constant. If frequency measures are used without reference to these variables, overall performance is open to subjective interpretation. For example, frequency would be an appropriate measure if the student is consistently provided 30 math problems (the same opportunity to respond during each observation) to complete in 2 minutes (constant time during each observation). Frequency would not be appropriate if the number of problems varied from observation to observation, or if the amount of time to complete these problems varied from one observation to another.

Rate of behavior. Rate of behavior is a measure expressed as frequency per unit of time (usually per minute). Rate is calculated by dividing the total number of observed behaviors by the amount of time spent producing those behaviors (in minutes) and multiplying by 60 (due to the fact that there are 60 seconds in a minute). Rate of response is considered the basic datum of the science of behavior (Skinner, 1966).

Percentage of behavior. Percentage of behavior is a ratio that expresses the amount of a behavior as a certain number of responses per every 100 opportunities. Percentage is obtained by dividing the total opportunities for a specific behavior (e.g., 50 intervals) into the number of times the behavior was actually observed (e.g., the specific behavior was observed in 10 of those intervals) and multiplying that result by 100 (10/50 = .20 x 100 = 20%).

FIGURE 4. Use of a line graph on which two behaviors are monitored concurrently.

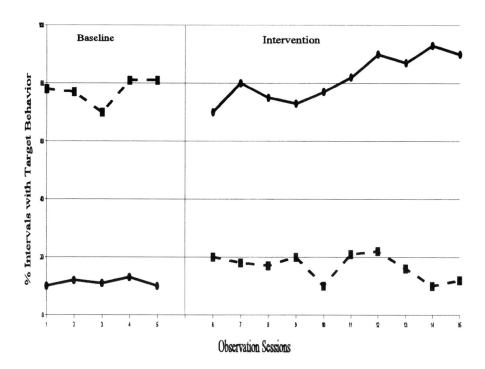

Graphic Display of the Data

The line graph is the most commonly used graphic display for presenting daily data. Figure 4 shows a simple line graph on which tow behaviors (academically engaged and off-task) are concurrently monitored across time.

The line graph has several advantages, the most important being that it is familiar to, and therefore easily understood by most teachers. In addition, it is easy to construct and permits the school psychologist and teacher to evaluate continuously the effect an intervention has on the target behavior, thus facilitating formative evaluation and the decision to maintain or modify the intervention (Tawney & Gast, 1984).

SUMMARY

Significant effort has been made over the last decade in shifting the role of the school psychologist toward a problem solver rather than a problem identifier. To problem solve successfully, school psychologists must have methodologies that match this function. Systematic observation provides one of the most useful assessment strategies to accomplish this goal. Its emphasis on the links between assessment and intervention are clear. It remains focused on identifying socially valid and meaningful behavior change. Additionally, systematic observation provides a means for psychologists to be highly accountable for their recommendations and to offer direct feedback to teachers regarding the effectiveness of these recommenda-

tions. Further, the emphasis in systematic observation on data collection under the conditions and in the setting where the problem behavior has arisen places the psychologist in close contact with the teacher's perspective of the problem.

Like any new skill, use of systematic observation will take time to learn. School psychologists should not be fooled by its apparent simplicity; it is wise to devote as much time in training to the use of these strategies as is typically devoted to learning a newly published, standardized norm-referenced test of intelligence. With continued use, however, school psychologists will find systematic observation to be an important and crucial asset to the services they can offer on behalf of helping teachers work better with children.

REFERENCES

Alessi, G. (1988). Direct observation methods for emotional/behavior problems. In E. S. Shapiro & T. R. Kratochwill (Eds.), *Behavior assessment in schools: Conceptual foundations and practical applications* (pp. 14–75). New York: Guilford.

Angle, H. V., Hay, L. R., Hay, W. M., & Ellinwood, E. H. (1977). Computer assisted behavioral assessment. In J. D. Cone & R. P. Hawkins (Eds.), *Behavioral assessment: New directions in clinical psychology* (pp. 369–380). New York: Brunner/Mazel.

Baer, D. M., Wolf, M. M., & Risely, T. (1968). Current dimensions of applied behavior analysis. *Journal of Applied Behavior Analysis, 1,* 91–97.

Cooper, J. O. (1987). Measuring and recording behavior. In J. O. Cooper, T. E. Heron, & W. L. Heward (Eds.), *Applied behavior analysis* (pp. 59–80). Columbus, OH: Merrill Publishing.

Fuqua, R. W., & Schwade, J. (1986). Social validation of applied behavioral research: A selective review and critique. In A. Poling & R. W. Fuqua (Eds.), *Research methods in applied behavior analysis: Issues and advances* (pp. 265–292). New York: Plenum.

Gresham, F. M. (1985). Behavior disorder assessment: Conceptual, definitional, and practical considerations. *School Psychology Review, 14*, 495–509.

Hawkins, R. P. (1986). Selection of target behaviors. In R. O. Nelson & S. C. Hayes (Eds.), *Conceptual foundations of behavioral assessment* (pp. 331–385). New York: Guilford.

Hawkins, R. P. (1991). Is social validity what we are interested in? Argument for a functional approach. *Journal of Applied Behavior Analysis, 24*, 205–213.

Hawkins, R. P., & Dobes, R. W. (1977). Behavioral definitions in applied behavior analysis: Explicit or implicit? In B. C. Etzel, J. M. LeBlanc, & D. M. Baer (Eds.), *New developments in behavioral research: Theory, method, and application* (pp. 167–188). Hillsdale, NJ: Lawrence Erlbaum.

Heward, W. L. (1987). Selecting and defining target behavior. In J. O. Cooper, T. E. Heron, & W. L. Heward (Eds.), *Applied behavior analysis* (pp. 36–58). Columbus: Merrill Publishing.

Kratochwill, T. R., & Bergan, J. R. (1990). *Behavioral consultation in applied settings.* New York: Plenum Press.

Larry P. et al. v. Wilson Riles et al. United States District Court, Northern District of California, Case No. C-71-2270 RFP, 1974, 1979.

Nelson, R. O., & Hayes, S. C. (1979). Some current dimensions of behavioral assessment. *Behavioral Assessment, 1*, 1–16.

O'Leary, K. D. (1972). The assessment of psychopathology in children. In H. C. Quay & J. S. Werry (Eds.), *Psychopathological disorders of childhood* (pp. 234–272). New York: John Wiley & Sons.

Ollendick, T. H., Shapiro, E. S., & Barrett, R. P. (1982). Effects of vicarious reinforcement in normal and severely disturbed children. *Journal of Consulting and Clinical Psychology, 50*, 63–70.

PASE (Parents in Action on Special Education) v. Joseph P. Hannen. 506 F Supp. 831 (N.D., Ill., 1980).

Shapiro, E. S. (1987). *Behavioral assessment in school psychology.* Hillsdale, NJ: Lawrence Erlbaum Associates.

Skinner, B. F. (1966). Operant behavior. In W. K. Honig (Ed.), *Operant behavior: Areas of research and application* (pp. 12–32). New York: Appleton-Century-Crofts.

Tawney, J. W., & Gast, D. L. (1984). *Sintle subject research in special education.* New York: Macmillan Publishing Company.

Tharp, R. G., & Wetzel, R. J. (1969). *Behavior modification in the natural environment.* New York: Academic Press.

Warren, S. F., Rogers-Warren, A., & Baer, D. M. (1976). The role of offer rates on controlling sharing by young children. *Journal of Applied Behavior Analysis, 9*, 491–497.

Witt, J. C., Martens, B. K., & Elliot, S. N. (1984). Factors affecting teachers' judgments of the acceptability of behavioral interventions: Time involvement, behavior problem severity, and type of intervention. *Behavior Therapy, 15*, 204–209.

ANNOTATED BIBLIOGRAPHY

Alessi, G. (1988). Direct observation methods for emotional/behavioral problems. In E. S. Shapiro & T. R. Kratochwill (Eds.), *Behavioral assessment in schools: Conceptual foundations and practical applications* (pp. 14–75). New York: Guilford.
This chapter provides an excellent summary of both conceptual and practical issues related to conducting direct observations. Discussions of technical and practical problems related to using direct observations are included. A case example of an actual observation on a referred child is also provided.

Greenwood, C. R., & Carta, J. J. (1987). An ecobehavioral interaction analysis of instruction within special education. *Focus on Exceptional Children, 19*(9).
This volume describes in detail the abbreviated version of the CISSAR code. The instrument described here is easy to use and very applicable as a measure to systematically and directly assess the instructional environment. Definitions of behavior categories, copies of the code, and examples on how to analyze and interpret the resulting data are provided.

Lentz, F. E., Jr., & Shapiro, E. S. (1986). Functional assessment of the academic environment. *School Psychology Review, 15*, 336–345.
This article describes the importance of assessing the instructional environment. A conceptual model for the assessment is provided as well as examples of specific methods to conduct such an assessment.

56

Best Practices in Individualized Education Programs

Nancy A. McKellar
Wichita State University

OVERVIEW

The individualized education program (IEP) is the legally prescribed mechanism for designing and monitoring student-specific education and is required for all students receiving special education services. Kaye and Aserlind (1979) have proposed that the IEP should be considered as both a product and a process.

The elements that must be included in the written product are specified in the rules and regulations (U.S. Office of Education, 1977) that govern the implementation of the Education for All Handicapped Children Act of 1975 (Public Law 94-142). These elements include the student's present levels of educational performance; annual goals and short-term instructional objectives; specific special education and related services; extent of the student's participation in regular education programs; initial dates and duration of services; and criteria, procedures, and schedules for evaluating attainment of the short-term objectives. This document must be reviewed and revised at least annually. A sample abbreviated IEP is available in *Best Practices–II* (McKellar, 1990).

When the federal law was amended in 1990 and renamed the Individuals with Disabilities Act (IDEA; Public Law 101-476), a new requirement was added. No later than when the student is 16 years old, the IEP and each revision of it thereafter must include a statement of the transition services needed by the student upon leaving school and entering adult life.

The IEP document reflects the decisions made by a team of persons who are important to the student's education. Legally, the team must include the student's teacher (regular education teacher for a student who has not been receiving special education services and special education teacher for students who have); an administrator with authority to commit the educational agency's resources to implement the IEP; and one or both parents. The student and other persons may be included on the team at the discretion of the parent(s) or the agency. Also, one of the persons who conducted the comprehensive evalua-

tion or someone knowledgeable about the evaluation and the results must be included on the IEP team the first time the student is evaluated.

The history of treatment of the IEP in the professional literature has been described as consisting of three major phases (Smith, 1990b). In the first phase, many authors described and explained the IEP norms and standards. In the next phase, researchers focused on the process of developing the IEP document. The final phase is one in which efforts have been made to manage IEP document development with computer-assisted systems.

Hopefully, the next phase will be one in which the relevance of the IEP to improving students' educational experiences is emphasized. The IEP is the logical link between assessment and intervention. Also, many states are considering and implementing outcomes-based education for all students. The short-term objectives and annual goals of the IEP represent the expected educational outcomes for the student receiving special education services.

School psychologists are likely to be the only experts in measurement on the IEP team. Also, they are trained in many of the skills that are required for problem-solving groups such as IEP teams to function effectively. These skills include knowledge of team strategies, problem-solving skills, and interpersonal factors (Zins, Curtis, Graden, & Ponti, 1988). School psychologists can help other team members to develop the IEP by assisting with integrating the data, planning the individualized program, and promoting generalization and maintenance of skills. This role is consistent with ethical standards for school psychologists (National Association of School Psychologists, 1992; see principles in Section IV.B.).

BASIC CONSIDERATIONS

Problems with the Product

Research has shown that the IEP is not always a working document that guides the student's educational program. Lytle (1992) reported that the majority of special education teachers who were studied in

Philadelphia found the IEPs of students entering their classrooms of "little or no value in planning instruction" (p. 192). Dudley-Marley (1985) studied teachers who said that IEPs were seldom referred to and often were locked away or otherwise not readily accessible to them.

To become more useful to teachers, the IEP should build on information about the student gained in the comprehensive evaluation. If the assessment procedures have included a consideration of the conditions under which the student learns best, and not just focused on special education eligibility issues, then the recommendations from the assessment should be reflected in IEP goals. However, Fiedler and Knight (1986) reported that only 0–25% of diagnostic recommendations are translated into IEP goals. In a study of the IEPs of male elementary school students with behavior disorders or learning disabilities, Smith (1990a) found that only 62% of the time was there a match between an identified need of the student and an annual goal.

Another problem with IEP documents is that they are sometimes not uniquely geared to the individual student. If the IEP represents a program that truly is individualized for the student, then IEPs should differ from one another to the extent that students differ from one another in their educational needs. When Nutter, Algozzine, and Lue (1982) compared IEPs for students within the same disability areas, they did not find significant differences. In *Board of Education v. Rowley* (1982), the U.S. Supreme Court included in the criteria for appropriate education of students with disabilities the existence of an IEP that is "reasonably calculated to enable the child to receive educational benefits" (p. 207). If IEPs are not blueprints for individually designed instruction, the appropriateness of the education received by the students is suspect (Smith, 1990b).

Problems with the Process

Parents, regular education teachers, and other persons with information relevant to designing student-specific education do not always attend and/or fully participate in the IEP conference. In the Collaborative Study of Children with Special Needs (Silverstein, 1988), five large metropolitan school districts throughout the United States were studied for over 5 years. Less than half the parents attended their child's IEP meeting. The reasons for the low parental involvement were varied, including intimidation of parents by the process, scheduling conflicts, lack of childcare, and burnout from parenting a handicapped child.

Attendance by the school psychologist at IEP meetings appears to vary considerably, according to such factors as geographic location and district policy. In a study of initial IEP planning conferences for mildly handicapped children in five North Carolina school districts (Vacc et al., 1985), only 13% of the meetings were attended by all the persons required in the federal guidelines. Those typically absent from the meeting were the local education agency representative and a professional, such as the school psychologist, who was qualified to interpret assessment data. In contrast, Vaughn, Bos, Harrell, and Lasky (1988) found that the school psychologist attended all of the initial placement/IEP meetings for students suspected of having learning disabilities in a large southwestern school district.

The participation among those at the IEP conference typically varies, with parents and regular education teachers participating less and in more passive ways than special education teachers (Vacc et al., 1985). These inequalities in participation may be influenced by the practice of writing the IEP document prior to the actual meeting. Parents feel that they are being presented with decisions rather than recommendations for a plan to which they also can provide input (Gartner & Lipsky, 1992). Also, parents' incomplete understanding of their child's handicapping conditions and the nature of the decisions to be made during the conference may contribute to parents' sparse, passive participation (Vaughn et al., 1988).

Parents can be caught in a no-win situation (Gartner & Lipsky, 1992). On the one hand, if they complain that their child is not receiving adequate educational or related services, the school personnel may respond by stereotyping the parents as overprotective. If the parents, for whatever reason, have less time to be involved in their child's education and/or therapy, then they may be labeled as in denial. In both of these views of parents, they are seen as being part of the problem rather than a valuable resource who can provide knowledge about the student and support for the educational program.

Vaughn and her colleagues (1988) found that some parents expressed uncertainty about how to explain to their child the learning problem and the planned changes in the child's educational program. The law allows the student to attend the IEP conference but this rarely happens.

A final problem with the IEP process is that plans for implementation and for integrating students into the regular classroom are discussed very little at IEP conferences (Vacc et al., 1985). Perhaps that is why so little correspondence has been found between the content of the IEP and the observed instructional activities in which the student engages (Lynch & Beare, 1990). Information on what to do once the IEP document is prepared, signed, and filed is noticeably lacking in the IEP literature. Methods of monitoring and evaluating the interventions prescribed in the IEP document have not received sufficient attention. It is only by completing the problem-solving process that the IEP can be instrumental in students' attainment of their educational goals.

BEST PRACTICES IN INDIVIDUALIZED EDUCATION PROGRAMS

Improving the Product

Important decisions for the IEP team have to do with which behaviors, set to what criteria levels, are to be described by the goals. When selecting the behaviors for improvement, the IEP team should consider those behaviors that are most central to the student's education. Such diverse behaviors as decoding unfamiliar words, feeding oneself with a spoon, and expressing one's anger in appropriate language might be included. Typically, the behaviors identified in the IEP goals will be ones in which the student is most discrepant in comparison with nondisabled peers. Norm-referenced comparisons will be required to make such judgments.

Criterion-referenced comparisons also could be the basis of goal selection. Skills that the student performs at the independent level would be considered an academic or social strength. In contrast, a skill on which the student performs no higher than the instructional level, or with 80% success, might be considered a weakness that should be the basis of an IEP goal.

In general, the annual goal represents the amount of progress that the IEP team expects the student to make in a single year. The author has asked teachers, in both special and regular education, how the IEP teams on which they serve determine how much progress it is reasonable to expect of a special education student in the time span for which the IEP is written. A common response has been, "It's a mystery to me." One option for the goal is that the student acquire a specific skill. This option requires the team to define the skill in such a way that it is clear to all what success looks like when it occurs. The goal could be that the student simply show any improvement. In this case, the team only needs to know the student's current level of performance.

Several other options for defining the expected improvement require information about the performance of the student's regular education peers (Fuchs & Shinn, 1989; Shinn, 1986). One option is to expect the special education student to catch up with regular education peers by reaching grade level performance. This criterion level is unrealistic because it means that the student will have to progress at a faster rate than the other students. Keep in mind that this expectation would be placed on a student who by virtue of his/her eligibility for special education has been recognized already as progressing at a rate less than her or his peers. Another option for the level of improvement expected of the special education student is to maintain the same rate of improvement as the nondisabled peers. This standard would keep the student at the same relative position with respect to the peers. McKellar and Jeffrey (1993) have proposed that improvement relative to one's own previous rate

of progress could be considered a reasonable goal for a student. This approach requires that data on the student's rate of previous change be used by the IEP team in establishing the criterion level. Teams should be cautioned against "playing it safe" by setting goals low, because goal ambitiousness has been shown to be positively correlated with students' achievement (Fuchs, Fuchs, & Deno, 1985).

Implicit in the development of the goals is a comparison of the student's current performance with the desired performance represented by the goal. A determination needs to be made as to whether the student cannot or will not perform the desired behavior at this time. It can be helpful to ask, "Has anyone observed the student performing the desired behavior at any time under any conditions?" If the answer is yes to this question, then the focus of the intervention should be on getting the student to perform the behavior when and where desired. This approach has a performance focus for addressing a "won't do" problem. If the answer to the question is no, then a skill deficit may exist and the student "can't do" the desired behavior at the present time. Task analysis can reveal any prerequisite skills that need to be taught to move the student toward goal attainment.

The short-term behavioral objectives related to each goal on the IEP represent steps for dealing with a performance or a skill deficit. Suppose that the goal is for the student to add two-digit numbers. If an examination of the student's current behavior reveals that he or she performs this behavior correctly when given only this type of problem and not a sheet with several types of problems, then the short-term objectives might represent a series of steps to shape the student to perform the goal under more varied conditions. On the other hand, if error analysis reveals that the student does not regroup correctly, then the short-term objectives might represent skill instruction in place value and the algorithm of regrouping.

Weisenfeld (1986) recommends that the IEP contain no more than 10 annual goals, with fewer being appropriate for many students. Once the goals are selected, task analysis and error analysis are required to determine the student's current skills and knowledge in the areas addressed by the goals and to identify and sequence the objectives needed to achieve each goal. The short-term objectives should be written as behavioral objectives. The use of specific behavioral descriptions is important so that there is no misunderstanding of the skill to be achieved and the behavior can be measured.

One consideration in selecting the objectives for a student is whether the programming represents active or passive instruction. Downing (1988) defined active IEP objectives as those "that specify behaviors/skills the student is expected to acquire upon completion of instruction" and passive IEP objectives as those "that state what staff will do to student . . . and/or provide general information on what activities will be provided" (p. 198). Active programming has been shown to improve the likelihood that students with severe disabilities will participate in their environments in functional, age-appropriate activities. Care must be taken to insure that IEP objectives for these students are age-appropriate and functional and represent active, rather than passive, instruction.

A critical component of the short-term objectives is the criterion level included in each. As a general rule, the criterion should not be set at 100% accuracy. With the exception of behaviors related to safety, there is no need to have that high a level of performance. Setting a criterion of 100% ensures failure to reach the objective. Instead, set the criterion level so that the student will have sufficient competency on that objective for it to be a realized prerequisite skill in the attainment of more advanced objectives.

Improving the Process

The development, implementation, and evaluation of the IEP are part of the overall problem-solving process that is required to provide education that meets the needs of students with disabilities. The problem-solving process can be enhanced by the school psychologists' use of good consultation skills (McKellar, 1991). These skills include actively listening to the concerns of parents, teachers, and other IEP team members. It may be necessary to help other team members understand the role of the school psychologist in the IEP process and also the limits of confidentiality in the consultation relationship. School psychologists should be familiar with the empirically demonstrated effectiveness of different interventions so they can assist the teacher in selecting the methods to use to move the student toward attainment of the IEP goals.

IEP team members should become aware of other members' competencies and their relationship to IEP development. The differing perspectives of group members may help bring about a solution for the targeted problem. Written policy statements on the responsibilities of the team members during IEP development, implementation, and evaluation are recommended. The process of IEP development can be improved by providing IEP team members with training in decision making (Poland, Thurlow, Ysseldyke, & Mirkin, 1982) and in how to use the competencies of each team member to enhance IEP development (McKellar, 1991).

The fact that some districts have rates of parent attendance at IEP meetings as high as 95% (Singer & Butler, 1992) indicates that it is possible to develop formats for IEP meetings that are parent-friendly. Special attention should be given to ways of helping parents and teachers participate as partners equal to administrators and support personnel in the IEP process. Parents and teachers usually lack formal training in problem solving or consultation (McKellar,

1991). They can be provided with a brochure prior to the IEP development meeting that gives the agenda, the meeting participants, and the role that each, including parents and teachers, will be asked to take. They can be helped to prepare for the IEP meeting with a written outline of the discussion topics and important decisions, on which space has been left between items for questions that they might want to ask. At all meetings the discussions and written materials should be free of educational jargon. Those who participate on the IEP team less infrequently, as is the case with parents and regular education teachers, should be given the name and telephone number of another IEP team member who can provide clarifications and answer questions before and after the meeting.

Determining the student's needs should occur at the beginning of the problem-solving process as part of identifying and clarifying the presenting problem, a crucial step in successful problem resolution (Bergan & Tombari, 1976). Whether the problem is attributed to factors internal to or external to the child affects expectations about whether the interventions are likely to succeed (Zins et al., 1988). The way in which the problem is defined will determine which interventions are selected. A useful technique in identifying the problem is to discuss the specific behaviors of concern that the student is exhibiting. This discussion can lead to a separation between what the student actually is doing and the meanings that different team members may be attributing to the behavior.

An important topic to discuss at the IEP meeting is how the results will be communicated to the student. This explanation will help students make adjustments to the planned changes more easily. A preferable procedure is to include the student in the IEP problem-solving process whenever possible, in order to increase the student's commitment to the interventions selected (Maher & Yoshida, 1985). Peters (1990) has provided specific suggestions for facilitating student involvement in each phase of the IEP process. For example, students can be asked to share their likes and dislikes, and this information can be used to determine present and potential reinforcers. Also, prior to the IEP meeting the student can roleplay with another team member the appropriate and expected behaviors to use at the conference.

IEPs can impact the students for which they are written only when they are implemented. The specific interventions that will be used to move the student to attainment of the IEP goals are not part of the IEP document. The interventions that are considered can be ones aimed at changes in the environment as well as changes in the student. The persons who have the most relevant information about the student's functioning and/or who will implement the interventions required to achieve the goals in the IEP need to participate in the IEP planning meeting. Incorporating the ideas of parents and teachers into the intervention plans increases their commitment to carrying out the plans. Providing a consultant to help teachers incorporate instruction related to students' IEP objectives into the existing classroom program results in concomitant increases in attainment of the IEP objectives (Peck, Killen, & Baumgart, 1989).

The means for evaluating the attainment of the IEP goals and objectives are a required part of the IEP document. For example, if the IEP objective is that Mary will read aloud correctly 90% of the words from a specified word list, then the objective should be evaluated by having Mary read the word list and computing the accuracy of her performance. Curriculum-based assessment, performance assessment, and portfolio assessment are among the assessment approaches that are particularly well suited to monitoring students' performance. The evaluation process with these methods is ongoing.

The system that will be used for monitoring progress in attaining the objectives should be discussed at the time that the IEP is developed. Ongoing data collection is essential to the IEP monitoring process. An effective practice is to graph the data so that change is apparent visually. An aimline can be drawn from the student's beginning level of performance at the left of the graph to the criterion performance at the right, to signify the rate of progress necessary to reach the goal. If the student's performance as the interventions are implemented is lower than the aimline, either the criterion level of the goal or the intervention being used will need to be changed. The former requires the approval of the IEP team. Before giving up on the planned criterion, however, it is probably best to change or alter the intervention. Error analysis of skill performance and functional analysis of behavioral sequences can be very useful at this point in identifying how or what to change with respect to the intervention. It is important, however, not to continue to do something that the data show is not working. Howell, Fox, and Morehead (1993) present a lengthy table relating possible decisions on how to change an intervention to the data that would support each specific change. Without ongoing data collection during the implementation of the interventions for reaching the IEP goals and objectives, it may not be readily apparent that an intervention is not working as expected until much of the student's valuable educational time has passed.

Rosenfield (1987) advises that teachers should be expected to adapt interventions to fit the situation. An important role of the school psychologist consultant is to assist and support teachers while guarding the integrity of the interventions. This requires frequent contact between the consultant and the teacher, whether in person or by telephone. Since this type of support is vital to the intervention's success, the IEP development meeting should include a discussion of who will implement the various interventions and who will act as the consultant.

If short-term objectives are being met, even if somewhat off schedule from the timetable listed in the IEP, the intervention process probably should continue. If the persons implementing the interventions find it necessary to add or delete objectives, such a change in the IEP must have the approval of the IEP team.

SUMMARY

The IEP is the means required by law for designing education for students with disabilities that is "special," meaning that it is uniquely appropriate to the student's needs. Much has been written about the form of the IEP document and the basic steps in developing the IEP. In this chapter, emphasis is on some of the more difficult issues faced by IEP teams in selecting the behaviors targeted for improvement, setting the criterion levels of the short-term objectives, and determining how much progress to expect of the student during the period covered by the IEP. Also presented are practical suggestions for improving the problem-solving process through more meaningful participation by all IEP team members, careful problem identification, and the monitoring, adjustment, and evaluation of resultant interventions. Only when the problem-solving process is completed with successful interventions is the student's education impacted positively by the IEP as Congress intended.

REFERENCES

Bergan, J., & Tombari, M. (1976). Consultant skill and efficiency and the implementation and outcomes of consultation. *Journal of School Psychology, 14*, 3–14.

Board of Education v. Rowley, 458 U.S. 176 (1982).

Downing, J. (1988). Active versus passive programming: A critique of IEP objectives for students with the most severe disabilities. *Journal of the Association for Persons with Severe Handicaps, 13*, 197–201.

Dudley-Marley, C. (1985). Perceptions of the usefulness of the IEP by teachers of learning disabled and emotionally disturbed children. *Psychology in the Schools, 22*, 65–67.

Fiedler, J. F., & Knight, R. R. (1986). Congruence between assessed needs and IEP goals of identified behaviorally disabled students. *Behavioral Disorders, 12*, 22–27.

Fuchs, L. S., Fuchs, D., & Deno, S. L. (1985). Importance of goal ambitiousness and goal mastery to student achievement. *Exceptional Children, 52*, 63–71.

Fuchs, L. S., & Shinn, M. R. (1989). Writing CBM IEP objectives. In M. R. Shinn (Ed.), *Curriculum-based measurement: Assessing special children* (pp. 130–152). New York: Guilford.

Gartner, A., & Lipsky, D. K. (1992). Beyond special education: Toward a quality system for all students. In T. Hehir & T. Latus (Eds.), *Special education at the century's end: Evolution of theory and practice since 1970* (pp. 123–157). Cambridge, MA: Harvard Educational Review.

Howell, K. W., Fox, S. L., & Morehead, M. K. (1993). *Curriculum-based evaluation: Teaching and decision making* (2nd ed.). Pacific Grove, CA: Brooks/Cole.

Kaye, N. L., & Aserlind, R. (1979). The IEP: The ultimate process. *Journal of Special Education, 13,* 137–143.

Lynch, E. C., & Beare, P. L. (1990). The quality of IEP objectives and their relevance to instruction for students with mental retardation and behavioral disorders. *Remedial and Special Education, 11,* 48–55.

Lytle, J. H. (1992). Is special education serving minority students? A response to Singer and Butler. In T. Hehir & T. Latus (Eds.), *Special education at the century's end: Evolution of theory and practice since 1970* (pp. 191–197). Cambridge, MA: Harvard Educational Review.

McKellar, N. A. (1990). Best practices in individualized education programs. In A. Thomas & J. Grimes (Eds.), *Best practices in school psychology–II* (pp. 383–392). Washington, DC: National Association of School Psychologists.

McKellar, N. A. (1991). Enhancing the IEP process through consultation. *Journal of Educational and Psychological Consultation, 2,* 175–187.

McKellar, N. A., & Jeffrey, S. L. (1993, April). *The effectiveness of special education as reflected in group achievement test scores.* Paper presented at the meeting of the National Association of School Psychologists, Washington, DC.

National Association of School Psychologists. (1992). *Principles for professional ethics.* Silver Spring, MD: Author.

Nutter, R. E., Algozzine, B., & Lue, M. S. (1982). An evaluation model of the implementation of individualized education programs. *Planning & Changing, 13,* 172–180.

Peck, C. A., Killen, C. C., & Baumgart, D. (1989). Increasing implementation of special education instruction in mainstream preschools: Direct and generalized effects of nondirective consultation. *Journal of Applied Behavior Analysis, 22,* 197–210.

Peters, M. T. (1990). Someone's missing: The student as an overlooked participant in the IEP process. *Preventing School Failure, 34,* 32–36.

Poland, S. F., Thurlow, M. L., Ysseldyke, J. E., & Mirkin, P. K. (1982). Current psychoeducational assessment and decision-making practices as reported by directors of special education. *Journal of School Psychology, 20,* 171–179.

Rosenfield, S. A. (1987). *Instructional consultation.* Hillsdale, NJ: Erlbaum.

Shinn, M. R. (1986). Does anyone care what happens after the refer–test–place sequence: The systematic evaluation of special education program effectiveness. *School Psychology Review, 15,* 49–58.

Silverstein, J. A. (1988). *Serving handicapped children: A special report* (No. 1). Princeton, NJ: Robert Wood Johnson Foundation.

Singer, J. D., & Butler, J. A. (1992). Singer and Butler reply to Lytle. In T. Hehir & T. Latus (Eds.), *Special education at the century's end: Evolution of theory ad practice since 1970* (pp. 197–202). Cambridge, MA: Harvard Educational Review.

Smith, S. W. (1990a). Comparison of individualized education programs (IEPs) of students with behavioral disorders and learning disabilities. *Journal of Special Education, 24,* 85–100.

Smith, S. W. (1990b). Individualized Education Programs (IEPs) in special education – From intent to acquiescence. *Exceptional Children, 57,* 6–14.

U.S. Office of Education. (1977). Education of handicapped children: Implementation of Part B of the Education of the Handicapped Act. *Federal Register, 42,* 42474–42518.

Vacc, N. A., Vallecorsa, A. L., Parker, A., Bonner, S., Lester, C., Richardson, S., & Yates, C. (1985). Parents' and educators' participation in IEP conferences. *Education & Treatment of Children, 8,* 153–162.

Vaughn, S., Bos, C. S., Harrell, J. E., & Lasky, B. A. (1988). Parent participation in the initial placement/IEP conference ten years after mandated involvement. *Journal of Learning Disabilities, 21,* 82–89.

Weisenfeld, R. B. (1986). The IEPs of Down Syndrome children: A content analysis. *Education and Training of the Mentally Retarded, 21,* 211–219.

Zins, J. E., Curtis, M. J., Graden, J. L., & Ponti, C. R. (1988). *Helping students succeed in the regular classroom: A guide for developing intervention assistance programs.* San Francisco: Jossey-Bass.

ANNOTATED BIBLIOGRAPHY

Howell K. W., Fox, S. L., & Morehead, M. K. (1993). *Curriculum-based evaluation: Teaching and decision making* (2nd ed.). Pacific Grove, CA: Brooks/Cole.
This book is intended to help teachers make educational decisions about what to teach and how to teach. The first decision, what to teach, underlies much of the IEP team's work. The second decision, how to teach, must be made by the teacher in order to implement the IEP.

Ortiz, A. A., & Yates, J. R. (1989). Staffing and the development of Individualized Education Programs for the bilingual exceptional student. In L. M. Baca & H. T. Cervantes (Eds.), *The bilingual special education interface* (2nd ed.; pp. 183–203). St. Louis: Mosley.
As our nation becomes increasingly multilingual, more school psychologists will be participating on IEP teams that are making decisions about the educational programs of bilingual exceptional students. The special considerations in developing and implementing IEPs for these students and in working with their families are discussed in this chapter.

Rosenfield, S. A. (1987). *Instructional consultation.* Hillsdale, NJ: Erlbaum.
Good consultation skills are required by the school psychologist to assist in the development, implementation, and evaluation of the IEP. This book contains many practical suggestions for the consultant, particularly when selecting and implementing interventions.

Shore, K. (1986). *The special education handbook: A comprehensive guide for parents and educators.* New York: Teachers College Press.
The special education process, including the IEP document and its development, is explained by a school psychologist in a clear and well-organized manner. Specific suggestions are offered to enable parents to become more active contributors to their child's individualized education program.

Zins, J. E., Curtis, M. J., Graden, J. L., & Ponti, C. R. (1988). *Helping students succeed in the regular classroom: A guide for developing intervention assistance programs.* San Francisco: Jossey-Bass.
Many practical suggestions are offered for working with teachers in a problem-solving process to assist students. The orientation is toward teacher assistance teams working in regular education, but the process is also applicable to the IEP development, implementation, and evaluation sequence.

57

Best Practices in Collaborative Problem Solving for Intervention Design

Sarah J. Allen
Janet L. Graden
University of Cincinnati

OVERVIEW

This chapter describes a *process* that can guide assessment and intervention procedures used in addressing academic and behavior concerns of students. The primary focus is on the two basic components of the term *collaborative problem solving. Collaborative* refers to the nature of the relationship between the participants in problem solving, the teacher(s), parent(s), student, and the school psychologist, who are *equal participants* in the process. *Problem solving* refers to the *systematic approach* used to conceptualize a problem situation, identify needs, design strategies to meet those needs, and implement and evaluate the strategies. Moreover, collaborative problem solving describes a way for school psychologists to organize their approach to service delivery — assessment and intervention, consultation for systems-level concerns such as school-wide discipline and school crises, counseling, and program planning and evaluation. Collaborative problem solving, with a foundation in consultation as a services delivery approach, has been long described in the school psychology literature as an effective and efficient way of providing services because it aims to help more students, focuses on *solving* problems in direct ways, involves relevant individuals in the intervention planning, and ultimately, enhances classroom and school situations for students.

Collaborative problem solving as a model for organizing services delivery has taken on renewed importance with the growing concerns about special education and increasing application of general education reforms in assessment and instructional approaches. Now, more than ever before, educators and parents are looking for ways to more directly assess student learning and performance (e.g., authentic assessment, performance-based assessment, outcome assessment). Parents of children with disabilities are seeking assessment that focuses more on describing specific skill, intervention, and support needs rather than on documenting deficits for the purposes of accessing services (e.g., Ahearn, 1993). Educators, in both general and special education, are desiring instructional, behavioral, and social-support approaches that meet the needs of *all* learners and accommodate the diversity existing among learners in all classrooms (e.g., Roach, 1992).

As a method for systematically approaching assessment and intervention design, collaborative problem solving also represents a useful way for school psychologists to rethink and reconceptualize their own approach to service delivery and the ways they can address these and other needs of students and teachers. By using a systematic approach in collaboration with others to clearly identify concerns, analyze and evaluate the factors affecting the concern, and design and evaluate specific interventions intended to remediate or eliminate the problem situation, school psychologists can provide an underlying framework for addressing the many different problems occurring in schools today, potentially at any of several levels within the organization.

In a time when students are experiencing more disturbing problems and facing increasing challenges and schools are struggling to meet diverse needs with sometimes fewer resources, school psychologists can be seen as vital when they help to address the problems of students and teachers. This will require a shift from the perception of school psychologists functioning to diagnose and assess problems to being seen more as a problem-solving facilitator and participant. However, the national context is conducive to such a shift. Major national reports and policy reviews have advocated for such changes (e.g., National Association of School Psychologists, 1994; Roach, 1992) and some states have already begun to systematically reform services delivery to more of a problem-solving and intervention focus (e.g., Iowa, Pennsylvania, Ohio).

BASIC CONSIDERATIONS

Collaborative problem solving as a framework for approaching problem situations has its foundations in many interrelated literatures in school psychology,

psychology, education, and special education. Among its key foundations are the scientist-practitioner approach; ecological and behavioral approaches to conceptualizing problems, assessing, and intervening; and consultation.

Scientist-Practitioner Approach

In the scientist-practitioner approach to psychological services delivery (described in detail in Barlow, Hayes, & Nelson, 1984), the practitioner relies on theory and research to guide assessment and intervention decisions, and intervention choices are treated as testable hypotheses. In this framework, all assessment is linked *directly* to intervention — assessment serves the purpose of gathering information to answer specific questions to inform intervention choices. One specific method for guiding this question-driven, hypothesis-testing process linking assessment to intervention, the Referral Question Consultation Method (RQC), is described in more detail in Batsche and Knoff (this volume). Interventions are selected based on determining (a) the most supportable hypotheses and (b) those predictions regarding interventions judged to have potential for success, based on prior research or founded in theoretical conceptions.

Another important feature is that interventions, as testable hypotheses, must be systematically monitored to assess whether they produce desired outcomes. Thus, informed decision making, question-focused assessment, a rationale for intervention selection, and a reliance on systematic data collection to monitor intervention outcomes are central features of a problem-solving approach to intervention design premised on a scientist-practitioner model.

Behavioral and Ecological Foundations

Although a generic problem-solving approach to child-related problems is not linked solely to behavioral and ecological foundations, behavioral and ecological approaches to assessment and intervention planning provide a strong, direct foundation for problem solving. Behavioral approaches stress the importance of

- Specifically defining and clarifying concerns.

- Analyzing both contexts in which behaviors occur and variables that are hypothesized to effect, control, and reinforce the behavior.

- *Directly* (versus indirectly) assessing the behaviors of concern in relevant environments.

- Intervening directly and in relevant environments.

- Directly assessing intervention outcomes.

This approach can be contrasted with, for example, a diagnostic-prescriptive approach in which the focus is on assessing to determine a diagnostic label or cat-

egory (e.g., learning disability, attention deficit disorder) that leads to a general prescription presumed to be related to the label. In contrast, a behavioral approach focuses on specific behaviors, skills, deficits, excesses, and environmental supports needed to enhance skills and support desired behaviors and performance. Also, in a behavioral model, the individual (within specific environments) is the level of analysis, whereas in other assessment approaches, there is more emphasis on normative comparisons and descriptions. Knutson and Shinn (1991), Lentz and Shapiro (1986), and Shapiro (1989) all include more detailed descriptions of behavioral foundations of problem solving.

Obviously, behavioral approaches include an examination of the context in which behaviors occur and therefore are ecological in nature. A problem-solving approach relies heavily on this ecological foundation in recognizing the importance of systematically and directly assessing *contexts* and including these contextual variables, not primarily child deficits, in the intervention plan. By emphasizing a problem *situation*, the ecological approach moves away from a primary emphasis on a problem as child focused and toward an understanding of a behavior or situation in a context. Major features of an ecological approach are described in more detail in Conoley and Conoley (1992) and Haynes (1992).

Consultation

Consultation has long been promoted as a way to organize service delivery and to assist teachers and parents to develop interventions for children. The consultation literature includes descriptions of several consultation models (e.g., behavioral consultation, Bergan, 1977; Bergan & Kratochwill, 1990; mental health consultation, Caplan, 1963; Meyers, Parsons, & Martin, 1979; collaborative consultation, Conoley & Conoley, 1982; Idol & West, 1987; collaborative problem-solving consultation, Gutkin & Curtis, 1990). However, as described in major consultation texts (e.g., Brown, Pryzwansky, & Schulte, 1987), these various approaches for organizing and describing consultation share many common characteristics. All emphasize, to some extent, relationship building and interpersonal variables, including developing a collaborative relationship. All also use a systematic approach to problem solving that involves the basic steps of problem identification, analysis of relevant features affecting the problem situation, intervention planning and development, and evaluation of progress toward desired outcomes.

Although the consultation literature was used heavily for the framework of this chapter, this chapter's authors have come to prefer the term *collaborative problem solving* to *consultation*. It seems to us that the former term

- Is more descriptive of what actually occurs in the consultative process.

- Emphasizes the collaborative nature of the problem solving across all phases.

- Avoids some terms used in the consultation literature (e.g., consultant, consultee) that by their very nature imply an expert/recipient model, with the consultant being the expert and the teacher or parent being the more passive recipient of the process.

In collaborative problem solving as described here, all participants engage actively in the process and share power in decision making. The notion of mutual problem solving, shared power, and active engagement in the process have been described as critical components of problem solving by others (e.g., Gutkin & Curtis, 1990), so this is not a novel idea. However, this chapter emphasizes and describes the process very specifically throughout the ensuing sections on problem solving.

ASSUMPTIONS UNDERLYING THE PROBLEM-SOLVING APPROACH

Careful consideration of the features of a collaborative problem-solving approach to intervention design reveals a number of assumptions that underlie this model of service delivery, both in theory and in practice. Practitioners adopting this approach to intervention design will find that endorsing these basic assumptions is prerequisite.

All Children Can Learn

A guiding principle of the National Association of School Psychologists (NASP) review of policy and practices regarding assessment and eligibility in special education is the premise that "all children can learn" (NASP, 1994, p. 2). Some children learn faster or slower, and some learn best differently than others. However, all children have the potential to learn. Further, federal legislation dictates that all children have a right to a free and appropriate education regardless of categorical label. As a result, it is incumbent upon education systems and school professionals to deliver services responsive to the needs of all children — with and without disabilities.

The implication of this assumption for a problem-solving approach is that it becomes the task of problem solving and the responsibility of the problem solvers to discover the interventions and supports that will enable children to learn. In this view, identification of a deficit or a need is only the first step in problem solving, not a goal in itself.

Learning is an *Interaction* Between Learner and Environment

Also underlying a collaborative problem-solving approach to intervention design is the premise that learning and behavior problems are a result of an *interaction* between a particular learner and his or her environment. The focus is on identifying a child's *needs* and the environmental *supports* required to meet those needs. This is fundamentally different from an internal child attribution, deficit-focused approach that underlies the current categorical model. A focus on interactions between learner and the environment has obvious implications for assessment in a problem-solving model. In this approach, assessment is focused on both learner characteristics and environmental variables as they affect the learner, skills, and performance. Environmental factors such as classroom features, instructional methods used, task demands, and responses and reinforcers are systematically assessed for the purpose of designing interventions that modify environmental variables.

Assessment and Intervention Must be Multidimensional

This principle stems logically from the person–environment interaction. Because learning is the result of an interaction between a learner and his or her environment, any procedures aimed at understanding that situation must be multidimensional and include consideration of both the learner and the environmental context and the interaction between them. Although the nature of and procedures for collecting data will depend upon the characteristics of each problem situation, some of the critical variables that need to be addressed include

1. Child variables, such as current skills and behaviors (e.g., academic, social), performance versus skill deficits, competing behaviors, response style.

2. Curricular variables, such as scope and sequences of objectives, placement versus expected placement in curriculum.

3. Instructional variables, such as teaching strategies, opportunity to respond, practice time, contingencies both during and after work is completed, feedback procedures.

4. Classroom context, such as class size, physical arrangement and structure, equipment, materials, and other resources available.

5. Peer intervention and support.

6. Teacher interaction, such as teaching strategies, classroom management strategies, instruction giving, and feedback format.

7. School and/or district variables, such as policies and resources available.

8. Family variables, such as support systems, stressors, interactions, and parenting skills.

9. Community variables.

More detailed descriptions of the focus and procedures of multidimensional assessment for intervention design are available in Lentz and Shapiro (1986) and Shapiro (1989).

Problem *Solving*, not Problem Finding, Sorting, Labeling, or Admiring

All too often the delivery of services to children with needs gets stalled at the point of "admiring the problem" (see footnote); that is, focusing on student deficits rather than solving the problem through specific interventions. Considerable time and energy can be devoted to assessing and diagnosing a problem for the purpose of determining a categorical label. However, with a primary focus on determining *what* the problem is or which label the child is eligible for, little or no time is spent in designing, implementing, and evaluating interventions to provide supports for student needs. In contrast, the primary purpose of the collaborative problem-solving approach to service delivery is to identify and provide the support, services, and/or accommodations needed to resolve the current problem situation.

Needs-Based, not Eligibility-Driven Model

A problem-solving approach to service delivery urges that for specific needs of children, rather than categorical labels with questionable implications for intervention, serve as the basis for design and delivery of supports and services. This conceptualization of the term *problem solving* focuses not on problems or deficits within and belonging only to children (NASP, 1993/94), but rather on addressing children's needs, which may include needs for improved competence in children as well as needs for environmental or instructional modifications.

Assessment and Intervention: Necessarily Idiosyncratic

Assessment refers to a process of gathering information needed to answer questions about a specific problem situation. Information derived from the assessment process should form the basis of intervention design. Based on the unique characteristics, experiences, and needs of each child and the distinctive nature of the environmental context in which each problem situation is occurring, both assessment and intervention are necessarily idiosyncratic. Throughout each phase of problem solving, the focus should remain on situation-specific solutions to situation-specific problems.

IMPORTANT ASPECTS OF PROBLEM SOLVING

Collaboration

An important aspect of the problem-solving approach to service delivery is collaboration among all participants (e.g., professionals and parents) at every step in the process. Unlike the medical model of service delivery in which the person functioning in the role of consultant is regarded as an "expert" who will dominate decision making, the problem-solving approach assumes that the knowledge and expertise of all participants are essential in the development and implementation of effective intervention strategies. As a result, parents, teachers, principals, school psychologists, and others must work together to clearly understand identified concerns. Giving consideration to both individual (e.g., student, teacher) and situational (e.g., classroom, school, community) variables that may affect performance, responsibility for planning and implementing interventions also are shared by all participants. Ultimately, however, final decision-making power regarding selection of intervention strategies is given to the person(s) assuming responsibility for implementation. Lastly, evaluating outcomes and considering needed modifications are also cooperative efforts.

Multilevel Service Delivery System for Problem Solving

Reflecting the need for and availability of support, efforts to intervene with student-related problem situations can occur at different levels within the school organization. Curtis, Curtis, and Graden (1988) provided a framework for conceptualizing the implementation of problem-solving efforts within a multilevel service delivery system resembling a pyramid.

Personal problem solving. Initially, teachers attempt to intervene with student-related problem situations through personal problem-solving efforts. In recognition of that fact, the first level of service delivery depicted on the Figure 1 pyramid involves classroom teachers collaborating in problem solving with another teacher. At this level, problem-solving steps and activities (e.g., delineating plans, monitoring changes) tend to be informal and unstructured.

One-to-one problem solving. At the next pyramid level, classroom teachers engage in collaborative problem solving through one-to-one consultation with individual special services personnel. Adhering to a systematic approach to problem-solving steps, Curtis et al. (1988) recommended that specific intervention plans be recorded and outcome data be monitored.

Group problem solving. Within this multilevel system, the highest level of service delivery is repre-

FIGURE 1.

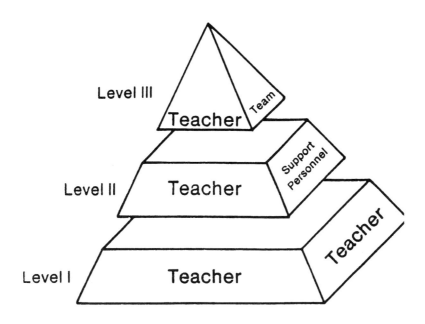

Level III   Group Problem Solving
Level II   Individual Consultation
Level I   Personal Problem Solving

sented by group problem solving. The composition and function of the group may vary, such that all members of the group may problem solve as a team, or the group could engage in problem clarification and then assign one member as a collaborator to assist the teacher. Certainly group problem solving is the most costly configuration of these service delivery options in terms of personnel time and resources and, therefore, is best used only to address the most complex and difficult problem situations.

Data-Based Decision Making

Finally, data-based decision making is an important aspect of collaborative problem solving. In fact, at each phase of the problem-solving process, assessment data generated from direct measures relevant to the problem situation form the basis for making decisions about the subsequent course(s) for action. For example, rather than making comparisons with a normative reference group, data generated from direct measures and tools is used to set goals and monitor progress toward attaining desired behavior relative to this problem situation. Further, brief, repeated measures of progress towards these goals are used to evaluate the success of interventions and to deter-

mine the need to change interventions when they are not resulting in the desired progress toward goals.

**BEST PRACTICES/
PROBLEM-SOLVING STEPS**

Although the literature includes descriptions of many different models of problem solving, all undertake the same basic phases. For the purposes of this discussion the four-step model of problem solving outlined by Bergan (1977; Bergan & Kratochwill, 1990) will be used. Those steps are problem identification, problem analysis, plan development and implementation, and problem evaluation. Also, to at least some extent, all approaches to consultative problem solving emphasize the importance of developing a collaborative relationship. Because this chapter's authors believe it is vitally important to collaborate meaningfully with teachers, parents, and students in problem solving, this chapter highlights the importance of collaboration at each step in problem solving.

This problem-solving process can be successfully applied to a whole spectrum of problem situations occurring in schools. Because of space limitations, this chapter will be devoted to an overview of the model as applied to problems of individual student performance, which might be addressed at either the individual or group consultation levels of problem-solving service delivery. It is important to note, however, that the same model and decision-making processes can be used to address problem situations applicable to different organizational levels, such as classroom- or building-level issues. For example, occasionally a school may repeatedly experience the same type of referral problems. When this occurs, it may be decided that some sort of programmatic interventions need to be implemented. Such a decision also is well within the purpose of a problem-solving approach to intervention design. Although the context to be examined differs to some degree, the decisions that have to be made by problem solvers are extremely similar.

The following discussion is intended to provide a clear understanding of the sequence and type of decisions that problem solvers must make when presented with a student who is not meeting expectations. The decisions that need to be made are the same for students with and without disabilities as well as for academic or behavioral problems. For each step in the problem-solving process, the *questions* that must be answered, the *tasks* that need to be completed to answer these questions, some *methods* for accomplishing the tasks, and the *outcomes* of the step are highlighted. Links between assessment and intervention will occur as the implications of decisions made at each step of problem solving must be used to inform the subsequent steps. That is, the design, implementation, and evaluation of interventions aimed at resolving problem situations are presented.

Problem Identification: What is the Problem?

The objective of the first phase of problem solving is specific problem identification. Premised on the assumption that the problem is situation-centered within an educational environment, the intent of this initial phase is to clearly define the discrepancy between expected and actual performance in a particular setting. Specifically, the problem is defined based on the mismatch between what people expect of the student to be successful in the environment and the student's current level of performance.

Questions to be asked at this phase include: What is the problem? Specifically, what is the student doing (or not doing) that has caused someone to perceive a problem? In defining and clarifying the problem to systematically include environmental factors in the problem identification, the question is broadened to: What is the problem situation? For example, a student is out of his assigned seat during large-group instruction periods, or a student is hitting other children when she does not receive an item requested. Rather than identifying problems such as a student is

"unmotivated" or "learning disabled," it is necessary to ask what the student is doing (or not doing) that the teacher has come to label in these general terms. In this case, it may be that the student does not turn in her assigned paper at the end of class or that he looks down and does not respond when called on during a class discussion.

To answer these questions, a number of *tasks* need to be accomplished during this phase of problem solving. Conceptualized as a funnel, the problem identification process should begin from a broad base to identify all concerns regarding a problem situation. First, problems may be described in general, global terms. As the funnel narrows, however, the problem(s) being identified must also be defined and clarified in more specific terms. For example, because problem situations often are complex in nature, it may be necessary to break the problem into component parts and, subsequently, to prioritize them either in terms of sequence (e.g., short-term and long-term) or importance (e.g., most critical based on potential for harm). Additionally, research (Bergan & Tombari, 1976) has shown that when problem situations are defined in observable, operational terms, the probability of successful problem resolution is significantly higher. Conversely, when a consultant introduced a medical-model label or internal child attribution or explanation into the interaction (e.g., child has ADHD), the teacher took less responsibility for problem resolution and problem solving efforts were less successful (Tombari & Bergan, 1978).

Therefore, beginning with top priority problems, specific target behaviors should be defined for each. Each problem should be stated in concrete, behavioral terms that can be both observed and measured. In addition to being representative of the problem area, specific target behaviors should also be socially valid and meaningful. That is, if these behaviors were changed, the primary caregiver's concerns would be alleviated. As a result, the input of the primary caregiver is critical to this and each of the remaining stages of problem solving.

Lastly, it is important that positive replacement behaviors be specified for each identified problem. Also stated in concrete, easy-to-measure, behavioral terms, goals should be generated as a criterion for assessing intervention effect. What is the expected outcome? What level of performance will the student need to reach (or not reach) to meet expectations? The target behaviors that will be increased and/or decreased also should be clearly defined and agreed upon by all participants.

Incorporated into all phases of collaborative problem solving, assessment may not be extensive during this phase but it does begin during problem identification. Because the concerns identified as part of this initial phase of problem solving represent what is perceived to be the problem and what must be changed if intervention is to be regarded as successful, assessment may be used to gather information needed in defining and clarifying a child's current performance or skills as well as environmental variables. Particular *methods* of assessment that may be used include interviews with teacher, parents, and/or the child; review of school grades and other records; review of work samples; direct observations; and behavioral rating. Finally, the *outcome* of this step is specific delineation of the problem situation in terms of target behavior(s) and replacement behavior(s).

Throughout problem identification, collaboration occurs by the consultant eliciting from the teacher, parent, and/or student their specific concerns and goals, and clarifying understanding of these. The consultant's role in this collaboration is to facilitate the problem-solving process and completion of the steps. The participant's role is to provide the best information he or she can about the concern. In terms of decision making, the person presenting the concern, not the consultant, makes the decision about which problems are priorities and which targets to include. Thus, the primary ownership for defining the situation of concern rests with the persons experiencing the problem situation (e.g., the teacher, student, parents).

Problem Analysis: Why is the Problem Situation Occurring?

Making decisions regarding why the problem situation is occurring corresponds to the second phase of problem solving, problem analysis. In answering questions about what "causes" a student to fail to meet expectations, the objectives are to understand the behavior in context and to form a hypothesis about why the problem situation is occurring so that an appropriate intervention can be developed. If the interventions developed later are to match the reasons that the problem exists, the decisions made here obviously are important. The selection, use, and interpretation of assessment tools are critical in determining the validity and reliability of information derived from the problem-analysis phase of problem solving. The focus is on *direct* assessment of variables that help guide intervention choices. Information is collected to answer specific questions in a direct and parsimonious manner. Assessment that does not have direct implications for intervention design is not completed.

The processes of problem solving in general, and problem analysis in particular, are not necessarily linked to any theoretical orientation. Problem solving does provide a systematic process for addressing problem situations; however, the application of this framework can be useful in guiding service delivery premised on various theoretical models. Neither the process, the questions to be answered, nor the tasks that need to be accomplished at each step in the problem-solving process will change dependent upon one's theoretical orientation. However, the hypothe-

ses and the answers that result will be different dependent upon the theoretical orientation of problem solvers due to the way each conceptualizes the issues, interprets the information gathered, and so forth. Given that this chapter's authors endorse an ecological orientation, for example, our conceptualization of a problem situation and the factors causing it would not be limited to sole focus on child variables. Rather, our analysis of the causes of the problem situation would include consideration of the skills and behavior of the child, his/her teacher, and the environmental context in which the problem situation is occurring.

The *questions* that need to be answered during the problem analysis phase of problem solving include: Why is this problem situation occurring? What factors are contributing to the mismatch that exists between actual and desired levels of performance for each target behavior? What resources are available to help resolve this problem situation?

To answer these questions, all of the factors possibly related to the problem situation need to be analyzed — both those factors serving as obstacles inhibiting desired performance and those which might serve as supportive factors or resources in resolving the problem situation. In particular, attention should be given to variables directly relevant to the problem situation and, therefore, possible areas for intervention planning. Readers are referred to the Batsche and Knoff chapter in this book for a discussion of domains or conditions that need to be considered when attempting to understand why the problem situation is occurring. Complete descriptions of behavioral approaches to problem analysis can be found in texts devoted to elaborating these procedures (for example, Martin & Pear, 1992; Shapiro, 1989; Shapiro & Lentz, 1986).

There are several general *considerations and tasks* for assessment at this stage of problem solving. First, the situational context in which problems are occurring should be carefully assessed. For example, a functional analysis of the problem situation could be conducted to examine antecedents, behaviors, and consequences. Second, exceptions to the problem situation might be examined. That is, what are the environmental conditions when the problem behavior is not occurring or when performance is better? Particular note should be made of conditions that can be altered as they may be useful targets for change in intervention planning. Finally, resources or factors supportive of resolving the problem situation should be identified.

In general, the goal of problem analysis is to determine a functional relationship between independent and dependent variables within this environmental context (Greenwood, Carta, & Atwater, 1991). There are various types and approaches to assessment that might be used during the problem analysis phase. Together participants must decide how best to answer the questions being asked about the cause of this problem situation. As a rule, however, comprehensive assessment within a problem-solving framework includes multiple procedures and sources of information. That is, for the purposes of problem analysis, assessment should be conducted across multiple environments, domains and times, and use multiple methods.

As additional information is needed to clearly understand the cause of the problem situation, specific questions should be generated collaboratively to guide further assessment. It is important to remember that assessment is the process of asking questions and generating information to answer questions. Therefore, assessment questions should focus on solving the current problem situation rather than just "admiring" it. That is, assessment questions and methods must be intervention oriented. In this framework, if assessment will not have direct intervention links, it is not completed. Examples of *methods* most directly useful for intervention purposes include systematic and directed observation, structured interviewing with those most familiar with the problem situation, functional analysis, curriculum-based assessment and measurement, behavioral rating scales, performance-based assessment, review of records, and permanent products such as classwork.

Collaboration as a method underlies all that is accomplished at this step. All data collected and all questions generated must be developed collaboratively and must serve the purpose of helping to develop interventions to improve the situation. The consultant does not serve in an expert role of deciding what information needs to be collected and how it will be collected. Nor does the consultant own the assessment information and its interpretation once it is collected. Rather, the teacher or intervenor should ideally be the "expert" in terms of a thorough understanding of the problem and its context. If assessment information is seen as the domain of an outside expert such as the school psychologist, the teacher or parent cannot be an active partner in problem analysis. From this collaborative perspective on problem analysis, all decisions about what data to collect, how to collect it, and how to use it are driven by collaboration. Thus, classroom observation data are collected to answer a specific intervention-related question, not to "verify" a teacher observation.

For example, observation could occur when there is a mutually agreed upon decision that more specific data are needed on a variable such as time on task, number of interruptions, or triggers for disruptive behavior. In this collaborative model, all forms of data collection are seen as answering questions generated earlier by the collaborators. It should be obvious that much of the data that school psychologists routinely collect for the purpose of determining special education eligibility as mandated by state rules and regulations do not serve the collaborative model.

However, in this situation, the school psychologist can make clear distinctions between data collected for intervention design and data collected to meet mandates. Also, the emphasis can be on data that help with intervention design.

From information generated during problem analysis, the *outcomes* of this step will be (a) an identification of the discrepancy between actual and desired level for each target behavior, (b) the setting of a specific outcome goal(s) for the intervention that will follow, and (c) a sufficient understanding of the problem situation and contextual variables to decide on an intervention plan to improve the situation. Based on this result of problem analysis, it sometimes is necessary to refine the target behavior.

Plan Implementation: What Can Be Done to Resolve the Current Problem Situation?

Once the problem situation is clearly identified and understood, the focus of the problem-solving process turns to the task of designing an intervention to resolve the problem. Related to the task of intervention planning, this next step in the problem-solving process can be divided into several phases, each with their own questions to be answered and tasks to be accomplished. Specifically, these phases include exploring alternative intervention strategies, selecting intervention(s), clarifying intervention plans, and implementing the chosen intervention(s).

Explore alternative intervention strategies.
In posing the *questions*, "what needs to be changed and how is that going to be done?" the first phase of intervention planning aims to explore alternative intervention strategies that could be tried to improve the problem situation. In so doing, the intent is to generate and explore a wide range of possible strategies for consideration by the person(s) responsible for implementing the intervention.

To be effective, interventions must be logically related to the identified problem and to the reasons that the problem situation exists. Therefore, the exploration and selection of intervention strategies is based on specific information derived from problem analysis. By discussing the factors that contribute to the mismatch between current and expected performance, problem-solving participants should begin to identify strategies for intervention. Consideration is given both to changing relevant context variables within the environment and to changing relevant skills or behavior of the student, teacher, and others.

Participants are encouraged to think creatively in generating possible intervention strategies and beyond the traditional use of resources such as placing a child in an existing program or classroom. At the same time, it is important to explore interventions within the control of those in the situation. That is, intervention strategies should consist of actions that participants can either prepare for or begin implementing tomorrow. When identifying strategies, all participants assume responsibility for contributing ideas and considering options so that the process remains collaborative. Instead of presenting primary caregivers with the "solution," participants should offer ideas as possibilities for consideration.

In collaborative problem solving, the school psychologist does not recommend action plans to the teacher as has been done in traditional psychoeducational reports. Rather, like each of the other participants, the school psychologist has the responsibility to contribute his or her knowledge and expertise so that participants can consider and evaluate alternatives. Ultimately, it will be the primary caregiver(s) who assumes responsibility for implementation of the intervention plan. As such, she or he will also be the person best able to determine the appropriateness or acceptability of proposed strategies. In fact, often some of the best ideas are generated by the persons most familiar with the problem situation. Certainly they are in the best position to evaluate their ability and willingness to implement a proposed intervention plan.

Select intervention plan(s). From among the many alternatives considered, specific intervention strategies must be chosen and an intervention plan outlined. Answers generated to the questions posed in previous steps are used to respond to the **question** that must be answered at this phase in the problem-solving process — "what intervention(s) should be tried to improve the problem situation?"

With regard to the *task* of selecting an intervention plan, there are several important issues to be considered. First, consistent with the notion of collaboration, responsibility for selecting an intervention strategy must rest with the person(s) who eventually will implement it. Given the collaborative nature of the problem-solving process, all participants share responsibility for brainstorming and evaluating alternative interventions. However, because the person(s) most directly involved in the problem situation assume primary responsibility for plan implementation, they are given final choice in the selection of intervention plans. Clearly, if an intervention is unacceptable to the person who is supposed to implement it, it is unlikely that it will ever be implemented as intended.

Another important consideration relative to the task of selecting an intervention plan is the likelihood of success in changing the problem situation. Based on the findings from problem analysis, a determination is made regarding what should be changed and what can be changed. With a focus on "alterable" variables, the selection of interventions should consider what are the most natural, least intrusive, and most effective strategies for accomplishing change. That is, to what extent do these strategies fit with current classroom routine and teaching practices? What, if any, positive effects are likely to result in other stu-

dents? Finally, in judging the potential efficacy of an intervention plan, consideration is given to issues of feasibility, including the availability of resources.

Clarify the intervention plan. Once an intervention plan has been selected, it is important to clarify all aspects of the procedures. In particular, all participants should agree on a written action plan that specifies (a) every component of the intervention plan, (b) person(s) responsible for each component, (c) setting(s) where the intervention will be conducted, and (d) beginning and review dates. Simply stated, the action plan needs to answer the *question* of "How will the intervention occur to improve the problem situation?" by considering who will do what, when, where, and how.

Also, clearly outlined as a portion of the intervention plan are procedures and a schedule for monitoring progress toward goals. Specifically, participants will need to answer the important *questions* of "How will we know that the intervention is working?" and "How will we show others that the intervention is working?"

In addition to establishing a brief repeated measure that may be used to assess target behaviors, a progress monitoring plan must include a timeline for intervention, goals or criteria for performance, and a decision-making system that allows for interventions to be changed when they do not produce the desired outcome.

Implement intervention plan. The primary responsibility for implementation of the chosen intervention plan is assumed by the individual(s) (e.g., teacher, parent) who spends the most time in setting(s) when interventions are being implemented rather than by support personnel such as school psychologists. However, it is the responsibility of *all* participants during the implementation phase to provide ongoing support for the intervention plan and for their collaborators. In our experience with implementing collaborative problem solving in schools, collaboration is most evident when all of the individuals who helped to develop the intervention plan also have a role in its implementation. For example, the teacher could direct implementation of the instructional strategy, the school psychologist could help set up the data-monitoring plan, and chart and direct data collection, the student could chart and self-monitor goal attainment, and the parents could reinforce goal attainment through rewards at home. The *question* to be answered at this phase in the problem-solving process is "How can we best support the intervention and the intervenor(s) during implementation?"

In response to this question, the *tasks* that need to be accomplished include providing ongoing support and systematic follow-up with intervention implementation. For example, it is important to provide those participants directly involved with implementation of the planned intervention with encouragement and positive feedback for their efforts. Additionally, support may be needed in gathering resources and collecting data. To ensure that interventions are being implemented as outlined, certain participants may need to provide support by trouble-shooting with the intervenor(s), providing technical assistance with intervention procedures, and/or monitoring treatment integrity.

Problem Evaluation: Is the Intervention Plan Working or Does It Need to be Changed?

In the problem-solving approach, an intervention is treated as a testable hypothesis, not a known solution. As such, assessment is an ongoing process and progress toward attainment of desired outcomes is monitored continually. After giving interventions sufficient time to be implemented, participants evaluate data regarding target behaviors and make decisions about whether the degree of progress being made toward each goal is adequate.

The principal *question* to be answered during the problem evaluation step is "How well is the intervention working?" Depending on the answer received, participants may need to ask follow-up questions. Specifically, if the goals of the intervention program are met, the focus of questions that follow will address issues in maintenance and/or generalization. For example, "Is the problem resolved or is there a need to continue an intervention?" "How will the intervention be faded in order to maintain the improvement?" and "How can the intervention strategies be applied to other settings in which the problem occurs?" If intervention outcomes are not satisfactory, it will be necessary to answer questions such as, "Is it certain that the intervention plan was implemented consistently as outlined?" and "What information was missed during problem analysis?"

To decide whether the intervention plan is working, problem solvers need to undertake several *tasks*. Specifically, the data collected through ongoing assessment needs to be examined to determine if the progress toward meeting goals is adequate. Subsequently, participants need to examine the implementation of the intervention plan, discuss problems, and decide if any changes are needed.

Based on the determinations made regarding the adequacy of the current intervention strategies meeting goals, problem solvers should undertake one of several alternative *tasks*. Specifically, if the intervention has been successful, it will be necessary to decide whether to (a) continue with the current intervention plan; (b) outline strategies to phase out the current intervention procedures, with consideration for generalizing to alternative settings or target behavior, or for maintenance within the natural setting; or (c) progress toward the next goal.

However, if it is decided that the interventions have not been effective in producing the desired changes in the problem situation, it may be necessary to recycle to an earlier step in the problem-solving process. If so, the tasks facing participants include reconsidering the questions addressed in an earlier step, such as target behaviors, situational variables contributing to the problem situation, or the nature of an intervention strategy. Alternatively, if the outcomes of an intervention plan are not effective, it may be necessary for participants to pursue more in-depth or extended problem solving. That is, it may be necessary to access additional resources and supports by taking the problem to a higher level on the continuum of service delivery options (e.g., request consultative assistance at group problem-solving level rather than at individual level).

Consistent with a problem-solving approach, progress toward desired outcomes is monitored through ongoing assessment. Data are used to determine whether interventions are working, whether goals are being met, or if the intervention plan needs to be changed. Based on the information derived from assessment data, all participants work cooperatively to evaluate outcomes, and decide both whether and how intervention plans may need to be modified in order to enhance progress. Having agreed, during the initial stages, about what the problem situation was and which behavior changes would indicate improvement, participants should find this question easy to answer.

Flexibility in Problem-Solving Sequence Implementation

Actual problem solving rarely proceeds in a sequence as orderly as described. Rather it is often necessary to move back and forth between steps, or, sometimes, to recycle to an earlier step in the process as new information is gathered, communication among participants improves, and the like. Nevertheless, the model described provides a framework that may be used as a flexible guideline for the ordering of steps, not as a rigid sequence of events.

SUMMARY

Given our common interest in supporting and addressing the needs of students, it becomes incumbent upon us (e.g., school professionals, parents, community members) to work together to solve problems. Recognizing that each participant will make different contributions to the process, it is important to realize that each also enhances the probability of reaching an effective solution to this particular problem situation. For school psychologists, perhaps the most important contributions that can be made are through facilitating the process used to address problem situations. Rathr than directing our energy at producing "the" right answer, school psychologists can work to establish ongoing relationship with and among other concerned individuals. And secondly, we have the expertise to guide the use of a framework that all participants can use in systematically addressing the problem situation. A collaborative problem solving approach to intervention design provides a model school psychologists might use in doing so.

REFERENCES

Ahearn, E. M. (1993). *Re-examining eligibility under IDEA: A background paper prepared for the Policy Forum Re-Examining Eligibility under IDEA.* Alexandria, VA: National Association of State Directors of Special Education.

Barlow, D. H., Hayes, S. C., & Nelson, R. O. (1984). *The scientist-practitioner: Research and accountability in clinical and educational settings.* New York: Pergamon Press.

Bergan, J. R. (1977). *Behavior consultation.* Columbus, OH: Charles E. Merrill.

Bergan, J. R., & Kratochwill, T. R. (1990). *Behavioral consultation and therapy.* New York: Plenum.

Bergan, J. R., & Tombari, M. L. (1976). Consultant skill and efficiency and the implementation of outcomes of consultation. *Journal of School Psychology, 14,* 3–14.

Brown, D., Pryzwansky, W. B., & Schulte, A. (1987). *Psychological consultation: Introduction to theory and practice.* Boston: Allyn & Bacon.

Caplan, G. (1963). Types of mental health consultation. *American Journal of Orthopsychiatry, 33,* 470–481.

Conoley, J. C., & Conoley, C. W. (1992). *School consultation: A guide to practice and training* (2nd ed.). New York: Pergamon Press.

Conoley, J. C., & Haynes, G. (1992). Ecological perspectives. In R. D'Amato & B. Rothlisberg (Eds.), *Psychological perspectives on intervention* (pp. 177–189). White Plains, NY: Longman Publishing.

Curtis, M. J., Curtis, V. A., & Graden, J. L. (1988). Prevention and early intervention through intervention assistance programs. *School Psychology International, 9,* 257–264.

Greenwood, C. R., Carta, J. J., & Atwater, J. (1991). Ecobehavioral analysis in the classroom: Review and implications. *Journal of Behavioral Education, 1,* 59–77.

Gutkin, T. B., & Curtis, M. J. (1990). School-based consultation: Theory, techniques, and research. In T. B. Gutkin & C. R. Reynolds (Eds.), *The handbook of school psychology* (2nd ed., pp. 577–611). New York: Wiley.

Idol, L., & West, J. F. (1987). Consultation in special education: Part 2. Training and practice. *Journal of Learning Disabilities, 20,* 474–497.

Knutson, N., & Shinn, M. R. (1991). Curriculum-based measurement: Conceptual underpinnings and integration into problem-solving assessment. *Journal of School Psychology, 29,* 371–393.

Lentz, F. E., & Shapiro, E. S. (1986). Functional assessment of the academic environment. *School Psychology Review, 15,* 346–357.

Martin, G., & Pear, J. (1992). Behavior modification: What it is and how to do it (4th ed.). Englewood Cliffs NJ: Prentice-Hall.

Meyers, J., Parson, R. D., & Martin, R. (1979). *Mental health consultation in the schools: A comprehensive guide for psychologists, social workers, psychiatrists, counselors, educators, and other human services professionals.* San Francisco: Jossey-Bass.

National Association of School Psychologists. (1994). *Assessment and eligibility in special education: An examination of policy and practice with proposals for change.* Alexandria, VA: National Association of State Directors of Special Education.

Roach, V. (1992). *Winners all: A call for inclusive schools.* Alexandria, VA: National Association of State Boards of Education.

Shapiro, E. S. (1989). *Academic skills problems: Direct assessment and intervention.* New York: Guilford.

Tombari, M. L., & Bergan, J. R. (1978). Consultation cues and teacher verbalizations, judgements, and expectations concerning children's adjustment problems. *Journal of School Psychology, 16,* 212–219.

ANNOTATED BIBLIOGRAPHY

Conoley, J. C., & Conoley, C. W. (1992). *School consultation: Practice and training* (2nd ed.). New York: Macmillan.

Written with the needs of practitioners in mind, this book provides a practical, straightforward guide to consultation in the schools that can be useful to both experienced and beginning problem solvers. Although each of the major approaches to consultation are presented, an ecological model provides the basis for discussions of implementation and ethical issues, necessary skills, pragmatic ways of evaluating effectiveness, and common obstacles to practice. Annotated case transcripts, suggested readings and references are used to expand upon the information discussed in the chapters.

Friend, M., & Cook, L. (1992). *Interactions: Collaboration skills for school professionals.* New York: Longman.

With an emphasis on interpersonal interactions among individuals and groups, this practical volume provides a detailed overview of collaboration skills. Both collaboration contexts, and interpersonal skills essential to effective consultative problem solving — listening, communicating, questioning, framing statements, and providing feedback — are covered in detail with practical application examples and practice activities for each. This book is an excellent introduction for educators without specific training in interpersonal aspects of collaboration and a useful refresher for experienced school psychologists regarding communication skills as applied to collaborative problem solving.

Kratochwill, T. R., & Bergan, J. R. (1990). *Behavioral consultation in applied settings: An individual guide.* New York: Plenum Press.

Intended to be a skill-training guidebook for practitioners interested in learning a behavioral consultation approach to the design and delivery of behavioral interventions in applied settings, this book can be used independently or as a supplement to a text by the same authors (Bergan & Kratochwill, 1990) and/or supervised training in collaborative problem solving. Objectives and procedures are detailed for each of the four stages in the problem solving process, along with some sample interview formats. The content presented in each chapter is expanded with examples and discussion of transcripts from consultation interviews, discussion questions, and self-quizzes.

Shapiro, E. S. (1989). *Academic skill problems: Direct assessment and intervention.* New York: Guilford.

Effective collaborative problem solving for the purpose of intervention design requires that problem solvers have a strong foundation in direct, intervention-oriented assessment, knowledge of effective classroom interventions, and skills in the use of methods to systematically plan and monitor assessment and interventions. This book is an excellent source of extensive, detailed information on each of these topics, with a particular emphasis on academic skills assessment and intervention. Practical guidelines, steps to follow in the process, and coverage of the knowledge base in several areas important to understanding classrooms (e.g., ecological assessment, interviewing frameworks for focusing on academic variables) are included. Helpful information is included on several specific assessment and data monitoring strategies, including curriculum-based assessment.

ACKNOWLEDGMENTS

The conceptualizations and examples found in this chapter have been shaped by the influence of many colleagues, and we want to gratefully acknowledge their contributions to our thinking. These individuals include our colleagues at the University of Cincinnati, David Barnett and F. Edward Lentz, as well as our many skilled students and graduates, whom we thank for their contributions to how we view problem solving. We also are indebted to the many educators and parents we have worked with in schools who continue to teach us about practical implementation of collaborative problem solving.

FOOTNOTE

We attribute the phrase "admiring the problem" to James Ysseldyke from whom we first heard this term several years ago. We believe it accurately captures the essence of many of the activities of multifactored evaluation teams that focus on finding and documenting student deficits, which Seymour Sarason has referred to previously as a "search for pathology."

58

Best Practices in Assessing Environmental Factors That Impact Student Performance

Maura L. Roberts
Illinois State University

OVERVIEW

Many procedures and measures have been used to assess academic performance throughout the years. The field of school psychology has been represented by different theoretical approaches which affect the selection of assessment instruments and interpretation of target behaviors. Regardless of these differences, the overall goal of assessment should be to design interventions. To achieve this goal, assessment procedures must be directly linked to an intervention for the target behavior. This link, however, can only be established by assessing the relationship between academic problems and critical variables in the classroom. In fact, to design and implement effective interventions, all factors that influence learning outcomes need to be assessed. Therefore, this chapter discusses the best practices for an alternative service delivery model that links assessment to intervention and highlights some of the most important environmental variables that impact student performance. Specifically, best practices for assessing the classroom environment will include the use of teacher interviews, direct observations, permanent products, curriculum-based measurement probes, and the evaluation of interventions/treatment procedures. Important environmental variables related to student, classroom, and instructional variables will also be discussed.

BASIC CONSIDERATIONS

Historically, educators have characterized traditional psychoeducational assessment and decision-making practices as a "search for pathology." These procedures tend to use instruments that primarily focus on within-student variables and processing deficits related to academic difficulties termed poor cognitive abilities (Lentz & Shapiro, 1986). Often school failure is attributed to these within-student characteristics. In other words, the emphasis of a diagnosis implies that something is "wrong" with the child rather than environmental variables. Therefore, psychoeducational evaluations are often administered for the purpose of identifying within-student deficits or disabilities that are presumed to "cause" educational difficulties (Algozzine, Ysseldyke, & Hill, 1982; Ysseldyke & Christenson, 1987; Ysseldyke, Regan, Thurlow, & Schwartz, 1981). Unfortunately, this type of assessment ignores environmental and instructional factors within the classroom that influence a student's performance. To remediate problems, school psychologists need to use assessment procedures that analyze the relationship of an academic problem to critical variables within the classroom environment.

Because of the limitations of traditional assessment, researchers and educators have designed new approaches to evaluate students in an academic environment — standardized observational codes and curriculum-based assessment. This alternative service delivery model has emphasized a direct link between assessment and intervention in primarily three ways:

1. Assessment information must be directly linked to interventions specifically designed for the target student's needs.

2. Assessment must examine the relationship between academic skills and the classroom environment.

3. The assessment process should be continuous to determine the success of interventions and make treatment modifications when necessary (Lentz & Shapiro, 1986).

Psychologists also need to assess and have a clear understanding of the complex interactions of the academic environment. Later in the chapter some of the critical variables in a structured environment that can impact student performance will be discussed. These variables fall into three groups: (a) student characteristics, (b) classroom environments, and (c) instructional practices.

BEST PRACTICES

In order to understand students in a structured environment, the psychologist should include in the assessment process (a) teacher interviews, (b) direct classroom observations, (c) analysis of permanent products, (d) the administration of curriculum-based measurement probes, and (e) treatment evaluation. Each of these assessment methods is designed to evaluate particular variables related to academic performance. Furthermore, these assessment techniques determine academic performance as well as their interaction with critical factors within the classroom. These procedures also provide information that can be directly linked to interventions and remediation of target behaviors.

Teacher Interviews

The primary objective of the teacher interview is to obtain a clear, operational definition of the target behavior and the classroom environment. Bergan's (1977) behavioral consultation model provides an excellent structure for psychologists conducting teacher interviews. This model explicitly outlines four types of interviews: problem identification, problem analysis, plan implementation, and plan evaluation. Each interview format allows the psychologist to analyze the structured environment and identify specific variables that may interfere with performance. These interviews not only help identify the problem, but each interview works toward planning and implementing interventions. In fact, Lentz and Shapiro (1986) recommend the use of the problem identification and analysis interviews for assessment and remedial planning, and the plan implementation and evaluation interviews for assessing treatment effectiveness.

In addition to Bergan's interview formats, Shapiro (1989) provides an excellent structure for conducting the teacher interview. The objectives of Shapiro's teacher-interview format are to help psychologists identify the problem, analyze the critical variables related to the problem (e.g., antecedent and consequences), and provide some indication of student skill level in reading, math, spelling, and written expression. Again, this format is designed to help psychologists obtain a clear definition of the presenting academic difficulties and related environmental events. Other variables specifically related to the target behavior that should be included in the teacher interview include instructional procedures, current level and placement in the curriculum, child performance, contingencies for performance, and classroom participation. Once a problem has been analyzed, additional interviews can permit teachers and psychologists to plan and evaluate interventions.

Direct Observations.

Following the problem identification interview, repeated observations need to be conducted to collect objective data on the student's interaction in the academic environment. Ideally, direct observations of the referred student should be conducted during the part of the school day in which the referral concern or target behavior occurs. The primary goal of direct observations is to obtain data that verify the teacher reports and establish an accurate and objective picture of the student's typical classroom behavior. Direct observations also enable psychologists to analyze the relationship between antecedents and consequences that may be maintaining the target behavior in the classroom.

When conducting classroom observations, the psychologist would do well to use highly standardized observational codes with protocols and standard definitions and procedures. Standardization helps ensure that the data collected are reliable, valid, and clearly communicated. The State-Event Classroom Observation System (Saudargas & Creed, 1982), Code of Instructional Student and Academic Responses (Stanley & Greenwood, 1981), and The Instructional Environment Scale (Ysseldyke & Christenson, 1987b) are all examples of standardized observation codes that can be used for direct classroom observations. All of these codes systematically describe the extent to which a student's academic or behavior problems are a function of the factors in the structured environment and help identify starting points in designing appropriate interventions. Observational data, such as out-of-seat behavior and on-task behavior, can also be collected subsequent to the assessment process to evaluate interventions' effectiveness.

Permanent Products

Whenever a direct observation is made, it is imperative that psychologists examine work produced during that time and compare these products to less direct measures of engagement (e.g., time on-task and orientation to material). Permanent products provide excellent samples of written responses of skills that students are required to perform or master. Other examples of permanent products include daily independent worksheets, homework, tests, and progress evaluations. Permanent products can be utilized during the initial teacher interview to help identify target skill areas. In fact, it is recommended that teachers maintain copies of the referred child's work products throughout the assessment and intervention process to measure changes in performance. Psychologists can also assess permanent products to determine the quality of response opportunities during independent seatwork. Specifically, permanent products can be analyzed to determine the types of errors typically made by the students (e.g., forgetting the beginning or ending of spelling words or difficulties regrouping math problems). Information obtained from an error analysis can help specify the interventions to remediate the problem. Furthermore, psychologists can continue to analyze the number of error responses to evaluate the success of interventions that are implemented (Lentz & Shapiro, 1986; Shapiro, 1989).

Curriculum-Based Measurement

Psychologists often administer various kinds of tests to determine a student's learning or academic achievement in the schools. More recently, educators have cited some limitations of traditional standardized norm-referenced measures (Deno, 1985; Tucker, 1985). A primary limitation is their inadequacy in measuring the outcomes of educational decisions, because they do not reflect small changes in student academic progress (Marston, Fuchs, & Deno, 1986). Secondly, these tests provide little information to help facilitate appropriate and effective interventions for academic difficulties within the classroom (Deno, 1985). Based on the limitations of traditional assessment, researchers and educators have begun to design new approaches to educational evaluation that provide objective long-term measurement of learning. Each of these measures attempts to link the assessment process to the curriculum and instruction, to allow on-going monitoring of progress in the curriculum, and to help identify a student's instructional needs (Shapiro & Derr, 1990).

Among the recently developed approaches to educational evaluation is curriculum-based assessment (CBA). CBA can be defined as "any set of measurement procedures that use direct observation and recording of a student's performance in the local curriculum as a basis for gathering information to make instructional decisions" (Deno, 1985, p. 41). These assessment procedures are derived directly from the curriculum material in which the child is being instructed to determine how much of that material the child has mastered. Furthermore, CBA procedures require only a series of brief, timed-skill probes which can be conducted in the areas of reading, spelling, mathematics, and written expression. In addition, CBA procedures can be used to create local normative samples and serve as a basis for making education decisions regarding student academic performance and growth at the local (school or classroom) level.

Since the conceptualization of CBA, different models have been developed, each with a different focus and/or set of procedures, and each designed to address different aspects of a student's academic performance (Shapiro, 1990). However, all CBA models are designed to: (a) provide improved links between the assessment and intervention processes, (b) employ direct measurement procedures, (c) use frequent and repeated measurement, and (d) rely on test administration of short duration. For example, Deno's (1985) model of curriculum-based measurement (CBM) is designed to decrease the gap between measurement and instruction by integrating a student's

achievement data with a teacher's daily instructional decisions. The four major assumptions of CBM are:

1. Modifications in instructional programs for individual students should be empirically tested before their effectiveness can be evaluated.

2. Time-series research designs are appropriate for monitoring and evaluating instructional program changes.

3. Applying time-series designs requires the specification of data representing academic progress in school years.

4. Time-series designs can discriminate between students who are in special and regular education programs (Deno, 1985).

In comparison to CBM measures, standardized achievement tests yield only norm-referenced scores, reflecting a student's relative standing within some reference group. Such measures do not yield any information regarding student competence within the curriculum and also fail to reflect a student's performance within the curriculum relative to his or her peer group. Similarly, achievement tests cannot generate data points frequently enough to establish the actual rate of student growth. Furthermore, CBM is sensitive to specific academic progress, unlike standardized achievement measures, which fail to show any student growth for up to 16 weeks (Friedman, 1990; Marston, Fuchs, & Deno, 1986). Within a short duration of time, CBM data reflect changes in a student's performance (as displayed in slope of improvement) which allow teachers and psychologists to frequently monitor academic performance.

In relation to special education placement decisions (Deno, Marston, & Tindal, 1986), CBM data can be used for screening and identification of students in need of special services by evaluating ratios between actual and expected performance as determined through collection of peer performance. Current performance levels can also be the basis for developing appropriate goals for the Individualized Education Plan and progress can be evaluated to facilitate timely and appropriate modifications in the program (Deno et al., 1986). Clearly, data already exist on the effectiveness of CBM, thus providing a strong support for its continued use and importance in educational assessment.

Direct Measurement of Intervention Effectiveness

Once the assessment process is completed, the repeated use of observations and CBM data can be used to determine the effectiveness of interventions. In particular, CBM data can be used to construct progress/performance graphs. These procedures allow psychologists to regularly obtain brief samples of student performance. These data can be graphically displayed in a series of repeated measures to describe a student's current level of performance. For example, the dependent measures, such as words read correctly, of CBM data can be graphed and the slope of these data can estimate the student's rate of curricular progress (Deno, 1985). Thus, CBM yields a slope of improvement unobtainable when using standardized achievement tests. These graphs also help clearly and effectively communicate a student's rate of achievement to teachers, parents, and students. Therefore, CBM allows teachers and psychologists to frequently monitor and evaluate the instructional effectiveness of interventions in order to efficiently solve a student's achievement problems.

ENVIRONMENTAL VARIABLES IMPORTANT TO ASSESSMENT

Student Characteristics

In order to understand and remediate academic problems, psychologists must examine student characteristics, as well as the classroom and instructional variables that influence learning. The most successful technologies for remediating academic problems involve direct instruction for skill deficits and/or manipulation of environmental variables impinging on student performance (Lentz & Shapiro, 1986). Academic skills, time needed to learn, and motivational factors are three examples of student characteristics that are often cited in the professional literature.

When assessing academic skills, psychologists need to differentiate between a skill and a performance deficit; this information is crucial for designing interventions. A skill deficit would indicate that a child's academic repertoire does not include the necessary skill or skills required to complete an academic task. For these children, variables such as the pace of instruction, opportunities for practice, and missing entry-level skills may be factors contributing to the skill deficit. On the other hand, a performance deficit would suggest a child has the academic skill or skills in his or her repertoire, but is not exhibiting the required behavior in the environment. For these children, contingencies for accuracy, completion of schoolwork, motivation, off-task behavior, and understanding the expectations for the assignment may be interfering with performance. Once the variables impinging on a child's skill or performance acquisition are identified, interventions specifically designed to meet a student's needs can be constructed.

Another student characteristic related to academic performance is the time each student requires to learn new information. Although research suggests that student rates of acquisition are considerably different, there seems to be a direct relationship between a student's cognitive ability, as measured by IQ, and the number of repetitions to acquire new material. Research suggests that students with high IQs (120–129) need fewer repetitions (20) compared to students with lower IQs (60–69; repetitions = 55). There is also evidence to suggest that students with IQs between 90–109 should be provided with 35 repetitions to achieve rapid and accurate recognition of new academic material. Clearly, automaticity and accuracy of responding can be greatly enhanced by increasing the number of repetitions of new information (Gates, 1930; Hargis, Terhaar-Yonkers, Williams, & Reed, 1988).

Lastly, the effect of motivation on student learning and performance is a crucial variable that needs to be assessed in the classroom. Although student motivation is often conceptualized as an internal process, it can be externally managed to dramatically affect change by using incentives for accuracy and completion of task-related assignments. Reinforcement programs and self-management techniques (e.g., contingency contracting, self-monitoring) can effectively motivate students in the classroom. Ysseldyke and Christenson (1987a) suggest the following strategies to increase a student's motivation to learn: vary assignments, set individual goals for learning and performance, assign tasks at a child's appropriate instructional level, clearly define contingencies for completing or not completing work, and regularly schedule conferences with students regarding performance. Given the importance of these motivation factors, psychologists need to determine the extent to which these practices are implemented and/or influence a student's target behavior. Suggested methods for assessing these student variables can be found in Table 1.

Classroom Environment

Many variables within the classroom environment can affect a student's classroom behavior and academic performance. For example, large group-size classrooms with minimal teacher supervision have been found to result in increases in classroom misbehavior (Jason & Nelson, 1980). Other research indicates that different classroom environments result in different student motivational goals (Covington & Omelich, 1984). When assessing the classroom environment, psychologists should pay particular attention to assessing variables related to academic engaged time (allocated time, on-task, opportunities to respond), classroom management (transitions, rules, physical arrangement) and the direction and frequency of teacher attention. Often these factors can interact with learning and can affect performance in the classroom.

Academic engaged time represents one of the most potent classroom variables affecting student achievement. Academic engagement can be defined as making frequent, accurate responses to stimuli or to relevant tasks to be learned, maintained, generalized, or adapted. The three variables related to academic engagement are: (a) allocated instructional

TABLE 1
Suggested Assessment Methods for
Student Characteristics Related to Academic Performance

	Interviews	Direct Observation	Permanent Product	Skill Probes
Motivation	X	X		
Prior Knowledge	X		X	X
Task Persistence	X	X		
Time needed to learn	X	X		
Cognitive types	X			
Cognitive abilities			X	X
Cognitive behaviors			X	X
Entry behavior/skills			X	X
Level of skill development	X		X	X
Learning rate	X		X	X
Pupil characteristics (sex, race, etc.)	X	X		
Ability to understand instruction	X	X	X	
Affective characteristics	X	X		

time, (b) on-task behavior, and (c) opportunities to respond (Lentz & Shapiro, 1986). Regardless of a student's characteristics or cognitive abilities, academic engagement is required to make adequate progress in the curriculum (Rosenshine, 1981).

Allocated instructional time is a general concept of academic engagement which refers to the amount of time actually available for students to work in the classroom (e.g., 30 minutes of math instruction). It consists of the time scheduled for instruction and the time available for students to work. In general, the amount of time a student can be academically engaged in the classroom is determined by allocated time. Therefore, the relationship between achievement and engagement is directly related to the amount of time allocated to work, and, more specifically, to the student's orientation to the task and appropriateness of academic responding.

In order to determine a student's use of allocated time, school psychologists should assess a child's on-task or "attention to task" behavior during instruction and work time, especially since such behaviors seem to be an important predictor of student achievement (Good & Brophy, 1984). There are many considerations and clues in this variable. For example, there may be differences between the percentage of time on-task during independent seatwork and during group instruction. Or a child who is off-task a high percentage of the time may have difficulty completing assignments or may not take advantage of opportunities to practice and acquire a new skill. Yet, a child may be on-task a high percentage of the time and still have lower rates of academic responding or task

completion (Ferritor, Buckholdt, Hamblin, & Smith, 1972). This may indicate a deficit in the child's academic skill repertoire. For example, a child who has just acquired a new skill may not be fluent in performing the skill and, therefore, need a longer period of time to complete an assignment.

The most specific and important variable related to academic engagement, however, is the number of opportunities to respond academically (Greenwood, Delquadri, & Hall, 1984). Opportunities to respond is defined as the number and type of student academic responses per time unit. Some examples include independent seatwork, cooperative learning, and accurate responses in small- and large-group instruction. Implementing strategies to increase opportunities to respond can greatly improve academic performance in the classroom (Rosenshine & Berliner, 1978). For example, establishing specific contingencies following completion of academic work can strengthen academic engagement. These contingent activities may include free time, access to desirable activities, public feedback about performance, and feedback to parents about the quality of student academic work during the school day. Altering some of the factors related to academic engagement can help ensure high rates of active, productive student involvement throughout the learning process (Fuchs, 1986).

Classroom Management

Another important part of assessing the classroom environment involves the examination of classroom management. Disruptive or inappropriate behaviors, such as misbehavior, out-of-seat, talking or looking around, are examples of competing responses that must be eliminated or minimized to enhance the learning environment. In fact, a student's achievement is often decreased by classroom noise and distractions. Effective classroom management can reduce disruption and increase the amount of allocated time for instruction. Three factors of effective classroom management are the use of classroom rules, sufficient transition time, and the efficient physical arrangement of the classroom.

There are at least two important reasons to use consistent classroom rules. First, rules help communicate the teacher's expectations regarding student behavior in the classroom. Secondly, rules provide an opportunity for students to receive attention from teachers for observing the rules (Paine, Radicchi, Roselinni, Deutchman, & Darch, 1983). In fact, rules can be established for different activities or desired behavior, such as social conduct (e.g., in your seat, work on assigned task, raise your hand before speaking), academic performance (e.g., 90% or more correct for a passing grade or to earn a reward) or instruction time (e.g., keep your hands/feet to yourself, talk only when it is your turn). When developing rules, Paine et al. (1983) offer the following guidelines: (a) use only three to four rules for any given activity, (b) keep wording of rules simple, (c) state the rules positively, (d) use different rules for different situations (e.g., transition time versus group instruction), and (e) post the rules in a prominent location in the classroom. Consistent implementation of classroom rules decreases disruptions (i.e., less noise, out-of-seat behavior, time off-task) and increases allocated time.

Transition time, another aspect of classroom management often overlooked when assessing the structured environment, is the amount of time it takes to change from one activity to another. The effective use of transition time leads to fewer student behavior problems during unstructured time. Clearly stated and implemented procedures for transition time can help minimize the amount of nonacademic time that children spend in school. It provides teachers with more time for academic instruction and decreases the number of behavior problems that often occur during this unstructured time (Paine et al., 1983). Therefore, the effective use of transition time can maximize allocated instructional time and minimize distractions which can indirectly influence academic performance.

The classroom's physical arrangement, defined as the organization of classroom space (i.e., furniture, teaching activities area, room dividers), can also have an effect on student behavior and academic performance. Ideally, this physical arrangement should facilitate optimum student performance. For example, classrooms in which desks are grouped together often have a higher incidence of student talking, which can indirectly affect a student's time spent on task. Properly organizing classroom space can improve the level and quality of student interactions. Undesirable student interactions, such as excessive talking, can be decreased by separating the desks, while effective classroom arrangements can increase desirable student interaction. For example, open areas within the classroom can help facilitate student participation in a variety of activities in order to develop creativity, sharing, communication, and friendship skills. Factors such as the location of students' and the teacher's desks, classroom partitions, and the placement of teaching materials and stations can all play an important part in classroom management and the effectiveness of student learning (Paine et al., 1983). For example, student desks should be separated in rows, facing the chalkboard (not the window). Classroom partitions can help structure small-group instructional activities to minimize distractions from the rest of the class. Teaching stations can be positioned in any unoccupied corner of the room, whereas self-correction stations can be placed against one wall with a few tables or chairs. Materials stations can be placed in the front of the room for easy access in distribution or collection.

Within the classroom environment, teacher attention is probably one of the most powerful ways of managing a student's behavior. Teachers who provide attention or acknowledgment for appropriate task behaviors increase the probability of a student demonstrating that behavior in the future (Bernhard & Forehand, 1975; Broden, Bruce, Michelle, Carter, & Hall, 1970; Kazdin & Kloch, 1973). Teachers can positively affect academic performance by providing praise for on-task behaviors. Likewise, problematic behaviors, such as looking around and off-task behaviors, can also be maintained by contingent teacher attention. Therefore, teachers' attention can enhance academic acquisition, as well as decrease problematic behaviors, by providing frequent, brief contacts to students who are on-task. The use of modeling and teacher feedback (verbal or written) can also affect the accuracy of completed work. Error correction procedures, provided immediately upon completion of work, can increase academic performance and minimize future errors. Therefore, it is important to consider teacher attention and feedback to the target student when examining the academic ecology (Paine et al., 1983). Methods for assessing classroom variables are found in Table 2.

Instructional Practices

The last broad category of variables to assess in the structured academic environment is the instructional practices related to student outcomes. Practices such as planning procedures, teaching procedures, and monitoring and evaluation procedures can affect a student's achievement. Academic achievement requires students to learn and progress through

TABLE 2
Environmental Factors Related to Academic Performance
and Methods for Assessing Them

	Interviews	Direct Observation	Permanent Product	Skill Probes
Engaged time	X	X	X	
Allocated time	X	X		
Scheduled time	X	X		
On-task	X	X	X	
Opportunities to respond	X	X		
Response rate	X	X	X	X
Classroom rules	X	X		
Classroom procedures	X	X		
Contingencies for behaviors	X	X		
Accuracy feedback	X	X		
Teacher attention	X	X		
Expectations for performance	X	X		
Class size	X	X		
Class structure	X	X		
Extent of discipline problems	X	X		

the curriculum at the expected pace. Students who have academic difficulties, however, are often unable to meet the curricular demands. In fact some educators believe that the curriculum pace moves too quickly for these students, in relation to their repertoire of skills. This creates a downward spiral in which these children get further and further behind academically (Gickling & Havertape, 1981).

Instructional material can be altered to ensure that a particular level of success is experienced (Dickinson & Butt, 1989). Gickling and Havertape (1981) suggest that the delivery of instruction can be altered to carefully control the difficulty level of curriculum materials. They recommend an instructional match be based on the student's performance rather than the chosen type of assignments. They have suggested three levels of instruction that represent the degree of instructional match or mismatch between the student's skills and the learning demands of the instructional task. If an assignment is entirely too challenging or at a frustrational level for a student, the ratio would approach 0% known items to 100% unknown items. An assignment far too easy or at an independent level would approach a ratio of 100% known to 0% unknown items. Student's daily performances are based on a continuum between these two extremes (Gickling & Havertape, 1981). Therefore, a student's performance can also be objectively measured via curriculum-based measurement procedures to determine the effectiveness of a teacher's instructional decisions, and the instructional ratios can be

readjusted to maximize a student's academic progress (Gickling & Thompson, 1985).

Based on this assumption, they suggest that students acquire and retain new materials best if the ratio of known to unknown items are controlled while students are learning. Known responses are emitted rapidly and correctly all the time, whereas unknown responses are defined as either errors or hesitant responses. They recommend that instructional ratios for comprehension be 93–97% known to 3–7% unknown. Under conditions of drill and practice, however, instructional levels should contain 70–85% known and 15–30% unknown material. For example, students trying to learn 10 new vocabulary words should receive 8 known words and 2 unknown words or an instructional ratio of 80% known to 20% unknown or 8:2 (within Gickling's suggested ratio for drill and practice). Presented items exceeding these limits would be viewed at an independent level (e.g., 90% known to 10% unknown or 9:1 — too easy), while material below these levels would be considered to be at a frustrational level (e.g., 20% known to 80% unknown or 2:8 — too difficult). Since instructional mismatch is often a major contributor to the poor academic performance of low-achieving students, assessment procedures need to evaluate and, if necessary, alter the match between student acquisition and instruction.

In addition to matching a student's skill and instructional materials, other variables that enhance learning and influence a person's learning of new ma-

TABLE 3
Instructional Practices Related to Academic Performance
and Possible Assessment Methods

	Interviews	Direct Observations	Permanent Product	Skill Probes
Sufficient time allocated to academic activities	X	X	X	
Task matched to a student's skill level		X	X	X
Instructional decision making (grouping material, ongoing diagnostic ability)		X	X	X
Lesson presentation	X			
Practice opportunities	X	X	X	
Review material		X		
Kind of curriculum	X			
Pacing of instruction		X	X	X
Accuracy of student responses	X	X	X	X
Active monitoring of seatwork activities		X		
Use of error correction procedures	X	X		
Frequent, direct measurement of pupil progress		X	X	X

terial involve practice, temporal continuity, and cumulative versus rapid material presentation (Gleason, Carnine, & Vala, 1988; Johnson, Gersten, & Carnine, 1987). An important consideration regarding acquisition of new material is the time delay between learning and reviewing difficult items. Although students may learn difficult information, they may not have ample opportunities to review this newly acquired information. If a student is taught a word but does not have subsequent chances to practice, this may impede the rate of learning. A delayed review may also increase the likelihood that mistakes will occur in the future. To minimize possible future errors, students should review difficult material within a day or two of initial learning. Ysseldyke and Christenson (1987a) also highlight the following requirements for providing relevant practice opportunities: (a) assignment of practice tasks at an instructional level appropriate for the student (i.e., instructional levels mentioned by Gickling and his associates for drill and practice — previously discussed), (b) modification of task requirements when necessary so that a student can complete the work successfully, (c) careful monitoring of student performance, and (d) frequent feedback during practice. Furthermore, opportunities for practice should be implemented until a student makes only infrequent mistakes.

Teacher planning and evaluation is another important instructional practice related to learning. Teachers who set discrete academic performance goals for remedial students and collect periodic data on student progress are able to affect greater achieve-

ment (Fuchs, Deno, & Mirkin, 1984). Ongoing progress evaluation facilitates formative modification of instructional procedures. Self-management techniques, such as self-charting, self-monitoring, self-evaluation, and contingency contracting, can also increase academic performance, and, therefore, should be considered when assessing the academic environment (Ysseldyke & Christenson, 1987a). Suggested methods for assessing instructional variables can be found in Table 3.

SUMMARY

Analyzing the relationship between student characteristics, environmental variables and instructional practices is crucial to understanding students in a structured classroom environment. It enables psychologists to determine the interaction between these variables and the presenting problem. Furthermore, predictions about classroom events and student performance can help determine appropriate intervention strategies for academic success. Alternative strategies, such as interviewing, direct observations, analysis of permanent products, CBM probes, and treatment evaluation, allow psychologists to directly assess and remediate academic skills. These direct methods not only provide intervention strategies, but also offer ways to evaluate the success of treatment programs. Therefore, the alternative service delivery model discussed in this chapter links assessment to intervention to provide an understanding of the relationship between environmental factors that impact student performance.

REFERENCES

Algozzine, B., Ysseldyke, J. E., & Hill, C. (1982). Psychoeducational decision-making as a function of the number of devices administered. *Psychology in the Schools, 19*, 328–334.

Bergan, J. (1977). *Behavioral consultation.* Columbus, OH: Merrill.

Bernhard, A., & Forehand, R. (1975). The effects of labeled and unlabeled praise upon lower and middle class children. *Journal of Experimental Child Psychology, 19*, 536–543.

Broden, M., Bruce, C., Mitchell, N., Carter, B., & Hall, R. (1970). Effects of teacher attention and a token reinforcement system in a junior high school special education class. *Exceptional Children, 36*, 341–349.

Christenson, S. L., Ysseldyke, J. E., & Thurlow, M. L. (1989). Critical instructional factors for students with mild handicaps: An integrated review. *Remedial and Special Education, 10*, 21–31.

Covington, M. V., & Omelich, C. L. (1984). Task-oriented vs. competitive learning structures: Motivational and performance consequences. *Journal of Educational Psychology, 76*, 1038–1050.

Deno, S. (1985). Curriculum-based measurement. The emerging alternative. *Exceptional Children, 52*, 219–232.

Deno, S. L., Marston, D., & Tindal, G. (1986). Direct and frequent curriculum-based measurement: An alternative for educational decision making. *Special Services in the Schools, 6*, 5–27.

Dickinson, D. J., & Butt, J. A. (1989). The effects of success and failure on the on-task behavioral of high achieving students. *Education and Treatment of Children, 12*, 243–253.

Ferritor, D., Buckholdt, D., Hamblin, R., & Smith, J. (1972). The non-effects of contingent reinforcement for attending behavior on work accomplished. *Journal of Applied Behavior Analysis, 5*, 7–17.

Friedman, J. (1990). *An evaluation of the relative sensitivity to student growth in reading and spelling of standardized achievement tests and curriculum-based measures.* Unpublished doctoral dissertation, Lehigh University, Bethlehem, PA.

Fuchs, L. (1986). Formative evaluation of mildly handicapped children. *Remedial and Special Education, 7*, 5–12.

Fuchs, L. S., Deno, S. L., & Mirkin, P. K. (1984). The effects of frequent curriculum-based measurement and evaluation on pedagogy, student achievement, and student awareness of learning. *American Educational Research Journal, 21*, 449–460.

Gates, A. (1930). *Interest and ability in reading.* New York: Macmillan.

Gickling, E., & Havertape, S. (1981). *Non-test based assessment training manual.* National School Psychology Inservice Training Network, Minneapolis, MN.

Gickling, E. E., & Thompson, V. P. (1985). A personal view of curriculum-based assessment. *Exceptional Children, 52*, 205–218.

Gleason, M., Carnine, D., & Vala, N. (1988). Cumulative versus rapid introduction of new information. *Exceptional Children, 5*, 353–358.

Good, T., & Brophy, J. (1984). *Looking in classrooms.* New York: Harper & Row.

Greenwood, C., Delquadri, J., & Hall, R. (1984). Opportunities to respond and student academic performance. In W. Heward, T. Heron, D. Hall, & J. Trap-Porter (Eds.), *Focusing on behavior analysis in education* (pp. 58–88). Columbus, OH: Merrill.

Hargis, C. H., Terhaar-Yonkers, M., Williams, P. C., & Reed, M. T. (1988). Repetition requirements forward recognition. *Journal of Reading, 3*, 320–327.

Jason, L. A., & Nelson, T. (1980). Investigating relationships between problem behaviors and environmental design. *Corrective and Social Psychiatry, 26*, 53–57.

Johnson, G., Gersten, R., & Carnine, D. (1987). Effects of instructional design variables on vocabulary acquisition of LD students: A student of computer-assessment instruction. *Journal of Learning Disabilities, 20*, 206–213.

Kazdin, A., & Shields, F. (1972). The effect of nonverbal teacher approval on student attentive behavior. *Journal of Applied Behavior Analysis, 6*, 643–654.

Lentz, F. E., & Shapiro, E. S. (1986). Functional assessment of the academic environment. *School Psychology Review, 15*, 346–357.

Marston, D., Fuchs, L. S., & Deno, S. L. (1986). Measuring pupil progress: A comparison of standardized achievement tests and curriculum-related measures. *Diagnostiqué, 11*, 77–90.

Paine, S. C., Radicchi, J., Rosellini, L., Deutchman, L., & Darch, C. B. (1983). *Structuring your classroom for academic success.* Champaign, IL: Research Press Company.

Rosenshine, B. V. (1981). Academic engaged time, content covered, and direct instruction. *Journal of Education, 3*, 38–66.

Rosenshine, B. V., & Berliner, D. C. (1978). Academic engaged time. *British Journal of Teacher Education, 4*, 3–16.

Saudargas, R. A., & Creed, V. (1980). *State-Event Classroom Observation System.* Knoxville, TN: University of Tennessee, Department of Psychology.

Shapiro, E. S. (1989). *Academic skills problems: Direct assessment and interventions.* New York: Guilford Press.

Shapiro, E. S. (1990). An integrated model for curriculum-based assessment. *School Psychology Review, 19*, 331–400.

Shapiro, E. S., & Derr, T. F. (1990). Curriculum-based assessment. In T. B. Gutkin & C. R. Reynolds (Eds.), *The handbook of school psychology* (2nd ed., pp. 365–387). New York: Wiley.

Stanley, S., & Greenwood, C. (1981). *CISSAR, code for instructional structure and student academic reasons: Observer's manual.* Kansas City, KS: Juniper Gardens Children's Project, Bureau of Child Research, University of Kansas.

Tucker, J. A. (1985). Curriculum-based assessment: An introduction. *Exceptional Children, 52*, 199–204.

Ysseldyke, J. E., & Christenson, S. L. (1987a). Evaluating students' instructional environments. *Remedial and Special Education, 8*, 17–24.

Ysseldyke, J. E., & Christenson, S. L. (1987b). *The instructional environment scale.* Austin, TX: Pro-Ed.

Ysseldyke, J. E., & Christenson, S. L. (1988). Curriculum-based measurement. In J. Graden, J. Zins, & M. Curtis (Eds.), *Alternative educational delivery systems: Enhancing instructional options for all students* (pp. 111– 135). Washington, DC: National Association of School Psychologists.

Ysseldyke, J. E., Regan, R. R., Thurlow, M. L., & Schwartz, S. Z. (1981). Current assessment practices: The cattle dip approach. *Diagnostiqué, 6*, 16–27.

ANNOTATED BIBLIOGRAPHY

Graden, J. L., Zins, J. E., & Curtis, M. J. (1988). *Alternative educational delivery systems: Enhancing instructional options for all students.* Washington, DC: National Association of School Psychologists.

This is an excellent source for information on alternative service delivery in psychology. The book is organized into three major parts corresponding to the need for alternatives, information on possible alternative frameworks, and means of facilitating the change process to implement alternative service delivery systems. Alternative practices related to referral, assessment, and intervention as well as an alternative organizational framework for providing a broad-based service to school and district levels are discussed. It also covers special topics relative to alternative services for individuals with severe disabilities, infants and toddlers, and preschoolers.

Paine, S. C., Radicchi, J., Rosellini, L., Deutchman, L., & Darch, C. B. (1983). *Structuring your classroom for academic success.* Champaign, IL: Research Press Company.
This book provides guidance in managing the classroom successfully. It presents an overview of important variables related to management skills. The authors' recommendations are based on empirical research and teacher experiences. Overall, the book is a valuable resource for psychologists and can serve as the basis for inservice teacher training programs.

Shapiro, E. S. (1989). *Academic skills problems: Direct assessment and intervention.* New York: Guilford Press.

This book provides methods for direct assessment and intervention of academic problems. It is written with the practitioner in mind and offers step-by-step instructions for using these methods. In particular, procedures for direct observation and curriculum-based assessment procedures are discussed and forms for many parts of the evaluation process are included in the book.

Zins, J. E., Curtis, M. J., Graden, J. L., & Ponti, C. R. (1988). *Helping students succeed in the regular classroom: A guide for developing intervention assistance programs.* San Francisco: Jossey-Bass, Inc.
All the ingredients for understanding and effectively implementing and operating an intervention assistance program in the schools are presented in this book. They present a practical yet necessary conceptual background to understand the intervention assistance process. Sufficient detail is also provided to enable practitioners to make intervention assistance programs an integral component of a psychologist's current educational system. Additionally, the development of interventions for individual students as well as the implementation of intervention assistance programs in the school organization are discussed.

59

Best Practices in Developing Local Norms in Behavioral Assessment

Andrea Canter
Minneapolis Public Schools

The use of local norms in the assessment of academic skills has received considerable attention in recent years, particularly in the professional literature regarding Curriculum-Based Measurement. This chapter addresses the application of local norms to the assessment of social and functional skills. An overview will be followed by a discussion of basic considerations in the development of locally normed procedures, recommended practices, and a case study of the development of a locally normed functional skills assessment procedure at the district and state level.

OVERVIEW

For nearly a century, the practice of school psychology has been characterized by nationally normed assessment procedures used to diagnose and classify intellectual, academic, and behavioral problems. In recent years, researchers and practitioners have implemented significant alternatives to traditional approaches for measuring academic skills, such as Curriculum-Based Assessment and Curriculum-Based Measurement. This new generation of direct assessment procedures is more strongly linked to intervention than to classification, more relevant to instruction than to diagnosis, and more tied to local than to national standards of performance.

While the call to *replace* traditional approaches with alternative models is the source of much controversy in the profession (e.g., Braden & Reschly, 1993), the development of direct assessment and other new procedures has unquestionably resulted in improved professional practice linked to students' academic outcomes. The shortcomings of traditional assessment are certainly as evident in the domains of social and adaptive behavior as in the domains of cognition and achievement: Student performance is compared to statistical national norms regardless of relevance to local cultural norms and home/school expectations and without a direct link to intervention.

A Rationale for Local Norms

One alternative approach to traditional assessments is the use of local, rather than national, norms. Local norms have been cited as essential to developing instructionally and ecologically relevant assessments (Bardon, 1988), as more realistic and, for some purposes, as more appropriate than "nonequivalent national norms" (Anastasi, 1988). Locally normed measures provide a means of overcoming some of the criticisms of traditional procedures, as they can address social standards and environmental contexts, lead to intervention, and reduce ethnic and cultural bias. Local norms also can provide an essential perspective to the special education eligibility and placement process as they "operationalize the expectations of the mainstream environment" (Shinn, 1989).

Even within the context of traditional assessment purposes of diagnosis and classification, the use of a local frame of reference is essential in addressing functional and social skills which are typically defined in terms of social significance or social validity. Recognition of the social significance of behavior has been recommended as a component of state definitions of emotional/behavioral disorder (Cullinen, Epstein, & McLinden, 1986). Gresham (1983) defines social skills as "situationally specific behaviors that predict important social outcomes for children and youth."

To best understand the student's functioning, one must consider the social norms or expectations of the classroom, school, and community in which the student is asked to perform. In fact, Achenbach, McConaughy, and Howell (1987) cite the situational specificity of behavior, rather than measurement error, as the basis of relatively low inter-rater reliability of behavior scales. Deno (1989) notes the importance of situational specificity in understanding the concept of "handicap."

Handicaps can only be defined in terms of the relationship between what a person can do and what a person must do to succeed in a given environment. . . . Teachers do not make judgments . . . based only on the universal norms of the culture; instead, their judgments are also based on the behavior of the students in classrooms and schools within which they are working. (p. 5, 10)

Local Norms, Expectations, and Intervention

The concept of social validity is closely tied to local expectations — the standards of one's community, culture, neighborhood, school, or peer group. National norms provide information about the individual's functioning relative to what are assumed to be universal standards. Yet, in a diverse society, such assumptions can lead to cultural and regional bias in measurement, one of the strongest criticisms of norm-referenced testing.

Locally developed norms, on the other hand, should reflect what is relevant for success within the local context; procedures reflecting local standards should more fairly identify individuals in need of intervention in order to perform successfully. Such measures directly relate to referral concerns, as teacher referrals likely reflect a discrepancy between student performance and teacher *expectation*, rather than an absolute deficit in skills (Ritter, 1989; Shinn, Tindal, & Spira, 1987). Furthermore, congruence with teacher expectations for classroom functioning is highly related to mainstream success for at-risk students and those with disabilities (Hersh & Walker, 1983).

Assessment approaches reflecting local standards are more readily applied to designing intervention strategies than are global, nationally normed procedures. Such procedures allow comparison of a referred student with relevant peer groups, facilitating informed decisions regarding (a) the most appropriate and least restrictive placement, (b) the degree of discrepancy between the student's behavior and the expectations of a potential placement, and (c) areas requiring intervention prior to transition to a less restrictive or mainstream placement.

These characteristics are consistent with the concept of "template matching" described by Hoier, McConnell, and Pallay (1987), in which assessment information is used to develop a "template" (behavioral profile) of individual classrooms. When the situational specificity of student performance is measured and understood, intervention strategies can better focus on generalization across settings. Thus, assessment based on local standards can help to promote successful transitions from special to regular education classrooms (McConnell, 1987; Horn & Fuchs, 1987) as well as successful inclusion efforts.

Importance to School Psychology Practice

School psychologists are generally trained to serve as problem solvers, yet traditional practice tends to emphasize problem *identification*. School psychologists seeking expanded roles should find that the implementation of locally normed assessment procedures enhances opportunities for problem-solving consultation by directly addressing teacher expectations and referral concerns. By offering alternative or supplemental information which can be interpreted in the local cultural context, local norms also can help alleviate ethical dilemmas created by the potentially discriminatory nature of nationally normed procedures. Furthermore, the design and development of locally normed procedures provides an ideal opportunity for school psychologists to use their training and expertise in measurement and applied research within the practical scope of a single classroom, school, or district.

Limitations of Local Norms

Use of local norms is hardly a cure for all problems associated with traditional measures. Many of the criticisms of nationally normed tests apply to local norms as well. A norm-referenced measure of any sort may not fit the assessment purpose; even a locally normed procedure may not fairly represent a given individual; technical adequacy can be a significant problem with locally normed procedures if samples are small. If the behaviors measured vary significantly across settings, it may be difficult to identify sufficiently consistent environments from which to draw an adequate sample for norming purposes. Furthermore, when data reflect local values and/or local samples, one can not generalize with much confidence beyond the immediate context.

BASIC CONSIDERATIONS

To effectively design and implement a locally based assessment model, the school psychologist must consider a number of factors, including (a) the purpose of the assessment procedure(s); (b) the "measurement net" or domain(s) of the assessment; (c) the definition and characteristics of the local population; (d) the format of the assessment; (e) data collection procedures, including standardization and psychometric properties; and (f) the availability of administrative and technical support for the design and implementation of the procedure. These factors are addressed sequentially, as presented in Figure 1.

Purpose of Assessment

Prior to embarking on the development of a locally normed assessment procedure, school psychologists should determine the reasons why the measure is needed and the level of inference to be made from

FIGURE 1. Developing local norms for behavioral assessment.

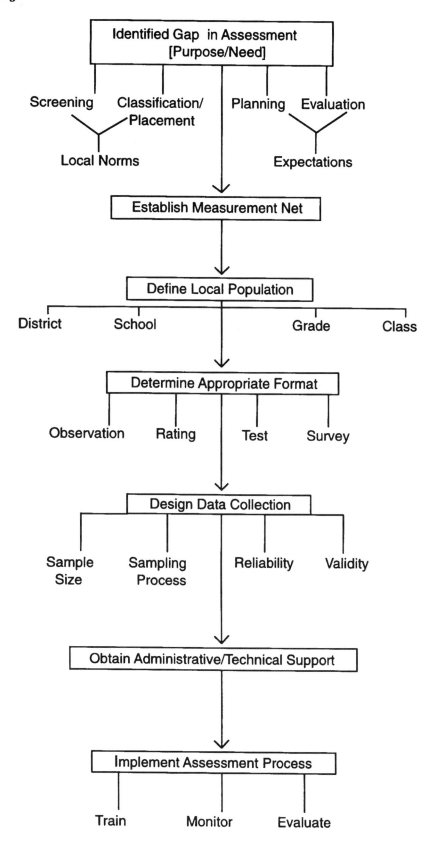

the data. In designing the measure, educators need to consider:

- What referral concerns/school problems will the measure address?

- What types of educational decision (eligibility, placement, instructional strategies) will be made?

- What level of decision making is desired (e.g., screening versus diagnosis)?

- Is a new tool needed or just local norming of an existing measure?

For reasons just noted, locally normed procedures are well-suited for the assessment of social and functional behaviors, as these are frequently situation-specific and tend to reflect localized cultural and community values and expectations. Normative measures typically are most appropriate for identifying, classifying, and sorting individuals, and are less often appropriate for specific intervention planning or progress monitoring.

The use of locally normed measures enables school personnel to directly address the *need* for special services as well as *eligibility*. If most students in a third-grade class are unable to independently exhibit social problem-solving skills and all score below the 25th percentile on a nationally normed scale of social skills, John's "below average" performance on that scale will not be regarded as discrepant from his classmates. Rather than identify all as in need of remedial or special education, as might be indicated using nationally normed tests, the locally normed procedure indicates that John is functioning like his classmates or is meeting most of the demands of his current class placement. However, if John's areas of deficit are dissimilar to those of his classmates, some type of intervention would be warranted to enable him to meet the expectations of his teacher and to avoid referral for more restrictive programming.

Is the procedure intended to serve as a screening device, with students who fall below some set criterion to be referred for more in-depth assessment? Or is the procedure intended to be used to make placement/programmatic decisions? Local norms can be appropriately applied to both purposes, but should not be used in isolation to make diagnostic decisions or special placements. Locally normed measures can help limit the number of students for whom more complete diagnostic information will be obtained by sorting out a group who appears to be at risk relative to the typical students in the local population. Both absolute and relative performance data should be obtained prior to making placement decisions.

Depending upon the format and content of the procedure, some locally normed measures may be appropriate for program planning, with the normative data serving as a "benchmark" or criterion level of performance. Students who fall below this benchmark might be identified for intervention. For example, if most fifth graders are able to use a problem-solving approach to resolving peer conflict, those who are rated low on this skill might be referred to a conflict resolution program.

Generally, norm-referenced measures can not be repeated at frequent intervals to measure progress or response to intervention. At annual intervals, or perhaps twice per year, teacher ratings of a student's skills on a locally normed scale might provide useful data regarding the degree of discrepancy between a student and his peer group following implementation of intervention services.

The "Measurement Net"

In a problem-solving model, educators develop questions which the assessment will attempt to answer. Questions which might be appropriately addressed by a locally normed measure of social/functional skills include:

- How do the student's social skills compare to those of her classmates?

- Are the student's deficits in areas where staff expectations are high or low?

- Has the student's relative performance of locally desired social skills improved following the social skills group training program?

The assessment tool must address the behaviors/skills relevant to the question or problem area. Using the examples just listed, "social skills" is the apparent domain of concern; to find answers, both the skill level of the referred student and the expectations of school staff must be addressed by the assessment.

Whatever the area of concern, the skills or behavior of that domain must be clearly defined and adequately sampled within the boundaries of the measure's intended purpose. What skills and behaviors will be included in "social skills?" Is an in-depth, task-analyzed sampling of these skills needed or will a more superficial sampling of general skills suffice? Are multiple skill areas (domains) needed, such as adult-directed interaction versus peer-directed interaction, or will a single domain such as interpersonal interaction be adequate? Decisions in regard to these questions will help determine the content and length of the measure.

Shinn (1989) describes the establishment of a "measurement net" to identify specific skills to be included in locally normed measures. A pool of possible skills/test items is generated by requesting information from teachers and surveying available curriculum and research literature. Surveying teachers regarding the behaviors of typical, successful students versus unsuccessful students will provide a starting point for developing a school- or classroom-based behavior rating scale. A review of the objectives of a social skills training curriculum will also contribute tasks/skills to the measurement net. This pool of potential items can then be reviewed by teachers and others, and field tested prior to final decisions regarding the content of the measure. A similar approach can be taken when considering local norming of an existing test or scale; review and piloting will be necessary to determine if the tool's content has local relevance.

Defining the Local Population

Who will be the subject of the assessment? Generally, one considers developing local norms or new locally normed procedures because some or all of the population of concern is inadequately served by existing norms and measures of the relevant behavioral domains. Defining the "local" population is critical. If a fair measure of the adaptive behavior skills of Native American students is desired, it would make little sense to randomly sample from the entire school population in a district of only 12% Native American students: The new norms would still reflect a very limited number of the target group. If the target group is "urban midwest children," then the normative group might be randomly drawn from an entire midwest, urban district.

Some behavioral concerns are so situationally specific that the target population appropriately is an individual classroom or school building. Even in situations where the behavior may have more generalized consequences, *intervention* may be most appropriate when it addresses skills needed in the immediate environment of the classroom. Therefore, it would be appropriate to use the typical behavior of students in that classroom as the standard for comparison, rather than the behavior of students in the school or district as a whole.

Defining the population to serve as the "standard" is critical to the design of the measure, to the development of reliable and valid norms, and to the ultimate usefulness of the measure as a problem-solving tool.

Appropriate Formats for the Assessment

The format selected for any assessment tool must be appropriate for the assessment's purpose, desired domains, and target population. In behavioral and functional skills areas, observation is often the most practical direct assessment approach; indirect methods such as checklists and rating scales are commonly used and more easily developed at the local level than standardized individual tests. Rating scales can serve as criterion measures and/or as normative measures in behavioral and functional assessments. While third-party data is inevitably vulnerable to some subjective judgment, parent and teacher ratings of specific behaviors can be highly reliable and valid

(e.g., Gresham, 1981; Hersh & Walker, 1983). When developed and normed locally, such procedures reflect the community standards and expectations for performance.

An alternative means of establishing local norms is to obtain ratings of expected or preferred performance rather than the direct ratings of individuals from a representative sample. For example, instead of rating the social behaviors of 10 "typical" or randomly selected students, a sample of teachers would be asked to rate the importance or desirability of those social behaviors as related to classroom success. Referred students' behaviors would then be rated and compared to the established expectations for that school or district; this approach could also be limited to one classroom and one teacher's expectations. While teacher expectations are not necessarily realistic or consistent with the rated behaviors of "typical" students, these expectations tend to be stable over time and are highly related to referral to special education (Hersh & Walker, 1983).

Once the type of measure is determined, the specific format must be considered. Rating scales, for example, can require yes/no responses, ratings of the frequency or severity of problem behavior, or ratings of the degree of independence or success of the individual's performance. The specificity of the ratings and format for responding will vary with the level of inference desired in relation to the scale's purpose: Psychologists must seek the most practical balance between precision and user-friendliness.

For the purpose of classification or screening for more detailed assessment, the most simple and global ratings may be sufficient. However, for intervention planning, effective measures typically differentiate deficits in skill versus deficits in performance (Gresham, 1984). Multipoint rating scales more reliably reflect important differences in the frequency and quality of target behaviors compared to dichotomous scales (Edelbrock, 1983), although complex ratings can be overly demanding for the rater and possibly limit the usefulness of the results. Furthermore, highly demanding rating tasks could significantly reduce the level of cooperation needed for data collection.

Similar considerations apply to the development of standardized observational systems from which local norms are derived. Complex coding procedures may yield more specific data but also require extensive training for reliable use. Systems commonly used in research may be unnecessarily complex for classroom implementation and the intended level of decision-making.

Data Collection

Developing local norms requires careful consideration of the level of technical adequacy needed for decision-making. Special education labelling and placement have obvious long-term implications for the student, and a higher level of technical confidence is necessary than in the case of screening. The general considerations of reliability and validity of norm-referenced procedures apply to the development of locally normed measures. It is typically impractical, however, to hold locally normed measures to the same standards of technical adequacy used to judge nationally normed procedures. Generalization from locally normed data should address inherent limitations of smaller samples, restricted sampling procedures, and situational specificity.

Local norms should appropriately reflect the population of concern, be it a classroom, school building, or school district. The standardization sample should have proportionate representation according to relevant demographic factors such as age, grade, gender, economic status, and ethnicity. Depending upon the tool's purpose, students with disabilities may or may not be appropriately included in normative samples. If norms are desired for the entire school district, adequate geographic representation is necessary, as well as sampling across the various curricula and organization options present in the district. Particularly when the norms are to be derived from a single classroom or grade level, the normative group might include all students from that population rather than a random sample.

What norms will be available for the interpretation of results? Separate norms for groups known to differ significantly on the target behaviors are preferred for classification and placement purposes, but collecting sufficiently large samples for multiple norming groups is often impractical. Age or grade-level norms tend to be the easiest to construct, assuming that development is a significant factor. Some problematic and social behaviors do not appear to be highly related to age within the school population; gender-specific norms may be more appropriate for some behavioral domains. Ethnic group norms may also be desirable for some purposes, but often the smaller cultural groups can not be adequately sampled within a school or district.

What type of normative scores are desired? Percentiles are often the easiest scores to report and interpret, but eligibility criteria often require the use of standard scores. Standard scores can be derived from any distribution, but distributions significantly skewed away from the normal curve yield standard scores that can be misleading.

Sample sizes will dictate reliability of norms and generalizability to similar students in the population. Obviously, larger samples should be more reliable than smaller samples, but how large a sample is necessary for the purpose of the procedure? If percentiles are desired, measurement experts generally recommend that at least 100 individuals be included in each comparison group (e.g., each grade level) so that "true percentiles" can be derived. Smaller groups require "smoothed" percentiles using linear interpolation in order to determine values at each percentile point. Groups of less than 100 may nevertheless yield useful norms if sampling is conducted carefully, but the scores should be interpreted with greater caution.

It clearly is impossible to determine true percentiles for single classroom samples, and groups of 25 to 30 students will certainly not yield the stable normative data possible with significantly larger groups. However, means and standard deviations can be derived and used for screening, planning, and evaluating student progress at the classroom or building level. Such samples can be used effectively for screening purposes and can serve as a practical alternative approach for developing classroom norms for each class or grade level in a school. Samples of 5 to 10 typical students from each classroom can serve as a standard for comparison with referred students in order to obtain a gross estimate of deviation from the norm. Such data can help teams prioritize referral for more extensive assessment or serve as a first-level screening to identify students for intervention. Depending upon the type of measurement, small classroom samples may offer the only practical means of collecting normative data without external funding resources.

Initial piloting of a new measure or new norming procedure with small classroom or building samples may be desirable even if the ultimate goal is district-level norms: The smaller investigation provides a cost-effective means of field-testing materials, procedures, scoring, and decision making. Small investigations can also be effective in establishing teacher expectations as a practical alternative to true norms.

The collection of normative data should, to the extent possible, include data regarding internal consistency, stability of results, and validity relative to the assessment purpose. Depending upon sample size, some or all of the sample can serve as a test-retest group. Appropriate criterion measures, such as similar scales or class grades, can be included to examine concurrent and predictive validity. Less formal procedures, such as referral rates, placement rates, and observed response to intervention, can also be useful in validating local norms. With sufficiently large samples, statistical tests of discriminant validity can be applied to determine if the locally normed procedure adequately differentiates groups of students for eligibility or treatment purposes.

When developing normative observation systems and third-party rating scales, one must consider inter-rater agreement. Typically this is determined by comparing the results of two independent observers/raters, such as teacher and parent, reading teacher and math teacher, or two trained observers making simultaneous observations. Behavior scales are often criticized if inter-rater agreement is only moderate. However, if the target behaviors are assumed to be situationally specific, a high degree of inter-rater agreement may not be realistic; in fact, differences between raters may be of both diagnostic and prescriptive value. Some assessment systems are designed to obtain two or more sets of ratings or observations of the same student in order to provide such comparisons. The degree of acceptable inter-rater difference will of course depend upon the purpose of the assessment and level of inference desired.

Administrative and Technical Support

The development of local measures and local norms is typically carried out by school district personnel, such as school psychologists, sometimes with the assistance of grants and in collaboration with university researchers. Regardless of the scope of the project, individuals developing these procedures need the support of school administrators. Professional time must be allocated to the project, and the project must thus be regarded as a priority among the many tasks of the school psychologist. The administration must therefore understand and support the rationale for developing local norms and perceive the proposed project as a cost-effective means of impacting student outcomes.

General support from the school district administration is an essential first step, but support from building principals is critical to implementing data collection. Parents and teachers will ultimately be involved in data collection, either directly by responding to rating scales or administering tests, or indirectly through the consent process. The endorsement and cooperation of the building principal will help to secure the cooperation of parents, staff, and students, and lend credibility to the project. However, directives from administrators are not sufficient to ensure cooperation of subjects and respondents. Teachers and parents must also perceive that the project leads to better services for students and involves minimal time, effort, and disruption of the normal school routine.

Finally, to implement and successfully complete a local norming project, the school psychologist needs access to sufficient technical support. Very small studies (such as classroom norming projects) may require minimal clerical support, data entry, and data analysis. Larger scale projects such as district-wide norming may require additional funding (such as grants) to secure computer time, data entry personnel, consultants with statistical expertise, and, in some cases, data collection personnel.

Large school districts often have research departments with adequate support for such projects, while smaller districts may have to seek (and purchase) expertise elsewhere. Local universities often offer opportunities for collaboration, shared computer access, and pools of inexpensive labor for data collection.

When external funding is needed, local sources often offer the best opportunities for relatively small grants. State departments of education, local corporations, and private foundations often provide grants for projects directed toward at-risk and special needs populations. Larger school districts often employ one or more individuals to identify such funding sources and to assist staff in applying for grants.

Implementation Issues

The final step in establishing local norms is the development of an implementation plan. The plan should address relevant timelines for training staff in the new procedure(s), a system of monitoring the use of the procedure(s), and methods of evaluating the impact of the procedure(s) in the context of the assessment's intended purpose. Monitoring can be accomplished through periodic surveys or reporting systems which help determine if procedures are appropriately followed. Depending upon the assessment's purpose, evaluation plans might address referral and/or placement rates, impact on decision making, teacher satisfaction, and so forth. If resources are available, evaluation might also include validation through discriminant analysis and replication studies.

BEST PRACTICES

The development and implementation of a locally normed assessment procedure unfolds as a problem-solving approach to decision making (see Figure 1). At each step, the school psychologist is confronted with questions to answer in order to best shape the final product (measure) to the needs of the classroom, school, or district. Regardless of the domains of behavior measured or of the type of measure developed, this sequence of decisions allows the school psychologist to adapt the assessment tool to the identified needs, local population, and available resources.

For the purpose of this chapter, this decision-making sequence will be described in the context of a case-study illustration (Figure 2), using as the example the development of the Mainstream Survival Skills Assessment (MSSA, Canter & Heistad, 1990). While the MSSA is a multimethod system addressing functional and social behavior through ratings, observation, and interviews, this discussion will include only the locally normed rating-scale components.

Purpose: Identifying a Gap in Assessment

- *What is the rationale for developing a locally normed procedure?*
- *What is (are) the purpose(s) of the measure for the local population?*

In the process of identification, placement, and program planning for at-risk students, school psy-

FIGURE 2. Development of the Mainstream Survival Skills Assessment.

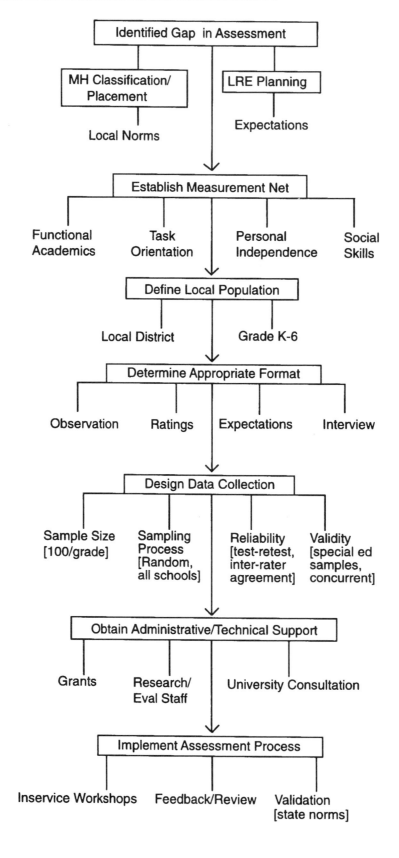

chologists and other team members are frequently confronted with dilemmas resulting from gaps in assessment technology. One such problem encountered repeatedly during the mid-1980s was the apparent discrepancy between the behaviors which prompted special education referral and those behaviors which our available tools were designed to assess. Furthermore, recent changes in state and federal rules mandated assessment of adaptive behavior in school as well as home/community settings as part of the identification of "mental handicaps"; yet there were very few measures published and none appeared to be specifically relevant to the diverse local population. During the 1986–87 school year, school psychologists in a midwest urban school district initiated a project to address this gap in technology through the development of a local assessment procedure.

After reviewing literature and informally surveying local teachers regarding factors related to school success and failure, "school survival skills" were identified as the general target behaviors for the new assessment. Researchers have described as "survival skills" task-related behaviors such as academic engagement, following directions, seeking assistance, and organizing materials, as well as functional academic, personal, and social competencies (Cobb & Hops, 1973; Hops & Cobb, 1974), and have found these skills to effectively differentiate successful from nonsuccessful mainstream students (McConnell et al., 1984). It was therefore hypothesized that assessment of school-based functional skills would contribute important data to classification and placement decisions, to predicting student outcomes in alternative settings, and, subsequently, to promoting the development and implementation of curricula to improve survival skills for all students.

It was highly desirable that the procedure be sufficiently robust to be useful in eligibility decisions and that student performance be readily compared to teacher expectations.

Establishing the Measurement Net

- *What skills and behaviors will be assessed?*

After defining the generic set of target behaviors as "school survival skills," the next problem facing scale developers was identification of the specific skills, tasks, and behavior to be measured. The overriding criterion for inclusion in the "net" was the relationship of the skill to successful and independent functioning in mainstream classrooms and to available remediation/intervention strategies. Furthermore, it was essential that the skill was readily observable in school and classroom environments.

In addition to an extensive review of relevant literature on the behavioral correlates of school success and failure, K–8 teachers from a sample of local schools were surveyed regarding their expectations and observations. Currently available measures of functional and problematic behavior were also reviewed. From these sources, a preliminary set of skills was generated and reviewed by a panel of teachers (regular and special education), school social workers, and school psychologists. These skills were then organized into four (and later condensed into three) general domains of functional academics, task orientation, personal independence, and social skills.

Defining the Local Population

- *What student population(s) will be the target of this assessment procedure?*

- *Who will be included in the normative sample?*

The assessment concerns which prompted this project were not unique to any one school in the district. Because 90% of the district's students were bussed for desegregation purposes, there was considerable heterogeneity across schools regardless of neighborhood differences. It was therefore desirable that the new measure be applicable district-wide.

After trying out items and discussing the procedure with teachers, it was decided to limit the scope of the measure to the elementary (K–6) population. Skills judged relevant for school success appeared to be acquired by fifth or sixth grade; for adolescents, vocational interests/skills and a very different set of social expectations appeared relevant, making a K–12 tool impractical.

It was also decided to include representative samples of *all* district students who participated in mainstream programs, including those with mild disabilities and with Limited English Proficiency. Of critical importance was a representative sampling of the district's nonwhite ethnic populations, who at that time accounted for nearly half of the total enrollment. Similarly, it was important that the district's economic diversity be reflected in the norming sample.

Because the measure was to be used district-wide, students from every K–6 school in the district were included in the normative sample, ensuring geographic representation throughout the city as well as sampling across all organizational and curricular structures in the district, such as open and "magnet" schools.

Research and test development regarding the construct of adaptive behavior, including socialization, indicated a strong relationship between these skills and age across the school years. Norms for each grade level were therefore necessary for the MSSA. Reviewing the enrollment records of many students indicated that there was often an age range in excess of 18 months in any given classroom. Therefore, norms for *age* groups as well as grade levels were desirable. While gender-specific norms are often included with nationally normed measures, developing gender norms for the MSSA would require doubling of the size of each age/grade sample, an impractical consideration given available resources. However, gender differences were to be studied to help interpret results.

Determining Appropriate Formats

- *What is the most cost-effective means of measuring target skills, in the context of available resources, population needs, and assessment purpose?*

- *What format will minimize resistance to data collection?*

For both the purpose of cost-effective test development and the ultimate goal of implementing a practical data collection procedure, a rating-scale format was selected, using a three-point scale reflecting independence in typical functioning. Two forms of this rating scale were devised — one for teachers to rate an individual student's competencies, and a second with identical items for teachers to rate the skills' importance to classroom success. The teacher rating scale would provide normative data relative to other district students. The teacher expectations scale would provide a template for that classroom, which could then be compared to an individual student's skills for the purpose of identifying intervention targets or matching students to potential environments. Scale items were written as positive descriptors based upon the list of skills established earlier for each domain.

Designing Data Collection

- *What level of technical adequacy and representative sampling is acceptable for the purpose of this assessment procedure?*

- *How will appropriate samples be obtained?*

The MSSA rating scales followed traditional test-development procedures, including experimentation with item content and format (pilot testing), standardization with a random sample of mainstream students, tests of reliability and validity, and discriminant analyses using special population samples. Published scales of similar behaviors were reviewed to determine a range of acceptable sample sizes, reliability, and validity data.

The normative sample was derived through random sampling of each elementary school's enrollment lists, including a number of students proportionate to that school's contribution to the total district enrollment. Because of the desegregation efforts across the district, it was assumed that random sampling at each grade level at each school would yield a total sample representative of the district in terms of gender, ethnicity, socioeconomic status (SES), and disability. To obtain the desired target samples of 100 students per grade level, samples of 140 to 150 were selected for the norming pool. Subsamples of this total were included in test-retest reliability (second grade), inter-rater agreement (using students in team-teaching situations), and concurrent validity (third grade) samples, using the Vineland Adaptive Behavior Scales, Classroom Edition as the criterion measure.

Discriminant validity samples were drawn from special education enrollment lists of students in resource and self-contained classroom programs for children with mental handicaps, learning disabilities, and emotional/behavioral disorders. Another sample was selected from the Limited English Proficiency program.

The original rating scale included 138 items in four subdomains. Following statistical analyses of the normative data, 20 items were discarded for failing to meet criteria of developmental validity (correlations with age), discriminant validity (differentiation of disabled versus nondisabled students), reliability (internal consistency or test-retest), or social validity (ratings of importance by teachers). The 50 items with the highest concordance with these criteria formed the teacher expectations scale. A sample of district teachers at each grade level (K–6) was asked to complete the expectations scale.

Extensive analyses were conducted to examine age, gender, ethnic, and SES differences in teachers ratings, as well as to examine different special education samples. Norms tables were constructed using smoothed percentiles with linear interpolation for the final normative samples of 80 to 90 students per grade level.

Rationale, data collection procedures, norms tables, technical data, and recommendations for applying data to educational decisions were included in a manual published by the district for school personnel (Canter & Heistad, 1990).

Administrative and Technical Support

- *What resources (funding, personnel) will be necessary to support the desired technical design?*

Within the local district, many sources of support were tapped for this project. The Research and Evaluation staff included a school psychologist well versed in experimental design, data analysis, and computer technology. Psychological Services staff included an individual assigned half-time to research and evaluation projects. Principals and special education administrators expressed interest in the development of the MSSA and encouraged teacher participation. To accomplish the goals of the project in a timely manner, however, required additional funding for project coordination, teacher incentives (stipends for each scale completed), materials, and data entry. A proposal to the state department of education for funding as an innovative assessment project resulted in a grant of approximately $30,000.

Implementation Issues

- *Does the new procedure fulfill its intended purpose?*

- *What training and monitoring is needed to ensure appropriate implementation?*

The MSSA project resulted in a teacher-rating scale that meets accepted standards of reliability and validity and is in fact technically comparable to many published, nationally normed measures of adaptive and social behavior (Canter & Heistad, 1990). The norming population very closely reflects the demographic characteristics of the district, and, as predicted, ratings differentiated disabled from nondisabled and mildly disabled from more severely disabled students. As a contingency for securing funding, the MSSA was normed at the state level in a replication of the district-level norming project. This statewide study served to further validate the data obtained in the earlier project (Canter, Schrot, & Heistad, 1990).

The MSSA scales have been used extensively in the district as components of special education eligibility assessments and as fundamental data in planning interventions and placements for mildly disabled students who participate in inclusion programs or who are making the transition to less restrictive programs. To ensure appropriate implementation, numerous presentations have been made to school personnel, particularly to special education personnel. Over time, additional data have been collected to enhance understanding of survival skills relative to specific groups, including students with severe emotional/behavioral disorders, students with Limited English Proficiency, and Native American students.

As the local district moves toward adopting a problem-solving model to address academic and behavior referrals, the MSSA offers a locally normed behavioral complement to the academic procedures of Curriculum-Based Measurement (also locally normed) as well as to more traditional norm-referenced measures and direct observation systems which comprise the comprehensive assessment arsenal. Of particular value to the problem-solving model has been the comparison of teacher expectation ratings to teachers' ratings of referred students' performances. School psychologists have been able to identify targets for intervention that are specific to the interaction between the referred student and the classroom environment or to the potential interaction between the student and a future environment. Such interventions then become key to planning transitions to less restrictive settings or to developing skills necessary to maintain the student in the mainstream. At times, these data have also been used to help identify specific classrooms where students are most likely to succeed.

SUMMARY

This chapter has presented a rationale for the use of local norms and standards in the assessment of school-based functional and social behaviors, a set of basic considerations in the development of local procedures, and best practice guidelines using a case-study example. School psychologists are ideally suited to the roles of test development consultants and project coordinators: They possess knowledge of educational and psychological measurement and basic research design, as well as intimate knowledge of the purposes of assessment in education and of the gaps between our technology and student/teacher needs.

The use of local norms for identifying and understanding achievement problems has been promoted among researchers and practitioners, particularly regarding implementing Curriculum-Based Measurement strategies. The advantage of locally normed procedures for identifying and understanding behavioral and functional skills problems has been well-stated in the literature but appears to be less widely implemented in practice. Even very small projects at the classroom or building level can provide the local frame of reference necessary for appropriate identification of target behaviors which are essential to positive student outcomes.

Skills that are basic to daily functioning in significant settings must be identified, analyzed, and directly taught if students are to be ready for mainstream schooling and, ultimately, the demands of independent living.

Many published, norm-referenced procedures offer technical advantages over locally developed measures but rely upon national norms and assumptions of commonality in their criteria for success. There is no doubt that such general standards for performance should be considered in the assessment process. However, the importance of ecologically valid assessment to effective intervention can not be overstated. By including local standards and situationally specific performance criteria in the comprehensive assessment plan, school psychologists can help promote better practices in both problem identification and intervention for a broad student population.

REFERENCES

Achenbach, T., McConaughy, S., & Howell, C. (1987). Child/adolescent behavioral and emotional problems: Implications of cross-informant correlations for situational specificity. *Psychological Bulletin, 101,* 213–232.

Anastasi, A. (1988). *Psychological testing* (6th ed.). New York: MacMillan.

Bardon, J. I. (1988). Alternative educational delivery approaches: Implications for school psychology. In J. L. Graden, J. E. Zins, & M. C. Curtis (Eds.), *Alternative educational delivery systems: Enhancing instructional options for all students* (pp.

563–571). Washington, DC: National Association of School Psychologists.

Braden, J., & Reschly, D. (1993, February). The future of assessment in public schools. *Communiqué, 21*(5), 9.

Canter, A. S., & Heistad, D. (1990). *Mainstream Survival Skills Assessment: Administration and technical manual* (Minneapolis Schools Edition). Minneapolis: Minneapolis Public Schools.

Canter, A. S., Schrot, D., & Heistad, D. (1990). *Mainstream Survival Skills Assessment: Administration and technical manual* (Minnesota Schools Edition). Minneapolis: Minneapolis Public Schools/Minnesota Department of Education.

Cobb, J. A., & Hops, H. (1973). Effects of academic survival skills training on low achieving first graders. *Journal of Educational Research, 67,* 108–113.

Cullinen, D., Epstein, M., & McLinden, D. (1986). Status and change in state administrative definitions of behavior disorder. *School Psychology Review, 15,* 383–392.

Deno, S. (1989). Curriculum-Based Measurement and special education services: A fundamental and direct relationship. In M. R. Shinn (Ed.), *Curriculum-Based Measurement: Assessing special children* (pp. 1–17). New York: Guilford.

Edelbrock, C. (1983). Problems and issues in using rating scales to assess child personality and psychopathology. *School Psychology Review, 12,* 293–299.

Gresham, F. (1981). Assessment of children's social skills. *Journal of School Psychology, 19,* 120–129.

Gresham, F. (1983). Social skills assessment as a component of mainstreaming placement decisions. *Exceptional Children, 49,* 331–336.

Gresham, F. (1984). Social skills assessment and training. In J. Ysseldyke (Ed.), *School psychology: State of the art* (pp. 57–80). Minneapolis: National School Psychology Inservice Training Network.

Hersh, R. H., & Walker, H. M. (1983). Great expectations: Making schools effective for all students. *Policy Studies Review, 2,* 147–188.

Hoier, T. S., McConnell, S. R., & Pallay, A. G. (1987). Observational assessment for planning and evaluating educational transitions: An analysis of template matching. *Behavioral Assessment, 9,* 6–20.

Hops, H., & Cobb, J. A. (1974). Initial investigations into academic survival skills training, direct instruction, and first grade achievement. *Journal of Educational Psychology, 66,* 548–553.

Horn, E., & Fuchs, D. (1987). Adaptive behavior in assessment and intervention: An overview. *Journal of Special Education, 21,* 11–26.

McConnell, S. R. (1987, February). Planning for school transitions. Presentation to the Minnesota School Psychologists Association, Brainerd, Minnesota.

McConnell, S. R., Strain, P., Kerr, M., Staff, V., Lenkner, D., & Lambert, D. (1984). An empirical definition of elementary school adjustment. *Behavior Modification, 8,* 451–473.

Ritter, D. (1989). Teacher's expectations of problem behavior in general and special education. *Exceptional Children, 55,* 559–564.

Shinn, M. R. (1989). Identifying and defining academic problems: CBM screening and eligibility procedures. In M. R. Shinn (Ed.), *Curriculum-Based Measurement: Assessing special children* (pp. 90–129). New York: Guilford.

Shinn, M. R., Tindal, G., & Spira, D. (1987). Special education referrals as an index of teacher tolerance: Are teachers imperfect tests? *Exceptional Children, 54,* 32–40.

ANNOTATED BIBLIOGRAPHY

Canter, A. S., & Heistad, D. (1990). *Mainstream Survival Skills Assessment: Administration and technical manual* (Minneapolis Schools Edition). Minneapolis: Minneapolis Public Schools.
This manual includes a review of relevant research, an extensive description of the process of developing a locally normed assessment procedure, and detailed technical data, as well as administration and interpretation guidelines. Age and grade norms tables for the rating scale are included. The companion manual (Canter, Schrot, & Heistad, 1990) describes the statewide replication project. (Both manuals can be obtained at cost [$10 each] from the Prescriptive Instruction Center, Minneapolis Public Schools, 807 N.E. Broadway, Minneapolis, MN 55413.)

Hersh, R. H., & Walker, H. M. (1983). Great expectations: Making schools effective for all students. *Policy Studies Review, 2,* 147–188.
Hersh and Walker examine components of effective schooling in the context of serving children with disabilities in the mainstream classroom. Their extensive literature review focuses on the expectations and standards of classroom teachers and on "social behavior survival" – preparing special education students for the realities of regular education.

Hoier, T. S., McConnell, S. R., & Pallay, A. G. (1987). Observational assessment for planning and evaluating educational transitions: An analysis of template matching. *Behavioral Assessment, 9,* 6–20.
This article reports an observational study of behavioral conditions in mainstream versus special education classrooms which can be linked to intervention. Of particular relevance to local norming efforts is the review of research regarding local contingencies which impact teacher and student behavior and the description of data collection methods.

Shinn, M. R. (1989). Identifying and defining academic problems: CBM screening and eligibility procedures. In M. R. Shinn (Ed.), *Curriculum-Based Measurement: Assessing special children* (pp. 90–129). New York: Guilford.
This chapter, while specifically addressing CBM procedures, has useful applications to the development of local norms in general. Shinn discusses the creation of the "measurement net," alternative approaches to gathering local norms at the classroom/building/district levels, sampling procedures, data collection, and options for establishing norms.

60

Best Practices in Developing Local Norms for Problem Solving in the Schools

Lisa Habedank
University of Oregon

OVERVIEW

A sample of student behavior in isolation is no more useful than a photograph of a stranger found on the street. Without a meaningful context, student performance may be momentarily interesting but will not have utility in solving educational problems. So, student performance is placed in a context, often the context of (a) the student's own past performance and (b) how that student compares to what is expected of all students. For example, if a school psychologist were told that Ricky read 50 words a minute in grade-level reading material, he or she would likely ask "How does that compare to his reading in the past?" and "What do other students in his grade read like?" or "How many words per minute would we like Ricky to be reading?" Normative comparisons are used to help answer the latter two questions, questions about what is expected of a student in relation to how other students perform on the same task.

A norm is a description of a population's performance on a set of tasks. It is usually made up of the performance of a sample of people selected to represent the whole population. For example, the norm sample may be designed to represent students across the whole nation (e.g., the national norm sample of the Woodcock Reading Mastery Test), students with a particular background or disability (e.g., the visually impaired norm sample on the Blind Learning Aptitude Test), or students from a specific educational system (e.g., the local norms of Wild Rice Elementary school on Curriculum-Based Measures of basic skills). Comparisons made using norms should always be phrased so it is clear which population the norm sample represents. In this chapter, the term *local norms* describes norms developed to represent students from a particular educational system. As such, they provide a comparison for where a student's performance stands locally — in the student's own education cooperative, district, building, or even classroom. Local norms would not provide information on how a student compared to a national standard and vice versa.

The use of norms in the schools is not a new phenomenon. Since the early 1900s normative comparisons have been used extensively in the schools to describe individual differences (Bergan, 1985). These comparisons, typically involving nationally normed, published achievement and intelligence tests, have been used widely as part of the special education screening and eligibility process. The concept of local norms, likewise, is not new. Many psychological measurement texts (e.g., Anastasi, 1988; Kubiszyn & Borich, 1990) describe local norms as norms developed by the test users themselves to represent a narrowly defined population. "These local norms are more appropriate than broad national norms for many testing purposes, such as the prediction of subsequent job performance or college achievement, the comparison of a child's relative achievement in different subjects, or the measurement of an individual's progress over time" (Anastasi, 1988, p. 97).

Many of the local norm references in the school psychology literature describe local norms developed on nationally normed, published tests in order to represent a specific region's population (Kamphaus & Lozano, 1984). For example, local norms created on the WISC in a school district with a large Mexican-American, Spanish-speaking population (Elliott & Bretzing, 1980) provide an alternative to the WISC's national norm comparison standard. Again, these local norms developed on nationally normed, published tests typically were used as part of the special education screening and eligibility process.

The use of local norms that more directly represent the goals and outcomes of general education, however, is a relatively recent phenomenon. For example, as part of a series of projects in the 1970s for the University of Minnesota's Institute for Research on Learning Disabilities, a normative database was developed for the Pine County Education Cooperative. The normative information was collected on basic-skills academic tasks normed on students sampled from several Pine County schools (Tindal, Germann, & Deno, 1983). Both the tasks normed and the way the data were conceptualized and used differed from past documentation of local norms in the school psychology literature.

The tasks — brief, standardized fluency measures in the areas of reading, math, spelling, and written expression — became known as Curriculum-Based Measures (CBM, Deno, 1985; 1986). The tasks represented "vital signs" of learning in important educational areas for all students in the education cooperative. The normative data collected on these tasks were used to describe the expectations for a student's basic skill performance in general education. Instead of taking a student in isolation and using normative comparisons to document a within-child discrepancy (e.g., a student's achievement-ability discrepancy) for eligibility purposes only, the Pine County norms were used in a way similar to peer referencing in behavioral observation. A behavioral observer uses a peer reference to define what is expected of the student in his or her environment and then uses that information for several purposes. For example, a target student's level of engagement could be compared to a peer's level of engagement to determine if a problem exists. The peer level of engagement could be used as the goal, and when the student's engagement once again fell within the range of the peer's, the problem would be solved. The Pine County CBM local norms provided a normative comparison, on relevant educational tasks, that could be used in this way. The performance of general education peers was compared to an individual student's performance to determine if a discrepancy between what was expected (the norm) and what occurred (the student's performance) existed (Deno, 1988). This same local norm could be used in goal setting and determining when problems were solved.

It is this application of local norms — selecting behaviors that are important in the general education environment, developing local norms that represent the range of performance in general education, and using norms and norm tasks as part of a problem-solving system — that will be the focus of this chapter.

BASIC CONSIDERATIONS

Strengths of Local Norms

Although developing norms does involve time and resources, the strengths of local norms can make this a wise investment. For most educational decision making, local norms are representative of a meaningful comparison group on tasks relevant to the problems at hand. Specifically, local norms may decrease the likelihood of bias in decision making and increase testing/teaching overlap and norm utility across educational decisions.

Decreasing the likelihood of bias in decision making. Test bias is a hotly contested political and legal issue in school psychology (Reynolds & Kaiser,

1990). Although much has been written about developing culture-free or culture-fair tests, bias can be conceptualized as a function of the decision-making process rather than an inherent quality of the tests themselves (Ysseldyke, 1979). Local norms can decrease the likelihood of bias in decision making because they represent a meaningful comparison group. Local norms represent how a student performs in relation to others from his or her grade and school, a comparison likely to be representative of the age, grade, race, educational background, geographic, and socioeconomic factors relevant for educating this student (Shinn, 1988). Gerber and Semmel (1984) argue that general education teachers already use their own "local norms," where a student's performance falls in relation to the other students in the class, to determine who gets referred for more intensive services. Local norms make this comparison part of systematic and data-based decision making.

Local norms also can decrease the likelihood of bias in decision making because they promote the identification of educational needs and a problem-solving orientation. When education professionals base decisions on agreed upon, important educational outcomes operationalized in the form of locally normed educational tasks, they can identify and help students who perform significantly below their peers and thus are at risk for failure in the schools and in society. Furthermore, local norms can be used to demonstrate whether the special instruction or intervention designed by the problem-solving team is working. Although having local norms will not guarantee a nonbiased assessment and decision-making process or effective programs for students, selecting students for special services based on reliable measurement of educational needs and then having an accountable system for addressing those needs is not likely to be considered biased and unfair.

Opportunity for greater teaching/testing overlap. One of the complaints about the use of nationally normed, published tests is the lack of teaching/testing overlap. In an analysis of the data from two research projects, Leinhardt (1983) concluded that the amount of overlap between the nationally normed tests and curriculum not only was minimal, but also was an important predictor of end-of-the-year test performance. Several other studies have documented that differing levels of test-content overlap with the curriculum affects student performance (Jenkins & Pany, 1978; Shapiro & Derr, 1987; Good & Salvia, 1988).

Local norms give the school system flexibility for developing comparison data on educational outcomes and tasks that students have been exposed to in the school curriculum. Instead of making decisions based on questions that may or may not reflect content taught as part of the school's curriculum — and often assessed using bubble sheets or requiring a small number of responses — schools can base decisions about students on tasks related to curricular content. This flexibility means that the norm comparison data is directly relevant for making decisions about a student's performance compared to local expectations.

Utility across educational decisions. Deno (1988) proposes that educating tough-to-teach students is a problem-solving process and "systematic efforts in problem solving require the organization and sequencing of activities — the use of a problem-solving model" (p. 12). He outlines five problem-solving steps, or decisions, that correspond to the administrative steps of most special programs. The five steps are (a) problem identification, (b) problem certification, (c) exploring solutions, (d) evaluating solutions, and (e) problem solution. Problem identification and certification correspond to referral/screening and eligibility/need decisions. Exploring solutions includes setting long- and short-term goals and establishing and implementing an instructional plan. Evaluating solutions involves monitoring student progress toward goals and making instructional changes when students are not making adequate progress. Problem solution corresponds to program exit decisions or movement to a less restrictive setting.

Normative comparisons typically are used in educational decision making only to identify and describe the severity of a problem (e.g., problem identification and certification decisions). Local norms can be used in these initial problem-solving steps to determine what is expected of the student. In addition, local norms tied to curricular goals and student outcomes are parsimonious with the information needed to set good educational goals, evaluate student programs, and make other important educational decisions for that student. For example, CBM data used in problem identification and problem certification provide the foundation for goal setting, progress monitoring, and further assessment for instructional planning. Throughout this process, comparisons to other students via local norms provide a context for decision making. Local norm utility across educational decisions will be discussed further in a later section of this chapter. (Two other chapters in this volume also describe the use of CBM local norms.)

A related strength of local norms is that all local educators can use the same general education outcomes "ruler" or decision-making framework for many types of educational programs such as Chapter I, English as a Second Language (ESL), Talented and Gifted (TAG), general education, and special education. Normative comparisons are already used to identify students for many types of educational programs. However, the tests used between and within these programs may differ, making it difficult to compare the achievement of one group of students (e.g., students served in Chapter I programs) to another

(e.g., students identified as learning disabled with an Individualized Education Plan) and separating the decision making for special programs from general education expectations. Local norms can provide a consistent general education outcomes "ruler" that allows for a variety of comparisons between and within all of an educational system's programs.

Limitations of Local Norms

The limitations of local norms fall into three broad categories: (a) the potential for misinterpretation, (b) limitations on the use of local norms to define acceptable student performance and curricula, and (c) replicated effort.

Misinterpretation. Because not all educators are familiar with the use of local norms, it is important to define them. As with any type of educational assessment and normative comparison, parents, teachers, and others should be informed about who is represented in the normative sample and what the students were asked to do. It should be explained that the norm represents how students in this particular sample performed, what tasks were included, and how the scores were derived.

Using local norms with a small number of cases in the norm sample (e.g., fewer than 100 students per grade) can be problematic. If the sample size is small, the norm may be unstable and should not be used as the most important normative comparison for making eligibility decisions. Also, with a small sample size, infrequent elements in a population may not be represented. Small or limited sample size is not necessarily a problem, however, as long as the norm is interpreted appropriately. For example, if a classroom norm is used to help define what is expected of the student in that classroom, a statement should be made about the possibility that expectations of student performance in another classroom may differ. This does not mean the classroom comparison is not meaningful, however; it may be quite useful in understanding the difficulty a teacher is having in accommodating a student's needs.

Local norms and defining acceptable performance and curricula. Shinn (1988), in his description of developing Curriculum-Based Measurement (CBM) local norms for use in special education decision making, expressed concern that local normative performance would be seen as the goal for all students. "Another potential disadvantage exists when local normative performance is accepted as a goal for all children, which may suggest mediocrity" (Shinn, 1988, p. 76). Using a local norm to describe general education expectations does not mean that local normative performance is necessarily acceptable. For example, if a student's oral reading fluency is within the range of his third-grade peers — but his or her peers are reading a median of 20 words correctly per minute in typical grade-level material (1 word correct every 3 seconds) — the conclusion would be that the student is not different from peers. However, all the students are in trouble if they are expected to learn from that material. Regionally or nationally normed general achievement tests may be used periodically to assess the skills of the local school population and provide data about how the school population as a whole compares to regional or national standards.

A related concern is that developing local norms will somehow advocate the use of a particular published curriculum. Local norms tasks should reflect important educational outcomes. The norming materials themselves may or may not be derived directly from the school's adopted published curricula. Using local norm materials drawn from the published books and workbooks students use in the general education classroom is appealing because it makes the connection between general education expectations and the norming process more concrete. Right or wrong, success in these published materials is what the general education teacher sees in the classroom. "It is argued that regardless of quality of curriculum, it becomes *de facto* the decision-making standard for regular education. Students who fail to profit from the regular education curriculum, regardless of its quality, are viewed often as handicapped" (Shinn, 1988, p. 77). Having local norms drawn from published curricular materials does not mean that the adopted curriculum is the most effective, only that students are expected to learn from the adopted materials.

Replicated effort. Best practices in local norms development involves not only norming a task on the local population but taking a fresh look at the purpose and framework for assessment. By using local norms to define the expectations for students in the general education curricula, educational problems can be placed in a problem-solving context. Local norms used for problem identification and problem certification, however, will not provide a distinct advantage over national norms without a link between the locally normed tasks and (a) further assessment of the student's educational environment and performance and (b) goal setting and ongoing progress monitoring.

BEST PRACTICES

Selecting Important and Valid Behaviors to Norm

Prior to developing local norms, decisions must be made about the behaviors or educational tasks that will be normed. Examples of local norms in the recent school psychology literature and in this chapter have been associated with Curriculum-Based Measures (Marston & Magnusson, 1988; Shapiro & Derr, 1990; Shinn, 1988, 1989; Shinn, Nolet, & Knutson, 1990). Developing local norms using behaviors im-

portant in the general education environment could include other areas of assessment and norming tasks. For example, local norms could be developed on social behaviors, prereading tasks, physical education skills, or the use of basic skills or content tasks other than CBM tasks. What is most important in making decisions about what to norm is that the data are relevant and valid for decision making.

Choosing relevant areas of assessment. To be relevant, local norm data must be related to *important* educational outcomes for students. Developing local norms on spelling in first grade, for example, would be relevant in a school that had determined spelling skills were important in first grade and therefore were part of the first-grade curriculum. First grade spelling norms would not be relevant in a school that did not emphasize or teach spelling to first graders. This chapter has focused on norms that reflect general education expectations. Local norms in basic academic skill areas are a logical place to begin because these areas generally have been the most "important," well-defined, and accepted educational outcomes in our schools.

Norms of behaviors not tied to general education expectations will have limited utility across programs and educational decisions. For example, local norms could be developed on basic skills in languages other than English, even if those other languages are not part of the general education curriculum. Non-English norms provide a potentially useful comparison for decision making and goal setting for students in English as a Second Language (ESL) programs (Baker, 1992). However, Non-English norms would not be useful for any other group of students in the school, and there is a danger that the norms and norm tasks would promote a separate standard or decision-making process for ESL students. Assessment utilizing norms reflecting both general education students and tasks and a more limited group of students and tasks would be helpful in this situation. Using typical general-education student performance in English as one long-term goal, typical Spanish-speaking or ESL student performance in Spanish as another long-term goal and monitoring progress in both would be one example of combining the two.

Choosing valid measurement tasks. To be valid, local norm data must be reliable and accurate, have relatively normal distributions, and be sensitive to educational change. To increase the likelihood that a local norm has these qualities, tasks that are normed must have standardized administration and scoring procedures, with proven test-retest reliability and content validity. To be useful in decision making, the norms must reliably differentiate students' levels of skill on the task (e.g., performance on the tasks needs to be relatively normally distributed). The further a distribution is from being normal, the more difficult it becomes to use the norm to set goals or determine if a student being assessed is different from peers. The tasks being normed also must provide enough opportunities for responses to show an increase when that skill is taught in the classroom.

The use of Curriculum-Based Measurement tasks. It is a challenge to find measurement tasks that (a) fulfill the validity requirements, (b) are time-efficient and affordable, and (c) provide data tied to important general education expectations. This challenge is one reason that local norming in the basic skill areas developed in conjunction with CBM. CBM tasks have a database documenting their reliability, validity, sensitivity (Marston, 1989), and relatively normal distributions in local norm data collection (Tindal et al., 1983; Magnusson, 1986). Furthermore, CBM is not just a technology but a measurement system designed for use in a problem-solving system. Using local norms to operationalize the expectations of the general education environment is one of the defining characteristics of CBM (Deno, 1985; 1986). Because CBM tasks are so closely tied to the concept of developing and using local norms in a problem-solving system and have a database supporting their use, the examples in this chapter will be based on CBM data in the basic skills areas of reading, math, spelling, and written expression. However, the underlying concepts and steps of norm development could be applied to other behaviors that provide relevant and valid data for decision making.

STEPS IN DEVELOPING LOCAL NORMS

Once decisions have been made about what behaviors will be normed, a series of steps can be followed to develop the norms themselves (Ball, 1993). The steps are presented in Figure 1.

Select a Level of Norm

The three basic levels of local norms are classroom, school-building, and school-district norms. Classroom norms are developed by sampling students from an individual classroom and testing them. Building norms are developed by sampling students from each grade in a school building and testing them. School-district norms can be developed in two ways: (a) selecting a sample of students in each grade from the entire school district population or (b) developing norms in each building and then aggregating all the building norms. The former is generally less expensive, but aggregated district norms provide the benefit of having both building and district norms at your disposal. Each level of norm has its own characteristics.

Classroom, building, and district norm characteristics. Classroom norms are a great way to get started and provide the most direct measure of what is expected of a student in his or her own classroom.

However, with such a small norm sample, estimates of the variability within the classroom are problematic and stable percentile ranks cannot be developed. Classroom norms can be used in the prereferral or IEP process to identify problems and prioritize student needs. They are useful for setting goals for a student or group of students. For example, the goal for low readers in a class could be to perform within the typical range on spring reading norms by the end of the year. Classroom norms also have been used in determining when a student may be transitioned to a less restrictive environment, for example, from a resource room setting to the general education classroom (Shinn, Habedank, Rodden-Nord, & Knutson, 1993).

District norms, on the other hand, provide a more consistent estimate of the performance level and variability of the students within the district. The disadvantages of district norms are that they are a less precise measure of the least restrictive environment for a particular student (e.g., that student's classroom) and require relative homogeneity of curricular objectives across schools. District norms, like classroom norms, can be used to identify problems, set goals, and prioritize needs. If the district norm sample is 100 per grade or larger, the norms are stable enough to be used in problem certification decisions as well. Aggregated district norms also could be used to compare the performance of students in different schools for resource allocation and system-wide programmatic purposes.

Building norms' characteristics lie somewhere between classroom and district norms. They are a more precise estimate of the least restrictive environment than district norms and provide a more stable estimate of performance than classroom norms. Building norms can be used for the same general purpose as district norms, including problem certification if the student sample has at least 100 students per grade.

Factors in level of norm decisions. Important factors when selecting a level of norm are the (a) characteristics of the local population, (b) amount of curriculum chaos in the district, (c) political and economic structure of the area, (d) decisions for which the data will be used, and (e) economic and other resources available (Ball, 1993). As alluded to in the characteristics of different levels of norms, these five factors must be considered and balanced in order to determine which level of norm is both meaningful and feasible.

If the school district has relatively homogeneous school populations, district norms are appropriate. When the district is characterized by heterogeneous schools, such as schools that differ in terms of student's language, cultural, and/or socioeconomic backgrounds, district norms may not provide the most meaningful representation of student expectations. If

FIGURE 1. Steps in developing local norms.

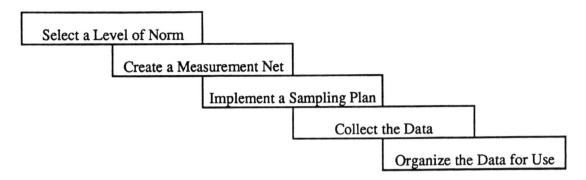

the curricula (e.g., grade-level educational goals and scope and sequence of instruction) across a district are relatively consistent, then district norms are appropriate. However, if the curricula are very different, then district norm data would not be relevant to many building decisions and building norms may be more appropriate. Schools that have a different structure, get funded differently, or have a history of functioning independently from the district "norm" would warrant the development of building norms. If the funds or personnel are unavailable for district norming, building norms may be more feasible. If resources for building norms are unavailable, norms can be developed one classroom at a time.

Determining the level of norming will be dependent on the circumstances in the school district. Each school district will have differing resources and needs that will change over time as well. Once a group of people have some experience developing one level of norm, they can use the knowledge they have gained to develop other levels of norms.

Create a Measurement Net

The second step in developing local norms is creating a measurement net. A measurement net is a grid of the grade levels and representative materials used in norming. The materials should represent the domain of the school year curriculum for *typical* general education students. For example, if a local norms comparison is desired for mathematic computation at Wild Rice Elementary School, a measurement net could be developed that detailed the grade levels where a math norm comparison would be useful in decision making. At each of these grade levels, the mathematic operations and problem types that best represent student expectations at that grade can be determined and grade-level math probes developed. When completed, the measurement net provides a guide for the student stimulus materials that must be developed. A CBM local norm measurement net for the four basic skill areas is presented in Table 1.

Identifying typical material. It is important that the measurement net truly represent *typical* material in each area and grade, not end-of-the-year goals nor preskill mastery objectives. Not every skill or level of difficulty can be represented in the norm materials, but choosing materials that best represent typical skills and levels of difficulty will allow for meaningful norm data. Many people and resources may be used to operationally define "typical." District curriculum specialists, adopted curriculum scope and sequence charts, and teachers provide the resources for answering questions such as: "What material is most frequently used?" "What levels of material are most representative of each grade's goals and objectives?" and "What materials are the majority of the students placed in for most of the school year?" The actual norming materials can be drawn directly from the adopted published curricular materials identified as typical or can be *generic* materials created to reflect typical materials at each grade level. The Monitoring Basic Skills reading maze, spelling, and math materials (Fuchs, Hamlett, & Fuchs, 1990) and the Test of Reading Fluency passages (Deno, Deno, Marston, & Marston, 1987) are examples of generic materials that may coincide with typical materials in use in the schools.

Measurement net dos and don'ts. Some hints for creating a measurement net will help avoid problems later. Field test your materials. Avoid material that is too easy (no variance) or too difficult (nothing to measure). Keep in mind the decisions you want to make using local norms. For example, if you are not interested in using normative comparisons for decisions about kindergarten students, then do not include kindergarten in your measurement net. Measurement nets should differ according to differences in the curriculum and level of norming.

Implement a Sampling Plan

"The normative sample is important because it is the group of individuals with whom a tested person is compared. Norms should be representative of the

TABLE 1
Sample Curriculum-Based Measurement Local Norms Measurement Net, Grades K–6

Grade	Readiness Skills	Reading	Math	Spelling	Written Expression
K	<u>Tool Movements</u> Write Letters Write Numbers <u>Identification</u> Read Numbers Read Letters <u>Phonological Awareness</u> Segmenting	--	--	--	--
1	<u>Identification</u> Read Numbers Read Letters <u>Phonological Awareness</u> Segmenting	Scribner Level 1 (Winter/Spring) Scribner Word List (Winter/Spring)	Basic Facts (+, -) Mixed Probe (+, -)	--	--
2	—	Scribner Level 2-2 Scribner Word List	Basic Facts (+, -) Mixed Probe (+, -)	Words from Laidlaw Spelling Level 2	Age appropriate story starters
3	---	Scribner Level 3-2 H-J Word List	Basic Facts (+, -) Mixed Probe (+, -, x)	Words from Laidlaw Spelling Level 3	Age appropriate story starters
4	---	Scribner Level 4 H-J Word List	Basic Facts (x, +) Mixed Probe (+, -, x, +)	Words from Laidlaw Spelling Level 4	Age appropriate story starters
5	---	Scribner Level 5 H-J Word List	Basic Facts (x, +) Mixed Probe (+, -, x, +)	Words from Laidlaw Spelling Level 5	Age appropriate story starters
6	---	Scribner Level 6 H-J Word List	Basic Facts (x, +) Mixed Probe (+, -, x, +)	Words from Laidlaw Spelling Level 6	Age appropriate story starters

population to which comparisons are made" (Salvia & Ysseldyke, 1991, p. 118). One of the strengths of local norms is that the data represent a meaningful comparison population: the students in the same school, curricula, age, grade, geographical area, and the like as the student being compared. A local norm does not necessarily mean norming the entire population, however. It is usually much more efficient to sample from the local population. A sampling plan must be developed that balances the resources available, representativeness of the sample, and information desired.

For classroom norms, a minimum of 7 to 10 students is necessary. Three methods of sampling students for classroom norms have been used: (a) creating a random subset of 7 to 10 students chosen from the entire class, (b) creating a subset of 7 to 10 students randomly selected from a pool of "typical" students identified by the teacher, and (c) a combination of testing all the students in the class for group administered tasks and selecting a subset of 7 to 10 students for more time-consuming individually administered tasks (e.g., oral reading). Choosing every nth name in the list from an alphabetized roster of student names or having a computer-generated random selection of students are the most typical ways to obtain a random sample of students.

At the building level, 15% to 20% of the students at each grade level, with a minimum of 20 students per grade, should be randomly sampled (Tindal et al., 1983). If building-level percentile ranks are desired, a sample of 100 students per grade is needed. Aggregated district norms can be developed by combining building norms if standard measurement materials have been used. If district-only norms are developed, a random sample of 100 students per grade is needed (aggregating across years if necessary to get 100 students).

Collect the Data

Data collection begins once the foundation has been laid for collecting well-developed norms: the level of norms has been selected, the measurement net filled in, and a sampling plan has been used to identify which students will be tested. Successful data collection hinges on the development of student testing materials, training data collectors, and scheduling when and where data collection will take place.

Materials and training. Student materials need to be prepared that are clear and time-efficient, for example, in booklet form with a place to summarize the data on the cover. Data collectors must be recruited and trained. Getting people involved in the data collection can be a good way of making the data meaningful for them. Parent volunteers, teachers, aides, school psychologists, principals, and school board members can be data collectors. Training materials should be developed so that the training itself is clear and consistent, and the data collectors leave training reliable and efficient in performing the norming administration and scoring procedures. Standardized administration and scoring, clear scheduling and materials, and monitoring integrity of data collection through spot checks or checklists also are key aspects in the collection of reliable norms.

Scheduling. The dates and logistics for norming must be scheduled as far in advance as possible to avoid conflicts. To get a picture of student performance throughout the year, trimester norming (e.g.,

Fall, Winter, Spring) is recommended, using equivalent but not identical norming materials each time (Shinn, 1989). Of course, classroom norms can be collected almost spontaneously if a classroom comparison is relevant to a decision being made and the materials and trained personnel are available. Norming can take place either within individual classrooms or at a central location in the school(s) such as a cafeteria or media center.

Organize the Data for Use

Because there are many potential uses for local norms and different consumers of norming information (e.g., parents, teachers, administrators), the norm data need to be organized so that they are easily and accurately interpreted. The data can be summarized at four different levels: (a) individual student raw scores; (b) classroom ranges of scores, medians, and rank orderings; (c) building-level ranges of scores, medians, rank orderings, and perhaps percentile ranks; and (d) school-district-level ranges of scores, percentile ranks, descriptive statistics, within-grade frequency distributions, and across-grade comparisons. One rule of thumb is that pictures communicate more clearly than tables and lists of numbers, so graphs that accurately represent the data are highly desirable.

Tables and graphs. Examples of tabular and graphic displays of classroom norm data are presented in Table 2 and Figures 2 and 3. Similar tables and graphs could be used to organize building and district norms. Table 2 presents a rank order of the students by raw score and also gives the range and median. Students in general education only, Chapter I, and special education in reading are separated so that comparisons of the achievement levels of students in these programs can be made. Additional descriptive statistics such as group averages and standard deviations could be added to the table for building and district norms. These same data are then presented in the form of a histogram or bar chart (Figure 2), and a frequency polygon (Figure 3). The histogram reflects the rank order information in visual form. The frequency polygon makes the norm distribution visible.

Percentile ranks are useful when making problem identification, certification, goal setting, and problem-solution decisions. For example, the district may determine that all students who are at or below the nth percentile on local norms are in need of further assessment, and students at or below the nth percentile are eligible for a particular program. The actual percentile cut-offs used by the district would be determined by considering several factors such as program intent, resources, federal or state guidelines, historical data, and so forth. Percentile rank data may be organized on tables by listing the raw scores and corresponding percentiles for each grade and norm-

TABLE 2
Sample Classroom Norms Table

Wild Rice Elementary: Grade 5-Mrs. Smith

CBM Oral Reading 9/14/94

Student	Rank Order	Raw Score		
		General Ed.	Chapter One	Special Ed.
BOWLER, WALTER	1	167		
SANCHEZ, JOSE	2	164		
LONGSTOCKING, THEA	3	139		
STENERSON, DALE	4	134		
GLEG, GLEN	5	129		
STORM, LISA	6	127		
SMITH, TERRY	7	125		
JENSON, KARLA	8	122		
CASS, CLAY	9	122		
SMITHEN, JOSHUA	10	119		
JOHNSON, HEIDI	11	111		
JACOBSON, DEBI	12	109		
DAHLEN, MEGAN	13	105		
THOMPSON, KRIS	14		103	
BERG, LAURA	15	102		
CHEW, NATHAN	16	90		
HERDMAN, STEVE	17	89		
COOPER, JENELL	18	88		
BLANDEN, MARY	19	88		
CARVER, JOSHUA	20		88	
PRESTON, WILLIAM	21			87
SIGERT, RICHARD	22	83		
CARVER, ZAK	23	75		
FREEMONT, SEAN	24	73		
JOHNSON, CORY	25	67		
ROSE, CONCETTA	26		57	
WILSON, BRUCE	27			50
FRAME, NAOMI	28		45	
HOMESCHMIDT, JUSTIN	29			23

Range		Low Score= 23		High Score=167

Median	102
General Ed. Median	110
Chapter One Median	72.5
Special Ed. Median	50

ing task. Percentiles also can be represented on "cut-off" charts that provide a visual display of where a child's performance falls in relation to the local norm (Gilbert & McKibben, 1993; Tindal & Marston, 1990). An example of a percentile rank cut-off chart is presented in Figure 4.

Also, percentile ranks could be used to determine which score corresponds to the Spring 50th percentile, and therefore what the goal would be for a student expected to be reading like an "average" student by the end of the year. A useful graphic for representing "typical performance" across grades is presented in Figure 5. The shaded bands represent performance between the 16th and 84th percentile at each grade level, with a line at the 50th percentile (Gilbert & McKibben, 1993). This same type of figure could be used to summarize typical performance within a grade across the three norming periods.

FIGURE 2. Sample classroom norm rank order histogram.

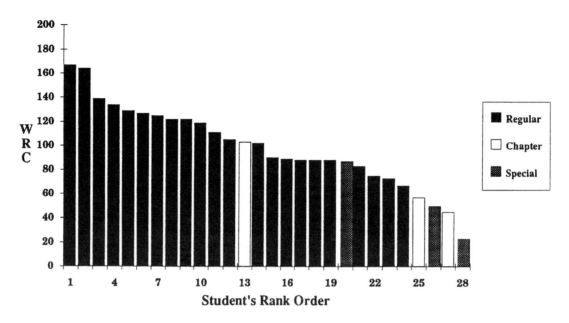

Computer programs. Many other types of graphs and tables could be used to organize and summarize the data; only a few of the possibilities have been provided. Regardless of the format chosen, however, having the normative data entered into a computer spreadsheet will make data presentation easier. Some type of computerized data organization and management usually is necessary for building and district norms, and desirable even for classroom norms data presentation. The programming and charting capabilities of spreadsheet programs such as Microsoft Excel (1993) have been used to organize and summarize local norms data. Zephyrus (Tilly, 1993) is a computer program designed specifically for local norming. Data entry and the creation of tables, histograms, and reports can be individualized to the behaviors and grade levels normed using the Zephyrus program.

Summary

The steps involved in developing local norms follow a logical sequence. Selecting a level of norm provides an opportunity for reviewing the purpose for developing the norm and the unique characteristics and needs of the local school(s). The completed measurement net is a blueprint for developing norming materials and forces the norm developers to closely examine the local curriculum content, instructional focus, and goals and expectations. The sampling plan identifies the students who will make up the norm sample and allows for further logistical planning such as scheduling and final materials preparation. The normative performance data is finally obtained by collecting and organizing it for use in educational decision making.

UTILIZING LOCAL NORMS IN A PROBLEM-SOLVING SCHOOL SYSTEM

One of the strengths of local norms is increased utility across educational decisions. What national norm comparisons often lack is (a) the ability to consider the student's immediate environment in defining problems and (b) a tie between the information used to define the problem and other decisions in the public school system. Local norms operationalize the expectations for a student's immediate educational surroundings and can be useful across the range of educational decisions, from problem identification to problem solution. A summary of local norm utility across decisions is presented in Table 3.

Problem Identification and Certification

Like national norms, local norms may assist in problem identification and certification decision making. A problem can be defined as the difference between what is expected and what occurs (Deno, 1988). Local norms can be used to define what is expected of a student. For example, comparing a student's score to a local oral reading norm can determine if the student's reading score falls within the average range of other student's in that district, building, or classroom. That average range represents what the teachers see as typical reading performance in the classroom. If the student's reading falls below that average range, educational personnel may con-

FIGURE 3. Sample classroom norm frequency polygon.

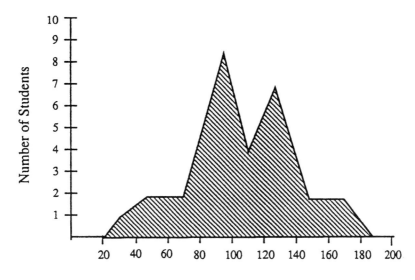

Words Read Correct Per Minute Interval Midpoints

clude that the student's performance does not meet expectations and therefore a problem exists. In this case, more intensive assessment, and perhaps educational services, are warranted. If, upon further assessment, the student's reading scores continue to fall far below typical students' performance in the local norm, evidence that the problem is important and warrants intensive school services (e.g., special education) is supported. This further corroboration of the importance of the problem is part of a multifaceted assessment for making problem certification decisions about students.

Exploring and Evaluating Solutions

Local norms can be useful at several other levels of a school's problem-solving framework. Once the problem has been validated, goals are set and services are provided to meet the student's needs. These services must be evaluated for their effectiveness and modifications made if goals are not being met. Local norms can be used to help set goals. IEP and Chapter I goals, for example, can be based on the typical performance of students in the local norm sample. Tying student goals to typical general education performance maintains congruence between what the student is expected to accomplish and what performance is needed to fit into the general education setting. Local norms also can be used to clarify placement in, and organization of, the variety of special services available in the school. By obtaining a picture of the local student population's range of skills (the local norm) and knowing which sections of that population are served by the resources available (e.g., where students in Chapter I, ESL, special education,

TAG, and at-risk programs perform on the norming tasks), decisions about services for individual students and the organization of programs can be more data based.

Problem Solution

Finally, local norms can be used in determining when a student can be exited from a program or moved to a less restrictive environment (i.e., problem solution or reintegration). Student performance within the range of typical students suggests consideration of exit from the special program. Relatedly, student performance within the range of the lowest achieving general education students in the classroom, school, or district sample could be used to determine when a student could be reintegrated into a less restrictive setting (Shinn et al., 1993).

Local Norms and Program Evaluation

Although not directly tied to decisions about individual students, local norms collected across years also can be used to evaluate program/curriculum effects, given fairly stable student population and demographics. Likewise, local norms collected across years could be used to evaluate the effects of population or demographic shifts, given fairly stable service delivery systems and program/curriculum. Local norms collected for the purpose of program evaluation or other administrative purposes may require a higher level of expertise and more standard set of tasks and measurement materials than local norms developed for student-centered decision making (Tindal, 1988; Tindal & Marston, 1990).

FIGURE 4. Sample district norm problem identification cut-off chart.

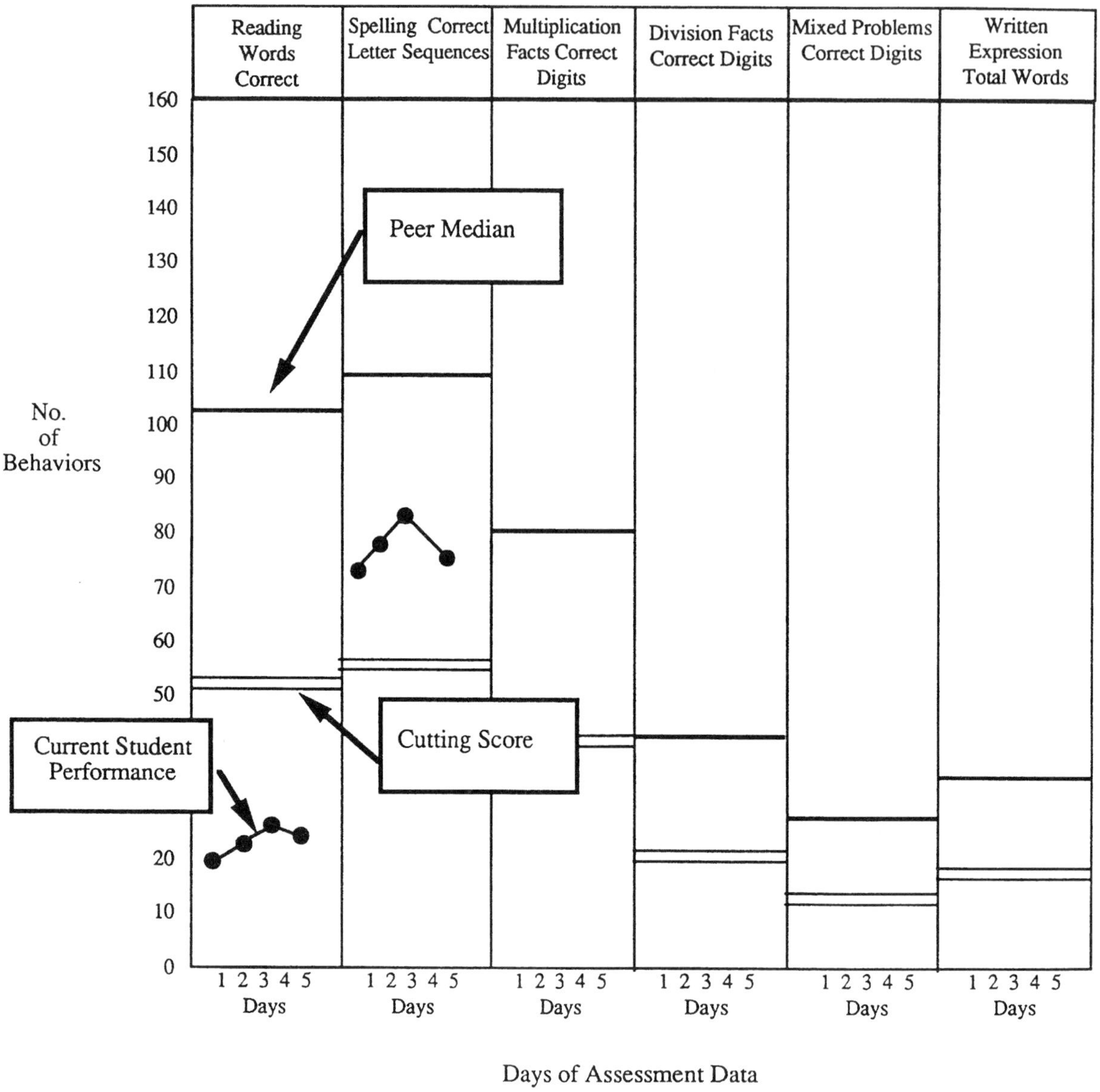

Days of Assessment Data

SUMMARY

Although the use of normative comparisons in the schools is common, developing and using local norms as part of a problem-solving system is still a relatively new area for school psychologists. A problem-solving system requires analysis of the educational context as well as the individual student. The context of the educational system — the class size, educational background, socioeconomic factors, student achievement levels, and so forth — will differ from district to district, school to school, and even classroom to classroom. For the school psychologist working with the staff and students in a particular system, local norms can provide a representative sample for local decision making and offer flexibility in which types of tasks are normed. These characteristics contribute to the strengths of local norms: decreased bias in decision making, increased teaching/testing overlap, and norm utility across educational decisions.

Developing local norms is a process of focusing on what information is most useful for educational problem solving and then implementing the five steps of norm development: (a) selecting a level of norm, (b) creating a measurement net, (c) implementing a sampling plan, (d) collecting data, and (e) organizing the data for use.

FIGURE 5. Sample district spelling norm across-grade distribution.

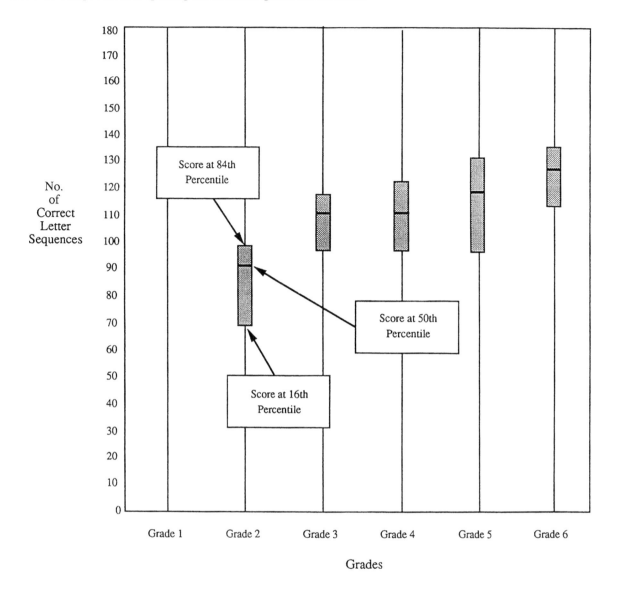

For maximizing norm utility in problem solving, best practices in local norm development would involve norming behaviors that are important in the general education environment and developing local norms that represent the range of performance in general education. By selecting important and valid behaviors tied to general education (e.g., Curriculum-Based Measures of reading, math, spelling, and written expression), the norm can be used to operationalize general education expectations. The process of problem solving then involves: (a) identifying a problem by examining if a particular student's performance or behavior is outside of the expectations of general education, (b) certifying a problem by showing whether the student's performance is so discrepant from peers that special services are war-ranted, (c) setting goals to get the student's performance back within the range of his or her general education peers, (d) monitoring student progress, and (e) determining when the student's performance is no longer outside of the general education expectations and the problem is solved. Throughout this problem-solving process, local norms provide a context for making educational decisions.

AUTHOR'S NOTES

This chapter was supported in part by Grant No. H02980051 awarded to the University of Oregon by the U.S. Department of Education, Special Programs Office. The views expressed within this chapter are not necessarily those of the USDE. The author wishes to thank Drs. Mark Shinn, Scott Baker, and Susan Green for their support in writing this chapter.

TABLE 3
Local Norms Utility Across Problem-Solving Decisions

Problem-Solving Decision	Use of Local Norms
Problem Identification (Screening)	Use local norms to determine if a performance discrepancy exists between a particular student and grade-level peers.
Problem Certification (Eligibility Determination)	Use local norms to decide if discrepancies are important enough that special services may be needed for problem resolution.
Exploring Solutions (Goal Setting and Intervention Planning)	Use local norms to facilitate goal setting. Select the level of skills required for success.
Evaluating Solutions (Progress Monitoring and Program Modification)	
Problem Solution (Exit from Programs)	Use local norms to decide if existing discrepancies are important or if alternative services are no longer warranted.

REFERENCES

Anastasi, A. (1988). *Psychological testing* (6th ed.). New York: Macmillan.

Baker, S. K. (1992). *The reliability and validity of a direct measure of English reading fluency for students who are bilingual.* Unpublished doctoral dissertation, University of Oregon, Eugene.

Ball, P. (Ed.). (1993). *CBA training institute: Developing local norms for use in problem-solving* (4th ed.). (Available from University of Oregon, School Psychology Program, DSER College of Education, Eugene, Oregon 97402).

Bergan, J. R. (1985). *School psychology in contemporary society: An introduction.* Columbus, OH: Merrill.

Deno, S. L. (1985). Curriculum-based measurement: The emerging alternative. *Exceptional Children, 52*(3), 219–232.

Deno, S. L. (1986). Formative evaluation of individual student programs: A new role for school psychologists. *School Psychology Review, 15*(3), 348–374.

Deno, S. L. (1988). Curriculum-based measurement and special education services: A fundamental and direct relationship. In M. R. Shinn (Ed.), *Curriculum-based measurement: Assessing special children* (pp. 1–17). New York: Guilford.

Deno, S. L., Deno, D., Marston, D., & Marston, D. (1987). *Test of read fluency: Measures for screening and progress monitoring.* Minneapolis, MN: Children's Educational Services, Inc.

Elliott, S. E., & Bretzing, B. (1980). Using and updating local norms. *Psychology in the Schools, 17,* 196–201.

Fuchs, L., Hamlett, C., & Fuchs, D. (1990). *Monitoring Basic Skills Program* [Computer Program]. Austin, TX: Pro-Ed.

Gerber, M., & Semmel, M. (1984). Teachers as imperfect tests: Reconceptualizing the referral process. *Educational Psychologist, 19*(3), 137–148.

Gilbert, M., & McKibben, M. (Eds.). (1993). *CBA training institute: Problem identification and problem certification using curriculum-based measures* (4th ed.). (Available from University of Oregon, School Psychology Program, DSER College of Education, Eugene, Oregon 97403.)

Good, R. H., & Salvia, J. (1988). Curriculum bias in published, norm-referenced reading tests: Demonstrable effects. *School Psychology Review, 17*(1), 51–60.

Jenkins, J., & Pany, D. (1978). Curriculum biases in reading achievement tests. *Journal of Reading Behavior, 10*(4), 345–357.

Kamphaus, R. W., & Lozano, R. (1984). Developing local norms for individually administered tests. *School Psychology Review, 13,* 346–357.

Kubiszyn, T., & Borich, G. (1990). *Educational testing and measurement: Classroom application and practice* (3rd ed.). Glenview, IL: Scott, Foresman.

Leinhardt, G. (1983). Overlap: Testing whether it is taught. In G. F. Madaus (Ed.), *The courts validity, and minimum competency testing* (pp. 153–170). Boston: Kluwer-Nijhoff Publishing.

Magnusson, D. (1986). *A comparison of school and district norms in making special education eligibility decisions.* Unpublished doctoral dissertation. University of Minnesota, Minneapolis.

Marston, D. (1989). Curriculum-based measurement: What is it and why do it? In M. R. Shinn (Ed.), *Curriculum-based measurement: Assessing special children* (pp. 18–78). New York: Guilford.

Marston, D., & Magnusson, D. (1988). Curriculum-based measurement: District-level implementation. In J. S. Graden & M. Curtis (Eds.), *Alternative educational delivery systems: Enhancing instructional options for all students* (pp. 137–172). Washington, DC: National Association of School Psychologists.

Microsoft Corporation. (1993). *Microsoft Excel* [Computer Program]. Microsoft Corporation.

Reynolds, C. R., & Kaiser, S. M. (1990). Test bias in psychological assessment. In T. B. Gutkin & C. R. Reynolds (Eds.), *The handbook of school psychology* (2nd ed.; pp. 487–525). New York: Wiley.

Salvia, J., & Ysseldyke, J. E. (1991). *Assessment in special and remedial education* (4th ed.). Boston: Houghton Mifflin.

Shapiro, E. S., & Derr, T. F. (1990). Curriculum-based assessment. In T. B. Gutkin & C. R. Reynolds (Eds.), *The handbook of school psychology* (2nd ed.; pp. 365–387). New York: Wiley.

Shapiro, E. S., & Derr, T. F. (1987). An examination of overlap between reading curricula and standardized achievement tests. *The Journal of Special Education, 21*(2), 59–67.

Shinn, M. R. (1988). Development of curriculum-based local norms for use in special education decision-making. *School Psychology Review, 17*(1), 61–80.

Shinn, M. R. (1989). Identifying and defining academic problems: CBM screening and eligibility procedures. In M. R. Shinn (Ed.), *Curriculum-based measurement: Assessing special children* (pp. 90–129). New York: Guilford.

Shinn, M. R., Habedank, L., Rodden-Nord, K., & Knutson, N. (1993). Using curriculum-based measurement to identify potential candidates for reintegration into general education. *Journal of Special Education, 27*(2), 202–221.

Shinn, M. R., Nolet, V., & Knutson, N. (1990). Best practices in curriculum-based measurement. In A. Thomas & J. Grimes (Eds.), *Best practices in school psychology–II* (pp. 287–307). Washington, DC: National Association of School Psychologists.

Tilly, D. W. (1993). *Zephyrus* [Computer Program]. Iowa State University, Des Moines, IA: Author.

Tindal, G. (1988). Evaluating the effectiveness of educational programs at the systems level using curriculum- based measurement. In M. R. Shinn (Ed.), *Curriculum-based measurement: Assessing special children* (pp. 202–238). New York: Guilford.

Tindal, G., Germann, G., & Deno, S. (1983). *Descriptive research on the Pine County norms: A compilation of findings* (Research Report 132). Minneapolis: University of Minnesota, Institute for Research on Learning Disabilities.

Tindal, G. A., & Marston, D. B. (1990). *Classroom-based assessment: Evaluating instructional outcomes.* Columbus, OH: Merrill.

Ysseldyke, J. E. (1979). Issues in psychoeducational assessment. In G. Phye & D. Reschly (Eds.), *School psychology: Perspectives and issues* (pp. 87–121). New York: Academic Press.

ANNOTATED BIBLIOGRAPHY

Shinn, M. R. (1988). Development of curriculum-based local norms for use in special education decision making. *School Psychology Review, 17*(1), 61–80.

This journal article describes the development and use of Curriculum-Based Measurement (CBM) local norms. Examples of applying CBM local norms in special education decision making are provided throughout. The use of CBM in decision making is presented as an opportunity to expand the role of the school psychologist. Technical adequacy and logistical issues in developing a local database are discussed.

Tindal, G. A., & Marston, D. B. (1990). *Classroom-based assessment: Evaluating instructional outcomes.* Columbus, OH: Merrill

This basic assessment text addresses many of the issues involved in developing and using local norms. Tindal and Marston give guidelines for test reliability and validity that include sections on the size and comparability of the norm group (Chapter 6). The text provides a good overview of norm-referenced evaluation (Chapter 13), including examples of local norms. Different formats for local norm data display also are demonstrated.

61

Best Practices in the Assessment of Written Expression

Scott Baker
Dawn Hubbard
University of Oregon

OVERVIEW

As Connally (1983) notes "education is inextricably linked with the capacity to produce visible language" (p. xi). Functional literacy is a cultural imperative for all students (Deno, 1989), and although the development of reading skills has received the bulk of the literacy focus during the latest reform movement in education, the development of writing skills has also generated considerable attention. At least three reasons justify a chapter for school psychologists devoted to the assessment of written expression.

First, many students are not acquiring adequate written expression skills. According to the results of the latest National Assessment of Educational Progress (cited in Hooper et al., 1994), only 1% of fourth-grade students and 8% of eighth-grade students wrote a well-developed narrative, and only 22% of eighth-graders could develop an argumentative report. Writing problems surface early and in many cases remain with students throughout their educational experiences (Isaacson, 1985). In addition, written expression in the early grades is a good predictor of overall school success, and in many cases becomes the first indication of academic difficulty noticed by teachers (Isaacson, 1985). Along with reading, failure to acquire adequate skills in written expression constitute the greatest number of referrals to, and placements in, special and remedial education programs (Hallahan & Kauffman, 1986; Howell, Fox, & Morehead, 1993).

Second, writing instruction is beginning to play a more prominent role in general education classrooms. In many ways, effective written expression represents the culmination of formal educational experiences (Salvia & Ysseldyke, 1991). Writing is an extremely complex task and its development is significantly influenced by the kinds of opportunities students have in school to write (Hillocks, 1984). Teachers are moving away from instruction that focuses exclusively on the mechanics of writing to instruction that focuses on the range of tasks involved during the writing process (Raphael & Englert, 1990). To write well requires that students have an adequate knowledge base from which to draw content ideas, the skills to organize their ideas and present them in print according to established conventions, and sufficient self-monitoring strategies to guide the recursive writing process. School psychologists need assessment procedures that reflect the richness and complexity of the written expression process.

The third reason for a chapter on the assessment of written expression is that the very act of sequencing skills (i.e., gaining access to the relevant knowledge base, generating and sequencing ideas, and using strategies of self-monitoring to evaluate performance) is traditionally a source of difficulty for low-performing students, including students with disabilities (Englert & Raphael, 1989). If school psychologists are to play a prominent role in structuring general education environments so that more students develop effective writing skills, they will need assessment strategies that reflect the degree to which students are acquiring the range of skills being emphasized in classroom settings.

BASIC CONSIDERATIONS

The goal of this chapter is to provide a framework for assessing written expression, a framework adaptable to the diverse writing expectations and formats that characterize classroom settings. Two assumptions are made that serve to structure the assessment of written expression. First, assessment procedures should be guided by a decision-making purpose and the data collected should reflect that purpose (Deno, 1989; Salvia & Ysseldyke, 1991; Shinn & Hubbard, 1993; Shinn, Nolet, & Knutson, 1990). In this context, the purpose and relevance of assessment data should be clear to the readers, parents, and students who may be affected by the outcome.

The second assumption is that comprehensive assessment procedures should address not only student writing performance but also the environmental variables that may be contributing to writing problems or that can otherwise serve as intervention targets. Converging evidence in education and psychology indicates that student performance on academic tasks is the result of complex interdependent factors. The belief that student performance reflects strengths and weaknesses attributable exclusively to within-student factors is being replaced by models of achievement that stress the influence of student skills *and* environmental variables in achievement outcomes (Lentz & Shapiro, 1986). For that reason, environmental variables associated with the content of the classroom writing curriculum and the procedures the teacher uses to deliver the writing content are discussed in this chapter (Howell et al., 1993).

BEST PRACTICES

Assessing Written Expression within a Decision-Making Context

Best practices in the assessment of written expression should center on activities to make specific educational decisions. For example, decisions regarding individual students range from determining the validity of a student referral to evaluating the effectiveness of an intervention aimed at improving student writing performance. A decision-making model proposed by Deno (1989) is sufficiently both broad and comprehensive to allow school psychologists from a variety of theoretical orientations to conduct assessments of written expression within a common decision-making context. In Deno's (1989) data-based problem-solving model, five types of decisions are identified. These decisions are depicted in Table 1, along with the assessment variables associated with each decision and general strategies for data collection.

In assessing written expression, the type of data collected and the ways the data are used depends on the decision being made. Although there is clear continuity from one decision to the next, the model does not need to be used in a lock-step fashion. For example, data-based decisions about student progress can be undertaken without first determining that a student is eligible for special education services. The majority of school psychologists, however, need comprehensive assessment strategies they can use in a step-by-step sequence. For this reason, a brief description of each decision is presented in a way that highlights the sequential nature in which the model can be used.

Screening decisions. The primary purpose of a screening decision is to determine if a student's performance in written expression is of sufficient concern to warrant a comprehensive writing assessment. The primary assessment task at this stage is to compare the target student's performance with typical peers from the same class, grade, or district. In addi-

tion, it is important to clarify the teacher's primary areas of concerns and to determine if instructional attempts to address the problems have been attempted. As with any assessment, more than one source of data should be collected to make a decision involving an individual student (Salvia & Ysseldyke, 1991). This is especially true in written expression because writing measures tend to be supported by lower reliability and validity data than other basic skill areas (Marston, 1989). Thus, a screening decision might be based on a direct measure of writing performance as well as student performance on a group-administered published test.

Program-eligibility decisions. The primary goal in making an eligibility decision is to determine if the resources in general education are sufficient to meet the instructional needs of the student or if additional resources, such as special education, are required. Achieving this goal requires a comprehensive assessment involving the collection of additional data on the student's writing performance as well as assessing the environmental variables that might be manipulated to improve student performance. Before anyone collects additional measures of student writing, a student interview should be conducted to determine if the student understands what the teacher expects in writing and has the knowledge preskills necessary to accomplish the writing objectives. For example, if some students are working on writing stories, do they understand the various elements that go into making a story?

An individual student's writing performance is assessed using multiple direct measures of writing. In addition, because of the importance of an eligibility decision, a published, individually administered measure of writing achievement should be administered to support the severity of the writing problem. The first step in assessing the writing environment involves conducting a teacher interview to confirm (a) the teacher's specific concerns regarding the target student's writing performance and (b) the content of the writing curriculum the teacher expects students to learn. The second step is to conduct classroom observations to determine the procedures the teacher uses to teach students the writing content and to observe the student's behavior during instruction.

Instructional-planning decisions. When the target student is found eligible for special education services, the purposes of instructional planning decisions are to determine (a) appropriate goals and objectives for improving student writing performance, (b) the procedures that will be used to monitor writing progress, and (c) the curriculum content and instructional delivery procedures that will be used to help the student meet his or her writing goals and objectives (Fuchs & Shinn, 1989). Additional assessment data do not have to be collected during this stage. The data collected to determine if the student

TABLE 1
Decision-Making Context for Students Experiencing Writing Problems

Problem-Solving Decision	Decision Outcome	Assessment Variables	Assessment Strategies
Screening	Determine whether the writing problem requires a comprehensive assessment	• Environmental • Student Performance	• Teacher clarification of concern • Direct measures of student and peer writing performance
Program Eligibility	Determine if the severity of the writing problem requires resources beyond general education for remediation	• Environmental • Student Performance	• Teacher interview using IPF • Systematic classroom observations • Direct and indirect measures of student writing performance
Instructional Planning	• Determine writing goals and objectives • Determine intervention components	Data from program eligibility decision	Data from program eligibility decision
Progress Monitoring and Intervention Implementation	• Determine whether student is making adequate progress toward writing goals and objectives • Determine changes when student progress is not adequate	• Student performance • Environmental	• Direct formative measures of student performance • Review IPF with teacher • Systematic classroom observations*
Program Evaluation	• Summarize student progress toward writing goals and objectives • Determine if the severity of the writing problem continues to require resources beyond general education for remediation	• Student Performance • Environmental	• Direct measures of student and peer writing performance • Review and revise IPF with teacher • Systematic classroom observation*

Adapted from: Shinn, M. R., Nolet, V., and Knutson, N. (1990). Best practices in Curriculum-Based Measurement. In A. Thomas and J. Grimes (Eds.), *Best practices in school psychology–II* (pp. 287–307). Washington, DC: National Association of School Psychologists.

* Optional

was eligible for special services should be sufficient to plan the student's writing program and establish a progress-monitoring system.

Progress-monitoring and intervention-implementation decisions. The primary purpose in monitoring student progress is to determine the adequacy of student growth toward the specific writing goals and objectives identified in the instructional planning stage. The more frequently student progress data are collected, the sooner changes can be made in

writing programs leading to insufficient rates of progress. Thus, measures of student progress should be sensitive to small changes in student performance and capable of frequent administration. When student progress is not adequate, the intervention should be evaluated and changes made in environmental variables in an attempt to increase the rate of student progress. Evaluating the implementation of the intervention typically involves an interview with the student's teacher to review the intervention and discuss changes that might facilitate student progress. Additional classroom observations can provide a more accurate assessment of how the writing program is being delivered and possible environmental variables that might be manipulated to enhance student progress.

Program-evaluation decisions. The two primary purposes of making program evaluation decisions are to summarize the overall effectiveness of the writing program at two levels and to determine if the student's writing performance continues to require services beyond general education. The first level of evaluating the effectiveness of the writing program is to summarize student progress toward individually referenced goals and objectives. At a second level, direct measures of a student's writing performance are compared to peers from the same class, grade, or district to determine how the severity of the student's writing discrepancy from peers has changed over time. The student's teacher also should be interviewed to determine the degree to which the writing program was implemented as planned and discuss changes the teacher would like to see in the student's writing program. Classroom observations also can be conducted to evaluate how additional environmental variables may be facilitating or inhibiting a student's writing progress. The combination of the two levels of summarizing student writing performances and the analyses of environmental variables are used by a multidisciplinary team to determine if services beyond general education are still needed for the student to make adequate writing progress (Allen, 1989).

Assessing Environmental Variables

Assessing variables in the writing environment is important to determine if a student is eligible for services beyond general education, to identify potential intervention targets in planning instruction, and to evaluate the extent to which interventions have been implemented as planned. An interview with the student's teacher is the best way of gathering data about the content of the writing curriculum and the methods the teacher plans to use to teach writing. Classroom observations are necessary to assess the instructional delivery procedures the teacher actually uses to teach writing, as well as to gather information about the student's behavior during instruction.

The instructional planning form. Writing instruction varies considerably from classroom to classroom (Hillocks, 1984). An instructional planning form (IPF) is used to gather information from teachers regarding the content and delivery of writing instruction. The interview format of the IPF involves a framework for identifying possible intervention targets when student progress is not adequate. The completed IPF in Table 2 details what might be a writing program for a student in the third grade. The five major headings (i.e., Instructional Procedures, Mate-

rials, Arrangements, Time, and Motivational Strategies) address variables in writing instruction that can be manipulated to increase student writing performance. For example, one possibility for increasing the student's writing fluency referred to in Table 2 might be to increase the amount of time the student spends in journal writing from 10 to 20 minutes per day.

The IPF should be completed by having teachers "talk through" their typical classroom writing routines. Discerning the primary writing skill and the strategies the teacher uses to teach the skill is the most difficult component to fill out on the IPF. Because there are many ways to describe a particular focus or skill, it is important to clarify with teachers what their description of activities in those two categories mean. A completed IPF serves as a description of the initial writing program to help a student meet specific writing goals and objectives. When student progress is inadequate, the school psychologist and teacher should use the IPF to identify where and how changes might be made to increase student growth. Classroom observation procedures are used to document the extent to which the components on the IPF are implemented and to supply additional information concerning possible interventions that might be successful in increasing student performance. Although it cannot be predicted in advance that a particular writing program will succeed with a given student, regardless of how well the program is planned and implemented (Deno, 1990), research evidence suggests that certain types of classroom writing environments have a higher probability of improving writing proficiency than others.

Traditional classroom writing environments. Traditional classroom writing environments frequently focus on student adherence to writing conventions such as spelling, punctuation, grammar, and handwriting (Englert & Mariage, 1992). On the IPF, these would be identified under *Focus or Skill*. In the early elementary grades, for example, the focus tends to be on punctuation skills. Students frequently practice punctuation skills by filling in blanks on worksheets (Bridge & Hiebert, 1985). Occasionally, there is verbatim copying of letters and sentences. During later elementary grades, more attention is directed to copying activities designed to improve punctuation skills and develop proficiency in identifying parts of speech (Bridge & Hiebert, 1985). At the secondary level, the focus tends to be primarily on the completion of grammar exercises (Applebee, 1981). On the IPF in Table 2, 15 minutes per day is allocated to grammar and conventions. More time is allocated to this activity than any other, which is an accurate reflection of what occurs in typical classrooms (Isaacson, 1987).

School psychologists should be aware of at least three problems associated with traditional classroom

TABLE 2
Instructional Planning Form for a Student in Grade 3

Instructional Procedures		Materials	Arrangements	Time	Motivational Strategies
Focus or Skill	*Teaching Strategy*				
Writing fluency	Student directed	Student journals	Independent	10 min. daily	• Praise • Student-selected topic
Grammar and Conventions	Teacher-led Instruction	Houghton-Mifflin Curriculum	Small Group (11:1)	15 min. daily	• Praise • Feedback • Group and individual points
Writing Process/ Narrative Text Structure	Teacher-led Instruction	• Overheads • Workbooks • Notebooks	Whole group (22:1)	20 min. M/W	• Praise • Feedback • Group and individual points
Writing Process	• Computer Program • Peer Editing	• Writing to Write Programs • Student writings	• Individualized at computer • Pairs of writers	20 min. T/Th	• Praise • Feedback • Group and individual points
Oral presentation of written products	Author's Chair	Student's written product	Whole group	20 min. Friday	• Peer praise • Feedback • Group and individual points

writing environments (Englert & Mariage, 1991; Isaacson, 1987). First, many traditional classroom environments allocate insufficient opportunities for students to engage in meaningful writing activities (Englert & Mariage, 1992). Research indicates that focusing on writing conventions does not result in overall improvements in students' written compositions (Hillocks, 1984). Second, many teachers rely heavily on published writing curricula to teach writing. Published writing curricula focus heavily on conventions, especially grammar, and studies conducted during the past 50 years clearly indicate that a predominant focus on grammar does not result in improvements in the overall quality of student writing (Hillocks, 1984). Third, traditional writing environments place nearly complete emphasis on product variables. Minimal attention is devoted to the critical skills needed for the development of overall writing proficiency (Isaacson, 1987). According to Isaacson (1987), writing environments should take into account *process* variables, such as selecting, combining, arranging, and developing ideas, as well as *product* variables, such as sentences and paragraph construction.

Changes in classroom writing environments.
Recent changes in classroom writing environments

offer numerous possibilities for facilitating instructional planning decisions in written expression. Many of these changes were fueled by Hillocks' (1984) meta-analysis of 60 experimental studies on written expression. Hillocks (1984) found that effective writing instruction was characterized by clear and specific writing objectives and activities in which students could interact with each other on writing tasks, such as small-group discussions focusing on the components of text structure. Hillocks (1984) also found that the most effective writing instruction consistently provided students with specific background information about a selected topic. Planned activities then were used to help students organize that information for the purpose of writing about the topic. Less effective environments included more traditional activities in which students practiced combining simple sentences into more complex sentences or applied evaluative criteria to a writing sample. Even less effective were methods in which students wrote about whatever interested them or analyzed features of exemplary writing samples to recognize and imitate those features in their own writing. The instructional approaches that resulted in the poorest writing performance were those that focused on studying parts of speech and sentences. Important changes in classroom writing environments influenced by Hillocks' (1984) findings include addressing the importance of text structure and making explicit the stages of the writing process.

Text structure. Awareness that written text involves recurring structures and patterns is an important prerequisite to mastering the writing process (Englert & Mariage, 1992). In many classrooms, students will be expected to develop writing skills to match different types of text structure. School psychologists should be familiar with the components of different text structures as they assess environmental variables that may be affecting student performance. For example, students may be expected to write proficiently using narrative text structure and many types of expository text structures such as compare/contrast, description, explanation, and persuasion (Englert & Mariage, 1992).

Narrative text structure is one of the earliest forms of communication acquired by children and contains a number of standard components (Englert & Mariage, 1992). Typical story grammar elements in narrative text include setting events, episodes, and conclusions. In some classrooms, teachers may expect students to include story grammar elements in their writing without providing explicit instruction on how that is done. In other classrooms, explicit instruction may occur on as many as eight or more elements (Simmons et al, in press).

Many students become implicitly aware of story grammar elements before they begin school, primarily through story reading at home. Even at the high school level, however, many low achieving students do not have a basic understanding of story grammar elements and, not surprisingly, the writing these students produce tends to be extremely poor compared to their classroom peers (Graves, Montague, & Wong, 1990; Meyer, Brandt, & Bluth, 1980). Recent developments in integrated curricula highlight one way to teach text structure elements in the context of written expression that may be useful in planning instructional programs (Langer & Applebee, 1987). For example, in an integrated reading and writing curriculum, students might learn about story grammar elements during reading instruction and then integrate those elements into their own written compositions (Raphael & Englert, 1990).

A study by Graham and Harris (1989) includes a number of components for planning instructional programs to meet the needs of students with poor writing skills. Graham and Harris (1989) taught students a question-asking strategy to improve their narrative writing. Their program began with prewriting activities that focused on identifying and generating story grammar elements using a mnemonic for seven story grammar questions. After students were able to recite the mnemonic and discuss its meaning, they generated story grammar elements while looking at a picture (Graham & Harris, 1989). A five-step learning strategy was used to help students write stories using the picture prompt. The teacher first demonstrated the strategy by using a "think aloud" technique. Students then practiced the five-step learning strategy as they wrote their own stories independently. To provide feedback, the stories were read by the teacher and students as a group, and if any of the story elements were missing, the group discussed how and where they could be added. The stories were returned to their authors for revision based on teacher and student recommendations.

The writing process. In general, environments that address the writing process attempt to make explicit the different stages of written expression, which can be used across different types of text structure. These stages include (a) establishing a purpose for writing, (b) generating and organizing ideas about what to write, (c) translating writing ideas into print according to established conventions, and (d) revising and editing drafts of the written product to match the writer's ultimate intent (Isaacson, 1985). Research evidence indicates that students make better writing gains when each of these stages is taught explicitly (Howell, Fox, & Morehead, 1993). In assessing the writing environment, school psychologists should document on the IPF and through direct observations the extent that explicit instruction is provided for each stage of the writing process. In many classrooms, the focus will be primarily on the third stage, that is, generating a writing product that adheres to established conventions. Little instructional attention typically is directed toward how to generate and organize ideas for writing nor on how to improve a written product through revision. Providing explicit instruction in the stages of the writing process should be considered a potentially valuable intervention when planning instructional programs for students.

Englert and her colleagues (Englert & Mariage, 1992; Englert & Raphael, 1989) have documented the effectiveness of explicitly teaching the stages of the writing process. For example, Englert and Mariage (1992) taught students a mnemonic strategy to help them learn to plan, organize, write, edit, and revise (POWER) their written products. After ensuring that students had learned the basics of text structure, they taught students the stages of the writing process through a sequence of explicit instructional activities. First, teachers modeled each stage of the writing process by "thinking aloud." For example, in modeling planning, teachers used self-talk and other overt procedures to clearly identify their audience and the purpose for writing. Then, to activate background knowledge teachers modeled brainstorming strategies to generate writing ideas, and ways to organize those ideas for content inclusion during the transcribing stage. After teachers modeled each stage of the writing process, they worked with students to write a class paper using the POWER strategy. Over time, students assumed more and more control of the writing process. Eventually they were required to complete writing projects independently, while continuing to demonstrate mastery of each stage of the writing process.

In summary, assessing environmental variables is conducted primarily to facilitate decisions regarding instructional planning. Typically, the data used to determine student eligibility for services beyond general education can be used to facilitate instructional planning decisions. However, it is not necessary to make an eligibility decision before gathering assessment data useful in planning instructional programs. The effectiveness of any program or intervention should be based primarily on student performance data. There are a number of ways to assess student writing. The methods vary in how students are asked to respond and the implications the data have for decision making.

Assessing Student Performance Variables

Direct and indirect measures can be used to assess student writing, Direct assessment measures (e.g., holistic judgments, objective indices, analytic ratings) are actual samples of student writing and provide for a rich analysis of student skills. In contrast, indirect measures are characterized by selection-type or contrived-response formats (e.g., multiple choice, matching, fill in the blank). Scoring indirect measures often involves determining if a response is correct or incorrect, and little information is obtained regarding how a student arrived at a particular answer. Although many indirect measures tap skills similar to those tracked by direct measures (Breland & Gaynor, 1979), the data typically are not useful beyond screening and eligibility decisions. A comprehensive review of indirect measures of written expression is provided by Bradley-Johnson and Lesiak (1989).

The remainder of this chapter will focus on the way direct assessment measures of student writing can be used to enhance decision making. All the procedures described can be used as part of a comprehensive assessment. Because there are few technically sound measures of written expression available, best practices in the assessment of written expression involves converging evidence among multiple measures of student performance (e.g., support from direct and indirect measures). This is particularly important when making eligibility decisions. Many of the procedures described next are best used for identifying student strengths and needs to plan instructional programs and monitor student progress toward short-term objectives.

Depending on the decision being made, student writing samples can be collected using standardized (e.g., curriculum-based measures, published norm-referenced tests) or nonstandardized procedures (e.g., portfolio samples, writing projects). When peer-referenced assessment data are needed for screening, eligibility, or program evaluation decisions, standardized procedures should be used. The writing samples generated to facilitate screening and eligibility decisions also can be used to facilitate instructional-planning and progress-monitoring decisions, but they may need to be supplemented with additional writing samples to obtain an accurate indication of student writing performance. Once the data are collected, assessment procedures are used to judge the student's overall writing proficiency and to identify skills in need of remediation.

Six components of written expression distinguish skilled from unskilled writers and provide an organizer for a comprehensive assessment of student writing skills. These six components are: (a) fluency, (b) grammar, (c) conventions, (d) content, (e) penmanship, and (f) student knowledge of the writing process (Graham, 1982; Isaacson, 1985). Students may have difficulty in one or more of these areas and assessment procedures should reflect the classroom teacher's concerns regarding student writing problems, as well as actual student performance on writing tasks. Techniques for assessing each component will be presented with a brief description of the scoring procedure and its primary application in decision making.

Writing fluency. Fluent writing is the ability to generate words, simple sentences, and compositions of gradually increasing length. Overall, the compositions of students with mild disabilities contain fewer words and shorter sentences than the compositions of students in general education (Myklebust, 1973; Nodine, Barenbaum, & Newcomer, 1985; Deno, Mirkin, & Marston, 1980). Fluency can be assessed by determining the number of words written in a specified time period or the average length of the sentences written. Fluency techniques can be illustrated using the writing sample provided in Figure 1.

Total words written. The number of words students write in 3 minutes in response to a story starter has been found to be a reliable and valid indicator of student writing proficiency (see Marston, 1989, for a summary of technical adequacy evidence). This measure of fluency has been examined in research on curriculum-based measurement (CBM) conducted during the past 13 years (Shinn, 1989). Writing fluency can be used to facilitate screening and eligibility decisions, student progress toward long-term goals, and program evaluation decisions.

Average sentence length. Average sentence length provides a general indication of variety and uniformity of sentences written. Average sentence length is calculated by totaling the number of words in the writing sample and then dividing that sum by

FIGURE 1. Katie's writing sample assessed using techniques related to fluency.

Katie, Grade 2

This morning a spaceship landed on the playground and ...

And a little green guy walked
out and entered my house. And then he
came up to my room. And draged me out
of bed. And I foled Him To the ship.

Fluency

Total Words Written = 32

Average Sentence Length (total words written ÷ # of sentences) = 32/4 = 8 words per sentence

---

the number of sentences in the sample. Cartwright (1969) suggests that mature writing is characterized by longer sentences (i.e., as students become more skilled in writing, their sentences become longer and more complex). Average sentence length can be used primarily to monitor progress toward short-term objectives.

Grammar. Poor grammar is the most frequent complaint about students' writing (Larsen, 1987). Appropriate grammar includes the correct use of words and combinations of words within sentences. Grammar can be assessed by examining vocabulary and sentence structure. All the techniques described are useful primarily for planning instructional programs and monitoring progress toward short-term objectives. Bonnie's writing sample in Figure 2 is used to demonstrate techniques to assess grammar.

Vocabulary. Selection of vocabulary to express meaning and communicate knowledge is critical to good writing. Research suggests that students with mild disabilities tend to use less "rich" vocabulary when they write than students without disabilities (Deno et al., 1980; Morris & Crump, 1982). Two ways to assess vocabulary include determining the variety and maturity of words used in a writing sample.

A type/token ratio can be used to examine the variety of words used in a writing sample. A higher type-token ratio indicates that the student is using a variety of words, with few words used repeatedly. The ratio is calculated by dividing the number of different words by the total number of words contained in a writing sample. If the student's ratio is compared to other students, or to previous samples of his or her own writing, the length of the writing sample should be the same for each comparison. For example, Cartwright (1969) recommended that the first 50 or

100 words from each writing sample be used. Use of mature words typically refers to words that contain seven or more letters (Howell et al., 1993). The proportion of large words is calculated by dividing the number of words containing seven or more letters by the total number of words.

Sentence structure. Numerous techniques can be used to examine the appropriateness of the words contained within a sentence. Two of the most common are sentence variety and syntactic maturity. Sentence variety refers to the types of sentences produced by the student, including sentences that are incomplete, simple, compound, complex, run-on, and fragmented (Cartwright, 1969; Howell et al., 1993). Tallying the types of sentences contained in a sample and summarizing the data in terms of percentages allows for comparisons across samples of varying length. As a student's writing matures, an increase in the percentage of compound and complex sentences should occur, along with a corresponding decrease in the number of simple, run-on, and fragmented sentences.

Syntactic maturity (i.e., the appropriate use of syntax and grammar) is most commonly measured by T-units (Hunt, 1965). A T-unit is described as "the minimal group of words that stands on its own as a sentence, with nothing left over" (Isaacson, 1985, P. 411). Compared to peers in general education, students with mild disabilities have been found to demonstrate difficulty with syntactical competence (Myklebust, 1973). For example, syntactical errors account for a large percentage of the expository writing errors made by students with learning disabilities (Thomas, Englert, & Gregg, 1987). To calculate syntactic maturity, average T-units are derived by dividing the number of T-units by the total number of words. To facilitate interpretation, T-units should be described in the

FIGURE 2. Bonnie's writing sample assessed using techniques related to grammar.

Bonnie, Grade 7

Story Writing Assignment

Once upon a time
Nadine was walking on
the street, all of the sudden
she got hit by a car, I
ran to call the cops because
I saw what happened. They
told me to stay calm, they
will be right there. They took
Nadine to the hospital and I
went with them. Nadine
got well soon After that we went
to the mall and bought some
clothes and we found our boyfriends!

GRAMMAR

Vocabulary

Type/Token Ratio (# of different words ÷ total # of words) = 54/73 = .7

Proportion of Large Words (# of words 7 letters or longer ÷ total # of words) = 6/73 = .08

Sentence Structure

T–Units = 11

Mean T–Units (total # of words ÷ total T–units) = 73/11 = 7

Sentence Type	Count
Incomplete	2
Simple	1
Compound	2
Complex	1

Paragraph Structure Checklist

1. Are the paragraphs properly indented?   No
2. Does each paragraph deal with a single topic?   Yes
3. Is a topical sentence used?   Yes
4. Are all the sentences related to the topic?   Yes
5. Are the sentences presented in a logical order?   Yes
6. Does the paragraph end with a logical conclusion?   Yes

FIGURE 3. Vance's writing sample assessed using techniques related to conventions.

Vance, Grade 3

Yesterday a monkey climbed through the window at school and ...

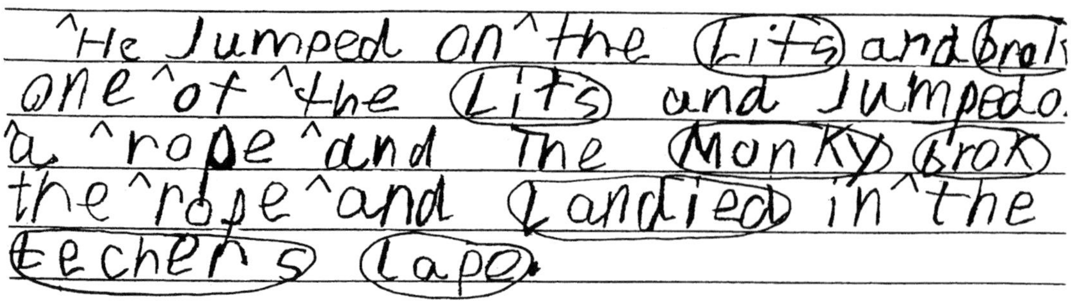

Conventions

Total Words Written = 28

Words Spelled Correctly = 20*

Correct Writing Sequences = 10**

*Words spelled incorrectly are circled.

**Correct Writing Sequences are marked with a carat.

---

context of the types of sentences produced in the writing sample.

Related to examining the appropriateness of words within sentences is examining the appropriateness of sentences within a paragraph. Bradley-Johnson and Lesiak (1989) recommend assessing a paragraph structure by attending to (a) the use of topical sentences, (b) the relation between sentences to topic, (c) the logical order of both sentences within a paragraph and paragraphs within an essay, and (d) adequacy of transitional sentences.

Conventions. Many students with mild disabilities have difficulty attending to writing conventions, especially in the areas of spelling, capitalization, and punctuation (MacArthur & Graham, 1987; Thomas et al., 1987). Significant differences have been demonstrated between students with mild disabilities and general education peers in the number of words spelled correctly and correct writing sequences within a writing sample (Deno, Marston, & Mirkin, 1982; Tindal & Parker, 1991). Further, mechanical errors (e.g., punctuation and capitalization) are shown to interfere with the quality and quantity of student writing (MacArthur & Graham, 1987) and strongly influence teacher ratings (Moran, 1982). Techniques to assess the adequacy of writing conventions include determining the (a) number of words spelled correctly, (b) proportion of errors by category, and (c) number of correct writing sequences. Vance's writing sample in Figure 3 illustrates these three techniques.

Words spelled correctly. CBM procedures use the number of words spelled correctly as an index of student writing proficiency (Marston, 1989). A word is counted as spelled correctly if it can stand alone as a word in the English language. This measure may be used to facilitate screening and eligibility decisions, plan instructional programs, monitor student progress toward long-term goals, and evaluate the effectiveness of writing programs.

Proportion of errors per category. With writing samples that contain excessive mechanical errors, Howell et al. (1993) provide a summary form that includes over 50 capitalization and punctuation conventions. Errors are tallied and transformed into a percentage of errors per 100 words. Categorizing student errors may be useful to plan instructional programs and write short-term objectives.

Correct writing sequence. Determining the number of correct writing sequences is a CBM procedure designed to provide a general quantitative index of writing that considers grammar, fluency, and conventions (Videen, Deno, & Marston, 1982). A Correct Writing Sequence is earned for each pair of adjacent writing units (i.e., words and punctuation marks) that fits the context of what is written. This index may be used to assist with making screening and eligibility decisions, writing long-term goals, monitoring student progress, and evaluating the effectiveness of writing programs.

Content. Increased emphasis is being placed on improving the content of student writing. Students with mild disabilities tend to experience particular difficulty in (a) gathering original, related responses (Nodine et al., 1985), (b) including the basic elements of a minimal story (Nodine et al., 1985), (c) conforming to the topic and including elements of text structure (Englert & Thomas, 1987), and (d) using organizational strategies (Englert, Raphael, Fear, & Anderson, 1988). The content of written expression can be assessed using an analytic rating scale and ascertaining the degree to which specific text structure components are present in a writing sample.

Analytic rating. Several analytic rating scales exist for assessing the content of student writing. Generally, analytic scales provide an index of writing content by comparing a student's writing to other writing samples that have been rated according to a particular content dimension. For example, the dimensions included in a scale by Tindal and Hasbrouck (1991) are story-idea, organization-cohesion, and conventions-mechanics. Each dimension uses a five-point rating scale, with definitions for each point on each dimension used to judge the sample papers. Information from analytic rating scales may be useful for supplementing screening decisions and planning instructional programs.

Text structure components. The degree to which students include important writing components can be evaluated for different text structures. The specific components and text structures depend on the classroom instructional focus and content described earlier. Based on the teacher interview, assessment of text structure components can be accomplished by developing a checklist of the critical elements and rating or judging the student's demonstration of each element in the writing sample. This technique is most appropriate for planning instructional programs and evaluating progress toward short-term objectives.

Penmanship. A student's handwriting must be legible for a message to be effectively communicated. In the early grades, a great deal of classroom writing instruction may be focused on writing legibility (Graham, 1982). Student writing can be evaluated to determine if it contains appropriate (a) spacing between letters and words, (b) letter size, (c) alignment (i.e., proportion of parts of letters in relation to the top, middle, and bottom line), (d) line quality (i.e., pressure consistency), (e) letter slant, (f) letter formation (i.e., correctly formed upper and lower case letters and discrimination when and when not to capitalize), and (g) style (i.e., cursive vs. manuscript). When assessing handwriting, it is important to find out what form of handwriting is expected in the classroom (e.g., D'Nealian handwriting) as well as the type of paper used for writing projects (e.g., wide ruled, college ruled). Assessment results are most useful for planning instruction and evaluating progress toward short-term objectives. An example of assessing handwriting is provided in Figure 4 using Cleo's writing sample.

Student knowledge of the writing process. Because a process approach to writing is increasingly emphasized in general education classrooms, assessment techniques should examine student understanding and demonstration of critical process variables. Student interviews can provide important information concerning the degree to which students have acquired the necessary background knowledge to meet classroom writing expectations. For example, students can discuss their knowledge of the stages of the writing process and the strategies they use to complete each stage. In addition, they can describe the various components included in narrative and expository text structures. To determine if students can apply their knowledge, they might edit a sample of their writing and discuss additional ways they could improve their writing (e.g., identify strengths and areas in need of improvement related to process and content variables). Similarly, if the teacher has established a peer-editing or "community of writers" program, a student might be asked to describe how they would edit a peer's story. Information gathered from these approaches can be used primarily for planning instructional programs and evaluating progress toward short-term objectives.

SUMMARY

Best practices in the assessment of written expression involves the systematic collection of data to facilitate educational decision making. This chapter explores the use of a problem-solving model to contextualize and guide data collection and decision making. Sources of data collection include environmental and student-performance variables. Assessing environmental variables is important to determine the writing expectations in the general education classroom, the procedures the teacher uses to teach students how to write, and which variables might be manipulated to increase student writing performance. Structured teacher interviews and classroom observational procedures are the two primary methods of gathering data on environmental variables. Direct and indirect procedures are available to collect data on student writing proficiency. Because direct writing measures provide actual samples of student writing, the results can be used to make a range of decisions including screening and program eligibility, planning instructional programs, monitoring student progress, and evaluating the effectiveness of writing programs and interventions. Many methods are available to analyze direct measures of student writing performance. The specific method or methods chosen should reflect the purpose of the assessment,

FIGURE 4. Cleo's writing sample assessed using techniques related to penmanship.

Cleo, Grade 5

I looked around the space capsule and …

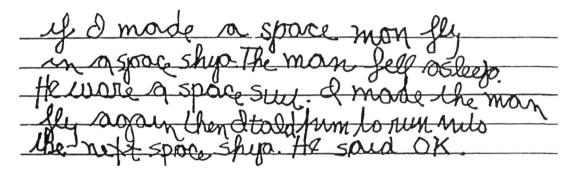

Alignment
Cleo's mid-line, tail-line, and headline alignment look properly displayed on this sample. The letters that go to the headline could be raised and the footline alignment could use additional work.

Line Quality/Spacing
Cleo applies pressure evenly and spacing between letters is good. Left hand margin used consistently.

Beginning and Ending Strokes
Cleo uses correct beginning and ending strokes for most letters. The ending stroke for "y," beginning stroke for "t" when at the beginning of the word, and "a" could use some work.

Connections
Cleo does a nice job with words that utilize the flow between letters (e.g., fly, run). In words that require Cleo to make trace back connections, his technique is not as smooth (e.g., again, space).

Slant
Cleo's writing is inconsistently slanted. Most of his lettes are written very vertical. In addition, the spacing between lettes is more consistent than it is between words.

Letter Formation
Cleo displays some good skills in forming cursive letters. It is not clear whether Cleo has been taught all the capital letters in cursive. He appears to write in manuscript when a letter is not known (e.g., T, H, x, and s). Letters that could use some work include a, f t, and i.

---

classroom expectations for writing performance, and evidence of student writing problems.

AUTHOR NOTES

We would like to thank Lynn Bain, Sean Carey, Tracey Hall, Mary Ann Kester, and two anonymous reviewers for their comments on earlier drafts of this chapter.

REFERENCES

Allen, D. (1989). Periodic and annual reviews and decisions to terminate special education services. In M. R. Shinn (Ed.), *Curriculum-based measurement: Assessing special children* (pp. 184–203). New York: Guilford.

Applebee, A. N. (1981). *Writing in the secondary school.* Urbana, IL: National Council of Teachers of English.

Barenbaum, E., Newcomer, P., & Nodine, B. (1987). Children's ability to write stories as a function of variation in task, age, and developmental level. *Learning Disability Quarterly, 10*(3), 175–188.

Bradley-Johnson, S., & Lesiak, J. L. (1989). *Problems in written expression: Assessment and remediation.* New York: Guilford Press.

Breland, H. M., & Gaynor, J. L. (1979). A comparison of direct and indirect assessments of writing skill. *Journal of Educational Measurement, 16,* 119–128.

Bridge, C. A., & Hiebert, E. H. (1985). A comparison of classroom writing practices, teachers' perceptions of their writing instruction, and textbook recommendations on writing practices. *Elementary School Journal, 86,* 155–172.

Cartwright, G. P. (1969). Written expression and spelling. In R. M. Smith (Ed.), *Teacher diagnosis of educational difficulties.* Columbus, OH: Merrill.

Connelly, K. (1983). Foreword to M. Martlew (Ed.), *The psychology of written language: Developmental and educational perspectives.* Chichester, England: John Wiley & Sons.

Deno, S. L. (1989). Curriculum-based measurement and special education services: A fundamental and direct relationship. In M. R. Shinn (Ed.), *Curriculum-based measurement: Assessing special children* (pp. 1–17). New York: Guilford Press.

Deno, S. L. (1990). Individual differences and individual difference: The essential difference of special education. *The Journal of Special Education, 24*(2), 160–173.

Deno, S. L., Marston, D., & Mirkin, P. (1982). Valid measurement procedures for continuous evaluation of written expression. *Exceptional Children, 48*(4), 368–371.

Deno, S. L., Mirkin, P. K., & Marston, D. (1980). *Relationships among simple measures of written expression and performance on standardized achievement tests* (Research Report No. 22). Minneapolis: University of Minnesota, Institute for Research on Learning Disabilities.

Englert, C., & Mariage, T. (1992). Shared understandings: Structuring the writing experience through dialogue. In D. Carnine & E. Kameenui (Eds.), *Higher order thinking* (pp. 107–137). Austin, TX: Pro-Ed.

Englert, C. S., & Raphael, T. (1989). Developing successful writers through cognitive strategy instruction. In J. Brophy (Ed.), *Advances in research on teaching* (Vol. 1, pp. 105–151). Greenwich, CT: JAI Press.

Englert, C. S., Raphael, T. E., Fear, K. L., & Anderson, L. M. (1988). Students' metacognitive knowledge about how to write informational texts. *Learning Disabilities Quarterly, 11*, 18–46.

Englert, C. S., & Thomas, C. C. (1987). Sensitivity to text structure in reading and writing: A comparison between learning disabled and non-learning disabled students. *Learning Disabilities Quarterly, 10*, 93–105.

Fuchs, L. S., & Shinn, M. R. (1989). Writing CBM IEP Objectives. In M. R. Shinn (Ed.), *Curriculum-based measurement: Assessing special children* (pp. 132–154). New York: Guilford.

Graham, S. (1982). Measurement of handwriting skills: A critical review. *Diagnostique, 8*, 32–42.

Graham, S., & Harris, K. (1989). Components analysis of cognitive strategy instruction: Effects on learning disabled students' compositions and self-efficacy. *Journal of Educational Psychology, 81*, 353–361.

Graves, A., Montague, M., & Wong, Y. (1990). The effects of procedural facilitation on the story composition of learning disabled students. *Learning Disabilities Research, 5*, 88–93.

Hallahan, D. P., & Kauffman, J. M. (1986). *Exceptional Children* (3rd ed.). Englewood Cliffs, NJ: Prentice-Hall.

Hayes, J., & Flower, L. (1986). Writing research and the writer. *American Psychologist, 41*, 1106–1113.

Hillocks, G. (1984). What works in teaching composition: A meta-analysis of experimental treatment studies. *American Journal of Education, 93*, 133–170.

Hooper, S. R., Swartz, C. W., Montgomery, J. W., Reed, M. S., Brown, T. T., Wasileski, T. J., & Levine, M. D. (1993). Prevalence of writing problems across middle school samples. *School Psychology Review, 22*, 610–662.

Howell, K. W., Fox, S. L., & Morehead, M. K. (1993). *Curriculum-based evaluation: Teaching and decision making* (2nd ed.). Pacific Grove, CA: Brooks/Cole.

Hunt, K. W. (1965). *Grammatical structures written at three grade levels* (NCTE Research Report No. 3). Urbana, IL: National Council of Teachers of English. (ERIC Document Reproduction Service No. ED 113 735)

Isaacson, S. (1985). Assessing written language skills, In C. S. Simon (Ed.), *Communication skills and classroom success: Assessment of language-learning disabled students* (pp. 403–424). San Diego: College-Hill Press.

Isaacson, S. L. (1987). Effective instruction in written language. *Focus on Exceptional Children, 19*(6), 1–12.

Langer, J., & Applebee, A. (1987). *How writing shapes thinking.* Urbana, IL: National Council of Teachers of English.

Larsen, S. C. (1987). *Assessing the writing abilities and instructional needs of students.* Austin, TX: Pro-Ed.

Lentz, F., & Shapiro, E. (1986). Functional assessment of the academic environment. *School Psychology Review, 15*, 346–357.

MacArthur, C. A., & Graham, S. (1987). Learning disabled students' composing under three methods of text production: Handwriting, word processing, and dictation. *The Journal of Special Education, 21*(3), 22–42.

Marston, D. (1989). A curriculum-based measurement approach to assessing academic performance: What it is and why do it. In M. R. Shinn (Ed.), *Curriculum-based measurement: Assessing special children* (pp. 18–178). New York: Guilford Press.

Meyer, B. J., Brandt, D. H., & Bluth, G. J. (1980). Use of authors' textual schema: Key for ninth-graders' comprehension. *Reading Research Quarterly, 16*, 72–103.

Moran, M. R. (1982). Analytical evaluation of formal written language skills as a diagnostic procedure. *Diagnostique, 8*, 17–31.

Morris, N. T., & Crump, W. D. (1982). Syntactic and vocabulary development in the written language of learning disabled and non-learning disabled students at four age levels. *Learning Disability Quarterly*, 163–172.

Myklebust, H. R. (1973). *Development and disorders of written language: Studies of normal and exceptional children.* New York: Grune & Stratton.

Nodine, B. F., Barenbaum, E., & Newcomer, P. (1985). Story composition by learning disabled, reading disabled, and normal children. *Learning Disability Quarterly, 8*, 167–179.

Raphael, T., & Englert, C. (1990). Writing and reading: Partners in constructing meaning. *The Reading Teacher, 43*, 388–400.

Salvia, J., & Ysseldyke, J. E. (1991). *Assessment.* Boston: Houghton Mifflin.

Shinn, M. R. (Ed.). (1989). *Curriculum-based measurement: Assessing special children.* New York: Guilford.

Shinn, M. R., & Hubbard, D. D. (1993). Curriculum-based measurement and problem-solving assessment: Basic procedures and outcomes. In E. L. Meyen, G. A. Vergason, & R. J. Whelan (Eds.), *Challenges facing special education* (pp. 193–226). Denver: Love.

Shinn, M. R., Nolet, V., & Knutson, N. (1990). Best practices in curriculum-based measurement. In A. Thomas & J. Grimes (Eds.), *Best practices in school psychology–II* (pp. 287–308). Washington, DC: National Association of School Psychologists.

Simmons, D. C., Kameenui, E. J. Dickson, S., Chard, D., Gunn, D., & Baker, S. K. (in press). Integrating narrative reading comprehension and writing instruction for all learners. *The Yearbook of the National Reading Conference.*

Thomas, C. C., Englert, C. S., & Gregg, S. (1987). An analysis of errors and strategies in the expository writing of learning disabled students. *Remedial and Special Education, 8*, 21–30.

Tindal, G., & Hasbrouck, J. (1991). Analyzing student writing to develop instructional strategies. *Learning Disabilities Research & Practice, 6*, 237–245.

Tindal, G., & Parker, R. (1991). Identifying measures for evaluating written expression. *Learning Disabilities Research & Practice, 6*, 211–218.

Videen, J., Deno, S., & Marston, D. (1982). *Correct word sequences: A valid indicator of proficiency in written expression* (Research Report No. 84). Minneapolis: University of Minnesota, Institute for Research on Learning Disabilities.

ANNOTATED BIBLIOGRAPHY

Howell K. W., Fox, S. L., & Morehead, M. K. (1993). *Curriculum-based evaluation: Teaching and decision making* (2nd ed.). Pacific Grove, CA: Brooks/Cole.

The authors of this book discuss assessing student performance based on a functional teaching-oriented evaluation. Of particular interest are the chapters related to language, written expression, and written mechanics. For each chapter, flow-charts are provided to guide data collection and decision making. Each flowchart includes procedures, decisions, and teaching recommendations. This book is highly recommended for school psychologists and teachers.

Bradley-Johnson, S., & Lesiak, J. L. (1989). *Problems in written expression: Assessment and remediation*. New York: Guilford Press.

This book examines a variety of approaches for the evaluation and remediation of writing problems. Chapter topics include: (a) handwriting, (b) capitalization and punctuation, (c) spelling, (d) vocabulary and word usage, (e) sentence and paragraph structure, (f) production and quality, and (g) remediation of writing problems. The authors provide useful checklists, interview forms, and considerations for assessing student writing samples. A review of 13 norm-referenced tests and 6 criterion-referenced tests is provided in the appendix

Englert, C., & Mariage, T. (1992). Shared understandings: Structuring the writing experience through dialogue. In D. Carnine & E. Kameenui (Eds.), *Higher order thinking* (pp. 107–137). Austin, TX: Pro-Ed.

This chapter provides a good description of environmental components that are likely to lead to student success in developing writing skills. Numerous intervention ideas are imbedded throughout the chapter, related primarily to the writing process and making the components of different text structures explicit. Particular attention is paid to strategies that can used with difficult-to-teach students and ways teachers can improve the writing atmosphere in their classrooms to make writing more enjoyable and beneficial for all students.

Berninger, V. W., & Hooper, S. R. (Eds.). (1993). Preventing and remediating writing disabilities: Interdisciplinary frameworks for assessment, consultation, and intervention (Mini-series). *School Psychology Review, 22*(4).

This mini-series addresses issues related to the assessment of, and interventions for, writing problems from multiple perspectives. A strong focus is placed on prevention of writing problems and the use of assessment and remediation techniques that stem from a theory-driven model of writing development. Articles include a discussion of the relation between oral and written language, evidence of writing problems among middle-school students, and a multilevel diagnostic procedure to assess writing performance. In addition, two articles on interventions address the use of student self-regulated procedures to monitor writing performance and the use of word processors and integrated instructional strategies to increase student proficiency.

62

Best Practices in Assessing Mathematics Skills

Christopher H. Skinner
Mississippi State University

Hannelore H. Schock
The University of Alabama

OVERVIEW

The majority of students referred to school psychologists are experiencing mild learning problems. Although the most common learning problems faced by students are related to reading, McCleod and Armstrong (1982) found that over 66% of the students with learning problems experience some deficits in mathematics. In an effort to prevent and remedy students' mathematics skills deficits, educators, school psychologists, and researchers have attempted to develop alternative assessment procedures. These procedures have been designed to assess students' current skills, monitor students' progress through sequential curricula objectives, assess retention of mastered skills, and lead to more effective and efficient interventions and instructional procedures.

BASIC CONSIDERATIONS: MAT TEACHES HIS TEACHER

The following scenario is loosely based on one of the authors' experiences with a student. Mat, a 10th-grade student with learning disabilities and behavior disorders, was placed in a special education resource room approximately 13 weeks into the school year. Mat had been receiving educational services via homebound instruction. Mat's individualized education program (IEP) recommended beginning Mat's instruction about halfway through the fourth-grade-level curricula. This recommendation was based on Mat's 4.5 grade-equivalent score on a standardized achievement test administered less than 3 weeks before Mat arrived at the resource room. Mat's teacher obtained a copy of the fourth-grade text, workbook, and test booklet. When Mat's teacher showed Mat which book he would be placed in, Mat became angry. He stated that he had the same book in fourth grade and that his younger sister had finished this same book 2 years ago. Mat refused to start at the middle of the fourth-grade book.

Best practice indicates that assessment procedures, techniques, and materials be selected according to their purpose. Standardized, norm-referenced achievement tests are often used to help determine if students are eligible for special education services. Standardized tests are often selected based on their psychometric properties (reliability, validity, normative sample). However, as school psychologists attempt to become involved in activities designed to prevent and remedy students' problems, the weaknesses of standardized achievement testing procedures become more evident.

Standardized mathematics achievement tests primarily assess accuracy on mathematics operations. Most mathematics curricula include over 100 separate, sequential skills to be mastered between grades 1 and 8. Across curricula publications, the objectives and sequence of objectives may vary. Shriner and Salvia (1988) compared the objectives across two different curricula and found that the Distar curricular objectives differed significantly from the Scott-Foresman curricula objectives for grades 1–3. In addition, they found what they termed a "chronic non-correspondence" between the objectives of these curricula and the assessment items on the Key Math Diagnostic Arithmetic Test and the Iowa Tests of Basic Skills. Given this lack of overlap between test items and curriculum objectives, standardized test results should not be used to assess students' ability to learn mathematics because students have not been taught all of the skills assessed. These assessment devices also neglect assessing other skills that have been taught.

Standardized, norm-referenced, achievement testing procedures have several other weaknesses. First, it is impossible for these one-shot assessment procedures to adequately assess the large number of mathematics skills taught across grades 1–8 because they cannot provide enough opportunities for students to perform those skills. Second, because assessment responses are often presented in multiple-choice format, students may respond correctly to some items they have not yet mastered. Finally, although standardized achievement tests assess student ability to perform mathematical operations, most tests do not allow for assessment of other mathematics skills including fluency, adaptation, and generalization. Due to the poor overlap with instructional objectives and the limited scope of skills assessed, standardized mathematics achievement tests do not provide enough data for determining students' learning rates or identifying skills that have been mastered and skills that require additional instruction.

Most curricula include assessment materials (text-provided practice tests and assignments; workbook practice tests and assignments; and test booklets for chapters, units, and grade levels) which have several advantages over standardized, norm-referenced achievement tests. First, these materials provide assessment of skills in a sequence that matches the curricula. This prevents teachers from assuming students have mastered prerequisite skills that have not in fact been mastered or maintained. Second, curricula-provided assessment materials often contain page numbers that allow one to easily and quickly determine which objectives require remediation and where they are covered in the curricula. Third, because some tests only assess one grade level, one chapter, or several chapters (often called units), a larger sample of students' performance across a more limited range of skills can be obtained. Fourth, the responses to these items are not multiple choice and therefore prevent concluding that students have acquired skills when they guessed or estimated correct answers. If students are asked to show their work on these assessments, some permanent product-assessment data are gathered that may reveal error patterns and therefore lead to more effective and efficient interventions. Finally, because the curricula contain many different sources of assessment across skills, teachers may be able to obtain multiple assessments of student performance across each skill allowing the teacher to monitor students' progress and performance through curricula objectives and assess the maintenance of skills learned.

Mat was angry because he was placed in a text which he had completed several years ago, but his case is not unique. Many students with mathematics skill deficits have mastered some skills targeted at various curricula levels throughout their education but failed to acquire other skills at similar levels. These mastered skills are sometimes called splinter skills. Although standardized assessment results show that Mat is functioning at a 4.5 grade level, Mat probably has mastered many skills in the fourth-grade and subsequent curricula. Mat is already behind in mathematics achievement and needs to spend instructional time improving his proficiency on skills he has not mastered, rather than working on objectives he has mastered and maintained. In addition, Mat may not possess all the skills assumed to be mastered

in the earlier curricula. Because many mathematics skills require mastery of earlier, prerequisite skills, Mat may have difficulty mastering some objectives in the fourth-grade curriculum. Mat was motivated to learn new material. By placing Mat in the 4.5 curricula the teacher risked ruining Mat's motivation and occasioning behavior problems by requiring Mat to work on skills he has already mastered or can not perform because he lacks the prerequisite skills.

The teacher could have attributed Mat's anger to his emotional problems and/or learning disability and attempted to begin teaching Mat at the 4.5 level. Instead, the teacher met with the school psychologist to discuss Mat's case. The school psychologist and the teacher used curriculum-based measurement procedures to determine Mat's placement within the curricula and monitor his progress through curricula objectives.

BEST PRACTICE IN PROGRESS GRAPHING: AN APPLIED SOLUTION

Before any instruction began, Mat's teacher had to identify which curricula objectives Mat had mastered and which he had not. The most readily available source of assessment materials was contained within the mathematics curricula.

During the next two mathematics class periods, Mat completed the end of book tests for grades 3–6. These tests were taken from workbooks. Based on Mat's errors on items which assessed specific objectives, the school psychologist constructed a sequential list of objectives for Mat from the curricula for grades 3–6. For grade 3 there were two objectives, for grade 4 five objectives, for grade 5 six objectives, and for grade 6 nine objectives. These 22 objectives comprised Mat's instructional objectives. Mat and the school psychologist then constructed a progress graph to monitor Mat's progress through the curricula (Fuchs, 1989).

Figure 1 shows Mat's progress graph. The objectives are assigned letters and listed in sequence on the vertical axis of the graph. The horizontal axis shows the remaining 22 weeks of school. In Figure 1 the broken line represents Mat's progress through curriculum objectives and the solid line represents Mat's goal or aim line. The school psychologist showed Mat how to monitor his progress using this graph. Mat was taught to place a dot on the graph when objectives were mastered and fill in the progress line. This ritual served as a stimulus for the teacher to reinforce Mat socially for his mastery of objectives and allowed Mat to self-monitor his rate of progress through curriculum objectives.

Before beginning to teach instructional objectives, Mat's teacher used the unit test (units were comprised of three or four related chapters) to ensure that Mat had mastered all the other skills contained within the unit which contained Mat's first ob-

FIGURE 1. Mat's progress graph.

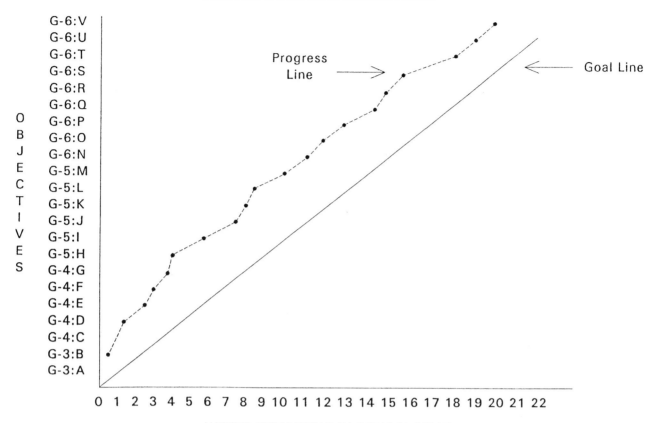

jective (subtracting three-digits from three-digits with borrowing) and second objective (subtracting four-digits from four-digits with borrowing). Mat correctly completed all of the items in this unit, except when borrowing from 0 was required in the tens and/or hundreds column. Mat's teacher began to teach the procedures and rationale for borrowing when a 0 was in the tens column. About 2 minutes into the direct instruction Mat responded, "Oh, yeah, I remember this!" and successfully completed this type of problem. Mat's teacher instructed Mat to do another problem and verbalize the steps and rationale for these steps. Mat completed these tasks successfully. Mat's teacher then gave Mat a four-digit minus four-digit problem with 0's in the tens and hundreds columns. Again Mat completed this problem accurately and explained each step.

Mat was more excited than his teacher. Mat's teacher assigned 20 subtraction problems for in-class work. Some problems contained subtraction with borrowing, some did not. Some problems had 0's in the tens and/or hundreds column, others did not. Mat finished all these problems in 10 minutes, and all were accurate. Mat was given the practice tests from

the ends of chapters 10 and 12 for homework. Chapter 12 was assigned because it contained subtracting four-digits from four-digits.

Before leaving, Mat told his teacher that he liked this system but would prefer not to take the text home because he would be embarrassed if his family saw he was placed in the same text his younger sister finished 2 years ago. Mat's teacher changed his assignment to the practice test in his workbook, removed these assessments from Mat's workbook, and gave them to Mat to take home. When Mat returned the next day, his teacher checked his work, found that Mat had completed it accurately, and gave Mat three in-class tests (the chapter 10 test, the chapter 12 test, and the end-of-third-grade test). Mat scored 100% on all, graphed his mastery of the first two objectives, turned in his grade 3 materials, and began similar test-teach-test procedures for grade 4 objectives the next school day.

Mat's situation appears to be a best case scenario. However, students with mathematics skills deficits can re-acquire objectives with little direct instruction. Mat probably spent substantial amounts of time learning borrowing from 0's earlier in his education.

Unfortunately, he did not master and/or maintain these skills. However, his previous instruction made it easy for him to re-learn these skills. Further, remedying his inaccuracies in borrowing 0's from the tens column also helped remedy his problem with borrowing 0's from the hundreds column. Because mathematics objectives are sequenced and assume students have prerequisite skills, often problems missed later in the sequence are caused by failure master or maintain skills targeted earlier.

If Mat were to continue to progress at this rate, he could be expected to acquire all objectives in 44 school days. This should not be expected. Students with splinter skills often make rapid progress with little direct instruction in the early skills. However, as higher level material is covered, mastery of objectives may be slowed.

Figure 1 shows how Mat's progress slowed as he began to learn higher level skills. However, he successfully attained all his objectives through grade six before the school year ended. The next step would be to assess grade seven and possibly grade eight objectives using the same end-of-text, end-of-chapter, and end-of-unit tests.

When students are failing to make progress or master objectives, the difference between goal lines and progress lines can signal teachers to alter instructional techniques so that students can reach year-end goals (Fuchs, 1989). Typically, a vertical line is drawn on the graph at the point where new instructional procedures are implemented. By comparing the slope of the student's progress line before and after new instructional techniques are added, the relative effects of instructional procedures can be evaluated (Fuchs, 1989). However, the slopes of the progress lines only provide a rough estimate of relative learning rates under the different instructional procedures because the target behaviors differ as students progress through curriculum objectives.

Because it is impossible to predict an individual's rate of learning across each and every objective, goal lines are not fixed. Original goal lines can be altered when students are making progress much faster than anticipated (objectives can be added yielding a steeper goal line). When students are progressing much slower than anticipated, objectives can be subtracted (flatter goal line). Fuchs (1989) suggests that using consistent rules for altering goal lines may result in increases in progress rates. However, researchers have not clearly indicated which rules result in the greatest increase in progress. Since the unit of measurement is an individual student's progress, it is not likely that any one decision rule for altering goal lines and changing instructional interventions will result in the highest rate of learning for all students across all objectives.

Figure 1 shows that Mat's progress was always above the goal line. However, a new progress graph with additional objectives and a steeper goal line was not constructed because the graphs and the process of progress graphing seemed to be motivating Mat. Mat often commented to his teacher and would show other students and school personnel his progress graphs indicating that he was ahead of his academic goals. Mat's teacher felt that it was important to keep Mat confident and enthusiastic about his progress through mathematics objectives. Therefore, goal lines were not adjusted but the teacher continued to attempt to keep Mat's progress ahead of his goal line.

Mat's problem is not unique. Many students with difficulties in mathematics have mastered some skills and not others. The causes of this can include being absent or not paying attention when material was covered, failing to retain material previously mastered, paying poor attention due to family problems, having different curricula covering different objectives in different sequences, and so forth. For Mat and his teacher, uncovering the causes of Mat's failure to learn was not the primary goal. Rather, the goal was to determine which skills had been mastered and retained and which had not. Mat was already behind in mathematics achievement. The standardized test showed this. However, the test did not pinpoint which skills needed to be targeted for remediation.

If Mat were placed in the 4.5 curriculum, as his standardized test score indicated, he was likely to experience problems with other mathematics skills that require borrowing from 0. Through these assessment procedures Mat's teacher was able to teach only those skills which required remediation and was able to skip skills and even entire chapters of curriculum objectives. Repeated curriculum-based assessments using chapter, unit, and end-of-book tests from workbooks, textbooks, and test booklets allowed Mat to practice skills that he had mastered. In addition, Mat's graphing his progress through the curriculum may have helped keep Mat motivated. These graphs also allowed Mat's teacher to evaluate the effects of different instructional interventions.

BEST PRACTICE IN ASSESSING MASTERY

Stages of Learning

In Mat's case, curricula materials (end-of-chapter questions, units, text tests, workbook practice test, and test booklet test) were used to assess his mathematics skills. However, mathematics curricula have been criticized for lacking in scope of skills and concepts covered and assessment of those skills and concepts (Hopkins, 1986). Mastery of mathematics skills implies being able to do much more than solve rote and meaningless computation problems. Haring and Eaton (1978) describe a learning hierarchy where the first stage of learning is acquisition and the goal is to increase accuracy. Traditionally, teachers and school psychologists have concentrated solely on assessing students' accuracy on mathematics problems. However, if the goal is for students to learn socially valid mathematics skills, they must also be able to respond accurately and quickly. This second level of learning involves increasing students' speed of accurate responding. Haring and Eaton (1978) call this *fluency*. After increasing students' accuracy and fluency, teachers and educators must ensure students can discriminate when these skills should be applied and when they should not be applied. Haring and Eaton (1978) call this the *generalization* stage of learning. If students can only respond accurately to printed numerical problems, then they are not likely to generalize these skills to applied situations. Haring and Eaton's (1978) final stage of learning is adaption. Students who can adapt their responses can go beyond what they were taught directly. These students have the ability to apply principles and procedures to new problems in novel ways. Some educators call this constructing new knowledge. A final measure of learning is maintenance. If students can not maintain increases in accuracy, fluency, generalization, discrimination, and adaption, then all the learning taking place inside the classroom will not be useful in building new skills or applying skills in natural situations. Mastery of mathematics skills requires students to be able to perform all of these tasks, not just complete numerical operations accurately.

Assessing Speed of Accurate Responding

Curriculum-based measurement procedures have also been developed for monitoring student performance. Performance goals are based on fluency or speed of accurate responding (Marston, 1989). Increasing students' speed of accurate responding is important for several reasons. Students who can perform basic addition, subtraction, multiplication, and division facts both accurately and rapidly may require less effort to make these responses than those who require more time or artificial prompts to complete these tasks. Horner and Day (1991) have shown that responses requiring less effort are more likely to be made than responses requiring more effort. Therefore, students who can respond both accurately and rapidly may be more likely to use these skills in classroom and applied environments.

Students who must count on their fingers to solve 1 digit by 1 digit times tables are faced with a long and arduous task when they must complete 10 multiplication problems with multiple digit factors (i.e., 6874 x 3957 =   ). Students who can perform basic addition and multiplication operations quickly and accurately may receive a larger number of opportunities to practice the new steps involved in solving these complex, multistep problems. These additional and higher rate opportunities to respond may increase students' acquisition, fluency, and maintenance of higher level mathematics skills. These additional opportunities to respond also allow these students more exposure to

trials designed to promote generalization, discrimination, and adaption.

Cognitive information processing theorists use the term *automaticity* to describe this goal of increasing speed of accurate responding. Some cognitive scientists believe that if skills are practiced, students will take less time to complete responses accurately and require less cognitive processing capacity and attention (Hasselbring, Goin, & Bransford, 1987). If skills are automatic, more cognitive attention is available to apply to other tasks, such as learning a complex new skill requiring students to perform these basic prerequisite skills. In the previous paragraph's multiplication example, the student is required to learn the steps to solving multidigit multiplication problems. However, if the student is spending so much time and cognitive energy working the basic facts, little energy can be devoted to learning the new steps or algorithms for solving the multistep problems.

Assessment of automaticity for specific facts. Speed of accurate responding has been measured in several ways. Hasselbring and Goin (1986) developed a computer program that measures speed of accurate responding to basic mathematics facts. Hasselbring, Goin, and Bransford (1987) describe a similar procedure for measuring automaticity in basic mathematics facts using flashcards. Using this system, students are shown a flashcard with a basic problem (e.g., 6 + 3 =   ). The student is observed and response time recorded. When students respond accurately within 1–2 seconds they are considered automatic. When student responses take longer or they use obvious counting strategies, they are considered nonautomatic. These procedures can then be used to assess automaticity across each and every basic mathematics fact.

If the digits 0–9 are considered the basic fact pool, a 10 x 10 matrix emerges for each basic operation (multiplying, dividing, subtracting, and adding). Because these four one-digit by one-digit operations are required for most higher level mathematics operations, it is important for students to become automatic or fluent in these skills. However, assessing 360 different facts in isolation is time consuming, especially if a computer is not available. One way to increase the efficiency of these assessments would be to have students assess each other. Another procedure would be to present mathematic fact problems to the entire class every two seconds.

Assessment of fluency for general problems. Curriculum-based measurement procedures provide a more molar system for evaluating speed of accurate responding (Marston, 1989). Under this system, students are given assessments containing many different computation problems. Students are timed and their number of digits correct per minute is calculated. A digit is considered correct if the correct numeral appears in the correct column. For example, if the problem is 6 x 8 =   , a response of 48 is scored as two digits correct. A response of 84 is scored as two digits incorrect, and responses of 42 or 78 would both be scored as one digit correct and one digit incorrect. Any skipped digits or problems are scored as incorrect. Only digits that occur after the equals symbol are counted. The number of digits correct per minute is then calculated by dividing the total number of digits correct, multiplying by the number of seconds required to complete the problems and dividing by 60 seconds.

By providing time limits and a large number of problems, curriculum-based-measurement procedures allow teachers to assess the fluency of large groups of students. For example, students could be supplied with sheets containing 100, one-digit by one-digit multiplication problems and instructed to complete as many problems as they can in 1 minute. After 1 minute, teachers can collect all of the sheets and determine each student's accuracy and fluency levels. Because fluency measures are very sensitive, if a student makes one mistake and goes back to correct it, much time is lost and his number of digits correct per minute will be dramatically reduced. Therefore, three separate assessments should be conducted and median scores should be used as fluency measures. These measures can be used to assess one set of skills (i.e., one-digit by one-digit multiplication) or multiple skills (addition, subtraction, and multiplication).

Deno and Mirkin (1977) supply some normative data on students' fluency. In grades 1–3, 0–9 digits correct per minute or 8 or more errors per minute is considered frustrational level. Mastery of a skill is obtained when 20 or more digits are correct per minute with 2 or fewer errors per minute. In between these levels are instructional levels. In grades 4 and above, mastery requires students to complete 40 or more digits correct per minute with frustrational level below 20 digits correct per minute. In grades 4 and above the error criteria are the same as for grades 1–3. Interested readers can find additional curriculum-based-measurement normative data in Shapiro (1989). Fuchs and Shinn (1989) provide procedures for developing local normative data. Local norms can be used to determine an individual student's performance in relation to other students in specific classrooms. These norms can be used to help set IEP goals and as criteria for determining readiness for placement in specific classrooms or general grade-levels placements (Fuchs & Shinn, 1989). When the school psychologist assessed Mat's performance on the end of book test, Mat was also given separate skill probes for basic addition, subtraction, multiplication, and division. Median scores across these probes showed that Mat was working at mastery levels on addition and subtraction but was functioning at instructional levels in multiplication and division. Results of these assessments showed that Mat made very few errors

in multiplication and division, but his digits correct per minute fell between 20 and 30. Therefore, the school psychologist and Mat's teacher developed several procedures designed to increase Mat's rate of accurate responding across these areas. Graphing procedures similar to those employed for Mat's progress monitoring were used to evaluate the effects of these interventions and determine when Mat had reached his fluency goals. Marston (1989) provides a detailed description of the procedures for progress monitoring.

Assessing Discrimination, Generalization, and Adaption

If students are to use mathematics skills in applied situations, they must be able to do more than perform mathematics operations on numerical problems containing signs and symbols. Students must also be able to discriminate when specific operations are required and when they are not required. One danger in the program designed to remedy Mat's mathematical skill deficits is that many of the skills may be taught in isolation. When students learn concepts and procedures in isolation, they may not be able to apply these appropriately to novel or even similar context because they have not acquired an understanding of the interrelatedness of the mathematical ideas (Hopkins & Dorsey, 1992). Successful problem solvers are able to perform procedures correctly and also choose appropriate procedures in which to engage (Herman, 1992).

In Mat's case, if the teacher had concluded that Mat had mastered different procedures based solely on his accuracy on specific numerical operations, the teacher would have run the risk of teaching Mat only mathematics operations. Rather, the teacher used other assessment procedures to determine if Mat had obtained an understanding of these concepts which will allow him to determine when these operations should be performed and when they should not.

One way to help determine if students have acquired the ability to generalize and discriminate is to assess students' performances on problems requiring newly learned skills while also assessing their performance on similar problems which require different, already mastered operations. In Mat's case, the teacher used end-of-chapter, end-of-unit, and end-of-grade tests to assess Mat's mastery. These tests are superior to assessments which target only single skills because they typically require different operations on similar problems.

Assessments contained within the curricula may provide some indication of students' ability to generalize and discriminate. However, mathematics textbooks have been criticized for teaching primarily logarithmic numerical operations and not providing enough instruction or assessment of students' ability to apply skills to novel situations (Remillard, 1992).

Therefore, teachers and school psychologists may want to supplement both their assessment and instructional procedures with additional activities.

Teacher-constructed tests. Teachers and school psychologists can use a variety of assessment procedures to determine whether students have gained enough understanding of mathematics concepts to generalize, discriminate, and adapt those concepts. One procedure is for teachers to construct their own written assessments. More than simple operations, problems should also include word problems, graph or figure problems, and applied problems that have some meaning to students. Before constructing these items teachers must ensure that students have the prerequisite skills necessary to comprehend word problems and interpret graphs, figures, and the like. Teacher-made assessments should include clear direction and adequate sampling of the types of problems target skills can be generalized to, as well as problems that are similar but require students to apply different skills. Problems requiring multistep operations having more than one correct answer, and including unnecessary information also allow one to assess students' abilities to discriminate, generalize, and adapt concepts and operations. Items on these tests should be designed to give useful information not only about the product or answer but also about students' conceptual knowledge and understanding of mathematical relationships (Trafton, 1987). Therefore, students should be encouraged to show their work and adequate space should be provided so that teachers can analyze student errors and conceptual understanding.

Error analysis. Mat's teacher was able to detect a particular error pattern that Mat was having. One of Mat's deficits related to borrowing from 0. Error analysis of students' written work samples can strengthen the link between ongoing daily assessment and instruction. Often teachers assume that students miss problems because they do not know their basic facts when actually students are making procedural errors. Remediation may be more successful when the specific error patterns can be identified, especially if these error patterns are identified and corrected before these patterns become ingrained. Because some errors are random and/or caused by basic computation errors, at least three to five examples of a type of problem should be present in a sample in order for an error pattern to surface (Fowler, 1978; Hopkins, 1986). Again, it is important that enough work space be provided so that the teacher can easily analyze students' procedures.

To ease the task of detection, several authors have listed common errors (Ashlock, 1983; Enright, 1990; Hopkins, 1985). Becoming familiar with these common errors can enhance and accelerate the error analysis and remediation process. Hopkins (1986) suggests using an error pattern matrix to make error analysis more efficient. This involves creating a matrix for a particular test or assignment and anticipating the incorrect answers that students will give on each specific problem if they fall prey to particular error patterns. For example, students often have difficulty borrowing. If a student answers 14 to the problem 23 − 17 = _____, the student may have subtracted the larger number from the smaller number in the ones column. While grading, the teacher can quickly determine which error patterns are evident for individuals as well as groups of students by simply looking at the incorrect answers and noting the specific error pattern (Hopkins, 1986).

Error analysis procedures are not limited to basic arithmetic computations. Fowler (1978) describes error analysis procedures for tasks as varied as geometry and statistics. Neither should this activity be limited to a focus on algorithms. Sometimes students miss problems because of a limited number or inappropriate use of strategies in their repertoire.

Interviews. Analyzing students' written calculations for error patterns can suggest interventions, but sometimes written work does not reveal the extent of the student's thinking (Szetela & Nicol, 1992). Mathematics interviews are one tool for assessing a student's problem-solving strategies and gaps in conceptual knowledge. Requiring students to verbally communicate their problem-solving steps may assist teachers in assessing appropriate and inappropriate problem-solving strategies.

Interviews can involve simply asking students to explain the procedures they used in solving a particular problem and what the answer means, as was done for Mat. Interviews can also be detailed and structured. Guidelines for conducting these interviews have been described by Lindquist (1988), Labinowicz (1987), Bartel (1986), and Hammill and Bartel (1982). These guidelines include starting interviews with problems that students have already mastered to build students' confidence, audio-taping interviews to obtain permanent product data, and allowing students to describe their thinking and problem-solving behaviors using their own words rather than specific terminology in order to avoid stifling, interrupting, or discouraging their thinking and description of thoughts. Some students may rush the interview process by giving the teacher what they feel is the desired information in order to please the teacher. For this reason, interviews should be conducted in a manner free from judgment and hints about correct responses.

Activities-based assessment procedures. Mathematics problem solving can require a great deal of higher order thinking, but it is often difficult for students to communicate both verbally and nonverbally how they solved a problem (Szetela & Nicol, 1992). Therefore, educators may need to provide some activities designed to help students identify and communicate their covert thinking behaviors.

Wadlington, Bitner, Partridge, and Austin (1992) suggest using other specific activities designed to help students express their covert problem-solving behaviors. These activities include asking students to write explanations and justifications of their procedures as a part of the problem-solving process and having students keep mathematics journals for personal reflections about their abilities and reactions to specific problems.

Other data which can help determine students' understanding of mathematics relationships can be gained by engaging in classroom discussion about constraints and different applications of various mathematical concepts and procedures. Requiring students to generate their own examples of general areas and specific problems where concepts can be applied may allow one to assess students' understanding of mathematics concepts and their ability to generalize these concepts to meaningful situations. Requiring students to explain their cognitive problem-solving behaviors to other students using cooperative learning or peer tutoring techniques can also improve students' mathematical communication skills and provide valuable assessment data regarding students' understanding of mathematics rules and concepts (McKillip & Stanic, 1988). Students' understanding of the problem-solving process can also be assessed by asking students to analyze various aspects of problems, generate multiple alternative procedures for solving problems, and justify their solutions and their choice of procedures to arrive at solutions.

Authentic assessment procedures, which have become popular in response to the limitations of standardized tests, emphasize the potential for meaningful and rich, real-life contexts for assessment activities. Sometimes referred to as performance assessment or dynamic assessment, authentic assessment strives to achieve close ties between assessment, the curriculum, and the world outside the classroom where the skills will eventually be tested. Problems should be presented in a simulated, contrived, or natural format so that their relevance is obvious to students and requires students to go beyond isolated skill performance (Herman, 1992; Hopkins & Dorsey, 1992). Students can be allowed to use textbooks and other resources to help them find solutions (Wiggins, 1992). Though assessment of performance in this rich context is preferred, it is important to remember that emphasis on assessing the students' understanding of the concepts underlying the activities should not fall to the wayside because of an emphasis on performance outcomes.

BEST PRACTICE IN PREVENTING SKILL DEFICITS

If the goal is to prevent mathematics skill deficits, assessment procedures must be developed that allow continuous monitoring of students' mastery and retention of objectives. Mastery criteria should include more than the ability to perform mathematical operations: They should also include the ability to perform these procedures quickly, to choose appropriate operations, to maintain these skills, and to apply these skills to novel situations.

One system that allows regular education teachers to continuously assess general education students' mastery of curriculum objectives has been developed by Fuchs (1992). Under this system, students are given a test at least every 2 weeks. The tests have been constructed so that each test contains one operations and one applications problem for each objective across an entire grade level. Students are given a limited amount of time to complete the test. Teachers are then given feedback regarding each students' performance on the test. This feedback allows teachers to monitor who has mastered and maintained objectives.

Mastery includes fluency because time limits are in place. Mastery also includes generalization, discrimination, and adaption because many different application problems for each operation are provided over the course of the year. Maintenance is measured because each and every objective is assessed every 2 weeks.

This type of system is similar to curriculum-based-measurement procedures discussed earlier. A major difference is that this system uses computer-generated monitoring procedures and preconstructed assessments which allow teachers to identify students who are experiencing problems with current mathematics objectives and ensure that they get help before they fall too far behind. In addition, by repeatedly assessing earlier objectives, these tests allow teachers to monitor student maintenance of specific objectives. When individual students fail to retain specific skills, teachers can implement procedures designed to re-teach those skills before too much time elapses. This reteaching of unretained skills prevents teachers from assuming students have prerequisite skills needed to perform new objectives. Because tests are given frequently, students are also given opportunities to practice skills that have been mastered. Therefore, the assessment procedures also serve as retention drills.

SUMMARY

Recently school psychologists have begun to question the educational validity of traditional assessment procedures. Educationally valid assessment procedures are said to provide information on how to better teach students. Diagnostic error-analysis procedures described in this chapter may lead to effective interventions for specific concept and operations deficits. In addition, the methods provided here for assessing accuracy, speed, generalization, discrimination, and adaption may help educators specify the types of problems students are experiencing and suggest general procedures designed to remedy those problems. Haring and Eaton (1978) suggest different interventions for different stages of learning. Students acquiring new skills need demonstrations, models, cues, and routine drills to increase their accuracy rates. Students who are working on increasing their speed of accurate responding need repeated novel drills and reinforcement for increased rates of accurate responding. To increase students' ability to generalize new skills, training across different stimuli conditions is needed. Increasing students' ability to adapt responses can be occasioned through problem-solving training, simulation training, cooperative group techniques, and exposure to novel applied problems.

Using the assessment techniques described in this chapter may allow one to select interventions designed to remedy specific skills deficits (i.e., interventions designed to increase acquisition versus interventions designed to increase fluency). Although these types of assessment may suggest a general class of interventions, school psychologists must evaluate the effects of all interventions. Currently there is no assessment system that allows one to determine what will definitely be the most effective instructional strategy for each student (Deno, 1985). Therefore, different techniques should be tried and their outcomes must be assessed on an ongoing basis.

Retention of mastered objectives is too often assumed. One reason why students experience mathematics learning problems is their failure to maintain skills. Fuchs' (1992) system offers an efficient and practical procedure for monitoring individual student progress through objectives and maintenance of skills over time. School psychologists and other education professionals must continue to develop and refine assessment procedures that allow for repeated or continuous assessments so that educators can ensure students have maintained previously mastered skills and remedy deficits that are not mastered or maintained. In this manner, mathematics learning problems may be prevented before they become severe.

REFERENCES

Ashlock, R. (1983). *Error patterns in computation: A semi-programmed approach* (3rd ed.). Columbus, OH: Merrill.

Bartel, N. (1986). Problems in mathematics achievement. In D. D. Hammill & N. R. Bartel (Eds.), *Teaching students with learning and behavior problems* (pp. 289–344). Boston: Allyn & Bacon.

Deno, S. L. (1985). Curriculum-based measurement: The emerging alternative. *Exceptional Children, 52*, 219–232.

Deno, S. L., & Mirkin, P. K. (1977). *Data-based program modification: A manual.* Reston, VA: Council for Exceptional Children.

Enright, B. E. (1990). Mathematics assessment tips: A checklist of common errors. *Diagnostique, 16*, 45–48.

Fowler, M. A. (1978). Why did he miss that problem? *Academic Therapy, 14*, 23–33.

Fuchs, L. S. (1989). Evaluating solutions: Monitoring progress and revising intervention plans. In M. R. Shinn (Ed.), *Curriculum-based measurement: Assessing special children* (pp. 153–181). New York: Guilford.

Fuchs, L. S. (1992). Classwide decision making with computerized curriculum-based measurement. *Preventing School Failure, 4*, 30–33.

Fuchs, L. S., & Shinn, M. R. (1989). Writing CBM IEP objectives. In M. R. Shinn (Ed.), *Curriculum-based measurement: Assessing special children* (pp. 130–152). New York: Guilford.

Hammill, D., & Bartel, N. (1982). *Teaching children with learning and behavior disorders* (3rd ed.). Boston: Allyn & Bacon.

Haring, N. G., & Eaton, M. D. (1978). Systematic instructional procedures: An instructional hierarchy. In N. G. Haring, T. C. Lovitt, M. D. Eaton, & C. L. Hansen (Eds.), *The fourth R: Research in the classroom* (pp. 23–41). Columbus, OH: Merrill.

Hasselbring, T. S., & Goin, L. I. (1986). *CAMS: Chronometric analysis math strategies.* Computer program. Nashville, TN: Expert Systems Software, Inc.

Hasselbring, T. S., Gin, L. I., & Bransford, J. D. (1987). Developing automaticity. *Teaching Exceptional Children, 1*, 30–33.

Herman, J. L. (1992). What research tells us about good assessment. *Educational Leadership, 49*, 74–78.

Hopkins, M. H. (1985). A classroom model for diagnosing the problem-solving skills of elementary school students. (Doctoral dissertation, Florida State University, 1984). *Dissertation Abstracts International, 45*, 279.

Hopkins, M. H. (1986). Assessment for instruction in mathematics. *The Pointer, 30*(2), 31–36.

Hopkins, M. H., & Dorsey, C. M. (1992). Math is everywhere – If only we could find it! *Preventing School Failure, 37*, 10–13.

Horner, R. H., & Day, H. M. (1991). The effects of response efficiency on functionally equivalent competing behaviors. *Journal of Applied Behavior Analysis, 24*, 719–732.

Labinowicz, E. (1987). The interview method. *Arithmetic Teacher, 35*, 22–23.

Lindquist, M. M. (1988). Assessing through questioning. *Arithmetic Teacher, 35*, 16–18.

Marston, D. B. (1989). A curriculum-based measurement approach to assessing academic performance: What it is and why do it. In M. R. Shinn (Ed.), *Curriculum-based measurement: Assessing special children* (pp. 18–78). New York: Guilford.

McCleod, T., & Armstrong, S. (1982). Learning disabilities in mathematics-skill deficits and remedial approaches at the intermediate and secondary grades. *Learning Disabilities Quarterly, 5*, 305–311.

McKillip, W. D., & Stanic, G. M. A. (1988). Putting the value back into evaluation. *Arithmetic Teacher, 35*, 37–38, 52.

Remillard, J. (1991). *Is there an alternative? An analysis of commonly used and distinctive elementary mathematics curricula (Series No. 31).* East Lansing, MI: Center for the Learning and Teaching of Elementary Subjects.

Shapiro, E. S. (1989). *Academic skills problems: Direct assessment and intervention.* New York: Guilford.

Shriner, J., & Salvia, J. (1988). Chronic noncorrespondence between elementary math curricula and arithmetic tests. *Exceptional Children, 55,* 240–248.

Szetela, W., & Nicol, C. (1992). Evaluating problem solving in mathematics. *Educational Leadership, 49,* 42–45.

Trafton, P. (1987). Tests – A tool for improving instruction. *Arithmetic Teacher, 35,* 17, 18, 44.

Wadlington, E., Bitner, J., Partridge, E., & Austin, S. (1992). Have a problem? Make the writing-mathematics connection! *Arithmetic Teacher, 40,* 207–209.

Wiggins, G. (1992). Creating tests worth taking. *Educational Leadership, 49,* 26–33.

ANNOTATED BIBLIOGRAPHY

Fuchs, L. S. (1992). Classwide decision making with computerized curriculum-based measurement. *Preventing School Failure, 4,* 30–33.

This article summarizes Dr. Fuchs' procedures for monitoring general education students' progress through mathematics curricula. Dr. Fuchs' research in this area is still in progress and interested readers should follow the literature and read future professional publications describing her findings regarding this applied prevention research.

Hopkins, M. H. (1986). Assessment for instruction in mathematics. *The Pointer, 30,* 31–36.

This article discusses various types of mathematics assessment techniques and instruments. Of particular interest is the example of an error pattern matrix.

Lesh, R., & Lamon, S. J. (Eds.). (1992). *Assessment of authentic performance in school mathematics.* Washington, DC: American Association for the Advancement of Science.

This edited book provides detailed chapters on authentic assessment of mathematics procedures and issues. The text grew out of a conference sponsored by the Educational Testing Service and the University of Wisconsin Center for Research in Mathematical Sciences Education. The text was not written for school psychologists but provides thorough and informed coverage of authentic assessment procedures and future direction in authentic assessment.

Shinn, M. R. (Ed.). (1989). *Curriculum-based measurement: Assessing special children.* New York: Guilford.

This edited book provides empirical data on curriculum-based-measurement systems and procedures. It is an excellent reference for anyone interested in using curriculum-based-measurement procedures or just learning more about these procedures. Chapters are written by most of the leading researchers of and advocates for curriculum-based measurement.

63

Best Practices in Vocational Assessment in the Schools

Edward M. Levinson
Indiana University of Pennsylvania

OVERVIEW

Work plays an important role in our lives. Research has suggested that positive adjustment to work is associated with increased self-esteem and a positive self-concept (Dore & Meachum, 1983; Erickson, 1968; Kalanidi & Deivasenapathy, 1980), reduced frequency of physical and mental health problems (Portigal, 1976), and increased satisfaction with one's life (Schmitt & Mellon, 1980). It is clear that the adequacy of our choice of occupation and the degree to which we adjust to work, has an impact on our overall happiness and quality of life. For this reason, it is important to ensure that individuals possess the knowledge and skills necessary for making realistic and informed career decisions, and to assist those who may be unable to make such decisions on their own. Information gleaned from vocational assessment is a critical component of this process.

The school population with whom school psychologists work most frequently, persons with disabilities, continue to be at high risk in regard to securing and maintaining employment. The President's Committee on the Employment of the Handicapped reports that only 21% of persons with disabilities will become fully employed, 40% will be underemployed and at the poverty level, and 26% will be on welfare (Pennsylvania Departments of Education and of Labor and Industry, 1986). Studies have indicated that 67% of persons with disabilities in the United States between the ages of 16 and 64 years are not working (Harris & Associates, 1986; Rusch & Phelps, 1987). Of those who are working, 75% are employed on a part-time basis, and of those who are not employed, 67% indicated that they would like to be employed. Similarly, statewide surveys in Florida (Fardig, Algozzine, Schwartz, Hengel, & Westling, 1985), Washington (Edgar, 1987), Colorado (Mithaug, Horiuchi, & Fanning, 1985), Vermont (Hasazi, Gordon, & Roe, 1985), and Nebraska (Schalock & Lilley, 1986) have indicated that the employment rate for persons with disabilities ranges between 45% and 70%, depending upon disability and geographical location. Between 64% and 82% of this population report living at home with a parent or guardian.

More recent data corroborate these findings but suggest some encouraging trends as well. D'Amico and Marder (1991), in a longitudinal study that included a nationally representative sample of youths with disabilities out of school at least 1 month and no more than 2 years, reported that 52% of youths with disabilities were employed in 1987. However, this employment rate had increased to 67% in 1989. While employment rates had increased in almost all disability categories, the rates varied by disability category. Although 67% of learning-disabled persons were employed in 1989, only 48% of emotionally disturbed, 56% of mildly and moderately retarded, and 10% of multiply handicapped youths were reported to be employed (Marder & D'Amico, 1992). In all disability categories other than learning disability and speech impairment, the employment rates of youths with disabilities was significantly lower than the employment rate of nondisabled youths (Marder & D'Amico 1992).

In addition to the high unemployment and underemployment rates, persons with disabilities also demonstrate an elevated high school attrition rate. Edgar (1987) reports that 42% of students with learning and behavioral disabilities leave school before graduating, as do 18% of mentally retarded students. More recently, the *Twelfth Annual Report to Congress on the Implementation of the Education of the Handicapped Act* (U.S. Department of Education, Office of Special Education and Rehabilitative Services, 1990) indicated that 47% of all students with disabilities do not graduate from high school with either a diploma or certificate of completion. These data are corroborated by data gathered by Wagner and Shaver (1989), who found that 44% of students with disabilities failed to graduate from high school and 36% of the students with disabilities dropped out of school.

There is little doubt that, given the high unemployment and underemployment rates among persons with disabilities, the high percentage who continue to live at home, and the elevated dropout rate of students with disabilities, efforts in the area of special education have not resulted in their successful integration into society. The resulting economic cost to society is staggering. Published reports have suggested that 15 million of the 16 million unemployed, noninstitutionalized disabled persons of working age were employable at a potential cost savings of $114 billion per year (Poplin, 1981; Batsche, 1982). The social, physical, and emotional benefits to be gained by persons with disabilities from successful adjustment to work are not to be eclipsed by consideration of the economic benefits to be derived by society. Just as successful adjustment to work is likely to be accompanied by increased feelings of self worth, greater overall life satisfaction, and a higher quality of life among the non-disabled population, so too are these likely to be benefits derived by those with disabilities.

To address the problems just outlined, considerable legislation designed to improve the vocational and career assistance provided to persons with disabilities has been passed in the last 10–15 years. The Vocational Rehabilitation Act, the Education of the Handicapped Act, the Vocational Education Amendments Act, and the Career Education Incentive Act have combined to provide federal funding assistance to assist those with disabilities to prepare for work.

More recently, the Carl D. Perkins Vocational Education Act, and the Individuals With Disabilities Education Act have contributed to the development of vocational and career assessment services in the schools. The Perkins Act requires that information about vocational education opportunities be provided to parents and students no later than the beginning of the ninth grade or at least 1 year before the student enters the grade in which vocational education is offered. The act also requires that information about eligibility requirements for enrolling in vocational education programs be provided to parents and students and that, once enrolled in vocational education, students receive an assessment of interests, abilities, and special needs and other special services designed to facilitate transition from school to postschool employment or training.

The Individuals with Disabilities Education Act (IDEA) was passed in 1990 and reauthorizes and expands many of the provisions of Public Law 94-142 (the Education for All Handicapped Children Act). IDEA incorporates requirements for the establishment of services designed to assist students in making a successful transition from school to work and community living. Under this law, plans for a student's transition from school to work and community living must be initiated by age 16. Readers who are interested in additional information on transition services are referred to the chapter on transition by Levinson elsewhere in this volume.

For the purposes of this chapter, the terms *career assessment, vocational assessment, vocational evaluation,* and *work evaluation* will be considered synonymous, although distinctions have been made among them in the literature. While the purpose of all of these processes is to generate information that can be used to assist the individual in making decisions regarding career choice, their differences have largely to do with the professional group involved in the process, the setting in which the process occurs, or the instrumentation or methodology utilized to complete this process.

School psychologists report spending only a small percentage of their time in vocational activities despite attaching great importance to them (Shepard & Hohenshil, 1983). Studies have indicated that approximately one third of school psychologists have had some involvement in vocational assessment (Levinson, 1988). Regardless, NASP has provided considerable support for school psychologists' involvement in vocational activities, and it incorporates both vocational assessment and vocational intervention in its *Professional Conduct Manual.*

In its description of Standards for the Provision of School Psychological Services, NASP (1992) prescribes that "psychologists and psychoeducational assessments include evaluation, as appropriate, of the areas of . . . vocational development, aptitude, and interests" (p. 44).

In reference to consultation, the standards state that "school psychologists provide skill enhancement activities (such as . . . vocational development . . .) to school personnel, parents, and others in the community, regarding issues of human learning, development, and behavior" (p. 44). As to direct services, the standards specify that "School psychologists design direct service programs to enhance . . . vocational development" (p. 45).

Hence, if school psychologists are going to practice their profession in a manner consistent with their professional standards, they *should* be involved in vocational assessment and programming in the schools. In fact, given their particular expertise as compared with that of other professionals in the schools, the school psychologist's involvement in the vocational assessment process may be critical to the success of such programs. The school psychologist's psychometric expertise and knowledge of measurement theory can safeguard against the inappropriate selection and use of assessment devices and against the inappropriate interpretation and use of assessment data (historically a problem in vocational assessment programs in the schools). Their skills in assessment can be used to generate data (e.g., in the realms of intelligence, achievement, personality, and social skills) that are critical to vocational planning; and their knowledge of learning and behavior theory, and of adolescent psychology, can be used in the effective development and implementation of services.

BASIC CONSIDERATIONS

The planning and implementation of vocational assessment services should be guided by two overriding concerns: (a) vocational/career development theory, and (b) the skills needed by individuals for successful employment. While the latter determines which traits should be assessed as part of a comprehensive vocational assessment, the former determines when these traits should be assessed and how the resulting data will be interpreted.

Vocational/Career Development Theory

Development theory underlies and guides the appropriateness of any assessment or educational intervention. Just as our interpretation of letter reversals and transpositions in writing is influenced by our understanding of perceptual–motor development (that is, we wouldn't be overly concerned about a 6-year-old who evidenced letter reversals but would be concerned about a 12-year-old who did), so too is our interpretation and use of vocational data influenced by vocational/career development theory. To design and implement a vocational assessment program for the schools, one must understand vocational development theory and use such knowledge in deciding what traits will be measured in a particular individual at any given grade or age level. Similarly, vocational development theory will allow results to be placed in perspective and will allow users of the data to generate developmentally appropriate recommendations for the student.

While there are numerous theories of vocational development, Figure 1 depicts the various stages of development that span the school years as suggested by Super (1957) and Ginzberg, Ginsburg, Axelrad, and Herma (1951). Not all individuals progress through the various stages listed at the same rate, and not all students are capable of accomplishing the objectives at each stage without assistance. One purpose of vocational assessment is to determine whether a student is progressing through the developmental stages at an acceptable rate or in fact might need assistance in accomplishing the objectives associated with each stage.

During the elementary school years, children begin to learn, through play, about themselves and the world of work. They fantasize themselves to be police officers, teachers, doctors, ballerinas, and so forth and "try on" various life roles. They also begin to learn about the value and importance of work and how to interact and work with others. As children get older and move into middle school or junior high school, self-awareness and occupational awareness are refined, decision-making skills begin to develop, and tentative interests and aptitudes emerge. In high school, students begin to combine their knowledge of themselves with their understanding of occupations and, utilizing their decision-making skills, begin to make tentative career choices.

Skills Needed for Employment

Clearly, different jobs require different sets of skills for success. For example, success as a school psychologist is more dependent upon general cognitive ability and verbal skill than it is upon manual dexterity and spatial aptitude. The opposite is true of success as a carpenter or plumber. However, there are some traits that are important for success in any employment. The ability to get along with others (social skills) and the ability to make good decisions (decision-making skills) are general skills that are important in all jobs.

A comprehensive vocational assessment incorporates an evaluation of psychological, social, educational/academic, physical/medical, and vocational functioning. Figure 2 depicts the domains that should be part of a comprehensive vocational assessment, and the information within each domain that might be gathered. It is important to note that much of the information that needs to be gathered as part of a comprehensive vocational assessment is typically obtained by school psychologists when they conduct psychoeducational evaluations. Intelligence test data, academic achievement test data, personality data, and so on all have relevance in vocational planning. As it is beyond the scope of this chapter to discuss the vocational implications of traditional psychoeducational test data, readers interested in a more detailed discussion of this are referred to Levinson (1993).

A variety of techniques are employed to collect information in vocational assessment programs. Interviews, observations, and paper-and-pencil tests are commonly employed, being techniques with which school psychologists are familiar. Additionally, performance tests, work samples, and situational assessment are often used in such programs. *Performance tests* are manipulative tasks that, while minimizing the use of language (Anastasi, 1982), are designed to evaluate a specific ability believed to be related to successful job performance. A performance task may measure manual dexterity — an ability related to the performance of many trade and technical occupations — by requiring a student to assemble a series of nuts and bolts (Anderson, Hohenshil, Buckland-Heer, & Levinson, 1990). *Work samples* are samples of actual work that allow the subject to experience work activities related to a particular job. An automotives work sample might require the subject to change the oil in a car; a clerical work sample might require the subject to file papers, type a memo, and so on. Work samples usually consist of demonstration, training, and assessment phases. The task is first demonstrated to the person being assessed; the subject is then trained to perform the task; finally, he or she per-

FIGURE 1. Developmental tasks by stage of career development age.

STAGE	GROWTH			EXPLORATION		
Substage	Fantasy	Interest (What do I like?)	Capacity (What am I good at?)	Tentative (What will I do	Transition . . . .)	Trial
Estimated age range	0–10	11–12	13–14	15–17	18–21	22–24
Tasks		1. Gain awareness of personal qualities and develop a healthy self-concept. 2. Appreciate and consider the broad variety of careers and acquire knowledge of workers, their roles, and the value of work. 3. Develop a broad, flexible, and satisfying sex role identity. 4. Develop attitudes that are conducive to competence, cooperation, and achievement.	1. Gain awareness of aptitudes and values. 2. Develop decision-making, planning, and problem-solving skills. 3. Realize that different occupations have different requirements and provide different rewards. 4. Become aware of imminent academic choices and their relationship to post-high-school alternatives. 5. Assume responsibility for own career-related decisions.	1. Gain awareness of aspiration. 2. Develop tentative career goals and identify vocational options. 3. Explore tentative career goals and vocational options.	1. Specify a choice. 2. Acquire necessary skills for entry-level employment.	1. Implement vocational choice (acquire a job).

From Children and career development, by E. M. Levinson. In A. Thomas & J. Grimes (Eds.), *Children's needs: Psychological perspectives,* 1987. Copyright National Association of School Psychologists.

FIGURE 2. Type of information in vocational assessment.

Psychological Functioning	Social Functioning	Educational Academic Functioning
— Emotional Stability — Needs — Temperament — Values — Intelligence — Behavioral Tendencies	— Adaptive Behavior — Social/Interpersonal Skills — Independent Living Skills — Hygiene	— Receptive/Expressive Language (Oral, Written) — Reading Skills — Mathematics Skills — Range of Knowledge (General Information)

Physical/Medical Functioning	Vocational Functioning
— Vision — Hearing — Health — Strength — Dexterity/Motor Skills — Endurance	— Vocational Interests — Vocational Aptitudes — Work Habits/Attitudes — Vocatonal/Career Maturity

From *Transdisciplinaryy vocational assessment: Issues in school-based programs* (p. 24), by E. M. Levinsin, 1993, Brandon VT: Clinical Psychology Publishing Co. Copyright 1993 by Clinical Psychology Publishing Co. Reprinted by permission.

forms the task while being observed and evaluated. Performance may be compared to industrial and age-based norms, and interest and motivation to perform the task are observed and measured. *Situational assessment* techniques are designed to test a person's interests, aptitudes, and work habits in a real or simulated work situation. A student who is interested in sales occupations might be employed in a school store and be observed and evaluated by a business education instructor. A student who is interested in a food service job might be employed in the school cafeteria and be observed and evaluated by cafeteria workers and/or an occupational foods instructor.

While not frequently employed in vocational assessment programs in the schools, curriculum-based assessment (CBA) may prove to be a particularly useful strategy in evaluating a student's potential to acquire the competencies necessary to enter or to successfully complete a vocational program. In that many vocational programs are competency-based in structure and design, these programs would appear to lend themselves to the use of CBA.

BEST PRACTICES

The following section will discuss best practices in establishing vocational assessment programs in the schools, program models that have been developed and implemented, and roles for school psychologists and other professionals in the vocational assessment process. The nature and type of vocational assessment program to be established will depend on sev-

eral factors, including the available resources, the characteristics and expertise of available personnel, the population targeted for services, the nature and type of vocational and postsecondary training and placement options available in the community, and the nature of auxiliary services available.

Steps in Program Development and Implementation

The steps involved in planning and implementing school vocational assessment programs subtend three phases: planning and development; implementation; and evaluation and improvement (Levinson, 1993). Figure 3 summarizes the program development process.

The first step in program development is to set up a task force that adequately represents all school and community personnel who are likely to be involved in or affected by the assessment program. The task force conducts a needs assessment, which identifies school and community resources and services that can be utilized in the program and potential obstacles to successful vocational planning. Then an assessment model is developed that makes use of local resources and minimizes the potential obstacles. Formal interagency agreements are established between school and community agencies that clearly identify what services will be provided by which agencies, to which students, at what points in time. Funding requirements are identified, and sources of funding are secured, if necessary.

FIGURE 3. Steps involved in program development.

Phase 1 — Planning and Development

1. Develop a Task Force
2. Conduct a Needs Assessment
3. Develp a Program Model and Establish Objectives
4. Develop Local Interagency Agreements/Action Plans
5. Identify Funding Requirements and Sources

Phase 2 — Implementation

1. Hire a Vocational Assessment Program Coordinator
2. Select Vocational Assessment Site(s)
3. Develop a Procedure Manual
4. Select/Purchase Materials and Equipment
5. Train Personnel
6. Conduct Inservice Workshops with School Staff/Community
7. Pilot-Test the Assessment Program
8. Revise and Implement the Program

Phase 3 — Evaluation

1. Identify Aspects of Program in Need of Evaluation
2. Identify Standards for Evaluation
3. Hire/Identify a Program Evaluator
4. Conduct Evaluation
5. Plan and Implement Program Improvements

From *Transdisciplinary vocational assessment: Issues in school based program.* by E. M. Levinson. Copyright Clinical Psychology Publishing Co., 1993. Reprinted by permission.

A coordinator is appointed to oversee the implementation of the assessment program, who with the assistance of other involved personnel, identifies sites at which assessments will be conducted, develops a manual that clearly describes procedures, selects and purchases equipment, and trains involved personnel. Following workshops designed to acquaint school and community personnel with the program, the program is pilot-tested on a small, select target group, modified and revised, and then fully implemented.

In the final phase, after the program has been in operation for a predetermined period of time, the program is evaluated and revised as necessary.

Program Models

Most school vocational assessment programs employ several levels. At different levels, the assessment process has different purposes, uses different assessment techniques and strategies, and is designed to gather different types of information. The nature and purpose of assessment at a particular level is directly related to the developmental objectives discussed previously. Programs usually consist of either two or three levels of assessment. As summarized by Anderson et al. (1990), Level 1 assessments begin during the

elementary school years, focus upon children's understanding of themselves, interpersonal skills, and decision-making skills, utilize vocational and career exploration activities, and have the goal of building self-awareness. Level 2 assessments generally occur during the middle school or junior high school years; focus on interests, aptitudes, work habits, and career maturity; utilize interviews, observations, and standardized norm-referenced assessment instruments; and have the goal of continuing to encourage career exploration and assisting students in making tentative choices regarding educational and career goals. A Level 3 assessment generally occurs during the high school years, often employs more experiential devices like work samples and situational assessment, and focuses upon the specific training needed to obtain post-school education or employment. Level 3 assessments are also designed to determine what skills a person may need in order to make a successful transition from school to work and community living.

Transdisciplinary School-Based Vocational Assessment

Transdisciplinary school vocational assessment (TVA) (Levinson, 1993) is defined as follows:

A comprehensive assessment conducted within a school setting whose purpose is to facilitate educational and vocational planning in order to allow a student to make a successful adjustment to work and community living. The assessment is conducted by educational, community agency, and state agency personnel, in cooperation and consultation with the student's parents, and incorporates an assessment of the student's psychological, social, educational/academic, physical/medical, and vocational functioning.

The term *transdisciplinary* is used instead of *multidisciplinary* in order to depict the need to involve professionals "across disciplines" (and outside of the schools) in the vocational assessment and planning process. Figure 4 depicts the transdisciplinary school-based vocational assessment program model, which links assessment and intervention and involves school and professionals in the community in both the planning and development of the program, and in the gathering and use of data. Four phases that embody two levels of assessment are included in the TVA model. Phase 1 involves planning, organizing, and implementing the assessment program. Community agency and school personnel are involved in this planning.

Phase 2 involves an initial Level 1 vocational assessment, which is conducted at some point between Grades 6 and 9. This yields data that are used to establish educational and vocational objectives to be included in students' individual education plans. These data are used to tentatively identify vocational training options for the students — options that can form the basis for further vocational exploration. Data are also used to identify residential options for the students, curricula modifications that might be necessary to the students' success in vocational training, and school or community services the students might require to make a successful transition from school to work and community living.

Phase 3, carried out during Grades 10–12, consists of specific vocational training (which can take place in a variety of settings). Should additional problems or questions arise about the appropriateness of this training, a Level 2 vocational assessment can be conducted. Following this assessment, a revised educational/vocational plan can be developed for the student, and modifications in training can be initiated.

Phase 4 follows this training, and involves placement in a job, a postsecondary institution, and/or a residential facility. To facilitate successful transition from school to work and community living, follow-up and ongoing support can be provided as part of this phase.

A Model Developed in Virginia

The Virginia Special Education Consortium (VSEC) assessment program is a two-phase model that integrates vocational and special education triennial reevaluation processes. Federal regulations require that students in special education programs be reevaluated once every 3 years or sooner if necessary. Many of the professionals involved in this reevaluation process are the same as the personnel involved in the vocational assessment process, and much of the information can be a part of a comprehensive vocational assessment. As Levinson and Capps (1985) have noted, integrating these two processes has the following advantages: (a) It provides for a time- and cost-efficient assessment process, reduces redundant information gathering, and conserves personnel time; (b) the special education reevaluation process provides a framework for the multidisciplinary cooperation required by a vocational assessment program; and (c) integrating the vocational assessment and special education reevaluation processes ensures a holistic evaluation of the student (that is, vocational assessment will not be completed in isolation, but will be combined with psychological, educational, social, medical, and other data to provide a total picture of the student).

The VSEC's interfacing of the vocational assessment and special education reevaluation processes is described in Figure 5. A Phase I vocational assessment is conducted at the time of a student's triennial special education reevaluation (or initial special education evaluation used to identify the student as handicapped for the first time) in Grades 6, 7, or 8. All students who are identified as handicapped prior to their ninth-grade year are thus guaranteed a Phase I vocational assessment. The process is jointly conducted by teachers, counselors, psychologists, nurses, and other school personnel; it utilizes interviews, observations, and standardized tests.

A Phase II assessment is conducted during the 9th, 10th, or 11th grades upon referral only. It is conducted at a regional vocational assessment center staffed by vocational evaluators. This assessment is conducted over a period of 4 1/2 days and is designed for students who need additional evaluation or who might need an assessment composed of more work-oriented, experiential devices. The evaluation utilizes work samples, situational assessment, work behavior observation, and to a lesser extent, psychometric testing.

Roles for School Psychologists

The role of the school psychologist in a vocational assessment program will vary, depending upon the nature of the vocational services available in the district and the expertise of other involved school personnel. In a best-practice scenario, a school vocational assessment program similar to one of the models previously described will be in operation, and the school psychologist will be one of several school and community-based professionals involved in assessment and individual vocational planning. The school

FIGURE 4. Transdisciplinary school-based vocational assessment model.

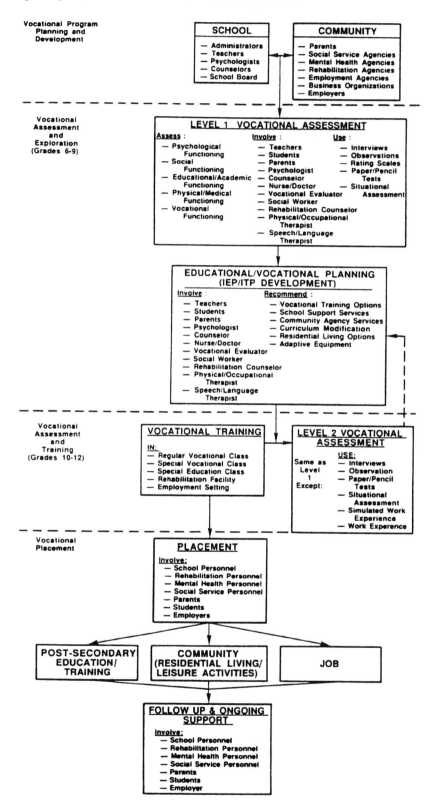

From *Transdisciplinary vocational assessment: Issues in school-based programs* by E. M. Levinson. Copyright Clinical Psychology Publishing Co., 1993. Reprinted by permission.

FIGURE 5. Virginia Special Education Consortium (VSEC) vocational assessment and programming continuum.

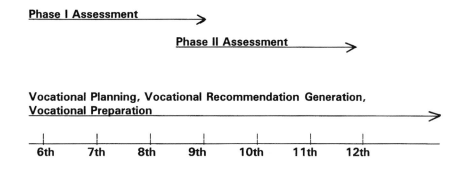

Interfacing of Vocational Assessment with Special Education Triennial Re-Evaluation

Student's Triennial Special Education Re-Evaluation	Phase I Assessment	Phase II Assessment
6th Grade	6th Grade	9th Grade--or when needed
7th Grade	6th-7th Grade	10th Grade--or when needed
8th Grade	7th-8th Grade	11th Grade--or when needed

psychologist might be responsible for gathering information regarding a student's intellectual, academic, and social functioning and for interpreting these data from a vocational perspective. The school psychologist's skills in CBA can prove to be particularly useful in both Phase I and Phase II vocational assessments. In a Phase I assessment, CBA can be used to determine if a student has acquired the academic skills requisite for success in a particular vocational program, or to estimate how long it might require a student to acquire these skills. This information can be used to help determine how realistic and appropriate a future vocational placement might be for a student. In both Phase 1 and Phase 2 assessments, school psychologists can employ CBA to evaluate the amount of time a student might need to acquire all of the competencies necessary for entry-level employment in a particular occupational area, and what modifications or interventions might promote their acquisition. As mentioned earlier, the competency-based structure of many vocational programs lends itself to use of CBA.

When working with adolescents, the school psychologist can include measures of vocational interests and aptitudes, as well as clinical interviews to gather vocationally relevant data. As team members, it is prudent for school psychologists to share their psychometric knowledge with others, in order to assist in the selection of instruments and techniques to be used and in the interpretation and use of the results. School psychologists' knowledge of learning theory and adolescent psychology also allows them to assist in individual vocational planning and to act as consultants for others who are involved in vocational programming.

Where an organized school vocational assessment program is not in operation, school psychologists might assume the lead in the development of such a program or assist others in such development. School psychologists' expertise in psychometrics can be used to design an assessment program that incorporates sound, reliable, and valid instrumentation. If the development of a comprehensive vocational assessment program involving several professionals is not possible, school psychologists may find themselves to be the sole person involved in vocational assessment. In such a case, they may wish to consider incorporating a vocational component in each evaluation conducted with an adolescent. Such a component could include measures of vocational interests, aptitudes, work habits, and career maturity, as well as traditional psychoeducational measures. There are many time and cost efficient instruments available to assess these traits, and school psychologists are referred to this chapter's annotated bibliography for references summarizing these instruments.

SUMMARY

Work is a integral aspect of human life. The extent to which one successfully adjusts to work influences physical and psychological well-being, and overall quality of life. It is important to ensure that students develop the skills they need in order to secure and maintain satisfying and productive work once they leave school.

As a result of nearly two decades of federal and state legislation, schools have come to assume a major responsibility for preparing their students for the world of work. Statistics indicate that the population with whom school psychologists most frequently work, students with disabilities, are at particularly high risk in respect to securing and maintaining satisfying and productive work once they leave school. Persons with disabilities are overrepresented among this country's underemployed and unemployed. The economic cost to society, and the personal costs to the disabled individual, of providing support for these unemployed persons is considerable.

Vocational assessment is designed to provide the information needed by school personnel to facilitate educational and vocational planning for their students, the goal of which is to allow the students to acquire the skills they need to make a successful transition to work and community life. This assessment involves a variety of school and community personnel and includes an evaluation of the students' psychological, educational/academic, physical/medical, vocational, and social functioning.

School psychologists have a critical role to play in the vocational assessment process. In particular, the school psychologist's psychometric expertise and knowledge of measurement theory can safeguard against the inappropriate selection and use of assessment devices in assessment programs, and against inappropriate interpretation and use of assessment data; their skills in assessment can be used to generate the data (e.g., in regard to intelligence, achievement, personality, social skills) that are necessary for effective vocational planning; and their knowledge of learning and behavior theory, and of adolescent psychology, can be used in the effective development and implementation of services.

REFERENCES

Anastasi, A. (1982). *Psychological testing* (5th ed.). New York: Macmillan.

Anderson, W. T., Hohenshil, T. H., Buckland-Heer, K., & Levinson, E. M. (1990). Best practices in vocational assessment of students with disabilities. In A. Thomas & J. Grimes (Eds.), *Best practices in school psychology–II*. Washington, DC: National Association of School Psychologists.

Batsche, C. (1982). *Handbook for vocational school psychology.* Des Moines, IA: Iowa Department of Education.

D'Amico, R., & Marder, C. (1991). *The early work experiences of youth with disabilities: Trends in employment rates and job characteristics.* Menlo Park, CA: SRI International.

Dore, R., & Meachum, M. (1983). Self-concept and interests related to job satisfaction of managers. *Personnel Psychology, 26,* 49–59.

Edgar, E. (1987). Secondary programs in special education: Are they justifiable? *Exceptional Children, 53*(6), 555–561.

Erickson, E. H. (1968). *Identity: Youth and crises.* New York: W. W. Norton.

Fardig, D. B., Algozzine, R. F., Schwartz, S. E., Hensel, J. E., & Westling, D. L. (1985). Postsecondary vocational adjustment of rural, mildly handicapped students. *Exceptional Children, 52*(2), 115–121.

Ginzberg, E., Ginsburg, S. W., Axelrad, S., & Herman, J. L. (1951). *Occupational choice: An approach to a general theory.* New York: Columbia University Press.

Harris, L., & Associates. (1986). *ICD survey of disabled Americans: Bringing disabled Americans into the mainstream: A nationwide survey of 1,000 disabled people.* New York: International Center for the Disabled (ICD).

Hasazi, S. B., Gordon, L. R., & Roe, C. A. (1985). Factors associated with the employment status of handicapped youth exiting high school from 1979 to 1983. *Exceptional Children, 51*(6), 455–469.

Kalanidi, M. S., & Deivasenapathy, P. (1980). Self-concept and job satisfaction among the self-employed. *Psychological Studies, 25*(1), 39–41.

Levinson, E. M. (1988). Correlates of vocational practice among school psychologists. P*sychology in the Schools, 25*(3), 297–305.

Levinson, E. M. (1993). *Transdisciplinary vocational assessment: Issues in school-based programs.* Brandon, VT: Clinical Psychology Publishing Co.

Levinson, E. M., & Capps, C. F. (1985). Vocational assessment and special education triennial reevaluations at the secondary school level. *Psychology in the Schools, 22,* 283–292.

Marder, C., & D'Amico, R. (1992). *How well are youth with disabilities really doing? A comparison of youth with disabilities and youth in general.* Menlo Park, CA: SRI International.

Mithaug, D. E., Horiuchi, C. N., & Fanning, P. N. (1985). A report on the Colorado statewide follow-up survey of special education students. *Exceptional Children, 51*(5), 397–404.

National Association of School Psychologists. (1992). *Professional conduct manual.* Silver Spring, MD: National Association of School Psychologists.

Pennsylvania Departments of Education and Labor and Industry. (1986). *Pennsylvania Transition from School to the Workplace,* pp. 3, 7, 83.

Poplin, P. D. (1981). The development and execution of the vocational IEP: Who does what, when, to whom. In T. H. Hohenshil & W. T. Anderson (Eds.), *School psychological services in secondary vocational education.* Blacksburg, VA: Virginia Polytechnic Institute and State University.

Portigal, A. H. (1976). *Towards the measurement of work satisfaction.* Paris: Organization for Economic Cooperation and Development.

Rusch, F. R., & Phelps, L. A. (1987). Secondary special education and transition from school to work: A national priority. *Exceptional Children, 53,* 487–492.

Schalock, R. L., & Lilley, M. A. (1986). Placement from community-based mental retardation programs: How well do clients do after 8 to 10 years? *American Journal of Mental Deficiency, 90*(6), 669–676.

Schmitt, N., & Mellon, P. M. (1980). Life and job satisfaction: Is the job central? *Journal of Vocational Behavior, 16*(1), 51–58.

Shepard, J. W., & Hohenshil, T. H. (1983). National survey of career development functions of practicing school psychologists. *Psychology in the Schools*, *20*(4), 445–449.

Super, D. E. (1957). *The psychology of careers*. New York: Harper.

U.S. Department of Education, Office of Special Education and Rehabilitative Services. (1990). *Twelfth annual report to Congress on the implementation of the Education of the Handicapped Act*. Washington, DC: U.S. Government Printing Office.

Wagner, M., & Shaver, D. M. (1989). *The transition experiences of youth with disabilities: A report from the National Longitudinal Transitional Study*. Menlo Park, CA: SRI International.

ANNOTATED BIBLIOGRAPHY

Bolton, B. (1987). *Handbook of measurement and evaluation in rehabilitation* (2nd ed.). Baltimore, MD: Paul H. Brooks Co.
This edited text discussed vocational assessment from a rehabilitation perspective, provides reviews of various assessment instruments, and includes separate chapters on the vocational assessment of mentally retarded, deaf, and visually impaired persons.

Kapes, J. T., & Mastie, M. M. (1988). *A counselor's guide to career assessment instruments* (2nd ed.). Alexandria, VA: National Career Development Association.
This book summarizes uses and technical characteristics of frequently used vocational assessment instruments. Measures of interests, aptitudes, work values, and career maturity are included, as well as sections on test selection and instruments for use with persons with disabilities.

Levinson, E. M. (1993). *Transdisciplinary vocational assessment: Issues in school-based programs*. Brandon, VT: Clinical Psychology Publishing Co.
This book summarizes various theories of vocational development, discusses the advantages, disadvantages, and uses of different vocational assessment techniques, provides brief reviews of tests that can be used to assess different vocational assessment domains, and discusses the development of school vocational assessment programs from both a theoretical and a practical perspective. Six school vocational assessment program models are described, as are the roles of curriculum-based and community-referenced assessment in vocational planning. The book addresses the use of assessment data in vocational planning and includes sample forms that can be adapted for use in vocational assessment programs. A bibliography of references for professionals is also included.

Levinson, E. M. (1987). Children and career development. In A. Thomas & J. Grimes (Eds.), *Children's needs: Psychological perspectives*. Washington, DC: NASP.
This chapter summarizes the career development stages through which school-age children progress, identifies a career planning model that incorporates assessment as a means of gathering information necessary for effective decision making, and briefly discusses actions that can be taken by parents and professionals to facilitate vocational development among students.

Seligman, L. (1980). *Assessment in developmental career counseling*. Cranston, RI: Cranston Press.
This book discusses the career development needs of persons at different life stages and discusses the various assessment instruments and techniques that are appropriate for use at these different stages. Case studies provided for each life stage are discussed to illustrate the career development issues, assessment techniques, and counseling strategies applicable to each stage.

64

Best Practices in the Assessment of Adaptive Behavior

Patti L. Harrison
Bettina Robinson
University of Alabama

Adaptive behavior represents an extremely important component of every person's life. All people, regardless of age, gender, disability status, or other characteristics, must have a repertoire of day-to-day adaptive skills in order to function effectively and to meet the various demands of many environments and situations. Examples of adaptive skills used by most people on a daily basis include dressing, eating, and communicating and interacting with other people. Deficits in adaptive behavior can greatly impact on people's lives and can become major problems for children and youths.

Adaptive behavior assessment has been emphasized for many years in the definition of mental retardation, and professionals have called for the application of the construct of adaptive behavior to assessment and intervention for all students with disabilities (Harrison, 1990; Reschly, 1990). However, adaptive behavior assessment may not have reached its potential, and adaptive behavior scales may often be administered simply because they are "required." Recent changes in assessment practices in special education, with a de-emphasis of global test scores and of indirect measurement of underlying traits, have resulted in an increased emphasis on functional skills and on direct assessment of behavior (Elliott, 1991). The changes in assessment practices will hopefully result in a reconsideration of the purposes of adaptive behavior assessment and greater use of adaptive behavior assessment to design and monitor interventions for functional, adaptive skills.

The purpose of this chapter is to present adaptive behavior assessment as an important application of the problem-solving model of school psychology services, the theme of this book. The problem-solving model is particularly applicable for assessing adaptive skills, identifying deficits or problems in adaptive behavior, designing and implementing interventions for increasing adaptive behavior, and monitoring the effectiveness of adaptive behavior interventions. A problem-solving approach to adaptive behavior assessment will hopefully result in an abandonment of the use of adaptive behavior scales simply to meet requirements for special education placement and in the more appropriate use of adaptive behavior assessment that is tied to interventions.

OVERVIEW

The following elements form the foundations for using adaptive behavior assessment within a problem-solving framework: definition and characteristics of adaptive behavior, historical perspectives, and the current perspective of American Association on Mental Retardation ([AAMR], 1992).

Definition and Characteristics

Traditionally, adaptive behavior has been defined as personal independence and social responsibility, or the skills that are necessary to take care of oneself and get along with others (AAMR, 1992; Horn & Fuchs, 1987). The concept of adaptive behavior has been incorporated into broader models of *general competence* or personal competence, the Greenspan model of competence being the most widely utilized. According to one of the latest descriptions of the Greenspan model (Greenspan & Granfield, 1992), general competence consists of instrumental and social competence. Both instrumental and social competence have nonintellectual and intellectual aspects, as summarized below:

Instrumental competence:
  Intellectual aspects: processing and
  conceptual intelligence

  Nonintellectual aspects: state and
  motor functioning

Social competence:
  Intellectual aspects: practical and
  social intelligence

  Nonintellectual aspects: temperament
  and character

The intellectual aspects of social competence, practical and social intelligence, work together to develop adaptive behavior (AAMR, 1992). McGrew and Bruininks (1990) provided evidence to support the inclusion of adaptive behavior into a Greenspan global model of general competence.

Adaptive behavior is characterized by several elements, as summarized by Harrison (1990). Adaptive behavior is considered to be *developmental,* and adaptive skills increase in number and complexity as individuals grow older and encounter the demands of new environments and situations. Adaptive behavior comprises *several specific domains,* including self-help skills, interpersonal/socialization skills, physical and motor skills, communication, applied cognitive/academic skills, domestic skills, vocational/occupational skills, and responsibility. A person's adaptive skills are judged by the *expectations and standards of other people;* the other people include groups of people, such as communities, cultures, and ethnic groups, as well as specific persons of particular significance in a person's life, such as parents, teachers, and peers. Similarly, adaptive behavior is influenced by the demands of *specific situations and environments,* including home, school, community, and workplace. Finally, *ability and performance* are both important parts of adaptive behavior; a person's adaptive skills are considered to be deficient if he or she has the ability to perform a task but does not perform it as needed on a routine basis.

Historical Perspectives

The history of adaptive behavior assessment is closely tied to professional practice, legislation, and litigation in respect to serving the needs of persons with mental retardation (Harrison, 1990; Horn & Fuchs, 1987; Reschly, 1990). Prior to the early 1900s, definitions of mental retardation emphasized social competence, social norms, and adaptability to the environment. The development of intelligence tests in the early 1900s led to the widespread use of IQ scores to define mental retardation and a de-emphasis of adaptive behavior and social competence.

The practice of basing diagnosis and classification of mental retardation solely on scores from IQ tests was highly criticized. Throughout the mid 1900s professionals called for a return to consideration of adaptive behavior. The first official definition of mental retardation by the AAMR in 1959 indicated that deficits in adaptive behavior, in addition to low intelligence, must be substantiated for a diagnosis of mental retardation. Unfortunately, IQ test scores continued to be used as the sole criterion for mental retardation for many years.

Several significant events occurred in the 1960s and 1970s that impacted on the definition of mental retardation. A number of lawsuits across the country addressed problems in large, custodial facilities for persons with mental retardation. As a result, less restrictive, community programs were developed, and rehabilitation programs began to focus on identifying strengths and weaknesses in adaptive behavior and providing adaptive skills training that would allow individuals with mental retardation to function in the mainstream.

The practice of using only IQ scores to diagnose and classify mental retardation, concern about bias in IQ tests, and evidence of disproportionate numbers of students from minority groups in special education programs for mental retardation led to a number of lawsuits in the 1960s and 1970s. Although the overall decisions from lawsuits such as *Larry P. v. Riles* and *Marshall v. Georgia* differed, the conclusions about adaptive behavior assessment were consistent, and adaptive behavior was identified as an integral component of the classification of mental retardation. Education legislation, including the Education for all Handicapped Children Act in 1975 and the later Individuals with Disabilities Education Act in 1991, defined mental retardation in terms of both below-average intelligence and deficits in adaptive behavior.

Although the history of adaptive behavior assessment has been closely tied to diagnosis and classification of mental retardation, adaptive behavior assessment is also important for individuals with other disabilities (Reschly, 1990). Harrison (1990) summarized research supporting adaptive behavior deficits for individuals with learning disabilities, emotional disturbances, and sensory impairments and described the need for adaptive skills training for all individuals with disabilities. Historically, however, adaptive behavior assessment has been emphasized for diagnosis and classification of mental retardation and not for diagnosis and classification of other disabilities. In addition, adaptive behavior measures are typically used only for diagnosis and classification and are seldom used for planning interventions (AAMR, 1992).

Current Perspective: New AAMR Definition of Mental Retardation

The latest definition of mental retardation by the AAMR (1992) places greater emphasis on adaptive behavior than any previous definition for the following reasons: (a) IQ scores may have questionable validity in the diagnosis of mental retardation for an individual and diagnoses should show a more balanced consideration of IQ and adaptive behavior; and (b) assessment of adaptive skills provides confirmation of functional limitations of an individual and can promote linkage between functional limitations and an individual's need for services. The definition of mental retardation, according to AAMR, is as follows:

> Mental retardation refers to substantial limitations in present functioning. It is characterized by significantly subaverage intellectual functioning, existing

concurrently with related limitations in two or more of the following applicable adaptive skill areas: communication, self-care, home living, social skills, community use, self-direction, health and safety, functional academics, leisure, and work. Mental retardation manifests before age 18. (AAMR, 1992, p. 5)

The AAMR definition is accompanied by four essential assumptions, two assumptions being directly related to adaptive skills. First, cultural, linguistic, communication, and behavioral factors must be considered for assessment of an individual to be valid. Second, adaptive skills limitations must be considered in the context of environments in the community that are typical of the age-peers of an individual and in relation to individualized needs and supports within the environments. Third, adaptive skills limitations may coexist with adaptive skills strengths or strengths in other areas. Fourth, the functioning of an individual with mental retardation is likely to improve if appropriate supports are provided.

As seen by the assumptions, a strong emphasis of the latest AAMR definition is identifying needs and planning and providing supports and services for individuals with mental retardation. Previous AAMR definitions identified four levels, or degrees of severity, of mental retardation: mild, moderate, severe, and profound. Instead of levels of mental retardation, the 1992 AAMR manual identifies four possible intensities of needed supports for individuals with mental retardation: intermittent, limited, extensive, and pervasive. Resources of supports for individuals may include personal supports, other people, technology, behavioral support, employee assistance, in-home living assistance, and community access.

BASIC CONSIDERATIONS IN ADAPTIVE BEHAVIOR ASSESSMENT

Adaptive Behavior Assessment Methods

A number of different methods can be used to assess adaptive behavior, including traditional, norm-referenced instruments and a number of important alternative methods.

Norm-referenced instruments. There are numerous standardized, norm-referenced adaptive behavior scales available for use. Brief descriptions of several instruments follow.

The *Vineland Adaptive Behavior Scales* (Sparrow, Balla, & Cicchetti, 1984a, 1984b, 1985) is composed of three forms. The Classroom Edition is a questionnaire designed for teachers to complete for children from the ages of 3 through 12 years. The Survey Form and the Expanded Form are in interview format administered to parents and guardians of infants and children through the age of 18 and to low functioning adults. In addition the Expanded Form contains a sequential guide for planning intervention

programs and furnishes information about specific deficits.

The Vineland Adaptive Behavior Scales assesses four domains and 11 subdomains. The four domains include Communication, Daily Living Skills, Socialization, and Motor Skills. The domains are combined to provide an overall Adaptive Behavior Composite score. The Expanded Form and Survey Form contain a maladaptive behavior domain that is administered for children aged 5 years and older.

The *Scales of Independent Behavior* (Bruininks, Woodcock, Weatherman, & Hill, 1984) is designed for individuals from infancy through adulthood. The Scales of Independent Behavior require a highly structured interview with a third-party informant, such as parent or teacher, who is familiar with the child. The scale also may be administered to the examinee. The scale contains four adaptive behavior clusters: Motor Skills, Social Interaction and Communication Skill, Personal Living Skill, and Community Living Skills. The four clusters make up the Broad Independence Score. The Scales of Independent Behavior also include a Problem Behavior Scale that produces four maladaptive indexes.

The *Comprehensive Test of Adaptive Behavior* and Normative Adaptive Behavior Checklist (Adams, 1984a, 1984b, 1986) are scales intended for individuals from birth through 21 years of age. The Comprehensive Test of Adaptive Behavior assesses behavior by direct observation or through third-party informants when observation is not possible. The Normative Adaptive Behavior Checklist is composed of selected items from the Comprehensive Test of Adaptive Behavior and consists of a questionnaire completed by an informant, such as parent or teacher. Each instrument measures six areas: Language Concepts and Academic Skills, Sensory and Motor Skills, Self-Help Skills, Social Skills, Home Living Skills, and Independent Living Skills. The categories are combined to obtain a general adaptive score.

The *Adaptive Behavior Inventory* (Brown & Leigh, 1986) is a questionnaire designed for completion by teachers of individuals 5–18 years of age. The Adaptive Behavior Inventory assesses five categories of skills: self-care skills, communication skills, social skills, academic skills, and occupational skills. Scores in the five skill areas are combined to create the Adaptive Behavior Quotient.

The *Adaptive Behavior Scale–School Edition* (Lambert, 1981; Lambert & Windmiller, 1981) can be used to evaluate children aged 3–17 years. The scale is divided into two parts, Part 1 evaluating personal independence and Part 2 measuring problem behaviors. The Adaptive Behavior Scale–School Edition can be administered by two possible methods: conducting an interview with the informant or having an informant complete a questionnaire. The Adaptive Behavior Scale–School Edition contains 21 subdomains that are combined into scores for five categories: Personal Self-Sufficiency, Personal–Social Responsibility, Community Self-Sufficiency, Social Adjustment, and Personal Adjustment.

Alternative methods. The most traditional and widely used method of adaptive behavior assessment is to administer norm-referenced rating scales. Although norm-referenced instruments may provide useful information about adaptive behavior, these scales have a number of limitations. Many of the limitations are related to the reliance on ratings by third-party informants. The informants selected to complete the instruments may not be familiar with the all-inclusive environment of the subject or may present inaccurate information. For example, research suggests that teachers are often aware only of behavior in the school setting and have little knowledge about skills in the home or community (Harrison, 1985; Holman & Bruininks, 1985). Norm-referenced adaptive behavior scales usually focus on only the skills that can be assessed through a rating scale or questionnaire completed by an informant; the skills assessed by adaptive behavior scales may not adequately sample the many adaptive skills needed to function in a variety of environments. Norm-referenced adaptive behavior scales that utilize third-party informants may simply provide an assessment of the informant's *perceptions* of the subject's general adaptive behavior. Although informants' perceptions may represent important and useful information, they may provide very little information about specific adaptive skills.

Because of the inherent limitations of norm-referenced instruments, alternative methods of adaptive behavior assessment should be routinely used with norm-referenced scales to provide a more comprehensive adaptive behavior assessment. Methods that may be useful additions in comprehensive adaptive behavior assessment are informal interviews and observations, structured observations, sociometric techniques, and self-reports. Each of these four alternative methods of assessment should emphasize the identification of strengths and weaknesses in the major adaptive skill areas defined by the AAMR (1992). In addition, the alternative methods should be used systematically by all members of multidisciplinary teams to conduct ongoing monitoring and evaluation of improvements in students' adaptive behavior.

Informal interviews and observations can assist in answering a number of important questions about a person's adaptive skills and may help guide additional, more structured assessment. Informal interviews with significant others, such as parents and teachers, may assist in determining whether parenting and teaching styles or other environmental factors are potential reasons for children's adaptive behavior weaknesses (Harrison, 1991). Informal observations of subjects allow for assessing them in a variety of environments and suggesting possible avenues for additional analysis of behavior (Elliott & Gresham, 1987; Harrison, 1991). Norm-referenced adaptive behavior instruments depend a great deal on an informant's perception and memory, and informal observation allows an observer to view subjects firsthand and assess the validity of informants' responses to a norm-referenced instrument (Harrison, 1991).

Structured observations focus on direct and systematic observations of individuals in natural settings, such as the classroom, home, lunchroom, and workplace. According to Elliott and Gresham (1987), naturalistic observation is one of the most valid means of measuring a person's social skills. Shapiro and Skinner (1990) described two types of observational methods that can be applied to measuring adaptive behavior: the descriptive method and the quantitative method. The descriptive method requires observers to give narrative explanations of the adaptive behavior observed. Common collection techniques include daily logs, antecedent–behavior–consequent (A–B–C) evaluation, and narrative time sampling. The use of daily logs requires observers to record general, daily adaptive behavior; the reports generate an overall picture of behavior, including inconsistency and frequency of behavior. The second type of descriptive recording, the A–B–C method, provides more detailed information than daily logs concerning events that occur prior to the behavior and events that transpire following the behavior. Narrative time sampling requires observers to record the observance of adaptive skills at predetermined intervals and to provide a general description of overall behavior during the interval.

The second type of structured observation method, the quantitative method, allows observers to obtain countable data about specific behaviors. Quantitative procedures utilize the following techniques: event recording, duration recording, and time-sampling techniques. Event recording requires the observer to record the exact number of occurrences of a target adaptive behavior within a specific time frame. Duration recording is designed to measure the precise length, from beginning to end, of occurrences of an adaptive behavior. The final technique, time sampling, includes measurement of the number of times a behavior occurs during a specified amount of time, such as recording the presence or absence of a behavior every 15 seconds.

Sociometric techniques are frequently used to assess social acceptance of individuals by their contemporaries and can be useful in determining the impact of adaptive behavior deficits on the perceptions of peers. Sociometric assessment has two basic components, peer nominations and peer ratings, which may correspond to either behavioral or nonbehavioral standards (Gresham & Elliott, 1987). The standards for the peer nominations and ratings can focus on the adaptive skills of individuals. Behavioral criteria can be based on peers' perception of the specific adaptive behaviors demonstrated by individuals.

Nonbehavioral standards for sociometric techniques can focus on general activities or attributes or on the overall competence of individuals and not on specific adaptive behaviors.

A final alternative method is the use of *self-report* in measuring adaptive behavior. Self-report techniques rely on information obtained from interviews with individuals themselves, rather than relying on informants such as teachers and parents. According to Voelker et al. (1990), self-report measures have the advantage of obtaining firsthand information from the subjects themselves that otherwise might be unattainable from other informants.

Issues in Adaptive Behavior Assessment

A number of important issues relate to the assessment of adaptive behavior and use of adaptive behavior assessment in problem solving and decision making by school psychologists.

Psychometric issues. Although alternative assessment techniques are garnering attention and gaining in popularity, traditional, norm-referenced techniques remain the most widely used method of adaptive behavior assessment. The psychometric properties of norm-referenced adaptive behavior instruments must be carefully evaluated, and the psychometric limitations of norm-referenced instruments must be taken into account. Issues concerning norm samples, reliability, and validity have particular relevance for selecting the adaptive behavior instrument to be used and for interpreting the results of adaptive behavior scales (AAMR, 1992; Harrison, 1987; Kamphaus, 1987; Reschly, 1990).

Historically, many adaptive behavior instruments have been characterized by norm samples that may not serve as adequate comparison groups for many of the individuals with whom the scale is used. Some instruments were normed with a sample of individuals intended to represent the United States population, but the norm sample had a number of limitations (e.g., only specific regions of the country were represented; some socioeconomic status groups were underrepresented). Other adaptive behavior instruments were normed with samples of persons with disabilities but were represented only by individuals in specific settings (e.g., only residential settings; only school settings). When an adaptive behavior instrument is selected for use with an individual and the results are interpreted, the appropriateness of the norm group as a comparison for the person under evaluation must be considered. More recently, the norm samples for adaptive behavior instruments have improved, and many instruments have norm samples that can serve as adequate comparison groups for most individuals.

Reliability is another psychometric issue that must be considered when norm-referenced adaptive behavior scales are used. Although the global scores of many adaptive behavior scales may show evidence of adequate internal consistency reliability, many subtest scores have inadequate internal consistency. Subtest scores of adaptive behavior scales should be used with caution during interpretation of assessment results, and strengths and weaknesses suggested by subtests should be assessed more comprehensively with alternative methods of adaptive behavior assessment. Adaptive behavior scales, like most rating scales that rely on third-party informants, may be characterized by low stability and interrater reliability.

Validity of adaptive behavior scales has been investigated in a number of ways. Predictive validity research indicates that scores from adaptive behavior instruments exhibit low to moderate correlations with measures of school achievement, but higher correlations with criteria such as vocational placement, job performance, and other important "life achievement" criteria for individuals with mental retardation. The correlations between adaptive behavior and achievement instruments are expected to be relatively low, because the two types of instruments measure fairly distinct constructs. However, the low relationship between adaptive behavior and achievement scores and the higher relationship between intelligence and achievement scores could potentially contribute to the reliance on intelligence test scores in diagnosis of school-related problems.

A psychometric consideration of adaptive behavior assessment is factorial validity, or the number of dimensions found through factor analysis of the results of different adaptive behavior scales. Factor analysis has revealed inconsistent results concerning the number of dimensions measured by each scale (Harrison, 1987). Most adaptive behavior instruments claim a multidimensional perspective and offer scores for many dimensions. However, research has suggested that most adaptive behavior scales may measure only one dimension, a general factor that gauges personal independence (McGrew & Bruininks, 1989). The mixed results appear to be caused by differences in the theoretical frameworks that comprise each instrument and the factoring method that was employed (Harrison, 1987; McGrew & Bruininks, 1989). Practitioners should choose more than one instrument and several alternative, supplemental methods to obtain needed information, because of the lack of multidimensionality of a single adaptive behavior scale.

A final psychometric issue related to adaptive behavior instruments is treatment validity. Little research has been conducted that investigates the validity of using adaptive behavior scales in planning effective treatments, but research has supported the effectiveness of training adaptive skills (Bruininks, Thurlow, & Gilman, 1987; Holman & Bruininks, 1985). AAMR (1992) emphasizes the importance of determining needed supports for deficits in adaptive skill area and stresses the assumption that the life functioning of a person with mental retardation will improve if supports are provided for the adaptive skills areas. However, AAMR notes the need for development of adaptive measures that have programmatic implications.

Direct versus indirect assessment. Shapiro and Skinner (1990) described the continuum of indirect and direct assessment. The most direct form of assessment is observing behaviors of individuals in their natural environment. Movement along the continuum to indirect assessment results in assessment that does not take place in individuals' natural environment, that focuses on inferences about abilities and not direct observation of behavior, or that does not involve the actual participation of the individuals in their own assessment. Adaptive behavior can be assessed directly (for example, through structured observation) or indirectly (for example, through third-party ratings on a norm-referenced adaptive behavior scale). Both types of assessment should be utilized in a comprehensive adaptive behavior assessment, but each type has advantages and disadvantages. School psychologists must consider the strengths and limitations of each method when using adaptive behavior assessment during problem solving and decision making.

Although direct assessment relies on actual observation of another person and provides information not obtainable in using third-party informants, difficulties arise in accurate recording of behaviors. Problems that are often encountered in direct observation include timing errors, failure to provide enough accurate descriptive information, measurement of behaviors that occur infrequently, and subjectivity in reporting behaviors (Shapiro & Skinner, 1990). Direct assessment may also present a number of practical difficulties, such as the amount of time and training required for observers to assess behaviors in natural environments. However, as noted by AAMR (1992), direct assessment must be part of a comprehensive adaptive behavior assessment in order to evaluate subjects' skills and limitations, the strengths and limitations of the settings in which they are required to function, and the supports that they need within the settings.

Indirect measures of adaptive behavior, typically through interviews and norm-referenced questionnaires completed by parents, teachers, and staff members, offer general measures of adaptive behavior that can be obtained in a short amount of time. However, the use of indirect measures must take into account the limitations of informant-based instruments. Many studies have supported the low correlations between reports from different informants. For example, studies have found low correlations between parents' and teachers' ratings of a number of different behaviors, including adaptive skills, social

skills, and problem behaviors (e.g., Gresham & Reschly, 1987; Harrison, 1989). Bracken and Barnett (1987) concluded that adaptive behavior scales have little convergent validity and interrater reliability. However, inconsistency between informants' ratings of behavior may simply reflect differences between informants' perceptions of the subjects or different expectations in the home, school, work, and other environments (Harrison, 1989). There is also evidence to support that self-reports of adaptive skills for older persons with mental retardation may provide useful information and may be similar to reports given by staff members (Voelker et al., 1990). Because of the concerns about informant ratings, it is recommended that indirect assessment of adaptive behavior routinely include two or more informants (AAMR, 1992; Reschly, 1990).

Decision making for special education eligibility. Several specific issues related to adaptive behavior assessment must be considered during special education decision making by multidisciplinary teams. The first issue is the continued, inappropriate emphasis on intelligence test scores in determining a classification of mental retardation, despite the inclusion of deficits in adaptive behavior, in addition to limitations in intellectual functioning, in legal and professional definitions of mental retardation. Reschly and Ward (1991) found that intelligence test scores continue to be used as the primary criterion in special education decision making about mental retardation. Multidisciplinary teams must use a more balanced consideration of intellectual levels, school achievement, and adaptive behavior during decision making about classification of mental retardation, and they must emphasize adaptive behavior strengths and weaknesses in intervention planning.

A question that often arises during decision making about classification of mental retardation is "What is a deficit in adaptive behavior?" Unlike guidelines for intelligence tests, few guidelines specify an operational definition of an adaptive behavior deficit or provide a cut score to indicate a limitation in adaptive behavior. AAMR (1992, p. 42) cautions against reliance on a precise cut score for operationalizing a deficit in adaptive behavior, for three reasons. First, AAMR recommends that information about a person's adaptive behavior must come from a number of sources and methods of assessment; the use of a single cut score would probably promote the use of only one norm-referenced instrument. Second, AAMR recognizes that individuals with mental retardation typically have strengths as well as weaknesses in adaptive behavior; the use of a single cut score would mask important intraindividual differences in adaptive functioning. Third, AAMR suggests that single cut scores provide little or information for planning treatments and interventions, and the focus of adaptive behavior assessment should include planning interventions and not just special education eligibility.

When adaptive behavior assessment is considered in addition to intelligence test scores during special education decision making about mental retardation, "declassification" may occur (Reschly, 1985). Declassification may result for students who would be given a classification of mental retardation if intelligence test scores were used alone, but who are found to have no adaptive behavior deficits and thus do not meet the criteria for the classification. Declassification may also result for students who have met the criteria for classification in the past, but who no longer meet the criteria because intervention has increased their adaptive skills. Multidisciplinary teams must carefully consider the potential effect of declassification on students and must include students' needs for intervention in addition to criteria for classification in determining eligibility for special education. In addition, teams must take into account AAMR's recommendation to focus on strengths and weaknesses in adaptive skills, rather than on a single cut score, when adaptive behavior assessment results are being considered for classification of mental retardation. Unfortunately, special education regulations for some states may have stringent criteria for adaptive behavior deficits in the classification of mental retardation. If so, declassification may occur even for students with special education needs.

Reschly (1982, 1990) described an important distinction for adaptive behavior of students in school: in-school adaptive behavior, which includes skills and behaviors necessary in a school environment, and out-of-school adaptive behavior, which includes skills and behavior necessary at home and in the community. Both in-school and out-of-school adaptive behavior should be addressed in special education decision making. Until recently, the distinction between in-school and out-of-school adaptive behavior has been rather blurred in special education decision making. For example, the Vineland Adaptive Behavior Scales has a version for parent informants and a version for teacher informants; both versions primarily measure out-of-school adaptive behavior, but the teacher's version is often used alone in determining special education eligibility. Teachers are asked to rate children's performance of a number of out-of-school adaptive behaviors about which they have little direct knowledge (Harrison, 1985). The new AAMR definition of adaptive behavior skills deficits, with its inclusion of in-school skills such as self-direction and functional academics and out-of-school skills such as self-care and home living, may be useful for planning comprehensive assessment of both in-school and out-of-school skills and for bringing both type of skills into consideration in determining special education eligibility.

Planning and monitoring interventions. An important feature of the AAMR (1992) manual is its emphasis on assessment and intervention for adaptive, functional skills and its problem-solving approach to providing educational services for students with mental retardation. AAMR prescribes that multidisciplinary assessment teams in schools must expand their assessment to include identification of supports and services that are consistent with adaptive skills needs. Furthermore, AAMR recommends that assessment must be ongoing and multifaceted, cannot be limited to norm-referenced assessment, and must be tied to devising and monitoring interventions.

Assessment for planning and monitoring interventions for adaptive skills can be viewed as a problem-solving sequence. AAMR (1992, pp. 116–119) suggests that one of the first steps should be to identify the functions that the student's assessment is to provide. AAMR provides several examples of assessment functions that may be included in an assessment plan: to determine priorities for adaptive skills needs to be addressed in an intervention plan, to plan transition to a vocational program, to assess progress toward meeting the objectives of the intervention plan, and to assess problem behaviors that may be interfering with attainment of skills.

Once the function of assessment have been determined, a broad assessment should be planned and conducted and assessment information should be analyzed. AAMR provides examples of a number of assessment methods that can be used to meet the assessment functions. For example, the priorities of an individualized educational plan (IEP) can be obtained with an ecological inventory, which may make use of structured interviews and norm-referenced adaptive behavior scales with informant services provided by parents, teachers, peers, or self-reports, as well as direct observation in home, school, work, and community settings. Assessment that is conducted to plan transition to a vocational program may include interviews and observations to determine the subject's current skills and the skills needed in the vocational setting.

AAMR then recommends that the assessment information should be translated into a description of needed supports to provide interventions for the student's limitations and weaknesses. The educational services and other needed supports should be planned and delivered. Finally, the student's progress is evaluated and modifications to supports and services should be made.

When planning interventions to provide the supports and services specified in the IEP, AAMR recommends that interventions be selected to provide widespread use of the skills to be developed within the student's environment, including home, school, leisure, and work setting. Interventions should strengthen the student's independence, community integration, and productivity. The techniques designed for the student should be age-specific and planned according to the student's strengths and limitations. Younger students with mental retardation may benefit from interventions that expose them to association with other children in the regular classroom and are more performance-oriented. Interventions that may be considered for younger students include the following: modeling, in which the student duplicates a task performed by another person; behavior rehearsal, in which the student practices a learned task over and over; and coaching procedures, which use direct verbal instruction with discussion of the desired behavior (Elliott, Sheridan, & Gresham, 1989).

Older students may benefit more from interventions that focus on job skills and independent living. Interventions for older students may include community-based instruction. McDonnell, Hardman, Hightower, Keifer-O'Donnell, and Drew (1993) found that community-based instruction is an effective technique for generalization of classroom-learned skills to natural settings. Other interventions that may be effective with older students include problem-solving training and self-motivational methods, such as self-instruction, self-management, and self-monitoring (Hughes, 1992; Lovett & Haring, 1989; Misra, 1992; Foss, Auty, & Irvin, 1989).

BEST PRACTICES IN ADAPTIVE BEHAVIOR ASSESSMENT

1. School psychologists should incorporate adaptive behavior assessment into a comprehensive problem-solving framework of conducting assessment and planning intervention. They should never conduct adaptive behavior assessment simply because it is "required" for a classification of mental retardation. They must view adaptive behavior assessment as an integral component of assessment of functional skills.

2. School psychologists should incorporate comprehensive adaptive behavior assessment into the assessment plan for *all* children experiencing learning and behavior problems, and not just children suspected of having mental retardation. Most children who are experiencing problems also have concurrent deficits in adaptive skills. Increases in adaptive skills represent important intervention goals for many children.

3. School psychologists should carefully plan adaptive behavior assessment to answer important questions about children's functioning and service needs. They should incorporate different methods of adaptive behavior assessment, including traditional, norm-referenced scales and alternative methods of assessment, in order to obtain ecologically valid information about children's functional strengths and limitations.

4. School psychologists may carefully select one or more norm-referenced scales for use in a comprehensive adaptive behavior assessment for a child. They should select scales based on consideration of the individual child's needs for assessment and the specific information provided by the scales. School psychologists should never make a practice of using the same adaptive scale for every child.

5. Norm-referenced adaptive behavior scales may have a number of practical and psychometric limitations. School psychologists should carefully evaluate norm-referenced scales before selecting them for use. Because no scale will overcome all limitations, school psychologists must carefully consider the limitations when evaluating and interpreting results.

6. School psychologists should always incorporate alternatives to norm-referenced scales into comprehensive adaptive behavior assessment. Methods such as informal interviews and observations, structured observations, sociometric techniques, and self-report by the client are necessary during adaptive behavior assessment in order to obtain more detailed information about strengths and weaknesses in a variety of settings and to plan and monitor interventions.

7. School psychologists should routinely include both direct assessment (e.g., informal observations, structured observations) and indirect assessment (e.g., informal interviews, self-reports, informant rating scales) so as to obtain a comprehensive ecological inventory of adaptive behavior. Although both direct and indirect assessment have strengths and limitations, the use of both allows assessment in multiple environment and with multiple sources of information.

8. School psychologists should encourage consideration of the following issues during decision-making for special education eligibility:

a. Multidisciplinary teams must always use a balanced consideration of adaptive behavior, intellectual, and achievement assessment results when making decisions about a mental retardation classification. An emphasis on intelligence test scores, with an accompanying de-emphasis on adaptive behavior assessment, violates legal and professional guidelines and does not meet the needs of children.

b. Multidisciplinary teams should not attempt to apply a single cut score on an adaptive behavior scale as part of the criteria for mental retardation. Although the use of a single cut score on an intelligence test is often used, such a practice should not be used with adaptive behavior assessment. Instead, multidisciplinary teams should emphasize multifaceted information from a number of sources and methods of assessment in order to identify strengths and weaknesses in adaptive skills.

c. "Declassification" may occur with individuals who have low scores on intelligence tests but no adaptive behavior deficits, especially if a multidisciplinary team emphasizes a single cut score on an adaptive behavior scale. Multidisciplinary teams should focus on children's needs for services during special education decision making, instead of just focusing on criteria for classification, and they should emphasize information about multiple adaptive skills, instead of just emphasizing a single, global cut score.

d. Multidisciplinary teams should consider both in-school and out-of-school adaptive behavior when making decisions. Students may have limitations in either or both areas, and either or both areas may pose needs for services for children.

9. School psychologists should never conduct adaptive behavior assessment solely for the purpose of classification of a disability. Adaptive behavior assessment should be conducted for planning and monitoring interventions. School psychologists should make careful and detailed plans in order to incorporate all important functions of assessment, conduct broad assessment to address the functions, and analyze assessment information to identify children's needs and provide supports and services.

SUMMARY

This chapter has described adaptive behavior assessment as a problem-solving activity for school psychologists. The current perspective provided by the AAMR (1992) provides a framework for assessing adaptive skills in order to gather information about an individual's functional limitations and needs for services. Comprehensive adaptive behavior assessment must include an ecological approach, in which norm-referenced and alternative methods and direct and indirect assessment are integrated. The adaptive skills of individuals across a number of settings and environments must be emphasized. Most importantly, the goal of adaptive behavior assessment should be to plan and monitor interventions for students. Adaptive behavior should never be conducted simply to provide a required assessment for a special education placement.

REFERENCES

Adams, G. L. (1984a). *Comprehensive Test of Adaptive Behavior.* Columbus, OH: Charles E. Merrill.

Adams, G. L. (1984b). *Normative Adaptive Behavior Checklist.* Columbus, OH: Charles E. Merrill.

Adams, G. L. (1986). *Comprehensive Test of Adaptive Behavior and Normative Adaptive Behavior Checklist: Technical manual.* Columbus, OH: Charles E. Merrill.

American Association on Mental Retardation. (1992). *Definitions, classifications, and systems of supports* (9th ed.). Washington, DC: Author.

Bracken, B., & Barnett, D. (1987). The technical side of preschool assessment: A primer of critical issues. *Preschool Interests*, 6–7, 9.

Brown, L., & Leigh, J. E. (1986). *Adaptive Behavior Scale.* Austin, TX; PRO-ED.

Bruininks, R. H., Thurlow, M., & Gilman, C. J. (1987). Adaptive behavior and mental retardation. *Journal of Special Education, 21*, 69–88.

Bruininks, R. H., Woodcock, R. W., Hill, B. K., & Weatherman, R. (1984). *Scales of Independent Behavior.* Allen, TX: DLM Teaching Resources.

Elliott, S. N. (1991). Authentic assessment: An introduction to a neobehavioral approach to classroom assessment. *School Psychology Quarterly, 6*, 273–278.

Elliott, S. N., & Gresham, F. M. (1987). Children's social skills: Assessment and classification practices. *Journal of Counseling and Development, 66*, 96–99.

Elliott, S. N., Sheridan, S. M., & Gresham, F. M. (1989). Assessing and treating social skills deficits: A case study for the scientist-practitioner. *Journal of School Psychology, 27*, 197–222.

Foss, G., Auty, W. P., & Irvin, L. K. (1989). A comparative evaluation of modeling, problem-solving, and behavior rehearsal for teaching employment-related interpersonal skills to secondary students with mental retardation. *Education and Training of the Mentally Retarded, 24*, 17–27.

Greenspan, S., & Granfield, J. M. (1992). Reconsidering the construct of mental retardation: Implications of a model of social competence. *American Journal of Mental Retardation, 96*, 442–453.

Gresham, F. M., & Elliott, S. N. (1987). The relationship between adaptive behavior and social skills: Issues in definition and assessment. *Journal of Special Education, 21*, 169–181.

Gresham, F. M., & Reschly, D. J. (1987). Dimensions of social competence: Method factors in the assessment of adaptive behavior, social skills, and peer acceptance. *Journal of School Psychology, 25*, 367–381.

Harrison, P. L. (1985). *Vineland Adaptive Behavior Scales, Classroom Edition manual.* Circle Pines, MN: American Guidance Service.

Harrison, P. L. (1987). Research with adaptive behavior scales. *Journal of Special Education, 21*, 37–61.

Harrison, P. L. (1989). Adaptive behavior: Research to practice. *Journal of School Psychology, 27*, 301–317.

Harrison, P. L. (1990). Mental retardation, adaptive behavior assessment, and giftedness. In A. S. Kaufman (Ed.), *Assessing adolescent and adult intelligence* (pp. 533–585). Boston: Allyn and Bacon.

Harrison, P. L. (1991). Assessment of adaptive behavior. In B. A. Bracken (Ed.), *The psychoeducational assessment of preschool children* (2nd ed.) (pp. 168–186). Boston: Allyn and Bacon.

Holman, J., & Bruininks, R. (1985). Assessing and training adaptive behaviors. In K. C. Lakin & R. H. Bruininks (Eds.), *Strategies for achieving community integration of developmentally disabled citizens* (pp. 73–104). Baltimore, MD: Paul H. Brookes.

Horn, E., & Fuchs, D. (1987). Using adaptive behavior in assessment and intervention: An overview. *Journal of Special Education, 21*, 11–25.

Hughes, C. (1992). Teaching self-instruction utilizing multiple exemplars to produce generalized problem-solving among individuals with severe mental retardation. *American Journal of Mental Retardation, 97*, 302–314.

Kamphaus, R. W. (1987). Conceptual and psychometric issues in the assessment of adaptive behavior. *Journal of Special Education, 21*, 27–35.

Lambert, N. M. (1981). *AAMD Adaptive Behavior Scale, School Edition: Diagnostic and technical manual.* Monterey, CA: Publishers Test Service.

Lambert, N. M., & Windmiller, M. (1981). *AAMD Adaptive Behavior Scale, School Edition.* Monterey, CA: Publishers Test Service.

Lovett, D. L., & Haring, K. A. (1989). The effects of self-management training on the daily living of adults with mental retardation. *Education and Training of Mental Retardation, 24*, 306–323.

McDonnell, J., Hardman, M. L., Hightower, J., Keifer-O'Donnell, R., & Drew, C. (1993). Impact of community-based instruction on the development of adaptive behavior of secondary-level students with mental retardation. *American Journal of Mental Retardation, 97*, 575–584.

McGrew, K., & Bruininks, R. (1989). The factor structure of adaptive behavior. *School Psychology Review, 18*, 64–81.

McGrew, K. S., & Bruininks, R. H. (1990). Defining adaptive and maladaptive behavior within a model of personal competence. *School Psychology Review, 19*, 53–73.

Misra, A. (1992). Generalization of social skills through self-monitoring by adults with mild mental retardation. *Exceptional Children, 58*, 495–507.

Reschly, D. J. (1982). Assessing mild mental retardation: The influences of adaptive behavior, sociocultural status, and prospects for nonbiased assessment. In C. R. Reynolds & T. R. Gutkin (Eds.), *The handbook of school psychology* (pp. 209–242). New York: Wiley.

Reschly, D. J. (1985). Best practices in adaptive behavior assessment. In A. Thomas & J. Grimes (Eds.), *Best practices in school psychology–II* (pp. 353–368). Washington, DC: National Association of School Psychologists.

Reschly, D. J. (1990). Best practices in adaptive behavior. In A. Thomas & J. Grimes (Eds.), *Best practices in school psychology–II* (pp. 29–42). Washington, DC: National Association of School Psychologists.

Reschly, D. J., & Ward, S. M. (1991). Use of adaptive behavior measure and overrepresentation of black students in programs for students with mild mental retardation. *American Journal of Mental Retardation, 96*, 257–268.

Shapiro, E. S., & Skinner, C. H. (1990). Principles of behavioral assessment. In C. R. Reynolds & R. W. Kamphaus (Eds.), *Handbook of psychological and educational assessment of children personality, behavior, and context* (pp. 343–363). New York: Guilford.

Sparrow, S. S., Balla, D. A., & Cicchetti, D. V. (1984a). *Vineland Adaptive Behavior Scales, Expanded Form.* Circle Pines, MN: American Guidance Service.

Sparrow, S. S., Balla, D. A., & Cicchetti, D. V. (1984b). *Vineland Adaptive Behavior Scales, Survey Form.* Circle Pines, MN: American Guidance Service.

Sparrow, S. S., Balla, D. A., & Cicchetti, D. V. (1985). *Vineland Adaptive Behavior Scales, Classroom Edition.* Circle Pines, MN: American Guidance Service.

Voelker, S. I., Shore, D. L., Brown-Moore, C., Hill, L. C., Miller, L. T., & Perry, J. (1990). Validity of self-report of adaptive behavior skills by adults with mental retardation. *Mental Retardation, 28*, 305–309.

ANNOTATED BIBLIOGRAPHY

American Association on Mental Retardation. (1992). *Definitions, classifications, and systems of supports* (9th ed.). Washington, DC: Author.

The AAMR manual is an excellent resource concerning all important aspects of assessment, diagnosis, and intervention for individuals with mental retardation. The manual emphasizes new approaches in identifying support systems, multifaceted adaptive behavior assessment, and problem-solving techniques for providing services for individuals with mental retardation.

American Journal on Mental Retardation. (1992). Volume 96, special issue on "Social Competence."

The special issue of the leading journal in the field of mental retardation contains a variety of articles related to the social competence of individuals with mental retardation. Young children, adolescents, and adults are discussed in the articles, and topics include problem- solving strategies, self-perceptions, family roles, social skills, and new models of social competence.

Journal of Special Education. (1987). Volume 21, special issue on "Adaptive Behavior."

The series of articles contain a wealth of information pertaining to different aspects of adaptive behavior. The issue contains information about assessment, intervention, and adaptive behavior of individuals with different disabilities.

McGrew, K. S., & Bruininks, R. H. (1990). Defining adaptive and maladaptive behavior within a model of personal competence. *School Psychology Review, 19*, 53–73.

The article describes one of the few empirical studies investigating the theoretical aspects of adaptive behavior. The results of the study support a model of personal competence that includes adaptive behavior.

Reschly, D. J. (1990). Best practices in adaptive behavior. In A. Thomas & J. Grimes (Eds.), *Best practices in school psychology–II* (pp. 29–42). Washington, DC: National Association of School Psychologists.

This chapter should remain on school psychologists' reading lists for many, many years! The chapter is one of the best sources of information about adaptive behavior assessment owing to the outstanding discussion of key issues and the practical recommendations.

65

Best Practices in
Intellectual Assessment

Daniel J. Reschly
Iowa State University

Jeffrey P. Grimes
Iowa Department of Education

School psychology was born in the prison of the IQ test. This controversial thesis was advanced by a prominent American psychologist in a commentary on school psychology two decades ago (Sarason, 1975). In this chapter, the appropriate role for intellectual assessment will be considered as school psychology emerges from this prison. Although our analysis will suggest a diminished role for intellectual assessment in the future, we recognize the necessity of best practices when intellectual assessments are conducted because these results typically are used in crucial decisions about children and youth.

INFLUENCES ON CURRENT PRACTICES

The dominance of intellectual assessment in current practice was apparent from the results of national surveys of school psychologists in 1986–87 and 1991–1992 (Reschly, Genshaft, & Binder, 1987; Reschly & Wilson, in press). In both surveys practitioners indicated that about two-thirds of their time was devoted to various aspects of special education eligibility determination. Intellectual assessment was nearly always a part of eligibility determination. The typical practitioner administered approximately 17 intellectual measures per month, most often one of the Wechsler scales. Intellectual assessment appears to be a virtual daily activity for school psychologists.

Historical Influences

The development of school psychology and special education are closely intertwined (Fagan, 1992). The earliest roots of school psychology were in a university-based clinic where psychological studies of children with learning problems were conducted. As school psychology developed from these early roots, services were provided most often by itinerant professionals in clinic-like settings; that is, children were brought to psychologists who studied them individually *outside* of the natural setting in which behaviors

of concern occurred. This pattern of service continues today.

Standardized tests of intelligence and achievement were well suited to conducting analyses of learning problems in these clinic or clinic-like settings. Standardized procedures were used to obtain samples of behavior that became meaningful through comparisons to normative groups. These comparisons typically resulted in: (a) estimations of likely level of achievement; (b) identification of the cause(s) of low achievement; and (c) consideration of eligibility for a disability diagnosis (e.g., learning disability) and special education placement.

The measures were *indirect*; that is, they did not measure the actual behaviors of concern to the referral agent and the sample of behavior occurred outside of the natural setting. Direct samples of behavior in natural settings were not feasible due to the limitations in the availability of personnel and in the technology for obtaining reliable and valid direct behavioral samples. Although indirect samples of behavior were useful for many years and undoubtedly led to more appropriate educational services for many students, several disadvantages have become increasingly apparent over the past 10 years. The most important disadvantage is that the commonly used indirect measures are not closely related to interventions (see later section on reform themes).

Graduate Education

School psychology's history of using indirect measures in clinic or clinic-like settings was strongly established through graduate programs. In typical programs, the courses on administration, scoring, and interpretation of individual measures of cognitive functioning were emphasized more than courses on various intervention methods such as consultation, counseling, behavioral therapy, and behavioral assessment (Brown & Minke, 1986; Reschly & McMaster-Beyer, 1991). The nature of school psychology graduate education is changing, however, with many graduate programs now in various stages of initiating greater emphasis on assessment procedures that have direct connections to interventions.

Legal Regulations

Legal provisions in federal and state legislation and court cases are another significant source of influence on the use of intellectual assessment. The enactment of mandatory special education legislation at the state and federal levels in the 1970s had several influences including guaranteeing the access of persons with disabilities to educational services, thus expanding the numbers of students needing evaluations for possible diagnosis as disabled and subsequent special education placement. This legislation also established general standards for assessment practices that have had far reaching influences on intellectual assessment (Reschly, 1987).

Compliance with legal provisions is an ethical imperative; however, legal provisions are sometimes misinterpreted in ways that lead to rigid practices not in the best interests of children. For example, the critical federal regulation regarding the content of the multifactored assessment in initial placement or reevaluations states, "The child is assessed in all areas related to the suspected disability, including *if appropriate*, health, vision, hearing, social and emotional status, general intelligence, academic performance, communicative status, and motor abilities" (Individuals with Disabilities Education Act, 34 CFR 300.532; emphasis added).

The words "if appropriate" are crucial in this regulation. Professional judgment is needed in determining whether general intelligence information should be gathered regarding decisions to be made in individual cases. General intelligence information is not needed with many students referred for social-emotional or behavioral problems because (a) other information on cognitive functioning usually is available in school records and (b) IQ test results are unlikely to be directly related either to the emotional disturbance or behavior disorder diagnosis or to the development of interventions. Similarly, repeated administrations of IQ tests as part of triennial reevaluations, particularly for older students or students with severe disabilities, may be unnecessary because the results are not directly related to decisions that need to be made.

Legal regulations are not intended to eliminate professional judgment. The key federal regulation regarding the content of a multifactored assessment clearly requires that choices be made regarding which areas to include in initial eligibility determination and reevaluations. In a later section recommendations will be made that these choices be related closely to explicit questions established with the referral agent.

Disability Diagnostic Constructs

The conception and classification criteria in disability diagnostic constructs have enormous influences on the use of measures of intellectual functioning. Disability diagnostic constructs typically are formed by establishing critical dimensions of behavior and specifying criteria for decision making with individual cases. The traditional conceptions of mental retardation (MR) and specific learning disability (SLD) have used the dimension of intellectual functioning as a key component of the diagnostic construct. Classification criteria for MR and SLD in the special education rules of most states require that general intelligence be assessed as part of the eligibility determination evaluation. A substantial proportion of the use of intellectual assessment measures today occurs in the context of determining whether referred students meet the classification criteria for MR or SLD.

The conceptions and criteria related to diagnostic constructs change over time with the accumulation of research evidence as well as the development of different or expanded purposes of classification. Recent changes in the American Association on Mental Retardation classification scheme reflect somewhat less emphasis on general intelligence with more emphasis on adaptive skills and assessment of treatment needs (Luckasson et al., 1992). Other recent commentaries have suggested alternative ways to conceptualize and diagnose MR and SLD (Reschly, 1988a; Shinn, 1988; Siegel, 1989). These conceptions would place less emphasis on general intelligence and more emphasis on direct measures of student performance in natural settings. Implementation of these conceptions or other alternatives for conceptualizing traditional diagnostic constructs could markedly influence the use of intellectual assessment by school psychologists.

Reform Themes

Over the past five years increasing emphasis has been placed on the reform of school psychology through changes in the overall special education classification/placement system and in efforts to broaden services to low-achieving at-risk students. The capstone of the reform movement is less emphasis on eligibility determination and greater emphasis on the design and delivery of interventions to students within regular education settings (Graden, Zins, & Curtis, 1988; Reschly, 1988b). Significant changes are suggested in the roles of school psychologists and the kind of assessment information needed to address questions of interventions rather than questions of eligibility. Assessment in the new systems suggested will involve descriptions of problems in natural settings and information useful for designing, monitoring, and evaluating interventions. The kind of information useful for those purposes will necessarily involve curriculum-based measurement and behavioral assessment using techniques such as observation, direct measures of academic performance, ratings of social skills, direct and indirect measures of academic survival skills, and interviews with significant others such as teachers and parents.

As reform plans are implemented, we anticipate declining use of intellectual assessment. The current pattern of administering an intellectual assessment measure nearly every day by school psychologists will change with far greater emphasis given to more functional, that is more intervention-related, assessment procedures. However, intellectual assessment will continue, and that is as it should be. However, when intellectual assessment is used, it must be carried out in ways consistent with the theories and research on intellectual assessment and with well-recognized best practices. It is to these topics that the rest of the chapter is devoted.

BASIC CONSIDERATIONS

The voluminous literature pertaining to intellectual assessment cannot be reviewed in detail in this chapter. Thousands of journal articles, hundreds of book chapters, and scores of books have been written on topics related to intellectual assessment. This review, therefore, will cover only general findings that relate directly to best practices considerations. Readers are referred to other sources such as Sternberg (1982) and Sattler (1988/1992) for further information on theories, developmental patterns, research on various groups and tests, and reviews of measures.

Nature of Current Measures

The intellectual measures used most frequently in school psychology are composed of a variety of complex tasks ranging from items requiring simple memory to abstract problem solving. Most are atheoretical in the sense that the items and scales are not derived from applications of theories of cognitive development or information processing. Analysis of their psychometric structure typically yields a general factor, not unlike the concept of Spearman's "g," with one to three group factors (Vernon, 1979).

Although current measures such as the WISC-R and the Stanford-Binet Fourth Edition (SB) yield numerous scores, the most meaningful scores based on factor analytic investigations, as well as concurrent validity studies, are a composite of overall score and two or three scores reflecting group factors such as verbal comprehension and visual spatial problem solving. Scores on subtests, typically composed of similar items, are considerably less meaningful and substantial variation on the subtest scores is typical. The relationship of performance to important indices such as school achievement is typically best for the composite score and the primary or group factor scores. Relationships between important criteria and subtest scores tend to be highly variable and considerably weaker.

Meaning of Current Measures

Interpretation of the results of measures of intellectual functioning can be highly controversial. Perhaps the most widely accepted view is that measures of general intellectual functioning reflect the results of incidental learning through exposure to the general culture. The emphasis is on incidental learning because little if anything on the test is taught directly. However, schooling and the quality of educational experiences do influence intellectual development.

Academic performance. Intellectual measures are useful because of their relationship to other critical indices of human functioning. The most common use is to attempt to estimate likely level of performance in educational settings or to attempt to identify causes of poor school performance. This use of intellectual measures is supported by the well-known substantial correlation between intellectual functioning and school achievement. This relationship, ranging from a correlation of about .4 to .7 depending on the achievement criterion measure, reflects a substantial, but by no means perfect, association between intellectual functioning and school performance.

Occupational attainment. Intellectual measures are also correlated with occupational attainment. Although there is a broad range of ability associated with each occupational category, such as attorney or carpenter, there is a clear relationship with the average level of ability in occupational categories. Generally, the more prestigious the occupation the higher the average level of ability. This fundamental relationship rarely has direct applicability to school psychology decision making.

Cognitive processes. Performance on intellectual measures is also related to a variety of indices of cognitive processing. Campione, Brown, and Ferrara (1982) provided an excellent discussion of these relationships. Although their review focused primarily on studies of persons with mild mental retardation, the relationships they reported in the literature reviewed were interpreted as, for the most part, applying to all ranges of ability. According to Campione et al., performance on intellectual measures is positively related to the speed and efficiency of information processing, to the individual's knowledge base, to the spontaneous use of appropriate strategies in problem-solving tasks, to metacognitive operations whereby the individual exerts control over approaches to problem solving, and to the transfer of problem-solving skills to novel situations.

Perhaps the most salient result in the Campione et al. (1982) review was the interpretation of intellectual differences in terms of the capability of profiting from incomplete instruction. In general, the higher the level of measured ability, the greater the individual's capability of learning through indirect or incomplete instruction. The latter bears strong relationships to the concept of incidental learning, cited earlier as the process through which much of the knowledge or problem-solving strategies on intellectual measures are learned.

It should be noted that the most widely used measures of intellectual functioning do not provide direct assessment of any of the cognitive processes. Rather, the complex types of items included on current measures require each of the cognitive processes to varying degrees. Furthermore, the scores on current measures, whether from subtests or from composite scales, cannot be interpreted directly, with few exceptions, as pure measures of any of the cognitive processes. Rather, these scores represent the products rather than the processes whereby individuals recall information, explain concepts, or solve problems.

Measured Intelligence versus Intelligent Behavior

The discrepancy between what is assessed on intellectual measures and effective, intelligent behavior has been recognized for many decades. In a 1921 symposium on the meaning of intelligence, E. L. Thorndike suggested three major facets of intelligence, social, mechanical (practical), and abstract thinking. He noted that the tests at that time, like most current measures, focused primarily on abstract thinking. A similar insight was offered by David Wechsler in his emphasis on intelligent behavior as the overall capacity to think rationally, act purposely, and deal effectively with the environment. Recently Sternberg (1985) has identified different components of intelligent behavior including social and practical intelligence (an aspect of which is tacit knowledge). All of these formulations recognize the distinction between what is measured on current measures and intelligent behavior. Intelligent behavior, if defined simply as the effectiveness in dealing with the environment, clearly involves a variety of intellectual and nonintellectual competencies. The IQ score from a well-standardized instrument such as one of the Wechsler scales represents some, but by no means all, of these competencies. It is critical for users of measures of general intellectual functioning to understand this distinction and to communicate the distinction to consumers of test results, that is, students, teachers, and parents. As Wechsler pointed out, a high level of measured intelligence, perhaps reflecting primarily abstract thinking, capabilities, is rendered quite useless in the absence of goal-directedness, motivation, persistence, or sufficient mental health stability to allow concentrated effort.

Variations in Performance: Intra-Individual Differences

Intellectual measures are designed to identify individual differences. Two perspectives can be used in examining these variations: Intra-individual differences involve variations within the individual over different tasks or items; inter-individual differences, between persons on the same tasks or items. Both types of differences have been used widely in intellectual assessment.

Intra-individual differences over subtests have often been used in making diagnostic decisions about individuals. For example, it was widely believed that larger subtest variations or unique patterns were typical of persons with various disabilities or neuropsychological deficits. It turns out that these assertions were and are still almost certain to be incorrect because a high degree of variation across item types or tasks is typical of normal persons. Kauffman (1976a, b) noted that large variations among the Wechsler subtests or in the verbal and performance scores were typical of persons in the standardization sample. Therefore, such variations could not be a defining or unique feature of any diagnosis that occurred infrequently in the general population.

Difference scores are nearly always less reliable than the separate scores on which the difference is based. This fact explains to a large degree why the intra-individual differences used in profile or scatter analysis are not useful bases for diagnoses or specification of treatment. If the reason for difference scores being less reliable is not immediately apparent, consider this analogy. If one is uncertain about when a vacation period begins and also uncertain about when the vacation ends, then, there must be even greater uncertainty about the length of the vacation. Similarly, if we are somewhat uncertain of the individual's Block Design score, also somewhat uncertain about the individual's Vocabulary score, then we are, by necessity, even less certain of the difference between the two scores.

Norms for subtest and scale differences are available for the most widely used tests (Sattler, 1988/1992). The norms often are organized around the size of the difference between two scores that is statistically significant at the .05 or .01 levels. These results are widely misunderstood. For example, on a Wechsler scale the Verbal-Performance Scale difference of about 10 points is statistically significant at the .01 level. Does this mean that only one per cent of the standardization sample obtained Verbal and Performance scores at that magnitude of difference? No! In fact, nearly 25% of persons in the standardization obtained Verbal and Performance scores that were different by 15 points or more. The statistical significance indicates the likelihood that a difference of that magnitude would occur by chance. The .01 or .05 levels indicate that the difference is likely to be real, not whether the difference is unusual or unique. It is essential to keep in mind that real differences in profiles of scores do occur frequently.

Developmental Changes

The performance of individuals also varies over time. IQ test results are relatively stable for many individuals after approximately age five to seven; however, the IQ scores for a significant percentage of individuals (at least 20%) change by 15 points or more between age 6 and maturity, and considerably larger changes of 30 to 40 points have been reported in a few cases. When large changes do occur, they tend to be associated with significant changes in the individual's environment or overall adjustment (McCall, Appelbaum, & Hogarty, 1973). The fact that IQ test results do change as a function of changes in the individual or the environment can be seen as evidence to support the most common interpretation of test results as reflecting *current* intellectual functioning. School psychologists need to be conscious of, and inform others about, the fact that scores do change and that inferences about future intellectual status of the individual are tentative.

Measures of Cognitive Processes

In recent years intellectual measures reflecting theoretical formulations of cognitive processes have begun to appear accompanied by suggestions that these measures replace some of the uses of traditional measures (Naglieri, Das, & Jarman, 1990). To date these measures have not been used frequently by psychologists although two distinct types have appeared. The Kaufman Assessment Battery for Children (K-ABC) is an example of a measure that attempts to assess cognitive processing for the purpose of improving learning through selecting an instructional method that capitalizes on processing strengths (Kaufman & Kaufman, 1983). In much the same fashion, attempts are made in neuropsychological assessment to match instructional method with "intact" neurological functions which are inferred from profiles of performance on various measures of cognitive and noncognitive behaviors (Reynolds, 1992). The major problem with these approaches is the absence of treatment validity (Kavale, 1990; Reschly & Gresham, 1989; Teeter, 1987, 1989). Although attractive, the idea of matching instructional method to cognitive or neuropsychological strengths has little empirical support.

A second use of cognitive process measures is represented by dynamic assessment procedures that attempt to identify strengths and weaknesses in the individual's problem-solving strategies. Attempts are then made to overcome deficits in strategies through direct cognitive modification (Lidz, 1987). Thus far, dynamic assessment and cognitive training have not had much impact on the practice of school psychol-

ogy, in part because the dynamic assessment procedures have not been well standardized and the effectiveness of interventions related to improving cognitive processing are as yet unproved.

Inter-Individual Differences

The central purpose in most administrations of individual IQ tests is to determine how the individual performs in relation to a group of persons with similar characteristics. The standard scores and percentile ranks that give meaning to the performance and form the basis for the interpretation are based on the normative group. Obviously, the quality of the norms is crucial to the usefulness of the test. When we interpret the performance of individuals using the common scores such as IQs and percentile ranks, we are implicitly concluding that the normative group on which these scores were based constituted an appropriate comparison group for that individual. Careful consideration of that group's appropriateness is crucial to accurate interpretation of measures of intellectual performance.

Perhaps the most controversial finding related to intellectual assessment is that sociocultural groups differ in level and pattern of performance on measures of intellectual performance. These findings have appeared for many years (Kaufman & Doppelt, 1976; Lesser, Fifer, & Clark, 1965). The variations in level typically are confounded with group differences in socioeconomic status, rendering difficult interpretation of the source(s) of level and pattern differences. For that reason, extreme caution should be used in attributing causality to group differences as well as in interpreting the results of intellectual test performance for persons from groups that are culturally different. Mercer (1979) gives an excellent discussion of conditions that must be met before attributing intellectual test differences to hereditary causes. In fact, those criteria cannot be met for individuals, and estimations of their effects for groups are fraught with many possible sources of error. For these reasons, it is unwise to make inferences about causation in the everyday interpretations of inter-individual differences on measures of intellectual functioning.

Bias and Litigation

Allegations of bias are perhaps the most controversial issues related directly to the use of intellectual measures by school psychologists. Bias concerns are related to two populations: economically disadvantaged minority students and students with sensory or motor disabilities. Issues of possible bias need to be considered carefully when selecting intellectual assessment instruments, administering them, and interpreting the results.

Bias against minorities. Bias concerns are most often expressed regarding populations of minority students, particularly African-American, Latino, and Native American students. Considerable research was devoted to topics of bias in the 1970s and 1980s. The voluminous results generated from this research led to complex conclusions about intellectual assessment with minority students. First, there are multiple definitions of bias with varied meanings. The results of studies of bias depend heavily on the definition used. Definitions of bias include the following conceptions: (a) mean differences; (b) item bias; (c) psychometric characteristics of tests; (d) factor analysis of underlying test structure; (e) atmosphere or examiner/examinee interaction effects; (f) prediction; (b) selection ratios or disproportionate classification of students; and (h) social consequences, particularly use of test results to support racist interpretation of differences.

Most conventional tests, for example the WISC-R, are not biased according to the conventional definitions related to properties of items, psychometric characteristics, factor analysis, atmosphere effects, and prediction (Jensen, 1980; Reschly, 1979; Reynolds & Kaiser, 1990). Specifically, there is no evidence that conventional tests underpredict the actual performance of minority students. Conventional tests typically are found to be biased on the less well-accepted definitions such as mean differences, selection ratios/disproportionate classification, and social consequences.

The mean differences and disproportionate classification definitions, along with several conventional definitions, were key features of extremely costly and divisive litigation over the past twenty years. Four trials over these issues occurred in federal district courts between 1979 and 1986 (Reschly, Kicklighter, & McKee, 1988a, b). Three of the trials concluded that conventional measures of intellectual functioning were not biased, despite overrepresentation of minority students in special education programs, if certain crucial standards were met: (a) rigorous implementation of procedural safeguards in the referral, classification, and placement process; (b) implementation of a multifactored assessment designed to identify specific educational needs by a group of professionals; and (c) classification, placement, and programming decisions made by a team that included professionals and parents. The famous *Larry P* case in California resulted in a different decision on essentially the same facts (see Reschly et al., 1988a, b for an analysis of the cases and a discussion of implications for school psychology).

Bias against persons with sensory impairments. A slightly different concern about bias was reflected in the Federal Protection in Evaluation Procedures Provisions (IDEA, 34 CFR 300.530–534). This concern had to do with the use of measures that un-

fairly penalized students due to their sensory, motor, or language handicaps/differences. For example, the standard administration of the Wechsler verbal scale to a student with a hearing impairment or deafness likely measures the effect of the disability to a greater extent than the underlying construct of intellectual functioning. Similarly, use of highly verbal measures in the English language unduly penalizes students with mixed language capabilities (e.g., Spanish and English) or students with limited exposure to English. The population most frequently involved with the latter concern are of Hispanic origin, an increasing segment of the United States population and school psychologists' caseloads. Intellectual assessment of students with sensory or motor disabilities or language differences should, to the greatest extent possible, use administration procedures and response modes that do not merely reflect the effects of the disability or language difference. Use of special scales designed specifically for particular populations or non-language measures generally are preferred procedures.

Treatment Validity

The use of intellectual assessment is expected to decline because the results of intellectual measures are not related closely to treatment selection, planning, or evaluation. Witt and Gresham's evaluation of the treatment validity of the most widely used scale is a good metaphor for all such intellectual measures, "In short, the WISC-R lacks treatment validity in that its use does not enhance remedial interventions for children who show specific academic skill deficiencies . . . For a test to have treatment validity, it must lead to better treatments (i.e., better educational programs, teaching strategies, etc.)" (Witt & Gresham, 1985, p. 1717).

Of course, many respected school psychology professionals may disagree with the view of treatment validity stated here. Regrettably, space limitations do not permit a full representation of all views. It should be noted that the principal use of intellectual measures has been the classification of a child with disabilities leading to placement in special education. The reader may, therefore, wish to explore Kavale's (1990) analysis of the efficacy of special education programs organized around disability labels. From these results, as well as the negative findings on matching instruction to cognitive or neuropsychological strengths, many school psychologists have concluded that alternatives should be considered.

Alternative assessment procedures that focus on direct measures of behaviors in natural settings appear to be promising for use in classification decisions. Existing information confirms the value of these measures in intervention planing, implementation, monitoring, and evaluation. The move to alternative assessment procedures appears to provide better services to children and youth, as well as exciting and challenging opportunities for school psychologists to establish broader roles that utilize the full range of the psychological knowledge base.

Appropriate and Inappropriate Uses of Intellectual Assessment

Intellectual assessment may have a positive or negative impact on the individual depending on the context that leads to assessment and the outcomes of decisions made using intellectual assessment information. The importance of these context and outcome conditions was emphasized in a report of the National Research Council on equity in special education placement (Heller, Holtzman, & Messick, 1982). Consideration of alternatives to special education referral, classification, and placement — and, if these steps are necessary, focusing on the outcomes of classification and placement — moves the discussion of bias beyond arguments about test items and prediction equations (Reschly, 1979; Reschly et al., 1988b). Consideration of alternatives and outcomes is the central focus of system-reform efforts now underway.

Context. The typical context of intellectual assessment for school psychologists often involves determining eligibility for possible special education classification and placement. A two-pronged classification-placement process is established in federal and state special education legislation determining: (a) the need for special education, and (b) eligibility of classification. All too often the eligibility determination, rather than the need for special education, is addressed in the multifactored assessment that precedes classification and placement.

The least restrictive environment (LRE) principle from federal and state legislation places emphasis on attempts to resolve problems and to provide necessary services in regular education settings. Application of this principle implies that intellectual assessment and eligibility determination should not be the first choice in efforts to address learning or behavior problems.

The first phase of a system within which intellectual assessment can be used appropriately involves concerted efforts to resolve problems in regular education settings. This phase must include careful consideration of prior efforts to resolve the problem and systematic, high quality interventions. Typically, intervention quality at the prereferral stage is poor, lacking such essential features as behavioral definition of the problem, collection of baseline data, design of systematic interventions, and intervention implementation, monitoring, and evaluation. School psychologists have critical roles and essential contributions to ensuring the delivery of high-quality prereferral interventions.

Choice of measure and decision making. If the problem behavior is pervasive and persistent and beyond the purview of regular education, even with high-quality prereferral interventions, then consideration of special education eligibility is appropriate. At this stage, depending on state rules concerning classification of students as disabled, intellectual assessment may be part of the multifactored assessment. Intellectual assessment should not dominate the assessment process; rather, it should be one component of a comprehensive evaluation tailored to the referral problem and oriented to determining specific intervention need(s). Consideration of other aspects or dimensions of behavior should receive equal or more attention and decision making about eligibility and placement should reflect a clear balance between intellectual assessment and other important information.

The choice of intellectual assessment measure(s) must be based on the characteristics of the student. Student characteristics such as age, sensory status, language competencies, and acculturation are crucial factors that must be considered carefully when professionals select specific intellectual measures. For some students, few if any good choices exist due to various combinations of language differences, sensory impairments, and acculturation. In some of these cases, intellectual assessment should be avoided. In other cases, interpretations should be extremely cautious and decisions considered highly tentative.

The best measures available should be used when intellectual assessment results are part of significant decisions such as disability classification. Practitioners should base instrument choices on published critical reviews in authoritative sources such as the Buros Mental Measurement Yearbooks (also see Salvia & Ysseldyke, 1991) as well as their thorough study of the available technical and clinical information. Instruments that are short forms of more comprehensive measures, tests with a single-item type, and measures with dubious technical adequacy should be avoided.

Additional challenges arise when the effects of various disabilities such as sensory impairments or complex conditions such as autism or traumatic brain injury have to be considered in instrument choice and interpretation. Familiarity with a variety of instruments and knowledge of various disabling conditions is essential to choice of measures and interpretation of results in these complex cases.

Decision making. Information on intellectual functioning is used most often in decisions about classification of students as MR or SLD. Most students considered for these classifications will be performing near the margins of the classification criteria; that is, they will perform at levels where they are just eligible or just ineligible for classification. For example, an IQ less than 70 or 75 is used frequently as part of the criteria for a diagnosis of MR. The vast majority of the persons for whom an MR diagnostic decision is necessary will perform within a few points of the cut off score of 70 or 75. There are, for example, more students with IQs between 70 and 75 than have IQs below 70! A substantial proportion of cases will be within one standard error of measurement — often regarded as three to four points on the composite score of the most widely used instruments — of the cutoff established by the state rules.

The mechanical application of scores to classification criteria is inappropriate in MR and SLD eligibility decisions; rather, complex judgments are required. These complex judgments should reflect application of the convergent validity principle described by Gresham (1985), that is, the consistency of information over settings, sources, and data collection methods. Application of the convergent validity principle provides a means to integrate information from the multifactored assessment. For students performing near cut-off points, a pattern of information consistent with the underlying diagnostic construct should lead to classifying the child as disabled. On the other hand, one or more sources of information that are not consistent with the diagnostic construct should lead to not classifying the student as disabled.

Inappropriate or Questionable Uses of Intellectual Assessment

An array of inappropriate or questionable uses of measures of general intellectual functioning will be described briefly in this section. An obvious inappropriate use is to reach conclusions about the individual using only the results from a measure of intellectual functioning, without considering a wide variety of other information. It is not generally known how frequently this inappropriate use occurs, but it was of sufficient concern to merit a special sentence in federal regulations pertaining to assessment of students (IDEA, 34 CFR 300.532). We suspect that the results of an intellectual measure overshadow other important information quite frequently and that this other information, so valuable in developing interventions, is not used fully or is ignored.

Profile analysis. A frequent inappropriate use of a standard tool is to conduct a profile analysis for the purpose of differential diagnosis (e.g., determining whether the student is learning disabled or emotionally disturbed). As noted previously, a considerable degree of subtest score variation is typical. Differences between scales or subtests, because they occur frequently, simply cannot be a unique feature of any diagnostic category nor, therefore, the basis for distinguishing between diagnostic categories.

Group differences. Results from studies of groups of students also need to be interpreted cautiously with individuals. For example, the WISC-R

ACID profile has been reported frequently in contrasts of learning disabled and normal achieving students (Sattler, 1988/1992). However, these findings are based on mean differences, developed from distributions of scores for normal achieving and learning disabled groups. The overall distributions overlap considerably. Therefore, a specific normal achieving child may obtain the ACID profile and a specific student accurately characterized as learning disabled may not obtain that profile. Therefore, conformance or nonconformance with the particular profile reported for groups is not an accurate indicator of the appropriate diagnosis for an individual child.

Personality or neuropsychological status. Profile analysis to determine neurological strengths or weaknesses or psychodynamic personality characteristics is also fraught with significant errors of logic and probably unreliable. These interpretations have a long history in applied areas of psychology including school and clinical. The empirical basis for the interpretations typically is weak or nonexistent. In virtually all instances, careful studies have not been done with individuals known to possess the underlying neurological or psychodynamic characteristics inferred from the test profile. Rather, analogical reasoning of the form, "what would this most likely mean," has been applied to analysis of the profile resulting in largely unsubstantiated inferences about the meaning of various subtests or scale discrepancies. These interpretations in the absence of empirical support are likely to be inaccurate, unreliable and, in any case, not related to effective intervention methodology or techniques (Reschly & Gresham, 1989).

Structured observations. One of the most frequent justifications for administering an IQ test to nearly all students with learning and/or behavioral problems is the opportunity provided for structured observations. The problem with this use is that the observations occur in an unnatural setting, on a one-to-one basis, with an adult who may have little continuing involvement, using tasks that do not reflect directly the difficulties that prompted the referral. Most important, the behavioral observations in the testing setting do not predict accurately behavior in other settings (Glutting, Oakland, & McDermott, 1989).

In contrast, structured observations in natural settings are enormously useful if gathered through use of direct measures of the behavior or concern and related to crucial environmental or instructional variables that can be used in interventions. The question is, in large part, whether we adapt to the client's setting or whether we require the client to adapt to our setting. Use of the IQ test for structured observations is also time consuming, usually requiring 3 to 4 hours for test administration, scoring, interpretation, and report preparation. Time is precious; the professional's time as well as the client's. Time devoted to

IQ testing inevitably reduces or eliminates the opportunity to conduct other assessment activities.

Inferences about group differences. The final inappropriate use relates to the use of results on measures of general intellectual functioning to support inferences about innate abilities of individuals or groups. Although these questions are investigated, sometime rigorously and sometimes not, the varied and controversial inferences from this research have little relationship to the day-to-day practice with diverse groups of students. The most popular conclusions from this research have varied throughout psychology's history and will likely continue to be modified as new information is generated and more sophisticated investigative techniques are developed and applied. Concern for accurate interpretation for individuals must include efforts to protect individuals from unwarranted inferences about innate abilities that may further diminish efforts to remediate problems and to intervene effectively.

Surgeon General's Warning

A kind of "Surgeon General's" warning can be formulated to protect children and youth from unwarranted inferences about their intellectual abilities and to remind all involved of the developmental nature of measured abilities (Reschly, 1979). This warning is far from perfect and concerned practitioners can develop appropriate modifications. However, the essential ideas are to protect students from inappropriate inferences such as the beliefs that (a) intellectual abilities are determined by genetic factors; (b) intellectual abilities are unitary; (c) IQ scores reflect all of intelligent behavior; and (d) performance on intellectual measures is fixed or unchanging. A statement such as the following should appear on test reports and be attached to test protocols if the latter are likely to be reviewed by other important parties such as teachers, other members of the multidisciplinary team, or parents.

> *IQ tests measure only a portion of the competencies involved with human intelligence. The IQ results are best seen as estimates of likely performance in school and reflections of the degree to which children have mastered the middle class cultural symbols and broad culturally rooted facts, concepts, and problem solving strategies. This information is useful but limited. IQ tests do not reflect innate genetic capacity and the scores are not fixed. Some persons do exhibit significant increases or decreases in their measured intellectual abilities.* (Reschly, 1979, p. 224)

BEST PRACTICES

Best practices considerations require careful judgments about (a) *when* and *how* intellectual assessment instruments are used; (b) the selection, administration, and interpretation of measures; and (c) prevention of misuses and misconceptions.

1. *Appropriate use requires a context that emphasizes prevention and early intervention rather than eligibility determination as the initial phase in services to students with learning and behavior problems.* The context within which the intellectual assessment occurs is crucial. The typical context is the investigation of the causes and correlates of learning problems. Special education eligibility may be a concern, but that concern should be investigated after, not before, the development, implementation, and evaluation of interventions within regular education settings.

2. *Intellectual assessment should be used when the results are directly relevant to well defined referral questions, and other available information does not address those questions.* Evaluations should be goal directed. The goal of the evaluation should be to address significant questions developed jointly between the psychologist and the referral agent. Some referral questions require consideration of current intellectual functioning, many do not.

3. *Mandatory use of intellectual measures for all referrals, multifactored evaluations, or reevaluations is not consistent with best practices.* It is not uncommon for all referred students to receive IQ tests, regardless of referral questions or behavioral problems. IQ test results simply are not relevant to many referral questions or reevaluation issues. A critical question is, "How would the intervention, classification decision, or selection of placement option change if an IQ test is or is not administered?"

4. *Intellectual assessment must be part of a multifactored approach, individualized to a child's characteristics and the referral problems.* The practice of using a standard battery, often dominated by IQ tests, for all children regardless of referral questions must be avoided. The standard battery typically involves an intellectual measure such as a Wechsler scale, a brief screening measure of achievement such as the Wide Range Achievement Test, and a brief measure of visual motor skills such as the Bender Visual Motor Gestalt. Standard batteries provide superficial information over very limited areas of functioning. In most instances, the standard battery does not relate directly to referral problems and is not well matched to characteristics of the child. Consideration and systematic assessment of other important areas of functioning using technically adequate measures is essential in order to develop a comprehensive perspective on the child and to address significant referral questions. The development of well refined referral questions should dictate the components of the comprehensive evaluation, rather than attempting to answer all questions through a limited set of instruments.

5. *Intellectual assessment procedures must be carefully matched to characteristics of children and youth.* A variety of instruments are available and no instrument is appropriate for all students. Special consideration needs to be devoted to choices of instruments with students exhibiting sensory or motor disabilities, language differences, or significant cultural differences. Basal and ceiling problems need to be considered. For example, a low functioning youngster close to the bottom age of the test norms will not be assessed adequately by the instrument because very few items will be administered due to ceiling rules.

6. *Score reporting and interpretation must reflect the known limitations of tests, including technical adequacy, measurement error, and general performance ranges.* Test scores should always be presented as ranges around an obtained score using confidence intervals. Furthermore, limitations in the norms for the test, in reliability or stability of scores, and questionable or undemonstrated validity, must be carefully considered and communicated to consumers of test information. Finally, the overall performance needs to be interpreted within broad categories, established by the test developer or established by other sources, for example, state special education rules.

7. *Interpretation of performance and decisions concerning classification must reflect consideration of overall strengths and weaknesses in intellectual performance and performance on other relevant dimensions of behavior, age, family characteristics, and cultural background.* Present behavior is described. Interpretations and descriptions of likely future performance are inferred from the sample of current behavior. The sample of current behavior may need to be regarded with varying degrees of tentativeness depending on age, family characteristics, and cultural background. Furthermore, overall pattern of strengths and weaknesses in intellectual performance as well as the individual's performance on other relevant dimensions such as adaptive behavior and social skills must be incorporated in interpretations and recommendations.

8. *Professionals should adopt strategies to prevent misuse and misconceptions about the results of intellectual measures.* Many consumers of test results including teachers and parents often view the findings as reflecting a predetermined characteristic and regard the results as fixed. Many do not see the distinction between the results of measures of intellectual measures and the much broader construct of intelligent behavior. A "Surgeon General's Warning" should appear on test protocols and reports as a means to reduce the likelihood of misuse and misconceptions (see previous section).

REFERENCES

Brown, D. T., & Minke, K. M. (1986). School psychology graduate education: A comprehensive analysis. *American Psychologist, 14,* 1328–1338.

Campione, J. C., Brown, A. L., & Ferrara, R. A. (1982). Mental retardation and intelligence. In R. J. Sternberg (Ed.), *Handbook of human intelligence* (pp. 392–490). Cambridge, England: Cambridge University Press.

Fagan, T. K. (1992). Compulsory schooling, child study, clinical psychology, and special education: Origins of school psychology. *American Psychologist, 47,* 236–243.

Glutting, J. J., Oakland, T., & McDermott, P. A. (1989). Observing child behavior during testing: Constructs, validity, and situational generality. Journal of School Psychology, 27, 155–164.

Graden, J. L., Zins, J. E., & Curtis, M. J. (Eds.). (1988). *Alternative educational delivery systems: Enhancing instructional options for all students.* Washington, DC: National Association of School Psychologists.

Gresham, F. (1985). Behavior disorder assessment: Conceptual, definitional, and practical considerations. *School Psychology Review, 14,* 495–509.

Grimes, J. P. (1981). Shaping the future of school psychology. In J. Ysseldyke & R. Weinberg (Eds.), The future of psychology in the schools: Proceedings of the Spring Hill Symposium. *School Psychology Review, 10,* 206–231.

Heller, K., Holtzman, W., & Messick, S. (Eds.). (1982). *Placing children in special education: A strategy for equity.* Washington, DC: National Academy Press.

Individuals with Disabilities Education Act. (1991). 20 U.S.C. Chapter 33; Department of Education Regulations for IDEA at 34 CFR 300 and 301 (September 29, 1992).

Jensen, A. R. (1980). *Bias in mental testing.* New York: Free Press.

Kaufman, A. (1976a). A new approach to interpretation of test scatter on the WISC-R. *Journal of Learning Disabilities, 9,* 160–168.

Kaufman, A. (1976b). Verbal-performance IQ discrepancies on the WISC-R. *Journal of Consulting and Clinical Psychology, 44,* 739–744.

Kaufman, A., & Doppelt, J. (1976). Analysis of the WISC-R standardization data in terms of stratification variables. *Child Development, 47,* 165–171.

Kaufman, A., & Kaufman, N. (1983). *Kaufman Assessment Battery for Children* (K-ABC). Circle Pines, MN: American Guidance Service.

Kavale, K. (1990). The effectiveness of special education. In T. B. Gutkin & C. R. Reynolds (Eds.), *The handbook of school psychology* (2nd ed.; pp. 868–898). New York: Wiley.

Lesser, G., Fifer, G., & Clark, D. (1965). Mental abilities of children from different social class and cultural group. *Monographs of the Society for Research in Child Development, 30*(4), 1–115.

Lidz, C. S. (Ed.). (1987). *Dynamic assessment: An interactional approach to evaluating learning potential.* New York: Guilford.

Luckasson, R., Coulter, D. L., Polloway, E. A., Reiss, S., Schalock, R. L., Snell, M. E., Spitalnik, D. M., & Stark, J. A. (1992). *Mental retardation: Definition, classification, and systems of support* (9th ed.). Washington, DC: American Association on Mental Retardation.

McCall, R., Appelbaum, M., & Hogarty, P. (1973). Developmental changes in mental performance. *Monographs of the Society for Research in Child Development*, *38* (Whole No. 150), 1–83.

Mercer, J. (1979). *System of multicultural pluralistic assessment: Technical manual.* New York: Psychological Corporation.

Naglieri, J. A., Das, J. P., & Jarman, R. F. (1990). Planning, attention, simultaneous, and successive cognitive processes as a model for assessment. *School Psychology Review*, *19*, 423–442.

Reschly, D. (1979). Nonbiased assessment. In G. Phye & D. Reschly (Eds.), *School psychology: Perspectives and issues* (pp. 215–253). New York: Academic Press.

Reschly, D. J. (1987). Assessing educational handicaps. In A. Hess & I. Weiner (Eds.), *The handbook of forensic psychology* (pp. 155–187). New York: Wiley.

Reschly, D. J. (1988a). Assessment issues, placement litigation, and the future of mild mental retardation classification and programming. *Education and Training of the Mentally Retarded*, *23*, 285–301.

Reschly, D. J. (1988b). Special education reform: School psychology revolution. *School Psychology Review*, *17*, 459–475.

Reschly, D. J., Genshaft, J., & Binder, M. S. (1987). *The NASP survey: Comparison of practitioners, NASP leadership, and university faculty on key issues.* Washington, DC: National Association of School Psychologists. (ERIC Document Reproduction Service No. 300 733)

Reschly, D. J., & Gresham, F. M. (1989). Current neuropsychological diagnosis of learning problems: A leap of faith. In C. R. Reynolds & E. Fletcher-Janzen (Eds.), *Child neuropsychology techniques of diagnosis and treatment* (pp. 503–519). New York: Plenum.

Reschly, D. J., Kicklighter, R. H., & McKee, P. (1988a). Recent placement litigation Part II, Minority EMR overrepresentation: Comparison of Larry P. (1979, 1984, 1986) with Marshall (1984, 1985) and S-1 (1986). *School Psychology Review*, *17*, 20–36.

Reschly, D. J., Kicklighter, R. H., & McKee, P. (1988b). Recent placement litigation Part III: Analysis of differences in Larry P., Marshall, and S-1 and implications for future practices. *School Psychology Review*, *17*, 37–48.

Reschly, D. J., & McMaster-Beyer, M. (1991). Influences of degree level, institutional orientation, college affiliation, and accreditation status on school psychology graduate education. *Professional Psychology: Research and Practice*, *22*, 368–374.

Reschly, D. J., & Wilson, M. S. (in press). School psychology faculty and practitioners: 1986–1991 trends in demographic characteristics, roles, satisfaction, and system reform. *School Psychology Review*.

Reynolds, C. R., & Kaiser, S. M. (1990). Test bias in psychological assessment. In T. B. Gutkin & C. R. Reynolds (Eds.), *The handbook of school psychology* (2nd ed.; pp. 487–525). New York: Wiley.

Reynolds, C. R. (1992). Two key concepts in the diagnosis of learning disabilities and the habilitation of learning. *Learning Disability Quarterly*, *15*, 2–12.

Salvia, J., & Ysseldyke, J. (1991). *Assessment in special and remedial education* (5th ed.). Boston: Houghton-Mifflin.

Sarason, S. (1975). The unfortunate fate of Alfred Binet and school psychology. *Teachers College Record*, *77*, 579–592.

Sattler, J. M. (1988/1992). *Assessment of children* (3rd ed., rev.). San Diego, CA: Jerome Sattler Publisher.

Shinn, M. R. (1988). Development of curriculum-based local norms for use in special education decision-making. *School Psychology Review*, *17*, 61–80.

Siegel, L. S. (1989). IQ is irrelevant to the definition of learning disabilities. *Journal of Learning Disabilities*, *22*, 469–479.

Sternberg, R. J. (Ed.). (1982). *Handbook of human intelligence.* Cambridge, England: Cambridge University Press.

Sternberg, R. J. (1985). *Beyond IQ: A triarchic theory of human intelligence.* Cambridge, England: Cambridge University Press.

Teeter, P. A. (1987). Review of neuropsychological assessment and intervention with children and adolescents. *School Psychology Review*, *16*, 582–583.

Teeter, P. A. (1989). Neuropsychological approaches to the remediation of educational deficits. In C. R. Reynolds & E. Fletcher-Janzen (Eds.), *Handbook of clinical child neuropsychology* (pp. 357–376). New York: Plenum Press.

Vernon, P. E. (1979). *Intelligence: Heredity and environment.* San Francisco: W. H. Freeman.

Witt, J. C., & Gresham, F. M. (1985). Review of the Wechsler Intelligence Scale for Children-Revised. In J. Mitchell (Ed.), *Ninth Mental Measurement Yearbook* (pp. 1716–1719). Lincoln, NE: Buros Institute.

ANNOTATED BIBLIOGRAPHY

Aiken, L. R. (1987). *Assessment of intellectual functioning.* Boston: Allyn & Bacon.
Aiken provides an overview of intellectual assessment with interesting and useful information on patterns of intellectual abilities for various groups.

Kaufman, A. (1990). *Assessing adolescent and adult intelligence.* New York: Allyn and Bacon.
Kaufman provides an authoritative review of the research on adolescent and adult intellectual development and assessment.

Lidz, C. S. (Ed.). (1987). *Dynamic assessment: An interactional approach to evaluating learning potential.* New York: Guilford.
A well-organized overview of cognitive processing approaches to intellectual assessment is provided through chapters written by several leading figures.

Sattler, J. M. (1988/1992). *Assessment of children* (3rd ed., rev.). San Diego, CA: Jerome Sattler, Publisher.
Sattler provides an excellent text as well as an essential reference for individuals responsible for conducting intellectual assessments of children. Extensive information is provided on the most commonly used intellectual assessment measures with suggested guidelines for interpretation.

Sternberg, R. J. (Ed.). (1982). *Handbook of human intelligence.* Cambridge, England: Cambridge University Press.

Sternberg, R. J. (1985). *Beyond IQ: A triarchic theory of human intelligence.* Cambridge, England: Cambridge University Press.
The edited volume provides complex but extremely thorough treatments of essential topics related to human intelligence including chapters on attention, perception, learning, memory, reasoning, problem solving, personality, mental retardation, education, social policy, culture, genetics, development, and theories. Collectively, these chapters provide one of the best available treatments of the meaning of intelligence. Sternberg's paperback, *Beyond IQ*, provides an excellent treatment of his triarchic theory. Sections on social and practical intelligence and exceptional intelligence are especially useful in distinguishing between what current tests assess and the broader notion of intelligent behavior.

66

Best Practices
Assessing Infants and Toddlers

Karleen K. Preator
Joseph R. McAllister
Children's Hospital of Pittsburgh
University of Pittsburgh

J. K. was born at 25 weeks gestation weighing 794 grams (1 lb. 12 oz.). He was the first baby born to his parents who had been married 9 years and he was the product of in vitro fertilization. J. K.'s parents were told that he had less than a 50% chance of surviving birth and the immediate neonatal period and, that if he did survive, he had a chance of having a range of disabilities from learning disabilities and hyperactivity to severe cerebral palsy and mental retardation.

J. K. survived delivery and was intubated in the delivery room. He had immature lung development and spent 30 days on a ventilator. Because of his prolonged oxygen requirement, he developed chronic lung disease and required supplemental oxygen through a tube in his nose for an additional 20 days. Head sonar revealed bleeding within the ventricles of his brain which resolved before discharge from the hospital. Other medical diagnoses during J. K.'s first 3 months of life included jaundice requiring phototherapy and anemia requiring blood transfusions. He passed his hearing screening. Ophthalmology screening revealed that he had immature retinas.

J. K. was discharged after 4 months of hospitalization. By then, J. K.'s parents were fluent in medical jargon and understood the multiple diagnoses as discussed by the neonatologists: hyaline membrane disease, bronchopulmonary dysplasia, bilateral grade III intraventricular hemorrhage, hyperbilirubinemia, and stage 3 retinopathy of prematurity.

At 16 months of age, only 2 months after discharge from the hospital, J. K. was referred to the school psychologist by his pediatrician for his first evaluation.

OVERVIEW

Changing and expanding roles provide school psychologists with ongoing challenges. With the implementation of Public Law 99-457, psychologists and educators throughout the United States are responsible for evaluating children from birth to 5 years of age for screening and diagnosis, eligibility for early intervention services, and program planning.

Emphasis on team assessment/intervention and family-centered decision making challenges traditional methods of the evaluation and eligibility process. Working with the medical community provides yet another challenge, and the children themselves present significant challenges: They do not answer questions, do not respond to instructions, are hard to motivate, and do not stay on task. Learning to interact comfortably with young children is an essential skill in mastering the art and the science of assessing infants and toddlers. Communication skills, in general, are also needed as the school psychologist may be called upon to serve as team coordinator.

Infant and toddler assessment involves an ecological approach to assessment and intervention and requires a broadened range of clinical skills. Instead of evaluation for eligibility purposes only, infant and toddler assessment is an ongoing process that begins the intervention process for the family during the first contact. Satisfaction with this first professional encounter may increase compliance with intervention recommendations and decrease the tendency to shop for alternative treatments (Parker & Zuckerman, 1990).

This chapter provides practicing school psychologists a resource to assist in the assessment of infants and toddlers. It is not a substitute for specialized training and the extensive experience needed for competence in this task, but rather an overview of infant/toddler assessment and an orientation to the literature to provide a base of best practices from which school psychologists can expand their existing knowledge and skills to include assessment and intervention of infants and very young children.

BASIC CONSIDERATIONS IN ASSESSING INFANTS AND TODDLERS

The first consideration in assessing infants and toddlers is the skill and training of the examiner. The goal of infant and toddler assessment is not to administer a test, but to gain a clear picture of the children's skills and limitations and a comprehensive understanding of family needs to facilitate intervention (Bailey & Simeonsson, 1988). Psychologists must be willing to observe and interact rather than test. The focus belongs on children's skills in the natural environment — what they do on a regular basis and what they can do given support and encouragement — not on the test.

Need for Psychologist Involvement

At present, the involvement of school psychologists in providing services to infants and toddlers is limited. Although the Individuals with Disabilities Education Act (IDEA) states that psychological services should be available to infants and toddlers, the role of school psychologists is not specified (McLinden & Prasse, 1991). Often it is educators, nurses, or other professionals who have the responsibility for assessment and program planning with this population, which bothers some school psychologists not at all. For them, infant/toddler assessment has as much appeal as changing a dirty diaper. Nor, historically, have school psychology training programs addressed the preschool population, leaving the average school psychologist ill-prepared to provide infant/toddler services (Epps & Jackson, 1991). However, the essential skills that make the school psychologist valuable in assessing school-aged children are no less critical in evaluating infants and toddlers. They include:

- Knowledge of psychometric methods and their limitations.

- Skills in working with parents.

- Observational skills.

- Understanding of typical and atypical development.

- Knowledge of current research and its application to intervention.

The generalist's background is insufficient for effective functioning as an infant/toddler school psychologist. Comprehensive training, including both specific academic preparation and extensive applied experience (Shonkoff & Meisels, 1991), is needed so that those assessing infants and toddlers acquire the requisite skills (see Figure 1). McLinden and Prasse (1991) suggest that "specialized preservice training is the best option" (p. 46) for developing expertise in infant/toddler school psychology. All this means that the postdegree individual moving into infant/toddler services faces formidable though not insurmountable challenges.

The traditional training and employment ground for school psychologists has been the school building. Other settings in which school psychologists are employed, however, include hospitals, neonatal intensive care units, outpatient diagnostic and treatment clinics, private practice, and mental health/mental retardation centers. Even within the confines of public or private schools, the role of the school psychologist is changing. With infants and toddlers, it is important to provide expanded services: assessment of development, behavior, and family resources; case management; coordination of interdisciplinary efforts; program planning; and evaluation of the effectiveness of intervention.

The well-prepared school psychologist can be an invaluable asset to the infant/toddler assessment team. No other discipline is likely to prepare its practitioners for the full range of responsibilities involved in infant/toddler assessment, particularly the job of discussing results with the family. As a profession, school psychology has two responsibilities regarding infant/toddler assessment: (a) ensuring that a sufficient number of competent individuals are prepared for the role, and (b) advocating for inclusion of school psychologists in assessment and intervention with infants and toddlers.

PUBLIC LAW 102–119

The 1986 amendments to the Education of the Handicapped Act, Public Law (PL) 99-457, have been called "the most important piece of federal legislation affecting special education since the passage of PL 94-142" (NASDE, 1986). PL 99-457 mandated availability of free, public, early intervention programs for children from birth to 3 years of age and a free, appropriate public education (FAPE) for children from 3 to 5 years of age. In 1991, PL 99-457 was combined with other legislation, passed as Public Law 102-119, and renamed the Individuals with Disabilities Education Act (or IDEA). Infants and toddlers experiencing developmental delays in one or more developmental domains are eligible for services under IDEA. These domains include expressive language, receptive language, fine motor, gross motor, cognitive, self-help, or socialization skills. In addition, children are eligible for early intervention services if they have a documented physical or mental condition which carries a high probability of resulting developmental delays. These conditions include genetic disorders such as Downs Syndrome, Williams Syndrome, Fragile X, tuberous sclerosis; inborn errors of metabolism such as Tay-Sachs disease; cerebral palsy or other neuromuscular disorders; medical diagnoses such as symptomatic congenital cytomegalovirus; or exposure to toxic substances such as in fetal alcohol exposure. At the state's discretion, children who are at risk medically or environmentally for substantial developmental delays if services are not provided may or may not be included as eligible for early intervention services. These children may be those raised by mothers with mental health problems, living in extreme poverty, homeless, or having medical conditions which place them at risk for developmental delays (e.g., prematu-

FIGURE 1. Skills required in infant/toddler assessment.

- Knowledge of the range of normal development.

- Ability to distinguish delays from aberrant development.

- Ability to write functional reports for families and early childhood educators.

- Familiarity with a variety of specialized instruments and techniques.

- Comfort with working in integrated, team format.

- Familiarity with early childhood curricula.

- Knowledge of related concerns such as medical issues.

- Expertise in working with families.

rity, asymptomatic congenital infection, chronic lung disease, or failure to thrive).

IDEA mandates a family focus to early intervention programming, stating that all early intervention services be guided by an Individual Family Service Plan (IFSP), developed jointly by service providers and families. The regulations for Part H (the Handicapped Infant and Toddler Program) of IDEA suggest a clear distinction between evaluation and assessment. *Evaluation* refers to the initial and periodic procedure to determine eligibility for early intervention or special education services. The term *assessment* is used to describe the ongoing process of monitoring a child's developmental progress, family strengths and needs, and the early intervention services required. Assessment occurs throughout the period during which early intervention services are provided (Campbell, 1991).

Eligibility for Programs Under IDEA

Most states require norm-referenced testing to determine eligibility for early intervention or special education services (Harbin, Gallagher, & Terry, 1991). Nevertheless, formal and standardized procedures are insufficient for understanding the child and must be supplemented. Infant assessment should employ "integrated strategies" (Campbell, 1991) as part of a covergent assessment program (Bagnato & Neisworth, 1991). Information is "gathered from several sources, instruments, settings, and occasions to produce the most valid appraisal of developmental status and to accomplish the related assessment purpose of identification, prescription, and progress evaluation" (Bagnato & Neisworth, 1991, p. 57). The result is richer and more informative data than a single score from a standardized test given under artificial conditions. At least one-half of the children evaluated for eligibility purposes and perhaps as many as 90% are declared "untestable" using traditional measures and

standardized procedures (Bagnato & Neisworth, in press; 1991). Best practices in assessing young children demand expansion of our skills to include a combination of assessments — norm-based, ecologic, curriculum-based, judgment-based, and play-based — in addition to thorough parent interview and behavioral observation (Paget, 1990).

Bagnato and Neisworth (1991) provide comprehensive tables describing assessment batteries for specific developmental ages and handicapping conditions or disorders (pp. 245–251). These tables present examples of norm-referenced, curriculum-based, judgment-based, and eco-based assessment procedures such as the Bayley Scales of Infant Development, the Battelle Developmental Inventory, and the Hawaii Early Learning Profile.

Under IDEA, eligibility can often be determined on a *prima facie* basis. Genetic diagnoses and other medical conditions may have been identified prior to the initial evaluation and suffice in determining eligibility. Furthermore, many of the children referred for evaluation will function at a level or in a manner that precludes the use of standardized instruments. Thus the need for norm-referenced instruments to determine eligibility may be restricted to a relatively small percentage of the cases referred.

However, having already answered the eligibility question does not excuse the infant/toddler psychologist from the evaluation process. The evaluation serves other equally important functions including program planning, establishing a baseline against which future progress can be gauged, determining family needs and resources, and helping the family begin the acceptance and coping process. When there is a need to determine eligibility, the most appropriate course of action may be use of both norm-referenced and curriculum-based measures to address the multiple functions of the evaluation (i.e., "covergent assessment" or "integrated strategies").

BEST PRACTICES IN ASSESSMENT OF INFANTS AND TODDLERS

Best practices in infant/toddler assessment include:

- Understanding the referral.
- Specifying the purpose of the assessment.
- Effective collaboration with the medical community.
- Choosing assessment strategies.
- Interactive strategies.
- Working with families as team members.
- Assessment as an intervention.

Understanding the Referral

Children referred to school psychologists for evaluation and early intervention services in infancy or early childhood are likely to have less common conditions, more severe delays, or more severe disabilities than those referred at school age (Parker & Zuckerman, 1990).

Because of the nature of infant and toddler assessment, the referral for the initial evaluation may be parents' first experience discussing specific concerns and delays with a professional other than their physician. Parents may have wondered about their child's apparent delays and discussed them with their pediatrician or family physician, but the assessment process brings these concerns into focus. This experience can be frightening for families, especially if their worse fears are confirmed — fears that something is "wrong" with their child. In this respect, assessment and intervention begin simultaneously with the referral. "Intervention should begin with an assessment that informs and initiates the therapeutic process through its sensitivity to the parents' emotional state" (Parker & Zuckerman, 1990, p. 353).

J. K.'s parents called the school psychologist at the request of the physician to schedule an evaluation. Although the next screening appointment had been scheduled for 6 months from that date, J. K.'s pediatrician was having concerns about his motor development and wanted him to be evaluated earlier. J. K. was now 8 months old and his parents were becoming much more comfortable with him. They expressed much less fear about the medical issues prevalent when he was in the hospital and immediately after his discharge and were able to enjoy playing and interacting with him as they would with a large, healthy, full-term baby. They occasionally expressed concerns to each other about waiting for the "next shoe to drop," knowing that, even though J. K. survived many significant problems during his neonatal period, he could still be affected by learning problems, cerebral palsy, or other developmental disabilities. The school psychologist arranged to visit J. K. at his home when both of his parents were able to be there. This required scheduling the appointment 3 weeks in advance to accommodate the busy work schedules of both J. K.'s parents and the psychologist. On the morning of the assessment, J. K.'s mother called to cancel the appointment — something had come up and they would be unavailable for the next 2 weeks.

Parent fears are often expressed in indirect ways: they may miss appointments, have difficulty identifying specific concerns, or report that "everything is fine."

Referrals may originate from physicians, preschools, day-care centers, or from parents themselves. Regardless, at an early stage of the assessment/intervention process, it is important to enlist support and help from parents whose concerns may be very different from those of the referring physician or day-care staff. If a child is referred for assessment because of motor delays but, according to the parents, cries constantly and is extremely irritable, the referral question is expanded by the dual concerns. Attending first to the parents' concerns about the irritability by providing suggestions and recommendations about behavior and calming may help enlist the support and trust of the parents. They may find it easier to listen to discussion about motor delays if they feel they have been heard when describing their own concerns. By listening to parent concerns first and intervening at that level, the school psychologist may find the parents more supportive and accepting of other concerns or questions.

When J. K.'s rescheduled evaluation took place, the parents expressed concern about J. K.'s fussy period in the evenings and his poor sleep schedule. They reported that J. K. was inconsolable between 6 and 8 PM and would wake three or four times each night for a few sips from a bottle.

A phone call to J. K.'s physician prior to the evaluation revealed concern about J. K.'s cognitive development. The doctor reported that J. K. was not yet cooperating with his parents in games of peek-a-boo. The physician noted that J. K. also stiffens his legs when he is picked up and would rather stand with his parent's support than sit.

The school psychologist discussed with J. K.'s parents several ideas to console J. K. during his fussy period and was empathetic in discussing their frustrations and exhaustion after 4 months without a full night's sleep. The school psychologist also discussed the importance of the mother's and father's relationship and offered ideas that would allow them to go out for dinner and leave J. K. with his grandparents once a month.

On the second visit, the psychologist was able to discuss concerns about cognitive and motor development with the assistance of an early intervention specialist and a physical therapist, providing suggestions to encourage J. K. to play and interact more consistently. The physical therapist cautioned against the use of a walker or other equipment that would make

J. K. want to straighten his legs. Early intervention services were also discussed as a possibility if J. K.'s development did not improve. A third visit was scheduled in 2 months.

Specifying the Purpose of Assessment

Assessment goals may range from developmental monitoring or screening of children in high risk categories to a complete diagnostic evaluation to reveal underlying causes of developmental delays, to determine eligibility for services, and to provide ongoing program planning and monitoring of program efficacy and child progress. Before launching into "testing," the school psychologist is responsible for determining the goals of the assessment in conjunction with the child's family and the referral source. Determining the assessment goals both aids the school psychologist in selecting assessment strategies and tools needed to provide the desired information and involves the parents as participants in the assessment/intervention process. Parents' hopes, fears, and unrealistic expectations can be addressed if their expectations for the evaluation process are discussed openly (Parker & Zuckerman, 1990).

Medical Considerations

Working with the medical community. An increasing number of low-birth-weight infants and children with medically complex conditions are surviving as a result of advancing medical technology (National Center for Clinical Infant Programs, 1985). Because these children are at increased risk for having special needs, psychologists should receive additional professional preparation concerning medical conditions. When families have questions concerning the development of their young children, they typically turn first to their family physician or pediatrician (McAllister, 1987). Therefore, many referrals originate from pediatricians or other physicians and many evaluation teams include medical input. Subsequently, it often falls to school psychologists to assume responsibility for integrating information from transdisciplinary team evaluations. They may also serve as a consultant for educational personnel working with children with medically complex conditions. It is imperative, therefore, that school psychologists receive training and experience with medical risk factors as well as behavioral characteristics associated with medical conditions, and that they feel comfortable communicating with health care professionals. This underscores the need for open and clear communication between schools and the medical community. Education and health care systems sometimes have difficulty interacting because of a different frame of reference and base of acquired knowledge (Morse, 1990) and a poor understanding of what can be reasonably provided by professionals in different fields (Marshall, Wuori, Hudler, & Cranston, 1987).

Why do physicians refer children for assessment/intervention? Some children are referred because parents have expressed concerns about delayed developmental milestones. Some are referred for developmental monitoring because of significant risk factors. Often, developmental screening and observation suggests developmental problems. Because of the physician's focus on health care, developmental screening is only one (albeit a very important one) component of health care. Physicians must rely on the expertise of psychologists and educators to identify specific needs and strengths of a particular child (see Figure 2). They may have questions about appropriate intervention strategies, behavior management strategies, or early intervention programs available to a family.

The importance of communicating with a child's physician cannot be over-emphasized. It may be the responsibility of the school psychologist and educational staff to make the first contact with the physician to meet a child's and family's developmental, medical, and educational needs. Some physicians who are with patients much of the day prefer to be interrupted when a professional phone call concerning a patient is announced; some prefer that the professional leave a detailed message. Informing the physician's receptionist of the child's name, the purpose of the call, and the psychologist's available hours will allow the physician to be prepared with the child's chart in hand for the return call. Physicians often appreciate hearing about psychologists' concerns, observations, and recommendations following assessment/intervention.

Prematurity. When evaluating development during the first 2 years of life, researchers and clinicians often think of premature infants in terms of their due dates or age post-conception rather than their actual birth dates or chronologic age. For example, a baby who is 6 months old but was born 3 months early has an "adjusted age" of 3 months. When comparing developmental milestones and skills with other children, this infant should be compared with other 3-month-old children instead of with 6-month-old age mates. The infant brain continues to develop at a rapid rate during the neonatal period (Gould, 1977). An enormous amount of energy is spent on growth and development, fighting infection, and adapting to a neonatal nursery with its frequent alarms, buzzers, urgent voices, crying babies, and glaring 24-hour lighting. Children who have been very ill during the neonatal period may lag behind even their adjusted ages (Harrison, 1983).

J. K.'s first evaluation took place when he was 6-months old — according to his actual birth date. Because he was born nearly 4 months early and spent his first 4 months of life in the Neonatal Intensive Care Unit, we would expect him to demonstrate developmental skills at approximately a 2-month level.

FIGURE 2. Services school psychologists can provide to child's physician following assessment.

- Explain educational services available in the community, mandated procedures, the roles of educational personnel, and ways teachers and school psychologists can help monitor a child's developmental progress and physical well-being.

- Send a letter that can be kept in a child's chart concerning evaluation findings and recommendations made following referral for assessment/intervention. Highlight medical needs and questions. Do not send more detailed documents, such as IEPs and IFSPs unless specifically requested.

- Alert physician to suspected medical conditions by providing symptoms, characteristics, or observations that bring a specific medical disorder to mind.

Although J. K.'s chronologic age is 6 months, his "adjusted" or "corrected" age is 2 months.

Although, in many respects, the development of infants born prematurely is similar to that of infants born at term, there are some significant differences. In general, the motor skill development of premature babies tends to lag behind other skills. Shoulders may be retracted and premature infants may keep their arms and hands pulled back in line with or behind their shoulders rather than relaxed at the midline. Increased muscle tone may be seen, especially in the first year (Harrison, 1983). In the case of these developmental differences, assessment must focus on the child's functional skills: Do increased tone and shoulder retractions interfere with functional movements? Can the infant bring hands to midline to grasp a cookie or an attractive toy placed in front? Are stiff legs interfering with the infant's ability to roll or sit comfortably?

Most premature infants do not have lasting medical or developmental problems. However, very low birthweight babies (|3\\i|||1 1500 grams/approximately 3 lbs. 5 oz.) and babies who have experienced severe perinatal complications may develop significant handicapping conditions. These conditions may include sensory impairments, cerebral palsy, or mental retardation (Harrison, 1983) or more subtle learning problems such as learning disabilities, attention deficit hyperactivity disorder, or other academic problems (Sameroff & Chandler, 1975). Although it is impossible to predict a newborn child's future development, the prevalence of significant physical, mental, or sensory impairment increases as birthweight and gestational age decrease (Harrison, 1983). The addition of significant medical complications may also increase the likelihood of future developmental problems.

Babies born prematurely have several medical needs and complications (Figure 3), some of which are more common or more serious than others. School psychologists working with infants and toddlers should be aware of these medical problems. Although there are many other medical problems frequently associated with prematurity, school psychologists should pay close attention to neurologic information (presence of intraventricular hemorrhages or cysts, history of seizure, evidence of sensory impairment) and the level of lung disease in children. Grade IV intraventricular hemorrhages are often associated with neuromotor disorders such as cerebral palsy; severe chronic lung disease and prolonged requirements for supplemental oxygen may result in more diffuse brain dysfunction and mental retardation or specific learning disabilities.

Medical diagnoses. School psychologists must make an effort to learn about the developmental and behavioral implications of a syndrome, medical condition, or risk factor before observing the child or interacting with the family. This information can be obtained from the child's physician or school nurse. It is important to know whether the condition is static or degenerative, understand the effects of medications on the child's state control, and know whether the child requires special handling because of a medical condition. It is also important to know the limits of a medical diagnosis as an indicator of future functioning levels. For example, a child with a diagnosis of Apert Syndrome may have substantial physical malformations and require extensive physical and occupational therapy services but may have normal intelligence.

Working with Families as Team Members

IDEA requires that families be an integral part of the evaluation and intervention process. The infant/toddler psychologist should strive to include the family in all aspects of the evaluation, including:

1. Using the family as a source of information about the child.

2. Determining family needs and resources for the IFSP.

3. Including the family in direct assessment.

4. Developing program recommendations which fit with family priorities for services.

FIGURE 3. Terms associated with premature infants.

- **Apnea** — lack of breathing for longer than 15 or 20 seconds.

- **Bradycardia** — Slower than normal heartbeat.

- **Hyaline membrane disease or respiratory distress syndrome** — Immature lungs. Some premature babies lack sufficient amounts of surfactant, the substance that keeps the lungs' air sacs from collapsing, causing difficulty with breathing. Many premature infants require intubation and mechanical ventilation after birth: A tube is inserted into the trachea and oxygen is pumped into the lungs.

- **Bronchopulmonary dysplasia** — Mechanical ventilation and supplemental oxygen delivered to immature lungs can produce damage to the lungs over an extended period of time. This condition is called BPD, a form of chronic lung disease.

- **Intraventricular hemorrhage** — Brain bleeds. Tiny blood vessels in the brain have fragile walls in premature babies. These blood vessels may burst with fluctuations in the baby's blood pressure and bleeding can occur into the ventricles. These bleeds are graded by severity: Grade I is the least severe indicating that bleeding is limited to a small area within the ventricle to grade IV in which blood fills the ventricles and may be associated with bleeding in the brain tissue.

- **Retinopathy of prematurity** (formerly called retrolental fibroplasia) — Abnormal blood vessels in immature retina. In its most severe stage, it is associated with detached or detaching retinas. Treatment may include cyro surgery to stop the tearing.

Note. Adapted from *The Premature Baby Book: A Parents' Guide to Coping and Caring in the First Years* by H. Harrigan, 1983. New York: St. Martin's Press. Copyright © 1983 by St. Martin's Press.

---

5. Presenting findings and recommendations to parents in a therapeutic manner to facilitate the process of acceptance and coping.

Information source. Parents can provide an additional source of information about the child to partially obviate the limitations of direct assessment and observation. Specifically, there is an increased risk that the sample of behavior seen in direct assessment is not representative due to fatigue, wariness, or a host of other factors, hence the need for cultivating "multiple sources" of information in assessing infants and toddlers (Bagnato & Neisworth, 1991). Some instruments, such as the Battelle (Newborg, Stock, Wnek, Guidubaldi, & Svinicki, 1988) have been structured to permit any combination of direct assessment, observation, and parent report when scoring items, thus allowing the school psychologist to include information not available through direct assessment. Many parent report measures are also available for quantifying parental perceptions such as the Assessment, Evaluation, and Programming System for Infants and Children (Bricker, 1993) and the MacArthur Communicative Development Inventory (Fenson et al., 1991). While some have suggested that parents tend to have inflated estimates of their child's abilities (e.g., Rogers, Booth, Duffy, & Hassan, 1992), others have found parents to be reliable reporters of their children's developmental level (Bricker, Squires, Kaminski, & Mounts, 1988), perhaps even more accurate than professionals (Gradel, Thompson, & Sheehan, 1981). In part, the accuracy of parents may be a function of how the information is elicited. Parent report measures that tap current, observable behavior and do not require interpretation generally provide the most reliable results (Lichtenstein & Ireton, 1984). Thus, the supposed lack of parental objectivity may in fact be "the result of the professional's lack of clarity and specificity in the questions asked" (Lichtenstein & Ireton, 1984, p. 87). Similarly, Bailey and Wolery (1989) have noted the "high level of skill required both to formulate appropriate interview questions that will evoke specific assessment data and to support qualitative, non-judgmental interpersonal relationships" (p. 257).

Individual family service plan. Because of the importance placed on the family as the focus of infant/toddler special education services, each child must have an Individual Family Service Plan (IFSP). Like the Individualized Education Plan (IEP), the IFSP specifies current levels, necessary services, duration of services, and methods for evaluation. The IFSP differs from the IEP in that it includes a statement of the family's strength and needs as they relate to the child's developmental needs. Furthermore, the IFSP must address both child and family outcomes anticipated as a result of the intervention. The IFSP is intended to be the instrument for enabling and empowering families (McGonigel, Kaufman, & Johnson, 1991). It provides the structure in which information is integrated, including family priorities. It is not intended to be intrusive; the family can freely decline or limit family assessment.

A number of instruments are available for family assessment (e.g., the Family Needs Scale in Dunst, Cooper, Weeldreyer, Snyder, & Chase, 1988). However, informal discussions with families may be the most appropriate and efficient way of determining needs and strengths (Beckman & Bristol, 1991) and are required according to IDEA regulations.

Inclusion in assessment. Parents' direct participation in the evaluation program has many payoffs. Developing rapport with the parent sets the stage for family-focused intervention. Family involvement serves to make them participants in the first stage of the intervention process, increasing the likelihood that they will find the team's conclusions and recommendations acceptable. Parents can be asked to attempt evaluation tasks with the child; this may elicit the child's best performance by increasing his or her comfort level and compliance (Parker & Zuckerman, 1990). The course of the evaluation also provides frequent opportunities for the psychologist to demonstrate optimal approaches for working with the child. Modeling approaches to interaction with an infant with disabilities can improve parent behavior more than verbal instruction alone (Minor, Minor, & Williams, 1983). Active parent involvement (as opposed to passive observing) can enhance the quality of parent–infant interactions (Parker & Zuckerman, 1990).

Program recommendations. Family life situations and family needs must be a focus of early intervention program recommendations. Many families of children who are eligible for early intervention services will have clear ideas about the most appropriate educational alternatives for their children. Program planning and IFSP development should meet child educational goals while taking into account family life situations for educational placement. For example, if a family is expecting a new baby, home-based services may be more appropriate for the first year; if family priorities include increasing peer interactions, toddler play groups in which parents are actively involved may be the best program alternative.

Feedback. Parker and Zuckerman (1990) note that the distinction between assessment and intervention is relatively arbitrary, and, in fact, intervention begins with the assessment. In discussing the results of the evaluation with the family, the infant/toddler psychologist is often the first professional to raise sensitive issues about developmental status, needs, and (to the extent feasible and appropriate) prognosis. Perhaps the most difficult and challenging task for the infant/toddler psychologist is the initial discussion of a disabling condition with the family. Many parents express frustration and anger regarding their initial contacts with professionals (Teglasi, 1985). This conflict may stem partially from a gap between what parents expect and what a professional

can legitimately provide. Parents often come seeking "answers," wanting to know the reason for the disability and what can be expected. Yet, except in cases of profound disabilities and some genetic disorders, it is seldom appropriate for a definitive diagnosis at the infant/toddler stage, thus uncertainty and ambiguity are prevalent (Calnan, 1984). This gap between what the parents expect and what professionals are able to provide may leave the parents unsatisfied and delay the process of acceptance and coping. Recently, various factors have been identified that can decrease parental dissatisfaction with the process (see Figure 4; Krahn, Hallum, & Kime, 1993).

Regardless of how sensitively the psychologist presents information, an additional session may be needed to present additional and more detailed information because parents may not "hear" anything after discussion of diagnosis (Parker & Zuckerman, 1990). The process of accepting that one has a child with disabilities has been compared to the stages passed through in dealing with death: denial, anger, bargaining, depression, and acceptance (Kubler-Ross, 1969; Murray, 1985). Professionals should not attempt to "work through" the entire acceptance process with parents in the course of a single discussion. Generally, the process will take years and significant life events (such as moving from a toddler to a preschool program) may cause previously resolved issues to resurface (Harris & Powers, 1984).

The professional confronted with the denying or angry parent may feel frustrated by the parent's failure to accept the "obvious." The temptation may be to convince the parent of the severity of the child's deficits. But the tenacity with which parents cling to an idealized concept of their child suggests that the phases of acceptance may serve an adaptive purpose (McAllister & Vanden Heuvel, 1989). At least initially, there may be a relationship between acceptance of the disability and acceptance of the child. Too rapid a shift toward acceptance of the disability may change the nature of the parent–child relationship. Rather than "pushing" the parents into acceptance, a more appropriate professional role may be to help parents achieve a balance between maintaining hope for their child's future and coping with the child's current status. Providing the parents with direction and with functional roles in the intervention process may also facilitate the coping process.

Choosing an Assessment Strategy

Staging an assessment is much more difficult for infants and toddlers than for school-aged children. To ensure optimal child performance, the school psychologist must be a master at arranging the environment, selecting materials, and adjusting language and style to sustain the child's attention (Bagnato & Neisworth, 1991). For children with mild disabilities, the testing environment is an important factor. Factors

FIGURE 4. Providing feedback to parents.

- Both parents and/or other supporting family members should be present, if possible.

- The infant should be present.

- The psychologist should show acceptance of the infant as a person through physical contact and statements regarding the child's strengths and positive characteristics.

- Jargon, including relatively common professional terms, should be avoided.

- The limits of prognostication and the range of possible outcomes should be explained.

- The family should have as much time as needed to ask questions.

- Parents should be provided with the opportunity to express their feelings but not be required to do so.

- Additional sources of information should be provided.

- The oportunity to contact other parents should be facilitated.

- A follow-up session should be offered.

- The family should be provided with private time at the conclusion of the discussion.

---

that can help elicit ecologically valid information for diagnosis and prescription include:

- A friendly and familiar setting with minimal distractions.

- A small table and chair in which a child can sit with feet on the floor for toddlers or a mat or large blanket for infants.

- The presence of parents to reassure the child.

For children with severe disabilities, adequate seating or body positioning and a variety of multisensory, response-contingent toys as well as sensitivity to the child's strengths may mean the difference between a description of the child's needs and a statement that the child is "untestable."

Staging an assessment for children from birth to three is based on multiples: multiple purposes, multiple measures, multiple sources, multiple settings, and multiple occasions (Bagnato & Neisworth, 1991).

Multiple purposes. Multiple purposes of infant/toddler assessments include confirmation of a developmental problem, description of functioning levels in developmental domains, diagnosis of a developmental disability such as autism or cerebral palsy, and facilitation of appropriate intervention strategies. These goals are not mutually exclusive and diagnosis and prescription should be addressed simultaneously throughout the assessment/intervention process (Teti & Gibbs, 1990).

Multiple measures. To provide diagnostic and prescriptive information based on an accurate assessment of a child's strengths and limitations, a covergent assessment approach is imperative. Norm-ref-

erenced tests for infants and toddlers have been criticized on numerous grounds including:

- Limited utility in program planning and evaluation (Bagnato & Neisworth, 1991).

- Lack of theoretical underpinnings, insensitivity (Cicchetti & Wagner, 1990).

- An overly narrow, unitary construct of development (Cicchetti & Wagner, 1990).

- Lack of adaptation for individuals with various disabilities.

- Exclusion of individuals with disabilities from the norming group (McCune, Kalmanson, Fleck, Glazewski, & Sillari, 1990).

- Developmentally inappropriate expectations for performance "on demand" (Zelazo, 1982).

However, the ability of a test to discriminate children with disabilities from nondisabled children may be more important than the stability of scores over time for the entire population (Ross, 1989). The Bailey Scales of Infant Development and the Mullen Scales of Early Learning are among those norm-referenced instruments that satisfy this criterion (e.g., Maisto & German, 1986).

Play-based assessment and curriculum-based assessment are more useful for identifying instructional strategies and educational goals (Bagnato & Neisworth, 1991; Campbell, 1991). Curriculum-based assessments are also useful for monitoring child progress and the impact of early intervention or special education services on a child's developmental skills. Judgment-based scales allow parents and professionals to quantify their perceptions of a child's developmental skills and progress. These scales are helpful in clarifying ambiguous information provided during more formal observation and assessment. Ecological scales focus on the needs of the family and the quality of the learning and living environment for the child.

By staging an effective covergent assessment, a school psychologist can provide diagnostic information to determine a child's present level of developmental functioning in several different domains or skill areas in addition to a clear understanding of the child's strengths and limitations for determining goals and objectives to be included on the IFSP or IEP.

Testing without tests. LeVan (1990) proposes that standardized testing is an unnatural approach to the assessment of children with special needs. He suggests that observations of a child's natural skills, keeping a clear idea of typical and atypical developmental skills in mind, will provide the school psychologist and infant/early childhood educator with a rich source of diagnostic and prescriptive information. Using grocery shopping as an analogy, LeVan recommends that developmental evaluations can be completed using a shopping list of developmental expectations.

> In the market, goods are shelved in a somewhat orderly fashion based upon group or use. Although the precise arrangement may vary from market to market, there is a general pattern of organization that is recognized by most shoppers. To promote efficiency, the shopper prepares a list to guide the pursuit. Knowing the layout of the market may be helpful in preparation of the list and in procuring the goods. Of course, the list does not map out an exact route. You can start at any point, pick up items as you go, and come back to get what you missed. Bargains can be selected from special displays in any aisle and at any time. (p. 69)

Shopping for developmental skills can be accomplished in much the same way. Developmental skills may be considered in "orderly fashion" according to domain:

- Receptive language skills
- Expressive language skills
- Fine motor skills
- Gross motor skills
- Cognitive/play/early problem solving skills
- Social development
- Temperament

Understanding the "layout" or the patterns of typical development helps in preparing a list of developmental skills to be sampled, and the list ensures that assessment time is used efficiently to gain the necessary information. However, the "route" through the child's developmental skills is not dictated by an instrument or standardized set of procedures and "bargains" are frequent when a child exhibits behaviors spontaneously. Although a school psychologist or other evaluator can develop a list of domains and developmental skills, norm-referenced and curriculum-based measures can also provide samples of skills to be measured. Again, the emphasis in this approach is on the child's behavior and performance with a variety of tools and materials, not on a score on a test.

Neuromotor assessment. School psychology training programs generally do not include assessment of motor development. However, because rolling, sitting, crawling, and walking are major developmental milestones during the first 18 months of life, referral concerns for infant/toddler assessment and intervention often include motor delays. School psychologists can include neuromotor screening or assessment as a part of a comprehensive covergent assessment prior to making a referral to a physician or physical therapist. Several neuromotor screening or assessment tools are available to school psychologists including the Movement Assessment of Infants (Chandler, Andrews, & Swanson, 1980), the Chandler Movement Assessment of Infants-Screening Test (Chandler, in press), and the Milani-Comparetti Motor Development Screening Test (Milani-Comparetti & Gidoni, 1967). Although all require specialized training and extensive experience, neuromotor assessment falls well within the realm of a thorough developmental evaluation. A physical therapist can be helpful in assisting school psychologists with neuromotor screening.

Multiple sources. Information from parents, daycare providers, and medical charts or reports should be included as part of assessment/intervention. Multidisciplinary, transdisciplinary, and interdisciplinary assessment/intervention teams, mandated by IDEA, have become widely accepted methods of identifying the multifaceted needs of very young children. Information from assessment/intervention teams comprised of school psychologists, early intervention developmental specialists, speech pathologists, occupational therapists, physical therapists, and parents can provide a comprehensive view of a child's and family's strengths and needs. At times, two members may want to employ a "four-handed" approach to assessment (two professionals working with the child at the same time). One can keep the child engaged while the other observes, prepares materials, plans assessment strategies, interprets assessment procedures to parents, or elicits comments from the parent. Physical therapists and occupational therapists can be especially helpful to school psychologists working with children with physical disabilities by providing positioning and handling techniques to ensure optimal performance (Bagnato & Neisworth, 1991).

Arena evaluations. Transdisciplinary assessment programs may employ an "arena" approach to assessment/intervention (Woodruff & McGonigel, 1988). Although only one professional and the parent(s) interact with the child during an arena assessment, all members of a transdisciplinary team are present to observe and record information concerning the child's behavior and skills. While the child is expected to interact with only one unfamiliar adult, several or all team members have the opportunity to observe the entire evaluation and can offer a variety of behavioral and developmental perspectives to the assessment.

Multiple settings. The assessment environment can have a profound impact on a very young child's behavior. Infant/toddler assessment takes place in one or more of several locations including the child's home or day care setting, the public or private school building, and/or the clinic or hospital setting. Because young children usually perform better at home than in a school, clinic, or hospital setting, and because assessment of the home environment can be helpful in determining IFSP goals, the preferred assessment setting is in the more familiar environment. However, it can be helpful to observe the child's reaction to an unfamiliar setting during clinic/school/hospital evaluations.

Multiple occasions. Working with children over several sessions is essential with infants and young children. Accurate predictions and diagnostic information can be provided only in the context of progress with intervention over time. Patterns in skills can be observed only with multiple observations and assessment opportunities and will prevent inappropriate labeling and underestimating skill levels in children with developmental delays or disabilities (Bagnato & Neisworth, 1991). In addition, multiple assessment opportunities will allow the school psychologist to observe the dynamics of parent/infant interactions.

Not only are infants and young children sensitive to their environment, they are driven by their basic needs and states. Babies are often available for interaction for very short periods of time. They cannot perform for an evaluator if they are hungry, sleepy, or need a diaper change. Developmental evaluations can occur between diaper changing and bottles, but are seldom completed before an infant fusses for milk and a nap. Toddlers are often tired and fussy during the afternoons, especially if their regular routine includes an afternoon nap. Infant/toddler school psychologists must allow the child's state, needs, and regular routine to dictate the parameters of the assessment/observation session.

Interactive Strategies

Now for the "art" of working with young children: the quality of school psychologist/educator interactions with infants and toddlers during assessment can result in a range of possible outcomes from a clear image of a child's skills and needs on one end of the continuum to a frustrating and unproductive session on the other end. Fear of unfamiliar adults is developmentally appropriate for infants and toddlers. School psychologists can reduce this fear by interacting first with the parents. Children benefit when they have the opportunity to explore the environment or sit on the parent's lap for a few minutes before the evaluator attempts to begin the evaluation. For very slow-to-warm-up children seen in a clinic or school setting, the parents and the child may enter the examining room 5 to 10 minutes before the examiner to allow unrestricted exploration. Figure 5 provides additional interaction strategies to further reduce the effects of stranger anxiety.

> At 10 months of age (6 months adjusted age), J. K. was evaluated by the school psychologist. Although J. K.'s parents reported that he was able to reach out with both hands to grasp a rattle, the school psychologist found that J. K. kept his hands and arms back on the mat and did not reach out for the red ring when he was supine. The school psychologist attempted to encourage J. K. to reach for other, more attractive toys, but to no avail. J. K.'s mother offered her assistance by sitting on the floor and supporting J. K. in a sitting position between her legs. In this position, J. K. reached out actively for the rattle, the red ring, and his own stuffed dog, using smooth and symmetric movements.
>
> J. K. was again evaluated at 30 months of age. When the school psychologist rang the doorbell at J. K.'s home, J. K. ran to hide behind his mother's leg and refused to let go for the first 20 minutes of the visit. The school psychologist talked with J. K.'s mother, smiling occasionally at J. K. as J. K. reached around his mother's legs for a toy. The school psychologist moved to the floor and began exploring J. K.'s toys. When J. K. approached, to provide instructions about his favorite truck, the school psychologist listened attentively and introduced a toy from the bag of developmental assessment materials. J. K. cooperated with the school psychologist for approximately 40 minutes until he became hungry for lunch. Another appointment was scheduled within the week to complete the evaluation.

Report Preparation

Psychological reports are often organized according to tests administered to identify cognitive abilities, academic achievement, processing deficits, and/or emotional disabilities. This traditional format is not appropriate for infant/toddler reports because it fails to communicate information that would be applicable for early intervention programming. Developmentally based reports (Bagnato & Neisworth, 1991) work better because they are organized with headings identifying developmental domains, medical information and recommendations, behavioral obser-

FIGURE 5. Working with very young children.

- Incorporate the child's toys into the developmental evaluation.

- Encourage parents and siblings to assist in eliciting developmental skill. Provide explicit instructions about the developmental skill and possible ways to detect that skill.

- Begin with a brief warm-up period. This period should be long enough to allow the child to engage with the examiner but not so long that the attention span of the child is overtaxed (Paget, 1983).

- INfants and children with significant physical needs perform to the best of their ability when they are placed in comfortable positions in which their attention and physical movements are not restricted. Infants should be placed in the most mature position possible; children with significant physical needs should be positioned with the assistance of parents or physical therapists.

- Infants and very young children provide a small window of opportunity for assessment. Close attention to timing of item presentation is essential to maintain the child's attention and willingness to work. Developmental tasks should be introduced quickly enough to retain the child's attention but not so quickly that the child is overstimulated. Although the examienr should be ready with the next task, the child should not be rushed to move on before completing work with the previous task.

- When working with very young infants or those with significant developmental delays, it is often helpful to dim the lights and reduce extraneous noise or other stimuli. Gentle handling can increase the observation opportunities by reducing the amount of time the examienr or parent must spend comforting a crying or upset baby.

- Some toddlers, especially those who are noncompliant to instructions, will perform when given a choice of activities. In a clinic or school setting, developmental activities can be distributed throughout a large room. The school psychologist can gain a great deal of useful information by observing how children make choices among the activities, how they move from one activity to another, and how long they are able to maintain attention to a single task before moving onto the next activity.

---

vations, and curricular/family goals. Under each heading, information from difference sources can be integrated to provide a clear description of a child's strengths, limitations, and programming needs.

Professional reports seldom communicate in "parent friendly" terms (Bagnato & Neisworth, 1991). Clinical jargon and the use of technical language must be avoided in reports. Even commonly used terms such as "expressive and receptive language," "muscle tone," or "etiology" can be intimidating for parents (Parker & Zuckerman, 1990).

SUMMARY

School psychologists are a valuable resource in the evaluation process with infants and toddlers. Adequate preparation is critical, because evaluating infants and toddlers requires different skills and expectations than those taught in traditional training programs. With appropriate training and experience, school psychologists can be fully prepared for the responsibilities involved in infant/toddler assessment and can function as valuable members of the assessment team.

Because of dramatic developmental changes and behavioral fluctuations of infants and toddlers, psychologists are asked to rely more on professional judgment and the knowledge of parents and other team members in understanding a child's develop-

mental needs. The limited utility of traditional assessment instruments at this level requires the use of multiple measures, sources, settings, and occasions to address the assessment goals. Families must have the opportunity to be full participants in all phases of the evaluation/intervention process. The emphasis is on family-centered decision making and assessment as an initial step in the intervention process. Providing an additional challenge, infant/toddler school psychologists must be comfortable with medical issues that confront young children with disabilities. Participating in the team assessment/intervention process of infants and toddlers is an exciting and important new role for school psychologists.

REFERENCES

Bagnato, S. J., & Neisworth, J. T. (1991). *Assessment for early intervention: Best practices for professionals.* New York: Guilford.

Bagnato, S. J., & Neisworth, J. T. (1994). A national study of the social and treatment "invalidity" of intelligence testing for early intervention. *School Psychology Quarterly, 9*(2), 81–102.

Bailey, D. B., & Simeonsson, R. J. (1988). Assessing the needs of families with handicapped infants. *Journal of Special Education, 22,* 117–127.

Bailey, D. B., & Wolery, M. (1989). *Assessing infants and preschoolers with handicaps.* Columbus, OH: Merrill.

Beckman, P. J., & Bristol, M. M. (1991). Issues in developing the IFSP: A framework for establishing family outcomes. *Topics in Early Childhood Special Education, 11*(3), 19–31.

Bricker, D. (1993). *The assessment, evaluation, and programming system for infants and children. Vol. 1: AEPS measurement for birth to three years.* Baltimore: Paul H. Brookes.

Bricker, D., Squires, J., Kaminski, R., & Mounts, L. (1988). The validity, reliability, and cost of a parent-completed questionnaire system to evaluate at-risk infants. *Journal of Pediatric Psychology, 13*(1), 55–68.

Calnan, M. (1984). Clinical uncertainty: Is it a problem in the doctor–patient relationship? *Sociology of Health and Illness, 6,* 74–85.

Campbell, P. H. (1991). Evaluation and assessment in early intervention for infants and toddlers. *Journal of Early Intervention, 15*(1), 36–45.

Chandler, L. S. (in press). *The Chandler Movement Assessment of Infants-Screening Test: A manual.* Rolling Bay, WA: Infant Movement Research.

Chandler, L. S., Andrews, M., & Swanson, M. (1980). *The Movement Assessment of Infants: A manual.* Rolling Bay, WA: Infant Movement Research.

Cicchetti, D., & Wagner, S. (1990). Alternative assessment strategies for the evaluation of infants and toddlers: An organizational perspective. In S. J. Meisels & J. P. Shonkoff (Eds.), *Handbook of early childhood interventions* (pp. 219–245). New York: Cambridge University Press.

Dunst, C. J., Cooper, C. S., Weeldreyer, J. C., Snyder, K. D., & Chase, J. H. (1988). Family needs scale. In C. J. Dunst, C. M. Trivette, & A. G. Deal (Eds.), *Enabling and empowering families: Principals and guidelines for practice* (p. 151). Cambridge, MA: Brookline.

Epps, S., & Jackson, B. (1991). Professional preparation of psychologists for family-centered service delivery to at-risk infants and toddlers. *School Psychology Review, 20*(4), 498–509.

Fenson, L., Dale, P. S., Reznick, J. S., Thal, D., Bates, E., Hartung, J. P., Pethick, S., & Reilly, J. S. (1991). *Technical Manual for the MacArthur Communicative Development Inventories.* San Diego, CA: San Diego University.

Gould, S. J. (1977). *Ontogeny and phylogeny.* Cambridge, MA: Belknap Press.

Gradel, K., Thompson, M. S., & Sheehan, R. (1981). Parental and professional agreement in early childhood assessment. *Topics in Early Childhood Special Education, 1*(2), 31–39.

Harbin, G. L., Gallagher, J. J., & Terry, D. V. (1991). Defining the eligibility population: Policy issues and challenges. *Journal of Early Intervention, 15*(1), 13–20.

Harris, S. L., & Powers, M. D. (1984). Behavior therapists look at the impact of an autistic child on the family system. In E. Schopler & G. B. Meisbov (Eds.), *Effects of autism on the family.* New York: Plenum Press.

Harrison, H. (1983). *The premature baby book: A parents' guide to coping and caring in the first years.* New York: Martin's Press.

Krahn, G. L., Hallum, A., & Kime, C. (1993). Are there good ways to give "bad news"? *Pediatrics, 91*(3), 578–582.

Kubler-Ross, E. (1969). *On death and dying.* London: Macmillan.

LeVan, R. (1990). Clinical sampling in the assessment of young, handicapped children: Shopping for skills. *Topics in Early Childhood Special Education, 10*(3), 65–79.

Lichtenstein, R., & Ireton, H. (1984). *Preschool screening.* New York: Grune & Stratton.

Maisto, A. A., & German, M. L. (1986). Reliability, predictive validity, and interrelationships of early assessment indices used with developmentally delayed infants and children. *Journal of Clinical Child Psychology, 15*(4), 327–332.

Marshall, R. M., Wuori, D. F., Hudler, M., & Cranston, C. S. (1987). Physician/school teacher collaboration. *Clinical Pediatrics, 26*(1), 524–527.

McAllister, J. R. (1987, March). Identifying special needs preschoolers: Child care workers' perceptions. Paper presented at the National Association of School Psychologists Convention, New Orleans.

McAllister, J. R., & Vanden Heuvel, E. K. (1989). Support groups for parents of young handicapped children. *Preschool Interests, 5,* 3–4, 6.

McCune, L., Kalmanson, B., Fleck, M. B., Glazewski, B., & Sillari, J. (1990). An interdisciplinary model of infant assessment. In S. J. Meisels & J. P. Shonkoff (Eds.), *Handbook of early childhood intervention* (pp. 219–245). New York: Cambridge University Press.

McGonigel, M. J., Kaufman, R. K., & Johnson, B. H. (1991). A family-centered process for the individualized family service plan. *Journal of Early Intervention, 15*(1), 46–56.

McLinden, S. E., & Prasse, D. P. (1991). Providing services to infants and toddlers under PL 99-457: Training needs of school psychologists. *School Psychology Review, 20*(1), 37–48.

Milani-Comparetti, A., & Gidoni, E. (1967). Routine developmental examination in normal and retarded children. *Developmental Medicine and Child Neurology, 9,* 631–638.

Minor, S., Minor, J., & Williams, P. (1983). A participant modeling procedure to train parents of developmentally disabled infants. *Journal of Psychology, 115,* 107–111.

Morse, M. T. (1990). P.L. 94-142 and P.L. 99-457: Considerations for coordination between the health and the educational system. *Children's Health Care, 19*(4), 213–218.

Murray, J. N. (1985). Best practices in interpreting psychological assessment data to parents. In A. Thomas & J. Grimes (Eds.), *Best practices in school psychology* (pp. 415–429). Kent, OH: National Association of School psychologists.

National Center for Clinical Infant Programs. (1985). *Training and manpower issues in services to disabled and at-risk infants, toddlers and their families.* Washington, DC: Author.

National Association of State Directors of Special Education Incorporated (NASDE). (1986). "EHA Amendments of 1986" become law; Establishes new partnerships for early intervention programs. *Liaison Bulletin, 12*(12), 1–15.

Newborg, J., Stock, J. R., Wnek, L., Guidubaldi, J., & Svinicki, J. (1988). *Battelle Developmental Inventory.* Allen, TX: DLM.

Paget, K. D. (1983). The individual examining situation: Basic considerations for preschool children. In K. D. Paget & B. A. Bracken (Eds.), *Psychoeducational assessment of preschool children* (pp. 51–61). New York: Grune & Stratton.

Paget, K. D. (1990). Best practices in the assessment of competence in preschool-age children. In A. Thomas & J. Grimes (Eds.), *Best practices in school psychology–II* (pp. 107–119). Washington, DC: National Association of School Psychologists.

Parker, S. J., & Zuckerman, B. S. (1990). Therapeutic aspects of the assessment process. In S. J. Meisels & J. P. Shonkoff (Eds.), *Handbook of early childhood intervention* (pp. 350–369). New York: Cambridge University Press.

Rogers, B. T., Booth, L. J., Duffy, L. C., & Hassan, M. B. (1992). Parents' developmental perceptions and expectations for their high-risk infants. *Journal of Developmental and Behavioral Pediatrics, 13*(2), 102–107.

Ross, G. (1989). Some thoughts on the value of infant tests for assessing and predicting mental ability. *Journal of Developmental and Behavioral Pediatrics, 10*(1), 44–47.

Sameroff, A. J., & Chandler, M. J. (1975). Reproductive risk and the continuum of caretaking casualty. In F. D. Horowitz, M. Hetherington, S. Scarr-Salapatek, & G. Siegel (Eds.), *Review of child development research* (Vol. 4, pp. 187–244). Chicago: University of Chicago Press.

Shonkoff, J. P., & Meisels, S. J. (1991). Defining eligibility for services under PL 99-457. *Journal of Early Intervention, 15*(1), 21–35.

Teglasi, H. (1985). Best practices in interpreting psychological assessment data to parents. In A. Thomas & J. Grimes (Eds.), *Best practices in school psychology* (pp. 415–429). Kent, OH: National Association of School Psychologists.

Teti, D. M., & Gibbs, E. D. (1990). Infant assessment: Historical antecedents and contemporary issues. In E. D. Gibbs & D. M. Teti (Eds.), *Interdisciplinary assessment of infants: A guide for early intervention professionals* (pp. 3–13). Baltimore: Paul H. Brookes.

Woodruff, G., & McGonigel, M. J. (1988). Early intervention team approaches: The transdisciplinary model. In J. B. Jordan, J. J. Gallagher, P. L. Hutinger, & M. B. Karnes (Eds.), *Early childhood special education: Birth to three* (pp. 164–181). Reston, VA: The Council for Exceptional Children.

Zelazo, P. R. (1982). Alternative assessment procedures for handicapped infants and toddlers: Theoretical and practical issues. In D. Bricker (Ed.), *Intervention with at-risk and handicapped infants: From research to application* (pp. 107–128). Baltimore: University Park Press.

ANNOTATED BIBLIOGRAPHY

Bagnato, S. J., & Neisworth, J. T. (1991). *Assessment for early intervention: Best practices for professionals.* New York: Guilford Press.
The role of the family in assessment and intervention of infants and toddlers is emphasized in IDEA. This book, which has been described as "essential reading" for school psychologists and early intervention specialists, provides a clear understanding of how parents and professionals can work together to assess a child's needs and design an appropriate educational program. The focus of the book is assessment for early intervention; the scope of the book moves beyond test administration and interpretation to describe family-focused assessment in which the child's developmental skills and needs are the emphasis. Covergent assessment is discussed in detail as well as testing without tests, curriculum-based developmental assessment, and professional/family collaboration.

Blackman, J. A. (1990). *Medical aspects of developmental disabilities in children birth to three (2nd ed.).* Rockville, MD: Aspen.
School psychologists involved in infant/toddler assessment/intervention will meet a new challenge in dealing with the significant medical needs of these children. This book provides a summarized compilation of medical information related to children with special needs. In clear, easily understood chapters, Blackman provides descriptions, causes, incidence, methods of detection, and implications for education of nearly 40 medical conditions that occur in infants and toddlers with developmental delays or disabilities. Included in the chapter are prevalent conditions with which school psychologists often have knowledge and experiences including Down syndrome, myelomeningocele, anemia, and sensory impairments in addition to some conditions which may be new to psychologists just becoming involved in early intervention including congenital infections, bronchopulmonary dysplasia, environmental teratogens, and perinatal injury.

Cohen, M. A., & Gross, P. J. (1979). *The developmental resource: Behavioral sequences for assessment and program planning (Vol. 1).* New York: Grune & Stratton.
Cohen and Gross translate the literature on a variety of developmental skills into sequences of developmental tasks from birth to 6 years of age across multiple domains, including sensorimotor/early cognitive, gross and fine motor, language, social, and self-help/adaptive living skills. This book provides a base of typical infant/child development from which to build a "shopping list" of skills to observe during developmental evaluation.

Flehmig, I. (1992). *Normal infant development and borderline deviations: Early diagnosis and therapy.* New York: Thieme.
School psychologists must be familiar with normal and deviant patterns of development when evaluating infants and toddlers. This book details normal motor development from birth to 18 months, neuromotor assessment strategies, and clear descriptions of deviating motor development in infancy. Photographs of infants provide clear understanding of primitive reflexes and normal and aberrant motor development. A chapter on handling includes tips for appropriate and inappropriate handling of infants, especially those with neuromotor problems. This is an excellent guide for school psychologists who will be involved with infant assessment.

Gibbs, E. D., & Teti, D. M. (1990). *Interdisciplinary assessment of infants: A guide for early intervention professionals.* Baltimore: Paul H. Brookes.
Assessment/intervention with infants involves understanding a variety of skills and behaviors. Information concerning infant neuromotor assessment, cognitive/language/developmental assessment, social assessment, and the assessment process is comprehensively compiled in this book, providing a valuable resource for educators and school psychologists.

Harrison, H. (1983). *The premature baby book: A parents' guide to coping and caring in the first years.* New York: St. Martin's Press.
Premature babies comprise a large subsection of the infants and toddlers considered "at-risk" under IDEA. Although many premature babies develop normally, developmental and neuromotor monitoring is important during the first years of a premature baby's life. This book is designed for parents of premature babies but can be useful to school psychologists or other team members who are involved with assessment and intervention of infants and children. Chapters include information about how parents cope with the birth of a premature baby, medical problems that arise with premature deliveries, and developmental delays associated with prematurity.

67

Best Practices in the Academic Assessment of Secondary Students

Kathryn Clark Gerken
The University of Iowa

OVERVIEW

"Ten years after *A Nation at Risk*, we still lack the will and commitment to reduce the risks that imperil our children" (Crosby, 1993, p. 598). Crosby also states that it is as if society is allowing a school bus full of screaming children to slide out of control down an icy hill. I believe that school bus contains children of all ages, but the adolescents in that bus may be at an even greater risk than the other children. Adolescence is typically associated with great risks in the area of health and education. Takanishi (1993b) reports that adolescents today face greater risks to their current and future health than ever before. For example, mental disorders are the major cause of disabilities among adolescents ages 10 to 18 (National Center for Education in Maternal and Child Health, 1990); more adolescents, especially before age 15, are experimenting with drugs (Gans & Blyth, 1990); U.S. adolescents are unique among adolescents in developed nations in their exposure to violence, especially homicide (Hammond & Yung, 1993) and in their rates of pregnancy (Moore, 1992). Poverty, homelessness, and disintegration of families have all increased. A current review of research on adolescent development suggests that the early adolescent years mark the beginning of a downward spiral for some individuals, a spiral leading to academic failure and school dropout (Eccles et al., 1993). Hahn (1987) reports that overall dropout rates for adolescents may not have increased, but the dropout rates in large cities range from 40 to 60% of the population. Dropout rates are much higher for adolescents who (a) come from low-income and single-parent households; (b) are behind in grade level and older than classmates; (c) have poor academic performance; (d) have frequent detentions and suspensions; (e) are pregnant; (f) believe that work or military service is their only alternative to failure in school; or (b) have learning disabilities, emotional problems, and language difficulties.

Whether the situations confronting today's children are called "childhood genocide" (Reynolds, 1992) or a waste of lives (Hahn, 1987; Takanishi, 1993a), it is clear that changes are needed. Multiple layers of structural change are needed. Only by working together across the boundaries created by society (school vs. community vs. family, etc.) can today's educators hope to effect positive changes in the lives of a large number of adolescents. It is imperative that all education professionals make a commitment to support the full development of all adolescents into productive adults. Crosby (1993) states that in the land of the free, many of our children are not free:

> Some are not free to receive equal opportunities. Some are not free because they are minorities. Some are not free because of poverty. Some are not free because they are teenage mothers. Some are not free because their families have disintegrated. Some are not free because of violence, drugs, and guns in their environment. All of them are not free because we are not willing to free them. (p. 604)

The seriousness of the problems encountered during adolescence is magnified for those adolescents already at risk. The results of the 1992 National Assessment of Educational Progress (NAEP; Elliott, 1993) shows that, for students in the eighth grade, there were significant decreases in mathematics performance for "disadvantaged urban" students' average proficiency as well as for the proportion of these students at or above the basic level. Foertsch's (1992) report on the 1990 NAEP reading assessment focused on the factors influencing literacy achievement. She found that the amount of reading students did in school and the amount of reading that students did out of school were positively related to their reading achievement. Yet, students reported doing relatively little reading in school or out of school. It was also found that students who reported more home support for literacy had higher average achievement. Students reported somewhat less access to reading materials in the home in 1990 than in 1988. Foertsch (1992) also reported that in spite of extensive research suggesting that effective reading instruction includes moving toward more opportunities for combining reading and writing activities, workbooks remain a prevalent approach to instruction in reading. Students in fourth, eighth, and twelfth grades all had difficulty in constructing thoughtful responses to questions asking them to elaborate or defend their interpretations. Also, as the grade level increased, the frequency of the use of the library decreased. The majority of the eighth graders said they went to the library on a monthly basis and most twelfth graders reported only yearly use of the library.

School psychologists who work with adolescents can begin to "free" some of the at-risk adolescents by utilizing a problem-solving approach in which interventions are student specific and outcome focused. There are a variety of problem-solving models in existence. However, the steps in the IDEAL (Bransford & Stein, 1984) model are the basic steps in every model: **I**dentify the behavior; **D**efine the Problem; **E**xplore intervention options; **A**ct on the plan; and **L**ook at results. The Department of Education, State of Iowa (1993) believes that the critical components of the problem-solving process are parent involvement, problem statement, systematic data collection, problem analysis, goal, intervention plan development, intervention plan implementation, progress monitoring, and decision making. Problem-solving practices can be used to identify problems and intervene with large numbers of students or with individual students, but they must be adapted to fit the nature of the problem. Solving one problem at a time in cooperation with the adolescent, his or her family, and the community should lead over time to the desired structural changes in America's schools, families, and communities.

The purpose of this chapter is to provide guidelines for assessing the academic skills of adolescents. It is apparent that academic assessment should not be done in isolation. Therefore, a comprehensive assessment process that leads to effective intervention is presented.

BASIC CONSIDERATIONS

Huebner (1993) reporting on the results of a national survey of school psychologists serving secondary schools, noted that approximately three-quarters of them were satisfied with their functioning in the secondary schools. The data suggested that job satisfaction increased as time spent conducting individual and family counseling increased and time spent in assessment decreased. Thus these results appear similar to those in the 1970s that said psychologists were dissatisfied with spending much of their time conducting assessment. An unknown regarding this survey is how assessment was defined. It is also interesting to note which special skills or knowledge the school psychologists thought should be in a training program and what the psychologists perceived as their three greatest needs in terms of professional development. Counseling was the most frequently listed component for a training program (73 persons), then crisis intervention (36) and consultation (29). (In fifth

place was adolescent psychology [19]. Despite the fact that professionals increasingly recognize how little is known about adolescent development, these respondents were more interested in specific learning techniques than the foundation upon which these techniques should be based.) The greatest needs the psychologists reported were, in order, general counseling skills (46), crisis intervention (26), and consultation (23). Huebner (1993) concluded that school psychologists need to be prepared to offer a diversified array of professional services.

The best way to be prepared to offer a diversified and appropriate array of services is to

- Have an understanding of the school environment and the social environments in which adolescents live.

- Have knowledge of current research in adolescent development, theories of learning, basic measurement theory, and the theories underlying skill development in reading, writing, and arithmetic.

- Have supervised experience in applying this knowledge during coursework and field experiences.

A psychologist working with adolescents needs to be interested in adolescents and knowledgeable about their interests and needs if he or she hopes to prevent the steep decline in academic and social behavior observed in many adolescents (those already receiving special services; those not identified earlier; those already lost to dismal, intractable academic failure; and those who have serious social/emotional problems). Eccles et al. (1993) argue that optimal development takes place when there is a good stage-environment fit between the needs of developing individuals and the opportunities afforded them by their social environments. It is the responsibility of school psychologists and other professionals who work with adolescents to try to help teachers and parents provide an environment that changes in the right way and at the right place. This is a difficult task, but one school psychologists should be academically and experientially prepared to handle. A needs assessment within the school, classroom, and home should be conducted to determine the interest and support of administrators, support personnel, classroom teachers, and parents for improving academic assessment and intervention for adolescents. Junior and senior high school teachers often feel overworked and harried and unable to give individual attention to students (feelings often shared by parents of adolescents). To be effective in meeting the needs of adolescents with academic problems, the school psychologist must first be effective in determining ways to "fit" improved assessment and intervention into the already existing culture of the school and home rather than assuming the culture can be changed.

School psychologists need to continuously update themselves relative to research on adolescent development; academic and social curricula for adolescents; and technology used to set up screening, assessment, and intervention programs.

BEST PRACTICES

Screening and diagnosis of academic problems must be improved because too many adolescents have academic skills far below their age-mates before intervention is attempted. There is no reasonable justification for this because empirical support exists for providing early intervention to prevent or at least reduce some of the negative effects of academic difficulties.

Definitions

There are numerous terms for referring to the collection of data used to describe an individual's or group's level of knowledge, performance, or achievement. *Assessment, evaluation, measurement,* and *test* are the terms most frequently used. Sometimes they are used interchangeably when they should not be. Wood (1987) states that "assessment is regarded as providing a comprehensive account of an individual's functioning in the widest sense — drawing on a variety of evidence, qualitative as well as quantitative, and therefore going beyond the testing of cognitive skills by pencil-and-paper techniques, which for many people is measurement" (p. 2). Webb (1992) states that in education the term measurement is restricted to a quantitative description of student behavior. He believes evaluation is the systematic collection of evidence to help make decisions regarding students' learning, material development, and program. For the purpose of this chapter, problem-solving assessment refers to the comprehensive accounting of an individual's functioning within the academic areas or in the application of academic skills. Problem-solving assessment is an approach used to collect the data needed to solve problems for individuals or groups. Testing, measurement, and evaluation are important aspects of that approach.

Disability versus Deficiency

Many adolescents exhibit significant difficulties in academic work. It is extremely important to pinpoint the sources of these difficulties and identify and define the specific problem. Appropriate intervention may be dependent on whether the student is having difficulties due to

- Environmental factors such as limited exposure to the material, cultural expectations based on student characteristics, and inadequate instruction.

- Individual characteristics such as limited ability to think abstractly, anxiety and other affective concerns, inefficient learning strategies, inability to retrieve information, poor attention span, low motivation, impaired communication, and the like.

- The interaction of environmental and individual variables.

The intervention plan for a student with a deficiency in math due to not ever having spent the time necessary to master the basic multiplication facts will differ from the plan for the student who has spent considerable time attempting to master the multiplication facts but has a specific disability in retrieving nonmeaningful material. A specific disability would require that in addition to a positive and effective instructional environment, compensatory skills be developed. Whereas, a student who has an academic deficiency but not a specific disability may simply need to receive effective instruction for the existing gaps in academic skills and/or be taught appropriate study skills. Assessment and intervention in the 1990s still need to be individualized.

Screening

Reynolds (1992) believes that literacy, social and civic behavior, and self-dependence are the cultural imperatives in modern America. Schools are being challenged to teach all students in the domains of these cultural imperatives; yet many times the students' difficulties in these areas are not identified at the incipient stage and become "serious" or "severe" before intervention begins. The information needed to screen for problems in these areas is usually already available as is the technology to make such information accessible. Four curriculum areas appear to accommodate the needs of all secondary age students: (a) academic knowledge and skills; (b) vocational knowledge and skills; (c) independent living knowledge and skills; and (d) social knowledge and skills. A thorough assessment and intervention plan for an adolescent must begin with screening for problems in each of these areas and then focus on the area of greatest need. (Assessments of adaptive behavior, social/emotional status and vocational skills are covered in other chapters in this book.) A screening system should be in place at every school level, but it is imperative for adolescents. Educational professionals cannot wait for adolescents to be referred or be placed in more restrictive environments before attempting to pinpoint their academic problems and effecting positive changes for them.

Gerken and Winslow-Garvin (1993) created an "early warning system" to identify at-risk students:

- Classroom teachers completed a School Behavior Rating Scale for every student.

- Support teaching staff (art, media, music, and physical education) selected students the staff believed to be "at risk."

- Parents were asked to complete a Home Behavior Rating Scale.

- The students in Grades 2 to 6 completed the Piers-Harris Children's Self-Concept Scale.

- File reviews were conducted to record absences, number of school changes, health problems, frequent trips to the office because of health complaints, information on whether the students were on medication, reports of academic difficulties, test scores, reported social/emotional difficulties, removal from classroom, parent and teacher comments regarding academic and/or social difficulties, classroom management plans, intervention within the classroom, intervention outside of the school, letters to and from parents regarding academic and/or behavioral concerns, removal from the classroom and/or school, referrals for special services within or outside the school (child study team, speech, Chapter 1, ESL, school psychologist, guidance counselor, social worker, etc.).

The four major sources of information about the students were teachers, parents, self, and cumulative folders. Students were identified as "in need of intervention" if their names appeared on the at-risk list from at least two of the four sources. Verification of need for intervention was done by communicating with all concerned persons. Reynolds, Zetlin, and Wang (1993) created a "20/20 Analysis" to identify students showing the least (below 20th percentile) and most (above 20th percentile) progress toward important objectives of education in a school. The steps for performing 20/20 analysis were

1. Select a dimension of learning to be used.

2. Identify the grade and school-wide percentile distribution compared to national norms.

3. Identify the percentile cutoffs of the high 20% and the low 20% for each grade level.

They chose reading as the dimension of school learning for analysis because it was a major concern of the school staff with whom they were working. Although some students receiving special education services were not identified via this method, it did uncover others not receiving services who would benefit from intensive help in basic subjects. Of the students scoring below the 6th percentile (national) in reading, 68% ($n = 89$) were not receiving any intensive forms of instruction. A secondary school could build other steps into this approach which would verify the need for intervention. This chapter's Appendix A presents a model for assessing the academic skills of secondary students that is based on the research presented here and on the author's experiences working with students and schools.

It is necessary to check health, vision, and hearing before initiating other assessment. Task-related skills, vocational goals and skills, and social skills of secondary students are all part of the academic assessment process.

Diagnosis

If the secondary school has a screening process in place, the general problem area will be identified. However, with or without the screening process, it will be necessary to pinpoint the problem area, conduct appropriate assessment, determine priorities and resources for intervention, initiate changes needed, monitor progress, and initiate additional changes if needed. The purpose of assessment at any level is to effect positive changes for the person with the presenting problem. The assessment "tool box" of school psychologists should contain many different tools, as the actual assessment conducted should be dependent on the specific problem that needs to be solved. Far too often information is collected that education staff already possess, do not need, or will not use. Many times assessment may never need to go beyond direct observation and record review.

Numerous individual and group achievement tests were developed or revised in the 1980s in an attempt to improve their standardization procedures, make the format and content more relevant to what is being taught in the schools, and use alternative techniques to pinpoint areas of concern. Many students' academic needs are being ignored because there is insufficient direct observation, review of work samples and past records, use of interviews, error pattern analysis, task analysis, checklists, self-report inventories, and curriculum-based assessment. Valencia, McGinley, and Pearson's 1990 chapter on literacy assessment provides basic guidelines for good assessment across all basic skill areas. They state that assessment needs to be put back in the hands of those most affected by it — students and teachers — and that assessment should be a natural part of the teaching/learning process, not something added on or imposed as an afterthought. The emphasis in the 1990s is on contextualized assessment (Ruddell, 1993; Valencia et al., 1990) that has the following attributes:

1. Focuses on learning.

2. Is equitable.

3. Is consistent with the aims of the system, the school, and the curriculum.

4. Recognizes the limitations of assessment methods.

5. Reduces competition and increases cooperation in the classroom.

6. Includes participation by students.

7. Includes consistent and meaningful reporting.

8. Is continuous.

9. Is multidimensional.

10. Is collaborative.

11. Must be grounded in knowledge.

12. Must be anchored in genuine tasks and purposes (authentic).

Appropriate assessment should result in

1. Insight into the substance and extent of students' content knowledge.

2. Understanding of which literacy skills students need to learn in order to function effectively in various subject areas.

3. An indication of what the teacher needs to do to assist or guide students in the classroom.

4. Identification of students who may need additional evaluation or assistance outside the classroom.

If the screening process has indicated a student has an academic problem, the diagnostic process in Appendix A needs to be implemented. Parents/guardians should be involved in the screening process and in every step of the diagnostic process. A decision must be made as to which additional techniques will be used to collect data and who will collect the data. School psychologists, parents, other support personnel, and classroom teachers need to work together to determine what information each will gather. The classroom teacher will usually be better prepared to do curriculum-based assessment in a content area than the school psychologist. But the school psychologist may have a better understanding of the psychology of learning and can serve as a consultant in both the assessment and intervention phases.

Reading

The most essential basic skill needed in any school curriculum is reading; yet content area teachers often find themselves confronted by students who vary considerably in their development of and ability to apply the skills necessary to read and understand content area materials. Thus, it becomes imperative that content area teachers learn to recognize the extent to which students can apply reading skills to the printed materials they encounter. Farr, Tully, and Pritchard (1989) state that there are six categories of information content area teachers need to know about their students in order to plan for instruction:

- Students' instructional reading levels.

- Strategies that students use when they encounter specialized or technical vocabulary.

- Students' competence with literal, inferential, and critical levels of comprehension.

- Students' background knowledge of the subject area.

- Students' skills with study techniques.

- Students' interests and attitudes.

Often, content area teachers have not had coursework on the reading process or on the assessment of reading skills. Thus, school psychologists need to assist the teachers in determining if students have the skills necessary to succeed in a particular content area. How can such determinations be made? Henk (1993) believes that the contemporary view of reading has forced education professionals to look beyond diverse aspects of the reader to other critical reader variables such as prior knowledge of the topic; attitude towards reading; school and home-based reading habits; topical interests; and the use of before-, during-, and after-reading strategies. He also makes it clear that the analysis does not stop with the reader. Text variables such as conceptual difficulty, genre, organization of the text, its physical features, author's style and intent, and the appeal of the text must be examined along with contextual variables such as where and when reading takes place, the purpose of the reader, the nature of the task, and the reader's previous or current instruction.

The contemporary view of reading is that it is a dynamic interaction among the characteristics of the particular reader, the attributes of a specific text, and the context in which the reading occurs (Henk, 1993). The assessment of reading must go beyond the administration of any one assessment tool. It has been generally accepted that assessment of prior knowledge will contribute to a reading diagnosis, but no one method of assessment has been agreed on. Reading strategies are also viewed as important components of the reading process, but there has been little done on assessing reading strategies.

Three assessment tools that aspire to assess reading processes versus products are miscue analysis, a system for evaluating oral reading errors; think alouds, a form of verbal self-report; and inserted questions, questions embedded within a passage to assess hypothesis testing and prediction abilities. Miscue analysis and think alouds have been used in reading assessment, whereas inserted questions have been used more for instruction than assessment. Additional assessment tools that have recently emerged are the use of authentic texts; assessment of reading habits and attitudes; and informal, dynamic, and portfolio assessments.

Informal Reading Inventories (IRIs). The assessment of the reading skills of secondary students can be done thoroughly only if the informal reading inventory used is based on the student's content area skills. A format developed by Readence, Bean, and Baldwin (1983) contains the sections of a typical Content Area Reading Inventory (CARI):

I. Textual Reading/Study Aids

  A. Internal aids

    1. Table of contents

    2. Index

    3. Glossary

    4. Chapter introduction/summaries

    5. Pictorial information

    6. Other pertinent aids

  B. External aids

    1. Card catalog

    2. Reader's guide

    3. Encyclopedias

    4. Other pertinent aids

II. Vocabulary Knowledge

  A. Recall

  B. Contextual meanings

III. Comprehension

  A. Text-explicit information

  B. Text-implicit information

  C. Author organization

Farr, Tully, and Pritchard (1989) report that each main section of a CARI contains 20 to 25 questions. Each section uses the student's textbooks. The comprehension section is a passage about 3 or 4 pages in length taken from the textbook. Both literal and inferential questions are to be asked. The CARI is used to examine performance in responding to the different kinds of tasks. The teacher sets the criteria for determining whether the students can successfully complete the reading and study tasks required in a course or unit of instruction.

Other Informal Reading Inventories (IRIs) are developed from students, textbooks, or any other reading materials. The IRIs are used to determine independent, instructional, and frustrational levels of reading. General guidelines for developing more traditional IRIs are available in Hammill and Bartel (1990). Critical reviews of the use of IRIs suggest that several problems limit their use:

- The criteria for evaluating IRI performance are subjective and arbitrary.

- Selecting passages from a graded reading will not accurately guarantee a progressing range of reading difficulty.

- The examiner needs to have considerable knowledge about reading in order to record errors and make judgments about a student's performance.

- IRIs are not as useful at the upper grade levels as they are at the lower grade levels because of differences in reading material.

- Background information takes on greater importance.

- Oral and silent reading appear to be less similar at the upper grade levels (Farr & Carey, 1986).

Decoding. The relationship between decoding and comprehension is not a simple one, as each enables the other and neither should be ignored. The four subskill areas that need to be examined in word recognition skills are basic sight vocabulary, phonics, structural analysis, and word meaning. When measured, word recognition should be assessed in a way that enhances instruction. A majority of reading tests contain word recognition subtests, but just as there are numerous theories and methods of teaching word recognition, there are numerous testing methods also. Knowledge of the meaning of words is considered by many to be the most important of the word recognition skills. Word recognition skills should be assessed on context as much as possible. Therefore, do not use nonsense words to determine the word recognition skills of adolescents. Any word recognition test should be considered just a sample of the many word recognition behaviors that could be tested. The test should be of adequate length to ensure stable results.

Howell and Morehead (1987) provide a format for evaluating decoding that was adapted here for assessing the secondary-age student (see Appendix B).

Comprehension. There are six common approaches to measuring comprehension: (a) asking questions requiring either recall or recognition answers; (b) having students paraphrase; (c) having students retell a story exactly as heard; (d) having students fill in missing words (cloze technique); (e) having students select the correct word to complete a sentence (mazes); and (f) asking students to read for one minute each of three different 250-word passages that have been selected from their own curriculum (oral reading rate).

Howell, Fox, and Morehead (1993) indicate that there is no simple best procedure for assessing comprehension and that one needs to use more than one method across texts of various styles. They have developed a "Comprehension Status Sheet" which helps identify the comprehension strategies and enabling skills a student has. If the results of survey tests indicate that comprehension is a problem, comprehension within the student's own materials should be assessed. Is the student having comprehension problems because of a deficit in background knowledge, decoding skills, vocabulary, language syntax, or comprehension strategies? General and specific guidelines for determining the cause of the problem (Choate et al., 1992; Howell et al., 1993) and for planning interventions (Choate et al., 1992; Howell et al., 1993; Masters, Mori, & Mori, 1993) are available.

Written Expression

Poteet (1980) defines written expression as "a visual representation of thoughts, feelings, and ideas using symbols of the writer's language system for the purpose of communication or recording" (p. 88). The components of written expression are usually thought of as handwriting, spelling, mechanics, usage, and ideation. It has been generally accepted that there is a hierarchy of written expression and that the expression of ideas through writing is the last of the skill areas acquired by students. However, a view of writing as an interrelated set of motoric, cognitive, and social responses has emerged during the 1980s and 1990s. This view has had an impact on the way writing is taught (Morocco, Dalton, & Tivnan, 1992) and should have an impact on the way it is assessed.

The minimum desired competencies in written expression are that students write legibly and express their thoughts in writing well enough for others to understand them. If concern about any aspect of written expression is noted during the screening process, the steps outlined in Appendix A need to be carried out.

It is necessary for the psychologist to know (a) which writing skills have already been introduced to the student, (b) which skills are appropriate for the student's grade placement, (c) the requirements of the writing tasks the student has failed, (d) the intervention programs and techniques available to the student, and (e) the student's desire to perform writing tasks.

It is possible to use the student's role in communication as an instructional and assessment tool. Students need to make the purpose of their writing clear; participate in the processes of planning, reviewing, revising, and transcribing; and produce a product that is accurate and easily understood. Fluency, syntactic maturity, vocabulary, content, and writing conventions can each be observed and measured. Formal and informal assessment techniques have been used to assess these products. If writing is viewed as an integrated process, then the assessment of it should occur when students are completing a variety of writing tasks.

Morocco, Dalton, and Tivnan (1992) report that good writing instruction includes (a) engaging students in the full composing process; (b) engaging them in a real intent to communicate; (c) helping students become fluent in expressing their ideas; and (d) fostering listening and peer response skills. These principles can be met only if there is balanced in-

struction which includes explicit instruction in the writing process and explicit instruction in the mechanics of writing. Fluency, sentence combining, and accuracy are also aspects of writing that must be taught. Choate et al. (1992), Howell et al. (1993), Ruddell (1993), and Valencia et al. (1993) contain excellent inventories, surveys, scales, checklists, charts, and sample items that can be used in writing instruction and assessment. "Assessment, Consultation and Intervention for Writing Problems" is a useful annotated bibliography (Berninger & Hooper, 1993).

Mathematics

Despite the general improvement in students' mathematics performance on the National Assessment of Educational Progress (NAEP) between 1990 and 1992 (Mullis, Dossey, Owen, & Phillips, 1993), large disparities exist across demographic groups. More than one-third of the students at Grades 4, 8, and 12 did not reach the lowest level of performance and no statistically significant increases were found at the Advanced Level. Seniors from the bottom-performing one-third of the schools appeared to be less mathematically proficient than the eighth graders in the top one-third performing schools.

Bottge and Hasselbring (1993) report that adolescents with a history of difficulties in mathematics have a greater risk of finishing school without the necessary skills to function in everyday life. Therefore, it is imperative that appropriate mathematics assessment take place. Webb and Briars (1990) state that assessment should occur in a variety of situations, include a variety of mathematical representations, and involve the use of calculators and computers. The assessment information should be used to determine students' perceptions of mathematical ideas and processes, determine their ability to function in a mathematical context, and guide instruction.

Changes in mathematics assessment procedures have been influenced by the overall movement in the assessment arena to make assessment more "authentic." However, the Curriculum and Evaluation Standards (National Council of Teachers of Mathematics [NCTM], 1989) and the Professional Standards for Teaching Mathematics (NCTM, 1992) have had a more powerful influence on the persons who should know most about mathematics teaching and assessment, the classroom teachers. Thus, the assessment likely to be most effective is an interaction between teacher and student, with the teacher continually seeking to understand what a student can do and how the student is able to do it, and then using that information to guide instruction.

If the screening process had indicated that a student has a problem in mathematics, the steps outlined in Appendix A under the diagnostic process need to be carried out: determination of academic expectations in mathematics, observations, interviews, curriculum-based assessment, and informal analysis of responses. The results of the most recent group achievement test would give a general idea of a student's functional level in mathematics. An individually administered standardized mathematics test should be given only if there is a technically adequate one available that assesses the important components of mathematics that this student is expected to master. Numerous tests have been developed as diagnostic math tests, but few provide enough information regarding strengths and weaknesses to plan intervention.

The guidelines for teachers' assessing students' understanding of mathematics (NCTM, 1991) should be followed by anyone conducting mathematics assessment: (a) use a variety of assessment methods; (b) match assessment with the developmental level, mathematical maturity, and cultural background of the student; (c) analyze the student's understanding of and disposition to do mathematics and provide this information to students, parents, and pertinent school personnel; and (e) base instruction on assessment.

These guidelines can best be followed by assessing the student in his or her own curriculum. Various alternatives to standardized formal mathematics assessment are available and should be used if they provide a much better assessment/instruction match.

Just as a new assessment vocabulary developed in the 1980s, constructivism became a widely accepted theoretical position in mathematics education. What that means from a practical instructional view is that teaching skills from explaining or telling to facilitating the development of students' knowledge structure or co-constructing knowledge with the student. Although this approach is not new to everyone, it does require a significant shift in the teacher's responsibilities to the student and an increase in the complexity of decision making in teaching. When does one "tell" versus "co-construct?" How does one decide what a student does or does not understand? It is a lot easier to teach and assess via a strict behaviorist approach in which the product or response is what is important, not the process or understanding of the response. However, such teaching and assessment is not considering the students' prior knowledge and the processes that may already be in place. Arcavi and Schoenfeld (1992) state that, above all, the constructivist approach demands that educators listen very carefully to what students have to say. This is also true in the assessment arena.

Lesh, Lamon, Behr, and Lester (1992) discuss future directions in mathematics assessment and provide a very detailed table that summarizes some of the important differences between traditional standardized testing and performance assessment activities. They point out that, in general, traditional types of standardized tests have only dealt with a narrow range of decision-making issues and have been based on outdated conceptions of mathematics. Yet, the alternative assessment movement has focused on using the measures as a leverage point for curriculum reform and given little attention to issues such as fairness and reliability in scoring, the usefulness and credibility of results for some decisions and the scope and representativeness of the constructs that are measured when looking at the quality of a collection of tasks. Lesh and Lamon (1992) believe that curriculum reform efforts (and in turn assessment efforts) need to

- Go beyond testing (for screening) to assessment (for informal decision making).

- Go beyond a few discrete assessment events to the seamless integration of instruction and assessment.

- Go beyond behavioral objectives to cognitive objectives.

- Go beyond multiple-choice tasks to realistic tasks.

- Go beyond right answers to reasoned answers.

- Go beyond one-number scores to multi-dimensional profiles.

- Go beyond report cards to learning progress maps. (Lesh & Lamon, 1992, p. 15)

Relative to assessment and instruction/remediation in mathematics, technological aids (calculators, computers, interactive videos) have proven to be useful (Bottge & Hasselbring, 1993; Fey & Hirsch, 1992; Hopkins, 1992; Thomas, 1992). Numerous resources for mathematics projects and activities can be used as assessment and intervention techniques (Choate et al., 1992; Cooney, 1990; Fey & Hirsch, 1992; Hammill & Bartel, 1990; Howell et al., 1993; Mathematical Sciences, 1993; Thomas, 1992).

Science, Social Studies, and Other Academic Courses

If there is concern about any other academic area, the steps outlined in Appendix A should be carried out with the specific or personalized assessment focusing on the content of these courses and on determining skills in reading, vocabulary, problem solving, use of graphic aids, study strategies, and social skills.

Task-Related Skills/Strategies

Terms such as study skills, habits, tactics, and strategies have been used to describe techniques and strategies that assist a student in adequately and efficiently completing the educational tasks associated with the learning components. Hoover (1988) identifies several learning components affected by the use of study skills: (a) acquisition, (b) recording, (c) location, (d) organization, (e) synthesis, (f) memorization, and (g) integration of these components. The assessment of task-related skills and strategies can be done via norm-referenced and/or informal assessment techniques. Most of the multiskill group achievement tests have a study skill component. However, just as in every other area discussed in this chapter, the most effective assessment tool is one that is personalized and specific to the needs of the student or class involved. The steps outlined in Appendix A should be followed. Rakes (1992), Hammill and Bartel (1990) and Howell et al. (1993) contain excellent guidelines for assessing task-related skills/strategies. For example, Hammill and Bartel (1990) have created a Study Skills Inventory; Choate et al. (1990) a Teacher Survey and an appendix with study strategy objectives and sample test items; and Howell et al. (1993) a Status Sheet for Task Related Knowledge. (Also, the chapter in this book by Harvey contains guidelines for teaching study skills.)

Vocational Goals and Skills

A significant number of adolescents leave school without having mastered the skills needed to successfully obtain and maintain employment. Vocational goals and skills should be assessed long before a student is ready to enter the world of work. Information about vocations and integration of interests, aptitudes, and goals should be introduced no later than middle school. Levinson's chapter in this book deals specifically with vocational assessment, but the steps in Appendix A should be carried out with any secondary student with academic concerns. Such assessment can be done via formal and informal assessment techniques, but if done in the context of students' regular coursework, then informal techniques would be most appropriate.

Social Skills

Gresham covers the area of social skills training and assessment of social/emotional functioning in this text. I have introduced the topic in this chapter because direct observation in classrooms with adolescents has made it clear that academic achievement problems and social/emotional difficulties are not easy to separate. They may be acting directly or indirectly on each other, have no relationship whatsoever, or be so intertwined that it is not possible to determine which came first. Long-term problems without intervention in either area are likely to affect the other. There are far too many students with a history of academic difficulties being identified as students with behavior difficulties when they reach adolescence. Assessment and intervention in this area is a necessary part of the procedures for appropriate academic assessment of secondary students. Make sure that the steps in Appendix A have been carried out. Hammill and Bartel (1990) and Howell et al. (1993)

offer assessment and intervention guidelines for social/emotional difficulties.

SUMMARY

There are numerous demands placed on students in secondary classrooms such as (a) bring necessary materials to class; (b) read from materials at or above grade level; (c) listen to lectures and take notes; (d) follow directions; (e) complete assignments; (f) work independently; (g) participate in discussion; (h) spell and write; (i) take tests; and (j) follow classroom rules. Problems with any of these demands can interfere with academic success. Therefore, academic assessment must be comprehensive, give recognition to all valued learning experience, be sensitive to process as well as products, and use a problem-solving approach to assessment — an approach that **I**dentifies and **D**efines the problem, **E**xplores alternative solutions, **A**cts on the plan, and **L**ooks at results (IDEAL).

Clarke, Clarke, and Lovitt's list of major uses for assessment information is appropriate for all levels of students and all academic areas as well as nonacademic areas:

- To improve instruction by identifying the specific sources of a student's error that requires remediation or the specific learning behaviors that might need to be encouraged and developed or discouraged and replaced.

- To improve instruction by identifying those instructional strategies that are most successful.

- To inform the pupil of identified strengths and weaknesses both in knowledge and in learning strategies so that the most effective strategies might be applied where most needed.

- To inform subsequent teachers of the student's competencies so that they can more readily adapt their instruction to the student's needs.

- To inform parents of their child's progress so that they can give more effective support. (Clarke, Clarke, & Lovitt, 1990, p. 199)

REFERENCES

Arcavi, A., & Schoenfeld, A. H. (1992). Mathematics tutoring through a constructivist lens: The challenges of sense-making. *Journal of Mathematical Behavior, 11,* 321–335.

Ashlock, R. B. (1990). *Error patterns in computation: A semi-programmed approach* (5th ed.). Columbus, OH: Merrill.

Berninger, V. W., & Hooper, S. R. (1993). Mini-series — Preventing and remediating writing disabilities: Interdisciplinary frameworks for assessment consultation and intervention. *School Psychology Review, 22*(4), 590–686.

Bottge, N. S., & Hasselbring, T. S. (1993). A comparison of two approaches for teaching complex, authentic mathematics problems to adolescents in remedial math classes. *Exceptional Children, 59*(6), 556–566.

Bransford, J. D., & Stein, B. S. (1984). *The IDEAL problem solver.* New York: W. H. Freeman.

Choate, J. S., Enright, B. E., Miller, L. J., Poteet, J. A., & Rakes, T. A. (1992). *Curriculum-based assessment and programming* (2nd ed.). Boston: Allyn & Bacon.

Clarke, D. J., Clarke, D. M., & Lovitt, C. L. (1990). Changes in mathematics teaching call for assessment alternatives. In T. J. Cooney (Eds.), *Teaching and learning mathematics in the 1990s.* Reston, VA: National Council of Teachers of Mathematics.

Cooney, T. J. (Ed.). (1990). *Teaching and learning mathematics in the 1990s* (190 Yearbook). Reston, VA: National Council of Teachers of Mathematics.

Crosby, E. A. (1993). The "at-risk" decade. *Phi Delta Kappan, 74*(8), 598–604.

Eccles, J. S., Midgely, C., Wigfield, A., Buchanan, C. M., Reuman, D., Flanagan, C., & MacIver, D. (1993). Development during adolescence: The impact of stage-environment and fit on young adolescents' experiences in school and in families. *American Psychologist, 48*(2), 90–101.

Elliott, E. J. (1993). *A preliminary report of national estimates from the National Assessment of Educational Progress 1992 Mathematics Assessment.* Washington, DC: U. S. Department of Education.

Farr, R., & Carey, R. F. (1986). *Reading. What can be measured?* (2nd ed.). Newark, DE: International Reading Association.

Farr, R., Tully, M. A., & Pritchard, R. (1989). Assessment instruments and techniques used by content area teachers. In D. Lapp, J. Flood, & N. Farnan (Eds.), *Content area reading and learning.* Englewood Cliffs, NJ: Prentice Hall.

Feldman, S. S., & Elliott, G. R. (Eds.). (1990). *At the threshold: The developing adolescent.* Cambridge, MA: Harvard University Press.

Fey, J. T., & Hirsch, C. R. (1992). *Calculators in mathematics* (1992 Yearbook). Reston, VA: National Council of Teachers of Mathematics.

Foertsch, M. A. (1992). *Reading in and out of school.* Washington, DC: U.S. Office of Education.

Gans, J. E., & Blyth, D. A. (1990). *American's adolescents: How healthy are they?* AMA Profiles of Adolescent Health Series. Chicago: American Medical Association.

Gerken, K. C., & Winslow-Garvin, B. (1993). *The early warning system.* Iowa City, IA: Iowa City Collaborative Integration Project.

Graham, S., Harris, K. R., & MacArthur, C. A. (1993). Improving the writing of students with learning problems: Self-regulated strategy development. *School Psychology Review, 22*(4), 656–670.

Hahn, A. (1987). Reaching out to American's dropouts: What to do? *Phi Delta Kappan, 69*(4), 256–263.

Hammill, D., & Bartel, N. R. (1990). *Teaching students with learning and behavior problems* (5th ed.). Boston: Allyn & Bacon.

Hammond, W. R., & Yung, B. (1993). Psychology's role in the public health response to assaultive violence among young African-American males. *American Psychologist, 48*, 142–154.

Henk, W. A. (1993). New directions in reading assessment. *Reading and Writing Quarterly, 9*, 103–120.

Hooper, S. R., Swartz, C. W., Montgomery, J. W., Reed, M. S., Brown, T. T., Wasileski, T. J., & Levine, M. D. (1993). Prevalence of writing problems across three middle school samples. *School Psychology Review, 22*(4), 610–621.

Hoover, J. J. (1988). *Teaching handicapped students study skills.* Lindale, TX: Hamilton Publications.

Hoover, J. J. (1990). Teaching students to use study skills. In D. D. Hammill & N. R. Bartel (Eds.), *Teaching students with learning and behavior problems* (5th ed.). Boston: Allyn & Bacon.

Hopkins, M. H. (1992). The use of calculators in the assessment of mathematics achievement. In J. T. Fey (Ed.), *Calculators in mathematics education.* Reston, VA: National Council of Teachers of Mathematics.

Howell, K. W. (1991). Curriculum-based evaluation: What you think is what you get. *Diagnostique, 16*(4), 193–202.

Howell, K. W., & Morehead, M. K. (1987). *Curriculum-based evaluation for special and remedial education.* Columbus, OH: Merrill.

Howell, K. W., Fox, S. L., & Morehead, M. K. (1993). *Curriculum-based evaluation* (2nd ed.). Pacific Grove, CA: Brooks/Cole.

Hudson, F., & Colson, S. (1988). *Hudson Education Skills Inventory.* Austin, TX: Pro-Ed.

Huebner, E. S. (1993). Psychologists in secondary schools in the 1990s: Current functions, training, and job satisfaction. *School Psychology Quarterly, 8*(1), 50–56.

Lesh, R., & Lamon, S. J. (1993). Assessing authentic mathematical progress. In R. Lesh & S. J. Lamon (Eds.), *Assessment of authentic performance in school mathematics.* Washington, DC: AAAS Press.

Lesh, R., Lamon, S., Behr, M., & Lester, F. (1992). Future directions for mathematics assessment. In R. Lesh & S. J. Lamon (Eds.), *Assessment of authentic performance in school mathematics.* Washington, DC: AAAS Press.

Leslie, L. (1993). A developmental-interactive approach to reading assessment. *Reading and Writing Quarterly, 9*, 5–30.

Leslie, L., & Caldwell, J. (1990). *Qualitative Reading Inventory.* Glenview, IL: Scott, Foresman.

Masters, L. F., Mori, B. A., & Mori, A. A. (1993). *Teaching secondary students with mild learning and behavior problems* (2nd ed.). Austin, TX: Pro-Ed.

Mathematical Sciences Education Board National Research Council. (1993). *Measuring up.* Washington, DC: National Academy Press.

Moore, K. (1992). *Facts at a glance.* Washington, DC: Childtrends.

Morocco, C. C., Dalton, B., & Tivnan, T. (1992). The impact of computer-supported writing instructions on fourth-grade students with and without learning disabilities. *Reading and Writing Quarterly, 8*, 87–113.

Mullis, I. V. S., Dossey, J. A., Owen, E. H., & Phillips, G. W. (1993). *NAEPP 1992 report card for the nation and the states.* Washington, DC: U.S. Department of Education.

National Center for Education in Maternal and Child Health. (1990). *The health of America's youth.* Washington, DC: Author.

National Council of Teachers of Mathematics. (1989). *Curriculum and evaluation standards for school mathematics.* Reston, vA: Author.

National Council of Teachers of Mathematics. (1992). *Professional standards for teaching mathematics.* Reston, VA: Author.

Poteet, J. A. (1980). Informal assessment of written expression. *Learning Disabilities Quarterly, 3*, 88–98.

Rakes, T. A. (1992). Content and study strategies. In J. C. Choate, B. E. Enright, L. J. Miller, J. A. Poteet, & T. A. Rakes (Eds.), *Cur-*

riculum-based assessment and programming. Boston: Allyn and Bacon.

Readence, J. E., Bean, T. W., & Baldwin, R. S. (1985). *Content and reading: An integrated approach* (2nd ed.). Dubuque, IA: Kendall/Hunt.

Reynolds, M. (1992). Students and programs at the school margins: Disorder and needed repair. *School Psychology Quarterly, 7*(4), 233–244.

Reynolds, M. C., Zetlin, A. G., & Wang, M. C. (1993). 20/20 analysis: Taking a close look at the margins. *Exceptional Children, 59*(4), 294–300.

Ruddell, M. R. (1991). Authentic assessment: Focused observation as a means for evaluating language and literacy development. *The California Reader, 24,* 2–7.

Ruddell, M. R. (1993). *Teaching content reading and writing.* Boston: Allyn & Bacon.

Salvia, J., & Ysseldyke, J. E. (1991). *Assessment* (5th ed.). Boston: Houghton Mifflin.

Schmitt, M. C. (1990). A questionnaire to measure children's awareness of strategic reading processes. *The Reading Teacher, 7,* 454–461.

Shinn, M. R., & Hubbard, D. D. (1992). Curriculum-based measurement and problem-solving assessment: Basis procedures and outcomes. *Focus on Exceptional Children, 24*(5), 1–20.

Takanishi, R. (Ed.). (1993a). Adolescence [Special issue]. *American Psychologist, 48*(2), 85–201.

Takanishi, R. (1993b). The opportunities of adolescence-research interventions and policy. *American Psychologist, 48*(2), 85–87.

Thomas, D. A. (1992). *Teenagers, teachers, and mathematics.* Boston: Allyn & Bacon.

Valencia, S. W., McGinley, W., & Pearson, P. D. (1990). Assessing reading and writing. In G. G. Duffy (Ed.), *Reading in the middle schools.* Newark, DE: International Reading Association.

Wade, E. S. (1990). Using think-alouds to assess comprehension. *The Reading Teacher, 7,* 442–451.

Webb, N., & Briars, D. (1990). Assessment in mathematics classrooms, K–8. In T. J. Cooney (Ed.), *Teaching and learning mathematics in the 1990s.* Reston, VA: National Council of Teachers of Mathematics.

Webb, N. L. (1992). Assessment of students' knowledge of mathematics: Steps toward a theory. In D. A. Grouws (Ed.), *Handbook of research on mathematics teaching and learning.* New York: Macmillan.

Webb, N. L. (1993). *Assessment in the mathematics classroom* (1993 Yearbook). Reston, VA: National Council of Teachers of Mathematics.

Wood, R. (1987). *Measurement and assessment in education and psychology.* London: The Falmer Press.

ANNOTATED BIBLIOGRAPHY

Choate, J. S., Enright, B. E., Miller, L. J., Poteet, J. A., & Rakes, T. A. (1992). *Curriculum-based assessment and programming* (2nd ed.). Boston: Allyn & Bacon.
The second edition of this book emphasizes the bond between curriculum-based assessment and curriculum-based programming. Step-by-step practical assessment and programming procedures are provided that will enable the assessor/interventionist to personalize instruction based on assessed needs. The appendices contain skill objectives and sample test items.

Howell, K. W., Fox, S. L., & Morehead, M. K. (1993). *Curriculum-based evaluation* (2nd ed.). Pacific Grove, CA: Brooks/Cole.
The basic concepts of evaluation and instruction are integrated with current research knowledge in order to generate productive tools for classroom use. Functional classroom-based evaluation is explained and demonstrated across academic, social, and task-related skills. Teaching recommendations are made for each of these skill areas.

Lesh, R., & Lamon, S. J. (Eds.). (1992). *Assessment of authentic performance in school mathematics.* Washington, DC: AAAS Press.
Most of the chapters in this book focus on clarifying and articulating the goals of assessment and instruction. The content of assessment is stressed vs. the mode of delivery. "Portfolio," "performance," "authentic," and other forms of assessment are viewed as means to an end, not as ends themselves.

Masters, L. F., Mori, B. A., & Mori, A. A.(1993). *Teaching secondary students with mild learning and behavior problems* (2nd ed.). Austin, TX: Pro-Ed.
This book is an excellent instructional resource. It covers assessment and evaluation of student progress; specific instructional methods, techniques, and materials for remedial, compensatory, tutorial, and strategic-oriented programs; vocational and transitional training; social skills training; and computer and technological classroom applications. It also contains checklists for instructional modifications and transition planning.

Takanishi, R. (Ed.). (1993). Adolescence [Special issue]. *American Psychologist, 48*(2), 85–201.
This issue highlights the knowledge base in specific areas of adolescent development, assesses the intervention experience, and attempts to strengthen the role of research and professional practice in the development of public policies. Article authors address how this period of great risks can be turned into opportunities for well-being.

Appendix A

Academic Assessment of Secondary-Age Students (7th–12th Grades)

I. The Screening Process

  A. Indirect Student Assessment

    1. Develop a brief rating form for sixth-grade teachers to complete that indicates students' current academic and behavioral adjustment and projected adjustment to junior high.

    2. Check health records for current and past health information such as acute or chronic illness, frequent trips to the office for health complaints, and medication.

    3. Check attendance records. Screening team determines standards for excessive absences. The files of any student demonstrating excessive absences will be reviewed.

    4. Check the cumulative folder for current and past special services such as Chapter 1, resource help, counseling, speech and language, and the like.

    5. Review grade reports. The files of any student failing one or more subjects will be reviewed.

    6. Review standardized group test data. Screening team develops cut-off scores. The files of any student whose scores are below this will be reviewed.

    7. Develop a checklist summary sheet that can be completed for all students identified during the screening process. Questions to be answered on the checklist include:

      a. Is there concern about academic skills or problems in specific content areas?

      b. Are there descriptive samples of behavior and work samples available?

      c. What is known about school-related and outside-of-school variables?

      d. What if any, intervention efforts have been attempted?

    8. Ask for current information from teachers and parents about the students identified during the first stage of the screening process. Create your own checklist of questions to ask parents and teachers. Or use a checklist or survey already created such as the "General Teacher Survey" in Choate et al. (1992).

  B. Direct Student Assessment

    1. Administer a survey-level assessment instrument in any area where additional information is needed before proceeding with a specific level assessment such as self-esteem, study habits, skills, and strategies.

    2. Interview the students identified during the first stage of the screening process.

    3. Observe the students identified during the first stage of the screening process.

  C. Interpret the Screening Data

    1. Establish weighting for each piece of information gathered.

    2. Establish the inclusion/exclusion criteria for proceeding with a specific level or personalized assessment and intervention.

    3. Establish priorities based on significant need for intervention (**I**dentify the **P**roblem).

II. The Diagnostic Process

  A. Determining Academic Expectations/Conducting Curriculum Analyses

    1. Review district/school/teacher goals in the academic or content area.

    2. Review textbook objectives, content, reading level, and so forth.

    3. Review specific classroom requirements.

    4. Check readability level of informal inventory and curriculum materials available.

B. Indirect Student Assessment

   1. Review classroom work.

   2. Check: reports from parents, teachers, school psychologists.

   3. Interview the student: conducted by classroom teacher or school psychologist.

   4. Perform curriculum-based assessment: conducted by classroom teacher, special teacher, or school psychologist.

   5. Do an informal analysis of responses — error pattern analysis, task analysis.

   6. Assess instructional environment.

C. Direct Student Assessment

   1. Check skill levels in the academic or content area.

      a. word recognition (sight vocabulary, phonetic analysis, structural analysis, word meaning)

      b. reading comprehension (literal, interpretive, critical, and words in context)

      c. mathematics (integration of mathematical knowledge, problem solving, communication, reasoning, mathematical concepts, mathematical procedures, mathematical disposition)

      d. written expression (mechanics, usage, ideation)

      e. spelling and handwriting

      f. science (vocabulary, problem solving)

      g. social studies (vocabulary, graphic aids)

   2. Check task-related skills/strategies.

      a. organization

      b. categorization

      c. alphabetizing

      d. directions

      e. book use

      f. references

      g. study habits

         1. outlines

         2. study strategies

         3. adjustment of reading rate

      h. test-taking skills

   3. Check vocational goals and skills.

      a. interest

      b. aptitude

      c. opportunities

   4. Check social skills.

      a. observation
      b. self-report or third-party report

III. The Intervention Process.

    A.   Describe present level of performance (**D**efine the Problem).

    B.   Set goals/priorities.

    C.   Select content.

    D.   Select methods and materials (**E**xplore Intervention Options).

    E.   Program for subskills.

        1. Development strategies

        2. Corrective strategies

        3. Maintenance strategies

    F.   **A**ct on the Plan.

    G.   Evaluate effectiveness/Monitor progress (**L**ook at Results).

    H.   Recycle if necessary.

Appendix B
Assessment of Word Recognition Skills

Known Information	Probable Causes	Assessment	Intervention
Oral reading is slow but accurate	Lack of practice in reading quickly	Ask student to reread passage	If rate increases work on improving rate
	Poor use of passage content	Same as above	Same as above
	Poor use of phonics; speed would increase errors	Analyze decoding errors	Teach the use of skills emphasizing rate
Oral reading is inaccurate	Not reading for accuracy	Tell student the purpose for reading and have student reread passage	Emphasizing reading for accuracy
	Poor use of context	Check the use of text	Emphasize accuracy; teach higher-level strategies
	Learned error patterns	Categorize decoding errors by strategy	Correct the error patterns
	Poor use of decoding	Categorize decoding errors by content	Teach the use of skills within passage reading

Note. Adapted from *Curriculum-based Evaluation for Special and Remedial Education* by K. W. Howell and M. K. Morehead, 1987. Columbus, OH: Merrill.

68

Best Practices in Assessment with Persons Who Have Severe or Profound Handicaps

Wendy K.Berg
University of Iowa

David P. Wacker
University of Iowa

Mark W. Steege
University of Southern Maine

OVERVIEW

Students who are severely to profoundly handicapped constitute a diverse group of individuals. The label *severely handicapped* is applied to students who display severe deficits in adaptive skills and may include students with moderate to profound mental retardation and those who have severe sensory or physical impairments. Within the past 10 years, the use of this label in public school programs has been expanded to include students with severe health impairments and students who engage in extreme forms of aberrant behavior such as self-injury. As a result, the label provides the practitioner with limited information regarding the student to be served.

The diversity of the students who are included by this label is exemplified by the variety of educational programs that serve this population. For example, within different school systems, students with severe disabilities may attend segregated schools, be taught in regular education classrooms with same-age nonhandicapped peers, or spend the majority of the school day in community-based programming. The majority of students with severe disabilities, however, are served in self-contained with integration classrooms located in regular public school programs. It is not unusual for the children in self-contained classrooms to represent an age span of several years, to range in speech skills from those who speak in brief sentences to those who display no expressive skills, and to range from those who are independent in all self-care skills to those who are dependent. Because of the variations in programming and the unique characteristics of each student, it is important for the school psychologist to become familiar with the student's classroom as well as with the student.

Regardless of the type or level of disability the student displays, the goal for education remains fairly constant. The student should be able to participate as independently as possible in activities that are typical of other students of the same chronological age. This goal reflects two standards for educational programs serving students with severe disabilities: (a) age-appropriate activities and (b) a continuum of partial participation to complete, independent participation in educational, social, and vocational activities.

The standard denoted by *age-appropriate* refers to providing the student with activities and materials that are typical of those engaged in by students of the same chronological age but who have not been diagnosed as having a disability. The second standard reflects the principle that independence in an activity is a goal, not a requirement for participation in classroom activities. Although some students may not be capable of performing every component of an activity, every student should be capable of performing at least some components. Allowing students to participate, with whatever level of assistance they require, is referred to as partial participation.

Classroom activities for students with severe disabilities should occur in settings with other students of the same age, who may or may not be disabled, with ample opportunities for social interactions and the formation of friendships. Attendance and participation in classrooms and activities with nonhandicapped students of the same chronological age is referred to as integration or inclusion. Inclusion for students with severe disabilities may range from participation in nonacademic class periods, such as music and art, to full inclusion as a student enrolled in a regular education classroom with same-age peers. The diagnosis of the student does not dictate the setting in which education is best provided.

Finally, the skills developed in the educational setting should build on the student's strengths and lead toward the opportunity for gainful employment as an adult. The priority of any given educational goal in a student's individual education plan (IEP) depends on the age of the student and the wishes of the student and his or her parents. It is simply not possible to prioritize goals in an a priori fashion without conducting an individualized assessment.

The purpose of this chapter is to present some of the current methodologies available for conducting assessments and effective intervention procedures for students who are severely to profoundly disabled. Traditionally, the role of the school psychologist has been limited to assessing students' intellectual or developmental functioning and determining their eligibility for various special education programs. In this chapter we are proposing a different role: to assess the environmental conditions under which a student will be most successful in achieving individualized education goals within the educational setting of choice. Identifying the environmental conditions that promote optimal performance necessitates that the school psychologist observe the impact that different antecedent and consequence variables have on the student's ability or motivation to respond correctly to task directions or social cues. This is in contrast to determining if the student meets initial baseline criteria for participation in a specific educational program.

Thus, we are suggesting that participation be based on IEP goals, not on assessed abilities. When participation in a situation has been agreed on by the interdisciplinary team, the goal of assessment is to identify environmental conditions that facilitate success. This is not to suggest that we see no role for IQ or other forms of psychometric testing. As will be seen in one of the case examples, we believe that psychometric assessment can be a useful evaluation, but not as the only or primary form of assessment. Also, school psychologists tend to know much more about psychometric than behavioral assessment; therefore, we devote more space to assessment of environmental (antecedent and consequence) variables.

The procedures are presented in the context of three case examples (Table 1) illustrating issues you are likely to encounter while serving programs for students with severe/profound disabilities. The first example, Katie, is a referral for an evaluation of cognitive abilities and overall level of functioning. Katie is typical of many referrals in that she does not engage in many adaptive behaviors, nor does she communicate effectively; however, she is responsive to the people and activities in her environment. For Bill and Renee, the purpose of referral is to change the student's behavior. In Bill's case, assessment focuses on reducing the occurrence of head banging and increasing his participation in adaptive behaviors. The assessment designed for Renee focuses on identifying environmental factors that will increase her participation in classroom activities.

BASIC CONSIDERATIONS

Purpose of Assessment

The first step in any assessment is to determine the purpose of assessment from the perspectives of the parents, teachers, other educational staff, and, when appropriate, the student being evaluated. The involvement of parents and teachers in the assessment process is critical, because they provide valuable information regarding the history of the student, previous approaches to assessment and treatment, and the current goals for the student. For Katie, the referral question centers on identifying the most appropriate classroom placement for the next school year. For Bill, the reason for referral is to obtain an intervention procedure that will reduce or eliminate self-injury. For Renee, the goal is to improve work performance.

Each referral question requires collecting a different set of information to satisfactorily address the issues raised. The assessment question dictates the type of information that is needed and, therefore, the units of behavior to be examined. For example, Katie's assessment will focus on her performance on selected standardized tests to determine her level of intellectual functioning. Renee's teacher is not interested in evaluating her intellectual functioning but, rather, in identifying an intervention procedure that will result in better work habits. For Bill, assessment will focus initially on the frequency of his self-injurious behavior under different environmental conditions.

BEST PRACTICES

Diagnostic Assessment

Prior to conducting the evaluation, the school psychologist should first consult with parents, classroom teachers, and therapists to determine the student's most reliable means of communication (e.g., verbalization, signing, pointing to pictures, augmentative communication). Having identified the student's means of communication, the school psychologist then selects the assessment procedure that is matched to the student's style of communication. For example, with a student who evidences little, if any, verbal skills but who has a reliable reach-and-point response, the Peabody Picture Vocabulary Test–Revised or the Test of Nonverbal Intelligence might be used to estimate cognitive abilities. Similarly, preferred positioning and level of stamina are important considerations in conducting assessments with students who have significant physical disabilities or medical conditions. With these students, it is often helpful to ask the parent or classroom teacher to participate in the assessment to assist in determining the degree to which the student is attending and responding to the questions/test stimuli. Salvia and Ysseldyke (1988) and Sattler (1988) provide guidelines

TABLE 1
Case Descriptors and Assessment Approach

Student	Description	Referral Issue	Assessment Approach
1. Katie	A 3-year-old with multiple handicaps; has limited use of arms and legs; uses no formal communication. Appears to be attentive to activities and people in environment.	Most appropriate placement: adaptive skills, general level of functioning.	Intellectual and adaptive behavior assessment.
2. Bill	A 12-year-old diagnosed as profoundly mentally retarded; uses no formal communication system; has 10-year history of self-injurious behavior.	Decrease self-injurious behavior; increase participation in adaptive activities.	Functional analysis of behavior.
3. Renee	A 6-year old diagnosed as severely mentally retarded; communicates with 1–2 word statements; does not participate in assigned activities.	Increase participation in adaptive activities.	1. Reinforcer assessment. 2. Structural assessment of conditions promoting on-task behavior.

and information regarding the use of specific standardized assessments for persons with severe handicaps.

In most cases, the results of assessment of intellectual functioning for students with severe, multiple disabilities yields *global estimates* of cognitive functioning. Subtest analysis and hypotheses about cognitive strengths and weaknesses are rarely clinically significant. Adaptive behavior assessments, particularly curriculum-based assessments, will result in information that is useful to the interdisciplinary team for designing habilitative programs. (See chapter by Harrison and Robinson [this volume] for a thorough review of adaptive behavior assessment.)

In most cases, the results of adaptive behavior assessments also indicate significant deficits across a variety of domains (e.g., expressive language, domestic activity, personal living, vocational, leisure, social). However, global assessments are often an insensitive measure of the student's level of functioning with respect to specific but complex skills such as bedmaking, toothbrushing, laundering, meal preparation, operating a microcomputer, and so forth. A comprehensive analysis of the student's degree of mastery of these types of tasks needs to be individually tailored. For example, task analysis data could be collected to identify mastery or the level of assistance (type of prompts) that a student needs within and across tasks. By themselves, the results of norm-referenced adaptive behavior assessment, although useful in describing a student's current level of global functioning, are not particularly useful in prescribing individually designed habilitative programs.

Another method of describing a student's current level of functioning involves the use of a semistructured interview with parents, teachers, and others who provide services to the student. We suggest focusing the interview on the following: (a) behavioral assets (i.e., behaviors that the student performs independently or with minimal assistance), (b) behavioral deficits (i.e., behaviors that the student has not learned or mastered), (c) behavioral excesses (i.e., behaviors that are considered aberrant), (d) survey of reinforcers (e.g., types of activities, foods, and social attention that appear to be preferred by the student), (e) means of communicating wants and needs (e.g., signing, language board, verbalizations), and (f) primary concerns (i.e., behaviors to be targeted for skill development and, if any, behaviors targeted for elimination). The interview should be focused throughout on behaviors that are both functional and age-appropriate. This analysis not only yields information about the student's strengths and weaknesses, but also sets the stage for more comprehensive assessments.

In the case of Katie, the school psychologist consulted with family members and school personnel about her communication skills, positioning, and stamina. Given Katie's limitations with respect to verbal and motor abilities, the school psychologist administered the Peabody Picture Vocabulary Test–Revised. Katie accurately pointed to several pictures that corresponded to stimulus words presented by the school psychologist. Katie's performance was significantly below age level expectations, suggesting that she evidenced significant deficits in relation to one-word receptive language skills. The school psychologist next administered the American Association on Mental Retardation (AAMR) Adaptive Behavior Scale–School Version, with the classroom teacher serving as the informant. The results of adaptive behavior assessment suggested significant deficits across all domains. On the basis of this evaluation, the school psychologist offered the diagnosis of Mental Retardation, Severe. To further evaluate Katie's adaptive behavior skills, the school psychologist conducted a semistructured interview and identified several behavioral strengths, no maladaptive behaviors, and specific skills deficits.

Behavioral Assessment

Behavioral assessments are conducted to identify the conditions that guide and maintain a subject's behavior. The goal of assessment is to describe current behavior and identify effective interventions.

Behavior is always defined in a specific context, which is composed of both antecedents and consequences to behavior. Antecedent variables include contextual and instructional stimuli that precede or coincide with participation in targeted activities. Contextual variables typically include environmental stimuli such as the presence or absence of peers, noise, or other factors in the environment that might facilitate instruction or be distracting to the student. Among instructional stimuli are the manner in which the task is presented, such as one-to-one versus group instruction, the amount of work to be completed within one work session, and the presence or absence of prompts or cues to promote task performance.

Consequences are stimuli that follow a behavior. For example, *positive reinforcement* refers to what a student gains, such as tangible items, points, or praise; and *negative reinforcement* refers to what a student avoids or escapes, such as the assignment of additional work, ongoing task demands, or reprimands.

Defining and Measuring Behavior

Behavioral definitions describe the specific behavior a student exhibits in such a way that two or more individuals can agree that the target behavior has occurred. A behavioral definition is focused on the behavior displayed by a student and on the situation in which the behavior occurs, but not on the presumed causes or intent of the behavior.

When the behaviors of interest have been identified, the next step is to identify an observation system or instrument that will most accurately quantify the occurrence of these behaviors. For Renee, assessment will focus on determining the conditions under which she will actively and appropriately participate in classroom activities. In determining the conditions under which Renee will work most effectively, we are not interested so much in whether appropriate or inappropriate behavior occurs in a given situation, but rather in the relative frequencies with which the different behaviors occur across different types of activities and environmental manipulations. Similarly, the assessment for Bill will not focus on whether self-injury occurs during the school day, but rather on the relative frequency with which self-injury occurs across different antecedent and consequent conditions.

Time-based systems. Several different dimensions of behavior can be measured, but it is most common to measure behavior in terms of its frequency or duration. Frequency, how often the target behavior occurs, involves the use of event or interval recording. With event and interval recording systems, the student is observed for a fixed amount of time (e.g., 5–30 minutes) across observation sessions (Kazdin, 1982). Event recording consists of scoring each time the behavior occurs within that time period. Because the observer counts how often the target behavior occurs, the behavior must be a discrete event with a clear beginning and ending (e.g., Bill's striking his head against a table). If the behavior is not discrete, an interval recording system might be used. With an interval recording system, the time period is further divided into fixed intervals that range from seconds to minutes. In general, the smaller the interval the better. We often use a 6-second interval because 100 intervals occur in 10 minutes, which makes computations of percentages easy. The occurrence or nonoccurrence of the target behaviors is then recorded within each interval, with "percentage of intervals" being the outcome of interest. Duration recording measures the time that elapses from the onset of the response until the response ends. Unlike repetitive, discrete behaviors, which can be measured easily by event recording, the behaviors that are most appropriate for duration recording can be broadly considered as measures of persistence. The duration of a student's hand biting, for example, could be recorded with a stopwatch. This requires defining a certain unit of time (e.g., 5 seconds) that separates the occurrence of one behavior from the next.

The selection of event, interval, or duration recording is based on the occurrence of behavior and the purposes of instruction. Event recording is useful for high-frequency behaviors that are discrete. Interval recording is useful for high-frequency behaviors that are not discrete or when multiple behaviors are occurring. Duration recording is preferred when the time spent in a behavior or activity is important or when low-frequency responses persist for extended time periods.

Task analysis. In some cases, the question of interest revolves around how accurately or how completely a student performs tasks or activities. Task analysis data provide a direct assessment of these measures. With tasks analysis measures, a given task or assignment is divided into the component behaviors required to complete each part of the task. These

TABLE 2
Task Analysis for Sorting Silverware

_____	1. Pick up three containers.
_____	2. Set containers behind the silverware tub.
_____	3. Take a utensil (e.g., knife) out of the silverware tub.
_____	4. Place the utensil into Tub A.
_____	5. Take a different type of utensil (e.g., fork) out of silverware tub.
_____	6. Place the utensil into Tub B.
_____	7. Take the third type of utensil (e.g., spoon) out of silverware tub.
_____	8. Place the utensil into Tub C.
_____	9. Take a utensil out of the silverware tub.
_____	10. Place it with the matching utensil in the correct tub.

Repeat Steps 9 and 10 until silverware tub is empty.

Number of knives sorted correctly: _____/_____ Total number of knives.

Number of spoons sorted correctly: _____/_____ Total number of spoons.

Number of forks sorted correctly: _____/_____ Total number of forks.

components are referred to as steps in the task analysis, and the student is scored on his or her performance for each task step. An example of a task analysis for sorting silverware is provided in Table 2.

For each step, the student is given a score of either + (completed the step correctly) or − (did not complete the step correctly). By dividing the total number of steps in the task analysis by the number of + scores, one can determine the percentage of the task or activity that the student performed correctly.

An alternative method for scoring performance by a task analysis is to indicate the level of assistance the student requires to complete each task step correctly. Assistance may range from no assistance to complete physical guidance (i.e., hand-over-hand guidance). A number or letter can be assigned for each level of assistance, and this score replaces the score of + or − for each step of the task analysis. Progress is measured by documenting the student's movement from more to less restrictive levels of prompting (Steege, Wacker, & McMahon, 1987).

Task analysis data are particularly useful in educational settings because they provide information regarding the types of errors the student makes as well as a score for overall accuracy. For example, by reviewing the student's performance on a silverware sorting task, you can determine if the student has difficulty in starting the task but performs well once started, or if the student has difficulty in sorting throughout the entire work period. Task analysis data are also useful for determining if poor performance is due to a lack of skills or a lack of motivation. If a student attempts to perform most of the steps in a task analysis but performs these steps incorrectly, a skill deficit is indicated. On the other hand, if the student does not even attempt to perform the assigned tasks, the problem may be one of motivation instead of, or in addition to, a skill deficit. In these cases, assessment needs to focus on identifying positive reinforcers to be provided to the student contingent on task performance.

Assessment Procedures

Hypothesis formulation. For students such as Bill and Renee, the purpose of assessment is to identify specific interventions to change their behavior. Depending on the referral question, the primary goal of assessment may be either to increase the frequency of a low-rate appropriate behavior, such as Renee's engagement in classroom activities, or to decrease the occurrence of a high-rate aberrant behavior, such as Bill's head banging. When the referral question centers on a low-rate response, such as the lack of a desired behavior, task analysis and reinforcer assessment data may provide the most useful information. When high-rate problematic behavior is the issue, assessment should focus on identifying, by a functional analysis, the variables in the school environment that are maintaining the behavior (Iwata, Dorsey, Slifer, Bauman, & Richman, 1982).

In order to increase or decrease the frequency of any behavior, you need to know what environmental factors influence the occurrence of the behavior. For example, Renee's completion of classroom activities might be affected by the presence or absence of peers and by the amount of the teachers' attention she receives, but the type of activity assigned might not have any observable effect on her behavior. Because the number of environmental variables that may influence behavior is unlimited, you will need to de-

TABLE 3
Classroom Observation of Renee's Task Performance

Task	Conditions	% Task Step Completed	% Task Steps Completed Independently
Brush teeth	1:1 Teacher assistance with no peers	70	65
Sort silverware	Alone	15	15
Clear snack items	Teacher assistance with peers	92	75
Puzzles	Alone	20	20
Hands-on math	Teacher assistance with peers	95	60

velop specific hypotheses to guide your assessment efforts (Repp, Felce, & Barton, 1988).

Hypotheses can be based on information obtained through interviews with the parents and teachers, or through direct observation of students across different situations. We recommend a combination of the two procedures. Interviewing the people who have frequent, direct contact with the students will provide information regarding the situations in which the behaviors of concern are most likely to occur as well as the parents' and teachers' perspectives on why the children behave the way they do. Direct observation of the children across different classroom activities will allow you to form your own hypotheses and to refine those developed from parent and teacher interviews. Table 3 provides an example of what an initial classroom observation might reveal regarding Renee's task performance.

Hypothesis testing. After a hypothesis is developed regarding the factors that influence a student's behavior, the next step is to directly test that hypothesis. To evaluate the effects that a given variable has on a student's behavior, observe the student across situations in which the hypothesized variable is present and situations in which it is absent. If the variable influences behavior, behavior will change reliably as the variable is introduced and removed.

There are at least three assessment procedures for testing hypotheses regarding the role of different environmental variables on a student's behavior. The first procedure, reinforcement assessment, focuses on identifying positive reinforcers that the student is willing to work for. Such an approach is useful for identifying consequences that would increase Renee's motivation to perform assigned activities. The second approach, functional analysis of consequences, provides a means for evaluating the effects that positive and negative reinforcers have on a student's behavior. This approach is typically reserved for aberrant be-

havior that occurs at high frequencies; it would be an effective assessment procedure for addressing Bill's head banging. The final procedure, functional analysis of antecedents, is used to evaluate the impact of different antecedent stimuli. This approach would provide another method for obtaining information regarding the impact of different environmental stimuli on either Renee's or Bill's behavior.

Reinforcer assessment. Reinforcer assessments are based on the operant principle that a reinforcer is something that increases the frequency of the behavior that it follows. In the case of Renee, the purpose of a reinforcer assessment is to identify consequences to behavior that Renee is willing to work for. In Renee's case, provision of the desired consequences is to be contingent on participation in classroom activities.

A reinforcer assessment begins with developing hypotheses, which in this case involve identifying activities, toys, food items, and social consequences, such as conversation, that Renee not only likes, but is willing to work to earn. From interviews of Renee's teacher and parents a list of potential reinforcers is identified, and the items are presented to Renee contingent on a desired response. By comparing the frequencies with which Renee engages in the desired response across different consequences, you can determine which consequences are positive reinforcers for Renee.

There are numerous methods for conducting reinforcer assessments. The procedure that we have found to be the most effective for students with severe to profound handicaps is a forced-choice procedure developed by Fisher et al. (1992). The assessment is conducted in two phases and begins with the identification of potential reinforcers. Typically, five to six items that are available in the classroom and that can be provided immediately following brief instances of a desired response are sufficient.

TABLE 4
Results of a Reinforcer Assessment for Renee

Phase 1: Activity/item offered	% of offers in which item was selected
Praise	85
High-5 hand shake	80
Juice	25
Sticker	25
Book	10

Phase 2: Consequences for completing task steps	% of task steps completed
Praise	92
Book	6
No consequence	18

At the beginning of each assessment session for Phase 1, the students are provided with a brief sample of each potential reinforcer. For example, if the list includes music, students are shown a radio and allowed to listen to music for 5–10 seconds. Similarly, for consumable items, such as graham crackers and juice, they receive a small bite or drink of the item. The purpose of sampling the items is to present the options and to familiarize the students with the symbol (usually the item itself) used to represent each option. After the students briefly sample each item, the formal assessment begins.

During Phase 1, the potential reinforcers are presented two at a time to the students, who are given 5 seconds to choose one of the items. Depending on their respective abilities, they indicate a selection by taking the item from the examiner's hand, reaching, pointing, or leaning towards or gazing at the item. When an item is selected, the students receive a sample of the item (e.g., a small bite, brief access to an activity, or several seconds of interaction). When the item has been consumed or the specified time elapses, another choice of two items is offered. A student who does not select either option within 5–10 seconds loses that choice and another set of two options is presented. Thus, it is critical that a choice response be within a student's repertoire.

Each item identified as a potential reinforcer should be paired at least one time with each of the other options. Also, the position of each item should be randomized across right and left locations to control for a position bias on the part of the student. Furthermore, the assessment should be repeated at least two or three times on different days to determine the stability of students' preferences. By comparing the frequency with which students select each item across assessment sessions, you can achieve a ranking of most preferred (most frequently chosen) to least preferred (least frequently chosen) items (see Table 4).

Identifying items that a student appears to prefer completes the first phase of this assessment. Then it is necessary to determine if the preferred item will serve as a reinforcer for the desired behavior. In Renee's case, the desired behavior is participation in class activities. To complete this second phase, Renee is provided with an activity to complete for 10 minutes. During that 10-minute period, Renee receives a brief sample of the most preferred stimuli (based on Phase 1) upon the completion of each step of the task analysis, following the least restrictive level of prompting that she requires for accurate performance. Her performance of task steps completed during this condition is compared with a similar 10-minute session in which she receives one of the least preferred stimuli for completing each task step, or in which she works without receiving any consequence for completing task steps.

Each of the conditions is presented in a counterbalanced order at least three times across at least 2 days. If Renee consistently completes more task steps when she receives the consequence identified as most preferred, then that stimulus is identified as a positive reinforcer for Renee and can be used for intervention. If Renee performs similarly across both consequences, then a reinforcer has not necessarily been identified. Remember, preference does not equal reinforcer. Phase 2 must continue with additional stimuli until (hopefully) a reinforcer is identified.

If time on task is of more interest than task completion or accuracy of performance, then an interval recording system can be used to measure the percentage of intervals in which Renee remains on task during the 10-minute assessment sessions. A comparison is made of the percentage of intervals in which

TABLE 5
Behavioral Assessment Protocols for Assessment of Self-Injurious Behavior (SIB)
by Functional Analysis of Consequences

Condition	Task Setup	Activity	Contingency
Alone, no task	None	None	None
Alone, with task	None	Recreation; leisure task.	None
Demand	Psychologist presents instructional demands; ignores appropriate behavior.	Training in educational task.	Psychologist provides brief time-out from task contingent on SIB.
Social attention	Psychologist in room; ignores appropriate behavior.	Recreation; leisure task.	Psychologist provides social attention ("Don't do that; you'll hurt yourself") contingent on SIB.
Tangible	Psychologist in room; ignores appropriate behavior.	None	Psychologist presents preferred toys, objects, etc., contingent on SIB.

Note: Conditions based on Iwata, Dorsey, Slifer, Bauman, & Richman (1982) and Carr & Durand (1985).

Renee engages in on-task behavior across the different consequence conditions.

Functional analysis of consequences. Functional analysis is a special form of assessment reinforcer that is typically used to address aberrant behaviors that occur at a high frequency. As with other forms of reinforcer assessment, functional analysis is conducted by manipulating the consequences of behavior. However, it serves to identify what currently maintains an undesired behavior rather than what will increase an adaptive behavior. The basic premise of this type of assessment is that the behavior serves a function: to obtain the specified consequence. By systematically providing and withholding specific consequences for a problematic behavior across different conditions and comparing changes in the frequency of the behavior across sessions, we can determine which consequences result in the highest frequency of the behavior.

The consequences that are manipulated in a functional analysis represent different outcomes the child might experience as a result of aberrant behavior. For example, the consequences of Bill's head banging, although quite varied, can be divided among three general categories: (a) those that result in the gain of a desired outcome, such as social attention, a preferred toy, or a desired activity (positive reinforcement); (b) those that result in the removal of something not desired, such as physical contact or task-related demands (negative reinforcement); and (c) those that are not socially mediated but, rather, are maintained by intrinsic variables (automatic reinforcement) (see

Table 5). By identifying the consequence that results in the highest frequency of the behavior, we can determine what is reinforcing (or maintaining) the behavior.

The first step in a functional analysis is the same as with reinforcer assessments: formulation of hypotheses about what is maintaining the behavior. When a hypothesis is formulated, the next step is to determine how to assess it directly. For example, if Bill's teacher notes that head banging occurs primarily during times of one-to-one instruction such as grooming tasks, it might be hypothesized that escape from task (negative reinforcement) is the maintaining event for head banging.

This hypothesis can be tested directly by engaging Bill in a grooming task. Each time he attempts to bang his head against the counter, his teacher might back away from him and remove the grooming materials. After a pause of 20–30 seconds, the teacher resumes the grooming task. The withdrawal from the activity described above is repeated each time head banging reoccurs. This analogue condition can be alternated with one in which attention is provided (e.g., "Don't do that, you'll hurt yourself") *only* when Bill engages in self-injury. That is, the teacher ignores Bill until Bill bangs his head.

Assessment involves recording the occurrence and nonoccurrence of Bill's self-injurious (head banging) and appropriate (task-directed) behaviors by either an event or an interval recording system across a fixed amount of time (e.g., 10-minute sessions). From repeating each of the analogue conditions at least twice and comparing the rates of self-injury across conditions, the maintaining conditions of Bill's self-injury may become apparent. If self-injury occurs more often during the condition in which all demands and task materials are removed, the assessment supports the hypothesis that escape from task demands serves as a reinforcer for head banging. By alternating the escape with the attention condition and recording each occurrence of self-injury, we have met the two criteria for a functional analysis: direct observation and experimental control. In this case, experimental control is demonstrated through an alternating treatments design. (See chapter by Keith [this volume] for a description of single-case designs.)

Functional analysis of antecedent stimuli: Structural analysis. The final approach to evaluating the role of different environmental stimuli on a student's behavior is to conduct a functional analysis that manipulates the antecedent stimuli rather than the consequences (Carr & Durand, 1985). For the purposes of this discussion, we refer to this assessment as a structural assessment, because it focuses on the effects of the structural or contextual variables on behavior. A structural analysis requires that we observe the behavior under different environmental conditions. For example, we can observe behavior as it occurs naturally in the classroom. We can observe Renee's behavior under the natural classroom conditions and compare her rate of on-task behavior during individual versus group work periods so as to evaluate the effects of having peers in close proximity to her. We could also observe behavior across preferred and nonpreferred tasks to determine if task preference affects behavior.

When we observe different frequencies of behavior across different situations or activities, we can develop hypotheses regarding which variables account for those differences. If we observe that Renee remains on task for 80% of the intervals during group projects but only 20% of the intervals for independent work, we might hypothesize that Renee prefers working within a group rather than working alone.

Although the presence of peers is one variable that might be associated with different frequencies of on-task behavior, there are other factors that might confound the results of our assessment. It is plausible, for example, that different types of tasks are associated with individual versus group activities. Furthermore, group and independent activities might be associated with different amounts of attention from teachers as well as peers.

To test the roles of the different variables that might be influencing Renee's behavior, we could set up conditions either within or outside the classroom to look at very specific relationships between the presence or absence of different antecedent stimuli and the occurrence of on-task behavior. We can test the role of peer presence, for example, by comparing Renee's behavior across two different conditions —

having her work on a task at a table with and without peers — in neither condition receiving the teacher's attention. Thus, the activity and amount of teacher attention are held constant across the two assessment conditions that directly vary the amount of peer attention. If differences in behavior occur reliably across the two conditions, the role of peers as a variable associated with high rates of on-task behavior is confirmed. In addition, the influence of peers is assessed without having to instruct them on how to behave, as would be needed in a functional analysis.

Each type of assessment presented in this section is conducted prior to intervention to help us identify which interventions might be most useful. The results of assessment permit us to match intervention to the specific environmental conditions guiding a student's behavior.

Matching Intervention to Assessment

The primary purpose of assessment is to provide guidance for ongoing instruction. When the initial assessment is completed, it is possible to begin intervention immediately, because the results of assessment constitute the first phase of intervention. The following examples of Renee and Bill demonstrate how the assessment data can be translated directly into ongoing instruction. Notice how many options arise for different types of treatment.

Use of reinforcer assessment data for Renee. The goal of assessment for Renee is to increase her participation in assigned classroom activities. The results obtained from the reinforcer assessment provide two sets of information that can be used to develop an intervention plan. First, the results of the assessment identify a reinforcer, or perhaps several reinforcers, that can be used to increase the amount of time Renee spends engaged in classroom activities. The stimuli that result in the highest frequency of on-task behavior (i.e., praise) or the highest accuracy in performance can be provided to Renee contingent on participation in the assigned activity.

Intervention begins by placing Renee in the context of an assigned activity. As soon as Renee complies with a teacher request or participates in the activity for a specified amount of time, she receives the reinforcer. After the reinforcer is consumed or after a brief amount of time (up to 1 or 2 minutes), Renee is returned to the task and allowed another opportunity to earn the reinforcer. Over time, and with ongoing success, the amount of time required of Renee before she receives reinforcement can be increased slightly.

The second set of information derived from a reinforcer assessment is a list of consequences that Renee will not work for; that may, in fact, be aversive to her and function as punishers! For example, it is not unusual for an item listed initially (e.g., books) as a potential reinforcer to result in lower frequencies of target behavior than when no consequence is provided. In short, that consequence is inhibiting performance and is, therefore, punishing. Thus, a reinforcer assessment can also help you avoid the inadvertent use of punishment.

If a student is suddenly or unexpectedly performing poorly, it may be helpful to evaluate the effects of the stimuli that typically follow the completion of the target task to determine if that activity is preferred or nonpreferred. For instance, the teacher may typically send students back to their desks to play quietly or look at books when they've completed their assigned task. If Renee prefers to be with the teacher, she is in effect being given a choice between (a) completing her work and leaving the teacher to return to her desk (i.e., punished for working), or (b) dawdling over her work and remaining in the presence of the teacher (i.e., reinforced for remaining off-task). In fact, if Renee remains off-task long enough, she may gain one-to-one instruction with the teacher.

Use of structural assessment results for Renee. The results of the structural assessment provide information that can be used to augment an intervention based on another form of assessment (e.g., reinforcer assessment or functional analysis) or to develop a separate intervention. In Renee's case, the results of the structural assessment can be used to arrange assigned activities in such a way that the likelihood of participation is maximized.

If the results of the structural assessment indicate that Renee performs better within a peer group than at her seat, two options are available. First, the reinforcement program can be implemented only during times in which Renee is required to work at her seat. In this scenario, the reinforcer is used to compensate for the differences in the two task arrangements. This option would be a logical intervention if Renee's off-task behavior occurs primarily during seatwork.

A second option is to implement the reinforcement program within group activities to maximize the likelihood that Renee experiences the reinforcer. During the initial stages of this intervention, seatwork is minimized. After Renee consistently participates in the group activities for an acceptable amount of time, the reinforcement program is transferred to seatwork. Renee's success with the program in group settings may generalize to the seatwork situation. This is a logical intervention if Renee's off-task behavior occurs across both group work and seatwork.

A third option of incorporating the reinforcement program across both types of activities may appear attractive. However, such an extensive program is likely to be too cumbersome to be implemented with good integrity. Whenever a choice must be made between good integrity and increased frequency of treatment sessions, select the option that promotes good integrity.

Structural assessments can be used to develop interventions that are separate from other assessments. For example, Renee's teacher can structure the classroom routine so that tasks that are less preferred by Renee, but which must be completed, are presented in group situations. Alternatively, group activities might be used as warm-ups for independent seatwork. With a warm-up, Renee starts out working within a group but then is required to work at her seat for the remaining time. Seatwork is then followed (reinforced) by more group activity. As Renee's performance improves, the amount of time spent in seatwork is increased in proportion to the amount of time spent in group work until an acceptable balance between the two types of activities is achieved.

Use of functional analysis results for Bill. The results of the functional analysis demonstrate that Bill's head banging is maintained by negative reinforcement; that is, Bill bangs his head to escape from task demands. Thus, when Bill is provided with a demanding task such as grooming, he bangs his head against a counter, which results in time-out (removal from the grooming area). Given these findings, at least three intervention strategies are possible, depending on their acceptability to the IEP team and parents: (a) providing Bill with only nondemanding or preferred tasks, which requires a complete restructuring of his education program and the development of a plan to reintroduce demanding tasks; (b) providing him with brief "work breaks" that are contingent on appropriate behavior; or (c) teaching him to sign "stop" or "break" to indicate that he wants a brief break and providing a break for this appropriate communicative response (Durand & Carr, 1985). With each intervention plan, time-out must be stopped; Bill must not be allowed a break from the task when self-injury occurs. In fact, if Bill continues to gain a break from task (e.g., in the form of time-out) for head banging, then head banging will be reinforced, and you can expect Bill to continue to engage in self-injury.

Evaluation intervention. Each intervention is based directly on the results of assessment. The outcomes of intervention will ultimately confirm the validity of the assessment. For this reason, when intervention is first initiated, there is a need to develop an ongoing evaluation plan that teachers and parents can use to monitor the progress of the student. (See chapter by Tilly & Flugham [this volume] for a description of evaluation.) For both Renee and Bill, the goal of intervention is that they will participate in the desired tasks in the selected environment with as little intrusion as possible. If intervention is successful, Renee and Bill will be able to perform assigned activities under the same conditions as the other students in the classroom or perhaps as students in a less restrictive classroom placement. Thus, any components of an intervention that add to the classroom routine should be restricted to those that are essential.

For Renee, this could be accomplished by periodically probing her performance across group work and seatwork when additional reinforcement for participation is not provided. With Bill, regardless of the intervention plan selected, intervention will ultimately involve requiring Bill to participate in demanding activities for increasing amounts of time or until set amounts of work are completed. Probing Bill's performance to these ultimate criteria will make it possible to adjust the intervention protocol to facilitate acquisition of that goal. Evaluating the effectiveness of an intervention is discussed in the chapter by Tilly and Flugham (this volume).

SUMMARY

Most commonly, school psychologists have their first contact with students who are severely handicapped when they conduct some type of assessment. It is critical that the primary purpose of assessment be identified and discussed with the parents and IEP team. Assessment can be conducted to describe current functioning, to predict future functioning, or to prescribe intervention plans. Each type of assessment approach leads to different assessment strategies and outcomes. The approach selected should be based on the reason for referral, previous assessment results, and ultimately on the instructional goals for the student.

Assessment and intervention of students diagnosed as severely handicapped might be best conceptualized as constituting a continuum, ranging from initial assessment that prepares for direct intervention to ongoing evaluation of intervention that leads to documentation of improvement or changes in the intervention plan. Even when placement is the major outcome, assessment and intervention are driven by the educational goals developed for the student and by hypotheses developed about the student's responding in certain conditions. The initial assessment results serve to confirm or refute these hypotheses. If confirmed, intervention is initiated that serves to further substantiate original hypotheses or to modify initial conclusions. If refuted, further assessment may be needed. In either case, assessment is the first step of intervention. Ultimately, the outcomes of intervention provide the final analysis of assessment.

REFERENCES

Carr, E., & Durand, V. M. (1985). Reducing behavior problems through functional communication training. *Journal of Applied Behavior Analysis, 18,* 111–126.

Durand, V. M., & Carr, E. (1985). Self-injurious behavior: Motivating conditions and guidelines for treatment. *School Psychology Review, 14*(2), 171–176.

Fisher, W., Piazza, C., Bowman, L., Hagopian, L., Owens, J., & Slevin, I. (1992). A comparison of two approaches for identifying reinforcers for persons with severe and profound disabilities. *Journal of Applied Behavior Analysis, 25,* 491–498.

Iwata, B., Dorsey, M., Slifer, K., Bauman, K., & Richman, G. (1982). Toward a functional analysis of self-injury. *Analysis and Intervention in Developmental Disabilities, 2,* 3–20.

Kazdin, A. (1982). *Single-case research designs: Methods for clinical and applied settings.* New York: Oxford University Press.

Repp, A., Felce, D., & Barton, L. (1988). Basing the treatment of stereotypic and self-injurious behaviors on hypotheses of their causes. *Journal of Applied Behavior Analysis, 21,* 281–289.

Salvia, J., & Ysseldyke, J. (1988). *Assessment in special and remedial education* (4th ed.). Boston: Houghton Mifflin.

Sattler, J. M. (1988). *Assessment of children* (3rd ed.). San Diego: Jerome M. Sattler.

Steege, M., Wacker, D., & McMahon, C. (1987). Evaluation of the effectiveness and efficiency of two stimulus prompt strategies with severely handicapped students. *Journal of Applied Behavior Analysis, 20,* 293–299.

ANNOTATED BIBLIOGRAPHY

Iwata, B. A., Vollmer, T. R., & Zarcone, J. R. (1990). The experimental (functional) analysis of behavior disorders: Methodology applications and limitations. In A. Repp & N. Singh (Eds.), *Nonaversive and aversive interventions for persons with developmental disabilities* (pp. 301–330). Sycamore: Sycamore.
As the title implies, this chapter presents a thorough discussion of both the conceptual and applied issues related to the use of functional analysis procedures. The chapter begins with a discussion of the rationale for using functional analysis, followed by a complete description of the assessment procedure including options for data collection. Guidelines are provided regarding the interpretation of assessment results and development of interventions. In addition, the authors discuss possible confounding factors and limitations to the procedure.

Berg, W. K., & Wacker, D. P. (1991). The assessment and evaluation of reinforcers for individuals with severe mental handicap. In B. Remington (Ed.), *The challenge of severe mental handicap* (pp. 25–45). London: John Wiley & Sons Ltd.
This chapter provides an overview of a variety of reinforcer assessment procedures that have been successfully applied to persons with severe mental disabilities. Issues related to identifying reinforcers for persons with severe disabilities are discussed. Appropriate reinforcer assessment procedures are described and a discussion of their applications to educational settings is provided. The reinforcer assessment procedures are presented in the framework of those appropriate for low-rate behavior and those appropriate for high-rate behavior.

Fisher, W., Piazza, C., Bowman, L., Hagopian, L., Owens, J., & Slevin, I. (1992). A comparison of two approaches for identifying reinforcers for persons with severe and profound disabilities. *Journal of Applied Behavior Analysis, 25,* 491–498.
A forced-choice reinforcer assessment procedure is compared with one developed by Pace, Ivancic, Edwards, Iwata, and Page (1985). Prior to this article, the procedure developed by Pace et al. served as the standard for reinforcer assessments for persons with severe disabilities. Fisher et al. discuss the limitations of the Pace et al. procedures and present the forced-choice procedure as an alternative approach for identifying reinforcers. We consider the forced-choice approach to be a best practice for identifying reinforcers for persons with severe disabilities.

Repp, A., Felce, D., & Barton, L. (1988). Basing the treatment of stereotypic and self-injurious behaviors on hypotheses of their causes. *Journal of Applied Behavior Analysis, 21,* 218–289.
In this article, the process of developing and testing hypotheses regarding the cause of maladaptive behaviors is presented and discussed. Experimental analyses demonstrating the effectiveness of this approach are presented for three subjects.

Rusch, F., Rose, T., & Greenwood, C. (1988). *Introduction to behavior analysis in special education.* Englewood Cliffs, NJ: Prentice-Hall.

This book describes an alliance between special education and applied behavior analysis, reviews the practical and conceptual issues relative to behavior assessment and intervention with special education populations, and describes the application of behavior analysis to adaptive and maladaptive behaviors. The chapter describing the use of single-case designs to evaluate student progress is very useful.

69

Best Practices in the Assessment of Children with Attention Disorders

Steven Landau
Illinois State University

Barbara G. Burcham
University of Kentucky

OVERVIEW

Most school psychologists are already quite familiar with children who have deficits in attention, and this disorder by whatever name, is easy to conceptualize. Unfortunately, efforts at consistent communication have been more elusive. Historically, the disorder has been known as "brain damage syndrome," "minimal brain dysfunction," "hyperkinetic reaction to childhood" (i.e., hyperactivity), "attention deficit disorder" (with and without hyperactivity; ADD), and "attention-deficit hyperactivity disorder." Although frustrating for some, this trend of changing nomenclature does represent improved understanding of the population of children with ADHD (Schaughency & Rothlind, 1991).[1]

Children with attention deficits belong to a relatively large male-dominated group (prevalence estimates suggest about 5% of school-age children) who have serious difficulties in concentrating, inhibiting inappropriate responses, and getting along in the everyday world (Whalen, 1989). Therefore, their presenting problems clearly put them at great risk for difficulties at school, in terms of both academic performance and interactions with adults and peers. Thus, the school psychologist may be in a better position than any other professional to conduct a comprehensive assessment of the child with ADHD.

However, school psychologists are faced with the arduous task of reconciling confused communication among parents, medical and mental health clinicians, and school personnel due to discrepant classification models. Family physicians, pediatricians, psychiatrists, and all other mental health professionals use the psychiatric taxonomy found in the *Diagnostic and Statistical Manual of Mental Disorders* for the purpose of labeling. In contrast, classification by school personnel is the product of legal mandate, such as the reauthorized Public Law 94-142 (now the Individuals with Disabilities Education Act). Thus, school-based assessment of children with attentional difficulties should not be undertaken to address the diagnostic criteria for ADHD. Instead, the assessment objective for school psychologists is to determine the extent to which attentional problems are interfering with the child's academic, affective, and social needs, such that an appropriate intervention plan can be developed.

BASIC CONSIDERATIONS

Primary Characteristics of the Disorder

The evolving terminology characterizing children with attention deficits indicates a shift in emphasis regarding what is considered most central to the disorder. Most researchers agree that a deficit in *sustained attention*, the inability to remain vigilant, represents a significant difficulty for the child with ADHD (Douglas, 1983). Thus, these children appear much less persistent than their classmates. Even though many teachers use the term "distractible" to characterize their observations of a student's school performance, distractibility implies that the child seems unable to focus on task-relevant stimuli. It would seem that some students' attentions are seduced by extraneous and irrelevant events more aptly termed *selective attention deficit*. However, the bulk of current research indicates that their greatest difficulty stems from an inability to sustain a response long enough to accomplish assigned tasks. Thus, they lack perseverance in their efforts. As a consequence, parents and teachers attribute to them characterizations such as "doesn't seem to listen," "fails to finish assigned tasks," "can't concentrate," "can't work independently of supervision," "requires more redirection," and "confused or seems to be in a fog" — all apparently the result of this inability to sustain attention (Barkley, 1990).

However, it is important to stress that, even though inattention may be the source of some difficulty in a less structured, free-play setting, it is the more restrictive academic setting that creates the greatest problem for these youngsters (Milich, Loney,

& Landau, 1982). Thus, the specific expectations within a setting, and its relative degree of structure, play an important role in determining how truly deviant the child with an attention deficit might actually be. This may explain, in part, why limited correspondence exists when parents and teachers rate the symptoms of these children (Achenbach, McConaughy, & Howell, 1987). Expectations in the home environment are clearly quite different from those at school. This point was recently reinforced in a study by Landau, Lorch, and Milich (1992), who were intrigued by the surprising but frequent anecdote from parents that their child with ADHD is able to attend to television (for example, "He sits glued to the TV for hours!"). In fact, a pediatrician's recent advice column in *Parents* magazine suggested to parents that they could rule out thoughts of ADHD if their youngster was able to pay attention to television. Results of the Landau et al. study indicated that boys with an ADHD diagnosis, who are known to be extremely inattentive in the classroom, were able to attend to educational television to an extremely high degree and were indistinguishable from normal age-mates under some conditions. It seems evident that television holds greater intrinsic appeal than academic work for the child with ADHD and does not represent the historical source of frustration and failure associated with the classrooms. Thus, the Landau et al. (1992) study highlights the notion that measures of attention must be evaluated in terms of their ecological validity; that is, the nature of the task, and the assessment setting, must be representative of the criterion being predicted. As such, one would not necessarily expect measures of attention in the laboratory to correspond with attentional performance in the classroom.

The second primary symptom, *impulsivity*, involves behavioral disinhibition (Barkley, 1990) or problems with inhibitory control. As with inattention, impulsivity is a multidimensional construct, and it can be defined in several ways (Olson, 1989). For example, children with attention deficits can be impulsive in their problem solving when confronted with academic tasks. They are extremely quick to issue a response without considering or scanning all response alternatives. As such, they become known as fast but careless and inaccurate problem solvers. Obviously, this failure to engage a more reflective response style can have a deleterious influence on the child's academic achievement.

Unfortunately, impulsive responding, when considered as a manifestation of cognitive tempo, is extremely difficult to operationalize and quantify with objective methods. Even though laboratory procedures have been developed to evaluate this impulsive response style, empirical evidence for its construct validity is lacking (Milich & Kramer, 1984). In fact, performance on one laboratory measure frequently does not correspond with performance on another.

Besides cognitive tempo, impulse control problems can also manifest as an inability to suppress inappropriate behavior (also known as behavioral disinhibition). As such, children with attention deficits can be high risk takers (e.g., running out in traffic) and may be unable to delay gratification. In school, they experience difficulty waiting their turn in line, blurt out answers in class, constantly touch other children, and tend to be undesirable playmates because of their difficulty with turn-taking, sharing, cooperation, and a low tolerance for frustration while playing games (Landau & Moore, 1991). Here, too, problems exist regarding the clarity of the impulsivity construct, and there has been much debate regarding the central importance of this symptom. However, recent laboratory advances developed by Newman and Wallace (1993) to investigate behavioral disinhibition seem to offer an intriguing explanation for the difficulties experienced by children with ADHD (see Milich, Hartung, Martin, & Haigler, in press).

Finally, there is little controversy that many children with attention deficits engage in high-energy motor excess or *overactivity*. As with the other symptoms, overactivity can take many forms but is especially apparent as excessive body movements (both major and minor motor) and vocalizations. Thus, for example, these children are described as "always on the go," "squirmy and fidgety," "can't sit still," "hums and makes other odd noises," "talks incessantly," and "climbs excessively" (Barkley, 1990). When children with ADHD attempt academic seatwork, they may constantly get up and down from the desk (or do all seatwork while standing). In addition, many show minor motor fidgeting, such as pencil tapping or leg shaking, and seem unable to keep their hands off objects unrelated to the task before them. During individual psychological testing, children with attention deficits can be extremely challenging subjects, as they stand during testing or, if they do remain seated, rock the chair back and forth until it falls over. In addition, they may strive to handle the school psychologist's test materials throughout the evaluation, thereby disrupting all attempts at a standardized administration. However, the presence or absence of these behaviors during testing is not diagnostic in itself. It is critical to realize that children with ADHD may, or may not, be symptomatic during an office evaluation — be it during psychoeducational testing or a visit to the physician considering medication for the child.

Lastly, these children are often overactive and incessantly talkative in the context of social play — behaviors that can have a negative effect on peer relations (Landau & Moore, 1991). However, from an assessment perspective, it is important to remember that setting demands — in particular, the degree of structure in the environment — can influence the extent to which these children are considered deviant (Jacob, O'Leary, & Rosenblad, 1978). Thus, in a highly structured academic setting, where desks are placed in rows and all work is to be accomplished in one's seat, the child who is overactive may be considered extremely troublesome. In contrast, the same motor excess may be more tolerable in the open classroom setting, where cooperative learning is encouraged and students are expected to move about and collaborate with their classmates.

Associated Features

Children with attention deficits may experience numerous difficulties that go beyond the primary symptoms and diagnostic criteria. However, it is important to note that not all children with attentional disturbance experience these additional difficulties. This fact may account for the extreme heterogeneity among children who have received an ADHD diagnosis.

The most obvious secondary characteristic is conduct disorder, and many children with ADHD meet the special education eligibility criteria for Seriously Emotionally Disturbed (SED). Although the rates of overlap vary across studies, most investigators agree that up to one-half of all children with ADHD are comorbid for conduct disorder and/or oppositional-defiant disorder. Thus, many may be extremely stubborn, noncompliant, and hostile, and engage in rule violations, stealing, lying, and aggressive acts (Hinshaw, 1987). Follow-up studies of children with ADHD indicate that those who also show conduct disorder not only are more difficult to manage as children but will also have more serious adolescent and adult adjustment problems (Weiss & Hechtman, 1986).

Second, children with attention deficits are at elevated risk for achievement difficulties, and many meet special education placement criteria as learning disabled (McGee & Share, 1988). Because children with ADHD in the classroom are typically off task, noisy, disruptive, and out-of-seat, and do not finish school work or homework, both parents and teachers complain of underachievement. These children's work can be highly inefficient and disorganized, and their performance often shows great fluctuations. Consequently, there may be a grave discrepancy between a child's estimated potential for learning and actual achievement in school. To make matters worse, there is suggestive evidence that children with ADHD may score an average of one-half to one full standard deviation below age-mates on standardized tests of intelligence. Even though there are competing explanations for this discrepancy (see Barkley, 1990), there is reason to worry that these children do experience a delay in the development of some cognitive strategies (Whalen, 1989). Because of academic difficulties, many of these children experience grade retentions and other school failures. These failures combined with their problem behaviors and tendency

to alienate peers place them at great risk for negative feedback from parents, teachers, and the peer group. It is little wonder that they are also at risk for low self-esteem and depression as they mature. Even though this is a relatively new area of inquiry, the possibility of internalizing disorders must also be considered during the assessment process.

Third, many children with ADHD experience disturbed peer relations and are considered by others to be highly aversive playmates (Landau & Moore, 1991). As a consequence, they are frequently rejected by peers. Indeed, negative reputation can be established after only brief contact with unfamiliar children (Pelham & Bender, 1982). This rejected status is not surprising, as these children can be bossy, intrusive, disruptive, and easily frustrated while in the play group. They appear to have few, if any, friends. Peer rejection is a serious outcome for children with ADHD, as children who experience rejection early in life are known to be at high risk for many adult outcome difficulties, including job dismissals, bad conduct discharge from the military, police contact and incarcerations, and psychiatric hospitalizations (Parker & Asher, 1987).

Legal Requirements that Guide Assessment

It is important for school psychologists to understand relevant legal issues pertaining to the assessment of children with attention deficits. Evaluators must adhere to a careful and systematic identification plan to ensure that referred children suspected of having ADHD are not misidentified, overidentified, or underidentified. Schifani, Essex, and Wright (1992) even suggest that mistakes in assessment may lead to academic injury and, ultimately, charges of educational malpractice.

The process of assessment is complex and exacerbated by many variables. First, the characteristics of the disorder (i.e., inattention, impulsivity, and overactivity) are common to many children in the general population. However, it is only when these characteristics are excessive and/or developmentally inappropriate that a child should be identified as having a significant attention deficit. Second, children who do have an attention deficit may not present all symptoms representative of the disorder. Thus, there is extreme heterogeneity among children with ADHD. Third, the symptoms of ADHD often co-occur with a number of other disorders such as conduct disorder, and the symptoms may also be mimicked by associated problems such as abuse.

In 1991, the U.S. government issued a memorandum that clarified how children with ADHD qualify for special educational services as mandated by the Individuals with Disabilities Education Act (IDEA) and Section 504 of the 1973 Rehabilitation Act. Certainly, students who meet eligibility criteria for learning disabilities or serious emotional disturbances could receive services through those categorical placements. However, this memorandum made clear that children with ADHD may also qualify for special education support — under the Other Health Impaired category — as well as related services, solely on the basis of the attention deficit when it impairs educational performance (Aronofsky, 1992). The term attention deficit disorder does not appear in the IDEA, but this law does not attempt to provide an exhaustive list of chronic or acute health problems in the definition of "other health impairments." Thus, even though this category had long been available to serve children with health problems, it had largely been overlooked as a method of accessing special education services for children with attentional deficits (Latham & Latham, 1992).

The IDEA and Section 504 supply the foundation for identifying our responsibilities for proper school-based assessment of children with ADHD. However, school psychologists should be familiar with other laws regarding the education of these children. The Federal Civil Rights Act and the new Americans with Disabilities Act are examples of federal legislation that stress the requirement of schools to appropriately address the needs of children with disabilities. Also, awareness of the current litigation surrounding the issue of ADHD is important. Information about these laws and litigation is available through a variety of sources (Aronofsky, 1992; Latham & Latham, 1992; Martin, 1991). In addition, the Individuals with Disabilities Education Law Report can be obtained from LRP Publications, 747 Dresher Road, P.O. Box 980, Horsham, PA 19044-0980, (215) 784-0860.

The evaluation requirements under the IDEA and Section 504 for children with attention deficits are not unlike those for children with any suspected disability:

- A child must be evaluated before school personnel can begin programming.

- The parents must be involved in the evaluation process.

- The child must be evaluated in all areas related to the suspected disability.

- The evaluation team must include at least one specialist with knowledge in the area of the suspected disability.

In addition, evaluations must be kept current and are required at least every three years, or more often if (a) a parent or teacher request it, (b) if other conditions warrant it, or (c) if significant changes are to occur in the child's program. If a parent disagrees with the school's evaluation, the parent may obtain an independent evaluation which the school must use in educational programming decisions. Schools may even utilize identical evaluation processes and proce-

dural safeguards for both the IDEA and Section 504 compliance.

The IDEA requires public schools to use a multidisciplinary team to identify and evaluate children having, or suspected of having, a difficulty. The purpose of the IDEA is to ensure that all children with disabilities have access to a free, appropriate public education that emphasizes special education and related services designed to meet their individual needs. Additionally, it ensures that the rights of children with disabilities and their families are protected. The purpose of Section 504 is to end discrimination against individuals with disabilities and to improve educational services for them. It requires that:

1. Students with disabilities be educated to the maximum extent possible with nondisabled peers.

2. Educational agencies identify unserved children with disabilities.

3. Evaluation procedures be improved in order to avoid the inappropriate education that results from misclassifying students.

The intervention implications of Section 504 are somewhat different than those of the IDEA, in that they do not require a need for special education as an eligibility condition. Thus, children who do not meet the criteria for services under the IDEA may be served under Section 504 if their attention deficit limits one or more major life activities, such as learning. In either case, careful attention to assessment issues is essential as a basis for providing appropriate services to these children.

Issues of Diversity

As school psychologists begin to design their assessment protocol for children with attentional deficits, it is imperative to maintain an understanding and appreciation of the diversity inherent in our society. Diversity extends beyond race and ethnicity, to differences in language, socioeconomic status, gender, age, religion, and ability. Schools are filled with all types of children, some of whom need support to be successful learners and, ultimately, contributing members of their community. The consensus is that the prevalence of ADHD is neither higher nor lower among different cultures (Barkley, 1990). It is clear, however, that social, cultural, and economic factors can play a significant role in the adjustment of children with ADHD and the impact they have on their families. Parents' level of education, family income, and family stability often dictate the resources available to deal with the medical, educational, and behavioral challenges these children present. Cultural and religious factors may also affect the perspective taken towards the child's problems. Thus, when assessing these children, consideration must also be given to these issues.

In 1992, the Office of Special Education Programs (OSEP) initiated an effort to identify critical issues that must be addressed to provide a free appropriate public education for children from culturally and linguistically diverse backgrounds. This initiative includes children with ADHD from diverse backgrounds. The final task force report identified "assessment as a critical issue" of concern, suggesting that certain groups are over- or under-represented in programs for children with disabilities and for gifted and talented students. This task force identified several strategies for change including:

- Utilize assessment and placement procedures that do not use a model designed to find and fix deficits.

- Ensure that all assessment procedures and tests used for sorting individuals have been validated on a population representative of the culture of the individual being assessed.

- Utilize authentic, reliable, and valid multilingual, multicultural techniques designed to promote student growth and development.

- Ensure that alternative assessment techniques are sensitive to culturally and linguistically diverse students.

- Utilize instructionally relevant assessment in schools that focuses primarily on process and outcomes of education.

- Provide educational personnel with the resources to become effective participants in authentic assessment processes that consider the cultural background of the students being evaluated (Federal Resource Center, 1993).

These suggestions are appropriate for any assessment protocol designed for children with attention deficits. As school psychologists, we must remain sensitive to differences among children and advocate the use of assessment procedures that do not misidentify, over-identify, or under-identify children with ADHD because of their background.

BEST PRACTICES

Assessment in a Problem-Solving Paradigm

As suggested by the recent position statement on students with attention disorders by the National Association of School Psychologists (National Association of School Psychologists, 1992), many school psychologists have approached the assessment of children with attention deficits as a diagnosis-driven undertaking, while investing significantly less attention to the development and monitoring of school-based interventions. Thus, some teachers may be well aware of the fact that enrolled in their classroom is a child with a diagnosable attention disorder. Unfortu-

nately, they receive little collaborative efforts or support after the classification has been determined. However, the consultative model of Bergan and Kratochwill (1990) offers a useful problem-solving paradigm that can be translated into a flexible and dynamic assessment strategy to be directly linked to intervention planning and implementation. Thinking in terms of problem identification, problem analysis, plan implementation, and problem evaluation, school psychologists can collaborate with parents, school personnel, and community professionals to address the needs of children with attention deficits. In this way assessment is extended well beyond ADHD as a diagnosis and becomes, instead, an ongoing, problem-solving process.

The *problem identification* stage involves multiple objectives. For example, the school psychologist needs to determine precisely which behaviors evoke concern from significant others. Parent and teacher interviews, as well as omnibus rating scales completed by these informants, represent excellent strategies to accomplish this. By reflecting a normative perspective, rating scales also permit the school psychologist to determine the child's symptom severity or degree of deviance from age-mates regarding the behaviors of concern. Assessment during this phase continues until enough data are assembled to determine that a discrepancy exists between the child's current and desired levels of functioning (Bergan & Kratochwill, 1990). Direct observations in the natural setting can also prove useful for this purpose, especially if contrast observation data are collected on nonreferred same-gender classmates.

During the *problem analysis* stage, the school psychologist would identify the variables leading to the problem solution and develop an intervention plan to meet the stated objectives. During this phase, there are two major foci of the assessment process. The first is to establish the child's present abilities and resources to assist in meeting the objectives of the intervention (i.e., to determine if the concerns are due to a skill deficit or a performance deficit). In this case, individual psychoeducational testing may be warranted — both traditional norm-referenced and nontraditional curriculum-based measures. Second, variables external to the child, but within the environment and responsible for maintaining problem behaviors, would be assessed. For this purpose, further interviewing of teachers and parents about relevant events (e.g., the nature and timing of eliciting stimuli surrounding the presentation of inappropriate behavior), plus direct observations to precisely determine controlling variables, would be conducted. At this point, the specific intervention plan would be designed. In addition, tactics of implementation would be formulated, and the intervention evaluation would be planned (Bergan & Kratochwill, 1990).

During the *plan implementation* stage, the role of assessment is to ensure that the plan is being dispensed as formulated and to permit sensitivity to un-intended consequences of the intervention. Thus, for example, child or consultee (parent, teacher) behavior would be monitored for the purpose of establishing treatment integrity (i.e., to determine that the intervention is being dispensed as planned). Additionally, if the child with attention deficits was to receive psychopharmacological treatment in school, a checklist or rating scale designed to assess treatment-emergent symptoms (i.e., medication side-effects) should be administered.

Finally, during the *problem evaluation* stage, assessment continues to determine the extent to which intervention objectives have been met. Thus, assessment data would compare the child's performance at this stage with the desired goals previously specified during the problem identification stage (Bergan & Kratochwill, 1990). As before, interviews, rating scales, and direct observations could all be used to assess treatment efficacy. If, however, the assembled data reveal that some goals have not been met, further assessment would be indicated for the purpose of returning to problem analysis.

The preceding discussion highlights the fact that a comprehensive and efficient assessment of children with attention deficits involves procedures serving multiple purposes. The same assessment method could be repeated several times as the reasons for conducting the assessment change. Thus, for example, direct observation of behavior may:

- Indicate potential areas of concern during the problem identification state.

- Reveal controlling variables in the environment to facilitate problem analysis.

- Serve as a measure of treatment efficacy during problem evaluation.

In addition, a comprehensive assessment of children with attention deficits must reflect a protocol comprised of several necessary components. First, it must engage *multiple methods* of assessment. Each method (interview, rating scale, or direct observation) can account for only a portion of the description of the child. Thus, a sufficient assessment uses numerous and diverse procedures. Second, assessment should depend on *multiple informants*. Parent(s), every teacher, the child, and even peers can each contribute unique information about the problem. Multiple sources are critical in the assessment of children with attention deficits because:

- Different informants may evoke different behaviors from the same child.

- Informants vary in terms of their respective expectations and demands placed on the child.

- Each informant is embedded in a unique environment (i.e., parents are primarily exposed to home-based problems, whereas peers are more familiar with problem behaviors in the free-play setting).

It is known, for example, that mothers of ADHD boys may experience more serious discipline problems at home than do fathers (Barkley, 1990).

Finally, children with attention deficits should be assessed in the context of *multiple settings*, as data are consistent in documenting that these children do not present the same problem in a trans-situational fashion. Teacher reports, for example, may vary considerably as a function of differences in classroom structure and curricular demands. Also, children with ADHD may be relatively unremarkable on the playground but quite distinctive in the classroom. And, the child's behavior during individual testing in the school psychologist's office may have no implications for classroom behavior. Obviously, specific setting differences need to be integrated in the details of problem identification, problem analysis, and ultimately, problem evaluation.

Specific Assessment Procedures

Given the view presented earlier, assessment is an ongoing process and progresses with various objectives in mind. Throughout this process, school psychologists need to consider the entire range of potential difficulties that could be experienced by the child with attention deficits. Thus, it is not sufficient to determine the extent to which the child exhibits inattentive, overactive, and impulsive behaviors (plus a specification of settings and situations in which these problems present): One must also focus inquiry on the potential for secondary characteristics typically found in samples of children with attention deficits. These include conduct disorder, academic difficulties, disturbed peer relations, and the internalizing problems of self-esteem deficits and depression. If the school psychologist concludes that the child does, indeed, have problems in any of these areas, the determination should be based upon a developmental perspective (i.e., the child was found to behave in age-inappropriate fashion). This means that the school psychologist must have a sound knowledge of normative or age-appropriate behavior and use assessment procedures that include components with adequate normative data. Ultimately, this developmental perspective also provides relevant and realistic goals for the intervention plan (i.e., the child will be expected to behave in age-appropriate ways).

Rating scales. Behavior rating scales are an important component in the assessment of children with ADHD. The reader is encouraged to consult Barkley (1990) for a summary of the psychometric properties of numerous scales as well as their advantages and disadvantages. Rating scales allow practitioners to determine the degree to which a child exhibits certain characteristics relative to same-age and same-gender students. In addition, they collapse information across situations and time, and provide insight into concerns experienced by those individuals who work and live with a child. This also permits a cost-effective method of data collection on infrequently occurring behaviors likely to be missed by more direct methods. However, the weaknesses of rating scales must be acknowledged. For example, results from these scales simply represent the opinions of others and do not capture the uniqueness of the child's style nor the strengths he or she presents. In addition, rating scales reflect the limitations of any retrospective report, such as distortions in memory, misunderstanding of scale items, and informant bias. These data may also be influenced by cognitive, social, emotional, or educational characteristics of the rater. Thus, the results of these indirect measures should be interpreted with caution: They do not portray the child's actual behaviors but, instead, the informant's impressions of that behavior.

Dykman, Raney, and Ackerman (1993) have identified 42 rating scales that have been used to describe or diagnose children with ADHD. Some of these instruments were developed to assess the primary symptoms associated with the disorder, while others were designed to evaluate situational variation in problem behavior. In addition to the many scales identified by Dykman et al. (1993), numerous other rating scales may be useful in assessing comorbid symptoms and disorders or targeting adjustment factors within the family. Instruments such as the IOWA-Conners Scale (Loney & Milich, 1982), the Revised Behavior Problem Checklist (Quay & Peterson, 1987), Social Skills Rating System (Gresham & Elliott, 1990), and the Children's Depression Inventory (Kovacs, 1980/81) may provide valuable information regarding potential secondary characteristics exhibited by children with ADHD.

Due to the extensive array of currently available rating scales, selecting an appropriate scale can be a confusing task. One must carefully evaluate the psychometric properties of a particular scale as well as consider the age of the child and the quality of the norms. In addition, the particular questions to be addressed by that stage of the assessment process must be taken into account. If, for example, ratings were to focus on problem identification, an omnibus scale such as the Child Behavior Checklist would seem appropriate. However, if one needed to assess the child's response to medication, the Conners (1969) Teacher Rating Scale, known to be drug sensitive, would be a better choice. School psychologists should never allow preference for a particular scale to drive the assessment process: The questions under investigation determine instrument selection.

During the first stage of assessment, problem identification, school psychologists should select and utilize rating scales as a strategy to delineate specific reported concerns about the child. Because rating scales are quite sensitive to setting effects, it is helpful to have as many individuals as possible having direct contact with the student complete these. They give the school psychologist a better understanding of who views which behaviors as problematic and how perceived differences in degree of deviance vary as a function of setting effects. In order to have confidence in the reliability of the data, teachers should have at least 6 weeks of familiarity with the student being rated (Edelbrock, 1983).

During problem analysis, a careful review of data collected from rating scales can be invaluable in developing intervention plans. Not only can these data reveal specific concerns as a function of informant (e.g., the mother reports significantly more oppositional and defiant behavior than her husband), but differences in symptom severity as a function of setting may indicate where interventions must be implemented. For example, a child with attention deficits may have difficulty following directions and completing assignments only with the math teacher. This determination would evoke an hypothesis (to be further assessed by other methods) that the problem behavior may be situational or setting-specific in nature.

For problem evaluation, rating scales are invaluable as an objective method of assessing the child's response to intervention. By readministering the same rating scales to those informants who previously provided data for problem identification, the school psychologist will be able to make a baseline versus response-to-treatment comparison. Indeed, these scales should be administered intermittently throughout the intervention to ensure their continued potency.

Cognitive and educational assessment. Because the attentional difficulties presented by children with ADHD can interfere with the educational process, assessment of academic functioning must be considered. Standardized tests of cognitive ability and achievement can be useful for problem identification. Also, many states require these norm-referenced tests to determine eligibility for special education services, including those for the learning disabilities frequently experienced by students with ADHD. Unfortunately, tests such as the *WISC-III, Stanford Binet—4th Edition, Kaufman Assessment Battery for Children*, or any norm-referenced achievement test can not be used to reliably identify students as ADHD. In addition, they have limited value for the development of a remedial plan. However, in combination with a teacher interview and record review, standardized test data will assist in determining that an achievement problem does exist.

If the child with ADHD does exhibit academic problems, criterion-referenced tests and curriculum-based measures show much promise in delineating the student's academic needs and strengths. Being the most sensitive to academic growth, these nontraditional methods of academic assessment should be used for problem analysis and are also appropriate for problem evaluation. A compilation of the academic portfolio (i.e., a collection of work samples over time) will also reflect changes in the student's performance and, therefore, is extremely useful in monitoring progress and evaluating the effects of intervention.

Interviewing. Interviewing procedures are essential in the assessment of children with attention deficits and can serve multiple objectives. Interviews with parents and teachers are an effective means of building rapport and, for problem identification, highlight specific areas of concern about home- and school-based problems. Although frequently overlooked, interviews also provide parents and teachers an opportunity to say what they like about the child. Second, for problem analysis, interviews can reveal controlling variables and the settings and situations in which the problems occur. Third, interviews permit the school psychologist to determine potential reinforcers that parents and teachers consider most salient to the child and to tap into the resources of parents and teachers functioning as consultees during plan implementation. Another often ignored value of interviews is in helping the school psychologist discover parents' and teachers' attitudes about, and acceptability of, a particular intervention (see Elliott, 1988), thereby having implications for treatment integrity. Thus, interviews not only offer specific information about the challenges presented by the child with attention deficits and have direct relevance for the design of an intervention, they also permit the school psychologist to gain better understanding of the consultees who may implement the intervention. It is important to note that those respected standardized interview schedules currently in use that are organized to reflect psychiatric diagnostic criteria, even those that facilitate differential diagnosis, have limited value for designing an intervention and are best reserved for research purposes.

Some features specific to parent interviews need to be considered. Clearly, parents are the best informants regarding the child's developmental and medical histories. For example, specific thought should be given to establishing the presence of tics in the child or history of tic disorders in biological relatives, as this fact can affect the suitability of psychostimulant treatment for the child. Second, because many children with attention deficits present oppositional and coercive behaviors at home, the parent interview should be designed to reveal potential problems in the parent–child relationship. Consistent with Barkley's (1990) suggestion, this should be done in terms of the eliciting activities or situations about which the parents experience the greatest difficulty. Thus, the school psychologist will learn not only which problem behaviors are presented by the child,

but also where, and under what circumstances, they are presented, information crucial to the development of an intervention. In addition, differences between parents regarding their respective management strategies should be explored.

Because many children with ADHD can be extremely stressful to parents and may contribute significantly to marital discord (Fisher, 1990), it is important for the school psychologist to be sensitive to the impact that the child has on the entire family system. Parents should be asked questions pertaining to peer and sibling relationships which can be a source of great difficulty. Also, the child's general emotional state should be the focus of inquiry, and questions pertaining to self-esteem deficits and depression should be presented. Finally, the school psychologist should ask a series of questions to establish a prioritized list of parental concerns (i.e., which problems are most important to address first), the most salient reinforcers available to the parents, and the parents' motivation and ability to follow through on home-based recommendations. The reader is advised to consult Barkley (1989; 1990) for detailed guidelines on developing a parent interview.

Just as with parents, there are issues specific to the teacher interview that should be pursued. For example, to establish a functional analysis of behavior, the school psychologist should query teachers about inappropriate classroom behavior as a function of varying settings and structure. Given that many children with ADHD experience problems adjusting behavior as environmental expectations change (Landau & Milich, 1988), questions about transition time (e.g., going from recess to the classroom; lining up for lunch) should be included in the interview. Questions from the School Situations Questionnaire (Barkley, 1990) provide numerous other activities that could be the focus of this interview, and the teacher should be asked about the child's work habits and style of academic performance. Questions should target difficulties related to carelessness, disorganization, sloppy handwriting, and problems related to inefficiency. In addition, the teacher interview should pursue the child's ability to comply with commands at school and establish if problems in the peer group are present. If any of the above areas emerge as potential indicators of a difficulty, then further assessment is necessary to permit problem analysis. The interview should permit the school psychologist to assess resources available to the teacher to permit an effective school-based intervention, and special consideration should be made regarding the teacher's need for collaborative support from the school psychologist and other professionals working with the child.

Finally, some mention should be made of a direct interview with the child. Obviously, the purpose of this interview will depend on the age and maturity of the child, but it is a good practice for several reasons. First, this contact will facilitate rapport for subsequent sessions and will permit the school psychologist to observe the child directly. In this context, one should consider the child's language development, ability to comply with directions, and the degree of overactive/fidgety symptoms and inattention during the interview. However, it is important to remember that the presence or absence of particular behaviors during the interview may not be diagnostic of the child's actual problems outside the psychologist's office. And, the school psychologist must remain cautious when interpreting what the child actually says about problems at home or school. Children's self-reports are notoriously less reliable than reports from other informants, and children with ADHD have been found to deny about 50% of the problems attributed to them by their mothers (Landau, Milich, & Widiger, 1991).

Direct observation. Based upon informant concerns that emerge from the use of interviews and ratings scales, the school psychologist should then conduct systematic observations of the child with attention deficits, as these data will provide unique information. If the school psychologist observes the target child and all same-gender classmates engaged in the same activity, the resulting data can contribute to problem identification. For example, if the teacher complains about a boy who "never seems to get his math workbook problems completed; he daydreams constantly instead of doing his work," this boy's duration of on-task behavior can be contrasted with the average duration of all male classmates. These contrast data will not only establish if a problem does, in fact, exist but also suggest a realistic level of performance to serve as the intervention objective. Second, direct observations are necessary for problem analysis: They further clarify what the child is actually doing, and provide important information about the settings and situations in which problems occur. Thus, observations represent the best method of identifying controlling variables in the environment, a necessary component of the intervention design. Third, observation data can be used for plan implementation and provide information about treatment integrity. For example, the school psychologist may observe in the classroom to determine if the teacher is dispensing strategic feedback as prescribed. Finally, direct observations can establish the efficacy of an intervention (i.e., problem evaluation). Thus, direct observations can serve multiple assessment purposes and offer the most direct and ecologically valid behavioral data.

Unfortunately, no single observation system considered appropriate for all children with attention deficits exists. Instead, selection of particular code categories, specific recording methods to use (e.g., duration versus event recording), and the various settings for observation should depend on the informant concerns that emerged during problem identification.

In any case, it is crucial to observe the child with ADHD in multiple settings and situations. For example, the school psychologist may seek to determine differences in classroom performance as a function of small- versus large-group activities, teacher-directed versus self-paced academic seatwork, highly structured versus informal classroom settings, and restricted academic versus freeplay activities. Because different situations account for much of the variance in observed child behavior, resulting data should always be considered in the context of a particular setting.

When selecting a particular observation system, the system's potential to capture relevant information about specific areas of concern serves as the single most important criterion. In most cases, the system should at least be sensitive to the occurrence of inattention, motor excess, and impulsive responding in the classroom. The interval recording system described by Abikoff, Gittelman-Klein, and Klein (1977) is one excellent example. In addition, if problem identification reveals difficulties with peer relations, observations should be conducted when the child is engaged in freeplay behavior (e.g., on the playground; see, for example, Landau, Milich, & Whitten, 1984). Even though the use of these systems requires some training prior to implementation, they can provide data for the design of interventions not readily available through any other method of assessment.

Laboratory methods of assessment. During the past two decades, much interest (and money) have been invested in laboratory and computer-driven methods to assess children with attention deficits. For example, Kagan's Matching Familiar Figures Test — a match-to-sample procedure — is a standard lab measure of impulsive responding, albeit with serious problems (see Milich & Kramer, 1984). In addition, numerous versions of the Continuous Performance Task (the most marketed one being Gordon's Diagnostic System) have been used to quantify vigilance or attention in the lab. Even though their putative objectivity and efficiency is appealing, several inherent limitations should be kept in mind. Obviously, school psychologists must consider the psychometric properties of these various procedures. Equally important, but significantly more daunting, is the question of ecological validity. Under the best of circumstances (i.e., adequate normative data and sufficient reliability and validity), knowing the child's performance on one or more of these lab techniques contributes little to an understanding of how the child functions in the classroom. In addition, these procedures are incapable of revealing controlling variables that could be targeted for intervention. Thus, even though these computer-driven devices may have heuristic appeal to some and are considered by others appropriate for problem identification, they have questionable utility for problem analysis and should not be used for an intervention evaluation.

Assessment of medication effects. Since most children with ADHD experience a trial of psychopharmacological therapy sometime during their childhood, the school psychologist should be familiar with the best practice in the assessment of medication effects. This is particularly important, as it is known that a given dose of psychostimulant medication does not exert the same therapeutic effect on all domains of functioning for a given child or across children. In addition, many prescribing physicians tend to rely on parent anecdotal reports to determine proper dosage, especially if systematically collected data are not available. Thus, dose effects must be considered as part of the assessment process for children with attention deficits. The reader is encouraged to consult Gadow, Nolan, Paolicelli, and Sprafkin (1991) for a description of a school-based model of medication evaluation involving rating scales and direct observation data.

Whichever assessment protocol is ultimately adopted, the school psychologist should supplement it with the use of a Parent Daily Report sent home at the end of each school day (see Pelham, 1993). This procedure has high ecological validity and is designed to directly reflect the concerns of parents and teachers. It provides for the specification of agreed-upon and operationalized targets of intervention (both academic and social) and presents the child's daily performance in these areas. For example, the number of workbook problems correctly completed or frequency of inappropriate rough play during recess could be evaluated among several targets. As recommended by Pelham (1993), one person in the school (usually the school psychologist) should be identified as coordinator of medication assessment, and would be responsible for establishing collaboration among parents, teachers, and physician regarding the specification of targets. With the use of a Parent Daily Report, the child's performance is monitored on a daily basis (rather than the more typical once-weekly use of ratings and observation), and the parents are given daily feedback regarding the child's response to medication.

Clearly, any intervention applied to the child with ADHD should be monitored for the purpose of problem evaluation. However, with psychopharmacological therapy, there exists an additional concern that must also be assessed; that is, the possibility of treatment-emergent symptoms or side effects. To this end, Pelham (1993) provides an example of the standard side effects rating scale appropriate for school use.

Guidelines

The following guidelines, which have been modified from Barkley (1990), are suggested for the school-based assessment of children with attention deficits. These guidelines should not be considered a rigid chronology for the assessment process but, instead, a flexible model for decision making that can be linked directly to the planning and evaluation of interventions.

1. Identify the major concerns of referral sources, and apply a developmental perspective to establish degree of deviance from age-mates. Rating scales and interviews are efficient and appropriate methods here.

2. Begin to cluster specific concerns into areas of developmental domains of functioning (e.g., motor, language, social, emotional, academic) and into settings or situations of occurrence (home, school, free play with peers, community).

3. Conduct direct observations in all settings in which problems reportedly occur. This is done to (a) verify informant concerns, (b) further establish degree of deviance and treatment goals by concurrently observing child and same-gender classmates, (c) determine relevant situation/setting effects that may account for differences in informant reports, and (d) isolate controlling variables in each setting that may be suitable targets for intervention.

4. Rank-order the apparent problems and developmental concerns into a hierarchy of troublesomeness/seriousness for this case. This will help establish which interventions should be applied first and which can come later.

5. Identify unique aspects of this case that may have implications for treatment planning. Some examples include:

- Make note of particular features in the classroom environment that could compromise a prescribed behavioral intervention.

- Develop an understanding of parent and teacher acceptance of potential interventions being considered.

- Assess parent and teacher ability to serve as consultees during the intervention process.

- Establish child characteristics that could relate directly to the selection of a particular intervention (e.g., social skills training designed to increase rates of interaction will not be suitable for an assaultive child).

These unique aspects can be identified through the use of interviews and direct observations.

6. In collaboration with parents and teachers, list all interventions that seem appropriate to each area of dysfunction or delay, and make determination based on previously established resources, treatment acceptability attitudes, and strengths noted in the child.

7. Design and apply specific interventions according to hierarchical list of concerns and the unique features of this case.

8. Assess treatment integrity using direct observations.

9. Conduct problem evaluation with rating scales, direct observations, and Parent Daily Report.

10. Conduct posttreatment follow-up using previously applied assessment methods.

A BEST PRACTICE MODEL

The Broward County Public Schools in Ft. Lauderdale, Florida, which is committed to meeting the needs of children with attention deficits in the regular classroom, has developed an assessment model based on the use of the Intervention Assistance Team (IAT). As such, the following does not reflect an assessment protocol for school psychologists per se; it represents a problem-solving approach applied by school personnel, including the school psychologist.

Each school designates a contact person to whom all requests for assistance are made. This school-based contact person reviews each request and then channels it to the school's multidisciplinary team (IAT). The school psychologist and the team then enters into problem identification/problem analysis phases by reviewing records, conducting interviews and observations, collecting rating scale data, and consulting with the child's teacher to develop a plan of action. This plan may include such strategies as further clarifying child characteristics or environmental factors that could be interfering with the child's progress, implementing and evaluating classroom interventions, or referring the child and/or family to an outside service agency. If this level of intervention does not prove sufficient to meet the child's needs, the case is further reviewed by the IAT.

When the IAT reconvenes, they evaluate the problem based upon the data collected and, in collaboration with the family, determine if the student meets the 504 classification as a qualified individual with disabilities. If the child is considered an appropriate candidate for 504 services, parents, teachers, and support personnel collaborate in planning accommodation strategies that meet the child's needs and develop a 504 Accommodation Plan. This plan specifically addresses the kind of modifications needed:

- Physical arrangements of the classroom.

- Nature of lesson presentation and work assignments.

- Test-taking methods.

- Ways to help the student get organized.

- Suggestions for managing the child's behavior (including medication needs).

- Special considerations. For example, does the bus driver need support in managing the child with ADHD? Does the child's teacher need more information about the disorder?

Thus, the team extends its consideration to all others with whom the child has contact.

Once the 504 Accommodation Plan has been developed, a school-based case manager, responsible for completing a Section 504 record form is assigned to the child. This accommodation record form indicates the specific areas of difficulty for the child, the accommodations to be made, the date to start the accommodations, the person responsible for implementing the accommodation, as well as a specification of the means of outcome evaluation. It is the case manager's job to monitor the plan and set timelines for implementing and evaluating the accommodations. Parents receive copies of the Accommodation Plan and the Section 504 record, along with a formal notice of the rights afforded to them by Section 504.

If the accommodations described on the Section 504 record form are ineffective, the case is resubmitted to the school-based assistance team for review. The team, along with the family, makes one of two decisions at this point. First, it is determined whether to redesign and modify the accommodations on the Section 504 record form. If this decision is made, the student continues services with monitoring by the case manager. The other options available to the team may include: psychoeducational evaluation, a dropout prevention program, alternative educational services, and remedial services.

Broward County has taken a clear position that most students with ADHD can be educated in the regular program with the help of appropriate interventions. Evaluation of these interventions is viewed as an essential component of the assessment process, regardless of whether the child is served in the regular program or receives support through special education.

The Broward County Public Schools have developed a range of materials that describe its assessment model. These include a handbook outlining procedures used to implement Section 504 of the Rehabilitation Act of 1973, a series of forms enabling schools to comply with the guidelines, and a videotape illustrating the process. For further information and/or copies of these materials contact Dr. Merrick Kalan, 600 S.E. 3rd Ave., 8th Floor, Ft. Lauderdale, FL 33301. Send $25.00 to cover the cost of the materials and make checks payable to School Board of Broward County.

SUMMARY

Assessing students who exhibit notable difficulty with sustaining attention, impulsivity, and overactivity represents a challenge for school psychologists. Many of these children present not only the primary characteristics associated with ADHD, they also have co-existing conditions such as conduct disorder, learning disabilities, and significant problems with peer relationships. Schools are required to provide a free, appropriate education to children with ADHD, which includes an evaluation if attention problems are interfering with the child's ability to be educated.

A problem-solving paradigm, based upon Bergan and Kratochwill's (1990) consultative model, is proposed to guide the evaluation process for students whose attentional problems are negatively impacting their school performance. The paradigm encompasses

1. Problem Identification: The school psychologist determines specific behaviors causing concern in the school setting.

2. Problem Analysis: Variables that permit attainment of a solution are identified. They may include intervention development and psychoeducational testing.

3. Plan Implementation: Accommodations are made and treatment integrity is monitored.

4. Problem Evaluation: The assessment process continues in order to determine the extent to which objectives have been met.

Specific school-based assessment strategies are discussed including rating scales, direct observation techniques, and interviewing techniques, as well as intellectual and achievement testing. In addition, a description of a model program in a local school system is described.

REFERENCES

Abikoff, H., Gittelman-Klein, R., & Klein, D. (1977). Validation of a classroom observation code for hyperactive children. *Journal of Consulting and Clinical Psychology, 45,* 772–783.

Achenbach, T. M., McConaughy, S. H., & Howell, C. T. (1987). Child/adolescent behavioral and emotional problems: Implications of cross-informant correlations for situational specificity. *Psychological Bulletin, 101,* 213–232.

Aronofsky, D. (1992). ADD: A Brief Summary of School District Legal Obligations and Children's Educations Rights. In M. Fowler (Ed.), *CH.A.D.D. Educators Manual* (pp. 57–60). Plantation, FL: CH.A.D.D.

Barkley, R. A. (1989). Attention-deficit hyperactivity disorder. In E. J. Mash & L. G. Terdal (Eds.), *Behavioral assessment of childhood disorders* (2nd ed., pp. 69–104). New York: Guilford.

Barkley, R. A. (1990). *Attention-deficit hyperactivity disorder: A handbook for diagnosis and treatment.* New York: Guilford.

Bergan, J. R., & Kratochwill, T. R. (1990). *Behavioral consultation and therapy.* New York: Plenum.

Conners, C. K. (1969). A teacher rating scale for use in drug studies with children. *American Journal of Psychiatry, 126,* 884–888.

Douglas, V. I. (1983). Attentional and cognitive problems. In M. Rutter (Ed.), *Developmental Neuropsychiatry* (pp. 280–329). New York: Guilford.

Dykman, R. A., Raney, T. J., & Ackerman, P. T. (1993). *Forum report: Review of assessment tools.* Office of Special Education Programs, U.S. Department of Education: National ADD Forum.

Edelbrock, C. (1983). Problems and issues in using rating scales to assess child personality and psychopathology. *School Psychology Review, 12,* 293–299.

Elliott, S. N. (1988). Acceptability of behavioral treatments in educational settings. In J. C. Witt, S. N. Elliott, & F. M. Gresham (Eds.), *Handbook of behavior therapy in education* (pp. 121–150). New York: Plenum.

Federal Resource Center. (1993). *Task force report: Cultural and linguistic diversity in education.* Washington, DC: Office of Special Education Programs, U.S. Department of Education.

Fisher, M. (1990). Parenting stress and the child with attention-deficit hyperactivity disorder. *Journal of Clinical Child Psychology, 19,* 337–346.

Gadow, K. D., Nolan, E. E., Paolicelli, L. M., & Sprafkin, J. (1991). A procedure for assessing the effects of methylphenidate on hyperactive children in public school settings. *Journal of Clinical Child Psychology, 20,* 268–276.

Gresham, F. M., & Elliott, S. N. (1990). *Social skills rating system.* Circle Pines, MN: American Guidance Service.

Hinshaw, S. P. (1987). On the distinction between attentional deficits/hyperactivity and conduct problems/aggression in child psychopathology. *Psychological Bulletin, 101,* 443–463.

Jacob, R. B., O'Leary, K. D., & Rosenblad, C. (1978). Formal and informal classroom settings: Effects on hyperactivity. *Journal of Abnormal Child Psychology, 6*(1), 47–59.

Kovacs, M. (1980/1981). Rating scales to assess depression in children. *Acta Paedopsychiatria, 46,* 305–315.

Landau, S., Lorch, E. P., & Milich, R. (1992). Visual attention to and comprehension of television in attention-deficit hyperactivity disordered and normal boys. *Child Development, 63,* 928–937.

Landau, S., & Milich, R. (1988). Social communication patterns of attention-deficit-disordered boys. *Journal of Abnormal Child Psychology, 16,* 69–81.

Landau, S., Milich, R., & Whitten, P. (1984). A comparison of teacher and peer assessment of social status. *Journal of Clinical Child Psychology, 13,* 44–49.

Landau, S., Milich, R., & Widiger, T. A. (1991). Conditional probabilities of child interview symptoms in the diagnosis of attention deficit disorder. *Journal of Child Psychology and Psychiatry, 32,* 501–513.

Landau, S., & Moore, L. (1991). Social skill deficits in children with attention-deficit hyperactivity disorder. *School Psychology Review, 20,* 235–251.

Latham, P. S., & Latham, P. H. (1992). *Attention deficit disorder and the law: A guide for advocates.* Washington, DC: JKL Communications.

Loney, J., & Milich, R. (1982). Hyperactivity, inattention, and aggression in clinical practice. In D. K. Routh & M. Wolraich (Eds.), *Advances in developmental and behavioral pediatrics* (Vol. 3, pp. 113–147). Greenwich, CT: JAI Press.

Martin, R. (1991). *Extraordinary children, ordinary lives.* Champaign, IL: Research Press.

McGee, R., & Share, D. L. (1988). Attention deficit disorder-hyperactivity and academic failure: Which comes first and what should be treated? *Journal of the American Academy of Child and Adolescent Psychiatry, 27,* 318–325.

Milich, R., Hartung, C. M., Martin, C., & Haigler, E. D. (in press). Behavioral disinhibition and underlying processes in adolescents with disruptive behavior disorders. In D. K. Routh (Ed.), *Disruptive behavior disorders in childhood.* New York: Plenum.

Milich, R., & Kramer, J. (1984). Reflections on impulsivity: An empirical investigation of impulsivity as a construct. In K. D. Gadow (Ed.), *Advances in learning and behavioral disabilities* (Vol. 3, pp. 57–94). Greenwich, CT: JAI Press.

Milich, R., Loney, J., & Landau, S. (1982). The independent dimensions of hyperactivity and aggression: A validation with playroom observation data. *Journal of Abnormal Psychology, 91,* 183–198.

National Association of School Psychologists. (1992, May). Position statement on students with attention deficits. *Communiqué, 20,* 5.

Newman, J. P., & Wallace, J. F. (1993). Diverse pathways to deficient self-regulation: Implications for disinhibitory psychopathology in children. *Clinical Psychology Review, 13,* 699–720.

Olson, S. L. (1989). Assessment of impulsivity in preschoolers: Cross-measure convergence, longitudinal stability, and relevance to social competence. *Journal of Clinical Child Psychology, 8,* 176–183.

Parker, J. G., & Asher, S. R. (1987). Peer relations and later personal adjustment: Are low-accepted children at risk? *Psychological Bulletin, 102,* 357–389.

Pelham, W. E. (1993). Pharmacotherapy for children with attention-deficit hyperactivity disorder. *School Psychology Review, 22,* 199–227.

Pelham, W. E., & Bender, M. E. (1982). Peer relationships in hyperactive children: Description and treatment. In D. D. Gadow & I. Bialer (Eds.), *Advances in learning and behavioral disabilities: A research annual* (Vol. 1, pp. 365–436). Greenwich, CT: JAI Press.

Quay, H. C., & Peterson, D. R. (1987). *Manual for the Revised Behavior Problem Checklist.* Unpublished manuscript, University of Miami, Coral Gables, FL.

Schaughency, E. A., & Rothlind, J. (1991). Assessment and classification of attention deficit hyperactive disorders. *School Psychology Review, 20,* 187–202.

Schifani, J., Essex, N. L., & Wright, J. (1991–92). Attention deficit disorder: A growing legal problem for educators. *Administrator's Notebook, 35*(2), 1–4.

Whalen, C. K. (1989). Attention deficit and hyperactivity disorders. In T. H. Ollendick & M. Hersen (Eds.), *Handbook of child psychopathology* (2nd ed., pp. 131–169). New York: Plenum.

Weiss, B., & Hechtman, L. T. (1986). *Hyperactive children grown up.* New York: Guilford Press.

ANNOTATED BIBLIOGRAPHY

Barkley, R. A. (1990). *Attention-deficit hyperactivity disorder: A handbook for diagnosis and treatment.* New York: Guilford.
  The most comprehensive and scholarly text pertaining to children with attention deficits. Although some of it seems more suitable for clinic-based practitioners, many chapters are extremely relevant for the school psychologist. These include an exhaustive review of rating scales and an excellent discussion of classroom-based modifications and interventions.

Welsh, R., Burcham, B., DeMoss, K., Martin, C., & Milich, R. (1992). *Attention-deficit hyperactivity disorder diagnosis and management: A training program for teachers.*
  This is an excellent in-service training program that school psychologists can use to enhance the knowledge base of teachers regarding the assessment and treatment of children with ADHD. Developed by the collaborative efforts of the University of Kentucky's Departments of Psychiatry and Psychology, it is available from the Kentucky Department of Education, Nancy LaCount, Division of Special Learning Needs, 500 Mero Street, Frankfort, KY 40601.

CHADDER, published by Children with Attention Deficit Disorders (CH.A.D.D.), 1859 North Pine Island Road, Suite 185, Plantation, FL 33322, (305) 587-3700.
  This newsletter, published by the active parent-support group for children with ADHD, can provide helpful information to parents and teachers regarding assessment, treatment, and legal/placement issues.

DuPaul, G. J., & Stoner, G. (1994). *Assessment and treatment of attention deficit hyperactivity disorder in the schools.* New York: Guilford.
  This text provides a comprehensive review of ADHD in the context of a school setting. Issues of school-based identification and intervention are thoroughly discussed. In addition, the authors review topics such as how to involve families, as well as students, in the educational process.

AUTHOR NOTE

Sincere appreciation is extended to Richard Milich and Mark Swerdlik whose helpful comments and suggestions contributed significantly to this chapter.

FOOTNOTE

[1]The term ADHD will be used throughout this chapter to refer to children and youth with attention-deficit hyperactivity disorder or undifferentiated attention deficit disorder.

70

Best Practices in Assessment and Intervention with Children with Low Self-Esteem

E. Scott Huebner
University of South Carolina

OVERVIEW

School psychologists often are asked to consult with teachers who view children's problems as a manifestation or result of low self-esteem. In support of such concern, numerous psychological theories emphasize the importance of positive views of oneself and one's capabilities as a prerequisite to favorable psychological and educational adjustment. Indeed, research has demonstrated that children with high self-esteem are active, expressive individuals who tend to be successful in academic and interpersonal contexts. They display confidence and optimism about their abilities, social skills, and personal qualities. They initiate rather than passively listen in group discussions, are eager to express their opinions, and are not particularly sensitive to criticism. Overall, they experience a greater internal locus of control.

In contrast, children with low self-esteem tend to report feelings of isolation, anxiety, and self-consciousness. They are more sensitive to criticism and are thus less likely to assert their opinions or needs. They are more readily discouraged, giving up easily in the face of difficulties or avoiding challenges altogether. Finally, they experience greater difficulty in accepting others, leading to interpersonal conflicts. In summary, children with negative views of themselves will likely be at a considerable disadvantage compared to their counterparts with average or high self-esteem. (See J. A. Hattie, 1992, and Silvernail, 1987, for reviews.)

This chapter provides an overview of (a) selected self-concept measures, (b) special issues in the assessment of self-concept (e.g., use with special populations), (c) correlates of self-concept (e.g., demographics, family variables), and (d) intervention studies. These topics will be addressed within a general problem-solving framework; which has previously been applied to such areas as personality assessment (Knoff, 1990), consultation (Bergan & Kratochwill, 1990), and individual therapy (Goldfried & Davison, 1976).

BASIC CONSIDERATIONS

Definitional Issues

The past several decades have seen increasing interest in the theory and measurement of self-concept. Crain and Bracken (1993) report that more than 11,000 studies of self-concept have been published from 1974 to 1992 alone. Along with the increase in research, a proliferation of self-concept scales has emerged.

Before providing a brief historical overview of changes in self-concept theory and measurement, I should at this point define "self-concept." This is no easy task; numerous authors have provided a variety of definitions. Some authors distinguish between self-concept and self-esteem. For example, Rosenberg (1979) has defined self-concept as "the totality of the individual's thoughts and feelings having reference to himself as object" (p. 7). Self-concept is thus defined broadly to include an individual's total set of possible descriptions of herself or himself, not all of which may be evaluative in nature. The term "self-esteem" is restricted by some to the descriptions or beliefs to which a person attaches a positive or negative evaluation (e.g., Coopersmith, 1967). Self-concept thus describes individuals' perceptions of themselves, and self-esteem reflects their evaluations of their perceptions (Silvernail, 1987). Although these terms can be distinguished conceptually, research has not supported their differentiation (Shavelson, Hubner, & Stanton, 1976; Bracken & Howell, 1991). Rather, the research suggests that self-concept and self-esteem are "in fact a single construct or two very closely related constructs" (Bracken & Howell, 1991, p. 325). Thus, the terms will be used interchangeably throughout the chapter.

Changing Models of Self-Concept

Early self-concept research was based upon models that posited a unidimensional construct (e.g., Coopersmith, 1967). Self-concept was thought to be best conceptualized and assessed by combining an individual's self-evaluations across items tapping a diverse range of content domains (e.g., behavior, competence, affect, physical appearance, peer acceptance). The items were given equal weights and summed to derive a total score reflecting an individual's global self-concept. However, different instruments emphasized different domains during test construction, often yielding measures producing equivocal results.

Unidimensional models have been challenged by those who argue that such approaches mask important distinctions that individuals make in evaluating themselves in relation to various facets or domains in their lives (e.g., Harter, 1982; Wylie, 1974, 1979). Current research has provided strong support for the multidimensionality of self-concept (see Bracken, 1992; Harter, 1989; Marsh, 1988; Shavelson, Hubner, & Stanton, 1976). Such approaches yield profiles of self-evaluations across the particular domains included in the self-concept measures. For example, in a conceptual review of the self-concept literature, Bracken (1992) identified six specific domains that have been supported empirically in numerous research studies of children from age 8 to 18 approximately. These domains included family, social, competence, academic, affect, and physical. Evaluation of each of these domains, in addition to a global evaluation, enables a more differentiated assessment of children's self-concepts, which can produce more focused intervention plans. Obviously, interventions would differ for a child whose self-concept difficulties were limited to the family domain, compared to one whose difficulties involved primarily the academic and competence domains. The greater specificity of the multidimensional models has generated much support for their use in applied work.

BEST PRACTICES

Problem Identification

Problem identification requires the assessment of self-concept from a multidimensional framework. During the problem-identification stage of the problem-solving model, the school psychologist must determine in which domain(s) the child manifests negative self-perceptions. In the next section, six of the major self-concept measures are described, and issues related to their use are discussed.

Measures of Self-Esteem

Piers-Harris Children's Self-Concept Scale (The Way I Feel About Myself) (PHCS) (Piers, 1984). The PHCS is a widely used 80-item self-report questionnaire that has been researched extensively. It consists of simple declarative sentences (e.g., I like being the way I am; I have many friends) to which the child responds "yes" or "no." Reading difficulty is at approximately the third grade level; thus the scale is not recommended for students below the fourth grade level.

The PHCS was normed on 1183 children in grades 4–12 from one Pennsylvania school district. Internal consistency reliabilities for the total score range from .88 to .93. Test-retest correlations range from .42 (eight months) to .96 (three to four weeks). Concurrent validity estimates in the form of correlations with other self-concept measures range from .32 to .85. Although this scale was originally conceptualized as unidimensional, the manual provides six subscale scores: Behavior, Intellectual and School Status, Physical Appearance, Anxiety, Popularity, and Happiness/Satisfaction. However, because factor analytic studies have yielded inconsistent findings, Piers (1984) encourages caution in interpreting the subscales.

The Self-Esteem Inventory (SEI) (Coopersmith, 1984). The SEI School Form is a 58-item self-report scale designed "to measure evaluative attitudes toward the self in social, academic, family, and personal areas of experience" (Coopersmith, 1984, p. 1). There is an eight-item Lie Scale incorporated within the scale as well. The items are worded as brief statements (e.g., My parents and I have a lot of fun together; I'm pretty sure of myself) to which the student must respond with "like me" or "unlike me." Also available is a 25-item short form that correlates .86 with the long form.

The manual includes data from several large, but inadequately described normative samples. Users are strongly encouraged to develop local norms. Internal consistency reliabilities are reported as ranging from .87 to .92 for the total score for children in grades 4–8. Test-retest reliability for the SEI was originally reported by Coopersmith (1967) to be .88 (five-week interval) for a sample of 50 fifth graders and .70 (three-year interval) for a sample of 56 children. Fullerton (1972) reported a correlation coefficient of .64 (one-year interval) for a sample of 104 children in grades 5 and 6. Numerous studies support the concurrent validity of the SEI total score. Factor analytic studies have not provided consistent support for the hypothesized subscale scores, thus leading Harter (1990) to conclude that "the Coopersmith Inventory total score will provide a general estimate of self-esteem that may be fruitfully used as a first screening assessment, but will not provide a meaningful profile of domain-specific evaluations" (p. 297).

The Self-Perception Profile for Children. (SPPC) (Harter, 1985). The SPPC, which is available from the author, is a revision of the Perceived Competence Scale for Children (Harter, 1982). This 36-item scale, designed for students from ages 8 to 15, yields subscale scores for five competency or skill domains. Scholastic Competence, Social Acceptance, Athletic Competence, Physical Appearance, and Conduct/Behavior. Internal consistency estimates for the various subscales range from .73 to .86.

Concurrent validity has been demonstrated with a variety of self-concept scales. Factor analytic studies reported in the manual consistently have revealed a five-factor structure. Its most controversial feature is its unique item format. Children must respond by marking "really true for me" or "sort of true for me" to one of two alternative statements for each item (e.g., Some kids are happy with themselves as a person; Other kids are often not happy with themselves). Although designed to reduce social desirability responding, this response format is difficult for some children to understand, thus limiting its usefulness (Witt, Cavell, Heffer, Carey, & Martens, 1988). It should be noted that there are separate versions for younger children (The Scale of Perceived Competence and Social Acceptance for Young Children [Harter & Pike, 1984]) and adolescents (The Self-Perception Profile for Adolescents [Harter, 1988]).

Self-Description Questionnaire–1 (SDQ–1) (Marsh, 1988). The SDQ–1 is a 76-item self-report scale designed for use with students ages 6 to 11. Based upon Shavelson, Hubner, and Stanton's (1976) multidimensional self-concept model, it consists of eight subscales: Physical Abilities, Physical Appearance, Peer Relationship, Parent Relationship, Reading, Math, General-School, General Self. The SDQ–1 displays good internal consistency, with coefficient alphas all in the .80s and .90s for its subscales. Numerous studies are reported in the manual demonstrating convergent and discriminant validity. Extensive factor analytic research has supported its hypothesized factor structure, providing support for the usefulness of the various subscale scores. There are separate versions for adolescents (SDQ–II [Marsh, 1990]) and college students (SDQ–III [Marsh, 1991]). To date, the major limitation of the SDQs is that the normative data for all three versions have been obtained exclusively from students in Australia.

Self-Esteem Index (Brown & Alexander, 1991). The Self-Esteem Index is an 80-item self-report instrument based on a multidimensional model incorporating four domains: familial acceptance, academic competence, peer popularity, and personal security. An estimate of global self-esteem is derived by summing the responses to all 80 items. The test was standardized in 1988 and 1989 on 2455 students age 8–10 and 11–18 from 19 states. The demographic characteristics of the sample compare favorably to comparative U.S. population statistics with respect to gender, race, domicile, geographic region, ethnicity, and parental educational attainment. In short, the standardization data were excellent.

In contrast to the standardization, less effort was expended on reliability and validity research. Internal consistency estimates were acceptable, most falling in the .80s and .90s throughout the age range. However, test-retest data were not reported. Concurrent validity studies demonstrated encouraging correlations with similar measures (Piers-Harris, Coopersmith); nevertheless, all of the studies included less than 30 subjects from restricted age ranges. Finally, although preliminary factor analytic data supported the multidimensionality of the subscales, the correlations between the subscales and criterion measures were unacceptable in several instances (e.g., .04 between Academic Competence and Coopersmith's School-Academic scale; .29 between Peer Popularity and the Piers-Harris Popularity scale). Although this instrument is highly promising, additional validation work is needed before it can be used confidently in diagnostic decision making with individuals.

Multidimensional Self Concept Scale (MSCS) (Bracken, 1992). The MSCS is the most recent addition to the plethora of self-concept scales potentially available to the school psychologist. The 150-item scale is appropriate for students between 9 and 19 years of age. The scale requires students to rate items by degree of agreement using a modified Likert format with no neutral option (i.e., strongly agree, agree, disagree, strongly disagree). The MSCS was designed to assess individual's self-perceptions across six contexts: Social, Competence, Affect, Academic, Family, and Physical. An equal number of items is included in each scale.

The standardization data were obtained from 2501 students (ages 9–19) from 17 sites located in all major regions of the United States. The MSCS sample closely matches U.S. population demographic characteristics. Total scale internal consistency reliabilities range from .97 to .99 for each age level and the total sample. Subscale reliabilities range from .87 to .97. Test-retest reliabilities are reported as .90 for the Total scale score and .73–.81 for the subscales. Several studies have supported the convergent and discriminant validity of the scales. A large-scale joint factor analysis of the MSCS with the Coopersmith Self-Esteem Inventory, Piers-Harris Self-Concept Scale, Self-Esteem Index, and the Tennessee Self-Concept Scale has provided support for the six dimensions (Bracken, Bunch, Keith, & Keith, 1992). Although research with the MSCS is just beginning, the instrument appears especially promising as an individual clinical assessment tool, particularly given its outstanding norms and careful development.

Issues in the Assessment of Self-Concept

The use of any of the above measures must be tempered by several considerations. The first issue involves developmental differences in the structure and content of the self-domains. Regarding the structure, some researchers (Harter, 1989; Marsh, 1990) have provided tentative empirical support for the notion that an increasing number of domains can be differentiated by children as they mature. For example, Harter's self-perception scale for adolescents includes three domains (close friendships, romantic relationships, and job competence) that are not included in the preadolescent version. The addition of these domains is thought to reflect not only developmental advances but also changes in the concerns of adolescents.

Another developmental limitation is demonstrated in the fact that "young children are incapable of making judgments about their global self-worth" (Harter, 1990, p. 303). That is, it is not until middle childhood (approximately age 8 and above) that children can make conscious, reliable verbalizations about global self-esteem. Taken together, these developmental issues suggest limitations in the use of any *one* instrument with children of all ages. A given instrument may be particularly appropriate to the concerns of one age range, but not appropriate to the concerns of another age group. Thus, sensitive assessment of the self-concept across different age groups may require different assessment strategies and instruments.

The second issue involves the use of self-report measures of self-concept with special populations, such as children with handicapping conditions or children from different cultural settings. Because self-concept measures have been developed mostly for use with "normal" school children, their use may present unique problems with special populations. Some children may not possess the skills to respond to the self-report scales as intended. Among children with mild mental handicaps and learning disabilities, Harter and her associates (Renick & Harter, 1989; Silon & Harter, 1985) have found differences in the factor structures of her instruments compared to nonhandicapped children. For example, she obtained a two-factor solution to the SPPC with a group of mildly mentally retarded children, ages 9 to 12. This finding suggests that mildly mentally handicapped children differentiate among fewer domains than their nonhandicapped agemates. With students with learning disabilities, additional factors have been defined. Not only is scholastic competence differentiated from athletic competence (as well as the other SPPC domains), but general intellectual ability is differentiated from the specific skills involved in particular school subjects (e.g., reading). As a result of such findings, Harter revised the SPPC for use with learning disabled (LD) students to assess academic and general cognitive perceptions independently. Without separate subscales, a user might inadvertently derive the wrong conclusions regarding the cognitive self-perceptions of an LD child.

Although little cross-cultural research has been done, particularly with regard to the specific domains of self-concept (J. A. Hattie, 1992), similar cautions likely apply. That is, users of popular self-concept scales must be especially cautious with handicapped and culturally different children.

The final caveat involves the use of self-report scales of any kind with children and adolescents. Self-report scales have long been considered suspect by some because of problems such as social desirability, unclear observable referents, and poor agreement with ratings by others and with observed behavior (see LaGreca, 1990; Witt, Heffer, & Pfeiffer, 1990). Nevertheless, the difficulties surrounding the assessment of children's covert, internal states via other assessment techniques (e.g., teacher and parent report, direct observation) have prompted the development of more psychometrically sophisticated self-report methods such as those described above. Thus, at present, the school psychologist would be wise to conduct a multimethod, multiperson assessment. Multiple methods and raters are desirable to overcome the limitations of any one procedure or individual's perspective. Thus, comprehensive, multimodal approaches, including such procedures as parent and teacher interviews and/or ratings and behavioral observations, are likely to be essential in developing the most accurate picture of the child's self-concept.

School psychologists must be cautious, however, in extrapolating from self-evaluations to behavior. As J. A. Hattie (1992) has noted, self-perceptions may guide behavior, but in many instances it does not. Also, not all individuals monitor or control their self-presentations consistently (Snyder, 1987). Different children may manifest low self-esteem with disparate behaviors (e.g., acting-out behaviors, withdrawn behaviors). Since many factors mediate the relationship between self-concept and behavior, it should be apparent that a strong, one-to-one correspondence between a child's self-concept ratings and particular behavior(s) across situations is unlikely.

Not surprisingly, few formal, standardized behavioral measures of self-concept have been developed (Chiu, 1987; Hughes, 1984). Those that have been developed have received little research attention. Also, to my knowledge, no multidomain behavioral measures have been developed. Consequently, the school psychologist must rely upon behavioral indicators specific to the individual case. Possible behavioral examples from Chiu's (1987) research include: hesitates to speak up in class, adapts poorly to new situations or new tasks, becomes upset by failures (e.g., by pouting, whining, withdrawing), gets along poorly with peers, gives in to others easily, tends to dominate or bully other children.

Finally, self-concept data need to be integrated with all other assessment and background data. For example, Bracken (1992, Appendix D) in a useful table describes the overlap between his MSCS domains and more than 100 commonly used psychoeducational instruments, such as behavior rating scales, adaptive behavior inventories, omnibus personality and adjustment inventories (e.g., MMPH) and projectives (e.g., sentence completion, apperception tests).

PROBLEM ANALYSIS

Problem analysis encompasses a description of the child's areas of low self-concept and an understanding of the variables that might cause, support, or maintain the low self-concept. This process is accomplished through an analysis of intrapersonal and environmental forces that may be influential for a given individual. One may develop working hypotheses concerning possible antecedent variables by examining the existing research base on self-concept and its correlates. The following discussion will focus on research related to demographic, family process, school, and cognitive process variables.

The relationship between demographic variables and self-concept has been investigated in several studies. There is little evidence for consistent, systematic differences in global or domain-specific self-concepts as a function of age, gender, race, or socioeconomic status, as measured by occupational status or income (Bracken, 1992; Wylie, 1979). Thus, there is insufficient support for the widely held notions that self-concept decreases when children enter adolescence or that disadvantaged children show lower levels of self-concept than middle-class children.

Although social status variables have little, if any, direct relationship with self-concept, J. A. Hattie (1992) suggests that their effects may be indirect, operating through family process variables. J. A. Hattie's review shows considerable support garnered for Coopersmith's (1967) conclusions about the family antecedents of self-concept: acceptance of children by their parents, clearly defined and enforced limits, and respect and latitude for children's behavior within defined limits. Self-concept is thus related to parental evaluations, interests, and expectations, all of which provide stimulation for the child's developing self-concept.

Self-concept also has been investigated in relationship to school variables. For the most part, this literature has revealed few meaningful, reliable findings. However, there are suggestions that teacher expectations as well as students' perceptions of their teachers' expectations relate to self-esteem. For example, some evidence suggests that students who feel liked and respected by their teachers have high self-concepts, while those who believe they are disliked by their teachers have lower self-concepts. Also, teachers described as displaying democratic leadership techniques coupled with a relatively low degree of negative evaluations have been associated with students with higher self-concepts (for reviews of the influences of school variables, see J. A. Hattie, 1992; Silvernail, 1987). These findings are not surprising in light of the findings regarding family influences.

Finally, various intrapersonal variables have been found to relate to self-concept. Most important, research suggests that high self-concept is correlated significantly with cognitive processes, such as attributions for success to ability and to effort (Marsh, Cairns, Relich, Barnes, & Debus, 1984). Students with higher academic self-concepts tend to demonstrate a more internal locus of control, attributing outcomes to their own actions rather than to external events or chance. In contrast, students with low self-concepts tend to blame others or external conditions or chance. Low self-concept students have also been found to self-reinforce less frequently than do high self-concept students (Ames & Felkner, 1979).

INTERVENTION

Although many standardized intervention programs have been designed to improve self-concept, few have demonstrated validity. Self-concept intervention studies have been categorized by J. Hattie (1992) as falling into three general categories: cognitive-behaviorally oriented programs, affectively oriented programs, and programs neither cognitively nor affectively oriented.

Cognitive-behaviorally oriented programs assume that changing an individual's thought patterns (e.g., negative self-statements) will change the feelings and behavior that characterize and maintain low self-concepts. For example, rational-emotive therapy (RET), in which children are taught specific strategies to dispute unrealistic, irrational cognitions related to low self-concepts, has been applied to children and adolescents (DiGuiseppe & Bernard, 1990).

Attribution retraining approaches also assume that an individual's cognitions influence the intervention process. Specifically, attribution styles theory maintains that a low self-concept is mediated by global, stable internal attributions for failures. Change efforts therefore attempt to modify attributions based upon failure to reflect attributions based upon lack of effort, coupled with positive statements about ability, whereas attributions based on success are modified by encouraging self-reinforcement based on effort and ability (Craven, Marsh, & Debus, 1991).

Cognitive-behavioral approaches also include personal development programs (e.g., social skills training, vocational training, values clarification) communications skills courses, and transactional analysis approaches. See Pope, McHale, and Craighead (1988) for an example of a *multidimensional* cognitive-behavioral approach.

Affectively oriented programs rely upon efforts to increase an individual's awareness of her or his feelings, which presumably impede the development of a positive self-concept. Such methods also focus heavily on the interpersonal relationships between clients and the therapist/change agent. J. Hattie (1992) described approaches based upon Adlerian, client-centered, and Gestalt models in this category, including such structured programs as the

Development of Understanding of Self and Others (DUSO) (Dinkmeyer, 1970) and the Human Development Program (HDP) (Human Development Training Institute, 1970).

Programs neither cognitively nor affectively oriented involve programs in which the intervention is not directed specifically at improving the self-concept. These include academic programs and physical fitness programs. Academic programs include those in which specific academic skills are taught. Such programs are based upon the assumption that improved academic competence will result in improved self-concepts (Scheirer & Kraut, 1979).

Programs with a focus on physical fitness and awareness (e.g., camp programs) have been developed to attempt to increase self-concepts. One of the most popular is the Outward Bound Program, in which outdoor activities provide the context for increased mastery and improved self-perceptions (Marsh & Richards, 1988).

Following a comprehensive review of the literature, J. Hattie (1992) conducted a meta-analysis to evaluate the overall effectiveness of the self-concept modification techniques. Using studies involving both children and adults, she obtained 485 effect sizes from 89 studies suitable for inclusion in the analysis. The average effect size for the interventions was .37, and the average effect for the control group was .12. Based upon the assumption of a normal distribution, the data suggested that "65% of the people who undertook a program to enhance self-concept experienced change, whereas 55% of people involved in the control groups experienced change. This difference indicates that 10% of those who had some intervention had enhanced conceptions of self compared with those in the control groups" (J. Hattie, 1992, p. 227).

J. Hattie also compared the differential effectiveness of the three intervention approaches. The results revealed that the cognitive-behaviorally oriented approaches were the most effective, while the affectively oriented approaches were the least effective. The efficacy estimates of programs that were neither cognitively nor affectively oriented overall fell in between the other two categories; however, there was considerable variation among the approaches. For example, on the one hand, the intense outdoor programs, implemented in extra non-school residential settings (e.g., Outward Bound) had the highest average effect sizes. On the other hand, academic programs that attempted to enhance self-concepts by increasing academic achievement were typically ineffective.

Additional conclusions from the meta-analysis revealed that the self-concept interventions for children were most effective when the interventions used (a) therapists rather than teachers, (b) lower socioeconomic groups, (c) and domain-specific measures of self-concept rather than global measures. Overall, J.

Hattie (1992) concluded that "it is possible to enhance self-concept using some form of intervention, although this change was not as great as many researchers would claim" (p. 236).

One shortcoming of many of the intervention studies conducted to date is that global self-concepts rather than specific facets have been targeted for change. Likewise, such studies have employed poorly defined global measuring instruments, rather than selecting multidimensional instruments with demonstrated construct validity that include the dimensions specifically pertinent to the intervention. As a result it is not surprising that the measured effects have been modest and/or ambiguous, because such measures may have masked improvement in specific domains of self-concept. Future studies that compare the effects of treatments on targeted specific domains with effects on nontargeted domains may further clarify the differential effectiveness of various interventions.

The implications for school psychologists are clear. They must assess multiple domains of self-concept to determine which *specific* domains to target in their intervention efforts. Subsequently, intervention efforts must be tailored to match the unique profile of self-perceptions of the particular student under consideration.

A useful example of a successful cognitive-behaviorally oriented self-concept intervention study is provided by Craven et al. (1991). This study will be explored in detail because it incorporated many of the aforementioned methodological improvements as well as illustrating several validated, specific strategies for enhancing particular facets of self-concept. The primary purpose of this intervention study was to enhance reading and mathematics self-concepts. They used a multidimensional self-concept instrument (i.e., the SDQ–1) to examine the effects of the intervention. Two forms of interventions, performance feedback and attributional feedback, were employed together to develop a more powerful intervention. Similar interventions based upon the two types of feedback were administered to late elementary age students, one by teachers and one by researchers over an eight-week period. The researcher-administered interventions were conducted in individual and small group settings, while the teacher-administered interventions were conducted in regular classrooms. Statements that focused on positive ability (Shunk, 1985) were coupled with statements that focused on performance feedback in order to encourage students to generate appropriate self-reinforcers. Such feedback, which has been termed internally focused performance feedback, was used to train students to transform low self-concept judgments to high self-concept judgments. Using Brophy's (1981) guidelines for praise, the internally focused feedback was contingent only upon appropriate gains in performance. Examples of internally focused feedback were "look at all the skills you have in mathematics. You can do lots of things well in mathematics. You must feel good about your abilities in mathematics."

Attributional feedback was also used to enhance self-concept. Attributional feedback involved attributing success on graded mathematics and reading tasks to ability or effort; and attributing failure to lack of effort, coupled with ability statements. Feedback was made contingent upon success or failure on tasks consistent with the ability level of the students. Examples of such feedback statements were "No, that's not right. You have the ability to do well and will do well when you try harder."

The results of this brief intervention demonstrated that the researcher-administered interventions were successful in enhancing academic areas of self-concept. Furthermore, the treatment effects were specific to the targeted areas (i.e., reading and math self-concepts), with no effects for nontargeted areas (e.g., physical, appearance, family self-concepts), with one exception (peer self-concept). In contrast, the interventions administered by teachers in the context of ongoing, every day classroom activities, did not produce significant changes in self-concept. The reasons for the differences between the success of the researcher- and teacher-administered interventions were unclear, but possibly reflected differences in the frequency of feedback that the teachers and the researchers were able to administer. Specifically, perhaps as a consequence of implementing the program with individuals or small groups outside the regular classroom, the researchers were able to administer almost twice as many verbal reinforcers as the teachers were over the course of the treatment.

Whatever the case, this study provides an example of a brief, relatively simple intervention that could be applied efficiently and effectively by school psychologists working with individuals or small groups of children. This study also underscores the benefits of highly focused self-concept intervention efforts. Furthermore, the study demonstrates the usefulness of careful and systematic assessment efforts. By specifying *a priori* predictions about which facets of self-concept should be affected by the interventions, as well as which facets should *not* be affected, the researchers established greater confidence in the specific links between the intervention and its outcomes. Finally, the study demonstrated the advantage of including measures of the processes (i.e., frequency of feedback statements) that were expected to be responsible for the self-concept changes. The inclusion of such measures enabled generation of a plausible, data-based hypothesis regarding the differential effectiveness of the treatment as a function of the particular intervention agent.

Research also has highlighted the importance of considering a student's particular frame of reference for his or her global and specific self-concepts (see Harter, 1985; Marsh, 1988). Researchers have long recognized that self-concepts are constructed with respect to one or more reference groups that serve as a basis of comparison. Consideration of this finding helps clarify seemingly paradoxical findings in the literature — for example, the lack of mean differences in the self-concepts of disadvantaged minority children and nondisadvantaged children. Such knowledge also points to an important caveat in designing interventions for children. Intervention agents must keep in mind possible changes in self-concept that may follow from changes in a student's reference group. For example, a student who is highly competent in academics in comparison to his regular class peers may suffer a decrease in academic self-concept when placed in a program for gifted students. Although the student's academic competence might actually increase during the program, his academic self-concept might decrease as a result of comparisons with his new, more gifted peers (J. Hattie, 1992). Similarly, a student who is performing well in comparison to his peers in a special education program may lower particular facets of academic self-concept following mainstreaming attempts.

The implication for school psychologists is that they should not simply administer a self-concept scale and then formulate "educated guesses" about a child's relevant reference groups. To the contrary, school psychologists should *directly* explore children's bases for comparisons. For example, Harter (1985) provides examples of age-appropriate, open-ended questions that can be used to ask students about relevant social comparison groups. Using such techniques, school psychologists will be in a better position to make predictions about changes that might be expected in a given child's self-concept as a result of potential intervention efforts.

EVALUATION

In the evaluation phase, the school psychologist must address the problem-solving process in general and the associated intervention specifically. The evaluation of a self-concept change program will likely involve repeated, direct assessment of a child's self-perceptions (e.g., changes on a self-concept scale, teacher behavior ratings) as well as any related change expectations (e.g., increased academic achievement, increased peer acceptance). As underscored in the previous sections, the school psychologist must select instruments and techniques that tap the specific areas of interest from a multimethod, multiperson perspective. In this manner, assessment is performed within a construct validation approach, thus assuring greater confidence in the assessment findings. For further information regarding general formative and summative program evaluation techniques, the reader is referred elsewhere (e.g., Maher & Bennett, 1984).

With regard to the intervention evaluation stage, one additional concern bears mentioning. The evaluator must be careful to distinguish between the validity of a self-concept measure and the accuracy of an individual's self-judgments (Harter, 1990). Consider the following example: Objective indicators of school performance (e.g., grades, teacher ratings) are moderately, but significantly correlated with students' perceived academic competence. Nevertheless, students are often referred who do not demonstrate the expected relationship between their actual competence and their perceived competence. Some children perceive themselves as "stupid" even though they are performing at the top of their class. Similarly, students may perceive themselves as unattractive despite obvious evidence to the contrary. Rather than simply interpreting the child's perceptions as inaccurate, it will likely be more fruitful to investigate the reasons for the lack of association between the child's perceptions and the more "objective" conditions. For example, in the former example, perhaps overly high parental expectations have been internalized by the child so that s/he perceives herself in an unduly negative light. In such a case, the school psychologist may need to target intervention efforts toward changing the parents' behavior and expectations as well as the child's (Bracken, 1992).

SUMMARY

This chapter has summarized the literature on self-concept and formulated a best practices approach to enhancing children's self-concepts from a problem-solving paradigm. Self-concept was defined broadly to include an individual's descriptions of her or himself, including evaluative descriptions. In contrast to early unidimensional theories of self-concept, the multidimensional perspective has received the most empirical support to date. Six frequently used multidimensional self-report measures of self-concept were reviewed, including the Piers-Harris, Coopersmith's SEI, Harter's SPPC, Marsh's SDQs, Brown and Alexander's Self-Esteem Index, and Bracken's MSCS. Given the outstanding national standardization and preliminary evidence of psychometric properties, Bracken's MSCS is an especially promising new addition to self-concept assessment.

Differences in the structure of self-concept have been reported for special populations, such as the handicapped. The integration of self-report instruments with other assessment data was proposed as essential to a construct validation approach and thus consistent with a best practices approach.

Self-concept has not been consistently related to age, gender, race, or socioeconomic status, but rather to a variety of family process variables, school environment variables, and intrapersonal cognitive variables.

Based upon a multidimensional perspective,

interventions must be tailored to a student's unique profile of self-perceptions. The intervention for a student who displays negative family self-perceptions will need a qualitatively different treatment approach and different treatment context from that for a student who displays primarily negative academic self-perceptions. Likewise, a student who displays a circumscribed self-concept problem (e.g., negative self-concept in one domain) will perhaps require a less intensive intervention than a student who displays a more pervasive negative self-concept. In general, cognitive-behavioral interventions have proven more successful than affectively oriented interventions. The most successful self-concept programs have involved strategies aimed at enhancing self-concept (e.g., attributions retraining) along with direct academic instruction.

REFERENCES

Ames, C., & Felkner, D. (1979). Effects of self-concept on children's causal attributions and self-reinforcement. *Journal of Educational Psychology, 70,* 345–355.

Bergan, J. R., & Kratochwill, T. R. (1990). *Behavioral consultation and therapy.* New York: Plenum Press.

Bracken, B. A. (1992). Multidimensional Self Concept Scale. Austin, TX: Pro-Ed.

Bracken, B. A., Bunch, S., Keith, T. Z., & Keith, P. B. (1992, August). *Multidimensional self concept: A five instrument factor analysis.* Paper presented at the annual conference of the American Psychological Association, Washington, DC.

Bracken, B., & Howell, K. K. (1991). Multidimensional self concept validation: A three-instrument investigation. *Journal of Psychoeducational Assessment, 9,* 319–328.

Brophy, J. (1981). Teacher praise: A functional analysis. *Review of Educational Research, 51,* 5–32.

Brown, L., & Alexander, J. (1990). *Self-Esteem Index.* Austin, TX: Pro-Ed.

Chiu, L. (1987). Development of the Self-Esteem Rating Scale for Children (Revised). *Measurement and Evaluation in Counseling and Development, 23,* 36–41.

Coopersmith, S. (1967). *The antecedents of self-esteem.* London: Freeman.

Coopersmith, S. (1984). *Self-Esteem Inventories.* Palo Alto, CA: Consulting Psychologists Press.

Crain, R. M., & Bracken, B. (1993). *Age, race, and gender differences in child and adolescent self-concept: Evidence from a nine-year cross-sectional study.* Manuscript submitted for publication.

Craven, R. G., Marsh, H. W., & Debus, R. L. (1991). Effects of internally focused feedback on enhancement of academic self-concept. *Journal of Educational Psychology, 83,* 17–27.

DiGuiseppe, R., & Bernard, M. E. (1990). The application of rational-emotive theory and therapy to school-aged children. *School Psychology Review, 19,* 268–286.

Dinkmeyer, D. (1970). *Developing Understanding of Self and Others* (Educational program). Circle Pines, MN: American Guidance Service.

Fullerton, W. S. (1972). *Self-disclosure, self-esteem, and risk-tak-*

ing: A study of their convergent and discriminant validity in elementary school children. Unpublished doctoral dissertation, University of California, Berkeley.

Goldfried, M. R., & Davison, G. C. (1976). *Clinical behavior therapy.* New York: Holt, Rinehart, and Winston.

Harter, S. (1982). The perceived competence scale for children. *Child Development, 53,* 3–15.

Harter, S. (1985). *Manual for the Self-Perception Profile for Children.* Unpublished manuscript. University of Denver.

Harter, S. (1988). *Manual for the Self-Perception Profile for Adolescents.* Unpublished manuscript. University of Denver.

Harter, S. (1989). Causes, correlates, and functional role of global self-worth: A life-span perspective. In J. Kolligan & R. Sternberg (Eds.), *Perceptions of competence and incompetence across the life-span* (pp. 67–100). New Haven: Yale University Press.

Harter, S. (1990). Issues in the assessment of the self-concept of children and adolescents. In A. M. LaGreca (Ed.), *Through the eyes of the child* (pp. 292–325). Needham Heights, MA: Allyn & Bacon.

Harter, S., & Pike, R. (1984). The pictorial scale of perceived competence and social acceptance for young children. *Child Development, 55,* 1969–1982.

Hattie, J. A. (1992). *Self-concept.* Hillsdale, NJ: Erlbaum.

Hattie, J. (1992a). Enhancing self-concept. In J. A. Hattie, (Ed.), *Self-concep* (pp. 221–240). Hillsdale, NJ: Erlbaum.

Hughes, H. M. (1984). Measures of self-concept and self-esteem for children ages 3–12 years: A review and recommendations. *Clinical Psychology Review, 4,* 657–692.

Human Development Training Institute. (1970). *The Human Development Program* (Educational program). Los Angeles: Author.

Knoff, H. M. (1990). Best practices in personality assessment. In A. Thomas & J. Grimes (Eds.), *Best practices in school psychology–II* (pp. 547–562). Washington, DC: National Association of School Psychologists.

LaGreca, A. M. (1990). *Through the eyes of the child.* Needham Heights, MA: Allyn & Bacon.

Maher, C. A., & Bennett, R. E. (1984). *Planning and evaluating educational services.* Englewood Cliffs, NJ: Prentice-Hall.

Marsh, H. W. (1988). *Self-description questionnaire – I.* San Antonio, TX: The Psychological Corporation.

Marsh, H. W. (1990). *Self-description questionnaire – II* San Antonio, TX: The Psychological Corporation.

Marsh, H. W. (1991). *Self-description questionnaire (SDQ) III: A theoretical and empirical basis for the measurement of multiple dimensions of late adolescent self-concept.* Macarthur: Faculty of Education, University of Western Sydney.

Marsh, H. W., Cairns, L., Relich, J., Barnes, J., & Debus, R. L. (1984). The relationship between dimensions of self-attribution and dimensions of self-concept. *Journal of Educational Psychology, 76,* 3–32.

Marsh, H. W., & Richards, G. E. (1988). The Outward Bound Bridging Course for low achieving high school males: Effect on academic achievement and multidimensional self-concepts. *Australian Journal of Psychology, 40,* 281–298.

Piers, E. (1984). *A manual for the Piers-Harris Children's Self-Concept Scale.* Los Angeles: Western Psychological Services.

Pope, A. W., McHale, S. M., & Craighead, W. E. (1988). *Self-esteem enhancement with children and adolescents.* Needham

Heights, MA: Allyn & Bacon.

Renick, M. J., & Harter, S. (1989). Impact of social comparison on the developing self-perceptions of learning disabled students. *Journal of Educational Psychology, 81,* 631–638.

Rosenberg, M. (1979). *Conceiving the self.* New York: Basic Books.

Scheirer, M. A., & Kraut, R. E. (1979). Increasing educational achievement via self-concept change. *Review of Educational Research, 49,* 131–150.

Shavelson, R. J., Hubner, J. J., & Stanton, G. C. (1976). Self-concept: Validation of construct interpretations. *Review of Educational Research, 46,* 407–441.

Shunk, D. (1985). Self-efficacy and classroom learning. *Psychology in the Schools, 22,* 208–223.

Silon, E. L., & Harter, S. (1985). Assessment of perceived competence, motivational orientation, and anxiety in segregated and mainstreamed educably mentally retarded children. Journal of Educational Psychology, 77, 217–230.

Silvernail, D. L. (1987). *Developing positive student self-concept.* Washington, DC: National Education Association.

Snyder, M. (1987). *Public appearances/private realities.* New York: Freeman.

Witt, J. C., Cavell, T., Heffer, R. W., Carey, M. P., & Martens, B. K. (1988). Child self-report: Interviewing techniques and rating scales. In E. S. Shapiro & T. R. Kratochwill (Eds.), *Behavioral assessment in schools: Conceptual foundations and practical applications (pp.* 384–454). New York: Guilford.

Witt, J. C., Heffer, R. W., & Pfeiffer, J. (1990). Structured rating scales: A review of self-report and informant rating processes, procedures, and issues. In C. R. Reynolds & R. W. Kamphaus (Eds.), *Handbook of psychological and educational assessment of children: Personality, behavior, and context* (pp. 364–394). New York: Guilford.

Wylie, R. C. (1974). *The self-concept: A review of methodological considerations and measuring instruments* (Vol. 1, 2nd rev. ed.). Lincoln: University of Nebraska Press.

Wylie, R. C. (1979). *The self-concept* (Vol. 2). Lincoln: University of Nebraska Press.

ANNOTATED BIBLIOGRAPHY

Canfield, J., & Wells, H. C. (1976). *100 Ways to enhance self-concept in the classroom: A handbook for teachers and parents.* Englewood Cliffs, NJ: Prentice-Hall.
This classic curriculum guide for teachers and parents includes 100 activities that can easily be implemented in regular and special education classrooms of all grade levels.

Craven, R. G., Marsh, H. W., & Debus, R. L. (1991). Effects of internally focused feedback and attributional feedback on enhancement of self-concept. *Journal of Educational Psychology, 83,* 17–27.
This well-written article describes a brief group intervention that successfully improved elementary school children's academic self-concepts. The authors describe thoroughly the intervention, which could be implemented by school psychologists.

Harter, S. (1990). Issues in the assessment of the self-concept of children and adolescents. In A. M. LaGreca (Ed.), *Through the eyes of the child* (pp. 292–325). Needham Heights, MA: Allyn & Bacon.

This chapter provides a well-written scholarly discussion of issues in the assessment of the self-concepts of children and adolescents from a developmental perspective. Based upon much of this leading researcher's own work, this chapter provides thoughtful discussions of such complex topics as self-concept theories, developmental considerations, assessment with special populations (e.g., handicapped students), psychometric concerns, and children's awareness of self-processes.

Hattie, J. A. (1992). *Self-concept.* Hillsdale, NJ: Erlbaum.
This book provides a comprehensive, scholarly overview of self-concept research, including the author's own significant contributions. Included are chapters on theory, history, measurement, correlates, interventions, and dimensionality.

Pope, A. W., McHale, S. M., & Craighead, W. E. (1988). *Self-esteem enhancement with children and adolescents.* Needham Heights, MA: Allyn & Bacon.
This text describes a cognitive-behavioral intervention for self-esteem enhancement of children and adolescents. An overview of the theoretical and research support for the treatment approach is included, as is practical information, such as specific techniques for the identification of target children and recommendations for handling "unexpected difficulties" during intervention.

71

Best Practices in the Use of Standardized Assessments

Brian J. Stone
Wichita State University

OVERVIEW

Standardized tests alone do not provide complete and sufficient information for designing, implementing, and monitoring individual education programs. However, standardized tests can provide objective information that is unobtainable through other means. In particular, standardized tests quantify information through reference group comparisons. When funding is targeted for a specific percentage of the population, it is possible with standardized tests to identify the correct proportion. In addition, the scores (or estimates) can be used to generate ideas about problems and competencies that are *internal* to the child. Standardized tests can be used with other forms of assessment, such as ecological assessment (which provides information about problems external to the child). Indeed, different approaches can provide complementary information and are compatible, rather than mutually exclusive.

Every child possesses unique characteristics. Assessment of these characteristics allows us to reliably determine a child's inter- and intraindividual strengths and weaknesses. When tempered with information regarding a child's background, standardized test information can help provide an understanding of the child's current functioning and educational needs.

Regrettably, use of standardized tests is often dictated by state and district interpretation of federal policy. This has led to an overreliance on such tests for qualification scores. Further, more is expected of tests than tests can reasonably be expected to provide. Simply put, tests **sometimes** help to clarify the reasons for a child's learning problem; sometimes they do not. When used properly, tests are merely a means to an end, not the end itself. Because tests have been overused or misused in the past is no reason to discard them totally. Standardized tests are capable of providing relevant information in many circumstances (Reschly & Grimes, 1990).

There has been discussion in school psychology about a need for less emphasis on standardized assessment (e.g., Batsche, 1992) with a shift to curriculum-based assessment (which incidentally, can also be standardized). Fagan and Wise (1993) have argued for a continuation of the existing assessment framework, with the addition of other roles. Indeed, public law compliance mandates that the school psychologist's role include standardized testing. Rather than shift completely our role, chances are we will merely add to it (Fagan & Wise, 1993). Thus, informed use of standardized tests will continue to play a major part for the school psychologist.

The IQ test remains the most frequently administered standardized test in school psychology. However, over the past 10 years school psychologists have tended to use fewer IQ tests and more tests of achievement and adaptive behavior and behavioral checklists (Hutton, Dubes, & Muir, 1992). This trend will continue, as demonstrated in the lowered use of IQ tests in reevaluation situations (Reschly & Grimes, 1990).

Standardized testing information should not be overinterpreted. In order to avoid this trap it is important to be aware of psychometric characteristics of tests. Scores can sometimes reflect more of the attributes of a test than of a child. The first part of this chapter covers the psychometric attributes of test interpretation; the second part introduces the fourfold goal of test interpretation in clinical judgment: (a) Reliable inter- and intraindividual comparisons; (b) generation and cross-validation of hypotheses; (c) need determination; and (d) appropriate intervention decisions.

BASIC CONSIDERATIONS

Standardized Tests

Standardized (or norm-referenced) tests must be administered and scored according to uniform procedures in order for children to be compared with their representative reference group. Standardized tests include tests of ability, achievement, personality, and adaptive behavior. Assessment is a more general term than test, and typically refers to a broad range or battery of tests or procedures, covering more than one domain.

Standards

Standardized tests should meet certain criteria of test development, administration, and interpretation (Anastasi, 1988). As school psychologists trained in the scientist-practitioner model, we should make sure tests meet standards of reliability and validity before blindly placing faith in them to provide relevant information. The school psychologist is responsible to know the standards of empirical reliability and validity, as well as ethical guidelines for test use and interpretation — see *Standards for Educational and Psychological Testing* (AERA, 1985), *Ethical Principles of Psychologists* (American Psychological Association, 1992), and *NASP Principles for Professional Ethics*, Appendix I (NASP, 1984). This is particularly true for serving as an expert witness or participating in due process hearings. One has to be able to defend what one has done, both in the areas of psychometrics and clinical judgment.

Measurement Error

All tests have some error, as tests are merely samples of behavior used to estimate a theoretical true score. The accuracy of the estimate is a function of the reliability of the test and is operationalized by the standard error of measurement. The standard error of measurement is used to create confidence intervals. All obtained scores should be bracketed by confidence intervals in order to acknowledge the degree of error in the test. In this way, we not only admit that no score is exact, but we also quantify our degree of error.

Some tests bracket the estimated true score with asymmetrical confidence intervals (e.g., Wechsler Intelligence Scale for Children–Third Edition [WISC III; Wechsler, 1991], and the Differential Ability Scales [DAS; Elliott, 1990]), while others simply bracket the obtained score with symmetric intervals. The former technique is more sophisticated than the latter because it takes into account regression to the mean. The assumption is made that a person with an extreme score is likely to have a true score somewhat closer (regressed) to the mean. Therefore, the most accurate confidence limits are asymmetrical about the obtained score rather than being the same number of points above and below (symmetrically distant from) the obtained score.

Group Tests

Standardized group achievement testing can provide an objective reference point of how a child is doing outside the day-to-day curriculum of the classroom. Group achievement tests can be misused when there is no specified a priori plan for their use. If a district wants to see how it compares nationally, it would be more cost-effective to test a random sample from the district, rather than test all students. If there is a planned use for each individual's score, then all children should be tested. It is important to keep in mind, however, that if group and individual results seem discrepant, more confidence can be placed in the individual results (Hood & Johnson, 1991).

Sometimes a district uses group achievement testing results to evaluate teachers rather than the students. This is an inappropriate use of tests. Interestingly, quality teaching spreads the distribution (top students make great gains; poor students make very modest gains), which results in a larger standard deviation, but only a slight increase in the mean. If a district wishes to increase its mean, it should concentrate resources on top students to increase high outliers, which will pull the mean up. If the district desires to decrease variability, resources should be concentrated on poor students, which moves them up slightly (but does not do much to the mean).

Generalizability

A major assumption of standardized test data is that the results are generalizable. In other words, subjects' performance on the IQ or achievement test reflects their problem-solving level and style outside the testing situation (Sattler, 1988). The power of test scores in predicting relevant criteria such as school or work success is well established. Indeed, IQ tests are one of the few instruments that have predictive ability that extends years into the future. While IQ tests are less reliable and predictive for very young children, it should be noted that IQ scores are fairly stable for handicapped infants and toddlers (Kamphaus, 1993).

A child's behavior during the individual testing session is far less generalizable than the actual scores, however (Glutting, Oakland, & McDermott, 1989). This makes sense in that the classroom setting is much different from a one-on-one session with an examiner attempting to elicit the child's optimal performance.

User Friendliness versus Psychometric Sophistication

Interestingly, tests show a trade-off between user friendliness and psychometric sophistication. For example, the Kaufman Assessment Battery for Children (K-ABC; Kaufman & Kaufman, 1983) at the subtest level is user-friendly but psychometrically poor. The item sets within subtests allow a ceiling to be reached with only one failure if that is the last item within the set for a given age. While this is a very user-friendly technique for both the examiner and the child (allowing quick administration and limited frustration, respectively), it is poor measurement. Accurate measurement requires the child to obtain at least a few right *and* a few wrong items in order to estimate the child's ability level on any subtest. A child who gets all items right may have had "barely enough" ability to get them right, or far more ability than is needed. Conversely, a child who misses all the items may have had almost enough ability or not nearly enough ability to get one right. The same is basically true for only one right or one wrong — we simply do not have enough information to get an accurate measure of the child's ability.

This point obviously has relevance for floors and ceilings. Indeed, tests may have limited floors and ceilings at different age and ability levels. For example, Pattern Analysis on the Stanford-Binet IV (SB IV; Thorndike, Hagen, & Sattler, 1986) has an excellent floor and ceiling for young children and children at average ability levels (most children will obtain some correct and some incorrect responses). However, for gifted teens the ceiling is poor, as high-ability older children tend to "top out," receiving correct credit for all items. The obtained score is then a low estimate and can artificially lower the overall composite score.

Except for Pattern Analysis the SB IV seems to show the opposite problem in regard to high-ability teens: a high degree of psychometric sophistication (accurate measurement) at the expense of limited user friendliness (very lengthy testing session). For gifted teens the test can take well over 2 hours, yielding a very accurate score at the expense of examiner and examinee fatigue. The bottom line is that school psychologists should be aware of the trade-off between user friendliness and psychometric sophistication.

More Trade-offs

Assuming we have accurate measurement, what is the construct that is being accurately measured, and how do we intend to use it? For example, the Mental Processing Composite (MPC) of the K-ABC is obviously not highly g-loaded. Therefore, gifted children will tend to score closer to the mean on the K-ABC, and retarded children will tend to score higher than they would on the Wechsler Scales. The MPC will not be as predictive as a Wechsler Full Scale IQ (FSIQ). Knowing this, I still chose to use the K-ABC with Native American children of the Ute nation because verbal tests seemed to affect rapport and trigger defensiveness in some of these children. The Wechsler scales may have provided more useful information in a predictive sense, but at the expense of rapport. Therefore, clinical judgment and working with these children day to day mandated the use of the psychometrically poorer test!

Constructs

Some would argue that since the SB IV includes memory subtests in the overall composite, it is a poor measure of reasoning for the gifted child. Gifted children typically score lower (closer to the mean) on memory tests than on general mental ability tests, just as low-ability children score higher on memory tests

(again, closer to the mean). This regression to the mean occurs because memory tests are lower on g, the general mental ability factor. In other words, people high on g regress to the mean on tests that are less g-loaded. Similarly, people low on g score slightly higher on tests that are low on g-loading. This phenomenon could lower a gifted child's score on the SB IV (or raise a mentally retarded child's score). Indeed, this phenomenon helps us to aticipate and explain why certain composites (e.g., processing speed) are closer to the mean than highly g-loaded composites (e.g., Verbal IQ) for extreme scorers such as gifted and retarded children.

It is a delicate business to balance between adequate psychometric measurement and user friendliness. However, the best tests manage to balance the need for psychometric sophistication with the need for user friendliness while making it clear to the user exactly what is being measured.

Outdated Tests

A frequently encountered ethical consideration in testing is use of an older test after a revision has been published. Outdated tests are not appropriate for placement decisions. This is because the child is compared with a noncurrent norm group. This practice results in inflated scores. School psychologists are sometimes guilty of saying a new test (e.g., WISC III) gives "lower scores." This is false. The new test yields correct scores. The older version of the test gives *inflated* scores. This is a very important point and school psychologists should be aware of it.

Interestingly, gifted children will seem to have even more of a "drop" on a new revision of a test. This is because regression to the mean is also at work. In other words, when an obtained score is extreme, there is a high likelihood that the true score is slightly closer to the mean.

Bias

Bias occurs when a test unfairly favors one group over another (Jensen, 1980). For example, the standardization version of the DAS (Elliott, 1990) had a picture of a cactus and the subject was asked to name it. Not surprisingly, children from the Southwest had greater familiarity with cacti and did much better on this item than children from the Northeast and North Central regions. The difference in item difficulty scores was not due to differences in ability level, but merely to differences in exposure to cacti. Thus, the item was regionally biased and was dropped from the final version.

Bias can also be operationally tested in a fairness-of-prediction model. A test would be biased if it had different predictive accuracy for one group than for another. Most IQ tests by this definition are not biased. For example, an IQ of 70 predicts difficulty at school no matter what the race or sex of the subject.

Similarly, a IQ of 130 predicts school success for a member of any group. Under this model, bias does not exist when two groups with unequal means on the predictor also have unequal means on the criterion (Stone, 1992).

IQ tests tend to remove or reduce the achievement content in problem solving. IQ tests actually avoid, or entail only in reduced measure, some of the perceived bias in achievement tests (i.e., mean differences in achievement test scores that result when one group has been exposed to less or allegedly poorer schooling).

Most modern IQ tests have succeeded in vastly reducing culture bias. For example, matrices-type tasks ("this shape goes to that shape as this other shape goes to . . .") are not specifically a part of any culture. The same goes for newer measures of intelligence, such as reaction time in simple information-processing tasks (Jensen, 1993). Even tests on which a great deal of verbal and cultural knowledge is required on nonverbal tasks (e.g., the performance subtests of the Wechsler scales) have not been shown to be empirically biased. Vocabulary tasks can be argued as being cultural, but among native speakers of the particular language from which the vocabulary is drawn, they are also probably the best single measure of intellectual functioning. This is because they require the integration of many high-level cognitive tasks; one must learn words through exposure, deduce meaning through context, and recall and express coherently their meaning. Highly *g*-loaded tasks appear to be important for successfully functioning in a complex technological society.

It is important to remember that low ability is just one hypothesis for explaining why a child has scored low on a test of ability. There are many other hypotheses (and combinations of hypotheses) to explain a low score (e.g., lack of environmental stimulation, limited exposure to educational materials and settings, distractibility, anxiety, major emotional trauma). However, most explanations for a low score would also tend to predict poor performance on a relevant criterion. There are exceptions, however, particularly when the contributing factors are more situational than chronic.

One area of potential bias that is often misunderstood is the standardization sample. Obviously, the sample should be selected so as to reflect the population. Some educators are concerned when the sample does not include persons with specific mildly handicapping conditions, or some other low-base-rate group. The inclusion of low-frequency groups does not change scores (a child who would obtain a score of 100, would also obtain a 100 if the entire sample were redone to include, for example, a 3% sample of Conduct Disordered children or Moravian immigrants). The intent is to compare scores with those of representative sample of the population. The inclusion of any low-incidence group in the sample will simply not change the normative scores to any great degree.

Summary

Before interpreting a test it is important to keep in mind certain things about both the test and the subject. Regarding the test one should be aware of measurement error, the floor or ceiling of the test, regression to the mean, and the relevance and validity of the test for the specific use employed. Regarding the child, factors to consider include the child's background, environment, language use, and social, medical, and educational history, as well as the past and current family situation.

BEST PRACTICES

Test Selection

Tests should be selected on the basis of specific referral question to be answered. The attributes of the test for the pertinent age and ability level should be known by the examiner. For example, a child 6 years, 1 month of age suspected of low ability would be better measured by the DAS (Elliott, 1990) or Wechsler Preschool and Primary Scales of Intelligence–Revised (WPPSI–R; Wechsler, 1989) than by the WISC III (Wechsler, 1991). The child would receive more correct responses on the first two in comparison with the latter, on which too few correct responses might be made to accurately gauge ability level. That is, better measurement for this child would come from the first two tests because of the attributes of both the child and the tests considered together.

Furthermore, one might have to look into the problem of including to the composites subtest raw scores of zero. While it is true that too many raw scores of zero give a poor measurement, to discard those subtests could falsely inflate the overall score. Each test handles this situation differently; information should be provided in the manual. While school psychologists are legally and ethically held responsible to follow manual recommendations, keep in mind that these recommendations are made by human beings and therefore sometimes come more from desperation than inspiration.

The child aged 6 years, 1 month would be in the very first norms table on the WISC III, which is the least accurate. Norms tables at 4-month intervals (such as on the WISC III) change a great deal from 6 years 3 months 30 days to 6 years 4 months 0 days. The DAS solves this by using 3-month-interval norms tables up to age 8 (beyond which less drastic raw score increases occur), after which 6-month-interval tables are used. The SB IV has 4-month intervals to age 6, then 6-month intervals to age 11, 1-year intervals through age 17, and a final 6-year norms table through age 23. Ideally, the most accurate norms would be computerized versions that could conceivably have a different norms table for every day.

Explaining Constructs

It is a leap of faith to say that a test that requires a child to put cartoons in order measures "social planning." The test merely requires a child to put cartoons in order. The construct "social planning" is what we infer (however inappropriately) to be an underlying process. Sometimes our labels for constructs serve to confuse or overintellectualize the task. It is best to literally and succinctly describe what an assigned task is — for example, "On the Developmental Test of Visual–Motor Integration (VMI; Beery, 1989), *a test of copying increasingly more difficult shapes*, John scored in the range of . . ." This should be done prior to, or instead of, assigning a construct name to the task in the report (try to avoid jargon, e.g., "integrative visuo-spatial motor skills"). Our constructs quickly become confusing to parents and other professionals, hindering rather than facilitating communication.

Empirical versus Clinical Interpretation

Just as the various questions discussed above involved the psychometric and clinical attributes of assessment, test interpretation also makes use of this interactive dichotomy. An empirical approach is purely psychometric, while a clinical approach is more subjective and intuitive. Ideally, best practices would require a blend of the two. However, a wary eye must always be kept upon the psychometric aspects of a test to avoid being fooled into thinking that a test attribute is a child attribute. In the absence of sufficient knowledge of psychometrics it is easy to fall victim to overinterpretation and too much non-scientific thinking. However, in the absence of clinical knowledge it is easy to fall victim to identifying people with mere scores. When psychometric particularities are kept firmly in mind, clinical judgment makes a good companion.

Intelligence Testing with the WISC–R (Kaufman, 1979) set the standard for the empirical top-down approach to test interpretation. The most reliable score is the full scale composite score (because it has the most items). Therefore it is the score you can put the most trust in. The other composites and factors are somewhat less reliable. Less reliable still are the individual subtests, and finally, the individual items. The *Introductory and Technical Handbook for the DAS* (Elliott, 1990) goes a step further psychometrically, and demonstrates how reliability is a function of the ability level of a child. For example, the DAS subtest Early Number Concepts (ages 2:6 through 7:11) is reliable for all children ages 3 through 6. However, it is not reliable for low ability two-year olds, as they will

not obtain enough correct responses to accurately measure their ability. Similarly, it is not reliable for high ability seven-year olds as they tend not to receive any incorrect items, therefore their ability is not accurately measured.

On the clinical side, the shared-abilities approach is a legitimate although admittedly "armchair" method of deriving meaning from a group of tests. It is assumed that subtests are measuring various abilities and that the child's pattern of subtest strengths and weaknesses reveals his or her underlying abilities and deficits. There is less empirical research in this area but it makes sense. However, one should not turn their back on psychometric knowledge when employing shared ability procedures.

Ideally, one would start psychometrically, but also be able to employ the shared-abilities method to generate hypotheses about the child. In addition, it is sometimes useful to "test limits" to further investigate hypotheses. For example, if time limitations seem to be an impediment, time limits can be avoided. However, this would not be according to standardized procedure and could not be scored as such. Incidentally, some tests (such as Pattern Construction on the DAS) are normed with and without bonus points for speed so that one can score it either way.

The psychometric and shared-abilities approaches can be combined. For example on the DAS, the subtest Copying (similar to the VMI: copying increasingly more difficult shapes) can be contrasted with Recall of Designs (copying increasingly difficult shapes from memory). We can assume that a child who does well on Copying but poorly on Recall of Designs has the requisite visual–motor skills but falls down in the area of visual memory. This hypothesis can be further explored and cross-validated on other tests of visual memory. This processing deficit in visual memory could explain why a child of average or above average ability shows far below average achievement. It is still only a hypothesis, however, no matter how much support we have from other tests. Our best guess would be that this processing deficit apparently is responsible for the lower than expected achievement. Furthermore, there is no magical way to teach a child with this (or any) particular pattern of strengths and weaknesses. Research has consistently shown the only way to improve a child's reading is by spending more time on reading (Kavale & Forness, 1987). Typically we look for ways to compensate (note-taking strategies, taping lectures, etc.) rather than to remediate. A child with this deficit might qualify as learning-disabled; and sometimes a label can help parents and teachers be more accepting, patient, and understanding of a child's uniqueness.

Some newer tests combine the psychometric quantification with the clinical processing style approach. For example, the California Verbal Learning Test for Children (CVLT-C; Delis & Kramer, 1993) quantifies simple verbal memory across trials, while also producing standardized information regarding memory strategy and learning curve. The CVLT-C gives scores that explain whether the child was remembering mainly the first or last things heard (primacy vs. recency), and to what extent the child uses semantic category grouping as a memory strategy. The CVLT-C offers promise for the future in terms of information that standardized tests can provide.

Significance versus Frequency of the Difference

An important psychometric consideration in comparing scores across tests is significance versus frequency of the difference. Significance of the difference between scores is the probability that the theoretical underlying true scores are equal. This is useful in seeing if a discrepancy between ability and achievement scores is "real" (meaning unlikely to have occurred by chance). In other words significance of the difference is a computation of how often the obtained difference in scores could occur from underlying true scores that are the same. The bottom line is that it merely tells us whether our underlying true score on one measure is probably different from our underlying true score on another measure. It is not the most useful clinical measure.

A more practical measure is frequency of the difference, which tells us exactly what percentage of the population walks around with this difference. Quite often we will find a difference to be statistically significant (say, $p < .01$), yet perhaps 20% of the population have such a difference (the underlying scores may be different but the magnitude of that difference is fairly common). Frequency of the difference gives us important real-world information.

Problem-Solving Model

Within the problem-solving model, standardized tests help us to (a) make reliable inter- and intraindividual comparisons; (b) generate and cross-validate hypotheses; (c) participate in needs determination; and (d) take appropriate action (e.g., intervention and placement decisions).

With a representative norm sample and accurate measurement of a reliable construct, both inter- and intraindividual comparisons are valid. It is useful to compare individuals with the reference group (nomothetic comparison), which provides information on relative strengths and weaknesses within the child. This information may help diagnose a certain condition, which can create a link to a data base (e.g., mental retardation, developmental learning disability). It will also provide information as to how extreme a condition is, as all our diagnoses in education exist on a continuum (there are no blood tests for the presence or absence of learning disability, behavior disorder, etc.).

Intraindividual (or ipsative) comparison refers to looking at the pattern of a child's scores for relative strengths and weaknesses. This can become complicated because people may have different reasons for having similar scores.

Many neuropsychologists use the "levels of inference" model. This model has four levels, and is very similar to Kaufman's approach (Kaufman, 1979). First is the general level, at which overall functioning (from IQ or other total composites) is compared with the reference group. Second, lesser composites and individual subtests are examined for patterns within the individual. Third, specific pathognomonic signs are noted (e.g., perseveration, echolalia, "constructional dyspraxia"). Finally left versus right distinctions within the individual are examined (grip strength, finger-tapping speed, etc.). This model builds in both nomothetic and ipsative approaches. The two approaches are complementary, not mutually exclusive.

We should not overinterpret from a single measure, particularly if that measure has questionable reliability and validity. For example, we might ask, "Does evidence for low self-esteem exist across diverse measures such as the Draw-A-Person, sentence completion tasks, social interaction, and so on, or do we just see a very small and lightly drawn Draw-A-Person without indications of low self-esteem across other measures and settings? The more settings and tests by which the hypothesis is supported, the more confidence we can place in it. On the other hand, too much testing can be redundant (there is usually no need to give a child two or three IQ tests).

Standardized tests do not specifically determine a child's educational needs unless the testing is linked to the curriculum. However, certainly knowing a child's age and grade level and what the child can and cannot do is relevant to needs determination. The information provided by tests is often summarized by the school psychologist in a team meeting. Intervention decisions are team decisions; therefore the school psychologist must use the relevant data provided by the tests and testing situation and express it without jargon to the other professionals.

We must have some faith (as well as some empirical knowledge) about the interventions prescribed. Prognosis is difficult when reduced to the individual level, and is more difficult the farther into the future prediction is to be made. Yet at some level we should be aware that the information we have gathered is fairly predictive of future functioning. Knowledge of predictive validity helps us to plan goals and objectives for the child. This information can also allow us to help the parent(s) to accept the child's exceptionality and its consequences.

SUMMARY

Standardized testing does not answer all the questions that arise in individual educational program planning, and sometimes it merely raises more questions (Is it indeed the child's weakness in visual/verbal memory that is causing the learning problem in reading?). Testing is useful for generating hypotheses that can describe the severity of a problem. Standardized testing does not address all information that is relevant for intervention decisions, such as what the child finds rewarding, whether the child has object permanence, and so forth.

Once a problem is clearly defined, standardized assessment can help to determine the nature of the problem (e.g., Is the child mentally retarded or is there a specific language delay?). This is useful information for designing and implementing interventions. However, in some instances IQ may be irrelevant (e.g., behavioral problems when ability to do the school work is not in question). Jensen (1980) has pointed out that it is far more relevant for a teacher to know how well a child has learned what has been taught than to know the child's IQ. Sometimes, though, standardized tests are useful for ruling out certain causal hypotheses such as severe cognitive deficits.

No single approach or test can supply more than a fraction of the information and insight necessary for investigating a child's learning problems. All forms of assessment are merely samples of behavior and therefore have limitations. Standardized tests can be used with other forms of assessment. Different approaches may provide complementary information. Indeed, it is best practice not to rely solely on any single approach, but to be prepared to combine all approaches to investigate the referral question most effectively and to develop information useful for interventions.

REFERENCES

AERA (American Educational Research Association, American Psychological Association, & National Council on Measurement in Education). (1985). *Standards for educational and psychological testing.* Washington, DC: American Psychological Association.

American Psychological Association. (1992). *Ethical principles of psychologists.* Washington, DC: Author.

Anastasi, A. (1988). *Psychological testing* (6th ed.). New York: Macmillan.

Batsche, G. M. (1992). President's message: Training in school psychology: Future oriented or mired in the past? *NASP Communiqué, 20*(7), p. 2.

Beery, K. (1989). *Manual for the Developmental Test of Visual–Motor Integration.* Cleveland, OH: Modern Curriculum Press.

Bracken, B. (1988). Ten psychometric reasons why similar tests produce dissimilar results. *Journal of School Psychology, 26,* 155–166.

Delis, D., & Kramer, J. (1993). *Manual for the California Verbal Learning Test for Children.* San Antonio: Psychological Corporation.

Elliott, C. D. (1990). *Introductory and technical handbook for the Differential Ability Scales.* San Antonio: Psychological Corporation.

Fagan, T. K., & Wise, P. S. (1993). *School psychology: Past, present, and future.* White Plains, NY: Longman.

Glutting, J. J., Oakland, T., & McDermott, P. A. (1989). Observing child behavior during testing: Constructs, validity, and situational generality. *Journal of School Psychology, 27,* 155–164.

Hood, A. B., & Johnson, R. W. (1991). *Assessment in counseling: A guide to the use of psychological assessment procedures.* Alexandria, VA: American Association for Counseling and Development.

Hutton, J. B., Dubes, R., & Muir, S. (1992). Assessment practices of school psychologists: Ten years later. *School Psychology Review, 21,* 271–284.

Jensen, A. R. (1980). *Bias in mental testing.* New York: Free Press.

Jensen, A. R. (1993). Spearman's hypothesis tested with chronometric information-processing tasks. *Intelligence, 17,* 47–77.

Kamphaus, R. (1993). *Clinical assessment of children's intelligence.* Boston: Allyn & Bacon.

Kaufman, A. (1979). *Intelligent testing with the WISC–R.* New York: Wiley-Interscience.

Kaufman, A., & Kaufman, N. (1983). *Manual for the Kaufman Assessment Battery for Children.* Circle Pines, MN: American Guidance Service.

Kavale, K. A., & Forness, S. R. (1987). Substance over style: Assessing the efficacy of modality testing and teaching. *Exceptional Children, 54,* 228–239.

NASP. (1984). *NASP Principles for Professional Ethics.* Washington, DC: Author.

Reschly, D. J., & Grimes, J. P. (1990). Best practices in intellectual assessment. In A. Thomas & J. P. Grimes (Eds.), *Best practices in school psychology* (2nd ed.; pp. 425–439). Washington, DC: NASP.

Sattler, I. (1988). *Assessment of children* (3rd ed.). San Diego, CA: Author.

Stone, B. J. (1992). Prediction of achievement by Asian-American and white children. *Journal of School Psychology, 30,* 91–99.

Thorndike, R. I., Hagen, E. P., & Sattler, J. (1986). *Manual for the Stanford-Binet* (4th ed.). Chicago: Riverside.

Wechsler, D. (1989). *Manual for the Wechsler Preschool and Primary Scale of Intelligence–Revised.* San Antonio: Psychological Corporation.

Wechsler, D. (1991). *Manual for the Wechsler Intelligence Test for Children* (3rd ed.). San Antonio: Psychological Corporation.

ANNOTATED BIBLIOGRAPHY

Bracken, B. A. (1991). *Psychoeducational assessment of preschool children* (2nd ed.). Boston: Allyn & Bacon.
Bracken provides a very thorough, in-depth analysis of major tests in the preschool assessment area. He balances ability and school readiness debates with a firm command of psychometric issues.

Kamphaus, R. (1993). *Clinical assessment of children's intelligence.* Boston: Allyn & Bacon.
The new standard in the field. A very thorough and readable work, well-written and succinct. The breadth of general topics covered is outstanding. Kamphaus shows an excellent knowledge of psychometrics and statistics. He provides an excellent reference on all major IQ tests. The organization of current re-

search and practice is superb. Overall, this book is an excellent text and reference for all school psychologists.

Sattler, J. (1991). *Assessment of children* (3rd ed.). San Diego: Author.

The standard in the field. In addition to the lengthy text, Sattler provides excellent summaries at the end of chapters that are veritable Cliff's notes for the field of assessment. The tables provided are indispensable. In general, the depth and breadth are remarkable.

Witt, J., Elliott, S., Gresham, F., & Kramer, J. (1988). *Assessment of special children: Tests and the problem-solving process.* Boston: Scott, Foresman.

Provides a thorough discussion of tests within the problem-solving model. The emphasis is on linking assessment to intervention in school settings. Also provides a valuable general reference on all aspects of testing, from psychometrics to the law.

72

Best Practices in Personality Assessment

Howard M. Knoff
University of South Florida

OVERVIEW

The assessment of child and adolescent personality remains an important activity for the school psychologist, given the mandate of the Individuals with Disabilities Education Act (IDEA; Public Laws 94-142 and 99-457 and subsequent reauthorizations) to identify and provide services to severely emotionally disturbed (SED) students. Beyond IDEA, however, the personality assessment process helps us to better understand the significant number of social-emotional and behavioral problems that non-special education students manifest in today's schools and communities. Clearly, through personality assessment school psychologists can provide parents and educators with insight and direction into such problems as truancy, drug abuse, dropping out, teenage pregnancy, suicide, and the emotional impact of divorce, poverty, rejection, and academic failure. But, most important, school psychologists can provide these individuals with recommendations and action plans that decrease or resolve current child and adolescent problems and help prevent them in the future. This is the bottom line of personality assessment. Personality assessment is a process of collecting valid data to explain the causes for or contingencies relevant to a child's social-emotional, behavioral, or affective difficulties. This assessment is useless in isolation; it must be linked with viable, acceptable, and socially valid interventions that are successfully implemented with ongoing attention to treatment integrity and evaluation (Knoff, 1986).

Within a context of comprehensive school psychological service delivery, it is essential that school psychologists understand normal and abnormal personality development and apply this information to empirical models that explain children's social-emotional, behavioral, and affective development. In addition, school psychologists must identify what they want to accomplish from the personality assessment process, as well as what their school districts and multidisciplinary teams want from this process. Then, they must determine whether these two sets of goals converge. While the ultimate personality assessment goal is to develop and implement effective intervention programs for referred students, the following are also goals of the school psychologist: to determine who "owns" a specific referred problem (e.g., the referred child, a referring teacher or parent, a dysfunctional system, or a combination thereof); to validate hypotheses explaining how a referred child's behaviors are being caused, encouraged, reinforced, or supported; to create a sound baseline of data so that intervention can be evaluated from an appropriate context and so that an accurate presenting history can be documented; and to identify the referred child's behavioral assets and the home's and school's resources so that they may be integrated into an intervention program.

Relative to the school district, the primary goal of personality assessment often is to determine a student's eligibility for special education services. This is a national tragedy, because it reinforces the serious misconception that a special education placement is, in and of itself, an intervention. Special education is a setting — ideally, the optimal setting in which to deliver an intervention program needed by a student. And if a special education placement is made in the absence of a functional personality assessment that clearly identifies the program in need, then the placement is, in essence, unethical.

School psychologists must discourage districts from requesting personality assessments primarily as a means to qualify students for a placement in a class for the severely emotionally disturbed. The following are more appropriate district-related uses of personality assessment: to identify and analyze recurring patterns of student behavior or affect so that effective preventive programs can be developed; to understand the severity and demands of students' social-emotional problems so that optimal staffing patterns can be organized; to investigate the relationship between unrealistic academic expectations and inappropriate student behavior so that curricular restructuring as appropriate can occur; and to address student problems that do not require formal referrals or special education placements through teacher consultation, staff development, and prereferral interventions. Ultimately, the best criterion for an SED special education placement is the student's resistance to intervention. Because a "best practice" personality assessment process determines needed intervention programs, placement decisions then can be related more to the success of these interventions than to an assessment process linked to supposedly measurable eligibility criteria.

Under ideal circumstances, school psychologists' professional goals for personality assessment will closely match those of their school districts. However, school psychologists often assess students from a perspective that integrates both psychology and education, while their school colleagues often focus only on an educational perspective. While this may create some tension within the school, the psychology-by-education context is the most effective through which to understand and respond to most referrals for personality assessment. Yet, parenthetically, this difference in perspective explains why school psychologists' assessment conclusions and program and placement recommendations for SED-referred students often differ from their colleagues on the multidisciplinary team: school psychologists are independently and interdependently analyzing referred students' psychological and educational status and outcomes, while others are assessing only the academic impact of these students' referred behaviors or interactions.

The need to analyze referred students from a psychology-by-education perspective is a "best practice" behavior for school psychologists. Children's behavior and affect are the interdependent products of the many institutions, settings, people, and contingencies with which they interact. Personality assessment must reflect these interactions through multitrait, multisetting, and multimethod analyses that necessarily involve data collection from home, school, and community sources (Gresham, 1983). School psychologists should never yield to an educational perspective that is not in the best interests of a student's educational and *psychological* needs and future. School psychologists must look at the child's entire ecology; the school setting is but one part of that ecology (Knoff, 1983).

Given the discussion above, it seems critical that school psychologists work from an empirical model that explains children's social-emotional, behavioral, and affective development from a psychology-by-education and ecological perspective. While this model must be sensitive to situation-specific behavior (Kenrick & Funder, 1988), it should nonetheless guide the school psychologist's thinking so that personality assessment becomes an empirically based problem-solving process that links directly to intervention and that integrates referred problems into a realistic and wholistic context. Significantly, a number of empiri-

cally derived models have been developed to synthesize the research literature and to explain certain specific student outcomes (Centra & Potter, 1980; McKee & Witt, 1990; Rosenfield, 1987). These models have been synthesized into a single, summary model in which student outcomes have been operationalized as (a) academic skill outcomes, (b) cognitive/metacognitive skill outcomes, (c) social skill outcomes, and (d) adaptive behavior skill outcomes. While all four outcome areas can relate to personality assessment, b and c are the two that most directly relate.

As can be seen in Figure 1, the four outcome areas are directly and indirectly impacted (via the arrows shown) by eight different conditions or domains that exist in most students' worlds: family, neighborhood, and community conditions; school and school district conditions; within school and classroom conditions; teacher characteristics or conditions; teacher performance and teacher effectiveness conditions; curricular characteristics and conditions; student characteristics and conditions; and student academic behavior conditions. The point here is that it is usually very easy to identify the specific behaviors, emotions, or affects that are of concern with a specific referred student. What is not always easy to determine is *why* the behaviors are occurring. Using this model, hypotheses explaining why a student's behaviors are occurring can be generated and, once confirmed, they can be directly linked to specific interventions. The personality assessment process, then, focuses on the confirmation or rejection of hypotheses generated using this empirically derived model (Knoff & Batsche, 1991a).

Briefly, the six areas of the empirical model, as described previously (Knoff & Batsche, 1991b, pp. 177–180), are as follows:

1. *Family, neighborhood, and community conditions.* These involve characteristics or conditions of a referred student's family, neighborhood, and community as they relate ultimately to effective discipline and behavior management approaches and student social skills, self-esteem, and self-management outcomes. They emphasize the importance of a positive and proactive home environment and its impact on a student's school readiness, social-emotional development, and success.

2. *Within-classroom/school/district conditions.* These involve favorable and unfavorable characteristics and conditions within a referred student's classroom and school building, such as the physical plant, the pupil–teacher ratio, the presence of mental health resources (e.g., school psychologists and guidance programs), professional development opportunities for staff, the administrative and instructional organization of the building, and other conditions that explain teacher effectiveness. This area also extends to characteristics and conditions within the school dis-

FIGURE 1. Summary of ecological characteristics and conditions that impact student learning outcomes.

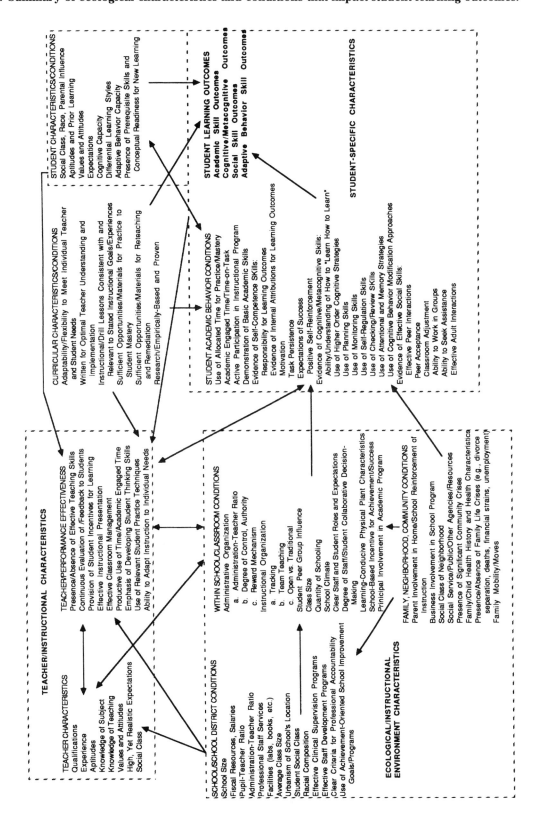

trict that impact classroom management and instruction and successful student achievement.

3. *Teacher characteristics/performance/effectiveness conditions.* These involve characteristics and conditions that teachers bring to the classroom that ultimately translate into the effective management and instructional skills and behaviors that support student learning and development (e.g., background characteristics, professional training). Also involved are those empirically identified skills, activities, and conditions of teachers that make their instruction effective and impactful (e.g., their ability to adapt instruction, their use of social skills curricula and behavior management techniques).

4. *Curricular characteristics and conditions.* These involve characteristics and/or conditions of the curricula being used and include content as well as the processes that are used to ensure student learning and mastery. Curricula here include the self-esteem, social skills, and other behavior management curricula that lead to student learning in the areas of self-control, self-management, and self-efficacy.

5. *Peer characteristics and conditions.* These are characteristics and interactions with a referred student's peer group that function as either antecedent or consequent stimulus control conditions for specific behaviors. While these peer characteristics may be real or simply perceived by the referred student, they do nonetheless have some impact on a referred situation.

6. *Student characteristics and conditions.* These often are preexisting characteristics and conditions, including neurological, physiological, genetic, and biochemical conditions, that relate primarily to a student's behaviors, emotions, affects, and cognitions. Cognitions here include a student's attitudes, expectation, beliefs, attributions, thoughts, and internal processes. All of the characteristics or conditions in this area should directly link to the social-emotional development of students and their ability to conform to social and situational demands. These characteristics and conditions also involve the behaviors that students exhibit that directly support their academic and social learning and progress such as their motivation, their self-competence skills, and their use of appropriate social skills.

Using the model above, school psychologists can generate hypotheses that explain why specific behaviors or emotional responses are occurring. Their personality assessment then can be guided by these hypotheses, not by some random search for eligibility or pathology. Unfortunately, even when assessing for eligibility or pathology, many school psychologists use a test-by-test approach rather than a strategic approach in which assessment is used to answer specific questions that lead to interventions. School psy-

chologists must make this paradigm shift; otherwise personality assessment will remain a random, subjective, and disconnected process that does not lead to effective or defensible interventions or services.

The best practice cited above create a foundation for sound personality assessment. Below, these approaches are extended and operationalized by focusing on the classification systems, pragmatic beliefs, applied approaches, and fundamental procedures that translate into effective personality assessment. After reading this chapter, school psychologists should have not only an updated perspective as to how to link personality assessment and intervention but also a working model that helps them to implement this important process.

BASIC CONSIDERATIONS

Assuming a psychological and educational perspective of personality assessment, school psychologists must attend to the available classification systems that are used to categorize referred child and adolescent behavior. While a functional analysis of a student's behavior and affect will be more relevant to planning viable and effective intervention programs, the presence of these classification systems cannot be ignored, given their widespread use and their determination of much of our diagnostic nomenclature. Three different classification systems, with their strengths and weaknesses briefly will be reviewed: The IDEA definition of SED, DSM-IV, and empirically based classification approach.

The IDEA Definition

Most states (approximately 75%) use the actual or an adapted IDEA definition of SED, even though they may not use the label seriously emotionally disturbed. Despite the apparent consensus, the fact remains that the IDEA definition (a) is predominantly an educational definition that does not lend itself to psychological differentiation or analysis, (b) requires behavioral operationalization in order to be used in a consistent manner, (c) necessitates only a yes or no diagnostic decision, and (d) encourages a medical model perspective of disturbed behavior. For example, the IDEA definition focuses on conditions that "adversely affect educational performance," desensitizing our schools to children who progress educationally but still need socialization or mental health services. The definition leaves vague phrases — e.g., "inappropriate types of behaviors or feelings," "under normal circumstances," "for a long period of time," and "to a marked degree" — to the state, school district, or individual multidisciplinary team to interpret and operationalize. This creates, at best, a great potential for inconsistency across referred children and, at worst, conditions allowing unchecked bias, inequity, and prejudice. Finally, the definition permits a simplistic "yes, the child qualifies as an SED child" or "no, the child does not qualify" mentality, which suggests that the child owns or does not own the causal pathology. This discourages an ecological perspective that focuses more on functional assessment, intervention, and problem resolution.

Over the past 4 years, the Mental Health and Special Education Coalition, made up of numerous special education, mental health, and parent advocacy associations and groups (including NASP), has crafted a new definition that is a marked improvement, both conceptually and functionally, over the current SED definition. Submitted to Congress (but not yet approved), this proposed definition is written as follows:

I. The term *emotional or behavioral disorder* means a disability characterized by behavioral or emotional responses in school programs so different from appropriate age, cultural or ethnic norms that they adversely affect educational performance. Educational performance includes academic, social, vocational or personal skills. Such a disability —

   A. is more than a temporary expected response to stressful events in the environment;

   B. is consistently exhibited in two different settings, at least one of which is school-related; and

   C. persists despite individualized interventions within educational settings unless the education agency and the parent(s) agree that the child or youth would not benefit from such interventions.

II. Emotional or behavioral disorders can co-exist with other disabilities.

III. This category may include children or youth with schizophrenic disorders, affective disorders, anxiety disorders or other sustained disorders of conduct or adjustment when they adversely affect educational performance in accordance with Section I. (Forness & Knitzer, 1992)

While further operationalization is needed even with this definition, it clearly addresses many of the cultural, normative, clinical, developmental, situational, and behavioral issues missing from the current SED definition. Further, this proposed definition is more consistent with the multimethod, multisource, multisetting perspective advocated in the field.

While the coalition definition is a great improvement, the school psychologist still must take a leadership role at the district and individual multidisciplinary team levels to operationalize and systematize the SED definition currently in use. This will require discussions with all team members as to (a) what is typical and expected behavior in the classroom and school building from both a developmental perspective and a normative (school or community) perspective; (b) what types of behaviors, affects, and interactions fall under the SED definition, thereby requiring programmatic intervention (regardless of its setting); (c) what curricular, instructional, and mental health support services are available to "wrap around" an SED student so that regular classroom placement can continue; and (d) what behavioral frequencies, intensities, and durations are needed for regular versus special education classroom placement decisions. Only by having clear SED procedures and definitions can a multidisciplinary team make consistent, objective, and functional decisions, simultaneously overcoming the weaknesses of the current IDEA definition. Only by operationalizing at a local level can a multidisciplinary team evaluate referred children; be sensitive to a community's individual strengths, weaknesses, history, and problems; and determine what constitutes SED behavior for a specific community.

DSM-IV

The most recent revision of the *Diagnostic and Statistical Manual of Mental Disorders*, the DSM-IV (APA, 1994), was published in May of 1994. Continuing its attempts to describe disorders as behaviorally as possible, the DSM-IV describes the following disorders of infancy, childhood, and adolescence: Mental Retardation, Learning Disorders, Motor Skill Disorders, Pervasive Developmental Disorders, Attention-Deficit Disorders and Disruptive Behavior, Feeding and Eating Disorders of Infancy or Early Childhood, Tic Disorders, Communication Disorders, Elimination Disorders, and Other Disorders of Infancy, Childhood, or Adolescence. Critically, there are other disorders that extend from infancy, childhood, and/or adolescence through adulthood that are classified elsewhere in the DSM-IV.

The DSM-IV was published after extensive committee work, research reviews, and clinical trials, and it continues the behavioral and functional focus of its predecessor, the DSM-III–R. Significantly, as the DSM-IV is evaluated during the next few years, it will be important to determine whether the concerns previously expressed for the DSM-III–R exist for its newer version. For example, will the DSM-IV be more able to demonstrate its reliability and validity across all its diagnostic areas? Will the adapted psychosocial stressor and adaptive functioning scales (and axes) of the DSM-IV be more functional and socially valid? Will the adaptations especially to the diagnoses listed under Disruptive Behavior and Attention-Deficit Disorders prove any more applicable or useful to the school setting?

As an example of this latter point, the inattention subset of DSM-IV's Attention-Deficit/Hyperactive Disorder (AD/HD) diagnosis is made for a disturbance of at least 6 months duration, beginning no later than age 7, and involving at least six of nine specific manifestations. Critically, the psychologist does not need to specify which six of the nine behaviors exist when the diagnosis is made, and some of these behaviors (e.g., "often has difficulty organizing tasks and activities," "often forgetful in daily activities," "often does not seem to listen to what is being said to him or her") are behaviorally imprecise and dependent at times on situation-specific factors. Thus, one AD/HD diagnosis could be functionally different from another, and there would be no way for a psychologist to determine which of the various AD/HD behaviors were present unless they were specified in a psychological report. Without specifying the behaviors of concern, then, the AD/HD diagnosis is of limited use, especially in the development of appropriate intervention strategies and programs. When the behavioral manifestations are specified, the AD/HD label is basically unnecessary — school psychologists' interventions will address these problematic behaviors, not the so-called diagnostic labels.

In summary, there are few, if any, compelling reasons why school psychologists need to use the DSM system. While some feel that their ability to label a referred problem means that they understand it and are ready to successfully resolve it, this has never been empirically demonstrated. What has been demonstrated is that the identification of behavioral skill deficits, performance deficits, and self-management deficits and their behavioral contexts and contingencies can be successfully addressed, and that these approaches are often more parsimonious, efficient, and well-accepted by referral sources and referred individuals.

Empirically Based Classification Approaches

An empirically based classification system can be developed from the factor analytic results of the many researchers (e.g., Edelbrock & Achenbach, 1980; Quay, 1983) who have analyzed the characteristics of emotionally disturbed and behaviorally disordered children and adolescents. At a broad-band level, two factors — Internalizing or Overcontrolled and Externalizing or Undercontrolled — have consistently been identified. These factors broadly describe children who demonstrate depressed, withdrawing, or uncommunicative behavioral styles versus hyperactive, aggressive, or delinquent behavioral styles, respectively. At a narrow-band level, many different behavioral clusters have been identified, some of which vary developmentally across age, sex, and research sample. To date, the following narrow-band factors have been most consistently identified: Aggressive, Delinquent, Attention Problems, Thought Problems, Social Problems, Anxious/Depressed, Somatic Complaints, and Withdrawn Behavior (Achenbach, 1991), and Conduct Disordered, Socialized Aggression, Attention Problems/Immaturity, Anxiety-Withdrawal, Psychotic Behavior, and Motor Excess (Quay, 1983).

From a psychometric perspective, the factor analytic approach, with its broad-band and narrow-band factors, represents a sophisticated approach to clas-

sifying behavior. However, this classification approach does not facilitate accurate identification of all problems or the development of appropriate interventions in every case. In fact, it must be emphasized that (a) the factors derived from this approach are statistical clusters of correlated behaviors or characteristics, (b) there are numerous theoretically and empirically based decisions made by the researcher that influence which items appear on which factors, and (c) the factors ultimately are named by the researcher. By way of implication, this suggests that (a) some factors may be multidimensional in nature despite the fact that a single factor is presented, (b) the presence of an item within a factor does not imply a causal relationship relative to the diagnostic label of the factor, and (c) there is a level of subjectivity involved in finalizing or naming any factor, especially at the narrow-band level.

While the empirically based classification approaches have some limitations, they do provide a functional framework from which to organize a sound, school-based classification system that differentiates among referred students' primary social-emotional problems and that facilitates a link between assessment and intervention. One excellent example of an empirically based classification system that has been adapted into a state special education definition for behaviorally disordered students exists in Iowa. There, a behaviorally disordered student is defined in this way:

1. Behaviorally disordered is the inclusive term for patterns of situationally inappropriate behavior which deviate substantially from behavior appropriate to one's age and significantly interfere with the learning process, interpersonal relationships, or personal adjustment of the pupil to such an extent as to constitute a behavioral disorder.

2. Clusters of behavior characteristics of pupils who are behaviorally disordered include: Cluster I — Significantly deviant disruptive, aggressive or impulsive behaviors; Cluster II — Significantly deviant withdrawn or anxious behaviors; Cluster III — Significantly deviant thought processes manifested with unusual communication or behavioral patterns or both; and Cluster IV — Significantly deviant behavior patterns characterized by deficits in cognition, communication, sensory processing or social participation or a combination thereof that may be referred to as autistic behavior. A pupil's behavior pattern may fall into more than one of the above clusters.

3. The determination of significantly deviant behavior is the conclusion that the pupil's characteristic behavior is sufficiently distinct from his or her peer group to qualify the pupil as requiring special education programs or services on the basis of a behavioral disorder. The behavior of concern shall be observed in the school setting for school-age pupils. It must be determined that the behavioral disorder is not maintained by primary intellectual, sensory, cultural or health factors.

4. In addition to those data required within the comprehensive educational evaluation for each pupil requiring special education, the following areas of data collection shall be gathered when identifying a pupil as behaviorally disordered which describe the qualitative nature, frequency, intensity, and duration of the behavior of concern. If it is determined that any of the areas of data collection are not relevant in assessing the behavior of concern, documentation must be provided explaining the rationale for such a decision. (Wood, Smith, & Grimes, 1985)

This definition emphasizes many of the critical best practices points discussed so far in this chapter. The definition (a) validates referred children's atypical behavior by comparing it to behavior that is developmentally expected at their chronological age levels and to those behaviors normatively observed in their classroom- or community-based peer group; (b) emphasizes students' behavioral, affective, and interpersonal progress from a psychological perspective and their learning and instructional progress from an educational perspective; (c) acknowledges and synthesizes the empirical literature by specifying four major clusters of atypical behavior; and (d) recognizes that behavioral and emotional handicaps can be situation- and setting-specific and that referred behaviors occur within an environmental context that must be incorporated into the intervention program. While this definition is admittedly behavioral in orientation and nature, it is clear that behavioral assessment and intervention approaches are now the national norm (Grosenick, George, & George, 1987). As with any special education SED definition, this definition will need further operationalization by school psychologists within their individual school districts as part of a comprehensive approach to effective service delivery for referred and identified SED students.

Pragmatic Beliefs

As a review and extension of the discussion above, five pragmatic beliefs are essential to a best practices approach to personality assessment (Knoff, 1986). These beliefs, critical both to the conceptualization and operationalization of the assessment process, involve the following.

1. The need for an ecological/environmental orientation to personality assessment suggests that referred students are best understood by investigating the family, school, and community systems in which they have been and are now interacting. In most cases, these systems have determined or influenced referred students' developmental progress, and analyses of the interdependent relationships between these systems and students may explain certain behaviors, affects, and interactions of concern. Clearly, a child's anxious or phobic behavior toward school is best understood when it is known that the child has been corporally punished and embarrassed in full view of her or his peer group for forgetting to bring in her or his homework. Similarly, a child who never attended preschool and has been in four different kindergartens and first grades due to frequent moves may never have learned appropriate play or socialization behavior. The ecological/environmental assessment efficiently helps to explain many referred problems, while decreasing the tendency to assume that the child should be the exclusive focus of the assessment process. This perspective also increases the probability that the ecological/environmental contingencies that explain referred problems will be recognized and directly addressed with appropriate intervention approaches.

2. The need for multimethod, multisource, multisetting assessments suggests that the identification and analysis of referred problems are more accurate when the assessment procedures used involve multiple techniques and approaches from multiple informants who have interacted with the referred student in multiple situations and settings (Gresham, 1983). This process minimizes diagnostic and analytical errors and poorly developed intervention programs that have occurred because (a) only one assessment technique was used (e.g., a projective test) rather than a more comprehensive assessment battery (e.g., behavioral observations plus behavior rating scales plus home and school interviews plus appropriate developmental scales); (b) only one assessment source (e.g., the mother) was used, when multiple sources might have indicated that the mother had excessively high expectations for the child; and because (c) the child was evaluated in only one setting, when a multiple setting evaluation might have indicated that the child experienced a traumatic event in a different setting and generalized the emotional response across settings. While some problems are legitimately related to specific individuals or settings, the multimethod, multisource, multisetting process increases assessment and intervention reliability and validity while assuring attention to the ecological/environmental considerations described above.

3. The need for a developmental context to assessment suggests that school psychologists must be knowledgeable and sensitive to the typical and atypical developmental characteristics that occur for the independent variables of age, sex, multicultural status, and socioeconomic status, and that all personality assessment data must be analyzed and interpreted from this perspective. For example, it makes no sense to interpret projective drawings as psychologically significant when a child has obvious visual-motor deficiencies or when developmental norms indicate that a student cannot form meaningful, interactive figures in such drawings at that age. It is also somewhat dangerous for school psychologists to depend on their

own, or others', subjective interpretations of any assessment method if no sound empirical base exists to guide and support those conclusions. Finally, it is important to consider referred children's cognitive-developmental status when interpreting any personality assessment data gathered directly or indirectly. Clearly a mildly retarded child's social skills and emotional reaction to frustration may be closely related to his or her cognitive skills and developmental status.

In this context, it is important to note that much of the projective drawing literature depends on clinically based, rather than empirically based, studies and case examples (Knoff, 1990). While projective drawings may provide insight into a student's behavioral cognitions and belief systems, their results can only be interpreted as hypotheses that are in need of objective and multimodal validation. In contrast, even though a common set of narrow-band scales have been created, the various Achenbach (1991) behavior rating scales have been factor-analyzed across age and sex, and the problems scales are scored separately by gender and age (ages 4–11 and 12–18).

4. The need for a problem-solving and hypothesis-testing approach to assessment suggests that the personality assessment process should systematically involve a problem identification, problem analysis, intervention, and evaluation sequence so that problems are accurately (and ecologically) identified and then comprehensively analyzed (using multimethod, multisource, and multisetting assessments) before any intervention is attempted. This process explicitly and logically links assessment results with intervention programs, and ensures that these programs are not implemented until an explanation as to why a referred problem or situation is occurring has been found. Within the problem-solving process, then, it is important to behaviorally operationalize referral problems, to generate hypotheses to explain why the problem exists, to empirically confirm (through personality assessment) these hypotheses, and then to develop and implement the interventions that are logically linked to the confirmed hypotheses.

Using this approach, the most critical step in the personality assessment process is the generation of hypotheses. In trying to explain a student's verbal aggression toward her or his teachers, for example, a number of potential hypotheses concerning the cause (student, teacher, classroom/school, peer, curricular, home/community) exist. However, if a diagnostic interview suggested that the referred student verbally lashes out at teachers when confronted with work at too high an academic level (the hypothesis), and this hypothesis was empirically confirmed, then the intervention is obvious: give this student academic material at an academic level where she or he can succeed. At this point, the only questions are whether this intervention can be accommodated in the regular classroom and whether the intervention decreases the frequency, duration, and intensity of the verbal aggression.

In the example above, note that (a) the need for a classification decision is independent of the reasons explaining the referred problem, and dependent only on the intensity of the behavior when compared developmentally and normatively and its resistance to intervention; (b) a placement decision would be needed only if it was determined that the intervention program (i.e., providing material at the student's instructional level) would be more successfully implemented in a special education setting; and (c) there is a definite link between the assessment process and the interventions recommended. To summarize, this problem-solving hypothesis-testing process allows school psychologists to strategically choose which assessment instruments and approaches are needed to confirm the hypotheses generated. In this way, the school psychologist controls the entire process; personality assessment instruments are used to facilitate rather than dictate all interpretations and conclusions.

5. The need for objective and observable assessment strategies emphasizes that all assessment hypotheses must be validated objectively and, ideally, through observable means. While objectivity is clearly relative, school psychologists must use instruments and techniques that have demonstrated their ability to validly and reliably generate the desired data and information. Thus the psychometric properties of all personality assessment instruments must be investigated on an ongoing basis, and only the soundest instruments should be used among those that advertise similar assessment purposes or domains. In context, comprehensive behavioral observation is still the best way to assess the presence of specific social-emotional skills or deficits. Behavioral observation requires a clear operationalization of targeted skills or deficits, and the results include the frequency, intensity, and duration of a referred student's behavior and the antecedent, consequent, and ecological conditions that exist when these behaviors are exhibited. Collecting accurate and useful data through behavioral observation requires training, organization, and practice; it is a learned skill. But when done effectively, behavioral observation becomes the cornerstone of any personality assessment, and the source of the objective data that can confirm or reject many important hypotheses about a referred student.

BEST PRACTICES IN PERSONALITY ASSESSMENT

Rather than describing the various personality assessment approaches, tools, and techniques in a somewhat random, categorical form, this section will discuss the assessment process from the beginning to the end using the Referral Question Consultation (RQC) process (Knoff & Batsche, 1991a). Assumed throughout this entire discussion are the beliefs that (a) school psychologists have the professional training and autonomy to determine what personality assessment procedures are necessary for any SED (or related) referral; (b) school psychologists ultimately identify and implement intervention programs that offer the highest probability of treatment success; and (c) service delivery is provided within the context of consultee acceptability, social validity, treatment integrity, and transfer of training and generalization. While some states and school districts require the completion of certain personality assessment techniques (e.g., projective tests) with any SED referral regardless of the circumstances surrounding the referral, this is not a best practices approach. Personality assessment is an individualized process that should be fully in the hands of the professional school psychologist, and the requirement that certain techniques be used is personally and professionally appalling and potentially unwise or even damaging to the referred student.

RQC Process

The RQC process involves 10 interdependent steps after an individual student has been referred.

1. Review all existing data available on the referred student and collect any additional background data as appropriate.

2. Meet with the referral source in a consultative interview to behaviorally define his or her initial concerns, to identify the need for additional data to finalize the behavioral operationalization of these concerns, to informally test some initial hypotheses, and to determine the referral source's assessment goals and commitment to the RQC process.

3. Develop hypotheses to explain the initial concerns as behaviorally operationalized.

4. Develop prediction statements from the generated hypotheses.

5. Develop data-based referral questions that will guide the assessment process and confirm or reject the generated hypotheses.

6. Select multitrait, multimethod assessment procedures that will specifically answer the referral questions and facilitate the link between assessment and intervention.

7. Apply the assessment and background data so as to answer the referral questions and to confirm or reject the generated hypotheses.

8. Select and implement intervention strategies consistent with those hypotheses that have been confirmed.

9. Monitor change in the area of the initial concern to determine the impact of the intervention.

10. Develop a written report that documents the RQC process, the interventions tried, and the intervention outcomes as they relate to the resolution of the initial referred concerns.

Review of the data. When a school psychologist receives a referral from a teacher, the first step in the RQC process is to review essential information about the referred student and to collect any additional background data that may be important to know before interviewing the teacher. The review of essential information typically centers around an analysis of four possible existing student areas or folders: (a) the student's cumulative folder, (b) the administrative/discipline folder, (c) relevant teachers' academic work sample folders, and (d) the special education/remedial education (e.g., Chapter I) folder. In addition to the information available in already-existing records and student folders, it may be time- and cost-efficient to collect other data from teachers and other sources prior to an initial consultation interview. This information may be collected through behavior checklists, behavior rating scales, ecological or developmental status surveys or questionnaires, or objective personality scales or inventories, and it may, for example, provide the answers to routine developmental (and other) status questions so that precious interview time can focus on the areas most relevant to the referral concerns. Significantly, this information also may facilitate a more accurate and in-depth behavioral operationalization of the teacher's initial concerns, identify possible correlates of those concerns, identify possible student assets and strengths, and generally prepare the school psychologist more thoroughly for the consultation interview and the teacher's (and others') perception of the referral problem.

Behavior rating scales. Behavior rating scales are one of the most efficient, sound, and effective ways (a) to identify a referred student's behavioral strengths and weaknesses, (b) to validate a referral source's initial concerns, (c) to evaluate the severity of a wide range of specific behaviors, (d) to assess for atypical patterns of behaviors or clinical entities, and (e) to complete one facet of a multisource, multisetting evaluation. With literally hundreds of rating scales on the market, school psychologists' ability to choose the rating scales that will best accomplish their assessment goals without sacrificing psychometric quality is critical. To that end, Edelbrock (1983) noted that behavior rating scales differ dramatically across a number of critical dimensions, and he provided the following suggestions to help school psychologists become better consumers of behavior rating scales.

1. School psychologists need to match their RQC and assessment goals to the results that a particular behavior rating actually provides. Some behavior rat-

ing scales (a) assess clinical, home, or school concerns; (b) are descriptive, prescriptive, or diagnostic; (c) evaluate specific behaviors or simply provide a checklist indication that they exist; (d) are unidimensional or multidimensional in scope; (e) rate actual student behaviors or characteristics that correlate with certain behavioral conditions; (f) focus exclusively on behavioral deficits or problems, or assess both behavioral deficits and assets (Wood, Smith, & Grimes, 1985). School psychologists must consider these rating scale characteristics, the referred problem, and the diagnostic and intervention questions to be answered. Clearly, behavior rating scales must be chosen in an informed manner with proper consideration for their purposes and intended uses.

2. School psychologists need to recognize that the technical adequacy of behavior rating scales varies greatly and needs to be analyzed prior to their use. Among the variables to evaluate are (a) how items were selected during the development of the behavior rating scale, (b) what response scaling approach was used (e.g., true/false, often/sometimes/never), (c) how the scale was developed and constructed, (d) the scale's standardization and norming procedures, and (e) the scale's validity and reliability data.

3. School psychologists need to evaluate whether behavior rating scales evaluate global or specific levels of manifested behavior, the time frames within which referred students are evaluated (e.g., every 1, 3, or 6 months), and who the optimal respondent should be. To clarify this point, some behavior rating scales require that the informant be the target child's mother or teacher, others can be completed simply by an individual who genuinely knows the child or who has interacted with the child over a long period of time.

4. Finally, school psychologists must assess how behavior rating scales control for response bias — for example, for halo effects, leniency or severity effects, and central tendency or range restriction effects. Without sufficient controls for bias, a behavior rating scale's results are of extremely limited use.

From an RQC perspective, school psychologists must strategically use all of the potential information generated by a behavior rating scale. School psychologists also must recognize that behavior rating scales measure the perceptions of the scale's respondent and that these perceptions must be validated. Finally, too often school psychologists simply use the broad-band and narrow-band results of a behavior rating scale, concluding and writing in their personality assessment reports, for example, that a referred child "has significantly high externalizing or acting-out tendencies, and that he manifests hyperactive, aggressive, and delinquent behavior" by virtue of elevated scores on those scales. Unfortunately, conclusions

like these are simplistic at best and downright inaccurate and damaging at worst. A best practices approach to behavior rating scale interpretation (a) begins at the individual item level to determine what specific behaviors or behavioral correlates are of greatest concern to the scale respondent; (b) continues at the narrow-band scale level, first to determine if the significant items are consistent with the label of the specific scale that contains them, and then to determine if the scale's scores indicate a statistical or clinical problem; and (c) ends at the broad-band scale level where the most global interpretations of a referred student's behavior are considered. Significantly, the data generated in this manner are compared with other information at this first step of the RQC process and then integrated into the consultation interview for further confirmation and analysis.

Objective personality scales. Objective personality assessment scales assess specific diagnostic areas (e.g., self-concept, anxiety, depression) or multidimensional areas of referred children's personality functioning. At this RQC stage, it may be best to use the latter type of objective scale, so that a broad range of psychological problems or concerns can be sampled for later, more in-depth investigation. Currently, a number of multidimensional objective scales are available, including the Personality Inventory for Children and for Youth, the Children's Personality Questionnaire, the Early School and High School Personality Questionnaires, the Minnesota Multiphasic Personality Inventory–Adolescents, and the Millon Adolescent Personality Inventory. The Personality Inventory for Children, for example, has 12 clinical scales — Achievement, Intellectual Screening, Development, Somatic Concerns, Depression, Family Relations, Delinquency, Withdrawal, Anxiety, Psychosis, Hyperactivity, and Social Skills — all of which can stand alone as separate clinical entities.

Like behavior rating scales, the development and psychometric properties of all objective scales must be investigated, and only those scales that have clinical (as opposed to research) validation and utility should be used. Also, like the behavior rating scales, analyses of individual items on these instruments — as opposed to unconditional acceptance of scale and profile results — are more likely to facilitate the development of effective interview questions and hypotheses for later validation through the RQC process.

The consultative interview. The consultation interview, involving those individuals referring and relevant to a specific child, is the most important activity in the RQC process. While the long-term impact of the consultation interview focuses on intervention planning and implementation, the interview has the following goals as the second step of the RQC process:

1. To engage the teacher (and/or parents) in the comprehensive problem-solving process, so that they are committed to the entire process and to the service delivery directions that result from the process.

2. To obtain additional relevant information beyond that already collected during the review of data step and to integrate and apply all of the data to the next steps of the RQC process.

3. Using all the data collected, to clarify the initial concerns of the referral source resulting in a behavioral definition and operationalization of the behavior(s) of concern.

4. To determine what interventions have already been attempted and to evaluate the treatment integrity and impact of those interventions.

5. To begin to generate tentative hypotheses that explain the clarified concern and to outline the remainder of the RQC assessment process for the consultee.

Armed with the teacher- and parent-completed referral and background information forms, behavior rating scales, and objective rating scales, the school psychologist can begin the diagnostic interview process at a much higher level of sophistication than when starting the process with a simple statement of concern. In fact, with the social, behavioral, developmental, educational, and familial history of the student already documented by both teachers and parents, a great many background questions are unnecessary, and the school psychologist need only pursue those questions that are directly or indirectly related to the referral problem. Thus the school psychologist now can listen to teachers' and parents' descriptions of the referral problem, match them to the behavior and objective rating scale data that has already been completed, behaviorally define and operationalize the stated problems and the behavioral ecology where they exist, and begin to generate hypotheses that explain the referred behavior or situation.

Development of hypotheses. After completing the needed consultation interviews and collecting the necessary relevant information, the RQC process proceeds to the development of hypotheses that explain the now-clarified and behaviorally operationalized referral concerns. At this point in the process, the school psychologist and others have a great deal of information about the referred behavior, the settings within which this behavior occurs, and other significant ecological environments and contexts that are related to the referred student and the referral situation. Now it is time to integrate all of this information and generate hypotheses that answer the question "Why is this referral situation happening?" These hypotheses are generated using the variables and conditions in Table 1, and they conform to the principle

that hypotheses must be relevant, predictive, and measurable.

Development of predictions. The next step in the RQC process is the development of predictions. Predictions are statements, developed from specific hypotheses, that identify what should or should not happen if a hypothesis is true or untrue, respectively. For example, if we hypothesize "A child aggresses because his peers verbally taunt him," then our prediction statements would be "When peers verbally taunt the child, then the child will aggress against the peers," and "When peers do not verbally taunt the child, then the child will not aggress against the peers."

Prediction statements are set up to evaluate the hypothesis and its converse. That is, it is necessary to demonstrate that the referral concern exists when our explanatory hypothesis is true, and it is also necessary to demonstrate that the concern does not exist in the absence of our hypothesis. For example, given the example above we need to demonstrate that the child aggresses only when his peers verbally taunt him. If he aggresses when the peers ignore him, then our hypothesis is not true in that the verbal taunting is not consistently related to an aggressive response.

Another important point about predictions is that they must be evaluated without changing the student's natural environment whenever possible. That is, predictions should be tested, as much as possible, without implementing new interventions and thus without changing the referral setting. If a student, for example, is referred because she is out of her seat a great deal of the time, and your hypothesis is that she gets out of her seat during unstructured times in the classroom, then your prediction statements would be "When unstructured time occurs in the classroom, then the student will get out of her seat" and "When structured time occurs in the classroom, then the student will stay in her seat." In order to evaluate these prediction statements in a naturally occurring way, we would need to observe during times when the teacher routinely allows the classroom to be structured and unstructured. If we asked the teacher to artificially plan special structured and unstructured times, this would constitute an intervention that changes the normally occurring classroom routine. When such changes occur, in the absence of baseline data and a multiple baseline or reversal research design, we cannot truly be sure whether the referred student's behavior is a function of the classroom structure (or lack of structure) or the change in the classroom routine.

Development of referral questions. Referral questions are data-based questions, derived from the prediction statements, that quantitatively confirm or reject the original hypotheses related to a referral concern. More specifically, referral questions are typically yes or no questions, or questions related to fre-

TABLE 1
Conditions that Relate Directly/Indirecty to Student Learning

1. FAMILY/NEIGHBORHOOD, COMMUNITY DOMAIN
    :   Home Conditions
    :   Parenting Style
    :   Peers in the Community
    :   Home/Community Values
    :   Cultural/Language Differences

2. SCHOOL/SCHOOL DISTRICT DOMAIN
    :   Resources Available
    :   Rules In School vs Rules at Home
    :   Major Changes in Curriculum--School/District Based
    :   Busing Issues--Behavior/Distance/Time/Peers

3. CLASSROOM DOMAIN
    :   Number of Students
    :   Classroom Environment--seating etc
    :   Format of Instruction--centers not compatible with student

4. TEACHER CHARACTERISTICS
    :   Teaching Style
    :   Management Style
    :   Skills with Academic Curriculum--Learning Problems
    :   Expectations/Flexibility/Philosophy

5. CURRICULUM
    :   Difficulty/format
    :   Related to Student Background/Prior Experiences
    :   Skills Required (writing/long worksheets) vs Student Skills

6. STUDENT CHARACTERISTICS
    :   Attention Span/ Listening Skills/ Ability/ Writing Skills
    :   Academic Skills Level
    :   Social Skills Level

quency, duration, latency, or intensity. Referral questions are important for a number of reasons. First, referral questions actually drive the assessment and decision-making process. While assessment procedures must be reliable, valid, and psychometrically sound, the form and format of the referral questions actually determine what assessment methodologies must be used. Second, referral questions provide an internal check for the RQC process to ensure that the parents' or teachers' referral concerns still are being addressed. Third, referral questions help to organize the report-writing process. In fact, reports documenting the confirmation of hypotheses, the development of interventions, and the successful results of those interventions can be structured in a question-and-answer format around the referral questions. Thus reports should do more than describe the referred student; they should answer questions that lead to and relate to interventions.

To be effective and appropriate, referral questions must have the following characteristics:

1. Referral questions must be clearly defined, they must be directly related to the previous prediction statements, and they must require data that are observable and measurable.

2. Referral questions must be agreed upon by the referral source and other evaluation team members,

and they must lead to or have the potential to lead to interventions, not labels.

3. Referral questions should result in clear, definitive answers. Ideally, referral questions should be answered in a yes-or-no or other data-based format, and they should be able to directly confirm or reject hypotheses generated to explain the referred problem.

For the scenario above with an aggressive child, the referral questions should be:

1. Do peers verbally taunt the child? (yes or no?)

2. Is the child aggressive with peers? (yes or no?)

3. Do peers ignore or leave the child alone? (yes or no?)

4. Is the child aggressive with peers? (yes or no?)

To confirm the hypothesis in this situation, questions 1, 2, and 3 would have to be answered yes and question 4 would have to be answered no.

Assessment. Once referral questions are developed, assessment begins. It is important to note that only those assessment instruments and processes needed to answer the referral questions are necessary. This discourages the random use of personality assessment tools in a search for pathology, and it makes the RQC process both efficient and effective. In this context, most RQC referral questions will be answered jointly by the school psychologist and the classroom teacher, and they will most likely involve direct assessment in the setting where the referred student's behavior or problem is occurring. These assessments involve low-inference procedures (e.g., the use of behavioral observation), use multitrait, multimethod assessment procedures, and directly link assessment and intervention.

Briefly, there are four behavioral observation approaches commonly noted in the literature: naturalistic free behavior, naturalistic role-play, analog free behavior, and analog role-play observations (Cone, 1978; Keller, 1986). Naturalistic observation involves observing referred students in the actual settings where their behaviors of concern or the conditions that most influence those behaviors are exhibited. When used to confirm hypotheses generated to explain well-identified behaviors, naturalistic observations are both time- or cost-efficient. In addition, they are the most ecologically sound of the behavioral approaches, and they are the least inferential relative to interpretation within the personality assessment context. Analog observation involves observing referred students in controlled situations that simulate particular environments or circumstances of behavioral concern. These situations are used to objectively evaluate a priori hypotheses that explain referred behaviors or situations and to provide detailed and comprehensive functional analyses of significant facets of a referred student's behavior. Significantly, analog ob-

servations attempt to maximize the ecological accuracy of simulated situations so that interpretation requires as little inference as possible. They are also very time-efficient, given their intent to elicit behaviors that test the referral-related hypotheses.

Free behavior observations occur when referred students are allowed to freely react and interact within environments that are either unmanipulated and naturalistic or simulated and analog. No artificial rules or constraints are placed on the students, and they respond to situations in any way that they choose. Role-play observations occur as referred students are requested to follow preconceived and semistructured scripts that focus on interactions or situations relevant to particular hypotheses. These observations involve more inference than free behavior observations, because the students' role-played behavior is assumed to represent behavior that would be exhibited if the situation actually occurred in a real-life situation. Once again, role-play observations can occur in both naturalistic or classroom-based settings and analog or simulated settings; naturalistic observations are assumed to require less interpretive inference than analog observations.

While behavioral observations may appear to be the easiest and most objective of all personality assessment approaches, they actually involve very complex processes. In addition to choosing which observational approach to use, school psychologists must decide which recording method to use (e.g., narrative, interval, event, ratings), and how to best assess the antecedent conditions, environmental characteristics and interactions, overt and covert contingencies, planned and unplanned consequent conditions, and unintended effects of a referred behavior within its unique ecology. While behavioral observation is one of the most effective ways to validate hypotheses generated during the problem identification phase of the personality assessment process, it also can be misused or abused. School psychologists must recognize that it is a learned skill that requires training, practice, and more practice.

Once data are collected, the referral questions can be answered and the original hypotheses can be confirmed or rejected. At this point, the multidisciplinary team can take the confirmed hypotheses, begin to develop intervention plans, and outline a formative report organized around the hypotheses tested, the referral questions generated, and the data collected.

Other assessment techniques. Beyond behavioral observation, there are a number of other personality techniques that can be used during the assessment process to answer specific RQC questions. These include objective personality assessment techniques that focus on single diagnostic dimensions when needed — e.g., self-concept, anxiety, depression — and family assessment techniques (Knoff, 1986). Projective instruments, to a large degree, cannot validate a priori hypotheses; they only generate additional hypotheses that need subsequent validation and thus are useful only (if at all) in the earliest stages of the RQC process. The reader is strongly encouraged to read Knoff's (1990; 1993) research review and analyses of projective drawing approaches. The primary conclusions from these reviews are that projective instruments do not have sufficient empirical validation for clinical use, they are both time- and cost-inefficient, and their use necessitates additional assessments to validate their assertions.

A Brief RQC Case Study

To quickly illustrate the RQC process in action, let's consider a fourth-grade boy (Jason), who has been referred by his regular classroom teacher because of a number of incidents in which he becomes verbally angry, pushes his desk violently away from himself and toward other students, and refuses to calm down and follow teacher directions. Typically, we would behaviorally operationalize this problem in more specific detail by completing a series of consultative interviews, making some classroom observations, and perhaps having the teacher complete a behavior rating scale or two. But, for the purposes of this example, let's just generate one hypothesis for each of the six hypothesis areas delineated in Table 1 that potentially explain this behavior. Putting these hypotheses in the recommended format, we would say that Jason becomes verbally angry, pushes his desk violently away from himself and toward other students, and refuses to calm down and follow teacher directions because:

- *Family-oriented hypothesis:* He sees his father respond similarly to his mother when she asks him to do something around the house.

- *Classroom-oriented hypothesis:* There is so much noise in the classroom that he can't attend to and complete his work.

- *Teacher-oriented hypothesis:* The teacher constantly orders him around, giving him five negative comments for every one positive comment.

- *Curriculum-oriented hypothesis:* His mathematics text and assignments are above his instructional level.

- *Peer-oriented hypothesis:* His peers reinforce him with attention and laughter each time he does this.

- *Student-oriented hypothesis:* He forgets to use the "stop and think" steps of his prosocial skills/problem-solving self-management intervention.

At this point, we would generate prediction statements and referral questions for each of these hypotheses, and then proceed to collect the data to confirm or reject each hypothesis. Continuing our example for just one of the hypotheses above, the curriculum-oriented hypothesis, we would predict that when Jason's mathematics assignments are above his instructional level, then he will become verbally angry, push his desk violently away from himself and toward other students, and refuse to calm down and follow teacher directions. Conversely, when Jason's mathematics assignments are at his instructional level, then he will not become verbally angry, not push his desk violently away from himself and toward other students, and not refuse to calm down and follow teacher directions.

The data-based referral questions needed to assess this hypothesis, drawn from the prediction statements, are these: "Are Jason's mathematics assignments above his instructional level?" and "Does Jason become verbally angry, push his desk violently away from himself and toward other students, and refuse to calm down and follow teacher directions?"

At this point, the school psychologist or the teacher can collect the data to answer these questions through (a) an assessment of the instructional level of Jason's math assignments over time, and (b) observations of Jason's behavior during math. If the data demonstrate that Jason acts out when math assignments are above his instructional level, but does not act out, is calm, and appropriately follows teacher directions when math assignments are at his instructional level, then the hypothesis has been confirmed. If the data do not support one or both of these situations, then the hypothesis should be rejected. For the confirmed hypothesis, the intervention program would focus on (a) ensuring that current math assignments are at Jason's instructional level, (b) working with Jason to increase his mathematics skill levels so that his instructional level progresses, and (c) teaching Jason coping skills so that he is able to more adaptively handle the academic and personal frustration that occurs when he receives a mathematics assignment above his instructional level. If the hypothesis is rejected, then another hypothesis must be generated, assessed, and validated — intervention programs cannot be developed without one or more confirmed hypotheses.

SUMMARY

Once the referral problem has been comprehensively identified and analyzed from ecological, developmental, and environmental perspectives using a hypothesis-testing, problem-solving process in which hypotheses are evaluated using objective, multimethod, multisource, multisetting methods, the school psychologist is ready to develop an intervention program. Intervention should be clearly linked to the assessment process, the referral concerns identified and confirmed by the personality and behavioral assessments, and the factors that interact and influence the referral concerns. As noted earlier, intervention is useless unless viable, acceptable, and socially valid approaches are successfully implemented with ongoing attention to treatment integrity and treatment evaluation. In the end, the success of the personality assessment process will be evaluated most clearly through the behavioral and treatment changes resulting from the intervention program.

To summarize, personality assessment is a process, not a product. It is simply not enough to understand a child's behavioral or social-emotional problems. School psychologists must move from problem analysis to interventions that resolve these problems and facilitate children's normal development and positive mental health. This chapter has been devoted to this ultimate best practice. Hopefully, we will soon see the day when school psychologists provide comprehensive services, when intervention success is valued over special education placement, and when social, emotional, and behavioral success is an explicit educational goal and emphasis.

REFERENCES

Achenbach, T. M. (1991). *Manual for the Child Behavior Checklist and Revised Child Behavior Profile.* Burlington, VT: University of Vermont Department of Psychiatry.

American Psychiatric Association. (1994). *The diagnostic criteria from DSM-IV.* Washington, DC: Author.

Centra, J. A., & Potter, D. A. (1980). School and teacher effects: An interrelational model. *Review of Educational Research, 50,* 273–291.

Cone, J. D. (1978). The Behavioral Assessment Grid (BAG): A conceptual framework and a taxonomy. *Behavior Therapy, 9,* 882–888.

Edelbrock, C. S. (1983). Problems and issues in using rating scales to assess child personality and psychopathology. *School Psychology Review, 12,* 293–299.

Edelbrock, C. S., & Achenbach, T. M. (1980). A typology of child behavior profile patterns: Distribution and correlates for disturbed children aged 6–16. *Journal of Abnormal Child Psychology, 8,* 441–470.

Forness, S. R., & Knitzer, J. (1992). A new proposed definition and terminology to replace "Serious Emotional Disturbance" in Individuals with Disabilities Education Act. *School Psychology Review, 21,* 12–20.

Gresham, F. M. (1983). Multitrait-multimethod approach to multifactored assessment: Theoretical rationale and practical application. *School Psychology Review, 12,* 26–34.

Grosenick, J. K., George, M. P., & George, N. L. (1987). A profile of school programs for the behaviorally disordered: Twenty years after Morse, Cutler, and Fink. *Behavior Disorders, 12,* 159–168.

Keller, H. R. (1986). Behavioral observation approaches. In H. M. Knoff (Ed.), *The assessment of child and adolescent personality* (pp. 353–397). New York: Guilford.

Kenrick, D. T., & Funder, D. C. (1988). Profiting from controversy: Lessons from the person-situation debate. *American Psychologist, 43,* 23–34.

Knoff, H. M. (1983). Personality assessment in the schools: Issues and procedures for school psychologists. *School Psychology Review, 12,* 391–398.

Knoff, H. M. (Ed.). (1986). *The assessment of child and adolescent personality.* New York: Guilford.

Knoff, H. M. (1990). Evaluation of projective drawings. In C. R. Reynolds & R. W. Kamphaus (Eds.), *Handbook of psychological and educational assessment of children: Volume 2. Personality, behavior, and context* (pp. 89–146). New York: Guilford.

Knoff, H. M. (1993). The utility of human figure drawings in personality and intellectual assessment: Why ask why? *School Psychology Quarterly, 8,* 191–196.

Knoff, H. M., & Batsche, G. M. (1991a). *The Referral Question Consultation process: Addressing system, school, and classroom academic and behavioral problems.* Tampa, FL: Authors.

Knoff, H. M., & Batsche, G. M. (1991b). Integrating school and educational psychology to meet the educational and mental health needs of all children. *Educational Psychology, 26,* 167–183.

McKee, W. T., & Witt, J. C. (1990). Effective teaching: A review of instructional and environmental variables. In T. B. Gutkin & C. R. Reynolds (Eds.), *The handbook of school psychology* (2nd ed.; pp. 821–846). New York: John Wiley & Sons.

Quay, H. C. (1983). A dimensional approach to behavior disorder: The Revised Behavior Problem Checklist. *School Psychology Review, 12,* 244–249.

Rosenfield, S. (1987). *Instructional consultation.* Hillsdale, NJ: Erlbaum.

Wood, F. H., Smith, C. R., & Grimes, J. (1985). *The Iowa assessment model in behavioral disorders: A training manual.* Des Moines, IA: State Department of Public Instruction.

ANNOTATED BIBLIOGRAPHY

Knoff, H. M., & Batsche, G. M. (1991b). *The Referral Question Consultation process: Addressing system, school, and classroom academic and behavioral problems.* Tampa, FL: Authors.
An introductory manual to the Referral Question Consultation process, which utilizes a systematic problem-solving process to address referred problems. Using consultation processes as a foundation, this process ensures a direct link between case-related assessment and intervention by generating hypotheses that explain the referred behavior, confirming behavioral predictions based on these hypotheses, and developing interventions that address these behavioral explanations. This manual describes this decision-making process and relates it to use by support teams, team reports, and triennial reevaluations. It also provides a step-by-step teaching of the RQC process complete with numerous case examples and practice exercises to facilitate reader mastery.

Knoff, H. M. (Ed.). (1986). *The assessment of child and adolescent personality.* New York: Guilford.
A comprehensive volume on personality assessment specifically with children and adolescents written in four parts. Part 1 discusses the theoretical bases underlying the personality assessment process; Part 2 describes the development, administration, scoring, and interpretation of the predominant techniques now used in personality assessment from behavioral to projective to family assessment; Part 3 describes how to communicate and translate personality assessment results into effective intervention strategies; and Part 4 summarizes the issues currently in the field and presents future directions and needs. A single-authored update of this book is currently in preparation and should be available in 1996 or 1997.

Knoff, H. M. (1990). Evaluation of projective drawings. In C. R. Reynolds & R. W. Kamphaus (Eds.), *Handbook of psychological and educational assessment of children: Vol. 2. Personality, behavior, and context* (pp. 89–146). New York: Guilford.

A critical chapter in an important edited volume devoted to personality assessment and sound clinical and school practice. The chapter reviews all of the current research on projective drawings and concludes that much of the "evidence" is provided through case studies or research containing serious methodological flaws. Projective drawings are put into a problem-solving context that suggests limiting their use while increasing their accountability – for those who still want to use them. While the debate on projectives rages on, this chapter provides an objective and empirical perspective in the midst of the storm.

Martin, R. P. (1988). *Assessment of personality and behavior problems: Infancy through adolescence.* New York: Guilford.
An important book that approaches perso/*Assessment of personality and behavior problems: Infancy through adolescence.*/nality assessment from a developmental and integrative perspective. It is divided into four sections, which discuss issues and assumptions implicit in the personality assessment process, techniques and decisions underlying the design of assessment instruments, and actual instruments and procedures used from infancy through adolescence. The book reviews specific personality assessment tools, presents case study examples, and addresses the advantages and disadvantages of different assessment and interpretation approaches.

Sattler, J. M. (1990). *Assessment of children.* San Diego, CA: Author.
The third edition of Sattler's comprehensive volume covering all facets of the assessment process with children and adolescents has some critical chapters related to personality assessment: assessment of adaptive behavior and behavior problems; assessment of behavior by interview methods; assessment of behavior by observational methods; assessment of ethnic minority children; and others related to consultation, conferencing, and report writing. Sattler balances theory, empirical research, and pragmatic best practices approaches in a way that facilitates appropriate assessment processes and a clear assessment to intervention linkage.

73

Best Practices in Multidimensional Assessment of Emotional or Behavioral Disorders

Stephanie H. McConaughy
University of Vermont

David R. Ritter
Burlington (Vermont) School District

OVERVIEW

When the district school psychologist read the referral for evaluation, it was clear that the student's classroom behavior warranted concern. The student was not completing assignments and was disruptive in class. Teachers also reported episodes of defiance and refusal to comply with requests and school rules. The student was often sent out of class as a disciplinary procedure and as a result, missed instruction and was falling behind in academic performance. On the playground, the student frequently fought with others, though it was not always clear who initiated the fights. Such behavior was understandably disturbing to others. Whether the same problems constituted an emotional or behavioral disorder was another question.

The school psychologist recalled that children are often labeled emotionally or behaviorally disordered because their behavior is bothersome to teachers (Algozzine, 1977). (The term "children" includes adolescents.) Indeed, teachers have applied the terms "behavior disorder" to as many as 22% and "emotional handicap" to 16% of children in regular classes (Tisdale & Fowler, 1983). Certain types of problems appear to be especially disturbing to teachers, such as noncompliant, defiant, or oppositional behaviors (Coleman & Gilliam, 1983; Mattison, Morales, & Bauer, 1992). More passive behaviors, such as withdrawal or anxiousness, appear to be less disturbing to teachers, probably because they do not interfere as much with classroom activity (Coleman & Gilliam, 1983).

In formulating an assessment plan, the school psychologist considered three different perspectives on emotional or behavioral disorders. One perspective views *child psychopathology* as the basis for disorder. This viewpoint seeks to identify emotions and behaviors exhibited by the child that are symptoms or characteristics of different patterns of psychopathology. It also acknowledges that familial and environmental factors may contribute to the development of child psychopathology. Examples are mental illness in a parent, parental alcohol or drug abuse, low socioeconomic status, life stress, and divorce (Jensen, Bloedau, & Davis, 1990; Jensen et al., 1990; Stanger, McConaughy, & Achenbach, 1992).

A second perspective focuses on *behavioral-environmental interactions* as the basis for disorder. Instead of identifying symptoms or characteristics of psychopathology in the child, this perspective emphasizes reciprocal interactions between the child's behavior and the environment (Bandura, 1986). Behavioral excesses or deficits are then thought to constitute emotional or behavioral disorders. This viewpoint considers family factors as well but from a different angle, such as incompatibility between parents' and children's interactional styles, parents' maladaptive reactions to the needs or problems of children, and parents' attributions about intentionality, consequences, and circumstances surrounding behavior (Grotevant, McRoy, & Jenkins, 1988). Aspects of the school environment and interactions with teachers are also important considerations within this perspective (Ysseldyke, Christenson, & Thurlow, 1987).

Yet a third perspective emphasizes the effectiveness of *interventions* for emotional or behavioral problems, directly linking assessment of "disorders" to prior individual educational programming (Mowder, 1980). This viewpoint defines emotional or behavioral disorders by the extent to which the child's behavior proves to be resistant to interventions (Gresham, 1991).

In our case example, the school psychologist recognized that the three perspectives were not mutually exclusive. Each perspective needed to be considered in evaluating the referred student's problems and determining the extent to which such problems constituted an "emotional or behavioral disorder" (EBD). The school psychologist also recognized that the primary goals for assessments of EBD should be to identify students' needs and to assist in developing and implementing interventions, when they are warranted (National Association of School Psychologists, 1993). To accomplish these general goals, school-based assessments of EBD can serve several different purposes:

1. Help teachers better cope with behavior problems in regular education classrooms.

2. Help students improve their behavior and school performance.

3. Determine a student's eligibility for special education services.

4. Refer children (and perhaps families) for mental health services outside of the school setting.

Depending on the purposes of assessment, the school psychologist may emphasize each of the three perspectives on EBD to different degrees. To help teachers cope with classroom behavior, the behavioral-environmental interaction or intervention-focused views of EBD are likely to offer the most effective strategies. In such cases, the school psychologist could employ behavioral consultation methods (see Kratochwill, this volume) to determine specific excesses or deficits in the student's behavior. Specific antecedents and consequences of the problem behaviors would also be identified. In consultation with teachers, the school psychologist could then evaluate the effectiveness of prior interventions and the feasibility of alternative interventions in the regular education setting. The behavioral-environmental interaction or intervention-focused views of EBD are also likely to be effective for working directly with students to improve their behavior and school performance. In such cases, the school psychologist may provide individual or group counseling to a student as well as consult with teachers. For these purposes, it is usually not necessary to label or classify a student's problems into categories that represent different patterns of psychopathology.

In contrast, to determine eligibility for special education services, federal and state laws require classifying children's problems according to categories of psychopathology or "disabilities." Providing mental health services outside of school may also require some form of classification of psychopathology, for example, in order to obtain third party insurance payments. Making appropriate classifications requires assessing the severity of problems and different patterns of behavior, as well as considering behavioral-environmental interactions and the effectiveness of prior interventions. Basic considerations regarding the classification process are discussed in the next section. A subsequent section describes "best practice" procedures for assessing and classifying emotional or behavioral disorders in order to determine special education eligibility.

BASIC CONSIDERATIONS

Two different approaches have been taken toward classifying children's emotional or behavioral disorders: categorical systems and quantitative taxonomies (Achenbach, 1993; McConaughy & Skiba, 1993). Categorical systems classify problems in a *dichotomous* present-versus-absent fashion. In a categorical system, specific criteria are listed to describe features of a disorder. If all of the required features are met, an individual is judged to have the disorder; if all of the required features are not met, the individual is judged not to have the disorder.

In quantitative taxonomies, individuals are scored according to the *degree* to which they manifest a given feature or behavior. Rather than judging features as present or absent, features are scored on quantitatively graded scales that represent frequency, duration, and/or intensity. In empirically based taxonomies, statistical procedures, such as principal components or factor analysis, are employed to derive syndromes or groupings of problems that tend to co-occur. Scores for the groupings of features are then summed to produce an overall score for each syndrome. Standard scores can also be used to indicate how an individual scores on a syndrome relative to normative reference groups.

Quantitative taxonomies and categorical classification systems are not incompatible. Scores on quantitative scales can be dichotomized to define normal versus clinical ranges. However, because it is not assumed that each syndrome represents a distinct or separate disorder, profiles of high and low scores are also possible across a set of syndromes. Thus, quantitative taxonomies can provide a more differentiated method than categorical systems for assessing the severity and patterning of children's problems.

The DSM-III-R and DSM-IV

The American Psychiatric Association's *Diagnostic and Statistical Manual of Mental Disorders* (DSM-III-R; 1987; DSM IV, 1994) is one of the most widely used categorical systems for classifying adult and childhood psychopathology. The DSM-III-R and DSM-IV list specific features describing over 40 numerically coded disorders of childhood and adolescence, as well as several adult disorders applicable to children. In each case, defining features of disorders are judged to be present or absent. Children judged to meet the requisite number of features (or symptoms) are diagnosed as having a DSM disorder. Common childhood diagnoses include conduct disorder, oppositional defiant disorder, attention deficit hyperactivity disorder, and separation anxiety disorder (which can include school phobia). Examples of adult diagnoses that can be applied to children include major depression, dysthymia (a chronic form of sad affect), schizophrenia, obsessive compulsive disorder, anxiety disorder, and phobias.

The utility of the DSM for determining special education eligibility has been questioned (Gresham & Gansle, 1992; Sinclair & Forness, 1988). There is general agreement that DSM diagnoses are *not* required by federal law for assessing emotional or behavioral disorders or determining eligibility for special education services. However, DSM diagnoses may be useful for communicating with mental health professionals providing services outside of the school setting, and they are sometimes required for mental health administrative purposes.

Empirically Based Taxonomies

The profiles scored from the *Child Behavior Checklist* (CBCL; Achenbach, 1991b) and its related forms are examples of a quantitative taxonomy (Achenbach, 1991a, 1993). The CBCL is designed to obtain parents' ratings of emotional or behavioral problems of children aged 4 to 18. Parents rate their child on each of 118 items according to a 3-point scale. The *Teacher's Report Form* (TRF; Achenbach, 1991c), covering ages 5 to 18, and the *Youth Self-Report* (YSR; Achenbach, 1991d), covering ages 11 to 18, are designed to obtain teachers' ratings and adolescents' self-ratings of problems. The CBCL and YSR profiles also provide scores for social competencies, while the TRF profile provides scores for academic performance and school adaptive functioning.

To provide a quantitative taxonomy, the 1991 CBCL, TRF and YSR scoring profiles each contain eight empirically based cross-informant syndrome scales: Withdrawn, Somatic Complaints, Anxious/Depressed, Social Problems, Thought Problems, Attention Problems, Delinquent Behavior, and Aggressive Behavior. The profiles also provide scores for higher order groupings of Internalizing and Externalizing problems, as well as total problems. In this taxonomic system, the names of the syndrome scales describe the problems they represent and are not considered to be "diagnostic" labels. (For details of the derivation of syndromes, see Achenbach, 1991a, 1993, and McConaughy, 1993a). Cutpoints for defining normal, borderline, and clinical range scores on the problem scales can be used for judging the deviance of a child's reported problems relative to nationally representative normative samples.

Several other rating scales also contain empirically based syndromes for assessing children's emotional or behavioral problems. For example, the *Behavior Assessment System for Children* (BASC; Reynolds & Kamphaus, 1992) is scored on 10 clinical syndromes: Aggression, Anxiety, Attention Problems, Atypicality, Conduct Problems, Depression, Hyperactivity, Learning Problems (teacher form only), Somatization, and Withdrawal. The BASC also contains four scales assessing positive traits: Adaptability, Leadership, Social Skills, and Study Skills (teacher form only). The *Revised Behavior Problem Checklist*

(RBPC; Quay & Peterson, 1987) is scored on six syndromes: Anxiety-Withdrawal, Attention Problems-Immaturity, Motor Tension-Excess, Psychotic Behavior, Socialized Aggression, and Conduct Disorder. The *Walker Problem Behavior Identification Checklist* (WPBIC; Walker, 1983) is scored on five syndromes: Acting Out, Distractibility, Disturbed Peer Relations, Immaturity, and Withdrawal. Other rating scales, such as the *Behavior Evaluation Scale–2* (BES–2; McCarney & Leigh, 1990), may provide quantitative scores for problems, but they do not contain empirically based syndrome scales derived through statistical procedures.

Special Education Classification

The Individuals with Disabilities Education Act (IDEA, 1990; formerly the Education of the Handicapped Act, EHA) represents another form of categorical classification. The IDEA defines 10 types of disability that entitle children to special education services. Although general criteria are described for each disability area, a categorical decision must be made regarding the presence or absence of a given disability.

Children with emotional or behavioral disorders are most likely to qualify for special education under the IDEA category of serious emotional disturbance (SED), originally defined in the EHA as follows:

(i) The term means a condition exhibiting one or more of the following characteristics over a long period of time and to a marked degree, which adversely affects educational performance:

   A. An inability to learn which cannot be explained by intellectual, sensory, or other health factors;

   B. An inability to build or maintain satisfactory interpersonal relationships with peers and teachers;

   C. Inappropriate types of behavior or feelings under normal circumstances;

   D. A general pervasive mood of unhappiness or depression;

   E. A tendency to develop physical symptoms or fears associated with personal or school problems.

(ii) The term includes children who are schizophrenic. The term does not include children who are socially maladjusted unless it is determined that they have a serious emotional disturbance (20 U.S.C. § 1401 [a] [1]; 34 C.F.R. § 300.7 [g])

To meet the criteria for SED according to the above definition, a child must exhibit *one or more* of the five characteristics A through E *or* have a diagnosis of schizophrenia. In addition, *all three* qualifying conditions listed in paragraph (i) must apply to at least one of the identified characteristics. That is, the characteristic(s) must exist over *a long period of time, to a marked degree,* and must *adversely affect educational performance.* A child exhibiting at least one of the five characteristics or schizophrenia, and meeting all three qualifying conditions, is judged to have SED. A child who does not meet criteria for SED is judged to be ineligible for special education on the basis of an emotional or behavioral disorder.

Professionals and advocacy groups have criticized the IDEA definition of SED as being overly restrictive and not supported by legal precedent or educational and clinical research (Forness, 1992; Forness & Knitzer, 1992; Skiba & Grizzle, 1992). Accordingly, a National Mental Health and Special Education Coalition has proposed the following new definition of "emotional or behavioral disorder" (EBD) as a substitute for the current IDEA definition of SED:

> (1) The term "emotional or behavioral disorder" means a disability that is characterized by behavioral or emotional responses in school programs so different from appropriate age, cultural, or ethnic norms that the responses adversely affect educational performance, including academic, social, vocational or personal skills; more than a temporary, expected response to stressful events in the environment; consistently exhibited in two different settings, at least one of which is school-related; and unresponsive to direct intervention applied in general education, or the condition of a child is such that general education interventions would be insufficient.

> The term includes a disability that co-exists with other disabilities.

> The term includes a schizophrenic disorder, affective disorder, anxiety disorder, or other sustained disorder of conduct or adjustment, affecting a child if the disorder affects educational performance as described in paragraph (1) (*Federal Register,* 1993, Vol. 58, No. 26, p. 7938).

The National Association of School Psychologists has endorsed the proposed definition of EBD (National Association of School Psychologists, 1993). After receiving public comments, Congress must decide whether to substitute the proposed definition of EBD for the current definition of SED in its reauthorization of the IDEA. The next section describes "best practice" procedures for special education assessments that are applicable to both definitions. While the focus is primarily on special education evaluations, most of the procedures described can also be utilized for the other assessment purposes discussed earlier.

BEST PRACTICES FOR ASSESSMENT OF SED/EBD

A multidisciplinary team is required for all special education evaluations. Because of their special expertise regarding emotional and behavioral problems,

school psychologists should serve as members of multidisciplinary teams in all school-based assessments of SED/EBD. (Other evaluations such as special educators, classroom teachers, and speech/language pathologists, are also likely to assess additional areas of concern.) In practice, school psychologists may become involved with children exhibiting behavioral or emotional problems long before they are referred for special education evaluations. For example, a school psychologist may have already consulted with teachers to develop classroom interventions or provided counseling to such children (or their families). The school psychologist's role in assessment of SED/EBD may involve any or all of the following:

- Reviewing referral and screening information.
- Planning assessment and/or interventions.
- Conducting screening or assessment procedures.
- Interpreting assessment data.
- Linking assessment data to intervention planning, implementation, and evaluation. (National Association of School Psychologists, 1993.)

Professional ethics require that all evaluators be familiar with relevant instruments and procedures and select only those they are trained to administer and interpret with confidence. However, not all measures produce quantifiable data or meet psychometric standards for reliability and validity. Thus, evaluators must be aware of the advantages and limitations of various procedures and report their findings accordingly. No single measure or procedure should be considered definitive in providing evidence of SED/EBD. Instead, determination of SED/EBD must be based on an integration of findings from a multidimensional approach to assessment, as discussed in the following sections.

Multidimensional Assessment

Educational and mental health professionals concur that multidimensional assessment is necessary to obtain a full view of children's emotional and behavioral functioning (Achenbach, 1991a; Gresham, 1985; Marsh & Terdal, 1988; McConaughy, 1993b, 1993c). Multidimensional assessment has the additional advantage of not limiting data gathering to only one source or one informant. "Best practice" for assessing SED/EBD dictates some combination of the following procedures: standardized behavioral rating scales; standardized self-reports; interviews with parents, teachers, and the child; direct observation of the child; and reviews of relevant background information. Personality assessment may also be included to assess social and emotional functioning, as described by Knoff (this volume). As the first step in multidimensional assessment, data should be gathered from three major sources, as outlined in Table 1: parent reports, teacher reports, and direct assessment of the child. Instruments and procedures are discussed below for each data source listed in Table 1.

Standardized Behavioral Rating Scales

Standardized behavioral rating scales provide efficient methods for obtaining parent and teacher reports of children's emotional and behavioral problems. Numerous rating scales have been developed for this purpose. Some instruments are "omnibus" measures that assess a wide range of potential problems. Examples are the CBCL, TRF, BASC, RBPC, and WPBIC described earlier. Other instruments are more narrow in their focus, such as the Conners (1990) scales for assessing attention deficits and hyperactivity. Instruments of choice for assessment of SED/EBD are those with empirically based problem scales, large normative samples covering a wide age range for both sexes, and demonstrated reliability and validity. Standardized behavioral rating scales meeting these criteria have the following advantages:

1. Information is quantifiable and thus amenable to psychometric standards of reliability and validity.

2. Information is organized in a systematic way by aggregating problems according to different scores and scales.

3. Empirically based syndromes cluster problems that co-occur in large samples of referred children, rather than being based on assumed diagnostic categories.

4. Normative data provide a standard for judging the severity of problems by comparing an individual to large samples of nonreferred children.

5. Multiple items on omnibus measures provide data on a broad range of potential problems, rather than limiting the focus only to referral concerns or behaviors in one area.

6. Rating scales are economical and efficient because most can be completed by the relevant information in 10 to 15 minutes and can be scored quickly by hand or computer.

7. Sets of related rating scales can be used to compare similar data from multiple informants, such as parents, teachers, children's self-reports, and observers.

When choosing a standardized behavioral rating scale, it is important that it meet acceptable psychometric standards of reliability and validity. It is equally important that the scale provide useful information for assessing SED/EBD and planning appropriate interventions. To accomplish these goals, the following criteria should be considered:

1. Do the items on the rating scale pertain directly to the child's observable behavior rather than consequences of behavior (e.g., often in trouble), inferences about behavior (e.g., lacks social skills), or family situations (e.g., on welfare)?

2. How are the items scaled? Simple yes/no scaling is less effective than multiple point scales, since most behaviors vary in degree. In general, 3- or 4-point scales have shown better discriminatory power than dichotomous scales (e.g., yes/no or true/false) or scales where 0 equals "never."

3. Are the items on the scale appropriate for the particular situation? For example, some behavior is more likely to be observed by teachers (e.g., can't follow directions), while other behavior is better observed by parents (e.g., has nightmares).

4. Are there procedures or forms for comparing information from multiple raters who observe the child under different conditions in and outside of school?

While standardized behavioral rating scales provide quantifiable data on children's problems, they also have the following limitations:

1. Rating scale results do not identify the etiology or causes of children's problems. Most rating scales assess current functioning over a limited time frame, such as 2 or 6 months. To identify factors that may precipitate and sustain identified problems, evaluators must obtain additional information on factors, such as biological conditions, earlier development, social interactions, and environmental circumstances.

2. Rating scale results do not dictate choices for interventions. While results are useful for identifying specific areas of concern, additional data are necessary to determine appropriate and feasible interventions in each case.

3. Rating scales are not "objective" measures of children's problems. Like most other assessment procedures, rating scales involve people's perceptions of problems. Perceptions can vary from one rater to the next and can be influenced by the rater's memory, values, attitudes, and motivations, as well as situational factors.

Research has shown that similar informants in similar settings are more likely to agree on ratings of children's problems than are informants in different situations (Achenbach, McConaughy, & Howell, 1987). For this reason, it is important to obtain ratings from multiple informants so that variations in perceptions can be compared and integrated with other findings. As "best practice," it is recommended that an omnibus standardized behavioral rating scale be completed by at least one parent and a teacher who knows the child well. If a child has multiple teachers,

TABLE 1
Components of Multidimensional Assessment of SED/EBD

Parent Reports	Teacher Reports	Direct Assessmnt of the Child
Standardized Behavioral Rating Scales	Standardized Behavioral Rating Scales	Standardized Self-Reports
Parent Interview	Teacher interview	Child interview
a. Details of presenting problems	a. Details of presenting problems	a. Child's view of problems
b. History related to problems	b. History related to problems	b. Observed behavior and coping skills
c. Other possible problem areas	c. Feasibility of interventions	c. Workability for interventions
d. Family factors and stressors	d. Initial goals and intervention plans	d. Diagnoses (when appropriate)
e. Feasibility of interventions		
Questionnaires/Forms	Questionnaires/Forms	Direct Observations
	School Records	Personality Assessment

it is useful to obtain ratings from several teachers to compare problems across different school environments. Rating scale results must then be integrated with results from other procedures discussed in the following sections.

Standardized Self-Reports

Standardized self-reports are valuable for obtaining older children's perceptions of their own competencies and problems. Respondents are usually asked to rate their feelings or behaviors on dichotomous or multistep scales. The *Youth Self-Report* (YSR; Achenbach, 1991d) is an example of a standardized omnibus self-report for children aged 11 to 18. Examples of standardized self-reports for more targeted problems include the *Child Depression Inventory* (CDI; Kovacs, 1992), the *Reynolds Adolescent Depression Scale* (RADS; Reynolds, 1987), and the *Piers-Harris Children's Self-Concept Scale* (Piers, 1984).

Scores on standardized self-reports can be compared with reports from other informants, such as parents and teachers. To facilitate cross-informant comparisons, the 1991 YSR profile has the same eight empirically based syndromes as the CBCL and TRF, plus Internalizing, Externalizing, and total problem scales. When interpreting results from self-reports, evaluators should consider how responses might be affected by a child's reading ability, insight, motivation, and willingness to disclose sensitive personal information.

Interviews

In both clinical and school settings, interviews are frequently used to assess children's emotional and behavioral problems (Gresham & Davis, 1988; Hughes & Baker, 1990; McConaughy, in press). As "best practice," parent, teacher, and child interviews are all recommended for assessment of SED/EBD. If standardized behavioral rating scales and self-reports are obtained, as recommended, interviews can be tailored to gather information that may prove less accessible by these other procedures.

The first and second columns of Table 1 list general areas to be covered in parent and teacher interviews. Each interview begins with questions regarding details of a child's presenting problems. Behavioral interviewing techniques are usually applicable for this process (e.g., see Batsche, this volume; Kratochwill, this volume). Behavioral interviewing elicits information on behaviors to be targeted for interventions. Once specific behaviors have been identified, interviewers should ask about antecedent, sequential, and consequent conditions that precipitate and sustain the behaviors. Interviewers should also inquire about parents' and teachers' feelings toward targeted problems, their usual responses to the problems, and their expectations and preferences for children's behaviors. While the focus of parent and teacher interviews is primarily on children's current behavior, historical information about identified problems should be obtained as well. It is also important to explore other possible problem areas. This can be accomplished by discussing scores and profile patterns obtained from standardized behavioral rating scales, assuming these instruments were completed by parents and teachers in advance of the interviews.

Parents should also be asked about family factors and stressors that may be related to their children's problems. Examples are:

1. Has there been any change in family structure or relationships, such as divorce or a death in the family?

2. Has the child experienced significant or upsetting changes in school?

3. Has there been a significant change in residence or the economic status of the family?

4. Have any members of the family had psychological or psychiatric problems or received mental health services?

5. Has the child experienced significant losses, such as death of a loved one, break-up of peer or romantic relationships, or loss of a pet?

6. Has the child or members of the family experienced any medical traumas, hospitalizations, or serious illnesses?

7. Is there any evidence of alcohol or drug use/abuse by the child or members of the family?

8. Has the child experienced any traumatic episodes, such as a suicide attempt, sexual or physical abuse, violence, or serious accident?

9. Has the child or members of the family ever had trouble with the law or been involved in the juvenile justice system or social service agencies?

To assess the feasibility of different interventions, it is also useful to ask parents and teachers about their typical strategies for coping with identified problems, such as discipline and reward procedures.

The third column in Table 1 lists general areas to be covered in child interviews. Several methods for interviewing children have been developed, including structured interviews, semistructured interviews, and unstructured or nondirective play interviews (Hughes & Baker, 1990; McConaughy, in press). For assessment of SED/EBD, unstructured interviews are the least useful, because it is difficult to quantify their results and clinicians vary widely in their interpretations of children's responses. As a result, unstructured interviews are less amenable to psychometric tests of reliability and validity than are semistructured or structured interviews.

Several structured child (and parent) interviews have been developed for epidemiologic studies and clinical uses. Highly structured interviews require strict adherence to standard procedures for asking questions, rating responses, and ordering items. An example is the NIMH *Diagnostic Interview Schedule for Children* (DISC–2.3; Shaffer, 1992). Less structured interviews also utilize standard question formats but allow the interviewer to adjust the length and order of items to create a more conversational approach. Examples are the *Child Assessment Schedule* (CAS; Hodges, et al., 1982) and the *Schedule for Affective Disorders and Schizophrenia for School-Age Children* (K-SADS; Puig-Antich & Chambers, 1978). The DISC, CAS, and K-SADS, however, have limited utility for special education evaluations of SED/EBD, because they are designed primarily for obtaining DSM diagnoses (for reviews, see Hodges, 1993; McConaughy, in press; McConaughy & Achenbach, 1994).

A well designed semistructured child interview, on the other hand, can provide important information for assessments of SED/EBD (Hughes, 1989; McConaughy, in press). The child interview should be conducted by the school psychologist, or another professional with appropriate clinical training and experience interviewing children. Such interviews offer unique opportunities for evaluating children's coping strategies and their perceptions of significant persons and events related to their problems. They can also provide opportunities for directly observing children's behavior, especially behavior that may impinge on different treatment options. Hughes (1989) cited several important behaviors to note during child interviews, such as response to limit setting, impulsivity, distractibility, reaction to frustration or praise, language skills, responsiveness to the interviewer, emotional reactions, nervous mannerisms and range of affect. The child's behavior and responses during the interview can then be compared to reports from other informants, such as parents and teachers. Finally, a well conducted child interview can serve as the initial step for establishing the rapport necessary for treatment. In this respect, the child interview can serve as a bridge between assessment and intervention.

The *Semistructured Clinical Interview for Children and Adolescents* (SCICA; McConaughy & Achenbach, 1994) is an example of an interview designed for children aged 6 to 18. The SCICA utilizes a semistructured protocol covering different content areas but also has structured rating scales for scoring observed behavior and children's self-reports. The SCICA scoring profile contains eight empirically based syndrome scales, plus Internalizing, Externalizing, and total problem scales for ages 6 to 12. Separate syndromes were derived for scoring observed behavior and self-reports. Profiles for adolescents are being developed. Data obtained from the SCICA can be compared with parent ratings on the CBCL, teacher ratings on the TRF, and self-ratings on the YSR by older children.

Besides providing relevant assessment information, child interviews can be used to assess the feasibility of different school-based interventions and to determine whether referral for mental health or social services outside of school is warranted. For certain purposes, special interviewing techniques or protocols may be indicated, such as assessment of danger to self or others or possible physical or sexual abuse.

Direct Observations

Direct observations are strongly recommended for assessment of SED/EBD. For some children with emotional or behavior problems, direct observations may have already been performed by the school psychologist as part of behavioral consultation with teachers. After a child has been referred for a special education evaluation, additional direct observations should be conducted. These can be done once again by the school psychologist or by other members of the school staff trained in observational techniques. Observations should occur in relevant settings where problems are occurring. It may also be useful to observe the student in other less problematic situations for comparison. Because children's behavior is apt to vary from day to day, it is important to obtain more than one observation. It may be more appropriate to make several observations of short duration (e.g., 10-minute samples on different days), rather than a single lengthy observation. Observing one or two randomly selected "control" children in the same setting affords a comparison with peers in the same environment. Finally, the validity of direct observations may become suspect if children are aware of being observed. This problem can be reduced by using an observer who is not known by the child or who is a regular visitor to the classroom. If the observer is also one of the evaluators, then it is advisable to conduct observations prior to assessing the child.

Direct observations require an independent observer who can record overt behaviors and environmental conditions surrounding the behaviors (see Shapiro, this volume). For optimal effectiveness, direct observations should focus on target behaviors amenable to change. Antecedent and consequent events should also be noted. Observations may utilize narrative recording or empirical methods.

To obtain narrative recordings, an observer writes a description of events that occurred within a given time frame. Methods for narrative recording include descriptive time sampling, antecedent-behavior-consequent (A-B-C) analysis, or daily logs. Narrative recordings are then used to operationally define behaviors that can be targeted for intervention.

Empirical methods require operationally defined behaviors that can be recorded or rated by an independent observer. Once operational definitions have been established, several different techniques can be employed. Continuous recording methods count the number of times that a behavior (or event) occurs within a given period or record the duration of time in which the behavior (or event) was observed. Continuous recording is most effective when behaviors have discreet beginnings and ends, have low to moderate rates of occurrence, and are present only briefly. Time sampling records the presence or absence of operationally defined behavior within short specified time intervals. Time sampling is useful when multiple simultaneous target behaviors hinder continuous recording or when samples of behavior are observed across several different settings.

The *Direct Observation Form* (DOF; Achenbach, 1986) is an example of a standardized rating scale for obtaining time samples. The DOF contains 96 items scored over 10-minute intervals. The DOF scoring profile contains six empirically based syndromes, plus Internalizing, Externalizing, and total problem scales. Children's on-task behavior is also rated at 1-minute intervals over each 10-minute sample. Examples of other procedures and formats for obtaining direct observations are discussed by Batsche (this volume); Rhode, Jenson, and Reavis (1982); and Shapiro (this volume).

Personality Assessment

In some instances, personality assessment can provide additional information on broader aspects of social-emotional functioning. Personality assessment is described in detail by Knoff (this volume). It should be noted, however, that while scoring procedures exist for many personality measures, the interpretation of their results still relies heavily on clinical judgment. Moreover, normative data, reliability, and validity are limited for certain types of procedures, such as projective techniques. Personality assessment, therefore, should be conducted only by psychologists specifically trained in this methodology. Even then, results should be interpreted with caution. Because different examiners often disagree in their interpretations of personality measures, such procedures should *not* be used as primary data sources for assessment of SED/EBD.

Social Skills and Social Reasoning

Assessing children's social skills and social reasoning can be an important dimension in assessment of SED/EBD. Methods most frequently used include behavior observations, rating scales, students' self-reports, and sociometric techniques (see Gresham, this volume). A number of standardized rating scales have been specifically developed to measure social skills. Examples are the *School Social Behavior Scales* (Merrell, 1993), *Social Skills Rating System* (Gresham & Elliott, 1990), and the *Walker-McConnell Scale of Social Competence and School Adjustment* (Walker & McConnell, 1988).

Observations of children's behavior with peers and adults in natural settings, such as the regular classroom or at recess, can also provide information about social skills and relationships. Observing children's behavior during social skills intervention programs or role-playing situations provides a more direct method for assessing specific areas of social reasoning, such as empathy or problem solving, and specific social behaviors, such as giving and receiving praise or criticism.

Co-occurring Conditions

Children with emotional or behavioral problems may also exhibit other problems. Thus, SED/EBD can be an overlapping or *co-occurring* condition with other disabilities. Children who have attention deficit disorders or learning disabilities, for example, frequently display emotional and/or behavioral problems (Barkley, 1990; McConaughy, 1986; McConaughy & Ritter, 1986; Ritter, 1989). Several chronic or acute medical conditions, such as allergies, seizure disorders, traumatic brain injury, and Tourette's syndrome, may have related behavioral characteristics that might prompt referral for evaluation of SED/EBD. Children with intellectual or communication impairments may also exhibit behavior problems. In certain cases, children with other identified disabilities may also be determined to have SED/EBD, if they meet necessary IDEA criteria. However, behavior that is clearly a function of another medical, learning, cognitive, or communication disorder does not necessarily constitute an additional behavioral or emotional disorder.

Achievement and Educational Performance

As with all other special education evaluations, assessment of SED/EBD must include assessment of the child's current academic achievement and educational performance. This information is necessary to determine if identified behavioral or emotional problems adversely affect educational performance, which is one of the qualifying conditions for special education eligibility. Evidence regarding academic achievement can be obtained from standardized tests, curriculum-based assessment, grade reports, and work samples. Evaluation of broader educational performance can focus on school adaptive functioning and academic behaviors, such as productivity. Standardized teacher rating scales, such as the BASC and TRF, provide ratings of academic performance and school adaptive functioning, as well as behavior problems.

Social Maladjustment

Paragraph (ii) of the current IDEA definition of SED specifically excludes "children who are socially maladjusted unless it is determined that they are seriously emotionally disturbed." Certain authors have argued that children with externalizing problems, such as DSM diagnoses of oppositional defiant disorder and conduct disorder, are socially maladjusted, and therefore should be excluded from special education (Slenkovich, 1992a, 1992b). Others disagree, arguing there is no theoretical or empirical basis to exclude youth with externalizing problems from special education (Forness, 1992; Skiba & Grizzle, 1991, 1992).

Research based on quantitative taxonomies, as well as categorical classification systems, has demonstrated high co-occurrence or "comorbidity" between externalizing and internalizing problems (McConaughy, Mattison, & Peterson, 1994; McConaughy & Skiba, 1993). Based on the current IDEA definition

of SED, children with comorbid externalizing and internalizing problems should qualify for special education, even if they are considered to be socially maladjusted, if they also meet the SED criteria. As a general guideline, once SED criteria are met, further evidence of social maladjustment is irrelevant for purposes of determining eligibility for special education. The presence of social maladjustment along with SED, however, is an important factor to consider in planning interventions, because children with such problems often require mental health and/or social services in addition to special education to meet their needs (Duchnowski, Johnson, Hall, Kutash, & Friedman, 1993).

Written Psychological Reports

After data gathering has been completed, the school psychologist must integrate relevant findings into a written psychological report. The report should provide specific information that addresses the characteristics and qualifying conditions of the IDEA definition of SED or proposed definition of EBD, if it is adopted. It is not sufficient to merely state that a child has "SED/EBD." The report should provide clear and specific descriptions of the child's emotional or behavioral problems, as reported by parents and teachers and directly assessed through clinical interviews, observations, self-reports, and other measures. Scores on standardized behavioral rating scales and standardized self-reports, in particular, can provide quantitative evidence of the extent to which a child exhibits characteristics of SED/EBD. Accordingly, Table 2 outlines relations between the IDEA criteria for SED and empirically based syndromes scored from the CBCL, TRF, & YSR, BASC, RBPC, and WPBIC. For each instrument, Table 2 lists the syndromes containing problem items that are most closely related to each characteristic of SED. (McConaughy, 1993b, describes applications of CBCL, TRF, and YSR results to the IDEA criteria for SED.)

The written psychological report should also provide information on the duration of identified problems and severity of problems compared to norms for peers of the same age and sex. Standard scores and clinical cutpoints can be examined to determine the degree to which a child's identified problems deviate from problems reported for large normative reference samples. It is also important to indicate how the identified problems may adversely affect academic achievement and other aspects of educational performance. In most cases, additional evidence regarding learning and academic performance will be provided by other evaluators.

Finally, as "best practice," the psychological report should contain specific recommendations that link assessment results to interventions. Examples include recommendations for consultation with teachers, home-school collaboration, behavioral contracts

TABLE 2
Relations between IDEA Criteria for SED and Empirically Based Sundromes

IDEA Criteria for SED	CBCL, TRF, & YSR	BASC	RBPC	WPBIC
Inability to learn	Attention Problems	Attention Problems	Attention Problems-Immaturity	Distractibility
Inability to build or maintain relationships	Social Problems Withdrawn	Withdrawal	Anxiety-Withdrawal	Withdrawal Disturbed Peer Relations
Inappropriate types of behavior or feelings	Aggressive Behavior Thought Problems	Aggression Atypicality	Conduct Disorder Psychotic Behavior	Acting Out Immaturity
General pervasive mood of unhappiness	Anxious/Depressed	Depression	—	—
Tendency to develop physical symptoms or fears	Anxious/Depressed Somatic Complaints	Anxiety Somatization	Anxiety-Withdrawal	Immaturity

Note: CBCL = Child Behavior Checklist; TRF = Teacher's Report Form; BASC = Behavior Assessment System for Children; RBPC = Revised Behavior Problem Checklist; WPBIC = Walker Problem Behavior Identification Checklist; YSR = Youth Self-Report.

with students, classroom accommodations, schedule alterations, adaptations in teaching strategies, social skills training, and individual or group counseling. The psychological report may also contain recommendations for monitoring the student's behavioral and academic progress, evaluating outcomes of chosen interventions, and making adjustments in interventions as needed to ensure their efficacy and validity. The school psychologist may be directly or indirectly involved in several of the recommended activities.

Need for Special Education Services

If a child exhibits a specific disability, such as SED/EBD, this in itself is not sufficient to qualify him or her for special education services. *Need* for special education must also be documented. That is, the multidisciplinary team must demonstrate that the child needs interventions that cannot be accomplished through remedial education or supplemental services. For many children with behavioral or emotional problems, an array of educational and behavioral interventions may have been undertaken prior to referral for a special education evaluation. If prereferral interventions have produced minimal positive effects on the child's behavior or school performance, then such resistance to change would be evidence of the need for special education services. School psychologists who have been involved in prereferral and regular education interventions can play a key role in multidisciplinary team decisions regarding need for special education and other more intensive interventions.

SUMMARY

"Best practice" procedures were presented for assessing children's emotional or behavioral disorders. A multidimensional approach was recommended, which requires coordinating and integrating information from multiple informants and data sources. Multidimensional assessment assumes that no single method or informant can capture all relevant aspects of children's emotional or behavioral problems. While school-based assessments of emotional or behavioral disorders can serve several purposes, a major emphasis in this chapter was on determining special education eligibility.

Procedures were described for obtaining parent reports, teacher reports, and direct assessment of the child. As "best practice," some combination of the following procedures was recommended: standardized behavioral rating scales; standardized self-reports; parent, teacher, and child interviews; direct observations of the child; and reviews of relevant background information. Some cases may require additional assessment of intellectual ability and communication skills, social skills, and broader aspects of personality. All special education evaluations require assessing the impact of an identified disability on academic achievement and educational performance.

After all necessary data have been gathered, the school psychologist must integrate information in a written psychological report. The report should present specific findings that address the eligibility criteria for serious emotional disturbance (SED), as currently defined in the IDEA, or Emotional or Behavioral Disorders (EBD), if a new proposed definition is adopted. Scores on empirically based syndromes of standardized behavioral rating scales and self-reports can provide quantitative evidence of the characteristics of SED/EBD. Parent, teacher, and child interviews, as well as direct observations, can also contribute evidence of SED/EBD. Normative comparisons on standardized behavioral rating scales and standardized self-reports can determine whether identified problems deviate from expected behavior "to a marked degree." Duration of problems and their adverse effect on educational performance must be documented. The psychological report should also contain specific recommendations that tie assessment results to interventions.

Although major emphasis was placed on assessment of SED/EBD for special education services, many of the evaluation procedures and problem-solving strategies described as "best practice" can also be applied in regular education settings. The recent emphasis on regular education initiatives and total inclusion models call for expansion of the school psychologist's role beyond assessment for special education (e.g., see Batsche, this volume; Graden, this volume). Consultation between school psychologists and classroom teachers can facilitate inclusion of children with emotional or behavioral disorders within regular education settings. Involving school psychologists more directly in regular education interventions should also reduce the need for more restrictive special education placements for many children with emotional or behavioral disorders.

Once interventions have been implemented, it is important to monitor student progress and evaluate outcomes in a rigorous and meaningful fashion. For children with emotional or behavioral disorders, standardized behavioral rating scales and standardized self-reports can be used to obtain baseline data and follow-up assessments of identified problems. Comparison of Time 1 and Time 2 scores on similar measures can determine whether there has been any change in identified problems. To determine whether changes are associated with specific interventions, it is also necessary to make comparisons with other comparable samples of children who have not received the interventions. Monitoring student progress and evaluating outcomes are essential steps for ascertaining which interventions are most effective for which types of problems.

ACKNOWLEDGMENTS

Portions of this chapter were adapted from McConaughy, S. H. (1993). *Vermont Guidelines for Identifying Students Experiencing Emotional-Behavioral Disabilities.* Montpelier, VT: Vermont Department of Education. Preparation of this chapter was supported in part by Grant H133G00061 to Dr. McConaughy from the National Institute on Disability and Rehabilitation Research (NIDRR) of the U.S. Department of Education. The opinions and statements are those of the authors and in no way represent positions of the U.S. Department of Education. Address correspondence to Dr. Stephanie H. McConaughy, Department of Psychiatry, University of Vermont, One South Prospect St., Burlington, VT 05401.

REFERENCES

Achenbach, T. M. (1986). *Direct Observation Form.* Burlington, VT: University of Vermont, Department of Psychiatry.

Achenbach, T. M. (1991a). *Integrative Guide for the 1991 CBCL/4–18, YSR & TRF Profiles.* Burlington, VT: University of Vermont, Department of Psychiatry.

Achenbach, T. M. (1991b). *Manual for the Child Behavior Checklist/4–18 and 1991 Profile.* Burlington, VT: University of Vermont, Department of Psychiatry.

Achenbach, T. M. (1991c). *Manual for the Teacher's Report Form and 1991 Profile.* Burlington, VT: University of Vermont, Department of Psychiatry.

Achenbach, T. M. (1991d). *Manual for the Youth Self-Report and 1991 Profile.* Burlington, VT: University of Vermont, Department of Psychiatry.

Achenbach, T. M. (1993). *Empirically based taxonomy: How to use syndromes and profile types derived from the CBCL/4–18, TRF, and YSR.* Burlington, VT: University of Vermont, Department of Psychiatry.

Achenbach, T. M., McConaughy, S. H., & Howell, C. T. (1987). Child/adolescent behavioral and emotional problems: Implications of cross-informant correlations for situational specificity. *Psychological Bulletin, 101,* 213–232.

Algozzine, B. (1977). The emotionally disturbed child: Disturbed or disturbing? *Journal of Abnormal Child Psychology, 5,* 205–211.

American Psychiatric Association. (1987, 1994). *Diagnostic and statistical manual of mental disorders* (3rd rev. ed., 4th ed.). Washington, DC: Author.

Bandura, A. (1986). *Social foundations of thought and action: A social cognitive theory.* Englewood Cliffs, NJ: Prentice-Hall.

Barkley, R. A. (1990). *Attention deficit hyperactivity disorder: A handbook for diagnosis and treatment.* New York: Guilford Press.

Coleman, M., & Gilliam, J. (1983). Disturbing behaviors in the classroom: A survey of teacher attitudes. *Journal of Special Education, 17,* 121–129.

Conners, K. C. (1990). *Conners' Rating Scales Manual.* North Tonawanda, NY: Multi-Health Systems.

Duchnowski, A., Johnson, M. J., Hall, K. S., Kutash, K., & Friedman, R. M. (1993). The Alternatives to Residential Treatment Study: Initial findings. *Journal of Emotional and Behavioral Disorders, 1,* 17–26.

Forness, S. (1992). Legalism versus professionalism in diagnosing SED in the public schools. *School Psychology Review, 21,* 29–34.

Forness, S., & Knitzer, J. (1992). A new proposed definition and terminology to replace "serious emotional disturbance" in Individuals with Disabilities Education Act. *School Psychology Review, 21,* 12–20.

Gresham, F. (1991). Conceptualizing behavior disorders in terms of resistance to intervention. *School Psychology Review, 20,* 23–36.

Gresham, F. M., & Davis, C. J. (1988). Behavioral interviews with teachers and parents. In E. S. Shapiro & R. R. Kratochwill (Eds.), *Behavioral assessment in schools: Conceptual foundations and practical applications* (2nd ed.; pp. 455–493). New York: Guilford Press.

Gresham, F. M., & Elliott, S. N. (1990). *Social Skills Rating System*. Circle Pines, MN: American Guidance Service.

Gresham, F. M., & Gansle, K. A. (1992). Misguided assumptions of the DSM–III–R: Implications for school psychological practice. *School Psychology Quarterly, 7*, 79–95.

Grotevant, H., McRoy, R., & Jenkins, V. (1988). Emotionally disturbed adopted adolescents: Early patterns of family adaptation. *Family Process, 27*(4), 439–457.

Hodges, K. (1993). Structured interviews for assessing children. *Journal of Child Psychology and Psychiatry, 34*, 49–68.

Hodges, K., Kline, J., Stern, L., Cytryn, L., & McKnew, D. (1982). The development of a child assessment interview for research and clinical use. *Journal of Abnormal Child Psychology, 10*, 173–189.

Hughes, J. N. (1989). The child interview. *School Psychology Review, 18*, 247–259.

Hughes, J., & Baker, D. B. (1990). *The clinical child interview*. New York: Guilford Press.

Individuals with Disabilities Act. (1990). Public Law 101–476. 20 U.S.C. § 1401.

Invitation to comment on the regulatory definition of "serious emotional disturbance" and the use of this term in the Individuals with Disabilities Education Act. (1993). *Federal Register, 58*, No. 26, p. 7938.

Jensen, P. S. Bloedau, L., & Davis, H. (1990). Children at risk: II. Risk factors and clinic utilization. *Journal of the American Academy of Child and Adolescent Psychiatry, 29*, 804–812.

Jensen, P. S., Bloedau, L., Degroot, J., Ussery, T., & Davis, H. (1990). Children at risk: I. Risk factors and child symptomatology. *Journal of the American Academy of Child and Adolescent Psychiatry, 29*, 51–59.

Kovacs, M. (1992). *Children's Depression Inventory Manual*. North Tonawanda, NY: Multi-Health Systems.

Mash, E. J., & Terdal, L. G. (Eds.). (1988). *Behavioral assessment of childhood disorders* (2nd ed.). New York: Guilford Press.

Mattison, R., Morales, J., & Bauer, M. (1992). Distinguishing characteristics of elementary schoolboys recommended for SED placement. *Behavioral Disorders, 17*, 107–114.

McCarney, S. B., & Leigh, J. E. (1990). *Manual for the Behavior Evaluation Scale–2*. Columbia, MO: Educational Services.

McConaughy, S. H. (1986). Social competence and behavioral problems of learning disabled boys aged 12–16. *Journal of Learning Disabilities, 19*, 101–106.

McConaughy, S. H. (1993a). Advances in empirically based assessment of children's behavioral and emotional problems. *School Psychology Review, 22*, 285–307.

McConaughy, S. H. (1993b). Evaluating behavioral and emotional disorders with CBCL, TRF, and YSR cross-informant scales. *Journal of Emotional and Behavioral Disorders, 1*, 40–52.

McConaughy, S. H. (1993c). *Vermont guidelines for identifying students experiencing Emotional-Behavioral Disabilities*. Montpelier, VT: Vermont Department of Education.

McConaughy, S. H. (in press). Behaviorally oriented assessment: The interview process. In M. Breen & C. Fiedler (Eds.), *Behavioral approach to the assessment of emotionally disturbed youth: A handbook for school-based practitioners*. Austin, TX: Pro-Ed.

McConaughy, S. H., & Achenbach, T. M. (1994). *Manual for the Semistructured Clinical Interview for Children and Adolescents*. Burlington, VT: University of Vermont, Department of Psychiatry.

McConaughy, S. H., Mattison, R. E., & Peterson, R. (1994). Behavioral/emotional problems of children with serious emotional disturbance and learning disabilities. *School Psychology Review 23*, 81–98.

McConaughy, S., & Ritter, D. (1986). Social competence and behavior problems of learning disabled boys aged 6–11. *Journal of Learning Disabilities, 19*, 39–45.

McConaughy, S. H., & Skiba, R. (1993). Comorbidity of externalizing and internalizing problems. *School Psychology Review, 22*, 419–434.

Merrell, K. W. (1993). Using behavior rating scales to assess social skills and antisocial behavior in school settings: Development of the School Social Behavior Scales. *School Psychology Review, 22*, 115–133.

Mowder, B. (1980). Pre-intervention assessment of behavior disordered children: Where does the school psychologist stand? *School Psychology Review, 9*, 5–13.

National Association of School Psychologists. (1993). *Position statement on students with emotional/behavioral disorders*. Silver Spring, MD: Author.

Piers, E. V. (1984). *Piers-Harris Children's Self-Concept Scale Revised Manual*. Los Angeles, CA: Western Psychological Services.

Puig-Antich, J., & Chambers, W. (1978). *The Schedule for Affective Disorders and Schizophrenia for School-aged Children (Kiddie–SADS)*. New York: New York State Psychiatric Institute.

Quay, H. C., & Peterson, D. R. (1987). *Manual for the Revised Behavior Problem Checklist*. Coral Gables, FL: University of Miami, Department of Psychology.

Reynolds, C. R., & Kamphaus, R. W. (1992). *Behavior Assessment System for Children (BASC)*. Circle Pines, MN: American Guidance Service.

Reynolds, W. M. (1987). *Reynolds Adolescent Depression Inventory*. Odessa, FL: Psychological Assessment Resources.

Rhode, G., Jenson, W. R., & Reavis, H. K. (1992). *The tough kid book*. Longmont, CO: Sopris West, Inc.

Ritter, D. R. (1989). Social competence and problem behavior of adolescent girls with learning disabilities. *Journal of Learning Disabilities, 22*, 460–461.

Shaffer, D. (1992). *Diagnostic Interview Schedule for Children, Version 2.3*. New York: Columbia University, Division of Child and Adolescent Psychiatry.

Sinclair, E., & Forness, S. (1988). Special education classification and its relationship to DSM–III. In E. S. Shapiro & T. R. Kratochwill (Eds.), *Behavioral assessment in schools* (pp. 494–521). New York: Guilford.

Skiba, R., & Grizzle, K. (1991). The social maladjustment exclusion: Issues of definition and assessment. *School Psychology Review, 20*, 577–595.

Skiba, R., & Grizzle, K. (1992). Qualifications v. logic and data: Excluding conduct disorders from the SED definition. *School Psychology Review, 21*, 23–28.

Slenkovich, J. (1992a). Can the language of "social maladjustment" in the SED definition be ignored? *School Psychology Review, 21*, 21–22.

Slenkovich, J. (1992b). Can the language of "social maladjustment" in the SED definition be ignored? The final words. *School Psychology Review, 21*, 43–44.

Stanger, C., McConaughy, S., & Achenbach, T. (1992). Three-year course of behavioral/emotional problems in a national sample of 4- to 16-year olds: II. Predictors of syndromes. *Journal of the American Academy of Child and Adolescent Psychiatry, 31,* 941–950.

Tisdale, P., & Fowler, R. (1983). Effects of labels on teachers' perceptions of the prevalence of emotionally disturbed children and youth. *Education, 103*(3), 278–280.

Walker, H. M. (1983). *Walker Problem Behavior Identification Checklist.* Los Angeles, CA: Western Psychological Services.

Walker, H. M., & McConnell, S. R. (1988). *Walker-McConnell Scale of Social Competence and School Adjustment.* Austin, TX: PRO-ED.

Ysseldyke, J., Christenson, S., & Thurlow, M. (1987). *Instructional factors that influence student achievement: An integrative review.* (Monograph No. 7). Minneapolis MN: University of Minnesota, Instructional Alternatives Project.

ANNOTATED BIBLIOGRAPHY

Achenbach, T. M. (1991). *Integrative guide for the 1991 CBCL/4–18, YSR, and TRF profiles.* Burlington, VT: University of Vermont, Department of Psychiatry.
Describes relations among instruments for obtaining parent ratings, self-ratings, and teacher ratings of children's and adolescents' competencies and problems. Early chapters describe relations among the 1991 profiles of the Child Behavior Checklist (CBCL) for ages 4 to 18, Youth Self-Report (YSR), and Teacher's Report Form (TRF), including procedures for deriving empirically based syndromes common to all three instruments. Later chapters present research and practical applications for coordinating assessment of children and adolescents from multiple data sources. A good resource for users of the CBCL, YSR, and TRF for multimethod assessment.

Breen, M., & Fiedler, C. (1994). *Behavioral approach to the assessment of emotionally disturbed youth: A handbook for school-based practitioners.* Austin, TX: Pro-Ed.
Describes behaviorally oriented procedures for assessing children's emotional and behavioral disorders. Early chapters address theoretical and legal requirements for school-based assessment of emotional and behavioral disorders, including eligibility for special education services. Later chapters cover empirically based behavioral rating scales; direct observation methods; parent teacher, and child interviews; and consultation strategies. A comprehensive and practical resource for school-based practitioners involved in assessment and programming for children with emotional and behavioral problems.

Hughes, J. N., & Baker, D. B. (1990). *The clinical child interview.* New York: Guilford.
Describes various procedures for interviewing children and adolescents for clinical and school-based assessments. Early chapters cover developmentally sensitive interviewing techniques for children of varying ages. Later chapters describe different interviewing procedures, including structured diagnostic interviews, psychodynamic approaches, behavioral interviewing, and problem-specific interviews. An excellent resource for school-based practitioners and clinicians involved in child assessment and therapy.

Knoff, H. M. (Ed.). (1986). *The assessment of child and adolescent personality.* New York: Guilford.
Describes procedures for assessing personality and emotional and behavioral problems of children and adolescents. Early chapters address theoretical bases underlying the assessment process. Later chapters cover development and administration of various tests and procedures, including behaviorally oriented assessment, personality measures, and projective techniques. A pragmatic, applied view of assessment of emotional and behavioral disorders and personality in school and community settings.

74

Best Practices in School Reintegration

Douglas Fuchs
Samuel Dempsey
Holley Roberts
Anja Kintsch
George Peabody College of Vanderbilt University

OVERVIEW

During the past 5 years, special educators have engaged in rancorous debate about what is wrong with the field and how best to fix it. Although the controversy has appeared wide ranging, including such diverse topics as tests, labels of exceptionality, accountability, fragmentation of services, and teacher referrals, it has pivoted on a basic issue: Should special education abolish or conserve the cascade of services? This question creates a meaningful divide among the major players in the debate, producing *conservationists* and *abolitionists* (see D. Fuchs & L. S. Fuchs, 1991; D. Fuchs & L. S. Fuchs, in press; and Figure 1).

Conservationists versus Abolitionists

Conservationists. By definition, conservationists support the preservation of the cascade (see, for example, Kauffman, Gerber, & Semmel, 1988; Keogh, 1988; Lieberman, 1985; National Education Association, 1992; Singer, 1988). They do so because they believe it represents a rich array of placement options necessary for schools to meet the wide-ranging cognitive, behavioral, social, and physical needs of its students with disabilities. Moreover, the degree of many students' disabilities, such as those with severe behavior disorders, requires unique and intensive support. This help, say the conservationists, often can be delivered more efficiently and effectively in settings separate from the mainstream (e.g., Kauffman, 1989; Walker & Bullis, 1991). And if too few special-needs students move up the cascade, it is not the fault of the model; rather, it is the responsibility of those who use it incorrectly.

As reflected in Figure 1, we distinguish between mild and strong conservationists. Mild conservationists (e.g., Gottlieb, Alter, & Gottlieb, 1991) differ from strong conservationists on at least two related counts: First, they are more likely to call attention to

special education problems; second, they have a penchant for issuing strident calls for reforms (which, nevertheless, presume a continuation of the cascade of services).

Abolitionists. At loggerheads with both mild and strong conservationists are abolitionists who argue that increasing numbers of children in special education are proof that the cascade model is unworkable, that it represents a trap for most students with disabilities, whereby initial placements become terminal assignments in their educational careers (e.g., Taylor, 1988). Abolitionists and The Association for Persons with Severe Handicaps, the organization with which they are most closely connected, work to eliminate the cascade and for the immediate integration, or "full inclusion," of all students with disabilities into regular classrooms (e.g., Biklen, Lehr, Searl, & Taylor, 1987; Giangreco, Dennis, Cloninger, Edelman, & Schattman, 1993; Lipsky & Gartner, 1989; S. Stainback & W. Stainback, 1992; Thousand & Villa, 1990; York & Vandercook, 1991). Facilitating full inclusion would be support staff (e.g., physical therapists, speech clinicians, vocational instructors) bought with savings realized through an elimination of the cascade's special settings. Abolitionist optimism over this ambitious, if not revolutionary, plan is based on a belief that much of special education is expendable because regular education has become more expandable, that is, more willing and able to accommodate greater student diversity, including the integration of all students with disabilities (e.g., Lipsky & Gartner, 1991).

Like the conservationists, abolitionists can also claim a kindred group that espouses a milder doctrine. Mild abolitionists like Gersten and Woodward (1990), Maheady and Algozzine (1991), Pugach and Lilly (1984), Reynolds, Wang, and Walberg (1987), and Will (1986) tend to focus their criticism of special education on services provided students with milder disabilities. Reynolds (1991), for example, argues that

FIGURE 1. Continuum of opinion regarding the cascade of special education services.

ABOLITIONISTS		CONSERVATIONISTS	
Strong	**Mild**	**Mild**	**Strong**
The Assn. for Persons with Severe Handicaps (1992)	Dunn (1968)	California Teachers Assn. (1990)	Braaten, Kauffman, Braaten, Polsgrove, & Nelson (1988)
Biklen, Lehr, Searl, & Taylor (1987)	Gartner & Lipsky (1987)	Council for Exceptional Children (1993)	Commission on the Education of the Deaf (1988)
Gartner & Lipsky (1989)	Gersten & Woodward (1990)	Deno (1970)	Council for Children with Behavioral Disorders (198)
Giangreco, Dennis, Cloninger, Edelman, & Schattman (1993)	Jenkins, Pious, & Peterson (1988)	Gottlieb, Alter, & Gottlieb (1991)	Hallahan, Keller, McKinney, Lloyd, & Bryan (1988)
Gilhool (1989)	Maheady & Algozzine (1991)	New Jersey Education Assn. (1991)	Illinois State Board of Education (1990)
Lipsky & Gartner (1989)	Pugach & Lilly (1984)	Pugach & Raths (1987)	International Reading Assn. (1986)
National Assn. of State Boards of Education (1992)	Reynolds, Wang, & Walberg (1987)		Iowa State Education Assn. (n.d.)
Sapon-Shevin (1988)	Stainback & Stainback (1984)		Kauffman, Gerber, & Semmel (1988)
Snell (1991)	Stainback & Stainback (1985)		Keogh (1988)
Stainback & Stainback (1992)	Will (1986)		Learning Disabilities Assn. (1993)
Taylor (1988)			Lerner (1987)
Thousand & Villa (1990)			Lieberman (1985)
York & Vandercook (1991)			McKinney & Hocutt (1988)
			Megivern (1987–88)
			National Education Assn. (1992)
			National Joint Committee on Learning Disabilities (1993)
			Singer (1988)
			Vergason & Anderegg (1989)
			Walker & Bullis (1991)

categorical approaches to the education of such children cannot be justified, whereas he implies elsewhere (e.g., Reynolds, 1988) that they are justified for children with more severe disabilities. In other words, mild abolitionists tend to push for a partial rollback of the cascade of services, not a total elimination of all special education placement options.

Reintegration: Case-by-Case and Large-Scale

Case-by-case. Although conservationists and abolitionists agree that integration, or inclusion, is an important goal, they disagree fundamentally about what rightly should be called integration and how one

best accomplishes it. For conservationists, the targeted integration setting may be the mainstream, but it also may be a self-contained class for a student currently attending a special day school. Implicit is a belief that mainstreaming — reintegration into regular classes — is not necessarily for all students with disabilities.

For some, say the conservationists, an appropriate education must be delivered by a specially trained teacher in a setting removed and different from regular education, a setting where students presumably receive intensive, systematic, and data-based instruction unattainable in regular education. Many conservationists believe in a case-by-case approach to integration, by which movement up the cascade of services into a less restrictive setting, or reintegration into a regular classroom, is planned, implemented, and evaluated individually — on a case-by-case basis. Each student's strengths and weaknesses are considered in conjunction with various features of the student's future setting. A fit or match is explored. And a child is not reintegrated unless he or she can adapt academically, behaviorally, and otherwise to the expectations in the new setting. Advocates of a case-by-case approach see its individualized nature as the embodiment of that which is quintessentially special about special education and as consonant with federal law, which requires the provision of individualized educational programs (see Huefner, 1994).

Large-scale. In contrast to the conservationists' case-by-case strategy, the abolitionists' large-scale approach calls for large groups, or literally all students, to be reintegrated simultaneously into nothing short of regular education settings. Implicit is the view that it is not the child that needs to be changed, but rather the mainstream setting. Such change may involve adoption of cooperative learning structures or more sweeping arrangements like open-classroom, constructivist approaches to teaching and learning (see S. Stainback & W. Stainback, 1992). Advocates of the large-scale approach also assume support staff will provide considerable help to facilitate such change and that they will be available on an "as-needed" basis to work with integrated students.

In comparison with the case-by-case alternative, large-scale integration is more efficient, say proponents. For example, it presumably circumvents the time-consuming and costly process of testing, labeling, placing, and reevaluating. More important, with everyone in regular education, the need for and high cost of a second, partly duplicative, special education system — separate teachers, administrators, credentialling process, programs, and budgets — is eliminated (see Wang, Reynolds, & Walberg, 1988). Moreover, say the advocates, large-scale mainstreaming will force regular education to reform itself because it no longer will have the proverbial "dumping ground" of special education to which it once sent students it deemed "unteachable" (see Fuchs, D., & Fuchs, L. S., 1994, for discussion of this point).

We Choose Case-by-Case, But . . .

Despite these purported benefits, we adhere to the traditional case-by-case approach — not for the sake of tradition, but because its individualized approach to integration increases the likelihood that students' unique needs will be addressed, that they and their parents will have a choice of placements, and that teachers and parents of students with disabilities will not be required to engage in the high-stakes gamble that regular education will indeed ac-

complish the revolutionary reforms it must for large-scale mainstreaming to work. Moreover, there currently is a very small body of research on the efficacy of large-scale mainstreaming; we do not have the technical know-how to implement it and expect success. In fairness, however, the same can be stated about our preferred alternative, case-by-case reintegration.

Where's the research? Few studies of the case-by-case strategy exist. In a recent review of eight special education journals for 16 years and of the ERIC computer data base, Scott and D. Fuchs (in preparation) found only nine investigations that attempted to validate an explicit process for moving students from a more restrictive to less restrictive setting. Many educational researchers and policymakers do not recognize that reintegration has been understudied because such investigations are often equated incorrectly with the more numerous mainstreaming studies. Mainstreaming studies, by definition, explore the effects on students with disabilities of *being there;* the students have already re-entered before such studies start. Reintegration studies, by contrast, focus on the process of *getting there:* They begin with the student participants in special education, not regular education, settings. Thus, we know precious little about how effectively to move students with disabilities from special education to regular education, irrespective of our preference for case-by-case or large-scale. All of which leads to the Peabody Reintegration Project.

Peabody Reintegration Project. For several years we and our colleagues at Vanderbilt University, in collaboration with local educators, have been trying to develop an effective, efficient, and responsible process for transferring students with learning and behavior problems from various special education settings (especially resource rooms) to less restrictive settings (mostly regular classrooms). As part of this work, which is known as the Peabody Reintegration Project, we have conducted a series of quasi-experimental studies, several of which have been published in scholarly journals (e.g., D. Fuchs, L. S. Fuchs, & Fernstrom, 1992; D. Fuchs, L. S. Fuchs, & Fernstrom, 1993; D. Fuchs, L. S. Fuchs, Fernstrom, & Hohn, 1991). Together with our unpublished studies, these have involved scores of schools and more than 100 teachers and students with disabilities in several contiguous districts in Middle Tennessee. Research findings indicate that our methods help special educators prepare their students for reintegration into mainstream math and reading classrooms. The following sections outline our research results in somewhat more detail after an initial description of the interventions and the process by which teachers participating in the Peabody Reintegration Project work to achieve successful integration for some of their students in the area of reading.

BASIC CONSIDERATIONS: CURRICULUM-BASED MEASUREMENT AND TRANSENVIRONMENTAL PROGRAMMING

Curriculum-Based Measurement (CBM)

CBM is a set of standardized procedures for obtaining reliable and valid measures of student achievement, which in turn facilitate teachers' formative evaluation of their teaching effectiveness. CBM procedures have been developed for measuring progress in reading, spelling, written expression, and math and represent an alternative to commercially distributed achievement tests (see Deno, 1985). Research demonstrates that instructional programs designed with CBM can result in greater student achievement, improved teacher decision making, and enhanced student awareness of their own performance (L. S. Fuchs, Deno, & Mirkin, 1984; L. S. Fuchs & D. Fuchs, 1986).

CBM and reintegration. There are two reasons for special and regular educators to use CBM in reading instruction. First, it permits them to conduct frequent assessments of academic progress, with which they may judge readiness for and adaptation to mainstream reading on a student-by-student basis. Second, CBM data are used by special and regular educators to develop more effective instructional interventions.

CBM reading "maze" assessment. Special educators determine an appropriate reading level on which to establish each reintegration candidate's year-end goal, that is, the level of reading material that the teacher hopes the student will master by April or May of the current year. Teachers assess the reintegration candidate's reading performance two or three times weekly, each time on a different passage, a random sample from the goal-level pool of passages. These reading assessments are administered and scored automatically by computers. Students are permitted 2.5 minutes to complete a maze (i.e., cloze procedure) of a 400-word passage displayed on a computer screen. The first sentence is presented intact; thereafter, every seventh word is deleted and replaced with three choices. Only one is semantically correct. The student must use the space bar and <RETURN> key. Performance is scored as the number of correct replacements. (For more description, see L. S. Fuchs, D. Fuchs, Hamlett, & Ferguson, 1992). Reliability and validity of this computerized assessment may be found in Espin, Deno, Maruyama, and Cohen (1989), L. S. Fuchs and D. Fuchs (1990), and Jenkins and Jewell (1992).

Transenvironmental Programming (TP)

TP (e.g., Anderson-Inman, 1986) is a process to reintegrate pupils into mainstream settings. Although it has been the focus of several single-subject reintegration studies (e.g., Anderson-Inman, 1981; Anderson-Inman, Walker, & Purcell, 1984), we are unaware of prior, larger-scale efforts (excepting our own) to explore its effectiveness or to study it in combination with CBM use. TP comprises four phases, the first of which is *environmental assessment*. Because it is assumed that effective preparation of a student with disabilities for mainstreaming can be accomplished best by first identifying the academic and behavioral expectations of this environment, the purpose of the first phase is to ascertain the specific skills and behaviors required for success in the regular classroom. This knowledge then can be used to help plan the content of instruction in the special education setting.

In the second phase, *intervention and preparation*, the special educator teaches the skills identified during the preceding phase. Next, in *promoting transfer across settings*, the special education teacher helps ensure that the reintegrating student actually uses the newly acquired skills in regular education. In the final phase, *evaluation in the mainstream*, data are collected on the extent to which the student has adjusted academically and socially.

BEST PRACTICES

In the following description, participants are the special and regular educators; the student targeted for reintegration, hereafter referred to as the "reintegration candidate"; and project staff. This last group consists of Peabody/Vanderbilt graduate students trained to provide technical assistance to facilitate the successful completion of project activity. Because it is football season as we write this chapter, and because the first author is a devotee and aficionado (his preferred terms for "fanatic"), you will notice and hopefully forgive allusions to that sport.

Step #1: Recruiting the Players

The special educator is responsible for selecting one or more students who could be ready to reintegrate into a regular class for reading instruction at some point during the school year. That is, the student need not be ready for mainstreaming right away, but maybe in 2 to 4 months, following work in reading or efforts to improve his or her school behavior or social skills. Choosing a student for possible reintegration does not commit the student (or the special educator) to reintegration. If, after some time, the teacher believes insufficient progress has been made, he or she can decide against mainstreaming. The decision to mainstream, then, is ultimately a teacher decision, or teacher-parent decision, or teacher-parent-student decision. To facilitate the selection of appropriate reintegration candidates, we give special educators two "true story profiles" of successfully reintegrated students. ("True Story Profiles" are available from the first author.)

For each selected reintegration candidate, the special educator also identifies a mainstream reading teacher. If two or more such teachers are available for a given student, the special educator chooses the one most likely to be receptive to mainstreaming. The special educator is reminded that this teacher need not be a "perfect" teacher or his or her best friend. Instead, the regular educator should be open-minded and willing to accept responsibilities associated with project involvement.

This teacher is invited to a meeting with project staff and the special education teacher, who communicates the project's purpose, describes the reintegration process, and specifies the roles and obligations of each participant. The special educator provides evidence that the reintegration candidate is currently, or soon will be, ready for return to a mainstream reading class. Such evidence includes the student's level of reading performance and a description of his or her classroom behavior. To facilitate this communication, the special educator shares a "profile" form on the student completed prior to the meeting. (A "Reintegration Student Profile" form may be obtained from the first author.) As reflected by the items on this form, the special educator is encouraged to present a balanced view of the candidate, documenting both strengths and weaknesses. The regular educator is then asked whether reintegrating the student during the current school year seems feasible. After the teacher's (generally positive) response, the special educator makes clear that such a solicited judgment is not binding and that reintegration need not be immediate.

Step #2: Identifying the Competition

During this same first meeting, project staff states that successful reintegration often requires knowledge about both the student and the general education classroom. The staff person indicates that a frequently useful question about the regular classroom is, "What's the lowest acceptable level of academic performance?" In this vein, the mainstream teacher is asked to think of two current students who, although low achievers, are not in jeopardy of referral for possible special education placement. These students will become the standard or, in a sense, the "competition" against which the reintegration candidate's academic progress will be compared. Hereafter, they are referred to as "lowest achieving peers," or "LAPs."

Step #3: Scouting with a Classroom Inventory

The special and general educators and project staff meet a second time to (a) discuss the reintegration candidate's legitimacy and the general educator's willingness to participate in the reintegration process, (b) share information about the candidate and their respective instructional settings, and (c) identify aspects of the student's performance and the two classrooms that require modification to enhance

the likelihood of the student's successful transfer to the mainstream setting. Toward these ends, each teacher completes a three-part Classroom Inventory during their second meeting. (A complete copy of the "Classroom Inventory" may be obtained from the first author.)

Part 1. Part 1 of the inventory is meant to provide a snapshot of a classroom's instructional environment, for reasons explained later. It uses a combined checklist and Likert-type format and addresses a potpourri of instructional issues, such as permissible student behavior (e.g., how much movement and talking is allowed); expected student performance (e.g., how often students are required to respond orally); the ways a student gets directions about in-class and out-of-class assignments and help from the teacher when experiencing difficulty; and so forth.

Part 2. Contrastingly, Part 2 makes use of open-ended items and asks many more questions that, in aggregate, explore in depth how instruction gets delivered. Questions in Part 2 concern allocating time for reading; grouping students for instruction; naming primary and supplementary reading texts; presenting new skills and vocabulary; assigning independent in-class work and homework; determining student grades; doling out rewards and punishment; modifying instruction when students do not understand; and so forth. This second part of the inventory makes use of a double-column response format; both special and regular educators answer the same question so that their answers appear side by side. Responding to the same questions in each other's company, and recording answers side by side, is expected to increase teachers' awareness of the similarities and differences between their respective instructional settings and the possible implications of these between-setting differences for the reintegration candidate.

Part 3. Part 3, also completed during the second meeting, taps teachers' expectations for performance and classroom deportment. Reflecting the influence of Walker and Rankin's (1983) SBS, this part of the inventory makes use of a rating scale (where 1 = "critically important," 2 = "desirable but not critical," and 3 = "unimportant"). Teachers use it to communicate the relative salience of various student characteristics and actions. For example, teachers rate the importance of assuming responsibility for materials, listening and complying with directions, using appropriate means to seek teacher attention, ignoring distractions, cooperating with peers, and so on.

CBM training and classroom observations. Completion of the inventory generates rich descriptions of the reintegration candidate's current and (presumably) future classrooms. Completion also triggers two important activities that must be undertaken prior to a third meeting between the two teachers and project staff. First, the reintegration candidate and LAPs are trained to take CBM probes in reading at the computer, and they begin these once (LAPs) or twice (reintegration candidate) weekly. Second, using Part 1 of the inventory as a guide, the special educator observes the mainstream teacher's reading class. Project staff encourages the mainstream teacher to reciprocate if his or her schedule permits. This observing in one another's class familiarizes both teachers with the reintegration candidate's current and future settings and helps the teachers identify discontinuities across instructional environments.

Step #4: The Game Plan

A third meeting of teachers and project staff has four objectives: (a) to assess the progress and validate the choice of the reintegration candidate; (b) to identify salient discrepancies between the two classrooms and between the reintegration candidate's performance/behavior and the mainstream teacher's expectations; (c) to select interventions addressing the discrepancies, which would be implemented in special education and/or the mainstream reading classroom; and (d) to secure the participation of all parties for the duration of the project. The first objective (assessing the progress and validating the legitimacy of the student as a reintegration candidate) is addressed by reviewing the student's CBM performance since the last meeting and comparing it to that of the LAPs. If the student's progress is judged less than satisfactory, this is a last opportunity for the special educator to recommend an alternate child. On the other hand, if the student's performance is as strong as or superior to that of the LAPs, the teachers may decide to transfer him or her at once to a regular classroom. In this case, the teachers would schedule an IEP meeting and discuss instructional interventions and CBM monitoring in the mainstream.

Addressing discrepancies between settings. If the teachers agree on the appropriateness of the candidate — that he or she might require additional time and work in special education, but eventual mainstreaming is likely — the two review their completed inventories and discuss their observations in one another's class to determine whether, and if so which, features of the classes are different. Furthermore, they try to ascertain whether these differences represent potential problems for the reintegration candidate. If salient differences are found, one or more becomes the focus of change. Let us say the special educator observed the mainstream teacher to monitor and praise student work infrequently. By contrast, the regular educator noted the special educator to monitor and praise student work with regularity. Responding to these disparities, the two might decide that the special educator should encourage the reintegration candidate to work more independently and with less encouragement. In so doing, they

would be attempting to align special education instruction more closely with mainstream instruction and, presumably, facilitate a smoother student transition.

Addressing discrepancies between teacher expectations and student performance: Impact Strategies. A similar process is followed when exploring possible discrepancies between the reintegration candidate's performance/behavior and the mainstream teacher's expectations. It is often the case that both teachers express concern about the reintegration candidate's reading performance. For this reason, project staff gives teachers a set of "Impact Strategies" — techniques based on the research literatures in reading and special education instruction that address fluency and comprehension development (see Figure 2). Each strategy is described on one or two typed pages, which offer a rationale and directions for implementation. Oral Preview, Silent Review, and Repeated Reading strategies address fluency; Sequencing, Main Idea, Story Mapping, and Content Webbing are the comprehension activities. In addition to a rationale for and description of these strategies, staff also provides practice materials. However, staff does not require teachers to use these strategies and materials; teachers are encouraged to generate their own.

Discrepancy Plan Sheets. To help the teachers conceptualize their "game plan," and to provide a means of recording who would be doing what to whom, they also receive Discrepancy Plan Sheets (see Figure 3). These encourage formulation of an explicit "plan of action," "expected outcomes," and "maintenance" activities in the mainstream classroom. The Discrepancy Plan Sheets represent something of a contract between the teachers, whereby the special educator pledges to implement strategies and setting modifications to prepare the student for reintegration and the regular educator agrees to various modifications to make the mainstream more hospitable once the student transfers.

Step #5: Executing the Game Plan in Special Education

In a word, the purpose of this step is "preparation." The special educator is expected to use the Impact Strategies, or some other instructional strategies, with the reintegration candidate to promote reading growth, which, as mentioned, is indexed by twice-weekly CBM probes. If such feedback indicates insufficient progress relative to the LAPs' growth, the special educator is expected to modify the instructional approach. The student, meanwhile, tries to best previous performance on the probes. If necessary, the teacher and student work together to modify the student's classroom behavior, bringing it into closer conformity with the future teacher's expectations. The

FIGURE 2. Impact Strategies.

FLUENCY

The fluency packets provide the student with repeated exposure to text which should increase automaticity of word recognition skills, enabling the student to focus on the meaning of text rather than reading the words correctly. Oral Preview is designed for a very dysfluent reader who needs to hear a model of fluent reading. Silent preview and repeated reading are designed for more fluent readers. All three processes are designed to enhance the student's ability to read the passage smoothly, with few mistakes, and to increase comprehension.

Oral Preview

Provides students repeated practice on text by allowing the student to hear a model of fluent reading before reading orally.

Silent Preview

Provides students repeated practice on text by allowing the student practice reading text silently before reading orally.

Repeated Reading

Provides students repeated practice on text by allowing the student practice reading with a fluent model before reading a passage independently.

COMPREHENSION

The comprehension packets are arranged in a hierarchy of difficulty. Students should master sequencing before proceeding to the main idea and so on. The end goal in the comprehension series is for students to master the Story Mapping packet for fictional text and Content Webbing for nonfiction.

Sequencing

Has been identified as a critical skill for comprehending text and as a prerequisite skill for more complex comprehension strategies such as story mapping.

Main Idea

Provides practice with identifying the main idea of a passage, which is a critical skill for comprehending text.

Story Mapping

Enables a student to identify the major structural features of a story, thereby strengthening his or her understanding of the text.

Content Webbing

Assists students in organizing content area text and can result in increased comprehension. It incorporates a number of reading and reasoning skills such as identifying the main idea and supporting details and classifying and organizing information.

"game plan," then, has a relatively narrow focus. It is based on the salient discrepancies identified jointly by special and regular educators; the plan is not to "fix" the whole child, nor to make him or her perfect prior to mainstreaming. Across several years, special educators participating in the reintegration project take, on average, 2 to 3 months to help prepare their students for transition.

Step #6: On the Road

Transition from special education to regular education is coordinated with a fourth meeting at which it is determined whether the reintegration candidate has achieved sufficient progress to warrant either full-time or gradual inclusion in the regular reading classroom. If the decision is affirmative for one or the other, the teachers (a) review the mainstream teacher's planned accommodations for the new student, (b) discuss what supports, if any, are required, and (c) plan for follow-up communication. If this transition requires a change in the student's special education status, project staff propose that a multidisciplinary team meeting be held. Whether such a meeting occurs is left to the discretion of the teachers. If the teachers decide against reintegration at this time, they review both their goals and intervention strategies for the student.

Step #7: Executing the Game Plan in the Mainstream

The regular educator's adherence to the game plan, developed during Step #4 and revisited in Step

FIGURE 3. Discrepancy Plan Sheet.

DISCREPANCY PLAN SHEET

Name _____

School _____

Special Education Teacher _____

Regular Education Teacher _____

Discrepancy # _____

_____

_____

A. Plan of action

1. What: _____

_____

2. When: _____

3. Who: _____

B. Expected Outcome

1. Academic/Behavior: _____

_____

_____

2. Weekly Reading Test: _____

C. Maintenance

1. What: _____

_____

_____

2. When: _____

3. Who: _____

#6, is monitored by either project staff or the special educator once or twice each week for about 8 weeks. Staff also helps the mainstream teacher to ensure that the reintegrated student and LAPs continue on a weekly basis to take their CBM probes. About 8 weeks after the student's transition, the teachers meet for a fifth time to evaluate his or her progress in the regular classroom. This meeting occasionally represents an IEP meeting, to which the student's parents and others, sometimes the student, are invited to deliberate about changing the student's special education status.

EVALUATING CASE-BY-CASE MAINSTREAMING

Building Half a Bridge

For several years, we have implemented and evaluated experimental procedures for reintegrating stu-

dents in reading and math mainstream classes, always searching for effectiveness and efficiency. Findings from this research and development program have been both encouraging and disappointing. During the 1988–89 school year, for example, we assigned 42 students with mild disabilities to experimental and control groups. We assisted special and regular educators in the experimental condition to implement CBM and TP to prepare selected students for reintegration into mainstream math classrooms. Math progress was measured by pre- versus posttreatment and ongoing curriculum-based achievement data obtained in special and regular education settings and by teacher reports. Findings indicated that experimental students substantially reduced time spent in special education math, whereas control students' time in special education math was unchanged. Experimental students' pre-to-posttreatment achievement was greater than that of controls and was similar to the progress of lowest-achieving nondisabled students in mainstream classes. Time-series analysis revealed, however, that experimental students' improved performance occurred only in special education; once in the mainstream, their progress ceased (see D. Fuchs, L. S. Fuchs, & Fernstrom, 1992; D. Fuchs, L. S. Fuchs, & Fernstrom, 1993).

These findings were replicated in reading in 1992–93 in the same school districts. On the computerized reading assessment (described previously), 11 reintegration candidates registered an average gain of 3.71 maze restorations, or words chosen correctly to complete a passage, in approximately 2.5 months in special education. Control students' math gain was only 1.25 maze restorations. In contrast to their progress in special education, the experimental students' average gain in regular reading classes during an equal interval of time was a mere .27 maze restorations.

How might we explain the experimental students' disappointing performance in mainstream reading and math classrooms? Anecdotal evidence suggests at least two reasons: First, in the districts in which we were operating, special and general educators have little time to talk with each other. Once reintegration candidates were mainstreamed, very high pupil–teacher ratios in special education and an absence of structured consultation time militated against a continuing dialogue about the student with disabilities. Second, regular educators may think individualized instruction is valuable in principle, or when someone else is doing it, but, like the proverbial domestic who draws the line when it comes to windows, general educators with whom we have worked typically "don't do individualized instruction." It is something for which they were not trained and for which they have little patience (see Baker & Zigmond, 1990; Zigmond & Baker, 1993). Thus, once the reintegration student transferred to the mainstream, she or he failed to obtain the tailor-made accommodations in instruction, curriculum, behavior management, and so forth provided through CBM and TP in special education.

Irrespective of why, our reintegrated students' inadequate performance in the mainstream prompts this question: How long will they be tolerated before their academic progress or behavior is (once again) viewed as too discrepant from class norms to justify their continued presence? A follow-up study we conducted provides a sobering answer. During the 1989–90 academic year, 32 students who had experienced TP or CBM or both in special education were transferred full time to regular education math classrooms. One year later, only 56% of these children were still in the mainstream; 44% were once again receiving their math instruction in special education.

Thus, we and our school-based colleagues have succeeded in building half a bridge: We have demonstrated that by the use of CBM and TP, special educa-

tors can boost selected students' achievement levels in reading and math to a point recognized by all parties as commensurate with mainstream expectations. The rub comes following reintegration when the students' reading and math progress stops. To build the second half of the bridge, we have turned to classwide peer tutoring.

Classwide Peer Tutoring (CWPT)

CWPT was first developed at the Juniper Gardens Children's Project in the early 1980s as a technique for improving children's learning in urban schools (e.g., Delquadri, Greenwood, Stretton, & Hall, 1983). It was found to increase students' opportunities to practice reading and to permit teachers greater flexibility in the use of reading texts (Greenwood, Carta, & Kamps, 1990). Reading procedures focused on developing students' fluency by requiring them to read connected text while being supervised by a peer. During the past 5 years, we and our colleagues at Peabody/Vanderbilt have attempted to extend the Juniper Gardens' model. The Peabody CWPT version (D. Fuchs, Mathes, & L. S. Fuchs, 1993) includes three reading activities: Partner Reading, Paragraph Shrinking, and Prediction Relay. The focus is on enhancing comprehension by directing students to engage in processing strategies designed to help them understand and remember text and monitor their comprehension. These strategies include (a) cumulatively reviewing information read, (b) sequencing information, (c) summarizing paragraphs and pages, (d) stating main ideas in as few words as possible, and (e) predicting and checking outcomes.

In Peabody CWPT all students in a teacher's class are paired. Each pair includes a higher and lower performing student. The roles of tutor and reader are reciprocal; that is, each student in a pair serves as reader for part of the time and as tutor for an equal portion of time. The higher performing reader reads first for each activity and serves as a model for the lower performing reader. Pairs are assigned to one of two teams for which they earn points. Points are awarded for engaging in reading activities and for behaving appropriately during tutoring. At the end of an instructional week, points are reported to the teacher; total points for each team are determined; and the winning team is announced. After 4 weeks, new pair and team assignments are made so that no team is consistently better or worse. Paris are always assigned to the same team. Thus, the motivational procedures combine competitive and cooperative features. Research indicates that Peabody CWPT promotes markedly better reading achievement than does conventional instruction in a wide range of learner types, including those with learning disabilities and low-achieving and average-achieving students (D. Fuchs, L. S. Fuchs, & Mathes, 1993).

Our hope is that CWPT will help make the mainstream somewhat more responsive and hospitable to the reintegration student and provide some of the individualization of instruction and nurturance necessary for the returning student's continued academic growth. This academic year, we are exploring experimentally the "value added" of CWPT by comparing a CBM + TP + CWPT condition to a CBM + TP condition to controls.

Serious problems are associated with developing an effective case-by-case approach to reintegration. No doubt about it. But so, too, are there many unanswered questions connected to large-scale mainstreaming. Because case-by-case reintegration embodies the individualization principle and exemplifies what's special about special education, and because case-by-case reintegration is supported by federal law, we hold that it is the more responsible way to try to move children into more integrated settings.

SUMMARY

Few special education teachers, administrators, teacher-trainers, or researchers are satisfied with the low frequency with which students with disabilities are transitioned into less restrictive educational settings. For these professionals the question is not whether many of these children should be prepared for reintegration, but how to do it in a responsible manner. During the last decade, cooperative learning models have been developed that aim to mainstream — all at once — large numbers of special-needs students. This chapter describes an alternate strategy: case-by-case reintegration that combines CBM and TP. It was developed to facilitate the successful transition of students with mild and moderate disabilities into regular reading and math classes. By "successful" we mean reintegrating students in such a manner that (a) they have the skills and behaviors required by the mainstream setting prior to entry, and (b) the regular educators are familiar with their strengths and weaknesses and confident that they are prepared to perform adequately and behave appropriately. In several years of research, we have shown that by use of CBM and TP, special educators can boost students' achievement levels to a point recognized by all parties as commensurate with mainstream expectations. However, we also have found that, once in the regular classroom, these students' academic progress typically ceases. Thus, we, and the teachers with whom we have been working, have succeeded in building half a bridge. To complete it, we have turned to CWPT with the expectation that it will help make mainstream instruction more responsive and hospitable to the reintegrating student.

AUTHORS' NOTE

Preparation of this chapter was supported in part by the Office of Special Education Programs in the U.S. Department of Education (Grant No. H023C10086-93) and by the National Institute of Child Health and Human Development (Core Grant HD15052). The chapter does not necessarily reflect the position or policy of the funding agencies, and no official endorsement by them should be inferred.

We thank the special and regular education teachers who have worked with us on our reintegration project, and Sue Dutka, Jill Howard, Wendy Locke, Patricia Mathes, and Marcia Stewart, whose help has been invaluable during project implementation.

Inquiries should be addressed to Douglas Fuchs, Department of Special Education, Box 328, George Peabody College, Vanderbilt University, Nashville, TN 37203.

REFERENCES

Anderson-Inman, L. (1981). Transenvironmental programming: Promoting success in the regular class by maximizing the effect of resource room instruction. *Journal of Special Education Technology, 4,* 3–12.

Anderson-Inman, L. (1986). Bridging the gap: Student-centered strategies for promoting the transfer of learning. *Exceptional Children, 52,* 562–572.

Anderson-Inman, L., Walker, H. M., & Purcell, J. (1984). Promoting the transfer of skills across settings: Transenvironmental programming for handicapped students in the mainstream. In W. L. Heward, T. E. Heron, D. S. Hill, & J. Trap-Porter (Eds.), *Focus on behavior analysis in education* (pp. 17–35). Columbus, OH: Merrill.

The Association for Persons with Severe Handicaps. (1992, July). CEC slips back; ASCD steps forward. *TASH Newsletter, 18,* 1.

Baker, J. M., & Zigmond, N. (1990). Are regular education classes equipped to accommodate students with learning disabilities? *Exceptional Children, 56,* 515–526.

Biklen, D., Lehr, S., Searl, S. J., & Taylor, S. J. (1987). Purposeful integration: Inherently equal [Manual prepared by the Center on Human Policy, Syracuse University]. (Available from Technical Assistance for Parent Programs [TAPP] Project, 312 Stuart Street, Boston, MA 02116)

Braaten, S., Kauffman, J. M., Braaten, B., Polsgrove, L., & Nelson, C. M. (1988). The Regular Education Initiative: Patent medicine for behavioral disorders. Exceptional Children, 55(1), 21–27.

California Teachers Association, Coalition for Students with Special Needs. (1990). Foundation of excellence for special education programs. Burlingame, CA: Author.

Commission on the Education of the Deaf. (1988, February). *Toward equality: Education of the deaf.* Washington, DC: U.S. Government Printing Office.

Council for Children with Behavioral Disorders, Executive Committee. (1989). Position statement on the Regular Education Initiative. *Behavioral Disorders, 14,* 201–207.

Council for Exceptional Children. (1993, April). *Statement on inclusive schools and communities.* Reston, VA: Author.

Delquadri, J. C., Greenwood, C. R., Stretton, K., & Hall, R. V. (1983). The Peer Tutoring Spelling Game: A classroom procedure for increasing opportunity to respond and spelling performance. *Education and Treatment of Children, 6,* 225–239.

Deno, E. (1970). Special education as developmental capital. *Exceptional Children, 37,* 229–237.

Deno, S. L. (1985). Curriculum-based measurement: The emerging alternative. *Exceptional Children, 52,* 219–232.

Dunn, L. M. (1968). Special education for the mildly retarded: Is much of it justifiable? *Exceptional Children, 34,* 5–22.

Espin, C., Deno, S. L., Maruyama, G., & Cohen, C. (1989). *The Basic Academic Skills Survey (BASS): An instrument for screening and identification of children at risk for failure in general education classrooms.* Paper presented at the annual meeting of the American Educational Research Association, San Francisco.

Fuchs, D., & Fuchs, L. S. (1991). Framing the REI debate: Abolitionists versus conservationists. In J. W. Lloyd, A. C. Repp, & N. N. Singh (Eds.), *The Regular Education Initiative: Alternative perspectives on concepts, issues, and models* (pp. 241–255). Sycamore, IL: Sycamore.

Fuchs, D., & Fuchs, L. S. (1994). Inclusive schools movement and the radicalization of special education reform. *Exceptional Children, 60,* 294–309.

Fuchs, D., & Fuchs, L. S. (in press). Sometimes separate is better. *Educational Leadership.*

Fuchs, D., Fuchs, L. S., & Fernstrom, P. (1992). Case-by-case reintegration of students with learning disabilities. *The Elementary School Journal, 92,* 261–281.

Fuchs, D., Fuchs, L. S., & Fernstrom, P. (1993). A conservative approach to special education reform: Mainstreaming through transenvironmental programming and curriculum-based measurement. *American Educational Research Journal, 30,* 149–177.

Fuchs, D., Fuchs, L. S., Fernstrom, P., & Hohn, M. (1991). Toward a responsible reintegration of behaviorally disordered students. *Behavioral Disorders, 16,* 133–147.

Fuchs, D., Fuchs, L. S., & Mathes, P. (1993, April). *Peer-mediated learning strategies: Effects on learners at different points on the achievement continuum.* Paper presented at the annual meeting of the American Educational Research Association, Atlanta, GA.

Fuchs, D., Mathes, P., & Fuchs, L. S. (1993). *Peabody Classwide Peer Tutoring reading methods.* Unpublished teacher's manual. (Available from Douglas Fuchs, Box 328, George Peabody College, Vanderbilt University, Nashville, TN 37203.)

Fuchs, L. S., Deno, S. L., & Mirkin, P. K. (1984). The effects of frequent curriculum-based measurement and evaluation on pedagogy, student achievement, and student awareness. *American Educational Research Journal, 21,* 449–460.

Fuchs, L. S., & Fuchs, D. (1986). Effects of systematic formative evaluation: A meta-analysis. *Exceptional Children, 53,* 199–209.

Fuchs, L. S., & Fuchs, D. (1990). *Identifying an alternative reading measure for curriculum-based measurement.* Nashville, TN: George Peabody College, Vanderbilt University.

Fuchs, L. S., Fuchs, D., Hamlett, C. L., & Ferguson, C. (1992). Effects of expert system consultation within curriculum-based measurement using a reading maze task. *Exceptional Children, 58,* 436–450.

Gartner, A., & Lipsky, D. K. (1987). Beyond special education: Toward a quality system for all students. *Harvard Educational Review, 57,* 367–395.

Gartner, A., & Lipsky, D. K. (1989). *The yoke of special education: How to break it. Working Paper.* Rochester, NY: National Center on Education and the Economy. (ERIC Document Reproduction Service No. ED 307 792)

Gersten, R., & Woodward, J. (1990). Rethinking the Regular Education Initiative: Focus on the classroom teacher. *Remedial and Special Education, 11*(3), 7–16.

Giangreco, M. F., Dennis, R., Cloninger, C., Edelman, S., & Schattman, R. (1993). "I've counted Jon": Transformational experiences of teachers educating students with disabilities. *Exceptional Children, 59,* 359–372.

Gilhool, T. K. (1989). The right to an effective education: From *Brown* to PL 94-142 and beyond. In D. K. Lipsky & A. Gartner (Eds.), *Beyond separate education: Quality education for all* (pp. 243–253). Baltimore, MD: Brookes Publishing.

Gottlieb, J., Alter, M., & Gottlieb, B. W. (1991). Mainstreaming academically handicapped children in urban schools. In J. W. Lloyd, A. C. Repp, & N. N. Singh (Eds.), *The Regular Education Initiative: Alternative perspectives on concepts, issues, and models* (pp. 95–112). Sycamore, IL: Sycamore.

Greenwood, C. R., Carta, J. J., & Kamps, D. (1990). Teacher versus peer-mediated instruction: A review of educational advantages and disadvantages. In M. Foot, F. Morgan, & R. Shute (Eds.), *Children helping children* (pp. 177–205). Sussex, England: Wiley Ltd.

Hallahan, D. P., Keller, C. E., McKinney, J. D., Lloyd, J. W., & Bryan, T. (1988). Examining the research base of the Regular Education Initiative: Efficacy studies and the Adaptive Learning Environments Model. *Journal of Learning Disabilities, 21,* 29–35, 55.

Huefner, D. S. (1994). The mainstreaming cases: Tensions and trends for school administrators. *Educational Administration Quarterly, 30*(1), 27–55.

Illinois State Board of Education. (1990). *See* Lieberman, G. (1990).

International Reading Association. (1986). *See* IRA. (1986–87).

Iowa State Education Association. (n.d.). Renewed Service Delivery System Task Force Report.

IRA president makes statement on education of the handicapped. (1986, December/1987, January). *Reading Today, 4*(3), p. 2.

Jenkins, J. R., & Jewell, M. (1992). An examination of the concurrent validity of the Basic Skills Samples (BASS). *Diagnostique, 17,* 273–288.

Jenkins, J. R., Pious, C. G., & Peterson, D. L. (1988). Categorical programs for remedial and handicapped students: Issues of validity. *Exceptional Children, 55,* 147–158.

Kauffman, J. M. (1989). The Regular Education Initiative as Reagan-Bush education policy: A trickle-down theory of education of the hard to teach. *Journal of Special Education, 23,* 256–278.

Kauffman, J. M., Gerber, M. M., & Semmel, M. I. (1988). Arguable assumptions underlying the Regular Education Initiative. *Journal of Learning Disabilities, 21,* 6–11.

Keogh, B. K. (1988). Perspectives on the Regular Education Initiative. *Learning Disabilities Focus, 4,* 3–5.

Krasner, M. (1991, March 9). Report of the Exceptional Children Committee to the Delegate Assembly [New Jersey Education Association].

Learning Disabilities Association. (1993). Position paper on full inclusion of all students with learning disabilities in the regular education classroom. *Journal of Learning Disabilities, 26,* 594–596.

Lerner, J. W. (1987). The Regular Education Initiative: Some unanswered questions. *Learning Disabilities Focus, 3*(1), 3–7.

Lieberman, G. (1990, August). Choices in special education. *Administrative Bulletin,* No. 90–2AB. Illinois State Board of Education, Department of Special Education.

Lieberman, L. M. (1985). Special education and regular education: A merger made in heaven? *Exceptional Children, 51,* 513–516.

Lipsky, D. K., & Gartner, A. (1989). *Beyond separate education: Quality education for all.* Baltimore: Paul Brookes.

Lipsky, D. K., & Gartner, A. (1991). Restructuring for quality. In J. W. Lloyd, A. C. Repp, & N. N. Singh (Eds.), *The Regular Education Initiative: Alternative perspectives on concepts, issues, and models* (pp. 43–56). Sycamore, IL: Sycamore.

McKinney, J. D., & Hocutt, A. M. (1988). Policy issues in the evaluation of the Regular Education Initiative. *Learning Disabilities Focus, 4*, 15–23.

Maheady, L., & Algozzine, B. (1991). The Regular Education Initiative – Can we proceed in an orderly and scientific manner? *Teacher Education and Special Education, 14*(1), 66–73.

Megivern, K. (1987a, October). The war within. *AER Report.* (Reprinted in *Yearbook of the Association for Education and Rehabilitation of the Blind and Visually Impaired,* 1987, *5*, 29–30. Washington, DC)

Megivern, K. (1987b, December). Update from the front. *AER Report.* (Reprinted in *Yearbook of the Association for Education and Rehabilitation of the Blind and Visually Impaired,* 1987, *5*, 31–32. Washington, DC)

Megivern, K. (1988a, February). A statement of conscience could get a person fired! *AER Report.* (Reprinted in *Yearbook of the Association for Education and Rehabilitation of the Blind and Visually Impaired,* 1987, *5*, 33–34. Washington, DC)

Megivern, K. (1988b, February). Least restrictive environment revisited. *AER Report.* (Reprinted in *Yearbook of the Association for Education and Rehabilitation of the Blind and Visually Impaired,* 1987, *5*, 33–34. Washington, DC)

National Association of State Boards of Education. (1992, October). *Winners all: A call for inclusive schools.* Washington, DC: Author.

National Education Association. (1992). *Resolution B-20: Education for all students with disabilities.* Washington, DC: Author.

National Joint Committee on Learning Disabilities. (1993). A reaction to "full inclusion": A reaffirmation of the right of students with learning disabilities to a continuum of services. *Journal of Learning Disabilities, 26*, 594–596.

New Jersey Education Association. (1991). *See* Krasner (1991).

Pugach, M., & Lilly, M. S. (1984). Reconceptualizing support services for classroom teachers: Implications for teacher education. *Journal of Teacher Education, 35*(5), 48–55.

Pugach, M., & Raths, J. D. (1987, April). *Prelude to merger: An analysis of teaching roles in general and special education.* Paper presented at the annual meeting of the American Educational Research Association, Washington, DC.

Reynolds, M. C. (1988). Reaction to the JLD special series on the Regular Education Initiative. *Journal of Learning Disabilities, 21*, 352–356.

Reynolds, M. C. (1991). Classification and labeling. In J. W. Lloyd, A. C. Repp, & N. N. Singh (Eds.), *The Regular Education Initiative: Alternative perspectives on concepts, issues, and models* (pp. 29–41). Sycamore, IL: Sycamore.

Reynolds, M. C., Wang, M. C., & Walberg, H. J. (1987). The necessary restructuring of special and regular education. *Exceptional Children, 53*, 391–398.

Sapon-Shevin, M. (1988). Working towards merger together: Seeing beyond distrust and fear. *Teacher Education and Special Education, 11*(3), 103–110.

Scott, S., & Fuchs, D. (in preparation). *A critical review of studies that reintegrate students with disabilities into mainstream settings.*

Singer, J. D. (1988). Should special education merge with regular education? *Educational Policy, 4*, 409–424.

Snell, M. E. (1991). Schools are for all kids: The importance of integration for students with severe disabilities and their peers. In J. W. Lloyd, A. C. Repp, & N. N. Singh (Eds.), *The Regular Education Initiative: Alternative perspectives on concepts, issues, and models* (pp. 133–148). Sycamore, IL: Sycamore.

Stainback, S., & Stainback, W. (1985). *Integration of students with severe handicaps into regular schools.* Reston, VA: The Council for Exceptional Children.

Stainback, S., & Stainback, W. (1992). *Curriculum considerations in inclusive classrooms: Facilitating learning for all students.* Baltimore: Paul Brookes.

Stainback, W., & Stainback, S. (1984). A rationale for the merger of special and regular education. *Exceptional Children, 51*, 102–111.

Taylor, S. J. (1988). Caught in the continuum: A critical analysis of the principle of least restrictive environment. *Journal of the Association of Persons with Severe Handicaps, 13*, 41–53.

Thousand, J. S., & Villa, R. A. (1990). Strategies for educating learners with severe disabilities within their local home schools and communities. *Focus on Exceptional Children, 23*, 1–24.

Vergason, G. A., & Anderegg, M. L. (1989). Save the baby!: A response to "Integrating the children of the second system." *Phi Delta Kappan, 71*, 61–63.

Walker, H. M. & Bullis, M. (1991). Behavior disorders and the social context of regular class integration: A conceptual dilemma? In J. W. Lloyd, A. C. Repp, & N. N. Singh (Eds.), *The Regular Education Initiative: Alternative perspectives on concepts, issues, and models* (pp. 75–93). Sycamore, IL: Sycamore.

Walker, H. M., & Rankin, R. (1983). Assessing the behavioral expectations and demands of less restrictive settings. *School Psychology Review, 12*, 274–284.

Wang, M. C., Reynolds, M. C., & Walberg, H. J. (1988). Integrating the children of the second system. *Phi Delta Kappan, 70*, 248–251.

Will, M. (1986). *Educating students with learning problems – A shared responsibility: A report to the Secretary.* Washington, DC: Office of Special Education and Rehabilitative Services, U.S. Department of Education. (ERIC Document Reproduction Service No. ED 279 149)

York, J., & Vandercook, T. (1991). Designing an integrated program for learners with severe disabilities. *Teaching Exceptional Children, 23*(2), 22–28.

Zigmond, N., & Baker, J. (1993, October). *An examination of the meaning and practice of special education in the context of full-time mainstreaming of students with learning disabilities.* Paper presented at the Policy Conference on the Meaning and Practice of Special Education in the Context of Inclusion. Nemacolin Woodlands, PA.

ANNOTATED BIBLIOGRAPHY

Fuchs, D., Fuchs, L. S., & Fernstrom, P. (1993). A conservative approach to special education reform: Mainstreaming through transenvironmental programming and curriculum-based measurement. *American Educational Research Journal, 30*, 149–177

This article provides a detailed description of how transenvironmental programming and curriculum-based measurement may be combined to strengthen case-by-case reintegration efforts. The article also reports results from a year-long experimental study of the mainstreaming approach.

Mathes, P. G., Fuchs, D., Fuchs, L. S., Henley, A. M., & Sanders, A. (1994). Increasing strategic reading practice with Peabody Classwide Peer Tutoring. *Learning Disabilities Research & Practice, 9*(1), 44–48.

Written for practitioners, this article describes Peabody Classwide Peer Tutoring's three principal activities: partner reading, paragraph shrinking, and prediction relay. It also discusses materials, scheduling, use of points, training, and other nuts-and-bolts issues associated with implementing Peabody Classwide Peer Tutoring.

Slavin, R. E., & Stevens, R. J. (1991). Cooperative learning and mainstreaming. In J. W. Lloyd, A. C. Repp, & N. N. Singh (Eds.), *The Regular Education Initiative: Alternative perspectives on concepts, issues, and models* (pp. 177–191). Sycamore, IL: Sycamore.

This book chapter describes cooperative learning approaches to mainstreaming, specifically, Team Assisted Individualization – Mathematics and Cooperative Integrated Reading and Composition.

75

Best Practices in Individual Counseling of Elementary-Age Students

Deborah Tharinger
Mary Stafford
The University of Texas at Austin

This chapter provides a theoretically integrated and pragmatically oriented framework for the provision of school-based individual counseling to children by school psychologists. Other important intervention services that can be provided by school psychologists — such as group counseling, crisis counseling, family counseling, milieu counseling (e.g., in school-based day treatment programs), and teacher support programs, although they are necessary to an integrated approach and the concept of a continuum of care of school-based health and mental health services — are not addressed here. The chapter is addressed to school psychologists who desire to engage in direct and coordinated interventions with children to promote their development and learning by helping to alleviate their distress and behavioral dysfunction.

When addressing "best practices" in counseling children, it is important to recognize that school psychologists come from varied training and practice traditions, function in uniquely defined roles within different school districts, practice in distinct ways within the same roles (e.g., counseling children), and have different views of the future practice of school psychology. Although the practice of school psychology in most schools continues to be dominated by an assessment role, a counseling role often is available. This role for the school psychologist can be limited to counseling that is provided exclusively to children designated as seriously emotionally disturbed in the special education system or can be as extensive as including all children in need, services being prioritized through a screening and referral system. In addition, a school psychologist may be the only provider of mental health services in his or her school site, or may work collaboratively with school counselors, social workers, nurses, and prevention specialists. Furthermore, one school psychologist may have adopted a model of child counseling with extensive parent and teacher involvement, while another may focus primarily or exclusively on the child. These many differences among school psychologists reflect philosophical, theoretical, and pragmatic influences that impact on attitudes and the sense of "best practices" of counseling in the field.

In this chapter, the position is taken that for school psychologists who counsel children individually in the schools there is not a single best practice that can be specified in terms of a particular theoretical framework or implementation method. However, there is a best practice in terms of functioning from a theoretically, ethically, scientifically, and humanly driven orientation that maximizes competent and effective service delivery. Thus, what is presented in this chapter is best viewed as *one* such integration that offers guidelines to those who are currently counseling children or who aspire to do so. It is acknowledged that the perspective and integration proposed will appeal to some, but certainly not all, practitioners and trainers. In particular, in light of the problem-solving approach being stressed throughout this volume, a problem-solving orientation is central to this chapter in the sense that the counseling process involves constant hypothesis testing and adjustment. However, any use of a formal problem-solving approach or curriculum is seen as one of the many possible therapeutic techniques that can be employed in the context of the counseling relationship. Counseling with children as presented in this chapter is informed but not limited or unduly determined by a problem-solving approach.

This chapter is influenced by the view that school psychologists can be primary providers of mental health services for children (and their teachers and caretakers) within the health provision system of the schools. A child–school–family philosophy is stressed that involves home and school caregivers, in addition to the child, in the counseling process. Theoretically, the chapter is guided by an integrated model of counseling that emphasizes a developmentally and culturally sensitive relationship approach, influenced by attachment theory and buttressed by recent innovations in cognitive behavioral and systems/ecological theory. Central to this view is the perception that the counseling relationship provides the child with a secure base from which to explore her or his relational, physical, cognitive, and internal world and from which to choose to make or respond to changes. The relationships the school psychologist establishes with the child's caregivers and teachers also can provide them with a secure base from which to explore their attitudes, influences, and reactions to the child, as well as their motivation to engage in and support change for the child and themselves. In this model, the child is seen as the primary client, with secondary relationships established with parents and teachers.

The remainder of this chapter is divided into three parts. The first, an overview, examines children's unmet mental health needs, the uniquenesses and challenges involved in counseling children in the schools, considerations in selecting children for counseling, the process and general goals of counseling, and characteristics conducive to being a counselor to children. The second section addresses basic considerations, with a focus on developmental and cultural influences, and discusses the essential knowledge necessary for counseling children. The final section provides a seven-stage model designed to guide school psychologists in constructing their own best practices in counseling elementary-age children.

OVERVIEW

It has been acknowledged widely that there has been a failure to respond to the mental health needs of the vast majority of children in all settings, including the schools. This point has been brought home strongly in the past decade by Jane Knitzer in her 1982 book, *Unclaimed Children: The Failure of Public Responsibility to Children and Adolescents in Need of Mental Health Services*, and in her more recent book (1990) written with colleagues Steinberg and Fleisch, *At the Schoolhouse Door: An Examination of Programs and Policies for Children with Behavioral and Emotional Problems*. It is estimated that at least 12% of children and adolescents suffer from emotional and behavioral disorders and at least 5% are thought to suffer from serious emotional and behavioral problems. Furthermore, it is estimated that at least 70%–80% of these children are not receiving necessary mental health services, and that the children from minority groups are the most underserved (Tuma, 1989). The large majority (80%) of children and adolescents with serious emotional disturbances and mental health needs attend the public schools (Knitzer et al., 1990). Currently the schools are being viewed as a key setting for the delivery of many of the mental health services, both intervention and prevention, that children may need (Holtzman, 1992), and school psychologists can be central providers. It is useful to review many of the unique and challenging aspects of delivering mental health services to children in the schools.

Unique and Challenging Aspects of School-Based Counseling with Children

There are unique and challenging aspects to how children, the environment of the school, and a collaborative framework affect the counseling process. It is important to examine these influencing factors, as they impact on the effectiveness of counseling and the receptivity of the system to counseling services. Clarizio and McCoy (1983) have described unique aspects of counseling children and conclude: (a) that children are unlikely to seek help voluntarily or to initiate entry into counseling; (b) that most children lack an explicit understanding of counseling, the purpose and goals of treatment, and the role they are to assume; (c) that children's verbal and cognitive abilities, as well as the organization of their personalities are in development; and (d) that children are extremely dependent on and influenced by their immediate environments, most specifically their families and their schooling experience. Although these characteristics of children may appear to be limitations, they also can be viewed as opportunities for practitioners to educate the adults in children's lives as well as the children about the potential benefits of counseling, to work with children early in their personality development, and to influence the significant others in children's lives while they are still energized, motivated, and committed.

One major advantage to counseling children within the school setting is that one is working in the child's world — a natural setting where children come every day. One has access to children's teachers, administrators, and other personnel who interact with the child. In addition, one has the opportunity to experience a complete cohort of children in a particular school, and to get a sense of where and how a particular child does and does not fit in. In other words, there are inherent local norms in the schools for comparison purposes. In addition, involvement and feedback from teachers about the child's progress can be obtained. There also may be the opportunity, depending on the continuum of services available in the school, to provide a child with a combination of individual, group, and family-related services. Moreover, it may be possible to coordinate a variety of services with other professionals in the school, such as a school counselor or social worker. Lastly, there is an opportunity for long-term follow-up, even over several years, to track the development of an individual child and his or her family.

The challenges involved in counseling children in the school include finding a good fit between the goals and process of the educational system and the goals and process of counseling, with its origins in the psychology and mental health arenas. The educational and the mental health systems, although similarly invested in promoting growth in children, have somewhat different perspectives and priorities.

These differences have the potential for raising conflicts among the school psychologist, teachers, administrators, other school personnel, and parents. The primary goal of the schooling perspective is to educate all children, with a focus on academic progress, group socialization, and appropriate behavior. The primary goal from the mental health perspective in the school environment is to assist individuals in solving emotional, behavioral, and interpersonal problems that are impinging upon their being able to take full advantage of academic and socialization experiences. Though the end goals are the same, the means may be quite distinctive. The school psychologist needs to impart to teachers, administrators, and parents that children will profit from the educational environment only if their mental health needs are reasonably met.

Another challenge to a model of school-based counseling that includes consultation with teachers and parents is finding effective ways to involve them. Teachers usually will cooperate in order to alleviate the child's emotional and/or behavioral distress in the classroom, and they often are more than willing to collaborate on classroom interventions in conjunction with individual counseling. However, the teacher's available time for consultation may be minimal and proposed solutions must consider the target child's needs in relation to the needs of the rest of the children in the classroom. In addition, the teacher's role and responsibilities are influenced by the direction the school's leadership takes, affecting what type of changes are acceptable in the child's classroom. Involvement of parents in a child's counseling allows for the formation of a partnership between the family and school that may not have existed previously (Christenson & Conoley, 1992). Many parents want to be involved in the process of deciding their children's educational programs and involvement in counseling. However, the factors that interfere with the school psychologist's efforts to facilitate the development of partnerships between families and schools include (a) work schedules that limit parents' availability to meet during the day, and childcare responsibilities that interfere with their availability during the evening; (b) some parents' belief that schools should handle school matters, including managing the child's school behavior and discipline, rather than asking parents to intervene; (c) resistant communication because parents often receive only negative feedback from the school about their child; and (d) some parents' belief that their children should spend school time in academic activities rather than in other activities, including counseling. While beliefs often are hard to change, there are some things that schools and school psychologists can do to increase parents' involvement and to facilitate partnerships. It is important for school personnel to provide an atmosphere that is family-friendly and scheduled so that families can more easily be involved. Providing child-

care for younger siblings during meetings, scheduling meetings at late or very early hours, overtly recognizing the parent as the most knowledgeable person about the child, and structuring a program for the child that includes communication of the child's positive accomplishments and strengths may facilitate the formation of the home–school partnership.

Pragmatic challenges to counseling in the schools consist of managing the many changes and disruptions that happen in the school day and securing private, child-friendly physical space. Counseling in many other settings consists of a clinical hour in a private, quiet office and perhaps a playroom where interruptions are held to a minimum. In these settings, consistency in time and physical location are symbolic of the psychological safety and security being offered to the child. In contrast, space is at a premium in many of today's schools, and schedules are affected by school-wide standardized testing, field trips, assemblies, classroom tests, and detention, as well as meetings and crises that are imposed upon the school psychologist. Efforts must be made to secure and maintain a physical environment and schedule where respect can be shown to both the child and to the counseling process. For example, educating others not to interrupt a session by knocking on the door and having a phone with a silent ring that takes messages can control many of the intrusions to the process. For counseling children individually, the office space does not need to be large, but it does need to be equipped in a way that welcomes children and promotes safety and security. It also is important to provide materials and toys that allow for the expression of anger and aggression, as children have few releases for these feelings, especially at school. Recommended materials and toys for working with elementary-age children in counseling include paper, crayons, magic markers, scissors, clay, puppets, dolls, games (of various developmental levels), stuffed animals, building blocks, plastic animals, monsters, and if possible, a doll house and a blow-up "bobo" punching bag. In addition, a collection of books that address childhood stressors, such as divorce and death, are good to have and to use with children and their parents, as are problem-solving curricula, usually based on a cognitive behavioral orientation (Kendall, 1991). Fortunately, counseling materials, games, and curricula are readily available through many publishers' catalogs.

A final challenge to counseling in the school involves maintaining whatever level of confidentiality was offered to the child and his or her parents and teachers. Working in a school is a bit like working in a fishbowl: There can be constant pressure to share one's work with other professionals also working with the child. Although collaboration can be extremely useful, school psychologists in these positions must work very hard to respond respectfully to the interests and needs of others involved while at the same time retaining offered confidentiality and privacy. The school psychologist can function as a role model when it comes to respecting confidentiality in the complex system of the school, particularly as it applies to information obtained from parents.

Children to Consider for Individual School-Based Counseling

Children whose behavioral, cognitive, emotional, and/or interpersonal functioning causes them or others moderate to serious distress and interferes with their development or learning are good candidates for individual counseling. Children's difficulties that may indicate needed counseling can include (but are not limited to) coping with attention deficit–hyperactivity disorder, having learning or language disabilities, experiencing family divorce and disruption, being the victim of child abuse and neglect, witnessing family or community violence, experiencing unrealistic parent or peer expectations, experiencing multiple losses, living with parents affected with psychopathology or drug and alcohol abuse, and being the objects of prejudice or stigma. These difficulties may manifest themselves as depression, suicidal thoughts, anxiety, out-of-control behavior, distorted cognitions and emotions, disorganization, and/or impaired relationships. Children who experience these difficulties chronically may be assessed as seriously emotionally disturbed and may be entitled to associated services, such as counseling as part of their individualized educational plan. However, as only 1%–2% of children are so identified in the schools (Knitzer et al., 1990), there are many more children in need who are not being identified through the special education channels. School psychologists with the necessary education and training are in an excellent position to help identify these children, prioritize their needs, and plan appropriate interventions, which may include individual counseling.

Determining whether a child is best served through *individual* counseling services, rather than or in addition to other psychological services, requires attention to a variety of indicators gleaned from information provided by multiple sources, including the child, teachers, and parents. The school psychologist needs to consider the nature of the child's problem, its severity and acute or chronic state, the level of negative forces relative to positive resources acting upon and available to the child, and the child's level of stability at the present time. For example, inclusion in group counseling requires a higher level of stability in the child than that required for individual counseling. In cases of crisis (such as potential for suicide, current breakup of the family, or similar events) or severe disturbances, the child may not be stable enough initially to tolerate or benefit from group counseling. A decision may be made to provide individual counseling initially, followed by group counseling as the child stabilizes and is able to receive feedback from peers constructively, with teacher and family consultation services provided concurrently to both interventions. The factors that influence decisions regarding the appropriateness of individual counseling (either alone or in conjunction with other interventions) also can affect the counseling process and provide a basis for determining counseling goals.

Counseling Process and General Goals

Individual counseling with children can be described as the process of ongoing, planned interactions between a mental health professional and a child who has sought, or for whom someone else has sought, help for a particular problem or set of problems. The professional agrees to attempt to provide conditions to alleviate the child's distress and to improve the child's psychological functioning by directly facilitating change in the child and by promoting and supporting change in the child's environment, most centrally the school and family systems. Psychological functioning includes the child's cognitions, perceptions, emotions, behavior, and relational capacities. The general goals of counseling can include alleviating the child's emotional and cognitive distress, changing the child's behavior, assisting with self-understanding, helping the child meet current developmental tasks successfully, supporting needed environmental changes, and promoting a more positive fit between the child and the systems in which she or he resides (e.g., school and family).

The goals of counseling are achieved through a combination of interpersonal relationships with the child and significant others in the child's life, and the implementation of therapeutic techniques that allow for expression, self-examination, building new skills, and promoting adaptation. The relationship with the child allows for the establishment of a safe place that builds trust, where the child can explore himself or herself and learn and practice new ways of feeling, thinking, and behaving that are designed to promote healthier adaptations and increased options. The relationships with significant others are designed to promote a new understanding of the child, support for change in the child, and hopefully a commitment to examination and change within the adults themselves. The therapeutic techniques applied usually reflect the theoretical orientation and integration of the practitioner and are drawn from psychodynamic, object relations, attachment, humanistic, behavioral, cognitive-behavioral, and family systems theories. Techniques are chosen to fit the needs of a particular child at a given time and to address the goals of counseling. Modalities for working with children are many and include verbal interactions, such as talking, story telling, and dialogue during play; action play; game playing; work with art materials; and use of books and journals. Social skills and self-management training are examples of additional interventions that can complement the individual counseling process.

Being a Counselor of Children

Practitioners who provide counseling to children in the schools are likely to be very diverse; however, it is beneficial if they are hopeful, enjoy being in children's worlds, can create a sense of security, are non-judgmental, can be playful, are flexible, can be innovative and creative with space and materials, and are talented at getting access to children's thoughts and feelings. Comfortableness with the modalities of talking, play, games, role playing, art, skill building, and sports activities also is needed. It is important to be able to engage in the art of counseling while at the same time being informed by the science of counseling. In addition, being able to balance the crises that occur in the school that compete with regular counseling sessions is essential. The school-based counselor also has to be able to deal with the pressure to change children's behavior very quickly. This type of pressure usually leads to nothing more than "talking at kids" and trying to "straighten kids out," a job best left to an adult in charge of school discipline matters. And finally, the counselor must be effective with children as well as adults, including parents, teachers, and administrators.

Counselors, through training and supervision, need to develop and refine an array of interpersonal and counseling skills as well as develop a sense of themselves as counselors. The skills needed include demonstrating empathy, regard, respect, and caring for other persons, as well as listening, reflecting, confronting, and interpreting — all skills originally described by the humanistic tradition. In addition, informal and formal assessment skills, interviewing skills, consultation skills, capacity to effectively and empathically provide feedback, and limit-setting abilities need to be mastered. It is essential for counselors to be comfortable with their knowledge and skills, and to know when they are outside their areas of competence. In that case, it is important to refer or to obtain supervision and consultation from professionals with the desired expertise. Knowing when the material in a counseling case with a child may be too close to home in respect to a counselor's own pain or unresolved issues (countertransference) is another time for referral, consultation, and/or supervision. With continuing education, training, experience, and professional and personal integration the developing counselor will function confidently in more and more areas of competence.

Thus, just as counseling with a child is a developmental process, counselors themselves undergo a developmental process from a novice counselor to a more expert one. It may be helpful to consider that counselors also need a secure base from which to develop and maintain their counseling expertise; without it, the ability to offer security to others may be compromised. Unfortunately, tremendous external and internal demands are placed on personnel who attempt to address children's mental health needs in many of today's schools, challenging the counselor's own secure base. It has been recognized that secondary trauma and/or burnout can result if providers do not acknowledge and address the level of stress in their worksites and set boundaries between what is possible and what is not. Thus, school psychologists need to foster health within themselves and their workplace that is then reflected in their relationships with children, families, and teachers.

BASIC CONSIDERATIONS

Besides the set of sustaining characteristics described above, counselors of children need to possess a core body of knowledge in order to develop as effective practitioners. Areas that make up this integration include developmental and cultural considerations, theoretical models for counseling, knowledge of the research and clinical literatures, familiarity with children's play and play therapy, psychopharmacology, and professional ethics.

Developmental and Cultural Perspectives

Counseling with children demands a developmental perspective, regardless of the other theoretical influences that may guide the goals and process of counseling. Also, the cultural features of the child must be attended to if counseling is to be effective with the wide variety of children in schools.

Developmental theory and a developmental perspective. Theory organizes and gives meaning to facts, provides a framework for them, and assigns more importance to some facts than others. In addition, a theory provides a framework for raising questions, guiding observations, and generating new information. Theories are useful to the practitioner because they provide heuristics to guide problem solving. Knowledge of developmental theories and frameworks can prevent tunnel vision among practitioners working with children. A rigid perspective on children's behavior can be avoided if one incorporates multiple theoretical perspectives in an attempt to understand children's behavior within a view of the whole child. For example, combining and integrating Freud's concern with underlying motivations and emotions, Erikson's concern with the mastery of psychosocial crises. Piaget's findings on cognitive capabilities, social learning theory's concern with modeling and observation, Bowlby's focus on the quality of attachment and internalized working models, and Bronfenbrenner's concern with transactions between the child and multiple environmental systems produces a powerful perspective for understanding children's development and the forces that effect such development. A developmental perspective is useful for conceptualizing, choosing, and evaluating specific and appropriate counseling goals for each child (Tharinger & Lambert, 1990). In addition, by understanding normal developmental progressions as well as culture- and gender-designated developmental tasks, the practitioner can match the process of counseling to the child's developmental levels.

Although developmental theories are useful for understanding normative development, what is challenging about children who receive counseling is that they are typically outside of the norm in one or more areas of development. Although an understanding of where they "ought" to be or "where most children their age are" is useful, familiarity with approaches that examine individual differences in the developmental process also is essential. For example, the work in the field of developmental psychopathology has raised questions about the continuity and discontinuity in development and has emphasized how normal development can inform abnormal development and vice versa (Achenbach, 1990; Cicchetti, 1990; Lewis, 1990; Rutter, 1990). Also of keen interest has been the child who appears to overcome extreme odds to function in an adaptive, competent manner (Garmezy, Masten, & Tellegen, 1984). What is apparent from this collected work is the complexity of the developmental process in respect to a course of health or a course of pathology, or a weaving in and out between the two. Notions of a fixed continuity of either health or pathology have been shown to be naive, and it is widely accepted that the majority of individuals who have mental health problems as children do not show problems as adults and that the majority of adults who present with mental health problems did not show difficulties as children (Richters & Weintraub, 1990). This general finding supports the concept of discontinuity of development as well as the malleability of the individual, which in turn supports prevention and intervention efforts. Thus, an awareness of risk and protective factors of underlying mechanisms (Rutter, 1990) can help inform the school psychologist about varied developmental paths, enhancing the understanding of each individual child.

Cultural considerations. Developmental perspectives and environmental impacts can be areas of difference between majority and minority group children that may add complexity to the counseling process. Definitions of normal behavior are culturally determined, and thus differ for various cultural groups. Non-western children may differ in the schedule and expression of certain behaviors considered age- and gender-appropriate for U.S. children (Vargas & Koss-Chioino, 1992). For example, some cultures encourage autonomy at earlier ages than others. In addition, environmental impacts, such as poverty, racism and prejudice, and level of acculturation may serve to increase environmental stresses, cause confusion for minority children, and add complexity to the counseling process. Furthermore, if the counselor's culture is different from the child's, misperception and miscommunication on the part of both the counselor and the child may interfere with the counseling process.

The purpose of counseling usually is to bring the child's thoughts, feelings, or behaviors into the healthy range, as well as to alleviate distress and promote more optimal adaptation. However, definitions of normality, distress, and adaptation differ among cultures. Obtaining information from relevant sources about norms for various cultures (e.g., Sue, 1990; Sue & Sue, 1990; Vargas & Koss-Chioino, 1992), as well as gathering information from the child's parents and community members concerning their expectations for normal behavior provide vital data for the counselor to consider in developing counseling goals.

Poverty, racism, and prejudice often intertwine to create feelings of powerlessness and helplessness for the minority child (Vargas & Koss-Chioino, 1992). When poverty is a part of the child's life, often it is accompanied by inadequate housing, nutrition, and consequent poor health. Racism and prejudice often are subtle and may not be overtly recognized by the person delivering or receiving the negative messages. However, even the most subtle statements and actions may be felt severely by the targeted child. Sensitivity to the meaning of statements and actions is likely to result from repeated experiences with even the most subtle forms of racism, resulting in an inability to trust others, especially members of the group delivering the message. When the counselor is a member of a cultural group with whom the child has had negative experiences, interference in the development of the counseling relationship may result for both the counselor and the child. Additionally, the minority child's development of a sense of identity is more complex than that of children from the majority group (Vargas & Koss-Chioino, 1992). Finding one's sense of self in a society where advantages are enjoyed at a greater rate by the majority group is complex and difficult. The counseling process may need to address both the problem areas that interfere with the child's fitting in and the development of a healthy identity within the child's own cultural group.

Levels of acculturation also impact the minority child. First-generation children, who were born of parents in another country have learned behaviors that were considered appropriate in that country. As with all children, their experiences in the early years of their life influence the way they view the world and interpret situations. These children literally are caught between two cultures (Vargas & Koss-Chioino, 1992). It is essential when working with these children, as well as second-or third-generation minority children, to assess strengths of the child and family and culturally specific responses to mental health problems (Lee, 1988).

Counseling children from minority cultures requires an understanding of the child's culture (e.g., value systems, family structure, socialization patterns, verbal and nonverbal language systems), as well as the impact on present functioning of the child's level of acculturation and language proficiency in both the native language and English. Sensitivity to the effect of the counselor's culture on the child and her or his family, as well as the effect of the child's culture on the counselor is necessary for effective counseling. Inclusion of spirituality and other cultural aspects in the counseling process and use of ethnically relevant toys and materials reflects this sensitivity. Models for understanding culturally responsive psychotherapies can be found in Sue (1990), Sue and Sue (1990), Sue and Zane (1987), and Vargas and Koss-Chioino (1992).

Knowledge of Theoretical Models for Counseling: The Need for Integration

Counseling and psychotherapy with children have a rich history influenced by multiple sources (Koocher & D'Angelo, 1992). At the present time there are many recent books (within the past 5 years) on the topic, from a variety of theoretical perspectives, that address general practice as well as counseling and psychotherapy with children with specific disorders or needs (e.g., see Allan, 1988; Barkley, 1990; D'Amato & Rothlisberg, 1992; Dennison, 1989; Dennison & Glassman, 1987; Hodges, 1991; James, 1989; Kazdin, 1988; Keat, 1990; Kendall, 1991; Kernberg & Chazan, 1991; Kratochwill & Morris, 1991; Mordock, 1991; Shirk, 1988; Siegel, 1991; Spiegel, 1989; Stark, 1990; Thompson & Rudolph, 1992; Vargas & Koss-Chioino, 1992; Vernon, 1989; Webb, 1991).

Models adopted to guide counseling usually correspond with the practitioner's explicit or implicit theories of developmental change. Each of the major developmental theories proposes a model of change that can be applied to the counseling process (Tharinger & Lambert, 1990). From the psychodynamic perspective, the goal is to promote emotional and behavior change by interpreting the child's defenses so as to bring unconscious elements that have been impeding development into consciousness. From the psychosocial perspective the goal is to promote resolution of developmentally salient conflict to allow the child an increased sense of mastery, good judgment, and capacity "to do well." From the cognitive developmental perspective the goal is to promote progression to higher stages of cognitive reasoning, thus allowing the child greater cognitive flexibility, a wider range of application of her or his new structural organization, the ability to coordinate more per-

spectives, and an increased capacity to handle new, unfamiliar problems.

From the social learning and cognitive behavioral perspectives the goal of counseling is to promote behavior change directly by reinforcing desired behavior, by providing positive models and positive vicarious experiences, and by changing children's cognitions — for example, by helping them learn cognitive mediation to control impulsive behavior or by helping them alter negative self-evaluations. From the attachment perspective the goal is to promote interpersonal change by providing a secure base for exploration, by establishing a positive relationship with the children, and by aiding them in understanding the quality of their earlier attachments and the significance of their losses in relation to current behavior. From the ecological and the transactional organism perspectives the goal is to promote behavioral, cognitive, emotional, and interpersonal change by bringing about changes in the children (using the above methods) and in the children's environment. Environment targets include parents (e.g., through parent consultation), family (e.g., through family therapy), teachers (e.g., through teacher consultation), and peers (e.g., through classroom interventions and group counseling). From the developmental psychopathology perspective, the goal of counseling is to facilitate getting the child back on developmental track through addressing the multiple child and environmental transactional factors that may be adversely impacting the child.

Although each of the above models of change is applicable with children and will help promote change if matched with the children's needs and their developmental levels, an integrated perspective provides the most flexible and comprehensive model for change in counseling with children in schools. Arkowitz (1992) provides a useful discussion on integrative theories of therapy, and D'Amato and Rothlisberg (1992) illustrates eight different theoretical perspectives' views on providing psychological intervention for an adolescent. If one accepts that the practitioner cannot effect change optimally by focusing on only one domain of functioning, be it emotional, interpersonal, cognitive, or behavioral, or by ignoring individual difference factors and mechanisms underlying development, then a counselor needs to work simultaneously on cognitive, emotional, and behavioral change, taking into account uniqueness within the individual and his or her environment and culture. In addition, with few exceptions the counselor needs to work with significant adults in the child's world, especially parents and teachers, to carry out change in the child's environment. For an excellent example, see Nathan (1992).

Knowledge of Research and Clinical Literatures

It is also important for school psychologists to be knowledgeable about the clinical and research literature available on treatment guidelines for specific disorders of childhood. There are many reference materials available that specifically address prevalence, specific features, etiology, and treatment guidelines for children who have childhood DSM-III-R mental disorders that frequently lead to a counseling referral, such as attention deficit–hyperactivity disorders, conduct disorders, anxiety disorders, and mood disorders (Barkley, 1990; Hughes, 1988; Kendall, 1991; Kernberg & Chazan, 1991; Kratochwill & Morris, 1991; Stark, 1990). It also is important to have available literature on children's reactions, adjustment, and recovery in relation to such life stressors as loss, abuse, and handicaps. Children dealing with these issues are likely counseling candidates. Fortunately, there is a growing body of research findings on the effects of life events as stressors that negatively affect children's development (Cook & Dworkin, 1992; Johnson, 1986). The literature on the effects of divorce of parents on children's development (Hodges, 1991) and death of parents (Blom, Cheney, & Snoddy, 1986) are important resources offering useful perspectives. As more children experience a portion of their lives in single-parent homes and with stepparents, researchers are investigating the impact of each (Whitehead, 1993). In addition, as professionals have become aware of the high incidence and grave impact of child sexual abuse, conceptual models, research findings, and applications to counseling have been forthcoming (Cicchetti & Carlson, 1989; James, 1989; Tharinger, 1990; Tharinger & Horton, 1992; Webb, 1991).

Knowledge of Children's Play and Play Therapy

Play in a counseling relationship is to the child what verbalization is to the adult (Garbarino et al., 1989). Play is the natural and comfortable medium of expression for children. It is a medium for expressing feelings, exploring relationships, describing experiences, disclosing wishes, and building solutions. Children may not discuss their feelings, but may act them out. Thus, play can be the natural medium for much of counseling or therapy with children. Play therapy does not belong to a particular theoretical orientation. It is a medium, a method of expression and communication. The use of play in therapy has been described from many theoretical perspectives (Kissel, 1990; Schaefer & O'Connor, 1983), including a psychoanalytic perspective (Esan, 1983), a client-centered perspective (Guerney, 1983), a cognitive-behavioral perspective (Meichenbaum, 1977), and a cognitive-developmental perspective (Harter, 1983). The use of play therapy has also been hearalded in work with traumatized children (James, 1989) and children in crises (Webb, 1991).

Erikson (1977) has described play in a broad sense to mean the use of imagination to try out ways of mastering and adapting to the world, to express emotion, to recreate past situations or imagine future situations, and to develop new models of existence. From Erikson's view, problems that cannot be solved in reality can be resolved through doll play, dramatics, sports, art, or playing house. Similarly, Bettelheim (1987) states that to understand children, their play must be understood. Children use play to work through and master quite complex psychological difficulties of the past and the present. From children's play an understanding of how they see and construe the world, what they would like it to be, and a sense of their concerns and problems are gained. Through play, children express what they cannot put into words. Children do not play spontaneously only to pass time: What children choose to play is motivated by their inner processes, desires, problems, and anxieties (Bettelheim, 1987).

It is essential that a counselor working with children respect their need for expression through play. The presence and use of toys and play materials in a counselor's office indicates to children that it is a place for children, that their world is understood there, and that they can be children there. Play materials invite children to participate and establish a natural means of communication that does not require or depend upon verbal interaction. Children's play becomes the medium of exchange and is utilized by the counselor to build a therapeutic relationship, to understand the child, to solve problems, and to practice solutions.

Knowledge of Psychopharmacology

Children are increasingly being treated by practitioners in the medical community with medication, particularly for seizure disorders, attention deficit–hyperactivity disorder, and depression. It is important that practitioners counseling in the schools have a working knowledge of the effects of medication on children, how they can be used as an adjunct to counseling, and how to assist children in helping them understand and be in compliance with medication (for resources, see Barkley, 1990; Dulcan, 1992; Gadow & Pomeroy, 1881; Green, 1991).

Knowledge of Professional Ethics

It is extremely important for school psychologists delivering counseling services in the schools to have and apply a working knowledge of professional ethics. Both the NASP Principles for Professional Ethics (this volume, Appendix I) and the newly revised Ethical Principles of Psychologists and Code of Conduct (APA, 1992) provide guidelines in the areas of competence, integrity, responsibility, and respect and concern for others, which guide general practice. More specific standards on assessment, therapy, privacy, and confidentiality that apply to the practice of counseling also are included in these guidelines.

BEST PRACTICES

A seven-stage model of best practices in school-based individual counseling with elementary students is presented below, giving a step-by-step guide from referral to termination and evaluation of the counseling intervention (see Table 1). To facilitate discussion, the counseling process has been divided into stages; however, boundaries between stages may not be clearly evident in practice.

Stage 1: Assess Appropriateness of Referral for Individual School-Based Counseling

When a referral for school-based counseling is received, an evaluation of the referral needs to be made. A review of both the child's school records and information from the referral source about the reason for referral, presenting problem(s), and steps already taken to alleviate the problem(s) precedes a judgment about the appropriateness of the referral for intervention in general, and individual counseling in particular. Alternative interventions, such as changing the child's classroom assignment or routine, consulting with the child's teachers, creating a behavior management plan, working with the child's family, group counseling, designing a joint home–school management plan, or referring the child for assistance outside school, may be more appropriate choices than individual school-based counseling, as discussed earlier.

Observations, interviews, and sometimes formal psychological assessment conducted by the likely counselor or another member of the psychological services team also may be needed to inform these decisions. The level of necessary assessment is determined, in part, by the nature and degree of severity of the problem the child is exhibiting. Informal assessment may provide enough information to determine the child's need for individual counseling. In other cases formal assessment may be necessary. Assessment information gathered at this stage also may be used as a pretest to provide the basis from which to develop goals and, during the course of individual counseling, to judge whether goals have been met.

During this first stage, the child's parents or guardians need to be contacted to gain information and, if the decision is made to pursue counseling, to obtain their permission. It is recommended that the school psychologist arrange to meet with the child's parents or contact them by phone to begin developing a relationship that is likely to be vital to the effectiveness of the counseling intervention. Parents can pro-

vide the school psychologist with important information about family, developmental, and cultural factors that could influence the success or failure of the counseling intervention. In addition, it is vitally important that the parents, teachers, and other important people in the child's life provide input that influences the counseling plan. Consideration should be given to their needs, viewpoints, and relationships with the child, and provisions need to be made for continuing communication with them during the course of counseling.

Stage 2: Plan for Counseling and Construct General and Specific Goals

To begin planning the counseling intervention, information gathered in Stage 1 provides the basis for understanding the child's needs. Viewing the child from a variety of theoretical orientations provides the basis for hypothesizing about underlying needs and for developing counseling goals and interventions. A theoretical framework, methods, and techniques that are appropriate for the child's difficulties and developmental level and are compatible with the personality and philosophy of the counselor must be chosen. The general counseling goals and methods chosen to attempt to meet those goals need to match the child's cognitive and emotional development. For example, the difficulty that young children have in taking another person's point of view or understanding abstract concepts must be considered when the plans for counseling with them are formulated. Additionally, possible cultural factors that may contribute both to the problem or to constructing an effective intervention should be considered (see, e.g., Vargas & Koss-Chioino, 1992). The level of intervention also must be considered at this stage. The level of intervention relates to the depth in which the counselor delves into emotional issues. Considerations about length of available time relative to the counselor's case load and the school year's end, as well as depth of intervention necessary to bring about positive change, are necessary.

Specific goals for the child may include lessening depression, anger, or anxiety; improving self-concept, interpersonal skills, or impulse control; or developing a repertoire of alternative appropriate behaviors for situations causing the child distress. The specific goals may be developed for the child within the school environment (such as reducing physical aggression in school or increasing participation in class) and within the home environment (such as increasing positive communication with parents or decreasing outbursts of anger at home). These specific goals would necessitate teachers' and parents' participation in modifying the environment, gathering data about the occurrences of behaviors, providing opportunities that make appropriate response by the child

TABLE 1
A Seven-Stage Model for Individual School-Based Counseling

Stage 1: Assess Appropriateness of Referral for Counseling

Evaluate referral to judge appropriateness
Consider alternative interventions to individual counseling
Contact child's parents to obtain information
Observe interview, and/or assess child
Decide on individual counseling
Contact child's parents to obtain permission, develop relationship, and gain input

Stage 2: Plan for Counseling and Construct Goals

Use assessment data as pretest/basis for developing specific counseling goals
Initiate counseling goals
Determine framework and methods to be used
Determine depth of counseling intervention

Stage 3: Begin Counseling

Educate child about counseling
Involve child in planning process
Instill expectation of hope that counseling will benefit
Provide feedback from assessment process
Discuss confidentiality
Discuss rules and limits

Stage 4: Establish a Working Relationship and Implement Plan for Change

Work to develop counselor–child relationship
Listen with empathy
Make emotional connections
Communicate understanding of emotions
Offer emotional support
Summarize, reflect, and be consistent in setting limits
Maintain communication with parents, teachers
Propose environmental interventions as necessary
Be aware of one's own emotional reactions and seek assistance

Stage 5: Continue Counseling and Adjust the Plan for Change

Reevaluate original plan and goals
Administer interim measures and compare to pretest results
Update goals and adjust methods
Provide feedback to child, parents, and teachers

Stage 6: Assess Progress, Develop Plan for Termination, and Terminate

Administer posttest measures and compare to pretest results
Determine whether goals have been met and functioning stabilized
Plan termination, providing adequate time for ending relationship
Terminate counseling
Provide feedback to parents and/or teachers

Stage 7: Evaluate Effectiveness of the Counseling Intervention

Evaluate effectiveness of counseling intervention
Write summary of initial assessment, counseling goals, course of counseling relationship, and evaluation
   of progress
Follow-up with parents/ teachers about continued progress and needs

more likely, and providing positive reinforcers. The level of specificity, wording, and measurement of goals may differ according to the theoretical orientation of the school psychologist. Thus, the measurement of specific goals requires input from the child, teachers, and parents.

Stage 3: Begin Counseling

The primary work at Stage 3 involves preparing the child for the counseling intervention. Eliciting the child's knowledge, feelings, and beliefs about counseling in order to discuss them, and using developmentally appropriate language to share the initial goals and expectations, are part of preparing the child for counseling. It is desirable to give consideration to the child's needs, to involve him or her in the planning process, and to work at instilling an expectation of hope that counseling involves working together to remedy matters that are troubling to the child. It can also be very effective to provide the child feedback from the informal or formal assessment process. An approach taken by Fischer (1985) on individualizing assessment and providing meaningful feedback may be helpful.

Also at this stage guidelines concerning confidentiality need to be explained to everyone involved. Different counselors adopt different policies regarding this issue. For example, some share information with parents concerning the child's general progress while striving to keep the specific content of the counseling sessions confidential. Other counselors inform the child that the parents will have access to information from sessions, but agree to respect the confidentiality of any information the child specifically requests to be kept private. Whatever policy is adopted, parents' legal rights to information about counseling with their children and the legal obligation of counselors to take appropriate action if a threat of harm to the child or others is revealed needs to receive primary consideration. During the beginning phase of counseling, it also is appropriate to discuss limits and rules with the child, such as time and length of sessions and rules about breakage of toys, toy's remaining in the playroom, and the like. However, care should be taken not to overwhelm the child with a long list of rules. Often, limits are understood more easily when they are discussed as the occasion for them arises.

Stage 4: Establish a Working Relationship and Implement the Plan for Change

One of the primary bases for change in counseling lies in the development of the counselor–child relationship. The relationship provides the foundation for improvement and meeting the counseling goals. In order for progress to be made, a base of trust and security in the counseling relationship must be built. Guidelines for establishing the trust necessary for an effective counseling relationship can be found in sev-

eral sources that discuss person-oriented approaches (Thompson & Rudolph, 1992; Wright, Everett, & Roisman, 1986). Listening with empathy, making emotional connections by striving to see and feel the child's world, communicating that understanding, and offering emotional support are essential to building a relationship of trust. Through trust, threatening feelings and thoughts can be examined and new ways of thinking, behaving, and relating can be attempted. Personal characteristics, such as warmth and the counselor's ability to be comfortable with the child's and her or his own thoughts and feelings, will help to establish the conditions necessary for building a relationship of trust with the child. Personal skills for establishing a working relationship with the child also include the ability to summarize, to reflect, and to be consistent, especially with respect to setting limits.

While developing a working relationship, the plan for effecting change is implemented. The qualities and skills used to build the relationship will continue to remain relevant throughout the course of counseling. Among the skills utilized by counselors in this and the following stages are the ability to play, to communicate a sense of humor, to use self-disclosure to promote the child's growth, to use interpretation to make connections among patterns and themes in the child's life, and to use confrontation when necessary. Techniques from various theoretical frameworks need to be implemented — for example, problem-solving strategies from a cognitive-behavioral orientation. It is necessary to maintain communication with parents, teachers, and others working with the child throughout the counseling process. Environmental influences on the child need to be noted and environmental interventions made when necessary. Rather than attempting to take over the roles of others in the child's life, the counselor should encourage the caring and competence of others in relation to the child.

Throughout the counseling process it is essential for the counselor to consider his or her feelings in relation to the child and others involved with the child. Careful and consistent attention to personal feelings will help to clarify emotional reactions related to the counseling relationship, to understand the child's feelings, and to understand the reactions of others to the child. It is common for counselors to experience emotional reactions in their professional relationships that echo past relationships. Awareness that this is happening can help the counselor react to the present child and situation rather than reacting blindly to remnants of past persons and situations. The counselor should not hesitate to arrange for consultation with a colleague if difficulties in understanding and managing emotions within the counseling relationship are encountered. The value that consultation with colleagues holds for improving the practice of school-based counseling cannot be emphasized enough. Awareness that results from meeting to discuss particular cases, theories, methods, techniques, and personal feelings in relation to a particular child is a vital part of one's development as an effective counselor.

Stage 5: Continue Counseling and Adjust the Plan for Change

During the course of counseling, a reevaluation of the original plan, the goals, and progress to date needs to be performed. Mistakes in planning, lack of understanding of the child's culture, changes in the child and the child's environment, and the counseling process itself make ongoing adjustment of the goals and methods that are chosen for counseling essential. Utilization of measures to determine progress and gather further information about the appropriateness of working hypotheses will aid in making decisions about effectiveness of methods and degree of progress toward goals. Periodically during the course of counseling feedback about the progress of the intervention (within the guidelines of confidentiality) needs to be given to the child, the parents, and others who work with the child. Feedback should be honest and be designed to maximize the potential for future improvement.

Stage 6: Assess Progress, Develop a Plan for Termination, and Terminate

In theory, counseling should end when goals have been met and the child's functioning has improved and stabilized. In practice, the decision to end counseling is seldom simple, or ideally planned. Partially met goals, lack of cooperation by significant persons in the child's life, a family move to another city, the psychologist's move to another school or job, and the end of the school year are often the primary reasons for termination of counseling. When few goals have been met and the child is not functioning well, more intensive counseling than the school is able to provide or an entirely different type of intervention may be necessary. If the goals have been met partially, enough progress may have been made so that interactions between the child and significant others are healthier, thus creating an environment more likely to support continued progress. To determine whether progress toward meeting goals has occurred, posttest measures similar to those initially used to develop goals need to be administered and the results compared with initial assessment results.

In planning for termination it is vitally important for the counselor to be sensitive to the significance that the relationship has for the child. Negative feelings, such as anger and sadness, may be evident at the termination of a meaningful relationship. Some children may experience problems associated with earlier separations and losses. Adequate time during the final counseling sessions should be taken to discuss feelings associated with ending the counseling rela-

tionship. Attention also should be paid to positive feelings associated with the child's improvement and plans for the future. Reassurances that the child will be remembered and exchanging keepsakes such as photographs, artwork, or stories written for the child are examples of strategies used by counselors to help the child manage feelings associated with termination. Gradual reduction of counseling time may be helpful in some situations, for example, by scheduling sessions every other week or once a month during the termination phase. Henderson (1987) and Schmukler (1991) thoroughly address the termination process with children and adolescents.

Stage 7: Evaluate Effectiveness of the Counseling Intervention

Systematic evaluation of the effectiveness of school-based counseling interventions is essential in order to improve counseling methods and outcomes (for further information, see Ehly & Dustin, 1989). Attention to concurrent interventions, environmental changes, case progress notes, data from pre- and postassessment measures, and measures of the child's behavior in natural contexts relative to the goals of the counseling intervention provides the information necessary for determining the extent to which counseling has been effective. After termination, a written summary of the precounseling assessment, the counseling goals, and the course of the counseling relationship, as well as an evaluation of the progress made by the child, need to be completed and placed in the appropriate records. Periodic follow-up with parents and/or teachers is recommended in order to trace the child's adjustment and progress after the counseling intervention has ended.

SUMMARY

Children are an underserved population with respect to their mental health needs. Multiple and coordinated interventions designed for children, their families, and their teachers are needed, and school psychologists can play a key role in the delivery of a continuum of school-based psychological services. The provision of individual school-based counseling is one piece of the complex response needed. Fortunately, there currently is a wealth of scholarly and pragmatic material available to the counselor to guide intervention efforts. This chapter presented a developmentally and culturally sensitive orientation to counseling, strongly influenced by a relationship model and strengthened by the therapeutic techniques of attachment, cognitive-behavioral, and systems theories. The adoption of a child–school–family philosophy, involving home and school caregivers in the counseling process, was emphasized throughout. Cultural considerations were strongly emphasized because of the need to provide more relevant services to children from minority groups. The unique and challenging aspects of providing counseling to children in schools were discussed. The many elements necessary to the process of becoming, and developing as, a counselor were stressed, including: extensive education and training in a developmental perspective, cultural considerations, integration of theoretical models for counseling, pertinent research findings, play therapy psychopharmacology, and professional ethics. Finally, a seven-stage framework was offered as a step-by-step guide to *best practices* in school-based counseling with elementary-age children. School psychologists are challenged to integrate their knowledge, skills, and self development as they continue to address the extensive mental health needs of children in the schools.

REFERENCES

Achenbach, T. M. (1990). Conceptualization of developmental psychopathology. In M. Lewis & S. M. Miller (Eds.), *Handbook of developmental psychopathology* (pp. 3–14). New York: Plenum.

Allan, J. (1988). Inscapes of the child's world: Jungian counseling in schools and clinics. Dallas, TX: Spring Publications.

American Psychological Association. (1992). Ethical principles of psychologists and code of conduct. *American Psychologist, 47*(12), 1597–1611.

Arkowitz, H. (1992). Integrative theories of therapy. In D. K. Freedheim, H. J. Freudenberger, J. W. Kessler, S. B. Messer, D. R. Peterson, H. H. Strupp, & P. L. Wachtel (Eds.), *History of psychotherapy: A century of change* (pp. 261– 303). Washington, DC: American Psychological Association.

Barkley, R. A. (1990). *Attention-deficit hyperactivity disorder: A handbook for diagnosis and treatment.* New York: Guilford.

Bettleheim, B. (1987, March). The importance of play. *Atlantic Monthly,* pp. 34–46.

Blom, G. E., Cheney, B. D., & Snoddy, J. E. (1986). *Stress in childhood: An intervention model for teachers and other professionals.* New York: Teachers College Press.

Christenson, S. L., & Conoley, J. C. (Eds.). (1992). *Home-school collaboration: Enhancing children's academic and social competence.* Silver Spring, MD: National Association of School Psychologists.

Cicchetti, D. (1990). A historical perspective on the discipline of developmental psychopathology. In J. Rolf, A. S. Masten, D. Cicchetti, K. H. Nuechterlein, & S. Weintraub (Eds.), *Risk and protective factors in the development of psychopathology* (pp. 2–28). New York: Cambridge University Press.

Cicchetti, D., & Carlson, V. (1989). Child maltreatment: Theory and research on the causes and consequences of child abuse and neglect. New York: Cambridge University Press.

Clarizio, H. F., & McCoy, G. F. (1983). *Behavior disorders in children* (3rd ed.). New York: Harper and Row.

Cook, A. S., & Dworkin, D. S. (1992). *Helping the bereaved: Therapeutic interventions for children, adolescents, and adults.* New York: Basic Books.

D'Amato, R. C., & Rothlisberg, B. A. (1992). *Psychological perspectives on intervention: A case study approach to prescriptions for change.* New York: Longman.

Dennison, S. T. (1989). *Twelve counseling programs for children at risk.* Springfield, IL: Charles C Thomas.

Dennison, S. T., & Glassman, C. K. (1987). *Activities for children in therapy: A guide for planning and facilitating therapy with troubled children.* Springfield, IL: Charles C Thomas.

Dulcan, M. K. (1992). Information for parents and youth on psychotropic medications. *Journal of Child and Adolescent Psychopharmacology, 2*(2), 81–101.

Ehly, S., & Dustin, R. (1989). *Individual and group counseling in schools.* New York: Guilford.

Erikson, E. H. (1977). *Toys and reasons.* New York: Norton.

Esman, A. H. (1983). Psychoanalytic play therapy. In C. E. Schaefer & K. J. O'Connor (Eds.), *Handbook of play therapy* (pp. 11–20). New York: Wiley.

Fischer, C. T. (1985). *Individualizing psychological assessment.* Monterey, CA: Brooks/Cole.

Gadow, K. D., & Pomeroy, J. C. (1991). An overview of psychopharmacotherapy for children and adolescents. In T. R. Kratochwill & R. J. Morris (Eds.), *The practice of child therapy* (2nd ed.; pp. 367–409). New York: Pergamon.

Garbarino, J., Stott, F. M., & the faculty of the Erikson Institute. (1989). *What children can tell us.* San Francisco, CA: Jossey-Bass.

Garmezy, N., Masten, A. S., & Tellegen, A. (1984). The study of stress and competence in children: A building block for developmental psychopathology. *Child Development, 55,* 97–111.

Green, W. H. (1991). *Child and adolescent clinical psychopharmacology.* Baltimore, MD: Williams & Wilkins.

Guerney, L. F. (1983). Client-centered (nondirective) play therapy. In C. E. Schaefer & K. J. O'Connor (Eds.), *Handbook of play therapy* (pp. 21–64). New York: Wiley.

Harter, S. (1983). *Cognitive-developmental considerations in the conduct of play therapy.* In C. E. Schaefer & K. J. O'Connor (Eds.), *Handbook of play therapy* (pp. 95–127). New York: Wiley.

Henderson, P. A. (1987). Terminating the counseling relationship with children. *Elementary School Guidance and Counseling, 22*(2), 143–148.

Hodges, W. F. (1991). *Interventions for children of divorce: Custody, access, and psychotherapy* (2nd ed.). New York: John Wiley & Sons.

Holtzman, W. (1992). *School of the future.* Washington, DC: American Psychological Association.

Hughes, J. N. (1988). *Cognitive behavior therapy with children in schools.* Oxford, England: Pergamon.

James, B. (1989). *Treating traumatized children: New insights and creative interventions.* Lexington, MA: D. C. Heath.

Johnson, J. H. (1986). *Life events as stressors in childhood and adolescence.* Beverly Hills, CA: Sage.

Kazdin, A. E. (1988). *Child psychotherapy: Developing and identifying effective treatments.* New York: Pergamon.

Kazdin, A. E. (1993). Psychotherapy for children and adolescents: Current progress and future research directions. *American Psychologist, 48,* 644–657.

Keat, D. B. (1990). *Child multimodal therapy.* Norwood, NJ: Ablex.

Kendall, P. C. (1991). *Child and adolescent therapy: Cognitive-behavioral procedures.* New York: Guilford.

Kernberg, P. F., & Chazan, S. E. (1991). *Children with conduct disorders: A psychotherapy manual.* New York: Basic Books.

Kissel, S. (1990). *Play therapy: A strategic approach.* Springfield, IL: Charles C Thomas.

Knitzer, J. (1982). *Unclaimed children: The failure of public responsibility to children and adolescents in need of mental health services.* Washington, DC: Children's Defense Fund.

Knitzer, J., Steinberg, Z., & Fleisch, B. (1990). *At the schoolhouse door: An examination of programs and policies for children with behavioral and emotional problems.* New York: Bank Street College of Education.

Koocher, G. P., & D'Angelo, E. J. (1992). Evolution of the practice in child psychotherapy. In D. K. Freedheim (Ed.), *History of psychotherapy: A century of change* (pp. 457–492). Washington, DC: American Psychological Association.

Kratochwill, T. R., & Morris, R. J. (Eds.). (1991). *The practice of child therapy* (2nd ed.). New York: Pergamon.

Lee, E. (1988). Cultural factors in working with Southeast Asian refugee adolescents. *Journal of Adolescence, 11,* 167–179.

Lewis, M. (1990). Challenges to the study of developmental psychopathology. In M. Lewis & S. M. Miller (Eds.), *Handbook of developmental psychopathology* (pp. 29–40). New York: Plenum.

Meichenbaum, D. (1977). *Cognitive-behavioral modification: An integrative approach.* New York: Plenum.

Mordock, J. B. (1991). *Counseling children: Basic principles for helping the troubled and defiant child.* New York: Continuum.

Nathan, W. A. (1992). Integrated multimodal therapy with children with ADHD. *Bulletin of the Menninger Clinic,* pp. 283–312.

Richters, J., & Weintraub, S. (1990). Beyond diathesis: Toward an understanding of high-risk environments. In J. Rolf, A. S. Masten, D. Cicchetti, K. H. Nuechterlein, & S. Weintraub (Eds.), *Risk and protective factors in the development of psychopathology* (pp. 67–96). New York: Cambridge University Press.

Rutter, M. (1990). Psychosocial resilience and protective mechanisms. In J. Rolf, A. S. Masten, D. Cicchetti, K. H. Nuechterlein, & S. Weintraub (Eds.), *Risk and protective factors in the development of psychopathology* (pp. 181–214). New York: Cambridge University Press.

Schaefer, C. E., & O'Connor, K. J. (Eds.). (1983). *Handbook of play therapy.* New York: Wiley.

Schmukler, A. G. (Ed.). (1991). *Saying goodbye: A casebook of termination in child and adolescent analysis and therapy.* Hillsdale, NJ: Analytic Press.

Shirk, S. R. (Ed.). (1988). *Cognitive development and child psychotherapy.* New York: Plenum.

Siegel, E. V. (1991). *Middle class waifs: The psychodynamic treatment of affectively disturbed children.* Hillsdale, NJ: Analytic Press.

Spiegel, S. (1989). *An interpersonal approach to child therapy: the treatment of children and adolescents from an interpersonal point of view.* New York: Columbia University Press.

Stark, K. D. (1990). *Childhood depression: School-based intervention.* New York: Guilford.

Sue, D. W. (1990). Culture-specific strategies in counseling: A conceptual framework. *Professional Psychology: Research and Practice, 21*(6), 424–433.

Sue, D. W., & Sue, D. (1990). *Counseling the culturally different: Theory and practice* (2nd ed.). New York: Wiley.

Sue, S., & Zane, N. (1987). The role of culture and cultural techniques in psychotherapy: A critique and reformulation. *American Psychologist, 42*(1), 37–45.

Tharinger, D. (1990). The impact of child sexual abuse on developing sexuality. *Professional Psychologist: Research and Practice, 21,* 331–337.

Tharinger, D., & Horton, C. B. (1992). Family–school partnerships: The response to child sexual abuse as a challenging example. In S. L. Christenson & J. C. Conoley (Eds.), *Home–school collaboration: Enhancing children's academic and social competence* (pp. 467–486). Silver Spring, MD: National Association of School Psychologists.

Tharinger, D., & Lambert, N. (1990). Contributions of developmental psychology to school psychology. In T. Gutkin & C. Reynolds (Eds.), *Handbook of school psychology* (2nd ed.). New York: Wiley.

Thompson, C. L., & Rudolph, L. B. (1992). *Counseling children* (3rd ed.). Pacific Grove, CA: Brooks/Cole.

Tuma, J. M. (1989). Mental health services for children: The state of the art. *American Psychologist, 44,* 188–199.

Vargas, L. A., & Koss-Chioino, J. D. (Eds.). (1992). *Working with culture: Psychotherapeutic interventions with ethnic minority children and adolescents.* San Francisco, CA: Jossey-Bass.

Vernon, A. (1989). *Thinking, feeling, behaving: An emotional education curriculum for children grades 1–6.* Champaign, IL: Research Press.

Webb, N. B. (1991). *Play therapy with children in crisis: A casebook for practitioners.* New York: Guilford.

Whitehead, B. D. (1993, April). Dan Quayle was right. *Atlantic Monthly,* pp. 47–84.

Wright, L., Everett, F., & Roisman, L. (1986). *Experimental psychotherapy with children.* Baltimore: Johns Hopkins University Press.[TO]

ANNOTATED BIBLIOGRAPHY

Dennison, S. T. (1989). *Twelve counseling programs for children at risk.* Springfield, IL: Charles C Thomas.
This book presents the author's model for therapy practice, which combines several theoretical orientations but primarily derives from behavioral therapy. Process and content goals, as well as suggested means of attainment, are presented for both individual and group therapy. Additionally, presenting symptoms, treatments of choice, possible goals, assessment instruments, possible session focuses, and suggested techniques are presented for twelve problem areas (school-related problems, low self-esteem, aggressive/acting-out problems, children in crisis, childhood depression, family life changes, children of substance abusers, sexually abused children, peer relationship problems, hyperactivity/short attention span, physically abused children, and neglected children). This book provides a variety of activity ideas for the beginning counselor.

James, B. (1989). *Treating traumatized children: New insights and creative interventions.* Lexington, MA: D. C. Heath.
This book provides an in-depth view of states that result from trauma and guidelines for treatment. The traumagenic states that are discussed and for which treatment is suggested include self-blame, powerlessness, loss and betrayal, fragmentation of bodily experience, stigmatization, eroticization, destructiveness, dissociative/multiple disorder, and attachment disorder. This book is an excellent source for both beginning counselors and those working with traumatized children.

Kissel, S. (1990). *Play therapy: A strategic approach.* Springfield, IL: Charles C Thomas.

This book provides a broad approach to play therapy that can be used by clinicians from a variety of theoretical orientations. Suggested techniques include the use of modeling, drawing, construction, cameras, computers, board games, storytelling, and relaxation. Specific activities make this book an excellent resource for the beginning counselor.

Spiegel, S. (1989). *An interpersonal approach to child therapy: The treatment of children and adolescents from an interpersonal point of view.* New York: Columbia University Press.

This book presents therapy from an interpersonal and developmental perspective. The use of play and metaphors is discussed, and a description of the course of therapy from initial sessions and limit setting to termination provides an easily read guide for the beginning therapist.

Vargas, L. A., & Koss-Chioino, J. D. (Eds.). *Working with culture: Psychotherapeutic interventions with ethnic minority children and adolescents.* San Francisco: Jossey-Bass.

Working with Culture discusses therapeutic issues and suggested intervention techniques when working with African American, Hispanic American, Asian American, and Native American children. It presents culture-related issues that affect therapy, including developmental and environmental perspectives (i.e., poverty, racism, acculturation, and normative behavior) and provides a model for understanding culturally responsive psychotherapies. This book is an excellent source for all counselors, especially those who work with children of culturally diverse backgrounds.

76

Best Practices in Transition Services

Edward M. Levinson
Indiana University of Pennsylvania

OVERVIEW

It is late one Friday afternoon in the dead of winter. The snow has just begun to fall as you leave Testa U. Child High School. You have just participated in a multidisciplinary staffing on Susan, a 16-year-old special education student who was due for her triennial reevaluation. You had first recommended that Susan be placed in a special education program when she was 10 years old, and this was the third time you had evaluated her. This evaluation was no different than any of the others: curriculum-based assessment results, standardized test scores, and observational and interview data continued to suggest functioning within the range of educable mental retardation; no evidence of social or emotional difficulties; recommendation for continued placement in the current special education class. The multidisciplinary team has relied heavily on you for program planning, and has accepted your recommendation for continued special education programming.

As you walk down the steps of the school, your thoughts begin to shift to your imminent week-long vacation to Hawaii. It is a vacation for which you had been preparing for years. As you begin to dream of white sand beaches and lais, you are interrupted by a coworker who has just participated with you in the staffing on Susan. Your colleague asks, "What do you think Susan's life will be like next year when she leaves school?" There is a bit of silence. "I don't know." There is more silence; then your colleague bids you farewell. Your mind wanders back to your work with Susan and then abruptly shifts to all the thought and effort that went into planning your vacation. Your mind wanders back to Susan and your stomach feels empty. What will happen to Susan . . .

Until recently, evidence suggests that for students with disabilities like Susan, little effort has gone into post-school planning. As Halloran (1989) has said:

> Some students reach the end of their public school experience poorly prepared for competitive employment or independent living. As students approach the end of their formal schooling, we frequently ask what

they will be doing after school ends. Unfortunately, when we look back to determine what preparations have been made for students to live and work in our communities, we often see a series of disjointed efforts lacking a focus on skills necessary to confront the new expectations of adult life. (p. xiii)

Statistics clearly support Halloran's assertion. The President's Committee on the Employment of the Handicapped reports that following the completion of school, only 21% of persons with disabilities become fully employed, 40% will be underemployed and at the poverty level, and 26% will be on welfare (Pennsylvania Departments of Education and of Labor and Industry, 1986). Similarly, Rusch and Phelps (1987) have reported that 67% of persons with disabilities in the United States between the ages of 16 and 64 years are not working. Of those persons with disabilities who are working, 75% are employed on a part-time basis, and of those who are not employed 67% indicate that they would like to be employed. Similarly, statewide surveys in Florida (Fardig, Algozzine, Schwartz, Hensel, & Westling, 1985), Washington (Edgar, 1987), Colorado (Mithaug, Horiuchi, & Fanning, 1985), Vermont (Hasazi, Gordon, & Roe, 1985), and Nebraska (Schalock & Lilley, 1986) have indicated that the employment rate for persons with disabilities ranges between 45% and 70%, depending upon disability and geographical location. Between 64% and 82% of this population report living at home with a parent or guardian. According to Edgar (1987), 42% of learning-disabled and behaviorally disturbed students leave school before graduating, as do 18% of mentally retarded students.

More recently, the *Twelfth Annual Report to Congress on the Implementation of the Education of the Handicapped Act* (U.S. Department of Education, Office of Special Education and Rehabilitative Services, 1990) indicated that 47% of all students with disabilities do not graduate from high school with either a diploma or certificate of completion. These data are corroborated by Wagner and Shaver (1989), who found that 44% of students with disabilities failed to graduate from high school and 36% of students with disabilities dropped out of school. As Ysseldyke, Algozzine, and Thurlow (1992) report, studies that have compared special education dropout rates with control group dropout rates or normative data have consistently shown that students with disabilities leave school more often than students without disabilities.

More recent data corroborate these findings but suggest some encouraging trends as well. D'Amico and Marder (1991), in a longitudinal study that included a nationally representative sample of youths with disabilities out of school at least 1 month and no more than 2 years, reported that 52% of youths with disabilities were employed in 1987. However, this employment rate increased to 67% in 1989. Whereas employment rates increased in almost all disability categories, rates varied by disability category. While 67% of learning-disabled persons were employed in 1989, only 48% of emotionally disturbed, 56% of mildly and moderately retarded, and 10% of multiply handicapped persons were reported to be employed (Marder & D'Amico, 1992). In all disability categories other than learning disability with speech impairment, the employment rates of youths with disabilities was significantly lower than the employment rate of nondisabled youths (Marder & D'Amico, 1992).

There is little doubt that, given the high unemployment and underemployment rates among persons with disabilities, the high percentage who continue to live at home following the completion of school, and the elevated dropout rate among students with disabilities, efforts in the area of special education have not resulted in their successful integration into society. School psychologists, who have historically played an integral part in the special education process, must assume some responsibility for such a dismal state of affairs. Historically, school psychologists have had little involvement in the vocational or career planning of students with disabilities (Shepard & Hohenshil 1983; Levinson, 1988, 1990), despite the fact that they possess skills that, it can be argued, are critical to effective vocational planning, and despite the standards set by the National Association of School Psychologists (NASP, 1992). (For citation of these standards, see NASP [1992] or Levinson, this volume, on Vocational Assessment.)

In an effort to promote successful transition from school to work and community living, federal and state governments have made transition services a priority for all students with disabilities. In the landmark document "OSERS Programming for the Transition of Youth with Disabilities: Bridges from School to Working Life" Madeline Will, of the Office of Special Education and Rehabilitative Services, defined transition as follows:

> The transition from school to working life is an outcome-oriented process encompassing a broad array of services and experiences that lead to employment. Transition is a period that includes high school, the point of graduation, additional postsecondary education or adult services, and the initial years of employment. Transition is a bridge between the security and structure offered by the school and the opportunities and risks of adult life. Any bridge requires both a solid span and a secure foundation at either end. The transition from school to work and adult life requires sound preparation in the secondary school, adequate support at the point of school leaving, and secure opportunities and services, if needed, in adult situations. (Will, 1986, p. 10)

Will's document is the generic root from which transition programs have developed. In October 1990, Congress enacted the Education of the Handicapped Act Amendments of 1990 (Public Law 101—476), an amendment of PL 94-142, the Education of the Handicapped Act (EHA). Under this new law, the name EHA has been changed to the Individuals With Disabilities Education Act (IDEA). IDEA requires that transition plans be developed for all students with disabilities and be included in the students' IEPs by the time the students reach age 16. Section 602(a) of IDEA defines transition services as

> a coordinated set of activities for a student, designed within an outcome-oriented process, which promotes movement from school to post-school activities, including post-secondary education, vocational training, integrated employment (including supported employment), continuing and adult education, adult services, independent living, or community participation. The coordinated set of activities shall be based upon the individual student's needs, taking into account the student's preferences and interests, and shall include instruction, community experiences, the development of employment and other post-school adult living objectives, and, when appropriate, acquisition of daily living skills and functional vocational evaluation. (Education of the Handicapped Act Amendments of 1990, pl 101-476, Section 602(a) [20 USC 1401(a)]

PL 101-476 requires that a student's IEP address the issue of transition and that transition planning be initiated by at least age 16. Specifically, IDEA lists the following additional requirements for the IEP:

> . . . a statement of needed transition services for students beginning no later than age 16 and annually thereafter (and, when determined appropriate for the individual, beginning at age 14 or younger), including when appropriate, a statement of the interagency responsibilities or linkages (or both) before the student leaves the school setting, and . . . in the case where a participating agency, other than the educational agency, fails to provide the agreed-upon services, the educational agency shall reconvene the IEP team to identify alternative strategies to meet the transition objectives.

BASIC CONSIDERATIONS IN TRANSITIONAL PROGRAMMING

While the professional literature has generally treated transition planning separately from vocational assessment, the two are intimately related. Successful transition planning cannot occur without the information gleaned from a comprehensive, functional, vocational assessment. Conversely, vocational assessment data have little value if they are not used to recommend services designed to facilitate successful transition from school to work and community living. Given the clear relationship between vocational assessment and transition planning, it makes little sense to discuss each separately. Transition planning should be embedded in an overall vocational assessment and planning model. The transdisciplinary vocational assessment (TVA) model advocated by this author (Levinson, 1993) and discussed in the chapter on vocational assessment elsewhere in this volume essentially integrates the two processes. The data gathered through TVA can be used to recommend the services a student needs to make a successful adjustment to work and community living. Based upon the results of the TVA, a transition plan can be developed and included in a student's individual education plan.

As to the information needed by a school psychologist or other school professional to facilitate the transition process of students with disabilities, one must first consider what skills the student needs to adjust to community living and to obtain and maintain employment. Generally, these skills can be broken down into three major areas: *daily living skills*, *personal/social skills*, and *occupational/vocational skills* (Wehman, Moon, Everson, Wood, & Barcus, 1988). The daily living skills that are necessary for independent living include managing finances, maintaining a home, caring for personal needs, buying and preparing food, buying and caring for clothing, engaging in recreation and leisure pursuits, and being mobile within the community. Personal/social skills include maintaining hygiene and appearance, accepting praise and criticism, and exhibiting situationally appropriate behavior, appropriate interpersonal skills, adequate problem-solving skills, and adequate communication skills. Occupational/vocational skills include understanding and exploring occupational and vocational alternatives, exhibiting appropriate work habits and behaviors, possessing marketable vocational skills, and exhibiting appropriate job-seeking skills. The assessment of these areas, in addition to those traditionally assessed by school psychologists, is especially critical to the development of a transition plan.

Having identified the individual needs of a particular student and having determined the particular skills that this student needs to learn to make a successful transition, school personnel must structure the educational curriculum accordingly. Generally, this will involve the development of a "functional curriculum." A functional curriculum is one in which the goals and objectives are based upon the demands of adult life across a variety of settings (Wehman et al., 1988). In such a curriculum, the particular skills a student lacks across the domains cited previously (daily living, personal/social, occupational/vocational) are taught in a way that enables the student to utilize them in the workplace, in leisure and residential settings, and in community facilities. Given the difficulty that persons with severe disabilities have in generalizing skills across settings, it is sometimes necessary to conduct instruction appropriate to a particular setting in that setting itself. Consequently, professionals involved in transition services must be familiar with residential and community-based educational programs. For more information on Life-Centered Career Education, Functional Community-Based Special Education, Work Adjustment, Training Programs, and other organized programs designed to accomplish the goals listed above, the reader is referred to Levinson, Peterson, and Elston (in press).

Knowledge of local employment options available for individuals with disabilities is also necessary for professionals developing transition plans for students. Generally, the options include *competitive employment*, *supported employment*, and *sheltered employment*. The appropriateness of each of these employment options for a particular student depends upon that student's individual skills. Competitive employment options are those in which individuals are placed in competitively salaried community jobs without the provision of ongoing support services. Supported employment options are those in which individuals are placed in jobs with special assistance from "job coaches" who provide ongoing support (including training, retraining, problem resolution, etc.). Sheltered employment options are those in which individuals are placed in businesses operated by human service agencies (typically termed *sheltered workshops* or *work activity centers*). The various residential options that are available for persons with disabilities in the community must also be considered by transition personnel when planning for students. Residential options may include independent living in single-family or group homes and apartments, living with family or friends, foster homes, nursing homes, and other private and public residential facilities. Again, the appropriateness of each of these alternatives will be determined by the unique needs and circumstances of each student.

Finally, school psychologists and other professionals involved in transition services must be knowledgeable about the support service agencies in the local community, and they must understand the nature of the services provided by these agencies and the extent to which these agencies can assist in the transition process. As will be discussed shortly, the transition process involves a variety of school and community professionals working together as a team to provide for the needs of persons with disabilities. To the extent that various team members understand, respect, and utilize the expertise and services provided by one another, the transition process will be greatly facilitated.

BEST PRACTICES IN TRANSITION PROGRAMMING

Components of Effective Transition Programs

Halloran (1989) suggests that effective transition programs have three essential components: (a) The program involves the families of persons with disabilities as equal partners in planning and implementing activities that are designed to facilitate independent functioning; (b) the program is community-based, providing persons with disabilities with opportunities to succeed in employment and other aspects of community life; and (c) the program is based upon working partnerships among schools, businesses, and community agencies. Additionally, effective programs ensure that planning for postschool adjustment begins early in a student's educational career; that written, individualized plans specifying transition services are a part of each student's IEP; that attempts are made to integrate persons with disabilities with persons without disabilities; that the educational curriculum focuses upon instruction of relevant and functional life skills; and that a large part of instruction takes place in the community.

Development of Transition Programs

As has been suggested earlier, transition programming involves a variety of school and community professionals. Consequently, the initial step in developing a transition program at the local level is to identify, organize, and mobilize these various professionals and agencies. Wehman et al. (1988) advocate the establishment of a local core transition team to include such professionals as a special education administrator, a vocational education administrator, a vocational rehabilitation administrator, the director of mental health/mental retardation, a developmental disabilities planning council member, and a parent and/or client advocate. According to Wehman et al. (1988), this local core team has the responsibility of conducting a needs assessment to determine the extent to which existing school, employment, and adult service programs are capable of providing the services which persons with disabilities require to make a successful transition from school to community living. For example, school programs must be evaluated to determine the extent to which educational/vocational programs are providing students with the skills necessary to obtain employment available in the local

community. Employment programs must be evaluated to determine the extent to which they are successful in placing persons with disabilities in jobs. Adult service programs must be evaluated to determine the type of vocational assessment and postsecondary training services that are provided and the availability of supported and sheltered employment opportunities. The quality of community living arrangements, transportation, recreational and leisure programs, and medical and psychological services that are available in the local area must also be evaluated.

On the basis of the needs assessment data that are gathered, the team recommends improvements in school and community services and begins developing transition planning procedures. Decisions such as the age at which to begin formal transition planning, the types of students to receive transition services, the professionals to be involved in transition planning, the roles of these professionals, and so forth are made by this local core team.

A major responsibility of the core planning team is to establish formal, written interagency agreements, which have the purpose of further defining the various roles school and community agencies will assume in transition programming. Because many such interagency agreements have been developed at the state level, these should be reviewed and considered when local agreements are developed. According to Wehman et al. (1988), the core team identifies and verifies participation of key agencies and organizations, establishes flow patterns of handicapped students across local agencies and organizations (i.e., when a particular student is likely to be serviced by a particular agency and the nature of the services likely to be provided), and identifies the means by which services will be evaluated.

Individualized Transitional Programming

Once interagency agreements have been established that specify the kinds of transition services to be provided by the various agencies (school and community) involved and the population to whom these services are provided, individual transition programming can be initiated. According to Wehman et al. (1988), the first step in implementing this programming is to set up individual transition planning teams (ITPTs) for all students for whom plans are to be developed. Both school and community agency personnel participate on these teams. Appropriate school personnel include teachers (regular, special education, and vocational education), counselors, psychologists, and administrators. Representatives from community agencies such as mental health/mental retardation, vocational rehabilitation, and social services also participate on the ITPT. Parents need to be involved in these meetings, since research has indicated that parental participation increases the effectiveness of transitional services (Hasazi et al., 1985; Schalock & Lilley, 1986).

Since an overlap obviously exists between the school professionals who are involved in development of the student's individual education plan and those who are to be involved in transition planning, it makes sense to conduct transition planning as a part of annual IEP meetings for students with disabilities (as stated previously, PL 101-476 now requires that IEPs address transition by age 16). At a certain designated point during a student's educational career (the point at which transition planning is to be initiated, and no later than age 16), the IEP team should be expanded to include relevant community agency personnel. Although the age at which transition planning should begin is debatable, it is the author's opinion that it should be initiated at least 4 years before the student leaves school. In that the transition planning process for students with severe disabilities may be more involved and time-consuming than it is for other students, transition planning should probably be initiated earlier in the educational career of these students.

Roles for School Psychologists

It is likely that school psychologists will become increasingly involved in transition planning as a result of their extensive involvement in the assessment and programming of students with disabilities. Although the specific role that school psychologists will assume in the process is still undefined, it is clear that the skills possessed by school psychologists are critical to the development and implementation of successful transition plans.

At the present time, a variety of professionals assume major responsibility for the development and implementation of transition programs. Although no agreement currently exists as to who should assume this major responsibility, there are a number of "transition specialist" training programs for professionals with such titles as job coach, individual living specialist, supported employment, specialist, rehabilitation counselor, and special education teacher. The competencies acquired in these programs clearly overlap with the knowledge and skills of school psychologists. In their study of the competencies taught in 13 university "transition specialist" training programs across the country, Baker, Geiger, and deFur (1988) found that general knowledge of learning theory (particularly behavioral theory) and assessment were areas in which an extensive amount of training was concentrated. Both Baker et al. (1988) and Marinelli, Tunic, and LeConte (1988) agree that adolescent psychology is a frequently omitted but important area in the training of transition specialists. Clearly, the school psychologist's expertise in assessment, learning and behavior theory, and adolescent

psychology may be particularly useful in transition planning.

From an assessment perspective, school psychologists have much to contribute to transition planning. As mentioned previously, particularly important in transition planning will be evaluation of interpersonal and social skills, independent living skills, and vocational skills. School psychologists working at the secondary school level may wish to alter their assessment strategies somewhat in order to emphasize these areas. For example, school psychologists might choose to incorporate measures of vocational interests and aptitudes and social skills (through interviews, observations, and paper-and-pencil tests) into their assessments. A number of time- and cost-efficient procedures for gathering this information are available to school psychologists and are discussed elsewhere (Levinson, 1993; Kapes & Mastie, 1988). Likewise, school psychologists might also wish to incorporate an evaluation of functional living skills into their assessments. An instrument such as the Social and Prevocational Information Battery (Halpern, Rafeld, Irvin, & Link, 1975) provides functional skills assessment data that can be utilized in transition programming.

School psychologists' knowledge of learning and behavior theory and of adolescent psychology allows them to serve as effective consultants to teachers (regular, special education, vocational education), rehabilitation counselors, job coaches, and employers relative to the conditions under which optimum learning and performance might be attained. Because a substantial amount of training may occur outside the school in job, community, or residential settings, school psychologists will have to prepare themselves to provide consultative services in settings other than the office or classroom. As a consultant, the school psychologist may also function as a liason among parents, other team members, community service agencies, and employers; or, in some cases, they may actually initiate the development of transition planning.

Other roles for school psychologists in the transition process are direct intervention, in-service, and research. From a direct intervention perspective, the school psychologist can facilitate transition by initiating development of social skills training programs. Such programs might be most effective when implemented in residential, community, or employment settings. School psychologists might conduct in-service workshops on the use of assessment data in transition programming for those involved in the development of transition plans, and on basic issues in adolescent psychology or learning for those professionals involved in direct training of skills necessary for successful transition. Finally, the effectiveness of the various programs designed to promote acquisition of the skills required for successful transition needs to be determined and the success that local school and community services have in facilitating the transition of students from school to work and community must be evaluated.

SUMMARY

As the final impact of recent federal legislation aimed at facilitating the transition between school and adult living is realized, it is likely that an increased number of school psychologists will become involved in transition planning. School psychologists, working as part of a transition team comprised of both school and community professionals, will need to upgrade their knowledge of vocational and independent living skills assessment, functional curricula, and community-based education; as well as the various employment and residential options available in their local community. Although the exact role school psychologists will assume in transition planning is still undefined, their assessment, counseling, consultation, and research skills will prove to be valuable assets to the development, implementation, and evaluation of transition programs.

REFERENCES

Baker B. C., Geiger, W. L., & deFur, S. (1988, November). *Competencies for transition personnel*. Paper presented at the Mid-East Regional Conference of the Career Development Division of the Council for Exceptional Children, White Sulphur Springs, WV.

D'Amico, R., & Marder, C. (1991). *The early work experiences of youth with disabilities: Trends in employment rates and job characteristics*. Menlo Park, CA: SRI International.

Edgar, E. (1987). Secondary programs in special education: Are many of them justifiable? *Exceptional Children, 53*(6), 555–561.

Fardig, D. B., Algozzine, R. F., Schwartz, S. E., Hensel, J. E., & Westling. D. L. (1985). Postsecondary vocational adjustment of rural, mildly handicapped students. *Exceptional Children, 52*(2), 115–121.

Halloran, W. (1989). Foreword. In D. E. Berkell & J. M. Brown (Eds.), *Transition from school to work for persons with disabilities* (pp. xiii–xvi). New York: Longman.

Halpern, A. S., Raffeld, P., Irvin, L. K., & Link, R. (1975). *Social and prevocational information battery*. Monterey, CA: Publishers Test Service.

Hasazi, S. B., Gordon, L. R., & Roe, C. A. (1985). Factors associated with the employment status of handicapped youth exiting high school from 1979 to 1983. *Exceptional Children, 51*(6), 455-469.

Kapes, J. T., & Mastie, M. M. (1988). *A counselor's guide to career assessment instruments* (2nd ed.). Alexandria, VA: National Career Development Association.

Levinson, E. M. (1988). Correlates of vocational practice among school psychologists. *Psychology in the Schools, 25*(3), 297–305.

Levinson, E. M. (1990). Vocational assessment involvement and use of the Self-Directed Search by school psychologists. *Psychology in the Schools, 27*(3), 217–227.

Levinson, E. M. (1993). *Transdisciplinary vocational assessment: Issues in school-based programs*. Brandon, VT: Clinical Psychology Publishing Co.

Levinson, E. M., Peterson, M., & Elston, R. (in press). Vocational counseling with the mentally retarded. In D. C. Strohmer & H. T. Prout (Eds.), *Counseling and psychotherapy with mentally retarded persons*. Brandon, VT: Clinical Psychology Publishing.

Marder, C., & D'Amico, R. (1992). *How well are youth with disabilities really doing? A comparison of youth with disabilities and youth in general*. Menlo Park, CA: SRI International.

Marinelli, R. P., Tunic, R. H., & Leconte, P. (1988, November). *Vocational evaluation education: Regional programs*. Paper presented at the Mid-East Regional Conference of the Career Development Division of the Council for Exceptional Children, White Sulphur Springs, WV.

Mithaug, D. E., Horiuchi, C. N., & Fanning, P. N. (1985). A report on the Colorado statewide follow-up survey of special education students. *Exceptional Children, 51*(5), 397–404.

National Association of School Psychologists. (1992). *Professional conduct manual*. Washington, DC: NASP.

Pennsylvania Departments of Education and of Labor and Industry. (1986). *Pennsylvania Transition From School to the Workplace*, 3, 7, 83.

Rusch, F. R., & Phelps, L. A. (1987). Secondary special education and transition from school to work: A national priority. *Exceptional Children, 53*(6), 487–492.

Schalock, R. L., & Lilley, M. A. (1986). Placement from community-based mental retardation programs: How well do clients do after 8 to 10 years? *American Journal of Mental Deficiency, 90*(6), 669–676.

Shepard, J. W., & Hohenshil, T. H. (1983). Career development functions of practicing school psychologists: A national study. *Psychology in the Schools, 20*, 445–449.

U.S. Department of Education, Office of Special Education and Rehabilitative Services. (1990). *Twelfth annual report to Congress on the implementation of the Education of the Handicapped Act*. Washington, DC: Government Printing Office.

Wagner, M., & Shaver, D. M. (1989). *The transition experiences of youth with disabilities: A report from the National Longitudinal Transitional Study*. Menlo Park, CA: SRI International.

Wehman, P., Kregel, J., & Barcus, J. M. (1985). From school to work: A vocational transition model for handicapped students. *Exceptional Children, 52*(1), 25–37.

Wehman, P., Moon, M. S., Everson, J. M., Wood, W., & Barcus, J. M. (1988). *Transition from school to work: New challenges for youth with severe disabilities*. Baltimore, MD: Paul H. Brooks Publishing Co.

Will, M. (1986). OSERS programming for the transition of youth with disabilities: Bridges from school to working life. In J. Chadsey-Rusch & C. Hanley-Maxwell (Eds.), *Enhancing transition from school to the workplace for handicapped youth: Personnel preparation implications* (pp. 9–24). Champaign, IL: National Network for Professional Development in Vocational Special Education.

Ysseldyke, J. E., Algozzine, B., & Thurlow, M. L. (1992). *Critical issues in special education* (2nd ed.). Boston: Houghton Mifflin

ANNOTATED BIBLIOGRAPHY

Brolin, D.(Ed.). (1986). *Transition from school to work and adult life*. Columbia, MO: Division on Career Development, Council for Exceptional Children.
This volume, which contains abstracts of more than 80 projects, curricula, teaching methods, and transition models, is a useful

reference guide for professionals and parents interested in the development of transition programs.

Levinson, E. M. (1993). *Transdisciplinary vocational assessment: Issues in school-based programs.* Brandon, VT: Clinical Psychology Publishing Co.

This book presents a model that integrates the vocational assessment and transition planning processes and discusses the development of such a program from both a theoretical and practical perspective. Six school vocational assessment program models are described, as are the roles of curriculum-based and community-referenced assessment in vocational and transition planning. The book addresses the use of assessment data in vocational and transition planning and includes sample forms that can be adapted for use in programs. A bibliography of references for professionals is also included.

McCarthy, P., Everson, J. M., Moon, S., & Barcus, J. M. (Eds.). (1985). *School-to-work transition for youth with severe disabilities.* Richmond: Virginia Commonwealth University, Project Transition Into Employment.

This compendium of articles by various authors describes step-by-step procedures for the development and implementation of transitional programs for severely handicapped students.

Wehman, P., Moon, M. S., Everson, J. M., Wood, W., & Barcus, J. M. (1988). *Transition from school to work: New challenges for youth with severe disabilities.* Baltimore, MD: Paul H. Brooks Publishing Co.

This text provides a comprehensive overview of transition services, including a discussion of the initial planning process and development of interagency agreements, professional and parent roles in the transition process, and individualized transitional planning.

Technical Assistance for Special Populations Program (TASPP), The National Center for Research in Vocational Education, Department of Vocational and Technical Education, The University of Illinois–345 Education Building 1310 South Sixth St., Champaign, IL 61820. Dr. Carolyn Maddy-Bernstein, Director. 217-333-0807.

TASPP is a resource center specifically designed to assist in the transition of special needs learners to workplaces and continuing education programs; it can provide professionals with information on model programs, project materials, and so forth.

77

Best Practices in Counseling Programs for Secondary Students

Pauline M. Pagliocca
Tulane University

Steve R. Sandoval
University of Nebraska–Lincoln

OVERVIEW

School Psychologists and Counseling

At the secondary level, school psychologists function in a variety of professional roles such as psychoeducational evaluator, consultant, student services coordinator, community liaison, in-service trainer, and supervisor. In addition to these traditional roles, practitioners report that they are increasingly being called upon to provide individual and group counseling services to students (Huebner, 1993). As with other areas of practice, psychologists not only provide direct service to pupils but also participate in the design, development, and evaluation of counseling programs.

At the same time that many academic trainers are advocating an indirect/consultative services model in the schools (e.g., Conoley & Gutkin, 1986; Elliott & Witt, 1986), practitioners in the field, such as principals (Hartshorne & Johnson, 1985), special education directors (Cheramie & Sutter, 1993), and school psychologists themselves (Huebner, 1993) are calling for school psychologists to play a more active role in student counseling. Despite such interest in "psychologists as counselors," time and skill demands often preclude school psychologists from providing counseling directly to the number of students in need. But psychologists need not choose one end of the direct–indirect continuum over the other. Instead, they can apply their skills at multiple levels of any comprehensive counseling program.

Whether directly involved in student counseling or designing a school's counseling agenda, psychologists can expect their activities to interact and overlap with other professionals in the system. School counselors, social workers, administrators, nurses, and teachers are involved in counseling initiatives (Ehly & Dustin, 1989). And, increasingly, community mental health professionals and paraprofessional volunteers are delivering their services in school settings. Thus, school psychologists will not necessarily enjoy a "unique" role within a counseling program; rather, they can expect to share responsibilities with colleagues equally (and sometimes better) qualified to counsel adolescents and develop school- and system-wide counseling programs.

Use of this Chapter

School psychologists may wish to consult this chapter when considering the counseling needs of students, families, and professionals in their particular schools and the array of program components necessary to meet those needs. No survey of counseling or psychotherapy theories will be provided; other sources (e.g., Corsini & Wedding, 1989) offer more comprehensive and detailed information than can be included here. This chapter also will not advocate any particular approach to intervention; reviews of child and adolescent psychotherapy outcome research (Casey & Berman, 1985; Kazdin, 1990) offer little support favoring any one theoretical model (e.g., psychodynamic, cognitive-behavioral) or method (e.g., individual, group, family) of treatment. Instead, this chapter will discuss the expanding counseling role assumed by many school psychologists and will emphasize the importance of actively collaborating in the development of comprehensive counseling programs at the secondary level. Consistent with the position that school psychologists comprise but one profession involved in counseling secondary school students, the generic term "counselor" will be used throughout this chapter in reference to any professional providing such services in school settings. Finally, this chapter will present a broad range of issues for consideration in determining whether to counsel, who should counsel, and what the scope of the total counseling program should be.

BASIC CONSIDERATIONS

Counseling or Psychotherapy?

When assisting students with emotional and behavioral difficulties, do school psychologists practice *counseling* or do they practice *psychotherapy?* How easily can distinctions be made between the two endeavors? And is it important to do so? A comparison of Patterson and Eisenberg's (1983) account of "counseling" with Kazdin's (1988) description of "psychotherapy" illustrates the difficulties inherent in attempting to differentiate clearly between the two and suggests that dwelling on carefully crafted definitions may not lead to any notable distinctions in actual practice.

> *Counseling* [italics added] is an interactive process characterized by a unique relationship between counselor and client leading to change in the client in one or more of the following areas: (1) Behavior; (2) Personal constructs (ways of construing reality, including self) or emotional concerns relating to these perceptions; (3) Ability to cope with life situations so as to maximize opportunities and minimize adverse environmental conditions; (4) Decision-making knowledge and skill. (Patterson & Eisenberg, 1983, p. 22)

> *Psychotherapy* [italics added] consists of a special interaction between two (or more) individuals where one person (the patient, or client) has sought help for a particular problem, and where another person (the therapist) provides conditions to alleviate that person's distress and to improve functioning in everyday life. The interaction is designed to alter the feelings, thoughts, attitudes, or actions of the person who has sought or has been brought to treatment. (Kazdin, 1988, p. 1)

Obviously, it is difficult to determine where counseling ends and therapy begins. In fact, with the growing popularity of interventions such as short-term therapy, cognitive-behavioral counseling, solution-focused therapy, parent education, and various types of support groups, distinctions once considered informative may no longer serve any useful function. Thus, throughout the remainder of this chapter, the terms "counseling" and "therapy" will be used interchangeably. Generally, however, most school intervention literature relies on the term "counseling," irrespective of the particular discipline or theoretical orientation of the practitioner.

Who Provides Counseling?

Many personnel are involved in counseling in schools. Generally, however, three groups — school psychologists, counselors, and social workers — provide the majority of such services. While acknowledging overlap in functions, Sandoval and Davis (1992) argue for a "unique" counseling role for the school psychologist: "crisis counseling, brief counseling, brief family therapy, vocational counseling for special education children, and social and other skills training" (p. 245). The only support they offer, however, is the extended length of training for the school psychologist, without further reference to any particular component of training (e.g., specialized counsel-

ing course work) that would qualify the psychologist in any of these areas.

Humes and Hohenshil (1987) approach the "uniqueness" issue from a different perspective. While acknowledging certain differences in expertise (e.g., the school psychologist's preparation as a diagnostician), they highlight similarities in training and actual practice which are applicable to the question of who should provide counseling services in the schools.

> All these personnel [counselors, school psychologists, and social workers] provide counseling services, are involved in primary mental health prevention, assist in curricular adaptations for individual pupils, and engage in outcome-oriented efforts to evaluate the productivity of the helping relationships. (Humes & Hohenshil, 1987, p. 39)

Like the blurred lines between counseling and psychotherapy, role distinctions based on professional discipline may reflect little of the actual practice of psychosocial treatment in secondary schools.

Rather than professional identity, the primary criterion for determining who should provide therapeutic services should be competence. That is, who is qualified to provide a particular type of intervention to a specific student or group of students? Both the American Psychological Association (APA, 1992) and the National Association of School Psychologists (NASP, 1992) suggest "competence" as a basic ethical principle in guiding psychological practice. Thus, one school psychologist may be competent to provide crisis counseling while another is not. Training (or certification) as a school psychologist does not, *per se*, qualify an individual to provide any particular form of intervention. The experience of the individual counselor should determine who provides services.

An emphasis on competence, rather than on profession-determined roles, suggests the need for cooperation and collaboration at both the building and system levels. The various counseling professions must work together as a team, assessing their collective competencies and determining areas for further professional development. By functioning in this way, they will be more likely to address effectively the counseling needs presented by their students.

Characteristics of School-Based Counseling

School-based counseling involves several characteristics which differentiate it from interventions practiced in other settings, such as community mental health centers or the offices of private practitioners. Maher and Springer (1987) provide a useful summary of "distinguishing features":

> 1. School-based counseling provides an opportunity to counsel students in a natural setting.

2. It is provided over a finite period of time and within circumscribed time parameters.

3. It is targeted to a clearly defined set of school-related goals.

4. It can be provided in one-to-one or in group modes.

5. It can be provided by a range of different school personnel.

6. It has limited confidentiality.

7. It involves assisting some involuntary clients. (p. 101)

Such school-based treatment also focuses on changing school and family systems and allows an opportunity for early intervention in many cases. Although not all school personnel agree that mental health intervention should take place in the schools, often this is an ideal setting for providing direct service to troubled children and families. In many communities (both urban and rural) few other services are available or accessible, parents may not avail themselves of those that do exist (Sandoval & Davis, 1992), and parents and adolescents may view involvement in school services as less stigmatizing than those offered in other public settings. Thus, students and parents may be more likely to actually follow through on referrals and *participate* in school-based intervention services.

Comprehensive Counseling Programs

General approaches to counseling in the schools. Textbooks on school counseling vary in their presentations of approaches to counseling. Some focus on program components while others describe a range of theoretical approaches to intervention. Myrick (1987) described four general approaches to guidance and counseling used in school settings: (a) *crisis*, (b) *remedial*, (c) *preventive*, and (d) *developmental*. "Each approach has a salient theme which influences program direction, the type of services provided to students, and how professional personnel spend their time" (Myrick, 1987, p. 11). Although counseling programs often incorporate all of these approaches to some extent, it is likely that, without careful planning and coordination, a particular approach will dominate, leaving only limited time and resources for the others. A comprehensive counseling program at the secondary level should include all of these approaches.

• *The crisis approach.* In the crisis approach to counseling, the focus is usually short-term (sometimes involving only one session) and specific to defusing the immediate danger or threat. This orientation is all too familiar to experienced school psychologists. Programs dominated by this approach respond to students and staff only when problems have escalated to the point of jeopardizing individual psychological and/or physical welfare. While all programs must develop the capacity to respond to crisis situations, those that rely on this as the primary scheme are likely to be costly, inefficient (Myrick, 1987), and guilty of allowing problems to reach a crisis level before warranting a response. In the meantime, other students and problems may be ignored. Interestingly, as Myrick points out, "while counselors complain that they do not have time to see all the students who need their help, there is always time to react to a crisis" (1987, p. 13).

• *The remedial approach.* In the remedial approach, perhaps the most common in school counseling programs, specific academic or psychosocial needs of the student body are identified. Intervention strategies are then designed and implemented in an effort to avoid repeated, but predictable, crises (see Myrick, 1987). For example, a series of counseling groups may be established in response to a large number of students being identified as having problems in day-to-day social interaction with peers. Referral to the group program, then, would be based on identified deficits in social skills with the goal of making up for such deficiencies. Counseling programs dominated by the remedial approach involve more planning than those with a primarily crisis orientation, but generally, they still operate in a reactive mode.

• *The preventive approach.* As in other areas of mental health, the preventive approach has enjoyed much popularity, if not demonstrated success. This approach relies on considerable planning and anticipation of student and staff problems. It places the counseling staff in a more favorable position, compared to those operating in a primarily reactive mode. Unfortunately, the list of what should be prevented could be endless (Myrick, 1987) and subject to political pressures from the most vocal elements of the school community and to which "causes" are most popular at a particular time. And as Myrick suggests, the preventive approach "concentrates on what we do not want (e.g., drug abuse, violent behavior, poor study habits), instead of what we do want to happen" (1987, p. 15).

• *The developmental approach.* The developmental approach to guidance and counseling (e.g., Gysbers & Henderson, 1988), while perhaps unfamiliar to many school psychologists, has played a prominent role in the training and experience of school counselors. This approach includes the other three (i.e., crisis, remedial, and preventive) and views the guidance and counseling "curriculum" as complementing the academic curriculum. Such a comprehensive counseling program "attempt[s] to identify certain skills and experiences that students need to have as part of their going to school and being successful" (Myrick, 1987, p. 15). Schools that develop comprehensive counseling programs, such as those suggested by the developmental approach, are able to provide "counseling" by integrating it into the academic curriculum as well as by providing more specialized interventions.

Essential services of a comprehensive counseling program. The term "counseling" usually brings to mind a picture of an adult professional meeting with one or more troubled individuals to discuss and work toward solutions to identified or suspected problems. Such activity would constitute only one service, however, in a comprehensive counseling program. Schmidt (1993) identified four major components of such a program:

1. *Counseling* — individual and group, with students, parents, and teachers.

2. *Consulting* — including individual student planning, classroom guidance, parent education, and teacher in-service.

3. *Coordinating* — data collection and sharing, referrals and follow-up, and school-wide events and programs.

4. *Appraising* — individual, group, and family assessment including testing, observations, and interviews.

While schools may provide all of these services, frequently they are offered through separate departments or divisions of the school district, resulting in overlapping (and sometimes uncoordinated) services to the same students and staff. In a comprehensive counseling program, all four components are considered essential and offered in a single agenda rather than as separate, or even interconnected, pieces.

When is Counseling Warranted?

Adolescents whose "behavioral, cognitive, emotional, and/or interpersonal functioning causes them or others distress and interferes with their development and learning" are those likely to be referred for counseling (Tharinger & Koranek, 1990, p. 407, regarding younger children). In addition, students experiencing academic problems are frequently referred by teachers and administrators in an attempt to "fix" such problems. Counselors are then in a position to determine if counseling, rather than other forms of intervention such as consultation with the classroom teacher or remedial instruction, is warranted and likely to be the most appropriate means of addressing identified or suspected problems. A scheme for classifying problems which may lend

themselves to counseling intervention is discussed more fully below.

Ethical and Legal Concerns

Counseling inevitably involves ethical and legal questions that must be addressed by individual counselors as well as program developers. While professional organizations provide ethical principles and standards of practice as guidelines for their membership (e.g., APA, 1992; NASP, 1986, 1992), each state applies its own statutes and regulations governing professional conduct. Sometimes, laws that apply to practitioners in private practice may not apply directly to those operating in public schools. Similarly, statutes and regulations governing the practice of "licensed" psychologists may not extend to "certified" school psychologists. For example, a state which grants a right of "privileged communication" to treatment with licensed psychologists may not extend this same privilege to treatment with a certified, but not licensed, school psychologist. (Privileged communication has been defined as "those statements made by certain persons within a protected relationship such as husband–wife, attorney–client, priest–penitent … which the law protects from forced disclosure on the witness stand at the option of the witness, client, penitent, spouse" [Black, 1991]. In some states, this privilege may also apply to the psychotherapist–client relationship. The privilege belongs to the client, not to the professional.) When this is the case, such a distinction should be made clear to any client. In addition, individual school systems develop specific policies related to the ethical and legal practice of all school staff, including psychologists. Given this variety of rules that may direct, as well as limit, the scope of practice, it is imperative that school psychologists become thoroughly familiar with all that apply to them.

Although this chapter advocates cross-disciplinary collaboration in the provision of counseling services, it must be made clear that the law may not operate from such a perspective. Instead, psychologists will be expected to adhere to laws and ethical principles governing the professional behavior of *psychologists* and not those of any other related profession, regardless of the specific activities they undertake.

Written policies and procedures and in-service education for all staff may well be the best vehicles for ensuring that counseling-related policies are developed and followed. For example, all staff should be aware of the system's policies related to confidentiality and its limitations, parental notification, feedback to classroom teachers, voluntary participation in counseling, emergency hospitalization, and reporting of suspected child abuse. Procedures should not be determined on a case-by-case basis but should follow from the guidelines established in the development of the overall counseling program as well as from state statutes and regulations governing professional practice in each of these areas.

School Psychologists' Training in Counseling and Program Development

Related to ethical practice, counseling should be provided only by those professionals with the appropriate preparation to do so. "School psychologists, provided that they possess the necessary education, training, and supervised experience, are in an excellent position to help identify [students in need of counseling] and, if appropriate, to offer them counseling services" (Tharinger & Koranek, 1990, p. 407). But are school psychologists adequately prepared to provide counseling at the secondary level?

When surveyed, practicing school psychologists repeatedly report that they have received insufficient training in counseling in general and in counseling secondary students, in particular (e.g., Carroll, Bretzing, & Harris, 1981; Huebner, 1993). And yet they are increasingly expected to provide counseling services (Fisher, Jenkins, & Crumbley, 1986; Hartshorne & Johnson, 1985; Huebner, 1993). Consequently, when called upon to provide individual or group counseling to adolescents, many school psychologists may be not only ill-prepared but also at risk of crossing the ethical bounds of their professional competence.

The findings of the surveys cited here support the arguments of Curtis and Batsche (1991) that in order for psychologists to be prepared to work effectively at the secondary level, school psychology programs may need to increase the level of training in direct intervention services with adolescents. Practicing school psychologists must also avail themselves of course work and training in approved programs, as well as supervised experience, in order to meet clinical, ethical, and legal obligations when delivering counseling services to students.

In addition to direct services, psychologists are frequently involved in the design, development, and evaluation of counseling programs in school settings. But again, field surveys reveal that school psychologists receive limited preservice training in program development and evaluation (e.g., Huebner, 1993; Moore & Carlson, 1988) and see this as an important training need of secondary school practitioners (Huebner, 1993). Graduate programs should attend to this feedback from experienced practitioners in modifying and improving training curricula and standards.

Problems Faced by Contemporary Adolescents

Recent research shows that the number of stressors for children has increased substantially over the past two decades, and once children make the transition into adolescence, that number increases dramatically (Simmons & Blyth, 1987). Today's adolescents face a host of psychosocial problems that reflect the rapid pace of societal change (Barona & Garcia, 1990). Secondary students, themselves, identify numerous school-related sources of stress, ranging from difficulty of classroom tests (Bauwens & Hourcade, 1992) to interpersonal aggression (Armacost, 1989). In one study, the stressors of greatest concern to students were the ability-grouping system, the need to keep up with school work while holding a job, and theft of personal belongings (Armacost, 1989).

Given the pressures perceived by adolescents, which issues might psychologists anticipate addressing in developing and providing counseling services in secondary schools? A study conducted by Hutchinson and Reagan (1989), noting the most common problems for which high school seniors seek counseling services in school, suggests some answers to this question. They found that high school students seek counseling for a host of concerns, many of which might be addressed by school psychologists (see Table 1). Given the nature and variety of problems today's adolescents face, school personnel must be prepared to meet such needs by providing a range of services in the school setting.

Consistent with the notion that school problems reflect society's problems (Packard, 1983), psychologists might also anticipate issues of sexual orientation, ethnic/cultural identity, and gender equality in developing and providing counseling services at the secondary level. Contemporary authors have provided insight into the specific stressors that many homosexuals (Rotheram-Borus, Rosario, & Koopman, 1991), adolescents of color (Sandoval, Gutkin, & Naumann, 1994; Smith, 1986) and females (Dornbusch, Mont-Reynaud, Ritter, Chen, & Steinberg, 1991) must confront in a society which many experience as oppressive. Such marginalized students are expected to adjust to traditional school settings and expectations, and likewise, schools must accommodate and adjust to students who do not fit neatly into the mainstream.

Rotheram-Borus et al. (1991) maintain that gay and lesbian youth experience stress from the fear that their sexual orientation will be discovered by family and friends or cause significant others to "disown" them and that "coming out of the closet" will create chronic stress. In fact, one- to two-thirds of homosexual youths have reported experiencing stressors directly related to their sexual orientation (Dornbusch et al., 1991).

Among adolescents of color, the stressors are numerous as well. For example, Hale-Benson (1986) observed that, on the one hand, the "emphasis of traditional education has been upon molding and shaping Black children so that they can fit into an educational process designed for Anglo-Saxon middle class children" (p. 1), but on the other hand, they have to deal with pressures from their own cultural group to avoid "acting White" (Fordham & Ogbu, 1986). For many students of color, this potential clash between the demands of mainstream culture and those of their own ethnic group may lead to mental, emotional, and so-

TABLE 1
Rank Order of Issues for Which High School Seniors Would Seek Counseling Services

Rank	Reason	Percentage
1	Information about college, etc.	89.6
2	Graduation requirements	89.1
3	Registering for classes	89.0
4	Assistance in changing a class	87.3
5	Information about career opportunities	83.5
6	Scholarships/financial aid	81.0
7	Interpretation of test results	74.6
8	Deciding on a career	68.8
9	Assistance in job hunting	62.2
10	Conflicts with teachers	61.3
11	Orientation to a new school	60.9
12	Discipline problems	55.8
13	Truancy problems	47.0
14	Awareness of feelings and values	45.6
15	Alcohol or drug education	41.6
16	Conflicts with peers	39.6
17	General personal problems	39.5
18	How to get along in life	34.2
19	Alcohol or drug problems	33.3
20	Sexual, physical, or emotional abuse	32.2
21	Conflicts with parents	30.7
22	Relieving tension	26.5
23	Boyfriend/girlfriend relationships	19.5
24	Questions about sex	11.1

Note. Based on Hutchinson and Reagan (1989, p. 277). Rank order indicates the percentage of students checking either "Strongly Agree" or "Agree" to each item.

cial stress that warrants attention from school counseling personnel (Sandoval et al., 1994).

With regard to gender equality, Rosser (1990) pointed out that economic and social structures, including schools, suppress female students' achievement, self-worth, and self-esteem. For example, according to the recent report by the American Association of University Women (AAUW, 1993), many U.S. schools do not encourage female students to pursue science, mathematics, or other disciplines that are typically male dominated; sexual harassment of girls by boys has increased at an alarming rate; and female students do not receive as much attention from their teachers (male and female) as do boys. As a result, the AAUW posited, many young high school women lag behind their male counterparts in confidence and self-esteem.

A Framework for Addressing Adolescent Problems

In attempting to meet the psychological and social needs of secondary students presenting such a wide range of problems, psychologists must utilize approaches that are as multifaceted as the problems students bring into the counseling room. Sigmon (1988) offers a convenient (but not all-encompassing) framework for understanding the severity of adolescent problems and planning for a continuum of services. He proposes a five-level framework to guide school psychologists in deciding when, and how intensely, to counsel public school students. His scheme provides an organization for both practitioners and program planners.

- A *Level I* student is considered to be "normally" adjusted with occasional mild problems requiring a counselor's attention, for example, academic or career choices. Other than perhaps needing someone to lend an ear to his or her concerns, this student is not likely to need any formal psychological intervention.

- At *Level II*, a student may experience academic, personal, or behavioral problems that are situational, intermittent, and only mildly problematic. A school psychologist may offer counseling or classroom behavioral intervention when situations arise but would not typically consider this student for special education due to emotional or behavioral factors.

- At *Level III*, students experience mild to moderate psychosocial problems and are most likely to be referred for counseling intervention. These students are generally not self-destructive or severely pathological but instead exhibit behaviors that may be considered oppositional or defiant. Typical interventions might include group training in social skills, problem solving, or anger control.

- *Level IV* students present moderate to severe psychological problems that have persisted for a relatively long period. They may experience hallucinations, delusions, or exaggerated phobias and may be better served by community agencies that provide long-term therapy or medical attention, if necessary. In addition to identifying and monitoring Level IV students, school psychologists may coordinate outreach and referral programs for students requiring community or private treatment.

- *Level V* is characterized as a severe or "crisis situation" in which the student has been traumatized or shown to have been injurious to self and/or others. For example, adolescents traumatized by rape, the death of a friend or family member, courtship or community violence, or substance abuse may require specialized and immediate attention from not only school counseling services but external services as well (e.g., rape/abuse crisis center, psychiatric emergency room, medical or psychiatric hospital, or substance abuse treatment program).

To meet the wide range of psychological challenges faced by today's secondary students, schools must be prepared to provide counseling services across all of Sigmon's five levels.

BEST PRACTICES IN COUNSELING PROGRAM DEVELOPMENT

Counseling programs may be described in many ways. Kruger (1988) defines a *program* as "a system of staff, materials, and procedures intended to improve or resolve a problem that a group of students

have in common" (p. 491). Schmidt (1993) more explicitly characterizes the comprehensive counseling program as providing "individual and group counseling, consulting, testing and assessment, group instruction, and referrals" and serving students, parents, and teachers "within the framework of an organized program" (pp. 31–32).

Psychologists need to think on the developmental program level so that the overall mental health and counseling needs of the school are not misunderstood or slighted in favor of reactive, case-by-case response. Psychologists must be more systematic in both identification and intervention, rather than allowing counseling activities to be governed by the interests of individual counselors or the transient, albeit serious, concerns of highly vocal groups of students, parents, or teachers. Instead, the needs of the entire school community must be considered when developing and allocating resources.

ESTABLISHING A COUNSELING PROGRAM: PROCEDURES IN PROGRAM DEVELOPMENT AND CHANGE

Professional conferences and catalogues abound with descriptions of predesigned educational programs, including those addressing the mental health needs of students. Kruger (1988) offers some sound advice for those considering such programs in their own schools. "Programs described in journals or books should not be merely adopted 'as is' by a school. All schools in their overall contexts are unique, and sometimes the variations make a difference in how change should occur" (Kruger, 1988, p. 491). It is unlikely that many psychologists will actually be involved in *establishing* a school counseling program from scratch. More likely is the psychologist's participation in program *modification* at the building and/or system level.

Reflecting a systems orientation, Schmidt (1993) presented a model for counseling program development, involving four basic phases: (a) planning, (b) organizing, (c) implementing, and (d) evaluating. Rather than functioning as sequential steps, these phases operate in a cyclical fashion, with each step feeding the next in an ongoing, developing system. For example, rather than serving as the final phase of a program, evaluation leads to planning of new or revised programs, and the cycle continues. Psychologists may wish to examine current practices in their own settings to determine in which phases their skills might best be utilized and how best to accommodate the unique needs and life challenges of adolescents in their own schools.

Program Planning

Program planning involves identifying and clarifying the problem(s); evaluating school-wide goals; and assessing the needs of students, staff, and parents. Illback, Zins, Maher, and Greenberg (1990) refer to the activities in this phase as "problem clarification," designed to "gather systematic information to place the problem(s) in context and to assure that the appropriate planning occurs based on a clear understanding of service needs" (p. 807). This requires two separate but compatible strategies: (a) initial contextual analysis and (b) formal needs assessment.

Contextual analysis. Using a variety of strategies, contextual analysis involves placing the problem "in context."

> Through preliminary interviews with involved persons, records reviews, direct observation, and similar methods, [the program planner] seeks … to obtain a general sense of the history and development of the concern, to understand what the present state of affairs appears to be, to know which individuals perceive that there is a problem, and to recognize there are multiple perspectives from which the problem may be viewed. (Illback et al., 1990, p. 807).

Whether engaged in initial program development or program modification, psychologists and other professionals involved in the process must understand the setting before deciding how (or whether) to proceed. It is crucial to assess, for example, whether change is needed, which characteristics of the setting and staff support and hinder change, and how a school might become more amenable to change (see Kruger, 1988, for further discussion). Answers to such questions can provide a clear understanding of the context and serve as a guide in the next step, formal needs assessment.

Needs assessment. In school settings, needs assessment for counseling frequently consists solely of surveys administered to students or teachers addressing the need or desire for specific types of services, for example, grief support groups following the death of a classmate. But, many other strategies are available for gathering multisource data that will inform the development of the overall program. Indeed, in a comprehensive counseling program, needs must be assessed across all four approaches to service — crisis, remedial, preventive, and developmental. Although the variety of needs assessment strategies cannot be discussed in detail here, Illback et al. (1990) suggest several which can be applied at the planning stage (see Table 2). Data collection from multiple sources (e.g., students, teachers, parents, administrators, existing documents) will then serve as the basis for clarifying the problem, defining the need(s), and negotiating with decision makers about competing needs and priorities. This process leads to setting relevant goals and objectives and designing an overall program structure to address the identified needs and problems.

Program Organization and Development

The program organization phase may be considered an extension of the planning stage, in which the focus shifts to identifying and developing the appropriate services and resources to support the program structure. Resources include personnel, participants, activities, skills, materials, space, and time. Basically, the task is to determine *who* will do *what* with *whom, when*. In making these determinations, planners must consider the various approaches (i.e., crisis, remedial, preventive, and developmental) included in the counseling program.

Even when readily available, resources may still require organization to coordinate them into the overall program, or policies outlining their usage may need to be written. When resources are not yet available, it may be necessary to hire or train staff, develop or purchase materials, and establish the timelines necessary to accomplish these tasks. In this phase, areas of responsibility are designated.

The skills required to conduct effective counseling are frequently overlooked as essential program resources. When assigning and training staff, however, their mastery of requisite knowledge and skills should receive primary consideration. The professional literature provides some guidance for hiring and training counseling staff suggesting that, to promote growth and change, psychologists should possess certain generic characteristics. For example, effective counselors are authentic, empathic, and warm in their interactions with clients. In addition, they serve as role models, display genuine concern, and instill hope that clients can and will change (Corey, 1986; Ivey, Ivey, & Simek-Downing, 1987). While not comprehensive in scope, these characteristics do provide a foundation from which to offer effective psychological services.

Although generic counseling knowledge and skills are essential, they are not sufficient for establishing and maintaining effective therapeutic relationships. To meet the psychological needs of students confronted with unique social challenges, counselors must be prepared to work with students whose life experiences may be different from their own. Accordingly, Sue et al. (1982) maintain that the professional repertoire of culturally competent counselors must include various fundamental beliefs/attitudes, knowledge, and skills (see Table 3). Although their model was aimed primarily at clinicians working specifically with ethnically diverse clients, similar characteristics may apply to those counseling students who are in any way different from the mainstream. Experience, expertise, sensitivity, and flexibility in a wide range of counseling skills should be considered in assessing available and needed resources, both in terms of personnel and training needs. However, rarely do all essential resources exist within the confines of the school building. Pro-

TABLE 2
Needs Assessment Strategies

Strategy	Description
Key informant approach	Interview those in central positions ("experts") in the organization who have knowledge about the problem
Indicators analysis	Use school's (and other organizations') existing data bases relevant to the problem
Analysis of demands for services and analysis of service resources	Use data and records that are already available, for example, number of individual counseling appointments, number of students on waiting lists
Survey/Questionnaire	Ask a sample of respondents about the problem, for example, particular counseling needs
Nominal group approach	Involve representatives of the various constituencies in group discussion and analysis of the problem
Delphi approach	Involve experts in systematic series of questionnaires
Community forums	Conduct open discussions of interested parties

Note. Based on Illback, R. J., Zins, J. E., Maher, C. A., & Greenberg, R. (1990). An overview of principles and procedures of program planning and evaluation. In T. B. Gutkin & C. R. Reynolds (Eds.), *The handbook of school psychology* (2nd ed.; pp. 799–820). New York: Wiley.

gram planners may also consider community agencies such as mental health centers, recreational programs, substance abuse treatment services, and university training programs as resources to be tapped. In some locales, partnerships have developed among schools, universities, and/or community organizations, resulting in services such as school-based clinics and social service programs (see, e.g., Godin, Jacobs, & Nowak, 1993; and the School Mental Health Project, Institute for Families in Society, University of South Carolina) and crisis teams invited into school settings on an as-needed basis to assist school-based teams (e.g., Boston Public Schools' collaboration with the multi-agency Community Crisis Response team of Cambridge Hospital).

Program Implementation

Schmidt (1993) described program implementation as the "action phase," in which services are delivered as designed. To those who prefer jumping into the cycle at this stage, without careful prior planning and organizing, Schmidt offers the following caution:

> Implementing a program that is void of clear goals and objectives is like piloting a plane without a flight plan. The plane is airborne, all instruments are working, but the pilot has no idea where the plane is heading or why it is going in that direction. (1993, p. 43)

And, it is likely that the pilot will not know when the plane has arrived.

Maher and Bennett (1984) proposed a model of program development which stresses ongoing inter-action among program planners, staff, and participants. Of particular relevance to the implementation phase, they highlight rewarding and adapting as important activities in fostering program success. Rewarding is not often cited in discussions of program development but may deserve special attention at the secondary level. While true in any setting, it may be in the high school, with its reliance on frequent class changes throughout the day, that the cooperation of teaching staff is most essential to service scheduling and delivery. Both written and in-person acknowledgment (Maher & Springer, 1987), as well as feedback about individual and group progress when appropriate, will contribute to ongoing, needed teacher support.

Modification and adaptation are also often needed, especially in the early stages of program implementation. For example, changes in scheduling, staffing, location, focus, or number of counseling services are not uncommon. Anticipating such changes, through ongoing discussion with administrators, staff, parents, and students, can prevent or at least reduce resistance and objections.

Program Evaluation

Frequently, program developers and practitioners are reluctant to participate in any form of evaluation, fearing that it will lead only to the dismantling of services. Cowen, however, described the value of program evaluation:

TABLE 3
Characteristics of the Culturally Competent Counselor

Areas of Competence	Description
Beliefs/Attitudes	Becomes aware of own cultural history and respects differences
	Becomes aware of own values and biases and how they may affect clients
	Comfortable with client despite racial and/or worldview differences
	Sensitive to circumstances (e.g., racial identity development) that may warrant referral to another counselor who is more culturally similar to client
Knowledge	Good understanding of the sociopolitical system's operation in the U.S. with respect to treatment of minorities
	Knowledge about client's racial/ethnic group
	Has explicit knowledge and understanding of the generic characteristics of counseling and psychotherapy
	Aware of the institutional barriers that prevent many people of color from using mental health services
Skills	Able to generate a wide variety of verbal and nonverbal responses
	Able to send and receive verbal and nonverbal messages accurately and appropriately
	Able to exercise institutional intervention skills on behalf of client when appropriate

Note. Based on "Position paper: Cross-cultural counseling competencies" by D. W. Sue, J. E. Bernier, A. Curran, L. Feinberg, P. Pedersen, E. J. Smith, & E. Vasquez-Nuttal, 1982, *Counseling Psychologist, 10,* 45–52.

If a program is not evaluated at all or is evaluated improperly, the major benefits to be derived from a carefully conceptualized and conducted program — indeed one with important positive outcomes — may be lost, and the program may incorrectly be dismissed as a failure. (1984, p. 489)

From this perspective, evaluation is considered an opportunity to demonstrate a program's effectiveness, rather than the first step toward its demise. Approaches to evaluation generally fall into two categories: (a) the process of implementation and (b) the assessment of outcome effectiveness (Illback et al., 1990).

Implementation evaluation. Before the effectiveness of a given program or intervention can be assessed, it must be demonstrated that the program has actually been implemented as originally planned or as intentionally revised. Otherwise, it may be some "other" program that is actually evaluated. This issue has been discussed elsewhere in terms of treatment or program integrity (see, e.g., Kazdin & Wilson, 1978). Unfortunately, many school programs fail to conduct a systematic assessment of the integrity of implementation. But such evaluation is crucial to program development in that it "increases confidence in the eventual assessment of program outcomes by ensuring that measured effects are attributable to an intervention that has been implemented as planned" (Illback et al., 1990).

In documenting implementation integrity, many issues should be considered, including the extent to which staff are carrying out planned program activities; the extent to which students and staff actually participate; the comparison of planned and actual costs; the development of written materials; and the perceptions of various constituencies or stakeholders regarding intended and unintended effects of the program (see e.g., Bennett, 1988; Illback et al., 1990). As with needs assessment, a multimethod approach is recommended at this stage. Interviews, paper-and-pencil measures, record reviews, and observations are frequently used (Bennett, 1988; Illback et al., 1990). Once questions about implementation have been answered, the focus of evaluation may shift to program effectiveness or outcome.

Outcome assessment. As already suggested, evaluation should not be conducted only as the final stage of program development, for the sole purpose of reporting the level of effectiveness (summative evaluation). It should also be conducted as a continuous process aimed at identifying and improving services and effective methods of service delivery (formative evaluation; Stake, 1991). Whether summative or formative in purpose and timing, evaluation may assess a variety of outcomes and serve a range of purposes.

In program evaluation, effectiveness does not have a single definition. Instead, program effectiveness is determined from the perspectives of the various stakeholders who, in the model described here, have also been involved in the development and implementation of the counseling program. Thus, multiple (and sometimes conflicting) definitions and measures of effectiveness may be operating simultaneously.

Based on Bennett's (1988) definitions of "outcome" and Illback et al.'s (1990) discussion of levels of decision making, a series of questions will serve to illustrate the various perspectives from which a program's outcome or value might be assessed:

1. Have the program goals been achieved? Have the identified unmet needs been satisfied? To what extent can the level of change be attributed to the program, rather than to some other event or resource?

2. Has the program generated any unintended "related effects," whether harmful or beneficial?

3. How do the various consumers (e.g., students, parents, staff, funding sources, service providers) rate the program's effectiveness? To what extent has the program met relevant government regulations?

4. How cost effective is the program? What other appropriate cost analyses (e.g., cost-benefit, cost-utility, cost feasibility) have been conducted?

Clearly no one evaluation procedure will address the different perspectives represented in these questions. In some cases, predetermined, standardized clinical measures may provide the most useful information. Others, such as unintended outcomes, may emerge from ongoing interviews, observations, self-report measures, or record reviews. Measures of satisfaction may be collected from all participants, a random sample, or only key informants. Evaluation designs may range from true experiments to quasi-experiments to intensive case studies (see Rossi & Freeman, 1985, for a more thorough discussion of evaluation design).

As expressed by Stake (1991), comprehensive program evaluations use a variety of data collection methods to determine the level of effectiveness as well as to illuminate program areas that need improvement. As is true with any school program, strategies for performing ongoing evaluation should be developed and implemented as an integral part of a comprehensive counseling program. As such, evaluation procedures are not used simply to appease decision makers or satisfy the public during "critical" times. Rather, evaluating should be viewed as an essential (and iterative) step in the process of designing, developing, and delivering counseling services to the school community.

SUMMARY

School psychologists serve in a broad range of direct and indirect service delivery roles in secondary schools. The unique psychosocial challenges faced by today's adolescents, however, call for expanding the responsibilities of school psychologists to include increased time for counseling students and greater attention to developing counseling programs. These efforts demand collaboration by all teaching, administrative, and mental health staff in order to capitalize upon their collective competencies, thereby more effectively addressing the needs of all members of the school community.

A comprehensive counseling program is designed to address the crisis, remedial, prevention, and developmental needs of students, parents, and staff. Developing such a program requires sufficient time, skill, and commitment to interdisciplinary collaboration. The extent to which a counseling program is successful depends largely on the questions and issues addressed in the planning and organizing phases, the quality and range of resources made available during implementation, and the rigor and commitment with which ongoing evaluation is conducted.

School psychologists, in their roles as counselors and program developers, are in an ideal position to apply their assessment, intervention, and consultation skills at the secondary level. Today's youth can benefit greatly from the services of well-trained and experienced school psychologists, working collaboratively with other school and community professionals to provide high quality counseling programs.

ACKNOWLEDGMENTS

The authors would like to thank Ronald E. Reeve and an anonymous reviewer for their helpful comments on earlier drafts of this chapter.

Support was provided, in part, for work on this chapter through a postdoctoral fellowship pursuant to a National Research Service Award from NIMH (Grant #5T32MH16156) to the University of Nebraska–Lincoln while the first author was a postdoctoral research fellow with the Center on Children, Families, and the Law.

REFERENCES

American Association of University Women. (1993). *Hostile hallways: The AAUW survey on sexual harassment in America's schools*. Washington, DC: Author.

American Psychological Association. (1992). Ethical principles of psychologists and code of conduct. *American Psychologist, 47,* 1597–1611.

Armacost, R. L. (1989). Perceptions of stressors by high school students. *Journal of Adolescent Research, 4,* 443–461.

Barona, A., & Garcia, E. E. (Eds.). (1990). *Children at risk: Poverty, minority status, and other issues in educational equity*. Washington, DC: National Association of School Psychologists.

Bauwens, J., & Hourcade, J. J. (1992). School-based sources of stress among elementary and secondary at-risk students. *The School Counselor, 40,* 97–102.

Bennett, R. E. (1988). Evaluating the effectiveness of alternative educational delivery systems. In J. L. Graden, J. E., Zins, & M. J. Curtis (Eds.), *Alternative educational delivery systems: Enhancing instructional options for all students* (pp. 513–524). Washington, DC: National Association of School Psychologists.

Black, H. C. (1991). *Black's law dictionary* (Abridged, 6th Ed.). St. Paul, MN: West Publishing.

Carroll, J. L., Bretzing, B. H., & Harris, J. D. (1981). Psychologists in secondary schools: Training and present patterns of service. *Journal of School Psychology, 19,* 267–277.

Casey, R. J., & Berman, J. S. (1985). The outcome of psychotherapy with children. *Psychological Bulletin, 98,* 388–400.

Cheramie, G. M., & Sutter, E. G. (1993). Role expansion in school psychology: The need for primary and secondary prevention services. *Psychology in the Schools, 30,* 53–59.

Conoley, J. C., & Gutkin, T. B. (1986). School psychology: A reconceptualization of service delivery realities. In S. N. Elliott & J. C. Witt (Eds.), *The delivery of psychological services in schools* (pp. 393–424). Hillsdale, NJ: Erlbaum.

Corey, G. (1986). *Theory and practice of counseling and psychotherapy.* Monterey, CA: Brooks/Cole.

Corsini, R. J., & Wedding, D. (Eds.). (1989). *Current psychotherapies* (4th ed.). Itasca, IL: Peacock Publishers.

Cowen, E. L., (1984). A general structural model for primary prevention program development in mental health. *The Personnel and Guidance Journal,* April, 485–490.

Curtis, M. J., & Batsche, G. (1991). Meeting the needs of children and families: Opportunities and challenges for school psychology training programs. *School Psychology Review, 20,* 565–577.

Dornbusch, S. M., Mont-Reynaud, R., Ritter, P. L., Chen, Z., & Steinberg, L. (1991). Stressful events and their correlates among adolescents of diverse backgrounds. In M. Curtis & S. Gore (Eds.), *Adolescent stress: Causes and consequences* (pp. 111–130). New York: Aldine DeGruyter.

Ehly, S., & Dustin, R. (1989). *Individual and group counseling in schools.* New York: Guilford.

Elliott, S. N., & Witt, J. C. (1986). *The delivery of psychological services in schools: Concepts, processes, and issues.* Hillsdale, NJ: Erlbaum.

Fisher, G. L., Jenkins, S. J., & Crumbley, J. D. (1986). A replication of a survey of school psychologists: Congruence between training, practice, preferred role, and competence. *Psychology in the Schools, 23,* 271–279.

Fordham, S., & Ogbu, J. U. (1986). Black students' school success: Coping with the "burden of 'acting white'." *The Urban Review, 18,* 176–206.

Godin, S., Jacobs, H., & Nowak, K. (1993). *Evaluation of the elementary and middle school youth services programs at the New Brunswick and Bridgeton Schools.* Research report (1993–6). Trenton, NJ: Department of Human Services.

Gysbers, N. C., & Henderson, P. (1988). *Developing and managing your school guidance program.* Alexandria, VA: American Association for Counseling and Development.

Hale-Benson, J. E. (1986). *Black children: Their roots, culture and learning styles.* Baltimore: Johns Hopkins University Press.

Hartshorne, T. S., & Johnson, M. C. (1985). The actual and preferred roles of the school psychologist according to secondary school administrators. *Journal of School Psychology, 23,* 241–246.

Huebner, E. S. (1993). Psychologists in secondary schools in the 1990s: Current functions, training, and job satisfaction. *School Psychology Quarterly, 8,* 50–56.

Humes, C. W., & Hohenshil, T. H. (1987). Elementary counselors, school psychologists, school social workers: Who does what? *Elementary School Guidance & Counseling, 22,* 37–45.

Hutchinson, R. L., & Reagan, C. A. (1989). Problems for which seniors would seek help from school counselors. *School Counselor, 36,* 271–280.

Illback, R. J., Zins, J. E., Maher, C. A., & Greenberg, R. (1990). An overview of principles and procedures of program planning and evaluation. In T. B. Gutkin & C. R. Reynolds (Eds.), *The handbook of school psychology* (2nd ed.; pp. 799–820). New York: Wiley.

Ivey, A. E., Ivey, M. B., & Simek-Downing, L. (1987). *Counseling and psychotherapy: Integrating skills, theory, and practice.* Englewood Cliffs, NJ: Prentice-Hall.

Kazdin, A. E. (1988). *Child psychotherapy: Developing and identifying effective treatments.* New York: Pergamon.

Kazdin, A. E. (1990). Psychotherapy for children and adolescents. *Annual Review of Psychology, 41,* 21–54.

Kazdin, A. E., & Wilson, .G. T. (197). *Evaluation of behavior therapy: Issues, evidence, and research strategies.* Cambridge, MA: Ballinger.

Kruger, L. J. (1988). Programmatic change strategies at the building level. In J. L. Graden, J. E. Zins, & M. J. Curtis (Eds.), *Alternative educational delivery systems: Enhancing instructional options for all students* (pp. 491–511). Washington, DC: National Association of School Psychologists.

Maher, C. A., & Bennett, R. E. (1984). *Planning and evaluating special education services.* Englewood Cliffs, NJ: Prentice-Hall.

Maher, C. A., & Springer, J. (1987). School-based counseling. In C. A. Maher & J. E. Zins (Eds.), *Psychoeducational interventions in the schools: Methods and procedures for enhancing student competence* (pp. 101–117). New York: Pergamon Press.

Moore, C. M., & Carlson, D. (1988, April). *Accountability: Practices and issues.* Paper presented at the annual meeting of the National Association of School Psychologists, Chicago.

Myrick, R. S. (1987). *Developmental guidance and counseling: A practical approach.* Minneapolis: Educational Media Corp.

National Association of School Psychologists. (1986). *Standards for training and field placement programs in school psychology.* Washington, DC: Author.

National Association of School Psychologists. (1992). *Principles for professional ethics.* Washington, DC: Author.

Packard, V. (1983). *Our endangered children.* New York: Free Press.

Patterson, L. E., & Eisenberg, S. (1983). *The counseling process* (3rd ed.). Boston: Houghton Mifflin.

Rosser, S. V. (1990). *Female-friendly science: Applying women's studies, methods, and theories to attract students.* New York: Pergamon Press.

Rossi, P. H., & Freeman, H. E. (1985). *Evaluation: A systematic approach.* Beverly Hills, CA: Sage.

Rotheram-Borus, M. J., Rosario, M., & Koopman, C. (1991). Minority youths at high risk: Gay males and runaways. In M. Colten & S. Gore (Eds.), *Adolescent stress: Causes and consequences* (pp. 181–200). New York: Aldine DeGruyter.

Sandoval, J., & Davis, J. M. (1992). Applications of social psychology to school counseling and therapy. In F. J. Medway & T. P. Cafferty (Eds.), *School psychology: A social psychological perspective* (pp. 245–268). Hillsdale, NJ: Erlbaum.

Sandoval, S. R., Gutkin, t. B., & Naumann, W. C. (1994). Racial identity attitudes and school performance among African-American high school students: A correlational study. Manuscript submitted for publication.

Schmidt, J. J. (1993). *Counseling in schools: Essential services and comprehensive programs*. Boston: Allyn & Bacon.

Sigmon, S. B. (1988). A framework to determine when the school psychologist should counsel. *Psychology in the Schools, 25*, 62–64.

Simmons, R., & Blyth, D. (1987). *Moving into adolescence: The impact of pubertal change and school context*. Hawthorne, NY: Aldine.

Smith, E. (1986). Cultural differences and academic achievement. *Pointer, 30*, 28–31.

Stake, R. E. (1991). Responsive evaluation and qualitative methods. In W. Shadish, Jr., T. Cook, & L. Leviton (Eds.), *Foundations of program evaluation: Theories of practice* (pp. 270–314). Newbury Park, CA: Sage.

Sue, D. W., Bernier, J. E., Durran, A., Feinberg, L., Pedersen, P., Smith, E. J., & Vasquez-Nuttal, E. (1982). Position paper: Cross-cultural counseling competencies. *Counseling Psychologist, 10*, 45–52.

Tharinger, D., & Koranek, M. (1990). Best practices in individual counseling with elementary students. In A. Thomas & J. Grimes (Eds.), *Best practices in school psychology–II* (pp. 407–423). Washington, DC: National Association of School Psychologists.

ANNOTATED BIBLIOGRAPHY

Colten, M. E., & Gore, S. (Eds.). (1991). *Adolescent stress: Causes and consequences*. New York: Aldine deGruyter.

The editors of this book bring together a series of well-written papers that illustrate the complex and multifaceted nature of adolescent stress and its implications for mental health and well-being. Topics include coping with contemporary stressors, stress as it relates to adolescents of diverse backgrounds, stress among adolescent females, adolescent–parent conflict, psychoactive substance abuse, and teenage pregnancy.

Ehly, S., & Dustin, R. (1989). *Individual and group counseling in schools*. New York: Guilford Press.

An ideal introduction for school psychologists new to counseling, this book reveals the elements of providing effective service to students at all age levels. A discussion of various theoretical orientations is provided to address students' concerns at either an individual or group counseling level. Program evaluation procedures are described, providing a comprehensive package of effective counseling service.

Kruger, L. J. (1988). Programmatic change strategies at the building level. In J. L. Graden, J. E. Zins, & M. J. Curtis (Eds.), *Alternative educational delivery systems: Enhancing instruction options for all students* (pp. 491–511). Washington, DC: National Association of School Psychologists.

This helpful chapter provides school psychologists detailed information in the development and implementation of any school-based program. In addition to presenting strong arguments for programmatic change at the building level, Kruger thoroughly describes the tacit knowledge (i.e., personal attitude, school culture, professional literature, planning skills, and interpersonal influence skills) needed by school psychologists before initiating change at the building level.

Meeks, J. E., & Bernet, W. (1990). *The fragile alliance: An orientation to the psychiatric treatment of the adolescent* (4th ed.). Malabar, FL: Krieger Publishing.

A classic in the field of adolescent psychotherapy, the most recent edition of this text, targeted at experienced clinicians, has expanded its focus on the real-world problems faced by contemporary high school students. In addition to basic clinical considerations in adolescent treatment, special topics include suicidal threat and behavior, runaways, violence, victimization, divorce, substance abuse, and medical problems. This book is highly recommended for any practitioner specializing in adolescent treatment.

Ramirez, M. (1991). *Psychotherapy and counseling with minorities: A cognitive approach to individual and cultural differences*. New York: Pergamon Press.

Ramirez challenges the mainstream therapeutic methods counselors and psychotherapists have used when working with people of color as perpetuating the "assimilationist" perspective. Instead, he offers a model of psychotherapy and counseling based on a multicultural perspective. Ramirez's use of case histories helps characterize the primary objectives of his multicultural treatment model.

Shadish, W., Jr., Cook, T. D., & Leviton, L. C. (1991). *Foundations of program evaluation: Theories and practice*. Newbury Park, CA: Sage Publications.

Shadish, Cook, and Leviton have collected a variety of chapters written by major contributors to the field of program evaluation. Although primarily theory driven, this book provides its readers an invaluable source of evaluation information that can be readily applied to any program.

Sue, D. W. (1988). *Counseling the culturally different*. New York: John Wiley Publishers.

This book is among the classic works in the cross-cultural counseling arena. It adds meaning to related issues of counseling all historically oppressed groups, identifies differences and similarities across racial/ethnic groups in relation to counseling practices, and perhaps most importantly, addresses our social-political system's impact on cross-cultural counseling delivery services. "Critical incidents" highlight and illustrate issues and concerns that are likely to arise in typical counseling situations.

78

Best Practices in Teaching Study Skills

Virginia Smith Harvey
University of Massachusetts Boston

OVERVIEW

Of the many factors that influence learning (family, socioeconomic class, innate intelligence, motivation, self-image, study skills), study skills are most easily changed, and they can be taught to students of all ages and levels of ability. Thus, assessing and improving a student's study skills can be one of the school psychologists's most effective interventions.

Study skills are defined as competence in acquiring, recording, organizing, synthesizing, remembering, and using information and ideas. They are frequently broken down into skills of organization, listening, reading, writing, research, and test taking. Although many of these skills are taught throughout the regular curriculum, often instruction in study skills is neglected because we assume that students learn these skills on their own, or that they have mastered them in an earlier grade (Devine, 1987). When students are not specifically, and repeatedly, taught these skills, a large proportion of referrals to school psychologists may be students whose study skills are not well developed. Often interventions to improve organization or study skills can take place in the pre-referral stage and prevent the need for more extensive assessments and interventions.

This chapter provides a framework for understanding study skills, assessment methods, and intervention strategies. The intervention techniques presented here are a small sample of effective interventions. Many additional intervention techniques, as well as resources for classroom interventions, are cited in the references (Graham & Robinson, 1989; Langan, 1978; Mannix, 1989; Segal, Chipman, & Glasser, 1985).

School psychologists' training greatly facilitates their work in assessing and improving students' study skills. Integral to work in this area is knowledge of human learning and memory, skill in assessing individual differences, knowledge of learning styles, skill in consulting with parents and teachers, and expertise in ecological assessment.

BASIC CONSIDERATIONS

Study skills are taught best in conjunction with regular coursework and homework. If taught in isolation, they are unlikely to be maintained or to transfer from one setting to another. Therefore, effective remediation requires that the school psychologist, teacher, and parent work closely together to determine appropriate procedures, designate responsibilities, and design techniques to encourage generalization to other tasks.

BEST PRACTICES

The school psychologist should assess study skills particularly when the referral question concerns academic effort or behavior. Referral questions that suggest deficiencies in study skills include "does not complete assignments," "doesn't complete homework," "doesn't follow directions," and "isn't organized." Poor grades in social studies and science, and poorer performance on tests than in discussions, also suggest poor study skills.

If the same referral questions arise repeatedly, one should investigate the adequacy of the teacher's and/or school's instruction in study skills. Often students are taught these skills only once, with the assumption that they will then practice the techniques independently. Actually, these skills must be reviewed every year, and often require ongoing monitoring.

Home-School Collaboration

Given that most studying takes place at home, home-school collaboration is imperative. Teachers, for example, need to communicate with parents about problems with homework. Similarly, parents need to help with homework and organization. Parents also should let the teacher know when excessive time is being spent on homework, so that the load can be reduced. Parents will find extremely helpful suggestions in *Homework Without Tears* (Canter & Canter, 1987) and *How to Help Your Child Achieve in School* (1988). In addition, this volume contains a chapter on improving home-school collaboration, to which the reader is referred.

Assessment of Existing Study Skills

Loene (1983) indicated the following steps when teaching study skills:

1. Conduct an assessment and define the area to be taught.

2. Determine the entire procedure, including assessment, monitoring, and reinforcement.

3. Teach the techniques.

4. Gradually increase the student's responsibility.

5. Practice for transfer to other classrooms and subjects.

6. Provide regular feedback.

7. Use alternative technique if setbacks occur.

8. Evaluate the process before termination.

Some formal instruments for assessing study skills exist (Brown & Holtzman, 1967; Demos, 1976). However, the most productive method uses the ecological approach of investigating in several domains and at several levels. The following steps should be taken:

1. Interview the teacher and parent during a pre-referral conference, using the Study Skills Assessment Checklist (Table 1) to determine general areas of weakness. During the interview most of the questions will be answered and the areas of significant deficiency should be apparent.

2. Observe the student in class and analyze work samples to obtain further information. Selectively use the Checklist of Classroom Qualities that Foster Study Skills (Table 2) during the observation.

3. Interview the student. Selectively use questions from the Study Skills Assessment Checklist and the Student Interview Questions (Table 3). Have the student complete work with you. While the student works, observe carefully and have the student describe his or her work method. Examine the student's notebooks, assignment books, and completed work. Have the student show and describe his textbook. Have the student write down his or her weekly schedule, or keep a log of activities for a week, to help determine when homework "fits in."

4. Determine appropriate intervention techniques. The remainder of this chapter expands on the Study Skills Assessment Checklist. Often the remedial step to be taken will be readily apparent, but some suggestions are supplied and many more can be found in the references. Instruction can be provided at the individual, small-group, or classroom level. Several commercial materials are available as curriculum guides, some of which are listed in Table 4. Other possible intervention approaches include teacher consultation, teacher training, and/or district curriculum consultation. As mentioned previously, teachers often assume that students already have acquired many of these skills in earlier grades. The school psychologist is in a good position to observe the extent of the need for study skills training and to consult with teachers and administrators in that area.

5. Develop a plan of maintenance and generalization for the interventions. The implementation of almost all interventions will require ongoing monitoring until they become habitual on the part of the student.

Basic Skills in School

Does the student understand that he or she has some control over his or her life and academic achievement? Students whose locus of control is completely external will need to be led through successful experiences to help them understand that the effort they expend relates to the outcome they experience, and that their success in school is not simply an effect of innate ability or luck. One method of linking personal success to effort can be to ask students "when" questions, such as "How old do you think you will be when you learn to read?" Another is to have each student keep a log of activities for a week to track time spent on tasks and resultant success level.

Are assignments turned in with a label, name, and date? Are they neat? Are they complete? Are assignments checked for errors, and corrected, before being turned in? Students need to develop the habit of checking their work before turning it in. One method is for the teacher to give the entire class time to check over their work before collecting it, and then fade active monitoring. On the individual level, papers can be turned back to the student (nonpunitively) when it is immediately apparent that checking is needed. The acronym COPS can be used to remind to check for Capitalization, Overall appearance, Punctuation, and Spelling (Wiens, 1983).

Are all materials necessary for homework completion brought home? "Forgetfulness" can be alleviated by home-school collaboration. At school, the teacher can remind students to check that they have their homework and necessary materials before the dismissal bell. At home, parents can implement a simple behavior-management system to reinforce bringing materials home. One effective technique is to require the student to spend time on academic activity even when homework was forgotten. Other parents solve the problem by having the child walk back to school to get forgotten materials, or by charging "gas money" for return trips to a distant school.

TABLE 1
Study Skills Assessment Checklist

Basic Skills in School

Does the student understand that he or she has some control over achievement?

Are assignments turned in with a label, name, and date, neat, complete, checked for errors, and corrected, before being turned in?

Are all materials necessary for homework completion brought home?

Are short-term assignments tracked in a book; long-term in a calendar?

Does the student (grades 4 and below) keep a folder for assignment sheets?

Does the student (grades 5 and agove) keep a loose-leaf notebook organized chronologically, by subject?

Does the teacher come to class with notebook, pencil, completed homework, books?

Is the student's desk, cubby, or locker neat?

Can the student use the catalogue in the library?

Can the student use the periodical index?

Basic Skills at Home

Where does the student prefer to do homework? Is there a place at home to study that is quiet and well lighted, with a table or desk? Are supplies, reference books, and a dictionary kept there?

Is there a regular, quiet time to study at home?

Does the student estimate how long it will take to complete an assignment? Is this estimate used to make a schedule? Is the schedule followed?

Does the student follow a schedule?

What does the student do when unable to understand something at home?

What kind of homework does the student enjoy? Dislike? Why?

What does the student like about the way he or she handles homework? Dislike?

Does the parent regularly check the assignment calendar/homework sheet?

Listening Skills

Are directions understood?

Are directions followed?

Does the student listen in class?

Are notes taken in class?

Are details added to class notes as soon as possible after class?

Is a note-taking system used?

Are abbreviations and symbols used while taking notes?

Is particular attention paid to important items cued by the lecture?

Are relevant reading materials preread before the lecture on the material?

Reading Study Skills

Is the purpose of reading the material understood?

Does the student preread?

When there are words taht the student doesn't understand in the reading, does the student detemine their meaning and write them down?

Is the student easily distracted or bored while reading?

Does the student know how to take notes in textbooks?

Is the student able to adjust reading speed to the material?

Is a reading technique used when reading difficult assignments?

Does the student outline reading assignments? Does the student know how to "map" a reading?

Does the student use headings and other typographical aids?

Can the student read tables, charts, and graphs?

Does the student know how to use the table of contents and index of a book?

(... Table 1, continued)

Is the student able to comprehend the textbooks?

Can the student predict outcomes, distinguish fact from opinion, discern emotional appeals, recognize bias, discern inference?

Reporting Skills

Does the student organize thoughts before beginning a written assignment? Does he or she write a first draft?

Does the student proofread for success/failure in answering the purpose of the assignment, legibility, neatness, spelling, complete sentences, and punctuation errors?

With which reporting techniques is the student most familiar? Most capable?

Which does he or she prefer?

Test-taking Habits

Does the student space learning over several sessions (vs. cramming)?

Does the student study using the SQ3R (see Reading Study Skills) or a similar method? Does the student use study guides while studying?

Does the student predict test questions?

Does the student know and use good test-taking strategies?

Does the student perform significantly better on practice than on actual tests?

Are short-term assignments kept track of in a book or log? Are long-term assignments, tests, reports, and projects kept track of in a calendar? Assignment books or sheets and calendars should be required of all students as soon as they are expected to complete work independently. Often teachers need to make sure that assignments are actually written down, and school psychologists often need to reinforce teachers for monitoring this procedure. If a student has considerable difficulty writing down assignments, even given careful monitoring by the teacher, a "buddy" can be seated next to the child to help make sure assignments are recorded.

Students need specific guidance in learning how to break long-term assignments into small components and integrate the components into their assignment books. The use of a calendar becomes critical as students become older and have multiple long-term assignments as well as multiple teachers.

Does the student (grades 4 and below) keep one folder for assignment sheets with "work to do" on the left and "work to turn in" on the right? This is an extremely effective method for managing work sheets in the lower grades. Often children at this age level find "Trapper-keepers" and notebooks too cumbersome and confusing.

Does the student (grades 5 and above) keep a loose-leaf notebook organized chronologically, by subject? Loose-leaf notebooks are most efficient because handouts and notes from the textbook can be added in chronological order. Each subject should be in a separate section. There should also be a pouch for supplies and a section for assignments.

Does the student come to class with notebook, pencil, completed homework, and textbook? Students need a certain place at home to keep materials "to go to school." It is important that this place not be cluttered with other materials. If a student does come to class unprepared, less desirable supplies should be given as substitutes to avoid reinforcing irresponsibility.

Is the student's desk, cubby, or locker neat enough that the student can locate required materials quickly? Teachers can provide specific times for the entire class to clean out both desks and notebooks. Students with severe organizational problems will need an adult or mature student buddy to help sort their papers. Unscheduled and scheduled notebook and desk checks, with rewards for good organization, are helpful. For students who become disorganized between classroom cleanups (for some students this can be daily), a cleaning routine should be established, with neatness criteria, timeline, and reinforcement for keeping neat enough so that major cleanups are not necessary.

Can the student use the catalogue in the library? Can the student use the periodical index? Surprisingly large numbers of older students are not independent in using these essential resources.

Basic Skills at Home

Where does the student prefer to do homework? Is there a place at home to study that is quiet and well lighted, with a table or desk? Are supplies, reference books, and a dictionary kept there? Where a

TABLE 2
Checklist of Classroom Qualities that Foster Study Skills

General:	The class climate is positive
	The teacher relates the material to students' experiences.
	Tasks are stimulating and challenging.
	Students are treated as individuals with varied needs and talents.
	Regular successes are experienced by the students, and displayed.
	The classroom is organized.
	The classroom is free from unnecessary distractions: quiet for independent work, with minimal visual distractions.
	Expectations for students are clear.
	Students are allowed to help set goals and choose reinforcers.
	Students are not subjected to public humiliation.
	Advance organizers are provided.
	Before speaking, the teacher gains the attention of the class.
Assignments:	Students are given prompt feedback.
	Work is collected, corrected, and returned promptly.
	The teacher gives assignments both orally and in writing.
	Assignments are clear.
	The teacher checks that students write assignments in an assignment book or long-term calendar when assigned.
	Homework assignments follow successful classroom practice.
	Worksheets have sufficient writing space (e.g., second grade arithmetic is not typewritten), are dark enough to read.
	Writing assignments are integrated into the curriculum.
Lectures:	Unfamiliar concepts are taught before lectures or readings.
	Students are taught to relate material to their own lives.
	Frequent examples are given in class.
	Visual aids are frequently used.
	Relevant material is distinguished from irrelevant material.
	The teacher frequently checks for students' understanding by asking open-ended questions related to the topic.
	When children do not understand, the teacher rephrases, substituting key words and simplifying grammar.
Reading and notetaking:	Students are taught to recognize a speaker's or writer's purpose.
	Students are taught to identify their own purposes in reading.
	Students are taught to note transitions in the talk or text.
	Students are taught to recognize main points.
	Students are taught to note supporting details and examples.
	Students are taught to note the sequence of ideas.
	Students are taught to take notes.
	Students are taught how to summarize.
	Students are taught how to draw conclusions.
	Students are taught how to make inferences.
Tests:	Tests are administered in a low-anxiety atmosphere.
	Students know test question formats before the test.
	The material to be covered on tests is clear to students.

TABLE 3
Student Interview Questions

About you:	What do you like to do best?
	What do you like to do least?
	What do you do especially well?
	What do you least well?
	What do you get praised for doing?
	What are your strongest skills and abilities?
	What are fve jobs you might like to have as an adult?
	What would you like to know, and know how to do, when you have finished school?
At school:	What are your favorite school activities?
	What do you dislike most about school?
	Why do you think you don't do well in school?
	What are five skills you believe are important to succeed in school?
	What grades do you want to get in school?
At home:	What grades do your parents want you to get in school?
	Do your parents praise you for your school work?
	Where do you like to study? When?
	How much sleep do you get each night?
	What type of exercise do you get? How often?
	What chores do you have at home?
	Keep a log of your activities for a week, blocked off in half-hour units.

student prefers to study needs to be taken into account. Some students find working in their own room too lonely, and constantly seek adult attention to alleviate loneliness. Such students may study better at the kitchen table while supper is prepared. Other students may prefer to work at the library, and transportation will need to be negotiated. The most effective strategy is for a student to study in only one place, so that efficient studying is associated with that location.

Is there a regular, quiet time to study at home? Helping parents and students agree upon a "study hour" is one of the simplest yet most effective interventions. Finding a quiet time to study can be very challenging in busy households, and the establishment of a daily study hour best takes into account already scheduled extracurricular activities, chores, and favorite TV shows. In addition to these factors, the student's ability to concentrate at different times of the day should be considered. Some can focus much better in the early morning, others after supper, and others right after school. Many elementary school children are too tired after dinner to be able to concentrate efficiently, and this is demonstrated by their being easily frustrated and slow to complete tasks. Ideally, the family agrees upon a study hour (perhaps 7:00 to 8:00 each night), the television and stereo are turned off, phone calls are not taken, and the entire family studies, reads, or completes paperwork.

Does the student estimate how long it will take to complete an assignment? Is this time estimate used to make a daily schedule? Is the schedule followed? Students often have unrealistic ideas of the length of time it takes to complete given tasks. Timing a student completing a worksheet or reading assignment can produce helpful planning guidelines. Daily schedules should be written down. If keeping to the schedule becomes problematic, a behavior management system can be implemented.

Does the student follow a schedule and do the same things at about the same time every day or week? A routine schedule, although difficult to achieve in many busy families, has many advantages. Most important, a routine reduces arguments between parents and students.

What does the student do when unable to understand something at home? Some parents are clearly more skilled at helping with homework than others, and some students have no one whom they feel comfortable asking for help. If this is the case, students will need help brainstorming how they might solve this dilemma. Sometimes a neighbor or another family member (older sibling, cousin, grandparent) can be helpful; some communities have a homework hotline; some students prefer to ask the teacher for help before or after school. Often it is helpful for students to have "study buddies," peers who have shared their telephone numbers and call one another for help.

TABLE 4
Study Skills Curriculum Materials

Publisher	Title	Level	Format
Academic Resources Corporation Acton, MA	*Effective Study Skills*	12–adult	video
American Guidance Service 4201 Woodland Rd. P.O. Box 99 Circle Pines, MN 55014-1796	*Homework Coach*	12–adult	video
	How to Study	12–adult	book
	Improving Your Study Skills	12–adult	book
	Programmed Study Techniques	12–adult	workbook
	Study Skills and Strategies	12–adult	book
Crowell Press 10 e. 53rd St. New York, NY 10022	*I Hate School: How to Hang in and When to Drop Out*	15–18	self-help manual
Curriculum Associates 5 Esquire Road N. Billerica, MA 01862	*Skills for School Success*	8–18	content area integration video and books available in Spanish
	Thirty Lessons in Outlining	8–18	booklets
	Brigance Prescriptive Study Skills: Strategies and Practice	8–adult	
	Organization Skills	10–13	booklets
	Following Directions	7–12	booklets
	Notetaking	10–13	booklets
	Research Reports	8–12	booklets
Hawthorne Press	*Study Skills for Students in Our Schools*	8–18	worksheets and teacher interventions
Lakeshore Learning Materials 2695 E. Dominguez St. P.O. Box 6261 Carson, CA 90749	*Basic Study Skills Workbooks*	8–12	workbooks
	Getting Smarter: The Study Skills Improvement Program	8–12	workbooks
	Improve Your Grades	12–18	booklet
	Strategies for Study	10–12	
	Study Skills for People Who Hate to Study	12–18	video
Rosen Publishing Group 29 E. 21st Street New York, NY 10010	*Coping with Academic Anxiety*	12–adult	self-help book
Thinking Publications P.O. Box 163 Eau Claire, WI	*Study Smart*	10–18	game
United Learning 6633 W. Howard St. Niles, IL	*Developing Effective Study Skills*	8–12	filmstrips, worksheets
	High School Study Skills	12–18	multi-media
William & Morrow & Co., NY 105 Madison Ave. New York, NY 10016	*How to Take Tests*	12–18	self-help handbook
	How to Be School Smart: Secrets of Successful Schoolwork	8–12	handbook
Write Source Educational Pub. Box 460 Burlington, WI 53105	*Write Source 2000*	10–18	student handbook and classroom materials

What kind of homework does the student enjoy? Dislike? Why? Asking students what kind of homework they like is interesting because most students assume they dislike all types of homework, when they actually do have homework they like (projects, perhaps). Knowing homework preferences helps in developing a homework schedule. Some students prefer to get the disliked homework done first, while others prefer to do their easier work first. Students can be made aware that when they dislike a subject, they can find ways to make it less frustrating. For example, they might set themselves a goal of doing five math problems and then taking a stretch.

What does the student like about the way he handles homework? Dislike? Whatever students dislike about the way they handle homework can be subjected to a brainstorming session. Then one of the solutions brainstormed can be chosen, tried, and evaluated. For example, a student may dislike a habit of procrastinating, and may decide to try rewarding himself with a telephone call to a friend or shooting baskets after completing an assignment.

Does the parent regularly check the assignment calendar/homework sheet with the child, as well as checking for notices, permission slips, and other school communication? Does the parent monitor homework completion? Students generally need help from their parents in prioritizing activities, establishing consistent homework and bedtime routines, and organizing books, notebooks, and papers for return to school. Even more important, they need their parents to provide structure and praise. Generally, students need less supervision as they get older, and by junior high they often make and keep their own homework schedule. Some adolescents, particularly students with LD, will continue to need considerable parental involvement.

Listening Skills

Are directions understood? The comprehension of oral communications is often assumed, yet students frequently do not understand what is said to them. Comprehension of directions can be checked by having students tell you, in their own words, what needs to be done. It is helpful for students to write (circle, if the directions are written) each action word, number each action, and cross off each number after completion (Kuepper, 1990).

Are directions followed? If students understand the directions yet still do not follow them, perhaps they do not attend to directions, or they do not want to follow directions. The former can be remedied by having the student read the directions subvocally before starting the paper. Lack of desire to follow directions needs to be further explored in an expanded student interview to determine the benefits (such as adult attention) the student gains from noncompli-

ance, and to delineate alternate methods to obtain the same benefit.

Does the student listen in class? Not listening in class can be caused by many factors, including chronic or intermittent hearing loss, preoccupation with personal issues, a boring presentation, or weak listening skills. Many studies have demonstrated that listening skills can be taught (Devine, 1987); a number of strategies to improve listening skills are provided by Devine (1987) and Williams et al. (1993).

Listening skills can be assessed through the use of standardized instruments, including the Woodcock-Johnson Psychoeducational Battery (Woodcock & Johnson, 1989). The Test of Language Competence (Wiig & Secord, 1989) assesses the knowledge a student has of the deep meaning of language, including idioms, making inferences, and understanding dual meanings. The Clinical Evaluation of Language Fundamentals-Revised (Semel, Wiig, & Secord, 1989) assesses comprehension of oral directives, sentence structure, linguistic concepts, and oral paragraphs. If one determines that the student has a deficiency in one of these areas, efforts toward remediation and compensation will be appropriate.

Are notes taken in class? Does each page of notes have the date and topic written at the top? Notetaking has several advantages, including improving acquisition of material and improving the ability of students to listen. Students' ability to take orderly notes needs to be assessed by every teacher, and students often need supervised practice. Notes should be orderly, labeled, and legible, written in the student's own words, and contain all key words and some supporting details. Many of the materials included in Table 4 have specific methods to teach these skills.

Are details added to class notes as soon as possible after class? Completing notes right after class is extremely beneficial because it provides another learning trial, and because students are better able to remember and correct details if only a short time has elapsed. It is very beneficial if the teacher allows time for this at the end of the class period, so students can ask questions about unclear material at that time.

Is a note-taking system used? Many students find it helpful to divide each page by a vertical line, taking notes on the right side and later writing "key ideas" (to be used as a study guide) on the left side.

Are abbreviations and symbols used while taking notes? Students should be encouraged to develop their own "shorthand" system.

Is particular attention paid to important items cued by the lecture? Verbal cues include repetition, foreshadowing ("We will now discuss"), consensus ("Many agree"), issues ("It's a point of debate"), absolutes ("No one," "It is certain"), summaries, and reviews. Nonverbal cues include gestures, blackboard writing, and changes in movement, tempo, and volume.

Are relevant reading materials preread before the lecture on the same material? Prereading greatly increases understanding of a lecture. It also is another method to space learning trials, and produces much better retention. It has the added advantage of encouraging the student to focus on unfamiliar words or concepts, and ask about them in class.

Reading Study Skills

Is the purpose of reading the material understood? To increase motivation and the ability to comprehend reading material, students need to understand the purpose for the material. This includes why the teacher has assigned the material and how the reading assignment relates to students' learning goals. It also includes generally understanding the author's intentions, being able to ask questions, and reading actively to answer questions.

Does the student preread? Prereading takes very little time but is one of the most important techniques to aid in understanding material. Nonfiction is preread by reviewing nontextual cues (title, author, publication date, headings and subheadings, picture, graphs, charts), reading the introduction, preface, and conclusion, and skimming the body. Fiction is preread by reading the front cover, back cover, and introduction, and skimming the first 25% of the material to determine setting, character, and plot.

When there are words that the student doesn't understand in the reading, does the student determine their meaning and write them down? SSCD (Devine, 1987) provides four approaches to unfamiliar words: Sound (students sound out the word to see if it is already in their listening vocabulary), Structure (analyze the word for familiar prefixes, suffixes, and roots), Context (guess at the meaning using clues in the surrounding passages), and Dictionary (use the dictionary or glossary to look up unfamiliar words). An alternative to using the dictionary might be asking a peer or adult.

Is the student easily distracted or bored while reading? If a student is easily bored or distracted, it can be helpful to determine how long the student can concentrate and have him or her take a brief break every so often. Taking notes, outlining, mapping, and writing down questions while reading also aid attention. Other techniques include relating something known to the topic being read, guessing what will come next, visualizing the material (making a mental movie), and making time lines or flow charts to track events while reading.

Are personal copies of textbooks available to the student? Does the student know how to take notes in textbooks by highlighting or making margin nota- tions? Personal copies of textbooks enable students to use them as much more effective learning tools. Writing margin notes in reaction to the text is more effective than highlighting because it is more active. Only one or two sentences per paragraph should be highlighted.

Is the student able to adjust reading speed to the material? Is a reading technique used when reading difficult assignments? Effective readers vary their reading speed according to the difficulty of the material. Particular care needs to be taken with difficult assignments; several techniques enable students to better understand complex reading material. The best known, SQ3R (Robinson, 1961) has these steps:

Survey: Look over the material before beginning to read to obtain a general framework in which to store supporting details. Particular attention should be given to the title, chapter headings and subheadings, charts and pictures, the introductory paragraphs, and the conclusion.

Question: Write down questions about the material before beginning to read. These questions should reflect curiosity about the topic. Another source of questions is converting headings and subheadings into questions.

Read: Read through the material in the normal way. Add unknown words to the list of questions.

Recite and Write: Give the answers to the questions to another person, or write them down. Summarize the material in writing.

Review: Go over the material several times before being tested, attending particularly to the author's purpose and key points, until overlearning occurs.

Does the student outline reading assignments? Does the student know how to "map" a reading? Outlining is one of the most effective recording techniques. It is frequently taught in the intermediate grades, but a student's ability to outline should be checked at the secondary level as well. To "map," the main topic is placed in the middle of a blank sheet of paper. Subheadings branch from the main topic, and supporting details branch from the subheadings. This creates a highly effective visual aid that increases organization and comprehension (Sebranek, Meyer, & Kemper, 1992).

Does the student use headings and other typographical aids? Can the student read tables, charts, and graphs? Does the student know how to use the table of contents and index of a book? These abilities can be checked by having the student show the psychologist his textbook, read some of the graphs and charts, and find items using the table of contents and index.

Is the student able to comprehend the textbook? Several methods may determine a student's ability to comprehend the assigned textbook. First, it is very useful to have the student review his textbook orally, explaining the pictures, graphs, and general material in a previously studied chapter. Second, have the student read aloud a passage from the text. The student should be able to read with 90% word calling accuracy and 75% accuracy in answering comprehension questions.

A second method to assess a student's ability to comprehend content material is to devise a Cloze test. This is done by photocopying approximately 260 running words from the text. The first sentence is left complete; then one of the first five words in the second sentence is blanked out, as is every fifth word until there are fifty blanks. Finish with a complete sentence. The student then reads the passage, guessing the missing words. The student should be able to guess at least 60% of the missing words (Jacobson, 1990).

A third method is to determine the readability level of the textbook and compare this score with the score obtained on a standardized reading test, such as the Test of Comprehension of the Woodcock Reading Mastery Test-Revised (Woodcock, 1987) or the Test of Reading Comprehension (Brown, Hammill, & Wiederholt, 1986). Publishers often calculate readability through one of the several indices. The problem with this method is that the scores vary considerably and even when the score is at the student's reading level there is no guarantee that the student can actually understand the text.

Several strategies can be used when a student is unable to comprehend a text: audiocassette-taping the textbook, using high-interest low-vocabulary materials, teaching textbook structure, preteaching, providing advance organizers (which might include the teacher's notes), and teaching textbook reading strategies (Meese, 1992). Devine (1987) and Robin (1983) also suggest multiple methods of dealing with students who are unable to read content area materials.

Can the student predict outcomes, distinguish fact from opinion, discern emotional appeals, recognize bias, discern inference? If not, the student will find it difficult to understand reading material at the secondary level. These critical thinking skills typically are taught in the intermediate grades, but most students will require additional instruction throughout their schooling.

Reporting Skills

Does the student organize papers, by outlining or using a story map, before writing? Does the student write a first draft? Does the student proofread for success/failure in answering the purpose of the assignment, legibility, neatness, spelling, complete sentences, and punctuation errors? Again, these skills typically are taught in the intermediate grades,

but most students will require additional instruction throughout their schooling.

With which reporting techniques is a student familiar? Most capable? Which does he or she prefer? Besides the traditional oral and written reports, nonverbal reporting techniques are available. These include preparing charts and graphs, making models, making maps, dramatic presentation, pictures, or photographs. The use of these techniques is not limited to the traditional subject: For example, maps can be employed in English class to indicate dialect use (Devine, 1987). Many students, particularly those with learning disabilities, prefer using nonverbal reporting techniques, and the school psychologist can consult with the classroom teacher to help develop appropriate nonverbal reporting techniques in various content areas.

Test-Taking Habits

Does the student space learning over several sessions (vs. cramming) and use a study plan? Does the student conduct weekly reviews? Studying for a test should be spread over several days and divided into several small units. A great deal of research has demonstrated that spaced practice results in better learning than massed practice (What works: Research about teaching and learning, 1986).

Does the student study using the SQ3R (see Reading Study Skills) or a similar method? Does the student use study guides while studying? In addition to using study guides provided by teachers and in the textbook, it is helpful for the student to group information into meaningful units. "Mapping" and other visual aids are particularly helpful to this end.

Does the student predict test questions? Having a student make up test questions while studying, including multiple choice, short answer, and essay questions, is a very effective study technique.

Does the student know and use good test-taking strategies? These include coming to the exam with everything needed; reviewing the directions carefully, including any sample items; skimming through the entire test to determine its scope; setting up and keeping a schedule; reading each question carefully (on essays, responding precisely to words such as discuss, describe, illustrate, explain, evaluate; on multiple choice, being wary of words such as always, never, everyone); outlining the important points to be covered before responding to an essay question; postponing an extremely difficult question; attempting to answer every question; writing neatly; and rechecking work before handing it in (Deese & Deese, 1979).

Does the student perform significantly better on practice tests than on actual tests? If so, anxiety may be reducing test performance; relaxation and/or slow breathing exercises may be helpful. Cognitive behavioral strategies outlined by Ottens (1984) also may be useful.

SUMMARY

Study skills significantly affect students' school functioning and can be taught at all ages and levels of ability. Teachers often do not provide instruction in study skills because they assume that students already have mastered them. Frequently diagnosis and interventions to improve organization or study skills can take place in the prereferral stage and prevent the need for more extensive assessments and interventions. School psychologists' training greatly facilitates their work in improving students' study skills.

The most productive assessment method uses an ecological approach, involving classroom observations, analyses of work samples, consultations with teachers and parents, student interviews, observing the student at work and having him describe his work method, and examining the student's notebooks, assignment books, and completed work. One must precisely identify areas of weakness to design effective remediation. This chapter groups study skill assessments and interventions into five areas: Basic Skills, Listening Skills, Reading Study Skills, Reporting Skills, and Test-Taking Habits. In addition, questions to supplement clinical interviews are provided, as well as a checklist of classroom characteristics facilitating good study skills. Effective remediation requires that the school psychologist, teacher, and parent work together closely to determine appropriate procedures, designate responsibilities, and design techniques to encourage generalization.

REFERENCES

Brown, V. L., Hammill, D. D., & Wiederholt, J. L. (1986). *Test of reading comprehension*. Circle Pines, MN: American Guidance Service.

Brown, W. F., & Holtzman, W. H. (1967). *Survey of study habits and attitudes*. San Antonio, TX: Psychological Corporation.

Canter, L., & Canter, M. (1987). *Homework without tears*. Santa Monica, CA: Canter & Associates.

Deese, J., & Deese, E. K. (1979). *How to study* (3rd ed.). New York: McGraw-Hill.

Demos, G. D. (1976). *Study skills counseling evaluation*. Los Angeles, CA: Western Psychological Corporation.

Devine, T. G. (1987). *Teaching study skills* (2nd ed.). Boston: Allyn & Bacon.

Graham, K. G., & Robinson, H. A. (1984). *Study skills handbook: A guide for all teachers*. Newark, DE: International Reading Association.

How to help your child achieve in school. (1988). Pueblo, CO: Consumer Information Center (Dept. 109M).

Jacobson, J. M. (1990). Group vs. individual completion of a cloze passage. *Journal of Reading, 33*, 244–250.

Kuepper, J. E. (1990). Best practices in teaching study skills. In A. Thomas & J. Grimes (Eds.), *Best practices in school psychol-ogy–II* (pp. 711–721). Washington, DC: National Association of School Psychologists.

Langan, J. (1978). *Reading and study skills*. New York: McGraw-Hill.

Loene, P. (1983). Teaching learning disabled adolescents to monitor their behavior. *Pointer, 27*(2), 14–17.

Mannix, D. (1989). *Be a better student: Lessons and worksheets for teaching behavior management in grades 4–9*. West Nyack, NY: Center for Applied Research in Education.

Meese, R. L. (1992). Adapting textbooks for children with learning disabilities in mainstreamed classrooms. *Teaching Exceptional Children, 24*, 49–51.

Ottens, A. J. (1984). *Coping with academic anxiety*. New York: Rosen.

Robinson, F. P. (1961). *Effective study* (4th ed.). New York: Harper & Row.

Rubin, D. (1983). *Teaching reading and study skills in content areas*. New York: Holt, Rinehart, and Winston.

Sebranek, P., Meyer, V., & Kemper, D. (1992). *Write source 2000*. Burlington, WI: Write Source Educational Publishing House.

Segal, J., Chipman, S., & Glasser, R. (1985). *Thinking and learning skills, Vol. 1: Relating instruction to research*. Hillsdale, NJ: Erlbaum.

Semel, E. M., Wiig, E. H., & Secord, W. (1989). *The clinical evaluation of language fundamentals-revised*. San Antonio, TX: Psychological Corporation.

What works: Research about teaching and learning. (1986). Washington, DC: U.S. Department of Education.

Wiens, W. (1983). Why teach cognitive strategies to adolescents? *Pointer, 27*(2), 5–7.

Wiig, E. H., & Secord, W. (1989). *Test of Language Competence*. San Antonio, TX: Psychological Corporation.

Williams, W., Blythe, T., White, N., Li, J., Sternberg, R., & Gardner, H. (1993). *Practical intelligence for schools*. Cambridge, MA: Harvard University, Department of Education, Project Zero.

Woodcock, R. W. (1987). *Woodcock Reading Mastery Test-Revised*. Circle Pines, MN: American Guidance Service.

Woodcock, R. W., & Johnson, M. B. (1989). *Woodcock-Johnson psycho-educational battery*. Allen TX: DLM Teaching Resources.

ANNOTATED BIBLIOGRAPHY

Williams, W., Blythe, T., White, N., Li, J., Sternberg, R., & Gardner, H. (1993). *Practical intelligence for schools.*. Cambridge, MA: Harvard University, Department of Education, Project Zero.
This middle school curriculum focuses on increasing "practical intelligence" in reading, writing, organizing, and test taking. Many creative classroom activities are suggested, including leading students to assess their areas of strength and weakness.

Canter, L., & Canter, M. (1987). *Homework without tears*. Santa Monica, CA: Canter & Associates.
This book is a parents' guide for motivating children to do homework.

Devine, T. G. (1987). *Teaching study skills: A guide for teachers* (2nd ed.). Boston, MA: Allyn and Bacon.
This text provides guidelines and multiple strategies for the improvement of listening, textbook reading, thinking process, vocabulary, notetaking, homework, research skills, comprehension, reporting, remembering, test taking, and motivation.

Mannix, D. (1989). *Be a better student: Lessons and worksheets for teaching behavior management in grades 4–9.* West Nyack, NY: Center for Applied Research in Education.
This book suggests strategies to use in teaching students to identify problem behaviors and devise, implement, and evaluate action plans regarding organization, motivation, listening skills, and homework.

McCarney, S. B., & Wunderlich, K. K. (1988). *The pre-referral intervention manual.* Columbia, MO: Hawthorne Educational Services.
The manual contains hundreds of intervention techniques to help students of all ages improve memory, organization, listening, speaking, reading, writing, performance, motivation, and behavior.

79

Best Practices for Increasing Academic Learning Time

Maribeth Gettinger
University of Wisconson–Madison

OVERVIEW

There continues to be considerable interest among educational researchers in examining time variables that are related to school achievement. One of the most consistent findings from research on learning time is that the amount of time students devote to active engagement in appropriate learning activities is significantly related to their achievement outcomes (Gettinger, 1986). Time has been accorded special significance by teachers and classroom consultants because of the well-documented relationship between time and learning. In addition, time, unlike less malleable determinants of achievement such as student ability, is viewed as a manipulable facet of school and classroom life that teachers are able to control. Indeed, research has shown that certain teacher behaviors and classroom practices can, in fact, influence the amount of time students are engaged in learning (Brophy & Good, 1986).

For classroom teachers, time is a limited and critical resource. There is only a finite amount of time in which to accomplish multiple educational goals, often for academically diverse groups of students. Although most teachers acknowledge the importance of using instructional time efficiently and effectively to improve learning, many may not fully appreciate or understand their own role in the management of classroom time. According to Goodman (1990), "the master variable of pedagogy is the amount and intensity of student engagement in appropriate learning tasks. Effective learning time depends heavily on the atmosphere of the classroom and on the teacher's leadership skills in managing the instructional tasks" (pp. 10–11). This statement underscores the significance of instructional time, appropriate learning tasks, and teachers' instructional and managerial skills for enhancing classroom learning.

One recommendation that emerges from recent research on instructional time is that teachers should try to minimize the extent of discrepancy between allocated learning time and engaged learning time in their classrooms. Such a recommendation, however, is not helpful unless classroom consultants can provide more specific guidelines about how to engage students and how to use instructional time effectively. Because of their evolving role as classroom-based, instructional consultants, school psychologists need to be aware of, and must be able to apply, findings from research that link specific teaching practices with high levels of engaged learning time. The purpose of this chapter is to describe best practices for working with classroom teachers to improve their use of instructional time to maximize student engagement and achievement. In accordance with the problem-solving approach adopted for this volume, the following discussion of basic considerations focuses on defining academic learning time and its components, and on describing procedures for assessing current levels of learning time, for setting reasonable goals for change, and for monitoring progress or improvement. The subsequent section on best practices describes strategies for increasing academic learning time that can be offered to classroom teachers through collaboration and consultation with school psychologists.

BASIC CONSIDERATIONS

School psychologists' ability to help teachers maximize academic learning time among students is predicated on several basic considerations. The first is an understanding of the concept of *academic learning time* (ALT) and its relationship to learning. Of all the time variables that have been investigated in recent years (e.g., time-on-task, allocated time), ALT has been shown to be most consistently associated with students' achievement (Fisher & Berliner, 1985). A complex concept related to a number of other dimensions of instructional time, ALT is defined as the portion of instructional time allocated to a subject-matter area during which students are engaged actively and successfully in instructional activities. Three individual elements collectively constitute ALT: (a) allocated time, (b) engagement time, and (c) success rate.

Allocated time is the amount of instructional time made available by the teacher for learning. It represents the upper limit of students' in-class opportunities to be engaged in learning activities. One requirement of effective teaching is to be able to allocate and organize instructional time effectively. Because teachers differ in their ability to manage instructional activities, allocated time may vary considerably across classrooms. Furthermore, allocated learning time may differ from student to student even in the same classroom because of variable outside-of-class time that learners devote to individual study or homework. For example, one student may self-allocate 20 minutes of study time for spelling every night, whereas another may only spend 5 minutes. Over a five-day period, this will result in a range of allocated study time from 25 to 100 minutes. For purposes of this chapter, only in-class, instructional time allocated by teachers will be considered.

Engagement rate is the proportion of allocated instructional time during which students appear to be learning, as evidenced by observable behaviors such as paying attention, completing written problems, or interacting with peers about assigned work. Whether students are engaged in learning depends not only on how academic content is presented by the teacher and for how long, but also on how much time students actively study it. Teachers do not produce active or engaged learning time directly; they provide opportunities to learn that students then exploit to a greater or lesser extent. Even in classrooms where students have the same opportunity to learn, disparities exist among students in their individual levels of engagement. In one sixth-grade classroom, for example, Smyth (1985) found that engagement rates among individual students ranged from as low as 38% of the allocated time to as high as 78%. When these rates are extrapolated to an entire school year, the differences between low- and high-achieving students in their accumulated hours of engaged learning time could be expected to range from 46 hours to 280 hours.

Although they are important classroom variables, neither allocated time nor engagement rate impute any specific value to the learning activities involved. For example, it is possible that some students may spend time engaged in learning activities that are so easy or so difficult as to be of little educational value. Notwithstanding the need to provide a certain amount of challenging material, research indicates that children gain most of their engaged learning time when they experience a relatively high level of success (Myers, 1990). In addition, students spend more time engaged in tasks that match their current level of knowledge and skill. Therefore, *success rate* is another critical component of ALT.

Success rate represents the proportion of allocated instructional time that students are engaged in tasks providing high, medium, or low levels of success. The ratio between the number of correct re-

sponses and the number of incorrect responses on a designated assignment constitutes the success rate for the student's performance. Although success rate guidelines vary across different researchers, a high success rate is commonly viewed as at least 80% accuracy, in such assignments as responding to teachers' questions during class discussions, completing math problems, or spelling words. In other words, students should encounter a preponderance of success in their daily work, and the ratio between correct and incorrect responding should favor success by at least a 4-to-1 margin. Ensuring a high success rate depends, in part, on the teacher's ability to match the difficulty of learning tasks to students' ability level. In fact, the teacher's ability to assess the knowledge and skill level of individual students relative to academic tasks is a strong predictor of ALT.

In light of its complexity, efforts to increase ALT require that (a) teachers maximize their allocations of instructional time, (b) students have high engagement rates, and (c) students experience a high level of success on assigned academic tasks. Although it is not possible to prescribe an optimal level of ALT, the consistency of the relationship between ALT and achievement across a number of different studies suggests that the more ALT a student experiences, the greater the learning that presumably has occurred.

A second basic consideration for school psychologists is familiarity with assessment strategies for evaluating use of instructional time in classrooms as well as academic learning time among students. Such an undertaking, seen as a problem-solving task, entails helping teachers to analyze their own use of time and to target potential areas for change.

Figure 1 presents a framework for examining time use in classrooms that includes the three elements of ALT described above. First, allocated time is examined as a function of two variables: (a) opportunity time, which is the total amount of time available in the school day, and (b) actual instructional time, or the amount of opportunity time that is actually allocated to instruction by teachers. Second, engaged time is examined as a portion of allocated time; this requires an estimate of the amount of time during which students are actively involved in learning activities. Finally, ALT, or the amount of engaged time in which students are experiencing at least 80% success, is examined.

Best practices for increasing ALT begin with a comprehensive analysis of ALT in schools and individual classrooms using the framework presented in Figure 1. Such an analysis can serve to heighten teachers' awareness of their use of instructional time and to help them see for themselves that a considerable loss of potential learning time can occur during the day. Two types of time analysis procedures can be conducted. For the first procedure, the school psychologist facilitates discussions among small groups of teachers who teach similar grade levels or subject-

FIGURE 1. Framework for analyzing instructional time use.

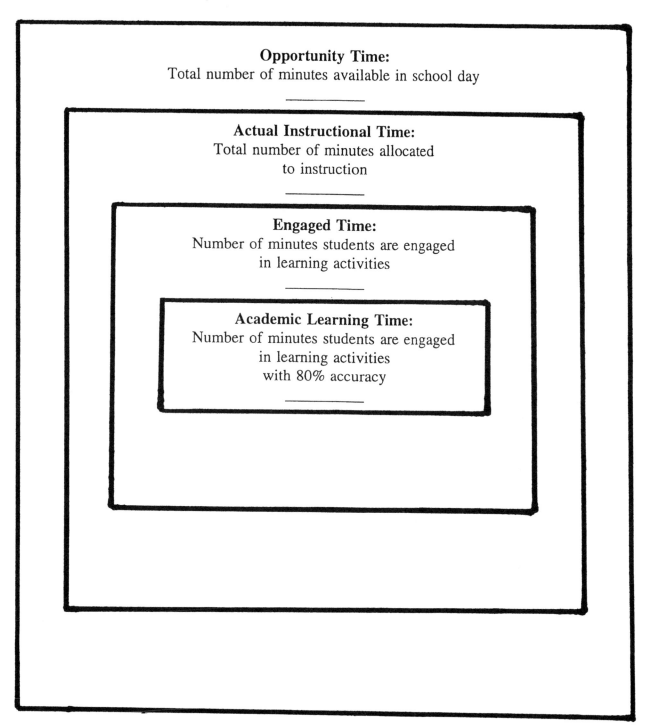

matter areas. Teachers work through the framework in Figure 1 using their existing knowledge about school operations and estimates of how they allocate class time. As a group, the teachers begin by placing the number of minutes available in a school day in the outer box. Then they examine ways that potential instructional time is lost (e.g., lunch, recess, transitions, early dismissals). When this lost time is subtracted from opportunity time, the amount that remains is available instructional time. This analysis procedure continues through the various dimensions of time until a number is determined for the inner box (ALT). Mutual analysis of time usage among teachers in small groups can provide a forum for collective dialogue on ways of modifying classroom practices in order to increase ALT.

The second procedure entails a more extensive, individualized analysis of time use in classrooms. As with the first procedure, this analysis uses the framework presented in Figure 1. However, rather than guide discussions among small groups of teachers to arrive at estimates of time allocations at the four levels, school psychologists devise and implement strategies to measure actual time usage in the individual classroom. Although this is more time-consuming than a group procedure, teachers may be more likely to view time analyses as useful when data are included from their own classrooms. Assessment strategies include reviewing existing documents such as lesson plans or daily/weekly schedules, having teachers keep personal logs or diaries of how they use class time during a typical 1- or 2-week period, interviewing teachers and students about time usage, and conducting observations of student engagement and success rates during classroom activities. When possible, it is useful for teachers to collect this type of information themselves. For example, having teachers identify and observe one or two "typical" or above average and below average students during ongoing activities can provide rich and revealing windows on students' engagement in learning.

Because of the importance of analyzing instructional time use on the basis of student engagement and success rate, school psychologists will need to develop protocols to assess the extent of students' engagement in the teaching-learning process. Figure 2 provides one example of a format for integrating data on student engagement and success.

Another self-monitoring procedure that teachers can use to analyze their class schedules and time usage was recommended by Paine (1983). For this procedure, teachers construct a written schedule of all classroom activities and compute the percentages of available class time they devote to each activity. Activities are then ranked from highest to lowest based on the percentage of time devoted to each one. These rankings indicate teachers' priorities for time use, as reflected by their schedules. It is also useful for teachers to rate overall achievement among students in each curricular area on their schedule. This allows them to determine whether there is a relationship between achievement and the amount of time they allocate to various areas. This type of classroom schedule analysis is useful in finding ways to increase or reallocate time devoted to particular activities or content.

Subsequent to an analysis of the use of classroom time, it is helpful to pursue with teachers their organizational or teaching activities. The same duration of allocated learning time and similar engagement and success rates may yield quite different learning outcomes. This occurs because some ways of organizing instructional time are more efficient than others for learning. For example, one researcher asked a group of middle school teachers to sort statements describ-ing teaching activities that ranged from "keeping on track" activities to "squandering time" activities (Murphy, 1992). In effect, all of the activities could be organized along a managerial dimension of being teacher-controlled versus student-controlled. Teacher-controlled activities were more structured and kept students engaged ("on track"). The activities had a definite goal and a definite time in which to achieve the goal. Examples included note-taking by students during a teacher-presented lesson and accomplishing assigned problems while seated at their desks. Student-controlled activities, on the other hand, had greater potential for the squandering of time, but they also had relatively higher intrinsic benefit and motivational value for the students. Examples included students' taking measures for a science experiment and discussing readings in a small group. Inherent in student-controlled learning activities are long-range gains relative to motivation and engagement that must be balanced against the potential immediate loss of instructional time. According to Wang, Gennari, and Waxman (1985), effective management of classroom activities integrates both types of activities (termed "prescriptive" and "discovery" learning activities in their model of classroom instruction) in order to maximize students' involvement in learning.

In sum, school psychologists can initiate teachers' thinking about instructional time through an analysis of the three elements that compose ALT by using the framework shown in Figure 1. Based on evaluations of current time use and overall management of classroom activities, best practices for increasing ALT in individual classes can be identified and implemented.

BEST PRACTICES

The nexus between ALT and learning outcomes, in many respects, is a commonsense notion. Classroom teachers often acknowledge that the proportion of time students spend actively and successfully engaged in learning is positively related to their achievement. Confirmation of commonsense notions, however, does not necessarily imply widespread or common acceptance. Many teachers may not possess the necessary skills or knowledge of instructional approaches that have been shown to increase ALT. In addition, they simply may not recognize the long-term impact of their allocations and use of classroom time. The way in which teachers choose to allocate time and the way in which their students are allowed to spend that time provide insights into the values teachers hold with respect to learning. Thus, it is important for school psychologists to target teachers' skills, knowledge, and values in their efforts to work collaboratively with teachers to increase students' ALT.

In recent years, research on effective instruction has focused on identifying demonstrably best prac-

FIGURE 2. Protocol for evaluating engagement and students' success levels during instruction characterized by content, instructional activity, grouping structure, and allocated time.

	Number of Students Engaged [observed every 5 mins.]	**Achievement: Productivity**	**Achievement: Success rate**
Content Area: math			
Instructional Activity: solving problems	Approximately 15 students engaged in small-group activities across five small groups.	Average of 6 problems completed for each of five small groups.	Average of 80% accuracy on problems for each of five small groups.
Grouping Structure: small-group			
Allocated Time: 20 minutes			
Content Area:			
Instructional Activity:			
Grouping Structure:			
Allocated Time:			

tices for increasing ALT. Several proven methods of classroom management and instructional approaches can be implemented to increase ALT (Hawley & Rosenholtz, 1984). Research has demonstrated that teachers can be provided with direct training or con-

sultation related to specific instructional procedures that, if implemented, will lead to more engaged learning time and higher achievement among students.

Much of the research can be organized around three paradigms: (a) the process–product paradigm,

TABLE 1
Best Practices for Increasing Academic Learning Time

Process-Product Research Paradigm: Interactive Teaching Behaviors

- Academic focus
- Interactive instructional activities
- Active academic responding
- Teacher-selected activities
- Student–teacher interactions
- Delivery of instruction approaches
- Classroom management strategies

Classroom Ecology Research Paradigms: Structure of Learning Activities

- Adaptive instruction
- Flexible grouping practices
- Integrated curriculum approach

Mediating Process Research Paradigm: Student Strategies

- Cognitive-behavioral training
- Independent learner strategies
- Self-management

---

which looks at the relationship between teachers' behaviors and students' learning; (b) the classroom–ecology paradigm, which considers the structure and characteristics of the classroom as important factors in explaining students' learning; and (c) the mediating–process paradigm, which views variations in learning as a function of activities carried out during the learning process; these activities are viewed as mediating between teacher behavior and student learning outcomes. All three strands of instructional research have contributed to our understanding of classroom learning. Best practices for increasing ALT, therefore, can be discussed relative to three general groups of recommendations: (a) teacher behaviors, (b) structural arrangement of classrooms and learning situations, and (c) student strategies and self-monitoring. The following sections present a number of teaching practices and management strategies that are supported by research as strongly associated with ALT. These are intended to serve as guidelines for school psychologists in their role as classroom consultants. These best practices for increasing ALT are summarized in Table 1 and discussed below.

Teacher Behaviors

Certain teacher behaviors and instructional management strategies can have an impact on student behavior so as to promote ALT. Collectively, these behaviors reflect what has been termed a directive or *interactive teaching style*. Interactive teaching encompasses a constellation of specific teaching behaviors related to high levels of ALT.

The primary characteristic of interactive teaching is a strong *academic focus*. Academic focus is re-flected in the amount of time devoted to academic versus nonacademic activities and in the type of instructional interaction that prevails in the classroom. Rosenshine and Stevens (1986) described classrooms with a strong academic focus as incorporating the following teaching characteristics: (a) systematic, goal-related activities; (b) lessons and content related to attaining specific goals; (c) rapid pacing of lessons; (d) ready availability of teaching materials; (e) high levels of student participation and responding; (f) efficient use of time; (g) student accountability for homework; (h) frequent monitoring of students' performance through weekly and monthly tests; and (i) positive encouragement of good work habits. There is some concern that a strong academic emphasis may be gained at the expense of affective outcomes. Research indicates, however, that classrooms with an academic focus are also characterized by warmth, friendliness, high levels of student motivation, and positive attitudes among students toward school and themselves (Berliner, 1988).

The nature of teaching activities and instructional methods is also related to ALT. Research suggests that not all academic activities are of equal instructional value. Specifically, *interactive activities*, such as discussion, review, reading aloud, and providing supportive corrective feedback, are more positively related to ALT than are noninteractive activities, such as silent reading or assignment of seatwork. Research by Stallings and her colleagues (Stallings, 1980) has consistently shown that interactive instructional activities are associated with higher levels of ALT and achievement. Spending a greater proportion of time in interactive instructional activities may be initiated after teachers first analyze their classroom activities and then think about ways to convert or modify some activities to be more interactive. For example, math problems might be solved collectively by small groups of students rather individually as an independent seatwork assignment.

Another important aspect of interactive teaching is the nature of children's participation or involvement in academic activities. Children's participation during instruction can be characterized as either active or passive. These two types of responding are not equally beneficial for students or equally related to ALT and achievement. *Active academic responding* on the part of students is related to high levels of ALT (Anderson, 1984). Active responding involves children's practicing academic tasks (e.g., answering a question, reading a text, performing the steps in solving a problem). Examples of passive responding include general attending behavior, such as listening to another child read or watching another child complete a problem. ALT can be increased by incorporating some element of active student responding into every learning activity and encouraging oral responses from all students during group lessons and discussion. Again, a careful analysis of classroom tasks might reveal how active responding can be built into particular activities. For example, students could be encouraged to ask questions and respond to answers from peers as well as answer their classmates' questions, rather than having the teacher do so. Beyond fostering active participation, this strategy allows students to practice good listening skills. In addition to maximizing ALT, active academic responding on the part of children affords the teacher numerous opportunities to monitor the students' progress and provide corrective feedback about their performance.

Inherent in an interactive teaching style is the emphasis on *teacher-selected activities*. Research has consistently shown that students are engaged more and learn more when the teacher, not the students, selects and directs learning activities (Brophy & Good, 1986). Although students continue to take responsibility for their own learning, in an interactive teaching model, the teacher has leadership in determining and structuring learning activities for students.

Interactive teaching, as the name implies, involves a high level of *student–teacher interactions*. And frequent student–teacher interactions are specifically associated with high levels of ALT. As the teacher interacts with and directs questions to students, it is important that all children be given an opportunity to participate, not just those who are eager to respond. There is ample evidence that low-functioning students, in particular, accrue lower amounts of ALT because of fewer student–teacher interactions and fewer opportunities to respond (Thurlow, Ysseldyke, Graden, & Algozzine, 1984).

Many teachers state that maintaining engagement among all students during whole-class discussions is one of the most difficult aspects of interactive teaching. An effective questioning technique for circumventing this problem is for the teacher to direct questions to students randomly or in ordered turns, moving in sequence among all children in the group or class. Random selection in calling on students has the effect of keeping students attentive, particularly if the teacher occasionally returns to a student who has recently answered a question.

Another recommendation for maintaining engagement during student–teacher interactions is to wait at least 5 seconds before providing a correct answer to a question or calling on another student to respond. Research indicates that, on the average, teachers wait only 1 second for a student to respond (Rowe, 1974). To make this finding more believable, school psychologists should ask teachers to consider a typical type of question they might ask in their classroom and then silently count to five to experience a 5-second wait. If teachers want to maintain students' engagement and increase willingness and ability to answer questions, they must provide all students adequate time to answer. When teachers fail to provide sufficient time for responding, students may learn that they can remain uninvolved simply by failing to respond immediately.

A final aspect of student–teacher interactions is feedback. Children perform better and maintain high levels of ALT when they are given frequent feedback concerning how they are doing. Feedback to students that is characterized by specificity and academic relevance has been found to be highly associated with ALT. Thus, information given to students about their performance should indicate whether responses are correct or incorrect as well as provide specific suggestions for rethinking or redoing the work. Modeling appropriate feedback to students and effective student–teacher interactions by classroom consultants is an effective way of demonstrating to teachers the positive effects of these modifications on ALT.

A number of procedures related to the actual *delivery of instruction* in an interactive teaching approach also influence levels of ALT among students. For example, valuable instructional time is often lost in classrooms because teachers may have difficulty obtaining students' attention and getting started on lessons, or making smooth transitions between activities. Several strategies can reduce the amount of time needed to start new activities. One is to select a discriminative stimulus or cue that foreshadows a new activity. The phrase or cue can be thematic, may vary every month, and can be selected by the students themselves. Teachers should be encouraged to record the time it takes students to pay attention following the cue, and to monitor the reduction in the amount of time needed across weeks. Children can be challenged to reduce the time it takes the class to get ready for a lesson from the previous time. Another guideline is to wait to begin instruction until everyone is paying attention in order to prevent having to repeat presentation of content or directions for completing work. The amount of time targeted for students to "get ready" should be optimal, allowing slower students sufficient time to attend while maintaining readiness among the faster ones.

Still another recommendation related to the delivery of instruction is to stimulate interest in a new lesson or activity by relating it to a previous lesson or experience, or starting with a motivating activity to make the initial contact with the lesson as positive as possible. We know that students' motivation and engagement in tasks can be heightened by simply indicating why the material is being learned and by suggesting ways in which the new learning may be related to other events or experiences in their lives. Another effective approach to delivery of instruction is to give precise instructions that clearly describe the goals, the activities to be completed by students relative to their goals, and the evaluation procedures associated with the lesson being presented. A significant amount of lost time stems from students' not knowing how they are to proceed with assigned tasks. To ensure that students understand instructions, teachers can ask students to paraphrase the directions, state any problems that might occur in understanding or following them, and make an oral or written commitment to follow the directions carefully. In addition, whenever possible, directions should be written and placed where they can be seen and referred to continuously by students as needed. It may also be necessary to distribute outlines, definitions, or study guides to help students organize their thoughts and focus their attention on lessons or assigned work.

Finally, interactive teaching is characterized by effective *classroom management strategies* designed to conserve instructional time. For example, the best management strategy for noninstructional transitions is to instill a routinized awareness in students of the classroom rules and procedures for such activities. Teachers whose classrooms are examples of good management invest considerable time and effort, particularly early in the year, in training students in the rules and procedures necessary for smooth classroom operation. The degree of loss of instructional time is closely tied to the teacher's management skills. Therefore, teachers may benefit from consultation or direct training in leadership and organizational skills as well as guidelines for establishing expectations for students with clear contingencies for performance. Some time loss to managerial needs is inevitable in every classroom, but the goal should be to keep lost time to a minimum. An analysis of time usage as described earlier can facilitate targeting areas for change.

In summary, interactive teaching occurs when the classroom teacher assumes a central, active, and direct role in the instructional process. Teachers who emphasize academic goals and display high levels of actual involvement with students on learning tasks generate high levels of ALT. The teacher selects the academic activities and leads students through academic tasks to accomplish specific instructional objectives. There is a high level of student–teacher interaction, most of which is initiated by the teacher. The majority of instructional time is devoted to the teacher's presentation, explanation, and demonstration. Practice, feedback, the teacher's questioning, and review of activities also figure prominently in daily instruction. The teacher monitors student progress and provides corrective feedback. The teacher holds and conveys high expectations for student performance. Finally, clarity of directions on how to undertake learning tasks, praise, and feedback on correctness of responses are all associated with high levels of ALT.

Helping teachers to think about their activities may contribute to or detract from students' engagement is a critical component of school psychologists' efforts to increase ALT. School psychologists can take an active role in encouraging teachers to evaluate their own classrooms as to how effectively time is being used. A problem often associated with recommendations to enhance ALT is a tendency, even with acknowledgment of their value, not to implement them in actual classroom teaching. It is unreasonable for school psychologists to expect that teachers will adopt several new teaching methods at one time. Therefore, it is important to encourage classroom teachers to identify one to three approaches that maximize ALT during instruction. In collaboration with a school psychologist, teachers can write one specific method that they do not currently use and that they believe could be implemented in their classroom to help increase engaged learning time among their students. For example, a teacher might write, "Place directions where they can be seen and referred to by students." After identifying and formalizing viable strategies, teachers and school psychologists together should develop a plan for implementing the procedure, specifying when teachers will begin using the method, the length of time for implementation before evaluating its effectiveness, and a method for evaluating effectiveness.

School psychologists can play an important role in helping teachers collect data to evaluate the effectiveness of a new approach. Whenever possible, teachers should generate some form of evaluative data to assess the results of using new methods. For example, during a question-and-answer period when a teacher is implementing a 5-second wait strategy to increase engagement among students, the school psychologist or teacher can count the number of hands that are raised to answer each question and compare this with the typical number of students who raise their hands during a time when a 5-second wait strategy is not used.

Structural Arrangement of Classrooms and Learning Situations

Increasing ALT among students also requires incorporating innovative practices to restructure and reorganize classroom learning that extend beyond individual teacher behaviors. The heterogeneity of most classrooms today poses a unique challenge to teachers in their efforts to increase ALT among all students. Therefore, school psychologists should work with teachers through individual consultation or in-service training to structure learning activities in accordance with approaches that have been shown to promote high levels of ALT and achievement among diverse students. Collectively, these approaches are called *adaptive instruction.* Adaptive classrooms are designed to accommodate a wide range of individual differences among students. Conceptually, adaptive instruction is viewed as a two-way enterprise between the classroom environment, on one hand, and the students themselves. Hence, efforts to adapt to student diversity have a dual focus: (a) to structure the learning environment to accommodate students' needs, and (b) to provide students with independent learning strategies to improve their capability to adapt to the demands of the classroom. In this section, two strategies that entail the modification of classroom structure are described: (a) flexible grouping practices, and (b) integrated curriculum approaches. Student strategies for independent learning are discussed in the final section.

Flexible grouping practices represent a resolution to a paradox that school psychologists are likely to confront as they assist teachers in attempting to maximize ALT. Whole-class instruction has the potential for enhancing overall engagement by virtue of the teacher's ability to collectively monitor and foster active responding among all students at one time. Whole-class instruction, however, may not provide individual students with sufficient opportunities to respond or with material at an appropriate level of difficulty in order to ensure the high success rate necessary for ALT. Individual seatwork, on the other hand, lends itself to providing high levels of student success, but it may minimize students' engagement. Furthermore, individual teaching and learning activities may not always represent the most efficient use of allocated instructional time. Teaching students in small groups or having students work cooperatively in groups can circumvent some of the problems inherent in individual or whole-class teaching.

The key to grouping practices that are successful in increasing ALT is flexibility. In other words, membership in groups should change on the basis of specific needs of students and the nature of the learning activity. The decisions made about grouping for instruction are important because of their management implications and instructional impact. For example, heterogeneous grouping arrangements foster high levels of engagement in activities that are designed to be cooperative — that is, activities in which students coordinate their individual skills and efforts to achieve a group goal. Typically, exploratory tasks lend themselves to heterogeneous grouping. These are tasks designed to foster social development and to enrich or apply basic skills, such as playing games or solving problems. For group activities to maintain a high level of student involvement, tasks must be selected to allow each student to function as a contributing member. Every student needs the opportunity to be both challenged and successful on the learning task (necessary components of ALT), which may require adding easier or smaller components for low-ability students as well as more difficult or complex ones for high-ability students.

Homogeneous grouping, on the other hand, allows students to work on material according to their achievement level. Homogeneous grouping arrangements allow the teacher to provide assistance geared to the level of students in the group, thus maximizing their ALT. Prescriptive tasks are more appropriate for homogeneous groups, such as completing independent seat work problems, receiving teacher-directed explanations or instruction, or being tutored in basic skills.

Table 2 provides an example of a math lesson that incorporates flexible grouping to increase individual levels of engaged learning time among heterogeneous learners. By selectively incorporating whole-class, small-group, and individual teaching, the classroom teacher is able to increase the efficiency of the time allocated for teaching this math lesson. An important role for the classroom consultants is to work collaboratively with classroom teachers to adjust lessons and teaching formats to be more flexible.

In sum, decisions about how children are best grouped for instruction to maximize ALT, particularly children who are experiencing academic difficulty, should reflect teachers' knowledge of engagement patterns in their classrooms and of how to make the best use of instructional time. Each grouping option impacts differently on students' engagement. Whole-group instruction may be easiest to manage because the teacher can supervise all students at one time. Small-group instruction entails greater management skills on the part of the teacher, but it is more effective in engendering high levels of student–teacher interaction. Finally, individualized instruction facilitates matching instruction to each child's unique needs and skill level to maximize success rate. Efforts to increase ALT reside in the careful and selective application of whole-class, small-group, or individualized teaching according to the particular needs of students.

TABLE 2
Example of Flexible Grouping for Math Instruction

Grouping	Activity
Whole-class grouping	Explain concept of two-digit subtraction with borrowing.
Heterogeneous groups	Play game "Break the Bank" in groups of 4–5 students. Game provides opportunity to perform operation at concrete level.
Homogeneous groups	Independent skill practice on computation problems.
Individual instruction	Individual assistance from teacher on computation problems as needed.
Heterogeneous groups	Choice of enrichment activities: (1) Create own game. (2) Write own story problems.
Whole-class grouping	Review concept. Student presentations of group enrichment activity product.

The recommendation for an *integrated curriculum strategy* emerges from the lack of adequate instructional time for content-area teaching that is often encountered, particularly in the upper elementary grades. Lack of instructional time is often identified as a major limiting factor in improving the quality of instruction in content areas such as science, history, and social studies. For example, within the restricted instructional time available, many elementary science programs include only assigned reading activities in science textbooks. Educators attribute the generally negative attitudes displayed by students at the secondary level toward specific content areas, such as science and history, to the lack of in-depth instruction in elementary school that includes hands-on activities. At the same time, educators stress the importance of content-based reading activities as vehicles for developing applied reading comprehension and thinking skills, but they also acknowledge the limited amount of instructional time available for such activities.

An integrated curriculum strategy that teaches applied reading skills across a range of content areas is one approach to circumvent this problem – that is, to increase ALT in content-area reading and, simultaneously, provide additional time for in-depth thinking activities. The goal of such a strategy is to improve the quality of both the content-area and reading instruction within an integrated time frame that reallocates the combined instructional time assigned to all curriculum areas. For example, Romance and Vitale (1992) described an integrated curriculum strategy designed to increase the time allocated for in-depth science teaching by replacing the district-adopted basal reading program with science-content-based instruction that concomitantly facilitated reading comprehension skills. They found that ALT in both science and reading activities increased for students as well as their achievement, attitudes toward science and reading, and academic self-confidence.

Student Strategies and Self-Monitoring

The concept of ALT implies instructional, managerial, and cognitive-behavioral concerns. Achievement is in large part a function of discrepancies between time allocated by teachers for learning and time spent by students cognitively engaged with the content of learning tasks. Even when students appear to be actively engaged in learning, their ALT may not be optimal because they may have difficulty allocating attention efficiently to information within tasks. This may be particularly true for students with learning problems whose slower rates of acquisition and subsequent lower achievement have been linked to inefficient cognitive-behavioral strategies (Goodman, 1990). Best practices for increasing ALT implicate procedures to improve not only how teachers allocate and structure available time (instructional efficiency), but also how students use instructional time (cognitive efficiency).

According to Corno and Mandinach (1983), cognitive engagement refers to students' processing of task-oriented information as well as some degree of cognitive regulation. To maximize cognitive engagement, students need to receive training in general problem-solving skills. By teaching students to attend to and apply strategies common to all problem-solving situations, teachers can increase students' self-regulated ALT across several different learning tasks. For example, Hallahan and his colleagues (Hallahan et al., 1983) have shown that when students with learning disabilities are trained to self-monitor and self-record their attention during independent seatwork periods, they demonstrate higher levels of on-task behavior as well as gains in academic productivity (number of correct responses per unit of allocated time). Gerber (1988) obtained similar positive effects on both level of attending and achievement when students were taught to monitor the quality of their performance (e.g., "Am I checking my spelling?") rather than simply attention to the task (e.g., "Am I paying attention?"). Finally, Palincsar and Brown (1984) concluded from a series of studies that to be successful, cognitive training must direct students to be cognitively engaged during learning tasks, must provide corrective feedback on appropriate use of trained strategies, and must provide instruction concerning when and why such strategies should be *applied.*

The systematic application of cognitive-behavioral training (CBT) as part of instruction that enhances self-regulation during learning can increase ALT. By providing a self-managed problem-solving routine, CBT reduces the difficulty of tasks in terms of information load. If students can be taught to approach learning tasks in a more structured, organized fashion, it is reasonable to expect that they also will be more efficient with their learning time. By facilitating students' ability to organize information more efficiently, CBT increases the probability of correct responses (high success rate) during learning activities.

Another factor that contributes to an increase in individual ALT is students' *independent functioning* in the classroom. To try to manage the range of ability levels in heterogeneous classrooms and to enable each child to exhibit maximum ALT for specified time periods, a systematic approach toward developing independent learners is necessary (Cohen & de Bettencourt, 1988). Students can be taught directly to guide themselves through much of their day with minimal assistance from a teacher and with minimal loss of engaged learning time.

There are several best practices for teaching and encouraging students to become independent learners. For example, students able to perform tasks may not approach them systematically, which often results in time lost while they are getting started on an assignment. Teaching children a systematic task approach can be accomplished by using a step-by-step sequence that helps children structure that behavior. The procedure may consist of having students ask themselves a series of questions listed on an individualized job card (e.g., What materials do I need?; How much time do I have?). Before beginning an assigned task, students use their job cards to determine what needs to be done and whether they have the knowledge, skills, materials, and time to complete it.

Another way in which students can enhance the efficiency of classroom use of time is through *self-management.* A growing body of research shows that students are capable of fulfilling some instructional functions typically carried out by the teacher. Training students to assume a degree of responsibility for their own instruction has been shown to increase ALT (Cole, 1987). Furthermore, to the extent that students can self-manage aspects of their own instructional program, teachers will have greater flexibility in the use of their time for other tasks and for students who may require additional instructional time. One example of self-management is the use of self-correcting techniques. Several types of self-correcting materials

have been shown to be effective, including the use of flash cards, answer tapes, overlays, or checking stations with scoring keys.

In summary, students are capable, given the proper training and supervision, of assuming a degree of instructional autonomy through the use of CBT, independent learning strategies, and self-management. The use of these procedures consistently produces enhanced student attending and ALT.

SUMMARY

There are several approaches to classroom management and instruction that have been shown to maximize academic learning time, which directly affects students' achievement. Best practices for helping teachers increase their students' ALT begin with an awareness of the components of ALT, an understanding of the relationship between ALT and achievement, and an analysis of use of classroom time to target specific activities, content areas, or instructional periods for change. Allocating more time to instruction alone does not ensure that students will exhibit higher ALT and achievement. If, for example, academic tasks are so difficult that students do not experience sufficient success during their study time, providing more time to the same tasks will fail to have a positive effect on either students' ALT or achievement.

Best practices for increasing ALT have emerged from three separate strands of instructional research. The first is process–product research, which identifies teachers' behaviors (process) that are associated with higher ALT and achievement (product). An interactive teaching style, for example, is associated with high levels of ALT. The second strand is classroom environment research, which examines the way in which classroom activities and instruction are structured. Flexible grouping practices and integrated curriculum approaches have been identified as procedures that foster higher levels of ALT. The third area is mediating-process research, which identifies students' mediating behaviors that are related to ALT. Specifically, cognitive-behavioral approaches, independent learning strategies, and self-management are student strategies that mediate between teaching and student behaviors that increase ALT. Through collaborative instructional consultation, in-service training, and direct modeling of specific procedures in classrooms, school psychologists can promote teachers' implementation of the best practices for increasing ALT described in this chapter.

REFERENCES

Anderson, L. W. (1984). Attention, tasks and time. In L. W. Anderson (Ed.), *Time and school learning* (pp. 46–68). New York: St. Martin's Press.

Berliner, D. C. (1988). Effective classroom management and instruction: A knowledge base for consultation. In J. L. Graden, J.

E. Zins, & M. C. Curtis (Eds.), *Alternative educational delivery systems: Enhancing instructional options for all students* (pp. 309–325). Washington, Dc: National Association of School Psychologists.

Brophy, J. E., & Good, T. L. (1986). Teacher behavior and student achievement. In M. C. Wittrock (Ed.), *Handbook of research on teaching* (3rd ed.; pp. 328–375). New York: Macmillan.

Cohen, S., & de Bettencourt, L. (1988). Teaching children to be independent learners: A step-by-step strategy. In E. L. Meyen, G. A. Vergason, & R. J. Whelan (Eds.), *Effective instructional strategies for exceptional children* (pp. 78–94). Denver, CO: Love.

Cole, C. L. (1987). Self-management. In C. R. Reynolds & L. Mann (Eds.), *Encyclopedia of special education* (pp. 337–347). New York: John Wiley.

Corno, L., & Mandinach, E. B. (1983). The role of cognitive engagement in classroom learning and motivation. *Educational Psychologist, 18*, 88–108.

Fisher, C. W., & Berliner, D. C. (1985). *Perspectives on instructional time.* New York; Longman.

Gerber, M. M. (1988). Cognitive-behavioral training in the curriculum: Time, slow learners, and basic skills. In E. L. Meyen, G. A. Vergason, & R. J. Whelan (Eds.), *Effective instructional strategies for exceptional children* (pp. 45–64). Denver, CO: Love.

Gettinger, M. (1986). Issues and trends in academic engaged time of students. *Special Services in the Schools, 2*(2), 1–17.

Goodman, L. (1990). *Time and learning in the special education classroom.* Albany, NY: State University of New York Press.

Hallahan, D. P., Hall, R. J., Ianna, S. O., Kneedler, R. D., Lloyd, J. W., Loper, A. B., & Reeve, R. E. (1983). Summary of research findings at the University of Virginia Learning Disabilities Research Institute. *Exceptional Education Quarterly, 4*, 95–114.

Hawley, W. D., & Rosenholtz, S. J. (1984). Effective teaching. *Peabody Journal of Education, 61*, 15–52.

Murphy, J. (1992). Instructional leadership: Focus on time to learn. *NASSP Bulletin, 76*, 19–26.

Myers, S. S. (1990). The management of curriculum time as it relates to student engaged time. *Educational Review, 42*, 13–23.

Paine, S. (1983). *Structuring your classroom for academic success.* Champaign, IL: Research Press.

Palincsar, A. S., & Brown, A. L. (1984). Reciprocal teaching of comprehension-fostering and comprehension-monitoring activities. *Cognition and Instruction, 1*, 117–175.

Romance, N. R., & Vitale, M. R. (1992). A curriculum strategy that expands time for in-depth elementary science instruction by using science-based reading strategies: Effects of a year-long study in grade four. *Journal of Research in Science Teaching, 29*, 545–554.

Rosenshine, B., & Stevens, R. (1986). Teaching functions. In M. C. Wittrock (Ed.), *Handbook of research on teaching* (3rd ed.; pp. 376–391). New York: Macmillan.

Rowe, M. B. (1974). Wait-time and rewards as instructional variables, their influence on language, logic, and fate control: Part 1. Wait-time. *Journal of Research in Science Teaching, 4*, 81–94.

Smyth, W. J. (1985). A context for the study of time and instruction. In C. W. Fisher & D. C. Berliner (Eds.), *Perspectives on instructional time* (pp. 3–27). New York: Longman.

Stallings, J. (1980). Allocated academic learning time revisited, or beyond time on task. *Educational Researcher, 9*(1), 11–16.

Thurlow, M., Ysseldyke, J., Graden, J., & Algozzine, R. (1984). Opportunity to learn for learning disabled. *Learning Disability Quarterly, 6*, 283–288.

Wang, M. C., Gennari, P., & Waxman, H. C. (1985). The adaptive learning environments model: Design, implementations and effects. In M. C. Wang & H. J. Walberg (Eds.), *Adapting instruction to individual differences* (pp. 191–235). Berkeley, CA: McCutchan.

ANNOTATED BIBLIOGRAPHY

Gettinger, M. (1986). Issues and trends in academic engaged time of students. *Special Services in the Schools, 2*(4), 1–17.
This article describes several theoretical views of time and learning, including Carroll's model. It provides a review of major empirical time-and-learning studies that document a relationship between academic learning time and achievement. Finally, it addresses the implications of research for increasing learning time among students.

Goodman, L. (1990). *Time and learning in the special education classroom.* Albany, NY: State University of New York Press.
The purpose of this book is to encourage and help teachers of students with special educational needs to analyze their own teaching and look for ways to improve their effectiveness for all students. In addition to providing an overview of research related to time and learning, the author derives many practical classroom applications from the research findings, including strategies for conserving instructional time and enhancing academic learning time among students with learning problems.

Paine, S. C. (1983). *Structuring your classroom for academic success.* Champaign, IL: Research Press.
This book was written for teachers and classroom consultants. It focuses on important management skills every teacher needs to keep students actively engaged in learning and to make the most efficient use of class time. A unique feature of this book's practical approach is the use of actual scripts that outline specifically how to implement techniques in classrooms.

80

Best Practices in Preventing Problems in Unstructured Situations

Ann Casey
University of Minnesota/Minneapolis Public Schools

OVERVIEW

All children need a certain degree of structure in order to maximize their ability to be successful in an environment. The degree of structure necessary varies based upon an individual child's needs. However, when groups of children are placed together, a certain degree of structure, including rules and consequences, is helpful so that there is a sense of orderliness. While individual teachers may maintain a highly structured classroom environment, less structure is typically evident in the large-group activities of lunch, recess, passing periods, and on the school bus. Problems are waiting to happen in these environments. Many classrooms usually have lunch and recess at the same time, so that the sheer number of students in a given place is substantially increased. If attention is not given to increasing the structure in activities where the numbers of children are increased, one can predict that some kinds of behavior problems will evolve. When problems do occur, they often carry over into the classroom environment because they were not resolved in the occurring environment. Thus, it is an excellent idea for school psychologists to assist schools in prevention.

BASIC CONSIDERATIONS

This chapter looks at the behavior of children in large-group settings: playground, lunchroom, school bus, and hallways during passing periods. Teachers often express concern about how children behave in these settings, and the degree to which prosocial behavior is exhibited in these settings can contribute to the overall climate or feel of a school. Rowdy lunchrooms contribute to the characterization of a school as rowdy. Further, even in the most structured classrooms, spillover effects of unsolved playground confrontations can contribute to classroom behavior problems. Thus, it behooves school psychologists to plan for and anticipate potential problems in these settings and devise systems to reduce behavior problems.

Functional analysis of behaviors in these settings can lead to helpful information for intervention planning. Specifically, a functional analysis requires investigation of antecedent, situational, and consequent events through systematic observation and interview. In more pragmatic terms, it is important to investigate the events that precede the problem behavior, occur concurrently, and follow a problem behavior. Situational and consequent events are fairly easy for most observers to spot; however, antecedent events are not always so obvious. Antecedents can consist of a wide variety of things such as stated rules, directions given, number of adults assigned to supervision, and the number of students in the setting. All these antecedent variables exist prior to a problem occurring and, thus, can be potential contributors to behavior problems. In the discussion that follows, interventions will be discussed as either antecedent or consequent events.

Consultation skills are extremely important for any school psychologist attempting to work with schools to solve problems occurring in large-group settings. Consultation can take place on two levels: a system level (e.g., school building) or an individual teacher level. Sometimes an individual teacher may request help for a particular student who is experiencing difficulty at lunch or recess; however, upon inspection and observation the school psychologist may find that a significant number of children, not just the one referred student, could benefit from an intervention. In any case, the features of collaboration and shared decision-making inherent in consultation are also important to successful intervention.

Behavioral interviewing as described by Bergan and Kratochwill (1990) is a good introduction to functional analysis of behavior through a behavioral consultation framework. The methods these authors describe provide one with questions that can be used to specify antecedent, situational, and consequent events.

BEST PRACTICES — SYSTEM INTERVENTIONS

For purposes of discussion, "system" as it is used in this section, refers to a school building. Most of the interventions discussed here apply primarily to elementary school buildings, although a number of suggestions could be adapted for use with secondary students. How does a school psychologist get involved in implementing interventions at the systems level? While there are a wide variety of ways, one of the best is to get involved in school-based committee work. Many schools are moving toward a site-based management approach to school governance. This philosophy requires more staff and parent participation in determining problems and solutions. Thus, if school psychologists become more involved in the site-based management of the school, they can influence the direction some of the intervention planning will take.

The environments of the lunchroom, playground, hallways, and school bus will be discussed here from a building level with attention to both antecedent and consequent events. In order to reduce behavior problems in these settings, it is recommended that plans be made to attempt to prevent problems as well as have plans ready to deal with behaviors when they occur. After the discussion of building plans for the playground, lunchroom, hallways, and school buses, further discussion and suggestions for individual students with behavior problems in these settings will be presented.

Lunchroom

Problem behavior during the midday lunch period can be annoying for both staff and students trying to enjoy their meal. If significant problems are occurring, one consequence-focused intervention would be to use a group contingency. Students could be reinforced with extra recess time following their lunch, if there are no altercations during lunch. While this intervention has a nice appeal due to the immediacy of the consequence, it is not as easy to carry out as one might think. Schedules often dictate the school day. Typically, several classrooms share a lunch period with each following a different schedule once the lunch-recess period is completed. Thus, it may not always be possible to deliver the reinforcer of extra recess because students are likely to miss something else of importance. If this can be worked out, this intervention is a potentially powerful one. A variation would be to divide the lunch room into teams, and use the group contingency for each team. This variation includes the element of competition and may help improve behavior in some instances.

Another consequent event to consider would be the use of reductive techniques such as loss of recess time for behavioral problems. While this intervention may be worth a try, its implementation may cause other problems. Many teachers believe that students need recess time to expend pent-up energy so they can then focus on the remainder of the school day. Thus, if one deprives students of their recess, more

behavior problems might be evident in the afternoon. This is a hypothesis that could be tested.

A "timeout" lunch table could be set aside for violators of lunchroom rules. Throwing food, name-calling, and other disruptive behaviors would result in the children manifesting these behaviors being sent to this table. At this table, students would lose their talking privileges and be required to finish their lunch with no conversation. Because many students view lunch as a social activity, this punishment procedure might be quite effective in reducing behavioral incidents for a vast majority of the student body.

In many parts of the country with frequent inclement weather, the students are not able to go outside for a noon recess so the lunch period is often extended. This can create an undesirable situation for lunchroom supervisors. Students typically eat their lunches and still have 15 minutes or so of time on their hands. To prevent behavior problems in this scenario, schools should plan alternative activities for the students during the remaining time. Some suggested activities include showing entertaining videos in one part of the lunchroom and having board or card games available for students to play at the lunch tables. Team games could be devised requiring the participation of larger groups of children such as a spelling bee or a game of 20 questions. Because the weather is unpredictable, a file of activities should be prepared and available to lunchroom supervisors when needed.

Preventive-focused intervention procedures for the lunchroom focus on antecedent events. The lunchroom design and procedures can be devised in such a way as to minimize the likelihood of behavior problems. First, chaos can be avoided if all children enter the lunchroom from one point rather than multiple entrance points. For example, if the food line is at one end of the room, the door closest to the food could be designated as the entry point. All students would enter at that point, eliminating problems of multiple lines forming to get lunch. Coats and book-bags could be banned which should help diminish the problem of stealing food. Students could be assigned to specific tables so that supervisory staff could become acquainted with the students in their area. Enough staff should be deployed to the lunchroom so that no one person is asked to supervise more students than is feasible.

Playground

If a number of fights and scuffles are breaking out on the playground, it is a good idea to take serious account of the playground including some of the following aspects: the physical layout including a place for games requiring running and a place for students who choose not to participate in activities, ages of the students using the playground at the same time, number of supervisors assigned, and current playground rules. Playgrounds vary considerably in size and in the amount and kinds of equipment available. Given the financial constraints in which most school districts currently find themselves, it will be assumed that purchasing new equipment is not an option. A large space is optimal because the playground can then be divided into different play areas. For example, a soccer game can be played in one part of the playground while foot races are being held in another. Big kids could shoot baskets at one hoop, and smaller kids could be at a different hoop.

On smaller playgrounds, this luxury is not available, and games that require large spaces such as soccer are not possible. Staff will want to give serious consideration to whether running games should be allowed at all. Running in small spaces can be dangerous as well as prompt behavior difficulties when students start running into one another. Observing playground behaviors can help determine if running is contributing to behavior problems. If this seems to be the case, it might be in everyone's best interest to ban games of tag that promote random running. Foot races could still be held but would need to be confined to a specific area where only those racing were allowed.

If permanent playground equipment is minimal, other play options should be devised. Murphy, Hutchison, and Bailey (1983) found that organized playground activities in conjunction with logical consequences for misbehavior contributed to improved playground behavior. In the absence of a sufficient number of swings, slides, and jungle gyms, organized activities such as jumping rope, hopscotch, red rover, and captain may I, should be considered.

Playground staffing patterns are important. A sufficient number of staff need to be available in order that all parts of the playground are adequately supervised. Perhaps one of the better methods of supervision is to assign staff to specific playground zones. For example, one person would be in charge of the basketball court, another in charge of rope skipping and foot races, while another supervises students on playground equipment. A staffing pattern such as this works well because adults have specific assignments rather than having a more vague objective of supervising the playground. In addition to using a zone supervision approach, staff should be encouraged to roam throughout their zone rather than standing in one spot. Walking around and interacting with the children provides the students with the appearance of a more actively involved supervisor and contributes to a safer environment.

Consideration needs to be given to who will conduct the playground supervision. Often this role is relegated to paraprofessional staff. This can work well if some attention is given to training and preparing paraprofessional staff for this role. Knoff (1984) suggested using stimulus control techniques whereby the control exhibited by the classroom teacher is gradu-

ally transferred to a paraprofessional so that, ultimately, the good behavior exhibited in the presence of the teacher is also exhibited in the presence of the paraprofessional on the playground.

After consideration has been given to playground organization, activities, and supervision with the idea of preventing problems, a plan for handling the occasional playground behavior problem will still be required. Natural consequences seem to work well. Most children find recess a reinforcing activity and, thus, the loss of any recess time is viewed as punishment. For example, if a student is caught chasing after someone and this is a rule violation, the student would be told to take a 5-minute timeout. A timeout space could be designated by using a piece of chalk to draw a large circle on the blacktop. The student in "timeout" would need to sit or stand in the circle for 5 minutes. Some playgrounds have benches or fences that can be used for the same purpose. For more serious behavior problems such as deliberately hitting someone, a more serious consequence may be in order. Most school discipline policies have prespecified consequences for offenses such as this, and suspension may be appropriate.

Some schools are experimenting with alternatives to school discipline policies. Most notable in these efforts is the implementation of conflict-resolution programs. While mediation or conflict resolution can be used throughout the school day, one of the most helpful places for peer mediation to occur is on the playground. Peer mediation attempts to teach children negotiation skills so that they can mediate their own conflict rather than always relying on adult intervention or externally imposed consequences. A group of children are given intensive instruction in peer mediation. Once trained these students are assigned to the playground as peer-conflict mediators. Mediators are easily identified by the other students because of special t-shirts or badges they wear while on the playground. Mediators work in pairs and assist students having a conflict. The rules of mediation are straightforward, and both parties experiencing the conflict must first agree to mediation. Each party then has an opportunity to state his/her side of the story, and the mediators help the parties reach an agreement that is mutually acceptable.

Some schools using peer mediation have allowed school discipline procedures to be suspended if the parties can come to an acceptable agreement on how to resolve the conflict. For example, two students may end up in a fist fight due to name-calling between the two. A mediated solution is likely to lead to a real resolution of the presenting problem. Suspending the students from school provides a consequence that may diminish the future occurrence of the behavior, but it does not help resolve the original problem. Thus, the goal of peer mediation is to help students resolve their own problems — a skill that will be valuable in life.

School Hallways

Someone entering a school for the first time usually gets an immediate feel for the building climate by how the students behave in the hallways. Thus, hall behavior, although certainly only a small part of school climate, is not unimportant. Passing periods and arrival and dismissal times need to be structured in such a way that children are orderly and generally well-behaved in hallways. Arrival and dismissal times can be chaotic just by the sheer numbers of students in the hallways at one time. Prevention strategies which focus on arranging antecedents will be discussed first.

One of the first things to consider is traffic patterns. Kerr, Nelson, and Lambert (1987) found that traffic patterns in school hallways contributed to the noise level and behavior problems. Without specific direction, students can end up congregating, so that suddenly there are more students in one place than can be reasonably supervised. For safety reasons, this problem should be avoided if at all possible. Traffic patterns to some extent are dictated by the design of the school building. However, depending upon the number of entry doors and hallways in a school, a wide variety of traffic patterns can be established. If the goal is to prevent hallway behavior problems upon arrival, students should not be allowed to go to their lockers any way they wish. Rather, assign students a specific route to follow to get to their locker. Generally, the route should be the most expeditious one — or the shortest distance between the entry door and the lockers. Staff assigned to monitor the halls as the students enter for the day come to know the students who should and should not be in any given hall. For example, one hallway of lockers could be designated for sixth graders. Rather than taking any one of four staircases to reach this hallway, students would be told to use only the northeast stairway when arriving in the morning. This should cut down on students roaming the halls.

At dismissal time, many behavior problems could be avoided if classroom teachers escorted their students from their lockers to the school buses. Another consideration would be to use a staggered dismissal time. This might be preferred in a very large school where the hallways would have too many children in them if all were dismissed at the same time. The disadvantage of a staggered dismissal is that some children end up sitting on the bus for extended periods which might create another set of problems.

Bus Problems

The job of a school bus driver has been underestimated by many. Not only is the driver responsible for driving safely in all kinds of weather and traffic conditions, but the driver needs to ensure that students behave in such a way as to not hurt one another or distract the driver from the primary responsibility of driving. Ideally, school districts would hold inservice training programs on simple behavior management techniques that bus drivers could use. Such an inservice could include topics like group contingent reinforcement and timeout procedures. Campbell, Adams, and Ryabik (1974) found that the consequences of pulling the bus over to a stop (timeout) for any instance of unruly behavior was an effective intervention. Another study (Greene, Bailey, & Barber, 1981) demonstrated that a sound-recording device and accompanying light display installed on a bus were effective in reducing high noise levels on the bus. Even in the absence of sophisticated equipment, bus drivers could make listening to the bus radio contingent upon good behavior. When the bus becomes too noisy, the driver simply turns the radio off. When the behavior is under control, the radio goes back on.

BEST PRACTICES — INDIVIDUAL INTERVENTIONS

Many teachers complain of students who behave relatively well in a structured classroom environment but have special difficulty in the hallway, bus, or playground. In this section, strategies for interventions with individual students will be discussed. When only one or two children are experiencing a problem, a system-level intervention is probably not warranted. Thus, when planning an individual intervention, a problem-solving approach will be necessary. This involves defining the problem behavior in behavioral terms, measuring the frequency and/or duration of the behavior, designing an intervention, and monitoring the effects of the intervention upon the behavior.

Hallway Interventions for Individual Students

A typical problem reported by teachers is students who cannot keep their hands and feet to themselves and push, shove, and inappropriately touch others while walking or waiting in line. First, it is important to establish how much of a problem this really is. Baseline data could be gathered daily for several days. The exact data to be collected would consist of counting the number of pushes, shoves, and other inappropriate touches the individual student makes each time the class moves in the hall. These data would be aggregated for the day. Several days worth of data would be necessary to establish a good baseline because the number of times the class moves in the hall probably varies each day depending on the schedule. (See Hartman, 1984, for a description of behavioral assessment procedures.) Once the baseline is established the data can be reviewed to determine if a problem exists. Peer comparison data can be collected concurrently to determine how discrepant the target student's hall behavior is from typical peers. Reviewing the data can lead to one of three possible solutions: (a) low frequency and, thus, not really a problem; (b) low frequency, but high intensity when it does occur (e.g., a fight); and (c) high frequency and, thus, a problem to be solved.

For the purposes of this chapter, a problem of relatively high frequency will be discussed, and both antecedent and consequence interventions considered. From an antecedent point of view, the environment needs to be arranged in such a way as to avoid the occurrence of pushing, shoving, and the like. One such intervention is to have the student walk either at the front of the line or a few paces ahead so no one is within touching distance. Another antecedent approach would be to have the student always walk in the hall with his hands in his pockets or with her arms crossed in front of herself. This strategy would probably require prompting and reinforcement by the teacher but may be worth the extra effort if the student is compliant with the prompts. This is termed differential reinforcement of an incompatible behavior (DRI) approach: Having one's hands in pockets is an incompatible behavior with pushing and shoving.

Interventions focusing on the consequences would consist of either rewards for decreased inappropriate touching in line or punishment for continuation of this behavior. Punishment procedures alone are usually not in the best interest of children because they do not focus on teaching the appropriate behavior. Thus, either a response-cost procedure or a procedure with both rewards and costs is a better intervention. For example, one response-cost procedure would be to start the student's day with five tickets for hallway behavior. The student would lose a ticket for any instance of pushing, shoving, or hitting in the hallway. If there are any tickets remaining at the end of the day, the student could earn a reward. Once the student begins to earn the reward, the number of tickets available should be gradually diminished so that, ultimately, the student exhibits no pushing, shoving, or hitting in the hall.

Overcorrection can be a powerful consequence for misbehavior in the hallway. There are two kinds of overcorrection procedures: positive practice and restitution. Both might be useful depending upon the type of inappropriate hallway behavior being exhibited. In the case of a student running in the hall, a positive practice consequence could be applied. Every time the student runs in the hall, he/she is stopped and asked to return to the starting point and to walk in the hall. Depending on the frequency of the problem, the adult might have the student "practice" walking two or three times in a row. Overcorrection through restitution would be a good consequence for instances of vandalism such as drawing on lockers or ripping displays off hallway walls. In this case, the student would have to replace the display or remove the drawings from the lockers. Again, if the problem is of high frequency, the intervention might require the student to overcorrect by cleaning not only the

locker drawn on but also all other lockers in the hallway with drawings on them.

Individual Bus Plans

Some students have particular problems managing their behavior on the school bus. Usually, this comes to the attention of the school after the problem has escalated and the bus driver can no longer stand the misbehavior and asks to have the student suspended from the bus. Ideally, bus behavior problems would be dealt with before they become this severe. The bus driver is usually the only adult on the bus except for those cases where an educational assistant has been assigned to ride the bus with special education students. In either case, designing bus plans for individual students requires one to consult with the driver, the educational assistant, or both.

To get some idea of the severity of the problem, it would be best to ask one of the adults on the bus to collect some baseline data. First, it would be necessary to define the problem behavior. Then, if the driver is the consultee, a simple data-collection system will be needed that does not interfere with the job of driving the bus. Hand-held counters or stopwatches can be considered but may be unrealistic in many situations. At a minimum, the driver should be asked to estimate the level of behavior at the end of each trip and record or report it.

For purposes of illustration, the behavior of concern is identified as "name-calling" which typically results in other students on the bus getting angry and name-calling back to the target student. Name-calling is defined as any instance where the student uses a derogatory term to refer to others or others' mothers. In this case, the bus driver would keep track of the number of times the student name-called on each trip. The driver could use a counter to keep track and mark the number of name-calling events on a clipboard at the end of each trip. Baseline data should be collected for a minimum of three days or six trips in order to make some determination about whether there is a pattern. For example, upon inspection of the data, it may be discovered that only afternoon trips are problematic.

Assume the average number of name-calling events was five per trip, and the driver considered this a problem. Several intervention ideas could be considered. From an antecedent point of view, one possible intervention would be to change the student's seat arrangement so that he had to sit in the front row with no other students seated nearby. This might not be effective if the student is quite good at yelling out and attracting peers' attention. However, it might work to assign the student to the front row as a consequence. Thus, a system could be designed whereby the student was required to sit in the front row if the number of name-calling events from the previous trip was more than a prespecified criterion

— five to begin with, and then gradually reduced. The driver would continue to keep track of the number and record them on the clipboard after each trip. If the number of name-calling events decrease, we can assume that the intervention is working.

A more positive approach to improving an individual's bus behavior would be to use some form of a contract. The student and driver could write a contract for the student to earn some type of reward contingent upon improved conduct on the bus. For example, if the target behavior was out-of-seat, the contract could specify that if one or less instances of out-of-seat behavior occur in one week, the student would earn a reward. If the student cannot come up with an acceptable reward to earn, a menu of several items is suggested, some of which are tangible and some of which are activities. The menu might include bubble gum, a soft drink, the privilege of choosing the radio station listened to on the bus, extra free time in class, or a home/bus plan where the student earns the right to stay up an hour later on Friday nights.

If the behavior is of a very high frequency, a weekly reward is probably unrealistic, and a daily reinforcement plan should be considered. Once the behavior is under control, the amount of time to earn a reward could be gradually increased. Some drivers can handle the contract implementation on their own; however, as in any consultation case, it is best to follow up with the driver by checking daily to make sure that the plan is being implemented as intended and that some other unexpected effects are not occurring. Essentially, if the bus driver is being asked to put in the extra work to implement such a plan, it is best to ensure that he or she experiences success.

Similar individual plans can be developed for behavior problems in the lunchroom or on the playground. Natural consequences work well in these situations; however, one caution is important to mention. Denying a student lunch as a consequence for lunchroom behavior problems is not recommended, is of ethical concern, and considered illegal in many places. Delaying lunch may be appropriate in some circumstances, but the delay should probably be for no more than 30 minutes. As a general rule, it is best not to use lunch as a natural consequence and to assume that lunch is a right extended to all regardless of a student's behavior during the day.

Another variable to consider when designing an individual student program is whether the problem is due to a behavioral excess or a behavioral deficit. If the problem behavior appears to be an example of excess, then the procedures described for changing antecedent and/or consequent events should be helpful. However, if the problem is more of a deficit, that is the student does not have the appropriate skill in his or her repertoire, then a different approach may be more useful. Typically, students with behavioral deficits require direct teaching of prosocial skills. For

example, if a student does a lot of pushing and shoving it may be that the student has not learned appropriate ways of gaining peer attention and, thus, resorts to inappropriate means. In such a case, it is necessary to teach the student how to approach peers, how to engage in conversation, and other skills that peers will recognize as positive. Students who exhibit behavioral deficits will require an opportunity to learn and practice prosocial skills. In addition, prompting the student to use a newly acquired skill should help in transferring the skill to everyday situations.

The University of Oregon's Center for Research in the Behavioral Education of the Handicapped (CORBEH) developed a systematic package for teaching socially negative/aggressive children social interaction skills in the playground setting. This package, referred to as RECESS, focuses on teaching a student to discriminate appropriate versus inappropriate social behavior. It utilizes a response-cost procedure, adult praise for positive interactive behavior, and group and individual reinforcement contingencies. The packages developed by CORBEH are very specific, include plans for fading and maintenance, and are recommended to novices who have no previous experience in designing interventions of this type. For general information about the CORBEH packages, please refer to Walker, Hops, and Greenwood (1984) and the annotated bibliography.

CASE STUDY

Staff at a large (750 students) urban elementary school became concerned with the increasing amount of violent behavior that seemed to be occurring in the school. A task force of interested staff formed around this issue and began to discuss the perceived problem in earnest. One of the first things the task force accomplished was to review information the school was already collecting. Suspension data including the reason the student was suspended were compiled. In addition, Quiet Room data were reviewed. In this school, the Quiet Room was a place where teachers could send students if they were being disruptive in the classroom. The Quiet Room also kept data in terms of time of referral, reason for referral, and outcome. Both sets of data collected gave credence to the staff's concern that there was an increasing amount of physically as well as verbally aggressive behavior. In reviewing the data, however, an interesting trend was noted. Many behavior referrals seemed to occur during or immediately after the lunch recess.

The task force met informally once a week for approximately 1 hour and became increasingly more focused on the behavior problems at the lunch recess and their relation to the overall climate in the school being perceived as increasingly violent. This group had a number of goals in mind. A broad goal was to improve the school climate in such a way as to send a message that violence would not be tolerated, and that this school provided a safe and nurturing environment for children. A more specific goal was to develop a lunchroom and recess plan that would increase structure in order to minimize the opportunity for behavior problems.

In examining the current lunch and recess environments, a number of issues became evident. First, it became quite clear that the number of adults assigned to lunch and recess duty was not adequate to provide good supervision. Second, adults assigned to supervise were generally not familiar with the students they were asked to supervise and thus, generally knew few student names. The third thing that was clear upon inspection was that there were no consistent rules for what was acceptable and unacceptable behavior on the playground during recess.

The playground was not ideal in this school and perhaps typical compared to other inner-city schools where space is a premium. Because the playground was bounded by a busy street, it was fenced in. The space itself was about half the size one would prefer and so playground equipment (swings, basketball hoop, etc.) was at a minimum. Worst of all, the children were unable to play games such as soccer requiring a larger than available space. Given that the playground itself was far from ideal, a number of discussions occurred around how to improve the situation. One suggestion was that benches be built for children to sit upon if they chose not to play a game or use the equipment. Currently, the children either sat on the asphalt or leaned against the building. Essentially, the teachers were trying to make what improvements were possible within the given physical constraints of the playground.

The lunchroom/playground supervision was organized in the following way. Teachers were entitled to a duty-free lunch as per their contract. Because they ate at the same time as their students, the lunchroom was usually supervised by one administrator and several educational assistants (paraprofessionals). There were six 15-minute lunch periods with approximately 125 students per lunch. When students were finished eating, they were allowed to go outside to the playground where several more educational assistants supervised. One person monitored the hall route from the lunchroom to the playground. A typical behavior problem scenario looked like this: A student would leave the table without throwing away the milk carton or other trash. A supervisor would call out to the student but, not knowing the child's name, had little impact on getting the student to return to the table. Because there were many other children to watch over, the supervisor would rarely chase after the student and, thus, the student had no consequence for not following the rule of recycling and throwing trash away. The same situation existed on the playground. The educational assistants felt rather

powerless to enforce any kind of playground rules and, thus, there was a great deal of running, chasing, and other behavior that easily ended up in fights among students.

The task force set out to change the structure of the lunchroom and playground in order to improve general student behavior and diminish problems occurring in these settings. To do this, several school resources needed to be redeployed which, in turn, required the approval of the entire staff. The first thing requested was round lunch tables rather than the traditional long fold-up tables. Staff believed the round tables would promote the goal of more prosocial behavior at lunch. Second, the entire educational assistant staff for the school was deployed for lunchroom supervision. One assistant was assigned to supervise no more than two classes during lunch. Assistants were asked to make a point of getting to know all the students in their charge early on, and to converse with them during lunch. The educational assistants went to their assigned classroom 15 minutes prior to the student lunch period and took over the class so the teacher could leave and begin his or her own lunch. The purpose of this was to allow the teaching staff a 30-minute duty-free lunch, but one which ended when their students finished eating. The teachers, then, would go to the student lunch room, escort their students to the playground, and supervise the 15-minute recess. This eliminated the need for hall monitors as well as educational assistants on the playground.

In discussing rules for the playground, it was agreed that the primary concern was to enforce existing rules, particularly chasing on the playground — and, thus, games of tag were forbidden. Chasing was viewed as an antecedent to fighting, and by stopping chasing behavior it was hoped that some fighting could be prevented.

Behavioral data from suspensions and the Quiet Room continued to be kept so that comparisons could be made from the previous year. Some remarkable differences were noted. However, the lunch/playground plan alone did not necessarily contribute to the improvement in student behavior, because, in addition to this plan, the school implemented a schoolwide behavior plan with monthly programs to reinforce improved student behavior. Yet it was clear that the number of behavioral incidents during lunch/recess and immediately following were reduced. Initially, some teaching staff were not enthusiastic about having to perform recess supervision, but almost all were converted after they saw the positive effects it had on student behavior. Certainly, some stimulus control effects were evidenced. Most students had relatively good behavior in the classroom setting. By having teachers on the playground, some transfer of behavioral expectations from the classroom to the playground likely occurred.

SUMMARY

Unstructured settings such as school hallways, playground, lunchroom, and the bus typically account for a high percentage of behavior problems that occur in schools. These settings have a number of characteristics in common which likely account for the increased behavioral problems. First, large numbers of children are congregated in one setting, typically larger numbers than in the classroom. Second, the staff-to-student ratio is usually less than what exists in a classroom. These two factors combine to provide less structure than desired, and in the absence of structure, increases in behavior problems can be expected. This chapter provided a number of intervention ideas for these settings. Best practices suggest that antecedents to behavior problems in these settings be considered first. In determining antecedent events, it is possible to identify various aspects of the environment that could be changed or improved to prevent situations from occurring. The second aspect of good practice is being prepared with reasonable consequences for those occasions when behavior problems do arise. Thus, interventions were discussed from both an antecedent and consequent point of view.

REFERENCES

Bergan, J., & Kratochwill, T. (1990). *Behavioral consultation and therapy.* New York: Plenum Press.

Campbell, D. P., Adams, R. M., & Ryabik, J. E. (1974). Group-contingent timeout and behavior on a school bus. *Psychological Reports, 34,* 883–885.

Greene, B. F., Bailey, J. S., & Barber, F. (1981). An analysis and reduction of disruptive behavior on school buses. *Journal of Applied Behavior Analysis, 14,* 179–192.

Hartman, D. P. (1984). Assessment strategies. In D. Barlow & M. Hersen (Eds.), *Single case experimental designs: Strategies for studying behavior change* (2nd ed.; pp. 107–139). New York: Pergamon Press.

Kerr, M. M., Nelson, C. M., & Lambert, D. L. (1987). *Helping adolescents with learning and behavior problems.* Columbus, OH: Merrill Publishing.

Knoff, H. M. (1984). Stimulus control, paraprofessionals, and appropriate playground behavior. *School Psychology Review, 13,* 249–253.

Murphy, H. A., Hutchison, J. M., & Bailey, J. S. (1983). Behavioral school psychology goes outdoors: The effect of organized games on playground aggression. *Journal of Applied Behavior Analysis, 16,* 29–35.

Walker, H. M., Hops, H., & Greenwood, C. R. (1984). The CORBEH research and development model: Programmatic issues and strategies. In S. C. Paine, G. T. Bellamy, & B. Willcox (Eds.), *Human services that work: From innovation to standard practice.* Baltimore: Paul H. Brookes.

ANNOTATED BIBLIOGRAPHY

Campbell, D. P. Adams, R. M., & Ryabik, J. E. (1974). Group-contingent timeout and behavior on a school bus. *Psychological Reports, 34,* 883–885.
School bus behavior was significantly improved when the bus driver pulled the bus over and stopped whenever disruptive behavior occurred.

Center at Oregon for Research in the Behavioral Education of the Handicapped. (1977). *RECESS: Reprogramming Environmental Contingencies for Effective Social Skills.* Eugene, OR: University of Oregon.
This is one of four packages developed by CORBEH in the 1970s. The RECESS package was specifically developed for socially negative and aggressive children on the playground setting. Four components comprise the program: (a) discrimination training in appropriate versus inappropriate behavior, (b) response cost, (c) adult praise, and (d) group and individual reinforcement contingencies. This package can be obtained by writing to CORBEH, Clinical Services Building, Center on Human Development, University of Oregon, Eugene, OR 97403.

Greene, B. F., Bailey, J. S., & Barber, F. (1981). An analysis and reduction of disruptive behavior on school buses. *Journal of Applied Behavior Analysis, 14,* 179–192.
This article describes the use of a sound-recording device installed on a school bus. The device was activated when the noise level on the bus was above 500 Hz and a light panel was displayed which provided a visible cue to all the passengers. Students were allowed to listen to appealing music if they could keep the noise level below a specified criterion.

MacPherson, E. M., Candee, B. L., & Hohman, R. J. (1974). A comparison of three methods for eliminating disruptive lunchroom behavior. *Journal of Applied Behavior Analysis, 7,* 287–298.
Part of the tactic described here was for disruptive students to write what is described as a mediation essay. These students during their lunchroom timeout had to respond in writing to questions such as "What did I do wrong?" and "What should I have done?" Some written language teachers object to using writing as a punishment; however, this same tactic could be used but change the consequence to loss of recess or some other potentially motivating variable.

Murphy, H. A., Hutchison, J. M., & Bailey, J. S. (1983). Behavioral school psychology goes outdoors: The effect of organized games on playground aggression. *Journal of Applied Behavior Analysis, 16,* 29–35.
The conclusion reached by the authors was that when dealing with large groups, manipulating antecedent events may be more practical than trying to provide consequences. Thus, organized activities such as rope-skipping and foot races were implemented as a means of attending to antecedent events. Natural consequences were provided to students who did not follow the activity rules.

81

Best Practices in the Response to Child Maltreatment

Connie Burrows Horton
Illinois State University

The child trapped in an abusive environment is faced with formidable tasks of adaptation. She must find a way to preserve a sense of trust in people who are untrustworthy, safety in a situation that is unsafe, control in a situation that is terrifyingly unpredictable, power in a situation of helplessness.

Herman, 1992, p. 96

OVERVIEW

Given the nearly impossible tasks for abused children described above, the roles for school psychologists endeavoring to support the development and recovery of child victims may also be overwhelming. Yet school psychologists are increasingly being identified as among the critical respondents to the tragic phenomenon of child maltreatment. It is imperative, therefore, that all school psychologists maintain a basic level of awareness of issues regarding child abuse and neglect, so that they are prepared for identification, reporting, referring, and consulting roles. Others may choose to specialize in additional roles involving direct intervention and prevention activities. Thus, the purpose of this chapter is twofold: (a) to provide a brief summary of issues and roles that almost all school psychologists should be prepared to address, and (b) to provide a springboard from which those wishing to specialize may begin.

The maltreatment of children is currently recognized as a social problem of major proportion (Gil, 1980). National incidence studies, using conservative estimates of countable reported cases, reveal that more than 1.5 million children nationwide are victims of abuse or neglect each year (NCCAN, 1988). Given that many children do not report their abuse but attempt to protect parents and cover up injuries (Broadhurst, 1980), reported cases should always be viewed as gross underestimates of the actual number of abused children. Thus, even these "tip of the iceberg" statistics demonstrate the epidemic proportions of this national tragedy. Clearly, for many children, the family home is a dangerous place (Kolko, 1992). Given the now recognized increased vulnerability of children who have experienced maltreatment to immediate physical pain and emotional distress as well as long-term risks of delinquency, psychiatric disorders, school failure, self-destructive behavior, domestic violence, and sexual dysfunction — the costs to individuals, families, and society are increasingly being recognized as overwhelming (Garbarino, 1983).

While the maltreatment of children has been occurring for centuries (Garbarino, 1977), public acknowledgment of this tragedy is very recent. One might expect that the medical community would have recognized child abuse long ago, considering the many suspicious injuries physicians have treated. However, the medical field, too, responded slowly (Gil, 1991). Though there were a few physicians who raised questions about child abuse earlier, it was not until 1961 when Kempe coined the phrase "the battered child syndrome" at a medical conference presentation and published his findings, that the medical field considered the problem seriously (Kempe & Helfer, 1980). The passage of laws between 1963 and 1965 that required medical reporting of abuse led to the establishment of child protective agencies. In 1974 the Child Abuse Prevention and Treatment Act became law. This act established a National Center on Child Abuse and Neglect that has been involved in public education, the support of improved child protective services, and research to improve identification, prevention, and treatment of child maltreatment (Green, 1980).

By the 1980s, schools were recognized as potential resources in the response to child maltreatment. "As the major institution concerned with the development of children it seems natural that schools should assume a major responsibility in facilitating, reporting, and participating in the delivery of services to the abused" (Volpe, 1980, p. 3). Since school personnel operate under legal and ethical mandates, and the opportunity for abuse to be detected, identified, and reported exists in the school settings, it does seem appropriate to expect school professionals to be involved.

School psychologists, in particular, have been identified as having the position and expertise that uniquely enables them to respond to various forms of child maltreatment (Erickson & Egeland, 1987; Garbarino, 1987; Gelardo & Sanford, 1987; Tharinger, Russian, & Robinson, 1989; Vevier & Tharinger, 1986). Given their skills in communicating with children and adults who may have relevant information, their knowledge of child and family function and dysfunction, and their training in assessment, interviewing, and consultation, and given the perception by others that they are helpers and problem solvers (Vevier & Tharinger, 1986), the expectations that school psychologists will be leaders in the schools' response to child maltreatment seem reasonable.

BASIC CONSIDERATIONS

School psychologists must have a working knowledge of child maltreatment issues so that they are in a position to respond appropriately (Vevier & Tharinger, 1986). It is important to have a basic understanding about why child maltreatment occurs, as well as an awareness of issues regarding each form of abuse. Thus, the following is a brief review of models used to explain the phenomenon of abuse and a discussion of the four major types of child maltreatment: physical abuse, sexual abuse, neglect, and emotional abuse.

Models

Various models, including psychiatric (focusing on individual pathology of offenders), sociological (focusing on societal factors such as unemployment), and family systems (focusing on the function of abuse within the family) have been proposed to explain the occurrence of child maltreatment (see Gelardo & Sanford, 1987; Vevier & Tharinger, 1986). Increasingly, researchers and clinicians are recognizing that each of these models is too simplistic. More complex, ecological models that recognize the interplay between factors are needed to explain abuse (Garbarino & Gilliam, 1990). Ecological models acknowledge the contributions of the individual, family, community, and culture that contribute to the occurrence of child maltreatment (Belsky, 1980). Thus, school psychologists are reminded that causes are complex and that once they have an understanding of abuse issues, their response can be multifaceted.

Physical Abuse

Description. The physical abuse of children may take many forms and vary in both severity and duration. For example, some children are injured during extended physical altercations (e.g., hitting, kicking), others are physically harmed in brief, isolated incidents (e.g., being burned, or thrown down stairs). Additionally, there are many other children who may not meet legal definitions of physical abuse but suffer harsh physical discipline (Kolko, 1992). While the majority of abuse cases cause moderate injuries (those

that persist in observable form for 48 hours or more but are not life-threatening), over 1,000 children die annually at the hands of their abusers (NCCAN, 1988).

Incidence. The exact scope of the occurrence of physical abuse is unknown because of unreliable data, variety of sources, and variance in definitions (Gelardo & Sanford, 1987); however, conservative estimates reveal that over 350,000 children are physically abused annually (NCCAN, 1988). Male and female children seem equally at risk for this type of abuse, and while older children are more likely to be physically abused, very young children are more likely to suffer severe, even fatal, injuries (NCCAN, 1988).

Effects. Physical abuse affects a child in many ways. Direct physical injuries are perhaps the most obvious effects of this form of child maltreatment. Such injuries may include skin injury (such as bruises, welts, abrasions, puncture wounds, burns, and scaldings), skeletal injury (such as skull and bone fractures and dislocations), and internal injuries (such as brain damage or internal organ damage) (Gelardo & Sanford, 1987).

Psychological effects are also varied. While teachers are most aware of externalizing symptoms (Haskett & Kistner, 1991), internalizing symptmology is also often present. Internalizing symptoms that are commonly found among physically abused children include a lack of positive affect (Erickson & Egeland, 1987), withdrawal (Haskett & Kistner, 1991), depression (Kolko, 1992), and low self-esteem (Gelardo & Sanford, 1987). Externalizing symptoms include noncompliance (Erickson & Egeland, 1987), and instrumental aggression, even at young ages (Haskett & Kistner, 1991). Clearly, not all children who are physically abused will become aggressive. Just as in other pathologies, there may be a temperamental or genetic predisposition toward aggression or resiliency. However, living with aggressive adult models and experiencing physical assaults at the hands of one's parents greatly increases the odds that a child will become aggressive (Lewis, 1992). The aggressive tendencies may develop into more serious conduct problems in adolescence, including fighting, property offenses, other delinquent activities leading to arrests, and higher rates of alcohol and drug use (Kolko, 1992).

Given these symptom patterns, it is not surprising that children who have been physically abused are generally not popular among their peers (Erickson & Egeland, 1987). In fact, the social/peer domain is perhaps the most affected area for physically abused children (Kolko, 1992). Their interactions with familiar peers are markedly different from nonabused children's and tend to be marked by both withdrawal and aggression (Haskett & Kistner, 1991). They may exhibit a number of social skills deficits (Gelardo & Sanford, 1987). For example, children who have been the victims of physical abuse often show difficulty reacting appropriately to positive peer initiation. Furthermore, they often appear unable to respond supportively to peer distress, perhaps because of difficulty empathizing (Kolko, 1992). Therefore, even at very young ages, peers find children who have been abused to be less desirable playmates; thus, the abused child continues to be at risk for peer rejection (Haskett & Kistner, 1991).

Of particular note to school psychologists are the multiple academic problems that children who have been abused frequently experience, including poor school achievement, failing grades, and increased risk for retention or referrals for special education services (Erickson & Egeland, 1987; Gelardo & Sanford, 1987). There are multiple explanations for such academic difficulties. Clearly, emotional factors are critical considerations. It is difficult for a child to learn who is withdrawn, depressed, and having difficulty concentrating because of distress regarding recent abuse or fears of potential future abuse. Alternative or additional explanations may also apply. For example, if physical abuse involves head injuries, intellectual impairment may be a direct consequence (Gelardo & Sanford, 1987). Further, the academic careers of maltreated children are often marked by considerable discontinuity, because of frequent moves, school transfers, and tardiness (Kolko, 1992). Additionally, these children have also been noted to be disruptive, inattentive, and impatient in the classroom (Erickson & Egeland, 1987). In later years, abused children continue to have disciplinary problems at school and thus have higher rates of suspensions (Gelardo & Sanford, 1987). It is apparent that the school psychologist should consider multiple explanations for academic difficulties experienced by students who have been physically abused.

Sexual Abuse

Description. Sexual abuse has been defined as "the involvement of dependent, developmentally immature children in sexual activities that they do not fully comprehend and therefore to which they are unable to give informed consent and/or which violate the taboos of society" (Krugman & Jones, 1987, p. 286). Sexual abuse is not limited to sexual intercourse. Sexual assaults involving adult sexual contact with children may include fondling of breasts and genitals, oral sex, anal penetration, and vaginal intercourse. Additionally, some forms of child sexual abuse do not involve actual sexual contact with offenders. Examples of such noncontact abuse include encounters with exhibitionists, solicitation to engage in sexual activity when no physical contact occurs, and exposure to or involvement in pornography (Courtois, 1993; Peters, Wyatt, & Finkelhor, 1986). It is common for sexual abuse to progress from less to more invasive forms. For example, an offender may expose himself to a child, then move to fondling, oral sex, and then intercourse (Courtois, 1993).

Offenders may gain access to a child victim through deception or by direct approach through the use of psychological pressure, enticement, and encouragement. In some cases force, threats, or use of strength are involved (Burgess & Groth, 1980). Thus, a child victim will keep the secret of sexual abuse for a variety of complex reasons, which may include being deceived into thinking the experience is normal or educative, because she fears for her life or the life of her family, or because she gets some "benefits" or "payment" for participating.

The majority of sexual offenders are family members or those known to the child (Finkelhor, Hotaling, Lewis, & Smith, 1990). Males are apparently more likely to be sexually abused by someone outside of the family, whereas females are more likely to be sexually abused by someone within the family (Courtois, 1993). The vast majority of sexual abuse is perpetrated by males, though there are some cases in which females victimize male or female children (Finkelhor et al., 1990).

Incidence. Incidence and prevalence figures for this type of abuse vary widely depending on the source of the information, the definitions of abuse included, and the population studied (Vevier & Tharinger, 1986). Very conservative estimates suggest that over 150,000 new cases of child sexual abuse occur annually (NCCAN, 1988); underreporting of this type of abuse, however, has been characterized as "massive" (Kempe, 1980).

Retrospective studies of adults reporting on their childhood histories reveal alarming rates of sexual abuse. For example, a recent national survey of child sexual abuse found victimization reported by 27% of women and 16% of men (Finkelhor et al., 1990). While the ratio varies depending on the study, females appear to be at greater risk than males of becoming victims of sexual abuse, though most observers acknowledge that the abuse of boys is still significantly underreported (Finkelhor & Baron, 1986). While reported cases are approximately 5 females for every one male victim reported, retrospective studies find that an average of 2.5 females report a child sexual abuse experience for every male who reports victimization (Finkelhor & Baron, 1986).

Almost all studies report that children are most vulnerable to sexual abuse starting between the ages of 8 and 12 years (Finkelhor & Baron, 1986), though in some cases the abuse starts at much younger ages, even in infancy. The average length of intrafamilial sexual abuse is 4 years, while extrafamilial abuse is generally much shorter in length, probably owing to more limited access to the child victim (Courtois, 1993).

Effects. Because of the range of responses of victims of child sexual abuse, it is difficult to postulate a "post-sexual-abuse syndrome" with a specific course or outcome (Beitchman, Zucker, Hood, DaCosta, & Akman, 1991). While individual responses vary, there are a number of common symptoms found among child victims of sexual abuse.

Child victims of sexual abuse may suffer any number of physical effects, including bladder injuries, rectal and vaginal tears or bruising, lacerations on genitalia, and sexually transmitted diseases (Bates, 1980; Brassard, Tyler, & Kehle, 1983) and pregnancy. Child victims may experience a variety of somatic complaints (e.g., headaches, stomachaches), and sleep difficulties including insomnia and night terrors are also common (Vevier & Tharinger, 1986).

Emotionally, child victims of sexual abuse may initially experience fear, anxiety, depression, anger, or hostility (Browne & Finkelhor, 1986). Some observers have referred to the "sleeper" effect, describing many children who do not experience significant pathology until late adolescence or adulthood, at which point survivors are more likely to manifest depression, self-destructive behavior, anxiety, feelings of isolation and stigma, poor self-esteem, a tendency to experience further victimization, and substance abuse (Browne & Finkelhor, 1986).

Behaviorally, child victims of sexual abuse often regress and may engage in thumb-sucking, bedwetting, or other behaviors typical of younger children. Many sexually abused children internalize their distress and will be cooperative or overly compliant. Other victims, especially if they attempted to get help but were ignored, may act out their anger through a variety of behaviors (Vevier & Tharinger, 1986). Additionally, adolescents may engage in delinquent or runaway behaviors, play a parental role in the family, or exhibit suicidal behavior (Brassard et al., 1983).

School difficulties are also common among child victims of sexual abuse. Academic achievement often declines, apparently partially because of an inability to concentrate (Vevier & Tharinger, 1986). Grades also suffer from what may appear to be a rebellious attitude (e.g., refusal to change for gym class). Additionally, children who were developmentally delayed before the abuse, and thus were more vulnerable to being victimized (Tharinger, Horton, & Millea, 1990), may further deteriorate academically following the abuse (Beitchman et al., 1991).

Socially, victims of sexual abuse often have difficulties (Brassard et al., 1983). While children who have been sexually abused may not be as aggressive as their physically abused counterparts, they still tend to have inadequate peer relationships. These children often demonstrate an inability to make friends (Vevier & Tharinger, 1986). Thus, they become extremely dependent on adults (Erickson & Egeland, 1987) and may be excessively clingy and demonstrate a need for an unusual degree of reassurance (Brassard et al., 1983).

Finally, victims of sexual abuse may develop fear and anxiety regarding the opposite sex or sexual issues (Brassard et al., 1983) and may display inappropriate sexual behavior (Browne & Finkelhor, 1986). In young children, this tendency may be observed in heightened interest in, or a preoccupation with, sexuality that may be manifested in a number of ways including sexual play, excessive masturbation, sexually aggressive behavior, and age-inappropriate sexual knowledge. Adolescent sexual difficulties include sexual dissatisfaction, promiscuity, and an increased risk of further victimization (Beitchman et al., 1991).

Neglect

Description. The dynamics involved in situations of child neglect are significantly different than those involved in situations of physical or sexual abuse. Perhaps the greatest difference is that abused children receive attention (Gil, 1991). While it is true that the attention is negative and potentially very damaging, the child's presence is acknowledged. This is often not true for neglected children, who are often treated as if they do not exist. Neglect is more subtle, but it can cause irreparable damage (Bates, 1980).

Neglect has been defined as "a form of maltreatment characterized by a chronic lack of care in the areas of health, cleanliness, diet, supervision, education, or meeting of emotional needs that places the child's normal development at risk" (Ethier, Placio-Quintin, & Jourdan-Ionescu, 1992, p. 13). Since, by definition, neglect involves absence, definitions are complex and vague (Ethier et al., 1992). Although states may try to clarify some specifics such as at what age a child may be left unsupervised, it is difficult to define the point at which a child slips from satisfactory care to neglect (Helfer, 1987).

Neglect may be chronic or circumstantial (Ethier et al., 1992). Chronic situations may include a wide variety of situations such as intellectual handicap, drug abuse, or emotional immaturity on the part of parents (Ethier et al., 1992). It is important to note that while neglect may be more easily detected among poor families because, in those cases, there is more likely to be inappropriate dress, evidence of malnutrition, and the like, emotional neglect occurs across all socioeconomic groups.

National incidence studies conducted by the National Center for Child Abuse and Neglect include three types of neglect: physical, emotional, and educational. The definition of physical neglect includes the refusal or delay of health care, abandonment, and inadequate supervision. Emotional neglect includes inadequate nurturance/affection, chronic or extreme spouse abuse, permitted drug or alcohol abuse, other permitted maladaptive behavior, and refusal or delay of psychological care. Educational neglect includes permitted chronic truancy, failure to enroll, and inattention to special educational needs.

Incidence. Partially as a result of definitional complexities, and the ease with which some forms may be hidden, it is difficult to determine with any accuracy the incidence and prevalence of neglect (Ethier et al., 1992). Incidence studies conducted by the National Center for Child Abuse and Neglect report over one million cases of neglect annually (NCCAN, 1988). Physical neglect is the most documented form of neglect, accounting for 57% of the reported cases. Educational neglect accounted for 29% of the total of neglect cases, while emotional abuse accounted for 22% of the total cases of reported neglect.

Effects. Children who are victims of neglect often exhibit poor weight gain, delayed developmental growth, and varying degrees of malnutrition (Cantwell, 1980; Helfer, 1987). These children often suffer from frequent illness. While the illness may not be serious, they are often chronic (Helfer, 1987). The "failure to thrive" syndrome (i.e., failure over time to grow to accepted standards for height, weight, and development) has been used to describe children who have been neglected (Helfer, 1987).

Emotionally, children who have been neglected appear to be anxious and withdrawn, and they may repress their other feelings (Polansky, 1981). Such repression is understandable. If no one appears to be available to comfort, support, and protect, a child learns to silence feelings of aloneness, fear, or anger. Self-esteem, a fundamental basic to mental health, is of course greatly compromised.

Socially, the effects of neglect include disrupted attachment and an impaired ability to empathize with others. The latter can lead to violence and delinquency (Polansky, 1981). Some have suggested that the social competence of children who have been neglected is, as a result of a lack of experience, lower than that of children who have experienced physical or sexual abuse (Erickson & Egeland, 1987).

Children who have been neglected often have a very difficult time performing adequately in academic settings. At even very young ages, these children may exhibit developmental delays, especially in language (Cantwell, 1980), that continue to plague them in school. In fact, the academic skills of children who have been neglected are often lower than those of children who have experienced other forms of child maltreatment. One reason for academic difficulties may be that the psychologically unavailable parent does not provide the encouragement, participation, and responsiveness to school activities and achievements required for success (Helfer, 1987).

Emotional Abuse

Description. Emotional abuse includes treating a child in a way that is rejecting, degrading, terrorizing, isolating, corrupting, or exploiting, or that denies emotional responsiveness (Brassard & Gelardo, 1987). Some prefer to use the term *psychological maltreatment* rather than emotional abuse, since this type of maltreatment of children affects more than emotions and clearly has both cognitive and affective components. In some ways, definitions of emotional abuse are more vague than other types of abuse. That is, it is difficult to know where to draw the line and say that particular parental behavior is truly emotionally abusive. At the same time, this form of abuse relates to the core issues that are inherent in all forms of child maltreatment, and thus clarifies and unifies constructs (Brassard & Gelardo, 1987). That is, a child who is physically abused is clearly also emotionally abused. Likewise, a child who is sexually abused or is neglected is also affected emotionally and psychologically. Still, emotional abuse can occur in isolation. It is possible for a parent never to be physically violent, never cross sexual boundaries, and continually provide adequate nutrition, education, and supervision, and still be emotionally abusive, by making constant, degrading, hurtful comments.

Incidence. Since definitions are so unclear, many states do not keep records of emotional abuse (Gelardo & Sanford, 1987). However, approximately 211,000 cases of emotional abuse are reported annually (NCCAN, 1988). It should be noted, however, that reported cases generally include only extreme situations such as tortuous restriction of movement (e.g., tying a child to a bed), threats of abandonment, or attempted but not completed physical or sexual abuse. The more subtle forms of emotional abuse such as rejecting, degrading, or not responding to children are generally not detected or not reported.

Effects. Some have argued that the psychological effects that result from emotional abuse are the most long lasting (Brassard & Gelardo, 1987). Generally, physical injuries from abuse heal; however, deep psychological wounds are more persistent. In fact, it is possible that it is even more difficult for emotional abuse to heal when there are no physical injuries, experiences of neglect, or memories of sexual assaults. The lack of evidence of injury may confuse victims about the severity of their abuse. For example, although shouting and threatening might have completely terrorized a child (Ethier et al., 1992), the child (or adult survivor) has no proof of injury. Although she may feel horrible, she may be unable to identify that the feelings are the result of someone else's abusive behavior.

In sum, children who are emotionally abused feel abused, unwanted, angry, and bad (Bates, 1980). Psychological abuse has been demonstrated to be a critical variable in predicting levels of depressions, self-esteem, and attributional style. Children subjected to this form of abuse have not had important psychological needs met by significant adults and are affected accordingly (Brassard & Gelardo, 1987).

In addition to the emotional effects, psychological maltreatment is a threat to social competence. Being treated in an emotionally abusive manner distorts a child's concepts of social relationships, creates socially dysfunctional defenses, and elicits patterns of inappropriate behavior (Gross & Keller, 1992).

Overall Effects

As is evident from the description of emotional abuse, the various forms of maltreatment of children often do not occur in isolation. That is, abuse or neglect of one type often occurs simultaneously with other types of maltreatment. Furthermore, while specific types of abuse produce certain unique injuries and effects, there appear to be certain shared effects among various forms of maltreatment as well (Briere, 1992). Therefore, while it is important to consider various forms of abuse and neglect separately, it may also be beneficial to examine them in summary form.

In short, child victims of abuse tend to develop internalized symptom patterns that reflect an attempt "to negotiate the trauma themselves" or externalized behaviors in which the symptoms are directed toward others (Gil, 1991). Commonly noted internalizing symptoms among victims of child abuse include withdrawal, depression, a lack of spontaneity and playfulness, overcompliance, phobias, hypervigilance/anxiety, sleep disorders or night terrors, regressed behavior, somatic complaints, eating disorders, substance abuse, suicide gestures, self-mutilation, and dissociation. Externalized symptom patterns that are commonly found among abused children include behavior that is aggressive, destructive, provocative (eliciting abuse), violent, or sexualized. Specific behaviors such as fire setting and killing or torturing animals are also seen among some abused children (Gil, 1991).

Mediators of Effects

The effects discussed above are findings from group studies and are common findings among clinicians. It should be acknowledged, however, that not all child victims experience the same symptoms or the same severity of symptom patterns. There are a variety of factors that mediate the impact of child abuse, including the following: the age of the child at the time of the abuse, chronicity of the abuse, severity of the abuse, the relationship with the offender, the level of threat involved, the emotional climate of the family prior to the abuse, the child's emotional/mental health functioning prior to the abuse, the amount of guilt that the child feels, the sex of the victim, and parental response (Gil, 1991).

Another important mediator for school psychologists to consider is the response of significant others, including schools, towards the child victim and toward the offender (Hindman, 1989). Child victims who find that significant people in their lives believe and support them and clearly place the responsibility for the abuse with the offender are likely to experience less trauma. In a disturbing case example, Hindman (1989) reports a situation in which a male sixth-grade teacher sexually abused several children. The school personnel did not respond in a way that was supportive and affirming of the victims. Instead, the children were pulled out of classes, confronted by other teachers about their claims, and were allowed to be interviewed by the offender. At the same time, school personnel had a car wash and a baked food sale on school grounds to raise money for the teacher's legal defense: These responses had a tremendously negative effect on the boys: Two dropped out and one committed suicide (Hindman, 1989). Clearly this is an extreme example; however, it should remind school personnel that their response to the abuse of a child may make a positive difference that promotes that child's recovery or may be the last straw for a child who has experienced far too much maltreatment.

BEST PRACTICES

In considering the appropriate response and roles for school psychologists, an intervention framework, proposed for response to sexual abuse (Vevier & Tharinger, 1986), may be generalized to apply to response to all forms of child maltreatment. This model consists of two levels: one that incorporates roles for all school psychologists and another that particularizes roles for those wishing to specialize in working with these children.

General Roles

Detecting abuse. School personnel, including school psychologists, have been recognized as key respondents to child maltreatment, partially because they have the opportunity to detect child abuse in their work. Unfortunately, schools have not responded well to the tragedy of abuse. This is largely the case because school personnel do not recognize indicators of abuse and neglect (Broadhurst, 1980).

Commonly observed symptoms of maltreatment such as those discussed above, while not conclusive in isolation, are indicators of possible abuse (Gil, 1991) that school psychologists should consider. Awareness of the symptoms and prevalence of abuse allow school psychologists to consider abuse as a possible cause of some behaviors. For example, when a child is referred for an assessment because of his poor academic performance, does the school psychologist consider whether the child has eaten before coming to school? When an adolescent female is suspended for refusing to dress down for P.E., does the school psychologist consider that she may be experiencing shame and discomfort regarding her body following episodes of sexual abuse? When a kindergarten boy is extremely aggressive, does the school psychologist wonder about where he learned that behavior or what is behind the anger before developing a behavior modification plan? When a child is referred for suspected Attention Deficit Disorder in view of an inability to concentrate, does the school psychologist wonder about what possible distraction the child is concentrating on or working hard to forget? Clearly, school psychologists should not make conclusions about child maltreatment with only limited descriptions of symptoms, but they can use child maltreatment, along with other possible explanations, as a possible initial hypothesis in the assessment process. Once again, lists of effects of abuse are not conclusive in themselves but should be reminders of possible explanations for a child's behavior, affect, or school performance.

In recognizing indicators, school psychologists will need to work closely with other school personnel. For example, a school nurse might be the first to be aware of difficulty in walking or sitting; torn, stained, or bloody underclothing; complaints of pain or itching in the genital area; bruises or bleeding in external genital, vaginal, or anal areas; or veneral disease in cases of sexual abuse (Brassard et al., 1983). Teachers may be the first to recognize aggressive or withdrawn behavior as well as bruises or other injuries in children who have been physically abused. Thus, ongoing collaborative communication between school professionals is critical if child abuse is to be accurately detected.

School psychologists should be reminded to notice not only difficult, acting out, or overtly disturbed students. In addition, there should be equal concern for uncommunicative children, who are little trouble to their teachers but may be seriously depressed by abuse, neglect, or some other difficult home situation (Fewster & Bagley, 1986).

Child interviews. Often a school psychologist may have concerns regarding possible child maltreatment because of physical, emotional, or behavioral indicators but may need additional information. In other cases, a child may make a direct disclosure regarding abuse to the school psychologist or other school professional. In either of these situations, the school psychologist, if she or he has the skills to do so, may need to interview the child further to gain enough information to make a report (Brassard et al., 1983).

The school psychologist, whether following up on indicators of abuse (Brassard, et al., 1983) or responding to a child's disclosure (Johnson, 1989), should be careful to conduct a clinically sensitive, yet legally defensible, nonleading interview. The most important aspect of a child interview may be a warm, caring, nonjudgmental style. Although variations in individual style are acceptable (Johnson, 1989), some key points are important for all to consider.

First, the school psychologist must be clear about limits to confidentiality. Sometimes without mentioning anything about abuse, children will attempt to get school professionals to make promises of absolute confidentiality (e.g., "If I tell you something very, very private, will you promise not to tell?"). School psychologists are reminded not to naively agree, but to be clear with a child (in developmentally appropriate terms) about limits to confidentiality. A frank discussion regarding confidentiality at the outset may prevent a child from disclosing abuse at that time. However, upon further consideration, the child may appreciate the honesty, realize this is an adult who can be trusted, and disclose at a later date. In either case, being honest with a child is preferred to having to betray the child's trust by breaking a promise that never should have been made.

Interviews regarding suspected child maltreatment should be conducted in a private setting. Given the shame, embarrassment, and confusion that victims of abuse experience, the school psychologist must be especially sensitive to issues of privacy. While practical constraints may exist, it is imperative that the school psychologist find some place in the school where he or she can be alone with the child rather than using a corner of a classroom or an open space in a hallway where other students or school personnel may overhear the conversation. A child victim may be more likely to deny the abuse if he or she fears others may be listening to the conversation.

The school psychologist should maintain a somewhat informal, calm tone throughout the interview. Rather than immediately grabbing a clipboard to take notes, the school psychologist should more informally dialog with the child, starting with more general, nonthreatening subjects, and leading up to topics related to the suspected abuse. Once the child does begin discussing the abuse, it is important that the school psychologist remain calm. The interviewer should be careful not to alarm the child through the display of reactions of extreme disgust, horror, or shock. Often a child will tell about a limited aspect of the abuse experience initially, as if to test the interviewer. A child who concludes that the interviewer "can't handle it" may not go on to tell what else happened.

Basic, good listening and child-oriented communication skills are imperative throughout the interview. The school psychologist should listen carefully to what the child is saying, while at the same time, noticing nonverbal communication. The interviewer should work to use developmentally appropriate language and concepts, noticing and using the child's words. Open-ended questions that facilitate disclosure are preferable to closed-ended questions that can be answered yes or no and may lead the child or interrupt the child's story (Krugman & Jones, 1987). Thus, questions like "What happened next?" are generally better than "Then did he hit you?" More focused questions may be appropriate at the end of the interview to clarify information (e.g., "Do you know your Uncle John's last name?").

As with any sensitive clinical work, the school psychologist should listen and validate how the child feels rather than guessing or telling them how they must feel. Given the wide variety of abuse experiences children have suffered and the various stages of feeling that each child may go through, the school psychologist really cannot assume what the child feels. Thus, comments like "I'm sure you feel guilty, but you shouldn't" or "I know you're angry. You have a right to be," while well-intended, are generally not helpful.

Keeping in mind that children rarely lie about abuse and that it is important only to get enough information to make a report since others will do a more investigative interview to determine the accuracy of statements, school psychologists should generally assume a child is telling the truth and act accordingly. Direct or subtle messages of disbelief may squelch the child's further disclosure. Instead, the child should be reassured that telling someone was the right thing to do.

At the conclusion of the interview, it is important for the school psychologist to explain, as much as possible, what will happen next. For example, if the child has disclosed abuse, the school psychologist should inform the child that the abuse will be reported and what can be expected to happen. While the school psychologist clearly will not be able to say definitively how a child protection agency will proceed, a good working relationship with such agencies allows school psychologists to have some idea of the likely response for various types of abuse reports. The school psychologist might be able to tell an adolescent who has suffered mild physical abuse, "A social worker may call your parents and ask what has been going on or to suggest a counselor." On the other hand, a school psychologist might warn a young sexual abuse victim, "The policy may come to school to talk to you. That does not mean you are in trouble. They will be trying to help you." Another aspect of informing a child about what to anticipate next is to be clear with the child about what to expect from the school psychologist. It is important to be honest with oneself and with the child. As well-intended, caring people who are deeply concerned about child victims, some school psychologists may be tempted to volunteer for more than they can really do. A realistic explanation of "I'll be checking in with you every week or so, and you can ask your teacher to contact me in an emergency" may be more honest than "I'll stick with you through this whole thing. I'll go to court. I'll be with you wherever you go, whatever you need." Since most school psychologists are overburdened with multiple demands, clear boundaries are better for everyone concerned.

When the interview is completed, the interviewer should document the conversation in as much detail as possible. Without being obtrusive or overly formal, some school psychologists prefer to jot brief notes, including key phrases used by the child, during the interview and fill in extra details after the interview. Others, depending on state and district regulations, tape record the interview and take notes while listening to the tape. The child should be informed accordingly.

Given the importance and complexity of this work, whenever possible, school personnel should allow trained personnel from an abuse agency to handle the interviews (Brassard et al., 1983). School psychologists should conduct interviews only to gain information to make the report and thus involve abuse experts.

Reporting abuse. Once there is enough information from physical, behavioral, or emotional indicators, and/or child reports to suspect abuse, a school psychologist, as a mandated reporter, must draw up a report to the appropriate child protective agency. School psychologists should be familiar with the laws on reporting child abuse in their state (Brassard et al., 1983), since the specifics — such as which agency should be contacted, and the time frame within which the written report that follows the immediate oral report must be made — vary from state to state.

Certain important aspects are consistent across states, however. For example, school psychologists are generally mandated reporters, so the failure to report is considered a class B misdemeanor as a negligent party (Brassard et al., 1983). Further, no state requires proof of abuse, but rather only a "reason to suspect" (or some similar phrase) before a report is required. Thus, school psychologists are warned not to wait until they have irrefutable evidence. In fact, every state provides immunity from civil liability and/or criminal penalty for those who do report abuse, provided the report is made in good faith (Brassard et al., 1983).

While mandated to report, many professionals are reluctant to do so for a variety of reasons (Johnson, 1989). For example, many are afraid of testifying or getting involved because of potential physical or legal retribution. Others are reluctant to report because they do not trust the protective agency to respond appropriately. Thus, they fear there will be no enforcement, but just enough agency involvement to get the child in further trouble, or an overreaction by the system that will end in having the child pulled from secure, positive experiences, such as school, as a consequence of an out-of-home placement (Johnson, 1989). In sum, there is a fear that reporting will retraumatize the child.

Given the countless tragic cases nationally that have been handled inappropriately, such fears may be justified. On the other hand, school psychologists must keep the larger picture in mind. It is through public disclosure of child maltreatment and the involvement of social agencies that the abusive cycle can be broken and the healing cycle may begin (Johnson, 1989). Furthermore, while there may be some risks in reporting, there are also many risks, both legal and ethical, for not reporting suspected abuse. Imagine, for example, a case in which a school psychologist does not report the suspected physical abuse of a child because of some of the fears discussed above, and later the child is more severely injured or killed.

In addition to making their own difficult reporting decisions, school psychologists may find themselves in positions of advising others on reporting dilemmas. Within schools, teachers are most likely to suspect maltreatment and initiate child abuse reports; however, in many schools principals act as gatekeeper. In this common practice, teachers and other school personnel are asked to discuss suspected abuse with the principal, who will then decide whether to make the report (Zellman, 1990). Since some states require direct reports from the person who suspected abuse, the gatekeeper role, especially if the principal does not report situations that others believe are reportable, may not meet legal requirements. School psychologists may be in positions to consult, advise, or mediate in such situations. Furthermore, a school psychologist who keeps abreast of current legal requirements in the state may offer in-service training for both administrators and teachers (Brassard et al., 1983). State law and district policy should be examined to ensure congruence. Generally, however, school principals are good reporters who may need some additional support from school psychologists regarding difficult situations (Zellman, 1990).

Consultation with teachers. In addition to training and consultation regarding reporting decisions, teachers may appreciate the school psychologist's input regarding other aspects of dealing with a child victim. Abused children often need and can benefit greatly from a special attachment with a concerned teacher (Gelardo & Sanford, 1987), especially if they are able to spend the majority of the school day with one special teacher (Erickson & Egeland, 1987). At the same time, given the multiple symptom patterns described above, it is not always easy for a teacher to maintain a positive relationship with an abused child.

Although the awareness and sensitivity of teachers to the problem of child maltreatment is growing, many will still find it difficult to act upon their concerns. When children who have been maltreated act out in class, teachers find the situations to be upsetting emotionally (Milgram, 1984) and challenging to the classroom structure and routine. Teachers need support and encouragement for their persistent efforts to be patient and understanding of children who have been abused. School psychologists may assist by helping to reinterpret a child's behavior to a teacher, thus helping the teacher to avoid a classroom replication of the child's destructive family relationships (Erickson & Egeland, 1987). Behavioral and mental health consultation may be appropriate. In cases of sexually reactive children, teachers may need very specific suggestions and guidelines regarding supervision and appropriate interventions (Slater & Gallagher, 1989).

While the child's privacy must be respected, teachers sometimes need some information to respond sensitively to children who have been maltreated. The school classroom may be the most stable setting these children experience, and teachers may provide the empathy and positive regard needed to help children cope with their ordeal (Gerler, 1991). Thus, while maintaining professional standards of confidentiality, a school psychologist may elect to share some general information with a teacher who may have a need to know, so that the teacher can respond appropriately and supportively. Allowing the child the opportunity to be with one teacher who knows him or her well may increase the likelihood of promoting that child's adjustment (Erickson & Egeland, 1987).

Consultation with parents. School professionals may want to avoid contact with families once abuse has been reported. However, that response may be detrimental to the child. Supporting the families, even in the most difficult times, is a way of supporting children. School psychologists are urged to promote positive relationships between the child and caretaking parents.

Specifically, school psychologists must do what they can to support the positive mental health of caretaking parents. It is important to remember that most parents, even abusive ones, want to be good parents. Parents who may be stressed, overburdened, or ill-equipped for their roles, deserve caring, nonjudgmental support, just as children deserve protection when necessary (Gelardo & Sanford, 1987). School psychologists are advised to report what they need to report, but then let the legal and protective agencies handle prosecution decisions. Parents, even those believed to be abusive, should still be treated with respect.

Additionally, it is critical in cases in which only one parent is involved in the abuse, and even arrested and incarcerated, that the school psychologist do what is possible to support the nonoffending parent. Studies repeatedly demonstrate that the mental health of nonoffending caretaking parents is closely related to the recovery of their children who have been victimized (Tharinger & Horton, 1992). While school psychologists may hold to common myths that nonoffending caretaking parents in every case have somehow colluded in abuse of the child, this is not accurate. Research demonstrates that nonoffending parents are a heterogeneous group. While some may have had some knowledge or involvement in instances of abuse, other nonoffending parents were not involved or even aware of the abuse and took immediate protective action when they became aware of it (Tharinger, 1991). For the child's sake, nonoffending parents need support.

While school psychologists are clearly not in a role to be the primary therapist for parents, there may be situations in which crisis intervention with parents is appropriate (Tharinger, 1991). For example, in situations in which the reported child abuse is so severe that the perpetrator is arrested at work, and the child is taken to the police station to make a formal statement, someone must be there for the nonoffending parent. The school psychologist may be in a role to assist in explaining to the mother why her child has not yet arrived home from school, what is happening, and where she might get help. Further, there may be ongoing opportunities for education/consultation regarding the child's emotional, behavioral, or academic response to the trauma (Tharinger, 1991).

Making referrals. As noted above, school psychologists will not be the primary therapists for parents. In most cases, they should not serve as the primary therapist for children either. Most school psychologists do not possess the expertise or experience to deal effectively with the problem of abuse. Therefore, the most realistic intervention provided by a school psychologist may be an intelligent referral (Brassard et al., 1983). Helping parents locate available resources may be the most valuable service the school psychologist provides (Brassard et al., 1983).

Quality referral work does not simply mean giving the parents a long list of providers. Instead, school psychologists must build a network of community services (Gelardo & Sanford, 1987). They must keep current on which providers have the specific expertise needed, how long waiting lists are, and which agencies have sliding fee scales. Additionally, once the referral is made, the school psychologist will want to be aware of and cooperate with treatment plans developed by other mental health professionals.

Specific/Optional Roles

Direct interventions. Once again, the school psychologist who does not have the time, the interest, the therapeutic background and training, the personal therapeutic experience, and other professionals to consult with in time of crisis, should not attempt to treat a maltreated child (Brassard & Appilaniz, 1991). However, school psychologists who have such interests and resources may choose to specialize in this area.

Best practices regarding therapy with children who have been victims of maltreatment will address affective, cognitive, and behavioral concerns in the context of a safe, supportive relationship. Regardless of one's theoretical orientation, an important aspect of treatment is the attempt to demonstrate the potential for safe, rewarding human interaction in the relationship with the maltreated child (Gil, 1991). Until a child feels safe and connected to the therapist, there will not likely be much response to treatment (Friedrich, 1990). While such cautions are generally assumed in therapy with any child, for the maltreated child, who feels extremely vulnerable, they are of utmost importance (Gil, 1991). Not only is the relationship critical for the work to be done immediately, it contributes immeasurably in creating a positive and meaningful experience in case the need arises for future therapy (Friedrich, 1990).

In the context of a safe relationship, a child can begin to explore and ventilate affect, including anxiety, frustration, rage, anger toward the offender, and grief for all that has been lost (Brassard & Gelardo, 1987; Wheeler & Berliner, 1988). Play therapy techniques may be appropriate for the expression of such emotions (Gil, 1991). Initially, children may need to learn to recognize their own feelings of emotional pain, as well as the feelings of others (Lewis, 1992). Additionally, children may need assistance in specific coping techniques to handle overwhelming emotions outside of therapy. For example, relaxation techniques may be used to assist children in reducing anxiety. Bedtime rituals may be helpful with night terrors and insomnia (Wheeler & Berliner, 1988).

In addition to expressing the related emotions, children who have been maltreated must learn to make sense of what has happened to them. Distorted, harmful cognitions often result from abusive experiences. While each child's experience is unique, the following conclusions are common among children who are being abused:

1. I am being hurt, emotionally or physically by a parent or other trusted adult.

2. On the basis of how I think about the world thus far, this injury can only be due to one of two things: Either I am bad or my parent is bad (the abuse dichotomy).

3. I have been taught by other adults, wither at home or in school, that parents are always right, and always do things for your own good (any other alternative is very frightening). When they occasionally hurt you, it is for your own good, because you have been gad. This is called punishment.

4. Therefore, it must be my fault that I am being hurt, just as my parent says. This must be punishment. I must deserve this.

5. Therefore, I am as bad as whatever is done to me (the punishment must fit the crime; anything else suggests parental badness, which I have rejected). I am bad because I have been hurt. I have been hurt because I am bad.

6. I am hurt quite often, and/or quite deeply; therefore I must be very gad. (Briere, 1991, p. 28)

Clearly, such distortions are understandable, given the abuse experience, yet very destructive. Children must learn to process and make sense of the trauma in a way that can be tolerated (Gil, 1991).

Maltreated children must learn to understand the abuse experience differently and to view themselves differently (Friedrich, 1990). Specifically, it is important that children who have been abused alter their attribution of responsibility for the abuse so that they can explain the offender's behavior in a way that allows them to "get off the hook" and have a restored sense of self-efficacy (Wheeler & Berliner, 1988). Thus, various cognitive approaches, adapted to the child's level, may be appropriate for gently challenging previous interpretations and providing more useful cognitions. Additionally, cognitive interventions are also important as a precedent for behavioral interventions (Garbarino, 1987). As long as a child thinks "I must be bad," he has little motivation to learn to "act good." A restructured cognitive map may allow the child to incorporate new behaviors.

Behavioral interventions are appropriate in efforts to deal with maltreated children, largely to build up the elements of social competence (Garbarino, 1987). Enhancing a child's prosocial reportoire may be especially important, given the inappropriate models many children who have been abused have experienced (Kolko, 1992).

Specific behavior goals and techniques will vary depending on the child's current functioning (Friedrich, 1990). For some, social skills training may be imperative because of problems with impulsive, withdrawn, and/or aggressive behavior (Haskett & Kistner, 1991; Lewis, 1992). For others, sexualized behaviors must be addressed (Wheeler & Berliner, 1988). For most child victims, assertiveness training that includes a repertoire of specific coping techniques may be helpful in decreasing the likelihood of future abuse. While the burden of child abuse prevention should never rest on the shoulders of children (Tharinger et al., 1990), children may be able to learn to avoid specific high-risk situations and may learn how to disclose abuse more readily.

While a relationship-based intervention plan designed to address affective, cognitive, and behavioral aspects of a child's life may be very effective on an individual basis, group experiences, which are more time-efficient and allow victims to see they are not alone, may also address multiple effects. A good example of such a program is a structure-time-limited therapy group for sexually abused preadolescent children (Corder, Haizlip, & DeBoer, 1990). This program incorporates a balance of affective, cognitive, and behavioral interventions. Cathartic exploration of feelings is prompted through art and story-telling exercises. Cognitive relabeling and self-esteem building are addressed through role-play and chants and cheers. Structured group exercises are designed to develop specific coping skills. Resources that include additional specific therapeutic techniques are listed at the conclusion of this chapter.

Prevention. An additional role for school psychologists with the interest and resources for involvement is in the area of child abuse prevention. School psychologists may have the opportunity to develop and/or implement prevention programs for school districts.

If so, the school psychologist must be aware of strengths, limitations, and possible unintended consequences of existing prevention programs (Consentino, 1989). There are many issues to consider when selecting a prevention program, including the developmental sensitivity, empirical ground, and the complex mixed messages that some programs may unintentionally send (Tharinger et al., 1988).

School psychologists, hopefully on committees with other professionals, must carefully consider these issues. Further specific goals should be considered before a program is implemented and the needed support should be in place before beginning the program. For example, if schools are going to do a series of assemblies regarding child maltreatment, they should be sure that a reporting plan is clear and that the school mental health professionals are prepared to respond to disclosures (Tharinger et al., 1988).

Furthermore, committees should carefully consider decisions regarding format, length, and the incorporation of the program into a broader health curriculum. It is important that programs directed at children include special education children as well, since they may be more vulnerable to abuse (Tharinger et al., 1990).

Additionally, parents should be included in the prevention process. School psychologists should collaborate with parents regarding prevention programs for child audiences and should consider directing prevention efforts to parent audiences (Consentino, 1989). For example, schools may consider offering parent support groups to prevent physical abuse of children (Gerler, 1991).

In addition to providing specific prevention programs for children or parents, some school psychologists may be involved in larger national and cultural fronts. "We need to be activists in fighting for the psychological rights of current and future students in our schools" (Erickson & Egeland, 1987, p. 166). School psychologists should be involved in advocating for change at this level, since major societal change is necessary for real and lasting improvement (Brassard & Gelardo, 1987). Such efforts might include lobbying for specific legal changes through NASP and other professional organizations or lobbying for prosocial media presentations that directly address these concerns (Brassard & Gelardo, 1987).

Finally, in considering prevention, school psychologists must look at the schools themselves (Brassard & Gelardo, 1987). One should consider the psychological climate of the school. Is it positive? Does it promote mental health and/or recovery? Teachers may be targets of prevention efforts so that they do not develop a pattern of psychological maltreatment (rejecting, isolating, terrorizing, ignoring, or corrupting) but rather create a climate that bolsters self-esteem in students and that presents a model of nurturance (Garbarino, 1987).

Self-Care Issues

School psychologists who choose to specialize in a field of child maltreatment must take measures to protect themselves. Child abuse brings up feelings of hostility, sadness, and helplessness as well as protective impulses (Gil, 1991). Stress arises from personal investment in difficult situations (Johnson, 1989). For some, old personal issues are brought to the surface (Friedrich, 1990). Work in this field is simultaneously rewarding and demanding (Gil, 1991).

Clearly, there is a need for continuing education regarding child abuse (Tharinger et al., 1989). It is important to recognize, however, that attending conferences only on this subject and reading professional literature solely in the area of child maltreatment may be overwhelming. While there is an urgent need for experts in this area, professionals will survive longer if they also attend to other arenas of professional development as well to balance their caseloads (Gil, 1991). A school psychologist should not work only with severely abused children, but rather should balance the load with more minor behavioral or emotional concerns. Additionally, supportive collegial relationships are imperative for all that work in this disturbing field (Friedrich, 1990).

SUMMARY

School psychologists are increasingly being identified as among the critical respondents to the tragic phenomenon of child maltreatment. Physically, sexually, and emotionally abused and neglected children fill our schools. School psychologists, therefore, must maintain an awareness of issues regarding child abuse and neglect, so that they are prepared for multiple levels of response. All school psychologists should be prepared for roles involving detecting and reporting child maltreatment, consulting with teachers and parents, and making referrals for needed services. Additionally, those who wish to specialize may

provide direction intervention services and/or design and implement prevention programs. Because of the distressing nature of this work, school psychologists involved in the response to child maltreatment are urged to practice self-care by keeping balanced perspectives and case loads so that they can continue to respond effectively.

REFERENCES

Bates, R. P. (1980). Child abuse and neglect: A medical priority. In R. Volpe, M. Breton, & J. Mitton (Eds.), *The maltreatment of the school-aged child* (pp. 45–58). Lexington, MA: D. C. Heath.

Belsky, J. (1980). Child maltreatment: An ecological integration. *American Psychologist, 35,* 320–335.

Brassard, M. R., & Gelardo, M. S. (1987). Psychological maltreatment: The unifying construct in child abuse and neglect. *School Psychology Review, 16,* 127–356.

Brassard, M. R., Tyler, A., & Kehle, T. J. (1983). Sexually abused children: Identification and suggestions for intervention. *School Psychology Review, 12,* 93–96.

Briere, J. N. (1992). *Child abuse trauma: Theory and treatment of the lasting effects.* Newbury Park, CA: Sage.

Broadhurst, D. D. (1980). The effect of child abuse and neglect on the school-aged child. In R. Volpe, M. Breton, & J. Mitton (Eds.), *The maltreatment of the school-aged child* (pp. 19–27). Lexington, MA: D. C. Heath.

Burgess, A. W., & Groth, N. (1980). Sexual victimization of children. In R. Volpe, M. Breton, & J. Mitton (Eds.), *The maltreatment of the school-aged child* (pp. 79–90). Lexington, MA; D. C. Heath.

Cantwell, H. B. (1980). Child neglect. In C. H. Kempe & R. E. Helfer (Eds.), *The battered child* (pp. 183–197). Chicago: University of Chicago Press.

Corder, B. F., Haizlip, T., & DeBoer, P. (1990). A pilot study for a structured time-limited therapy group for sexually abused preadolescent children. *Child Abuse and Neglect, 14,* 243–251.

Consentino, C. E. (1989). Child sexual abuse prevention: Guidelines for the school psychologist. *School Psychology Review, 18,* 371–383.

Curtois, C. A. (1993). *Adult survivors of child sexual abuse.* Milwaukee: Families International.

Erickson, M. F., & Egeland, B. (1987). A developmental view of the psychological consequences of maltreatment. *School Psychology Review, 16,* 156–168.

Ethier, L. W., Palacio-Quinton, E., & Jourdan-Ionescu, C. (1992). Abuse and neglect: Two distinct forms of maltreatment? *Canada's Mental Health, 40,* 13–19.

Fewster, G., & Bagley, C. (1986). Detection and treatment of child sexual abuse: Mobilising schools. *Journal of Child Care* (2), vii–ix.

Finkelhor, D. (1986). *A sourcebook on child sexual abuse.* Beverly Hills, CA: Sage.

Finkelhor, D., & Baron, L. (1986). High-risk children. In D. Finkelhor (Ed.), *A sourcebook on child sexual abuse.* Beverly Hills, CA: Sage.

Finkelhor, D., Hotaling, G., Lewis, I. A., & Smith, C. (1990). Sexual abuse in a national survey of adult men and women: Prevalence, characteristics, and risk factors. *Child Abuse and Neglect, 14,* 19–28.

Garbarino, J. (1977). The human ecology of child maltreatment: A conceptual model for research. *Journal of Marriage and the Family, 39,* 721–736.

Garbarino, J. (1983). What we know about child maltreatment. *Children and Youth Services Review, 5,* 5–6.

Garbarino, J. (1987). What can the school do on behalf of the psychologically maltreated child and the community? *School Psychology Review, 16,* 181–187.

Gelardo, M. S., & Sanford, E. E. (1987). Child abuse and neglect: A review of the literature. *School Psychology Review, 16,* 137–155.

Gerler, E. R. (1991). *The changing world of the elementary school counselor.* Ann Arbor, MI: School of Education, University of Michigan, Ann Arbor. ERIC Clearinghouse on Counseling and Personnel Services. ED 328 824

Gil, D. (1980). Foreword. In R. Volpe, M. Breton, & J. Mitton (Eds.), *The maltreatment of the school-aged child* (pp. ix–xi). Lexington, MA: D. C. Heath.

Gil, E. (1991). *The healing power of play.* New York: Guilford.

Green, A. H. (1980). *Child maltreatment.* New York: Aronson.

Gross, A. B., & Keller, H. R. (1992). Long-term consequences of childhood physical and psychological maltreatment. *Aggressive Behavior, 18,* 171–185.

Haskett, M. E., & Kistner, J. A. (1991). Social interactions and peer perceptions of young physically abused children. *Child Development, 62,* 979–990.

Helfer, R. E. (1987). The litany of the smoldering neglect of children. In R. E. Helfer & C. H. Kempe (Eds.), *The battered child* (pp. 301–311). Chicago: University of Chicago Press.

Helfer, R. E. (1991). Child abuse and neglect: Assessment, treatment, and prevention, October 21, 2007. *Child Abuse and Neglect, 15,* 5–15.

Hindman, J. (1989). *Just before dawn: From the shadows of tradition to new reflections in trauma assessment and treatment of sexual victimization.* Ontario, OR: AlexAndria Associates.

Johnson, K. (1989). *Trauma in the lives of children.* Alameda, CA: Hunter House.

Kempe, C. H. (1980). Incest and other forms of sexual abuse. In C. H. Kempe & R. E. Helfer (Eds.), *The battered child* (pp. 198–214). Chicago: University of Chicago Press.

Kolko, D. J. (1992). Characteristics of child victims of physical violence: Research findings and clinical implications. *Journal of Interpersonal Violence, 7,* 244–276.

Krugman, R., & Jones, D. P. H. (1987). Incest and other forms of sexual abuse. In R. E. Helfer & R. E. Kempe (Eds.), *The battered child* (pp. 286–300). Chicago: University of Chicago Press.

Lewis, D. O. (1992). From abuse to violence: Psychophysiological consequences of maltreatment. *Journal of the American Academy of Adolescent Psychiatry, 31,* 383–391.

Milgram, J. (1984). Physical and sexual child abuse: Implications for middle level professionals. *NASSP Bulletin, 68,* pp. 58–62.

NCCAN (National Center on Child Abuse and Neglect). (1988). *Study findings: Study of national incidence and prevalence of child abuse and neglect* (DHHS Publication No. OHDS). Washington, DC: Government Printing Office.

Slater, B. R., & Gallagher, M. M. (1989). Outside the realm of psychotherapy: Consultation for intervention with sexualized children. *Journal of School Psychology, 18,* 400–411.

Tharinger, D., & Horton, C. B. (1992). Family–school partnerships: The response to child sexual abuse as a challenging example. In S. L. Christenson & J. C. Conoley (Eds.), *Home school collaboration: Enhancing children's academic and social competence* (pp. 467–486). Silver Spring, MD: NASP.

Tharinger, D., Horton, C. B., & Millea, S. (1990). Sexual abuse and exploitation of children and adults with mental retardation and other handicaps. *Child Abuse and Neglect, 14,* 301–312.

Tharinger, D. J., Krivacska, J. J., Laye-Donough, M., Jamison, L., Vincent, G. G., & Hedlund, A. D. (1988). Prevention of child sexual abuse: An analysis of issues, educational programs, and research findings. *School Psychology Review, 17,* 614–634.

Tharinger, D., Russian, T., & Robinson, P. (1989). School psychologists' involvement in the response to child sexual abuse. *School Psychology Review, 18,* 386–399.

Vevier, E., & Tharinger, D. J. (1986). Child sexual abuse: A review and intervention framework for the school psychologist. *Journal of School Psychology, 24,* 293–311.

Volpe, R. (1980). Schools and the problem of child abuse: An introduction and overview. In R. Volpe, M. Breton, & J. Mitton (Eds.), *The maltreatment of the school-aged child* (pp. 3–10). Lexington, MA: D. C. Heath.

Wheeler, J. R., & Berliner, L. (1988). Treating the effects of sexual abuse on children. In G. E. Wyatt & G. J. Powell (Eds.), *Lasting effects of child sexual abuse* (pp. 227–247). Newbury Park, CA: Sage.

Zellman, G. L. (1990). Linking schools and social services: The case of child abuse reporting. *Education and Policy Analysis, 12,* 41–55.

ANNOTATED BIBLIOGRAPHY

Briere, J. N. (1992). *Child abuse trauma: Theory and treatment of the lasting effects.* Newbury Park, CA: Sage.
This work provides a helpful review of relevant research and clinical literature and considers the interrelationships between all forms of child maltreatment, recognizing that they rarely occur in isolation. The treatment portions of the book, which are primarily focused on adult survivors, could be helpful to the school psychologist working with adolescents who have been victimized.

Friedrich, W. N. (1990). *Psychotherapy of sexually abused children and their families.* New York: Norton.
After reviewing literature regarding the impact of child sexual abuse and suggesting a model of coping, this work outlines treatment goals and gives specific suggestions for therapeutic work with sexually abused children. Throughout both assessment and intervention sections, family issues are carefully considered.

Garbarino, J., Stott, F. M., & the faculty of the Erickson Institute. (1989). *What children can tell us.* San Francisco: Jossey-Bass.
This book serves as a guide to help adults understand what children are trying to communicate, particularly in cases in which they may be attempting to disclose some type of abuse. Specific interview techniques are recommended, and other forms of communication (such as behavior, play, and psychological test responses) are addressed.

Gil, E. (1991). *The healing power of play: Working with abused children.* New York: Guilford.
Following a discussion of the impact of child maltreatment and the resulting therapeutic issues, Gil offers practical suggestions for play-based, child-oriented therapy with abused children. Clinical vignettes of treatment with victims of various forms of child maltreatment are included.

Hindman, J. (1991). *When mourning breaks.* Ontario, OR: AlexAn-
    dria Associates.
    Dispelling common myths with research, Hindman discusses
    factors that mediate the impact of child sexual abuse and pro-
    poses a model of trauma assessment. Also included is a compi-
    lation of over 100 specific treatment activities, indexed by age
    — many that could be appropriate for school-based individual
    or group sessions.

82

Best Practices in Assisting Families Who Move and Relocate

Frederic J. Medway
University of South Carolina

OVERVIEW

This chapter is intended to provide a framework and guidelines for deciding the best professional practices for school psychologists to follow in order to answer questions, make decisions, and take actions relevant to clinical situations in which family mobility is of concern. The chapter will attempt to clarify the impact of relocation on children and their parents and provide guidelines and resources for intervention. To develop this framework it is necessary to first operationalize, as best possible, the concept of mobility and describe various variables associated with it. Next, research studies on the effects of moving are described. Finally, ways that school psychologists can contribute to situations in which mobility is a factor are considered.

BACKGROUND

Each year more than 17% of all American families change residence. This figure includes nearly 9 million children of school age (U.S. Bureau of the Census, 1990). More strikingly, each year approximately 30% of families with preschool children change residence and some types of families, such as those associated with the military, often relocate every 2 years.

Although most families who move remain within the same city, county, or standard metropolitan statistical area (van Vliet, 1986), residential mobility often accompanies social mobility. Residential moves are made by upwardly mobile families who seek larger or more luxurious housing and lower income groups who move because of financial hardship. These short distance moves often result from family separations as well. Thus, even short distance moves can involve many family changes. These include parent occupational, social, and lifestyle changes, changes in children's familiar surroundings, and often, school changes.

About one in six moves is to a different state or country. Occupations in the corporate world, sales, academia, the clergy, government service, and the military often require such moves. Interstate and international moves also characterize migrant and immigrant families. Just during their school years children may relocate many times. One survey of nearly 7,000 high school students found that 5.5% moved seven or more times (Norford, 1991).

Even one act of relocation places many demands and challenges on individuals. It is difficult to leave friends, family, and familiar environments and develop new relationships. Feelings of anxiety, loneliness, a sense of loss, and uncertainty are common. For children these worries typically center around losing friends and making new ones rather than changing school or adjusting to a new place (Norford, 1991). At least theoretically it is assumed that a stable reference group of friends and associates is important in order to get feedback on one's abilities and thus to develop a stable self-concept. Although early studies of relocation tried to link it with social and psychiatric problems, the research literature generally shows that children who are well adjusted prior to relocating are well adjusted after relocating whereas children with academic or adjustment deficits preceding a move tend to be at risk for similar or greater problems after a move.

In short, as will be demonstrated subsequently, there is little evidence to support the widely held belief that moving has negative effects on average children. This belief basically is based on case study reports, clinical impressions, and methodologically flawed studies (e.g., small and selected samples, lack of experimental controls). It also tends to be validated by the personal experience of some individuals. It further is compounded by media accounts of moving as "traumatic" for children. Although these erroneous beliefs regarding children and moving have been challenged (Goldsmith & Clark, 1987), even school professionals continue to be unduly concerned about the negative side of moving.

BASIC CONSIDERATIONS

The Process of Moving and Relocation

There is general consensus that family relocation should be viewed as life-transition and adjustment processes. With this view relocation can potentially have either positive or negative effects on families and, in most instances, involves some combination of the two. These effects can be short-term and result in changes transient in nature or long-term and alter previously established behavior patterns for many years. The impact may be a direct effect of environmental change on the child. The impact of moving may be mediated by changes in the family system or more likely, the results of moving may reflect some combination of the two.

There also is general support for the notion that moving involves a series of interrelated stages. At each stage there may be adjustment difficulties and accordingly opportunities for school psychologists to provide assistance. These intervention opportunities are described in the closing section of this chapter. The stages of family relocation can be broken down as follows:

- *Stage One: Anticipation and Preparation.* This stage generally is marked by families' facing a moving situation and considering the advantages and disadvantages of relocating. It involves all aspects of decision-making regarding relocation (possibly including solicitation of the child's input), parents' attitudes, and ultimately communication of the decision to the child. Research is clear in indicating that the vast majority of children are unhappy, sad, or scared when they hear they have to move (Khleif, 1978). They conjure up all kinds of hypothetical negative events and minimize positive benefits. This likely is especially true of younger children who lack formal operations thinking. Adequate explanation of the reasons for the move, upbeat and optimistic parent attitudes, and child reassurance are essential first steps for making the transition successfully. In fact, parents' attitudes and the opportunity for forming new friendships are the two most important variables in ensuring a successful move.

- *Stage Two: Planning.* This stage involves all actions necessary to make the move smoothly. This may involve elements related to house sale, selection of neighborhoods and schools, inquiries about community resources, and transfers of school records. Without proper planning, parents may feel irritable, overwhelmed, and fatigued, and these feelings often affect child behavior.

- *Stage Three: Moving Day.* Moving day is characterized by the actual relocation of the family and its possessions. Because only one in four families uses a moving company, this day is highly stressful. Young children may be particularly upset during this time.

- *Stage Four: Initial Adjustment.* This stage, lasting upwards of 6 months, is characterized by those actions taken by the family, child, and community resources to deal with the stresses associated with

environmental change. This may involve increased financial responsibilities, securing new employment for family members, and adjusting to changing work or travel schedules of the breadwinner(s). Families hope that the child's behavior in the new home, school, and neighborhood will be similar to (or in some cases better than) the prior location. There is little disagreement among clinicians and researchers that initial adjustment difficulties are normal and expected.

- *Stage Five: Later Adjustment.* This stage involves the long-term impact of a move or series of relocations.

Many families feel relatively well equipped to deal with Stages Two and Three. Often they are assisted by businesses and moving professionals with these issues. By contrast, Stages One, Four, and Five have been the concern of social scientists.

Mobility Dimensions

Beyond acknowledging that moving represents a series of activities and subsequent adjustments school psychologists need to recognize that the events themselves vary dramatically from one moving situation to another. Even situations which appear similar on the surface such as a military transfer are not experienced the same by all children. Rather, moving and relocation vary across many different dimensions, and each of these, either singly or in combination with others, will influence moving-related reactions.

These dimensions are presented in Figure 1. Each of these can impact on various aspects of children's social adjustment, including peer relations and friendship networks, participation in social activities, mental health, including anxiety, self-concept, age-appropriate behavior, loneliness and susceptibility to depression, and school performance.

Mobility characteristics. Several variables associated with the move itself have the potential to impact on children. Three of particular importance are the distance moved, the degree of perceived choice, and the reason for the move. Although distance as measured by miles from old to new residence has little consistent impact on children, it must be recognized that even short moves can potentially exaggerate existing problems if they involve significant life changes such as an extended commute or a school change. Moving usually is hardest on family members who have had little say in the decision to move, the place of new residence, and other factors such as the school and neighborhood. Typically, this is the child and relocated spouse involved in corporate and military-related moves. Transplanted spouses are likely to have initial feelings of loneliness, depression, and loss, and these feelings in turn may affect their atti-

FIGURE 1.   Variables associated with family mobility.

Mobility Characteristics

Distance of Move
Timing of Move
Degree of Choice in Move
Reason to Move
Recency of Moving
Cultural Similarity Between Old and New Community
Number of Prior Moves
Pattern of Prior Moves

Child Characteristics

Age
Gender
Personality
Pre-existing Achievement or Adjustment Problems

Family Characteristics

Family Size
Family Support Mechanisms
Family Structure
Family Mobility History
Family Attitudes About Moving
Availability of Parents

School Factors

Time of Entry into Classroom
Curriculum
Size
Amount of Student Turnover
Programs to Address Relocation and Other Support Services
Degree of Student Retention

Community Factors

Availability of Child and Family Social Services
Availability of Community Supports
Economic Climate

tudes toward the move and parenting skills. Thus, children may develop problems because parents are less functional. In some cases, roles may be reversed, and the child may feel pressure to support the parent. Research also shows the important role of the reason for the move. Families may move because of financial hardship, the requirements of military duty, separation or divorce, occupational necessity, or simply to secure more adequate housing. Single-parent families move more often than two-parent families. Children who move as a result of divorce report less involvement in school social activities in the years following a move (Norford, 1991) compared to nonmovers, even when stressful life events are controlled.

Child characteristics. The stresses associated with moving affect children in different ways and this appears to be influenced by developmental levels, gender, and psychological risk factors. Several studies have directly examined children of different ages

following a move and found no clear developmental patterns. Nevertheless, the bulk of the literature suggests that the most vulnerable ages to moving-related stressors are the preschool years and during early adolescence (Vernberg, 1990). This is contrary to the general public view that the best time to move is before children start elementary school and that moving is hardest on high school students. Preschoolers have difficulty dealing with the changes in familiar surroundings, lack the coping skills of older children, and have trouble cognitively understanding the need for the move. Also, they are less likely than older children to understand abstract concepts of time such as "in six months" which may relate to when the move will occur. Young adolescents report about three times as much difficulty forming friendships as do children in the primary grades (Barrett & Noble, 1973).

Gender does not appear to have consistent effects on mobility reactions, although some have argued that males react more negatively than females to relocation (van Vliet, 1986; Vernberg, 1990) and to a variety of associated transitions (Rutter, 1981). Males appear to have a harder time leaving old friends and making new ones (Donahue & Gullotta, 1983). On the other hand, Brown and Orthner (1990) found that recent moves and frequency of mobility history were more strongly associated with low life-satisfaction among female than male adolescents. Second, males are more likely to rely on and experience rejection from peers than females. And, third, males are more negatively reactive to a variety of life transitions (Rutter, 1981).

Finally, it has been recognized that children with existing academic and behavioral problems require structure, consistency, and special attention. Typically, therefore, moving or any potential stressors is likely to impact such children to a greater extent than children without pre-existing problems. Kantor (1965), in one of the few studies to assess children both before and after moving, showed that negative mobility effects were attributable to initial behavioral differences between children, not mobility per se.

Family characteristics. It is virtually impossible to disentangle the effects of family variables from the impact of relocation. It is the family who informs the child of the move; deals with concerns and anxieties; makes the relocation decisions; and attempts to help the child through the transition period. If the family attitude toward moving or toward this particular move is negative it is likely that the child's will be as well. Several studies have underscored the importance of the mother's attitude toward the move on children. Norford (1991) reported that over 60% of mothers who had relocated their children an average of seven times reported moving as either "moderately" or "very" stressful. Further, if either parent becomes overanxious, withdrawn, physically stressed, or intolerant this too will affect the child, particularly if the child connects this behavioral change to the move. In corporate families the needs of the head of the household may so overshadow the needs of other family members that problems develop. Several studies indicate that moving can result in depression but only when family support and social cohesion is low. By contrast, selective attrition of service personnel in the military system may have resulted in large numbers of families basically accepting of the mobile lifestyle and therefore communicating these positive relocation expectations to their children.

School factors. School factors are an important, although unstudied, moderator of moving-related reactions. School size, quality of teacher–student interactions, opportunities for leadership roles, curriculum demands, policies and norms, and the nature of support services all would appear to impact on mobility adjustment. Occasionally school experiences

can certainly exacerbate moving reactions. For example, considering the effects of group cohesion, it is not surprising that elementary-age males who enter school late in the year are less likely to be accepted socially than boys who enter early in the year. Schools characterized by existing cliques create challenges for the newly relocated adolescent. However, in most cases, schools have had little systematic impact on mobility issues due to their general failure to address this population. One review found only two large-scale school intervention programs to ease the transition discussed in the literature (Blair, Marchant, & Medway, 1984). One program, known as the Summer Visitation Program (Keats, Crabbs, & Crabbs, 1981), used school counselors to (a) make new school families aware of school policies using home visitations; (b) involve these families in school and community activities by sponsoring various outings enabling the families to meet others in the community; and (c) develop support groups for recently relocated children. This program was successful in increasing social contacts and happiness and reducing absenteeism in participating students compared to nonparticipating controls. A second program, known as Students Assimilated into Learning (Panagos, Holmes, Thurman, Yard, & Spaner, 1981), also sought to increase parental involvement in the school and, in addition, made use of staff development activities and special learning centers to quickly assess the educational status of students moving into the school and provide assistance with academic deficiencies. Data obtained from this program indicated that served students showed increased achievement scores.

In one area, however, schools have played a questionable role regarding the mobile student. Many schools have policies or philosophies encouraging grade retention of new students and, in fact, research shows that highly mobile children are retained more often than nonmobile children. *Light's Retention Scale* is a questionable assessment tool which inappropriately includes mobility as a factor to consider in deciding whether to retain a child. A survey (Norford, 1991) of adolescents who had moved at least six times indicated that only 15% indicated feeling behind academically after moving. Given that retention itself is a questionable practice and that research indicates mobility generally is not a major stressor for most children, there is nothing to recommend retention of mobile students and much support for rejecting the practice.

Community factors. The similarity of new communities to old ones helps moderate the stress of relocation. Moves which subject children to cultural and subcultural differences are presumed to require greater adjustment. Along these lines it is often assumed that moving from one military base to another is generally not highly stressful because (a) bases tend to be similar and (b) the base tends to insulate the military family from the surrounding community. In addition, relocation support services are available through military-supported Family Service Centers. While this may be true, there is no empirical evidence that children in military-related moves do any better (or worse) than children in corporate moves.

The Impact of Relocation on Children

In attempting to understand the impact of relocation on families it is not only important to consider the stages of moving and the various elements associated with the process but also to realize that there are vast differences in the public view of mobility as compared to the scientific community. The following three excerpts are typical of how mobility is perceived by many citizens and by the media.

Sesame Street Magazine: Samantha and Robert Brown had been preparing for moving day for weeks. On the big day, Samantha left her one-year-old son with a neighbor while she and her husband supervised the movers. Eight hours later it was time for one last look around. With the baby in her arms, Samantha entered his now-bare room. He took one startled look and began to bawl. Brown was surprised at the force of her infant's reaction: "There was no question. He knew something was terribly wrong." Like most infants, Brown's baby suffered only momentarily, because the real center of his world was his parents . . . But for most kids, be they toddlers or teens, moving can be stressful. (Rouhana, 1990, p. 19–20).

Boston Globe: Whether you are relocating across town or across country, moving is traumatic for children of any age. The change in routine, parents' preoccupation with the move, giving up friends — these are all losses for the child. The worst mistake parents can make is to underestimate their importance. (Maltz, 1992, pp. 67, 71)

New York Times: Daniel and Gerry Barnett hadn't expected their children to react so strongly to the family's move from Oklahoma to suburban Chicago. Twelve-year-old Helen told her parents that she looked forward to the move because it was "a neat thing to do." . . . But as the move approached, she became more obstinate when an adult asked her to do something. She would overreact to ordinary events. Helen's school grades dropped slightly in the next marking period. (Kutner, 1988, p. 21)

In short, both the popular press and general opinion view moving as a potentially traumatic event that can have long-term consequences on children's mental health and school performance. This view tends to be shared by teachers and school administrators. By contrast, although research suggests that there may be some short-term impact of mobility on children, data obtained from more than 100 studies of children's relocation indicates that there is little evidence for any long-term negative impact. The following is a brief overview of research in this area drawn from earlier reviews by Norford (1991) and van Vliet (1986).

Academic achievement. Achievement of mobile versus nonmobile populations has been the most widely researched area. Across 18 of the most methodologically sound studies (out of over 40 conducted) there is virtually no effect of mobility on school achievement once initial achievement levels are controlled. Mobility does appear to hurt the academically underprepared student. Further, in six studies measuring grade retention, mobile students consistently are held back more often than nonmobile students, despite the fact that in three of these studies achievement levels of mobile and nonmobile students did not differ.

Social adjustment. Does frequent relocation undermine self-image, peer relations, participation in extracurricular activities, and other areas of social adjustment? Most research suggests that it does not. High-frequency and low-frequency movers have not been found to differ on traditional scales of self-concept and personality. There is some evidence that depression may be associated with higher levels of mobility in young adolescents. However, it is not clear if, in these studies, depression arose after the move or during earlier preparatory stages. In one recent, well-controlled study (Norford, 1991) there were no differences in depression and perceived social support among high school students varying in mobility history, including nearly 100 students who had moved seven times on average. Norford did find that frequent mobility after seventh grade did significantly affect participation in extracurricular activities. Norford measured potential positive adjustment indicators as well and found no consistent positive effects associated with high mobility.

BEST PRACTICES

With an awareness of the prior background information and appropriate training in assessment, child development, and intervention, school psychologists should have the basic skills to deal with relocation concerns. School psychologists are likely to encounter mobility issues in two primary contexts. First, in their capacities as school consultants, psychologists occasionally are asked to provide information about relocation to various sources. Those seeking this information most likely are parents (those considering relocation or those who have just relocated), teachers (faced with making decisions about newly transferred students), school administrators, and, occasionally, the media. Parents may be prone to worry about mobility effects far more than is warranted. Norford (1991) found that 27% of approximately 95 adolescents who had moved six times or more viewed moving as "very positive" for them compared to 15% of their mothers. Only 3% of the students viewed moving as "very negative" compared to 10% of their mothers.

Typically, however, families new to a community do not pose these questions to school psychologists. If their child has not had school problems in the past or if the parents are unfamiliar with school resources, it is unlikely that psychologists will be called. Best practice, therefore, dictates that school psychologists inform those in the community such as doctors, the clergy, and key people in school district administration of their knowledge in this area.

Second, in their roles as providing intervention services, school psychologists may be called upon directly to (a) develop programs to ease mobility transitions or (b) work with children having difficulty with mobility-related adjustments. The following section reviews several best practices and helpful sources to aid in both capacities.

Parent Consultation

Parents who contact school psychologists for information about moving may do so at any stage of the relocation process. Typically, these parents fear that moving will upset their child in some way and desire practical tips and resources to make the move easier. Figure 2 presents a list of practical information that families and the media can be provided. This list addresses many questions parents have about moving. Further tips are presented in books specifically designed for parents listed at the end of this chapter. These can be useful provided the reader keeps in mind that most popular books overdramatize the negative effects of mobility. In addition, school psychologists can encourage parents to use one or more of the children's story books listed in Figure 4 to clarify relocation feelings and let the children know that their feelings are not unique. Also, most of the major moving companies have materials to aid families with moving. A brochure entitled *Moving with Children* can be obtained from United Van Lines, One United Drive, Fenton, Missouri 63026. Ryder Truck Rental has a "Movers Advantage" package that includes games and activities for children. It can be obtained by calling 305-593-3183.

School Professional Consultation

School psychologists are encouraged to share the information in this article with school teachers, counselors, and administrators. Specific guidelines for teachers are presented in Figure 3. In addition, psychologists can be given the names of all recent movers and check with teachers on their progress after a period of time. Particular attention should be given to newly transferred males given research showing their greater vulnerability to moving-related stress and their decreased reliance on appropriate coping mechanisms compared to females.

Program Development

School psychologists can take the lead in developing school-based preventive programs centered around relocation issues. In particular, aspects of the Summer Visitation Program (Keats, Crabbs, & Crabbs, 1981) reviewed earlier, can be developed by special service teams, particularly in areas characterized by high transiency. Given the empirical validation of this program, it represents one of the few validated best practices in this area. In addition to interventions with students just entering school, counseling groups can be organized for elementary school children whose families will soon be moving to other communities. In such groups children can be given an opportunity to share feelings about moving and discuss specific strategies such as social skills training to use in saying good-bye and making new friends. Programs also can be developed for parents to help them understand the impact of moving as it relates to their own specific circumstances and the development of their child. It is very important to tailor intervention programs, teacher inservices, and parent education groups to the age of child clients.

Counseling and Therapy

As indicated previously, it is unlikely that school psychologists will encounter large numbers of students with serious problems such as depression, withdrawal, physical symptoms, or dramatic achievement declines that necessitate extended counseling. Adjustment problems are normal during the first 6 months after relocation and typically can be handled through family or teacher consultation. Unusual withdrawal, anxiety, anger, stress-related reactions, acting-out, or academic problems, however, do require early intervention. Several nonbehavioral techniques (cf. Medway, 1985) are particularly appropriate. These include play therapy, role playing to bring conflicts into awareness, and bibliotherapy. The children's literature on moving listed in Figure 4 is suited for treatment designed to help children gain insight into their problems and to develop alternative courses of action. The video *Let's Get a Move On!* is especially engaging and has won several educational awards. Additionally, social skills training can be used to aid in building friendship networks and dealing with negative remarks made by others. Because many contextual factors such as family dynamics and household economics may affect the child more than just environmental change and adjustment, consultation and therapy in cases involving relocation require extensive problem-identification activities prior to treatment.

FGURE 2. Parent tips on relocation.

1. Discuss the move openly and honestly with children once the decision to move is definite. Older children should be given at least 3 months notice, if possible, to prepare for the move. They should also be given some input into family decisions. For younger children, it is preferable to wait until moving is closer, such as when moving-related activities change family routines. For younger children, reading story books about moving may stimulate questions, elicit feelings, and easy any anxiety. Toys, such as trucks and wagons, can be used in "moving games" to illustrate the concept of moving to the 2- and 3-year-old child. Be clear the move is final and avoid promises you may not be able to keep.

2. Try not to move during other upheavals in the child's life such as right after a sibling birth or following a divorce or parent death. This will compound the stress and adjustment demands placed on children.

3. Get children involved in the move. Encourage children to take on projects designed to gather information on the new community. Subscribe to the newspaper in the new community.

4. Start building a new community network before the move. Inquire about religious groups, medical and social service facilities, educational opportunities, newcomer's assistance, and children's activities such as scouting. If relocation is due to corporate or military transfer, inquire about special assistance offered.

5. Recocognize your own stress level and don't take on more than you can handle. Moving yourself, looking for a house without an experienced real estate agent, or moving into a home requiring repairs and renovation can serve as added stressors. Recognize that your stress level as well as your attitude about moving will affect your child's behavior.

6. Make sure that all medical and school records are sent ahead. These should include a birth certificate, achievement tests, immunization records, and relevant school correspondence. Special education transfers should provide psychoeducational assessment results, health screenings, and Individual Education Plans.

7. Take responsibility for orienting your child to the new school and community. Have a meeting with your child's teacher to discuss the placement. Inquire about any special programs or assistance provided by psychologists and counselors for relocated students. Do not allow your child to repeat a grade just on the basis of a move. If retention is recommended, insist on a full, individually administered evaluation and, if necessary, a second opinion.

8. Although a move during the summer is less likely to be disruptive to children's school performance, a move during the school year brings children into immediate contact with others their age. Also, teachers and classmates are more likely to treat them as special when they enter during the year than at the start of a new year.

9. On moving day reassure children that their possessions are going to the new home. Allow children to pack a small suitcase to carry with them with special playthings, momentos, and pictures. Load the furniture of young children last so that these items are first to be unloaded and placed in the new home. Once in the new home, allow the child some say in how the room will be decorated or try to arrange it similarly to the last arrangement. Make the first night in the new home special by having some kind of party.

10. Goodbyes should be allowed to occur such as going-away parties. Encourage children to make scrap books with pictures of old friends and to keep up correspondence.

11. Take the initiative, especially during the initial weeks of a move, to actively explore the new environment. Make an effort to meet people. Invite neighbors over and volunteer at the school. Avoid staying indors and devoting all your time to unpacking and arranging the new house. This should be a time spent with children.

12. Try to find positive things in moves required by financial hardships.

13. Moving may diminish teenagers' feelings of independence and need for control. Therefore, aid teenagers in exploring social opportunities in the new environment. Resist the temptation to be overprotective due to unfamiliarity with the new community.

FIGURE 3. School staff tips on children and relocation.

1. Present children who are moving with photo albums of classmates and friends. Consider having a going-away party for moving students.
2. Announce the arrival of new students. Make sure they are included in yearbooks and the like.
3. Assign student "buddies" to new students. Buddies may also serve as guides and peer tutors.
4. Encourage recently moved students to do presentations on the places they have lived.
5. Be sensitive to family stresses that may be associated with mobility. Note in particular financial hardships and provide the family with information about support services if needed.
6. Do not retain new school enrollees. Retention decisions, if made at all, should not be based on family mobility history or the ability of the child to adjust to new school routines. If academic or behavior problems are present, consult the school psychologist.
7. Maintain particularly close contact with newly relocated families so as to enhance school–home communication.
8. Participate in and encourage school-sponsored meetings and social events for parents of newcomers to acquaint them with school policies and community services.

SUMMARY

Each year one out of five families relocate in the United States. The process of relocation involves several adjustment stages and each, in turn, is influenced by a host of contextual variables such as reasons for the move, child age and gender, and aspects of the new community. Because moving does involve changes and interruptions in children's schooling and friendships there is concern among the public and school professionals about the effects of moving on children and their families. Despite this concern, research indicates that family relocations are far less stressful on children than many people believe. Although mobility can cause children to be anxious, to develop behavior problems, and to have academic problems in the classroom these problems typically are short-lived. Most normal children ultimately handle moving transitions well. Those who do not typically have presenting problems which originate before rather than after a move. Within six months to a year it is virtually impossible to distinguish movers and nonmovers on traditional measures of personality and achievement.

The keys to successful moves lie in family behavior and attitudes and in the opportunities available for children to make new friends and experience a consistent, known environment. Schools can positively impact in both these areas. Unfortunately, with the exception of some isolated efforts, schools often have ignored their important role as a key community resource in aiding mobile families during the transition to a new neighborhood (Blair, Marchant, & Medway, 1984). Thus, school psychologists can serve an important function in both advocating for school-wide efforts and including personal efforts to aid relocating families among their activities. Several best practices have been described. Family mobility is an integral part of the American lifestyle. By providing planned consultation and intervention services centering around relocation issues, school psychologists can bring to bear a variety of assessment, consultation, and intervention skills to a potential family dilemma.

REFERENCES

Barrett, C. L., & Noble, H. (1973). Mother's anxieties vs. the effects of long distance moves on children. *Journal of Marriage and the Family, 35*, 181–188.

Blair, J. P., Marchant, K. H., & Medway, F. J. (1984). Aiding the relocated child and mobile family. *Elementary School Guidance and Counseling, 18*, 251–259.

Brown, A. C., & Orthner, D. K. (1990). Relocation and personal well-being among early adolescents. *Journal of Early Adolescence, 10*, 366–381.

Donahue, K. C., & Gullotta, T. P. (1983). The coping behavior of adolescents following a move. *Adolescence, 18*, 391–401.

Goldsmith, D. F., & Clark, E. (1987). Moving. In A. Thomas & J. Grimes (Eds.), *Children's needs: Psychological perspectives* (pp. 372–378). Washington, DC: National Association of School Psychologists.

Kantor, M. B. (1965). Some consequences of residential and social mobility for the adjustment of children. In M. B. Kantor (Ed.), *Mobility and mental health* (pp. 86–122). Springfield, IL: Charles C Thomas.

Keats, D. B., Crabbs, M. A., & Crabbs, S. K. (1981). Facilitating the adjustment process of new students. *Elementary School Guidance and Counseling, 15*, 319–323.

Khleif, B. B. (1978). The military dependent as a stranger in the public schools. *Sociologia Internationalis, 16*, 153–161.

Kutner, L. (1988, July 8). A move can shake children's confidence. *The New York Times*, p. 21.

Medway, F. J. (1985). Direct therapeutic intervention in school psychology. In J. R. Bergan (Ed.), *School psychology in contemporary society: An introduction* (pp. 207–229). Columbus, OH: Merrill.

Meltz, B. F. (1992, May 29). Helping kids handle the stress of moving. *Boston Globe*, pp. 67, 71.

Norford, B. C. (1991). The relationship of repeated geographical mobility to social adjustment and depression in high school students. Unpublished doctoral dissertation, University of South Carolina, Columbia.

Panagos, J. L., Holmes, R. L., Thurman, R. L., Yard, G. L., & Spaner, S. D. (1981). Opertion SAIL: One effective model for the assimilation of new students into a school district. *Urban Education, 15*, 451–468.

Rouhana, K. (1990, June). Smooth moves. *Sesame Street Magazine: Parent's Guide*, pp. 19–20.

Rutter, M. (1981). Stress, coping, and development: Some issues, some questions. *Journal of Child Psychology and Psychiatry, 22*, 323–356.

U.S. Bureau of the Census. (1990). *Statistical abstracts of the United States: 1990 (110th ed.)*. Washington, DC: U.S. Government Printing Office.

van Vliet, W. (1986). Children who move: Relocation effects and their context. *Journal of Planning Literature, 1*, 403–426.

Vernberg, E. M. (1990). Experiences with peers following relocation during early adolescence. *American Journal of Orthopsychiatry, 60*, 466–472.

ANNOTATED BIBLIOGRAPHY

Miller, Y. F., & Cherry, J. W. (1992). *Kids on the move*. Laurel, MD: National Association of School Psychologists.
A comprehensive source designed for professionals working with children who have encountered a variety of relocation-related problems, including both routine family moves and divorce-related changes.

Let's get a move on! (1990). Newton, MA: Kidvidz.
In this 25-minute video a variety of children share their feelings when they hear they have to move and discover ways of making new friends. The video is well produced and contains several original songs ranging in style from 60's rock to rap.

Artenstein, J. (1990). *Moving: How to be sure that your child makes a happy transfer to a new home*. New York: TOR.
This easy-to-read paperback is designed for families going through a move. It contains helpful tips to make parents more optimistic about moving. Several idealized stories of children moving can be used by parents to facilitate children's willingness to talk about their feelings about moving.

Blair, J. P., Marchant, K. H., & Medway, F. J. (1984). Aiding the relocated child and mobile family. *Elementary School Guidance and Counseling, 18*, 251–259.
This article reviews research on children and moving, and discusses several effective school-based programs designed to aid the mobile child. It contains tips for parents and a reading list for children.

BIBLIOGRAPHY AND READINGS ON RELOCATION

Suggested Readings for Parents

Artenstein, J. (1990). *Moving: How to be sure that your child makes a happy transfer to a new home*. New York: TOR.

Friedrich, B., & Hulstrand, S. (1978). *Did someone pack the baby?* Englewood Cliffs, NJ: Prentice-Hall.

Miller, Y. F., & Cherry, J. W. (1992). *Kids on the move*. Laurel, MD: Natonal Association of School Psychologists.

Porter, O. (1992). *From here to here: The workbook for families on the move*. Portland, OR: Niche Press.

Ruina, E. (1970). *Moving: A common sense guide to relocating your family*. New York: Funk & Wagnalls.

Books for Children: Preschool

Asch, F. (1986). *Goodbye house*. Englewood Cliffs, NJ: Prentice-Hall.

Books for Children: Elementary Grades

Brown, M. (1967). *Pip moves away*. San Francisco, CA: Golden Gate Press.

Fisher, A. L. (1966). *Best little house*. Scranton, PA: Harper & Row.

Hickman, M. (1975). *I'm moving*. Nashville, TN: Abington.

Hughes, S. (1979). *Moving Molly*. Englewood Cliffs, NJ: Prentice-Hall.

Hurwitz, J. (1979). *Aldo Applesauce*. New York: Morrow.

Iwasaki, C. (1973).*What's fun without a friend?* New York: McGraw-Hill.

Milford, S., & Milford, J. (1979). *Maggie and the goodbye gift*. New York: Lothrop, Lee, & Shepherd Books.

O'Donnell, E. L. (1987). *Maggie doesn't want to move*. New York: Four Winds.

Schulman, J. (1976). *Big Hellos*. New York: Greenwillow Books.

Sharmat, M. W. (1978). *Mitchell is moving*. New York: Aladdin.

Sharmat, M. W. (1980). *Gila monsters at the airport*. New York: Puffin.

Slote, A. (1974). *Tony and me*. Philadelphia: Lippincott.

Tobias, T. (1976). *Moving day*. New York: Knopf.

Zolotow, C. (1973). *Janey*. New York: Harper & Row.

Books for Adolescents

Nida, P. C., & Heller, W. M. (1985). *The teenager's ssurvival guide to moving*. New York: Atheneum.

Videotapes for Children

Let's get a move on! (1990). Newton, MA: Kidvidz (appropriate for ages 4–10).

83

Best Practices in Planning Interventions for Students with Attention Disorders

Margaret M. Dawson
The Center for Learning and Attention Disorders

OVERVIEW

With increased awareness on the part of parents, educators, clinicians, and researchers, concerning the nature of attention disorders and the effect they have on school performance and adjustment, school psychologists are becoming more involved in both identifying attention disorders and in developing effective interventions. Another chapter in this volume addresses diagnostic and assessment issues in the identification of students with Attention Deficit Hyperactivity Disorder (ADHD)[1]. This chapter delineates the range of interventions commonly used with students who have attention disorders.

This chapter addresses intervention needs of students diagnosed as having ADHD as well as those students who may not meet any formal definition of ADHD but who demonstrate problems in the classroom due to characteristics commonly associated with ADHD. By addressing a broad range of attention problems without undue emphasis on formal classification of students as ADHD, this chapter is congruent with NASP's Position Statement on Students with Attention Deficits (NASP, 1992). This statement acknowledges that reliable diagnosis of ADHD is difficult and recognizes "that it is difficult to distinguish attention deficits so severe as to require special education from the normal range of temperament and fluctuations in attention to which all students are susceptible." Furthermore, it is consistent with a consultation/problem-solving orientation toward the practice of school psychology. Problems with attention can be defined as deficits in a set of school-related behaviors. The task of the school psychologist is to work with teachers and parents to define those deficits, to develop interventions to address the deficits, and to help implement and evaluate those interventions. This chapter will describe briefly the behavior characteristics associated with attention disorders, delineate a problem-solving process to develop effective interventions, and then focus on the array of interventions that can be used to address the behavior and academic performance problems commonly associated with attention disorders.

BASIC CONSIDERATIONS

Characteristics of Students with Attention Disorders

The DSM-III-R (1987) provides the most commonly accepted definition of Attention Deficit Hyperactivity Disorder. This definition lists 14 characteristics, and requires that a student demonstrate at least eight of those characteristics for a duration of at least six months in order to meet the formal criteria for ADHD. The 14 characteristics primarily describe problems with inattention, impulsivity, and motoric hyperactivity.

Since DSM-III-R was published, many researchers and clinicians have argued that this definition of ADHD omits a significant population of students who exhibit attentional problems but may not be impulsive or motorically hyperactive. Frick and Lahey (1991), for instance, maintained that attention disorders and motor hyperactivity are two distinct behavioral dimensions, and that a significant number of students with attention problems do not have concomitant problems with hyperactivity or impulsivity.

Students with attention disorders *without* hyperactivity display the following characteristics: They often fail to finish tasks, they are easily distracted, they have difficulty listening, concentrating, and organizing their work, they require supervision to accomplish tasks, and they frequently shift activities. Students with attention disorders *with* hyperactivity display these same characteristics. However, they are also described as having difficulty remaining seated, exhibiting motor restlessness and excessive fidgeting, frequently calling out in class or interrupting, being always on the go, and often acting without thinking (Lahey, Pelham et al., 1988).

Another set of characteristics are associated with what Barkley (1990) called a "focused attention disorder," and these may make up a third distinct category of attention disorder. These characteristics include: "(1) often daydreams or is 'lost in a fog'; (2) is frequently 'spacey' or internally preoccupied; (3) is often confused or lost in thought; (4) often appears sluggish or slow moving; (5) often stares; and (6) often appears to be apathetic or unmotivated" (Barkley, 1990, p. 185). These youngsters are more often *underactive* than hyperactive, but can have attention problems that may profoundly affect school performance.

Although children with ADHD are commonly considered to have problems *paying attention*, for the purposes of developing effective interventions, it may be more useful to think of the disorder, as Barkley (1990) has postulated, as a biologically-based "motivational deficit." Youngsters with attention disorders appear to be insensitive to normal behavioral consequences, either positive or negative. Thus, the typical responses to behavior in school, such as praise, reprimands, or test grades, tend to be ineffective in shaping behaviors of children with attention disorders.

Viewing attention disorders in this light helps resolve some of the seeming inconsistencies these children display. Parents and teachers often comment, "But he has no trouble paying attention to things he enjoys!" (e.g., video games, favorite television shows). They also note that the quality of work these children produce in school can sometimes be exceptional, leading them to wonder why such children cannot produce work of high quality "all the time." A motivational deficit hypothesis would suggest that many of the problems these students encounter in school (and at home) occur because they have an inordinate amount of difficulty *making themselves do* tasks that are not intrinsically interesting to them.

This hypothesis would also account for another common characteristic of students with attention disorders: There is frequently an attention/task difficulty interaction, such that the students are most susceptible to attention problems on tasks that they find difficult. While people in general attend better to tasks that interest them, those with attention deficits show significantly greater problems attending to tasks that are tedious, difficult, or uninteresting to them. It takes students with attentional deficits an inordinate amount of effort (and hence requires greater motivation) for them to apply themselves to tasks and responsibilities that the ordinary student can accomplish with less effort and self-determination. An awareness of this characteristic can help the school psychologist develop more effective interventions to address motivational issues.

Additional characteristics of children with attention disorders, although they are not considered part of the disorder itself, co-occur frequently and thus may need to be the target of appropriate interventions. About 65% of children with attention disorders also display significant oppositional behaviors (Barkley, 1990). These children often resist authority figures and may become hostile and defiant in the face of requests for compliance.

Additionally, youngsters with attention deficits often have significant problems with peer relationships. Arising from impulsivity, problems reading social cues, and difficulty taking the perspective of others, these may make them appear self-centered and insensitive. And, as years of negative feedback from parents, teachers, and peers accumulate, children with attention disorders are at high risk for self-esteem problems as well.

Another common characteristic of students with attention disorders is academic underachievement. Although this sometimes is due to a concomitant learning disability that may cause skill deficits, more often these students have acquired basic academic skills but demonstrate difficulties with day-to-day classroom performance that stem from characteristics inherent in the attention disorder. Academic skills are delayed most often in written production, perhaps due to deficits in fine motor coordination, poor planning and organization, difficulty generating ideas, and problems sequencing thoughts. Some students with ADHD may also exhibit problems with reading comprehension — again, not because of skill deficits in either decoding or comprehension but because they have trouble concentrating on what they are reading sufficiently to grasp the meaning.

Finally, a significant number of youngsters with attention deficits exhibit problems with a constellation of behaviors referred to as "executive functions." Beside problems with sustained attention, executive function deficits may include problems with planning and organization, task initiation and follow-through, goal selection, anticipation of consequences of actions, and inhibition of impulsive responding.

It is important to recognize that all children with attention disorders (indeed, *all* children) bring a unique set of characteristics, both strengths and weaknesses, to any learning situation. While it is helpful to be aware of problems commonly associated with attention disorders, ultimately one must consider the specific needs of each child in order to develop interventions effectively tailored to those individual needs.

Designing Interventions

Effective interventions to meet the needs of students with attention disorders generally fall into three broad categories: modifying the attitudes and beliefs of those who work with students with ADHD; modifying the environments in which these youngsters live and learn; and modifying the behavior of the students themselves.

While it is generally assumed that the most effective way to help students with learning problems is to define clearly the skill deficits and then develop strategies to address those deficits, many experts in attention disorders believe that the place to start is with educating those who work with these students concerning the nature of the disorder itself. Barkley (1990) stated that "the actual initial target of intervention is the teacher's knowledge of and attitude toward the disorder of ADHD. For we have found that where teachers have a poor grasp of the nature, course, outcome, and causes of this disorder and misperceptions about appropriate therapies, attempting to establish behavior management programs within that classroom will have little impact" (p. 501).

Educating teachers and parents about ADHD can occur naturally while one works with individual students referred because of the disorder. School psychologists may accomplish this more efficiently, however, by conducting workshops and in-service training courses on ADHD. Conducting courses with sessions extending over several weeks may be more effective than doing "one-shot" workshops, particularly if time is built into these sessions for small group discussion and problem solving. This approach enables teachers to "live with" the concept of ADHD, to have more time to integrate new learning, and to have the opportunity to try out new skills and discuss the results with others.

It may be helpful to address attitudes and beliefs directly in these workshops. For instance, one small group activity might be to ask teachers to answer the following questions:

1. If you were the parent of a child with an attention disorder, of all the beliefs, attitudes, or values your child's teacher might have about ADHD, which do you think would be the most important?

2. If you were to walk into that teacher's classroom, what would you see that would let you know that your child's teacher has that value?

The resulting discussion would allow teachers to consolidate some of their thinking about attention disorders and to formulate beliefs and values that can have a positive effect on how they respond to children with attention problems.

Environmental modifications involve changing aspects of the student's environment to address learning or behavior problems. Examples might include seating the student near the teacher for whole-group instruction or allowing the student to come directly in from recess without having to wait in line. Behavioral modification consists primarily of developing incentive systems to increase the likelihood that the student will engage in appropriate classroom behaviors. These interventions are most effectively developed using a problem-solving format. This approach can be used in a one-to-one consultation between school psychologist and teacher or applied in a small group setting. Many school psychologists serve on teacher

assistance teams that function in this way. Such an approach generally follows the following steps: (a) define target behaviors specifically; (b) brainstorm possible solutions; (c) select an appropriate intervention; (d) implement the intervention; and (e) evaluate the results. The chapter on behavioral consultation elsewhere in this volume provides further information about this problem-solving model.

This approach can be used with students whose attention problems range from mild to severe, whose needs can be met in the regular classroom with minimal modifications, or who may require something more formal, such as a special education plan or a Section 504 plan. Where something more formal is desired, the outcome of such problem solving may be a written plan that delineates the problem behaviors, the appropriate interventions, or accommodations, and the person(s) responsible for implementing the interventions. Figure 1 provides an example of such a plan.

BEST PRACTICES

Incentive Systems

As noted above, youngsters with attention disorders frequently do not respond to the natural incentives, both positive and negative, that are effective with other students. Extensive research has clearly demonstrated that positive reinforcement is highly effective in addressing problem behaviors associated with attention disorders. Behaviors that have responded successfully to positive reinforcement include sustained attention, activity level, time on-task, response accuracy, disruptive behavior, and social skills (Fiore, Becker, & Nero, 1993).

In its simplest form, a positive reinforcement procedure involves administering a reinforcer upon demonstration of an appropriate target behavior. An example would be allowing a student to spend the last 15 minutes before lunch playing a computer game with a friend after completing all required morning seatwork.

Simple reinforcement procedures, however, often are ineffective with children with attention disorders. Experts in ADHD (e.g., Barkley, 1993) offer suggestions and guidelines for establishing incentive systems:

1. *Ensure that reinforcers are administered immediately and frequently.* Some research suggests that continuous reinforcement systems are significantly more effective than partial reinforcement systems for students with ADHD (Fiore, Becker, & Nero, 1993). Thus, systems need to be designed carefully to ensure that the reinforcer can be administered consistently.

2. *Build variety into the reinforcement system.* Youngsters with ADHD often crave novelty and satiate very quickly on specific reinforcers. This problem

FIGURE 1. Sample Section 504 plan.

Area of Concern	Intervention/Accommodation
1. Written expression	1. Provide assistance with prewriting activities (brainstorming/concept mapping) 2. Allow use of computer or dictation for longer assignments 3. Provide assistance with proofing, preparing final draft
2. Long assignments	1. Break down long assignments into shorter ones 2. Help student develop time lines for longer assignments 3. Reduce writing requirements by reducing length and allowing alternative methods of demonstrating learning
3. Following directions	1. Provide written as well as oral directions 2. Repeat group directions individually 3. Have student repeat directions to show understanding 4. Break down longer directions into smaller steps 5. Build in incentives for following directions and for asking fo help
4. Distractibility	1. Preferential seating during whole class work 2. Nonverbal signal from teacher to attend 3. Quiet place to work during seatwork 4. Cue for transitions 5. Incentives for timely work completion

can be addressed by developing a reinforcement menu so that the student can choose from a variety of attractive rewards.

3. *Assume that whatever system is designed will require adjustments.* The expectation that the system will likely require some "fine tuning" to make it work effectively should be communicated to those who implement the system, lest they decide too quickly that the system has failed and should be abandoned. Whenever such a system is designed, arrange a follow-up meeting within a week or two, to "troubleshoot" and refine the program.

4. *Involve the student in helping to design the incentive system.* To the extent possible depending on the age of the child, the student should be a full partner in this process, giving input on target behaviors, realistic goals, and appealing reinforcers. Students themselves often have good ideas about how the system can be administered, including how to keep records and how often and under what circumstances to give reinforcers. When the program needs to be revised, students often offer valuable insights into how it can be improved. When students are active participants in the process, not only are they more likely to "buy into" the system, but they also can learn valuable skills in task analysis, goal-setting, self-monitoring, and self-evaluation.

Various reinforcement systems have been effective with students with attention disorders. Some of the options to consider are presented below.

Token economies. The use of secondary, or token, reinforcers gives a teacher more flexibility in what rewards can be earned and when they will be given. By giving the student "tokens" (or more often, particularly with older children, "points") for demonstrating appropriate target behaviors, the teacher gives immediate feedback regarding performance without having to give the reward right away. Such a system allows the child to earn a variety of reinforcers of varying values, since specific points values can be attached to each reward. This approach can be used with an individual student or with groups of students, with different target behaviors and reinforcers assigned to each student if desired. Reinforcers should include a variety of activity as well as tangible reinforcers. By building in group rewards, the aid of the whole class can be enlisted in helping the youngster achieve his or her goals, since all will benefit from the child's earning rewards.

Response cost. With response cost, earned tokens are withdrawn when undesirable behaviors occur. This approach has been found particularly effective in increasing attention to task and work completion, and, as with many other interventions, it appears to be particularly effective when paired with medication (Fiore, Becker, & Nero, 1993). Studies using commercially available electronic desktop counters also have shown positive effects on attention and work completion, thus making it easier to administer a response cost system (e.g., Gordon, Thomason, Cooper, & Ivers, 1991).

Home-school report cards. This approach combines several important features that make it an effective intervention for youngsters with ADHD. In addition to incorporating the components of a token economy (e.g., defining target behaviors and assigning points that can be exchanged for an array of reinforcers), it also enables parents and teachers to collaborate, building communication between home and school. This enables home and school to work together on mutually agreed-upon behaviors, and may help reduce other problems associated with ADHD, such as keeping track of academic materials and assignments, forgetting homework assignments, and the like. Finally, it expands the variety of reinforcers available for students to earn, since parents often provide attractive rewards that are unavailable in school (e.g., the opportunity to play a game with dad, the chance to rent a video game, or go on a family outing to a favorite place).

The steps to develop a home-school report are as follows:

1. Identify between two and four target behaviors. These may include either appropriate behaviors that should be increased, such as work completion or participation in class discussions, or inappropriate behaviors that should be decreased, such as speaking out of turn or making derogatory comments to classmates. It may be helpful to have as at least one of the selected behaviors a skill that the child already possesses, in order to reinforce positive behavior and to increase the likelihood that reinforcers can be earned each day.

2. Develop a rating scale with which the teacher can judge the child's performance on the targeted behaviors. Higher numbers should be equated with more successful performance. In this way, the ratings the child is given can equal the number of points the child earns that day.

3. Develop a list of possible reinforcers, with point values attached to each. It is helpful to include reinforcers that can be earned daily, weekly, and on a longer-term basis. As students get older, they may be most interested in saving points over a longer period of time for more substantial rewards, while younger children will find smaller, daily rewards the most attractive.

4. At the end of each day, the teacher and student together review the student's behavior and complete the home-school report card form. Some teachers like to have students fill out their own forms independently and then compare the results with the

teacher's assessment. This builds into the process an important self-evaluation component.

5. If remembering to bring home the report card is a problem, the teachers at first have to ensure that the card is actually placed in the child's backpack. Additional points could be assigned for handing the report card to parents, and this added incentive is usually sufficient to ensure that the report card is transported safely between school and home. Alternatively, a response cost approach could be added, by allowing the child to earn points only for the days when he or she remembers to bring the report card home.

Figures 2 and 3 contain a sample report card and reinforcement menu.

Time-Out Procedures

With those youngsters with ADHD who are also disruptive or aggressive, the use of rewards or a response cost system alone may be insufficient to shape appropriate classroom behavior. For these youngsters, time-out is a common procedure. Technically, time-out is "the withdrawal of positive reinforcement contingent upon inappropriate behavior" (Barkley, 1990). In most cases, this means the removal of the child to a "time-out" area of the classroom away from the center of activity for a brief period of time (usually 2 to 10 minutes). If the disruptive behavior escalates, an additional consequence may be a loss of points or tokens or removal from the class (e.g., to another classroom or the principal's office).

Time-out can be very effective, particularly with young children such as preschoolers. Some cautions are worth noting, however:

1. The amount of time the student is expected to remain in time-out should be kept relatively brief. A general rule of thumb is 1–2 minutes per year of age. The clock does not start, however, until the child is sitting *quietly* in the time-out area.

2. The effectiveness of the procedure should be carefully monitored. If a child is being sent to time-out many times in a day and this frequency does not decrease over time, then one should assess why it is not having the desired effect. Some children are sent to time-out for behaviors that are not easily within their conscious control. An example of this might be sending a preschooler to time-out for impulsive behaviors in response to provocation by another child. Sometimes, the work children are being asked to do is so tedious, aversive, or difficult that being placed in time-out becomes a form of negative reinforcement (since it leads to the withdrawal of a stimulus that is even more aversive to them than time-out). Time-out may also be ineffective because the rewards that students can earn are not sufficiently powerful to induce them to avoid time-out, or the opportunities to earn

FIGURE 2. Sample home–school report card.

Child's Name: _____   Date: _____

	Scoring:	4 = Outstanding
		3 = Good
		2 = Acceptable
		1 = Improvement Needed
		0 = Unacceptable

Completes his assigned work   0 1 2 3 4

Listens carefully to directions   0 1 2 3 4

Follows adult directions without arguing   0 1 2 3 4

Uses appropriate language   0 1 2 3 4

TOTAL POINTS EARNED   _____

Comments:

---

rewards may be too limited. Whenever time-out is implemented, either at home or at school, it is a good idea to set up a reinforcement system first and to keep that system in place for a period of time before introducing time-out.

3. For some children, time-out is most effective when it is presented to the child not as a punishment but as a time for the child to "cool out" — to calm down, collect his or her thoughts, to do some relaxation exercises, and so on. Time-out then becomes an effective strategy to control anger. For this purpose, one can encourage the child to place him or herself in time-out voluntarily when it seems advantageous, rather than being sent by an adult.

Cognitive-Behavioral Interventions

Cognitive-behavioral interventions encompass many self-regulation strategies in which students learn to control their behavior by altering how they think about a task or situation. This section will address three approaches employed with youngsters with attention disorders.

Self-monitoring. These procedures involve training students to become aware of their own attending behavior, with the eventual goal being for them to cue themselves to attend. The most common training procedure is to employ an audio tape that sounds electronic tones at random intervals ranging from 15 to 90 seconds apart. When the tone sounds, students are instructed to ask themselves, "Was I paying attention?" Initially students are instructed to note their responses on a checklist. Eventually, they are weaned from both the checklist and the tape, but are instructed to note covertly whether they are attending. This approach has been demonstrated to increase attention to task (e.g., Hallahan, Lloyd, Kosiewicz, Kauffman, & Graves, 1979), and is a relatively easy intervention to introduce. It may be more effective when used as a whole-class procedure, since students sometimes feel singled out when such an approach is used individually. Self-monitoring tapes also can be employed effectively at home to increase attention to task during homework sessions.

Self-instruction. These procedures are more elaborate. Students are taught to "talk to themselves" as they perform a task. Self-instruction originally was developed as a strategy for helping impulsive children increase self-control through verbal mediation (Meichenbaum & Goodman, 1971). Numerous programs developed since have addressed both learning and behavior problems (see Wallace & Kauffman, 1986, for an overview of self-instructional strategies).

Self-instruction has been used with students with attention disorders to address problems with impulsivity, activity level, sustained attention, aggression,

FIGURE 3. Sample reinforcement menu.

Privileges	Cost
D A I L Y	
Extra half hour TV show	10
Extra snack	10
Practice soccer with dad	10
15 minutes video game time	10
W E E K L Y	
Rent a video game	50
Rent a movie	50
Have a friend sleep over	60
Go out for ice cream	60
L O N G T E R M	
Go bowling	200
Earn a new cassette tape	200
Take a friend to a movie	300
Eat at a Chinese restaurant	300

compliance, and social skills. An example of a commercially available program designed to improve self-control is the *Think Aloud* program (Camp & Bash, 1981). With this approach, young children are taught to ask themselves four questions as they attempt cognitive or academic tasks: "What is my problem?" "How can I do it?" "Am I using my plan?" and "How did I do?"

Self-instruction also is employed to teach students social skills. A commonly used program is the *Skillstreaming* model developed by Goldstein and his colleagues (e.g., Goldstein, Sprafkin, Gershaw, & Klein, 1980). With this approach, children are taught specific skills in small, structured learning groups following a sequence of steps that includes skill definition, modeling, role playing, feedback, and generalization (via homework assignments and a token economy). While this model often is used in small group settings apart from the regular classroom, it can be more effective when whole classrooms participate in the process, led by the regular classroom teacher with assistance from a school psychologist, resource room teacher, or guidance counselor.

Another specific skill-instructional strategy that has some promising research support is correspondence training. With this approach, students are rewarded for achieving a correspondence between statements and behaviors — in other words, they are rewarded for doing what they say they are going to do. In one study, for instance, a young hyperactive, conduct-disordered boy was able to reduce inattention, overactivity, and noise as a result of correspondence training. He was given tangible reinforcers for

making a verbal commitment, for following through on the commitment, and for consistent performance across observation trials (Paniagua, Morrison, & Black, 1990).

Self-evaluation. In this approach, students are taught to evaluate their progress on specific academic or behavioral goals — a simple example: a teacher would have reading group members rate how well they attended or how much they participated during the reading group session. Or teachers and students would separately rate targeted behaviors at the end of the day when a home-school report card is used, with subsequent discussion about agreement and disagreement of ratings.

Research has been somewhat equivocal about the effects of cognitive-behavioral techniques. Although clinicians have found them useful, the generalization of such methods to natural settings has been questioned, and their labor-intensive nature may make classroom use unrealistic (Fiore, Becker, & Nero, 1993).

However, questions have been raised as to whether cognitive-behavioral techniques can be sufficiently learned and successfully applied in the short amount of time most research studies employ. Developing a cognitive strategies curriculum that is taught over multiple years with collaborative efforts on the part of all teachers, such as the approach advocated by Deshler and his colleagues (Deshler & Schumaker, 1988) or the Benchmark program (Gaskins & Elliot, 1991) may be a more effective way to employ cognitive behavioral methodologies.

Parent Training

Often, just by becoming familiar with the characteristics associated with attention disorders, parents become more tolerant and accepting of their children and experience a reduction in stress which makes parenting easier and interactions between parents and children more positive.

Some parents, however, experience significant difficulty managing some of the more problematic behaviors of their children with attention disorders. They find that with younger children, compliance issues often are the most intractable, while with preadolescents and adolescents, setting limits and reasonable expectations for rights and responsibilities are of concern. Parent training to address these concerns is an effective approach that school psychologists can employ. With younger children, school psychologists may want to follow a model such as Barkley's *Defiant Children* (1987). This eight-week program follows a behavioral model, teaching parents to recognize and reinforce positive behaviors (including compliance with commands), to set up a home token economy, and to use time-out procedures appropriately both at home and in public. It can be used with individual families or with groups of parents. For older youngsters, school psychologists can train parents in negotiation strategies, such as those described by Robin and Foster (1989).

Parent training is most effective when it is one component of a multimodal approach to treating youngsters with attention disorders. It also enables school psychologists to develop nontraditional roles, strengthening the link between home and school.

Medication

Medication, primarily psychostimulants, is the most common treatment in this country for ADHD (Barkley, 1990). Stimulant medication also has been the subject of extensive research, concluding that "numerous studies have clearly demonstrated medication-induced, short-term enhancement of the behavioral, academic, and social functioning of the majority of children being treated" (Barkley, 1990, p. 573).

Although school psychologists are in an excellent position to monitor medication effects and to collect objective data that can help evaluate the efficacy of medication, they are sometimes in a difficult position with respect to recommending that parents consider medication as a possible treatment for ADHD. Parents often believe that school personnel advocate the use of medication as a way to avoid treating the behaviors of concern. When school psychologists evaluate youngsters for attention disorders, care should be taken to present the findings and recommendations to parents in such a way that medication is described as one of many possible intervention strategies. A decision regarding medication should be made by parents, in consultation with a physician experienced in treating youngsters with attention disorders. With teenagers, it is important to involve the youngsters themselves in making the decision about whether to use medication.

Medication should never be used as the sole treatment for ADHD, but should be employed in conjunction with other interventions. In most cases, other interventions, including behavior modification and classroom modifications, should be put in place before medication trials are begun. When this is done, the feedback mechanisms already developed to monitor the effectiveness of these interventions (e.g., points accumulated on a home-school report card) can be used to help evaluate medication effects as well.

Environmental Modifications

With appropriate modifications and accommodations, the educational needs of a majority of students with attention disorders can be met solely or primarily within a regular classroom environment. And while behavior modification strategies can be very effective in improving classroom performance and behavior, altering environmental variables and making task modifications are an important adjunct.

Research on task modifications for students with attention disorders has been conducted primarily by Zentall and her colleagues at Purdue University. Some of their findings that may be relevant to classroom settings are:

1. Stories presented at a faster-than-normal rate of speech resulted in improved listening comprehension and decreased activity level (Shroyer & Zentall, 1986).

2. Using color to highlight salient information increased accuracy and decreased activity level for students with ADHD (Zentall, 1985, 1986).

3. Tasks with a high degree of structure decreased activity level, compared to low-structured, more open-ended tasks (Zentall & Leib, 1985).

4. Active response (i.e., requiring a motor response) resulted in improved performance, compared to more passive response conditions (Zentall & Meyer, 1987).

5. Providing brief, global instructions, instead of lengthy, detailed instructions, produced shorter task completion time and fewer requests for cues (Zentall & Gohs, 1984).

6. Math and reading tasks presented in a low-noise environment created better performance and decreased activity levels than did a high-noise environment (Zentall & Shaw, 1980).

Effective classroom modifications include seating students preferentially, calling on the student fre-

FIGURE 4. School–based interventions for children with attentional problems.

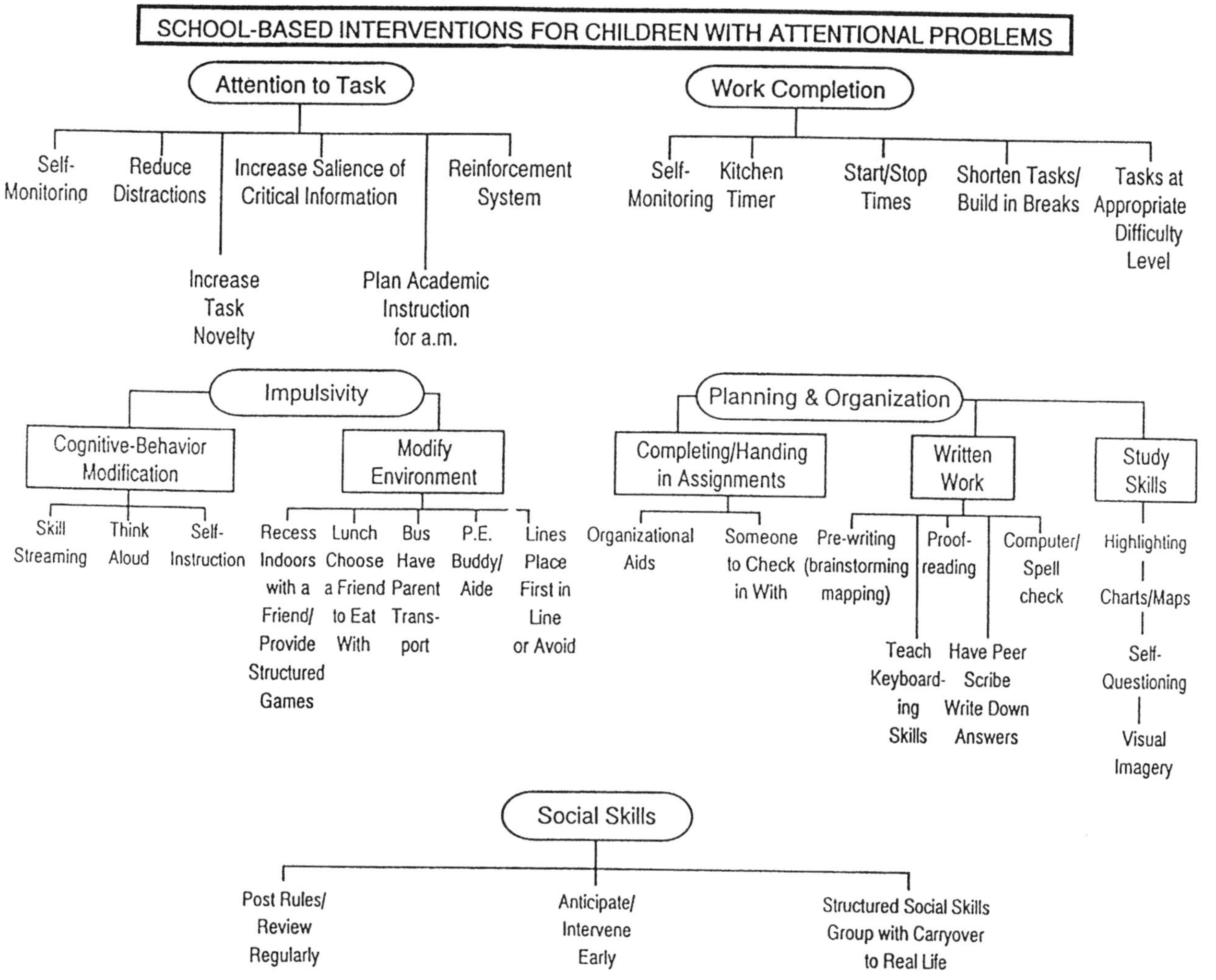

quently during class discussions, writing start and stop times for written work completion, using a kitchen timer as a motivator, and providing the student with a daily checklist of assignments to help organize work assignments. Children with attention disorders, particularly if they have concomitant executive skill deficits, may need help getting started on assignments. This can be done by walking them through the first few items or talking to them about the assignment to help them get oriented. They often do significantly better when tasks are modified to respond to their deficit areas, including presentation of briefer tasks, building in breaks, allowing the opportunity to stand up and move around, and, as noted above, providing high within-task stimulation.

Other modifications for youngsters with ADHD address the fact that they tend to do best when they have frequent opportunities to respond and receive immediate feedback. Peer tutoring and cooperative learning approaches both build in greater opportuni-

ties for individual response and immediate feedback than do more traditional classroom structures, such as lectures and individual seatwork activities. Computers also offer great promise for youngsters with ADHD, because levels of response and feedback are increased and because computer software can be novel, entertaining, and interactive.

Modifications that address difficulty in written production include reducing writing requirements, allowing students to dictate or tape record assignments, and allowing for alternative means of demonstrating knowledge or learning, such as projects and oral reports. Providing access to computers to learn word processing and to complete written assignments is an essential modification for many youngsters with ADHD.

Still other modifications address the fact that youngsters with ADHD do more poorly with tasks they find tedious, difficult, or uninteresting. These modifications include reducing repetitive seatwork and making tasks and assignments as appealing as possible. Youngsters with ADHD respond very well to activities with a game format or to lessons that are presented as problems to be solved, particularly if they have real-life applications. Project-oriented learning is ideally suited to the learning style of many youngsters. Others respond to the opportunity to design their own assignments. Independent learning projects can be particularly effective at the secondary level. Allowing students to negotiate their own learning contract can increase motivation and enhance performance — another modification that may be especially effective at the secondary level.

Giving these students choices — in terms of *what* assignments they will do, *how* they will do them, *in what order*, *where*, and *with whom* they will complete the work — can have a dramatic impact on productivity and task completion. And pairing youngsters with ADHD with other students allows them to use complementary strengths. A youngster with ADHD may have very creative ideas but have trouble putting them down on paper, while another student may be skilled at organizing work and writing but lack imagination; by pairing the two, both can benefit — and learn — from the strengths of the other.

While we generally think about classroom and task modifications in terms of the learning weaknesses of youngsters with attention disorders, the strengths these students have must not be neglected. It is critically important for those who work with these students to identify their skills, aptitudes, and talents, to find ways to encourage their development, and to ensure that these students are recognized for their accomplishments. Youngsters with attention disorders tend to receive negative feedback in greater quantities than their classmates. Special efforts must counteract these threats to self-esteem by finding areas where these students can shine.

This is a brief summary of the kinds of instructional and task modifications that are employed frequently with youngsters with attention disorders. Figures 4 and 5 contain examples of other modifications that may be appropriate.

Support Services

While the interventions described above may be sufficient for most youngsters with attention disorders, others will require additional support services to meet their needs. Students with attention disorders may qualify for these services either through Section 504 of the Rehabilitation Act (which protects students who have a physical or mental impairment "that substantially limits one or more major life activities," such as learning) or through the Individuals with Disabilities Education Act, IDEA, through the disability category Other Health Impaired. Under Section 504, school districts develop an accommodation plan that defines what services are needed and how they will be provided. Under IDEA, these services are specified in the student's Individual Education Plan (IEP).

While the need for special education or other services is often determined on the basis of a discrepancy between scores on measures of ability and achievement, with children with attention disorders, the central issue is more often a problem with *daily classroom performance*, and it is on this basis that the need for services should be determined.

Support services, provided either through Section 504 or IDEA, may include any of the following:

1. A monitor with whom the student can check in one or more times a day. This approach often is employed at the secondary level, where students change classes and have many teachers, and may, as a result, have difficulty keeping track of assignments, materials, and possessions. A monitor helps ensure that the student hands in homework assignments, is prepared for class, and has the necessary materials for class participation and homework completion. Monitors can also help manage home-school report cards when they are used.

2. Supervised study halls, to ensure that students use this time wisely and can receive assistance with assignments as needed.

3. Help with study and organizational skills, either through tutoring, in a supervised study hall, or through participation in study skills courses. This may include assistance with setting up and keeping an assignment notebook, using memory aids, planning long-term assignments, monitoring progress on long-term assignments, and learning note-taking skills, time-management skills, and study and test-taking skills.

4. A classroom aide to help make task modifications, increase student time on task, intervene in response to disruptive behavior, and administer reinforcement systems.

5. Remedial instruction in areas of academic skill deficit.

6. Counseling services to address social/emotional needs, such as participation in social skills groups.

While these are all direct services, students with attention disorders are also entitled to indirect services, such as consultation for the classroom teacher from a special education teacher, counselor, or school psychologist.

Other Roles for School Psychologists

The school psychologist can play a critical role in designing appropriate interventions for students with attention disorders. Other roles that are well suited to the skills and training of school psychologists include:

1. Acting as a liaison among the home, the school, and other service providers, such as mental health workers and physicians.

2. Case managing, including follow-up to assess intervention effectiveness, data collection to monitor medication effects, and help with transitions to the next grade level, school, and the like.

3. Providing training and information to parents concerning the management of attention disorders in the home.

4. Providing in-service training for teachers.

5. Becoming involved with advocacy groups for parents of children with attention disorders. Besides becoming a valuable resource to such groups, this can have good public relations benefits for the school psychologist and the school district where he or she is employed.

SUMMARY

Youngsters with attention disorders present with a variety of characteristics that pose problems for school adjustment and academic performance. Familiarity with these characteristics, as well as other academic and social problems associated with ADHD, can help the school psychologist develop effective interventions. A problem-solving orientation, in which target behaviors are identified and interventions selected from an array of possible solutions, is well suited to the task of helping students with ADHD achieve success in school.

Possible interventions include modifying the beliefs and attitudes of those who work with students with attention disorders, modifying the environments in which these students live and learn, and modifying the behavior of the students themselves. Commonly used strategies include incentive systems, response cost methods, time-out procedures, cognitive behavioral strategies, parent training, psychopharmocological interventions, and modifying classroom environments, including instructional and task variables, both to address students' weaknesses and to enhance their strengths.

School psychologists play a vital role in meeting the needs of students with attention disorders. By working with schools to develop multimodal treatment plans, school psychologists can extend their traditional roles and put *all* their training and skills to work. And developing effective interventions for children with attention disorders may have the broader effect of helping schools become more responsive to the individual needs of *all* children. The kinds of strategies that help students with attention disorders can help other students as well. Accommodating the needs of children with attention disorders thus may

help move us forward to a day when education can truly be personalized for *all* children.

FOOTNOTE

[1]The term ADHD is currently used to refer to all students with attention disorders. Although a significant number of students with attention disorders are *not* hyperactive, for ease of communication the term ADHD will be used in this chapter to refer to all students with attention deficit disorders.

REFERENCES

American Psychiatric Association. (1980). *Diagnostic and statistical manual of mental disorders* (3rd ed., rev.). Washington, DC: Author.

Barkley, R. A. (1987). *Defiant children: A clinician's manual for parent training.* New York: Guilford Press.

Barkley, R. A. (1990). *Attention-deficit hyperactivity disorder: A handbook for diagnosis and treatment.* New York: Guilford Press.

Barkley, R. A., (1993, April). Eight principles to guide ADHD children. *The ADHD Report,* p. 1.

Camp, B., & Bash, M. (1981). *Think aloud.* Champaign, IL: Research Press.

Deshler, D. D., & Schumaker, J. B. (1988). An instructional model for teaching students how to learn. In J. L. Graden, J. E. Zins, & Michael E. Curtis (Eds.), *Alternative educational delivery systems: Enhancing instructional options for all students.* Washington, DC: National Association of School Psychologists.

Fiore, T. A., Becker, E. A., & Nero, R. C. (1993). *Research synthesis on educational interventions for students with ADD.* Research Triangle Park, NC: Research Triangle Institute.

Frick, P. J., & Lahey, B. B. (1991). The nature and characteristics of attention-deficit hyperactivity disorder. *School Psychology Review, 20,* 163–173.

Gaskins, I., & Elliot, T. (1991). *Implementing cognitive strategy instruction across the school.* Cambridge, MA: Brookline Books.

Goldstein, A. P., Sprafkin, R. P., Gershaw, N. J., & Klein, P. (1980). *Skillstreaming the adolescent.* Champaign, IL: Research Press.

Gordon, M., Thomason, D., Cooper, S., & Ivers, C. L. (1991). Nonmedical treatment of ADHD/hyperactivity: The Attention Training System. *Journal of School Psychology, 29,* 151–159.

Hallahan, D. P., Lloyd, J., Kosiewicz, M. M., Kauffman, J. M., & Graves, A. W. (1979). Self-monitoring of attention as a treatment for a learning disabled boy's off-task behavior. *Learning Disability Quarterly, 2,* 24–32.

Lahey, B. B., Pelham, W. E., Schaughency, E. A., Atkins, M. S., Murphy, A., Hynd, G. W., Russo, M., Hartdagen, S., & Lorys-Vernon, A. (1988). Dimensions and types of attention deficit disorder. *Journal of the American Academy of Child and Adolescent Psychiatry, 27,* 330–335.

Meichenbaum, D., & Goodman, J. (1971). Training impulsive children to talk to themselves: A means of developing self-control. *Abnormal Psychology, 77,* 115–126.

National Association of School Psychologists. (1992, May). Position Statement on Students with Attention Deficits. *Communiqué, 20,* 5.

Paniagua, F. A., Morrison, P. B., & Black, S. A. (1988). Clinical effects of correspondence training in the management of hyperactive children. *Behavioral and Residential Treatment, 3,* 19–40.

Robin, A. L., & Foster, S. L. (1989). *Negotiating parent-adolescent conflict: A behavioral family systems approach.* New York: Guilford Press.

Shroyer, C., & Zentall, S. S. (1986). Effects of rate, nonrelevant information, and repetition on the listening comprehension of hyperactive children. *Journal of Special Education, 20,* 231–239.

Wallace, G., & Kauffman, J. M. (1986). *Teaching children with learning and behavior problems.* Columbus, OH: Merrill.

Zentall, S. S. (1985). Stimulus-control factors in the search performance of hyperactive children. *Journal of Learning Disabilities, 18,* 480–485.

Zentall, S. S. (1986). Effects of color stimulation on the performance and activity of hyperactive and nonhyperactive children. *Journal of Educational Psychology, 78,* 159–165.

Zentall, S. S., & Gohs, D. E. (1984). Hyperactive and comparison children's response to detailed vs. global cues in communication tasks. *Learning Disabilities Quarterly, 7,* 77–87.

Zentall, S. S., & Leib, S. L. (1985). Structured tasks: Effects on activity and performance of hyperactive and comparison children. *Journal of Educational Psychology, 79,* 91–95.

Zentall, S. S., & Meyer, M. J. (1987). Self-regulation of stimulation for ADD-H children during reading a vigilance task performance. *Journal of Abnormal Child Psychology, 15,* 519–536.

Zentall, S. S., & Shaw, J. H. (1980). Effects of classroom noise on the performance and activity of second-grade hyperactive and control children. *Journal of Educational Psychology, 72,* 830–840.

ANNOTATED BIBLIOGRAPHY

Barkley, R. A. (1990). *Attention-deficit hyperactivity disorder: A handbook for diagnosis and treatment.* New York: Guilford Press.
This comprehensive volume addresses both diagnostic and treatment issues related to ADHD. It is perhaps the most comprehensive single volume addressing attention disorders and is highly recommended for all professionals who work with students with ADHD. The book is divided into three sections, with Part 1 addressing the nature and diagnosis of ADHD, Part 2 addressing assessment issues, and Part 3 devoted to treatment issues. Part 3 includes chapters on counseling and training parents, educational placement and classroom management, social skills and peer relationship training, and medication therapy.

Fiore, T. A., Becker, E. A., & Nero, R. C. (1993). *Research synthesis on educational interventions for students with ADD.* Research Triangle Park, NC: Research Triangle Institute.
This volume, prepared by one of the federally funded ADD Intervention Centers, contains a comprehensive summary of research on educational interventions for students with ADHD. Research is divided into seven topics: positive reinforcement, behavior reduction, response cost, cognitive-behavioral interventions, parent training, task/environmental stimulation, and biofeedback. For each topic area, the authors present a brief synopsis of research findings with suggestions for educators and areas for further study and a chart summarizing each research study reviewed. The rest of the volume consists of an annotated bibliography of the research studies.

Guevremont, D. C. (1992, Fall/Winter). The parents' role in helping the ADHD child with peer relationships. *CHADDER,* p. 17
This article, written for parents by an associate of Russell Barkley, outlines the social behaviors common to children with ADHD and then gives parents useful suggestions for improving social skills and enhancing their children's ability to make and keep friends. It describes a home reward program that is relatively easy to administer and goes on to suggest practical ways that parents can arrange for positive experiences with peers both at home and in the community. It concludes with suggestions for how parents may work with teachers to enhance social skills and positive peer interactions. It makes a useful handout that school psychologists can give to parents.

Teeter, P. A. (Guest Ed.). (1991). Mini-series: Attention-deficit hyperactivity disorders in children: Clinical and treatment issues. *School Psychology Review, 20,* 161–281.
This volume of *School Psychology Review* contains nine articles on a variety of topics associated with ADHD, written by the leading researchers in the field. In addition to articles on diagnosis and assessment, four articles address treatment issues. These include therapeutic effects of medication, classroom-based behavioral interventions, remediating social skills deficits, and training for parents of children with ADHD. Each of these articles provides a concise synopsis of current thinking and research as well as practical information the practicing school psychologist will find useful.

84

Best Practices in Early Intervention Design

David W. Barnett
Kristal E. Ehrhardt
University of Cincinnati

Early intervention has considerable promise but successful results are not guaranteed. The traditional model is based on the identification of children with disabilities followed by special class placements. However, outcomes of traditional special education services that stem from federal legislative efforts have been ambiguous at best and subject to extensive criticism. This chapter describes the basics of an alternative model for preschool children that is guided by intervention design principles.

OVERVIEW: THE FOUNDATIONS OF INTERVENTION DESIGN

The model for intervention design suggested in this chapter is based upon (a) ongoing problem solving involving parents and teachers and (b) intervention research. Consultation, suggested as the foundation for the provision of alternative educational delivery systems (Curtis & Meyers, 1988), provides a framework to guide the problem-solving process. Behaviors of importance include those interfering with parenting or teaching and ones precluding positive peer relationships. In addition, environmental characteristics and setting events may receive critical attention.

BASIC CONSIDERATIONS

Features of Parent and Teacher Consultation

Consultation is a process of collaborative problem solving between a consultant such as a school psychologist, parents, and/or other educational personnel such as a teacher (Curtis & Meyers, 1988). The consultation process generally includes problem definition and clarification, problem analysis, plan development, implementation, and evaluation. These stages or steps are not necessarily executed in lockstep order but are utilized as the situation demands.

Rather than providing direct services to children, the early intervention consultant engages in problem solving with primary caregivers to develop effective, acceptable intervention strategies for use within natural settings. Consultation goals are (a) the improvement of current problem situations through the development of effective interventions and (b) the prevention of future problems through the enhancement of the caregiver's and/or children's skills. Intervention strategies arising out of parent/teacher consultation may be developed for the home, community, and school, and are designed to support and expand skill development, generalization, and maintenance.

When guided by intervention design and a problem-solving model, those involved emphasize the identification of *problem situations*, not problem children. Problem situations are defined in terms of barriers or behaviors that preclude the natural effective roles of parents, siblings, teachers, and peers in children's development. Because the focus is on problem situations, from the outset it should be clear that caregiver behaviors, as well as the child's behaviors and setting characteristics, are frequently the focal points in problem solving. Thus, the unit of analyses are reciprocal interactions between child and caregiver behaviors and demands and expectations related to situations.

Making Sound Early Intervention Decisions

It is best if professionals involved in early intervention are oriented by an analysis of intervention decisions and outcomes and not by traditional educational classifications (Barnett, Macmann, & Carey, 1992). Establishing a goal of intervention design is supported by very different theory, research, and practice than those employed when establishing developmental delay or other "profiles" of developmental skills. Most important, intervention design is dominated by assumptions of change whereas diagnostic decision making is dominated by assumptions of stability. The basic frameworks for intervention decisions are reviewed in the following paragraphs.

1. Intervention design is guided by sequential rather than diagnostic strategies. *Sequential decision making* consists of identifying the most reasonable steps in the assessment-intervention process with

each step subsequently evaluated. Thus, most simply, sequential decision making yields responses to the questions "what is the most reasonable first step, second, step," and so forth, generated through problem solving. The steps address the what, where, who, when, and how of planning interventions — essentially a set of goals and a map of how to achieve those goals. Sequential decision making allows for continued reframing or refinement of target behaviors and interventions. While "diagnosis" may be used in some form (i.e., generalizations from research for a child described as autistic), it is not a primary goal for professional practices from the child's view — the goal is effective service delivery.

Sequential decisions are established by: (a) collaborative "team" problem solving (i.e., parent, teacher, and consultant), (b) logical and/or research-based steps in assessment-intervention design (i.e., establishing a baseline for preintervention behavior), (c) developmental studies of performance (i.e., social skills), (d) task analysis, and (e) decision-making "checks" to help ensure the adequacy of the overall plan and process.

Figure 1 includes checkpoints for features of the child's environments necessary for many intervention decisions. If not in place, a checkpoint may become a focal point for assessment and intervention design — and a prerequisite for subsequent steps. If a checkpoint cannot be "passed through," consultation focuses on problem solving to improve or restore the conditions or to assist with coping efforts. However, in some cases, as for example children raised in families inaccessible to the consultant, interventions may focus on available settings such as the classroom. In sum, rather than establishing developmental delay or another classification, the problem-solving steps are oriented to basic intervention decisions.

When developing an intervention, perhaps one of the most significant steps is to ensure that a nurturing caregiver is available to a child. For example, professionals may be serving very young children who may have been in numerous foster homes in their lives (our high is 11 homes for one young child in a 3-year period). Clearly establishing some stability in the caregiving environment is a top priority. Numerous temporary placements preempt normal learning opportunities, but we have seen children in these circumstances "tested" first to develop "plans" related to a disability. The analysis of quality indicators in a preschool classroom may be another important step in consultation. Such analysis should establish that the environment will support needed interventions and that the curriculum is developmentally appropriate and functional. If needed, organizational consultation can be arranged as part of the early intervention services.

2. Intervention design ultimately rests on *professional judgment*, but ironically formal techniques (behavior rating scales, developmental scales, IQ tests) used by professionals to objectify and help with the decision process introduce a wide range of errors that may be exceedingly difficult to detect. While space does not permit more than mention here, consultants should be aware of sources of potential error pertaining to specific assessment techniques, cognitive activities of professionals, and intervention design (Barnett et al., 1992). A good way to bolster professional judgment is to take significant care with *problem structuring*. While there are no panaceas, problem structuring is essentially building a collaborative understanding of a problem situation through interviews, observations, and logical generalizations from pertinent intervention research and from systematically evaluating plans. Because problem structuring must be developed from understanding natural interactions in natural settings, it cannot be built upon traditional developmental assessment or play-based assessment in contrived settings. Potential *intervention bias* is treated by creating a range of promising intervention alternatives (discussed in a subsequent section).

3. Intervention recommendations can result in radical departure from normal routines. As a guiding principle, *naturalistic intervention design* may be defined as identifying the least intrusive, most robust intervention that will accomplish the goals of change within a natural setting (see Yeaton & Sechrest, 1981). Naturalistic intervention design applies problem-solving steps toward identifying (a) naturally occurring parent or teacher intervention strategies likely to be successful either as implemented or with only minor changes developed through consultation and feedback and (b) research-based interventions adaptable to evident styles of parenting or teaching within a problem context and setting.

4. There are three significant educational issues inherent in early interventions and naturalistic design. First, *inclusion* is a philosophical stance used to help make judgments about the soundness of decisions for children based on normalcy of environments and activities. Basic premises are that services should be provided in normal settings and that the most normal interventions capable of accomplishing the goals of change are preferred.

Another basic consideration for early intervention is to ensure the *developmental appropriateness* of professional practices and outcomes (Bredekamp, 1987). Learning takes place within an interpersonal context whereby the caregiver's warmth and responsiveness are of critical significance. The caregiver's roles include creating learning environments, selecting learning events, focusing children's attention on those that are important, and by following the children's lead, encouraging children's curiosity and skill development.

FIGURE 1. Examples of decision-making checkpoints.

- Responsive and nurturing caregiver is available.
- Basic family needs aremet.
- Well-conducted developmental and functional curriculum is in place in a well-managed classroom.
- Child is adapting to classroom activities and routines.
- Child is progressing at satisfactory rate.
- Child has satisfactory relationships with peers.

A third core-educational issue is *transitional* planning. The preschool years are times of great change, and planning for change is a significant theme. Vincent and colleagues wrote: "Traditional special educational programming may be incompatible with child success in least restrictive programs" (1980, p. 326). Basic strategies include planning for the next environment by teaching children functional adaptive classroom skills (Sainato & Lyon, 1989) and helping parents with problem solving and planning.

BEST PRACTICES IN DESIGNING PRESCHOOL INTERVENTIONS

Assessment for Intervention Design

We recommend the use of ecobehavioral and functional analyses to gather assessment information necessary to design interventions. The goal of ecobehavioral analysis is the determination of functional relationships between independent and dependent variables within a broad ecological context (Greenwood, Carta, & Atwater, 1991). Thus, units of analysis are natural systems (e.g., families and classrooms), setting characteristics and events, behaviors, and their contingent variables (Rogers-Warren, 1984).

Functional analysis involves determining the relationship between specific behaviors and environmental factors that trigger or maintain them. Functional analysis is used to develop predictions about the conditions under which behaviors are likely to occur.

There are three basic techniques useful for early intervention design: ecobehavioral interviews, observations, and curriculum-based assessment. Adapted from Wahler and Cormier (1970), the waking-day interview provides a detailed description of behaviors across settings and problem situations for caregivers. The problem-solving interview is used to identify target behaviors and to examine problem situations in detail. Previously attempted intervention strategies are also explored.

A three-step process is effective in developing appropriate observations for home, preschool, or community settings.

1. The results of waking-day and problem-solving interviews are used to help define behaviors, places, circumstances, times for observations, and potential intervention roles.

2. Real-time observations are used to document target behaviors, interactions, situations, sequences of events, and possible naturalistic interventions. This observational technique focuses on a child's behaviors, interactions, and situations. The observer records meaningful and complete units of behaviors in lines or sentences and records the clock time for each unit of behavior. A brief example follows.

11:12   Begins play alone at water table.
11:13   Approached by another child.

Data collected from real-time observations can yield frequency of behavior, rate of occurrence, duration, prevalence, and interresponse time.

3. Decisions are made about the use of other observation techniques based on findings from interviews and real-time observations. Relatively high-rate behaviors or those related to parent—child or teacher—child typically will benefit from consultant observation and perhaps from the use of a preschool observation code (e.g., Bramlett & Barnett, 1993), or an A-B-C (antecedent-behavior-consequence) analysis. Low-rate behaviors (i.e., infrequent tantrums, fire setting) usually require that parents or teachers serve as the primary observers. Observation techniques useful for preschool settings are described in more detail by Wolery (1989).

Criticism of traditional developmental assessment pertain not to the importance of developmental objectives but to how the skills are measured. Curriculum-based assessment enables ongoing observations of children's performance in preacademic, social, and other developmental areas and yields information needed to determine the conditions necessary for competent performance. Although not free of measurement problems, curriculum-based assessment involves the analysis of functional developmental skills within an instructional context.

Selecting Likely Interventions

Preschool consultants are usually needed, not to identify a specific intervention, but to expand the range of interventions that may be considered by parents and teachers. Thus, a fundamental question is "Where do we get intervention ideas?" Interventions are (a) generalized from developmental studies and intervention research, (b) founded on the realities of settings determined through problem analysis, and (c) based on the predicted success of the least intrusive intervention likely to accomplish the goals of change. Examples of well-established and promising research-based interventions are summarized in the following paragraphs.

1. *Fundamentals.* Simple, basic, and well-researched interventions should be considered before more obscure, radical, intrusive, or expensive interventions. In our work with Head Start children, the following interventions have been used extensively. While they may seem commonplace, they serve as a starting point for analysis and as foundations for intervention design for many preschool children across diverse problem situations for ethical and practical reasons.

    a. *Environmental enrichment, responsiveness, and monitoring:* Preschool psychologists may do well by assisting with ways to enhance "time-in" environments, and rule development and management procedures so that children may fully experience them.

    > An enriched environment . . . provides availability of and reinforcement for interacting with materials and activities, opportunity and reinforcement for the use of language and other forms of communication, a high interest curriculum, novelty in available stimuli, frequent reinforcement for adaptive behaviors, opportunities for structured and incidental social interaction, an adequate amount of personal space, choices within a predictable schedule, and the opportunity for community participation. (Schrader & Gaylord-Ross, 1990, p. 408–409)

    Responsiveness is a significant broad construct in early intervention research and generally pertains to caregiver attentiveness and interactions resulting from children's communication attempts. From the child's view, it is a feature of an enriched environment. Effective parents and teachers scan and monitor behavior with intensity appropriate for the child and task. These skills, responsiveness and monitoring, within an enriched environment, are keystones of intervention design.

    b. *Rules and consequences:* Rule learning is essential for self-regulation as well as family

and classroom management. The basic principle is that carefully selected, positively stated, learned, and enforced rules establish expectations for behavior. Paine at al. (1983) provided a thorough discussion about setting up classroom rules that we have frequently used and have adapted for many parent consultations.

c. *Differential attention:* Differential or systematic attention consists of approval contingent on desired behavior. It may be used to shape new behaviors and maintain or generalize behaviors. By definition, it is brief and may be nonintrusive. However, this intervention may be easily squandered or misapplied. Furthermore, studies show that appropriate behavior is frequently and inadvertently ignored and misbehavior may actually be rewarded. Thus, assessing caregivers' use of differential attention is often a necessary step for intervention design. Assessment for differential attention may be conducted through an A-B-C analysis.

d. *Modeling and opportunities to practice:* According to Bandura (1986), most behavior is learned through modeling. Thus, modeling appropriate and adaptive behavior and guiding, prompting, and reinforcing children to perform new or alternative behaviors are basic intervention strategies.

   One of the most powerful interventions for preacademics or social behavior is simply increasing "opportunities to practice" skill attainment (Greenwood, Delquadri, & Hall, 1985). Two steps are necessary: (a) analyzing occasions for learning and practice, and (b) increasing the chances for practice and feedback.

e. *Reprimands:* Children referred for behavior or learning problems may be experiencing very negative environments. Reprimands (and more harsh forms of discipline) are frequently overused and ineffective, and thus may be a critical point of consultation. We recommend routinely asking parents making referrals about misbehavior to describe their use of discipline and their feelings about it. One of the additional benefits of consultation regarding the ineffective use of reprimands is to improve family environment. However, if it is likely that reprimands will be used because of parental preference, we recommend procedures by Van Houten (1980) in addition to increasing positive experiences.

2. *Reducing maladaptive behaviors (including excessive activity changes) and increasing adaptive behaviors.* Back to the idea of "check-

points": All of the above interventions (time-in, rule development and implementation, etc.) constitute "gates" for referrals related to misbehaviors. In other words, children would not be referred, assessed, and labeled as behavior disordered, ADHD, or learning disabled (or other similar labels); rather, consultation would first occur to ensure that fundamental features of a supportive environment are in place. If environments are sound and maladaptive behavior continues, further intervention planning is in order. The next section gives examples of other techniques with the goal of expanding the range of intervention alternatives.

a. *Behavioral momentum:* Interventions need appropriate strength or power to accomplish desired change. Behavior momentum refers to the resistance of behavior to change. Resistance must be analyzed by behavioral factors (severity, chronicity, generalization, and teacher/parent tolerance of behavior) and intervention factors (strength of intervention, acceptability, treatment integrity, competing contingencies of reinforcement, and treatment effectiveness). Davis, Brady, Williams, and Hamilton (1992) give a simple example (and background references for those interested). They used high-probability commands — those likely to be complied with based on a child's history — like "touch your nose" to increase behavioral momentum of responding that would carry over to low-probability commands such as "pick up your toys."

b. *Teaching alternative responses and functional communication training.* Extending the discussion of differential reinforcement (related to differential attention, above), there are many positive intervention procedures to reduce maladaptive behaviors. Differential reinforcement means that certain responses are reinforced while others are not. (Because the procedures build on changes in reinforcement patterns, a functional analysis, discussed earlier, is a prerequisite.) "Differential reinforcement of alternative behavior" means a more acceptable behavior is substituted for the maladaptive behavior and occurrences of the acceptable behavior are reinforced. A common example is play engagement as an alternative for unoccupied time. Alternative responses may need to be first taught and practiced.

Carr and Durand (1985) argued that communication skills may offer significant possibilities as functional alternative skills for severe problem behaviors. They proposed a "communication hypothesis of child behavior problems" where behavior problems function as "nonverbal communication acts" (p. 124). Durand (1990) presents a detailed guide for professionals to assist with functional communication training.

c. *Differential reinforcement of diminishing (DRD) rates of behavior:* This tactic means that reinforcement is contingent on a pre-planned reduction in response rate (Sulzer-Azaroff & Mayer, 1991). Two examples should make it clear why this contingency arrangement may be valuable. A mother may be concerned with excessive yelling or the use of intense reprimands that occur with very high frequency. She may "self-reward" at the end of the day if self-monitoring demonstrates that 17 "yells" were recorded, down from 18 the day before. As another example, a child may show 10 "complaints" in play with other children; a decrease to 9 "complaints" is reinforceable during the next play period. Thus, on subsequent days, the mother and child in our examples would have to beat the prior days' accomplishments to be reinforced. Goal setting is critical (i.e., realistic goals for "yelling" should be established). DRD may be used for eliminating behaviors or reducing behaviors to suitably low levels. As with other differential reinforcement strategies, an important condition is that appropriate alternative behaviors need to be in the person's repertoire or must be taught.

d. *Intervention "packages" for parents and noncompliant children:* The term "package" in this context applies to a multicomponent intervention with strong evidence for wide applicability. Many parents have been referred to us for behaviors typically described as conduct disordered or oppositional. Earlier, we described work by Durand (1990) that falls under this category. Another intervention "package" is provided by Barkley (1987). Sanders and Dadds (1993) also provide a comprehensive model for parent consultation.

3. *Teaching language in natural settings.* Language and communication referrals are pervasive in preschool settings. Perhaps the best example of a naturalistic intervention is incidental teaching in facilitating language development (Warren, 1992). Incidental teaching capitalizes on important exchanges between a child and caregiver in relatively unstructured settings rich in materials or activities. The adult, following the child's lead, focuses attention on the child's verbalizations and encourages elaboration. The power of incidental teaching results from the

cumulative effects of numerous brief exchanges between child and caregiver (or siblings, peers).

Tirapelle and Cipani (1991) described an intervention termed a *missing-item format* that employs both incidental teaching and brief time-delays. Teachers provide opportunities to practice and motivation to do so by removing a necessary item from a natural activity. For example, in a game-like fashion, the spoon or cereal may be briefly removed giving the child an opportunity to make a functional request. Correct responses are prompted after an incorrect response or a delay of 5 seconds.

4. *Teaching functional skills.* Early intervention is not only concerned with the remediation of problems, but also involves enhancing child development through teaching functional skills. Bricker and Cripes (1992) proposed an activity-based approach to early intervention combining strategies from applied behavior analysis, early childhood education, and naturalistic intervention design.

5. *Intervening with groups and peers.* There are many significant reasons for considering environments, groups, and peers as targets for intervention efforts. First, "when a group is functioning well, it is extremely difficult for an individual child to behave in a disturbed way" (Hobbs, 1966, p. 1112). Second, environments may be changed to help support appropriate behaviors. Examples include availability of play materials and planning of play areas to help promote social, adaptive, and educational goals, or planning transitions between activities. Third, interventions related to social competence must have a social context such as play and sharing. Groups of children and peers may add power to intervention efforts by providing models for skills and behaviors and significant reinforcement for learning, generalizing, and maintaining behaviors. Odom and associates (1988) present a curriculum dedicated to these efforts.

Determining Reinforcement Preferences and Strategies

Reinforcers are contingent *events* that follow a response and increase the likelihood of further occurrence of behaviors in the same *response class*. Thus, reinforcers are defined by effects on behavior. The idea of a response class is critical because complex interrelated behaviors are typically the unit of analysis (i.e., whining, throwing, tantrums, crying following a parent request). Due to space limitations, discussion of types and schedules of reinforcers will be omitted. Rather, readers are referred to basic texts such as Sulzer-Azaroff and Mayer (1991).

Multiple assessment methods should be used to assess reinforcement preferences including interviewing teachers and parents, and observation. We concentrate on research-based strategies for selecting positive reinforcers for young children that build on direct observations. A general principle is to select the most natural reinforcer, and ideally the most subtle, that is effective for a problem behavior and situation. A basic strategy is functional analysis leading to rearrangement of contingencies for events that follow behavior.

Adding something to situations may frequently be necessary. The "something" can involve material reinforcers; social reinforcers ("Hugs," "Great," "Thank you for _____", which have added information value); or activity reinforcers which may be very potent and under natural teacher and parent control. In some cases, a set of strategies that stem from *reinforcer sampling* may be effective. A child can be given several samples of reinforcers, and preferences can be observed directly. Furthermore, reinforcement value may be increased by seeing other children play with the object.

An additional consideration is that children habituate to reinforcers. Mason, McGee, Farmer-Dougan, and Risley (1989) developed methods for *ongoing assessment of reinforcer preferences* that capitalize on novelty and variety — two other critical dimensions. Thus, choice making may be an important added component.

In considering other reinforcement strategies, do not forget *Grandma's Law* (Premack Principle): High-frequency behaviors (playing with favorite toys) are made contingent on low-frequency behaviors (completing preacademic task). Although it has a wicked sounding title, the *response deprivation hypothesis* is simply a more general statement of Grandma's Law and has may possibilities for reinforcer assessment: Almost any behavior in which children naturally engage in may be a potentially effective reinforcer, "proving access to that response can be restricted" (Sulzer-Azaroff & Mayer, 1991, p. 160). In fact, a low-probability behavior can function as a reinforcer for a high-probability behavior if there are restrictions placed on responses as assessed at baseline levels. Stollar, Dye-Collins, and Barnett (1994) reduced the inappropriately high activity levels of two children by placing some mild restrictions (and rules) on free play. Last, it is important to evaluate the reinforcement context. There may be competing contingencies and concurrent reinforcers that diminish intended reinforcer effects (Herrnstein's "Law of Effect"). Durand (1990) has an excellent section of identifying reinforcers.

Evaluating Preschool Interventions

Acceptability. Acceptability refers to judgments by caregivers regarding the appropriateness, fairness,

FIGURE 2. Script for redirection to appropriate activity and differengial attention.

Mark (Y) for yes, (N) for no, or (DN) for didn't need after each step below.

Steps	Date					
	Time					
1. Scott begins inappropriate activity						
2. Mom tells Scott "Don't do _____."						
3. Mom redirects him to an alternative activity, "Scott come here and play with this truck.						
4. Mom begins to play with toy. "Look how fast this blue truck goes."						
5. Scott plays with the truck.						
6. Mom praises Scott's appropriate play. "I like it when you sit quietly and play with the truck."						
7. If Scott continues inappropriate activity, Mom gives him a warning. "If you don't stop that, then you are going to sit in the chair."						
8. If Scott does not comply, Mom uses script for time out.						

reasonableness, intrusiveness, and normalcy of interventions (Kazdin, 1980). A purpose for evaluating acceptability is to anticipate and avoid rejection of an intervention and to provide information about variables that affect a consumer's use of an intervention.

Treatment integrity. Treatment integrity is the degree to which an intervention is carried out as planned (Yeaton & Sechrest, 1981). Achieving a high degree of treatment integrity is critical to ensuring intervention effectiveness. Many failures in interventions may be attributed to a lack of treatment integrity. Without assessment and monitoring of treatment integrity, any interpretations about the effectiveness of interventions are questionable.

Several factors may affect treatment integrity of interventions (Yeaton & Sechrest, 1981), including: (a) complexity of treatments, (b) time required to implement interventions, (c) materials/resources required, (d) number of treatment agents, (e) perceived and actual effectiveness, and (f) motivation of treatment agents. Also, interventions that require expensive materials, substantial changes in the classroom or home ecology, and/or atypical privileges may not be readily implemented. In sum, the more complex and time-consuming the intervention, the less likely that it will be implemented as intended. Conversely, naturalistic interventions may have greater treatment integrity because they are based upon existing caregiver competencies.

Scripts can be used as treatment integrity measures. Essentially they are personalized and detailed guidelines (written or pictorial) for providing instructions and/or managing behaviors to meet specified goals. Scripts are developed through collaborative consultation with caregivers using information from ecobehavioral interviews and/or real-time observations about interactions, naturalistic interventions, and goals. An example of a script is depicted in Figure 2.

Evaluating intervention outcomes. Evaluation is a continuous process that includes judgments of how reasonable the interventions are, whether they are sufficiently powerful to lead to desired changes, whether they are being carried out as planned, and whether they lead to desired changes. The adequacy of intervention design is determined at the individual-case level.

Single-case experimental designs are particularly appropriate for evaluating the effectiveness of individual interventions in professional practice (Barlow, Hayes, & Nelson, 1984). These designs emphasize repeated, ongoing measurement, and modification based upon data analysis. A critical feature of single-case design is that it provides measures of level, trend, and stability of behavior across baseline and intervention phases. Typically, these types of data are presented graphically and analyzed visually to determine intervention effectiveness or the need for modification.

CONCLUSIONS: MEETING PRESENT AND FUTURE FEDERAL GUIDELINES

Recent federal legislation (PL 99-457 amended by PL 101–476) attests to the importance of early intervention. However, intervention design builds on a collaborative problem-solving process, not disability evaluation. Interventions must be well conceived and well executed and linked to key adaptive and developmental outcomes. Children who remain at a particular level of a skill sequence, who have problems with rate of skill attainment, or who continue to exhibit behavior problems, may require a change in instructional and/or intervention strategies to progress adequately. If the child still has difficulty with progress, a "decision" should be made to provide additional consultation and more intensive measurement and intervention efforts. Following consultative services and well designed interventions, the children still not meeting goals may be described as resistant to intervention efforts and may be in need of special services. Specific plans (currently defined as IFSPs and IEPs) and additional resources to assist teachers and parents may be necessary.

REFERENCES

Bandura, A. (1986). *Social foundations of thought and action: A social cognitive theory.* Englewood Cliffs, NJ: Prentice-Hall.

Barkley, R. A. (1987). *Defiant children: A clinician's manual for parent training.* New York: Guilford.

Barlow, D. H., Hayes, S. C., & Nelson, R. O. (1984). *The scientist practitioner: Research and accountability in clinical and educational settings.* New York: Pergamon.

Barnett, D. W., Macmann, G. M., & Carey, K. T. (1992). Early intervention and the assessment of developmental skills: Challenges and directions. *Topics in Early Childhood Special Education, 12,* 21–43.

Bramlett, R. K., & Barnett, D. W. (1993). The development of a direct observation code for use in preschool settings. *School Psychology Review, 22,* 49–62.

Bredekamp, D. (Ed.). (1987). *Developmentally appropriate practices for children birth to age 8.* Washington, DC: National Association for the Education of Young Children.

Bricker, D. D., & Cripes, J. W. C. (1992). *Activity-based approach to early intervention.* Baltimore: Paul Brookes.

Carr, E. G., & Durand, V. M. (1985). Reducing behavior problems through functional communication training. *Journal of Applied Behavior Analysis, 18,* 111–126.

Curtis, M. J., & Meyers, J. (1988). Consultation: A framework for alternative service in the schools. In J. L. Graden, J. E. Zins, & M. J. Curtis (Eds.), *Alternative educational delivery systems: Enhancing instructional options for all students* (pp. 35–48.). Washington, DC: National Association of School Psychologists.

Davis, C. A., Brady, M. P., Williams, R. E., & Hamilton, R. (1992). Effects of high-probability requests on the acquisition and generalization of responses to requests in young children with behavior disorders. *Journal of Applied Behavior Analysis, 25,* 905–916.

Durand, V. M. (1990). *Severe behavior problems: A functional communication training approach.* New York: Guilford.

Greenwood, C. R., Carta, J. J., & Atwater, J. (1991). Ecobehavioral analysis in the classroom: Review and implications. *Journal of Behavioral Education, 1,* 59–77.

Greenwood, C. R., Delquadri, J. C., & Hall, V. R. (1984). Opportunities to respond and student academic performance. In W. L. Heward, T. E. Heron, D. S. Hill, & J. Trap-Porter (Eds.), *Focus on behavior analysis in education* (pp. 58–88). Columbus, OH: Merrill.

Hobbs, N. (1966). Helping disturbed children: Psychological and ecological strategies. *American Psychologist, 21,* 1105–1115.

Kazdin, A. E. (1980). Acceptability of alternative treatments for deviant child behavior. *Journal of Applied Behavior Analysis, 13,* 259–273.

Mason, S. A., McGee, G. G., Farmer-Dougan, V., & Risley, T. (1989). A practical strategy for reinforcer assessment. *Journal of Applied Behavior Analysis, 22,* 171–179.

Odom, S. L., Bender, M. K., Stein, M. L., Doran, L. P., Houden, P. M., McInnes, M., Gilbert, M. M., Deklyen, M., Speltz, M. L., & Jenkins, J. R. (1988). *The integrated preschool curriculum: Procedures for socially integrating young handicapped and normally developing children.* Seattle: University of Washington Press.

Paine, S. C., Radicchi, J., Rosellini, L. C., Deutchman, L., & Darch, C. B. (1983). *Structuring your classroom for academic success.* Champaign, IL: Research Press.

Rogers-Warren, A. K. (1984). Ecobehavioral analysis. *Education and Treatment of Children, 7,* 283–303.

Sainato, D. M., & Lyon, S. R. (1989). Promoting successful mainstreaming transitions for handicapped preschool children. *Journal of Early Intervention, 13,* 305–314.

Sanders, M. R., & Dadds, M. R. (1993). *Behavioral family intervention.* Boston: Allyn & Bacon.

Schrader, C., & Gaylord-Ross, R. (1990). The eclipse of aversive technology: A triadic approach to assessment and treatment. In A. C. Repp & N. N. Singh (Eds.), *Perspectives on the use of nonaversive and aversive interventions for persons with developmental disabilities* (pp. 403–417). Sycamore, IL: Sycamore Publishing.

Stollar, S. A., Dye-Collins, P. A. D., & Barnett, D. W. (1994). Structured free-play to reduce disruptive activity changes in a Head Start classroom. *School Psychology Review, 23,* 310–322.

Sulzer-Azaroff, B., & Mayer, G. R. (1991). *Behavior analysis for lasting change.* Troy, MO: Holt, Rinehart, & Winston.

Tirapelle, L., & Cipani, E. (1991). Developing functional requesting: Acquisition, durability, and generalization effects. *Exceptional Children, 58,* 260–269.

Van Houten, R. (1980). *How to use reprimands.* Austin, TX: Pro-Ed.

Vincent, L. J., Salisbury, C., Walter, G., Brown, P., Gruenewald, L. J., & Powers, M. (1980). Program evaluation and curriculum development in early childhood/special education: Criteria of the next environment. In W. Sailor, B. Wilcox, & L. Brown (Eds.), *Methods of instruction for severely handicapped students* (pp. 303–328). Baltimore: Paul Brookes.

Wahler, R. G., & Cormier, W. H. (1970). The ecological interview: A first step in outpatient child behavior therapy. *Journal of Behavior Therapy and Experimental Psychiatry, 1,* 279–289.

Warren, S. F. (1992). Facilitating basic vocabulary acquisition with milieu teaching procedures. *Journal of Early Intervention, 16,* 235–251.

Wolery, M. (1989). Using direct observation in assessment. In D. B. Bailey, Jr., & M. Wolery (Eds.), *Assessing infants and preschoolers with handicaps* (pp. 64–96). Columbus, OH: Merrill.

Yeaton, W. H., & Sechrest, L. (1981). Critical dimensions in the choice and maintenance of successful treatment: Strength, integrity, and effectiveness. *Journal of Consulting and Clinical Psychology, 49,* 156–167.

ANNOTATED BIBLIOGRAPHY

Bailey, D. B., & Wolery, M. (1992). *Teaching infants and preschoolers with disabilities* (2nd ed.). New York: Merrill.
Details broad and specific intervention strategies within an educational context. Source for pre- or inservice training for teachers and other professionals.

Barnett, D. W., & Carey, K. T. (1992). *Designing interventions for preschool learning and behavior problems.* San Francisco: Jossey-Bass.
Describes ecobehavioral assessment for intervention design and provides a comprehensive overview of naturalistic and research-based interventions for home and school settings.

Bricker, D. D., & Cripes, J. W. C. (1992). *Activity-based approach to early intervention.* Baltimore: Paul Brookes.
A "how to" guide for teaching functional, adaptive skills within the context of children's daily routines. Includes practical guidelines for selecting goals, developing intervention routines, and monitoring progress.

Meisels, S. J., & Shonkoff, J. P. (Eds.). (1990). *Handbook of early childhood intervention.* Cambridge: Cambridge University.
Provides a comprehensive collection of theoretical and empirical perspectives from disciplines that comprise the field of early intervention.

85

Best Practices in Preschool Social Skills Training

Stephen N. Elliott
Caroline N. Racine
R. T. Busse
University of Wisconsin–Madison

OVERVIEW

Developing skills for successful social relationships is one of the most important accomplishments of childhood. This interpersonal social process, although not fully understood, begins soon after birth and is influenced by personal variables (e.g., physical abilities, language, and communication skills) and environmental variables (e.g., family members' and peers' involvement and interactions). Unfortunately, not all children acquire adequate social skills and consequently, often experience negative child–adult or child–child relationships. Thus the identification and treatment of preschool children who are experiencing delays or deficiencies in social-emotional development warrant the attention of teachers, parents, and psychologists. This call for attention is congruent with recent research, which documents significant social skills deficits in young students with mild disabilities (Guralnick, 1986; Strain, Odom, & McConnell, 1984). Briefly, this literature indicates that students with disabilities frequently display fewer positive social and cooperative behaviors, show less initiative in peer interactions, and exhibit lower rates of peer reinforcement than their nondisabled peers. If untreated, these social skills deficits may remain relatively stable over time, be related to poor academic performance, and be predictive of social adjustment problems in adolescence and adulthood (Parker & Asher, 1987). Given these concerns, psychologists and educators are encouraged to include methods of assessing and treating social skills in their daily activities.

The purposes of this chapter are (a) to provide an overview of normal social development during the preschool years and the behavior expectations of adults for preschool children; (b) to briefly review the process of assessing social skills and identifying children in need of treatment; and then (c) to focus on practical assumptions and effective methods for promoting social skills in preschoolers. (Readers interested in more information on these topics are referred to the Annotated Bibliography at the end of this chapter.)

BASIC CONSIDERATIONS

Identification and Development of Socially Important Behaviors

Behaviors such as sharing, helping, initiating relationships, requesting help from others, giving compliments, and saying "please" and "thank you" are socially desirable behaviors that almost everyone would agree are examples of social skills. In general, social skills may be defined as socially acceptable learned behaviors that enable a person to interact with others in ways that elicit positive responses and assist the person in avoiding negative responses (Gresham & Elliott, 1984). When social skills are enacted successfully, the reactions generally are positive perceptions of social competence.

The acronym CARES has been offered by Gresham and Elliott (1990) to facilitate identifying and remembering five major behavioral clusters of social skills. These clusters are Cooperation, Assertion, Responsibility, Empathy, and Self-Control. Briefly, these clusters of social behaviors can be characterized for preschoolers as follows:

1. Cooperation — behaviors such as helping others, sharing materials with a peer, and complying with rules.

2. Assertion — initiating behaviors such as asking others for information and behaviors that are responses to others' actions such as responding to peer pressure.

3. Responsibility — behaviors that demonstrate ability to communicate with adults and concern about one's property.

4. Empathy — behaviors that show concern for peers' or significant adults' feelings.

5. Self-Control — behaviors that emerge in conflict situations such as responding appropriately to teasing or to corrective feedback from an adult.

Guevremont (1990) developed an alternative, but equally appealing, situational approach to characterizing clusters of target skills. Specifically, these skill clusters are referred to as social entry skills, conversational skills, conflict-resolution and problem-solving skills, and anger-control skills. Regardless of the terminology or approach one uses to characterize target behaviors, the behaviors of interest to most individuals conducting social skills interventions are those overt nonverbal and verbal interpersonal skills that maximize social engagement and social reinforcement.

What is the normal course of the development of social skills in young children? There is general agreement that older preschool children engage in socially cooperative activities with greater frequency than younger children. Having established the general agreement that social interaction does indeed increase ontogenetically, with interactive behaviors occurring very early in a child's life, investigators have directed attention to the behavioral components of successful social interactions. Findings from these investigations are relevant to efforts to remediate social skills deficits in children who have difficulty interacting effectively (cf. Eisenberg & Harris, 1984).

One area of interest concerns social initiation, that is, the manner in which a child attempts to initiate social interaction. Leiter (1977) found that requests to play accompanied by whining, crying, begging, or coercion were more likely to be denied; whereas, friendly, smiling initiations with suggestions for an activity were more likely to be accepted. This is not to say that children who are ingratiating always have successful social initiations. Rather, a judicious balance between assertiveness and accommodation to others' interests constitutes a more successful strategy (Lamb & Baumrind, 1978). Similarly, Hazen, Black, and Fleming-Johnson (1984) found popular children who were successful at entering others' play situations were able to flexibly alter their entry communications to fit the demands of ongoing play situations, which reflected not only the children's knowledge of a wide array of social initiation strategies but their adaptability in using the strategies appropriately. Further, in contrast to less socially successful children, popular children clearly indicated the children to whom they were addressing their entry statements, and they communicated to all children in the play situation they were trying to enter. It is apparent, then, that successful social initiation is characterized by specific nonverbal and verbal communication behaviors that clearly transmit the entering child's desire as well as awareness of contextual accommodations.

A second area of relevant developmental research is concerned with those skills that enhance the maintenance of social interaction. Asher (1978) describes the characteristics of the maintenance skills that are frequently used by socially successful children. These include complex perspective-taking abilities, such as adjusting the effectiveness of one's communications to other children's needs. In addition, more straightforward reinforcement strategies may be employed, such as offering other children praise and approval, as well as going along with another child's plan or wishes. Related to these maintenance skills is the manner in which interpersonal conflict is managed by children who exhibit successful interaction styles. In a study of preschool children's friendships, Hartup, Laursen, Stewart, and Eastenson (1988) found that conflicts among friends did not differ from conflicts among nonfriends in situational inducement, frequency, or duration. What did make conflicts distinct between friends and nonfriends was an effort to maintain the interaction with friends in spite of the disagreement. The children who were friends accomplished this by disengaging from each other temporarily, which served to reduce the intensity of the conflict and increased the likelihood of parity in outcome. This study exemplifies efforts to understand social skills within the context of perspective-taking. That is, behaviors that comprise successful peer interactions may be conceptualized as reflective of a maturing social-cognitive system in which children are developing the abilities to consider and coordinate their and others' points of view (LeMare & Rubin, 1987).

Whereas the above brief review illustrates some highpoints in the development of social skills, it does not address an additional issue of interest in the remediation of social skills deficits in preschool children, that is, the behaviors of young children. It is important to consider this issue, since an intervention program that addresses socially valid target behaviors and establishes goals has a greater chance of being used and maintained (Elliott, 1988). In a recent investigation, Elliott, Barnard, and Gresham (1989) asked the teachers and parents of a heterogeneous group of preschool children to rate the frequency and importance of over 50 discrete social behaviors from the Social Skills Rating System (SSRS). The collective ratings of parents indicate that they considered the following five social skills the most important for their preschool children at home: (a) requests permission before leaving the house, (b) reports accidents or minor emergencies to an adult, (c) shows concern for friends' and siblings' feelings, (d) pays attention to parent verbal instructions, and (e) communicates problems to a parent. Thus parents of preschoolers seem to place high value on basic communication skills and behaviors that indicate respect for others. For the teachers of these children, the following were the social skills of greatest importance for functioning in their classrooms: (a) attends to teacher's instructions, (b) complies with teacher's directions, (c) appropriately asks questions of the teacher when unsure of what to do in schoolwork, (d) finishes class assignments within time limits, and (e) cooperates with peers without prompting from the teacher. These teacher-valued social behaviors are indicative of compliance, cooperation, and orderliness.

Assessment of Social Skills and Identification of Children in Need of Social Skills Training

A number of methods, including rating scales, checklists, and sociometric nomination techniques, have been designed to identify children at risk for behavior problems. In general, the social skills assessment technology for preschoolers is not well developed. For example, there is only one published social skills rating scale (i.e., Social Skills Rating System) designed for use with preschoolers. Reviews of social skills assessment methods have been published by Gresham and Elliott (1989), Strain, Guralnick, and Walker (1986), and Demaray et al. (1993).

In general, the purposes of social skills assessments concern either identification/classification or intervention/program planning. From a behavioral perspective, the critical characteristic that differentiates assessment methods is the extent to which a method allows for a functional analysis of behavior (i.e., the extent to which an assessment procedure provides data on the antecedent, sequential, and consequent conditions surrounding a molecular behavior).

Process of assessment. As with the psychological assessment of any problem, the process of social skills assessment can be characterized by a series of hypothesis-testing sequences. Hypotheses are generated in an attempt to answer questions regarding identification, intervention, and evaluation of treatment effects.

A standard battery of tests or methods for assessing social skills does not exist. Rather, hypotheses generated dictate the direction of assessment, the questions to be answered, and the methods to be used. Assessment should proceed from global to specific to allow for appropriate planning of interventions. In contrast, evaluation of intervention success typically proceeds from behavior-specific outcomes to more global analyses of important social outcomes.

Ideally, practitioners should use assessment methods that possess the attributes of reliability (i.e., consistency of measurement), validity (i.e., capability of answering a given assessment question), and practicality (i.e., costs of collecting information). Unfortunately, few social skills assessment methods meet all of these criteria. Easily administered instruments that are useful for screening purposes generally are of lit-

tle help in designing interventions. Other methods that require considerably more effort from assessors and clients (e.g., naturalistic observations and self-monitoring) often have equivocal or unknown psychometric properties (Dodge, Murphy, & Buchsbaum, 1984; Gresham & Elliott, 1984). Moreover, there is a tendency for assessment data obtained from different sources to correlate moderately at best: often their correlation is quite low (Achenbach, McConaughy, & Howell, 1987). Still, as a safeguard, multiple sources of information are considered a best practice when assessing social skills.

To increase the likelihood of accurate identification and classification of social behavior problems, we recommend the use of direct observations of the target child and nontarget peers in multiple settings; behavioral interviews with the referral source and possibly the target child; rating scale data, preferably norm-referenced, from both a social skills scale and a problem behavior scale completed by the referral source; and sociometric data from the target child's classmates. Regarding intervention decisions, data contributing to a functional analysis of important social behaviors are imperative. These types of data usually result from multiple direct observations across settings; behavioral role-plays with the target child; and teacher and parent/guardian ratings of socially valid molecular behaviors. Behavioral interviews with the treatment agent(s) also will be important for assessing the treatment setting, the acceptability of the final treatment plan, and the integrity with which the plan is implemented. Table 1 provides a summary of an heuristic sequence for the assessment of social skills.

Basic Assumptions and Procedures for Linking Social Skills Assessments to Interventions

Social skills interventions focus on positive behaviors and most often use nonaversive methods (e.g., modeling, coaching, and reinforcement) to improve children's behavior. These also are the characteristics that teachers and parents report they like in interventions (Elliott, 1988). Therefore, use of these methods may enhance treatment acceptability and integrity. In addition, these programs can be built into the existing structure of a classroom or home environment, thus minimizing the time required for successful implementation and maximizing treatment generality. Finally, social skills interventions can be used with individuals or groups of students, and because they primarily concern increasing prosocial behaviors, all students can participate and benefit from the interventions.

The selection of social skills interventions rests heavily on the classification of social skills difficulties as resulting from either deficits in response acquisition or response performance (e.g., Bandura, 1977).

TABLE 1
Overview of Social Skills Assessment Methods and Their Characteristics

1. Teacher Ratings of Social Skills
   A. Estimation of frequency of behaviors
   B. Estimation of behavior's importance to teacher
   C. Tentative estimation of skill and performance deficits
   D. Guidance for teacher interview and direct observations

2. Parent Ratings of Social Skills
   A. Estimation of cross-setting generality of deficits
   B. Parent's perceived importance of social behaviors
   C. Guidance for parent interview

3. Teacher Interview
   A. Further delineation of target behaviors
   B. Functional analysis of behavior in specific situations
   C. Selection of target behaviors based upon importance ratings and teacher's rankings

4. Parent Interview
   A. Further delineation of target behaviors
   B. Functional analysis of behavior in specific situations
   C. Selection of target behaviors based upon importance ratings and teacher's rankings

5. Direct Observations of Classroom Behavior
   A. Functional analysis of behavior
   B. Direct measurement of behavior in applied setting
   C. Observation of peer reactions to target child's behavior

6. Sociometrics Using Liked Most and Liked Least Nominators
   A. Measurement of social preference and social impact
   B. Classification of sociometric status (rejected, neglected, controversial)

7. Self-Report of Social Skills — Obtain Child's Perception of Social Behavior

8. Child Interview

Note: Adapted from Elliott, Sheridan, and Gresham (1989).

Gresham and Elliott's (1990) Social Skills Rating System extended this two-way classification scheme to include areas of social skills problems, social skills strengths, and potential concurrent interfering problem behaviors. As shown in Figure 1, this scheme distinguishes whether a child possesses the ability to perform a target skill and whether interfering behaviors (e.g., aggression, anxiety) are present. Additionally, Figure 1 includes suggested treatments that have been found effective for various problem types.

Social skills acquisition deficits. This social skill problem characterizes children who have not acquired the necessary social skills to interact appropriately with others, or children who have not acquired a critical step in the performance of a given skill. Training in skill acquisition frequently uses direct treatment approaches, such as direct instruction, modeling, and coaching.

Social skills acquisition deficits with interfering problem behaviors. This social skills problem describes children with responses that interfere with skills acquisition; these responses can be emo-

tional (e.g., anxiety, sadness, impulsivity) and/or overt behavioral (e.g., verbal or physical aggression, tantrums, excessive movement). Thus, with social skills acquisition deficits accompanied by significant interfering behaviors, the intervention objectives are to teach and increase the frequency of prosocial behaviors while concurrently decreasing or eliminating interfering problem behaviors. Interventions designed to remediate emotional responses typically involve emotional-arousal reduction techniques such as desensitization or flooding, paired with self-control strategies such as self-talk, self-monitoring, and self-reinforcement (Kendall & Braswell, 1985; Meichenbaum, 1977). Interventions that can help reduce overt behaviors often are referred to as reductive procedures (Lentz, 1988). These procedures include the use of differential reinforcement (e.g., differential reinforcement of other behavior [DRO], differential reinforcement of alternative behaviors [DRA], and differential reinforcement of low rates of responding [DRL]), group contingencies, and mild aversive techniques (e.g., reprimands, time out from positive reinforcement, response cost, and overcorrection). If

FIGURE 1. A classification schema for conceptualizing and linking social behavior problems to interventions.

	No interfering problem behaviors	Interfering problem behaviors
Social skills acquisition deficits	Direct instructon Modeling Behavioral rehearsal Coaching	Modeling Coaching Differential reinforcement of a low rate of response (DRL) Differential reinforcement of other behavior (DRO) Reductive procedures to decrease interfering problem behaviors
Social skills performance deficits	Operant methods to manipulate antecedent or consequent conditions to increase the rate of existing behaviors.	Operant methods to manipulate antecedent or consequent conditions to increase the rate of existing prosocial behaviors Differential reinforcement of a low rate of response (DRL) Differential reinforcement of other behavior (DRO) Reductive procedures to decrease interfering problem behaviors
Social skills strengths	Reinforcement procedures to maintain desired social behavior Use student as a model for other students	Reinforcement procedures to maintain desired social behavior Reductive procedures to decrease interfering problem behaviors

aversive techniques are used, it is a best practice to couple aversives with socially positive procedures.

Social skills performance deficits. Children with social skills performance deficits have appropriate social skills in their behavior repertoires, but do not perform the behavior at acceptable levels, at appropriate times, and/or in appropriate settings. Interventions for social skills performance deficits typically use manipulations of antecedent and consequent contingencies such as peer initiations, social reinforcement, and group contingencies.

Social skills performance deficits with interfering problem behaviors. Children with social skills performance deficits accompanied by interfering problem behaviors have acquired given social skills, but performance of the skills is hindered by emotional or overt behavior responses and by problems in antecedent or consequent control. Self-control strategies to teach inhibition of inappropriate behavior, stimulus control training to teach discrimination skills, and contingent reinforcement to increase display of appropriate social behavior often are used to ameliorate this social skills problem. Occasionally, when the interfering behaviors persist, it may be nec-

essary to use reductive methods in addition to positive techniques.

Social skills strengths. Many children exhibit social skills strengths that often may be overlooked and may be undermined through lack of attention. Therefore, it is a best practice to take a proactive approach to maintaining those strengths through reinforcement of desired social behaviors. Children with strong social skills also can become part of a treatment strategy for children with social skills deficits by serving as models or as participants in peer pairing and peer initiation strategies.

Procedures for Promoting Social Skills

Teaching children social skills involves many of the same methods as teaching academic concepts. Effective teachers of both academic and social skills model correct behavior, elicit an imitative response, provide corrective feedback, and arrange for opportunities to practice the new skills (Cartledge & Milburn, 1986; Elliott & Gresham, 1991). A large number of intervention procedures have been identified as effective for social skills training with preschool children. These procedures can be classified into three approaches that highlight common treatment features and assumptions about how social behavior is learned. These approaches are operant, social learning, and cognitive-behavioral.

In practice, many researchers and practitioners have used procedures that represent combinations of these basic approaches. However, we will use the three groups of interventions to describe the basic procedures and to organize a review of their effectiveness. First, however, it is instructive to review five assumptions proposed by Michelson, Sugai, Wood, and Kazdin (1983, p. 3) that are fundamental to the conceptualization of social skills assessment and intervention plans:

Assumption 1: Social skills primarily are acquired through learning, which involves observation, modeling, rehearsal, and feedback.

Assumption 2: Social skills comprise specific and discrete verbal and nonverbal behaviors.

Assumption 3: Social skills entail both effective and appropriate initiations and responses.

Assumption 4: Social skills are interactive by nature and entail effective and appropriate responses.

Assumption 5: Social skills performance is influenced by the characteristics of an environment.

Collectively, these pragmatic assumptions provide direction for both assessment and intervention activities by stressing the multidimensional (verbal–nonverbal and initiating–responding), interactive, situation-specific nature of social skills. Thus, regardless of intervention approach, effective interventions most likely will need to address target behaviors that involve both verbal and nonverbal communications used to initiate or respond to others. With this in mind, we now examine the procedures that are germane to the operant, social learning, and cognitive-behavioral approaches to social skills interventions.

Operant intervention procedures. Operant intervention procedures focus on discrete, observable behavior and the antecedent and consequent events that maintain that behavior. Behavioral control is achieved most often through the use of reinforcement and/or punishment paradigms that are contingent upon a specified behavior. Many social behaviors, however, can be controlled by manipulating preceding events, such as having a peer ask another child to play or a teacher cuing a child to initiate play.

Young children often fail to interact successfully because of a nonresponsive or inhospitable social environment. Here the use of antecedent control can serve to facilitate a positive environment and elicit positive social interactions. With these procedures, a teacher or other intervention agent makes full use of cuing and prompting (Elliott & Gresham, 1991). The key assumption with antecedent control procedures

is that a child possesses the necessary social skills but is not performing them at an acceptable rate. Two of the most frequently used antecedent strategies are peer social initiation and cooperative learning.

Peer social initiations have been used by Fenning (1993) and Strain and his colleagues (Strain, 1977; Strain, Shores, & Timm, 1977; Strain & Timm, 1974) to increase the social interaction rates of socially withdrawn preschoolers. This intervention entails training similar-age peer confederates to initiate and maintain social interactions with a withdrawn or isolated child. Overall, this procedure has been effective in increasing positive social behavior in withdrawn preschoolers. It should be noted, however, that when a child's interaction rate approaches zero, peer initiations are likely to be less effective (Elliott & Gresham, 1991). Strain and Fox (1981) provided a detailed review of these procedures for preschoolers and older children.

Another procedure that focuses on manipulating antecedent events is cooperative learning. Cooperative learning provides a prosocial environment in which preschoolers work together to complete specified activities (Doescher & Sugawara, 1989). This procedure requires preschoolers to cooperate, share, and assist each other to complete a task and, as such, represents an effective method for increasing the likelihood of positive social behaviors. When implementing cooperative learning techniques, it is implicitly assumed that children know how to cooperate but are not doing so at optimal levels.

Many operant-learning procedures — that is, the manipulation of antecedents and consequents — have been used to decrease interfering problem behaviors while simultaneously increasing positive social behaviors. These procedures are based on the premise that behaviors are maintained by functional relationships. In other words, reinforcement contingencies (positive or negative) perpetuate low rates of positive social interactions and high rates of negative social interactions. For this reason, it is assumed that a child can perform positive social interaction skills but does not demonstrate the skills due to lack of reinforcement. Given the wealth of studies in this domain, only two of the most frequently used methods will be discussed: contingent social reinforcement and differential reinforcement. Group contingencies (Elliott & Gresham, 1991; McConnell, Sisson, Cort, & Strain, 1991; Litow & Pumroy, 1975) also are used frequently; however, since they have much in common with cooperative learning, they will not be discussed here.

Contingent social reinforcement involves publicly reinforcing a child's socially appropriate behaviors. Allen, Hart, Buell, Harris, and Wolf (1964) demonstrated the efficacy of this method long ago when they applied it to a 4-year-old socially isolated girl. Whenever she interacted with other children, an adult would publicly reinforce her social behavior. This procedure led to a sixfold increase in social interaction rates over baseline levels. Variations of this basic procedure have been successfully extended to children who are electively mute or severely and profoundly mentally retarded (Fenning, 1993; Mayhew, Enyart, & Anderson, 1978). Although this procedure has been found effective, it can require an extraordinary amount of time to ensure that the reinforcement is delivered on a consistent basis. Unless reinforcement is given in a consistent manner, it is doubtful that the intervention will be as effective. This type of contingent social reinforcement is perhaps best used to maintain social interaction rates established through the use of other social skills interventions.

Other operant-learning procedures used to modify social skills are DRO, DRA, and DRL. DRO and DRA are based on the omission rather than the commission of a specific behavior (Cooper, Heron, & Heward, 1987). Therefore, after a certain amount of time, reinforcement is given after any behavior except the target behavior. For example, if one wanted to decrease disruptive behavior while increasing socially appropriate behavior, any behavior exhibited except for disruptive behavior is reinforced after a certain amount of time has elapsed. Hence, this method serves to extinguish undesirable behaviors and increase all other behaviors. Pinkston, Reese, Le Blanc, and Baer (1973) successfully used DRO to decrease a boy's aggressive behavior while at the same time implementing contingent social reinforcement to increase his positive social interaction. In this study, the teacher differentially reinforced positive peer interaction while she ignored aggressive behavior.

Differential reinforcement of low rates of responding (DRL) involves reinforcement to achieve reduction in the frequency of a target behavior. Reinforcers may be delivered either for reduction in overall frequency of a response within a particular time period or for increased elapsed time between responses (interresponse time). For example, if the criterion limit for the DRL was six incidents per hour, the target child would receive reinforcement only if there were six or fewer incidents. Dietz and Repp (1973) successfully used a full-session DRL procedure to decrease the amount of inappropriate talking in an EMR classroom. The DRL contingency was five or fewer "talk outs" per 50-minute class period. This was also applied as a group contingency, because reinforcement was based on the behavior of the entire class.

The aforementioned studies demonstrate that DRO and DRL are effective in decreasing interfering problem behaviors. These procedures probably are most effective, however, when used in conjunction with other social skills interventions, whereby one decreases socially inappropriate behavior while concurrently teaching or reinforcing positive social behaviors.

Social learning intervention procedures. Social learning procedures can be traced back to the social learning theory of Bandura and Walters (1963) and Bandura (1977). From this perspective, social behavior is the result of two types of learning: observational learning and reinforced learning. Social learning theorists differentiate between the learning and the performance of a response. This distinction enables social learning theorists to advocate the process of modeling as a means to acquire new, socially appropriate behaviors. Modeling also affects previously learned responses through its disinhibitory and/or cueing effects. Therefore, children are vicariously reinforced (positively or negatively) by observing a model receive reinforcement for a behavioral performance. In essence, observers tend to inhibit responses that they see punished in others, whereas they are likely to perform modeled behaviors that elicit desired reinforcers.

That modeling promotes social skills in children and youths has substantial empirical support (Gresham, 1985; Wandless & Prinz, 1982). For social skills training, modeling can be divided into two types: (a) live modeling, in which the target child observes the social behaviors of models in naturalistic settings (e.g., the classroom); and (b) symbolic modeling, in which the target child observes the social behaviors of a model via film or videotape. Both types of modeling have been effective in remediating social skills deficits, but most research has focused on symbolic modeling due to the degree of experimental control afforded by videotaped models. Live modeling, however, may be more flexible and efficient in a classroom setting. For instance, Matson, Fee, Coe, and Smith (1991) used peer and puppet models as a novel way to effect a positive change in the social behaviors of preschoolers with developmental disabilities.

A recent development in the realm of social learning has been peer-mediated interventions. These interventions are based on the premise that peers can be effective change agents for children with social skills performance deficits. Empirically, it has been shown that peers can serve to differentially reinforce appropriate social interactions and influence the occurrence of positive social behaviors (Mathur & Rutherford, 1991). Peer-mediated interventions may be more successful than teacher-mediated interventions because peer confederates may be better able to consistently monitor and differentially reinforce their peers. Additionally, peer mediation can be cost-effective because it minimizes teacher involvement.

Cognitive-behavioral intervention procedures. Cognitive-behavioral intervention procedures are a loosely bound group of procedures that focus on children's internal regulation of their behavior. In particular, cognitive-behavioral approaches to social skills training emphasize a child's ability to problem solve and to self-regulate behavior. For preschoolers, two of the most frequently used cognitive-behavioral social skills procedures are coaching and problem solving.

Coaching, unlike modeling, is a direct verbal instruction technique that involves a coach (usually a teacher or a psychologist, occasionally a peer) who has knowledge about how to enact a desired behavior. Most coaching procedures involve three basic steps: (a) a student is presented with rules for or the standards of a specific behavior; (b) a selected social skill is rehearsed with the coach; and (c) the coach provides specific informational feedback during behavioral rehearsal and gives suggestions for future performances. In some instances, modeling may be included in the coaching procedure to give the child a better understanding of the topography of the social behavior and, if praise is given, reinforcement may occur. Therefore coaching, although conceptualized as a procedure that requires the child's cognitive skills to translate instruction into desired behaviors, can be enhanced with behavioral and/or social-learning procedures.

Coaching has received considerable empirical support as a social skills training procedure. For example, Oden and Asher (1977) used coaching to effectively teach participation, communication, cooperation, and peer reinforcement. In addition, sociometric ratings of coached students increased when compared to noncoached students. Ladd (1981) obtained similar results when using a coaching procedure to those of Gottman, Gonso, and Schuler (1976).

Several interventions have been developed that stress teaching children the process of solving social or interpersonal problems as a way to facilitate socially appropriate behaviors. As Weissburg (1985) pointed out, some of these intervention programs, which are largely classroom-based, have been called social problem-solving (SPS) programs, whereas others have been called interpersonal cognitive problem-solving (ICPS) programs. ICPS programs generally place greater emphasis on cognitions that parallel social problem situations and employ narrower training procedures than SPS approaches; however, both use a similar training sequence to help students identify and cope with social problems. Briefly, the steps can be described as (a) identify and define the problem, (b) determine alternate ways of reacting to the problem, (c) predict consequences for each alternative reaction, and (d) select the best or most adaptive alternative. Social problem-solving methods can be used with individual children or with entire classrooms. It should be noted, however, that these methods often are cognitively too complex for most preschoolers and do not focus on discrete social skills training; learning social skills generally requires more skill-oriented, externally reinforcing procedures than are offered by a strictly cognitive approach.

Effectiveness of Interventions and Suggestions for Practice

The popularity and widespread use of social skills training procedures have resulted in several major reviews of the effectiveness of these procedures with children (see Cartledge & Milburn, 1986; Elliott & Gresham, 1993; Gresham, 1981, 1985; Ladd & Mize, 1983; Schneider & Byrne, 1985). With regard to child characteristics, Schneider and Byrne, who conducted a large meta-analysis of social skills training studies, indicate that social skills interventions are more effective for preschoolers and adolescents than elementary children. No gender differences in effect sizes are noted, although few studies have treated gender as an independent variable. In addition, social skills training was found to be more effective for students exhibiting social withdrawal or learning disabilities than for aggressive students.

Based on the reviews of research by Elliott and Gresham (1993), Schneider and Byrne (1985), and Mastropieri and Scruggs (1985–86), there appears to be substantial support for the effectiveness of social skills training procedures in general, and in particular for operant and modeling procedures. Practical suggestions from the research literature for individuals interested in facilitating the development of social skills in young children include the extensive use of operant methods to reinforce existing social skills. These basic operant tactics include (a) the manipulation of environmental conditions to create opportunities for social interactions that prompt or cue socially desired behavior in a target child, and (b) the manipulation of consequences so that socially appropriate behavior is reinforced and socially inappropriate behavior, whenever possible, is ignored rather than punished. In addition, modeling of appropriate social behavior supplemented with coaching, feedback, and reinforcement should be a primary tactic in developing new social behaviors in children.

Facilitating Generalization of Social Skills

Social skills training often results in positive outcomes; however, treatment effects often are short-lived and fail to generalize (Berler, Gross, & Dabman, 1982). For treatments delivered in social skills training to be considered truly effective and valid, levels of change must evidence treatment generality. Treatment generality is comprised of maintenance (behavior change that persists over time) and generalization (behavior changes that occur under nontraining conditions) (Cooper et al., 1987). Although treatment generality often is evaluated as a hope-for-the-best side effect of social skills training, maintenance and generalization should be systemic facets of any training program. Several authors have discussed procedures to enhance treatment generality (e.g., Michelson et al., 1983; Stokes & Baer, 1977; Stokes & Osnes,

FIGURE 2. **A social skills intervention progress-monitoring record sheet.**

A Social Skills Intervention Progress-Monitoring Record

Student's Name _____ Teacher/Grade _____

Group Leader _____ Date Program Began _____

Skill Domains, Subdomains, and Behavioral Objectives	**Progress Assessment**				
	Check Skills to be taught	**No Progress**	**Improvement Observed**	**Mastered in Treatment Group**	**Generalized**
Cooperation					
1. Ignoring disractions	_____	_____	_____	_____	_____
2. Making transitions	_____	_____	_____	_____	_____
3. Using free time	_____	_____	_____	_____	_____
Classroom Interaction Skills					
1. Finishing assignments on time	_____	_____	_____	_____	_____
2. Keeping desk clean, putting away materials	_____	_____	_____	_____	_____
3. Producing correct work	_____	_____	_____	_____	_____
4. Paying attention and following directions	_____	_____	_____	_____	_____
5. Using time appropriately when waiting	_____	_____	_____	_____	_____
Assertion					
Conversation Skills					
1. Giving a compliment	_____	_____	_____	_____	_____
2. Introducing oneself	_____	_____	_____	_____	_____
3. Making positive self-statements	_____	_____	_____	_____	_____
4. Initiating conversation	_____	_____	_____	_____	_____
5. Telling an adult about unfair treatment	_____	_____	_____	_____	_____
Joining and Volunteering Skills					
1. Joining ongoing activities	_____	_____	_____	_____	_____
2. Volunteering to help peers	_____	_____	_____	_____	_____
3. Inviting others to join activities	_____	_____	_____	_____	_____
Responsibility					
1. Asking an adult for help	_____	_____	_____	_____	_____
2. Paying attention to a speaker	_____	_____	_____	_____	_____
3. Refusing unreasonable requests	_____	_____	_____	_____	_____
4. Answering the telephone	_____	_____	_____	_____	_____
5. Introducing oneself to new people	_____	_____	_____	_____	_____
6. Asking permission to use property	_____	_____	_____	_____	_____
7. Asking permission to leave house/property	_____	_____	_____	_____	_____
8. Reporting accidents to appropriate persons	_____	_____	_____	_____	_____
9. Questioning rules that may be unfair	_____	_____	_____	_____	_____
10. Responding to a compliment	_____	_____	_____	_____	_____

1989). These generality facilitators include (a) targeting behaviors that will be maintained by natural reinforcement contingencies; (b) training across different behaviors, settings, and persons; (c) training loosely, i.e., varying stimuli such as reinforcers, and tone of voice; (d) systematically withdrawing or fading intervention procedures to approximate the natural environment; (e) reinforcing behavior change in novel and appropriate settings; (f) including peers in training; and (g) providing booster sessions. Programming for generality should occur for both child and treatment agent (e.g., parent or teacher) behaviors. Incorporating as many generality facilitators as possible into social skills interventions should enhance the likelihood of treatment maintenance and generalization.

Evaluation of Intervention Effectiveness

The final leg of the social skills training journey invariably rests with the deceptively simple question, "Was the intervention effective?" Although many practitioners and researchers assess treatment effectiveness as a matter of course, methodologically sound measurement often is overlooked in evaluations of intervention effectiveness. Treatment evaluation extends beyond simply assessing changes in social skills at the completion of treatment. Evaluation should include ongoing assessments of acceptability, integrity, social validity, and generality. Ideally, assessments of intervention effectiveness will be multifaceted, involving multiple settings, informants, and methods.

Important advances in the monitoring and the evaluation of interventions have occurred recently. These advances include the use of goal attainment scaling, progress-monitoring records (Figure 2), reliability change indexing (Gresham, 1993), and the integration of visual and statistical analyses (Busse, Kratochwill, & Elliott, in press). The progress-monitoring record illustrated in Figure 2 often has been used as part of a goal-setting and self-monitoring process with elementary and middle school students; however, no reports of its use with preschoolers have been published.

SUMMARY: AN IMPLEMENTATION FRAMEWORK FOR SOCIAL SKILLS ASSESSMENT AND INTERVENTION

A general framework for social skills training can be described by the acronym DATE. First, behaviors are *defined* and stated in observable terms, as are also the conditions (antecedent and consequent) surrounding the behavior. Second, behaviors are *assessed*, preferably via multiple methods that include rating scales, direct observations of the child, interviews with teachers and/or parents, and occasionally a structured role-play to confirm deficits and to refine intervention plans. Third, *teaching* strategies are prescribed to fit the student's needs as determined by assessment results and the classification that best characterizes the child's social skills deficits. Fourth, the effects of the teaching procedures are *evaluated* empirically by using the assessment methods through which students were selected for training. This Define-Assess-Teach-Evaluate (DATE) model is applied continuously to each deficient social behavior the student exhibits.

The DATE model can be implemented by a teacher, psychologist, or other specialist through five steps: (a) establishing the need for performing the behavior, (b) identifying the specific behavioral components of the skill or task analysis, (c) modeling the behavior, (d) obtaining behavior rehearsal and response feedback, and (e) generalizing training. These five steps represent an easily implemented and generic approach to teaching positive social behavior by using the intervention procedures that consistently have been found to be most effective with young children.

REFERENCES

Achenbach, T. M., McConaughy, S. H., & Howell, C. T. (1987). Child/adolescent behavioral and emotional problems: Implications of cross-informant correlations for situational specificity. *Psychological Bulletin, 101,* 213–232.

Allen, K. E., Hart, B. M., Buell, J. S., Harris, F. R., & Wolf, M. M. (1964). Effects of social reinforcement on isolate behavior of a nursery school child. *Child Development, 35,* 7–9.

Asher, S. R. (1978). Children's peer relations. In M. E. Lamb (Ed.), *Social and personality development* (pp. 91–113). New York: Holt, Rinehart and Winston.

Bandura, A. (1977). *Social learning theory.* Englewood Cliffs, NJ: Prentice-Hall.

Bandura, A., & Walters, R. H. (1963). *Social learning and personality development.* New York: Holt, Rinehart and Winston.

Berler, E. S., Gross, A. M., & Drabman, R. S. (1982). Social skills training with children: Proceed with caution. *Journal of Applied Behavior Analysis, 15,* 41–53.

Busse, R. T., Kratochwill, T. R., & Elliott, S. N. (in press). Meta-analysis in single-case consultation outcome research. *Journal of School Psychology.*

Cartledge, G., & Milburn, J. F. (Eds.). (1986). *Teaching social skills to children: Innovative approaches* (2nd ed.). Elmsford, NY: Pergamon.

Cooper, J. O., Heron, T. E., & Heward, W. L. (1987). *Applied behavior analysis.* Columbus, OH: Merrill.

Demaray, M. K., Ruffalo, S. L., Carlson, J., Olson, A. E., McManus, S., Leventhal, A., & Busse, R. T. (1993). *Social skills assessment: A comparative evaluation of published rating scales.* Manuscript submitted for publication.

Dietz, S., & Repp, A. (1973). Decreasing classroom misbehavior through the use of DRL schedules of reinforcement. *Journal of Applied Behavior Analysis, 6,* 457–463.

Dodge, K., Murphy, R., & Buchsbaum, D. (1984). The assessment of intention-cue detection skills in children: Implications for developmental psychopathology. *Child Development, 55,* 163–173.

Doescher, S. M., & Sugawara, A. I. (1989). Encouraging prosocial behavior in young children. *Childhood Education, 65,* 213–216.

Eisenberg, N., & Harris, J. D. (1984). Social competence: A developmental perspective. *School Psychology Review, 13,* 267–277.

Elliott, S. N. (1988). Acceptability of behavioral treatments in educational settings. In J. C. Witt, S. N. Elliott, & F. M. Gresham (Eds.), *Handbook of behavior therapy in education* (pp. 121–150). New York: Plenum.

Elliott, S. N., Barnard, J., & Gresham, F. M. (1989). Preschoolers' social behavior: Teachers' and parents' assessments. *Journal of Psychoeducational Assessment, 7,* 223–234.

Elliott, S. N., & Gresham, F. M. (1991). *Social skills intervention guide: Practical strategies for social skills training.* Circle Pines, MN: American Guidance Service.

Elliott, S. N., & Gresham, F. M. (1993). Social skills interventions for children. *Behavior Modification, 17,* 287–313.

Elliott, S. N., Sheridan, S. M., & Gresham, F. M. (1989). Assessing and treating social skills deficits: A case study for the scientist-practitioner. *Journal of School Psychology, 27,* 197–222.

Fenning, P. A. (1993). *A combined peer-mediated and video-modeling social skills intervention for preschool children with developmental delays.* Unpublished dissertation, University of Wisconsin–Madison.

Gottman, J. M., Gonso, J., & Schuler, P. (1976). Teaching social skills to isolated children. *Journal of Abnormal Child Psychology, 4,* 179–197.

Gresham, F. M. (1981). Social skills training with handicapped children: A review. *Review of Educational Research, 51,* 139–176.

Gresham, F. M. (1985). Utility of cognitive-behavioral procedures for social skills training with children: A review. *Journal of Abnormal Child Psychology, 13,* 411–423.

Gresham, F. M. (1993). Moving beyond statistical significance in reporting consultation outcome research. In J. Zins, T. R. Kratochwill, & S. N. Elliott (Eds.), *Handbook of consultation services for children* (pp. 249–273). San Francisco: Jossey-Bass.

Gresham, F. M., & Elliott, S. N. (1984). Assessment and classification of children's social skills: A review of methods and issues. *School Psychology Review, 13,* 292–301.

Gresham, F. M., & Elliott, S. N. (1989). Social skills deficits as a primary learning disability? *Journal of Learning Disabilities, 22,* 120–124.

Gresham, F. M., & Elliott, S. N. (1990). *Social Skills Rating System.* Circle Pines, MN: American Guidance Service.

Gresham, F. M., & Reschly, D. J. (1988). Issues in the conceptualization, classification, and assessment of social skills in the mildly handicapped. In T. R. Kratochwill (Ed.), *Advances in school psychology* (vol. 6; pp. 203–247). Hillsdale, NJ: Lawrence Erlbaum Associates.

Guevremont, D. (1990). Social skills and peer relationship training. In R. A. Barkley (Ed.), *Attention deficit hyperactivity disorder: A handbook for diagnosis and treatment* (pp. 540–572). New York: Guilford.

Guralnick, M. J. (1986). The peer relations of young handicapped and nonhandicapped children. In P. S. Strain, M. J. Guralnick, & H. M. Walker (Eds.), *Children's social behavior: Development, assessment, and modification* (pp. 93–142). Orlando, FL: Academic Press.

Hartup, W. W., Laursen, B., Stewart, M. I., & Eastenson, A. (1988). Conflict and friendship relations of young children. *Child Development, 59,* 1590–1600.

Hazen, N., Black, B., & Fleming-Johnson, F. (1984). Social acceptance: Strategies children use and how teachers can help children learn them. *Young Children, 39,* 26–36.

Jones, R. N., Sheridan, S. M., & Binns, W. (1993). Schoolwide social skills training: Providing preventive services to students at-risk. *School Psychology Quarterly, 8,* 57–80.

Kendall, P. C., & Braswell, L. (1985). *Cognitive-behavioral therapy for impulsive children.* New York: Guilford.

Ladd, G. W. (1981). Effectiveness of a social learning method for enhancing children's social interaction and peer acceptance. *Child Development, 52,* 171–178.

Ladd, G. W., & Mize, J. (1983). A cognitive-social learning model of social skill training. *Psychological Review, 90,* 127–157.

Lamb, M. E., & Baumrind, D. (1978). Socialization and personality development in the preschool years. In M. E. Lamb (Ed.), *Social and personality development* (pp. 50–69). New York: Holt, Rinehart and Winston.

Leiter, M. P. (1977). A study of reciprocity in preschool play groups. *Child Development, 48,* 1288–1295.

LeMare, L. J., & Rubin, K. H. (1987). Perspective taking and peer interaction: Structural and developmental analyses. *Child Development, 58,* 306–315.

Lentz, F. (1988). Reductive techniques. In J. C. Witt, S. N. Elliott, & F. M. Gresham (Eds.), *The handbook of behavior therapy in education* (pp. 439–468). New York: Plenum Press.

Litow, L., & Pumroy, D. K. (1975). A brief review of classroom group-oriented contingencies. *Journal of Applied Behavior Analysis, 8,* 341–347.

Mastropieri, M. A., & Scruggs, T. E. (1985–86). Early intervention for socially withdrawn children. *Journal of Special Education, 19,* 429–441.

Mathur, S. R., & Rutherford, R. B. (1991). Peer-mediated interventions promoting social skills of children and youth with behavioral disorders. *Education and Treatment of Children, 14,* 227–242.

Matson, J. L., Fee, V. E., Coe, D. A., & Smith, D. (1991). A social skills program for developmentally delayed preschoolers. *Child and Family Behavior Therapy, 20,* 428–433.

Mayhew, G., Enyart, P., & Anderson, J. (1978). Social reinforcement and the naturally occurring social responses of severely and profoundly retarded adolescents. *American Journal of Mental Deficiency, 83,* 164–170.

McConnell, S. R., Sisson, L. A., Cort, C. A., & Strain, P. S. (1991). Effects of social skills training and contingency management on reciprocal interaction of preschool children with behavioral handicaps. *Journal of Special Education, 24,* 473–495.

Meichenbaum, D. (1977). *Cognitive-behavior modification: An integrative approach.* New York: Plenum Press.

Michaelson, L., Sugai, D. P., Wood, R. P., & Kazdin, A. E. (1983). *Social skills assessment and training with children: An empirically based approach.* New York: Plenum.

Oden, S. L., & Asher, S. R. (1977). Coaching children in social skills for friendship making. *Child Development, 48,* 495–506.

Parker, J. G., & Asher, S. R. (1987). Peer relations and later personal adjustment: Are low-accepted children at risk? *Psychological Bulletin, 102,* 357–389.

Pinkston, E. M., Reese, N. M., Le Blanc, J. M., & Baer, D. M. (1973). Independent control of a preschool child's aggression and peer interaction by contingent teacher attention. *Journal of Applied Behavior Analysis, 6,* 223–224.

Schneider, B. H., & Byrne, B. M. (1985). Children's social skills: A meta-analysis. In B. H. Schneider, K. H. Rubin, & J. E. Ledingham (Eds.), *Children's peer relations: Issues in assessment and intervention* (pp. 175–192). New York: Springer-Verlag.

Stokes, T. F., & Baer, D. M. (1977). An implicit technology of generalization. *Journal of Applied Behavior Analysis, 10,* 349–367.

Stokes, T. F., & Osnes, P. (1989). An operant pursuit of generalization. *Behavior Therapy, 20,* 337–355.

Strain, P. S. (1977). An experimental analysis of peer social initiations on the behavior of withdrawn preschool children: Some training and generalization effects. *Journal of Abnormal Child Psychology, 5,* 445–455.

Strain, P. S., & Fox, J. (1981). Peers as behavior change agents for withdrawn classmates. In B. B. Lahey & A. E. Kazdin (Eds.), *Advances in clinical child psychology* (vol. 4; pp. 167–198). New York: Plenum.

Strain, P. S., Guralnick, M. J., & Walker, H. M. (Eds.). (1986). *Children's social behavior: Development, assessment, and modification.* Orlando, FL: Academic Press.

Strain, P. S., Odom, S., & McConnell, S. (1984). Promoting social reciprocity of exceptional children: Identification, target behavior selections, and intervention. *Remedial and Special Education, 5,* 21–28.

Strain, P. S., Shores, R. E., & Timm, M. A. (1977). Effects of peer social initiations on the behavior of withdrawn preschool children. *Journal of Applied Behavior Analysis, 10,* 289–298.

Strain, P., & Timm, M. (1974). An experimental analysis of social interaction between a behaviorally disordered preschool child and her classroom peers. *Journal of Applied Behavior Analysis, 7,* 583–590.

Wandless, R. L., & Prinz, R. J. (1982). Methodological issues in conceptualizing and treating childhood social isolation. *Psychological Bulletin, 92,* 39–55.

Weissberg, R. P. (1985). Designing effective social problem-solving programs for the classroom. In B. H. Schneider, K. H. Rubin, & J. E. Ledingham (Eds.), *Children's peer relations: Issues in assessment and intervention* (pp. 225–242). New York: Springer-Verlag.

ANNOTATED BIBLIOGRAPHY

Cartledge, G., & Milburn, J. (Eds.). (1986). *Teaching social skills to children: Innovative approaches.* Elmsford, NY: Pergamon Press.
Oriented toward social skills training as a part of school curriculum. Part I sets out general assessment and teaching procedures. Part II focuses on specific populations: behavior disordered, young children, and adolescents.

Elliott, S. N., & Gresham, F. M. (1991). *Social skills intervention guide: Practical strategies for social skills training.* Circle Pines, MN: American Guidance Service.
This practical guidebook is an extension of the Social Skills Rating System (Gresham & Elliott, 1990) and provides lesson plans for 43 of the social skills assessed on the SSRS. The lessons are presented in a tell-show-do instructional group format. Psychologists, counselors, or teachers are considered group leaders. A rich assortment of tables and figures is provided to support implementation of the basic strategies and communication with parents and others.

Strain, P. S., Guralnick, M. J., & Walker, H. M. (Eds.). (1986). *Children's social behavior: Development, assessment, and modification.* Orlando, FL: Academic Press.
This volume is divided into three sections and provides up-to-date reviews and conceptual discussions of the development, assessment, and treatment of children's social skills problems. Chapters on peer relationships of young children, naturalistic observation, and sociometrics are the best available.

86

Best Practices in Social Skills Training

Frank M. Gresham
University of California–Riverside

OVERVIEW

The assessment and facilitation of social competence continues to be an important area of concern for school psychologists. Schools are one of the most important settings in which children acquire, develop, and refine the skills that are essential for establishing and maintaining interpersonal relationships. Successful and mutually beneficial interactions with peers and significant adults represent an important developmental accomplishment that is predictive of long-term life adjustment (Asher, 1990; Coie, 1990; Parker & Asher, 1987; Schneider, 1993).

Social skills are the tools with which positive and rewarding relationships are built and negative and pernicious relationships are modified or eliminated. Some children, however, lack the necessary tools to build, maintain, or terminate interpersonal relationships. Deficiencies in social competence have been related to poor academic performance, social maladjustment, peer rejection, and psychopathology (Kupersmidt, Coie, & Dodge, 1990; Parker & Asher, 1987). Relatively large mean differences in social competence have been found between nondisabled children and children with learning disabilities (Gresham, 1992; LaGreca & Stone, 1990; Swanson & Malone, 1992), mental retardation (Gresham & Reschly, 1987, 1988; Morrison, Forness, & MacMillan, 1983), behavior disorders (Coie & Koeppel, 1990; Stumme, Gresham, & Scott, 1982; Walker & McConnell, 1988), and attention deficit hyperactivity disorders (Landau & Moore, 1991). This literature suggests that children with mild cognition and behavioral disabilities experience substantial difficulties in social competence.

Schools as Settings for Social Skills Interventions

As a microcosm of society, the school is a place where children and adults work, play, eat, and live together for 6 hours per day, 5 days per week, and at least 180 days per year. At a minimum, children spend approximately 5,400 hours per year in school and are exposed to numerous social interactions. Schools, as social settings, represent environments that are ideal for teaching social behavior.

Social skills interventions in schools take place both informally and formally. Informal social skills instruction is based on the principle of incidental learning, which takes advantage of naturally occurring behavioral events or incidents to teach appropriate social behavior. Most social skills instruction in schools can be characterized as informal and incidental. Literally thousands of behavioral incidents occur in a classroom over the course of an academic year and these incidents can be used as the basis for social skills instruction. For this reason, informal and incidentally taught social skills have greater potential for generalization than social skills taught in more formal and less naturalistic settings.

Formal social instruction can take place in a classroom setting in which the entire class is exposed to a social skills "curriculum" or in a small group setting removed from the classroom. This chapter focuses upon incidental teaching of social skills and social skills instruction in small-group settings. For more detailed information regarding classwide social skills instruction readers should consult other comprehensive treatments of this literature (Elias & Clabby, 1992; Elias & Branden, 1988; Weissberg, Caplan, & Harwood, 1991).

Defining Social Competence

Part of the difficulty in defining social competence has been the failure by many to distinguish between social skills and social competence. McFall (1982) argued that *social skills* are behaviors exhibited in specific situations that result in judgments of *social competence*. Social skills are behaviors that lead others to judge whether a behavioral performance was competent. Therefore, social skills are behaviors and social competence represents "judgments" about those behaviors. These judgments may be based on opinions of significant others (e.g., teacher, parents, peers), comparisons with explicit criteria (e.g., number of social tasks performed correctly in relation to some criterion), or comparisons with an appropriate normative sample.

Gresham (1983) developed a *social validity* definition of social skills, in which social skills are defined as socially significant behaviors, exhibited in specific situations, that predict important social outcomes for children and youth. *Socially significant* behaviors are behaviors that treatment consumers consider important and desirable and that predict an individual's standing on socially important outcomes. *Socially important* outcomes are outcomes that treatment consumers judge to be important, adaptive, and functional. In most settings relevant for children and youths, important social outcomes include, but are not limited to, (a) peer acceptance, (b) friendships, (c) significant others' judgments of social skill, (d) positive feelings of self-worth, (e) academic achievement, and (f) positive adaptation to school, home, and community environments, as judged by significant others who regulate these environments.

The social validity concept of social skills has the advantage of specifying behaviors in which a child may be deficient, but it also can define these behaviors as socially skilled on the basis of their relationship to socially important outcomes. This social validity definition of social skills is broader than McFall's (1982) social competence definition, because it expands the concept of "judgment" to include additional criteria in defining social competence (e.g., peer acceptance, friendships, achievement, school adaptation, etc.). Social validity constitutes an important type of validity in interventions with children and youths and has been an important standard against which the success of behavioral interventions has been judged (Kazdin, 1977; Wolf, 1978).

Classification of Social Skills Deficits

An important distinction to be made in the assessment of social skills is the differentiation between *acquisition* and *performance* deficits (Gresham, 1981a, 1981b). This distinction is important because it suggests different intervention approaches in remediating social skills deficits. The notion of social skills *acquisition deficits* refers to the absence of particular social skills from a behavioral repertoire. Social skills acquisition deficits reflect the absence of knowledge for executing given social skills even under the optimal conditions. *Social performance deficits* represent the presence of social skills in a behavioral repertoire but the failure to perform these skills at acceptable levels in given situations.

Gresham and Elliott (1990) extended this two-way classification into a four-category classification scheme. Most children exhibit some social behaviors in each of these four categories. This scheme incorporates two dimensions of behavior: (a) social skills and (b) interfering problem behaviors. Children may have acquisition or performance deficits with or without problem behaviors. Interfering problem behaviors include internalizing (e.g., anxiety, depression, etc.) and externalizing (e.g., aggression, impulsivity, etc.) that prevent the acquisition or performance of socially skilled behavior. Figure 1 shows this four-category classification scheme.

The classification scheme shown in Figure 1 is pivotal in linking assessment results to interventions for social skills deficits. It does not make much sense to teach a social skill to children who already have the skill in their repertoires. This would be analogous to teaching single-digit addition to calculus students in high school. Many, if not most, children have social performance deficits. This being the case, the goal of the intervention should be to increase the frequency with which the behavior is exhibited in specific situations rather than teach the skill. Fewer students have acquisition deficits; thus intervention must emphasize promoting skills acquisition. These differential intervention strategies for acquisition and performance deficits are discussed in greater detail later in this chapter.

BASIC CONSIDERATIONS

An in-depth discussion of social skills assessment methods is beyond the scope of the present chapter. There are, however, several key factor that should be recognized in linking social skills assessment and intervention strategies. Table 1 presents 12 major goals of social skills assessment. These goals include the five major stages of the assessment/intervention sequence: (a) screening/selection, (b) classification, (c) target behavior selection, (d) functional analysis, and (e) evaluation of intervention.

Although a number of social skills assessment methods have been developed, three methods are the most commonly used: ratings by other, peer-referenced assessment, and naturalistic observations. These methods are discussed in greater detail in other sources (Gresham, 1986; Gresham & Little, 1993; LaGreca & Stark, 1986; McConnell & Odom, 1986).

Social skills training rests on the fundamental assumption that children learn social skills through the processes of observational, instrumental (operant), and respondent (classical) learning (Elliott & Gresham, 1991). There are numerous variables that may account for deficits in prosocial behavior; however, many of these variables either are highly inferential (e.g., repressed hostile feelings, poor ego controls, etc.) or are beyond anyone's control (e.g., developmental immaturity, inadequate cognitive abilities, etc.). Elliott and Gresham (1991, 1993) described a model of variables that influence social skills deficits and that can be used to remediate social skill deficiencies. This model suggests that social skills deficits may result from five factors: (a) lack of cues

FIGURE 1. Classificaton of social skills deficits.

	Acquisition Deficit	Performance Deficit
Interfering problem behaviors present	Social skills acquisition deficit with interfering problem behaviors	Social skills performance deficit with interfering problem behaviors
Interfering problem behaviors absent	Social skills acquisition deficit without interfering problem behaviors	Social skills performance deficit without interfering problem behaviors

or opportunities to learn or perform prosocial behaviors; (b) presence of interfering problem behaviors that block acquisition or impede performance of prosocial behaviors; (c) lack of knowledge; (d) lack of sufficient practice or feedback for prosocial behavioral performances; and (e) lack of reinforcement for performance of prosocial behaviors.

Social Skills Training Variables

Four fundamental processes underlie all social skills training techniques discussed in this chapter. These training variables are instruction, rehearsal, feedback/reinforcement, and reductive procedures; they are based, in part, on the theoretical work of Ladd and Mize (1983). Each of these variables is discussed briefly in the following sections.

Instruction. There are two types of instructions: verbal and modeled. Verbal instruction typically involves the use of spoken language to describe, prompt, explain, define, and/or request social behavior. Verbal instruction may involve the use of concrete or abstract concepts to facilitate the acquisition of social skills. The training procedures of coaching and direct instruction rely primarily on verbal instruction.

Modeled instruction involves the use of live or filmed performance or enactments of behaviors that illustrate social skills. The major advantage of modeled instruction is that children learn how to combine, chain, and sequence behaviors that make up particular social skills. The adage "a picture is worth a thousand words" captures the essence of modeled instruction.

Rehearsal. Rehearsal is the repeated practice of a social skill that promotes the retention of the skill concept and leads to more polished and effective behavioral performances. Rehearsal can be overt, covert, or verbal. *Overt rehearsal,* typically called behavioral rehearsal, is the repeated practice of the observable behaviors involved in the performance of a social skill. *Covert rehearsal* refers to thinking about or imagining behavioral performances of a social skill. Covert rehearsal of instructed social skills allows for retention of instructed information as well as

more effective behavioral performances of the social skill (Elliott & Gresham, 1993).

Verbal rehearsal entails the verbal report or recitation of the components of a particular social skill. The learner says what he or she might do in a particular social situation, whereas overt rehearsal requires the learner to actually enact or perform the social skill and covert rehearsal requires the learner to think about or imagine rather than say or perform a social skill.

Feedback and reinforcement. Feedback is the information that is provided a learner regarding the correspondence between a social skill performance and some standard of performance. Feedback can take two forms: evaluative and informative. *Evaluative feedback* informs the learner of the extent to which a given behavioral performance matched an external criterion or standard. *Informative feedback* gives the learner specific information regarding the reasons for effective and ineffective performances of a given social skill. Informative feedback is the preferred type of feedback to be used in social skills training, because it allows for modification of behavioral performances.

Reinforcement involves the presentation or removal of environmental events that increase the frequency of behavior. Reinforcement can be positive or negative. With positive reinforcement, an environmental event is presented that increases the frequency of a behavior. Positive reinforcement is perhaps the most frequently used social skills training strategy (Barton, 1986).

With negative reinforcement, an environmental event that increases the frequency of behavior is *removed.* Negative reinforcement always involves either escape or avoidance learning. That is, a person's behavior will be negatively reinforced if that behavior allows the person to escape or avoid an aversive stimulus. Escape learning results in termination of an ongoing aversive stimulus, whereas avoidance learning prevents the presentation of the aversive stimulus. For instance, some children in classrooms exhibit disruptive behavior to escape or avoid academic assignments that they consider aversive. Negative rein-

TABLE 1
Goals of Social Skills Assessment

Identify social skills strengths
Identify social skills acquisition deficits
Identify social skills performance deficits
Identify incompletely developed social skills
Identify poor quality social performances
Identify interfering problem behaviors
Conduct functional analyses of behavior
Determine importance of social skills
Select target behaviors
Develop intervention strategies
Evaluate effects of intervention
Assess generality/generalization of effects

forcement is not used as frequently as positive reinforcement in social skills training.

Reductive processes. Social skills training focuses on teaching prosocial behaviors to children. The presence of interfering problem behaviors, however, often prevents the acquisition or hinders the performance of social skills. Reductive procedures present or remove environmental events in order to *decrease* the frequency of problem behaviors. These procedures, to be discussed later, include response cost, overcorrection, and differential reinforcement techniques.

BEST PRACTICES IN SOCIAL SKILLS TRAINING

As an intervention process, social skills training has four objectives: (a) promoting skills acquisition, (b) enhancing skills performance, (c) removing interfering problem behaviors, and (d) facilitating generalization of prosocial behavior. These objectives reflect the type of social skills deficiency (i.e., acquisition versus performance deficit), the presence or absence of interfering problem behaviors, and the functional control of social behaviors in specific situations. Figure 2 lists specific social skills intervention strategies that are appropriate to each training objective. Specific step-by-step intervention procedures and recommendations can be found in the *Social Skills Intervention Guide* (Elliott & Gresham, 1993).

In social skills training it must be recognized that a given child may have some acquisition deficits, some performance deficits, and some interfering problem behaviors. Professionals in charge of social skills interventions must match appropriate intervention strategies with the particular deficits or behavioral excesses the child exhibits. Moreover, a common misconception is that one seeks to facilitate generalization after presenting procedures for acquisition or performance as part of a final stage of inter-

vention. The evidence is clear that best practice is to incorporate generalization from the very beginning of any social skills training program (Elliott & Gresham, 1991, 1993).

Promoting Skills Acquisition

Procedures designed to promote acquisition are applicable when children do not have a particular social skill in their repertoire, when they do not know a particular step in the performance of a behavioral sequence, or when their execution of the skill is awkward or ineffective. It should be noted that a relatively small percentage of children will need social skills interventions based on acquisition deficits: Far more children have performance deficits in the area of prosocial behavior (Gresham, 1981a; Gresham & Reschly, 1988).

Three procedures represent pathways to remediation of deficits in social skill acquisition: modeling, coaching, and behavioral rehearsal. Social problem solving is another pathway, but it is not discussed here owing to space limitations and the fact that it incorporates the three procedures discussed in this section. More specific information on social problem-solving interventions can be found in Elias and Clabby (1992) and Elias and Branden (1988).

Modeling is the process of learning a behavior by observing another person performing that behavior. Modeling instruction presents the entire sequence of behaviors involved in a particular social skill and teaches how to integrate specific behaviors in this sequence into a composite behavioral pattern. Modeling is one of the most effective and efficient ways of teaching social behavior (Gresham, 1985; Schneider, 1993).

Coaching is the use of verbal instruction to teach social skills. Unlike modeling, which emphasizes visual displays of social skills, coaching emphasizes a child's cognitive and language skills. Coaching is accomplished in three fundamental steps; (a) present-

FIGURE 2. Social skills interventions by type of social skills deficit.

	Acquisition Deficit	Performance Deficit
Interfering problem behaviors present	Modeling Coaching Behavioral Rhearsal DRO DRL DRI Positive practice Response cost Behavioral cost Behavioral contracting School/home notes Group contingencies	Proactive teaching Peer initiations Peer tutoring Cuing/prompting Behavioral rehearsal Reinforcement (+/–1) Behavioral contracting School/home notes DRO DRL DRI Positive practice Response cost Behavioral contracting School/home notes Group contingencies
Interfering problem behaviors absent	Modeling Coaching Behavioral rehearsal	Proactive teaching Peer initiations Peer tutoring Cuing/Prompting Behavoral Rehearsal Reinforcement (+/–) Behavioral contracting School/home notes

ing social concepts or rules, (b) providing opportunities for practice or rehearsal of a social skill, and (c) providing specific informational feedback on a behavioral performance.

With coaching, one can transmit general principles of social interaction, integrate behavioral sequences in performing a social skill, set social goals of an interaction sequence, and help children become aware of their social impact on others (Renshaw & Asher, 1983). It is assumed that children can use general principles of social interaction to guide their behavior in specific social situations. In this sense, coaching is based, in part, on the notion of "rule-governed" rather than "contingency-shaped" behavior. In rule-governed behavior, not every situation a child is likely to encounter has to be taught. Instead, the goal is to teach social rules that a child can apply in a variety of situations. Theoretically, this should lead to greater generalization of social skills.

Behavioral rehearsal refers to practicing a newly learned behavior in the structured, protective situation of role playing. In this way, children can enhance their proficiency in using social skills without experiencing adverse consequences. Social learning theory suggests that behavioral rehearsal is essential to learning social behavior (Bandura, 1977).

Three forms of behavioral rehearsal can be used in a number of ways and combinations. For example, one can ask children to imagine being teased by another child and then to imagine how they would respond (covert rehearsal). Next, one might combine covert rehearsal with verbal rehearsal by asking students to recite the specific behaviors they would exhibit in imagined situations. Finally, one might combine covert and verbal with overt rehearsal by asking students to role play the imagined situation.

Enhancing Performance of Social Skills

Most social skills interventions will involve procedures that increase the frequency of prosocial behaviors, because most social skills deficits, as has been noted, are performance (won't do) rather than acquisition (can't do) deficits. This suggests that most social skills interventions for most children will take place in naturalistic environments (e.g., classrooms, playgrounds, etc.) rather than in small "pullout" groups. Therefore, most social skills interventions can be facilitated by using a consultative framework for intervention. Failure to perform certain social skills in specific situations result from two fundamental factors: (a) inappropriately arranged an-

tecedents and/or (b) inappropriately arranged consequences. A number of specific procedures can be
classified under the broad rubrics of antecedent and
consequent strategies.

Antecedent strategies. Interventions based on
antecedent control assume that the environment does
not set the occasion for the performance of prosocial
behavior. That is, cues, prompts, or other stimuli are
either not present or the child does not discriminate
these stimuli in relation to the performance of prosocial behavior. Antecedent control techniques are
based on the principle of discrimination learning.
Briefly, a discrimination is made when a behavior is
reinforced in the presence of one stimulus, but not in
the presence of another stimulus. If these stimuli are
not present or if the learner does not discriminate
them, the behavior will not be performed. Intervention procedures based on the control of antecedents
focus on presenting and/or enhancing stimuli that set
the occasion for prosocial behavior.

Two general strategies fall under the category of
antecedent strategies: peer-mediated interventions
and cuing/prompting. Peer-mediated interventions
can include three techniques: (a) peer initiations, (b)
peer tutoring, and (c) peer modeling (Kohler & Strain,
1990). With peer initiation strategies, a child's peers
are used to initiate and maintain social interactions
with socially isolated or withdrawn students. These
strategies are effective for students who exhibit performance deficits and who evidence relatively low
rates of social interaction.

In using peer initiation, peer confederates are recruited and instructed in the specific behaviors that
are required to initiate and maintain a social interaction. Specific feedback is given to peer confederates
that is based on role-played examples of peer initiations. Finally, peer confederates are instructed to initiate interactions with targeted children and to report
any problems they encounter in their initiation efforts. Peer initiation strategies are effective in increasing the social functioning of socially withdrawn
children in naturalistic settings.

Peer tutoring traditionally has been used to teach
academic skills. Although there are no controlled
studies in the literature, peer tutoring is a potentially
effective strategy for teaching social behavior. In
many cases peers may be more realistic and convincing teachers of social skills than adults because of
their familiarity with peer group mores, values, and
customs. Peer tutoring is closely related to coaching
as an intervention strategy that relies on verbal instruction, role playing, and verbal feedback (Oden &
Asher, 1977).

Since peers serve as models for social behavior in
peer modeling, the techniques can be considered an
antecedent control strategy because a peer provides
discriminative stimuli for the performance of social

behavior. Peer modeling has been used extensively in
social skills interventions (Strain & Fox, 1981).

A cuing and prompting procedure uses verbal or
nonverbal cues or prompts to facilitate prosocial behaviors. Simple prompts or cues for some children
may be all that is needed to signal to children to engage in socially appropriate behaviors. Cuing and
prompting represent one of the easiest and most efficient social skills intervention strategies.

Consequent strategies. Intervention techniques that rely on consequent control techniques can
be classified into three categories: (a) reinforcement-
based strategies, (b) behavioral contracts, and (c)
school–home notes. Reinforcement-based strategies
assume that a child knows how to perform a social
skill but is not doing so because of little or nonexistent reinforcement for the behavior. Reinforcement
strategies include attention, tokens, points, and activity reinforcers, as well as group-oriented contingency
systems; more comprehensive discussion of these
procedures can be found in Martens and Meller
(1990).

Behavioral contracts are written agreements between students and intervention personnel that specify the relation between behavior and its consequences. Behavioral contracts should have the following five components: (a) specification of mutual
gains, (b) ways in which the child will demonstrate
observable behavior, (c) provisions for sanctions for
not meeting contract terms, (d) a bonus clause for
consistent performance of desired behaviors, and (e)
means of monitoring reinforcers given and received
(Stuart, 1971). Behavioral contracts are an effective
means of enhancing the performance or quality of
prosocial behavior.

School–home notes are written communications
sent by intervention personnel to parents on a daily
or weekly basis. School–home notes can be easily incorporated into behavioral contracts to enlist
parental involvement and cooperation in facilitating
prosocial behavior. More extensive discussion of
using school–home notes can be found in Kelley and
Carper (1988).

Removing Interfering Problem Behaviors

Students may not acquire or may not perform certain social skills because problem behaviors interfere
with or block their acquisition or performance. The
social skills classification model presented earlier
distinguishes between acquisition and performance
deficits that are associated with interfering problem
behaviors.

Three general strategies may be used to remove
or reduce interfering problem behaviors: (a) differential reinforcement, (b) positive practice, and (c) response cost. In differential reinforcement, a particular behavior is reinforced in the presence of one stimulus and is not reinforced in the presence of another

stimulus. In other words, the purpose of differential reinforcement is to get a behavior under stimulus control.

One differential reinforcement technique known as differential reinforcement of other behavior (DRO) refers to the delivery of a reinforcer after any appropriate behavior except the target behavior selected for reduction. The effect of DRO is to reduce a target behavior and increase other behaviors. Another differential reinforcement technique, known as differential reinforcement of low rates of behavior (DRL), a specific number of reductions in a target behavior in a specified time interval is reinforced. For example, reductions in a target behavior by 50% in a class period may be reinforced, thereby reducing the overall rate of the inappropriate target behavior. Finally, in differential reinforcement of incompatible behaviors of DRI, behaviors that are incompatible with the target behavior are reinforced. For instance, talking nicely to others is incompatible with yelling at others. Thus, if talking nicely is reinforced more frequently than yelling, talking will increase and yelling will decrease.

Positive practice is a component of overcorrection that reduces the frequency of problem behavior. It is the repeated practice of an appropriate behavior that is incompatible with an inappropriate behavior. If a student, for example, insulted another student (e.g., "You're really ugly"), he or she would have to practice saying nice things or giving compliments to the insulted child, to each person in the class, and perhaps even the teacher. Positive practice should be part of every social skills intervention program because intervention personnel can use
naturally occurring behavioral incidents to teach the prosocial alternative to inappropriate behavior.

Response cost is the removal of a specified amount of a positive reinforcer to decrease the frequency of a target behavior. In practice, response cost usually takes the form of fines or penalties for inappropriate behavior. Response cost can be used in conjunction with group contingency systems, school–home notes, and behavioral contracts. Response cost is more user-friendly than the labor-intensive reductive procedures of DRO, DRL, and DRI. A more detailed discussion of reductive procedures can be found in Lentz (1988).

Facilitating Generalization

Social skills would not be particularly functional if they did not occur outside the setting in which they were taught. The ultimate goal of social skills interventions is to have trained behaviors occur in diverse settings and situations, and to be maintained over time. Thus, three types of generalization are relevant for social skills interventions: (a) setting generalization, (b) behavior generalization, and (c) time generalization.

Setting generalization is the occurrence of a behavior in settings or situations other than those in which the social skill was taught. One reason behavior generalizes across settings or situations is that settings and situations often have common properties. The more closely the generalization setting resembles the training setting, the greater the degree of setting generalization.

Behavior generalization is changes in behavior that are not the direct focus of social skills training. For example, changes in sharing behavior may also produce changes in complimenting others even although complimenting was not a target behavior. If behaviors are members of the same functional response class, then behavior generalization can be facilitated by teaching only a subset of that response class.

Time generalization, or maintenance, is the continuation or maintenance of behavior after an intervention has been withdrawn. Several factors account for time generalization. Some social behaviors taught in social skills training have a high probability of being reinforced in the future. Some behaviors taught in social skills training produce their own reinforcing consequences. Finally, some behaviors may produce permanent changes in the behavior of significant others such as parents or teachers.

Stokes and Osnes (1989) presented a comprehensive discussion of 12 generalization programming strategies. These strategies are classified under three broad categories of generalization programming: (a) exploiting functional contingencies, (b) training diversely, and (c) incorporating functional mediators. A detailed discussion of these strategies is not possible, given the space constraints; however, several techniques can be highlighted.

Two strategies under the category of training diversely are useful generalization programming techniques: training sufficient stimulus exemplars and training sufficient response exemplars. Diverse stimulus exemplars incorporate varied stimulus conditions in teaching a social skill. This represents training for stimulus generalization. In training for response generalization, one provides sufficient response exemplars by teaching children as many ways as possible to respond in the same social setting or situation — in other words, by giving students sufficient "behavioral ammunition."

Teaching behavior that is relevant to a given environment is another way to promote generalization. To get a behavior to enter an environment that reinforces the behavior without any special programming, relevant behaviors should be taught. The relevance of a particular social skill depends on the behavioral standards, expectations, and requirements of particular social environments. In order to teach relevant behaviors for given environments, it is necessary to know what is relevant in those environments.

The behaviors taught to a child in social skills training should have social validity. That is, the behaviors should be socially significant behaviors as judged by significant others in the child's environment. By teaching behaviors that are considered by others to be socially significant, one increases the chances that these behaviors will enter a natural community of reinforcement. More detailed discussions of generalization can be found in other sources (Edelstein, 1989; Fox & McEvoy, 1993; Stokes & Osnes, 1989).

SUMMARY

Social skills are behavior that lead to judgment of social competence by others; they are the tolls by which children and youths build, maintain, and improve the quality of their interpersonal relationships. Social skills were defined in this chapter as socially significant behaviors, exhibited in specific situations, that predict important social outcomes for children and youths. Social skills deficits were classified as being either acquisition deficits or performance deficits, which may or may not be accompanied by interfering problem behaviors. This classification was seen as essential in determining the most appropriate social skills intervention strategy.

Four processes underlying all social skills training techniques were discussed: instruction, rehearsal, feedback/reinforcement, and reductive processes. These processes form the basis for social skills training strategies of modeling, coaching, behavioral rehearsal, reinforcement, and punishment. Social skills training was viewed as having four fundamental objectives: (a) promoting skill acquisition, (b) enhancing skill performance, (c) removing interfering problem behaviors, and (d) facilitating generalization of prosocial behavior. Specific strategies for accomplishing each of these four objectives were defined and discussed.

REFERENCES

Asher, S. (1990). Recent advances in the study of peer rejection. In S. Asher & J. Coie (Eds.), *Peer rejection in childhood* (pp. 3–16). New York: Cambridge University Press.

Bandura, A. (1977). *Social learning theory.* Englewood Cliffs, NJ: Prentice-Hall.

Barton, E. (1986). Modification of children's prosocial behavior. In P. Strain, M. Guralnick, & H. Walker (Eds.), *Children's social behavior: Development, assessment, and modification* (pp. 331–372). Orlando, FL: Academic.

Coie, J. D. (1990). Toward a theory of peer rejection. In S. Asher & J. Coie (Eds.), *Peer rejection in childhood* (pp. 365–401). New York: Cambridge University Press.

Coie, J., & Koeppel, G. (1990). Adapting intervention to the problems of aggressive and disruptive rejected children. In S. Asher & J. Coie (Eds.), *Peer rejection in childhood* (pp. 309–337). New York: Cambridge University Press.

Edelstein, B. (1989). Generalization: Terminological, methodological, and conceptual issues. *Behavior Therapy, 20,* 311–324.

Elias, M., & Branden, L. (1988). Primary prevention of behavioral and emotional problems in school-age populations. *School Psychology Review, 17,* 581–592.

Elias, M., & Clabby, J. (1992). *Building social problem solving skills: Guidelines from a school-based program.* San Francisco: Jossey-Bass.

Elliott, S. N., & Gresham, F. M. (1991). *Social skills intervention guide.* Circle Pines, MN: American Guidance Service.

Elliott, S. N., & Gresham, F. M. (1993). Social skills interventions for children. *Behavior Modification, 17,* 287–313.

Fox, J., & McEvoy M. (1993). Assessing and enhancing generalization and social validity of social-skills interventions with children and adolescents. *Behavior Modification, 17,* 339–366.

Gresham, F. M. (1981a). Assessment of children's social skills. *Journal of School Psychology, 19,* 120–134.

Gresham, F. M. (1981b). Social skills training with handicapped children: A review. *Review of Educational Research, 51,* 139–176.

Gresham, F. M. (1983). Social validity in the assessment of children's social skills: Establishing standards for social competency. *Journal of Psychoeducational Assessment, 1,* 297–307.

Gresham, F. M. (1985). Utility of cognitive-behavioral procedures for social skills training with children. *Journal of Abnormal Child Psychology, 13,* 411–423.

Gresham, F. M. (1986). Conceptual and definitional issues in the assessment of social skills: Implications for classification and training. *Journal of Clinical Child Psychology, 15,* 16–25.

Gresham, F. M. (1992). Social skills and learning disabilities: Causal, concomitant, or correlational? *School Psychology Review, 21,* 348–360.

Gresham, F. M., & Elliott, S. N. (1990). *Social Skills Rating System.* Circle Pines, MN: American Guidance Service.

Gresham, F. M., & Little, S. G. (1993). Peer-referenced assessment strategies. In T. Ollendick & M. Hersen (Eds.), *Handbook of child and adolescent assessment* (pp. 165–179). Boston: Allyn & Bacon.

Gresham, F. M., & Reschly, D. J. (1987). Sociometric differences between mildly handicapped and nonhandicapped black and white student. *Journal of Educational Psychology, 79,* 195–197.

Gresham, F. M., & Reschly, D. J. (1988). Issues in the conceptualization, classification, and assessment of social skills in the mildly handicapped. In T. Kratochwill (Ed.), *Advances in school psychology* (pp. 203–247). Hillsdale, NJ: Lawrence Erlbaum.

Kazdin, A. (1977). Assessing the clinical or applied importance of behavior change through social validation. *Behavior Modification, 1,* 427–451.

Kelley, M. L., & Carper, L. (1988). Home-based reinforcement procedures. In J. Witt, S. Elliott, & F. Gresham (Eds.), *Handbook of behavior therapy in education* (pp. 419–438). New York: Plenum.

Kohler, F., & Strain, P. (1990). Peer-assisted interventions: Early promises, notable achievements, and future aspirations. *Clinical Psychology Review, 10,* 441–452.

Kupersmidt, J., Coie, J., & Dodge, K. (1990). The role of peer relationships in the development of disorder. In S. Asher & J. Coie (Eds.), *Peer rejection in childhood* (pp. 274–308). New York: Cambridge University Press.

Ladd, G., & Mize, J. (1983). A cognitive-social learning model of social skill training. *Psychological Review, 90,* 127–157.

LaGreca, A., & Stone, W. (1990). Children with learning disabilities: The role of achievement in their social, personal, and behavioral functioning. In H. L. Swanson & B. Keogh (Eds.), *Learning disabilities: Theoretical and research issues* (pp. 333–352). Hillsdale, NJ: Lawrence Erlbaum.

LaGreca, A., & Stark, P. (1986). Naturalistic observations of children's social behavior. In P. Strain, M. Guralnick, & H. Walker (Eds.), *Children's social behavior: Development, assessment, and modification* (pp. 181–214). Orlando, FL: Academic.

Landau, S., & Moore, L. (1991). Social skill deficits in children with attention-deficit hyperactivity disorder. *School Psychology Review, 20,* 235–251.

Lentz, F. E. (1988). Reductive procedures. In J. Witt, S. Elliott, & F. Gresham (Eds.), *Handbook of behavior therapy in education* (pp. 439–468). New York: Plenum.

Martens, B. K., & Meller, P. (1990). The application of behavioral principles to educational settings. In T. Gutkin & C. Reynolds (Eds.), *The handbook of school psychology* (pp. 612–634). New York: Wiley.

McConnell, S., & Odom, S. (1986). Sociometric: Peer-referenced measures and the assessment of social competence. In P. Strain, M. Guralnick, & H. Walker (Eds.), *Children's social behavior: Development, assessment, and modification* (pp. 215–275). Orlando, FL: Academic.

McFall, R. (1982). A review and reformulation of the concept of social skills. *Behavioral Assessment, 4,* 1–33.

Morrison, G., Forness, S., & MacMillan, D. (1983). Influences on sociometric ratings of mildly handicapped children: A path analysis. *Journal of Educational Psychology, 75,* 63–74.

Oden, S., & Asher, S. (1977). Coaching children in social skills for friendship making. *Child Development, 48,* 495–506.

Parker, J., & Asher, S. (1987). Peer relations and later personal adjustment: Are low-accepted children at risk? *Psychological Bulletin, 102,* 357–389.

Renshaw, P., & Asher, S. (1983). Children's goals and strategies for social interaction. *Merrill-Palmer Quarterly, 29,* 353–374.

Schneider, B. (1993). *Children's social competence in context.* New York: Pergamon.

Stokes, T., & Osnes, P. (1989). An operant pursuit of generalization. *Behavior Therapy, 20,* 337–355.

Strain, P., & Fox, J. (1981). Peers as behavior change agents for withdrawn classmates. In B. B. Lahey & A. Kazdin (Eds.), *Advances in clinical child psychology* (Vol. 4, pp. 167–198). New York: Plenum.

Stuart, R. (1971). Behavioral contracting with families of delinquents. *Journal of Behavior Therapy and Experimental Psychiatry, 2,* 1–11.

Stumme, V., Gresham, F. M., & Scott, N. (1982). Validity of social behavior assessment in discriminating emotionally disabled from nonhandicapped students. *Journal of Behavioral Assessment, 4,* 327–341.

Swanson, H. L., & Malone, S. (1992). Social skills and learning disabilities: A meta-analysis of the literature. *School Psychology Review, 21,* 427–443.

Walker, H. M., & McConnell, S. (1988). *Walker-McConnell Scale of Social Competence and School Adjustment.* Austin, TX: PRO-ED.

Weissberg, R., Caplan, M., & Harwood, R. (1991). Promoting competency-enhancing environments: A systems-based perspective on primary prevention. *Journal of Consulting and Clinical Psychology, 59,* 830–841.

Wolf, M. M. (1978). Social validity: The case for subjective measurement or how applied behavior analysis is finding its heart. *Journal of Applied Behavior Analysis, 11,* 203–214.

ANNOTATED BIBLIOGRAPHY

Asher, S. R., & Coie, J. D. (Eds.). (1993). *Peer rejection in childhood.* New York: Cambridge University Press.

This edited volume presents and integrates knowledge about children's peer relationships with a particular focus on peer rejection. The book is composed of 13 chapters, written by leading developmental researchers in the area of peer relationships, that are organized under five headings: (a) behavioral characteristics of peer-rejected children (three chapters), (b) social-cognitive processes (two chapters), (c) parent–child relations and peer rejection (two chapters), (d) consequences of peer rejection (two chapters), and (e) issues in intervention research (two chapters). The book ends with a chapter detailing a developmental theory of peer rejection.

Elliott, S. N., & Gresham, F. M. (1992). *Social skills intervention guide.* Circle Pines, MN: American Guidance Service.

The *Social Skills Intervention Guide* (SSIG) is a systematic approach to teaching social skills to children between the ages of 6 and 16 years. A system for classifying social skills deficits based on acquisition/performance deficits and presence/absence of interfering problem behaviors is described. Implementation issues such as selection and grouping of students, establishing group rules, and a means of monitoring students' progress are described. Social skills training techniques based on instruction, rehearsal, reinforcement, and reductive processes are discussed in relation to accomplishing the objectives of promoting skill acquisition, enhancing skill performance, removing interfering problem behaviors, and facilitating generalization of prosocial behaviors.

Gresham, F. M., & Elliott, S. N. (1990). *Social Skills Rating System.* Circle Pines, MN: American Guidance Service.

The *Social Skills Rating System* (SSRS) is a broad, multirater assessment of student social behaviors that can affect teacher–student relations, peer acceptance, and academic performance. The SSRS is a nationally standardized, norm-referenced series of teacher, parent, and self-report rating scales for children and adolescents between the ages of 3 and 18 years. Norms are stratified into three developmental levels: preschool (ages 3–5 years), elementary (ages 5–12 years), and secondary (ages 13–18 years). The SSRS measures social skills in the domains of cooperation, assertion, responsibility, empathy, and self- control and interfering problem behaviors in the areas of externalizing, internalizing, and hyperactivity problems. The teacher scale also includes a rating measure of academic performance.

Hansen, D. J. (Ed.). (1993). Social-skills assessment and intervention with children and adolescents. [Special issue]. *Behavior Modification, 17*(3), 227–366.

This special issue discusses the evolving data base and best practices in social skills assessment and intervention. Five articles written by leading researchers in the field of social skills assessment and training are included; they address the following topics: (a) developmental issues in social skills assessment and intervention (b) assessing acceptance and social skills with peers, (c) social skills interventions with children, (d) social skills interventions with adolescents, and (e) assessing and enhancing generalization and social validity of social skills interventions.

Walker, H. M., Todis, B., Holmes, D., & Horton, G. (1988). *The Walker Social Skills Curriculum: The ACCESS Program*. Austin, TX: PRO-ED.
This curriculum is designed for adolescents with mild handicaps and is based on principles of direct instruction. The ACCESS program teaches 31 social skills distributed across three broad social skills domains: (a) peer-related social skills, (b) adult-related social skills, and (c) self-related social skills. The curriculum is designed for small-group (five or fewer) instruction and uses scripted lessons.

87

Best Practices in Working with Students with Autism

Lorna Volmer
Heartland AEA, Iowa

OVERVIEW

Students with autism have a diagnosis that is associated with a medical model (Reschly, 1992), although the diagnosis may be made by professionals in a variety of settings. Although the diagnosis is medical, problem solving provides a useful approach to the difficulties faced by these students. The problem-solving approach currently is being embraced over the classification system because diagnostic categorization has not enhanced treatment (Reschly, 1992). However, in working with students with autism, the problem-solving approach and a diagnosis complement each other: The diagnosis of autism creates an understanding of the unique characteristics of the student as well as interventions that can be used most effectively. The diagnosis also can be vitally important to families as they seek support and begin to understand the long-term implications.

For students with autism, the diagnosis is a critical step in developing appropriate educational interventions. These students perceive the world differently from the majority of the population. To teach them effectively, educators must acknowledge those differences and set up an environment that enables them to learn. Although the typical environment in the schools is not necessarily well suited for students with autism, it can be adapted to suit their needs. The diagnosis of autism does not predict an educational program. Interventions or programs should always consider the needs of the student; however, the diagnosis does suggest several strategies that have been successful with autistic students (Landrus & Mesibov, 1986; Szatmari, 1991).

The diagnosis can be important to educators and to families. The family of a student with autism shares with the families of other developmentally disabled individuals many frustrations and stresses. Yet families with an autistic child typically have borne a greater degree of misunderstanding and blame than other families (Cutler & Kozloff, 1987). These families have to deal on a daily basis with a child who may not be able to communicate wants and needs, has bizarre and ritualistic behaviors, and may not recognize dangers. They are forced to adopt a lifestyle that is generally far different from what family members would otherwise choose. Educators can help families understand that they are not to blame for their child's disorder. They can also help the family understand the implications of autism, link them to support systems, and help them understand how to implement at home interventions that are successful in the school setting. Families, in turn, can help educators understand idiosyncrasies of their child as well as techniques that have been useful in the home environment. The student ultimately will benefit from a cooperative and mutually supportive effort between educators and families.

Characteristics of Autism

The diagnostic criteria for autism have changed somewhat since those detailed by pioneer Leo Kanner (1943). The changes have reflected evolving concepts of the disorder, and have not been universally accepted (Szatmari, 1992). The DSM-III criteria (American Psychiatric Association, [APA], 1980) were criticized as too restrictive (Volkmar, Cohen, & Paul, 1986), while Szatmari (1992) suggested that the DSM-III-R (APA, 1987) criteria may lack specificity, and thus incorrectly overidentify students as having autism.

While the subtleties of the criteria for autism are debated, authorities agree that three areas of developmental difference exist. Wing (1991) noted that "both the World Health Organization (WHO) and the American Psychiatric Association (APA) emphasize the importance for the diagnosis of impairments of social interaction and communication and the presence of repetitive stereotyped routines" (p. 105). Additionally, Rutter and Schopler (1988) stressed that it is the deviance in the developmental process that sets autism apart from other disorders. Impaired language and socialization may be found in mentally retarded individuals or children with communication disorders, yet, while those individuals may demonstrate delay, they do not demonstrate the pattern of deviance that is distinctive to autism. Individuals with mental retardation or communication disorders also are unlikely to have significant repetitive stereotypical routines. Students with schizophrenia may show an assortment of bizarre behaviors but not the same deviance of language and social development that is characteristic of autism (Rutter & Schopler, 1988).

Impairment in reciprocal social interactions. Of the three characteristics of autism, several authors indicated that the qualitative impairment in reciprocal social interactions is the essential feature of the disorder (Frith, 1989; Gillberg, 1990). Kanner (1943) suggested that children with autism were happiest when left alone to engage in solitary activities. Young children with autism may not respond differentially to strangers and may act as if people, including their own parents, are not important. This contrasts markedly with the importance of social relationships for most children. It also contrasts with the sensitivity displayed by many children with autism to very small changes in their physical environment or in their routines. Social impairments can take many forms, and include a lack of awareness that others exist (for younger and lower functioning students) to interacting with others only in terms of the child's own obsessive interests (a characteristic demonstrated by older, less impaired students). The DSM-III-R (APA, 1987) delineates examples of how this impairment in social interactions is manifested; however, the key issue is not just that children with autism are socially isolated, but that they are very limited in the degree they are able to modify their social behavior to meet the demands of the environment (Gillberg, 1990).

Impairment in verbal and nonverbal communication. A second important feature is impairment in verbal and nonverbal communication (Gillberg, 1990). Some individuals with autism never develop speech (Paul, 1987), but even students who become verbally fluent have significant receptive and expressive communication differences. Kanner (1943) indicated that children with autism fail to use speech for communicative purposes. He also commented on the echoic repetition of whole phrases, pronominal reversals, primarily involving the child's reference to him or herself as "you," and of a literalness in interpretation (Kanner, 1943). Some very capable students with autism demonstrate more subtle communication deficits than those described by Kanner. They may exhibit large vocabularies and reasonable grammar. Some are described as talking like grownups in early childhood, although they tend to ramble. Very able students with autism are referred to as high-functioning. The term *high-functioning* describes individuals who have a diagnosis of autism and who also score within the average range on standardized intelligence tests; the usual intellectual quotient cutoff score mentioned is about 70 on either a verbal or performance measure (Szatmari, 1991; Yirmiya & Sigman, 1991).

For high-functioning individuals with autism, initiating and sustaining a conversation seems to be especially problematic. Language is used not for social interaction but as a means to a particular concrete end (Szatmari, 1991). Additionally, the speech of very verbal high-functioning individuals with autism, sometimes referred to as having Asperger's syndrome, is characterized by a lack of inflection in sentences, and conversation that is tangential, off the point, and circumstantial. Because few links are provided among thoughts in a conversation, the overall effect lacks cohesion (Szatmari, 1991).

Restricted repertoire of activities and interests. The third area of deviance that must exist for a student to be diagnosed as having autism concerns markedly restricted, repetitive, and stereotyped patterns of behaviors and interests (APA, 1987). The meaning of the tendency to impose rigidity and routine on a wide range of everyday occurrences remains obscure, and the ways in which the stereotypical patterns are evidenced vary (Rutter & Schopler, 1988). They may be reflected in distress over changes in small details of the environment, stereotypical and repetitive motor mannerisms, persistent preoccupation with parts of objects, attachment to unusual objects, compulsive rituals, and a markedly restricted range of interests as well as a preoccupation with one narrow interest. Specific examples of these patterns are detailed in the DSM-III-R (APA, 1987), but it is important to realize that the extreme interest can develop in subjects such as astronomy, meteorology, wrestling, or rock videos. The interests can shade into the interests of normal children. However, while such interests typically are used to interact with others, the individual with autism engages in the solitary interests for the sake of the interests, not as a means to interact (Szatmari, 1991).

The symptoms that comprise the triad of impairments in autism occur on a continuum. Wing (1991) has detailed the continuum concept by providing concrete examples of the manifestations of autism for eight symptoms on a four-point scale, ranging from most severe to least severe. For example, a very severely affected individual would demonstrate no formal language system. The most severe manifestation shades to somewhat less affected individuals who demonstrate limited formal language that is mostly echolalic. That level shades into individuals who demonstrate an incorrect use of pronouns and prepositions and idiosyncratic use of words and phrases. The least affected individuals use grammatically correct language but are long-winded and repetitive, and provide very literal interpretations (Wing, 1991).

BASIC CONSIDERATIONS

It is time to refute forever the notion that autism is caused by psychodynamic conflicts between mother and child! Autism has a biological cause. The exact nature of the cause is not known, but there is evidence for several contributing factors: genetic, pre- or perinatal brain damage, and immune dysfunction and/or viral infection (Frith, 1989). There appears to be no single biological cause, but rather a causal chain that produces varying degrees of harm. The basis of the disorder is important because parents need reassurance that their parenting in no way contributed to their child's having autism.

Role of the School Psychologist

Most, if not all, practicing school psychologists will encounter and serve students with autism. Research has demonstrated that autism occurs in somewhere between four to five children in 10,000 (APA, 1987) to one in every 1,000 children (Frith, 1989). What is the role of the school psychologist in serving these students? First, it may be to recognize students who reflect the triad of difficulties and refer them elsewhere for evaluation, or, if appropriate, base interventions on strategies that would be effective for a child with autism. Recognizing the subtle characteristics in higher-functioning students is especially difficult, but experience matters in making the diagnosis of autism at any level of functioning. Interpreting the significance of different, absent, or delayed behaviors depends on a sound clinical background and experience in autism. Making the diagnosis is not a reasonable expectation for all school psychologists, but recognizing the range of manifestations of autism is reasonable.

A second role for school psychologists is that of assessment. Behavioral assessment is the cornerstone of assessment when working with students with autism. Additionally, Reschly (1990) has emphasized the relevance of assessing adaptive behaviors for all students who are handicapped. It is certainly important to do so for students with autism, and it is vital to do so in adolescence as part of transition planning. The Scales of Independent Behavior (SIB), completed with parents or parent surrogates as respondents, have proved to be particularly helpful. The SIB assesses both adaptive and problem behaviors. It also provides prompts for discussing training objectives that the respondent would like to see implemented in each of the fourteen adaptive behavior areas. Completing the SIB affords an excellent opportunity for the respondent and psychologist to discuss goals and objectives in a structured format. Parents generally appreciate this opportunity to provide input, and a cooperative relationship is fostered.

The third role for school psychologists is that of providing consultation services. Any psychologist trained in behavioral consultation possesses most of the skills required to help in the classroom and at home. Consultation skills and a willingness to be of service are the only requisites to working with students with autism. An increased understanding of autism and training in the strategies and techniques that have proven to be helpful with these students do, however, increase the effectiveness and ease of interventions.

BEST PRACTICES

Schopler and Mesibov (1988) stress that children with autism perceive the world differently than do the majority of the population. To help them adapt, educational approaches should acknowledge and accommodate those differences. Students with autism have significant deficits in comprehending language (Cox, 1991a), so it is important to provide visual cues. Schopler and Mesibov (1988), like other teacher trainers and professionals in the field of autism, also discussed the fact that students with autism respond well to structure. Landrus and Mesibov (1986) operationally defined the important components that lend structure to the classroom environment while providing the visual cues that students with autism require. The components provide an approach to teaching students with autism that helps reduce behavior problems while developing independence in the students: Structured Teaching.

Structured Teaching

The student with autism will have fewer behavior problems and experience greater independence and success if the classroom is structured and organized and provides visual cues that help make expectations clear. The structure, organization, and visual cues are provided by Structured Teaching. Structured Teaching uses physical organization, scheduling, and specific teaching methods to promote success. While it is important to emphasize crucial elements of structure, all aspects of a student's environment and educational program are tailored to the needs of each student (Landrus & Mesibov, 1986).

Physical organization. The physical arrangement of the room can help a student be more independent and more compliant. Students with autism often have serious organizational problems and, because of comprehension difficulties, may not understand rules or directions. Additionally, most are very distractible. The physical organization of the classroom can help with these problems. Lower-functioning and younger students, as well as those with less self-control, will need more structure, boundaries, and cues than higher-functioning and older students. Having specific areas for various learning activities, marking clear boundaries, and making materials easily accessible helps students know where they are to be and permits them to get their own materials (Landrus & Mesibov, 1986).

A classroom for young students requires different areas for play, teaching, independent work, snack, and developing self-help skills (Landrus & Mesibov,

1986). A classroom for older students who require a special education classroom for much of the day typically has a leisure area, a work area, a domestic skills area, a grooming area, and places for individual teaching (Landrus & Mesibov, 1986). Additionally, classrooms need a place for students to put their personal belongings and an established place for the teacher's desk. Large rooms with totally separate areas for each activity are the ideal, but are uncommon. However, the key is to use visual cues to make expectations clear. If a room contains one table and it must serve multiple purposes, then it is important for the student to be able to discriminate visually each activity. For snack time there could be a sign that says "Snack" and a tray with the students' drinking glasses on the table. Art time at the same table could be differentiated by a sign saying "Art" and a pile of protective shirts that would subsequently be worn by the students. It is a good idea to provide the printed word and another visual cue that can be understood by nonreaders. Labeling the environment gives students with autism the opportunity to acquire reading skills in a very natural and meaningful way, and some children with autism learn to read and write before they communicate verbally.

In establishing the different areas in a classroom, consider the natural attributes of the room. Children with autism are distractible, so independent work areas need to minimize distractions. Having the desk face a blank wall can be effective, as can providing the student with a study carrel. Landrus and Mesibov (1986) also point out that "areas where students spend some independent time, such as play or leisure, are better off not being located near exits. This can take away a bit of worry about student 'escape' from the teacher's mind" (p. 3). The play area for younger children requires clear and sturdy boundaries that provide a safe environment for energetic little people. Play area boundaries can include walls, shelves for toys, or child-sized pretend sinks and appliances. Because of the nature of activities in a play area, boundaries need to be sturdy. In other areas, clear visual cues are often all that is needed. Rugs or tape on the floor can let a child know where he or she is to sit for story time or where to stand for washing hands or dishes. For the student with autism in a regular education classroom, a bit of tape can help him or her understand where to form lines or sit during group times. Another accommodation that can be helpful to the student in a regular education classroom is an additional desk for independent work. The student sits in a desk with classmates for group instruction and activities but can go to his or her other desk, situated to minimize distractions, to complete assigned tasks.

Schedules. Schedules and routines are both important because they provide a student with structure, understanding, and predictability. Classroom routines are good, but are not a substitute for schedules. Checking the daily schedule should become part of the student's routine; it is the schedule that provides flexibility. Students with autism typically do not accept changes in routine well, yet the day-to-day activities in classrooms do change. The student with autism will be able to accept those changes more easily if checking a schedule has become part of the student's routine, if the changes are on the schedule, and if the schedule is at a communication level that matches the level of the student.

We all depend on our personal schedules; they tell us who we are to see, what we are to do, where we are to be, and when we are to be there. The use of schedules for students with autism basically has the same function, but the communication system can vary. High-functioning students who read well are good candidates for written schedules. Students who do not yet read fluently benefit from a pictorial representation. The picture can be a line drawing (artistry is not critical — stick figures are very adequate) or a photograph, usually used with younger children who are learning the concept of schedules. The lowest level of schedule is an object schedule. The object schedule is helpful for young students, who must first learn that an item in hand can represent an event that will occur.

Children are often first started on an object schedule; they then move to a photo schedule, and the photo is frequently combined with a word, called a photo/word schedule. The next step is the line drawing schedule, again often combined with a word. Finally, there is the word system, similar to what we all use in our daily lives. An example of this progression would be to start by handing a child a diaper, to indicate that it is time to change a diaper. For a child on a picture schedule, a photo of the speech pathologist could indicate that it was time for speech, while a line drawing of a sink and dishes could indicate that it was time to do the dishes. The schedule that seems easiest for the teacher is the written word, but the system is supposed to enable the child to be independent. Thus, however tempting it may be, a written schedule should be used only when the student reads well.

Many classrooms use two types of schedules simultaneously — a general class schedule and an individual student schedule (Landrus & Mesibov, 1986). The general class schedule indicates what the teacher has planned for the entire class, while the schedule for an individual student would also note when the child was to see the speech pathologist and specifically what that child was to do.

Schedules can be individualized in many ways. As noted already, there are object schedules, two kinds of picture schedules, and written schedules. Schedules also differ in the time period they span. Some schedules list activities for the entire day, while others deal with short spans of time (Cox, 1991b). An example of the use of schedules for a young student might be to have the child's individual schedule on a clipboard he or she carries. The child's routine has him or her first put coat and book bag away and then check the schedule. The schedule might have a photograph of the play area first, so the child could turn that picture over and proceed to the play area. At the end of free play the child would be told again to check the schedule. The next photograph might be of the work station. Again, the child would turn the photograph over and go to the work area. At the student's independent work area there might be a strip of poster board with colored geometric shapes clipped to it in a vertical row. The student learns to take the topmost shape and match it to the same shape basket on work area shelves by his or her desk. The shape is turned over to indicate completion, and the basket is replaced on the shelf when the child has completed each task; this process is continued until all the shapes have been turned. The child then checks the schedule and finds a picture of the computer, so proceeds to the computer (a very much preferred activity).

An important point of good scheduling is the alternating of less preferred and more preferred activities. This employs the Premack principle, where the opportunity to do more preferred activities is contingent upon the completion of less preferred activities. The Premack principle, or First/Then sequencing, is a powerful way to maintain motivation in students. A final point about scheduling is that children need to be taught to use schedules.

Teaching methods. Teaching methods involve the use of visual cues to provide directions and prompts to the student (Landrus & Mesibov, 1986). In American classrooms, directions are usually given verbally; for the student with autism they also need to be given visually, at least to a large degree. Most important, directions always need to be given at the student's level of understanding. For example, to a child with limited expressive language, do not say "I want you to finish coloring the picture, and then when you finish, you can go select a game to play on the computer." Instead, minimize words, which can be confusing to the student with autism, and say, "First finish picture, then computer." Verbal directions should be accompanied by gestures and visual cues to help the student understand (Landrus & Mesibov, 1986). In the example above, the teacher could show the student the same picture, already colored, point to the child's uncolored picture, then point to the computer. Using gestures, as verbal directions are being given, helps the student with autism understand.

An important aspect of giving directions is having the student's attention prior to giving the direction (Landrus & Mesibov, 1986). For a student with autism this does not mean that eye contact must be established, but it does mean that the student needs to signal attention. That may be accomplished by body orientation, a verbal response, or by stopping other activities. "When giving directions, a teacher needs to make sure that expectations and consequences are clear and organized for the student. If a student does not know where materials are, how to start a task, or what to do when he is finished, then he is not likely to perform a task up to teacher standards" (Landrus & Mesibov, 1986, p. 9).

There are many ways to use visual cues and organizational strategies to help students with autism understand what is necessary to complete a task. For an adolescent, a laundry basket with several items of clothing to be ironed and an iron and ironing board convey quite clearly that ironing needs to be done. The goal is always to convey visually to the student four things: How much work? What work? When is the work done? and What is the reward for doing the work? (Landrus & Mesibov, 1986; Cox, 1991b). The laundry basket example clearly conveyed the first three things. Adding a picture of a can of pop or a computer would also indicate the reward. Organizational strategies that are helpful include working from right to left and from top to bottom (Cox, 1991b). Those strategies are equally applicable to washing floors, cleaning mirrors, vacuuming, reading, or doing work sheets.

As demonstrated with schedules, visual cues can be provided at several different levels. If one wanted to convey to a high-functioning teen all that needed to be done to clean a bathroom at home, a written list could be provided, and the student could check off each item cleaned. For a student not able to read, the same thing could be achieved pictorially by having a photo or line drawing of the mirror, sink, tub, toilet, and floor. An alternative, for a student who had previously learned a cleaning routine and who needed minimal prompting, would be to put the containers of glass cleaner, scouring powder or solution, toilet bowl cleaner, a detergent for the floor, and sponges all in the bathroom that was to be cleaned.

Visual cues are very helpful for students with autism, but these students still need direct instruction for new tasks. The visual cues help them to organize, sequence, and stay focused, but tasks need to be taught to the student with autism. In teaching tasks, or the use of visual cues, prompts help assure accuracy. A physical prompt involves physically assisting a student through the motions of the task; a visual prompt can take a variety of forms. It might be a plate, knife, fork, spoon, and drinking glass drawn on a placemat to assist in table setting, a list of two or three rules taped to a student's desk, or a gesture to point out a spot remaining on a mirror being cleaned. The final level of prompt is verbal. In using prompts, or giving other directions to students, you want to tell them what to do, not what not to do. Thus, if a rule were taped to a student's desk reminding the child not to swear, it should say something like "Use appropriate language." Prompts need to be clear, consistent, and directed to the student before an incorrect response occurs (Landrus & Mesibov, 1986). If a student used too much detergent when preparing to wash dishes, it is not helpful to say, "No, you used too much detergent. Only use a little next time." Far better is to say, as the student picks up the detergent on the next occasion, "Use only a little detergent, just enough to fill this lid." Then give the student a way to approximate the amount and help him or her measure the soap accurately. After several days of that sort of prompting, the student will be independent at the task (Landrus & Mesibov, 1986).

Students with autism need visual cues and structure. However, there are other programming considerations. School psychologists routinely work with teachers to target behaviors for change. In working with students with autism, special attention is warranted in selecting and prioritizing behaviors. For behaviors that are a part of autism and that are not a high priority in the developmental sequence of skill acquisition nor critical to the student's functioning, it may be appropriate to delay targeting the behavior, and instead focus on the most critical skills. Cases where target behaviors might be delayed include lack of eye contact in a young student or harmless and discrete self-stimulatory shirt rubbing in a low-functioning student. Additional programming considerations include the following general needs of young and lower-functioning students with autism: small classrooms; a curriculum designed to enhance communication skills; special training in leisure and prevocational skills; the appropriate use of behavior theory for managing behavior problems — especially an emphasis on an environment structured to promote success and on reinforcement of positive behaviors, rather than punishment of negative behaviors; and attention to problems of generalization (Schopler & Mesibov, 1988).

All students with autism need interventions to improve their adaptive skills and reduce symptoms that limit participation in normal activities. Rutter (1985) has suggested that it is not helpful to adopt a rigid response to diagnostic labels — to assume that because a child is diagnosed as having autism, the only suitable educational placement is a unit for other children with autism. Instead, Rutter (1985) and Szatmari (1991) believed that it is critical to maintain higher-functioning students in situations where they are integrated with nonhandicapped students. Szatmari (1991) indicated that a program without integration would produce very slow progress and perhaps inappropriate behavior. However, he cautioned that integrations require careful planning and extra resources. Szatmari (1991) discussed the educational programming needs of high-functioning students with autism more specifically by noting "areas that may require intervention include training in socialization, communication, and imagination, adaptive skills, and controlling aggressive behavior" (p. 89). Experience

suggests that a wide range of students with autism can be integrated successfully into regular education classes by employing structure and visual cues.

Behavior Management

The management of behavior is a part of all teaching, and teaching children with autism is no exception. But there are some different considerations in working with children with autism. Behavior modification techniques look at antecedents to a behavior but typically focus on the consequences of a behavior. For students with autism, the focus needs to be on the antecedents to the behavior and skill deficits that can characterize autism. If such a student has tantrums, it may be because of the receptive or expressive communication deficits; consequently, the intervention should focus on giving the student a more functional communication system. If a student with autism were not handing work in to the teacher, it would be important to consider the possibility of both an organizational problem and a social/communication problem. Some students with autism have difficulty initiating an interaction with the teacher to hand in an assignment. If that were the case, the only needed intervention might be to provide a basket where the student could place completed papers. Lots of praise and a corrective "no" with redirection are important techniques to influence the student with autism or any student. Certainly, positive reinforcement and mild punishment are effective strategies for students with autism (Schopler, Reichler, & Lansing, 1980). But for the student with autism, the focus of interventions needs to be on providing adequate structure and visual cues while understanding how autism may be affecting behavior.

Social Skills Training

Gresham (1990) has established the need to do social skills training for handicapped students, while Wooten and Mesibov (1986) have discussed that need in students with autism. Because the general topic of social skills training is thoroughly discussed by Gresham (1995) in this book, comments here are limited to those that pertain directly to working with students with autism. Students with autism have more trouble generalizing social skills than do other students, so social skills training with this population should focus on the generalization of skills. I have found it effective to positively reinforce the targeted skill(s) across several settings, in a cooperative effort with teachers, the speech pathologist, and parents. The additional efforts in assuring generalization of skills has meant that fewer skills, typically only four to six, were targeted in a year.

Wooten and Mesibov (1986) have used nonhandicapped peer tutors to do social skills training. Their approach, which met with success, also enhanced the generalization of skills. Cox and Schopler (1991) have emphasized that one of the major benefits of programs that use peer tutors is the change in the peer tutors. They note "one quickly develops an appreciation for the change in peer tutors' sensitivity to, acceptance of, and openness with their paired handicapped participant" (1991, p. 908). To improve the skills of the student with autism while helping nonhandicapped peers gain sensitivity and acceptance would be ideal!

Facilitated Communication

Facilitated communication (FC) is included in this section because an awareness of it is vital for psychologists dealing with students with autism. Basically, the technique involves a facilitator supporting the hand, wrist, elbow, or shoulder of the person with autism, or other disability, while he or she selects letters on a letter board, computer keyboard, or typewriter. The facilitator initially may help isolate the index finger and stabilize the hand of the person being assisted, but is not to aid in letter selection. The ultimate goal is to fade the use of the facilitator so the student is able to type independently (Wheeler, Jacobson, Paglieri, & Schwartz, 1992). The technique was pioneered in Australia, but has been refined in this country and enjoys a great deal of support from many enthusiastic parents and educators (Saks, 1992). However, research examining the validity of FC is less glowing than are the anecdotal reports. The research supports two major conclusions. First, it makes it "fairly clear that at least some, and possibly many, facilitators are unknowingly influencing (or producing) the communications that they believe to represent the individual's free expression" (Wheeler et al., 1992, p. 3). It is important to note here that there is no evidence that facilitator influence is purposeful or intentional! Second, some people do clearly benefit from FC and become skilled in independent, unassisted typing (Wheeler et al., 1992). The benefit to these individuals is clear. Additionally, "there may be secondary gains for people from increased socialization with facilitators, and perhaps, among peers if conversations are facilitated with peers" (Wheeler et al., 1992, p. 3).

This is currently one of the most controversial topics in the field of autism, if not the most. No one wants to deny a child every opportunity for success, yet no one wants to raise false hopes. The conclusion of the research — that FC helps some individuals become skilled, independent typists — raises a related point. Whether through FC, trial and error, keyboarding or typing classes, or independent study, typing skills and use of a computer can make an enormous difference in the written communication skills of high-functioning students with autism. The written language skills of many of these students are a problem, for various reasons. However, many have significantly improved their fluency and technical ade-

quacy when allowed to do writing assignments on the computer. Additionally, they have become less averse to writing; some even have found pleasure in it.

SUMMARY

Autism is a biologically based disorder that is characterized by qualitative impairments in reciprocal social interactions, qualitative impairment in verbal and nonverbal communication, and a markedly restricted repertoire of activities and interests.

The problem-solving approach is very effective in dealing with the difficulties faced by students with autism. However, in planning interventions, one must make sure that the classroom environment provides the structure and visual cues that are necessary accommodations for the student with autism. When behavior problems do occur, skill or performance deficits that are characteristic of autism may be the cause. In those cases, sometimes a skill, such as a different communication system, should be taught. At other times — such as with the student who would not initiate contact with a teacher to hand in assignments — a performance deficit can be overcome by finding a way to achieve the goal in a different manner. An alternative strategy would have been to positively reinforce compliance and mildly punish noncompliance; but in working with students with autism, it is preferable to save that strategy and use it only when an alternative strategy is not available. Finally, there are some behaviors that are a part of autism and not a priority in the developmental sequence of skill acquisition. The lack of eye contact in a young student with autism might well be such a behavior. It should be addressed at some point, but might not be a high-priority behavior to target immediately.

Most, if not all, practicing school psychologists will encounter and serve students with autism. The school psychologist has the skills to be of service to these intriguing students and their families.

REFERENCES

American Psychiatric Association. (1980). *Diagnostic and statistical manual of mental disorders.* Washington, DC: Author.

American Psychiatric Association. (1987). *Diagnostic and statistical manual of mental disorders* (3rd ed., rev.). Washington, DC: Author.

Cox, R. (1991a, March). *Characteristics of students with autism.* Week-long TEACCH Training conducted for Heartland AEA, Des Moines, IA.

Cox, R. (1991b, March). *Structured Teaching.* Week-long TEACCH Training conducted for Heartland AEA, Des Moines, IA.

Cox, R. D., & Schopler, E. (1991). Social skills training for children. In M. Lewis (Ed.), *Child and adolescent psychiatry: A comprehensive textbook* (pp. 903–909). Baltimore: Williams & Wilkins.

Cutler, B. C., & Kozloff, M. A. (1987). Living with autism: Effects on families and family needs. In D. J. Cohen & A. M. Donnellan

(Eds.), *Handbook of autism and pervasive developmental disorders* (pp. 513–527). New York: Wiley.

Frith, U. (1989). *Autism: Explaining the enigma.* Cambridge, MA: Basil Blackwell.

Gillberg, C. (1990). Infantile autism: Diagnosis and treatment. *Acta Psychiatrica Scandinavica, 81*(3), 209–215.

Gresham, F. M. (1900). Best practices in social skills training. In A. Thomas & J. Grimes (Eds.), *Best practices in school psychology–II* (pp. 29–42). Washington, DC: National Association of School Psychologists.

Gresham, F. M. (1995). Best practices in social skills training. In A. Thomas & J. Grimes (Eds.), *Best practices in school psychology–III*. Silver Spring, MD: National Association of School Psychologists.

Kanner, L. (1943). Autistic disturbances of affective contact. *Nervous Child, 2,* 217–250.

Landrus, R. I., & Mesibov, G. B. (1986). *Structured Teaching.* Unpublished manuscript. University of North Carolina, Division TEACCH, Chapel Hill.

Paul, R. (1987). Communication. In D. J. Cohen & A. M. Donnellan (Eds.), *Handbook of autism and pervasive developmental delays.* New York: Wiley.

Reschly, D. J. (1990). Best practices in adaptive behavior. In A. Thomas & J. Grimes (Eds.), *Best practices in school psychology–II* (pp. 29–42). Washington, DC: National Association of School Psychologists.

Reschly, D. J. (1992). *Classification of students for special education: Alternative models and criteria.* Policy Analysis Paper Developed for the California Department of Education, July, 1990. (Revised September, 1992)

Rutter, M. (1985). The treatment of autistic children. *Journal of Child Psychology and Psychiatry, 26,* 193–214.

Rutter, M., & Schopler, E. (1988). Autism and pervasive developmental disorders: Concepts and diagnostic issues. In E. Schopler & G. B. Mesibov (Eds.), *Diagnosis and assessment in autism* (pp. 2–33). New York: Plenum Press.

Saks, J. B. (1992). New approach stirs hope, controversy. *Counterpoint, 13,* 1, 7.

Schopler, E., & Mesibov, G. B. (1988). Overview of diagnosis and assessment in autism. In E. Schopler & G. B. Mesibov (Eds.), *Diagnosis and assessment in autism* (pp. 2–33). New York: Plenum Press.

Schopler, E., Reichler, R. J., & Lansing, M. (1980). *Individualized assessment and treatment for developmentally disabled children.* Austin, TX: PRO-ED.

Szatmari, P. (1991). Asperger's syndrome: Diagnosis, treatment, and outcome. *Psychiatric Clinics of North America, 14,* 81–93.

Szatmari, P. (1992). A review of the DSM-III-R criteria for autistic disorder. *Journal of Autism and Developmental Disorders, 22,* 507–523.

Volkmar, F., Cohen, D. J., & Paul, R. (1986). An evaluation of DSM-III criteria for infantile autism. *Journal of the American Academy of Child Psychiatry, 25,* 190–197.

Wheeler, D. L., Jacobson, J. W., Paglieri, R. A., & Schwartz, A. A. (1992). *An experimental assessment of facilitated communication* (TR # 92–TA1). Schenectady, NY: O. D. Heck/ER DDSO.

Wing, L. (1991). The relationship between Asperger's syndrome and Kanner's autism. In U. Frith (Ed.), *Autism and Asperger syndrome* (p. 122–146). Cambridge, MA: Cambridge University Press.

Wooten, M., & Mesibov, G. B. (1986). Social skills training for elementary school autistic children with normal peers. In E. Schopler & G. B. Mesibov (Eds.), *Social behavior in autism* (pp. 305–319). New York: Plenum Press.

Yirmiya, N., & Sigman, M. (1991). High-functioning individuals with autism: Diagnosis, empirical findings, and theoretical issues. *Clinical Psychology Review, 11,* 669–683.

ANNOTATED BIBLIOGRAPHY

Cohen, D. J., & Donnellan, A. M. (Eds.). (1987). *Handbook of autism and pervasive developmental delays.* New York: Wiley. Leaders in the field discuss the behavioral and biological characteristics of "autistic syndromes," behavioral and medical interventions, as well as societal issues affecting individuals with autism and their families.

Schopler, E., & Mesibov, G. B. (Eds.). (1983). *Autism in adolescents and adults.* New York: Plenum Press. Leaders in the field of autism discuss some of the unique difficulties faced by adolescents and adults with autism. Topics include recreation and leisure needs, sex education, the management of aggressive behavior, stress and coping in families, medical needs, legal needs, and social and interpersonal needs.

Schopler, E., & Mesibov, G. B. (Eds.). (1988). *Diagnosis and assessment in autism.* New York: Plenum Press. Major contributors to the field of autism discuss important diagnostic issues and delineate assessment considerations. The validity of intellectual assessment is addressed, a variety of instruments and approaches are described, and the assessment of special groups (adolescents, preschoolers, and low-functioning children) is included.

Schopler, E., Reichler, R. J., & Lansing, M. (1980). *Individualized assessment and treatment for developmentally disabled children.* Austin, TX: PRO-ED. This book contains numerous, specific suggestions for teaching the student with autism. It details aspects of setting goals and objectives as well as of structuring tasks to help students with specific difficulties. The book also contains an informative chapter on behavior management.

Szatmari, P. (1991). Asperger's syndrome: Diagnosis, treatment, and outcome. *Psychiatric Clinics of North America, 14,* 81–93. The relationship between pervasive developmental disorder not otherwise specified, autism, and Asperger's syndrome (AS) is explored. Szatmari reviews the diagnostic features of AS and delineates the differential diagnosis of autism in high-functioning individuals with autism. A strength of the paper is the emphasis on treatment, including the efficacy of medications.

88

Best Practices in Working with Children with Psychosis

Thomas J. Huberty
Indiana University

OVERVIEW

The terms *psychosis* or *childhood psychosis* refer to a group of psychological/psychiatric disorders that are considered to be the most severe forms of disturbance in children. For the professional, psychosis likely epitomizes "serious emotional disturbance" because of the type and extremes of behavior shown and the degree of impact that behavior has on the social, personal, family, and academic functioning of a child. Children with psychosis present behavioral, academic, and developmental challenges to parents, schools, and others in the attempt to meet their unique needs. This chapter will provide an overview of childhood psychosis with emphasis on describing its characteristics, what the school psychologist should know about working with these children, and suggestions for using a problem-solving approach to develop intervention approaches.

Childhood Psychosis as a Form of Developmental Psychopathology

The traditional approach to understanding children's abnormal behavior, including psychosis, emphasizes a medical model — i.e., one in which the locus of the problem is within the individual — and "look(s) to statistical norms, social rules and values, or various conceptions of ideal psychological adaptation to define standards of normality. Marked deviations from these standards are labeled as pathological or dysfunctional" (Cowan, 1988).

Conversely, *developmental psychopathology* emphasizes the development and change in behavior of the individual over time and factors that place him or her at increased risk for behavioral and emotional problems. Thus, even though a child might be diagnosed as psychotic at one point in time, it is conceivable that the diagnosis might change later, or that the diagnosis might remain but some of the initial behaviors might change or disappear. Developmental psychopathologists are interested in observing and studying changes over time, and do not view the child's behavior as static but as mutable, being a func-

tion of developmental processes and interventions designed to address problem areas. Childhood psychoses represent disorders that will persist throughout life, so the major focus of school psychologists is on the personal, academic, social, and family needs of the child over time. For further information about developmental psychopathology, the reader is referred to Achenbach (1982), Lewis and Miller (1990), and Nannis and Cowan (1988).

Characteristics of Childhood Psychosis

For many years, childhood psychosis comprised the disorders of schizophrenia, infantile autism, symbiotic psychosis, and severe, psychotic depression. It was not until Kanner (1943) described autism as a unique disorder separate from schizophrenia that efforts were intensified to more clearly define the nature of childhood psychosis. Currently, autism is considered to be a developmental disorder, although some of the behaviors may be similar to those seen in schizophrenia. Mahler (1952) described *symbiotic psychosis* as a unique disorder characterized by the psychotic behaviors of intense clinging to the mother, extreme emotional reactions when separated, and little personal identity. However, research has failed to support this distinction, and currently it is not considered to be a separate diagnostic category. Manic-depressive psychosis (now called bipolar disorder) also might be viewed as another category, but this disorder is rare in children and adolescents. Other disorders designated as psychotic (e.g., schizophreniform disorder) or having psychotic features (e.g., major depressive episode) also may occur in less frequent cases. Merrell (1994) includes three Axis I disorders described in the *Diagnostic and Statistical Manual of Mental Disorders*, 3rd ed., rev. (DSM-III-R; American Psychiatric Association, 1987) as representing psychotic disorders that might be seen in childhood or adolescence: schizophrenia, delusional (paranoid) disorder, and Psychotic Disorders Not Elsewhere Classified.

The DSM-III-R does not include a separate category for childhood schizophrenia in "Disorders Usually First Evident in Infancy, Childhood, or Adolescence," although the criteria for adult schizophrenia may be applied to children (p. 27). The DSM-III-R does not, however, apply the term *psychosis* to children's disorders but categorizes them as pervasive developmental disorders (PDD). The stated rationale for this global classification is that only autism has been defined as being a subgroup of PDD, and that childhood psychoses are not related to adult psychoses. The three major characteristics of PDD are "qualitative impairment in reciprocal interaction," "impairment in communication and imaginative skill," and "markedly restricted repertoire of activities and interests" (p. 34).

If adult criteria are applied to childhood psychoses, the characteristic symptoms are dysfunctions in the following areas:

- *Content of thought:* Delusions that may be multiple, fragmented, or bizarre.

- *Form of thought:* Loosening of associations, incoherent or tangential speech shown, or speech that shows poverty of content or communicates little information.

- *Perceptual disturbances:* Hallucinations; sensations of bodily change; hypersensitivity to sound, sight, and smell; illusions; synesthesia.

- *Affect disturbances:* Flat or inappropriate affect.

- *Sense of self disturbances:* Lack of feelings of individuality, uniqueness, and self-direction.

- *Volition:* Disturbance in self-initiated, goal-directed activity.

- *Impaired interpersonal functioning and relationship to the external world:* Difficulty with interpersonal relationships.

- *Psychomotor behavior difficulties:* Marked decrease in activity, spontaneous movements, and reactivity to the environment.

Clarizio and McCoy (1983) provide a list of "clinical manifestations" that are secondary characteristics of children with psychosis: bizarre body movements; repetitive, stereotypic movements; distorted use of body parts; nonhuman behaviors such as making animal noises; disturbances in speech structure and content; denial of the human quality of others; inappropriate affect, ranging from rather flat to explosive; special interest in a particular object or activity (such as remembering detailed statistics on sports figures); and a distorted sense of time, including difficulty in separating the present from the past or the future (pp. 360–361).

Rosenhan and Seligman (1989) differentiate Type I and Type II schizophrenia. Type I is described as manifesting "positive symptoms" — e.g., delusions, hallucinations, and prominent thought disorders —

which are reversible. Type II is described as showing "negative symptoms" — e.g., flat affect, poverty of speech, and loss of volition — which are not amenable to change. Type II schizophrenia has a much poorer prognosis than does Type I, and is associated with challenging, long-term care needs.

Cullinan, Epstein, and Lloyd (1983) list other characteristics associated with childhood schizophrenia:

- Ratio of 3:1, male to female

- Occurrence of about 1 in 1,000 live births

- Generally, low-average level of intelligence

- Earlier age of onset more likely to be associated with mental retardation

- Likelihood of a family history of schizophrenia, which may include a genetic basis

- Tendency to come from lower socioeconomic backgrounds

There have been many theories about the causes of childhood schizophrenia (including unresponsive and unattached mothers, chaotic environments, and neurological/neurochemical abnormalities), which are too extensive for discussion here. The predominant research suggests that the causes of most psychoses likely are based in neurochemical imbalances, specifically disruptions in neurotransmitters such as dopamine. Other theories suggest that there may be a specific gene or set of genes that lead to schizophrenia, or that an individual has a genetic predisposition for schizophrenia that emerges only when particular stressful conditions occur (i.e., the diathesis-stress model) (Rosenthal, 1970). Regardless of the causes of childhood psychosis, the most practical considerations for the school psychologist or other professional will involve working to improve the child's social, behavioral, and academic functioning.

BASIC CONSIDERATIONS

Impact of Childhood Psychosis

Academic performance. Children with psychosis often achieve less in most subject areas than their peers. Success in many school tasks requires sustained attention, concentration, and interest in objects and events beyond oneself, which are some of the abilities that the child with psychosis often lacks. Although the measured intelligence of these children can range from retarded to superior levels, most show lower than average ability. Performance in the classroom on a daily basis can be problematic, due to difficulties in responding to abstract material, receptive and expressive language problems, and lesser ability to participate. Most of these children receive special education services during their educational careers, either in separate classes or on a consultation basis. In general, children with schizophrenia or other forms of psychosis tend to be difficult to teach and to have learning problems (Clarizio & McCoy, 1983).

Interpersonal relationships. Perhaps the most salient aspect of children with psychosis is that, invariably, they show significant deficits in interpersonal relationships. They have difficulty in social situations, may make inappropriate comments, show stereotypic or ritualistic behavior, treat others as objects, exhibit perseverative behavior, withdraw from social situations, or demonstrate self-stimulatory behavior. They fail to perceive the subtle nuances of interpersonal situations or to make appropriate inferences or interpretations of the actions or words of others. Children with psychosis may show a preference for inanimate objects over peers and adults, and they may treat others primarily as instruments for meeting their needs, exhibiting little emotional attachment to them.

Family factors. Although early theorists tended to ascribe the causes of childhood psychosis to parents who were hostile, rejecting, or detached from the child, there is little evidence to suggest that children develop psychosis as a function of parental behavior. It is possible, however, that how these children are treated within the family may exacerbate their problems. In general, children with psychosis present a myriad of challenging behaviors that can have significant impacts on family functioning. In addition to unusual behaviors, they may have deficits in self-help skills, thereby requiring added attention in day-to-day activities. These children also may show social withdrawal, temper tantrums, needs for sameness, poor social skills, and concrete modes of thinking that contribute to stress among family members. If the parents or family members are unable to develop effective ways to cope with these behaviors and their effects, then problems are likely to become more complicated.

Areas of Emphasis for the Child with Psychosis

As indicated above, children with psychosis show a variety of maladaptive behaviors that may interact in complex ways. To effectively work with these children, the school psychologist must be able to assess and delineate the child's needs in four areas of functioning: personal, social, academic, and family domains. Personal assessment includes addressing the child's emotional and behavioral functioning within various settings. Knowledge of the level of cognitive development, language skills, overall adaptive behavior, motor skills, affective development, and school functioning is essential. Because the social functioning of children with psychosis invariably is impaired, it is important that a thorough knowledge of a child's social strengths and weaknesses be obtained. Obvi-

ously, school is an important part of children's lives, and intervention programs should consider the complexity, uniqueness, and challenges associated with psychosis. Family assessment often will be needed, because what happens at home may be manifested at school. In practice, there almost always will be an interaction among these four factors that creates unique challenges for those who work with these children.

Knowledge and Skills Needed by the School Psychologist

Principles of developmental psychopathology. As indicated above, knowledge of principles of developmental psychopathology will be helpful for the school psychologist in working with these children. For the child with psychosis, intervention should be based on the assumption that the child has the ability to progress in one or more developmental areas rather than on the assumption that psychotic processes are static and subject to little change. Although it is true that the progress of children with psychosis often is very slow (Achenbach, 1982), the well-informed school psychologist will focus on the need to help the child develop, regardless of a formal diagnosis.

Medications. Although medications are not used in every case, some children with psychosis are given psychotropic medications, such as antipsychotics or major tranquilizers. These medications may be given to reduce agitation, anxiety, hallucinations, aggressiveness, or other symptoms. Howlin and Yule (1990) suggest that medications may be essential to help prevent relapses that tend to occur with psychosis. The school psychologist should be aware of the general categories of these drugs, their intended effects, and possible side effects. It may be that the school psychologist will be the only person in a school system with the background and training in behavior disorders who can serve as a link with the prescribing physician and report changes in behavior or evaluate medication effectiveness. If the school psychologist is working with a child who is taking psychotropic medications, she or he should become familiar with the specific medications and their associated effects.

Assessment and intervention techniques. The preceding discussion points out that working with children having psychosis is a multifaceted process that requires high levels of individual skills and collaboration with others. The school psychologist should be thoroughly grounded in behavioral and developmental assessment, behavioral approaches to intervention, consultation skills, working with families, counseling, and working with community agencies and professionals. These areas will be discussed in more detail below.

BEST PRACTICES

Behavioral and Developmental Assessment

Because the characteristics of childhood psychosis often overlap with those of children having mental retardation, autism, organic brain dysfunction, or pervasive developmental disorders, it is important that the school psychologist have a background in the characteristics of these disorders. More specifically, the practitioner should have knowledge of how to conduct a functional assessment on the basis of the presenting behavior pattern, using a variety of assessment procedures including systematic observation, structured clinical interviews, educational assessment, objective personality measures, behavior rating scales, various self-report measures of specific problems, adaptive behavior scales, and developmental and family histories.

Of particular value will be thorough assessment of adaptive behavior, using instruments such as the Vineland Adaptive Behavior Scales (Sparrow, Balla, & Cichetti, 1984) or similar measures. The various domains of adaptive behavior will provide a more complete picture of the child's strengths and weaknesses, from which interventions may be developed. Although many of these children have been identified as having psychosis by the time they enter school, the school psychologist may need to make a comprehensive assessment or differential diagnosis. A differential diagnosis that results in a label may not have direct relevance for intervention, but may help to facilitate communication among the persons involved.

When conducting a psychological and educational assessment, the psychologist should emphasize multimethod, multitrait, and multisetting approaches (Martin, Hooper, & Snow, 1986). Multisource/multi-informant assessment also will be needed, because much of the information must come from third parties. The assessment should include this variety of approaches to ensure that sufficient information is gained prior to developing interventions. Determining the needs of these children often will depend upon observation, reports from others via structured or semistructured interviews or behavior ratings, and anecdotal/historical information.

Of particular help in this area are behavior rating scales, especially those that can reliably measure both internalizing and externalizing characteristics. The Child Behavior Checklist (CBCL; Achenbach & Edelbrock, 1983) is especially useful for assessing these children, because it identifies specific behavior patterns and their severity for children aged 2–18. Although it is not specifically designed to assess psychosis, the CBCL does contain items and subscales that may be related to the behavior of the child with psychosis, such as hearing voices (Merrell, 1994). Further, the CBCL has forms for both teacher and parent, thereby reducing the variance associated with using different instrumentation for these informants. Generally, data generated that can be compared across settings and informants will have the most utility.

A related objective inventory that can be completed by a parent or other informed person is the Personality Inventory for Children (PIC; Wirt, Lachar, Klinedinst, & Seat, 1984) that assesses behavior for ages 3–16. The PIC is a multidimensional measure of psychopathology and contains scales having both internalizing and externalizing items. Among the scales are Psychosis, Anxiety, and Depression, which can be valuable in assessing multiple facets of children with psychosis.

Observation of the child in a variety of settings is important to determine how the child functions in different settings and to understand better what environmental variables tend to have a positive or negative effect on the child's behavior. The child with psychosis may engage in unusual behaviors to such an extent that functioning is impaired. Therefore, interval, frequency, or duration recording will be valuable for generating baseline data about the child's functioning, and also can be used to verify data from interviews and behavior ratings.

Although there are a number of self-report personality measures available for depression, anxiety, and so forth, their utility with these children may range from none at all to moderate usefulness (Merrell, 1994). Language problems, concentration difficulties, inability to reflect on internal mood states or behavior, or perseveration with the same answer to several items are but some factors that may lead to invalid results. If self-reports are not appropriate, then observation, behavior rating scales, interviews, and anecdotal records will yield the most useful information.

Standardized achievement tests, while indicating overall achievement, may have relatively little utility for the classroom. More precise information about academic strengths and weaknesses may be gained from evaluating classroom performance and using curriculum-based measurement (CBM) in specific subject areas. The reader is referred to Shinn (1989) for more information about CBM.

Intervention Techniques

Because the child with psychosis often demonstrates needs in many areas, the school psychologist should have a broad background in various intervention methods. Skills in remediation of academic deficits, particularly as related to language skills, are essential. If the child shows language-related deficits in areas such as reading and spelling, consultation with the teacher and the school speech/language therapist may be indicated to develop strategies to address these problems. Language arts and mathematics may be particularly difficult for the child, because of the complex skills required and the need for sustained effort and concentration.

Knowledge and skill in behavioral interventions will be essential in working with these children. The most promising documented interventions for the behaviors shown tend to be operantly based, and may include variations of behavior modification, such as reinforcement methods, token economy systems, and the use of extinction methods for undesirable behaviors. These methods have been shown to be effective in enhancing eye contact, reducing stereotypic or repetitive behavior, increasing completion of tasks, enhancing prosocial skills development, and decreasing self-abusive or self-stimulatory behavior.

Cognitive-behavioral interventions refer to methods of cognitive behavior therapy (CBT) to modify thinking and problem-solving processes, and include self-instructional training, problem-solving, and self-monitoring techniques (Woody, LaVoie, & Epps, 1992). These techniques have been shown to be effective for many academic, behavioral, and social skills problems, and may include procedures such as modeling, self-recording, and self-monitoring. For children with psychosis, however, particular care must be used if CBT methods are to be considered. Woody et al. (1992) suggest that CBT methods are not appropriate for children who have low levels of cognitive functioning as well as difficulty in recognizing their own role, self-efficacy, and personal responsibility in the intervention. Even though a child with psychosis may have average to above intelligence, concreteness in thinking or other cognitive characteristics may render CBT methods of little value, at least in the initial stages of intervention. It is possible that the child might show a negative reaction to CBT, perceiving it as threatening to needs for sameness and structure. The psychologist should consider the developmental appropriateness of CBT for these children, and could do some preliminary trials of these methods before implementing a more detailed plan.

Behavior therapy and behavior modification methods have been shown to be effective with children having psychosis and developmental disabilities. The majority of these techniques can be implemented with children having a range of cognitive and social abilities, including children with psychosis. Several studies have demonstrated the effectiveness of these methods with the behaviors of psychotic children. Many techniques have utilized aversive procedures, which should be used with caution, particularly in a school setting. In general, however, these techniques likely will be the most useful, and can be applied to a number of problems.

Social skills interventions. Because children with psychosis characteristically show deficient social skills, the school psychologist should be prepared to assess and provide intervention in this area. Assessment of social skills can be accomplished by observation, assessment of adaptive behavior, or the completion of scales such as the Social Skills Rating System (Gresham & Elliott, 1990). Another method of assessing social relationships is to gather information about sociometric status (i.e., how the child is accepted by others), such as the system developed by Coie, Dodge, and Coppotelli (1982).

Gresham (1990) suggests that there are four steps in developing interventions for social skills problems: "(a) facilitation of skill acquisition, (b) enhancement of skill performance, (c) removal of interfering problem behaviors, and (d) generalization of trained social skills" (p. 706). Space limitations prohibit detailed discussion of these steps here, but these points should serve as a guide for developing social skills interventions for children with psychosis.

Counseling approaches. In the past, psychoanalytic and psychodynamic therapies were used to treat children with psychosis, on the assumption that the disorders had a psychogenic origin or that alteration of personality processes was necessary for improvement to occur. There is little convincing empirical evidence that counseling and therapy approaches directed toward changing personality processes have been successful with these children. Children with psychosis often lack sufficient self-awareness or ability to reflect upon their behavior or affect to make such intervention helpful. Counseling often is beneficial for families of these children by helping them to reduce the type and extent of behavioral problems shown, and to develop management skills. It can also help to reduce the tendency that some parents have to blame themselves for having a child with psychosis. Applications of techniques of family systems therapy also may be appropriate in some situations. Finally, counseling that emphasizes the child's adjustment in school, personal responsibility, and social relationships may be appropriate.

Variations such as play therapy are not likely to produce significant gains in behavior or development, but may give the child the opportunity to relate to an adult with whom he or she feels comfortable. If used in the school setting, play therapy probably should be viewed as being rather short-term and focused on specific goals. For more discussion of general counseling techniques with children, see Tharinger and Koranek (1990).

Behavioral consultation skills will prove valuable for the school psychologist working with these children. Although there are many models of consultation, the behavioral consultation model proposed by Bergan (1977) or a variation of it probably will be the most useful. Bergan proposes that there are four steps in the behavioral consultation process: (1) problem identification, (2) generation of possible solutions, (3) implementation of the plan, and (4) evaluation of efficacy. Huberty and Skiba (1992) have modified the basic model by including a component whereby the consultee also generates a list of contributing factors to a problem and decides which factors affect the child and her or his behavior. Then the consultee determines which contributing factors are the most salient and can be addressed in developing intervention plans. Following this stage, the last three steps of Bergan's model are implemented. Because there may be many factors operating in the evaluation of and intervention for children with psychosis, it is important to identify as many contributing factors as possible, determine the ones that are the most important and can be addressed, and then develop the interventions.

Perhaps the most challenging task in using behavioral consultation with these children is identifying the problem that is to be the focus of intervention. The problems presented may be complex and have a high degree of interrelatedness (e.g., social skill and cognitive deficits), making it necessary to clearly define the target behaviors while considering other contributing factors. Problem analysis and plan implementation should include consideration of contributing factors, such as the child's cognitive functioning and skill levels to determine the degree to which he or she can participate in and respond to the intervention. Planning evaluation for these children must account for the fact that progress often is slow, uneven, and of a long-term nature, therefore requiring patience and sometimes plan modifications.

Family interventions. When intervening at the family level, it is useful to identify goals, which could include (1) focusing on specific variables or behaviors that are related to or a product of family functioning, (2) enlisting the family's involvement to assist with a problem at school, e.g., task completion, (3) teaching parents how to manage behaviors of the child that are problematic at home or school, and (4) implementing a problem-solving approach for identifying and developing an intervention plan. A variety of interventions could be used, such as family therapy, parent management training, behavior modification, or other approaches. The interventions chosen would be determined by the goals established, the needs of the situation, the characteristics of the participants, the resources available (including family members), and the intended outcomes.

Modifications of curriculum, assignments, and tasks. A frequent method of intervention for children with psychosis has been to place them in special education classes, where they spend most or all of their instructional day. To the extent possible or appropriate, it is best to keep these children in the regular classroom, where they will be more likely to interact with normal peers and imitate desired behaviors. As with any child who has learning difficulties, consideration should be given to modifications of tasks, assignments, and instructions. Breaking assignments into smaller parts, repetition, specific instruc-

tions, and task analysis often are necessary. Individual and classwide peer tutoring, buddy systems, and similar peer interaction procedures may be of benefit, depending upon the child's skill levels, behavior, and acceptance by other students.

Liaisons with other professionals and agencies. The child with psychosis may have involvement with other professionals, such as physicians who prescribe medications. The school psychologist can provide valuable services to these professionals by serving as a link with the school. Accumulating behavioral data, observing medication effects, and implementing external recommendations are but some of the roles that are important. If a child has been hospitalized for an extended period of time, working with external professionals to devise plans for reintegration into school can make a major difference in the degree of success and adjustment shown by the child upon reentry. Children who have been away from school for a long time often have readjustment difficulties, which may be exacerbated in children with psychosis. See Colegrove (1990) for a good discussion of reintegration of children into school.

A Problem-Solving Approach

The child with psychosis will present unique challenges to parents and school personnel that likely will require a diversity of approaches toward understanding the nature of the problems and developing effective assessment and intervention approaches. The child with psychosis has a complex interaction among skills and behaviors, unlike problem areas for children who do not have psychosis. Behavioral problems exhibited by the child may have their basis in a variety of causal factors, such as language deficits, social skills problems, or extreme cognitive rigidity. Whereas the behavior problems of nonpsychotic children may be addressed directly, the child with psychosis may require a more complex approach to intervention. For example, a nonpsychotic child with average cognitive ability may respond well to a token reinforcement system for noncompliant behavior, but such an approach might not be effective for a child with psychosis if cognitive and language deficits interfere with understanding or responding to the contingencies or exchange rules. Because assessment and intervention for children with psychosis is complex and challenging, a systematic problem-solving approach is recommended.

The complex nature of these children's problems indicate that a problem-solving approach will facilitate assessment and intervention, and can be conceptualized as a series of steps to be addressed:

1. Identify the child's needs and problems in behavioral terms with adequate baseline data.

2. Prioritize and determine which of the child's needs or problems should be the focus of interventions.

3. Determine the factors that are causing or contributing to the identified problems or needs.

4. Generate possible intervention approaches for the problems.

5. Select the appropriate interventions.

6. Implement the selected interventions.

7. Evaluate the interventions and revise, if necessary.

Identifying the child's needs is accomplished by using a multiple-component approach in assessment, with particular attention to objective, behavioral approaches. At this stage, it is important to be as specific and thorough as possible, because behaviors that will become the focus for intervention will be specified during this assessment. Adequate baseline data should be determined from observation, rating scales, or other objective measures of behavior.

Prioritizing behaviors is a process of determining which behaviors are to be the focus of possible interventions. The primary factors in determining which behaviors to focus on are the degree to which they interfere with the child's functioning (or that of others) and the extent of intervention indicated. For example, the child may engage in self-stimulatory behavior that is not disruptive to the class and also may show frequent aggressiveness. Although the self-stimulatory behavior may be noticeable and annoying, the aggressiveness should be focused on first, because of its impact on the child and others.

Determining causal or contributing factors can be achieved by assessing individual child characteristics, environmental variables (e.g., curriculum), behavior management skills of parents or teachers, and other factors that may cause or maintain the problems. Of particular importance in this step is to determine which of these factors are the most amenable to change. For example, although a child's social skills deficits may be related to cognitive ability, emphasis should be placed upon the area most amenable to change, (i.e., social skills) while considering the impact of the cognitive problems.

Generating possible intervention approaches essentially can be a brainstorming process, i.e., considering a variety of possible interventions that may be appropriate. At this point, there is little attempt to select the best intervention; rather, the goal is to identify potential specific interventions.

Selecting the appropriate intervention should be determined by the specific goals to be accomplished, the resources needed to implement an intervention, the resources available, the degree to which the intervention can be implemented for the specific prob-

lems, and the degree to which efficacy can be evaluated. Careful attention to these factors will help to increase the probability of success. For example, time-out would not be chosen to treat withdrawal behavior but might be appropriate for aggressiveness.

Implementing the intervention will occur as the result of developing a clearly delineated plan of action that follows from the baseline data. Implementation should identify what is to be done, who will be responsible for each aspect of the intervention, and the plan for collection of evaluative data.

Evaluating the intervention is the last, but important, aspect of an intervention. By comparing current data to the baseline information, the school psychologist can determine if the intervention should continue or be modified in some way. If changes are to occur in the intervention, it may be necessary to gather more baseline data. An effective method is to do pre- and postintervention observations or behavior ratings that can be compared to determine the changes that have occurred.

SUMMARY

This chapter has focused on children with psychosis and issues regarding provision of quality school psychological services for them. These children present unique challenges to professionals because of the nature of their problems, which will persist through life. The greatest gains for these children likely will be in the educational arena, which is where the school psychologist can be of the most help. Particular areas of importance are improvement in social skills, interpersonal relationships, personal care and responsibility, and academic functioning. The practitioner should have knowledge about developmental psychopathology, psychotropic medications used, and a variety of assessment and intervention techniques. Of particular importance is an understanding and appreciation of the complex nature of childhood psychosis and the interactions among various problem areas. Assessment and interventions likely will be multifaceted and require considerable skill to develop and implement. Optimal interventions for these children should follow a problem-solving process, such as that described above.

In closing, an essential point to remember is that children with psychosis will experience problems throughout their lives. Cullinan et al. (1983) have summarized some research findings on children with psychosis that are pertinent to consider:

1. No treatment — psychodynamic, psychoeducational, behavioral, drug, megavitamin, or any other — can make psychotic children normal.

2. Except for drug therapy, which is rarely used alone, all interventions require great effort over a very long period of time.

3. Psychotic children have the best chance for meaningful improvement in *educational* programs — ones in which the therapists, parents, school teachers, and other interventionists teach needed skills and eliminate nonfunctional behaviors that interfere with the child's learning and social acceptability (pp. 242–243).

Progress can be expected to be slow, uneven, and long-term, and expecting the child to achieve "normalcy" is unrealistic. Nevertheless, with collaborative efforts by parents and professionals, some academic and social gains should be realized over time.

REFERENCES

Achenbach, T. M. (1982). *Developmental psychopathology* (2nd ed.). New York: Wiley.

Achenbach, T. M., & Edelbrock, C. S. (1983). *Child Behavior Checklist. Manual.* Burlington, VT: University Associates in Psychiatry.

American Psychiatric Association. (1987). *Diagnostic and statistical manual of mental disorders* (3rd ed., rev.). Washington, DC: Author.

Bergan, J. R. (1977). *Behavioral consultation.* Columbus, OH: Charles E. Merrill.

Clarizio, H. F., & McCoy, G. F. (1983). *Behavior disorders in children* (3rd ed.). New York: Harper and Row.

Coie, J., Dodge, K., & Coppotelli, H. (1982). Dimensions and types of social status: A cross-age perspective. *Developmental Psychology, 18,* 557–570.

Colegrove, R. W. (1990). Best practices in school reintegration. In A. Thomas & J. Grimes (Eds.), *Best practices in school psychology–II* (pp. 665–672). Washington, DC: National Association of School Psychologists.

Cowan, P. A. (1988). Developmental psychopathology: A nine-cell map of the territory. In E. D. Nannis & P. A. Cowan (Eds.), *Developmental psychopathology and its treatment* (pp. 5–29). San Francisco, CA: Jossey-Bass.

Cullinan, D., Epstein, M. H., & Lloyd, J. W. (1983). *Behavior disorders of children and adolescents.* Englewood Cliffs, NJ: Prentice-Hall.

Gresham, F. M. (1990). Best practices in social skills training. In A. Thomas & J. Grimes (Eds.), *Best practices in school psychology–II* (pp. 695–709). Washington, DC: National Association of School Psychologists.

Gresham, F. M., & Elliott, S. N. (1990). *Social Skills Rating System.* Circle Pines, MN: American Guidance Service.

Huberty, T. J., & Skiba, R. S. (1992). *Active consultation for teachers: A new model of consultation for at-risk students.* Paper presented at the annual convention of the American Psychological Association, Washington, DC.

Kanner, L. (1943). Autistic disturbances of affective contact. *Nervous Child, 2,* 217–250.

Lewis, M., & Miller, S. M. (Eds.). (1990). Handbook of developmental psychopathology. New York: Plenum.

Mahler, M. (1952). On child psychosis and schizophrenia: Autistic and symbiotic infantile psychosis. *Psychoanalytic study of the Child, 7,* 286–305.

Martin, R. P., Hooper, S., & Snow, J. (1986). Behavior rating scale approaches to personality assessment in children and adolescents. In H. M. Knoff (Ed.), *The assessment of child and adolescent personality.* New York: Guilford.

Merrell, K. W. (1994). *Assessment of behavioral, social, and emotional problems.* New York: Longman.

Nannis, E. D., & Cowan, P. A. (Eds.). (1988). *Developmental psychopathology and its treatment.* San Francisco, CA: Jossey-Bass.

Rosenhan, D. L., & Seligman, M. E. P. (1989). *Abnormal psychology* (2nd ed.). New York: W. W. Norton.

Rosenthal, D. (1970). *Genetic theory and abnormal behavior.* New York: McGraw-Hill.

Shinn, M. R. (1989). Identifying and defining academic problems. In M. Shinn (Ed.), *Curriculum-based measurement: Assessing special children* (pp. 90–129). New York: Guilford.

Sparrow, S. S., Balla, D. A., & Cichetti, D. V. (1984). *Vineland Adaptive Behavior Scales.* Circle Pines, MN: American Guidance Service.

Tharinger, D., & Koranek, M. (1990). Best practices in individual counseling with elementary students. In A. Thomas & J. Grimes (Eds.), *Best practices in school psychology–II* (pp. 407–423). Washington, DC: National Association of School Psychologists.

Wirt, R. D., Lachar, D., Klinedinst, J. K., & Seat, P. D. (1984). *Personality Inventory for Children.* Los Angeles, CA: Western Psychological Services.

Woody, R. H., LaVoie, J. C., & Epps, S. (1992). *School psychology: A developmental and social systems approach.* Boston: Allyn & Bacon.

ANNOTATED BIBLIOGRAPHY

Achenbach, T. M. (1982). *Developmental psychopathology* (2nd ed.). New York: Wiley.

This book gives a thorough description of the concepts of developmental psychopathology, and discusses individual disorders from a developmental perspective. Included are chapters on intervention, etiology, assessment, and classification of disorders. This book is a valuable resource for psychologists who wish to understand and apply principles of developmental psychopathology.

Clarizio, H. F., & McCoy, G. F. (1983). *Behavior disorders in children* (3rd ed.). New York: Harper and Row.

This book provides a comprehensive treatment of childhood disorders and includes good information about the impact of disorders on school performance. Each chapter describes well a specific disorder, and includes discussion of educational issues and possible methods for intervention. The book also is likely to be helpful in differential diagnosis situations, and would be a valuable reference for the practitioner.

Stoner, G., Shinn, M. R., & Walker, H. M. (Eds.). (1991). *Interventions for achievement and behavior problems.* Washington, DC: National Association of School Psychologists.

This volume of nearly 800 pages describes a wide range of school-based interventions for academic and social/emotional/behavioral problems for students of all ages. The book is divided into helpful sections: Evaluation Issues, General Intervention Strategies, Interventions for Target Areas by Level, Interventions for Specific Problems, and Training Intervention Oriented School Psychologists. The book is especially useful for working with children with psychosis, who present a variety of problems that need a multifaceted approach.

Thomas, A., & Grimes, J. (Eds.). (1990). *Best practices in school psychology–II.* Washington, DC: National Association of School Psychologists.

Like the NASP's *Interventions for achievement and behavior problems* described above, this book covers a wide array of top-ics pertinent to student problems. The topics are very specific and cover a range of conceptual and practical issues, many of which will apply directly to childhood psychosis and can be readily adapted. The book will be a valuable resource regarding best practice in many areas related to childhood psychosis.

89

Best Practices in Working with Culturally Different Families

Dawn P. Flanagan
St. John's University

Antoinette Halsell Miranda
The Ohio State University

Culture is akin to being the observer through the one-way mirror; everything we see is from our own perspective. It is only when we join the observed on the other side that it is possible to see ourselves and others clearly — but getting to the other side of the glass presents many challenges.

— Eleanor W. Lynch (1992, p. 35)

OVERVIEW

The United States is becoming an increasingly diverse nation. The number of children from nonwhite and non-Anglo white families is growing. This growth is expected to continue despite the fact that the percentage of children that make up the total U.S. population is decreasing (Counting the Children, 1989). It is estimated that by the year 2000, 38% of the U.S. population under the age of 18 will be non-Anglo whites and nonwhites (Research and Policy Committee of the Committee for Economic Development, 1987) and by the year 2030, the number of Latino children, African American children, and children of other races, will increase by 5.5, 2.6, and 1.5 million, respectively, while the number of white, non-Latino children will decrease by 6.2 million from the 1985 figure (Children's Defense Fund, 1989). These dramatic changes in the ethnic composition of the United States can be attributed to increasing birth rates among non-Anglo women and decreasing birth rates among the resident Anglo population; increasing numbers of non-Anglo women of childbearing age; increased immigration of non-Europeans; and increased longevity among ethnically diverse populations (Hanson, Lynch, & Wayman, 1990; Huang & Gibbs, 1992).

In addition to these demographic changes, today's families are also undergoing significant changes. First, the percentage of traditional, nuclear families in the United States is decreasing while the percentage of nontraditional families, including single parents, step parents, grandparents, adoptives, foster parents, and same-sex parents, is increasing

(Copeland & White, 1991; Masnick & Bane, 1980). Second, the percentage of young women having children is on the rise as well as the percentage of women electing to marry and bear children at later ages (Levitan, Belous, & Gallo, 1988). Third, family size has decreased in the past few decades among the U.S. Anglo population, while the average number of births per woman in other ethnic/cultural groups has increased (Hanson et al., 1990). Family size is also influenced by the number of individuals who reside in the same household but are not part of the nuclear family (e.g., grandparents). Many individuals who recently immigrated to the United States, for example, reside in large, extended families for cultural and economic reasons (Wayman, Lynch, & Hanson, 1990). Finally, although several sociohistorical events have had an effect on families in recent years, "the disproportionate decrease in the standard of living of many children and families in the United States is perhaps the single most significant sociohistorical change affecting families today" (Hanson & Lynch, 1992, p. 291). For example, in 1989, 41% of poor children resided in a household with an income below half of the poverty line (i.e., an income of $412 per month) (Children's Defense Fund, 1991, cited in Hanson & Lynch, 1992).

These powerful demographic and familial changes have culminated in a multitude of cultural patterns and characteristics, languages, values, beliefs, attitudes, and behaviors. As a result of the increasing ethnic/cultural diversity of the United States, the number of non-Anglo children and their families who require early intervention services is on the rise. Moreover, the recent enactment of Public Law 99-457 (Individuals With Disabilities Education Act, 1991) has served to increase the extent to which school psychologists form partnerships with families. Ideally, families requiring early intervention services should be matched with at least one service provider whose language and experience are similar to that of the family in order to ensure caring, sensitivity, and responsive service delivery. Unfortunately, the provision of services to culturally different families is not likely to include this ideal component in the near future.

Training programs that prepare professionals to work with children with disabilities and their families do not include large numbers of students from differing ethnic, cultural, and linguistic groups (Hanson, 1992). Although the number of non-Anglo children attending early intervention programs is increasing, by the year 2000 the persons providing services to these children and their families will be predominantly Anglo-whites (Hanson, 1990, 1992). This mismatch between families and service providers can result in "cultural clashes." That is, when the values and beliefs of culturally diverse families differ from the U.S. mainstream's values and beliefs held by service providers, conflict and/or miscommunication will likely ensue, thereby diminishing the effectiveness of service delivery. Thus, recruiting students from diverse backgrounds and expanding university curricula to include an emphasis on multicultural education (Banks, 1993; Hanson, 1992) must begin in earnest and remain a top priority well into the twenty-first century. In the meantime, school psychologists and other service providers must strive to develop a respect for the values of other cultures so that they can identify more effectively the concerns, priorities, needs, strengths, and resources of the families with whom they work (Hanson, 1992).

At present, many school psychologists are faced with the challenge of providing services to children of ethnically diverse backgrounds and to their families in the absence of prior training in multicultural education, in general, and prior experience in working with culturally different families, in particular. As a result of their lack of training and experience, many school psychologists are ill-prepared and therefore, reluctant to work with families whose cultural backgrounds differ from their own. The purpose of this chapter is to provide school psychologists with a foundation from which to build or enhance their skills in providing services to culturally different families and from which to begin exploring, understanding, and appreciating diversity. Specifically, this chapter will provide useful terms that need to be understood by school psychologists prior to working with culturally different families so that they can clearly delineate the dimensions along which difference is defined. In addition, this chapter will present a culture-oriented perspective of family systems and discuss how school psychologists can begin to develop cross-cultural awareness and competence. This chapter will conclude with a summary of guidelines for gathering culturally relevant data that can be used by school psychologists to learn more about the practices and functions of the families with whom they work.

BASIC CONSIDERATIONS

The phrase *culturally different* is used in this chapter to describe families who come from cultural backgrounds that differ from the school psychologist's, which in many instances means that they differ from mainstream U.S. culture. However, school psychologists should guard against treating "culturally different families" as a uniform group. They are *similar* only in that their respective cultural backgrounds differ from that of the professional. There are a number of salient dimensions along which families differ including culture, race, ethnicity, socioeconomic status (SES), and level of acculturation. School psychologists who assess a family's status along each of these dimensions will be more sensitive to the specific ways in which the family's priorities, strengths, resources, and needs differ from their own. Often, differences among families categorized as culturally different become clouded by the psychologist's tendency to view difference as unidimensional. Adopting a multidimensional way of thinking about difference will circumvent our tendency to generalize across a variety of cultures. The following definitions are offered to provide school psychologists with an understanding of the most salient dimensions along which families differ.

Terminology

Culture. There is often confusion over the connotative meaning of the term *culture* (Frisby, 1992a). According to Frisby (1992a), there are approximately six connotative meanings associated with the term in contemporary society. One meaning is the "characteristic patterns of living, customs, traditions, values, and attitudes that are associated with broad differences in intercontinental habitation or a society's level of technological sophistication" (Frisby, 1992a, p. 533). Thus, an industrialized society characterized by ongoing technological advancement is implied in the term *modern* as opposed to *primitive* culture. Another definition of culture refers to the unique contributions of the members of a given ethnic/racial group or ancestral homeland including humanitarian, scientific, or artistic accomplishments. Many U.S. schools, for example, have revised their social studies curriculums to include sociohistorical events that highlight the significant contributions of African civilizations or African American leaders in an attempt to provide all individuals with an educational foundation in "black culture" (Frisby, 1992a; Huang & Gibbs, 1992).

A third concept of culture has been labeled "race consciousness" by Hall and Allen (1989); it refers to behaviors, attitudes, and beliefs that serve to advance interest in and promote identification with one's race regardless of differing levels of education, social class status, or area of residence (Frisby, 1992b; McGhee, 1983). Sensitivity to and awareness of racial prejudice or discrimination is a component of racial consciousness. A fourth meaning of culture reflects the values, beliefs, and customs that are inherent in the environments in which a person receives information about society. Individuals who recently immigrated to the United States, for example, may find the "culture" of their family to be very different from the "culture" of U.S. schools. The remaining two concepts of culture are more superficial: Individuals may be regarded as "culturally different" because of their adherence to particular styles of dress, religious worship, culinary practices, and so on, or as a result of outer appearances alone (e.g., skin pigmentation) (Frisby, 1992a; McGoldrick, Pearce, & Giordano, 1982; Stewart & Bennett, 1991).

From the above definitions, it is evident that much information is conveyed through the casual use of the term "culture." Therefore, culture must not be viewed as "a rigidly prescribed set of behaviors or characteristics, but rather a framework through which actions are filtered or checked as individuals go about daily life" (Hanson, 1992, p. 3). Although individuals of the same cultural background share certain tendencies, they do not necessarily behave in the same way, since behavior is also influenced by such factors as gender, age, socioeconomic status, area of residence, and level of education (Hanson, 1992). The degree to which individuals follow a prescribed assemblage of cultural patterns varies considerably; there exists a vast continuum reflecting the extent to which individuals identify with a particular cultural group or groups (Frisby, 1992a; Gopaul-McNicol, 1992; Hanson, 1992). Thus, school psychologists must appreciate all the nuances inherent in the notion of culture, since their precision regarding its meaning directly impacts on how effectively they can communicate with diverse families.

Ethnicity and race. Related to culture but narrower in scope is the concept of *ethnic group*. Banks and McGee Banks (1993) define ethnic group as "a microcultural group or collectivity that shares a common history and culture, common values, behaviors, and other characteristics that cause members of the group to have a shared identity" (p. 357). It is important to note here that although the terms *ethnicity* and *race* are often used interchangeably, they are separate concepts. Race is a biological concept that refers to phenotypically distinct groups. Thus, cultural traits are the main attributes of an ethnic group while biological traits determine race (Banks & McGee Banks, 1993).

Minority. Another important concept to understand is minority group. The term *minority* may be used to refer to a small group of privileged individuals. However, it is more typically used to refer to a proportionately smaller group, in contrast to the majority group in a society, that is disadvantaged (due to such factors as limited opportunity for educational and/or economic advancement) and treated unfavorably by the majority group. Groups that differ from the majority group in race or ethnicity often are treated unfavorably by the majority group and as a result acquire an underprivileged minority status. Moreover, when a minority group is considered underprivileged because of unfavorable treatment or other variables related to deprivation and discrimination, the psychological well-being of the group's family life will likely be affected adversely (Tseng & Hall, 1991).

Socioeconomic status. An additional central concept to have knowledge of is *socioeconomic status* (SES), since it defines an individual's world. Membership in a particular social class has a profound impact on essentially every variable that influences an individual's physical and psychological growth and development. These variables range from educational attainment, occupational aspirations, and lifestyles to selection of friends, activities, and social roles. Thus, as social class varies, so do the range of opportunities, the kind of choices, and the degree of challenges that are available to individuals and their families (Huang & Gibbs, 1992).

Social class and its interrelationship with ethnicity and race complicate further the plight of culturally diverse families living in the United States. Essentially, being a member of white, Anglo-Saxon, middle-class families is reflective of high status whereas being a member of non-Anglo, or non-white, working-class families is reflective of low status. This means that "youth in many Asian, Black, Hispanic, and Indian families are triply stigmatized in American society because they differ from the ideal norm in three major respects: They are non-white by race (except for Spanish-speaking whites), non-Anglo-Saxon by ethnicity, and predominantly non-middle-class by socioeconomic status" (Huang & Gibbs, 1992, p. 85). Thus, the school psychologist's familiarity with the separate definitions of culture, ethnicity, race, minority group, and SES is not enough to ensure sensitivity and effective communication when working with culturally different families. School psychologists must also understand that the connotations inherent in these concepts are often inextricable and subsequently come to appreciate the interrelationships among them.

Acculturation. A final useful term that is necessary to understand before providing services to culturally different families is *acculturation*. Acculturation may be defined as the set of circumstances that result when two cultures experience, first hand, the subsequent alterations in the fundamental sociocultural system of one or both groups (Redfield, Linton, & Herskovits, 1936). When migrant families leave their homeland and move to new locations, they may find that the sociocultural system that obtains in their new place of residence differs significantly from the one they left behind. As a result, these families may feel pressure to conform to different ways of thinking that are characteristic of their new environment. In addition, they may have to adjust to a new way of life regarding occupation, financial resources, and social network (Tseng & Hsu, 1991).

This adjustment process is influenced by several factors, including the migrants' reason for migration, their occupational/educational attainment, the climate of reception in the new host society, and the degree of compatibility between the cultures of the migrants and the host society. Further complicating the adjustment process is the degree and pace of conformity to a new cultural system. For example, often young children are more adept at learning a new language and more amenable to assuming new social roles than their middle-aged parents. This differing pace of adjustment may create tension and disharmony within the family and disrupt the family hierarchy. That is, as a result of the child's more rapid pace of adjustment to a new cultural system, the roles and status of the parents and child may reverse, particularly when the child is forced to assume the role of emissary for the parents in certain social contexts (Huang, 1989; Huang & Gibbs, 1992; Tseng & Hsu, 1991).

The degree to which an individual acculturates influences her or his attitudes, values, and beliefs. Five stages or levels of acculturation have been proposed by Atkinson, Morten, and Sue (1989) and presented in Nuttall, De Leon, and Valle (1990) in an attempt to explain how minority individuals react to the dominant culture. Briefly, at the first level (Conformity), minority individuals do not like themselves or those who share membership in the same minority group; they admire members of the dominant group. The second level of acculturation (Dissonance) is seen as a time of conflict in which the migrant's preference for the views of the majority culture, vis a vis their previous views, waxes and wanes. At the third level (Resistance and Immersion), minority individuals have come to appreciate themselves and their affiliation with a minority group but have developed a dislike for the majority group. Also, at this level, empathic feelings for other minority groups are expressed; however, they are in direct conflict with feelings of ethnocentrism. At level 4 (Introspection), individuals begin to explore the grounds on which they can justify liking themselves and members of their minority group. Finally, at level 5 (Synergetic Articulation and Awareness), individuals come to appreciate themselves, their own group, other ethnic minority groups, and particular aspects of the majority culture.

Knowing a family's current level of acculturation provides an additional perspective from which the school psychologist can develop plans for service delivery. For example, a family that is functioning at level 1 or level 5 is likely to respond positively to interactions with service providers of the dominant culture, whereas a family functioning at level 3 will likely respond negatively or avoid such interactions (Nuttall et al., 1990). Also, it is important to understand that highly acculturated minority individuals may have more in common with members of the dominant culture than with members of their own group. Thus, a third generation Vietnamese family may have more in common with a white middle-class family than with a Vietnamese immigrant (Huang & Gibbs, 1992). Given the varying degrees of acculturation that may be experienced by ethnic minority individuals, and its resultant impact on the attitudes, values, and beliefs held by minority families, the importance of knowing the level that has been reached by the family or family members prior to service delivery cannot be overemphasized.

Family Systems

In addition to mastering the various concepts presented above, a consideration and basic understanding of the ways in which family systems function is also necessary to enable the school psychologist to work more effectively with families of various cultural backgrounds. There are numerous patterns of family systems that exist worldwide, many of which are influenced by external political, economic, and sociocultural factors as opposed to internal emotional and psychological (family) factors. Moreover, different family systems have emerged in response to different social contexts as well as to solutions to problems that reflect the psychological milieu in which they live, rather than by a predetermined evolutional course or by chance (Tseng & Hsu, 1991). It is beyond the scope of this chapter to examine all the cultural aspects of family systems, family development, and family function. Therefore, only a brief cross-cultural perspective of how family systems function will be presented here. (For a more comprehensive examination of culture and family systems, see Tseng & Hsu, 1991.)

The term *family* is defined by Tseng and Hsu (1991) as "the basic sociocultural unit . . . the nest for the growth of an individual, the resource for social support, and the institution through which culture is transmitted" (p. 1). Although the term takes on a variety of concepts and meanings across cultures, what is clear is that this social unit plays a significant role in cultivating the growth, development, and psychological well-being of its children (Lewis, Beavers, Gossett, & Phillips, 1976). When a family has a child with a disability or other at-risk condition, it is likely that they will come into contact with a school psychologist or other service provider. The family may seek out or welcome services from these professionals or they may have reservations regarding the need and desirability of services (Hanson, 1992). The perceived need for services may be influenced by a number of variables including the emotional state of the family at the time of referral; the attitudes, values, and belief systems of the family; the match between the culture of the family and the culture of the service provider; the family's level of acculturation; and the family's social support system, to name a few. School psychologists can provide culturally appropriate services to families of different cultural backgrounds only if they understand the fundamental cultural aspects of family systems and function. In order to begin to understand and distinguish between differing family patterns, it is helpful to examine the most salient parameters of family systems such as marriage forms, postmarital residence, kinship system, and family structure (Tseng & Hsu, 1991).

Marriage. Each society has its own rules regarding marriage. In the United States as well as in most contemporary developed societies, *monogamy* is the norm. However, in more than 80% of the societies worldwide (based on those listed in the *Ethnographic Atlas*, Murdock, 1967), monogamy with *polygyny* (i.e., having more than one wife) or only polygyny is preferred (Hoebel, 1972). In many societies, polygyny can increase a man's wealth, his social position, and his affiliations with various groups, especially when his wives are economically important. Although considerably less prevalent, *polyandry* (having more than one husband) is preferred among many tribes in India (e.g., Tibetans; Hoebel, 1972); in these societies, property is scarce and brothers often will marry a common wife to circumvent division of assets. Thus, although not common in the United States, polygyny and polyandry serve significant political and economic functions in many societies around the world (Tseng & Hsu, 1991).

Residence. Different patterns of postmarital residence are also evident across cultures. These patterns of residence are usually dictated by ecological factors. For example, when the primary means of support or livelihood rests with the male, the married couple will likely live near the husband's family. Conversely, when the woman plays a prominent role in subsistence, as is seen in horticultural societies where cooperation among women is important, then the couple will benefit from living near the wife's family. Finally, in societies that are characterized by a high degree of mobility and value independence within the nuclear family, such as the United States and other industrialized and urbanized societies, a married couple will typically live apart from the families of both spouses. Thus, the role(s) assumed by each spouse, the power distribution within the family, and the configuration of kinship relationships are impacted by the choice of residence following marriage (Stewart & Bennett, 1991; Tseng & Hsu, 1991).

Kinship. Another parameter of family systems that is useful to examine from a cross-cultural perspective is the kinship system. A *kinship system*, ac-cording to Tseng and Hsu (1991), is "the totality of relationships based on blood and marriage that links individuals, through a web of rights and obligations, to the kinds of groups formed in a society on the basis of kinship" (p. 9–10).

The perpetuation of any society is dependent on the functions of kinship. In the majority of societies, individuals are associated with sets of kin following certain rules of descent. For example, the most common type of descent system (i.e., *patrilineal*) associates individuals with both male and female kin through the males. Each generation of children belong to the father's kin group and carry his family name. Furthermore, an individual's lineage is traced through the grandfather, father, son, and grandson line. The far fewer societies that are characterized by a *matrilineal* descent system reflect the same rules of descent as the patrilineal system except that descent association is transferred through females (Ember & Ember, 1973; Tseng & Hsu, 1991).

In a third type of descent system, *ambilineal*, individuals are associated with both male and female kin through either males or females, resulting in a society in which some children belong to the father's kin group and some to the mother's kin group (Ember & Ember, 1973). These different types of descent groups appear to reflect the type of subsistence base that predominates in the associated societies (Tseng & Hsu, 1991). Thus, a subsistence base characterized by pastoralism is associated with a patrilineal descent system, one defined by developed agriculture with a matrilineal system, and one defined by hunting and gathering with an ambilineal system (Schneider & Gough, 1961).

Structure of the family. Related to the different descent systems that exist across cultures are the various configurations of family that assemble on the basis of kinship. For example, the *nuclear* family, composed of parents and their unmarried children, is the most frequently occurring family structure in modern industrialized and in hunter/gatherer societies (i.e., in societies that necessitate substantial mobility). However, in cultivating societies, *extended* families are widespread, primarily for economic reasons; since extended families may include a spouse's married siblings and their children, a greater number of workers are available through this type of kinship network than through nuclear families (Tseng & Hsu, 1991). The presumably "ideal" nuclear family actually exists in a very small percentage of societies worldwide (Nanda, 1980). Furthermore, although the nuclear family currently predominates in the United States, an increasing number of extended family systems are forming due to the impact that changing demographcis are having on U.S. society.

These changing demographics, for example, have resulted in a prevalence of extended families among Asian Americans, African Americans, and Native

Americans. In addition, the importance of the family and extended kinship bonds are securely established in the traditional values of Latino families who reside in the United States (Huang & Gibbs, 1992). It is important to note here that the methods by which societies categorize kin may or may not be dependent on biological ties (Cunningham, Cunningham, & O'Connell, 1986; Harry, 1992; Nanda, 1980). For example, strong kinship bonds among many African American families may result in a multitude of linkages between domestic units that include blood relatives and "fictive kin" (Huang & Gibbs, 1992). Through these coherent networks of extended families, mutual emotional and economic support is provided. Thus, a variety of individuals including friends, neighbors, siblings, and grandparents may participate in raising or caring for any one African American child, especially in times of economic stress or illness (Huang & Gibbs, 1992; Stack, 1975).

Another important element to consider when examining the structure of the family is which family member is given the power to make important decisions. In the United States, for example, an egalitarian family in which power and authority are distributed equally is preferred and practiced commonly. Conversely, in societies marked by patrilineal and matrilineal descent systems, the individuals who exercise authority in kin groups are male. In a patrilineal system, authority is typically delegated to the father or grandfather and in a matrilineal system, to the woman's brother(s). Although many decisions may be made jointly by both husband and wife in private, irrespective of the rules inherent in particular descent systems, it is important to recognize and respect the cultural patterns that are emphasized in public (Tseng & Hsu, 1991). For instance, in many Asian American families, "fathers are often the figurative heads . . . especially when dealing with the public, whereas the mother may actually be the driving force in the family and the decision maker behind the scene" (Huang & Gibbs, 1992, pp. 86–87). Unless professionals understand and defer to these cultural patterns in their interactions with families, they may be perceived as disrespectful and the effectiveness of service delivery will be hampered.

In summary, there are many different aspects of the family that need to be considered by the school psychologist from a cross-cultural perspective. An understanding of the economic, political, ecological, and social conditions that play a role in shaping a family's unique cultural patterns will aid in providing an individualized approach to service delivery, where intervention is tailored to the family's needs, as well as provide a foundation from which to help the family understand U.S. culture. Only through knowledge and awareness can school psychologists recognize the strengths of different family structures and respond sensitively and effectively to families whose cultural practices differ from their own.

BEST PRACTICES IN WORKING WITH CULTURALLY DIFFERENT FAMILIES

Developing Cultural Awareness and Competence

Until recently, little attention has been given to developing cross-cultural competence and to understanding the effects that cultural differences have on interpersonal relations. Achieving cross-cultural competence is an effortful process that requires individuals to take risks, lower their defenses, and set aside their own beliefs in an attempt to adopt another's viewpoint. For individuals who are just beginning to develop cross-cultural competence, it is likely that some encounters with culturally different families will be uncomfortable, especially when they require that we change our typical ways of thinking and behaving.

> For most people, including Americans, the distinguishing mark of cross-cultural interaction is the disappearance of the familiar guideposts that allow them to act without thinking in their own culture. Routine matters become problems that require planning or conscious decisions. They may not know when to shake hands, nod their heads, ask a question, express an opinion, or maintain silence. They may have to question the effectiveness of their techniques for giving advice and may need to search for proper channels of communication. (Stewart & Bennett, 1991, pp. 2–3

The rewards of developing effective skills for working with families whose cultures differ from our own, however, far outweigh the feelings of unfamiliarity and uncertainty that may be associated with initial cross-cultural interactions. That is, as we become more knowledgeable about other cultures and the nuances of our own culture, we will be better able to help families bridge the gap between two distinct cultures and be more effectual in our interpersonal communications (Lynch, 1992).

Developing cross-cultural competence does not happen overnight and we cannot expect to know everything there is to know about every culture. However, through an open mind and a willingness to implement new ideas, we can acquire specific strategies that will enable us to work effectively and sensitively with culturally different families, as well as enable families to feel comfortable about their interactions with service providers. Strategies that have been shown to be effective in working with culturally diverse families are interspersed throughout the psychology and special education literature (e.g., Allen & Boykin, 1992; Chan, 1990; Hanson et al., 1990; Harry, 1992; Lynch, 1992). The purpose of this section of the chapter is to present those strategies that will be most useful for school psychologists who are just beginning to develop cross-cultural competence.

Awareness. Cultural self-awareness is the first step to developing cross-cultural competence (Chan, 1990; Hanson et al., 1990; Harry, 1992; Lynch, 1992). In order for school psychologists and other service providers to completely comprehend and acknowledge the diversity that exists across cultures and, more specifically, among the families they serve, they must understand and appreciate their own culture. A beginning step in this process involves exploring one's own heritage, including place of origin, time of and reason for migration, and location of the family's first settlement in the United States. This may be accomplished through talking with the eldest family members or through document searches in county court houses, churches, or libraries. The goal here is to gain an appreciation of how one's own values, beliefs, attitudes, and customs have been molded by culture. In this way, values and beliefs that have been assumed to be universal can be viewed separately from those that are culture-specific (Chan, 1990; Lynch, 1992).

In addition to becoming knowledgeable about one's own cultural heritage, school psychologists should analyze the values and beliefs that are characteristic of mainstream U.S. culture. American values emphasize individualism, independence, autonomy, interpersonal competition, mastery, equality, punctuality, materialism, progress, and a future orientation. In addition, Americans prefer interactions that are informal rather than formal, have a high regard for achievement, and take pride in direct and assertive interactional styles (Althen, 1988; Pinderhughes, 1982). School psychologists who understand the extent to which they identify with each of these values will be in a better position to determine how the values that they adhere to most strongly affect their practice (Stewart & Bennett, 1991; Lynch, 1992).

School psychologists who value independence and autonomy in young children, for example, and who believe in promoting the attainment of developmental milestones and correcting slight deviations from the norm, may have difficulty understanding why some Native American and Latino parents have a relaxed attitude toward their children's achievement of self-reliance (Huang & Gibbs, 1992). School psychologists who value individual achievement and interpersonal competition may have difficulty working with families who come from a cultural background that values interpersonal affiliation, cooperation, and reciprocity (e.g., Latino families). School psychologists who believe that the source of a child's disability lies in physical phenomena rather than spiritual will likely experience discord with parents who are committed to spiritual rather than medical treatments (e.g., some Southeast Asian groups) (Chan, 1986; Harry, 1992). Determining the extent to which one's own cultural values differ from those of other cultures, as well as the extent to which adhering to these values affects the intervention and treatment of chil-

dren with disabilities and their families, will provide school psychologists with a more realistic perspective regarding their ability to engage in unbiased service. Thus, cultural self-awareness provides the foundation from which to discover the intricacies of other cultures and build effective relationships with culturally different families.

Knowledge and awareness of specific cultures. Once school psychologists have explored their own roots and examined the extent to which their cultural values and beliefs influence the ways in which they practice, they are ready to move into the second phase of developing cross-cultural competence — that is, learning about other cultures (Cross, 1981; Hanson et al., 1990; Lynch, 1992). This discussion is presented with two caveats. First, generalizations regarding the values, beliefs, or characteristics of a particular culture may obscure important differences within the cultural group. Second, the characteristics that determine a family's values, beliefs, and behaviors are numerous. In addition to culture, socioeconomic status, level of acculturation, level of education, reason for immigration, and geographic location are but a few of the important variables that influence and shape the values, beliefs, and behaviors embraced by culturally different families (Hanson, 1992; Harry, 1992; Lynch, 1992; Tseng & Hsu, 1991).

To illustrate, Puerto Rican families value spirituality and humanism over commercialism. However, these values are more typical of the lower-SES classes; Puerto Ricans who belong to middle and upper classes value possessions as highly symbolic of personal worth (Garcia-Preto, 1982). Thus, although an author's portrayal of a culture-specific paradigm necessitates generalizations, school psychologists should be cautious in making them and limit their generalizations from any given group to similar groups who have experienced similar circumstances.

Generalizations notwithstanding, specific information about a given culture aids in understanding the values, beliefs, and behaviors that are expressed in cross-cultural interactions. According to Lynch (1992) some of the most effective ways of gathering culture-specific information include the following: (a) acquiring knowledge about another culture through reading and studying, (b) interacting with individuals from another culture who can serve as guides or mediators, (c) engaging in the lifeways of another culture (e.g., through community activities or religious worship), and (d) learning the language of another culture.

The most efficient way for school psychologists to learn about the specific cultures of the families with whom they work is to read. In searching for reading materials, it is important to keep in mind that critical insights and viewpoints regarding any given culture may be communicated by authors who are from that culture. Therefore, it may be helpful to review several sources in order to appreciate and understand differing viewpoints regarding cultural values and cross-cultural interactions (Lynch, 1992). Viewing culture from the perspectives of many authors helps to orient school psychologists to a particular culture and increase their awareness regarding cultural differences. However, specific information pertaining to family patterns and practices is necessary to ensure that school psychologists appropriately match interventions to a family's unique lifestyle and needs.

Information related to a family's childrearing practices, family structure and function, perceptions of disability and its source, perceptions of interventions, and willingness or desire to change is useful for developing intervention plans that incorporate the family's values, beliefs, and ways of life (Hanson & Lynch, 1992; Hanson et al., 1990; Lynch, 1992). Suggesting that a behavior modification program be implemented by the parents of a young Native American child who is noncompliant may be perceived by the family as inappropriate and may even humiliate some family members. This is because, in many Native American tribes, information about a child's misbehavior is passed from the mother to an extended family member who has been appointed as the individual responsible for cultivating the child's character development; this direct communication serves to protect the parent–child bond as well as extended family connections (Huang & Gibbs, 1992).

In this example, the interventionist lacked adequate information concerning the family's childrearing practices, their patterns of communication, and the value that they place on the extended family system; therefore, a behavior program was selected that was incongruent with the family's values. The interventionist would have had a better chance of successfully implementing the behavior program if he or she had included influential family members, other than the parents, in its development. Thus, the more culture-specific information school psychologists obtain, the more sensitive they will be to different family systems and functions and the better equipped they will be to devise intervention plans that are congruent with the family's values, beliefs, traditional practices, and lifeways.

Although reading about a specific culture provides school psychologists with a wealth of information that will lead to a greater respect for and understanding of the values and beliefs that culturally different families embrace, it is not sufficient. Other enriching experiences are necessary to heighten one's awareness and understanding of different cultures. Interacting with and observing members of another culture, participating in various community activities of diverse cultures, and learning the language of another culture all provide additional opportunities to study different cultures and strengthen one's commit-

ment to developing cross-cultural competence (Hanson & Lynch, 1992; Hanson et al., 1990; Lynch, 1992).

The extent of one's commitment to developing cross-cultural competence, however, will likely be a direct reflection of the nature and diversity of the populations served. School psychologists who work *occasionally* with Muslim or Vietnamese children and their families, for example, will likely derive much of their information about these cultures through reading materials. On the other hand, school psychologists who work in areas encompassing large Asian American, African American, and/or Latino communities, may spend more time in open discussion and interpersonal sharing with members of these communities, as well as participating in holiday celebrations and other community activities, in an effort to increase their understanding of these specific cultures. Finally, school psychologists who work *primarily* with children and families whose cultural background differs from their own may choose to learn the language of that culture, since "much of what is described as culture is reflected in language" (Lynch, 1992, p. 41). The number of bilingual school psychology programs that have emerged within the last decade demonstrates the importance of language in understanding other cultures as well as a strong commitment to developing cross-cultural competence.

Communication. School psychologists who speak the same language as the families they serve may experience more effective interpersonal interactions than those who do not. However, an understanding of how different cultures transmit information *nonverbally* is also necessary for effective communication and will increase one's competence in cross-cultural interactions.

When working with culturally different families, it is important for school psychologists to understand that the amount of information that is communicated explicitly through words versus the amount of information that is communicated through contextual cues varies considerably from one culture to the next (Hall, 1976). In high-context cultures, such as Asian, Native American, African American, and Latino, meaning is derived typically through shared experience, history, and implicit messages. Conversely, in low-context cultures, such as the British, Swiss, German, and Scandinavian cultures, and those of their U.S. descendants, meaning is derived from direct, precise, and logical verbal interchanges. Misunderstandings between school psychologists and families may arise when the level of context that each party uses to communicate with one another differs. Individuals from high-context cultures, for example, may perceive specific verbal directions, detailed examples, and extensive elaboration as insensitive and mechanistic, whereas individuals from low-context cultures may feel uncomfortable with silence, obscure phrases, or unfamiliar gesturing. Thus, it is the school psychologist's responsibility to observe family communication patterns or consult with colleagues or other members of the family's culture to determine what level of reliance on context the family uses to communicate. This information will enable the school psychologists to adjust their style of communication to match those of the families with whom they work (Hanson et al., 1990; Lynch, 1992).

In addition to learning about culturally different communication patterns, school psychologists should become familiar with the meanings and uses of specific nonverbal behaviors across cultures. For example, prolonged eye contact between individuals in Latino cultures is considered disrespectful and eye contact between two strangers in some Asian cultures is regarded as shameful (Randall-David, 1989, cited in Lynch, 1992). Other nonverbal behaviors, such as specific facial expressions, amount of distance considered to be comfortable between two individuals engaged in conversation, type of physical contact permitted (e.g., a hand shake, hug, slap on the back), and gestural language, are influenced greatly by culture and differ as a function of age, gender, religion, and personal preference. Although the school psychologist cannot learn all the culturally appropriate ways of communicating and behaving, by acknowledging the most salient patterns of nonverbal communication within a given culture, they can interact and behave in ways that are respectable (Lynch, 1992). School psychologists interested in learning more about nonverbal communication across cultures may wish to begin by reading Lynch and Hanson (1992; see annotated bibliography).

In our zeal to learn as much as we can about a particular culture, gathering bits and pieces of information about unique family patterns, values, beliefs, and so forth, before an initial parent conference, we must not forget the most integral component of effective communication — the ability to view the world from the family's perspective. What is the family thinking, feeling, experiencing? The only way we are going to intervene effectively with families is to understand and respect their viewpoint, even when it is at odds with our own values and typical approaches to service delivery. Our interventions will be successful only in so far as they are culturally relevant to families.

Guidelines for Gathering Culturally Relevant Data

Understanding the cultural aspects of family systems and function will enable school psychologists to match intervention with the needs and lifestyles of families from diverse cultural backgrounds effectively. Several useful guidelines and suggestions have been offered in an attempt to assist service providers in gathering culturally relevant information from family members (Boyd-Franklin, 1989; Gopaul-McNicol,

1993; Hanson et al., 1990; Lynch, 1992; Lynch & Hanson, 1992; Ruiz & Padilla, 1979; Tseng & Hsu, 1991; Wayman et al., 1990). Although some of these guidelines were designed to be used with specific cultural groups (e.g., West Indians; Gopaul-McNicol, 1993) and others were designed to be used in early childhood settings (e.g., Wayman et al., 1990), they have direct relevance for *all* cultural groups and can be altered easily to fit families whose children are older and therefore likely to be seen by school psychologists rather than early interventionists. The following guidelines have been selected from the above sources and are useful for school psychologists to consider when structuring their interactions with culturally different families.

1. *Establish rapport and build trust.* School psychologists should attempt to put the family at ease. This requires patience, effective listening skills, and a willingness to take the time necessary to establish mutual goals. For example, Ruiz and Padilla (1979) suggest that when counseling Latinos, it is important to realize that in Latin American cultures there is a preference for personal contact and individualized attention when dealing with social institutions. Latino clients will be more comfortable and receptive to service providers who work to establish a personal relationship that is consistent with Latin American cultural characteristics. In an attempt to assist service providers in establishing this type of relationship, these authors offer the following suggestions. Greet the client on arrival, even though this may require interrupting briefly other activities. Extend your hand and introduce yourself, using your first name rather than your formal title. Finally, allow time for so-called "small talk." Moreover, continuing these informal interchanges at the beginning of subsequent sessions will help to maintain rapport.

When working with families who have recently immigrated to the United States, it may also be necessary to explain how other systems operate (e.g., educational, legal, political). To determine whether the provision of this information is necessary, school psychologists can assess (by an interview) the family's level of acculturation and understanding of relevant social institutions. There are also other tools available to assess a family's level of acculturation. For example, the West Indian Comprehensive Assessment Battery (WICAB) (Gopaul-McNicol, 1993) is designed to determine the extent to which a West Indian immigrant has assimilated into U.S. society.

2. *Identify the presenting problem.* School psychologists should listen to the family's perception of the problem and attempt to understand it from their perspective. It is also necessary to determine the family's past efforts to resolve the problem and to elicit their present understanding of treatment goals. Once these issues have been clarified, the school psycholo-

gist will be in a position to negotiate intervention strategies.

The following example, provided by Boyd-Franklin (1989), highlights the importance of taking the time to learn the client's presenting concerns. In this case, a 40-year-old African American woman began to cancel therapy appointments for herself and a 7-year-old boy, Carl, whom she had been caring for since he was 1-year-old. The client had stopped coming to appointments because she perceived the therapist as an extension of the child welfare agency, which was pressuring her to adopt her "son" or give him up so that another family could adopt him. This mother's fear that her child was going to be removed is common among many poor African American mothers. Fortunately, therapy was not terminated prematurely; the therapist's close attention to the client's perception of her role as well as the role of the child welfare agency led her to arrange a session with the client. The purpose of this session was to clarify these roles and create some distance between the therapist and the outside agency. As a result, the therapist discovered further that the client would not officially adopt Carl because "in her view and in Black culture one never terminates a mother's rights to her child even if someone else raises him and becomes his de facto mother" (p. 173). Once these issues were clarified and the roles of the therapist and the child welfare agency were delineated clearly, the therapist was able to regain the client's trust and continue with the proposed treatment plan.

3. *Learn the family system.* Before school psychologists can effectively match interventions with the needs of the family, it is necessary to determine the structure of the family system. The following areas of family functioning are particularly important to consider: family composition, family members' roles and responsibilities, family's interactional patterns, family's support system, family's childrearing practices, and the family's beliefs about the child's handicapping condition and its source. Once the school psychologist has determined the relevant aspects of the family system, interventions can be individualized and tailored to the particular needs and resources of the family.

For example, in considering family structure, Boyd-Franklin (1989) points out that African Americans will likely have at least some regular involvement with extended family members. For this reason, she emphasizes the need for any service provider working with African Americans to take the time to learn about the relationships that clients have with extended family members. Similarly, Ruiz and Padilla (1979) explain that when working with Latinos, it is important to remember that in addition to nuclear family relationships, Latino family relationships include certain formalized kinship relations such as that of the godfather.

SUMMARY

The purpose of this chapter was to provide school psychologists with a foundation from which to begin to build their skills in providing services to families whose cultural backgrounds differ from their own. Several key concepts were defined in an attempt to aid school psychologists in determining the important dimensions along which families differ, including ethnicity, race, socioeconomic status, and level of acculturation. In addition, a framework for understanding how family systems function was presented from a cross-cultural perspective, and strategies for developing cross-cultural competence were offered. The chapter concluded with a summary of useful guidelines for gathering culturally relevant information about families.

As a result of the rapidly changing demographics of the United States and the concomitant implementation of PL 99-457, school psychologists are faced with the challenge of providing services to culturally different children and their families. Many school psychologists feel ill-prepared to embark on this mission because they have not received adequate instruction or experience through their training programs. The strategies, guidelines, and suggestions offered in this chapter will provide school psychologists with useful ways to begin to develop the skills necessary for working effectively with culturally different families. It is important to understand that acquiring these skills is a lifelong process. Learning about another culture and developing the skills to communicate effectively with its members is a process that begins with the first family with whom we work and improves over time as our number of cross-cultural interactions and experiences increase. Once we make a commitment to developing cross-cultural competence, the knowledge that we gain about ourselves and others and the cross-cultural interactions that we experience will be forever enriching.

REFERENCES

Althen, G. (1988). *American ways — a Guide for foreigners in the United States.* Yarmouth, ME: Intercultural Press.

Atkinson, D. R., Morten, G., & Sue, D. W. (Eds.). (1989). *Counseling American minorities.* Dubuque, IA: W. C. Brown.

Allen, B. A., & Boykin, A. W. (1992). African-American children and the educational process: Alleviating cultural discontinuity through prescriptive pedagogy. *School Psychology Review, 21,* 586–596.

Banks, J. A. (1993). The canon debate, knowledge construction, and multicultural education. *Educational Researcher, 22,* 4–14.

Banks, J. A., & McGee Banks, C. A. (1993). *Multicultural education: Issues and perspectives* (2nd ed.). Boston: Allyn and Bacon.

Boyd-Franklin, N. (1989). *Black families in therapy: A multisystems approach.* New York: Guilford.

Chan, S. Q. (1986). Parents of exceptional Asian children. In M. K. Kitano & P. C. Chinn (Eds.), *Exceptional Asian children and youth* (pp. 36–53). Reston, VA: Council for Exceptional Children.

Chan, S. Q. (1990). Early intervention with culturally diverse families of infants and toddlers with disabilities. *Infants and Young Children, 3*(2), 78–87.

Children's Defense Fund. (1989). *A vision for America's future.* Washington, DC: Author.

Children's Defense Fund. (1991). *The state of America's children.* Washington, DC: Author.

Copeland, A. P., & White, K. M. (1991). *Studying families.* Newbury Park, CA: Sage.

Counting the children. (1989, May). *Education Week*, p. 3.

Cross, W. E. (1981). Black families and black identity development: Rediscovering the distinction between self-esteem and reference group orientation. *Journal of Comparative Family Studies, 12*, 19–49.

Cunningham, K., Cunningham, K., & O'Connell, J. C. (1986). Impact of differing cultural perceptions on special education service delivery. *Rural Special Education Quarterly, 8*(1), 2–8.

Ember, C. R., & Ember, M. (1973). *Anthropology.* New York: Appleton-Century-Crofts.

Frisby, C. L. (1992a). Issues and problems in the influence of culture on the psychoeducational needs of African-American children. *School Psychology Review, 21*, 532–551.

Frisby, C. L., (1992b). Parent education as a means for improving the school achievement of low-income African-American children. In S. L. Christenson & J. C. Conoley (Eds.), *Home–school collaboration* (pp. 127–155). Silver Spring, MD: National Association of School Psychologists.

Garcia-Preto, N. (1982). Puerto Rican families. In M. McGoldrick, J. K. Pearce, & J. Giordano (Eds.), *Ethnicity and family therapy* (pp. 164–186). New York: Guilford.

Gopaul-McNicol, S. (1992). Implications for school psychologists: Synthesis of the mini-series. *School Psychology Review, 21*, 597–600.

Gopaul-McNicol, S. (1993). *Working with West Indian families.* New York: Guilford.

Hall, M., & Allen, W. (1989). Race consciousness among African-American college students. In G. Berry & J. Asamen (Eds.), *Black students: Psychosocial issues and academic achievement* (pp. 172–197). Newbury Park, CA: Sage Publications.

Hall, E. T. (1976). *Beyond culture.* Garden City, NY: Anchor Press/Doubleday.

Hanson, M. J. (1990). *Final report: California Early Intervention Personnel Study Project.* San Francisco: San Francisco State University, Department of Special Education. (Available from Early Intervention Programs, Department of Developmental Services, 1600 9th Street, Sacramento, CA 95814.)

Hanson, M. J. (1992). Ethnic, cultural, and language diversity in intervention settings. In E. W. Lynch & M. J. Hanson (Eds.), *Developing cross-cultural competence* (pp. 3–18). Baltimore: Paul H. Brookes.

Hanson, M. J., & Lynch, E. W. (1992). Family diversity: Implications for policy and practice. *Topics in Early Childhood Special Education, 12*(3), 283–306.

Hanson, M. J., Lynch, E. W., & Wayman, K. I. (1990). Honoring the cultural diversity of families when gathering data. *Topics in Early Childhood Special Education, 10*(1), 112–131.

Harry, B. (1992). Developing cultural self-awareness: The first step in values clarification for early interventionists. *Topics in Early Childhood Special Education, 12*(3), 333–350.

Hoebel, E. A. (1972). *Anthropology: The study of man* (4th ed.). New York: McGraw-Hill.

Huang, L. N. (1989). Southeast Asian refugee children and adolescents. In J. T. Gibbs & L. N. Huang (Eds.), *Children of color: Psychological interventions with minority youth* (pp. 278–321). San Francisco: Jossey-Bass.

Huang, L. N., & Gibbs, J. T. (1992). Partners or adversaries? Home–school collaboration across culture, race, and ethnicity, In S. L. Christenson & J. C. Conoley (Eds.), *Home–school collaboration* (pp. 81–109). Silver Spring, MD: National Association of School Psychologists.

Levitan, S. A., Belous, R. S., & Gallo, F. (1988). *What's happening to the American family? Tensions, hopes, and realities* (rev. ed.). Baltimore: Johns Hopkins University Press.

Lewis, J. M., Beavers, W. R., Gossett, J. T., & Phillips, V. A. (1976). *No single thread: Psychological health in family systems.* New York: Brunner/Mazel.

Lynch, E. W. (1992). Developing cross-cultural competence. In E. W. Lynch & M. J. Hanson (Eds.), *Developing cross-cultural competence* (pp. 35–61). Baltimore: Paul H. Brookes.

Lynch, E. W., & Hanson, M. J. (1992). Steps in the right direction: Implications for interventionists. In E. W. Lynch & M. J. Hanson (Eds.), *Developing cross-cultural competence* (pp. 355–370). Baltimore: Paul H. Brookes.

Masnick, G., & Bane, M. J. (1980). *The nation's families: 1960–1990.* Boston: Auburn House.

McGhee, J. D. (1983). *Black solidarity: The tie that binds.* Washington, DC: National Urban League. (ERIC Document Reproduction Service No. 234117)

McGoldrick, M., Pearce, J. K., & Giordano, J. (1982). *Ethnicity and family therapy.* New York: Guilford.

Murdock, G. P. (1967). *Ethnographic atlas.* Pittsburgh.

Nanda, S. (1980). *Cultural anthropology.* New York: D. Van Nostrand.

Nuttall, E. V., De Leon, B., & Valle, M. (1990). Best practices in considering cultural factors. In A. Thomas & J. Grimes (Eds.), *Best practices in school psychology–II* (pp. 221–233). Washington, DC: National Association of School Psychologists.

Pinderhughes, E. (1982). Afro-American families and the victim system. In M. McGoldrick, J. K. Pearce, & J. Giordano (Eds.), *Ethnicity and family therapy* (pp. 108–122). New York: Guilford.

Randall-David, E. (1989). *Strategies for working with culturally diverse communities and clients.* Washington, DC: Association for the Care of Children's Health.

Redfield, R., Linton, R., & Herskovits, M. (1936). Memorandum on the study of acculturation. *American Anthropologist, 38*, 149–152.

Research and Policy Committee of the Committee for Economic Development. (1987). *Children in need — Investment strategies for the educationally disadvantaged.* New York: Author.

Ruiz, R. A., & Padilla, A. M. (1979). Counseling Latinos. In D. R. Atkinson, G. Morten, & D. W. Sue (Eds.), *Counseling American minorities: A cross cultural perspective* (2nd ed., pp. 213–231). Dubuque, IA: Wm. C. Brown.

Schneider, D. M., & Gough, K. (Eds.). (1961). *Matrilineal kinship.* Berkeley, CA: University of California Press.

Stack, C. (1975). *All our kin: Strategies for survival in the Black community*. New York: Harper & Row.

Stewart, E. C., & Bennett, M. J. (1991). American cultural patterns: A cross-cultural perspective (rev. ed.). Yarmouth, ME: Intercultural Press.

Tseng, W. S., & Hsu, J. (1991). *Culture and family: Problems and therapy*. New York: Haworth.

Wayman, K. I., Lynch, E. W., & Hanson, M. J. (1990). Home-based early childhood services: Cultural sensitivity in a family systems approach. *Topics in Early Childhood Special Education*, *10*(4), 56–75.

ANNOTATED BIBLIOGRAPHY

Lynch, E. W., & Hanson, M. J. (Eds.). (1992). *Developing cross-cultural competence: A guide for working with young children and their families*. Baltimore: Paul H. Brookes.
Part 1 of this book introduces several critical issues regarding the provision of services to families of diverse cultural, ethnic, and language groups. Several chapters in this section focus on developing intercultural effectiveness. Part 2 describes the history, values, and beliefs of the major cultural and ethnic groups that make up the U.S. population, while Part 3 offers suggestions and recommendations for interventionists who work with families whose cultural backgrounds differ from their own.

McGoldrick, M., Pearce, J. K., & Giordano, J. (1982). *Ethnicity and family therapy*. New York: Guilford.
This book provides a comprehensive view of ethnic differences in family patterns and common attitudes toward therapy. Positive and practical clinical suggestions are offered for working with 18 different ethnic families including African American, Native Americans, West Indian, Mexican, Puerto Rican, Cuban, Asian, French Canadian, German, Greek, Iranian, Irish, Italian, Jewish, Polish, Portuguese, Norwegian, and British.

Tseng, W. S., & Hsu, J. (1991). *Culture and family: Problems and therapy*. New York: Haworth.
This book offers a comprehensive overview of family systems from a cross-cultural perspective. Critical issues regarding family development, family subsystems, and family adjustment are discussed and cultural considerations in family assessment and therapy are presented.

Gibbs, J. T., Huang, L. N., & Associates. (1989). *Children of color: Psychological interventions with minority youth*. San Francisco: Jossey-Bass.
This book provides an up-to-date analysis of the state of knowledge and developmental/ecological and intervention issues with respect to culturally different children and families. A case study approach for assessing and treating culturally different children and adolescents is provided.

90

Best Practices in Working with Parents of Children with Disabilities

Marian C. Fish
Queens College of the City University of New York

OVERVIEW

Relationships between school professionals and parents of children with disabilities have changed dramatically over the last century. This shift in family–professional relationships has greatly influenced best practices of school psychologists working with parents of children with disabilities.

Prior to the 1960s parents were expected to follow the recommendations of professionals rather than to participate in decision making (Turnbull & Winton, 1984). Fine and Gardner (1994) remind us that parents were often blamed for their children's problems and treated poorly. They describe this phase of involvement as one of "passivity on the part of the parent" (p. 2).

As a result of the political advocacy of such parent organizations as the National Association for Retarded Children and other activist groups and greater interest by professionals in the rights of families, legislation passed in the 1970s reflected a shift in policy toward mandated parent participation in educational planning for children with disabilities. Rights given to parents in PL 94-142, the Education for All Handicapped Children Act of 1975, for example, included required notice and consent for evaluation and participation in decisions regarding evaluation results and at IEP conferences. While parent participation increased dramatically and many professionals recognized the importance of family involvement, parents were not always prepared for active participation and school policies often did not encourage parent involvement. During this second phase of family–professional interaction, the continued use of the medical model of help giving fostered dependency of parents on "professional prescribers." "Parents were typically expected to implement the treatment that was prescribed by experts" (Fine & Gardner, 1994).

The ideological shift that has brought us to the current phase of family–professional interaction is the acknowledgment of the rights of parents to participate in the development of programs for children and the recognition that parents and families have strengths, resources, and expertise that can and should be used to meet the needs of their children (Fine & Gardner, 1994). This new perspective can be seen clearly in the Part H requirements of PL 99-457 (1986); this extends PL 94-142 to children below age 5 and requires services to be directed at *families* through the Individualized Family Service Plan (IFSP) which includes a statement of family strengths as well as needs. The primary systems in the life of a child are the home and school, and the message of this legislation is that participation by each system and collaboration between these systems is necessary for the healthy development of the child.

School psychologists have always worked extensively with children with disabilities in special education and to varying degrees with their parents. The "inclusion" movement, which supports placement of children with disabilities into the mainstream whenever possible, will likely further expand the need for the school psychologist to work with parents of children with disabilities in developing viable educational programs.

This chapter describes how school psychologists can effectively apply the philosophy of parent–professional collaboration in their work with children with disabilities. It recognizes that there is not one type of relationship between parents of children with disabilities and school psychologists. The ultimate goal of the relationship is to promote healthy family functioning and parent decision making and to empower parents.

BASIC CONSIDERATIONS

When there is a child with a disability in the family, there is an impact on family functioning (Turnbull & Turnbull, 1990). "Children with disabilities inevitably challenge families by making inordinate demands on their time, psychological well-being, relationships, economic resources, and freedom of movement" (Brantlinger, 1991, p. 250). While there are many similarities in functioning in families with an exceptional child, adaptation of these families can vary greatly and is influenced by a number of factors including ethnic and cultural background, nature of the disability, and family position in the life cycle.

To work successfully with parents of children with disabilities, school psychologists need to be aware of commonalities in functioning and experiences of families with children with disabilities; that is, how are these families alike? Next, it is necessary to consider variables that may affect family adjustment and contribute to the uniqueness of each family. Finally, school psychologists should recognize adaptive coping responses: What does healthy adjustment look like in families with children with disabilities?

Common Family Experiences

Economic realities. Expenses related to a child with a disability often result in financial hardship for families (Turnbull & Turnbull, 1990). Although medical insurance may reduce some of the expenses for medical care, therapy, child care, and special equipment, it rarely provides for all needs (Darling, 1991). Transportation, laundry, or structural modifications for the home to accommodate a child (e.g., ramps) or to repair damage are often costly (Fish, 1991). There are also indirect costs for these families such as lost work time and interference with career advancement. A chance to relocate to another city might have to be rejected because needed child services are not available, and this may prevent a parent from moving upward in his or her company. Funds may not be available to provide for higher education and/or other needs of siblings.

Costs may be high not only for children with severe disabilities but also for those with mild and moderate disabilities; for example, a learning disabled child might need tutoring, summer programs, or a special computer (Turnbull & Turnbull, 1990). The economic impact on families with disabled children can be quite significant.

Daily care needs. The physical and health needs of children with disabilities often require great effort, particularly when the disabilities are severe or the illnesses are chronic. Daily care includes bathing, dressing, toileting, and feeding the youngster as well as cooking, cleaning, washing, and taking care of the household. Going to the doctor, supermarket, or to a fast food outlet can be a major undertaking. Once the child is dressed, he or she must be "taken" in and out of transportation (e.g., car or bus) and moved from place to place. The responsibility of daily care over many years is associated with increased parental stress (Turnbull & Turnbull, 1990). One parent describes a shopping trip with her daughter who is mentally retarded:

> When Beckie was little, such an excursion required only the extra energy needed to carry her on my hip and choose groceries one handed ...But, when she hit

her teens a completely new ingredient was added to the challenge. I took her shopping with me only if I felt up to looking groomed, cheerful, competent, and in command of any situation, so that when she bellowed and stamped as she did when we walked through the supermarket door, people who stared could quickly surmise that I would handle the situation, quiet my strange child, and get on with my shopping. (Turnbull & Turnbull, 1985, p. 144)

Socialization needs and recreational opportunities. It has been well documented that parents who have a child with a disability are less frequently engaged in leisure-time activities and interact socially less with friends (Fish, 1991). Parents express feelings of isolation and find it more difficult to go on family trips, out to dinner, or to the movies. Frequently, their social life is limited because of the difficulties in finding a babysitter or care giver who often must be specially trained.

Just as parents' social interactions are curtailed, children with disabilities are often lonely. Meeting the socialization needs of the child with a disability may be stressful as many of these youngsters have significant social handicaps. Negative attitudes of community members is often cited as a major barrier to socialization for the whole family (Turnbull & Turnbull, 1990). For example, when disabilities are very stigmatizing (e.g., severely impaired speech) parents often structure their lives to avoid social situations where the child would have to speak, limiting their social interaction as well (Darling, 1991).

Future planning considerations. A major issue that must be faced is planning for the child when he or she is no longer eligible for mandated services (Darling, 1991). "Most parents of disabled children have concerns about the future from the day they suspect that something is wrong with the child" (Darling, 1991, p. 81). They often ask, "what if something happens to us?" Uncertainty about the future with regard to employment, social opportunities, and legal/financial needs is a common worry that impacts on family planning.

Parent response. Theories that have been proposed to explain the response of parents when learning that their child has a disability include stage theory and nonsequential stage theory (Brantlinger, 1991; Darling, 1991). Stage theory suggests that all families go through a sequential series of stages such as shock, denial, sadness, anger or anxiety, adaptation, and reorganization before generally reaching a final acceptance stage. Nonsequential stage theorists agree that these reactions may be present but believe that the reactions do not necessarily occur in a set order, and may recur at different points in the life cycle. A variant of this view is held by Olshansky (1962) who describes "chronic sorrow" as a normal reaction to the birth of a child with a disability that remains with parents throughout life, often emerging when developmental milestones are reached. More recent opinions suggest that families may have similar responses, but if and when families pass through stages is dependent on a number of variables (Darling, 1991).

Variables Affecting Family Response

All families share many characteristics, and all children present a host of challenges and responsibilities to their parents, yet there is great diversity among families (Hanson & Hanline, 1990; Powers, 1991). A number of variables impact on the adjustment of a family to a child with a disability. For example, Hanson and Hanline (1990) list child characteristics (e.g., age, diagnostic categories, caregiving demands, behavioral characteristics), parent ability to cope with stressors in general, parental beliefs about the cause of the disability, and types and availability of both formal and informal systems and networks of support (e.g., family, friends, professionals) as contributing to the adaptation and stress experienced by families of children with disabilities. Other researchers have identified variables such as socioeconomic status, physician attitude, presence of other children and spouse in the home, prior information, religiosity, physical appearance of the child, and prognosis (Darling, 1991). For the purposes of this chapter, these variables have been combined and organized as follows: nature of disability, cultural background, family structure, and family's position in the life cycle.

Nature of the disability. The nature, severity, and demands of the disability play a critical role in family response (Turnbull & Turnbull, 1990). Each type of disability has distinctive characteristics and functional behaviors that impact on the family. For example, when a child has a language or speech disorder, everyday communication may be affected (Turnbull & Turnbull, 1990). In a recent study, 28% of parents of children with a wide variety of disabling conditions indicated that the disability impacted on the daily lives of the family; the effect was "clearly more pronounced among the families of children with more substantial handicaps and rises to 60% for families of children with physical/multiple impairment" (Palfrey, Walker, Butler, & Singer, 1989, p. 102).

The physical appearance of the person with disabilities can influence family reaction. A very visible handicap may affect not only the child's self-concept but also the attitudes of parents, siblings, and others in the community. Severe disabilities that are more visible may excuse inappropriate behavior or may cause social stigma (Turnbull & Turnbull, 1990). It is not clear, however, that parents always share a common view of severity of handicap (Blacher, 1984). Ambiguous conditions such as autism or those with uncertain prognoses are hypothesized to be the most

emotionally stressful for families as parents often keep searching for plausible diagnoses or appropriate treatment (Brantlinger, 1991). Genetic disorders have broad implications because parents may be carriers of the trait (Brantlinger, 1991). When parents have negative attitudes toward deviance prior to the birth of the child, a more difficult adjustment may occur (Seligman, 1991). This suggests that a thorough understanding of parents' feelings about the disability and of their expectations for the child is essential.

Of course, a most critical aspect of the disability is the functional behavior of the child. It is not the disability itself that is the key, but the resulting behavioral characteristics which impact on the family.

Cultural background. There is great diversity of reaction to childhood disability dependent on subcultural groups. A family's beliefs, values, customs, traditions, and the ways it accesses health care will affect its adjustment to disability. Seligman and Darling (1989) identify four major subcultural categories: (a) social class, (b) race/ethnicity, (c) religion, and (d) region. However, care must be taken not to stereotype any group.

The clearest examples of social class differences have occurred in studies of children within the mild ranges of retardation. Parents and professionals from middle- and upper-class families regarded even mild retardation as devastating, while lower-class parents "may not even define it as a disability" (Seligman & Darling, 1989, p. 189). Possible explanations are that lower-class families are not as achievement oriented and were able to envision their child in normal adult roles or that they have a higher tolerance for deviance. In the case of a physical disability, however, there appeared to be no differences by social class. A recent study reported that lower-class families had less family support and more physical, emotional, and financial problems than higher-class families (Seligman & Darling, 1989). It is hypothesized that when necessities are scarce, the child's disability is only one of a myriad of problems and may not get the same attention as in more affluent families. The results of still another study indicate that parents from different socioeconomic groups will report stress differently and will behave differently with regard to participating in program planning (Palfrey et al., 1989).

Attitudes toward disability in our society vary by ethnicity and religion, yet we must be careful not to stereotype any group as there is much intragroup variability. Also, there is considerable confounding in studies of ethnic groups, religious groups, and social class.

Research on African-Americans, for example, indicates that they place great importance on the extended family and the church as social support and that they report a greater number of significant others who assist families with a disabled child (Seligman & Darling, 1989). Hispanic subcultures include Mexicans, Puerto Ricans, and subgroups from many Latin American countries. Traditional Mexican culture values familism, male dominance, subordination of young to old, and person orientation rather than goal orientation (Seligman & Darling, 1989). These values and child-rearing attitudes may result in Mexican-American parents being more accepting of disability than Anglo parents. Similarly, family strength and support is very important in the Puerto Rican community along with submissiveness and acceptance of fate; such "fatalism may help parents cope with a child's disabilities" (Seligman & Darling, 1989, p. 200). Another situation where culture may play a role is among Asian-Americans. In Chinese culture the oldest son usually has more responsibilities than other children in the family, and if he is disabled, this may create difficulties (Seligman & Darling, 1989).

There is no clear relationship between any religious group and acceptance of disability. It is suggested, however, that more religious families may have support networks through their church or synagogue that may facilitate acceptance and coping (Seligman & Darling, 1989).

It is clear that cultural background is a significant factor in family adjustment to a child with a disability and that it also affects family responsiveness and receptivity to sources of help (Fine & Gardner, 1994).

Family structure. Family structure refers to the characteristics of the family, its members and organization. Persons in the family — mother, father, siblings, grandparents — join together to perform various tasks or functions; all have different roles and responsibilities (Fish & Jain, 1988; Powers, 1991).

An increasing number of children with disabilities are being raised in nontraditional households such as single-parent, blended, or multigenerational homes (Fish, 1991). For example, an overwhelming majority of single parents, 95%, are mothers who work outside the home (Lombana, 1983). While the functions of the single-parent family are the same as the two-parent family, when the custodial parent tries to carry out both functions, role strain may result (Fish, 1991). On the other hand, in blended families or step families, where one or both partners have been previously married, a major structural issue is the lack of clear role definition and clear boundaries (Fish, 1991): This is the opposite situation to a single-parent household because there are now more than two parents with potential conflict in such areas as visitation, life-style, and/or discipline (Fish, 1991). It is clear that alternative family structures must be carefully considered and play a critical role in adaptation when there is a child with a disability.

Factors such as the sex of the child, visibility, and/or severity of the disability may affect the responses of individual family members. There are data to suggest that mothers may have more demands placed on their time as a result of role division in the family (McLinden, 1990). Some research suggests that siblings of children with disabilities may be prone to adjustment problems (Hannah & Midlarsky, 1985). There is some evidence that when a sibling has excessive responsibility for a brother or sister with a disability, this is related to the development of anger, guilt, and resentment (Seligman, 1991). Several studies indicate that older female siblings in small families may have more extensive care-taking responsibilities than other siblings. It is apparent then that family subsystems, mother, father, parents, and siblings, all affect and are affected by the exceptional child in the family and contribute to the uniqueness of each family's adjustment.

Life-cycle position. Families progress through identifiable, predictable stages in their development (Carter & McGoldrick, 1989). Whether these are crises or transitions depends on the ability of a family to modify its structures to accommodate changing needs (Carlson, 1987). A survey of the literature suggests that major stages for families with a child with a disability are at preschool age (3–5 years), school age (6–8 years), adolescence (12–14 years), and chronological adulthood (19–21 years) (Beavers, Hampson, Hulgus, & Beavers, 1986; Powers, 1991). For example, with a retarded child during the early years, there are issues concerning the child's physical health and safety, parent adjustment to a diagnosis and readjustment of expectations (Powers, 1991). When the disabled child reaches school age, parents may be forced to acknowledge once again their child's widening differences from other youngsters. For parents of children with retarded development the onset of puberty increases their awareness of differences between their child's physical appearance and his or her mental and social abilities (Wikler, 1981). The adolescent may have increased wishes for independence, and his or her emerging sexuality is evident. At a time when the nondisabled adolescent is entering independent adulthood, the adolescent with a disability is often still dependent on the family. Parents who anticipated increased freedom and independence in personal, professional, and family areas must readjust their expectations (Dane, 1993). In one study of development and transition involving 30 parents of mentally retarded persons, their child's 21st birthday was characterized as the second most stressful of 10 predictable crises (Wikler, 1981).

Adaptive Coping

Despite oft-repeated statements of greater chronic dysfunction in families of children with disabilities, there is little evidence that supports the presence of greater psychopathology among these families (Hampson, Hulgus, Beavers, & Beavers, 1988). Although some families adapt better to the stress of a disabled child than others, most families manage to adapt quite well to the requirements of a child with special needs.

In a study of families with a retarded child, for example, observed family competence was within the adequate range and compared favorably to the non-clinical group of families (Hampson et al., 1988). Characteristics associated with healthy adaptation included (a) openness and directness of communication, (b) strong internal support systems, (c) a noticeable degree of autonomy and responsibility in all members, and (d) few signs of unresolved conflict. Expression of feelings did not necessarily have to be positive; it could be negative or ambivalent and still indicate good coping. In another study, family adaptation was promoted by clear diagnosis and information about the disability and the capability for positive contact with and response to other family members (Beavers et al., 1986). Families that acknowledged the extra needs and the differentness of the disabled member, while giving other family member needs and views equal weight, were most competent. In these families there was an effort made to balance the special needs of the disabled child with other family concerns (Beavers et al., 1986). Still other studies have reported that adequate social support and financial and personal resources such as family integration, parental self-esteem, and physical and emotional health were associated with fewer negative consequences (Todis & Singer, 1991). Morgan (1988) reports that family cohesion, expression, and recreational orientation as well as the mother's perception of adequacy of support from the husband and other relatives were associated with better adaptation to an autistic child.

In general, certain family characteristics appear to be associated with healthy adjustment. These include good communication among the family members, supportiveness of family members towards each other, and the ability to assume appropriate parent and child roles (Fine & Gardner, 1994).

Background and Training

Working successfully with parents of children with disabilities requires that school psychologists move from a child-centered model to a family-centered model. A family orientation in school psychology is not synonymous with family therapy but rather refers to consideration of the child within the family context. It recognizes that families have strengths and supports, and it appreciates their diversity and uniqueness. An understanding of similarities and differences among families and recognition of adaptive functioning as just discussed is essential. A knowledge base in family systems is required as all members of a family influence and are influenced by other members. The family is a dynamic entity and should be approached in a manner that recognizes the developmental and cyclical nature of adaptation (Bailey &

Simeonsson, 1988). A family orientation does not subscribe to a deficit model, but rather it builds on existing family competencies and helps develop new competencies so that a family can actively advocate for itself.

It is helpful if the school psychologist working with families with a disabled child not only has a systemic perspective but also has knowledge about (a) the contemporary family (e.g., single-parent, blended, extended); (b) the cultural/ethnic background of families within the district including their values, traditions, beliefs, and view of health care; (c) relevant community resources; and (d) the specific disability and the behavioral aspects of the disability.

A number of skills for effectively working with parents follow from the knowledge bases described. Fine and Gardner (1994) note five "process skills" that support the enactment of collaboration:

1. Interpersonal skills (e.g., accurate listening and communicating).

2. Language considerations (e.g., "we" rather than "I" statements, respect for others' views).

3. Problem-solving skills.

4. Recognition of family prerogatives.

5. Ability to personalize assessment (e.g., assess families with regard to structure, function, strengths, and resources). (p. 20)

Table 1 illustrates the types of helping behaviors likely to be enabling and have positive consequences (Dunst & Paget, 1991, p. 36).

In a fascinating study of low-income, black, single-mothers, behaviors in unempowering and empowering relationships were identified (Kalyanpur & Rao, 1991). Disrespect, a focus on deficits, and a discounting of differences in parenting styles led to unempowering relationships. Behaviors in empowering relationships included (a) responsiveness to parent's needs by providing emotional support and specific services and (b) establishment of rapport by being conversational, interpreting what was said, sharing stories, and expressing confidence in the mothers' ability to bring up their children.

It is also important for the school psychologist to be able to identify potential obstacles to a parent–professional relationship and have the skills to overcome them. Sometimes, however, these obstacles are bureaucratic and require major organizational change.

Finally, consultation skills, which are now an integral part of the curriculum of many training programs, will facilitate interactions with parents and the development of a collaborative relationship. These skills include expertise in communication and problem solving (Fine & Gardner, 1994).

TABLE 1
Help Giver Attitudes, Beliefs, and Behaviors Associated with
Empowering and Competency-Producing Influences

Prehelping attitudes and beliefs	Helping behaviors	Posthelping responses and consequences
1. Positive attributions toward help seekers and helping relationships.	1. Employs active and reflective listening skills.	1. Accepts and supports help seeker decisions.
2. Emphasis on help seeker responsibility for meeting needs and solving problems.	2. Helps client clarify concerns and needs.	2. Minimizes the help seeker's sense of indebtedness.
3. High expectations regarding the capacity of help seekers to become competent.	3. Pro-offers help in response to help seeker needs.	3. Permits reciprocity as part of help giver–help seeker exchanges.
4. Emphasis upon building on help seeker strengths.	4. Offers help that is normative.	4. Minimizes the psychological response costs of accepting help.
5. Proactive stance toward helping relationships.	5. Offers help that is congruent and matches the help seeker's appraisal of needs.	5. Enhances a sense of self-efficacy regarding active involvement in meeting needs.
6. Promotion emphasis as the focus of help giving.	6. Promotes acquisition of competencies to meet needs, solve problems, and achieve aspirations.	6. Maintains confidentiality at all times; shares information only with help seeker's permission.
	7. Employs partnerships and parent–professional collaboration as the mechanisms for meeting needs.	
	8. Allows locus of decision making to rest with the help seeker.	

Note. From "Parent–professional partnerships and family empowerment" by C. J. Dunst and K. D. Paget, 1991, p. 36. In M. J. Fine (Ed.), *Collaboration with parents of exceptional children,* Brandon, VT: Clinical Psychology Publishing Company, Inc. Copyright 1991; all rights reserved. Reprinted by permission.

BEST PRACTICES

Traditional means of working with parents of special needs children have often been paternalistic and have led to dependency on the professionals. Despite pleas for family involvement, there is often a disparity between the approach to helping which views the school psychologist as being the authority with all the answers and the behaviors necessary to promote greater participation on the part of the family (Dunst & Paget, 1991).

A number of models proposed for working with parents of special needs children have attempted to address this conflict. The model developed by Dunst, Johanson, Rounds, Trivette, and Hamby (1992), for example, sees parent–professional partnerships as a function of interactive time between parents and professionals and the display of different behavioral states and traits such as trust, honesty, and shared responsibility (p. 170). This model shows how relationships evolve from coordination to cooperation to collaboration and finally to a partnership "as parents and professionals work toward agreed upon goals" (p.

169). Reaching a true partnership relationship is a process that takes time. Table 2 (Dunst et al., 1992, p. 163) presents a categorization scheme for organizing the major characteristics of parent–professional partnerships as identified by *both* parents and professionals. These characteristics can be used by professionals as guidelines to evaluate their own performance with regard to attitudes, beliefs, and behaviors.

A model of collaborative consultation is presented by Fine (1990, 1991). Its objectives include (a) educating parents for decision making and including them in decision making, (b) assisting them therapeutically to improve coping behaviors, and (c) enabling and empowering parents to actively support their child. Multiple roles are seen for the school psychologist including mediator, advocate, therapist, and expert. As with the parent–professional partnership model of Dunst et al. (1992), collaboration is a desirable goal that takes time to achieve.

Laborde and Seligman (1991) propose a model of intervention for working with families of disabled children that has three counseling interventions: educative, personal advocacy, and facilitative counsel-

TABLE 2
A Categorization Scheme for Organizing the
Major Characteristics of Parent–Professional Partnerships

Category	Definition	Characteristics
Beliefs	Cognitive attributions about how one should act or ought to behave toward other people	Trust, mutual respect, honesty, acceptance, mutually supportive, nonjudgmental, presumed capabilities
Attitudes	Particular (emotional) feelings about a person, situation, or relationship	Caring, understanding, commitment, empathy, positive stance, humor, confidence
Communicative Style	Methods and approaches for information sharing between partners	Open communication, active listening, openness, understanding, full disclosure of information, information sharing
Behavioral Actions	Behaviors that reflect translation of attitudes and beliefs into actions	Mutual respect, openness, flexibility, understanding, shared responsibility, mutual support, reciprocity, mutual agreement about goals, dependability, equality, humor, problem solving

Note. From "Characteristics of parent–professional partnerships" by C. J. Dunst, C. Johanson, T. Rounds, C. M. Trivette, and D. Hamby. In S. L. Christenson & J. C. Conoley (Eds.), *Home–school collaboration: Enhancing children's academic and social competencies.* Silver Spring, MD: National Association of School Psychologists. Copyright 1992 by NASP. Reprinted by permission of the publisher.

ing (p. 348). The educative role is one of providing information to parents; personal advocacy refers to assisting parents in finding relevant information and locating appropriate services but being careful to help parents assume this role themselves. Facilitative counseling is similar to supportive counseling or psychotherapy to help parents deal with feelings or behaviors of concern and to build coping behaviors.

A review of these and other models suggests that there is considerable agreement as to what effective relationships between school psychologists and parents look like, and much consensus on the means to achieve these goals. Best practices in working with parents of children with disabilities has as its goal collaboration and/or partnership with parents using approaches that empower, encourage participatory involvement, and enhance competency (Dunst et al., 1992). Professionals move in and out of the life of the child, but parents provide constant support for their children and hold ultimate responsibility for their well-being.

Best practice in working with parents of children with disabilities include the following services:

Education/Information sharing. The role of providing information means that school psychologists help parents obtain information, understand and interpret information, or use information to help make decisions. The types of information can include behaviors associated with the disability, characteristic patterns of development, health or related services, and community resources. Care must be taken

to ensure that siblings and/or other family members are also informed during this process.

Information needs will vary at different age periods (Blacher, 1984). For example, diagnostic and prognostic information is generally conveyed at earlier ages (Seligman & Darling, 1989). On the other hand, information on sex management and sources of vocational training is more likely to be requested during adolescence. Other information needs are quite consistent across ages and include inquiries about respite services, financial assistance, support groups, and appropriate child-care providers.

At any age of the child, parents may want practical information regarding management, specialized equipment, or legal rights, all of which may be provided through books and other reading materials as well as through referrals to community organizations. A list of 60 books written by parents of children with many different disabilities has been prepared by Mullins (1987) and is an excellent bibliographic resource. The National Information Center for Children and Youth with Disabilities (NICHCY, P.O. Box 1492, Washington, DC 20013-1492) is a national information and referral clearinghouse and provides material for parents and professionals. Also, the Association for the Care of Children's Health Resource Catalogue (ACCH, 7910 Woodmont Avenue, Suite 300, Bethesda, MD 20814) lists a number of useful publications.

Because information may come from many sources, Powers (1991) sees one role of the school psychologist as facilitating and coordinating service access. As a liaison to medical, educational, social, and financial services, the school psychologist can slowly transfer this knowledge of services to the family. One father's plea for such a coordinator is seen here:

> It seems that ever since Joan was born, everything has changed . . . there always seems to be at least three experts around giving Judy advice on how to handle Joan . . . I know that my son Jimmy has been having some problems, but the thought of another expert . . . is more than I can take. I wish we could find one person who could pull all the information together. (Family Life, 1985, p. 50)

Once all the information is gathered, parents may choose to collaborate with the school psychologist in decision making. An essential aspect of this collaboration is that parents be given options whenever they exist so that they can make educated decisions on behalf of their child (Apter, 1992). A problem-solving approach involving problem identification and analysis, brainstorming alternatives, and choosing a plan of action not only is a collaborative process but also models the problem-solving procedure for families.

Helping to ensure an appropriate match between family needs and service opportunities is a critical responsibility of the school psychologist. Providing services congruent with the needs of family may mean problem solving with parents on the phone rather than in person so they do not miss work. Care must be taken not to overburden families but rather to reinforce their decision-making abilities.

Advocacy. Advocacy "refers to the process of aiding parents to actively and purposively work for their own and their child's welfare by obtaining the support and services they need" (Laborde & Seligman, 1991, p. 361). This may involve overcoming physical barriers such as stairs, cultural barriers such as prejudice, or social barriers such as needed services (Seligman & Darling, 1989). As seen in the education role described earlier in this chapter, the school psychologist has the requisite knowledge about how agencies operate and how referral services work. Powers (1991) suggests that the school psychologist move from being a direct advocate for the child and family to being a consultant to parents in the advocacy process. Once again this means a relinquishing of authority on the part of the school psychologist and supporting the family as it asserts itself.

Support. Social support has been identified repeatedly as a key component in healthy family adaptation and coping. Support networks can be formal, such as organized groups run by the National Association of Retarded Citizens or the local school, or informal such as family, extended family, and friends. Often families have resources other than the schools available to them. For example, the church or synagogue may be a nurturing environment for its members. Maintaining existing social networks and developing new social networks help reduce the social isolation and stresses of the family with a child with a disability. One useful source of information is the *Parent Resource Directory* available from the ACCH (address given earlier). This guide provides a listing by state of parents of children with special health needs who are willing to network. Of particular importance in all cases is to consider support not only for mothers but for fathers and siblings as well.

Facilitation of healthy family functioning. Promoting healthy family functioning requires school psychologists to support the structural balance within the family including clear boundaries between parental and child subsystems, the executive function of the parental subsystem and a healthy relationship between the parents (Powers, 1991). It is important to acknowledge the extra needs and differences of the child with the disability without neglecting other family members. Remember parents have needs beyond those of educating their children. Family competencies and resources can be assessed informally or through the use of specific assessment measures such as those described by Bailey and Simeonsson (1988). Noncustodial parents should be included in decision making when appropriate and information should be sent to all involved adults.

Parents must determine if they want help and what kinds of help they need. Some ways to assist families might include helping them to minimize or better manage time demands and/or to encourage parents to maintain their own health through such means as exercise and vacations. Another suggestion is to hold informal family meetings weekly to review household responsibilities and discuss concerns.

Individualization of services. In all cases the relationship between the school psychologist and the parents is an individualized one taking into consideration racial, ethnic, cultural, and socioeconomic diversity as well as the nature of the disability, family structure, and life cycle position. For example, early childhood consultation with families regarding young children with disabilities is qualitatively different from consultation when children are in elementary and secondary school settings (Mowder, 1994). These younger children are developmentally more dependent on parents and families for their care and protection (Mowder, 1994). Parents should never be expected to function in only one way, and school psychologists must match services to need.

Other best practices. Best practices in working with all parents should be applied to families with disabilities as well. Some examples include avoidance of jargon, flexible scheduling, addressing correspondence to both mother and father, considering siblings, and establishing a relationship before there is a crisis (e.g., Fish, 1990). Parent–teacher contacts will likely increase as a result of including more children with disabilities in mainstream classes. School psychologists can assist teachers and other school personnel in acquiring skills important for successful collaborative relationships with parents.

SUMMARY

This chapter has identified a number of common experiences among families with children with disabilities. These are economic constraints, daily care needs, socialization needs, and worries about the future. Though these families share many concerns, each family is unique and a number of variables impact on their adjustment including the nature of the disability, the cultural background, and family structure, and the family's position in the life cycle. Adaptive functioning in families with children with special needs is associated with good communication, strong support networks, and clear boundaries between subsystems.

Working successfully with parents requires school psychologists to adopt a family-centered approach to services. This is reflected in a nonblaming perspective where family strengths and resources are recognized and supported, and different methods of coping are respected. The goal is one of collaboration with parents to enable and empower them so that they may help themselves. This involves the development of trust, respect, mutual commitment, and sharing. Empowerment of parents is facilitated by the school psychologist through information sharing, advocacy, support, promoting healthy family functioning, and individualization of service to each family. In all of these roles the school psychologist aims to increase parents' involvement so that they assume the role of decision-makers for the family.

REFERENCES

Apter, D. (1992). Utilization of community resources: An important variable for the home–school interface. In S. L. Christenson & J. C. Conoley (Eds.), *Home–school collaboration: Enhancing children's academic and social competence* (pp. 487–498). Silver Spring, MD: National Association of School Psychologists.

Bailey, D. B., & Simeonsson, R. J. (1988). *Family assessment in early intervention.* Columbus, OH: Merrill.

Beavers, J., Hampson, R. B., Hulgus, Y. F., & Beavers, W. R. (1986). Coping in families with a retarded child. *Family Process, 25,* 365–378.

Blacher, J. (Ed.). (1984). *Severely handicapped young children and their families.* Orlando, FL: Academic Press.

Brantlinger, E. (1991). Home–school partnerships that benefit children with special needs. *The Elementary School Journal, 91,* 249–259.

Carlson, C. I. (1987). Resolving school problems with structural family therapy. *School Psychology Review, 16,* 457–468.

Carter, E. A., & McGoldrick, M. (Eds.). (1989). *The family life cycle: A framework for family therapy.* Boston, MA: Allyn & Bacon.

Dane, E. (1993). Family fantasies and adolescent aspirations: A social work perspective on a critical transition. *Family Community Health, 16,* 34–45.

Darling, R. B. (1991). Initial and continuing adaptation to the birth of a disabled child. In M. Seligman (Ed.), *The family with a handicapped child* (pp. 55–89). Boston, MA: Allyn & Bacon.

Dunst, C. J., Johanson, C., Rounds, T., Trivette, C. M., & Hamby, D. (1992). Characteristics of parent–professional partnerships. In S. L. Christenson & J. C. Conoley (Eds.), *Home–school collaboration: Enhancing children's academic and social competence* (pp. 157–174). Silver Spring, MD: National Association of School Psychologists.

Dunst, C. J., & Paget, K. D. (1991). Parent–professional partnerships and family empowerment. In M. J. Fine (Ed.), *Collaboration with parents of exceptional children* (pp. 25–44). Brandon, VT: Clinical Psychology Publishing.

Family Life. (1985, July). The thought of another expert is more than I can take. *Exceptional Parent, 15,* 48–52.

Fine, M. J. (1991). *Collaboration with parents of exceptional children.* Brandon, VT: Clinical Psychology Publishing.

Fine, M. J. (1990). Facilitating home–school relationships: A family orientation approach to collaborative consultation. *Journal of Educational and Psychological Consultation, 1,* 169–187.

Fine, M. J., & Gardner, A. (1994). Collaborative consultation with families of children with special needs – why bother? *Journal of Educational and Psychological Consultation, 5,* 283–308.

Fish, M. C. (1990). Best practices in family–school relationships. In A. Thomas & J. Grimes (Eds.), *Best practices in school psychology–II* (pp. 371–381). Washington, DC: National Association of School Psychologists.

Fish, M. C. (1991). Exceptional children in nontraditional families. In M. J. Fine (Ed.), *Collaboration with parents of exceptional children* (pp. 45–59). Brandon, VT: Clinical Psychology Publishing.

Fish, M. C., & Jain, S. (1988). Using systems theory in school assessment and intervention: A structural model for school psychologists. *Professional School Psychology, 3,* 291–300.

Hampson, R. B., Hulgus, Y. F., Beavers, W. R., & Beavers, J. S. (1988). The assessment of competence in families with a retarded child. *Journal of Family Psychology, 2,* 32–53.

Hannah, M. E., & Midlarsky, E. (1985). Siblings of the handicapped: A literature review for school psychologists. *School Psychology Review, 14,* 510–520.

Hanson, M. J., & Hanline, M. F. (1990). Parenting a child with a disability: A longitudinal study of parental stress and adaptation. *Journal of Early Intervention, 14,* 234–248.

Harris, S. L. (1987). The family crisis: Diagnosis of a severely disabled child. *Marriage and Family Review, 11,* 107–118.

Kalyanpur, M., & Rao, S. S. (1991). Empowering low-income black families of handicapped children. *American Journal of Orthopsychiatry, 61,* 523–532.

Laborde, P. R., & Seligman, M. (1991). Counseling parents with children with disabilities. In M. Seligman (Ed.), *The family with a handicapped child* (pp. 337–368). Boston, MA: Allyn & Bacon.

Lombana, J. H. (1983). *Home–school partnerships.* New York: Grune & Stratton.

McLinden, S. E. (1990). Mothers' and fathers' reports of the effects of a young child with special needs on the family. *Journal of Early Intervention, 14,* 249–259.

Morgan, S. B. (1988). The autistic child and family functioning: A developmental-family systems perspective. *Journal of Autism and Developmental Disorders, 18,* 263–280.

Mowder, B. A. (1994). Consultation with families of young at-risk and handicapped children. *Journal of Educational and Psychological Consultation, 5,* 309–320.

Mullins, J. B. (1987). Authentic voices from parents of exceptional children. *Family Relations, 36,* 30–33.

Olshansky, S. (1962). Chronic sorrow: A response to having a mentally retarded child. *Social Casework, 43,* 190–193.

Palfrey, J. S., Walker, D. K., Butler, J. A., & Singer, J. D. (1989). Patterns of response in families of chronically disabled children: An assessment of five metropolitan school districts. *American Journal of Orthopsychiatry, 59,* 94–104.

Powers, M. D. (1991). Intervening with families of young children with severe handicaps: Contributions of a family systems approach. *School Psychology Quarterly, 6,* 131–146.

Seligman, M. (1991). Siblings of disabled brothers and sisters. In M. Seligman (Ed.), *The family with a handicapped child* (pp. 181–201). Boston, MA: Allyn & Bacon.

Seligman, M., & Darling, R. B. (1989). *Ordinary families, special children.* New York: Guilford.

Todis, B., & Singer, G. (1991). Stress and stress management in families with adopted children who have severe disabilities. *JASH (Journal of the Association for Persons with Severe Handicaps), 16,* 3–13.

Turnbull, A. P., & Turnbull, H. R. (Eds.). (1985). *Parents speak out* (2nd ed.). Columbus, OH: Merrill.

Turnbull, A. P., & Turnbull, H. R. (1990). *Families, professionals, and exceptionality: A special partnership.* Columbus, OH: Merrill.

Turnbull, A. P., & Winton, P. J. (1984). Parent involvement policy and practice: Current research and implications for families of young, severely handicapped children. In J. Blacher (Ed.), *Severely handicapped young children and their families* (pp. 377–397). Orlando, FL: Academic Press.

Wikler, L. (1981). Chronic stress of families of mentally retarded children. *Family Relations, 30,* 281–288.

ANNOTATED BIBLIOGRAPHY

Bishop, K. K., Woll, J., & Arango, P. (1993). *Family/professional collaboration for children with special health needs and their families.* Available from Association for the Care of Children's Health (ACCH), 7910 Woodmont Avenue, Suite 300, Bethesda, MD 20814.
  This monograph reviews seven principles of family/professional collaboration that include behaviors, beliefs, attitudes, and values that must be present in a collaborative relationship. It gives specific family, community, state, and national examples of programs that use collaborative practice.

Christenson, S. L., & Conoley, J. C. (1992). *Home–school collaboration: Enhancing children's academic and social competence.* Silver Spring, MD: National Association of School Psychologists.
  This volume provides information to facilitate the development of successful home–school partnerships so that children's educational and mental health concerns can be addressed effectively. It includes both theoretical and practical chapters that provide information on specific programs and approaches to intervention.

Fine, M. J. (Ed.). (1991). *Collaboration with parents of exceptional children.* Brandon, VT: Clinical Psychology Publishing Co.
  This volume has as its theme the empowerment of parents so they can become active partners in meeting the needs of their own children. It begins with an overview of the family and exceptionality and then covers important educational and intervention considerations. There is a section on the impact of different exceptionalities on the family and a discussion of some critical topics such as sexuality, transitions, and advocacy.

Seligman, M. (Ed.). (1991). *The family with a handicapped child.* Boston, MA: Allyn & Bacon.
  The second edition of this book deals with all aspects of exceptional families and is written for professionals in mental health, educational, and medical settings. It includes chapters on siblings and fathers as well as chapters on specific types of disabilities.

Turnbull, A. P., & Turnbull, H. R. (1990). *Families, professionals, and exceptionality: A special partnership.* Columbus, OH: Merrill.
  This is an easy-to-read, comprehensive, and practical guide to understanding the special partnership of families with exceptional children and professionals who work with them. Its emphasis is on applying family-systems theory in professional practice. It is filled with clear and helpful examples.

91

Best Practices in Working with Students with Traumatic Brain Injury

J. Michael Havey
Eastern Illinois University

OVERVIEW

The recent revision and renaming of federal special education legislation mandated services for a new category of exceptionality, traumatic brain injury (TBI). Although the category is new, the disability is certainly not, nor is it rare. In fact, TBI is the number one killer and disabler of children and young adults in this country. The tragedy of this condition is intensified because it is unforeseen and unexpected. A young person can be inexorably robbed of abilities and skills overnight. As medical technology has improved so have survival rates of those who have sustained this type of injury. Increasing numbers of children with TBI are returning to schools who are then called upon to be major providers of long-term rehabilitation for these individuals. School psychologists knowledgeable about this disability can play a meaningful and important role in providing these services.

Educationally, TBI is defined as an acquired injury to the brain caused by an

external physical force, resulting in total or partial functional disability or psychosocial maladjustment that adversely affects educational performance. The term applies to open or closed head injuries resulting in mild, moderate, or severe impairments in one or more areas, such as cognition; language; memory; attention; reasoning; abstract thinking; judgment; problem-solving; sensory, perceptual and motor abilities; psychosocial behavior; physical functions; information processing; and speech. The term does not apply to injuries that are congenital or degenerative, or brain injuries induced by birth trauma (Individuals with Disabilities Education Act of 1990).

As do other categories of educational disability, this definition excludes some children. The present educational definition includes children who are adversely affected by "an external physical force." It explicitly excludes those children whose brains may have been affected by congenital or degenerative conditions (e.g., hydrocephaly, microcephaly) as well as those whose brains may have been injured by birth trauma. The definition also omits mention of those children who might suffer from an "internal" incident such as a vascular accident.

Brain injury caused by external physical force is typically divided into two major classes: open and closed. Open brain injury results when the skull is penetrated by a foreign body, as in gunshot or missile wounds. Resultant damage is often focal rather than diffuse. Closed brain injury, the most common type among children, results when a moving object (e.g., baseball bat) strikes the stationary head causing a sudden jolt (acceleration injury) or when the moving head is abruptly stopped or slowed by a stationary object (e.g., car dashboard; deceleration injury). In contrast to penetrating or open head injury, damage resulting from closed head injury is almost always diffuse due to both the nature of the physical agent involved and characteristics of the human brain and central nervous system.

The brain is of a gelatin-like consistency. Strong impacts cause the brain to move in a rippling manner inside the skull. Twisting and tearing of tissue often results from this movement. This damage is exacerbated by the fact that the inner surface of the skull is rough and rigid. The movement of the brain across this surface causes additional tearing.

Damage obviously occurs at the point of impact (coup) in a closed head injury. Additional damage also occurs to the area of the brain opposite the site of actual contact (contracoup). In addition to the mechanisms just described — collectively known as "primary" brain damage — closed head injury also often results in "secondary" injuries that can occur subsequent to the initial injury. These include bleeding, swelling of tissue, decreased blood flow, elevated pressure, and infection.

Even though children whose brains have been damaged through internal and congenital processes are excluded, large numbers of children will still potentially be eligible for services under this new category. Trauma to the head from external events such as motor vehicle accidents, abuse, and falls has been estimated to be one of the most common neurological disorders in children (Berg, 1986). Current estimates suggest that between 500,000 and 1,000,000 cases occur per year in the United States (e.g., Begali, 1987; Savage, 1991). Moreover, as medical technology and care have become more sophisticated, the survival rate from TBI has continued to increase. Although young people in the 15-to-24-year-old range are most at risk for TBI, children under 15 are afflicted at almost the same rate (Kalsbeek, McLaurin, Harris, & Miller, 1980; Rosen & Gerring, 1986). TBI occurs in males at a rate approximately twice that in females. Incidence rates are similar for whites and nonwhites. Motor vehicle accidents and falls are the most common causes (Kalsbeek et al., 1980).

BASIC CONSIDERATIONS

Issues of Severity

Because the forces responsible for TBI vary significantly, the severity of the injury varies from individual to individual. A convention among medical personnel is to rate TBI as mild, moderate, or severe based on length and depth of coma and duration of post-traumatic amnesia. Although common usage suggests that a dichotomy exists between coma and consciousness, reality is better represented as a continuum of degrees of consciousness. A metric frequently utilized to measure the severity of coma is the Glasgow Coma Scale (GCS). This technique grades eye, motor, and verbal responses within the first 24 hours following trauma. Numerical values are assigned to different levels of response and a total score (15 points possible) is obtained. Lower scores represent a lesser degree of response and are indicative of more severe injury. In addition to providing an indication of initial severity, the GCS is also employed for monitoring change.

Post-traumatic amnesia (PTA) is defined as the period of time following trauma when the patient is incapable of reliable, consistent, and accurate memory for ongoing events. Under a common classification system, PTA of less than 1 hour is considered mild, PTA of 1 to 24 hours is considered moderate, PTA that continues from 1 to 7 days is considered severe, and PTA of greater than 7 days is considered very severe.

Although these ratings are often employed to provide an estimate of severity of injury and physiological disruption, an important consideration for school psychologists and other school personnel to remember is that they often do not correlate well with future recovery nor provide information useful in predicting outcome. For example, Savage (1991) cited a study that found many children with mild head injury were experiencing serious problems in a variety of contexts. Also cited were many children with severe injury who, with the exception of motor difficulties, were doing as well as the mildly to moderately injured children. Traumatic brain injury is a complex phenomenon and recovery is impacted by a variety of

factors. Other variables such as age, causal agent, extent of damage, site of injury, and quality of rehabilitation all interact to influence outcomes for individuals (Begali, 1987). School personnel need to remember that severity of injury is only one bit of information needed to make accurate judgments about a child's potential for recovery.

A related issue of importance to school psychologists who might work with children with TBI is the concept of "plasticity." This term has been applied to the long-held notion that because children's brains are not completely developed, they can recover more rapidly and more completely from brain insult than can adults. Although some evidence does exist suggesting that children may recover language functioning more easily than do adults, other research evidence suggests that trauma to a brain incompletely developed prevents the development of a complete and competent behavioral repertoire (Berg, 1986). Moreover, other evidence suggests that early brain injury may result in more severe long-term deficits than injury sustained later (Shaw & Yingst, 1992). Current beliefs about the limits of cerebral plasticity in children argue against complacency in rehabilitation efforts.

Psychological Sequelae of TBI

As mentioned previously, TBI can vary greatly in severity and the rating of injury severity and physiological disruption does not provide a great deal of insight about recovery. Efforts to help a child be reintegrated into a school setting can be hindered by (a) the lack of correlation between severity of injury and cognitive and behavioral recovery and (b) the lack of consistency between physical and cognitive recovery. The potential often exists for sending a child back to school with little if any academic or social support before he or she has recovered sufficiently. Although apparently well, children who have sustained TBI often experience psychological sequelae that may not be apparent until they are returned to a school setting. According to Levin (1985) memory disorders are the most common and persistent psychological consequences of TBI. Problems of attention and concentration are also frequently experienced by these children as are problems with language production and processing (e.g., word finding, verbal fluency, reading comprehension, and writing; Begali, 1987). Other psychological and behavioral problems associated with TBI include impairments of judgment, flexibility, self-control, family relationships, and age-appropriate behavior (Savage & Wolcott, 1988).

Obviously, any of these impairments could pose serious problems within a school setting for a child who has sustained a brain injury. In addition, educators should be aware that many children are prescribed anticonvulsant medication — as a prophylactic measure to reduce the possibility of seizures —

and/or other medications to help manage behavioral excesses. The possibility exists of cognitive side effects that could influence learning. Therefore, educators should always know the medications prescribed and any possible side effects.

A number of physical deficits can also result from TBI. Rigidity of movement, loss of muscular control, weakness, and loss of balance and coordination are not uncommon sequelae of TBI. School psychologists need to be particularly aware of these factors because of their potential impact on assessment results and classroom performance, two areas of direct concern to the psychologist.

BEST PRACTICES

Best Practices in Assessment

The goal of the assessment process is to gather information and data that will allow educational personnel to address the following questions:

- What are the needs of the student with traumatic brain injury?

- What is the educational interference caused by the traumatic brain injury?

- What are the services and programs necessary to minimize interference . . . [and maximize learning]? (Roth, Harley, Havey, Probst, & Vaal, 1993)

To make the best educational plans and develop the best educational programs for children who have sustained TBI, the school psychologist and other school personnel must complete a broad-based evaluation that provides information relevant to the child's pre-trauma functioning, the nature of the trauma itself, and the child's level of post-trauma functioning. Information regarding pre-trauma functioning helps determine the educational impact of the trauma by providing a baseline against which post-trauma behavior can be judged. Because it is likely that a child who experienced TBI did not have a complete psychoeducational assessment prior to injury, this component of the evaluation focuses primarily on a review of the child's educational record and interviews with adults knowledgeable about the child's previous level of functioning. Group achievement scores, report cards, anecdotal records, and work samples are all important sources of data. Parents, teachers, and other school personnel can provide subjective information that may help shed light on the child's behavior and performance.

A review of medical records and/or interviews with medical personnel and parents can provide valuable information about the severity of the trauma and the overall medical situation surrounding the injury. Moreover, many children will have been evaluated by a hospital psychologist shortly before returning to school. A review of the report and personal contact with the hospital psychologist can also provide helpful information.

In most cases the school psychologist sill need to be directly involved with a complete case-study evaluation conducted by school personnel. Telzrow (1991) suggests that such assessment should incorporate several characteristics. First, she recommends that evaluations of these children incorporate techniques and procedures in compliance with federal and state regulations governing the assessment and education of students with disabilities. Telzrow (1991) also suggests that assessment of students with TBI should incorporate a neuropsychological framework. Because TBI involves neurological dysfunction, this point of view is logical. Although many school psychologists are not very knowledgeable about this branch of psychology, an increasing number are. And the number of graduate programs offering courses and practica in neuropsychology is growing (Hynd, 1981; Stone, Gray, & Dean, 1989). In addition, the National Association of School Psychologists and state associations offer continuing education opportunities to develop an understanding of basic neuropsychological principles and knowledge of TBI in particular. If school psychologists are to effectively serve this population of students they must avail themselves of these continuing education opportunities. School psychologists may also be able to increase their understanding of neuropsychology in general and TBI in particular through consultation with professionals based in a regional education center or a local medical facility.

Thirdly, Telzrow (1991) suggests that assessment of children with TBI be multidisciplinary in nature. Even though federal legislation mandates a multidisciplinary evaluation of all children suspected of a disability, a multidisciplinary evaluation is imperative for children with TBI. TBI affects each child differently and any aspect of the child's functioning can be affected. TBI can have an impact on cognitive processes, language, social behavior, and/or sensory and motor functioning. More so than with other disabilities, the expertise of professionals such as speech-language pathologists, occupational therapists, physical therapists, and medical doctors may be needed in order to develop a comprehensive picture of the child's abilities and needs. A fourth recommendation made by Telzrow (1991) is that assessment of children with TBI should also include contextual assessment. This includes a focus on "moderator" variables — social, environmental, and motivational factors — that influence the child's ability to cope and adjust to the presenting disorder (Ewing-Cobbs & Fletcher, 1990). These factors may not be obvious but they cannot be ignored because they can have a significant impact on the child's functioning in the school setting.

Telzrow (1991), in addition to several other authors (e.g., Ewing-Cobbs & Fletcher, 1990; Obrzut &

Hynd, 1990), suggests that school psychologists take a domain-specific approach to the assessment of children who have sustained TBI. This approach involves the identification and examination of several specific areas of domains of functioning. Although the nomenclature varies somewhat from author to author, domains typically specified include intelligence, language, memory and concentration, sensory recognition and perception, academic achievement, and behavior and personality (see Telzrow, 1991 for lists of major assessment domains suggested by seven experts or teams of experts). Figure 1 provides an illustrative list of instruments and procedures relevant to various domains.

The purpose of this domain-centered approach is "to obtain a comprehensive sampling of performance across the range of behaviors sensitive to neuropsychologic functioning" (Telzrow, 1991, p. 30). This approach is in keeping with the multidisciplinary philosophy because some areas are more appropriately assessed by a particular professional discipline than by another. Moreover, this approach is similar to that taken in many typical psychoeducational case-study evaluations. An advantage of this approach is that it allows for flexibility; the particularities of a child's case may call for an emphasis on some domains but not on others. Some domains only marginally related to performance in school may, nevertheless, provide information about factors that might interfere with the child's progress. The main focus of the assessment should, however, remain on those factors most closely related to school performance.

On a cautionary note, an overemphasis on domains may lead school personnel to ignore information directly related to interventions that can improve school performance and to shift their attention to areas of processing deficit that may provide little information useful for intervention. Caution also needs to be expressed because many of the instruments commonly employed in the assessment of some of these domains have been criticized for their psychometric inadequacies (Reschly & Gresham, 1989; Reynolds, 1989).

During the recovery process the child's level of functioning can change rapidly. For this reason, optimal assessment of the child with TBI will need to be periodic and ongoing. This does not mean that complete psychoeducational batteries need to be administered on a frequent basis. Indeed, many standardized assessment measures are subject to practice effects and tend to be insensitive to small, but important changes in skill level (Kranzler & Shaw, 1992). A methodical system for closely monitoring progress of the child will be important, however. Curriculum-based assessment (CBA) or measurement (CBM) techniques designed for ongoing assessment and for measuring discrete changes in functioning can be important tools in assessment of and program planning for children with TBI.

In addition, CBA and/or CBM techniques can be useful in documenting the adverse impact of the trauma on academic functioning (Shaw & Yingst, 1992) and in helping children and parents understand the need for a gradual and systematic return to school (Ylvisaker, Hartwick, & Stevens, 1991). By comparing performance on post-trauma measures with pre-trauma placement in the curriculum the school psychologist can determine if functioning has deteriorated. Shaw and Yingst (1992) recommend starting the CBA at the place within the curriculum where the child was placed prior to the trauma and testing through progressively lower levels until an instructional level is reached if evidence of decline is apparent.

Regardless of technique utilized, school psychologists assessing children who have sustained TBI need to be alert for signs of the cognitive and behavioral difficulties that are frequent sequelae of TBI. There are, however, several steps that school psychologists can take to surmount this problem. Spreading the assessment over more than one session will probably be appropriate with a child who has difficulty maintaining attention and concentration. "Testing the limits" procedures may also allow greater insight into a child's abilities and skills when test performance is impeded by one of the sequelae previously discussed. Information gained through observation and interview methods will be especially important in the assessment of a child whose behavioral limitations interfere with testing and interpretation of results. Finally, nonstandardized measures such as CBA that allow for greater flexibility in administration can be valuable sources of information.

Best Practices in Educational Planning

Although careful attention needs to be paid to the assessment of children with TBI, its main function is to provide educators with information that can be used to develop an educational program appropriate for the child's needs. An important and somewhat unique problem facing educators who develop educational plans for children with TBI is the transition between a medical environment (hospital or rehabilitation center) and an educational environment. The differences in philosophy, outlook, and system structure all too often contribute to inadequate communication and poorly coordinated services. The return of a student with TBI to a school setting is not a one-time process and may take several weeks. Savage and Carter (1988) identified four steps crucial to ensure a successful transition:

1. Involvement of the school-based special education team in the hospital or rehabilitation facility.

2. Inservice training for all school-based staff who will have contact with the student.

FIGURE 1. Domains and appropriate techniques for assessing children with Traumatic Brain Injury.

Cognition

Intelligence

> Age-Appropriate Wechsler Scale
> Differential Abilities Scale (DAS)
> Stanford-Binet: Intelligence Scale Fourth Edition (SB–IV)

Attention and Concentration

> Freedom from Distractibility Factor: Wechsler Scales
> ACTeRS
> Achenbach Parents' Report Form Profile
> Achenbach Teacher's Report Form Profile
> Behavioral Observation

Communication and Language

> Peabody Picture Vocabulary Test–Revised
> Test of Primary Language Development
> Test of Auditory Comprehension of Language

Memory

> Digit Span Subtest of Wechsler Scales
> Immediate and Delayed Mastery Subtests of the DAS
> Wechsler Memory Scales
> Wide Range Assessment of Memory and Learning

Problem Solving and Abstract Reasoning

> Verbal
> > Comprehension Subtest of Wechsler Scales
> > WJ–R Reasoning Cluster
> Nonverbal
> > Matrices Subtest of DAS
> > Mazes Subtest of Wechsler Scales

Social/Behavioral Functioning

Areas to be Assessed

> Relationships
> Self-Esteem
> Self-Control
> Age-Appropriate Behavior

Examples of Assessment Instruments and Procedures

> Interviews
> Observations
> Behavior Checklists
> > Achenbach Parents' Report Form Profile
> > Achenbach Teacher's Report Form Profile
> Adaptive Behavior
> > Scales of Independent Behavior
> > Vineland Adaptive Behavior Scale
> Other Personality Tests
> > Personality Inventory for Children

(Figure 1 continues . . .)

(. . . Figure 1, continued)

Sensorimotor

Areas to be Assessed

> Balance
> Equilibrium
> Fine and Gross Motor Skills
> Spatial Orientation
> Speech
> Speed and Coordination of Movement
> Strength
> Vision and Hearing
> Visual and Auditory Perception
> Visual-Motor Integration

Examples of Assessment Instruments and Procedures

> Development Test of Visual-Motor Integration
> SB–IV Abstract Visual Reasoning Cluster
> Brunicks-Oserestsky Test of Motor Proficiency

Achievement

Kaufman Test of Educational Achievement
Peabody Individual Achievement Test–Revised
Curriculum-Based Assessment/Measurement Techniques

---

3. Short- and long-term planning for the support services needed for the student.

4. Continued follow-up by the rehabilitation professionals.

The training and background of many school psychologists contribute to make them logical liaisons between schools and medical/rehabilitation facilities. Many school psychologists are knowledgeable about clinical and medical issues and have served as transition facilitator for children who have been hospitalized for psychiatric reasons. School psychologists who have developed expertise about TBI may also serve the transition process by providing inservice presentations for school personnel. Blosser and De-Pompei (1991) developed objectives and identified topics suitable for professional training and development programs for educators. General topics they designated as appropriate for such programs include identification of the nature of TBI; similarities and differences between students with TBI and other types of handicapping conditions; the impact of impairments resulting from TBI on the student's learning and performance; program decision making, including policy and administration; educational program development including assessment and management strategies; and consultation and collaboration between professionals (rehabilitation and education) and with families for effective program planning.

Another problem facing educators who plan for the return to school of a child with TBI is the fact that the medical designations of mild, moderate, and severe used to classify degree of physiological disrup-

tion often do not provide information useful in predicting educational need. It often happens that a child who has sustained a mild injury is returned to school before sufficient time has elapsed and without the support services necessary for monitoring behavior and progress. Frequently, the educational performance of children who have returned to school following a TBI is hampered by subtle cognitive and behavioral problems (Savage, 1991). Cohen, Joyce, Rhoades, and Welks (1985) identified the following behavioral criteria necessary for a return to school:

1. Attend to a task for 10 to 15 minutes.

2. Tolerate 20 to 30 minutes of general classroom stimulation.

3. Function within a group of two or more students.

4. Follow simple directions.

5. Engage in some type of meaningful communication.

6. Give evidence of learning potential.

These criteria should be viewed as guidelines only and interpreted in a manner flexible enough to effectively accommodate individual differences among children. Based on classroom observation and other sources of information the school psychologist could help establish individually appropriate entry-level criteria.

An important component of the transition process is the development of an Individualized Education Plan (IEP) that will determine the child's educational program after the return to school. Although not appropriate for every child with a disability, the "one-size-fits-all" IEP commonly developed for children with learning disabilities is especially inappropriate for children with TBI. Brain injury affects each child differently. Some children will be only mildly affected and need only minimal services. Other, more seriously affected children, however, will need more services and a more restrictive environment. And many children with TBI will need related services such as speech-language therapy or occupational therapy. Therefore, input from the complete multidisciplinary team is important in IEP development.

A key concept in the IEP development for a child with TBI is flexibility. Students with TBI often make rapid progress in the first few months following their injury. Future performance levels often are not consistent with nor can they be inferred from current levels of performance. Because the student's needs may change rapidly during the early stages of the recovery process, the recommendation has been made (e.g., Savage, 1991; Ylvisaker et al., 1991) that the initial IEP should be written for a shorter period of time, namely 6 to 8 weeks, rather than the more customary 1-year period. Because TBI often affects more than academic functioning, it is important that IEPs contain provisions for addressing the child's other needs as well. The IEP must view academic progress as a part of the process of achieving independent functioning and should include provisions to foster the development of adaptive and effective behaviors that will enable the child to meet with educational, social, and vocational success (Roth et al., 1993).

Ylvisaker et al. (1991) recommended that the IEP contain a "package" of services including as much regular education as possible and supported by an appropriate combination of resource room assistance, remedial programs, tutoring, classroom consultation, related services, and possible outpatient therapy. Ylvisaker et al. (1991) also assert that the unique characteristics and possible rapid recovery of children with TBI make the ongoing success of their educational programs dependent on careful case management. The responsibility of the manager would be to monitor the program, make recommendations for change, and ensure that all staff are properly oriented to the child and program. Oftentimes well-conceived programs can deteriorate and cease to be appropriate without careful monitoring and management.

Just as the "one-size-fits-all" IEP is inappropriate for children with TBI, the "one-educational-placement-suits-all" is also inappropriate. The wide variety of outcomes subsequent to TBI mandates that educators consider the complete continuum of services as they plan educational programs for children with TBI. Educators also need to be flexible enough to allow for changes in placement as the recovery process progresses. Two areas in which flexible programming

can be important include length of school day and length of time in a "regular" education classroom. Many children with TBI become fatigued easily; for many of these children a gradual return to a complete school day might be more appropriate than an abrupt reentry. In addition, as children recover they will need less restrictive educational environments and will be able to spend more time in "regular" classrooms. Systematic assessment and careful monitoring are essential to ensure that these changes are made in a timely and appropriate manner.

Although teaching methods and techniques uniquely beneficial for children with TBI have not been identified and educators are left to assume that sound teaching practices have the same chance of success for children with TBI as they do for other children with disabilities (Cruikshank, Bentzen, Ratzeburg, & Tannhauser, 1961; Heward & Oriansky, 1980), systemic factors do exist that can contribute to or detract from the quality of an educational placement once it has been made. Telzrow (1987) identified several characteristics of quality educational delivery systems for children who have sustained a TBI. Basing her assertions on successful rehabilitation programs, she suggested that school programs, at least initially, be provided in a self-contained classroom in which stress can be reduced by ensuring that adults, expectations, and the surroundings remain constant. In addition, she asserts that the need of the student with TBI for individual instruction and direct personal feedback mandates a low pupil-teacher ratio.

Brain injury impairs the capacity for learning. For this reason, a need exists to modify instructional program delivery and content as well as setting. Telzrow (1987) advocates that these programs be repetitive, provide for practice, and allow more time for learning to take place. Reducing time devoted to noninstructional activities is one method for achieving this end. The self-contained environment just described and an IEP provision for an extended school year can also allow more opportunities for repetition and practice. Telzrow (1987) also recommends that educational programs for children who have sustained TBI focus on learning process as well as academic content. Efforts to increase sustained attention, develop and follow a plan of study, and utilize memory clues were offered as examples of processes that might be incorporated into an educational program for children with TBI. Educational programs based on behavioral instructional strategies also appear to be most successful. Task analysis and systematic progression from goal to goal are key components to successful programs.

Because many children who have sustained TBI require related services as well as modified instruction, an integrated program that provides coordinated instructional and therapeutic services is viewed as preferable to a more segregated approach. One method of ensuring this integrated approach is to deliver related services in the primary instructional setting rather than via a "pull-out" design. According to Telzrow (1987) successful programs for children with TBI foster transfer of skills from setting to setting by providing opportunities to practice through simulation experiences. Utilization of the learning principles of cuing and fading is also recommended as beneficial for students with TBI, as is providing shadowing experiences for the student. Shadowing is a technique whereby the child is provided close and direct supervision during early trials at displaying a skill or participating in an activity. Because children who have sustained TBI often exhibit behavioral and emotional problems such as anxiety, depression, and/or acting out, the need to incorporate readjustment counseling into a child's program may exist. Finally, Telzrow (1987) recommends that because TBI can have a major impact on the family as well as the child, a formal system of communication between family members and school personnel should also be a part of an educational program for a child with TBI.

Programming for Behavioral and Emotional Needs

Post-traumatic cognitive difficulties can interfere with social as well as academic adjustment. Moreover, head injured children may lack the confidence to participate in social situations (Newton & Johnson, 1986). As previously described, a complete package of integrated related services can be an important part of a child's educational program. School psychologists may, therefore, be called upon to provide behavior management consultation or direct counseling as a part of the intervention package for children who have sustained TBI. Although each person who has incurred TBI displays a unique constellation of behaviors, enough commonality exists for Deaton (1990) to categorize behavioral deficits following TBI as problems in self-care, cognitive functioning (e.g., attention problems, impulsiveness), and interpersonal behaviors. Problems of behavioral generalization may also be apparent in these children and direct and explicit behavioral directives may be necessary for them to function in a school setting (Begali, 1987). Moreover, intrinsic reward and/or motivation is often insufficient in the head-injured population, and external reinforcement systems such as token economies may be necessary (Begali, 1987). In addition to positive reinforcement systems, timeout has proven particularly effective for disruptive and dangerous behavior exhibited by children with TBI (Newcombe, 1981). Begali (1987) adapted for use in schools Olson's general strategies for managing the behavior of head-injured clients. These guidelines and strategies include

- Promoting communication among staff.

- Permitting students to experience the logical consequences of their actions.

- Breaking long-range goals down into smaller steps.

- Providing clear and direct feedback.

- Serving as a role model of appropriate behavior.

- Manipulating the environment in order to reduce stress.

- Redirecting perseverative and organically based behaviors.

- Expecting variable performance from TBI students.

- Setting reasonable expectations.

- Involving the family in the behavioral plan (Begali, 1987).

In addition to the provision of indirect, behavioral consultation services, school psychologists may need to provide direct psychotherapeutic services to the student with TBI. A theme that runs through much of the literature dealing with psychoemotional issues surrounding TBI is "loss." The person recovering from a traumatic injury to the brain is, in many ways, different from the person who sustained the injury. Children who have sustained this type of injury may have particular difficulty adjusting to this circumstance because outwardly they may appear to be perfectly normal. A major goal of school psychologists and others who counsel children with TBI should be to help the individual accept the trauma, its consequence, and the new set of circumstances posed by the injury. Prigitano and Klonoff (1990) recommend a psychoeducational model that presents and explains clients' behavior in precise and concise units. Such a model provides not only information to clients, but also a framework in which to interpret behavior. Groups, if possible to establish, may be especially appropriate mechanisms for providing support and realistic feedback to students with TBI.

Working with Families

The changes caused by TBI in an individual's functioning extend their impact to other people with whom that individual interacts. Nowhere is this more obvious than within the family. The impact of TBI on the family, although often considered to be outside the purview of school psychologists, should be taken into account because the family is such an important part of any child's life and because their support and cooperation are essential for the child's success in school.

A family's response to the knowledge that a child has sustained a TBI has been likened to the classic bereavement reaction (Hall, 1989; Martin, 1990) through which family members progress through stages of grief on the way to an acceptance of the circumstance. Although a complete discussion of these stages is beyond the scope of this chapter, a brief description follows. Initial reaction to the accident is one of shock. Parents are often disoriented, may experience feelings of helplessness, and may have difficulty thinking rationally. After the initial shock subsides, parents often shift into a phase of denial that may last for months. Although Hall (1989) warns against attempts to destroy this protective mechanism, professionals should also guard against giving a falsely optimistic prognosis and be aware that persistent denial may drive parents to constantly search for treatments that they unrealistically believe could totally reverse the brain injury.

As parents come to grips with the reality of the situation, they may respond with a profound sense of sorrow. The grief or mourning reaction for a child with TBI has been likened to the grief that is experienced upon the birth of a child with severe disabilities: Both situations entail a loss and the substitution of an earlier perception of the child with another, less pleasant one. Oftentimes commingled with feelings of sorrow is a diffuse sense of anger at the injustice of the child's condition. It is not unusual for some of the anger to be turned inward; parents often experience feelings of guilt associated with the child's accident.

Finally parents reach a stage of acceptance and accommodation and begin to be able to deal with the child of present reality rather than the child as he/she was before the trauma. This process of coming to terms with the child's condition is not a one-time occurrence — it is often interrupted by fresh episodes of grief and anxiety. Although these generalizations have been proffered to help the professional formulate a response to the family that has experienced TBI, it is important to remember that they are generalizations and the reality of the situation for a particular family may be much more complex and variable.

In addition to leaving a child with diminished abilities and perhaps a different personality, severe TBI can affect the family in a variety of other ways as well. Children, who require long-term rehabilitation present their families with a different set of responsibilities and demands. The amount of time and energy expended simply transporting the child can be daunting as can the new and extra demands for home care presented by the child. Another source of stress for the parents of a child severely disabled by a head injury is the realization that their responsibility for the child will be ongoing and continue much longer than previously expected. The financial strain of providing for the needs of the child can also be a source of substantial stress. The new circumstances of the family of a child who has sustained a TBI often result in at least some social problems involving isolation, loss of emotional support, and restricted independence (Lezak, 1988).

In addition to the stresses and strains encountered by the parents of the child with TBI, specific problems are also associated with the child's siblings. Two common results of TBI for the uninjured sibling are a decrease in parental attention and an increase in responsibility. In addition, increased demands at home may prevent siblings and/or parents from participating in typical activities, therefore decreasing social contacts and support. Siblings often experience feelings of confusion, anger, shame, and guilt as a result of these changes in family roles and relationships.

School psychologists can assist families with their adjustment in several ways. Listening carefully and providing an empathic ear can provide an important service to family members. Oftentimes professionals are so intent on conveying information and directions that they do not take the time to listen to the concerns of the parents. A sensitivity to the parents' current stage in the bereavement process can lead the school psychologist to tailor his or her presentation according to the parent's needs at the time. For example, parents still in a state of shock may need information to be presented in small amounts and on more than one occasion. On the other hand, parents experiencing great sorrow at their child's condition may need assistance dealing with feelings of guilt. Because the personal and financial demands of caring for a child who has sustained a severe head injury can be so draining, school psychologists can help by providing information regarding respite care services as well as rehabilitation facilities that operate with sliding payment schedules or in other ways that could ease the families' financial burden. Hall (1989) offered suggestions that are helpful in working with parents of children who have incurred a TBI. These include giving important news to both parents simultaneously; providing a quiet, distraction-free environment for discussion; allowing ample time for questions; and encouraging parents to bring another adult for support and to reinforce the information provided by the professional.

Their location in the schools and subsequent availability to children provide school psychologists with a unique opportunity to help siblings adjust to their new family circumstances. Serving as a source of information about TBI and its effects can be helpful to many siblings. Others may experience greater adjustment difficulties and require therapeutic intervention. Group counseling may be a particularly effective method of providing support, but the low incidence of TBI may make the establishment of a group difficult.

SUMMARY

The two concepts that are probably central to effective service to children who have sustained traumatic brain injury are variability and flexibility. Children sustain TBI in any number of ways; the effects on the child's physical, cognitive, and behavioral functioning are completely idiosyncratic; the child's level of functioning can change from one day to the next; and the school and home environments to which children must return following a head injury vary widely. In order to effectively serve this population, school psychologists and other professionals must be aware of this variability and realize that TBI impacts each child and family in a different manner. Although some generalizations can be made and guidelines offered, flexibility must be a key principle guiding intervention efforts; effective service can be provided only by tailoring the efforts of the professional to the needs of the individual. Despite the fact that the need for flexibility is important when working with all children, it is especially important when working with children with TBI because of the variability of needs among the population and the rapidity with which their functioning levels can change.

Another concept important in working with children with TBI is multidisciplinary coordination. Because TBI can affect all aspects of children's functioning and development, effective services can only result from the coordinated efforts of representatives of different disciplines. Coordinating these services can require much effort, but the unique needs of these children can only be met if the expertise of educators and allied professionals is incorporated into the educational program.

School psychologists can play key roles in providing appropriate educational services to these children. One important function that the school psychologist can perform is to ensure that broad-based, comprehensive, and timely assessment provides a valid picture of the child's assets and deficits that can be incorporated into an appropriate educational plan. School psychologists can also serve the population with TBI by providing inservice presentations to teachers and other educators about the nature of the disability and the needs of the children. Providing ongoing consultation to teachers to help them effectively meet the educational and behavioral needs of these children is another important service that the school psychologist can render. Direct intervention in the form of counseling to help the child with TBI to come to terms with the disability may also be necessary. Finally, school psychologists need to be sensitive to the effects that TBI can have on the family and provide support for parents and siblings.

AUTHOR NOTE

The impetus behind this chapter was a best-practice document created for the Illinois School Psychologists Association. That document was written by a committee chaired by Gloria Roth and included Richard Harley, Jennie Probat, Joe Vaal, and myself. I thank Steven Shaw of Illinois State University for sharing his expertise as I prepared this manuscript.

REFERENCES

Begali, V. (1987). *Head injury and adolescents: A resource and review for school and allied professions.* Brandon, VT: Clinical Psychology Publishing Co.

Berg, R. A. (1986). Neuropsychological effects of closed-head injury in children. In J. E. Obrzut & G. W. Hynd (Eds.), *Child neuropsychology: Clinical practice* (pp. 113–135). Orlando, FL: Academic Press.

Blosser, J. L., & DePompei, R. (1991). Preparing education professionals for meeting the needs of students with traumatic brain injury. *Journal of Head Trauma Rehabilitation, 6,* 73–82.

Cohen, S. B., Joyce, C. M., Rhoades, K. W., & Welks, D. M. (1985). Educational programming for head injured students. In M. Ylvisaker (Ed.), *Head injury rehabilitation: Children and adolescents* (pp. 383–409). Boston: College Hill Press/Little, Brown & Co.

Cruikshank, W. M., Bentzen, F. A., Ratzeburg, F. H., & Tannhauser, M. T. (1961). *A teaching method for brain-injured and hyperactive children: A demonstration-pilot study.* Syracuse, NY: Syracuse University Press.

Deaton, A. V. (1990). Behavioral change strategies for children and adolescents with traumatic brain injury. In E. D. Bigler (Ed.), *Traumatic brain injury* (pp. 231–249). Austin, TX: Pro-Ed.

Ewing-Cobbs, L., & Fletcher, J. M. (1990). Neuropsychological assessment of traumatic brain injury in children. In E. D. Bigler (Ed.), *Traumatic brain injury* (pp. 107–128). Austin, TX: Pro-Ed.

Hall, D. (1989). Understanding parents. In D. Johnson, D. Utley, & M. Wyke (Eds.), *Children's head injury: Who cares* (pp. 171–182). Hillsdale, NJ: Lawrence Erlbaum.

Heward, W. L., & Orlansky, M. D. (1980). *Exceptional children.* Columbus, OH: Charles E. Merrill.

Hynd, G. W. (1981). Training the school psychologist in neuropsychology: Perspectives, issues, and models. In G. W. Hynd & J. E. Obrzut (Eds.), *Neuropsychological assessment and the school-age child: Issues and procedures* (pp. 379–404). San Diego: Grune & Stratton.

Hynd, G. W. (1988). *Neuropsychological assessment in clinical child psychology.* Newbury Park, CA: Sage Publications.

Individuals with Disabilities Education Act of 1990, Section 300 134 C.F.R. (1992).

Kalsbeek, W., McLaurin, R., Harris, B. S., & Miller, J. D. (1980). The national head and spinal cord injury survey: Major findings. *Journal of Neurosurgery, 53,* 19–31.

Kranzler, J. H., & Shaw, S. S. (1992). *The application of the techniques of mental chronometry to the study of learning disabilities.* Paper presented at the convention of the National Association of School Psychologists, Nashville, TN.

Levin, H. J. (1985). Neurobehavioral outcome. In D. B. Becker & J. T. Poulighouk (Eds.), *Central nervous system trauma status report* (pp. 108–129). Maryland, NIH.

Lezak, M. D. (1988). Brain damage is a family affair. *Journal of Clinical and Experimental Neuropsychology, 10,* 11–123.

Martin, D. A. (1990). Family issues in traumatic brain injury. In E. D. Bigler (Ed.), *Traumatic brain injury* (pp. 381–394). Austin, TX: Pro-Ed.

Newcombe, F. (1981). The psychological consequences of closed head injury: Assessment and rehabilitation. *Injury, 14,* 111–136.

Newton, A., & Johnson, D. A. (1986). Social adjustment after severe head injury: Performance, anxiety, or esteem? *British Journal of Clinical Psychology, 24,* 225–234.

Obrzut, J. E., & Hynd, G. W. (1990). Cognitive dysfunction and psychoeducational assessment in traumatic brain injury. In E. D. Bigler (Ed.), *Traumatic brain injury* (pp. 165–179). Austin, TX: Pro-Ed.

Prigitano, G. P., & Klonoff, P. S. (1990). Psychotherapy and neuropsychological assessment after traumatic brain injury. In E. D. Bigler (Ed.), *Traumatic brain injury* (pp. 313–329). Austin, TX: Pro-Ed.

Reschly, D. J., & Gresham, F. M. (1989). Current neuropsychological diagnosis of learning problems: A leap of faith. In C. R. Reynolds & E. Fletcher-Janzen (Eds.), *Handbook of clinical child neuropsychology* (pp. 503–519). New York: Plenum.

Reynolds, C. R. (1989). Measurement and statistical problems in neuropsychological assessment of children. In C. R. Reynolds & E. Fletcher-Janzen (Eds.), Handbook of clinical child neuropsychology (pp. 147–166). New York: Plenum.

Rosen, C. D., & Gerring, J. P. (1986). *Head trauma: Educational reintegration.* San Diego: College Hill Press.

Roth, G., Harley, R., Havey, M., Probst, J., & Vaal, J. (1993). *Reference manual for determining eligibility and best practices in assessment of traumatic brain injury (TBI).* Addison, IL: Illinois School Psychologists Association.

Savage, R. C. (1991). Identification, classification, and placement issues for students with traumatic brain injury. *Journal of Head Trauma Rehabilitation, 6,* 1–9.

Savage, R. C., & Carter, R. R. (1988). Transitioning pediatric patients into educational systems: Guidelines for rehabilitation professionals. *Cognitive Rehabilitation, 6*(4).

Savage, R. C., & Wolcott, G. F. (Eds.). (1988). *An educator's manual: What educators need to know about students with traumatic brain injury.* Southborough, MA: National Head Injury Foundation.

Shaw, S. S., & Yingst, C. A. (1992). Assessing children with traumatic brain injuries: Integrating educational and medical issues. *Diagnostique, 17,* 255–265.

Stone, B. J., Gray, J. W., & Dean, R. S. (1989). The school psychologist in neurologic settings. In R. C. D'Amato (Ed.), *The school psychologist in nontraditional settings* (pp. 139–157). Hillsdale, NJ: Erlbaum.

Telzrow, C. F. (1987). Management of academic and educational problems in head injury. *Journal of Learning Disabilities, 20,* 536–545.

Telzrow, C. F. (1991). The school psychologists perspective on testing students with traumatic brain injury. *Journal of Head Trauma Rehabilitation, 6,* 23–34.

Ylvisaker, M., Hartwick, P., & Stevens, M. (1991). School reentry following head injury: Managing the transition from hospital to school. *Journal of Head Trauma Rehabilitation, 6,* 10–22.

ANNOTATED BIBLIOGRAPHY

DePompei, R., & Blosser, J. L. (Eds.). (1991). School reentry following head injury [Special issue]. *Journal of Head Trauma Rehabilitation, 6*(1).

Provides articles relating to many issues associated with the reintegration of children with TBI into a public school setting. Of particular use to school-based professionals are a checklist of activities to ensure that a successful transition takes place and an outline useful as an aid in developing an inservice program regarding the educational needs of the child with TBI.

Begali, V. (1987). *Head injury and adolescents: A resource and review for school and allied professions.* Brandon, VT: Clinical Psychology Publishing Co.

A good overview of brain injury and its effects on children. Provides chapters concerning basic brain functions, mechanisms of brain injury, sequelae of brain injury, assessment of children with TBI, and treatment rationale and strategies for educational settings.

Bigler, E. D. (Ed.). *Traumatic brain injury: Mechanisms of damage, assessment, intervention, and outcome.* Austin, Tx: Pro-Ed.

The subtitle explicitly states the sections of this edited volume. Although many of the topics of discussion are similar to the Begali book described above, the presentation is more detailed and technical. Early chapters provide excellent photographs of CT scans and actual brains that depict effects of brain injury.

Savage, R. C., & Wolcott, G. F. (Eds.). (1988). *An educator's manual: What educators need to know about students with traumatic brain injury.* Southborough, MA: National Head Injury Foundation.

As the title states, this volume was created specifically for educators. It contains valuable information written in a style that can be understood by readers who possess little prior knowledge of the topic. Two useful components of this volume are a glossary worthwhile for educators unfamiliar with the medical terminology associated with TBI and a list of state head injury associations valuable for those wishing to become more involved or network with other professionals.

92

Best Practices in Gifted Education

Teresa Argo Boatman
Keith G. Davis
Camilla P. Benbow
Iowa State University

OVERVIEW

Providing educational programming that meets the academic and intellectual needs of gifted and talented students is a challenging task facing educators throughout the nation. With the increasing emphasis on serving children in the least restrictive environment and prereferral interventions, educators are charged with the task of serving increasingly heterogeneous classrooms. The changing roles of school psychologists, as evidenced by the focus of this volume, is moving away from its traditional roots of classification and toward an expanding role of problem solving in the general education classroom. School psychologists, more than ever before, find themselves involved with students at all points along the continuum of academic behaviors. Highly able students, commonly referred to in the school as talented and gifted (TAG), are a traditionally underserved population but may benefit greatly by the new problem-solving focus in education.

As school psychologists embrace the role of assessing and meeting the individual needs of students, problems may be conceptualized as discrepancies between the student's performance and the expectations of the educational environment (Tindal, Wesson, Deno, Germann, & Mirkin, 1985). This discrepancy may result from a student's performance or skill deficit or from inappropriate demands of the environment. Frequently, the successful resolution of the problem requires the consideration of both student and environmental factors. A fourth-grade student with severe reading difficulties provides a useful illustration. Not only is the student deficient in the requisite skills to function in the fourth-grade reading curriculum, but that curriculum level may be inadequate to remediate those skills. This student's deficit in basic reading skills may be more effectively remediated by instruction at the third- or second-grade level.

This example illustrates a principle that guides much of curriculum and teaching and is referred to by cognitive developmental psychologists as the moderate-discrepancy hypothesis (Siegler, 1991). Simply, learning is most effectively promoted when the child is presented material slightly more difficult than the child's current level of functioning. Thus, the second- or third-grade curriculum may be the appropriate academic placement and permit his reading skills to remediate without being overwhelmed by the demands of the fourth-grade curriculum for which he is not prepared. A parallel is the case of a highly able student functioning significantly beyond the level of her peers. Rather than receiving instruction in grade level materials, which she has previously mastered, her needs may be more appropriately met by instruction in curriculum moderately beyond her current level of mastery. Herein lies the "problem" that a problem-solving approach addresses in gifted education — serving the needs of gifted students through educational placements that address their special academic needs.

The role of gifted education in today's schools should be to identify the specific talents and abilities of gifted students and nourish those abilities through placing students in appropriate curricula. The challenge to school psychologists is to advocate for the identification of these individual needs of gifted students and the provision of effective interventions. To aid school psychologists in their challenge, this chapter's authors present an approach to assessment, intervention, and evaluation that integrates the best practices in the field of gifted education. The primary emphasis is toward appropriately identifying the specific patterns of abilities of each student and then providing educational placement based upon the specific abilities (not the chronological age) of each student. The process parallels the problem-solving approach used by school psychologists in working with developmentally challenged students, students who are usually the outliers in the classroom. Gifted students are also outliers distinguished from developmentally challenged students by their place at the opposite extreme of the developmental continuum. The school psychologist's role is similar with students at both ends of this continuum; only the interventions differ.

Definition of Giftedness

Among researchers interested in intellectual abilities, a framework that has received a remarkable degree of acceptance (cf. Lubinski & Dawis, 1992), is that cognitive abilities are organized around two dimensions. The first is the sophistication of the intellectual repertoire, commonly referred to as general intelligence. The second dimension is the content of the abilities, which are divided into three distinct factors: verbal/linguistic, numerical/quantitative, and spatial/pictorial. Giftedness, therefore, can be identified in verbal, numerical, and spatial abilities.

Considerable effort has been made to define and refine the construct of giftedness further. There is a general agreement within the field of gifted education that giftedness arises out of a mixture of advanced cognitive abilities, personality traits, and environmental circumstances (Feldhusen, 1986; Tannenbaum, 1983). Feldhusen, for example, identified giftedness as a composite of four general characteristics: general intellectual ability, which is characterized by higher order cognitive processes accessed in problem solving; specific talents such as verbal or mathematical ability, which may be based on curriculum demands; a self-concept of being competent and capable of new ideas, inventions, and performances; and motivation characterized by an achievement orientation.

Yet, within the school system, intellectual abilities have been more narrowly defined and traditionally identified via outstanding performance on national achievement tests, such as the Iowa Test of Basic Skills or the Iowa Test of Educational Development. Gifted programs typically set an inclusionary criterion of students scoring in the top three to ten percent of ability on these standardized tests of achievement. General measures of intelligence (e.g., the Weschler Intelligence Scale for Children–III) were used in the past and tended to define giftedness as two standard deviations above the mean (> 130 IQ). General intelligence measures, such as the WISC–III, are not used as frequently in school gifted programs today, however, due to the lower cost and availability of other assessment alternatives, the expanded view of giftedness, and the less clear applications of such scores with educational programming. One of the drawbacks of the standardized tests of achievement and the structure of the school system is that only two of the three content areas of cognitive abilities, the verbal/linguistic and numerical/quantitative, are adequately assessed. The spatial/pictorial content area is all but ignored within the current school system.

Within the school system, it is imperative to develop an operational definition of giftedness. The boundaries of the operational definition provide guidelines for making programming and administrative decisions and channeling resources. This chapter's operational definition is based on the one used by the 20-year-old Study of Mathematically Precocious Youth (SMPY) research program at Iowa State University and focuses upon the academic components of high ability. A child who shows exceptional ability within a specific talent area is identified as gifted within that area. While the authors recognize the poignant needs of children with talents in other areas, this chapter is restricted primarily to academic talents which can and should be served reasonably in the schools. Attention is concentrated especially upon the quantitative reasoning and verbal reasoning abilities as those two areas may be objectively, reliably, and validly measured within the school setting. Additionally, appropriate educational interventions have been demonstrated to strongly influence future performance in these areas.

School Psychologists' Role

As school psychologists utilize effective models of systematic problem solving, they encounter increasing opportunities to effect change in gifted education. Through consultation with teachers, parents, and administrators, school psychologists assist in the identification and interpretation of exceptional academic talent in young people, identify interventions that address the needs of the gifted learner, and help evaluate the effectiveness of these interventions for individual students. Serving the student, often indirectly through consultation, the psychologist advocates the utilization of best practices outlined in the research. The information provided herein, coupled with the school psychologist's knowledge of psychometrics and problem solving, should begin to provide the foundation for these consultation services.

The school psychologist as a consumer of research on gifted education will generally be led outside of the school psychology professional journals. This chapter's inclusion in this volume represents a growing trend in the field to serve all students who may require special curricular modifications through the problem-solving approach. As this trend continues and school psychologists become more involved in serving this population, additional research on the gifted will make its way into the professional school psychology journals. The annotated bibliography at the end of this chapter should provide an excellent resource for further research in appropriate educational options. In addition, four journals, *Gifted Child Quarterly, Journal for Educating the Gifted, Gifted Child Today,* and *Roeper Review* will provide current and relevant information for school psychologists interested in gifted education.

BASIC CONSIDERATIONS

Educational programming for talented and gifted children is currently driven by three educational models: acceleration, ability grouping, and enrichment (Feldhusen, 1989). Considerable research within the field of gifted education has been devoted to developing and implementing these models as well as evaluating their effectiveness in serving the needs of gifted students. As the academic needs of highly able students become more fully understood, it becomes clear that no one form of programming addresses the needs of all talented and gifted students. The following section highlights the basic components of acceleration, ability grouping, and enrichment to provide the school psychologist a framework of the educational options available in the schools.

Acceleration

Although acceleration has been used since the one-room school house as a means to meet the academic needs of advanced students, the true meaning of acceleration is often misunderstood. Some educators wrongly conclude that acceleration consists only of radical jumps from one grade to another. Acceleration, however, encompasses a much wider range of educational alternatives than just grade skipping. The goal of acceleration is curricular flexibility or curricular access without regard to age. Rather than subjecting a student to a lock-step approach, the curriculum can be modified for the purpose of meeting the individual needs of a student. Some of the accelerative educational options are

- Early admittance to school.
- Subject-matter acceleration.
- Grade skipping.
- Early entrance to college with or without a high school diploma.
- An International Baccalaureate.
- Course enrollment one or two years earlier than typical.
- Enrollment in college courses while still in high school.
- Curriculum compacting.
- Advanced Placement (AP) courses.

See Figure 1 for descriptions of these options, all of which are designed to provide an academic curriculum commensurate with individual ability and achievement levels. A definition encompassing this concept of acceleration was outlined by Feldhusen (1989) as "the process is really one of bringing gifted and talented youth up to a suitable level of instruction commensurate with their achievement levels and readiness so that they are properly challenged to

learn new material" (p. 8). Acceleration, therefore, provides the student the opportunity to utilize the standard curriculum at a pace and time that is appropriate for his/her ability level.

Interventions used when working with gifted students are highly focused upon accelerative opportunities, primarily because acceleration provides both short- and long-term benefits for academic performance. Additionally, research studies for over 60 years have identified acceleration as best practice for gifted students (Benbow, 1991; Benbow & Stanley, 1983; Feldhusen, 1989). Reviews of research on acceleration have shown that early entrants were at a comparable level as their classmates or had surpassed them (Proctor, Black, & Feldhusen, 1986) and that accelerated talented youngsters performed as well as talented, older pupils (Kulik & Kulik, 1984). Accelerated students also tend to earn high grades and win honors at the collegiate level (Swiatek & Benbow, 1992). The culmination of this research is that accelerative options have consistently proven to be the most effective intervention with highly talented youth. Further, accelerative options are economical, generally utilizing resources already available in the school.

A commonly held myth concerning acceleration is that the social and emotional development of the gifted child is affected adversely by accelerative options. Contrary to this belief, research indicates that acceleration is not detrimental and may even have some positive effects on social and emotional development. At different ages in their development, accelerants have been shown to be well-adjusted in comparison with same age counterparts (Robinson & Janos, 1986), report high self-esteem and internal locus of control (Richardson & Benbow, 1990), and exhibit advanced social maturity (Janos & Robinson, 1985). In all, there is not one empirical investigation that shows harmful effects of acceleration on social and emotional development, with no group of talented students at particular risk either (Swiatek & Benbow, 1992).

Ability Grouping

The second most effective educational intervention with gifted students is ability grouping. Students are grouped according to current level of mastery, ability, and/or achievement for the purpose of reducing the heterogeneity of the group and increasing the appropriateness of the instruction. Despite its utility, this intervention is frequently rejected as a viable educational option, often being misconstrued as conflicting with the special education goals of mainstreaming and least restrictive environments. These special education goals are important and, as illustrated throughout this volume, are directly tied to best practice and mandated by public law. However, the grouping eschewed by these goals is *disability*

FIGURE 1. Curricular flexibility options for gifted students.

The following educational options and score criteria were developed for junior high age students who have completed the ACT or SAT. The score criteria act as a guideline for educational planning. Additional factors such as student motivation, access to resources, and academic maturity should be taken into consideration.

SAT–Verbal	200–470	SAT–Verbal	430–480
SAT–Math	200–550	SAT–Math	520–800
ACT–English	0–23	ACT–English	21–36
ACT–Reading	0–23	ACT–Reading	23–36
ACT_Math	0–19	ACT–Math	18–36
ACT–Science Reasoning	0–25	ACT–Science Reasoning	23–36
ACT–Composite	0–22	ACT–Composite	21–36

Seventh-grade students scoring in this range may want to consider options for their educational plans.

1. *Enriching learning opportunities from a variety of areas.* Develop independent research projects, potentially with specific contests or competitions in mind. Students may attend a summer course in an area of interest or attend a lecture series at a local science center, art museum, or college.

2. *Early course entry.* Algebra I in the seventh or eighth grade or the intense study of a foreign language in junior high or elementary school. All course sequences should be continuous, without obvious breaks in sequence.

3. *Access to Advanced Placement (AP) and Honors courses.* AP and Honors courses may provide the appropriate level of educational challenges to gifted students. If AP courses are not offered in the local school, the option of preparing for and taking the AP exams is still available.

4. *Mentoring program.* Specific interests and abilities can be developed with assistance from an outstanding adult in that field. For example, students who excel in the social sciences may be paired with a professor completing research in that area.

5. *Involvement in contests and competitions.* Group and individual contests such as Science Bowl, MathCounts, Physics Olympiad, and History Day provide a community of peers with whom gifted students may choose to interact.

Seventh- and eighth-grade students scoring in this higher range may consider suggestions 1 through 5 with the following options.

6. *Self-paced instruction.* Current areas of strength in a subject can be identified and tested. Once areas of mastery have been identified, students should proceed through the remaining course work at the rate appropriate for the individual student.

7. *Attendance at summer academic programs.* Many summer courses offer an opportunity for students to complete a semester or year's worth of academic material in a 3- or 4-week time span, for which they may receive credit in their local school.

8. *Course skipping.* Students can be moved into courses appropriate for their level of academic ability and mastery. For example, a sixth-grade mathematically gifted child may take pre-algebra to prepare him or her for algebra in the seventh grade.

9. *Grade skipping.* This works best when it incorporates a natural break (e.g., skipping the last year of middle school by oing directly to high school). Grade skipping is reserved for those students who are achieving highly in all areas of the curriculum.

10. *Course compacting.* The completion of a course in a shorter amount of time may be accomplished by self-instruction or mentoring of the student.

11. *Early entrance to college.* Gifted students may consider leaving high school and attending college following the sophomore or junior year of high school.

---

grouping — not ability grouping. Grouping students by disabilities, which are unrelated to their educational needs, is truly a travesty. In contrast to grouping by disability, ability grouping strives to identify educationally critical characteristics such as current level of mastery, ability, and achievement, thereby increasing the appropriateness of instruction for the students grouped.

Ability grouping is commonly divided into two forms: within class and between class. For within-class groups flexible, independently paced instruction is offered for each student or student assignments based on ability level for specific curriculum. An example of within-class grouping is commonly seen in the divided reading curriculum at the elementary level. Between-class groups may be special classes assigned by ability level, subject-matter grouping across grade lines according to ability level, or flexible grouping according to performance rather than age. An example of between-class ability grouping is the precalculus mathematics series offered at the secondary level. The grouping of these students is related to their mastery of the earlier components in the series. The purpose of ability grouping is to provide students at a similar level of mastery, ability, and/or achievement educational instruction that is an optimal fit to their needs.

The meta-analysis research on the efficacy of ability grouping with gifted students has pointed to clear and consistent benefits (Kulik & Kulik, 1991; 1992). The benefits are most positive when grouping is accompanied by curriculum modification. Students who were grouped and then exposed to enriched or accelerative learning environments show moderate-to-large positive academic gains from grouping. A cross-grade grouping or within-class grouping that included curriculum matched to the group ability showed small positive effects in academic gains. Students who were exposed to multilevel grouping that included few planned adjustments to curriculum showed little academic gain (Kulik & Kulik, 1992). This evidence leads us to the same conclusion as Feldhusen and Moon (1992), who state that "the linkage among grouping, acceleration, and differentiated curriculum is an essential aspect of the instructional services that produces higher achievement among gifted and/or high-ability students" (p. 65).

Opponents of grouping purport that removing high-ability learners from the classroom will deprive the average-ability students of important positive academic role models. Shunk (1987) found that students tend to choose role models who are at their same ability level. Thus, the removal of the high ability students does not affect role model selection and may actually provide for an increase in positive role modeling among like-ability students. Despite the benefits of ability grouping, it tends to be the most infrequently used intervention in schools. This may be due to problems of allocating the additional resources needed for ability grouping or simply due to the misunderstandings associated with this intervention.

Enrichment

The concept of enrichment within the school setting not only has been misunderstood but also is troubled by inconsistency in definition (Treffinger, Callahan, & Vaughn, 1991). Broadly defined, enrichment includes any activity outside the regular curriculum that provides a richer and more varied educational experience. A wide range of educational activities, including field trips, independent research projects, artistic creations, science fair projects, and cultural experiences are categorized as enrichment. Most enrichment interventions are aimed at providing an avenue within a total school program to develop creative-thinking skills and problem-solving ability or to nurture talents and interests in an effort to build a foundation for more developed enrichment activities for advanced students (Renzulli & Reis, 1985). Most enrichment activities tend to occur in the "resource room," where gifted students have been pulled out of the regular classroom for one or two hours per week.

Pull-out is the most frequently used mechanism to serve gifted students in the United States.

It is critical that enrichment activities are carefully planned so as to avoid becoming just simply fun and games. There are numerous models and programs of enrichment that have been outlined (e.g., Renzulli, 1986). Renzulli and Reis's *Schoolwide Enrichment Model* (SEM; Renzulli & Reis, 1985) will be highlighted here to represent the specific components of an enrichment program because it is an extremely popular model in today's schools. SEM provides enrichment to a broad spectrum of students with a focus on providing creative productivity and integrating gifted education into the regular classroom. Three different types of enrichment are provided, each successively more challenging and integrative in nature. Type I activities provide general exploration of topics not available in the regular curriculum. Type II activities provide the tools for further learning by promoting thinking and feeling processes as well as enhancing general skills in creative thinking, skill usage, and use of reference materials. Type III activities provide practice in thinking, feeling, and acting like a professional and focus upon promoting advanced understanding of the content and process integral to the development of an authentic product through an in-depth investigation on a topic of choice. The SEM model suggests using curriculum compacting, an accelerative option through which teachers help students master the regular curriculum in a more economical and efficient manner, to enable students to use their additional educational time for enrichment activities.

Enrichment programs have been widely embraced by many school systems as the primary intervention to meet the needs of the gifted child. The overall results of Treffinger, Callahan, and Vaughn's (1991) comprehensive review of the limited literature indicated that enrichment program students achieve as well as peers and sometimes better than control groups. In addition, enrichment programs are effective in reaching program goals, parents and students have very positive attitudes toward enrichment activities, and participation in enrichment programs do not have an adverse effect on self-confidence. The overall conclusion of the review, however, indicated "a paucity of systematic, experimental research on the effectiveness, and particularly long term effectiveness, of enrichment efforts" (p. 40).

The school psychologist should remember, however, that within an individual school district, maximum benefit is achieved when appropriate components from each of the instructional theories are integrated into an individual educational plan.

BEST PRACTICES

Best practices of working with gifted children do not differ significantly from those used with other special needs students. A problem-solving model, in which the identification of educational needs of the student, development of an individual educational plan, access to educational opportunities within the school, and evaluation of the effectiveness of the individual educational plan provides a conceptual approach to working with gifted children and educators. A combination of acceleration, ability grouping, and enrichment practices, in which the appropriate options for the individual student are integrated as necessary, provide the best intervention options.

An understanding of best practices in gifted education may be illustrated by looking retrospectively at the educational placement decisions that could have been made for one young man, Jeffrey, given unlimited allocation of resources, support, and access to curricular options. It should be noted that this example combines a large number of potential interventions to provide illustration of the processes of integrating acceleration, ability grouping, and enrichment options. For each student, the configuration of instructional activities that provides the framework for the most appropriate individual educational plan will depend upon two components: a thorough evaluation of the individual student's current level of mastery, abilities, preferences, and motivation and a degree of creativity utilizing options available within the school district and community.

Jeffrey first came to our attention as a 10-year-old sixth-grade student at a local elementary school. When he was in the second grade, Jeffrey's school had identified him as gifted. Prior to beginning formal education, Jeffrey could complete mathematical calculations (subtraction and addition) and was interested in drawing maps that were proportionally correct. When we met Jeffrey, he was attending weekly astronomy lectures at the local university with his father and expressed interest in several other areas of the sciences as well as mathematics. Jeffrey enjoyed studying languages and had completed short, introductory courses in Spanish and German. His test scores in all subjects were superior; however, his grades were only average. The teachers reported that Jeffrey would commonly fail to turn in assignments or turn in incomplete assignments. It was obvious, however, that Jeffrey was not a mediocre student. Jeffrey's parents and teachers, as well as Jeffrey, were seeking answers. At what level was Jeffrey functioning intellectually? What curriculum would best challenge his abilities? Where would they find the educational challenges that would best meet his needs? So began the search for best practices in gifted education that would answer these and other questions.

Identification of Needs

As with all problem-solving approaches, the identification phase is the most important, as it lays the groundwork for the educational interventions that

follow. Identifying the academic needs of a gifted and talented child is a three-phase process: identifying abilities, assessing interests, and identifying suitable academic placement.

Assessment of abilities. The annual or bi-annual nationally standardized tests, such as the Iowa Test of Basic Skills (ITBS) and the Iowa Test of Educational Development (ITED), are good measures of overall level of performance within subject matter. These tests provide a mechanism of tracking student progress as well as serving as an initial screening tool for students who may be at the lower or higher end of the continuum of academic ability. Traditionally, students who score at or above the 97th percentile on nationally standardized tests are considered intellectually highly able. These tests, however, provide little information concerning specific abilities of a gifted child. Students who score lc3\\flla1 97th percentile on age-appropriate standardized tests are affected by the ceiling effect of the test. That is, the test is not difficult enough to accurately assess the true ability level of individuals scoring in the upper percentiles. In addition, the results of standardized achievement tests are scores of broad range achievement, measuring how well the students have accomplished academic goals as compared to peers in a national normative sample. Tests of aptitude, especially out-of-level examinations, are better measures for gifted students of actual potential for achievement and will serve as better indicators of specific strengths and weaknesses.

When faced with the dilemma of further defining the academic abilities of gifted students, Dr. Julian C. Stanley at Johns Hopkins University developed the Talent Search model of identification. Through the Talent Search model, students who score in the top 3% on national standardized achievement tests (e.g., ITBS) are invited to take an out-of-level test. In the original Talent Search and its subsequent offshoots, junior high students are invited to take the College Board Scholastic Aptitude Test (SAT). The SAT provides a SAT-Verbal and SAT-Mathematics score and is designed to measure verbal and mathematical reasoning abilities. The SAT traditionally is a college entrance examination completed during the junior or senior year of high school. When completed at the junior high school age, however, the SAT has proved to be an especially appropriate measure of the specific verbal/linguistic and quantitative reasoning abilities of a gifted individual (Benbow & Wollins, in press; Benbow, 1991). Among students who are in the top 3% on the ITBS, the distribution of scores on the SAT range from 200 (chance) to 800 (the top score). The mean score for this select group of junior-high-age students is comparable to the national sample of high school students. The Talent Search model has been implemented across the nation and over 150,000 junior high school age students participate annually (VanTassel-Baska, in press). In addition to the SAT, the American College Testing Program (ACT) Assessment recently has been used by some talent searches. How useful this instrument will be in assessing the abilities of gifted students remains to be determined. Recently, the Talent Search model also has been implemented for fourth through sixth grade students through various centers for gifted students, using out-of-level tests originally designed for typical eighth-grade students.

Although research has shown that best practice for screening gifted students is through standardized tests, other methods of assessment may be necessary for traditionally underrepresented populations. Behavioral observation by the teacher, parents, and school psychologist may identify characteristics that are common to gifted students. Baldwin, Gear, and Locito (1978 in Baldwin, 1991) provided an extensive list of exceptional characteristics to look for in children who are culturally diverse, socioeconomically deprived, or geographically isolated. These characteristics include good memory, intuitive grasp of situations, understanding of compromise, tolerance for ambiguities, insight, inventiveness, flexibility, originality, ability to think systematically, uncluttered thinking, insightfulness, special aptitudes in the arts, and skilled body movements. Inclusion of teacher and peer nomination also expands the scope of identification to include students not selected through standardized examinations. Although these behaviors and nominations are not objective measures of a high academic ability, they may be used effectively to screen students for further and more valid assessment of abilities.

Assessment of interests. Identification of interest areas has not been traditionally integrated into developing educational plans for gifted students. However, at the other end of the continuum, interests have been a primary component of vocational rehabilitation programming. Extending the Theory of Work Adjustment (TWA) developed by Dawis and Lofquist (1984) to appropriate educational placement indicates the need to assess the personal preferences of gifted students. According to TWA, optimal educational and work environments are those in which the individual corresponds with the environment on two levels, *satisfactoriness* and satisfaction. Satisfactoriness is the correspondence between an individual's abilities and the ability requirements of the environment. Satisfaction is the correspondence between an individual's preferences and the types of reinforcers provided by an occupational or educational track. The extent to which satisfactoriness and satisfaction are achieved determines the eventual educational choice, degree of commitment to this choice, and the eventuality of whether talents have the opportunity to be brought to fruition (Benbow & Lubinski, in press). Therefore, the identification of the individual's preferences in addition to his ability level may be an important consideration in academic placement decisions.

Assessing areas of interest may be a formal or informal process. Formally, there are several tools available to most school guidance counselors. The student may complete a career planning session, which involves assessment instruments such as the Strong Vocational Interest Blank, the DISCOVER computer program, or other nationally recognized career guidance systems. These systems provide information concerning the degree to which the individual's interests and traits match the interest patterns of a particular occupation or college major. Informal interviews, where additional information concerning pastimes, hobbies, and individual pursuits may be gathered, provide further clues to specific interest areas. Interest and preference data may then be used to identify projects in enrichment activities, the focus of mentorship experiences, or as data in designing an educational plan.

Assessment of curriculum. The school psychologist's expertise in working with educators to make academic placement decisions may play an important role in identifying the appropriate curriculum for the gifted child. An assessment of the correspondence between the curriculum level and a student's achievement level may be completed through curriculum-based assessments, comparison of classroom achievement and out-of-level test results, and diagnostic testing. Curriculum Based Measurement (CBM), although not typically used with gifted children, provides an easily understandable measure of the level of curriculum most appropriate for an individual student. Marston and Magnusson (1988) use the CBM technology of survey-level assessment to determine the needs of elementary-age students. This procedure identifies children as two years discrepant when they test below the 16th percentile (i.e., one standard deviation below the mean) one grade below their current grade level. A similar discrepancy could be noted for the gifted student performing above the 84th percentile (one standard deviation above the mean) one grade above her or his current grade level. School psychologists well versed in CBM technology with access to local normative data may make good use of this method of assessment for identifying the appropriateness of the curriculum for individual students.

A comparison of the performance of the student on the out-of-level testing and placement in the school curriculum provides important diagnostic information. A sixth-grade student whose mathematical reasoning is at the level of a high school senior, as identified by the SAT-Math, but who is in the sixth-grade curriculum is not in a mathematics curriculum that is meeting her needs. The out-of-level test results provide guidance as to the possible mismatch between the child and the existing curriculum. Programming options generated from out-of-level testing are presented in Figure 2. Further assessment (see diagnostic testing following) would be warranted to effectively plan for this student's curricular placement. As with all educational decisions impacting individual children, the school psychologist will want to collect multiple forms of assessment data across multiple settings and observers and establish appropriate decisions with convergent assessment data and professional judgment.

Another avenue of identifying the appropriate academic curriculum for a child is to complete diagnostic testing within specific subject matter. Diagnostic tests designed by the instructor or nationally standardized examinations are administered at the beginning of each unit, quarter, or semester. These tests are designed to assess student knowledge of specific subject matter prior to the presentation of the corresponding curriculum. High ability students frequently master large portions of a curriculum independently before it is presented formally. Using diagnostic testing, student mastery of subcomponents of the subject matter is identified and students are then taught only those areas of the curriculum which they have not mastered. The SMPY math courses have successfully used this Diagnostic Testing followed by Prescriptive Instruction for almost 20 years (Benbow, 1986).

Let us return to Jeffrey. Jeffrey scored in the 99th percentile on the Iowa Test of Basic Skills. To provide more information concerning Jeffrey's specific strengths and weaknesses, he completed the SAT. He scored 600 on the SAT-Math and 280 on the SAT-Verbal. These scores placed him in the 89th and 8th percentiles, respectively, in comparison to college-bound high school seniors. Jeffrey's mathematical reasoning ability was well above that of most college-bound high school seniors, with his verbal reasoning ability not as well developed as his mathematical reasoning ability. The teacher diagnostically tested Jeffrey and noted mastery of pre-algebraic skills in mathematics, well beyond the sixth-grade curriculum. Criterion-referenced assessment in social studies and language usage indicated average performance for the sixth-grade curriculum. In addition, Jeffrey completed an informal interest survey indicating a strong preference for scientific and task-oriented activities as well as blossoming interests in languages and foreign cultures.

An educational team then had the data — Jeffrey's level of mathematical and verbal reasoning ability, an informal measure of his interests and preferences, teacher observations, and the appropriateness of the curriculum in meeting his needs — with which to make educational decisions.

Developing an Educational Plan

Utilizing the data gathered through the identification phase, the team developed an educational plan for the coming school year and beyond, utilizing the various educational options available through the regular curriculum, accelerative options, enrichment activities, and resources outside the school. The educational plan provides the optimal educational placement based upon the skills, level of academic performance, and preferences of the individual student as well as the resources of the school and the community. As a side note, school psychologists should be aware that a large proportion of money within gifted programs is allocated to enrichment activities. This intervention, however, is the least cost effective and has surprisingly little research support. As will be described shortly, curricular flexibility (acceleration) provides the optimal educational placement for gifted students with little need to create new curriculum or differential programming. Instead, curricular flexibility adapts existing curriculum to meet the needs of the gifted learner.

Educational plan components. The development of an educational plan is an evolutionary process. An initial plan outlines the appropriate curricular placement, independent study, summer academic experiences, enrichment options, and extracurricular experiences (band, newspaper staff, mentoring experiences, volleyball, etc.) for the next 1 to 6 years. On a yearly basis, the plan is reviewed to respond to a developing individual and to integrate new educational opportunities, assessment results, or interests of the child.

When considering educational opportunities for the gifted child, the accelerative options outlined in Figure 2 have been shown to be effective (Benbow, 1991). Acceleration, or curricular flexibility, involves utilizing the existing curriculum in the school system or local community college and placing the child at the curriculum level consistent with her or his current level of functioning. This opens the curriculum designed for older students to younger, highly able students. Frequently, curricular flexibility options may be utilized by the school system and the child without incurring additional costs and with minimal time commitment from classroom teachers. One of the most effective curricular flexibility options is subject matter acceleration, wherein students are placed into courses based upon ability level, regardless of age. For example, a mathematically able seventh-grade student is identified as possessing the prerequisite skills for the advanced mathematics curriculum. The school places her in the ninth-grade algebra course. Her academic needs are met without developing a new curriculum and with the added benefit of providing her with peers at her intellectual ability level. Subject matter acceleration has been used successfully at all ages and grade levels to provide challenging curriculum for academically able students.

Subject-matter acceleration is also accomplished through compacting the curriculum (i.e., completing two years of a course in one year). For courses using diagnostic pretesting, the curriculum may be compacted by completing only those components not already mastered. Fast-paced summer academic courses provide students an opportunity outside of their school to complete up to a full year of a high school course during an intensive 3-week program. Local colleges and universities are increasingly opening their doors to high school students to complete courses in specific subject areas. This option has the added benefit of students accruing college credits prior to attending college as a full-time student.

Other curricular flexibility options to consider include condensing grades 9 through 12 into a 3-year time span or allowing the student to leave high school without a diploma and enter college early. A number of undergraduate institutions have specific programs for students who leave high school after the 10th or 11th grade. Advanced Placement courses provide collegiate level course work without leaving high school. AP courses are offered in over 30 disciplines; schools without formalized AP programs can offer supervised independent study arrangements using AP syllabi. Mentoring and internship opportunities with individuals from the community allow students to conduct research or explore other opportunities not available in the school curriculum.

When developing interventions, the team should consider the importance of grouping students by ability. When grouping is combined with appropriate accelerative and enrichment opportunities, as well as changes to the curriculum to accommodate for ability, significant gains in academic achievement have been demonstrated (Kulik & Kulik, 1992). Gifted students also benefit socially by having a peer group to interact with. The advantage of the educational team approach to gifted education is that often the team is able to provide guidance for a number of students, opening up the possibility that like-ability students may be grouped together and have access to similar educational experiences.

An educational plan. An educational plan may include the following components:

1. Courses to be completed during each semester as well as summer educational experiences.

2. Enrichment opportunities available through the school.

3. Extracurricular activities which will supplement educational experiences.

4. Community-based experiences such as mentoring programs, local science center courses, and art center courses.

5. Academic year correspondence courses from colleges and universities.

6. Academic year courses completed at local colleges.

As an example, examine the outcome of Jeffrey's educational plan developed during his sixth grade. For the remainder of the year, Jeffrey completed his sixth-grade courses in social studies and language arts with his classmates. His teacher designed an independent study course in mathematics compacting the seventh- and eighth-grade curriculum based upon the diagnostic testing results. Jeffrey completed the sixth-grade science curriculum and also worked with a mentor from the local science center to complete an independent project in astronomy. His parents transported him to the science center on two Saturdays a month for this experience. During that following summer, Jeffrey attended a language camp, which introduced him to Russian language and culture. He also completed Junior Great Books sponsored by the local library. During his seventh-grade year, Jeffrey was placed into Algebra I with the ninth-grade students. In addition, he was placed into ninth-grade Earth Science and Spanish I. He completed seventh-grade English and Social Studies with his enrichment activities focused upon those courses. Additionally, he participated in band, chorus, chess club, basketball, and track. During the summer after his seventh-grade year, he attended a summer academic program mastering two semesters of computer programming in 3 weeks. Future educational plans include continuing with his mathematics sequence through his sophomore year of high school and completing calculus at the local university during his junior and senior years. He will take AP History and AP Literature and Composition while in high school so is doubling up on courses in these areas during his freshman and sophomore year of high school. Jeffrey has considered compacting his high school course work into 3 years but is currently undecided concerning that option.

As is obvious from Jeffrey's plan, carefully selecting appropriate accelerative and enrichment activities based upon the data provided during the identification and assessment stage is critical to a manageable plan. During this phase of the intervention, the school psychologist may act as a consultant, working with the team, parents, and student to make effective educational decisions. To understand the opportunities for gifted students available in each state, a primary source of information is the state gifted and talented association as well as local associations for parents of gifted students. These organizations often act as clearinghouses of information concerning opportunities for gifted children.

Plan Implementation

Once the educational plan is complete, the student and educational team meet to organize a strategy for implementation and placement. Educators, administrators, and coordinators of summer programs may need to be contacted concerning the availability of curricular options or courses. University-based programs usually have eligibility requirements for summer programs and completion of college course work. Thus, parents or the student should inform themselves early of the appropriate tests or entrance requirements so that the student may complete the requirements during the school year.

Contact with administrators throughout the development of the educational plan is essential as it will ensure that the placement decisions and appropriate curriculum are available through the school or community. In some cases, the school's traditional policy concerning course sequence, grades for access to a course, and acceptance of outside course work may need to be reconsidered. In these situations, the school psychologist may act as an advocate for gifted learners with administrators and school board members, ensuring that these individuals have a professional understanding of the needs and academic abilities of the gifted student, as well as the research supporting the effectiveness of these options. The school psychologist may often choose to work with the gifted and talented teacher in the role of liaison between the teacher and the school officials, explaining the rationale behind the educational plan developed for the gifted child. It is critical that sufficient assessment data from multiple domains be collected to adequately plan the interventions and justify implementation.

Evaluation of Student Progress

Although teachers consistently and appropriately monitor student progress within the classroom, little research is available providing guidance in the evaluation of appropriate academic placement of gifted children. One difficulty in evaluating progress is the focus on enrichment. Enrichment programming is usually focused on increasing problem-solving and creative-thinking skills and completing appropriate projects and research activities. Few formalized assessment instruments validly measure growth in the skill areas. A strategy of assessing growth, however, using both formative and summative procedures focused upon academic performance may provide a system of effective progress monitoring for the gifted student's educational plan.

Formative evaluations, in which the teacher and student monitor growth regularly throughout the school year, provides the first indication of the level of success of the academic placement. Gifted students are excellent candidates to use self-assessment strategies, where the gifted student is responsible for the identification of strengths and weaknesses in the process and outcome of projects as well as academic performance in accelerative educational placements. Diagnostic testing followed by prescriptive instruc-

tion falls naturally into a formative evaluation strategy for the teacher and gifted student. Performance on end-of-chapter and end-of-section examinations compared with performance on pretests quantifies growth within the specific subject matter as well as tracks progress throughout the academic year. Finally, formative evaluations which draw upon teacher ratings of student's academic performance, as well as interpersonal and social functioning within the classroom, provide additional data which may be used to evaluate appropriateness of academic placement in meeting student needs.

Summative evaluations, which track progress from year to year, provide additional evidence of student growth and continued academic challenge. The same out-of-level tests used for identification (e.g., SAT, ACT) may be completed upon a yearly basis, providing evidence of continued academic growth. Additionally, performance in specific areas targeted for growth is one indication of success of academic placement. As a rule of thumb, when students are completing the SAT at the junior-high-school age, their scores increase approximately 40 points from one year to the next on the SAT-Math and SAT-Verbal. Tracking growth with out-of-level tests is problematic for those students who have achieved a high score on initial testing. Again, the ceiling of the test becomes problematic. For these students, higher level performance on out-of-level tests is an inappropriate expectation given the limitations of the test in measuring increased performance at the extremes.

The evaluative process also is an identification process, providing the data from which future educational placement decisions develop. Summative evaluations, such as out-of-level tests, provide data concerning both the abilities and needs of the student. Formative evaluation data provide evidence of the motivation and behavioral responses of the student to the academic placement decisions made during the previous school year. With this data, the educational team may revise and refine the individualized educational plan and make recommendations for appropriate placement for the upcoming year.

Jeffrey's evaluative procedure was a combination of formative and summative strategies. Throughout his seventh-grade year, Jeffrey's progress through algebra, earth science, and Spanish I was tracked by his teachers, who regularly conferenced with the TAG coordinator concerning his progress. Jeffrey's algebra teacher noted consistently high performance on assignments and end-of-chapter tests; Jeffrey was even asked to study with a group of the ninth-grade students for some of the examinations. Earth science was an academic challenge for Jeffrey, yet he willingly invested additional time into his homework to perform at an appropriate academic level. Moreover, he was consistently at the top of his seventh-grade class in English and social studies and the teacher and self-evaluations of his enrichment activities indicated he was rapidly developing strong critical thinking skills and verbal and written communication skills. In the spring, he completed the SAT for a second time, scoring 650 SAT-Math and 360 SAT-Verbal. He has shown adequate growth in both areas. His verbal abilities, however, have shown significant improvement from his previous performance.

Special Populations

The limited scope of this chapter precludes an indepth discussion of special populations of gifted students, students who are at risk for underachievement due to the occurrence of medical, intellectual, or environmental factors that complicate the development of that student's special abilities. Seeley (1993) provides an excellent chapter addressing the issue of gifted students who are at risk due to factors such as physical or medical disabilities (e.g., blindness, deafness, cerebral palsy), learning disabilities, emotional disorders, delinquency, low income or culturally diverse individuals (this category is confounded by race and ethnicity), and school environment. Additionally, information concerning learning disabled gifted students may be found in Silverman (1993). Educational planning for special populations within the gifted community, however, is approached with the same strategy and emphasis on appropriate educational placement. The consideration of alternative testing situations, individualized curricular materials or instruction, and focusing on the strengths of the special student allows the educational plan to meet the academic needs of each student.

The identification and inclusion of minority students within the gifted population has proven to be a politically sensitive task. Traditional methods of identification, such as academic achievement and performance on standardized tests, has resulted in an underrepresentation of minority students (Richert, Alvino, & McDonnell, 1982). Identification of gifted students through peer, teacher, and self-nomination may be an alternative solution. It must be noted, however, that these methods are not as psychometrically sound as standardized testing. Additionally, the Raven's Progressive Matrices is often promoted to be used in the identification of minority children. For further discussion of this topic, the reader may want to consult Baldwin (1991).

SUMMARY

School psychologists working with gifted students and their parents, teachers, and school administrators have the skills to ensure that this special population within the school is not underserved. As operationally defined in this chapter, a child who shows exceptional abilities within a specific talent area is identified as gifted in that area. Specifically, the discussion focused on the issues of serving students with identified academic talents and the ways

school psychologists, through consultation, problem solving, and advocacy, can aid schools in making appropriate educational decisions regarding gifted learners.

Three interventions are commonly used to facilitate the education of gifted students: acceleration, ability grouping, and enrichment. Of these three, acceleration will effectively and economically provide a means of serving students of high ability with resources readily available in the school. Additionally, it served as the focus here due to its widespread research support. Acceleration, which in actuality is the concept of curricular flexibility, meets the needs of gifted students by placing them in a curriculum commensurate with their current level of ability. The school psychologist, through guiding the process to screen, identify, and assess the current level of development of the gifted learner plays a critical role in assisting an educational team to develop an appropriate educational plan resulting in a better student/curriculum match. Finally, through progress monitoring and program evaluation the intervention's effectiveness can be determined and modifications made where needed.

These interventions used within gifted education also address an important component of working with gifted children, providing a peer group at the same intellectual and social level with whom the gifted child can interact. This appropriate peer interaction, which is focused upon peers at a similar intellectual level rather than age, fosters an atmosphere in which social development can proceed optimally. Although not directly addressed, this outcome of acceleration, ability grouping, and enrichment may provide another important intervention with gifted children. Therefore, using the framework provided, the school psychologist may begin to address both the academic and social needs of the gifted child within his or her school.

REFERENCES

Baldwin, A. Y. (1991). Ethnic and cultural issues. In C. Colangelo & G. A. Davis (Eds.), *Handbook of gifted education* (pp. 416–427). Boston: Allyn and Bacon.

Benbow, C. P. (1986). SMPY's model for teaching mathematically precocious students. In J. S. Renzulli (Ed.), *Systems and models in programs for the gifted and talented* (pp. 1–25). Mansfield Center, CT: Creative Learning Press.

Benbow, C. P. (1991). Meeting the needs of gifted students through the use of acceleration: A neglected resource. In M. C. Wang, M. C. Reynolds, & H. J. Walberg (Eds.), *Handbook of special education* (Vol. 4; pp. 23–26). New York: Pergamon Press.

Benbow, C. P., & Lubinski, D. (in press). Individual differences among the mathematically gifted: Their educational and vocational implications. In N. Colangelo, S. G. Assouline, & D. L. Ambroson (Eds.), *Talent development.* New York: Trillium Press.

Benbow, C. P., & Stanley, J. C. (Eds.). (1983). *Academic precocity. Aspects of its development.* Baltimore: Johns Hopkins University Press.

Benbow, C. P., & Wolins, L. (in press). Utility of out-of-level testing for gifted 7th & 8th graders using SAT-M: An examination of test bias. In C. P. Benbow & D. Lubinski (Eds.), *Psychometric and social issues concerning intellectual talent.* Baltimore: Johns Hopkins University Press.

Dawis, R. V., & Lofquist, L. H. (1984). *A psychological theory of work adjustment: An individual differences model and its applications.* Minneapolis: University of Minnesota Press.

Feldhusen, J. F. (1986). A conception of giftedness. In R. J. Sternberg & J. D. Davidson (Eds.), *Conceptions of giftedness* (pp. 112–127). Cambridge: Cambridge University Press.

Feldhusen, J. F. (1989). Synthesis of research on gifted youth. *Educational Leadership, 56,* 6–11.

Feldhusen, J. F., & Moon, S. M. (1992). Grouping gifted students: Issues and concerns. *Gifted Child Quarterly, 36*(2), 63–67.

Janos, P. M., & Robinson, N. M. (1985). Psychosocial development in intellectually gifted children. In F. D. Horowitz & M. O'Brien (Eds.), *The gifted and talented: Developmental perspectives* (pp. 149–196). Washington, DC: American Psychological Association.

Kulik, J. A., & Kulik, C. C. (1984). Effects of accelerated instruction on students. *Review of Educational Research, 54,* 409–425.

Kulik, J. A., & Kulik, C. C. (1991). Ability grouping and gifted students. In N. Colangelo & G. A. Davis (Eds.), *Handbook of gifted education* (pp. 178–196). Boston: Allyn & Bacon.

Kulik, J. A., & Kulik, C. C. (1992). Meta-analytic findings on grouping programs. *Gifted Child Quarterly, 36*(2), 73–77.

Lubinski, D., & Dawis, R. V. (1992). Aptitudes, skills, and proficiency. In M. D. Dunnette & L. M. Hough (Eds.), *The handbook of industrial/organizational psychology* (Vol. 3, 2nd ed.; pp. 3–59). Palo Alto, CA: Consulting Psychologists Press.

Marston, D., & Magnusson, D. (1988). Curriculum-based assessment: District level implementation. In J. Graden, J. Zins, & M. Curtis (Eds.), *Alternative educational delivery systems: Enhancing instructional options for all students* (pp. 137–172). Washington, DC: National Association of School Psychologists.

Proctor, T. B., Black, K. N., & Feldhusen, J. F. (1986). Early admissions of selected children to elementary school: A review of literature. *Journal of Educational Research, 80*(2), 70–76.

Renzulli, J. S. (Ed.). (1986). *Systems and models for developing programs for the gifted and talented.* Mansfield Center, CT: Creative Learning Press.

Renzulli, J. S., & Reis, S. M. (1985). *The schoolwide enrichment model: A comprehensive plan for educational excellence.* Mansfield Center, CT: Creative Learning Press.

Richardson, T. M., & Benbow, C. P. (1990). Long-term effects of acceleration on the social-emotional adjustment of mathematically precocious youths. *Journal of Educational Psychology, 82,* 464–470.

Richert, E. S., Alvino, J., & McDonnell, R. (1982). *The national report on identification: Assessment and recommendations for comprehensive identification of gifted and talented youth.* Seward, NJ: Educational Information and Resource Center for U.S. Department of Education.

Robinson, N. M., & Janos, P. M. (1986). Psychological adjustment in a college-level program of marked academic acceleration. *Journal of Youth and Adolescence, 15,* 51–60.

Seeley, K. (1993). Gifted students at risk. In L. K. Silverman (Ed.), *Counseling the gifted and talented* (pp. 263–276). Denver, CO: Love Publishing Co.

Shunk, D. H. (1987). Peer models and children's behavioral change. *Review of Educational Research, 57*(2), 149–174.

Siegler, R. S. (1991). *Children's thinking* (2nd ed.). Englewood Cliffs, NJ: Prentice-Hall.

Silverman, L. K. (Ed.). (1993). *Counseling the gifted and talented.* Denver, CO: Love Publishing Co.

Swiatek, M. A., & Benbow, C. P. (1992). Non academic correlates of satisfaction with acceleration: A longitudinal study. *Journal of Youth and Adolescence, 21,* 699–723.

Tannenbaum, A. J. (1983). *Gifted children: Psychological and educational perspectives.* New York: Macmillan.

Tindal, G., Wesson, C., Deno, S. L., Germann, G., & Mirkin, P. K. (1985). The Pine County model for special education delivery: A data-based system. In T. Kratochwill (Ed.), *Advances in school psychology: Volume IV* (pp. 223–250). Hillsdale, NJ: Lawrence Erlbaum Associates.

Treffinger, D. J., Callahan, C. M., & Vaughn, V. L. (1991). Research on enrichment efforts in gifted education. In M. C. Wang, M. C. Reynolds, & H. J. Walberg (Eds.), *Handbook of special education* (Vol. 4; pp. 37–55). Oxford, England: Pergamon Press.

VanTassel-Baska, J. (in press). Contributions to gifted education of the talent search concept. In C. P. Benbow & D. Lubinski (Eds.), *Psychometric and social issues concerning intellectual talent.* Baltimore: Johns Hopkins University.

ANNOTATED BIBLIOGRAPHY

Colangelo, N., & Davis, G. A. (Eds.). (1991). *Handbook of gifted education.* Boston: Allyn & Bacon
This edited volume contains contributions by eminent authors in gifted education. It is divided into six sections including the conceptions and identification of giftedness, instructional models and practices, creativity and thinking skills, psychological and counseling services, and special topics that apply to gifted education.

Gallagher, J. J., & Gallagher, S. A. (1994). *Teaching the gifted child* (4th ed.). Boston: Allyn & Bacon.
This volume provides guidance and practical suggestions for educators of the gifted. The most applicable chapters include specific curriculum and content modifications for the education of gifted students. Additionally, school psychologists working in a consultative role will find the chapter on administration particularly useful.

Heller, K. A., Monks, F. J., & Passow, A. H. (Eds.). (1993). *International handbook of research and development of giftedness and talent.* Oxford, England: Pergamon Press Ltd.
A world perspective on gifted education from respected researchers from different countries is provided within this edited volume. Specific sections include a focus upon nurturing gifts to their fulfillment, identification of giftedness, and the conception/development of giftedness.

Silverman, L. K. (Ed.). (1993). *Counseling the gifted and talented.* Denver: Love Publishing Company.

This edited volume delineates counseling and developmental strategies for a wide variety of populations of gifted students. Specific chapters focus on the emotional and social needs of learning disabled gifted, multicultural gifted students, at risk students, families of gifted children, and career guidance and group counseling with gifted students. The focus is on prevention rather than remediation.

Wang, M. C., Reynolds, M. C., & Walberg, H. J. (Eds.). (1991). *Handbook of special education*. New York: Pergamon Press.
Only one of the three sections within this handbook is focused upon gifted education; however, the carefully chosen authors and topics skillfully apply the current research in gifted education. Topics covered include acceleration, enrichment, social-emotional development, and special populations of gifted students.

Recommended Journals:

Gifted Child Today

Gifted Child Quarterly

Journal for Educating the Gifted

Roeper Review

93

Best Practices in Working with Single-Parent and Stepfamily Systems

Cindy Carlson
The University of Texas at Austin

OVERVIEW

It is no longer appropriate in the United States to consider the normative family environment for child rearing to be a household in which two biological parents reside with their children. Both single-parent and stepfamily systems have become increasingly common. Between 1960 and 1988 the proportion of families headed by single mothers more than doubled. It is projected that in the 1990s nearly half of all children alive today, and 85% of African-American children, will spend some portion of their life in a single-parent home; 40% of children are projected to live with a stepparent before age 18 (Glick, 1989). It is the purpose of this chapter to inform school psychologists about the most recent research findings associated with the adjustment of children in single-parent and stepparent homes and to provide recommendations regarding interventions at multiple system levels using a problem-solving framework.

ESSENTIAL BACKGROUND

Definitional Issues

In its narrowest definition *a single-parent family* refers to households in which an adult raises children alone without the presence of a second adult (Weiss, 1979). Single-parent homes may result from marital divorce or separation, death of a spouse, or a parent never marrying. When single parenting is the result of separation or divorce, these families are sometimes termed binuclear to reflect the reality of children visiting two linked households. Because over 90% of single-parent homes are headed by mothers, these homes are also frequently termed female-headed, mother-only, or fatherless families (Angel & Angel, 1993). Although most frequently mothers, a single parent may also be a father, a grandparent, or other relative or nonrelative. It is important to keep in mind that many families identified as single-parent by school or census records, for example, in fact have additional adults in residence who, to a greater or lesser extent, provide support to the household. Up to 34% of single parents have at least one additional adult relative in the home, with the highest percentages associated with young, never-married mothers (Hernandez, 1988). In addition, many single-parents have live-in partners. It should be expected that these diverse single-parent households are different psychologically, emotionally, and functionally for both adults and children (see Carlson, 1987, 1992 for further discussion).

A *stepfamily household* is one in which at least one adult is a stepparent to a child residing with them (Coleman & Ganong, 1991). This differs from the frequently used broader definition of *stepfamilies* referring to a family system created by marriage in which one or both of the spouses have children; however, the children may or may not reside full-time in the home (Ahrons & Wallisch, 1987, cited in Crosbie-Burnett & Skyles, 1989). Stepfamilies have multiple forms including the following: stepfather homes (mother with children marries a man with no children), stepmother homes (father with children marries a woman with no children), blended or complex families (both spouses have children), and binuclear home (single-parent whose spouse marries). In addition, numerous permutations of each of these stepfamily forms exist depending upon the custodial arrangements of the children. As with the heterogeneity of single-parent households, it is expected that each variation of stepfamily has distinctive features and emotional processes. (For further discussion see Carlson, 1985, 1990, 1991c).

In summary, both single-parent homes and stepfamilies are characterized by diversity, not homogeneity. The within-group variations in single-parent and stepfamily systems is seldom addressed in research. Thus, current knowledge of the complexities of these systems and their differential impact on the psychological well-being of children is quite limited. Information is most comprehensive for divorce, single, female-headed homes and for stepfather families. These family forms are most characteristic of the European-American population within the United States.

The Demographic Context

Race, ethnicity, and socioeconomic status dramatically influence the likelihood that a child will reside in a single-parent or stepparent home, the antecedents of such living arrangements, and the degree to which these living arrangements are associated with risk to children. The term *ethclass*, the combined influence of ethnicity, race, gender, and socioeconomic status, has been coined to underscore the importance of understanding how these variables combine to form a hierarchy of risk and resiliency for children in single-parent and stepparent homes (Kissman & Allen, 1993).

Single parenting is only rarely encountered among certain ethclasses, whereas in other groups it is encountered so frequently as to constitute the normative family form. By 1988, 12% of Asian-American children, 16% of European-American children, 27% of Hispanic children, 29% of American Indian children, and 51% of African-American children were living in female-headed, single-parent homes (Laosa, 1988). It is important to be cautious about possible racial biases related to these statistics as single parenting also varies as a function of residential ecology. There is a dramatic increase in single-parent homes across ethnic and racial groups, for example, as one moves from a rural to urban setting (Laosa, 1988). Thus, European-Americans located in the central cities show a higher incidence of single parenting than African-Americans living on farms.

Ethclass also dramatically influences the causes giving rise to single-parent homes. The most frequent precursor of single-parenting for European-Americans is divorce, for African-Americans out-of-wedlock births, and for Hispanics marital separation; only a small percentage of children reside in single-parent homes due to death of a parent — a finding consistent across racial and ethnic groups (Laosa, 1988). Laosa (1988) alerts us to the importance of considering within-group ethnic diversity in conjunction with family form. For example, there is an exceedingly high incidence of single parenting among Puerto Rican Hispanics comparable to the African-American population, whereas Cuban-Americans and Mexican-Americans have ratios of single-parenting closer to the European-American population.

Incidence of single fathering also varies with race and ethnicity. Although single fathers still represent only a small proportion of single-parent homes, the number had climbed from 616,000 households (approximately 2%) in 1980 to 1.1 million by 1989 (Downey & Powell, 1993). Single fathering is most common among Asian-American and European-American populations and least characteristic of African-American and Hispanic groups (Laosa, 1988). Another family composition characteristic associated with race is the relatively high proportion of African-American children (12%) who reside with neither parent in contrast with European-American (1.8%) and Hispanic (2.8%) children. This family pattern has been associated in the African-American culture with a broader, more informal and flexible kinship and social network structure that permits informal adoption of children by nonrelatives and/or relatives.

Remarriage rates resulting in the formation of stepfamilies also vary by ethclass (Hernandez, 1988). European-American parents are most likely to remarry; Hispanic parents are least likely to remarry; African-American parents form an intermediate group. Among both African-American and European-American groups, mothers who are less educated are most likely to remarry (Coleman & Ganong, 1991). As Catholicism is associated with lower remarriage rates, this is a likely factor among the Hispanic population. Among the urban poor, the lack of marriageable men is a factor in low remarriage rates (Angel & Angel, 1993). Regarding first marriages of adolescent mothers, European-Americans are almost twice as likely to marry within 5 years of the birth of the child as are African-American teenage mothers (Astone, 1993).

Not only do European-American individuals remarry at a high rate, they remarry relatively soon after a divorce. Th median interval between divorce and remarriage is only 3 years (Bumpass & Sweet, 1989, cited in Furstenberg & Cherlin, 1991). Moreover, it is common for a birth to occur in remarriage. Thus, 25% of preschool children gain a sibling in the first 18 months following remarriage (58% if the mother is under 25 years of age), and one-sixth of early adolescents gain a half-sibling (Bumpass, 1984, cited in Furstenberg & Cherlin, 1991). Each of these events — divorce, remarriage, sibling additions — represent significant family transitions for children.

Economic and Social Well-Being

Perhaps the most glaring difference between single-parent homes and two-parent systems, including stepfamilies, is disparity in economic well-being. *Single mothers and their children comprise the largest segment of the population in poverty in the United States.* Sixty-eight percent of African-American, more than 50% of Hispanic, and nearly 40% of non-Hispanic European-American female-headed households live in poverty (Angel & Angel, 1993). Although for a significant fraction serious poverty and welfare dependency is chronic (Angel & Angel, 1993), a sizable majority become poor at the time of marital disruption (McLanahan & Booth, 1991). Income following divorce has been found to drop approximately 70% for women, whereas the income for men remains about 90% of predivorce levels (Weitzmann, 1985). The feminization of poverty is maintained by the low earning capacity of women, lack of child support from the nonresidential father, and meager state welfare benefits (McLanahan & Booth, 1991). Single mothers face a double disadvantage — as women in the labor force their wages average 60% of males in comparable jobs, and as single parents they face alone the high costs of child-care while working (McLanahan & Booth, 1991). Not surprisingly, many deficits found for children reared in single-parent homes, when compared with children in intact homes, disappear when socioeconomic status is considered.

The economic situation is most serious for adolescent mothers, particularly minority adolescent mothers. The primary route out of poverty for single mothers is marriage o remarriage. Adolescent mothers have lower marriage rates than other women and thus are more likely to remain single and at economic disadvantage. Adolescent mothers are also more likely to divorce if they marry and thus to re-form economically at-risk mother-only families (Astone, 1993). Out-of-wedlock births, the interruption of schooling, the lack of marriageable (employable) males, fewer employment opportunities, and the emotional immaturity of adolescent mothers have serious social and economic consequences for both the mothers and their children. Children of young mothers have been found to be more likely to experience behavioral problems, do poorly in and drop out of school, nd face restricted employment opportunities (Angel & Angel, 1993). Adolescent girls who do poorly in school and reside in a single-parent home are more likely to become young single parents (Angel & Angel, 1993). Thus, there is fairly convincing evidence that early pregnancy and low educational attainment are the primary mechanisms through which poverty is transmitted from mother to children.

Social Bias

The demographic context of the single-parent and stepparent family might appropriately be considered a dimension of objective social reality. In contrast, constructed social reality reflects the degree to which objective facts about these family systems, which clearly are elusive given their diversity, are colored by social glasses. Two distinctive viewpoints have characterized discussion and research of the single-parent and stepparent family structures. The one is a *problem-oriented* or *deficit-comparison perspective*, whereas the other is a *normative adaptive perspective* (Coleman & Ganong, 1991). In the former there is the assumption that children in both single-parent and stepparent homes will be deficient in some manner when compared with children in nuclear families. Numerous hypotheses underlie the problem-oriented viewpoint. These include greater stress, differential socialization patterns, additional or deficient numbers of adults in family roles, differences in attachment related to biological discrimination, and incomplete institutional support for these family variations when contrasted with nuclear intact families. Despite the prevalence of single-parent and stepfamily homes, the problem-oriented perspective is deeply rooted in current American society.

The *deficit-comparison perspective* is also widespread within the public schools. Fuller (1986) found that teachers associated positive, conforming behaviors with children from intact homes and more often associated negative, disruptive behaviors with children from single-parent families. Teachers older than 36 years of age were most extreme in their biases. One exception to this bias was the greater likelihood of children in single-parent homes being perceived by teachers as independent. A similar negative bias in attitudes of school counselors and social workers was also found regarding children from stepfamilies, when compared with children in intact homes (Bryan, Ganong, Coleman, & Bryan, 1985, cited in Crosbie-Burnett & Skyles, 1989).

In contrast to the problem-oriented or deficit-comparison perspective, a *normative-adaptive perspective* considers single-parent and stepparent systems to be normative lifestyle choices that are firmly established in society. Rather than examining deficits in children's adjustment, understanding the ways in which competent children are reared in *diverse* family forms is the goal of this perspective. Far less research is available to guide interventions with children and families based on the normative-adaptive perspective. Every effort will be made within this chapter to examine single-parent and stepparent families as normative lifestyle choices, despite the fact that this is not the prevalent social viewpoint.

PROBLEM IDENTIFICATION: CHILD OUTCOMES ASSOCIATED WITH SINGLE-PARENT AND STEPPARENT HOUSEHOLDS

It is critical for practitioners to bear in mind that a sizable percentage of children in single-parent families and stepparent families thrive, and many children in intact families do not. As has been noted by multiple authors and studies, family structure does not, in and of itself, explain child and adolescent well-being. What matters most is what happens within the family. *On the average*, however, current research suggests that children fare better in intact, two-parent homes than in either single-parent or stepparent households, regardless of socioeconomic status. Differences, however, may be slight. Recent research suggests that outcomes associated with rearing in a single-parent or stepparent home are most strongly influenced by family processes and gender of the child.

SINGLE-PARENT HOMES

Educational Problems

Early research found rearing in a single-parent home to be associated with lower cognitive functioning, lower school achievement, lower achievement motivation, and a "feminine" cognitive style. Negative effects were consistently found to be more pronounced for boys than girls and most applicable to postdivorce, single-mother-headed homes (for review see Carlson, 1987; Emery, 1988). Several recent large-scale studies, which control the effects of socioeconomic status (SES), suggest that children in single-parent homes are at a slight, but practically speaking insignificant, disadvantage for educational attainment compared with children in intact homes. Of greater concern is their dramatically increased risk for school drop-out.

A large ($N = 58,000$), national, random probability sample of 10th and 12th graders found slight, but practically small, differences in achievement test scores and high school grades between children in single-parent homes and intact homes (Zimilies & Lee, 1991). Girls get better grades than boys in both intact and single-parent homes. Similar findings of statistically significant, but practically small, differences in school achievement were obtained in a meta-analysis of 92 studies of postdivorce children (Amato & Keith, 1991). In a noteworthy study of single-father homes, a large scale survey of eighth graders found educational benefits to girls living with fathers including higher educational expectations, better science and history test scores, and greater access to educational resources including home computers and newspapers.

Although differences in educational achievement are slight between children in single-parent and intact homes, disturbing data have emerged regarding the greater risk of children in single-parent homes to drop out of high school. Zimilies and Lee (1991) found students from single-parent homes to be *almost three times as likely to leave high school before graduation* as were those from intact families, despite the fact that their grades and achievement test scores were relatively comparable to students in intact families. This pattern persists after statistical adjustment for SES differences between the groups. Significant triple interactions between drop-out behavior, gender of the child, and family structure suggest complex relationships. Specifically, males, when residing in mother-headed single-parent homes, were found to be at greater risk of school drop-out than when residing in father-headed single-parent homes. In contrast, when females reside with a single-parent mother, drop-out rates are low whereas residing with a single father increases the risk of dropping out. Zimilies and Lee (1991) note that the higher drop-out risk of boys in single-mother homes and girls in single-father homes existed despite school achievement comparable to peers. In fact, girls in single-father homes who later dropped out of school actually had higher achievement test scores than their counterparts who stayed in school, leading these researchers to conclude that high school drop-out appears to be more a function of social deviance than cognitive deficiency (Zimilies & Lee, 1991).

Problems of Adjustment and Social Deviance

Earlier research on the social and personality effects of rearing in a single-parent home (for reviews see Carlson, 1987, 1990, 1992; Emery, 1988; Hetherington, Stanley-Hagan, & Anderson, 1989) found this family constellation to be associated in boys with greater difficulty with self-control, higher rates of antisocial and delinquent behavior, lower moral development and maturity, and a less secure masculine style. For girls, negative effects were seldom obtained; however, a few early studies found that maturing girls in single-parent homes may be at risk for early onset of sexual behavior in contrast with peers in intact homes.

Recent research, based on a large-scale survey, finds that adolescents in single-parent families are, *on the average*, clearly at more risk than those in two-parent, intact families (Benson & Roehlkepartian, 1993). Areas of greater risk for single-parent youth include alcohol use, tobacco use, depression, suicide, antisocial behavior, and sexual activity. On average, youth (both middle school and high school) in single-parent families were involved in 3.96 of 20 risk behaviors compared to 2.65 risk behaviors among youth in intact homes. These results remained when race, maternal education, and age and sex of the child were controlled. According to the researchers, the impact of rearing in a single-parent family, however, appeared to be more negative for European-American youth than for youth of color.

A meta-analysis of 92 studies (data from over 13,000 children) comparing children living in divorced single-parent families with children living in continuously intact families on measures of well-being, found children of divorce to score lower across a variety of outcomes (Amato & Keith, 1991). Although statistically significant, the differences in well-being between these groups were generally weak (.14 of one standard deviation on average).

A study of depressive affect in early adolescents in intact versus single-parent families found that youth in single-parent families were more likely to be depressed than their peers in intact homes (Feldman, Rubenstein, & Rubin, 1988). Further analyses revealed, however, that family structure was only related to adolescent depression when the adolescent also perceived his or her family to be lower in cohesion and parent–child communication to be unsatisfactory. Youth in single-parent homes were at particularly high risk for depression if these family conditions co-existed with low perceived friendship support. Friendship support clearly offset the negative impact of processes within the single-parent family. Family structure was not related to friendship support. Therefore, youth who lack both the support of friends and perceived family support may be at high risk for continued depression. In summary, the studies mentioned here clearly indicate statistically significant differences in the educational achievement and psychological adjustment of children in single-parent homes when compared with children in two-parent, never-divorced homes. These differences, however, are frequently quite small practically speaking except for high school dropout rates. The fact that differences exist at all, however, between these two family forms suggests factors which may operate to differentiate single-parent and two-parent, intact homes.

Family Processes Associated with Children's Problems

Research consistently finds that the quality of parenting is a stronger predictor of child competence in single-parent homes than any other variable. Single parents are vulnerable to permissive parenting styles characterized by few or inconsistent rules, low monitoring, and low involvement in school (Dornbusch et al., 1987). Whereas earlier studies found permissive parenting to be more characteristic of single mothers and viewed this as a key factor in the differential adjustment of boys versus girls in mother-headed families, recent research has found permissive parenting to be characteristic of both mother-headed and father-headed single-parent homes (Dornbusch et al., 1987).

Single parents are also more vulnerable to violence and abusive forms of parental control. Gelles (1989), in a national survey of 6,000 households, found that single parents were significantly more likely to use abusive forms of violence towards their children than parents in dual-caretaker homes and concluded that "the single parent household is at particularly high risk for physical abuse of children" (p. 498). Poverty and its associated stressors placed children at greatest risk of violence in single-mother-headed homes with these mothers reporting a 71% greater rate of very severe violence toward their children than did mothers in two-parent homes. Presence of another caretaker in the home (16% of single mothers lived in a household with one or more other adults) did not alter rates of violence toward children; in fact, rates of severe and very severe violence were actually higher in these homes. The rate of severe and very severe violence toward children, however, was highest in single-father families, particularly homes with incomes below $10,000. *The rate of very severe violence in low income single-father homes (406 per 1000) is higher than any rate of severe violence observed in any other subpopulation of parents* (Gelles, 1989).

In summary, children in single-parent homes, both mother-headed and father-headed, may experience adjustment problems associated with permis-sive parenting. When combined with poverty, these children may be at particularly high risk for severe and abusive violence. These risks were corroborated in a large-scale survey of adolescents (Benson & Roehlkepartain, 1993). The average youth in single-parent homes was more likely to have experienced home environmental deficits including physical abuse, sexual abuse, parental addiction, time alone, stress, and television overexposure when compared with youth in intact homes.

Interparental conflict is another family process that increases risk for children in single-parent homes. Amato and Keith (1991) concluded based on their meta-analysis of 92 studies, that family conflict was the most significant predictor of children's adjustment in postdivorce single-parent homes. Johnston (1990) found that hostile and noncooperative relationships between divorced spouses were related both to diminished parenting capacity and poorer child outcomes. Specifically, children's interpersonal competence and an absence of behavior problems were predicted where parents maintained a successful coparental alliance after divorce and where family role structure remained clear and parental warmth remained intact. In a similar study with adolescents, Fauber, Forehand, Thomas, and Wierson (1990) found interparental conflict to predict single-parent rejection/withdrawal, which, in turn, predicted adolescent adjustment problems. This was in contrast with the causal pathways for intact families where interparental conflict directly influenced adolescents negatively but did not affect parenting style.

In summary, these studies consistently point to the undermining role that interparental conflict has on the competence of the custodial single parent, which, in turn, relates to negative outcomes for children. Results suggest that noncustodial parents can most effectively promote the social competence of their children by supporting the parenting of the single custodial parent. Other factors contributing to ineffective parenting in single-parent homes are role strain and maternal depression. A study of never-married (66.7%) single mothers ($N = 225$) in poverty (more than 90% of sample had annual income levels below $10,000 despite the majority having completed high school) revealed a high rate of depressive symptoms (59.6% compared with the general population rate of 8.7%; Hall, Gurley, Sachs, & Kryscio, 1991). Maternal depressive symptoms and quality of th mother's primary intimate relationship predicted poor parenting attitudes, which, in turn, predicted child behavior problems. The more severe the mother's depressive symptoms, and the poorer the quality of her primary intimate relationship, the less favorable were maternal parenting attitudes. More severe depressive symptomatology was associated with greater numbers of everyday stressors, fewer social resources (i.e., functional social support and quality of family relationships), and greater use of avoidance coping strategies.

Family Processes Associated with Resiliency

While on average youth in single-parent families are more likely to be at risk than those in intact homes, this is clearly not inevitable. Benson and Roehlkeparten (1993) found $1/2$ of middle-school and $1/4$ of high-school-aged youth in single-parent homes to be at low risk. When the family assets are compared for single-parent homes with youth who thrive versus those who are at highrisk, thrivers were almost twice as likely to report living in homes characterized by family support (including turning to a parent for social support and having a parent involved in their schooling), parental control (including having explicit parental standards for behavior, discipline for broken rules, parental monitoring of whereabouts, and fewer than three nights out per week for fun). These same resilient youth expressed higher levels of internal assets including motivation to achieve, valuing of sexual restraint, and self-esteem. Resilient youth in single-parent homes were also more likely to report extrafamilial assets of positive peer influence, positive school climate, and involvement in structured activities (e.g., church, school extracurricular, lessons). These results lead the researchers to conclude that, "Many of the differences in assets between single-parent youth who thrive and those who do not point toward the support systems around families. It may be this external network of support is key to success in single-parenting" (Benson & Roehlkeparten, 1993, p. 9).

STEPPARENT FAMILIES

As with children in single-parent homes, although differences are seldom large, recent studies find stepchildren, when SES is controlled, to perform less capably on both educational and adjustment indices when compared with children in intact homes. When compared with children in single-parent homes, stepchildren seldom differ on these indices. Increasingly these differences are reliably associated with gender of the child and gender of stepparent such that the following conclusion appears warranted: The stepparent situation is comparatively beneficial for boys and comparatively detrimental for girls. The risk associated with remarriage appears to be heightened during early adolescence.

Educational Progress

Several large-scale studies have found children and adolescents in stepfamilies to demonstrate lower educational achievement than their cohorts in intact, nuclear families. When compared with children in intact homes, children and adolescents in stepfamilies have been found to earn lower grades (Dornbusch et al., 1987; Zimilies & Lee, 1991), have lower achieve-ment test scores (Zimilies & Lee, 1991), rank lower in their class (Zill, 1988), and be twice as likely to repeat a grade (Zill, 1988). Stepparents have also been found to be less active than biological parents in school affairs (Dornbusch et al., 1987). Gender of the child, however, influences these results. Both the achievement test scores and school grades of males have been found to be considerably enhanced by living in a stepfamily (Zimilies & Lee, 1991).

Regarding school drop-out, as with single-parent homes, adolescents in stepparent homes have been found to be significantly more likely to drop out of school before high school graduation, despite the fact that their grades and achievement test scores are relatively comparable to students in intact families (Zimilies & Lee, 1991). For adolescents in stepparent families, however, the pattern is reversed from that obtained within single-parent homes, with drop out more likely in homes with a like-gender custodial parent. Thus, females in a stepfather home and males in a stepmother home have been found to be at greatest drop-out risk. According to one study:

> Thus, these results may be summarized by stating that when a mother decides to remarry, the probability that her daughter will drop out of high school rises sharply, whereas the likelihood that her son will drop out is almost halved. Similarly, but to a lesser extent, drop-out behavior among boys increases when their fathers remarry, while the tendency for daughters to drop out declines upon their father's remarriage (Zimilies & Lee, 1991, p. 318).

These complex results were interpreted by the researchers as being consistent with attachment theory which proposes that a strong attachment develops between the adolescent and same-sex parent that is perceived to be lost or threatened when the like-sex parent remarries. This is particularly true for adolescent females. On the other hand, when remarriage brings a same-sex parent into the family unit (as with the remarriage of a single mother with sons), the probability of drop-out decreases. This suggests that relationships within parent–child dyads of dissimilar sex are particularly complex.

Adjustment and Deviance

Overall it can be concluded that children in stepfamilies show greater psychological adjustment problems when compared with children in intact homes. Comparisons between children in stepparent and single-parent homes yield conflictual results with some studies finding adjustment to be similar and others reporting stepchildren are at greater risk.

Teachers report more behavior problems and school counselors report more contact with stepchildren when compared with children in intact homes (Crosbie-Burnett, 1988, cited in Crosbie-Burnett & Skyles, 1989). Stepchildren are consistently reported by parents and teachers to have more internalizing behavior problems (e.g., anxiety and depression) and more externalizing problems (e.g., fighting, poor peer relations) than children in nuclear families (Bray, 1988; Zill, 1988). Results across 92 studies (Amato & Keith, 1991) found children in stepfamilies, compared with children in intact homes, to be significantly lower in behavioral conduct, psychological adjustment, self-esteem, social relations, and marginally lower in academic achievement. Compared with children in divorced single-parent families, children in stepfamilies were significantly lower in psychological adjustment and marginally lower in behavioral conduct. These results indicate that children living with a stepparent exhibit considerably more problems than children in intact homes and suggests that parental remarriage does not "solve" problems of an absent or single parent. However, these findings vary with the sex of the child. *Across all studies and all outcomes, boys in stepfather families scored above boys in single-parent, mother-headed homes, whereas girls in stepfather families scored below girls in single-parent, mother-headed homes.*

Family Processes Associated with Child Problems

Evidence is mounting that early adolescence appears to be a developmental period of particular risk and vulnerability for children's adjustment to remarriage (Hetherington, 1989). In a longitudinal study of children's adaptation during early adolescence to remarriage, with comparison groups of single-parent homes and intact homes, Hetherington and Clingempeel (1992) found that the course of adaptation to remarriage in stepfather families is a very difficult one that shows little improvement over a 2-year period. Disruptions in family functioning accompanying remarriage of a single mother were pervasive and affected sibling as well as parent–child relationships. Children's behavior problems in these stepfamilies persisted despite good marital adjustment (Bray, 1992; Hetherington & Clingempeel, 1992) and irregardless of authoritative parenting by both parents (Hetherington & Clingempeel, 1992). This indicates that coping with marital transitions is particularly difficult for young adolescents and that factors beyond the quality of parenting play an important role in the adjustment of adolescents to stepfamilies. Zill (1988), in a large-scale national survey, similarly concluded that stepchildren whose families were disrupted in early adolescence showed elevated behavior problem scores in comparison to those whose families were disrupted in middle childhood.

Other factors associated with risk for stepchildren include parents' education, income level, and having half-siblings in the household (Zill, 1988). Stepchildren are at greater risk when parent education is low, income is low, and when half-siblings (versus no siblings or biological siblings) are present in the home. In a surprising result regarding parents' education, Zill (1988) found that within father-stepmother families high parental education level (college degree) predicted greater stepchild problems. It was surmised that more highly educated stepmothers may be more apt to try to play an active role in the family, and, in effect, take over as the child's mother. Given the child's continuing bonds with the biological mother, active parenting on the part of the stepmother may create conflict and resentment in the child. Regular contact with the noncustodial biological parent was found to be important for stepchildren in father-stepmother families but not in mother-stepfather families (Zill, 1988). Thus, contact with the noncustodial mother was more critical than contact with the noncustodial father. Children in stepfamilies experience a disproportionately high rate of abuse and neglect when compared with children in intact families (Crosbie-Burnett & Skyles, 1989). Both the lack of bonding and reduced incest taboos between stepparents and children have been given as explanations.

Family Processes Associated with Resilience

Stepfamily conflict and child symptoms are reduced when discipline and supervision of children remains in the responsibility of the biological parent, whether mother or father, particularly in the early stages of remarriage. Younger children adjust more favorably to a stepfather when he first works to establish a warm (not parental) relationship with his stepchildren, support the mother's discipline, with gradual movement into an authoritative parenting role (Hetherington, 1989, cited in Hetherington & Clingempeel, 1992). When stepfathers engage in control and supervision of children, not only is the stepfather-stepchild relationship attenuated, but the biological mother–child relationship is of poorer quality (Fine, Voydanoff, & Donnelly, 1993). For adolescents, warm, supportive, noncoercive parents who monitored their early adolescents' behavior but granted them considerable autonomy had the most well-adjusted stepchildren (Hetherington & Clingempeel, 1992). In short, stepchildren resent supervision from an adult with whom they do not have a close affectional relationship. The development of a close affectional relationship between stepparent and stepchild appears easier for younger children, who typically adjust to remarriage within 2 to 2.5 years (Hetherington, 1989 and Bray, 1990, cited in Hetherington & Clingempeel, 1992). This is in contrast to stepfamilies with adolescents where it may take 6 to 9 years for family cohesion to approximate levels typical of intact homes (Visher & Visher, 1988).

PROBLEM ANALYSIS

See Carlson, 1990, 1991c, for a comprehensive assessment process for single-parent and stepfamilies, which evaluates family processes on the dimensions of systems organization, family life cycle stage, parent–child relationship quality, social support, and coping style. In addition, an interview procedure for single-parent and stepparent families is available in Carlson (1985) and Visher and Visher (1988). Guidelines for conducting family assessments, including appropriate measures and methods, appear in Carlson (1991a, 1991b). A comprehensive assessment of the family system should be considered a critical part of the child assessment procedure.

It has been recommended that, in addition to completing a family assessment as part of a child referral, school psychologists annually screen their student populations for high risk family situations. Factors associated with risk in single-parent and stepparent families, which have been previously discussed, are summarized in Table 1. In addition to the risk factors noted, screening the student population for any family changes that have occurred in the past year (i.e., separation, divorce, death of a parent or loved one) or are anticipated in the current year (i.e., remarriage) would be useful to the formation of voluntary, prevention-oriented support or education groups for children and/or parents.

PROBLEM SOLVING

The clear goal of screening and assessment is differential diagnosis and the matching of treatment. School psychologists have many intervention options ranging from prevention to intervention, indirect versus direct intervention, and targeting the child, parent, family, teacher, or school. For purposes of clarity, the following recommendations for problem solving with single-parent and stepparent families are organized by the focus of intervention: child, parent/family, or school.

Child Centered

Small, time-limited, structured, school-based support-group interventions with children have been found to be effective for children experiencing family change. Studies have documented the effectiveness of such programs in modifying beliefs and attitudes about family change and teaching coping behaviors (Anderson, Kinney, & Gerler, 1984), reducing depression (Crosbie-Burnett & Newcomer, in press, cited in Crosbie-Burnett & Skyles, 1989), reducing anxiety (Pedro-Carroll & Cowen, 1985), and improving self-concept (Stolberg & Garrison, 1985). These groups have been designed primarily as interventions for children experiencing divorce; however, it can be expected that such groups would also be effective for other forms of family transition as well. Recent data

on the difficulty associated with the transition to remarriage, particularly for children in middle childhood and early adolescence, would suggest that support groups for these children should be a high priority.

Individual counseling may be necessary for youth in crisis or in high levels of distress related to family conflict or transitions. Conflict between parents is common during family transitions which are marked by stress, anxiety, and loss. Clinicians have long noted that parents sometimes diffuse the stress of spousal conflict by "spilling" some of it onto children. Direct help should be provided to children specifically for coping with parental conflict, diminished parenting, and triangulation (Johnston, 1990). For all of these situations, it is important to help children (a) understand the reasons for parental behavior, (b) identify ways in which they exacerbate or ease the tension with their behavior, and (c) establish clear boundaries regarding their blame and responsibility for parents' actions. Self-help books may also be helpful to children and adolescents. Reviews of existing materials have been completed by Schlesinger (1986) on single-parent homes and Coleman and Ganong (1989) for stepparent homes.

In addition to child interventions targeted to the family situation, interventions facilitating general adjustment can also be expected to benefit children experiencing family stress. As noted previously, children fare better in family transitions when they are socially competent and academically capable and have friends (who do not get in trouble). Social skills interventions, tutoring, facilitating participation in extracurricular activities, and newcomer groups for children who have moved into the school district would all appear to be beneficial to youth in single-parent and stepparent homes.

Parent and Family Centered

The goal of parent and family problem solving is to enhance parenting skills despite the unique challenges of single-parent and stepparent homes. As noted in the previous discussion, issues associated with single parenting and stepparenting may diminish parental capacity and adversely affect children. In addition, research consistently demonstrates that authoritative parenting facilitates children's development in single-parent and stepparent homes. Parent interventions, therefore, should focus on developing the capacity of parents to engage in authoritative parenting. Methods of parent and family intervention include support and educational groups, parent skills training, parent/family consultation, and family counseling.

Group interventions have the advantage of cost-effectiveness and provide the opportunity to create social support for parents. Individual parent or family interventions are more costly but have the advantage

TABLE 1
Risk Factors in Single-Parent and Stepparent Homes

Lower Risk	Higher Risk
Both Family Types	
higher parental education	low parental education
economic well-being	low income
authoritative parenting	permissive/neglectful parenting
co-parental cooperation	co-parental conflict
later childbearing	adolescent parenthood
fewer children	more children
younger children	early adolescence
compliance during early adolescence	acting out in early adolescence
parental involvement in school	lack of school involvement
Single-Parent Homes	
mothers with daughters	mothers with sons
fathers with sons	fathers with daughters•
healthy custodial parent	custodial parent depressed
adequate social support	lack of social support
Stepparent Homes	
children younger at remarriage	remarriage with early adolescents
mother-son-stepfather families	mother-daughter-stepfather families
biological mother ties continue	stepmother replaces mother
no stepsiblings	stepsiblings

•Results of studies are suggestive but remain equivocal.

of more directly targeting a solution to the problem. Disadvantages of school-based parent and family interventions include getting parents to participate, role constraints on school psychologists, and adequacy of school psychologists' training in family dynamics and intervention (see Carlson & Sincavage, 1987). In the following discussion an overview of these intervention modalities will be provided followed by specific variations relevant to subpopulations.

Parent groups. Parent group interventions may take the form of support groups, education groups, and skills-training groups. Systematic skills training has been found effective in reducing child problems associated with both single-parent and stepparent homes. In a study evaluating the effectiveness of two treatment conditions (intensive parent training and parent training plus training in social problem-solving targeted for problems other than child management) with single mothers, it was found that both conditions produced improvement in children's externalizing disorders; however, the later condition produced greater decreases (Pfiffner et al., 1990). Systematic skills training with stepfamily parents found trained

parents increased frequency of desirable parenting responses to their children and became more verbally responsive (Nelson & Levant, 1991). Stepchildren noticed positive changes in parents as well as on pre-/posttest measures.

Although the effects have not been systematically examined, support groups for single parents and stepfamily parents may also be of value. Kissman and Allen (1993) define social support as "help that is available in difficult or stress-arousing situations and feeling valued and belonging to a group" (p. 58). Social support network building requires relationship skills, emotional energy, available time, motivation, and a pool of contacts. These are in short supply for many parents, particularly single parents. The availability of these resources in one location, that is, a support group, would be highly desirable. In addition to providing an opportunity for developing social support networks, support groups can help parents learn ways to cope with stress created by negative societal views of single-parent and stepfamily homes (Fuller, 1986) and the lack of clear role expectations for stepparents (Crosbie-Burnett & Skyles, 1989).

Parent consultation/family counseling. School psychologists may find brief parent consultation is useful to single parents and stepparents for normalizing the stressors of these family situations, providing information about how family relationships may influence their child's behavior, providing guidance regarding appropriate behavior with noncustodial parents, providing assistance with the establishment of authoritative parenting practices, and facilitating communication between parents and teachers regarding family concerns and the child's achievement. Key to successful parent consultation by the school psychologist is learning about single-parent and stepfamily issues and concerted attention to one's own biases so that challenges faced by these parents are not viewed and communicated as being reflective of lack of competence.

Family counseling or referral for family counseling is particularly appropriate when conflict is present and chronic between family members in the single-parent/stepfamily system. Counseling with these families most frequently involves resolution of conflicts between family members and the clarification of appropriate roles and responsibilities. Lack of agreement on roles and responsibilities can fuel conflict. Some family dyads are particularly susceptible to conflict in single-parent and remarried systems. These include custodial-noncustodial parents; single mothers–sons; single mothers–grandparents; stepparents–stepchildren (particularly of opposite sex); and biological parent–child during early adolescence. Availability of school personnel for counseling during evening hours for parents who work during the day is, of course, desirable.

Stepfamilies and single-parent families also bring unique issues to counseling. Key developmental issues during the first years of remarriage include arranging for discipline and parental authority for children; forming a strong marital bond; and developing a workable relationship with the noncustodial parent (Bray, 1992). Single-parent homes, as noted, are particularly vulnerable to permissive parenting, role strain, and depressive symptomatology. All these are exacerbated if there is a conflictual or unsupportive relationship between the custodial and noncustodial parent. Specific counseling strategies for this have been specified by Morrissette (1987) and Glenwick and Mowrey (1986).

Special considerations of single-parent mother-headed homes. The primary concern of intervention with single mothers should be the provision of support. These parents are overburdened financially and experience considerable role strain as the wage-earner, child caretaker, and household manager. As such, they are commonly isolated from emotional and recreational support from peers and vulnerable to depression, irritability, and diminished parenting. Sources of support should be explored within the family, the school, and the community and among peers of the parent. Acceptance of the need for support can be difficult for single-parent mothers as the prevailing social belief is that families should be able to care for themselves and not rely on outsiders. This appears particularly problematic for European-American single mothers; the African-American, Native-American, and Latino cultures are more accepting of supportive kinship networks. Persons of color are also more accustomed and accepting of informal and flexible systems of exchange. These diversity considerations are important to consider in assisting single mothers with social support.

Adolescent single parents. Adolescent single parents, as previously noted, constitute the subgroup of greatest risk for poor parenting, poverty, chronic family disorganization, and child abuse and neglect. Effective intervention with adolescent single parents requires a comprehensive service delivery package that includes opportunities to continue schooling, childcare provision, economic support, child development knowledge, parenting skills training, and life skills training (Kissman & Allen, 1993). In addition, adolescent mothers may benefit from individual therapy or professionally led groups in which the conflicting demands of adolescence and motherhood are confronted and problem-solving strategies encouraged.

It should also be noted that between 65% and 85% of pregnant and parenting teenagers live with their families. Moreover, reviews of the research indicate that families play a large role in decisions both leading to and consequences resulting from teen pregnancy: The consequences of teen pregnancy — school dropout, poverty, repeat pregnancies, and prolonged dependence — are considerably more negative for teen mothers living alone than for those living with their families who provide them with the majority of material and psychological support. These facts suggest that programs for teen parents would be optimized by viewing the family, including the infant's father, as the client to receive program services. Currently, only the teen mother is generally targeted for intervention. Data from three federal programs find that family involvement in interventions, regardless of how measured and defined, is related to positive outcomes for the infant and teen mother (Hanson, 1992). These data also suggest that teen mothers who live alone with their children are at extremely high risk and should be a priority for intensive wraparound intervention.

Single fathers. Single fathers report the following difficulties: insufficient knowledge of child development and gender differences in development, developing the ability to nurture as well as to discipline children, balancing work and childrearing, lack of organized social support, reluctance to seek therapy, and minimization of feelings. In addition, single fathers commonly report more discomfort raising daughters than sons and more ease raising younger children versus adolescents. Many of these difficulties reflect socialized gender-related role difficulties in our culture. Single fathers tend to be less confident of their ability to nurture in contrast with mothers who end to lack confidence in their ability to discipline effectively. Because a primary source of self-esteem for males in our culture is work, balancing work and childrearing may impose greater strain on single fathers. Of particular note is the failure of many men to recognize feelings of loss and depression (Kissman & Allen, 1993). Single fathers may act out these feelings in ways destructive to their children, for example, imposing rigid rules and restricting visitation with the noncustodial parent. It is critical for school psychologists to keep in mind that impoverished single fathers, as noted in earlier discussion, had the highest rates of severe and very severe child abuse of all population subgroups (Gelles, 1989). Grief (1990) emphasizes that the best interventions for single fathers are those that link them with other single parents in a group format.

School Centered

Schools provide an important source of information, acceptance, stability, and support to children and parents in single-parent and stepparent homes. Recommendations for schools in facilitating the coping of these families have been made previously (i.e., Crosbie-Burnett & Skyles, 1989; Fuller, 1986; Johnston, 1990; Kissman & Allen, 1993; Montemayor, 1983) and will be incorporated into this discussion. School interventions may focus on policy changes, practice changes, or attitude changes.

Policy recommendations.

1. Ensure consistency of school policies toward single parent and stepfamilies. At present, legally married stepparents are conceptualized as replacements of biological parents for purposes of financial policies (e.g., college financial aid, free school lunch) yet are denied legal rights and responsibilities of biological parents in other policies (e.g., school permission slips, medical emergency release forms, access to school records, signing report cards). These policies undermine the authority of the stepparent, which may be fostered in the home, and attenuate an already fragile stepparent–stepchild relationship (Stenger, 1986, cited in Crosbie-Burnett & Skyles, 1989). Similarly, single custodial parents are granted all legal rights and responsibilities regarding their child, which undermine the involvement and authority of the noncustodial parent.

2. Assume and promote cooperation among adults involved with the child. School policies (which frequently require that only one parent attend special education review meetings, teacher conferences, or open house) send the message to parents that it is unnecessary to involve or inform more the distal or conflictual co-parent. The school represents a powerful social institution which can model and require that parents cooperate in the best interest of the child. All parental figures involved with the child should be regularly provided information about the child and invited to all meetings and functions regarding the child. The expectation of schools should be that only in circumstances where two or more parents are unable to sit in the same room with each other without engaging in violence or abuse should separate meetings be conducted.

3. Mail report cards and important announcements to nonresidential parents with information stating they have the right to access their child's record, to talk with the child's teacher, and so forth.

4. Annually collect and update information on the family structures of each student.

5. Maintain library resources that focus on the experiences of children in single-parent and stepparent families.

6. Review existing curricula for nuclear, intact family bias.

7. Provide/require/make available training on family structures to all school personnel and provide incentives for attendance. Crosbie-Burnett and Pulvino (cited in Crosbie & Skyles, 1992) report changes in attitudes and beliefs and feelings of competence among teachers and counselors in dealing with stepchildren following a 4-hour training session.

8. Ask single-parent mothers if they would like their children placed with male teachers and single-parent fathers if they would like their children placed with female teachers.

9. Allow for the many variations of family forms in any data collected by the school, district, or state.

10. Provide after-school activities so children can avoid going home to an empty house or to a conflictual home environment. Virtually everyone agrees this is important for elementary school-age children, but it is viewed as less essential for middle-school-aged youth. As a result, early adolescents in single-parent and stepparent homes are more peer-oriented than those in nonconflictual intact homes. Adolescents who are peer oriented rely heavily on peers rather than parents for emotional gratification, advice, and companionship and engage in more antisocial activities, many of which are committed during the after-school, unsupervised hours.

11. Consider the needs of working single parents in scheduling school activities and events.

School psychology practice.

1. Be informed about single-parent and stepfamily issues; conduct presentations and develop/distribute handouts with useful information.

2. Be available to communicate with all parents or individuals of psychological importance to the child.

3. Include all parents and persons of psychological importance to the child in any assessment of the child's problem.

4. Screen the student population for high-risk family situations.

5. Offer support and education groups to single parents, stepparents, and their children and adolescents.

6. Provide parent consultation and family counseling at least one evening per week or identify local mental health professionals who specialize in these issues and have evening hours.

7. Conduct your professional practice to facilitate communication between parents and with the expectation that parents are able to cooperate in the best interests of the child.

Facilitating nonbiased attitudes. Although it is seldom the intention of schools to discriminate in their policies or for school personnel to express biased attitudes, research consistently finds that society views both the single parent and remarried family system as deficient in comparison with intact, nuclear families. As professionals, school psychologists bear the responsibility for examining their individual biases as well as the unintended biases inherent in school practices and policies because these may contribute to child deficits. The following are recommended ways to facilitate nonbiased attitudes:

1. Expand the narrow definition of parent as the biological parent or parent with whom the child resides. "Educators must recognize that a student's most important *psychological* parent(s) may not be synonymous with residential biological parent(s) and that all of the parental figures have the *potential* to contribute to the student's development in school" (Crosbie-Burnett & Skyles, 1989, p. 61).

2. Think about parental involvement as many dimensions on a continuum versus dichotomous categories of involved or uninvolved. Parents who monitor their children's homework, for example, would not be considered "involved" by most school definitions yet this is a significant message of concern and values to children.

3. Adopt a perspective that assumes it is the responsibility of the community, not just biological parents, to raise children.

SUMMARY

Demographic projections indicate that the majority of children in the United States will reside in either single-parent or stepparent homes. Dominant social attitudes view these homes as deficient when contrasted with stable, intact families. Recent large-scale studies support this perspective with data indicating that *on the average* children from single-parent and stepparent homes do not do as well on a variety of outcomes when compared with peers in harmonious intact homes. It is important to bear in mind, however, that differences, although often statistically significant, are frequently practically insignificant, particularly when socioeconomic status is controlled. Thus, the majority of children in these families, practically speaking, do as well as children in intact homes. Clearly they do better than children in conflictual intact homes.

The fact that differences in child outcomes are obtained, however, between intact homes and non-intact homes, is cause for concern. When differences are large and significant, as with high school drop-out rates, concern is even greater. Multiple hypotheses have been proposed to account for these differences (including greater stress, differential socialization patterns, additional or deficient numbers of adults in family roles, differences in attachment related to biological-discrimination, and incomplete institutional support). However, both the diversity among single-parent and stepparent families as well as the complexity and multiplicity of variables that contribute to resilience and vulnerability make simple equations inappropriate. As with intact homes, a consideration of risk factors for children, regardless of family form, appears more appropriate than an assumption of risk inherent in family structure. Alternatively, family structure can be expected to influence family processes; thus, an appreciation of the common developmental challenges faced by single-parent and stepparent families facilitates prevention and sensitive intervention.

Schools and school psychologists can play an important role in promoting the viewpoint that single-parent and stepparent homes are normative and adaptive, not negative and deficient. Altering the contemporary social construction of reality, so strongly biased by the two-parent family of the 1950s, is, however, challenging. Therefore, this chapter concludes with a recent, simple proposition for the 1990s from syndicated columnist Ellen Goodman (1994). *Every American child should be born and raised in a three-parent family.* Goodman notes that a three-parent family would allow one parent to serve as primary caretaker at any instance given the necessity of two parents working full-time to maintain an adequate standard of living. The three-parent family would permit greater division of labor as parenting becomes increasingly complex. For example, one parent could be Designated Chauffeur, another Designated Worrier, another Designated Emergency Back-up System, another Designated Homework Monitor. In fact, Goodman notes, why stop at three parents — four may be better.

In summary, for the family of the 1990s, even the common social ideal of the intact family with two parents is not enough. As such, the socially networked single-parent family system and the multiple parent roles of the stepfamily system may reflect more evolved forms of the family. The challenge to schools and to school psychologists is to promote competent parenting and to provide support and acceptance to parents and children, regardless of family form.

REFERENCES

Amato, P. R., & Keith, B. (1991). Parental divorce and the well-being of children: A meta-analysis. *Psychological Bulletin, 110*(1), 26–43.

Angel, R., & Angel, J. L. (1993). *Painful inheritance: Health and the new generation of fatherless families.* Madison, WI: The University of Wisconsin Press.

Astone, N. M. (1993). Are adolescent mothers just single mothers? *Journal of Early Adolescence, 3*(4), 353–371.

Benson, P. L., & Roehlkepartain, E. C. (1993). *Youth in single-parent families: Risk and resiliency.* Minneapolis, MN: Search Institute.

Bray, J. H. (1988). Children's development during early remarriage. In E. M. Hetherington & J. D. Arasteh (Eds.), *Impact of divorce, single parenting and stepparenting on children* (pp. 279–298). Hillsdale, NJ: Lawrence Erlbaum Associates.

Bray, J. H. (1992). Family relationships and children's adjustment in clinical and nonclinical stepfather families. *Journal of Family Psychology, 6*(1), 60–68.

Carlson, C. I. (1985). Best practices for working with single-parent and stepparent families. In A. Thomas & J. Grimes (Eds.), *Best practices in school psychology – Manual* (pp. 43–60). Kent, OH: National Association of School Psychologists.

Carlson, C. I. (1987). Children and single parent homes. In A. Thomas & J. Grimes (Eds.), *Children's needs: Psychological perspectives* (pp. 560–570). Washington, DC: National Association of School Psychologists.

Carlson, C. I. (1990). Best practices for working with single-parent and stepparent families. In A. Thomas & J. Grimes (Eds.), *Best practices in school psychology–II* (pp. 837–858). Washington, DC: National Association of School Psychologists.

Carlson, C. I. (1991a). Assessing the family context. In R. Kamphaus & C. R. Reynolds (Eds.), *Handbook of psychological and educational assessment of children. Vol. II: Personality, behavior, and context* (pp. 546–575). New York: Guilford Press.

Carlson, C. I. (1991b). Models and strategies for family–school assessment. In M. Fine & C. I. Carlson (Eds.), *Handbook of family–school intervention: A systems approach* (pp. 18–44). Boston: Allyn & Bacon.

Carlson, C. I. (1991c). Single parent and stepparent family systems: Problems, issues, and interventions. In M. Fine & C. I. Carlson (Eds.), *Handbook of family–school intervention: A systems approach* (pp. 188–214). Boston: Allyn & Bacon.

Carlson, C. I. (1992). Single parent families. In M. E. Procidano & C. B. Fisher (Eds.), *Families: A handbook for school professionals* (pp. 36–56). New York: Teachers College Press.

Carlson, C. I., & Sincavage, J. M. (1987). Family-oriented school psychology practice: Results of a national survey of NASP members. In W. P. Erchul (Ed.), Family systems assessment and intervention (Special issue). *School Psychology Review, 16*(4), 517–524.

Coleman, M., & Ganong, L. H. (1989). Stepfamily self-help books: Brief annotations and ratings. *Family Relations, 38*, 91–96.

Coleman, M., & Ganong, L. H. (1991). Remarriage and stepfamily research in the 1980s. In A. Booth (Ed.), *Contemporary families* (pp. 192–207). Minneapolis, MN: National Council on Family Relations.

Crosbie-Burnett, M., & Skyles, A. (1989). Stepchildren in schools and colleges: Recommendations for educational policy changes. *Family Relations, 38*, 59–64.

Dornbusch, S. M., Ritter, P. L., Leiderman, P. H., Roberts, D. F., & Fraleigh, M. J. (1987). The relation of parenting style to adolescent school performance. *Child Development, 58*, 1244–1257.

Downey, D. B., & Powell, B. (1993). Do children in single-parent households fare better living with same-sex parents? *Journal of Marriage and the Family, 55*(1), 55–71.

Emery, R. E. (1988). *Marriage, divorce, and children's adjustment.* Newberry Park, CA: Sage.

Fauber, R., Forehand, R., Thomas, A. M., & Wierson, M. (1990). A mediational model of the impact of marital conflict on adolescent adjustment in intact and divorced families: The role of disrupted parenting. *Child Development, 61*, 112–1123.

Feldman, S. S., Rubenstein, J. L., & Rubin, C. (1988). Depressive affect and restraint in early adolescents: Relationships with family structure, family process, and friendship support. *Journal of Early Adolescence, 8*(3), 279–296.

Fine, M. A., Voydanoff, P., & Donnelly, B. W. (1993). Relations between parental control and warmth and child well-being in stepfamilies. *Journal of Family Psychology, 7*(2), 222–232.

Fuller, M. L. (1986). Teachers' perceptions of children from intact and single-parent families. *The School Counselor*, May, 365–374.

Furstenberg, J., & Cherlin, A. J. (1991). *Divided families: What happens to children when parents part.* Cambridge, MA: Harvard University Press.

Gelles, R. J. (1989). Child abuse and violence in single-parent families: Parent absence and economic deprivation. *American Journal of Orthopsychiatry, 59*(4), 492–501.

Glenwick, D. S., & Mowrey, J. D. (1986). When parent becomes peer: Loss of intergenerational boundaries in single parent families. *Family Relations, 35*, 57–62.

Glick, P. (1989). Remarried families, stepfamilies, and stepchildren: A brief demographic analysis. *Family Relations, 38*, 24–27.

Goodman, E. (1994, April 14). Why stop with two parents? *Austin American Statesman*, p. A11.

Grief, G. L. (1990). *The daddy track and the single father.* Lexington, MA: Lexington Books.

Hall, L. A., Gurley, D. N., Sachs, B., & Kryscio, R. J. (1991). Psychosocial predictors of maternal depressive symptoms, parenting attitudes, and child behavior in single-parent families. *Nursing Research, 40*(4), 214–220.

Hernandez, D. J. (1988). The demographics of divorce and remarriage. In E. M. Hetherington & J. D. Arasteh (Eds.), *Impact of divorce, single parenting and stepparenting on children* (pp. 3–22). Hillsdale, NJ: Lawrence Erlbaum Associates.

Hetherington, E. M. (1989). Coping with family transitions: Winners, losers, and survivors. *Child Development, 60*, 114.

Hetherington, E. M., Hagan, M. S., & Anderson, E. R. (198). Marital transitions: A child's perspective. *American Psychologist, 44*(2), 303–312.

Hetherington, E. M., & Clingempeel, W. G. (1992). Coping with marital transitions. *Monographs of the Society for Research in Child Development*, vol. 57 (2–3).

Johnston, J. R. (1990). Role diffusion and role reversal: Structural variations in divorced families and children's functioning. *Family Relations, 39*, 405–413.

Kissman, K., & Allen, J. A. (1993). *Single-parent families.* Newberry Park, CA: Sage Publications.

Laosa, L. M. (1988). Ethnicity and single parenting in the Unites States. In E. M. Hetherington & J. D. Arasteh (Eds.), *Impact of divorce, single parenting and stepparenting on children* (pp. 23–49). Hillsdale, NJ: Lawrence Erlbaum Associates.

McLanahan, S., & Booth, K. (1991). Mother-only families. *Contemporary families: Looking forward, looking back* (405–428). Minneapolis, MN: National Council on Family Relations.

Montemayor, R. (1983). Picking up the pieces: The effects of parental divorce on adolescents with some suggestions for school-based intervention programs. *Journal of Early Adolescence, 4*, 289–314.

Morrissette, P. J. (1987). Altering problematic family hierarchy: A strategy for therapy with single-parent families. *Family Therapy, 14*(1), 53–59.

Nelson, W. P., & Levant, R. F. (1991). An evaluation of a skills training program for parents in stepfamilies. *Family Relations, 40*, 291–296.

Pedro-Carroll, J. L., & Cowen, E. L. (1985). The children of divorce intervention program: An investigation of the efficacy of a school-based prevention program. *Journal of Consulting and Clinical Psychology, 53*, 603–611.

Pfiffner, L. J., Jouriles, E. N., Brown, M. M., Etscheidt, M. A., & Kelly, J. A. (1990). Effects of problem-solving therapy on outcomes of parent training for single-parent families. *Child and Family Behavior Therapy, 12*(1), 1–11.

Schlesinger, B. (1986). Single parent families: A bookshelf: 1978–1986. *Family Relations, 35*, 199–204.

Stolberg, A. L., & Garrison, K. M. (1981). *Children's support group: A procedures manual.* (DHEW Publication No. 1 RO1MH 34462-02). Washington, DC: Government Printing Office.

Visher, E., & Visher, J. (1988). *Old loyalties, new ties.* New York: Brunner/Mazel.

Warren, N. J., & Amara, I. A. (1984). Educational groups for single parents: The parenting after divorce programs. *Journal of Divorce, 8*, 79–86.

Weiss, R. (1979). *Going it alone.* New York: Basic Books.

Weitzman, L. J. (1985). *The divorce revolution: The unexpected social and economic consequences for women and children in America.* New York: The Free Press.

Zill, N. (1988). Behavior, achievement, and health problems among children in stepfamilies: Findings from a national survey of child health. In E. M. Hetherington & J. D. Arasteh (Eds.), *Impact of divorce, single parenting and stepparenting on children* (pp. 325–368). Hillsdale, NJ: Lawrence Erlbaum Associates.

Zimilies, H., & Lee, V. E. (1991). Adolescent family structure and educational progress. *Development Psychology, 27*(2), 314–320.

ANNOTATED BIBLIOGRAPHY

Cohen, M. G. (1989). *Long distance parenting.* New York: New American Library.
Approximately half of divorced fathers have not seen their children in the past year. This book educates fathers regarding the importance of their involvement in their children's lives and provides tips on how to be an involved father regardless of geographic distance.

Furstenberg, Jr., & Cherlin, A. J. (1991). *Divided families: What happens to children when parents part.* Cambridge, MA: Harvard University Press.
This is a user friendly summary of the intervention implications of research on the effects on children of divorce, single-parenting, and remarriage. It is well-researched and authoritative but also clearly written without jargon. As such it is very useful background reading for both professionals and parents.

Grief, G. L. (1990). *The daddy track and the single father.* Lexington, MA: Lexington Books.
This is a self-help book for single fathers based on an updated survey of 1,100 fathers raising children alone. It provides both a view of characteristics of this growing population and information useful to single fathers. Chapters address common myths, running a household, parenting children, balancing work and family, conducting one's social life, getting along with the noncustodial mother, dealing with the courts and child support and joint custody, and fatherhood after death of a spouse.

Kissman, K., & Allen, J. A. (1993). *Single-parent families.* Newbury Park, CA: Sage Publications.
This book written primarily for professionals provides a comprehensive discussion of the heterogeneity of the single-parent family. Chapters are devoted to mother-headed families, ethnic families, adolescent parents, single-father-headed families, and noncustodial parents. Specific suggestions for intervention are provided. This book is unusually sensitive in discussion of issues of gender, ethnicity, race, and social class. As such, it is an invaluable resource on both single-parent families and professional cultural sensitivity.

94

Best Practices in Working with Bilingual Children

Emilia C. Lopez
Queens College, City University of New York

OVERVIEW

This chapter highlights best assessment and intervention practices for school psychologists working with bilingual students. It is also designed to heighten the awareness and sensitivity of school psychologists to students with linguistic and culturally different backgrounds.

The provision of assessment and intervention services for bilingual students is approached from a wide perspective; several factors that can influence how these students function in schools are examined. Those factors include internal or student-centered variables such as the student's language, cognitive, achievement, and socioemotional functioning as well as external variables such as the impact of culture, the instructional environment, and the classroom setting.

Recent statistics indicate that 5.3 million school-aged children in the United States enter school speaking a language other than English (Children's Defense Fund, 1989). Estimates for the 21st century indicate that the number of language minority children, including bilingual children in America's schools, will continue to rise.

Bilingual children live in homes where a language other than English is used either continuously or intermittently. The language proficiency profiles of these children may vary depending on their history of second language acquisition and the contexts in which they use each language (e.g., school vs. home).

Bilingual students may come from a multitude of cultural backgrounds and practices (Lynch, 1992). Although many culturally different families adhere to values and customs very close to those followed in the homeland, others may integrate into their repertoire some of the practices and values of the host culture while retaining some or many of their traditional patterns.

Children from bilingual homes may face a number of challenges including the severance of family ties and friendships as a result of migration; acculturation conflicts stemming from the clash between the family's more traditional values and the children's higher rate of acculturation into the host culture; higher levels of poverty associated with minority populations; and cultural conflicts resulting from subtle as well as major differences between the children's cultural values and those of the new adopted culture (Esquivel, 1985).

Bilingual students may encounter a number of educational barriers that can influence their performance in schools. These educational barriers may include prejudicial racial attitudes, intolerance to linguistic and cultural differences, lower levels of expectations from school professionals, a lack of access to adequate or higher level educational services due to tracking, and the implementation of policies and regulations insensitive to the needs of culturally different students (e.g., implementation of rigid assessment policies; Cummins, 1989).

BASIC CONSIDERATIONS

The Bilingual Child Within the Context of Language

Working successfully with bilingual children requires that all assessment and intervention practices should be based upon a well-developed knowledge base of first- and second-language (L1 and L2, respectively) development. Among the factors that need to be considered when interpreting assessment data are

1. The students' stage of L2 acquisition.

2. The students' language backgrounds (e.g., years of exposure to the English language, academic vs. informal exposure to L2).

3. The quantity and quality of exposure to L1 and L2.

4. The level of proficiency of L1 at the time L2 was introduced.

5. The age of the child at the time of L2 acquisition.

6. Personality factors (e.g., introversion vs. outgoing personality).

7. Motivation for learning L2 (e.g., internally vs. externally based).

8. The social distance between the student's culture and the culture of L2.

The planning and implementation of interventions for bilingual students must also be based on the knowledge of theory and research in language development, L2 acquisition, and effective language strategies. Some of this basic knowledge includes

1. The most effective strategies to help bilingual students learn L2 incorporate activities where language is used within natural, meaningful interactions.

2. "More language" (i.e., more English) is not better; what is important is exposure to comprehensible input in L2.

3. Bilingual children can develop high levels of literacy and proficiency in both languages.

4. High levels of proficiency and literacy in L1 can facilitate learning L2 because of the common underlying proficiency or interdependence across languages which facilitates the transfer of knowledge from one language to the other. (Cummins, 1984)

The Bilingual Child Within the Context of Culture

Culturally different families may differ from nonminority families along a number of complex variables that interact dynamically and may result in numerous cultural patterns or variations. (For a discussion of best practices in working with culturally different families, see the chapter by D. P. Flanagan and A. H. Miranda in this volume.)

According to Lynch (1992), culturally different families may differ in terms of their family composition; primary caregivers; childrearing practices; sleeping and eating patterns; response to disobedience and aggression; perceptions of disability, health, and healing; language; religion; communicative interaction styles; and help-seeking behaviors. These cultural characteristics and differences should be examined in the context of how they influence the students' functioning within assessment and classroom situations, schools, families, and communities. In planning and evaluating interventions, careful consideration should also be given to the benefits of incorporating activities, interaction styles, and instructional sequences that match the students' cognitive, emotional, and behavioral styles (Tharp, 1989).

The Bilingual Child Within the Context of the Classroom Setting

Bilingual children's poor academic achievement and behavioral difficulties are frequently, but inappropriately attributed to two factors: their lack of English language skills and their "culturally deficient" backgrounds (Cummins, 1989). School professionals' perceptions of bilingual children as poor academic achievers — and as language and culturally deficient — frequently result in referrals for special education assessment (Cummins, 1984). The special education assessment process currently employed in schools is student-oriented with assessment procedures geared towards identifying the internal or student-centered factors that have resulted in poor academic and behavioral functioning.

Recent trends in school psychology and special education emphasize a wider perspective or ecological model of assessment that views the student as part of many dynamically interacting systems which have a direct effect on students' performance in classroom situations (Cortes, 1986). Within this wider perspective, school psychologists can explore bilingual children's functioning in the areas of cognition, language, achievement, and socioemotional skills (i.e., internal variables) while also examining how instructional environments and classroom characteristics influence the bilingual students' behaviors and learning process. Information collected at the internal and external levels can be used to plan and implement interventions targeted at multiple sources (e.g., students, parents, teachers), settings (e.g., home, school), and situations (e.g., instruction, classroom management).

BEST PRACTICES IN THE ASSESSMENT OF BILINGUAL CHILDREN

Student-Centered Assessment

Bilingual children should be assessed by school psychologists who (a) are proficient in two languages; (b) have the prerequisite knowledge and skills in the nonbiased assessment of language proficiency, cognition, academic functioning, and socioemotional functioning; and (c) have intimate knowledge with the children's cultural backgrounds.

School psychologists working with bilingual students must maintain a culturally sensitive stance throughout all assessment activities by examining (a) the characteristics of culturally different individuals and families (i.e., the shared ideas, concepts, behaviors, and beliefs of a given cultural group); (b) the cultural values and practices that individual bilingual children adopt from their native culture and modify as a result of contact with the majority culture; and (c) the processes by which these cultural values and practices impact on bilingual children's functioning in the areas of cognition, language, thinking, learning, and socioemotional functioning.

Overall, normed instruments are not recommended in the assessment of bilingual children for a number of reasons including:

1. Norms are usually limited to small samples of minority children with the majority of children represented being of nonminority, middle class backgrounds.

2. Norming procedures routinely exclude students with limited English proficiency, a population of students frequently assessed by school psychologists.

3. Test items tap information that minority children may not be familiar with due to their linguistically and culturally different backgrounds.

4. Testing formats do not allow examiners the opportunity to provide feedback or to probe into the children's quality of responses.

5. The tests' scoring systems arbitrarily decide what are the correct responses based on majority culture paradigms.

6. The standardized testing procedures assume that the children have appropriate test-taking skills.

All of these criticisms are frequently cited as possible sources of bias in assessing bilingual students with continued debate as to the basis and evidence for bias (Reynolds & Kaiser, 1990).

Translated tests are often cited as an option because of the lack of instruments to assess children in languages other than English. However, this practice is strongly discouraged due to the inherent problems in translating test items. Difficulties in translating entail vocabulary and concepts that cannot be directly translated from one language to another, differences in dialects that can result in the same word being translated into several words in the other language, and concepts that change meaning once translated into a different language. Clearly, all these problems inherent to the process of translation render translated tests invalid as content changes may result in items that measure constructs and knowledge different from what was originally intended.

Alternative procedures for evaluating bilingual children include the collection of data from numerous sources (e.g., parent, children, school personnel) and the use of multiple procedures such as informal tasks, observations, interviews, checklists, and rating scales. Throughout the use of all these measures, school psychologists must proceed cautiously while attending to the students' familiarity with the content of the tasks and the test-taking skills they require.

Assessment of language proficiency. The assessment of language proficiency involves examining the bilingual student's expressive and receptive language skills in interpersonal as well as academic situations. Language proficiency tests for bilingual children are scarce and the few that are available are considered inadequate because of a lack of validity and reliability, a tendency to measure discrete aspects of language, and the use of arbitrary cutoff scores that vary from test to test (Mattes & Omark, 1984).

Among the practices recommended are parent, children, and teacher interviews to explore the history of language use, language development, and language background. Informal questionnaires may be helpful in collecting language-background data (for a sample of a language-background questionnaire useful with parents and teachers, see Payan, 1984). It is also important to collect language samples during informal situations (e.g., play, conversations) as well as in more formal academic tasks (e.g., classroom discussions). (See Prutting, 1983, for the assessment of language proficiency through language samples.)

Because language use and proficiency can vary along many dimensions, observations are also recommended across different languages (e.g., L1 and L2), situations (e.g., small group vs. large group), settings (e.g., classroom vs. school yard), topics (e.g., talking about math vs. talking about food), contexts (e.g., home vs. school) and individuals communicating with the assessment subjects (e.g., peers, adults, family). According to Mattes and Omark (1984), observations can be used to examine how bilingual children use their first and second languages to (a) comment on their own actions and the actions of others; (b) describe experiences; (c) recount events sequentially; (d) maintain topics; (e) answer questions; (f) request information, attention, clarification, and action; (g) express feelings and needs; (h) describe plans and solutions; and (i) support viewpoints.

Overall, all language proficiency tasks should be interpreted taking into consideration the following issues:

- As children are exposed to L2, they may demonstrate a loss of receptive and expressive language skills in L1. Thus, less developed skills in L1 may be due to the normal second language acquisition process and not to language disabilities.

- Bilingual students' proficiency may vary depending on the context in which the language is being used. For example, some bilingual children are well able to communicate in both languages in interpersonal situations but are more proficient in L2 within academic situations.

- Language proficiency includes Basic Interpersonal Communicative Skills (BICS) and Cognitive Academic Language Proficiency Skills (CALPS; Cummins, 1984). BICS entails the use of language during context-embedded, interpersonal situations whereas CALPS involves the use of language during context-reduced, academic situations. The L2 acquisition research indicates that BICS takes approximately 2 years to develop in L2 whereas CALPS takes 5 to 7 years. Language proficiency data based on tasks that assess BICS (e.g., observations during play activities, language samples during informal conversations) should not be used to determine bilingual children's ability to use language in cognitively demanding, academic situations. CALPS should be determined through tasks that assess bilingual students' abilities to use language in academic situations (e.g., observations of academic behaviors, collection of language samples in academic situations).

Assessment of intelligence. The intellectual assessment of bilingual children is perhaps the most debatable area in the assessment arena with supporters arguing that there are no empirical data justifying the critics' call of bias (Reynolds & Kaiser, 1990). Critics, however, question the existing research on bias because of methodological flaws failing to consider the effects of L2 on test scores (Figueroa, 1990a). Critics also point to inherent flaws in cognitive measures due to problems in defining and understanding (a) the construct of intelligence, (b) the constructs represented within the test items, (c) the processes underlying the test items, and (d) the skills assessed by the cognitive tasks in those tests (Reynolds & Kaiser, 1990). Perhaps one of the strongest criticisms is that cognitive tests fail to measure intellectual functioning and instead assess bilingual children's language ability. Also, intellectual measures may stress a set of cognitive processes relevant primarily to children from nonminority populations (Armour-Thomas, 1992). Thus, they fail to capture the idiosyncratic ways in which culture shapes an individual's thoughts, organization of knowledge, cognitive strategies, and learning modes used to solve complex intellectual tasks. Despite strong opposition, school psychologists continue to use cognitive tests in assessing bilingual children. Questionable practices such as the use of adjusted IQ scores and tests standardized in other countries also persist but are not recommended because of their lack of validity with bilingual students.

Dynamic assessment procedures such as Feuerstein's Learning Potential Assessment Device are often discussed as one alternative to validly measure cognitive function (Duran, 1989). Dynamic assessment procedures are designed to involve assessment subjects in test-teach-test approaches that evaluate children's cognitive deficiencies and examine under what learning conditions those deficiencies can be overcome. However, a lack of empirical evidence attesting to their validity continues to render dynamic assessment procedures as questionable with bilingual students.

Other alternative procedures include nonverbal tests and developmentally based tasks. Nonverbal tests should be used with caution as they usually assess a narrow set of cognitive strategies and the performance of bilingual students may still be dependent on their familiarity with test-taking skills and with the test content. Piagetian tasks such as the Cartoon Conservation Scales (DeAvila, 1977) are also a viable alternative but they too are limited in terms of the range of skills they evaluate.

Recent reviews of the literature are calling for new forms of cognitive assessment instruments based on the culturally sensitive models of Vygotsky and Cecic as well as on the multidimensional models of Gardner and Sternberg (e.g., Armour-Thomas, 1992). There is also a call for assessment models that explore individual cognitive functioning within the context of culture and experience. The adoption of such models would have serious implications for the training of school psychologists as programs would need to emphasize alternative assessment theories and practices.

Assessment of academic functioning. Currently available academic measures have questionable validity with bilingual populations because of basic flaws (e.g., norms inappropriate for minority student populations, rigid standardization and scoring systems) common to normed tests. As a general rule, academic measures in English tend to measure bilingual students' language proficiency in English and fail to assess achievement or knowledge of academic content (Figueroa, 1990a). Although some instruments are available in other languages, the validity of their results are usually limited because many bilingual children have never received instruction in their native or home language and the test results are confined to that interpretation. Other strong criticisms directed at academic tests include their lack of connection to the curriculum of the students, their tendency to assume that all children have the same background knowledge, and their emphasis on content unfamiliar to culturally different children.

Alternative procedures include Curriculum Based Assessment activities such as informal reading inventories, error analyses, and task analyses that use the students' curriculum materials as the basis of the assessment. Criterion-referenced tests, either publisher-constructed or self-made, can also be helpful when attempting to establish accomplished and future academic goals. Test-teach-test dynamic approaches may be most valuable when the assessor uses tasks and materials directly related to the students' academic functioning rather than more cognitively based procedures (e.g., Feuerstein's Instrumental Enrichment program), which are less pertinent to the classroom setting and demonstrate limited validity (Duran, 1989). Curriculum Based Measurement (CBM) procedures to measure bilingual students'

English language skills are now emerging and merit serious consideration as tools to measure these students' academic functioning (Baker & Good, 1993). Currently, the use of portfolio assessment is advocated for bilingual students because of its emphasis on examining students' permanent products (Canales, 1993). However, its validity has not been established and its usefulness largely depends on the kind of work included in the portfolio and the criteria used to evaluate them.

Overall, whichever alternative procedures are used to measure bilingual students' academic performance, school psychologists must give careful consideration to the interaction between the content of the procedures and the student's background. Bilingual students' performances on academic tasks are largely dependent on the type of previously established knowledge they bring to the testing situation. Thus, asking comprehension questions after they read a story they know little about limits their ability to understand the story and to respond appropriately to the questions in either language.

Assessment of socioemotional functioning. In general, there is a lack of emphasis on social-skills-assessment issues in the literature pertaining to bilingual students. Many unanswered questions remain concerning how linguistic and cultural differences affect bilingual students' ability to function adaptively in home, school, and community situations. Currently available instruments to measure adaptive behavior are mostly normed with nonminority samples and scored using majority-culture behavioral expectations, rendering them inappropriate for use with bilingual and bicultural students. In addition, many of these measures tend to be limited because they emphasize data collection in one setting, either home or school, and fail to examine the potential differences in children's performances across settings and cultural milieus (Scott, Mastenbrook, Fisher, & Gridley, 1982).

School psychologists are advised to use a variety of formal and informal techniques that include interviews, behavioral observations, self-reports, and rating scales to examine bilingual students' functioning across a number of settings (e.g., school, home, community). Interpreting the results derived from these measures may be facilitated by examining bilingual students' social skill deficits in terms of (a) their familiarity with the majority culture's behavioral expectations, and/or (b) the acculturation conflicts that may interfere with the student's ability to perform adequately within various social situations. Throughout the process of assessing social skills, school psychologists can minimize bias by comparing the performance of individual bilingual students to other children of the same age, socioeconomic level, and linguistic and cultural backgrounds.

The use of projective techniques to assess children's emotional functioning has generally been criticized for its lack of validity in intervention situations (Moran, 1990). Also, little is known about its usefulness with bilingual children because of a lack of research with this population. The few empirical studies currently available, comprised mostly of adult with only a few children's samples, have shown that minority subjects tend to perform differently than nonminority subjects on a number of projective measures. In general, minority subjects tend to score higher on items that typically indicate pathology. Studies with bilingual subjects also indicate that individual responses to projective stimuli can vary depending on the languages the subjects are using with different languages acquiring different affective meanings. Overall, these studies imply that projective techniques developed and normed with nonminority subjects fail to capture the influence of language and culture on bilingual children's belief systems; symptom manifestations; defensive styles; and patterns of coping with anxiety, depression, fear, guilt, and anger.

The projective assessment of bilingual children must be approached cautiously while taking into account the specific cultural and linguistic characteristics of each individual. A projective instrument that appears to have promising validity and reliability properties with Hispanic children is the Tell-Me-A-Story Test or TEMAS (Constantino, 1986), a projective technique which uses stimulus cards representing minority characters in urban settings and within culturally relevant themes. Based on the accumulated empirical support for TEMAS (e.g., Constantino & Malgady, 1983), the development of culture-specific tests seems a promising alternative to measure bilingual students' empirical functioning.

Assessment of the Classroom Situation

The traditional student-centered assessment orientation has been criticized for its failure to view bilingual children within the context of an array of other systems that interact dynamically and have a direct impact on bilingual children's learning and behaviors (Cortes, 1986). Some of those systems include the family, the community, and the instructional and classroom environments. Although it is beyond the purpose of this chapter to address each of the systems that impact on bilingual children's functioning in schools, the instructional and classroom environments are discussed as important components to examine within the assessment process.

Assessment of the instructional environment. The main purpose of assessing the instructional environment is to examine the appropriateness of the tasks and methods used in the instruction of bilingual children. School psychologists involved in assessing the instructional environments of bilingual children can base their assessment on the following questions:

- Are the appropriate languages being used for instruction?
- Is the level of the language used in the instructional tasks comprehensible to the student?
- Is language and content context-embedded?
- Are the classroom materials appropriate for the language and academic skills of the students?
- Do the students have the sufficient background knowledge to understand the content of the instructional materials?
- Can the students relate to the content of the instructional materials from a cultural perspective?
- Are instructional activities and materials used for the purposes of developing literacy skills?
- Is the curriculum being adapted to the needs of exceptional bilingual students?

Classroom observations, interviews, task analyses, and examination of students' permanent products (e.g., tests, assignments, homework) can be used to determine the effectiveness of the instructional materials and the need to modify existing instructional procedures.

Assessment of the classroom setting. The literature on classroom interactions, management, and organization is extensive but lacks emphasis on issues relevant to bilingual students. However, there are empirical data to support the hypothesis that teachers' expectations of minority students are related to the types of interactions occurring in classrooms: Low-achieving minority students tend to receive less positive feedback and less attention (Cummins, 1984). This line of research has also demonstrated a relationship between teacher expectations, differential teacher behavior, and minority students' low academic achievement in the classroom. There is also much concern that interactions in most classrooms, including bilingual classrooms, are described as teacher centered and with little student input (Ramirez, Yuen, & Ramey, 1991). Other empirical research exploring culturally relevant variables within classroom settings indicate that many language minority students perform poorly academically and behaviorally when classroom interventions do not match the cultural backgrounds of the students (Tharp, 1989).

Baca (1984) recommends that classroom interactions and management strategies should be evaluated in the context of (a) the bilingual students' cultural perspective and (b) the potential effects of using biased behavioral and classroom management strategies. School psychologists involved in assessing

classroom settings can use data from observations as well as teacher and student interviews to explore the following questions:

- Are there cultural disparities between the interactional styles of the teachers and bilingual students?
- Is the classroom managed using strategies sensitive to students' cultural differences in communication, attitudes, and values?
- What are the teachers' expectations towards the bilingual students?
- Are cultural differences recognized and valued in the classroom?
- Are the rewards and incentives used valued within the cultural backgrounds of the bilingual students?

Concluding Comments on Best Practices in Assessment

Assessing bilingual students is a time-consuming process that strives to explore language and cultural issues while collecting data from numerous sources in various contexts and through a variety of techniques. Throughout the assessment process, consideration should be given to the establishment of strong collaborative relationships with teachers and other school professionals. Assessment conducted through collaborative efforts can facilitate the process of data collection and establish a cooperative environment conducive to the planning and implementation of appropriate interventions (Conoley & Conoley, 1992).

BEST PRACTICES IN PLANNING AND IMPLEMENTING INTERVENTIONS FOR BILINGUAL CHILDREN

Planning and implementing effective intervention strategies for bilingual students is contingent on two factors. First, all assessment data collected should be directly linked to interventions by using assessment techniques that help identify specific intervention goals. Second, all interventions should be monitored continuously to establish their effectiveness and the need to make specific modifications.

Choosing the Language of Intervention

The issue of which language to choose for bilingual students' interventions is complicated and sparked by controversy. Factors to consider in determining the language of intervention include:

- The student's level of proficiency in the two languages.
- The student's age (e.g., high school students with low proficiency in English may need to receive vocational training in their native language).
- The student's length of time in the country.

- Type and severity of the handicapping condition (e.g., severely mentally retarded children may need to receive services in their native language).

- Cognitive demands of the subject matter taught.

- Programs available.

- Parent and student preferences.

- Local and national policies.

- Availability of bilingual personnel.

- Student performance within a given language (Ortiz, 1984).

Instructional Programs for Bilingual Students

The three instructional programs generally available for bilingual students include bilingual transitional, bilingual maintenance, and English-only programs. Each is usually accompanied by English as a Second Language (ESL) instruction. ESL instruction generally entails a variety of strategies to improve the English-language skills of L2 speakers (for a review of the literature on bilingual education and ESL see Wong-Fillmore & Valadez, 1986).

As their names imply, bilingual transitional and bilingual maintenance programs provide instruction in both English and the primary language of the students. However, the language models used within and across programs may differ. They include:

1. The alternate-days approach whereby each of the two languages is used every other day.

2. The alternate-subjects approach in which one language is used in a set of subjects while the second is used in a different set of subjects.

3. The phased approach with L2 being phased in progressively.

4. The preview-review technique in which the lesson is previewed in one language and expanded in the other language.

5. The translation approach whereby information is given in one language and translated to the other on a continuous basis.

6. The functional approach whereby translations are used only when the students are having difficulty grasping concepts and the teacher wishes to provide clarification or background information (Wong-Fillmore & Valadez, 1986).

The foundation for bilingual programs rests in the empirically supported, common underlying proficiency principle. This principle states that first and second language skills are strongly interdependent and that instruction in L1 is developing not just the first language but also a deeper conceptual and linguistic proficiency transferrable to L2 (Cummins, 1984). Thus, a student who learns and understands

the concept of "democracy" in L1 will be able to transfer that knowledge to L2.

Despite their commonalities, there are some major differences between bilingual transitional and maintenance programs. Bilingual transitional programs aim to develop English language proficiency and to transfer bilingual students to English monolingual classes after 2 or 3 years of instruction. Within transitional programs, the students are instructed in two languages until they can speak sufficient English to go into an English-only class. In contrast, bilingual maintenance programs have the goal of developing literacy and language skills in both the primary language and English. Thus, students in maintenance programs stay in bilingual classrooms for a longer period of time and continue to learn in both their primary and secondary languages.

The third type of program, the English-only program, entails placing students in English-speaking classrooms without any bilingual support. In the United States, these programs are sometimes referred to as immersion programs. However, contrary to popular belief, English-only programs are substantially different from the Canadian immersion programs which aim to develop bilingual skills in French and English by initially immersing the students in L2 and eventually introducing them to instruction in both languages (Cummins, 1984).

Bilingual maintenance programs have received strong opposition despite empirical evidence demonstrating that *quality* programs result in higher achievement for bilingual students (Ramirez et al., 1991; Wong-Fillmore & Valadez, 1986). The school psychology literature is noticeably devoid of discussions related to bilingual education. However, in the author's experience, practicing school psychologists constantly struggle with their assumptions and questions about bilingual education issues. Overall, school psychologists involved in recommending and planning programs for bilingual students should consider all the variables discussed in the previous section (i.e., Choosing the Language of Intervention), maintain a flexible attitude, and keep in mind that a position such as "children are unable to learn within bilingual milieus" negates the tremendous potential of the human organism to learn under a variety of conditions and circumstances.

Instructional and Classroom Interventions

The literature offers a variety of interventions recommended for bilingual children. Yet the scarcity of empirical studies validating the effectiveness of many interventions often renders those recommendations questionable. Some data are available to support general strategies reported as effective with bilingual children. According to Ortiz (1984, pp. 85–86), the process of L2 acquisition is facilitated for *all* second language learners by activities that:

1. Maximize student exposure to natural communication.

2. Focus on the message being conveyed, not the linguistic form of the message.

3. Incorporate a silent period at the beginning of the instructional program so that students can listen to the second language without being pressured to speak it.

4. Encourage and create situations in which students can interact with native speakers of the language.

5. Use concrete references to make the new language understandable to beginning students.

6. Devise specific techniques to relax students and to protect their egos. Less anxious, more motivated, more self-confident students experience greater success in second language acquisition.

7. Motivate students to learn.

8. Create an atmosphere where students are not embarrassed by their errors.

9. Do not refer to, or revert to, the students' native language when teaching the second language. To do so may create a situation in which the student, instead of focusing attention on the second language, simply waits for the teacher to repeat utterances in the native language. Under these circumstances, motivation for second language learning may be negatively affected.

Other strategies recommended for all bilingual children include the use of:

- Contextualized instruction that incorporates the students' experiences.

- Instructional sequences with meaningful interactions that facilitate comprehending the content of the material learned.

- Previously learned information to provide a bridge for students to learn new concepts and skills.

- Multicultural materials relevant to the students' backgrounds and experiences.

- Whole language and language experiences approaches that integrate writing, reading, and oral language activities.

- Peer teaching and cooperative learning activities that encourage student participation.

- Metacognitive (e.g., self-management, functional planning, advance organizers) and cognitive (e.g., note taking, inferencing, cooperation) strategies to facilitate the learning of language and content.

- A variety of writing activities that focus on learning clear communication as well as the mechanics of writing (e.g., punctuation, spelling).

- Thematic curriculum strategies that integrate the learning of language skills and content.

- Strategies that emphasize the use of higher order thinking skills (e.g., analyzing, synthesizing). (Cummins, 1984, 1989; Ortiz, 1984; Tharp, 1989).

Classroom environments conducive to learning for bilingual students have the characteristics of high on-task ratios with teachers who expect the children to succeed and achieve (Cummins, 1989). Dulay, Burt, and Krashen (1982) also recommend a low-anxiety classroom atmosphere where errors are expected and students are encouraged to question ideas and experiment with language. Rewards used in classroom situations, whether intrinsic or extrinsic, should be motivating on the basis of the students' individual and cultural preferences.

Finally, Tharp (1989) recommends integrating activities, interactions, and organizational structures that match the students' cultural backgrounds. To illustrate, Hawaiian children have been found to frequently engage in several types of classroom interactions including (a) high levels of seeking attention from peers, (b) low levels of seeking attention from teachers, and (c) "talk-story" sequences characterized by the children co-narrating and overlapping in conversations with adult narrators. According to Tharp, all those behaviors are based on Hawaiian cultural traditions in which cooperation, peer assistance, and sharing of experiences in story telling are valued behaviors. In classrooms with low-achieving Hawaiian children, the emphasis on cooperative activities, small-group classroom activities, and lively discussions have resulted in significantly higher academic achievement. In comparable programs with Navajo children, the introduction of classroom discussion patterns that emphasize the Navajo cultural traditions of turn-taking, a slow pace of talking, and longer discussions have also resulted in higher achievement and greater student participation.

Interventions for Social Skills and Emotional Functioning

In general, the school psychologist involved in providing social skills training to bilingual students is once again left with no specific guidelines as to how language and cultural variables affect the process of social skills training. Obviously, any social skills intervention program should be planned and implemented taking into account the social skills deemed appropriate within the students' cultural backgrounds.

Counseling services may be appropriate when bilingual students demonstrate social or emotional difficulties that interfere with their classroom functioning. A cross-cultural counseling perspective is recommended for school psychologists working with bilingual students. Cross-cultural counseling is especially relevant when language and cultural issues are influencing bilingual students' performance in school. According to Esquivel and Keitel (1989), bilingual students may struggle with acculturation issues, ethnic identity confusion, and culture shock reactions that can impact on classroom functioning. In addition, bilingual students may experience high levels of stress related to learning a second language and to racist attitudes within schools and communities. Among the culturally sensitive techniques recommended in the literature are (a) ethnotherapy whereby emphasis is placed on helping individuals to develop a positive sense of ethnic identity (Klein, 1976, cited in Esquivel & Keitel, 1989), (b) cuento therapy in which folk stories are used to explore cultural identity and ego development (Constantino, Malgady, & Rogler, 1986), and (c) the use of toys and materials that reflect the students' cultural and linguistic backgrounds. Group counseling approaches may also be appropriate but their usefulness must be evaluated for children whose cultural backgrounds do not encourage self-disclosure with individuals outside of the family structure. Finally, all social skills training and counseling activities should be delivered in the students' primary or most proficient language to facilitate the communication process.

Concluding Comments on Best Practices in Interventions

Planning and implementing effective interventions for bilingual students requires a cooperative and collaborative working relationship between school psychologists, teachers, and other school personnel. As such, consultation may facilitate the process of working with school personnel involved in delivering interventions to bilingual students. Consultation is defined as a collaborative process in which consultants such as school psychologists can help consultees (i.e., bilingual teachers, ESL teachers, as well as regular education and special education teachers instructing bilingual students) with students' classroom difficulties (Conoley & Conoley, 1992). Cross-cultural models of consultation are beginning to emerge in the literature and focus on delivering consultation services within a linguistic and culturally sensitive context (Lateer & Curtis, 1991; Lopez, 1993).

Intervention activities must also be framed within a home-school collaboration partnership. Empirical data are available demonstrating that bilingual students achieve in programs emphasizing parent involvement in (a) curriculum planning, (b) school organization, (c) classroom participation, and (d) home activities that promote literacy in the native language (Cummins, 1989). Consulting with parents may also

be beneficial in exploring with the family the appropriateness of the recommended interventions from a cultural perspective.

The Use of Interpreters During Assessment and Intervention Activities

The shortage of bilingual school psychologists has resulted in the frequent use of school interpreters. Little is known about the effects of using interpreters because of the lack of research in this area. However, there are some potential problems that school psychologists should keep in mind.

Preliminary findings of a recent study indicate that inexperienced and untrained interpreters can make errors in the process of translating IQ test questions from English to Spanish (Lopez, 1994). Many of these errors consist of substantial changes in the content and meaning of the test questions. School psychologists using interpreters will most likely not be aware of such errors and the ultimate outcome may be erroneous interpretations of assessment data and inappropriate classifications.

Well trained interpreters can certainly be an asset during assessment and intervention activities but most school interpreters lack training in a number of important areas (Lopez, 1992). Even if well trained interpreters are available, differences across languages as well as dialectical differences within languages (e.g., differences in dialects between Spanish speakers from Puerto Rico, Cuba, Santo Domingo, etc.) can still make the process of translation difficult and substantially change the validity of the measures and procedures used in assessing bilingual students.

The use of interpreters during intervention activities can hinder the establishment of rapport (Esquivel & Keitel, 1989). Their use adds another layer to the complexity of delivering intervention services, complicates issues of confidentiality and trust, and can create barriers in the communication of affect and in the establishment of the working alliance so necessary to the process of working with children and families.

In general, the process of working with interpreters during assessment and intervention activities is risky, speculative, and plagued with conjecture. They should therefore, be the absolute last resort. School psychologists who find themselves in situations where they must work with interpreters should adhere to the following best practices (Figueroa, 1990b; Langdon, 1985; Lopez, 1992):

• Choose interpreters who have prior experience as school interpreters, high proficiency in both languages, a high level of education, and are familiar with the field of education and special education and with the student's cultural and linguistic background.

- Train interpreters in issues related to test administration, assessment of exceptional children, and the special education process (e.g., due process, IEP meetings).

- Provide interpreters with the opportunity to translate written documents prior to meeting with parents (e.g., IEPs).

- Encourage interpreters to ask questions as the testing session or meeting is occurring.

- Prior to actual assessment sessions, provide interpreters with time to ask questions about test procedures and to discuss testing procedures and details related to the student's background (e.g., place of birth).

- During testing sessions or meetings, (a) speak in short, simple sentences; (b) avoid idioms, metaphors, or colloquialisms; (c) use specific terms and avoid jargon; (d) allow the interpreters time to translate all messages; and (e) do not speak to your colleagues while interpreters are in the process of translating.

- After the testing session or meeting, discuss any difficulties encountered during the process (e.g., words that could not be translated), and explore cultural factors that may have influenced the child's/parent's behaviors.

- Do not use interpreters for on-the-spot translation of test questions. Instead, rely on validated test translations.

- In psychological reports, provide details on how the interpreter was used and in which contexts. Also, report all data collected through interpreters in qualitative format and use extreme caution when interpreting the results obtained.

SUMMARY AND CONCLUSION

School psychologists involved in delivering assessment and intervention services must work in the context of examining the language and cultural issues that have a direct impact on bilingual students' performance in classroom situations. The performance of bilingual students should also be examined within the context of the instructional and classroom variables that inhibit or promote appropriate classroom performance. Many unanswered questions remain concerning the best assessment and intervention practices for bilingual students but some general guidelines can be followed to minimize bias during assessment and intervention activities. Those guidelines are best implemented when school psychologists become directly involved in advocating for bilingual children and substantially change existing school practices that limit bilingual students' potential to achieve and succeed.

REFERENCES

Armour-Thomas, E. (1992). Intellectual assessment of children from culturally diverse backgrounds. *School Psychology Review, 21,* 552–565.

Baca, L. (1984). Teacher education programs. In P. C. Chinn (Ed.), *Education of culturally and linguistically different exceptional children* (pp. 101–123). Reston, VA: Council for Exceptional Children.

Baker, S. K., & Good, R. (1993). *The reliability and validity of a direct and frequent measure of English reading fluency for Hispanic students who are bilingual.* Unpublished manuscript. University of Oregon, School Psychology Program, Eugene.

Canales, J. (1993). Innovative assessment in traditional settings. In J. V. Tinajero & A. F. Ada (Eds.), *The power of two languages: Literacy and biliteracy for Spanish-speaking students* (pp. 132–142). New York: Macmillan/McGraw-Hill.

Children's Defense Fund. (1989). *A vision for American's future.* Washington, DC: Author.

Conoley, J. C., & Conoley, C. W. (1992). *School consultation: Practice and training* (2nd ed.). Boston: Allyn & Bacon.

Constantino, G. (1986). *TEMAS (Tell Me a Story).* Los Angeles: Western Psychological Services.

Constantino, G., & Malgady, R. G. (1983). Verbal fluency of Hispanic, black, and white children on TAT and TEMAS, a new thematic apperception test. *Hispanic Journal of Behavioral Sciences, 5,* 199–206.

Constantino, G., Malgady, R. G., & Rogler, L. H. (1986). Cuento therapy: A culturally sensitive modality for Puerto Rican children. *Journal of Consulting and Clinical Psychology, 54,* 639–645.

Cortes, C. E. (1986). The education of language minority students: A contextual interaction model. In Bilingual Education Office, California State Department of Education (Ed.), *Beyond language: Social and cultural factors in schooling language minority students* (pp. 3–31). Los Angeles: Evaluation, Dissemination and Assessment Center, California State University.

Cummins, J. (1984). *Bilingualism and special education: Issues in assessment and pedagogy.* San Diego, CA: College-Hill.

Cummins, J. (1989). *Empowering minority students.* Sacramento, CA: California Association for Bilingual Education.

DeAvila, E. A. (1977). *The Cartoon Conservation Scales.* San Rafael, CA: Linguametrics.

Dulay, H., Burt, M., & Krashen, S. (1982). *Language two.* New York: Oxford University Press.

Duran, R. P. (1989). Assessment and instruction of at-risk Hispanic students. *Exceptional Children, 56,* 154–158.

Esquivel, G. (1985). Best practices in the assessment of limited English proficient and bilingual children. In A. Thomas & J. Grimes (Eds.), *Best practices in school psychology* (pp. 113–123). Kent, OH: National Association of School Psychologists.

Esquivel, G. B., & Keitel, M. A. (1989). Counseling immigrant children in the schools. *Elementary School Guidance and Counseling, 24,* 213–221.

Figueroa, R. A. (1990a). Assessment of linguistic minority group children. In C. R. Reynolds & R. W. Kamphaus (Eds.), *Handbook of psychological and educational assessment of children: Intelligence and achievement* (pp. 671–696). New York: Guilford.

Figueroa, R. A. (1990b). Best practices in the assessment of bilingual children. In A. Thomas & J. Grimes (Eds.), *Best practices in school psychology–II* (pp. 93–106). Washington, DC: National Association of School Psychologists.

Langdon, H. W. (1985, February). *Working with interpreters and translators in a school setting.* Paper presented at the Fordham University Bilingual Conference, New York, NY.

Lateer, A., & Curtis, M. (1991, April). *Cross-cultural consultation: Responding to diversity.* Paper presented at the National Association of School Psychologists, Dallas, TX.

Lopez, E. (1992, April). *A survey of school interpreters: Implications for practice and research.* Paper presented at the National Association of School Psychologists Conference, Nashville, TN.

Lopez, E. (1993, April). *The use of consultation with linguistically and culturally diverse students: Benefits and implications.* Paper presented at the National Association of School Psychologists Conference, Washington, DC.

Lopez, E. (1994, April). *A preliminary investigation of errors made by interpreters during on the spot translations of WISC-R questions.* Paper presented at the National Association of School Psychologists Conference, Seattle, WA.

Lynch, E. W. (1992). Developing cross-cultural competence. In E. W. Lynch & M. J. Hanson (Eds.), *Developing cross-cultural competence: A guide for working with young children and their families* (pp. 35–59). Baltimore, MD: Paul H. Brookes.

Mattes, L. J., & Omark, D. R. (1984). *Speech and language assessment for the bilingual handicapped.* Austin, TX: Pro-Ed.

Moran, M. P. (1990). The problem of cultural bias in personality assessment. In C. R. Reynolds & R. W. Kamphaus (Eds.), *Handbook of psychological and educational assessment of children: Personality* (pp. 524–545). New York: Guilford.

Ortiz, A. A. (1984). Language and curriculum development for exceptional bilingual children. In P. C. Chinn (Ed.), *Education of culturally and linguistically different exceptional children* (pp. 77–100). Reston, VA: Council for Exceptional Children.

Payan, R. (1984). Language assessment for bilingual exceptional children. In L. M. Baca & H. T. Cervantes (Eds.), *The bilingual special education interface* (pp. 125–137). St. Louis, MO: Times Mirror/Mosley.

Prutting, C. A. (1983). Assessing communicative behavior using a language sample. In D. R. Omark & J. G. Erickson (Eds.), *The bilingual exceptional child* (pp. 89–99). San Diego: College-Hill.

Ramirez, J. D., Yuen, S. D., & Ramey, D. R. (1991). *Executive summary, Final report: Longitudinal study of structured English immersion strategy, early-exit and late- exit transitional bilingual education programs for language- minority children* (Contract No. 300-87-0156). Submitted to the U.S. Department of Education. San Mateo, CA: Aguirre International.

Reynolds, C. R., & Kaiser, S. M. (1990). Bias in assessment of aptitude. In C. R. Reynolds & R. W. Kamphaus (Eds.), *Handbook of psychological and educational assessment of children: Intelligence and achievement* (pp. 611–653). New York: Guilford.

Scott, L. S., Mastenbrook, J. L., Fisher, A. T., & Gridley, G. C. (1982). Adaptive behavior inventory for children: The need for local norms. *Journal of School Psychology, 20*, 39–44.

Tharp, R. G. (1989). Psychocultural variables and constants. *American Psychologist, 44*, 349–359.

Wong-Fillmore, L., & Valadez, C. (1986). Teaching bilingual learners. In M. C. Wittrock (Ed.), *Handbook of research on teaching* (3rd ed.; pp. 648–685). New York: Macmillan.

ANNOTATED BIBLIOGRAPHY

Barona, A., & Garcia, E. E. (Eds.). (1990). *Children at risk: Poverty, minority status, and other issues in educational equity.* Washington, DC: National Association of School Psychology.
The various chapters cover topics dealing with bilingualism, educational interventions, and assessment. A good beginning step for school psychologists interested in getting an overview of issues related to bilingual students.

Geisenger, K. F. (Ed.). (1992). *Psychological testing of Hispanics.* Washington, DC: American Psychological Association.
The sections on technical and educational issues are of particular interest to school psychologists working with Hispanic children and other minority youngsters.

Gibbs, J. T., & Huan, L. N. (Eds.). (1989). *Children of color: Psychological interventions with minority youth.* San Francisco: Jossey-Bass.
Culturally relevant psychological interventions for a wide range of minority children are explored and analyzed by various authors.

Hamayan, E. V., & Damico, J. S. (Eds.). (1991). *Limiting bias in the assessment of bilingual students.* Austin: ProEd.
This book focuses on the variety of assessment issues confronting educators working with bilingual students.

Miller-Jones, D. (1989). Culture and testing. *American Psychologist, 44*, 360–366.
This article offers a review of the literature and a critical look at cultural issues in testing situations.

Tharp R. G., Jordan, C., Speidel, G. E., Au, K. H., Klein, T. W., Calkins, R. P., Sloat, K. C. M., & Gallimore, R. (1984). Product and process in applied developmental research: Education and the children of a minority. In M. E. Lamb, A. L. Brown, & B. Rogoff (Eds.), *Advances in developmental psychology, Volume III* (pp. 91–144). Hillsdale, NJ: Lawrence Erlbaum.
This is an excellent resource describing the process by which culturally relevant interventions can be applied to classroom situations to foster achievement and success with minority children.

95

Best Practices in Program Planning for Children Who Are Deaf or Severely Hard of Hearing

Susan Vess
University of Southern Maine

Laura Douglas
Colorado School for the Deaf and Blind

OVERVIEW

Since the implementation of Public Law 94-142 (Education for All Handicapped Children Act of 1975), many children who are deaf or severely hard of hearing (HOH) have been educated within their local public schools, generally through day classes within special education. Their schooling has also been affected by the educational reform movement of the 1980s, including its emphasis on academic achievement and other instructional modifications. However, issues related to efforts in integrating them into general education with the support of interpreters are complex.

According to Mertens (1989), proponents of mainstreaming claimed that integration provided children who are deaf or HOH with the opportunity to acquire social and communication skills needed to participate in the hearing community. Conversely, others supported a full range of educational options saying that mainstreaming isolated these children from members of the deaf community. Neither argument was supported by research, although observation indicated that proximity alone with hearing children did not translate directly into social interaction.

In 1988, the U.S. Presidential Commission on Education of the Deaf made the following observation about the impact of integration on children who are deaf and HOH:

> Of the children mainstreamed, only about half actually experience any true integration, even on a part-time basis. Due to a lack of understanding of the nature and diversity of hearing impairment, the unique communicative, linguistic, and social needs of the deaf child have seldom been met appropriately, particularly in the mainstream setting, despite the Education of the Handicapped Act. LRE has too often been regarded as synonymous with mainstreaming; the regular classroom, even with supplementary aids and services, is often inappropriate. (p. 9)

The Commission went on to recommend "the Department of Education should refocus the least restrictive environment concept by emphasizing appropriateness over least restrictive environment" (p. 27). This controversy confused parents of children who are deaf or HOH as they attempted to choose the best educational programs for their children. Further, it clearly indicated that the education of these children is far more complex than choosing among service delivery options.

BASIC CONSIDERATIONS

Frequently, deaf individuals were the subjects of studies focusing either on the presumed negative consequences of deafness on development and behavior or on identifying the best means of teaching children who are deaf, especially finding strategies that promoted the acquisition of speech and language. Findings of these studies suggested that the supposedly marginal behavior and abilities of persons who are deaf or severely HOH isolated them from the hearing society. Multiple negative personality traits such as immaturity, impulsivity, egocentricity, rigidity, irresponsibility, and noncompliance were identified and said to typify these individuals. Additionally, people who were deaf or HOH were described as more concrete and less intelligent than hearing persons because they performed less well on standard intelligence tests. Thus, conclusions derived from conventionally designed research projects often reflected an all or none perspective in which deafness represented either an overwhelming disability or a variation of normalcy.

Traditional research methods which attempted to isolate the operation of specific variables rarely captured the complexity and diversity of deafness and its impact on the child who is deaf or HOH and his or her family. Moreover, as Leigh and Stinson indicated (1991), it was not unusual for the hearing community to expect people who were deaf to learn speech and speech reading and to conform to social and behavioral expectations of the hearing world. When deaf or HOH persons did not comply with these demands, they were viewed as unwilling to belong to the dominant community.

Recently, conclusions drawn from research not only affirmed the essential normalcy of deaf individuals, but also acknowledged that children who are deaf or HOH are shaped by their soundless environment. From this perspective, people who are deaf or HOH are normal, but their unique environments contribute important differences in the development of cognitive, linguistic, and social behaviors. Because deaf and hearing children are exposed to qualitatively and quantitatively different environments, it is both erroneous to equate difference with deviance and unrealistic to lose sight of the importance of deafness for the child and his or her family (Marschark, 1993).

The overly simplistic deviance and normalcy perspectives failed to recognize the uniqueness of each child who is deaf or HOH, the etiology of his or her deafness, the impact of any additional handicaps, the role of family dynamics, the input of the child's school and community, and the importance of tricultural issues if the child was also a member of a minority group. Further, there was minimal consideration of (a) the contribution of a child who is deaf or HOH to the family system, (b) the importance of the family's structure and values on the child's development, and (c) ways in which the child who is deaf or HOH was similar to and different from family members. It is now understood that synergy and reciprocity in family and interpersonal relationships as well as integration across cognitive, socio-emotional, linguistic, and communicative areas of development are more critical factors than deafness itself in determining outcomes for the child.

Social-emotional functioning and compensatory strategies for learning are often not included in the evaluations of the child who is deaf or HOH. In developing a quality evaluation of hearing children, the following 20 questions are central in the ongoing process of planning and evaluating a comprehensive educational program for every deaf or HOH child and helping parents explore their child's specific academic, social, emotional, and linguistic needs:

1. What are the student's personal, nonlanguage, and nonacademic strengths and skills?

2. How does the child interact with deaf and hearing peers and deaf and hearing adults?

3. How does she or her react to frustration in communication, ask for help, develop and display coping mechanisms?

4. What are the child's work habits?

5. Does the student feel successful in and enjoy school?

6. Does the student feel that he or she is placed in classes that are neither too easy or too difficult?

7. What are the child's favorite and least favorite classes?

8. What reasons does the child cite for these preferences?

9. Does the child have friends?

10. Who are the student's friends and how do they communicate?

11. What leisure and recreational skills does the child have?

12. In which recreational activities does she or he participate?

13. Are there others the student would like to participate in and what would it take to accomplish that participation?

14. What are the child's roles in the immediate and extended family and in the neighborhood and community?

15. How does the student feel about himself or herself?

16. What personal goals has the student set?

17. What is the family's perspective on the child's progress, strengths, and needs?

18. How does the interpreter perceive the child's progress and needs?

19. What are the child's skill levels in the various academic areas as measured by curriculum based assessment (CBA)?

20. What specifically is needed to maximize the child's socio-emotional development, enable participation as a valued member of the family and community, integrate the child into the deaf and hearing communities, and promote acquisition of social, communicative, and academic skills?

The primary goal of each deaf or HOH child's education is development of a host of positive attributes, including self-confidence, pride in oneself and one's accomplishments, responsibility, independence, and self-determination (Kessler-Grimes & Prichett, 1988). In 1988, the Colorado Department of Education (CDE) developed a service design checklist to help school psychologists design and evaluate the educational programs of deaf or HOH children and to ensure that the schools address each child's social, emotional, recreational, and communication needs. The 20 questions combined with the service design checklist identify the critical program components that support the successful education of the child who is deaf or HOH.

FIGURE 1. Service Design Checklist.

Have you considered:

Family School Partnership
- Providing emotional support to the family
- Providing information to the family on:
  implications of hearing loss
  importance of communication
  assistive devices
  functions and publications specific to hearing impaired individuals
- Providing skill training in:
  speech, language, auditory skill development
  sign language
  hearing aid maintenance
  behavior management

Learning Environment
- altering the student's physical environment:
  room accommodations regarding noise, lighting, seating
  captioned films and videos
  assistive listening devices such as auditory trainers
  a telecommunication device for telephone usage
  flashing fire alarm
- Providing inservice training to all the student's teachers and peers
- Providing notetakers, interpreters, tutors; using a buddy system
- Providing specific teaching regarding rules and expectations

Communication
- Providing specific instruction in language development:
  communication intent and appropriateness
  language meaning and content
- Providing auditory training
- Providing training in speech production and refinement
- Utilizing manual communication

Instruction
- Utilizing a multisensory approach
- Teaching the exceptions of new concepts
- Assisting and limiting number of concepts to be learned
- Providing materials at appropriate reading levels
- Providing notetakers, interpreters, tutors, peer tutors, buddies
- Providing class outlines, vocabulary lists, class notes

Transition to Adulthood
- Providing information relating to independent living:
  obtaining and utilizing interpreters
  rights of a handicapped citizen
  telling employers and others about your hearing loss and needs
  hearing aids, TDDs, relay systems, assistive learning devices
  counseling and community mental health services available
  support groups for hearing impaired individuals
- Providing information, training, and experiences relating to career:
  specific information on postsecondary educational facilities, vocational rehabilitation,
    centers of deafness, etc.
  specific instruction on social skills, work habits, and work ethics
  shadowing and specific instruction at job entry
  exposure to jobs of other hearing impaired adults
- Providing information about recreation/leisure activities including social clubs for hearing
  impaired individuals

(... Figure 1, continued)

Development of Self
- Helping the student to understand him/herself, to share feelings, goals, etc.
- Encouraging and expecting the student to take responsibility for him/herself ... permitting failure as well as success
- Providing opportunities to learn about deaf culture and heritage
- Providing specific instruction in social skills

Note. From *Guidelines for Designing and Implementing Services* (pp. 14–15), by C. Amon, J. Sutera, C. Johnson, and C. Yoshinaga-Itano, 1988, Denver, Colorado Department of Education. Reprinted by permssion.

When designing an effective educational program for the child who is deaf or HOH, two additional points should be kept in mind. First, information about the deaf or HOH child's world and its impact on all facets of his or her life needs to be integrated with educational and social goals. Second, this child, like hearing peers, learns most effectively in naturally occurring conversations and social interactions and through modeling and context. From this information, the basic considerations for developing an effective program flow:

1. Select a program content that includes skills that a hearing child acquires indirectly through exposure to sounds coupled with experience.

2. Create experiential contexts for a deaf or HOH child isolated from regular interaction with deaf persons or fluent signers.

3. Evaluate how the child's development compares to that of a hearing child of the same developmental age.

4. Incorporate the observations, input, and preferences of the child and his or her parents.

Because eligibility for services for a child who is deaf or severely HOH rests primarily on acuity and other information provided by doctors, audiologists, and other professionals, school psychologists usually play a minimal role in its determination. However, they can be able advocates for the child and his or her family and knowledgeable participants in planning, evaluating, and modifying programs into which this child is placed. A willingness to incorporate the perspectives of parents, the child, and teachers into the educational plan is fundamental to the school psychologist's roles as child advocate, program planner, and evaluator.

BEST PRACTICES

Implementation of a program that allows each child who is deaf or HOH to participate in as many and varied environments as experienced by hearing peers constitutes the most fundamental recommendation (Colorado Department of Education, 1988).

Because sheltering a child who is deaf or HOH does not promote acquisition of the skills, attitudes, and behaviors she or he will need as an adult, full participation in multiple environments must include the opportunity to learn from both success and failure.

Partnerships between Parents and Professionals

Historically, many parents of a deaf or severely HOH child felt that they were forced to grant parent surrogate status to schools for the deaf and that residential counselors and teachers played a large role in raising their child. Some parents believed that professionals usurped parental prerogatives and focused more on the child's test scores and audiograms than on the actual child (Morgan-Redshaw, Wilgosh, & Bibby, 1989). Others were frustrated by the limited number and types of programs available in the public schools because inadequate local resources prevented them from taking a more active role in raising their deaf or HOH child. Finally, many parents encountered deaf educators who argued that a particular teaching or speech/language strategy was the only method that guaranteed the parents' goal of enabling their child to speak and participate in the hearing community but found that their hopes were seldom realized. Thomas (1989) illustrated this point in her description of oralism: "Oralism is the philosophy and method dedicated to making deaf people as undeaf as possible. Parents rush to it because they are provided no alternatives to believing that being 'like hearing' is the only way of being" (p. 8).

Parents' competency and preferences were increasingly recognized by deaf educators as children who are deaf or HOH remained at home to be educated in day classes within the public schools. As the experts on their child who is deaf or HOH, and the primary agents in that child's socialization, parents were now expected to speak with decisive voices as the educational programs for their child were planned and implemented. However, the pressure for parents of a child who is deaf or HOH to assume advocacy and teaching roles often required them to put aside their own reactions and inclinations as they advocated for their child in the educational system and larger community. Additionally, Schlesinger (cited in

Lederberg, 1993) identified three contributors to parents' sense of powerlessness and frustration in raising a child who is deaf or HOH: (a) their inability to cure their child's deafness, (b) the deaf or HOH child's lack of responsiveness to the parents' normal communication in English, and (c) the intrusion of professionals into the expression of parental rights.

Research has clarified parents' feelings and perspectives about raising a child who is deaf or HOH. Parenting this child produces all the normal stresses associated with child rearing and then adds stressors such as learning about deafness, making choices about the child's education, and serving as intermediaries between the child and the hearing world. Parents gladly adopt greater decision-making power in the education of their child who is deaf or HOH but also describe the enormous fatigue and frustration associated with parenting, teaching, advocating, and interpreting for that child. Some also expressed fear of alienating professionals essential to the child's education if they demand additional or different programming.

In addition to their emotional responses, parents are confronted by the task of raising a child who is deaf or severely HOH in the absence of useful information about deafness. Yet, if they are to become effective advocates for their child and informed decision-makers in the child's educational program, they needed to understand the impact of deafness on family interactions and on the child's education and cognitive, social, and linguistic development. Parents were best informed about these issues by other parents of deaf or HOH children.

In fact, research indicated that parents need regular contact with other parents of deaf or HOH children who can lend emotional and social support and may have faced similar decision points in the lives of their child who is deaf or HOH. These support systems allow parents to express their feelings about their child's deafness, alert them to choices on their child's academic horizon, and provide the opportunity to discuss and evaluate information about deafness and the plethora of programs, assistive devices, and "cures" for deafness. Additionally, parent groups acknowledge the legitimacy of parents' emotions and affirm parental perogatives in making decisions for their deaf or severely HOH child.

Calderon and Greenberg (1993) suggest the following strategies for helping hearing parents successfully parent their deaf or HOH child: (a) assess family dynamics and coping styles including the marital relationship as well as parents' adjustment and roles within the family; (b) expand parents' personal mastery and control and strengthen their roles as models for their child by increasing their problem-solving skills; (c) develop strong support networks for parents to meet their social, emotional, and informational needs; (d) encourage home-school collaboration throughout the child's school career; and (e) provide a developmentally appropriate continuum of services. Additionally, regular interaction and conversation with adult deaf persons are critical for helping hearing parents of a young child who is deaf or severely HOH understand the visual world within which that child lives.

Learning

Although there is little empirical information about deaf children as thinkers and learners, hearing loss apparently alters their learning styles so that they often depend on experiential/visual learning modalities. Further, because these children have no undistorted access to the flow of language and information in the environment, they quite reasonably can demonstrate gaps in vocabulary, language, and conceptual knowledge, especially understanding and using abstract concepts. These recurring differences in the learning of a child who is deaf or HOH highlight the necessity of specifically teaching concept generalization and transfer through direct instruction, repetition, review, simplification, and clarification.

In her observations of the interactions between children and their mothers, Lederberg (1993) found that children who are deaf constantly shifted their attention between the task and their mothers. In contrast, hearing children remained visually focused on the task while listening to their mothers' oral input. She observed that mothers of children who are deaf intruded on learning by forcing them to pay attention even when they could more appropriately focus on the task. Three suggestions arise from Lederberg's research:

1. Encourage parents and teachers of a deaf or HOH child to assist him to divide his attention between the task and the adult without impeding learning.

2. Follow the child's lead in learning, attracting attention to oneself at appropriate points during an activity and waiting for the child's attention before communicating.

3. Recognize when the deaf child is communicating and help her capture the parent's and others' attention.

When parents and the school communicate routinely, a deaf or HOH child's learning is enhanced because regular home–school interactions help ensure consistency in signs, behavioral expectations, and academic goals. Parents are encouraged to observe their child's classroom to see other children who are deaf or HOH and ways their child fits within the group. The school also bridges the gap between parents and community resources by assisting parents in obtaining adaptive equipment and contacting service organizations such as the Lions Club.

Finally, it is important that the individual child who is deaf or HOH have access to the educational services that match his cognitive abilities and communication capabilities. Evaluating the appropriateness of a deaf or HOH child's program includes using CBA and other tools to identify precisely her skill levels. Then, interpreters, notetakers, and adaptive equipment such as captioners and TDDs allow the child to participate fully in the instructional environment. School buildings must also be conducive to learning through attention to lighting, acoustics, and space needs and provision of a safe environment with equipment such as lighted fire alarms.

Emotional and Social Development

The child who is deaf or severely HOH often exhibits significant emotional and social needs at school and home. This leads parents and teachers to express concern about teaching him to conform to social expectations in the absence of a reliable means of communication and to sometimes even question the child's competency (Lederberg, 1993). Teachers in an integrated setting often describe a child who is deaf or HOH as immature, lazy, stubborn, aggressive, inattentive, physical, a loner, inappropriate, unable to complete assignments, unable to keep up with the class, and unable to understand directions and directives. Parents report the following behaviors in their young child who is deaf or HOH: hitting, pinching, biting, temper tantrums, screaming, wanting it now, lack of awareness of danger, short fuses, problems with social group interactions, difficulty generalizing behavior from one situation to another, exaggerating, and depending on mother. Therefore, it is vital to include a deaf or HOH child's emotional needs and the appropriate expression of those needs on her IEP.

The behavior of a child who is deaf or HOH, rather than suggesting pathology, more often indicates that he does not immediately understand the behavioral expectations of hearing adults. When verbal skills are limited, her behavior may serve as a physical expression of emotion. Additionally, a child who is deaf or HOH may experience risk factors such as lack of a common language with parents and others in the hearing community; lack of a nonhearing peer group at home, school, and in the neighborhood; and lack of opportunity to interact regularly with members of the deaf community. Of particular relevance to the development of social skills and self-esteem of a child who is deaf or HOH is his limited opportunity to control the environment or to observe deaf adults functioning successfully in both the hearing and deaf communities. Finally, a deaf or HOH child who is not proficient in either sign or speech is at risk of social and academic failure. Any of these factors alone or in combination may compromise the deaf or HOH child's optimal social development.

Leigh and Stinson (1991) identified interactions with others as the primary means through which a deaf or HOH child's social skills and language develop and the source of personal understanding, self-efficacy, and self-esteem. They concluded that social development proceeds along two tracks: (a) a vertical track where the child is mentored by experienced members of the culture, such as parents, teachers, neighbors, and older children who model and teach cultural expectations for behavior, and (b) a horizontal track in which the child learns to negotiate interpersonal relationships and communicate with children her own age, including siblings and peers.

Social Skills

Deaf and hearing children differ in typical peer interactive patterns. Compared to a hearing peer, a child who is deaf or HOH uses less communication when playing, engages in less imaginative and cooperative play, and prefers to play with one or two children (Lederberg, 1993). A child who is deaf or severely HOH is different, not deficient, in social interactions. He derives similar benefits from social interactions that a hearing child enjoys, including immediate satisfaction of social needs and acquisition of social skills which will be important to him as an adult.

A child who is deaf or HOH needs peers of comparable age and language with whom to interact and communicate and the opportunity to find models through whom to learn appropriate social behaviors and develop self-identity (CED, 1988). This child rarely interacts with both hearing and deaf peers, choosing instead peers and models selectively on the basis of language usage. The deaf or HOH child competent in oral skills often interacts with hearing peers, while the child who is competent in sign usually interacts with deaf peers. Further, because a mainstreamed child who is deaf or severely HOH interacts primarily with other deaf or HOH children or teachers, the goal of socially integrating this child with hearing peers is rarely accomplished unless she receives supportive services (Leigh & Stinson, 1991; Mertens, 1989). Whether the child who is deaf or HOH interacts with hearing or with deaf peers, language and social development are enhanced. Thus, the goal of learning to interact with both deaf and hearing peers is not realized for most children who are deaf or severely HOH.

A child who is deaf or severely HOH needs to be comfortable not only with the persons with whom to interact, but also with the content of those interactions. This child often feels left out of social interactions because he doesn't understand jokes, the connotations of words or the idioms, cliches, colloquialisms, and other symbolic and shorthand ways that hearing individuals communicate. Moreover, the child who is deaf or HOH does not follow or participate in formal group discussions and informal kidding around. Much of what hearing children talk about in groups such as the lyrics to popular songs, the story line and vocabulary of television and movies, and slang expressions is outside the experience of the child who is deaf or HOH. She must be directly taught the latest age-appropriate jokes and the "cool" language used by hearing peers as well as strategies for following and understanding the gist of conversations.

For a child who is deaf or severely HOH to express emotions appropriately, it is important to teach him behaviors and emotional expressions that are not only socially appropriate in the hearing world but also effectively assert the child's rights without offending others. This is best accomplished when parents and teachers model positive expression of feelings and also teach the child who is deaf or HOH the appropriate sign and/or word with which to communicate an emotion. Moreover, the child needs experience in identifying options for behavior and the consequences of those various options and then permission to choose a behavior on the basis of that information.

The child who is deaf or HOH often lacks the social amenities of the hearing world and may alienate hearing persons by repeatedly touching them or speaking bluntly. She is often awkward in social aspects of communication including initiating and exiting conversations, giving compliments, saying no, making friends, and tailoring conversations for social circumstances or the needs of participants. This child needs to learn the social conventions of conversation through programs such as Skillstreaming and guided practice in the art of casual and formal communication.

Teaching social expectations to a child who is deaf or HOH includes clarifying rules and the circumstances in which they apply. Behavioral contracts for appropriate social behavior are negotiated with the child and the rewards and consequences of the behavior applied in a timely and equitable manner. Additionally, as a means of relieving the tension and frustration that arise from communicating and interacting socially with the hearing world, a child who is deaf or HOH needs to learn relaxation and stress reduction techniques such as deep breathing, counting to ten, and sequentially relaxing muscles.

As the adolescent child who is deaf or HOH experiences the teenager's typical need to belong, he may want to dress like his hearing peers and sometimes even grow his hair somewhat longer to cover the hearing aids. Further, he needs to acquire the visually oriented leisure and recreational skills such as card, board, computer, and arcade games which are the vehicles of social interaction among hearing adolescents. The child should also learn sports such as swimming, skiing, and biking that provide exercise, recreation, and opportunities for social interaction.

Finally, the successful acquisition of social skills by persons who are deaf or HOH who attended schools for the deaf sheds light on how to enhance the social skill acquisition of the child who is deaf or HOH in public education. The experience of these individuals indicates that exposure to multiple persons who are deaf or severely HOH can provide open access to communication with peers through the use of signs. Further, the observations by deaf adults and adolescents provide the basis of suggestions for eliminating feelings of isolation, loneliness, and lack of connection with hearing students (Mertens, 1989). According to adults who are deaf, the benefits of attending a school for the deaf that later translate into successful experience in the deaf community included the signing skills of teachers, convenient socialization with peers, and the opportunity to participate in extracurricular activities (Mertens, 1989). Thus, the experience of socially competent persons who are deaf underscores the necessity of providing each child who is deaf or severely HOH with access to formal and social opportunities to communicate with others and model interpersonal interactions.

Self-Awareness

Deafness has a serious impact on a deaf or HOH child's development of a positive self-esteem (Kessler-Grimes & Prichett, 1988). Moreover, it is through their reflection in the eyes of mothers and other significant others that both hearing and deaf or HOH children develop self-concepts. If the child senses that others perceive her as valuable, capable, and lovable, then she is more likely to develop a positive self-concept. However, despite the positive regard of their mothers, a child who is deaf or severely HOH may equate her differences from siblings and peers with inferiority (Kessler-Grimes & Prichett, 1988). In effect, the experiences of a child who is deaf or HOH may override a parent's expressions of love and support.

It is not uncommon for a child who is deaf or severely HOH to describe himself as unimportant and dumb and express self-consciousness about hearing aids and other visible signs of difference from hearing siblings and peers. To counteract feelings of worthlessness and isolation, a child who is deaf or HOH often prizes physical attractiveness, sports prowess, or other external attributes as indicators of personal value. To develop positive self-esteem, this child must learn about his worth and competence through positive experiences rather than relying on superficial indicators of value.

Self-understanding is the key to the deaf or HOH child's distinction of difference from deficiency. A child who is deaf or severely HOH often feels "stupid" because she sees hearing peers respond quickly to teacher directions. She does not understand that her slower processing time is related to the inability to hear oral instructions. The child who is deaf or HOH must be directly told about the implications of the hearing loss and that deafness comes from the ears not from limitations in the brain.

Strategies for teaching a child who is deaf or HOH about himself include telling him about personal strengths and needs and explaining which areas such as vocabulary, speech, reading comprehension, and math applications are especially affected by the deafness. It is necessary to go beyond simply providing the child with this information and ensure that he understands and owns this information. Finally, a child who is deaf or HOH needs to identify his own personal characteristics, especially strengths, and then call upon those strengths by engaging in recreational, social, and educational activities.

Additional strategies that enable a child who is deaf or severely HOH to perceive self-worth and develop positive self-esteem include assigning her real responsibilities that can be carried out successfully and then providing frequent and legitimate feedback about her efforts. For example, the child should be encouraged to act independently by engaging in such activities as making a purchase at a convenience store, finding an item in the grocery store, or ordering from the menu at a fast food restaurant. Feedback includes information about the child's success in completing the task as well as evaluation of the effort and attention the child applied to the accomplishment. Further, a child who is deaf or HOH should be asked for her opinions, preferences, feelings, and ideas and included regularly in conversations at home and school. These opportunities must also include visually adapting the situation to maximize the child's understanding. Finally, it is important for parents and teachers to remember that several people talking at once will quickly discourage a child who is deaf or HOH from participating in group interactions.

Communication

Communication is not language, although language is among the most important means used to communicate (Garretson, 1990; iii). Communication is the interaction between two or more persons and includes encoding and decoding thoughts and feelings through any medium that conveys a message. Speech is the mechanical act of producing oral language. There may be considerable discrepancy among the communication, language, and speech skills of the child who is deaf or severely HOH. For example, he may have clear and intelligible speech, but language, the content of the message, may be significantly below the child's chronological age. Whether at home or at school, focusing on the deaf or HOH child's speech and language production to the exclusion of social, academic, or interactive needs emphasizes an area of special difficulty for the child and communicates to him that his value is intimately

tied to speech and language proficiency (Kessler-Grimes & Prichett, 1988).

Although signing is the natural language of persons who are deaf or severely HOH, this visual spatial language is not the natural language of most of their parents. Typically, a child who is deaf or HOH does not learn either signs or her parents' spoken language through natural exposure and imitation. Because she and her parents do not share a common language or communication system, she may not find the support and input which the family could provide (Rittenhouse, Jordan, Overton, Freeman, & Jaussi, 1991).

Parents of a child who is deaf or HOH expressed less concern about the mode of communication than the need to communicate with their child (Morgan-Redshaw, Wilgosh, & Bibby, 1989). Most found that their child adopted a means of communicating when parents resisted speaking for the child and allowed him to communicate on his own. Nevertheless, mothers and older siblings often act as interpreters for the child who is deaf or HOH, especially when listeners were unwilling to communicate directly with the child. Siblings expressed anger at the expectation that they not only must interpret for a deaf or HOH sibling, but also must account for and explain the behavior and needs of the child to others in the community.

American Sign Language

According to Newell (1990), American Sign Language (ASL) is a complete language system, including a variety of dialects that reflect regional, situational, personal, and interactive needs and styles. ASL is the fourth most commonly used language in the U.S. (Christensen, 1990). However, not all deaf individuals use ASL or one of its variants. Further, because few deaf children are born to deaf parents, ASL is rarely transmitted from parent to child but is often learned from interacting with peers at schools or other centrally based programs where there is a critical mass of students who are deaf or severely HOH.

Bragg (1990) cited several reasons why parents and teachers find learning, and by extension teaching, ASL difficult: (a) a defeatist attitude toward deafness, (b) fear of learning a new and different language, and (c) the awesome challenge of developing sufficient proficiency in ASL to communicate with and teach the child. Most parents and hearing teachers use a pidgin form of signed English that includes ASL vocabulary. Many lack proficiency in ASL, including dialectical variations, which restricts the deaf or HOH child's opportunity to learn this visual/spatial language system. Additionally, the attempts of these parent and teacher models to teach ASL in the artificial environment of the classroom and in the context of lessons further complicates its acquisition by the child who is deaf or severely HOH.

Proficiency in signing includes transmitting and receiving signs and fingerspelling proper words. However, Anderssen (1990) differentiated proficiency in signing from proficiency in communicating by stating that proficiency in communication meant that the person who is deaf or HOH understood what another said and also conveyed her emotions and ideas. In contrast, proficiency in signing is a technical skill that does not communicate if the signer is unwilling to convey a message because of a negative attitude. There are three basic requirements for a child who is deaf or severely HOH to develop communicative proficiency in ASL: (a) exposure to fluent users of ASL who sign regularly, (b) natural acquisition through communication rather than lessons in ASL, and (c) beginning learning of ASL during the preschool years (Cornett, 1990). Similar characteristics are relevant to the child who is deaf or HOH learning spoken English.

A child learns whatever language is modeled by significant others in his life. The deaf or HOH child who has limited exposure to adults proficient in ASL must rely on his hearing parents and teachers to model both sign language and spoken English. The success of this child's learning of either language depends, at least in part, on the language proficiency of the model.

Typically, the child who is deaf or HOH communicates during her formative years of language development with parents and teachers who are themselves just learning to sign. Parents who are beginning signers are awkward with signing and experience tremendous fatigue when communicating through this second language for them. Many are reasonably concerned that the signing skills of their deaf or HOH child will surpass their own. Parents' effort and commitment to signing to their child who is deaf or HOH need to be acknowledged and supported. Additionally, professionals who are competent signers should model signing for parents. Finally, parents should be taught stress management/relaxation techniques to relieve tension from trying to communicate with their child in an unfamiliar language.

For the child who is deaf or severely HOH to become fluent in sign as a means of communication and as an avenue to cognitive, social, and academic growth, he needs frequent opportunities to interact with fluent users of ASL. Regular interaction by the child and his parents with the deaf community helps shift part of the burden of the child's learning ASL to natural models of this language. Furthermore, contact with fluent users of ASL allows the child who is deaf or HOH to develop higher order thinking skills through modeling and participation in conversations (Nelson, Loncke, & Camarata, 1993).

Deaf Community

The deaf community is primarily an adult culture with identified members in schools or social organizations for the deaf. Like any culture, this community is not a monolith in which all members are the same; however, most members are proficient in ASL, abide by its rules and expectations for behavior and interactions, and share a common history and traditions. Facility in ASL is the cornerstone for acceptance and success in the deaf community and facility with ASL, as with any language, is the marker of social and cognitive competence.

Because of their difficulty communicating in spoken language, many persons who are deaf use spoken English as a vehicle for interacting with the hearing world. However, deaf educators and parents often emphasize the deaf or HOH child's reliance on residual hearing and communication skills, including listening and spoken language. The use of residual hearing and oral communication to the exclusion of ASL separates many persons who have a hearing loss from the deaf community, especially if the individual is thought to be trying to "pass" as hearing. A critical point to remember is that members of the deaf community frequently differ from parents and educators in judging who is socially and cognitively competent.

Recently, the deaf community affirmed its existence as a minority group. Like many minority groups, members of the deaf community rejected pressure to place themselves in the proverbial melting pot and merge with the dominant hearing society. Further, many in this group equate deaf education in the public schools with bilingual education and support the goal of teaching the child who is deaf or HOH to communicate in sign and spoken English. Therefore, although there is a preference for interaction with other members of the deaf community, most persons who are deaf recognize that bilingual education potentially expands their opportunities to interact with the hearing world.

The National Association of the Deaf's position statement on communication and language expresses the deaf community's goals for bilingual education for deaf children.

> Inherent in our Communication Position is our recognition of American Sign Language (ASL) as a language in its own right, fully deserving of respect because of its importance to deaf people for its communication, educational and cultural values. The NAD recognizes that two languages in the deaf community are ASL and English and that deaf individuals have the right to become fluent in both languages and the right to choose and utilize whichever language, communication approach, or combination of approaches that best meets their personal needs in varying situations.

Although most adolescents who are deaf or HOH explore the deaf community in their search for personal identity, this does not constitute rejection of the values of hearing parents. Parents' fears of losing their deaf or HOH child to the deaf community is minimized by routinely providing opportunities to interact with adolescents and adults in that community. Moreover, expecting the child who is deaf or HOH to choose between the hearing and deaf communities is an artificial choice in that optimally she is provided with the communication skills to flow back and forth between both groups.

In addition to having a language model, the child who is deaf or HOH needs consistent and regular exposure to deaf peers and adults because, without this contact, he shows limited social development (CED, 1988). This exposure is central to improving the emotional health and maturity of the deaf or HOH child who exhibits low self-esteem, withdrawal, or inappropriate behavior (CED, 1988). Lack of adult deaf role models results in the child drawing erroneous conclusions about the future such as believing that he will become hearing someday or will not survive into adulthood. In addition, he and his family need information about the deaf culture and deaf heritage, including access to deaf-focused magazines such as the *World Around You, Deaf America, and Deaf Life*. Further, the child who is deaf or HOH and her family should avail themselves of the opportunity of participating in activities and organizations for the deaf such as deaf olympics, the National Association of the Deaf (NAD), and junior NAD.

SUMMARY

This chapter is best summarized by a quote from Thomas (1989):

> There is another approach to deafness, which is a cultural, social definition. Instead of trying to cure it, and make people as hearing as possible, you accommodate it. This means that physiologically, psychologically, you start with the premise that a child is deaf and is going to stay deaf, and you embrace that premise. In other words, you allow the child to be who he or she is. (p. 25)

REFERENCES

Andersson, Y. (1990). Who should make decisions on communication among deaf people? In M. D. Garretson (Ed.), *Eyes, hands, voices: Communication issues among deaf people* (pp. 1–4). Deaf American Monograph, 40(1, 2, 3, 4).

Bragg, B. (1990). Communication and the deaf community: Where do we go from here? In M. D. Garretson (Ed.), *Eyes, hands, voices: Communication issues among deaf people* (pp. 9–14). Deaf American Monograph, 40(1, 2, 3, 4).

Calderon, R., & Greenberg, M. (1993). Considerations in the adaptation of families with school-aged deaf. In M. Marschark & M. D. Clark (Eds.), *Psychological perspectives on deafness* (pp. 27–48). Hillsdale, NJ: Erlbaum.

Christiansen, K. (1990). American sign language and English: Parallel bilingualism. In M. D. Garretson (Ed.), *Eyes, hands, voices: Communication issues among deaf people* (pp. 27–30). *Deaf American Monograph 40*(1, 2, 3, 4).

Colorado Department of Education. (1988). *Quality indicators for educating students with hearing impairment: Guidelines for designing and implementing services for students with hearing impairments.* Colorado Department of Education, Special Services Unit: Denver.

Cornett, R. O. (1990). The complete deaf person. In M. D. Garretson (Ed.), *Eyes, hands, voices: Communication issues among deaf people* (pp. 35–38). *Deaf American Monograph, 40*(1, 2, 3, 4).

Garretson, M. D. (1990). Introduction. In M. D. Garretson (Ed.), *Eyes, hands, voices: Communication issues among deaf people* (pp. iii–iv). *Deaf American Monograph, 40*(1, 2, 3, 4).

Kessler-Grimes, V., & Prichett, H. (1988). Developing and enhancing positive self concept in deaf children. *American Annals of the Deaf, 133*(4), 255–257.

Lederberg, A. (1993). The impact of deafness on mother-child and peer relations. In M. Marschark & M. D. Clark (Eds.), *Psychological perspectives on deafness* (pp. 93–119). Hillsdale, NJ: Erlbaum.

Leigh, I. W., & Stinson, M. S. (1991). Social environments, self perceptions, and identity of hearing impaired adolescents. *Volta Review, 93*(5), 7–22.

Marschark, M. (1993). Origins and interactions in the social, cognitive, and language development of deaf children. In M. Marschark & M. D. Clark (Eds.), *Psychological perspectives and deafness* (pp. 7–26). Hillsdale, NJ: Erlbaum.

Mertens, D. M. (1989). Social experiences of hearing-impaired high school youth. *American Annals of the Deaf, 134*(1), 15–19.

Morgan-Redshaw, M., Wilgosh, L., & Bibby, M. A. (1989). Hearing families with deaf children: Living with deafness. *ACEH/ACEDA, 15*(3), 105–113.

Nelson, K., Loncke, F., & Camarata, S. (1993). Implications of research on deaf and hearing children's language learning. In M. Marschark & M. D. Clark (Eds.), *Psychological perspectives on deafness* (pp. 123–152). Hillsdale, NJ: Erlbaum.

Newell, W. (1990). ASL is not a four-letter word: Deaf education can dance with the bogeyman. In M. D. Garretson (Ed.), *Eyes, hands, voices: Communication issues among deaf people* (pp. 97–102). *Deaf American Monograph, 40*(1, 2, 3, 4).

Rittenhouse, R. K., Johnson, C., Overton, B., Freeman, S., & Jaussi, K. (1991). The black and deaf movements in America since 1960: Parallelism and an agenda for the future. *American Annals of the Deaf, 136*(5), 392–400.

Thomas, R. (1989). A parent/professional speaks out. *Perspectives for teachers of the hearing impaired, 7*(4), 6–9.

U.S. Presidential Commission on Education of the Deaf. (1988). *Toward equality education of the deaf: A report to the President and Congress of the United States.* Washington, DC: Government Printing Office.

96

Best Practices in Planning Effective Instruction for Students Who Are Visually Impaired or Blind

Sharon Bradley-Johnson
Central Michigan University

OVERVIEW

Definitions

Few students classified as visually impaired are totally blind. Most are able to perceive light and see details to some extent. In the United States, more than 75% of persons who are blind have some usable vision (American Foundation for the Blind, undated).

The classification "legally blind" makes one eligible for government benefits. This classification applies when visual acuity is 20/200 or less in the better eye with correction or when there is restricted visual field with a diameter of no more than 20 degrees. The definition of legally blind is not helpful in educational planning because those students whose vision is 20/200 in the better eye often can use visual material in the classroom setting (Scholl, 1985). Hence, for clarity in this chapter, the term "blind" will be used to describe students who have to use senses other than vision for learning in the classroom setting.

Students who are blind will need tactile and auditory input for instruction. They will require specialized equipment and materials such as voice or Braille output computers, talking calculators, Braille material, recorded material, or raised line paper. For the purpose of determining eligibility for special education services, these students would be classified as visually impaired.

Other students classified as visually impaired who are not blind are those who need more than glasses in order to function well in the classroom. This group of students includes those described as having "low vision," who are able to see material that is held close to their eyes. Students classified as visually impaired may be able to read regular type or may require large-type materials. A number of these students use low vision equipment including magnifiers or closed circuit television (CCTV) where text is magnified electronically and shown on a television monitor. Even though these students have some vision that can be used for reading, some may require the use of tactile and auditory material for instruction.

Incidence

According to the U.S. Department of Education (1992), 17,783 students classified as visually impaired were served under the Individuals with Disabilities Education Act of 1990 (IDEA), Part B. These students comprised 0.4% of special education students between the ages of 6 and 21. During the 1989–90 school year, 84.1% of students classified as visually impaired attended regular schools, 4.5% attended a separate school, and 10.9% attended residential facilities. Students with multiple impairments were not included in these percentages.

Etiology

The group of students classified as visually impaired is very heterogeneous. There are many types and degrees of visual loss. Thus, there are numerous etiologies. Congenital losses can have genetic etiologies or result from prenatal damage. For school-age students, most visual losses are congenital (Scholl, 1985). The specific cause of a congenital loss, however, is frequently unknown (Finkelstein, 1989). Acquired visual losses can occur because of diseases or accidents.

The most frequent types of visual loss for school-age students are retrolental fibroplasia, congenital cataracts, optic nerve atrophy, and albinism (Hatfield, 1975).

Consultation with a student's medical specialist, teacher, and the consultant certified for working with students who have a visual loss should be helpful in understanding a particular student's condition. A multidisciplinary approach is essential in order to work effectively with these students.

Onset and Progression

Age at onset of the visual loss has implications for instruction. Children for whom the onset is after five years of age typically retain visual memories, such as memories for color and visual images. These memories can be used to facilitate acquisition of language concepts as well as other skills. For example, it is easier to instruct a child who remembers what a castle looks like than it is to have to teach such a concept to a child with little usable vision. Students unlikely to have visual memories may not have a satisfactory understanding of some concepts. Furthermore, some students who are visually impaired or blind may use concepts correctly but have learned the concepts only by rote. Hence, it is wise to probe questionable responses to ensure adequate understanding.

Whether the onset is gradual or sudden also has implications for instruction. When the loss is gradual, it is important to teach as much information as possible that requires vision while a student is still able to use visual input. Students who are experiencing a progressive loss may need support and counseling to help them adjust to their changing condition. Those students who experience a sudden loss of vision also are likely to require support and counseling, but this assistance would be to help them cope with this dramatic change in their lives. Those who experience a sudden loss of vision, leaving them with little usable vision, will need to adapt to the use of tactile and auditory input for instruction and, in many cases, to a new mode for written expression.

BASIC CONSIDERATIONS

Multidisciplinary by Necessity

In the large majority of cases, it is not possible to plan a comprehensive, effective instructional program for a student who is visually impaired or blind without using a multidisciplinary approach. When planning programs for these students, the three key disciplines with which a school psychologist must work are teachers certified in working with students who are visually impaired or blind, medical specialists, and orientation and mobility instructors.

A recent development in the education of students who are visually impaired or blind is the use of functional vision assessments. Such assessments are carried out by a teacher certified in working with these students, and the results have important implications for classroom instruction. Because such assessments are relatively new, they are not currently required in all states. Results from functional vision assessments describe how a particular student uses his or her vision when performing various academic and daily living tasks. In the school setting, these assessments are carried out with children from infancy through adolescence. The reports based on functional vision assessments contain recommendations regarding conditions, materials, and equipment needed for instruction for a particular student. For example, a report might provide information about appropriate lighting, viewing distance for materials, appropriate media for a student for reading and writing, size of type required, and recommendations for low-vision equipment.

Reviewing medical reports is critical to understanding a student's loss of vision. Ophthalmologists' and optometrists' reports will include a description of medical interventions needed, prescriptions, and any required restrictions on eye use.

Reading a medical report can be frustrating because of the terminology and the abbreviations encountered. Following is a list of common abbreviations and their meaning that may be useful when reading these reports.

- O.D. — ocular dexter (right eye)
- O.S. — ocular sinister (left eye)
- O.U. — oculi unitas (both eyes)
- W.N.L. — within normal limits
- S., S.S., S.C. — without correction
- C., C.C. — with correction
- N.L.P. — no light perception (totally blind)
- P.P. — near point
- P.R. — far point
- V.A. — visual acuity
- V.F. — visual field
- N.V. — near vision
- L.P. — light perception

Information in the medical report will describe visual acuity measured separately for each eye. Furthermore, visual acuity will be measured with and without correction, that is, with and without glasses. Typically such information is given for both near-vision and distance viewing.

Recommendations from a medical report may not apply to the classroom environment. Anxiety and the unfamiliar environment of a medical office may affect a student's use of vision. Thus, information from a functional vision assessment also is needed because this assessment is conducted within the school environment.

It is important that vision assessments are current — having been done within about a year — because visual conditions change resulting in changing needs for the student. Not only should vision assessments be current, but hearing reports must be up to date as well. Students who are visually impaired or blind rely so heavily on what they hear that it is important to ensure that hearing ability is maximized.

An orientation and mobility instructor has specialized training for teaching students who are visually impaired or blind how to travel about effectively and safely. When someone untrained in orientation and mobility observes a student who is visually impaired or blind travel about, he or she may think that the student does quite well considering the visual loss. An orientation and mobility specialist when making the same observation, however, may be able to suggest several things that could considerably increase a student's level of independent functioning. Hence, assessment and intervention by a specialist in this area is an important component of an educational program for a student who is visually impaired or blind. Training in orientation and mobility skills should begin as early as preschool. Examples of skills taught include appropriate gait and stride when walking and ways to travel safely and independently within both school and home environments and to seek help when assistance with orientation and mobility is needed.

Thus, to develop comprehensive, well coordinated educational programs that meet the needs of students who are visually impaired or blind, school psychologists must collaborate with other professionals, especially teachers certified in working with these students, medical specialists, and orientation and mobility specialists.

Family and Home Environments

Adjustment to having a child with a serious visual loss can be difficult, especially when family members have had little or no contact with persons who are visually impaired or blind. Family members are likely to go through the various stages of grieving when first informed of the condition. Parents may be very concerned, even frightened, about the prospect of raising a child who is visually impaired or blind. There are several things a school psychologist can do to assist the family in making the adjustment.

Besides providing support and counseling, the school psychologist can arrange for the family to talk with adults who are visually impaired or blind. These adults can share their experiences and discuss concerns the parents may have. The fact that most children who are visually impaired or blind grow up to be happy, productive adults needs to be emphasized. Also, arranging for family members to talk with other families who have children with serious visual losses can be helpful.

For families of infants, a family assessment must be conducted to determine the family's needs and interests with regard to their child. Such an assessment may be needed for preschoolers as well and can be of assistance to some families of older children also. For a comprehensive discussion of family assessment, see *Family Assessment in Early Intervention* (Bailey & Simeonsson, 1988).

A number of skills tend to be delayed for young children who are visually impaired or blind, though many of these delays can be lessened or eliminated with appropriate instruction. See Bradley-Johnson (1994) for a discussion of these areas. It is important for parents to be aware of these potential delays in development. Having this knowledge in advance may help parents cope when developmental milestones are not attained at the time they would be for sighted children. The component of family assessment that addresses such events is particularly important for families with children who are visually impaired or blind. Bailey et al. (1986) have developed a Critical Events Checklist to address concerns for families of infants and young children with disabilities.

Clearly it is important that parents are closely involved in educational planning for their child and that their interests and concerns are solicited and utilized in planning. Communication with parents will be enhanced during this planning process if professionals avoid the use of jargon.

BEST PRACTICES

Infants, Toddlers, and Preschoolers

There are several unique issues involved in planning instructional programs for infants who are visually impaired or blind. Some parents, especially those with little or no experience with others with a significant visual loss, may benefit from information regarding how to interact appropriately with their infant. Modeling appropriate interaction with their infant can be helpful.

Because infants who have little or no useful vision do not make eye contact or direct their gaze toward someone speaking to them, this can interfere with interactions. Parents may feel disappointed or even rejected in their attempts to interact with their infant and the frequency of their interaction may decrease because the baby is unable to make eye contact. Hence, these parents will benefit from learning to look for other behaviors indicating that their infant is responding to their attention. These behaviors can include any fairly consistent change in behavior following initiation of interaction by the parent. Examples include quieting, squirming, changes in facial expression, change in breathing rate, and increase in activity. Helping parents recognize these responses from their infant is important to enhance their relationship with the baby.

Young children learn a great deal through physical contact. This is especially true for children with a serious visual loss. Physical contact plays an important part in the development of social skills, language, cognition, and motor skills. If these children learn to find physical contact pleasurable, it will help to prevent the passivity and isolation that frequently characterize children with visual impairments. Thus, encouraging physical contact between the parents and infant or young child can be very beneficial. The use of infant sling carriers makes it easier for some parents to provide frequent physical contact. Their use also places the infant in an upright position making him or her more alert and providing a situation where the baby can experience varied stimulation.

It is important that parents consider how to initiate contact with their infant without producing a startle response from the baby. Because some infants with a visual loss are unable to see someone approach, contact should be made gradually (rather than suddenly), and it is helpful if the parent talks as he or she approaches.

Because children who are visually impaired or blind do not receive the visual input of sighted children, language development is slower for young children with a significant visual loss. Parents can help in this area by developing the habit of naming objects and describing their actions often, even for infants. For infants and young children up to the age of five years, the program *On the Way to Literacy* (Stratton & Wright, 1993) can be beneficial in terms of language development, parent–child interaction, and early book-handling skills. This program consists of a print handbook for parents or teachers and 10 tactile/visual storybooks to be read to children. The books are in Braille and print and include tactile and visual illustrations. For parents unsure of how to interact in ways helpful to their child who is visually impaired or blind, this program can provide a framework for interaction, while at the same time helping the parent teach useful language concepts and finger and hand skills.

Encouraging parents to use their child's name before saying something to the child is helpful for two reasons. Often these children are delayed in learning to respond to their names. Frequent use of the child's name provides practice in name recognition. Also, it lets the child know that what is about to be said is directed to her or him. Developing the habit of using the child's name first when speaking to an infant or young child is beneficial.

Safety is a primary concern for infants and young children, especially when there is impairment of vision or blindness. Interacting with the environment, however, is critical for these children in order to reduce passivity and enhance their learning. Often, in order to learn, these infants and children need more opportunities to explore the environment than a sighted child. Hence, a balance needs to be found between encouraging these children to explore their surroundings and ensuring their safety. Parents with children who are disabled often tend to be overprotective and thereby inhibit learning. Learning to avoid hazards and to respond appropriately to "no," are particularly important skills to teach these children. Consistency by parents will facilitate the acquisition of these skills, whereas inconsistency in responding to their child will interfere.

Unfortunately, social skills are delayed for many children who are visually impaired or blind. Often these infants and young children miss nonverbal cues such as gestures, facial expressions, and eye contact. Compared with sighted peers, they interact less, initiate fewer interactions, are less responsive and less re-

inforcing to others, and may display more negative affect (Preisler, 1988; Rogers & Puchalski, 1984; Skellenger, Hill, & Hill, 1992).

Clearly, social interaction is likely to require intervention to prevent delays and increase positive contact. To aid in goal setting and evaluation of program effects, the following measures should be of assistance:

- Systematic direct observation (such as interval or frequency recording).

- The General Social and Emotional Development section of the *Revised Brigance Diagnostic Inventory of Early Development* (Brigance, 1991), a criterion-referenced measure.

- The Self-Direction and Social Skills sections of *The Carolina Curriculum for Infants and Toddlers with Special Needs* (Johnson-Martin, Jens, Attermeier, & Hacker, 1991), a curriculum-based measure.

- The Socialization Skills section of the *Oregon Project for Visually Impaired and Blind Preschool Children* (Anderson, Boigon, & Davis, 1986), a curriculum-based measure.

These measures have either been designed for infants and young children with a visual loss or do not require vision.

Play skills are likely to require instruction as well. Parents can assist development in this area by providing appropriate toys. Toys that are large and make noise are easier for these infants and children to locate. Toys that are response contingent aid a child in learning that he or she is able to affect the environment, an important skill for a child with a physical or mental disability.

Parents should encourage an infant or young child who is passive to move and to explore the environment. Infants and children with little or no useful vision are not enticed by visual stimulation to explore their environment. Furthermore, because of extended stays in the hospital where they may have been restrained for medical reasons, some of these infants may be quite passive. These children will benefit from physical guidance to encourage them to move. It will be important to teach them to use their hands to turn and explore objects and also to search for objects that fall out of reach.

Measures for goal setting and monitoring progress of play skills include many items from measures listed for social skills as well as the Schemes for Objects scale from the *Ordinal Scales of Psychological Development* (Uzgiris & Hunt, 1989). The *Ordinal Scales* are appropriate for infants from birth to two years of age.

School-Age Students

A number of behaviors relevant to classroom functioning are important to consider when planning instruction for students who are visually impaired or blind. Because most of these students are likely to require more assistance than their sighted peers, they need to be able to request help, accept help, and refuse help appropriately. Classroom observation should indicate whether any of these behaviors should be targeted for instruction.

For efficient functioning in the classroom, they need organizational skills: keeping their desk well-organized, and routinely putting things away where they belong. These skills aid in avoiding frustration and unnecessary searches for materials. Such skills enable a student to function more independently.

Because of their reliance on auditory input, these students must have good listening skills. If attention and listening are problematic, instruction will be necessary and well worth the time required to remediate deficiencies.

Reading Braille takes about 2 1/2 times longer than reading regular type (Duckworth & Caton, 1986). Reading large type takes longer than regular type also. Furthermore, the use of limited vision is very tiring. Hence, additional time will be necessary for completing assignments and taking tests. Classroom performance and progress should be evaluated considering that fatigue is more of a factor for these students than for their sighted peers.

Goal setting and progress monitoring of classroom behavior can be done through the use of systematic direct observation. Also, the *Behavioral Rating Scale* (Swallow, Mangold, & Mangold, 1978), an informal checklist completed by teachers and designed specifically for students who are visually impaired or blind, can provide useful information on classroom behavior.

Because of potential delays, consideration of a student's social skills is an important part of instructional planning. The frequency and quality of interaction with peers should be examined. Participation in clubs, sporting events, and other after-school activities should be encouraged. Response to teasing may need to be addressed as well.

As noted earlier, social skills tend to be delayed for students who are visually impaired or blind. Several factors unique to students with a serious loss of vision may contribute to this delay. One of these factors has to do with their use of gestures and facial expressions. This type of nonverbal communication typically is learned from observation of others. Some students with a visual impairment are unable to observe such nonverbal communication. Hence, other people may find it somewhat difficult to interpret the emotions of these students because of their lack of typical gestures and facial expressions.

When speaking with someone, a sighted person turns his or her face toward the other person. Turning to this en face position is something that often must be taught to students with little or no useful vision. Orienting to a speaker may be difficult, especially when several people are speaking simultaneously. If a student has not learned to orient to a speaker or to the person to whom he or she is speaking, this should be targeted for instruction. If this skill is not taught, interactions with others could be unnecessarily awkward.

Though everyone engages in self-stimulation to some extent, students who are visually impaired or blind may self-stimulate at a higher frequency or by displaying some behaviors that make them appear unusual. These behaviors are most likely to occur when a student is bored or stressed. One type of self-stimulation seen in many of these children is eye pressing or poking. This behavior can begin around 12 months of age with frequent rubbing of the eyes, and by about 18 months can progress to a well-established habit of pressing the thumbs against the eyes (Scott, Jan, & Freeman, 1985). If allowed to continue, this can cause deeply depressed eyes discolored with dark circles which make a child look strange to others. Yet it can be a difficult habit to eliminate. Eye poking and body rocking are the most frequent forms of self-stimulation in young blind children and they tend to be quite stable behaviors (Brambring & Troster, 1992).

Of eye poking or rocking are observed, these behaviors should be targeted for remediation. Situations in which self-stimulation is likely to occur will need to be identified and programs developed to eliminate these behaviors. Ross and Koenig (1991) decreased head rocking in a child who was blind by use of a physical prompt. Brambring and Troster (1992) indicated that when these behaviors occur in children over 4 1/2 years of age they are particularly stable even if they are low frequency behaviors. Thus, intervention should begin as early as possible.

In addition to systematic direct observation, information from the *Social Skills Rating System* (SSRS; Gresham & Elliott, 1990) can be helpful in planning instruction in this area. The SSRS is completed by a teacher and each item is rated both for frequency of occurrence and for importance. This comprehensive system can be used with students from preschool through high school. No adaptations are required for students with a visual loss.

Well-researched programs for teaching social skills to school-age students include the *Social Skills Intervention Guide* (Elliott & Gresham, 1991), *The ACCEPTS Program: A Curriculum for Children's Effective Peer and Teacher Skills* (Walker et al., 1983), and *The ACCESS Program: Adolescent Curriculum for Communication and Effective Social Skills* (Walker, Todis, Holmes, & Horton, 1988).

Students who must read large-type material can be taught with regular basal readers where either the print is enlarged or magnifiers are employed. *Patterns* (Caton, Pester, & Bradley, 1980) is a basal reading program for teaching Braille reading and goes through a third-level reader. A systematic approach should be employed to teach Braille reading.

For goal setting and monitoring progress in reading, several useful options have been published. The *Braille Unit Recognition Battery* (Caton, Duckworth, & Rankin, 1985) is a criterion-referenced test for units of grade 2 literary Braille for students in grades 3 through 12. Examiners must be able to read Braille to use this test. The *Diagnostic Reading Scales* (Spache, 1981), are available in a Braille edition (Duckworth, 1992) or a large-type edition. This test provides information on a student's oral and silent reading levels (considering both decoding and comprehension), errors made in oral reading, and behaviors used when reading. Levels for the tests are mid-first to mid-seventh grade. Examiners do not need to be able to read Braille to use this test. For the *Comprehensive Diagnostic Inventory of Basic Skills* (Brigance, 1983), the *APH Tactile Supplement* (Duckworth & Abbot, undated) to this test can be used with Braille readers to obtain criterion-referenced information on a student's knowledge of phonics, structural analysis, and functional words. Finally, for monitoring progress in Braille reading, curriculum-based measurement (CBM) procedures seem to work well. If examiners have a regular-type copy of the material to be read, they do not have to be able to read Braille to use CBM with Braille readers.

In a study with elementary-age Braille readers, Morgan and Bradley-Johnson (in press) found that using the mean of three 2-minute samples of reading correlated better with results from a Braille transcription of the *Diagnostic Reading Scales* (Spache, 1981; r = .70 for decoding and .88 for comprehension) than the three 1-minute samples typically used with sighted students. This is not surprising, given that Braille takes about 2 1/2 times as long to read as regular type (Duckworth & Caton, 1986). Use of a 3-minute sample did not enhance the correlation. Test-retest reliability for the mean of the three 2-minute reading samples over a 2-week interval was .98. Hence, this appears to be both a reliable and valid measure of Braille reading performance. For more information on curriculum-based measurement, see Shinn (1989).

When planning instruction in the area of mathematics for young children who are visually impaired or blind, educators will need to use real objects. Because language concepts tend to be delayed for these children and some concepts may be learned only by rote, it is important to ensure that an adequate understanding of math concepts is acquired. Use of the quantitative and shape concepts sections of the *Revised Diagnostic Inventory of Early Development* (Brigance, 1991) can help in goal setting and progress monitoring for children up to the age of about 7 years.

For children with little or no vision, the *APH Tactile Supplement* (Duckworth & Stratton, 1992) also will be needed. These two measures can provide criterion-referenced information on numeral comprehension, reading of Braille numbers, and understanding of ordinal position. For children having difficulty with addition, checking for understanding of the steps for meaningful counting (Englemann, 1969) using real objects is important because these skills form the basis for beginning addition. The four steps are:

a) count 10 objects that are placed in a row, starting at either end, and answer the question "How many are there";

b) count to a given number, and count out a specified number of objects from a group of ten objects;

c) indicate the number that comes after any number in the 1–10 series;

d) predict the number of objects what will be in a group if one is added. (Englemann, 1969, p. 253)

In order to demonstrate these skills, a child must be able to rote count and synchronize touch-and-count.

To determine skills learned and those to be taught next in arithmetic and mathematics for older students, the *Diagnostic Comprehensive Inventory of Basic Skills* (Brigance, 1983), in conjunction with the *APH Tactile Supplement* (Duckworth & Abbott, undated) for this scale, can be used with Braille readers. Skills measured include math facts, operations, fractions, decimals, time, measurement, mathematics vocabulary, and money.

For carrying out arithmetic operations, some students who are visually impaired or blind may use an abacus. Use of the abacus would be comparable to sighted students using scratch paper to work out their problems.

Unfortunately, no studies have been published on the use of curriculum-based measurement for mathematics for Braille or large-type readers.

With regard to written expression, students who have lost their vision after having learned to write may be able to use script writing on raised-line paper. This paper, available from the American Printing House for the Blind (see address in bibliography), may be helpful to other students who are visually impaired as well. For students who cannot use script writing, however, another method will be needed. Some students may use a brailler (similar to a typewriter, but for Braille) or the more portable slate and stylus. Writing in Braille is very time consuming. Others may use a computer system with speech output, print, or Braille. The *Informal Assessment of Developmental Skills* (Swallow, Mangold, & Mangold, 1978) contains informal checklists developed by teachers of students who were visually impaired or blind to assess skills in Braille writing, script writing, and typing.

To set goals and monitor progress in other written language skills, the *Diagnostic Comprehensive Inventory of Basic Skills* (Brigance, 1983) along with the *APH Tactile Supplement* for Braille readers (Duckworth & Abbot, undated) can be given to obtain information on capitalization, punctuation, spelling, writing sentences, addressing envelopes, and writing letters.

If an assessment of cognitive development is required for eligibility purposes, *Psychoeducational Assessment of Students Who Are Visually Impaired or Blind: Infancy Through High School* (Bradley-Johnson, 1994) contains detailed information regarding special issues to consider, a description of appropriate procedures, and a review of relevant measures.

SUMMARY

Planning instruction for infants, children, and adolescents who are visually impaired or blind is a time-consuming process when done well. There are a number of unique issues that require consideration. Coordinated efforts by a multidisciplinary team, including parents of the child or adolescent, the teacher certified in working with these students, medical specialists, an orientation and mobility instructor, and the school psychologist can be helpful to students. Fortunately, there are a number of useful new materials for instruction as well as new measures and procedures to help in setting goals and monitoring progress. Further research on the use of curriculum-based measurement for Braille and large-type readers would be helpful in the areas of reading, mathematics, and written expression.

REFERENCES

American Foundation for the Blind. (Undated). *Facts about blindness.* New York: Author.

Anderson, S., Boigon, S., & Davis, K. (1986). *The Oregon Project for Visually Impaired and Blind Preschool Children* (5th ed.). Medford, OR: Jackson Education Service District.

Bailey, D. B., & Simeonsson, R. J. (1988). *Family assessment in early intervention.* Columbus, OH: Merrill.

Bailey, D. B., Simeonsson, R. J., Winton, P. J., Huntington, G., Comfort, M., Isbell, P., O'Donnell, K. J., & Helm, J. M. (1986). Family-focused intervention: A functional model for planning, implementing, and evaluating individualized family services in early intervention. *Journal of the Division for Early Childhood, 10,* 156–171.

Brambring, M., & Troster, H. (1992). On the stability of stereotyped behaviors in blind infants and preschoolers. *Journal of Visual Impairment and Blindness,* Feb., 105–110.

Bradley-Johnson, S. (1994). *Psychoeducational assessment of students who are visually impaired or blind: Infancy through high school* (2nd ed.). Austin, TX: PRO-ED.

Brigance, A. (1991). *Revised Diagnostic Inventory of Early Development.* North Billerica, MA: Curriculum Associates.

Brigance, A. (1983). *Diagnostic Comprehensive Inventory of Basic Skills.* North Billerica, MA: Curriculum Associates.

Caton, H., Duckworth, B., & Rankin, E. (1985). *Braille Unit Recognition Battery: Diagnostic Test of Grade 2 Literary Braille.* Louisville, KY: American Printing House for the Blind.

Caton, H., Pester, H., & Bradley, W. J. (1980). *Patterns: The primary Braille reading program.* Louisville, KY: American Printing House for the Blind.

Duckworth, B. (1992). Braille edition of the *Diagnostic Reading Scales.* Louisville, KY: American Printing House for the Blind.

Duckworth, B., & Abbot, D. (undated). *APH Tactile Supplement for the Diagnostic Comprehensive Inventory of Basic Skills.* Louisville, KY: American Printing House for the Blind.

Duckworth, B., & Caton, H. (1986). *Braille Reading Rate Scale.* Louisville, KY: American Printing House for the Blind.

Duckworth, B., & Stratton, J. M. (1992). *APH Tactile Supplement for the Brigance Diagnostic Inventory of Early Development.* Louisville, KY: American Printing House for the Blind.

Elliott, S. N., & Gresham, F. M. (1991). *Social skills intervention guide.* Circle Pines, MN: American Guidance.

Englemann, S. (1969). *Preventing failure in the primary grades.* Chicago, IL: Science Research Associates.

Finkelstein, S. (1989). *Blindness and disorders of the eye.* Baltimore: National Foundation of the Blind.

Gresham, F., & Elliott, S. (1990). *Social Skills Rating System.* Circle Pines, MN: American Guidance Service.

Hatfield, E. M. (1975). Why are they blind? *Sightsaving Review, 45,* 3–22.

Johnson-Martin, N. M., Jens, K. G., Attermeier, S. M., & Hacker, B. J. (1991). *The Carolina Curriculum for Infants and Toddlers with Special Needs* (2nd ed.). Baltimore, MD: Paul H. Brookes Publishing.

Morgan, S., & Bradley-Johnson, S. (in press). Technical adequacy of a curriculum-based measure for visually impaired Braille readers. *School Psychology Review.*

Preisler, G. G. (1988, August). *The development of communication in blind infants.* Paper presented at the International Symposium on Visually Impaired Infants and Young Children: Birth to Seven, Edinburgh, Scotland.

Rogers, S. J., & Puchalski, C. B. (1984). Social characteristics of visually impaired infants' play. *Topics in Early Childhood Special Education, 3,* 52–56.

Ross, D. B., & Koenig, A. J. (1991). A cognitive approach to reducing stereotypic head rocking. *Journal of Visual Impairment and Blindness, 85,* 17–19.

Scholl, G. T. (1985). Visual impairments. In G. T. Scholl (Ed.), *The school psychologist and the exceptional child* (pp. 203–218). Reston, VA: Council for Exceptional Children.

Scott, E. P., Jan, J. E., & Freeman, R. D. (1985). *Can't your child see?* Austin, TX: PRO-ED.

Shinn, M. (1989). *Curriculum based measurement: Assessing special children.* New York: Guilford Press.

Skellenger, A. C., Hill, M., & Hill, E. (1992). The social functioning of children with visual impairments. In S. L. Odom, S. R. McConnell, & M. A. McEvoy (Eds.), *Social competence of young children with disabilities* (pp. 165–188). Baltimore, MD: Paul H. Brookes Publishing.

Spache, G. (1981). *Diagnostic Reading Scales.* Monterey, CA: CTB/McGraw Hill.

Stratton, J. M., & Wright, S. (1993). *On the way to literacy: Early experiences for visually impaired children.* Louisville, KY: American Printing House for the Blind.

Swallow, R., Mangold, S., & Mangold, P. (1978). *Informal Assessment of Developmental Skills for Visually Handicapped Students.* New York: American Foundation for the Blind.

U.S. Department of Education. (1992). *Fourteenth Annual Report to Congress on the Implementation of the Individuals with Disabilities Education Act.* Washington, DC: Author.

Uzgiris, I., & Hunt, J. McVicor. (1989). *Ordinal Scales of Psychological Development.* Urbana, IL: University of Illinois Press.

Walker, H. M., McConnell, S., Holmes, D., Todis, B., Walker, J., & Golden, N. (1983). *The ACCEPTS program: A curriculum for children's effective peer and teacher skills.* Austin, TX: PRO-ED.

Walker, H. M., Todis, B., Holmes, D., & Horton, G. (1988). *The ACCESS program: Adolescent curriculum for communication and effective social skills.* Austin, TX: PRO-ED.

ANNOTATED BIBLIOGRAPHY

American Printing House for the Blind (APH). P.O. Box 6085, Louisville, KY 40206. (1-800-223-1839.)

APH has the latest in educational materials and assessment instruments. APH publishes adapted and transcribed materials in Braille or large type as well as recorded books and magazines. The Printing House is a national nonprofit organization that publishes materials solely for persons who are visually impaired or blind.

Blind Children's Center, 4120 Marathon Street, Los Angeles, CA 90029. (1-800-222-3566).

The Center publishes a number of helpful booklets for parents of infants and preschoolers who are visually impaired or blind. Some topics include play, language, and movement. Copies are free to parents and inexpensive for professionals. Most booklets are available in English or Spanish.

Bradley-Johnson, S. (1994). *Psychoeducational assessment of students who are visually impaired or blind: Infancy through high school* (2nd ed.). Austin, TX: PRO-ED.

This undated edition emphasizes information useful for planning instruction. Extensive checklists are included for organizing assessment information. Also, checklists of procedures for each phase of assessment are presented along with detailed reviews of tests for social skills, play, language, cognition, achievement, and adaptive behavior.

National Federation of the Blind. (undated). *The blind child in the regular preschool program.* Baltimore: Author.

This fact sheet presents useful recommendations for helping regular classroom teachers understand the needs of these children. The fact sheet is free from the National Federation of the Blind, 1800 Johnson Street, Baltimore, MD 21230. (310) 659-9314.

Stratton, J. M., & Wright, S. (1993). *On the way to literacy: Early experiences for visually impaired children.* Louisville, KY: American Printing House for the Blind.

This program enables sighted parents, or parents who are visually impaired or blind, to read to and with their children who are visually impaired or blind. It is designed for children from infancy to age five. The handbook contains suggestions on how to use the program. The 10 storybooks have both tactile and visual illustrations as well as Braille and print text.

Appendices

Principles for Professional Ethics

I. INTRODUCTION

The formal principles that guide the conduct of a professional school psychologist are known as *Ethics*. By virtue of joining the Association, each NASP member has agreed to act in a manner that shows respect for human dignity and assures a high quality of professional service. Although ethical behavior is an individual responsibility, it is in the interest of an association to adopt and enforce a code of ethics. If done properly, members will be guided towards appropriate behavior, and public confidence in the professional will be enhanced. Additionally, a code of ethics should provide due process procedures to protect members from potential abuse of the code. These *Principles* have been written to accomplish these goals.

The principles in this manual are based on the assumptions that: (1) school psychologists will act as advocates for their students/clients, and (2) at the very least, school psychologists will do no harm. These necessitate that school psychologists "speak up" for the needs and rights of their students/clients at times when it may be difficult to do so. School psychologists are also restrained to provide only those services for which they have acquired an acknowledged level of experience, training, and competency. Beyond these basic premises, judgment is required to apply the ethical principles to the fluid and expanding interactions between school and community.

There are many different sources of advice for the proper way to behave; local policies, state laws, federal laws, credentialing standards, professional association position statements, and books that recommend "Best Practices" are just a few. Given one's employment situation and the array of recommendations, events may develop in which the proper course of action is unclear.

As a general rule, the Association will seek to enforce the *Ethical Principles* upon members. The NASP *Standards for the Provision of School Psychological Services* are typically not enforced, although all members are encouraged to work towards achieving the hallmarks of quality services delivery that are described therein. Similarly, "position statements" and "best practices" documents are not adjudicated.

In other words, one may consider the guidance of *Ethical Principles* to be more general, yet more enduring than other documents that reflect short-term opinions about specific actions that are shaped by local events, popular trends, or recent developments in the field.

The principles in this manual are organized into several sections as a result of editorial judgment. Therefore, principles discussed in one section may also apply to other sections. Every school psychologist, regardless of position (e.g., practitioner, researcher, university trainer, supervisor, state or federal consultant, administrator of psychological services) or setting (e.g., public or private school, community agency, hospital, university, private practice) should examine the theme reflected in each ethical principle to determine the application to her/his individual situation. For example, although a given principle may specifically discuss responsibilities towards "clients," the intent is that the standard would also apply to supervisees, trainees, and research participants. To obtain additional assistance in applying these principles to your particular setting, consult with experienced school psychologists, and seek advice from the National Association of School Psychologists or your state school psychology association.

II. PROFESSIONAL COMPETENCY

A. General

1. School psychologists recognize the strengths and limitations of their training and experience, engaging only in practices for which they are competent. They must continually seek additional training with the welfare of children, families, the school community, and their trainees or supervisees in mind.

2. Competence levels, education, training, and experience are accurately represented to clients in a professional manner.

3. School psychologists do not use affiliations with persons, associations, or institutions to imply a level of professional competence which exceeds that which has actually been achieved.

4. School psychologists are aware of their limitations and enlist the assistance of other specialists in supervisory, consultative, or referral roles as appropriate in providing services.

5. School psychologists engage in continuing professional development. They remain current regarding developments in research, training, and professional practices that benefit children, families, and schools.

6. School psychologists refrain from any activity in which their personal problems or conflicts may interfere with professional effectiveness. Competent assistance is sought to alleviate conflicts in professional relationships.

III. PROFESSIONAL RELATIONSHIPS AND RESPONSIBILITIES

A. General

1. School psychologists are committed to the application of their professional expertise for the purpose of promoting improvement in the quality of life for students, their families, and the school community. This objective is pursued in ways that protect the dignity and rights of those involved. School psychologists accept responsibility for the appropriateness of their treatments and professional practices.

2. School psychologists respect all persons and are sensitive to physical, mental, emotional, political, economic, social, cultural, ethnic, racial, gender, sexual preference, and religious characteristics.

3. School psychologists are responsible for the direction and nature of their personal loyalties or objectives. When these commitments may influence a professional relationship, the school psychologist informs all concerned persons of relevant issues in advance.

4. School psychologists in all settings maintain professional relationships with students, parents, the school, and community. Consequently, parents and students are to be fully informed about all relevant aspects of school psychological services in advance. The explanation should take into account language and cultural differences, cognitive capabilities, development level, and age so that the explanation may be understood by the student, parent, or guardian.

5. School psychologists shall attempt to resolve situations in which there are divided or conflicting interests in a manner which is mutually beneficial and protects the rights of all parties involved.

6. School psychologists do not exploit clients through professional relationships nor condone these actions in their colleagues. Students, clients, employees, colleagues, and research participants will not be exposed to deliberate comments, gestures, or physical contacts of a sexual nature. School psychologists do not engage in sexual relationships with students, supervisees, trainees, or past or present clients.

7. School psychologists attempt to resolve suspected detrimental or unethical practices on an informal level. If informal efforts are not productive, the appropriate professional organization is contacted for assistance, and procedures established for questioning ethical practice are followed.

a. The filing of an ethical complaint is a serious matter. It is intended to improve the behavior of a colleague that is harmful to the profession and/or the public.

b. School psychologists enter into this process thoughtfully and with concern for the well-being of all parties involved. They do not file or encourage the filing of an ethics complaint that is frivolous or motivated by revenge.

8. School psychologists respect the confidentiality of information obtained during their professional work. Information is revealed only with the informed consent of the client, or the client's parent or legal guardian, except in those situations in which failure to release information would result in clear danger to the client or others.

9. School psychologists discuss confidential information only for professional purposes and only with persons who have a legitimate need to know.

10. School psychologists inform their clients of the limits of confidentiality.

B. Students

1. School psychologists understand the intimate nature of consultation, assessment, and direct service. They engage only in professional practices which maintain the dignity and integrity of students and other clients.

2. School psychologists explain important aspects of their professional relationships with students and clients in a clear, understandable manner. The explanation includes the reason why services were requested, who will receive information about the services provided, and the possible outcomes.

3. School psychologists understand their obligation to respect the rights of a student or client to initiate, participate in, or discontinue services voluntarily.

4. Recommendations for program changes or additional service will be discussed, including any alternatives which may be available.

C. Parents, Legal Guardians, and Appointed Surrogates

1. School psychologists explain all services to parents in a clear, understandable manner. They strive to propose a set of options which takes into account the values and capabilities of each parent.

2. School psychologists recognize the importance of parental support and seek to obtain this by assuring that there is direct parent contact prior to seeing the student/client. They secure continuing parental involvement by a frank and prompt reporting to the parent of findings and progress that conforms to the limits of previously determined confidentiality.

3. School psychologists respect the wishes of parents who object to school psychological services and attempt to guide parents to alternative community resources.

4. School psychologists discuss recommendations and plans for assisting the student/client with the parent. The discussion includes alternatives associated with each set of plans, showing respect for the ethnic/cultural values of the family. The parents are advised as to sources of help available at school and in the community.

5. School psychologists discuss the rights of parents and students regarding creation, modification, storage, and disposal of confidential materials that will result from the provision of school psychological services.

D. Service Delivery

1. School psychologists are knowledgeable of the organization, philosophy, goals, objectives, and methodologies of the setting in which they are employed.

2. School psychologists recognize that an understanding of the goals, processes, and legal requirements of their particular workplace is essential for effective functioning within that setting.

3. School psychologists attempt to become integral members of the client systems to which they are assigned. They establish clear roles for themselves within that system and the local community.

4. School psychologists who provide services to several different groups may encounter situations when loyalties are conflicted. As much as possible, the stance of the school psychologist is made known in advance to all parties to prevent misunderstandings.

5. School psychologists promote changes in their employing agencies that will benefit their clients.

E. Community

1. School psychologists are also citizens, thereby accepting the same responsibilities and duties as any member of society. They are free to pursue individual interests, except to the degree that these compromise professional responsibilities.

2. School psychologists may act as individual citizens to bring about social change in a lawful manner. Individual actions should not be presented as, nor suggestive of representing the field of school psychology.

3. As employees or employers, in public or private domains, school psychologists do not engage in or condone practices that discriminate against clients based on race, handicap, age, gender, sexual preference, religion, national origin, economic status, or native language.

4. School psychologists avoid any action that could violate or diminish the civil and legal rights of clients.

5. School psychologists adhere to federal, state, and local laws and ordinances governing their practice. If regulations conflict with ethical guidelines, school psychologists seek to resolve such conflict through positive, respected, and legal channels.

F. Related Professions

1. To best meet the needs of students and clients, school psychologists cooperate with other professional disciplines in relationships based on mutual respect.

2. School psychologists recognize the competence of other professionals. They encourage and support the use of all resources to best serve the interests of students and clients.

3. School psychologists strive to explain their field and their professional competencies, including roles, assignments, and working relationships to other professionals.

4. School psychologists cooperate with other professionals and agencies with the rights and needs of their client in mind. If a client is receiving similar services from another professional, school psychologists promote coordination of services.

5. The student or client is referred to another professional for services when a condition is identified which is outside the professional competencies or scope of the school psychologist.

6. When transferring the intervention responsibility for a student or client to another professional, school psychologists ensure that all relevant and appropriate individuals, including the student/client

when appropriate, are notified of the change and reasons for the change.

7. When school psychologists suspect the existence of detrimental or unethical practices, the appropriate professional organization is contacted for assistance in determining the procedures established by that profession for examining the practices in question.

G. Other School Psychologists

1. School psychologists who employ, supervise, or train other professionals accept the obligation to provide continuing professional development. They also provide appropriate working conditions, fair and timely evaluation, and constructive consultation.

2. School psychologists who supervise interns are responsible for all professional practices of the supervisees. They assure the students/clients and the profession that the intern is adequately supervised.

IV. PROFESSIONAL PRACTICES PUBLIC AND PRIVATE SETTINGS

A. Advocacy

1. School psychologists consider the students or clients to be their primary responsibility, acting as advocates of their rights and welfare. When choosing a course of action, school psychologists take into account the rights of each individual involved and the duties of the school personnel.

2. School psychologists' concerns for protecting the rights and welfare of students is communicated to the school administration and staff, and is the top priority in determining services.

B. Assessment and Intervention

1. School psychologists will maintain the highest standard for educational and psychological assessment.

   a. In conducting psychological, educational, or behavioral evaluation, or in providing therapy, counseling, or consultation services, due consideration will be given to individual integrity and individual differences.

   b. School psychologists respect differences in age, gender, socioeconomic, cultural, and ethnic backgrounds. They select and use appropriate assessment or treatment procedures, techniques, and strategies.

2. School psychologists collect relevant data using valued and reliable instruments and techniques that are applicable and appropriate for the benefit of the student or client.

3. School psychologists combine observations, background information, and information from other disciplines in order to reach comprehensive conclusions.

4. School psychologists use assessment techniques, counseling and therapy procedures, consultation techniques, and other direct service methods that the profession considers to be responsible, research-based practice.

5. School psychologists do not condone the use of psychological or educational assessment techniques by unqualified persons in any way, including teaching, sponsorship, or supervision.

6. School psychologists develop interventions which are appropriate to the presenting problems and are consistent with data collected. They modify or terminate the treatment plan when the data indicate the plan is not achieving the desired goals.

C. Use of Materials and Technology

1. School psychologists maintain test security, preventing the release of underlying principles and specific content that would undermine the use of the device.

2. School psychologists uphold copyright laws. Permission is obtained from authors to reproduce non-copyrighted published instruments.

3. School psychologists will obtain written prior consent or else remove identifying data presented in public lectures or publications.

4. When producing materials for consultation, treatment, teaching, public lectures, or publication, school psychologists acknowledge sources and assign credit to those whose ideas are reflected in the product. Recognition is given in proportion to the contribution. Plagiarism of ideas or product is a violation of professional ethics.

5. School psychologists do not promote or encourage inappropriate use of computer-generated test analysis or reports. For example, a school psychologist would not offer an unedited computer report as one's own writing, nor use a computer scoring system for tests in which one has no training.

6. School psychologists maintain full responsibility for any technological services used. All ethical and legal principles regarding confidentiality, privacy, and responsibility for decisions apply to the school psychologist and cannot be transferred to equipment, software companies, or data processing departments.

7. Technological devices should be used to improve the quality of client services. School psychologists will resist applications of technology that ultimately reduce the quality of service.

D. Research and Evaluation

1. In performing research, school psychologists accept responsibility for selection of topics, research methodology, subject selection, data gathering, analysis, and reporting.

2. In publishing reports of their research, school psychologists provide discussion of limitations of their data and acknowledge existence of disconfirming data, as well as alternate hypotheses and explanations of their findings.

E. Reporting Data and Conference Results

1. School psychologists ascertain that student or client information reaches only authorized persons.

    a. The information is adequately interpreted so that the recipient can better help the student or client.

    b. The school psychologist assists agency recipients to establish procedures to properly safeguard the confidential material.

2. School psychologists communicate findings and recommendations in language readily understood by the intended recipient. These communications describe potential consequences associated with the proposals.

3. School psychologists prepare written reports in such form and style that the recipient of the report will be able to assist the student or client. Reports should emphasize recommendations and interpretations; reports which present only test scores or brief narratives describing a test are seldom useful. Reports should include an appraisal of the degree of confidence which could be assigned to the information.

4. School psychologists review all of their written documents for accuracy, signing them only when correct.

5. School psychologists comply with all laws, regulations and policies pertaining to the adequate storage and disposal of records to maintain appropriate confidentiality of information.

V. PROFESSIONAL PRACTICES — PRIVATE SETTING

A. Relationship with School Districts

1. Some school psychologists are employed in both the public and private sectors, and in so doing, may create a conflict of interest. School psychologists operating in both sectors recognize the importance of ethical standards, the separation of roles, and take full responsibility for protecting and completely informing the consumer of all potential concerns.

2. A school psychologist, while working in the private sector, may not accept any form of remuneration from clients who are entitled to the same service provided by the same school psychologist while working in the public sector.

3. School psychologists in private practice have an obligation to inform parents of any free school psychological services available from the public or private schools prior to delivering such services for remuneration.

4. School psychologists working in both public and private sectors will conduct all private practice outside of the hours of contracted public employment.

5. School psychologists engaged in private practice do not use tests, materials, equipment, facilities, secretarial assistance, or other services belonging to the public sector employer, unless approved in advance through a written agreement.

B. Service Delivery

1. School psychologists conclude a financial agreement in advance of service delivery.

    a. School psychologists ensure to the best of their ability that the client clearly understands the agreement.

    b. School psychologists neither give nor receive any remuneration for referring clients for professional services.

2. School psychologists in private practice adhere to the conditions of a contract until service thereunder has been performed, the contract has been terminated by mutual consent, or the contract has otherwise been legally terminated.

3. School psychologists in private practice prevent misunderstandings resulting from their recommendations, advice, or information. Most often, direct consultation between the school psychologist in private practice and the school psychologist responsible for the student in the public sector will resolve minor differences of opinion without necessarily confusing the parents, yet keep the best interests of the student or client in mind.

4. Personal diagnosis and therapy are not given by means of public lectures, newspaper columns, magazine articles, radio and television programs, or mail. Any information shared through mass media activities is general in nature and is openly declared to be so.

C. Announcements/Advertising

1. Appropriate announcement of services, advertising, and public media statements may be necessary for school psychologists in private practice. Accurate representations of training, experience, services provided, and affiliation are done in a restrained manner. Public statements must be made on sound and accepted theory, research, and practice.

2. Listings in telephone directories are limited to the following: name/names, highest relevant degree, state certification status, national certification status, address, telephone number, brief identification of major areas of practice, office hours, appropriate fee information, foreign languages spoken, policy regarding third party payments, and license number.

3. Announcements of services by school psychologists in private practice are made in a formal, professional manner, using the guidelines of section 2, above. Clear statements of purposes with unequivocal descriptions of the experiences to be provided are given. Education, training, and experience of all staff members are appropriately specified.

4. School psychologists in private practice may use brochures in the announcement of services. The brochures may be sent to professional persons, schools, business firms, government agencies, and other similar organizations.

5. Announcements and advertisements of the availability of publications, products, and services for sale are professional and factual.

6. School psychologists in private practice do not directly solicit clients for individual diagnosis or therapy.

7. School psychologists do not compensate in any manner a representative of the press, radio, or television in return for personal professional publicity in a news item.

PROCEDURAL GUIDELINES FOR THE ADJUDICATION OF ETHICAL COMPLAINTS

Section I. Responsibility and Function

The Ethical and Professional Standards Committee shall be responsible for developing and maintaining a clearly defined position for the Association regarding the ethical and professional conduct principles to be adhered to by its members and also the members of the National School Psychology Certification System (NSPCS). The major area of particular ethical concern to the Committee will be that of the protection and general well-being of individuals served by school psychologists, in schools and in private practice, and in institutions or agencies through which the service is rendered. The Committee is fur-

ther charged to study and make recommendations to the Executive Board when it is alleged that a NASP or NSPCS member has failed to follow the ethical principles of the Association.

Members of the Ethical and Professional Standards Committee recognize that their role is an extremely important one, involving the rights of many individuals, the reputation of the profession, and the careers of individual professionals. They bear a heavy responsibility because their recommendations may alter the lives of others. Therefore, they must be alert to personal, social, organizational, financial, or political situations or pressures that might lead to misuse of their influence. The Ethical and Professional Standards Committee shall assure the responsible use of all information obtained in the course of an inquiry or investigation. The objective with regard to the individual shall, whenever possible, be constructive, rather than punitive in character.

The function of the Committee in investigating complaints of alleged ethical misconduct involves obtaining a thorough and impartial account of the behaviors or incidents in order to be able to evaluate the character of the behaviors in question. When responding to complaints, members of the Ethics and Professional Standards Committee have the responsibility to consider the competency of the complainant, to act in an unbiased manner, to work expeditiously and to safeguard the confidentiality of the Committee's activities. Committee members and their designees have the added responsibility to follow procedures which safeguard the rights of all individuals involved in the complaint process.

Section II. Scope and Authority

The Ethical and Professional Standards Committee shall address issues of ethical misconduct in an investigatory, advisory, educative, and/or remedial role. What constitutes ethical misconduct shall be determined on the basis of the provisions of the NASP *Principles for Professional Ethics* and any published advisory opinions that from time to time are developed by the Ethical and Professional Standards Committee. In applying the Principles, the authorized opinions of those charged by NASP with the administration and interpretation of the ethical principles shall be binding on all NASP members, individuals who hold a certificate issued by the National School Psychology Certification Board (NSPCB), and on the members of state associations affiliated with NASP.

When investigating and/or responding to a complaint or inquiry, the Ethical and Professional Standards Committee shall conduct itself in a manner consistent with the Bylaws of the Association and with the NASP *Principles for Professional Ethics* and shall also be bound by these procedures. The Ethical and Professional Standards Committee shall endeavor to settle cases informally, recommend disciplinary action when unethical conduct has occurred, report regularly to the Delegate Assembly on its activities and shall revise and amend (subject to ratification by the Delegate Assembly) the NASP Principles and these procedures in a timely manner. The Association may, at the recommendation of the Ethical and Professional Standards Committee, and in accordance with the Bylaws of the Association, expel a NASP member. The Ethical and Professional Standards Committee will also issue a recommendation to the NSPCB regarding charges filed against any nationally certified school psychologist.

When a complaint is received about a non-member, the Ethical and Professional Standards Committee shall respond only if the individual complained against is a member of the National School Psychology Certification System. Otherwise, the committee may act only in an advisory or educative fashion and shall have no authority to investigate the case or to discipline the individual in question.

Complaints that address concerns about professional standards, organizations, employers, and the like, shall be referred to the Ethical and Professional Standards Committee. Nevertheless, it should be recognized that in situations where an individual psychologist is being coerced to behave unethically, he/she bears certain ethical responsibilities and to fail to take appropriate action, e.g., refusing to behave ethically, could eventuate in charges of misconduct against the individual psychologist involved. However, as a rule, such "standards" concerns would not fall under the purview of this complaint process.

Complaints received by the Ethical and Professional Standards Committee shall be reviewed and judged on the basis of the *Principles for Professional Ethics* in force at the time of the alleged misconduct. Investigation and adjudication of ethical complaints shall be on the basis of the "Procedural Guidelines for the Adjudication of Ethical Complaints" in force at the time the complaint is received by the Committee.

Section III. Receipt and Acknowledgment of Complaints and Inquiries

A. The Ethical and Professional Standards Committee shall recognize and respond to all complaints and inquiries from any responsible individual or group of individuals in accordance with these procedures. The individual who petitions the Committee (hereinafter referred to as the *complainant*) need not be a member of NASP or the affiliated state association. Anonymous letters and phone calls will not be recognized. Complaints by members which are judged by the committee to be frivolous or revengeful may be cause for action against the complainant.

B. An oral complaint or inquiry may be informally handled, referred elsewhere when appropriate, or an Ethical and Professional Standards Committee chairperson may request that the complaint be for-

mally submitted in writing. Only written statements expressing the details of the alleged misconduct will be accepted for action. Such written statements shall be signed by the complainant and should state, in as much detail as practicable, the facts upon which the complaint is based. All the correspondence, records, and activities of the Ethical and Professional Standards Committee shall remain confidential.

C. Within 15 days of receipt of a written statement outlining the details of the alleged misconduct, the chairpersons of the Ethical and Professional Standards Committee shall do the following:

1. Determine if the individual against whom the complaint is made (hereinafter referred to as the *respondent)*, is a member of NASP or NCSP. If the respondent is not a member of NASP or NCSP, the complainant shall be so advised and when appropriate, referred to other agencies and/or associations who would have authority in the matter.

2. If the respondent is a member of NASP or NCSP, the Ethical and Professional Standards Committee chairpersons, with any advisory opinions deemed necessary, shall review the complaint. If it is determined that the alleged misconduct, even if true, would *not* constitute an actual violation of the NASP Principles, a chairperson shall notify the complainant.

3. If the information obtained from the complainant is insufficient to make a determination regarding the alleged misconduct, the chairpersons may send a written request to the complainant, asking for clarification and/or additional information as would be needed to make such a determination.

4. If it is determined that the alleged misconduct, if substantiated, would constitute an actual violation of NASP Principles, the Ethical and Professional Standards Committee chairpersons shall direct a letter to and advise the complainant that the allegation will be investigated by the Committee. The complainant shall be asked to sign a release, authorizing that his/her name be revealed to the respondent.

5. If the complainant refuses to permit his/her identity to be made known to the respondent, such refusal will serve as a basis for forfeiting the complaint process. However, the Ethical and Professional Standards Committee may proceed on its own volition when a member appears to have engaged in ethical misconduct that tends to injure the Association or to adversely affect its reputation, or that is clearly inconsistent with or destructive of the goals and objectives of the Association.

Section IV: Conduct of an Informal Inquiry

A. Within 15 days of receipt of the signed release, the Ethical and Professional Standards Committee shall inform the respondent, in writing, with the envelope marked "confidential," that a complaint has been filed against him/her. This letter shall describe the nature of the complaint, indicate the principle(s) which appear to have been violated, and request the respondent's cooperation in obtaining a full picture of the circumstances which led to the allegations. A copy of the NASP *Principles for Professional Ethics*, these procedures, and any pertinent advisory opinions of the Ethical and Professional Standards Committee shall also be enclosed. Ordinarily the respondent shall be informed of the name of the complainant, when written permission to do so has been obtained. (See Section III, C-5 above, for exception.)

B. The respondent shall be asked to provide a written statement outlining his/her view of the situation in order that the Committee may be cognizant of all relevant aspects of the case.

C. Whenever possible, the Ethical and Professional Standards Committee shall attempt to resolve differences privately and informally through further correspondence with all parties involved. An attempt shall be made to bring about an adjustment through mediative efforts in the interest of correcting a general situation or setting the particular issues between the parties involved.

D. If the respondent does not respond to the original inquiry within 30 days, a follow-up letter shall be sent to the respondent by registered or certified mail, marked "confidential," with a return receipt requested.

E. If the respondent refuses to reply to the Committee's inquiry or otherwise cooperate with the Committee, the Committee may continue its investigation, noting in the record the circumstances of the respondent's failure to cooperate. The Committee shall also inform the respondent that his/her lack of cooperation may result in action which could eventuate in his/her being dropped from membership in the Association.

F. As a rule, if the complainant wishes to withdraw the complaint, the inquiry is terminated, except in the extreme cases where the Committee feels the issues in the case are of such importance as to warrant completing the investigation in its own right and in the interest of the public welfare or that of the Association. (See Section III, C-5.)

G. The Association will not recognize a respondent's resignation from membership while there is a complaint pending before the Ethical and Professional Standards Committee or before an ethics committee of a state association unless he/she submits an affidavit stating that:

    1. The resignation is free and voluntary;

    2. He/she is aware of a pending investigation into allegations of misconduct;

    3. He/she acknowledges that the material facts upon which the complaint is based are true; and;

    4. He/she submits the resignation because he/she knows that if charges are predicated on the misconduct under investigation, he/she could not defend him/herself successfully against them.

H. Within 30 days of receipt of the written statement from the respondent, or (in the event the respondent fails to reply or otherwise cooperate), within 30 days of receipt of the return receipt requested from the second notification by the Committee (Section IV, D, E), the chairpersons, through advice of the Committee, shall determine if a violation may have occurred, and if so, what principles have potentially been violated.

I. If, in the opinion of the Committee, the complaint has a basis in fact but is considered likely to be corrected without further action, the chairpersons shall so indicate in the record and shall so inform all parties involved.

J. If, in the opinion of the chairpersons, the issues raised by the complaint would, if true, constitute a violation of the principles, and if it appears that the complaint cannot be resolved by less formal means, the chairpersons shall, in coordination with the appropriate State Delegate, appoint two impartial NASP members from the state in which the respondent practices to form an Ad Hoc Committee, together with the chairpersons of the Ethical and Professional Standards Committee. The purpose of this Ad Hoc Committee is to investigate the case, to evaluate the character of the behavior(s) in question, and to make recommendations to the Ethics and Professional Standards Committee for final disposition of the case.

K. The Ethical and Professional Standards Committee chairpersons shall transmit to the members of the Ad Hoc Committee, by registered or certified mail, in envelopes marked "confidential," copies of the following:

    1. The original complaint or material;

    2. The letter to the respondent apprising him/her of the nature of the alleged violation;

    3. The response from the respondent; and

    4. Any such further facts related to the case as the chairpersons can assemble from sources of evident reliability.

L. The Ad Hoc Committee shall then determine whether;

    1. The case shall be closed;

    2. Further investigation by correspondence is indicated;

    3. Further investigation by a Fact-Finding Committee is indicated (see Section VI);

    4. The respondent and/or complainant shall be asked to appear before the Ad Hoc Committee; or

    5. Some other action or a combination thereof shall be taken.

Section V. Recommendations of the Ad Hoc Committee

A. When the Ad Hoc Committee has obtained sufficient information with which to reach a decision, or in any event, in not more than 60 days from the formation of the Ad Hoc Committee, the Ethical and Professional Standards Committee chairpersons shall request that the Ad Hoc Committee vote on the disposition of the case.

B. If, in the unanimous opinion of the Ad Hoc Committee members, a violation of the NASP Principles has occurred and if, in the opinion of the Ad Hoc Committee, the unethical behavior can be terminated by action of the Committee itself, one or more of the following recommendations shall be made:

    1. The Ad Hoc Committee shall request, in writing, that the respondent take corrective measures to modify or stop certain activities or practices;

    2. The Ad Hoc Committee shall, in writing, censure or reprimand the respondent;

    3. The Ad Hoc Committee shall require that the respondent provide restitution to or apologize, in writing, to an individual, group of individuals, or organization harmed by the respondent's unethical conduct.

    4. The Ad Hoc Committee shall recommend that the respondent be placed under a period of probation of membership or surveillance under fixed terms agreed to by the respondent;

    5. The Ad Hoc Committee may recommend a combination of the above four recommendations. (NOTE — In all cases, supervision of the member's behavior for a period of time will be a required component of the corrective action.)

C. Within 5 days, the Ethical and Professional Standards Committee chairpersons shall inform the respondent of the Ad Hoc Committee's determination and recommendations. The respondent shall be notified that he/she may make a request for a hearing on the charges within 30 days from the receipt of a statement of the charges and the Committee's findings and recommendations. Such a request shall be in writing and directed to the President of the Association.

D. The Ethical and Professional Standards Committee chairpersons shall draft a report summarizing the findings and recommendations of the Ad Hoc Committee, copies of which shall be distributed to the two other Ad Hoc Committee members, the respondent, and, at the Committee's discretion, the complainant. This report shall be transmitted in envelopes marked "confidential" in the case of the respondent, by registered or certified mail with a return receipt requested.

E. A summary report shall then be edited by the Ethical and Professional Standards Committee chairpersons, ensuring the confidentiality of all persons involved is strictly maintained, for purposes of reporting to the Delegate Assembly at the next regularly scheduled meeting on the activities and recommendations of the Ethical and Professional Standards Committee and its designees, e.g., any Ad Hoc Committee so convened in the interim.

F. The unanimous decision by the Ad Hoc Committee shall be binding on the Association unless overturned by the Hearing Committee, Executive Board, or Delegate Assembly in accordance with the procedures outlined herein. (See Section VIII.)

Section VI. Conduct of a Formal Investigation

A. A formal investigation shall be undertaken if any one of the following circumstances prevails:

    1. The Ad Hod Committee finds that it lacks sufficient data with which to proceed;

    2. The Ad Hoc Committee is unable to reach consensus;

    3. The recommendations of the Ad Hoc Committee do not lead to resolution of the problem; or

    4. The facts alleged in the complaint, if substantiated, would likely require action leading to termination of the respondent's membership in the Association, or revocation of a National Certificate.

B. When a formal investigation is warranted under these procedures, the Ethical and Professional Standards Committee chairpersons, in coordination with the President of the Association, shall appoint a Fact-Finding Committee, which shall appoint its own chairperson, to consist of not less than three nor more than five members of the Association, for the specific purpose of more fully investigating the charges. No member previously involved in reviewing the case may serve on the Fact-Finding Committee. The Ethical and Professional Standards Committee chairpersons shall serve on the Fact-Finding Committee in ex-officio status in order to apprise the Fact-Finding Committee of the procedures by which they are bound and to serve in an advisory capacity.

C. The Fact-Finding Committee shall be bound by the same procedures and timelines as outlined in Sections III and IV of these procedures. In addition, the Fact-Finding Committee may, at the discretion of the Executive Board, retain a legal advisor as counsel to the committee while investigating its case.

D. The respondent may seek advice from any individual, including an attorney or another member of the Association, for assistance in preparing and presenting documentary evidence requested by the Fact-Finding Committee.

Section VII. Recommendations of the Fact-Finding Committee

A. If the formal investigation was convened following a decision by consensus of the Ad Hoc Committee, and if the Fact-Finding Committee unanimously concurs with the Ad Hoc Committee's findings and recommendations, all parties shall be so informed and this decision shall be binding on the Association unless overturned by the Hearing Committee, Executive Board, or Delegate Assembly, in accordance with the procedures outlined herein.

B. If the case was not resolved at the Ad Hoc Committee level, the Fact-Finding Committee must announce its findings and recommendations within the prescribed timelines. The Fact-Finding Committee may exercise any of the recommendations open to the Ad Hoc Committee (Section V, B) and in addition may also recommend that the respondent's membership in the Association be terminated.

C. Should the Fact-Finding Committee so recommend, the chairpersons of the Ethical and Professional Standards Committee must present the findings and recommendations of the Fact-Finding Committee to the NASP Executive Board and Delegate Assembly. A summary report shall be prepared, such that the confidentiality of all parties involved, i.e., identifying information of the informer, is strictly maintained. The case shall be reviewed in sufficient detail so as to allow the Executive Board and the Delegate Assembly members to vote to concur or overrule the decision of the Fact-Finding Committee.

D. In accordance with NASP Bylaws, cases involving a recommendation for expulsion from the Association by the Ethical and Professional Standards Committee shall be confirmed by a 2/3 vote of the Ex-

ecutive Board, with a member of the NSPCS, the expulsion shall be reported to the NSPCB along with a recommendation for further action, if any, the NSPCB should take.

E. At the discretion of the Executive board and Delegate Assembly, the respondent may be allowed to voluntarily resign his/her membership in the Association.

F. Within five days, the Ethical and Professional Standards Committee chairpersons shall inform the respondent of the decision of the Executive Board and Delegate Assembly in the same manner as provided in Section V, C of these procedures.

G. If the Executive board and/or the Delegate Assembly do not concur with the Committee's recommendation for expulsion from membership, the case shall be remanded back to the Fact-Finding Committee for consideration of a lesser penalty.

Section VIII. Conduct of the Hearing Committee

A. Within 30 days of receipt of a statement of the charges against him/her and a statement of the Committee's findings and recommendations, the respondent has the right to request from the President of the Association a hearing on the charges. This right shall be considered waived if such request is not made in writing within the 30 day period.

B. If the respondent does request a hearing, the President shall select a panel of ten members of the Association, none of whom shall be members of the Ethical and Professional Standards Committee or have had any prior connection with the case. From the panel, the respondent shall have 30 days in which to choose a Hearing Committee of five members. If he/she does not make a selection, the President shall choose the five members to comprise the Hearing Committee.

C. The President shall select a chairperson of the Hearing Committee who shall conduct the hearing and assure that the procedures are properly observed. There shall be no communication between the members of the Hearing Committee and the Ethical and Professional Standards Committee or any of its representatives prior to the hearing itself.

D. A date for the hearing shall be set by the President with the concurrence of the respondent. In no event shall the hearing take place later than 90 days from the date of the respondent's request for a hearing.

E. At least 30 days prior to the hearing, the respondent and the Hearing Committee members shall be provided with copies of all documents to be presented and the names of all witnesses that will be offered by the Ethical and Professional Standards Committee in support of the charges.

F. Presentation of the case against the respondent shall be the responsibility of the Ethical and Professional Standards Committee, or such others as the Ethical and Professional Standards Committee has designated to investigate the complaint. Legal counsel for the Association may participate fully in the presentation of the case.

G. All evidence that is relevant and reliable, as determined by the chairperson of the Hearing Committee, shall be admissible. Evidence of mitigating circumstances may be presented by the respondent.

H. The respondent shall have the right to counsel, to present witnesses and documents, and to cross-examine the witnesses offered by the Ethical and Professional Standards Committee.

I. The hearing may be adjourned as necessary and the Ethical and Professional Standards Committee may introduce rebuttal evidence.

J. In the interest of obtaining a full and accurate record of the hearing, a tape recorder or other transcription device may be used, at the discretion of the Hearing Committee and the respondent.

Section IX. Recommendations of the Hearing Committee

A. At the conclusion of the hearing, the Hearing Committee shall have 30 days in which to issue its report and recommendations.

B. If the Hearing Committee recommends that the respondent be dropped from membership or that the respondent be permitted to resign, the matter shall be referred to the Executive Board. A recommendation that the respondent be expelled or be allowed to resign must be made by 4 of the 5 committee members. Other disciplinary measures would be decided upon per individual case and would require a simple majority vote.

C. Only the disciplinary measures specified by the Ethical and Professional Standards Committee in the formal statement of charges, or a lesser penalty, shall be recommended by the Hearing Committee. Although the Ethical and Professional Standards Committee recommendations may be modified by the Hearing Committee, it may not increase the penalty recommended.

D. The Hearing Committee shall submit its report and recommendations simultaneously to the Executive Board and to the respondent.

E. The respondent shall have 15 days from receipt of the Hearing Committee's report in which to file a written statement with the Executive Board.

The Ethical and Professional Standards Committee shall then have 15 days in which to file a response.

F. After consideration of the record, the recommendations of the Hearing Committee and any statements that may be filed, the Executive Board shall adopt the recommendations of the Hearing Committee unless it determines that:

1. The NASP Principles and/or the procedures herein stated have been incorrectly applied;

2. The findings of fact of the Hearing Committee as stated in the report are not supported by the evidence, or;

3. The procedures followed were in violation of the Bylaws of the Association.

G. The Ethical and Professional Standards Committee shall inform the respondent and, at its discretion, may inform the complainant of any final action taken by the Executive Board. The Ethical and Professional Standards Committee shall report to the Delegate Assembly at its next regularly scheduled meeting, in Executive Session, the names of those members who have been allowed to resign or who have been expelled from membership, and the ethical principle(s) involved. Actions involving individuals who hold a certificate issued by the NSPCB will be reported to the national certification board in a timely manner.

H. The Ethical and Professional Standards Committee shall report annually and in confidence to the Delegate Assembly and Executive Board, in Executive Session, the names of members who have been expelled from the Association and the ethical principle(s) involved.

I. In severe cases and when the welfare of the public is at stake, and when the Ethical and Professional Standards Committee deems it necessary to maintain the principles of the Association and the profession, it may also notify affiliated state and regional associations and state and local licensing and certification boards of the final disposition of the case. Other interested parties, including the respondent's employer, may be notified of the final action when, in the opinion of the Ethical and Professional Standards Committee, notification is necessary for the protection of the public or the profession.

REFERENCES

American Psychological Association. (1980, February 22–23). "Amendments in CSPEC's Rules and Procedures," as documented in the non-confidential minutes of CSPEC's Action Agenda.

American Psychological Association. 1977. *Ethical Standards of Psychologists.* Washington, DC: American Psychological Association, Inc.

American Psychological Association. (1974, September). "Rules and Procedures — Committee on Scientific and Professional Ethics and Conduct." *American Psychologist,* 703–710.

Bersoff, D. N. (1980, February 6). "Review of CSPEC Rules and Procedures." American Psychological Association Memorandum.

Illinois Psychological Association. (1975, January–March). "Revised Procedural Guidelines for Ethic Committee." *Illinois Psychologist,* 23–31.

Illinois School Psychologists Association. (1980, September). "Procedures for Handling Complaints of Alleged Violations of Ethical Principles."

National Association of School Psychologists. (1980, April). "National School Psychology Certification System." *NASP Operations Handbook.*

National Association of School Psychologists. (1974, October). *Principles for Professional Ethics.*

National Association of School Psychologists. (1974, October). "Procedures for Handling of Complaints of Alleged Violations of Ethical Principles."

PROCEDURAL GUIDELINES FOR THE
ADJUDICATION OF ETHICAL COMPLAINTS

A COMPLAINT IS RECEIVED BY THE COMMITTEE

Is the complaint anonymous?	If so, take no action.

Is the complaint oral?	If so, advise only.

Is the complaint about *Standards?*	If so, advise only.

Is the complaint frivolous or vengeful?	If so, consider action against complainant.

Is the ethical complaint about a NASP member or a member of the National Certification system?	If not, advise complainant that the situation is out of NASP jurisdiction.

WITHIN 15 DAYS OF THE COMPLAINT:

The committee reviews the written complaint.	

Is there a potential violation of NASP ethics?	If not, notify complainant and get more information, or stop.

Complainant is advised that an informal investigation will occur, and is asked for a release so that respondent may know who issued the complaint.

Is the release obtained?	If not, the committee must decide whether to proceed on its own volition.

WITHIN 15 DAYS OF SIGNED RELEASE:

Inform the respondent, describe the complaint and the principles believed to be involved, request cooperation, and send a copy of the *Ethics.* Ask for a written response.

Attempt to resolve the situation informally, if possible.

IF NO ANSWER WITHIN 30 DAYS:

Follow up with another request for a written response, using a certified letter with return receipt requested.

If there is still no reply, or if the respondent refuses to cooperate, note this in the record and inform the respondent that a lack of cooperation could result in expulsion from NASP.

WITHIN 30 DAYS OF THE WRITTEN STATEMENT:

If the facts seem to suggest that a violation may have occurred, is the situation likely to correct itself without further action?	If so, inform all parties and monitor the situation.

WITHIN THE NEXT 60 DAYS:

Contact the state delegate, appoint two impartial NASP members in the respondent's state, and form an Ad Hoc committee.

Ad Hoc committee receives copies of the original complaint materials, the committee's letter to the respondent, the respondent's written response, and other pertinent material.

Can the situation be settled at the informal level?	If so, contact the parties and monitor the situation.
Can the needed information be obtained through correspondence?	If so, the Ad Hoc committee continues to gather the facts.
Does the Ad Hoc committee need for the complainant and the respondent to appear?	If so, arrange for them to appear before the committee.
Does the Ad Hoc committee have enough information to decide the issues at hand?	If not, begin fact finding procedures.
Is the Ad Hoc committee unanimous in its decision?	If not, begin formal investigation procedures.

THE COMMITTEE ISSUES A DECISION, WHICH IS BINDING UNLESS OVERTURNED BY A HEARING; SUPERVISION IS REQUIRED:

Order corrective action.	Censure or reprimand.	Require an apology or restitution	Require probation	Determine no violation occurred.

WITHIN 5 DAYS:

Notify the respondent of the decision.

WAIT 30 DAYS FOR RESPONDENT TO REQUEST A HEARING:

If there is no request for a hearing, draft a report and advise the Delegate Assembly of the actions of the committee. Make recommendations to National Certification Board if respondent holds national certification.

FORMAL INVESTIGATION PROCEDURES

Follow these steps if:
- The Ad Hoc committee lacks the data to proceed.
- The Ad Hoc committee cannot reach a consensus.
- The solutions available to the Ad Hoc committee are unlikely to resolve the problem.
- The facts, if substantiated, could lead to the expulsion of a NASP member or a member of the NSPCS.

The chairs of the Ethical and Professional Standards Committee, along with the NASP President, appoint members of a fact finding committee. This committee follows the same basic procedures as the Ad Hoc committee.

| Does the fact finding committee concur unanimously with the Ad Hoc Committee? | If so, the Ad Hoc Committee decisions are binding unless overturned by a hearing, Executive Board, or Delegate Assembly. |

The fact finding committee reaches its own conclusions. The recommendations may include expulsion.

If expulsion is advised, the Ethical and Professional Standards chairs will present the findings to the NASP Executive Board and the Delegate Assembly, with all due consideration for matters of confidentiality.

| Is the expulsion recommendation confirmed by a 2/3rd vote of the Executive Board and ratified by a majority of the Delegates? | If not, have the fact finding committee review the situation and consider a lessor penalty. |

WITHIN 5 DAYS:

Notify the respondent.

WAIT 30 DAYS FOR RESPONDENT TO REQUEST A HEARING:

If there is no request for a hearing, draft a report and advise the Delegate Assembly and the National Certification Board (if necessary) of the actions of the committee.

CONDUCT OF THE HEARING COMMITTEE

Upon receipt of a written decision by the Ad Hoc or the Fact Finding committee, a respondent has thirty days in which to ask for a hearing. Should a hearing be requested within the 30 days:

> The NASP President selects a panel of 10 impartial NASP members. From this group, the respondent selects 5 to serve on the committee. The President then selects the Chair.

NO LATER THAN 90 DAYS FROM THE DATE OF THE HEARING REQUEST:

> The date for the hearing is set.

AT LEAST 30 DAYS BEFORE THE HEARING:

> Hearing committee members and respondent receive copies of all relevant documents.

AT THE HEARING:

> The Ethical and Professional Standards committee chair, or designee, presents the facts in the complaint. The respondent has the right to counsel, to present witnesses and documents, and to cross-examine witnesses. The Ethical and Professional Standards committee may offer rebuttal.

WITHIN 30 DAYS:

> The hearing committee issues a report and recommendations to the respondent and the NASP Executive Board.

WITHIN 15 DAYS:

> The Ethical and Professional Standards Committee and the respondent may file comments on the hearing committee report.

AT THE NEXT EXECUTIVE BOARD MEETING:

Does the NASP Executive Board believe that there is no evidence of ethical misconduct, or that there was a problem with the application of the principles or procedures for investigation?	If yes, the matter is ended.

> The Executive Board adopts the findings and recommendations of the Hearing Committee.

> The Ethical and Professional Standards Committee informs the respondent, and has the discretion to inform the complainant or not. The EB/DA is notified of members expelled and the ethical principles involved. The National School Psychology Certification System will be notified if the proceedings involve an NSPCS member.

> When the welfare of the public is at stake, NASP may notify other interested parties of the final disposition of the case.

Appendix II

Standards for the Provision of School Psychological Services

1.0 Definitions

1.1 A *School Psychologist* is a professional psychologist who has met all requirements for credentialing as stipulated in the appropriate NASP standards. The credential is based upon the completion of a school psychology training program which meets the criteria specified in the NASP *Standards for Training and Field Placement Programs in School Psychology.*

1.2 A *Supervising School Psychologist* is a professional psychologist who has met all NASP requirements for credentialing, and who has been designated by an employing agency as a supervisor responsible for school psychological services in the agency. Coursework or other training in the supervision of school personnel is desirable.

1.3 *Parent(s)*, as used in these *Standard*, includes both biological parent(s) and legal guardian(s) or appointed surrogates.

2.0 Standards for Administrative Agencies

The purpose of this section of the standards is to provide guidance to federal and state administrative agencies in regard to administrative organization, laws, policies, and regulations as they pertain to the provision of school psychological services.

2.1 Federal Level Administrative Agency

2.1.1. The federal education agency should employ a supervising school psychologist in order to accomplish the following objectives:

2.1.1.1 To provide professional leadership and assistance to the federal education agency, state education agencies, and the school psychology profession in regard to standards, policies, and procedures for program delivery, and for utilization, funding, education and training, and inservice education of school psychological services personnel.

2.1.1.2 To participate in the administration of federal programs providing funding for school psychological services in state, intermediate, and local education agencies, and for the education and training of school psychologists.

2.1.1.3 To encourage and assist in evaluation, research, and dissemination activities; to determine the effectiveness of school psychological education, training, and service programs; to determine needed changes; and to identify and communicate exemplary practices to training and service units.

2.1.1.4 To assure that consistent communication is established and maintained among professional organizations, federal, state, and local education agencies, and university training programs involved in providing and developing school psychological services.

2.1.2 Laws

2.1.2.1 The Congress of the United States should ensure that the rights of all parents and children are protected by the creation and modification of laws which provide for the services of school psychologists. These services include, but are not limited to, consultation, assessment, research, program planning/evaluation, and direct service for individuals, groups, and systems. These services should be available to all children, their families, and school personnel.

2.1.2.2   The Congress should ensure that school psychological services are provided in a free and appropriate manner to all children, their families, and school personnel in need of such services.

2.1.2.3   The Congress should ensure that federal laws recognize the appropriate involvement of school psychologists in educational programs and that adequate federal funding is made available for the education, training, services, and continuing professional development of school psychologists in order to guarantee appropriate and effective services.

2.1.2.4   The Congress should create no laws which effectively prohibit the credentialed school psychologist from the ethical and legal practice of his/her profession in the public or private sector, or which would be in violation of these standards.

2.1.3   Regulations

2.1.3.1   All federal agencies should utilize the services of the federal educational agency school psychologist in developing and implementing regulations pursuant to all relevant federal laws.

2.1.3.2   All federal agencies should seek the advice and consultation of the National Association of School Psychologists prior to the adoption of regulations pursuant to any federal law which involves or should reasonably involve the profession of school psychology.

2.1.3.3   Federal agencies should promulgate regulations consistent with the principles set forth in these *Standards* and the NASP *Principles for Professional Ethics.*

2.2   State Level Administrative Agencies

2.2.1   **Organization.** Each state educational agency (SEA) should employ at least one full-time supervising school psychologist for each 500 (or fewer) school psychologists within the state. An equivalent ratio should be maintained if there are more than 500 school psychologists. It is recognized that this ratio may vary based upon administrative structures, available resources, and types of programs served, however the intention is to assign the individual(s) full-time (1FTE) to the supervision of school psychology. Appropriate objectives to be accomplished by the SEA school psychologist(s) include the following:

2.2.1.1   To provide professional leadership assistance to the SEA, local educational agencies, and the profession with regard to standards, policies, and procedures for school psychology program delivery.

2.2.1.2   To support the utilization, funding, education, training, and in-service education of school psychologists.

2.2.1.3   To participate in the administration of state and federal programs providing funding for school psychological services in intermediate and local educational agencies, and for the education and training of school psychologists.

2.2.1.4   To encourage and assist in evaluation, research, and dissemination activities to determine the effectiveness of school psychological education, training, and service programs; to determine needed changes; and to identify and communicate exemplary practices to training and service units.

2.2.1.5   To maintain communication with and assure the input of state school psychological associations into the policy making of the SEA.

2.2.1.6   To communicate with the federal education agency school psychologist to ensure recognition of state issues and to facilitate input into federal policy.

2.2.2   Laws

2.2.2.1   All state legislative bodies should ensure that the rights of all parents and children are protected by the creation and modification of laws which provide for the services of school psychologists. These services include, but are not limited to, consultation for individuals, groups, and systems, assessment, program planning/evaluation, research, and direct service. These services are available to all children, their families, and school personnel.

2.2.2.2   The state legislature should ensure that school psychological services are provided in a free and appropriate way to all children, their families, and school personnel in need of such services.

2.2.2.3   The state legislature should ensure that state laws recognize the appropriate involvement of school psychologists in educational programs.

2.2.2.4   The state legislature should ensure that adequate funding is made available for the education, training, services, and continuing professional development of school psychologists in order to guarantee appropriate and effective services.

2.2.2.5   The state legislature should ensure that state laws provide for the credentialing of school psychologists consistent with NASP standards.

2.2.2.6   The state legislature should create no laws which prohibit the school psychologist from the ethical and legal practice of his/her profession in the public or private sector, or that prevent the school psychologist from practicing in a manner consistent with these *Standards*.

2.2.2.7   The state legislature should ensure that there are sufficient numbers of adequately prepared and credentialed school psychologists to provide services consistent with these *Standards*. In most settings, this will require at least one full-time school psychologist for each 1,000 children served by the LA, with a maximum of four schools served by one school psychologist. It is recognized that this ratio may vary based upon the needs of children served, the type of program served, available resources, distance between schools, and other unique characteristics.

2.3.3   Regulations

2.2.3.1   All state agencies should utilize the services of the SEA school psychologist(s) in developing and implementing administrative rules pursuant to all relevant state laws, federal laws, and regulations.

2.2.3.2   All state agencies should seek the advice and consultation of the state school psychologists' professional association prior to the adoption of rules pursuant to any state law, federal law, or regulation which involves or should reasonably involve the profession of school psychology.

2.2.3.3   All state education agencies should utilize the services of the SEA school psychologist(s) and the school psychologists' professional association in the SEA review and approval of school psychology training programs.

2.2.3.4   All state education agencies should utilize the services of the SEA school psychologist(s) and the school psychologists' professional association in developing and implementing administrative rules for credentialing school psychologists. Such rules shall be consistent with NASP *Standards for the Credentialing of School Psychologists*.

2.2.3.5   State education agencies should promulgate regulations consistent with the principles set forth in the *Standards* and the NASP *Principles for Professional Ethics*.

3.0 Standards for Employing Agencies

The purpose of these standards is to provide employing agencies with specific guidance regarding the organization, policies, and practices needed to assure the provision of adequate school psychological services.

3.1. Comprehensive Continuum of Services

Employing agencies assure that school psychological services are provided in a coordinated, organized fashion, and are deployed in a manner which ensures the provision of a comprehensive continuum of services as outlined in Section 4.0 of these *Standards*. Such services are available to all students served by the agency and are available to an extent sufficient to meet the needs of the population served.

Breadth or availability of services should not be dictated by the funding source. (For example, some Districts have been known to limit services to special education students only because the school psychology budget came from special education sources. Similarly, other Districts provided assessment services only because funds were taken from State or Federal assessment grants. Both cases are considered to be mistakes in the attempt to provide comprehensive school psychological services to all students.)

3.2   Professional Evaluation, Supervision, and Development

3.2.1   Supervision. Employing agencies assure that an effective program of supervision and evaluation of school psychological services exists. School psychologists, in cooperation with their employing agencies, are responsible for the overall development, implementation, and professional supervision of school psychological service programs, and are responsible for articulating those programs to others in the employing agency and to the agency's constituent groups.

3.2.2   Supervisor(s). The school psychological services program is supervised by a designated school psychologist who meets the requirements for a supervising school psychologist (Section 1.2) and who demonstrates competencies needed for effective supervision.

3.2.3   Availability of Supervision. Supervision is available to all school psychologists to an extent sufficient to ensure the provision of effective and accountable services (see Section 4.6 for specific requirements). In most cases, one supervising school psychologist should be employed for every ten school psychologists to be supervised (an equivalent ratio should be maintained for part-time supervisors). It is recognized that this ratio may vary based upon the type of program served, staff needs, and other unique characteristics.

3.2.4   Intern Supervision. A credentialed school psychologist meeting the requirements of a supervising school psychologist, with at least one year of experience at the employing agency, supervises no more than two school psychology interns at any given time (consistent with the NASP *Standards for Training and Field Placement Programs in School Psychology*), unless the supervising school psychologist has no other assigned duties. In such cases, a maximum of six school psychology interns may be supervised at any given time.

3.2.5   Peer Review. After initiating independent practice status (see Section 4.5), school psychologists continue to receive appropriate supervision. The independent practitioner should also engage in peer review with other school psychologists. Peer review involves mutual assistance with self-examination of services and the development of plans to continue professional growth and development. Employing agencies assure that school psychologists are given appropriate time and support for peer review activities.

3.2.6   Accountability and Program Evaluation. Employing agencies assure that school psychologists develop a coordinated plan for accountability and evaluation of all services provided in order to maintain and improve the effectiveness of services. Such plans include specific, measurable objectives pertaining to the planned effects of services on all relevant elements of the system. Evaluation and revision of these plans occurs on a regular basis.

3.2.7   Continuing Professional Development. Employing agencies recognize that all school psychologists, not just those holding national certification, are obligated to continue their professional training and development through participation in a recognized Continuing Professional Development (CPD) program (see Section 4.6). Employing agencies provide release time and financial support for such activities. They recognize documented continuing professional development activities in the evaluation and advancement of school psychologists. Private practitioners who contract to provide services are responsible for their own CPD program, and these activities should also be encouraged by employing agencies.

3.3   Conditions for Effective Service Delivery

In order to assure that employment conditions enable school psychologists to provide effective services, employing agencies adopt policies and practices ensuring that Section 3.3.1 through 3.3.4 are met.

3.3.1.   School psychologists are not subjected to administrative constraints which prevent them from providing services in full accordance with these *Standards* and NASP *Principles for Professional Ethics*. When administrative policies conflict with these *Standards* or the NASP *Ethics*, the principles outlined in the *Standards* or *Ethics* take precedence in determining appropriate practices of the school psychologist.

3.3.2 School psychologists have appropriate input into the general policy making of the employing agency and the development of programs affecting the staff, students, and families they serve.

3.3.3 School psychologists have appropriate professional autonomy in determining the nature, extent, and duration of services they provide. Specific activities are defined within the profession, although school psychologists frequently collaborate and seek input from others in determining appropriate service delivery. Legal, ethical, and professional standards and guidelines are considered by the practitioner in making decisions regarding practice (see Section 4.4).

3.3.4 School psychologists have access to adequate clerical assistance, appropriate professional work materials, sufficient office and work space, and general working conditions that enhance the delivery of effective services. Included are test materials, access to private telephone and office, secretarial services, therapeutic aids, professional literature (books, journals), computers and related technology, and so forth.

3.4 Contractual Services

It is recognized that employing agencies may obtain school psychological services on a contractual basis in order to ensure the provision of adequate services to all children. However, each student within the educational system must be assured the full range of school psychological services necessary to maximize his/her success and adjustment in school. When an employing agency utilizes contractual services, the following standards are observed:

3.4.1. Contractual school psychological services encompass the same comprehensive continuum of services as that provided by regularly employed school psychologists. Overall, psychological services are not limited to any specific type of service and include opportunities for follow-up and continuing consultation appropriate to the needs of the student. Individual contracts for services may be limited as long as comprehensive services are provided overall.

3.4.2 Persons providing contractual psychological services are fully credentialed school psychologists as defined by these *Standards*. In specific limited instances, however, services by psychologists in other specialty areas (e.g., clinical, industrial/organizational) might be used to supplement school psychological services in a coordinated manner.

3.4.3 Contractual school psychological services are not to be utilized as a means to decrease the amount and quality of school psychological services provided by an employing agency. They may be used to augment programs but not to supplant them.

3.4.4 School psychologists providing contractual services are given appropriate access and information. They are familiar with the instructional resources of the employing agency to ensure that students they serve have the same opportunities as those served by regularly employed school psychologists.

3.4.5 Contractual school psychological services are provided in a manner which protects the due process rights of students and their parents as defined by state and federal laws and regulations.

3.4.6 Contracting for services is not to be used as a means to avoid legitimate employee rights, wages, or fringe benefits.

3.4.7 Psychologists providing contractual school psychological services provide those services in a manner consistent with these *Standards*, NASP *Principles for Professional Ethics*, and other relevant professional guidelines and standards.

3.4.8 Psychologists providing contractual school psychological services will encourage regular evaluation of the continued need for the service as well as the quality of the service.

3.5 Non-Biased Assessment and Program Planning

Employing agencies should adopt policies and practices in accordance with the following standards:

3.5.1 General Principles

3.5.1.1   School psychologists use assessment techniques to provide information which is helpful in maximizing student achievement, educational success, psychological adjustment, and behavioral adaptation.

3.5.1.2   School psychologists have autonomous decision-making responsibility (as defined in Section 4.4) to determine the type, nature, and extent of assessment techniques they use in student evaluation.

3.5.1.3   School psychologists have autonomy (as defined in Section 4.4) in determining the content and nature of reports.

3.5.1.4   Whenever possible, school psychologists use assessment techniques and instruments which have established validity and reliability for the purposes and populations for which the procedures are intended. In addition, certain clinical procedures and measures at the "research" stage of development may be used by practitioners trained in their use provided the reliability and validity of the procedures are reported and clearly distinguished from those techniques which meet standards.

3.5.1.5   School psychologists use, develop, and encourage assessment practices which increase the likelihood of the development of effective educational interventions and follow-up.

3.5.2   Professional Involvement

3.5.2.1   A multi-disciplinary team is involved in assessment, program decision-making, and evaluation. The team conducts periodic evaluations of its performance to ensure continued effectiveness.

3.5.2.2   The multi-disciplinary team includes a fully trained and certified school psychologist.

3.5.2.3   The school psychologist communicates a written minority position to all involved when in disagreement with the multi-disciplinary team position.

3.5.3   Non-Biased Assessment Techniques

3.5.3.1   Assessment procedures and program recommendations are chosen to maximize the student's opportunities to be successful in the general culture, while respecting the student's ethnic background.

3.5.3.2   Multifaceted assessment batteries are used which include a focus on the student's strengths.

3.5.3.3   Communications are held in the client's dominant spoken language or alternative communication system. All student information is interpreted in the context of the student's socio-cultural background and the setting in which she/he is functioning.

3.5.3.4   Assessment techniques (including computerized techniques) are used only by personnel professionally trained in their use and in a manner consistent with these *Standards*.

3.5.3.5   School psychologists promote the development of objective, valid, and reliable assessment techniques.

3.5.3.6   Interpretation of assessment results is based upon empirically validated research.

3.5.4   Parent/Student Involvement

3.5.4.1   Informed written consent of parent(s) and/or student (if the student has reached the age of majority) is obtained before assessment and special program implementation.

3.5.4.2   The parent(s) and/or student is fully informed of all essential information considered and its relevancy to decision-making.

3.5.4.3   The parent(s) and/or student is invited to participate in decision-making meetings.

3.5.4.4   The parent(s) and/or student is routinely notified that an advocate can participate in conferences focusing on assessment results and program recommendations.

3.5.4.5   A record of meetings regarding assessment results and program recommendations is available to all directly concerned.

3.5.5   Educational Programming and Follow-Through

3.5.5.1   School psychologists are involved in determining options and revisions of educational programs to ensure that they are adaptive to the needs of students.

3.5.5.2   The contributions of diverse cultural backgrounds should be emphasized in educational programs.

3.5.5.3   School psychologists follow-up on the efficacy of their recommendations.

3.5.5.4   Student needs are given priority in determining educational programs.

3.5.5.5   Specific educational prescriptions result from the assessment team's actions.

3.5.5.6   Where a clear determination of the student's needs does not result from initial assessment, a diagnostic intervention or teaching program is offered as part of additional assessment procedures.

3.5.5.7   Regular, systematic review of the student's program is conducted and includes program modifications as necessary.

3.6   School Psychological Records

3.6.1   The employing agency's policy on student records is consistent with state and federal rules and laws, and ensures the protection of the confidentiality of the student and his/her family. The policy specifies the types of data developed by the school psychologist which are classified as school or pupil records.

3.6.2.   Parents may inspect and review any personally identifiable data relating to their child which were collected, maintained, or used in his/her evaluation. Although test protocols are part of the student's record, school psychologists protect test security and observe copyright restrictions.

3.6.3   Access to psychological records is restricted to those permitted by law who have legitimate educational interest in the records.

3.6.4   School psychologists interpret school psychological records to non-psychologists who qualify for access.

3.6.5   School psychological records are only created and maintained when the information is necessary and relevant to legitimate educational program needs and when parents (or student if age of majority has been attained) have given their informed consent for the creation of such a record. This consent is based upon full knowledge of purposes for which information is sought, and the personnel who will have access to it. The school psychologist assumes responsibility for assuring the accuracy and relevancy of the information recorded.

3.6.6   School psychological records are systematically reviewed, and when necessary purged, in keeping with relevant federal and state laws in order to protect children from decisions based on incorrect, misleading, or out-of-date information.

4.0 Standards for the Delivery of Comprehensive School Psychological Services

The purpose of these standards is to ensure the delivery of comprehensive services by school psychologists.

4.1   Organization of School Psychological Services

4.1.1   School psychological services are planned, organized, directed, and reviewed by school psychologists.

4.1.2   School psychologists participate in determining the recipients and the type of school psychological services offered.

4.1.3   The goals and objectives of school psychological services are available in written form.

4.1.4   A written set of procedural guidelines for the delivery of school psychological services is followed and made available upon request.

4.1.5   A clearly stated referral system is in writing and is communicated to parents, staff members, students, and other referral agents.

4.1.6   The organization of school psychological services is in written form and includes lines of responsibility, supervisory, and administrative relationships.

4.1.7   Where two or more school psychologists are employed, a coordinated system of school psychological services is in effect within that unit.

4.1.8   Units providing school psychological services include sufficient professional and support personnel to achieve their goals and objectives.

4.2   Relationship to Other Units and Professionals

4.2.1   The school psychological services unit is responsive to the needs of the population that it serves. Psychological services are periodically and systematically reviewed to ensure their conformity with the needs of the population served.

4.2.2   School psychologists establish and maintain relationships with other professionals (e.g., pediatricians, bilingual specialists, audiologists) who provide services to children and families. They collaborate with these professionals in prevention, assessment, and intervention efforts as necessary. They also cooperate with advocates representing children and their families.

4.2.3   Providers of school psychological services maintain a cooperative relationship with colleagues and co-workers in the best mutual interests of clients, in a manner consistent with the goals of the employing agency. Conflicts should be resolved in a professional manner.

4.2.4   School psychologists develop plans for the delivery of services in accordance with best professional practices.

4.2.5   School psychologists employed within a school setting help coordinate the services of mental health providers from other agencies (such as community mental health centers, child guidance clinics, or private practitioners) to ensure a continuum of services.

4.2.6   School psychologists are knowledgeable about community agencies and resources. They provide liaison and consulting services to the community and agencies regarding psychological, mental health, and educational issues.

    4.2.6.1   School psychologists communicate as needed with state and community agencies and professionals (e.g., child guidance clinics, community mental health centers, private practitioners) regarding services for children, families, and school personnel. They refer clients to these agencies and professionals as appropriate.

    4.2.6.2   School psychologists are informed of and have the opportunity to participate in community agency staffings of cases involving their clients.

    4.2.6.3   Community agency personnel are invited to participate in school system conferences concerning their clients (with written parental permission).

4.3   Comprehensive School Psychological Services Delivery

School psychologists provide a range of services to their clients. These consist of direct and indirect services which require involvement with the entire educational system: (a) the students, teachers, administrators, and other school personnel; (b) the families, surrogate caretakers, and other community and regional agencies, and resources which support the educational process; (c) the organizational, physical, temporal, and curricular variables which play major roles within the system; and (d) a variety of other factors which may be important on an individual basis.

The intent of these services is to promote mental health and facilitate learning. Comprehensive school psychological services are comprised of diverse activities. These activities complement one another and therefore are most accurately viewed as being integrated and coordinated rather than discrete services. However, for descriptive purposes, they will be listed and described separately. The following are the services that comprise the delivery system:

4.3.1   **Consultation:** the act of meeting to discuss, decide, or plan, typically regarding primary prevention or the reasons for an identified problem, and the resulting intervention(s). The school psychologist usually does not personally provide the intervention, but guides those who do. (See **direct service** for contrast.)

4.3.1.1 School psychologists consult and collaborate with parents, school, and outside personnel regarding mental health, behavioral, and educational concerns.

4.3.1.2 School psychologists design and develop procedures for preventing disorders, promoting mental health and learning, and improving educational systems.

4.3.1.3 School psychologists provide skill enhancement activities (such as inservice training, organizational development, parent counseling, program planning and evaluation, vocational development, and parent education programs) to school personnel, parents, and others in the community, regarding issues of human learning, development, and behavior.

4.3.1.4 School psychologists facilitate the delivery of services by assisting those who play major roles in the educational system (i.e., parents, school personnel, community agencies).

4.3.2 Psychological and Psychoeducational Assessment: the process of obtaining data about human functioning according to the current practices of the fields of psychology and education for the purpose of identifying critical factors and evaluating their importance for answering referral questions.

4.3.2.1 School psychologists conduct multifactored psychological and psychoeducational assessments of children and youth as appropriate.

4.3.2.2 Psychological and psychoeducational assessments include evaluation, as appropriate, of the areas of: personality, emotional status, social skills and adjustment, intelligence and cognitive functioning, scholastic aptitude, adaptive behavior, language and communication skills, academic knowledge and achievement, sensory and perceptual-motor functioning, educational setting, family/environmental-cultural influences, career and vocational development, aptitude, and interests.

4.3.2.3 School psychologists utilize a variety of instruments, procedures, and techniques. Interviews, observations, and behavioral evaluations are included in these procedures.

4.3.2.4 When conducting psychological and psychoeducational assessments, school psychologists have explicit regard for the context and setting in which their assessments take place and will be used.

4.3.2.5 School psychologists adhere to the NASP resolutions regarding non-biased assessment and programming for all students (see Section 3.5.3). They also are familiar with and consider the *Standards for Educational and Psychological Tests* (developed by APA. AERA, and NCME) and other related publications in the use of assessment techniques.

4.3.3 Direct Service: techniques applied in a face-to-face situation designed to enhance the mental health, behavior, personality, social competency, academic or educational status of the student/client. (Contrast with **consultation**.)

4.3.3.1 School psychologists provide direct service to facilitate the functioning of individuals, groups, and/or organizations.

4.3.3.2 School psychologists design direct service programs to enhance cognitive, affective, social, and vocational development.

4.3.3.3 School psychologists develop collaborative relationships with their clients and involve them in the assessment, direct service, and program evaluation procedures.

4.3.4 Supervision: the process of overseeing and managing the activities of a school psychologist for the purpose of quality assurance, assistance with difficult assignments, and the improvement of performance.

4.3.4.1 School psychologists provide and/or engage in supervision, peer review, and continuing professional development as specified in Section 3.2 and 4.6.

4.3.5   Research: the process of careful, systematic investigation to discover or establish facts.

4.3.5.1   School psychologists design, conduct, report, and utilize the results of research of a psychological and educational nature. All research conducted is in accordance with relevant ethical guidelines of the profession (e.g., APA *Ethical Principles in the Conduct of Research with Human Participants)*, with particular concern for obtaining informed consent, notifying subjects of the expected length of participation, and protecting subjects from breach of confidentiality, coercion, harm, or danger. Applied and/or basic research should be pursued, focusing on:

(a)   psychological functioning of human beings;

(b)   Psychoeducational assessment tools and procedures;

(c)   Educational programs and techniques applied to individual cases and groups of various sizes;

(d)   Educational processes;

(e)   Social system interactions and organizational factors associated with school communities; and

(f)   Psychological treatments and techniques applied to individual cases or groups.

4.3.5.2   School psychologists' involvement in research can range from support or advisory services to having direct responsibility for one or more major components of a research project. These components may include planning, data collection, data analyzing, disseminating, and translating research into practical applications within the school community.

4.3.6   Program Planning and Evaluation: the process of designing and judging the effectiveness of educational structures at all levels.

4.3.6.1   School psychologists provide program planning and evaluation services to assist in decision-making activities.

4.3.6.2   School psychologists serve on committees responsible for developing and planning educational and educationally-related activities.

4.4   Autonomous Functioning

School psychologists have professional autonomy in determining the nature, scope, and extent of their specific services. These activities are defined within the profession, although school psychologists frequently collaborate with and seek input from others in determining appropriate services delivery. Legal, ethical, and professional standards and guidelines are considered by the practitioner in making decisions regarding practice. All practice is restricted to those areas in which the school psychologist has received formal training and supervised experience.

4.4.1   Professional Responsibility and Best Practices. Professional autonomy is associated with professional responsibility. The ultimate responsibility for providing appropriate comprehensive school psychological services rests with the individual practitioner.

While being cognizant of the fact that there often are not explicit guidelines to follow in providing comprehensive school psychological services, the individual practitioner has a responsibility to adhere to the best available and most appropriate standards of practice. There is no substitute for sensitive, sound, professional judgment in the determination of what constitutes best practice. Active involvement in supervision and other continuing professional development activities will assist the practitioner in adhering to best professional practices.

4.5   Independent Practice

A credentialed school psychologist who has completed a school psychology training program which meets the criteria specified in the NASP *Standards for Training and Field Placement Programs in School Psychology* and three years of satisfactory, properly supervised experience is considered qualified for unsupervised practice with peer review, regardless of work setting. (NOTE: "independent practice" as used in this paragraph refers to the character of supervision needed. Contrast this with the licensure rules various states have for "private practice.")

4.6 Continuing Professional Development

The practice of school psychology has and will continue to undergo significant changes as new knowledge and technological advances are introduced. The development of new intervention techniques, assessment procedures, computerized assistance, and so forth, will require that practitioners keep abreast of these innovations as well as obtain appropriate professional education and training in these areas. All school psychologists actively participate and engage in activities designed to continue, enhance, and upgrade their professional training and skills and to help ensure quality service provision. These efforts are documented by participation in the NASP or other formal Continuing Professional Development (CPD) programs, although they are not limited to such activities. Memberships in professional organizations, reading of professional journals and books, discussions of professional issues with colleagues, and so forth, are also an integral component of a school psychologist's overall CPD activities.

4.6.1 Participation in CPD activities and the maintenance of high professional standards and practice are continuing obligations of the school psychologist. These obligations are assumed when one initially engages in the practice of school psychology and should be required for continued credentialing.

4.6.2 School psychologists receive supervision by a supervising school psychologist for the first three years of full-time employment (or the equivalent) as a school psychologist. The supervisor shares professional responsibility and accountability for the services provided. While the level and extent of supervision may vary, the supervisor maintains a sufficiently close relationship to meet this standard. Individual face-to-face supervision is engaged in for a minimum of one hour per week or the equivalent (e.g., two hours bi-weekly). Standards for intern supervision are contained in the NASP *Standards for Training and Field Placement Programs in School Psychology.*

4.6.3 After completion of the first three years of supervision, all school psychologists continue to engage in supervision and/or peer review on a regular basis, and further their professional development by actively participating in CPD activities. The level and extent of these activities may vary depending on the needs, interests, and goals of the school psychologist, with more comprehensive service delivery requiring more extensive related professional exchanges. At a minimum, however, these activities are at the level required for successful participation in an appropriate CPD program.

4.6.4 School psychologists, who after three years no longer have required supervision, engage in peer review activities. These may include discussion of cases and professional issues designed to assist with problem solving, decision-making, and appropriate practice.

4.6.5 School psychologists readily seek additional assistance from supervisors, peers, or colleagues with particularly complex or difficult cases, and/or when expanding their services into new areas or those in which they infrequently practice (e.g., low incidence assessment).

4.6.6 Nationally Certified School Psychologists engage in continuing professional development as a requirement of certificate renewal.

4.7 Accountability

4.7.1 School psychologists perform their duties in an accountable manner by keeping records of these efforts, evaluating their effectiveness, and modifying their practices and/or expanding their services as needed.

4.7.2 School psychologists devise systems of accountability and outcome evaluation which aid in documenting the effectiveness of intervention efforts and other services they provide.

4.7.3 Within their service delivery plan, school psychologists include a regular evaluation of their progress in achieving goals. This evaluation should include consideration of the cost effectiveness of school psychological services in terms of time, money, and resources, as well as the availability of professional and support personnel. Evaluation of the school psychological delivery system is conducted internally, and when possible, externally as well (e.g., through state educational agency review, peer review). This evaluation includes an assessment of effectiveness, efficiency, continuity, availability, and adequacy of services.

4.7.4   School psychologists are accountable for their services. They should make information available about their services, and provide consumers with the opportunity to participate in decision-making concerning such issues as initiation, termination, continuation, modification, and evaluation of their services. Rights of the consumer should be taken into account when performing these activities.

4.8 Private Practice

4.8.1   School psychologists practicing in the private sector provide comprehensive services and adhere to the same standards and guidelines as those providing services in the public sector.

4.8.2   School psychologists document that they have formal training, supervised experience, licensure and/or certification, and demonstrated competence, in any areas of service they intend to deliver to clients within the private sector. They also have a responsibility to actively engage in CPD activities.

4.8.3   School psychologists in private practice adhere to the NASP *Principles for Professional Ethics*, and practice only within their area of competence. If the services needed by clients fall outside the school psychologist's area of competence, they are referred elsewhere for assistance.

4.8.4   It is the responsibility of the school psychologist engaging in private practice to inform the client that school psychological services are available without charge from the client's local school district.

4.8.5   School psychologists do not provide services on a private basis to students who attend the school(s) to which the school psychologist is assigned, or would normally be expected to serve. This includes students who attend non-public schools served by the school psychologist.

4.8.6   School psychologists offering school psychological services in the private sector ensure that, prior to the commencement of treatment/services, the client fully understands any and all fees associated with the services, and any potential financial assistance that may be available (i.e., third-party reimbursement).

4.8.7   Parents must be informed by the school psychologist that if a private school psychological evaluation is to be completed, this evaluation constitutes only one portion of a multi-disciplinary team evaluation. Private services must be equally comprehensive to those described in Section 4.3

4.8.8   School psychologists in private practice provide and maintain written records in a manner consistent with Section 3.6.

4.9 Professional Ethics and Guidelines

Each school psychologist practices in full accordance with the NASP *Principles for Professional Ethics*, and these *Standards*.

5.0 Standards for School Psychology Training Programs

Each school psychology training program should meet the criteria specified in the NASP *Standards for Training and Field Placement Programs in School Psychology*.

Standards for Training and Field Placement Programs in School Psychology (1994)

The National Association of School Psychologists (NASP) is committed to the development of comprehensive and effective psychological services for all children and youth. The NASP *Standards for Training and Field Placement Programs in School Psychology* contribute to the development of services through the identification of critical content and training experiences needed by students preparing for careers in school psychology. These *Standards* serve to guide the design of school psychology graduate education, as a basis for program evaluation, and as the foundation for the recognition of strong programs through the program approval process.

I. VALUES AS A PROGRAM FOUNDATION

As a specialty within the profession of psychology, school psychology is founded in respect for the dignity and worth of each individual and in a commitment to further the understanding of human behavior for the purpose of promoting human welfare. The values that serve as a foundation for this field should also provide a foundation for graduate education and professional practice in school psychology.

   1.1   Standard: A commitment to understanding and responsiveness to human diversity is articulated and practiced throughout all aspects of the program, including admissions, faculty, coursework, practica, and internship experiences. Human diversity is recognized as a strength which is valued and respected. The program promotes recognition and valuing of the uniqueness of each individual, an affirmation of the inherent worth of all human beings, and a commitment to the enhancement of human development and capability through the application of school psychological services.

   1.2   Standard: The program fosters a commitment to enhancing the strengths of critical socialization institutions such as families and schools through the delivery of school psychological services that are sensitive to the unique needs of systems and organizations, as well as effective in promoting mental health and the acquisition of competencies.

II. KNOWLEDGE BASE, TRAINING PHILOSOPHY, GOALS & OBJECTIVES

The essential knowledge base for the professional practice of school psychology encompasses psychological foundations, educational foundations, interventions and problem solving, statistics and research methodologies, and professional school psychology. That knowledge base should be delivered within a context of commonly held and publicly known values, and clearly articulated training philosophy, goals, and objectives for the preparation of future school psychologists. The same knowledge base standards apply to both specialist-level and doctoral programs. However, there shall be a clear distinction between the two levels. Additionally, doctoral programs shall ensure greater breadth or depth in each of the areas.

   2.1   Standard: An integrated and sequential program of study and supervised practice shall be provided to all trainees that reflect the values and training philosophy of the program, ensuring the preparation of all trainees in accordance with clearly articulated goals and objectives. There shall be a direct and obvious relationship between the components of the curriculum and the goals and objectives of the program.

NOTE: The specification of content areas in Standards 2.2–2.8 does not necessarily require that an entire graduate-level course be devoted to each of the areas. The criterion for program approval purposes will be "substantive" preparation in each of the areas. Substantive preparation, depending on the area and the organization of the program, may mean an entire course, portions of one or more courses, didactic components of practica or internship, or practica or internship experiences.

2.2 Standard: Psychological Foundations

The program employs a systematic process that ensures that all students have a foundation in the knowledge base for the discipline of psychology. That knowledge base shall include:

Biological Bases of Behavior (e.g., biological bases of development, neuropsychology, physiological psychology, psychopharmacology)

Human Learning

Social and Cultural Bases of Behavior (e.g., cross-cultural studies, social development, social and cultural diversity, social psychology)

Child and Adolescent Development

Individual Differences (e.g., human exceptionalities, developmental psychopathology)

2.3 Standard: Educational Foundations

The program employs a systematic process that ensures that all students have a foundation in the knowledge base for education. That knowledge base shall include:

Instructional Design

Organizational and Operation of Schools (including, but not limited to, education of exceptional learners, school and community-based resources, alternative service delivery systems)

2.4 Standard: Interventions/Problem Solving

The Program employs a systematic process that ensures that all students possess the knowledge and professional expertise to collaborate with families and school- and community-based professionals in designing, implementing, and evaluating interventions that effectively respond to the educational and mental health needs of children and youth. Areas of knowledge and practice shall include:

Assessment (diverse models and methods linked to direct and indirect interventions)

Direct Interventions, both Individual and Group (including counseling and behavior management)

Indirect Interventions (including consultation, systems and organizational change)

2.5 Standard: Statistics and Research Methodologies

The program employs a systematic process that ensures that all students are competent consumers of research and new knowledge, and are able to use diverse methodologies (e.g., ethnographic, single subject designs, quantitative methods) to evaluate professional practices (e.g., interventions) and/or programs. That knowledge base shall include:

Research and Evaluation Methods
Statistics
Measurement

2.6 Standard: Professional School Psychology

The Program employs a systematic process that ensures that all students have a knowledge base specific to the professional specialty of school psychology. That knowledge base shall include:

History and Foundations of School Psychology
Legal and Ethical Issues
Professional Issues and Standards
Alternative Models for the Delivery of School Psychological Services
Emergent Technologies
Roles and Functions of the School Psychologist

III. PRACTICA

Practica are an essential component in the professional preparation of school psychologists. They provide opportunities for students to practice, under supervision, the application of knowledge and specific skills in the resolution of individual, group, and system-level problems. Practica are consistent with the values and training model of the program. Laboratory or field-based practica are used to evaluate a trainee's mastery of distinct skills as one measure of preparedness to enter the internship.

3.0 Standard: The program provides a sequence of closely supervised practica experiences through which students practice and are evaluated regarding their mastery of distinct skills consistent with the goals and objectives of the program. Practica include, but are not necessarily limited to, orientation to the educational process, assessment for intervention, direct intervention methods including counseling and behavior management, and indirect intervention methods including consultation.

Practica reflect the following characteristics:

a. Practica experiences shall include: (1) orientation to the educational process; (2) assessment for intervention; (3) direct intervention (including counseling and behavior management); and (4) indirect intervention (including consultation). Student performance shall be systematically evaluated in each area.

b. Practica experiences shall be distinct from and occur prior to the internship.

c. Practica occur at time(s), are in settings, and are of sufficient length to be appropriate to the specific training objectives of the program.

d. There is a direct and obvious relationship between practica experiences and the objectives for which the practica are intended.

e. Practica experiences occur under conditions of supervision appropriate to the specific training objectives of the program.

f. Practica experiences are provided appropriate recognition through the awarding of academic credit.

g. Practica experiences occur with university involvement appropriate to the specific training objectives of the program.

h. The quality of practica experiences are systematically evaluated in a manner consistent with the specific training objectives of the program.

i. Practica experiences are conducted in accordance with current legal-ethical standards for the profession.

IV. INTERNSHIP

The internship is the culminating experience in school psychology graduate preparation. It is a comprehensive experience through which the student is required to integrate the knowledge base and applied skills of school psychology in promoting positive educational and mental health practices and in resolving individual, group, and system-level problems. The internship affords the student the opportunity to demonstrate knowledge and skills acquired through coursework and practica, as well as to acquire new knowledge and skills. Internship settings shall be appropriate for the goals and objectives of the training program; all students shall complete at least one-half of their internship in a school setting. (See Standard 6.10).

4.0 Standard: A comprehensive internship experience is provided through which all students are required to demonstrate, under supervision, their ability to integrate knowledge and skills in providing a broad range of school psychological services. The internship is conceptualized as the culminating component in school psychology graduate education. It affords the student the opportunity to work with diverse client populations, a range of problems, and different types of human service programs, using varied intervention methodologies.

The internship experience reflects the following characteristics:

a. The internship experience is provided at or near the end of the formal training period.

b. The internship experience occurs on a full-time basis over a period of one academic year, or on a half-time basis over a period of two consecutive academic years.

c. The internship experience is designed according to a written plan that provides the student opportunities to gain experience in the delivery of a broad range of school psychological services. Services include, but are not limited to assessment for intervention, counseling, behavior management, and consultation.

d. The internship experience occurs in a setting appropriate to the specific training objectives of the program.

e. The internship experience is provided appropriate recognition through the awarding of academic credit.

f. The internship experience occurs under conditions of appropriate supervision. Field-based internship supervisors hold a valid credential as a school psychologist for that portion of the internship that is in a school setting. That portion of the internship which appropriately may be in a non-school setting requires supervision by an appropriately credentialed psychologist.

g. Field-based internship supervisors are responsible for no more than two interns at any given time. University internship supervisors are responsible for no more than twelve interns at any given time.

h Field-based internship supervisors provide, on average, at least two hours per week of direct supervision for each intern.

i. The internship is based on a positive working relationship and represents a collaborative effort between the university program and field-based supervisors to provide an effective learning experience for the student. University internship supervisors provide at least one on-site contact per semester with each intern and supervisor.

j. The internship placement agency provides appropriate support for the internship experience including: (a) a written contractual agreement specifying the period of appointment and the terms of compensation, (b) a schedule of appointment consistent with that of agency school psychologists (e.g., calendar, participation in in-service meetings, etc.), (c) provision for participation in continuing professional development activities, (d) expense reimbursement consistent with policies pertaining to agency school psychologists, (e) an appropriate work environment including adequate supplies, materials, secretarial services, and office space, (f) release time for internship supervisors, and (g) a commitment to the internship as a training experience.

k. The quality of the internship experience is systematically evaluated in a manner consistent with the specific training objectives of the program.

l. The internship experience is conducted in a manner consistent with the current legal-ethical standards of the profession.

V. PERFORMANCE-BASED PROGRAM ACCOUNTABILITY

Systematic evaluation of coursework, practica, internship experiences, faculty, supervisors, and institutional resources is essential to monitoring and improving program quality. It is essential that programs also demonstrate accountability with regard to the overall effectiveness of the total curriculum. That accountability is demonstrated through the ability of the program's graduates to provide school psychological services that effectively respond to the educational and mental health needs of children and youth, their families, and the educational and mental health agencies that serve them.

5.1 Standard: Systematic evaluation procedures are used to ensure the integrity and quality of the program. Different sources of information (e.g., tests of knowledge, observations of skills, instructional evaluation, performance portfolios, perceptions of students or supervisors), are used, as appropriate, to evaluate components of the program.

5.2 Standard: The program employs a systematic process to ensure that all students, prior to the conclusion of the internship experience, are able to integrate domains of knowledge and applied professional skills in delivering a comprehensive range of services that result in measurable positive changes regarding the educational and mental health needs of children and youth.

5.3 Standard: The program systematically collects, analyzes, and interprets process and performance evaluation data; results are used to improve the program.

VI. PROGRAM LEVEL AND STRUCTURAL REQUIREMENTS

Standards 6.1–6.5 Apply to Both Doctoral and Specialist-Level Programs

6.1   Standard: The program shall limit the number of credit hours acquired through courses, seminars, and other learning experiences not open exclusively to graduate students to no more than one-third of the student's program.

6.2   Standard: Program requirements exclude credit for undergraduate study, study which is remedial, or study which is designed to remove deficiencies in meeting requirements for program admission.

6.3   Standard: A full-time continuous residency or an alternate planned experience is required for all students. Programs allowing alternate planned experiences as a substitute for full-time residency must demonstrate how those experiences are equivalent to experiences commonly associated with residency requirements.

6.4   Standard: The program shall provide an active continuing professional development program for practicing school psychologists.

6.5   Standard: The program shall meet established approval standards for the appropriate state credentialing body(ies).

Requirements for Specialist-Level Programs (6.6–6.7)

6.6   Standard: Specialist-level programs shall consist of a minimum of three years of full-time study or the equivalent at the graduate level. The program shall include at least 60 graduate semester hours or the equivalent, at least 54 hours of which are exclusive of credit for the supervised internship experience. Institutional documentation of program completion shall be provided.

6.7   Standard: Specialist-level programs shall include at least one academic year of supervised internship experience, consisting of a minimum of 1200 clock hours, at least one-half of which must be in a school setting.

Requirements for Doctoral Programs (6.8–6.10)

6.8   Standard: Doctoral programs shall provide greater breadth and depth in knowledge domains and applied competencies. NOTE: Doctoral programs are encouraged to provide opportunities for doctoral study for practicing school psychologists and to allow credit for prior training to the greatest extent possible.

6.9   Standard: Doctoral programs shall consist of a minimum of four years of full-time study or the equivalent at the graduate level. The program shall include a minimum of 90 graduate semester hours or the equivalent, at least 78 of which are exclusive of credit for the predoctoral supervised internship experience and any terminal doctoral project (e.g., dissertation) and shall culminate in institutional documentation.

6.10 Standard: Doctoral programs shall include at least one academic year of predoctoral supervised internship experience, consisting of a minimum of 1500 clock hours, at least one-half of which must be in a school setting.

NOTE: Doctoral students who have met the school-based internship requirement through a specialist-level internship or equivalent experience may complete the predoctoral internship in a non-school setting. Program policy shall specifically define equivalent experiences and explain their acceptance with regard to doctoral internship requirements. Demonstration of policy implementation in practice also shall be provided.

Standards for the Credentialing of School Psychologists (1994)

Credentialing is the process which authorizes the use of the title School Psychologist, or related titles, by those professionals meeting accepted standards of training and experience who seek to provide school psychological services. The purpose of this document is to provide guidelines to state and national bodies for the establishment of, and procedural processes involved in, implementing credentialing standards. These guidelines were developed and approved by the National Association of School Psychologists (NASP) pursuant to its mission to further the mental health and educational development of children and youth and to advance the standards of the profession of school psychology.

The National School Psychology Certification System (NSPCS) was created by NASP to establish a nationally recognized standard for credentialing school psychologists. The title to be used by persons accepted into the NSPCS is Nationally Certified School Psychologist, or NCSP. Among the purposes of this national credentialing system are to promote uniform credentialing standards across states, agencies, and training institutions, and to facilitate credentialing of school psychologists across states through the use of reciprocity or equivalence. The NASP *Standards for the Credentialing of School Psychologists* are used by the NSPCS and are considered to be appropriate for states to use in executing their authority in credentialing school psychologists.

CREDENTIALING STRUCTURE

1. Legal Basis for Credentialing

   1.1 Credentialing is the process whereby a state authorizes the provision of school psychological services and the use of the title School Psychologist (or related titles such as School Psychology Specialist) by professionals meeting acceptable standards of training and experience. The basis of a state's credentialing authority is found in its statutory laws, whereby all providers of school psychological services and all users of the title School Psychologist must hold a current credential, and legal sanctions and sanctioning procedures are provided for violators.

2. Credentialing Body

   2.1 The state legislature shall empower one or more bodies to administer the credentialing (certification and/or licensure) process. Administrative codes and regulations adopted by such bodies shall comply with these *Standards for the Credentialing of School Psychologists*, and shall carry the weight of law.

3. Nature of the Credential

   3.1 The credential shall be issued in writing and expressly authorize both the practice of school psychology and the exclusive use of the title School Psychologist in all settings, public and private.

   3.2 The credential shall allow for the practice of school psychology as defined by NASP's *Standards for the Provision of School Psychological Services* (1992) in public and private settings (e.g., school, educational, mental health-related, or university-based child study clinics).

   3.3 Where a state empowers more than one body to issue more than one type of credential, such as for the separate regulation of school psychological services in the public schools and in private practice, the lowest entry levels of all such credentials shall conform to these standards.

CREDENTIALING REQUIREMENTS

4. Criteria for Credential

   4.1 The minimum requirement for credentialing shall be a sixth year/specialist program, with a 60 graduate semester hour minimum, consisting of coursework, practica, internship, and an appropriate graduate degree from an accredited institution of higher learning. Criteria for *each area shall be consistent with* NASP's *Standards for Training and Field Placement Programs in School Psychology* (1994).

4.2 The credentialing criteria shall require that competency be demonstrated in three areas: professional work characteristics, knowledge base, and applied professional practice. Each area is listed below and detailed in NASP's *Standards for Training and Field Placement Programs in School Psychology* (1994).

4.3 Professional Work Characteristics

The applicant's professional work characteristics shall be evaluated and verified by the applicant's school psychology training program through information collected during courses, practica, internship, and other appropriate means. Professional work characteristics shall include:

1. Communication Skills
2. Effective Interpersonal Relations
3. Ethical Responsibility
4. Flexibility
5. Initiative and Dependability
6. Personal Stability
7. Respect for Human Diversity

4.4 Knowledge Base

The applicant shall complete an integrated and sequential program of study that is explicitly designed to develop knowledge and competencies in the domains of psychological foundations, educational foundations, intervention and problem-solving, statistics and research methodologies, and professional school psychology.

Psychological Foundations

The applicant for the credential has a foundation in the knowledge base for the discipline of psychology, including:

Biological Bases of Behavior (e.g., biological bases of development, neuropsychology, psychopharmacology, physiological psychology)

Human Learning

Social And Cultural Bases of Behavior (e.g., social development, social and cultural-diversity, social psychology, cross-cultural studies)

Child and Adolescent Development

Individual Differences (including human exceptionalities and developmental psychopathology)

Educational Foundations

The applicant for the credential has a foundation in the knowledge base for education, including:

Instructional Design

Organization and Operation of Schools (including, but not limited to, education of exceptional learners, school- and community-based resources, alternative service delivery systems)

Intervention/Problem-Solving

The applicant for the credential has demonstrated knowledge and professional expertise to collaborate with families, schools, and community-based professionals in designing, implementing, and evaluating interventions that effectively respond to the educational and mental health needs of children and youth.

Assessment (diverse models and methods linked to direct and indirect interventions)

Direct Interventions (individual and group, including counseling and behavior management)

Indirect Interventions (including consultation, systems, and organizational change)

Statistics and Research Methodologies

The applicant for the credential is a competent consumer of research and new knowledge, and is able to use diverse methodologies (e.g., ethnographic, single-subject designs, quantitative methods) to evaluate professional practices (e.g., interventions) and/or programs.

Research and Evaluation Methods

Statistics

Measurement

Professional School Psychology

The applicant for the credential has a knowledge base specific to the professional specialty of school psychology and is able to demonstrate the application of that knowledge base to professional practice, including:

History and Foundations of School Psychology

Legal and Ethical Issues

Professional Issues and Standards

Alternative Models for Delivery of School Psychological Services

Emergent Technologies

Roles and Functions

4.5   Applied Professional Practice

The applicant shall provide written evidence of his/her ability to perform competently as a school psychologist. Such evidence shall consist minimally of successful completion and documentation of practicum experience and internship consistent with criteria outlined in NASP's *Standards for Training and Field Placement Programs in School Psychology* (1994).

A.   The practica shall consist of a sequence of supervised experiences that occur prior to internship, are conducted in laboratory or field-based settings, and provide for application of knowledge and mastery of distinct skills.

B.   The internship experience shall consist of a full-time experience over one year, or half-time over two years, with a minimum of 1200 clock hours, at least one-half of which must be in a school setting. Other acceptable internship experiences include private, state-approved educational programs, or other appropriate mental health-related programs or settings for the education of children and youth.

C.   Other practicum and internship criteria are outlined in NASP's *Standards for Training and Field Placement Programs in School Psychology* (1994).

IMPLEMENTATION OF CREDENTIALING PROCEDURES

Only graduates from NASP approved training programs, or programs consistent with NASP training standards, shall be eligible for credentialing. A complete listing of NASP approved programs, *Approved Programs in School Psychology*, is published annually. Each approved program shall be responsible for assessing a candidate's competency in the areas of professional work characteristics, knowledge base, and applied professional practice. The responsibility for the final determination of minimum professional competencies in all credentialing areas, however, rests with the credentialing body. All assessment methods by both the training program and the cre-

dentialing body shall rely on the most objective, quantifiable, and accountable procedures available.

5.   Type of Credential - State and National

5.1   State Credential

The state credential shall be granted to individuals who meet the requirements described in Standard 4, including an appropriate graduate degree, professional work characteristics, knowledge base, and applied professional practice.

Upon initial granting of the credential, the individual shall arrange supervision and mentoring to assure that entry level qualifications are translated into ongoing competency in the provision of school psychological services. Supervision shall consist of a minimum of one face-to-face contact hour per week or two consecutive face-to-face contact hours once every two weeks for the initial academic year of full time practice, or the equivalent. Supervision and mentoring shall be provided by a school psychologist with a minimum of three years of experience. For any portion of the experience which is accumulated in a non-school setting, supervision and mentoring shall be provided by a psychologist or school psychologist appropriately credentialed for practice in that setting.

Subsequent to the completion of the supervision requirement, an individual holding the credential shall participate in an organized program of continuing professional development.

Upon completion of the initial year of post-degree supervision, the credential shall allow psychologists to have professional autonomy in determining the nature, scope, and extent of their specific services in all settings, public and private. These services shall be consistent with the NASP definitions of school psychological services and shall be delivered within the bounds of the school psychologist's training, supervised experience, and demonstrated expertise as specified in NASP's *Standards for the Provision of School Psychological Services* (1992) and *Principles for Professional Ethics* (1992).

Individual states may choose to grant a continuing credential to persons who have met the criteria for supervision and continuing professional development, and have a minimum of three years of experience.

5.2   Nationally Certified School Psychologist

The credential, Nationally Certified School Psychologist (NCSP), is granted to persons who have successfully met national training standards by:

A. Completion of a sixth year/specialist level program or higher in school psychology, with a 60 graduate semester hour minimum, consisting of coursework, practica, internship, and an appropriate graduate degree from an accredited institution of higher education.

B. Successful completion of a 1,200 clock hour supervised internship in school psychology, at least one-half of which must be in a school setting.

C. Achieving a passing score on the National School Psychology Examination administered by the Educational Testing Service (ETS).

Persons who hold the credential Nationally Certified School Psychologist (NCSP) meet the criteria for an initial state credential. For renewal, all persons holding the NCSP must complete at least 75 contact hours of continuing professional development activities within a three year period.

6. Credential Renewal/Continuing Education

   6.1 State Credential

   The credential shall be issued for a period of three years. *Initial renewal* of the state credential shall be contingent upon the applicant providing verified evidence of one year of supervision as described in Standard 5.1 and continuing professional development activities. *Subsequent renewals* shall be granted to applicants meeting the following criteria:

   A. Evidence of public, private, or university-based practice for a minimum of one academic year of full-time equivalent (F.T.E.) experience during the previous three years.

   B. Evidence of continuing professional development for a minimum of 75 clock hours in the previous three year period during which the credential was in effect.

7. Withdrawal/Termination of the Credential

   7.1 The credentialing body has the right to cancel, revoke, suspend, or refuse to renew the credential of any school psychologist, or to reprimand any school psychologist, upon proof that the school psychologist has engaged in unprofessional conduct as defined by NASP's *Principles for Professional Ethics* (1992) or *Standards for the Provision of School Psychological Services* (1992). Such action must be based on a formal finding of guilt by the appropriate adjudicating body after following a documented procedure ensuring that the due process rights of all parties involved have been fully observed.

8. New Application for Credentialing

   8.1 All school psychology trainees completing an approved program on or after January 1, 1998 and all other new applicants, shall be trained and credentialed in accordance with these standards. All practitioners currently credentialed shall be recredentialed in an appropriate state or national renewal cycle.

APPENDIX A
Definition of Terms Included in Standards for the Credentialing of School Psychologists

STANDARD 3.2:

NASP *Standards for the Provision of School Psychological Services* (1992): The current standards document from the National Association of School Psychologists (NASP) describing the delivery of appropriate and comprehensive school psychological services for administrative and employing agencies.

Public Setting: Any setting (e.g., school, educational, mental health-related, or university-based) which is legislated, regulated, and/or supported by public funds and whose staff serve, without bias or special selection processes, individuals primarily from the public domain.

Private Setting: Any setting (e.g., school, educational, mental health-related, or university-based) which is supported in whole or in part by private funding sources, which may be for profit, and whose staff can specifically select the populations that it serves.

STANDARD 4.1:

NASP *Standards for Training and Field Placement Programs in School Psychology* (1994): The current standards document from the National Association of School Psychologists (NASP) describing procedural standards supporting the comprehensive training of school psychologists at the doctoral and sixth year/specialist levels.

STANDARD 4.5:

Practica Experiences, as defined in the NASP *Standards for Training and Field Placement Programs in School Psychology* (1994): Practica experiences include orientation to the educational process, assessment for intervention, and direct and indirect intervention methods; are distinct from and occur prior to internship; occur at times appropriate to the specific training objectives of the program; shall be of sufficient length and in settings that are appropriate to specific training objectives of the program; are provided appropriate recognition through the awarding of academic credit; are systematically evaluated in a manner consistent with the specific training objectives of the program; are conducted in accordance with current legal and ethical standards for the profession.

Internship experiences, as defined in the NASP *Standards for Training and Field Placement Programs in School Psychology* (1994): A comprehensive internship experience is required for students to demonstrate, under supervision, their ability to integrate knowledge and skills in providing a broad range of outcome-based school psychological services. Internship experiences are provided at or near the end of the formal training period; occur on a full-time basis over a period of one academic year, or on a half-time basis over a period of two consecutive academic years; are designed according to a written plan that provides a broad range of experiences; occurs in a setting appropriate to the specific training objectives of the program; are provided appropriate recognition through the awarding of academic credit; occur under conditions of appropriate supervision; are systematically evaluated in a manner consistent with the specific training objectives of the program; are conducted in accordance with current legal and ethical standards for the profession.

School Setting (from Appendix B of the NASP *Standards for Training and Field Placement Programs in School Psychology*, 1994): Has the availability of (a) children of all school ages, (b) pupil personnel services functioning within a team framework, (c) regular and special education services at the preschool, elementary, and secondary levels, (d) full-range of services for children with high incidence and low incidence disabilities, (e) at least one credentialed school psychologist having a minimum of three years of full-time school psychology experience, or the equivalent who serves as internship supervisor. It is not essential that the above all be provided within the context of the local educational agency to which the intern is assigned. However, it is essential that all elements be available and integrated into the internship experience.

STANDARD 5:

Approved Programs in School Psychology: The National Association of School Psychologists (NASP) publishes annually a list of training programs in school psychology that have been determined to meet NASP *Standards for Training and Field Placement Programs in School Psychology* (1994). A copy of the Approved Program list can be obtained by contacting the office of the National Association of School Psychologists, 8455 Colesville Road, Suite 1000, Silver Spring, Maryland 20910.

Mentoring and Continuing Professional Development: In addition to the one year of post-degree supervision described in Standard 5.1, it is recommended that individuals enter an organized program of mentoring and continuing professional development. This recommendation is made in recognition of the complex problems in today's schools and the need to continue, enhance, and upgrade school psychologists' professional training and skills in an effort to ensure quality service delivery. Mentoring should be provided by a school psychologist with at least three years experience, and should involve, as is needed, elements of supervision, collegial discussion, and support regarding professional issues. Mentoring is often one component of a continuing professional development plan, and should be arranged in an organized manner to enhance and develop an individual's professional skills and knowledge. Continuing professional development and mentoring may include, but are not limited to, discussions of professional issues with colleagues, readings of professional journals and books, memberships in professional organizations, and participation in formal continuing professional development programs.

STANDARD 7.1:

NASP *Principles for Professional Ethics* **(1992):** The current document of principles from the National Association of School Psychologists (NASP) describing guidelines for ethical behavior including professional competency, professional relationships and responsibilities, and professional practices in public and private settings.

NASP Continuing Professional Development Program

1.0 PHILOSOPHY AND INTENT

With the inception of the National Certification System for School Psychologists, NASP has, for the first time, a mechanism for advocating its long established position regarding appropriate standards for the provision of school psychological services as it pertains to Continuing Professional Development:

> The practice of school psychology has and will continue to undergo significant changes as new knowledge and technological advances are introduced. The development of new intervention techniques, assessment procedures, computerized assistance, and so forth, will require that practitioners keep abreast of these innovations as well as obtain appropriate professional education and training in these areas. **All school psychologists actively participate and engage in activities designed to continue, enhance, and upgrade their professional training and skills and to help ensure quality service provision** [emphasis added]. These efforts are documented by participation in NASP or other formal Continuing Professional Development (CPD) programs, although they are not limited to such activities. Membership in professional organizations, reading of professional journals and books, discussions of professional issues with colleagues, and so forth, are also an integral component of a school psychologist's overall CPD activities. ["Standards for the Provision of School Psychological Services," *Professional Conduct Manual*, NASP, 1984, Section 4.6]

It is assumed that all school psychologists, and particularly those participating in the National School Psychology Certification System, have a common ethic and goal to grow professionally by keeping abreast of trends and new research in order to enhance their services. Because the knowledge base of the field is broad, training and skill levels are varied, and the professional role has many dimensions, individuals will want to have a personal plan for professional development. The plan should be designed to include a broad range of experiences and should be unique to the needs of the individual. Meeting the requirements of the NASP CPD program (which is part of the National School Psychology Certification System) provides an opportunity to reach this goal.

Inasmuch as school psychologists function in a variety of job assignments in a number of diverse locations, it is important to recognize the variables in availability of formal and informal inservice opportunities. **The intent of the CPD requirement, therefore, is not to limit the school psychologist's continuing professional development by approving only specific activities, but rather to acknowledge and encourage participation in the variety of activities that are available to each individual.**

2.0 PROCESS

Consistent with the *NASP Standards for the Provision of School Psychological Services* (1984), participation in activities designed to maintain and expand skills and to insure quality service provision is the continuing obligation of school psychologists. For renewal of national certification, it is expected that school psychologists will enhance their skills in the following areas as defined in the *Standards* (see Appendix A):

CONSULTATION
PSYCHOLOGICAL AND PSYCHOEDUCATIONAL ASSESSMENT
INTERVENTION
SUPERVISION
RESEARCH
PROGRAM PLANNING AND EVALUATION

The emphasis of CPD is upon recency and regularity of participation in skill development activities. It is also expected that the effective practice of school psychology reflects, at its most basic level, a broad knowledge base, and that, for continued effective delivery, school psychologists enhance their skills in a variety of areas.

2.1 Professional Development Activities

2.1.1 CPD Activities include (see Appendix B for specific explanations):

2.1.3.1 National , state and local school psychology association conferences, workshops, and inservice training

2.1.3.2 Related professional conferences, workshops, and inservice training

2.1.3.3 Completion of college and university courses beyond those required for entry-level certification as a school psychologist

2.1.3.4 Teaching courses and provision of workshops and inservice training when not an ordinary aspect of employment

2.1.3.5 Research

2.1.3.6 Publication

2.1.3.7 Presentations

2.1.3.8 Intern Supervision

2.1.3.9 Post-graduate supervised experiences, when not an ordinary aspect of employment

2.1.3.10 Program planning/evaluation when not an employment requirement

2.1.3.11 Sequenced programs of self-study

2.1.3.12 Informal programs of self-study

2.1.3.13 Professional organization leadership

2.1.2 Activities should be chosen as part of an overall professional development plan devised by the participant to enhance knowledge in several foundation areas. While submission of a formal plan is not required, participants are encouraged to devise such a plan for their own use.

2.1.3 Participation time must be accrued **in at least three of the six specific skill areas** (see Section 2.0).

2.1.4 The individual will participate in a variety of activities which emphasize learning, including coursework or workshop experiences and instruction, presentations, program development, or research. These activities go beyond the ordinary aspects of employment.

2.2 CPD Credits

2.2.1 Maintenance of National School Psychology Certification requires the completion of **75 CPD credits,** or 75 contact hours or their equivalency of professional development activity.

2.2.2 A contact hour is defined as an actual clock hour (60 minutes) spent in direct participation in a structured educational format as a learner.

2.2.3 When college or university courses are taken to fulfill the CPD requirement, the following equivalencies shall be used: 1 semester hour = 15 CPD credits; 1 quarter hour = 10 CPD credits.

2.2.4 Some organizations may represent CPD activities through the use of Continuing Education Units (CEUs). One CEU is typically equivalent to *10 contact hours.*

2.2.5 When CPD activities cannot be represented by contact hours, CPD credit equivalencies and ceiling limits have been established (see Appendix B).

2.2.6 For purposes of Nationally Certified School Psychologists (NCSP) renewal, all activities should be reported in terms of CPD credits.

2.3 Claiming CPD Credit for Activities

2.3.1 Individuals may claim CPD credits for a variety of activities. The activities may be evaluated and selected by the individual, as described in 2.3.2.

2.3.2 Individuals may evaluate and select CPD activities and may claim the activities for CPD credit *without contacting NASP for pre-approval of these activities*. The following steps should be used:

    2.3.2.1 Evaluate an activity to determine if it may be claimed for CPD credit. Only activities for which each of the following questions can be answered with a "yes" by the individual may be claimed for CPD credit.

- Did the activity enhance or add to my knowledge base?
- Was the activity relevant to the professional practice of school psychology?
- Did the activity fit into my personal plan for continuing professional development?
- Did the activity go beyond the ordinary aspects of my employment?

    2.3.2.2 Determine the activity category for the activity by referring to the descriptions in Appendix B. If the activity does not fall into an activity category, do not claim the activity for CPD credits.

    2.3.2.3 Determine the skill area for the activity by referring to the descriptions in Appendix A and selecting the skill area(s) that was most enhanced or upgraded by the activity.

    2.3.2.4 Determine the number of CPD credits to claim for the activity by referring to the CPD credit equivalencies and credit ceilings in Appendix B.

    2.3.2.5 Verify the activity with the required documentation listed in 3.1 and Appendix B.

    2.3.2.6 File the verification of the activity to submit with other materials at the time of NCSP renewal.

3.0 PROCEDURES

3.1 Documentation

3.1.1 Participation in CPD activities must be documented.

3.1.2 For purposes of NCSP renewal, the NASP CPD Summary Sheet (see Appendix C) must be completed and all CPD activities and credits must be listed on the Summary Sheet.

3.1.3 Verification of participation for each activity listed must be submitted with the NASP CPD Summary Sheet(s). Several forms of verification will be acceptable (see Appendix B).

    3.1.3.1 Certificates or log sheets of participation provided by the CPD sponsor may be submitted as verification.

    3.1.3.2 When CPD involves college or university coursework, a copy of the course transcript will serve as verification.

    3.1.3.3 In states where professional development is required for maintenance of certification or licensure, or in school districts or other agencies and organizations where professional development is required, summary reports or activity validation forms generated by the state board of education, credentialing agency, school district, or other agency or organization may be submitted as verification of participation.

    3.1.3.4 Any activity not otherwise documented per the above instructions is to be documented through completion of an Activity Documentation Form (see Appendix D). A separate Activity Documentation Form is to be submitted for each activity claimed.

3.1.4 If an individual participates in a state or local school psychology association's CPD program *that has been pre-approved by NASP*, the individual may submit a state or local association's CPD summary report(s) for NCSP renewal instead of NASP's CPD Summary Sheet and verification of each individual activity. A list of CPD programs that have been pre-approved by NASP is available from the NASP National Headquarters.

3.2   Submission of Documentation for National Certification Renewal

If CPD activities are used to renew status as an NCSP, the following procedures must be followed:

3.2.1   NCSP renewal occurs on a three year cycle. CPD credit must be accrued within the three year cycle prior to renewal.

3.2.2   Prior to each third anniversary of the individual's national certification, the National School Psychology Certification Board (NSPCB) will notify the participant of renewal procedures.

3.2.3   Documentation of CPD activities will be submitted as part of the renewal procedure.

3.2.4   Documentation to be submitted will include the NASP CPD Summary Sheet, verification of participation for each activity listed on the CPD Summary Sheet, the NCSP renewal questionnaire, the Directory Listing and the appropriate renewal fee.

3.2.5   Questions regarding the acceptability of a specific activity should be directed to the NASP Professional Development Committee prior to application for renewal.

3.2.6   The documentation submitted for NCSP renewal will be reviewed and approved according to procedures established by the Professional Development Committee.

3.2.7   Documentation will not be returned to the NCSP. Therefore, copies, rather than original documents, are acceptable.

APPENDIX A
Continuing Professional Development Skill Area Definitions

The areas of skill development cited in Section 2.0 of the NASP Continuing Professional Development Program document are those defined in the NASP *Standards for the Provision of School Psychological Services* (1984) Section 4.3. The salient points of that section of the document are reprinted here to assist the participant in determining the skill area(s) under which a specific CPD activity might fall.

CONSULTATION

1. Activities which enhance the school psychologist's skill in:
   a. mental health consultation
   b. behavioral consultation
   c. educational consultation with parents, school personnel, or outside agencies.

2. Training in the promotion of:
   a. mental health and learning
   b. prevention of disorders
   c. improving educational systems

3. Provision of inservice in the areas of:
   a. human learning
   b. human development
   c. behavior to parents, school personnel, and others in the community

4. Development of skills to enhance collaborative relationships with clients, including:
   a. students
   b. school personnel
   c. parents
   d. outside agencies

PSYCHOLOGICAL AND PSYCHOEDUCATIONAL ASSESSMENT

1. Development of skills in multifactored assessment

2. Enhancement of skills in specific assessment areas, including:
   a. personal-social adjustment
   b. intelligence
   c. scholastic aptitude
   d. adaptive behavior
   e. language and communication skills
   f. academic achievement
   g. sensory and perceptual motor functioning
   h. environmental-cultural influences
   i. vocational development, aptitude and interests

3. Development of skills in non-test based measurement, including:
   a. observation
   b. behavioral measurement

4. Development of skill in non-biased assessment

5. Activities that promote ethical considerations and conduct regarding evaluation of students

INTERVENTION

1. Skill development in both direct and indirect intervention strategies that will enhance or facilitate the functioning of:
   a. individuals
   b. groups
   c. systems

2. Enhancement of theory and practice in designing programs to enhance:
   a. cognitive development
   b. affective development
   c. social development
   d. vocational development

3. Assisting others within the community to enhance service delivery skills through such avenues as:
   a. inservice
   b. organizational development
   c. parent counseling
   d. parent education

SUPERVISION

1. Participation in specific activities which enhance the school psychologist's supervisory and administrative skills

2. Provision of practicum and/or internship experiences to school psychology graduate students

RESEARCH

1. Designing or conducting research of a psychological and educational nature, including:
   a. psychological functioning of human beings
   b. psychoeducational assessment tools and procedures
   c. educational programs and techniques applied to individual cases and groups of various sizes
   d. educational processes
   e. social system interactions and organizational factors associated with school communities
   f. psychological treatments and techniques applied to individual cases or groups

PROGRAM PLANNING AND EVALUATION

1. Development of skills in the area of program planning and evaluation

2. Provision of program planning and evaluation services that assist in decision-making

3. Serving on committees responsible for developing and planning educational and educationally-related activities

APPENDIX B
CPD Credit Equivalencies and Credit Ceilings

The NASP Continuing Professional Development Program lists a variety of activities which have potential for enhancing a school psychologist's knowledge and the quality of service provision. These activities are listed in the *CPD Program* document in Section 2.1.1 CPD credit equivalencies and credit ceilings for activities are described in the following sections of Appendix B.

Group A: Hour-for-Hour Activities:

All workshop, conference, and inservice training activities earn one hour of CPD credit for each contact hour of participation:

2.1.3.1 National, state, and local school psychology association conferences, workshops, and inservice training

2.1.3.2 Related professional conferences, workshops, and inservice training

An Example: Two hours of attendance at a NASP Convention miniskills workshop = 2 contact hours or 2 CPD credits.

Group B: Standard Conversions:

Taking or teaching college/university courses and provision of workshops and inservice training are credited on a standard basis as follows:

2.1.3.3 Completion of college courses and university courses beyond those required for entry level certification

    a. The participant earns 10 CPD credits for each hour of course credit if the course is for *one quarter*

    An Example: A 3-quarter credit course in consultation earns 30 CPD credits

    b. If the course is for *one semester*, then one hour of course credit is worth 15 CPD credits

    An Example: A course in advanced research earns 3-semester hours = 45 CPD credits

2.1.3.4 Teaching courses and provision of workshops and inservice training when not an ordinary aspect of employment

CPD credit should not be claimed for activities which are a part of the school psychologist's regular job requirements. However, credit may be claimed for those teaching/presenting activities which go beyond the normal demands of that psychologist's job setting. Additionally, although the course or inservice training may be reported, credit may only be claimed once. Credit claimed is equal to the number of contact hours obtained by those attending the course or workshop, as described in items 1–3 above.

Examples: A university trainer presents a workshop on curriculum-based assessment at a state conference. The workshop is 4 hours long. Participants obtain 4 CPD hours of credit. The presenter may also claim 4 CPD credits. However, credit may only be claimed *once* for workshops on this subject.

A school psychologist teaches one course as a guest lecturer at a local university. Students taking the course earn 3 semester hour credits. The lecturer can earn 45 CPD credits for teaching the course. However, the school psychologist may only obtain those credits the *first* time the course is taught.

Group C: Conversions and Limitations:

Other types of activities are also valuable in professional development. However, participation in these activities is *not covered on a per hour basis alone*. These activities might:

1. require more actual time than the credit that may be earned

2. be limited in the credit they offer

Limited activities include the following:

2.1.3.5   Research

2.1.3.6   Publication

2.1.3.7   Presentation

To claim credit in these categories, it is necessary for the participant to reasonably estimate the amount of time spent and claim those actual hours up to the maximum specified. Also, the participant should claim credit *only once for any project.*

- Unpublished Research — up to 10 CPD credits
- Research *and* publication or presentation on a topic — up to 25 CPD credits
- Non-research based published articles with references *or* poster presentation at a state or national convention — up to 10 CPD credits
- Published theoretical or editorial articles — up to 5 CPD credits

2.1.3.8   Supervision of interns in field placements by school psychologists.

For purposes of claiming CPD credits, field supervisors should consider the extent to which this role leads to professional growth on the part of the supervisor. Up to 10 CPD credits may be obtained for supervising one or two interns for one academic year. Credit for supervision may be claimed *no more than twice* (two years) during a three-year renewal period.

An Example: A school psychologist supervised an intern for 1 academic year. They decided to lead a group at one of the elementary schools for children whose parents were divorced. This and several other activities involved new learning for both the supervisor and intern. The supervisor may claim 10 CPD credits.

2.1.3.9   Post-graduate supervised experiences when not an ordinary aspect of employment, including post-graduate fellowships, internships, or supervised work experiences.

Following completion of their school psychology degrees, many school psychologists participate in supervised fellowships, internships, or other experiences in order to acquire new knowledge and skills. The supervised experiences may occur in settings outside the school psychologist's regular job setting or may occur as part of a planned and sequential program on the job. For purposes of claiming CPD credit for this activity category, school psychologists should consider the extent to which the supervised experience leads to professional growth and new knowledge and skills. CPD credit may *not* be claimed for regular supervised experiences that are required as part of the school psychologist's typical employment. CPD credit may be claimed according to the percentage of the school psychologist's time spent in the supervised experience, according to the following:

Quarter time for one academic year — 5 CPD credits

Half time for one academic year — 10 CPD credits

Three-quarters time for one academic year — 15 CPD credits

Full time for one academic year — 20 CPD credits

Credit for supervised experiences may be claimed *no more than twice* (two years) during a three year renewal period. *Note:* If the experience is taken for university/college course credit, activity category 2.1.3.3 should be used instead of activity category 2.1.3.9. In addition, some activities during the supervised experience, such as attendance at conferences or inservice training or informal programs of self-study may earn CPD credits in other activity categories listed in Appendix B.

Examples: A school psychologist wishes to enhance her skills in family counseling and intervention. She makes arrangements with her school district to spend 25% of her time for one academic year to receive training and experience in this area, under the supervision of a qualified school psychologist in another school. She may claim 5 CPD credits for this activity.

A school psychologist takes a one academic year leave of absence from her job to participate in a full-time, supervised fellowship program at a children's hospital. She may claim 20 CPD credits for this activity.

2.1.3.10 Program planning/evaluation, when not an ordinary aspect of employment

As with the research/publication categories above, actual hours should be claimed, but *no more than* 25 CPD credits for one project may be obtained in this area, and no more than one project may be claimed in a three year period.

An Example: A school psychologist promotes the development of teacher assistance teams in the district. Considerable time is spent planning for the program, training staff, developing procedures, etc. The psychologist estimates 80 actual hours of work. A total of 25 CPD credits are claimed.

2.1.3.11 Sequenced programs of self-study

Programs developed and published to provide training in a specific knowledge or skill area are valued for obtaining CPD credits. *No more than two topics may earn credit in this category during a three-year renewal period.* Credit may be determined by:

- obtaining the CPD designated by program developers.

  An Example: A course on non-biased assessment is developed by NASP for Continuing Professional Development. It involves purchasing a course manual and video tapes. The credit offered is 20 CPD credits.

- estimation of credit based on time spent mastering the material. Credit obtained in this manner is limited to 15 CPD credits.

  An Example: A course on Counseling Techniques with Children involved 20 hours of reading, 3 hours of audio tapes, and 3 written exercises. A total of 15 CPD credits may be claimed.

2.1.3.12 Informal programs of self-study

When a school psychologist pursues a topic of interest by systematically reviewing the literature, developing a comprehensive list of resources and studying these resources, CPD credits may be obtained. Included in this category would be book, journal, and manual reading. To obtain credit, the psychologist must provide the reading list with the Activity Documentation Form (see Appendix D). At least 4 resources should be included on any one topic. Actual hours claimed in this activity are not to exceed 15 CPD hours per topic. *No more than two topics may earn credit in this category during a three-year renewal period.*

An Example: A school psychologist decides to study "collaborative consultation." A review of the literature reveals 5 well-known authors on this topic. Additionally, the *School Psychology Review* lists four recent articles. The psychologist spends 20 hours reading these and earns 15 hours of CPD credit.

2.1.3.13 Professional organization leadership

A school psychologist who holds a position in a local, state, or national professional organization may earn:

- 10 CPD credits as president
- 5 CPD credits as other officer
- 5 CPD credits as committee chair, delegate, or regional director

Credit may be obtained for no more than *one position, per year, per organization.* No more than 20 CPD credits may be obtained in this category during a three-year renewal period.

An Example: A school psychologist serves as treasurer of the state school psychology association one year and holds a NASP delegate position for all three years of a renewal period. She may claim 5 credits for the treasurer's position and 15 hours for the delegate's position (5 CPD credits for each of three years) for a total of 20 hours. This activity should be claimed under the area of Program Planning and Evaluation.

CPD CREDIT EQUIVALENCIES AND CREDIT CEILINGS SUMMARY TABLE

ACTIVITY CATEGORY	CPD CREDIT CONVERSION	CEILING LIMITS	DOCUMENTATION REQUIRED
2.1.3.1 School psychology workshops/conferences/inservice training	Each hour = 1 CPD	None	Certificate of Attendance or Activity Documentation Form and receipt
2.1.3.2 Other professional workshops/conferences/inservice training	Each hour = 1 CPD	None	Certificate of Attendance or Activity Documentation Form and receipt
2.1.3.3 College/university courses	One quarter hour = 10 CPD One semester hour = 15 CPD	None	Transcript
2.1.3.4 Teaching/workshop and inservice presentation	Hour-for-hour or university credits as defined in 2.1.3.1-3 above	Credit may be claimed only first time content is taught.	Copy of syllabus for course <u>or</u> copy of program flyer <u>or</u> Activity Documentation Form
2.1.3.5 Research 2.1.3.6 Publication 2.1.3.7 Presentations	Actual hours, up to ceilings established	Unpublished research=10 CPD. Research & publication or presentation=25 CPD. Article published or poster presented = 10 CPD. Theoretical/editorial article = 5 CPD. Each project may only be claimed once.	Activity Documentation Form <u>and</u> Abstract of Program, if possible
2.1.3.8 Intern supervision	1 year of supervision = 10 CPD	Only one intern claimed per year. No more than 2 interns in 3 years.	Activity Documentation Form
2.1.3.9 Post-graduate supervised experiences	1/4 time = 5 CPD 1/2 time = 10 CPD 3/4 time = 15 CPD full time = 20 CPD	No more than 2 supervised experiences in 3 years	Activity Documentation Form
2.1.3.10 Program planning/evaluation	Actual hours, up to ceiling	1 project = 25 CPD	Activity Documentation Form
2.1.3.11 Sequenced self-study	Actual hours, up to ceiling	1 project = 15 CPD (or other as established). No more than 2 topics in 3 years.	Activity Documentation Form
2.1.3.12 Informal self-study	Actual hours, up to ceiling	1 topic = 15 CPD. No more than 2 topics in 3 years.	Activity Documentation Form
2.1.3.13 Professional organization leadership	President = 10 CPD Other officer = 5 CPD Committee Chair/delegate/regional director = 5 CPD	No more than one activity per organization per year. No more than 20 CPD in this category in 3 years.	Activity Documentation Form

NATIONAL ASSOCIATION OF SCHOOL PSYCHOLOGISTS

8455 Colesville Road
Suite 1000
Silver Spring, MD 29010

APPENDIX C

CONTINUING PROFESSIONAL DEVELOPMENT SUMMARY SHEET

INSTRUCTIONS: This form is to be completed, signed, and submitted with NCSP renewal materials after the renewal notice is received. Verification for each activity claimed on this CPD Summary Sheet must be attached. If more space is needed, attach additional sheets. Activities must be listed for at least three of the six skill areas on this form.

NAME: _____

ADDRESS: _____

NCSP NUMBER: _____

DAYTIME PHONE NO: _____

Activities listed on this form were completed

between _____ and _____ .
                (starting date)   (ending date)

PRIMARY ROLE (check only one): ☐ Practitioner   ☐ University Trainer
                                ☐ Administrator/Supervisor ☐ Other (specify): _____

Skill Area	Activity Title	Date	Activity Category Number and Title (see Appendix B)	CPD Credits Claimed (see Appendix B)
Consultation				
	Consultation Skill Area Subtotal			

CPD Summary Sheet Page 1

Continued Next Page

Name _____ NCSP Number _____

CPD Summary Sheet Continued

Skill Area	Activity Title	Date	Activity Category Number and Title (see Appendix B)	CPD Credits Claimed (see Appendix B)
Assessment				

Assessment Skill Area Subtotal

Skill Area	Activity Title	Date	Activity Category Number and Title (see Appendix B)	CPD Credits Claimed (see Appendix B)
Intervention				

Intervention Skill Area Subtotal

CPD Summary Sheet Page 2

Continued Next Page

CPD Summary Sheet Continued

Name _____ NCSP Number _____

Skill Area	Activity Title	Date	Activity Category Number and Title (see Appendix B)	CPD Credits Claimed (see Appendix B)
Supervision				

Supervision Skill Area Subtotal

Skill Area	Activity Title	Date	Activity Category Number and Title (see Appendix B)	CPD Credits Claimed (see Appendix B)
Research				

Research Skill Area Subtotal

Continued Next Page

CPD Summary Sheet Continued

Name _____ NCSP Number _____

Skill Area	Activity Title	Date	Activity Category Number and Title (see Appendix B)	CPD Credits Claimed (see Appendix B)
Program Planning/ Evaluation				
Program Planning/Evaluation Skill Area Subtotal				

☐

TOTAL CPD CREDITS ☐

I attest that the activities reported on this form reflect actual activities in which I participated. I understand that falsification of this information is an ethical violation and may result in my being ineligible for future certification and/or legal action may be taken against me.

_____
(signature)

NATIONAL ASSOCIATION OF SCHOOL PSYCHOLOGISTS

8455 Colesville Road
Suite 1000
Silver Spring, MD 20910

APPENDIX D

ACTIVITY DOCUMENTATION FORM

INSTRUCTIONS: This documentation form is to be used to report activities for which no other standard documentation form exists. A separate form must be used for each activity.

NAME: _____   NCSP Number: _____

ADDRESS: _____   Daytime Phone No.: _____

_____

Title of Activity: _____

Description of Activity:

Date(s) of Activity: _____ Location: _____

Skill Area(s) Addressed Through This Activity:

_____Consultation   _____Supervision
_____Assessment   _____Research
_____Intervention   _____Program Planning/Evaluation

Activity Category Number (Appendix B): _____

Activity Category Title (Appendix B): _____

Actual Number of Clock Hours of Participation: _____

CPD Credits Claimed (See allowed equivalencies/limits in Appendix B): _____

I certify that this activity merits CPD credit in that it meets the following criteria:

1. This activity enhanced or upgraded my professional skills or added to my knowledge base.
2. This activity was relevant to the professional practice of school psychology.
3. This activity fits into my personal plan for continuing professional development.
4. This activity went beyond the ordinary aspects of my employment.

_____
(signature)

Reproduce this form as needed

NASP Position Statements

Ability Grouping

To ensure educational equity and excellence for all America's youth. NASP supports the creation of inclusive classrooms that are based on the belief that all students can learn — a core value of all schools in a democracy. NASP believes that tracking, or whole class ability grouping, is not consistent with that core value.

Extensive research on ability grouping has documented the following negative effects:

- Students with lower ability achieve less in lower track classes than in mixed ability classes.

- Students with higher ability do not achieve more in tracked classes than in mixed ability classes.

- Placing students with lower ability in tracked classrooms reduces self-esteem, with a particularly negative effect on students' sense of their own academic competence.

- Tracking students reduces the likelihood that students placed in lower track classes will choose college preparatory courses.

- Tracking students reduces opportunities to develop relationships among students from other racial, ethnic, and socioeconomic groups and has a negative effect on race relations.

- The placement decision concerning ability grouping is often made very early in a student's school career, is often based on questionable data, and is enduring.

NASP believes that grouping students heterogeneously offers advantages unavailable in schools that track. When implemented appropriately, heterogeneous grouping:

- gives all students equal access to an enriched curriculum and the highest quality instruction schools have to offer;

- avoids labeling and stigmatizing students with lower ability;

- promotes higher expectations for student achievement;

- reduces in-school segregation based on socioeconomic status, race, gender or ethnicity, or disability;

- encourages teachers to accommodate individual differences in students' instructional and social needs;

- enables students to learn from their peers, including students whose background may be very different from their own; and

- emphasizes effort more than ability.

NASP recognizes that heterogeneous grouping will not automatically guarantee all students a quality education. "Watering down" the curriculum or "teaching to the middle" will create disadvantages for able students and should be avoided. While NASP believes that all students can benefit from a more challenging curriculum, we also strongly support the development of a curriculum which recognizes and accommodates individual differences in learning styles, abilities, and interests. To be successful, mixed ability grouping must occur within the context of such a curriculum.

NASP also recognizes that heterogeneous classes require instructional and organizational innovations to accommodate a wide range of learners. Such approaches include cooperative learning groups, peer tutors, flexible grouping practices, team teaching, multi-age groupings, and instruction in higher order thinking and problem-solving skills. Where teachers do not currently possess competencies to enable them to work effectively with mixed ability classes, a commitment to further training is essential.

NASP believes that "untracking" schools requires careful planning and collaboration among constituent groups, including teachers, administrators, support personnel, students, and parents. Planned change can best take place using a model that includes the following:

- a steering committee composed of educators, parents, community members and school board representatives whose task is to study grouping practices and make policy recommendations to the school board;

- local self-study to assess the impact of grouping practices within the school community;

- wide dissemination of local and national studies of ability grouping effects;

- implementation of a strategic plan that allows for a phase-in process and ensures monitoring troubleshooting, and evaluation.

NASP believes that school psychologists can play a central role in helping schools develop appropriate alternatives to tracking. School psychologists have access to research, understand good instructional practices that enhance learning for all students, and possess group problem-solving skills that make them valuable as members of steering committees and strategic planning groups and as staff trainers.

School psychologists can contribute to the process of untracking schools by:

- making research available to administrators and central office personnel;

- leading informal study groups to explore alternative grouping practices;

- becoming members of steering committees assembled to study tracking and to develop policy recommendations; and

- participating in strategic planning and staff development to prepare for untracking.

NASP recognizes that schools cannot simply eliminate tracking but must develop viable alternatives. Developing alternatives to tracking will take patience and careful planning. In order for schools to live up to the promise of educating all students to become productive citizens of the 21st century, NASP believes these alternatives must be characterized by fairness and challenge, with equity and excellence equally available to all learners.

Adopted by the NASP Delegate Assembly, April 17, 1993.

This position statement drew on material from George P. (1992), Alexandria, VA: Association for Supervision and Curriculum Development.

Goals 2000

The National Association of School Psychologists (NASP) strongly supports the creation of national education goals. Goals 2000 sets forth eight National Education Goals:

1. All children in America will start school ready to learn.

2. The high school graduation rate will increase to at least 90 percent.

3. American students will leave grades four, eight, and twelve having demonstrated competency in challenging subject matter, including English, mathematics, science, history, and geography, and every school in America will ensure that all students learn to use their minds well, so they may be prepared for responsible citizenship, further learning, and productive employment in our modern economy.

4. The Nation's teaching force will have access to programs for the continued improvement of their professional skills and the opportunity to acquire the knowledge and skills needed to instruct and prepare all American students for the next century.

5. United States students will be first in the world in science and mathematics achievement.

6. Every adult American will be literate and will possess the knowledge and skills necessary to compete in a global economy and exercise the rights and responsibilities of citizenship.

7. Every school in the United States will be free of drugs, violence, and unauthorized presence of firearms and alcohol and will offer a disciplined environment conducive to learning.

8. Every school will promote partnerships that will increase parental involvement and participation in promoting the social, emotional, and academic growth of children.

The broad purposes outlined in these eight National Education Goals and the nine year strategy to achieve these goals are important steps in committing the United States to develop a world class education system.

To achieve these goals the focus of education must extend beyond academic goals alone. The impact of social-emotional, health, and mental needs of children and youth on school achievement must be addressed if the desired outcomes are to be achieved. Students who are not motivated to learn, who are abused or neglected, who come from backgrounds in which education is not a priority, who are part of highly mobile families, or who are otherwise at risk are not in a position to achieve these goals without the proper levels of support. History has shown us that each time academic standards are raised in this country, at-risk student groups are further alienated unless specific strategies are developed to prevent their disenfranchisements. Pupil services personnel, including school psychologists, are in the best position to identify and respond to those concerns and to facilitate the attainment of these goals by all children and youth.

The NASP position statement, "At Risk Students and Excellence in Education: The Need for Educational Restructuring," sets forth the view that minor adjustments to the current educational system is no longer a credible solution. As an example, increased academic time is essential but simply adding more hours, standards, and requirements will not meet the goals of either equity or excellence.

To arrive at effective solutions to address the weaknesses of our educational system, the National Educational goals must incorporate the following values and guiding principles:

- **Provide high quality education for *all* children.** To do this we must take into account the special needs of students with disabilities, students at risk for school failure, children and youth of poverty, children and youth of diverse backgrounds, and students with gifts and talents.

- **Provide community and family support for educational readiness.** All children must be given a legitimate opportunity to learn. Reaching the National Educational Goals requires competent and committed parents, wanted and healthy children, adequate nutrition, appropriate nurturing, decent housing, and freedom from abuse, neglect, and exploitation. Children must be provided with environments that encourage their eager participation, exploration, and curiosity about the world.

- **Address the diverse needs of students.** Academic success, the social and emotional, developmental and family needs of all students must be addressed. Academic gains will be made only after these other "basic" needs of students have been met. Education in the 21st century must expand its "curriculum" to include these needs.

- **Support intervention and prevention programs.** Prevention and early identification of problems combined with immediate intervention are the most effective methods to make school a success for all children and youth. Such programs are essential for the success of the National Education Goals.

- **Emphasize the parental role in children's school success.** Home–school collaboration goes hand-in-hand with efforts to redesign education for children and youth. These family-oriented efforts will promote the critical linkages between school and home in the areas of effective parenting, methods of working and communicating with children, inclusion of students with disabilities, and ensuring effective home-communication with schools.

- **Promote alternatives to corporal punishment.** If schools are truly to be "safe havens" for learning and growing for all students, corporal punishment must be abolished. Students must be safe from physical harm from those adults who are entrusted with their care. Teachers can be prepared to use positive alternatives to corporal punishment that are more effective in establishing appropriate classroom discipline and promoting academic achievement.

School psychologists are essential personnel in the schools. Their presence will directly facilitate the attainment of education goals by all students. To help reach the National Education Goals, school psychologists can:

- Design, implement and evaluate prevention and early intervention programs.

- Address a wide range of behavioral problems through the implementation of programs such as substance abuse prevention, violence reduction, social skills training, crisis intervention, school-wide effective discipline programs, etc.

- Work with parents by providing parents education and facilitating home–school collaboration.

- Provide information on how individual differences affect school achievement and have knowledge of instructional methods to address diversity in the classroom and to promote critical thinking and problem-solving in all students.

- Provide collaborative professional development to enable an increasingly diverse student population to utilize their strengths and learning skills.

- Assist in classroom management and behavior management essential for increasing academic engaged time and enhancing effective classroom instruction.

- Provide information about the factors that place students at risk for school failure and have the skills to implement programs to prevent school failure and reduce school dropout.

- Help school personnel understand the developmental education needs of children and youth; and

- Develop a collaborative support system so that teachers and other instructional staff are able to teach to the "fullest."

No important social aims are ever achieved by rhetoric. The strategies to restructure American education must be predicated on strong and continuing federal leadership, investment in human and related capital, and collaboration among families, service providers, government, and the private sector. Coordination of the separate efforts of the individual states, localities, and the private sector is essential if the National Educational Goals are to be achieved in a way that promotes and ensures excellence and equality.

The National Association of School Psychologists believes that the federal government must provide adequate financial support to ensure the achievement of the National Education Goals. States and localities throughout the country are experiencing unprecedented fiscal crises of such proportion that education budgets are being severely slashed. These realities profoundly affect the ability to plan and implement change. Even under the optimal financial circumstances, states and localities are likely to devote differing amounts of resources to restructuring education. The values exemplified in Goals 2000 must be matched with a willingness to invest the fiscal resources of the United States to make achievement of the National Goals a reality.

Adopted by the NASP Delegate Assembly, March 1992.

Advocacy for Appropriate Educational Services for All Children

PL 94-142 (The Education of All Handicapped Children Act) has achieved major goals in serving handicapped children, many of whom had been previously excluded from appropriate educational programs. Since its enactment in 1975, all handicapped children have been guaranteed a free and appropriate education, the right to due process, and individualization of program according to need. We strongly support the continuation of legislation which has mandated these guarantees.

We also recognize that serious problems have been encountered as school districts strive to meet these mandates and that quality education is still an elusive goal. some of these problems reflect difficulties within special education; others appear to be special education issues but have their origins in the regular education system.

One major set of problems involves reverse sides of the issue of access to appropriate education: (1) On the one hand, access to special eduction must be assured for all significantly handicapped children who need and can benefit from it. (2) Conversely, children are being inappropriately diagnosed as handicapped and placed in special education because of: (a) a lack of regular education options designed to meet the needs of children with diverse learning styles; (b) a lack of understanding, at times, of diverse cultural and linguistic backgrounds; and (c) inadequate measurement technologies which focus on labels for placement rather than providing information for program development.

It is not a benign action to label as "handicapped" children who are low achievers but are not, in fact, handicapped, even when this is done in order to provide them with services unavailable in general education. Special personnel often resort to labeling because it seems the only way to obtain needed services for children. This is an unfortunate result of categorical models which attach funding to classifications. Other problems originating in the classification system include:

- Labels that are often irrelevant to instructional needs.

- Categories, based on deficit labels, that are rather arbitrarily defined, particularly for mildly handicapped and low achieving students, but which seem to be accepted as "real" and may prevent more meaningful understanding of the child's psychoeducational needs. The intent of this statement is not necessarily to endorse mixing children with different moderate to severe handicaps in a single special education classroom.

- Reduced expectations for children who are placed in special needs programs.

- Assessment processes aimed at determining eligibility which often deflects limited resources from the determination of functional educational needs and the development of effective psychoeducational programs.

- A decreased willingness on the part of regular education, at times bordering on abdication of responsibility to modify curricula and programs in order to better meet the diverse needs of all children.

As increasing numbers of children are classified as handicapped and removed from regular classrooms for special instruction, there has been a dramatic reduction in the range of abilities among children who remain within the general education system. Concurrently, as national standards for excellence are being raised, the number of children at risk for school failure is growing dramatically. Without provisions to prepare students for higher expectations through effective instructional programs, many of these children may also be identified as handicapped and placed in special education. This climate, in which children are tested and labeled as failures or as handicapped in increasing numbers, creates an urgent need for reexamination and change in the system which provides access to services.

In view of these problems, and based upon the commitment to see that all children receive effective and appropriate education irrespective of race, cultural backgrounds, linguistic background, socioeconomic status, or educational need, we believe:

- All children can learn. Schools have a responsibility to teach them, and school personnel and parents should work together to assure every child a free and appropriate education in a positive social environment.

- Instructional options, based on the individual psychoeducational needs of each child, must be maximized within the general education system. Necessary support services should be provided within general education, eliminating the need to classify children as handicapped in order to receive these services.

- Psychoeducational needs of children should be determined through a multi-dimensional, non-biased assessment process. This must evaluate the match between the learner and his or her educational environment, assessing the compatibility of curriculum and system as they interact with the child, rather than relying on the deficit based model which places the blame for failure within the child. Referral to the assessment and placement process must always relate directly to services designed to meet psychoeducational needs.

- In addition to maintaining current protection for handicapped children, protections and safeguards must be developed to assure the rights of children who are at risk for school failure and require services while remaining in general education without classification as handicapped.

We propose a new national initiative to meet the educational needs of all children:

We propose the development and piloting of alternatives to the current categorical system. This requires reevaluation of funding mechanisms, and advocacy for policy and funding waivers needed for the piloting of alternative service delivery models. It also requires the development of increased support systems and extensive retraining of all school personnel to enable them to work effectively with a broad range of children with special needs within the regular education system.

This initiative will encourage greater independence for children by enabling them to function within the broadest possible environment, and independence for school personnel by providing them with training and support so they can help a wide range of children.

The types and extent of change we are suggesting should be made cautiously. Targeted funds intended for children with moderate and severe handicapping conditions must be protected. Similarly, resources for children who are not handicapped, but who experience learning difficulties, must be protected even though these children are served within general education. We need to assure that no child is put at risk for loss of services while the change process is occurring.

Our task is to reduce the rigidities of the current system without taking away the protections offered by PL 94-142. All experimentation and research must take place within a framework of maximum protection for children. It is highly likely that this may require the development of temporary parallel systems — the traditional system of classification and placement under PL 94-142, and a system of experimental programs, primarily within general education — until satisfactory models can be developed which meet the requirement of accountability, due process, and protection of students' and parents' rights, and provide funding for students in need of services. In addition, while these recommended modifications might reduce the risk of misclassification due to cultural or linguistic differences, we caution that these issues must continue to be monitored and discussed during the transition period and beyond.

Because of the complexity of these issues, the generation of effective solutions will require a national effort of interested persons and organizations which we hope to generate through this task force. We will actively work toward the collaboration of a wide variety of individuals and organizations, joining together to develop a strong base of knowledge, research, and experience in order to establish new frameworks and conceptualizations on which to base decisions, design feasible service delivery options, advocate for policy and funding changes needed to implement these alternatives, and coordinate efforts and share information for positive change. We invite you to join us.

This statement issued jointly by the National Association of School Psychologists and the National Coalition of Students.

AIDS

Acquired Immune Deficiency Syndrome (AIDS) currently threatens the physical and mental health and the civil liberties of many persons in America. Children and youth particularly may be at risk. Many teenagers engage in high-risk activities. Over 70 percent of our teenagers have had sexual intercourse by the age of twenty, many with more than one partner. Nearly one-half of all sexually transmitted disease patients are under 25 years of age. In 1986, approximately 1.1 percent of high school seniors reported having used heroin. Certain populations hold even higher risk; approximately 80 percent are Black and Hispanic.

School systems have a major responsibility both in the acceptance of children who have AIDS and in the education about risk reduction. Because a cure will not be available in the foreseeable future, education about risk reduction is the primary prevention strategy currently available.

Rights to an Education

NASP affirms the right of children who have AIDS to an appropriate education in the least restrictive environment. Toward that end, school psychologists have an active role in working with other educators to sensitize and educate the community, school staff, and students to the needs of these children.

AIDS Education and Related Services

Education currently is the only effective weapon in the battle against AIDS. NASP supports the U.S. Surgeon General C. Everett Koop's recommendations for early and continuing AIDS education in our schools.

Transmission of AIDS information alone will not be adequate to establish and maintain appropriate behaviors that reduce the risk of HIV transmission. Research has shown that educational programs designed to effect behavior change should address the topics of decision making, risk assessment, attitude change, group norms, and other social and psychological processes, as well as factual knowledge.

All responses of the school must be tailored to the individual needs of students. AIDS education must be culturally sensitive, gender-relevant, and appropriate to the level of intellectual, emotional, and social development of the student. AIDS education must be appropriate for handicapped students, students with low literacy levels, and non-English speaking students.

AIDS education should be integrated into dropout prevention, school reentry, and community-based outreach programs.

Developmentally appropriate AIDS education must start as early as the lower elementary grades in order to establish appropriate attitudes and behaviors. AIDS education must be incorporated into a comprehensive health education program that includes sex education, family life education, and drug education. Specific behaviors through which the virus can be transmitted must be addressed.

Related services — including counseling of students and parents about feelings, behaviors, and decision-making — must be available.

School community programs must be developed with the active involvement of parents. Parent education should be provided so that parents can discuss factual information with their children within the context of their own family values.

Staff development for school personnel should be available and should include accurate factual information, as well as helping them deal with their own fears and feelings about AIDS.

Role of the School Psychologist

Because of their training in human development, psychological processes, learning processes, and educational systems, school psychologists can play an important role in the integration of children with AIDS into schools and in the education for risk reduction. School psychologists should be aware that the issue of AIDS education is controversial. NASP encourages all school psychologists to learn the necessary information and to provide their expertise in order to facilitate the provision of effective AIDS education and to provide necessary related services to students with AIDS and/or high risk students.

In collaboration with other support and education personnel, school psychologists can:

- Assist in the development, implementation, and evaluation of AIDS education that is appropriate for age, gender, ability level, and cultural group;

- Facilitate parental involvement in AIDS education in the school, home, and community;

- Participate in the decisions about educational and related services for a child infected with HIV;

- Respond to the educational and psychological needs of students, parents, and school personnel who are concerned about school attendance of a student known to be HIV-infected, at perceived high risk of infection, or who has a family member with HIV infection;

- Provide counseling for students who have a family member or friend with AIDS, students at high risk or perceived high risk of HIV infection, or students with AIDS.

- Help teachers, administrators, and parents recognize and address their general feelings and personal concerns regarding AIDS.

- Work with other support and education personnel to establish and maintain appropriate AIDS-related behaviors and attitudes in students.

Adopted by the NASP Delegate Assembly, April 1988

At-Risk Students and Excellence in Education: The Need for Educational Restructuring

The Imperative for Change

Significant changes in social and economic contexts have rendered traditional school structures ineffective. Numerous reports calling for educational reform have been published in recent years; and educators, citizens, and policy makers alike now recognize the serious problems inherent in our current educational system. Some reports have recommended higher standards and expectations, greater emphasis on basic skills or technological training, and increased accountability. Others have called for more widespread application of effective schools and teaching research.

More recently, concern has focused on the increased numbers of students in our schools at-risk for academic and personal problems. Educators and the community at large acknowledge the devastating economic and social impact of high student dropout rates, students graduating without functional skills, and students experiencing serious academic and personal problems which prevent them from becoming productive members of society. Schools are facing increasing numbers of students with multiple risk factors — children from single parent homes, from immigrant families, from poor families, from dysfunctional families — as well as ethnic minorities who historically have been denied access to the training and employment needed to participate in an increasingly complex society. Social-personal problems confronting students, such as teenage pregnancy, substance abuse, neglect, peer pressures, and family stress, contribute to increasingly complex educational needs.

It has become clear that striving for excellence in education without also ensuring equity leaves large numbers of students disenfranchised. NASP is committed to finding the most effective ways to educate all students. The NASP position statement, Advocacy for Appropriate Education for All Students (1985), recognized the limitation of categorical approaches in meeting the needs of students with learning problems and called for careful piloting of alternative delivery systems that increase access and reduce barriers to effective instruction for all students. We renew and expand this call for alternatives to the current educational delivery system.

NASP believes that many of our basic assumptions about schooling need to be reconsidered. Given the magnitude of the problems, making minor adjustments to the current educational system is no longer a credible solution. While increased academic time is essential, simply adding more hours, more standards, and more requirements will not meet the goals of either equity or excellence.

Among the traditional assumptions that need to be questioned are age-graded, lock-step classes, extensive use of retention and tracking, emphasis on norm-referenced comparisons, and categorical eligibility requirements for special assistance that are unrelated to instructional needs. The knowledge to facilitate a thoughtful and effective restructuring of our system of schooling is available and is continuing to grow. Schools must be altered significantly to be relevant to a changing society and a changing population.

Considerations in Restructuring Education

There is no single model for restructuring schools. Decisions about restructuring should be made by partnerships of policy makers, administrators, and school personnel working within the goals and purposes of education shared by the community. However, a number of principles and underlying beliefs should be considered in any implementation efforts. Restructured schools should:

- Ensure a single educational system for all students that integrates special services and support programs with the regular education program.

- Ensure the rights of all students to an appropriate education and involve parents at all levels of decision making. An appropriate education should emphasize student outcomes that include maximized achievement, productive work attitudes and skills, and healthy personal and skill development.

- Involve parents in the education of their children and in schools in meaningful ways.

- Support meaningful school-based decision making and local flexibility. However, redesigned schools should be based on the most current psychological knowledge about learning and development, as well as effective instruction. Local decision making without an empirical base may lead to less than optimal results and even move in harmful directions.

- Ensure a challenging curriculum for all students that can be adapted individually as appropriate. High expectations should be held for all students. Instructional effectiveness should be the hallmark feature.

- Promote heterogeneous age-grade grouping and competency standards, such that all students of all given ages are not expected to master the same objectives in the same period of time. Seek alternatives to the use of retention as an academic intervention.

- Recognize that children learn in different ways and incorporate experiential and participative learning strategies into instruction that promotes understanding and problem-solving. Emphasize heterogeneous classes, cooperative learning, peer-assisted learning, and other adaptive education strategies that meet individual learning needs in diverse group settings.

- Ensure a caring personalized school environment that supports the social/emotional needs, as well as the academic needs of students. This environment should be reflected in design of programs, curriculum and attitudes of all staff. High quality youth–adult relationships should be evident.

- Encourage prevention and early intervention, including developmental early childhood programs for socio-economically disadvantaged children and other at-risk children.

- Emphasize assessment that focuses on the instructional and functional needs of the student, including progress in the curriculum, rather than assignment to categories or groups. Normative group assessment should be minimized in making decisions for and about students. Outcome measures should directly reflect success of specific school and student efforts and provide for direct and frequent monitoring of student progress.

- Maintain or expand existing levels of federal, state, and local funding, which provide instructional and support services in a manner that endures their availability for all students.

- Encourage active private/public cooperation, but not at the expense of adequate government funding of educational programs and services.

- Recognize that schools cannot accomplish their goals alone. Community supports to youth must be expanded: coordination among schools and community services to meet the health, welfare, and social needs of children and their families must be ensured, increased attention to school-work transitions for many students is essential.

- Find creative and new ways to recognize and reward excellence among teachers and students.

Next Steps

NASP joins other groups in recognizing the need to reexamine existing educational assumptions and systems. We believe the knowledge and research base is available to educate effectively all students in the mainstream of education. It is only through the united efforts of the many public and private stakeholders in the education of our youth that meaningful restructuring can occur. As we work collaboratively to explore viable options and alternatives, several dimensions that will influence the change process must be considered.

- Funding mechanisms must be examined for their impact on the access to and utilization of programs and services. If necessary, pilot efforts should be granted waivers from funding source regulations that restrict innovation on the basis of accountability for outcomes. Dual systems of record keeping and operation may be necessary until success of new models and paradigms can be demonstrated. In all cases, due process rights of students and parents must be protected.

- Policies at the local, state, and federal levels must be examined for the extent to which they constrain or facilitate effective instructional and schooling processes. Again, waivers for pilot efforts based on outcomes may be necessary.

- Attitudes of educators, parents, students, and the community are a significant factor in the speed and ease of organizational change. They must be considered and addressed so that they better support the restructuring process. Effective systems change requires efforts to empower those who are involved in it. All participants involved must feel some ownership for new programs and procedures and be part of the planning to restructure systems.

- Effective preservice and inservice training for all public school personnel is critical. New systems will require new skills. University training programs in all areas must be consistent with the most current knowledge base in order to prepare personnel with essential skills and attitudes for restructured schools. Substantive and ongoing inservice training must be provided for existing personnel to address skills required in restructured schools. The nature and delivery of preservice and inservice training may need to be redesigned.

NASP is eager to participate in discussion, planning, implementation, and evaluation of pilot restructuring efforts with schools, other organizations, and policy makers.

The Role of School Psychology in Educational Restructuring

For restructuring to occur, all education professions must work collaboratively in planning, implementing, and evaluating shared goals and outcomes. Each profession has important skills to bring to the process. NASP identifies here the knowledge and skills that school psychologists can contribute to educational restructuring. The knowledge base for the practice of school psychology provides an important empirical foundation for educational practice. Professional school psychologists are trained in human behavior, including learning, social, and emotional development. As data-oriented problem solvers, they are trained to approach problems from a systemic perspective and to consider the many interacting factors that influence educational attainment. As children's lives become more complex and as family, school, and other social structures change, this systemic view assumes greater importance. Working collaboratively with other educators, policy makers, parents, and students, school psychologists can make an important contribution to school effectiveness.

As an integral part of educational restructuring, school psychologists can:

- facilitate the process of planning for restructuring by applying expertise in organizational consultation, group process, problem solving and planning;

- integrate their services fully into the "general" education system;

- provide consultation and planning for effective classroom organization and social structures, as well as implementation of effective teaching principles;

- assist in modifying instructional practices to make them more appropriate to the social and academic needs of students with diverse backgrounds and characteristics;

- develop functional assessment procedures that measure instructional progress and learning outcomes;

- participate in developing curricula which promote mentally healthy children and adolescents, including topics of substance abuse prevention, sexuality, child care, relationship building, personal problem solving, suicide prevention and others;

- establish procedures for early identification of an intervention for learning, social, and emotional difficulties;

- help develop meaningful, collaborative partnerships between school and home and provide interventions, including parent education to families where needed.

- develop collaborative relationships with relevant community agencies, including medical, social, economic, and family support systems; and

- apply their training in psychology and research to studying practical problems of instructional and organizational effectiveness and to evaluating the outcomes of educational innovations.

Implementing New Roles

School psychological services should be examined in terms of their impact on students. Although extremely difficult to address, outcome measures also must be applied to psychological services and programs. In applying their own skills, school psychologists must seek to utilize the knowledge and skills of other education professionals in pursuing the challenge of restructuring schools to enhance the academic and personal success of all students. In addition, schools should strive to create the opportunities for school psychologists to perform these roles by implementing policies and funding strategies that promote services to all students.

Adopted April, 1989

Corporal Punishment

As the purpose of the National Association of School Psychologists is to serve the mental health and educational needs of all children and youth; and

The use of corporal punishment as a disciplinary procedure in the schools negatively affects the social, educational, and psychological development of students; and

The use of corporal punishment by educators reinforces the misconception that hitting is an appropriate and effective technique to discipline children; and

Corporal punishment as a disciplinary technique can be easily abused and thereby contribute to the cycle of child abuse; and

School psychologists are legally and ethically bound to protect the students they serve; and

Research indicates that punishment is ineffective in teaching new behaviors, that a variety of positive and effective alternatives are available to maintain school discipline, and that children learn more appropriate problem solving behavior when provided with the necessary models;

Therefore, it is resolved that the National Association of School Psychologists joins other organizations in opposing the use of corporal punishment in the schools and in other institutions where children are cared for or educated;

And will work actively with other organizations to influence public opinion and legislative bodies in recognizing the consequences of corporal punishment, in understanding and researching alternatives to corporal punishment, and in prohibiting the continued use of corporal punishment;

And will encourage state affiliate organizations and individual members to adopt positions opposing corporal punishment, to promote understanding of and research on alternatives to corporal punishment including preventive initiatives, and to support abolition of corporal punishment at state and federal levels.

Adopted by the NASP Delegate Assembly, April, 1986

Early Childhood Assessment

The purpose of the National Association of School Psychologists is to serve the educational and mental health needs of all children and youth, including infants and young children. Because the preschool and primary school years represent a period of rapid development, early identification and intervention for these children's psychological and developmental difficulties are essential, beneficial, and cost-effective. Furthermore, the accurate and fair identification of the developmental needs of young children is critical to the design, implementation, and success of appropriate interventions.

Relative to preschool and primary school children, evidence from research and practice indicates that:

- a limited number of technically adequate assessment procedures are available to conduct appropriate developmental assessments;

- standardized assessment procedures should be applied with great caution to decisions regarding school readiness, as such tools are inherently less accurate and less predictive when used with young children;

- multidisciplinary team assessments must include multiple sources of information, multiple procedures, and multiple settings in order to yield a comprehensive understanding of children's abilities;

- assessments should address family systems and home environments, which substantially influence the development of young children;

- parent–professional collaboration is crucial to decision-making as well as to the identification of child and family service needs;

- traditional categories of exceptionality are inappropriate for use in identifying special needs of young children;

- assessment of young children requires specialized training and skills beyond those required for the assessment of older children;

- longitudinal assessment is needed to evaluate and document progress or response to intervention over time; and

- functional assessment of an infant, young child, or family system's adaptive skills must guide early intervention strategies in meaningful ways.

Therefore, the National Association of School Psychologists will *promote* the following:

1. Early childhood assessment practices that are:

- developmentally appropriate, ecological, comprehensive, curriculum-based, and family-focused;

- conducted by a multi-disciplinary team;

- directly linked to intervention strategies designed for young children, rather than to categorical classification;

- based upon comprehensive, educational and/or behavioral concerns, rather than isolated deficits identified by individual scales;

- nondiscriminatory in terms of gender, ethnicity, native language, family composition, and/or socioeconomic status; and

- technically adequate and validated for the purpose(s) for which they are used.

2. Adoption of the philosophy of "parents as partners" to promote assessments and interventions for young children that include:

- full integration of parents into the assessment and intervention components of early childhood services;

- methods of naturalistic and systematic observation and information gathering;

- involvement of the family, home environment, daycare/preschool, and the community ecology as part of the comprehensive assessment to gather information and input from parents and caregivers.

3. Preservice and inservice education for school psychologists to address:

- normal as well as atypical developmental patterns of young children;

- practices, procedures, and instrumentation appropriate for screening and assessment of young children, their families, and their environments;

- the use of empirically sound procedures and technically adequate instruments with demonstrated treatment utility;

- the selection of assessment techniques and utilization of findings from such assessments for the design, implementation, and efficacy evaluation of interventions;

- standards for early childhood psychological and educational assessment, including legal, ethical, and professional issues; and

- noncategorical service delivery for young children and their families.

Adopted by the NASP Delegate Assembly March 24, 1991

ANNOTATED BIBLIOGRAPHY

Barnett, D., & Paget, K. (1988).Alternative service delivery in preschool settings: Practical and conceptual foundations. In J. Graden, J. Zins, & M. Curtis (Eds.), *Alternative service delivery systems: Enhancing educational options for all students.* Washington, DC: NASP.

This chapter provides the essentials for alternative assessment and intervention design for young children. The empirical foundations of early intervention, an appraisal of traditional preschool service delivery, and practitioner issues are discussed.

Danielson, E., Lynch, E., Moyano, A., Johnson, R., & Bettenburg, A. (1988). *Assessing young children.* Washington, DC: NASP.

This document was acquired from the Minnesota Department of Education and offers information about best practice in screening and assessment of young children. A critique of commonly used procedures is included, as well as standards for selecting and interpreting appropriate procedures. Naturalistic observation and family assessment are encouraged.

McLoughlin, C., & Rausch, E. (1990). Best practices in kindergarten screening. In A. Thomas & J. Grimes (Eds.), *Best practices in school psychology–II.* Washington, DC: NASP.

This chapter summarizes appropriate approaches and skill areas to consider as part of a kindergarten screening program. Problems unique to this age group are included, as well as specific techniques that will lead to developmentally appropriate decision-making.

NASP. (1987). *Early Intervention Services* (Position Statement adopted by the Delegate Assembly, September 1987).

This position statement calls for developmentally appropriate intervention services, comprehensive evaluation of all important aspects of the development of young children, reliable and valid screening, flexible assessment procedures, noncategorical services, and training opportunities for professionals. A supporting paper citing research and policy accompanies this position statement.

Ohio Department of Education. (1988). *Early childhood identification process; A manual for screening and assessment.* Washington, DC: NASP.

This manual uses an intervention framework to describe a wide range of approaches to early identification and referral of at-risk preschool children.

Paget, K. D. (1990). Best practices in the assessment of competence in preschool-age children. In A. Thomas & J. Grimes (Eds.), *Best practices in school psychology–II.* Washington, DC: NASP.

The author summarizes best practices in preschool assessment from an ecological perspective and within the provisions of PL 99-457. Qualitative differences in the approach to assessing young children versus older children are emphasized, along with areas where school school psychologists may need additional training. Support is provided for regarding the family and the child's natural environment as appropriate contexts for assessment.

School Psychology Review, 15(2). (1986). Mini-series on preschool assessment.

This mini-series offers articles covering conceptual as well as practical issues, emphasizing an ecological model. A full range of issues is addressed, including family, curriculum-based developmental procedures, cognition, social-emotional development, and neuropsychology.

Early Childhood Care and Education

The National Association of School Psychologists recognizes that the futures of children are affected by factors that occur early in life. Affordable, high quality early childhood care and education represent major needs of today's and tomorrow's children and families and can benefit children, their families, and society in terms of prevention of later learning and behavior problems, increased family self-sufficiency, and reduced costs for special education, welfare, and other public assistance.

The need for affordable, quality early childhood education and care is supported by the following findings:

- The majority of families in the United States have two parents or a single head of household who work outside the home because of economic necessity and only 7% of households now fit the pattern of a breadwinner father and housewife mother, with dependent children.

- Poverty rates in the United States have increased from 11.6% in 1979 to 14% in 1985. In 1983, 22% of all children lived in households below the poverty level. About 20% of economically disadvantaged children are poor even though they have two parents or a single head of household who work full-time.

- Governmental support for child care has decreased. Many families, particularly single-parent families, cannot afford quality child care, even when parents work. The average yearly child care cost of $3,000 represents 45% of the annual income for one parent working at minimum wage. The cost of child care results in a system where low-income families have few child care choices.

- Many children are left unsupervised or in poor quality child care and may be vulnerable to psychological and physical risks that affect their development and safety. Estimates indicate that 2 to 7 million children aged 6 to 11 years are unsupervised after school. About 70% of family day care programs are not licensed or are not required to be licensed.

- Inadequate child care options can have a broad and costly social impact by contributing to parents' inability to acquire or maintain employment, inability to participate fully in job-assistance programs, and higher absenteeism and lower productivity on the job.

Affordable, high quality early childhood care and education can benefit children, families, and society. Positive outcomes of quality child care and education programs are most pronounced for economically disadvantaged children and families. Although more research is needed, existing research findings support potential benefits in each of these areas:

Children

Participation in quality early childhood programs can result in:

- prosocial behaviors of young children such as more self-regulation, verbalization, and competent play and exploration;

- short-term gains in intelligence test scores, especially by economically disadvantaged children; and

- long term benefits for economically disadvantaged children such as decreased placement in special education and lower retention rates.

Families

- Participation in early childhood programs, particularly those which provide family services, can result in factors such as more positive maternal attitudes regarding their children and themselves and better mother–child interactions.

- Availability of early childhood programs can promote increased family financial self-sufficiency.

Society

Availability of early childhood programs can result in:

- reduction of costs to society, such as costs related to special education, public assistance, crime, and welfare; and

- increased business productivity related to less turnover and absenteeism and improved job productivity in parents.

The benefits identified above are associated with high quality programs. Advanced development of children in early childhood programs is associated with the quality of the programs in terms of factors such as group size, adult–child ratios, curriculum, adult–child interaction, and training and education of the staff. Family involvement, interventions, and services can also be effective components of early childhood programs.

Research concerning participation in after-school care programs by school-aged children is extremely limited at this time, but suggests promising benefits of these programs, including increased social adjustment and academic achievement.

The need for early childhood care and education cannot be denied; furthermore, affordable, high quality child care can promote the futures of children and their families. Therefore, it is resolved that the National Association of School Psychologists will:

1. Support programs and government funding which provide equal access to affordable, high quality early childhood care and education for all children and their families. Tax rebates and credits are not substitutes for government funding of accessible, quality programs.

2. Encourage the development, implementation, and ongoing evaluation of standards for child care quality including:

a. developmentally appropriate curricula.

b. appropriate group sizes and adult–child ratios.

c. adequate staff selection, education, training, and compensation.

d. appropriate physical facilities.

e. responsiveness to individual differences and cultural and language diversity.

f. appropriate access to special and related services or specialists.

g. non-discriminatory practices.

3. Support and assist with the development of alternative forms of child care, including in-home and out-of-home care, that meet the preferences and needs of families.

4. Support public regulation of all forms of out-of-home care to insure the quality of programs and safety of children.

5. Support comprehensive programs, beginning at the prenatal period, which include involvement of and interventions for parents and families, and health, nutrition, and related services.

6. Support continued research investigating factors related to child care, including effects of day care and family dynamics on children's development, methods of improving child care, effects of alternative forms of child care and family services, long-term benefits of child care for children and families, and economic benefits of child care for society.

7. Encourage the development of programs which help families evaluate their child care needs and goals and provide families with information about child care arrangements and standards for quality.

8. Encourage the establishment of partnerships between schools and other programs and organizations which provide accessible, comprehensive early childhood services for all families who need them.

9. Support continued research investigating the effectiveness of after-school care programs for school-aged children.

10. Encourage state affiliate organizations to adopt this position statement and school psychologists to participate in developing affordable, quality child care programs and delivering effective services within the programs.

Adopted by the NASP Delegate Assembly April, 1989

Early Intervention Services

Whereas the purpose of the National Association of School Psychologists is to serve the mental health and educational needs of all children and youth; and

Research has shown that early intervention with handicapped and at-risk infants, toddlers, and preschool children is effective in terms of benefits to children, benefits to their families, and long-term cost savings to school districts and society; and

Many public schools are now or will soon be involved in providing special education and related services to these children and their families as a result of federal and state legislation;

It is is resolved that the National Association of School Psychologists supports the expansion and improvements of services to handicapped and "at-risk" infants, toddlers, and preschool children.

NASP will encourage school psychologists to take part in efforts of national, state, and local levels to:

1. Assure that programs for young children are built on recognition of the needs and developmental characteristics of these children which make them different from older children.

2. Work with school administrators, teachers, and parents to develop programs that attend to all important aspects of the development of young children, including cognitive, motor, self-help, socioemotional, and communication development.

3. Promote programs which provide reliable and valid means of screening young children for possible handicapping and "at-risk" conditions as early as possible.

4. Encourage the use of flexible team assessment approaches which take into account the unique attributes and variability of young children and the influence of home and family factors on their development.

5. Support the provision of necessary individualized services without attempting to assign labels for specific handicapping conditions.

6. Work toward establishing programs which provide a broad spectrum of options for intervention, opportunities for parents to receive support and assistance, and mainstreaming opportunities wherever possible.

7. Encourage university programs, professional associations, public schools and other continuing education providers to provide opportunities for practitioners to receive professional developmental experiences that adequately prepare them to serve the needs of young children and their families.

8. Help establish networks of communication and collaboration among the many agencies that provide service to infants, toddlers, and preschool children.

9. Advocate for the provision of state and federal funding to assure that appropriate programs for infants, toddlers, and preschoolers are provided.

Adopted by the NASP Delegate Assembly September, 1987.

Students with Attention Deficits

The National Association of School Psychologists advocates appropriate educational and mental health services for all children and youth. NASP further advocates noncategorical models of service delivery within the least restrictive environment for students with disabilities and students at risk for school failure.

NASP recognizes that there are students in schools with academic and adjustment problems who exhibit a constellation of behaviors commonly associated with ADD/ADHD (Attention Deficit Disorder/Attention Deficit Hyperactivity Disorder). NASP believes that attention deficits are not a unitary condition, and that they are not reliably diagnosed. NASP also recognizes that it is difficult to distinguish attention deficits so severe as to require special education to which all students are susceptible.

Longitudinal data suggest that the problems associated with attention deficits present at an early age, may change over time, and that they may persist into adulthood. Therefore, NASP believes that interventions must be designed within a developmental framework. Furthermore, recognizing that these students are at particular risk for developing social-emotional and learning difficulties, NASP believes problems should be addressed early to reduce the need for long-term special education.

NASP believes that students with attention deficits can be provided special education services as appropriate under disability categories currently existing in EHA/IDEA. While concern has been expressed that children with attention deficits served in existing categories will not receive the most appropriate instruction for their unique needs, research indicates that disability categories or areas of teacher certification have no significant effect on instructional methods or on effectiveness of service.

NASP believes that excessive emphasis on assessment and diagnosis at the expense of developing and monitoring effective interventions is not in the best interests of children. Assessment of youngsters with possible attention deficits should include intervention assistance to students and their teachers as prerequisites to a formal assessment process.

NASP believes that effective interventions should be tailored to the unique learning strengths and needs of every student. For children with attention deficits, such interventions will often include the following:

1. Classroom modifications to enhance attending, work production, and social adjustment;

2. Behavior management systems to reduce problems in areas most likely to be affected by attention deficits (e.g., unstructured situations, large group instruction, transitions, etc.);

3. Direct instruction in study strategies and social skills, within the classroom setting whenever possible to increase generalization;

4. Consultation with families to assist in behavior management in the home setting and to facilitate home–school cooperation and collaboration;

5. Monitoring by a case manager to ensure effective implementation of interventions, to provide adequate support for those interventions, and to assess programs in meeting behavioral and academic goals;

6. Education of school staff in characteristics and management of attention deficits to enhance appropriate instructional modifications and behavior management;

7. Access to special education services when attention deficits significantly impact school performance;

8. Working collaboratively with community agencies providing medical and related services to students and their families.

NASP believes appropriate treatment may or may not include medical intervention. When medication is considered, NASP strongly recommends:

1. That instructional and behavioral interventions be implemented before medication trials are begun;

2. That behavioral data be collected before and during medication trials to assess baseline conditions and the efficacy of medication; and

3. That communication between school, home, and medical personnel emphasize mutual problem solving and cooperation.

NASP believes school psychologists have a vital role to play in developing, implementing, and monitoring effective interventions with students with attention deficits. As an association, NASP is committed to publishing current research on attention deficits and to providing continuing professional development opportunities to enhance the skills of school psychologists to meet the diverse needs of students with attention deficits.

Adopted by NASP Delegate Assembly September, 1991.

Students with Emotional/Behavioral Disorders

The National Association of School Psychologists is committed to promoting effective services to meet the educational and mental health needs of all students. Students with emotional and/or behavioral problems constitute an underserved population within the American educational and mental health systems. These problems interfere with the acquisition of academic and social skills and negatively impact adult adjustment. Therefore, early identification and intervention for students with emotional and/or behavioral problems are essential.

Definition

The National Association of School Psychologists has endorsed the following definition of Emotional/Behavioral Disorders developed by the National Mental Health and Special Education Coalition:

Emotional or Behavioral Disorder (EBD) refers to a condition in which behavioral or emotional responses of an individual in school are so different from his/her generally accepted, age-appropriate, ethnic, or cultural norms that they adversely affect educational performance in such areas as self-care, social relationships, personal adjustment, academic progress, classroom behavior, or work adjustment.

- EBD is more than a transient, expected response to stressors in the child's or youth's environment and would persist even with individualized interventions, such as feedback to the individual, consultation with parents or families, and/or modification of the educational environment.

- The eligibility decision must be based on multiple sources of data about the individual's behavioral or emotional functioning. EBD must be exhibited in at least two different settings, at least one of which is school-related.

- EBD can co-exist with other handicapping conditions, as defined elsewhere in this law (i.e., Education of Handicapped Act).

- This category may include children or youth with schizophrenia, affective disorders, anxiety disorders, or with other sustained disturbances of conduct, attention, or adjustment.

Assessment and Identification

The identification of a student as emotionally/behaviorally disordered is a serious event that can have lifelong educational, social, and vocational consequences. It is essential that the identification reflects a true handicapping condition, and not the intolerance or insensitivity to individual differences, the impact of unrelated disabilities, or temporary situational factors. The primary purpose of the assessment should be identification of needs/goals and related intervention, not labeling.

The identification process should proceed from the least intrusive to more intrusive procedures. Many behavior problems can be addressed through simple non-intrusive means within the regular education setting. Should behavior problems be more pervasive and intense, more intrusive procedures will be needed, involving personnel beyond the regular education setting. A small number of students will require comprehensive special education assessment, placement, and intervention.

Assessment of emotional/behavioral problems under the above definition should address duration, severity, and pervasiveness of problem manifestations, and response to intervention. Furthermore, the assessment should be collaborative and interdisciplinary, and include:

- Multiple sources of information, including such procedures as structured interviews, systematic and structured observations, behavior checklists and rating scales, self-reports, work samples, and standardized assessment instruments when appropriate. These methods should be demonstrably reliable and valid, and developed for the purposes for which they are used.

- Information from the home and community in relation to the child's behavioral and emotional functioning, cultural norms and expectations, and relevant family, health, and developmental history.

- The determination of a significant impairment in at least one area of school adaptive behavior (such as social skills, organizational skills) and significant impairment in adaptive behavior outside of the school setting (such as vocational skills or interpersonal relationships).

- The analysis of alternative factors underlying the child's behavioral or emotional responses.

- Documentation of the student's response to intervention(s).

- A direct link to intervention planning.

The school psychologist should be involved in all school-based emotional/behavioral disorder assessments. This involvement could include any or all of the following:

- Review of referral and screening information.

- Consultation in the planning of assessment and/or intervention.

- Interpretation of assessment data.

- Linking assessment data to intervention planning, implementation, and evaluation.

Intervention

Emotional/Behavioral Disorder is a dimensional rather than categorical condition. Emotional and/or behavioral disorders that impair school performance exist along a continuum of severity. Most students will experience behavioral and/or emotional difficulties at some time in response to transient situational and developmental stressors. Many students' needs can be effectively addressed through prevention programs, consultation with teachers and parents, short-term counseling, and/or interventions within the regular classroom setting. Such interventions should be empirically-based interventions and of sufficient duration to maximize opportunities for success. Systematic evaluation of interventions is also needed to determine effectiveness, treatment integrity, and the need for modification or additional strategies.

Characteristics of interventions for emotional and behavioral problems should include the following:

- Choice and planning of interventions based on empirical data documenting effectiveness in dealing with identified problems;

- A direct relationship to assessment information;

- A plan to evaluate effectiveness in yielding desired results; and

- Continuous monitoring and adjustment as needed to ensure efficiency and accuracy of services.

Program Placement

Identification is not synonymous with placement in a special education program; and identification does not negate the school's obligation to provide services in the Least Restrictive Environment (LRE). The LRE is the learning environment that best meets the academic and social needs of the student with any appropriate modification and/or related services. The LRE may be the regular education classroom or another setting. Special education programs exist on a continuum from least to most restrictive in relation to the regular education classroom, including resource rooms, self-contained classrooms, and residential programs. Frequently, students requiring more specialized interventions and placements also require coordination of services between school-based and community-based programs.

At each level, school psychologists should consult with teachers, parents, and agencies; provide counseling and social skills training; and continue to develop, implement, and evaluate intervention procedures. Furthermore, school psychologists endorse alternatives to categorical labeling and placement and help ensure that only those students who cannot be served appropriately in the regular classroom, based upon reliable and valid data, are considered for more restrictive programs.

In determining the student's need for placement in a more restrictive setting, the following conditions must be considered.

- Duration — The condition must exist for an extended period of time and not be a short-term response to specific situational stressors.

- Severity — The condition must significantly effect school performance as reflected by academic achievement, acquisition of social skills, and interpersonal relationships within the school setting.

- Pervasiveness — The behaviors of concern occur across situations.

- Resistance to Intervention — The behaviors of concern continue despite the appropriate, individualized application of intervention strategies provided within the regular classroom.

- Exclusionary Factors — The behaviors of concern are not due to transient situational variables, cultural or linguistic differences, or primarily the result of other handicapping conditions. Furthermore, intervention and placement are not sought primarily as disciplinary actions or as efforts to resolve conflicts between individuals or agencies.

Importance of Collaboration

The provision of appropriate services to students with Emotional/Behavioral Disorders requires efficient and effective coordination of assessment and intervention strategies. The multi-disciplinary team is essential to the comprehensive evaluation process and to the determination of eligibility for special education and related services. The National Association of School Psychologists recognizes the importance of collaboration across all service providers to ensure that services are designed and carried out in a manner that is empirically-based, culturally sensitive, and of the greatest benefit to the student and family. The National Association of School Psychologists endorses alternatives to categorical labeling. School psychologists are aware of the long-term harmful effects of such labeling. Thus, only those students who cannot be educated appropriately in the regular classroom, based on reliable and valid data, are considered for more restrictive placements.

REFERENCES

Dwyer, K. P. (1990, Spring). Making the least restrictive environment work for children with serious emotional disturbance: Just say NO to segregated placements. *Preventing School Failure*, 14–21.

Forness, S. R., & Knitzer, J. (1990, June). *A new proposed definition and terminology to replace "serious emotional disturbance" in education of the handicapped act.* Paper developed by the Workgroup of the National Mental Health and Special Education Coalition, Alexandria, VA.

Gresham, F. M. (1991). Conceptualizing behavior disorders in terms of resistance to intervention. *School Psychology Review, 20,* 23–36.

Ranes, R. (1990, March). *Standards for blue ribbon quality: Substantive and evaluative issues in the treatment of seriously emotionally disturbed students.* Paper presented at the California Association of School Psychologists Convention, Irvine, CA.

Employing School Psychologists for Comprehensive Service Delivery

The National Association of School Psychologists supports policies and practices which enhance the education of all students. NASP is concerned about staffing policies which are detrimental to the best interests of the child, family, and school system as a whole. During times of economic crisis and personnel shortages, school districts may consider alternatives to employing their own school psychologists, such as contracting out for services or general staff reductions It is essential that administrators and policy-makers understand the nature and potential limitations of these options and the importance of maintaining professional standards in order to make cost-effective decisions which do not sacrifice the quality or availability of services to students.

Independent contracting for school psychological services includes a variety of arrangements, such as privatization and subcontracting through other public agencies. Some school districts have implemented contracts with agencies or individuals which shift the delivery of services from the public to the private sector, or may contract services through public cooperative (intermediate) units, or may supplant school-based services with "co-located" services of community agencies.

NASP does not oppose the provision of comprehensive school psychological services through intermediate educational agencies. In fact, NASP recognizes that such units often represent the most viable means of ensuring appropriate services. However, NASP opposes independent contracting as a general practice if it compromises the delivery of comprehensive services as required by professional standards and federal law and if contracting supplants or decreases the availability of services delivered by district-employed school psychologists.

NASP's professional standards require that "employing agencies assure that school psychological services are provided in a coordinated, organized fashion, and are deployed in a manner which ensures the provision of a comprehensive continuum of services . . ."[1] In addition, the federal mandates of the Individuals with Disabilities Education Act (IDEA), formerly PL 94-142, require that the evaluation and placement of students with disabilities is comprehensive, multi-faceted, and determined by a multidisciplinary team. This process stresses the need for educational specialists to work with each other in the educational environment and to gather input from numerous sources, including observation of the student within the learning environment, consultation with school personnel regarding educational performance, consultation with parents, and individualized assessment of the student's skills.

Both NASP and the American Psychological Association recognize the specialized training in school psychology as different from the specialized training in other specialty areas, such as clinical and industrial psychology. The independent contractor who is not a trained school psychologist may be a skillful clinician, but lack essential knowledge, expertise, and experience to gather appropriate data in the school context and to facilitate a collaborative, comprehensive approach with the other members of the educational team.

School psychologists employed by school districts:

- offer cost-effective services including early prevention and intervention activities which can eliminate the need for many costly evaluations and placements;

- are readily available to school personnel and students in times of crisis;

- understand school issues form a systems perspective;

- are sufficiently familiar with the students, staff, legal requirements, and policies of the school system to provide support, consultation, and intervention where day-to-day knowledge is essential to communication and to defusing potential dangerous or adversarial situations; and

- provide a wide range of services not easily or cheaply purchased via private contracts, such as reviews of records, consultation with parents and school personnel, ongoing systematic classroom observations, inservice training, program planning and evaluation, and participation on multidisciplinary teams.

Contractual services may be appropriate in limited circumstances in which an outside contractor supplements the regular services of the district's school psychologists or provides services which are otherwise unavailable or impractical. Such circumstances include:

- specific situations where specialized training and experience beyond what is typically available in the school district is required in order to provide appropriate service to the student or district, such as with low incidence disabilities or the provision of clinical home-based services through shared funding;

- situations where a very small district is unable to support the funding of a full-time psychologist and must seek an alternative arrangement such as contracting through an independent services provider; and

- situations where a personnel shortage creates a temporary need to obtain services from available sources such as private providers.

Any contractual agreement should meet the standards established by NASP (Standards for the Provision of School Psychological Services, 1992, Section 3.4, "Contractual Services") and follow the guidelines of the APA/NASP Inter-organizational Council, and ensure that:

- due process rights of students are upheld;
- the amount and quality of psychological services is increased, not decreased; and
- the agreement does not result in any loss of legitimate employee rights, benefits, or wages.

Psychologists hired under independent contract to provide services in the schools should hold at least the same credentials and should be expected to practice within the same professional and ethical standards as school-employed psychologists.

The National Association of School Psychologists is committed to enhancing educational opportunities for all students through the organized delivery of comprehensive school-based psychological services. NASP further recognizes that such services can be delivered in a variety of ways without compromising the rights and needs of students. However, in most situations, the most cost-effective, professionally accountable services will be those delivered from employees within the school district.

NASP therefore urges school administrators and school board members to consider the legal, educational, and long-term financial ramifications of any shift of services away from the school district, and to seek more cost-effective models of service delivery which do not decrease the availability of school-based psychologists. We further urge school psychologists to work with administrators, collective bargaining units, and professional associations to help develop strategies for the delivery of cost-effective services which maintain their rights as employees and enhance educational outcomes for all students.

Finally, NASP urges school psychologists and other educators to empirically evaluate the cost-effectiveness of current and proposed models of service delivery and to establish ongoing program evaluation of all providers of school psychological services.

Standards for the Provision of School Psychological Services, National Association of School Psychologists, 1992.

Guidelines: Contractual Services in School Psychology. Statement developed by the APA/NASP Inter-Organizational Council (IOC). Endorsed by the NASP Delegate Assembly, March 27, 1992.

Adopted by the NASP Delegate Assembly, April 18, 1993.

Home–School Collaboration

The National Association of School Psychologists is committed to increasing the academic, behavioral, and social competence of all children and youth. To meet the educational and mental health needs of all students, partnerships between parents and educators are needed. Collaboration between home and school is essential if students are to benefit optimally from the schooling process. Early implementation of home–school partnerships helps to focus efforts toward prevention.

Parents play an important role in school, and research has demonstrated that:

- home environment influences student performance in school;

- parent participation in education is associated with students' positive attitudes and behavior, long-term achievement gains, better attendance, increased completion of school work, higher grades, and improved test scores;

- specific intervention programs have successfully used parents to change their children's academic and behavioral performance;

- family involvement is essential to address specific referral concerns; and

- children achieve more when there is a match between expectations, rules, and interaction styles in the home and school environments.

Educators need to support families, and research has demonstrated that:

- parents want their children to be successful in school, but some parents do not know how to assist their children;

- parents seek guidance from educators;

- parents want to be partners with educators in the education of their children;

- parents' participation in education includes involvement at home and at school; and

- parents' participation increases when they see their participation directly linked to the success of their children.

Societal factors impinge upon children's school performance, including:

- increased cultural diversity;

- increased poverty and unemployment;

- increased drug abuse, crime, and violence; and

- change in the concept of family (e.g., divorce, remarriage, single parenting, extended families, neighbors).

Society is increasingly recognizing that schools cannot meet the educational and socialization needs of all children without the sharing of resources provided by the family and community. The National Association of School Psychologists supports creating collaborative partnerships between parents and educators for the purpose of increasing students' academic, behavioral, and social competence. Collaborative partnerships are characterized by:

- meaningful dialogue and sharing of information;

- mutually agreed upon goals;

- sharing of resources; and

- shared decision-making

The philosophy of partners working together toward a common goal with shared power characterizes home–school collaboration. Home–school collaboration is an attitude, not an activity and occurs when parents and educators share common goals and responsibilities, and are seen as equals. Effective partnerships recognize that all parent/families have strengths rather than identifying deficits. Effective partnerships between parents and educators have an additive, positive effect on students' performance.

NASP encourages school psychologists to take part in national, state, and local efforts to:

- define parent involvement in education to include true partnerships between home, school, and community;

- advocate, with school systems, for increased collaboration between educators and parents regarding the schooling process.;

- reach out to all parents and identify strategies to encourage participation by uninvolved parents;

- recognize parents as experts in relationship to their children's behavior;

- avoid labeling families by using an approach which builds on family strengths;

- work with other organizations to promote home–school–community partnerships to increase students' performance in school;

- pursue continuing education on such topics as family interventions, models of home–school collaboration, models of parent education/training, child development and family developments, and understanding cultural and ethnic differences;

- develop parent involvement programs that provide parents with options to be meaningfully involved and are sensitive to individual parents' needs, resources, and time constraints, including those parents who may have been disenfranchised from the school due to their own negative experiences;

- promote communication among families, community, and school personnel to increase students' success in school;

- provide training and support to parents from all cultures on effective strategies for communicating with educators;

- provide training to educators to increase their understanding of culturally and ethnically diverse families;

- develop home–school collaboration programs that facilitate family–school meetings as parents and educators engage in problem solving about individual students;

- provide direct services to parents regarding techniques to promote students' academic and behavioral success in school and the community; and

- consult with parents and teachers to coordinate home and school efforts and serve as a liaison to maintain information exchange and sharing of resources between home, school, and community.

Adopted by the NASP Delegate Assembly, September, 1992.

Inclusive Programs for Students with Disabilities

The Individuals with Disabilities Education Act (IDEA) created significant educational opportunities for students with disabilities and established important safeguards that ensure the provision of a free, appropriate education to students with special needs. NASP strongly supports the continuation and strengthening of this mandate. NASP also recognizes the need to continually evaluate the effectiveness of all aspects of our educational system and to promote reform when needed.

Problems with the Current System

NASP also recognizes that the special education system that evolved under this mandate includes a number of problems that create unintended negative outcomes for some students. These include:

- A referral and evaluation system that does not function as originally intended. Some of the weaknesses of this system include: (a) an inability to reliably differentiate among categories of students with disabilities; (b) a lack of evidence that students grouped by category learn differently or are taught differently; and (c) a classification system that lacks reliability, utility, and acceptance by many parents and professionals.

- Inequities in implementation of the least restrictive environment provisions of IDEA. Data suggests that the restrictiveness of many special education placements is not based upon the severity of students' disabilities, but may instead result from the configuration of the service delivery system that is available in the community.

- Concerns that traditional special education programs are not effective in terms of learner outcomes.

- Overly restrictive special education programs housed in separate schools or "cluster" sites that result in social segregation and disproportionate numbers of students with disabilities being grouped together. For example, some students, especially those with more severe disabilities, must attend separate schools to receive appropriate special services. Many parents and professionals feel that it is inherently inequitable that some students must leave their neighborhood schools and communities to receive appropriate services.

A Call for Inclusive Schools

NASP, in its continuing commitment to promote more effective educational programs for ALL students, advocates the development of inclusive programs for students with disabilities. Inclusive programs are those in which students, regardless of the severity of their disability, receive appropriate specialized instruction and related services within an age-appropriate general education classroom in the school that they would attend if they did not have a disability. *NASP believes that carefully designed inclusive programs represent a viable and legitimate alternative on the special education continuum that must be examined for any student who requires special education.*

Potential Benefits

Some of the benefits of inclusive programs include:

- typical peers serving as models for students with disabilities;

- the development of natural friendships within the child's home community;

- learning new skills within natural environments, facilitating generalization of skills;

- students with disabilities existing in "natural" proportions within the school community;

- all students learning to value diversity; and

- general education classrooms that are better able to meet the needs of all students as a result of additional instructional resources, a more flexible curriculum, and adapted instructional delivery systems.

Developing Inclusive Programs

In advocating for the development of these programs, NASP takes the position that:

- Inclusive programs must provide all the services needed to ensure that students make consistent social and academic gains.

- General education teachers, special education teachers, school psychologists, other related services providers, and parents must collaborate to ensure appropriate services for all students and to ensure that all programs are based upon a careful analysis of each student's needs.

- Outcome-based data on inclusive programs must be collected to ensure that students with and without disabilities are making consistent educational progress.

- All educators involved in implementing inclusive programs must participate in planning and training activities. Knowledge and skills in effective collaboration, curriculum adaptation, developing supportive social relationships, and restructuring special services are but a few of the areas in which skills are needed. Training based upon the needs of the staff involved in planning these programs is essential.

The Role of the School Psychologist

School psychologists can provide effective leadership in the development of inclusive programs. School psychologists have training and experience in collaborative consultation, disabilities, intervention design and curriculum adaptation, modification of learning environments, program evaluation, and other issues critical to effective inclusive programs. Because of this expertise, school psychologists are in a unique position to assist schools in assessing student needs, reallocating existing resources, and restructuring service delivery systems to better meet the educational and mental health needs of all students. School psychologists can foster the development of inclusive schools by:

- providing meaningful support and consultation to teachers and other educators implementing inclusive programs;

- distributing articles and research to fellow educators and district committees responsible for educational restructuring;

- leading or serving as members of groups that are evaluating or restructuring education programs;

- planning and conducting staff development programs that support inclusion;

- providing information on needed changes to legislators and state and federal policy-makers; and

- collecting and analyzing program evaluation and outcome-based student data.

Changing our Schools

NASP recognizes that the current framework of special education policies and regulations is often incompatible with inclusive programs. Consequently, NASP joins with the National Association of State Boards of Education in calling for a fundamental shift in the policies which drive our compensatory education system. Changes are required in:

- The system used to identify and evaluate students with special needs. Categorical labeling systems are not only unreliable and stigmatizing, they are unnecessary in an inclusive system.

- The current special education funding system. The link between funding and placements must be severed. Many aspects of the funding system are driven by labels and program locations rather than by student needs.

NASP recognizes that the shift toward more inclusive schools will require profound changes in the ways in which schools are organized. We are committed to working with parents, other professional groups, and state and national policy-makers in creating new funding and regulatory mechanisms that promote effective programs within neighborhood schools and ensure that students with special needs continue to receive appropriate resources. We endorse a process of planned change that involves all stakeholders in research, planning, and training to ensure that our nation's schools can attain excellence for *all* of our children.

Adopted by the NASP Delegate Assembly, April 17, 1993.

Minority Recruitment

As the purpose of the National Association of School Psychologists is to serve the mental health and educational interests of all youth,

As the proportion of ethnic minority children is increasing in the total school population, and

As there are disproportionately few ethnic minority school psychologists to serve both regular and special education students, and

As NASP is committed to the recruitment of ethnic minority group members,

Therefore, it is resolved that the National Association of School Psychologists will work actively to increase the numbers of ethnic minority school psychologists working with children and as trainers in school psychology programs;

And will advocate the use of recruitment procedures that are known to be successful, such as flexible admission standards, financial support, and active outreach efforts;

And will encourage its membership to assist school psychology training programs in recruiting ethnic minority group members into the profession;

And will encourage school psychology training programs to conduct research and develop the most appropriate strategies to recruit, train, and graduate greater numbers of ethnic minority individuals from their programs.

Adopted by the NASP Delegate Assembly, September, 1987.

Pupil Services: Essential Education

The goal of education is to prepare young people to become literate and motivated workers, caring family members and responsible citizens. Professionals concerned with education further recognize that — in addition to intellectual challenges — students must overcome personal, social, organizational, and institutional challenges that could place them at risk for educational failure. Intervention that addresses these challenges is essential.

Pupil service teams that include professional counselors, school psychologists, and school social workers are trained in such interventions and in removing barriers to learning. These professionals are partners with other educators, parents and the community in accomplishing this objective and in providing optimum teaching and learning conditions for all students in a total education program.

The value of pupil services has long been recognized by federal, state, and local governments. In 1988, the pupil services team concept was again reinforced in federal law. In the Hawkins-Stafford Elementary and Secondary School Improvement Amendments of 1988 (PL 100-297), the following definition was included:

> "The terms 'pupil services personnel' and 'pupil services' mean school counselors, school social workers, school psychologists, and other qualified professional personnel involved in providing assessment diagnosis, counseling, education, therapeutic, and other necessary services as part of a comprehensive program to meet student needs, and the services provided by such individuals."

Clearly, pupil services are most effectively delivered through the team approach. The complex needs of students demand the comprehensiveness implied by uniting the skills of trained professionals. Through teamwork, school psychologists, school social workers, school counselors, and other pupil services providers work together to provide coordinated services for students and their families. The pupil services team approach is based on the following concepts:

- Pupil services programs should be developed from identified needs of students, parents, staff, and administrators.

- All pupil services are related and must be coordinated for optimum effectiveness.

- Pupil services demand developmental, preventive, and remedial emphases, thus requiring the contributions of skilled professionals.

- Pupil services facilitate effective linkages between the school community and external community resources.

- Program evaluation is critical to pupil services teamwork.

- The teamwork required for achievement of pupil service objectives mandates trust, open communication, mutual respect, ongoing collaboration, and effective coordination.

We believe that this team approach for pupil services can establish a national precedent for state and local initiatives. Such initiatives would be designed to provide vital services to all young people in our schools. Our purpose is to support the efforts of counselors, psychologists, social workers, and other pupil service professionals in providing a coordinated delivery system designed to serve this country's school-aged youth.

Through this statement, our respective organizations reaffirm the pupil services team approach as integral to the educational process. We further signify our commitment to continue collaborative efforts. We invite other pupil service professionals to join with us in this alliance.

This statement issued jointly by the American Association for Counseling and Development, the American School Counselor Association, the National Association of School Psychologists, and the National Association of Social Workers.

Racism, Prejudice, and Discrimination

The National Association of School Psychologists is committed to promoting the rights, welfare, educational, and mental health needs of all students. This can only be accomplished in a society which ensures that all people, including children and youth, are treated equitably without reference to race, ethnicity, religion, or gender. NASP believes that racism, prejudice, and discrimination are harmful to children and youth because they can have a profoundly negative impact on school achievement, self-esteem, personal growth, and ultimately the welfare of all American society.

A discussion of multicultural issues requires a definition of terms. The following definitions apply to the terms used in this position statement (adopted from the Multicultural Project for Community Education, Cambridge, MA and Washington, DC).

Prejudice: Prejudice is an attitude, opinion, or feeling formed without prior knowledge, thought, or reason.

Discrimination: Discrimination is differential treatment that favors one individual, group, or object over another. The source of discrimination is prejudice, and the actions are not systematized.

Racism: Racism is racial prejudice and discrimination — supported by institutional power and authority — used to the advantage of one race and the disadvantage of other race(s). The critical element of racism which differentiates racism from prejudice and discrimination is the use of institutional power and authority to support prejudice and endorse discriminatory behaviors in systematic ways with far-reaching outcomes and effects.

Research indicates that students who are the victims of racism, prejudice, and discrimination develop feelings of worthlessness; deny membership within their own group, identify with the dominant group, develop prejudice against other ethnic minorities, achieve less in school and have lower aspirations for the future, and drop out of school in increased numbers.

As a nation, we must be committed to replacing racism, discrimination, and prejudice with attitudes and behaviors that reflect fairness and cooperation. Children must learn tolerance and cooperation, and this learning must begin at an early age. The National Association of School Psychologists urges all educators and community leaders to:

- promote policies to establish and maintain racial and cultural diversity among school personnel;

- take an active role in teaching students pluralistic values, using strategies such as cultural sensitivity training, cooperative learning, and conflict resolution training;

- discuss racism, prejudice, and discrimination with students of all ages;

- provide students with an opportunity to learn about culturally and ethnically diverse groups;

- employ curricula which give students the opportunity to explore issues of self-identity; and

- develop self-esteem programs for all students to promote self-respect and respect for others.

As mental health professionals, it is our charge to understand the effects of racism, discrimination, and prejudice — how they impact on our own performance as school psychologists and how they affect every facet of the lives of children in America. The practice of school psychology must be informed by this knowledge and understanding, and NASP supports all efforts, at both a preservice and inservice level, to ensure that this occurs. NASP believes that school psychologists have a critical role to play in making schools culturally sensitive environments. Ultimately, the welfare of all students — and our nation — is at stake.

Adopted by the NASP Delegate Assembly, March, 1993.

Rights without Labels

The Rights without Labels concept has been developed to address problems associated with the classification and labeling of children as "handicapped" for educational purposes. This classification establishes certain legal rights for children and parents, often including funds for schools offering specialized services.

Problems permeate this system: unreliability of classification; lack of instructional relevance for some classifications; exclusion of children from regular education; and the stigmatization of classified children. Moreover, removing these classifications and labels to return a student to regular education has proved very difficult.

The Rights without Labels guidelines presented here have special significance for children with academic and/or behavioral difficulties who are frequently classified as learning disabled, educable mentally retarded, or behavioral disordered/emotionally disturbed. Our intention, however, is to apply these guidelines to as broad a range of exceptionalities as is feasible and in no way to diminish opportunities for even the severely/profoundly handicapped student to be served in settings with their non-handicapped peers.

The Rights without Labels guidelines are based on the assumption that it would be desirable at this time to conduct programs wherein efforts are made to serve children who have special needs without labeling them or removing them from regular education programs. Research indicates that several factors are critical to the success of such experimental programs.

Pre-referral Screening/Intervention

Attempts must be made at the very outset to ameliorate educational difficulties through the use of pre-referral screening/intervention methods conducted by regular school personnel with the support of resources typically limited to special education (i.e., school psychologists, teachers, social workers, speech therapists, etc.). This benefits all children, especially those experiencing educational problems, while helping to identify students with characteristics consonant with legal definitions of handicapped conditions. Such practices will engender an abiding respect for students' rights under the law not to be evaluated in the absence of genuine suspicion of a handicap.

Curriculum Based Assessment

Secondly, identification and evaluation methods must include curriculum based assessment procedures. Research demonstrates these procedures provide reliable measures of student performance and produce relevant information for instructional planning. Most importantly, they fulfill the evaluation protection criteria set out in PL 94-142. The primary purpose of these procedures is not to classify or label children, but rather to identify specific curriculum and instructional deficits and strengths in order to provide a framework to develop appropriate educational programs. Individualized Education Programs (IEPs) continue to be required, as well as related services provided in accordance with current legal guidelines.

Special Resources in Regular Settings

The traditional array of special education supplementary aids, services and resources (including teachers/aides) are available to children only outside the regular classroom. Our goal is to broaden the classroom situation within which special education resources can be used and to reverse the practice of moving handicapped students to special education situations outside regular classes and schools. Instead, special education resources can be transferred into the non-categorically identified student's regular classroom setting.

RIGHTS WITHOUT LABELS GUIDELINES

These guidelines are stated positively as principles for programs which professionals, advocates, and parents may wish to examine. The checklist format is provided for use in developing experimental programs in local or state systems.

I. ASSURANCES: Any proposed alternatives non-categorical program or system shall:

A. Ensure that the fundamental rights afforded handicapped students and their parents under PL 94-142 are maintained and safeguarded. These include, but are not limited to:

1. Standards for fair and unbiased identification and evaluation of children who would qualify as "handicapped" in a categorical system.

2. Individualized Education Programs (IEPs) for all students who would otherwise qualify under a categorical system.

3. Specialized instruction and related services for students who would otherwise qualify under a categorical system.

4. Least Restrictive Environment (LRE) standards in determining educational placements.

5. Appointment of surrogate parents when appropriate.

6. Non-discriminatory discipline procedures.

7. All timeline standards governing the above practices and procedures.

8. Parental rights in the identification, evaluation, IEPs, and placement of students who would otherwise qualify under a categorical system.

9. Due Process rights for parents and students who wish to pursue concerns/complaints regarding educational evaluations, programs, and placements.

10. Local advisory boards to assist (LEAs) in planning for the provision of appropriate educational services.

B. Provide parents of handicapped students with an alternative to selecting a traditional categorical approach to classification.

C. Provide full disclosure of the non-categorical system to parents including an explanation of resources, services, and rights that will be afforded students in this system.

II. GENERAL QUALITY OF ALTERNATIVE PROGRAM: Any proposed non-categorical program or system shall:

A. Employ pre-referral screening/intervention measures and utilize evaluation procedures that include curriculum-based assessments.

B. Employ methodology known to be associated with effective teaching/learning (for example, provide students with orderly and productive environments, ample learning/teaching time, systematic and objective feedback on performance, well sequenced curricula, etc.).

C. Focus attention on basic skills as priority areas for instruction (for example, language, self-dependence, reasonable social behavior, mathematics, health and safety, etc.).

D. Provide procedures to identify and respond to the individual needs of all students, and in particular, those who may need modifications in their school programs.

E. Provide for special education aids, services, and resources to be delivered in regular education settings.

III. ASSESSMENT OF OUTCOMES: Any proposed non-categorical program shall:

A. Have an objective methodology for assessing the educational progress of students in major curriculum domains (including academic, social, motivational, and attitudinal variables) and for comparing such progress with results in traditional programs.

B. Contain and utilize a cost-benefit analysis to compare costs with traditional programs.

IV. TEACHING STAFF AND FACILITIES: Any proposed non-categorical program shall:

A. Include instruction and services by teachers and staff who are qualified in accordance with current state certification standards.

B. Include a delivery system that provides continuing staff development responsive to the training needs of the teaching staff and administrative personnel who will be implementing the requirements of the non-categorical program.

C. Include appropriate instructional materials and other resources.

D. Include assurances that funding levels and personnel allocations will not be decreased during the experimental period or as a result of successful alternative service delivery.

To provide these assurances it is assumed that as part of the experimental procedures, it would be common to conduct a dual classification system, whereby, for example, a student who might be classified as "learning disabled" in a traditional system would actually be so identified. Although the student's record would reflect the traditional classification, the student would be considered in need of "supplemental services" (ie., regular and special education services) for purposes of his/her participation in the non-categorical program. Only by such a dual system could assurances concerning "rights" be offered and safeguarded. Over the long term, the traditional classification system might be modified if all stakeholders are satisfied with the new procedure.

School Psychologists: Assessment Experts for Restructured Schools

School psychologists have long been recognized for their expertise in developing, conducting, and interpreting individual and program assessment procedures; and

School psychologists are specifically trained in psychometric theory, assessment procedures, and the application of assessment data to educational decisions; and

School psychologists have expertise in norm-referenced assessment techniques that are well grounded in research; and

School psychologists promote the use of technically adequate assessment tools which are directly linked to instruction and intervention; and

Initiatives for school restructuring, such as inclusion, outcome-based education, and site-based management, have significant implications for the evaluation of student and program outcomes; and

New models of schools may require new approaches to student and program evaluation; and

The current empirical base for new approaches such as authentic assessment is very limited; and

Furthermore, be it relayed that the National Association of School Psychologists will work with school psychologists to refine the appropriate use of norm-referenced assessment techniques and expand their understanding and utilization of alternative assessment techniques. NASP will work with training programs to ensure that alternative models of assessment are included in the revision and updating of core curriculum to prepare school psychologists for their roles in restructured schools. NASP affirms its commitment to ensure that practicing school psychologists have opportunities to learn and develop skills in functional and problem-solving assessment through ongoing professional development.

Adopted by the NASP Delegate Assembly, April 17, 1993.

Three Year Evaluations for Handicapped Students

Three-year reevaluation of students in special education placements is a critical assessment concern of school psychologists. Reevaluations are often mechanical, bureaucratic processes which do not address the unique needs of students. Specific problems with current reevaluation practices include excessive emphasis on reestablishing eligibility, rote replication of initial evaluation procedures, excessive reliance on unnecessary psychoeducational tests, and a lack of variation in assessment team membership to reflect the unique concerns of the reevaluation.

Federal law and regulations on reevaluations have been misinterpreted by many state and local school systems. State and local policies often require that the same assessment procedures used for initial evaluation be used for reevaluation and/or that "tests" per se must be administered. In fact, although the same assessment "domains" must be addressed, federal law and regulations allow alternative assessment procedures. Reevaluation practices among professionals vary widely due to these state and local interpretations and to varying understanding of the purposes for conducting the reevaluations. A change in the focus and process of reevaluations as conducted in many places is needed in order to serve the best interests of students and to better utilize time and skills of involved school personnel.

NASP supports, and federal regulations allow, a flexible approach to three-year reevaluations based on the unique needs of the student and the specific questions that need to be answered. Federal guidelines and professional standards call for meaningful, individualized, multifaceted reevaluations which serve the best interests of students. The following factors should be considered in conducting and in shaping the nature of reevaluations.

- The purposes and specific questions for reevaluation should guide the selection of assessment methods. Three broad purposes of reevaluation are:

  1. evaluating the effectiveness of the student's individual education program,

  2. evaluating the appropriateness of the student's current interventions and determining his/her future needs, and

  3. determining whether the student continues to be eligible for special education services.

- Additional factors influence the choice of specific assessment procedures, including the student's age, severity, and nature of handicap(s), progress in school, years in special education, availability of data from many sources (e.g., school and home), and the consistency of the results of previous evaluations.

- Sources of information that may be considered in an assessment include, but are not limited to, review of records, interviews, observations, curriculum-based measures, rating scales, and psychoeducational tests. Some areas of assessment may require procedures from several of these data sources, whereas others may use only one source.

- When any student is placed in a special education program, the ultimate goal whenever feasible should be that student's return to general education. Exit criteria for special programs should include functional assessment of the student's performance in special program/placement options. Criteria written solely in terms of initial eligibility standards do not address the best interest of the child.

In order to implement reevaluation processes that are useful in meeting student and program needs, NASP encourages school psychologists, school administrative units, and state education agencies to develop flexible and meaningful approaches to reevaluation. School psychologists have unique training and expertise in assessment, and their knowledge is crucial in the selection of appropriate, reliable, and valid assessment procedures. They should be available to assist the multidisciplinary team in selecting and conducting assessments which address the efficacy and appropriateness of the student's current program, future program needs, and program eligibility. Of primary importance is the need for school psychologists to assist in developing appropriate instructional strategies in general education settings so that handicapped students may successfully return to the mainstream as soon as possible.

Adopted by the NASP Delegate Assembly, April, 1989.

Student Grade Retention

The National Association of School Psychologists is committed to promoting educational practices that are demonstrably effective in enhancing the educational attainment of all children. The retention of students, while widely practiced, is in large measure not substantiated by sound research.

The cumulative evidence indicates that retention decisions cannot be validated using any standardized or competency-based tests and that retention can negatively affect achievement and social-emotional adjustment.

Retention has not been shown to be successful:

- When it is employed in lieu of other more effective interventions when students fail to learn;

- When it is used to postpone or supplant special education services;

- When it is used at the secondary level where it correlates positively with student drop-out rates;

- When retention or delayed school entrance is used with students with social or behavioral deficits linked to "developmental immaturity."

Retention is least likely to be harmful when students:

- lack serious deficits in the year prior to retention;

- have positive self-esteem and good social skills;

- show signs of difficulty in school because of lack of opportunity for instruction rather than lack of ability;

- do not have serious social, emotional, or behavioral deficits.

Therefore, it is resolved that the National Association of School Psychologists will:

1. Encourage early identification and intervention of academic, behavioral, and/or emotional difficulties to avoid the inappropriate use of retention.

2. Encourage use of interventions other than retention for students in academic difficulty.

3. Promote and publicize research comparing retention to alternative practices at the kindergarten and first grade level with children determined to be at risk for school failure.

4. Encourage school psychologists to assist in the decision-making process about retention of individual students by examining:

   a. the child's school and developmental history.

   b. reasons for school failure (e.g., emotional problems, low ability, frequent school moves or absences).

   c. the effectiveness of instruction (e.g., teaching practices, the match between teaching and learning style and between student achievement level and curricular demands).

   d. the type and quality of alternative strategies (e.g., direct instruction, remedial services, cooperative learning, peer tutoring, etc.).

   e. student attitude toward retention and level of parental support, and

   f. the extent of alternative programming available in both the new and repeated grade.

5. Encourage NASP's state affiliate organizations and individual members to adopt positions and support research which promote alternative interventions to retention.

Approved by the NASP Delegate Assembly, July, 1988.

A Summary of Credentialing Requirements for School Psychologists in Public School Settings

Joseph Prus
Winthrop University

Ashlyn Draper
Winthrop University

Michael J. Curtis
University of South Florida

Sawyer Hunley
University of Cincinnati

Psychoeducational problem solving and related services provided by psychologists in the schools require substantial breadth and depth of training. School psychologists must be adequately prepared to respond to increasingly diverse and intensive needs of children, youth, and families in a rapidly changing world. Credentialing standards such as certification and licensure requirements are intended to ensure that school psychologists possess minimum qualifications needed to be effective providers of professional services to the public. Requirements for certification or licensure also regulate who may use the title "school psychologist" or legally provide school psychological services, and may affect the level of independent professional functioning and career opportunities available to school psychologists. Thus, familiarity and compliance with the requirements for being certified or licensed are important prerequisites for school psychologists and aspiring school psychologists.

Licensure and certification requirements affect the roles and functions of most educators, health care practitioners, and human service providers, including school psychologists. They are part of the mechanism by which governments and professional regulating bodies protect the health, safety, and welfare of citizens (Council of State Governments, 1952). The existence of credentialing requirements for school psychologists in all 50 states and the District of Columbia as well as certification at the national level thus reflects the perceived importance of our profession in its potential benefit, as well as harm, to members of the public.

There has been a consistent interest in certification and licensure requirements for school psychologists for nearly 50 years (Horrocks, 1946; Clayton, 1950; Hodges, 1960; Gross, Bonham, & Bluestein, 1966; Graff & Clair, 1973; Sewall & Brown, 1976; Brown, Horn, & Lindstrom, 1980; Prus, White, & Pendleton, 1987; Curtis, Hunley, & Prus, 1995). Since its inception, the National Association of School

Psychologists (NASP) has been the primary source of review and dissemination of such requirements (Sewall & Brown, 1976; Brown, Horn, & Lindstrom, 1980; Prus, White, & Pendleton, 1987; Curtis, Hunley, & Prus, 1995). In addition, NASP created the National School Psychology Certification System (NSPCS) in 1988 for the purpose of promoting nationally recognized standards for credentialing school psychologists.

In order to qualify to use the designation Nationally Certified School Psychologist, or NCSP, individuals must meet a variety of entry level requirements based on *Standards for the Credentialing of School Psychologists* (NASP, 1994). Requirements include:

- Completion of a sixth year/specialist or higher level degree program in school psychology, with a sixty (60) graduate semester hour minimum consisting of coursework, practica, internship and an appropriate graduate degree from an accredited institution of higher learning;

- Preparation in psychological foundations, educational foundations, assessment, interventions, statistics/research design, and professional school psychology;

- Successful completion of a 1200 hour internship in school psychology, of which 600 hours must be in a school setting. The internship must be supervised by a credentialed school psychologist or a psychologist appropriately credentialed for an alternate setting and be recognized through institutional (transcript) documentation;

- Attainment of a passing score on the National School Psychology Examination administered by Educational Testing Service (ETS/NTE Test #40, which is now part of ETS's PRAXIS series).

As is indicated by the summary of certification and licensure requirements presented later in this chapter, some states have adopted the NCSP credential as a mechanism by which applicants are certified or licensed to practice in the public schools. Others are in the process of considering formal recognition of the NCSP credential in state education regulations.

This chapter presents a summary of certification and licensure requirements for school psychologists in public school settings. It is based on the most recent national review of such requirements completed by NASP in 1994. A risk inherent in any summary is that misinterpretation may occur due to the lack of potentially important details in the summary. The highly detailed information contained in the certificate and licensure regulations of many states, along with ongoing modifications of such regulations, suggest the need for caution in using this summary for professional planning or decision making. The reader interested in the requirements of a particular state should refer to the latest edition of NASP's *Handbook of Certification and Licensure Requirements for School Psychologists* (Curtis, Hunley, & Prus, 1995) or obtain the actual state credentialing requirements (names, addresses, and phone numbers of state contacts are included in the *Handbook*).

Data Collection and Validation

Standardized survey protocols and copies of state credentialing summaries from the Fourth Edition of the *Handbook of Certification and Licensure Requirements for School Psychologists* (Prus, White, & Pendleton, 1987) were mailed to departments of education, certification/licensure offices, and similar departments and offices which oversee state level credentialing for school psychologists. An initial mailing list of state contacts was compiled through the previous edition of NASP's *Handbook*. Phone calls to state offices were conducted in order to update the list prior to mailing.

Respondents were asked to complete the survey, review and revise as needed a written summary of their state standards, and provide copies of administrative codes and statutes for the credentialing of school psychologists in the public schools. Follow-up phone calls and mailings were made to nonrespondents. Ninety-four (94) percent of states responded by completing the survey and reviewing draft summaries of their requirements. Previous summaries, reviews of state regulations obtained through alternate methods, and consultation with state school psychology consultants and trainers were used to summarize the requirements of four states which had not responded to written requests. These states are noted in the summary tables that appear later in this chapter.

Every effort has been made to ensure the presentation of valid summary information regarding certification and licensure requirements. Ultimately, however, the responsibility and authority to provide and interpret credentialing requirements lie with the appropriate agencies within individual states. Consequently, individuals interested in credentialing within a given state should contact the designated official within that state.

Interpretation of Summary Tables

Considerable variation exists in the content and terminology of state credentialing laws and regulations. Most commonly, "licensure" refers to the process of regulation applicable to practice of psychology or school psychology in the private sector or outside the public educational system. The licensure process in this sense is typically administered by state boards of psychology or psychological examiners. "Certification" usually refers to the process of credentialing public school professionals including school psychologists. This process is most often regulated and administered by state departments of education.

The above descriptions of licensure and certification are not universally applicable. For example, some state boards of psychology *certify* psychologists for private practice while some state departments of education refer to their credentialing process as *licensure*. Recent discussions and efforts to promote state *licensure* and national *certification* in education have the potential to add to the confusion regarding these terms. Thus, those seeking credentials are advised to clarify the nature and scope of the credential they desire and the setting in which they plan to work. *Licensure* and *certification* requirements as summarized in this chapter refer to credentials issued by state departments of education and similar agencies and departments for the practice of school psychology in the public schools.

The basic requirements for state credentials for school psychologists in public school settings are summarized in Table 1. This table includes the title and levels of the credential(s) by state, minimum degree and graduate credit hours required, internship and field experience requirements, and whether or not an exam must be passed. It is suggested that the reader review the notes appearing at the end of the table as these define terms and abbreviations used to clarify information in the table.

School psychologists concerned with the "mobility" of their training and credentials should be aware of the processes of credentialing that states utilize for out-of-state applicants wishing to work in the public schools. Some states offer reciprocity, which is a process through which an individual may become credentialed in one state by virtue of possessing a comparable or equivalent credential in another state. Other state departments of education certify or license school psychologists who have completed a training program approved by the state of origin or by an accrediting body or specialty organization such as

NASP. A more recent trend has been the adoption by some states of certification by the National School Psychology Certification Board as a means by which to attain state credentials. State options for school psychology credentialing of out-of-state applicants are summarized in Table 2.

Finally, Table 3 summarizes processes by which in-state applicants are credentialed in school psychology. These processes often differ from the credentialing processes for out-of-state applicants (e.g., a state may require completion of a state-approved training program in school psychology for in-state applicants but accept the NCSP credential or have a reciprocity agreement in granting certification or licensure to those trained in other states). Tables 2 and 3 contain information regarding examination requirements for credentialing school psychologists for work in the public schools.

REFERENCES

Brown, D. T., Horn, A. J., & Lindstrom, J. P. (1980). *The handbook of certification/licensure requirements for school psychologists* (Third Edition). Washington, DC: National Association of School Psychologists.

Council of State Governments. (1952). *Occupational licensing legislation in the states: A study of state legislation licensing in practice of professions and other occupations.* Chicago: Author.

Curtis, M., Hunley, S., & Prus, J. (1995). *Handbook of certification and licensure requirements for school psychologists* (Fifth Edition). Silver Spring, MD: National Association of School Psychologists.

Graff, M. P., & Clair, T. N. (1973). Requirements for certification of school psychologists: A survey of recent trends. *American Psychologist, 8,* 704–709.

Gross, F. P., Bonham, S. J., & Bluestein, V. W. (1966). Entry requirements for state certification of school psychologists: A review of the past nineteen years. *Journal of School Psychologists, 4,* 43–51.

Hodges, W. (1960). State certification of school psychologists. *American Psychologist, 6,* 346–349.

Horrocks, J. E. (1946). State certification requirements for school psychologists. *American Psychologist, 1,* 399–401.

National Association of School Psychologists. (1984). *Standards for the credentialing of school psychologists.* Silver Spring, MD: Author.

Prus, J. S., White, G. W., & Pendleton, A. (1987). *Handbook of certification and licensure requirements for school psychologists* (Fourth Edition). Washington, DC: National Association of School Psychologists.

Sewall, T. J., & Brown, D. T. (1976). *The handbook of certification requirements for school psychologists.* Washington, DC: National Association of School Psychologists.

TABLE 1
Summary of Basic Credentialing Requirements

STATE	TITLE LEVEL/TYPE	MINIMUM DEGREE	CREDIT HOURS	EXPERIENCE		EXAM
				INTERNSHIP	FIELD	
Alabama	School Psychometrist (A) School Psychometrist (AA) School Psychologist (AA)	Master's Master's Master's	33 66 66	10 weeks 10 weeks 300 hours	2 years (T) 2 years (T) 2 years (T)	AP AP AP
Alaska	School Psychologist	Master's	AP	AP		no
Arizona	School Psychometrist (I) Assistant School Psychologist (II) School Psychologist (III)	Master's Master's Master's	30 50 70	1 semester (e) 1 year (e) 1 year (e)		no no no
Arkansas	School Psychology Specialist	Master's	60	1200 hours		yes
California	Pupil Personnel Services - School Psychology	Master's	60	required		yes
Colorado	Special Services Certificate (E)	6th year		required		yes
Connecticut	School Psychologist (Initial Educator) School Psychologist (Provisional Educator) School Psychologist (Professional Educator)	Master's Master's	45 60	10 school months	 1 year (c) 3 years (c)	yes yes yes
Delaware	School Psychologist	Master's	60	1200 hours		yes
District of Columbia *	School Psychologist (Class 3)	Master's	45	300 hours (e)		no
Florida	School Psychologist	Master's	60	1 year (e)		yes
Georgia	Nonrenewable Service Certificate in School Psychology (NS-5) Professional Service Certificate (S-6) Professional Service Certificate (S-7)	Master's Education Specialist Doctorate	60 quarter hours or 45+thesis 100 quarter hours or 45 + thesis	10 quarter hours credit 1000 hours (e) 1200 hours (e)		yes yes yes
Hawaii *	Psychological Examiner (II) Psychological Examiner (III) Psychological Examiner (IV) School Psychologist	Bachelor's Bachelor's Bachelor's Doctorate			 1 year (e) 1 year (e) 1 year	no no no no
Idaho	School Psychologist	Master's	AP	300 hours		no
Illinois	School Service Personnel Certificate with School Psychologist Endorsement	Master's	60	1 year/1200 hours		yes

TABLE 1
Summary of Basic Credentialing Requirements

STATE	TITLE LEVEL/TYPE	MINIMUM DEGREE	CREDIT HOURS	EXPERIENCE		EXAM
				INTERNSHIP	FIELD	
Indiana	School Psychologist (I) School Psychologist (II)	Master's Ed.D/Ph.D	60	3 sem. hours 1 year	3 years (T) or coursework	no no
Iowa	School Psychologist	Master's	60	600 hours		no
Kansas	School Psychologist	Master's	AP	1 year		no
Kentucky	School Psychologist (Provisional) School Psychologist (Standard)	Master's Master's	48 60	 1200 hours		yes yes
Louisiana *	School Psychologist (B) School Psychologist (A)	Master's or Specialist Doctorate	60 60	1225 hours 1225 hours		no no
Maine	School Psychologist	Doctorate		750 hours		no
Maryland	School Psychologist (I) School Psychologist (II) Supervisor of School Psychological Services	Master's Specialist Doctorate	45 (G&U) 60	500 hours 1000 hours	3 years (c)	no no no
Massachusetts	School Psychologist	Bachelor's	60	600 hours		no
Michigan	Preliminary School Psychologist (I) School Psychologist	Bachelor's Specialist	45 60	600 hours 600 hours		no no
Minnesota	School Psychologist	Education Specialist	90 quarter hours	600 hours		no
Mississippi	School Psychologist (AAA) School Psychologist (AAAA)	Educational Specialist Doctorate		6 sem. hours		yes yes
Missouri	School Psychologist	Master's	60		2 years (T) or AP	no
Montana	School Psychologist (Class 6)	Master's		6 quarter hours credit		no
Nebraska	School Psychologist	Bachelor's	60	1000 hours		yes
Nevada	School Psychologist	Master's	60	1000 hours		yes
New Hampshire	Associate School Psychologist (One) School Psychologist (Two)	Master's Master's	 60 or AP	 1 year (e)	 1 year (c)	no no
New Jersey	School Psychologist	Bachelor's	60 or AP	450 hours		no

TABLE 1
Summary of Basic Credentialing Requirements

STATE	TITLE LEVEL/TYPE	MINIMUM DEGREE	CREDIT HOURS	EXPERIENCE		EXAM
				INTERNSHIP	FIELD	
New Mexico	Entry Level School Psychologist (I)	Master's	60	1200 hours (e)		yes
	Independent School Psychologist (II)	Master's	60	1200 hours (e)		yes
	Clinical Supervising School Psychologist (3A)	Doctorate		875 hours (e)		yes
New York	School Psychologist (Provisional)	Bachelor's	60	required		no
	School Psychologist (Permanent)	Master's	60	required	2 years	no
North Carolina	School Psychologist (II)	Master's	AP	AP		yes
	School Psychologist (III)	Doctorate	AP	AP		yes
North Dakota	Credential in School Psychology	Master's		350 hours		no
Ohio	School Psychologist	Master's	60	9 months		yes
Oklahoma	School Psychologist (Standard)	Master's	60	1000 hours		yes
Oregon	School Psychologist	Master's	75 quarter hours	9 weeks (e)		yes
Pennsylvania	School Psychologist (Educational Specialist I)	Bachelor's		1000 hours		no
	School Psychologist (Educational Specialist II)	Bachelor's	24 hours + BA		3 years (c)	no
Rhode Island	School Psychologist (Provisional)	Master's	AP			no
	School Psychologist (Professional)	Master's	AP		3 years (c)	no
	School Psychologist (Life Professional)	Doctorate or C.A.G.S	AP		6 years (c)	no
South Carolina	School Psychologist (I)	Master's	AP	AP		yes
	School Psychologist (II)	Specialist	AP	AP		yes
	School Psychologist (III)	Doctorate	AP	AP		yes
South Dakota	School Psychological Examiner	Master's	30 (G&U)			no
	School Psychologist	Master's	AP			no
Tennessee	School Psychologist	Master's		1 semester		yes
Texas	Intermediate Associate School Psychologist	Master's				no
	Professional Associate School Psychologist	Master's			1 year	no
	Intermediate School Psychologist Certificate	Doctorate				no
	Professional School Psychologist Certificate	Doctorate			1 year	no

TABLE 1
Summary of Basic Credentialing Requirements

STATE	TITLE LEVEL/TYPE	MINIMUM DEGREE	CREDIT HOURS	EXPERIENCE		EXAM
				INTERNSHIP	FIELD	
Utah	School Psychologist	Master's		1 year		no
Vermont	School Psychologist	Master's		1200 hours		no
Virginia *	School Psychologist	Master's	60	1 year		no
Washington	School Psychologist (Initial)	Master's (except thesis)		240 hours		yes
	School Psychologist (Continuing)	Master's			1 year (c)	
West Virginia	Professional Service Certificate (Provisional)	Master's	AP	AP		yes
	Professional Service Certificate	Master's			3 years	yes
	Permanent Professional Service Certificate	Master's			5 years	yes
Wisconsin	Provisional School Psychologist	Master's	48	600 hours		no
	School Psychologist	Specialist	60	1 year		no
Wyoming	Educational Diagnostician	Master's	45		2 years (T)	no
	School Psychologist	Doctorate	60	1 year (e)		no

NOTES:

Levels and types of certificates that vary in basic training or experience are presented. In some states, additional types of certificates (e.g., a temporary certificate provided to an applicant who lacks one requirement) are available.

Credit hours are given in graduate semester hours unless otherwise designated. "G&U" indicates that a combination of graduate and undergraduate credits may be applied to certification requirements.

In the "Experience" column, "Internship" refers to pre-degree field experience which may be referred to as practica, externships, or internships. Although typically consisting of post-degree experience, the experience listed under the "Field" column may at least in-part include pre-degree experience in some states. An "(e)" indicates that experience can be accepted as an alternative to the internship requirement.

"AP" indicates the existence of a requirement applied to completion of an "approved program".

"C.A.G.S.," Certificate of Advanced Graduate Study, which is typically equivalent to a Specialist degree or Master's plus additional credit hours.

"T" indicates experience that at least partly must be in teaching or its equivalent. In some cases the completion of an approved program or additional coursework is accepted as an alternative to teaching.

"c" indicates experience that must be attained while holding the next "lower" level or type of school psychology certification. For example, Maryland requires 3 years of experience under the level II certificate before awarding the Supervisor of School Psychological Services title.

"*" indicates that the summary of state requirements is based on previous information or on a review of state materials conducted by the authors due to a lack of response on the part of state officials to survey.

TABLE 2
Processes of Credentialing/Reciprocity for Out-of-State Applicants

STATE	STATE APPROVED PROGRAM	NASDTEC	NCATE/ NASP	NCSP	INTERSTATE RECIPROCITY AGREEMENT	COURSE REVIEW	EQUIVALENT TRAINING & CERTIFICATE	OTHER	EXAM
Alabama			X		X				
Alaska			X	X				APA	
Arizona			X			X			
Arkansas									NTE
California							X		X
Colorado	X								X
Connecticut							X		X
Delaware		X	X			X		APA	X
District of Columbia		X			X	X			
Florida		X	X	X		X	X		X
Georgia	X		X						X
Hawaii						X			
Idaho		X	X			X	X		
Illinois						X	X		X
Indiana						X	X		
Iowa	X						X		
Kansas	X		X						
Kentucky	X	X	X						NTE
Louisiana			X						
Maine		X	X			X			
Maryland			X	X		X			
Massachusetts					X				
Michigan					X				
Minnesota	X					X			
Mississippi		X	X				X		NTE
Missouri	X								
Montana		X	X			X			
Nebraska	X				X				
Nevada			X			X			X
New Hampshire	X								
New Jersey						X			
New Mexico	X					X			NTE
New York	X				X	X			
North Carolina	X	X	X				X		NTE
North Dakota		X	X			X			
Ohio						X			NTE
Oklahoma						X			X
Oregon	X					X	X		NTE
Pennsylvania	X					X			
Rhode Island		X			X				
South Carolina	X								NTE
South Dakota	X					X			
Tennessee	X				X				X
Texas				X				X	

(Table 2, continued)

STATE	STATE APPROVED PROGRAM	NASDTEC	NCATE/ NASP	NCSP	INTERSTATE RECIPROCITY AGREEMENT	COURSE REVIEW	EQUIVALENT TRAINING & CERTIFICATE	OTHER	EXAM
Utah		X	X		X				
Vermont						X			
Virginia				X				X	
Washington	X								NTE
West Virginia	X	X	X		X				
Wisconsin	X					X			
Wyoming			X			X			

NOTES/DEFINITIONS:

"State Approved Program" - Completion of an approved training program in state of origin.

"NASDTEC" - Completion of a program approved via the standards of the National Association of State Directors of Teacher Education and Certification.

"NCATE/NASP" - Completion of a program approved by the National Association of School Psychologists in an institution or unit accredited by the National Council for Accreditation of Teacher Education.

"NCSP" - Attainment of certification from the National School Psychology Certification Board

"Interstate Reciprocity Agreement" - A reciprocity agreement with other states

"Equivalent Training & Certificate" - Documentation of training and certification equivalent to that in the state in which certification is desired.

"Other" - Some other method of review. "APA" refers to completion of a program accredited by the American Psychological Association. An "NA" in this column indicates that, although a process may be in place for certifying in-states applicants, the state reports having no approved school psychology training programs at present.

"Exam" - An examination is required. The designation "NTE" indicates that the School Psychology Specialty Area Test of the National Teachers' Examination (Part of the Praxis Series Professional Assessments for Beginning Teachers administered by the Educational Testing Service) is required or is one option for meeting the exam requirement.

TABLE 3
Processes of Credentialing for Graduates of In-State Programs

STATE	STATE APPROVED PROGRAM	NASDTEC	NCATE/ NASP	NCSP	COURSE REVIEW	OTHER	EXAM
Alabama	X						
Alaska						NA	
Arizona	X		X		X		
Arkansas			X			NA	NTE
California	X						X
Colorado	X						X
Connecticut	X						X
Delaware		X					X
District of Columbia	X	X			X		
Florida	X	X	X		X		X
Georgia	X						X
Hawaii					X		
Idaho	X	X					
Illinois	X						X
Indiana	X	X	X				
Iowa	X						
Kansas	X						
Kentucky	X	X	X				NTE
Louisiana	X						
Maine					X		
Maryland		X	X	X	X		
Massachusetts	X						
Michigan	X						
Minnesota	X						
Mississippi	X	X	X				NTE
Missouri	X						
Montana	X	X	X		X		
Nebraska	X						
Nevada			X		X		X
New Hampshire	X						
New Jersey	X				X		
New Mexico	X						NTE
New York	X						
North Carolina	X						NTE
North Dakota						NA	
Ohio	X						NTE
Oklahoma	X				X		X
Oregon	X						NTE
Pennsylvania	X						
Rhode Island		X					
South Carolina	X	X					NTE
South Dakota	X				X	NA	
Tennessee	X						X
Texas	X						

(Table 3, continued)

STATE	STATE APPROVED PROGRAM	NASDTEC	NCATE/ NASP	NCSP	COURSE REVIEW	OTHER	EXAM
Utah	X						
Vermont	X	X				NA	
Virginia	X						
Washington	X						
West Virginia	X						X
Wisconsin	X						
Wyoming			X		X		

See notes for Table 2

A Summary of Licensure Requirements for Independent Practice in Psychology and School Psychology

Joseph Prus
Winthrop University

Kelly Mittelmeier
Winthrop University

Although most school psychologists are employed in public schools, increasing numbers are working in nontraditional settings, including private practice (D'Amato & Dean, 1989; Graden & Curtis, 1991). One reason for this may be the desire for professional role expansion often offered by non-public school settings (Rosenberg & Wonderly, 1990). Another may be increased opportunities for practice in employment settings other than schools due to compromises in psychology licensing acts (Pryzwansky, 1993) and to increased recognition of the expertise and potential contributions of school psychologists. In any case, school psychologists interested in non-public school practice must be familiar with the professional credentials required for such work.

Despite differences from state to state in the terminology and administration of credentials relevant to school psychologists, the process of credentialing psychologists and school psychologists for independent practice is usually called "licensure." Licensure is typically required if psychological services are provided independently to individuals (i.e., "private practice") and may be required for the provision of such services in particular settings (usually exclusive of schools, for which *certification* is usually required). Licensing laws restrict service or practice activity to those professionals holding a certain title or protect professionals in regard to the legitimacy of their offering particular services (Pryzwansky, 1993). As opposed to the credentialing of school psychologists for work in the public schools, which is usually administered by state departments of education or teacher certification divisions or boards, licensure of psychologists is administered by state boards of psychology or psychological examiners.

The purpose of this chapter is to provide a brief summary of the licensure requirements for independent practice in psychology and school psychology. Those interested in more in-depth discussions of licensure and its applications to school psychology are encouraged to read Prasse (1988) and Pryzwansky

(1993). Batsche (1990), Batsche, Knoff, and Peterson (1989), Fagan and Wise (1994), and Pryzwansky (1993) also provide useful recent overviews of school psychology credentialing.

Sources of Information on State Licensure Requirements

Although the National Association of School Psychologists (NASP) has since its inception been the primary source of review and dissemination of state credentialing requirements for school psychologists (Sewall & Brown, 1976; Brown, Horn, & Lindstrom, 1980; Prus, White, & Pendleton, 1987; Curtis, Hunley, & Prus, 1995), licensure requirements for the independent practice of psychology have been influenced and more closely monitored by the American Psychological Association (APA) and the Association of State and Provincial Psychology Boards (ASPPB). The ASPPB conducts an annual update of licensure/certification requirements for psychologists in North America.

The summary of licensure requirements for the independent practice of psychology and school psychology presented in this chapter was prepared by using ASPPB's *Handbook of Licensing and Certification Requirements for Psychologists in North America* (1994) to update and supplement information contained in NASP's *Handbook of Certification and Licensure Requirements for School Psychologists* (Prus, White, & Pendleton, 1987). The resulting product should be a useful general guide to state licensure requirements. However, readers interested in a more in-depth, state-by-state description of licensure requirements and other information and materials related to licensure are encouraged to contact ASPPB (P.O. Box 4389, Montgomery, Alabama 36103).

Interpretation of Licensure Information

Table 1 contains a state-by-state summary of psychology licensure requirements. As is evident in the information presented in the table, considerable variation exists from state to state in the terminology and requirements pertinent to licensure by state psychology boards. This variability makes the tabular presentation of data somewhat of a challenge. The condensing of information into table format, while useful for purposes of comparison and summarizing, required the elimination of details that may be relevant to individuals seeking licensure. Thus, readers interested in the licensure requirements of a particular state are strongly advised to contact the state board of psychology or psychological examiners in that state to obtain complete, valid information.

In interpreting the information in Table 1, blank spaces signify the lack of a specified requirement. Since the statutes in many states grant licensure boards some or considerable autonomy in administering requirements, however, the lack of a specified requirement may mean that either no requirement exists or that the details are left to the discretion of the state board. The following descriptions of each heading are provided as aids to the interpretation of Table 1.

Title: Psychologists credentialed to provide independent or private services to the public may be described by a number of different titles, including "psychologist," "licensed psychologist," or "certified psychologist." Terms such as "clinical psychologist" or "health services provider" may be used to describe psychologists in applied specialties such as clinical, counseling, or school psychology who provide health-related or clinical services. In such cases, licensure as a psychologist may be a prerequisite to a clinical psychologist or health service provider credential. Some states also offer licensure specifically as a "school psychologist." Others recognize a variety of specialties, including school psychology, but issue licensure under one title such as "psychologist."

Minimum Degree: The minimum degree required for each credential is listed in the third column of the table. Although the degree requirements are summarized as "Masters" or "Doctorate," states often specify the particular degrees (e.g., Ph.D., Ed.D., Psy.D.) and fields of study required. Twenty-five states now have provisions for licensure at the masters degree or equivalent level. Such credentials typically include restrictions of function and/or supervision requirements.

Experience: The experience required for each licensure is summarized in three columns as described below.

Post-Degree: The number of years or hours of experience acquired after a degree is awarded.

Supervised: The number of years or hours of supervised experience. Most states further specify the required amount and/or conditions of supervision.

Total: The total number of years or hours of experience required for license.

In cases where states require a minimum number of years *and* hours of experience, only years are reported in the table.

It may be helpful to read the "Experience" columns in the table from right to left. For example, Alabama requires one year of experience, all of which must be supervised, whereas Florida requires 4000 hours of experience, 2000 hours of which must be post-degree and 4000 hours of which must be supervised.

Mandatory Exam: All states require at least one examination for licensure and most require both national and state exams. The Examination for the Professional Practice of Psychology (EPPP) is required by all states for at least one type or level of license. Some states that offer a school psychologist licensure require the School Psychology examination of the National Teachers Examination (NTE) for such licensure. Where a "board exam" is required, the examination may include an oral exam, written exam, or both. The designation "Must be Licensed" in the table indicates that an examination is required by virtue of having another type of licensure as a prerequisite.

Continuing Education Requirement: Most states require a minimum number of continuing education hours for licensure renewal. The required hours, "credits," or "CEUs" for each renewal period are listed in the far right column of Table 1. Renewal periods vary from state to state. For example, Arkansas requires completion of 20 hours of continuing education every year whereas Oregon requires 50 hours every two years. "Hours," "credits," or "CEUs" typically refer to hours or contact hours in approved continuing education activities.

ACKNOWLEDGMENTS

The authors are grateful to the Association of State and Provincial Psychology Boards for making available the information that served as a basis for this summary.

REFERENCES

Association of State and Provincial Psychology Boards (1994). *Handbook of licensing and certification requirements for psychologists in North America.* Montgomery, AL: Author.

Batsche, G. M. (1990). Best practices in credentialing and continuing professional development. In A. Thomas & J. Grimes (Eds.), *Best practices in school psychology–II* (pp. 887–898). Washington, DC: National Association of School Psychologists.

Batsche, G. M., Knoff, H., & Peterson, D. (1989). Trends in credentialing and practice standards. *School Psychology Review, 18,* 193–202.

Brown, D. T., Horn, A. J., & Lindstrom, J. P. (1980). *The handbook of certification/licensure requirements for school psychologists* (3rd ed.). Washington, DC: National Association of School Psychologists.

Curtis, M., Hunley, S., & Prus, J. (1995). *Handbook of certification and licensure requirements for school psychologists* (5th ed.). Silver Spring, MD: National Association of School Psychologists.

D'Amato, R. C., & Dean, R. S. (Eds.). (1989). *The school psychologist in nontraditional settings: Integrating clients, services, and settings.* Hillsdale, NJ: Lawrence Erlbaum.

Fagan, T. K., & Wise, P. S. (1994). *School psychology past, present, and future.* White Plains, NY: Longman Publishing Group.

Graden, J., & Curtis, M. (1991, September). *A demographic profile of school psychology: A report to the Delegate Assembly of the National Association of School Psychologists.* Washington, DC: National Association of School Psychologists.

Prasse, D. P. (1988). Licensing, school psychology and independent private practice. In T. R. Kratochwill (Ed.), *Advances in school psychology: Vol. 6* (pp. 49–80). Hillsdale, NJ: Lawrence Erlbaum.

Prus, J. S., White, G. W., & Pendleton, A. (1987). *Handbook of certification and licensure requirements for school psychologists* (4th ed.). Washington, DC: National Association of School Psychologists.

Pryzwansky, W. B. (1993). The regulation of school psychology: A historical perspective on certification, licensure, and accreditation. *Journal of School Psychology, 33,* 219–235.

Rosenberg, R. L., & Wonderly, D. M. (1990). Best practices in establishing an independent practice. In A. Thomas & J. Grimes (Eds.), *Best practices in school psychology–II* (pp. 339–352). Washington, DC: National Association of School Psychologists.

Sewall, T. J., & Brown, D. T. (1976). *The handbook of certification/licensure requirements for school psychologists.* Washington, DC: National Association of School Psychologists.

TABLE 1
Summary of Basic Licensure Requirements

State	Title	Minimum Degree	Experience Post-Degree	Experience Supervised	Experience Total	Mandatory Exam	Continuing Education Requirement
Alabama	Psychologist	Doctorate		1 yr.	1 yr.	EPPP/Board Exam	20 hrs./yr.
Alaska	Psychologist	Doctorate	1 yr.	1 yr.	1 yr.	EPPP/Board Exam	20 hrs./yr.
	Psychological Associate	Masters	3 yrs.	3 yrs.	3 yrs.	EPPP/Board Exam	20 hrs./yr.
Arizona	Psychologist	Doctorate	1500 hrs.	3000 hrs.	3000 hrs.	EPPP	30 hrs./yr.
Arkansas	Psychologist	Doctorate			2,000 hrs.	EPPP/Board Exam	20 hrs./yr.
	Psychological Examiner	Masters			500 hrs.	EPPP/Board Exam	20 hrs./yr.
California	Psychologist	Doctorate	1500 hrs.	3000 hrs.	3000 hrs.	EPPP/Board Exam	18 hrs./yr.
	Registered Psychological Assistant	Masters					
Colorado	Psychologist	Doctorate	1 yr.	1 yr.	1 yr.	EPPP/Board Exam	none
Connecticut	Psychologist	Doctorate	1 yr.		1 yr.	EPPP/Board Exam	none
Delaware	Psychologist	Doctorate	2 yrs.	2 yrs.	2 yrs.	EPPP/Board Exam	40 hrs./2 yrs.
	Registered Psychological Assistant	Masters					20 hrs./2 yrs.
District of Columbia	Psychologist	Doctorate	2 yrs.	2 yrs.	2 yrs.	EPPP/Board Exam	none
Florida	Psychologist	Doctorate	2000 hrs.	4000 hrs.	4000 hrs.	EPPP/Board Exam	40 hrs./2 yrs.
Georgia	Psychologist	Doctorate	2000 hrs.		4000 hrs.	EPPP/Board Exam	40 hrs./2 yrs.
Hawaii	Psychologist	Doctorate			2 yrs.	EPPP/Board Exam	none
Idaho	Psychologist	Doctorate	1 yr.	2000 hrs.	2000 hrs.	EPPP	20 hrs./yr.

State	Title	Minimum Degree	Experience			Mandatory Exam	Continuing Education Requirement
			Post-Degree	Supervised	Total		
Illinois	Clinical Psychologist	Doctorate	1 yr.	2 yrs.	2 yrs.	EPPP	none
Indiana	Licensed Psychologist	Doctorate				EPPP/Board Exam	none
	Health Service Provider	Doctorate	1 yr.	2 yrs.	2 yrs.	Must be Licensed	40 hrs./2 yrs.
Iowa	Psychologist	Doctorate	1 yr.	2 yrs.	2 yrs.	EPPP/Board Exam	40 hrs./2 yrs.
Kansas	Licensed Psychologist	Doctorate	2 yrs.		2 yrs.	EPPP	100 hrs./2 yrs.
	Registered Master's Psychologist	Masters		750 hr. practicum or 1500 hrs. post-degree			25 hrs./2 yrs.
Kentucky	Licensed Psychologist	Doctorate	1yr.	2 yrs.	2 yrs.	EPPP/Board Exam	30 hrs./3 yrs.
	Certified Psychological Associate	Masters		600 hrs.	600 hrs.	EPPP	30 hrs./3 yrs.
Louisiana	Psychologist	Doctorate	1 yr.	2 yrs.	2 yrs.	EPPP/Board Exam	30 hrs./2 yrs.
Maine	Psychologist	Doctorate	1 yr.	2 yrs.	2 yrs.	EPPP/Board Exam	40 credits/2 yrs.
	Psychological Examiner	Masters		1 yr.	1 yr.	EPPP/Board Exam	40 credits/2 yrs.
Maryland	Psychologist	Doctorate	1 yr.	2 yrs.	2 yrs.	EPPP/Board Exam	30 hrs./yr.
Massa-chusetts	Psychologist	Doctorate	1600 hrs.	3200 hrs.	3200 hrs.	EPPP	20CEU/2 yrs.
Michigan	Full License Psychologist	Doctorate	4000 hrs.	2000 hrs.	6000 hrs.	EPPP	none
	Limited License Psychologist	Masters	2000 hrs.	500 hrs.	2500 hrs.		none
Minnesota	Licensed Psychologist	Doctorate	2 yrs.	2 yrs.	2 yrs.	EPPP/Board Exam	40 hrs./2 yrs.
	Psychological Practitioner	Masters				EPPP/Board Exam	40 hrs./2 yrs.
Mississippi	Psychologist	Doctorate		1 yr.	1 yr.	EPPP/Board Exam	10 hrs./yr.

State	Title	Minimum Degree	Experience			Mandatory Exam	Continuing Education Requirement
			Post-Degree	Supervised	Total		
Missouri	Licensed Psychologist	Doctorate	1 yr.	1 yr.	1 yr.	EPPP	None
	Licensed Psychologist	Masters	3 yrs.	3 yrs.	3 yrs.	EPPP	None
	Certified Health Services Provider	Doctorate	1 yr.	1 yr.	1 yr.	Must be licensed	None
Montana	Psychologist	Doctorate	1 yr.	2 yrs.	2 yrs.	EPPP/Board Exam	40 hrs./2 yrs.
Nebraska	Licensed Psychologist	Doctorate				EPPP/Board Exam	none
	Certified Clinical Psychologist	Doctorate	1 yr.	1 yr.	1 yr.	Must be Licensed	none
Nevada	Licensed Psychologist	Doctorate	1750 hrs.	3500 hrs.	3500 hrs.	EPPP/Board Exam	30CEU/2 yrs.
	Licensed Psychological Assistant	48 Graduate cr. hrs.		1750 hrs.	1750 hrs.		None
New Hampshire	Certified Psychologist	Doctorate	1 yr.	2 yrs.	2 yrs.	EPPP	20 hrs./yr.
	Registered Psychological Assistant	Masters		1 yr.	1 yr.		20 hrs./yr.
New Jersey	Psychologist	Doctorate	1750 hrs.		3500 hrs.	EPPP/Board Exam	none
New Mexico	Psychologist	Doctorate	1 yr.	1 yr. (2 yrs. if non-APA internship)	1 yr.	EPPP/Board Exam	20 hrs./yr.
	Psychological Associate	Masters		1 yr.	5 yrs.	EPPP/Board Exam	12 hrs./yr.
New York	Psychologist	Doctorate	1 yr.	2 yrs.	2 yrs.	EPPP	none
North Carolina	Licensed Psychologist	Doctorate	1 yr.	2 yrs. (none for provisional license)	2 yrs.	EPPP/Board Exam	none
	Psychological Associate	Masters				EPPP/Board Exam	none
North Dakota	Psychologist	Doctorate		1 yr.	1 yr.	EPPP/Board Exam	40 hrs./2 yrs.
Ohio	Psychologist	Doctorate	1 yr.	2 yrs.	2 yrs.	EPPP/Board Exam	none
	School Psychologist	Masters	3 yrs.	4 yrs.	4 yrs.	Board Exam/ NTE	none

State	Title	Minimum Degree	Experience			Mandatory Exam	Continuing Education Requirement
			Post-Degree	Supervised	Total		
Oklahoma	Licensed Psychologist	Doctorate		2 yrs.	3 yrs.	EPPP/Board Exam	20 hrs./yr.
	Certified Health Services Provider	Doctorate	1 yr.	1 yr.	2 yrs.	Must be licensed	20 hrs./yr.
	Psychological Technician	Masters					none
Oregon	Psychologist	Doctorate	1 yr.	2 yrs.	2 yrs.	EPPP/Board Exam	50 hrs./2 yrs.
	Psychological Associate	Masters	3 yrs.	4 yrs.	4 yrs.	EPPP/Board Exam	50 hrs./2 yrs.
Penn-sylvania	Psychologist	Doctorate	1 yr.	2 yrs.	2 yrs.	EPPP/Board Exam	30 hrs./yr.
	Psychologist	Masters	3 yrs.	3 yrs.	3 yrs.	EPPP/Board Exam	none
Rhode Island	Psychologist	Doctorate	1 yr.	2 yrs.	2 yrs.	EPPP/Board Exam	40 hrs./2 yrs.
South Carolina	Psychologist	Doctorate	1 yr.	2 yrs.	2 yrs.	EPPP/Board Exam	12 hrs./yr.
South Dakota	Psychologist	Doctorate	1 yr.	2 yrs.	2 yrs.	EPPP/Board Exam	none
Tennessee	Psychologist	Doctorate	1 yr.	1 yr.	2 yrs.	EPPP/Board Exam	none
	Psychologist Examiner	Masters				EPPP/Board Exam	none
Texas	Licensed Psychologist	Doctorate	1 yr.	2 yrs.	2 yrs.	EPPP/Board Exam	12 hrs./yr.
	Certified Psychologist	Doctorate				EPPP/Board Exam	12 hrs./yr.
	Licensed Psychological Associate	Masters		450 hrs.	450 hrs.	EPPP/Board Exam	12 hrs./yr.
Utah	Licensed Psychologist	Doctorate	2000 hrs.	4000 hrs.	4000 hrs.	EPPP/Board Exam	48 hrs./2 yrs.
	Registered Psychological Assistant	Bachelors					
Vermont	Psychologist	Doctorate		2 yrs.	2 yrs.	EPPP	60 credits/2 yrs.
	Psychologist	Masters		2 yrs.	2 yrs.	EPPP	60 credits/2 yrs.

| State | Title | Minimum Degree | Experience | | | Mandatory Exam | Continuing Education Requirement |
			Post-Degree	Supervised	Total		
Virginia	Nonclinical Psychologist	Doctorate				EPPP/Board Exam	none
	Clinical Psychologist	Doctorate	1 yr.	1 yr.	1 yr.	EPPP/Board Exam	none
	School Psychologist	Masters	1 yr.	1 yr.	1 yr.	EPPP/Board Exam	none
Washington	Psychologist	Doctorate	1500 hrs.	1500 hrs.	3000 hrs.	EPPP/Board Exam	150 hrs./3 yrs.
West Virginia	Licensed Psychologist	Masters	5 yrs. (1-2 yrs. required for doctorates)	5 yrs.	5 yrs.	EPPP/Board Exam	20 CEU/2 yrs.
	School Psychologist I	Masters	3 yrs.	3 yrs.	3 yrs.	NTE/Board Exam	75 CEU/3 yrs.
	School Psychologist II	Masters	5 yrs.	5 yrs.	5 yrs.	NTE/Board Exam	75 CEU/3 yrs.
Wisconsin	Psychologist	Doctorate	1500 hrs.	3000 hrs.	3000 hrs.	EPPP/Board Exam	40 hrs./2 yrs.
	Private Practice School Psychologist	Masters		1 yr.	1 yr.	Board Exam/ NTE	40 hrs./2 yrs.
Wyoming	Psychologist	Doctorate	1500 hrs.	2000 hrs.	3500 hrs.	EPPP	none
	School Psychologist	Doctorate	1500 hrs.	2000 hrs.	3500 hrs.	EPPP	none
	Masters Psychological Practitioner	Masters	4500 hrs.	4950 hrs.	4950hrs.	EPPP	none
	Masters Specialist in School Psychology	Masters	4500 hrs. (must be nationally certified school psychologist)	4950 hrs.	4950 hrs.	EPPP	none

Resources on the Training of School Psychologists

Douglas K. Smith
University of Wisconsin–River Falls

Thomas K. Fagan
Memphis State University

Published listings of programs specifically for the preparation of school psychologists date to at least the early 1940s when, in an official publication, the New York State Education Department identified several programs. Perhaps the first nationwide listing was that appearing in the Thayer Conference proceedings published in 1955. Since the 1960s, articles have been regularly published on the growth of training programs. Though these studies identified the program institutions, they often conveyed little information about program philosophy, goals, content, and characteristics. A summary of these studies indicated that the number of institutions offering one or more levels of training grew from about 28 in the 1950s to more than 100 by 1970 and more than 200 by the 1980s (Fagan, 1986). There are now about seven times as many training institutions as existed in 1960.

NASP published the results of its first survey of training programs in 1972 (Patros, et al., 1972). The pamphlet identified 153 United States and 4 Canadian training institutions and included information about degree levels and financial assistance. The first formal directory of training programs was published by NASP in 1977 (Brown & Lindstrom, 1977), with two subsequent revisions (Brown & Minke, 1984; McMaster, Reschly, & Peters, 1989). The original 1977 directory identified 203 United States and 17 Canadian institutions; subsequent revisions have included U.S. institutions only. The 1984 revision described 210 institutions, and the 1989 *Directory* revision identified 203 institutions which provided information on their programs and 28 which failed to respond. The NASP directories have included increasingly greater information about the characteristics of preparation programs. The directories serve as the only national listing of preparation programs exclusively in school psychology. The most recent *Directory* revision (Smith & Henning, in press) is the most comprehensive resource of school psychology program information. It identifies 212 training institu-

tions, which suggests a pattern of stability since the mid-1980s, and provides detailed information on the 208 programs responding to the directory survey.

Other resources have been available to assist prospective students in identifying training programs and/or in making a career decision to enter the field of school psychology. These include: the American Psychological Association's *Graduate Programs in Psychology*, an annual publication which includes departmental information on each type of graduate program' accreditation listings and information available from APA and NCATE/NASP; and several published items related to training (Curtis & Zins, 1989; Fagan, 1990; Gerner & Genshaft, 1981; Knoff, 1986; National School Psychology Inservice Training Network, 1984).

The data tables in this appendix are drawn from a 1993 NASP survey which appears in the 1994 NASP directory (Smith & Henning, 1994) and represent information based on the 1992–1993 year. This appendix provides a tabular summary of that survey related to the following data:

a. An alphabetical list, by states, of programs including name, address, phone, contact person, degrees offered, and NASP accreditation status.

b. A NASP regional listing of programs by name only, organized alphabetically by state and program name.

c. Maps of the United States identifying the location of masters, specialist, and doctoral programs.

The appendix serves as a resource of program information for prospective and current students, and for persons researching the status and history of school psychology training.

REFERENCES

Brown, D. T., & Lindstrom, J. P. (1977). *Directory of school psychology training programs in the United States and Canada.* Washington, DC: National Association of School Psychologists.

Brown, D. T., & Minke, K. M. (1984). *Directory of school psychology training programs.* Washington, DC: National Association of School Psychologists.

Curtis, M. J., & Zins, J. E. (1989). Trends in training and accreditation. *School Psychology Review, 18,* 182–192.

Fagan, T. K. (1986). The historical origins and growth of programs to prepare school psychologists in the United States. *Journal of School Psychology, 24,* 9–22.

Fagan, T. K. (1990). Best practices in the training of school psychologists: Considerations for trainers, prospective entry-level and advanced students. In A. Thomas & J. Grimes (Eds.), *Best practices in school psychology* (pp. 723–741). Washington, DC: National Association of School Psychologists.

Gerner, M., & Genshaft, J. (1981). *Selecting a school psychology training program.* Washington, DC: National Association of School Psychologists.

Knoff, H. M. (1986). *Graduate training in school psychology: A national survey of professional coursework.* Washington, DC: National Association of School Psychologists.

McMaster, M. D., Reschly, D. J., & Peters, J. M. (199). *Directory of school psychology graduate programs.* Washington, DC: National Association of School Psychologists.

National School Psychology Inservice Training Network. (1984). *School psychology: A blueprint for training and practice.* Minneapolis, MN: Author.

Patros, P. G., Gross, F. P., & Bjorn, M. (1972). *A survey of institutions offering graduate training in the area of school psychology.* Washington, DC: National Association of School Psychologists.

Smith, D. K., & Henning, A. (in press). *Directory of school psychology graduate programs* (4th Edition). Washington, DC: National Association of School Psychologists.

ANNOTATED BIBLIOGRAPHY

Brown, D. T., & Minke, K. M. (1986). School psychology graduate training: A comprehensive analysis. *American Psychologist, 41,* 1328–1338.
From both historical and contemporary perspectives, the authors describe the decline in master's level programs with attendant increases in specialist and doctoral programs. It is estimated that half the graduate students in school psychology will be enrolled in doctoral programs by 1990. The content analyses of specialist and doctoral programs suggest the practical proximity of the specialist to the doctorate and the need for greater job opportunities for some programs to acquire the doctoral status. Implications for the issues of entry-level titles and credentials are presented.

Curtis, M. J., & Zins, J. E. (1989). Trends in training and accreditation. *School Psychology Review, 18,* 182–192.
Written as part of the "NASP at Twenty" mini-series, this article chronicles the growth of school psychology and training during NASP's first twenty years. A strong trend is identified for practitioners and students to acquire increased levels of preparation with the specialist and doctoral levels showing considerable growth. The influence of NASP in the development of training standards, especially for nondoctoral programs, is emphasized. NASP's accreditation relationship to NCATE is also discussed. Future challenges identified included personnel shortages, the need for greater minority student enrollments, quality assurance through NCATE accreditation mechanisms, and standards revisions. The specialist level standards are perceived as inadequate to meet future needs for alternative school psychological services. Expansion and revision of these standards will be needed, and perhaps two or more levels of practice will emerge in the future.

Fagan, T. K. (1986). The historical origins and growth of programs to prepare school psychologists in the United States. *Journal of School Psychology, 24,* 9–22.
A survey of the quantitative growth of school psychology training programs across the twentieth century. Identifies the earliest training institutions and the scarcity of such institutions prior to the 1960s. A tabular summary of published studies indicates the growth of program institutions from 28 in 1954, to 79 in 1964, to 147 in 1974, and 211 in 1984. Information regarding training content and enrollments are also provided.

National School Psychology Inservice Training Network. (1984). *School psychology: A blueprint for training and practice.* Minneapolis, MN: Author.
Employing the *Nation At Risk* study published in 1983, this publication identifies several problematic areas of education and special education and their relationship to school psychological services. Following a reconceptualization of the functions of the school psychologist, the report identifies several areas of needed training and retraining for the future. The reconceptualization is along lines of consultation, and curriculum-based assessment, while disbanding functions associated with classification in the categories of learning disabled, educably mentally retarded, and behavior disordered or emotionally disturbed.

Reschly, D. J., & McMaster-Beyer, M. (1991). Influence of degree level, institutional orientation, college affiliation, and accreditation status on school psychology graduate education. *Professional Psychology: Research and Practice, 22,* 368–374.
Based on survey responses associated with the 1989 NASP *Directory of School Psychology Graduate Programs,* comparisons are made among programs based on program levels, institutional orientation, academic department (e.g., education vs. arts and sciences), and type of accreditation. After alerting the reader to the study's limitations, the authors contend that the specialist and doctoral level data support the "long-standing APA policy that restricts the independent, unsupervised practice of psychology in varied settings to doctoral-level professional psychologists" (p. 373). The authors also interpreted the data to favor research oriented institutions, though differences associated with academic location and accreditation were not observed.

TABLE 1
School Psychology Programs by State[1]

ALABAMA

Alabama A&M University
Box 143
Normal, AL 35762
205-851-5330
Gail S. Gibson
Ed.S.

Auburn University
Haley Center 2014
Auburn, AL 36849
205-844-5160
Joseph A. Buckhalt
M.Ed., Ed.S., Ph.D.

University of Alabama
Area of Professional Studies
P.O. Box 870231
Tuscaloosa, AL 35487-0231
205-348-7583
Patti L. Harrison
M.A., Ed.S., Ph.D., Ed.D.
SL-Full; DL-Full

University of Alabama–Birmingham
119 School of Education
Birmingham, AL 35294
205-934-7598
Gary L. Sapp
Ed.S.

ARIZONA

Arizona State University
Division of Psychology in Education
Tempe, AZ 85287-0611
602-965-3384
Jerry Harris
Ph.D.
DL-Full

Northrn Arizona University
Educational Psychology
Box 5774
Flagstaff, AZ 86011
602-523-6757
William E. Martin, Jr.
MA, Ed.D
SL-Full

University of Arizona
College of Education
Tucson, AZ 87521
602-621-7825
Richard J. Morris
Ph.D.
SL-Conditional; DL-Full

ARKANSAS

University of Central Arkansas
Department of Psychology
P.O. Box 4915
Conway, AR 72032
501-540-3193
Ron Bramlett
MS
SL-Conditional

CALIFORNIA

California State University–Chico
Department of Psychology
Chico, CA 95929-0234
916-898-5147
Neil Schwartz

California State University–Fresno
Educational Psychology
5310 N. Campus Drive
Fresno, CA 93740-0011
209-278-2478
Karen T. Carey
MA
SL-Full

California State University–Hayward
Educational Psychology
25800 Carlos Bee Blvd.
Hayward, CA 94542
510-881-3011
Mary DiSibio
MS
SL-Conditional

California State University–Humboldt
Department of Psychology
Arcata, CA 95521
707-826-3755
Richard A. Langford
MA

California State University–Long Beach
Educational Psychology
1250 Bellflower
Long Beach, CA 90840
310-985-4998
Thomas J. Kampwirth
MS

California State University–Los Angeles
Div. of Administration & Counseling
5151 State University Drive
Los Angeles, CA 90032
213-343-4250
Margaret Garcia
MS
SL-Conditional

California State University–Northridge
Department of Psychology
Northridge, CA 91330
818-885-2827
Joseph Morris
MA

California State University–Sacramento
Department of Special Education, Rehabilitation & School Psychology
6000 J Street
Sacramento, CA 95819
916-278-6118; 916-278-6310
William R. Merz
MS

Chapman College
333 North Glassell St.
Orange, CA 92666
714-997-6781; 714-997-6950
Ron Lackey
MA

La Sierra University
4700 Pierce St.
Riverside, CA 92515
909-785-2267
Leonard Jorgensen
MA, Ed.S.

Loyola Marymount University
School of Education
Loyola Blvd. at W. 80th St.
Los Angeles, CA 90045
310-338-2863
Scott W. Kester
MA

San Diego State University
Department of Counseling and School Psychology
San Diego, CA 92182
619-594-7730
Valerie Cook-Morales
MS
SL-Full

University of California–Berkeley
School of Education
Berkeley, CA 94720
415-642-7581
Nadine Lambert
MA, Ph.D.

University of Caifornia–Davis
Department of Education
Davis, CA 95616-8579
916-752-3198
Jonathan Sandoval
Ph.D.

University of California–Riverside
School of Education
Riverside, CA 95616
909-787-4516
Frank M. Gresham
Ph.D.

University of California–
Santa Barbara
Department of Education
Santa Barbara, CA 93106
805-893-3375
Gale Morrison
M.Ed., Ph.D.

University of the Pacific
Department of Education and
Counseling Psychology
Stockton, CA 95211
209-946-2559
Mari G. Irvin
MA, Ph.D.

COLORADO

University of Colorado–Boulder
School of Education
Campus Box 106, P.O. Box 173364
Denver, CO 80217
303-556-8448
Beth Doll
MA
SL-Conditional

University of Denver
School of Education, AH #233
Denver, CO 80208
303-871-2481
Raymond Kluever
Ph.D.

University of Northern Colorado
McKee 248
Division of Professional Psychology
Greeley CO 80639
303-351-2731
Rik Carl D'Amato
Ed.S., Ph.D.
SL-Full; DL-Full

CONNECTICUT

Fairfield University
Graduate School of Education
and Alllied Professions
Fairfield, CT 06430-7524
203-254-4000
Daniel Geller
MA

Southern Connecticut State
University
501 Crescent Street, DA 143
New Haven, CT
203-392-5910
Michael Martin
MS

University of Connecticut
Department of Educational
Psychology 4-64
Storrs, CT 0629-2064
203-486-0166
Thomas J. Kehle
MA, Ph.D.
SL-Full; DL-Full

University of Hartford
Department of Psychology
200 Bloomfield Avenue
West Hartford, CT 06117
203-768-4544; 203-768-5230
Howard S. Rosenblatt
MS

DELAWARE

University of Delaware
Educational Studies
Willard Hall Education Building
Newark, DE 19716
302-831-2321
Kathleen Minke
MA

DISTRICT OF COLUMBIA

Galludet University
Department of Psychology
800 Florida Avenue, NE
Washington, DC 20002
202-651-5540
Anne Spragins
MA, Ed.S.
SL-Full

Howard University
Department of Psychoeducational
Studies
2400 6th St., NW
Washington, DC 20059
202-806-5196
Essie Knuckle
MA, M.Ed., Ph.D., Ed.D
DL-Conditional

FLORIDA

Florida A&M University
Department of Psychology
GECC, Room 305
Tallahassee, FL 32307
904-599-3014; 904-599-3468
Seward Hamilton
MS

Florida International University
University Park, DM 216-B
Miami, FL 33199
304-348-2552; 305-348-2725
Philip J. Lazarus
Ed.S.

Florida State University
HSS/COE, 215 Stone Building
Tallahassee, FL 32306-1051
904-644-6485
E. Thompson Prout
Ed.S.

University of Central Florida
College of Education
Orlando, FL 32816
407-823-2596
David J. Mealor
Ed.S.
SL-Full

University of Florida
1403 Norman Hall
Gainesville, FL 32611-2053
904-392-0724 ext. 231
Craig L. Frisby
MA, Ed.S., Ph.D.
SL-Full; DL-Full

University of South Florida
Department of Psychological
Foundations, FAO 268
Tampa, FL 33620
813-974-3246
Howard Knoff
Ed.S., Ph.D.
SL-Full; DL-Full

University of West Florida
Department of Psychology
1100 University Parkway
Pensacola, FL 32504
Peter Prewett
MA

GEORGIA

Georgia Southern University
Landrum Box 8131
Statesboro, GA 30460-8131
912-681-5301
Robert Martin
M.Ed., Ed.S.

Georgia State University
Department of Counseling and
Psychological Services
Atlanta, GA 30303
404-651-2550
R. Wayne Jones
Ed.S., Ph.D.
SL-Conditional

University of Georgia
325 Aderhold Hall
Athens, GA 30602
706-542-4110
Roy P. Martin
Ed.S., Ph.D.
SL-Full; DL-Full

Valdosta State University
Valdosta, GA 31698-0100
912-333-5930
Larry Hilgert
Ed.S.
SL-Full

IDAHO

Idaho State University
Box 8059
Pocatello, ID 83209
Gerald J. Spadafore
Ed.S.
SL-Conditional

University of Idaho
Department of Counseling and
  Special Education
Moscow, ID 83843
208-885-6159
Thomas N. Fairchild
Ed.S.

ILLINOIS

Eastern Illinois University
Department of Psychology
Lincoln Avenue, SB 104C
Charleston, IL 61920
217-581-2127
Michael Havey
Ed.S.

Governors State University
Department of Psychology and
  Counseling
University Park, IL 60466
708-534-5000
David Prasse
MA

Illinois State University
Department of Psychology
Box 4620
Normal, IL 61740-4620
309-438-5720; 309-438-8651
Mark Swerdik
SSP, Ph.D.
SL-Full

Loyola University of Chicago
820 N. Michigan Ave.
Chicago, IL 60611
312-915-6007
Ronald R. Morgan
M.Ed., Ph.D.

National-Louis University
2840 N. Sheridan Rd.
Evanston, IL 60201-1796
800-443-5522; 800-624-8521 (IL)
Shani Beth-Halachmy
Ed.S., Ed.D.

Northern Illinois University
Department of Psychology
Dekalb, IL 60115
815-753-3508
Gregory A. Waas
MA
SL-Full

Southern Illinois University
Psychology Department
Box 1121
Edwardsville, IL 62026
618-692-3542
Robert E. Lamp
MS, Ed.S.

Western Illinois University
Department of Psychology
Macomb, IL 61455
309-298-1919
Paula S. Wise
Ed.S.

INDIANA

Ball State University
Department of Educational
  Psychology, TC 524
Muncie, IN 47306
317-285-8500
Barbara Rothlisberg
MA, Ed.S., Ph.D.
SL-Full; DL-Full

Indiana State University
Porter School Psychology Center
SOE 622
Terre Haute, IN 47809
812-237-3588
Liam Grimley
MS, Ed.S., Ph.D.
DL-Full

Indiana University
W. W. Wright School of Education
Bloomington, IN 47405
812-856-8332
Thomas J. Huberty
Ed.S., Ph.D.
SL-Full; DL-Full

Valparaiso University
Kretzman Hall
Valparaiso, IN 46383
219-464-5440
Stanley Hughes
MA

IOWA

Iowa State University
Department of Psychology
Ames, IA 50011-3180
515-294-1742; 515-294-1487
Daniel J. Reschly
Ed.S., Ph.D.
SL-Full

University of Iowa
N336 Lindquist Center
Iowa City, IA 52442
319-335-5335
Stewart Ehly
Ph.D.
DL-Full

University of Northern Iowa
617 Education Center
Cedar Falls, IA 50614
319-273-3384
Donald Schmits
Ed.S.

KANSAS

Emporia State University
1200 Commercial
Emporia, KS 66801-5087
316-341-5317
Sharon Karr
MS, Ed.D.

Fort Hays State University
600 Park Street
Hays, KS 67601-4099
913-628-4405
Tom Jackson
Ed.S.

Pittsburg State University
1701 South Broadway
Pittsburg, KS 66762
316-235-4522
C. O. Lindskog
Ed.S.

University of Kansas
213 Bailey Hall
Lawrence, KS 66045
913-864-4526
Steven W. Lee
Ed.S., Ph.D.
SL-Full

Wichita State University
Campus Box 123
Wichita, KS 67260
316-689-3326
Nancy McKellar
Ed.S.

KENTUCKY

Eastern Kentucky University
Department of Psychology
102 Camack
Richmond, KY 40475-0937
606-622-1105
James Batts
PsyS

University of Kentucky
Educational and Counseling
  Psychology
237 Dickey Hall
Lexington, KY 40506-0017
606-257-1381
Stephen T. DeMers
Ed.S., Ph.D.
SL-Full; DL-Full

Western Kentucky University
Department of Psychology
Bowling Green, KY 42103
502-745-2696
Elizabeth Jones
Ed.S.
SL-Conditional

LOUISIANA

Louisiana State University
Psychology Department
Baton Rouge, LA 70803-5501
504-388-4111
Joseph Witt
Ph.D.

Louisiana State University–
  Shreveport
Department of Psychology
One University Place
Shreveport, LA 71115
318-797-5044
Marikay M. Ringer
Ed.S.
SL-Full

McNeese State University
Department of Psychology and
  Special Education
Lake Charles, LA 70609
318-475-5457
Jerry Whiteman
MA

Nicholls State University
Department of Psychology and
  Counselor Education
P.O. Box 2075
Thibodaux, LA 70310
504-448-4370
J. Stevens Welsh
Ed.S.
SL-Full

Northeast Louisiana University
Department of Psychology
Monroe, LA 71209
318-342-4147
E. H. Baker
MS
SL-Full

Tulane University
Psychology Department
2007 Stern Hall
New Orleans, LA 70118
504-865-5331
C. Chrisman Wilson
Ph.D.

MAINE

University of Southern Maine
400 Bailey Hall
Gorham ME 04038
207-642-4269
Mark W. Steege
MA
SL-Conditional

MARYLAND

Towson State University
Psychology Department
Towson, MD 21204
401-830-2634
Mary Brizzolara
MA

University of Maryland
Counseling and Personnel Services
3214 Benjamin Building
College Park, MD 20742-1125
301-405-2858
William Strein/Hedy Teglasi
MA, Ph.D.
SL-Full; DL-Full

MASSACHUSETTS

American International College
1000 State Street
Springfield, MA 01109
413-747-6302
Antoinette Spinelli-Nannen
MA

Northeastern University
Bouve College of Pharmacy and
  Health Sciences
203 Mugar Life Science Building
Boston, MA 02115
617-373-2708
Ena Vazquez-Nuttal
MS, Ed.D.
SL-Conditional

Tufts University
Lincoln Filene Center
Medford, MA 02155
617-628-0500 ext. 2393
Caroline H. Wandle
MA
SL-Conditional

University of MA–Amherst
School of Education
151 Hills South
Amherst, MA 01003-4150
413-545-3610
Marla Brassard
Ph.D.
SL-Full; DL-Full

University of MA–Boston
Wheatley Hall
100 Morrissey Blvd.
Boston, MA 02125-3393
617-287-7602
Vincent A. Cristiani
M.Ed.
SL-Full

MICHIGAN

Andrews University
Bell Hall, Room 160
Berrien Springs, MI 49104
616-471-3113
Elsie P. Johnson
Ed.S., Ph.D., Ed.D.

Central Michigan University
Department of Psychology
Mt. Pleasant, MI 48859
517-774-3001
Timothy S. Hartshorne
Ed.S., Psy.D.
SL-Full

Eastern Michigan University
227 Rackham
Ypsilanti, MI 48197
313-487-0026
Gary B. Navarre

Michigan State University
439 Erickson Hall
East Lansing, MI 48824-1034
517-355-8502
Harvey F. Clarizio
Ph.D.
DL-Full

University of Detroit–Mercy
4001 W. Michigan Rd., P.O. Box
  19900
Detroit, MI 48219-3599
313-927-1267
Mary E. Hannah
Ed.S.

Wayne State University
355 Education Building
Detroit, MI 48202
313-577-1671
John A. George
MA

Western Michigan University
Department of Psychology
Kalamazoo, MI 49008
616-387-4478
Howard A. Farris
Ed.S., Ph.D.
SL-Full; DL-Full

MINNESOTA

Moorhead State University
Morhead, MN 56563
218-236-2802
Elizabeth Danielson
MS, Ed.D.
SL-Full

University of Minnesota
N548 Elliott Hall
Minneapolis, MN 55455
612-624-4156
James E. Ysseldyke
Ed.S., Ph.D.
SL-Conditional
DL-Full

MISSISSIPPI

University of Southern Mississippi
Southern Station, Box 5025
Hattiesburg, MS 39406-5025
601-266-4604
Daniel Tingstrom
MS, MA, Ph.D.
DL-Full

MISSOURI

University of Missouri–Columbia
16 Hill Hall
Columbia, MO 65211
314-882-7731
James R. Koller
MA, MEd., Ed.S., Ph.D.

MONTANA

University of Montana
Psychology Department
Missoula, MT 59812
406-243-4521
George C. Camp
MA, Ed.S.
SL-Full

NEBRASKA

University of Nebraska–Kearney
Founders Hall Room 2102
Kearney, NE 68849
308-234-8508
Max A. McFarland
Ed.S.
SL-Conditional

University of Nebraska–Lincoln
117 Bancroft Hall
Lincoln, NE 68588-0345
402-472-2210
Terry Gutkin
Ed.S., Ph.D.
SL-Full; DL-Full

University of Nebraska–Omaha
347 Arts & Sciences Hall
Omaha, NE 68134-0274
402-554-2592
Robert E. Woody
Ed.S.

NEVADA

University of Nevada–Las Vegas
College of Education
Las Vegas, NV 89154
702-895-1110
Joe N. Crank
Ed.S.

NEW JERSEY

Jersey City State College
2039 Kennedy Boulevard
Jersey City, NJ 07035-1597
201-200-3309
Dale Kahn

Kean College of New Jersey
Department of Psychology
Union, NJ 07083-9982
201-527-2170
Gary I. Danielson

Montclair State College
Psychology Department
Upper Montclair, NJ 07043
201-655-7233; 201-655-5147
Joan Silverstein

Rider College
2083 Lawrenceville Rd.
Lawrenceville, NJ 08648
609-895-5449
James P. Murphy

Rowan College of New Jersey
Robinson Hall, 201 Mullica Rd.
Glassboro, NJ 08028
609-863-7092
John W. Klanderman
MA
SL-Conditional

Rutgers University
P.O. Box 819, Busch Campus
Piscataway, NJ 08855-0819
908-445-2008; 908-445-2325
Kenneth Schneder
PsyD

Seton Hall University
400 S. Orange Avenue
South Orange, NJ 07075
201-761-9451
Steven Korner
Ed.S.

NEW YORK

Alfred University
26 N. Main St.
Alfred, NY 14802-1232
607-871-2212
Carla M. Narrett
MA, PsyD
SL-Full

Brooklyn College of City University
2900 Bedford Avenue
1105 James Hall
Brooklyn, NY 11210
718-951-5876
Laura Barbanel
MS
SL-Full

City University of NY–City College
North Academic Center, 33227
Convent Ave. at 138th St.
New York, NY 10031
212-650-7987; 212-650-5484
Sybil Gottlieb
MS

College of New Rochelle
Graduate Psychology Program
New Rochelle, NY 10805
914-632-5300; 914-654-5561
Jerri L. Frantzre
MS

Fordham Universty–Lincoln Center
113 West 60th St.
New York, NY 10023
212-636-6460
Anthony Cancelli
Ph.D.
SL-Full; DL-Full

Hofstra University
127 Hofstra University
Hempstead, NY 11550
516-463-5662
Kurt Salzinger
Ph.D.
DL-Full

New York University
239 Greene Street, 5th Floor
New York, NY 10003
212-998-5370
Iris Fodor
Ph.D., PsyD
DL-Full

Pace University
Psychology Department
One Pace Plaza
New York, NY 10038
212-346-1506
Barbara Mowder
M.Ed., Psyd

Queen's College of City University
of New York
052A PH
Flushing, NY 11367
718-997-5230
Marian Fish
MS

Rochester Institute of Technology
18 Lomb Memorial Drive
Rochester, NY 14623-5604
716-475-2765
Virginia Costenbader
MS
SL-Full

St. John's University
8000 Utopia Parkway
Jamaica, NY 11439
718-990-6369
Ray DiGuiseppe
MS

State University College–Platsburgh
Psychology Department,
Beaumont Hall
Platsburgh, NY 12901
518-564-3076
Ronald Dumont
MA

State University of New York–Albany
Education 232
Albany, NY 12222
518-442-5052
Joel Meyers
MS, Ph.D., PsyD

State University of New York–Buf-
falo
409 Baldy Hall
Buffalo, NY 14260
716-645-3154
LeAdelle Phelps
MA, Ph.D.
SL-Full

State University of New York–
Oswego
CPS #13
Oswego, NY 13126
315-341-4051

Syracuse University
430 Huntington Hall
Syracuse, NY 13244-2340
315-443-1015
Lawrence Lewandowski
Ph.D.

Teachers College, Columbia
University
Box 120
New York, NY 10027
212-678-3084
Stephen Peverly
M.Ed., Ph.D., Ed.D.

Yeshiva University
Ferkauf Graduate School of
Psychology
1300 Morris Park Ave.
Bronx, NY 10461
212-430-4201
Abraham Givner
PsyD

NORTH CAROLINA

Appalachian State University
Department of Psychology
Boone, NC 28607
704-262-2297
James Deni
MA
SL-Full

East Carolina University
Department of Psychology
Rawl 105
Greenville, NC 27858-4353
919-757-6800; 919-757-6202
Raymond E. Webster
MA

North Carolina State University
Department of Psychology
Box 7801
Raleigh, NC 27695-7801
919-515-2251
William P. Erchul
Ph.D.
DL-Full

University of North Carolina–
Chapel Hill
Campus Box 3500
Chapel Hill, NC 27599-3500
919-966-5266
John C. Brantley
MA, M.Ed., Ph.D.
SL-Full; DL-Full

Western Carolina University
327 Killian Building
Cullowhee, NC 28723
704-227-7361
Lu Juan Gibson
MA

NORTH DAKOTA

Minot State University
Department of Psychology
Minot, ND 58707
701-857-3138
Philip Hall
MS

OHIO

Bowling Green State University
EDSE #403, Education Building
Bowling Green, OH 43403-0255
419-372-9498
Audrey Ellenwood
M.Ed.
SL-Full

Cleveland State University
Psychology Department
E. 24th & Euclid Avenue
Cleveland, OH 44115
216-687-2551
Constance Hollinger
SL-Full

John Carroll University
Department of Education
Administration Building
Cleveland, OH 44118
216-397-4656
Jeanne E. Jenkins
M.Ed.
SL-Conditional

Kent State University
310 White Hall
Kent, OH 44240
216-672-2928
Caven S. McLoughlin
Ed.S., Ph.D.
SL-Full; DL-Full

Miami University
201 McGuffey Hall
Oxford, OH 45056
513-529-6632
Alex Thomas
MS, Ed.S.
SL-Full

Ohio State University
356 ARPS Hall
1945 North High St.
Columbus, OH 43210
614-292-8148
James L. Collins
MA, Ph.D.
SL-Full; DL-Full

University of Akron
115 Carroll Hall
Akron OH 44325-5007
216-972-8150
James F. Austin
MA
SL-Full

University of Cincinnati
522 Teachers College
P.O. Box 210002
Cincinnati, OH 45221-0002
513-556-3335
Janet Graden
M.Ed., Ph.D.
SL-Full; DL-Full

University of Dayton
300 College Park
Dayton, OH 45469-0530
513-229-3644
James H. Evans
MS
SL-Conditional

University of Toledo
Department of Counselor and
    Human Services Education
2801 W. Bancroft Street
Toledo, OH 43606
419-537-2013
Robert W. Wendt
MS, Ed.S., Ph.D.
SL-Full; SL-Full

OKLAHOMA

University of Central Oklahoma
Department of Psychology and
    Personnel Services
Edmond, OK 73034
405-341-2980
Peggy Kerr

Oklahoma State University
301 N. Murray Hall
Stillwater OK 74078
405-744-6036
Paul G. Warden
Ph.D.

OREGON

Lewis and Clark College
Department of Counseling
    Psychology
Box 93
Portland, OR 97219
503-768-7730
Mary Henning-Stout
MS

University of Oregon
Division of Counseling and
    Educational Psychology
Eugene, OR 97403
503-346-2144
Mark R. Shinn
MS, Ph.D.
SL-Conditional; DL-Conditional

PENNSYLVANIA

Bryn Mawr College
Department of Psychology
101 N. Merion St.
Bryn Mawr, PA 19010
215-527-5190
Leslie Rescorla

Bucknell University
Department of Education
Lewisburg, PA 17837
717-524-1133
Robert Midkiff, Jr.
MS

California University of Pennsylvania
317 Learning Research Center
California, PA 15419
412-938-4100
Sylvia Williams
MS

Duquesne University
Canevin Hall
Pittsburgh, PA 15282
412-396-6102
Al Rizzo
MS

Edinboro University of Pennsylvania
B3422
Edinboro, PA 16444
814-732-2523
Dean Stoffer
M.Ed.

Immaculata College
Graduate Division
Immaculata, PA 19345
215-647-4400 ext. 3503
Jed Yalof
MA

Indiana University of Pennsylvania
246 Stouffer Hall
Indiana, PA 15705
412-357-2316
Mary Ann Rafoth
MS, Ed.S.
SL-Full

Lehigh University
111 Research Drive
Iacocca Hall
Bethlehem, PA 18015
610-758-3256
Edward Shapiro
Ed.S., Ph.D.
SL-Full; DL-Full

Marywood College
2300 Adams Avenue
Scranton, PA 18509
717-348-6211
Elizabeth Pearson

Millersville University of
    Pennsylvania
Byerly Hall
Millersville, PA 17551
717-872-3093
Katherine Green
SL-Full

Pennsylvania State College
227 Cedar Building
University Park, PA 16802-3109
814-865-1881
Joseph L. French
MS, Ph.D.
DL-Full

Temple University
262 Ritter Annex
Philadelphia, PA 19122
215-204-8075
Joseph Rosenfeld
M.Ed., Ph.D., Ed.D.
DL-Full

University of Pennsylvania
3700 Walnut St.
Philadelphia, PA 19104-6216
215-898-4790
John Fantuzzo
Ph.D.

RHODE ISLAND

Rhode Island College
Department of Counseling and
    Educational Psychology
Providence, RI 02908
401-456-8023
Mary Wellman
MA

University of Rhode Island
Department of Psychology
Chafee Social Science Center
Kingston, RI 0281-0808
401-792-5321
Janet Kulberg
MS, Ph.D.
SL-Full; DL-Full

SOUTH CAROLINA

The Citadel
Capers Hall 102
Charleston, SC 24049
803-953-5321
Michael Politano
Ed.S.
SL-Full

University of South Carolina
Department of Psychology
Columbia, SC 29208
803-777-4137
Frederic Medway
Ph.D.
SL-Full
DL-Full

Winthrop University
124 Kinard
Rock Hill, SC 29733
803-323-2117
Joseph Prus
MS, Ed.S.
SL-Full

SOUTH DAKOTA

University of South Dakota
Division of Educational Psychology
    and Counseling
Vermillion, SD 57069
605-677-5250
Hee-sook Choi
Ed.S., Ph.D.

TENNESSEE

Austin Peay State University
Department of Psychology
Clarksville, TN 37044
615-648-7233
Susan Kupisch
MA, Ed.S.

Middle Tennessee State University
Box 533, MTSU Station
Murfreesboro, TN 37132
615-898-2319
James O. Rust
MA, Ed.S.
SL-Full

Tennessee State University
3500 John A. Merritt Blvd.
Nashville, TN 37209-1561
615-321-1275
Cornell Lane
MS, Ed.D.

Tennessee Technological University
Box 5181
Cokeville, TN 38505
615-372-3457
Jann Cupp

The University of Memphis
Department of Psychology
Memphis, TN 38152
901-678-4676
Thomas K. Fagan
MA, Ed.S., Ph.D.
SL-Full

University of Tennessee–
    Chattanooga
Division of Graduate Studies in
    Education
Chattanooga, TN 37403
615-755-4272
George Helton
MS

University of Tennessee–Knoxville
108 Claxton Building
Knoxville, TN 37996
601-974-5131
Donald J. Dickinson
Ed.S., Ph.D.

TEXAS

Abilene Christian University
Box 8011
Abilene, TX 79699
915-674-2287
T. Scott Perkins
MS

East Texas State University
Department of Psychology and
    Special Education
Commerce, TX 75429
903-886-5596; 903-886-5594
William G. Masten
MA, MS

Our Lady of the Lake University
411 SW 24th St.
San Antonio, TX 78207-4666
210-431-3914
Nadene Peterson
MS

Sam Houston State University
Psychology Department
Huntsville, TX 77341
409-294-1178
Richard F. Eglsaer
MA

Southwest Texas State University
Education Building Room 4011
San Marcos, TX 78666
512-245-3083
Edward Scholwinski
M.Ed.

Texas A & M University
701 Harrington
College Station, TX 77843-4225
409-845-2324
Jan Hughes
Ph.D.
DL-Full

Texas Women's University
Department of Psychology &
    Philosophy
P.O. Box 22996
Denton, TX 76204-0996
817-898-2306
Frank Vitro
MA, Ph.D.
SL-Conditional; DL-Full

Trinity University
715 Stadium Drive
San Antonio, TX 78212
210-736-7501
Albert Riestar
MA

University of Houston-Clear Lake
2700 Bay Area Blvd.
Houston, TX 77058
713-283-3392
Gail Cheramie
MA
SL-Full

University of North Texas
Psychology Department
Denton, TX 76203
817-565-2761
Sander Martin
MS, MA, Ph.D.

University of Texas–Austin
Department of Educational
    Psychology
E.D.B. 504
Austin, TX 78712
512-471-4407
Kevin Stark
Ph.D.
DL-Full

University of Texas–Pan American
Department of Educational
    Psychology
Edinburg, TX 78539
210-381-3466
Ralph Carlson
MA

University of Texas–Tyler
Department of Psychology
3900 University Boulevard
Tyler, TX 75701
214-566-7130
Robert McClure
MS

UTAH

Brigham Young University
320-E MCKB
Provo, UT 84602
801-378-3931
Gail W. Brown
MS

University of Utah
Department of Educational
    Psychology
MBH 327
Salt Lake City, UT 84112
801-581-7148
Elaine Clark
MS, Ph.D.
DL-Full

Utah State University
Department of Psychology
Logan, UT 84322-2810
801-797-1460
Kenneth W. Merrell
MS

VIRGINIA

College of William and Mary
School of Education
P.O. Box 8795
Williamsburg, VA 23187-8795
804-221-2356
Sandra Wood
M.Ed., Ed.S.
SL-Full

George Mason University
Psychology Department
4400 University Drive
Fairfax, VA 22030-4444
703-993-1366
John Blaha
MA
SL-Full

James Madison University
Department of Psychology
Harrisonburg, VA 22807
703-568-6834
Harriett Cobb
MA, Ed.S.
SL-Full

Radford University
Department of Psychology
P.O. Box 5761
Radford, VA 24142
703-831-5521
Joseph Montuori
Ed.S.
SL-Full

University of Virginia
Curry School of Education
405 Emmet Street
Charlottesville, VA 22903
804-924-3334
Ronald E. Reeve
Ph.D.
DL-Full

WASHINGTON

Central Washington University
Psychology Department
Ellensburg, WA 98926
509-963-2501
Gene Johnson
M.Ed.
SL-Full

Eastern Washington University
Department of Psychology, MS 94
Cheney, WA 99004
509-359-2478
Connie Raybuck
MS

Eastern Washington University
Department of Applied Psychology
MS 92
Cheney, WA 99004
509-458-6227
Brenna Beedle
MS

Seattle University
Education Department
12th and Madison
Seattle, WA 98122
206-296-5767
Bonnie Denoon
Ed.S.

University of Washington
322 Miller Hall, DQ-12
Seattle, WA 98195
206-543-1846
Virginia W. Burniger
M.Ed., Ph.D.

WEST VIRGINIA

West Virginia Graduate College
P.O. Box 1003
Institute, WV 25112-1003
304-766-1932
Stephen L. O'Keefe
Ed.S.
SL-Full

WISCONSIN

Marquette University
Schroeder Complex 176
Milwaukee, WI 53233
414-288-7375; 414-288-1430
Rebecca Bardwell
MA, M.Ed., Ph.D.

University of Wisconsin–Eau Claire
Department of Psychology
Eau Claire, WI 54702
715-836-2429
William Frankenberger
MSE
SL-Full

University of Wisconsin–LaCrosse
Department of Psychology
1725 State Street
LaCrosse, WI 54601
608-785-8441
Robert E. Arthur
MS
SL-Conditional

University of Wisconsin–Madison
333 Educational Sciences
1025 Johnson Street
Madison, WI 53706
608-262-1427
Thomas R. Kratochwill
Ph.D.
DL-Full

University of Wisconsin–Milwaukee
Department of Educational
  Psychology
P.O. Box 413
Milwaukee, WI 53201
414-229-4998
Anne Teeter
MS, Ph.D.

University of Wisconsin–River Falls
410 South Third Street
River Falls, WI 54022-5001
715-425-3889
Douglas K. Smith
MSE
SL-Full

University of Wisconsin–Stout
226 Vocational Rehabilitation Bldg.
Menomonie, WI 54751
715-232-1442
Calvin L. Stoudt
MSE
SL-Conditional

University of Wisconsin–Superior
Old Main 324
1800 Grand Ave.
Superior, WI 54880
715-398-8381; 715-394-8316
Janice E. Kuldau
MS

University of Wisconsin–Whitewater
800 West Main St.
Whitewater, WI 53190
414-472-1026
James Larson
MS

---

[1]This Table contains a program listing by state. The listing indicates the name of the university, address, phone number, name of the program director, degree(s) offered, and NASP accreditation status. This information is current as of December 30, 1994. NASP accreditation status is on a voluntary basis and some programs have not been reviewed. Thus, it cannot be assumed that a program does not meet national training standards because it is not included as having NASP accreditation. Compliance with national standards should be verified directly with the program (Program Level: SL = Specialist Level and DL = Doctoral Level).

TABLE 2
Regional Listing of School Psychology Programs

NORTHEASTERN REGION

Connecticut

Fairfield University, Fairfield, CT
Southern Connecticut University, New Haven, CT
University of Connecticut, Storrs, CT
University of Hartford, West Hartford, CT

Delaware

University of Delaware, Newark, DE

Maine

University of Southern Maine, Gorham, ME

Massachusetts

American International College, Springfield, MA
Northeastern University, Boston, MA
Tufts University, Boston, MA
University of Massachusetts–Amherst, Amherst, MA
University of Massachusetts–Boston, Boston, MA

New Jersey

Jersey City State College, Jersey City, NJ
Kean College of New Jersey, Union, NJ
Montclair State College, Upper Montclair, NJ
Rider College, Lawrenceville, NJ
Rowan College of New Jersey, Glassboro, NJ
Rutgers University, Piscataway, NJ
Seton Hall University, South Orange, NJ

New York

Alfred University, Alfred, NY
Brooklyn College of the City University Brooklyn, NY
City University of New York–City College,
    New York, NY
College of New Rochelle, New Rochelle, NY
Fordham University–Lincoln Center, New York, NY
Hofstra University, Hempstead, NY
New York University, New York, NY
Pace University, New York, NY
Queens College, City University of New York,
    Flushing, NY
Rochester Institute of Technology, Rochester, NY
St. John's University, Jamica, NY
State University College–Plattsburgh, Plattsburgh, NY
State University of New York–Albany, Albany, NY
State University of New York–Buffalo, Buffalo, NY
State University of New York–Oswego, Oswego, NY
Syracuse University, Syracuse, NY
Teachers College, Columbia University, New York, NY
Yeshiva University, Bronx, NY

Pennsylvania

Bryn Mawr College, Bryn Mawr, PA
Bucknell University, Lewisburg, PA
California University of Pennsylvania, California, PA
Duquesne University, Pittsburgh, PA
Edinboro University of Pennsylvania, Edinboro, PA
Immaculata College, Immaculata, PA
Indiana University of Pennsylvania, Indiana, PA
Lehigh University, Bethlehem, PA
Marywood College, Scranton, PA
Millersville University of Pennsylvania, Millersville, PA

Pennsylvania State University, University Park, PA
Temple University, Philadelphia, PA
University of Pennsylvania, Philadelphia, PA

Rhode Island

Rhode Island College, Providence, RI
University of Rhode Island, Kingston, RI

SOUTHEASTERN REGION

Alabama

Alabama A & M University, Normal, AL
Auburn University, Auburn, AL
The University of Alabama, Tuscaloosa, AL
University of Alabama–Birmingham, Birmingham, AL

Florida

Florida A & M University, Tallahassee, FL
Florida International University, Miami, FL
Florida State University, Tallahassee, FL
University of Central Florida, Orlando, FL
University of Florida, Gainesville, FL
University of South Florida, Tampa, FL
University of West Florida, Pensacola, FL

Georgia

Georgia Southern University, Statesboro, GA
Georgia State University, Atlanta, GA
University of Georgia, Athens, GA
Valdosta State University, Valdosta, GA

Kentucky

Eastern Kentucky University, Richmond, KY
University of Kentucky, Lexington, KY
Western Kentucky University, Bowling Green, KY

Maryland

Towson State University, Towson, MD
University of Maryland, College Park, MD

Mississippi

University of Southern Mississippi, Hattiesburg, MS

North Carolina

Appalachian State University, Boone, NC
East Carolina University, Greenville, NC
North Carolina State University, Raleigh, NC
University of North Carolina–Chapel Hill,
    Chapel Hill, NC
Western Carolina University, Cullowhee, NC

South Carolina

The Citadel, Charleston, SC
University of South Carolina, Columbia, SC
Winthrop University, Rock Hill, SC

Tennessee

Austin Peay State University, Clarksville, TN
Middle Tennessee State University, Murfreesboro, TN
Tennessee State University, Nashville, TN
Tennessee Technological University, Cokesville, TN
The University of Memphis, Memphis, TN

University of Tennessee–Chattanooga, Chattanooga, TN
University of Tennessee–Knoxville, Knoxville, TN

Virginia

College of William and Mary, Williamsburg, VA
George Mason University, Fairfax, VA
James Madison University, Harrisonburg, VA
Radford University, Radford, VA
University of Virginia, Charlottesville, VA

District of Columbia

Gallaudet University, Washington, DC
Howard University, Washington, DC

West Virginia

West Virginia Graduate College, Institute, WV

NORTH CENTRAL REGION

Illinois

Eastern Illinois University, Charleston, IL
Governors State University, University Park, IL
Illinois State University, Normal, IL
Loyola University of Chicago, Chicago, IL
National-Louis University, Evanston, IL
Northern Illinois University, DeKalb, IL
Southern Illinois University–Edwardsville,
   Edwardsville, IL
Western Illinois University, Macomb, IL

Indiana

Ball State University, Muncie, IN
Indiana State University, Terre Haute, IN
Indiana University, Bloomington, IN
Valparaiso University, Valparaiso, IN

Michigan

Andrews University, Berrien Springs, MI
Central Michigan University, Mt. Pleasant, MI
Eastern Michigan University, Ypsilanti, MI
Michigan State University, East Lansing, MI
University of Detroit–Mercy, Detroit, MI
Wayne State University, Detroit, MI
Western Michigan University, Kalamazoo, MI

Ohio

Bowling Green State University, Bowling Green, OH
Cleveland State University, Cleveland, OH
John Carroll University, University Heights, OH
Kent State University, Kent, OH
Miami University, Oxford, OH
Ohio State University, Columbus, OH
University of Akron, Akron, OH
University of Cincinnati, Cincinnati, OH
University of Dayton, Dayton, OH
University of Toledo, Toledo, OH

Wisconsin

Marquette University, Milwaukee, WI
University of Wisconsin–Eau Claire, Eau Claire, WI
University of Wisconsin–La Crosse, La Crosse, WI
University of Wisconsin–Madison, Madison, WI
University of Wisconsin–Milwaukee, Milwaukee, WI
University of Wisconson–River Falls, River Falls, WI
University of Wisconsin–Stout, Menomonie, WI

University of Wisconson–Superior, Superior, WI
University of Wisconsin–Whitewater, Whitewater, WI

WEST CENTRAL REGION

Arkansas

University of Central Arkansas, Conway, AR

Iowa

Iowa State University, Ames, IA
University of Iowa, Iowa City, IA
University of Northern Iowa, Cedar Falls, IA

Kansas

Emporia State University, Emporia, KS
Fort Hays State University, Fort Hays, KS
Pittsburg State University, Pittsburg, KS
University of Kansas, Lawrence, KS
Wichita State University, Wichita, KS

Louisiana

Louisiana State University, Baton Rouge, LA
Louisiana State University–Shreveport,
   Shreveport, LA
McNeese State University, Lake Charles, LA
Nicholls State University, Thibodaux, LA
Northeast Louisiana University, Monroe, LA
Tulane University, New Orleans, LA

Minnesota

Moorhead State University, Moorhead, MN
University of Minnesota, Minneapolis, MN

Missouri

University of Missouri–Columbia, Columbia, MO

Nebraska

Kearney State College, Kearney, NE
University of Nebraska–Lincoln, Lincoln, NE
University of Nebraska–Omaha, Omaha, NE

North Dakota

Minot State University, Minot, ND

Oklahoma

University of Central Oklahoma, Edmond, OK
Oklahoma State University, Stillwater, OK

South Dakota

University of South Dakota, Vermillion, SD

Texas

Abilene Christian University, Abilene, TX
Baylor University, Waco, TX
East Texas State University, Commerce, TX
Our Lady of the Lake University, San Antonio, TX
Sam Houston State University, Huntsville, TX
Southwest Texas State University, San Marcos, TX
Texas A & M University, College Station, TX
Texas Women's University, Denton, TX
Trinity University, San Antonio, TX
University of Houston–Clear Lake, Houston, TX
University of North Texas, Denton, TX
University of Texas–Austin, Austin, TX
University of Texas–Pan American, Edinburg, TX
University of Texas–Tyler, Tyler, TX

WESTERN REGION

Arizona

Arizona State University, Tempe, AZ
Northern Arizona University, Flagstaff, AZ
University of Arizona, Tucson, AZ

California

Califoria State University–Chico, Chico, CA
California State University–Fresno, Fresno, CA
California State University–Hayward, Hayward, CA
California State University–Humboldt, Humboldt, CA
California State University–Long Beach,
    Long Beach, CA
California State University–Los Angeles,
    Los Angeles, CA
California State University–Northridge,
    Northridge, CA
California State University–Sacramento,
    Sacramento, CA
Chapman College, Orange, CA
La Sierra University, Riverside, CA
Loyola Marymount University, Los Angeles, CA
San Diego State University, San Diego, CA
University of California–Berkeley, Berkeley, CA
University of California–Davis, Davis, CA
University of California–Riverside, Riverside, CA
University of California–Santa Barbara,
    Santa Barbara, CA
University of the Pacific, Stockton, CA

Colorado

University of Colorado–Denver, Denver, CO
University of Denver, Denver, CO
University of Northern Colorado, Greeley, CO

Idaho

Idaho State University, Pocatello, ID
University of Idaho, Moscow, ID

Montana

University of Montana, Missoula, MT

Nevada

University of Nevada–Las Vegas, Las Vegas, NV

Oregon

Lewis and Clark College, Portland, OR
University of Oregon, Eugene, OR

Utah

Brigham Young University, Provo, UT
University of Utah, Salt Lake City, UT
Utah State University, Logan, UT

Washington

Central Washington University, Ellensburg, WA
Eastern Washington University, Cheney, WA
Seattle University, Seattle WA
University of Washington, Seattle, WA

FIGURE 1. Distribution of school psychology training programs in the United States according to NASP region (NE, SE, NC, WC, W). Code: 1–Master's degree only; 2–Specialist degree or level; 3–Doctoral and nondoctoral degrees; 4–Doctoral degree only.

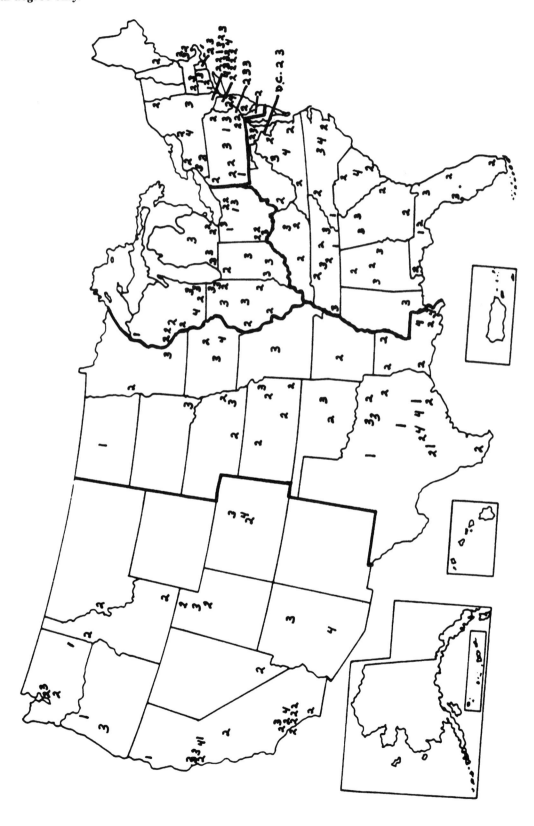

Medications Commonly Used to Treat Children and Adolescents with Convulsive Disorders, Juvenile Rheumatoid Arthritis and Respiratory Illnesses

Susan Vess
University of Southern Maine

OVERVIEW

School psychologists encounter children and adilescents with health problems who take prescribed medication. Their problems and the medications used to treat them may hinder or change the child's or adolescent's academic performance, behavior, and social interactions. Therefore, it is reasonable that school psychologists know how medications work in general, basic information about categories of medications, and preliminary facts about specific drugs.

BASIC CONSIDERATIONS

Drugs are chemicals which produce a variety of effects on the body as they circulate through the blood stream. No drug is completely safe. Every drug has desired effects, meaning it treats the symptoms or disorder for which it was prescribed and also produces undesired effects. Every drug has multiple effects so one person's desired effect is someone else's undesired effect. Individual drugs vary in degree and type of therapeutic effects and negative reactions. Their influence on the organs of the body accounts for both desired and undesired effects. Drugs never act as bullets speeding to the precise site where a desired action will occur.

When prescribing medication, it is important to wiegh the potential benefits of the drug against its negative effects. Additionally, the patient must be told about the benefits and possible risks of a drug, alternative treatments, and the implications of no treatment.

Some body systems are immature until adolescence, while others are adultlike in childhood (Bindler, Tso, & Howry, 1986; Pagliaro & Pagliaro, 1986). The maturity of a particular organ influences the speed with which the drug is absorbed, distributed, achieves its desired effect, or is excreted (Bindler, Tso, & Howry, 1986). Thus, the general principles of pharmacology and pharmakinetics (study of the processes of absorption, distribution, and excretion of drugs) apply to children and adults (Malseed & Harrigan, 1989).

Calculations using rules taking into account a child's age, height, weight, and/or body surface area are used to select dosage (Pagliaro & Pagliaro, 1986). Each method suggests a slightly different pediatric dose. Adult dosages are exceeded if the drug specifically requires a greater amount to treat children effectively.

Although age may be used to estimate the child's developmental level, the size of the child is an important factor. Small children may be overmedicated and large children undermedicated when dosage level is based on age alone. Surface area of the body is the preferred means of establishing dosage because this metric provides the best information about the efficiency of the child's metabolism, the amount of blood and other fluids, and the effectiveness of the kidneys in ridding the body of waste (Bindler, Tso, & Howry, 1986).

Other factors also contribute to difficulty in predicting and recommending pediatric dosages (Malseed & Harrigan, 1989). There are few controlled studies of drugs with children because of the relatively small numbers treated with any drug and the expense of this kind of research. Additionally, the potential for short-term side effects and negative long-term consequences of drug treatment of children ethically and practically limits the use of medication.

Depending on their ages, children tolerate drugs differently (Bindler & Howry, 1991). Moreover, the therapeutic dosage level and effect of a drug given to children may differ from those of adults. Generally, treatment of children begins with the lowest effective dosage and then the amount is increased as tolerance for the drug increases or a higher dosage is necessary to achieve therapeutic efficacy. However, side effects may occur in children at lower doses than with adults. Further, unique effects such as stained teeth from tetracyclines and growth suppression from corticosteroids are found with children (Friesen, 1987).

Compliance

Compliance or treatment adherence is defined as the ability and willingness to subscribe to recommended medication, including the number of doses and duration of therapy (Feist & Brannon, 1988; Reiss & Melick, 1987). It presumes that the condition is accurately diagnosed and treatable and that the physician selects an appropriate medication. It is also assumed that the drug is taken at a therapeutic level and the use of multiple drugs has not altered the effectiveness of any medication. Compliance with treatment does not assume either symptomatic relief or cure of the condition.

La Greca (1988) concluded from her review of the literature that a significant percentage of children and their caregivers fail to comply with treatments of acute ailments, such as otitis media and upper respiratory infections (URIs) and chronic disorders, such as epilepsy and asthma. Mothers are only as compliant with their children's treatments as they are with their own (Feist & Brannon, 1988). The overall predicted rate of compliance for children and adults approximates 50% (Feist & Brannon, 1988; La Greca, 1988). It is not possible to predict who will and will not comply with prescribed treatment.

Generally, people adhere to treatments when there is an immediate reduction in symptoms or relief from pain. With acute illnesses, they often discontinue medication when symptoms abate. Other manifestations of noncompliance include taking less medicine than prescribed, taking more medicine than prescribed in the hope of achieving a quicker or more effective response, doubling up on doses to make up for a missed dose, and hoarding drugs to treat a similar condition in the future.

People fail to comply with prescribed treatment for a variety of reasons, including inadequate understanding of the disorder or the medication, dissatisfaction with the doctor, cost of medication, annoying side effects, rejection of the diagnosis, or belief that taking medication is a sign of personal weakness. An additional concern is fear of addiction and dependence.

Regardless of the illness, chronicity is associated with poorer compliance (La Greca, 1988). Compliance is jeopardized when the treatment alters the person's life style, is prescribed for an extended period, includes multiple drugs, involves different schedules of administration or multiple medications, and/or works by preventing the appearance of the disorder/symptoms (Feist & Brannon, 1988; La Greca, 1988).

Side Effects

Side effects are the result of exaggerated pharmacological action of the drug in which the patient is drug toxic either from acute overdose or from accumulation of the drug in the body (Spunt, Hermann, & Rousseau, 1986). They are usually annoying, mild, and unavoidable (Malseed & Harrigan, 1989). Most side effects are well-known and are attributed to the pharmacological properties of the drug. Evaluating patients for side effects includes their subjective report and monitoring with objective measures such as serum concentrations.

Some drugs produce adverse reactions which are toxicities from high concentrations of the drug in the body. These negative effects involve severe reactions involving multiple systems in the body and may be unexpected. Adverse reactions include addiction, allergic reactions, anaphylactic shock, convulsions, hearing impairment, photosensitivity, psychosis, and respiratory depression (Malseed & Harrigan, 1989).

Some drugs produce non-dose dependent idiosyncratic reactions. These reactions are drug allergies in which histamines produce allergic symptoms from skin rashes to fatal toxicities. Non-dose dependent adverse effects include over or under responsiveness to the drug, abnormal tolerance, or a qualitatively different effect such as excitation with a sedative (Malseed & Harrigan, 1989; Spunt, Hermann, & Rousseau, 1986). Symptoms range from mild to severe and from local to widespread and appear immediately to days after administration of the drug.

When an idiosyncratic reaction occurs, the drug is discontinued immediately and is unlikely to be tried again. The patient is described as allergic only in the case of an idiosyncratic response to a drug. To confuse or label annoying side effects as signs of an allergy may mean that a safe, effective drug is not tried again.

Polypharmacy, the administration of multiple drugs to the same person, is usually avoided. However, advantageous administration of multiple drugs is designed to improve symptoms better than any drug achieves alone. The number of possible negative effects increases greatly as drugs are added to treatment (Malseed & Harrigan, 1989). This may result in drug interactions, side effects where the action of one drug influences or negates the action of another.

Of particular concern with children and adolescents are problems such as treating them with distasteful medications or with painful or frightening routes of administration, teaching them about their disorder and its treatment, and helping them develop ownership of their treatment. Pagliaro and Pagliaro (1986) identified the following ways of misadministering drugs to children: (a) choosing a drug that requires multiple doses when single dose drugs are available, (b) giving drugs with important foods because of the risk of associating food with an unpleasant medicinal taste, and (c) making drugs tasty or equating them with candy. Treating children and adolescents with drugs requires understanding of treatment, recognizing desired and negative effects of a particular drug, patience, finesse, and recognition of the child's level of development.

Seizure Disorders

Epilepsy is a group of central nervous system (CNS) seizure disorders that are manifestations of abnormal electrical activity in the brain, especially the cerebral cortex. Each seizure type has a characteristic electroencephalogram (EEG) and symptom pattern. The electrical activity is usually episodic and may occur spontaneously or may be triggered by stimuli such as stress, fever and illness, hyperventilation, photosensitivity, poor nutrition, and hormonal imbalances.

Status epilepticus is an exception in which multiple generalized convulsions continue without interruption or return to consciousness or normal muscle tone. Status epilepticus is dangerous, even life threatening, because of impaired respiration or lack of oxygen getting to the brain.

When seizures are secondary to another medical condition, their treatment involves resolving the underlying disorder. Seizures not secondary to another disorder are treated with anticonvulsants. These chemically diverse drugs depress abnormal neuronal discharges in the CNS. Anticonvulsants differ in how they control seizures and what kinds of seizures they treat.

Side effects of anticonvulsants are expected because of their long-term use, their relatively high doses, and their frequent combination (Spunt, Hermann, & Rousseau, 1986). They are classified according to three criteria: (a) intoxification from high concentrations in the blood, (b) common side effects associated with therapeutic dosages, and (c) idiosyncratic reactions (Gadow, 1986). It is always important to monitor the achievement and behavior of children taking anticonvulsants.

Although chronic seizure activity has been associated with problems in learning, behavior, and mood, anticonvulsants are not recommended to treat childhood behavior disorders (Biederman & Steingard, 1991). Nevertheless, Dilantin and Tegretol have been used to treat aggression, impulsivity, and restlessness even in the absence of seizures (Biederman & Steingard, 1991).

Arthritic Conditions

Arthritis is a disease of the joints which occurs in over 100 forms, especially osteoarthritis and rheumatoid arthritis (RA). Arthritis is characterized by inflammation in the joints, surrounding tissues, or both. Inflammation is indicated by redness, swelling, warmth to the touch, and tenderness (Phillips, 1988). Because of this inflammation, the patient experiences pain, stiffness, and reduced mobility (Phillips, 1988).

There are several different forms of arthritis in children, but the most common is Juvenile Rheumatoid Arthritis (JRA). Approximately 250,000 children have JRA (DHHS, 1991). The major symptom of JRA is inflammation of the joints which may have a negative effect on bone growth and physical development during active phases of the disease.

Arthritis is neither preventable nor curable. The treament of adult and child forms of arthritis is very similar and shares goals including relief of symptoms such as inflammation, pain and fever, and maintenance or restoration of functioning of the joints. To achieve these objectives, drugs are combined with good nutrition and physical therapy.

Antiarthritis drugs demonstrate one or more of the following effects: (a) antiinflammatory, (b) antipyretic in the presence of fever, (c) analgesic, and (d) anti-coagulant. Generally, medication is required for several months to years with the primary goals of reducing inflammation and pain and allowing greater mobility. Over the long term, drugs may alter the progress of the arthritis and halt destruction of bones and soft tissues.

Nonsteroidal and Antiinflammatory Drugs (NSAIDs) such as aspirin and other salicylates and medications including ibuprofen are the first tried in the treatment of arthritic symptoms. Most of the drugs used to treat arthritis require weeks to months for treatment effects to become apparent. These non-narcotic analgesics relieve the fever of arthritis within hours, although several weeks may be needed to control the high fevers of JRA. Relief of pain and stiffness occurs next and then reduction in swelling and inflammation follows several weeks of treatment. Improvement in these symptoms of arthritis is accompanied by improved mobility.

NSAIDs without salicylates are similiar to aspirin in effectiveness in relieving the symptoms of RA, but require a prescription and produce somewhat different side effects. Some are also used as analgesics and antipyretics to treat dental extractions, athletic injuries, and dysmenorrhea. NSAIDs without salicylates became more important in the treament of JRA when the connection between aspirin and Reye's syndrome became apparent. Reye's syndrome rarely occurs now in either the United States or in countries that continued to use aspirin (Brewer & Angel, 1992).

There are 15 NSAIDs on the market (DHHS, 1991). Brewer and Angel (1992) estimated that the first NSAID prescribed for a particular patient has only a 50% chance of being effective and reported that several drugs are tried before the most effective medication is identified. NSAIDs approved for use with children include aspirin, Advil, Motrin, Nuprin, Naprosyn, and Tolectin.

NSAIDs are rarely used or studied with children, but may be safely prescribed because no NSAID has been found more toxic with children than with adults (Brewer & Angel, 1992). No NSAID is more effective or more toxic than another, but each is somewhat more or less effective with a particular individual. NSAIDs are similar in pain relief, but differ in side effects (NIA, 1990). Common side effects include stomach pain and cramps, nausea, heartburn, vomiting, diarrhea, and constipation. Fewer than 5% of children experience side effects from NSAIDs that are sufficiently severe to stop treatment (Brewer & Angel, 1992). Non-aspirin NSAIDs produce anemia in 2 to 3 percent of children (Brewer & Angel, 1992). Aspirin affects one-sixth of children and damages liver functioning in 10% of children (Brewer & Angel, 1992).

Second-line drugs, including disease modifiers, immunosuppressants, and corticosteroids are used to treat arthritis when NSAIDs are inadequate in the reduction of pain and inflammation. They are used when drastic measures are needed to treat stiff, painful, or damaged joints, when other joints and organs are affected, when fatigue increases and is prolonged, or when low grade fevers persist (Phillips, 1988). These drugs take months to achieve their effects so are called slower-acting anti-rheumatic drugs (Brewer & Angel, 1992).

Disease modifiers, including gold, d-penicillamine and antimalarial agents are used to treat RA when the patient has experienced symptoms for at least six months without relief from NSAIDs (DHHS, 1991). Although not useful for osteoarthritis, these drugs slow the progress of RA.

RA is an autoimmune disease. Hence, drugs which suppress the immune system relieve the symptoms of RA and JRA. Immunosuppressants include methotrexate, the anti-cancer (cytotoxic) drugs and steroids. Cytotoxic drugs used to treat arthritis include Imuran (azathioprine), Cytoxan (cyclophosomide), and Leukeran (cholorambucil). In serious incapacitating cases of JRA, steroids rapidly control high fever, severe pain, and joint swelling and reduce inflammation in the eyes and around the heart (Brewer & Angel, 1992).

Immunosuppressant drugs are used in the treatment of RA when other drugs do not work, the RA is so severe that other organs of the body such as the eyes and heart are involved, or when the child is at risk of death or loss of sight (Brewer & Angel, 1992). By suppressing the body's immune system, these drugs reduce the body's overall effectiveness in resisting infections and may mask symptoms such as fever and pain which are diagnostically important and common to both infections and arthritis.

Allergic Reactions

Allergies are immune system dysfunctons in which there is an exaggerated response to substances, called allergens, to which most people show no reaction. These allergies enter the body through inhalation (pollen, dust, mold, and pet dander), ingestion (milk, eggs, wheat, shrimp, peanuts and other nuts), injection (penicillin and other shots and insect bites), and absorption through the skin (poison ivy, sumac, poison oak, cosmetics, and othe plant and environmental substances) (Lockey, Fox, & Ledford,

nd). The most common allergic disorders include: (a) allergic rhinitis (hay fever) with symptoms such as nasal stuffiness and itching, repeated and often violent sneezing, clear nasal discharge, red, runny eyes, and itching of the ears or roof of the mouth; (b) allergic asthma with symptoms such as wheezing, coughing, and shortness of breath; (c) allergic conjunctivitis with symptoms such as red, itchy eyes with a mucus-related discharge; (d) allergic eczema or skin rash; and (e) allergic contact dermatitis caused by poison ivy, deodorants, dyes, metals, and other allergens (Lockey, Fox, & Ledford, nd). Allergic skin reactions include atopic dermatitis/eczema, hives, and contact dermatitis (Steinmann, 1992). They may also include angioma, a swelling of the underlying tissues of the body. In skin allergies, this swelling usually involves the eyes, lips, and ears.

Anaphylaxis is the term used to describe any severe, body wide allergic reaction to food, drugs, and the venom of stinging insects. It occurs most often with antibiotics, especially penicillin, but may not be caused by the drug itself as much as a constituent part such as eggs or horse serum. Allergies rarely cause anaphylaxis. In anaphylaxis, the tissues of the airways swell which may threaten life. It is indicated by an extreme drop in blood pressure and body temperature, irregular heartbeat, palpitations, flushing, itching, throbbing in the ears, swelling, coughing, sneezing, and difficulty breathing. The person may become unconscious and go into shock.

Antihistamines prevent the release of and block the action of histamines which cause allergic reactions. Hence, they are most effective when taken at the first appearance of symptoms and only provide relief as long as they are taken (Clayton & Stock, 1993). They are most often prescribed to relieve the symptoms of allergies such as allergic and seasonal rhinitis, urticaria (hives), and conjunctivitis. Antihistamines treat allergies by drying up secretions in the nose, throat, and broncial tree.

Antihistamines are not part of the treatment of the comon cold or viruses because they are not caused by histamines. However, because antihistamines produce mild anticholinergic effects including reduction of mucus secretions, they may be used to provide symptomatic relief of colds. Due to their anticholinergic effects on the respiratory tract, they re not used in the treatment of children with asthma unless they also have nasal and skin allergies. Antihistamines work in about 30 minutes to relieve itching, sneezing, watery eyes, runny nose, and other symptoms of allergies.

Decongestants purchased over the counter (OTC) or by prescription control the symptoms of allergies and asthma, prevent acute attacks of these disorders, and reduce or even prevent inflammation. They also treat colds, acute and chronic inflammations, hay fever, and middle ear infections. Tolerance develops rapidly to decongestants and a rebound effect may occur.

Nasal decongestants temporarily relieve nasal stuffiness, inflammation, and sinus congestion due to the common cold, alergic rhinitis, hay fever, and other acute and seasonal disorders (Julien, 1988). They are used to reduce nasal congestion or discharge from increased secretion in the nose (Steinmann, 1992; Bindler, Tso, & Howry, 1991). Decongestants are structurally related to amphetamines, but differ in their impact on heart rate, breathing, and the degree of stimulation produced (Julien, 1992). Because these drugs are stimulants, the child may become more active for several hours after taking the drug and experience insomnia (Steinmann, 1992).

Coughing is the body's natural protective action to expel foreign particles from its respiratory tract (Julien, 1988). It may also be a reflex response to irritation, inflammation, and thick or accumulated secretions (Malseed & Harrigan, 1989; Julien, 1988). However, in a nonproductive cough, the coughing reflex is triggered, but the irritant is not eliminated. Continued nonproductive coughing irritates the respiratory tract and perpetuates coughing (Clayton & Stock, 1993).

Antitussives include both narcotic and nonnarcotic drugs that relieve dry, unproductive coughing through suppression of the cough reflex. They do not completely eliminate coughing, but provide enough relief to enable the person to carry on routine activities or sleep.

Coughs that are productive in expelling excess mucus from the respiratory tract are allowed to continue. Expectorates are drugs that increase mucus formation, liquefy thickened bronchial secretions and stimulate their flow (Julien, 1988). They are used to treat obstructive pulmonary diseases such as asthma, chronic bronchitis, and emphysema and to reduce dry irritating coughs of the common cold. Glyceryl guaiacolate is the most widely used drug in expectorates and is found in common cough medicines.

Upper Respiratory Disorders

Upper respiratory infections (URIs) such as the common cold and coughs are treated with decongestants, cold preparations, and cough supressants (Julien, 1988). Numerous combination products have been formulated to treat the symptoms of minor URIs. These medications are composed of at least two of the following pharmacological groups: antitussives, expectorants, antihistamines, nasal decongestants, and bronchodilators (Julien, 1988). Combination products should be used only when multiple symptoms are present and the particular combination is designed to treat those specific symptoms. These symptoms must be severe enough to warrant treatment. Julien (1988) recommends additional guideliens in evaluating the potential use of

combination cold products: (a) inclusion of no more than three drugs from the above-mentioned pharmacological groups, (b) each individual ingredient in the amount to provide safe and effective treatment of a specific symptom, and (c) consideration of the side effects of each drug.

Asthma, chronic bronchitis, and emphysema are identified as pulmonary or lower tract disorders. They are characterized by bronchospasms (Julien, 1988). Other symptoms include coughing, shortness of breath, wheezing, and chest tightness. Symptoms are often worse at night and may interrupt sleep.

Asthma is a common respiratory disease with a variety of characteristics. It is characterized by hyperresponsiveness of the trachea and airways to multiple stimuli, airway narrowing (source of wheezing, dyspnea, and cough), and airway inflammation. Attacks are triggered by exercise, irritants such as cigarette smoke, the common cold, and allergens such as pollen, dust, animal dander, and some foods (Busse, 1990). The airways narrow so that the amount of air entering and leaving the lungs is reduced. Bronchospasms, mucus formation, inflammation and edema of the lung contribute to airway obstruction (Busse, 1990; Pagliaro & Pagliaro, 1986).

Bronchodilators, drugs that expand the breathing passages in the lungs, are common in the treatment of asthma and other chronic lung obstructions. They relax tight bronchial muscles and dilate constricted airways. Bronchodilators reverse respiratory obstructions due to narrowed air passages and relieve and/or prevent spasms of the breathing passages in the lungs.

Mucolytics are used to treat chronic obstructive pulmonary diseases. They liquefy tenacious mucus secretions so that they are less sticky and thick. This reduces bronchiolar obstruction, improves ventilation, and facilitates removal of these secretions from the respiratory passages by coughing. These drugs relieve the abnormal, viscous mucus accumulation due to chronic lung diseases such as asthma, asthmatic bronchitis, tuberculosis, and complications of cystic fibrosis.

There are four groups of drugs used to treat asthma and other chronic pulmonary diseases. These include the xanthine (caffeine) derivatives such as theophylline, the adrenaline-like drugs, cromolyn and steroids. The xanthines have stimulant properties that may cause a child to act as though several cups of coffee were consumed. The adrenergic-like drugs are the growth area of asthma pharmacology. Even at normal doses, these drugs may produce nervousness and muscle tremors which may be manifested by shaking hands and deteriorating penmanship (Clayton & Stock, 1993). They may also act as stimulants in some children.

The corticosteroids are synthetics of hormones such as cortisone produced by the adrenal gland. They are not the same as the male steroid taken to increase strength. The dosage of steroids used to treat medical disorders exceeds the amount of cortisol secreted by the body daily.

Because they have antiinflammatory, metabolic, and immunosuppressant effects, steroids are used to treat multiple chronic, disabling medical disorders including collagen, endocrine, cardiovascular, and rheumatoid disorders; allergic states such as asthma and drug hypersensitivity reactions; acute leukemia; gastrointestinal diseases, and respiratory distress syndrome that are refractory to other treatment. They are most frequently used to treat accute flareups of inflammatory conditions such as arthritis and bronchial asthma, especially when aggressive, systemic therapy is required. They produce the best response when used to treat autoimmune diseases (Clayton & Stock, 1993). Steroids provide relief of symptoms, but do not change the course of diseases.

Steroids' usefulness stems from their antiinflammatory and antiallergic properties. They are the most effective antiinflammatories known and are most often used to treat local inflammatory conditions affecting the skin such as dermatitis and psoriasis (Phillips, 1988). As antiinflammatory drugs, the corticosteroids work by suppressing the immune system (Brewer, 1992). Hence, steroids are used to reduce rejection of transplants (Julien, 1988). Moreover, they quickly reduce pain and inflammation, allergic reactions, and asthma and colitis attacks (Phillips, 1988). Within days of treatment, steroids restore mobility and relieve the pain of arthritis (Phillips, 1988). However, the immunosuppressant effects of steroids also lower the body's resistance to infections and facilitate their spread (Julien, 1988).

Corticosteroids are among the most powerful drugs used in the treatment of allergies and asthma. Steroids prevent triggering inflammation of the airways and also reduce ongoing inflammation. Because several weeks are needed to achieve effectiveness, they are preventative medications only. Inhaled corticosteroids used in the treatment of bronchial asthma include **beclomethazone, flunisolide, and triamcinolone.**

Corticosteroids are also used to reduce inflammation and reduce the discomfort of inflammatory, ocular conditions, trauma to the eye and allergic disorders. Side effects from prolonged use include glaucoma; damage to the structure of the eye, including the optic nerve; cataract formation; and increased susceptibility to infections.

Steroids are safest when applied locally through inhalation, injection, or topical applications such as creams, but produce the same side effects irrespective of the means of administration. Topical steroids include **hydrocortisone, methylprednisolone, dexamethasone,** and **betamethasone.** The most common side effects associated with topical applications include local itching and irritation.

The side effects of steroids are directly related to length of treatment and dosage levels. Behavioral side effects coinciding with extended treatment include nervousness, insomnia, changes in mood or psychoses. Other side effects include lowered resistance to infection, indigestion, weight gain, loss of muscle mass and strength, mood changes, blurred vision, cataracts, diabetes, osteoporosis, and increased blood pressure. Fluid retention in the abdomen and cheeks producing the characteristic moon face is a serious concern. Children may gain 10 to 20 pounds when treated with steroids for JRA (Brewer & Angel, 1992). Steroids may retard growth which explains why they are drugs of last resort in the treatment of JRA. After chronic use, too rapid withdrawal of corticosteroids may result in acute adrenal insufficiency or a rebound effect (Friesen, 1987).

The following is a listing of drugs used to control epileptic seizures, to reduce the discomfort and other symptoms of arthritis, and to prevent or provide relief of respiratory illness, especially allergies and asthma. None cure the disorder. Trade names are listed first with the generic name in parentheses. Drugs are listed alphabetically by their generic names. Treatment comments are included in the right hand column. This listing is incomplete in both the number of drugs and their indications, side effects, and other treatment comments. Medical professionals and pharmacists, the most current *Physician's Desk Reference* (PDR) and other resources should be consulted for more complete information.

Anticonvulsants

Diamox (**acetazolamide**)	Diamox, a diuretic, is infrequently used as an anticonvulsant to great petit mal, grand mal, and focal seizures. Women with epilepsy associated with menstruation may be given this drug several days before the beginning of the menstrual cycle. Common side effects include diarrhea, increased frequency of urination, anorexia, and a metallic taste.
Tegretol (**carbamazepine**)	Tegretol is used to treat grand mal, psychomotor, and mixed seizures and may be used to treat seizures refractory to other anticonvulsants. It has also been used in the treatment of pain associated with tic douloureux. Investigational uses of Tegretol include bipolar affective and schizoaffective disorders, resistant schizophrenia, and rage reactions. Tegretol is chemically related to the TCAs so produces similar adverse effects and precautions, but is less sedating than other anticonvulsants. It is among the newest and most used anticonvulsants. Although the safety of this drug has not been established for children under 6, Tegretol is often preferred to phenobarbital in their treatment. The most frequent short-term side effects include blurred vision, nystagmus, drowsiness, dizziness, and nausea. Some tolerance to these side effects develops with continued use. Ataxia and nystagmus are associated with toxic levels of Tegretol. Several blood disorders are associated with the use of Tegretol (Friesen, 1987).
Klonopin (**clonazepam**)[4]	Klonopin is a primary drug of choice in the treatment of myoclonic seizures and is used to treat petit mal seizures and variants refractory to other drugs. In oral form, it is used to treat absence seizures in children. Nonapproved uses include control of grand mal, psychomotor and infantile spasm seizures. The effectiveness of Klonopin has been investigated for panic attacks. Its safety has not been established for long-term use with children. Common dose-related side effects of Klonopin include sedation and severe drowsiness in about 50% of epileptics and ataxia in about one third (Gadow, 1986). These effects usually disappear with continued use. Behavioral effects such as aggression, hyperactivity, irritability and difficulty concentrating occur in about 25% of patients (Friesen, 1987). Klonopin is removed slowly to reduce the likelihood of status epilepticus. If used alone with persons with mixed types of epilepsy, it may increase the frequency of grand mal seizures (Townsend, 1990).
Tranxene (**clorazepate**)[4]	Tranxene is used to treat anxiety and as an adjunct in the management of partial seizures. It It is contraindicated in children under 9.
Valium (**diazepam-IV**)[4]	Valium is used primarily to treat status epilepticus, but is not recommended for long-term control of epilepsy. Its most common side effects include drowsiness and ataxia. Grand mal seizures are exacerbated in some patients (Friesen, 1987).
Depakote (**divalprox sodium**)	Depakote is used to treat petit mal, grand mal, and myoclonic seizures primarily and may be used with complex partial seizures.
Zarontin (**ethosuximide**)[3]	Zarontin is used primarily in the treatment of petit mal seizures, but is also used for grand mal and psychomotor seizures. Its sole use in patients with mixed types of epilepsy may increase the incidence of grand mal seizures (Townsend, 1990). Tolerance develops with continued use. Zarontin is withdrawn if dyskinesias or psychiatric disorders occur (Friesen, 1987).
Peganone (**ethotoin**)[2]	Peganone is used to treat grand mal and psychomotor seizures. It is both the least toxic and least potent of the hydatoins.
Mesantoin (**mephenytoin**)[2]	Mesantoin is used to treat grand mal, psychomotor, focal, and Jacksonian seizures when less toxic anticonvulsants fail. It is the most toxic anticonvulsant. Its most common side effect is drowsiness.
Mebaral (**mephobarbital**)[1]	Mebaral is used to treat grand mal and petit mal seizures and moderate anxiety states. It is less likely to produce sedation or behavior problems than phenobarbital.
Gemonil (**metharbital**)[1]	Gemonil is used to treat grand mal, petit mal, myoclonic, and mixed types of seizures. It is usually combined with other anticonvulsants.
Paral (**paraldehyde**)	Paral is a sedative hypnotic used to treat seizures associated with emergency situations such as status epilepticus, tetanus, and drug poisoning.
Paradione (**paramethadione**)[5]	Paradione is used to treat petit mal seizures refractory to other anticonvulsants.

Luminal **(phenobarbital)**[1]	Phenobarbital is used to treat moderate anxiety states, insomnia, and status epilepticus. It is also used for the long-term management of seizures, especially grand mal, myoclonic jerking, and infantile spasms. It is the most commonly used barbituate in the treatment of epilepsy. Of all anticonvulsants, phenobarbital is least likely to produce serious side effects. Its most common side effect is sedation which necessitates monitoring school performance and achievement. Drowsiness usually subsides after several weeks of treatment. About 15% of young children may experience paradoxical CNS excitement or hyperkinetic-like syndrome (Friesen, 1987).
Milontin **(phensuximide)**[3]	Milontin is used in the treatment of petit mal seizures. Its sole use in patients with a mixed type of epilepsy may increase the incidence of grand mal seizures (Townsend, 1990).
Dilantin **(phenytoin)**[2]	Dilantin is used to treat grand mal and psychomotor seizures, grand mal seizures associated with neurosurgery or status epilepticus and to control seizures not caused by epilepsy (Julien, 1992; Bindler & Howry, 1991). It is contraindicated in the treatment of petit mal and seizures associated with hypoglycemia (Townsend, 1990). Fetal abnormalities have occurred when Dilantin was taken during pregnancy (Julien, 1992). At therapeutic levels, Dilantin is less sedating than barbituates. The side effects of Dilantin are related to the length of treatment, dosage or plasma levels, and mode of administration. The most common side effects of Dilantin include gingival hyperplasia which may result in dental problems, GI tract disturbances, and hirsutism. Overmedication with Dilantin produces a variety of CNS effects such as sedation, lethargy, nystagmus, ataxia, and diplopia. Behavioral indicators of toxicity include silliness, hyperactivity, drowsiness, hallucinations, and confusion. Increased frequency of seizures, confusion, slurred speech, vertigo, and hallucinations indicate more severe toxicity. Dilantin is discontinued if a skin rash occurs.
Mysoline **(primidone)**	Mysoline is used in the treatment of psychomotor, grand mal, and elementary focal seizures when other anticonvulsants were not effective. It is also used cautiously in the treatment of children with ADD and other disorders. It converts to phenobarbital in the body. Mysoline's primary side effect is drowsiness, especially early in treatment. Other reactions include ataxia, dizziness, skin rash, and GI distress (Malseed & Harrigan, 1989). It is often used with Dilantin.
Tridione **(trimethadione)**[5]	Tridione is used to treat petit mal seizures refractory to other anticonvulsants.
Depakene **(valporic acid)**	Depakene is used to treat petit mal seizures and as an alternative treatment of multiple seizures. It has investigational use in the management of other types of seizures, especially grand mal, myclonic, atonic, psychomotor, and infantile spasm seizures. It is among the newest and most used anticonvulsants, especially when other anticonvulsants are not effective. About 75% of epileptics respond favorably to Depakene (Julien, 1992). GI tract disorders, such as anorexia, nausea, vomiting, indigestion, and diarrhea occur often at beginning of treatment. Temporary hair loss, fine tremors, and sleep disturbance may also occur. There are few serious toxicities associated with Depakene.

Barbituates[1] produce selective depression of the CNS with relatively little toxicity (Julien, 1992). They are among the most frequently prescribed drugs for all types of epilepsy, but are most effective in the treatment of generalized seizures. Long acting barbituates are often combined with other anticonvulsants. Barbituates used in the treatment of epilepsy include Gemonil (**metharbital**), Mebaral (**mephobarbital**), Mysoline (**primidone**), and **phenobarbital.**

Because of their side effects, barbituates are used cautiously to treat children with behavior problems (Biederman & Steingard, 1991). Common side effects include overacivity, irritability, aggression, excitability, and a hangover effect. These effects may interfere with learning which is among the major disadvantages in using barbituates with children (Julien, 1992; Gadow, 1986).

Hydantoins[2] are used primarily in the treatment of generalized major motor seizures. They are also used in the treatment of psychomotor, elementary focal, and Jacksonian seizures. They are not CNS depressants nor do they interfere with normal sensory functioning. Adverse reactions include ataxia, confusion, slurred speech, diplopia, nystagmus, a skin rash, gingival hyperplasia, epigastric distress, and anemia (Malseed & Harrigan, 1989). Hydatoins used in the treatment of convulsive disorders include Dilantin (**phenytoin**), Mesantoin (**mephenytoin**), and Peganone (**ethotoin**).

Succinimides[3] are rarely used drugs prescribed for the treatment of petit mal seizures. In mixed seizure types, they increase the frequency of grand mal seizures. The most common side effects include nausea, gastric upset, anorexia, epigastric pain, hiccups, headaches, minor behavioral disturbances, and skin eruptions (Malseed & Harrigan, 1989). The side effects of Celontin and Milontin are similar to those of Zarontin, but are more likely to produce drowsiness. Succinimides used in the treatment of seizure disorders include Celontin (**methsuximide**), Milontin (**phensuximide**), and Zarontin (**ethusoximide**).

Benzodiazepines[4] are used to treat difficult-to-control seizures, particularly petit mal, myoclonic, and akinetic seizures. They work by controlling the spread of seizures (Clayton, 1987). Their use is periodically evaluated because of the possibility of drug-induced personality changes and learning problems (Julien, 1992). Common side effects include ataxia, drowsiness, blurred vision, and behavioral changes

(Malseed & Harrigan, 1989). Benzodiazepines used to treat seizure disorders include Klonopin (**clonazepam**), Tranxene (**clorazepate**), and Valium (**diazepam**).

Oxazolidinediones[5] are alternate drugs used in the treatment of petit mal seizures, but are rarely prescribed because of their side effects. Their most comon side effects include headaches, photophobia, diplopia, irritability, rash, drowsiness, hiccups, and abdominal pain (Malseed & Harrigan, 1989). The oxazolidinediones used to treat epilepsy include Paradione (**paramethadione**) and Tridione (**trimethadione**).

Non-Narcotic Analgesics

Tylenon, Datril (**acetaminophen**)	Tylenol and Datril are used in the treatment of fever and mild to moderate pain due to headaches, toothaches, influenza, and muscle skeletal distress. They are useful in the treatment of children and persons unable to tolerate aspirin. They are not associated with Reye's syndrome and cause fewer side effects than aspirin. Tylenol and Datril have analgesic and antipyretic actions similar to aspirin in equivalent doses, but are not effective as antiinflammatory agents. Therefore, they are not useful in the treatment of arthritis and acute inflammation. When used in recommended dosages, they are almost free of side effects. Hypersensitivity is often characterized by skin reactions (Friesen, 1987).
aspirin (**acetylsalic acid**)	Aspirin is most useful in the treatment of low intensity pain such as headaches and skeletal muscle discomfort; but, at higher doses, also reduces inflammation. Increased dosages of aspirin do not correspond to increased pain relief. Aspirin is the drug of choice in the treatment of inflammatory disorders, including all types of arthritis (Reiss & Melick, 1987). It is used to treat acute rheumatic fever. Described as the most important drug in the world, it is effective in treating about half the cases of RA with no additional medications (Phillips, 198). The most common side effects of aspirin involve GI upset such as epigastric distress, nausea, and vomiting. Toxicity is indicated by ringing in the ears, auditory and visual difficulties, mental confusion, thirst, and hyperventilation (Julien, 1992). Chronic use of aspirin may increase the chance of peptic ulcers (Friesen, 1987). The use of aspirin by children with chicken pox, influenza, or viral infections is associated with Reye's syndrome. Fatalities occur in about 40% of children with Reye's syndrome (Friesen, 1987). Aspirin is associated with increased bleeding during surgery, peptic ulcers, trauma, and blood disorders (Friesen, 1987). It is avoided when patients have peptic and other ulcers and is discontinued for at least a week before surgery.
Ascriptin (**acetylsalic acid**)	Ascriptin is sometimes prescribed to reduce the side effects of aspirin, especially those related to stomach upset.
Ridaura (oral gold/**auranofin**), Solganol (gold injection/ **aurothioglucose**), Myochrysine (gold injection/**sodium thiomalate**)	Arthritis has been treated with gold since the 1920s. Gold compounds are the most effective second-line drug in the treatment of mild to moderate RA when other treatments such as rest, physical therapy, and other drugs are not effective. It is not effective in the treatment of other forms of arthritis. Gold has been replaced by methotrexate as the primary second-line drug used to treat JRA. The first effect of gold, which occurs within two to four months of treatment, is reduction of morning stiffness (Brewer & Angel, 1992). Joint swelling, pain and tenderness are reduced after four to six months. Gold is not effective in reducing the high fevers of JRA (Brewer & Angel, 1992). About 10% of children stop taking gold because of intolerable side effects (Brewer & Angel, 1992). Side effects of gold include anemia, low white blood cell count, and liver function test abnormalities. Others include blood in the urine, easy bruising, sores in the mouth, skin rashes, and numbness of the hands and feet. There are few serius side effects, but if white blood cells are not made, the body becomes open to infections. Gold is added to treatment with NSAIDs, aspirin or corticosteroids, not substituted for it. If gold works, the other drugs may be eliminated. It is effective in about 50% of cases of RA (Brewer & Angel, 1992; DHHS, 1991). After five years of use, gold is effective only in 5 to 15% of persons with arthritis (DHHS, 1991).
Arthropan (**choline salicylate**)	Arthropan is a liquid salicylate that is used with children and others who have difficulty swallowing pills and capsules.

Dolobid **(diflunisal)**	Dolobid is an antiinflammatory analgesic used to reduce mild to moderate pain and osteoarthritis. It has little antipyretic effects.

Plaquenil **(hydroxychloroquine)**

Plaquenil is used primarily in the treatment of malaria. It is thought to work on the immune system to reduce pain, swelling, stiffness, and flare-ups of arthritis due to weather or illness (Brewer & Angel, 1992; NIA, 1990). It is orally administered for months before treatment effects become apparent. It reduces the need for steroids.

Side effects of Plaquenil include low blood count, blood or protein in the urine, and abnormal liver function. Other side effects include diarrhea, headaches, loss of appetite, skin rash, and stomach pain. At high doses, it may damage the retina.

Mitrin, Rufen and OTCs such as Advil, Nuprin **(ibuprofen)** **(fenoprofen)**

These prescription and OTC drugs are used to treat mild to moderate pain and fever of RA, including JRA and osteoarthritis. They are not for use in home treatment of minor discomfort in children. These drugs produce aspirin-like antiinflammatory and analgesic effects at high doses. They produce side effects in the GI tract similar to, but less severe than those caused by aspirin. Common CNS side effects include headaches and dizziness. Skin rashes and itching may be fairly common.

Naproxin, Anaprox, Naprosyn **(naproxen)**

Naproxen is used to treat mild to moderate pain and inflammation of diseases such as JRA and RA. It is similar to ibuprofen, but requires a prescription.

The side effects of naproxen involve the GI tract. They are similar to, but less severe than those associated with aspirin. Common CNS effects include headaches and dizziness. Skin rashes and itching may be fairly common. Information about side effects is derived from experience with adults.

Ibuprofen, fenoprofen, and naproxen show analgesic, antipyretic, and antiflammatory effects. Their effectiveness is comparable to other non-narcotic analgesics and Darvon (Julien, 1992). They are used with caution in persons with peptic ulcers and bleeding disorders.

Indocin **(indomethacin)**

Indocin is used in the treatment of several types of active arthritis, including JRA. It reduces pain, stiffness, swelling, and tenderness of joints, but only 25% show significant improvement (Clayton, 1987). It is not used unless the arthritis is unresponsive to aspirin or safer nonsteroidal antiinflammatory drugs (Friesen, 1987).

Indocin produces many side effects with chronic use incuding GI symptoms. CNS side effects occur frequently. They include headaches, dizziness, vertigo, and mental confusion (Friesen, 1987).

Abitrexate, Folex, Mexate **(methotrexate)**

Methotrexate is used primarily in the treatment of leukemia and other cancers. It is also used experimentally in the treatment of autoimmune disorders. It works on the immune system, reduces cell proliferation, and has antiinflammatory effects.

Methotrexate is a rapid acting second-line drug used in low doses for the treatment of JRA. Because of lower doses, there are fewer side effects than found with cancer treatment. It does not retard the child's growth. It presents the same profile of side effects as other arthritis medications.

Depen, Curpimine **(penicillamine)**

Penicillamine is an orally administered drug that is used in conjunction with NSAIDs or other drugs to treat severe RA and JRA. Penicillamine works on the immune system. This drug is the least often used medication in the treatment of JRA and is only tried when others are not effective. After several months of treatment, it relieves joint pain, swelling, and stiffness. Side effects of penicillamine are very similar to those of injected gold.

Tolectin **(tolmetin)**

Tolectin is used in the treatment of osteoarthritis and rheumatoid arthritis, including JRA. It produces GI tract disturbances similar to but less severe than those of aspirin. Common side effects include headache, dizziness, skin rashes, and itching.

Antihistamines, Decongestants, and Antitussives

Bromarest, Chlorphed,
Dimetane, Dimetapp
Rolabromophen,
Veltane
(brompheniramine)

Antihistamine used in the treatment of rhinitis and allergy, including respiratory congestion with runny or stuffy nose and watery eyes. As an injection, brompheniramine is used to prevent allergic reactions to blood and plasma and to halt anaphylactic reactions (Bindler & Howry, 1991). It is contraindicated in asthma attacks.

Clistin
(carbinoximine),
Rondec
**(carbinoximine,
pseudoephedrine)**

Antihistamine used to provide relief of allergic or vasomotor rhinitis. This drug acts as an antiemetic and has strong anticholinergic action.

Aller-Chlor,
Chlor-Trimeton
Chlormene, Histapan,
Novahistine, Teldrin
(chlorpheniramine)

Antihistamine used in the treatment of rhinitis and allergy. As an injection, it is used to prevent allergic reactions to blood and plasma and anaphylactic reactions (Bindler & Howry, 1991). This drug has antiemetic, antitussive, and some local anesthetic actions. It is contraindicated in acute asthma attacks.

Marezine
(cyclizine)

Antihistamine and antiemetic used primarily to treat and prevent the nausea, vomiting, and dizziness of motion sickness and vestibular disorders.

Periactin
(cyproheptadine)

Antihistamine and antipyretic used in the treatment of seasonal allergic rhinitis, conjunctivities, pruritus, and cold urticaria. It also relieves angiodema (the pronounced swelling of allergies from food and airborne allergens) and minor drug or serum reactions. Its unapproved uses include anorexia nervosa, somatrotropin deficiency, and Cushing's syndrome (Bindler & Howry, 1991). This drug has been used as an appetite stimulant in children (Clayton, 1987).

Pertussin 8-Hour,
Romilars
(dextromethorphan)

Antitussive that is also used in combination cough remedies such as Formula 44-D, Nyquill, Robitussin DM, and Vicks. This nonnarcotic antitussive (OTC) does not relieve pain or produce addiction.

Drammamine and
others
(dimenhydrinate)

Antihistamine and antiemetic used to prevent nausea and vomiting from motion sickness and to control dizziness and vertigo.

Benadryl, Benylin,
Nordryl, Valdrene
and others
(diphenhydramine)

Antihistamine, antiemetic, and antivertigo drug used to prevent and treat symptoms of itching and swelling of skin from allergy and bug bites, milk allergies, vertigo, and motion sickness, and to suppress coughing and induce sleep. It relieves mild blood and transfusion reactions characterized by angioedema, urticaria, and pruritus. In combination products, it is used to treat URIs and colds. In topical form, it is used to treat pruritus and pain from sunburn, insect bites, and minor skin irritations.

Decapryn
(doxyamine)

Antihistamine used to treat allergy symptoms and rhinitis. It is a component of cough and cold preparations.

Anti-Tuss, Robitussin,
and others
(guaifensin)

Antitussive that works as an expectorant to liquefy secretions in the lungs, promote productive coughing, and prevent the accumulation of tenacious airway secretions. It relieves dry, nonproductive coughing from minor throat and bronchial irritation of URIs.

Atarax, Vistaril
and others
(hydroxyzine)

Antihistamine, sedative, analgesic, and anxiolytic used to control pre-operative anxiety and to treat allergic pruritus, nausea, and vomiting of surgery and motion sickness. It is also used to treat emotional states characterized by anxiety, tension, and agitation. This drug may be combined with opiates and analgesics.

Bonine, Antivert
(mecilizine)

Antihistamine and antinauseant used to control nausea, vomiting, and dizziness due to motion sickness and diseases of the vestibular system.

Tacaryl
(methdilazine)

Antihistamine used to treat pruritus.

Allerest, Eye Drops,
Clear Eyes, Privine
(naphazoline)

Vasoconstrictor and nasal decongestant used to provide relief of nasal congestion or rhinitis. As an ophthalmic decongestant, it reduces redness in the eyes by decreasing swelling of the sclera due to minor eye irritations. Its use should be avoided in children.

Afrin, Dristan, Duration, Neosynephrine 12-hour **(oxymetazoline)**	Antihistamine and nasal decongestant used to relieve nasal congestion or rhinitis. It relieves a stuffy nose by reducing the swelling of the mucous membranes in the nose. Excess use may produce rebound stuffiness.
Neo-Synephrine, Alconefrin drops, Allerest Nasal, Coricidin Nasal Mist, Isophrin, Sinarest Nasal and others **(phenylephrine)**	Decongestant used as an oral inhalation to constrict bronchioles and relieve congestion. In a topically applied nasal form, this drug reduces congestion of the mucus membrane (stuffy nose) during an URI. In the form of eyedrops, it reduces redness of the eyes by reducing swelling of the sclera.
Decongestant P, Dimetapp, Propardine **(phenylpropanolamine)**	Widely used oral decongestant that is commonly found in OTC products such as Allerest, Contac, Sinutab, and Triaminic which provide relief of nasal congestion and rhinitis.
Phenergan and others **(promethazine)**	Antihistamine and antiemetic related to the phenothiazines used in the management of allergy and motion sickness. It is used pre-operatively for its sedative and antiemetic effects.
Sudafed, Novafed Afrinol, Neosynephrol **(pseudoephedrine)**	Alone, this drug is used as a nasal decongestant and vasoconstrictor to shrink swollen nasal mucus membranes and to allow the airways to open and sinuses to drain. It is combined with antihistamines, expectorants, and antitussives to treat allergies and provide symptomatic relief of colds and viral infections. Hypertension may occur at effective dosages.
Neo-Antegran, Allerest, Triaminic **(pyrilamine)**	Antihistamine used in combination cold remedies such as Allerest to provide symptomatic relief of allergic and vasomotor rhinitis. Because it produces sleepiness, this drug is also used in sleep aids such as Nytol and Sominex to treat insomnia.
Seldane **(terfenadine)**	Antihistamine used to relieve the symptoms of chronic allergic disorders, seasonal and perennial allergic rhinitis and dermatological disorders, including primary urticaria and eczema from histamine release and pruritus. It compares favorably in effectiveness with other anthistamines; but produces less drowsiness, sedation, and anticholinergic effects.
Tyzine, Murine Visine **(tetrahydrozoline)**	Nasal decongestant used to relieve nasal congestion and rhinitis. In the form of eyedrops, drug reduces redness of the eye by reducing swelling of the sclera from minor eye irritations. It produces significantly more side effects than other decongestants.
Temaril **(trimeprazine)**	Antihistamine used to treat pruritus.
Pyribenzamine PBZ **(tripelennamine)**	Anthistamine.
Actidil, Actifed **(triprolidine)**	Antihistamine used to provide symptomatic relief of allergic and vasomotor rhinitis. It has a rapid onset and few side effects. This drug may cause paradoxical irritability and excitation.
Otrivin drops, Sinutab, Neosynephrine 2 **(xylometazoline)**	Nasal decongestant at used to relieve stuffy nose.

Antihistamines

Mucomist (**acetylcysteine**)	This drug reduces the visocisity of purulent and nonpurulent secretions of the lungs from pneumonia, bronchitis, emphysema, tuberculosis, and pulmonary complications of cystic fribrosis. It enables removal of secretions by coughing, postural drainage, and mechanical means.
Proventil, Ventolin (**albuterol**)	Bronchodilator and adrenergic used to treat bronchospasms of asthma, brochitis, emphysema, and crystic fibrosis by dilating the smooth bronchial muscle and relieving obstructive bronchospasms. Common side effects include tachycardia, nervousness, tremors, and heaches. CNS excitement is common in children between 2 and 5 years (Bindler & Howry, 1991). Paradoxical airway resistance may develop with repeated, excessive use of inhaled albuterol (Friesen, 1987). Tolerance may develop with long-term use.
Aminophylline, Amoline, Somophyllin, and others (**aminophylline**)	Bronchodilator used for symptomatic relief of bronchial asthma and bronchospasms of bronchitis and emphysema. This drug is also used to treat status asthmaticus and congestive heart failure. It is meant to control asthma only under medical supervision.
Tornalate (**bitolterol**)	Bronchodilator, which metabolizes into colterol, used to treat bronchial asthma and to relieve the bronchospasms of bronchitis and emphysema. When compared to similar drugs, it has a longer duration of action with similar side effects.
Intal, Aarane, Opticrom and others (**cromolyn sodium**)	Anti-asthmatic and anti-allergy medication used in the prevention of severe bronchial asthma and bronchospasms and the prevention and treatment of allergic rhinitis, allergic ocular disorders and food allergies with symptoms such as runny nose, itching, and sneezing. It is also used to treat inflamed bowel diseases. It is among the safest drugs in the treatment of children. Cromolyn is an antiinflammatory drug, but has no direct bronchodilating effect. It may be used in the treatment of colds and exercise-induced asthma. It is a prophylactic whose effects do not become apparent until 4 weeks after the beginning of therapy (Friesen, 1987). There are few side effects of cromolyn, but those that occur often include local itching and burning. The most common side effects relate directly to the irritative properties of the inhaled powder, including bronchospasms, wheezing, cough, nasal congestion, and pharyngeal irritation (Friesen, 1987).
Lufyllin, Dilor, Neothylline (**diphylline**)	Bronchodilator used to treat acute bronchial asthma and the reversible bronchospasms of bronchitis and emphysema.
Vaponefrin, AsthmaHaler (**epinephrine/ adrenaline**)	Adrenergic used to treat reversible airway obstrctions in allergies and acute asthma attacks and to provide systemic relief from anaphylaxis. It dilates and relaxes the smooth bronchial muscle to relieve the bronchospasms of acute and chronic asthma and reduce congestion within the bronchial mucosa. A cardiac stimulant, epinephrine may cause elevated blood pressure, cardiac stimulation, and other cardiac symptoms (Julien, 1988; Friesen, 1987). Paradoxical airway resistance may develop with repeated, excessive use of inhalation products (Friesen, 1987).
Teldral, Histadyl EC, Bronkaid, Bronkotabs, Mudrane (**ephedrine**)	Bronchidilator, vasodilator and nasal decongestant used to treat reversible airway obstruction due to mild forms of chronic pulmonary disease and to provide relief of nasal mucosal congestion. Ephedrine may cause cardiac symptoms such as elevated blood pressure and tachycardia (Friesen, 1987). CNS excitement is characterized by nervousness, occasional anxiety, and insomnia. Paradoxical airway resistance may develop with repeated, excessive use of inhalation products.
Bronkephrine (**ethylorephedrine**)	Bronchodilator used to treat reversible airway obstruction and relieve bronchospasms. It is often available in combination products. Cardiac symptoms include tachycardia. CNS excitement is chacterized by nervousness, occasional anxiety and insomnia. Paradoxical airway resistance may develop with repeated, excessive use of inhalation products.

Bronkephrine (**ethylnorephedrine**)	Bronchodilator used to treat reversible airway obstruction and relieve bronchospasms. I tis often available in combination products. Cardiac xymptoms include tachycardia. CNS excitement is characterized by nervousness, occasional anxiety and insomnia. Paradoxical airway resistance may develop with repeated, excessive use of inhalation products.
Arma-a-Med Isoetharine, Bronkometer, Bronkosol (**isoetharine**)	Bronchodilator used to treat reversible airway obstruction and relieve the bronchial smooth muscle. Cardiac symptoms include tachycardia. CNS excitement is characterized by nervousness, occasional anxiety, and insomnia. Paradoxical airway resistance may develop with repeated, excessive use of inhalation products. Tolerance may develop with prolonged or excessive use.
Medihaler-Iso, Isuprel, Norisodrine, Adrenaline, Sus-prine (**isoproterenol**)	Bronchodilator and adrenergic used to relieve bronchospasms, acute and chronic bronchospasms, bronchitis, and emphysema. It relaxes the smooth bronchial muscle and relieves bronchial constriction. Cardiac symptoms include tachycardia. CNS excitement is characterized by nervousness, occasional anxiety, and insomnia. Paradoxical airway resistance may develop with repeated, excessive use of inhalation product. Tolerance and rebound bronchospasms result from frequent use.
Alupent, Metaprel (**metaproterenol**)	Adrenergic and bronchodilator used to treat reversible airway obstruction in the management of asthma, to prevent exercise-induced asthma, or to enhance the therapeutic effect of theophylline. Cardiac symptoms include tachycardia. CNS excitement is characterized by nervousness, occasional anxiety, and insomnia. Paradoxical airway resistance may develop with repeated, excessive use of inhalation roducts. The safety of inhalation products wth metaproterenol is not established for children under 12. Side effects of the inhalation form include nervousness, tremor, and weakness. Tolerance can develop with long-term use.
Choledyl (**oxtriphylline**)	Bronchodilator used in the long-term treatment of bronchospasms of acute asthma, chronic bronchitis, and emphysema.
Adrenalin, Asthma Meter, Medihaler-Epi, Primatene Mist, Bronkaid Mist, Astj,amefrin, Duo-Medihaler (**phenyleprine with isoproterenol**)	Decongestant and bronchodilator. As a decongestant, it is a topically applied nasal preparation used to reduce congestion of URIs. As an oral inhalation, this drug causes constriction of the bronchioles and relieves congestion.
Bricanyl, Brethine, Brethaire (**terbutaline**)	Adrenergic and bronchodilator that dilates the smooth bronchial muscle. It is used to treat the symptoms of asthma and the bronchospasns of emphysema and chronic bronchitis. Cardiac symptoms include tachycardia. CNS excitement is characterized by nervousness, occasional anxiety, and insomnia. Paradoxical airway resistance may develop with repeated, excessive use of inhalation products. Its safety is not established for children under 12. Tolerance can develop from long-term use.
Theodur, Sl-Phyllin, Elixophyllin, Aerolate, Sustaire, Theolaire, Theobid, Theovent, Somophyllin, Slo-bid and others (over 50) (**theophylline**)	Bronchodilator used to treat bronchial asthma, status asthmaticus, and reversible bronchospasms of chronic bronchitis, emphysema and cystic fribrosis. It is available in combination with antitussives, expectorants, sedatives, and sympathominetics. There is a narrow band between therapeutic and toxic dosages. At therapeutic levels, theophylline may produce CNS excitation and seizures (Friesen, 1987). Theophylline is used cautiously with children. Toxicity is most often related to failure to take the medication, then double dosing (Steinmann, 1992). Common side effects of theophylline include nausea, loss of appetite, hyperactivity, and insomnia. Major side effects include persistent vomiting, vomiting blood, disorientation, and severe headache. Symptoms of overdose include nausea, vomiting, headache, tachycardia, dysrhythmias, hypotension, and hypoglycemia (Friesen, 1987).

Corticosteroids

Beconase, Vanceril and others (**beclomethazone aerosol**)	Steroid used to treat allergic rhinitis and asthma which are not responsive to traditional treatment and to treat steroid dependent asthma when it is necessary to reverse adverse effects or decrease the use of systemic steroids.
Cortelan, Cortone (**cortisone**)	Steroid used to treat severe seasonal and chronic bronchial asthma.
Decadron, Hexadrol, Heradrol (**dexamethasone**)	Steroid found in many combinations that is used to treat collagen and dermatologic diseases, allergies, acute leukemia and fetal respiratory distress syndrome. As an inhalation, it controls the symptoms of bronchial asthma and seasonal or perennial rhinitis when there is a poor response to traditional treatment.
Aerobid (**flunisolide**)	Steroid used to control the symptoms of bronchial asthma and seasonal or perennial rhinitis when there is a poor response to traditional treatment.
Cortisol, Cortef (**hydrocortisone**)	Steroid used to treat severe seasonal allergies. It is short acting and the least potent steroid used topically. It may be found in OTC products.
Medral, Wynacort (**methylprednisolone**)	Steroid used to treat opthalmic conditions such as allergic conjunctivitis as well as allergies and dermatological conditions.
Colisone, Cortan, Meticortin (**prednisone**)	Steroid used to treat collagen and dermatologic disorders, allergies, acute leukemia, RA, rheumatoid diseases, bursitis, and respiratory distress syndrome.
Cortalone, Delta-Cortef (**prednisolone**)	Steroid used to treat eye ailments, cancer, acute rheumatoid conditions, bronchial asthma, and post-operative dental inflammation.
Azmacort, Aristospan, Aristocort, Kenalog, Kenacort, Nasacort (**triamcinolone**)	Steroid used to treat collagen and dermatologic diseases, allergies, acute leukemia and other disorders. As an oral inhalation, it is used to treat bronchial asthma.

REFERENCES

Biederman, J., & Steingard, R. (1991). Pediatric psychopharmacology. In A. J. Gelenberg, E. L. Bassuk, & S. C. Schoonover (Eds.), *The practitioner's guide to psychoactive drugs* (3rd ed.) (pp. 341–388). New York: Plenum.

Bindler, R. M., & Howry, L. B. (1991). *Pediatric drugs and nursing implications*. Norwalk, CT: Appleton and Lange.

Bindler, R. M., Tso, Y., & Howry, L. B. (1986). *The parent's guide to pediatric drugs.* New York: Harper Row.

Brewer, E. J., & Angel, K. C. (1992). *Parenting a child with arthritis.* Chicago: Contemporary Books.

Busse, W. W. (1990). *What is asthma?* (Advance PLUS). Washington, DC: Allergy and Asthma Foundation of America.

Clayton, B. D. (1987). *Mosby's handbook of pharmacology* (4th ed.). St. Louis: C. V. Mosby.

Clayton, B. D., & Stock, Y. N. (1993). *Basic pharmacology for nurses.* St. Louis: C. V. Mosby.

Department of Health and Human Services. (1991). *Arthritis: Modern treatment for that old pain in the joints.* DHHS Publication No. (FDA) 92–1190. Washington, DC: USDHHS.

Feist, J., & Brannon, L. (1988). *Health psychology: An introduction to behavior and health.* Belmont, CA: Wadsworth.

Friesen, A. J. D. (1987). Adverse drug reactions in infants and children. In L. A. Pagliaro & A. M. Pagliaro (Eds.), *Problems in pediatric drug therapy* (2nd ed.) (pp. 303–363). Hamilton, IL: Drug Intelligence Publications.

Gadow, K. D. (1986). *Children on medication: Epilepsy, emotional disturbance and adolescent disorders* (Vol. 2). San Diego: College Hill.

Julien, R. M. (1992). *A primer of drug action* (6th ed.). New York: W. H. Freeman.

Julien, R. M. (1988). *Drugs and the body.* New York: W. H. Freeman.

LaGreca, A. (1988). Adherence to prescribed medical regimens. In D. K. Routh (Ed.), *Handbook of pediatric psychology* (pp. 299–320). New York: Guilford Press.

Lockey, R. F., Fox, R. D., & Ledford, D. K. (nd). *What is an allergy?* (Advance PLUS). Washington, DC: The Allergy and Asthma Foundation of America.

Malseed, R. T., & Harrigan, G. S. (1989). *Textbook of pharmacology and nursing care: Using the nursing process.* Philadelphia: Lippincott.

National Institute on Aging. (1990). *Arthritis medicines.* Gaithersburg, MD: U.S. Food and Drug Administration (Age Press).

Pagliaro, A. M., & Pagliaro, L. A. (1986). Drugs used to treat psychotic disorders. In A. M. Pagliaro and L. A. Pagliaro (Eds.), *Pharmacological aspects of nursing* (pp. 325–351). St. Louis: C. V. Mosby.

Phillips, R. H. (1988). *Coping with rheumatoid arthritis.* Garden City Park, NY: Avery Publishing Group.

Reiss, B. S., & Mellick, M. E. (1987). *Pharmacological aspects of nursing care* (2nd ed.). Albany, NY: Delmar Publishers.

Spunt, A. L., Hermann, B. P., & Rousseau, A. M. (1986). Epilepsy. In M. Hersen (Ed.), *Pharmacological and behavioral treatment: An integrative approach* (pp. 178–196). New York: Wiley.

Steinmann, M. (1992). *A parent's guide to allergies and asthma.* New York: Delta.

Townsend, M. C. (1990). *Drug guide for psychiatric nursing.* Philadelphia: F. A. Davis, Company.

Medications Commonly Used to Treat Children with Behavior Disorders: Antipsychotics, Anxiolytics, Antidepressants and Stimulants

Susan Vess
University of Southern Maine

OVERVIEW

In 1937, when a study was published on the effectiveness of d-amphetamine in the treatment of agitated children, the field of psychopharmacology began (Biederman & Steingard, 1991). Although more information about the usefulness of stimulants has been developed, there were few other major breakthroughs in pediatric psychopharmacology during the next 50 years (Biederman & Steingard, 1991).

BASIC CONSIDERATIONS

Psychotropic drugs such as antipsychotics, anxiolytics, antidepressants, and stimulants are medications designed to alter the behavior or emotions of children, adolescents, and adults with severe disturbances (Martin & Agran, 1988). These drugs change the individual's behavior in positive and negative ways, but do not cure the disorder. Although psychotropic medications are used in the treatment of many childhood disorders, relatively few children and adolescents are treated with drugs.

There are very few studies evaluating the long-term consequences of psychotropic drugs on children and their behavior, health, or learning (Schatzberg & Cole, 1991). Thus the effectiveness and safety of psychotropic medications with children and adolescents are almost never known prior to their introduction in treatment (Schatzberg & Cole, 1991). Most information about psychotropic drugs comes from adult-oriented research, clinical experience with adult patients, poorly formulated studies with children or anecdotes about the treatment effectiveness of a psychotropic drug with children and adolescents. Consequently, the FDA has not granted approval for the use of most psychoactive drugs with children or adolescents (Biederman & Steingard, 1991).

Despite the lack of FDA approval of these medications, psychotropic drugs are routinely prescribed. Crnic and Reid (1989) label the combination of medication with behavior management as the skills and pills approach to treatment.

Which particular drug is prescribed depends on the doctor's evaluation of how and how well a drug works to treat a particular disorder, what side effects accompany its use, health and other information about the patient, and the doctor's experience with the particular medication. The physician also considers the usual dosage of the drug, its route and schedule of administration, and its interaction with other drugs.

Because of the limited knowledge about the effectiveness and toxicity of medication in pediatric uses, psychotropic drugs should be prescribed only after other interventions such as psychotherapy and behavior management show limited or only short-term effectiveness (Biederman & Steingard, 1991). When prescribing these medications, the potential benefits must be constantly weighed against the long and short term risks of the drug.

Children tolerate higher dosages of psychotropic medications for their weight than adults tolerate because children's livers efficiently metabolize drugs (Schatzberg & Cole, 1991). Additionally, when drugs are used with accurately diagnosed disorders and at appropriate dosages, psychotropic medications produce small, but important, benefits (Biederman & Steingard, 1991).

Antipsychotics

Antipsychotics are indicated only for the treatment of childhood psychoses, but have been used to control behaviors such as severe agitation, aggression, self abuse, and insomnia associated with mental retardation and autism. They have been used to treat hospitalized nonpsychotic children and adolescents with angry, impulsive behavior (Schatzberg & Cole, 1991). Finally, these drugs have been tried in the management of Tourette's syndrome, Attention Deficit Disorder (ADD), and aggressive forms of Conduct Disorder (CD).

Children with autism and schizophrenia are frequently treated with antipsychotics, but demonstrate only modest improvement, especially when under 15 years (Schatzberg & Cole, 1991). In autistic children, antipsychotic medication is used to control stereotyped behavior and to reduce anxiety (Keltner, 1991).

In schizophrenic children, antipsychotic medication is used to reduce disordered thinking and to re-establish more normal behavior (Keltner, 1991). In both groups, these medications are used in the management of assaultive, aggressive, or self destructive behaviors (Keltner, 1991).

According to Keltner (1991), antipsychotics produce both neuroleptic and antipsychotic effects. Neuroleptic effects include sedation, emotional quieting, and psychomotor slowing. These effects are more relevant to autistic patients. Antipsychotic effects involve normalizing the patient's thoughts, moods, and behaviors (Keltner, 1991). These effects are more pertinent for schizophrenics.

Symptoms most responsive to antipsychotics include motor agitation, aggressiveness, tics, stereotypies, delusions, and hallucinations. Overactive, disorganized behavior in children may decrease (Schatzberg & Cole, 1991).

Children, adolescents, and adults are similar in their tolerance of antipsychotics and demonstrate similar side effects. Common short-term side effects of antipsychotic medication include drowsiness, weight gain, and increased appetite. Some also produce sedation and cognitive blunting which jeopardizes a child's opportunity to learn.

Additionally, all antipsychotics produce neurological side effects which are most often associated with the high potency medications. These side effects involve the extrapyramidal system and include dystonia, pseudoparkinsonianism, akinesias, and tardive dyskinesia.

To some extent, the specific array of side effects depends on whether a high potency versus a low potency drug was administered. High potency antipsychotics including Haldol and Stelazine produce neurological/extrapyramidal effects. Low potency antipsychotics including Thorazine and Mellaril produce side effects such as lowered blood pressure, drowsiness, and anticholinergic effects (constipation, dried mouth and nose, blurred vision, and difficulty urinating).

Because children show little improvement with antipsychotics and because these drugs produce important side effects, antipsychotics are used cautiously. As children grow into late adolescence, their schizophrenia becomes similar to that of adults. This results in similar effectiveness and safety considerations in the use of antipsychotic medications.

Anxiolytics

Anxiolytics treat anxiety and its symptoms primarily through generalized CNS depression (Townsend, 1990). Because they may produce behavioral inhibition, antianxiety drugs should be used cautiously in the treatment of children whose behavior is already inhibited (Biederman & Steingard, 1991). Four groups of drugs are used to treat anxiety: (a) barbituates, (b) antihistamines, (c) carbamates, and (d) benzodiazepines (Reiss & Melick, 1987). However, only antihistamines and benzodiazepines are used with sufficient frequency with children to merit discussion.

There is little information about the safety or effectiveness of antianxiety drugs in the treatment of children (Biederman & Steingard, 1991). Anxiolytics, especially the antihistamines, are used in the treatment of young children with poorly diagnosed insomnia and agitation (Biederman & Steingard, 1991). They are also used in the treatment of separation anxiety disorder, overanxious disorder, and avoidant disorder, the childhood anxiety disorders described in DSM III R. Anxiolytics are not used in the treatment of child sleep disorders such as night terrors and somnambulism.

Common short-term side effects of antianxiety medication include drowsiness, decreased mental acuity, and confusion at higher doses. These drugs should not be combined nor should they be stopped suddenly.

Antidepressants

Antidepressants are used along with psychotherapy in the treatment of affective disorders. However, their use with children is very limited. The antidepressants most often used with children are imipramine and amitriptyline. The side effects of these drugs most commonly involve their anticholinergic and sedative effects.

Persons who are seriously ill with disorders such as AIDS and cancer may take stimulants to treat their depression. Stimulants are also tried with persons who were not treated successfully with conventional antidepressants and psychotherapy.

Stimulants

CNS stimulants are used in the treatment of behavior problems such as impulsivity, inattentiveness, off-task behavior, and excess activity associated with ADHD in children and the mentally disabled and ADD in children and adults. They are the best studied and most understood drugs used in the treatment of childhood disorders. Stimulants are also indicated for the treatment of narcolepsy and obesity in adults.

The stimulant drugs most commonly used in the treatment of children are Ritalin and the amphetamines. Ritalin, Dexedrine, or Cylert have been used to treat 1 to 2% of children in elementary school and 80 to 90% of children with ADD (Pelham & Murphy, 1986). They are useful in treating ADHD in children over 5 years of age (Barkley, 1989). These drugs control the overt symptoms of ADHD, but should be used only in conjunction with other treatments such as behavior modification and social skills training. Not all children show improvements when administered stimulant medications.

D-amphetamine, Ritalin, and Cylert improve behavior and learning of 50–75% of children correctly diagnosed with ADHD (Julien, 1992). Learning may improve with stimulant medication because the child's attention span is improved. However, stimulants are insufficient to produce normal academic and social functioning.

Ritalin and d-amphetamine produce their effects within 30 to 60 minutes and reach their peak effectiveness in 1 to 3 hours after administration (Biederman & Steingard, 1991). Several daily dosages are required of these two short-acting drugs. Of the three, Cylert is somewhat less effective and less safe; however, it may be administered in a single dose each day (Schatzberg & Cole, 1991). Its effectiveness may not be apparent for several weeks (Biederman & Steingard, 1991).

Current practices suggest that children, especially those with severe ADHD or CD, should be medicated throughout the week and during vacations (Barkley, 1989). While drug holidays allow evaluation of the usefulness of stimulant medication, interruptions in treatment may have negative consequences for the child's relationships with family and peers and for learning outside school.

Stimulants are used cautiously with psychotic children and persons with Tourette's syndrome or motor tics because these drugs increase the likelihood of a tic disorder, even when medication is discontinued (Biederman & Steingard, 1991). They are contraindicated in the presence of anorexia, insomnia, and other disorders. Stimulants may aggravate anxiety in some patients. They may also inhibit the metabolism of anticoagulants, anticonvulsants, and tricyclic antidepressants (TCAs).

The most commonly reported side effects of stimulants are insomnia and delayed sleep onset due to late afternoon or early evening administration of the drug. Others include tremors, weight loss, slight suppression of growth rate, nervousness, mild increases in heart rate and blood pressure, and changed mood with irritability, weepiness or oversensitivity. Some may aggravate seizure disorders (Friesen, 1987). There may be a rebound effect or transient behavior problems with discontinuation of stimulant medication (Biederman & Steingard, 1991). Prolonged use may result in psychological or physical dependence.

Psychoactive drugs are widely prescribed in the treatment of the mentally disabled, especially hospitalized adults with severe, antisocial, debilitating behavior (Crnic & Reid, 1989). Antipsychotic medications such as Thorazine, Navane, and Haldol are used to control aggression, destructiveness, hyperactivity, and antisocial behavior (Crnic & Reid, 1989). Stimulants are commonly prescribed to treat moderately and mildly disabled children enrolled in the public schools to improve their learning, attending, impulse control, and activity level (Crnic & Reid, 1989). Finally, anticonvulsants are administered to the mentally disabled to control behavior problems despite no evidence that these drugs improve cognition or behavior (Crnic & Reid, 1989). A large percentage of mentally disabled who receive anticonvulsants show no evidence of seizure activity (Crnic & Reid, 1989).

Information about psychotropic medications is listed in chart form for convenient access. The trade name appears first, then the generic name in parentheses. Drugs are ordered alphabetically by their generic names. Additional information is located in the treatment comments column. Medical professionals such as doctors and pharmacists and other resources such as the latest *Physician's Desk Reference* (PDR) should be consulted for more complete information about a disorder and its medical treatment.

Psychoses

Thorazine **(chlorpromazine)**[2]	Thorazine is used to treat acute and chronic psychosis such as schizophrenia, to control children with agitated or very excited behavior and excessive motor activity, and to manage children with severe behavioral problems such as explosiveness, hyperexcitability, or combativeness (Townsend, 1990; Clayton, 1987). Because of its sedative effects, it may be used with the severely or profoundly mentally disabled or to treat those who are violent or agitated (Thomas, 1988). It is the most well-known and well-researched of the phenothiazines (Julien, 1992). There is a low incidence of extrapyramidal effects with Thorazine.
Catapres **(clonidine)**[3]	Catapres is an antihypertensive drug used to treat severe Tourette's syndrome, including explosive violent behavior (Schatzberg & Cole, 1991). Its side effects include dry mouth, constipation, sedation, and hypotension.
Haldol **(haloperidol)**[1]	Haldol is a tranquilizer used to treat agitated states of psychosis in children and adults. Other uses include control of motor and vocal tics of Tourette's syndrome as well as hyperactivity and severe behavior problems of children (Townsend, 1990). It is also prescribed in the short-term management of ADD (Bindler & Howry, 1991). Although showing limited effectiveness in the treatment of children with autism, Haldol is used with autistic children with serious management problems to decrease maladaptive behavior and to increase discriminative learning (Schatzberg & Cole, 1991; Perry & Meislas, 1988). It is used to treat autism with alternating hyperactivity and hypoactivity. It reduces high levels of stereotypies and increases orienting reactions in children who previously showed little orientation (Perry & Meislas, 1988). It has been used in the treatment of persons not responding to phenothiazines (Julien, 1992). Haldol may cause extrapyramidal side effects (Martin & Agran, 1988).
Inderol **(propranolol)**[3]	Inderol, a beta blocker, has not been approved for use with children. However, its usefulness in the treatment of severe aggressive and self injurious behaviors, schizophrenia, anxiety disorders, and Tourette's syndrome has been investigated (Biederman & Steingard, 1991). Reduction of explosive behavior in children and adolescents as well as aggression in the mentally disabled have been reported (Biederman & Steingard, 1991). Its most common side effects include nausea, vomiting, constipation, and mild diarrhea.
Mellaril **(thioridazine)**[2]	Mellaril is used to treat hyperkinesis, combativeness, aggression, and severe behavior problems in children (Bindler & Howry, 1991; Townsend, 1990). It is among the most frequently used antipsychotics with children (Gittelman & Kanner, 1986). It may be used to control aggression and hostile and self injurious behavior in the mentally retarded (Martin & Agran, 1988). Because of its sedative effects, Mellaril may be used with the mentally disabled or profoundly retarded (Thomas, 1988). This tranquillizer reduces psychomotor agitation and tension from psychoses and neuroses (Clayton, 1987). It has the least extrapyramidal effects of the phenothiazines.
Stelazine **(trifluoperazine)**[2]	Stelazine is used to treat anxiety, tension, and agitation due to psychoses. It may control head banging, self injury, hyperactivity, and assaultiveness in the mentally disabled (Thomas, 1988). The patient is monitored for extrapyramidal effects, especially when taking large doses. However, it produces less sedation, blurred vision, and hypotension than other phenothiazines.

Butryophenones[1] are similar to phenothiazines, but work more quickly. In children, they frequently produce the extrapyramidal effects of akathisia and dystonia (Pagliaro & Pagliaro, 1986).

Phenothiazines[2] which include both high and low potency medications, are the oldest, most studied and most widely used group of antipsychotics with both adults and children.

Other drugs[3] have been used in the management of psychosis and other disorders frequently treated with antipsychotic medications.

Anxiety

Xanax (**alprazolam**)[2]	Xanax is used to treat the symptoms of anxiety and anxiety with mild symptoms of depression and panic disorders. It is not approved by the FDA for treatment of depression, but some doctors find the drug helpful. Xanax is contraindicated in children under 18 (Townsend, 1991).
Librium (**chlordiazepoxide**)[2]	Librium is a tranquilizer used to treat mild to moderate anxiety and tension. It has been used along with psychological treatment with adolescents and young adults showing anxiety disorders (Martin & Agran, 1988). This drug has antiepileptic properties.
Tranxene (**clorazepate**)[2]	Tranxene is used in the treatment of anxiety and epilepsy. It is contraindicated in children under 9 (Townsend, 1990).
Valium (**diazepam**)[2]	Valium is a tranquilizer and anxiolytic used to treat mild to moderate anxiety disorders and tension, perhaps Generalized Anxiety Disorder (GAD), skeletal muscle spasms of cerebral palsy, convulsive disorders and status epilepticus. Its effectiveness in the treatment of night terrors has been investigated (Townsend, 1990). It has been used along with psychological treatment with adolescents and young adults showing anxiety disorders (Martin & Agran, 1988). This drug has antiepileptic properties.
Atarax, Vistaril (**hydroxyzine**)	This antihistamine is used in the treatment of anxiety, especially from allergic reactions due to pruritus or asthma and to produce sedation prior to surgery.

Antihistamines[1] have been used to treat anxiety because of their sedative effects. They are successful in the treatment of anxiety that accompanies skin disorders with severe itching (Reiss & Melick, 1987). Two antihistamines used to treat anxiety are Atarax (**hydroxyzine chloride**) and Vistaril (**hydroxyzine pamoate**). These drugs are safe and produce minimal negative reactions so are often used to treat children as a preoperative sedative and to relieve itching (Malseed & Harrigan, 1989).

Benzodiazepines[2] are used in the treatment of anxiety and epilepsy, as muscle relaxants and as an aid to sleep. These drugs, especially Librium, Valium, and Xanax are the anxiolytics used most often with children. They may result in increased activity or aggravate behavior disorders, especially in children with ADHD (Schatzberg & Cole, 1991).

Benzodiazepines are relatively safe drugs, unless combined with other substances. About half of patients treated with benzodiazepines experience symptoms of withdrawal such as nervousness, insomnia, and loss of appetite when these drugs are stopped.

Benzodiazepines are CNS depressants whose individual derivatives have their effects on different sites in the brain. Therefore, specific drugs are used to treat specific types of disorders. Benzodiazepines are often grouped on the basis of their clinical use: (a) anticonvulsants (**diazepam, clonazepam,** and **clorazepate**), (b) antianxiety, and (c) hypnotics (**flurazepam, triazolam,** and **tomazepam**).

Affective Disorders

Amitrill, Elavil, Endep, and others (**amitriptyline**)	This drug is used to treat major depression, especially with anxiety. It has also been used to treat severe chronic depression in children with normal intelligence and may be used to treat hperactivity (Martin & Agran, 1988). It has been investigated in the control of chronic pain and the prevention of migraines. Nonapproved uses in children include treatment of anorexia and bulimia, ADD, enuresis, and pruritus in cold urticaria.
Wellbutrin (**bupropion**)[2]	Wellbutrin is used to treat major depression in patients who did not respond adequately to or could not tolerate other antidepressants (Townsend, 1990). Wellbutrin has been tried successfully in the treatment of children with ADD (Julien, 1992; Schatzberg & Cole, 1991). Its safety in children under 18 has not been established. Persons with bulimia or anorexia show a high incidence of seizures with this medication (Townsend, 1990). The side effects of Wellbutrin include behavior stimulation, anxiety, restlessness, tremor, and insomnia.
Anafranil (**clomipramine**)[1]	Anafranil is not FDA approved because it seems to increase the risk of seizures. It has been found effective in the treatment of obsessive compulsive disorder (OCD) in both children and adolescents (Schatzberg & Cole, 1991). This drug has been used in Europe to treat depression and OCD.
Norpramine, Pertofane (**desipramine**)[1]	This drug has been used to treat major depression in children and adults. Its effectiveness in the treatment of ADD in children is under investigation (Townsend, 1990).

Prozac
(fluoxetine)[2]

Prozac is used to treat depression, especially when the depression is mild or the person is an outpatient (Julien, 1992). Its effectiveness in the treatment of exogenous obesity is under investigation. Prozac has been tried in the treatment of persons with OCD, bulimia, and panic and anxiety disorders (Julien, 1992). Its safety in children has not been established. Prozac is now the most widely prescribed antidepressant (Julien, 1992). The side effects of Prozac include nervousness, anxiety, sexual dysfunction, motor restlessness, and muscle rigidity. It lacks the anticholinergic or cardiac effects of the TCAs.

Tofranil
(imipramine)[1]

Tofranil, the first antidepressant identified, is used in the treatment of major depression with melancholia or psychotic symptoms. It is the only TCA approved for use with children and the most frequently studied TCA with children. Tofranil has been FDA approved only for the treatment of enuresis in disabled and nondisabled children. Apparently, its success in treating enuresis rests on its anticholinergic effects. Behavior treatment of enuresis is often more effective and results in fewer relapses (Schatzberg & Cole, 1991).

Tofranil soothes adult panic attacks (Gittelman & Kanner, 1986). It has been used to treat depression in children who are not mentally disabled. This drug is the most studied TCA in the treatment of childhood depression and is sometimes used to treat separation anxiety disorders (Thomas, 1988; Gittelman & Kanner, 1986). Tofranil's effectiveness in the treatment of ADD in children is under investigation (Bindler & Howry, 1991; Townsend, 1990). Additionally, high dosages of Tofranil have been tried in the treatment of school phobia (Biederman & Steingard, 1991).

(Lithium carbonate)

Lithium is used to treat bipolar disorders. Its usefulness in the treatment of children with a mixed bipolar disorder, aggressive behavior, and hyperactivity with psychotic or neurotic components has been investigated (Townsend, 1990). Lithium may be useful in the treatment of resistant depression, OCD, and some schizophrenia (Julien, 1992).

There is little documentation of lithium's usefulness in treating children, but it has been tried in the treatment of children with ADD, CD, anorexia, and schizophrenia when family members show a history of manic depression. It may also be used to treat a childhood behavior disorder that includes emotional lability and aggression when family members demonstrate bipolar or major depressive disorders. It is used to treat aggression, hyperactivity, or self-injurious behavior in mentally disabled children (Thomas, 1988).

The side effects of lithium are related to plasma concentrations. They include nausea, vomiting, diarrhea, tremor, and increased output of urine. These side effects are the same in persons of all ages, but children may tolerate lithium better than adults.

The therapeutic dose of lithium is very close to the toxic dosage, but the safety and adequacy of dosage is easily monitored by measuring serum lithium levels in the blood (Biederman & Steingard, 1991; Schatzberg & Cole, 1991) As the concentration level of lithium increases, toxic effects such as fatigue, muscle weakness, slurred speech, and tremors also increase. The use of lithium may result in serious complication when combined with electroshock therapy or Haldol. Infrequently, persons not responding well to or tolerating lithium have been treated with anticonvulsants, especially Tegretol and Depakane (Julien, 1992).

Tricyclic Antidepressants[1] (TCAs) are used primarily in the treatment of major depression in adults, but they have been used for over 30 years to treat depression in both adults and children (Carlson, 1988). They are the most widely studied of the antidepressants for use with children (Kazdin, 1989). These drugs, especially imipramine, are effective when they reach therapeutic levels of plasma concentration.

The TCAs have been found effective in the treatment of enuresis (imipramine), ADHD, childhood depression and juvenile anxiety disorders (Biederman & Steingard, 1991). These drugs, especially imipramine and desipramine, are used to treat children with ADHD for whom stimulants are contraindicated or for whom ADHD is combined with a significant mood disorder (Barkley, 1989). They have been used in the treatment of anorexia, bulimia, OCD, panic disorder, chronic pain, migraine headaches, post-traumatic stress disorder, and peptic ulcers (Julien, 1992). Finally, the TCAs may also be useful in the treatment of Tourette's syndrome and anxiety disorders (Biederman & Steingard, 1991).

Generally, TCAs are slow-acting drugs which require 4 to 8 weeks of administration to demonstrate effectiveness. Children with enuresis or ADHD respond within days to TCAs, but take several weeks to respond to TCAs in the treatment of mood disorders. Children are treated with TCAs for 3 to 6 months (Martin & Agran, 1988).

The most frequently administered TCAs are **imipramine, desipramine, amitriptyline,** and **nortriptyline.** Of these, amitriptyline produces the most side effects, especially sedation. A particular TCA is selected because of its effectiveness, side effects, and duration of action (Julien, 1992). Of the TCAs, the most is known about the effectiveness and safety of imipramine in the treatment of children. In addition to treating enuresis, TCAs may be effective in the treatment of children with major depression (Biederman & Steingard, 1991).

The effectiveness and side effects of TCAs when used with children are similar to those found with adults (Biederman & Steingard, 1991). The most common side effects relate to the TCAs' anticholinergic effects such as constipation, dry mouth and nasal passages, blurred vision, and urinary hesitancy. Because of limited salivation due to anticholinergic effects of TCAs, some children may experience tooth decay. Other side effects include increased sensitivity to sun light, dizziness on standing quickly, increased heart rate, increased sweating, weight gain, and drowsiness. However, the effectiveness and safety of these drugs is often unpredictable with children.

TCAs lower the seizure threshold so should be used with caution in the treatment of epileptics. Because they decrease their metabolism, combining anticonvulsants or antipsychotics with TCAs may increase their toxicity (Biederman & Steingard, 1991). TCAs may also exacerbate the psychotic and manic symptoms of schizophrenia and mania (Biederman & Steingard, 1991). There is little information about the safety and effectiveness of **Second Generation (Atypical) Antidepressants**[2] with children.

Monamine Oxidase Inhibitors (MAOIs) preceeded TCAs in treatment of depression. Forms that are effective and less toxic are being developed (Julien, 1992). There is minimal information on the safety and effectiveness of MAOIs in the treatment of children. However, they may be useful in the treatment of major depression, CD, childhood schizophrenia, autism, phobic anxiety states, and OCD.

The use of MAOIs is limited by their side effects, especially interactions with drugs such as cold medications and nasal decongestants and foods with tyramine such as aged cheese, red wine, aged meat (sausages and corned beef), aged fish (pickled herring), broad beans, etc. These interactions may produce a hypertensive crisis, including a severe increase in blood pressure, severe headaches, increased heart rate, and palpitations. Hypertensive crisis may lead to stroke, other severe problems, and even death. Because of the above interactions and because they interact with stimulants, MAOIs are rarely used with children.

Stimulants

Dexedrine **(dextroamphetamine sulfate)**	Dexedrine is used in the treatment of ADHD, narcolepsy, and exogenous obesity. It is used cautiously with psychotic children and persons with Tourette's syndrome.
Pondimen **(fenfluramine)**	Pondimen is used in the treatment of exogenous obesity. An investigational use includes treatment of autistic children with elevated serotonin. It is a promising drug in the treatment of autism to improve the behavior of children with severe management problems. Autistic children with IQs over 40 and extreme agitation demonstrate greater social awareness, communication, and cognitive functioning and show less hyperactivity, sensorimotor symptoms, irritability, temper tantrums, aggression, and self mutilation with Pondimen (Biederman & Steingard, 1991). The safety of Pondimen has not been established for children under 12. This drug reduces appetite with little behavioral stimulation.
Desoxyn **(metamphetamine)**	Desoxyn is used to treat ADHD, narcolepsy, and exogenous obesity.
Ritalin **(methylphenidate)**	Ritalin is used to treat narcolepsy and ADHD. It is contraindicated in persons with motor tics or diagnosis/family history of Tourette's syndrome and severe depression. Its safety on children under 6 has not been established. Ritalin may lower the seizure threshold (Reiss & Melick, 1987).
Cylert **(pemoline)**	Cylert is used to treat ADHD. Investigational uses include narcolepsy and excessive daytime sleepiness. It is contraindicated in persons with Tourette's syndrome or history of tics. Cylert is chemically different from Ritalin and Dexedrine and produces less CNS stimulation. It is sometimes associated with liver abnormalities.

REFERENCES

Barkley, R. A. (1989). Attention deficit-hyperactivity disorder. In E. J. Mash & R. A. Barkley (Eds.), *Treatment of childhood disorders* (pp. 39–72). New York: Guilford.

Biederman, J., & Steingard, R. (1991). Pediatric psychopharmacology. In A. J. Gelenberg, E. L. Bassuk, & S. C. Schoonover (Eds.), *The practitioner's guide to psychoactive drugs* (3rd ed., pp. 341–388). New York: Plenum.

Bindler, R. M., & Howry, L. B. (1991). *Pediatric drugs and nursing implications.* Norwalk, CT: Appleton and Lange.

Carlson, G. A. (1988). Depression: Pharmacotherapies. In J. L. Matson (Ed.), *Handbook of treatment approaches in childhood psychopathology* (3rd ed., pp. 345–363). New York: Plenum.

Clayton, B. D. (1987). *Mosby's handbook of pharmacology* (4th ed.). St. Louis, MO: C. V. Mosby.

Crnic, K. A., & Reid, M. (1989). Mental retardation. In E. J. Mash & R. A. Barkley (Eds.), *Treatment of childhood disorders* (pp. 247–285). New York: Guilford.

Friesen, A. J. D. (1987). Adverse drug reactions in infants and children. In L. A. Pagliaro & A. M. Pagliaro (Eds.), *Problems in pediatric drug therapy* (2nd ed., pp. 303–363). Hamilton, IL: Drug Intelligence Publications.

Gittelman, R., & Kanner, A. (1986). Psychopharmacology. In H. C. Quay & J. S. Werry (Eds.), *Psychopathological disorders of childhood* (3rd ed., pp. 455–495). New York: John Wiley & Sons.

Julien, R. M. (1992). *A primer of drug action* (6th ed.). New York: W. H. Freeman.

Kazdin, A. (1989). Childhood depression. In E. J. Mash & R. A. Barkley (Eds.), *Treatment of childhood disorders* (pp. 135–166). New York: Guilford.

Keltner, N. (1991). Psychopharmacology. In P. Clunn (Ed.), *Child psychiatric nursing* (pp. 380–395). St. Louis: Mosby.

Malseed, R. T., & Harrigan, G. S. (1989). *Textbook of pharmacology and nursing care: Using the nursing process.* Philadelphia: Lippincott.

Martin, J. E., & Agran, M. (1988). Pharmacotherapy. In J. L. Matson (Ed.), *Handbook of treatment approaches in childhood psychopathology* (pp. 327–344). New York: Plenum.

Pagliaro, A. M., & Pagliaro, L. A. (1986). Drugs used to treat psychotic disorders. In A. M. Pagliaro & L. A. Pagliaro (Eds.), *Pharmacological aspects of nursing* (pp. 325–351). St. Louis: C. V. Mosby.

Pelham, W. E., & Murphy, H. A. (1986). Attention deficit and conduct disorders. In M. Hersen (Ed.), *Pharmacological and behavioral treatment: An integrative approach* (pp. 108–148). New York: Wiley.

Perry. R., & Meislas, K. (1988). Infantile autism and childhood schizophrenia. In J. L. Matson (Ed.), *Handbook of treatment approaches in childhood psychopathology* (pp. 301–325). New York: Plenum.

Reiss, B. S., & Melick, M. E. (1987). *Pharmacological aspects of nursing care* (2nd ed.). Albany: Delmar Publishers.

Schatzberg, A. F., & Cole, J. O. (1991). *Manual of clinical psychopharmacology* (2nd ed.). Washington, DC: American Psychiatric Press.

Thomas, M. (1988). Mental retardation and learning disability: Pharmacotherapies. In J. L. Matson (Ed.), *Handbook of treatment approaches in childhood psychopathology* (pp. 503–524). New York: Wiley.

Townsend, M. C. (1990). *Drug guide for psychiatric nursing.* Philadelphia: F. A. Davis Company.

ANNOTATED BIBLIOGRAPHY

Gelenberg, J. A., Bassuk, E. L., & Schoonover, S. C. (Eds.). (1991). *The practitioner's guide to psychoactive drugs* (3rd ed.). New York: Plenum.
This volume is particularly useful in many ways. First, this book is a very readable and complete discussion of the major psychological disorders. Second, it provides background on other topics such as the use of medications with children and geriatric populations. Third, it describes the various treatments used with a particular disorder in addition to medication.

Julien, R. M. (1992). *A primer of drug action* (6th ed.). New York: W. H. Freeman.

Julien, R. M. (1988). *Drugs and the body.* New York: W. H. Freeman.
These two books are very useful in describing how the body functions and various physical and psychological disorders. They also explain how drugs work and provide basic information about categories of medication. These are only two of Freeman's excellent books about drugs and psychological disturbances.